The Catholic Encyclopedia

VOLUME ELEVEN
New Mexico—Philip

THE CATHOLIC ENCYCLOPEDIA

AN INTERNATIONAL WORK OF REFERENCE
ON THE CONSTITUTION, DOCTRINE,
DISCIPLINE, AND HISTORY OF THE
CATHOLIC CHURCH

EDITED BY
CHARLES G. HERBERMANN, Ph.D., LL.D.
EDWARD A. PACE, Ph.D., D.D.   CONDÉ B. PALLEN, Ph.D., LL.D.
THOMAS J. SHAHAN, D.D.   JOHN J. WYNNE, S.J.
ASSISTED BY NUMEROUS COLLABORATORS

IN FIFTEEN VOLUMES
VOLUME XI

New York
ROBERT APPLETON COMPANY

Nihil Obstat, June 1, 1911

REMY LAFORT

CENSOR

Imprimatur

✠ JOHN M. FARLEY

ARCHBISHOP OF NEW YORK

Copyright, 1911

By ROBERT APPLETON COMPANY

The articles in this work have been written specially for The Catholic Encyclopedia and are protected by copyright. All rights, including the right of translation and reproduction, are reserved.

Contributors to the Eleventh Volume

AHAUS, HUBERT, S.T.D., Ph.D., St. Joseph's College, Mill Hill, London: Orders, Holy.

AHERNE, CORNELIUS, Rector, Professor of New Testament Exegesis, St. Joseph's College, Mill Hill, London: Pasch or Passover.

AHERNE, JAMES, South Omaha, Nebraska: Omaha, Diocese of.

ÁLDÁSY, ANTAL, Ph.D., Archivist of the Library of the National Museum, Budapest: Oláh, Nicolaus.

ALLARIA, ANTHONY, C.R.L., S.T.D., Abbot of S. Teodoro, Lector of Philosophy and Theology, Genoa: Peter de Honestis; Peter Fourier, Saint; Peter Nolasco, Saint; Peter of Arbues, Saint; Peter of Verona, Saint.

ALMOND, JOSEPH CUTHBERT. O.S.B., Superior of Parker's Hall, Oxford: Oates's Plot; Oblati; Olivetans.

AMADO, RAMÓN RUIZ, S.J., LL.D., Ph.L., College of St. Ignatius, Sarria, Barcelona: Orense, Diocese of; Orihuela, Diocese of; Osma, Diocese of; Oviedo, Diocese of; Palencia, Diocese and University of; Pamplona, Diocese of.

ANGLIN, HON. FRANCIS ALEXANDER, K.C., Puisne Judge, Supreme Court of Canada, Ottawa: Ontario.

ARENDZEN, J. P., Ph.D., S.T.D., M.A. (Cantab.), Professor of Sacred Scripture, St. Edmund's College, Ware, England: Occult Art, Occultism.

ATTERIDGE, ANDREW HILLIARD, London: Periodical Literature, Catholic, England.

AUGUSTINE, FATHER, O.S.F.C., Franciscan Capuchin Monastery, Dublin: Nugent, Francis.

AUSTIN, SISTER MARY STANISLAUS, St. Catharine's Convent of Mercy, New York: O'Reilly, Hugh.

AVELING, FRANCIS, S.T.D., London: Phenomenalism.

BACCHUS, FRANCIS JOSEPH, B.A., The Oratory, Birmingham, England: Pachomius, Saint; Pammachius, Saint; Pamphilius of Cæsarea, Saint; Pantænus; Paul the Hermit, Saint; Paul the Simple, Saint; Peter of Alexandria, Saint; Philastrius, Saint.

BANDELIER, AD. F., Hispanic Society of America, New York: Pedro de Cordova.

BANGHA, ADALBERT V., S.J., Member of the Catholic Philosophical Society of Thomas Aquinas (Budapest), Innsbruck, Austria: Pázmány, Peter.

BARNES, Mgr. ARTHUR STAPYLTON, M.A. (Oxon. and Cantab.), Cambridge, England: Passion of Jesus Christ in the Four Gospels.

BARRETT, MICHAEL, O.S.B., Buckie, Scotland: Ogilvie, John, Venerable.

BARRY, WILLIAM CANON, S.T.D., Leamington, England: Oxford Movement; Parables.

BAUMBERGER, GEORG, Knight of the Order of St. Sylvester, Editor-in-Chief, "Neue Züricher Nachrichten", Zurich: Periodical Literature, Catholic, Switzerland.

BAUMGARTEN, Mgr. PAUL MARIA, J.U.D., S.T.D., Rome: Old Catholics.

BECHTEL, FLORENTINE, S.J., Professor of Hebrew and Sacred Scripture, St. Louis University, St. Louis: Noe; Paralipomenon, The Books of; Pharao.

BENIGNI, Mgr. UMBERTO, Prothonotary Apostolic Partecipante, Professor of Ecclesiastical History, Pontificia Accademia dei Nobili Ecclesiastici, Rome: Nicastro; Nicosia; Nicotera and Tropea, Diocese of; Nocera, Diocese of; Nocera dei Pagani, Diocese of; Nola, Diocese of; Non Expedit; Norcia, Diocese of; Noto, Diocese of; Novara, Diocese of; Nusco, Diocese of; Ogliastra, Diocese of; Oppido Mamertina, Diocese of; Oria, Diocese of; Oristano, Diocese of; Orvieto, Diocese of; Osimo, Diocese of; Ostia and Velletri, Diocese of; Otranto, Archdiocese of; Pacca, Bartolommeo; Padua, Diocese and University of; Pagano, Mario; Palermo, Archdiocese and University of; Palestrina, Diocese of; Parma, Diocese of; Paruta, Paolo; Passaglia, Carlo; Passionei, Domenico; Patti, Diocese of; Pavia, Diocese and University of; Penne and Atri, Diocese of; Periodical Literature, Catholic, Italy; Perugia, Archdiocese of; Pesaro, Diocese of; Pescia, Diocese of.

BERTRIN, GEORGES, Litt.D., Fellow of the University, Professor of French Literature, Institut Catholique, Paris: Olivier de la Marche; Ozanam, Antoine-Frédéric.

BEWERUNGE, H., Professor of Church Music, Maynooth College, Dublin: Organ.

BIHL, MICHAEL, O.F.M., Lector of Ecclesiastical History, Collegio San Bonaventura, Quaracchi, Florence: Orbellis, Nicolas d'; Pacificus of Ceredano; Pacificus of San Severino, Saint.

BLANC, JOSEPH, S.M., Nukualofa, Tonga Islands: Oceania, Vicariate Apostolic of.

BLANCHIN, F., O.M.I., S.T.D., Oblate Scholasticate, Ottawa, Canada: Oblates of Mary Immaculate.

BLENK, JAMES H., S.M., S.T.D., Archbishop of New Orleans, Louisiana: Peñalver y Cardenas, Louis.

BOUDINHON, AUGUSTE-MARIE, S.T.D., D.C.L., Director, "Canoniste Contemporain", Professor of Canon Law, Institut Catholique, Paris: Nomination; Nomocanon; Notaries; Notoriety, Notorious; Ordinariate; Ordinary; Parish; Parochial Mass; Penitential Canons.

BOWDEN, HENRY SEBASTIAN, The Oratory, London: Oratory of St. Philip Neri, The.

CONTRIBUTORS TO THE ELEVENTH VOLUME

BRAUN, JOSEPH, S.J., St. Ignatius College, Valkenburg, Holland: Pallium; Pectorale.

BRAUNSBERGER, OTTO, S.J., St. Ignatius College, Valkenburg, Holland: Peter Canisius, Blessed.

BRÉHIER, LOUIS-RENÉ, Professor of Ancient and Medieval History, University of Clermont-Ferrand, Puy-de-Dôme, France: Nogaret, Guillaume de; Palæography; Pastoureaux, Crusade of the; Peter de Blois; Peter the Hermit.

BRENNAN, M. H., Devil's Lake, North Dakota: North Dakota.

BRIDGE, JAMES, S.J., M.A. (Oxon.), Liverpool, England: Norris, Sylvester; Persecution.

BROWN, CHARLES FRANCIS WEMYSS, Lochton Castle, Perthshire, Scotland: Perugia, University of.

BRUCKER, JOSEPH, S.J., Editor of "Etudes", Paris: Parrenin, Dominique.

BRUNAULT, J. S. HERMANN, S.T.D., Bishop of Nicolet, Province of Quebec, Canada: Nicolet, Diocese of.

BRUNET, FRANCIS XAVIER, Vice-Chancellor, Archdiocese of Ottawa, Canada: Ottawa, Archdiocese of.

BURTON, EDWIN, S.T.D., F.R.Hist.Soc., Vice-President, St. Edmund's College, Ware, England: Nicholson, Francis; Noble, Daniel; Northcote, James Spencer; Norwich, Ancient Diocese of; Odo, Saint, Archbishop of Canterbury; Offa, King of Mercia; Old Hall (St. Edmund's College); Oldham, Hugh; Palmer, William; Pandulph; Panzani, Gregorio; Paulinus, Saint, Archbishop of York; Pecock, Reginald; Penal Laws, I. In England, II. In Scotland; Pendleton, Henry; Peyto, William.

BYRNE, JEROME FRANCIS, Superior General, Brothers of St. Patrick, Tullow, Ireland: Patrician Brothers.

CABROL, FERNAND, O.S.B., Abbot of St. Michael's, Farnborough, England: Nocturns; None; Occurrence; Octavarium Romanum; Octave; Office, Divine; Office of the Dead; Pax in the Liturgy.

CALÈS, JEAN, S.J., Professor of Old Testament Exegesis, Enghien, Belgium: Osee.

CALLAN, CHARLES J., O.P., S.T.L., Professor of Philosophy, Dominican House of Studies, Washington: Orthodoxy.

CAMERLYNCK, ACHILLE, S.T.D., Member of the "Société Belge de Sociologie", Professor of Sacred Scripture and Sociology, Episcopal Seminary, Bruges, Belgium: Philemon.

CARROLL, JAMES J., S.T.D., Bishop of Nueva Segovia, Philippine Islands: Nueva Segovia, Diocese of.

CASTETS, J., S.J., Professor of Philosophy and Political Science, St. Joseph's College, Trichinopoly, India: Nobili, Robert de'.

CHAPMAN, JOHN, O.S.B., B.A. (Oxon.), Prior, St. Thomas's Abbey, Erdington, Birmingham, England: Novatian and Novatianism; Optatus, Saint; Papias, Saint; Patrology; Paul of Samosata; Peregrinus.

CHISHOLM, JOSEPH ANDREW, K.C., M.A., LL.B., Halifax, Nova Scotia: Nova Scotia.

CLUGNET, JOSEPH-LÉON-TIBURCE, Litt.L., Bourg-la-Reine, Seine, France: Ouen, Saint; Perpetuus, Saint.

CONWAY, KATHERINE ELEANOR, Boston: O'Reilly, John Boyle.

COSSIO, ALUIGI, S.T.D., S.S.D., J.U.D., Baccalaureus and Licentiatus of the University of Padua, Rome: Paulinus II, Saint, Patriarch of Aquileia.

CRAM, RALPH ADAMS, F.R.G.S., F.Am.Inst. Architects, President, Boston Society of Architects, Boston: Niche; Palladio, Andrea.

CRATIN, SISTER M. MAGDALEN, Baltimore, Maryland: Oblate Sisters of Providence.

CRIVELLI, CAMILLUS, S.J., Professor of General History, Instituto Científico, City of Mexico: Periodical Literature, Catholic, Mexico.

CROFT, Mgr. WILLIAM PROVOST, P.A., V.G., Diocese of Nottingham, Lincoln, England: Nottingham, Diocese of.

CROFTON, K., New York: Parahyba, Diocese of.

CRONIN, Mgr. CHARLES JOHN, S.T.D., Vice-Rector, English College, Rome: Petitions to the Holy See.

CROW, FREDERICK AIDAN CANON, O.S.B., Llanishen, Cardiff, Wales: Newport, Diocese of.

CUTHBERT, FATHER, O.S.F.C., Crawley, Sussex, England: Persico, Ignatius.

D'ALTON, E. A., LL.D., M.R.I.A., Athenry, Ireland: C'Connell, Daniel; O'Fihely, Maurice; O'Hanlon, John; O'Neill, Hugh; O'Neill, Owen Roe; O'Reilly, Edmund; Ossory, Diocese of; O'Sullivan Beare, Philip; Penal Laws, III. In Ireland.

DALY, JOSEPH J., S.J., Professor of English Literature, Ateneo de Manila, Philippine Islands: Nueva Cáceres, Diocese of.

DEASY, JOHN A., M.A., LL.B., Cincinnati, Ohio: Ohio.

DEDIEU, JOSEPH, Litt.D., Institut Catholique, Toulouse, France: Peter of Auvergne; Peterssen, Gerlac.

DEGERT, ANTOINE, Litt.D., Editor, "La Revue de la Gascoigne", Professor of Latin Literature, Institut Catholique, France: Nicolas, Auguste; Noailles, Louis-Antoine de; Nonnotte, Claude-Adrien; Ossat, Arnaud d'.

DELAMARRE, LOUIS N., Ph.D., Instructor in French, College of the City of New York: Nicéron, Jean-Pierre; Paris, Alexis-Paulin; Paris, Gaston-Bruno-Paulin; Perrault, Charles.

DELANY, JOSEPH, S.T.D., New York: Obedience; Occasions of Sin; Omission; Parents; Perjury.

DEVINE, ARTHUR, C.P., St. Paul's Retreat, Mount Argus, Dublin: Passionists; Passionist Nuns; Passions; Paul of the Cross, Saint; Perfection, Christian and Religious.

DE WULF, MAURICE, Member of the Belgian Academy, Professor of Logic and Æsthetics, University of Louvain: Nominalism, Realism, Conceptualism.

CONTRIBUTORS TO THE ELEVENTH VOLUME

DOUGLAS, ROBERT MARTIN, M.A., LL.D., GREENSBORO, NORTH CAROLINA: North Carolina.

DRISCOLL, JAMES F., S.T.D., NEW ROCHELLE, NEW YORK: Nicodemus; Ointment in Scripture; Onias; Oriental Study and Research; Ozias; Patriarch; Pectoral; Pharisees.

DRISCOLL, JOHN THOMAS, M.A., S.T.L., FONDA, NEW YORK: O'Callaghan, Edmund Baily.

DRUM, WALTER, S.J., PROFESSOR OF HEBREW AND SACRED SCRIPTURE, WOODSTOCK COLLEGE, MARYLAND: Parallelism; Patrizi, Francis Xavier; Paul of Burgos; Pereira, Benedict; Perrone, Giovanni; Pesch, Tilmann.

D'SOUZA, ANTHONY XAVIER, BOMBAY, INDIA: Passos (Santos Passos).

DUBRAY, C. A., S.M., S.T.B., PH.D., PROFESSOR OF PHILOSOPHY, MARIST COLLEGE, WASHINGTON: Nourrisson, Jean-Felix.

DUHEM, PIERRE, PROFESSOR OF THEORETICAL PHYSICS, UNIVERSITY OF BORDEAUX: Oresme, Nicole.

DUNN, JOSEPH, PH.D., PROFESSOR OF CELTIC LANGUAGES AND LITERATURE, CATHOLIC UNIVERSITY OF AMERICA, WASHINGTON: O'Braein, Tighernach; O'Growney, Eugene; O'Hussey, Maelbright.

EGAN, ANDREW, O.F.M., PROFESSOR OF THEOLOGY, THE FRIARY, FOREST GATE, LONDON: Pecham, John.

ENGELHARDT, ZEPHYRIN, O.F.M., SANTA BARBARA, CALIFORNIA: Padilla, Juan de; Palou, Francisco; Pareja, Francisco; Payeras, Mariano; Perez, Juan.

ESPINOSA, AURELIO MACEDONIO, M.A., PH.D., PROFESSOR OF THE SPANISHUAENGAG L, LELAND STANFORD UNIVERSITY, SAN FRANCISCO, CALIFORNIA: New Mexico; Penitentes, Los Hermanos.

EWING, JOHN GILLESPIE, M.A., NEW YORK: Newton, John.

FANNING, WILLIAM H. W., S.J., PROFESSOR OF CHURCH HISTORY AND CANON LAW, ST. LOUIS UNIVERSITY, ST. LOUIS: Obreption; Oratory; Papal Elections; Parish, In English Speaking Countries; Pension, Ecclesiastical.

FENLON, JOHN F., S.S., S.T.D., PRESIDENT, ST. AUSTIN'S COLLEGE, WASHINGTON; PROFESSOR OF SACRED SCRIPTURE, ST. MARY'S SEMINARY, BALTIMORE: Olier, Jean-Jacques.

FERET, P. CANON, SAINT-MAURICE, FRANCE: Paris, University of.

FISCHER, JOSEPH, S.J., PROFESSOR OF GEOGRAPHY AND HISTORY, STELLA MATUTINA COLLEGE, FELDKIRCH, AUSTRIA: Nicolaus Germanus; Ortelius (Oertel), Abraham.

FLAHERTY, MATTHEW J., M.A. (HARVARD), CONCORD, MASSACHUSETTS: O'Meara, Kathleen.

FLOOD, JAMES, NEW NORCIA, AUSTRALIA: New Norcia.

FORD, JEREMIAH D. M., M.A., PH.D., PROFESSOR OF THE FRENCH AND SPANISH LANGUAGES, HARVARD UNIVERSITY, CAMBRIDGE, MASSACHUSETTS: Ojeda, Alonso de; Parini, Giuseppe; Pellico, Silvio; Petrarch, Francesco.

FORGET, JACQUES, PROFESSOR OF DOGMATIC THEOLOGY AND THE SYRIAC AND ARABIC LANGUAGES, UNIVERSITY OF LOUVAIN: Nicole, Pierre.

FORTESCUE, ADRIAN, PH.D., S.T.D., LETCHWORTH, HERTFORDSHIRE, ENGLAND: Nikon, Patriarch of Moscow; Nilus, Saint; Nilus the Younger; Nonnus; Œcumenius; Offertory; Orate Fratres; Oremus; Orientius; Orsisius; Orthodox Church; Orthodoxy, Feast of; Palladius; Patriarch and Patriarchate; Paulicians; Peter Mongus.

FOX, WILLIAM, B.Sc., M.E., ASSOCIATE PROFESSOR OF PHYSICS, COLLEGE OF THE CITY OF NEW YORK: Nollet, Jean-Antoine; Palmieri, Luigi; Peuerbach, Georg von.

FREELAND, JOHN, BEDFORD, ENGLAND: Northampton, Diocese of.

FRERI, MGR. JOSEPH, D.C.L., DIRECTOR GENERAL IN THE UNITED STATES OF THE SOCIETY FOR THE PROPAGATION OF THE FAITH, NEW YORK: Peter-Louis-Marie Chanel, Blessed.

FUENTES, VENTURA, B.A., M.D., INSTRUCTOR, COLLEGE OF THE CITY OF NEW YORK: Pérez de Hita, Ginés.

GABRIELS, HENRY, S.T.D. (LOUVAIN), BISHOP OF OGDENSBURG, NEW YORK: Ogdensburg, Diocese of.

GARESCHÉ, EDWARD FRANCIS, S.J., ST. LOUIS UNIVERSITY, ST. LOUIS: Nicholas of Tolentino, Saint; Nicolas, Armella.

GEDDES, LEONARD WILLIAM, S.J., ST. BEUNO'S COLLEGE, ST. ASAPH, WALES: Person; Personality.

GERARD, JOHN, S.J., F.L.S., LONDON: Perry, Stephen Joseph.

GEUDENS, FRANCIS MARTIN, C.R.P., ABBOT TITULAR OF BARLINGS, CORPUS CHRISTI PRIORY, MANCHESTER, ENGLAND: Norbert, Saint; Park, Abbey of the.

GHELLINCK, JOSEPH DE, PROFESSOR OF PATROLOGY AND MEDIEVAL THEOLOGICAL LITERATURE, LOUVAIN: Pétau, Denis; Peter Cantor; Peter Comestor; Peter Lombard.

GIETMANN, GERARD, S.J., TEACHER OF CLASSICAL LANGUAGES AND ÆSTHETICS, ST. IGNATIUS COLLEGE, VALKENBURG, HOLLAND: Niessenberger, Hans; Nimbus; Oppenordt, Giles-Marie; Orme, Philibert de l'; Perrault, Claude; Peruzzi, Baldassare.

GILLET, LOUIS, PARIS: Painting, Religious; Perugino.

GILLOW, EULOGIO GREGORIO, S.T.D., ARCHBISHOP OF OAXACA, MEXICO: Oaxaca, Archdiocese of.

GLOUDEN, ATHANASE, PH.D., LITT.D., PROFESSOR OF LITERATURE, COLLÈGE ST-MICHEL, EDITOR, "LE PATRIOTE", BRUSSELS: Periodical Literature, Catholic, Belgium.

GOYAU, GEORGES, ASSOCIATE EDITOR, "REVUE DES DEUX MONDES", PARIS: Nice, Diocese of; Nîmes, Diocese of; Normandy; Odo, Bishop of Bayeux; Ollé-Laprune, Léon; Oran, Diocese of; Oriflamme; Orléans, Councils of; Orléans, Diocese of; Pamiers, Diocese of; Paris, Archdiocese of; Périgueux, Diocese of; Periodical Literature, Catholic, France; Perpignan, Diocese and University of.

CONTRIBUTORS TO THE ELEVENTH VOLUME

GRATTAN-FLOOD, W. H., M.R.I.A., Mus.D., Rosemount, Enniscorthy, Ireland: O'Hagan, Thomas; O'Loghlen, Michael; O'Reilly, Myles William Patrick; Periodical Literature, Catholic, Ireland.

GREY, FRANCIS W., LL.D., Ottawa, Canada: Ottawa, University of.

HAGEN, JOHN G., S.J., Vatican Observatory, Rome: Nicholas of Cusa; Paul of Middelburg.

HANDLEY, MARIE LOUISE, New York: Niccola Pisano; Nola, Giovanni Marliano da.

HANNA, EDWARD J., S.T.D., Professor of Dogmatic Theology and Patrology, St. Bernard's Seminary, Rochester, N. Y.: Penance.

HANSEN, NIELS, M.A., Copenhagen, Denmark: Olaf Haraldson, Saint.

HARENT, STÉPHANE, S.J., Professor of Dogmatic Theology, Ore Place, Hastings, England: Original Sin.

HARTIG, OTTO, Assistant Librarian of the Royal Library, Munich: Nubia.

HASSETT, Mgr. MAURICE M., S.T.D., Harrisburg, Pennsylvania: Orans; Orientation of Churches; Palm in Christian Symbolism; Paphnutius.

HEALY, PATRICK J., S.T.D., Assistant Professor of Church History, Catholic University of America, Washington: Nicolaites; Parabolani.

HECKMANN, FERDINAND, O.F.M., Lector of Church History, Franciscan Monastery, Washington: Nicholas Pieck, Saint; Peter Baptist and Twenty-five Companions, Saints; Peter de Regalado, Saint.

HENRY, H. T., Litt.D., Rector of Roman Catholic High School for Boys, Professor of English Literature and of Gregorian Chant, St. Charles Seminary, Overbrook, Pennsylvania: Nunc Dimittis; O Antiphons; O Deus Ego Amo Te; O Filii et Filiæ; O Salutaris Hostia; Pange Lingua Gloriosi.

HERBERT, JOHN ALEXANDER, Assistant in the Department of MSS., British Museum, London: Odo of Cheriton.

HIGHLEY, MONT F., Assistant Attorney General, Oklahoma City, Oklahoma: Oklahoma.

HILGERS, JOSEPH, S.J., Rome: Novena.

HOEBER, KARL, Ph.D., Editor, "Volkszeitung" and "Akademische Monatsblätter", Cologne: Otho, Marcus Salvius; Pertinax, Publius Helvius; Pescennius Niger.

HOFMANN, MICHAEL, S.J., Professor of Canon Law, University of Innsbruck, Austria: Nilles, Nikolaus.

HOLWECK, FREDERICK G., St. Louis, Missouri: Our Lady, Help of Christians, Feast of; Paschal Tide; Passion of Christ, Commemoration of the.

HUDLESTON, GILBERT ROGER, O.S.B., Downside Abbey, Bath, England: Ninian, Saint; Obedientiaries; Odo of Cambrai, Blessed; Peterborough Abbey.

HUGHES, JAMES, Liverpool, England: Nugent, James.

HULL, ERNEST R., S.J., Editor, "The Examiner", Bombay, India: Parsis (Parsees).

HUNTER-BLAIR, SIR D. O., Bart., O.S.B., M.A., Fort Augustus Abbey, Scotland: Oxford; Oxford, University of; Periodical Literature, Catholic, Scotland.

HYDE, DOUGLAS, LL.D., Litt.D., M.R.I.A., Frenchpark, Co. Roscommon, Ireland: O'Carolan, Torlogh; O'Conor, Charles; O'Curry, Eugene; O'Daly, Donogh Mor; O'Dugan, John.

HYVERNAT, HENRY, S.T.D., Professor of Semitic Languages and Biblical Archæology, Catholic University of America, Washington: Persecutions, Coptic.

INGOLD, A. M. P., Director, "Revue d' Alsace", Colmar, Germany: Oratory, French Congregation of the.

ISENRING, JOHN JAMES, O.S.F.S., Childs, Maryland: Oblates of St. Francis de Sales; Orange River, Vicariate Apostolic of.

JARRETT, BEDE, O.P., B.A., (Oxon.); S.T.L., St. Dominic's Priory, London: Papal Arbitration.

JIMÉNEZ, ENRIQUE, S.J., Lic.Sc., Professor of Mathematics, Instituto de Artes é Industrias, Madrid: Periodical Literature, Catholic, Spain.

JONES, ARTHUR EDWARD, S.J., Corresponding Member of the Minnesota, Ontario, and Chicago Historical Societies; Hon. Member of the Missouri Historical Society; Member of the International Congress of Americanists; Archivist of St. Mary's College, Montreal: Petun Nation.

JOYCE, GEORGE HAYWARD, S.J., M.A. (Oxon.), St. Beuno's College, St. Asaph, Wales: Papacy.

JUNGUITO, F. X., Bishop of Panama: Panama, Republic and Diocese of.

KAMPERS, FRANZ, Ph.D., Professor of Medieval and Modern History, University of Breslau: Notker Physicus; Notker, nephew of Notker Physicus; Notker, Provost of St. Gall; Otto I; Otto II; Otto III; Otto IV; Pepin the Short; Peter de Vinea.

KAUFMANN, CARL MARIA, Editor "Forschungen zur Monument. Th. und vergleichenden Rel.-Wiss.", Frankfort-on-the-Main: Ostraka, Christian; Overbeck, Friedrich.

KEILY, JARVIS, M.A., Grantwood, New Jersey: Penal Laws in the English Colonies in America.

KELLY, BLANCHE M., New York: Norton, Christopher; Notre Dame de Sion, Congregation of.

KELLY, JOSEPH IGNATIUS, Ph.D., LL.D., Late Professor of Law and Dean of the Law School, Louisiana State University, Chicago, Illinois: Pandects.

KENNEDY, DANIEL J., O.P., S.T.M., Professor of Sacramental Theology, Catholic University of America, Washington: Ory, Matthieu; Paludanus, Peter; Pelargus, Ambrose; Peter of Bergamo.

CONTRIBUTORS TO THE ELEVENTH VOLUME

KENNEDY, THOMAS, B.A. (NATIONAL UNIVERSITY OF IRELAND), LONDON: New Pomerania, Vicariate Apostolic of; Osaka, Diocese of.

KIRSCH, MGR. JOHANN P., S.T.D., PROFESSOR OF PATROLOGY AND CHRISTIAN ARCHÆOLOGY, UNIVERSITY OF FRIBOURG: Nicephorus, Saint; Nicetas, Bishop of Remesiana; Nicetius, Saint, Bishop of Trier; Nicholas I, Saint, Pope; Nicomedes, Saint; Notitia Dignitatum; Notitia Provinciarum et Civitatum Africæ; Nuncio; Nunciature Reports; Odilia, Saint; Oldoini, Augustino; Olympias, Saint; Ordeals; Orosius, Paulus; Orsi, Giuseppe Agostino; Orsini; Palatini; Pallavicino, Pietro Sforza; Paschal I, Pope; Paul I, Pope; Pelagia; Peter, Saint; Peter of Sebaste, Saint; Peter Urseolus, Saint; Petronilla, Saint; Petronius, Saint; Petrus Bernardinus; Petrus de Natalibus; Philip, Saint, Apostle.

KRUITWAGEN, BONAVENTURE, O.F.M., PROFESSOR OF ECCLESIASTICAL HISTORY, CONVENT OF THE FRIARS MINOR, WOERDEN, HOLLAND: Periodical Literature, Catholic, Holland.

LAPPIN, HENRY P. A., O.C.C., CARMELITE COLLEGE, TRENURE, IRELAND: Paoli, Angelo, Venerable.

LATASTE, JOSEPH, LITT.D., SUPERIOR OF THE SEMINARY, AIRE-SUR-ADOUR, LANDES, FRANCE: Pascal, Blaise; Pellissier, Guillaume; Perraud, Adolphe; Peter of Poitiers.

LAUCHERT, FRIEDRICH, PH.D., AACHEN: Nihus, Barthold; Nikolaus von Dinkelsbühl; Œcolampadius, Johann; Ohler, Aloys Karl; Pfefferkorn, Johannes; Pfister, Adolf; Philanthropinism.

LECLERCQ, HENRI, O.S.B., LONDON: Nicæa, Councils of.

LEJAY, PAUL, FELLOW OF THE UNIVERSITY OF FRANCE, PROFESSOR, INSTITUT CATHOLIQUE, PARIS: Paulinus of Pella.

LEROY, ALEXANDER A., C.SS.P., BISHOP OF ALINDA, SUPERIOR GENERAL OF THE CONGREGATION OF THE HOLY GHOST, PARIS: Nigeria, Upper and Lower.

LETANG, H. E., B.C.L., B.D., PEMBROKE, PROVINCE OF ONTARIO, CANADA: Pembroke, Diocese of.

LETELLIER, A., S.S.S., SUPERIOR, FATHERS OF THE BLESSED SACRAMENT, NEW YORK: Perpetual Adoration, Religious of the; Perpetual Adoration, Sisters of the; Perpetual Adorers of the Blessed Sacrament.

LINDSAY, LIONEL ST. GEORGE, B.Sc., PH.D., EDITOR-IN-CHIEF, "LA NOUVELLE FRANCE", QUEBEC: Peltrie, Madeleine de la; Periodical Literature, Catholic, Canada.

LINEHAN, PAUL H., B.A., INSTRUCTOR, COLLEGE OF THE CITY OF NEW YORK: Nunez, Pedro; Ozanam, Jacques; Pacioli (Paciuolo), Lucas.

LINS, JOSEPH, FREIBURG, GERMANY: Nuremberg; Osnabrück, Diocese of; Paderborn, Diocese of; Palatinate, Rhenish; Passau, Diocese of.

LOEHR, AUGUST OCTAV RITTER VON, PH.D., ASSISTANT DIRECTOR, IMPERIAL COLLECTION OF COINS AND MEDALS, VIENNA: Numismatics.

LÖFFLER, KLEMENS, PH.D., LIBRARIAN, UNIVERSITY OF MÜNSTER: Notker, Balbulus; Notker, Labeo; Odilio, Saint; Odo, Saint, Abbot of Cluny; Ostrogoths; Otto, Saint; Overberg, Bernhard Heinrich; Pannartz, Arnold; Pantaleon, Saint; Paschasius, Saint; Paulinus, Saint, Bishop of Nola; Peasants, War of the; Periodical Literature, Catholic, Germany; Pez, Bernhard and Hieronymus; Pforta.

*LOUGHLIN, MGR. JAMES F., S.T.D., PHILADELPHIA: Paschal II, Pope; Paul III; Paul IV, Paul V, Popes; Philadelphia, Archdiocese of.

MAAS, A. J., S.J., RECTOR, WOODSTOCK COLLEGE, MARYLAND: Pentateuch.

MacERLEAN, ANDREW A., NEW YORK: Northern Territory, Prefecture Apostolic of the; Nyassa, Vicariate Apostolic of; Olinda, Diocese of; Pasto, Diocese of; Pelotas, Diocese of; Perth, Diocese of.

MacERLEAN, JOHN, S.J., PROFESSOR OF HEBREW AND ECCLESIASTICAL HISTORY, JESUIT SCHOLASTICATE, MILLTOWN PARK, DUBLIN: O'Bruadair, David.

McGAHAN, FLORENCE RUDGE, M.A., YOUNGSTOWN, OHIO: Paulists; Penitential Orders; Penitents, Confraternities of.

McGUIRE, EDWARD J., M.A., LL.B., NEW YORK: New York, State of.

McHUGH, JOHN AMBROSE, O.P., S.T.D., LECTOR OF PHILOSOPHY, DOMINICAN HOUSE OF STUDIES, WASHINGTON: Omnipotence.

McKENNA, CHARLES F., PH.D. (COLUMBIA), VICE-PRESIDENT, CATHOLIC HOME BUREAU, NEW YORK: Orphans and Orphanages.

McNEILL, CHARLES, DUBLIN: O'Brien, Terence Albert; O'Cullenan, Gelasius; O'Devany, Cornelius; O'Donnell, Edmund; O'Hely, Patrick; O'Herlahy, Thomas; O'Hurley, Dermod; O'Queely, Malachias.

MACPHERSON, EWAN, NEW YORK: Nicaragua, Republic and Diocese of.

MacSHERRY, HUGH, TITULAR BISHOP OF JUSTINIANOPOLIS, VICAR APOSTOLIC OF EASTERN DISTRICT OF THE CAPE OF GOOD HOPE: Orange Free State.

MacSWEENEY, PATRICK, M.A. (N.U.I.), LECTURER IN ENGLISH, MAYNOOTH COLLEGE; PROFESSOR OF MODERN LITERATURE, HOLY CROSS COLLEGE, CLONLIFFE, DUBLIN: O'Donovan, John.

MAGNIER, JOHN, C.SS.R., LONDON: Passerat, John, Venerable; Perpetual Succour, Our Lady of.

MANN, HORACE K., HEADMASTER, ST. CUTHBERT'S GRAMMAR SCHOOL, NEWCASTLE-ON-TYNE, ENGLAND: Pelagius I, Pope; Pelagius II.

MARIQUE, PIERRE JOSEPH, INSTRUCTOR IN FRENCH, COLLEGE OF THE CITY OF NEW YORK: Nothomb, Jean-Baptiste.

MARSH, ERNEST, S.C., NEW YORK: Patagonia.

MARTIN, CAROLINE L., REL. OF THE PERPETUAL ADOR., WASHINGTON: Perpetual Adoration, Religious of the.

* Deceased.

CONTRIBUTORS TO THE ELEVENTH VOLUME

MARTINDALE, CYRIL C., S.J., B.A. (Oxon.), Ore Place, Hastings, England: Oracle; Paganism.

MARY JOSEPHINE, SISTER, Notre Dame Convent, Milwaukee, Wisconsin: Notre Dame, School Sisters of.

MEEHAN, ANDREW B., S.T.D., J.U.D., Professor of Canon Law and Liturgy, St. Bernard's Seminary, Rochester, New York: Pall; Pax.

MEEHAN, THOMAS F., New York: Oertel, John James Maximilian; O'Hara, Theodore; O'Higgins, Ambrose Bernard; O'Reilly, Bernard; O'Rorke, Patrick Henry; Parmentier, Antoine-Augustin; Periodical Literature, Catholic, United States; Peter, Sarah.

MERSHMAN, FRANCIS, O.S.B., S.T.D., Professor of Moral Theology, Canon Law and Liturgy, St. John's College, Collegeville, Minnesota: Othlo; Otto of Passau; Palm Sunday; Passion Offices; Passion Sunday; Passiontide; Patronage of Our Lady, Feast of the; Peter Gonzales, Saint; Pflug, Julius von.

MEYNELL, ALICE, London: Patmore, Coventry.

MIDDLETON, THOMAS COOKE, O.S.A., S.T.M., Lector in Philosophy, Villanova College, Pennsylvania: Our Lady of Good Counsel, Feast of.

MOLONEY, WILLIAM A., C.S.C., Notre Dame, Indiana: Notre Dame du Lac, University of.

MOONEY, JAMES, United States Ethnologist, Bureau of American Ethnology, Washington: Pakawá Indians; Pano Indians; Pápago Indians; Pcba Indians; Penelakut Indians; Penobscot Indians; Peoria Indians; Pericui Indians.

MOONEY, JOSEPH F., LL.D., Ph.D., Prothonotary Apostolic, Vicar-General of the Archdiocese of New York: New York, Archdiocese of.

MOORE, THOMAS V., C.S.P., St. Thomas College, Washington: Occasionalism; Optimism; Panpsychism.

MORAN, PATRICK FRANCIS CARDINAL, Archbishop of Sydney, Primate of Australia: Palladius, Saint; Patrick, Saint.

MORENO-LACALLE, JULIAN, B.A., Editor, "Pan-American Union", Washington: Paraguay; Peru.

MULLALY, CHARLES, S.J., Tortosa, Spain: Oriol, Joseph, Saint.

O'BOYLE, FRANCIS JOSEPH, S.J., St. Louis University, St. Louis: Omer, Saint.

OBRECHT, EDMOND M., O.C.R., Abbot of Gethsemani, Kentucky: Obazine, Monastery of.

O'CONNOR, JOHN B., O.P., St. Louis Bertrand's Convent, Louisville, Kentucky: Nicholas of Gorran.

O'CONNOR, RICHARD ALPHONSUS, S.T.D., Bishop of Peterborough, Province of Ontario, Canada: Peterborough, Diocese of.

O'HAGAN, THOMAS, M.A., Ph.D., Chicago, Illinois: Pardons of Brittany.

O'HARA, EDWIN V., Portland, Oregon: Oregon; Oregon City, Archdiocese of.

OJETTI, BENEDETTO, S.J., Consultor, S.C.P.F., Consultor, S.C.C., Consultor of the Commission on the Codification of Canon Law, Gregorian University, Rome: Palmieri, Domenico.

O'LEARY, EDWARD, M.R.I.A., Portarlington, Ireland: O'Leary, Arthur.

OLIGER, LIVARIUS, O.F.M., Lector of Ecclesiastical History, Collegio S. Antonio, Rome: Nicholas of Osimo; Obregonians; Olivi, Pierre Jean; Pacificus; Panigarola, Francesco; Papini, Nicholas; Parkinson, Anthony; Paulinus a St. Bartholomæo; Peter of Aquila.

OTT, MICHAEL, O.S.B., Ph.D., Professor of the History of Philosophy, St. John's College, Collegeville, Minnesota: Nicholas Justinani, Blessed; Nicholas of Flüe, Blessed; Nicholas of Myra, Saint; Nirschl, Joseph; Nonontola; Notburga, Saint; Odo of Glanfeuil; Oettingen; Oil of Saints; Olesnicki, Zbigniew; Oliva; Orlandini, Niccolò; Orval; Othmar, Saint; Ottobeuren; Our Lady of the Snow, Feast of; Pagi, Antoine; Palafox y Mendoza, Juan de; Panvinio, Onofrio; Peter Cellensis; Peter Fullo; Petit-Didier, Matthieu.

OTTEN, JOSEPH, Pittsburg, Pennsylvania: Okeghem, Jean d'; Oratorio; Palestrina, Giovanni Pierluigi da; Passion Music; Pergolesi, Giovanni Battista; Petrucci, Ottavio dei.

OUSSANI, GABRIEL, Ph.D., Professor, Ecclesiastical History, Early Christian Literature, and Biblical Archæology, St. Joseph's Seminary, Dunwoodie, New York: Persia.

PACE, EDWARD A., Ph.D., S.T.D., Professor of Philosophy, Catholic University of America, Washington: Pantheism.

PALMIERI, AURELIO, O.S.A., S.T.D., Rome: Nihilism; Periodical Literature, Catholic, Poland.

PAPI, HECTOR, S.J., Ph.D., B.C.L., S.T.D., Professor of Canon Law, Woodstock College, Maryland: Pastor.

PARKER, E. STANISLAUS ANSELM, O.S.B., M.A., Master of Parker's Hall, Oxford: Norfolk, Catholic Dukes of; Odo of Canterbury; Osbald; Osbern; Osmund, Saint; Oswald, Saint, Archbishop of York; Oswald, Saint, King; Oswin, Saint; Owen, Nicholas.

PARKINSON, HENRY, S.T.D., Ph.D., Rector, Oscott College, Birmingham, England: Oscott (St. Mary's College); Patron Saints.

PARSONS, J. WILFRID, S.J., Boston: Oostacker, Shrine of.

PÉREZ GOYENA, ANTONIO, S.J., Editor, "Razón y Fe", Madrid: Nieremberg y Otin, Juan Eusebio.

*PÉTRIDÈS, SOPHRONE, A.A., Professor, Greek Catholic Seminary of Kadi-Keui, Constantinople: Nyssa; Obba; Olba; Olympus; Orcistus; Pacandus; Paleopolis; Panemotichus; Parætonium; Parlais; Parnassus; Parœcopolis; Patara; Pednelissus; Perge; Pessinus; Petinessus; Phaselis; Philadelphia.

* Deceased.

CONTRIBUTORS TO THE ELEVENTH VOLUME

PFEIL, NICHOLAS, B.A., Cleveland, Ohio: Notre Dame, Sisters of (Cleveland).

PHILLIMORE, JOHN SWINNERTON, M.A. (Oxon.), Professor of Humanities, University of Glasgow: Paley, Frederick Apthorp.

PHILLIPS, EDWARD C., S.J., Ph.D., Woodstock College, Maryland: Odington, Walter; Oriani, Barnaba; Pardies, Ignace-Gaston.

PILCZ, ALEXANDER, Member of the French Academy, Extraordinary Professor, University of Vienna: Pathology, Mental.

PLASSMAN, THOMAS, O.F.M., Ph.D., S.T.D., St. Bonaventure's Seminary, St. Bonaventure, New York: Nicholas of Lyra.

POHLE, JOSEPH, S.T.D., Ph.D., J.C.L., Professor of Dogmatic Theology, University of Breslau: Paschasius Radbertus, Saint; Pelagius and Pelagianism.

POINTS, MARIE LOUISE, Editor, "The Morning Star", New Orleans, Louisiana: New Orleans, Archdiocese of.

POLLEN, JOHN H., S.J., London: Oaths, English Post-Reformation; Odescalchi, Carlo; Oldcorne, Edward, Venerable; Percy, John; Persons, Robert; Petre Family.

POYET, CLAUDIO, Paraná, Argentine Republic: Paraná, Diocese of.

PRAT, FERDINAND, S.J., Member of the Biblical Commission, Collège St. Michel, Brussels: Origen and Origenism; Paul, Saint.

PRESTAGE, EDGAR, B.A. (Oxon.), Commendador, Portuguese Order of S. Thiago; Corresponding Member of the Lisbon Royal Academy of Sciences and the Lisbon Geographical Society, Bowdon, England: Oporto, Diocese of; Periodical Literature, Catholic, Portugal.

RANDOLPH, BARTHOLOMEW, C.M., M.A., Teacher of Philosophy and Church History, St. John's College, Brooklyn, New York: Odin, John Mary.

REAGAN, P. NICHOLAS, O.F.M., Collegio S. Antonio, Rome: Peter of Alcántara, Saint.

REILLY, THOMAS À KEMPIS, O.P., S.T.L., S.S.L., Professor of Sacred Scripture, Dominican House of Studies, Washington: Nicholas of Strasburg; Pagnino, Santes.

REMY, ARTHUR F. J., M.A., Ph.D., Adjunct-Professor of Germanic Philology, Columbia University, New York: Otfried of Weissenburg; Peutinger, Conrad.

ROMPEL, JOSEF HEINRICH, S.J., Ph.D., Stella Matutina College, Feldkirch, Austria: Parlatore, Filippo.

RUSSELL, MATTHEW, S.J., Dublin; O'Hagan, John; O'Reilly, Edmund.

SACHER, HERMANN, Ph.D., Editor, "Konversationslexikon", Assistant Editor, "Staatslexikon" of the Görresgesellschaft, Freiburg, Germany: Oldenburg.

SÄGMÜLLER, JOHANNES BAPTIST, Professor of Theology, University of Tübingen: Patron and Patronage.

ST. EUPHROSINE, SISTER, Montreal: Notre Dame de Montreal, Congregation of.

ST. IGNACE DE LOYOLA, SISTER, St. Damien, Province of Quebec, Canada: Perpetual Help, Sisters of Our Lady of.

SALTET, LOUIS, S.T.D., Litt.Lic., Professor of Church History, Institut Catholique, Toulouse, France: Paula, Saint.

SALZER, ANSELM, O.S.B., Seitenstetten, Austria: Passion Plays.

SAUVAGE, G. M., C.S.C., S.T.D., Ph.D., Professor of Dogmatic Theology, Holy Cross College, Washington: Ontologism; Pelisson-Fontanier, Paul; Perreyve, Henri.

SCANNELL, THOMAS B. CANON, S.T.D., Weybridge, England: Nicholas V, Pope.

SCHEID, N., S.J., Stella Matutina College, Feldkirch, Austria: Pauli, Johannes.

SCHEUER, PIERRE, S.J., Professor of Philosophy, College of St. John Berchmans, Louvain: Para du Phanjas, François.

SCHLAGER, HEINRICH PATRICIUS, O.F.M., St. Ludwig's College, Dalheim, Germany: Nithard; Nuyens, Wilhelmus; Ostiensis; Otto of Freising; Otto of St. Blaise; Paulus Diaconus.

SCHROEDER, JOSEPH, O.P., St. Dominic's Priory, Benicia, California: Nicolaï, Jean; Niger, Peter George.

SCHWICKERATH, ROBERT, S.J., Holy Cross College, Worcester, Massachusetts: Pachtler, Georg Michael; Pestalozzi and Pestalozzianism.

SCOTT, JOHN ASKEW, M.A., LL.B., Editor, "New Zealand Tablet", Dunedin, New Zealand: New Zealand.

SENFELDER, LEOPOLD, M.D., Teacher of the History of Medicine, University of Vienna: Paracelsus, Theophrastus; Peré, Ambroise.

SHANNON, JAMES, Peoria, Illinois: Peoria, Diocese of.

SHARPE, ALFRED BOWYER, M.A. (Oxon.), London: Pessimism.

SIEGFRIED, FRANCIS PATRICK, Professor of Philosophy, St. Charles Seminary, Overbrook, Pennsylvania: Ontology.

SLATER, T., S.J., St. Beuno's College, St. Asaph, Wales: Obligation.

SLOANE, CHARLES WILLIAM, New York: O'Conor, Charles; Partnership.

SLOANE, THOMAS O'CONNOR, M.A., E.M., Ph.D., New York: Pelletier, Pierre-Joseph; Pelouze, Théophile-Jules.

SMITH, IGNATIUS, O.P., Dominican House of Studies, Washington: Nider, John; Peter Chrysologus, Saint.

SMITH, SYDNEY F., S.J., London: Nonconformists; Non-Jurors.

SMITH, WALTER GEORGE, M.A., LL.B. (U. of P.), Philadelphia: Peace Congresses; Pennsylvania.

SOLLIER, JOSEPH FRANCIS, S.M., S.T.D., San Francisco: Paraclete; Pavillon, Nicolas; Perseverance, Final.

CONTRIBUTORS TO THE ELEVENTH VOLUME

SORTAIS, GASTON, S.J., Assistant Editor, "Etudes", Paris: Orcagna (Andrea di Cione); Palma Vecchio; Parmigiano, Il.

SOUVAY, CHARLES L., C.M., S.T.D., Ph.D., Professor of Sacred Scripture, Hebrew, and Liturgy, Kenrick Seminary, St. Louis: Offerings (Oblations); Olivet, Mount; Ophir; Parasceve; Patmos; Pentapolis; Pentecost (of the Jews), Feast of; Phasga.

STANISFORTH, OSWALD, O.M.Cap., Lector of Dogmatic Theology and Sacred Scripture, Capuchin Monastery, Olton, England: Pascal Baylon, Saint.

SUAU, PIERRE, S.J., Castres, France: Olivaint, Pierre; Peter Claver, Saint; Peter Faber, Blessed.

TACCHI VENTURI, LUIGI, LL.D., Commendatore of the Order of the Crown of Italy, Rome: Oliva, Gian Paolo.

THURSTON, HERBERT, S.J., London: Numbers, Use of, in the Church; Ordines Romani; Ostensorium; Paris, Matthew; Paschal Candle; Passion of Jesus Christ, Devotion to the; Paten; Peterspence.

TIERNEY, JOHN J., M.A., S.T.D., Professor of Sacred Scripture and Semitic Studies, Mt. St. Mary's College, Emmitsburg, Maryland: New Year's Day.

TOKE, LESLIE ALEXANDER ST. LAWRENCE, B.A., Stratton-on-the-Fosse, Bath, England: Peter Damian, Saint.

TOURSCHER, FRANCIS E., O.S.A., Regent, St. Thomas's College, Villanova, Pennsylvania: Noris, Henry; Paulus Venetus.

TRABERT, WILHELM, Ph.D., Director of the Imperial Royal Central Institute of Meteorology and Geodynamics, Vienna: Pernter, Joseph Maria.

URIBE, ANTONIO JOSÉ, Bogotá, Colombia: Nueva Pamplona, Diocese of.

URQUHART F. F., Fellow and Lecturer in Modern History, Balliol College, Oxford: Northmen; Ordericus Vitalis.

VAILHÉ, SIMÉON, A.A., Member of the Russian Archæological Institute of Constantinople, Professor of Sacred Scripture and History, Greek Catholic Seminary of Kadi-Keui, Constantinople: Nicæa; Nicomedia; Nicopolis (Armenia); Nicopolis, Diocese of; Nicopolis (Epirus); Nicosia, Titular Archdiocese of; Nilopolis; Nisibis; Notitiæ Episcopatuum; Olenus; Ombus; Oropus; Orthosia; Ostracina; Oxyrynchus; Palmyra; Paltus; Panopolis; Paphos; Paralus; Parium; Patras; Pella; Pelusium; Pentacomia; Pergamus; Petra; Phacusa; Pharbætus; Pharsalus.

VAN DER ESSEN, LÉON, Litt.D., Ph.D., Professor of History, University of Louvain: Pamelius.

VAN DER HEEREN, ACHILLE, S.T.L. (Louvain), Professor of Moral Theology and Librarian, Grande Séminaire, Bruges, Belgium: Oaths; Peter, Epistles of Saint.

VAN HOVE, A., D.C.L., Professor of Church History and Canon Law, University of Louvain: Nicolò de' Tudeschi; Œconomus, Episcopal; Option, Right of; Paleotti, Gabriel; Papiensis, Bernardus; Peña, Francisco; Person, Ecclesiastical.

VERMEERSCH, ARTHUR, S.J., LL.D., Doctor of Social and Political Sciences, Professor of Moral Theology and Canon Law, College of St. John Berchmans, Louvain: Novice; Nuns; Obedience, Religious.

VOGEL, JOHN, Vicar Provincial of the Pious Society of Missions, Brooklyn, New York: Pollotti, Vincent Mary, Venerable.

WAAGEN, LUKAS, Assistant State Geologist, Vienna: Palæontology.

WAINEWRIGHT, JOHN BANNERMAN, B.A. (Oxon.), London: Nichols, George, Venerable; Nutter, Robert, Venerable; Osbaldeston, Edward, Venerable; Page, Anthony, Venerable; Palasor, Thomas, Venerable; Patenson, William, Venerable.

WALKER, LESLIE J., S.J., M.A. (Lond.), St. Beuno's College, St. Asaph, Wales: Parallelism, Psycho-Physical.

WALSH, JAMES J., M.D., Ph.D., LL.D., Dean of the Medical School, Fordham University, New York: Nussbaum, Johann Nepomuk von; O'Dwyer, Joseph; Pasteur, Louis.

WALSH, REGINALD, O.P., S.T.D., Professor of Theology, S. Clemente, Rome: O'Daly, Daniel.

WARD, Mgr. BERNARD, Canon of Westminster, F.R.Hist.Soc., President, St. Edmund's College, Ware, England: Oakeley, Frederick; Old Chapter, The; Oliver, George; Oxenham, Henry Nutcombe.

WARREN, KATE MARY, Lecturer in English under University of London at Westfield College, Hampstead, London: Occleve, Thomas; Oxenford, John.

WEBER, N. A., S.M., S.T.D., Professor of Fundamental Theology and Church History, Marist College, Washington: Nicholas II, Nicholas III, Nicholas IV, Popes; Orange, Councils of; Paul II, Pope; Permaneder, Franz Michael; Peter Igneus, Blessed; Petrobrusians; Petrus, Diaconus; Petrus Alfonsus.

WEIMAR, ANTON, Vienna: Periodical Literature, Catholic, Austria.

WELCH, SIDNEY READ, S.T.D., Ph.D., J.P., Editor, "The Catholic Magazine for South Africa", Cape Town: Pfanner, Franz.

WILHELM, JOSEPH, S.T.D., Ph.D., Battle, England: Nicene and Niceno-Constantinopolitan Creed.

WILLIAMSON, GEORGE CHARLES, Litt.D., London: Oggione, Marco D'; Orley, Barent van; Ortolano Ferrarese; Passignano, Domenico.

WITTMANN, PIUS, Counsellor for the Archives and Archivist for Prince Ysenburg-Büdingen, Royal Bavarian Counsellor for the Archives, Büdingen, Germany: Norway; Orkneys.

WOLFSGRUBER, COELESTINE, O.S.B., Vienna: Olmütz, Archdiocese of; Parenzo-Pola, Diocese of.

ZELLE, JOSEPH, S.J., Paray-le-Monial, France: Paray-le-Monial.

ZEVELY, J., New York: Petropolis, Diocese of.

xii

Tables of Abbreviations

The following tables and notes are intended to guide readers of THE CATHOLIC ENCYCLOPEDIA in interpreting those abbreviations, signs, or technical phrases which, for economy of space, will be most frequently used in the work. For more general information see the article ABBREVIATIONS, ECCLESIASTICAL.

I.—GENERAL ABBREVIATIONS.

a. . . . . article.
ad an. . . . . at the year (Lat. *ad annum*).
an., ann. . . . . the year, the years (Lat. *annus, anni*).
ap. . . . . in (Lat. *apud*).
art. . . . . article.
Assyr. . . . . Assyrian.
A. S. . . . . Anglo-Saxon.
A. V. . . . . Authorized Version (i.e. tr. of the Bible authorized for use in the Anglican Church—the so-called "King James", *or* "Protestant Bible").
b. . . . . born.
Bk. . . . . Book.
Bl. . . . . Blessed.
C., c. . . . . about (Lat. *circa*); canon; chapter; *compagnie*.
can. . . . . canon.
cap. . . . . chapter (Lat. *caput*—used only in Latin context).
cf. . . . . compare (Lat. *confer*).
cod. . . . . codex.
col. . . . . column.
concl. . . . . conclusion.
const., constit. . . . Lat. *constitutio*.
curâ. . . . . by the industry of.
d. . . . . died.
dict. . . . . dictionary (Fr. *dictionnaire*).
disp. . . . . Lat. *disputatio*.
diss. . . . . Lat. *dissertatio*.
dist. . . . . Lat. *distinctio*.
D. V. . . . . Douay Version.
ed., edit. . . . . edited, edition, editor.
Ep., Epp. . . . . letter, letters (Lat. *epistola*).
Fr. . . . . French.
gen. . . . . genus.
Gr. . . . . Greek.
H. E., Hist. Eccl. . Ecclesiastical History.
Heb., Hebr. . . . . . . Hebrew.
ib., ibid. . . . . in the same place (Lat. *ibidem*).
Id. . . . . the same person, *or* author (Lat. *idem*).

inf. . . . . below (Lat. *infra*).
It. . . . . Italian.
l. c., loc. cit. . . . . . at the place quoted (Lat. *loco citato*).
Lat. . . . . Latin.
lat. . . . . latitude.
lib. . . . . book (Lat. *liber*).
long. . . . . longitude.
Mon. . . . . Lat. *Monumenta*.
MS., MSS. . . . . . . manuscript, manuscripts.
n., no. . . . . number.
N. T. . . . . New Testament.
Nat. . . . . National.
Old Fr., O. Fr. . . . Old French.
op. cit. . . . . in the work quoted (Lat. *opere citato*).
Ord. . . . . Order.
O. T. . . . . Old Testament.
p., pp. . . . . page, pages, *or* (in Latin references) *pars* (part).
par. . . . . paragraph.
passim. . . . . in various places.
pt. . . . . part.
Q. . . . . Quarterly (a periodical), e.g. "Church Quarterly".
Q., QQ., quæst. . . question, questions (Lat. *quæstio*).
q. v. . . . . which [title] see (Lat. *quod vide*).
Rev. . . . . Review (a periodical).
R. S. . . . . Rolls Series.
R. V. . . . . Revised Version.
S., SS. . . . . Lat. *Sanctus, Sancti*, "Saint", "Saints"—used in this Encyclopedia only in Latin context.
Sept. . . . . Septuagint.
Sess. . . . . Session.
Skt. . . . . Sanskrit.
Sp. . . . . Spanish.
sq., sqq. . . . . following page, *or* pages (Lat. *sequens*).
St., Sts. . . . . Saint, Saints.
sup. . . . . Above (Lat. *supra*).
s. v. . . . . Under the corresponding title (Lat. *sub voce*).
tom. . . . . volume (Lat. *tomus*).

TABLES OF ABBREVIATIONS.

tr. . . . . translation *or* translated. By itself it means "English translation", *or* "translated into English by". Where a translation is into any other language, the language is stated.
tr., tract . . . . tractate.
v. . . . . see (Lat. *vide*).
Ven. . . . . Venerable.
Vol. . . . . Volume.

II.—Abbreviations of Titles.

Acta SS. . . . . *Acta Sanctorum* (Bollandists).
Ann. pont. cath. . . . . Battandier, *Annuaire pontifical catholique.*
Bibl. Dict. Eng. Cath. Gillow, Bibliographical Dictionary of the English Catholics.
Dict. Christ. Antiq. . . Smith and Cheetham (ed.), Dictionary of Christian Antiquities.
Dict. Christ. Biog. . . . Smith and Wace (ed.), Dictionary of Christian Biography.
Dict. d'arch. chrét. . . . Cabrol (ed.), *Dictionnaire d'archéologie chrétienne et de liturgie.*
Dict. de théol. cath. . . Vacant and Mangenot (ed.), *Dictionnaire de théologie catholique.*
Dict. Nat. Biog. . . . . Stephen and Lee (ed.), Dictionary of National Biography.
Hast., Dict. of the Bible . . . . Hastings (ed.), A Dictionary of the Bible.
Kirchenlex. . . . . Wetzer and Welte, *Kirchenlexicon.*
P. G. . . . . Migne (ed.), *Patres Græci.*
P. L. . . . . Migne (ed.), *Patres Latini.*
Vig., Dict. de la Bible. Vigouroux (ed.), *Dictionnaire de la Bible.*

Note I.—Large Roman numerals standing alone indicate volumes. Small Roman numerals standing alone indicate chapters. Arabic numerals standing alone indicate pages. In other cases the divisions are explicitly stated. Thus "Rashdall, Universities of Europe, I, ix" refers the reader to the ninth chapter of the first volume of that work; "I, p. ix" would indicate the ninth page of the preface of the same volume.

Note II.—Where St. Thomas (Aquinas) is cited without the name of any particular work the reference is always to "Summa Theologica" (not to "Summa Philosophiæ"). The divisions of the "Summa Theol." are indicated by a system which may best be understood by the following example: "I-II, Q. vi, a. 7, ad 2 um" refers the reader to the *seventh* article of the *sixth* question in the *first* part of the *second* part, in the response to the *second* objection.

Note III.—The abbreviations employed for the various books of the Bible are obvious. Ecclesiasticus is indicated by *Ecclus.*, to distinguish it from Ecclesiastes (*Eccles.*). It should also be noted that I and II Kings in D. V. correspond to I and II Samuel in A. V.; and I and II Par. to I and II Chronicles. Where, in the spelling of a proper name, there is a marked difference between the D. V. and the A. V., the form found in the latter is added, in parentheses.

Full Page Illustrations in Volume XI

	PAGE
New Orleans—St. Roch's Chapel and Cemetery, etc.	14
St. Patrick's Cathedral, New York	26
Norwich Cathedral	122
Typical Coins of Twenty-five Centuries	152
Daniel O'Connell	202
Church of Santa Maria de Naranco, Oviedo	364
Oxford—Balliol, Christ Church, the Sheldonian, and Brasenose	368
Basilica of S. Antonio, commonly called The Santo, Padua	384
The Empress Theodora and her Suite	394
Altar-piece of the Lamb, Hubert and Jan Van Eyck, Ghent	398
Among the Lowly—Léon Lhermitte	402
Cathedral, Palencia	416
Cathedral, Palermo	420
Notre-Dame de Paris	494
Cathedral and Baptistery, Parma	504
The Crucifixion—From the Passion Play of Oberammergau	530
Louis Pasteur in his Laboratory—A. Edelfelt	536
St. Paul—Ribera (Spagnoletto)	572
Paul III and his Nephews, Alessandro and Ottavio Farnese—Titian	578
The Certosa, near Pavia	592
Perugia—The Porta Urbica Etrusca, etc.	736
Perugino—Madonna with Four Saints, etc.	738
St. Peter—Ribera (Spagnoletto)	750
Blessed Peter Canisius—C. Fracassini	758

Coloured Plates

St. Genevieve—Puvis de Chavannes	486
St. Peter Martyr Enjoining Silence—Fra Angelico	772
Triumph of Fame	780

Map

Panama	438

THE CATHOLIC ENCYCLOPEDIA

N

New Mexico, a territory of the United States now (Jan., 1911) awaiting only the completion of its Constitution and the acceptance thereof by the Federal authorities to rank as a state. It lies between 31° 20' and 37° N. lat., and between 103° 2' and 109° 2' W. long.; it is bounded on the north by Colorado, on the east by Oklahoma and Texas, on the south by Texas and the Republic of Mexico, and on the west by Arizona. It is about 370 miles from east to west, 335 from north to south, and has an area of 122,580 sq. miles, with mountain, plateau, and valley on either side of the Rio Grande. The average rainfall is 12 inches, usually between July and September, so that spring and summer are dry, and agriculture and grazing suffer. The climate is uniform, the summers, as a rule, moderate, and, the atmosphere being dry, the heat is not oppressive. In the north-west and north-east the winters are long, but not severe, while in the central and southern portions the winters are usually short and mild. In the United States census of 1900 the population was 141,282, of which 33 per cent was illiterate; in the census of 1910 the population was 327,396. About one-half of the inhabitants are of Spanish descent.

The soil in the valleys is a rich and sandy loam, capable, with irrigation, of producing good crops. It is also rich in gold and silver, and important mines have been opened near Deming, Silver City, and Lordsburg, in the south-western part of the state. There are copper mines near Glorieta in the north, and near Santa Rita in the south; while coal is found in great abundance near Gallup, Cerillos, and in the north-west. The mineral production of New Mexico for 1907 was $7,517,843, that of coal alone amounting to $3,832,128. In 1909 the net product in coal, shipped from the mines, was 2,708,624 tons, or a total value of $3,881,508. A few forests exist in the eastern plains, and abundant timber is found in the north-western and central districts. Though mining and commerce as well as agriculture are now in process of rapid development, New Mexico is still a grazing country. Sheep-farming is the most important and lucrative industry; cattle-farming is also of importance. In 1908 and 1909 severe droughts caused the sheep industry to decline somewhat. In 1909 New Mexico shipped 700,800 head of sheep; in 1908, 835,800; in 1907, 975,800. The wool shorn in 1909, from over 4,000,000 sheep, was 18,000,000 lbs., which brought an average of 19 cents per lb., yielding a cash production of $3,420,000. The shipments of cattle in the same year amounted to 310,326, and 64,380 hides were handled in the same period. Farming is successfully carried on in the Rio Grande and other valleys, Indian corn, wheat, and garden products being the principal crops. For the year 1907 the territorial governnor's report placed the value of the agricultural products at $25,000,000, but this was a gross overestimate. The important manufacturing interests are those connected with mining, railroads, etc. Lumbering is being developed by capital brought from the East, and large lumber mills are now in operation, notably at Albuquerque. There are 75 banks (41 national and 34 territorial) in the state, with an aggregate capital of $3,274,086. The bonded debt of the state is $1,002,000, of which $89,579.49 is covered by the sinking fund.

GENERAL HISTORY.—In April, 1536, there arrived at Culiacán, in the Mexican Province of Sinaloa, Alvar Núñez Cabeza de Vaca, Andrés Dorantes, Alonso del Castillo Maldonado, and the negro Estevanico, the only survivors of the ill-fated expedition of Narváez which had left Spain in 1528. Mendoza, the Viceroy of Mexico was told astonishing tales by Cabeza de Vaca concerning the wealth of the country to the north, and he forthwith commanded Coronado, governor of the Province of Nueva Galicia, to prepare an expedition.

SEAL OF NEW MEXICO

The preparations went slowly, and Mendoza ordered Friar Marcos de Niza to make a preliminary exploration of the northern country. The Franciscan left Culiacán in 1539, accompanied by Estevanico and a few Indians. After untold hardships he reached the famous *pueblo* of Zuñi, took possession of all the surrounding country, planted the cross, and named the territory "The New Kingdom of St. Francis". Marcos de Niza is, therefore, rightly called the discoverer of New Mexico and Arizona. He then returned to Mexico, and his narrative, especially what he said about the seven cities of Cibola, was an incentive to Coronado, who set out from Culiacán in 1540, accompanied by Marcos and a large body of Spaniards and Indians. Coronado crossed Sonora (now Arizona) and entered New Mexico in July, 1540. The expedition returned in 1542, but, although many regions were discovered, no conquests were made nor colonies established. In 1563 an expedition was led into New Mexico by Francisco de Ibarra: it is worth mentioning only for the reason that de Ibarra returned in 1565 with the boast that he had discovered "a new Mexico", which was, probably, the origin of the name. Espejo entered New Mexico in 1581, but accomplished nothing. In this same year a Franciscan Friar, Augustín Rodríguez, entered with a few companions, and lost his life in the cause of Christianity. In 1581 Espejo called New Mexico Nueva Andalucia. By 1598 the name Nuevo Méjico was evidently well known, since Villagrá's epic is called "Historia del Nuevo Méjico".

The expeditions of Espejo and Father Agustín Rodríguez were followed by many more of an unimportant character, and it was not until 1598, when Don Juan de Oñate, accompanied by ten Franciscans under Father Alonso Martínez, and four hundred men, of whom one hundred and thirty were accompanied by their wives and families, marched up alongside the Rio Grande, and settled at San Juan de los Caballeros, near the junction of the Chama with the Rio Grande, thirty miles north of Santa Fé. This was the first permanent Spanish settlement in New Mexico. Here was established, also, the first mission, and San Juan de los Caballeros (or San Gabriel a few miles west on the Chama river?) was the capital of the new province until it was moved to Santa Fé some time between 1602 and 1616. The colony prospered, missions were established by the Franciscans, new colonists arrived, and by the middle of the seventeenth century general prosperity prevailed. In the year 1680, however, a terrible Indian rebellion broke out under the leadership of Pope, an Indian of the *pueblo* of San Juan. All the Spanish settlements were attacked, and many people massacred. The survivors fled to Santa Fé, but, after three days' fighting, were compelled to abandon the city and were driven out of the province.

Thus was destroyed the work of eighty years. The Spaniards did not lose courage: between 1691 and 1693 Antonio de Vargas reconquered New Mexico and entered it with many of the old colonists and many more new ones, his entire colony consisting of 800 people, including seventy families and 200 soldiers. The old villages were occupied, churches rebuilt, and the missions re-established. A new *villa* was founded, Santa Cruz de la Cañada, around which most of the families which had come with De Vargas under Padre Farfán were settled. The colonies, no longer seriously threatened by the Indians, progressed slowly. By the end of the eighteenth century the population of New Mexico was about 34,000, one-half Spaniards. The first half of the nineteenth century was a period of revolutions—rapid transformations of government and foreign invasions, accepted by the Spanish inhabitants of New Mexico in an easy-going spirit of submission unparalleled in history.

In 1821 the news of Mexican independence was received, and, although the people of New Mexico were ignorant of the events which had preceded it, and knew absolutely nothing of the situation, they celebrated the event with great enthusiasm and swore allegiance to Iturbide. In 1824, just three years after independence, came the news of the fall of Iturbide and the inauguration of the Republic of Mexico: throngs gathered at Santa Fé, the people were harangued, and the new regime was applauded as a blessing to New Mexico. When war was declared between the United States and Mexico—an event concerning which the New Mexicans were ignorant—General Stephen Watts Kearny was sent to conquer New Mexico. In 1846 he entered the territory, and General Armijo, the local military chief, fled to Mexico. Kearny took possession of the territory in the name of the United States, promising the people all the rights and liberties which other citizens of the United States enjoyed. The people joyfully accepted American rule, and swore obedience to the Stars and Stripes. At one stroke, no one knew why or how, a Spanish colony, after existing under Spanish institutions for nearly three centuries, was brought under the rule of a foreign race and under new and unknown institutions. After the military occupation by Kearny in 1846, Charles Bent was civil governor. He was murdered at Taos, in 1847, by some Spaniards whom he had grossly offended. In 1847–48 Donaciano Vigil was civil governor.

In 1848, by the treaty of Guadalupe Hidalgo, New Mexico was formally ceded by Mexico to the United States, and in 1850 it was regularly organized as a territory (which included Arizona until 1863), and James S. Calhoun was the first territorial governor. The first territorial Legislative Assembly met at Santa Fé in 1851: most of the members were of Spanish descent, and this has been true of all the Assemblies until the end of the century. Up to 1910 the proceedings of the Legislature were in Spanish and English, interpreters being always present. During the years 1861–62 the Texan Confederates entered New Mexico, to occupy Albuquerque and Santa Fé, but Federal troops arrived from Colorado and California and frustrated the attempt. During the years from 1860 to 1890 New Mexico progressed very slowly. Education was in a deplorable state (no system was established until 1890), the surrounding Indians continually harassed the inhabitants, and no railroad was constructed until after 1880. In 1860 the population was 80,567; in 1870, 90,573; in 1880, 109,793. Nine-tenths of the population in 1880 was of Spanish descent: at present (1911) this element is only about one-half, owing to the constant immigration from the other states of the Union. Since 1890 New Mexico has progressed rapidly. Education is now enthusiastically supported and encouraged, the natural resources are being rapidly developed, and the larger towns and cities have all the marks of modern civilization and progress. Since 1850 many unsuccessful attempts have been made to secure statehood; at last, in June, 1910, Congress passed an Enabling Act: New Mexico is to adopt a Constitution, subject to the approval of Congress.

MISSIONS OF NEW MEXICO.—The Franciscan Friar Marcos de Niza, as we have seen above, reached New Mexico near the *pueblo* of Zuñi in 1539. This short expedition may be considered, therefore, as the first mission in New Mexico and what is now Arizona. With the expedition of Coronado (1540–42) several Franciscans under Marcos de Niza entered New Mexico. There is some confusion about their exact number and even about their names. It seems reasonably certain, however, that Marcos had to abandon the expedition after reaching Zuñi, and that two Franciscan priests, Juan de Padilla and Juan de la Cruz, and a lay brother, Luis de Escalona, continued with the expedition into New Mexico, remained as missionaries among the Indians when Coronado returned in 1542, and were finally murdered by them. These were the first three Christian missionaries to receive the crown of martyrdom within the present limits of the United States. Forty years after the Niza and Coronado expeditions of 1539–42, it was again a Franciscan who made an attempt to gain the New Mexico Indians to the Faith. This was Father Agustín Rodríguez, who, in 1581, left San Bartolomé in Northern Mexico and, accompanied by two other friars, Juan de Santa María and Fr. Francisco López, and some seventeen more men, marched up the Rio Grande and visited many of the *pueblos* on both sides of the river. The friars decided to remain in the new missionary field when the rest of the expedition returned in 1582, but the Indians proved intractable and the two friars received the crown of martyrdom.

When news of the fate of Agustín Rodríguez reached San Bartolomé in Nueva Vizcaya, Father Bernardino Beltrán was desirous of making another attempt to evangelize New Mexico, but, being alone, would not remain there. It was in 1598 that Don Juan de Oñate made the first permanent Spanish settlement in New Mexico, at San Juan de los Caballeros. Ten Franciscan friars under Father Alonso Martínez accompanied Oñate in his conquest, and established at San Juan the first Spanish Franciscan mission. Missionary work was begun in earnest, and in 1599 Oñate sent a party to Mexico for re-enforcements. With this party went Fathers Martínez, Salazar, and Vergara to obtain more friars. Salazar died on the way, Martínez did not return, but a new Franciscan *comisario*, Juan de Escalona, returned to New Mexico with Vergara and eight more Franciscans. New missions were being established in the near *pueblos*, and prosperity was at hand, but Oñate's ambitions proved fatal: in 1601 he desired to conquer the country to the north and west, and started on an expedition with a small force, taking with him two Franciscans. The people who remained at and near San Juan de los Caballeros were left unprotected. Civil discord followed, and the newly-settled province was abandoned, the settlers, with the friars, moving south. Father Escalona remained, at the risk of his life, to await the return of Oñate; but he had written to the viceroy, asking that Oñate should be recalled. Oñate, with a new *comisario*, Francisco Escobar, and Father San Buenaventura, set out on another counter expedition, and Escalona and the other friars continued their missionary work among their neophytes. New re-enforcements arrived between 1605 and 1608, in spite of Oñate's misrule. In 1608 Father Alonso Peinado came as *comisario* and brought with him eight more friars. By this time 8000 Indians had been converted. By 1617 the Franciscans had built eleven churches and had converted 14,000 Indians.

In 1620 Father Gerónimo de Zárate Salmerón, a very zealous missionary, came to New Mexico. There he worked for eight years, and wrote a book on Christian doctrine in the language of the Jémez. By 1626 the missions numbered 27; 34,000 Indians had been baptized, and 43 churches built. Of the friars only 16 were left. In 1630 Fr. Benavides desired to establish a bishopric in New Mexico, and went to Spain to lay his petition before the king. In his memorial he says that there were in New Mexico, in 1630, 25 missions, covering 90 *pueblos*, attended by 50 friars, and that the Christian natives numbered 60,000. The missions established in New Mexico in 1630, according to this memorial, were the following: among the Piros, or Picos, 3 missions (Socorro, Senecú, Sevilleta); among the Liguas, 2 (Sandia, Isleta); among the Queres, 3; among the Tompiros, 6; among the Tanos, 1; among the Pecos, 1; among the Toas, or Tehuas, 3; at Santa Fé, 1; among the Taos, 1; among the Zuñi, 2. The other two are not mentioned. However, the wrongs perpetrated by local governors exasperated the Indians, and the missionaries were thus labouring under difficulties. By 1680 the number of missions had increased to 33, but the Indian rebellion broke out. All the missions and settlements were destroyed, the churches burned, and the settlers massacred. The number of victims among the Spaniards was 400. Of the missionaries, 11 escaped, while 21 were massacred.

With Don Diego de Vargas, and the reconquest of New Mexico in 1691-95, the Franciscans entered the province again. Father San Antonio was the guardian, but in 1694 he returned to El Paso, and, with Father Francisco Vargas as guardian, the missions were re-established. Not only were most of the old missions again in a prosperous condition, but new ones were established among the Apaches, Navajos, and other tribes. Towards the middle of the eighteenth century, petty disputes arose between the friars and the Bishop of Durango, and the results were unfavourable to the missions, which at this time numbered from 20 to 25, Father Juan Mirabal being guardian. In 1760 Bishop Tamarón of Durango visited the province. From this time on the Franciscan missions in New Mexico changed, the friars in many cases acted as parish priests, and their work did not prove so fruitful.

During the last half of the eighteenth century, and during the last years of Spanish rule (1800-1821), the missions declined more and more. The Franciscans still remained, and received salaries from the Government, not as missionaries but as parish priests. They were under their guardian, but the Bishop of Durango controlled religious affairs, with a permanent vicar in New Mexico. The Mexican rule of 1821-1846 was worse than the Spanish rule, and the missions existed only in name. At the time of the American occupation, in 1846, the missions, as such, no longer existed.

CHURCH AT PUEBLO OF ISLETA, NEW MEXICO

The missionary work in what is now Arizona was in some cases that of the New Mexican friars, who from the beginning of their labours extended their missions among the Zuñi and the Moquis. A few of these missions, however, had no connexion whatever with the missionary work of New Mexico. After Niza's exploration in 1540, we know little of the missionary work in Arizona proper, until 1633, when Fray Francisco Parras, who was almost alone in his work, was killed at Aguatevi. In 1680 four Franciscans, attending three missions among the Moquis, were killed during the New Mexican rebellion of that year. In Northern Mexico, close to the Arizona line (or, as then known, Pimeria Alta), the Jesuits were doing excellent mission work in 1600-1700. It was a Jesuit, also, Father Eusebio Francisco Kino, who explored what is now southern Arizona, in 1687. No missions were established, however, in Arizona before Father Kino's death in 1711, though churches were built, and many Indians converted. The work of Father Kino was abandoned after his death, until 1732, when Fathers Felipe Segesser and Juan B. Grashoffer established the first permanent missions of Arizona at San Xavier del Bac and San Miguel de Guevavi. In 1750 these two missions were attacked and plundered by the Pimas, but the missionaries escaped. In 1752 the missions were reoccupied. A rivalry between the Franciscans and the Jesuits hindered the success of the missions.

In 1767, however, the controversy between Jesuits and Franciscans was ended, and the Jesuits expelled. The Government, not content with their expulsion, confiscated the mission property, though the Franciscans were invited to the field. Four Franciscans arrived in 1768 to renew the missionary work and found the missions in a deplorable state, but they persuaded the Government to help in the restoration and to restore the confiscated property. It is to be observed that these missions of Arizona, as well as many of those of Sonora in Mexico, were, until 1873, under the control of the College of Santa Cruz (just across the Arizona line in Northern Mexico), separated from 1783 to 1791, and united in 1791. The two important Arizona Missions, San Xavier del Bac and San Miguel de Guevavi, became prosperous, the former under the famous Franciscan, Father Francisco Garcés from 1768 to 1774. Father Garcés laboured continually among the Indians until he lost his life, in 1781, in his missionary work near the Colorado River in California. The missions of Arizona declined after 1800, and in 1828 the Mexican Government ordered their abandonment. From this time until 1859, when Bishop Lamy of Santa Fé sent the Rt. Rev. J. P. Macheboeuf to minister to the spiritual needs of Arizona, there were no signs of Christianity in Arizona other than abandoned missions and ruined churches.

PRESENT CONDITIONS (1910).—Pending the full admission of New Mexico to statehood, its government is still that of a territory of the United States, regulated by the provisons of the Federal Statutes. Accordingly, the governor and other executive officers are appointed by the executive authority of the United States and paid by the Federal Treasury; the Legislature (House of Representatives and Council) is elected by the people of the territory; the Territorial Judiciary (a chief justice and five associate justices) is appointed by the President of the United States for a term of four years, but justices of the peace are elected for two years.

Education.—The educational system of New Mexico dates from 1890 and is still in process of development. The public-school system is governed by a territorial Board of Education consisting of seven members. This board apportions the school funds, prepares teachers' examinations, selects books, etc. There are also the usual county and district officers. At present there are approximately 1000 public schools in New Mexico, with about 50,000 pupils, of whom 20,000 are Spanish and 100 negroes. There are 70 denominational schools, with 5,000 pupils, and 18 private schools, with 288 pupils. Futhermore, there were, in 1908, 25 Indian schools with 1933 pupils.

The Catholic schools of the territory number 23, with about 100 teachers and about 1500 pupils (estimated in 1910; 1,212 in 1908). The most important Catholic school in New Mexico is St. Michael's College at Santa Fé, founded in 1859 by Bishop J. B. Lamy. The sisters' charitable institutions (hospitals, etc.) are state-aided. In 1909 the appropriations for these purposes amounted to $12,000. The other denominational schools are distributed as follows: Presbyterian, 25; Congregational, 9; Methodist, 11; Baptist, 2. The territorial (or state) university was established in 1889 at Albuquerque. It is supported by territorial appropriations and land revenues. For the year 1909–10 the income was $40,000. Its teaching force consisted, in 1909–10, of 16 professors, associate professors, and instructors, and the number of students in attendance was 130. There are three normal schools, one at Las Vegas, one at El Rito, and one at Silver City; a military school at Roswell; a school of mines at Socorro; and a college of agriculture and mechanic arts at Mesilla Park—the best equipped and most efficient school in New Mexico, receiving both federal and territorial aid aggregating $100,000 a year (1909–10), having a teaching force of 40 professors, assistant professors, and instructors, and an attendance of 285 students (1909–10). The combined valuation of the territory's educational institutions is about $1,000,000, while the annual expenditures aggregate $275,000.

Religion.—In 1850, when New Mexico was organized as a territory of the United States, it (including, till 1863, Arizona and part of Colorado) was made a vicariate Apostolic, under the Rt. Rev. John B. Lamy. In 1853 New Mexico (with exceptions noted below) was made the Diocese of Santa Fé, and the vicar Apostolic became its first bishop. In 1865 this diocese became the Archdiocese of Santa Fé, and Bishop Lamy became its first archbishop. The archdiocese includes all of New Mexico, except Doña Ana, Eddy, and Grant Counties, which belong to the Diocese of Tucson. The present Archbishop of Santa Fé is the Rt. Rev. John B. Pitaval. The Catholic population of the territory in 1882 was 126,000; in 1906 it was 121,558 (U. S. Census Bulletin, no. 103, p. 36). But the figures for 1882 (given by H. H. Bancroft) must include the Catholic population of Arizona and probably also of Colorado. In 1906 the Catholics were more than 88 per cent of the church membership of the territory, which was 137,009, distributed as follows:—

Roman Catholics	121,558
Methodists	6,560
Presbyterians	2,935
Baptists	2,403
Disciples, or Christians	1,092
Protestant Episcopalians	869
Unclassified	1,592
Total	137,009

At present (1910) the total Catholic population of New Mexico may be estimated at not less than about 130,000, about 120,000 being of Spanish descent. No definite statistics are available on this last point. The large Catholic population of New Mexico is due to its having been colonized by the Spaniards, whose first thought on founding a colony was to build churches and establish missions. The recent Catholic immigration has been from the Middle West, and this is largely Irish.

Catholics distinguished in Public Life.—The fact that until about the year 1890 the population of the territory was mostly Spanish, and therefore Catholic, is the reason why most of the men who have figured prominently in the history of New Mexico have been Catholic Spaniards. Among the more prominent may be mentioned: Donaciano Vigil, military governor, 1847–48; Miguel A. Otero, territorial secretary, 1861; delegates to the Federal Congress, José M. Gallegos, 1853–54; Miguel A. Otero, 1855–60; Francisco Perea, 1863–64; José F. Chaves, 1865–70; José M. Gallegos, 1871–72; Trinidad Romero, 1877–78; Mariano S. Otero, 1879–80; Tranquilino Luna, 1881–82; Francisco A. Manzanares, 1883–4. The treasurers and auditors from 1863 to 1886 were all, with but one exception, Catholic Spaniards.

Legislation affecting Religion.—(1) Absolute freedom of worship is guaranteed by the Organic Act constituting the territory, and by statute preference to any religious denomination by law is forbidden. (2) Horse-racing and cock-fighting on Sunday are forbidden; labour, except works of necessity, charity, or mercy, prohibited, and the offence is punishable by a fine of from $5 to $15. (3) No religious test shall be required as a qualification to any office or public trust in this territory. Oaths are administered in the usual fashion, but an affirmation may be used instead when the individual has conscientious scruples against taking an oath. (4) No statutory enactment punishing blasphemy or profanity has ever been passed in this territory. (5) It is customary to open the sessions of the Legislature with an invocation of the Supreme Being, but there is no statutory authority either for or against this ceremony. Until the present time (1910) this function has always been discharged by a Catholic priest. (6) Christmas is the only religious festival observed as a legal holiday in New Mexico. New Year's Day is also a legal holiday, but Good Friday, Ash Wednesday, All Souls' Day, etc., are not recognized. (7) There has been no decision in the courts of New Mexico regarding the seal of confession, but it is to be presumed that, in the absence of any statutory provision covering the point, the courts of the territory would follow the general rule: that confession to a priest is a confidential communication and therefore inviolable. (8) Churches are, in the contemplation of the laws of New Mexico, in the category of charitable institutions. (9) No religious or charitable institution is permitted to hold more than $50,000 worth of property; any property acquired or held contrary to the above prohibition shall be forfeited and escheat to the United States. The property of religious institutions is exempt from taxation when it is being used and devoted exclusively to its appropriate objects, and not used with a view to pecuniary profit. The clergy are exempt from jury and military service. (10) Marriage may be either by religious or by civil ceremony. The male must be eighteen years of age, and the female fifteen, for marriage with parents' consent; after the male is twenty-one and the female eighteen they may marry regardless of parents' consent. Marriages between first cousins, uncles, aunts, nieces and nephews, half-brothers and sisters, grandparent and grandchildren, are declared incestuous and absolutely void. (11) Education in the public schools must be non-sectarian. (12) No charitable or religious bequests are recognized unless made in writing duly attested by the lawful number of witnesses. (13) There are no restrictions as to cemeteries other than that they must not be near to running streams. (14) Divorce may be obtained for cruelty, adultery, desertion, and for almost every ground recognized as sufficient in any state of the Union. The party seeking divorce must have been a *bona fide* resident of the territory for more than a year prior to the date of filing the action. Service on the defendant must be personal, if the defendant is within the territory; but may be by publication, if the whereabouts of the defendant are unknown. Trials of divorce are without a jury.

BANCROFT, H. H., *History of New Mexico and Arizona* (San Francisco, 1888); *Biennial Report of the State Superintendent of Public Instruction of New Mexico* (Santa Fé, 1908); BLACKMAR, *Spanish Institutions in the Southwest* (Baltimore, 1891); *Compiled Laws of New Mexico* (Santa Fé, 1897 and 1908); *Catholic Directory for 1910*; U. S. CENSUS BUREAU, *Bulletin no. 103* (Washington, 1906); ENGELHARDT, *The Missions and Missionaries of California*, I (San Francisco, 1908); II (San Francisco, 1910); VILLAGRÁ, *Historia de la Nueva Méjico* (Alcalá de Henares, 1610; Mexico, 1900); *Illustrated History of New Mexico* (Los Angeles, 1907); COUES, *On the Trail of a Spanish Pioneer* (tr. of the diary of Father Francisco Garcés) (New York, 1900); *Report of the Governor of New Mexico to the Secretary of the Interior* (Washington, 1909); SHEA, *History of the Catholic Church in the United States* (New York, 1892); *Register of the University of New Mexico, 1909–10* (Albuquerque, 1910); *Register of the New Mexico College of Agriculture and Mechanic Arts* (Santa Fé, 1910); PINO, *Noticias históricas y estadísticas sobre la antigua provincia del Nuevo Méjico* (Cadiz, 1812; Mexico, 1839; 1849); *The Journey of Antonio de Vargas and Conquest of New Mexico in 1691–3* (MS. in Library of the New Mexico Historical Society, Santa Fé); *Publications of the New Mexico Historical Society* (Santa Fé, 1898–1910).

AURELIO M. ESPINOSA.

New Norcia, a Benedictine abbey in Western Australia, founded on 1 March, 1846, by a Spanish Benedictine, Rudesindus Salvado, for the christianizing of the Australian aborigines. It is situated eighty-two miles from Perth, the state capital; its territory is bounded on the south and east by the Diocese of Perth, and on the north by the Diocese of Geraldton. This mission at first had no territory. Its saintly founder, like the Baptist of old, lived in the wilderness, leading the same nomadic life as the savages whom he had come to lead out of darkness. His food was of the most variable character, consisting of wild roots dug out of the earth by the spears of his swarthy neophytes, with lizards, iguanas, even worms in times of distress, or, when fortunate in the chase, with the native kangaroo. After three years of unparalleled hardships amongst this cannibal race, Salvado came to the conclusion that they were capable of Christianity. Assisted by some friends, he started for Rome in 1849 to procure auxiliaries and money to assist him in prosecuting his work of civilization. While in Rome he was appointed Bishop of Port Victoria in Northern Australia, being consecrated on 15 August, 1849. Before he left Rome, all his people of Port Victoria had abandoned the diocese for the goldfields. Bishop Salvado thereupon implored the pope to permit him to return to his beloved Australian blacks. He set out for Spain, and obtained there monetary assistance and over forty young volunteers. All these afterwards became Benedictines. They landed in Australia in charge of their bishop on 15 August, 1852.

Bishop Salvado, with his band of willing workers, commenced operations forthwith. They cleared land for the plough, and introduced the natives to habits of industry. They built a large monastery, schools and orphanages for the young, cottages for the married, flour-mills to grind their wheat, etc. An important village soon sprang up, in which many natives were fed, clothed, and made good Christians. On 12 March, 1867, Pius IX made New Norcia an abbey *nullius* and a prefecture Apostolic with jurisdiction over a territory of 16 square miles, the extent of Bishop Salvado's jurisdiction until his death in Rome on 29 December, 1900, in the eighty-seventh year of his age and the fifty-first of his episcopate. Father Fulgentius Torres, O.S.B., was elected Abbot of New Norcia in succession to Bishop Salvado on 2 October, 1902. The new abbot found it necessary to frame a new policy for his mission. Rapid changes were setting in; agricultural settlers were taking up the land, driving out the sheep and cattle lords, and absorbing the labour of the civilized natives. The mission had now to provide for the spiritual wants of the white population, and Abbot Torres boldly faced the situation by entering upon a large scheme of improvements in and around the monastery. With the approbation of the Holy See, he had the boundaries of the abbey extended to embrace the country between 30° and 31° 20′ S. latitude, and between the sea and 120° E. longitude— a territory of over 30,000 sq. miles (nearly as large as Ireland or the State of Maine). Abbot Torres brought out many priests and young ecclesiastics for the monastery and parochial work, and built churches in the more settled districts of his new territory. Since Abbot Torres became superior in 1901, the number of churches has increased from one to ten. To foster higher education, Abbot Torres has erected a magnificent convent and ladies' college, and has in hand a similar institution for boys. He has already completed a large and commodious girls' orphanage. All these works have been accomplished at the expense of the Benedictine community. Abbot Torres has not confined his energies solely to New Norcia. He founded the "Drysdale River Aborigines Mission", 2000 miles away, in the extreme north-west of Australia, an unexplored land inhabited only by the most treacherous savages. This mission was opened on 12 July, 1908, with a party of fifteen in charge of two priests.

Abbot Torres was consecrated bishop in Rome on 22 May, 1910. On the fourth of the same month, by a Decree of the Propaganda, he was appointed administrator Apostolic of Kimberley, and had the "Drysdale Mission" erected into an abbey *nullius*. He has now under his jurisdiction a territory of 174,000 sq. miles— an area nearly as large as five important states of the United States—viz., Pennsylvania, Ohio, Indiana, W. Virginia, and Maine. The present position (1910) of the mission is: churches, 10; priests, 17 (secular, 7); monastic students, 9; other religious, 33; nuns, 18; high school, 1; primary schools, 4; charitable institutions, 2; children attending Catholic schools, 350; Catholic population, 3000.

JAMES FLOOD.

New Orleans, ARCHDIOCESE OF (NOVÆ AURELIÆ), erected 25 April, 1793, as the Diocese of Saint

Louis of New Orleans; raised to its present rank and title 19 July, 1850. Its original territory comprised the ancient Louisiana Purchase and East and West Florida, being bounded on the north by the Canadian line, on the west by the Rocky Mountains and the Rio Perdito, on the east by the Diocese of Baltimore, and on the south by the Diocese of Linares and the Archdiocese of Durango. The present boundaries include the State of Louisiana, between the twenty-ninth and thirty-first degree of north latitude, an area of 23,208 square miles. The entire territory of Louisiana has undergone a series of changes which divide its history into four distinct periods.

I. EARLY COLONIAL PERIOD.—The discoverers and pioneers, De Soto, Iberville, La Salle, Bienville, were accompanied by missionaries in their expeditions through the Louisiana Purchase, and in the toilsome beginnings of the first feeble settlements, which were simply military posts, the Cross blazed the way. From the beginning of its history, Louisiana had been placed under the jurisdiction of the Bishop of Quebec; in 1696 the priests of the Seminary of Quebec petitioned the second Bishop of Quebec for authority to establish missions in the West, investing the superior sent out by the seminary with the powers of vicar-general. The field for which they obtained this authorization (1 May, 1698) was on both banks of the Mississippi and its tributaries. They proposed to plant their first mission among the Tamarois, but when this became known, the Jesuits claimed that tribe as one already under their care: they received the new missionaries with personal cordiality, but felt keenly the official action of Bishop St-Vallier, in what they regarded as an intrusion. Fathers Jolliet de Montigny, Antoine Davion, and François Busion de Saint-Cosme were the missionaries sent to found the new missions in the Mississippi Valley. In 1699 Iberville, who had sailed from France, with his two brothers Bienville and Sauvolle, and Father Du Ru, S.J., coming up the estuary of the Mississippi, found Father Montigny among the Tensas Indians. Iberville left Sauvolle in command of the little fort at Biloxi, the first permanent settlement in Louisiana. Father Bordenave was its first chaplain, thus beginning the long line of zealous parish priests in Louisiana.

In 1703 Bishop St-Vallier proposed to erect Mobile into a parish, and annex it in perpetuity to the seminary; the seminary agreed, and the Parish of Mobile was erected 20 July, 1703, and united to the Seminary of Foreign Missions of Paris and Quebec. Father Roulleaux de la Vente, of the Diocese of Bayeux, was appointed parish priest and Father Huve his assistant. The Biloxi settlement being difficult of access from the sea, Bienville thought it unsuitable for the headquarters of the province. In 1718, taking with him fifty men, he selected Tchoutchouma, the present site of New Orleans, about 110 miles from the mouth of the Mississippi River, where there was a deserted Indian village. Bienville directed his men to clear the ground and erect buildings. The city was laid out according to the plans of the Chevalier Le Blond de La Tour, chief engineer of the colony, the plans including a parish church, which Bienville decided to dedicate under the invocation of St. Louis. The old St. Louis cathedral stands on the site of this first parish church, and the presbytery in Cathedral Alley is the site of the first modest clergy house. Bienville called the city New Orleans after the Duc d'Orléans, and the whole territory Louisiana, or New France.

In August, 1717, the Duc d'Orléans, as Regent of France, issued letters patent establishing a joint-stock company to be called "The Company of the West", to which Louisiana was transferred. The company was obliged to build churches at its own expense wherever it should establish settlements; also to maintain the necessary number of duly approved priests to preach, perform Divine service, and administer the sacraments under the authority of the Bishop of Quebec. Bienville experienced much opposition from the Company of the West in his attempt to remove the colony from Biloxi. In 1721 Father François-Xavier de Charlevoix, S.J., one of the first historians of Louisiana, made a tour of New France from the Lakes to the Mississippi, visiting New Orleans, which he describes as "a little village of about one hundred cabins dotted here and there, with little attempt at order, a large wooden warehouse in which I said Mass, a chapel in course of construction and two storehouses". But under Bienville's direction the city soon took shape, and, with the consent of the company, the colony was moved to this site in 1723. Father Charlevoix reported on the great spiritual destitution of the province occasioned by the missions being scattered so far apart and the scarcity of priests, and this compelled the council of the company to make efforts to improve conditions. Accordingly, the company applied to the Bishop of Quebec, and on 16 May, 1722, Louisiana was divided into three ecclesiastical sections. The district north of the Ohio was entrusted to the Society of Jesus and the Priests of the Foreign Missions of Paris and Quebec; that between the Mississippi and the Rio Perdito, to the Discalced Carmelite Fathers, with headquarters at Mobile. The Carmelites were recalled, not long after, and their district was given to the Capuchins.

A different arrangement was made for the Indian and new French settlements on the lower Mississippi. Because of the remoteness of this district from Quebec, Father Louis-François Duplessis de Mornay, a Capuchin of Meudon, was consecrated, at Bishop St-Vallier's request, coadjutor Bishop of Quebec, 22 April, 1714. Bishop St-Vallier appointed him vicar-general for Louisiana, but he never came to America, although he eventually succeeded to the See of Quebec. When the Company of the West applied to him for priests for the lower Mississippi Valley he offered the more populous field of colonists to the Capuchin Fathers of the Province of Champagne, who, however, did not take any immediate steps, and it was not till 1720 that any of the order came to Louisiana. Father Jean-Matthieu de Saint-Anne is the first whose name is recorded. He signs himself in 1720 in the register of the parish of New Orleans. The last entry of the secular clergy in Mobile was that of Rev. Alexander Huve, 13 January, 1721. The Capuchins came directly from France and consequently found application to the Bishop of Quebec long and tedious; Father Matthieu therefore applied to Rome for special powers for fifteen missions under his charge, representing that the great distance from the Bishop of Quebec made it practically impossible for him to apply to the bishop. A brief was really issued (Michael a Tugio, "Bullarium Ord. FF. Minor. S.P. Francisci Capucinorum", Fol. 1740–52; BLI., pp. 322, 323), and Father Matthieu seems to have assumed that it exempted him from episcopal jurisdiction, for, on 14 March, 1723, he signs the register "Père Matthieu, Vicaire Apostolique et Curé de la Mobile".

In 1722 Bishop de Mornay entrusted the spiritual jurisdiction of the Indians to the Jesuits, who were to establish missions in all parts of Louisiana with residence at New Orleans, but were not to exercise any ecclesiastical function there without the consent of the Capuchins, though they were to minister to the French in the Illinois District, with the Priests of the Foreign Missions, where the superior of each body was a vicar-general, just as the Capuchin superior was at New Orleans. In the spring of 1723 Father Raphael de Luxembourg arrived to assume his duties as superior of the Capuchin Mission in Louisiana. It was a difficult task that the Capuchins had assumed. Their congregations were scattered over a large area; there was much poverty, suffering, and ignorance of religion. Father Raphael, in the cathedral archives, says that when he landed in New Orleans he could hardly secure a room for himself and his brethren to occupy pending the rebuilding of the presbytery, much less one to convert into a chapel; for the population seemed indifferent to all that savoured of religion. There were less than thirty persons at Mass on Sundays; yet, undismayed, the missionaries set to work and soon saw their zeal rewarded with a greater reverence for religion and more faithful attendance at church. In 1725 New Orleans had become an important settlement, the Capuchins having a flock of six hundred families. Mobile had declined to sixty families, the Apalache Indians (Catholics) numbered sixty families, there were six at the Balize, two hundred at St. Charles or Les Allemandes, one hundred at Point Coupée, six at Natchez, fifty at Natchitoches and the other missions which are not named in the "Bullarium Capucinorum" (Vol. VIII, p. 330).

The founder of the Jesuit Mission in New Orleans was Father Nicolas-Ignatius de Beaubois, who was appointed vicar-general for his district. He visited New Orleans and returned to France to obtain Fathers of the Society for his mission. Being also commissioned by Bienville to obtain sisters of some order to assume charge of a hospital and school, he applied to the Ursulines of Rouen, who accepted the call. The royal patent authorizing the Ursulines to found a convent in Louisiana was issued 18 Sept., 1726. Mother Mary Tranchepain of St. Augustine, with seven professed nuns from Rouen, Le Havre, Vannes, Ploermel, Hennebon, and Elbœuf, a novice, Madeline Hauchard, and two seculars, met at the infirmary at Hennebon on 12 January, 1727, and, accompanied by Fathers Tartarin and Doutreleau, set sail for Louisiana. They reached New Orleans on 6 August to open the first convent for women within the present limits of the United States of America. As the convent was not ready for their reception, the governor gave up his own residence to them. The history of the Ursulines from their departure from Rouen through a period of thirty years in Louisiana, is told by Sister Madeline Hauchard in a diary still preserved in the Ursuline Convent of New Orleans, and which forms, with Father Charlevoix's history, the principal record of those early days. On 7 August, 1727, the Ursulines began in Louisiana the work which has since continued without interruption. They opened a hospital for the care of the sick and a school for poor children, also an academy which is now the oldest educational institution for women in the United States. The convent in which the Ursulines then took up their abode still stands, the oldest conventual structure in the United States and the oldest building within the limits of the Louisiana Purchase. In 1824 the Ursulines removed to the lower portion of the city, and the old convent became first the episcopal residence and then the diocesan chancery.

Meanwhile Father Mathurin le Petit, S.J., established a mission among the Choctaws; Father Du Poisson, among the Arkansas; Father Doutreleau, on the Wabash; Fathers Tartarin and Le Boulenger, at Kaskaskia; Father Guymonneau among the Metchogameas; Father Souel, among the Yazoos; Father Baudouin, among the Chickasaws. The Natchez Indians, provoked by the tyranny and rapacity of Chopart, the French commandant, in 1729 nearly destroyed all these missions. Father Du Poisson and Father Souel were killed by the Indians. As an instance of the faith implanted in the Iroquois about this time there was received into the Ursuline Order at New Orleans, Mary Turpin, daughter of a Canadian father and an Illinois mother. She died a professed nun in 1761, at the age of fifty-two with the distinction of being the first American born nun in this country. From the beginning of the colony at Biloxi the immigration of women had been small. Bienville made constant appeals to the mother country to send honest wives and mothers. From time to time ships freighted with girls would arrive; they came over in charge of the Grey Nuns of Canada and a priest, and were sent by the king to be married to the colonists. The Bishop of Quebec was also charged with the duty of sending out young women who were known to be good and virtuous. As a proof of her respectability, each girl was furnished by the bishop with a curiously wrought casket; they are known in Louisiana history as "casket girls". Each band of girls, on arriving at New Orleans, was confided to the care of the Ursulines until they were married to colonists able to provide for their support. Many of the best families of the state are proud to trace their descent from "casket girls".

The city was growing and developing; a better class of immigrant was pouring in, and Father Charlevoix, on his visit in 1728, wrote to the Duchesse de Lesdiguières: "My hopes, I think, are well founded that this wild and desert place, which the reeds and trees still cover, will be one day, and that not far distant, a city of opulence and the metropolis of a rich colony." His words were prophetic: New Orleans was fast developing, and early chronicles say that it suggested the splendours of Paris. There was a governor with a military staff, bringing to the city the manners and splendour of the Court of Versailles, and the manners and usages of the mother country stamped on Louisiana life characteristics in marked contrast to the life of any other American colony. The Jesuit Fathers of New Orleans had no parochial residence, but directed the Ursulines, and had charge of their private chapel and a plantation where, in 1751, they introduced into Louisiana the culture of the sugar-cane, the orange, and the fig. The Capuchins established missions wherever they could. Bishop St-Vallier had been succeeded by Bishop de Mornay, who never went to Quebec, but resigned the see, after five years. His successor, Henri-Marie Du Breuil de Pontbriand, appointed Father de Beaubois, S.J., his vicar-general in Louisiana. The Capuchin Fathers refused to recognize Father de Beaubois' authority, claiming, under the agreement of the Company of the West with the coadjutor bishop, de Mornay, that the superior of the Capuchins was, in perpetuity, vicar-general of the province, and that the bishop could appoint no other. Succeeding bishops of Quebec declared, however, that they could not, as bishops, admit that the assent of a coadjutor and vicar-general to an agreement with a trading company had forever deprived every bishop of Quebec of the right to act as freely in Louisiana as in any other part of his diocese. This incident gave rise to some friction between the two orders which has been spoken of derisively by Louisiana historians, notably by Gayarré, as "The War of the Capuchins and the Jesuits". The archives of the diocese, as also the records of the Capuchins in Louisiana, show that it was simply a question of jurisdiction, which gave rise to a discussion so petty as to be unworthy of notice. Historians exaggerate this beyond all importance, while failing to chronicle the shameful spoliation of the Jesuits by the French Government which suddenly settled the question forever.

In 1761 the Parliaments of several provinces of France had condemned the Jesuits, and measures were taken against them in the kingdom. They were expelled from Paris, and the Superior Council of Louisiana, following the example, on 9 June, 1763, just ten years before the order was suppressed by Clement XIV, passed an act suppressing the Jesuits throughout the province, declaring them dangerous to royal authority, to the rights of the bishops, and to the public safety. The Jesuits were charged with neglecting their mission, with having developed their plantation, and with having usurped the office of vicar-general. To the first charge the record of their labours was sufficient refutation; to the second, it was assuredly to the credit of the Jesuits that they made their plantation so productive as to maintain their missionaries; to the third, the action of the bishops of Quebec in appointing the vicar-general and that of the Superior Council itself in sustaining him was the answer. Nevertheless, the unjust decree was carried out, the Jesuits' property was confiscated, and they were forbidden to use the name of their Society or to wear their habit. Their property was sold for $180,000. All their chapels were levelled to the ground, leaving exposed even the vaults where the dead were interred. The Jesuits were ordered to give up their missions, to return to New Orleans and to leave on the first vessel sailing for France. The Capuchins forgetting their difference interfered in behalf of the Jesuits; and finding their petitions unavailing went to the river bank to receive the returning Jesuits, offered them a home alongside of their own, and in every way showed their disapproval of the Council's action. The Jesuits deeply grateful left the Capuchins all the books they had been able to save from the spoilation.

Father Boudoin, S.J., the benefactor of the colony, who had introduced the culture of sugar-cane and oranges from San Domingo, and figs from Provence, a man to whom the people owed much and to whom Louisiana to-day owes so much of its prosperity, alone remained. He was now seventy-two years old and had spent thirty-five in the colony. He was broken in health and too ill to leave his room. They dragged him through the streets when prominent citizens intervened and one wealthy planter, Etienne de Boré, who had first succeeded in the granulation of sugar, defied the authorities, and took Father Boudoin to his home and sheltered him until his death in 1766. The most monstrous part of the order of expulsion was that, not only were the chapels of the Jesuits in lower Louisiana—many of which were the only places where Catholics, whites and Indians, and negroes, could worship God—levelled to the ground, but the Council carried out the decree even in the Illinois district which had been ceded to the King of England and which was no longer subject to France or Louisiana. They ordered even the vestments and plate to be delivered to the king's attorney. Thus was a vast territory left destitute of priests and altars, and the growth of the Church retarded for many years. Of the ten Capuchins left to administer to this immense territory, five were retained in New Orleans; the remainder were scattered over the various missions. It is interesting to note that the only native Louisiana priest at this time and the first to enter the holy priesthood, Rev. Bernard Viel, born in New Orleans 1 October, 1736, was among the Jesuits expelled from the colony. He died in France, 1821. The inhabitants of New Orleans then numbered four thousand.

II. SPANISH PERIOD.—In 1763 Louisiana was ceded to Spain, and Antonio Ulloa was sent over to take possession. The colonists were bitterly opposed to the cession and finally rose in arms against the governor, giving him three days in which to leave the town. (See LOUISIANA.) The Spanish Government resolved to punish the parties who had so insulted its representative, Don Ulloa, and sent Alexander O'Reilly to assume the office of governor. Lafrénière, President of the Council, who chiefly instigated the passing of the decree expelling the Jesuits from the colony, and the rebellion against the Government, was tried by court martial and with six of his partners in his scheme, was shot in the Place d'Armes. O'Reilly reorganized the province after the Spanish model. The oath taken by the officials shows that the doctrine of the Immaculate Conception was then officially recognized in the Spanish dominions. "I ———— appointed ———— swear before God . . .to maintain . . . the mystery of the Immaculate Conception of Our Lady, the Virgin Mary."

The change of government affected ecclesiastical jurisdiction. The Province of Louisiana passed under the jurisdiction of the Bishop of Santiago de Cuba, the Right Rev. Jaime José de Echeverría, and Spanish Capuchins began to fill the places of their French brethren. Contradictory reports reached the new bishop about conditions in Louisiana and he sent Father Cirilo de Barcelona with four Spanish Capuchins to New Orleans. These priests were Fathers Francisco, Angel de Revillagades, Louis de Quintanilla, and Aleman. They reached New Orleans, 19 July, 1773. The genial ways of the French brethren seemed scandalous to the stern Spanish disciplinarian, and he informed the Bishop of Cuba concerning what he considered "lax methods of conduct and administration". Governor Unzaga, however, interfered in behalf of the French Capuchins, and wrote to the bishop censuring the Spanish friars. This offended the bishop and both referred the matter to the Spanish Court. The Government expressed no opinion, but advised the prelate and governor to compromise, and so preserve harmony between the civil and ecclesiastical authorities. Some Louisiana historians, Charles Gayarré among others, speak of the depravity of the clergy of that period. These charges are not borne out by contemporary testimony; the archives of the cathedral witness that the clergy performed their work faithfully. These charges as a rule sprang from monastic prejudices or secular antipathies. One of the first acts of Father Cirilo as pastor of the St. Louis Cathedral was to have the catechism printed in French and Spanish.

The Bishop of Santiago de Cuba resolved to remedy the deplorable conditions in Louisiana, where confirmation had never been administered. In view of his inability to visit this distant portion of his diocese, he asked for the appointment of an auxiliary bishop, who would take up his abode in New Orleans, and thence visit the missions on the Mississippi as well as those in Mobile, Pensacola, and St. Augustine. The Holy See appointed Father Cirilo de Barcelona titular Bishop of Tricali and auxiliary of Santiago. He was consecrated in Cuba in 1781 and proceded to New Orleans where for the first time the people enjoyed the presence of a bishop. A saintly man, he infused new life into the province. The whole of Louisiana and the Floridas were under his jurisdiction. According to official records of the Church in Louisiana in 1785, the church of St. Louis, New Orleans, had a parish priest, four assistants; and there was a resident priest at each of the following points: Terre aux Bœufs, St. Charles, St. John the Baptist, St. James, Ascension, St. Gabriel's at Iberville, Point Coupee, Attakapas, Opelousas, Natchitoches, Natchez, St. Louis, St. Genevieve, and at Bernard or Manchac (now Galveston). On 25 November, 1785, Bishop Cirilo appointed as parish priest of New Orleans Rev. Antonio Ildefonso Morenory Arze de Sedella, one of the six Capuchins who had come to the colony in 1779. Father Antonio (popularly known as "Père Antoine") was destined to exert a remarkable influence in the colony. Few priests have been more assailed by historians, but a careful comparison of the ancient records of the cathedral with the traditions that cluster about his memory show that he did not deserve on the one hand the indignities which Gayarré and Shea heap upon him, nor yet the excessive honours with which tradition has crowned him. From the cathedral archives it has been proven that he was simply an earnest priest striving to do what he thought his duty amid many difficulties.

In 1787 a number of unfortunate Acadians came at the expense of the King of France and settled near Plaquemines, Terre aux Bœufs, Bayou Lafourche, Attakapas, and Opelousas, adding to the already thrifty colony. They brought with them the precious Register of St. Charles aux Mines in Acadia extending from 1689 to 1749, only six years before their cruel deportation. These were deposited for safe keeping with the priest of St. Gabriel at Iberville and are now in the diocesan archives. St. Augustine being returned to Spain by the treaty of peace of 1783, the King of Spain made efforts to provide for the future of Catholicism in that ancient province. As many English people had settled there and in West Florida, notably at Baton Rouge and Natchez, Charles III applied to the Irish College for priests to attend the English-speaking population. Accordingly Rev. Michael O'Reilly and Rev. Thomas Hasset were sent to Florida. Catholic worship was restored, the city at once resuming its own old aspect. Rev. William Savage, a clergyman of great repute, Rev. Michael Lamport, Rev. Gregory White, Rev. Constantine Makenna, Father Joseph Denis, and a Franciscan with six fathers of his order, were sent to labour in Louisiana. They were distributed through the Natchez and Baton Rouge districts, and were the first Irish priests to come to Louisiana, the pioneers of a long and noble line to whom this archdiocese owes much. In 1787, the Holy See divided the Diocese of Santiago de Cuba, erected the Bishopric of St. Christopher of Havana, Louisiana, and the Floridas, with the Right Rev. Joseph de Trespalacios of Porto Rico as bishop, and the Right Rev. Cirilo de Barcelona as auxiliary, with the special direction of Louisiana and the two Floridas. Louisiana thus formed a part of the Diocese of Havana.

Near Fort Natchez the site for a church was purchased on April 11, 1788. The earliest incumbent of whom any record was kept was Rev. Francis Lennan. Most of the people of Natchez were English Protestants or Americans, who had sided with England. They enjoyed absolute religious freedom, no attempt to proselytize was ever made. On Good Friday, 21 March, 1788, New Orleans was swept by a conflagration in which nine hundred buildings, including the parish church, with the adjoining convent of the Capuchins, the house of Bishop Cirilo and the Spanish School, were reduced to ashes. From the ruins of the old irregularly built French City rose the stately Spanish City, Old New Orleans, practically unchanged as it exists to-day. Foremost among the public-spirited men of that time was Don Andreas Almonaster y Roxas, of a noble Andalusian family and royal standard bearer for the colony. He had made a great fortune in New Orleans, and at a cost of $50,000 he built and gave to the city the St. Louis Cathedral. He rebuilt the house for the use of the clergy and the Charity Hospital at a cost of $114,000. He also rebuilt the town hall and the Cabildo, the buildings on either side of the cathedral, the hospital, the boys' school, a chapel for the Ursulines, and founded the Leper Hospital.

Meanwhile rapid assimilation had gone on in Louisiana. Americans began to make their homes in New Orleans and in 1791 the insurrection of San Domingo drove there many hundreds of wealthy noble refugees. The archives of the New Orleans Diocese show that the King of Spain petitioned Pope Pius VI on 20 May, 1790, to erect Louisiana and the Floridas into a separate see, and on April 9, 1793, a decree for the dismemberment of the Diocese of Havana, Louisiana, and the Provinces of East and West Florida was issued. It provided for the erection of the See of St. Louis of New Orleans, which was to include all the Louisiana Province and the Provinces of East and West Florida. The Bishops of Mexico, Agalopli, Michoacan, and Caracas were to contribute, *pro rata*, a fund for the support of the Bishop of New Orleans, until such time as the see would be self-sustaining. The decree left the choice of a bishop for the new see to the King of Spain, and he on 25 April, 1793, wrote to Bishop Cirilo relieving him of his office of auxiliary, and directing him to return immediately to Catalonia with a salary of one thousand dollars a year, which the Bishop of Havana was to contribute. Bishop Cirilo returned to Havana and seems to have resided with the Hospital Friars, while endeavouring to obtain his salary, so that he might return to Europe. It is not known where Bishop Cirilo died in poverty and humiliation.

The Right Rev. Luis Peñalver y Cárdenas was appointed first bishop of the new See of Saint Louis of New Orleans. He was a native of Havana, born 3 April, 1719, and had been educated by the Jesuits of his native city, receiving his degree in the university in 1771. He was a priest of irreproachable character, and a skillful director of souls. He was consecrated in the cathedral of Havana in 1793. The St. Louis parish church, now raised to the dignity of a cathedral, was dedicated 23 December, 1794. A letter from the king, 14 August, 1794, decreed that its donor, Don Almonaster, was authorized to occupy the most prominent seat in the church, second only to that of the viceregal patron, the intendant of the province, and to receive the kiss of peace during the Mass. Don Almonaster died in 1798 and was buried under the altar of the Sacred Heart.

Bishop Peñalver arrived in New Orleans, 17 July, 1795. In a report to the king and the Holy See he bewailed the indifference he found as to the practice of religious duties. He condemned the laxity of morals among the men, and the universal custom of concubinage among the slaves. The invasion of many persons not of the faith, and the toleration of the Government in admitting all classes of adventurers for purposes of trade, had brought about disrespect for religion. He deplored the establishment of trading posts, and of a lodge of French Freemasons, which counted among its members city officials, officers of the garrison, merchants and foreigners. He believed the people clung to their French traditions. He said that the King of Spain possessed "their bodies but not their souls". He declared that "even the Ursuline Nuns, from whom good results were obtained in the education of girls, were so decidedly French in their inclinations that they refused to admit Spanish women, who wished to become members of their order and many were in tears because they were obliged to read spiritual exercises in Spanish books". It was a gloomy picture he presented: but he set faithfully to work and on 21 December, 1795, called a synod, the first and only one held in the diocese of colonial New Orleans. He also issued a letter of instruction to the clergy deploring the fact that many of his flock were more than five hundred leagues away, and how impossible it was to repair at one and the same time to all. He enjoined the pastors to walk in the footsteps of Jesus Christ and in all things to fulfil their duties. This letter of instruction bearing his signature is preserved in the archives of the diocese, and, with the call for the synod, forms the only documents signed by the first Bishop of New Orleans.

Bishop Peñalver everywhere showed himself active in the cause of educational progress and was a generous benefactor of the poor. He was promoted to the See of Guatemala, 20 July, 1801. Before his departure he appointed, as vicars-general, Rev. Thomas Canon Hasset and Rev. Patrick Walsh, who became officially recognized as "Governors of the Diocese".

Territorially from this ancient see have been erected the Archbishoprics of St. Louis, Cincinnati, St. Paul, Dubuque, and Chicago, and the Bishoprics of Alexandria, Mobile, Natchez, Galveston, San Antonio, Little Rock, St. Augustine, Kansas City, St. Joseph, Davenport, Cheyenne, Dallas, Winona, Duluth, Concordia, Omaha, Sioux Falls, Oklahoma, St. Cloud, Bismarck, and Cleveland.

Right Rev. Francis Porro y Peinade, a Franciscan of the Convent of the Holy Apostles, Rome, was appointed to succeed Bishop Peñalver. But he never took possession of the see. Some old chronicles in

Louisiana say that he was never consecrated; others that he was, and died on the eve of leaving Rome. Bishop Portier (Spalding's "Life of Bishop Flaget"), says that he was translated to the See of Tarrazona. The See of New Orleans remained vacant many years after the departure of Bishop Peñalver.

In 1798 the Duc d'Orléans (afterwards King Louis-Philippe of France) with his two brothers, the Duc de Montpensier and the Count de Beaujolais, visited New Orleans. They were received with honour, and when Louis-Philippe became King of France he remembered many of those who had entertained him when in exile, and was generous to the Church in the old French province.

III. FRENCH AND AMERICAN PERIOD.—By the Treaty of San Ildefonse, the Spanish King on 1 October, 1800, engaged to retrocede Louisiana to the French Republic six months after certain conditions and stipulations had been executed on the part of France, and the Holy See deferred the appointment of a bishop.

On 30 April, 1803, without waiting for the actual transfer of the province, Napoleon Bonaparte by the Treaty of Paris sold Louisiana to the United States. De Laussat, the French Commissioner, had reached New Orleans on 26 March, 1803, to take possession of the province in the name of France. Spain was preparing to evacuate and general confusion prevailed. Very Rev. Thomas Hasset, the administrator of the diocese, was directed to address each priest and ascertain whether they preferred to return with the Spanish forces or remain in Louisiana; also to obtain from each parish an inventory of the plate, vestments, and other articles in the Church which had been given by the Spanish Government. Then came the news of the cession of the province to the United States. On 30 April, 1803, De Laussat formally surrendered the colony to the United States commissioners. The people felt it keenly, and the cathedral archives show the difficulties to be surmounted. Father Hasset, as administrator, issued a letter to the clergy on 10 June, 1803, announcing the new domination and notifying all of the permission to return to Spain if they desired. Several priests signified their desire to follow the Spanish standard. The question of withdrawal was also discussed by the Ursuline Nuns. Thirteen out of the twenty-one choir nuns were in favour of returning to Spain or going to Havana. De Laussat went to the convent and assured them that they could remain unmolested. Notwithstanding this Mother St. Monica and eleven others, with nearly all the lay sisters applied to the Marquis de Casa Calvo to convey them to Havana. Six choir nuns and two lay sisters remained to begin again the work in Louisiana. They elected Mother St. Xavier Fargeon as superioress, and resumed all the exercises of community life, maintaining their academy, day school, orphan asylum, hospital and instructions for coloured people in catechism. Father Hasset wrote to Bishop Carroll, 23 December, 1803, that the retrocession of the province to the United States of America impelled him to present to his consideration the present ecclesiastical state of Louisiana, not doubting that it would soon fall under his jurisdiction. The ceded province consisted of twenty-one parishes some of which were vacant. "The churches were", to use his own words, "all decent temples and comfortably supplied with ornaments and everything necessary for divine services. . . . Of twenty-six ecclesiastics in the province only four had agreed to continue their respective stations under the French Government; and whether any more would remain under that of the United States only God knew." Father Hasset said that for his own part he felt that he could not with propriety, relinquish his post, and consequently awaited superior orders to take his departure. He said that the Rev. Patrick Walsh, vicar-general and auxiliary governor of the diocese, had declared that he would not abandon his post providing he could hold it with propriety. Father Hasset died in April 1804. Father Antonio Sedella had returned to New Orleans in 1791, and resumed his duties as parish priest of the St. Louis Cathedral to which he had been appointed by Bishop Cirilo. After the cession a dispute arose between him and Father Walsh, and the latter, 27 March, 1805, established the Ursuline Convent as the only place in the parish for the administration of the sacraments and the celebration of the Divine Office. On 21 March, 1804, the Ursulines addressed a letter to Thomas Jefferson, President of the United States, in which they solicited the passage of an Act of Congress guaranteeing their property and rights. The president replied reassuring the Ursulines. "The principles of the constitution of the United States", he wrote, "are a sure guaranty to you that it will be preserved to you sacred and inviolate, and that your Institution will be permitted to govern itself according to its own voluntary rules without interference from the civil authority. Whatever diversity of shades may appear in the religious opinions of our fellow citizens, the charitable objects of your Institution cannot be of indifference to any; and its furtherance of the wholesome purpose by training up its young members in the way they should go, cannot fail to insure the patronage of the government it is under. Be assured that it will meet with all the protection my office can give it."

Father Walsh, administrator of the diocese, died on 22 August, 1806, and was buried in the Ursuline chapel. The Archiepiscopal See of Santo Domingo, the metropolitan of the province, to which the Diocese of Louisiana and the Floridas belonged, was vacant, and not one of the bishops of the Spanish province would interfere in the New Orleans Diocese, though the Bishop of Havana extended his authority once more over the Florida portion of the diocese. As the death of Father Walsh left the diocese without any one to govern it, Bishop Carroll, who had meanwhile informed himself of the condition of affairs, resolved to act under the decree of 1 Sept., 1805, and assume administration. Father Antoine had been openly accused of intriguing against the Government; but beyond accusations made to Bishop Carroll there is nothing to substantiate them. He was much loved in New Orleans and some of his friends desired to obtain the influence of the French Government to have him appointed to the Bishopric of Louisiana. However, there is in the archives of the New Orleans cathedral a letter from Father Antoine to the Bishop of Baltimore declaring that having heard that some members of the clergy and laity had applied to Rome to have him appointed to the Bishopric of Louisiana, he hereby declared to the Bishop of Baltimore that he could not consider the proposition, that he was unworthy of the honour and too old to do any good. He would be grateful to the bishop if he would cut short any further efforts in that direction.

Bishop Carroll wrote to James Madison, secretary of State (17 November, 1806) in regard to the Church in Louisiana, and the recommending of two or three clergymen one of whom might be appointed Bishop of New Orleans. Mr. Madison replied that the matter being purely ecclesiastical the Government could not interfere. He seemed, however, to share the opinions of Bishop Carroll in regard to the character and rights of Father Antoine. In 1806 a decree of the Propaganda confided Louisiana to the care of Bishop Carroll of Baltimore, and created him administrator Apostolic. He appointed Rev. John Olivier (who had been at Cahokia until 1803), Vicar-General of Louisiana and chaplain of the Ursuline Nuns at New Orleans. Father Olivier presented his documents to the Governor of Louisiana, and also wrote to Father Antoine Sedella apprising him of the action of the Propaganda. Father Antoine called upon Father Olivier, but he was not satisfied as to Bishop Carroll's authorization. The vicar-general published the decree and the bishop's letter at the convent chapel. The Rev. Thomas Flynn wrote from St. Louis, 8 Nov., 1806, that the trustees were about to install him. He describes the church as a good one with a tolerably good bell, a high altar, and commodious pews. The house for the priest was convenient but in need of repair. Except Rev. Father Maxwell there was scarcely a priest in Upper Louisiana in 1807.

As the original rescript issued by the Holy See to Bishop Carroll had not been so distinct and clear as to obviate objections, he applied to the Holy See asking that more ample and distinct authorization be sent. The Holy See placed the Province of Louisiana under Bishop Carroll who was requested to send to the New Orleans Diocese either Rev. Charles Nerinckx or some secular or regular priest, with the rank of administrator Apostolic and the rights of an ordinary to continue only at the good will of the Holy See according to instructions to be forwarded by the Propaganda. Bishop Carroll did not act immediately, but on 18 August, 1812, appointed the Rev. Louis G. V. Dubourg Administrator Apostolic of the Diocese of Louisiana and the two Floridas. Dr. Dubourg's authority was at once recognized by Father Antoine and the remainder of the clergy. The war between the United States and Great Britain was in progress and as the year 1814 drew to a close, Dr. Dubourg issued a pastoral letter calling upon the people to pray for the success of the American arms. During the battle of New Orleans (8 January, 1815) Gen. Andrew Jackson sent a messenger to the Ursuline Convent to ask for prayers for his success. When victory came he sent a courier thanking the sisters for their prayers, and he decreed a public thanksgiving; a solemn high Mass was celebrated in the St. Louis Cathedral, 23 January, 1815. The condition of religion in the diocese was not encouraging, seven out of fourteen parishes were vacant. Funds were also needed, and Dr. Dubourg went to Rome to ask for aid for his diocese. There the Propaganda appointed him bishop, 18 September, 1818, and on 24 September he was consecrated by Cardinal Joseph Pamfili (see DUBOURG).

Bishop Dubourg proposed the division of the diocese and the erection of a see in Upper Louisiana, but the news of troubles among the clergy in New Orleans and the attempt of the trustees to obtain a charter depriving the bishop of his cathedral so alarmed him that he solicited the Propaganda to allow him to take up his residence in St. Louis and establish his seminary and other educational institutions there. He sailed from Bordeaux for New Orleans (28 June, 1817), accompanied by five priests, four subdeacons, eleven seminarians, and three Christian Brothers. He took possession of the church at St. Genevieve, a ruined wooden structure, and was installed by Bishop Flaget. He then established the Lazarist Seminary at Bois Brule ("The Barrens"), and brought from Bardstown, where they were temporarily sojourning, Father Andreis, Father Rosati, and the seminarians who had accompanied him from Europe. The Brothers of the Christian Doctrine opened a boys' school at St. Genevieve. At his request the Religious of the Sacred Heart, comprising Mesdames Philippe Duchesne, Berthold, André, and two lay sisters reaching New Orleans, 30 May, 1818, proceeded to St. Louis and opened their convent at Florissant. In 1821 they established a convent at Grand Coteau, Louisiana. The Faith made great progress throughout the diocese. On 1 January, 1821, Bishop Dubourg held the first synod since the Purchase of Louisiana. Where he had found ten superannuated priests there were now forty active, zealous men at work. Still appeals came from all parts of the immense diocese for priests; among others he received a letter from the banks of the Columbia in Oregon begging him to send a priest to minister to 1500 Catholics there who had never had any one to attend to them. The Ursuline Nuns, frequently annoyed by being summoned to court, appealed to the Legislature claiming the privileges they had enjoyed under the French and Spanish dominations. Their ancient rights were recognized and a law was passed, 28 January, 1818, enacting that where the testimony of a nun was required it should be taken at the convent by commission. It had a far-reaching effect in later days upon legislation in the United States in similar cases.

Spain by treaty ceded Florida to the United States, 22 February, 1818, and Bishop Dubourg was then able to extend his episcopal care to that part of his diocese, the vast extent of which prompted him to form plans for the erection of a metropolitan see west of the Alleghanies. This did not meet with the approval of the bishops of the United States; he then proposed to divide the Diocese of Louisiana and the Floridas, establishing a see at New Orleans embracing Lower Louisiana, Mississippi, Alabama, and Florida. Finally, 13 August, 1822, the Vicariate Apostolic of Mississippi and Alabama was formed with the Rev. Joseph Rosati, elected Bishop of Tenagra, as vicar Apostolic. But Archbishop Maréchal of Baltimore remonstrated because in establishing this vicariate, the Propaganda had inadvertently invaded the rights of the Archbishop of Baltimore as the whole of those States except a small portion south of the thirty-first degree between Perdido and Pearl River belonged to the Diocese of Baltimore. Bishop Rosati also wrote representing the poverty and paucity of the Catholics in Mississippi and Alabama, and the necessity of his remaining at the head of the seminary. Finally his arguments and the protests of the Archbishop of Baltimore prevailed, and the Holy See suppressed the vicariate, appointing Dr. Rosati coadjutor to Bishop Dubourg to reside at St. Louis. Bishop Rosati was consecrated by Bishop Dubourg at Donaldsonville, 25 March, 1824, and proceeded at once to St. Louis. In 1823 Bishop Dubourg took up the subject of the Indian Missions and laid before the Government the necessity of a plan for the civilization and conversion of the Indians west of the Mississippi. His plan met with the approval of the Government and an allowance of $200 a year was assigned to four or five missionaries, to be increased if the project proved successful.

On 29 August, 1825, Alabama and the Floridas were erected into a vicariate Apostolic, with the Rev. Michael Portier the first bishop. The Holy See divided the Diocese of Louisiana (18 July, 1826) and established the See of New Orleans with Louisiana as its diocese, and the Vicariate Apostolic of Mississippi to be administered by the Bishop of New Orleans. The country north of Louisiana was made the Diocese of St. Louis, Bishop Rosati being transferred to that see. Bishop Dubourg, though a man of vast projects and of great service to the Church, was little versed in business methods; discouraged at the difficulties that rose to thwart him he resigned his see and was transferred to Montauban. Bishop Rosati, appointed to the See of New Orleans, declined the appointment urging that his knowledge of English qualified him to labour better in Missouri, Illinois, and Arkansas, while he was not sufficiently versed in French to address the people of New Orleans with success. On 20 March, 1827, the papal Brief arrived permitting him to remain in St. Louis but charging him for a while with the administration of the See of New Orleans. He appointed the Rev. Leo Raymond de Neckere, C.M., vicar-general, and strongly recommended his appointment for the vacant see. Father de Neckere, then in Belgium whither he had gone to recuperate his health, was summoned to Rome and appointed bishop. Returning to New Orleans he was consecrated, 16 May, 1830. Bishop de Neckere was born, 6 June, 1800, at Wevelghem, Belgium, and while a seminarian at Ghent, was accepted for the Diocese of New Orleans by Bishop Dubourg. He joined the Lazarists and was ordained in St. Louis, Missouri, 13 October, 1822. On 23 February, 1832, he convoked a synod attended by twenty-one priests. Regulations were promulgated for better discipline and steps were taken to form an association for the dissemination of good literature.

Americans were now pouring into New Orleans. The ancient French limits had long since disappeared. Such was the enterprise on all sides that in 1830 New Orleans ranked in importance immediately after New York, Philadelphia, and Boston. It was the greatest cotton and sugar market in the world. Irish emigration also set in, and a church for the English-speaking people was an absolute necessity as the cathedral and the old Ursuline chapel were the only places of worship in New Orleans. A site was bought on Camp Street near Julia, a frame church, St. Patrick's, was erected and dedicated on 21 April, 1833. Rev. Adam Kindelon was the pastor of this, the first English-speaking congregation of New Orleans. The foundation of this parish was one of the last official acts of Bishop de Neckere. The year was one of sickness and death. Cholera and yellow fever raged. The priests were kept busy day and night, and the vicar general, Father B. Richards, and Fathers Martial, Tichitoli, Kindelon fell victims to their zeal. Bishop de Neckere, who had retired to a convent at Convent, La., in hope of restoring his shattered health, returned at once to the city upon the outbreak of the epidemic, and began visiting and ministering to the plague-stricken. Soon he too was seized with fever and succumbed ten days later, 5 September, 1833. Just before the bishop's death there arrived in New Orleans a priest who was destined to exercise for many years an influence upon the life and progress of the Church and the Commonwealth, Father James Ignatius Mullen; he was immediately appointed to the vacant rectorship of St. Patrick's. Upon the death of Bishop de Neckere, Fathers Anthony Blanc and V. Lavadière, S.J., became the administrators of the diocese. In November, undismayed by the epidemic which still continued, a band of Sisters of Charity set out from Emmitsburg, to take charge of the Charity Hospital of New Orleans. The sisters had come into the diocese about 1832 to assume the direction of the Poydras Asylum, erected by Julian Poydras, a Huguenot. Seven of the new colony from Emmittsburg were sent to the Asylum and ten to the Charity Hospital. Bishop de Neckere had invited the Tertiary Sisters of Mount Carmel to make a foundation in New Orleans, which they did on 22 October, 1833, a convent school and orphanage being opened.

Father Augustine Jeanjean was selected by Rome to fill the episcopal vacancy, but he declined and Father Anthony Blanc was appointed and consecrated on 22 November, 1835 (see BLANC, ANTHONY). Bishop Blanc knew the great want of the diocese, the need of priests, whose ranks had been decimated by age, pestilence, and overwork. To meet this want Bishop Blanc asked the Jesuits to establish a college in Louisiana. They arrived on 22 January, 1837, and opened a college at Grand Coteau on 5 January, 1838. He then invited the Lazarists and on 20 December, 1838, they arrived and at once opened a diocesan seminary at Bayou Lafourche. In 1836, Julian Poydras having died, the Asylum which he founded passed entirely under Presbyterian auspices, and the Sisters of Charity being compelled to relinquish the direction, St. Patrick's Orphan Asylum, now New Orleans Female Orphan Asylum, was founded and placed under their care. In 1841 the Sisters Marianites of Holy Cross came to New Orleans to assume charge of St. Mary's Orphan Boys' Asylum. They opened also an Academy for young ladies and the Orphanage of the Immaculate Conception for girls. The wants of the coloured people also deeply concerned Bishop Blanc, and he worked assiduously for the proper spiritual care of the slaves. After the insurrection of San Domingo in 1793 a large number of free coloured people from that island who were slave-holders themselves took refuge in New Orleans. Thus was created a free coloured population among which successive epidemics played havoc leaving aged and orphans to be cared for. Accordingly in 1842 Bishop Blanc and Father Rousselon, V.G., founded the Sisters of the Holy Family, whose duty was the care of the coloured orphans and the aged coloured poor. It was the first coloured sisterhood founded in the United States, and one of the only two that exist.

Bishop Blanc planned the erection of new parishes in the City of New Orleans, and St. Joseph's and the Annunciation were founded in 1844. The foundation of these parishes greatly diminished the congregation of the cathedral and the trustees seeing their influence waning entered upon a new war against religion. Upon the death of Father Aloysius Moni, Bishop Blanc appointed Father C. Maenhaut rector of the cathedral, but the wardens refused to recognize his appointment, claiming the right of patronage formerly enjoyed by the King of Spain. They brought an action against the bishop in the parish court, but the judge decided against the trustees, and the case was appealed to the Supreme Court. The Supreme Court decided that the right to nominate a parish priest, or the *jus patronatus* of Spanish law, was abrogated in the state, and the decision of the Holy See was sustained. But the wardens refused to recognize this decision and the bishop ordered the clergy to withdraw from the cathedral and parochial residence. One of the members of the board, who was a member of the city council, obtained the passage of a law punishing by fine any priest who should perform the burial service over a dead body except in the old mortuary chapel erected in 1826 as part of the cathedral parish. Under this ordinance Rev. Bernard Permoli was prosecuted. The old chapel had long outlived its purpose, and on 19 December, 1842, Judge Preval decided the ordinance illegal, and the Supreme Court of the United States sustained his decision. The faithful of St. Patrick's parish having publicly protested against the outrageous proceedings, the tide of public opinion set in strongly against the men who thus defied all church authority. In January, 1843, the latter submitted and received the parish priest appointed by the bishop. Soon after the faithful Catholics of the city petitioned the Legislature to amend the Act incorporating the cathedral, and bring it into harmony with ecclesiastical discipline. Even after the decision of the Legislature the bishop felt that he could not treat with the wardens as they defied his authority by authorizing the erection of a monument to Freemasons in the Catholic cemetery of St. Louis. To free the faithful, he therefore continued to plan for the organization of parishes and the erection of new churches. Only one low Mass was said at the cathedral, and that on Sunday. Bishop Blanc convened the third synod of the diocese on 21 April, at which the clergy were warned against yielding to the illegal claims of trustees, and the erection of any church without a deed being first made to the bishop was forbidden. For the churches in which the trustees system still existed special regulations were made, governing the method of keeping accounts. At the close of 1844 the trustees, defeated in the courts and held in contempt by public opinion throughout the diocese, yielded completely to Bishop Blanc.

This controversy terminated, a period of remarkable activity in the organization of parishes and the building of new churches set in. The cornerstone of St. Mary's, intended to replace the old Ursuline chapel attached to the bishop's house, was laid on 16 Feb., 1845; that of St. Joseph's on 16 April, 1846; that of the Annunciation on 10 May, 1846. The Redemptorists founded the parish of the Assumption, and were installed in its church on 22 Oct., 1847. The parish of Mater Dolorosa at Carrollton (then a suburb) was founded on 8 Sept.; that of the Holy Name of Mary at Algiers on 18 Dec., 1848. In 1849 St. Stephen's parish in the then suburb of Bouligny under the Lazarist Fathers and Sts. Peter and Paul came into existence. The corner-stone of the Redemptorist church of St. Alphonsus was laid by the famous Apostle of Temperance, Father Theobald Mathew, on 11 April, 1850; two years later it was found necessary to enlarge this church, and a school was added. In 1851 the foundation-stone of the church of the Immaculate Conception was laid, on the site of a humbler edifice erected in 1848. This is said to have been the first church in the world dedicated to the Immaculate Conception. The parishes of St. John the Baptist in the upper town and of St. Anne in the French quarter were organized in 1852.

The French congregation of Notre-Dame de Bon Secours was organized on 16 Jan., 1858. In the midst of great progress yellow fever broke out and five priests and two Sisters of Charity swelled the roll of martyrs. The devoted services of the Sisters of Charity, especially during the ravages of the yellow fever, in attending the sick and caring for the orphans were so highly appreciated by the Legislature that in 1846 the State made them a grant of land near Donaldsonville for the opening of a novitiate, and a general subscription was made throughout the diocese for this purpose. The sisters established themselves in Donaldsonville the same year.

In 1843, anxious to provide for the wants of the increasing German and Irish emigration, Bishop Blanc had summoned the Congregation of the Redemptorists to the diocese and the German parish of St. Mary's Assumption was founded by Rev. Czackert of that congregation. In 1847 the work of the Society of Jesus in the diocese, which had been temporarily suspended, was resumed under Father Maisounabe as superior, and a college building was started on 10 June. In the following year Father Maisounabe and a brilliant young Irish associate, Father Blackney, fell victims to yellow fever. The population of New Orleans now numbered over fifty thousand, among whom were many German immigrants. Bishop Blanc turned over the old Ursuline chapel to the Germans of the lower portion of the city, and a church was erected, which finally resulted in the foundation of the Holy Trinity parish on 26 October, 1847. In 1849 the College of St. Paul was opened at Baton Rouge. On 13 July, 1852, St. Charles College became a corporate institution with Rev. A. J. Jourdan, S.J., as president. In 1849 Bishop Blanc attended the Seventh Council of Baltimore at which the bishops expressed their desire that the See of New Orleans be raised to metropolitan rank. On 19 July, 1850, Pius X established the Archdiocese of New Orleans, Bishop Blanc being raised to the archiepiscopal dignity. The Province of New Orleans was to embrace New Orleans with Mobile, Natchez, Little Rock, and Galveston as suffragan sees. The spirit of Knownothingism invaded New Orleans as other parts of the United States, and Archbishop Blanc found himself in the thick of the battle. Public debates were held, conspicuous among those who did yeoman service in crushing the efforts of the party in Louisiana being the Hon. Thos. J. Semmes, a distinguished advocate, Rev. Francis Xavier Leray and Rev. N. J. Perche, both afterwards Archbishop of New Orleans. Father Perche founded (1844) a French diocesan journal "Le Propagateur Catholique", which vigorously assailed the Knownothing doctrines. On 6 June a mob attacked the office of the paper, and also made a fierce attack on the Ursuline Convent, breaking doors and windows and hurling insults at the nuns.

In 1853 New Orleans was desolated by the worst epidemic of yellow fever in its history, seven priests and five sisters being among its victims. On 6 March, 1854, the School Sisters of Notre Dame arrived in New Orleans to take charge of St. Joseph's Asylum, founded to furnish homes for those orphaned by the epidemic. St. Vincent's Orphan Asylum was also opened as a home for foundlings and infant orphans, and entrusted to the Sisters of Charity. On 29 July, 1853, the Holy See divided the Diocese of New Orleans, which at that time embraced all Louisiana, and established the See of Natchitoches (q. v.). The new diocese contained about twenty-five thousand Catholics, chiefly a rural population, for whom there were only seven churches. The Convent of the Sacred Heart at Natchitoches was the only religious institution in the new diocese. In 1854 Archbishop Blanc went to Rome and was present at the solemn definition of the dogma of the Immaculate Conception. In his report to the Propaganda he describes his diocese as containing forty quasi-parishes, each with a church and one or two priests and a residence for the clergy; the city had eighteen churches. The diocese had a seminary under the Priests of the Mission with an average of nine students; the religious orders at work were the Jesuits with three establishments, Priests of the Mission with three, and Redemptorists with two. The Catholic population of 95,000 was made up of natives of French, Spanish, Irish, or American origin, French, Germans, Spaniards, and Italians. Distinctive Catholic schools were increasing. The Ursulines, Religious of the Sacred Heart, Sisters of Holy Charity, Marianites of the Holy Cross, Tertiary Carmelites, School Sisters of Notre Dame, and the Coloured Sisters of the Holy Family were doing excellent work. Many abuses had crept in especially with regard to marriage, but after the erection of new churches with smaller parochial school districts, religion had gained steadily and the frequentation of the sacraments was increasing.

In 1855 the Fathers of the Congregation of the Holy Cross came to New Orleans to establish a manual industrial school for the training of the orphan boys who had been rendered homeless by the terrible epidemic of 1853. They established themselves in the lower portion of New Orleans, and became inseparably identified with religious and educational progress. In 1879 they opened their college, which is now one of the leading institutions of Louisiana. On 20 January, 1856, the First Provincial Council of New Orleans was held, and in January, 1858, Archbishop Blanc held the fourth diocesan synod. In 1859 the Sisters of the Good Shepherd were called by Archbishop Blanc to New Orleans to open a reformatory for girls. Bishop Blanc opened another diocesan seminary in the same year, and placed it in charge of the Lazarist Fathers. He convoked the second provincial council on 22 January, 1860. Just before the second session opened he was taken so seriously ill that he could no longer attend the meetings; he rallied and seemed to regain his usual health, but he died 20 June following.

Right Rev. John Mary Odin, Bishop of Galveston, was appointed successor to Archbishop Blanc, and arrived in New Orleans on the Feast of Pentecost, 1861. The Civil War had already begun and excitement was intense. All the prudence and charity of the archbishop were needed as the war progressed. An earnest maintainer of discipline, Archbishop Odin found it necessary on 1 January, 1863, to issue regulations regarding the recklessness and carelessness that had prevailed in the temporal management of the churches the indebtedness of which he had been compelled to assume to save them from bankruptcy. The regulations were not favourably received, and the archbishop visited Rome returning in the spring of 1863, when he had obtained the approval of the Holy See for his course of action. It was not till some time later that through his charity and zeal he obtained the cordial support he desired. His appeals for priests while in Europe were not unheeded and early in 1863 forty seminarians and five Ursulines arrived with Bishop Dubuis of Galveston. Among the priests were Fathers Gustave A. Rouxel, later Auxiliary Bishop of New Orleans under Archbishop Chapelle, Thomas Heslin, afterwards Bishop of Natchez, and J. R. Bogaerts, vicar-general under Archbishop Janssens. In 1860 the Dominican Nuns from Cabra, Ireland, came to New Orleans to take charge of St. John the Baptist School and open an academy. In 1864 the Sisters of Mercy came to the city to assume charge of St. Alphonsus' School and Asylum and open a convent and boarding-school, and the Marists were offered the Church of St. Michael at Convent, La. On 12 July, 1864, they assumed charge of Jefferson College founded by the State in 1835, and donated to them by Valcour Aime, a wealthy planter. The diocese was incorporated on 15 August, 1866, the legal name and title being "The Roman Catholic Church of the Diocese of New Orleans". In 1867 during a terrible epidemic of yellow fever and cholera, Fathers Spiessberger and Seelos of the Redemptorists died martyrs of charity. Father Seelos was regarded as a saint and the cause of his beatification has been introduced in Rome (1905). In 1866, owing to financial trials throughout the South, the diocesan seminary was closed. In February, 1868, Archbishop Odin founded "The Morning Star" as the official organ of the Archdiocese, which it has continued to be.

During the nine years of Bishop Odin's administration he nearly doubled the number of his clergy and churches. He attended the Council of the Vatican, but was obliged to leave Rome on the entry of the Garibaldian troops. His health was broken and he returned to his native home, Ambierle, France, where he died on 25 May, 1870. He was born on 25 February, 1801, and entered the Lazarists. He came as a novice to their seminary, The Barrens, in St. Louis, where he completed his theological studies and received ordination (see GALVESTON, DIOCESE OF). He was an excellent administrator and left his diocese free from debt.

Archbishop Odin was succeeded by the Rev. Napoleon Joseph Perche, born at Angers, France, January, 1805, and died on 27 December, 1883. The latter completed his studies at the Seminary of Beaupré, was ordained on 19 September, 1829, and sent to Murr near Angers where he worked zealously. In 1837 he came to America with Bishop Flaget and was appointed pastor of Portland. He came to New Orleans with Bishop Blanc in 1841, and he soon became famous in Louisiana for his eloquence and learning. Archbishop Odin petitioned Rome for the appointment of Father Perche as his coadjutor with the right of succession. His request was granted and, on 1 May, 1870, Father Perche was consecrated in the cathedral of New Orleans titular Bishop of Abdera. He was promoted to the see on 25 May, 1870. One of his first acts was the re-establishment of the diocesan seminary. The Benedictine Nuns were received into the diocese in 1870.

The Congregation of the Immaculate Conception, a diocesan sisterhood, was founded in the year 1873 by Father Cyprien Venissat, at Labadieville, to afford education and assistance to the children of families impoverished by the war. In 1875 the Poor Clares made a foundation, and on 21 November, 1877, the Discalced Carmelite Nuns of St. Louis sent two members to make a foundation in New Orleans, their monastery being opened on 11 May, 1878. In 1878 the new parish of the Sacred Heart of Jesus was organized and placed in charge of the Holy Cross Fathers from Indiana. On 12 October, 1872, the Sisters of Perpetual Adoration opened their missions and schools in New Orleans. In 1879 the Holy Cross Fathers opened a college in the lower portion of the city. Owing to the financial difficulties it was necessary to close the diocesan seminary in 1881. Archbishop Perche was a great scholar, but he lacked administrative ability. In his desire to relieve Southern families ruined by the war, he gave to all largely and royally, and thus plunged the diocese into a debt of over $600,000. He was growing very feeble and an application was made to Rome for a coadjutor.

Bishop Francis Xavier Leray of Natchitoches was transferred to New Orleans as coadjutor and Apostolic administrator of affairs on 23 October, 1879, and at once set to work to liquidate the immense debt. It was during the administration of Archbishop Perche and the coadjutorship of Bishop Leray that the Board of Trustees of the cathedral which formerly had caused so much trouble passed out of existence in July, 1881, and transferred all the cathedral property to Archbishop Perche and Bishop Leray jointly, for the benefit and use of the Catholic population. Archbishop Leray was born at Château Giron, Brittany, France, 20 April, 1825. He responded to the appeal for priests for the Diocese of Louisiana in 1843, and completed his theological studies at the Sulpician seminary in Baltimore. He accompanied Bishop Chanche to Natchez and was ordained by him on 19 March, 1852. He was a most active missionary in the Mississippi district and in 1860 when pastor of Vicksburg he brought the Sisters of Mercy from Baltimore to establish a school there. Several times during his years of activity as a priest he was stricken with yellow fever.

During the Civil War, he served as a Confederate chaplain; and on several occasions he was taken prisoner by the Federal forces but released as soon as the sacred character of his office was established. On the death of Bishop Martin he was appointed to the See of Natchitoches, and consecrated on 22 April, 1877, at Rennes, France; on 23 October, 1879, he was appointed coadjutor to Archbishop Perche of New Orleans and Bishop of Janopolis. His most difficult task was the bringing of financial order out of chaos and reducing the enormous debt of the diocese. In this he met with great success. During his administration the debt was reduced by at least $300,000. His health, however, became impaired, and he went to France in the hope of recuperating, and died at Château Giron, on 23 September, 1887.

The see remained vacant for nearly a year, Very Rev. G. A. Rouxel administering the affairs of the diocese, until the Right Rev. Francis Janssens, Bishop of Natchez, was promoted to fill the vacancy on 7 August, 1888, and took possession on 16 September, 1888. Archbishop Janssens was born at Tilburg, Holland, on 17 October, 1843. At thirteen he began his studies in the seminary at Bois-le-Duc; he remained there ten years, and in 1866 entered the American College at Louvain, Belgium. He was ordained on 21 December, 1867, and arranged to come to America. He arrived at Richmond in September, 1868, and became pastor of the cathedral in 1870. He was administrator of the diocese pending the appointment of the Right Rev. James (later Cardinal) Gibbons to the vacant see; Bishop Gibbons appointed him vicar-general, and five years later when he was appointed to the Archiepiscopal See of Baltimore, Father Janssens became again administrator of the diocese. On 7 April, 1881, the See of Natchez became vacant by the promotion of Right Rev. Wm. Elder as Archbishop of Cincinnati and Father Janssens succeeded. While Bishop of Natchez he completed the cathedral commenced forty years before by Bishop Chanche. Not the least of the difficulties that awaited him as Archbishop of New Orleans was the heavy indebtedness resting upon the see and the constant drain thus made which had exhausted the treasury. There was no seminary and the rapid growth of the population augmented the demand for priests. He at once called a meeting of the clergy and prominent citizens, and plans were formulated for the gradual liquidation of the debt of the diocese, which was found to be

NEW ORLEANS

JACKSON SQUARE AND CATHEDRAL OF ST. LOUIS
THE OLD VAULTS OF ST. LOUIS CEMETERY
ST. ROCH'S CHAPEL AND CEMETERY
THE ARCHBISHOP'S PALACE, THE OLDEST HOUSE IN NEW ORLEANS

$324,759. Before his death he had reduced it to about $130,000. Notwithstanding this burden, the diocese, through the zeal of Archbishop Janssens, entered upon a period of unusual activity. One of his first acts, March, 1890, was to found a little seminary, which was opened at Pontchatoula, La., 3 September, 1891, and placed under the direction of the Benedictine Fathers. He went to Europe in 1889 to secure priests for the diocese and to arrange for the sale of bonds for the liquidation of the debt. In August, 1892, after the lynching of the Italians who assassinated the chief of police, the Missionary Sisters of the Sacred Heart, founded in Italy by Mother Cabrina for work among Italian emigrants, arrived in New Orleans and opened a large mission, a free school, and an asylum for Italian orphans, and began also mission work among the Italian gardeners on the outskirts of the city and at Kenner, La. The same year a terrific cyclone and storm swept the Louisiana Gulf coast, and laid low the lands along the Caminada Cheniere where there was a settlement of Italian and Spanish and Malay fishermen. Out of a population of 1500 over 800 were swept away. Rev. Father Grimaud performed the burial services over 400 bodies as they were washed ashore. Father Bedel at Buras buried over three hundred, and went out at night to succour the wandering and helpless. Archbishop Janssens in a small boat went among the lonely and desolate island settlements comforting the people and helping them to rebuild their broken homes.

In 1893, the centenary of the diocese was celebrated with splendour at the St. Louis Cathedral; Cardinal Gibbons and many of the hierarchy were present. Archbishop Janssens was instrumental, at this time, in establishing the Louisiana Lepers' Home at Indian Camp, and it was through his offices that the Sisters of Charity from Emmittsburg took charge of the home. He was deeply interested in the work of the coloured Sisters of the Holy Family, now domiciled in the ancient Quadroon Ball Room and Theatre of *antebellum* days, which had been turned into a convent and boarding-school. Through the generosity of a coloured philanthropist, Thomy Lafon, Archbishop Janssens was enabled to provide a larger and more comfortable home for the aged coloured poor, a new asylum for the boys, and through the legacy of $20,000 left for this purpose by Mr. Lafon, who died in 1883, a special home, under the care of the Sisters of the Good Shepherd, for the reform of coloured girls. The St. John Berchman's chapel, a memorial to Thomy Lafon, was erected in the Convent of the Holy Family which he had so befriended. At this time Archbishop Janssens estimated the number of Catholics in the diocese at 341,613; the value of church property at $3,861,075; the number of baptisms a year 15,000 and the number of deaths, 5000.

In 1896 the Catholic Winter School of America was organized and was formally opened by Cardinal Satolli, then Apostolic Delegate to the United States. After the death of Archbishop Janssens the lecture courses were abandoned. The active life led by the archbishop told heavily upon him. Anxious to liquidate entirely the debt of the diocese he made arrangements to visit Europe in 1897, but died aboard the steamer Creole, 19 June, on the voyage to New York.

Most Rev. Placide Louis Chapelle, D.D., Archbishop of Santa Fé, was appointed to the vacant See of New Orleans, 1 December, 1897. Shortly after coming to New Orleans he found it imperative to go to Europe to effect a settlement for the remainder of the diocesan debt of $130,000. While he was in Europe war was declared between Spain and the United States, and, upon the declaration of peace, Archbishop Chapelle was appointed Apostolic delegate extraordinary to Cuba and Porto Rico and chargé d'affaires to the Philippine Islands. Returning from Europe he arranged for the assessment of five per cent upon the salaries of the clergy for five years for the liquidation of the diocesan debt. In October 1900 he closed the little seminary at Ponchatoula and opened a higher one in New Orleans, placing it in charge of the Lazarist Fathers. The Right Rev. G. A. Rouxel was appointed auxiliary bishop for the See of New Orleans, and was consecrated 10 April, 1899. Right Rev. J. M. Laval was made vicar-general and rector of the St. Louis Cathedral on 21 April, and Very Rev. James H. Blenk was appointed Bishop of Porto Rico and consecrated in the St. Louis Cathedral with Archbishop Barnada of Santiago de Cuba, 2 July, 1899. Archbishop Chapelle was absent from the diocese during the greater part of his administration, duties in the Antilles and the Philippines in connexion with his position as Apostolic Delegate claiming his attention, nevertheless he accomplished much for New Orleans. The diocesan debt was extinguished, and the activity in church work which had begun under Archbishop Janssen continued; returning to New Orleans he introduced into the diocese the Dominican Fathers from the Philippines. In the summer of 1905, while the archbishop was administering confirmation in the country parishes, yellow fever broke out in New Orleans, and, deeming it his duty to be among his people, he returned immediately to the city. On the way from the train to his residence he was stricken, and died 9 August, 1905 (see CHAPELLE, PLACIDE LOUIS). Auxiliary Bishop Rouxel became the administrator of the diocese pending the appointment of a successor. The Right Rev. James Hurbert Blenk, S.M., D.D., Bishop of Porto Rico, was promoted to New Orleans, 20 April, 1906.

IV. CONTEMPORARY CONDITIONS. — Archbishop Blenk was born at Neustadt, Bavaria, 28 July, 1856, of Protestant parentage. While a child, his family came to New Orleans, and it was here that the light of the true Faith dawned upon the boy; he was baptized in St. Alphonsus Church at the age of twelve. His primary education having been completed in New Orleans, he entered Jefferson College where he completed his classical and scientific studies under the Marist Fathers. He spent three years at the Marist house of studies in Belley, France, completed his probationary studies at the Marist novitiate at Lyons, and was sent to Dublin to follow a higher course of mathematics at the Catholic University. Thence he went to St. Mary's College, Dundalk, County Louth, where he occupied the chair of mathematics. Later he returned to the Marist house of studies in Dublin where he completed his theological studies. 16 August, 1885, he was ordained priest, and returned that year to Louisiana to labour among his own people. He was stationed as a professor at Jefferson College of which he became president in 1891 and held the position for six years. In 1896, at the invitation of the general of the Marists, he visited all the houses of the congregation in Europe, and returning to New Orleans in February, 1897, he became the rector of the Church of the Holy Name of Mary, Algiers, which was in charge of the Marist Fathers. He erected the handsome presbytery and gave a great impetus to religion and education in the parish and city, being chairman of the Board of Studies of the newly organized Winter School. He was a member of the Board of Consultors during the administration of Archbishop Janssens and of Archbishop Chapelle; the latter selected him as the auditor and secretary of the Apostolic Delegation to Cuba and Porto Rico. He was appointed the first bishop of the Island of Porto Rico under the American occupation 12 June, 1899. A hurricane overswept Porto Rico just before Bishop Blenk left to take possession of his see; through his personal efforts he raised over $30,000 in the United States to take with him to alleviate the sufferings of his new people. The successful work of Bishop Blenk is a part of the history of the reconstruction along

American lines of the Antilles. He returned to New Orleans as archbishop, 1 July, 1906, and new life was infused into every department of religious and educational and charitable endeavour. Splendid new churches and schools were erected, especially in the country parishes. Among the new institutions were St. Joseph's Seminary and College at St. Benedict, La.; St. Charles College, Grand Coteau, built on the ruins of the old college destroyed by fire; Lake Charles Sanitarium; Marquette University; and the Seaman's Haven, where a chapel was opened for sailors. The new sisterhoods admitted to the diocese were the Religious of the Incarnate Word in charge of a sanitarium at Lake Charles; the Religious of Divine Providence in charge of the school in Broussardville; and the French Benedictine Sisters driven from France, who erected the new Convent of St. Gertrude at St. Benedict, La., destined as an industrial school for girls. A large industrial school and farm for coloured boys under the direction of the Sisters of the Holy Family was opened in Gentilly Road, and two new parishes outlined for the exclusive care of the coloured race. In 1907, the seminary conducted by the Lazarist Fathers was closed and Archbishop Blenk opened a preparatory seminary and placed it in charge of the Benedictine Fathers. The diocese assumed full charge of the Chinchuba Deaf-mute Institute, which was established under Archbishop Janssens and is the only Catholic institute for deaf-mutes in the South. It is in charge of the School Sisters of Notre Dame.

New Orleans' priesthood, like the population of Louisiana, is cosmopolitan. The training of the priesthood has been conducted at home and abroad, the diocese owing much to the priests who came from France, Spain, Ireland, Germany, and Holland. Several efforts were made to establish a permanent seminary and recruit the ranks of the priesthood from the diocese itself. At various times also the diocese had students at St. Mary's and St. Charles Seminary, Baltimore, the American College, Louvain, and has (1910) twelve theological students in different seminaries of Europe and America. Each parish is incorporated and there are the corporate institutions of the Jesuits and other religious communities. The houses of study for religious are the Jesuit scholasticate at Grand Coteau, and the Benedictine scholasticate of St. Benedict at St. Benedict, La. The Poor Clares, discalced Carmelites, Benedictine Nuns, Congregation of Marianites of the Holy Cross, Ursuline Nuns, Religious of the Sacred Heart, Sisters of St. Joseph, Sisters of Perpetual Adoration, Sisters of the Immaculate Conception, Sisters of the Holy Family (coloured), Sisters of Mount Carmel, have mother-houses with novitiates in New Orleans. In early days there were distinctive parishes in New Orleans for French-, English-, and German-speaking Catholics, but with the growing diffusion of the English language these parish lines have disappeared. In all the churches where necessary, there are French, English, and German sermons and instructions; there are churches and chapels for Italian emigrants and Hungarians, a German settlement at St. Leo near Rayne, domestic missions for negroes under the charge of the Holy Family Sisters and Josephite Fathers and Lazarists at New Orleans and Bayou Petite, Prairie.

The educational system is well organized. The principal institutions are: the diocesan normal school; the Marquette University under the care of the Jesuits; 7 colleges and academies with high school courses for boys with 1803 students; 17 academies for young ladies, under the direction of religious communities, with 2201 students; 102 parishes with parochial schools having an attendance of 20,000 pupils; 117 orphan asylums with 1341 orphans; 1 infant asylum with 164 infants; 1 industrial school for whites with 90 inmates; 1 industrial school for coloured orphan boys; 1 deaf-mute asylum with 40 inmates; 3 hospitals; 2 homes for the aged white, and 1 for the aged coloured poor; 1 house of the Good Shepherd for the reform of wayward girls; a Seaman's Haven. The state asylums for the blind, etc., hospitals, prisons, reformatories, almshouses, and secular homes for incurables, consumptives, convalescents, etc., are all visited by Catholic priests, Sisters of Mercy, conferences of St. Vincent de Paul, and St. Margaret's Daughters. There is absolute freedom of worship. The first St. Vincent de Paul conference was organized in 1852.

The diocese has one Benedictine abbey (St. Joseph's, of which Right Rev. Paul Schäuble is abbot); 156 secular priests, 123 priests in religious communities, making a total of 279 clergy; 133 churches with resident priests and 90 missions with churches, making a total of 223 churches; 35 stations and 42 chapels where Mass is said. The total Catholic population is 550,000; yearly baptisms include 15,155 white children, 253 white adults, 3111 coloured children, and 354 coloured adults (total number of baptisms 18,873); the communions average 750,180; confirmations 11,215; converts, 817; marriages, 3533 (including 323 mixed). The large centres of church activity are the cities of New Orleans, Baton Rouge, Plaquemine, Donaldsonville, Thibodeaux, Houma, Franklin, Jeannerette, New Iberia, Lafayette, Abbeville, Morgan City, St. Martin, Crowley, Lake Charles. The churches and schools are all insured; an association for assisting infirm priests, the Priests' Aid Society, has been established and mutual aid and benevolent associations in almost every parish for the assistance of the laity. Assimilation is constantly going on among the different nationalities that come to New Orleans through intermarriage between Germans, Italians, French, and Americans, and thus is created a healthy civic sentiment that conduces to earnest and harmonious progress along lines of religious, charitable, educational, and social endeavour. The Catholic laity of the diocese is naturally largely represented in the life and government of the community, the population being so overwhelmingly Catholic; Catholics hold prominent civil positions, such as governor, mayor, and member of the Bar, State Legislature, and United States Congress. A Catholic from Louisiana, Edward D. White, has been recently (1910) appointed Chief Justice of the Supreme Court of the United States. Catholics are connected with the state normal schools and colleges, are on the board of the state universities and public libraries, and are represented in the corps of professors, patrons, and pupils of the Louisiana State and Tulane universities. Three fourths of the teachers of the public schools of Louisiana are Catholics.

The laity take a very active interest in the religious life of the diocese. Every church and convent has its altar society for the care of the tabernacle, sodalities of the Blessed Virgin for young girls and women. The Holy Name Society for men, young and old, is established throughout the diocese, while conferences of St. Vincent de Paul are established in thirty churches. St. Margaret's Daughters, indulgenced like the Society of St. Vincent de Paul, has twenty-eight circles at work, and the Total Abstinence Society is established in many churches. Besides the Third Order of St. Francis, the diocese has confraternities of the Happy Death, the Holy Face, the Holy Rosary, and the Holy Agony; the Apostleship of Prayer is established in nearly all the churches, while many parishes have confraternities adapted to their special needs. The Catholic Knights of America and Knights of Columbus are firmly established, while the Holy Spirit Society, devoted to the defence of Catholic Faith, the diffusion of Catholic truth, and the establishment of churches and schools in wayside places, is doing noble work along church extension lines. Other societies are the Marquette League, the Society for the Propagation of the Faith, which traces its origin to Bishop Dubourg of Louisiana, the Society of the Holy Childhood, and the Priests' Eucharistic League. Religious life in the diocese is regular and characterized by strict discipline and earnest spirituality. Monthly conferences are held and ecclesiastical conferences three times a year.

The religious communities in the diocese are: (1) *Male:* Benedictines, Fathers and Brothers of the Holy Cross, Dominicans, Jesuits, Josephites, Lazarists, Marists, Redemptorists, and Brothers of the Sacred Heart; (2) *Female:* Sisters of St. Benedict, French Benedictine Sisters, Discalced Carmelite Nuns, Sisters of Mount Carmel, Poor Clares, Sisters of Charity, Sisters of Charity of the Incarnate Word, Sisters of Christian Charity, Sisters of Divine Providence, Dominican Sisters, Sisters of the Good Shepherd, Sisters of the Holy Family, Sisters of the Immaculate Conception, Sisters of St. Joseph, Little Sisters of the Poor, Sisters Marianites of the Holy Cross, Sisters of Mercy, School Sisters of Notre Dame, Sisters of Our Lady of Lourdes, Religious of the Sacred Heart, Ursuline Sisters, Missionary Sisters of the Sacred Heart, Sisters of Perpetual Adoration of the Blessed Sacrament. Coloured Catholics: The works in behalf of the coloured race began in the earliest days in Louisiana, when the Jesuits devoted themselves especially to the care of the Indians and negroes. After the expulsion of the Jesuits the King of Spain ordered that a chaplain for negroes be placed on every plantation. Although this was impossible owing to the scarcity of priests, the greatest interest was taken in the evangelization of negroes and winning them from superstitious practices. The work of zealous Catholic masters and mistresses bore fruit in many ways, and there remains to-day in New Orleans, despite the losses to the Faith occasioned by the Civil War and during the Reconstruction Period when hordes of Protestant missionaries from the north flocked into Louisiana with millions of dollars to proselytize the race, a strong and sturdy Catholic element among the coloured people from which much is hoped. The Sisters of the Holy Family, a diocesan coloured order of religious, have accomplished much good. In addition to their academy and orphanages for girls and boys and homes for the coloured aged poor of both sexes, located in New Orleans, they have a novitiate and conduct an academy in the cathedral parish and schools in the parishes of St. Maurice, St. Louis, Mater Dolorosa, St. Dominic, and St. Catherine in New Orleans, and schools and asylums in Madisonville, Donaldsonville, Opelusas, Baton Rouge, Mandevilles, Lafayette, and Palmetto, Louisiana. Schools for coloured children are also conducted by the following white religious orders: Sisters of Perpetual Adoration, Sisters of Mercy, Mount Carmel Sisters, Religious of the Sacred Heart, Sisters of St. Joseph. Six coloured schools in charge of lay Catholic teachers in various parishes, St. Catherine's church in charge of the Lazarist Fathers, and St. Dominic's in charge of the Josephite Fathers in New Orleans are especially established for Catholic negroes.

Archives of the Diocese of New Orleans; Archives of the St. Louis Cathedral; SHEA, *The Cath. Church in Colonial Days* (New York, 1886); IDEM, *Life and Times of Archbishop Carrol* (New York, 1888); IDEM, *Hist. of the Cath. Church in the U. S., 1808–85* (2 vols., New York, 1892); GAYARRE, *Hist. de la Louisiane* (2 vols., New Orleans, 1846–7); CHARLEVOIX, *Journal d'un Voyage dans l'Amérique Septentrional,* VI (Paris, 1744); DE LA HARPE, *Journal Hist. de l'Etablissement des Français à la Louisiane* (New Orleans, 1831); KING, *Sieur de Bienville* (New York, 1893); DIMITRY, *Hist. of Louisiana* (New York, 1892); DUMONT, *Mémoires Histor. sur la Louisiane* (Paris, 1753); LE PAGE DU PRATZ, *Hist. de la L.* (3 vols., Paris, 1758); FORTIER, *L. Studies* (New Orleans, 1894); IDEM, *Hist. of L.* (4 vols., New York, 1894); MARTIN, *Hist. of L. from the earliest Period* (1727); KING AND FICKLEN, *Hist. of L.* (New Orleans, 1900); *Archives of the Ursuline Convent, New Orleans, Diary of Sister Madeleine Hachard* (New Orleans, 1727–65); *Letters of Sister M. H.* (1727); *Archives of Churches, Diocese of New Orleans* (1722–1909); *Le Propagateur Catholique* (New Orleans), files; *The Morning Star* (New Orleans, 1868–1909), files; *Le Moniteur de La Louisiane* (New Orleans, 1794–1803), files; French and Spanish manuscripts in archives of Louisiana Historical Society; CHAMBON, *In and Around the Old St. Louis Cathedral* (New Orleans, 1908); *The Picayune* (New Orleans, 1837–1909), files; CAMILLE DE ROCHEMENTEIX, *Les Jésuites et la Nouvelle France au XVIIIᵉ Siècle* (Paris, 1906); CASTELLANOS, *New Orleans as it Was* (New Orleans, 1905); MEMBER OF THE ORDER OF MERCY, *Essays Educational and Historic* (New York, 1899); LOWENSTEIN, *Hist. of the St. Louis Cathedral of New Orleans* (1882); MEMBER OF THE ORDER OF MERCY, *Cath. Hist. of Alabama and the Floridas; Centenaire du Père Antoine* (New Orleans, 1885); HARDEY, *Religious of the Sacred Heart* (New York, 1910).

MARIE LOUISE POINTS.

New Pomerania, VICARIATE APOSTOLIC OF.—New Pomerania, the largest island of the Bismarck Archipelago, is separated from New Guinea by Dampier Strait, and extends from 148° to 152° E. long. and from 4° to 7° S. lat. It is about 348 miles long, from 12½ to 92¼ miles broad, and has an area of 9650 sq. miles. Two geographical regions are distinguishable. Of the north-eastern section (known as the Gazelle Peninsula) a great portion is occupied by wooded mountain chains; otherwise (especially about Blanche Bay) the soil is very fertile and admirably watered by rivers (e. g. the Toriu and Kerawat), which yield an abundance of fish. The white population is practically confined to the northern part of this section, in which the capital, Herbertshöhe, is situated. The western and larger section also has extensive mountain chains, which contain numerous active volcanoes. The warlike nature of the natives, who fiercely resent as an intrusion every attempt to land, has left us almost entirely ignorant of the interior.

The natives are finely built, coffee brown in colour, have regular features, and, when well cared for as at the mission stations, approach the European standard, though their lips are somewhat thick and the mouth half or wide open. While resembling the south-eastern Papuan, they use weapons unknown to the latter—e. g. the sling, in the use of which they possess marvellous dexterity, skilfully inserting the stone with the toes. They occupy few towns owing to the constant feuds raging among them. One of their strangest institutions is their money (*dewarra*), composed of small cowrie shells threaded on a piece of cane. The difficulty of procuring these shells, which are found only in very deep water, accounts for the value set on them. The unit is usually a fathom (the length of both arms extended) of *dewarra*. The tribes have no chiefs; an individual's importance varies according to the amount of *dewarra* he possesses, but the final decision for peace or war rests with the tribe. This entire absence of authority among the natives is a great obstacle in the way of government. The natives are very superstitious: a demon resides in each volcano, and marks his displeasure by sending forth fire against the people. To propitiate the evil spirits, a piece of *dewarra* is always placed in the grave with the corpse. The celebrated institution of the Duk-Duk is simply a piece of imposture, by which the older natives play upon the superstitions of the younger to secure the food they can no longer earn. This "spirit" (a native adorned with a huge mask) arrives regularly in a boat at night with the new moon, and receives the offerings of the natives. The standard of morality among the natives of New Pomerania is high compared with that observed in New Mecklenburg (the other large island of the Bismarck Archipelago), where the laxity of morals, especially race suicide and the scant respect shown for marriage, seems destined rapidly to annihilate the population. In Nov., 1884, Germany proclaimed its protectorate over the New Britain Archipelago; New Britain and New Ireland were given the names of Neupommern and Neumecklenburg, and the whole group was renamed the Bismarck Archipelago. The great obstacle to the development of the islands is their poisonous climate, neither native nor European being immune from the ravages of fever. The native population is estimated at about 190,000; the foreign population (1909) at 773

XI.—2

(474 white). About 13,464 acres are under cultivation, the principal products being copra, cotton, coffee, and rubber.

The vicariate Apostolic was erected on 1 Jan., 1889, and entrusted to the Missionaries of the Sacred Heart of Issoudun. Since Sept., 1905, when the Marshall Islands were made a separate vicariate, its territory is confined to the Bismarck Archipelago. The first and present vicar Apostolic is Mgr Louis Couppé, titular Bishop of Leros. The mission has already made remarkable progress, and numbers according to the latest statistics 15,223 Catholics; 28 missionaries; 40 brothers; 27 Sisters of Our Lady of the Sacred Heart; 55 native catechists; 77 churches and chapels; 90 stations (26 chief); 29 schools with over 4000 pupils; 13 orphanages.

Monatshefte des Missionshauses von Hiltrup; Deutsche Kolonialblatt (1908), suppl. ,78 sqq.

THOMAS KENNEDY.

Newport (ENGLAND), DIOCESE OF (NEOPORTENSIS).—This diocese takes its name from Newport, a town of about 70,000 inhabitants, situated at the mouth of the river Usk, in the county of Monmouth. Before the restoration of hierarchial government in England by Pius IX in 1850, the old "Western District" of England had, since 1840, been divided into two vicariates. The northern, comprising the twelve counties of Wales with Monmouthshire and Herefordshire, was called the Vicariate of Wales. When the country was divided by an Apostolic Brief dated 29 Sept., 1850, into dioceses, the six counties of South Wales, with Monmouthshire and Herefordshire, became the Diocese of Newport and Menevia. Menevia is the Latin name for St. David's, and the double title was intended to signify that at some future day there were to be two distinct dioceses. The first bishop of the Diocese of Newport and Menevia was the Right Reverend Thomas Joseph Brown, O.S.B., who had already, as vicar Apostolic, ruled for ten years the Vicariate of Wales. A further re-adjustment of the diocese was made in March, 1895, when Leo XIII separated from it five of the counties of South Wales, and formed a new vicariate, which was to consist of all the twelve Welsh counties except Glamorganshire. Since that date the name of the diocese has been simply "Newport", and it has consisted of Glamorganshire, Monmouthshire, and Herefordshire. The Catholic population (1910) is about 45,000, the general population being about 1,050,000.

The diocesan chapter, in virtue of a Decree of the Congregation of Propaganda, 21 April, 1852, issued at the petition of Cardinal Wiseman and the rest of the hierarchy, was to consist of monks of the English Benedictine Congregation resident in the town of Newport. As the congregation, up to this date (1910), have not been able to establish a house in Newport, permission from the Holy See has been obtained for the members of the chapter to reside at St. Michael's pro-cathedral, Belmont, near Hereford. The chapter comprises a cathedral prior and nine canons, of whom four are allowed to be non-resident. Their choral habit is the *cuculla* or frock of the congregation with a special almuce. In assisting the bishop they dispense with the *cuculla*, and wear the almuce over the surplice. The present bishop, the Right Reverend John Cuthbert Hedley, O.S.B., was consecrated as auxiliary on 29 September, 1873, and succeeded in February, 1881, to Bishop Brown. He resides at Bishop's House, Llanishen, Cardiff. The pro-cathedral is the beautiful church of the Benedictine priory at Belmont. There are in the diocese about 40 secular diocesan priests, 21 Benedictines (of whom 15 work on the Mission), and 14 Rosminian Fathers. There are five deaneries. The principal towns are Cardiff, Newport, Swansea, and Merthyr Tydvil. The only religious house of men is the Cathedral Priory, Belmont, which is the residence of the cathedral prior and chapter, and is also a house of studies and novitiate for the English Benedictines. Of religious women there are houses of Poor Clares, Our Lady of Charity, the Good Shepherd, Sisters of Nazareth, Ursulines of Chavagnes, St. Joseph of Annecy, St. Vincent de Paul, and others. There are four certified Poor Law schools: one for boys, at Treforest, and three for girls—two, at Hereford and Bullingham respectively, conducted by the Sisters of Charity, one at Cardiff, conducted by the Sisters of Nazareth. There are 50 churches in the diocese, besides several school chapels and public oratories. There are about 11,000 children in the Catholic elementary schools. There are four secondary schools for girls, and one centre (in Cardiff) for female pupil teachers.

TINTERN ABBEY
Exterior—South-west

F. A. CROW.

Newport, RICHARD, VENERABLE. See SCOT, WILLIAM, O.S.B., VENERABLE.

New Testament. See TESTAMENT, THE NEW.

Newton, JOHN, soldier and engineer, b. at Norfolk, Virginia, 24 August, 1823; d. in New York City, 1 May, 1895. He was the son of General Thomas Newton and Margaret Jordan. In 1838 he was appointed from Virginia a cadet in the U. S. Military Academy, and graduated in 1842, standing second in a class that included Rosencrans, Pope, and Longstreet. Commissioned second lieutenant of engineers, he was engaged as assistant professor of engineering at West Point, and later in the construction of fortifications and other engineering projects along the coasts of the Atlantic and the Gulf of Mexico. Commissioned first lieutenant in 1852 and promoted captain in 1856, he was appointed chief engineer of the Utah Expedition in 1858. At the opening of the Civil War he was chief engineer of the Department of Pennsylvania, and afterwards held a similar position in the Department of the Shenandoah. Commissioned major on 6 August, 1861, he worked on the construction of the defences of Washington until March, 1862. He was commissioned on 23 Sept., 1861, brigadier-general of volunteers, and received command of a brigade engaged in the defence of the city. He served in the army of the Potomac under McClellan during the Peninsular Campaign, and distinguished himself by his heroic conduct in the actions of West Point, Gaines Mills, and Glendale. He led his brigade in the Maryland campaign, taking part in the forcing of Crampton Gap and in the battle of Antietam, and was for his gallant services brevetted lieutenant-colonel of regulars. He led a division at Fredericksburg in the storming of Marye Heights, and was rewarded on 20 March, 1863, with the rank of major-general of volunteers. He commanded divisions at Chancellorsville and Salem Heights, and, at the death of Reynolds on 2 July, 1863, was given command of the First Army Corps, which he led on the last two days of the battle of Gettysburg. On 3 July, 1863, for gallant service at Gettysburg, he was brevetted colonel of regulars. He engaged in the pursuit of the Confederate forces to Warrenton, Virginia, and towards the end of 1863 was active in the Rapidan Campaign. In May, 1864, he was transferred to the Army of the Cumberland, and commanded under General Thomas the Second Division, Fourth Corps. He fought in all the actions during the invasion of Georgia up to the capture of Atlanta. For his gallantry in this campaign, especially in the battle of Peach Tree Creek, he was brevetted on 13 March, 1865, major-general of volunteers and brigadier-general and major-general of regulars. He then took command of various districts in Florida until, in January, 1866, he was mustered out of the volunteer service.

Commissioned lieutenant-colonel of engineers in the regular service on 28 December, 1865, Newton was ordered in April, 1866, to New York City, where he thenceforth resided, engaged on the engineering labours that made his name famous. He was superintendent engineer of the construction of the defences on the Long Island side of the Narrows, of the improvements of the Hudson River, and of the fortifications at Sandy Hook. He was also one of the board of engineers deputed to carry out the modifications of the defences around New York City. The proposed enlargement of the Harlem River, and the improvements of the Hudson from Troy to New York, of the channel between New Jersey and Staten Island, and of the harbours on Lake Champlain were put under his charge. On 30 June, 1879, he was named colonel, and on 6 March, 1884, chief of engineers in the regular service with the rank of brigadier-general. Among Newton's achievements, the most notable was the removal of the dangerous rocks in Hell Gate, the principal water-way between Long Island Sound and the East River. To accomplish this task successfully, required the solution of difficult engineering problems never before attempted, and the invention of new apparatus, notably a steam drilling machine, which has since been in general use. Newton carefully studied the problem, and the accuracy of his conclusions was shown by the exact correspondence of the results with the objects sought. Hallett's Reef and Flood Rock, having been carefully mined under his directions, were destroyed by two great explosions (24 September, 1876; 10 October, 1885). This engineering feat excited the universal admiration of engineers, and many honours were conferred upon him. On Newton's voluntary retirement from the service in 1886, Mayor Grace of New York, recognizing his superior skill, appointed him commissioner of public works on 28 Aug. This post he voluntarily resigned on 24 Nov., 1888. On 2 April, 1888, he accepted the presidency of the Panama Railroad Company, which position he filled until his death. In 1848 General Newton married Anna M. Starr of New London, Connecticut. In his early manhood he became, and until his death remained, an earnest and devout member of the Catholic Church.

POWELL, *List of Officers of the U. S. Army, 1776–1900*; CULLUM, *Biographical Register of the Officers and Graduates of the U. S. Military Academy*; *Appleton's Encycl. Amer. Biog.*, s. v.; SMITH, *In Memoriam of General John Newton* (New York, 1895).

JOHN G. EWING.

New Westminster. See VANCOUVER, ARCHDIOCESE OF.

New Year's Day.—The word *year* is etymologically the same as *hour* (Skeat), and signifies a going, movement etc. In Semitic, שנה, year, signifies "repetition, sc. of the course of the sun" (Gesenius). Since there was no necessary starting-point in the circle of the year, we find among different nations, and among the same at different epochs of their history, a great variety of dates with which the new year began. The opening of spring was a natural beginning, and in the Bible itself there is a close relationship between the beginning of the year and the seasons. The ancient Roman year began in March, but Julius Cæsar, in correcting the calendar (46 B. C.), made January the first month. Though this custom has been universally adopted among Christian nations, the names, September, October, November, and December (i.e. the seventh, eighth, ninth, and tenth), remind us of the past, when March began the year. Christian writers and councils condemned the heathen orgies and excesses connected with the festival of the *Saturnalia*, which were celebrated at the beginning of the year: Tertullian blames Christians who regarded the customary presents—called *strenæ* (Fr. *étrennes*) from the goddess Strenia, who presided over New Year's Day (cf. Ovid, "Fasti", 185–90)—as mere tokens of friendly intercourse (Dé Idol. xiv), and towards the end of the sixth century the Council of Auxerre (can. I) forbade Christians "strenas diabolicas observare". The II Council of Tours held in 567 (can. 17) prescribes prayers and a Mass of expiation for New Year's Day, adding that this is a practice long in use (*patres nostri statuerunt*). Dances were forbidden, and pagan crimes were to be expiated by Christian fasts (St. Augustine, Serm., cxcvii–viii in P. L., XXXVIII, 1024; Isidore of Seville, "De Div. Off. Eccl.", I, xli; Trullan Council, 692, can. lxii). When Christmas was fixed on 25 Dec., New Year's Day was sanctified by commemorating on it the Circumcision, for which feast the Gelasian Sacramentary gives a Mass (*In Octabas Domini*). Christians did not wish to make the celebration of this feast very solemn, lest they might seem to countenance in any way the pagan extravagance of the opening year.

Among the Jews the first day of the seventh month, *Tishri* (end of September), began the civil or economic year "with the sound of trumpets" (Lev., xxiii, 24; Num., xxix, 1). In the Bible the day is not mentioned as New Year's Day, but the Jews so regarded it, so named it, and so consider it now (Mishnah, Rosh Hash., I, 1). The sacred year began with Nisan (early in April), a later name for the Biblical *abhibh*, i. e. "month of new corn", and was memorable "because in this month the Lord thy God brought thee out of Egypt by night" (Deut., xvi, 1). Barley ripens in Palestine during the early part of April; and thus the sacred year began with the harvest, the civil year with the sowing of the crops. From Biblical data Josephus and many modern scholars hold that the twofold beginning of the year was pre-exilic, or even Mosaic (cf. "Antiq.", I, iii, 3). Since Jewish months were regulated by the moon, while the ripening barley of Nisan depended upon the sun, the Jews resorted to intercalation to bring sun and moon dates into harmony, and to keep the months in the seasons to which they belonged (for method of adjustment, see Edersheim, "The Temple, Its Ministry and Services at the Time of Jesus Christ", x).

Christian nations did not agree in the date of New Year's Day. They were not opposed to 1 January as the beginning of the year, but rather to the pagan extravagances which accompanied it. Evidently the natural opening of the year, the springtime, together with the Jewish opening of the sacred year, Nisan, suggested the propriety of putting the beginning in that beautiful season. Also, the Dionysian method (so named from the Abbot Dionysius, sixth century) of dating events from the coming of Christ became an important factor in New Year calculations. The Annunciation, with which Dionysius began the Christian era, was fixed on 25 March, and became New Year's Day for England, in early times and from the thirteenth century to 1 Jan., 1752, when the present custom was introduced there. Some countries (e. g. Germany) began with Christmas, thus being almost in harmony with the ancient Germans, who made the winter solstice their starting-point. Notwithstanding the movable character of Easter, France and the Low Countries took it as the first day of the year, while Russia, up to the eighteenth century, made September the first month. The western nations, however, since the sixteenth, or, at the latest, the eighteenth century, have adopted and retained the first of January. In Christian liturgy the Church does not refer to the first of the year, any more than she does to the fact that the first Sunday of Advent is the first day of the ecclesiastical year.

In the United States of America the great feast of the Epiphany has ceased to be a holyday of obligation, but New Year continues in force. Since the mysteries of the Epiphany are commemorated on Christmas —the Orientals consider the feasts one and the same in import—it was thought advisable to retain by preference, under the title "Circumcision of Our Lord Jesus Christ", New Year's Day as one of the six feasts of obligation. The Fathers of the Third Plenary Council of Baltimore petitioned Rome to this effect, and their petition was granted (Con. Plen. Balt., III, pp. 105 sqq.). (See CIRCUMCISION, FEAST OF THE; CHRONOLOGY; CHRISTMAS.)

SCHROD in *Kirchenlex.*, s. v. *Neujahr*; WELTE, *ibid.*, s. v. *Feste*; ABRAHAMS in HASTINGS, *Dict. of the Bible*, s. v. *Time*; MACDONALD, *Chronologies and Calendars* (London, 1897); EDERSHEIM, *The Temple, Its Ministry and Services at the time of Jesus Christ*, x, xv; BROWNE in *Dict. Christ. Antiq.*, s. v.; *Harper's Classical Dict.* (New York, 1897), s. v. *Calendarium*; FEASEY, *Christmastide* in *Amer. Eccl. Rev.* (Dec., 1909); *The Old English New Year*, *ibid.* (Jan., 1907); THURSTON, *Christmas Day and the Christian Calendar*, *ibid.* (Dec., 1898; Jan., 1899). For Rabbinic legends see *Jewish Encycl.*, s. v. *New Year*.

JOHN J. TIERNEY.

New York, ARCHDIOCESE OF (NEO-EBORACENSIS); see erected 8 April, 1808; made archiepiscopal 19 July, 1850; comprises the Boroughs of Manhattan, Bronx, and Richmond in the City of New York, and the Counties of Dutchess, Orange, Putnam, Rockland, Sullivan, Ulster, and Westchester in the State of New York; also the Bahama Islands (British Possessions); an area of 4717 square miles in New York and 4466 in the Bahama Islands. The latter territory was placed in 1886 under this jurisdiction by the Holy See because the facilities of access were best from New York; it formerly belonged to the Diocese of Charleston. The suffragans of New York are the Dioceses of Albany, Brooklyn, Buffalo, Ogdensburg, Rochester, and Syracuse in the State of New York, and Newark and Trenton in New Jersey. All these, in 1808, made up the territory of the original diocese. The first division took place 23 April, 1847, when the creation of the Dioceses of Albany and Buffalo cut off the northern and western sections of the State; and the second, in 1853, when Brooklyn and Newark were erected into separate sees.

New York is now the largest see in population, and the most important in influence and material prosperity of all the ecclesiastical divisions of the Church in Continental United States.

I. COLONIAL PERIOD.—Nearly a century before Henry Hudson sailed up the great river that bears his name, the Catholic navigators Verrazano and Gomez, had guided their ships along its shores and placed it under the patronage of St. Anthony. The Calvinistic Hollanders, to whom Hudson gave this foundation for a new colony, manifested their loyalty to their state Church by ordaining that in New Netherland the "Reformed Christian religion according to the doctrines of the Synod of Dordrecht" should be dominant. It is probable, but not certain, that there were priests with Verrazano and Gomez, and that from a Catholic altar went up the first prayer uttered on the site of the present great metropolis of the New World. While public worship by Catholics was not tolerated, the generosity of the Dutch governor, William Kieft, and the people of New Amsterdam to the Jesuit martyr, Father Isaac Jogues, in 1643, and after him, to his brother Jesuits, Fathers Bressani and Le Moyne, must be remembered to their everlasting credit. Father Jogues was the first priest to traverse the State of New York; the first to minister within the limits of the Diocese of New York. When he reached Manhattan Island, after his rescue from captivity in the summer of 1643, he found there two Catholics, a young Irishman and a Portuguese woman, whose confessions he heard.

St. Mary's, the first rude chapel in which Mass was said in the State of New York, was begun, on 18 November, 1655, on the banks of the lake where the City of Syracuse now stands, by the Jesuit missionaries, Fathers Claude Dablon and Pierre Chaumonot. In the same year another Jesuit, Father Simon Le Moyne, journeyed down the river to New Amsterdam, as we learn from a letter sent by the Dutch preacher, Megapolensis (a renegade Catholic), to the Classis at Amsterdam, telling them that the Jesuit had visited Manhattan "on account of the Papists residing here, and especially for the accommodation of the French sailors, who are Papists and who have arrived here with a good prize." The Church had no foothold on Manhattan Island until after 1664, when the Duke of York claimed it for an English colony. Twenty years later, the Catholic governor, Thomas Dongan, not only fostered his own faith, but enacted the first law passed in New York establishing religious liberty. It is believed that the first Mass said on the island (30 October, 1683) was in a chapel he opened about where the custom house now stands. With him came three English Jesuits, Fathers Thomas Harvey, Henry Harrison, and Charles Gage, and they soon had a Latin school in the same neighbourhood. Of this Jacob Leisler, the fanatical usurper of the government, wrote to the Governor of Boston, in August, 1689: "I have formerly urged to inform your Honr. that Coll Dongan, in his time did erect a Jesuite Colledge upon cullour to learn Latine to the Judges West—Mr. Graham, Judge Palmer, and John Tudor did contribute their sones for sometime but no boddy imitating them, the colledge vanished" (O'Callaghan, "Documentary Hist. of N. Y.", II, 23).

With the fall of James II and the advent of William of Orange to the English throne, New York's Catholic colony was almost stamped out by drastic penal laws (see NEW YORK, STATE OF). In spite of them, however, during the years that followed a few scattered representatives of the Faith drifted in and settled down unobstrusively. To minister to them there came now and then from Philadelphia a zealous German Jesuit missionary, Father Ferdinand Steinmayer, who was commonly called "Father Farmer". Gathering them together, he said Mass in the house of a German fellow-countryman in Wall Street, in a loft in Water Street, and wherever else they could find accommodation. Then came the Revolution, and in this connexion, owing to one of the prominent political issues of the time, the spirit of the leading colonists was intensely anti-Catholic. The first flag raised by the Sons of Liberty in New York was inscribed "No Popery". When the war ended, and the president and Congress resided in New York, the Catholic representatives of France, Spain, Portugal, with Charles Carroll, his cousin Daniel, and Thomas Fitz Simmons, Catholic members of Congress, and officers and soldiers of the foreign contingent, merchants and others, soon made up a respectable congregation. Mass was said for them in the house of the Spanish minister, Don Diego de Gardoqui, on Broadway, near the Bowling Green, in the Vauxhall Gardens, which was a hall on the river front near Warren Street, and in a carpenter's shop in Barclay Street. Finally, an Irish Capuchin, Father Charles Whelan, who had served as a chaplain in De Grasse's fleet, and was acting as private chaplain to the Portuguese consul-general, Don José Roiz Silva, took up also the care of this scattered flock, which numbered less than two hundred, and only about forty of them practical in the observances of their faith.

Through efforts led by the French consul, Hector St. John de Crèvecœur (q. v.), an act of incorporation was secured, on 10 June, 1785, for the "Trustees of the Roman Catholic Church of the City of New York," in which José Roiz Silva, James Stewart, and Henry Duffin were associated with him as the first board. An unexpired lease of lots at Barclay and Church streets was bought from the trustees of Trinity church, Thomas Stoughton, the Spanish Consul-general, and his partner Dominick Lynch, advancing the purchase money, one thousand pounds, and there on 5 Oct., 1785, the corner-stone of St. Peter's, the first permanent structure for a Catholic church erected in the State of New York, was laid by the Spanish minister, Gardoqui. The church was opened 4 Nov., 1786. The first resident pastor was Father Whelan, who, however, was forced to retire owing to the hostility of the trustees and of another Capuchin, the Rev. Andrew Nugent, before the Church was opened. The prefect Apostolic, the venerable John Carroll, then visited New York to administer confirmation for the first time, and placed the church in charge of a Dominican, Father William O'Brien, who may be regarded as the organizer of the parish. He had as his assistants Fathers John Connell and Nicholas Burke, and, in his efforts to aid the establishment of the church, went as far as the City of Mexico to collect funds there under the auspices of his old schoolfellow, the archbishop of that see. He brought back $5920 and a number of paintings, vestments, etc. Father O'Brien and his assistants did heroic work during the yellow fever epidemics of 1795, 1799, 1801, and 1805. In 1801 he established the parish school, which has since been carried on without interruption. The church debt at this time was $6500; the income from pew rents, $1120, and from collections, $360, a year. The Rev. Dr. Matthew O'Brien, another Dominican, the Rev. John Byrne, and the Rev. Michael Hurley, an Augustinian, were, during this period, assistants at St. Peter's. In July, 1807, the Rev. Louis Sibourd, a French priest, was made pastor, but he left in the following year, and then the famous Jesuit, Anthony Kohlmann (q. v.), was sent to take charge. It was at this time that the Holy See determined to erect Baltimore into an archbishopric and to establish the new Dioceses of New York, Philadelphia, Boston, and Bardstown, Ky.

II. CREATION OF THE DIOCESE.—We have a picture of the situation in New York when the first bishop was named: a letter sent on 8 Nov., 1808, by Father Kohlmann, who was then acting as the administrator of the diocese, to his friend Father Strickland, S. J., of London, England, says, "Your favour of the 6th Sept. was delivered to me at the beginning of October in the City of New York, where our Right Rev. Bishop Carroll has thought proper to send me in the capacity of rector of this immense congregation and Vicar General of this diocese till the arrival of the Right Rev. Richard Luke Concanen, Bishop of New York. The congregation chiefly consists of Irish, some hundreds of French, and as many Germans, in all, according to the common estimation, of 14,000 souls. Rev. Mr. Fenwick, a young Father of our society, distinguished for his learning and piety, has been sent along with me. I was no sooner arrived in the city and, behold, the trustees, though before our arrival they had not spent a cent for the reparation and furniture of their clergyman's house, laid out for the said purpose above $800. All men seem to revive at the very name of the Society of Jesus, though yet little known in this part of the country." What rapid progress was made, he indicates, two years later, when, again writing to Father Strickland, on 14 Sept., 1810, he tells him: "Indeed it is but two years that we arrived in this city without having a cent in our pocket, not even our passage money, which the trustees paid for Father Fenwick and me . . . and to see things so far advanced as to see not only the Catholic religion highly respected by the first characters of the city, but even a Catholic college established, the house well furnished both in town and in the college improvements made in the college [sic] for four or five hundred dollars . . . is a thing which I am at a loss to conceive and which I cannot ascribe but to the infinite liberality of the Lord, to whom alone, therefore, be all glory and honour. The college is in the centre not of Long Island but of the Island of New York, the most delightful and most healthy spot of the whole island, at a distance of four small miles from the city, and of half a mile from the East and North rivers, both of which are seen from the house; situated between two roads which are very much frequented, opposite to the botanic gardens which belong to the State. It has adjacent to it a beautiful lawn, garden, orchard, etc."—This spot is now the site of St. Patrick's Cathedral on Fifth avenue.

OLD ST. PETER'S CHURCH, BARCLAY ST. (1785)

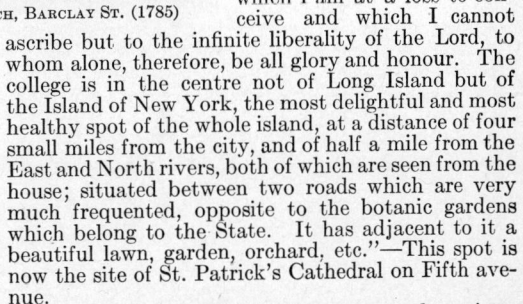

We can judge from the family names on the register of St. Peter's church that the early Catholics of New York were largely Irish; next in number come the French, then the Germans, followed by those of Italian, Spanish and English origin. There were enough Germans in 1808 to think themselves entitled to a church and pastor of their own nationality, for on 2 March of that year Christopher Briehill, John Kneringer, George Jacob, Martin Nieder, and Francis Werneken signed a petition which they sent to Bishop Carroll praying him "to send us a pastor who is capable of undertaking the spiritual Care of our Souls in the German Language, which is our Mother Tongue.

Many of us do not know any English at all, and these who have some knowledge of it are not well enough versed in the English Language as to attend Divine Service with any utility to themselves. As we have not yet a place of worship of our own we have made application to the Trustees of the English Catholic Church in this city to grant us permission to perform our worship in the German Language in their church at such times as not to interfere with their regular services. This permission they have readily granted us. During the Course of the year we shall take care to find an opportunity to provide ourselves with a suitable building of our own, for we have no doubt that our number will soon considerably increase." Nothing came of this petition, and no separate German congregation was organized in New York until a quarter of a century after its date. But Father Kohlmann saw to it that another church should be started, and St. Patrick's was begun "between the Broadway and the Bowery road" in 1809, to meet the needs of the rapidly increasing number of Catholics on the east side of the city. It was also to serve as the cathedral church of the new diocese. The corner-stone was laid 8 June, 1809, but, owing to the hard times and the war of 1812 with England, the structure was not ready for use until 4 May, 1815, when it was dedicated by Bishop Cheverus who came from Boston for that purpose. It was then far on the outskirts of the city, and, to accustom the people to go there, Mass was said at St. Peter's every other Sunday. The ground on which it was built was purchased in 1801 for a graveyard, and the interments in it from that time until the cemetery was closed in 1833 numbered 32,-153. Some of the Catholic laymen prominent during this period were Andrew Morris, Matthew Reed, Cornelius Heeney, Thomas Stoughton, Dominick Lynch, Benjamin Disobrey, Peter Burtsell, uncle of the Rev. James A. Neil, the first native of New York to be admitted to the priesthood, Joseph Icard, merchant and architect, Hugh McGinnis, Dennis Doyle, Miles F. Clossey, Anthony Trapanni, a native of Meta, Italy, pioneer Italian merchant and the first foreigner to be naturalized under the Constitution, Francis Varet, John B. Lasala, Francis Cooper, George Gottsberger, Thomas O'Connor, Thomas Brady, Dr. William James Macneven, and Bernard Dornin, the first Catholic publisher, for whose edition of Pastorini's "History of the Church," issued in 1807, there were 318 New York City subscribers.

RICHARD LUKE CONCANEN
First Bishop of New York

III. THE HIERARCHY.—A. When Bishop Carroll learned that it was the intention of the Holy See to recognize the growth of the Church in the United States by dividing the Diocese of Baltimore and creating new sees, he advised that New York be placed under the care of the Bishop of Boston till a suitable choice could be made for that diocese. Archbishop Troy of Dublin, however, induced Pius VII to appoint as New York's first bishop an Irish Dominican, Father Richard Luke Concanen, who had resided many years in Rome as the agent of the Irish bishops and was much esteemed there. He was prior of St. Clement's at Rome, librarian of the Minerva, and distinguished for his learning. He had refused a nomination for a see in Ireland and was much interested in the missions in America, about which he had kept up a correspondence with Bishop Carroll. It was at his suggestion that Father Fenwick founded the first house of the Dominicans in Kentucky. He was consecrated first Bishop of New York at Rome, 24 April, 1808, and some time after left for Leghorn on his way to his see, taking with him the pallium for Archbishop Carroll. After waiting there for a ship for four months he returned to Rome. Thence he went to Naples, expecting to sail from that port, but the French military forces in possession of the city detained him as a British subject, and, while waiting vainly to be released, he died of fever, 19 June, 1810. Finding that he could not leave Italy, he had asked the pope to appoint the Rev. Ambrose Maréchal to be his coadjutor bishop in New York. The American bishops cordially endorsed this choice and considered that the appointment would be made. Archbishop Carroll, writing to Father C. Plowden, of London, 25 June, 1815, said: "It was known here that before the death of Dr. Concanen his Holiness at the Dr's entreaty intended to assign to him as his coadjutor the Rev. Mr. Maréchal, a priest of St. Sulpice, now in the Seminary here, and worthy of any promotion in the Church. We still expected that this measure would be pursued; and that we made no presentation or recommendation of any other for the vacant see."

B.—Archbishop Troy, of Dublin, however, with the other Irish bishops, proposed to the pope another Irish Dominican, the Rev. John Connolly, for the vacant see of New York, and he was consecrated at Rome, 6 Nov., 1814 (see CONNOLLY, JOHN). It was a selection which might have proved embarrassing to American Catholics, for Bishop Connolly was a British subject, and the United States was then at war with Great Britain. "I wish," wrote Archbishop Carroll to Father Plowden, 25 June, 1815, "this may not become a very dangerous precedent fruitful of mischief by drawing upon our religion a false opinion of the servility of our principles." Owing to his own views of the situation in the diocese, Bishop Connolly did not announce his appointment to his fellow-members of the hierarchy or to the administrator of the diocese. Father Kohlmann was, therefore, in anticipation of the bishop's arrival, recalled by his superiors to Maryland, the college was closed, and the other Jesuits soon after left the diocese. Finally, Bishop Connolly arrived in New York unannounced, and without any formal local welcome, 24 Nov., 1815, his ship taking sixty-eight days to make the voyage from Dublin. In the diocese he found that everything was to be created from resources that were very small and in spite of obstacles that were very great. The diocese embraced the whole State of New York and half of New Jersey. There were but four priests in this territory. Lay trustees had become so accustomed to having their own way that they were not disposed to admit even the authority of a bishop.

JOHN CONNOLLY
Second Bishop of New York

Dr. Connolly was not wanting in firmness, but the pressing needs of the times, forcing an apparent concession to the established order of things, subjected him to much difficulty and many humiliations. He was a missionary priest rather than a bishop, as he wrote Cardinal Litta, Prefect of Propaganda, in February, 1818, but he discharged all his laborious duties with humility and earnest zeal. His diary further notes that he told the cardinal: "I found here about 13,000 Catholics. . . . At present there are about 16,000 mostly Irish; at least 10,000 Irish Catholics arrived at New York only within these last three years. They spread through all the other states of this confederacy, and make their religion known everywhere. Bishops ought to be granted to whatever here is willing to erect a Cathedral, and petition for a bishop. . . . The present dioceses are quite too extensive. Our Cathedral owes $53,000 borrowed to build it. . . . This burden hinders us from supporting a sufficient number of priests, or from thinking to erect a seminary. The American youth have an invincible repugnance to the ecclesiastical state."

He made a visitation of the diocese, no mean accomplishment at that time; provided churches for the people in Brooklyn, Buffalo, Albany, Utica, and Paterson; introduced the Sisters of Charity, started the orphan asylum, and encouraged the opening of parish schools. He died at his residence, 512 Broadway, 5 Feb., 1825, worn out by his labours and anxieties. Notable men of this period were Fathers Michael O'Gorman and Richard Bulger—the latter the first priest ordained in New York (1820) — Charles D. Ffrench, John Power, John Farnan, Thomas C. Levins, Philip Larisey and John Shannahan. There were several distinguished converts, including Mother Seton, founder of the American branch of the Sisters of Charity; the Rev. Virgil Barber and his wife, the Rev. John Richards, the Rev. George Kewley, the Rev. George E. Ironside, Keating Lawson, and others. Two years elapsed before the next bishop was appointed, and the Rev. Dr. John Power during that period governed the diocese as administrator. Brooklyn's first church was organized during this time. It was during Bishop Connolly's administration also, that New York's first Catholic paper "The Truth Teller" was started, on 2 April, 1825.

C.—The choice of the Holy See for the third bishop was the Rev. Dr. John Dubois, president of Mount St. Mary's College, Emmitsburg (see DUBOIS, JOHN), and he was consecrated at Baltimore, 29 October, 1826. The Rev. William Taylor, a convert who had come from Cork, Ireland, in June, 1818, at the suggestion of Bishop England of Charleston, endeavoured to be himself made bishop, going to Rome in January, 1820, for that purpose. This visit to Rome being fruitless, Taylor went to Boston, where he remained several years with Bishop Cheverus, returning to New York when that prelate was transferred to France. He was exceedingly popular with non-Catholics because of his liberality. He preached the sermon at the consecration of Bishop Dubois and used the occasion to expatiate on what he called "disastrous experiences which resulted to religion from injudicious appointments", hinting at coming trouble for the bishop in New York. He left New York simultaneously with the arrival of the bishop there, and sailed for France, where his old friend Mgr Cheverus, then Archbishop of Bordeaux, received him. He died suddenly, while preaching in the Irish college, Paris, in 1828.

None of the predicted disturbances happened when Bishop Dubois took possession of his see, though the abuse of trusteeism, grown more and more insolent and unmanageable by toleration, hampered his efforts from the very start. Fanaticism was aroused among the Protestant sects, alarmed at the numerical increase of the Church through the immigration attracted by the commercial growth of the State. But in spite of all, he went on bravely visiting all parts of the State, building and encouraging the building of churches wherever they were needed, obtaining aid from Rome and from the charitable in Europe. He found but two churches in the city when he came; to these he added six others and multiplied for his flock the facilities for practising their religion, his constant endeavour being to give his people priests, churches, and schools. With the trustees in New York City and in Buffalo he had many sad experiences, but he unflinchingly upheld his constituted authority. In 1834 he organized, with the Rev. John Raffeiner as pastor, the first German Catholic congregation in New York in a small disused Baptist church at Pitt and De Lancey Streets, which became the church of St. Nicholas. It was about this time, too, that a public controversy over Catholic doctrine raged between the Calvinist ministers, Rev. John Breckenridge and Rev. William Brownlee, and the vicar-general, Rev. Dr.

NEW YORK LITERARY INSTITUTION (1809)
Fifth Avenue and Fiftieth Street, New York. Site of the present Cathedral

Power, assisted by Fathers Varela, Levins, and Schneller. It was followed by the fanatical attack on Catholic religious communities known as "The Awful Disclosures of Maria Monk". Dr. Dubois "had then reached the age of seventy and, though still a vigorous combatant when necessary, was disinclined to religious controversy. Perhaps he did not understand the country and the people as well as the younger men who had grown up in America; perhaps he was deterred by his memories of the French Revolution" (Herbermann, "Hist. Records and Studies", I, Pt. 2, 333).

At length the many burdens and anxieties of his charge told on the bishop, and he asked for a coadjutor, naming the Right Rev. P. F. Kenrick, Coadjutor of Philadelphia, as his first choice, and the Rev. Thomas F. Mulledy, S.J., and the Rev. John Hughes, of Philadelphia, as alternates. Father Hughes, of Philadelphia, who had been his pupil at Emmitsburg, was selected and consecrated titular Bishop of Basileo, 7 January, 1838. His youth and vigour soon put new life into the affairs of the Church in New York, and were especially efficient in meeting the aggressions of the lay trustees. Bishop Hughes had fully realized the dangers of the system as shown in Philadelphia, and he lost no time in meeting and crushing it in New York. Bishop Dubois, through ill health, had to relinquish the details of his charge more and more to his youthful assistant, whose activity he warmly welcomed. Several attacks of paralysis warned him to give up the management of the diocese. His remaining days he spent quietly preparing for the end, his coadjutor ever treating him with respectful kindness and sympathy. He died 20 December, 1840, full of years and merits. Those of his assistants who were notably prominent were Father Felix Varela, an eminently pious and versatile priest, an exile from Cuba, and the Revs. Joseph Schneller, Dr. Constantine C. Pise, Alexander Mupietti, John Raffeiner, the pioneer German pastor; Hatton Walsh, P. Malou, T. Maguire, Michael Curran, Gregory B. Pardow, Luke Berry, John N. Neumann, later a Redemptorist and Bishop of Philadelphia, and John Walsh, long pastor of St. James, Brooklyn.

D.—Bishop Hughes, the administrator, at once assumed the title of the see as its fourth bishop, and is the really great figure in the constructive period of New York's history. "It was a day of great men in the civil order", says the historian, Dr. John Gilmary Shea, "the day of Clay, Webster, Calhoun, yet no man of that era spoke so directly or so effectively to the American people as Bishop Hughes. He was not an ordinary man. It had been well said that in any assemblage he would have been notable. He was full of noble thoughts and aspirations and devoted to the Church; every plan and every project of his mind aimed at the greater good of the country". The story of his eventful career is told in a separate article (see HUGHES, JOHN), and it will suffice to mention here some of the many distinguished men who helped to make his administration so important in local records. Among them were the Rev. William Quarter, afterwards first Bishop of Chicago, and his brother, the Rev. Walter J. Quarter, the Rev. Bernard O'Reilly, first Bishop of Hartford; the Rev. John Loughlin, first Bishop of Brooklyn; the Rev. James R. Bayley, first Bishop of Newark and Archbishop of Baltimore; the Rev. David Bacon, first Bishop of Portland; the Rev. William G. McCloskey, first rector of the American College at Rome and fourth Bishop of Louisville, Ky., son of one of the Brooklyn pioneers; the Rev. Andrew Byrne, first Bishop of Little Rock; the Rev. John J. Conroy, Bishop of Albany; the Rev. William Starrs, vicar-general; the Rev. Dr. Ambrose Manahan, the Rev. Dr. J. W. Cummings, Archdeacon McCarron, the Rev. John Kelly (Eugene Kelly's brother), who went as a missionary to Africa and then became first pastor at Jersey City. These are only a few of the names that are prominent. Among the notable converts of this period may be mentioned the Rev. Thomas S. Preston, J. V. Huntington, F. E. White, Donald McLeod, Isaac T. Hecker, A. F. Hewit, Alfred Young, Clarence Walworth, and Edgar P. Wadhams, later Bishop of Ogdensburg.

JOHN DUBOIS
Third Bishop of New York

E.—As the successor of Archbishop Hughes, Bishop John McCloskey of Albany was promoted to be the second archbishop. He had been consecrated Coadjutor of New York, with the right of succession, in 1844, but resigned both offices to become the first Bishop of Albany in 1847 (see McCLOSKEY, JOHN). He returned to New York in spite of his own protests of unworthiness, but with the unanimous approval and rejoicing of the clergy and laity. He was born in Brooklyn, 10 March, 1810, and was therefore the first native bishop, as he was the second native of New York to be ordained to the priesthood. He was a gentle, polished, amiable prelate, and accomplished much for the progress of Catholic New York. The Protectory, the Foundling Asylum, and the Mission of the Immaculate Virgin for homeless children were founded under his auspices; he resumed work on the new Cathedral, and saw its completion; the provincial seminary at Troy was organized; churches, schools, and charitable institutions were everywhere increased and improved. In the stimulation of a general appreciation of the necessity of Catholic education the cardinal (he was elevated to the Purple in 1875) was incessant and most vigorous. He saw that the foundations of the structure, laid deep by his illustrious predecessor, upheld an edifice in which all the requirements of modern educational methods should be found. Like him, also, as years crept on, he asked for a coadjutor, and the Bishop of Newark, Michael Augustine Corrigan, was sent to him.

F.—Born in Newark, 31 August, 1839, his college days were spent at Mt. St. Mary's, Emmitsburg, and at Rome. Ordained in 1863, Bishop Corrigan became president of Seton Hall College in 1868, Bishop of Newark in 1873, Coadjutor of New York in 1880, and archbishop in 1885 (see CORRIGAN, MICHAEL A.). He died, from an accidental fall during the building of the Lady Chapel at the Cathedral, 5 May, 1902. It was said of him by the New York "Evening Post": "The memory of his life distils a fragrance like to that of St. Francis." By some New Yorkers he was for a time a much misunderstood man, whose memory time will vindicate. Acute thinkers are appreciating his worth as a civilian as well as a churchman, and the fact that, for Catholics, he grappled with the first menacing move of Socialism and effectually and permanently checked its advance. He was an administrator of ability and, socially, a man of winning personality. To the serious problem of providing for the spiritual need of the inrushing thousands of European immigrants he gave successful consideration. The splendid seminary at Dunwoodie is his best memorial. Its beautiful chapel he built at a cost of $60,000—his whole private inherited fortune. During his administration controversy over the school question was waged with a certain amount of acrimony. He was regarded as the leader of those all over the country who stood for uncompromising Catholic education. Archbishop Corrigan was also drawn into conflict with the Rev. Dr. Edward McGlynn, rector of St. Stephen's church, a man of considerable ability, but whose radical views on the ownership of land had brought on him the official censure of Cardinal Simeoni, Prefect of Propaganda. In the municipal election of 1886, in spite of the archbishop's warnings, he became the open partisan of Henry George who was the candidate for mayor of the Single Tax party. As a consequence, he was suspended, and, as an alumnus of the College of Propaganda, was summoned to Rome to answer the charges made against him. He refused to go and was excommunicated.—For details and text of official letters, see Archbishop Corrigan's statement to New York papers (21 January, 1887) and Dr. McGlynn's formal answer in Henry George's "Standard" (5 February, 1887).—Dr. McGlynn's partisans organized themselves into what they called the Anti-Poverty Society. He addressed this body every Sunday until about Christmas, 1892, when, having willingly accepted the conditions laid down by the pope, he was absolved from censure and reconciled by Mgr Satolli, the Apostolic delegate. According to a published statement by Mgr Satolli, the conditions were in this form: "Dr. McGlynn had presented a brief statement of his opinions on moral-economic matters, and it was judged not contrary to the doctrine constantly taught by the Church, and as recently confirmed by the Holy Father in the encyclical 'Rerum Novarum'. Also it is hereby made known that Dr. McGlynn, besides publicly professing his adherence to all the doctrines and teachings of the Catholic Church, has expressed his regret (saying that he would be the first to regret it) for any word or act of his that may have seemed lacking in the respect due to ecclesiastical authority, and he hereby intends to repair as far as he can any offense which may have been given to Catholics. Finally, Dr. McGlynn has of his own free will declared and promised that, within the limits of a not long period of time, he will go to Rome in the spirit and intention which are becoming to a good Catholic and a priest." In 1894 Dr. McGlynn was appointed pastor of St. Mary's church, Newburg, where he remained quietly until his death in 1901.

Archbishop Corrigan made his last visit *ad limina* in 1890 and after his return, until his death in 1902, devoted himself entirely to the duties of his high office. His death brought out the fact that he was the foremost figure of the community in the respect and affection of his fellow-citizens. His unassuming personality and his gentle method, his considerate kindness and his unaffected piety were pathways to the love and veneration of his own flock. His steadfast adherence to principle, as well as his persuasive manner of, not only teaching, but also of acting out the doctrines of his religion, his profound scholarship, his experienced judgment, were ever employed when there was question of a religious, moral, or civil import to his fellow-men. The truth of this is to be found in the testimony of Leo XIII, himself, of the civil dignitaries of the land, of his brethren in the episcopate, of his own clergy and laity, on the mournful occasion of his death. Under the second and third archbishops, Mgr William Quinn, V.G., was a prominent figure, and among his associates of this era were Mgr Thomas S. Preston, Mgr Arthur J. Donnelly, Mgr James McMahon, Mgr P. F. McSweeny, Fathers M. Curran, William Everett, W. H. Clowry, Felix H. Farrelly, Eugene McGuire, Thomas Farrell, Edward J. O'Reilly, M. J. O'Farrell (later Bishop of Trenton), and Edmund Aubril.

G.—As fourth archbishop, the Holy See confirmed the choice of the diocesan electors, and appointed to fill the vacancy the auxiliary, the Right Rev. John Murphy Farley, titular Bishop of Zeugma, who was promoted to the archbishopric 15 September, 1902. He was born at Newton Hamilton, County Armagh, Ireland, 20 April, 1842. His primary studies were made at St. McCartan's College, Monaghan, and, on his coming to New York, were continued at St. John's College, Fordham. Thence he went to the provincial seminary at Troy for his philosophy course, and after this to the American College, Rome, where he was ordained priest 11 June, 1870. Returning to New York, he ministered as an assistant in St. Peter's parish, Staten Island, for two years, and in 1872 was appointed secretary to the then Archbishop McCloskey, in which office he served until 1884, when he was made pastor of St. Gabriel's church, New York City. He accompanied the cardinal to Rome in 1878, for the election of Leo XIII, which event, however, took place before their arrival. In 1884 he was made a private chamberlain; in 1892 he was promoted to the domestic prelacy, and in 1895 to be prothonotary apostolic. In 1891 he was chosen vicar-general of the diocese by Archbishop Corrigan, and, on 21 December, 1895, was consecrated as his auxiliary, with the title of Bishop of Zeugma. At the death of Archbishop Corrigan, he was appointed his successor, 15 Sept., 1902, and Pius X named him assistant at the pontifical throne in 1904. He made progress in Catholic education in the diocese the keynote of his administration, and within the first eight years added nearly fifty parochial schools to the primary list, encouraged the increase also of high schools, and founded Cathedral College as a preparatory seminary.

In the proceedings of the annual convention of the Catholic Educational Association held in New York in 1903, and of the National Eucharistic Congress in 1904, Archbishop Farley took a most active and directive part. Synods were held regularly every third year, and theological conferences quarterly, to give effect to every instruction and legislative act of the Holy See. A monthly recollection for all the priests of the diocese assembled together was instituted. Provision was made for the religious needs of Italians and other Catholic immigrants—the Italian portion of his flock numbering about 400,000 souls. The great work of issuing THE CATHOLIC ENCYCLOPEDIA owed its inception and progress to his help and stimulus. The centenary of the erection of the diocese was celebrated under his direction by a magnificent festival lasting a week (April 27–May 2, 1908); the Lady Chapel of the Cathedral was completed, the Cathedral debt was paid off, and the edifice consecrated 5 October, 1910, Cardinal Vincenzo Vannutelli, papal legate to the Twenty-first Eucharistic Congress, Cardinal Logue, Primate of All Ireland, Cardinal Gibbons of Baltimore, 70 prelates, 1000 priests, and an immense congregation of the laity being present at the Mass of the day.

MICHAEL AUGUSTINE CORRIGAN
Third Archbishop of New York

Archbishop Farley was given an auxiliary in the Right Rev. Thomas F. Cusack, who was consecrated titular Bishop of Themiscyra, 25 April, 1904. Bishop Cusack was born in New York, 22 Feb., 1862, and made his classical course at St. Francis Xavier's College where he graduated in 1880. His theological studies were pursued at the provincial seminary, Troy, where he was ordained priest in 1885. He was a very successful director of the Diocesan-Apostolate (1897–1904) before his consecration as bishop, after which he was appointed Rector of St. Stephen's parish.

IV.—DIOCESAN INSTITUTIONS.—*The Cathedral.*— St. Patrick's Cathedral, standing on the crest of New York's most magnificent thoroughfare, is the noblest temple ever dedicated, in any land, to the honour of the Apostle of Ireland. It is an edifice of which every citizen of the great metropolis is justly proud. Its style is the decorated and geometric Gothic of which the cathedrals of Reims, Amiens, and Cologne are prominent examples. It was planned in 1853 by James Renwick of New York; construction was begun in 1858, and the building was formally opened and dedicated on 25 May, 1879 (building operations having been suspended, owing to the Civil War, from 1861 –66). The site of the cathedral, the block bounded by Fifth Avenue, Fiftieth Street, Fourth Avenue, and Fifty-first Street, has been in the possession of the church authorities, and used for ecclesiastical purposes, except during a very brief interval (1821–1828), since 1 March, 1810. The block on which the Cathedral stands was purchased at its then marketable value and therefore never was a gift or donation from the city, as has been said sometimes, either ignorantly or even with conscious malice. The corner-stone was laid on the afternoon of Sunday, 15 August, 1858, by Archbishop Hughes, in the presence of an assemblage estimated at one hundred thousand. The address delivered by the archbishop is regarded as one of the most eloquent and memorable he ever uttered. The gathering may be considered the first public manifestation of that great Catholic New York which became the wonder and admiration of the nineteenth century, and it lent inspiration and power to the magic of his ringing words of joy and triumph.

St. Patrick's Cathedral is the eleventh in size among the great churches of the world. Its dimensions are as follows, the Lady Chapel excluded: Exterior:—Extreme length (with Lady Chapel), 398 feet; extreme breadth, 174 feet; general breadth, 132 feet; towers at base, 32 feet; height of towers, 330 feet. Interior:— Length, 370 feet; breadth of nave and choir (excluding chapels), 96 feet; breadth of nave and choir (including chapels), 120 feet; length of transept, 140 feet; central aisle, 48 feet wide, 112 feet high; side aisles, 24 feet wide, 54 feet high; chapels 18 feet wide, 14 feet high, 12 feet deep. The foundations are of very large blocks of blue gneiss, which were laid in cement mortar up to the level of the surface. Above the ground-line, the first base-course is of granite, as is also the first course under all the columns and marble works of the interior. Above this base-course the whole exterior of the building is of white marble. The cost of the building was about four million dollars. In the original plan there was an apsidal Lady Chapel, but work on this was not begun until 20 July, 1901, during the administration of Archbishop Corrigan. It was finished by Archbishop Farley in 1906. The architect was Charles T. Mathews whose design was thirteenth-century French Gothic. This chapel is 56½ feet long by 28 feet wide and 56 feet high. The building of the Lady Chapel was started by a memorial gift for that purpose from the family of Eugene Kelly, the banker, who died in New York, 19 Dec., 1894. Eugene Kelly was born in County Tyrone, Ireland, 25 Nov., 1808, and emigrated to New York in 1834. Here he engaged in the drygoods business, and later at St. Louis, Mo., whence he went to California in 1850 during the gold excitement. As a banker and merchant there, he amassed a considerable fortune the interests of which took him back to New York to live in 1856. He was a trustee of the Cathedral for several terms and indentified with the Catholic charitable, educational, and social movements of the city. In the crypt of the chapel the deceased archbishops are buried, and the vault of the Kelly family is at the rear of the sacristy under the Chapel.

Education.—In the cause of Catholic education the Diocese of New York can claim the proud distinction of being the pioneer, the unceasing and uncompromising advocate. In 1685 the Jesuit Fathers Harvey and Harrison began the first Catholic educational institution in the state; the New York Latin School, which stood near the present site of Trinity Church, Wall Street and Broadway, and was attended by the sons of the most influential colonial families. This school was closed by the fanatical intolerance which followed the Dongan administration in 1638. In 1801, Father Matthew O'Brien, O.P., pastor of St. Peter's church, opened the free school of the parish which has been carried on ever since without interruption. During the first five years it was supported entirely by the people of the parish, but in 1806 the legislature of the state, by an act passed 21 March, placed the school on the same footing as those of other religious denominations in the city; all of them received state support at the time, and Father O'Brien's school received its share of the public money. After St. Patrick's church was commenced, Father Kohlmann, S.J., began the New York Literary Institution, the first collegiate school of the diocese, in a house on Mott Street opposite the church. It was an immediate success, and was soon removed to a house on Broadway, and then, in March, 1812, to a suburban site in the village of Elgin, now Fiftieth Street and Fifth Avenue, the site of St. Patrick's Cathedral. Although well patronized by the best families of the city, the inability of the Jesuit community to keep up the teaching staff forced the abandonment of the enterprise in 1815. To supply teachers for girls, Father Kohlmann secured several Ursuline Nuns from Cork, Ireland, who arrived in the city 9 April, 1812. Their convent was located near the Literary Institution, and the Legislature, by the Act of 25 March, 1814, incorporated "The Ursuline Convent of the City of New York", by which "Christine Fagan, Sarah Walsh, Mary Baldwin and others are incorporated for the purpose of teaching poor children". After a year, as no other subjects joined their community, and they were not satisfied with the location, which was too remote from the city for them to receive daily spiritual direction from a chaplain, these nuns gave up the school and returned to Ireland.

With the advent of Bishop Connolly to the diocese (24 November, 1815) St. Patrick's parochial school was opened in the basement of the cathedral. The "Catholic Almanac" for 1822 relates that "there are in this city two extensive Catholic schools conducted upon a judicious plan and supported partly by the funds of the State and partly by moneys raised twice a year by the two congregations". The report of the trustees of St. Peter's church to the superintendent of common schools, in 1824, states that the average number of scholars in St. Peter's and St. Patrick's schools from their opening had been about 500 each. These two were the pioneer schools of that great Catholic parochial system of free schools throughout the diocese which has been the example and stimulus for Catholic education all over the United States. On 28 June, 1817, three Sisters of Charity, sent to her native city by Mother Seton, arrived in New York from Emmitsburg to take charge of the orphan asylum and school of St. Patrick's church. In 1830 these Sisters of Charity took charge of St. Peter's school and opened two academies. In 1816, owing to the conflict between the French rule of their institute, forbidding the care of boys, and other details of discipline which greatly interfered with diocesan progress, Bishop Hughes received permission to organize an independent community with diocesan autonomy. This was established 8 December, 1846, with the election of Mother Elizabeth Boyle as the first superior. The noviliate was opened at 35 East Broadway, but in 1847 was moved to Fifth Avenue and One Hundred and Fifth Street, where the academy for girls and mother-house of Mount St. Vincent was established. Ten years later the city took this property for Central Park, and the community moved to the banks of the Hudson, just below Yonkers, where the College of Mount St. Vincent, and the headquarters of the community now are. There are about eighteen hundred of these sisters teaching in more than sixty parish schools and in charge of diocesan institutions.

In 1841 a community of the Religious of the Sacred Heart was sent to the diocese by Mother Barat, and established their first school at Houston and Mulberry Streets. A year later this was moved to Astoria, Long Island, and in 1846 to the present site of the convent at Manhattanville, where, under the direction, for many years, of the famous Mother Mary Aloysia Hardey, it became, not only a popular educational institution but the centre whence radiated most of the progress made by the Institute throughout the United States. When the first Religious of the Sacred Heart arrived in New York, 31 July, 1827, on their way from France to make the first foundation in the

ST. PATRICK'S CATHEDRAL, NEW YORK

United States at St. Louis, Missouri, Bishop Dubois was most favourably impressed by them, and wished to have a community for New York also. A letter which he wrote to Mother Barat in the following October expresses this desire and gives a view of his charge at that time. "It was my intention", he says, "to visit you and your pious associates in Paris in order to give you a better idea of our country before asking you to establish a house in New York. There is no doubt as to the success of an order like yours in this city; indeed it is greatly needed; but a considerable sum of money would be required to supply the urgent needs of the foundation. The Catholic population, which averages over thirty thousand souls, is very poor, besides chiefly composed of Irish emigrants. Contributions from Protestants are so uncertain and property in this city so expensive that I cannot promise any assistance. All I can say is that I believe one of your schools, commenced with sufficient money to purchase property and support itself until the ladies have time to make themselves known, would succeed beyond all our expectations. . . . I have the sorrow of witnessing an abundant harvest rotting in the earth, through lack of Apostolic labourers and the necessary funds to organize the various needs of the diocese." Although Bishop Dubois was not able to accomplish his desire to have a school then established, his prophecy as to its success when it was opened was amply justified by subsequent results.

The Sisters of Mercy, Sisters of St. Dominic, School Sisters of Notre Dame, and other teaching communities followed in the course of the succeeding years, until now (1910) the parish schools of the archdiocese are in charge of twenty-six different religious communities, twenty-two of Sisters and four of Brothers. In 1829 an Irishman named James D. Boylan with the approbation of Bishop Dubois attempted to establish a religious community on the lines of the Irish Brothers of Charity to teach the boys' schools, and opened two schools. The attempt failed in the course of the year, owing to want of business tact and the inimical spirit of trusteeism. The Christian Brothers opened their first school in New York in September, 1848, in St. Vincent de Paul's parish, at 16 East Canal Street. La Salle Academy was opened in Canal Street in 1850, moved to Mulberry Street in 1856 and East Second Street in 1857. Manhattan College was opened in 1853. These Brothers have charge also of the De La Salle Institute, the Classon Point Military Academy, twenty-six parish schools, and the great Catholic Protectory. Bishop Hughes, in 1846, invited the Jesuits to return to the diocese and take charge of St. John's College and Seminary at Fordham, which he had opened there in the old Rose Hill manor house, 24 June, 1841. The seminary was moved to Troy in 1864, and St. John's remained as part of Fordham University. St. Francis Xavier's College was begun at the school of the church of the Holy Name of Jesus, Elizabeth Street, in 1847. It was burned down in the following year, reopened in Third Avenue near Twelfth Street, and finally located in West Sixteenth Street in 1850. Loyola School was opened by the Jesuits in 1899 at Park Avenue and Fifty-third street.

As has been said, the state appropriation for education was divided at first among all schools. Public education in New York, at the opening of the nineteenth century, was denominational, and under the direction of the Public School Society organized in 1805 "to provide a free school for the education of poor children in the city who do not belong to, or are not provided for by any religious denomination". In 1808 the name was changed to the "Free School Society of New York" and again in 1826 to the "Public School Society of New York", with power "to provide for the education of all children not otherwise provided for". This society gradually became, under the control of intolerant sectarian ministers, a combination against Catholic interests so that, when, in 1840, the eight Catholic parish schools, with an attendance of about 4000 pupils, made a demand for the share of the school appropriations to which the law entitled them, it was refused by the Board of Aldermen after a memorable hearing of the Catholic petition in the City Hall on 29–30 October, 1840, at which Bishop Hughes made one of his greatest oratorical efforts. As a result of this contest the Public School Society was soon after abolished, and the present system of public school control was enacted. The Catholics of New York also determined to organize and maintain their own system of free parish schools. "Go", Bishop Hughes told them, "build your own schools; raise arguments in the shape of the best educated and most moral citizens of the Republic, and the day will come when you will enforce recognition".

ST. JOSEPH'S SEMINARY, DUNWOODIE

To supply priests for the diocese Bishop Dubois established a seminary at Nyack-on-Hudson, in 1833, but it was burned down just as it was ready to be opened. Cornelius Heeney then offered the bishop the ground in Brooklyn on which St. Paul's church now stands, refusing, however, to give the diocese the title to the property immediately, and the design to build in Brooklyn was abandoned. In 1838 the estate of John Lafarge, Grovemont, in Jefferson County, was purchased and the seminary begun there. The place was then so inaccessible and impracticable that it was given up, and, on 24 June, 1841, Bishop Hughes, administrator of the diocese, opened with thirty students the new St. John's seminary and college at Fordham, then a village just outside the city. The Rev. John McCloskey, later Archbishop of New York and first cardinal in the United States, was its first president. The seminary remained at Fordham until 24 Oct., 1864, when it was moved again to Troy, where St. Joseph's seminary began with fifty-seven students transferred from Fordham. The faculty was composed of secular priests from Ghent, Belgium, under the direction of the Very Reverend H. Vanderhende. Here the seminary remained until 1896, during which period more than 700 priests were ordained there. The building was then given over to the Sisters of St. Joseph of the Diocese of Albany as a novitiate and training-school, and, on 12 August, 1896, the new provincial seminary at Dunwoodie was solemnly dedicated by Cardinal Satolli, then Apostolic delegate to the United States. The care of this seminary was entrusted to the Sulpician Fathers, but these retired in 1906, and the work was continued by the secular clergy of the archdiocese. A further step in providing facilities for seminary training was taken up by Archbishop Farley in September, 1903, by the opening of Cathedral College for the preparatory studies of ecclesiastical students.

In the cause of education the work done by the Catholic publishers must be noted; for New York, with the increase of its Catholic population, developed also into a great producing and distributing centre for Catholic literature of all kinds. It is claimed for Bernard Dornin who arrived in New York in 1803, an exile from Ireland, that he was the first publisher of exclusively Catholic works in the United States. His edition of Pastorini's "History of the Christian Church" (1807) was the first Catholic book published in New York. The next year he issued an edition of Dr. Fletcher's "Reflections on the Spirit of Religious Controversy", for which he had 144 city subscribers. There were 318 for the Pastorini book, and these two lists make an interesting directory of Catholic New York families at the opening of the nineteenth century. Dornin left New York for Baltimore in 1809. He was followed in New York by Matthew Field who published "at his library 177 Bowery within a few doors of Delancey St." the first American year book, "The Catholic Laity's Directory to the Church Service: with an almanac for the year 1817". About 1823 John Doyle began to publish books at 237 Broadway, and, up to 1849, when he went to San Francisco, he had issued many books of instruction and devotion. Most of the Doyle plates were taken over by Edward Dunigan, who had associated with him in business his half-brother James B. Kirker. He was the first publisher to encourage Catholic authors to give him their writings. John Gilmary Shea's early histories were published by this firm, as was a fine edition of Haydock's Bible (1844) and many school-books and standard works. In 1837 Dennis and James Sadlier began to issue Butler's "Lives of the Saints" and an edition of the Bible in monthly parts, and thus commenced what later developed into one of the largest book concerns in the United States. The list of their publications is as varied as it is lengthy, and remarkable for the time was their series of "Metropolitan" school books. Patrick O'Shea, who had been associated with the Dunigan concern, began for himself in 1854 and, until his death, in 1906, was a very industrious producer of Catholic books, his publications including, besides a great number of school books, many editions of valuable works, such as Darras' "History of the Church", Digby's "Mores", Brownson's "American Republic", Lingard's "History of England", Wiseman's and Lacordaire's works. Benziger Brothers, in 1853, opened the branch of their German house that developed into the great concern, covering all branches of the trade. Father Isaac T. Hecker, C.S.P., as part of his dream for the evangelization of his non-Catholic fellow-countrymen, founded, in 1866, the Catholic Publication Society. Into this enterprise his brother, George V. Hecker, also a convert, unselfishly put thousands of dollars. Its manager was Lawrence Kehoe, a man well versed in all the best ideals of the trade, who sent out its many books, bound and printed in a lavishness of style not attempted before.

Charities.—New York gave early evidence of the characteristic of heroic charity. In a letter written by Father Kohlmann, 21 March, 1809, he mentions "applications made at all houses to raise a subscription for the relief of the poor by which means $3000 have been collected to be paid constantly each year". New York then had only one church for its 16,000 Catholics. An orphan asylum was opened in 1817 in a small wooden house at Mott and Prince Streets, the "New York Catholic Benevolent Society", for its support and management, was incorporated the same year by the Legislature—the first Catholic Society so legalized in the state—and Mother Seton sent three of her Sisters of Charity from Emmitsburg to take care of the children. This asylum was moved in 1851 to the block adjoining the Cathedral in Fifth Avenue and remained there until this property was sold and the institution located in Westchester County, in 1901. A Union Emigrant Society, to aid immigrants, the precursor of the Irish Emigrant Society and the Emigrant Industrial Savings Bank (see EMIGRANT AID SOCIETIES) was organized in 1829. St. Patrick's, the first New York Conference of the Society of St. Vincent de Paul, was affiliated to the Paris Council in 1849, and in the steady increase of the organization throughout the diocese opened a new field for Catholic charity. The sturdy fight that had to be made against the raids on poor and neglected Catholic children in the public institutions was mainly through its members, and out of their efforts, in great measure, also grew the great Catholic Protectory, the Mission of the Immaculate Virgin, the Foundling Asylum, and the more recent Fresh Air and Convalescent Homes, Day Nurseries, and other incidental details of modern philanthropy.

V. STATISTICS.—The following religious communities now have foundations in the diocese (1910): *Men.*—Augustinians, Augustinians of the Assumption, Fathers of the Blessed Sacrament, Benedictines, Capuchins, Carmelites, Dominicans, Franciscans, Jesuits, Fathers of Mercy, Fathers of the Pious Society of Missions, Missionaries of St. Charles, Missionary Society of St. Paul the Apostle, Redemptorists, Salesian Fathers, Brothers of Mary, Christian Brothers, Marist Brothers, Brothers of the Christian Schools, Missionaries of La Salette. *Women.*—Sisters of St. Agnes, Little Sisters of the Assumption, Sisters of St. Benedict, Sisters of Bon Secours, Sisters of Charity, Sisters of Christian Charity, Sisters of the Divine Compassion, Sisters of Divine Providence, Sisters of St. Dominic, Sisters of the Order of St. Dominic, Felician Sisters, Missionary Sisters of the Third Order of St. Francis, Sisters of the Poor of St. Francis, Sisters of St. Francis, Franciscan Missionaries of Mary, Sisters of the Good Shepherd, Helpers of the Holy Souls, Sisters of the Holy Child Jesus, Marianite Sisters of Holy Cross, Sisters of the Holy Cross, Sisters of Jesus Mary, Sisters of the Sacred Heart of Mary, Sisters of Mercy, Sisters of Misericorde, School Sisters of Notre Dame, Sisters of the Congregation of Notre Dame, Little Sisters of the Poor, Sisters of the Atonement, Reparatrice Nuns, Religious of the Cenacle, Presentation Nuns, Religious of the Sacred Heart, Religious of the Visitation, Missionary Sisters of the Sacred Heart, Ursuline Sisters, Missionary Franciscan Sisters of the Immaculate Conception, Mission Helpers of the Sacred Heart.

The progress of the diocese is shown by the records kept of the gradual growth of population which made a great metropolis out of the small provincial city. The notable increase begins with the immigration during the canal and railroad-building period, after 1825, the exodus from Ireland following the famine year of 1847, and the German flight after the Revolutionary disturbances of 1848. In 1826 in New York City there were but three churches and 30,000 Catholics; and in the whole diocese (including New Jersey) only eight churches, eighteen priests, and 150,000 Catholics. The diocesan figures for 1850 are recorded as follows: churches, 57; chapels, 5; stations, 50; priests, 99; seminary, 1, with 34 students; academies, 9; hospital, 1; charitable institutions, 15; Catholic population, 200,000. In 1875 the increase is indicated by these figures: churches, 139; chapels, 35; priests, 300; ecclesiastical students in seminary, 71; colleges, 3; academies, 22; select schools, 18; hospitals, 4; charitable institutions, 23; religious communities of men, 17, of women, 22; Catholic population, 600,000.

In 1900 we find these totals: churches, 259 (city, 111; country, 148); chapels, 154; stations, 34; priests, 676 (regulars, 227); 112 ecclesiastical students; 60 parish schools for boys in city, with 18,953 pupils; 61 for girls, with 21,199 pupils; parish schools outside city for boys, 32, with 3743 pupils; for girls, 34, with 4542 pupils; in colleges and academies, 2439 boys and 2484 girls; schools for deaf mutes, 2; day nurseries, 4; emigrant homes, 5; homes for aged, 3; hospitals, 15; industrial and reform schools, 26; infant asylum, 1; orphan asylums, 6; total of young people under Catholic care, 68,269; Catholic population, 1,000,000. The figures for 1910 are: archbishop, 1; bishop, 1; churches, 331 (city, 147; country, 184); chapels, 193; stations (without churches) regularly visited, 35; priests, 929 (secular, 605; regular, 324); theological seminary (Dunwoodie), 1; students, 165; students (Rome), 11; preparatory seminary, 1; students, 235; pupils in colleges and academies for boys, 3407; in academies for girls, 3812; parish schools, New York City, for boys, 90, with 27,899 pupils; for girls, 90, with 31,004 pupils; outside New York City, 58, with 6377 male pupils, 6913 female; total in parish schools, 72,193; schools for deaf mutes, 3; day nurseries, 15; emigrant homes, 5; homes for the aged, 4; hospitals, 23; industrial and reform schools, 36; orphan asylums, 7; asylums for the blind, 2; total of young people under Catholic care, 101,087; Catholic population, 1,219,920. Besides those for English-speaking Catholics, there are now churches and priests in New York for Germans, Italians, Poles, French, Hungarians, Bohemians, Lithuanians, Greek Albanese, Greek Syrians, Greek Ruthenians, Slovaks, Spaniards, Chinese, for coloured people and for deaf mutes.

SHEA, *Hist. of Cath. Ch. in U. S.* (New York, 1886); IDEM, *Cath. Ch's of N. Y.* (New York, 1878); *Ecclesiastical Records, State of New York* (Albany, 1902); O'CALLAGHAN, *Documentary Hist. of New York* (Albany, 1849–51); BAYLEY, *Brief Sketch of the Early Hist., Cath. Ch. on the Island of New York* (New York, 1854); FINOTTI, *Bibliographia Americana* (New York, 1872); FLYNN, *The Cath. Ch. in New Jersey* (Morristown, 1904); WHITE, *Life of Mrs. Eliza A. Seton* (New York, 1893); CLARKE, *Lives of the Deceased Bishops, U. S.* (New York, 1872–86); SETON, *Memoir, Letters and Journal of Elizabeth Seton* (New York, 1869); FARLEY, *History of St. Patrick's Cathedral* (New York, 1908); SMITH, *Hist. Cath. Ch. in New York* (New York, 1905); REUSS, *Biog. Cycl., Cath. Hierarchy, U. S.* (Milwaukee, 1898); *The Catholic Directory*; U. S. CATH. HIST. SOCIETY, *Historical Records and Studies* (New York, 1899–1910); *Memorial, Most Rev. M. A. Corrigan* (New York, 1902); HASSARD, *Life of the Most Rev. John Hughes* (New York, 1866); BRANN, *Most Rev. John Hughes* (New York, 1892); CAMPBELL, *Pioneer Priests of North America* (New York, 1909–10); *Mary Aloysia Hardey* (New York, 1910); *New York Truth Teller*, files; *Freeman's Journal*, files; *Metropolitan Record*, files; *Tablet*, files; *Catholic News*, files; BROWNSON, H. F., *Brownson's Early, Middle and Later Life* (Detroit, 1898–1900); BENNETT, *Catholic Footsteps in Old New York* (New York, 1909); ZWIERLEIN, *Religion in New Netherland* (Rochester, 1910).

JOSEPH F. MOONEY.

New York, STATE OF, one of the thirteen colonies of Great Britain, which on 4 July, 1776, adopted the Declaration of Independence and became the United States of America.

BOUNDARIES AND AREA.—The State of New York lies between 40° 29′ 40″ and 45° 0′ 2″ N. lat. and between 71° 51′ and 79° 45′ 54″ W. long. It is bounded by Lake Ontario, the St. Lawrence River, and the Dominion of Canada on the north; by Vermont, Massachusetts, and Connecticut on the east; by Pennsylvania, New Jersey, and the Atlantic Ocean on the south, and by Pennsylvania, Lake Erie, and the Niagara River on the west. It has an area of 49,170 square miles, of which 1550 square miles is water surface. From east to west it is 326·46 miles in width; it is 300 miles long on the line of the Hudson River.

PHYSICAL CHARACTERISTICS.—The physical geography of New York is very varied. It includes the high range of the Adirondack Mountains in the northern part. In the southern and eastern part lie important portions of the Appalachian system, of which the principal branches are: the Catskill Mountains on the west bank of the Hudson River below Albany; the ranges of the Blue Ridge, which cross the Hudson at West Point and form the Litchfield and Berkshire Hills and the Green Mountains on the eastern boundary of the State and in Connecticut, Massachusetts, and Vermont, and the foothills of the Alleghanies in the south-western portion. The highest peak in the State is Mount Marcy in the Adirondacks, which has an altitude of 5344 feet. The valley of the Mohawk divides the mountainous district in the eastern part of the State, and forms a natural channel in which the Erie Canal now lies, and which affords easy communication by water and rail between the Great Lakes and the Hudson River valley. On the Niagara River is one of the great cataracts of the world, Niagara Falls, which is a mile wide and 164 feet high. The preservation of its natural beauty has been ensured by the erection of a State Park, which adjoins a similar park established by the Canadian Government.

Geologically, the State of New York is most interesting. The Hudson River valley and the Adirondacks form part of the Archæan continent, which is regarded as the oldest portion of the earth's surface. The Hudson River rises in the Adirondack country. It is navigable for 151 miles, from Troy to the sea. The Palisades of the Hudson are among the most interesting and important examples of basaltic rocks in the world. The principal rivers of the State, besides

SEAL OF NEW YORK

the great Hudson River and its tributary, the Mohawk, are the Susquehanna River, which rises in Lake Otsego in the central part of the State; the Delaware, which rises on the western slope of the Catskill mountain country, and the Allegheny, which rises in the south-western corner of the State. None of these is of commercial importance within the State of New York, all passing on to form the principal rivers of Pennsylvania. The series of large inland lakes in central New York form a marked feature of its physical geography. They are of great natural beauty, besides being of importance for transportation and commerce, and many of the large cities and towns of the State have grown up on their banks. The land surrounding them and the valleys of the brooks and small rivers which form their feeders and outlets are of remarkable fertility. The forests of the State are extensive. They lie principally in the Adirondack, Catskill, and Blue Ridge country. They are the remnants of the primeval forests that once covered most of the State. The State has established by constitutional provision and statutory enactments an extensive system of forest preserves. They are the Adirondack Preserve, containing approximately 1,500,000 acres, and the Catskill Preserve, containing 110,000 acres. Provision is made by law for increasing their area from year to year. The beautiful valleys of the Hudson and its tributaries extend from the sea into the foothills of the Adirondacks at Lake George. The valley of Lake Champlain on the eastern slope of the Adirondacks adjoins the valley of Lake George, and continues it, except for a divide of about two miles at its beginning, into the Dominion of Canada and the St. Lawrence valley. The great central plain of the State, lying between the mountainous districts of the south and west and the Great Lakes and the Adirondacks and the eastern mountain ranges on the north and east, is renowned for the fertility of its soil and the extent of its manufactures.

The only sea-coast of the State is formed by Long Island, and extends for 130 miles from New York Harbour to Montauk Point, which is nearly opposite the boundary line between the States of Connecticut and Rhode Island. The waters lying between Long Island and the mainland form Long Island Sound, one of the most important waterways of the United States. From the head of navigation on the Hudson River at Troy, a distance of 151 miles from the sea, there extends across the State to Lake Erie one of its great possessions, the Erie Canal, completed in 1825. It is 387 miles long. From Troy to Whitehall at the head of Lake Champlain extends another of the State's great works, the Champlain Canal, establishing water connexion with the St. Lawrence valley on the north. Ample communication by water from the Lake States on the west and from Canada on the north to the Atlantic Ocean at New York Bay is provided by this canal system. There are also three other important interior canals owned by the State, the Oswego, the Cayuga and Seneca, and the Black River canals. In 1909 the goods carried free on these state canals valued nearly sixty million dollars. There is now under construction by the State the Great Barge Canal, which it is estimated will cost more than $60,000,000. It is intended to provide navigation for modern canal barges of 1000 tons from Lake Erie to New York City.

The physical geography of the State has been an important factor in its growth. The easy communication afforded by its great rivers and its convenient waterways has made it the favoured highway for domestic trade and commerce and emigration for more than a century, while its possession of the greatest seaport of the North Atlantic Ocean has made the State the principal gateway for the world's trade with North America. The ice-free and deep-channelled port of New York, lying at the mouth of the Hudson River, with its wide roadsteads and anchorages and vast transportation facilities is indeed the greatest property of the State of New York. The port has a total water front of 444 miles.

MEANS OF COMMUNICATION.—The means of communication within the State are admirable.

Railroads.—In 1907 there were 8505 miles of railway and 3950 miles of electric railway tracks. The great railroad of the State is the New York Central system between New York and Buffalo which provides communication between New York City and the principal places in all parts of the United States by its own lines and their direct connexions. The great New England system, the New York, New Haven and Hartford Railroad, besides having its terminal in New York City, crosses the southern part of the State into the coal and iron country of Pennsylvania. It controls also the extensive New York, Ontario, and Western Railroad, extending diagonally across the State from Oswego on Lake Ontario to the Hudson River at Weehawken, opposite New York. The Erie system, in addition to being one of the trunk lines to Chicago, is probably the greatest freight carrier in the Union. Its passenger traffic around New York City is also of great extent. Its terminal is in Jersey City opposite New York. The Delaware and Hudson Railroad extends from its connexion with the Grand Trunk of Canada, at Rouse's Point on Lake Champlain, to Albany, where it forms a connexion with a network of roads extending into many of the important centres of central and western New York. The Delaware, Lackawanna, and Western Railroad runs parallel to the southern boundary of the State in New Jersey and Pennsylvania, and has its eastern terminal at Hoboken on the Hudson River also opposite New York City. It extends also to the north a most important line from Binghamton to Buffalo, Utica, and Oswego. It is the greatest of the anthracite coal carriers. The Buffalo, Rochester, and Pittsburg Railroad connects the three large cities named in its title, and serves one of the important agricultural, manufacturing, and mining districts of the States of New York and Pennsylvania. The Pennsylvania Railroad, one of the great national trunk lines, with its Hudson tunnels and its new vast terminal in New York City, is one of the great institutions of New York. Its main lines centre about Philadelphia. It owns and operates in addition to its other properties the entire railroad system of populous Long Island, whose wonderful growth in population and industry seems but a presage of still more extensive development. The Hudson Tunnels under the Hudson River connect the City of New York with the terminals of most of the railroads on the New Jersey side of the Hudson; recently opened (1910) tunnels under the East River bring the Long Island Railroad into direct connexion with the Pennsylvania system, and thus with the rest of the continent. These tunnels are a marvellous achievement in subaqueous construction. The development of the terminals of these trunk lines and of their accessories especially about the port of New York is a great object lesson in the astounding development of the Western Hemisphere in less than eighty years. The first railroad in the State, the Hudson and Mohawk, was built in 1831. It was 17 miles long and ran from Albany to Schenectady on the Mohawk. It was one of the earliest steam railroads in the world.

Water Routes.—The communication by water within New York State is not less wonderful. To the ocean navigation that fills the port of New York must be added the traffic on the rivers, lakes, and canals of the State and upon Long Island Sound. The prosperous cities and towns which are ranged along the banks of the Hudson River, across the State on the lines of the canals and lakes and rivers, and upon the shores of Lake Erie, Lake Ontario, and the St. Lawrence River are sustained largely by it.

Wagon Roads.—The improved system of State highways, begun in late years, has given modern highways to many of the rural districts and laid out avenues between the cities. It is based upon subventions of highway improvements by means of loans and aids from the State treasury to the various local authorities. The growth of vehicular traffic by electric tramways and by automobiles has greatly promoted this work.

CLIMATE.—The climate of the State is salubrious, and corresponds generally with that of the north temperate zone. In 1909—which was somewhat abnormal, it is true—the extremes of temperature were 102° above zero maximum and 35° below zero minimum. For 1909 the mean annual temperature of the entire State was 45.8°. The average rainfall throughout the State for the same year was 36·03 inches. New York State is divided by the Department of Agriculture of the United States into three climatological districts: (1) the Hudson, Delaware, and Susquehanna basins, (2) the Allegheny River, and (3) the Great Lakes and the St. Lawrence. The great extent of the State causes very variable climatic conditions within its boundaries. In 1909 the mean annual temperature for one part of the Adirondack region was 39° and for the vicinity of New York City 52°. The rainfall during the year 1909 averaged from 18·10 inches in Livingston County to 62·7 inches in Jefferson County. The winters in the Adirondack country, the St. Lawrence, and the Champlain valleys are generally severe, while the Hudson Valley, Long Island, and the vicinity of New York City have moderate winters and hot summers.

POPULATION.—New York has been since 1820 the most populous state in the Union. The Federal Census returns of 1910 place the population at 9,113,279; the State Census of 1905 placed it at 8,067,308. The City of New York in 1910 comprised 4,766,883 souls. It is one of the centres of the population of the world. In a circle of 680 square miles area with its centre at the Battery (the same area as that of Greater London) there are dwelling six millions of people, or scarcely a million less than in the London district, which it is to be remembered is not a municipality. This metropolitan district is the most cosmopolitan community in the world. Its urban character is most varied and interesting. One division of it, the City of New York proper, is so large that if divided it would make three cities such as Chicago, Philadelphia, and Pittsburg. Yet nearly a million and a half of people live outside the limits of the city and within the indicated area.

The cities of Buffalo, Rochester, Syracuse, Albany, and Troy are the five next in size; according to the census of 1910 they include respectively 423,715, 218,149, 137,249, 100,253, and 76,813 people. In 1905 there were 4821 Indians still on the State Reservations. There were 47 municipalities in New York in 1900 having a population of more than 8000 people, and in them 68·5 per cent of the people dwelt. In 1900 there were 3,614,780 males and 3,654,114 females in the State. There were 99,232 coloured people. 1,900,425 of the population or a little less than one quarter were foreign born. Of these there were 480,026 Germans, 425,553 Irish, 182,248 Italians, 165,610 Russian (mostly Hebrews), and 135,685 English—to mention only the largest groups. The population of the whole State in 1790 was 340,120 by the first Federal Census. In 120 years it has increased more than twenty-six times.

In 1906, according to the Federal Census Bureau, there were 2,285,768 Roman Catholics in New York, forming 63.6 per cent of the total of 3,591,974 religious communicants or church members in the State of New York. It is the largest religious denomination in the State. However, only 43·7 per cent of the people of the State claimed membership in any church or denomination. In 1906 there were 278 Roman Catholics for each 1000 of the population, a gain of 8·6 per cent over the figures of the census reports of 1890. The number of Protestant Episcopalian communicants at the same date in the State was 24 for each 1000 of the population. In 1906 the Federal Census reports show that in the State of New York the number of churches and halls for worship was 9193, having a seating capacity of 3,191,267. There were also presbyteries valued at $22,283,225. The Sunday schools were 8795 in number and attended by 1,247,051 scholars. The entire value of all church property was $255,166,284, on which the debt was $28,382,866. The Catholic Annual for 1910 shows the following carefully gathered for the dioceses of New York State. All these dioceses, it should be noted, are wholly included within the State boundaries and together comprise the whole State:

Dioceses	Catholic Population	Churches	Priests	Parochial Schools	Young People under Catholic Care
New York....	1,219,820	331	929	148	101,087
Albany......	193,525	171	232	47	20,362
Brooklyn,...	700,000	195	426	76	78,567
Buffalo......	244,739	194	346	111	36,405
Ogdensburg...	92,000	154	135	15	4,079
Rochester....	121,000	129	163	54	19,779
Syracuse......	151,463	106	119	18	9,141
Totals......	2,722,547	1280	2350	469	269,420

These Catholic estimates are interesting for the purposes of comparison with those of the official documents, and particularly as being in advance of the results of the Federal Census of 1910, which are now being prepared but cannot be published in detail for some years to come. The present population of the State of New York, according to the census of 1910, is 9,113,279, about one-tenth of the entire population of the United States.

WEALTH AND RESOURCES.—New York is the wealthiest State in the Union. The aggregate value of all the property within the State in 1904, as estimated by the Federal Census Bureau, was $14,769,042,207, of which $9,151,979,081 represented real property and improvements. The revenue of the State Government in 1908–9 was $52,285,239. The City of New York received the enormous revenue of $368,696,334 in 1908, and had in the same year a funded debt of $598,012,644. The resources of the State of New York lie first in its commerce, and then in its manufactures, agriculture, and mining.

Commerce.—In 1908 New York City was the third shipping port of the world, being surpassed only by London and Liverpool. Its imports were of the value of approximately 780 millions and its exports 600 millions. The tonnage movement of foreign trade for the year ending 30 June, 1909, was: entered,12,528,723 tons; cleared, 11,866,431 tons. The shipping of the inland waters and of the Great Lakes controlled by the State of New York is of equally vast extent. Buffalo, with a population of over 400,000, receives in its port on Lake Erie a large portion of the shipping trade of Canada and of the Lake States of the Union. The other ports of Lakes Erie and Ontario are similarly prosperous.

Manufactures.—New York is the leading State of the Union in manufactures. In 1905 it had invested in manufactures more than $2,000,000,000, and the value of its manufactures products was approximately $2,500,000,000. In the same year it produced 47 per cent of the men's and 70 per cent of the women's clothes made in the United States. The value of its textile output in the same year was $114,371,226.

Agriculture.—In 1900 there were in New York 226,720 farms of a total area of 22,648,100 acres, of which 15,599,986 acres were improved land. The principal crops are maize, wheat, oats, potatoes, and hay. The wool clip in 1908 was estimated at 5,100,000 pounds. The largest dairy interests in the United States are within the State of New York.

Mining.—The mines of the state in 1908 yielded products valued at $45,609,861; the quarries produced building stone valued at $6,137,279. The Onondaga salt springs produced in the same year products of the value of $2,136,738, while the petroleum wells yielded $2,071,533 worth of crude petroleum.

PUBLIC DEBT.—The State of New York has no funded debt except for canals and highways. Its outstanding bonds for these purposes on 30 September, 1909, aggregated $41,230,660. It has no direct taxation. It has a surplus in its treasury. The assessed valuation of the taxable property within the State for 1909 was just short of $10,000,000,000. The title of "Empire State", given to New York by common consent, is well deserved.

EDUCATIONAL SYSTEM.—The public educational system of New York is extensive and arranged upon broad plans. It is governed by a general revised statute of more than 2000 sections called "Education Law", adopted in 1910. This law provides for a central organization called the "Education Department" composed of the regents of the University of the State of New York, who are the legislative branch, and the Commissioner of Education, who is made the chief executive officer of the system and of the regents. The work of the Educational Department is divided into three parts, the common schools, the academic or secondary schools, and the colleges and universities. The head of the regents of the university is the chancellor. Executive control, however, is entrusted to the commissioner of education, who, with his assistants and subordinates, has charge of the enormous details of the entire educational system of the State under the legislative control of the regents and the direction of the statutes of the State passed by the legislature. The colleges and universities of the State are separate corporations, formed either by the regents or by special statutes. They are under either private or municipal control. There is no State university as such, although Cornell University has been given many of the privileges and State aids usually granted to such an institution. These corporations are subject, however, to the provisions of the Education Law and the jurisdiction of the Education Department. The academies or secondary schools are also either private or public. The public secondary schools are directly in charge of the school boards and boards of education of the various divisions of the State. The private academies may enroll themselves under the Department of Education, and receive the privileges of the public academies in respect to examinations and certificates from the Education Department. There is, however, no legal compulsion put upon them in this respect. The common schools of the State are divided generally into those which are controlled by the local boards of education in the cities and more populous centres, and those which are controlled by the local school officers elected by the people in the school districts in other parts of the State. Woman suffrage is granted in school officers' elections. In the great cities of the State the common and secondary schools are usually placed in charge of school boards and officers provided for in the city charters, which are in the form of statutes enacted by the legislature.

In New York City is situated the large college known as the College of the City of New York, maintained at public expense. It has the most extensive buildings for educational purposes in the city and an enrolment of more than 3736 pupils. On the Hudson, at West Point, is situated the famous United States Military Academy for the training of officers for the army. It is entirely under Federal control through the War Department, and has 525 cadets in attendance. The professional schools of the State of all classes are controlled by the Education Department under stringent provisions. Admission to the secular professions generally is granted by State certificates awarded after rigid examinations by State examining boards. The schools for the training of teachers are also either under departmental control or, in the more populous centres, under the control of the several boards of education of the localities. Primary education is compulsory between the ages of seven and sixteen years. The state does not interfere, however, with the liberty of choice of schools by parents. No discrimination is made against parochial and private schools, which have enrolled themselves with the Education Department: they receive, however, no public financial aid, if the small grant made by the Department to defray the cost of examinations in the enrolled secondary schools be excepted.

In 1908 there were 1,841,638 children between five and eighteen years of age in New York State; there were 1,273,754 pupils and 36,132 teachers in the public schools. The academies or secondary schools of the State had 95,170 pupils and 1523 teachers; the colleges and universities 22,097 students and 2699 teachers. There were 12,068 public school buildings, 144 public secondary schools or academies, and 30 colleges and universities. The appropriation of public moneys for educational purposes in New York State for the year 1907 was $71,838,172. The City of New York alone paid in 1909 for public school education $36,319,624. Its schools contained 730,234 pupils and had 17,073 teachers and directors. The public statistics of the Department of Education of New York available show that 451 parochial schools, besides numerous academies and colleges, were conducted under the auspices of the Catholic Church in New York in 1908. The number of pupils in the Catholic educational institutions of the State cannot be ascertained with certainty. A large number of Catholic schools and academies make no public reports, but it is conservatively estimated that 210,000 pupils were in the Catholic schools in 1908. The State Education Department reported that in 1907, 179,677 pupils were registered as in the Roman Catholic Elementary Schools alone. The Catholic Annual of 1910 estimates the number of young people under Catholic care including the orphans and other inmates of charitable institutions as 269,420.

There are many excellent high schools and academies in the State conducted by the Catholic teaching orders of men and women and by secular priests and laymen. The colleges under Catholic auspices are: Fordham University, St. Francis Xavier College, Manhattan College, Brooklyn College, St. Francis College, St. John's College, Brooklyn—all in New York City; Canisius College at Buffalo, Niagara University at Niagara Falls, and the College of New Rochelle, a flourishing college for women in charge of the Ursuline Nuns. All of these institutions are under the jurisdiction of the Education Department of the State of New York. In 1894 there was inserted in the Constitution of the State a provision that neither the State nor any subdivision thereof should use its property or credit or any public money or authorize or permit either to be used directly or indirectly in aid or maintenance other than for examination or inspection of any school or institution of learning wholly or in part under the control or direction of any religious denomination or in which any denominational tenet or doctrine is taught. The Catholic seminaries for the education of priests are flourishing. The great novitiates of the Jesuits, Redemptorists, and Christian Brothers, and several others maintained by various religious orders, are in the Hudson Valley, south of Albany. The seminary of the Archdiocese of New York at Dunwoodie, Westchester County, which is the monument of the late Archbishop Corrigan, is one of the leading seminaries of the United States. The diocesan seminaries of St. John's at Brooklyn, St. Bernard's at Rochester, and the Seminary of Our Lady of Angels, conducted by the priests of the Mission at Niagara Falls, in the Diocese of Buffalo, are of the highest standing for scholarship and training.

MILITIA.—The militia of the State, which is composed exclusively of volunteers, numbers 17,038 trained officers and men in all the arms of the military service. It is intended to form the nucleus of a military force in time of need by training volunteer citizen-soldiers in the military art. It is most liberally supported by the State and most carefully trained in co-operation with the Federal Government.

LIBRARIES.—The libraries of the State are numerous and important. The Education Department maintains a generous system for the establishment of libraries and provides generous State aid for their support. The great library of the State is the New York Public Library in the City of New York, which in 1909 owned 1,549,260 books and 295,078 pamphlets, in all 1,844,338 volumes. It will soon (in 1911) occupy the magnificent building erected by the City of New York in Bryant Square at Fifth Avenue and Forty-second Street, which has just been completed. It is largely endowed by the testamentary gifts of John Jacob Astor, James Lenox, and Samuel J. Tilden, and receives aid from the City Treasury.

HISTORY.—The territory which now forms the State of New York may, as regards its history, be divided into two parts. The first part includes the Hudson River valley, the valley of the Mohawk, the land around Newark Bay and New York Harbour, and the western end of Long Island—which, speaking generally, were, together with the sparse Delaware River settlements, the only portions of New Netherland actually occupied by the Dutch when the province was granted by the English Crown to the Duke of York in 1664. The second part comprises the rest of the State excluding eastern Long Island: this was the Indian country, the home of the Iroquois and the other tribes forming the Five Nations, now mostly remembered from the old romances, but a savage and fierce reality to the Dutch and English colonists. As late as 1756 there were only two counties to be found in the entire province west of the Hudson River. Interposed between the French and the Dutch (and afterwards the English), and brought from time to time into their quarrels for supremacy, the Indians kept the land between the Great Lakes, the Hudson, and the St. Lawrence truly "a dark and bloody ground" until the end of the eighteenth century, when, as part of the military operations of the Revolution, the expedition of the American forces, sent by Washington under command of General John Sullivan, finally broke their power at the Battle of Newton near Elmira in 1779.

Although their military power was thus destroyed, the Indians still remained a menace to the settlers in remoter districts for many years. Gradually, however, their opposition was overcome, and they finally became the wards of the State, living on reservations set apart for their exclusive occupancy. A remnant of them (4821 in the year 1905) still survives. Early in the nineteenth century large grants of land began to be made by the State at small prices to land companies and promoters for the purpose of fostering occupation by settlers. Systematic colonization was immediately undertaken, and a large emigration from Vermont, Massachusetts, Connecticut, and the Dutch settlements in the Hudson Valley began to flow into the Iroquois country. This continued prosperously, but not rapidly until De Witt Clinton, one of the great figures in the history of New York, upon his taking the office of Governor in 1818, pressed forward vigorously the long-standing plans for the construction and completion of the great artificial waterways of the State, the Erie and the Champlain canals. European immigration then became essential to supply the labour needed for the success of these plans. Stalwart men and women flocked from the British Islands and Germany in astounding numbers, and in forty years the population of New York City increased more than six times (from 33,131 in 1790 to 202,589 in 1830). The labouring men, who worked outside the cities on the public works, with their families became settlers in the villages and towns that grew up along the canals. The general prosperity which succeeded the successful completion of these works and their operation, and the consequent enormous development of the State's resources, drew others into the territory. The population of the State of New York itself increased from 340,120 in 1790 to 1,918,608 in 1830.

The European immigration thus begun included of course a large proportion of Catholics. Bishop Dubois estimated that in 1830 there were 35,000 Catholics in New York City and 150,000 throughout the rest of the State and in northern New Jersey, made up chiefly of poor emigrants. The Irish element was very large, and the first Catholic congregations in New York were in some cases almost wholly Irish. To them soon came their devoted missionary priests to minister to them in the Faith which had survived among their race and grown even brighter in the night of the iniquitous penal days, which had then but just begun to pass away. The State of New York, because of the uncertain boundaries of the old Dutch province of New Netherland, at first laid claim to the country which now comprises the State of Vermont, and also to part of the land now lying in western Massachusetts and Connecticut. These claims were settled by mutual agreement in due course and the boundaries were fixed. The State of Vermont thereupon became the fourteenth State of the Union in 1791, being the first admitted after the adoption of the United States Constitution in 1789. The first complete State Constitution framed after the Revolution was that of New York. It was adopted on 20 April, 1777, at Kingston on the Hudson. John Jay, George Clinton, and Alexander Hamilton were its principal framers. The City of New York became the capital of the State after the Revolution, as it had been the capital of the Province of New York before. Upon the adoption of the United States Constitution in 1789 it became the capital of the United States. President Washington was inaugurated there at Federal Hall at the head of Broad Street, the first capital of the United States. His house stood at the foot of Broadway. Its site is now occupied by the Washington Building. In 1790 the capital of the United States was removed to Philadelphia, and in 1797 the capital of the State was removed to Albany where it has since remained. Since 1820 the City of New York has been the commercial and financial centre of the continent of North America.

ECCLESIASTICAL HISTORY.—On 8 April, 1808, the Holy See created the Diocese of New York coincidently with the establishment of the American Hierarchy by the erection of Baltimore to be an Archiepiscopal See with New York, Philadelphia, Boston, and Bardstown (now Louisville) as suffragan sees. Doctor Richard Luke Concanen, an Irish Dominican resident in Rome, was appointed first Bishop of New York, but died at Naples in 1809, while awaiting an opportunity to elude Napoleon Bonaparte's embargo and set out for his see. After a delay of six years his successor Bishop John Connolly, also a Dominican, arrived at New York in November, 1815, and ministered as the first resident bishop to his scattered congregations of 17,000 souls (whom he describes as "mostly Irish") in union with the four priests, who were all he had to help him throughout his immense diocese. He died on 5 February, 1825, after a devoted and self-sacrificing episcopate, and is buried under the altar of the new St. Patrick's Cathedral. During the vacancy of the see, preceding the arrival of Bishop Connolly (1808–15), the diocesan affairs were administered by Father Anthony Kohlmann (q. v.). He rebuilt St. Peter's church in Barclay Street, and in 1809 bought the site of old St. Patrick's Cathedral in Mott Street, the building of which he finished in 1815. He also bought in 1809 the land and old residence in the large block on Fifth Avenue at Fiftieth Street—part of which is the site of the present St. Patrick's Cathedral—and there established a flourishing boys' school called the New York Literary Institution.

In 1822 the diocesan statistics were: two churches in New York City, one in Albany, one in Utica, one in Auburn, one at Carthage on the Black River, all of which were served by one bishop and eight priests. Bishop Connolly was succeeded on 29 October, 1826, by John Dubois (q. v.), a Frenchman who had been a fellow student of Robespierre and was one of the *émigré* priests of the French Revolution. He was one of the founders of Mount St. Mary's, Emmitsburg, Maryland—"the mother of priests", as it has been called—and passed through the cholera epidemic of 1832, when 3000 people died in the City of New York between July and October. He increased the churches and brought to his diocese zealous priests. It is noteworthy that he ordained to the priesthood at St. Patrick's in June, 1836, the Venerable John N. Neuman (q. v.), afterwards the saintly Bishop of Philadelphia. After a life of arduous labour, trial, and anxiety both as a missionary, an educator, and a pioneer bishop, his health broke down, and he was granted in 1837 as coadjutor John Hughes (q. v.), who justly bears the most distinguished name in the annals of the American hierarchy even to this day.

Bishop Hughes was consecrated on 9 February, 1838. A stroke of paralysis attacked the venerable Bishop Dubois almost immediately afterwards, and he was an invalid until his death on 20 December, 1842, whereupon he was succeeded by his coadjutor as Bishop of New York. In April, 1847, the Sees of Albany and Buffalo were created. Bishop John McCloskey (q. v.), afterwards the first American cardinal, who was then Coadjutor Bishop of New York, was transferred to Albany, and Reverend John Timon, Superior of the Congregation of the Mission, was made Bishop of Buffalo. In October, 1850, the Diocese of New York was erected into an archiepiscopal see with the Sees of Boston, Hartford, Albany, and Buffalo as its suffragans. Archbishop Hughes sailed for Rome in the following month, and received the pallium from the hands of Pius IX himself.

The career of Archbishop Hughes and the history of his archdiocese and its suffragan sees are fully treated under their appropriate titles, and need not be discussed here. The life of Archbishop Hughes marked the great formative period in the history of the pioneer Church in New York. His great work in the cause of education, in the establishment of the parochial schools, the establishment of the great teaching and other religious orders, and the erection of seminaries and colleges for the training of candidates for the priesthood, as well as in the solution of the tremendous problems connected with the building up of the churches and charities and the preservation of the Faith, had a profound effect upon the attitude of the State of New York towards religious institutions and persons and ecclesiastical affairs. The Knownothing movement of the fifties (see KNOWNOTHINGISM) was profoundly felt in New York, but the number and importance of the Catholic population protected them from the cowardly assaults made upon the Catholics in other places. The presence of Archbishop Hughes was ever a tower of strength in the conflict and in producing the overwhelming defeat which this un-American movement met. The only effect of this sectarian agitation upon the legislation of the State was the passage in 1855 of a plainly unconstitutional statute which sought to prevent Catholic bishops from holding title to property in trust for churches or congregations. It proved of no avail whatever. In 1862, after the Civil War began, it was quietly repealed.

In 1853 the Dioceses of Brooklyn in New York and of Newark in New Jersey were established, the first Bishop of Brooklyn being Reverend John Loughlin and the first Bishop of Newark Reverend James Roosevelt Bayley (q. v.), who later became Archbishop of Baltimore. In 1868 the Diocese of Rochester was separated from Albany, and the venerable and beloved apostle of Catholicism in north-western New York, Bishop Bernard J. McQuaid (q. v.), appointed its first bishop.

In 1872 the Diocese of Ogdensburg was created, and in November, 1886, the youngest diocese of the State, Syracuse. It is unnecessary to sketch further here the history of Catholicism in New York State during the incumbency of the archiepiscopal office by Cardinal McCloskey, Archbishop Hughes's successor, and that of his successor Archbishop Corrigan, or of his Grace, John M. Farley, its present archbishop. It is sufficient to record the continual progress in the advancement of Catholic interests, in the building up of the Church, and in adjusting its activities to the needs of the people.

DISTINGUISHED CATHOLICS.—The Catholics of New York State have produced their full proportion of persons of distinction in the professions, commercial, political, and social life. Of the ninety-seven justices who now sit in the Supreme Court seventeen are of the Catholic faith. Among the justices of the lower courts are many Catholics. Since 1880 three mayors of New York City (Messrs. Grace, Grant, and Gilroy) have been Catholics. Francis Kernan was United States Senator for New York from 1876–82. Denis O'Brien closed a distinguished career as Judge of the Court of Appeals, the court of last resort, by his retirement for age in 1908 after a continuous service of eighteen years. The first Catholic Justice of the Supreme Court was John R. Brady, elected in 1859, and loyal sons of the Church have been on that bench ever since. Mayors of the great cities of the State, senators, assemblyman, State officers and representatives in Congress, and a multitude of other public officers have been chosen from the Catholic citizenship ever since the beginning of the nineteenth century and have rendered distinguished service to the State. For many years the two brilliant leaders of the New York Bar were Charles O'Conor and James T. Brady, sons of Irish Catholic emigrants. In medicine Gunning S. Bedford and Thomas Addis Emmet kept for many years the Catholic name at the top of the profession, and they have now worthy successors. In the great public works and industries of the State Catholics have had more than their share of the labour and its rewards. In the commercial life of New York some of the largest fortunes have been honourably gathered by Catholic men, who have been most generous to the religious and charitable works of the State.

LEGAL.—The State of New York has a constitutional government. It was the model of that of the United States of America. The union of the executive, legislative, and judicial branches of government under a written constitution is its principle. Its executive head is the governor. The legislature has two houses, the Senate and Assembly, which meet annually at Albany, the State capital. Its courts are composed principally of a Court of Appeals (the highest court) and the Supreme Court, which is divided into four Appellate Divisions, and numerous courts of first instance, divided into districts throughout the State. There are many minor and local courts supplementing the Supreme Court.

The State of New York has always been foremost in the pursuit of freedom of worship and religious toleration. It is true, however, that her first Constitution in 1777 excluded all priests and ministers of the Gospel from her legislature and offices, and put a prohibitory religious test upon foreign-born Catholics who applied for citizenship. Herein we find an echo of the bitter intolerance of the eighteenth century, which was strongly opposed in the Convention. The naturalization disability disappeared very soon on the adoption of the Federal Constitution in 1789, and, by subsequent constitutional amendments, all these remnants of ancient bigotry were formally abolished. It is remarkable to find John Jay, otherwise most earnest in the fight for civil liberty, the leader in these efforts to impose religious tests and restraints of liberty of conscience upon his Catholic fellow-citizens. This Constitution, nevertheless, proclaimed general religious liberty in unmistakable terms. The provision is as follows: "The free exercise and enjoyment of religious profession and worship without discrimination or preference shall forever hereafter be allowed within this State to all mankind provided that the liberty of conscience hereby granted shall not be so construed as to excuse acts of licentiousness or justify practices inconsistent with the peace or safety of this State." The statutes of the State which permitted the formation of religious corporations without restraint, and gave to them when formed, freedom to hold property and conduct their affairs unhampered by the civil power, are contemporaneous with the restoration of order within its borders after the British evacuation in November, 1783, and were among the first statutes adopted by the legislature in 1784. The laws of New York which relate to matters of religion have been in many instances models for the other States. The Dutchmen who settled in

New Netherland, and the other emigrants and their descendants who came within their influence in the Province of New York, early learned the value and reason of religious toleration. The Dutchmen in America did not persecute for religion's sake.

The present civil relations of the Catholic Church to the State of New York and their history form an interesting study. The Dutch Colony of the seventeenth century was officially intolerantly Protestant, but was, as has been noted, in practice tolerant and fair to people of other faiths who dwelt within New Netherland. When the English took the province from the Dutch in 1664, they granted full religious toleration to the other forms of Protestantism, and preserved the property rights of the Dutch Reformed Church, while recognizing its discipline. The General Assembly of the province held in 1682 under the famous Governor Thomas Dongan, an Irish Catholic nobleman, adopted the Charter of Liberties, which proclaimed religious liberty to all Christians. Although this charter did not receive formal royal sanction, the fact of religious toleration was nevertheless universally recognized. In 1688 the Stuart Revolution in England reversed this policy of liberality, and the Province of New York immediately followed the example of the mother-country in all its bitter intolerance and persecution by law of the Catholic Church and its adherents. In 1697, although the Anglican Church was never formally established in the Province of New York, Trinity Church was founded in the City of New York by royal charter, and received many civil privileges and the munificent grants of land which are the source of its present great wealth. The Dutch Reformed Churches continued, however, to enjoy their property and the protection of their rights undisturbed by the new Anglican foundation, the inhabitants of Dutch blood being then largely in the ascendant. This condition continued many years, for it is a fact that, when the Revolution occurred in 1776, the majority of the inhabitants of the Province of New York were, contrary to general belief, not of English descent.

The political conditions at home, and also the long contest between England and France for the control of North America resulted, as has been stated, in the enactment by the provincial legislature from time to time of proscriptive laws against the Catholic Faith and its adherents—laws which are savage in their malignity. Catholic priests and teachers were ordered to keep away from the province or, if they by any chance came there, to depart at once. Severe penalties were provided for disobedience to these laws, extending to long imprisonment or even death. These laws were directed in many cases principally against the Catholic missionaries among the Iroquois, who were almost exclusively Frenchmen. They were adopted also, it is consoling to think, against the protest of many of the best of the colonial legislators and under the urging of authority, and were rarely enforced. This was not so in the case of the unfortunate schoolmaster John Ury, however. In the disturbances and panic of the so-called Negro Plot of 1741 he was actually tried in New York and executed under these statutes for the crime of being a "Popish priest" and teaching his religion. Although it is held by some that Ury was not a Catholic priest, Archbishop Bayley gives good reason for believing the contrary, citing especially the fact that the record shows that he never denied the accusation at any time, and therefore died as a priest. The entire body of this legislation was formally repealed at the first session of the Legislature of the State of New York.

The condition of the few Catholics who dared proscription and persecution in the province of New York before the Revolution of 1776 was deplorable from a religious point of view. These Catholics must have been recruited in numbers from time to time from seafaring people, emigrants, Spanish negroes from the West Indies, and at least part of the 7000 Acadians, who were distributed along the Atlantic seaboard in 1755 after the awful expatriation which that devoted people suffered, although the annals are almost bare of references even to their existence. Father Farmer from Philadelphia came to see the oppressed Catholics during his long service on the missions between 1752–86, but his visits have no history. They had no church or institutions of any kind. As Archbishop Bayley truly said, a chapel, if they had had means to erect one, would have been torn down. The first mention of their public worship shows them hearing Mass in a carpenter shop, and afterwards in a public hall in Vauxhall Garden (a pleasure ground on the Hudson near Warren Street), New York, between the years 1781–83 when they had begun to take heart because of the religious liberty which was to be theirs under the new republican government whose arms had already triumphed over England at Yorktown. Their number at this time was reported as being about two hundred, with only twenty odd communicants, as Father Farmer lamented.

The Revolution of 1776 overthrew entirely the system of government churches and all religious proscription by law, and the State Constitution of 1777 provided, as has been seen, for general religious liberty. The Legislature in 1784 carried out the declaration. It provided "that an universal equality between every religious denomination, according to the true spirit of the Constitution, toward each other shall forever prevail", and followed this by a general act providing for the incorporation of churches and religious societies under clear general rules, few, simple, and easy for all. This law made a most unusual provision in aid of justice for the vesting in these corporate bodies immediately of "all the temporalities granted or devised directly to said church, congregation or society, or to any person or persons in trust to and for their use and although such gift, grant or devise may not have strictly been agreeable to the rigid rules of law, or might on strict construction be defeated by the operation of the statutes of mortmain." It made provision also with great prescience for the protection of clergymen from the exercise of arbitrary power by the lay directors of religious corporations by taking from the trustees of the church the power to fix the salary of the clergyman and by requiring the congregation to fix it at special meetings. To prevent abuses, however, and in accordance with legal tradition and precedent, restrictions upon the amount of real estate and personal property which a church could hold were made, and the Court of Chancery was placed in control of all such matters by requiring that annual reports should be made by the churches to it. The final clause of the act crystallized the principle of the Constitution, that, while the State protects and fosters religion in its beneficent work, it must not interfere in religious matters. It is as follows: "Nothing herein contained shall be construed, adjudged, or taken to abridge or affect the rights of conscience or private judgment or in the least to alter or change the religious constitutions or governments of either of the said churches, congregations or societies, so far as respects or in any wise concerns the doctrine, discipline or worship thereof."

The Constitution of 1777 and the legislation of the Revolutionary period in aid of it are remarkable for deep sagacity and great grasp of principles, as well as for the conservative and sane treatment of the innovations and novelties which the radical changes in the government made necessary. This is the more remarkable when it is remembered that this Constitution was adopted in time of war by delegates who laid down their arms in most cases to join in the deliberations upon it, and that the Legislature first met immediately after the close of this war time. It was besides a venture in an almost virgin field. Its wisdom, knowledge, and broadness are priceless treasures of the citizens of New York. The wisdom of the Constitution is shown particularly in the provision creating the body of the law for the State. It enacted that the law of the State should be constituted of the Common Law of England and of the Acts of the Legislature of the Colony of New York, as together forming the law of the colony on 19 April, 1775 (the day of the battle of Concord and Lexington). It was expressly declared, however, "that all such parts of the said Common Law and all such of the said Statutes and Acts aforesaid or parts thereof as may be construed to establish or maintain any particular denomination of Christians or their ministers, are repugnant to this constitution and hereby are abrogated and rejected."

To New York belongs the honour of having been the first of all English-speaking states from the time of the Protestant Reformation, to protect by its courts and laws, the secrecy and sanctity of auricular confession. In June, 1813, it was judicially determined that auricular confession as a part of church discipline protects the priest from being compelled in a court of law to testify to statements made to him therein. The decision was made by De Witt Clinton, presiding in the Mayor's Court of New York City on the trial of one Phillips for theft, and the priest, whose protest was there considered, was the revered Father Anthony Kohlmann mentioned above. The decision is more remarkable because it was contrary to the principles of the English cases, and the opposite view had the support of respectable authorities.

Although no form of religion is considered by the State of New York as having rights superior to any other, yet the fact of the existence of the Christian religion as the predominating faith of the people has been uniformly recognized by the courts, constitutional conventions, and legislatures. As early as 1811, Chancellor Kent, writing the opinion of the Court in the case of People vs. Ruggles (8 Johnson 294), made the celebrated dictum: "We are a Christian people and the morality of the country is deeply ingrafted upon Christianity." This famous case arose on the conviction of the defendant for blasphemy in maliciously reviling Jesus Christ in a public place. In the absence of a specific statute the question was presented whether such an act was in New York a crime at common law. The Court held that it was, because to vilify the Author of Christianity under the circumstances presented was a gross violation of decency and good order, and blasphemy was an abuse of the right of religious liberty. The court further held that, though the Constitution discarded religious establishments, it did not forbid judicial cognizance of those offences against religion and morality which have no reference to any such establishment or to any particular form of government, but are punishable because they strike at the root of moral obligation and weaken social ties; that the Constitution never meant to withdraw religion in general, and with it the best sanctions of moral and social obligation, from all consideration and notice of the law; and that the framers intended only to banish test oaths, disabilities and the burdens, and sometimes the oppressions, of Church establishments, and to secure the people of the State freedom from coercion and an equality of right on the subject of religion.

This decision of the Supreme Court that, although Christianity is not the religion of the State, considered as a political corporation, it is nevertheless closely interwoven into the texture of society and is intimately connected with all the social habits, customs, and modes of life of the people, gave offence in certain quarters. In view of this Ruggles case, an amendment was proposed in the Constitutional Convention of 1821 to the effect that the judiciary should not declare any particular religion to be the law of the land. It was rejected after a full debate in which its opponents, while differing in details, agreed "that the Christian religion was engrafted upon the law and entitled to protection as the basis of morals and the strength of Government." In 1861 a similar question was presented for decision in the well-known case of Lindenmuller vs. People (33 Barbour Reports 548). The plaintiff sought from the court an injunction to restrain the police of New York City from interfering with theatrical performances on Sunday. The opinion of the Supreme Court was written by Justice William F. Allen, a most distinguished jurist, and was afterwards (1877) adopted by the Court of Appeals as the decision of the highest court. It contains an admirable and exhaustive study of the Sunday laws. It takes the claim of the plaintiff, stated broadly, to be that "the Bible, and religion with all its ordinances, including the Sabbath, are as effectually abolished by the Constitution as they were in France during the Revolution, and so effectually abolished that duties may not be enforced as duties to the State because they have been heretofore associated with acts of religious worship or connected with religious duties." It then proceeds: "It would be strange that a people, Christian in doctrine and worship, many of whom or whose forefathers had sought these shores for the privilege of worshipping God in simplicity and purity of faith, and who regarded religion as the basis of their civil liberty and the foundation of their rights, should, in their zeal to secure to all the freedom of conscience which they valued so highly, solemnly repudiate and put beyond the pale of the law the religion which was as dear to them as life and dethrone the God, who, they openly and avowedly profess to believe, had been their protector and guide as a people." The Court announced the broad decision that every act done, maliciously tending to bring religion into contempt, may be punished at common law, and the Christian Sabbath, as one of the institutions of religion, may be protected from desecration by such laws as the Legislature in their wisdom may deem necessary to secure to the community the privilege of an undisturbed worship, and to the day itself that outward respect and observance which may be deemed essential to the peace and good order of society, and to preserve religion and its ordinances from open reviling and contempt. It further held that this must be considered, not as a duty to God, but as a duty to society and to the State. This decision firmly established the proposition that, as a civil and political institution, the establishment and regulation of a Sabbath are within the just powers of civil government. It remains the law of the State confirmed by many decisions up to this time.

Many interesting questions have arisen from time to time in the courts as to how far the English doctrines as to "superstitious uses", mortmain, and charities, especially in relation to the ownership of lands by religious corporations and charitable corporations and as to their capacity to take charitable bequests and devises, remained the law of the State under the Constitution. As to superstitious uses, it has been expressly held that that English post-Reformation doctrine has no place in this State; that those professing the Roman Catholic Faith are entitled in law to the same respect and protection in their religious observances as those of any other denomination, and that these observances cannot be condemned as superstitious by any court as matter by law. The right to make provision for Masses for the dead by contracts made *inter vivos* was expressly proclaimed by the Court of Appeals. Direct bequests for Masses are in law "charities" and to be considered as such. As to these charities generally, the Court of Appeals in 1888 settled finally after much discussion that the English doctrine of trusts for charitable uses, with all its refinements, was not the law in New York; that the settled policy of the State was clear, and consisted in the creation of a system of public charities to be administered through the medium of corporate bodies, created by legislative power and endowed with the same legal capacity to hold property for their corporate purposes, as a private person or an ordinary private corporation had to receive and hold transfers of property. It was decided, therefore, in the leading case of Holland vs. Alcock (108 New York Reports 329), that direct bequests for Masses cannot be made definitely as such except to incorporated churches or other corporations having legal power to take property for such purposes. There is no difficulty in practice, however, in this regard, as Mass legacies are now either given to an incorporated church directly, or are left as personal bequests accompanied by requests, which in law do not derogate from the absolute quality of the gift.

However, it is to be noted that the rules laid down by the Court of Appeals in the matter of charities have been radically changed by legislation since 1888. The decision of the Court of Appeals in the Tilden will case, by which the elaborate plans for public charity made by Samuel J. Tilden were defeated by the application of these rules, was followed almost immediately by Chapter 701 of the Laws of 1893, which provides that gifts by will for charitable purposes shall not be defeated because of indefiniteness in designating the beneficiaries, and that the power in the regulation of the gifts for charitable purposes formerly exercised by the Court of Chancery under the ancient law of England should be restored and vested in the Supreme Court as a Court of Equity. The Court of Appeals construing this statute has held that the existence of a competent corporation or other definable trustee with power to take is no longer necessary for the validity of a trust for charitable uses, and that any legal trust for such purposes may be executed by proper trustees if such are named, and, if none are named, the trust will be administered by the Supreme Court. It is important to note, however, that this act must be confined to the cases to which it applies, and that it does not enable an unincorporated charity or association to take bequests or devises.

There exist, however, notwithstanding the liberality of the New York system, some important restrictions upon the conduct of religious and charitable corporations. The better opinion and the weight of judicial authority are, that, notwithstanding the repealing act of the Legislature of 1788 above noted, the English statutes of Elizabeth, which restricted religious and charitable corporations, may hold in the alienation and encumbering of their real estate, have been adopted as the law of this State, and that such acts can only be lawfully done under the order of the Supreme Court. Limitations upon the value of the property and the amount of the income of religious and charitable corporations have also been uniformly made by the New York Statutes. The present law, however, is most liberal in this respect, the property of such corporations being limited to $6,000,000 and the annual income to $600,000, and provision is also made that no increase in the value of property arising otherwise than from improvements made thereon by the owners shall be taken into account. By recent act also the strict requirements for accounting to the Supreme Court, the successor of the Court of Chancery, as to their property and income, which in the early statutes controlled such corporations, are confined to cases where the attorney-general intervenes for the purpose by petition to the Supreme Court upon proper cause being shown.

The law of New York on the general subject of the Church and the legal position of the latter before the law has been defined by the statutes and numerous decisions. The results may be briefly stated as follows: Religious societies as such are not legal entities, although as an aggregation of the individuals composing them, for motives of convenience, they are recognized as existing in certain cases. They can neither sue nor be sued in civil courts. They cannot hold property directly, although they may control property held by others for their use or upon trusts created by them. The existence, however, of the Church proper, as an organized legal entity, is not recognized by the municipal law of New York. There is no statute which authorizes the incorporation of the Church at large. The incorporation is generally made of the congregation or assemblage of persons accustomed stately to meet for Divine worship, although provision has been made for the incorporation of special ecclesiastical bodies with governing authority over churches. For example, the Catholic dioceses of Albany, Buffalo, and Brooklyn have been thus incorporated formally. The general plan provides specially for the incorporation and government of the churches of the separate denominations, as gathered into congregations. Each important denomination, therefore, has its own particular provisions in the Religious Corporation Law, the general statute of the State which has codified these laws and decisions. In the case of the Roman Catholic Church, incorporation is obtained in this way. A certificate of incorporation must be executed by the archbishop or bishop, the vicar-general of the diocese, the rector of the congregation, and two laymen thereof, selected by such officials or a majority of them. It must state the corporate name of the church, and also the municipality where its principal place of worship exists or is intended to be located. On filing such certificate with the clerk of the county in which the principal place of worship is or is intended to be, or with the Secretary of State in certain cases, the corporation is created.

Questions of the civil rights of persons, relating either to themselves or to property, whatever may be their relations to church organizations, are as a matter of course the subject of adjudication in the civil tribunals. But judicial notice will be taken of the existence of the church discipline or government in some cases, and it is always the subject of evidence. When, therefore, personal rights and rights of property are in cases in the courts dependent upon questions of doctrine, discipline, church government, customs, or law, the civil court will consider as controlling and binding the determinations made on such questions by the highest tribunal within the Church to which they have been presented. While a clergyman, or other person, may always insist that his civil or property rights as an individual shall be determined according to the law of the land, his relations, rights, and obligations arising from his position as a member of some religious body must be determined according to the laws and procedure enacted by that body for such purpose. Where it appeared, therefore, in one case that questions growing out of relations between a priest and his bishop had been submitted by the parties to an ecclesiastical tribunal which the church itself had organized for hearing such causes and was there decided by it, it was held by the Court of Appeals that the civil courts were justified in refusing to proceed further, and that the decision of the Church judicatory in the matter was a bar and a good defence (Baxter vs. McDonnell, 155 New York, 83). The Church at large, however, under the law of New York depends wholly upon moral power to carry on its functions, without the possibility of appeal to the civil authorities for aid either through the Legislature or the Court. Where there is no incorporation, those who deal with the Church must trust for the performance of civil obligations to the honour and good faith of the members. The congregations formed into civil corporations are governed by the principles of the common law and statute law. With their doctrinal peculiarity and denominational character the courts have nothing to do, except to carry out the statutes which protect their rights in this respect. However, these statutory rights are, as will be seen, very extensive. Generally speaking, whatever the corporation chooses to do that is within their corporate power is lawful except where restricted by express statute.

Control of Churches.—From time to time important restrictions upon the general power of the religious corporations in particular denominations have been made. The present Religious Corporation Law, for example, requires the trustees of such a body to administer the temporalities of the church in accordance with the discipline, rules, and usages of the religious denomination or ecclesiastical governing body, if any, with which the corporation is connected, and in accordance with the provisions of law relating thereto, and further for the support and maintenance of the corporation and its denominational or charitable work. It requires also the consent of the bishops and other officers to the mortgage, lease, or conveyance of the real property of certain churches. In the case of Catholic churches it is expressly provided also that no act or proceeding of the trustees of any such church shall be valid without the express sanction of the archbishop or bishop of the diocese or, in case of his absence, of the vicar-general or administrator. To prevent the creation of abuses from the generality of any of its provisions, the statute contains a further section directing that no provision thereof shall authorize the fixing or changing of the time, nature, or order of public or social or other worship of any church in any other manner or by any other authority than in the manner and by the authority provided in the laws, regulations, practice, discipline, rules, and usages of the religious denomination or ecclesiastical governing body, if any, with which the church corporation is connected, except in churches which have a congregational form of government.

Ecclesiastical Persons.—The relations of ecclesiastical persons one to the other have also been considered by the courts. It has been held that the personal contracts of a bishop are the same as those of a layman as far as their form, force, and effect are concerned. It has been determined, however, that the relation of master and servant does not exist between a bishop and his priests, but only that of ecclesiastical superior and inferior. Finally, the courts have ruled that a priest or minister in any church by assuming that relation necessarily subjects his conduct in that capacity to the law and customs of the ecclesiastical body from which he derives his office and in whose name he exercises his functions.

Marriage.—Until very recent times New York followed the common law respecting marriage. All that was required for a valid marriage was the deliberate consent of competent parties entering into a present agreement. No ceremony or intervention of a civil authority was necessary.

However, it is now provided that, although the contract of marriage is still in law a civil contract, marriages not ceremonial must be proven by writings authenticated by the parties under strict formalities and in the presence of at least two witnesses and recorded in the proper county clerk's office. It is now provided also that ceremonial marriages must not be celebrated without first obtaining a marriage licence. It is to be noted, however, that a failure to procure the marriage licence does not invalidate a ceremonial marriage, but only subjects the offending clergyman or magistrate who officiates thereat to the penalties of the statute. All clergymen and certain magistrates are given power to solemnize marriages. No particular form is required except that the parties must expressly declare that they take each other as husband or wife. In every case one witness besides the clergyman or magistrate must be present at the ceremony. It is provided, however, that modes of solemnizing marriage adopted by any religious denomination are to be regarded as valid notwithstanding the statute. This amending statute was passed at the session of 1907, and there are as yet no important adjudications upon it.

Annulment of Marriage.—An action to annul her marriage may be brought by a woman where she was under sixteen years of age at the time of the marriage and the consent of her parents or guardian was not had and the marriage was not consummated and not ratified by mutual assent after she attained the age of sixteen years. Either the husband or wife may sue for annulment of marriage for lunacy, nonage, prior valid marriage, or because consent was obtained by force, duress, or fraud, and finally for physical incapacity under certain rigid restrictions. The tendency of the courts of late years is to construe the provision as to fraud liberally, and annulment has been granted on this ground where the husband has been convicted of a felony and concealed the fact before the marriage, and again where false representations had been made before the marriage by the woman as to the birth of a child to the plaintiff. The Court of Appeals in the last case held, as the reasonable construction of the statute, that the essential fact to be shown was that the fraud was material to the degree that, had it not been practised, the party deceived would not have consented to the marriage (Di Lorenzo vs. Di Lorenzo, 174 New York, 467 and 471). This decision, it should be noted, was put squarely on the ground that in New York marriage is a civil contract to which the consent of parties capable in law of contracting is essential, and, where the consent is obtained by legal fraud, the marriage may be annulled as in the case of any other contract. Condonation of the force, duress, or fraud is required to be assumed from the fact of voluntary cohabitation after knowledge of the facts by the innocent party, and will, if established, defeat the action. Provision is also made for an action for the annulment of a marriage in certain cases at the instance of any relative having an interest in having it annulled or by a parent or guardian or next friend either in the lifetime of a party or after his or her death, where such an action will further the cause of justice.

Divorce.—Actions for absolute divorce and the dissolution of marriage can be maintained only for the cause of adultery. The New York Courts will hear no action for divorce unless both parties were residents of the State when the offence was committed, or were married within the State, or the plaintiff was a resident of the State at the time of the offence and is resident when the action is commenced, or finally when the offence was committed within the State and the injured party is a resident of the State when the action is commenced. Divorces obtained by citizens of New York in the courts of foreign jurisdiction are not recognized as valid in the State of New York unless personal jurisdiction of both of the parties is properly obtained by the foreign courts. Collusion of the parties is strictly guarded against. Condonation of the offence is made a defence. The action must be brought within five years after the discovery of the offence. Adultery by the plaintiff is a complete defence to the action. The provisions for the custody of the children of a dissolved marriage and for the maintenance of the innocent wife and children are very detailed and effective. Remarriage is forbidden to the guilty party during the life of the spouse, unless, after five years have elapsed, proof is made of his or her uniform good conduct, when the defendant may be permitted by the Court to marry again. The practical effect of these prohibitions is very slight because the entire validity of the subsequent marriages of guilty parties in New York divorce actions, when they are made out of the State of New York, is recognized by the New York courts, the only penalty provided for the disobedience to the decree being the punishment of the offender for contempt of court, and the infliction of this penalty is unheard of at the present day. The divorce law of New York, it may be noted, is more conservative than that of any other state in the Union except South Carolina, where no divorce *a vinculo* is permitted. Limited divorce or decree of separation *a mensa et thoro* is granted for numerous causes, viz: cruel and inhuman treatment, abandonment, neglect or refusal to provide for the wife, and conduct making it unsafe and improper for the plaintiff to cohabit with the defendant. The usual purpose of actions for limited divorce is to provide support for the children and alimony for the wife out of the husband's funds after the husband and wife have separated. These actions are comparatively infrequent. The judgment in them has of course no effect upon the validity of the marriage bond. It is granted only for grave cause, and the necessary bona fide residence of the parties in the State is of strictest proof, under the terms of the statute.

Charities.—The system of charities which has grown up within the State of New York, whether religious or secular, is one of the features of its social life. As was said by the Court of Appeals in 1888 in the famous case of Holland vs. Alcock above noted: "It is not certain that any political state or society in the world offers a better system of law for the encouragement of property limitations in favour of religion and learning, for the relief of the poor, the care of the insane, of the sick and the maimed, and the relief of the destitute, than our system of creating organized bodies by the legislative power and endowing them with the same legal capacity to hold property which a private person has to receive and hold transfers of property." A charitable or benevolent corporation may be formed under the Membership Corporation Law by five or more persons for any lawful, charitable, or benevolent purpose. It is subject in certain respects to the supervision of the State Board of Charities and of the Supreme Court, but this power of visitation is not oppressive and never exercised except in case of gross abuse and under strict provisions as to procedure. State and municipal aid to private charitable corporations is permitted by law. Some of the great private charities of the Catholic Church receive such aid in large amounts, particularly in the great cities. The public subvention of private charitable corporations is an old custom in the State, beginning when almost all charities were in Protestant hands and the Catholic charities were very few and poor. Although vigorously attacked in the Constitutional Convention of 1904, it was sustained and continued by the action of that convention and ratified by the people of the State. The system has done much for the cause of the education and maintenance of defective, dependent, and delinquent children, and for the building up of the hospitals for the destitute sick and aged in all the religious denominations. The Catholic protectories of New York and Buffalo and the Catholic foundling and infant asylums throughout the State are the models for such institutions in the whole United States. The charities under Catholic auspices which receive no State aid are, however, in the vast majority, and are found in great numbers in every quarter of the State, caring for the children and the aged, the sick and the destitute. They are served by an army of devoted religious, both men and women. The State institutions for the care of the insane and juvenile delinquents are numerous, and the almshouses, hospitals, and other charitable agencies under the care of the counties and other municipalities abound throughout the State. There are alone sixteen great State hospitals for the insane, conducted most carefully and successfully.

Restrictions on Bequests and Devises.—No person having a parent, husband, wife, or child can legally devise or bequeath more than one-half his estate to benevolent, charitable, or religious institutions, but such disposition is valid to the extent of one-half. In addition, certain kinds of corporations are still further restricted in respect to the portion of the estate of such persons which they may receive: in some cases it is only one-fourth. In respect to the invalidity by statute of legacies or devises made by wills executed within two months of the testator's death, this limitation was formerly widely applicable. Recent amendments, however, have restricted it to the corporations formed under the old statutes, and it applies now to very few others, and these mostly corporations created by special statutes. Bequests and devises to unincorporated churches or charities, are, as has been stated, invalid. Foreign religious and charitable corporations, however, may take bequests and devises if authorized to do so by their charters. They are also permitted to carry on unhampered their work in the State of New York. The legacies and devises to religious, charitable, and benevolent corporations are exempt from the succession tax assessed upon legacies and devises in ordinary cases.

Exemption from Taxation.—The Tax Law provides that the real and personal property of a "corporation or association organized exclusively for the moral or mental improvement of men or women or for religious, Bible, tract, charitable, benevolent, missionary, hospital, infirmary, educational, scientific, literary, library, patriotic, historical, or cemetery purposes or for the enforcement of law relating to children or animals or for two or more such purposes and used exclusively for carrying out thereupon one or more of such purposes", shall be exempt from taxation. Great care is taken, however, to protect against the abuse of this right of exemption. In some few cases further exemptions are also made; thus, for example, real property not in exclusive use for the above corporate purposes is exempt from taxation, if the income therefrom is devoted exclusively to the charitable use of the corporation. Property held by any officer of a religious denomination is entitled to the same exemption under the same conditions and exceptions as property held by a religious corporation itself.

Freedom of Worship.—It is expressly provided by statute that all persons committed to or taken charge of by incorporated or unincorporated houses of refuge, reformatories, protectories, or other penal institutions, receiving either public moneys or a *per capita* sum from any municipality for the support of inmates, shall be entitled to the free exercise and enjoyment of religious profession and worship without discrimination or preference, and that these provisions may be enforced by the Supreme Court upon petition of any one feeling himself aggrieved by a violation of it (Prison Law Section 20). It is further provided that all children committed for destitution or delinquency by any court or public officer shall, as far as practicable, be sent to institutions of the same religious faith as the parents of the child.

Liquor Law.—The excise legislation of the State is treated in an elaborate general statute called the "Liquor Tax Law", but better known as the "Raines Law" from the name of the late Senator John Raines who drafted it. In substance it provides for a State Department of Excise presided over by a commissioner of excise, appointed by the governor and confirmed by the Senate, who is given charge of the issuance of all licences to traffic within the State in intoxicating liquor, and also of the collection of the licence fees and the supervision of the enforcement of the drastic penalties provided for violations of the law. Its purpose was to take away the granting of excise licences by the local authorities, who had in some cases greatly abused the power, and also to subject local peace and police officers to the scrutiny, and in some cases the control of the State authorities in excise matters. It has resulted generally in a great improvement in excise conditions throughout the State, as well as incidentally in an enormous increase in the revenue of the State from this source. It has caused the almost complete disappearance of unlicenced liquor-selling, and has improved general order and decency in the business of trafficking in liquor, especially in the congested parts of the cities. The principle of high licence is carefully followed. The fee for a saloon licence, for example in the Borough of Manhattan, is $1200 per annum, the charge decreasing, according to the circumstances, to $150 per annum in the rural districts. The State is divided into excise districts which are in charge of deputy commissioners supervised by the staff of the commissioner of excise at Albany. Although it is an unusual provision which thus centralizes the power over the liquor traffic at Albany, and it seems to violate the principle of home rule adopted by all the public parties, the experiment is on the whole regarded with satisfaction. It should be noted that this law has created a very great abuse because of its provision attaching the right to sell liquor on Sunday to the keeping of hotels. There have thus sprung into existence the "Raines Law Hotels", which, satisfying the very inadequate provisions of the statute, obtain hotel licences without any legitimate business reason, and primarily for the purpose of selling liquor on Sunday. They are generally conducted as to their hotel accommodations in such a way as to be a menace to public order and decency in the poorer residential districts of the large cities of the State. They often defy police control, and their legal status makes their regulation or supervision most difficult. Earnest efforts have been made for many years to remedy the evil, but have met with but partial success. Ample provision is also made for local option as to prohibitive liquor licences in all localities of the State excepting the larger cities. It has worked well in practice.

Clergymen.—Priests and ministers of the Gospel are exempted from service on juries and from service in the militia of the State. A clergyman's real and personal property to the extent of $1500 is exempt from taxation, if he is regularly engaged in performing his duty, is permanently disabled by impaired health, or is over seventy-five years old. The dwelling-houses and lots of religious corporations, actually used by the officiating clergymen thereof, are also exempt to the extent of $2000. Any clergyman is empowered at his pleasure to visit all county jails, workhouses, and State prisons when he is in charge of a congregation in the town where they are located.

Holidays.—The legal holidays of the State are New Year's Day, Lincoln's Birthday (12 February), Washington's Birthday (22 February), Memorial Day (30 May), Independence Day (4 July), Labour Day (first Monday of September), Columbus Day (12 October), and Christmas Day. If any of these days fall on Sunday, the day following is a public holiday. The statute also provides that the day of the general election, and each day appointed by the President of the United States or by the Governor of the State as a day of "general thanksgiving, general fasting and prayer, or other general religious observances", shall be holidays. Each Saturday, which is not a holiday, is a half-holiday. There is of course no religious significance in the creation of any of these holidays, as far as the State is concerned. Good Friday, by general custom, is observed as a holiday throughout the State, although it is not designated as a legal holiday. The rules of the local school boards throughout the State also provide liberty to both Christian and Jewish scholars to take time from the school attendance for religious observances on their respective holydays.

LAMB, *Hist. of City of New York* (New York, 1877); BAYLEY, *Hist. of Cath. Church on Island of N. Y.* (New York, 1869); *U. S. Catholic Historical Society, Records and Studies* (New York), especially for Oct., 1900, and Nov., 1907; *United States Census 1900; New York State Census 1905;* LINCOLN, *Constitutional Hist. of N. Y.* (Rochester, 1906); ALEXANDER, *Political Hist. of the State of N. Y.* (New York, 1906); WILSON, *Memorial Hist. of City of N. Y.*, *Statesman's Year Book for 1910* (New York, 1910); *Report of N. Y. Chamber of Commerce* (New York, 1910); *U. S. Census Bulletin, Religious Bodies 1906* (Washington, 1909); O'CALLAGHAN, *Laws and Ordinances of New Netherland, Colonial Laws of N. Y.* (Albany); *Documents relating to Colonial Hist.* (Albany, 1853–87); FOWLER, *Introduction to Bradford's Laws* (New York, 1894); SAMPSON, *Catholic Question in America* (New York, 1813); *Debates of the Constitutional Convention of 1821;* BIRDSEYE, CUMMING AND GILBERT, *Consolidated Laws of N. Y.* (New York, 1909); *Ecclesiastical Records of N. Y.* (1901–5); *Revised Statutes; Reports of Revisers;* SMITH, *N. Y. City in 1789* (New York, 1889); *Report of Commissioner of Excise* (Albany, 1910); SHEA, *Hist. of Cath. Church in the U. S.* (New York, 1886); CLARKE, *Lives of the Deceased Bishops of the Cath. Church in the U. S.* (New York, 1872); BOOTH, *Hist. of the City of N. Y.* (New York, 1880); *Ecclesiastical Records of N. Y.* (official) (Albany, 1901); DECOURCY-SHEA, *Pages of Hist. of Cath. Church in U. S.* (New York, 1857); FARLEY, *Hist. of St. Patrick's Cathedral* (New York, 1908); ZWIERLEIN, *Religion in New Netherland* (Rochester, 1910).

EDWARD J. MCGUIRE.

New Zealand, formerly described as a colony, has, since September, 1907, by royal proclamation, been granted the style and designation of "Dominion", the territory remaining, of course, as before under British sovereignty. It consists of three main islands (North Island, South Island, sometimes also called Middle Island, and Stewart Island) and several groups of smaller islands lying at some distance from the principal group. The smaller groups included within the dominion are the Chatham, Auckland, Campbell, Antipodes, Bounty, Kermadec, and Cook Islands, along with half a dozen atolls situated outside the Cook Group. The total area of the dominion—104,751 square miles—is about one-seventh less than the area of Great Britain and Ireland. The quantity and quality of the grazing land available has made New Zealand a great wool, meat, and dairy-produce country. Its agricultural capabilities are very considerable; its forests yield excellent timber; and its mineral resources, though as yet but little developed and not very varied in character, form one of the country's most valuable assets. Volcanoes, one of which, Ngauruhoe, the highest cone of Mount Tongariro, was in active eruption in 1909, and a volcanic belt mark the centre of the North Island. In the North Island also is the wonderland of the boiling geysers—said by geologists to be the oldest in the world, with the exception of those in Wyoming and Idaho—and the famous "Hot Lakes" and pools, which possess great curative virtue for all rheumatic and skin diseases. An Alpine chain, studded with snow-clad peaks and mantled with glaciers of greater magnitude than any in the Alps of Europe, descends along the west coast of the South Island. In the South Island also are the famous Otago lakes (Wanaka, Wakatipu, Te Anau, and Manapouri) of which the late Anthony Trollope wrote, "I do not know that lake scenery could be finer". The south-west coast of the island is pierced by a series of sounds or fiords, rivalling in their exquisite beauty the Norwegian and Alaskan fiords; in the neighbourhood is a waterfall (the Sutherland Falls) over 1900 feet in height. Judged by mortality statistics the climate of New Zealand is one of the best and healthiest in the world. The total population of the dominion on 31 December, 1908, was 1,020,713. This included the Maori population of 47,731, and the population of Cook and other Pacific islands, aggregating 12,340.

I. CIVIL HISTORY.—Tasman discovered the islands in 1642 and called them "Nova Zeelanda", but Captain Cook, who surveyed the coasts in 1769 and following years, first made them known. The colony was planted in 1840 by a company, formed in England and known first as the New Zealand Company, afterwards as the New Zealand Land Company, which with auxiliary associations founded successively the settlements of Wellington, Nelson, Taranaki, Otago, and Canterbury. New Zealand was then constituted a dependency of the Colony of New South Wales

(Australia), but on 3 May, 1841, was proclaimed a separate colony. A series of native wars, arising chiefly from endless disputes about land, began in 1843 and ended in 1869, since which time unbroken peace has prevailed. A measure of self-government was granted in 1852, and full responsible government in 1856. The provincial governments created by the Constitution Act were abolished in 1876, and one supreme central government established. The Government consists of a governor, appointed by the crown, and two houses of Parliament—the legislative council, or upper chamber, with members nominated by the governor for life (except those nominated subsequently to September 17, 1891, after which date all appointments are for seven years only), and the house of representatives with members elected triennially on an adult suffrage. The first Speaker of the New Zealand House of Representatives (1853–60), the late Sir Charles Clifford, was a Catholic, and his son, Sir George Clifford, one of New Zealand's prominent public men, though born in the dominion was educated at Stonyhurst College, and has shown his fidelity to old ties by naming his principal New Zealand residence "Stonyhurst". There are a number of Catholic names in the list of past premiers, cabinet ministers, and members of Parliament who have helped to mould the laws and shape the history of the dominion. The present premier (1910), the Right Hon. Sir Joseph Ward, P.C., K.C.M.G., is a Catholic, and out of a legislative council of forty-five members five are Catholics.

The prominent feature of the political history of the past twenty years has been the introduction and development of that body of "advanced" legislation for which the name of New Zealand has become more or less famous. The mere enumeration of the enactments would occupy considerable space. It must suffice to say that, broadly speaking, their purpose is to fling the shield of the State over every man who works for his livelihood; and, in addition to regulating wages, they cover practically every risk to life, limb, health, and interest of the industrial classes. It should be mentioned that there is no strong party of professed State-Socialists in the dominion, and the reforms and experiments which have been made have in all cases been examined and taken on their merits, and not otherwise. Employers have occasionally protested against some of the restrictions imposed, as being harassing and vexatious; but there is no political party in the country which proposes to repeal these measures, and there is a general consensus of opinion that, in its main features, the "advanced legislation" has come to stay. In 1893 an Act came into force which granted the franchise to women. The women's vote has had no perceptible effect on the relative position of political parties; but it is generally agreed that the women voters have been mainly responsible for the marked increase in recent years of the no-licence vote at the local option polls. Elections are quieter and more orderly than formerly.

II. THE MAORIS.—The New Zealand natives, or Maoris, as they call themselves, are generally acknowledged to be intellectually and physically the finest aboriginal race in the South Sea Islands. Their magnificent courage, their high intelligence, their splendid physique and manly bearing, the stirring part they have played in the history of the country, the very ferocity of their long-relinquished habits, have all combined to invest them with a more than ordinary degree of interest and curiosity. Of their origin it can only be said, broadly, that they belong to the Polynesian race—ethnologists have tried to trace a likeness to the Red Indians of North America—and according to tradition they came to New Zealand about twenty-one generations ago (i. e., about five hundred and twenty-five years) from Hawaiki, an island of the Pacific not identified with any certainty. After being robbed and despoiled by the early white civilization and by trader-missionaries, tardy justice has at length been done to the native race. To-day the Maoris have four members in the house of representatives and two in the legislative council, all men of high lineage and natural orators. Until recent years it was supposed that the Maoris were dying out, but later statistics show the contrary. The official figures show that the Maori population fell from 41,993 in 1891 to 39,854 in 1896, increased to 43,143 in 1901, and further to 47,731 in 1906 (last census year).

III. THE CATHOLIC CHURCH IN NEW ZEALAND.— The first Catholic settler in New Zealand was an Irishman named Thomas Poynton, who landed at Hokianga in 1828. Until ten years later the footsteps of a Catholic priest never pressed New Zealand soil. Poynton's brave and pious wife, a native of Wexford County, took her first two children on a journey of over two thousand weary miles of ocean to be baptized at Sydney. Through Poynton's entreaties for a missionary the needs of the country became known, first at Sydney and next at Rome. In 1835 New Zealand was included in the newly created Vicariate Apostolic of Western Oceanica. In the following year its first vicar Apostolic, Mgr Jean Baptiste François Pompallier, set out for his new field of labour with seven members of the Society of the Marist Brothers, which only a few months before had received the approval of Pope Gregory XVI. On 10 January, 1838, he, with three Marist companions, sailed up the Hokianga River, situated in the far north-west of the Auckland Province. The cross was planted in New Zealand, and the first Mass celebrated in the house of the first Catholic settler of the colony. Irish peasant emigrants were the pioneers of Catholic colonization in New Zealand; the French missionaries were its pioneer apostles. Four years later (in 1842) New Zealand was formed into a separate vicariate, Mgr Pompallier being named its first vicar Apostolic. From this time forward events moved at a rapid pace. In 1848 the colony was divided into two dioceses, Auckland with its territory extending to 39° of south latitude forming one diocese, Wellington with the remaining territory and the adjoining islands forming the second. (See AUCKLAND, DIOCESE OF.) Bishop Pompallier remained in charge of Auckland, and Bishop Viard, who had been consecrated his coadjutor in 1846, was appointed administrator of the Diocese of Wellington, which was entrusted to the Society of Mary. By Brief of 3 July, 1860, Bishop Viard ceased to be coadjutor and was constituted first Bishop of Wellington. In 1869 the Diocese of Dunedin, comprising Otago, Southland, and Stewart's Island, was carved out of the Diocese of Wellington, and the Right Rev. Patrick Moran who died in 1895 was appointed its first bishop. His successor (the present occupant of the see), the Right Rev. Dr. Verdon, was consecrated in 1896. In 1887, at the petition of the Plenary Synod of Australasia, held in Sydney in 1885, the hierarchy was established in New Zealand, and Wellington became the archiepiscopal see. The Most Rev. Dr. Redwood, S.M., who had been consecrated Bishop of Wellington in 1874, was created archbishop and metropolitan by papal brief, receiving the pallium from the hands of the Right Rev. Dr. Luck, Bishop of Auckland. The same year (1887) witnessed the erection of the Diocese of Christchurch. The first and present bishop is the Right Rev. Dr. Grimes, S.M., consecrated in the same year. Ten years later New Zealand, hitherto dependent on Australia, was made a separate ecclesiastical province.

Some idea of the rapid growth of the Catholic population, both in numbers and in activity, may be gathered from the following figures. In 1840, when New Zealand was declared a colony, the number of Catholic colonists was not above 500 in a total population of some 5000. Eleven years later they numbered 3472 in a total population of 26,707. At the last Government census (1906) the Catholic total had amounted to 126,995. The total population of the dominion (exclusive of Maoris), according to the same census, was 888,578, so that the Catholic population is slightly over one-seventh of the whole. To-day (1910) the estimated Catholic population of New Zealand is over 130,000, with 4 dioceses, 1 archbishop, 3 suffragan bishops, 212 priests, 62 religious brothers, 855 nuns, 333 churches, 2 ecclesiastical seminaries (comprising 1 provincial ecclesiastical seminary and 1 ecclesiastical seminary for members of the Marist Order), 2 colleges for boys, 32 boarding and high schools, 18 superior day schools, 15 charitable institutions, and 112 Catholic primary schools. According to the "New Zealand Official Year-Book" for 1909 (a Government publication) the total number of Catholic schools in the dominion is 152 and the number of Catholic pupils attending is 12,650. New Zealand has added one new religious congregation (the Sisters of Our Lady of Compassion), founded in 1884 by Mother Mary Aubert, to "Heaven's Army of Charity" in the Catholic Church. Under the direction of their venerable foundress the members of the order conduct schools for the Maoris at Hiruharama (Jerusalem) on the Wanganui River, a home for incurables, Wellington, and a home for incurable children, Island Bay, Wellington. The order has quite recently extended its operations to Auckland.

The ordinary organizations of the laity, as usually found in English-speaking countries, are well and solidly established throughout the dominion. For benefit purposes New Zealand formed a separate district of the Hibernian Australasian Catholic Benefit Society. Thanks to capable management, due to the fact that the society has drawn to its ranks the ablest and most representative of the laity, the organization is making remarkable progress. On 30 January, 1910, the membership was reported at 2632; the funeral fund stood at £7795:2:2 (nearly $40,000) and the sick fund amounted to £12,558:5:0 (over $62,000). The Society of St. Vincent de Paul was probably the earliest lay organization established in New Zealand, a conference formed at Christchurch in July, 1867, by the Rev. Fr. Chastagner, S.M., being the first founded in Australasia. In almost every parish there are young men's clubs, social, literary, and athletic; in connexion with these a federation has been formed under the name of the Federated Catholic Clubs of New Zealand. In 1909 a Newman Society, on the lines of the Oxford University Newman Society, but with wider and more directly practical objects, was inaugurated by the Catholic graduates and undergraduates of New Zealand University. As the number of university men amongst New Zealand Catholics is now very considerable, the new society promises to prove an important factor in the defence and propagation of the faith.

IV. MISSIONS TO THE MAORIS.—From the outset, the conversion of the native race was set in the forefront of the Church's work in this new land. When the Marist Fathers, having been withdrawn to the Diocese of Wellington, left the Diocese of Auckland in 1850, they had in that part of the North Island 5044 neophytes. In 1853 there were about a thousand native Christians in the Diocese of Wellington. Homes and schools for native children were founded by the Sisters of Mercy at Auckland and Wellington; and in 1857 the governor, Sir George Grey, in his official report to Parliament, gave high praise to the Catholic schools among the Maoris. Up until 1860 the Maori mission was most flourishing. Then came the long-drawn years of fierce racial warfare, during which the natives kept their territory closed against all white men; and the Catholic missions were almost completely ruined. They are being steadily built up once more by two bodies of earnest and devoted men, the Marist Fathers in the Archdiocese of Wellington and Diocese of Christchurch, and the Mill Hill Fathers in the Diocese of Auckland. The progress made during the last twenty-five years may be gathered from the following summaries. (a) The Archdiocese of Wellington and Diocese of Christchurch (districts: Otaki, Hiruharama, Raetihi, Wairoa, and Okato) have about 40 stations and 19 churches, served by 7 priests. There are also 4 native schools; 1 highly efficient native high school, maintained by the Sisters of Our Lady of the Missions; and 1 orphanage, conducted by the Sisters of Our Lady of Compassion. The total number of Catholic Maoris is about 2000. Several very successful conventions of Maori tribes have been held in Otaki since 1903. At the last (held in June, 1909), which was attended by His Grace Archbishop Redwood, the institution of a Maori Catholic magazine was decided upon and has since been carried out. (b) The Diocese of Auckland (districts: Rotorua, headquarters of the provincial of the mission, Matata, Tauranga, Hokianga, Okaihau, Whangaroa, Whangarei, Dargaville, and Coromandel) has 57 stations and 22 churches, served by 16 priests, of whom 9 are wholly and 7 are partly engaged on the Maori mission. There are 4 native schools conducted by the Sisters of St. Joseph. The total number of Catholic Maoris is about 4000. Throughout the three dioceses the Maori population is extremely scattered, and the missionaries have frequently to travel great distances. As the deleterious influence of Maori *tohungaism* (belief in wizards and "medicine-men") is on the wane, and the rancorous feelings engendered by the war are now subsiding, the prospect in this distant outpost of the mission field is most hopeful and promising.

V. EDUCATION.—Primary education is compulsory in New Zealand; and of every 100 persons in the dominion at the time of the census of 1906, 83.5 could read and write, 1.6 could read only, and 14.9 could neither read nor write. As mentioned above, New Zealand became a self-governing colony in 1852. Each province had its separate legislature and the control of education within its borders, and most of the provinces subsidized denominational schools. The provincial legislatures were abolished by the Acts of 1875-6, and one of the early measures (1877) of the centralized New Zealand Government was to abolish aid to denominational schools and to introduce the (so-called) national system known as "free, secular, and compulsory". From that day to this the entire public school system of New Zealand has remained, legally, purely secular.

From the first Catholics have protested against the exclusion of Christian teaching from the schools; and they have refused, and continue to refuse (unless where forced by circumstances) to send their children to schools from which their religion is excluded. As in other countries, so here, Catholics have shown the sincerity of their protest by creating, at enormous and continual sacrifices, a great rival system of education under which some 13,000 Catholic children are nurtured into a full and wholesome development of the faculties that God has bestowed upon them. With scarcely an exception, Catholic primary schools follow precisely the same secular curriculum as that prescribed under the Education Act for the public schools; and they are every year inspected and examined, under precisely the same conditions as are the public schools, by the State inspectors. The cost of carrying on the public school system is not derived from any special rate or tax, but the amount is paid out of the Consolidated Fund, to which Catholics, as taxpayers, contribute their share. Catholics are thus subjected to a double impost: they have to bear the cost of building, equipping, and maintaining their own schools, and they are compelled also to contribute their quota of taxation for the maintenance of the public school system, of which, from conscientious motives, they cannot avail themselves. New Zealand Catholics have never asked or desired a grant for the religious education which is imparted in their schools. But they have urged, and they continue to urge, their claim to a fair share of that taxation to which they themselves contribute, in return for the purely secular instruction which, in accordance with the Government programme, is given in the Catholic schools. Their standing protest against the injustice so long inflicted on them by the various governments of the country, and their unyielding demand for a recognition of the right of Christian taxpayers to have their children educated in accordance with Christian principles, constitute what is known, *par excellence*, as "the education question" in New Zealand. It is unhappily necessary to add that of late years, for no very obvious or adequate reason, Catholic agitation on the subject has not been so active as it once was; and unless a forward movement is made, the prospects of success for the cause, on behalf of which such splendid battles have been fought and such heroic sacrifices have been endured, are exceedingly remote.

VI. LITERATURE AND CATHOLIC JOURNALISM.— There is no New Zealand literature in the broad and general acceptation of the term. The usual reason assigned is that so young a country has not yet had time to evolve a literature of its own; but perhaps an equally important factor in producing and maintaining the existing condition of things is the smallness of the market for literary wares, in consequence of which New Zealand writers possessing exceptional talent inevitably gravitate towards Sydney or London. In general literature the one conspicuous name is that of Thomas Bracken, Irishman and Catholic, author of several volumes of poems, which have attained great popularity both in Australia and in New Zealand. Amongst scientific writers, notable Catholic names are those of the late W. M. Maskell, formerly Registrar of New Zealand University, and the Very Rev. Dr. Kennedy, S.M., B.A., D.D., F.R.A.S., present Rector of St. Patrick's College, both of whom have made many valuable contributions to the pages of scientific journals and the proceedings of learned societies.

As usually happens in countries that are overwhelmingly Protestant, by far the greater portion of the purely Catholic literature that has been published in New Zealand is apologetic in character. "What True Free-masonry Is: Why it is condemned", published in 1885 by the Rev. Thomas Keane, is a detailed and extremely effective treatment of the subject. "Disunion and Reunion", by the Rev. W. J. Madden, is a popular and ably written review of the course and causes of the Protestant Reformation. One of the most learned and certainly the most prolific of the contributors to Catholic literature in New Zealand was the Very Rev. T. Le Menant des Chesnais, S.M., recently deceased. His works include "Nonconformists and the Church"; "Out of the Maze"; "The Temuka Tournament" (a controversy); a volume on "Spiritism"; "The Church and the World"; etc. The last-named work, published only a few years before the venerable author's death, was very favourably reviewed by English and American papers. A notable addition to the Catholic literature of the dominion has been the recent publication of three volumes from the pen of the editor of the "New Zealand Tablet", the Rev. H. W. Cleary, D.D. These works, "Catholic Marriages", an exposition and defence of the decree "Ne temere", "An Impeached Nation; Being a Study of Irish Outrages"; and "Secular versus Religious Education: A Discussion", are thorough in the treatment of their respective subjects and possess value of a permanent character. A modest beginning has been made towards the compilation of a detailed history of the Catholic Church in the dominion by the publication, a few months ago, of "The Church in New Zealand: Memoirs of the Early Days", by J. J. Wilson.

The history of Catholic journalism in New Zealand is in effect the history of the "New Zealand Tablet", founded by the late Bishop Moran in 1873, the Catholics of this country having followed the principle that it is better to be represented by one strong paper than to have a multiplicity of publications. From the first the paper has been fortunate in its editors. In the early days the work done by its revered founder, in his battle for Catholic rights, and by his valued lay assistant, Mr. J. F. Perrin, was of a solid character. The prestige and influence of the paper was still further enhanced by the Rev. Henry W. Cleary, D.D., who made the "New Zealand Tablet" a power in the land, and won the respect of all sections of the community not only for the Catholic paper but for the Catholic body which it represents. In February, 1910, Dr. Cleary was appointed Bishop of Auckland, and was consecrated on 21 August in Enniscorthy cathedral, Co. Wexford, Ireland. It is safe to say that there are few countries in the world in which, in proportion to size and population, the Catholic press has a higher status than in New Zealand.

POMPALLIER, *Early History of the Catholic Church in Oceania* (E. T., Auckland, 1888); MORAN, *History of the Catholic Church in Australasia* (Sydney); *Australasian Catholic Directory for 1910;* WILSON, *The Church in New Zealand: Memoirs of the Early Days* (Dunedin, 1910); DILKE, *Greater Britain* (1885); DAVITT, *Life and Progress in Australasia* (London, 1898); REEVES, *New Zealand* (London, s. d.); JOSE, *History of Australasia* (Sydney, 1901); REEVES, *The Long White Cloud* (London, 1898); WRIGHT AND REEVES, *New Zealand* (London, 1908); *New Zealand Official Year-Book* for 1906 (last census year) and for 1909; DOUGLAS, *The Dominion of New Zealand* (London, 1909); HOCKEN, *A Bibliography of the Literature Relating to New Zealand* (Wellington, 1909), issued by the New Zealand Government—the most complete bibliography that has been published. It is no mere list of books, but gives a full account of each item, from TASMAN'S *Journal* of 1643 onwards, with explanatory notes, biographical information and criticism, synopsis of important periodicals, and a full index.

J. A. SCOTT.

Nicæa, titular see of Bithynia Secunda, situated on Lake Ascanius, in a fertile plain, but very unhealthful in summer. It was first colonized by the Battæi and was called Ancora or Helicora. Destroyed by the Mysians, it was rebuilt about 315 B. C. by Antigonus, after his victory over Eumenius, and was thenceforth called Antigonia. Later Lysimachus enlarged it and called it Nicæa in honour of his wife. At first the kings of Bithynia resided there almost as often as at Nicomedia between which and Nicæa arose a struggle for influence. It was the birthplace of the astronomer Hipparchus and the historian Dio Cassius. Pliny the Younger frequently mentions the city and its public monuments. Numerous coins of Nicæa attest the interest of the emperors. After the first Œcumenical Council, held there in 325, Constantine gave it the title of metropolis, which Valens afterwards withdrew, but which it retained ecclesiastically. In the fifth century it took three suffragans from the jurisdiction of Nicomedia, and later six. In 787 a second Œcumenical Council (the seventh) was held there against the Iconoclasts, which, like the first, assembled more than 300 bishops. Among its archbishops, of whom Le Quien (Oriens Christ., I, 639–56) names forty-six, those worthy of mention are Theognis, the first known bishop, a partisan of Arius at the council of 325; Anastasius, a sixth-century writer; Sts. Peter and Theophanes Graptos, two victims of the Iconoclasts in the ninth century; Ignatius, the biographer of the patriarchs Tarasius and Nicephorus; Gregory Asbestus, former metropolitan of Syracuse and the consecrator of Photius; Eustratius, commentator on Aristotle and polemist under Alexius Comnenus; and Bessarion, afterwards cardinal.

Nicæa grew more important during the Middle Ages. Captured by the Seljukids at an unknown date, perhaps subsequent to the revolt of Melissenus against Nicephorus Botaniates, it was afterwards ceded to the Turks by Alexius Comnenus. In 1096 the troops of Peter the Hermit, having attempted to capture the town, were completely defeated and massacred. In June, 1097, the city was taken, after a memorable siege, by the Crusaders and ceded by them to the Greek Emperor Alexius I. It was retained, but with great difficulty, during the twelfth century. After the capture of Constantinople by the Latins in 1204 Nicæa, restored, fortified, and embellished, became until 1261 the capital of the new Byzantine Empire of the Lascari or Palæologi. For nearly sixty years it played a most important part. It was finally captured by the Turkish Sultan Orkhan in 1333, from which time it has formed a part of the Ottoman Empire. To-day Nicæa is called Isnik. It is a village of 1500 Greek and Turkish inhabitants in the sandjak of Erthogrul and the vilayet of Brusa. The Greek metropolitan resides at Ghemlek, the ancient Chios. The ramparts, several times restored and now in a good state of preservation, are 4841 yards in circumference. There are 238 towers, some of them very ancient. Four ancient gates are well preserved. Among the monuments may be mentioned Yechil-Djami, the Green Mosque, and the church of the Assumption, probably of the ninth century, the mosaics of which are very rich.

SMITH, *Dict. Greek and Roman Geog.*, II (London, 1870), 422; TEXIER, *Asie Mineure* (Paris, 1862), 91–110; CUINET, *La Turquie d'Asie*, IV (Paris, 1894), 185–90; WULF, *Die Koimesis Kirche in Nicæa und ihre Mosaïken* (Strasburg, 1890).

S. VAILHÉ.

Nicæa, COUNCILS OF, respectively the First and Seventh Œcumenical Councils, held at Nicæa in Bithynia (see above).

I. THE FIRST COUNCIL OF NICÆA (First Œcumenical Council of the Catholic Church), held in 325 on the occasion of the heresy of Arius (see ARIANISM). As early as 320 or 321 St. Alexander, Bishop of Alexandria, convoked a council at Alexandria at which more than one hundred bishops from Egypt and Libya anathematized Arius. The latter continued to officiate in his church and to recruit followers. Being finally driven out, he went to Palestine and from there to Nicomedia. During this time St. Alexander published his "Epistola encyclica", to which Arius replied; but henceforth it was evident that the quarrel had gone beyond the possibility of human control. Sozomen even speaks of a Council of Bithynia which addressed an encyclical to all the bishops asking them to receive the Arians into the communion of the Church. This discord, and the war which soon broke out between Constantine and Licinius, added to the disorder and partly explains the progress of the religious conflict during the years 322–23. Finally Constantine, having conquered Licinius and become sole emperor, concerned himself with the re-establishment of religious peace as well as of civil order. He addressed letters to St. Alexander and to Arius deprecating these heated controversies regarding questions of no practical importance, and advising the adversaries to agree without delay. It was evident that the emperor did not then grasp the significance of the Arian controversy. Hosius of Cordova, his counsellor in religious matters, bore the imperial letter to Alexandria, but failed in his conciliatory mission. Seeing this, the emperor, perhaps advised by Hosius, judged no remedy more apt to restore peace in the Church than the convocation of an œcumenical council.

The emperor himself, in very respectful letters, begged the bishops of every country to come promptly to Nicæa. Several bishops from outside the Roman Empire (e. g., from Persia) came to the Council. It is not historically known whether the emperor in convoking the Council acted solely in his own name or in concert with the pope; however, it is probable that Constantine and Silvester came to an agreement (see SILVESTER I, SAINT, POPE). In order to expedite the assembling of the Council, the emperor placed at the disposal of the bishops the public conveyances and posts of the empire; moreover, while the Council lasted he provided abundantly for the maintenance of the members. The choice of Nicæa was favourable to the assembling of a large number of bishops. It was easily accessible to the bishops of nearly all the provinces, but especially to those of Asia, Syria, Palestine, Egypt, Greece, and Thrace. The sessions were held in the principal church, and in the central hall of the imperial palace. A large place was indeed necessary to receive such an assembly, though the exact number is not known with certainty. Eusebius speaks of more than 250 bishops, and later Arabic manuscripts raise the figure to 2000—an evident exaggeration in which, however, it is impossible to discover the approximate total number of bishops, as well as of the priests, deacons, and acolytes, of whom it is said that a great number were also present. St. Athanasius, a member of the council, speaks of 300, and in his letter "Ad Afros" he says explicitly 318. This figure is almost universally adopted, and there seems to be no good reason for rejecting it. Most of the bishops present were Greeks; among the Latins we know only Hosius of Cordova, Cecilian of Carthage, Mark of Calabria, Nicasius of Dijon, Donnus of Stridon in Pannonia, and the two Roman priests, Victor and Vincentius, representing the pope. The assembly numbered among its most famous members St. Alexander of Alexandria, Eustathius of Antioch, Macarius of Jerusalem, Eusebius of Nicomedia, Eusebius of Cæsarea, and Nicholas of Myra. Some had suffered during the last persecution; others were poorly enough acquainted with Christian theology. Among the members was a young deacon, Athanasius of Alexandria, for whom this Council was to be the prelude to a life of conflict and of glory (see ATHANASIUS, SAINT).

The year 325 is accepted without hesitation as that of the First Council of Nicæa. There is less agreement among our early authorities as to the month and day of the opening. In order to reconcile the indications furnished by Socrates and by the Acts of the Council of Chalcedon, this date may, perhaps, be taken as 20 May, and that of the drawing up of the symbol as 19 June. It may be assumed without too great hardihood that the synod, having been convoked for 20 May, in the absence of the emperor held meetings of a less solemn character until 14 June, when after the emperor's arrival, the sessions properly so called began, the symbol being formulated on 19 June, after which various matters—the paschal controversy, etc.—were dealt with, and the sessions came to an end 25 August. The Council was opened by Constantine with the greatest solemnity. The emperor waited until all the bishops had taken their seats before making his entry. He was clad in gold and covered with precious stones in the fashion of an Oriental sovereign. A chair of gold had been made ready for him, and when he had taken his place the bishops seated themselves. After he had been addressed in a hurried allocution, the emperor made an address in Latin, expressing his will that religious peace should be re-established. He had opened the session as honorary president, and he assisted at the subsequent sessions, but the direction of the theological discussions was abandoned, as was fitting, to the ecclesiastical leaders of the council. The actual president seems to have been Hosius of Cordova, assisted by the pope's legates, Victor and Vincentius.

The emperor began by making the bishops understand that they had a greater and better business in hand than personal quarrels and interminable recriminations. Nevertheless, he had to submit to the infliction of hearing the last words of debates which had been going on previous to his arrival. Eusebius of

Cæsarea and his two abbreviators, Socrates and Sozomen, as well as Rufinus and Gelasius of Cyzicus, report no details of the theological discussions. Rufinus tells us only that daily sessions were held and that Arius was often summoned before the assembly; his opinions were seriously discussed and the opposing arguments attentively considered. The majority, especially those who were confessors of the Faith, energetically declared themselves against the impious doctrines of Arius. (For the part played by the Eusebian third party, see EUSEBIUS OF NICOMEDIA. The adoption of the term ὁμοούσιος by the Council is fully treated under HOMOOUSION. For the Creed of Eusebius, see EUSEBIUS OF CÆSAREA: *Life*.) St. Athanasius assures us that the activities of the Council were nowise hampered by Constantine's presence. The emperor had by this time escaped from the influence of Eusebius of Nicomedia, and was under that of Hosius, to whom, as well as to St. Athanasius, may be attributed a preponderant influence in the formulation of the symbol of the First Œcumenical Council, of which the following is a literal translation:—

We believe in one God the Father Almighty, Maker of all things visible and invisible; and in one Lord Jesus Christ, the only begotten of the Father, that is, of the substance [ἐκ τῆς οὐσίας] of the Father, God of God, light of light, true God of true God, begotten not made, of the same substance with the Father [ὁμοούσιον τῷ πατρί], through whom all things were made both in heaven and on earth; who for us men and for our salvation descended, was incarnate, and was made man, suffered and rose again the third day, ascended into heaven and cometh to judge living and dead. And in the Holy Ghost. Those who say: There was a time when He was not, and He was not before He was begotten; and that He was made out of nothing (ἐξ οὐκ ὄντων); or who maintain that He is of another hypostasis or another substance [than the Father], or that the Son of God is created, or mutable, or subject to change, [them] the Catholic Church anathematizes.

The adhesion was general and enthusiastic. All the bishops save five declared themselves ready to subscribe to this formula, convinced that it contained the ancient faith of the Apostolic Church. The opponents were soon reduced to two, Theonas of Marmarica and Secundus of Ptolemais, who were exiled and anathematized. Arius and his writings were also branded with anathema, his books were cast into the fire, and he was exiled to Illyria. The lists of the signers have reached us in a mutilated condition, disfigured by faults of the copyists. Nevertheless, these lists may be regarded as authentic. Their study is a problem which has been repeatedly dealt with in modern times, in Germany and England, in the critical editions of H. Gelzer, H. Hilgenfeld, and O. Contz on the one hand, and C. H. Turner on the other. The lists thus constructed give respectively 220 and 218 names. With information derived from one source or another, a list of 232 or 237 fathers known to have been present may be constructed.

Other matters dealt with by this council were the controversy as to the time of celebrating Easter and the Meletian schism. The former of these two will be found treated under EASTER, *Easter Controversy;* the latter under MELETIUS OF LYCOPOLIS.

Of all the Acts of this Council, which, it has been maintained, were numerous, only three fragments have reached us: the creed, or symbol, given above (see also NICENE CREED); the canons; the synodal decree. In reality there never were any official acts besides these. But the accounts of Eusebius, Socrates, Sozomen, Theodoret, and Rufinus may be considered as very important sources of historical information, as well as some data preserved by St. Athanasius, and a history of the Council of Nicæa written in Greek in the fifth century by Gelasius of Cyzicus. There has long existed a dispute as to the number of the canons of First Nicæa. All the collections of canons, whether in Latin or Greek, composed in the fourth and fifth centuries agree in attributing to this Council only the twenty canons, which we possess to-day. Of these the following is a brief résumé: Canon i: On the admission, or support, or expulsion of clerics mutilated by choice or by violence. Canon ii: Rules to be observed for ordination, the avoidance of undue haste, the deposition of those guilty of a grave fault. Canon iii: All members of the clergy are forbidden to dwell with any woman, except a mother, sister, or aunt. Canon iv: Concerning episcopal elections. Canon v: Concerning the excommunicate. Canon vi: Concerning patriarchs and their jurisdiction. Canon vii confirms the right of the bishops of Jerusalem to enjoy certain honours. Canon viii concerns the Novatians. Canon ix: Certain sins known after ordination involve invalidation. Canon x: *Lapsi* who have been ordained knowingly or surreptitiously must be excluded as soon as their irregularity is known. Canon xi: Penance to be imposed on apostates of the persecution of Licinius. Canon xii: Penance to be imposed on those who upheld Licinius in his war on the Christians. Canon xiii: Indulgence to be granted to excommunicated persons in danger of death. Canon xiv: Penance to be imposed on catechumens who had weakened under persecution. Canon xv: Bishops, priests, and deacons are not to pass from one church to another. Canon xvi: All clerics are forbidden to leave their church. Formal prohibition of bishops to ordain for their diocese a cleric belonging to another diocese. Canon xvii: Clerics are forbidden to lend at interest. Canon xviii recalls to deacons their subordinate position with regard to priests. Canon xix: Rules to be observed with regard to adherents of Paul of Samosata who wished to return to the Church. Canon xx: On Sundays and during the Paschal season prayers should be said standing.

The business of the Council having been finished Constantine celebrated the twentieth anniversary of his accession to the empire, and invited the bishops to a splendid repast, at the end of which each of them received rich presents. Several days later the emperor commanded that a final session should be held, at which he assisted in order to exhort the bishops to work for the maintenance of peace; he commended himself to their prayers, and authorized the fathers to return to their dioceses. The greater number hastened to take advantage of this and to bring the resolutions of the council to the knowledge of their provinces.

II. SECOND COUNCIL OF NICÆA (Seventh Œcumenical Council of the Catholic Church), held in 787. (For an account of the controversies which occasioned this council and the circumstances in which it was convoked, see ICONOCLASM, I, II.) An attempt to hold a council at Constantinople, to deal with Iconoclasm, having been frustrated by the violence of the Iconoclastic soldiery, the papal legates left that city. When, however, they had reached Sicily on their way back to Rome, they were recalled by the Empress Irene. She replaced the mutinous troops at Constantinople with troops commanded by officers in whom she had every confidence. This accomplished, in May, 787, a new council was convoked at Nicæa in Bithynia. The pope's letters to the empress and to the patriarch (see ICONOCLASM, II) prove superabundantly that the Holy See approved the convocation of the Council. The pope afterwards wrote to Charlemagne: "Et sic synodum istam, secundum nostram ordinationem, fecerunt" (Thus they have held the synod in accordance with our directions).

The empress-regent and her son did not assist in person at the sessions, but they were represented there by two high officials: the patrician and former consul, Petronius, and the imperial chamberlain and logothete John, with whom was associated as secretary the former patriarch, Nicephorus. The acts represent as constantly at the head of the ecclesiastical members the two Roman legates, the archpriest Peter and the abbot Peter; after them come Tarasius, Patriarch of Constantinople, and then two Oriental monks and priests, John and Thomas, representatives of the Patriarchs of Alexandria, Antioch, and Jerusalem. The operations of the council show that Tarasius, properly speaking, conducted the sessions. The monks John and Thomas professed to represent the Oriental patriarchs, though these did not know that the council had been convoked. However, there was no fraud on their part: they had been sent, not by the patriarchs, but by the monks and priests of superior rank acting *sedibus impeditis*, in the stead and place of the patriarchs who were prevented from acting for themselves. Necessity was their excuse. Moreover, John and Thomas did not subscribe at the Council as vicars of the patriarchs, but simply in the name of the Apostolic sees of the Orient. With the exception of these monks and the Roman legates, all the members of the Council were subjects of the Byzantine Empire. Their number, bishops as well as representatives of bishops, varies in the ancient historians between 330 and 367; Nicephorus makes a manifest mistake in speaking of only 150 members: the Acts of the Council which we still possess show not fewer than 308 bishops or representatives of bishops. To these may be added a certain number of monks, archimandrites, imperial secretaries, and clerics of Constantinople who had not the right to vote.

The first session opened in the church of St. Sophia, 24 Sept., 787. Tarasius opened the council with a short discourse: "Last year, in the beginning of the month of August, it was desired to hold, under my presidency, a council in the Church of the Apostles at Constantinople; but through the fault of several bishops whom it would be easy to count, and whose names I prefer not to mention, since everyone knows them, that council was made impossible. The sovereigns have deigned to convoke another at Nicæa, and Christ will certainly reward them for it. It is this Lord and Saviour whom the bishops must also invoke in order to pronounce subsequently an equitable judgment in a just and impartial manner." The members then proceeded to the reading of various official documents, after which three Iconoclastic bishops who had retracted were permitted to take their seats. Seven others who had plotted to make the Council miscarry in the preceding year presented themselves and declared themselves ready to profess the Faith of the Fathers, but the assembly thereupon engaged in a long discussion concerning the admission of heretics and postponed their case to another session. On 26 September, the second session was held, during which the pope's letters to the empress and the Patriarch Tarasius were read. Tarasius declared himself in full agreement with the doctrine set forth in these letters. On 28, or 29, Sept., in the third session, some bishops who had retracted their errors were allowed to take their seats; after which various documents were read. The fourth session was held on 1 October. In it the secretaries of the council read a long series of citations from the Bible and the Fathers in favour of the veneration of images. Afterwards the dogmatic decree was presented, and was signed by all the members present, by the archimandrites of the monasteries, and by some monks; the papal legates added a declaration to the effect that they were ready to receive all who had abandoned the Iconoclastic heresy. In the fifth session on 4 October, passages from the Fathers were read which declared, or seemed to declare, against the worship of images, but the reading was not continued to the end, and the council decided in favour of the restoration and the veneration of images. On 6 October, in the sixth session, the doctrines of the *concilia-* *bulum* of 753 were refuted. The discussion was endless, but in the course of it several noteworthy things were said. The next session, that of 13 October, was especially important; at it was read the ὅρος, or dogmatic decision, of the council [see IMAGES, VENERATION OF (6)]. The last (eighth) session was held in the Magnaura Palace, at Constantinople, in presence of the empress and her son, on 23 October. It was spent in discourses, signing of names, and acclamations.

The council promulgated twenty-two canons relating to points of discipline, which may be summarized as follows: Canon i: The clergy must observe "the holy canons," which include the Apostolic, those of the six previous Œcumenical Councils, those of particular synods which have been published at other synods, and those of the Fathers. Canon ii: Candidates for bishop's orders must know the Psalter by heart and must have read thoroughly, not cursorily, all the sacred Scriptures. Canon iii condemns the appointment of bishops, priests, and deacons by secular princes. Canon iv: Bishops are not to demand money of their clergy: any bishop who through covetousness deprives one of his clergy is himself deposed. Canon v is directed against those who boast of having obtained church preferment with money, and recalls the Thirtieth Apostolic Canon and the canons of Chalcedon against those who buy preferment with money. Canon vi: Provincial synods are to be held annually. Canon vii: Relics are to be placed in all churches: no church is to be consecrated without relics. Canon viii prescribes precautions to be taken against feigned converts from Judaism. Canon ix: All writings against the venerable images are to be surrendered, to be shut up with other heretical books. Canon x: Against clerics who leave their own dioceses without permission, and become private chaplains to great personages. Canon xi: Every church and every monastery must have its own œconomus. Canon xii: Against bishops or abbots who convey church property to temporal lords. Canon xiii: Episcopal residences, monasteries, and other ecclesiastical buildings converted to profane uses are to be restored their rightful ownership. Canon xiv: Tonsured persons not ordained lectors must not read the Epistle or Gospel in the ambo. Canon xv: Against pluralities of benefices. Canon xvi: The clergy must not wear sumptuous apparel. Canon xvii: Monks are not to leave their monasteries and begin building other houses of prayer without being provided with the means to finish the same. Canon xviii: Women are not to dwell in bishops' houses or in monasteries of men. Canon xix: Superiors of churches and monasteries are not to demand money of those who enter the clerical or monastic state. But the dowry brought by a novice to a religious house is to be retained by that house if the novice leaves it without any fault on the part of the superior. Canon xx prohibits double monasteries. Canon xxi: A monk or nun may not leave one convent for another. Canon xxii: Among the laity, persons of opposite sexes may eat together, provided they give thanks and behave with decorum. But among religious persons, those of opposite sexes may eat together only in the presence of several God-fearing men and women, except on a journey when necessity compels.

HEFELE-LECLERCQ, *Hist. des Conciles* (Paris, 1906); BRAUN, *De s. Nicæna synods: Syrische Texte* (1898); REVILLOUT, *Le Concile de Nicée d'après les textes coptes* (Paris, 1889) (these two referring to the First Nicæa).—For the literature of the Arian, the Easter, and the Iconoclastic controversies, see bibliographies given under ARIANISM; ATHANASIUS, SAINT; HOMOOUSION; EASTER, *Easter Controversy;* ICONOCLASM; IMAGES, VENERATION OF.

H. LECLERCQ.

Nicaragua, REPUBLIC AND DIOCESE OF (DE NICARAGUA).—The diocese, suffragan of Guatemala, is coextensive with the Central American Republic of Nicaragua. This republic (see CHILE, MAP OF SOUTH

AMERICA), lying between Honduras and Costa Rica, the Pacific Ocean and the Caribbean Sea, has an area of 49,200 square miles and a population of about 600,000 inhabitants. The great mass of the inhabitants are either aborigines, or negroes, or of mixed blood, those of pure European descent not exceeding 1500 in number. The legislative authority is vested in a single chamber of thirty-six members, elected for six years; the executive, in a president, whose term of office is also six years, exercising his functions through a cabinet of nine responsible ministers The country is traversed by a deep depression, running parallel to the Pacific coast, within which are a chain of volcanoes (among them, Monotombo, 7000 feet) and the great lakes, Managua and Nicaragua (or Cocibolga). From the latter (a body of water 92 miles long and, at its widest, 40 miles wide) the country takes its name, derived from Nicarao, the name of the aboriginal chief who held sway in the regions round about Lake Cocibolga when the Spaniards, under Dávila, first explored the country, in 1522. From that time, or soon after, until 1822 Nicaragua was a Spanish possession, forming part of the Province of Guatemala. From 1822 until 1839 it was one of the five states constituting the Central American Federation; from 1840 until the present time (1911) it has been an independent republic, with its capital at Managua (pop., about 35,000). The aborigines of the Mosquito Coast, a swampy tract extending along the Nicaraguan shores of the Caribbean, were nominally under British protection until 1860, when, by the Treaty of Managua, this protectorate was ceded by Great Britain to the republic; in 1905, another treaty recognized the absolute sovereignty of Nicaragua over what had been, until then, known as the Mosquito Reservation. Since the time of its acquiring political independence, Nicaragua has been in almost continuous turmoil. Commercially, the country is very poorly developed; its chief exports are coffee, cattle, and mahogany; a certain amount of gold has been mined of recent years, and the nascent rubber industry is regarded as promising.

The Diocese of Nicaragua was canonically erected in 1534 (according to other authorities, 1531), with Diego Alvarez for its first bishop. It appears to have been at first a suffragan of Mexico, though some authorities have assigned it to the ecclesiastical Province of Lima, but in the eighteenth century Benedict XIV made it a suffragan of Guatemala. The episcopal residence is at Léon, where there is a fine cathedral. A concordat between the Holy See and the Republic of Nicaragua was concluded in 1861, and the Catholic is still recognized as the state religion, though Church and State are now separated, and freedom is constitutionally guaranteed to all forms of religious worship. After 1894 the Zelaya Government entered upon a course of anti-Catholic legislation which provoked a protest from Bishop Francisco Ulloa y Larrios, and the bishop was banished to Panama. Upon the death of this prelate, in 1908, his coadjutor bishop, Simeone Pereira, succeeded him. The returns for 1910 give the Diocese of Nicaragua 42 parishes, with 45 priests, a seminary, 2 colleges, and 2 hospitals.

GAMEZ, *Archivo Histórico de la Republica de Nicaragua* (Managua, 1896); SQUIER, *Nicaragua* (London, 1852); BELT, *The Naturalist in Nicaragua* (London, 1873); *The Statesman's Year Book* (London, 1910).
E. MACPHERSON.

Nicastro (NEOCASTRENSIS), a city of the Province of Catanzaro, in Calabria, southern Italy, situated on a promontory that commands the Gulf of St. Euphemia; above it is an ancient castle. The commerce of the port of Nicastro consists of the exportation of acid, herbs, and wine. The cathedral, an ancient temple, with the episcopal palace, was outside the city; having been pillaged by the Saracens, it was restored in the year 1100, but it was destroyed in the earthquake of 1638, with the episcopal palace, under the ruins of which most valuable archives were lost. For a long time, the Greek Rite was in use at Nicastro. The first bishop of this city of whom there is any record was Henry (1090); Bishop Tancredo da Monte Foscolo (1279) was deposed by Honorius IV for having consecrated John of Aragon, King of Sicily, but he was reinstated by Boniface VIII; Bishop Paolo Capisucco (1533) was one of the judges in the case of the marriage of Henry VIII of England; Marcello Cervino (1539) became Pope Marcellus II; Giovanni Tommaso Perrone (1639) built the new cathedral. In 1818 the ancient See of Martorano, the former Mamertum (the first bishop of which was Domnus, in 761), was united to the Diocese of Nicastro. The diocese is a suffragan of Reggio in Calabria; it has 52 parishes, with 110,100 inhabitants; 71 churches and chapels, 2 convents of the Capuchins, and one orphan asylum and boarding-school, directed by the Sisters of Charity.

CAPPELLETTI, *Le Chiese d'Italia*, XXI (Venice, 1870), 200.
U. BENIGNI.

Niccola Pisano, architect and sculptor, b. at Pisa about 1205-07; d. there, 1278. He was the father of

CHURCH OF S. NICCOLA
The leaning tower, containing the remarkable winding stairs unsupported at the centre, is the work of Niccola Pisano

modern plastic art. When barely past adolescence, he came to the notice of Frederick II of Swabia who took him to attend his coronation in Rome, thence to Naples, to complete Castel Capuano and Castel dell' Uovo (1221-31). In 1233 Niccola was in Lucca; the *alto-rilievo* of the Deposition over the side door of the cathedral may be of this date. The marble urn or *Arca* made to contain the body of St. Dominic in the church bearing his name in Bologna, is said to be an early work, but shows maturity; the charming group of the Madonna and Child upon it, foreshadows all the Madonnas of Italian art. From Niccola's designs was built the famous basilica of St. Anthony in Padua, the church of the Feari in Venice is also attributed to him, possibly on insufficient grounds. In Florence he designed the interior of Sta. Trinità which Michelangelo loved so much that he called it his lady, "la mia Dama". Having been ordered by the Ghibellines to destroy the Baptistery frequented by the Guelphs, Niccola undermined the tower called *Guardo-morto*, causing it to so fall that it did not touch the precious edifice. On his return to Pisa, the architect erected the campanile for the church of S. Niccolò which contains the remarkable winding stair unsupported at its centre; an invention repeated by Bramante for the "Belvedere", and by San Gallo in the renowned well at Orvieto. In 1242 Niccola superintended the building of the cathedral of Pistoja, and in 1263 the restoration of S. Pietro Maggiore. He remodelled S. Domenico at Arezzo, the Duomo at Volterra, the Pieve and Sta. Margherita at Cortona. Much of his work at Pisa is believed to have perished in the fire of 1610. A wonderful creation (1260) is the hexagonal, insulated pulpit of the Baptistery. It is supported by seven columns, three of them resting on lions. The panels have reliefs from the New Testament; the pediments, figures of virtues; the spandrels, prophets and evangelists. The architectural part is Italian Gothic: the sculptures are mainly pure reproductions of the antique. A second pulpit for the Duomo of Siena followed in 1266. Niccola's early sculpture shows clumsiness, if we are to believe that the figures outside the Misericordia Vecchia in Florence are his. In later life, whether from Rome or from his own Camposanto at Pisa (Roman sarcophagus used for the Countess Beatrice of Tuscany; Greek vase with figures he reproduced) he learned to create with the freedom, beauty, and power of ancient art. Ruhmer suggests aptly that he may have used clay for his initial model, a method then unpractised in Italy. One of Niccola's last works in architecture was the abbey and church of La Scorgola, commemorating Charles of Anjou's victory at Tagliacozzo, now in ruins; in sculpture, the statuettes for the famous Fonte Maggiore at Perugia, erected after his design (1277–80).

PULPIT IN THE CATHEDRAL, SIENA—NICCOLA PISANO

CICOGNARA, *Storia della scultura* (Venice, 1813); PERKINS, *Tuscan sculptors* (London, 1864); LÜBKE, *History of sculpture*, tr. BURNETT (London, 1862–72).

M. L. HANDLEY.

Nice, DIOCESE OF (NICIENSIS), comprises the Department of Alpes-Maritimes. It was re-established by the Concordat of 1801 as suffragan of Aix. The Countship of Nice from 1818 to 1860 was part of the Sardinian States, and the see became a suffragan of Genoa. When Nice was annexed to France in 1860, certain parts which remained Italian were cut off from it and added to the Diocese of Vintimille. In 1862 the diocese was again a suffragan of Aix. The arrondissement of Grasse was separated from the Diocese of Fréjus in 1886, and given to Nice which now unites the three former Dioceses of Nice, Grasse, and Vence.

I. DIOCESE OF NICE.—Traditions tell us that Nice was evangelized by St. Barnabas, sent by St. Paul, or else by St. Mary Magdalen, St. Martha, and St. Lazarus; and they make St. Bassus, a martyr under Decius, the first Bishop of Nice. The See of Nice in Gaul existed in 314, since the bishop sent delegates to the Council of Arles in that year. The first bishop historically known is Amantius who attended the Council of Aquileia in 381. Cimiez, near Nice, where still can be seen the remains of a Roman amphitheatre, and which was made illustrious by the martyrdom of the youthful St. Pontius about 260, had also a see, held in the middle of the fifth century by St. Valerianus; a rescript of St. Leo the Great, issued after 450 and confirmed by St. Hilarus in 465, united the Sees of Nice and Cimiez. This newly-formed see remained a suffragan of Embrun up to the time of the Revolution (see GAP, DIOCESE OF). Mgr Duchesne has not discovered sufficient historical proof of the episcopate at Nice of St. Valerianus (433–43), of St. Deutherius (490–93), martyred by the Vandals, of St. Syagrius (d. 787), Count of Brignoles and son-in-law perhaps of Charlemagne. St. Anselm, a former monk of Lérins, is mentioned as Bishop of Nice (1100–07). Bishops of Nice bore the title of Counts of Drap since the donation of property situated at Drap, made in 1073 by Pierre, Bishop of Vaison, a native of Nice, to Raymond I, its bishop, and to his successors. Charlemagne, when visiting Cimiez devastated by the Lombards in 574, caused St. Syagrius to build on its ruins the monastery of St. Pontius, the largest Alpine abbey of the Middle Ages.

II. DIOCESE OF GRASSE.—The first known Bishop of Antibes is Armentarius who attended the Council of Vaison in 442; Mgr Duchesne admits as possible that the Remigius, who signed at the Council of Nîmes in 396 and in 417 received a letter from Pope Zosimus, may have been Bishop of Antibes before Armentarius. About the middle of the thirteenth century the See of Antibes was transferred to Grasse. Bishops of Grasse worthy of mention are: Cardinal Agostino Trivulzio (1537–1648); the poet Antoine Godeau (1636–53), one of the most celebrated habitués of the Hôtel de Rambouillet, where he was nicknamed "Julia's dwarf" on account of his small stature.

III. DIOCESE OF VENCE.—The first known Bishop of Vence is Severus, bishop in 439 and perhaps as early as 419. Among others are: St. Veranus, son of St. Eucherius, Archbishop of Lyons and a monk of Lérins, bishop before 451 and at least until 465; St. Lambert, first a Benedictine monk (d. 1154); Cardinal Alessandro Farnese (1505–11). Antoine Godeau, Bishop of Grasse, was named Bishop of Vence in 1638; the Holy See wished to unite the two dioceses. Meeting with opposition from the chapter and the clergy of Vence Godeau left Grasse in 1653, to remain Bishop of Vence, which see he held until 1672.

The following saints are specially honoured in the Diocese of Nice: The youthful martyr St. Celsus, whom certain traditions make victim of Nero's persecution; St. Vincentius and St. Orontius, natives of Cimiez, apostles of Aquitaine and of Spain, martyrs under Diocletian; St. Hospitius, a hermit of Cap Ferrat (d. about 581); Blessed Antoine Gallus (1300–92), a native of Nice, one of St. Catherine of Siena's confessors. The martyr St. Reparata of Cæsarea in Palestine is the patroness of the diocese. The chief pilgrimages of the diocese are: Our Lady of Laghet, near Monaco, a place of pilgrimage since the end of the seventeenth century; the chapel of the Sacred Heart of Jesus at Roquefort near Grasse; Our Lady of Valcluse; Our Lady of Brusq; Our Lady of Vie.

Prior to the application of the law of 1901 against associations, the diocese counted Assumptionists, Capuchins, Cistercians of the Immaculate Conception, Jesuits, Priests of the Christian Doctrine, Franciscans, Lazarists, Discalced Carmelites, Oblates of Mary Immaculate, Salesians of Dom Bosco, Camillians, several orders of teaching Brothers. The Sisters of St. Martha, devoted to teaching and nursing and founded in 1832, have their mother-house at Grasse. At the beginning of the twentieth century religious congregations of the diocese conducted 4

THE CATHEDRAL, NICE

crèches, 16 day nurseries, 2 institutions for crippled children, 1 boys' orphanage, 10 girls' orphanages, 3 sewing rooms, 11 hospitals or asylums, 4 convalescent homes, 6 houses for the care of the sick in their own homes, 1 insane asylum, 1 asylum for incurables. The Diocese of Nice, whither every year the warm and balmy climate of the Côte d'Azur attracts innumerable foreigners, counted in 1909 about 260,000 inhabitants, 32 parishes and 185 succursal parishes.

Gallia Christiana (nova, 1725), III, 1160-87, 1212-33, 1267-96, and *Instrumenta*, 189-200, 212-52; DUCHESNE, *Fastes Episcopaux*, I, 99, 279, 285-8; TISSERAND, *Chronique de Provence: hist. civ. et relig. de la cité de Nice et du département des Alpes-Maritimes* (2 vols., Nice, 1862); ALBIN DE CIGALA, *Nice chrét., guide hist. et artist. des paroisses* (Paris, 1900); CAIS DE PIERLAS AND SAIGE, *Chartrier de l'abbaye de Saint-Pons hors les murs de Nice* (Monaco, 1903); CAIS DE PIERLAS, *Cartulaire de l'ancienne cathédrale de Nice* (Turin, 1888); CHAPON, *Statuts synodaux* (Nice, 1906); TISSERAND, *Hist. de Vence, cité, évêché, baronnie* (Paris, 1860).

GEORGES GOYAU.

Nicene and Niceno-Constantinopolitan Creed.—The origin and history of the Nicene Creed are set forth in the articles: NICÆA, COUNCILS OF; ARIUS; ARIANISM; EUSEBIUS OF CÆSAREA; FILIOQUE. As approved in amplified form at the Council of Constantinople (381) q. v., it is the profession of the Christian Faith common to the Catholic Church, to all the Eastern Churches separated from Rome, and to most of the Protestant denominations. Soon after the Council of Nicæa new formulas of faith were composed, most of them variations of the Nicene Symbol, to meet new phases of Arianism. There were at least four before the Council of Sardica in 341, and in that council a new form was presented and inserted in the Acts, though not accepted by the council. The Nicene Symbol, however, continued to be the only one in use among the defenders of the Faith. Gradually it came to be recognized as the proper profession of faith for candidates for baptism. Its alteration into the Nicene-Constantinopolitan formula, the one now in use, is usually ascribed to the Council of Constantinople, since the Council of Chalcedon (451), which designated this symbol as "The Creed of the Council of Constantinople of 381" had it twice read and inserted in its Acts. The historians Socrates, Sozomen, and Theodoret do not mention this, although they do record that the bishops who remained at the council after the departure of the Macedonians confirmed the Nicene faith. Hefele (II, 9) admits the possibility of our present creed being a condensation of the "Tome" ($\tau \acute{o} \mu o s$), i. e. the exposition of the doctrines concerning the Trinity made by the Council of Constantinople; but he prefers the opinion of Rémi Ceillier and Tillemont tracing the new formula to the "Ancoratus" of Epiphanius written in 374. Hort, Caspari, Harnack, and others are of the opinion that the Constantinopolitan form did not originate at the Council of Constantinople, because it is not in the Acts of the council of 381, but was inserted there at a later date; because Gregory Nazianzen who was at the council mentions only the Nicene formula adverting to its incompleteness about the Holy Ghost, showing that he did not know of the Constantinopolitan form which supplies this deficiency; and because the Latin Fathers apparently know nothing of it before the middle of the fifth century.

The following is a literal translation of the Greek text of the Constantinopolitan form, the brackets indicating the words altered or added in the Western liturgical form in present use:—

"We believe (I believe) in one God, the Father Almighty, maker of heaven and earth, and of all things visible and invisible. And in one Lord Jesus Christ, the only begotten Son of God, and born of the Father before all ages. (God of God) light of light, true God of true God. Begotten not made, consubstantial to the Father, by whom all things were made. Who for us men and for our salvation came down from heaven. And was incarnate of the Holy Ghost and of the Virgin Mary and was made man; was crucified also for us under Pontius Pilate, suffered and was buried; and the third day he rose again according to the Scriptures. And ascended into heaven, sitteth at the right hand of the Father, and shall come again with glory to judge the living and the dead, of whose Kingdom there shall be no end. And (I believe) in the Holy Ghost, the Lord and Giver of life, who proceedeth from the Father (and the Son), who together with the Father and the Son is to be adored and glorified, who spake by the Prophets. And one holy, catholic and apostolic Church. We confess (I confess) one baptism for the remission of sins. And we look for (I look for) the resurrection of the dead and the life of the world to come. Amen".

In this form the Nicene article concerning the Holy Ghost is enlarged; several words, notably the two clauses "of the substance of the Father" and "God of God", are omitted as also are the anathemas; ten clauses are added; and in five places the words are differently located. In general the two forms contain what is common to all the baptismal formulas in the early Church. Vossius (1577-1649) was the first to detect the similarity between the creed set forth in the "Ancoratus" and the baptismal formula of the Church of Jerusalem. Hort (1876) held that the symbol is a revision of the Jerusalem formula, in which the most important Nicene statements concerning the Holy Ghost have been inserted. The author of the revision may have been St. Cyril of Jerusalem (315-386, q. v.). Various hypotheses are offered to account for the tradition that the Niceno-Constantinopolitan symbol originated with the Council of Constantinople, but none of them is satisfactory. Whatever be its origin, the fact is that the Council of Chalcedon (451) attributed it to the Council of Constantinople, and if it was not actually composed in that council, it was adopted and authorized by the Fathers assembled as a true expression of the Faith. The history of the creed is completed in the article FILIOQUE.

DENZINGER, *Enchiridion Symbolorum* (10th ed., Freiburg, 1908), for texts of creeds in Greek and Latin; HEFELE, *Conciliengeschichte*, I and II, Fr. tr. LECLERQ, II, pt. I, 11–13 (translator's note); HARNACK in *Realencyclopädie für protest. Theologie* (Leipzig, 1907), s. v. *Konstantinopolitanisches Symbol;* KÖLLNER, *Symbolik aller Confessionen* (1837), 28–52; LUMBY, *Hist. of Creeds* (2nd ed., London, 1880); CASPARI, *Quellen zur Gesch. d. Taufsymbols*, I-IV (Christiania, 1866 sq.); SWAINSON, *The Nicene and Apostles' Creeds*, etc. (London, 1875); HORT, *Two Dissertations, II: on the Constantinopolitan Creed and the other Eastern Creeds of the fourth century* (Cambridge, 1876); KUNZE, *Das n. k. Symbol* in *Studien zur Gesch. der Theol. u. Kirche* (Leipzig, 1898); IDEM, *Martin Eremita, ein neuer Zeuge für das altkirchl. Taufbekenntniss* (Leipzig, 1895).
J. WILHELM.

Nicephorus, SAINT, Patriarch of Constantinople, 806–815, b. about 758; d. 2 June, 829. This champion of the orthodox view in the second contest over the veneration of images belonged to a noted family of Constantinople. He was the son of the imperial secretary Theodore and his pious wife Eudoxia. Eudoxia was a strict adherent of the Church and Theodore had been banished by the Emperor Constantine Copronymus (741–75) on account of his steadfast support of the teaching of the Church concerning images. While still young Nicephorus was brought to the court, where he became an imperial secretary. With two other officials of high rank he represented the Empress Irene in 787 at the Second Council of Nicæa (the Seventh Œcumenical Council), which declared the doctrine of the Church respecting images. Shortly after this Nicephorus sought solitude on the Thracian Bosporus, where he had founded a monastery. Here he devoted himself to ascetic practices and to the study both of secular learning, as grammar, mathematics, and philosophy, and the Scriptures. Later he was recalled to the capital and given charge of the great hospital. Upon the death of Patriarch Tarasius (25 February, 806), there was great division among the clergy and higher court officials as to the choice of his successor. Finally, with the assent of the bishops Emperor Nicephorus (802–11) appointed Nicephorus as patriarch. Although still a layman, he was known by all to be very religious and highly educated. He received Holy Orders and was consecrated bishop on Easter Sunday, 12 April, 806. The direct elevation of a layman to the patriarchate, as had already happened in the case of Tarasius, aroused opposition in the ecclesiastical party among the clergy and monks. The leaders were the abbots, Plato of Saccadium and Theodore of Studium, and Theodore's brother, Archbishop Joseph of Thessalonica. For this opposition the Abbot Plato was imprisoned for twenty-four days at the command of the emperor.

Nicephorus soon gave further cause for antagonism. In 795 a priest named Joseph had celebrated the unlawful marriage of Emperor Constantine VI (780–97) with Theodota, during the lifetime of Maria, the rightful wife of the emperor, whom he had set aside. For this act Joseph had been deposed and banished. Emperor Nicephorus considered it important to have this matter settled and, at his wish the new patriarch, with the concurrence of a synod composed of a small number of bishops, pardoned Joseph and, in 806, restored him to his office. The patriarch yielded to the wishes of the emperor in order to avert more serious evil. His action was regarded by the strict church party as a violation of ecclesiastical law and a scandal. Before the matter was settled Theodore had written to the patriarch entreating him not to reinstate the guilty priest, but had received no answer. Although the matter was not openly discussed, he and his followers now held virtually no church communion with Nicephorus and the priest, Joseph. But, through a letter written by Archbishop Joseph, the course which he and the strict church party followed became public in 808, and caused a sensation. Theodore set forth, by speech and writing, the reasons for the action of the strict party and firmly maintained his position. Defending himself against the accusation that he and his companions were schismatic, he declared that he had kept silent as long as possible, had censured no bishops, and had always included the name of the patriarch in the liturgy. He asserted his love and his attachment to the patriarch, and said he would withdraw all opposition if the patriarch would acknowledge the violation of law by removing the priest Joseph. Emperor Nicephorus now took violent measures. He commanded the patriarch to call a synod, which was held in 809, and had Plato and several monks forcibly brought before it. The opponents of the patriarch were condemned, the Archbishop of Thessalonica was deposed, the Abbots Plato and Theodore with their monks were banished to neighbouring islands and cast into various prisons.

This, however, did not discourage the resolute opponents of the "Adulterine Heresy". In 809 Theodore and Plato sent a joint memorial, through the Archimandrite Epiphanius, to Pope Leo III, and later, Theodore laid the matter once more before the pope in a letter, in which he besought the successor of St. Peter to grant a helping hand to the East, so that it might not be overwhelmed by the waves of the "Adulterine Heresy". Pope Leo sent an encouraging and consolatory reply to the resolute confessors, upon which they wrote another letter to him through Epiphanius. Leo had received no communication from Patriarch Nicephorus and was, therefore, not thoroughly informed in the matter; he also desired to spare the eastern emperor as much as possible. Consequently, for a time, he took no further steps in the matter. Emperor Nicephorus continued to persecute all adherents of Theodore of Studium, and, in addition, oppressed those of whom he had grown suspicious, whether clergy or dignitaries of the empire. Moreover, he favoured the heretical Paulicians and the Iconoclasts and drained the people by oppressive taxes, so that he was universally hated. In July, 811, the emperor was killed in a battle with the Bulgarians. His son Stauracius, who had been wounded in the same fight, was proclaimed emperor, but was deposed by the chief men of the empire because he followed the bad example of his father. On 2 October, 811, with the assent of the patriarch, Michael Rhangabe, brother-in-law of Stauracius, was raised to the throne. The new emperor promised, in writing, to defend the faith and to protect both clergy and monks, and was crowned with much solemnity by the Patriarch Nicephorus. Michael succeeded in reconciling the patriarch and Theodore of Studium. The patriarch again deposed the priest Joseph and withdrew his decrees against Theodore and his partisans. On the other side Theodore, Plato, and the majority of their adherents recognized the patriarch as the lawful head of the Byzantine Church, and sought to bring the refractory back to his obedience. The emperor had also recourse to the papacy in reference to these quarrels and had received a letter of approval from Leo. Moreover, the patriarch now sent the customary written notification of his induction into office (*Synodica*) to the pope. In it he sought to excuse the long delay by the tyranny of the preceding emperor, interwove a rambling confession of faith, and promised to notify Rome at the proper time in regard to all important questions.

Emperor Michael was an honourable man of good intentions, but weak and dependent. On the advice of Nicephorus he put the heretical and seditious Paulicians to death and tried to suppress the Iconoclasts.

The patriarch endeavoured to establish monastic discipline among the monks, and to suppress double monasteries which had been forbidden by the Seventh Œcumenical Council. After his complete defeat, 22 June, 813, in the war against the Bulgarians, the emperor lost all authority. With the assent of the patriarch, he resigned and entered a monastery with his children. The popular general, Leo the Armenian, now became emperor, 11 July, 813. When Nicephorus demanded the confession of faith, before the coronation, Leo put it off. Notwithstanding this, Nicephorus crowned him, and later, Leo again refused to make this confession. As soon as the new emperor had assured the peace of the empire by the overthrow of the Bulgarians his true opinions began gradually to appear. He entered into connexion with the opponents of images, among whom were a number of bishops; it steadily grew more evident that he was preparing a new attack upon the veneration of images. With fearless energy the Patriarch Nicephorus now proceeded against the machinations of the Iconoclasts. He brought to trial before a synod several ecclesiastics opposed to images and forced an abbot named John and also Bishop Anthony of Sylæum to submit. Bishop Anthony's acquiescence was merely feigned.

In December, 814, Nicephorus had a long conference with the emperor on the veneration of images but no agreement was reached. Later the patriarch sent several learned bishops and abbots to convince him of the truth of the position of the Church on the veneration of images. The emperor wished to have a debate between representatives of the opposite dogmatic opinions, but the adherents of the veneration of images refused to take part in such a conference, as the Seventh Œcumenical Council had settled the question. Then Nicephorus called together an assembly of bishops and abbots at the Church of St. Sophia at which he excommunicated the perjured Bishop Anthony of Sylæum. A large number of the laity were also present on this occasion and the patriarch with the clergy and people remained in the church the entire night in prayer. The emperor then summoned Nicephorus to him, and the patriarch went to the imperial palace accompanied by the abbots and monks. Nicephorus first had a long, private conversation with the emperor, in which he vainly endeavoured to dissuade Leo from his opposition to the veneration of images. The emperor received those who had accompanied Nicephorus, among them seven metropolitans and Abbot Theodore of Studium. They all repudiated the interference of the emperor in dogmatic questions and once more rejected Leo's proposal to hold a conference. The emperor then commanded the abbots to maintain silence upon the matter and forbade them to hold meetings. Theodore declared that silence under these conditions would be treason and expressed sympathy with the patriarch whom the emperor forbade to hold public service in the church. Nicephorus fell ill; when he recovered the emperor called upon him to defend his course before a synod of bishops friendly to iconoclasm. But the patriarch would not recognize the synod and paid no attention to the summons. The pseudo-synod now commanded that he should no longer be called patriarch. His house was surrounded by crowds of angry Iconoclasts who shouted threats and invectives. He was guarded by soldiers and not allowed to perform any official act. With a protest against this mode of procedure the patriarch notified Leo that he found it necessary to resign the patriarchal see. Upon this he was arrested at midnight in March, 815, and banished to the monastery of St. Theodore, which he had built on the Bosporus.

Leo now raised to the patriarchate Theodotus, a married, illiterate layman who favoured iconoclasm. Theodotus was consecrated 1 April, 815. The exiled Nicephorus persevered in his opposition and wrote several treatises against iconoclasm. After the murder of the Emperor Leo, 25 December, 820, Michael the Amorian ascended the throne and the defenders of the veneration of images were now more considerately treated. However, Michael would not consent to an actual restoration of images such as Nicephorus demanded from him, for he declared that he did not wish to interfere in religious matters and would leave everything as he had found it. Accordingly Emperor Leo's hostile measures were not repealed, although the persecution ceased. Nicephorus received permission to return from exile if he would promise to remain silent. He would not agree, however, and remained in the monastery of St. Theodore, where he continued by speech and writing to defend the veneration of images. The dogmatic treatises, chiefly on this subject, that he wrote are as follows: a lesser "Apology for the Catholic Church concerning the newly arisen Schism in regard to Sacred Images" (Migne, P. G., C, 833–849), written 813–14; a larger treatise in two parts; the first part is an "Apology for the pure, unadulterated Faith of Christians against those who accuse us of idolatry" (Migne, loc. cit., 535–834); the second part contains the "Antirrhetici", a refutation of a writing by the Emperor Constantine Copronymus on images (loc. cit., 205–534). Nicephorus added to this second part seventy-five extracts from the writings of the Fathers [edited by Pitra, "Spicilegium Solesmense", I (Paris, 1852), 227–370]; in two further writings, which also apparently belong together, passages from earlier writers, that had been used by the enemies of images to maintain their opinions, are examined and explained. Both these treatises were edited by Pitra; the first 'Ἐπίκρισις in "Spicilegium Solesmense", I, 302–335; the second 'Ἀντίρρησις in the same, I, 371–503, and IV, 292–380. The two treatises discuss passages from Macarius Magnes, Eusebius of Cæsarea, and from a writing wrongly ascribed to Epiphanius of Cyprus. Another work justifying the veneration of images was edited by Pitra under the title "Antirrheticus adversus iconomachos" (Spicil. Solesm., IV, 233–91). A final and, as it appears, especially important treatise on this question has not yet been published. Nicephorus also left two small historical works, one known as the "Breviarium", the other the "Chronographis", both are edited by C. de Boor, "Nicephori archiep. Const. opuscula historica" in the "Bibliotheca Teubneriana" (Leipzig, 1880). At the end of his life he was revered and after death regarded as a saint. In 874 his bones were translated to Constantinople with much pomp by the Patriarch Methodius and interred, 13 March, in the Church of the Apostles. His feast is celebrated on this day both in the Greek and Roman Churches; the Greeks also observe 2 June as the day of his death.

Vita Nicephori auctore Ignatio diacono in Acta SS., March, II, 294 sqq. (Latin), 704 sqq. (Greek), and in MIGNE, P. G., C., 37 sqq.; Bibliotheca hagiographica græca, ed. BOLLANDISTS (2nd ed.), 186; HERGENRÖTHER, Photius, I (Ratisbon, 1867), 261 sqq.; IDEM, Kirchengeschichte (4th ed. KIRSCH), II, 31 sqq.; KRUMBACHER, Gesch. der byzantinischen Litt. (2nd ed. EHRHARD), 71 sqq., 349 sqq.

J. P. KIRSCH.

Nicephorus Blemmydes. See BLEMMIDA, NICEPHORUS.

Nicephorus Gregoras. See HESYCHASM.

Nicéron, JEAN-PIERRE, French lexicographer, b. in Paris, 11 March, 1685, d. there, 8 July, 1738. After his studies at the Collège Mazarin, he joined the Barnabites (August, 1702). He taught rhetoric in the college of Loches, and soon after at Montargis, where he remained ten years. While engaged in teaching, he made a thorough study of modern languages. In 1716 he went to Paris and devoted his time to literary work. His aim was to put together, in a logically arranged compendium, a series of biographical and bibliographical articles on the men who had distinguished themselves in literature and sciences since the time of the Renaissance. It required long research as well as great industry. After eleven years he published the first volume of his monumental work under the title of "Mémoires pour servir à l'histoire des hommes illustres de la république des lettres avec le catalogue raisonné de leurs ouvrages" (Paris, 1727). Thirty-eight volumes followed from 1728 to 1738. The last volume from his pen was published two years after the author's death (Paris, 1740). Father Oudin, J.-B. Michauld, and Abbé Goujet later contributed three volumes to the collection. A German translation of it was published in 1747–1777. It has been often repeated that this work lacks method, and that the length of many articles is out of proportion to the value of the men to whom they are devoted. This criticism, however true it may be, does not impair the genuine qualities and importance of the whole work. Even now, these "Mémoires" contain a great amount of information that could hardly be obtained elsewhere. Moreover, they refer to sources which, but for our author, would be easily overlooked or ignored. Besides this original composition, he translated various books from English, among which should be mentioned: "Le voyage de Jean Ovington à Surate et en divers autres lieux de l'Asie et de l'Afrique, avec l'histoire de la révolution arrivée dans le royaume de Golconde" (Paris, 1725); "La Conversion de l'Angleterre au Christianisme comparée avec sa prétendue réformation" (Paris, 1729).

D'ARTIGNY, *Mémoires d'histoire et de littérature*, I (Paris, 1749); GOUJET, *Eloge de J. P. Nicéron* in vol. XL of *Mémoires* (Paris, 1840); CHAUFFEPIÉ, *Dict. historique et critique* (Amsterdam, 1850–56).

LOUIS N. DELAMARRE.

Nicetas (NICETA), Bishop of Remesiana (Romatiana) in what is now Servia, b. about 335; d. about 414. Recent investigations have resulted in a more definite knowledge of the person of this ecclesiastical writer. Gennadius of Marseilles, in his catalogue of writers ("De viris illustribus", xxii) mentions a "Niceas Romatianæ civitatis episcopus" to whom he ascribes two works: one, in six books, for catechumens, and a little book on a virgin who had fallen. Outside of this reference no writer and bishop of the name of Niceas is known. This Niceas, therefore, is, without doubt, the same as Nicetas, "Bishop of the Dacians", the contemporary and friend of St. Paulinus of Nola. The identity is shown by a comparison of Gennadius (loc. cit.) with Paulinus in his "Carmina" (xvii, xxvii), and, further, by the agreement in time. In Dacia, where, according to Paulinus, his friend Nicetas was bishop, there was a city called Romatiana (now Bela Palanka) on the great Roman military road from Belgrade to Constantinople, and this was the see of Nicetas. He is mentioned a number of times in the letters and poems of St. Paulinus of Nola, especially in Carmen xxvii (ed. Hartel in "Corp. Script. eccl. lat.", XXX, 262 sqq.), and in Carmen xvii "Ad Nicetam redeuntem in Daciam" (op. cit., 81 sqq.), written on the occasion of Nicetas's pilgrimage to Nola, in 398, to visit the grave of St. Felix. In this latter poem Paulinus describes how his friend, journeying home, is greeted everywhere with joy, because in his apostolic labours in the cold regions of the North, he has melted the icy hearts of men by the warmth of the Divine doctrine. He has laid the yoke of Christ upon races who never bowed the neck in battle. Like the Goths and Dacians, the Scythians are tamed; he teaches them to glorify Christ and to lead a pure, peaceable life. Paulinus wishes his departing friend a safe journey by land and by water. St. Jerome, too, speaks of the apostolic labours of Nicetas and says of him that he spread Christian civilization among the barbarians by his sweet songs of the Cross (Ep. lx, P. L., XXII, 592).

This is all that is known concerning the life of Nicetas. Particulars concerning his literary activity are also given by Gennadius and Paulinus. The tradition concerning his writings afterwards became confused: his works were erroneously ascribed to Bishop Nicetas of Aquileia (second half of the fifth century) and to Nicetius of Trier. It was not until the researches of Dom Morin, Burn, and others that a larger knowledge was attained concerning the works of Nicetas. Gennadius (loc. cit.) mentions six books written by him in simple and clear style (*simplici et nitido sermone*), containing instructions for candidates for baptism (*competentes*). The first book dealt with the conduct of the candidates; the second treated of erroneous ideas of heathens; the third, of belief in one Divine Majesty; the fourth, of superstitious customs at the birth of a child (calculating nativities); the fifth, of confession of faith; the sixth, of the sacrifice of the paschal lamb. The work has not been preserved in its entirety, yet the greater part is still extant. Four fragments are known of the first book, one fragment of the second, the third probably consists of the two treatises, usually separated, but which undoubtedly belong together, namely, "De ratione fidei" and "De Spiritus sancti potentia" (P. L., LII, 847, 853). Nothing is known of the fourth book. The fifth, however, is most probably identical with the "Explanatio symboli habita ad competentes" (P. L., LII, 865–74); in the manuscripts it is sometimes ascribed to Origen, sometimes to Nicetas of Aquileia, but there are very strong reasons for assigning it to the Bishop of Remesiana. Nothing is known of the sixth book. Gennadius mentions another treatise addressed to a fallen virgin, "Ad lapsam virginem libellus", remarking that it would stimulate to reformation any who had fallen. This treatise used to be wrongly identified with the "De lapsu virginis consecratæ" (P. L., XVI, 367–84), traditionally assigned to St. Ambrose. Dom Morin has edited a treatise, unknown until he published it, "Epistola ad virginem lapsam" [Revue Bénédictine, XIV (1897), 193–202], which with far more reason may be regarded as the work of Nicetas.

Paulinus of Nola praises his friend as a hymn-writer; from this it is evident that Gennadius has not given a complete list of the writings of Nicetas. It is, therefore, not impossible that further works, incorrectly ascribed by tradition to others, are really his. Morin has given excellent reasons to prove that the two treatises, "De vigiliis servorum Dei" and "De psalmodiæ bono", which were held to be writings of Nicetius of Trier (P. L., LXVIII, 365–76), are in reality the work of Nicetas ["Revue Biblique Internat.", VI (1897), 282–88; "Revue Bénédictine", XIV (1897), 385–97, where Morin gives for the first time the complete text of "De psalmodiæ bono"]. Particularly interesting is the fresh proof produced—again by Morin—to show that Nicetas, and not St. Ambrose, is the author of the "Te Deum" [Revue Bénédictine, XI (1894), 49–77, 377–345]. Paulinus, like Jerome, speaks of him particularly as a hymn-writer. (See TE DEUM.) According to the testimony of Cassiodorus (De instit. divinarum litterarum, xvi) the "Liber de Fide" of Nicetas was, in his time, included in the treatise "De Fide" written by St. Ambrose, which shows that at an early date some were found to credit the great Bishop of Milan with works due to the Dacian bishop. The first complete edition of the works of Nicetas is that of Burn (see bibliography below).

BURN, *Niceta of Remesiana, His Life and Works* (Cambridge, 1905); WEYMAN, *Die Editio princeps des Niceta von Remesiana* in *Archiv für lateinische Lexikographie*, XIV (1905), 478–507; HÜMPEL, *Nicetas Bischof von Remesiana* (Erlangen, 1895); CZAPLA, *Gennadius als Literarhistoriker* (Münster, 1898), 56–61; TURNER, *Niceta and Ambrosiaster* in *Journal of Theological Studies*, VII (1906), 203–19, 355–72; PATIN, *Niceta Bischof von Remesiana als Schriftsteller und Theolog.* (Munich, 1909); BARDENHEWER, *Patrology*, tr. SHAHAN (St. Louis, 1907); KIHN, *Patrologie*, II (Paderborn, 1908), 134–36.

J. P. KIRSCH.

Nicetas Akominatos. See AKOMINATOS.

Nicetius, SAINT, Bishop of Trier, b. in the latter part of the fifth century, exact date unknown; d. in 563 or more probably 566. Saint Nicetius was the most important bishop of the ancient See of Trier, in the era when, after the disorders of the Migrations, Frankish supremacy began in what had been Roman Gaul. Considerable detail of the life of this vigorous and zealous bishop is known from various sources, from letters written either by or to him, from two poems of Venantius Fortunatus (Poem., Lib. III, ix, x, ed. Leo, in Mon. Germ. Hist.: Auct. antiq., IV (1881), Pt. I, 63–64 sq.) and above all from the statements of his pupil Aredius, later Abbot of Limoges, which have been preserved by Gregory of Tours (De vitis Patrum, xvii; De Gloria Confessorum, xciii–xciv). Nicetius came from a Gallo-Roman family; his home was apparently in Auvergne. The Nicetius mentioned by Sidonius Apollinaris (Epist. VIII, vi) may have been a relative. From his youth he devoted himself to religious life and entered a monastery, where he developed so rapidly in the exercise of Christian virtue and in sacred learning that he was made abbot. It was while abbot that King Theodoric I (511–34) learned to know and esteem him, Nicetius often remonstrating with him on account of his wrong-doing without, however, any loss of favour. After the death of Bishop Aprunculus of Trier, an embassy of the clergy and citizens of Trier came to the royal court to elect a new bishop. They desired Saint Gallus, but the king refused his consent. They then selected Abbot Nicetius, whose election was confirmed by Theodoric. About 527 Nicetius set out as the new bishop for Trier, accompanied by an escort sent by the king, and while on the journey had opportunity to make known his firmness in the administration of his office.

Trier had suffered terribly during the disorders of the Migrations. One of the first cares of the new bishop was to rebuild the cathedral church, the restoration of which is mentioned by the poet Venantius Fortunatus. Archæological research has shown, in the cathedral of Trier, the existence of mason-work belonging to the Frankish period which may belong to this reconstruction by Nicetius. A fortified castle (*castellum*) with a chapel built by him on the river Moselle is also mentioned by the same poet (Poem., Lib. III, n. xii). The saintly bishop devoted himself with great zeal to his pastoral duty. He preached daily, opposed vigorously the numerous evils in the moral life both of the higher classes and of the common people, and in so doing did not spare the king and his courtiers. Disregarding threats, he steadfastly fulfilled his duty. On account of his misdeeds he excommunicated King Clotaire I (511–61), who for some time was sole ruler of the Frankish dominions; in return the king exiled the determined bishop (560). The king died, however, in the following year, and his son and successor Sigebert, the ruler of Austrasia (561–75), allowed Nicetius to return home. Nicetius took part in several synods of the Frankish bishops: the synod of Clermont (535), of Orléans (549), the second synod of Clermont (549), the synod of Toul (550) at which he presided, and the synod of Paris (555).

Nicetius corresponded with ecclesiastical dignitaries of high rank in distant places. Letters are extant that were written to him by Abbot Florianus of Romain-Moûtier (Canton of Vaud, Switzerland), by Bishop Rufus of Octodurum (now Martigny, in the Canton of Valais, Switzerland), and by Archbishop Mappinius of Reims. The general interests of the Church did not escape his watchful care. He wrote an urgent letter to Emperor Justinian of Constantinople in regard to the emperor's position in the controversies arising from Monophysitism. Another letter that has been preserved is to Clodosvinda, wife of the Lombard King Alboin, in which he exhorts this princess to do everything possible to bring her husband over to the Catholic faith. In his personal life the saintly bishop was very ascetic and self-mortifying; he fasted frequently, and while the priests and clerics who lived with him were at their evening meal he would go, concealed by a hooded cloak, to pray in the churches of the city. He founded a school of his own for the training of the clergy. The best known of his pupils is the later Abbot of Limoges, Aredius, who was the authority of Gregory of Tours for the latter's biographical account of Nicetius. Nicetius was buried in the church of St. Maximin at Trier. His feast is celebrated at Trier on 1 October; in the Roman Martyrology his name is placed under 5 December. The genuineness of two treatises ascribed to him is doubtful: "De Vigiliis servorum Dei" and "De Psalmodiæ Bono".

Nicetius Opera in P. L. LXIII, 361 sqq.; HONTHEIM, *Historia Trevirensis diplomatica*, I (Augsburg, 1750), lx, 35 sqq.; IDEM, *Prodromus historiæ Trevirensis*, I (Augsburg, 1757), 415 sqq.; MABILLON, *Acta Sanct. ord. S. Benedicti*, I (Paris, 1668), 191 sqq.; MARX, *Geschichte des Erzstifts Trier*, I (Trier, 1858), 82 sq.; II, 377 sq.; MANDERNACH, *Die Schriften des hl. Nicetius, Bischof von Trier* (Mainz, 1850); KAYSER, *Leben und Schriften des hl. Nicetius* (Trier, 1873); MORIN in *Revue bénédictine* (1897), 385 sqq.

J. P. KIRSCH.

Niche, a recess for the reception of a statue, so designed as to give it emphasis, frame it effectively, and afford some measure of protection. It hardly existed prior to the twelfth century, and is one of the chief decorative characteristics of Gothic architecture. The constant and often lavish use of sculptured images of the saints was an essential part of the great style that was so perfectly to express the Catholic Faith, and that had its beginnings in Normandy as a result of the great Cluniac reformation; and from the moment the roughly chiselled bas-relief swelled into the round and detached figure, the unerring artistic instinct of the medieval builders taught them—as it had taught the Greeks—that figure sculpture becomes architectural only when it is incorporated with the building of which it is a part, by means of surrounding architectural forms that harmonize it with the fabric itself. In Romanesque work this frame is little more than flanking shafts supporting an arch, the statue being treated as an accessory, and given place wherever a space of flat wall appeared between the columns and arches of the structural decoration. The convenience, propriety and beauty of the arrangement were immediately apparent, however, and thenceforward the development of the niche as an independent architectural form was constant and rapid. Not only did the canopied niche assimilate the statue in the architectural entity and afford it that protection from the weather so necessary in the north; it also, in conjunction with the statue itself, produced one of the richest compositions of line, light, and shade known to art. The medieval architects realized this and seized upon it with avidity, using it almost as their chief means for obtaining those spots and spaces of rich decoration that gave the final touch of perfection to their marvellous fabrics. In the thirteenth century the wall became recessed to receive the statue, the flanking shafts became independent supports for an arched and gabled canopy, while a pedestal was introduced, still further to tie the sculpture into the architecture. Later the section of the embrasure became hexagonal or octagonal, the arched canopy was cusped, the gable enriched with crockets and pinnacles, and finally in the fourteenth and fifteenth centuries the entire feature became almost an independent composition, the canopy being developed into a thing of marvellous complexity and richness, while it was lavished on almost every part of the building, from the doors to the spires, and within as well as without. Protestant and revolutionary iconoclasm have left outside of France few examples of niches properly filled by their original statues, but in such masterpieces of art as the cathedrals of Paris, Chartres, Amiens, and Reims, one may see in their highest perfection these unique manifestations of the subtility and refinement of the perfect art of Catholic civilization.

RALPH ADAMS CRAM.

Nicholas I, SAINT, POPE, b. at Rome, date unknown; d. 13 November, 867; one of the great popes of the Middle Ages, who exerted decisive influence upon the historical development of the papacy and its position among the Christian nations of Western Europe. He was of a distinguished family, being the son of the Defensor Theodore, and received an excellent training. Already distinguished for his piety, benevolence, ability, knowledge, and eloquence, he entered, at an early age, the service of the Church, was made subdeacon by Pope Sergius II (844–47), and deacon by Leo IV (847–55). He was employed in all important matters during the pontificate of his predecessor, Benedict III (855–58). After Benedict's death (7 April, 858) the Emperor Louis II, who was in the neighbourhood of Rome, came into the city to exert his influence upon the election. On 24 April Nicholas was elected pope, and on the same day was consecrated and enthroned in St. Peter's in the presence of the emperor. Three days after, he gave a farewell banquet to the emperor, and afterwards, accompanied by the Roman nobility, visited him in his camp before the city, on which occasion the emperor came to meet the pope and led his horse for some distance.

Christianity in Western Europe was then in a most melancholy condition. The empire of Charlemagne had fallen to pieces, Christian territory was threatened both from the north and the east, and Christendom seemed on the brink of anarchy. Christian morality was despised; many bishops were worldly and unworthy of their office. There was danger of a universal decline of the higher civilization. Pope Nicholas appeared as a conscientious representative of the Roman Primacy in the Church. He was filled with a high conception of his mission for the vindication of Christian morality, the defence of God's law against princes and dignitaries, and of ecclesiastical law against powerful bishops. Archbishop John of Ravenna oppressed the inhabitants of the papal territory, treated his suffragan bishops with violence, made unjust demands upon them for money, and illegally imprisoned priests. He also forged documents to support his claims against the Roman See and maltreated the papal legates. As the warnings of the pope were without result, and the archbishop ignored a thrice-repeated summons to appear before the papal tribunal, he was excommunicated. Having first visited the Emperor Louis at Pavia, the archbishop repaired, with two imperial delegates, to Rome, where Nicholas cited him before the Roman synod assembled in the autumn of 860. Upon this John fled from Rome. Going in person to Ravenna, the pope then investigated and equitably regulated everything. Again appealing to the emperor, the archbishop was recommended by him to submit to the pope, which he did at the Roman Synod of November, 861. Later on, however, he entered into a pact with the excommunicated Archbishops of Trier and Cologne, was himself again excommunicated, and once more forced to make his submission to the pope. Another conflict arose between Nicholas and Archbishop Hincmar of Reims: this concerned the prerogatives of the papacy. Bishop Rothad of Soissons had appealed to the pope against the decision of the Synod of Soissons, of 861, which had deposed him; Hincmar opposed the appeal to the pope, but eventually had to acknowledge the right of the papacy to take cognizance of important legal causes (*causæ majores*) and pass independent judgment upon them. A further dispute broke out between Hincmar and the pope as to the elevation of the cleric Wulfad to the archiepiscopal See of Bourges, but here, again, Hincmar finally submitted to the decrees of the Apostolic See, and the Frankish synods passed corresponding ordinances.

Nicholas showed the same zeal in other efforts to maintain ecclesiastical discipline, especially as to the marriage laws. Ingiltrud, wife of Count Boso, had left her husband for a paramour; Nicholas commanded the bishops in the dominions of Charles the Bold to excommunicate her unless she returned to her husband. As she paid no attention to the summons to appear before the Synod of Milan in 860, she was put under the ban. The pope was also involved in a desperate struggle with Lothair II of Lorraine over the inviolability of marriage. Lothair had abandoned his lawful wife Theutberga to marry Waldrada. At the Synod of Aachen, 28 April, 862, the bishops of Lorraine, unmindful of their duty, approved of this illicit union. At the Synod of Metz, June, 863, the papal legates, bribed by the king, assented to the Aachen decision, and condemned the absent Theutberga. Upon this the pope brought the matter before his own tribunal. The two archbishops, Günther of Cologne and Thietgaud of Trier, who had come to Rome as delegates, were summoned before the Lateran Synod of October, 863, when the pope condemned and deposed them as well as John of Ravenna and Hagano of Bergamo. The Emperor Louis II took up the cause of the deposed bishops, while King Lothair advanced upon Rome with an army and laid siege to the city, so that the pope was confined for two days in St. Peter's without food. Yet Nicholas did not waver in his determination; the emperor, after being reconciled with the pope, withdrew from Rome and commanded the Archbishops of Trier and Cologne to return to their homes. Nicholas never ceased from his efforts to bring about a reconciliation between Lothair and his lawful wife, but without effect. Another matrimonial case in which Nicholas interposed was that of Judith, daughter of Charles the Bold, who had married Baldwin, Count of Flanders, without her father's consent. Frankish bishops had excommunicated Judith, and Hincmar of Reims had taken sides against her, but Nicholas urged leniency, in order to protect freedom of marriage. He commanded Hincmar to bring about a reconciliation between father and daughter, and succeeded in obtaining Charles's consent to the marriage. In many other ecclesiastical matters, also, he issued letters and decisions, and he took active measures against bishops who were neglectful of their duties.

In the matter of the emperor and the patriarchs of Constantinople Nicholas showed himself the Divinely appointed ruler of the Church. In violation of ecclesiastical law, the Patriarch Ignatius was deposed in 857 and Photius illegally raised to the patriarchal see. In a letter addressed (8 May, 862) to the patriarchs of the East, Nicholas called upon them and all their bishops to refuse recognition to Photius, and at a Roman synod held in April, 863, he excommunicated Photius. He also encouraged the missionary activity of the Church. He sanctioned the union of the Sees of Bremen and Hamburg, and confirmed to St. Anschar, Archbishop of Bremen, and his successors the office of papal legate to the Danes, Swedes, and Slavs. Bulgaria having been converted by Greek missionaries, its ruler, Prince Boris, in August, 863, sent an embassy to the pope with one hundred and six questions on the teaching and discipline of the Church. Nicholas answered these inquiries exhaustively in the celebrated "Responsa Nicolai ad consulta Bulgarorum" (Mansi, "Coll. Conc.", XV, 401 sqq.). The letter shows how keen was his desire to foster the principles of an earnest Christian life in this newly-converted people. At the same time he sent an embassy to Prince Boris, charged to use their personal efforts to attain the pope's object. Nevertheless, Boris finally joined the Eastern Church.

At Rome, Nicholas rebuilt and endowed several

churches, and constantly sought to encourage religious life. His own personal life was guided by a spirit of earnest Christian asceticism and profound piety. He was very highly esteemed by the citizens of Rome, as he was by his contemporaries generally (cf. Regino, "Chronicon", ad an. 868, in "Mon. Germ. Hist.: Script.", I, 579), and after death was regarded as a saint. A much discussed question and one that is important in judging the position taken by this pope is, whether he made use of the forged pseudo-Isidorian papal decretals. After exhaustive investigation, Schrörs has decided that the pope was neither acquainted with the pseudo-Isidorian collection in its entire extent, nor did he make use of its individual parts; that he had perhaps a general knowledge of the false decretals, but did not base his view of the law upon them, and that he owed his knowledge of them solely to documents which came to him from the Frankish Empire [Schrörs, "Papst Nikolaus I. und Pseudo-Isidor" in "Historisches Jahrbuch", XXV (1904), 1 sqq.; Idem, "Die pseudoisidorische 'Exceptio spolii' bei Papst Nikolaus I" in "Historisches Jahrbuch", XXVI (1905), 275 sqq.].

Roy, *St. Nicholas I* (London, 1901), in *Saints Series; Nicolai pp. I. Epistolæ*, in Jaffé, *Regesta Rom. Pont.*, I (2nd ed.), 342 sqq., and in Mansi, *Coll. Conc.*, XV, 143 sqq.; *Liber Pontificalis*, ed. Duchesne, II, 151 sqq.; Laemmer, *Papst Nicolaus I. und die byzantinische Staatskirche seiner Zeit* (Berlin, 1857); Thiel, *De Nicolao I commentationes duæ historico-canonicæ* (Braunsberg, 1859); Greinacher, *Die Anschauungen des Papstes Nikolaus I. über das Verhältnis von Staat und Kirche* (Berlin, 1909); Langen, *Geschichte der römischen Kirche*, III: *Von Nikolaus I bis Gregor VII* (Bonn, 1892), 1 sqq.; Hefele, *Conciliengeschichte*, II (4th ed.), 112 sqq., ed. Kirsch; 236 sqq. See also bibliography to Hincmar, Archbishop of Reims; Ignatius of Constantinople, Saint; Photius.
J. P. Kirsch.

Nicholas II, Pope (Gerhard of Burgundy), b. at Chevron, in what is now Savoy; elected at Siena, December, 1058; d. at Florence 19 or 27 July, 1061. Like his predecessor, Stephen X, he was canon at Liège. In 1046 he became Bishop of Florence, where he restored the canonical life among the clergy of numerous churches. As soon as the news of the death of Stephen X at Florence reached Rome (4 April, 1058), the Tusculan party appointed a successor in the person of John Mincius, Bishop of Velletri, under the name of Benedict X. His elevation, due to violence and corruption, was contrary to the specific orders of Stephen X that, at his death, no choice of a successor was to be made until Hildebrand's return from Germany. Several cardinals protested against the irregular proceedings, but they were compelled to flee from Rome. Hildebrand was returning from his mission when the news of these events reached him. He interrupted his journey at Florence, and after agreeing with Duke Godfrey of Lorraine-Tuscany upon Bishop Gerhard for elevation to the papacy, he won over part of the Roman population to the support of his candidate. An embassy dispatched to the imperial court secured the confirmation of the choice by the Empress Agnes. At Hildebrand's invitation, the cardinals met in December, 1058, at Siena and elected Gerhard who assumed the name of Nicholas II. On his way to Rome the new pope held at Sutri a well-attended synod at which, in the presence of Duke Godfrey and the imperial chancellor, Guibert of Parma, he pronounced deposition against Benedict X. The latter was driven from the city in January, 1059, and the solemn coronation of Nicholas took place on the twenty-fourth of the same month. A cultured and stainless man, the new pontiff had about him capable advisers, but to meet the danger still threatening from Benedict X and his armed supporters, Nicholas empowered Hildebrand to enter into negotiations with the Normans of southern Italy. The papal envoy recognized Count Richard of Aversa as Prince of Capua and received in return Norman troops which enabled the papacy to carry on hostilities against Benedict in the Campagna. This campaign did not result in the decisive overthrow of the opposition party, but it enabled Nicholas to undertake in the early part of 1059 a pastoral visitation to Spoleto, Farfa, and Osimo. During this journey he raised Abbot Desiderius of Monte Cassino to the dignity of cardinal-priest and appointed him legate to Campania, Benevento, Apulia, and Calabria. Early in his pontificate he had sent St. Peter Damiani and Bishop Anselm of Lucca as his legates to Milan, where a married and simoniacal clergy had recently given rise to a reform-party known as the "Pataria". A synod for the restoration of ecclesiastical discipline was held under the presidency of these envoys who, in spite of a tumultuous uprising which endangered their lives, succeeded in obtaining from Archbishop Guido and the Milanese clergy a solemn repudiation of simony and concubinage.

One of the most pressing needs of the time was the reform of papal elections. It was right that they should be freed from the nefarious influence of the Roman factions and the secular control of the emperor, hitherto less disastrous but always objectionable. To this end Nicholas II held in the Lateran at Easter, 1059 a synod attended by one hundred and thirteen bishops and famous for its law concerning papal elections. Efforts to determine the authentic text of this decree caused considerable controversy in the nineteenth century. That the discussions did not result in a consensus of opinion on the matter need not surprise, if it be remembered that thirty years after the publication of the decree complaints were heard regarding the divergency in the text. We possess to-day a papal and an imperial recension and the sense of the law may be stated substantially as follows: (1) At the death of the pope, the cardinal-bishops are to confer among themselves concerning a candidate, and, after they have agreed upon a name, they and the other cardinals are to proceed to the election. The remainder of the clergy and the laity enjoy the right of acclaiming their choice. (2) A member of the Roman clergy is to be chosen, except that where a qualified candidate cannot be found in the Roman Church, an ecclesiastic from another diocese may be elected. (3) The election is to be held at Rome, except that when a free choice is impossible there, it may take place elsewhere. (4) If war or other circumstances prevent the solemn enthronization of the new pope in St. Peter's Chair, he shall nevertheless enjoy the exercise of full Apostolic authority. (5) Due regard is to be had for the right of confirmation or recognition conceded to King Henry, and the same deference is to be shown to his successors, who have been granted personally a like privilege. These stipulations constituted indeed a new law, but they were also intended as an implicit approbation of the procedure followed at the election of Nicholas II. As to the imperial right of confirmation, it became a mere personal privilege granted by the Roman See. The same synod prohibited simoniacal ordinations, lay investiture, and assistance at the Mass of a priest living in notorious concubinage. The rules governing the life of canons and nuns which were published at the diet of Aix-la-Chapelle (817) were abolished, because they allowed private property and such abundant food that, as the bishops indignantly exclaimed, they were adapted to sailors and intemperate matrons rather than to clerics and nuns. Berengarius of Tours, whose views opposed to the doctrine of Christ's real presence in the Eucharist, had repeatedly been condemned, also appeared at the Council and was compelled to sign a formula of abjuration.

At the end of June, 1059, Nicholas proceeded to Monte Cassino and thence to Melfi, the capital of Norman Apulia, where he held an important synod and concluded the famous alliance with the Normans (July-August, 1059). Duke Robert Guiscard was invested with the sovereignty of Apulia, Calabria, and Sicily in case he should reconquer it from the Saracens; he bound himself, in return, to pay an annual tribute, to hold his lands as the pope's vassal, and to protect the Roman See, its possessions, and the freedom of papal elections. A similar agreement was concluded with Prince Richard of Capua. After holding a synod at Benevento Nicholas returned to Rome with a Norman army which reconquered Præneste, Tusculum, and Numentanum for the Holy See and forced Benedict X to capitulate at Galeria (autumn of 1059). Hildebrand, the soul of the pontificate, was now created archdeacon. In order to secure the general acceptance of the laws enacted at the synod of 1059, Cardinal Stephen, in the latter part of that year, was sent to France where he presided over the synods of Vienne (31 January, 1060) and Tours (17 February, 1060). The decree which introduced a new method of papal election had caused great dissatisfaction in Germany, because it reduced the imperial right of confirmation to the precarious condition of a personal privilege granted at will; but, assured of Norman protection, Nicholas could fearlessly renew the decree at the Lateran synod held in 1060. After this council Cardinal Stephen, who had accomplished his mission to France, appeared as papal legate in Germany. For five days he vainly solicited an audience at court and then returned to Rome. His fruitless mission was followed by a German synod which annulled all the ordinances of Nicholas II and pronounced his deposition. The pope's answer was a repetition of the decree concerning elections at the synod of 1061, at which the condemnation of simony and concubinage among the clergy was likewise renewed. He lies buried in the church of St. Reparata at Florence of which city he had remained bishop even after his elevation to the papal throne. His pontificate, though of short duration, was marked by events fraught with momentous and far-reaching consequences.

JAFFÉ, *Regesta Pontif. Roman.*, I (2nd ed., Leipzig, 1885), 557–66; *Diplomata, Epistolæ, Decreta* in *P. L.*, CXLIII, 1301–66; CLAVEL, *Le Pape Nicolas II* (Lyons, 1906); DELARC, *Le Pontificat de Nicolas II* in *Rev. des Quest. Hist.*, XL (1886), 341–402; WURM, *Die Papstwahl* (Cologne, 1902), 24–8; HEFELE, *Conciliengeschichte*, IV (2nd ed., Freiburg, 1879), 798–850; MANN, *Lives of the Popes*, VI (St. Louis, 1910), 226–60; FUNK, tr. CAPPADELTA, *Church History*, I (St. Louis, 1910), 263–4, 274. For bibliography of the election decree, see HERGENRÖTHER-KIRSCH, *Kirchengeschichte*, II (Freiburg, 1904), 342–4.

N. A. WEBER.

Nicholas III, POPE (GIOVANNI GAETANI ORSINI), b. at Rome, c. 1216; elected at Viterbo, 25 November, 1277; d. at Soriano, near Viterbo, 22 August, 1280. His father, Matteo Rosso, was of the illustrious Roman family of the Orsini, while his mother, Perna Gaetana, belonged to the noble house of the Gaetani. As senator Matteo Rosso had defended Rome against Frederick II and saved it to the papacy. He was a friend of St. Francis of Assisi and belonged to his third order, facts not without influence on the son, for both as cardinal and pope the latter was ever kindly disposed towards the Franciscans. We have no knowledge of his education and early life. Innocent IV, grateful for the services rendered to the Holy See by his father, created the young Orsini (28 May, 1244) cardinal-deacon with the title of St. Nicholas in Carcere Tulliano, and gave him benefices at York, Laon, and Soissons. Probably at an earlier date the administration of the Roman churches of San Lorenzo in Damaso and of San Crisogono had been entrusted to him. One of five cardinals, he accompanied Innocent IV in his flight from Civitá Vecchia to Genoa and thence to Lyons (29 June, 1244). In 1252 he was dispatched on an unsuccessful mission of peace to the warring Guelphs and Ghibellines of Florence. In 1258 Louis IX paid an eloquent tribute to his independence and impartiality by suggesting his selection as equally acceptable to England and to France for the solemn ratification of the peace concluded between the two countries. His integrity was likewise above reproach, for he never accepted gifts for his services. So great was his influence in the Sacred College that the election of Urban IV (1261) was mainly due to his intervention. Urban named him general inquisitor (1262) and protector of the Franciscans (1263). Under Clement IV (1265–68) he was a member of the delegation of four cardinals who invested Charles of Anjou with the Kingdom of Naples (28 June, 1265). Later he played a prominent part at the elections of Gregory X, who received the tiara at his hands, and of John XXI, whose counsellor he became and who named him archpriest of St. Peter's. After a vacancy of six months he succeeded John as Nicholas III.

ARMS OF NICHOLAS III

True to his origin he endeavoured to free Rome from all foreign influence. His policy aimed not only at the exclusion of the ever-troublesome imperial authority, but also sought to check the growing influence of Charles of Anjou in central Italy. At his request Rudolf of Habsburg renounced (1278) all rights to the possession of the Romagna, a renunciation subsequently approved by the imperial princes. Nicholas took possession of the province through his nephew, Latino, whom he had shortly before (12 March, 1278) raised to the cardinalate. He created Berthold, another nephew, Count of the Romagna, and on other occasions remembered his relatives in the distribution of honourable and lucrative places. He compelled Charles of Anjou in 1278 to resign the regency of Tuscany and the dignity of Roman Senator. To insure the freedom of papal elections, he ordained in a constitution of 18 July, 1278, that thenceforward the senatorial power and all municipal offices were to be reserved to Roman citizens to the exclusion of emperor, king, or other potentate. In furtherance of more harmonious relations with the Byzantine court, the pope also aimed at restricting the power of the King of Naples in the East. To his efforts was due the agreement concluded in 1280 between Rudolf of Habsburg and Charles of Anjou, by which the latter accepted Provence and Forcalquier as imperial fiefs and secured the betrothal of his grandson to Clementia, one of Rudolf's daughters. The much-discussed plan of a new division of the empire into four parts is not sufficiently attested to be attributed with certainty to Nicholas. In this partition Germany, as hereditary monarchy, was to fall to Rudolf, the Kingdom of Arles was to devolve on his son-in-law, Charles Martel of Anjou, while the Kingdoms of Lombardy and Tuscany were to be founded in Italy and bestowed on relatives of the pope. Nicholas's efforts for the promotion of peace between France and Castile remained fruitless. Unable to carry out his desire of personally appearing in Hungary, where internal dissensions and the devastations of the Cumani endangered the very existence of Christianity, he named, in the fall of 1278, Bishop Philip of Fermo his legate to that country. A synod, held at Buda in 1279 under the presidency of the papal envoy, could not complete its deliberations owing to the violent interference of the people. King Ladislaus IV, instigator of the trouble, was threatened in a papal letter with spiritual and temporal penalties if he failed to reform his ways. The king temporarily heeded this solemn admonition, and at a later date suppressed the raids of the Cumani. The appointments of worthy incumbents to the Archbishoprics of Gran and Kalocsa-Bacs made under this pontificate further helped to strengthen the cause of Christianity.

The task of Nicholas III in his dealings with the Eastern Church was the practical realization of the union accepted by the Greeks at the Second Council of Lyons (1274), for political reasons rather than out of dogmatic persuasion. The instructions to the legates whom he sent to Constantinople contained, among other conditions, the renewal by the emperor of the oath sworn to by his representatives at Lyons. The maintenance of the Greek Rite was granted only in so far as papal authority did not consider it opposed to unity of faith; those of the clergy opposed to reunion were required to obtain absolution of the incurred censures from the Roman envoys. These were more rigorous conditions than had been imposed by his predecessors, but the failure of the negotiations for reunion can hardly be attributed to them, for the Greek nation was strongly opposed to submission to Rome and the emperor pursued temporal advantages under cover of desire for ecclesiastical harmony. At the request of Abaga, Khan of the Tatars, the pope sent him in 1278 five Franciscan missionaries who were to preach the Gospel first in Persia and then in China. They encountered considerable obstacles in the former country and it was not until the pontificate of Nicholas IV that their preaching produced appreciable results. The realization of the pope's desire for the organization of a Crusade was frustrated by the distracted state of European politics. On 14 August, 1279, he issued the constitution "Exiit qui seminat", which is still fundamental for the interpretation of the Rule of St. Francis and in which he approved the stricter observance of poverty (see FRANCIS, RULE OF SAINT). While the Vatican had been occupied from time to time by some of his predecessors, Nicholas III established there the papal residence, remodelled and enlarged the palace, and secured in its neighbourhood landed property, subsequently transformed into the Vatican gardens. He lies buried in the Chapel of St. Nicholas, built by him in St. Peter's. He was an ecclesiastically-minded pontiff of great diplomatic ability and, if we except his acts of nepotism, of unblemished character.

GAY, *Les Registres de Nicolas III* (Paris, 1898–1904); POTTHAST, *Regesta Pontif. Roman.*, II (Berlin, 1875), 1719–56; SAVIO, *Niccolò III* in *Civiltà Cattolica*, ser. XV–XVI (Rome, 1894–5); DEMSKI, *Papst Nikolaus III* (Münster, 1903); STERNFELD, *Der Kardinal Johann Gaetan Orsini (1244–77)* (Berlin, 1905); MIRBT in *The New Schaff-Herzog Encyclopedia*, s. v.

N. A. WEBER.

Nicholas IV, POPE (GIROLAMO MASCI), b. at Ascoli in the March of Ancona; d. in Rome, 4 April, 1292. He was of humble extraction, and at an early age entered the Franciscan Order. In 1272 he was sent as a delegate to Constantinople to invite the participation of the Greeks in the Second Council of Lyons. Two years later he succeeded St. Bonaventure in the generalship of his order. While he was on a mission to France to promote the restoration of peace between that country and Castile, he was created cardinal-priest with the title of Santa Pudenziana (1278) and in 1281 Martin IV appointed him Bishop of Palestrina. After the death of Honorius IV (3 April, 1287), the conclave held at Rome was for a time hopelessly divided in its selection of a successor. When fever had carried off six of the electors, the others, with the sole exception of Girolamo, left Rome. It was not until the following year that they reassembled and on 15 February, 1288, unanimously elected him to the papacy. Obedience and a second election however (22 February) were alone capable of overcoming his reluctance to accept the supreme pontificate. He was the first Franciscan pope, and in loving remembrance of Nicholas III he assumed the name of Nicholas IV.

ARMS OF NICHOLAS IV

The reign of the new pope was not characterized by sufficient independence. The undue influence exercised at Rome by the Colonna is especially noteworthy and was so apparent even during his lifetime that Roman wits represented him encased in a column—the distinctive mark of the Colonna family—out of which only his tiara-covered head emerged. The efforts of Rudolf of Habsburg to receive the imperial crown at the hands of the new pope were not successful. His failure was partly due to the estrangement consequent upon the attitude assumed by the pope in the question of the Sicilian succession. As feudal suzerain of the kingdom, Nicholas annulled the treaty, concluded in 1288 through the mediation of Edward I of England, which confirmed James of Aragon in the possession of the island. He lent his support to the rival claims of the House of Anjou and crowned Charles II King of Sicily and Naples at Rieti, 29 May, 1289, after the latter had expressly acknowledged the suzerainty of the Apostolic See and promised not to accept any municipal dignity in the States of the Church. The action of the pope did not end the armed struggle for the possession of Sicily nor did it secure the kingdom permanently to the House of Anjou. Rudolf of Habsburg also failed to obtain from the pope the repeal of the authorization, granted the French king, to levy tithes in certain German districts for the prosecution of the war against the House

NICHOLAS IV
Benozzo Gozzoli, Church of S. Francesco, Montefalco

MONUMENT OF NICHOLAS IV
St. Mary Major's, Rome

of Aragon. When he appointed his son Albert to succeed Ladislaus IV of Hungary (31 August, 1290), Nicholas claimed the realm as a papal fief and conferred it upon Charles Martel, son of Charles II of Naples.

In 1291 the fall of Ptolemais put an end to Christian dominion in the East. Previous to this tragic event, Nicholas had in vain endeavoured to organize a crusade. He now called upon all the Christian princes to take up arms against the Mussulman and instigated the holding of councils to devise the means of sending assistance to the Holy Land. These synods were to discuss likewise the advisability of the union of the Knights Templars and Knights of St. John, as the dissensions among them had partly caused the loss of Ptolemais. The pope himself initiated the preparations for the crusade and fitted out twenty ships for the war. His appeals and his example remained unheeded, however, and nothing of permanent value was accomplished.

Nicholas IV sent missionaries, among them the celebrated John of Montecorvino (q. v.), to the Bulgarians, Ethiopians, Tatars, and Chinese. By his constitution of 18 July, 1289, the cardinals were granted one half of the revenues of the Apostolic See and a share in the financial administration. In 1290 he renewed the condemnation of the sect known as the Apostolici (q. v.). Nicholas was pious and learned; he contributed to the artistic beauty of Rome, building particularly a palace beside Santa Maria Maggiore, the church in which he was buried and where Sixtus V erected an imposing monument to his memory.

LANGLOIS, *Les Registres de Nicolas IV* (Paris, 1886–93); POTTHAST, *Regesta pontificum Romanorum*, II (Berlin, 1875), 1826–1915; KALTENBRUNNER, *Aktenstücke zur Gesch. des Deutschen Reiches unter Rudolf I und Albrecht I* (Vienna, 1889); REUMONT, *Gesch. der Stadt Rom*, II (Berlin, 1867), 611–14; SCHIFF, *Studien zur Gesch. Papst Nikolaus*, IV (Berlin, 1897); MASSI, *Niccolò IV* (Sinigaglia, 1905); SCHAFF, *History of the Christian Church*, V, pt. I (New York, 1907), 207, 287, 410.

N. A. WEBER.

Nicholas V, POPE (TOMMASO PARENTUCELLI), a name never to be mentioned without reverence by every lover of letters, b. at Sarzana in Liguria, 15 November, 1397; d. in Rome, 24–5 March, 1455. While still a youth he lost his father, a poor but skilful physician, and was thereby prevented from completing his studies at Bologna. He became tutor in the families of the Strozzi and Albizzi at Florence, where he made the acquaintance of the leading Humanist scholars of the day. In 1419 he returned to Bologna, and three years later took his degree as master of theology. The saintly bishop of Bologna, Niccolò Albergati, now took him into his service. For more than twenty years Parentucelli was the bishop's factotum, and in that capacity was enabled to indulge his passion for building and that of collecting books. Unlike many bibliophiles he was as well acquainted with the matter contained within his volumes as with their bindings and value. Some of them are still preserved, and contain many marginal notes in his beautiful writing. His knowledge was of the encyclopedic character not unusual at a time when the learned undertook to argue *de omni re scibili*. His mind, however, was receptive rather than productive. Nevertheless, he could make good use of what he had studied, as was shown at the Council of Florence where his familiarity with Patristic and Scholastic theology gave him a prominent place in the discussions with the Greek bishops. He accompanied Albergati in various legatine missions, notably to France, and was always watchful for rare and beautiful books. Eugene IV wished to attach such a brilliant scholar to his own person; but Parentucelli remained faithful to his patron. On the death of the latter he was appointed to succeed him in the See of Bologna, but was unable to take possession owing to the troubled state of the city. This led to his being entrusted by Pope Eugene with important diplomatic missions in Italy and Germany, which he carried out with such success that he obtained as his reward a cardinal's hat (Dec., 1446). Early next year (23 Feb.) Eugene died, and Parentucelli was elected in his place, taking as his name Nicholas in memory of his obligations to Niccolò Albergati (6 March, 1447).

ARMS OF NICHOLAS V

As soon as the new pontiff was firmly seated on his throne, it was felt that a new spirit had come into the papacy. Now that there was no longer any danger of a fresh outbreak of schism and the Council of Constance had lost all influence, Nicholas could devote himself to the accomplishment of objects which were the aim of his life and had been the means of raising him to his present exalted position. He designed to

MONUMENT OF NICHOLAS V (XV CENTURY)
The Vatican, Rome

make Rome the site of splendid monuments, the home of literature and art, the bulwark of the papacy, and the worthy capital of the Christian world. His first care was to strengthen the fortifications, and restore the churches in which the stations were held. Next he took in hand the cleansing and paving of the streets. Rome, once famous for the number and magnificence of its aqueducts, had become almost entirely dependent for its water supply on the Tiber and on wells and cisterns. The "Aqua Virgo", originally constructed by Agrippa, was restored by Nicholas, and is to this day the most prized by the Romans, under the name of "Acqua Trevi". But the works on which he especially set his heart were the rebuilding of the Leonine City, the Vatican, and the Basilica of St. Peter. On this spot, as in a centre, the glories of the papacy were to be focused. We cannot here enter into a description of the noble designs which he entertained (see Pastor, "History of the Popes", II, 173 sqq., Eng. tr.). The basilica, the palace, and the fortress of the popes are not now what he would have made them; but their actual splendours are due in no small measure to the lofty aspirations of Nicholas V. He has been severely censured for pulling down a portion of the old St. Peter's and planning the destruction of the remainder. He defended his action on the ground that the buildings were on the verge of ruin (Müntz, "Les Arts à la Cour des Papes", p. 118); but the almost equally ancient Basilica of San Paolo fuori le Mura was preserved by judicious restorations until it was destroyed by fire in 1823. The pontiff's veneration for antiquity may have yielded to his desire to construct an edifice more in harmony with the classical taste of the Renaissance school, of which he himself was so ardent an adherent. Nothing but praise, however, can be given to him for his work in the Vatican Palace. Indeed it was he who first made it the worthy residence of the popes. Some of his constructions still remain, notably the left side of the court of St. Damasus and the chapel of San Lorenzo, decorated with Fra Angelico's frescoes.

Though a patron of art in all its branches, it was literature that obtained his highest favours. His life-long love of books and his delight in the company of scholars could now be gratified to the full. His immediate predecessors had held the Humanists in suspicion; Nicholas welcomed them to the Vatican as friends. Carried away by his enthusiasm for the New Learning, he overlooked any irregularities in their morals or opinions. He accepted the dedication of a work by Poggio, in which Eugene was assailed as a hypocrite; Valla, the Voltaire of the Renaissance, was made an Apostolic notary. In spite of the demands on his resources for building purposes, he was always generous to deserving scholars. If any of them modestly declined his bounty, he would say: "Do not refuse; you will not always have a Nicholas among you." He set up a vast establishment in the Vatican for translating the Greek classics, so that all might become familiar with at least the matter of these masterpieces. "No department of literature owes so much to him as history. By him were introduced to the knowledge of western Europe two great and unrivalled models of historical composition, the work of Herodotus and the work of Thucydides. By him, too, our ancestors were first made acquainted with the graceful and lucid simplicity of Xenophon and with the manly good sense of Polybius" (Macaulay, Speech at Glasgow University). The crowning glory of his pontificate was the foundation of the Vatican Library. No lay sovereigns had such opportunities of collecting books as the popes. Nicholas's agents ransacked the monasteries and palaces of every country in Europe. Precious manuscripts, which would have been eaten by the moths or would have found their way to the furnace, were rescued from their ignorant owners and sumptuously housed in the Vatican. In this way he accumulated five thousand volumes at a cost of more than forty thousand *scudi*. "It was his greatest joy to walk about his library arranging the books and glancing through their pages, admiring the handsome bindings, and taking pleasure in contemplating his own arms stamped on those that had been dedicated to him, and dwelling in thought on the gratitude that future generations of scholars would entertain towards their benefactor. Thus he is to be seen depicted in one of the halls of the Vatican library, employed in settling his books" (Voigt, quoted by Pastor, II, 213).

His devotion to art and literature did not prevent him from the performance of his duties as Head of the Church. By the Concordat of Vienna (1448) he secured the recognition of the papal rights concerning bishoprics and benefices. He also brought about the submission of the last of the antipopes, Felix V, and the dissolution of the Synod of Basle (1449). In accordance with his general principle of impressing the popular mind by outward and visible signs, he proclaimed a Jubilee which was the fitting symbol of the cessation of the schism and the restoration of the authority of the popes (1450). Vast multitudes flocked to Rome in the first part of the year; but when the hot weather began, the plague which had been ravaging the countries north of the Alps wrought fearful havoc among the pilgrims. Nicholas was seized with a panic; he hurried away from the doomed city and fled from castle to castle in the hope of escaping infection. As soon as the pestilence abated he returned to Rome, and received the visits of many German princes and prelates who had long been upholders of the decrees of Constance and Basle. But another terrible calamity marred the general rejoicings. More than two hundred pilgrims lost their lives in a crush which occurred on the bridge of Sant' Angelo a few days before Christmas. Nicholas erected two chapels at the entrance of the bridge where Mass was to be said daily for the repose of the souls of the victims.

On this occasion, as in previous Jubilees, vast sums of money found their way into the treasury of the Church, thus enabling the pontiff to carry out his designs for the promotion of art and learning, and the support of the poor. As the Jubilee was the proof that Rome was the centre towards which all Christendom was drawn, so at its conclusion Nicholas sent forth his legates into the different countries to assert his authority and to bring about the reform of abuses. Cardinal D'Estouteville was sent to France; Cardinal Nicholas of Cusa, one of the most devout and learned men of his day, was sent to North Germany and England; and the heroic Franciscan, St. John Capistran, to South Germany. They held provincial and other synods and assemblies of the regular clergy, in which wholesome decrees were made. Nicholas of Cusa and St. John preached the word in season and out of season, thereby producing wonderful conversions among both clergy and laity. If they did not succeed in destroying the germs of the Protestant revolt, they certainly postponed for a while the evil and narrowed the sphere of its influence. It should be noted that Cusa never reached England, and that D'Estouteville initiated the process for the rehabilitation of Bl. Joan of Arc. The restored authority of the Holy See was further manifested by the coronation of Frederick III as Sovereign of the Holy Roman Empire —the first of the House of Habsburg raised to that dignity, and the last of the emperors crowned in Rome (1452).

Meantime the pontiff's own subjects caused him great anxiety. Stefano Porcaro, an able scholar and politician, who had enjoyed the favour of Martin V and Eugene IV, made several attempts to set up a republic in Rome. Twice he was pardoned and pensioned by the generous Nicholas, who would not sacrifice such an ornament of the New Learning. At last he was seized on the eve of a third plot, and condemned to death (Jan., 1453). A deep gloom now settled down on the pontiff. His magnificent designs for the glory of Rome and his mild government of his subjects had not been able to quell the spirit of rebellion. He began to collect troops and never stirred abroad without a strong guard. His health, too, began to suffer seriously, though he was by no means an old man. And before the conspiracy was thoroughly stamped out a fresh blow struck him from which he never recovered. We have seen what a prominent part Parentucelli had taken in the Council of Florence. The submission of the Greek bishops had not been sincere. On their return to Constantinople most of them openly rejected the decrees of the council and declared for the continuance of the schism. Eugene IV vainly endeavoured to stir up the Western nations against the ever-advancing Turks. Some help was given by the Republics of Venice and Genoa; but Hungary and Poland, more nearly menaced, supplied the bulk of the forces. A victory at Nish (1443) had been followed by two terrible defeats (Varna, 1444, and Kosovo, 1449). The whole of the Balkan peninsula, except Constantinople, was now at the mercy of the infidels. The emperor, Constantine XII, sent messages to Rome imploring the pope to summon the Christian peoples to his aid. Nicholas sternly reminded him of the promises made at Florence, and insisted that the terms of the union should be observed. Nevertheless the fear that the Turks would attack Italy, if they succeeded in capturing the bulwark of the east, induced the pontiff to take some action—especially as the emperor professed his readiness to accept the decrees of the council. In May, 1452, Cardinal Isidore, an enthusiastic Greek patriot, was sent as legate to Constantinople. A solemn function in honour of the union was celebrated on 12 Dec., 1452, with prayers for the pope and for the patriarch, Gregorius. But the clergy and the populace cursed the Uniates and boasted that they would rather submit to the turban of the Turk than to the tiara of the Roman Pontiff. After many obstacles and delays a force of ten papal galleys and a number of vessels furnished by Naples, Genoa, and Venice set sail for the East, but before they reached their destination the imperial city had fallen and the Emperor Constantine was no more (29 May, 1453). Whatever may have been the dilatoriness of Nicholas up to this point—and it must be acknowledged that he had good reason for not helping the Greeks—he now lost no time. He addressed a Bull of Crusade to the whole of Christendom. Every sort of inducement, spiritual and temporal, was held out to those who should take part in the holy war. Princes were exhorted to sink their differences and to unite against the common foe. But the days of chivalry were gone: most of the nations took no notice of the appeal; some of them, such as Genoa and Venice, even solicited the friendship of the infidels.

The gloom which had settled upon Nicholas after Porcaro's conspiracy grew deeper as he realized that his warning voice had been unheeded. Gout, fever, and other maladies warned him that his end was at hand. Summoning the cardinals around him, he delivered to them the famous discourse in which he set before them the objects for which he had laboured, and enumerated with pardonable pride the noble works which he had accomplished (Pastor, II, 311). He died on the night between 24 and 25 of March, 1455, and was laid in St. Peter's by the side of Eugene IV. His splendid tomb was taken down by Paul V, and removed to the crypt, where some portions of it may still be seen. His epitaph, the last by which any pope was commemorated, was written by Æneas Sylvius, afterwards Pius II.

Nicholas was small in stature and weakly in constitution. His features were clear-cut; his complexion pale; his eyes dark and piercing. In disposition he was lively and impetuous. A scholar rather than a man of action, he underrated difficulties, and was impatient when he was not instantly understood and obeyed. At the same time he was obliging and cheerful, and readily granted audience to his subjects. He was a man of sincere piety, simple and temperate in his habits. He was entirely free from the bane of nepotism, and exercised great care in the choice of cardinals. We may truly say that the lofty aims, the scholarly and artistic tastes, and the noble generosity of Nicholas form one of the brightest pages in the history of the popes.

PLATINA, *Lives of the Popes* (English translation, London); VESPASIANO DA BISTICCI, *Vite di uomini illustri del secolo XV* (Rome, 1839); SFORZA, *Ricerche su Niccolò V* (Lucca, 1884); MÜNTZ, *Les Arts à la cour des papes pendant le xve et le xvie siècle* (Paris, 1878–9); PASTOR, *History of the Popes*, II, 1–314, very complete and well documented (Eng. tr., London, 1891); GREGOROVIUS, *Gesch. der Stadt Rom* (Stuttgart, 1894); REUMONT, *Gesch. der Stadt Rom*, III (Berlin, 1867–70); CREIGHTON, *History of the Papacy*, III (London, 1897); GUIRAUD, *L'église romaine et les origines de la renaissance* (Paris, 1904); MILMAN, *History of Latin Christianity*, VIII (London, 1867).

T. B. SCANNELL.

Nicholas Justiniani, BLESSED, date of birth unknown, became monk in the Benedictine monastery of San Niccolò del Lido at Venice in 1153. When, in a military expedition of the Venetians in 1172, all the other members of the family of the Justiniani perished in the Ægean Sea near the Island of Chios, the Republic of Venice mourned over this disaster to so noble a family as over a public calamity. In order that the entire family might not die out, the Venetian Government sent Baron Morosin and Toma Falier as delegates to Alexander III, with the request to dispense Nicholas from his monastic vows. The dispensation was granted, and Nicholas married Anna, the daughter of Doge Michieli, becoming through her the parent of five new lines of his family. Shortly after 1179 he returned to the monastery of San Niccolò del Lido, having previously founded a convent for women on the Island of Aniano, where his wife took the veil. Both he and his wife died in the odour of sanctity and were venerated by the people, though neither was ever formally beatified.

GENNARI, *Notizie spettanti al B. Niccolo Giustiniani, monaco di S. Nicclo del Lido* (Padua, 1794; Venice, 1845); GIUSTINIANO, *Epistola ad Polycarpum, virum clarissimum in qua B. Nicholai Justiniani Veneti monachatus a fabulis vanisque commentis asseritur* (Trent, 1746); MURATORI, *Rerum Italicarum scriptores*, XII, 293 and XXII, 503 sq.

MICHAEL OTT.

Nicholas of Clemanges. See CLEMANGES, MATHIEU-NICOLAS POILLEVILLAIN DE.

Nicholas of Cusa, German cardinal, philosopher, and administrator, b. at Cues on the Moselle, in the Archdiocese of Trier, 1400 or 1401; d. at Todi, in Umbria, 11 August, 1464. His father, Johann Cryfts (Krebs), a wealthy boatman (*nauta*, not a "poor fisherman"), died in 1450 or 1451, and his mother, Catharina Roemers, in 1427. The legend that Nicholas fled from the ill-treatment of his father to Count Ulrich of Manderscheid is doubtfully reported by Hartzheim (Vita N. de Cusa, Trier, 1730), and has never been proved. Of his early education in a school of Deventer nothing is known; but in 1416 he was matriculated in the University of Heidelberg, by Rector Nicholas of Bettenberg, as "Nicolaus Cancer de Coesze, cler[icus] Trever[ensis] dioc[esis]". A year later, 1417, he left for Padua, where he graduated, in 1423, as doctor in canon law (*decretorum doctor*) under the celebrated Giuliano Cesarini. It is said that, in later years, he was honoured with the doctorate in civil law by the University of Bologna. At Padua he became the friend of Paolo Toscanelli, afterwards a celebrated physician and scientist. He studied Latin, Greek, Hebrew, and, in later years, Arabic, though, as his friend Johannes Andreæ, Bishop of Aleria, testifies, and as appears from the style of his writings, he was not a lover of rhetoric and poetry. That the loss of a lawsuit at Mainz should have decided his choice of the clerical state, is not supported by his previous career. Aided by the Archbishop of Trier, he matriculated in the University of Cologne, for divinity, under the rectorship of Petrus von Weiler, in 1425. His identity with the "Nicolaus Trevirensis", who is mentioned as secretary to Cardinal Orsini, and papal legate for Germany in 1426, is not certain. After 1428, benefices at Coblenz, Oberwesel, Münstermaifeld, Dypurgh, St. Wendel, and Liège fell to his lot, successively or simultaneously.

His public career began in 1431, at the Council of Basle, which opened under the presidency of his former teacher, Giuliano Cesarini. The cause of Count Ulrich of Manderscheid, which he defended, was lost and the transactions with the Bohemians, in which he represented the German nation, proved fruitless. His main efforts at the council were for the reform of the calendar and for the unity, political and religious, of all Christendom. In 1437 the orthodox minority sent him to Eugene IV, whom he strongly supported. The pope entrusted him with a mission to Constantinople, where, in the course of two months, besides discovering Greek manuscripts of St. Basil and St. John Damascene, he gained over for the Council of Florence, the emperor, the patriarch, and twenty-eight archbishops. After reporting the result of his mission to the pope at Ferrara, in 1438, he was created papal legate to support the cause of Eugene IV. He did so before the Diets of Mainz (1441), Frankfort (1442), Nuremberg (1444), again of Frankfort (1446), and even at the court of Charles VII of France, with such force that Æneas Sylvius called him the Hercules of the Eugenians. As a reward Eugene IV nominated him cardinal; but Nicholas declined the dignity. It needed a command of the next pope, Nicholas V, to bring him to Rome for the acceptance of this honour. In 1449 he was proclaimed cardinal-priest of the title of St. Peter ad Vincula.

His new dignity was fraught with labours and crosses. The Diocese of Brixen, the see of which was vacant, needed a reformer. The Cardinal of Cusa was appointed (1450), but, owing to the opposition of the chapter and of Sigmund, Duke of Austria and Count of the Tyrol, could not take possession of the see until two years later. In the meantime the cardinal was sent by Nicholas V, as papal legate, to Northern Germany and the Netherlands. He was to preach the Jubilee indulgence and to promote the crusade against the Turks; to visit, reform, and correct parishes, monasteries, hospitals; to endeavour to reunite the Hussites with the Church; to end the dissensions between the Duke of Cleve and the Archbishop of Cologne; and to treat with the Duke of Burgundy with a view to peace between England and France. He crossed the Brenner in January, 1451, held a provincial synod at Salzburg, visited Vienna, Munich, Ratisbon, and Nuremberg, held a diocesan synod at Bamberg, presided over the provincial chapter of the Benedictines at Würzburg, and reformed the monasteries in the Dioceses of Erfurt, Thuringia, Magdeburg, Hildesheim, and Minden. Through the Netherlands he was accompanied by his friend Denys the Carthusian. In 1452 he concluded his visitations by holding a provincial synod at Cologne. Everywhere, according to Abbot Trithemius, he had appeared as an angel of light and peace, but it was not to be so in his own diocese. The troubles began with the Poor Clares of Brixen and the Benedictine nuns of Sonnenburg, who needed reformation, but were shielded by Duke Sigmund. The cardinal had to take refuge in the stronghold of Andraz, at Buchenstein, and finally, by special authority received from Pius II, pronounced an interdict upon the Countship of the Tyrol. In 1460 the duke made him prisoner at Burneck and extorted from him a treaty unfavourable to the bishopric. Nicholas fled to Pope Pius II, who excommunicated the duke and laid an interdict upon the diocese, to be enforced by the Archbishop of Salzburg. But the duke, himself an immoral man, and, further, instigated by the antipapal humanist Heimburg, defied the pope and appealed to a general council. It needed the strong influence of the emperor, Frederick III, to make him finally (1464) submit to the Church. This took place some days after the cardinal's death. The account of the twelve years' struggle given by Jäger and, after him, by Prantl, is unfair to the "foreign reformer" (see Pastor, op. cit. infra, II). The cardinal, who had accompanied Pius II to the Venetian fleet at Ancona, was sent by the pope to Leghorn to hasten the Genoese crusaders, but on the way succumbed to an illness, the result of his ill-treatment at the hands of Sigmund, from which he had never fully recovered. He died at Todi, in the presence of his friends, the physician Toscanelli and Bishop Johannes Andreæ.

The body of Nicholas of Cusa rests in his own titular church in Rome, beneath an effigy of him sculptured in relief, but his heart is deposited before the altar in the hospital of Cues. This hospital was the cardinal's own foundation. By mutual agreement with his sister Clare and his brother John, his entire inheritance was made the basis of the foundation, and by the cardinal's last will his altar service, manuscript library, and scientific instruments were bequeathed to it. The extensive buildings with chapel, cloister, and refectory, which were erected in 1451–56, stand to this day, and serve their original purpose of a home for thirty-three old men, in honour of the thirty-three years of Christ's earthly life. Another foundation of the cardinal was a residence at Deventer, called the *Bursa Cusana*, where twenty poor clerical students were to be supported. Among bequests, a sum of 260 ducats was left to S. Maria dell' Anima in Rome, for an infirmary. In the archives of this institution is found the original document of the cardinal's last will.

The writings of Cardinal Nicholas may be classified under four heads: (1) juridical writings: "De concordantia catholica" and "De auctoritate præsidendi in concilio generali" (1432–35), both written on occasion of the Council of Basle. The superiority of the general councils over the pope is maintained; though, when the majority of the assembly drew from these writings startling conclusions unfavourable to Pope Eugene, the author seems to have changed his views, as appears from his action after 1437. The political reforms proposed were skilfully utilized by Görres in 1814. (2) In his philosophical writings, composed after 1439, he set aside the definitions and methods of the "Aristotelean Sect" and replaced them by deep speculations and mystical forms of his own. The best known in his first treatise, "De docta ignorantia" (1439–40), on the finite and the infinite. The Theory of Knowledge is critically examined in the treatise "De conjecturis" (1440–44) and especially in the "Compendium" (1464). In his Cosmology he calls the Creator the *Possest* (*posse-est*, the possible-actual), alluding to the argument: God is possible, therefore actual. His *microcosmos* in created things has some similarity with the "monads" and the "emanation" of Leibniz. (3) The theological treatises are dogmatic, ascetic, and mystic. "De cribratione alchorani" (1460) was occasioned by his visit to Constantinople, and was written for the conversion of the Mohammedans. For the faithful were written: "De quærendo Deum" (1445), "De filiatione Dei" (1445), "De visione Dei" (1453), "Excitationum libri X" (1431–64), and others. The favourite subject of his mystical speculations was the Trinity. His concept of God has been much disputed, and has even been called pantheistic. The context of his writings proves, however, that they are all strictly Christian. Scharpff calls his theology a Thomas à Kempis in philosophical language. (4) The scientific writings consist of a dozen treatises, mostly short, of which the "Reparatio Calendarii" (1436), with a correction of the Alphonsine Tables, is the most important. (For an account of its contents and its results, see LILIUS, ALOISIUS.) The shorter mathematical treatises are examined in Kästner's "History of Mathematics", II. Among them is a claim for the exact quadrature of the

House in which Cardinal Nicholas of Cusa was born, Cues, Germany

circle, which was refuted by Regiomontanus [see MÜLLER (REGIOMONTANUS), JOHANN]. The astronomical views of the cardinal are scattered through his philosophical treatises. They evince complete independence of traditional doctrines, though they are based on symbolism of numbers, on combinations of letters, and on abstract speculations rather than observation. The earth is a star like other stars, is not the centre of the universe, is not at rest, nor are its poles fixed. The celestial bodies are not strictly spherical, nor are their orbits circular. The difference between theory and appearance is explained by relative motion. Had Copernicus been aware of these assertions he would probably have been encouraged by them to publish his own monumental work. The collected editions of Nicholas of Cusa's works are: *Incunabula* (before 1476) in 2 vols., incomplete; Paris (1514) in 3 vols.; Basle (1565), in 3 vols.

DÜX, *Der deutsche Kardinal Nikolaus von Cusa und die Kirche seiner Zeit* (Ratisbon, 1847); CLEMENS, *Giordano Bruno u. Nikolaus von Cusa* (Bonn, 1847); ZIMMERMANN, *Der Kardinal N. C. als Vorläufer Leibnizens* in *Sitzungsber. Phil. Kl.*, VIII (Vienna, 1852); JÄGER, *Der Streit des Kardinals N. v. C.* (Innsbruck, 1861); HEFELE, *Conciliengeschichte*, VII (Freiburg, 1869); SCHARPFF, *Der Kardinal u. Bischof N. v. C.* (Tübingen, 1871); GRUBE in *Hist. Jahrb. d. Görres-Gesellschaft*, I (1880), *Die Legationsreise*; UEBINGER, *Philosophie d. N. C.* (Würzburg, 1880), dissert.; IDEM in *Hist. Jahrb. d. Görres-Ges.*, VIII (1887), *Kardinallegat N. v. C.*; IDEM, *ibid.*, XIV (1893), *Zur Lebensgesch. des N. C.*; IDEM, *Die Gotteslehre des N. C.* (Münster and Paderborn, 1888); BIRK in *Theol. Quartalschr.*, LXXIV (Tübingen, 1892); JANSSEN, *Geschichte des deutschen Volkes*, I (Freiburg, 1897), 3–6, tr. CHRISTIE (London and St. Louis, 1908); PASTOR, *Geschichte der Päpste*, II (Freiburg, 1904), tr. ANTROBUS (St. Louis, 1902); MARX, *Verzeichniss der Handschr. des Hospitals zu Cues* (Trier, 1905); IDEM, *Geschichte des Armen-Hospitals . . . zu Cues* (Trier, 1907); VALOIS, *La Crise religieuse du XVe siècle* (Paris, 1909).

J. G. HAGEN.

CARDINAL NICHOLAS OF CUSA
Portrait in the hospital at Cues, which he founded

Nicholas of Flüe (DE RUPE), BLESSED, b. 21 March, 1417, on the Flüeli, a fertile plateau near Sachseln, Canton Obwalden, Switzerland; d. 21 March, 1487, as a recluse in a neighbouring ravine, called Ranft. He was the oldest son of pious, well-to-do peasants and from his earliest youth was fond of prayer, practised mortification, and conscientiously performed the labour of a peasant boy. At the age of 21 he entered the army and took part in the battle of Ragaz in 1446. Probably he fought in the battles near the Etzel in 1439, near Baar in the Canton of Zug in 1443, and assisted in the capture of Zürich in 1444. He took up arms again in the so-called Thurgau war against Archduke Sigismund of Austria in 1460. It was due to his influence that the Dominican Convent St. Katharinental, whither many Austrians had fled after the capture of Diessenhofen, was not destroyed by the Swiss confederates. Heeding the advice of his parents he married, about the age of twenty-five, a pious girl from Sachseln, named Dorothy Wyssling, who bore him five sons and five daughters. His youngest son, Nicholas, born in 1467, became a priest and a doctor of theology. Though averse to worldly dignities, he was elected cantonal councillor and judge. The fact that in 1462 he was one of five arbiters appointed to settle a dispute between the parish of Stans and the monastery of Engelberg, shows the esteem in which he was held. After living about twenty-five years in wedlock he listened to an inspiration of God and with the consent of his wife left his family on 16 October, 1467, to live as a hermit. At first he intended to go to a foreign country, but when he came into the neighbourhood of Basle, a divine inspiration ordered him to take up his abode in the Ranft, a valley along the Melcha, about an hour's walk from Sachseln. Here, known as "Brother Klaus", he abode over twenty years, without taking any bodily food or drink, as was established through a careful investigation, made by the civil as well as the ecclesiastical authorities of his times. He wore neither shoes nor cap, and even in winter was clad merely in a hermit's gown. In 1468 he saved the town of Sarnen from a conflagration by his prayers and the sign of the cross. God also favoured him with numerous visions and the gift of prophecy. Distinguished persons from nearly every country of Europe came to him for counsel in matters of the utmost importance. At first he lived in a narrow hut, which he himself had built with branches and leaves, and came daily to Mass either at Sachseln or at Kerns. Early in 1469 the civil authorities built a cell and a chapel for him, and on 29 April of the same year the chapel was dedicated by the vicar-general of Constance, Thomas, Bishop of Ascalon. In 1479 a chaplain was put in charge of the chapel, and thenceforth Nicholas always remained in the Ranft. When in 1480 delegates of the Swiss confederates assembled at Stans to settle their differences, and civil war seemed inevitable, Henry Imgrund, the pastor of Stans, hastened to Nicholas, begging him to prevent the shedding of blood. The priest returned to the delegates with the hermit's counsels and propositions, and civil war was averted. Nicholas was beatified by Pope Clement IX in 1669. Numerous pilgrims visit the chapel near the church of Sachseln, where his relics are preserved. His feast is celebrated on 21 March.

MING, *Der selige Nicolaus von Flüe, sein Leben und Wirken* (4 vols., Lucerne, 1861–78); VON AH, *Des seligen Einsiedlers Nikolaus von Flüe wunderbares Leben* (Einsiedeln, 1887); BAUMBERGER, *Der sel. Nikolaus von Flüe* (Kempten and Munich, 1906); *Acta SS.*, III, March, 398–439; WETZEL, *Der sel. Nikolaus von Flüe* (Einsiedeln, 1887; Ravensburg, 1896) tr. into Italian, MONDADA (Turin, 1888); DE BELLOC, *Le bienheureux Nicolas de Flüe et la Suisse d'autrefois* (Paris, 1889); BLAKE, *A hero of the Swiss Republic* in *The Catholic World*, LXV (New York, 1897), 658–673.

MICHAEL OTT.

Nicholas of Gorran (or GORRAIN), medieval preacher, and scriptural commentator; b. in 1232 at Gorron, France; d. about 1295. He entered the Dominican Order in the convent of his native town and became one of its most illustrious alumni. His talents singled him out for special educational opportunities, and he was sent accordingly to the famous convent of St. James in Paris. In this convent he subsequently served several terms as prior. His piety and sound judgment attracted the attention of Philip IV of France, whom he served in the double capacity of confessor and adviser. In most of his ecclesiastical studies he does not seem to have excelled notably; but in preaching and in the interpretation of the Scriptures he was unsurpassed by any of his contemporaries. His scriptural writings treat of all the books of the Old and the New Testament, and possess more than ordinary merit. Indeed, in such high esteem were they held by the doctors of the University of Paris that the latter were wont to designate their author as *excellens postulator*. The commentaries on the Books of Ecclesiastes, Ezechiel, and Daniel, while generally attributed to Nicholas of Gorran, have at times been ascribed to a different authorship. His commentary on the Epistles of St. Paul is remarkably well done, and his gloss on the Apocalypse was deemed worthy of the highest commendation. Besides his Scriptural writings he commented on the Lombard's Book of Sentences and on the Book of Distinctions. His commentaries on the Gospels were published in folio at Cologne (1573) by Peter Quentel; and at Antwerp (1617) by John Keerberg. His commentaries on the Epistles of St. Paul were published at Cologne (1478); Hagenau (1502); Paris (1521); Antwerp (1617).

QUÉTIF-ECHARD, SS. Ord. Præd., I; LAJARD, Histoire litt. de France, XX (Paris, 1842), 324–56; DENIFLE AND CHATELAIN, Chartularium Univ. Parisien., II (Paris, 1891).

JOHN B. O'CONNOR.

Nicholas of Lyra (*Doctor planus et utilis*), exegete, b. at Lyra in Normandy, 1270; d. at Paris, 1340. The report that he was of Jewish descent dates only from the fifteenth century. He took the Franciscan habit at Verneuil, studied theology, received the doctor's degree in Paris and was appointed professor at the Sorbonne. In the famous controversy on the Beatific Vision he took sides with the professors against John XXII. He laboured very successfully, both in preaching and writing, for the conversion of the Jews. He is the author of numerous theological works, some of which are yet unpublished. It was to exegesis that Nicholas of Lyra devoted his best years. In the second prologue to his monumental work, "Postillæ perpetuæ in universam S. Scripturam", after stating that the literal sense of Sacred Scripture is the foundation of all mystical expositions, and that it alone has demonstrative force, as St. Augustine teaches, he deplores the state of Biblical studies in his time. The literal sense, he avers, is much obscured, owing partly to the carelessness of the copyists, partly to the unskilfulness of some of the correctors, and partly also to our own translation (the Vulgate), which not infrequently departs from the original Hebrew. He holds with St. Jerome that the text must be corrected from the Hebrew codices, except of course the prophecies concerning the Divinity of Christ. Another reason for this obscurity, Nicholas goes on to say, is the attachment of scholars to the method of interpretation handed down by others who, though they have said many things well, have yet touched but sparingly on the literal sense, and have so multiplied the mystical senses as nearly to intercept and choke it. Moreover, the text has been distorted by a multiplicity of arbitrary divisions and concordances. Hereupon he declares his intention of insisting, in the present work, upon the literal sense and of interspersing only a few mystical interpretations. Nicholas utilized all available sources, fully mastered the Hebrew and drew copiously from the valuable commentaries of the Jewish exegetes, especially of the celebrated Talmudist Rashi. The "Pugio Fidei" of Raymond Martini and the commentaries of St. Thomas Aquinas were laid under contribution. His exposition is lucid and concise; his observations are judicious and sound, and always original. The "Postillæ" soon became the favourite manual of exegesis. It was the first Biblical commentary printed. The solid learning of Nicholas commanded the respect of both Jews and Christians.

Luther owes much to Nicholas of Lyra, but how widely the principles of Nicholas differed essentially from Luther's views is best seen from Nicholas's own words: "I protest that I do not intend to assert or determine anything that has not been manifestly determined by Sacred Scripture or by the authority of the Church.... Wherefore I submit all I have said or shall say to the correction of Holy Mother Church and of all learned men..." (Prol. secund. in Postillas., ed. 1498). Nicholas taught no new doctrine. The early Fathers and the great schoolmen had repeatedly laid down the same sound exegetical principles, but, owing to adverse tendencies of the times, their efforts had partly failed. Nicholas carried out these principles effectively, and in this lies his chief merit—one which ranks him among the foremost exegetes of all times.

ST. NICHOLAS OF MYRA (OR OF BARI) BEFORE THE BLESSED VIRGIN
Bonvicino (Il Moretto), Pinacoteca, Brescia

WADDING, Annales (Rome, 1733), V, 264–7; VI, 237–9; IDEM, Scriptores (Rome, 1906), s. v.; SBARALEA, Supplementum (Rome, 1806), s. v.; FABRICIUS, Bibl. lat. et inf. latinitatis, V (Hamburg, 1736), 114 sqq.; HAIN, Repertorium. bibl. (Paris, 1826–38), s. v.; COPINGER, Supplement to Hain's Repert. bibl. (London, 1895–1902), s. v.; DENIFLE AND CHATELAIN, Chartul. Universit. Paris. II (Paris, 1891), passim; FERET, La faculté de théol. de Paris et ses docteurs les plus célèbres, III (Paris, 1894–96), 331–9; SIMON, Hist. crit. des commentaires d. V. T. (Rotterdam, 1683); IDEM, Hist. crit. des princip. commentateurs d. N. T. (Rotterdam, 1693); BERGER, Quam notitiam linguæ hebr. habuerunt Christiani med. ævi in Gallia (Nancy, 1893); CORNELY, Hist. et crit. Introd. in utr. Test. libros sacros, I (Paris, 1885), 660–2; GIGOT, Gen. Introd. to the study of the Scriptures (New York), 444 sq.; NEUMANN, Influence de Rachi et d'autres commentateurs juifs sur les postilles de Lyra in Revue des études juives, XXVI (1893), 172 sqq.; XXVII (1893), 230 sqq.; MASCHKOWSKI, Raschis Einfluss auf N. v. L. in d. Ausleg. d. Exodus in Zeitschr. f. alttestam. Wissenschaft, XI (1891), 268 sqq.; LABROSSE, Biogr. et œuvres de N. v. L. in Etudes franciscaines, XVI (1906), 383 sqq.; XVII (1907), 489 sqq., 593 sqq.; XIX (1908), 41 sqq., 153 sqq., 368 sqq.; BIHL, Hat N. v. L. in Erfurt doziert? in Zeitschr. d. Vereins f. thüring. Gesch. u. Altertum., XXVI (1908), 329 sqq.; see also a paper on Nicholas of Lyra by MARCHAL in Annuaire de l'université cath. de Louvain (1910), 432 sq.

THOMAS PLASSMANN.

Nicholas of Myra (or OF BARI), SAINT, Bishop of Myra in Lycia, d. 6 December, 345 or 352. Though he is one of the most popular saints in the Greek as well as the Latin Church, there is scarcely anything historically certain about him except that he was Bishop of Myra in the fourth century. Some of the main points in his legend are as follows: He was born at Parara, a city of Lycia in Asia Minor; in his youth he made a pilgrimage to Egypt and Palestine; shortly after his return he became Bishop of Myra; cast into prison during the persecution of Diocletian, he was released after the accession of Constantine, and was present at the Council of Nicæa. In 1087 Italian merchants stole his body at Myra, bringing it to Bari in Italy.

The numerous miracles St. Nicholas is said to have wrought, both before and after his death, are outgrowths of a long tradition. There is reason to doubt his presence at Nicæa, since his name is not mentioned in any of the old lists of bishops that attended this council. His cult in the Greek Church is old and especially popular in Russia. As early as the sixth century Emperor Justinian I built a church in his honour at Constantinople, and his name occurs in the liturgy ascribed to St. Chrysostom. In Italy his cult seems to have begun with the translation of his relics to Bari, but in Germany it began already under Otto II, probably because his wife Theophano was a Grecian. Bishop Reginald of Eichstädt (d. 991) is known to have written a metric, "Vita S. Nicholai". The course of centuries has not lessened his popularity. The following places honour him as patron: Greece, Russia, the Kingdom of Naples, Sicily, Lorraine, the Diocese of Liege; many cities in Italy, Germany, Austria, and Belgium; Campen in the Netherlands; Corfu in Greece; Freiburg in Switzerland; and Moscow in Russia. He is patron of mariners, merchants, bakers, travellers, children etc. His representations in art are as various as his alleged miracles. In Germany, Switzerland, and the Netherlands they have the custom of making him the secret purveyor of gifts to children on 6 December, the day on which the Church celebrates his feast; in the United States and some other countries St. Nicholas has become identified with the popular Santa Claus who distributes gifts to children on Christmas eve. His relics are still preserved in the church of San Nicola in Bari; up to the present day an oily substance, known as *Manna di S. Nicola*, which is highly valued for its medicinal powers, is said to flow from them.

The traditional legends of St. Nicholas were first collected and written in Greek by METAPHRASTES in the tenth century. They are printed in *P. G.*, CXVI sq. A Latin translation by GIUSTINIANI (Venice, 1502 and 1513) is printed in SURIUS, *De probatis sanctorum historiis*, 6 December. There is an immense amount of ancient and modern literature. The following modern authorities are noteworthy: GAETA, *S. Nicolò di Bari, vescovo di Mira* (Naples, 1904); BERTANI, *Vita di s. Nicolò, vescovo di Mira* (Monza, 1900); GEMMA, *La capsella delle reliquie di s. Nicolò di Bari in Bassarione*, X (Rome, 1906), 317–328; SCHNELL, *St. Nickolaus der heil. Bischof u. Kinderfreund* (Brünn, 1883–5, and Ravensburg, 1886); PRAXMARER, *Der h. Nikolaus u. seine Verehrung* (Münster, 1894); LAROCHE, *Vie de s. Nicholas, évêque de Myre, patron de la Lorraine* (Paris, 1886, 1893); IDEM, *La manne de s. Nicholas* in *Revue Suisse Catholique*, XXI (Freiburg, 1890), 56–68, 122–137; KAYATA, *Monographie de l'église grecque de Marseille et vie de s. Nicholas de Myre* (Marseilles, 1901).

MICHAEL OTT.

Nicholas of Osimo (AUXIMANUS), celebrated preacher and author, b. at Osimo, Italy, in the second half of the fourteenth century; d. at Rome, 1453. After having studied law, and taken the degree of doctor at Bologna, he joined the Friars Minor of the Observants in the convent of San Paolo. Conspicuous for zeal, learning, and preaching, as companion of St. James of the Marches in Bosnia, and as Vicar-Provincial of Apulia (1439), Nicholas greatly contributed to the prosperity of the Observants for whom (1440) he obtained complete independence from the Conventuals, a privilege shortly after revoked according to the desire of St. Bernardine. He was also appointed Visitator and afterwards Superior, of the Holy Land, but many difficulties seem to have hindered him from the discharge of these offices. Nicholas wrote both in Latin and Italian a number of treatises on moral theology, the spiritual life, and on the Rule of St. Francis. We mention the following: (1) "Supplementum Summæ Magistratiæ seu Pisanellæ", a revised and increased edition of the "Summa" of Bartholomew of San Concordio (or of Pisa), O.P., completed at Milan, 1444, with many editions before the end of the fifteenth century: Venice, 1473 sqq.; Genoa, 1474; Milan, 1479; Reutlingen, 1483; Nuremberg, 1494. (2) "Quadriga Spirituale", in Italian, treats in a popular way what the author considers the four principal means of salvation, viz. faith, good works, confession, and prayer. These are like the four wheels of a chariot, whence the name. The work was printed at Jesi, 1475, and under the name of St. Bernardine of Siena in 1494.

WADDING, *Scriptores Ord. Min.* (Rome, 1806), 179 (Rome, 1906), 176; IDEM, *Annales Minorum ad an. 1427*, n. 13–16, 2nd ed., X (Rome, 1734), 119–30; *ad an. 1438*, n. 21–23, XI (Rome, 1734), 39–46; *ad an. 1440*, n. 29, XI (Rome, 1734), 111 passim; SBARALEA, *Supplementum* (Rome, 1806), 550; SPEZI, *Tre Operette volgari di Frate Niccolo da Osimo, testi di lingua inediti tratti da' codici Vaticani* (Rome, 1865), preface; LUIGI DA FABRIANO, *Cenni cronologico-biografici della Osservante Provincia Picena* (Quaracchi, 1886), 161, 221; HAIN, *Repertorium Bibliographicum* (Paris, 1826), I, i, n. 2149–75; VON SCHULTE, *Die Geschichte der Quellen und Literatur des Canonischen Rechtes von Gratian bis auf die Gegenwart*, I (Stuttgart, 1877), 435–37; DIETTERLE, *Die Summæ Confessorum* in *Zeitschrift für Kirchengeschichte*, ed. BRIEGER, XXVII (Gotha, 1906), 183–88.

LIVARIUS OLIGER.

Nicholas of Strasburg, mystic, flourished early in the fourteenth century. Educated at Paris, he was later on lector at the Dominican convent, Cologne. Appointed by John XXII, he made a canonical visitation of the German Dominican province, where great discord prevailed. Relying on two papal briefs dated 1 August, 1325, it appears that the sole commission received from the pontiff was to reform the province in its head and members, and to act as visitor to the sisters. Nicholas, however, assumed the office of inquisitor as well, and closed a process already begun by Archbishop Heinrich (Cologne) against Master Eckhart, O.P., for his teachings on mysticism, in favour of the latter (1326). In January, 1327, the archbishop renewed the cause and arraigned Nicholas as a patron of his confrère's errors. Almost simultaneously, Hermann von Höchst, a discontented religious on whom Nicholas had imposed a well-merited penalty, took revenge by having him excommunicated. Nicholas, however, was soon released from this sentence by Pope John, that he might appear as definitor at the general chapter of his order convened at Perpignan, May 31, 1327. He is last heard of after the settlement of the process against Eckhart as vicar of the German Dominicans, 1329. Thirteen extant sermons show him to have been of a rather practical turn of mind.

Having realized the inherent necessity of solid piety being based upon the principles of sound theology, he urges in clear, pregnant, and forceful style the sacred importance of good works, penitential practices and indulgences, confession and the Holy Eucharist. Only by the use of these means can the love of God be well-regulated and that perfect conversion of the heart attained which is indispensable for a complete remission of guilt. Built up on so firm a groundwork, there is nothing to censure but much to commend in his allegorical interpretations of Sacred Scripture, which are otherwise consistent with his fondness for parable and animated illustration. "De Adventu Christi", formerly attributed to Nicholas, came originally from the pen of John of Paris.

PREGER, *Meister Eckhart und die Inquisition* (Munich, 1869); IDEM, *Gesch. der deutsch. Mystik im Mittelalter*, II (Leipzig, 1881); DENIFLE, *Actenstücke zu Meister Eckharts Prozess* in *Zeitschr. f. deutsches Altertum u. deutsche Literatur*, XXIX (XVII) (1885); IDEM, *Der Plagiator, Nich. von Strassb.* in *Archiv f. Lit. u. Kirchen-*

gesch., IV (1888); PFEIFFER, *Deutsche Mystiker des 14. Jahrh.*, I (Leipzig, 1845).

THOS. À K. REILLY.

Nicholas of Tolentino, SAINT, b. at Sant' Angelo, near Fermo, in the March of Ancona, about 1246; d. 10 September, 1306. He is depicted in the black habit of the Hermits of St. Augustine—a star above him or on his breast, a lily, or a crucifix garlanded with lilies, in his hand. Sometimes, instead of the lily, he holds a vial filled with money or bread. His parents, said to have been called Compagnonus de Guarutti and Amata de Guidiani (these surnames may merely indicate their birth-places), were pious folk, perhaps gentle born, living content with a small substance. Nicholas was born in response to prayer, his mother being advanced in years. From his childhood he was a model of holiness. He excelled so much in his studies that even before they were over he was made a canon of St. Saviour's church; but hearing a sermon by a hermit of St. Augustine upon the text: "Nolite diligere mundum, nec ea quæ sunt in mundo, quia mundus transit et concupiscentia ejus", he felt a call to embrace the religious life. He besought the hermit for admittance into his order. His parents gave a joyful consent. Even before his ordination he was sent to different monasteries of his order, at Recanati, Macerata etc., as a model of generous striving after perfection. He made his profession before he was nineteen. After his ordination he preached with wonderful success, notably at Tolentino, where he spent his last thirty years and gave a discourse nearly every day. Towards the end diseases tried his patience, but he kept up his mortifications almost to the hour of death. He possessed an angelic meekness, a guileless simplicity, and a tender love of virginity, which he never stained, guarding it by prayer and extraordinary mortifications. He was canonized by Eugene IV in 1446; his feast is celebrated on 10 September. His tomb, at Tolentino, is held in veneration by the faithful.

Acta SS., Sept., III, 636; BUTLER, *Lives of the Saints*, III (Baltimore), 440; HÄGELE in *Kirchenlex.*, s. v.

EDWARD F. GARESCHÉ.

Nicholas Pieck (also spelled PICK), SAINT, Friar Minor and martyr, b. at Gorkum, Holland, 29 August, 1534; d. at Briel, Holland, 9 July, 1572. He came of an old and honourable family. His parents, John Pieck and Henrica Clavia, were deeply attached to the Catholic faith, and the former on several occasions distinguished himself by his zeal against the innovations of Calvinism. Nicholas was sent to college at Bois-le-Duc ('S Hertogenbosch), and as soon as he had completed his classical studies he received the habit of the Friars Minor at the convent in that town. After his profession he was sent to the convent at Louvain to follow the course of study at the celebrated university there. Nicholas was ordained priest in 1558 and thenceforth devoted himself to the apostolic ministry. He evangelized the principal towns of Holland and Belgium, combating heresy everywhere, strengthening Catholics in their faith, and distinguishing himself by his singular humility, modesty, charity, and zeal for the honour of God and the salvation of souls. He was of an open disposition, gay and genial, and his whole bearing inspired affection and respect. His superiors, appreciating his fine qualities, appointed him guardian of the convent at Gorkum, his native town.

When this place was threatened by the Calvinists, Nicholas delivered several discourses to his fellow-townsmen, forewarning them against the dangerous errors of Calvinism. In particular, he proved by unanswerable arguments the dogma of the Real Presence, showing it to be a marvellous extension of the Incarnation, and he left nothing undone to bring his two brothers back to the true fold. When the citadel of Gorkum was taken by the Watergeuzen, the heretics detained the priests and religious, and confined them in a dark and foul dungeon. (See GORKUM, THE MARTYRS OF.) During the first night the Calvinists vented their rage particularly against Nicholas. Tying about his neck the cord which girded his loins, they first suspended him from a beam and then let him fall heavily to the ground. This torture was prolonged till the cord broke, and the martyr, seemingly lifeless, fell to the floor. They then applied a burning torch to his ears, forehead, and chin, and forced open his mouth to burn his tongue and palate, either to find out whether he was still alive or in order to torture him. Meanwhile, the two brothers of Nicholas were busy taking steps to obtain the deliverance of the captives. This was promised them only on condition that the prisoners would renounce the authority of the pope, and, as nothing could make Nicholas and his companions waver in their faith, they were taken to Briel, where they all gained the crown of martyrdom. Nicholas and his companions were beatified by Clement X, 24 November, 1675, and canonized by Pius IX, 29 June, 1867.

CLARY, *Lives of the Saints and Blessed of the Three Orders of Saint Francis*, II (Taunton, 1886), 457–65; SEDULIUS, *Historia Seraphica* (Antwerp, 1613), 671 sq.; SCHOUTENS, *Martyrologium Minoritico-Belgicum* (Antwerp, 1901), 114–15; ESTIUS, *Historiæ Martyrum Gorcomiensium* in *Acta SS.*, II, July (ed. 1867), 804–808; WADDING, *Annales Minorum*, XX, 381–418. (For further bibliography see GORKUM, THE MARTYRS OF.)

FERDINAND HECKMANN.

Nichols (or NICOLLS), GEORGE, VENERABLE, English martyr, b. at Oxford about 1550; executed at Oxford, 19 October, 1589. He entered Brasenose College in 1564 or 1565, and was readmitted 20 August, 1567, and supplicated for his B.A. degree in 1570–1. He subsequently became an usher at St. Paul's School, London. He arrived at Reims with Thomas Pilchard (q. v.), 20 Nov., 1581; but went on to Rome, whence he returned 21 July, 1582. Ordained subdeacon and deacon at Laon (probably by Bishop Valentine Douglas, O.S.B.) in April, 1583, and priest at Reims (by Cardinal Archbishop Louis de Guise) 24 Sept., he was sent on the mission the same year. Having converted many, notably a convicted highwayman in Oxford Castle, he was arrested at the Catherine Wheel Inn, opposite the east end of St. Mary Magdalen's Church, Oxford, together with Humphrey Prichard, a Welsh servant at the inn, Thomas Belson (q. v.), and Richard Yaxley. This last was a son (probably the third, certainly not the sixth) of William Yaxley of Boston, Lincolnshire, by Rose, daughter of John Langton of Northolme. Arriving at Reims 29 August, 1582, he received the tonsure and minor orders 23 Sept., 1583, and the subdiaconate 5 or 6 April, 1585, from the cardinal archbishop. Probably the same hand conferred the diaconate on 20 April. The priesthood was conferred at Reims by Louis de Brezé, Bishop of Meaux, 21 Sept., 1585. Yaxley left Reims for England 28 January, 1585–6. All four prisoners were sent from Oxford to the Bridewell prison in London, where the two priests were hanged up for five hours to make them betray their hosts, but without avail. Yaxley was sent to the Tower as a close prisoner 25 May, 1589, and appears to have been racked frequently. Belson was sent to the Gatehouse. The other two remained in Bridewell, Nichols being put into "a deep dungeon full of venomous vermin". On 30 June all four were ordered back to Oxford to take their trial. All were condemned, the priests for treason, the laymen for felony. Nichols suffered first, then Yaxley, then Belson, and last Prichard. The priests' heads were set up on the castle, and their quarters on the four city gates.

CHALLONER, *Memoirs of Missionary Priests*, I, nos. 73–5; POLLEN, *Catholic Record Society*, V (London, 1908), *passim*; DASENT, *Acts of the Privy Council*, XVII (London, 1890–1907), 203, 329; KNOX, *First and Second Diaries of English College, Douai* (London, 1878), *passim*; *Harleian Society Publications*, LII (London, 1904),

1124; *Oxford Historical Society Publications*, XXXIX (Oxford, 1899), 109, 110; LV (Oxford, 1910), 33.
JOHN B. WAINEWRIGHT.

Nicholson, FRANCIS, a controversial writer; b. at Manchester, 1650 (baptized 27 Oct.); d. at Lisbon, 13 Aug., 1731. The son of Henry or Thomas Nicholson, a Manchester citizen, when sixteen he entered University College, Oxford, as a servitor, and took his degrees as Bachelor of Arts (18 June, 1669) and Master of Arts (4 June, 1673). Ordained an Anglican clergyman, he officiated, first about Oxford, afterwards near Canterbury, where he gained some success in reconciling Nonconformists to the Church of England. A sermon preached at St. Mary's, Oxford, on 20 June, 1680, led to his being charged with unorthodox doctrine and the fact that he had been a pupil of Obadiah Walker caused him to be suspected of Catholic tendencies. The actual date of his reception into the Church is unknown, but during the reign of James II (1685–88) he was a professed Catholic and busied himself in the king's interests. At this time he wrote the appendix on the doctrine of the Church of England concerning the Real Presence, and the "Vindication of two recent discourses" on the same subject, added to Abraham Woodhead's "Compendious Discourse on the Eucharist", published in 1688. After the revolution he joined the Carthusians at Nieuport in Flanders, but his health was unequal to this austere life, and in 1692 he returned to England. There he entered the service of the Queen Dowager, Catharine of Braganza, whom he accompanied back to Portugal. For some years he resided at the Portuguese Court and then retired to an estate which he had bought at Pera, half a league south of the Tagus, and not, as the writer in the "Dictionary of National Biography" oddly asserts, the "suburb of Constantinople". He spent a considerable period there in devotion and study, until reaching his seventieth year he made over all his real and personal property to the English College at Lisbon, subject to the discharge of his debts, the provision of board and lodging for the remainder of his life, and a small annuity. Three years before his death at the college he sent back to the Catholic antiquary, Dr. Cuthbert Constable, all the surviving MSS. of Abraham Woodhead, which had passed into his hands as executor of Obadiah Walker. With them also he sent his MS. life of Constable, published with additions in his edition of that author's "Third Part of a Brief Account of Church Government".

ANTHONY À WOOD, *Athenæ Oxonienses*, II, reprinted from DODD, *Church History*, III, 402, *Catholic Magazine*, VI (May, 1835), 208; FOSTER, *Alumni Oxonienses* (Oxford, 1891); GILLOW, *Bibl. Dict. Eng. Cath.*, s. v. *Nicholson* and *Constable;* SUTTON in *Dict. Nat. Biog.*; CROFT, *Kirk's Historical Account of Lisbon College* (London, 1902).

EDWIN BURTON.

Nicodemus, a prominent Jew of the time of Christ, mentioned only in the Fourth Gospel. The name is of Greek origin, but at that epoch such names were occasionally borrowed by the Jews, and according to Josephus (Ant. of the Jews, XIV, iii, 2) Nicodemus was the name of one of the ambassadors sent by Aristobulus to Pompey. A Hebrew form of the name (נקדימון, *Naqdimôn*) is found in the Talmud. Nicodemus was a Pharisee, and in his capacity of sanhedrist (John, vii, 50) was a leader of the Jews. Christ, in the interview when Nicodemus came to him by night, calls him a master in Israel. Judging from John, xix, 39, Nicodemus must have been a man of means, and it is probable that he wielded a certain influence in the Sanhedrim. Some writers conjecture from his question: "How can a man be born when he is old?", that he was already advanced in years, but the words are too general to warrant such a conclusion. He appears in this interview as a learned and intelligent believer, but timid and not easily initiated into the mysteries of the new faith. He next appears (John, vii, 50, 51) in the Sanhedrim offering a word in defence of the accused Galilean; and we may infer from this passage that he embraced the truth as soon as it was fully made known to him. He is mentioned finally in John, xix, 39, where he is shown co-operating with Joseph of Arimathea in the embalming and burial of Jesus. His name occurs later in some of the apocryphal writings, e. g. in the so-called "Acta Pilati", a heterogeneous document which in the sixteenth century was published under the title "Evangelium Nicodemi" (Gospel of Nicodemus). The time of his death is unknown. The Roman Martyrology commemorates the finding of his relics, together with those of Sts. Stephen, Gamaliel, and Abibo, on 3 August.

CONYBEARE, *Studia Biblica*, IV (Oxford, 1896), 59–132; LE CAMUS, *La vie de N.-S. Jésus-Christ* (Paris, 1883), I, 251 sqq.; II, 24 sqq., 577 sqq., tr. HICKEY (3 vols., New York, 1906–08).

JAMES F. DRISCOLL.

Nicodemus, GOSPEL OF. See ACTA PILATI.

Nicolaï, JEAN, celebrated Dominican theologian and controversialist, b. in 1594 at Mouzay in the Diocese of Verdun, France; d. 7 May, 1673, at Paris. Entering the order at the age of twelve, he made his religious profession in 1612, studied philosophy and theology in the convent of St. James at Paris, obtained (1632) the doctorate in theology at the Sorbonne, and taught these branches with distinction in various houses of the order. He was highly esteemed for strict observance of the rule, prudence, rare erudition, and power of penetration. Besides Latin and Greek he was conversant with Italian, Spanish, and Hebrew. He was a member of the commission appointed to examine the works and teachings of the Jansenists and to prevent the further dissemination of their doctrine in the Sorbonne. In the disputes on grace between the Thomists and Molinists, which the teaching of Jansenius revived, he adhered strictly to the Thomistic doctrine. His numerous works fall into three classes: (a) new editions of older theologians which he supplied with commentaries and explanatory notes; (b) his own theological works; (c) his poetical and political writings. The most important of the first class are "Raineri de Pisis [1351] ord. Fr. Præd. Pantheologia sive universa theologia ordine alphabetico per varios titulos distributa" (Lyons, 1670): to each of the three volumes of this work he added a dissertation against the Jansenists; "S. Thomæ Aq. Expositio continua super quatuor evangelistas" (Lyons, 1670); "S. Thomæ Aq. commentaria in quatuor libros sententiarum P. Lombardi" (Lyons, 1659); "Commentarius posterior super libros sententiarum" (Lyons, 1660); "S. Thomæ Aq. quæstiones quodlibetales" (Lyons, 1660); "S. Thomæ Aq. Summa theologica innumeris Patrum, Conciliorum, scripturarum ac doctorum testimoniis ad materias controversas vel ad moralem disciplinam pertinentibus . . . illustrata" (Lyons, 1663); "S. Thomæ Aq. explanatio in omnes d. Pauli Ap. epistolas commentaria" (Lyons, 1689). His important theological works are: "Judicium seu censorium suffragium de propositione Ant. Arnaldi sorbonici doctoris et socii ad quæstionem juris pertinente" (Paris, 1656); "Theses theologicæ de gratia seu theses molinisticæ thomisticis notis expunctæ" (Paris, 1656); "Apologia naturæ et gratiæ" (Bordeaux, 1665). Against Launoy, the champion of the "Gallican Liberties", he wrote: "De jejunii christiani et christianæ abstinentiæ vero ac legitimo ritu" (Paris, 1667); "De Concilio plenario, quod contra Donatistas baptismi quæstionem ex Augustini sensu definivit" (Paris, 1667); "De plenarii Concilii et baptismatis hereticorum assertione dissertatio posterior anteriorem firmans" (Paris, 1668); "De baptismi antiquo usu ab Ecclesia instituto, dissertatio" (Paris, 1668); "De Constantini baptismo, ubi, quando et a quibus fuerit celebratus historica dissertatio" (Paris, 1680). The purpose of his poetical and political writings seems to have been to extol the dignity and glory of France and her kings. Thus, he delivered in Rome in 1628 a panegyric in honour of the victory of Louis XIII at La Rochelle and in 1661 composed a poem in honour of the son of Louis XIV. He was highly esteemed at the royal court and received a pension of 600 francs. He was buried in the chapel of the convent of St. James in Paris, and a marble stone beside the grave bears a long inscription recounting his virtues, his learning, and his services to his country.

QUÉTIF-ECHARD, *SS. Ord. Præd.*, II, 647; *Journal des Savants*, II, 340, 482.

JOSEPH SCHROEDER.

Nicolaites (NICOLAITANS), a sect mentioned in the Apocalypse (ii, 6, 15) as existing in Ephesus, Pergamus, and other cities of Asia Minor, about the character and existence of which there is little certainty. Irenæus (Adv. Hær., I, xxvi, 3; III, xi, 1) discusses them but adds nothing to the Apocalypse except that "they lead lives of unrestrained indulgence". Tertullian refers to them, but apparently knows only what is found in St. John (De Præscrip. xxxiii; Adv. Marc., I, xxix; De Pud., xvii). Hippolytus based his narrative on Irenæus, though he states that the deacon Nicholas was the author of the heresy and the sect (Philosoph., VII, xxvi). Clement of Alexandria (Strom., III, iv) exonerates Nicholas, and attributes the doctrine of promiscuity, which the sect claimed to have derived from him, to a malicious distortion of words harmless in themselves. With the exception of the statement in Eusebius (H. E., III, xxix) that the sect was short-lived, none of the references in Epiphanius, Theodoret etc. deserve mention, as they are taken from Irenæus. The common statement, that the Nicolaites held the antinomian heresy of Corinth, has not been proved. Another opinion, favoured by a number of authors, is that, because of the allegorical character of the Apocalypse, the reference to the Nicolaitans is merely a symbolic manner of reference, based on the identical meaning of the names, to the Bileamites or Balaamites (Apoc., ii, 14) who are mentioned just before them as professing the same doctrines.

HILGENFELD, *Ketzergeschichte des Urchristentums* (Leipzig, 1884); SEESEMAN, *Die Nikolaiten. Ein Beitrag zur älteren Häresiologie* in *Theol. Studien und Kritiken* (1893).

P. J. HEALY.

Nicolas, ARMELLA, popularly known as "La bonne Armelle", a saintly French serving-maid held in high veneration among the people, though never canonized by the Church, b. at Campenéac in Brittanny, 9 September, 1606, of poor peasants, George Nicolas and Francisca Néant; d. 24 October, 1671. Her early years were spent in the pious, simple life of the hard-working country folk. When she was twenty-two years of age her parents wished her to marry, but she chose rather to enter service in the neighbouring town of Ploërmel, where she found more opportunity for her pious works and for satisfying her spiritual needs. After a few years she went to the larger town of Vannes, where she served in several families, and for a year and a half was portress at the Ursuline monastery. She here formed a special friendship with a certain sister, Jeanne de la Nativité, to whom she told from time to time many details of her spiritual life, and who noted down these communications, and afterwards wrote the life of Armella, who could herself neither read nor write. Even the lowly work at the convent did not satisfy her craving for toil and humiliation, and she returned to one of her former employers, where she remained to the end of her life. To her severe trials and temptations she added many works of penance and was rewarded by the growth of her inner life and her intimate union with God. During the last years of her life a broken leg caused her great suffering, patiently borne. Many recommended themselves to her prayers and her death-bed was surrounded by a great number of persons who held her in special veneration. Her heart was preserved in the Jesuit church, and her body was buried in the church of the Ursulines. Near her grave was erected a tablet to "La bonne Armelle"; her tomb is a place of pilgrimage. Armella has been claimed, but without good grounds, as an exponent of Quietism (q. v.). If some of her expressions seemed tinged with Quietist thought, it is because the controversy which cleared and defined many notions concerning Quietism had not yet arisen. On the other hand her simple, laborious life and practical piety make any such aberrations very unlikely.

JUNGMANN in *Kirchenlexikon*, s. v. *Nicolas*; STOLTZ, *Legende der Heiligen*, 24 October; BUSSON, *Vie d'Armelle Nicolas etc.* (Paris, 1844); TERSTEEGEN, *Select Lives of Holy Souls*, I, 2nd ed. (1754).

EDWARD F. GARESCHÉ.

Nicolas, AUGUSTE, French apologist, b. at Bordeaux, 6 Jan., 1807; d. at Versailles 18 Jan., 1888. He first studied law, was admitted as an advocate and entered the magistracy. From 1841–49 he was justice of the peace at Bordeaux; as early as 1842 he began the publication of his apologetical writings which soon made his name known among Catholics. When in 1849 M. de Falloux became minister of public worship he summoned Nicolas to assist him as head of the department for the administration of the temporal interests of ecclesiastical districts. He held this office until 1854 when he became general inspector of libraries. In 1860 he was appointed judge of the tribunal of the Seine and finally councillor at the Paris court of appeals.

Nicolas employed his leisure and later his retirement to write works in defence of Christianity taken as a whole or in its most important dogmas. He showed his accurate conception of apologetics by adapting them to the dispositions and the needs of the minds of his time, but he lived in a period when Traditionalism still dominated many French Catholics, and this is reflected in his works. He aimed no doubt at defending religion by means of philosophy, good sense, and arguments from authority; but he also often appeals to the traditions and the groping moral sense of mankind at large. The testimonies, however, which he cites, are often apocryphal, and frequently also he interprets them uncritically and ascribes to them a meaning or a scope which they do not possess. Besides, his apologetics speedily grew out-of-date when ecclesiastical and critical studies were revived in France and elsewhere. His writings also betray at times the layman lacking in the learning and precision of the theologian, and some of his books were in danger of being placed on the Index. Some bishops, however, among them Cardinals Donnet and Pie, intervened in his behalf and certified to the uprightness of his intentions. Otherwise the author addressed himself to the general public and especially to the middle classes which were still penetrated with Voltairian incredulity, and he succeeded in reaching them. His books were very successful in France and some of them even in Germany, where they were translated. Among his works may be mentioned: "Etudes philosophiques sur le Christianisme" (Paris, 1841–45), a philosophical apology for the chief Christian dogmas, which reached a twenty-sixth edition before the death of the author; "La Vierge Marie et le plan divin, nouvelles études philosophiques sur le Christianisme" (4 vols., Paris, 1852, 1853, 1861), in which is explained the rôle of the Blessed Virgin in the plan of Redemption, and which was translated into German, and reached the eighth edition during the author's lifetime; "Du protestantisme et de toutes les hérésies dans leur rapport avec le socialisme" (Paris, 1852, 2 vols., 8 editions); "L'Art de croire, ou préparation philosophique au Christianisme" (Paris, 1866–67), translated into German; "La Divinité de Jésus-

Christ, démonstration nouvelle" (1864); "Jésus Christ introduction à l'Evangile étudié et médité à l'usage des temps nouveaux" (Paris, 1875). As semi-religious and semi-political may be mentioned: "La Monarchie et la question du drapeau" (Paris, 1873); "La Révolution et l'orde chrétien" (Paris, 1874); "L'Etat contre Dieu" (Paris, 1879); "Rome et la Papauté" (Paris, 1883); and finally the works in historico-philosophic vein: "Etude sur Maine de Biran" (Paris, 1858); "Etude sur Eugénie de Guérin" (Paris, 1863); "Mémoires d'un père sur la vie et la mort de son fils" (Paris, 1869); "Etude historique et critique sur le Père Lacordaire" (Toulouse, 1886).

LAPEYRE, *Auguste Nicolas, sa vie et ses œuvres d'après ses Mémoires inédits, ses papiers et sa correspondance* (Paris, 1892).

ANTOINE DEGERT.

Nicolaus Germanus (often called "Donis" from a misapprehension of the title "Donnus" or "Donus" an abbreviated form of "Dominus"), a fifteenth-century cartographer, place of birth, and date of birth and death unknown. The first allusion to him of authentic date is an injunction of Duke Borso d'Este (15 March, 1466) to his referendary and privy counsellor, Ludovico Casella, at Ferrara, to have the "Cosmographia of Don Nicolò" thoroughly examined and then to determine a recompense for it. The duke, on the thirtieth of the same month, called upon his treasurers for 100 florins in gold "to remit as a mark of his appreciation to Donnus Nicolaus Germanus for his excellent book entitled 'Cosmographia'". On 8 April, 1466, the duke again drew thirty golden florins to present to the Rev. Nicolaus, who "in addition to that excellent Cosmography" (ultra illud excellens Cosmographie opus) had dedicated to the duke a calendar made to cover many years to come ("librum tacuini multorum annorum"). The "Cosmographia" as preserved in the Bibliotheca Estensis at Modena comprises a Latin translation of the Geography of Ptolemy with maps. The version of the geographical text is substantially the same as that dedicated in 1410 to Pope Alexander V by Jacopo Angelo, a Florentine. In the execution of the maps, however, Nicolaus, instead of adhering to the flat projection of Ptolemy, chose what is known as the "Donis-projection", because first worked out by him, in which the parallels of latitude are equidistant, but the meridians are made to converge towards the pole. He likewise introduced new modes in delineating the outlines of countries and oceans, mountains and lakes, as well as in the choice of cartographic proportions. He reduced the awkward size to one which was convenient for use; the obscure and often unattractive mode of presentation he replaced by one both tasteful and easily intelligible; he endeavoured to revise obsolete maps in accordance with later information and to supplement them with new maps. While his first recension embraced only the twenty-seven maps of Ptolemy (one map of the world, ten special maps of Europe, four of Africa, twelve of Asia), the second comprised thirty (including in addition modern maps of Spain, Italy, and the Northern countries: Sweden, Norway, and Greenland). The last-named enlarged recension he dedicated as priest to Pope Paul II (1464-71). He dedicated to the same pontiff his third recension, containing thirty-two maps, adding modern maps of France and the Holy Land. The works of the German cartographer were of great value in diffusing the knowledges of Ptolemy's Geography. The first recension, probably the very copy in the Lenox Library (New York), is the basis of the Roman editions of Ptolemy bearing the dates 1478, 1490, and 1507; on the third, certainly the copy preserved in Wolfegg Castle, are based the Ulm editions of 1482 and 1486. By combining the Roman and Ulm editions Waldseemüller produced the maps of Ptolemy in the Strasburg edition of 1513, which was frequently copied. The modern map of the Northern countries, made by Claudius Clavus, which Nicolaus embodied in his second recension of Ptolemy, was perhaps the source of the Zeni map which had such far-reaching influence, and likewise of the maritime charts of the Canerio and Cantino type. The revised map of the Northern countries in the third recension of Nicolaus, which placed Greenland north of the Scandinavian Peninsula, was a powerful factor in cartography for a century, especially as Waldseemüller gave the preference to this representation in his world and wall map of 1507, "the baptismal certificate of America". Because of these and other services to geography and cartography, as for example, by the revision of Buondelmonte's "Insularium", it would be desirable to have it established whether Nicolaus was really, as I conjecture, a Benedictine father of the Badia at Florence.

FISCHER, *Nicolaus Germanus* in *Entdeckungen der Normannen in Amerika* (Freiburg, 1902), 75-90, 113 sqq. (Eng. tr., London, 1903), 72-86, 108 sqq.

JOSEPH FISCHER.

Nicole, PIERRE, theologian and controversialist, b. 19 October, 1625, at Chartres; d. 16 November, 1695, at Paris. He studied at Paris, became Master of Arts, 1644, and followed courses in theology, 1645-46. Under Sainte-Beuve's direction he applied himself earnestly to the study of St. Augustine and St. Thomas, devoting part of his time to teaching in the schools of Port-Royal. In 1649 he received the degree of Bachelor of Theology, and then withdrew to Port-Royal des Champs, where he fell in with the Jansenistic leaders, especially Antoine Arnauld, who found in him a willing ally. He returned to Paris in 1654 under the assumed name of M. de Rosny. Four years later, during a tour in Germany, he translated Pascal's "Provinciales" into classic Latin, adding notes of his own and publishing the whole as the work of William Wendrock. In 1676 he sought admission to Holy orders, but was refused by the Bishop of Chartres and never got beyond tonsure. A letter, which he wrote (1677) to Innocent XI in favour of the Bishops of Saint-Pons and Arras, involved him in difficulties that obliged him to quit the capital. In 1679 he went to Belgium and lived for a time with Arnauld in Brussels, Liège, and other cities. About 1683 de Harlay, Archbishop of Paris, to whom he had sent a sort of retractation, authorized Nicole to return to Chartres, then to Paris. Here he took part in two celebrated controversies, the one involving Quietism in which he upheld Bossuet's views, the other relating to monastic studies in which he sided with Mabillon against the Abbé de Rancey. His last years were saddened by painful infirmities and his death came after a series of apoplectic attacks.

Pierre Nicole was a distinguished writer and a vigorous controversialist, and, together with Pascal, contributed much to the formation of French prose. As a controversialist, he too frequently placed his talent at the service of a sect; however, many are of the opinion that he did not wholly share the errors of the majority of the Jansenists. At any rate, we generally find in him only a mitigated expression of these errors clothed in great reserve. On the other hand, he started the resistance fund known as "la boîte à Perrette". (See JANSENIUS.) Niceron (Mémoires, XXIX, Paris, 1783) enumerates no less than eighty-eight of his works, several of which were, however, very short. The principal works of Nicole relating either to Protestantism or Jansenism are: "Les imaginaires et les visionnaires" or "Lettres sur l'hérésie imaginaire", namely, that of the Jansenists (Liège, 1667); "La perpétuité de la foi catholique touchant l'Eucharistie", published under Arnauld's name, but the first three volumes of which (Paris, 1669-76) are by Nicole, the fourth and fifth (Paris, 1711-13) by the Abbé Renaudot; "Préjugés légitimes contre les Calvinistes" (Paris, 1671); "La défense de l'Eglise" (Cologne,

1689), being a reply to the "Défense de la Réformation" written by the minister, Claude, against the "Préjugés légitimes"; "Essais de morale" (Paris, 1671–78); "Les prétendus Réformés convaincus de schisme" (Paris, 1684); "De l'unité de l'Eglise" or "Réfutation du nouveau système de M. Jurieu" (Paris, 1687), a condensed and decisive criticism of the theory of the "fundamental articles"; "Réfutation des principales erreurs des Quiétistes" (Paris, 1695); "Instructions théologiques et morales sur les sacrements" (Paris, 1706), "sur le Symbole" (Paris, 1706), "sur l'Oraison dominicale, la Salutation angélique, la Sainte Messe et les autres prières de l'Eglise" (Paris, 1706), "sur le premier commandement du Décalogue" (Paris, 1709); "Traité de la grâce générale" (Paris, 1715), containing all that Nicole had written at different times on grace; "Traité de l'usure" (Paris, 1720).

GOUJET, *Histoire de la vie et des ouvrages de Nicole* (Paris, 1733); BESOIGNE, *Vie de Nicole* in the *Histoire de Port-Royal*, V; (Both of these authors are Jansenists and write as such.) an anonymous *Biography* of Nicole in the *Continuation des essais de morale* (Luxemburg, 1732); CERVEAU, *L'esprit de Nicole* (Paris, 1765); MERSAN, *Pensées de Nicole* (Paris, 1806); FLOSS in *Kirchenlex.*, s. v.; HURTER, *Nomenclator*, II.

J. FORGET.

Nicolet, DIOCESE OF (NICOLETANA), in the Province of Quebec, Canada, suffragan of Quebec. It comprises the counties of Nicolet, Yamaska, Arthabaska, Drummond, and a small part of Shefford and Bagot. The see takes its name from the town of Nicolet (population 3915), situated on the south bank of the St. Lawrence, opposite Trois-Rivières.

It was erected into a bishopric on 11 July, 1885, by separation from the Diocese of Trois-Rivières, the first occupant of the see being Mgr Elphège Gravel. He was born on 12 October, 1838, at Saint-Antoine de Richelieu, Quebec; consecrated at Rome on 2 August, 1885, and died, 28 January, 1904. His successor, Mgr Joseph-Simon-Herman Brunault, the present occupant of the see, was born at St-David, Quebec, on 10 January, 1857; educated at the seminary of Nicolet and the Canadian College, Rome; ordained, 29 June, 1882. Having ministered two years in the cathedral of St. Hyacinth and taught for many years in the seminary of Nicolet, first as professor of literature, and then of theology, he was named coadjutor to Mgr Gravel and consecrated titular Bishop of Tubuna, 27 December, 1899; and succeeded as Bishop of Nicolet, 28 January, 1904. The seminary of Nicolet was founded in October, 1803, and affiliated to the Laval University of Quebec, in 1863; it contains over 320 students; a *grand séminaire*, likewise affiliated to the University of Laval, was established at Nicolet, 22 February, 1908.

The religious in the diocese are as follows: Sœurs de l'Assomption de la Sainte-Vierge, teachers, founded at St-Grégoire (Nicolet) in 1853, have eighteen houses in the diocese; Sœurs Grises (de Nicolet), hospitallers, three houses; Congrégation de Notre-Dame (of Montreal), teachers, at Arthabaskaville, and Victoriaville; Sœurs de la Présentation de la Bienheureuse Vierge Marie, teachers, at St-David and Drummondville; Sœurs Grises de la Croix (of Ottawa), teachers and nurses, with academy and school of house-keeping at St-François du Lac, and a school at Pierreville (Abenaki Indian village); Religieuses hospitalières de St-Joseph (of Montreal), hospitallers, at Arthabaskaville; Sœurs du Précieux-Sang, and Sœurs de la Sainte-Famille at Nicolet; the Frères des Ecoles Chrétiennes have schools at Nicolet, Arthabaskaville, La Baie, and St-Grégoire; the Frères de la Charité are at Drummondville; and the Frères du Sacré-Cœur teach at Arthabaskaville, and Victoriaville. *General Statistics.*—Secular priests, 140; brothers, 120; sisters, 400; churches with resident priests, 65; mission, 1; theological seminary, 1; college seminary, 1; commercial colleges and academies for boys, 11; students, 1500; academies for young ladies in charge of sisters, 28; students, 1800; normal school for young ladies, 1; parochial schools, 500; children attending parochial schools, 20,000; orphan asylums, 1; orphans, 120; hospitals, 3; population: Catholic French Canadians, 90,000; Irish Canadians, 600; Protestants, 1800; total population, 92,400.

J.-S.-HERMAN BRUNAULT.

Nicolò de' Tudeschi ("abbas modernus" or "recentior", "abbas Panormitanus" or "Siculus"), a Benedictine canonist, b. at Catania, Sicily, in 1386; d. at Palermo, 24 February, 1445. In 1400 he entered the Order of St. Benedict; he was sent (1405–06) to the University of Bologna to study under Zabarella; in 1411 he became a doctor of canon law, and taught successively at Parma (1412–18), Siena (1419–30), and Bologna (1431–32). Meanwhile in 1425, he was made abbot of the monastery of Maniacio, near Messina, whence his name "Abbas", to which has been added "modernus" or "recentior" (in order to distinguish him from "Abbas antiquus", a thirteenth century canonist who died about 1288); he is also known as "Abbas Siculus" on account of his Sicilian origin. In 1433 he went to Rome where he exercised the functions of auditor of the Rota and Apostolic referendary. The following year he relinquished these offices and placed himself at the service of Alfonso of Castile, King of Sicily, obtaining the See of Palermo in 1435, whence his name "Panormitanus". During the troubles that marred the pontificate of Eugene IV, Nicolò at first followed the party of this pontiff but subsequently allied himself with the antipope Felix V who, in 1440, named him cardinal. In his "Tractatus de concilio Basileensi" he upheld the doctrine of the superiority of a general council to the pope. It was his canonical works, especially his "Lectura in Decretales" "In Sextum", and "In Clementinas", that won him the title of "lucerna juris" (lamp of the law) and insured him great authority; he also wrote "Consilia", "Quæstiones", "Repetitiones", "Disputationes, disceptationes et allegationes", and "Flores utriusque juris". A fine edition of his works appeared at Venice in 1477; among later, frequent editions, that published in 1617–18 (Venice) in 10 folio volumes is especially notable.

SCHULTE, *Die Gesch. der Quellen u. Lit. des canonischen Rechtes*, II (Stuttgart, 1877), 312–313; SABBADINI, *Storia documentata della Reale Università di Catania* (Catania, 1898), 10 sq. BRANDILEONE, *Notizie su Graziano e su Niccolò de Tudeschi's tratte da una cronaca inedita. Studi e memorie per la storia dell' Università di Bologna*, I (Bologna, 1909), i, 18–21.

A. VAN HOVE.

Nicomedes, SAINT, martyr of unknown era, whose feast is observed 15 September. The Roman Martyrologium and the historical Martyrologies of Bede and his imitators place the feast on this date. The Gregorian Sacramentary contains under the same date the orations for his Mass. The name does not appear in the three oldest and most important MSS. of the "Martyrologium Hieronymianum", but was inserted in later recensions ("Martyrol. Hieronymianum", ed. De Rossi-Duchesne, in Acta SS., Nov., II, 121). The saint is without doubt a martyr of the Roman Church. He was buried in a catacomb on the Via Nomentana near the gate of that name. Three seventh century Itineraries make explicit reference to his grave, and Pope Adrian I restored the church built over it (De Rossi, "Roma Sotterranea", I, 178–79). A titular church of Rome, mentioned in the fifth century, was dedicated to him (*titulus S. Nicomedis*). Nothing is known of the circumstances of his death. The legend of the martyrdom of Sts. Nereus and Achilleus introduces him as a presbyter and places his death at the end of the first century. Other recensions of the martyrdom of St. Nicomedes ascribe the sentence of death to the Emperor Maximianus (beginning of the fourth century).

Acta SS., Sept., V, 5 sqq.; *Analecta Bollandiana*, XI, 268–69; MOMBRITIUS, *Sanctuarium*, II, 160–61; *Bibliotheca hagiographica latina*, ed. BOLLANDISTS, II, 901–02; DUFOURCQ, *Les Gesta Martyrum romains*, I (Paris, 1900), 209–10; MARUCCHI, *Les catacombes romaines* (Rome, 1900), 254–56.

J. P. KIRSCH.

Nicomedia, titular see of Bithynia Prima, founded by King Zipoetes. About 264 B. C. his son Nicodemes I dedicated the city anew, gave it his name, made it his capital, and adorned it with magnificent monuments. At his court the vanquished Hannibal sought refuge. When Bithynia became a Roman province Nicomedia remained its capital. Pliny the Younger mentions, in his letters to Trajan, several public edifices of the city,—a senate house, an aqueduct which he had built, a forum, the temple of Cybele, etc. He also proposed to join the Black Sea with the Sea of Marmora by a canal which should follow the river Sangarius and empty the waters of the Lake of Sabandja into the Gulf of Astacus. A fire then almost destroyed the town. From Nicomedia perhaps, he wrote to Trajan his famous letter concerning the Christians. Under Marcus Aurelius, Dionysius, Bishop of Corinth, addressed a letter to his community warning them against the Marcionites (Eusebius, "Hist. Eccl.", IV, xxiii). Bishop Evander, who opposed the sect of the Ophites (P. L., LIII, 592), seems to have lived at the same time. Nicomedia was the favourite residence of Diocletian, who built there a palace, a hippodrome, a mint, and an arsenal. In 303 the edict of the tenth persecution caused rivers of blood to flow through the empire, especially in Nicomedia, where the Bishop Anthimus and a great many Christians were martyred. The city was then half Christian, the palace itself being filled with them. In 303, in the vast plain east of Nicomedia, Diocletian renounced the empire in favour of Galerius. In 311 Lucian, a priest of Antioch, delivered a discourse in the presence of the judge before he was executed. Other martyrs of the city are numbered by hundreds. Nicomedia suffered greatly during the fourth century from an invasion of the Goths and from an earthquake (24 Aug., 354), which overthrew all the public and private monuments; fire completed the catastrophe. The city was rebuilt, on a smaller scale. In the reign of Justinian new public buildings were erected, which were destroyed in the following century by the Shah Chosroes. Pope Constantine I visited the city in 711. In 1073 John Comnenus was there proclaimed emperor and shortly afterwards was compelled to abdicate. In 1328 it was captured by the Sultan Orkhan, who restored its ramparts, parts of which are still preserved.

Le Quien (Oriens Christ., I, 581–98) has drawn up a list of fifty metropolitans, which may easily be completed, for Nicomedia has never ceased to be a metropolitan see. Some Latin archbishops are also mentioned by Le Quien (III, 1017) and by Eubel (Hierarchia Catholica medii ævi, I, 381). As early as the eighth century the metropolitan See of Nicomedia had eight suffragan sees which disappeared by degrees. Among its bishops, apart from those already mentioned, were: the three Arians, Eusebius, Eudoxius, and Demophilus, who exchanged their see for that of Constantinople; St. Theophylactus, martyred by the Iconoclasts in the ninth century; George, a great preacher and a friend of Photius; Philotheus Bryennios, the present titular, who discovered and published Διδαχὴ τῶν ἀποστόλων. To-day Nicomedia is called Ismidt, the chief town of a sanjak directly dependent on Constantinople. It has about 25,000 inhabitants, who are very poor, for the German port of Haïdar Pacha has completely ruined its commerce. Since 1891 the Augustinians of the Assumption have a mission and school, and the Oblates of the Assumption, a school and a dispensary. The Latin Catholics number about 250 in the region of the mission, seventy of them living in the city. The Armenian Catholic parish numbers 120.

TEXIER, *Asie Mineure* (Paris, 1862), 60–68; CUINET, *La Turquie d'Asie* (Paris), IV, 355–64.

S. VAILHÉ.

Nicopolis, a titular see, suffragan of Sebasteia, in Armenia Prima. Founded by Pompey after his decisive victory over Mithridates, it was inhabited by veterans of his army and by members of the neighbouring peasantry, and was delightfully situated in a beautiful, well-watered plain lying at the base of a thickly-wooded mountain. All the Roman highways intersecting that portion of the country and leading to Comana, Polemonium, Neocæsarea, Sebasteia, etc., radiated from Nicopolis which, even in the time of Strabo (XII, iii, 28), boasted quite a large population. Given to Polemon by Anthony, in 36 B. C., Nicopolis was governed from A. D. 54, by Aristobulus of Chalcis and definitively annexed to the Roman Empire by Nero, A. D. 64. It then became the metropolis of Lesser Armenia and the seat of the provincial diet which elected the Armeniarch. Besides the altar of the Augusti, it raised temples to Zeus Nicephorus and to Victory. Christianity reached Nicopolis at an early date and, under Licinius, about 319, forty-five of the city's inhabitants were martyred; the Church venerates them on 10 July. St. Basil (P. G., XXXII, 896) calls the priests of Nicopolis the sons of confessors and martyrs, and their church (P. G., XXXII, 834) the mother of that of Colonia. About 472, St. John the Silent, who had sold his worldly goods, erected a church there to the Blessed Virgin.

In 499 Nicopolis was destroyed by an earthquake, none save the bishop and his two secretaries escaping death (Bull. Acad. de Belgique, 1905, 557). This disaster was irreparable, and although Justinian rebuilt the walls and erected a monastery in memory of the Forty-five Martyrs (Procopius, "De Ædificiis", III, 4), Nicopolis never regained its former splendour. Under Heraclius it was captured by Chosroes (Sebeos, "Histoire d'Heraclius", tr. Macler, p. 62) and thenceforth was only a mediocre city, a simple see and a suffragan of Sebasteia in Lesser Armenia, remaining such at least until the eleventh century, as may be seen from the various "Notitiæ episcopatuum". To-day the site of ancient Nicopolis is occupied by the Armenian village of Purkh, which has a population of 200 families and is near the city of Enderes, in the sanjak of Kara-Hissar and the vilayet of Sivas. Notable among the eight bishops mentioned by Le Quien is St. Gregory who, in the eleventh century, resigned his bishopric and retired to Pithiviers in France. The Church venerates him on 14 March.

LE QUIEN, *Oriens christianus* (Paris, 1740), I, 427–30; *Acta Sanctorum*, July, III, 34–45; CUMONT, *Studica Pontica* (Brussels, 1906), 304–14.

S. VAILHÉ.

Nicopolis, DIOCESE OF (NICOPOLITANA), in Bulgaria. The city of Nicopolis (Thrace or Mœsia), situated at the junction of the Iatrus with the Danube, was built by Trajan in commemoration of his victory over the Dacians (Ammianus Marcellinus, XXXI, 5; Jornandès, "De rebus geticis", ed. Savagner, 218). Ptolemy (III, xi, 7) places it in Thrace and Hierocles in Mœsia near the Hæmus or Balkans. In the "Ecthesis" of pseudo-Epiphanius (Gelzer, "Ungedruckte . . . Texte der Notitiæ episcopatuum", 535), Nicopolis figures as an autocephalous archbishopric about 640, and then disappears from the episcopal lists, owing to the fact that the country fell into the hands of the Bulgarians. Le Quien (Oriens christianus, I, 1233) has preserved the names of two ancient bishops: Marcellus in 458, and Amantius in 518. A list of the Latin titulars (1354–1413) may be found in Eubel (Hierarchia catholica medii ævi, Münster, I, 381). The city is chiefly noted for the defeat of the French and Hungarian armies (25 September, 1396) which made the Turks masters of the Balkan peninsula.

The Latin mission of Bulgaria, subject during the sixteenth century to the Archbishops of Antivari, afterwards received Franciscan missionaries from Bosnia, and in 1624 formed an independent province called "custodia Bulgariæ". In 1763 it was confided to the Baptistines of Genoa and in 1781, to the Passionists who have no canonical residences in the country, simply parishes. One of them is usually appointed Bishop of Nicopolis. The Franciscan bishops formerly resided at Tchiprovetz, destroyed by the Turks in 1688, but after the war and the pestilence of 1812, the bishop established himself at Cioplea, a Catholic village which the Bulgarians had just founded near Bucharest and where his successors resided until 1883, when the Holy See created the Archbishopric of Bucharest. The Bishop of Nicopolis, ceasing then to be apostolic administrator of Wallachia, chose Roustchouk as his residence and still lives there. In the diocese there are 13,000 Catholics; 24 priests, 5 of whom are seculars; 17 Passionists and 2 Assumptionists; 15 churches, and 3 chapels. The Assumptionists have a school at Varna, the Oblates of the Assumption a boarding-school in the same city, and the Sisters of Our Lady of Sion a boarding-school at Roustchouk.

Ptolemy, ed. MÜLLER, I (Paris), 481; LE ROULX, La France en Orient au XIVe siècle, I (Paris, 1886), 211–99; Echos d'Orient, VII (Paris), 207–9; Missiones catholicæ (Rome, 1907).

S. VAILHÉ.

Nicopolis, a titular see and metropolis in ancient Epirus. Augustus founded the city (B. C. 31) on a promontory in the Gulf of Ambracia, in commemoration of his victory over Anthony and Cleopatra at Actium. At Nicopolis the emperor instituted the famous quinquennial Actian games in honour of Apollo. The city was peopled chiefly by settlers from the neighbouring *municipia*, of which it was the head (Strabo III, xiii, 3; VII, vii, 6; X, ii, 2). According to Pliny the Elder (IV, 2) it was a free city. St. Paul intended going there (Tit., iii, 12) and it is possible that even then it numbered some Christians among its population; Origen sojourned there for a while (Eusebius, "Hist. eccl.", VI, 16). Laid waste by the Goths at the beginning of the fifth century (Procopius, "Bell. goth.", IV, 22), restored by Justinian (Idem, "De Ædificiis", IV, 2), in the sixth century it was still the capital of Epirus (Hierocles, "Synecdemus", ed. Burckhardt, 651, 4). The province of ancient Epirus of which Nicopolis was the metropolis, constituted a portion of the western patriarchate, directly subject to the jurisdiction of the pope; but, about 732, Leo the Isaurian incorporated it into the Patriarchate of Constantinople. Of the eleven metropolitans mentioned by Le Quien (Oriens christianus, II, 133–38) the most celebrated was Alcison who, early in the sixth century, opposed the Monophysite policy of Emperor Anastasius. The last known of these bishops was Anastasius, who attended the Œcumenical Council in 787, and soon afterwards, owing to the decadence into which Nicopolis fell, the metropolitan see was transferred to Naupactus which subsequently figured in the Notitiæ episcopatuum. Quite extensive ruins of Nicopolis are found three miles to the north of Prevesa and are called Palaio-Prevesa.

SMITH, Dict. Greek and Roman Geography, II (London, 1870), 426; LEAKE, Northern Greece, I, 185; WOLFE, Journal of Geographical Society, III, 92 sq.

S. VAILHÉ.

Nicosia, a city of the Province of Catania, in Sicily, situated at a height of about 2800 feet above the level of the sea. In its neighbourhood are salt mines and sulphur springs. The town is believed to stand on the site of the ancient Otterbita, which was destroyed by the Arabs. It has a fine cathedral, with a magnificent portal and paintings by Velasquez. Santa Maria Maggiore, also, is a beautiful church. The episcopal see was erected in 1818, its first prelate being Mgr Cajetan M. Averna. Nicosia was the birthplace of the Blessed Felix of Nicosia, a Capuchin lay brother. Within the diocese is the ancient city of Triona, which was an episcopal see from 1087 to 1090. Nicosia is a suffragan of Messina, from the territory of which that of Nicosia was taken; it has 23 parishes, with 60,250 inhabitants, 4 religious houses of men, and 5 of women, and 3 schools for girls.

CAPPELLETTI, Le Chiese d'Italia, XXI (Venice, 1857).

U. BENIGNI.

Nicosia, TITULAR ARCHDIOCESE OF, in the Province of Cyprus. It is now agreed (Oberhummer, "Aus Cypern" in "Zeitschrift der Gesellschaft für Erdkunde", 1890, 212-14), that Ledra, Leucotheon, Leucopolis, Leucosia, and Nicosia are the same city, at least the same episcopal see. Ledra is first mentioned by Sozomen (H. E., I, 11) in connexion with its bishop, St. Triphyllius, who lived under Constantine and whom St. Jerome (De scriptoribus ecclesiasticis), pronounced the most eloquent of his time. Mention is made also of one of his disciples, St. Diomedes, venerated on 28 October. Under the name of Leucosia the city appears for the first time in the sixth century, in the "Synecdemus" of Hierocles (ed. Burckhardt, 707–8). It was certainly subsequent to the eighth century that Leucosia or Nicosia replaced Constantia as the metropolis of Cyprus, for at the Œcumenical Council of 787 one Constantine signed as Bishop of Constantia; in any case at the conquest of the island in 1191 by Richard Cœur de Lion Nicosia was the capital. At that time Cyprus was sold to the Templars who established themselves in the castle of Nicosia, but not being able to overcome the hostility of the people of the city, massacred the majority of the inhabitants and sold Cyprus to Guy de Lusignan, who founded a dynasty there, of which there were fifteen titulars, and did much towards the prosperity of the capital. Nicosia was then made a Latin metropolitan see with three suffragans, Paphos, Limassol, and Famagusta. The Greeks who had previously had as many as fourteen titulars were obliged to be content with four bishops bearing the same titles as the Latins but residing in different towns. The list of thirty-one Latin archbishops from 1196 to 1502 may be seen in Eubel, "Hierarchia catholica medii ævi", I, 382; II, 224. Quarrels between Greeks and Latins were frequent and prolonged, especially at Nicosia, where the two councils of 1313–60 ended in bloodshed; but in spite of everything the island prospered. There were many beautiful churches in the possession of the Dominicans, Franciscans, Augustinians, Carmelites, Benedictines, and Carthusians. Other churches belonged to the Greeks, Armenians, Jacobites, Maronites, Nestorians etc. In 1489 Cyprus fell under the dominion of Venice and on 9 November, 1570, Nicosia fell into the power of the Turks, who committed atrocious cruelties. Nor was this the last time, for on 9 July, 1821, during the revolt of the Greeks in the Ottoman Empire, they strangled many of the people of Nicosia, among them the four Greek bishops of the island. Since 4 June, 1878, Cyprus has been under the dominion of England. Previously Nicosia was the residence of the Mutessarif of the sandjak which depended on the vilayet of the Archipelago. Since the Turkish occupation of 1571 Nicosia has been the permanent residence of the Greek archbishop who governs the autonomous church of Cyprus. The city has 13,000 inhabitants. The Franciscans administer the Catholic mission which is dependent on the Latin Patriarchate of Jerusalem, and has a school for boys. The Sisters of St. Joseph have a school for girls.

LE QUIEN, Oriens christianus, II (Paris, 1740), 1076; Acta Sanctorum, III Junii, 174–78; Analecta Bollandiana (Brussels, 1907), 212–20; MAS LATRIE, Histoire des Archevêques latins de l'île de Chypre (Genoa, 1882); HACKETT, A History of the Orthodox Church of Cyprus (London, 1901), passim; PHRANGOUDES, Cyprus (Athens, 1890), in Greek; CHAMBERLAYNE, Lacrimæ Nicosienses (Paris, 1894).

S. VAILHÉ.

Nicotera and Tropea, DIOCESE OF (NICOTEREN-SIS ET TROPEIENSIS), suffragan of Reggio di Calabria. Nicotera, the ancient Medama, is a city of the Province of Catanzaro, in Calabria, Italy; it was destroyed by the earthquake of 1783. Its first known bishop was Proculus, to whom, with others, a letter of St. Gregory the Great was written in 599. With the exception of Sergius (787), none of its bishops is known earlier than 1392. Under Bishop Charles Pinti, the city was pillaged by the Turks. In 1818, it was united on equal terms (*æque principaliter*) with the Diocese of Tropea. This city is situated on a reef, in the gulf of St. Euphemia connected with the mainland by a narrow strip. It is the birthplace of the painter Spanò, the anatomists Pietro and Paolo Voiani, and the philosopher Pasquale Galluppi. It has a beautiful cathedral, restored after its destruction by the earthquake of 1783. Here the Greek Rite was formerly used. Only three bishops before the Norman conquest are known; the first, Joannes, is referred to the year 649; among its other prelates was Nicolò Acciapori (1410), an eminent statesman. The diocese has 72 parishes, with 78,000 inhabitants, a Franciscan nouse, and a house of the Sisters of Charity.

CAPPELLETTI, *Le Chiese d'Italia*, XXI.

U. BENIGNI.

Nictheroy, DIOCESE OF. See PETROPOLIS.

Nider, JOHN, theologian, b. 1380 in Swabia; d. 13 August, 1438, at Colmar. He entered the Order of Preachers at Colmar and after profession was sent to Vienna for his philosophical studies, which he finished at Cologne where he was ordained. He gained a wide reputation in Germany as a preacher and was active at the Council of Constance. After making a study of the convents of his order of strict observance in Italy he returned to the University of Vienna where in 1425 he began teaching as Master of Theology. Elected prior of the Dominican convent at Nuremberg in 1427, he successively served as socius to his master general and vicar of the reformed convents of the German province. In this capacity he maintained his early reputation of reformer and in 1431 he was chosen prior of the convent of strict observance at Basle. He became identified with the Council of Basle as theologian and legate, making several embassies to the Hussites at the command of Cardinal Julian. Sent as legate of the Council to the Bohemians he succeeded in pacifying them. He journeyed to Ratisbon (1434) to effect a further reconciliation with the Bohemians and then proceeded to Vienna to continue his work of reforming the convents there. During the discussion that followed the dissolution of the Council of Basle by Eugene IV, he joined the party in favour of continuing the Council in Germany, abandoning them, however, when the pope remained firm in his decision. He resumed his theological lectures at Vienna in 1436 and was twice elected dean of the university before his death. As reformer he was foremost in Germany and welcomed as such both by his own order and by the Fathers of the Council of Basle. As a theologian his adherence to the principles of St. Thomas and his practical methods made him distinguished among his contemporaries. The most important among his many writings is the "Formicarius" (5 vols., Douai, 1602) a treatise on the philosophical, theological, and social questions of his day. Among his theological works are the following: "Commentarius in IV libros Sententiarum" (no longer extant); "Præceptorum divinæ legis" (Douai, 1612, seventeen other editions before 1500); "Tractatus de contractibus mercatorum" (Paris, 1514, eight editions before 1500); "Consolatorium timoratæ conscientiæ" (Rome, 1604); "De Morali lepra" (Regia, 1830); "Manuale ad instructionem spiritualium Pastorum" (Rome, 1513); "Alphabetum Divini Amoris" (Antwerp, 1705, in works of Gerson); "De modo bene vivendi" (commonly atttributed to St. Bernard); "De Reformatione Religiosorum Libri Tres" (Paris, 1512; Antwerp, 1611). Besides these there are several letters written to the Bohemians and to the Fathers of the Council of Basle, printed in "Monum. Concil. General., sæc. XV, Concil. Basil. Scrip.", I (Vienna, 1857).

QUÉTIF-ECHARD, *Scriptores O. P.*, I, 792 sqq.; II, 822; TOURON, *Histoire des Hommes illustres de l'ordre de St. Dominique*, III, 218–76; SCHIELER in *Kirchenlex.* q. v. *Nider*; COLVENERIUS, *J. Nider Formicarius* (Douai, 1602); STEILL, *Ord. Præd. Ephemerides Domincano-sacræ*, II (Dilling, 1692), 230; SCHIELER, *Magister Johannes Nider, aus dem Orden der Prediger-Brüder* (Mainz, 1885); *Année Dominicaine*, VII (1895), 731–46; HAIN, *Rep. Bibl.*, III (1831); BRUMER, *Predigerorden in Wien* (1867); CHEVALIER, *Répertoire des Sources historiques du Moyen Age*, II, 3360.

IGNATIUS SMITH.

Nieremberg y Otin, JUAN EUSEBIO, noted theologian and polygraphist, b. of German parents at Madrid, 1595; d. there, 1658. Having studied the classics at the Court, he went to Alcalá for the sciences and from there to Salamanca for canon law, where he entered the Society of Jesus in 1614, much against the wishes of his father who finally obliged him to leave the novitiate of Villagarcía. He remained firm in his resolution and was permitted to return to Madrid to finish his probation. He studied Greek and Hebrew at the Colegio de Huete, arts and theology at Alcalá, and was ordained in 1623, making his profession in 1633. At the Colegio Imperial of Madrid he taught humanities and natural history for sixteen years and Sacred Scripture for three. As a director of souls he was much sought, being appointed by royal command confessor to the Duchess of Mantua, granddaughter of Philip II. Remarkable for his exemplary life, and the heights of prayer to which he attained, he was an indefatigable worker, and one of the most prolific writers of his time. Seventy-three printed and eleven manuscript works are attributed to him; of these, twenty-four at least are in Latin. Though his works are distinguished for their erudition, those in Spanish being characterized according to Capmani, by nobility and purity of diction, terse, well-knit phrases, forcible metaphors, and vivid imagery, certain defects mar his style, at times inelegant and marked by a certain disregard for the rules of grammar and a too pronounced use of antithesis, paronomasia, and other plays upon words. Lack of a true critical faculty often detracts from the learning. The Spanish Academy includes his name in the "Diccionario de Autoridades". His principal works are: (1) "Del Aprecio y Estima de la Divina Gracia" (Madrid, 1638), editions of which have been issued at Saragossa, Barcelona, Seville, Majorca, also a second edition of the Madrid edition; it has been translated into Italian, French, Latin, German, Panayano, and condensed into English (New York, 1866, 1891); (2) "De la Diferencia entre lo Temporal y Eterno" (Madrid, 1640), of which there are fifty-four Spanish editions, and translations into Latin, Arabic, Italian, French, German, Flemish, and English (1672, 1684, 1884), Portuguese, Mexican, Guaranian, Chiquito, Panayano; (3) "Opera Parthenica" (Lyons, 1659), in which he defends the Immaculate Conception of the Blessed Virgin, basing it upon new, although not always absolutely reliable, documents; (4) "Historia naturæ maxime peregrinæ Libris XVI, distincta" (Antwerp, 1635); (5) "De la afición y amor de Jesús . . . Idem de Maria" (Madrid, 1630), of which there are five Spanish editions and translations into Latin, Arabic, German, Flemish, French, Italian, Portuguese, and an English translation of the first edition (1849, 1880); one edition of (6) "Obras Christianas espirituales y filosóficas" (Madrid, 1651, fol. 3 vols.), and one of (7) "Obras Christianas" (Madrid, 1665, fol. 2 vols.), are still extant. It was customary in many of the Spanish churches to read selections from these books every Sunday.

ANDRADE, *Varones ilustres de la Compañía de Jesús*, VIII (2nd ed., Bilbao (1891), 699–766; CAPMANI Y DE MONTPALAU, *Teatro*

Histórico crítico de la Elocuencia española, V (Barcelona, 1848), 271; R. P. *Joannis Eusebii Nierembergii e Societate Jesu Opera Parthenica. . . . Vita Ven. Patris. . . . Collecta ex his quæ hispanice scripserunt PP. Alphonsus de Andrade et Joannes de Ygarza ejus. Soc.* (Lyons, 1659); SOMMERVOGEL, *Bibliot.*, V, 1725; GUILHERMY, *Ménologe de la Compagnie de Jésus, Assistance d'Espagne*, pt. I (Paris, 1902).

ANTONIO PÉREZ GOYENA.

Niessenberger, HANS, an architect of the latter part of the Middle Ages, whose name is mentioned with comparative frequency in contemporaneous literature. But information about his personality and his works is somewhat more difficult to find. It seems however, that he was born in Gratz, Styria ("Seckauer Kirchenschmuck", 1880, p. 56). He worked on the choir of the Freiburg cathedral from 1471 to 1480; in the latter year he was compelled to leave the task of building and to swear that he would not try to revenge himself for this. In 1480 he worked on the church of St. Leonhard at Basle; in 1482, on the cathedral at Strasburg; and in the following year he probably was engaged on the great cathedral of Milan with a yearly salary of 180 guilders—at least there is a "Johannes of Graz" mentioned as architect in Ricci, "Storia dell' archit. italiana", II, 388. The choir at Freiburg was turned over to him in 1471; the contract is interesting and instructive, showing as it does the manner in which buildings of this kind were erected during the latter part of the Middle Ages, and how the working hours, wages, etc., were determined upon (Schreiber, "Münster zu Freiburg", Appendix, 15 sq.). The choir possesses great beauty, but it also manifests the peculiarities of Late Gothic. It is long, like the main church, with the nave higher, the side aisles lower and somewhat narrower than in the front, and surrounded by twelve chapels, enclosed on two sides by fluted columns. The arched roof, supported by beautifully carved columns, forms a network. The windows are characteristically Late Gothic, and the arches are wonderfully delicate. The whole is the work of a master.

SCHREIBER, *op. cit.*; KUGLER, *Gesch. der Baukunst*, II (1859); OTTE, *Kunst-Archäologie* (5th ed., 1884); KEMPF, *Das Münster zu Freiburg im Breisgau* (Freiburg, 1898).

G. GIETMANN.

Niger (NIGRI, Ger. SCHWARTZ), PETER GEORGE, Dominican theologian, preacher and controversialist, b. 1434 at Kaaden in Bohemia; d. between 1481 and 1484. He studied at different universities (Salamanca, Montpellier, etc.), entered the order in 1452 at Eichstätt, Bavaria, and after his religious profession took up philosophy and theology at Leipzig, where he also produced his first literary work "De modo prædicandi" (1457). In 1459 he defended publicly in Freiburg a series of theses so successfully that the provincial chapter then in session there sent him to the University of Bologna for advanced courses in theology and canon law. Recalled after two years, he was made lector of theology and engaged in teaching and preaching. In 1465 he taught philosophy and was regent of studies in Cologne; in 1467 taught theology at Ulm; in 1469 or 1470 was elected prior in Eichstätt; on 31 May, 1473, the newly founded University of Ingolstadt conferred on him the degree of Doctor of theology; in 1474 he taught theology in the convent at Ratisbon and in 1478 became professor of Old-Testament exegesis in the University of Ingolstadt. Shortly after, upon the invitation of the patron of learning, Matthias Corvinus, King of Hungary, he became rector of his newly-erected Academy of philosophy, theology, and Sacred Scripture at Buda, in gratitude for which honour he dedicated to his royal friend his "Clypeus Thomistarum adversus omnes doctrinæ doctoris angelici obtrectatores" (Venice, 1481), in which he defends the teaching of St. Thomas against the Scotists and Nominalists. Niger ranks among the most eminent theologians and preachers of the latter half of the fifteenth century. He was a keen disciple of St. Thomas, zealous for the integrity of his teachings and adhering strictly to the traditions of his school. In his few theological works he limits himself almost entirely to the discussion of abstract questions of logic and psychology. He devoted most of his time to preaching to the Jews. He had learned their language and become familiar with their literature at Salamanca and Montpellier by associating with Jewish children and attending the lectures of the rabbis. At Ratisbon, Worms, and Frankfort-on-the-Main he preached in German, Latin, and Hebrew, frequently challenging the rabbis to a disputation. He wrote two anti-Jewish works, one in Latin, "Tractatus contra Perfidos Judæos" (Esslingen, 1475), which is probably the earliest printed anti-Jewish work, and in which he severely attacked the Jews and the Talmud. The other, written in German, is entitled "Stern des Messias" (Esslingen, 1477). Reuchlin in his "Augenspiegel" declared them absurd. Both works are furnished with appendices giving the Hebrew alphabet in Hebrew and Latin type, rules of grammar and for reading Hebrew, the Decalogue in Hebrew, some Messianic texts from the Old Testament, etc. They are among the earliest specimens of Hebrew printing in Germany, and the first attempt at Hebrew grammar in that country by a Christian scholar. They were afterwards published separately as "Commentatio de primis linguæ Hebraicæ elementis" (Altdorf, 1764). Peter Teuto, O.P. (Quétif, I, 855), and Peter Eystettensis (Eck, "Chrysopassus Cent.", XLIX) are most probably to be identified with Peter Niger.

QUÉTIF-ECHARD, *SS. Ord. Præd.*, I, 861 sqq.; TOURON, *Hom. Ill. de l'ordre de S. Dom.*, III, 532–31; REUSCH, *Allg. d. Biogr.*, XXXIII, 247 sq.; JOCHER, *Allg. Gelehrtenlexikon*, s. v.; PRANTL, *Gesch. der Logik im Abendl.* (Leipzig, 1870), 221 sq.; *Katholik*, I (1891), 574; II (1902), 310; *Analecta Ord. Præd.*, II, 367; WOLF, *Bibliotheca Hebraica* (Hamburg, 1721), II, 17, 1037, 1110 sqq.; IV, 525 sqq.

JOSEPH SCHROEDER.

Nigeria, UPPER AND LOWER, a colony of British East Africa extending from the Gulf of Guinea to Lake Chad (from 4° 30' to 7° N. lat., and from 5° 30' to 8° 30' E. long.), is bounded on the north and west by French Sudan, on the south-west by the English colony of Lagos, on the south by the Atlantic, on the east by German Kamerun. It derives its name from the River Niger, flowing through it. The Niger, French from its source in the Guinean Sudan to the frontier of Sierra Leone and Liberia, enters Nigeria above Ilo, receives the Sokoto River at Gomba, and the Benue at Lokodja, the chief tributaries in English territory. Though the establishment of the English dates only from 1879, numerous explorers had long before reconnoitred the river and the neighbouring country. Among the most famous were Mungo Park (1795–1805), Clapperton (1822), René Caillé (1825), Lander, Barth, Mage, and recently the French officers Galliéni, Mizon, Hourst, and Lenfant. In 1879, on the initiative of Sir George Goldie, the English societies established in the region purchased all the French and foreign trading stations of Lower Niger and in 1885 obtained a royal charter which constituted them the "Royal Company of the Niger". The Royal Company developed rapidly and acquired immense territories, often at the cost of bloodshed. The monopoly of navigation which it claimed to exercise, contrary to the stipulations of the General Act of Berlin, its opposition to the undertakings of France and Germany, its encroachments on neighbouring territories, aroused numerous diplomatic quarrels which finally brought about the revocation of its privileges (1 Jan., 1900). It then became a simple commercial company with enormous territorial possessions; the conquered lands, reunited to the old Protectorate of the Niger Coast organized in 1884, constituted the British colony of

Nigeria. France, however, retained two colonies at Badjibo-Arenberg and at Forcados; navigation was free to all.

Politically Nigeria is divided into two provinces, Southern or Lower Nigeria, Northern or Upper Nigeria, separated by the parallel which passes through Ida. Each division is governed by a high commissioner named directly by the Crown. Northern Nigeria with an area of over 123,400 square miles is as yet only partly settled, and has nine constituted provinces. The ancient capital, Gebha, is now replaced by Wushishi on the Kaduna. The chief cities are Lokodja, Ilo, Yola, Gando, Sokoto, Kano, etc. Kano, situated two hundred miles to the north, is a remarkable city and one of the largest markets of the whole world. For more than a thousand years the metropolis of East Africa, Kano contains about fifty thousand inhabitants, is surrounded by walls built of hardened clay from twenty to thirty ft. high and fifteen miles in circumference. Every year more than two million natives go to Kano to exchange their agricultural products or their merchandise. The chief articles of commerce are camels, cattle, ivory, sugar, ostrich plumes, and kola nuts. Kano is also a great industrial centre, renowned for its hides and its cotton materials; sorghum and many kinds of vegetables and cereals are cultivated. The natives are very good workmen, especially in the cultivation of the fields. Although nominally subject to England, some chiefs, or sultans, have remained almost independent, for instance those of Sokoto and Nupe. English money, however, has circulated everywhere and three-penny pieces are very popular. Northern Nigeria has a population of about fifteen million inhabitants, divided into several tribes, each speaking its own tongue, the chief of which are the Yorubas, the Nupes, the Haussas, and the Igbiras. English is the official language of the administration.

Constantly pressing to the south, Islam has penetrated as far as the markets of the Lower Niger, and carries on a vigorous proselytism, aided by the representatives of the English Government. Mussulman chiefs and instructors are often appointed for the fetishistic population. Powerful English Protestant missions have unsuccessfully endeavoured to gain a foothold. Catholic missionaries explored a portion of these same regions as early as 1883, but only now have they undertaken permanent establishments. Nigeria is divided into two prefectures Apostolic; that of the Upper Niger is confided to the Society of African Missions of Lyons (1884), and that of the Lower Niger to the Fathers of the Holy Ghost (1889). The first comprises all the territory west of the Niger from Forcados and north of the Benue to Yola. Its limits were only definitively constituted by the decrees of 15 January and 10 May, 1894. The prefect Apostolic resides at Lokodja. The mission is chiefly developed in the more accessible part of Southern Nigeria, where Islam is still almost a stranger. Its chief posts, besides Lokodja, are Assaba, Ila, Ibsélé, Ibi, Idu, etc. The twenty missionaries are assisted by the Religious of the Queen of the Apostles (Lyons); in 1910 there were about 1500 Catholics and an equal number of catechumens. The Prefecture Apostolic of the Lower Niger comprises all the country situated between the Niger, the Benue, and the western frontier of German Kamerun. Less extensive than that of the Upper Niger, its population is much more dense, almost wholly fetishistic, and even cannibal. Towns of five, ten, and twenty thousand inhabitants are not rare; the population is chiefly agricultural, cultivating the banana and the yam. In the delta and on Cross River the palm oil harvest is the object of an active commerce. Several tribes are crowded into these fertile districts; the Ibo, Nri, Munchis, Ibibio, Ibani, Ibeno, Efik, Akwa, Aro, etc. Their religion is fetishism, with ridiculous and cruel practices often admitting of human sacrifices, exacted by the *ju-ju* (a corruption of the native word *egugu*), a fetish which is supposed to contain the spirit of an ancestor; but purer religious elements are found beneath all these superstitions, belief in God, the survival of the soul, distinction between good and evil, etc.

The Mussulmans are located in important centres such as the market of Onitcha. Moreover, wherever the English Government employs Haussas as militia the latter carry on an active propaganda, and where they are, a movement towards Islam is discernible. This is the case at Calabar, Lagos, Freetown, and numerous points in the interior and on the coast. English Protestant missions have long since penetrated into this country and have expended, not without results, enormous sums for propaganda. Native churches with pastors and bishops have even been organized on the Niger, constituting what is called the native pastorate. At Calabar the United Presbyterian Church dates from 1846, strongly established throughout the country. In 1885 the Catholic missionaries of Gabon established themselves at Onitcha, the centre of the Ibo country and a city of twenty thousand inhabitants. Several native kings, among them the King of Onitcha, have been converted, numerous schools have been organized, towns and villages everywhere have asked for missionaries, or lacking them, for catechists. Until 1903 no establishment could be made at Calabar, the seat of the Government and the most important commercial centre of Southern Nigeria, but once founded the Catholic mission became very popular, adherents came in crowds, the schools were filled to overflowing. There is need of labourers and resources for the immense harvest. The Fathers of the Holy Ghost are seconded in their efforts by the Sisters of St. Joseph of Cluny. The progress of evangelization seems to necessitate in the near future the division of the mission into two prefectures, one of which will have its centre at Onitcha, the other at Calabar.

Missions catholiques au XIXe siècle; Missions d'Afrique (Paris, 1902); *Missiones Catholicæ* (Rome, 1907).

A. Le Roy.

Nihilism.—The term was first used by Turgeniev in his novel, "Fathers and Sons" (in "Russkij Věstnik", Feb., 1862): a Nihilist is one who bows to no authority and accepts no doctrine, however widespread, that is not supported by proof. The nihilist theory was formulated by Cernysevskij in his novel "Cto delat" (What shall be done, 1862–64), which forecasts a new social order constructed on the ruins of the old. But essentially, Nihilism was a reaction against the abuses of Russian absolutism; it originated with the first secret political society in Russia founded by Pestel (1817), and its first effort was the military revolt of the Decembrists (14 Dec., 1825). Nicholas I crushed the uprising, sent its leaders to the scaffold and one hundred and sixteen participants to Siberia. The spread (1830) of certain philosophical doctrines (Hegel, Saint-Simon, Fourier) brought numerous recruits to Nihilism, especially in the universities; and, in many of the cities, societies were organized to combat absolutism and introduce constitutional government.

Theoretical Nihilism.—Its apostles were Alexander Herzen (1812–70) and Michael Bakunin (1814–76), both of noble birth. The former, arrested (1832) as a partisan of liberal ideas, was imprisoned for eight months, deported, pardoned (1840), resided in Moscow till 1847 when he migrated to London and there founded (1857) the weekly periodical, "Kolokol" (Bell), and later "The Polar Star". The "Kolokol" published Russian political secrets and denunciations of the Government; and, in spite of the police, made its way into Russia to spread revolutionary ideas. Herzen, inspired by Hegel and Feurbach, proclaimed the destruction of the existing order; but he did not advocate violent measures. Hence his younger followers wearied of him; and on the other hand his defense of the Poles during the insurrection of 1863 alienated many of his Russian sympathizers. The "Kolokol" went out of existence in 1868 and Herzen died two years later. Bakunin was extreme in his revolutionary theories. In the first number of "L'Alliance Internationale de la Démocratie Socialiste" founded by him in 1869, he openly professed Atheism and called for the abolition of marriage, property, and of all social and religious institutions. His advice, given in his "Revolutionary Catechism", was: "Be severe to yourself and severe to others. Suppress the sentiments of relationship, friendship, love, and gratitude. Have only one pleasure, one joy, one reward—the triumph of the revolution. Night and day, have only one thought, the destruction of everything without pity. Be ready to die and ready to kill any one who opposes the triumph of your revolt." Bakunin thus opened the way to nihilistic terrorism.

PROPAGANDA (1867-77).—It began with the formation (1861-62) of secret societies, the members of which devoted their lives and fortunes to the dissemination of revolutionary ideas. Many of these agitators, educated at Zurich, Switzerland, returned to Russia and gave Nihilism the support of trained intelligence. Prominent among them were Sergius Nečaev, master of a parochial school in St. Petersburg, who was in constant communication with nihilist centers in various cities, and Sergius Kovalin who established thirteen associations in Černigor. These societies took their names from their founders—the Malikovcy, Lavrists, Bakunists, etc. They enrolled seminarists, university students, and young women. Among the working men the propaganda was conducted in part through free schools. The promoters engaged in humble trades as weavers, blacksmiths, and carpenters, and in their shops inculcated nihilist doctrine. The peasantry was reached by writings, speeches, schools, and personal intercourse. Even the nobles shared in this work, e. g., Prince Peter Krapotkin, who, under the pseudonym of Borodin, held conferences with workingmen. As secondary centres, taverns and shops served as meeting-places, depositories of prohibited books, and, in case of need, as places of refuge. Though without a central organization the movement spread throughout Russia, notably in the region of the Volga and in that of the Dnieper where it gained adherents among the Cossacks. The women in particular displayed energy and self-sacrifice in their zeal for the cause. Many were highly cultured and some belonged to the nobility or higher classes, e. g., Natalia Armfeld, Barbara Batiuškova, Sofia von Herzfeld, Sofia Perovakaja. They co-operated more especially through the schools.

The propaganda of the press was at first conducted from foreign parts: London, Geneva, Zurich. In this latter city there were two printing-offices, established in 1873, where the students published the works of Lavrov and of Bakunin. The first secret printing-office in Russia, founded at St. Petersburg in 1861, published four numbers of the Velikoruss. At the same time there came to Russia, from London, copies of the "Proclamation to the New Generation" (Kmolodomu pokoleniju), and "Young Russia" (Molodaja Rosija), which was published in the following year. In 1862, another secret printing-office, established at Moscow, published the recital of the revolt of 14 December, 1825, written by Ogarev. In 1862, another secret press at St. Petersburg published revolutionary proclamations for officers of the army; and in 1863, there were published in the same city a few copies of the daily papers, "Svoboda" (Liberty) and "Zemlja i Volja" (The Earth and Liberty); the latter continued to be published in 1878 and 1879, under the editorship, at first, of Marco Natanson, and later of the student, Alexander Mihailov, one of the ablest organizers of Nihilism. In 1866, a student of Kazan, Elpidin, published two numbers of the "Podpolnoe Slovo", which was succeeded by the daily paper, the "Sovremennost" (The Contemporary), and later, by the "Narodnoe Dělo" (The National Interest), which was published (1868-70), to disseminate the ideas of Bakunin. Two numbers of the "Narodnaja Rasprava" (The Tribunal of Reason) were published in 1870, at St. Petersburg and at Moscow. In 1873, appeared the "Vpred" (Forward!), one of the most esteemed periodicals of Nihilism, having salient socialistic tendencies. A volume of it appeared each year. In 1875-76, there was connected with the "Vpred", a small bi-monthly supplement, which was under the direction of Lavrov until 1876, when it passed under the editorship of Smironv, and went out of existence in the same year. It attacked theological and religious ideas, proclaiming the equality of rights, freedom of association, and justice for the proletariat. At Geneva, in 1875 and 1876, the "Rabotnik" (The Workman) was published, which was edited in the style of the people; the "Nabat" (The Tocsin) appeared in 1875, directed by Thačev; the "Narodnaja Volja" (The Will of the People), in 1879, and the "Cernyi Pereděl", in 1880, were published in St. Petersburg. There was no fixed date for any of these papers, and their contents consisted, more especially, of proclamations, of letters from revolutionists, and at times, of sentences of the Executive Committees. These printing offices also produced books and pamphlets and Russian translations of the works of Lassalle, Marx, Proudhon, and Büchner. A government stenographer, Myškin, in 1870, established a printing-office, through which several of Lassalle's works were published; while many pamphlets were published by the Zemlja i Volja Committee and by the Free Russian Printing-Office. Some of the pamphlets were published under titles like those of the books for children, for example, "Děduška Egor" (Grandfather Egor), "Mitiuška", Stories for the Workingmen, and others, in which the exploitation of the people was deplored, and the immunity of capitalists assailed. Again, some publications were printed in popular, as well as in cultured, language; and, in order to allure the peasants, these pamphlets appeared at times, under such titles as "The Satiate and the Hungry"; "How Our Country Is No Longer Ours". But all this propaganda, which required considerable energy and sacrifice, did not produce satisfactory results. Nihilism did not penetrate the masses; its enthusiastic apostles committed acts of imprudence that drew upon them the ferocious reprisals of the Government; the peasants had not faith in the preachings of those teachers, whom, at times, they regarded as government spies, and whom, at times, they denounced. The books and pamphlets that were distributed among the country people often fell into the hands of the činovniki (government employees), or of the popes. Very few of the peasants knew how to read. Accordingly, Nihilism had true adherents only among students of the universities and higher schools, and among the middle classes. The peasants and workmen did not understand its ideals of destruction and of social revolution.

NIHILIST TERRORISM.—Propagation of ideas was soon followed by violence: 4 April, 1866, Tsar Alexander II narrowly escaped the shot fired by Demetrius Karakozov, and in consequence took severe measures (rescript of 23 May, 1866) against the revolution, making the universities and the press objects of special vigilance. To avoid detection and spying, the Nihilists formed a Central Executive Committee whose sentences of death were executed by "punishers". Sub-committees of from five to ten members were also organized and statutes (12 articles) drawn up. The applicant for admission was required to consecrate his life to the cause, sever ties of family and friendship, and observe absolute secrecy. Disobedience to the head of the association was punishable with death. The Government, in turn, enacted stringent laws against secret societies and brought hundreds before the tribunals. A notable instance was the trial, at St. Petersburg in October, 1877, of 193 persons: 94 went free, 36 were sent to Siberia; the others received light sentences. One of the accused, Myskin by name, who in addressing the judges had characterized the procedure as "an abominable comedy", was condemned to ten years of penal servitude. Another sensational trial (April, 1878) was that of Vera Sassulio, who had attempted to murder General Frepov, chief of police of St. Petersburg. Her acquittal was frantically applauded and she found a refuge in Switzerland. Among the deeds of violence committed by Nihilists may be mentioned the assassination of General Mezencev (4 Aug., 1878) and Prince Krapotkin (1879). These events were followed by new repressive measures on the part of the Government and by numerous executions. The Nihilists, however, continued their work, held a congress at Lipeck in 1879, and (26 Aug.) condemned Alexander II to death. An attempt to wreck the train on which the Tsar was returning to St. Petersburg proved abortive. Another attack on his life was made by Halturin, 5 Feb., 1880. He was slain on 1 March, 1881, by a bomb, thrown by Grineveckij. Six conspirators, among them Sofia Perovskaja, were tried and executed. On 14 March, the Zemlja i Volja society issued a proclamation inciting the peasants to rise, while the Executive Committee wrote to Alexander III denouncing the abuses of the bureaucracy and demanding political amnesty, national representation, and civil liberty.

The reign of Alexander III was guided by the dictates of a reaction, due in great measure to the counsels of Constantine Poběnoscev, procurator general of the Holy Synod. And Nihilism, which seemed to reach its apogee in the death of Alexander II, saw its eclipse. Its theories were too radical to gain proselytes among the people. Its assaults were repeated; on 20 March, 1882, General Strělnikov was assassinated at Odessa; and Colonel Sudežkin on the 28th of December, 1883; in 1887, an attempt against the life of the tsar was unsuccessful; in 1890, a conspiracy against the tsar was discovered at Paris; but these crimes were the work of the revolution in Russia, rather than of the Nihilists. The crimes that reddened the soil of Russia with blood in constitutional times are due to the revolution of 1905–07. But the Nihilism, that, as a doctrinal system, proclaimed the destruction of the old Russia, to establish the foundations of a new Russia, may be said to have disappeared; it became fused with Anarchism and Socialism, and therefore, the history of the crimes that were multiplied from 1905 on are a chapter in the history of political upheavals in Russia, and not in the history of Nihilism.

ISKANDER (the pseud. of HERZEN), *Du développement des idées révolutionnaires en Russie* (Paris, 1851); SCHEDO-FERROTI, *Etudes sur l'avenir de la Russie* (Berlin, 1867); ALEXÉI, *Les nihilistes ou les dames russes émancipées* (London, 1867); MAX NETTLAU, *Life of Michael Bakunin* (3 vols., London); GOLOVIN, *Der russische Nihilismus* (Leipzig, 1880); LAVIGNE, *Introd. à l'hist. du nihilisme en Russie* (Paris, 1880); LUBOMIRSKI, *Le nihilisme en Russie* (Paris, 1879); ARMANDO, *Il nihilismo* (Turin, 1879); IDEM, *Was ist der Nihilismus?* (Leipzig, 1881); GERBET-KARLOWITSCH, *Die Attentats-Period in Russland* (Heilbronn, 1881); GALLY-BOUTTEVILLE, *Tzarisme et nihilisme* (Paris, 1881); LEROY-BEAULIEU, *L'empire des tzars et les russes*, II (Paris, 1882), 544–66; STEPNIAK (pseud.), *La Russia sotterranea* (Milan, 1882); *Les nihilistes et la révolution en Russie* (Paris, 1882); *Der Czarenmord am 13. März 1881* (Dresden, 1882); BOUGARD, *Les nihilistes russes* (Zurich, 1881); THUN, *Gesch. der revolutionären Bewegungen in Russland* (Leipzig, 1883), tr. Polish (London, 1893), Russian (Moscow, 1905); SCHERR, *Die Nihilisten* (Leipzig, 1885); IEGOROV, *Aus den Mysterien des russ. Nihilismus* (Leipzig, 1885); STEPNIAK, *Le tzarisme et la révolution* (Paris, 1866); THOMIROV, *Conspirateurs et patriciens* (Paris, 1887); FRÉDÉ, *La Russie et le nihilisme* (Paris, 1887); OLDENBERG, *Der russ. Nihilismus von seinen Anfängen bis zur Gegenwart* (Leipzig, 1888); MILINKOV, *La crise russe* (Paris, 1907); MICHELET, *Essai sur l'hist. de Nicolas II, et le début de la révolution russe* (Paris, 1907); SCHLESINGER, *Russland im XX. Jahrh.* (Berlin, 1908); *Istorja molodoi Rossii* [*History of Young Russia*] (Moscow, 1908); RUDOLF URBA, *Die Revolution in Russland;* (2 vols., Prague, 1906); LOGNET AND SILBER, *Terroristes et policiers* (Paris, 1909); *Byloe* (*The Past*), I-XII (Paris, 1908–9), review conducted by Boucerv, contains documents bearing on the history of Nihilism.

A. PALMIERI.

Nihus, BARTHOLD, convert and controversialist, b. at Holtorf in Hanover, 7 February, 1590 (according to other sources in 1584 or 1589, at Wolpe in Brunswick); d. at Erfurt, 10 March, 1657. He came from a poor Protestant family, obtained his early education at Verden and Goslar, and from 1607 studied philosophy and medicine at the University of Helmstedt, where, on account of his poverty, he was the *famulus* of Cornelius Martini, professor of philosophy. Having become master of philosophy in 1612, his inclinations then led him to study Protestant theology. Contentions among the professors at Helmstedt made further stay there unpleasant, and when two students of noble family went in 1616 to the University of Jena, he accompanied them as preceptor. Later he became instructor of the young princes of Saxe-Weimar, among whom was the subsequently famous Bernhard of Saxe-Weimar. The inability of the Protestant theologians to agree upon vital questions caused him first to doubt and then to renounce Protestantism. He went to Cologne in 1622, and entered the House of Proselytes founded by the Brotherhood of the Holy Cross; in the same year he accepted the Catholic Faith and, after due preparation, was ordained priest. Chosen director of the House of Proselytes, and in 1627 provost of the nunnery of the Cistercians at Althaldensleben near Magdeburg, two years later he became abbot of the monastery of the Premonstratensians, from which he was expelled after the battle of Breitenfeld in 1631. He fled to Hildesheim where he became canon of the church of the Holy Cross, thence to Holland where he came into close relation with Gerhard Johann Vossius. In 1645 Nihus was called to Münster by the papal nuncio, Fabio Chigi (later Alexander VII), then in Münster attending the Westphalian Peace Congress. A few years later he was induced to come to Mayence by Johann Philip von Schönborn, Archbishop of Mayence, at whose request he went to Ingolstadt in 1654 to obtain information regarding the Welt-Priester-Institut of Bartholomew Holzhauser, and to report to the archbishop. Schönborn, in 1655, appointed him his suffragan bishop for Saxony and Thuringia, with residence in Erfurt, where he died.

After his conversion Nihus had sent to the Helmstedt professors, Calixtus and Hornejus, a letter in which he presented his reasons for embracing Catholicism; his chief motive was that the Church needs a living, supreme judge to explain the Bible and to settle disputes and difficulties. Calixtus attacked him first in his lectures and later in his writings, whence originated a bitter controversy between Nihus and the Helmstedt professors The most important of Nihus' numerous writings are: (1) "Ars nova, dicto S. Scripturæ unico lucrandi e Pontificiis plurimos in partes Lutheranorum, detecta non nihil et suggesta Theologis Helmstetensibus, Georgio Calixto præsertim et Conrado Hornejo" (Hildesheim, 1633); (2) "Apologeticus pro arte nova contra Andabatam Helmstetensem" (Cologne, 1640), in answer to the response of Calixtus to the first pamphlet: "Digressio de arte nova contra Nihusium"; (3) "Hypodigma, quo diluuntur nonnulla contra Catholicos disputata in Cornelii Martini tractatu de analysi logica" (Cologne, 1648). Assisted by his friend Leo Allatius (q. v.) he devoted considerable time to researches pertaining to the "Communion" and the "Missa præsanctificatorum" of the Greeks, and also took charge of the editing and publishing of several works of Allatius, some of which—as the "De Ecclesiæ occidentalis et orientalis perpetua consensione" (Cologne, 1648) and "Symmicta"

(Cologne, 1653)—he provided with valuable additions and footnotes.

KOCH, *Die Erfurter Weihbischöfe* in *Zeitschrift für thüringische Gesch.*, VI (Jena, 1865), 104–9; RÄSS, *Die Convertiten seit der Reformation*, V (Freiburg im Br., 1867), 97–103; WESTERMAYER in *Kirchenlex.* s. v.; IDEM in *Allg. deutsche Biog.*, XXIII, 699 sq.

FRIEDRICH LAUCHERT.

Nikolaus von Dinkelsbühl, theologian, b. c. 1360, at Dinkelsbühl; d. 17 March, 1433, at Mariazell in Styria. He studied at the University of Vienna, where he is mentioned as baccalaureus in the faculty of Arts in 1385. Magister in 1390, he lectured on philosophy, mathematics, and physics until 1397, and from 1402 to 1405. From 1397 he was dean of the faculty; he studied theology, lecturing until 1402 on theological subjects, first as *cursor biblicus*, and later on the "Sentences" of Peter Lombard. In 1405 he became bachelor of Divinity, in 1408 licentiate, and in 1409 doctor and member of the theological faculty. Rector of the university, 1405–6, he declined the honour of a re-election in 1409. From 1405 he was also canon at the cathedral of St. Stephen. The supposition of several early authors that he was a member of the Order of the Hermits of St. Augustine is incorrect, for he could not have been rector of the university had he been a member of any order. Eminent as teacher and pulpit orator, Nikolaus possessed great business acumen, and was frequently chosen as ambassador both by the university and the reigning prince. He represented Duke Albert V of Austria at the Council of Constance (1414–18), and the University of Vienna in the trial of Thiem, dean of the Passau cathedral. When Emperor Sigismund came to Constance, Nikolaus delivered an address on the abolition of the schism ("Sermo de unione Ecclesiæ in Concilium Constantiense," II, 7, Frankfort, 1697, 182–7). He took part in the election of Martin V, and delivered an address to the new pope (Sommerfeldt, "Historisches Jahrbuch", XXVI, 1905, 323–7). Together with John, Patriarch of Constantinople, he was charged with the examination of witnesses in the proceedings against Hieronymus of Prague. Returning to Vienna in 1418, he again took up his duties as teacher at the university, and in 1423 directed the theological promotions as representative of the chancellor. Duke Albert V having chosen him as his confessor in 1425, wished to make him Bishop of Passau, but Nikolaus declined the appointment. During the preparations for the Council of Basle, he was one of the committee to draw up the reform proposals which were to be presented to the council. His name does not appear thereafter in the records of the university.

His published works include "Postilla cum sermonibus evangeliorum dominicalium" (Strasburg, 1496), and a collection of "Sermones" with tracts (Strasburg, 1516). Among his numerous unpublished works, the manuscripts of which are chiefly kept in the Court library at Vienna and in the Court and State library at Munich, are to be mentioned his commentaries on the Psalms, Isaias, the Gospel of St. Matthew, some of the Epistles of St. Paul, the "Sentences" of Peter Lombard, and "Questiones Sententiarum"; a commentary on the "Physics" of Aristotle, numerous sermons, lectures, moral and ascetic tracts.

ASCHBACH, *Gesch. der Wiener Universität*, I (Vienna, 1865), 430–40; STANONIK in *Allg. deut. Biog.*, XXIII (1886), 622 sq.; ESSER in *Kirchenlex.*, s. v. *Nicolaus von Dinkelsbühl;* HURTER, *Nomen.*, II (Innsbruck, 1906), 830–32.

FRIEDRICH LAUCHERT.

Nikon, Patriarch of Moscow (1652–1658; d. 1681). He was of peasant origin, born in the district of Nishni-Novgorod in 1605, and in early life was known as Nikita. Educated in a monastery, he married, became a secular priest, and for a time had a parish in Moscow. After ten years of married life, his children having died, he persuaded his wife to become a nun and he entered the Solovetski monastery on the White Sea, according to Orthodox custom, changing his name to Nikon. In accordance also with a common custom he next became a hermit on an island near by, dependent on the monastery. But a disagreement about the alleged misuse of some alms caused him to break with the Solovetski monks and join the Kojeozerski community in the same neighbourhood, of which he became hegumen in 1643. Later he made a great impression on the emperor, Alexis, who made him Archimandrite of the Novospaski Laura at Moscow in 1646, and in 1649 Metropolitan of Novgorod. Here he founded almshouses, distinguished himself by his many good works, and succeeded in putting down a dangerous revolt in 1650. Meanwhile he was in constant correspondence with the Tsar, at whose court he spent part of each year. Already during this time he began to prepare for a revision of the Slavonic Bible and Service books. In 1652 the Patriarch of Moscow died and Nikon was appointed his successor.

As head of the Church of Russia Nikon set about many important reforms. One of the first questions that engaged his attention was the reunion of the Ruthenians (Little Russians) with the Orthodox Church. When Poland held Little Russia, the Synod of Brest (1596) had brought about union between its inhabitants and Rome. Under Alexis, however, the tide turned; many Ruthenians arose against Poland and united with Russia (1653). A result of this was that the Russians were able without much difficulty to undo the work of the Synod of Brest, and to bring the Metropolitan of Kief with the majority of his clergy back to the Orthodox Church. This greatly increased the extent of the Russian patriarch's jurisdiction. Nikon was able to entitle himself patriarch of Great, Little, and White Russia. During the reign of Alexis, Nikon built three monasteries, one of which, made after the model of the Anastasis and called "New Jerusalem," is numbered among the famous Lauras of Russia.

The chief event of Nikon's reign was the reform of the service books. The Bible and books used in church in Russia are translated from Greek into old Slavonic. But gradually many mistranslations and corruptions of the text had crept in. There were also details of ritual in which the Russian Church had forsaken the custom of Constantinople. Nikon's work was to restore all these points to exact conformity with the Greek original. This reform had been discussed before his time. In the sixteenth century the Greeks had reproached the Russians for their alterations, but a Russian synod in 1551 had sanctioned them. In Nikon's time there was more intercourse with Greeks than ever before, and in this way he conceived the necessity of restoring purer forms. While Metropolitan of Novgorod he caused a committee of scholars to discuss the question, in spite of the patriarch Joseph. In 1650 a Russian theologian was sent to Constantinople to inquire about various doubtful points. One detail that made much trouble was that the Russians had learned to make the sign of the cross with two fingers instead of three, as the Greeks did. As soon as he became patriarch, Nikon published an order introducing some of these reforms, which immediately called forth angry opposition. In 1654 and 1655 he summoned Synods which continued the work. Makarios, Patriarch of Antioch, who came to Russia at that time was able to help, and there was continual correspondence with the Patriarch of Constantinople. At last, with the approval of the Greek patriarchs, Nikon published the reformed service books and made laws insisting on conformity with Greek custom in all points of ritual (1655–1658). A new Synod in 1656 confirmed this, excommunicated every one who made the sign of the cross except with three fingers, and forbade the rebaptizing of Latin converts (still a peculiarity of the Russian Church). This aroused a strong party of opposition. The patriarch was accused of anti-national sentiments, of trying to Hellenize the Russian Church, of corrupting the old faith. Nikon's strong will would have crushed the opposition, had he not, in some way not yet clearly explained, fallen foul of the tsar. It is generally said that part of his ideas of reform was to secure that the Church should be independent of the state and that this aroused the tsar's anger. In any case in the year 1658 Nikon suddenly fell. He offered his resignation to the tsar and it was accepted. He had often threatened to resign before; it seems that this time, too, he did not mean his offer to be taken seriously. However, he had to retire and went to his New Jerusalem monastery. A personal interview with Alexis was refused. The patriarchate remained vacant and Nikon, in spite of his resignation, attempted to regain his former place. Meanwhile the opposition to him became stronger. It was led by a Greek, Paisios Ligarides, Metropolitan of Gaza (unlawfully absent from his see), who insisted on the appointment of a successor at Moscow. All Nikon's friends seem to have forsaken him at this juncture. Ligarides caused an appeal to be made to the Greek patriarchs and their verdict was against Nikon. In 1664 he tried to force the situation by appearing suddenly in the patriarchal church at Moscow and occupying his place as if nothing had happened. But he did not succeed, and in 1667 a great synod was summoned to try him. The Patriarchs of Alexandria and Antioch came to Russia expressly for this synod; a great number of Russian and Greek metropolitans sat as judges. The tsar himself appeared as accuser of his former friend. Nikon was summoned and appeared before the synod in his patriarch's robes. He was accused of neglecting his duties since 1658, of having betrayed his Church in a certain letter he had written to the Patriarch of Constantinople (in which he had complained of the Russian clergy), of harsh and unjust conduct in his treatment of the bishops. Nikon defended himself ably; the synod lasted a week; but at last in its eighth session it declared him deposed from the patriarchate, suspended from all offices but those of a simple monk, and sentenced him to confinement in a monastery (Therapontof) on the White Sea. The archimandrite of the Trinity Laura at Moscow, Joasaph, was elected his successor (Joasaph II, 1667–72). Joasaph confirmed Nikon's reform of the Service books and rites. The party that opposed it formed the beginning of the Russian dissenting sects (the Raskolniks).

For a time Nikon's imprisonment was very severe. In 1675 he was taken to another monastery (of St. Cyril) and his treatment was lightened. Alexis towards the end of his life repented of his harsh treatment of the former patriarch, and from his death-bed (1676) sent to ask his forgiveness. The next tsar, Feodor II (1676–82) allowed him to return to his New Jerusalem monastery. On the way thither Nikon died (17 August, 1681). He was buried with the honours of a patriarch, and all decrees against him were revoked after his death. His tomb is in the Cathedral church of Moscow. Nikon's fall, the animosity of the tsar, and of the synod that deposed him remain mysterious. The cause was not his reform of the Service books, for that was maintained by his successor. It has been explained as a successful intrigue of his personal enemies at the court. He certainly had made enemies during his reign by his severity, his harsh manner, the uncompromising way he carried out his reforms regardless of the intensely conservative instinct of his people. Or, it has been said, Nikon brought about his disgrace by a premature attempt to free the Russian Church from the shackles of the state. His attitude represented an opposition to the growing Erastianism that culminated soon after his time in the laws of Peter the Great (1689–1725).

This is no doubt true. There are sufficient indications that Alexis' quarrel with Nikon was based on jealousy. Nikon wanted to be too independent of the tsar, and this independence was concerned, naturally, with ecclesiastical matters. Some writers have thought that the root of the whole matter was that he became at the end of his reign a Latinizer, that he wanted to bring about reunion with Rome and saw in that reunion the only safe protection for the Church against the secular government. It has even been said that he became a Catholic (Gerebtzoff, "Essai", II, 514). The theory is not impossible. Since the Synod of Brest the idea of reunion was in the air; Nikon had had much to do with Ruthenians; he may at last have been partly convinced by them. And one of the accusations against him at his trial was that of Latinizing. A story is told of his conversion by a miracle worked by Saint Josaphat, the great martyr for the union. In any case the real reason of Nikon's fall remains one of the difficulties of Russian Church history. He was undoubtedly the greatest bishop Russia has yet produced. A few ascetical works of no special importance were written by him.

PALMER, *The Patriarch and the Tsar* (6 vols., London, 1871–76); SUBBOTIN, *The Trial of Nikon*, in Russian (Moscow, 1862); MAKARIOS, *The Patriarch Nikon*, Russian (Moscow, 1881); PHILARET, *Geschichte der Kirche Russlands*, German tr. by BLUMENTHAL (Frankfort, 1872); MOURAVIEFF, *A History of the Church of Russia*, English tr. by BLACKMORE (Oxford, 1842); NIKON in *Lives of Eminent Russian Prelates* (no author) (London, 1854); GEREBTZOFF, *Essai sur l'histoire de la civilisation en Russie* (Paris, 1858).

ADRIAN FORTESCUE.

Nile, VICARIATE APOSTOLIC OF THE UPPER. See UPPER NILE, VICARIATE APOSTOLIC OF THE.

Nilles, NIKOLAUS, b. 21 June, 1828, of a wealthy peasant family of Rippweiler, Luxemburg; d. 31 January, 1907. After completing his gymnasium studies brilliantly, he went to Rome where from 1847 to 1853, as a student of the Collegium Germanicum, he laid the foundation of his ascetic life and, as a pupil of the Gregorian University, under the guidance of distinguished scholars (Ballerini, Franzelin, Passaglia, Perrone, Patrizi, Schrader, Tarquini), prepared the way for his subsequent scholarly career. When he left Rome in 1853, he took with him, in addition to the double doctorate of theology and canon law, two mementoes which lasted throughout his life: his grey hair and a disease of the heart, the result of the terrors which he had encountered in Rome in the revolutionary year 1848–9. From 1853 to 1858 he laboured in his own country as chaplain and parish priest, and during this time made his first literary attempts. In March, 1858, he entered the Austrian Province of the Society of Jesus and, in the autumn of 1859, was summoned by his superiors to Innsbruck to fill the chair of canon law in the theological faculty, which Emperor Francis Joseph I had shortly before entrusted to the Austrian Jesuits. Nilles lectured throughout his life—after 1898 usually to the North American theologians, to whom he gave special instructions on canonical conditions in their country, for which task no one was better qualified than he. His "Commentaria in Concilium Baltimorense tertium" (1884–90) and his short essay, "Tolerari potest", gained him a wide reputation.

His literary achievements in the fields of canon law, ascetics, and liturgy were abundant and fruitful. Martin Blum enumerates in his by no means complete bibliography fifty-seven works, of which the two principal are: "De rationibus festorum sacratissimi Cordis Jesu et purissimi Cordis Mariæ libri quatuor" (2 vols., 5th ed., Innsbruck, 1885) and "Kalendarium manuale utriusque Ecclesiæ orientalis et occidentalis" (2 vols., 2nd ed., Innsbruck, 1896). Through the latter work he became widely known in the world of scholars. In particular Protestants and Orthodox Russians expressed themselves in terms of the highest praise for the Kalendarium or Heortologion. Professor Harnack of Berlin wrote of it in the "Theologische Literaturzeitung" (XXI, 1896, 350–2): "I have . . . frequently made use of the work . . . and it has always proved a reliable guide, whose information was derived from original sources. There is scarcely another scholar as well versed as the author in the feasts of Catholicism. His knowledge is based not only on his own observations, but on books, periodicals, papers, and calendars of the past and present. The Feasts of Catholicism! The title is self-explanatory; yet, though the basis of these ordinances is uniform, the details are of infinite variety, since the work treats not only of the Latin but also of the Eastern Rites. The latter, it is well known, are divided into Greek, Syriac, Coptic, Armenian . . ." Of the second volume Harnack wrote (ibid., XXXIII, 1898, 112 sq.): "Facts which elsewhere would have to be sought under difficulties are here marshalled in lucid order, and a very carefully arranged index facilitates inquiry. Apart from the principal aim of the work, it offers valuable information concerning recent Eastern Catholic ecclesiastical history, also authorities and literature useful to the historian of liturgy and creeds. . . . His arduous and disinterested toil will be rewarded by the general gratitude, and his work will long prove useful not only to every theologian 'utriusque', but also 'cuiusque ecclesiæ'". The Roumanian Academy at Bucharest awarded a prize to this work. Soon after the appearance of the second edition of the "Kalendarium", the Russian Holy Synod issued from the synodal printing office at Moscow a "Festbilderatlas" intended to a certain extent as the official Orthodox illustrations for the work. Nilles was not only a distinguished university professor, but also a meritorious director of ecclesiastical students. For fifteen years (1860–75) he presided over the theological seminary of Innsbruck, an international institution where young men from all parts of Europe and the United States are trained for the priesthood.

BLUM, *Das Collegium Germanicum zu Rom u. seine Zöglinge aus dem Luxemburger Lande* (Luxemburg, 1899); *Zeitschr. für kath. Theol.* (Innsbruck, 1907), 396 sqq.; *Korrespondenzblatt des Priester-Gebets-Verein*, XLI (Innsbruck), 37 sqq.

M. HOFMANN.

Nilopolis, a titular see and a suffragan of Oxyrynchos, in Egypt. According to Ptolemy (IV, v, 26) the city was situated on an island of the Nile in the Heraclean nome. Eusebius ("Hist. eccl.", VI, xli) states that it had a bishop, Cheremon, during the persecution of Decius; others are mentioned a little later. "The Chronicle of John of Nikiou" (559) alludes to this city in connexion with the occupation of Egypt by the Mussulmans, and it is also referred to by Arabian medieval geographers under its original name of Delas. In the fourteenth century it paid 20,000 *dinars* in taxes, which indicates a place of some importance. At present, Delas forms a part of the *moudirieh* of Beni-Suef in the district of El-Zaouiet, and has about 2500 inhabitants of whom nearly 1000 are nomadic Bedouins. It is situated on the left bank of the Nile about forty-seven miles from Memphis.

LE QUIEN, *Oriens christianus*, II (Paris, 1741), 587; AMÉLINEAU, *La géographie de l'Égypte à l'époque copte* (Paris, 1893), 136–138.

S. VAILHÉ.

Nilus, SAINT (Νεῖλος), the elder, of Sinai (d. c. 430), was one of the many disciples and fervent defenders of St. John Chrysostom. We know him first as a layman, married, with two sons. At this time he was an officer at the Court of Constantinople, and is said to have been one of the Prætorian Prefects, who, according to Diocletian and Constantine's arrangement, were the chief functionaries and heads of all other governors for the four main divisions of the empire. Their authority, however, had already begun to decline by the end of the fourth century.

While St. John Chrysostom was patriarch, before his first exile (398–403), he directed Nilus in the study of Scripture and in works of piety (Nikephoros Kallistos, "Hist. Eccl.", XIV, 53, 54). About the year 390 (Tillemont, "Mémoires", XIV, 190–91) or perhaps 404 (Leo Allatius, "De Nilis", 11–14), Nilus left his wife and one son and took the other, Theodulos, with him to Mount Sinai to be a monk. They lived here till about the year 410 (Tillemont, ib., p. 405) when the Saracens, invading the monastery, took Theodulos prisoner. The Saracens intended to sacrifice him to their gods, but eventually sold him as a slave, so that he came into the possession of the Bishop of Eleusa in Palestine. The Bishop received Theodulos among his clergy and made him door-keeper of the church. Meanwhile Nilus, having left his monastery to find his son, at last met him at Eleusa. The bishop then ordained them both priests and allowed them to return to Sinai. The mother and the other son had also embraced the religious life in Egypt. St. Nilus was certainly alive till the year 430. It is uncertain how soon after that he died. Some writers believe him to have lived till 451 (Leo Allatius, op. cit., 8–14). The Byzantine Menology for his feast (12 November) supposes this. On the other hand, none of his works mentions the Council of Ephesus (431) and he seems to know only the beginning of the Nestorian troubles; so we have no evidence of his life later than about 430.

From his monastery at Sinai Nilus was a well-known person throughout the Eastern Church; by his writings and correspondence he played an important part in the history of his time. He was known as a theologian, Biblical scholar and ascetic writer, so people of all kinds, from the emperor down, wrote to consult him. His numerous works, including a multitude of letters, consist of denunciations of heresy, paganism, abuses of discipline and crimes, of rules and principles of asceticism, especially maxims about the religious life. He warns and threatens people in high places, abbots and bishops, governors and princes, even the emperor himself, without fear. He kept up a correspondence with Gaina, a leader of the Goths, endeavouring to convert him from Arianism (Book I of his letters, nos. 70, 79, 114, 115, 116, 205, 206, 286); he denounced vigorously the persecution of St. John Chrysostom both to the Emperor Arcadius (ib., II, 265; III, 279) and to his courtiers (I, 309; III, 199).

Nilus must be counted as one of the leading ascetic writers of the fifth century. His feast is kept on 12 November in the Byzantine Calendar; he is commemorated also in the Roman martyrology on the same date. The Armenians remember him, with other Egyptian fathers, on the Thursday after the third Sunday of their Advent (Nilles, "Kalendarium Manuale", Innsbruck, 1897, II, 624).

The writings of St. Nilus of Sinai were first edited by Possinus (Paris, 1639); in 1673 Suarez published a supplement at Rome; his letters were collected by Possinus (Paris, 1657), a larger collection was made by Leo Allatius (Rome, 1668). All these editions are used in P. G., LXXIX. The works are divided by Fessler-Jungmann into four classes:—(1) Works about virtues and vices in general:—"Peristeria" (P. G., LXXIX, 811–968), a treatise in three parts addressed to a monk Agathios; "On Prayer" (περὶ προσευχῆς, ib., 1165–1200); "Of the eight spirits of wickedness" (περὶ τῶν θ΄ πνευμάτων τῆς πονηρίας, ib., 1145–64); "Of the vice opposed to virtues" (περὶ τῆς ἀντιζύγους τῶν ἀρητῶν κακίας, ib., 1140–44); "Of various bad thoughts" (περὶ διαφόρων πονηρῶν λογισμῶν, ib., 1200–1234); "On the word of the Gospel of Luke", xxii, 36 (ib., 1263–1280). (2) "Works about the monastic life":—Concerning the slaughter of monks on Mount Sinai, in seven parts, telling the story of the author's life at Sinai, the invasion of the Saracens, captivity of his son, etc. (ib., 590–694); Concerning Albianos, a Nitrian monk whose life is held up as an example (ib., 695–712); "Of Asceticism" (Λόγος ἀσκητικός, about the monastic ideal, ib., 719–810); "Of voluntary poverty" (περὶ ἀκτημοσύνης, ib., 968–1060); "Of the superiority of monks" (ib., 1061–1094); "To Eulogios the monk" (ib., 1093–1140). (3) "Admonitions" (Γνῶμαι) or "Chapters" (κεφάλαια), about 200 precepts drawn up in short maxims (ib., 1239–62). These are probably made by his disciples from his discourses. (4) "Letters":—Possinus published 355, Allatius 1061 letters, divided into four books (P. G., LXXIX, 81–585). Many are not complete, several overlap, or are not really letters but excerpts from Nilus' works; some are spurious. Fessler-Jungmann divides them into classes, as dogmatic, exegetical, moral, and ascetic. Certain works wrongly attributed to Nilus are named in Fessler-Jungmann, pp. 125–6.

NIKEPHOROS KALLISTOS, *Hist. Eccl.*, XIV, xliv; LEO ALLATIUS, *Diatriba de Nilis et eorum scriptis* in his edition of the letters (Rome, 1668); TILLEMONT, *Mémoires pour servir à l'histoire ecclésiastique*, XIV (Paris, 1693–1713), 189–218; FABRICIUS-HARLES, *Bibliotheca græca*, X (Hamburg, 1790–1809), 3–17; CEILLIER, *Histoire générale des auteurs sacrés*, XIII (Paris, 1729–1763), iii; FESSLER-JUNGMANN, *Institutiones Patrologiæ*, II (Innsbruck, 1896), ii, 108–128.

ADRIAN FORTESCUE.

Nilus the Younger, of Rossano, in Calabria; b. in 910; d. 27 December, 1005. For a time he was married (or lived unlawfully); he had a daughter. Sickness brought about his conversion, however, and from that time he became a monk and a propagator of the rule of St. Basil in Italy. He was known for his ascetic life, his virtues, and theological learning. For a time he lived as a hermit, later he spent certain periods of his life at various monasteries which he either founded or restored. He was for some time at Monte Cassino, and again at the Alexius monastery at Rome. When Gregory V (966–999) was driven out of Rome, Nilus opposed the usurpation of Philogatos (John) of Piacenza as anti-pope. Later when Philogatos was tortured and mutilated he reproached Gregory and the Emperor Otto III (993–1002) for this crime. Nilus' chief work was the foundation of the famous Greek monastery of Grottaferrata, near Frascati, of which he is counted the first abbot. He spent the end of his life partly there and partly in a hermitage at Valleluce near Gaeta. His feast is kept on 26 September, both in the Byzantine Calendar and the Roman martyrology.

Viti S. Nili abbatis Cryptæ Ferratæ, probably by BARTHOLOMEW, Abbot of Grottaferrata (d. 1065), in the *Acta Sanctorum*, VII, Sept., 283–343; *P. L.*, LXXI, 509–588; *P. G.*, IV, 616–618; MINASI, *S. Nilo di Calabria* (Naples, 1892); KRUMBACHER, *Byzantinische Litteratur* (2nd ed., Munich, 1897), 195, 198.

ADRIAN FORTESCUE.

Nimbus (Lat., related to *Nebula*, νεφέλη, properly vapour, cloud), in art and archæology signifies a shining light implying great dignity. Closely related are the halo, glory, and aureole.

IN NATURE.—All such symbols originate in natural phenomena, scientifically accounted for in textbooks on physics (Müller-Peter, "Lehrbuch der kosmischen Physik"; Pernter, "Meteorologische Optik"). There are circular phenomena of light in drops or bubbles of water and in ice crystals which by the refraction of light reveal in greater or less degree the spectral colours. Of the accompanying phenomena the horizontal and vertical diameters, the "column of light", may be mentioned. The curious rings of light or colour similar to the above, which often form themselves before the iris of the eye even in candle light, are more gorgeous on the mountain mist (Pilatus, Rigi, and Brocken), if the beholder has the sun behind him; they surround his shadow as it is projected upon the clouds. The dewdrops in a meadow can produce an appearance of light around a shadow, without, however, forming distinct circles. Occasionally one even sees the planet Venus veiled by a disc of light. The phenomena of discs and broad rings are more usual in the sun and moon. The Babylonians studied them diligently (Kugler, "Sternkunde und Sterndienst in Babel", II, 1). The terminology of these phenomena is vague. The disc or circle around the sun can be correctly called "anthelia", and the ring around the moon "halo". A more usual name is "aureole", which in a restricted sense means an oval or ellipitical ray of light like a medallion. If the brightness is merely a luminous glow without definitely forming ring, circle, or ellipse, it is usually spoken of as a "glory". The types in nature in which rays or beams of light with or without colour challenge attention, suggested the symbolical use of the nimbus to denote high dignity or power. It is thus that Divine characteristics and the loftiest types of humanity were denoted by the nimbus.

IN POETRY, this symbol of light is chiefly used in the form of rays and flames or a diffused glow. Holy Writ presents the best example: God is Light. The Son of God, the Brightness of His Father's glory (Hebr., i, 3). An emerald light surrounds God and His throne (Apoc., iv, 3), and the Son of Man seems to the prophet a flame of fire (Apoc., i, 14 sq.). So also He appeared in His Transfiguration on Tabor. On Sinai, God appeared in a cloud which at once concealed and revealed Him (Ex., xxiv, 16, sq.) and even the countenance of Moses shone with a marvellous light in the presence of God (Ex., xxxiv, 29, sq.). Such descriptions may have influenced Christian artists to distinguish God and the saints by means of a halo, especially around the head. They were also familiar with the descriptions of the classical poets whose gods appeared veiled by a cloud; e. g. according to Virgil, divinity appears "nimbo circumdata, succincta, effulgens" (bathed in light and shining through a cloud).

IN ART.—In the plastic arts (painting and sculpture) the symbolism of the nimbus was early in use among the pagans who determined its form. In the monuments of Hellenic and Roman art, the heads of the gods, heroes, and other distinguished persons are often found with a disc-shaped halo, a circle of light, or a rayed-fillet. They are, therefore, associated especially with gods and creatures of light such as the Phœnix. The disc of light is likewise used in the Pompeian wall paintings to typify gods and demigods only, but later, in profane art it was extended to cherubs or even simple personifications, and is simply a reminder that the figures so depicted are not human. In the miniatures of the oldest Virgil manuscript all the great personages wear a nimbus (Beissel, "Vatikanische Miniaturen"). The custom of the Egyptian and Syrian kings of having themselves represented with a rayed crown to indicate the status of demi-gods, spread throughout the East and the West. In Rome the halo was first used only for deceased emperors as a sign of celestial bliss, but afterwards living rulers also were given the rayed crown, and after the third century, although not first by Constantine, the simple rayed nimbus. Under Constantine the rayed crown appears only in exceptional cases on the coin, and was first adopted emblematically by Julian the Apostate. Henceforth the nimbus appears without rays, as the emperors now wished themselves considered worthy of great honour, but no longer as divine beings. In early Christian art, the rayed nimbus, as well as the rayless disc were adopted in accordance with tradition. The sun and the Phœnix received, as in pagan art, a wreath or a rayed crown, also the simple halo. The latter was reserved not only for emperors but for men of genius and personifications of all kinds, although both in ecclesiastical and profane art, this emblem was usually omitted in ideal figures. In other cases the influence of ancient art tradition must not be denied.

The Middle Ages scarcely recognized such influence, and were satisfied to refer to Holy Writ as an example for wreath and crown or shield shaped discs as marks of honour to holy personages. Durandus writes: "Sic omnes sancti pinguntur coronati, quasi dicerunt. Filiæ Jerusalem, venite et videte martyres cum coronis quibus coronavit eas Dominus. Et in Libro Sapientiæ: Justi accipient regnum decoris et diadema speciei de manu Domini. Corona autem huiusmodi depingitur in forma scuti rotundi, quia sancti Dei protectione divina fruuntur, unde cantant gratulabundi: Domine ut scuto bonæ voluntatis tuæ coronasti nos" (Thus all the saints are depicted, crowned, as if they would say: O Daughters of Jerusalem, come and see the martyrs with the crowns with which the Lord has crowned them. And in the Book of Wisdom: The Just shall receive a kingdom of glory, and a crown of beauty at the hands of the Lord. And a crown of this kind is shown in the form of a round shield, because they enjoy the divine protection of the Holy God, whence they sing rejoicingly: O Lord, Thou hast crowned us as with a shield of Thy good-will.) (Rationale divin. offic., I, 3, 19, sq.). Furthermore the Middle Ages are almost exclusively accredited with the extension of symbolism inasmuch as they traced, sometimes felicitously, allusions to Christian truths in existing symbols, of which they sought no other origin. Durandus adds to the passage quoted above, the nimbus containing a cross, usual in the figures of Christ, signifying redemption through the Cross, and the square nimbus which was occasionally combined with it in living persons, to typify the four cardinal virtues. Judging by the principal monuments, however, the square nimbus appears to be only a variant of the round halo used to preserve a distinction and thus guard against placing living persons on a par with the saints. The idea of the cardinal virtues, the firmness of a squared stone, or the imperfection of a square figure as contrasted with a round one was merely a later development. In the cross nimbus the association of the nimbus with an annexed cross must be conceded historical; but that this cross is a "signum Christi crucifixi" Durandus probably interprets correctly.

ORIGIN.—As stated above the nimbus was in use long before the Christian era. According to the exhaustive researches of Stephani it was an invention of the Hellenic epoch. In early Christian art the nimbus certainly is not found on images of God and celestial beings, but only on figures borrowed from profane art, and in Biblical scenes; in place of the simple nimbus, rays or an aureole (with the nimbus) were made to portray heavenly glory. Hence it follows that Holy Writ furnished no example for the bestowal of a halo upon individual saintly personages. As a matter of fact the nimbus, as an inheritance from ancient art tradition, was readily adopted and ultimately found the widest application because the symbol of light for all divine, saintly ideals is offered by nature and not infrequently used in Scripture. In contemporary pagan art, the nimbus as a symbol of Divinity had become so indefinite, that it must have been accepted as something quite new. The nimbus of early Christian art manifests only in a few particular drawings, its relationship with that of late antiquity. In the first half of the fourth century, Christ received a nimbus only when portrayed seated upon a throne, or in an exalted and princely character; but it had already been used since Constantine, in pictures of the emperors, and was emblematic, not so much of divine as of human dignity and greatness. In other scenes, however, Christ at that time was represented without this emblem. The "exaltation" of Christ as indicated by the nimbus, refers to His dignity as a teacher and king rather than to His Godhead. Before long the nimbus became a fixed symbol of Christ and later (in the fourth century), of an angel or a lamb when used as the type of Christ. The number of personages who were given a halo increased rapidly, until towards the end of the sixth century the use of symbols in the Christian Church became as general as it had formerly been in pagan art.

Miniature painting in its cycle represents all the most important personages with haloes, just as did the Virgil codex, so that the continuity of the secular and Christian styles is obvious. This connexion is definitively revealed when royal persons, e. g. Herod, receive a nimbus. Very soon the Blessed Virgin Mary always, and martyrs and saints usually, were crowned with a halo. More rarely the beloved dead or some person conspicuous for his position or dignity, were so honoured. Saints were so represented if they constituted the central figure or needed to be distinguished from the surrounding personages. The nimbus was used arbitrarily in personification, Gospel types, and the like. Official representations clearly show a fixed system, but outside of these there was great variety. Works of art may be distinctly differentiated according to their birthplace. The nimbus in the Orient seems to have been in general use at an early period, but whether it was first adopted from ecclesiastical art is uncertain. In general the customs of the East and West are parallel; for instance, in the West the personifications appear with a nimbus as early as the third century and Christ enthroned no later than in the East (in the time of Constantine). Their nature makes it apparent that in every department of plastic art the nimbus is more rarely used than in painting.

FORM AND COLOUR.—The form of the symbol was first definitely determined by Gregory the Great, who (about 600) permitted himself to be painted with a *square nimbus*. Johannus Diaconus in his life of the pope, gives the reason: "circa verticem tabulæ similitudinem, quod viventis insigne est, præferens, non coronam" (bearing around his head the likeness of a square, which is the sign for a living person, and not a crown.) (Migne, "P. L.", 75, 231). It appears to have already been customary to use the round nimbus for saints. In any event the few extant examples from the following centuries show that, almost without exception, only the living, principally ecclesiastics, but also the laity and even women and children, were represented with a square nimbus. The *aureole*, that is the halo which surrounds an entire figure, naturally takes the shape of an oval, though if it is used for a bust, it readily resumes the circular form. The radiation of light from a centre is essential and we must recognize the circle of light of the sun-god in ancient art as one of the prototypes of the aureole. The medallion form was for a long time in use among the ancient Romans for the *Imagines clipeatæ*. The gradations of colour in the aureole reveal the influence of Apoc., iv, 3, where a rainbow was round about the throne of God. Indeed, in very early times the aureole was only used in representations of God as the Dove or Hand, or of Christ when the divinity was to be emphatically expressed.

In early Christian times (as now) the *round* nimbus was by far the most usual designation of Christ and the saints. The broad circle is often replaced by the ring of light or a coloured disc, especially on fabrics and miniatures. In pictures without colour the nimbus is shown by an engraved line or a raised circlet, often by a disc in relief. In the aureole blue indicates celestial glory, and it is used in the nimbus to fill in the surface, as are yellow, gray, and other colours while the margins are sharply defined in different tints. In many haloes the inner part is white. In mosaics, since the fifth and sixth centuries, blue has been replaced by gold. From this period also, the frescoes show a corresponding yellow, as seen for instance, in paintings in the catacombs. Gold or yellow prevails in miniatures, but there is a great deal of variety in illustrated books. Blue as a symbol of heaven has the preference, but gold, which later became the rule, gives a more obvious impression of light. The explanation of the *cross* nimbus variety is obvious. Since the sixth century it has characterized Christ and the Lamb of God, but occasionally it is given to the other Persons of the Trinity. In connexion with it, in the fourth and fifth centuries, there was a *monogram* nimbus. The cross and the monogram of Christ were beside or above the head of Christ and the Lamb. In the fifth century they were brought to the upper edge of the nimbus and finally both were concentrically combined with it. In more recent times the monogram and the monogram nimbus have become more rare. The letters A and Ω for Christ and M and A for Mary, were intended for monograms and frequently accompanied the nimbus.

DEVELOPMENT.—In order to understand the nimbus and its history, it is necessary to trace it through the different branches of art. The frescoes in the catacombs have a peculiar significance inasmuch as they determine the period when the nimbus was admitted into Christian art. The numerous figures lacking this symbol (Christ, Mary, and the Apostles) show that before Constantine, representations of specifically Christian character were not influenced by art traditions. Only pictures of the sun, the seasons, and a few ornamental heads carried a nimbus at that date. The single exception is found in a figure over the well-known "Ship in a Storm" of one of the Sacrament chapels. But it is to be observed that in this case we are not dealing with a representation of God, but merely with a personification of heavenly aid, which marked a transition from personifications to direct representations of holy personages. The figure seems to be copied from pictures of the sun god. On the other hand, several pictures of Christ in the catacombs, dating from the fourth century, indicate the period when the nimbus was first used in the way familiar to us. Besides the Roman catacombs, others, especially that of El Baghaouat in the great oasis of the Libyan desert, must be taken into account. For the period succeeding Constantine, mosaics furnish important evidence since they present not only very numerous and usually definite examples of the nimbus, but have a more official character and give intelligent portrayals of religious axioms. Although allowance must be made for later restorations, a constant development is apparent in this field. The treatment of the nimbus, in the illuminating and illustrating of books, was influenced by the caprices of the individual artist and the tradition of different schools. In textiles and embroidery the most extensive use was made of the nimbus, and a rich colour scheme was developed, to which these technical arts are by nature adapted. Unfortunately the examples which have been preserved are only imperfectly known and the dates are often difficult to determine.

Sculpture presents little opportunity for the use of the nimbus. In some few instances, indeed, the nimbus is painted on ivory or wood carvings, but more often we find it engraved or raised in relief. Figures with this emblem are rare. On the sarcophagi we find that Christ and the Lamb (apart from the sun) alone appear with a circle or disc, the Apostles and Mary, never. In ivory neither Mary nor Christ is so distinguished.

In the course of centuries the Christian idea that God, according to Holy Scripture the Source of Light and Divine things, must always be given a halo, became more pronounced. This applied to the three Divine Persons and their emblems, as the Cross, Lamb, Dove, Eye, and Hand; and since, according to Scripture, saints are children of Light (Luke, xvi, 8; John, xii, 36), as such they should share the honour. Preference was shown for the garland or crown (*corona et gloriæ corona*) of Christ which was also bestowed by God as a reward upon the saints, either spiritually in this life or in the Kingdom of Heaven (Ps. xx, 4; Heb., ii, 7 sq.). Garlands and crowns of glory are frequently mentioned in Holy Writ (I Peter, v, 4; Apoc., iv 4, etc.). The nimbus also takes the form of a shield to emphasize the idea of Divine protection (Ps. v, 13). A truly classic authority for the explanation of the nimbus may be found in Wis., v, 17: the Just shall "receive a kingdom of glory, and a crown of beauty at the hands of the Lord: for with His right hand He will cover them, and with His holy arm He will defend them." (In Greek, "Holds the shield over them".) Whereas in pagan art, the rayless nimbus signified neither holiness nor Divine protection, but merely majesty and power, in Christian art it was more and more definitely made the emblem of such virtue and grace, which, emanating from God, extends over the saints only. Urban VIII formally prohibited giving the nimbus to persons who were not beatified. Since the eighteenth century the word "halo" has been incorporated into the German language. In Western countries John the Baptist is the only saint of the Old Testament who is given a halo, doubtless because before his time the grace of Christ had not yet been bestowed in its fullness.

We have already found that the aureole may be considered exclusively a device of Christian art, especially as it was reserved at first for the Divinity, and later extended only to the Blessed Virgin. Instead of simple beams it often consists of pointed flames or is shaded off into the colours of the rainbow. This form as well as the simple nimbus, by the omission of the circumference, may be transposed into a garland of rays or a glory. A glory imitating the sun's rays was very popular for the monstrances; in other respects the *lunula* suggests the nimbus only because the costliness of the material enhances the lustre. The aureole obtained the Italian name of *mandorla* from its almond shape. In Germany the fish was agreed upon for the symbol of Christ, or a fish bladder if it had the shape of a figure 8. God the Father is typified in later pictures by an equilateral triangle, or two interlaced triangles, also by a hexagon to suggest the Trinity. If there is no circle around the cross nimbus, the three visible arms of the cross give the same effect. Occasionally the *mandorla* is found composed of seven doves (type of the Seven Gifts of the Holy Ghost), or of angels. The latter are used in large pictures of the Last Judgment or heaven, for instance in the "glories" of Italian domes. In painting, haloes of cloud are sometimes used for delicate angel heads, as in Raphael's works. Angels also form a nimbus around the head of the Mother of God. She is also given the twelve stars of Apoc., xii, 1. Saint John Nepomucene has five or seven stars because of the great light which hovered over his body when he was drowned in the Moldau by order of King Wenceslaus. Artists have developed many varieties of the nimbus and aureole. Since the Renaissance it has been fashioned more and more lightly and delicately and sometimes entirely omitted, as the artists thought they could suggest the characteristics of the personage by the painting. It is true that the nimbus is not intrinsically a part of the figure and at times even appears heavy and intrusive. A distinguishing symbol may not, however, be readily dispensed with and with the omission of this one the images of the saints have often degenerated into mere *genre* pictures and worldly types. A delicate circlet of light shining or floating over the head does not lessen the artistic impression, and even if the character of Christ or the Madonna is sufficiently indicated in the drawing, yet it must be conceded that the nimbus, like a crown, not only characterizes and differentiates a figure but distinguishes and exalts it as well.

STEPHANI, *Ueber den Nimbus u. Strahlenkranz in den Werken der älteren Kunst* in *Mémoires de l'Académie de St.-Pétersbourg* (1859); KRÜCKE, *Der Nimbus u. verwandte Attribute in der früchristl. Kunst* (Strasburg, 1905); MENDELSOHN, *Heiligenschein in der italien. Malerei seit Giotto* (Berlin 1903); KRAUS, *Realenzyklopädie der christl. Altertümer* (1882–86); various works by DIDRON and MENZEL.

G. GIETMANN.

Nîmes, DIOCESE OF (NEMAUSENSIS), suffragan of Avignon, comprises the civil Department of Gard. By the Concordat of 1801 its territory was united with the Diocese of Avignon. It was re-established as a separate diocese in 1821, and a Brief of 27 April, 1877, grants to its bishops the right to add Alais and Uzès to their episcopal style, these two dioceses being now combined with that of Nîmes.

That Nîmes (Nemausus) was an important city in Roman antiquity is shown by the admirable *Maison Carrée*, the remains of a superb amphitheatre, and the *Pont du Gard*, four and a half leagues from the city. Late and rather contradictory traditions attribute the foundation of the Church of Nîmes either to Celidonius, the man "who was blind from his birth" of the Gospel, or to St. Honestus, the apostle of Navarre, said to have been sent to southern France by St. Peter, with St. Saturninus (Sernin), the apostle of Toulouse. The true apostle of Nîmes was St. Baudilus, whose martyrdom is placed by some at the end of the third century, and, with less reason, by others at the end of the fourth. Many writers affirm that a certain St. Felix, martyred by the Vandals about 407, was Bishop of Nîmes, but Duchesne questions this. There was a see at Nîmes as early as 396, for in that year a synodical letter was sent by a Council of Nîmes to the bishops of Gaul. The first bishop whose date is positively known is Sedatus, present at the Council of Agde in 506. Other noteworthy bishops are: St. John (about 511, before 526); St. Remessarius (633–40); Bertrand of Languissel (1280–1324), faithful to Boniface VIII, and for that reason driven from his see for a year by Philip the Fair; Cardinal Guillaume d'Estouteville (1441–49); Cardinal Guillaume Briçonnet (1496–1514); the famous pulpit orator Fléchier (1687–1710); the distinguished polemist Plantier (1855–75) whose pastoral letter (1873) called forth a protest from Bismarck; the preacher Besson (1875–88). Urban II, coming to France to preach the crusade, consecrated the cathedral of Nîmes in 1096 and presided over a council. Alexander III visited Nîmes in 1162. Clement IV (1265–68), born at Saint Gilles, in this diocese, granted the monastery of that town numerous favours. St. Louis, who embarked at Aigues-Mortes for his two crusades, surrounded Nîmes with walls. In 1305, Clement V passed through the city on his way to Lyons to be crowned. In consequence of disputes about the sale of grapes to the papal household, Innocent VI laid an interdict on Nîmes in 1358. The diocese was greatly disturbed by the Religious Wars: on 29 Sept., 1567, five years before the Massacre of St. Bartholemew, the Protestants of Nîmes, actuated by fanaticism, perpetrated the massacre of Catholics known in French history as the Michelade. Louis XIII at Nîmes issued the decree of religious pacification known as the Peace of Nîmes.

The first Bishop of Uzès historically known is Constantius, present at the Council of Vaison in 442. Other bishops were St. Firminus (541–53) and St. Ferréol (553–81). In the sixteenth century, Bishop Jean de Saint Gelais (1531–60) became a Calvinist. The celebrated missionary Bridaine (1701–67) was a native of the Diocese of Uzès. This little city was for seventy days the enforced residence of Cardinal Pacca, after his confinement at Fenestrelles (1812). The town of Pont Saint Esprit, on the Rhône, owes its names to a bridge built there between 1265 and 1309 with the proceeds of a general collection made by the monks.

About 570, Sigebert, King of Austrasia, created a see at Arisitum (Alais), taking fifteen parishes from the Diocese of Nîmes. In the eighth century, when Septimania was annexed to the Frankish Empire, the Diocese of Alais was suppressed and its territory returned to the Diocese of Nîmes. At the request of Louis XIV, a see was again created at Alais by Innocent XII, in 1694. The future Cardinal de Bausset, Bossuet's biographer, was Bishop of Alais from 1784 to 1790. After the Edict of Nantes, Alais was one of the *places de sureté* given to the Huguenots (see HUGUENOTS, *History*). Louis XIII took back the town in 1629, and the Convention of Alais, signed 29 June of that year, suppressed the political privileges of the Protestants.

The chief pilgrimages of the present Diocese of Nîmes are: Notre Dame de Grâce, Rochefort, dating

THE CATHEDRAL, NÎMES
Consecrated by Urban II in 1093

from Charlemagne, and commemorating a victory over the Saracens. Louis XIV and his mother, Anne of Austria, established here a foundation for perpetual Masses. Notre Dame de Grâce, Laval, in the vicinity of Alais, dating from not later than 900. Notre Dame de Bon Secours de Prime Combe, Fontanès, since 887. Notre Dame de Bonheur, founded 1045 on the mountain of l'Aigoual in the vicinity of Valleraugues. Notre Dame de Belvezet, a shrine of the eleventh century, on Mont Andavu. Notre Dame de Vauvert, whither the converted Albigenses were sent, often visited by St. Louis, Clement V, and Francis I. The shrine of St. Vérédème, a hermit who died Archbishop of Avignon, and of the martyr St. Baudilus, at Trois Fontaines and at Valsainte near Nîmes. The following Saints are especially venerated in the present Diocese of Nîmes: St. Castor, Bishop of Apt (fourth to fifth century), a native of Nîmes; the priest St. Theodoritus, martyr, patron saint of the town of Uzès; the Athenian St. Giles (Ægidius, sixth cent.), living as a recluse near Uzès when he was accidentally wounded by King Childeric, later abbot of the monastery built by Childeric in reparation for this accident, venerated also in England; Blessed Peter of Luxemburg who made a sojourn in the diocese, at Villeneuve-lez-Avignon (1369–87).

Prior to the Associations Law of 1901 the diocese had Augustinians of the Assumption (a congregation which originated in the city of Nîmes), Carthusians, Trappists, Jesuits, Missionaries of the Company of

Mary, Franciscan Fathers, Marists, Lazarists, Sulpicians, and various orders of teaching brothers. The Oblates of the Assumption, for teaching and foreign missions, also founded here, and the Besançon Sisters of Charity, teachers and nurses, have their motherhouses at Nîmes. At the beginning of the century the religious congregations conducted in this diocese: 3 crèches, 53 day nurseries, 6 boys' orphanages, 20 girls' orphanages, 1 employment agency for females, 1 house of refuge for penitent women, 6 houses of mercy, 20 hospitals or asylums, 11 houses of visiting nurses, 3 houses of retreat, 1 home for incurables. In 1905 the Diocese of Nîmes contained 420,836 inhabitants, 45 parishes, 239 succursal parishes, 52 vicariates subventioned by the State.

Gallia Christiana Nova, VI (1739), 426–516; 608–53, 1118–1121, 1123, and Instrumenta, 165–226, 293–312; DUCHESNE, Fastes Episcopaux, I (1900), 299–302; GERMAIN, Histoire de l'église de Nîmes (Paris, 1838–42); GOIFFON, Catalogue analytique des évêques de Nîmes (1879); DURAND, Nemausiana, I (Nîmes, 1905); BOULENGER, Les protestants à Nîmes au temps de l'édit de Nantes (Paris, 1903); ROUX, (Paris, 1908); DURAND, L'église Ste Marie, ou Notre Dame de Nîmes, basilique cathédrale (Nîmes, 1906); CHARVET, Catalogue des évêques d'Uzès in Mémoires et Comptes rendus de la Société Scientifique d'Alais, II (1870), 129–59; TAULELLE, L'abbaye d'Alais: histoire de S. Julien de Valgalgue (Toulouse, 1905).

GEORGES GOYAU.

Nimrod. See NEMROD.

Ninian, SAINT (NINIAS, NINUS, DINAN, RINGAN, RINGEN), bishop and confessor, date of birth unknown; d. about 432; the first Apostle of Christianity in Scotland. The earliest account of him is in Bede (Hist. Eccles., III, 4): "the southern Picts received the true faith by the preaching of Bishop Ninias, a most reverend and holy man of the British nation, who had been regularly instructed at Rome in the faith and mysteries of the truth; whose episcopal see, named after St. Martin the Bishop, and famous for a church dedicated to him (wherein Ninias himself and many other saints rest in the body), is now in the possession of the English nation. The place belongs to the province of the Bernicians and is commonly called the White House [Candida Casa], because he there built a church of stone, which was not usual amongst the Britons". The facts given in this passage form practically all we know of St. Ninian's life and work.

The most important later life, compiled in the twelfth century by St. Aelred, professes to give a detailed account founded on Bede and also on a "liber de vita et miraculis eius" (sc. Niniani) "barbarice scriptus", but the legendary element is largely evident. He states, however, that while engaged in building his church at Candida Casa, Ninian heard of the death of St. Martin and decided to dedicate the building to him. Now St. Martin died about 397, so that the mission of Ninian to the southern Picts must have begun towards the end of the fourth century. St. Ninian founded at Whithorn a monastery which became famous as a school of monasticism within a century of his death; his work among the southern Picts seems to have had but a short-lived success. St. Patrick, in his epistle to Coroticus, terms the Picts "apostates", and references to Ninian's converts having abandoned Christianity are found in the lives of Sts. Columba and Kentigern. The body of St. Ninian was buried in the church at Whithorn (Wigtownshire), but no relics are now known to exist. The "Clogrinny", or bell of St. Ringan, of very rough workmanship, is in the Antiquarian Museum at Edinburgh.

BEDE, Hist. Eccles., tr. SELLAR, III (London, 1907), 4; AELRED, Vita S. Niniani in FORBES, Historians of Scotland, V; Acta SS., Sept., V, 321–28; CAPGRAVE, Nova Legenda Angliæ (London, 1516); O'CONOR, Rerum Hibernicarum Scriptores (Dublin, 1825); COLGAN, Acta SS. Hibern. (Louvain, 1647), 438; CHALLONER, Britannia Sancta, II (London, 1745), 130; STANTON, Menology of England and Wales (London, 1887), 448, 669; MACKINNON, Ninian und sein Einfluss auf die Ausbreitung des Christenthums in Nord-Britannien (Heidelberg, 1891), this is the most authoritative work on the subject; see also IDEM, Culture in Early Scotland; Analecta Bollandiana, XII, 82; Revue Bénédictine, IX, 526.

G. ROGER HUDLESTON.

Ninive (NINEVEH). See ASSYRIA.

Nirschl, JOSEPH, theologian and writer, b. at Durchfurth, Lower Bavaria, 24 February, 1823; d. at Würzburg, 17 January, 1904. He was ordained in 1851 and graduated as doctor of theology in 1854 at Munich. He was appointed teacher of Christian doctrine at Passau in 1855 and in 1862 professor of church history and patrology. In 1879 he became professor of church history at Würzburg, and was appointed dean of the cathedral in 1892. Of his numerous works, mostly on patristics, the most important are: "Lehrbuch der Patrologie und Patristik" (3 vols., Mainz, 1881-5); "Ursprung und Wesen des Bösen nach der Lehre des hl. Augustinus" (Ratisbon, 1854); "Das Dogma der unbefleckten Empfängnis Maria" (Ratisbon, 1855); "Todesjahr des hl. Ignatius von Antiochien" (Passau, 1869); "Die Theologie des hl. Ignatius von Antiochien" (Passau, 1869, and Mainz, 1880); Das Haus und Grab der hl. Jungfrau Maria (Mainz, 1900). He translated into German the letters and the martyrium of St. Ignatius of Antioch (Kempten, 1870) and the Catecheses of St. Cyril of Jerusalem (Kempten, 1871). He defended the genuineness of pseudo-Dionysius and of the apocryphal letter of King Abgar of Edessa to Jesus.

LAUCHERT in Biogr. Jahrb. und deutscher Nekrolog (Vienna, 1904), 169 sq.

MICHAEL OTT.

Nisibis, titular Archdiocese of Mesopotamia, situated on the Mygdonius at the foot of Mt. Masius. It is so old that its original name is unknown. In any case it is not the Achad (Accad) of Genesis, x, 10, as has been asserted. When the Greeks came to Mesopotamia with Alexander they called it Antiochia Mygdonia, under which name it appears for the first time on the occasion of the march of Antiochus against the Molon (Polybius, V, 51). Subsequently the subject of constant disputes between the Romans and the Parthians, it was captured by Lucullus after a long siege from the brother of Tigranes (Dion Cassius, XXXV, 6, 7); and by Trajan in 115, which won for him the name of Parthicus (ibid., LXVIII, 23). Recaptured by the Osrhoenians in 194, it was again conquered by Septimius Severus who made it his headquarters and established a colony there (ibid., LXXV, 23). In 297, by the treaty with Narses, the province of Nisibis was acquired by the Roman Empire; in 363 it was ceded to the Persians on the defeat of Julian the Apostate. The See of Nisibis was founded in 300 by Babu (d. 309). His successor, the celebrated St. James, defended the city by his prayers during the siege of Sapor II. At the time of its cession to the Persians, Nisibis was a Christian centre important enough to become the ecclesiastical metropolis of the Province of Beit-Arbaye. In 410 it had six suffragan sees and as early as the middle of the fifth century was the most important episcopal see of the Persian Church after Seleucia-Ctesiphon. A great many of its Nestorian or Jacobite titulars are mentioned in Chabot ("Synodicon orientale", Paris, 1902, 678) and Le Quien (Oriens christ., II, 995, 1195–1204) and several of them, e. g. Barsumas, Osee, Narses, Jesusyab, Ebed-Jesus, etc., acquired deserved celebrity in the world of letters. Near Nisibis on 25 June, 1839, Ibrahim Pasha, son of Mehemet Ali, Viceroy of Egypt, won a great victory over the troops of Mahmud II. To-day Nezib is a town of 3000 inhabitants in the sandjak of Orfa and the vilayet of Aleppo. Its oil is considered very fine.

The first theological school of Nisibis, founded at the introduction of Christianity into the town, was closed when the province was ceded to the Persians, great persecutors of Christianity. St. Ephraem reestablished it on Roman soil at Edessa, whither flocked all the studious youth of Persia. In the fifth century the school became a centre of Nestorianism.

Archbishop Cyrus in 489 closed it and expelled masters and pupils, who withdrew to Nisibis. They were welcomed by Barsumas, a former pupil of Edessa. The school was at once re-opened at Nisibis under the direction of Narses, called the harp of the Holy Ghost. The latter dictated the statutes of the new school. Those which have been discovered and published belong to Osee, the successor of Barsumas in the See of Nisibis, and bear the date 496; they must be substantially the same as those of 489. In 590 they were again modified. The school, a sort of Catholic university, was established in a monastery and directed by a superior called *Rabban*, a title also given to the instructors. The administration was confided to a majordomo, who was steward, prefect of discipline, and librarian, but under the supervision of a council. Unlike the Jacobite schools, devoted chiefly to profane studies, the school of Nisibis was above all a school of theology. The two chief masters were the instructors in reading and in the interpretation of Holy Scripture, explained chiefly with the aid of Theodore of Mopsuestia. The course of studies lasted three years and was entirely gratuitous; but the students provided for their own support. During their sojourn at the university, masters and students led a monastic life under somewhat special conditions. The school had a tribunal and enjoyed a civil personality, being able to acquire and possess all sorts of property. Its rich library possessed a most beautiful collection of Nestorian works; from its remains Ebed-Jesus, Metropolitan of Nisibis in the fourteenth century, composed his celebrated catalogue of ecclesiastical writers. The disorders and dissensions, which arose in the sixth century in the school of Nisibis, favoured the development of its rivals, especially that of Seleucia; however, it did not really begin to decline until after the foundation of the School of Bagdad (832). Among its literary celebrities mention should be made of its founder Narses; Abraham, his nephew and successor; Abraham of Kashgar, the restorer of monastic life; John; Babai the Elder; three *catholicoi* named Jesus-yab.

SMITH, *Dictionary of Greek and Roman Geography*, II (London, 1870), 440; GUIDI, *Gli Statuti della Scuola di Nisibi* in *Giornale della Società asiatica italiana*, IV, 165–195; CHABOT, *L'Ecole de Nisibe. Son histoire, ses statuts* (Paris, 1896); LABOURT, *Le christianisme dans l'empire perse* (Paris, 1904), passim; DUVAL, *La littérature syriaque* (Paris, 1899), passim; CUINET, *La Turquie d'Asie*, II (Paris), 269.

S. VAILHÉ.

Nithard, Frankish historian, son of Angilbert and Bertha, daughter of Charlemagne; d. about 843 or 844 in the wars against the Normans. Little is known about his early life, but in the quarrels between the sons of Louis the Pious he proved a zealous adherent of Charles the Bald, by whose command he went as ambassador to Lothair in 840, though without success. At the battle of Fontenoy, in 841, he fought bravely at the side of Charles, and afterwards wrote, at the request of that prince, the history of the period in order to establish the right of Charles the Bald. This work, which usually bears the title: "De dissensionibus filiorum Ludovici Pii ad annum usque 843, seu Historiarum libri quattuor 841-843", recites in rather uncouth language the causes of the quarrels and describes, minutely and clearly, the unjust behaviour of Lothair, sometimes a little partially, but with understanding and a clear insight into the conditions. He was the only layman of his time who devoted himself to the writing of a history, and he reported earnestly and truthfully what he himself had seen and heard. It is very probable that he was lay abbot of St. Riquier. His body was buried there, and when it was found, in the eleventh century, Mico, the poet of the abbey, composed a lengthy rhymed epitaph. Nithard's historical work has been published by Migne, in "P. L.", CXVI, 45–76; also in the "Mon. Germ. Hist.: Script.", II, 649–72, and in "Scriptores rerum Germanicarum in usum Scholarum" (Hanover, 1830, reprinted 1907). German translations by Jasmund appeared at Berlin, 1859; third edition, by Wattenbach, Leipzig, 1889.

WATTENBACH, *Deutschlands Geschichtsquellen*, I (Berlin, 1904), 233–37; POTTHAST, *Bibliotheca*, II (Berlin, 1896), 856 sq.

PATRICIUS SCHLAGER.

Noah. See NOE.

Noailles, LOUIS-ANTOINE DE, cardinal and bishop, b. at the Château de Teyssière in Auvergne, France, 27 May, 1651; d. at Paris, 4 May, 1729. His father, first Duc de Noailles, was captain-general of Roussillon; his mother, Louise Boyer, had been lady-in-waiting to Queen Anne of Austria. Louis de Noailles studied theology at Paris in the Collège du Plessis, where Fénelon was his fellow-student and friend, and obtained his doctorate at the Sorbonne, 14 March, 1676. Already provided with the Abbey of Aubrac (Diocese of Rodez), he was, in March, 1679, appointed to the Bishopric of Cahors, and in 1680 transferred to Châlons-sur-Marne, to which see a peerage was attached. He accepted this rapid removal only at the formal command of Innocent XI. In this office he showed himself a true bishop, occupying himself in all kinds of good works. He confided his theological seminary to the Lazarists, and founded a *petit séminaire*.

The regularity of his conduct, his family standing, and the support of Mme de Maintenon induced Louis XIV to make him Archbishop of Paris, 19 August, 1695. At Paris he was what he had been at Châlons. Lacking in brilliant qualities, he was possessed of piety, zeal, and activity. He was simple in manners and accessible to poor and rich alike. In 1709 he sold his silver plate to provide food for the famine-stricken. His generosity towards churches was also remarkable, and he spent large sums from his private fortune in decorating and improving Notre-Dame. The decorum of public worship and the good conduct of the clergy were the particular objects of his care. Inspired more by customs prevalent in France than by the prescriptions of the Council of Trent, he caused the Breviary, Missal, and other liturgical books of Paris already published by his predecessor de Harlay, to be reprinted. To these he added the Rituale, the Cæremoniale, and a collection of canons for the use of his Church. By decrees issued on his accession (June, 1696) he imposed for the first time on aspirants to the ecclesiastical state the obligation of residing in seminaries for several months before ordination. He organized ecclesiastical conferences throughout his diocese and conferences in moral theology once a week at Paris; priests were obliged to make an annual retreat, wise rules were drawn up for the good conduct and regularity of all ecclesiastics, the Divine service, the assistance of the sick, and the primary schools. Seminaries for poor clerics were encouraged and supported, and one was founded which served as a shelter for poor, old, or infirm priests.

While still Bishop of Châlons he took part in the conferences held at Issy to examine the works of Mme Guyon (q. v.). His part was only secondary, but he succeeded in having the accused's entire defence heard. Shortly afterwards he became involved in a controversy with Fénelon (q. v.) concerning the latter's "Maximes des Saints," which was condemned by the Bishops of Meaux, Chartres, and de Noailles himself. In 1700 he was made a cardinal by Innocent XII. Several months later de Noailles presided at the General Assembly of the French clergy. This assembly exerted great influence on the teaching of moral theology in France, and after Bossuet no one had so great a share as de Noailles in its decisions. He became prior of Navarre in 1704, head of the Sorbonne in 1710, and honorary dean of the faculty of law. Except for his attitude towards Jansenism the cardinal's career would be deserving only of praise. He always denied being a Jansenist, and condemned the five propositions constituting the essence of Jansenism, but he always inclined, both in dogma and morals, to opinions savouring of Jansenism; he favoured its partisans and was ever hostile to the Jesuits and the adversaries of the Jansenists. Shortly before his elevation to the See of Paris he had approved (June, 1695) the "Réflexions morales" of Père Quesnel, an Oratorian already known for his ardent attachment to Jansenism and destined soon to be its leader. He earnestly recommended it to his priests. This approbation was the source of all the cardinal's troubles.

Believing themselves thenceforth certain of his sympathy the Jansenists, on de Noailles' elevation to the See of Paris, published a posthumous work of de Barcos (q. v.), entitled "Exposition de la foy", really the explanation and defence of the Jansenistic doctrine of grace already condemned by Rome. De Noailles condemned the book (20 August, 1696), at least in the first part of his instruction, but in the second he set forth a theory on grace and predestination closely resembling that of de Barcos. No one was satisfied; the ordinance displeased both the Jansenists and the Jesuits. The former did not fail to call attention to the contradictory attitudes of the Bishop of Châlons, who approved Quesnel, and the Archbishop of Paris, who condemned de Barcos. An anonymous pamphlet published under the title "Problème ecclésiastique", placed side by side twenty-nine identical propositions which had been approved in the Quesnel's work and condemned in de Barcos'. Parliament condemned the lampoon to be burned; six months later it was put on the Index (2 June, 1699) and proscribed by the Holy Office.

The controversies occasioned by the publication of the "Cas de Conscience" and Quesnel's "Réflexions morales" (for which see JANSENIUS, in Vol. VIII, 291-2) involved de Noailles deeply in the Jansenist quarrel. In spite of repeated papal decisions of the Holy See, the cardinal, for many years, would not accept the Bull "Unigenitus". Finally he yielded in May, 1728, and on 11 October following published his unconditional acceptance of the Bull. He afterwards retracted various writings, which seemed to cast doubt on the sincerity of his submission; he restored to the Jesuits the faculties of which he had deprived them thirteen years before. He died two months later, aged 78, regarded by all with respect and esteem. His weak and uncertain character caused him to offend everybody—Jesuits and Jansenists, pope and king, partisans and adversaries of the Bull "Unigenitus". He lacked discernment in the choice of his confidants; he bore a great name, and played an important part in his time, but lacked many qualities of a great bishop. His works—diocesan ordinances and parochial instructions—are mostly collected in the "Synodicon ecclesiæ Parisiensis" (Paris, 1777).

DE BARTHÉLEMY, Le Card. de Noailles d'après sa correspondance (Paris, 1886); SAINT-SIMON, Mémoires, ed. BOILISLE, II (Paris, 1879); [VILLEFORE], Anecdotes ou Mémoires secrets (s.l., 1730); LAFITAU, Réfutation des Anecdotes (Aix, 1734); PICOT, Mém. pour servir à l'hist. ecclés. pendant le XVIIIe siècle (Paris, 1853), I, II; [GUILLON], Hist. gén. de l'église pendant le XVIIIe siècle (Besançon, 1823); LE ROY, La France et Rome de 1700 à 1715 (Paris, 1892); CROUSLÉ, Fénelon et Bossuet (Paris, 1895).

ANTOINE DEGERT.

Nobili, ROBERT DE', b. at Montepulciano, Tuscany, September, 1577; d. at Mylapore, India, in 1656. He entered the Society of Jesus in 1597, at Naples, and after a brilliant course of studies sailed for the Indian mission in October, 1604, arriving at Goa, 20 May, 1605. After a short stay at Cochin and the Fishery Coast, he was sent in November, 1606, to Madura to study Tamil. Within a year he had acquired a complete mastery of Tamil, Telugu, and Sanskrit. In his zeal to convert the Brahmins he adopted their mode of life and so had to cut himself off completely from intercourse with his fellow missionaries. He worked in Madura, Mysore, and the Karnatic till old age and almost complete blindness compelled him to retire to Mylapore. (For an account of his missionary methods see MALABAR RITES.) De' Nobili translated into Sanskrit or composed therein many prayers and several longer works, especially an abridgment of Christian Doctrine and a life of Our Lady, in Sanskrit verse. Nearly all these productions were lost during his imprisonment in Madura (1639–41). His principal work in Tamil is his "Larger Catechism", in four books, printed after his death (partly reprinted, Trichinopoly, 1891–1906). It is a course of theology adapted to the needs of the country. In addition he wrote: "A Treatise on the Eternal Life", "A Dialogue on the Faith", "A Disproof of Transmigration", "A Manual of Rules of Perfection", numerous hymns and several instructions not yet edited, two small catechisms still in actual use, "The Science of the Soul", and many prayers. He translated into Telugu several of his Tamil works, among them the two small catechisms. In Tamil and Telugu he enriched the vocabulary with appropriate Christian terms.

BERTRAND, La Mission du Maduré (Paris, 1847); Lettres édifiantes, Collection Martin, II, 263–66; for the pseudo-Veda, or rather pseudo-Veda hoax, see Asiatic Researches, XIV (London, 1818), 35; pseudo-Vedas seem clearly a non-Christian production; for diatribes on de' Nobili, see D'ORSAY, Portuguese Discoveries (London, 1893), 254–58.

J. CASTETS.

Noble, DANIEL, physician, b. 14 Jan., 1810; d. at Manchester, 12 Jan., 1885. He was the son of Mary Dewhurst and Edward Noble of Preston, a descendant of an old Yorkshire Catholic family. Apprenticed to a Preston surgeon named Thomas Moore, Noble was in time admitted a member of the Royal College of Surgeons and a licentiate of Apothecaries Hall. In 1834 he began to practise in Manchester, and soon showed the special interest in mental disease which afterwards distinguished his career. In the following year he published his first work, "An Essay of the Means, physical and moral, of estimating Human Character", the tendency of which is indicated by the fact that he is described as President of the Manchester Phrenological Society. His practise increased, and in 1840 he married Frances Mary Louisa Ward, of Dublin; they had eight children, one of them Frances, the novelist. Cardinal Wiseman stood sponsor to his eldest child. From the University of St. Andrews he received the degrees of M.D. and M.A., and in 1867 he was elected a fellow of the College of Physicians. His other works are:—"Facts and Observations relative to the influence of manufactures upon health and life" (London, 1843); "The Brain and its Physiology, a critical disquisition of the methods of determining relations subsisting between the structure and functions of the encephalon" (London, 1846); "Elements of Psychological Medicine: an Introduction to the practical study of Insanity" (London, 1853-55); "Three Lectures on the Correlation of Psychology and Physiology" (London, 1854); "The Human Mind in its relations with the Brain and Nervous System" (London, 1858); "On certain popular fallacies concerning the production of epidemic diseases" (Manchester, 1859); "On the fluctuations in the death-rate" (Manchester, 1863); "Evanescent Protestantism and Nascent Atheism, the modern religious problem" (London, 1877); "On causes reducing the effects of sanitary reform" (Manchester, 1878) and several contributions to various medical journals, the best-known of which was a paper called "Mesmerism True—Mesmerism False", which was translated into German and Dutch.

GILLOW, Bibl. Dict. Eng. Cath., V, 181.

EDWIN BURTON.

Nocera, DIOCESE OF (NUCERINENSIS), in Perugia, Umbria, Italy, near the sources of the Tina, famous for its mineral waters, especially the Fonte Angelica. According to a legend, the first Bishop of Nocera was St. Crispoldus, a disciple of the Apostles, but his Germanic name renders this doubtful; more credible is the tradition of the martyrdom of SS. Felix, Constance, and Felicissimus. The Bishops Felix, to whom Pope Innocent addressed a letter in 402, and Cœlius Laurentius, the competitor of Pope Symmachus (498), were not Umbrian prelates, but bishops of Nocera, near Naples (Savio, "Civ. Cattol.", 1907). The first authentic Bishop was Liutardus (824); other prelates were Blessed Rinaldo d'Antignano (1258) and Blessed Filippo Oderisi (1285), monks of Fonte Avellana; Blessed Alessandro Vincioli, O.M. (1363); Antonio Bolognini (1438) restored the cathedral; Varino Favorino (1514), a noted humanist; Gerolano Maunelli (1545), founder of the seminary; Mario Battaglini (1690), diocesan historian; Francesco Luigi Piervisani (1800), exiled in 1809 because he refused the oath of allegiance to Napoleon. It is immediately dependent on Rome, with 82 parishes; 59,731 inhabitants; 7 religious houses of men and 9 of women.

CAPPELLETTI, *Le Chiese d'Italia*, VI. U. BENIGNI.

Nocera dei Pagani (OF THE PAGANS), DIOCESE OF (NUCERIN PAGANORUM), in Salerno, Italy, at the foot of Mt. Albinio, on the Sarno River; it is the Nuceria Alfaterna of the Nuvkrinum coins, captured by Fabius Maximus in the Samnite War (307), and sacked by Hannibal (215). The appellation "of the pagans" dates probably from the ninth century, because of a Saracen colony established there with the connivance of the Dukes of Naples. In 1132 King Roger nearly destroyed the town because it took part with Innocent II, and in 1382 Charles of Durazzo besieged there Urban VI. Nocera is the birthplace of Hugo de Paganis (*Payus*), one of the founders of the Templars; St. Ludovico, Bishop of Tolosa, a son of Charles II of Anjou; Tommaso de Acerno, historian of Urban VI; and the painter Francesco Solimena. St. Alphonsus Liguori founded his order there. At Nocera is the sanctuary of *Mater Domini*, which contains the tomb of Charles I of Anjou; the ancient church was rebuilt in the eleventh century, and given to some hermits; Urban VIII gave it to the Basilians, and when these were driven away in 1809 and 1829, it came into the hands of the Franciscans. Among its bishops were St. Priscus, the first bishop, not St. Priscus of Nola; and Cœlius Laurentius, competitor of Symmachus (498). In 1260 the assassination of the bishop caused the suppression of the diocese, but Urban VI restored it in 1386. Later bishops were Giovanni Cerretani (1498), a jurist; the historian Paul Jovius (1528), succeeded by his nephew Julius and his great-nephew Paul, who rebuilt the episcopal palace; Simone Lunadoro (1602), diocesan historian. United to the See of Cava in 1818, it was re-established in 1834. A suffragan of Salerno, it has 28 parishes; 60,350 inhabitants; 4 religious houses of men, and 11 of women; a school for boys, and 5 for girls.

CAPPELLETTI, *Le Chiese d'Italia*, XX. U. BENIGNI.

PAOLO GIOVIO, BISHOP OF NOCERA DEI PAGANI (1528)
Painter Unknown, Uffizi, Florence

Nocturns (*Nocturni* or *Nocturna*), a very old term applied to night Offices. Tertullian speaks of nocturnal gatherings (Ad. Uxor., II, iv); St. Cyprian, of the nocturnal hours, "nulla sint horis nocturnis precum damna, nulla orationum pigra et ignava dispendia" (De orat., xxix). In the life of Melania the Younger is found the expression "nocturnæ horæ", "nocturna tempora" (Anal. Bolland., VIII, 1889, pp. 49 sq.). In these passages the term signifies night prayer in general, and seems synonymous with the word *vigiliæ*. It is not accurate, then, to assume that the present division of Matins into three Nocturns represents three distinct Offices recited during the night in the early ages of the Church. Durandus of Mende (Rationale, III, n. 17) and others who follow him assert that the early Christians rose thrice in the night to pray; hence the present division into three Nocturns (cf. Beleth, Rupert, and other authors cited in the bibliography). Some early Christian writers speak of three vigils in the night, as Methodius or St. Jerome (Methodius, "Symposion", V, ii, in P. G., XVIII, 100); but the first was evening prayer, or prayer at nightfall, corresponding practically to our Vespers or Complines; the second, midnight prayer, specifically called Vigil; the third, a prayer at dawn, corresponding to the Office of Lauds. As a matter of fact the Office of the Vigils, and consequently of the Nocturns, was a single Office, recited without interruption at midnight. All the old texts alluding to this Office (see MATINS; VIGIL) testify to this. Moreover, it does not seem practical to assume that anyone, considering the length of the Office in those days, could have risen to pray at three different times during the night, besides joining in the two Offices of eventide and dawn.

If it is not yet possible to assign exactly the date of the origin of the three Nocturns, or to account for the significance of the division, some more or less probable conjectures may be made. In the earliest period there was as yet no question of a division in the Office. The oldest Vigils, in as far as they signify an Office, comprised certain psalms, chanted or sung either as responses or as antiphons, intermingled with prayers recited aloud, or interrupted by a few moments' meditation and readings from the Old or the New Testament. On certain days the Vigil included the celebration of Mass.

It was during the second period, probably in the fourth century, that to break the monotony of this long night prayer the custom of dividing it into three parts was introduced. Cassian in speaking of the solemn Vigils mentions three divisions of this Office (De cœnob. instit., III, viii, in P. L., XLIX, 144). We have here, we think, the origin of the Nocturns; or at least it is the earliest mention of them we possess. In the "Peregrinatio ad loca sancta", the Office of the Vigils, either for week-days or for Sundays, is an uninterrupted one, and shows no evidence of any division (cf. Cabrol, "Etude sur La Peregrinatio Sylviæ", Paris, 1895, pp. 37 and 53). A little later St. Benedict speaks with greater detail of this division of the Vigils into two Nocturns for ordinary days, and three for Sundays and feast-days with six psalms and lessons for the first two Nocturns, three canticles and lessons for the third: this is exactly the structure of the Nocturns in the Benedictine Office to-day, and practically in the Roman Office (Regula, ix, x, xi). The very expression "Nocturn", to signify the night Office, is used by him twice (xv, xvi). He also uses the term *Nocturna laus* in speaking of the Office of the Vigils. The proof which E. Warren tries to draw from the "Antiphonary of Bangor" to show that in the Celtic Church, according to a custom older than the Benedictino-Roman practice, there were three separate Nocturns or Vigils, is based on a confusion of the three Offices, "Initium noctis", "Nocturna", and "Matutina", which are not the three Nocturns, but the Office of Eventide, of the Vigil, and of Lauds (cf. The Tablet, 16 Dec., 1893, p. 972; and Bäumer-Biron, *infra*, I, 263, 264).

The division of the Vigils into two or three Nocturns in the Roman Church dates back at least to the fifth century. We may conjecture that St. Benedict, who, in the composition of the monastic *cursus*, follows the arrangement of the Roman Office so closely, must have been inspired equally by the Roman customs in the composition of his Office. Whatever doubt there may be as to priority, it is certain that the Roman system bears a strong analogy to that of the Nocturns in the Benedictine Office even at the present time, and the differences subsisting are almost entirely the result of transformations or additions, which the Roman Office has been subjected to in the course of time. On Sundays and feast-days there are three Nocturns, as in the Benedictine Office. Each Nocturn comprises three psalms, and the first Nocturn of Sunday has three groups of four psalms each. The ferial days have only one Nocturn consisting of twelve psalms; each Nocturn has, as usual, three lessons. For the variations which have occurred in the course of time in the composition of the Nocturns, and for the different usages see MATINS. These different usages are recorded by Dom Martène. For the terms, "Nocturnales Libri", "Nocturnæ", see Du Cange, "Glossarium infimæ latinitatis", s. vv.

See MATINS; VIGIL; CASSIAN, *De cœnob. instit.*, II, x; BELETH, *Rationale*, xx; *Liber Diurnus*, P. L., CV, 71; DURANDUS OF MENDE, *Rationale*, III, n. 7; RUPERT, *De div. officiis*, I, x; MARTÈNE, *De antiquis Monach. rit.*, IV, 4 sq.; ZACCARIA, *Onomasticon*, 50, 51; BÄUMER-BIRON, *Histoire du Bréviaire*, I (Paris, 1905), 74 sq., 78, 99, 263, 358–361, etc.

F. CABROL.

Noe [Heb. נֹחַ (Nôaḥ), "rest"; Gr. Νῶε; Lat. *Noe*], the ninth patriarch of the Sethite line, grandson of Mathusala and son of Lamech, who with his family was saved from the Deluge and thus became the second father of the human race (Gen., v, 25—ix, 29). The name Nôaḥ was given to him because of his father's expectation regarding him. "This same", said Lamech on naming him, "shall comfort us from the works and labours of our hands on [or more correctly "from", i. e. which come from] the earth, which the Lord hath cursed." Most commentators consider Lamech's words as the expression of a hope, or as a prophecy, that the child would in some way be instrumental in removing the curse pronounced against Adam (Gen., iii, 17 sqq.). Others rather fancifully see in them a reference to Noe's future discovery of wine, which cheers the heart of man; whilst others again, with greater probability, take them as expressing merely a natural hope on the part of Lamech that his son would become the support and comfort of his parents, and enable them to enjoy rest and peace in their later years. Amid the general corruption which resulted from the marriages of "the sons of God" with "the daughters of men" (Gen., vi, 2 sqq.), that is of the Sethites with Cainite women, "Noe was a just and perfect man in his generations" and "walked with God" (vi, 9). Hence, when God decreed to destroy men from the face of the earth, he "found grace before the Lord". According to the common interpretation of Gen., vi, 3, Noe first received divine warning of the impending destruction one hundred and twenty years before it occurred, and therefore when he was four hundred and eighty years old (cf. vii, 11); he does not seem, however, to have received at this time any details as to the nature of the catastrophe. After he reached the age of five hundred years three sons, Sem, Cham, and Japheth, were born to him (vi, 10). These had grown to manhood and had taken wives, when Noe was informed of God's intention to destroy men by a flood, and received directions to build an ark in which he and his wife, his sons and their wives, and representatives, male and female, of the various kinds of animals and birds, were to be saved (vi, 13–21). How long before the Deluge this revelation was imparted to him, it is impossible to say; it can hardly have been more than seventy-five years (cf. vii, 11), and probably was considerably less.

Noe had announced the impending judgment and had exhorted to repentance (II Pet., ii, 5), but no heed was given to his words (Matt., xxiv, 37 sqq.; Luke xvii, 26, 27; I Pet., iii, 20), and, when the fatal time arrived, no one except Noe's immediate family found refuge in the ark. Seven days before the waters began to cover the earth, Noe was commanded to enter the ark with his wife, his three sons and their wives, and to take with him seven pairs of all clean, and two pairs of all unclean animals and birds (vii, 1–4). It has been objected that, even though the most liberal value is allowed for the cubit, the ark would have been too small to lodge at least two pairs of every species of animal and bird. But there can be no difficulty if, as is now generally admitted, the Deluge was not geographically universal (see DELUGE; ARK). After leaving the ark Noe built an altar, and taking of all clean animals and birds, offered holocausts upon it. God accepted the sacrifice, and made a covenant with Noe, and through him with all mankind, that He would not waste the earth or destroy man by another deluge. The rainbow would for all times be a sign and a reminder of this covenant. He further renewed the blessing which He had pronounced on Adam (Gen., i, 28), and confirmed the dominion over animals which He had granted to man. In virtue of this dominion man may use animals for food, but the flesh may not be eaten with the blood (viii, 20–ix, 17). Noe now gave himself to agriculture, and planted a vineyard. Being unacquainted with the effects of fermented grape-juice, he drank of it too freely and was made drunk. Cham found his father lying naked in his tent, and made a jest of his condition before his brothers; these reverently covered him with a mantle. On hearing of the occurrence Noe cursed Chanaan, as Cham's heir, and blessed Sem and Japheth. He lived three hundred and fifty years after the Deluge, and died at the age of nine hundred and fifty years (ix, 20–29). In the later books of Scripture Noe is represented as the model of the just man (Ecclus., xliv, 17; Ezech., xiv, 14, 20), and as an exemplar of faith (Heb., xi, 7). In the Fathers and tradition he is considered as the type and figure of the Saviour, because through him the human race was saved from destruction and reconciled with God (Ecclus., xliv, 17, 18). Moreover, as he built the ark, the only means of salvation from the Deluge, so Christ established the Church, the only means of salvation in the spiritual order.

The Babylonian account of the Deluge in many points closely resembles that of the Bible. Four cuneiform recensions of it have been discovered, of which, however, three are only short fragments. The complete story is found in the Gilgamesh epic (Tablet xi) discovered by G. Smith among the ruins of the library of Assurbanipal in 1872. Another version is given by Berosus. In the Gilgamesh poem the hero of the story is Ut-napishtim (or Ṣit-napishti, as some read it), surnamed Atra–ḥasis "the very clever"; in two of the fragments he is simply styled Atra-ḥasis, which name is also found in Berosus under the Greek form Xisuthros. The story in brief is as follows: A council of the gods having decreed to destroy men by a flood, the god Ea warns Ut-napishtim, and bids him build a ship in which to save himself and the seed of all kinds of life. Ut-napishtim builds the ship (of which, according to one version, Ea traces the plan on the ground), and places in it his family, his dependents, artisans, and domestic as well as wild animals, after which he shuts the door. The storm lasts six days; on the seventh the flood begins to subside. The ship steered by the helmsman Puzur-Bel lands on Mt. Niṣir. After seven days Ut-napishtim sends forth a dove and a swallow, which, finding no resting-place for their feet return to the ark, and then a raven, which feeds on dead bodies and does not return. On leaving the ship, Ut-napistim offers a sacrifice to the gods, who smell the goodly odour and gather like flies over the sacrificer. He and his wife are then admitted among the gods. The story as given by Berosus comes somewhat nearer to the Biblical narrative. Because of the striking resemblances between the two many maintain that the Biblical account is derived from the Babylonian. But the differences are so many and so important that this view must be pronounced untenable. The Scriptural story is a parallel and independent form of a common tradition.

HUMMELAUER, *Comm. in Gen.* (Paris, 1895), 257 sqq.; HOBERG, *Die Genesis* (Freiburg, 1908), 74 sqq.; SELBST, *Handbuch zur bibl. Gesch.* (Freiburg, 1910), 200 sqq.; SKINNER, *Critic. and Exeg. Comm. on Gen.* (New York, 1910), 133 sqq.; DILLMANN, *Genesis*, tr., I (Edinburgh, 1897), 228 sqq.; DHORME, *Textes religieux assyro-babyl.* (Paris, 1907), 100 sqq.; VIGOUROUX, *La bible et les découv. mod.*, I (6th ed., Paris, 1896), 309 sqq.; SCHRADER, *Die Keilinschrift. u. das A. T.* (2nd ed., Giessen, 1882), 55 sqq.; JENSEN in SCHRADER, *Keilinschriftl. Bibliothek*, VI, i (Berlin, 1889—), 228 sqq.; VIGOUROUX, *Dict. de la Bible*, s. vv. *Ararat, Arche*, and *Noé*; HILPRECHT, *The earliest version of the Babylonian deluge story* (Philadelphia, 1910).

F. BECHTEL.

Noel Alexandre. See ALEXANDER NATALIS.

Noetus and Noetianism. See MONARCHIANS.

Nogaret, GUILLAUME DE, b. about the middle of the thirteenth century at St. Felix-en-Lauragais; d. 1314; he was one of the chief counsellors of Philip the Fair, of France (1285–1314), said to be descended from an Albigensian family and was a *protégé* of the lawyer, Pierre Flotte. He studied law, winning a doctorate and a professorship, and was appointed, in 1294, royal judge of the seneschal's court of Beaucaire. In 1299 the title of knight was conferred on him by Philip the Fair. Imbued, from his study of Roman law, with the doctrine of the absolute supremacy of the king, no scruple restrained Nogaret when the royal power was in question, and his influence was apparent in the struggle between Philip and Boniface VIII. In 1300 Philip sent him as ambassador to the Holy See to excuse his alliance with Albert of Austria, usurper of the Empire. Nogaret, according to his own account, remonstrated with the pope, who replied in vigorous language. After the death of Pierre Flotte at the battle of Courtrai (1302), Nogaret became chief adviser and evil genius of the king. On the publication of the Bull "Unam Sanctam" he was charged with directing the conflict against the Holy See (February, 1303). At the Assembly of the Louvre (12 March, 1303), he bitterly attacked the pope, and later, allying himself with the pope's Italian enemies (the Florentine banker, Musciatto de Franzesi, and Sciarra Colonna, the head of the Ghibelline party), he surprised Boniface in his palace at Anagni and arrested him after subjecting him to outrageous treatment (7 September). But the inhabitants rescued the pope, whose death (11 October), saved Nogaret from severe retribution. Early in 1304, at Languedoc, he explained his actions to the king, and received considerable property as recompense. Philip even sent him with an embassy to the new pope, Benedict XI, who refused to absolve him from the excommunication he had incurred. Clement V, however, absolved him in 1311.

Nogaret played a decisive part in the trial of the Templars. On 22 September, 1307, at Maubuisson, Philip made him keeper of the seal and the same day the Royal Council issued a warrant for the arrest of the Templars, which was executed on 12 October; Nogaret himself arrested the Knights of the Temple in Paris and drew up the proclamation justifying the crime. It was he who directed all the measures that ended in the execution of Jacques de Molai and the principal Templars (1314). The same year Nogaret, who displayed untiring energy in drawing up the documents by which he sought to ruin his adversaries, undertook to justify the condemnation of the Templars by announcing the plans for a new crusade, the expenses of which were to be defrayed by the confiscated goods of the Order. In this Latin document, addressed to Clement V, the author attributes the failure of the crusades to the Templars and declares that Philip the Fair alone could direct them successfully, provided that he obtained the help of all the Christian princes to secure the funds required for the expedition; all the property of the Templars should be given to the king, likewise all legacies left for the crusades and all the benefices in Christendom should be taxed. The other military orders, the abbeys, the churches should retain only the property necessary for their support, the surplus should be given for the Crusade. No one took this document seriously, it was probably intended as a solemn hoax. Nogaret's influence may be seen in the trial for sorcery against Guichard, bishop of Troyes (1308). A zealous but unscrupulous royal partisan, a fierce and bitter enemy, Nogaret died before Philip the Fair, at the time when the regime he had devoted himself to establishing was beginning to be attacked on all sides.

Hist. de Languedoc, IV, 551–4; HOLTZMANN, *Wilhelm v. Nogaret* (Freiburg, 1898); BOUTARIC, *Notices et extraits des documents inédits relatifs à l'hist. de France sous Philippe le Bel*; IDEM, *Not. et extraits des manuscrits Bibl. Nat.*, XX, ii, 83; BOUTARIC AND RENAN, *Etude sur la politique religieuse du règne de Philippe le Bel* (Paris, 1899); cf. *Hist. litt. de la France*, XXVI–XXVII; RIGAULT, *Le procès de Guichard, évêque de Troyes* (Paris, 1896). Inventory of Nogaret's papers is in the Bibliothèque Nationale, Collect. Dupuy 635, f. 101; the list of his political writings is to be found in the *Hist. litt. de la France*, XXVII, 359–64.

LOUIS BRÉHIER.

Nola, DIOCESE OF (NOLANA), suffragan of Naples. The city of Nola in the Italian Province of Caserta, in Campania, is said to have been founded by the Etruscans or by Chalcideans from Cumæ. On the most ancient coins it is called Nuvlana. In the Samnite War (311 B. C.) the town was taken by the Romans, in the Punic War it was twice besieged by Hannibal (215 and 214), and on both occasions splendidly defended by Marcellus. In the war with the Marsi, the latter took Nola, in 90 B. C., but, notwithstanding their brilliant defence of the city, it was retaken from them in the year 89, and its recapture put an end to that war. The city was sacked by Spartacus, for which reason Augustus and Vespasian sent colonies there. In A. D. 410 it was sacked by Alaric, in 453 by the Vandals, in 806 and again in 904 by the Saracens. From the time of Charles I of Anjou to the middle of the fifteenth century, Nola was a feudal possession of the Orsini. The battle of Nola (1459) is famous for the clever stratagem by which John of Anjou defeated Alfonso of Aragon. Nola furnished a considerable portion of the antiquities in the museum of Naples, especially beautiful Greek vases. In the seminary there is a collection of ancient inscriptions, among which are some Oscan tablets. The ruins of an amphitheatre and other ancient remains are yet to be seen in this city, where the Emperor Augustus, who died there, had a famous temple. Nola was the birthplace of Giordano Bruno, of Luigi Tausillo, the philosopher and poet, of the sculptor Giovanni Merliano, whose work is well represented in the cathedral, and of the physician Ambrogio Leo.

The ancient Christian memories of Nola are connected with the neighbouring Cimitile, the name of which recalls the site of an ancient cemetery. There is the basilica of St. Felix, the martyr, built, and poetically described by St. Paulinus, bishop of the city, who shows that no sanctuary, after the tombs of the Holy Apostles Peter and Paul, was visited by as many pilgrims as came to this shrine. St. Felix, who lived between the middle of the second century and the middle of the third, was the first Bishop of Nola. The city has several other martyrs, among them, Sts. Reparatus, Faustillus, and Acacius, companions of St. Januarius, besides St. Felix, confessor. Other bishops of Nola were St. Marinus (about the year 300); St. Priscus, who died in 328 or, according to Mommsen, in

523; St. Quodvultdeus, who died in 387 and was succeeded by St. Paulinus. The body of the last-named saint was taken to Benevento in 839, and in the year 1000 was given to Otho III by the people of Benevento in exchange for the body of St. Bartholomew; in 1909 it was restored to Nola. In the fifth century the archpresbyter St. Adeodatus flourished at Nola; his metrical epitaph has been preserved. In 484 Joannes Taloias, Orthodox Patriarch of Alexandria, having been driven from his diocese, was made Bishop of Nola. It was St. Paulinus III (c. 505) who became a slave to free a widow's son; this heroic deed was afterwards attributed to St. Paulinus I. Bishop Lupicinus (786) restored several sacred buildings. Francis Scacciani (1370) erected the Gothic cathedral, which was finished by Bishop Gian Antonio Boccarelli (1469). Antonio Scarampi (1549) founded the seminary and introduced the reforms of the Council of Trent. Fabrizio Gallo (1585) founded several charitable institutions; G. B. Lancellotti (1615–56), who was Apostolic nuncio to Poland from 1622 to 1627, did much for the diocese; Francis M. Carafa (1704), a Theatine, was zealous for the education of the clergy; Traiano Caracciolo (1738) constructed the new seminary.

The diocese is a suffragan of Naples; has 86 parishes, with 200,000 inhabitants, 9 religious houses of men, and 19 of women, several educational establishments and asylums, and four monthly and bi-monthly periodicals.

CAPPELLETTI, *Le Chiese d'Italia*, XXI; REMONDINI, *Storia della città e diocesi di Nola* (Naples, 1747–57).

U. BENIGNI.

Nola, GIOVANNI MARLIANO DA, sculptor and architect, b., it is said, of a leather merchant named Giuseppe, at Nola, near Naples, 1488; d. 1558 (?). He studied under Agnolo Aniello Fiore and then went to Rome, being attracted by the fame of Michelangelo, whose work he studied closely. On his return to Naples he was employed in churches, palaces, and *piazze*. Among his works may be mentioned the monument of Galeazzo Pandono in S. Domenico (1514); the tombs of the three youths Jacopo, Ascanio, and Sigismondo (who died of poison) in their family church of S. Severino (1516); various sculptures in the church of Monte Oliveto (1524), notably a fine group of the Mother and Child with infant St. John and, in the choir, tombs of Alphonsus II and Guerrero Origlia; in the church of S. Chiara, the simple and touching recumbent figure of the girl Antonia Gandino (1530). Outside of Italy the noble monument of the Spanish Duke of Cardona (about 1532) in the Franciscan church of Belpuch is among the best known. The decorations made by Nola for the reception of Emperor Charles V in Naples (1535) are still to be seen on the *Porta Capuana*. In 1537 he carved a beautiful standing Madonna and two Saints for the church of S. Domenico Maggiore. In 1553 the Spanish viceroy, Peter of Toledo, caused him to erect the mausoleum to himself and his wife in the church of S. Giacomo degli Spagnuoli. Further works of Nola's, also in Naples, are the Pietà and tomb of a child, Andrea Cicara, in the church of S. Severino; a Madonna della Misericordia in S. Pietro ad Aram; an altar-piece at S. Aniello, representing the Mother and Child seated on a crescent moon; and a fine set of wooden bas-reliefs depicting the life of Christ, in the sacristy of the Annunziata. Nola is one of the most justly lauded representatives of a rather poor school of Renaissance sculpture in Naples.

CICOGNARA, *Storia della scultura* (Venice, 1813–); PERKINS, *Italian Sculptors* (London, 1868); LÜBKE, *History of Sculpture*, tr. BURNETT (London, 1872).

M. L. HANDLEY.

Noli. See SAVONA AND NOLI, DIOCESE OF.

Nollet, JEAN-ANTOINE, physicist, b. at Pimpré, Oise, France, 19 November, 1700; d. at Paris, 25 April, 1770. His peasant parents sent him to study at Clermont and Beauvais. He went later to Paris to prepare for the priesthood. In 1728 he received the deaconship and applied immediately for permission to preach. Soon love of science became uppermost and together with Dufay and Réaumur he devoted himself to the study of physics and especially to research work in electricity. Abbé Nollet was the first to recognize the importance of sharp points on the conductors in the discharge of electricity. This was later applied practically in the construction of the lightning-rod. He also studied the conduction of electricity in tubes, in smoke, vapours, steam, the influence of electric charges on evaporation, vegetation, and animal life. His discovery of the osmosis of water through a bladder into alcohol was the starting-point of that branch of physics.

In 1734 Nollet went to London and was admitted into the Royal Society. In 1735 he started in Paris, at his own expense, a course in experimental physics which he continued until 1760. In 1738 Cardinal Fleury created a public chair of experimental physics for Nollet. In 1739 he entered the Academy of Sciences, becoming associate member in 1742, and pensionary in 1758. In April, 1739 the King of Sardinia called him to Turin to instruct the Duke of Savoy, and to furnish the instruments needed for the new chair of physics at the university. After lecturing a short time at Bordeaux, he was called to Versailles to instruct the dauphin in experimental science. He was appointed professor of experimental physics at the Royal College of Navarre, in 1753. In 1761 he taught at the school of artillery at Mézières. Nollet was also a member of the Institute of Bologna and of the Academy of Sciences of Erfurt. He was calm and simple in manner, and his letters and papers showed that he had been devoted and generous to his family and his native village. Nollet contributed to the "Recueil de l'Académie des Sciences" (1740–67) and the "Philosophical Transactions of the Royal Society"; his larger works include among others:—"Programme d'un cours de physique expérimentale" (Paris, 1738); "Leçons de physique expérimentale" (Paris, 1743); "Recherches sur les causes particulières des phénomènes électriques" (Paris, 1749); "L'art des expériences" (Paris, 1770).

GRANDJEAN DE FOUCHY, *Eloge de J.-A. Nollet; Histoire de l'Académie Royale des Sciences* (Paris, 1773), 121–36.

WILLIAM FOX.

Nominalism, Realism, Conceptualism.—These terms are used to designate the theories that have been proposed as solutions of one of the most important questions in philosophy, often referred to as the problem of universals, which, while it was a favourite subject for discussion in ancient times, and especially in the Middle Ages, is still prominent in modern and contemporary philosophy. We propose to discuss in this article: I. The Nature of the Problem and the Suggested Solutions; II. The Principal Historic Forms of Nominalism, Realism, and Conceptualism; III. The Claims of Moderate Realism.

I. THE PROBLEM AND THE SUGGESTED SOLUTIONS.—The problem of universals is the problem of the correspondence of our intellectual concepts to things existing outside our intellect. Whereas external objects are determinate, individual, formally exclusive of all multiplicity, our concepts or mental representations offer us the realities independent of all particular determination; they are abstract and universal. The question, therefore, is to discover to what extent the concepts of the mind correspond to the things they represent; how the flower we conceive represents the flower existing in nature; in a word, whether our ideas are faithful and have an objective reality. Four solutions of the problem have been offered. It is necessary to describe them carefully, as writers do not always use the terms in the same sense.

A. *Exaggerated Realism* holds that there are universal concepts in the mind and universal things in nature. There is, therefore, a strict parallelism between the being in nature and the being in thought, since the external object is clothed with the same character of universality that we discover in the concept. This is a simple solution, but one that runs counter to the dictates of common sense.

B. *Nominalism.*—Exaggerated Realism invents a world of reality corresponding exactly to the attributes of the world of thought. Nominalism, on the contrary, models the concept on the external object, which it holds to be individual and particular. Nominalism consequently denies the existence of abstract and universal concepts, and refuses to admit that the intellect has the power of engendering them. What are called general ideas are only names, mere verbal designations, serving as labels for a collection of things or a series of particular events. Hence the term Nominalism. Neither Exaggerated Realism nor Nominalism finds any difficulty in establishing a correspondence between the thing in thought and the thing existing in nature, since, in different ways, they both postulate perfect harmony between the two. The real difficulty appears when we assign different attributes to the thing in nature and to the thing in thought; if we hold that the one is individual and the other universal. An antinomy then arises between the world of reality and the world as represented in the mind, and we are led to inquire how the general notion of flower conceived by the mind is applicable to the particular and determinate flowers of nature.

C. *Conceptualism* admits the existence within us of abstract and universal concepts (whence its name), but it holds that we do not know whether or not the mental objects have any foundation outside our minds or whether in nature the individual objects possess distributively and each by itself the realities which we conceive as realized in each of them. The concepts have an ideal value; they have no real value, or at least we do not know whether they have a real value.

D. *Moderate Realism*, finally, declares that there are universal concepts representing faithfully realities that are not universal. "How can there be harmony between the former and the latter? The latter are particular, but we have the power of representing them to ourselves abstractly. Now the *abstract* type, when the intellect considers it reflectively and contrasts it with the particular subjects in which it is realized or capable of being realized, is attributable indifferently to any and all of them. This applicability of the abstract type to the individuals is its universality" (Mercier, "Critériologie", Louvain, 1906, p. 343).

II. THE PRINCIPAL HISTORICAL FORMS OF NOMINALISM, REALISM, AND CONCEPTUALISM.—A. *In Greek Philosophy.*—The conciliation of the one and the many, the changing and the permanent, was a favourite problem with the Greeks; it leads to the problem of universals. The typical affirmation of Exaggerated Realism, the most outspoken ever made, appears in Plato's philosophy; the real must possess the attributes of necessity, universality, unity, and immutability which are found in our intellectual representations. And as the sensible world contains only the contingent, the particular, the unstable, it follows that the real exists outside and above the sensible world. Plato calls it εἶδος, idea. The idea is absolutely stable and exists by itself (ὄντως ὄν; αὐτὰ καθ' αὑτά), isolated (χωριστά) from the phenomenal world, distinct from the Divine and the human intellect. Following logically the directive principles of his Realism, Plato makes an idea-entity correspond to each of our abstract representations. Not only natural species (man, horse) but artificial products (bed), not only substances (man) but properties (white, just), relations (double, triple), and even negations and nothingness have a corresponding idea in the suprasensible world. "What makes one and one two, is a participation of the dyad (δύας), and what makes one one is a participation of the monad (μόνας) in unity" (Phædo, lxix). The exaggerated Realism of Plato, investing the real being with the attributes of the being in thought, is the principal doctrine of his metaphysics.

Aristotle broke away from these exaggerated views of his master and formulated the main doctrines of Moderate Realism. The real is not, as Plato says, some vague entity of which the sensible world is only the shadow; it dwells in the midst of the sensible world. Individual substance (this man, that horse) alone has reality; it alone can exist. The universal is not a thing in itself; it is immanent in individuals and is multiplied in all the representatives of a class. As to the form of universality of our concepts (man, just), it is a product of our subjective consideration. The objects of our generic and specific representations can certainly be called substances (οὐσίαι), when they designate the fundamental reality (man) with the accidental determinations (just, big); but these are δεύτεραι οὐσίαι (second substances), and by that Aristotle means precisely that this attribute of universality which affects the substance as in thought does not belong to the substance (thing in itself); it is the outcome of our subjective elaboration. This theorem of Aristotle, which completes the metaphysics of Heraclitus (denial of the permanent) by means of that of Parmenides (denial of change), is the antithesis of Platonism, and may be considered one of the finest pronouncements of Peripateticism. It was through this wise doctrine that the Stagyrite exercised his ascendency over all later thought.

After Aristotle Greek philosophy formulated a third answer to the problem of universals, Conceptualism. This solution appears in the teaching of the Stoics, which, as is known, ranks with Platonism and Aristoteleanism among the three original systems of the great philosophic age of the Greeks. Sensation is the principle of all knowledge, and thought is only a collective sensation. Zeno compared sensation to an open hand with the fingers separated; experience or multiple sensation to the open hand with the fingers bent; the general concept born of experience to the closed fist. Now, concepts, reduced to general sensations, have as their object, not the corporeal and external thing reached by the senses (τύγχανον), but the λεκτόν or the reality conceived; whether this has any real value we do not know. The Aristotelean School adopted Aristotelean Realism, but the neo-Platonists subscribed to the Platonic theory of ideas which they transformed into an emanationistic and monistic conception of the universe.

B. *In the Philosophy of the Middle Ages.*—For a long time it was thought that the problem of universals monopolized the attention of the philosophers of the Middle Ages, and that the dispute of the Nominalists and Realists absorbed all their energies. In reality that question, although prominent in the Middle Ages, was far from being the only one dealt with by these philosophers.

(1) *From the commencement of the Middle Ages till the end of the 12th century.*—It is impossible to classify the philosophers of the beginning of the Middle Ages exactly as Nominalists, Moderate and Exaggerated Realists, or Conceptualists. And the reason is that the problem of the Universals is very complex. It not merely involves the metaphysics of the individual and of the universal, but also raises important questions in ideology—questions about the genesis and validity of knowledge. But the earlier Scholastics, unskilled in such delicate matters, did not perceive these various aspects of the problem. It did not grow up spontaneously in the Middle Ages; it was bequeathed in a text of Porphyry's "Isagoge", a text

that seemed simple and innocent, though somewhat obscure, but one which force of circumstances made the necessary starting-point of the earliest medieval speculations about the Universals.

Porphyry divides the problem into three parts: (1) Do genera and species exist in nature, or do they consist in mere products of the intellect? (2) If they are things apart from the mind, are they corporeal or incorporeal things? (3) Do they exist outside the (individual) things of sense, or are they realized in the latter? "Mox de generibus et speciebus illud quidem sive subsistant sive in nudis intellectibus posita sint, sive subsistentia corporalia sint an incorporalia, et utrum separata a sensibilibus an in sensibilibus posita et circa hæc subsistentia, dicere recusabo." Historically, the first of those questions was discussed prior to the others: the latter could have arisen only in the event of denying an exclusively subjective character to universal realities. Now the first question was whether genera and species are objective realities or not: sive subsistant, sive in nudis intellectibus posita sint? In other words, the sole point in debate was the absolute reality of the universals: their truth, their relation to the understanding, was not in question. The text from Porphyry, apart from the solutions he elsewhere proposed in works unknown to the early Scholastics, is an inadequate statement of the question; for it takes account only of the objective aspect and neglects the psychological standpoint which alone can give the key to the true solution. Moreover, Porphyry, after proposing his triple interrogation in the "Isagoge", refuses to offer an answer (*dicere recusabo*). Boëthius, in his two commentaries, gives replies that are vague and scarcely consistent. In the second commentary, which is the more important one, he holds that *genera* and *species* are both *subsistentia* and *intellecta* (1st question), the similarity of things being the basis (*subjectum*) both of their individuality in nature and their universality in the mind; that *genera* and *species* are incorporeal not by nature but by abstraction (2nd question), and that they exist both inside and outside the things of sense (3rd question).

This was not sufficiently clear for beginners, though we can see in it the basis of the Aristotelean solution of the problem. The early Scholastics faced the problem as proposed by Porphyry: limiting the controversy to *genera* and *species*, and its solutions to the alternatives suggested by the first question: Do the objects of our concepts (i. e., *genera* and *species*) exist in nature (*subsistentia*), or are they mere abstractions (*nuda intellecta*)? Are they, or are they not, things? Those who replied in the affirmative got the name of Reals or Realists; the others that of Nominals or Nominalists. The former, or the Realists, more numerous in the early Middle Ages (Fredugisus, Rémy d'Auxerre, and John Scotus Eriugena in the ninth century, Gerbert and Odo of Tournai in the tenth, and William of Champeaux in the twelfth) attribute to each genus and each species a universal essence (*subsistentia*), to which all the subordinate individuals are tributary.

The Nominalists, who should be called rather the anti-Realists, assert on the contrary that the individual alone exists, and that the universals are not things realized in the universal state in nature, or *subsistentia*. And as they adopt the alternative of Porphyry, they conclude that the universals are *nuda intellecta* (that is, purely intellectual representations).

It may be that Roscelin of Compiègne did not go beyond these energetic protests against Realism, and that he is not a Nominalist in the exact sense we have attributed to the word above, for we have to depend on others for an expression of his views, as there is extant no text of his which would justify us in saying that he denied the intellect the power of forming general concepts, distinct in their nature from sensation. Indeed, it is difficult to comprehend how Nominalism could exist at all in the Middle Ages, as it is possible only in a sensist philosophy that denies all natural distinction between sensation and the intellectual concept. Furthermore there is little evidence of Sensism in the Middle Ages, and, as Sensism and Scholasticism, so also Nominalism and Scholasticism are mutually exclusive. The different anti-Realist systems anterior to the thirteenth century are in fact only more or less imperfect forms of the Moderate Realism towards which the efforts of the first period were tending, phases through which the same idea passed in its organic evolution. These stages are numerous, and several have been studied in recent monographs (e. g. the doctrine of Adélard of Bath, of Gauthier de Mortagne, Indifferentism, and the theory of the *collectio*). The decisive stage is marked by Abélard (1079–1142), who points out clearly the rôle of abstraction, and how we represent to ourselves elements common to different things, capable of realization in an indefinite number of individuals of the same species, while the individual alone exists. From that to Moderate Realism there is but a step; it was sufficient to show that a real fundamentum allows us to attribute the general representation to the individual thing. It is impossible to say who was the first in the twelfth century to develop the theory in its entirety. Moderate Realism appears fully in the writings of John of Salisbury.

C. From the Thirteenth Century.—In the thirteenth century all the great Scholastics solved the problem of the universals by the theory of Moderate Realism (Thomas Aquinas, Bonaventure, Duns Scotus), and are thus in accord with Averroes and Avicenna, the great Arab commentators of Aristotle, whose works had recently passed into circulation by means of translations. St. Thomas formulates the doctrine of Moderate Realism in precise language, and for that reason alone we can give the name of Thomistic Realism to this doctrine (see below). With William of Occam and the Terminist School appear the strictly conceptualist solutions of the problem. The abstract and universal concept is a sign (*signum*), also called a term (*terminus;* hence the name *Terminism* given to the system), but it has no real value, for the abstract and the universal do not exist in any way in nature and have no fundamentum outside the mind. The universal concept (*intentio secunda*) has as its object internal representations, formed by the understanding, to which nothing external corresponding can be attributed. The rôle of the universals is to serve as a label, to hold the place (*supponere*) in the mind of the multitude of things to which it can be attributed. Occam's Conceptualism would be frankly subjectivistic, if, together with the abstract concept, he did not admit within us intuitive concepts which reach the individual thing, as it exists in nature.

D. In Modern and Contemporary Philosophy.—We find an unequivocal affirmation of Nominalism in Positivism. For Hume, Stuart Mill, Spencer, and Taine there is strictly speaking no universal concept. The notion, to which we lend universality, is only a collection of individual perceptions, a collective sensation, "un nom compris" (Taine), "a term in habitual association with many other particular ideas" (Hume), "un savoir potentiel emmagasiné" (Ribot). The problem of the correspondence of the concept to reality is thus at once solved, or rather it is suppressed and replaced by the psychological question: What is the origin of the illusion that induces us to attribute a distinct nature to the general concept, though the latter is only an elaborated sensation? Kant distinctly affirms the existence within us of abstract and general notions and the distinction between them and sensations, but these doctrines are joined with a characteristic Phenomenalism which constitutes the most original form of modern Conceptualism. Universal and necessary representations have no contact with external things, since they are produced exclusively by the structural functions (a priori forms) of our mind. Time and space, in which we frame all sensible impressions, cannot be obtained from experience, which is individual and contingent; they are schemata which arise from our mental organization. Consequently, we have no warrant for establishing a real correspondence between the world of our ideas and the world of reality. Science, which is only an elaboration of the data of sense in accordance with other structural determinations of the mind (the categories), becomes a subjective poem, which has a value only for us and not for a world outside us. A modern form of Platonic or Exaggerated Realism is found in the ontologist doctrine defended by certain Catholic philosophers in the middle of the nineteenth century, and which consists in identifying the objects of universal ideas with the Divine ideas or the archetypes on which the world was fashioned. As to Moderate Realism, it remains the doctrine of all those who have returned to Aristoteleanism or adopted the neo-Scholastic philosophy.

III. THE CLAIMS OF MODERATE REALISM.—This system reconciles the characteristics of external objects (particularity) with those of our intellectual representations (universality), and explains why science, though made up of abstract notions, is valid for the world of reality. To understand this it suffices to grasp the real meaning of abstraction. When the mind apprehends the essence of a thing (quod quid est; τὸ τί ἦν εἶναι), the external object is perceived without the particular notes which attach to it in nature (esse in singularibus), and it is not yet marked with the attribute of generality which reflection will bestow on it (esse in intellectu). The abstract reality is apprehended with perfect indifference as regards both the individual state without and the universal state within: abstrahit ab utroque esse, secundum quam considerationem consideratur natura lapidis vel cujus cumque alterius, quantum ad ea tantum quæ per se competunt illi naturæ (St. Thomas, "Quodlibeta", Q. i, a. 1). Now, what is thus conceived in the absolute state (absolute considerando) is nothing else than the reality incarnate in any given individual: in truth, the reality, represented in my concept of man, is in Socrates or in Plato. There is nothing in the abstract concept that is not applicable to every individual; if the abstract concept is inadequate, because it does not contain the singular notes of each being, it is none the less faithful, or at least its abstract character does not prevent it from corresponding faithfully to the objects existing in nature. As to the universal form of the concept, a moment's consideration shows that it is subsequent to the abstraction and is the fruit of reflection: "ratio speciei accidit naturæ humanæ". Whence it follows that the universality of the concept as such is the work purely of the intellect: "unde intellectus est qui facit universalitatem in rebus" (St. Thomas, "De ente et essentia", iv).

Concerning Nominalism, Conceptualism, and Exaggerated Realism, a few general considerations must suffice. Nominalism, which is irreconcilable with a spiritualistic philosophy and for that very reason with Scholasticism as well, presupposes the ideological theory that the abstract concept does not differ essentially from sensation, of which it is only a transformation. The Nominalism of Hume, Stuart Mill, Spencer, Huxley, and Taine is of no greater value than their ideology. They confound essentially distinct logical operations—the simple decomposition of sensible or empirical representations with abstraction properly so called and sensible analogy with the process of universalization. The Aristoteleans recognize both of these mental operations, but they distinguish carefully between them. As to Kant, all the bonds that might connect the concept with the external world are destroyed in his Phenomenalism. Kant is unable to explain why one and the same sensible impression starts or sets in operation now this, now that category; his a priori forms are unintelligible according to his own principles, since they are beyond experience. Moreover, he confuses real time and space, limited like the things they develop, with ideal or abstract time and space, which alone are general and without limit. For in truth we do not create wholesale the object of our knowledge, but we beget it within us under the causal influence of the object that reveals itself to us. Ontologism, which is akin to Platonic Realism, arbitrarily identifies the ideal types in our intellect, which come to us from the sensible world by means of abstraction, with the ideal types consubstantial with the essence of God. Now, when we form our first abstract ideas we do not yet know God. We are so ignorant of Him that we must employ these first ideas to prove a posteriori His existence. Ontologism has lived its life, and our age so enamoured of observation and experiment will scarcely return to the dreams of Plato.

ZELLER, Die Philosophie der Griechen (5 vols., 5th ed., Tübingen, 1903), tr. COSTELLOE AND MUIRHEAD, Aristotle and the earlier Peripatetics (2 vols., London and New York, 1897); PIAT, Aristote (Paris, 1903); BROCHARD, Sur la logique des stoïciens in Archiv für Gesch. der Philos. (1892); LOEWE, Der Kampf zw. dem Realismus u. Nominalismus im Mittelalter in Abhandl. d. k. böhm. Gesellschaft d. Wissenschaft, VIII (1876); DE WULF, Hist. of Medieval Philos., tr. COFFEY (New York and London, 1909); IDEM, Le problème des universaux dans son évolution historique du IXe au XIIIe siècle in Archiv für Gesch. d. Philos., IX, iv (1896); TURNER, Hist. of Philos. (Boston, 1903); REINERS, Der aristotel. Realismus in d. Frühscholastik (Aachen, 1907); IDEM, Der Nominalismus in d. Frühscholastik in Beiträge zur Gesch. d. Philos., VIII, v (Münster, 1910); STÖCKL, Hist. of Philos., tr. FINLAY (Dublin, 1903); DEHOVE, Qui præcipui fuerint labente XII sæculo ante introductam arabum philosophiam temperati realismi antecessores (Lille, 1908); MERCIER, Critériologie générale (Louvain, 1905).

M. DE WULF.

Nomination.—The various methods of designating persons for ecclesiastical benefices or offices have been described under BENEFICE; BISHOP; ELECTION; INSTITUTION, CANONICAL. All these methods are more or less included in the ordinary sense of the term nomination; but in its strict canonical sense, nomination is defined as the designation of a person for an ecclesiastical benefice or office made by the competent civil authority and conferring on the person named the right to be canonically instituted by the ecclesiastical superior. It follows the rules of patronal presentation, being based on the same grounds as the right of patronage, viz. the endowment of churches or benefices by kings, princes, or communities. Its method of action is designed to keep the prerogatives of the two powers clearly separated, the intervention of the secular power taking effect in the free choice of a fit person, the spiritual jurisdiction being reserved intact to the ecclesiastical superior, who alone can give canonical institution. At the present time appointments to benefices by right of nomination, especially to bishoprics, is generally settled by negotiation and previous understanding between the two powers. Under the old regime the nominated person himself applied for canonical institution; the superior made inquiry as to the applicant and, unless the inquiry disclosed unworthiness or unfitness, granted canonical institution according to the customary forms—most often by consistorial preconization. Whatever procedure may be followed, the person named by the civil power has no spiritual jurisdiction until he has been canonically instituted; and if he should dare to intrude in the administration of the diocese with no other title than his nomination by the secular authority, not only would all his acts be null and void, but he, and with him those who should have consented to his acts, would incur excommunication and other penalties; moreover, he would forfeit the right resulting from his nomination (Const. "Romanus pontifex", 28 Aug., 1873, and the texts there cited. Cf. EXCOMMUNICATION, vol. V, p. 691, col. 1).

The most important application of the right of nomination by princes is, without doubt, that which relates to the major, or consistorial, benefices, especially bishoprics. Without going back to the intrusions of royal power in episcopal elections in the barbarian kingdoms, or in the Carlovingian Empire, or the Byzantine, it must be remembered that the Concordat of Worms (1121), which ended the Conflict of Investitures (q. v.), included an initial measure for the separation of the parts and prerogatives of the two powers in the choice of bishops. The emperor recognized the freedom of episcopal elections and consecrations; the pope, on his side, agreed that elections should be held in the emperor's presence, without simony or restraint, that the emperor should decide in case of dispute, that he should give temporal investiture, by the sceptre, to the bishop-elect, while investiture by ring and crosier, symbolic of ecclesiastical jurisdiction, should be combined with the consecration. The custom of election of bishops by chapters, which was the common law of the thirteenth century, left, officially, no opening for royal interference, but princes none the less endeavoured to have their candidates elected. This became more difficult for them when, by successive reservations, the popes had made themselves masters of all episcopal elections, thus occasioning serious inconveniences. While in Germany the Concordat of 1448 re-established capitular elections, in France, on the contrary, after the difficulties consequent upon the Pragmatic Sanction of Bourges (1438), the quarrel ended with the Concordat of 1516. In this instrument we find the right of nomination guaranteed to the kings of France for consistorial benefices, bishoprics, abbacies, and priorates; and thence the arrangement passed into most of the subsequent concordats, including that of 1801 (cf. Nussi, "Quinquaginta conventiones", Rome, 1869, tit. v). The royal ordinance of Francis I promulgating the Bull of Leo X says: "Such vacancy occurring, the King of France shall be bound to present and name [the Bull says only *nobis nominabit*] a master . . . and otherwise fit, within six months . . . that we may appoint his nominee to the vacant see." If this person is rejected, the king will nominate another within three months; if not, the pope can himself appoint. The same right of nomination is extended to abbacies and priorates, with some exceptions. The Concordat of 1801 (articles 4 and 5) accords to the First Consul the same right of nomination, but only for bishoprics, and without fixing a limit of time for its exercise. In other countries (e. g. Spain) the right of the temporal ruler includes other benefices besides bishoprics.

Such being the nature of the very definite right of nomination, nothing but malicious provocation can be discerned in the conflict brought on by M. Combes, when Prime Minister of France (1902–5), in regard to the *nobis nominavit*, the expression which figured in the Bulls for French bishops. By a note dated 21 Dec., 1902, the French Government demanded the suppression of the *nobis*, as if to make it appear that the head of the State nominated bishops absolutely, like government officials. The Vatican explained the true nature of the nomination as the designation of a person by the head of the State, the latter indicating to the pope the cleric whom he desires as head of such a diocese, the pope accordingly creating that candidate bishop by canonical institution. The fact was pointed out that the word *nobis* is found in the episcopal Bulls of all nations which have by concordat the right of nomination; also that, with very rare exceptions, it appears in all the Bulls for France under the Concordat of 1516 as under that of 1801; that previously, in 1871, the French Government having obtained without any difficulty the suppression of the word *præsentavit*, had, upon representations made by Rome, withdrawn its demand for the suppression of the *nobis;* above all, it was insisted on that the letters patent of the French Government to the pope had from time immemorial contained the words: "We name him [the candidate] and present him to Your Holiness, that it may please Your Holiness, upon our nomination and presentation, to provide for the said bishopric", etc. The Vatican nevertheless declared that it did not desire to refuse any satisfactory revision; various formulæ were proposed on either side, without success; at last the Holy See consented to suppress the word *nobis* in the Bulls, contenting itself with the Government's employing the usual formula in drafting letters patent. (On this conflict see the "Livre Blanc du Saint Siège"; "La séparation de l'Eglise et l'Etat en France", ch. vi, in "Acta S. Sedis", 15 Jan., 1906.) This concession, as we know, did not delay the separation which the French Government was determined to have at any price. (See BENEFICE; BISHOP; CONCORDAT; ELECTION; INSTITUTION.)

Canonists on the title *De prœbendis*, III, v; HÉRICOURT, *Loix ecclésiastiques de France*, E, IV; CAVAGNIS, *Institutiones juris ecclesiastici*, II (Rome, 1906), 13, 256; SÉVESTRE, *L'histoire, le texte et la destinée du Concordat de 1801* (Paris, 1905); VERING, *Kirchenrecht* (Freiburg im Br., 1893), § 86; SÄGMÜLLER, *Lehrbuch des kath. Kirchengeschichte* (Freiburg, 1909), § 73 sq.

A. BOUDINHON.

Nomocanon (from the Greek νόμος, law, and κάνων, a rule), a collection of ecclesiastical law, the elements of which are borrowed from secular and canon law. When we recall the important place given to ecclesiastical discipline in the imperial laws such as the Theodosian Code, the Justinian collections, and the subsequent "Novellæ", and "Basilica", the utility of comparing laws and canons relating to the same subjects will be readily recognized. Collections of this kind are found only in Eastern law. The Greek Church has two principal collections. The first, dating from the end of the sixth century, is ascribed, though without certainty, to John Scholasticus (q. v.), whose canons it utilizes and completes. He had drawn up (about 550) a purely canonical compilation in fifty titles, and later composed an extract from the "Novellæ" in eighty-seven chapters (for the canonical collection see Voellus and Justellus, "Bibliotheca juris canonici", Paris, 1661, II, 449 sqq.; for the eighty-seven chapters, Pitra, "Juris ecclesiastici Græcorum historia et monumenta", Rome, 1864, II, 385). To each of the fifty titles were added the texts of the imperial laws on the same subject, with twenty-one additional chapters nearly all borrowed from John's eighty-seven (Voellus and Justellus, op. cit., II, 603). In its earliest form this collection dates from the reign of Emperor Heraclius (610–40), at which time Latin was replaced by Greek as the official language of the imperial laws. Its two sections include the ecclesiastical canons and the imperial laws, the latter in fourteen titles.

This collection was long held in esteem and passed into the Russian Church, but was by degrees supplanted by that of Photius. The first part of Photius's collection contains the conciliar canons and the decisions of the Fathers. It is in substance the Greek collection of 692, as it is described by canon ii of the Trullan Council (see LAW, CANON), with the addition of 102 canons of that council, 17 canons of the Council of Constantinople of 861 (against Ignatius), and of 3 canons substituted by Photius for those of the œcumenical council of 869. The nomocanon in fourteen titles was completed by additions from the more recent imperial laws. This whole collection was commentated about 1170 by Theodore Balsamon, Greek Patriarch of Antioch residing at Constantinople (Nomocanon with Balsamon's commentary in Voellus and Justellus, II, 815; P. G., CIV, 441). Supplemented by this commentary the collection of Photius has become a part of the "Pidalion" (πηδάλιον, rudder), a sort of *Corpus Juris* of the Orthodox Church, printed in 1800 by Patriarch Neophytus VIII. In the eleventh century it had been also translated into Slavonic for the Russian Church;

it is retained in the law of the Orthodox Church of Greece, and included in the "Syntagma" published by Rhallis and Potlis (Athens, 1852-9). Though called the "Syntagma", the collection of ecclesiastical law of Matthew Blastares (c. 1339) is a real nomocanon, in which the texts of the canons and of the laws are arranged in alphabetical order (P. G., loc. cit.; Beveridge, "Synodicon", Oxford, 1672). A remarkable nomocanon was composed by John Barhebræus (1226-86) for the Syrian Church of Antioch (Latin version by Assemani in Mai, "Script. vet. nova collectio", X, 3 sqq.). Several Russian manuals published at Kiev and Moscow in the seventeenth century were also nomocanons.

VERING, *Lehrb. des Kirchenrechts* (Freiburg. 1893), §§ 17-19; SCHNEIDER, *Die Lehre von den Kirchenrechtsquellen* (Ratisbon, 1892), 50, 199; also bibliographies of LAW, CANON; JOHN SCHOLASTICUS; PHOTIUS, etc.

A. BOUDINHON.

Nonantola, a former Benedictine monastery and prelature *nullius*, six miles north-east of Modena, founded in 752 by St. Anselm, Duke of Friuli, and richly endowed by Aistulph, King of the Longobards. Stephen II appointed Anselm its first abbot, and presented the relics of St. Sylvester to the abbey, named in consequence S. Sylvester de Nonantula. After the death of Aistulph (756), Anselm was banished to Monte Cassino by the new king, Desiderius, but was restored by Charlemagne after seven years. In 883 it was chosen as the place of a conference between Charles the Fat and Marinus I. Up to 1083 it was an imperial monastery, and its discipline often suffered severely on account of imperial interference in the election of abbots. In the beginning of the Conflict of Investitures it sided with the emperor, until forced to submit to the pope by Mathilda of Tuscany in 1083. It finally declared itself openly for the pope in 1111. In that year the famous monk Placidus of Nonantola wrote his "De honore Ecclesiæ", one of the most able and important defences of the papal position that were written during the Conflict of Investitures. It is printed in Pez, "Thesaurus Anecdot. noviss." (Augsburg, 1721), II, ii, 73 sq. The decline of the monastery began in 1419, when it came under the jurisdiction of commendatory abbots. In 1514 it came into the possession of the Cistercians, but continued to decline until it was finally suppressed by Clement XIII in 1768. Pius VII restored it 23 Jan., 1821, with the provision that the prelature *nullius* attached to it should belong to the Archbishop of Modena. In 1909 the exempt district comprised 42,980 inhabitants, 31 parishes, 91 churches and chapels, 62 secular priests and three religious congregations for women. The monastery itself was appropriated by the Italian Government in 1866.

TIRABOSCHI, *Storia dell' augusta badia di S. Silvestro di Nonantola* (2 vols., Modena, 1784-5); GAUDENZI in *Bull dell' Istituto stor. ital.*, XXII (1901), 77-214; CORRADI, *Nonantola, abbazia imperiale* in *Rivista Storica Benedettina*, IV (Rome, 1909), 181-9; MURATORI, *Rer. Ital. Script.*, I, ii, 189-196; *Notitia codicum monasterii Nonantulani anni 1166* in MAI, *Spicilegium Romanum* (Rome, 1839-44), V, i, 218-221; BECKER, *Catalogi bibliothecarum antiqui* (Bonn, 1885), 220 sq.; GIORGI in *Rivista delle Biblioteche e degli archivi*, VI (Florence, 1895), 54 sq.

MICHAEL OTT.

Nonconformists, a name which, in its most general acceptation, denotes those refusing to conform with the authorized formularies and rites of the Established Church of England. The application of the term has varied somewhat with the successive phases of Anglican history. From the accession of Elizabeth to the middle of the seventeenth century it had not come into use as the name of a religious party, but the word "conform", and the appellatives "conforming" and "nonconforming", were becoming more and more common expressions to designate those members of the Puritan party who, disapproving of certain of the Anglican rites (namely, the use of the surplice, of the sign of the cross at baptism, of the ring in marriage, of the attitude of kneeling at the reception of the sacrament) and of the episcopal order of Church government, either resigned themselves to these usages because enjoined, or stood out against them at all costs. However from 1662, when the Fourth Act of Uniformity had the effect of ejecting from their benefices, acquired during the Commonwealth, a large number of ministers of Puritan proclivities, and of constraining them to organize themselves as separatist sects, the term "Nonconformist" crystallized into the technical name for such sects.

HISTORY.—The history of this cleavage in the ranks of English Protestantism goes back to the reign of Mary Tudor, when the Protestant leaders who were victorious under Edward VI retired to Frankfort, Zurich, and other Protestant centres on the continent, and quarrelled among themselves, some inclining to the more moderate Lutheran or Zwinglian positions, others developing into uncompromising Calvinists. When the accession of Elizabeth attracted them back to England, the Calvinist section, which soon acquired the nickname of Puritans, was the more fiery, the larger in numbers and the most in favour with the majority of the Protestant laity. Elizabeth, however, who had very little personal religion, preferred an episcopal to a presbyterian system as more in harmony with monarchism, and besides she had some taste for the ornate in public worship. Accordingly she caused the religious settlement, destined to last into our own times, to be made on the basis of episcopacy, with the retention of the points of ritual above specified; and her favour was bespoken for prelates like Parker, who were prepared to aid her in carrying out this programme. For those who held Puritan views she had a natural dislike, to which she sometimes gave forcible expression, but on the whole she saw the expediency of showing them some consideration, lest she should lose their support in her campaign against Catholicism.

These were the determining factors of the initial situation, out of which the subsequent history of English Protestantism has grown by a natural development. The result during Elizabeth's reign was a state of oscillation between phases of repression and phases of indulgence, in meeting the persistent endeavours of the Puritans to make their own ideas dominant in the national Church. In 1559 the third Act of Uniformity was passed, by which the new edition of the Prayer Book was enjoined under severe penalities on all ministering as clergy in the country. In 1566, feeling that some concession to the strength of the Puritan opposition was necessary, Archbishop Parker, on an understanding with the queen, published certain Advertisements addressed to the clergy, requiring them to conform at least as regards wearing the surplice, kneeling at communion, using the font for baptism, and covering the communion table with a proper cloth. These Advertisements were partially enforced in some dioceses, and led to some deprivations, but that their effect was small is clear from the boldness with which the Puritans took up a more advanced position a few years later, and demanded the substitution of a presbyterian régime. This was the demand of Thomas Cartwright in his First and Second Admonitions, published in 1572, and followed in 1580 by his Book of Discipline, in which he collaborated with Thomas Travers. In this latter book he propounded an ingenious theory of *classes*, or boards of clergy for each district, to which the episcopal powers should be transferred, to be exercised by them on presbyterian principles, to the bishops being reserved only the purely mechanical ceremony of ordination. So great was the influence of the Puritans in the country that they were able to introduce for a time this strange system in one or two places.

In 1588 the Marprelate tracts were published, and

by the violence of their language against the queen and the bishops stirred up the queen to take drastic measures. Perry and Udal, authors of the tracts, were tried and executed, and Cartwright was imprisoned; whilst in 1593 an act was passed inflicting the punishment of imprisonment, to be followed by exile in case of a second offence, on all who refused to attend the parish church, or held separatist meetings. This caused a division in the party; as many, though secretly retaining their beliefs, preferred outward conformity to the loss of their benefices, whilst the extremists of the party left the country and settled in Holland. Here they were for a time called Brownists, after one who had been their leader in separation, but later they took the name of Independents, as indicating their peculiar theory of the governmental independence of each separate congregation. From these Brownists came the "Pilgrim Fathers" who, on 6 December, 1620, sailed from Plymouth in the "Mayflower", and settled in New England.

With the death of Elizabeth the hopes of the Puritans revived. Their system of doctrine and government was dominant in Scotland, and they hoped that the Scottish King James might be induced to extend it to England. So they met him on his way to London with their Millenary Petition, so called though the signatories numbered only about eight hundred. In this document they were prudent enough not to raise the question of episcopal government, but contented themselves for the time with a request that the ritual customs which they disliked might be discontinued in the State Church. James promised them a conference which met the next year at Hampton Court to consider their grievances, and in which they were represented by four of their leaders. These had some sharp encounters with the bishops and chief Anglican divines, but, whilst the Puritans were set more on domination than toleration, the king was wholly on the side of the Anglicans, who in this hour of their triumph were in no mood for concessions. Accordingly the conference proved abortive, and the very same year Archbishop Bancroft, with the king's sanction, carried through Convocation and at once enforced the canons known as those of 1604. The purpose of this campaign was to restore the use of the rites in question, which, in defiance of the existing law, the Puritan incumbents had succeeded in putting down in a great number of parishes. This result was effected to some extent for the time, but a quarter of a century later, when Laud began his campaign for the restoration of decency and order, in other words, for the enforcement of the customs to which the Puritans objected, he was met by an opposition so widespread and deep-rooted that, though ultimately it had lasting results, the immediate effect was to bring about his own fall and contribute largely to the outbreak of the Rebellion, the authors of which were approximately co-extensive with the Puritan party.

During the Civil War and the Commonwealth the Puritan mobs wrecked the churches, the bishops were imprisoned and the primate beheaded, the supremacy over the Church was transferred from the Crown to the Parliament, the Solemn League and Covenant was accepted for the whole nation, and the Westminster Assembly, almost entirely composed of Puritans, was appointed as a permanent committee for the reform of the Church. Next the Anglican clergy were turned out of their benefices to make way for Puritans, in whose behalf the Presbyterian form of government was introduced by Parliament. But though this was now the authorized settlement, it was found impossible to check the vagaries of individual opinion. A religious frenzy seized the country, and sects holding the most extravagant doctrines sprang up and built themselves conventicles. There was licence for all, save for popery and prelacy, which were now persecuted with equal severity. When Cromwell attained to power a struggle set in between the Parliament which was predominantly Presbyterian, and the army which was predominantly Independent. The disgust of all sober minds with the resulting pandemonium had much to do with creating the desire for the Restoration, and when this was accomplished in 1660 measures were at once taken to undo the work of the interregnum. The bishops were restored to their sees, and the vacancies filled. The Savoy Conference was held in accordance with the precedence of Hampton Court Conference of 1604, but proved similarly abortive. The Convocation in 1662 revised the Prayer Book in an anti-Puritan direction, and the Declaration of Breda notwithstanding, it was at once enforced. All holding benefices in the country were to use this revised Prayer Book on and after the Feast of St. Bartholomew of that year. It was through this crisis that the term Nonconformist obtained its technical meaning. When the feast came round a large number who refused to conform were evicted. It is in dispute between Nonconformist and Anglican writers how many these were, and what were their characters: the Nonconformist writers (see Calamy, "Life of Baxter") maintain that they exceeded 2000, while Kennett and others reduce that number considerably, contending that in the majority of cases the hardship was not so grave. At least it must be acknowledged that the victims were suffering only what they, in the days of their power, had inflicted on their opponents, for many of whom the ejection of the Puritans meant a return to their own. The fact that they organized themselves outside the Established Church under the name of Nonconformists, naturally made them the more offensive to the authorities of Church and State, and, during the remainder of the reign of Charles II, they were the victims of several oppressive measures. In 1661 the Corporation Act incapacitated from holding office in any corporation all who did not first qualify by taking the sacrament according to the Anglican Rite; in 1664 the Conventicle Act inflicted the gravest penalties on all who took part in any private religious service at which more than five persons, in addition to the family, were present; in 1665 the Five Mile Act made liable to imprisonment any Nonconformist minister who, not having taken an oath of non-resistance, came within five miles of a town without obtaining leave; and in 1673 the scope of the Corporation Act was extended by the Test Act.

In 1672 Charles II attempted to mitigate the lot of the Nonconformists by publishing a Declaration of Indulgence in which he used in their favour the dispensing power, till then recognized as vested in the Crown. But Parliament, meeting the next year, forced him to withdraw this Declaration, and in return passed the Test Act, which extended the scope of the Corporation Act. James II, though despotic and tactless in his methods like all the Stuarts, was, whatever prejudiced historians have said to the contrary, a serious believer in religious toleration for all, and was, in fact, the first who sought to impress that ideal on the legislature of his country. By his two Declarations of Indulgence, in 1687–88, he dispensed Nonconformists just as much as Catholics from their religious disabilities, and his act was received by the former with a spontaneous outburst of gratitude. It was not to their credit that shortly after they should have been induced to cast in their lot with the Revolution on the assurance that it would give them all the liberties promised by King James without the necessity of sharing them with the Catholics. This promise was, however, only imperfectly carried out by the Toleration Act of 1689, which permitted the free exercise of their religion to all Trinitarian Protestants, but did not relieve them of their civil disabilities. Some, accordingly, of their number practised what was called Occasional Conformity, that is, received the

Anglican sacrament just once so as to qualify. This caused much controversy and led eventually in 1710 to the Occasional Conformity Act, which was devised to check it. This Act was repealed in 1718, but many of the Nonconformists themselves disapproved of the practice on conscientious grounds, and, though it was often resorted to and caused grave scandals, those who resorted to it cannot be fairly taken as representatives of their sects. The Test Act was not repealed till 1828, the year before the Catholic Emancipation Act was passed; the Catholics and the Nonconformists combined their forces to obtain both objects.

Although by the passing of the Toleration Act of 1689 the condition of the Nonconformists was so much ameliorated, they lapsed in the second quarter of the eighteenth century into the prevailing religious torpor, and seemed to be on the verge of extinction. They were rescued from this state by the outbreak of the great Methodist movement, which resulted both in arousing the existing Dissenting sects to a new vigour, and in adding another which exceeded them all in numbers and enthusiasm.

PRESENT CONDITION.—At the present day the Nonconformists in England, the only country to which this name with its implications applies, are very numerous and constitute a powerful religious, social, and political influence. As they have effectually resisted the taking of a religious census by the State Census department, it is impossible to ascertain their numbers accurately, for their own statistics are suspected of exaggeration. According to Mr. Howard Evans's statistics (as given in the Daily Mail "Year Book of the Churches" for 1908), the Baptists then reckoned 405,755 communicants, the Congregationalists 459,983, and the various denominations of Methodists 1,174,462—to which figures are to be added those of the highly indeterminate number of "adherents" who are not accepted as communicants. It will be seen from this list that the Methodists are by far the larger of these three principal denominations, but they are likewise the most subdivided. It will be noticed, too, that the Presbyterians, once so numerous in the country, have no place among the larger sects. The Society of Friends, commonly called Quakers, are allotted 17,767 communicants by Evans. Besides these there are innumerable small sects, of which the Plymouth Brethren and the Swedenborgians are the most conspicuous. (For the separate denominations see the special articles, BAPTISTS; CONGREGATIONALISM; METHODISM; PRESBYTERIANISM; FRIENDS, SOCIETY OF.)

NEAL, *Hist. of the Puritans, or Protestant Nonconformists, 1517–1688* (2nd ed., London, 1822); PRICE, *Hist. of Protestant Nonconformity in England from the Reformation under Henry VIII* (2 vols., London, 1836); BOGUE AND BENNETT, *Hist. of Dissenters, 1688–1808* (4 vols., London, 1808); BENNETT, *Hist. of Dissenters, 1808–1838* (London, 1839); WILSON, *Hist. and Antiquities of the Dissenting Churches* (4 vols., London, 1808); WAKEMAN, *The Church and the Puritans, 1570–1660* in CREIGHTON, *Epochs of Church History* (London, 1887); OVERTON, *Life in the English Church, 1660–1714* (London, 1885); ABBEY AND OVERTON, *The English Church in the Eighteenth Century* (London, 1878); SKEATS AND MIALL, *Hist. of the Free Churches of England, 1688–1851* (London, 1891); REES, *Hist. of Protestant Nonconformity in Wales, 1633–1861* (London, 1861); HETHERINGTON, *Hist. of the Westminster Assembly of Divines* (Edinburgh, 1878); GOULD, *Documents relating to the Settlement of the Church of England by the Act of Uniformity of 1662* (2 vols., London, 1862); CALAMY, *Abridgment of Mr. Baxter's Hist. of his Life and Times, with an account of many . . . ministers who were ejected . . . and a continuation of their history till the year 1691* (London, 1702); *The Nonconformist's Memorial, being an account of the Ministers who were ejected or silenced after the Restoration* (2 vols., London, 1775), abridged and corrected edition by PALMER (London, 1802); WALKER, *An attempt towards recovering an account of the numbers and sufferings of the clergy of the Church of England. . . in the late times of the Grand Rebellion* (London, 1714), a set-off against Calamy's account of the sufferers in 1662; KENNETT, *Register and Chronicle . . . containing matter of fact, with notes and references towards discovering and connecting the true history of England from the Restoration of Charles II* (London, 1728), a careful criticism of Calamy's statistics.

SYDNEY F. SMITH.

None.—This subject will be treated under the following heads: I. Origin of None; II. None from the Fourth to the Seventh Century; III. None in the Roman and Other Liturgies from the Seventh Century; IV. Meaning and Symbolism of None.

I. ORIGIN OF NONE.—According to an ancient Greek and Roman custom, the day was, like the night, divided into four parts, each consisting of three hours. As the last hour of each division gave its name to the respective quarter of the day, the third division (from 12 to about 3) was called the *None* (Lat. *nonus, nona,* ninth). For this explanation, which is open to objection, but is the only probable one, see Francolinus, "De tempor. horar. canonicar.", Rome, 1571, xxi; Bona, "De divina psalmodia", III (see also MATINS and VIGILS). This division of the day was in vogue also among the Jews, from whom the Church borrowed it (see Jerome, "In Daniel," vi, 10). The following texts, moreover, favour this view: "Now Peter and John went up into the temple at the ninth hour of prayer" (Acts, iii, 1); "And Cornelius said: Four days ago, unto this hour, I was praying in my house, at the ninth hour, and behold a man stood before me" (Acts, x, 30); "Peter went up to the higher parts of the house to pray, about the sixth hour" (Acts, x, 9). The most ancient testimony refers to this custom of Terce, Sext, and None, for instance Tertullian, Clement of Alexandria, the Canons of Hippolytus, and even the "Teaching of the Apostles". The last-mentioned prescribed prayer thrice each day, without, however, fixing the hours (Διδαχὴ τῶν Ἀποστολῶν, n. viii).

Clement of Alexandria and likewise Tertullian, as early as the end of the second century, expressly mention the hours of Terce, Sext, and None, as specially set apart for prayer (Clement, "Strom.", VII, vii, in P. G., IX, 455–8). Tertullian says explicitly that we must always pray, and that there is no time prescribed for prayer; he adds, nevertheless, these significant words: "As regards the time, there should be no lax observation of certain hours—I mean of those common hours which have long marked the divisions of the day, the third, the sixth, and the ninth, and which we may observe in Scripture to be more solemn than the rest" ("De Oratione", xxiii, xxv, in P. L., I, 1191–3).

Clement and Tertullian in these passages refer only to private prayer at these hours. The Canons of Hippolytus also speak of Terce, Sext, and None, as suitable hours for private prayer; however, on the two station days, Wednesday and Friday, when the faithful assembled in the church, and perhaps on Sundays, these hours were recited successively in public (can. xx, xxvi). St. Cyprian mentions the same hours as having been observed under the Old Law, and adduces reasons for the Christians observing them also ("De Oratione", xxxiv, in P. L., IV, 541). In the fourth century there is evidence to show that the practice had become obligatory, at least for the monks (see the text of the Apostolic Constitutions, St. Ephraem, St. Basil, the author of the "De virginitate" in Baümer-Biron, op. cit. in bibliography, pp. 116, 121, 123, 129, 186). The prayer of Prime, at six o'clock in the morning, was not added till a later date, but Vespers goes back to the earliest days. The texts we have cited give no information as to what these prayers consisted of. Evidently they contained the same elements as all other prayers of that time—psalms recited or chanted, canticles or hymns, either privately composed or drawn from Holy Writ, and litanies or prayers properly so-called.

II. NONE FROM THE FOURTH TO THE SEVENTH CENTURY.—The eighteenth canon of the Council of Laodicea (between 343 and 381) orders that the same prayers be always said at None and Vespers. But it is not clear what meaning is to be attached to the words λειτουργία τῶν εὐχῶν, used in the canon. It is likely that reference is made to the famous litanies, in which prayer was offered for the catechumens, sinners, the faithful, and generally for all the wants of the Church. Sozomen (in a passage, however, which is not considered very authentic) speaks of three psalms which the monks recited at None. In any case, this number became traditional at an early period (Sozomen, "Hist. eccl.", III, xiv, in P. G., LXVII, 1076-7; cf. Baümer-Biron, op. cit., I, 136). Three psalms were recited at Terce, six at Sext, and nine at None, as Cassian informs us, though he remarks that the most common practice was to recite three psalms at each of these hours (Cassian, "De cœnob. instit.", III, iii, in P. L., XLIX, 116). St. Ambrose speaks of three hours of prayer, and, if with many critics we attribute to him the three hymns "Jam surgit hora tertia", "Bis ternas horas explicas", and "Ter horas trina solvitur", we shall have a new constitutive element of the Little Hours in the fourth century in the Church of Milan (Ambrose, "De virginibus", III, iv, in P. L., XVI, 225).

In the "Peregrinatio ad loca sancta" of Etheria (end of fourth century), there is a more detailed description of the Office of None. It resembles that of Sext, and is celebrated in the basilica of the Anastasis. It is composed of psalms and antiphons; then the bishop arrives, enters the grotto of the Resurrection, recites a prayer there, and blesses the faithful ("Peregrinatio", p. 46; cf. Cabrol, "Etude sur la Peregrinatio Sylviæ", 45). During Lent, None is celebrated in the church of Sion; on Sundays the office is not celebrated; it is omitted also on Holy Saturday, but on Good Friday it is celebrated with special solemnity (Peregrinatio, pp. 53, 66, etc.). But it is only in the succeeding age that we find a complete description of None, as of the other offices of the day.

III. NONE IN THE ROMAN AND OTHER LITURGIES FROM THE SEVENTH CENTURY.—In the Rule of St. Benedict the four Little Hours of the day (Prime to None) are conceived on the same plan, the formulæ alone varying. The office begins with *Deus in adjutorium*, like all the Hours; then follows a hymn, special to None; three psalms, which do not change (Ps. cxxv, cxxvi, cxxvii), except on Sundays and Mondays when they are replaced by three groups of eight verses from Ps. cxviii; then the capitulum, a versicle, the Kyrie, the Pater, the oratio, and the concluding prayers (Regula S. P. Benedicti, xvii). In the Roman Liturgy the office of None is likewise constructed after the model of the Little Hours of the day; it is composed of the same elements as in the Rule of St. Benedict, with this difference, that, instead of the three psalms, cxxv-vii, the three groups of eight verses from Ps. cxviii are always recited. There is nothing else characteristic of this office in this liturgy. The hymn, which was added later, is the one already in use in the Benedictine Office—"Rerum Deus tenax vigor". In the monastic rules prior to the tenth century certain variations are found. Thus in the Rule of Lerins, as in that of St. Cæsarius, six psalms are recited at None, as at Terce and Sext, with antiphon, hymn, and capitulum.

St. Aurelian follows the same tradition in his Rule "Ad virgines", but he imposes twelve psalms at each hour on the monks. St. Columbanus, St. Fructuosus, and St. Isidore adopt the system of three psalms (cf. Martène, "De antiq. monach. rit.", IV, 27). Like St. Benedict, most of these authors include hymns, the capitulum or short lesson, a versicle, and an oratio (cf. Martène, loc. cit.). In the ninth and tenth centuries we find some additions made to the Office of None, in particular litanies, collects, etc. (Martène, op. cit., IV, 28).

IV. MEANING AND SYMBOLISM OF NONE.—Among the ancients the hour of None was regarded as the close of the day's business and the time for the baths and supper (Martial, "Epigrams", IV, viii; Horace, "Epistles", I, vii, 70). At an early date mystical reasons for the division of the day were sought. St. Cyprian sees in the hours of Terce, Sext and None, which come after a lapse of three hours, an allusion to the Trinity. He adds that these hours already consecrated to prayer under the Old Dispensation, have been sanctified in the New Testament by great mysteries—Terce by the descent of the Holy Ghost on the Apostles; Sext by the prayers of St. Peter, the reception of the Gentiles into the Church, or yet again by the crucifixion of Our Lord; None by the death of Christ ("De oratione", xxxiv, in P. L., IV, 541). St. Basil merely recalls that it was at the ninth hour that the Apostles Peter and John were wont to go to the Temple to pray ("Regulæ fusius tract.", XXXVII, n. 3, in P. G., XXXI, 1013 sq.). Cassian, who adopts the Cyprian interpretation for Terce and Sext, sees in the Hour of None the descent of Christ into hell (De cœnob. instit., III, iii). But, as a rule, it is the death of Christ that is commemorated at the Hour of None.

The writers of the Middle Ages have sought for other mystical explanations of the Hour of None. Amalarius (III, vi) explains at length, how, like the sun which sinks on the horizon at the Hour of None, man's spirit tends to lower itself also, he is more open to temptation, and it is the time the demon selects to try him. For the texts of the Fathers on this subject it will suffice to refer the reader to the above-mentioned work of Cardinal Bona (c. ix). The same writers do not fail to remark that the number nine was considered by the ancients an imperfect number, an incomplete number, ten being considered perfection and the complete number. Nine was also the number of mourning. Among the ancients the ninth day was a day of expiation and funeral service—*novemdiale sacrum*, the origin doubtless of the novena for the dead.

As for the ninth hour, some persons believe that it is the hour at which our first parents were driven from the Garden of Paradise (Bona, op. cit., ix, § 2). In conclusion, it is necessary to call attention to a practice which emphasized the Hour of None—it was the hour of fasting. At first, the hour of fasting was prolonged to Vespers, that is to say, food was taken only in the evening or at the end of the day. Mitigation of this rigorous practice was soon introduced. Tertullian's famous pamphlet "De jejunio", rails at length against the Psychics (i. e. the Catholics) who end their fast on station days at the Hour of None, while he, Tertullian, claims that he is faithful to the ancient custom. The practice of breaking the fast at None caused that hour to be selected for Mass and Communion, which were the signs of the close of the day. The distinction between the rigorous fast, which was prolonged to Vespers, and the mitigated fast, ending at None, is met with in a large number of ancient documents (see FAST).

FRANCOLINUS, *De temp. horar. canonicar.* (Rome, 1571), xxi; AMALARIUS, *De eccles. officiis*, IV, vi; DURANDUS, *Rationale*, V, i sq.; BONA, *De divina psalmodia*, ix; DU CANGE, *Glossarium infimæ Latinitatis*, s. v. *Horæ canonicæ*; IDEM, *Glossarium mediæ Græcitatis*, s. v. Ὧραι; MARTÈNE, *De monach. rit.*, IV, 12, 27, 28, etc.; HAEFTEN, *Disquisit. Monasticæ*, tract. ii, ix, etc.; PROBST, *Brevier u. Breviergebet* (Tübingen, 1868), 22 etc.; BAÜMER-BIRON, *Hist. du Bréviaire*, I, 63, 73, 116, etc.; CABROL AND LECLERCQ, *Monum. Liturg.* (Paris, 1902), gives the texts from the Fathers to the fourth century; TALHOFER, *Handbuch der kathol. Liturg.*, II (1893), 458..

F. CABROL.

Non Expedit (It is not expedient).—Words with which the Holy See enjoined upon Italian Catholics the policy of abstention from the polls in parliamentary elections. This policy was adopted after a period of uncertainty and of controversy which followed the promulgation of the Constitution of the Kingdom of Italy (1861), and which was intensified by laws hostile to the Church and, especially, to the religious orders (1865-66). To this uncertainty the Holy Penitentiary put an end by its decree of 29 February,

1868, in which, in the above words, it sanctioned the motto: "Neither elector nor elected". Until then there had been in the Italian Parliament a few eminent representatives of Catholic interests—Vito d'Ondes Reggio, Augusto Conti, Cesare Cantù, and others. The principal motive of this decree was that the oath taken by deputies might be interpreted as an approval of the spoliation of the Holy See, as Pius IX declared in an audience of 11 October, 1874. A practical reason for it, also, was that, in view of the electoral law of that day, by which the electorate was reduced to 650,000, and as the Government manipulated the elections to suit its own purposes, it would have been hopeless to attempt to prevent the passage of anti-Catholic laws. On the other hand, the masses seemed unprepared for parliamentary government, and as, in the greater portion of Italy (Parma, Modena, Tuscany, the Pontifical States, and the Kingdom of Naples), nearly all sincere Catholics were partizans of the dispossessed princes, they were liable to be denounced as enemies of Italy; they would also have been at variance with the Catholics of Piedmont and of the provinces wrested from Austria, and this division would have further weakened the Catholic Parliamentary group.

As might be expected, this measure did not meet with universal approval: the so-called Moderates accused the Catholics of failing in their duty to society and to their country. In 1882, the suffrage having been extended, Leo XIII took into serious consideration the partial abolition of the restrictions established by the *Non Expedit*, but nothing was actually done (cf. "Archiv für kathol. Kirchenrecht", 1904, p. 396). On the contrary, as many people came to the conclusion that the decree *Non Expedit* was not intended to be absolute, but was only an admonition made to apply upon one particular occasion, the Holy Office declared (30 Dec., 1886) that the rule in question implied a grave precept, and emphasis was given to this fact on several subsequent occasions (Letter of Leo XIII to the Cardinal Secretary of State, 14 May, 1895; Congregation of Extraordinary Affairs, 27 January, 1902; Pius X, *Motu proprio*, 18 Dec., 1903). Later, Pius X, by his encyclical "Il fermo proposito" (11 June, 1905) modified the *Non Expedit*, declaring that, when there was question of preventing the election of a "subversive" candidate, the bishops could ask for a suspension of the rule, and invite the Catholics to hold themselves in readiness to go to the polls. (See MARGOTTI, GIACOMO.)

Civiltà Cattolica (Rome), ser. VIII, IV, 652; VI, 51; VIII, 653; VIII, 362; *Questioni politico-religiose* (Rome, 1905).

U. BENIGNI.

Non-Jurors, the name given to the Anglican Churchmen who in 1689 refused to take the oath of allegiance to William and Mary, and their successors under the Protestant Succession Act of that year. Their leaders on the episcopal bench (William Sancroft, Archbishop of Canterbury, and Bishops Francis Turner of Ely, William Lloyd of Norwich, Thomas White of Peterborough, William Thomas of Worcester, Thomas Ken of Bath and Wells, John Lake of Chichester, and Thomas Cartwright of Chester) were required to take the oath before 1 August, under pain of suspension, to be followed, if it were not taken by 1 Feb., by total deprivation. Two of them died before this last date, but the rest, persisting in their refusal, were deprived. Their example was followed by a multitude of the clergy and laity, the number of the former being estimated at about four hundred, conspicuous among whom were George Hickes, Dean of Worcester, Jeremy Collier, John Kettlewell, and Robert Nelson. A list of these Non-jurors is given in Hickes's "Memoirs of Bishop Kettlewell", and one further completed in Overton's "Non-jurors". The original Non-jurors were not friendly towards James II; indeed five of these bishops had been among the seven whose resistance to his Declaration of Indulgence earlier in the same year had contributed to the invitation which caused the Prince of Orange to come over. But desiring William and Mary as regents they distinguished between this and accepting them as sovereigns, regarding the latter as inconsistent with the oath taken to James. Deprived of their benefices the bishops fell into great poverty, and suffered occasional though not systematic persecution. That they were truly conscientious men is attested by sacrifices courageously made for their convictions. Their lives were edifying, some consenting to attend, as laymen, the services in the parish churches. Still, when circumstances permitted, they held secret services of their own, for they firmly believed that they had the true Anglican succession which it was their duty to preserve. Hence they felt, after some hesitation, that it was incumbent on them to consecrate others who should succeed them. The first who were thus consecrated, on 24 Feb., 1693, were George Hickes and John Wagstaffe. On 29 May, 1713, the other Non-juring bishops being all dead, Hickes consecrated Jeremy Collier, Samuel Hawes, and Nathaniel Spinkes. When James II died in 1701, a crisis arose for these separatists. Some of them then rejoined the main body of their co-religionists, whilst others held out on the ground that their oath had been both to James and to his rightful heirs. These latter afterwards disagreed among themselves over a question of rites. The death of Charles Edward in 1788 took away the *raison d'être* for the schism, but a few lingered on till the end of the eighteenth century. In Scotland in 1689 the whole body of Bishops refused the oath and became Non-jurors, but the resulting situation was somewhat different. As soon as the Revolution broke out the Presbyterians ousted the Episcopalians and became the Established Kirk of Scotland. Thus the Non-jurors were left without rivals of their own communion, though they had at times to suffer penalties for celebrating unlawful worship. Their difficulties terminated in 1788, when on the death of Charles Edward they saw no further reason for withholding the oath to George III.

HICKES, *Memorials of the Life of John Kettlewell* (London, 1718); LATHBURY, *A history of the Non-jurors, their controversies, and writings* (London, 1845); GRUB, *An Ecclesiastical History of Scotland* (4 vols., Edinburgh, 1861); OVERTON, *William Law, Non-juror and Mystic* (London, 1881); PLUMPTREE, *Life of Thomas Ken* (2 vols., London, 1888); CARTER, *Life and Times of John Kettlewell* (London, 1895); OVERTON, *The Non-jurors, their Lives, Principles, and Writings* (London, 1902).

SYDNEY F. SMITH.

Nonna, SAINT. See GREGORY OF NAZIANZUS, SAINT.

Nonnotte, CLAUDE-ADRIEN, controversialist; b. in Besançon, 29 July, 1711; d. there, 3 September, 1793. At nineteen he entered the Society of Jesus and preached at Amiens, Versailles, and Turin. He is chiefly known for his writings against Voltaire. When the latter began to issue his "Essai sur les mœurs" (1754), an attack on Christianity, Nonnotte published, anonymously, the "Examen critique ou Réfutation du livre des mœurs"; and when Voltaire finished his publication (1758), Nonnotte revised his book, which he published at Avignon (2 vols., 1762). He treated, simply, calmly, and dispassionately, all the historical and doctrinal errors contained in Voltaire's work. Nonnotte's work reached the sixth edition in 1774. Voltaire, exasperated, retorted in his "Eclaircissements historiques", and for twenty years continued to attack Nonnotte with sarcasm, insult, or calumny. Nevertheless Nonnotte's publication continued to circulate, and was translated into Italian, German, Polish, and Portuguese. After the suppression of the Jesuits, Nonnotte withdrew to Besançon and in 1779 added a third volume to the "Erreurs de Voltaire", namely, "L'esprit de Voltaire dans ses écrits", for which it was impossible to obtain the approval of the

Paris censor. Against the "Dictionnaire philosophique", in which Voltaire had recapitulated, under a popular form, all his attacks on Christianity, Nonnotte published the "Dictionnaire philosophique de la religion" (Avignon, 1772), in which he replied to all the objections then brought against religion. The work was translated into Italian and German. Towards the end of his life Nonnotte published "Les philosophes des trois premiers siècles" (Paris, 1789), in which he contrasted the ancient and the modern philosophers. The work was translated into German. He also wrote "Lettre à un ami sur les honnêtetés littéraires" (Paris, 1766), and "Réponse aux Éclaircissements historiques et aux additions de Voltaire" (Paris, 1774). These publications obtained for their author a eulogistic Brief from Clement XIII (1768), and the congratulations of St. Alphonsus Liguori, who declared that he had always at hand his "golden works" in which the chief truths of the Faith were defended with learning and propriety against the objections of Voltaire and his friends. Nonnotte was also the author of "L'emploi de l'argent" (Avignon, 1787), translated from Maffei; "Le gouvernement des paroisses" (posthumous, Paris, 1802). All were published under the title "Œuvres de Nonnotte" (Besançon, 1819).

L'ami de la religion, XXV, 385; SABATIER DE CASTRES, Les trois siècles de la littérature française (The Hague, 1781); SOMMERVOGEL, Bib. de la C. de Jésus (Paris, 1894), V, 1803–7; IX, 722.

ANTOINE DEGERT.

Nonnus, of Panopolis in Upper Egypt (c. 400), the reputed author of two poems in hexameters; one, Διονυσιακά, about the mysteries of Bacchus, and the other the "Paraphrase of the Fourth Gospel". Dräseke proposes Apollinaris of Laodicea (Theolog. Litteraturzeitung, 1891, 332), and a fourteenth-century MS. suggests Ammonius as the author of the "Paraphrase", but the similarity of style makes it very probable that the two poems have the same author. Nonnus would then seem to have been a pagan when he wrote the first, and afterwards to have become a Christian. Nothing else is known of his life. The "Paraphrase" is not completely extant; 3750 lines of it, now divided into twenty-one chapters, are known. It has some importance as evidence of the text its author used, and has been studied as a source of textual criticism (Blass, "Evang. sec. Ioh. cum variæ lectionis delectu", Leipzig, 1902; Janssen in "Texte u. Untersuchungen", XXIII, 4, Leipzig, 1903). Otherwise it has little interest or merit. It is merely a repetition of the Gospel, verse by verse, inflated with fantastic epithets and the addition of imaginary details. The "Paraphrase" was first published by the Aldine Press in 1501. The edition of Heinsius (Leyden, 1627) is reprinted in P. G., XLIII, 749–1228. The best modern edition is by Scheindler: "Nonni Panopolitani paraphrasis s. evang. Ioannei" (Leipzig, 1881).

FABRICIUS-HARLES, Bibl. græca, VIII (Hamburg, 1802), 601–12; KOECHLY, Opuscula philologica, I (Leipzig, 1881), 421–46; KINKEL, Die Ueberlieferung der Paraphrase des ev. Ioh. von Nonnos, I (Zurich, 1870); TIEDKE, Nonniana (Berlin, 1883).

ADRIAN FORTESCUE.

Norbert, SAINT, b. at Xanten on the left bank of the Rhine, near Wesel, c. 1080; d. at Magdeburg, 6 June, 1134. His father, Heribert, Count of Gennep, was related to the imperial house of Germany, and his mother, Hadwigis, was a descendant of the ancient house of Lorraine. A stately bearing, a penetrating intellect, a tender, earnest heart, marked the future apostle. Ordained subdeacon, Norbert was appointed to a canonry at Xanten. Soon after he was summoned to the Court of Frederick, Prince-Bishop of Cologne, and later to that of Henry V, Emperor of Germany, whose almoner he became. The Bishopric of Cambray was offered to him, but refused. Norbert allowed himself to be so carried away by pleasure that nothing short of a miracle of grace could make him lead the life of an earnest cleric. One day, while riding to Vreden, a village near Xanten, he was overtaken by a storm. A thunderbolt fell at his horse's feet; the frightened animal threw its rider, and for nearly an hour he lay like one dead. Thus humbled, Norbert became a sincere penitent. Renouncing his appointment at Court, he retired to Xanten to lead a life of penance.

Understanding, however, that he stood in need of guidance, he placed himself under the direction of Cono, Abbot of Siegburg. In gratitude to Cono, Norbert founded the Abbey of Fürstenberg, endowed it with a portion of his property, and made it over to Cono and his Benedictine successors. Norbert was then in his thirty-fifth year. Feeling that he was called to the priesthood, he presented himself to the Bishop of Cologne, from whose hands he received Holy Orders. After a forty days' retreat at Siegburg Abbey, he celebrated his first Mass at Xanten and preached an earnest discourse on the transitory character of this world's pleasures and on man's duties towards God. The insults of some young clerics, one of whom even spat in his face, he bore with wonderful patience on that occasion. Norbert often went to Siegburg Abbey to confer with Cono, or to the cell of Ludolph, a holy and learned hermit-priest, or to the Abbey of Klosterrath near Rolduc. Accused as an innovator at the Council of Fritzlar, he resigned all his ecclesiastical preferments, disposed of his estate, and gave it all to the poor, reserving for himself only what was needed for the celebration of Holy Mass. Barefooted and begging his bread, he journeyed as far as St. Giles, in Languedoc, to confer with Pope Gelasius concerning his future life. Unable to keep Norbert at his court, Gelasius granted him faculties to preach wherever he judged proper. At Valenciennes Norbert met (March, 1119) Burchard, Bishop of Cambray, whose chaplain joined him in his apostolic journeys in France and Belgium. After the death of Pope Gelasius (29 January, 1119) Norbert wished to confer with his successor, Calixtus II, at the Council of Reims (Oct., 1119). The pope and Bartholomew, Bishop of Laon, requested Norbert to found a religious order in the Diocese of Laon, so that his work might be perpetuated after his death. Norbert chose a lonely, marshy valley, shaped in the form of a cross, in the Forest of Coucy, about ten miles from Laon, and named Prémontré. Hugh of Fosses, Evermode of Cambray, Anthony of Nivelles, seven students of the celebrated school of Anselm, and Ralph at Laon were his first disciples. The young community at first lived in huts of wood and clay, arranged like a camp around the chapel of St. John the Baptist, but they soon built a larger church and a monastery for the religious who joined them in increasing numbers. Going to Cologne to obtain relics for their church, Norbert discovered, through a vision, the spot where those of St. Ursula and her companions, of St. Gereon, and of other martyrs lay hidden.

Women also wished to become members of the new religious order. Blessed Ricwera, widow of Count Raymond of Clastres, was St. Norbert's first spiritual daughter, and her example was followed by women of the best families of France and Germany. Soon after this, Norbert returned to Germany and preached in Westphalia, when Godfrey, Count of Kappenberg, offered himself and gave three of his castles to be made into abbeys. On his return from Germany, Norbert was met by Theobald, Count of Champagne, who wished to become a member of the order; but Norbert insisted that God wished Theobald to marry and do good in the world. Theobald agreed to this, but begged Norbert to prescribe a rule of life. Norbert prescribed a few rules and invested Theobald with the white scapular of the order, and thus, in 1122, the Third Order of St. Norbert was instituted. The saint was soon requested by the Bishop of Cambrai to go and combat the infamous heresies which Tanchelin had propagated, and which had their centre at Antwerp. As a result of his preaching the people of the Low Countries abjured their heresies, and many brought back to him the Sacred Species which they had stolen and profaned. In commemoration of this, St. Norbert has been proclaimed the Apostle of Antwerp, and the feast of his triumph over the Sacramentarian heresy is celebrated in the Archdiocese of Mechlin on 11 July.

The rapid growth of the order was marvellous, and bishops entreated Norbert to found new houses in their dioceses. Floreffe, Viviers, St-Josse, Ardenne, Cuissy, Laon, Liège, Antwerp, Varlar, Kappenberg and others were founded during the first five years of the order's existence. Though the order had already been approved by the pope's legates, Norbert, accompanied by three disciples, journeyed to Rome, in 1125, to obtain its confirmation by the new pope, Honorius II. The Bull of Confirmation is dated 27 February, 1126. Passing through Würzburg on his return to Prémontré, Norbert restored sight to a blind woman: the inhabitants were so full of admiration for him that they spoke of electing him successor to their bishop who had just died, but Norbert and his companions fled secretly. Soon after this, on his way to Ratisbon, he passed through Spier, where Lothair, King of the Romans, was holding a diet, the papal legate being present. Deputies from Magdeburg had also come to solicit a successor to their late archbishop, Rudger.

The papal legate and Lothair used their authority, and obliged Norbert to accept the vacant see. On taking possession of it, he was grieved to find that much property belonging to the Church and the poor had been usurped by powerful men, and that many of the clergy led scandalous lives. He succeeded in converting some of the transgressors, but others only became more obstinate, and three attempts were made on his life. He resisted Pietro di Leoni, who, as antipope, had assumed the name of Anacletus and was master in Rome, exerting himself at the Council of Reims to attach the German Emperor and the German bishops and princes more firmly to the cause of Pope Innocent II.

Though his health was increasingly delicate, Norbert accompanied Lothair and his army to Rome to put the rightful pope on the Chair of St. Peter, and he resisted the pope's concession of the investiture to the emperor. Norbert, whose health was now much impaired, accompanied the Emperor Lothair back to Germany and for some time remained with him, assisting him as his chancellor and adviser. In March, 1134, Norbert had become so feeble that he had to be carried to Magdeburg where he died on the Wednesday after Pentecost. By order of the emperor, his body was laid at rest in the Norbertine Abbey of St. Mary, at Magdeburg. His tomb became glorious by the numerous miracles wrought there. The Bollandists say that there is no document to prove that he was canonized by Innocent III. His canonization was by Gregory XIII in 1582, and his cultus was extended to the whole church by Clement X.

On 2 May, 1627, the saint's body was translated from Magdeburg, then in the hands of Protestants, to the Abbey of Strahov, a suburb of Prague in Bohemia. The Chancery of Prague preserved the abjurations of six hundred Protestants who, on the day, or during the octave, of the translation, were reconciled to the Catholic Church. On that occasion the Archbishop of Prague, at the request of the civil and ecclesiastical authorities, proclaimed St. Norbert the Patron and Protector of Bohemia. (For history of the order, see PREMONSTRATENSIAN CANONS.)

Until the middle of the last century, the principal source for the biography of St. Norbert was a MS. usually attributed to HUGO, the saint's first disciple and successor, of which numerous copies had been made. That belonging to the Abbey of Romersdorf, near Coblentz, *Vita Norberti, auctore canonico praeadjuvante Hugone abbate, Fossense*, is now in the British Museum. An abridgment of this by SURIUS was printed in 1572; the whole MS., with variants, was published by ABBOT VANDER STERRE in 1656; again, with commentaries and notes, by PAPEBROCH in *Acta SS.*, XX. Then followed: VANDER STERRE, *Het leven van den H. Norbertus* (Antwerp, 1623); DU PRÉ, *La Vie de S. Norbert* (Paris, 1627); CAMUS, *L'Homme apostolique en S. Norbert* (Caen, 1640); C. L. HUGO, *La Vie de S. Norbert* (Luxemburg, 1704); ILLANA, *Historia del Gran Padre y Patriarca S. Norberto* (Salamanca, 1755).

In 1856 a MS. *Life of St. Norbert* discovered in the Royal Library, Berlin, was published in PERTZ, *Mon. Germ. Hist.*, differing in many particulars from the HUGO MSS. mentioned above. The discovery occasioned a great revival of interest in the subject, and there followed: TENKOFF, *De S. Norberto Ord. Praem. Conditore commentatio historica* (Münster, 1855); SCHOLZ, *Vita S. Norberti* (Breslau, 1859); WINTER, *Die Prämonstratenser der 12. Jahrh.* (Berlin, 1865); ROSENMUND, *Die ältesten Biographien des h. Norbertus* (Berlin, 1874); HERTEL, *Leben des h. Norbert* (Leipzig, 1881); MÜHLBACHER, *Die streitige Papstwahl des Jahres 1130* (Innsbruck, 1876). In the following three works, the publication of Pertz and other lately discovered documents have been used: GEUDENS, *Life of St. Norbert* (London, 1886); MADELAINE, *Histoire de S. Norbert* (Lille, 1886) (the fullest and best-written biography of the saint so far published); VAN DEN ELSEN, *Levensgeschiedenis van den H. Norbertus* (Averbode, 1890).

F. M. GEUDENS.

Norbertines. See PREMONSTRATENSIAN CANONS.

Norcia, DIOCESE OF (NORSIN), a city in Perugia, Italy, often mentioned in Roman history. In the ninth century it was a republic. The Dukes of Spoleto often contended with the popes for its possession; when, in 1453, the communes of Spoleto and Cascia declared war against Norcia, it was defended by the pope's general Cesarini. It was the birthplace of St. Benedict; the abbots St. Spes and St. Eutychius; the monk Florentius; the painter Parasole; and the physician Benedict Pegardati. The chief industry is preserving meats. The first known bishop was Stephen (c. 495). From the ninth century, Norcia was in the Diocese of Spoleto, as it appears to have been temporarily in the time of St. Gregory the Great. The see was re-established in 1820, and its first bishop was Cajetan Bonani. Immediately dependent on Rome, it has 100 parishes; 28,000 inhabitants; 7 religious houses of women; 3 schools for girls.

CAPPELLETTI, *Le Chiese d'Italia*, IV.

U. BENIGNI.

Norfolk, CATHOLIC DUKES OF, SINCE THE REFORMATION.—Under this title are accounts only of the prominent Catholic Dukes of Norfolk since the Reformation; a list of the Dukes, from the time the title passed to the Howard family, is prefixed.

1. John (1430–1485), created first duke of the Howard line in 1483, died in battle in 1485.
2. Thomas (1443–1524), son. Became duke in 1514.
3. Thomas (1473–1554), son. Succeeded in 1524.
4. Thomas (1536–1572), grandson. Succeeded in 1554. Beheaded in 1572.
5. Thomas (1627–1677), great-great-grandson. Dukedom restored in 1660.
6. Henry (1628–1684), brother. Succeeded in 1677.
7. Henry (1655–1701), son. Succeeded in 1684.
8. Thomas (1683–1732), nephew. Succeeded in 1701.
9. Edward (1685–1777), brother. Succeeded in 1732.
10. Charles (1720–1786), descendant of seventh duke. Succeeded in 1777.
11. Charles (1746–1815), son. Succeeded in 1786.
12. Bernard Edward (1765–1842), third cousin. Succeeded in 1815.
13. Henry Charles (1791–1856), son. Succeeded in 1842.
14. Henry Granville (1815–1860), son. Succeeded in 1856.
15. Henry Fitzalan (1847–   ), son. Succeeded in 1860.

THOMAS, THIRD DUKE, was the eldest son of Thomas Howard, the second duke, and Elizabeth, daughter of Sir F..Tilney of Ashwellthorpe Hall, Norfolk. In 1495 he was married to Lady Anne, daughter of Edward IV. He fought as captain of the vanguard at Flodden Field in 1513. In 1514 he was created Earl of Surrey, and joined his father in opposing Wolsey's policy of depressing the old nobility. In 1520–21 he endeavoured to keep peace in Ireland; recalled, he took command of the English fleet against France, and successfully opposed the French in Scotland. In 1524 he became duke, and was appointed commissioner to treat for peace with France. With peace abroad came the burning question of Henry's divorce. Norfolk, uncle of Anne Boleyn, sided with the king and, as president of the privy council, hastened the cardinal's ruin. He became Henry's tool in dishonourable purposes and he acquiesced in his lust for the spiritual supremacy. With Cromwell, he obtained a grant of a portion of the possessions of the Priory of Lewes and other monastic spoils. He was created earl-marshal in 1533. In 1535 Norfolk was a leading judge in the trial of Sir Thomas More. In 1536 he disbanded the "Pilgrimage of Grace" with false assurances, but returned next year to do "dreadful execution". In 1536 he hanged in chains, at York, Fathers Rochester and Walworth, two Carthusians. Drastic measures of devastation marked his whole career as a military leader. He shared the King's zeal against the inroads of German Protestantism. In 1534 he had "staid purgatory" and was always in favour of the old orthodoxy, as far as he might be allowed to support it. In 1539, when the bishops could not agree concerning the practices of religion, Norfolk proposed the Six Articles to the Lords, theology thus becoming matter for the whole House. As an old man he served against a rising in Scotland, and in the French wars of 1544. In 1546 he was accused of high treason. Evidence, however, was not conclusive against him until Hertford, and other keen enemies, prevailed upon him, as a prisoner in the Tower, to sign his confession and throw himself on the King's mercy. A bill of attainder was passed in Parliament, and orders for his immediate execution would have been carried into effect had not Henry died on the previous evening. He remained a prisoner in the Tower the whole of Edward VI's reign but was released on Mary's accession, and restored to the dukedom in 1553.

His long experience as lord high steward and lieutenant-general made him useful to the queen, but he lost favour by his rashness and his failure to crush Wyat's rebellion. [See Gairdner, "Lollardy and the Reformation" (London, 1908); Gairdner, "Hist. of Engl. Church in XVIth Century" (London, 1902); "Letters and Papers, Henry VIII", various volumes; Creighton, "Dict. of Nat. Biog.", X (London, 1908).]

THOMAS, FOURTH DUKE, was the son of Henry Howard, Earl of Surrey and Frances Vere, daughter of John, Earl of Oxford. After the execution of his father, in 1547, he was, by order of privy council, committed to the charge of his aunt, and Foxe, "the martyrologist", was assigned as his tutor, probably to educate him in Protestant principles. In 1553, when Mary released his grandfather from prison, Bishop White of Lincoln became his tutor. Thomas succeeded his grandfather, as duke, in 1554, and became earl-marshal. He married, in 1556, Lady Mary Fitzalan, daughter of Henry, twelfth Earl of Arundel; in 1558, Margaret, daughter of Thomas Lord Audley of Walden; and, in 1567, Elizabeth, widow of Thomas Dacre of Gilsland, who had three daughters. By obtaining a grant of their wardship and intermarrying with them his own three sons, the issue of former marriages, he absorbed the great estates of the Dacre family. In 1568, he was again a widower, the only English duke, the wealthiest man in England, popular and ambitious. Elizabeth was eager to win one of Norfolk's position and he was given a part in the expulsion of the French troops from Scotland. With other commissioners, he was appointed to sit at York and inquire into the causes of the variance between Mary Stuart and her subjects. Circumstances, at the beginning of 1569, combined to awaken the fears of English nobles, and Arundel, Pembroke, Leicester, and others saw the advantage to be gained by the marriage, first suggested by Maitland, between Norfolk and Mary; that when married she might be safely restored to the Scottish throne and be recognized as Elizabeth's successor. Protestant nobles, however, looked on the affair with suspicion, and Catholic lords in the north were impatient of long delay. But, even after the council had voted for the settlement of the English succession by Mary's marriage with an English noble, Norfolk proceeded with great caution, withdrew from court, aroused Elizabeth's suspicion and was committed to the Tower, in October, 1569. On his abject submission to the queen and renunciation of all purpose of his alliance with Mary, he was released in 1570. He did not keep his promise; he continued to correspond with the Queen of Scots, was found to be in negotiation with Ridolfi, and through him with Philip and the Catholic Powers abroad, concerning an invasion of England. He was arraigned for high treason in 1571. After eighteen weeks' confinement in the Tower, deprived of books, informed of the trial only on the previous evening, kept in ignorance of the charges until he heard the indictment at the bar, and refused the aid of counsel to suggest advice, on the evidence of letters and extorted confessions from others, he was condemned to death by the Earl of Shrewsbury, the Lord High Steward, and twenty-six peers as assessors (judges, all selected by the queen's ministers and many of them his known enemies). After much hesitation on the part of Elizabeth and a petition from Parliament, on 2 June, 1572, he was executed. His sympathy seemed to be always with the Catholic party, but his policy was two-faced, and he was a professed adherent of the Reformed religion. Circumstances made it expedient for him always to temporize. He seems to have been led on by the course of events and not to have realized the result of his actions. [See State Trials, I (London, 1776), 82; Froude, "Hist. of Eng.", IV (London, 1866), XX;

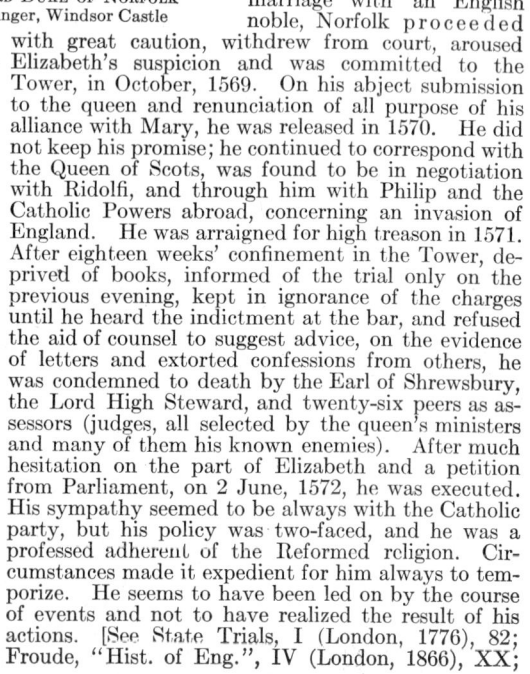

THOMAS HOWARD, THIRD DUKE OF NORFOLK
Hans Holbein the Younger, Windsor Castle

Labanoff, "Lettres, etc. de Marie Stuart" (1844), earlier ed. tr. (1842); Anderson, "Collections relating to Mary" (Edinburgh, 1727); Creighton in "Dict. of Nat. Biog.", X (London, 1908).

HENRY, SIXTH DUKE, the second son of Henry Frederick Howard, third Earl of Arundel and Lady Elizabeth Stuart, was educated abroad, as a Catholic. In 1669 he went as ambassador extraordinary to Morocco. In 1677 he succeeded his brother as duke, having previously been made hereditary earl-marshal. During the Commonwealth and Protectorate he lived in total seclusion. In January, 1678, he took his seat in the House of Lords, but in August the first development of the Titus Oates Plot was followed by an Act for disabling Catholics from sitting in either house of Parliament. He would not comply with the oath and, suspected of doubtful loyalty, withdrew to Bruges for three years. There he built a house attached to a Franciscan convent and enjoyed freedom of worship and scope for his munificence. He was a man of benevolent disposition and gave away the greater part of his splendid library, and grounds and rooms to the Royal Society, and the Arundelian marbles to Oxford University. Jealous of the family honour, he compounded a debt of £200,000 contracted by his grandfather. [See Evelyn's "Miscellaneous Writings" (London, 1825).]

HENRY, SEVENTH DUKE, son of Henry, sixth Duke, and Lady Anne Somerset, was at first a good Catholic and for four months held out against subscribing to the oath as a peer in the House of Lords. Afterwards he became a pervert.

THOMAS, EIGHTH DUKE, was brought up a Catholic but perverted on succeeding to the dukedom.

EDWARD, NINTH DUKE, did much to promote a more liberal treatment of Catholics by offering a home at Norfolk House to Frederick, Prince of Wales, and his wife at the time of the birth of their son, afterwards George III.

CHARLES, TENTH DUKE, son of Charles Howard of Greystoke, Cumberland, and Mary Paylward, was brought up a Catholic. Though he signed a petition for relief from the pressure of the penal laws, he led a very retired life. In 1764 he published "Considerations of the Penal Laws against the Roman Catholics in England and the new-acquired colonies in America"; and in 1768, "Thoughts, Essays, and Maxims, chiefly Religious and Political".

CHARLES, ELEVENTH DUKE, educated at the English College at Douai, was a man of dissolute life and had conformed to the State religion by 1780.

BERNARD EDWARD, TWELFTH DUKE, eldest son of Henry Howard of Glossop, and Juliana, daughter of Sir William Molyneux of Willow, Nottinghamshire. In 1789 he married Elizabeth Bellasis, daughter of Henry, Earl of Fauconberg, but was divorced, by Act of Parliament, in 1794. On the death of his third cousin, in 1815, he succeeded to the dukedom. Although a Catholic, he was allowed, by Act of Parliament in 1824, to exercise the hereditary office of earl-marshal. After the Relief Bill of 1829 he was admitted to the full exercise of his ancestral privileges; he took his seat in the House of Lords, where he was a steady supporter of the Reform Bill, and in 1830 was nominated as privy councillor. [See Gent. Mag., I (1842), 542.]

HENRY CHARLES, THIRTEENTH DUKE, only son of Bernard Edward and Elizabeth Bellasis. He was baptized a Catholic but did not practise his religion. In 1814 he married Lady Charlotte Leveson-Gower, daughter of George, Duke of Sutherland, and in 1815 he became, as heir, Earl of Arundel and Surrey. In 1829, after the Catholic Emancipation Act, he took the oath and his seat in the House of Commons (the first Catholic since the Reformation). In 1841 he sat in the House of Lords. In politics he was a stanch member of the Whig party. In 1842 he succeeded his father as Duke of Norfolk. He died at Arundel in 1856. Canon Tierney was chaplain at the time of his death. [See London Times (19 Feb., 1856); Gent. Mag. (April, 1856), 419.]

HENRY GRANVILLE FITZALAN, FOURTEENTH DUKE, eldest son of Henry Charles Howard and Charlotte, daughter of the Duke of Sutherland, was educated privately, and at Trinity College, Cambridge. He entered the army but retired on attaining the rank of captain. In 1839 he married the daughter of Admiral Sir Edmund (afterwards Lord) Lyons, the ambassador at Athens. From 1837 to 1842 he was a member of the House of Commons, a Whig, until he broke with his party on the introduction of the Ecclesiastical Titles Bill of 1850. In 1856, as Duke of Norfolk, he took his seat in the House of Lords. In 1839 he attended the services of Notre-Dame in Paris and made the acquaintance of Montalembert. This resulted in his conversion to Catholicism, and Montalembert describes him as "the most pious layman of our times". Cardinal Wiseman, in a pastoral letter, at the time of his death in 1860, referred to his benevolent nature: "There is not a form of want or a peculiar application of alms which has not received his relief or co-operation". He wrote: "Collections relative to Catholic Poor Schools throughout England", MS. folio, 134, pp. 1843; "A few Remarks on the Social and Political Condition of British Catholics" (London, 1847); Letter to J. P. Plumptre on the Bull "In Cœna Domini" (London, 1848); "Observations on Diplomatic Relations with Rome" 1848. He edited from original MSS. the "Lives of Philip Howard and Anne Dacres" (London, 1857 and 1861). [See "Gent. Mag." (Jan., 1861); "London Times" (27 Nov. and 4 Dec., 1860); "London Table" (1 Dec., 1860); H. W. Freeland, "Remarks on the Letters of the Duke of Norfolk" (1874); Montalembert, "Le Correspondant" (25 Dec., 1860), 766–776, tr. by Goddard at the end of his Montalembert, "Pius IX and France" (Boston, Mass., 1861).]

TIERNEY, Castle and Antiquities of Arundel (London, 1834); HOWARD, Memorials of the Howards (Corby Castle, 1834); GILLOW, Biog. Dict. of Engl. Catholics (London, 1885–1902); LINGARD, History of England (London, 1855); Dict. Nat. Biog. (London, 1908), s. v. Howard.

S. ANSELM PARKER.

Noris, HENRY, Cardinal, b. at Verona, 29 August, 1631, of English ancestry; d. at Rome, 23 Feb., 1704. He studied under the Jesuits at Rimini, and there entered the novitiate of the Hermits of Saint Augustine. After his probation he was sent to Rome to study theology. He taught the sacred sciences at Pesaro, Perugia, and Padua, where he held the chair of church history in the university from 1674 to 1692. There he completed "The History of Pelagianism", and "Dissertations on the Fifth General Council", the two works which, before and after his death, occasioned much controversy. Together with the "Vindiciæ Augustinianæ" they were printed at Padua in 1673, having been approved by a special commission at Rome. Noris himself went to Rome to give an account of his orthodoxy before this commission; and Clement X named him one of the qualificators of the Holy Office, in recognition of his learning and sound doctrine. But, after the publication of these works, further charges were made against him of teaching the errors of Jansenius and Baius. In a brief to the prefect of the Spanish Inquisition, 31 July, 1748, ordering the name of Noris to be taken off the list of forbidden books, Benedict XIV says that these charges were never proved; that they were rejected repeatedly by the Holy Office, and repudiated by the popes who had honoured him. In 1692 Noris was made assistant Librarian in the Vatican by Innocent XII. On 12 December, 1695, he was named Cardinal-Priest of the Title of S. Agostino. In 1700 he was given full charge of the Vatican Library. His works, apart from some minor controversial treatises, are highly valued for accuracy and thoroughness of research. In addition to those already named, the most important are: "Annus et Epochæ Syro-Macedonum in Vetustis Urbium Syriæ Expositæ"; "Fasti Consulares Anonimi e Manuscripto Bibliothecæ Cæsareæ Deprompti"; "Historia Controversiæ de Uno ex Trinitate Passo"; "Apologia Monachorum Scythiæ"; "Historia Donatistarum e Schedis Norisianis Excerptæ"; "Storia delle Investiture delle Dignità Ecclesiastiche". Select portions of his works have been frequently reprinted, at Padua, 1673–1678, 1708; at Louvain, 1702; at Bassano, edited by Berti, 1769. The best is the edition of all the works, in five vols. folio by the Ballerini Brothers, Verona, 1729–1741.

HURTER, *Nomenclator. Katholik*, I (1884), 181; PIETRO AND GIROLAMO BALLERINI, *Vita Norisii* in their ed. of Noris' works, IV (Verona, 1729–41); a shorter *Life* is prefixed to the edition of Padua, 1708; LANTERI, *Postrema Sæcula Sex Religionis Augustinianæ*, III (Tolentino, 1858), 64 sq.

FRANCIS E. TOURSCHER.

Normandy, ancient French province, from which five "departments" were formed in 1790: Seine-Inférieure (Archdiocese of Rouen), Eure (Diocese of Evreux), Calvados (Diocese of Bayeux), Orne (Diocese of Séez), Manche (Diocese of Coutances). The Normans, originally Danish or Norwegian pirates, who from the ninth to the tenth century made numerous incursions into France, gave their name to this province. In the Gallo-Roman period Normandy formed the so-called second Lyonnaise province (*Secunda Lugdunensis*). At Thorigny within the territory of this province was found an inscription very important for the history of the worship of the emperors in Gaul and of the provincial assemblies; the latter, thus meeting for this worship, kept up a certain autonomy throughout the conquered territory of Gaul. Under the Merovingians the Kingdom of Neustria annexed Normandy. About 843 Sydroc and his bands of pillagers opened the period of Northman invasions. The policy of Charles the Bald in giving money or lands to some of the Northmen for defending his land against other bands was unfortunate, as these adventurers readily broke their oath. In the course of their invasions they slew (858) the Bishop of Bayeux and (859) the Bishop of Beauvais. The conversion (862) of the Northman, Weland, marked a new policy on the part of the Carlovingians; instead of regarding the invaders as intruders it was admitted that they might become Christians. Unlike the Saracens, then disturbing Europe, the Northmen were admitted to a place and a rôle in Christendom.

The good fortune of the Northmen began with Rollo in Normandy itself. It was long believed that Rollo came by sea into the valley of the Seine in 876, but the date is rather 886. He destroyed Bayeux, pillaged Lisieux, besieged Paris, and reached Lorraine, finally establishing himself at Rouen, where a truce was concluded. His installation was considered so definitive that in the beginning of the tenth century Witto, Archbishop of Rouen, consulted the Archbishop of Reims as to the means of converting the Northmen. Rollo's settlement in Normandy was ratified by the treaty of St. Clair-sur-Epte (911), properly speaking only a verbal agreement between Rollo and Charles the Simple. As Duke of Normandy Rollo remained faithful to the Carlovingian dynasty in its struggles with the ancestors of the future Capetians. These cordial relations between the ducal family of Normandy and French royalty provoked under Rollo's successor William Long-sword (931–42) a revolt of the pagan Northmen settled in Cotentin and Bessin. One of their lords (*jarls*), Riulf by name was the leader of the movement. The rebels reproached the duke with being no longer a true Scandinavian and "treating the French as his kinsmen". Triumphant for a time, they were finally routed and the aristocratic spirit of the *jarls* had to bow before the monarchical principles which William Long-sword infused into his government.

Another attempt at a revival of paganism was made under Richard I *Sans Peur* (the Fearless, 942–96). He was only two years old at his father's death. A year later (943) the Scandinavian Setric, landing in Normandy with a band of pirates, induced a number of Christian Northmen to apostatize; among them, one Turmod who sought to make a pagan of the young duke. Hugh the Great, Duke of France, and Louis IV, King of France, defeated these invaders and after their victory both sought to set up their own power in Normandy to the detriment of the young Richard whom Louis IV held in semi-captivity at Laon. The landing in Normandy of the King of Denmark, Harold Bluetooth, and the defeat of Louis IV, held prisoner for a time (945), constrained the latter to sign the treaty of Gerberoy, by which the young Duke Richard was re-established in his possessions, and became, according to the chronicler Dudon de Saint-Quentin, a sort of King of Normandy. The attacks later directed against Richard by the Carlovingian King Lothaire and Thibaut le Tricheur, Count of Chartres, brought a fresh descent on France of the soldiers of Harold Bluetooth. Ascending the Seine these Danes so devastated the country of Chartres that when they withdrew, according to the chronicler Guillaume of Jumièges, there was not heard even the bark of a dog. When Eudes of Chartres, brother-in-law of Richard II the Good, again threatened Normandy (996–1020), it was once more the Scandinavian chieftains, Olaf of Norway and Locman, who came to the duke's aid. So attached were these Scandinavians to paganism that their leader Olaf, having been baptized by the Archbishop of Rouen, was slain by them. Although they had become Christian, all traces of Scandinavian paganism did not disappear under the first dukes of Normandy. Rollo walked barefoot before the reliquary of St. Ouen, but he caused many relics to be sold in England, and on his death-bed, according to Adhémar de Chabannes, simultaneously caused prisoners to be sacrificed to the Scandinavian gods and gave much gold to the churches. Richard I was a great builder of churches, among them St. Ouen and the primitive cathedral of Rouen, St. Michel du Mont, and the Trinity at Fécamp. Richard II, zealous for monastic reform, brought from Burgundy Guillaume de St. Bénigne; the Abbey of Fécamp, reformed by him, became a model monastery and a much frequented school.

All these dukes protected the Church, but the feudal power of the Church, which in many States at that time limited the central power, was but little developed in Normandy, and it was to their kinsmen that the dukes of Normandy most often gave the Archdiocese of Rouen and other sees. Ecclesiastical life in Normandy was vigorous and well-developed; previous to the eleventh century the rural parishes were almost as numerous as they are to-day. Thus Normandy for nearly a century and a half was at once a sort of promontory of the Christian world in face of Scandinavia and at the same time a coign of Scandinavia thrust into the Christian world. Henceforth those Danes and Scandinavians who under the name of Normans formed a part of Christendom, never called pagan Danes or Scandinavians to their aid unless threatened in the possession of Normandy; under their domination the land became a stronghold of Christianity. The monastery of Fontenelle (q. v.) pursued its religious and literary activity from the Merovingian period. The "Chronicon Fontanellense", continued to 1040, is an important source for the history of the period. The ducal family of Normandy early determined to have an historiographer whom they sought in France, one Dudon, dean of the chapter of St. Quentin, who between 1015–30 wrote in Latin half verse, half prose, a history of the family according to the traditions and accounts transmitted to him by Raoul, Count of Ivry, grandson of Rollo and brother of Richard I Alinea. Duke Robert the Devil (1027-35) was already powerful enough to interfere efficaciously in the struggles of Henry I of France against his own brother and the Counts of Champagne and Flanders. In gratitude the king bestowed on Robert the Devil, Pontoise, Chaumont en Vexin, and the whole of French Vexin. It was under Robert the Devil that the ducal family of Normandy first cast covetous glances towards England. He sent an embassy to Canute the Great, King of England, in order that the sons of Ethelred, Alfred and Edward, might recover their patrimony. The petition having been denied he made ready a naval expedition against England, destroyed by a tempest. He died while on a pilgrimage to the Holy Sepulchre.

It was reserved for his son William the Bastard, later called William the Conqueror, to make England a Norman colony by the expedition which resulted in the victory of Hastings or Senlac (1066). It seemed, then, that in the second half of the eleventh century a sort of Norman imperialism was to arise in England, but the testament of William the Conqueror which left Normandy to Robert Courte-Heuse and England to William Rufus, marked the separation of the two countries. Each of the brothers sought to despoil the other; the long strife which Robert waged, first against William Rufus, afterwards against his third brother Henry I Beauclerc, terminated in 1106 with the battle of Tinchebray, after which he was taken prisoner and brought to Cardiff. Thenceforth Normandy was the possession of William I, King of England, and while forty years previous England seemed about to become a Norman country, it was Normandy which became an English country; history no longer speaks of the ducal family of Normandy but of the royal family of England. Later Henry I, denounced to the Council of Reims by Louis VI of France, explained to Callistus II in tragic terms the condition in which he had found Normandy. "The duchy", said he, "was the prey of brigands. Priests and other servants of God were no longer honoured, and paganism had almost been restored in Normandy. The monasteries which our ancestors had founded for the repose of their souls were destroyed, and the religious obliged to disperse, being unable to sustain themselves. The churches were given up to pillage, most of them reduced to ashes, while the priests were in hiding. Their parishioners were slaying one another." There may have been some truth in this description of Henry I; however, it is well to bear in mind that the Norman dukes of the eleventh century, while they had prepared and realized these astounding political changes, had also developed in Normandy, with the help of the Church, a brilliant literary and artistic movement.

The Abbey of Bec was for some time, under the direction of Lanfranc and St. Anselm, the foremost school of northern France. Two Norman monasteries produced historical works of great importance; the "Historia Normannorum", written between 1070-87 by Guillaume Calculus at the monastery of Jumièges; the "Historia Ecclesiastica" of Ordericus Vitalis, which begins with the birth of Christ and ends in 1141, written at the monastery of St. Evroult. The secular clergy of Normandy emulated the monks; in a sort of academy founded in the second half of the eleventh century by two bishops of Lisieux, Hugues of Eu and Gilbert Maminot, not only theological but also scientific and literary questions were discussed. The Norman court was a kind of Academy and an active centre of literary production. The chaplain of Duchess Matilda, Gui de Ponthieu, Bishop of Amiens, composed in 1067 a Latin poem on the battle of Hastings; the chaplain of William the Conqueror, William of Poitiers, wrote the "Gesta" of his master and an extant account of the first crusade is due to another Norman, Raoul de Caen, an eyewitness. At the same time the Norman dukes of the eleventh century restored the buildings, destroyed by the invasions of their barbarian ancestors, and a whole Romance school of architecture developed in Normandy, extending to Chartres, Picardy, Brittany, and even to England. Caen was the centre of this school; and monuments like the Abbaye aux Hommes and the Abbaye aux Dames, built at Caen by William and Matilda, mark an epoch in the history of Norman art.

In the course of the twelfth century the political destinies of Normandy were very uncertain. Henry I of England, master of Normandy from 1106-35, preferred to live at Caen rather than in England. His rule in Normandy was at first disturbed by the partisans of Guillaume Cliton, son of Robert Courte-Heuse, and later by the plot concocted against him by his own daughter Matilda, widow of Emperor Henry V, who had taken as her second husband Geoffrey Plantagenet, Count of Anjou. When Henry I died in 1135 his body was brought to England; his death without male heirs left Normandy a prey to anarchy. For this region was immediately disputed between Henry Plantagenet, grandson of Henry I through his mother Matilda, and Thibaut of Champagne, grandson of William the Conqueror through his mother Adèle. After nine years of strife Thibaut withdrew in favour of his brother Stephen who in 1135 had been crowned King of England. But the victories of Geoffrey Plantagenet in Normandy assured (1144) the rule of Henry Plantagenet over that land, which being thenceforth subject to Angevin rule, seemed destined to have no further connexion with England. Suddenly Henry Plantagenet, who in 1152 had married Eleanor (Aliénor) of Aquitaine, divorced from Louis VII of France, determined to assert his rights over England itself. The naval expedition which he conducted in 1153 led Stephen to recognize him as his heir, and as Stephen died at the end of that same year Henry Plantagenet reigned over all the Anglo-Norman possessions, his territorial power being greater than that of the kings of France. A long series of wars followed between the Capetians and Plantagenets, interrupted by truces. Louis VII wisely favoured everything which paralyzed the power of Plantagenet, and supported all his enemies. Thomas à Becket and the other exiles who had protested against the despotism which Henry exercised against the Church, found refuge and help at the court of France; and the sons of Henry in their successive revolts against their father in Normandy, were supported first by Louis VII and then by Philip Augustus.

The prestige of the Capetian kings grew in Normandy when Richard Cœur de Lion succeeded Henry II in 1189. Philip Augustus profited by the enmity between Richard and his brother John Lackland to gradually establish French domination in Normandy. A war between Richard and Philip Augustus resulted in the treaty of Issoudun (1195) by which Philip Augustus acquired for the French crown Norman Vexin and the castellanies of Nonancourt, Ivry, Pacy, Vernon, and Gaillon. A second war between John Lackland, King of England in 1199 and Philip Augustus, was terminated by the treaty of Goulet (1200), by which John Lackland recovered Norman Vexin, but recognized the French king's possession of the territory of Evreux and declared himself the "liege man" of Philip Augustus. Also when in 1202 John Lackland, having abducted Isabella of Angoulême, refused to appear before Philip Augustus, the court of peers declared John a felon, under which sentence he no longer had the right to hold any fief of the crown. Philip II Augustus sanctioned the judgment of the court of peers by invading Normandy which in 1204 became a French possession. The twelfth century in Normandy was marked by the production of important works, chief of which was the "Roman de Rou" of Robert or rather Richard Wace (1100-75), a canon of Bayeux. In this, which consists of nearly 17,000 lines and was continued by Benoît de Sainte-More, Wace relates the history of the dukes of Normandy down to the battle of Tinchebray. Mention must also be made of the great French poem which the Norman Ambroise wrote somewhat prior to 1196 on the Jerusalem pilgrimage of Richard Cœur de Lion. As early as the twelfth century Normandy was an important commercial centre. Guillaume de Neubrig wrote that Rouen was one of the most celebrated cities of Europe and that the Seine brought thither the commercial products of many countries. The "Etablissements de Rouen" in which was drawn up the "custom" adopted by Rouen, were copied not only by the other Norman towns but by the cities with which Rouen maintained constant commercial intercourse, e. g. Angoulême, Bayonne, Cognac, St. Jean d'Angély, Niort, Poitiers, La Rochelle, Saintes, and Tours. The *ghilde* of Rouen, a powerful commercial association, possessed in England from the time of Edward the Confessor the port of Dunegate, now Dungeness, near London, and its merchandise entered London free.

Once in the power of the Capetians, Normandy became an important strategical point in the struggle against the English, masters of Poitou and Guyenne in the south of France. Norman sailors were enrolled by Philip VI of France for a naval campaign against England in 1340 which resulted in the defeat of Ecluse. Under John II the Good, the States of Normandy, angered by the ravages committed by Edward III of England on his landing in the province, voted (1348-50) subsidies for the conquest of England. The Valois dynasty was in great danger when Charles the Bad, King of Navarre, who possessed important lands in Normandy, succeeded in 1356 in detaching from John II of France a number of Norman barons. John II appraising the danger came suddenly to Rouen, put several barons to death, and took Charles the Bad prisoner. Shortly afterwards Normandy was one of the provinces of France most faithful to the Dauphin Charles, the future Charles V, and the hope the English entertained in 1359 of seeing Normandy ceded to them by the Preliminaries of London was not ratified by the treaty of Brétigny (1360); Normandy remained French. The victories of Charles V consolidated the prestige of the Valois in this province. In 1386 Normandy furnished 1387 vessels for an expedition against England never executed. In 1418 the campaign of Henry V in Normandy was for a long time paralyzed by the resistance of Rouen, which finally capitulated in 1419, and in 1420 all Normandy became again almost English.

The Duke of Clarence, brother of Henry V of England, was made lieutenant-general in the province. Henry VI and the Duke of Bedford founded a university at Caen which had faculties of canon and civil law, to which Charles VII in 1450 added those of theology, medicine, and arts. This last attempt at English domination in Normandy was marked by the execution at Rouen of Blessed Joan of Arc. English rule, however, was undermined by incessant conspiracies, especially on the part of the people of Rouen, and by revolts in 1435-36. The revolt of Val de Vire is famous and was the origin of an entire ballad literature, called "Vaux de Vire", in which the poet Oliver Basselin excelled. These songs, which later became bacchic or amorous in character, and which subsequently developed into the popular drama known as "Vaudeville", were in the beginning chiefly of an historical nature recounting the invasion of Normandy by the English. Profiting by the public opinion of which the "Vaux de Vire" gave evidence, the Constable de Richemont opposed the English on Norman territory. His long and arduous efforts in 1449-50 made Normandy once more a French province. Thenceforth the possession of Normandy by France was considered so essential to the security of the kingdom that Charles the Bold, for a time victorious over Louis XI, in order to weaken the latter, exacted in 1465 that Normandy should be held by Duke Charles de Berry, the king's brother and leader of those in revolt against him; two years later Louis XI took Normandy from his brother and caused the States General of Tours to proclaim in 1468 that Normandy could for no reason whatever be dismembered from the domain of the crown. The ducal ring was broken in the presence of the great judicial court called the Echiquier (Exchequer) and the title of Duke of Normandy was never to be borne again except by Louis XVII, the son of Louis XVI.

The Norman school of architecture from the thirteenth to the fifteenth century produced superb Gothic edifices, chiefly characterized by the height of their spires and bell-towers. Throughout the Middle Ages Normandy, greatly influenced by St. Bernard and the Cistercians, was distinguished for its veneration of the Blessed Virgin. It was under her protection that William the Conqueror placed his expedition to England. One of the most ancient mural paintings in France is in the chapel of the Hospice St. Julien at Petit-Quevilly, formerly the manor chapel of one of the early dukes of Normandy, portraying the Annunciation, the Birth of Christ, and the Blessed Virgin suckling the Infant Jesus during the flight into Egypt. As early as the twelfth century Robert or rather Richard Wace wrote the history of Mary and that of the establishment of the feast of the Immaculate Conception. The Norman students at Paris placed themselves under the patronage of the Immaculate Conception which thus became the "feast of the Normans"; this appellation does not seem to date beyond the thirteenth century. During the modern period the Normans have been distinguished for their commercial expeditions by sea and their voyages of discovery. As early as 1366 the Normans had established markets on the coast of Africa and it was from Caux that Jean de Béthencourt set out in 1402 for the conquest of the Canaries. He opened up to Vasco da Gama the route to the Cape of Good Hope and to Christopher Columbus that to America. Two of his chaplains, Pierre Bontier and Jean le Verrier, gave an account of his expedition in a manuscript known as "Le Canarien", edited in 1874. Jean Ango, born at Dieppe about the end of the fifteenth century, acquired as a ship-owner a fortune exceeding that of many princes of his time. The Portuguese having in time of peace, seized (1530) a ship which belonged to him, he sent a flotilla to blockade Lisbon and ravage the Portuguese coast. The ambassador sent by the King of Portugal to Francis I to negotiate the matter, was referred to the citizen of Dieppe. Ango was powerful enough to assist the armaments of Francis I against England. He died in 1551.

Jean Parmentier (1494-1543), another navigator and a native of Dieppe, was, it is held, the first Frenchman to take ships to Brazil; to him is also ascribed the honour of having discovered Sumatra in 1529. Poet as well as sailor, he wrote in verse (1536) a "Description Nouvelle des Merveilles de ce monde". The foundation by Francis I in 1517 of the "French City" which afterwards became Havre de Grace, shows the importance which French royalty attached to the Norman coast. Normandy's maritime commerce was much developed by Henry II and Catherine de Medicis. They granted to the port of Rouen a sort of monopoly for the importation of spices and drugs arriving by way of the Atlantic, and when they came to Rouen in 1550 the merchants of that town contrived to give to the nearby wood the appearance of the country of Brazil "with three hundred naked men, equipped like savages of America, whence comes the wood of Brazil". Among these three hundred men were fifty real savages, and there also figured in this exhibition "several monkeys and squirrel monkeys which the merchants of Rouen had brought from Brazil." The description of the festivities, which bore witness to active commercial intercourse between Normandy and America, was published together with numerous figures. After the Reformation religious wars interrupted the maritime activity of the Normans for a time. Rouen took sides with the League, Caen with Henry IV, but with the restoration of peace the maritime expeditions recommenced. Normans founded Quebec in 1608, opened markets in Brazil in 1612, visited the Sonda Islands in 1617, and colonized Guadeloupe in 1635. The French population of Canada is to a large extent of Norman origin. During the French Revolution Normandy was one of the centres of the federalist movement known as the Girondin. Caen and Evreux were important centres for the Gironde; Buzot, who led the movement, was a Norman, and it was from Caen that Charlotte Corday set out to slay the "montagnard" Marat. The royalist movement of "la Chouannerie" had also one of its centres in Normandy.

DUCHESNE, *Historiæ Normannorum scriptores antiqui* (Paris, 1619); LIQUET, *Histoire de la Normandie jusqu'à la conquête de l'Angleterre* (Paris, 1855); LABUTTE, *Hist. des ducs de Normandie jusqu'à la mort de Guillaume le Conquérant* (Paris, 1866); WAITZ, *Ueber die Quellen zur Gesch. der Begründung der normannischen Herrscher in Frankreich* in *Göttingische Gelehrte Anzeigen* (1866); BÖHMER, *Kirche und Staat in England und in der Normandie im XI. und XII. Jahrhundert* (Leipzig, 1900); SARRAZIN, *Jeanne d'Arc et la Normandie au XVᵉ siècle* (Rouen, 1896); LEGRELLE, *La Normandie sous la monarchie absolue* (Rouen, 1903); DE FÉLICE, *La Basse Normandie, étude de géographie régionale* (Paris, 1907); SION, *Les paysans de la Normandie Orientale: pays de Caux* (Paris, 1909); SOREL, *Pages normandes* (Paris, 1907); PRENTOUT, *La Normandie* (Paris, 1910); COCHET, *Normandie monumentale et pittoresque* (Rouen, 1894); BLACK, *Normandy and Picardy, their relics, castles, churches, and footprints of William the Conqueror* (London, 1904); MILTOUN, *Rambles in Normandy* (London, 1905); FREEMAN, *Hist. of the Norman Conquest of England* (Oxford, 1870–76); PALGRAVE, *Normandy and England* (2 vols., 1851–57); LAPPENBERG, *Anglo-Norman Kings*; NORGATE, *England under the Angevin Kings* (Oxford, 1887); KEARY, *The Vikings in Western Christendom A. D. 789 to A. D. 888* (London, 1891).

GEORGES GOYAU.

Norris, SYLVESTER (alias SMITH, NEWTON), controversial writer and English missionary priest; b. 1570 or 1572 in Somersetshire; d. 16 March, 1630. After receiving minor orders at Reims in 1590, he went to the English College, Rome, where he completed his studies and was ordained priest. In May, 1596, he was sent on the English mission, and his energetic character is revealed by the fact that he was one of the appellant clergy in 1600. In the prosecutions following upon the Gunpowder Plot, he was committed to Bridewell Gaol. From his prison he addressed a letter to the Earl of Salisbury, dated 1 Dec., 1605, in which he protests his innocence, and in proof of his loyalty promises to repair to Rome, and labour that the pope shall bind all the Catholics of England to be just, true, and loyal subjects, and that hostages shall be sent "for the afferminge of those things". He was thereupon banished along with forty-six other priests (1606), went to Rome, and entered the Society of Jesus. He was for some time employed in the Jesuit colleges on the Continent, but in 1611 returned to the English mission, and in 1621 was made superior of the Hampshire district, where he died.

He wrote: "An Antidote, or Treatise of Thirty Controversies; With a large Discourse of the Church" (1622); "An Appendix to the Antidote" (1621); "The Pseudo-Scripturist" (1623); "A true report of the Private Colloquy between M. Smith, alias Norriee, and M. Walker" (1624); "The Christian Vow"; "Discourse proving that a man who believeth in the Trinity, the Incarnation, etc., and yet believeth not all other inferior Articles, cannot be saved"(1625).

SOMMERVOGEL, *Bibl. de la C. de J.*, V (1808–09); FOLEY, *Records of the English Province, S. J.*, VI, 184; III, 301; OLIVER, *Collections towards Illustrating the Biography of S. J.*, s. v.; GILLOW, *Bibl. Dict. Eng. Cath.*, V, s. v.

JAMES BRIDGE.

Northampton, DIOCESE OF (NORTANTONIENSIS), in England, comprises the Counties of Northampton, Bedford, Buckingham, Cambridge, Huntingdon, Norfolk, and Suffolk, mainly composed of agricultural districts and fenlands, where Catholics are comparatively few (see, in article ENGLAND, Map of the Ecclesiastical Province of Westminster). The number of secular priests is 70, of regular 18, of chapels and stations, 73, and of Catholics, 13,308 (1910). Among the more important religious orders are the Benedictines, the Franciscans, the Carmelites, and the Jesuits. Of convents the most notable are those of the Benedictines at East Bergholt, the Sisters of Notre Dame at Northampton and Norwich, the Sisters of Jesus and Mary at Ipswich, the Poor Sisters of Nazareth at Northampton, and the Dames Bernardines at Slough, who at their own expense built a fine church for that parish. The principal towns are Norwich, Ipswich, and Cambridge, the university town where, according to tradition, St. Simon Stock, of the Order of Carmel, received the brown scapular from Our Lady. The Decorated Gothic Catholic church at Cambridge, one of the most beautiful in the kingdom (consecrated in 1890), is dedicated to Our Lady and the English Martyrs. It is the gift of Mrs. Lyne Stephens of Lynford Hall, Norfolk. Norwich possesses one of the grandest Catholic churches in England, built by the munificence of the present Duke of Norfolk in the Transitional Norman style, after the designs of Sir Gilbert Scott, and completed in 1910. The cathedral at Northampton is a commodious but unpretentious building designed by the younger Pugin. The first Bishop of Northampton, William Wareing, had been Vicar Apostolic of the Eastern District before the restoration of the Catholic hierarchy; he resigned the see in 1858, and died in 1865. His successor, Francis Kerril Amherst, was consecrated 4 July, 1858, and resigned in 1879, the see being occupied the following year by Arthur Riddell, who d. 15 Sept., 1907. The present Bishop of Northampton (1910), Frederick William Keating, b. at Birmingham, 13 June, 1859, was consecrated 25 Feb., 1908.

Northampton was the scene of the last stand made by St. Thomas of Canterbury against the arbitrary conduct of Henry II. Bury St. Edmund's, anciently so renowned as the place where the body of St. Edmund, King and Martyr, was enshrined and venerated as well as for its Benedictine abbey, has become familiar to the modern reader mainly through Carlyle's "Past and Present," in the pages of which Abbot Samson (1135–1211), the hero of Jocelin's Chronicle, occupies the central position. The Isle of Ely and St. Etheldreda are famous in English ecclesiastical history. Canute, King of England, was accustomed to row or skate across the fens each year to be present on the Feast of the Purification at the Mass in the Abbey Church of Ely, and Thomas Eliensis ascribes to him the well-known lines beginning, "Sweetly sang the monks of Ely". At Walsingham, also in this diocese, only ruins are now left of a shrine which, in the Middle Ages, was second only to the Holy House of Loreto, of which it was a copy. Many great names of the Reformation period are connected with the district covered by the Diocese of Northampton. Catherine of Aragon died at Kimbolton and was buried at Peterborough, where the short inscription, "Queen Catherine", upon a stone slab marks her resting-place. From Framlingham Castle, the ruins of which are still considerable, Queen Mary Tudor set out, on the death of Edward VI, to contest with Lady Jane Grey her right to the throne. At Ipswich, the birthplace of Cardinal Wolsey, is still to be seen the gateway of the College built by him. At Fotheringay, Mary Queen of Scots was beheaded (1587), and at Wisbech Castle, where so many missionary priests, during penal times, were imprisoned, William Watson, the last but one of the Marian bishops, died, a prisoner for the Faith (1584). Sir Henry Bedingfeld, the faithful follower of Queen Mary and the gentle "Jailor of the Princess Elizabeth", is associated with this diocese through Oxburgh Hall, his mansion, still occupied by another Sir Henry Bedingfeld, his direct descendant. The Pastons of Paston are memorable in connexion with the celebrated "Paston Letters". Many of the priests who suffered death under the penal laws belonged to the districts now included in the Diocese of Northampton, in particular, Henry Heath, born, 1600, at Peterborough; Venerable Henry Walpole, S.J., (d. 1595), a native of Norfolk, and Venerable Robert Southwell, S.J., (1560-95), the Catholic poet, also born in Norfolk. In more recent times Bishop Milner was connected with the preservation of the Faith in this part of England. Alban Butler, the hagiographer, was born in Northamptonshire and was resident priest at Norwich from 1754-56. Dr. Husenbeth resided for some years at Cossey, where he is buried (see HUSENBETH, FREDERICK CHARLES). Father Ignatius Spencer, the Passionist, son of Earl Spencer, and formerly Rector of Brington, was received into the Catholic Church at Northampton, and Faber, the Oratorian, held the Anglican living of Elton, Huntingdonshire, before his conversion.

The Catholic Directory (London); RIDDELL, *General Statistics*, MS.; BEDE, *Hist. Eccl.*; *Historia Eliensis*; WATERTON, *Pietas Mariana*.

JOHN FREELAND.

North Carolina, one of the original thirteen States of the United States, is situated between 33° 53' and 36° 33' N. lat., and 75° 25' and 84° 30' W. long. It is bounded on the north by Virginia, east and south-east by the Atlantic Ocean, south by South Carolina and Georgia, and west and north-west by Tennessee. Its extreme length from east to west is 503 miles, with an extreme breadth of 187 miles, and an average breadth of about 100 miles. Its area is 52,250 square miles, of which 3670 is water. Originally it included the present State of Tennessee, ceded to the United States in 1790. In 1784-5 the people of that section made an unsuccessful effort to set up an independent state named Franklin, with John Sevier as governor. It is divided into ninety-eight counties and has (1910) ten Congressional districts, with a population of 2,206,287. The capital is Raleigh, situated nearly in the geographical centre of the state; the principal cities are Wilmington, Charlotte, Asheville, Greensboro, and Winston.

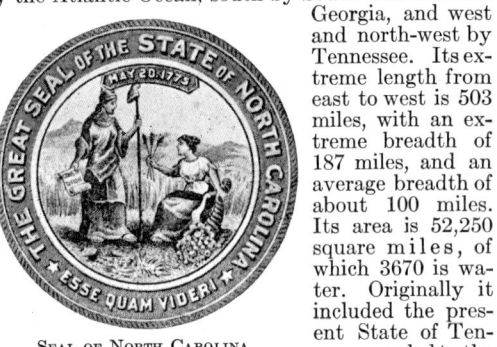

SEAL OF NORTH CAROLINA

PHYSICAL CHARACTERISTICS.—North Carolina has a remarkable variety of topography, soil, climate, and production and falls naturally into three divisions. The eastern or Tidewater section begins at the ocean and extends north-westwardly to the foot of the hills; the land is level, with sluggish streams and many marshes and swamps, including part of the great Dismal Swamp. It is the home of the long leaf pine, with its products of pitch, tar, and turpentine, long a source of wealth. The principal productions are cotton, corn, and rice; while "truck gardening" has recently grown into an important industry. The fisheries are also valuable. The central or Piedmont section, comprising nearly half the state and extending westward to the eastern foot of the Blue Ridge, is more or less hilly, but the rich intervening valleys produce practically all the general crops, including cotton and tobacco, with fruits of all kinds. The soil, though not naturally rich, is capable of a high degree of cultivation. The westward section, which runs to the Tennessee line, is mostly mountainous, with rich valleys and sheltered coves. Its principal productions are those of the central section, modified somewhat by its greater elevation. It contains some lofty peaks, Mount Mitchell being the highest peak east of the Rocky Mountains. The state is well watered, having numerous rivers, which, though not generally navigable, in their rapid descent furnish enormous waterpower, much of which has been recently developed. They may be divided into three classes, those flowing indirectly into the Mississippi, those flowing into the Great Pedee and the Santee, and those flowing into the Atlantic. The coast line, nearly four hundred miles long, includes Capes Fear, Lookout, and Hatteras; and, at varying distances from the ocean, run a series of sounds, chief of which are Currituck, Albemarle, and Pamlico. There are good harbours at Edenton, New Bern, Washington, Beaufort, and Wilmington, including Southport. The climate is generally equable, and North Carolina produces nearly all the crops grown in the United States with the exception of sub-tropical cane and fruits. Four of the wine grapes, the Catawba, Isabella, Lincoln, and Scuppernong, originated here. It has also large areas of valuable timber of great variety. With a few rare exceptions all the known minerals are found in the state. In 1905, taking the fourteen leading industries, including about 90 per cent of the total, there were 3272 manufacturing establishments, with a capital of $141,639,000, producing yearly products of the value of $142,520,776. The principal manufactured product was cotton, in which North Carolina ranked third among all the States, and tobacco, in which she ranked second.

RAILROADS AND BANKS.—There are in operation within the State 4387 miles of railroads, besides 911 miles of sidings, with a total valuation of $86,347,553, but capitalized for a much larger amount. The state has 321 banks organized under the state law; with an aggregate capital stock of $7,692,767; and 69 national banks with a capital of $6,760,000. The entire recognized state debt is $6,880,950, the greater part of which could be paid by the sale of certain railroad stock held by the state.

HISTORY.—North Carolina was originally inhabited by various tribes of Indians, the three principal ones being the Tuscaroras in the east, the Catawbas in the centre, and the Cherokees in the west. A small body of Cherokees is still located in the mountain section. In 1584 Queen Elizabeth granted to Sir Walter Raleigh the right to discover and hold any lands not inhabited by Christian people. This charter constitutes the first step in the work of English colonization in America. Five voyages were made under it, but without success in establishing a permanent settlement. In 1663 Charles II granted to Sir George Carteret and seven others a stretch of land on the Atlantic coast, lying between Virginia and Florida, and running west to the South Seas. The grantees were created "absolute lords proprietors" of the province of Carolina, with full powers to make and execute such laws as they deemed proper. This grant was enlarged in 1665 both as to territory and jurisdiction, and in 1669 the lords proprietors promulgated the "Fundamental Constitutions of Carolina", framed by John Locke, the philosopher, but they proved too theoretical for practical operation. The lords proprietors made every effort to colonize their province, which already contained one or two small settlements and for which they appointed governors at various times, frequently with local councils.

Albemarle, the name originally given to what now constitutes North Carolina, was augmented by settlements from Virginia, New England, and Bermuda. In 1674 the population was about four thousand. In 1729, Carolina became a royal province, the king having purchased from the proprietors seven-eighths of their domain. Carteret, subsequently Earl Granville, surrendered his right of jurisdiction, but retained in severalty his share of the land. It gained considerable accessions in population by a colony of Swiss at New Bern, of Scotch Highlanders on Cape Fear, of Moravians at Salem, and of Scotch-Irish and Pennsylvania Dutch, who settled in different parts of the state. For many years, however, there has been very little immigration and the population is now essentially homogeneous.

The people of North Carolina were among the earliest and most active promoters of the Revolution. The Stamp Tax was bitterly resented; a provincial congress, held at New Bern, elected delegates to the first Continental Congress in September, 1774, and joined in the declaration of Colonial rights. As early as 20 May, 1775, a committee of citizens met in Charlotte and issued the "Mecklenburg Declaration of Independence", formally renouncing allegiance to the British Crown. In December, 1776, the provincial congress at Halifax adopted a State constitution which immediately went into effect, with Richard Caswell as governor. The delegates from this state signed the Declaration of Independence and the Articles of Confederation. In 1786 the General Assembly elected delegates to the Federal Constitutional Convention and its delegates present signed the Constitution; but the General Assembly did not ratify it until 21 November, 1789, after the Federal Government had been organized and gone into operation. During the Revolution the state furnished the Continental army with 22,910 men. Important battles were fought at Guilford Court House (between Green and Cornwallis, 15 March, 1781), Alamance, Moore's Creek, Ramsour's Mill, and King's Mountain on the state line. There was a predominant Union sentiment in North Carolina in the early part of 1861; and at an election held 28 February, the people voted against calling a convention for the purpose of secession; but after the firing on Fort Sumter and the actual beginning of the war, a convention, called by the Legislature without submission to the people, met on 20 May, 1861, passed an ordinance of secession, and ratified the Confederate Constitution. Fort Fisher was the only important battle fought in the state. The State sent 125,000 soldiers into the Civil War, the largest number sent by any southern state. In 1865 a provisional government was organized by President Johnson, and later the state came under the Reconstruction Act passed by Congress, 2 March, 1867. On 11 July, 1868, the state government was restored by proclamation of the president.

The Constitution of 1776 had some remarkable provisions. It allowed free negroes to vote because they were "freemen", all slaves, of course, being disfranchised because in law they were considered chattels. Any freeman could vote for the members of the House of Commons; but must own fifty acres of land to vote for a senator, who must himself own at least three hundred acres, and a member at least one hundred acres. The governor must own a freehold of five thousand dollars in value. The borough towns of Edenton, New Bern, Wilmington, Salisbury, Hillsboro, and Halifax were each allowed a separate member in the House of Commons apart from the counties. It declared: "That all men have a natural and inalienable right to worship Almighty God, according to the dictates of their own conscience"; but that no person who denied the truth of the Protestant religion should hold any civil office of trust or profit. No clergyman or preacher of any denomination should be a member of either house of the Legislature while continuing in the exercise of his pastoral functions. All of these provisions, except the declaration of religious freedom, have since been abandoned. The Convention of 1835 adopted many amendments, ratified in 1836; among others, all persons of negro blood to the fourth generation were disfranchised; and the Protestant qualification for office omitted. The Constitution of 1868 restored negro suffrage, but in 1900 amendments, adopted by the Legislature and ratified by the people, provided that every qualified voter should have paid his poll tax and be able to read and write any section of the Constitution; but that any person entitled to vote on or prior to 1 January, 1867, or his lineal descendant, might register on a permanent roll until 1 November, 1908. This is called the "Grandfather Clause".

EDUCATION.—In early times there were no schools; private teachers furnishing the only means of education. Beginning about 1760, several private classical schools were established in different parts of the state, the most prominent being Queen's College at Charlotte, subsequently called Liberty Hall. The State University was opened for students in February, 1795; but want of means and a scattered population prevented any public school system until long after the Revolution. The Civil War seriously interfered with all forms of education; but the entire educational system is now in a high state of efficiency. The following are under State control, but receive aid from tuition fees and donations: the State University, situated at Chapel Hill, endowment, $250,000; total income, $160,000; annual State appropriation, $75,000; faculty, 101; students, 821; the North Carolina State Normal and Industrial College for women at Greensboro, founded in 1891, buildings, 13; annual State appropriation, $75,000; faculty, 63; students, 613; North Carolina College of Agricultural and Mechanic Arts at West Raleigh, opened in 1889, annual State appropriation, $37,000; annual Federal appropriation, $49,450; faculty, 42; students, 446; the Agricultural and Mechanical College for the coloured race at Greensboro, annual State appropriation, $10,000; annual Federal appropriation, $11,550; faculty, 14; students, 173. A training school for white teachers has just been established at Greenville. There are three State Normal Schools for the coloured race. The official reports of public schools for the year 1908–9 show a total school population of whites, 490,710; coloured, 236,855; schoolhouses, 7670; white teachers, 8129; coloured teachers, 2828; total available fund, $3,419,103. There are a large number of flourishing denominational colleges both for men and women, several of which belong to the coloured race. Among the State institutions are: a large central penitentiary, three hospitals for insane, three schools for deaf, dumb, and blind, and a tuberculosis sanitarium.

RELIGIOUS CONDITIONS.—Under the lords proprietors there was much religious discrimination and even persecution; but there was little under the Crown except as to holding office and celebrating the rite of matrimony. The disqualification for office involved in denying the truth of the Protestant religion remained in the Constitution until the Convention of 1835. In 1833 William Gaston, a Catholic of great ability and noble character, was elected associate justice of the Supreme Court for life. Regarding the religious disqualification as legally and morally invalid, he promptly took his seat without opposition. While still remaining on the bench, he was elected a delegate to the Constitutional Convention of 1835, and attended its session. His great speech against any religious discrimination was conclusive, and the obnoxious clause was stricken out of the Constitution. Since then there has been no legal discrimination against Catholics. All persons denying the existence of Almighty God have been disqualified from holding office under every constitution. The preamble to the present Constitution recognizes the dependence of the people upon Almighty God, and their gratitude to Him for the existence of their civil, political, and religious liberties. The Legislature is opened with prayer. The law requires the observance of Sunday, and punishes any disturbance of religious congregations. The following are legal holidays: 1 January; 19 January (Lee's birthday); 22 February; 12 April (anniversary of Halifax Resolution); 10 May (Confederate Decoration Day); 20 May (anniversary Mecklenburg Declaration of Independence); 4 July; 1st Monday in September (Labour Day); general election day in November; Thanksgiving; and Christmas. Neither Sundays nor holidays are regarded as *diei non* except in certain limited cases. Religious bodies may become incorporated either under the general law or by special act. If not specifically incorporated they are regarded as quasi corporations, and may exercise many corporate powers. The Protestant Episcopal bishop has been created a corporation sole by special act of the Legislature. All real and personal property used exclusively for religious, charitable, or educational purposes, as also property whose income is so used, is exempt from taxation. Ministers of the Gospel are exempt from jury duty and their private libraries from taxation. The only privileged communications recognized are those between lawyers and their clients, and physicians and their patients. There is no statute allowing this exemption to priests, and therefore they stand as at common law; but there is no recorded instance in which they have ever been asked to reveal the secrets of the confessional.

MARRIAGE AND DIVORCE.—Originally in this colony legally valid marriages could be solemnized only by ministers of the Church of England, of whom there were few, nearly all in the eastern part of the colony. In 1715 this power was conferred upon the governor; in 1741 upon justices of the peace; in 1766 upon ministers of the Presbyterian Church, and finally in 1778 upon the ministers of all denominations. The ceremony can now be performed by an ordained minister of any religious denomination or a justice of the peace; and the peculiar marriage custom of the Friends is recognized as valid. Males under sixteen and females under fourteen are legally incapable of marriage, and all marriages of those related by consanguinity closer than the degree of first cousin, and between whites and negroes or Indians are void. A marriage licence is required, and the Registrar is forbidden by law to issue licences for the marriage of any one under eighteen years of age without written consent of the parent or one standing *in loco parentis*. Absolute divorce (*a vinculo*) may be granted for the following causes: pre-existing natural and continued impotence of either party; if they shall have lived separate and apart continuously for ten years, and have no children; adultery by the wife, or pregnancy at the time of marriage unknown to husband and not by him; continued fornication and adultery by the husband. Either party may remarry, but no alimony is allowed. Divorce *a mensa et toro* may be granted with alimony for the following causes: if either party shall abandon his or her family, or turn the other out of doors, or shall by cruel and barbarous treatment endanger the life of the other, or shall offer such indignities to the person of the other as to make his or her life intolerable, or shall become an habitual drunkard. Upon such a divorce parties cannot remarry.

Bequests for charitable purposes must be clearly defined, as the *cy-près* doctrine is not recognized; and there must be some one capable of taking the bequest. Whether a bequest for Masses would be specifically enforced by the courts, has not been decided; but it is not probable that it would be interfered with, as the courts have never invoked the doctrine of Superstitious Uses. Cemeteries are provided for and protected by law. In administering oaths, the party sworn must "lay his hand upon the Holy Evangelists of Almighty God"; but those having conscientious scruples may appeal to God with uplifted hand; and "Quakers, Moravians, Dunkers, and Mennonites" may affirm.

PROHIBITION.—For many years prohibition sentiment has been growing until it culminated, in 1908, in the passage by the General Assembly of an act making it unlawful to make or sell any spirituous, vinous, fermented, or malt liquors within the state, except for sacramental purposes, or by a registered pharmacist on a physician's prescription. Native ciders may be sold without restriction; and native wines at the place of manufacture in sealed or crated packages containing not less than two and a half gallons each, which must not be opened on the premises.

RELIGIOUS STATISTICS
(From the Census of Religious Bodies, 1906)

Denomination	No. of Organizations	No. of Members	No. of Church Edifices	Value of Church Prop.
All denominations	8592	824,385	8188	$14,053,505
Baptist, white	2397	235,540	2305	3,056,889
Baptist, col.	1358	165,503	1192	1,266,227
Christian	192	15,909	188	194,315
Congregationalists	54	2,699	47	42,361
Disciples	130	13,637	128	151,605
Friends	63	6,752	63	90,525
Lutheran	179	17,740	173	445,525
Methodist, white	2141	191,760	2065	3,523,354
Methodist, col.	954	85,522	925	1,366,238
Presbyter. and Refor.	655	60,555	656	2,247,923
Protestant Episcopal	258	13,890	261	987,925
Roman Catholic	31	3,981	35	375,360
All other	180	10,897	150	305,258

In the above, the Catholic population was reduced by deducting 15 per cent for children under nine years of age.

NORTH CAROLINA, VICARIATE APOSTOLIC OF, was canonically established and separated from the Diocese of Charleston, South Carolina by Bull, 3 March, 1868, with James (now Cardinal) Gibbons as first vicar. It comprised the entire state until 1910, when eight counties were attached to Belmont Abbey. The latest statistics, for the entire state, show secular priests, 17; religious, 16; churches, 15; missions, 34; stations, 47; chapels, 5; Catholics, 5870. The Apostolate Company, a corporation of secular priests at Nazareth, maintains a boys' orphanage and industrial school, and publishes "Truth", a monthly periodical. There is a girls' school and sanatorium at Asheville, and hospitals at Charlotte (Sisters of Mercy) and Greensboro (Sisters of Charity). There are parochial schools at Asheville, Charlotte, Salisbury, Durham, Newton Grove, Raleigh, and Wilmington. The vicariate is subject to the Propaganda, and its present vicar is the Abbot Ordinary of Belmont.

Belmont Cathedral Abbey.—By Bull of Pius X, 8 June, 1910, the Counties of Gaston, Lincoln, Cleveland, Rutherford, Polk, Burke, McDowell, and Catawba were cut off from the vicariate to form the diocese of the Cathedral Abbey at Belmont, canonically erected by Mgr Diomede Falconio, Apostolic Delegate in the United States, on 18 October, 1910. The vicariate remains under the administration of the abbot ordinary at Belmont until a diocese can be formed in the state. Belmont Abbey, situated in Gaston County, was erected into an abbey by Papal Brief dated 19 December, 1884, its first abbot being Rt. Rev. Leo Haid. He was born at Latrobe, Pennsylvania, 15 July, 1849, ordained priest in 1872, and served as chaplain and professor in St. Vincent's Abbey until 1885. Appointed Vicar Apostolic of North Carolina in 1887, he was consecrated titular Bishop of Messene 1 July,

1888. The abbey itself has many extra-territorial dependencies, i. e. military colleges in Savannah, Georgia and Richmond, Virginia, and parishes in both of these cities, besides various missions in the state itself; and forms legal corporations in Virginia, North Carolina, and Georgia. To it also is attached a college for secular education and a seminary for the secular and regular clergy. To the abbey proper belong 32 priests, 2 deacons, 6 clerics in minor orders, and 37 lay brothers. At Belmont is also a college for the higher education of women under the Sisters of Mercy, with 60 pupils, an orphanage for girls and a preparatory school for little boys.

Prominent Catholics.—Though there are few Catholics in the state, an unusual proportion have occupied prominent official positions. Thomas Burke was governor, and William Gaston, M. E. Manly, and R. M. Douglas were associate justices of the Supreme Court. R. R. Heath, W. A. Moore, and W. S. O'B. Robinson were Superior Court judges, and R. D. Douglas attorney general. Prominent benefactors were Dr. D. O'Donaghue, Lawrence Brown, and Raphael Guasterino. Mrs. Francis C. Tiernan (Christian Reid) is a native of North Carolina.

SHEA, *Hist. of the Catholic Church* (New York, 1892); O'CONNELL, *Catholicity in the Carolinas and Georgia* (New York, 1879); *Official Catholic Directory* (New York, 1910); *Pub. of U. S. Bureaus of Census and Education; Ann. Rep. of State Officers* (Raleigh); BANCROFT, *Hist. of U. S.* (Boston, 1879); LAWSON, *Hist. of Carolina* (London, 1714; Raleigh, 1860); BRICKELL, *Natural Hist. of N. C.* (Dublin, 1737); WILLIAMSON, *Hist. of N. C.* (Philadelphia, 1812); MARTIN, *Hist. of N. C.* (New Orleans, 1829); WHEELER, *Hist. of N. C.* (Philadelphia, 1851); HAWKS, *Hist. of N. C.* (Fayetteville, N. C., 1857); MOORE, *Hist. of N. C.* (Raleigh, 1880); FOOTE, *Sketches of N. C.* (New York, 1846); REICHEL, *Hist. of the Moravians in N. C.* (Salem, N. C., 1857); BERNHEIM, *Hist. of the German Settlements in N. C.* (Philadelphia, 1872); CARUTHERS, *The Old North State in 1776* (Philadelphia, 1884); IDEM, *Life of Rev. David Caldwell* (Greensboro, N. C., 1842); HUNTER, *Sketches of Western N. C.* (Raleigh, 1877); VASS, *Eastern N. C.* (Richmond, Va., 1886); WHEELER, *Reminiscences and Memoirs of N. C.* (Columbus, Ohio, 1884); COTTON, *Life of Macon* (Baltimore, 1840); RUMPLE, *Hist. of Rowan County* (Salisbury, N. C., 1881); SCHENCK, *N. C.* (Raleigh, 1889); ASHE, *Hist. of N. C.* (Greensboro, N. C., 1908); BATTLE, *Hist. of the Univ. of N. C.* (Raleigh, 1907); ASHE, *Biog. Hist. of N. C.* (Greensboro, 1905); CLARK, *N. C. Regiments 1861–5* (Raleigh, 1901); CONNER, *Story of the Old North State* (Philadelphia, 1906); HILL, *Young People's Hist. of N. C.* (Charlotte, N. C., 1907); HAYWOOD, *Gov. Tryon* (Raleigh, 1903); JONES, *Defense of Revolutionary Hist. of N. C.* (Boston and Raleigh, 1834); *Pub. of N. C. Hist. Commission* (Raleigh, 1900–10); SMITH, *Hist. of Education in N. C.* (Govt. Printing Office, 1888); TARLETON, *Hist. of the Campaign of 1780–1* (London, 1787); *Princeton College during the Eighteenth Century* (New York, 1872); DE BOW, *Industrial Resources of the South and West* (New Orleans, 1852); POORE, *Constitutions, Colonial Charters and Organic Laws of the U. S.*, II (Govt. Printing Office, 1878), 1379; *Colonial and State Records of N. C.* (25 vols., 1886–1906); *Public Laws of N. C.*; *The Code of 1883*; *The Revisal of 1905* (published by State, Raleigh); CLARK, *The Supreme Court of N. C.* (Green Bag, Oct., Nov., Dec., 1892). There is also a large mass of valuable historical matter in magazine articles and published addresses both before and since 1895; see WEEKS, *Bibl. of the Hist. Lit. of N. C.* (issued by Library of Harvard Univ., 1895).

ROBERT M. DOUGLAS.

Northcote, JAMES SPENCER, b. at Feniton Court, Devonshire, 26 May, 1821; d. at Stoke-upon-Trent, Staffordshire, 3 March, 1907. He was the second son of George Barons Northcote, a gentleman of an ancient Devonshire family of Norman descent. Educated first at Ilmington Grammar School, he won in 1837 a scholarship at Corpus Christi College, Oxford, where he came under Newman's influence. In 1841 he became B.A., and in the following year married his cousin, Susannah Spencer Ruscombe Poole. Taking Anglican Orders in 1844 he accepted a curacy at Ilfracombe; but when his wife was received into the Catholic Church in 1845, he resigned his office. In 1846 he himself was converted, being received at Prior Park College, where he continued as a master for some time. From June, 1852, until September, 1854, he acted as editor of the "Rambler", and about the same time helped to edit the well-known "Clifton Tracts". After his wife's death in 1853 he devoted himself to preparation for the priesthood, first under Newman at Edgbaston, then at the Collegio Pio, Rome. On 29 July, 1855, he was ordained priest at Stone, where his daughter had entered the novitiate. He returned to Rome to complete his ecclesiastical studies, also acquiring the profound erudition in Christian antiquities which was later to be enshrined in his great work "Roma Sotterranea". In 1857 he was appointed to the mission of Stoke-upon-Trent, which he served until 1860, when he was called to Oscott College as vice-president, and six months later became president. Under his rule, which lasted for seventeen years, the college entered on an unprecedented degree of prosperity, and his influence on education was felt far outside the walls of Oscott. Failing health caused him to resign in 1876, and he returned to the mission, first at Stone (1878), and then at Stoke-upon-Trent (1881), where he spent the rest of his life revered by all for his learning, his noble character, and his sanctity. During the last twenty years of his life he suffered from creeping paralysis, which slowly deprived him of all bodily motion, though leaving his mind intact. He had been made a canon of the Diocese of Birmingham in 1861, canon-theologian in 1862, and provost in 1885. In 1861 the pope conferred on him the doctorate in divinity. Dr. Northcote's wide scholarship is witnessed to by many works, chief among which is "Roma Sotterranea", the great work on the Catacombs, written in conjunction with William R. Brownlow, afterwards Bishop of Clifton. This work has been translated into French and German; and it won for its authors recognition as being among the greatest living authorities on the subject. Other works were: "The Fourfold Difficulty of Anglicanism" (Derby, 1846); "A Pilgrimage to La Salette" (London, 1852); "Roman Catacombs" (London, 1857); "Mary in the Gospels" (London, 1867); "Celebrated Sanctuaries of the Madonna" (London, 1868); "A Visit to the Roman Catacombs" (London, 1877); "Epitaphs of the Catacombs" (London, 1878).

BARRY, *The Lord my Light* (funeral sermon, privately printed, 1907); *Memoir of the Very Rev. Canon Northcote* in *The Oscotian* (July, 1907); *Report of the case of Fitzgerald v. Northcote* (London, 1866).

EDWIN BURTON.

North Dakota, one of the United States of America, originally included in the Louisiana Purchase. Little was known of the region prior to the expedition of Lewis and Clark, who spent the winter of 1804–5 about thirty miles north-west of Bismarck. In 1811 the Astor expedition encountered a band of Sioux near the boundary of North and South Dakota on the Missouri. Settlement was long delayed on account of the numerous Indian wars, and the land was practically given up to hunters and trappers. In 1849 all that part of Dakota east of the Missouri and White Earth Rivers was made part of the Territory of Minnesota, and in 1854 all to the west of the said rivers was included in the Territory of Nebraska. Finally, 2 March, 1861, President Buchanan signed the bill creating the Territory of North Dakota, with Dr. William Jayne of Springfield, Ill., as first governor; and on 2 November, 1889, the State of North Dakota was formed. North Dakota is bounded on the north by Saskatchewan and Manitoba, on the south by South Dakota, on the east by Minnesota (the Red River dividing), and on the west by Montana. The surface is chiefly rolling prairie, with an elevation of from eight hundred to nine hundred feet in the Red

SEAL OF NORTH DAKOTA

River valley, from thirteen hundred to fifteen hundred feet in the Devil's Lake region and from two thousand to twenty-eight hundred feet west of Minot. The chief rivers are the Missouri, Red, Sheyenne, James, Mouse, and their tributaries. The state forms a rectangle, measuring approximately two hundred and fourteen miles from north to south and three hundred and thirty from east to west, and has an area of 70,795 square miles, of which 650 is water. The population (1910) was 577,056, an increase of 82.8 per cent. since 1900.

Resources.—Agriculture.—The number of farms in the state in 1910 was 64,442, number of acres in cultivation over 13 millions. Wheat is the dominant crop, the Red River Valley being perhaps the most famous wheat-producing region in the world. Oats flax, and barley are also produced in large quantities. The prairies offer fine ranching ground and the state has 1,315,870 head of live stock. Her forests aggregate 95,918 acres; there are 135,150 cultivated fruit trees, and 2381 acres of berries. Besides many natural groves, very rich in wild small fruit, there are a vast number of cultivated farm groves, and some fine nurseries, the largest of which is near Devil's Lake and consists of about 400 acres.

Mining.—In the western part of the state, North Dakota has a coal supply greater than that of any other state in the Union; coal is mined at Minot, Burlington, Kenmare, Ray, Dickinson, Dunseith, and other places; the supply is cheap and inexhaustible for fuel, gas, electricity, and power. In 1908 there were 88 mines in operation and 289,435 tons mined. Clays for pottery, fire and pressed brick abound in Stark, Dunn, Mercer, Morton, Hettinger, and Billings counties. Cement is found in Cavalier County on the border of Pembina. The artesian basin is in North Dakota sandstone at the base of the upper cretacean, at a depth of from eight hundred feet in the south-east to fifteen hundred feet at Devil's Lake. Good common brick clay may be found practically all over the state from deposits in the glacial lakes. North Dakota has 5012 miles of railroad, and four main lines cross the state. There is direct railway communication with Winnipeg, Brandon, and other points on the Canadian Pacific.

Matters Affecting Religion.—North Dakota is a code State. The civil and criminal codes prepared by the New York commission but not then adopted by that State, were adopted by Dakota Territory in 1865; a probate code was adopted the same year, and thus the Territory of Dakota was the first English-speaking community to adopt a codification of its substantive law. The territorial laws, compiled in 1887, were revised by the State in 1895, 1899, and 1905. Section 4, Article 1 of the State Constitution provides: "The free exercise and enjoyment of religious profession and worship, without discrimination or preference, shall be forever guaranteed in this State, and no person shall be rendered incompetent to be a witness or juror on account of his opinion on matters of religious belief; but the liberty of conscience hereby secured shall not be so construed as to excuse acts of licentiousness, or justify practices inconsistent with the peace or safety of this State." The statute makes it a misdemeanour to prevent the free exercise of religious worship and belief, or to compel by threats or violence any particular form of worship, or to disturb a religious assemblage by profane discourse, indecent acts, unnecessary noise, selling liquor, keeping open huckster shops, or exhibiting plays without licence, within a mile of such assemblages. Servile labour (except works of necessity or charity) is forbidden on Sunday; also public sports, trades, manufactures, mechanical employment, and public traffic (except that meats, milk, and fish may be sold before nine A. M., also food to be eaten on premises. Drugs, medicines, and surgical appliances may be sold at any time). Service of process except in criminal cases is prohibited on Sunday. A person uniformly keeping another day of the week as holy time, may labour on Sunday, provided he do not interrupt or disturb other persons in observing the first day of the week. The fine for Sabbath-breaking is not less than one dollar or more than ten dollars for each offence. It is a misdemeanour to serve civil process on Saturday on a person who keeps that day as the Sabbath.

Oaths.—Section 533 of the code of 1905, amended 1909, provides: "The following officers are authorized to administer oaths: each judge of the supreme court and his deputy, clerks of the district court, clerks of the county court with increased jurisdiction, county auditors and registers of deeds and their deputies within their respective counties, county commissioners within their respective counties, judges of the county court, public administrators within their respective counties, justices of the peace within their respective counties, notaries public anywhere in the State upon complying with the provisions of sections 545 and 546, city clerks or auditors, township clerks and village recorders within their respective cities, townships, and villages; each sheriff and his deputy within their respective counties in the cases provided by law; other officers in the cases especially provided by law". It is a misdemeanour to take, or for an officer to administer, an extra-judicial oath, except where the same is required by the provisions of some contract as the basis or proof of claim, or is agreed to be received by some person as proof of any fact in the performance of any contract, obligation or duty instead of other evidence. Blasphemy consists in wantonly uttering or publishing words, reproaches, or profane words against God, Jesus Christ, the Holy Ghost, the Holy Scripture, or the Christian religion. Profane swearing consists in any use of the name of God, Jesus Christ, or the Holy Ghost, either in imprecating Divine vengeance upon the utterer or any other person, in a light, trifling, or irreverent speech. Blasphemy is a misdemeanour, and profane swearing is punishable by a fine of one dollar for each offence. Obscenity in a public place or in the presence of females, or of children under ten years of age is a misdemeanour.

Exemptions from Taxation.—"All public school houses, academies, colleges, institutions of learning, with the books and furniture therein and grounds attached to such buildings, necessary for their proper occupancy and use, not to exceed forty acres in area and not leased or otherwise used with a view to profit; also all houses used exclusively for public worship and lots and parts of lots upon which such houses are erected; all land used exclusively for burying grounds or for a cemetery; all buildings and contents thereof used for public charity, including public hospitals under the control of religious or charitable societies used wholly or in part for public charity, together with the land actually occupied by such institutions, not leased or otherwise used with a view to profit, and all moneys and credits appropriated solely to sustaining and belonging exclusively to such institutions, are exempt from taxation." All churches, parsonages, and usual outbuildings, and grounds not exceeding one acre on which the same are situated, whether on one or more tracts, also all personal property of religious corporations, used for religious purposes, are exempt.

Matters Affecting Religious Work.—The law provides for corporations for religious, educational, benevolent, charitable, or scientific purposes, giving to such corporations power to acquire property, real and personal, by purchase, devise, or bequest and hold the same and sell or mortgage it according to the by-laws or a majority of votes of the members. Catholic church corporations, according to diocesan statutes, consist of the bishop, vicar-general, local pastor, and two trustees. No corporation or association for religious purposes shall acquire or hold real estate of greater value than $200,000 (laws of 1909). Charitable trusts are favoured if conformable to the statute against perpetuities, which forbids suspension of power or of alienations for a longer period than the lives of persons in being at the creation of condition (Hager vs. Sacrison, 123 N. W. Rep., 518). Cemetery corporation may be formed with powers of regulation. The net proceeds must go to protect and improve the grounds and not to the profit of the corporation or members. Interment lot inalienable, but any heir may release to another heir. Cemetery grounds are exempt from all process, lien, and public burdens and uses.

Marriage and Divorce.—Any unmarried male of the age of eighteen or upwards and any unmarried female of the age of fifteen or upwards, not otherwise disqualified, are capable of consenting to marriage, but if the male is under twenty-one or the female under eighteen, the licence shall not be issued without the consent of parents or guardian, if there be any. Marriages between parents and children including grandparents and grandchildren, between brothers and sisters, of half or whole blood, uncles and nieces, aunts and nephews, or cousins of the first degree of half or whole blood, are declared incestuous and absolutely void, and this applies to illegitimate as well as legitimate children and relations. A marriage contracted by a person having a former husband or wife, if the former marriage has not been annulled or dissolved, is illegal and void from the beginning, unless the former husband or wife was absent and believed by such person to be dead for five years immediately proceeding. Judges of all courts of record and justices of the peace, within their jurisdiction, "ordained ministers of the Gospel", and "priests of every church" may perform the marriage ceremony. The form used by Friends or Quakers is also valid. Licences, issued by the county judge of the county where one of the contracting parties resides, must be obtained and the persons performing the ceremony must file the certificate thereof, and such licence with the county judge within thirty days after the marriage, such certificate to be signed by two witnesses and the person performing the ceremony. Indians contracting marriage according to Indian custom and co-habiting as man and wife, are deemed legally married. All marriages contracted outside of the State and valid by the laws of the State where contracted, are deemed valid in this State. The original certificate and certified copy thereof are evidences of marriage in all courts. Marriages may be annulled for any of the following causes existing at the time: (1) if the person seeking annulment was under the age of legal consent, and such marriage was contracted without the consent of parent or guardian, unless after attaining the age of consent, they lived together as husband and wife; (2) when former husband or wife of either party was living and former marriage then in force; (3) when either party was of unsound mind unless after coming to reason the parties lived together as husband and wife; (4) when consent was obtained by fraud, unless after full knowledge of facts the party defrauded continued to live with the other in marriage relation; (5) when consent was obtained by force, unless afterwards they lived freely together; (6) incapacity.

Actions for annulment where former husband or wife is living, and where party is of unsound mind, may be brought at any time before the death of either party. Actions for annulment for other causes must be brought by the party injured within four years after arriving at age of consent or by parent or guardian before such time, also for fraud within four years after discovery. When a marriage is annulled children begotten before the judgment are legitimate and succeed to the estate of both parents. Marriages between white persons and coloured persons of one eighth or more negro blood are null and void by Act of 1907, and severe penalty is provided against parties, officials, and clergy for violation of the law. Divorce may be granted for (1) adultery, (2) extreme cruelty, (3) wilful desertion, (4) wilful neglect, (5) habitual intemperance, (6) conviction of felony. Neither party to a divorce may marry within three months after decree is granted. Wilful desertion, wilful neglect, or habitual intemperance must continue for one year before it is a cause for divorce. As to proof in divorce cases the Statute provides that no divorce can be granted on default of the defendant or upon the uncorroborated statement, admission, or testimony of parties, or upon any statement or finding of facts made by referee, but the court must in addition to any statement or finding of referee, require proof of facts alleged. The court has held that the fact of marriage alleged in complaint may be admitted in answer without other corroboration. The restriction as to corroboration applies to testimony, not to pleading, and is intended to prevent collusive divorce. This statute is more restrictive as to proof than the proposed resolution, No. 13, of proceedings of the National Congress on Uniform Divorce which reads: "A decree should not be granted unless the cause is shown by affirmative proof, aside from any admissions on the part of the respondent." A residence of one year in the State is required for the plaintiff in an action of divorce. Dower and Curtesy are abolished, and a deed of the homestead must be signed by both the husband and wife. Labour of children under fourteen years of age is prohibited, and stringent rules provide for regulation of those under sixteen, and no woman under eighteen years of age may be compelled to work over ten hours; age of consent is eighteen years.

Wills.—A woman is of age at eighteen, and any person of sound mind may, on arriving at that age, dispose of his or her real and personal property by will. A married woman may will her property without the consent of her husband. A *nuncupative* will is limited to $1000, and to cases where the testator is in military service in the field, or on board ship, and anticipates death, or where death is anticipated from a wound received that day. There must be two witnesses who are requested by the testator to act as such. An olographic will is one dated, written, and signed by the hand of the testator, and requires no other formalities. Other wills must be executed by the testator in presence of two witnesses, who in his presence and in the presence of each other, subscribe as witnesses.

Education.—The educational system in North Dakota is on a broad basis. Sections 16 and 36 of each Congressional township are given to the common schools by Congress, also 5 per cent of the net proceeds of the sale of public lands subsequent to admission, to be used as a permanent fund for schools, interest only to be expended for support of common schools. The enabling act also gives 72 sections for university purposes, to be sold for not less than ten dollars per acre, proceeds to constitute a permanent fund, interest only to be expended. Also 90,000 acres for the Agricultural College, 40,000 acres each for the School of Mines, Reform School, Deaf and Dumb School, Agricultural College, State University, two State Normal Schools; 50,000 acres for capital buildings and 170,000 acres for such other educational and charitable institutions as the legislature may determine. No part of the school fund may be used for support of any sectarian or denominational school, college, or university. The Normal Schools are located at Mayville and Valley City, the Industrial Training School at Ellendale, the School of Forestry at Bottineau, the Agricultural College at Fargo, the State University (Arts, Law, Engineering, Model High School, State School of Mines, Public Health Laboratory and

Graduate Departments) at Grand Forks; number of professors, instructors, and assistants, 68; lecturers, 13; students, 1000. Charitable institutions are the Deaf and Dumb School at Devil's Lake, the Hospital for Feeble Minded at Grafton, the Insane Asylum at Jamestown, the School for the Blind at Bathgate, the Soldiers' Home at Lisbon, the Reform School at Mandan. The permanent school and institutional fund amounted to about $18,000,000 in 1908; the apportionment from that fund in 1903 was $274,348.80; in 1908, $545,814.66. Ample provisions are made for State and county institutes, and teachers are required to attend. Third Grade Certificates are abolished. The minimum salary for teachers is $45 a month. Provisions are made for the extension of the High School system, and also for consolidated schools and transportation of children to the same. The legislative appropriation in 1909 for the university was $181,000.

Prisons and Reformatories.—The keeper of each prison is required to provide at the expense of the county for each prisoner who may be able and desires to read, a copy of the Bible or New Testament to be used by the prisoner at seasonable and proper times during his confinement, and any minister of the Gospel is permitted access to such prisoners at seasonable and proper times to perform and instruct prisoners in their moral and religious duties. Suitable provisions are made for reduction of time for good behaviour, for indeterminate sentences, and paroling prisoners.

Sale of Liquor.—The manufacture, importation, sale, gift, barter, or trade of intoxicating liquors by any person, association, or corporation as a beverage, is prohibited by Article 20 of the State constitution and by statute. Exceptions are made in favour of sale in limited quantities on affidavit of applicant by druggists for medicinal, mechanical, scientific, and sacramental purposes, under permit granted at the discretion of the district court. Not more than one-half pint may be sold to any one in one day and the purchaser must sign affidavit stating the particular disease for which the same is required. Sales to minors, habitual drunkards, and persons whose relatives forbid, are prohibited. Places where intoxicating liquors are sold or kept for sale or where persons are permitted to resort for purpose of drinking intoxicating liquors are declared to be common nuisances. The keeper is liable criminally and in an action the nuisance may be abated and the premises closed for one year. The statute also provides for civil liability against persons violating the law, in favour of those taking charge of and providing for intoxicated persons, and in favour of every wife, child, parent, guardian, employer, or other person injured in person or property or means of support by any intoxicated person.

Statistics of the Protestant Churches.—The *Episcopalian* Church has 4664 members; 1224 families; 97 Sunday School teachers; 741 pupils; 42 churches and chapels; 5410 sittings; 16 rectories; 795 members in guilds. The value of the churches, chapels, and grounds is $158,055; rectories $49,000; other property $42,850. There are 6 parishes; 36 organized missions; and 44 unorganized missions. Total offerings for all purposes for the year ending 1 June, 1910, were $32,496.28. The *Methodist Episcopal* Church had in the State in 1908, 223 church buildings valued at $600,000, and 101 parsonages valued at $150,000, with a membership of about 11,000. The most important fact in connexion with this organization is the affiliation of Wesley College with the State university, where the Methodists aim to give religious and other instruction in their own buildings and arrange for their pupils to get the benefit of secular instruction at the State university. The plan suggests a possible solution of the much vexed question of division of the school fund. The *Presbyterian* Church has 7 presbyteries; 175 ministers; 7185 members, 9411 Sunday School members. They contributed for all purposes in the past year $150,635. There are 185 church organizations; 50 preaching stations; 132 church buildings, and 62 manses. Value of church manses and educational property was estimated at $800,000 in 1908. This denomination has recently located at Jamestown, the Presbyterian university, said to have an endowment fund of about $200,000. The *Lutheran* Church is composed chiefly of Norwegians and other Scandinavians. According to the "Norwegian American", published in Norwegian at Minneapolis in 1907, there were in the State in 1905, of Norwegian birth and descent, 140,000. The Lutheran church had 380 congregations, and about 240 churches. The *Baptist* Church in 1908 had a membership of 4161, a Sunday School enrollment of 3164; 53 churches, valued at $191,430; and 28 parsonages valued at $35,772.

Ecclesiastical History.—The establishment of Catholic missions in North Dakota cannot be reliably traced to an earlier date than 1818. In that year Rt. Rev. J. Octave Plessis of Quebec sent Rev. Joseph Provencher and Rev. Josef Severe Dumoulin to Fort Douglas, as St. Boniface was then called, and after the grasshoppers had destroyed the crops, the Selkirk colonists went in large numbers to Pembina. Father Provencher sent Father Dumoulin in September, 1818, to minister to the spiritual wants of the colonists, with instructions to spend the winter at Pembina. When that place was found to be within the United States, Father Dumoulin was recalled. Rev. George Anthony Belcourt became the second resident priest of North Dakota. A gifted linguist, well versed in the Algonquin languages which included the Chippewa, he taught the latter to the young missionaries and composed an Indian grammar and dictionary, still standard works. He was resident priest from 1831-8 and often said Mass in every camping place from Lake Traverse to Pembina and in the interior of North Dakota. It was customary in the summer for the settlers to go to the south-western part of the State to hunt bison on the prairies, and to take their families with them. The priest always accompanied them and in those camps for the first time the children were given an opportunity of religious instruction. Father Belcourt is said to have evangelized the whole of the Turtle Mountain Chippewa, a circumstance which kept that tribe at peace with the government during the Sioux troubles following the Minnesota massacre in 1862. Father De Smet spent a few weeks with the Mandans on the Missouri in 1840 and baptized a number of their children. Father Jean Baptiste Marie Genin is credited with establishing a mission at St. Michael's, Fort Totten, in 1865. His name is honourably and extensively associated with much of the missionary history of the State. The first real missionary work among the Sioux of North Dakota dates from 1874 when Major Forbes (a Catholic), Indian Agent at Fort Totten, with the help of the Catholic Indian Bureau, induced the Sisters of Charity (Grey Nuns) of Montreal under Sr. Mary Clapin to establish themselves in his agency. Father Bonnin came as their chaplain. Rev. Claude Ebner, O.S.B., was stationed at Fort Totten, 1877-86. Rev. Jerome Hunt, O.S.B., has devoted his talent and zeal to the welfare of the Indians at Fort Totten Reservation since 1882, and has written and published in the Sioux language, a Bible history, prayerbook with instruction and hymns, and a smaller book of prayer, and for eighteen years has published an Indian paper in Sioux. The Grey Nuns at Fort Totten have conducted a school since 1874.

Rt. Rev. Martin Marty, O.S.B., was Vicar Apostolic of Dakota until 27 December, 1889, when Rt. Rev. John Shanley became Bishop of Jamestown; the see was later changed to Fargo. The number of churches increased from 40 in 1890 to 210 in 1908.

After the death of Bishop Shanley, the diocese was divided. Rt. Rev. James O'Reilly, as Bishop of Fargo, has charge of the eastern part, and Rt. Rev. Vincent Wehrle, O.S.B., rules over the western part as Bishop of Bismarck. According to the census of 1907, the Catholic population was 70,000 but a subsequent count shows the number much larger, and the latest estimate by Father O'Driscoll, secretary of the Fargo diocese, places it at about 90,000. There are in the two dioceses, 140 priests; 14 religious houses; 1 monastery; 7 academies; 5 hospitals; and about 250 churches. The Sisters of St. Joseph have a hospital at Fargo and one at Grand Forks, and an academy at Jamestown. The Sisters of St. Benedict have establishments at Richardton, Glen Ellen, Oakes, Fort Yates, and a hospital at Bismarck. The Presentation Nuns have an academy and orphanage at Fargo. Sisters of Mary of the Presentation are established at Wild Rice, Oakwood, Willow City, and Lisbon. The Ursuline Sisters conduct St. Bernard's Academy at Grand Forks. Three Sisters of Mercy opened a mission school at Belcourt in the Turtle Mountains among the Chippewa in 1884, and continued to teach until 1907, when their convent was destroyed by fire. They established at Devil's Lake, St. Joseph's hospital in 1895 and the Academy of St. Mary of the Lake in 1908. The State has several active councils of the Knights of Columbus and Courts of the Catholic Order of Foresters. Among the Catholics distinguished in public life are John Burke, three times elected governor; John Carmody, Justice of the Supreme Court; Joseph Kennedy, Dean of the Normal College, State University; W. E. Purcell, U. S. Senator; and P. D. Norton, Secretary of State.

State Hist. Society, I, II (Bismarck, 1906–8); *History and Biography of North Dakota* (Chicago, 1900); IRVING, *Astoria* (New York); WILLARD, *Story of the Prairies* (Chicago, 1903); *North Dakota Blue Books* (Bismarck, 1899–1909); *North Dakota Magazines*, pub. by Comm. of Agriculture (Bismarck, 1908); *Catholic Almanac* (1910); *Journal of the 26th Annual Convocation of the Episcopalian Church* (Fargo, 1910); *10th Biennial Report of Supt. Pub. Instruction* (Bismarck, 1908); *Minutes of Gen. Assembly of Presbyterian Church* (Philadelphia, 1910); LARNED, *Reference Digest; New American Ency.* (1876); *Norwegian American* in Norwegian (Minneapolis, 1907); CLAPP, *Clays of North Dakota* in *Economic Geology*, II, no. 6 (Sept. and Oct., 1907); *North Dakota Codes* (1905); *Session Laws* (1907–9); ROOSEVELT, *Winning of the West*, IV (New York, 1889–96); *University Catalogue* (1910); *The Bulletin*, a diocesan publication (Fargo, March and May, 1909).

M. H. BRENNAN.

Northern Missions. See GERMANY, VICARIATE APOSTOLIC OF NORTHERN; DENMARK; NORWAY; SWEDEN.

Northern Territory, PREFECTURE APOSTOLIC OF THE.—The Northern Territory, formerly Alexander Land, is that part of Australia bounded on the north by the ocean, on the south by South Australia, on the east by Queensland and on the west by Western Australia. It thus lies almost entirely within the tropics, and has an area of 523,620 square miles. It is crown land, but was provisionally annexed to South Australia, 6 July, 1863. It is practically uninhabited; the population is roughly estimated at between 25,000 and 30,000, of whom less than a thousand are Europeans, about 4000 Asiatics mostly Chinese, the remainder being aborigines. There are but two towns, Palmerston at Port Darwin, with a population of 600, and Southport on Blackmore River, twenty-four miles south. There is transcontinental telegraphic communication (over 2000 miles) established in 1872, between Palmerston and Adelaide, but railroad communication extends only 146 miles south of the former town, a distance of over 1200 miles from the northern terminal of the railway. There are large navigable rivers in the north, and Port Darwin is probably surpassed in the world as a deep water port by Sydney Harbour alone. The annual rainfall varies from sixty-two inches on the coast, where the climate resembles that of French Cochin China to six inches at Charlotte Waters. Droughts, cattle disease, and the financial crisis of 1891 have combined to retard the development of the country. John McDouall Stuart, the pioneer explorer, and his successors declare that large tracts in the interior are suitable for the cultivation of cotton and the breeding of cattle, while the government officials at Port Darwin have grown spices, fibre plants, maize, and ceara rubber with great success. The crown lands (only 473,278 of the total 334,643,522 acres have been leased) are regulated by the North Territory Crown Lands Act of 1890–1901.

Northern Territory has a varied ecclesiastical history. In 1847, by a decree of the Sacred Congregation (27 May), it was made a diocese (Diocese of Port Victoria and Palmerston), Joseph Serra, O.S.B., consecrated at Rome, 15 August, 1848, being appointed to the see. He, however, was transferred in 1849 before taking possession to Daulia, and nominated coadjutor "cum jure successionis", and temporal administrator of the Diocese of Perth; he retired in 1861 and died in 1886 in Spain. He was succeeded by Mgr Rosendo Salvator, O.S.B., consecrated at Naples on 15 August, 1849, but he was not able to take possession of his see, for in the meantime the whole European population had abandoned the diocese; consequently he returned to the Benedictine Abbey of New Norcia in Western Australia where he resided as abbot *nullius*. Resigning the See of Port Victoria, 1 August, 1888, he was appointed titular Bishop of Adrana, 29 March, 1889. Seven years previously the Jesuits of the Austrian Province were commissioned to establish a mission for the purpose of civilizing and converting the aborigines; about sixteen members of the order devoted themselves to the work and stations were established at Rapid Creek (St. Joseph's), seven miles north-east of Palmerston, Daly River (Holy Rosary) and Serpentine Lagoon (Sacred Heart of Jesus). There were 2 churches, 1 chapel, and 2 mixed schools. In 1891 there were about 260 Catholics in the mission. However the work did not thrive and after about twenty years' labour the Jesuits withdrew, Father John O'Brien, S.J., being the last administrator. On their withdrawal the diocese was administered by Bishop William Kelly of Geraldton. Somewhat later the mission was confided to the Missionaries of the Sacred Heart of Issoudun and established in 1906 as the Prefecture Apostolic of the Northern Territory. Very Rev. Francis Xavier Gsell, M.S.H., b. 30 October, 1872, was elected administrator Apostolic on 23 April, 1906. He resides at Port Darwin. At present there are in the prefecture 3 missionaries, 2 churches, and 1 chapel.

Missiones Catholicæ (Rome, 1907); *Australasian Catholic Directory* (Sydney, 1910); GORDON, *Australasian Handbook for 1891*; BASEDOW, *Anthropological Notes on the North-Western coastal tribes of the Northern Territory of South Australia* in *Trans., Proc. and Reports of the Royal Society of South Australasia*, XXXI (Adelaide, 1907), 1–62; PARSONS, *Historical account of the pastoral and mineral resources of the North Territory of South Australia* in *Proc. of the Royal Geog. Soc. of Australasia, South Australia Branch*, V (Adelaide, 1902), appendix, 1–16; HOLTZE, *Capabilities of the Northern Territory for tropical agriculture* (Adelaide, 1902), appendix, 17–27.

ANDREW A. MACERLEAN.

Northmen, the Scandinavians who, in the ninth and tenth centuries, first ravaged the coasts of Western Europe and its islands and then turned from raiders into settlers. This article will be confined to the history of their exodus.

Tacitus refers to the "Suiones" (Germ., xliv, xlv) living beyond the Baltic as rich in arms and ships and men. But, except for the chance appearance of a small Viking fleet in the Meuse early in the sixth century, nothing more is heard of the Scandinavians until the end of the eighth century, when the forerunners of the exodus appeared as raiders off the English and Scotch coasts. In their broad outlines the political divisions of Scandinavia were much as they are at the present day, except that the Swedes were confined to a narrower territory.

The Finns occupied the northern part of modern Sweden, and the Danes the southern extremity and the eastern shores of the Cattegat, while the Norwegians stretched down the coast of the Skager-Rack, cutting off the Swedes from the Western sea. The inhabitants of these kingdoms bore a general resemblance to the Teutonic peoples, with whom they were connected in race and language. In their social condition and religion they were not unlike the Angles and Saxons of the sixth century. Though we cannot account satisfactorily for the exodus, we may say that it was due generally to the increase of the population, to the breaking down of the old tribal system, and the efforts of the kings, especially of Harold Fairhair, to consolidate their power, and finally to the love of adventure and the discovery that the lands and cities of Western Christendom lay at their mercy.

The Northmen invaded the West in three main streams; the most southerly started from South Norway and Denmark and, passing along the German coast, visited both sides of the Channel, rounded the Breton promontory, and reached the mouths of the Loire and the Garonne. It had an offshoot to the west of England and Ireland and in some cases it was prolonged to the coasts of Spain and Portugal (where Northmen came into contact with Saracen) and even into the Mediterranean and to Italy. The midmost stream crossed from the same region directly to the east and north of England, while the northern stream flowed from Norway westwards to the Orkneys and other islands, and, dividing there, moved on towards Iceland or southwards to Ireland and the Irish Sea. The work of destruction which the first stream of Northmen wrought on the continent is told in words of despair in what is left of the Frankish Chronicles, for the pagan and greedy invaders seem to have singled out the monasteries for attack and must have destroyed most of the records of their own devastation. A Danish fleet appeared off Frisia in 810, and ten years later another reached the mouth of the Loire, but the systematic and persevering assault did not begin till about 835. From that date till the early years of the following century the Viking ships were almost annual visitors to the coasts and river valleys of Germany and Gaul. About 850 they began to establish island strongholds near the mouths of the rivers, where they could winter and store their booty, and to which they could retire on the rare occasions when the Frankish or English kings were able to check their raids. Such were Walcheren at the mouth of the Scheldt, Sheppey at that of the Thames, Oissel in the lower Seine, and Noirmoutier near the Loire. For over seventy years Gaul seemed to lie almost at the mercy of the Danes. Their ravages spread backwards from the coasts and river valleys; they penetrated even to Auvergne. There was little resistance whether from king or count. Robert the Strong did, indeed, succeed in defending Paris and so laid the foundations of what was afterwards the house of Capet, but he was killed in 866. In the end the success of the Danes brought this period of destruction to a close; the raiders turned into colonists, and in 911 Charles the Simple, by granting Normandy to Rollo, was able to establish a barrier against further invasion. Meanwhile, England had been assailed not only from the Channel and the southwest, but also by Viking ships crossing the North Sea. The Danes for a time had been even more successful than in Gaul, for Northern and Eastern districts fell altogether into their hands and the fate of Wessex seemed to have been decided by a succession of Danish victories in 871. Alfred, however, succeeded in recovering the upper hand, the country was partitioned between Dane and West Saxon, and for a time further raids were stopped by the formation of a fleet and the defeat of Hastings in 893.

To Ireland, too, the Northmen came from two directions, from south and north. It was one of the first countries of the West to suffer, for at the beginning of the ninth century it was the weakest. The Vikings arrived even before 800, and as early as 807 their ships visited the west coast. They were, however, defeated near Killarney in 812 and the full fury of the attack did not fall on the country till 820. Twenty years later there appear to have been three Norse "kingdoms" in Ireland, those of Dublin, Waterford, and Limerick, with an overking, but the Irish won a series of victories, while war broke out between the Danes coming by the Channel and the Norwegians descending from the north. For the next century and a half the Danish wars continued. Neither party gained a distinct advantage and both the face of the country and the national character suffered. Finally in 1014, on Good Friday, at Clontarf, on the shores of Dublin Bay, the Danes suffered a great defeat from Brian Boru. Henceforth they ceased to be an aggressive force in Ireland, though they kept their position in a number of the coast towns.

During the earlier attacks on Ireland the Scotch Islands and especially the Orkneys had become a permanent centre of Norse power and the home of those who had been driven to a life of adventure by the centralization carried out by Harold Fairhair. They even returned to help the king's enemies; to such an extent that about 885 Harold followed up a victory in Norway by taking possession of the Orkneys. The result was that the independent spirits amongst the Vikings pushed on to the Faroes and Iceland, which had been already explored, and established there one of the most remarkable homes of Norse civilization. About a hundred years later the Icelanders founded a colony on the strip of coast between the glaciers and the sea, which, to attract settlers, they called Greenland, and soon after occurred the temporary settlement in Vinland on the mainland of North America. But the prows of the Viking ships were not always turned towards the West. They also followed the Norwegian coast past the North Cape and established trade relations with "Biarmaland" on the shores of the White Sea. The Baltic, however, provided an easier route to the east and in the ninth and tenth centuries it was a Swedish Lake. By the middle of the ninth century a half-mythical Ruric reigned over a Norse or "Varangian" Kingdom at Novgorod and, in 880, one of his successors, Oleg, moved his capital to Kiev, and ruled from the Baltic to the Black Sea. He imposed on Constantinople itself in 907 the humiliation which

Viking Boat, Norway

had befallen so many of the cities of the West, and "Micklegarth" had to pay Danegeld to the Norse sovereign of a Russian army. The Varangian ships are even said to have sailed down the Volga and across the remote waters of the Caspian. There is, however, a second stage of Norse enterprise as remarkable, though for different reasons, as the first. The Norman conquests of Southern Italy and of England and in part the Crusades, in which the Normans took so large a share, prove what the astonishing vitality of the Northmen could do when they had received Christianity and Frankish civilization from the people they had plundered.

It is impossible to account for the irresistible activity of the Northmen. It is a mystery of what might be called "racial personality". Their forces were rarely numerous, their ships small and open, suited to the protected waters of their own coasts, most unsuitable for ocean navigation, and there was no guiding power at home. Their success was due to the indomitable courage of each unit, to a tradition of discipline which made their compact "armies" superior in fighting qualities and activity to the mixed and ill-organized forces which Frankish and English kings usually brought against them. Often they are said to have won a battle by a pretended flight, a dangerous manœuvre except with well-disciplined troops. Until Alfred collected a fleet for the protection of his coast they had the undisputed command of the sea. They were fortunate in the time of their attack. Their serious attacks did not begin till the empire of Charlemagne was weakened from within, and the Teutonic principle of division among heirs was overcoming the Roman principle of unity. When the period of reconstitution began the spirit of discipline, which had given the Northmen success in war, made them one of the great organizing forces of the early Middle Ages. Everywhere these "Romans of the Middle Ages" appear as organizers. They took the various material provided for them in Gaul, England, Russia, Southern Italy, and breathed into it life and activity. But races which assimilate are not enduring, and by the end of the twelfth century the Northmen had finished their work in Europe and been absorbed into the population which they had conquered and governed.

There is no complete history of the Northmen and their work in Europe. KEARY, *Vikings in Western Christendom*, can be consulted with profit; much is to be found in the histories of the countries they attacked, especially in PALGRAVE, *England and Normandy*, I; cf. HELMOLT, *World's History*, VI (London, 1907). The Saga literature is all of a later date and throws little trustworthy light on this early period of Norse history; cf. VIGFUSSON, *Prolegomena to the Sturlunga Saga* (Oxford, 1879).

F. F. URQUHART.

Northrop, HENRY P. See CHARLESTON, DIOCESE OF.

Norton, CHRISTOPHER, martyr; executed at Tyburn, 27 May, 1570. His father was Richard Norton of Norton Conyers, Yorkshire, and his mother, Susan Neville, daughter of Richard, second Baron Latimer. Richard Norton, known as "Old Norton", was the head of his illustrious house, which remained faithful to the Catholic religion. Despite this fact he held positions of influence during the reigns of Henry VIII and Edward VI, was Governor of Norham Castle under Mary, and in 1568–69 was sheriff of Yorkshire. He had been pardoned for joining in the Pilgrimage of Grace, but he and his brother Thomas, his nine sons, of whom Christopher was the seventh, and many of their relatives hastened to take part in the northern uprising of 1569. He was attainted and fled to Flanders with four of his sons, two of his sons were pardoned, another apostatized, Christopher and his father's brother having been captured proved themselves steadfast Catholics, were hanged, disembowelled, and quartered. Edmund, who apostatized, and a sister are the subject of Wordsworth's "White Doe of Rylstone".

SARTEES, *Hist. of Durham*, I, clx; LINGARD, *Hist. of Eng.* (ed. 1849), VI, 195; *Records of English Catholics* I, ii.

BLANCHE M. KELLY.

Norton, JOHN. See PORT AUGUSTA, DIOCESE OF.
Norton, JOHN, VENERABLE. See PALASOR, THOMAS, VENERABLE.

Norway, comprising the smaller division of the Scandinavian peninsula, is bounded on the east by Lapland and Sweden, and on the west by the Atlantic. The surface is generally a plateau from which rise precipitous mountains, as Snähätten (7566 feet) and Stora Galdhöppigen (about 8399 feet). The west coast is deeply indented by fiords. In eastern and southern Norway the valleys are broader and at times form extensive, fruitful plains. There are several navigable rivers, as the Glommen and Vormen, and lakes, of which the largest is Lake Myösen. The numerous islands along the coast, some wooded and some bare, promote shipping and fishing; in the Lofoten Islands alone twenty million cod are annually caught. The climate is only relatively mild, with rain almost daily. Agriculture consists largely in raising oats and barley, but not enough for home consumption. Rye and wheat are grown only in sheltered spots. Bread is commonly made of oats. The cultivation of the potato is widespread, a fact of much importance. There are in the country only about 160,000 horses; these are of a hardy breed. Cattle-raising is an important industry, the number of cattle being estimated at a million, that of sheep and goats at over two millions. Of late attention has been paid to the raising of pigs. The Lapps of the north maintain over a hundred thousand reindeer in the grassy pasture land of the higher plateaus. The most important trees are pine, fir, and birch; oak and beech are not so common.

Forestry was long carried on unscientifically; considerable effort has been made to improve conditions, and wood is now exported chiefly as wrought or partly wrought timber. Silver is mined at Kongsberg, and iron at Röraas, but the yield of minerals is moderate. Coal is altogether lacking. The peasants are skilful wood-carvers, and in isolated valleys still make all necessary household articles, besides spinning and weaving their apparel. The Northmen were always famous seamen, and Norwegians are now found on the ships of all nations. The merchant marine of about 8000 vessels is one of the most important of the world. Good roads and railways have greatly increased traffic. A constantly increasing number of strangers are attracted by the natural beauties. Although in this way a great deal of money is brought into the country, the morals and honesty of the people unfortunately suffer in consequence. The area is 123,843 sq. miles; the population numbers 2,250,000 persons.

The great majority belong officially to the Lutheran state Church, but on account of liberal laws there is a rapid development of sects. Catholics did not regain religious liberty until the middle of the nineteenth century. Reports as to their numbers vary from 1500, as given in the Protestant "Tägliche Rundschau", to 100,000, as given in the Catholic "Germania" (see below). Norway is a constitutional monarchy, its ruler since 18 November, 1905, has been King Haakon VII, a Danish prince. The colours of the flag are red, white, and blue. The country is divided into 20 counties and 56 bailiwicks. Justice is administered by district courts (*sörenskrifverier*). Eccleciastically the country is divided into 6 dioceses, with 83 provosts or deans, and 450 pastors. The largest city and the royal residence is Christiania (230,000 inhabitants), the seat of government, of the Parliament (Storthing), of the chief executive, of the state university, and of other higher schools. The most important commercial city is Bergen (80,000 inhabitants), important even in the Middle Ages and for a long time controlled by the Hanseatic League. Trondhjem, formerly Nidaros, a city of 40,000 inhabitants, was earlier the see of the Catholic archbishops, and the place where the Catholic kings were crowned and buried. Its fine cathedral, now in process of restoration, contains the bones of St. Olaf, the patron saint of Norway. The army is not highly trained; men between twenty-three and thirty-three years of age are liable for military duty. The modest well-manned navy is only used for coast defence.

HISTORY.—Unlike the Swedes and Danes, the Norwegians were not organized even so late as the ninth century. The name of king was borne by the chiefs and heads of separate clans, but their authority was limited and the rights of the subjects very extensive. Only by marauding expeditions were the Vikings able to gain honour and wealth, and at times also to acquire control of extensive districts. Their early history is lost in the fabulous tales of the bards. In 872, Harold Haarfager (Fair-Haired), after a decisive sea-fight near Stavanger, established his authority over all the clans. Those refusing to submit left the country and their possessions were confiscated. When Harold divided his kingdom among several sons, its permanence seemed once more uncertain, but Hakon the Good (q. v.) restored a transient unity and procured an entrance for Christianity. Olaf Trygvesson continued the work of union after Hakon's death, and promoted the spread of the new faith, but in a sea-fight with the united forces of the Danes and Swedes he was killed about 1000 near Svalder (of uncertain location). The kingdom now fell apart, some portions coming under Cnut the Great of Denmark.

Finally Olaf, son of Harold Grenske and a descendant of Harold Haarfager (1015), re-established the boundaries of Norway, and aided Christianity to its final victory. At a later date Olaf became the patron saint of Norway. His severity so embittered the great families that they combined with Cnut and forced him to flee the country. Returning with a small army from Sweden, he was defeated and killed in the battle of Stiklestad (29 July, 1030). His heroic death and the marvellous phenomena that occurred in connexion with his body completely changed the feeling of his opponents. His son, Magnus the Good, was unanimously chosen his successor (1035), and the Danish intruders were driven away. Magnus died childless in 1047, and the kingdom went to his father's half-brother Harold, son of Sigurd. Harold had won fame and wealth as a viking, and had been an important personage at the Byzantine Court. On account of his grimness he was called *Hardrada* (the Stern). Impelled by ambition, he first waged a bloody war with Denmark and then attacked England. On an incursion into Northumberland, he was defeated at the battle of Stamford Bridge (1066). His son, Olaf the Quiet, repaired the injuries caused the country by Harold Hardrada's policy. Olaf's successor, Magnus, conquered the Scotch islands, waged successful war with Sweden, and even gained parts of Ireland, where he was finally killed. One of his sons, Sigurd Jorsalafari (the traveller to Jerusalem), went on a crusade to the Holy Land, while another son, Eystein, peacefully acquired Jemtland, a part of Sweden. With Sigurd's death (1130) the kingdom entered upon a period of disorder caused partly by strife between claimants to the throne, partly by rivalry between the secular and ecclesiastical dignitaries, whose partisans (known as the Birkebeinar and the Baglar) perpetrated unbelievable outrages and cruelty on each other. The power of the king sank steadily, while that of the bishops increased. For a time Sverre (1177–1202) seemed successful, but lasting peace was not attained until the reign of his grandson, Hakon the Old (1217–63). Hakon ruled with wisdom and force and was highly regarded by the rulers of other countries. During his reign Norway reached its greatest extent, including Greenland and Iceland. He died in the Orkney Islands (1263) while returning from an expedition against the Scotch

His peace-loving son Magnus *Lagoboête* (the Law-Mender) tried to establish law and order and prepared a book of laws. His efforts to promote commerce and intercourse resulted unfortunately, as the Hanseatic League, to which he granted many privileges, used these to the detriment of the country, and gradually brought it into a state of grievous dependence. With the death (1319) of the vigorous younger son of Magnus, Hakon V, the male line of Harold Harfager became extinct. The crown went to the three year old King Magnus Eriksson of Sweden, son of Hakon's daughter, Ingeborg; this brought about for the first time a close union between the two kingdoms of northern Scandinavia. When King Magnus assumed the government (1332), it was soon evident that, although possessing many good qualities, he lacked force. He seldom came to Norway, and the Norwegians felt themselves neglected. They forced him, when holding court at Varberg (1343), to send his younger son Hakon as viceroy to Norway, where Hakon soon gathered an independent court, and in 1335 became the actual ruler. Seven years later he was elected King of Sweden by a part of the Swedish nobility, but had to yield to Duke Albert of Mecklenburg, chosen by an opposing faction. In 1363 Hakon married Margaret, daughter of King Waldemar of Denmark, and won with her a claim to the Danish throne. As Waldemar, when he died in 1375, left no male descendants, he was succeeded by their son, Olaf. Olaf also became King of Norway upon the death of his father, and died in 1387. His mother, an able and energetic ruler, entered at once upon the administration of Denmark. In Norway she was not only made ruler for life, but her nephew, Eric of Pomerania, was acknowledged as the lawful heir. Meanwhile, Albert of Mecklenburg, greatly disliked in Sweden and the estates, entered into negotiations with Margaret, whose troops took him prisoner (1389). The same year Eric was acknowledged King of Norway, and in 1395–6 as King of Denmark and Sweden. In 1397 the chief men of the three countries met at Kalmar to arrange a basis for a permanent legal confederation (the Union of Galmar). The plan failed, as no one country was willing to make the sacrifice necessary for the interest of all, but Eric was crowned king of the three united lands.

Up to 1408 Margaret was the real ruler. With unwearied activity she journeyed everywhere, watched over the administration of law and government, cut down the great estates of the nobles for the benefit of the crown, and protected the ordinary freeman. Denmark was always her first interest. She placed Danish officials in Sweden and forced the Church of that country to accept Danish bishops; the result was often unfortunate, as in the appointment of the Archbishop of Upsala (1408). Margaret's efforts to regain former possessions of the three Scandinavian countries were successful only in one case; she purchased the Island of Gotland from the Teutonic Knights. She died suddenly (1412) in the harbour of Flensburg whither she had gone to obtain Schleswig from the Counts of Holstein. Left to himself, the headstrong and hot-tempered Eric made one mistake after another and soon found all the Hanseatic towns on the Baltic against him. Conditions were still worse after the death of his one faithful counsellor, his wife Philippa, daughter of Henry IV of England. In Sweden increasing taxes, constant disputes with the clergy, and the appointment of bad officials aroused a universal discontent, which led later to dangerous outbreaks. Vain attempts were made (1436) to restore the tottering union. Disregarding his promises, Eric withdrew to Gotland, where he remained inactive. In 1438 his deposition was declared by Norway and Sweden, and his nephew, Duke Christopher of Bavaria, was elected king. Upon

Christopher's early death (1448) the union was virtually dissolved: the Swedes chose Karl Knutsson as king, and the Danes called Count Christian of Oldenburg to the throne. At first Norway wavered between the two, but Christian was able to retain control.

Of Christian's two sons Hans was at first only ruler of Denmark and Norway, but, by an agreement made at Calmar, he was able to gain Sweden also. Yet it was only after defeating Sten Sture that his position in Sweden was secure. King Hans I was succeeded (1513) in Denmark and Norway by his son, Christian II. Christian's cruelty to the conquered Swedes prepared the way for the defection of that country to Gustavus Vasa; consequently, he was indirectly responsible for the withdrawal of Sweden from Catholic unity. Christian soon aroused dissatisfaction in his own country. Undue preference granted to the lower classes turned the nobility against him, and his un-disguised efforts to open the way for the teachings of Luther repelled loyal Catholics. Serious disorders followed in Jutland, and Christian, losing courage, sought to save himself by flight. With the aid of the Hanseatic League his uncle, Duke Frederick of Schleswig-Holstein, soon acquired possession of his kingdoms. The new king and his son, Christian III, were fanatical adherents of the new doctrine, and by craft and force brought about its victory in Denmark (1539). In Norway Archbishop Olaf of Trondhjem laboured in vain for the maintenance of Catholicism and the establishment of national independence. The majority of the peasants were indifferent and the impoverished nobility, who hoped to benefit by the introduction of the "pure Gospel", urged Christian on. After the departure of the church dignitaries Christian acquired the mastery of the country (1537). Norway now ceased to be an independent state. While retaining the name of kingdom it was for nearly three hundred years (until 1814) only a Danish province, administered by Danish officials and at times outrageously plundered. Here, as in Sweden and Denmark, people were gradually and systematically turned away from the Catholic Faith, though it was long before Catholicism was completely extinguished. The last Bishop of Holum in Iceland, Jon Arason, died a martyr. The king and the nobility seized the lands of the Church. The chief nobles acquired inordinate influence, and the landed proprietors, once so proud of their independence, fell under the control of foreign tyrants.

As regards territorial development in the Middle Ages, Norway had a number of tributary provinces—in the north, Finmark, inhabited by heathen Lapps; various groups of islands south-west of Norway as: the Farve Islands, the Orkneys, the Shetlands, and the Isle of Man in the Irish Sea, to which were added later Iceland and Greenland. During the period of the union, Norway also included Bohuslän, Härjedalen, Jemtland, and some smaller districts, all now belonging to Sweden. With these islands and outlying territories the monarchy comprised about 7000 square miles. The Scotch islands were lost towards the end of the fifteenth century, and at a later period the colonies in Greenland were totally neglected. Originally the kingdom had consisted of four provinces, each with its own laws, but when a system of law for the entire country was introduced, it was divided into eleven judicial districts. The most closely settled districts were the fertile lowlands on the inlets of the sea, now Christiania and Trondhjem fiords. The waterway from Trondhjem to Oslo, near the present Christiania, was the most important route for traffic. There was also much intercourse by water between Oslo and Bergen. Through the mountain districts huts for the convenience of travellers (*Spälastugor*) were erected, and developed later into inns and taverns. The country was unprepared for war. The topography and economic conditions made it difficult to mobilize the land forces. The soldiers were not paid, but only fed. The chief state officials lived in Bohus, Akershus, Tunsberg, and the royal fortified castles on the harbours of Bergen and Trondhjem. Ecclesiastically, Norway was at first under the direction of the Archbishop of Lund (1103); later (1152) under the Archbishop of Trondhjem, who had jurisdiction over the Bishops of Bergen, Stavanger, Oslo, Hamar, Farvê, Kirkwall (Orkney Islands), Skalholt and Holar (Holum) in Iceland, and Gardar (Garde) in

THE CATHEDRAL, TRONDHJEM, NORWAY

Greenland. Jemtland was subject to the Swedish Archdiocese of Upsala. There were a thousand well-endowed churches, thirty monasteries, and various orders of women: Benedictines, Cistercians, Præmonstratensians, Dominicans, Franciscans, Augustinians, and Brigittines. Schools were attached to the cathedrals and to most of the monasteries. For higher education Norwegians went to foreign universities, especially to Paris.

From the reign of Christian III Norway shared the fortunes of Denmark. Christian's son, Frederick II (1559–88), paid no attention to Norway, but much was done for the country during the long reign of Christian IV (1588–1648), who endeavoured to develop the country by encouraging mining at Konsberg and Röraas, and to protect it from attack by improving the army. Jemtland and Herjudalen, however, had to be ceded to Sweden. Frederick III (1648–70) was also obliged to cede Bohuslan. Frederick V (1746–66) encouraged art, learning, commerce, and manufactures. Prosperity strengthened the self-reliance of the people and their desire for political independence. In 1807 they were granted autonomous administration, and in 1811 a national university was founded at Christiania. Political events enabled Sweden to force Denmark in the Treaty of Keil to relinquish Norway. Many of the Norwegians not being in favour of this, a national diet, held at Eidsvold (17 May, 1814), agreed upon a constitution and chose as king the popular Danish prince, Christian Frederick. But the Powers interfered and ratified the union with Sweden. The Swedish monarchs, Charles John XIV, Oscar I, Charles XV, and Oscar II, had a difficult position to maintain in Norway. Notwithstanding zealous and successful efforts to promote the material and intellectual prosperity of the land, they never attained popularity, nor could they reconcile national dislikes. Friction increased, the Norwegian parliament growing steadily more radical and even becoming the exponent of republican ideas. From 1884 the Storthing, which now possessed the real power, steadfastly urged the dissolution of the union, and on 7 June, 1905, declared it to be dissolved. The Swedish Government naturally was unwilling to consent to this revolutionary action. Negotiations were successfully concluded at the Convention of Karlstad, 23 September, 1905. The Norwegians elected as king Prince Charles of Denmark, who, under the title of Hakon VII, has since then reigned over the country.

ECCLESIASTICAL HISTORY.—Little is known of the religious ideas of the heathen Norwegians, and this little rests on later sources, chiefly on the Eddas of the thirteenth century. It seems certain that not only animals, but also human beings (even kings), were sacrificed to the gods, of whom first Thor (later Odin) was the most important. The early Norwegians were characterized by reckless courage and a cruelty that alternated with generosity and magnanimity. Hakon the Good and Olaf Tryggoesson laboured to introduce Christianity, and during the reign of Olaf Haroldsson Christianity became, nominally at least, the prevailing religion. Olaf Haroldsson was a zealous adherent of the new faith. He built churches, founded schools, and exerted influence by his personal example. After his death he was revered as a saint: the church built at Nidaros (now Trondhjem) over his grave was replaced later by the cathedral of Trondhjem, the finest building in Norway. The Dioceses of Nidaros, Bergen, Oslo, and Stavanger were soon founded, monks and nuns carried on successful missionary work, and in a short time the land was covered with wooden churches (*Stovkirken*) of singular architecture; the few that remain still arouse admiration. Gradually stone churches with a rich equipment were erected.

The Norwegian bishops were under the jurisdiction of the Metropolitan of Lund until 1152, when the papal legate, Nicholas of Albano, transferred the jurisdiction over the Norwegian Church to the Bishop of Trondhjem and his successors. The suffragans of the new archbishopric were: Hamar, Farve, and Kirkwall in the Orkneys, Skalholt, and Holar in Iceland, and Gardar in Greenland. The tithes, legally established before 1130 in the reign of Sigurd Jonsalafari, made possible the foundation of a large number of new parishes and strengthened those already existing. The Diocese of Oslo contained the largest number, namely 300 parishes; Nidaros had 280. There was a chapter for each see. Not much is known of the morals and religious spirit of the people; it is certain that in the Catholic period much more in proportion was given for purposes of religion than after the Reformation. There are few details of the pastoral labours of bishops and clergy, but the works of Christian charity, hospices, lazarettos, inns for pilgrims, bear ready testimony to their efforts for the advancement of civilization. Nor was learning neglected. As early as the twelfth century the monk Dietrich of Trondhjem wrote a Latin chronicle of the country, and in 1250 a Franciscan wrote an account of his journey to the Holy Land. Norwegian students who desired degrees went to the Universities of Paris and Bologna, or, at a later period, attended a university nearer home, that of Rostock in Mecklenburg. With the abandonment of the old Faith and its institutions was associated the loss of national independence in 1537. As early as 1519 Christian II had begun to suppress the monasteries, and Christian III abetted the cause of Lutheranism. Archbishop Olaf Engelloechtssen and other dignitaries of the Church were forced to flee; Mogens Lawridtzen, Bishop of Hamar, died in prison in 1642, and Jon Arason of Holar was executed on 7 November, 1550.

The large landed possessions of the Church went to the king and his favourites. Many churches were destroyed, others fell into decay, and the number of parishes was greatly reduced. The salaries of the preachers, among whom were very objectionable persons, were generally a mere pittance. Fanatics of the new belief thundered from the pulpit against idolatry and the cruelty of the "Roman Antichrist"; whatever might preserve the memory of earlier ages was doomed to destruction; the pictures of the Virgin were cut to pieces, burned, or thrown into the water; veneration of saints was threatened with severe punishment. Notwithstanding this, it was only slowly and by the aid of deception that the people were seduced from the ancestral faith. Catholicism did not die out in Norway until the beginning of the seventeenth century. The pope entrusted the spiritual care of Norway, first to the Nunciature of Cologne, and then to Brussels, but the Draconian laws of Denmark made Catholic ministration almost impossible. Whether the Jesuits appointed to Norway ever went there is unknown. A Dominican who reached the country was expelled after a few weeks. The Norwegian convert Rhugius was permitted to remain, but was not allowed to exercise his office. Conditions remained the same later, when the supervision was transferred from Brussels to Cologne, from Cologne to Hildersheim, and thence to Osnabrück.

There was no change until the nineteenth century when the laws of 1845 and succeeding years released all dissenters, including Catholics who had come into the country, from the control of the Lutheran state Church. From the time of its foundation the Lutheran Church had wavered between orthodoxy and rationalism, and was finally much affected by the Pietistic movement, led by Haugue. In 1843 a small Catholic parish was formed in Christiania, and from this centre efforts were made to found new stations. In 1869 Pius IX created an independent prefecture Apostolic for Norway. The first prefect was a Frenchman, Bernard, formerly prefect of the North Pole mission. He was followed by the Luxemburg priest

Fallize, later Bishop of Alusa, under whom the mission has steadily developed, although not yet large. Especially noteworthy among the men who of late years have been reconciled to the Church are the former gymnasial rector Sverenson, and the author Kroogh-Tonning, doctor of theology, originally a Lutheran pastor at Christiania. All monastic orders, Jesuits excepted, are allowed, but there are no monasteries for men. On the other hand the missionaries of the female congregations, Sisters of St. Elizabeth, Sisters of St. Francis, and Sisters of St. Joseph of Chambéry, numbering about thirty, have gained useful and active fellow-workers. There are a few thousands of Catholics, for whom there are churches in Christiania (St. Olaf and Halvard), in Bergen, Trondhjem, Fredrikshald, Tromsö. Fredrikstad, Altengaard, Hamerfest. Catholic hospitals exist in Christiania, Bergen, Drammen, and Christiansand, and there is a number of Catholic schools towards which the Protestant population has shown itself friendly. In 1897, for the first time in three hundred years, the feast of St. Olaf was celebrated at Trondhjem.

History of Art.—During the Middle Ages art was closely connected with religion, and its chief task was the building and embellishment of churches. Some twenty old wooden churches (*Stavkirker*), still in existence, show with what skill Norwegians made use of the wood furnished by their forests. At a comparatively early date, stone was used, first in the Romanesque, then in the Gothic buildings. Some of the work thus produced has a singular and characteristic charm. Besides primitive churches of one aisle with rude towers and belfries, as at Vossevanger, there are in existence churches of three aisles with pleasing, and at times relatively rich ornamentation. The façades of some of these are flanked by two towers, as at Akers, Bergen, and Stavanger. The most striking achievements of Norwegian architecture are the cathedral of St. Magnus at Kirkwall in the Orkneys, and, what is even finer, the cathedral at Trondhjem. The latter has had a chequered history. Built originally in 1077 by Olaf the Quiet (*Kyrre*) as a "Christ Church" of one aisle over the bones of St. Olaf, it served at first as the burial place of the kings. When in 1152 Trondhjem (Nidaros) was made an archdiocese, it became a place of pilgrimage for the entire kingdom, and the gifts of the faithful made possible the necessary enlargement of the cathedral. In 1161 Archbishop Eystein Erlandson began its restoration in the Romanesque style. Obliged to flee from King Sverri, he became acquainted during his stay in England with Gothic architecture and made use of this style on his return. This is especially evident in the unique octagon erected over St. Olaf's grave, evidently an imitation of "Becket's Crown" in Canterbury cathedral. Eystein's successors completed the building according to his plans. The cathedral was twice damaged by fire but each time was repaired (in 1328 and in 1432). It fell into almost complete ruin after the great fire of 5 May, 1531, and for several hundred years no attention was paid to it. A change came with the awakening of national pride, and the restoration of the cathedral is now nearing completion. Its most valuable treasures, the body of the great Apostle of Norway St. Olaf and the costly shrine that enclosed it, have disappeared. In 1537 the shrine was taken to Copenhagen, robbed of its jewels, and melted, while the bones of the saint were buried by fanatics in some unknown place to put an end forever to the veneration of them. The wood-carvings, paintings, and other objects of art, which formerly adorned Norwegian churches, have been either carried off or destroyed.

This was not so frequently the case in the northern part of the country, and in other districts some few objects escaped. Among the works of art especially interesting may be mentioned: (in wood-carving) the altar of the Virgin in the Church of Our Lady at Bergen, and the altar in the Ringsacker church on Lake Nysen; (in painting) the antependium at Gal; (in relief work) the doorways of the churches at Hyllestad and Hemsedal; the baptismal font at Stavanger, reliquaries, as at Hedal; censers, as at Hadsel; crucifixes and vestments. The finest medieval secular building is King Haakon's Hall, a part of the former royal palace at Bergen. Beautifully carved chairs, rich tapestries, and fine chased work are further proof of the degree of culture attained by Catholic Norway.

History of Literature.—Norway can hardly be said to have an indigenous literature. As regards material and arrangement, the chronicles and narratives are very much the same both in the north and the south (for Icelandic Sagas see Icelandic Literature). We here treat specifically Protestant literature only so far as individual writers, such as the brothers Munch, refer in poetry or prose to the Catholic era in Norway, and thus indirectly further the interests of the Church. The historical investigations and writings of Bang, Dietrichson, Daae, and Bugge have overthrown many historical misstatements and judgments prejudicial to Catholicism. These works have influenced even Protestant theology in Norway, so that its position towards Rome is relatively more friendly than in other countries. If heretofore no Norwegian Catholic has made a great contribution to the national literature the reason is obvious. Of late years, however, various books have been published of an edifying, apologetic, or of a polemical nature. There is a Catholic weekly, the "St. Olav".

When not otherwise noted, the place of publication is Christiania: *Diplomatarium Norwegicum* (1849—); Munch, *Det norske folkets historie* (8 vols., 1852–63); Sars, *Udsigt over den norske historie* (1893—); Odhner, *Lärobok i Sveriges, Norges och Danmarks historia* (7th ed., Stockholm, 1886); Zorn, *Staat u. Kirche in Norwegen bis z. 13. Jahrh.* (Munich, 1875); Keyser, *Den norske Kirkes Historie under Katolicismen* (2 vols., 1856–8); Bang, *Udsigt over den Norske Kirkes Historie under Katolicismen* (1887); Idem, *Udsigt over den Norske Kirkes Historie efter Reformationen* (1885); Storm, *Hist. topogr. Skrifter om Norge og norske Landsdele författede i Norge i det 16de Aarhundrade* (1895); Baumgartner, *Nordische Fahrten*, II (Freiburg, 1890); Dietrichson, *De Norske Stavkirker* (1892); Idem, *Vore Faedres Verk; Norges Kunst i Middelalderen* (1906); Idem, *Omrids af den norske Literatura Historie* (Copenhagen, 1866–9); Schweitzer, *Phil. Gesch. der skand. Literatur* (3 vols., Leipzig, 1886—); Oestergaard, *Illustreret Dansk Literaturhistorie* (1907); Halvorsen, *Norsk Forfatterlexikon 1874–1881* (1885—); *Kirkeleksikon for Norden* (Copenhagen, 1897—), 53 pts. already issued; *Die kathol. Missionen* (Freiburg, 1873—); Hermens and Kohlschmidt, *Protest. Taschenbuch* (Leipzig, 1905).

P. Wittmann.

Norwich (Nordovicum; Norvicum), Ancient Diocese of.—Though this see took its present name only in the eleventh century, its history goes back five hundred years earlier to the conversion of East Anglia by St. Felix in the reign of King Sigeberht, who succeeded to the kingdom of his father Redwald on the death of his half-brother Eorpweald in 628. St. Felix fixed his see at Dunwich, a sea-coast town since submerged, the site of which is in Southwold Bay. From Dunwich, St. Felix evangelized Norfolk, Suffolk, and Cambridgeshire, the counties which formed the diocese. He was succeeded by Thomas (647), Beorhtgils (Boniface), who died about 669, and Bisi, on whose death, in 673, St. Theodore, Archbishop of Canterbury, divided the see into two, with cathedrals at Dunwich and Elmham. The following are the lines of episcopal succession based on the most recent research, with approximate dates of accession where known:—

Dunwich: Ǣcci, 673; Alric; Ǣscwulf; Eardred; Ealdbeorht I; Eardwulf; Cuthwine; Ealdbeorht II; Ecglaf; Heardred; Ǣlfhun, 790; Tidfrith, 798; Waermund; Wilred, 825. *Elmham:* Beaduwine, 673; Nothbeorht; Heathulac; Ǣthelfrith, 736; Eanfrith; Ǣthelwulf; Ealhheard; Sibba; Hunfrith; St. Hunbeorht; Cunda (there is some doubt as to whether Cunda was Bishop of Elmham or Dunwich).

The See of Elmham came to an end about 870, when St. Edmund, King of the East Angles, and Bishop St. Hunbeorh were murdered by the Danes. The country was ravaged, the churches and monasteries destroyed, and Christianity was only practised with difficulty. Bishop Wilred of Dunwich seems to have reunited the dioceses, choosing Elmham as his see. His successors at Elmham were:—

Husa; Æthelweald; Eadwulf; Ælfric I; Theodred I; Theodred II; Æthelstan; Ælfgar, 1001; Ælfwine, 1021; Ælfric II; Ælfric III, 1039; Stigand, 1040; Grimcytel, 1042; Stigand (restored), 1043; Æthelmaer, 1047; Herfast, 1070. Bishop Herfast, a chaplain to William the Conqueror, removed his bishop's chair to Thetford. He died in 1084, and was succeeded by William de Bellofago (de Beaufeu), also known as William Galsagus (1086–91). William de Bellofago was succeeded by Herbert de Losinga, who made a simoniacal gift to King William Rufus to secure his election, but being subsequently struck with remorse went to Rome, in 1094, to obtain absolution from the pope. He founded the priory of Norwich in expiation for his sin and at the same time moved his see there from Thetford. The chapter of secular canons was dissolved and the monks took their place. The foundation-stone of the new cathedral was laid in 1096, in honour of the Blessed Trinity. Before his death, in 1119, he had completed the choir, which is apsidal and encircled by a procession path, and which originally gave access to three Norman chapels. His successor, Bishop Eborard, completed the long Norman nave so that the cathedral is a very early twelfth-century building though modified by later additions and alterations. The chief of these were the Lady chapel (*circa* 1250, destroyed by the Protestant Dean Gardiner 1573–89); the cloisters (*circa* 1300), the west window (*circa* 1440), the rood screen, the spire and the vault spanning the nave (*circa* 1450). The cathedral suffered much during the Reformation and the civil wars.

The list of bishops of Norwich, with the dates of their accession, is as follows:—

Herbert Losinga, consecrated in 1091, translated the see to Norwich in 1094; Eborard de Montgomery, 1121; William de Turbe, 1146; John of Oxford, 1175; John de Grey, 1200; Pandulph Masca, 1222; Thomas de Blunville, 1226; Ralph de Norwich, 1236; vacancy, 1236; William de Raleigh, 1239; vacancy, 1242; Walter de Suffield, 1245; Simon de Walton, 1258; Roger de Skerning, 1266; William de Middleton, 1278; Ralph de Walpole, 1289; John Salmon, 1299; William de Ayerminne, 1325; Anthony Bek, 1337; William Bateman, 1344; Thomas Percy, 1356; Henry le Despenser, 1370; Alexander de Totington, 1407; Richard Courtenay, 1413; John Wakering, 1416; William Alnwick, 1426; Thomas Brown, 1436; Walter Lyhart, 1446; James Goldwell, 1472; Thomas Jane, 1499; Richard Nykke, 1501; William Rugg (schismatic), 1536; Thomas Thirleby (schismatic but reconciled in Mary's reign), 1550; John Hopton, 1554, who died in 1558, being the last Catholic Bishop of Norwich.

The diocese, which consisted of Norfolk and Suffolk with some parts of Cambridgeshire, was divided into four archdeaconries, Norfolk, Norwich, Suffolk, and Sudbury. At the end of the seventeenth century there were 1121 parish-churches, and this number had probably not changed much since Catholic times.

The chief religious houses in the diocese were: the Benedictine Abbeys of Bury St. Edmund's, Wymondham, and St. Benet's of Hulm, the cathedral priory of Norwich, the Cistercian Abbey of Sibton, the abbeys of the Augustinian Canons at Wendling, Langley, and Laystone. The Dominicans and Franciscans were both found at Lynn, Norwich, Yarmouth, Dunwich, and Ipswich; the Dominicans also had houses at Thetford and Sudbury; the Franciscans at Bury St. Edmund's and Walsingham, where the great shrine of Our Lady was; the Carmelites were at Lynn, Norwich, Yarmouth, and Blakeney; and the Augustinian friars at Norwich, Lynn, and Orford. There were no Carthusians in the diocese. The arms of the see were azure, three mitres with their labels, or.

BRITTON, *Hist. of the See and Cath. of Norwich* (London, 1816); COTTON, *Hist. Anglicana necnon Liber de archiepiscopis et episcopis Angliæ* (London, 1859); JESSOPP, *Dioc. Hist. of Norwich* (London, 1884); QUENNELL, *Norwich: the Cath. and See* (London, 1898); *Visitations of the Diocese of Norwich, 1492–1532*, ed. JESSOPP (London, 1888); WINKLE, *Cathedral Churches of England and Wales*, II (London, 1851); GOULBURN AND SYMONDS, *Life, letters, and sermons of Herbert de Losinga* (London, 1878); ANSTRUTHER, *Epistolæ Herberti de Losinga* (London, 1846); *Hist. MSS. Commission, First Report* (giving a list of principal records in the bishop's registry); SEARLE, *Anglo-Saxon Bishops, Kings, and Nobles* (Cambridge, 1899).

EDWIN BURTON.

Notaries (Lat. *notarius*), persons appointed by competent authority to draw up official or authentic documents. These documents are issued chiefly from the official administrative bureaux, the chanceries; secondly, from tribunals; lastly, others are drawn up at the request of individuals to authenticate their contracts or other acts. The public officials appointed to draw up these three classes of papers have been usually called notaries.

Etymologically, a notary is one who takes notes. Notes are signs or cursory abbreviations to record the words uttered, so that they may be reproduced later in ordinary writing. Notaries were at first private secretaries, attached to the service of persons in positions of importance. It was natural for the science of notes to be in high esteem among those employed in recording the transactions of public boards, and for the name notary to be applied to these officials; so that before long the word was used to signify their occupation.

The title and office existed at the Imperial Court (cf. Cod. Theod., VI, 16, "De primicerio et notariis"), whence they passed into all the royal chanceries, though in the course of time the term notary ceased to be used. This was the case also with the chanceries of the pope, the great episcopal sees, and even every bishopric. There are grounds for doubting whether the seven regional notaries of the Roman Church, one for each ecclesiastical district of the Holy City, were instituted by St. Clement and appointed by him to record the Acts of the martyrs, as is said in the "Liber Pontificalis" ("Vita Clementis", ed. Duchesne, I, 123); they date back, however, to an early age. Not only were there notaries as soon as a bureau for ecclesiastical documents was established, but in very ancient days we find these notaries forming a kind of college presided over by a *primicerius;* the notice of Julius I in the "Liber Pontificalis" relates that this pope ordered an account of the property of the Church, intended as an authentic document, to be drawn up before the *primicerius* of the notaries.

The latter were in the ranks of the clergy and must have received one of the minor orders; for the notariate is an office and not an order. At intervals the popes entrusted the notaries of their *curia* with various missions. Their chief, the *primicerius*, with whom a *secundicerius* is sometimes found later, was a very important personage, in fact, the head of the pontifical chancery; during the vacancy of the papal chair, he formed part of the interim Government, and a letter in 640 (Jaffé, "Regesta", n. 2040) is signed (the pope being elected but not yet consecrated) by one "Joannes primicerius et servans locum s. sedis apostolicæ".

There were of course many notaries in the service of the pontifical chancery; the seven regional notaries preserved a certain pre-eminence over the others and became the prothonotaries, whose name and office

NORWICH CATHEDRAL

continued. The ordinary notaries of the chancery, however, were gradually known by other names, according to their various functions, so that the term ceased to be employed in the pontifical and other chanceries. The prothonotaries were and still are a college of prelates, enjoying numerous privileges; they are known as "participants", but outside of Rome there are many purely honorary prothonotaries. The official duties had insensibly almost ceased; but Pius X in his reorganization of the Roman Curia has appointed participant prothonotaries to the chancery (Const. "Sapienti", 29 June, 1908). A corresponding change occurred in the bureaux of the episcopal churches, abbeys, etc.; the officials attached to the chancery have ceased to be known as notaries and are called chancellor, secretary, etc. Lastly, mention must be made of the notaries of the synodal or conciliar assemblies, whose duties are limited to the duration of the assembly.

Society in former times did not recognize the separation of powers; so, too, in the Church the judicial authority was vested in the same prelates as the administrative. Soon, however, contentious matters were tried separately before a specially appointed body. The courts required a staff to record the transactions; these clerks were likewise notaries. In most civil courts they are, however, called registrars, clerks of the court, etc., but in the ecclesiastical tribunals they retain the name notary, though they are also called actuaries. Thus the special law of the higher ecclesiastical tribunals, the Rota and the Signatura, reorganized by Pius X, provides for the appointment of notaries for these two tribunals (can. v and xxxv). The reason why the head official charged with drawing up the documents of the Holy Office is called the notary, as were the clerks who in former times drew up the records of the Inquisition, is, doubtless, that of all the Roman Congregations the Holy Office is the only real judicial tribunal. The notaries of ecclesiastical tribunals are usually clerics; the duties may however be confided to laymen, except in criminal cases against a cleric.

Finally, there is the class of persons to whom the term notary is restricted in common parlance, to wit, those who are appointed by the proper authorities to witness the documentary proceedings between private persons and to impress them with legal authenticity. They are not engaged in the chanceries, in order that they may be within easy reach of private individuals; they have a public character, so that their records, drawn up according to rule, are received as authentic accounts of the particular transaction, especially agreements, contracts, testaments, and wills.

Consequently, public notaries may be appointed only by those authorities which possess jurisdiction *in foro externo*, and have a chancery, e. g. popes, bishops, emperors, reigning princes, and of course only within the limits of their jurisdiction; moreover, the territory within which a notary can lawfully exercise his functions is expressly determined. There were formerly Apostolic notaries and even episcopal notaries, duly commissioned by papal or episcopal letters, whose duty it was to receive documents relating to ecclesiastical or mixed affairs, especially in connexion with benefices, foundations, and donations in favour of churches, wills of clerics, etc. They no longer exist; the only ecclesiastical notaries at present are the officials of the Roman and episcopal *curiæ*. Moreover these notaries were layman, and Canon Law forbids clerics to acts as scriveners (c. viii, "Ne clerici vel monachi", l. III, tit. 50).

Du Cange, *Glossarium*, s. v. *Notarius*; Ferraris, *Prompta bibliotheca*, s. v. *Notarius*; Fagnani, *Commentaria* in c. *Sicut te*, 8, *Ne Clerici vel monachi*; and in c. *In ordinando*, I, *De simonia*; Héricourt, *Les lois ecclésiastiques de France* (Paris, 1721), E, xiii; Giry, *Manuel de diplomatique* (Paris, 1894).

A. Boudinhon.

Notary. See Prothonotary.

Notburga, Saint, patroness of servants and peasants, b. c. 1265 at Rattenberg on the Inn; d. c. 16 September, 1313. She was cook in the family of Count Henry of Rothenburg, and used to give food to the poor. But Ottilia, her mistress, ordered her to feed the swine with whatever food was left. She, therefore, saved some of her own food, especially on Fridays, and brought it to the poor. One day, according to legend, her master met her, and commanded her to show him what she was carrying. She obeyed, but instead of the food he saw only shavings, and the wine he found to be vinegar. Hereupon Ottilia dismissed her, but soon fell dangerously ill, and Notburga remained to nurse her and prepared her for death.

Notburga then entered the service of a peasant in the town of Eben, on condition that she be permitted to go to church the evenings before Sundays and festivals. One evening her master urged her to continue working in the field. Throwing her sickle into the air she said: "Let my sickle be judge between me and you," and the sickle remained suspended in the air. Meantime Count Henry of Rothenburg was visited with great reverses which he ascribed to the dismissal of Notburga. He engaged her again and thenceforth all went well in his household. Shortly before her death she told her master to place her corpse on a wagon drawn by two oxen, and to bury her wherever the oxen would stand still. The oxen drew the wagon to the chapel of St. Rupert near Eben, where she was buried. Her ancient cult was ratified on 27 March, 1862, and her feast is celebrated on 14 September. She is generally represented with an ear of corn, or flowers and a sickle in her hand; sometimes with a sickle suspended in the air.

Her legendary life was first compiled in Germany by Guarinoni, in 1646, Latin tr. Roschmann in *Acta SS.*, September, IV, 717–725; Hattler, *St. Notburg, die Magd des Herrn, den glaubwuerdigen Urkunden treuherzig nacherzaehlt*, 5th ed. (Donauwörth, 1902); Stadler, *Heiligen-Lexikon*, IV (Augsburg, 1875), 586–592; Dunbar, *Dictionary of Saintly Women*, II (London, 1905), 111–112; Baring-Gould, *Lives of the Saints*, 14 Sept.

Notburga, legendary daughter of Dagobert I, who is said to have lived in a cave near Hochhausen on the Neckar in Baden. Many legends are related as to the sanctity and holiness of her life. After her death her body was placed on a chariot drawn by two white oxen to the place of burial, where at present stands the church of Hochhausen. It is very probable that the legend of St. Notburga, the daughter of Dagobert I, is merely a distortion of that of St. Notburga of Rattenberg.

Du Blois, *La vie et la Légende de Madame Sainte Notburga* (Paris, 1868); Glock, *Ein Bield aus Badens Sagemvelt* (Karlsruhe, 1883); Stamminger, *Franconia Sancta* (Wurzburg, 1881), 22–34; Huffschmid, *Hochhausen am Neckar und die heil. Notburga* in *Zeitschrift für die Geschichte des Oberrheins*, new series, I (Freiburg im Br., 1886), 285–401; Dunbar, *Dictionary of Saintly Women*, II (London, 1905), 110.

Michael Ott.

Nothomb, Jean-Baptiste, Belgian statesman, b. 3 July, 1805, at Messancy, Luxemburg; d. at Berlin, 16 September, 1881. He received his secondary education at the *athénée* of Luxemburg, studied law in the University of Liège, and was awarded a doctor's degree in 1826. He practised law in Luxemburg, then in Brussels, where he took an active part in the war that was then waged in the press in behalf of the independence of Belgium. During the riots of August, 1830, he was in his native province; but hearing of the fight which had taken place between the patriots and the troops of the Prince of Orange he hurried back to the capital.

The provisional government appointed him secretary of the committee which was preparing the first draft of a new constitution. Three electoral districts of Luxemburg chose him as their representative in the first legislature of Belgium. He declared for the district of Arlon to which, in 1831, he gave proof of his gratitude by doing his utmost to prevent its union with Germany. Nothomb, who was the youngest member of the legislative assembly, was appointed one of its secretaries and a member of the committee on foreign affairs. In the chamber he strongly opposed the advocates of the union of Belgium with France and those who were for a republican government. His political ideal, which he defended with great eloquence, was a representative monarchy with two houses, liberty of the press, and complete independence, in their own spheres, of the secular and religious powers.

From 1831–36 he was general secretary for foreign affairs; with Devaux he went to London to carry on secret negotiations at the conference which had met in that city to settle the new state of affairs created by the Belgian revolution, and did much to remove the difficulties which had delayed the departure for Belgium of Leopold of Saxe-Coburg. He published in 1833 his "Essai historique et politique sur la révolution belge", a remarkable work which was translated into German and Italian and was reprinted three times in the same year. In 1836 Nothomb resigned as general secretary for foreign affairs and in 1837 became minister of Public Works in the Catholic administration of de Theux. He gave a powerful impetus to the construction of railroads and when he resigned in 1840 more than 300 kilometres had been built. In the same year he was sent as an extraordinary envoy to the German Confederation and in 1841 became minister of the interior in a unionist administration; but the positions of the parties were not what they had been in the preceding decade, and Nothomb soon realized that a union of the Catholics and Liberals was no longer possible. In 1845 he withdrew from the political arena to enter the diplomatic corps. He was for many years minister plenipotentiary of Belgium in Berlin. In 1840 he had become a member of the Royal Academy of Brussels; and he received many distinctions from foreign countries.

Nothomb, Alphonse, brother of Jean-Baptiste, b. 12 July, 1817; d. 15 May, 1898. He had a brilliant career in the magistracy, was minister of justice in 1855, and became a member of the lower house of Parliament in 1859. In 1884 he was made a minister of State. Like his brother he was a staunch Catholic; in the latter part of his life he had become a convert to the political creed of the new Catholic democratic party.

Juste, *Le Baron Nothomb* (Brussels, 1874); Thonissen, *Histoire du règne de Léopold I*er (Louvain, 1861); Hymans, *Histoire parlementaire de la Belgique* (Brussels, 1877–80).

P. J. Marique.

Notitia Dignitatum (Register of Offices), the official handbook of the civil and military officials in the later Roman Empire. The extant Latin form belongs to the early fifth century. The last addenda concerning the Eastern Empire point to the year 397 as the latest chronological limit, while supplementary notices concerning the Western Empire extend into the reign of Valentinian III (425–55). The bulk of the statements, however, point to earlier years of the fourth century, individual notices showing conditions at the beginning of this century. The first part of the "Notitia" gives a list of the officials in the Eastern Empire: "Notitia dignitatum omnium tam civilium quam militarium in partibus Orientis"; the second part gives a corresponding list for the Western Empire: "Notitia . . . in partibus Occidentis". Both give, first the highest official positions of the central administration, then the officials in positions subordinate to these, and also the officials of the various "dioceses" and provinces, the civil officials being regularly stated along with the military. In addition, the insignia of the officials and of the army divisions are shown by drawings. This register was used in the imperial chancery; the chief official of the chancery (*primicerius notariorum*) found in it all necessary information for drawing up the announcements of the appointment of officials and of their positions. The "Notitia", preserved as it is in an incomplete condition, is partly an abstract, partly an exact transcript of this official register. It shows that at various periods, extending as late as the first part of the fifth century, additions were made to the state register and gives the essential form of the list in the era just mentioned. It is, therefore, a very important authority for the divisions of the Empire, for an understanding of the Roman bureaucracy, and for the distribution of the army during the late Roman Empire. The first printed edition was "Notitia utraque cum Orientis tum Occidentis" (Basle, 1552); the latest editions were edited by Böcking (2 vols., Bonn, 1839–53), and O. Seeck, "Notitia dignitatum. Accedunt Notitia urbis Constantinopolitanæ et Laterculi provinciarum" (Berlin, 1876).

Seeck, *Quæstiones de Notitia dignitatum* (Berlin, 1872); Idem, *Die Zeit des Vegetius* in *Hermes*, XI (Berlin, 1876), 77 sqq.; Idem, *Zur Kritik der Notitia dignitatum* in *Hermes*, IX (1875), 217 sqq.; Steffenhagen, *Der Gottorfer Codex der Notitia dignitatum* in *Hermes*, XIX (1884), 458 sqq.; Mommsen, *Die Conscriptionsordnung der röm. Kaiserzeit* in *Hermes*, XIX (1884), 233 sqq.; Teuffel-Schwabe, *Gesch. der römischen Literatur* (5th ed., Leipzig, 1890), 1163.

J. P. Kirsch.

Notitiæ Episcopatuum, the name given to official documents that furnish for Eastern countries the list and hierarchical rank of the metropolitan and suffragan bishoprics of a Church. Whilst, in the Patriarchate of Rome, archbishops and bishops were classed according to the seniority of their consecration, and in Africa according to their age, in the Eastern patriarchates the hierarchical rank of each bishop was determined by the see he occupied. Thus, in the Patriarchate of Constantinople, the first metropolitan was not the longest ordained, but whoever happened to be the incumbent of the See of Cæsarea; the second was the Archbishop of Ephesus, and so on. In every ecclesiastical province, the rank of each suffragan was thus determined, and remained unchanged unless the list was subsequently modified. The hierarchical order included first of all, the patriarch; then the greater metropolitans, i. e., those who had dioceses with suffragan sees; the autocephalous metropolitans, who had no suffragans, and were directly subject to the patriarch; next archbishops who, although not differing from autocephalous metropolitans, occupied hierarchical rank inferior to theirs, and were also immediately dependent on the patriarch; then simple bishops, i. e., exempt bishops, and lastly suffragan bishops. It is not known by whom this very ancient order was established, but it is likely that, in the beginning, metropolitan sees and simple bishoprics must have been classified according to the date of their respective foundations, this order being modified later on for political and religious considerations. We here append, Church by Church, the principal of these documents.

A. Constantinople: The "Ecthesis of pseudo-Epiphanius", a revision of an earlier Notitia episcopatuum (probably compiled by Patriarch Epiphanius under Justinian), made during the reign of Heraclius (about 640); a Notitia dating back to the first years of the ninth century and differing but little from the earlier one; the "Notitia of Basil the Armenian", drawn up between 820 and 842; the Notitia compiled by Emperor Leo VI the Philosopher, and Patriarch Nicholas Mysticus between 901 and 907, modifying the hierarchical order which had been established in the seventh century, but had been disturbed by the incorporation of the ecclesiastical provinces of Illyricum and Southern Italy in the Byzantine Patriarchate; the Notitiæ episcopatuum of Constantine Porphyrogenitus (about 940), of Tzimisces (about 980), of Alexius Comnenus (about 1084), of Nil Doxapatris (1143), of Manuel Comnenus (about 1170), of Isaac Angelus (end of twelfth century), of Michael VIII Palæologus (about 1270), of Andronicus II Palæologus (about 1299), and of Andronicus III (about 1330). All these Notitiæ are published in Gelzer, "Ungedruckte und ungenügend veröffentlichte Texte der Notitiæ episcopatuum" (Munich, 1900); Gelzer, "Georgii Cyprii Descriptio orbis romani" (Leipzig, 1890); Gelzer, "Index lectionum Ienæ" (Jena, 1892); Parthey, "Hieroclis Synecdemus" (Berlin, 1866). The later works are only more or less modified copies of the Notitia of Leo the Philosopher, and therefore do not present the true situation, which was profoundly changed by the Mussulman invasions. After the capture of Constantinople by the Turks, another Notitia was written, portraying the real situation (Gelzer, "Ungedruckte Texte der Notitiæ episcopatuum", 613–37), and on it are based nearly all those which have been since written. The term *Syntagmation* is now used by the Greeks for these documents.

B. We know of only one "Notitia episcopatuum" for the Church of Antioch, viz. that drawn up in the sixth century by Patriarch Anastasius (see Vailhé in "Echos d'Orient", X, pp. 90–101, 139–145, 363–8). Jerusalem has no such document, nor has Alexandria, although for the latter Gelzer has collected documents which may help to supply the deficiency (Byz. Zeitschrift, II, 23–40). De Rougé (Géographie ancienne de la Basse-Egypte, Paris, 1891, 151–61) has published a Coptic document which has not yet been studied. For the Bulgarian Church of Achrida, see Gelzer, "Byz. Zeitschrift", II, 40–66, and "Der Patriarchat von Achrida" (Leipzig, 1902). M. Gerland has just announced for 1913 a critical and definitive new edition of all the Notitiæ episcopatuum of the Churches of Constantinople, Alexandria, Antioch, Jerusalem, Cyprus, Achrida, Ipek, Russia, and Georgia.

In addition to the works cited, a supplementary bibliography will be found in KRUMBACHER, *Gesch. der byz. Litt.* (Munich, 1897), 416.

S. VAILHÉ.

Notitia Provinciarum et Civitatum Africæ (List of the Provinces and Cities of Africa), a list of the bishops and their sees in the Latin provinces of North Africa, arranged according to provinces in this order: Proconsularis, Numidia, Byzacena, Mauretania Cæsariensis, Mauretania Sitifensis, Tripolitana, Sardinia. The cause of its preparation was the summoning of the episcopate to Carthage, 1 February, 484, by the Arian King of the Vandals, Hunerich (477–84). It names also the exiled bishops and vacant sees, and is an important authority for the history of the African Church and the geography of these provinces. It is incorporated in the only extant manuscript for the history of the Vandal persecution by Bishop Victor of Vita, and is printed in the editions of this work.

P. L., LVIII, 267 sqq.; *Victoris de Vita Opera*, ed. HALM in *Mon. Germ. hist.: Auct. antiq.*, III (Berlin, 1879), 63 sq.; ed. PETSCHENIG in *Corp. script. eccl. lat.*, VII (Vienna, 1881), xii, 117 sqq.

J. P. KIRSCH.

Notker.—Among the various monks of St. Gall who bore this name, the following are the most important:

(1) NOTKER BALBULUS (STAMMERER), BLESSED, monk and author, b. about 840, at Jonswil, canton of St. Gall (Switzerland); d. 912. Of a distinguished family, he received his education with Tuotilo, originator of tropes, at St. Gall's, from Iso and the Irishman Moengall, teachers in the monastic school. He became a monk there and is mentioned as librarian (890), and as master of guests (892–94). He was chiefly active as teacher, and displayed refinement of taste as poet and author. He completed Erchanbert's chronicle (816), arranged a martyrology, and composed a metrical biography of St. Gall. It is practically accepted that he is the "monk of St. Gall" (monachus Sangallensis), author of the legends and anecdotes "Gesta Caroli Magni". The number of works ascribed to him is constantly increasing. He introduced the sequence, a new species of religious lyric, into Germany. It had been the custom to prolong the *Alleluia* in the Mass before the Gospel, modulating through a skilfully harmonized series of tones. Notker learned how to fit the separate syllables of a Latin text to the tones of this jubilation; this poem was called the sequence (q. v.), formerly called the "jubilation". (The reason for this name is uncertain.) Between 881–887 Notker dedicated a collection of such verses to Bishop Liutward of Vercelli, but it is not known which or how many are his. Ekkehard IV, the historiographer of St. Gall, speaks of fifty sequences attributable to Notker. The hymn, "Media Vita", was erroneously attributed to him late in the Middle Ages. Ekkehard IV lauds him as "delicate of body but not of mind, stuttering of tongue but not of intellect, pushing boldly forward in things Divine, a vessel of the Holy Spirit without equal in his time". Notker was beatified in 1512.

CHEVALIER, *Bio-bibl.*, s. v.; MEYER VON KNONAU in *Realencyk. für prot. Theol.*, s. v.; WERNER, *Notker's Sequenzen* (Aarau, 1901); BLUME, *Analecta hymnica*, LIII (Leipzig, 1911).

(2) NOTKER LABEO, monk in St. Gall and author, b. about 950; d. 1022. He was descended from a noble family and nephew of Ekkehard I, the poet of Waltharius. "Labeo" means "the thick lipped", later he was named "the German" (*Teutonicus*) in recognition of his services to the language. He came to St. Gall when only a boy, and there acquired a vast and varied knowledge by omnivorous reading. His contemporaries admired him as a theologian, philologist, mathematician, astronomer, connoisseur of music, and poet. He tells of his studies and his literary work in a letter to Bishop Hugo of Sitten (998–1017), but was obliged to give up the study of the liberal arts in order to devote himself to teaching. For the benefit of his pupils he had undertaken something before unheard, namely translations from Latin into German. He mentions eleven of these translations, but unfortunately only five are preserved: (1) Boethius, "De consolatione philosophiæ"; (2) Marcianus Capella, "De nuptiis Philologiæ et Mercurii"; (3) Aristotle, "De categoriis"; (4) Aristotle, "De interpretatione"; (5) "The Psalter". Among those lost are: "The Book of Job", at which he worked for more than five years; "Disticha Catonis"; Vergil's "Bucolica"; and the "Andria" of Terenz. Of his own writings he mentions in the above letter a "New Rhetoric" and a "New Computus" and a few other smaller works in Latin. We still possess the Rhetoric, the Computus (a manual for calculating the dates of ecclesiastical celebrations, especially of Easter), the essay "De partibus logicæ", and the German essay on Music.

In Kögel's opinion Notker Labeo was one of the greatest stylists in German literature. "His achievements in this respect seem almost marvellous." His style, where it becomes most brilliant, is essentially poetical; he observes with surprising exactitude the laws of the language. Latin and German he commanded with equal fluency; and while he did not understand Greek, he was weak enough to pretend that he did. He put an enormous amount of learning and erudition into his commentaries on his translations. There everything may be found that was of interest in his time, philosophy, universal and literary history, natural science, astronomy. He frequently quotes the classics and the Fathers of the Church. It is characteristic of Notker that at his dying request the poor were fed, and that he asked to be buried in the clothes which he was wearing in order that none might see the heavy chain with which he had been in the habit of mortifying his body.

KELLE, *Gesch. der deut. Lit. bis zur Mitte des 11. Jahrhunderts*, I (Berlin, 1892), 232–63; KÖGEL, *Gesch. der deut. Lit. bis zum Ausgang des Mittelalters*, I, 2 (Strasburg, 1897), 598–626; PIPER, *Die Schriften Notkers*, I–III (Freiburg, 1882–3).

KLEMENS LÖFFLER.

(3) NOTKER PHYSICUS (surnamed PIPERIS GRANUM), physician and painter, d. 12 Nov., 975. He received his surname on account of his strict discipline. Concerning his life we only know that in 956 or 957 he became *cellarius*, and in 965 *hospitarius* at St. Gall. Ekkehard IV extols several of his paintings, and mentions some antiphons and hymns of his composition (e. g. the hymn "Rector æterni metuende secli"). He is probably identical with a "Notker notarius", who enjoyed great consideration at the court of Otto I on account of his skill in medicine, and whose knowledge of medical books is celebrated by Ekkehard. In 940 this Notker wrote at Quedlinburg the confirmation of the immunity of St. Gall. This is in accord with the great partiality later shown by the Ottos towards the monk, for example when they visited St. Gall in 972.

EKKEHART (IV), *Casus Sancti Galli*, ed. MEYER VON KNONAU in *Mitteil. zur vaterländ. Gesch.* (St. Gall, 1877), cxxiii, cxlvii; BURGENER, *Helvetia Sancta*, II (Einsiedeln, 1860), 132 sq.; SIRET, *Dict. des peintres etc.* (new ed., Paris, 1874), 640; WATTENBACH, *Deutschlands Geschichtsquellen*, I (7th ed., Stuttgart, 1904), 354; RAHN, *Gesch. der bildenden Künste in der Schweiz* (Zurich, 1876), 139 sqq.

(4) NOTKER, nephew of Notker Physicus, d. 15 Dec., 975. We have no documentary information concerning him until his appointment as Abbot of St. Gall (971). Otherwise also the sources are silent concerning him, except that they call him "abba benignus" and laud his unaffected piety.

EKKEHART (IV), *op. cit.*, cxxii; MABILLON, *Acta SS. O.S.B.*, V (1685), 21.

(5) NOTKER, Provost of St. Gall and later Bishop of Liège, b. about 940; d. 10 April, 1008. This celebrated monk is not mentioned by the otherwise prolix historians of St. Gall. He probably belonged to a noble Swabian family, and in 969 was appointed imperial chaplain in Italy. From 969 to 1008 he was Bishop of Liège. Through him the influence of St. Gall was extended to wider circles. He laid the foundation of the great fame of the Liège Schools, to which studious youths soon flocked from all Christendom. By procuring the services of Leo the Calabrian and thus making possible the study of Greek, Notker gave notable extension to the Liège curriculum. Among Notker's pupils, who extended the influence of the Liège schools to ever wider circles, may be mentioned Hubald, Gunther of Salzburg, Ruthard and Erlwin of Cambrai, Heimo of Verdun, Hesselo of Toul, and Adalbald of Utrecht. A noteworthy architectural activity also manifested itself under Notker.

In Folcwin's opinion Notker's achievements surpass those of any of his predecessors: among the buildings erected by him may be mentioned St. John's in Liège, after the model of the Aachen cathedral. Praiseworthy also were his services as a politician under Otto III and Henry II. He adhered faithfully to the cause of the romantic Otto, whom he accompanied to Rome. It was also he who brought back the corpse of the young emperor to Germany. The "Gesta episcoporum Leodiensium" have been frequently wrongly attributed to him, although he merely suggested its composition, and lent the work his name to secure it greater authority.

WATTENBACH, *Deutschlands Geschichtsquellen im Mittelalter*, I (7th ed., Stuttgart, 1904), 425 sqq. A *Vita Notkeri* (12th cent.) is partly preserved by ÆGIDIUS OF ORVAL; cf. KURTH, *Biogr. de l'évêque Notger au XII⁰ S.* in *Bull. de la Comm. royale d'hist. de Belgique*, 4th series, XVII (1891), n. 4.; *Biogr. de l'évêque N. au XII⁰ s.* in *Revue bénédictine*, VIII (1891), 309 sqq.

FRANZ KAMPERS.

Noto, DIOCESE OF (NETEN), the ancient Netum and after the Saracen conquest the capital of one of the three divisions of Sicily, was among the last cities to surrender to the Normans. Destroyed by an earthquake in 1693, it was rebuilt nearly five miles from its primitive site. It contains fine churches, like that of St. Nicholas, an archæological museum with a collection of Syracusan, Roman, and Saracen coins, and a library. Noto is the birthplace of the humanist John Aurispa, secretary of Eugene IV and Nicholas V. In the cathedral is the tomb of Blessed Conrad of Piacenza. The diocese was separated in 1844 from the Archdiocese of Syracuse, of which Noto is suffragan; the first bishop was Joseph Menditto. It has 19 parishes; 148,400 inhabitants; 11 religious houses of men, and 14 of women; a school for boys and three for girls; and a home for invalids.

CAPPELLETTI, *Le Chiese d'Italia*, XXI.

U. BENIGNI.

Notoriety, Notorious (Lat. *Notorietas*, *notorium*, from *notus*, known).—Notoriety is the quality or the state of things that are notorious; whatever is so fully or officially proved, that it may and ought to be held as certain without further investigation, is notorious. It is difficult to express exactly what is meant by notoriety, and, as the Gloss says (in can. Manifesta, 15, C. ii, q. 1), "we are constantly using the word *notorious* and are ignorant of its meaning". Ordinarily it is equivalent to public, manifest, evident, known; all these terms have something in common, they signify that a thing, far from being secret, may be easily known by many. Notoriety, in addition to this common idea, involves the idea of indisputable proof, so that what is notorious is held as proved and serves as a basis for the conclusions and acts of those in authority, especially judges. To be as precise as is possible, "public" means what any one may easily prove or ascertain, what is done openly; what many persons know and hold as certain, is "manifest"; what a greater or less number of persons have learnt, no matter how, is "known"; what is to be held as certain and may no longer be called in question is "notorious".

Authorities distinguish between notoriety of fact, notoriety of law, and presumptive notoriety, though the last is often considered a subdivision of the second. Whatever is easily shown and is known by a sufficient number of persons to be free from reasonable doubt is notorious in fact. This kind of notoriety may refer either to a transitory fact, e. g., Caius was assassinated; or permanent facts, e. g., Titius is parish priest of this parish; or recurring facts, e. g., Sempronius engages in usurious transactions. Whatever has been judicially ascertained, viz., judicial admissions, an affair fully proved, and the judgment rendered in a lawsuit, is notorious in law; the judge accepts the fact as certain without investigation; nor will he allow, except in certain well-specified cases, the matter to be called in question. "Notorious" is then used as more or less synonymous with "official". Such also are facts recorded in official documents, as civil or ecclesiastical registries of births, deaths, or marriages, notarial records. Lastly, whatever arises from a rule of law based on a "violent" presumption, for instance, paternity and filiation in case of a legitimate marriage, is presumptively notorious.

When a fact is admitted as notorious by the judge, and in general by a competent authority, no proof of it is required, but it is often necessary to show that it is notorious, as the judge is not expected to know every notorious fact. The notoriety has to be proved, like any other fact alleged in a trial, by witnesses or "instruments", that is, written documents. The witnesses swear that the fact in question is publicly known and admitted beyond dispute in their locality or circle. The documents consist especially in extracts from the official registries, in the copies of authentic judicial papers, for instance, a judgment, or of notarial papers, known as "notarial acts", drawn up by public notaries on the conscientious declarations of well-informed witnesses.

Canonists have variously classified the legal effects of notoriety, especially in matters of procedure; but, ultimately, they may all be reduced to one: the judge, and in general the person in authority, holding what is notorious to be certain and proved, requires no further information, and therefore, both may and ought to refrain from any judicial inquiry, proof, or formalities, which would otherwise be necessary. For these inquiries and formalities having as their object to enlighten the judge, are useless when the fact is notorious. Such is the true meaning of the axiom that in notorious matters the judge need not follow the judicial procedure (cf. can. 14 and 16, C. ii, q. 1; cap. 7 and 10, "De cohab. cleric.", lib. III, tit. ii; cap. 3, "De testib. cogend.", lib. II, tit. xxi). None of the essential solemnities of the procedure should ever be omitted. The most interesting application of the effect of notoriety in criminal matters is in connexion with the *flagrans delictus*, when the accused is caught in the criminal act, in which case the judge is dispensed from the necessity of any inquiry.

FAGNAN, *Comment. in cap. Vestra*, 7, lib. *III Decret.*, tit. ii; FERRARIS, *Prompta biblioth.*, s. v. *Notorium*; SMITH, *The Elements of Ecclesiastical Law* (New York, 1877–1889); TAUNTON, *The Law of the Church* (London, 1906), 452.

A. BOUDINHON.

Notre Dame, Congregations of.—I.—CONGREGATION OF NOTRE DAME DE MONTREAL.—Marguerite Bourgeoys, the foundress, was born at Troyes, France, 17 April, 1620. She was the third child of Abraham Bourgeois, a merchant, and Guillemette Garnier, his wife. In 1653 Paul Chomody de Maisonneuve, the founder of Ville Marie (Montreal), visited Troyes, and invited her to go to Canada to teach; she set out in June of that year, arrived at Ville Marie, and devoted herself to every form of works of mercy. She opened her first school on 30 April, 1657, but soon had to return to France for recruits, where four companions joined her. A boarding school and an industrial school were opened and sodalities were founded. In 1670 the foundress went back to France and returned in 1672 with letters from King Louis XIV and also with six new companions. In 1675 she built a chapel dedicated to Notre Dame de Bon Secours. To insure greater freedom of action Mother Bourgeoys founded an uncloistered community, its members bound only by simple vows. They had chosen 2 July, as their patronal feast-day. Modelling their lives on that of Our Lady after the Ascension of Our Lord, they aided the pastors in the various parishes where convents of the order had been established, by instructing children.

Although the community had received the approbation of the Bishop of Quebec, the foundress became very desirous of having the conditions of non-enclosure and simple vows embodied in a rule. To confer with the bishop, who was then in France, she undertook a third journey to Europe. She returned the next year, and resisted the many attempts made in the next few years to merge the new order in that of the Ursulines, or otherwise to change its original character. In 1683 a mission on Mount Royal was opened for the instruction of Indian girls. This mission, under the auspices of the priests of St. Sulpice, was removed in 1701 to Sault au Recollet, and in 1720 to the Lake of Two Mountains. It still exists. The two towers still standing on the grounds of Montreal College were part of a stone fort built to protect the colony from the attacks of their enemies; they were expressly erected for the sisters of that mission: one for their residence, the other for their classes.

The sisters continued their labours in the schools of Ville Marie, and also prepared a number of young women as Christian teachers. Houses were opened at Pointe-aux-Trembles, near Montreal, at Lachine, at Champlain and Château Richer. In 1685 a mission was established at Sainte Famille on the Island of Orléans and was so successful that Mgr de St. Vallier, Bishop of Quebec, invited the sisters to open houses in that settlement, which was done. In 1689 he desired to confer with Mother Bourgeoys in regard to a project of foundation. Though sixty-nine years of age, she set out at once on the long and perilous journey on foot to Quebec, and had to suffer all the inconveniences of an April thaw. Acceding to the demands of the bishop for the new foundation, she had the double consolation of obedience to her superior, and of keeping her sisters in their true vocation when, only four years later, the bishop himself became convinced that such was necessary. Mother Bourgeoys asked repeatedly to be discharged from the superiority, but not until 1693 did the bishop accede to her petition. Eventually on 24 June, 1698, the rule and constitution of the congregation, based upon those which the foundress had gathered from various sources, were formally accepted by the members. The next day they made their vows. The superior at the time was Mother of the Assumption (Barbier). Mother Bourgeoys devoted the remainder of her life to the preparation of points of advice for the guidance of her sisterhood. She died on 12 January, 1700. On 7 Dec., 1878, she was declared venerable. The proclamation of the heroicity of the virtues of the Venerable Marguerite Bourgeoys was officially made in Rome, 19 June, 1910. In 1701 the community numbered fifty-four members. The nuns were self-supporting and, on this consideration, the number of subjects was not limited by the French Government, as was the case with all the other existing communities. The conflagration which ravaged Montreal in 1768 destroyed the mother-house, which had been erected eighty-five years before. The chapel of Bon Secours, built by Mother Bourgeoys, was destroyed by fire in 1754, and rebuilt by the Seminary of St. Sulpice in 1771.

During the latter half of the nineteenth century, missions were established in various parishes of the Provinces of Quebec, Ontario, Nova Scotia, New Brunswick, Prince Edward Island, and in the United States; also, many new academies and schools were opened in the city of Montreal. The normal school in Montreal, under the direction of the congregation, begun in 1899, has worthily realized the hopes founded upon it. Of its three hundred and eighteen graduates, authorized to teach in the schools of Quebec, one hundred and eighty-four are actually employed there. The house, built after the fire of 1768, was demolished in 1844 to give place to a larger building. A still more commodious one was erected in 1880. This was burned down in 1893, obliging the community to return to the house on St. Jean-Baptiste Street. A new building was erected on Sherbrooke Street, and here the Sisters have been installed since 1908. The Notre Dame Ladies' College was inaugurated in 1908. To-day the institute, whose rules have been definitively approved by the Holy See, counts 131 convents in 21 dioceses, 1479 professed sisters, over 200 novices, 36 postulants, and upwards of 35,000 pupils.

The school system of the Congregation of Notre Dame de Montreal always comprised day-schools and boarding-schools. The pioneers of Canada had to clear the forest, to cultivate the land, and to prepare homes for their families. They were all of an intelligent class of farmers and artisans, who felt that a Christian education was the best legacy they could leave their children; therefore they seized the opportunity afforded them by the nascent Congregation of Notre Dame, to place their daughters in boarding-schools. The work, inaugurated in Canada, led to demands for houses of the congregation in many totally English parishes of the United States.

The schools of the Congregation of Notre Dame everywhere give instruction in all fundamental branches. The real advantages developed by the systematic study of psychology and pedagogy have been fully turned to account. The system begins with the kindergarten, and the courses are afterwards graded as elementary, model, commercial, academic, and collegiate. The first college opened was in Nova Scotia at Antigonish, affiliated with the university for young men in the same place: since the early years of its foundation it has annually seen a number of Bachelors of Arts among its graduating students. In 1909 the Notre Dame Ladies' College, in affiliation with Laval, was inaugurated in Montreal. The fine arts are taught in all the secondary schools and academies, while in the larger and more central houses these branches are carried to greater perfection by competent professors. The teaching in the very elements is in conformity with the best methods of the day.

DE CASSON, *Histoire de Montréal*, I (1673), 62 sq.; FAILLON, *Vie de la Sœur Bourgeoys*, II (1853); RANSONNET, *Vie de la Sœur Bourgeoys* (1728); DE MONTGOLFIER, *Vie de la Sœur Bourgeoys* (1818); SAUSSERET, *1er Éloge Historique de la Sœur Bourgeoys* (1864); IDEM, *2nd Éloge Historique de la Sœur Bourgeoys* (1879); SISTER OF THE CONGREGATION, *The Pearl of Troyes* (1878), 338-68; DRUMMOND, *The Life and Times of Marguerite Bourgeoys* (1907).

SISTER ST. EUPHROSINE.

II.—CONGREGATION OF NOTRE-DAME DE SION, a religious institute of women, founded at Paris in May, 1843, by Marie-Théodore and Marie-Alphonse Ratisbonne (q. v.). Théodore, at that time sub-director of the Archconfraternity of Our Lady of Victories, secured from Gregory XVI permission to work among the Jews for their conversion. His brother Marie-Alphonse was equally zealous and they established a congregation of sisters under the patronage of Our Lady of Sion, with its mother-house at Paris. The new body received warm encouragement from Mgr Affre, Mgr Sibour, and Cardinal Fornari, and, on 15 January, 1847, Pius IX showed his approbation of the work by granting many indulgences to the institute. Foundations were made in the Holy Land, the chief being the convent, orphan asylum, and school, near the Ecce Homo arch in Jerusalem. That of St. John's in the Mountains was founded from it. Connected with the orphanage in Jerusalem under the patronage of St. Peter are schools of art and manual-training. At the Ecce Homo there are 170 pupils, Jews, Mohammedans, and Greek schismatics, besides 100 day scholars.

There are foundations in London and also at Rome, Grandbourg near Versailles, Trieste, Vienna, Prague, Galatz, Bucharest, Jassy, Constantinople, Kadi-Koi, etc. At Munich the "Sionsverein" for the support of poor children in Palestine was founded in 1865 through the instrumentality of Baroness Thérèse von Gumppenberg and Hermann Geiger. The Sisters of Notre-Dame de Sion number 500, of whom fifty are at the Ecce Homo and St. John's, and seven at St. Peter's. They are directed spiritually by the Priests of Notre-Dame de Sion, a congregation of secular priests, which includes lay brothers. At St. Peter's in Jerusalem, there are six priests, nine lay brothers, and some scholastics. The German settlement of Tabgha, on the Lake of Genesareth, is in charge of a priest of Notre-Dame de Sion, assisted by a Lazarist. There is a foundation of Priests of Notre-Dame de Sion at Constantinople.

HEIMBUCHER, *Die Orden und Kongregationen*, III (Paderborn, 1908), 391; HÉLYOT, *Dict. des ordres religieux*.

BLANCHE M. KELLY.

III.—INSTITUTE OF NOTRE-DAME DE NAMUR, founded in 1803 at Amiens, France, by Bl. Julie Billiart (b. 1751; d. 1816) and Marie-Louise-Françoise Blin de Bourdon, Countess of Gézaincourt, in religion Mother St. Joseph (b. 1756; d. 1838). The formation of a religious congregation for the education of youth was the result of a formal order to Blessed Julie in the name of God by Père Joseph Varin, S.J., who discerned her fitness for such an enterprise. Mlle Blin de Bourdon offered to defray the immediate expenses. At Amiens, 5 August, 1803, they took a house in Rue Neuve, the cradle of the institute, with eight orphans, children confided to them by Père Varin. In the chapel of this house, at Mass on 2 February, 1803, the two foundresses and their postulant, Catherine Duchâtel of Reims, made or renewed their vow of chastity, to which they added that of devoting themselves to the Christian education of girls, further proposing to train religious teachers who should go wherever their services were asked for. Victoire Leleu (Sister Anastasie) and Justine Garçon (Sister St. John) joined the institute this year and with the foundresses, made their vows of religion 15 October, 1804. The Fathers of the Faith who were giving missions in Amiens sent to the five sisters women and girls to be prepared for the sacraments. Bl. Julie was successful and on the invitation of the missioners continued to assist them in the neighbouring towns.

Returning to Amiens, the foundress devoted herself to the formation of her little community. She taught the young sisters the ways of the spiritual life. To attain the double end of the institute, the foundress first secured teachers, among whom were Fathers Varin, Enfantin and Thomas, the last-named a former professor in the Sorbonne, and Mother St. Joseph Blin, to train the novices and sisters.

The first regular schools of the Sisters of Notre-Dame were opened in August, 1806. Pupils flocked into the class-rooms at once. The urgent need of Christian education among all classes of society in France at that time, led the foundresses to modify their original plan of teaching only the poor and to open schools for the children of the rich also. Simplicity, largeness of mind, and freedom from little feminine weaknesses, marked the training given to the higher classes. But the poorest and most forsaken were ever to remain the cherished portion of the institute, and the unwritten law that there may be in every mission free schools without pay schools, but not pay schools without free schools, still remains in force. Mother Julie did not require her postulants to bring a dowry, but a modest pension for the years of probation; a sound judgment, good health, aptitude for the work of the congregation, a fair education; these, with unblemished reputation, good morals, and an inclination to piety, were the qualifications she deemed indispensable. Within two years forty postulants were received.

The community lived under a provisional rule, based upon that of St. Ignatius, drawn up by Mother Julie and Father Varin, which was approved in 1805 by Mgr Jean-François Demandolx, Bishop of Amiens. The necessary recognition was accorded on 10 March, 1807. Though time and experience brought additions to those first constitutions, none of the fundamental articles have been changed: the sole exterior labour in the institute is the instruction of youth in schools in concert with the parochial clergy; a mother-house, a superior-general who appoints the local superiors, decides upon foundations and assigns their revenues, visits the secondary houses and moves subjects from one to another when necessary; one grade only of religious, no cloister, but no going out save for necessity, no visiting to relations, friends, or public buildings. It was for these points that the Blessed Foundress laboured and suffered, as the substance of the constitutions, solemnly approved by Gregory XVI in 1844, shows.

The first branch house was established at St. Nicholas, near Ghent. At the departure of these five missionaries, 15 December, 1806, the religious habit was assumed by the congregation, a private, religious ceremony, still unchanged. The taking of vows is also private, but takes place during Mass. St. Nicholas, as well as Mother Julie's five other foundations in France, were all temporary. Later and permanent foundations were made in Belgium: Namur, 1807, which became the mother-house in 1809; Jumet, 1808; St. Hubert, 1809; Ghent, 1810; Zele, 1811; Gembloux and Andennes, 1813; Fleurus, 1814; and all arrangements for Liège and Dinant, though the communities took possession of these convents only after 1816.

Mother St. Joseph Blin de Bourdon, the co-foundress, was elected superior-general in succession to Blessed Mother Julie. During her generalate the institute passed through the most critical period of its existence, owing to the persecutions of religious orders by William of Orange-Nassau, King of the Netherlands. To compel them to remain *in statu quo*, to hold diplomas obtained only after rigid examinations in Dutch and French by state officials, to furnish almost endless accounts and writings regarding convents, schools, finances, and subjects, were some of the measures adopted to harass and destroy all teaching orders; but Mother St. Joseph's tact, clear-sightedness, and zeal for souls saved the institute. During his tour in 1829, King William visited the establishment at Namur and was so pleased that he created the mother-general a Dutch subject. The Revolution of 1830 and the assumption of the crown of Belgium by Leopold of Saxe-Gotha put an end to the petty persecutions of religious. Mother St. Joseph founded houses at Thuin, 1817; Namur Orphanage, 1823; Hospital St. Jacques, 1823; Verviers, 1827; Hospital d'Harscamp and Bastogne, 1836, the latter having been for the past thirty years a state normal school; Philippeville, 1837. The most important work of her generalate was the compiling and collating of the present Rules and Constitution of the Sisters of Notre Dame. She has left an explanation of the rule; the particular rule of each office; the Directory and Customs. She had preserved a faithful record of all that Mother Julie had said or written on these points; hence the will of the foundress is carried out in the smallest details of daily life, and the communities are alike everywhere. Moreover, she drew up the system of school management which has been followed ever since, with only such modification of curricula and discipline as time, place, and experience have rendered indispensable. This system of instruction is based upon that of St. John Baptist de La Salle, and may be read broadly in the "Management of Christian Schools," issued by the Christian Brothers. The points of uniformity in the primary and secondary schools of all countries are chiefly: the emphasis laid upon thorough grounding in reading, writing, and arithmetic, grammar and composition, geography, and history; the half hour's instruction daily in Christian doctrine; the half-hourly change of exercise; the use of the signal or wooden clapper in giving directions for movements in class; the constant presence of the teacher with her class whether in the class-room or recreation ground; the preparation of lessons at home, or at least out of class hours. Vocal and chart music, drawing and needlework are taught in all the schools. No masters from outside may give lessons to the pupils in any of the arts or sciences.

Mother St. Joseph was twice re-elected superior-general, the term being at first fixed at ten years. To give greater stability to the government of the institute, a general chapter was convoked which should settle by ballot the question of life-tenure of the office of superior-general. The assembly unanimously voted in the affirmative. In 1819 a foundation was asked for Holland by Rev. F. Wolf, S.J., but, on account of political difficulties, Mother St. Joseph could not grant it. She offered, instead, to train aspirants to the religious life. Accordingly, two came to Namur, passed their probation, made their vows, and returned to labour in their own country. This is the origin of the congregation of Sisters of Notre Dame, whose mother-house is at Coesfield, and who have large schools in Cleveland, Covington, and other cities of the Middle West. Though not affiliated to Notre Dame of Namur, they follow the same rule and regard Blessed Mother Julie as their foundress.

XI.—9

Mother St. Joseph died on 9 February, 1838, in the eighty-third year of her age and the twenty-third of her generalate. The preliminary process of her beatification is well advanced.

The third superior-general was Mother Ignatius (Thérèse-Josephine Goethals, b. 1800; d. 1842). Her services during the persecution under King William were invaluable. Excessive toil, however, told upon her later, and she died in the fourth year of her generalate; but not before she had sent the first colony of sisters to America.

She was succeeded by Mother Marie Thérèse, who, on account of ill-health, resigned her office the following year and Mother Constantine (Marie-Jeanne-Joseph-Collin, b. 1802, d. 1875) was elected. She ruled the institute for thirty-three years, her term of office being marked by the papal approbation of the Rule in 1844, the first mission to England in 1845, to California in 1851, to Guatemala in 1859. Under Mother Aloysie (Thérèse-Joseph Mainy, b. 1817, d. 1888), fifth superior-general, the processes for the canonization of Mother Julie and Mother St. Joseph were begun in 1881; twenty houses of the institute were established in Belgium, England, and America. Under her successor, Mother Aimée de Jésus (Élodie Dullaert, b. 1825, d. 1907), the Sisters of Notre Dame, at the request of Leopold II of Belgium, took charge of the girls' schools in the Jesuit missions of the Congo Free State, where three houses were established. She also sent from England a community of eight sisters for the girls' schools in the Jesuit mission of Zambesi, Mashonaland. An academy and free school were opened later at Kronstadt, Orange River Colony, South Africa. Mother Aimée de Jésus was created by the King of Belgium a Knight of the Order of Leopold, and Sister Ignatia was accorded a similar honour after fourteen years of labour in the Congo. During this generalate Mother Julie Billiart was solemnly beatified by Pius X, 13 May, 1906. The present Superior-general, Mother Marie Aloysie, was elected in January, 1908.

The first foundation in America was made at Cincinnati, Ohio, at the request of the Right Reverend John B. Purcell, then Bishop and later the first Archbishop of Cincinnati. Sister Louise de Gonzague was appointed superior of the eight sisters who came here for this purpose. After firmly establishing the institute in America, failing health caused her recall to Namur, where she worked until her death in 1866. Upon Sister Louise, another of the original group, devolved in 1845 the charges of superiority not only of the house of Cincinnati, but also of the others then founded or to be founded east of the Rocky Mountains. Every year the sisters were asked for in some part of the country and the mother-house of Namur gave generously of subjects and funds until the convents in America were able to supply their own needs.

The two provincials who have followed Sister Louise continued the work along the lines she had traced out. Sister Julie (b. 1827, d. 1901) founded fifteen houses, including Trinity College, Washington, D. C., and a provincial house and novitiate at Cincinnati, Ohio. Sister Agnes Mary (b. 1840, d. 1910) made three foundations and built the first chapel dedicated to Blessed Mother Julie in America, a beautiful Gothic structure in stone, at Moylan, Pennsylvania.

In 1846 a colony of eight sisters left Namur under the care of Right Reverend F. N. Blanchet and Father de Smet, S.J., to labour among the Indians of the Oregon mission. Five years later these sisters, at the request of the Right Reverend J. S. Alemany, Bishop of San Francisco, were transferred to San José, California. The first establishment on the Pacific Coast was followed in course of time by ten others, which formed a separate province from Cincinnati. For thirty years it was under the wise care of Sister Marie Cornélie.

In 1851 two foundations were made in Guatemala, Central America, under government auspices and with such an outburst of welcome and esteem from the people as reads like a romance. In less than twenty years the reins of power having passed into the hands of the Liberals and Freemasons, the forty-one Sisters of Notre Dame were exiled.

There are three novitiates in America: at San José for the California Province, at Cincinnati for the central part of the United States, and at Waltham, Massachusetts, for the Eastern States. The rule has been kept in its integrity in America as in Europe. The union with Namur has been preserved, and a like union has even been maintained between all the houses of a province and its centre, the residence of the provincial superior. According to the needs of the schools, the sisters pass from house to house, and even from province to province as obedience enjoins.

It was through the Redemptorists that the Sisters of Notre Dame first went to England. Father de Buggenoms, a Belgian, superior of a small mission at Falmouth, felt the urgent need of schools for the poor Catholic children. He asked and obtained from the Superior of the Sisters of Notre Dame at Namur a community of six sisters, and with these he opened a small school at Penryn in Cornwall. It continued only three years, however, as the place afforded no means of subsistence to a religious house. The Redemptorists having established a second English mission at Clapham, near London, and having asked again for Sisters of Notre Dame for a school, the community of Penryn was transferred thither in 1848. Through the initiative of Father Buggenoms the Sisters of the Holy Child Jesus, a community in the Diocese of Northampton, about fifty in number, were affiliated in 1852 to the Institute of Notre Dame, with the consent of the Bishops of Namur and Northampton. Scarcely had the hierarchy been re-established in England when the Government offered education to the Catholic poor; the Sisters of Notre Dame devoted themselves earnestly to this work, under the guidance of Sister Mary of St. Francis (Hon. Laura M. Petre), who was to the congregation in England what Mother St. Joseph was to the whole institute. Before her death (24 June, 1886) eighteen houses had been founded in England. There are now twenty-one.

The most important of these English houses is the Training College for Catholic School-Mistresses at Mount Pleasant, Liverpool, the direction of which was confided to the Sisters of Notre Dame by the Government in 1856. The "centre system" which admits of the concentrated instruction of pupil teachers, now adopted by all the School Boards of the larger English cities, originated with the sisters at Liverpool.

At the request of the Scotch Education Department, the Sisters of Notre Dame opened the Dowanhill Training College for Catholic School-Mistresses at Glasgow in 1895. Its history has been an unbroken record of academic successes and material expansion. A second convent in Scotland has been opened at Dumbarton this year (1910).

Although "codes" differ in terms and requirements, it may be said in general that in England and America the schools of Notre Dame are graded from kindergarten all through the elementary, grammar, and high school classes. The academies carry the schedule of studies on to college work, while Trinity College, Washington, D. C., and St. Mary's Hall, Liverpool, are devoted exclusively to work for college degrees. To meet local difficulties and extend the benefit of Christian instruction, the sisters conduct industrial schools, orphanages for girls, schools for deaf mutes, and for negroes.

Annals of the Mother-House of Notre Dame, Namur, Belgium; SISTER OF NOTRE DAME, *Life of the Blessed Julie Billiart* (London, 1909); SISTER OF NOTRE DAME, *Life of the Rev. Mother St. Joseph* (Namur, 1850); MANNIX, *Memoir of Sister Louise* (Boston, 1906); CLARKE, *The Hon. Mrs. Petre, in religion Sister Mary of St. Francis* (London, 1899); *English Foundations of the Sisters of Notre Dame* (Liverpool, 1895); S.N.D., *Pages from the Records of Catholic Education (Sister Mary of St. Philip and the Training College at Mount Pleasant)* in *The Crucible*, I, no. 4, March, 1906. See JULIE BILLIART, BLESSED, and LOUISE, SISTER.

A SISTER OF NOTRE DAME.

STATISTICS FOR 1909:

	Belgium	England Scotland	America	Africa	Totals
Houses	49	18	47	4	118
Sisters	1,250	700	1,489	33	3,472
Free Scholars	15,954	36,510	31,010	1,586	85,060
Pay Scholars	5,969	2,845	2,595	50	11,459
Boarders	1,091	1,246	1,107	60	3,499
Industrial	618	93	54	....	765
Sunday Scholars	5,934	8,621	18,952	2,000	35,507
Sodalists	5,004	12,112	25,691	415	43,222

IV.—SCHOOL SISTERS OF NOTRE DAME, a religious community devoted to education. In 1910 they counted 3170 members in Europe and 3604 in America, a total of 6774, with about 115,300 pupils in America and 94,827 in Europe, a total of 210,127. In the United States they conduct parish schools in ten archdioceses and twenty-five dioceses, and have charge of eight orphanages; in addition they have parish schools and an orphanage in the Diocese of Hamilton, Canada; an Indian school at Harbor Springs, Mich.; a school for negroes at Annapolis; and a deaf-mute institute in Louisiana. Their principal boarding-schools are: Baltimore, Md.; Fort Lee, New Jersey; Quincy, Ill.; Longwood, Chicago; Prairie du Chien, Wis. Of their day and high schools the most prominent are at Baltimore, Md., Quincy, Ill.; Longwood and Chatawa, Miss.

The School Sisters of Notre Dame are a branch of the Congregation of Notre-Dame founded in France, by St. Peter Fourier in 1597. In the seventeenth and eighteenth centuries, several convents of the congregation were established in Germany. The one at Ratisbon was suppressed at the beginning of the nineteenth century, but it was soon restored and remodelled to meet the needs of modern times. Bishop Wittmann of Ratisbon and Father Job of Vienna effected the change. While retaining the essential features of the rule and constitutions given by St. Peter Fourier, they widened the scope of the Sisters' educational work. In 1834 their community consisted of one former pupil of the suppressed congregation, Caroline Gerhardinger, who became first Superior General (Mother Theresa of Jesus), and a few companions. The first convent was in Neunburg vorm Wald, Bavaria. In 1839 they removed to a suburb of Munich, and in 1843, into a former Poor Clare convent, built in 1284, and situated within the city limits. From this mother-house in the year 1847 six School Sisters of Notre Dame, on the invitation of Bishop O'Connor of Pittsburg, emigrated to America and landed at New York on 31 July. One of the Sisters succumbed to the heat of the season and died at Harrisburg, Pa., on the journey from New York to St. Mary's, Elk Co., Pa., destined to be the foundation-house in America. As St. Mary's was not the place for a permanent location the mother-general successfully negotiated to obtain the Redemptorists' convent attached to St. James' Church, Baltimore, Md. By 3 Nov., 1847, three schools were opened. The second and last colony of sisters, eleven in number, arrived from Munich, 25 March, 1848, and foundations were made at Pittsburg, Philadelphia, and Buffalo.

On 15 December, 1850, the mother-house was transferred to Milwaukee, with Mother Mary Caroline Friess as vicar-general of the sisters in America.

With money donated by King Louis I of Bavaria, a house was bought; this was absorbed later by Notre Dame Convent on St. Mary's Hill. On 2 January,

1851, St. Mary's parish school was opened and St. Mary's Institute for boarding and day pupils soon afterwards. On 31 July, 1876, owing to its growth and extension, the congregation was divided into two provinces: the Western, with mother-house at Milwaukee; and the Eastern with mother-house at Baltimore. A second division of the Western province became necessary, and on 19 March, 1895, the Southern province was formed, with its mother-house at St. Louis.

Government of the Congregation.—The Congregation of the School Sisters of Notre Dame is under the government of the mother-general at Munich; she and her four assistants form the generalate. In America the government is in the hands of the commissary-general and four assistants. The commissariate is elected for six years. All professed sisters of the teaching grade have a vote in this election. The congregation is divided into districts. The voting sisters in each district choose one chapter-sister. These chapter-sisters together with the provincials elect the commissary-general and assistants. The election is by secret ballot, and its results must be confirmed by the mother-general and the cardinal-protector. At the head of each province there is a mother provincial, elected with two assistants, by each province for three years. For the election of the mother-general and the general chapter, which meets every six years, a deputation of the sisters in America is sent to Munich, Bavaria. This deputation consists of the commissary-general and the mother provincial, ex officio, and a companion of each mother provincial elected by the respective province. In America a general congregation is convened every six years in the principal mother-house at Milwaukee.

Training of Members.—To train members for their future life the School Sisters have a candidature and a novitiate. The age for admission into the candidature is sixteen to twenty-seven. After two years' probation and study, the candidate enters the novitiate, and two years later makes temporal vows for seven years; she then makes perpetual vows and becomes a professed sister. The teaching sisters meet at specified periods and at appointed houses of the order for summer schools and teachers' institutes.

The principal houses of the congregation in the Western province are at Elm Grove, Waukesha Co., Wis., the home for aged, invalid, and convalescent sisters; at Prairie du Chien, Wis., founded in 1872, chartered in 1877, owing its origin to the generosity of Hon. John Lawler (died on 24 Feb., 1891) and his son, Thomas C. Lawler, of Dubuque, Iowa; at Longwood, Chicago, Ill., established and chartered in 1872. In 1903 the Legislature of Illinois granted the academy the right to add a college course and confer the degrees of A.B. and Ph.B. In the Eastern province at Baltimore, Md., chartered in 1864, charter amended and powers of corporation enlarged 1896. The sisters began their work in Baltimore in 1848; owing to the growth of their academy, more commodious quarters became necessary and the school, Notre Dame of Maryland, was transferred in 1873 to a magnificent estate of seventy acres obtained in the suburbs. To meet the continual demand for a more extensive curriculum for women, the sisters of the convent applied in January, 1896, to the State for the power of conferring academic degrees; this was granted by an Act of the Legislature, 2 April, 1896, and the convent has now a college with courses leading to the baccalaureate, an academy that prepares students for the college, and a grammar and primary department. There is a convent at Fort Lee on the Palisades of the Hudson, Bergen County, N. J., where a residence was purchased by the sisters on 2 Oct., 1879, the school being opened on 21 November, 1879, and chartered in June, 1890. In the Southern province the principal schools are at Quincy, Ill., founded on 28 Dec., 1859, as a parochial school, the academy opened in Sept., 1867; at Chatawa, Miss., founded on 15 October, 1874, a deaf-mute institution; at Chincuba, La., founded by Canon Mignot, 1 October, 1890, given in charge of the sisters 25 September, 1892.

Most prominent among the sisters in America was Mother M. Caroline Friess, who died on 22 July, 1892, after being superioress of the congregation for forty-two years. She was born near Paris, on 24 August, 1824, and was called at baptism by the name of Josephine. As a child she was brought to Eichstädt, Bavaria, under the tutelage of her uncle, Mgr Michael Friess. Even when only a novice she was given charge of very important schools in Munich. She was one of the first to volunteer for the missionary work in the New World, and emigrated to America in 1847. It soon became evident that it was Sister Caroline who was to develop the young congregation. She was appointed vicar of the mother-general in America and later on elected as the first commissary-general. Under her direction from four members in 1847, the sisterhood grew to two thousand in 1892. Her life was written by Mgr P. M. Abbelen. Mother M. Clara Heuck was the third commissary-general. When the Eastern province was established in 1876 Sister M. Clara was appointed as novice-mistress. Soon she became the superioress in Baltimore and the second mother provincial in the East, which position she held for three terms, after which she was elected commissary-general at Milwaukee on 13 May, 1899. She died at Milwaukee on 4 August, 1905, aged sixty-two.

SR. MARY JOSEPHINE.

V.—SISTERS OF NOTRE DAME (of Cleveland, Ohio), a branch of the congregation founded by Blessed Julie Billiart. In 1850, Father Elting of Coesfeld, Germany, aided by the Misses Hildegonda Wollbring and Lisette Kuehling, who became the first members of this community, introduced the Order of Notre Dame into Westphalia. The novices were trained by three sisters from the community of Amersfoort, Holland. Soon they were enabled to open a normal school and to take charge of parish schools. The Prussian Government objecting to teachers dependent on foreign authority, the sisters were compelled to sever their relations with the mother-house in Holland and to erect their own at Coesfeld. When in 1871, the Kulturkampf broke out in Germany, the Sisters of Coesfeld, though they had repeatedly received at the Prussian state examinations, the highest testimonials as most efficient teachers, were at once expelled. Thereupon, Father Westerholt, of St. Peter's Church, Cleveland, had Bishop Gilmour invite them to his diocese. On 5 July, 1874, the superioress-general accompanied by eight sisters arrived in New York, and the following day in Cleveland. Their first home was a small frame house near St. Peter's Church. Two months later they took charge of the parish school for girls. Presently Bishop Toebbe of Covington, Ky., invited them to his diocese, where they were first employed as teachers of the Mother of God schools in Covington. In the autumn of 1874, the sisters began to conduct the parish schools of St. Stephen's, Cleveland, and of St. Joseph's, Fremont. Within four years of their first arrival on the North American continent, two hundred sisters had been transferred to the missions in Ohio and Kentucky. The centre of the community was temporarily at Covington, where in 1875 a convent with an academy was erected. The same year the superioress-general came to Cleveland, where the mother-house was built and an academy founded in 1878. In 1883 a girls' boarding-school on Woodland Hills was opened. An academy was founded in Toledo, Ohio, and opened September, 1904. Since 1877 the Sisters of Notre Dame have been in charge of two orphanages, one at Cold Springs, Ky., and the other at Bond Hill in the Archdiocese of Cincinnati. In May, 1887, the Prussian Government allowed the sisters to return and their mother-house was established at Mühlhausen, Rhenish Prussia. The American branch is under the immediate direction of a provincial superioress, residing in Cleveland, and numbers 430 sisters. The sisters conduct also upwards of forty parish schools, mostly in Ohio and Kentucky, containing about 14,000 pupils.

ARENS, *Die selige Julie Billiart* (Freiburg im Br., 1908); *Annals of Notre Dame Convent in Cleveland* (manuscript).

NICHOLAS PFEIL.

Notre Dame du Lac, UNIVERSITY OF, in Northern Indiana near the boundary lines of Michigan and Illinois. It is owned and directed by the Congregation of Holy Cross, whose mother-house in the United States is located at Notre Dame, the name by which the university is most commonly known. Notre Dame was founded in 1842 by the Very Reverend Edward Sorin, C.S.C., late superior-general of his congregation, who came from France at the invitation of the Right Reverend Celestine A. L. Guynemer de La Hailandière, D.D., Bishop of Vincennes. Nearly two years passed before the first building was erected and a faculty organized. In 1844 the university received a charter from the State. By special act of the Legislature of Indiana, it was given legal existence and empowered to grant degrees in the liberal arts and sciences and in law and medicine. Though no medical faculty has been formed, all the other departments mentioned in the charter have been established, and collegiate and university degrees granted in each. At the outset only collegiate instruction was given in the studies then regarded as best furnishing a liberal education. The first faculty organized was that of the college of arts and letters, and chairs of philosophy, history, mathematics, and ancient and modern languages were established. But the educational conditions in the country near the university were primitive, and few students were ready to take up college work. Accordingly, there was soon founded a preparatory school at Notre Dame in which instruction was given, not only in subjects immediately preparing for college, but also in the rudiments. Soon after the college courses began, the needs of the North-West demanded a school for those preparing for the priesthood. The founder accordingly provided a faculty in theology, and six years after the State charter was granted, one-fifth of the students were pursuing theological studies. But as intercommunication between the more settled parts of the United States increased with more easy modes of travel, the theological faculty was maintained only for members of the Congregation of Holy Cross. To-day the university consists of five colleges, each with several departments—arts and letters, engineering, science, architecture, and law. At the head of each college is a dean. The faculties of the five colleges are directed by the president of the university, who governs in matters purely academic. All other affairs are administered by a board of trustees.

Though young as a university, Notre Dame has had distinct influence on movements of the Church in the Middle West from its foundation. Founded at a period when the need of missionaries was pressing and located in a centre of missionary activity, its aid in the spread of Catholicism in the North-West was strong. The work of the early French missionaries was continued by the religious at Notre Dame, who served both as professors and evangelists. They supplied, too, a Catholic literature by their doctrinal and scientific writings and by works of fiction. A university press was early established, from which has been issued weekly a literary and religious magazine, the "Ave Maria", contributed to by the best writers of Europe and America. By attracting, too, every year a large number of non-Catholic students, the university has greatly lessened antagonism to the Church and has quickened religious feeling among the indifferent. Moreover, in laws passed by the State Legislature affecting the Church, and especially in legislation regarding education, the university is usually consulted, and any protest from it is respectfully heeded. In these matters Notre Dame has merited consideration by the State not only by her position as a leading university, but also by a remarkable display of patriotism in the Civil War. At the first call for arms seven of her priests, who were acting as professors, were sent by Father Sorin to act as chaplains; and this at a time when the university could ill spare any of her faculty.

The progress of the university has been due largely to its presidents, who have been, in all cases, men of scholarly attainments and executive capabilities. Excepting the founder, who was the first president, each had served as professor at Notre Dame before being called to direct its affairs. In all there have been eight presidents—the Very Reverend Edward Sorin, the founder; Rev. Patrick Dillon, William Corby, Augustus Lemmonier, Patrick Colovin, Thomas Walsh, Andrew Morrissey, and John Cavanaugh, all members of the Congregation of Holy Cross. Among other professors who, by their writings and researches, have contributed to the sciences which they taught and have added lustre to Notre Dame, are Rev. J. A. Zahm, C.S.C., author of scientific works and professor of physics; Rev. Alex. Kirsch, C.S.C., professor of zoology; Rev. Jos. Carrier, C.S.C., professor of botany, William Hoynes and Timothy E. Howard, professors of law; Michael E. Shawe, Gardner Jones, Rev. N. H. Gillespie, C.S.C., Rev. Daniel Hudson, C.S.C., Charles Warren Stoddard, and Maurice Francis Egan, professors of English literature; James Farnham Edwards, librarian; Arthur J. Stace and Martin J. McCue, professors of engineering; Rev. John B. Scheier, C.S.C., professor of Latin; Rev. Louis Cointet, C.S.C., professor of philosophy.

Excepting the land on which it is built, donated by Bishop Hailandière, and a few lesser donations in money, Notre Dame has developed into a great university without financial aid. It opened as a college in September, 1843, in a modest brick structure erected to serve temporarily until a larger building was completed in 1844. This was enlarged in 1853. Farher Sorin was president continuously until 1865. The enrolment of students for many years was small, numbering sixty-nine in 1850, coming from four states in the Middle West and from New York and Pennsylvania. By 1861 the number had advanced to two hundred, and in that year the faculty of the college of science was organized. In 1865 the enlarged central building of 1853 gave way to a more pretentious structure; the corps of professors was augmented to forty; the university press was established; the main library was added to, and the equipment of the college of science enlarged. The college of law was formed in 1869, and the college of engineering in 1872. A fire in April, 1879, wiped out the labours of forty years, consuming all the university buildings except the church and the university theatre. Plans were at once made for rebuilding, and the present Notre Dame begun. In September, 1879, the administration building, a large structure, planned to form the centre of a group, was completed and classes resumed. A departure from the old system of student life was made in 1887 when the first residence hall containing private rooms was erected. Before that time the common-room system, modelled on college life in Europe, prevailed. In 1900 the college of architecture was established.

The growth of the University has been steady. At present (in 1911) over one thousand students are registered, from North and South America and from nearly all the countries of Europe. All the students live on the university grounds. The faculties are made up of eighty-five professors, including many laymen. Twenty buildings are devoted to university purposes, and these with their equipment and apparatus are valued at $2,800,000. The land belonging to Notre Dame is valued at $400,000. In the main library are sixty-five thousand volumes, while libraries in various departments have about ten thousand volumes.

WILLIAM ALAN MOLONEY.

Nottingham, DIOCESE OF (NOTTINGHAMIEN), one of the original twelve English Dioceses created at the time of the restoration of the hierarchy by Pius IX in 1850, embraces the counties of Nottingham, Leicester, Derby, Lincoln, and Rutland, which were comprised in the old Midland District or vicariate, when at the request of James II in 1685, the Holy See divided England into four vicariates, the London, the Northern, the Midland, and the Western. Prior to 1840 when the number of vicars Apostolic was increased from four to eight, the Midland District had consisted of fifteen counties. In 1850 Nottingham could count only twenty-four permanent missions, many of these little better than villages. For the most part they originated from chaplaincies which had through penal times been maintained by the Catholic nobility and gentry, or had been founded independently by them. Among these there existed foundations of several religious orders. In Derbyshire the Jesuits had missions at Chesterfield and Spink Hill; in Lincolnshire at Lincoln, Boston, and Market Rasen. The Dominicans were settled in Leicester, the Fathers of Charity carried on several missions in Leicestershire, and the Cistercians occupied their newly founded Abbey of Mount St. Bernard in Charnwood Forest.

From the appearance of the Jesuits in England in 1580 at the special request of Dr. Allen, they had done much by their devoted labours to keep alive the Faith in the Nottingham diocese. Of their missions mentioned above some were among the earliest of the Society in England dating back some three hundred years. Derby was included in the district or college of the Society called the "Immaculate Conception", founded by Father Richard Blount, about 1633, first Provincial of the English Province. Extinct for many years it was partially revived in 1842 as Mount St. Mary's College, when the present college and convictus was established by the then provincial, Father Randal Lythegoe. After the Reformation, the English Province of the Friars Preachers ceased to exist, until resuscitated at Bornhem in Flanders by Philip Howard (q. v.) later cardinal, who became the first prior of the Dominicans in 1675. The first introduction of the English Dominicans from Bornhem was at Hinckley, whence for many years Leicester was served by them at intervals. Their mission at Leicester was put on a permanent basis only in 1798 by the purchase of a house by Father Francis Xavier Choppelle. The present church of the Holy Cross was begun by Father Benedict Caestrick in 1815 and was opened in 1819. The dedication under the title of Holy Cross was adopted no doubt on account of the celebrated relic of the Holy Cross brought from Bornhem, and now in London. After the lapse of three centuries a monastery of the Cistercian Order was resuscitated in England by the foundation of the Abbey of Mount St. Bernard in Leicestershire, made possible by the assistance of Ambrose Phillips de Lisle of Grace Dieu Manor, who after his conversion in December, 1825, devoted all his energies to the spread of the Faith in England. This he hoped to accomplish by the re-establishment in the country of monastic institutions. In 1835 he purchased about two hundred and twenty-seven acres of wild uncultivated land in Charnwood Forest and presented it to the Cistercians. Beginning with one brother who lived alone in a four-roomed cottage, the community rapidly increased, and a larger building was erected as well as a small chapel, opened by Dr. Walsh 11 October, 1837. This also in a short time proving insufficient, the Earl of Shrewsbury generously offered them £2,000, but on condition that a new monastery should be erected, choosing for that purpose the present site of the abbey. It was built from designs by Augustus Welby Pugin. In 1848 by Brief of Pius IX the monastery of Mount St. Bernard was raised to the dignity of an abbey, and Father Bernard, the first mitred abbot in England since the Reformation, was consecrated 18 February, 1849. In introducing the Cistercians into England, de Lisle had hoped that they would undertake missionary work and with this view he had built three chapels, at Grace Dieu, Whitwick, and the abbey. On the score of their rule, however, they declined to take charge permanently of the missions. De Lisle then decided to bring from Italy members of the Order of Charity. After much negotiation with the head of the order, Father Gentili came to Grace Dieu as chaplain. This was the commencement of the settlement of this order in the diocese. In 1841 Dr. Walsh made over to them the secular mission of Loughborough founded in 1832 by Father Benjamin Hulme. The buildings were too small to permit of a novitiate and a college of their own which they were desirous to establish. To carry out this twofold object, about nine acres were purchased; here the foundation stone of the new buildings was laid in May, 1843, and in 1844 was opened the first college and novitiate house of the institute in England. The Sisters of Mercy had come to Nottingham in 1844, and in 1846 entered their convent in close proximity to the cathedral.

The first Bishop of Nottingham was the Rt. Rev. William Hendren, O.S.F., b. in 1792, consecrated 10 September, 1848, as Vicar Apostolic of the Western District, transferred to the Diocese of Clifton, 29 Sept., 1850, and to Nottingham, 22 June, 1851. The cathedral church of St. Barnabas is of the lancet style of architecture, and is considered one of the best specimens of the work of Augustus Welby Pugin. Owing to ill-health Dr. Hendren resigned in 1853 and was succeeded by Dr. Richard Roskell, b. at Gateacre near Liverpool, in 1817. He was sent to Ushaw and afterwards to Rome, where he took his degree and was ordained in 1840. He was consecrated in the cathedral by Cardinal Wiseman on 21 September, 1853. During his episcopate a number of missions were founded in the various counties of the diocese. In Lincolnshire, through the generosity of Thomas Arthur Young of Kingerby Hall, not only was there a church and presbytery built at Gainsborough and Grimsby, but the Premonstratensian order was re-introduced into England at Crowle and Spalding. In 1874, owing to Dr. Roskell's ill-health, the pope appointed the Rev. Edward Gilpin Bagshawe of the London Oratory his coadjutor. The same year, however, Dr. Roskell tendered his resignation and Dr. Bagshawe was consecrated at the London Oratory 12 November, 1874. Numerous missions necessitated by the development of the mining industry were opened during his administration, and various communities of nuns introduced into the diocese, which he ruled for twenty-seven years. He resigned in 1901 and in 1904 was transferred to the titular Archbishopric of Seleucia. Rt. Rev. Robert Brindle, D.S.O., his successor, was born at Liverpool, 4 November, 1837. The first Catholic chaplain to receive the pension for distinguished and meritorious service, as well as Turkish and Egyptian orders and medals, he was, on his retirement from the army in 1899, on the petition of Cardinal Vaughan, appointed his assistant, and on the resignation of Dr. Bagshawe, received his Brief to the See of Nottingham 6 November, 1901.

In 1910 there were in the diocese 32,000 Catholics; 84 secular, and 44 regular, priests; 75 churches with missions attached, 31 without missions; 6 convents for men, and 9 for women.

FOLEY, *Records*; PURCELL, *Life of Ambrose Phillips de Lisle; Priory Church of Holy Cross, Leicester;* JEWITT AND CRUIKSHANK, *Cistercian Records* in *Guide to Mt. St. Bernard's Abbey.*

W. CROFT.

Nourrisson, JEAN-FELIX, philosopher, b. at Thiers, Department of Puy-de-Dôme, 18 July, 1825; d. at Paris, 13 June, 1899. He received his education in the college of his native city and in the Collège Stanislas (Paris), where, at the age of nineteen, immediately after completing his studies, he was appointed professor. In accordance with the wishes of his father, he applied himself first to the study of law, but his own inclinations led him in another direction, and he finally decided to devote himself to philosophy. He was appointed to the chair of philosophy in the Collège Stanislas (1849), received the Doctorate (1852), and was made professor of philosophy successively in the Lycée de Rennes (1854), the University of Clermont-Ferrand (1855), the Lycée Napoléon, Paris (1858) and the Collège de France (1874). Nourrisson obtained three prizes in competitions on the philosophy of Leibniz (1860), and on the rôle of psychology in the philosophy of St. Augustine (1864), subjects proposed by the Institut de France. In 1870 he became a member of the Académie des Sciences morales et politiques in the section of philosophy. Nourrisson was one of the best representatives of French spiritualistic philosophy in the nineteenth century. Not only was he a deep thinker, a penetrating philosopher and historian, but a firm believer, convinced that "conscience remains hesitating, and that convictions come to nothing, unless the teachings of religion complete the data of reason" (letter to de Barante, 5 Dec., 1856).

Besides a number of reports, memoirs, and articles in the "Journal des Débats", "Revue des Deux Mondes", "Revue Contemporaine", "Correspondant", etc., Nourrisson's works are: "Quid Plato de ideis senserit" (Paris, 1852); "Essai sur la philosophie de Bossuet" (Paris, 1852); "Les Pères de l'Eglise latine" (Paris, 1856); "Le cardinal de Bérulle" (Paris, 1856); "Exposition de la théorie platonicienne des idées" (Paris, 1858); "Tableau des progrès de la pensée humaine depuis Thalès jusqu'à Leibniz" (Paris, 1858), the third edition was augmented and brought down to Hegel's time (1867); "Histoire et philosophie" (Paris, 1860); second enlarged edition under the title "Portraits et études" (Paris, 1863); "La philosophie de Leibniz" (Paris, 1860); "Le dix-huitième siècle et la Révolution française" (Paris, 1863), 2nd ed., 1873, under the title "L'ancienne France et la Révolution"; "La nature humaine: essais de psychologie appliquée" (Paris, 1865); "La philosophie de Saint-Augustin" (Paris, 1865); "Spinoza et le naturalisme contemporain" (Paris, 1866); "De la liberté et du hasard, essai sur Alexandre d'Aphrodisias" (Paris, 1870); "Machiavel" (Paris, 1875); "Trois révolutionnaires: Turgot, Necker, Bailly" (Paris, 1885); "Pascal, physicien et philosophe" (Paris, 1885); "Philosophes de la nature: Bacon, Bayle, Toland, Buffon" (Paris, 1887); "Défense de Pascal" (Paris, 1888); "Voltaire et le voltairianisme" (Paris, s. d.); "Rousseau et le rousseauisme" (Paris, 1904), a posthumous work edited by Paul Nourrisson.

THÉDENAT, *Une Carrière Universitaire, Jean-Félix Nourrisson* (Paris, 1901).

C. A. DUBRAY.

Nourry, LE. See LE NOURRY, DENIS-NICOLAS.

Novara, DIOCESE OF (NOVARIENSIS), the capital of the province of Novara, Piedmont, Italy, noted for the manufacture of wool, cotton, and silk textiles, and machinery. The cathedral originally Romanesque has been modified. The high altar is the work of Thorwaldsen, Marchesi, and Finelli; the baldachin is by Tenarini, and there are paintings by Bordine, Crespi, and other artists, besides some ancient mosaics; the baptistery dates from the fifth century. The cathedral archives contain codices and other documents from the eighth century. The church of St. Gaudentius, a work of Pellegrino Pellegrini, was begun in 1553 to replace the ancient basilica built by St. Gaudentius and torn down to make room for the fortifications; Renaissance in style, although the cupola does not harmonize, it contains valuable paintings and frescoes by Lombard, Caccia, Procaccini, Crespi, Gilardini, Sogni, Saletta, and Fiamminghino. The city has an institute of arts and trades, a museum of antiquities, and several private galleries, among them the Leonardi. Novara was the birthplace of the ancient jurist, C. Albucius Silo, Peter Lombard, the philologist Cattaneo, the painter Caccia, and the Jesuit Tornielli. Novara, formerly Novaria, was inhabited by Ligurians and Salassians. Under the Carolingians, it was the seat of a count, but the power of the counts passed gradually to the bishops, confirmed by Otho I (969), in the person of Bishop Aupaldus. From the time of Henry III, Novara was a commune, governed by two consuls and by a consul, called *Maggiore*. Frequently at war with Vercelli and Milan, it joined Frederick Barbarossa

THE CATHEDRAL, NOVARA

against the latter city, but in 1168 was compelled to join the Lombard League. After the peace of Constance it contended with the Counts of Biandrate, Vercelli, and its own bishops, unwilling to be deprived of their sovereign rights in which they had been again confirmed by Frederick Barbarossa. Upon the expulsion of the bishop in 1210, Innocent III threatened to suppress the diocese. Later, when Martin della Torre became lord of Milan, Novara gave its allegiance to him, then to the Visconti, from which time it formed part of the Duchy of Milan, with rare intervals; in 1536-38 it belonged to Monferrato, 1556-1602 to the Farnese of Parma, 1734 to the Savoy. Because of its position, Novara has been the scene of important battles: in April, 1500, Louis the Moor, Duke of Milan, intended to besiege here Trivulzi, appointed governor by the King of France, but abandoned by his Swiss troops, he was taken prisoner. On 6 June, 1513, the Swiss in the pay of the King of Spain, drove out the French; on 10 April, 1812, the troops that had rebelled against King Charles Felix were dispersed there; on 23 March, 1849, Radetzky inflicted upon the Piedmontese a defeat that compelled King Charles Albert to abdicate.

In the fourth century, Novara was in the Diocese of Vercelli; its first bishop, St. Gaudentius, was consecrated by St. Simplicianus, Bishop of Milan (397-400). St. Lawrence is said to have introduced the Faith into Novara. St. Julius and St. Julian assisted Gaudentius in the conversion of the diocese. The list of bishops has been preserved on two ivory diptychs, one in the cathedral dates from 1168; the other in the church of St. Gaudentius from 1343. Among the bishops were St. Agabius (417); St. Victor

(489); St. Honoratus (c. 500); St. Leo (c. 700), biographer of St. Gaudentius; Adalgisus (c. 840), called *Gemma Sacerdotum*; Albertus, killed by the Counts of Biandrate in 1081; Litifredus (1122) and Papiniano della Rovere (1296); Guglielmo Amidano (1343), a learned theologian and former general of the Augustinians; Pietro Filargo (1388), later the Antipope Alexander V; Bartolomeo Visconti (1429), deposed by Eugene IV, who suspected him of treachery, but finally reinstated; Cardinal Gian Angelo Arcimboldi (1525); Gian Antonio Serbelloni (1560), founder of the seminary; Francisco Rossi (1579), founder of a second seminary; Carlo Bescapé (1593), a Barnabite historian of the diocese; Benedetto Odescalchi (1650), later Innocent XI. Suffragan of Vercelli, it has 372 parishes; 408,000 inhabitants; 11 religious houses of men and 14 of women; 2 schools for boys, and 6 for girls; and 3 Catholic weekly publications.

SAVIO, *Gli antichi vescovi d'Italia*, I, *Piemonte*; CAPPELLETTI, *Le Chiese d'Italia*, XIV; MORBIO, *Storia di Novara* (Milan, 1833).

U. BENIGNI.

Nova Scotia.—I. GEOGRAPHY.—Nova Scotia is one of the maritime provinces of Canada. It forms part of what was formerly Acadie or Acadia and now consists of what is known as the peninsula of Nova Scotia proper and the Island of Cape Breton. The island is separated from the mainland by the Gut or Strait of Canso, an important international waterway connecting the Atlantic Ocean with the Gulf of St. Lawrence. This strait is about fifteen miles long and varies in width from half a mile to two miles. Sable Island, a dangerous sand ridge, on which in 1518 a Frenchman, named de Lery, made a fruitless attempt to form a settlement, was before the confederation of the provinces a part of the Province of Nova Scotia, but by the Union Act (British North America Act of 1867) this island came under the exclusive legislative authority of the Dominion Parliament. It is about twenty-five miles long and of varying width. In some places it is about a mile and a half wide. From the numerous shipwrecks that have occurred there, Sable Island has become known as "the graveyard of the Atlantic".

The Province of Nova Scotia lies between 43° 25' and 47° north latitude, and 59° 40' and 66° 35' west longitude. On the north it is bounded by the Bay of Fundy, Chignecto Bay, New Brunswick, Northumberland Straits, and the Gulf of Saint Lawrence, and on all other sides by the Atlantic Ocean. The peninsula is connected with the Province of New Brunswick by the Isthmus of Chignecto which is about twelve and a half miles wide. The total area of Nova Scotia is estimated at about 21,428 square miles. The surface is undulating. There are three mountain ranges, namely: the Cobequid Mountains, commencing at Cape Chignecto in Cumberland and running about one hundred miles through the Counties of Colchester, Pictou and Antigonish; the North Mountains extending from Cape Blomidon to Digby Neck, about one hundred and ten miles; and the South Mountains, a low range parallel with the North Mountains and with some interruptions running through the middle of the peninsula and through the Island of Cape Breton, the range being about three hundred and fifty miles long. The greatest height of these mountains is 1700 feet above sea-level. The rivers are small, and no part of the country is far from the sea. The lakes are numerous but not large. The Bras d'Or Lakes in Cape Breton divide the island into two parts and cover about 500 square miles. The coastline of Nova Scotia is about 1500 miles and there are numerous ports of refuge. The harbours of Halifax, Louisburg, and Sydney are among the best in North America. The average temperature ranges from 65° F. in summer to 25° F. in winter. The high tides on the Bay of Fundy constitute an unusual physical feature of the counties lying along the bay.

The resources of Nova Scotia are diversified. Farming, mining, fishing, lumbering, and manufacturing yield an ample return to the industry of the inhabitants. In the counties lying along the Bay of Fundy and penetrated by the inlets are valuable dike-lands begun by the early French settlers, and continued after the expulsion of the Acadians by the colonists from New England, who in 1760 and 1761 took possession of the lands of the expelled Acadians. The agricultural products of the country are hay, wheat, oats, barley, potatoes, and turnips, all of which obtain a local market. In the Annapolis Valley about 750,000 barrels of apples are annually produced and shipped to the English markets. There are large coal measures in the Counties of Cumberland, Pictou, Inverness, and Cape Breton. The coal is bituminous, and supplies the local demand and a large portion of the markets of the St. Lawrence River. Iron, copper, and gypsum are also mined. The coast fisheries are looked upon as very valuable. They consist of salmon, cod, shad, halibut, mackerel, herring, shellfish, and are exported to American and European markets. The forests produce maple, birch, hemlock, spruce, pine, and beech. The manufacturing interests are also extensive, the larger plants being the iron and steel works at Sydney and Sydney Mines.

II. ETHNOGRAPHY.—When the European colonists first came to Nova Scotia they found the country inhabited by a tribe of Indians known as the Micmacs. These savages were converted to Christianity by the early French missionaries. Their descendants, numbering 1542 at the time of the last official census (1901), belong to the Catholic Church. They live principally on reservations set aside for them by the Government. The duty of caring for the Indians has been assigned by the British North American Act to the Parliament of Canada. The descendants of the French settlers form an important body. They numbered at the time of the last census 45,161. They also are Catholics and are noted for their industry and frugality. The Germans form another important element. They are descended from the body of German settlers who arrived in Nova Scotia shortly after the founding of Halifax, and in 1753 removed to the County of Lunenburg. Principally Lutherans and Anglicans, they are thrifty and industrious. The English settlers came in after the defeat of the French, and after the Revolutionary War from twenty to thirty thousand loyalists left the United States and settled in Nova Scotia. Later on came accessions from Ireland and Scotland. At the last census these last-mentioned races were estimated as follows: English, 159,753; Scottish, 143,382; Irish, 54,710. There were also 5984 negroes in the province. They are descended from slaves who were brought to Nova Scotia before the abolition of slavery in British dominions. The total population of the Province of Nova Scotia in 1901 was 459,572, of whom 129,578 were returned as Catholics.

III. HISTORY.—John Cabot made his first voyage from Bristol in search of a westerly route to India in 1497. He made a landfall on the eastern coast of North America, but whether on Labrador, Newfoundland, or Nova Scotia is uncertain. No actual settlement immediately followed the voyages of the Cabots. In 1604 King Henry IV of France gave a commission to de Monts appointing him viceroy of the territory lying between the Gulf of St. Lawrence and the mouth of the Hudson River. De Monts arrived at the mouth of the La Have River on the coast of Nova Scotia and he then sailed up the Bay of Fundy and into the sheet of water which is now known as the Annapolis Basin. Here, near what is now the town of Annapolis, a site was chosen for a settlement and to the place de Monts gave the name of Port-Royal. Leaving some of his companions there he sailed along the northern shore of the Bay of Fundy, entered the St. John River and later made his winter quarters at the mouth of the St. Croix River. The companions whom he left at Port-Royal returned to France. The following year de Monts and the survivors of his party at St. Croix returned to Port-Royal. This was the beginning of European settlement in Canada, and the colony thus established is the oldest European settlement in North America with the exception of St. Augustine in Florida. The colony was temporarily abandoned in 1607, but in 1610 the French returned and remained in undisturbed possession until 1613, when a freebooter from Virginia named Argall made a descent upon the colony and totally destroyed it.

In 1621 King James I gave a grant of Acadia to Sir William Alexander and changed the name to Nova Scotia; but the efforts of Sir William Alexander to build up an English settlement were of little avail. After the capture of Quebec by David Kirke, peace was made between France and Great Britain by the Treaty of St-Germain-en-Laye (1632), and Quebec and Nova Scotia were given back to France. But in 1654 Cromwell sent out a fleet to capture the Dutch colony at Manhattan, and a portion of his fleet sailed into Annapolis Basin, and Port-Royal surrendered to them. After the accession of Charles II, by the Treaty of Breda, Nova Scotia was again restored to France. In 1690 Sir William Phips took command of a naval force from Massachusetts, and he easily took Port-Royal, but he left no garrison there and the French soon reoccupied it. After several years of war terms of peace were again arranged between Great Britain and France by the Treaty of Ryswick (1679) and Nova Scotia was once again placed under the rule of France. The final capture of Port-Royal took place in 1710 when the French surrendered to Colonel Nicholson, who named the settlement Annapolis in honour of Queen Anne. The long warfare between the two countries for the possession of Nova Scotia proper was brought to a close by the Treaty of Utrecht (1713), which provided that the peninsula should belong to England and the Island of Cape Breton to France. Annapolis became the capital of the colony and the only other English settlement was at Canso. Very few settlers arrived in the country for nearly forty years. The French to regain their position strongly fortified Louisburg on the south-east coast of Cape Breton. War again broke out and in 1745 a force was sent from Massachusetts under Colonel William Pepperell. After a siege of seven weeks the Governor of Louisburg was obliged to surrender. To recapture Louisburg the French in the year following sent out a powerful fleet under d'Anville. This expedition was unfortunate. The fleet encountered bad weather and after the remnants of it arrived at Chebucto (Halifax) Harbour, the commander and many of the men died; those who survived returned to France. Great Britain held Louisburg for three years after the first capture; and then terms of peace were arranged by the Treaty of Aix-la-Chapelle (1748) and Louisburg was given to France. To strengthen the position of the English in Nova Scotia it was determined to establish a permanent settlement on the shores of Chebucto Harbour. Accordingly in June, 1749, Colonel Cornwallis arrived with a number of settlers and founded the town of Halifax. The seat of government was transferred from Annapolis to the new town, and Cornwallis selected a council to assist him in the administration of the colony. Six years later occurred the cruel expulsion of the Acadians from their fertile lands along the Bay of Fundy. Several thousands of these people were banished from Nova Scotia and scattered in the English colonies from Massachusetts to Louisiana. In many cases families were separated and the event remains a dark blot on the reputation of the English governor of that day.

From 1749 to 1758 the governor of the colony administered its affairs with the assistance of a council, but there were no representatives directly chosen by the people. In the latter year the first representative Assembly was convened in Halifax. By the laws of that time Roman Catholics were disqualified from holding seats in the legislature.

In 1756 began the famous Seven Years' War; two years later the final capture of Louisburg, under General Amherst, took place. The siege lasted for seven weeks and at last the French governor was obliged to surrender unconditionally. By the Treaty of Paris (1763) France ceded Cape Breton, Prince Edward Island, and Canada to Great Britain, and the long duel in North America between the two great European powers came at last to an end. Cape Breton and Prince Edward Island became a part of Nova Scotia; but in 1770 Prince Edward Island severed its political connexion, as in 1784 did Cape Breton and New Brunswick. Cape Breton was reannexed to Nova Scotia in 1819. During the Revolutionary War Nova Scotia remained loyal to Britain. Many people in the United States who did not approve of the war migrated to the British provinces. These were known as United Empire Loyalists. In the province to which they removed they received free grants of land and they formed a valuable accession to the scant population.

At the first session of the Legislature of Nova Scotia a law was passed requiring all Catholic priests to leave the country; and any person who harboured a priest was liable to payment of a large fine. These laws were subsequently repealed. In 1827 a Catholic was permitted, for the first time, to take his seat as a member of the Assembly. While Nova Scotia had representative government as early as 1758, the executive was not in any way responsible to the people; affairs were so administered for about seventy years. Then arose a strong agitation under the brilliant leadership of Joseph Howe. After several years of discussion and negotiation, in 1848, responsible government was secured and thereafter the tenure of office of the government was made to depend upon the support of the representatives of the people in the Assembly. The next twenty years were years of continued progress. Steam communication was established with England; railways were built; and a revival of trade took place. In 1867 the Provinces of Nova Scotia, New Brunswick, Quebec, and Ontario were confederated as the Dominion of Canada, under the provision of the British North America Act. The legislative functions of the Dominion and of the provinces were separated, and subjects of local concern were assigned to the several provinces. Among the latter may be mentioned education and municipal institutions, solemnization of marriage, and property and civil rights. Among the powers assigned to the Dominion are the postal service, census and statistics, military and naval service and defence, navigation, banking, copyrights, marriage and divorce, and the regulations in regard to the Indians.

IV. CHURCH AND STATE.—The relations between Church and State do not give rise to much complaint. There is no state religion, and all religious denominations are placed on an equality by the law. The school system is undenominational. The Catholics have no separate schools, but in centres of population where they are numerous and in country districts where they predominate, they are permitted by usage to have teachers of their own belief. There is perfect freedom of worship in every respect.

V. DIVISION INTO DIOCESES, POPULATION, ETC.—The Province of Nova Scotia is divided into two dioceses: the Archdiocese of Halifax, which embraces the eleven westernmost counties of the province; and the Diocese of Antigonish, which embraces the four counties on Cape Breton Island, and the Counties of Guysborough, Pictou, and Antigonish on the peninsula. According to the last official census there were 54,301 Catholics in the Archdiocese of Halifax, and 75,277 in the Diocese of Antigonish. By chapter 31 of the Acts of the Legislature of Nova Scotia for the year 1849, the Roman Catholic Bishop of Halifax and his successors were incorporated under the name of "the Roman Catholic Episcopal Corporation of the City and County of Halifax" with perpetual succession, and power to hold, receive and enjoy real and personal estate. In 1888, by chapter 102 of the Acts of that year, s. 4, it was provided as follows:—"The Corporation may acquire by deed of conveyance or by devise or in any other manner for the time being recognized by law lands within Nova Scotia and may have, hold, possess and enjoy the same for the general uses and purposes eleemosynary, ecclesiastical or educational of the Archdiocese or of any portion thereof or for any such uses or purposes and may sell, alien, exchange, assign, release mortgage, lease, convey or otherwise dispose of such lands or any part thereof for such uses and purposes or any of them in the manner hereinafter provided". This statute also provides that all Church property, real and personal, shall be vested in the corporation and used as the property of the Roman Catholic Church within the archdiocese for eleemosynary, ecclesiastical, and educational purposes. The corporation executes a deed by its corporate seal and the signature of the archbishop, his coadjutor or vicar-general, and one other Roman Catholic clergyman of the archdiocese. The Diocese of Antigonish was formerly known as the Diocese of Arichat; by chapter 86 of the Acts of the Legislature of Nova Scotia for 1887 the name was changed from Arichat to Antigonish. The Roman Catholic Episcopal Corporation of Antigonish was created by Chapter 74 of the Acts of the Legislature of Nova Scotia (1854), and the legislative provisions with respect to this corporation are substantially the same as those relating to the Roman Catholic Episcopal Corporation of Halifax.

VI. TAXATION AND EXEMPTION OF CHURCHES, ETC.—The Assessment Act [R.S.N.S., 1900, c. 73, sec. 4, SS. (b)] exempts from taxation every church and place of worship and the land used in connexion therewith, and every church and burial ground. The same statute also exempts the real estate of every college, academy, or institution of learning and every schoolhouse. The statute mentioned applies to all property in Nova Scotia outside of the city of Halifax. Property within the city of Halifax is dealt with by the Halifax City Charter, S. 335, which exempts every building used as a college, incorporated academy, schoolhouse, or other seminary of learning, and every building used for public worship and the site, appurtenances and furniture of each. This charter also exempts every poorhouse, almshouse, orphans' home, house of industry, house of refuge, and infants' home, while used for the purposes indicated by their respective designations, and all their real and personal property.

VII. EXEMPTION OF THE CLERGY FROM PUBLIC SERVICES.—There are no obnoxious public duties required to be performed by clergymen. The Juries' Act (R. S. N. S., 1900, c. 162, s. 5) exempts from serving on juries "clergymen and ministers of the Gospel". The Militia Act (R. S., c. 41, s. 11) provides that the clergy and ministers of all religious denominations, professors in colleges and universities, and teachers in religious orders shall be exempt from liability to serve in the militia.

VIII. PRISONS AND REFORMATORIES.—These are maintained by the State and are non-denominational. The clergy are permitted to minister to the spiritual wants of the people of their own faith. At Halifax there are two reformatories conducted under Catholic auspices, namely, St. Patrick's Home for Boys, and the Good Shepherd Reformatory for women. Under the provisions of the Act relating to prisons and reformatories (R. S. C., c. 148), whenever a boy, who is a Catholic and under eighteen years, is convicted in Nova Scotia for an offence for which he is liable to imprisonment, the presiding justice may sentence such boy to be detained in St. Patrick's Home for a term not exceeding five years and not less than one year. The statute provides also that boys so detained shall be educated and taught a trade. This home is assisted from the public funds and is open at all time to public inspection. It is under the direction of the Christian Brothers. The statute provides also that juvenile offenders and vagrants may be sent to this reformatory. Similar provision is made in the case of a girl, being a Catholic and above the age of sixteen years, convicted of an offence punishable by imprisonment in the city prison or common jail for a term of two months or longer. She may be sentenced to the Good Shepherd Reformatory at Halifax, for an extended or substituted imprisonment subject to conditions: (a) if she is under the age of twenty-one, such extended imprisonment may be until she attains the age of twenty-one, or for any shorter or longer term not less than two and not more than four years; (b) if she is of the age of twenty-one or upwards, such extended imprisonment may be for any term not less than one year and not more than two years. Catholic girls under the age of sixteen may be sentenced in the same way to the Good Shepherd Industrial Refuge at Halifax, where the sisters are in charge and are obliged to instruct them in reading and writing and in arithmetic to the end of simple proportion, and also to teach them a trade or occupation suitable to their capabilities. The Good Shepherd Reformatory receives assistance from the public funds and is subject to inspection by a government official.

IX. WILLS AND CHARITABLE BEQUESTS.—Every person of the age of twenty-one years and upwards may dispose of his property by will. Such will must be signed by the testator in the presence of two witnesses who shall subscribe thereto as witnesses in his presence and in the presence of each other. By statute (R. S. N. S., 1900, c. 135) a devise or bequest of real or personal property to any religious or charitable corporation or any incorporated institution of learning is valid and effectual for the purpose of vesting the property in such body, notwithstanding that it was not by its act of incorporation empowered to take or hold real or personal property or notwithstanding any limit in such act as to the amount of real or personal property the incorporated body was empowered to take or hold—provided the statute shall not extend to render valid or effectual any devise or bequest that is to be void for another reason.

X. CEMETERIES.—By statute (R. S. N. S., 1900, c. 132) it is provided that any number of persons, not less than ten, may form themselves into a company for the purpose of establishing a public cemetery. Catholic cemeteries, however, are owned by the Episcopal Corporation of the diocese. Cemeteries are exempt from taxation and the lots or plots owned by individual proprietors cannot be seized or taken on execution.

XI. MARRIAGE LAWS.—By the provisions of the British North America Act, the subject of marriage and divorce is assigned to the Dominion Parliament, and that of the solemnization of marriage to the legislature of the province. The former body, under this distribution, deals with the capacity to contract marriage, and in pursuance of such power it has enacted (R. S. C., c. 105) that "a marriage is not invalid merely because the woman is a sister of a deceased wife of the man, or a daughter of a sister of a deceased wife of the man". The provincial statute (R.S.N.S., 1900, c. 111) deals with the mode of solemnizing a marriage within the province. It provides that every marriage shall be solemnized by a minister of a church or religious denomination, being a man and resident in Canada, who is recognized as duly ordained according to the rites and ceremonies of the church or denomination to which he belongs. Persons belonging to the society known as the Salvation Army may be married by any duly appointed male commissioner or staff officer of the society. No person shall officiate at the solemnization of any marriage unless publication has been made of the banns of the marriage or a licence has been obtained for the solemnization of the marriage. The banns shall be published in any church at the place in which one of the parties resides by the officiating clergyman in an audible voice during the time of Divine service, and if there is more than one public service in the church on each Sunday, such publication shall be made at three several services held on two or more Sundays; otherwise the publication may be at two several services on two Sundays. Every marriage shall be solemnized in the presence of at least two witnesses. After the solemnization of the marriage the clergyman solemnizing the same shall make out a certificate containing the date of the marriage, the place thereof, the date of the publication of the banns, the church in which and the clergyman by whom the banns were published, the names of the witnesses and his own name, and the religious denomination to which he belongs. The marriage register giving the above particulars, and also the names, ages, residences, etc., of the parties and their parents shall also be filled up. Returns in the prescribed form shall be made by the clergyman to the nearest issuer of marriage licences within ten days after the solemnization. Forms for that purpose are furnished by the issuer of marriage licences. Large penalties are provided for solemnizing marriage without banns of marriage or licence, for refusing to publish the banns, for solemnizing under an illegal licence, and for failing to return the marriage register.

XII. DIVORCE.—In Nova Scotia there is a court for divorce and matrimonial causes, and it has jurisdiction over all matters relating to prohibited marriages and divorce, and may declare any marriage null and void for impotence, adultery, cruelty, or kindred within the degrees prohibited in an Act made in the thirty-second year of King Henry the Eighth, entitled "An Act concerning pre-contracts, and touching degrees of Consanguinity"; and whenever a sentence of divorce shall be given, the court may pronounce such determination as it shall think fit on the rights of the parties or either of them to courtesy or dower. In the provinces of the dominion in which no divorce courts exist, applications for divorce are made to Parliament and the evidence is taken and considered by the members of the Senate of Canada. In Nova Scotia there is an appeal from the decision of the judge of the Divorce Court to the Supreme Court of Nova Scotia sitting *in banco*. When the final decree is for the dissolution of the marriage, the statute enables either of the parties to marry again as if the prior marriage had been dissolved by death; but no clergyman shall be liable to any penalty for refusing to solemnize the marriage of either of the parties who have been divorced. In cases of divorce the wife and husband are not competent to testify, but in proceedings by the wife, on account of adultery coupled with cruelty, the husband and wife are competent and compellable to give evidence of or relating to such cruelty.

XIII. RELIGIOUS ORDERS, SCHOOLS, ETC.—Several of the public schools of the province are taught by members of the religious orders. In such cases the teachers must be licensed in the same way as other public teachers, and they are paid out of the public funds. Besides the public schools there are many excellent private schools taught by members of religious orders. These do not receive any assistance from the public treasury. The public schools are maintained by a grant from the government and by local taxation upon the property holders of the section or municipality. They are otherwise free and all children of school age are entitled to be admitted to them.

BROWN, *History of the Island of Cape Breton* (London, 1869); the works of PARKMAN (Boston, 1882–4); CALKIN, *History of Canada* (Halifax, 1907); ROBERTS, *History of Canada* (Boston, 1897); CALKIN, *School Geography of the World* (Halifax, 1878); *Revised Statutes of Canada* (Ottawa, 1906); *Statutes of Nova Scotia* (various dates); *Statutes of Canada* (various dates); *Revised Statutes of Nova Scotia* (Halifax, 1900). For further bibliography see HALIFAX, ARCHDIOCESE OF.

JOSEPH A. CHISHOLM.

Novatian and Novatianism—Novatian was a schismatic of the third century, and founder of the sect of the Novatians; he was a Roman priest, and made himself antipope. His name is given as Novatus (Νοουάτος, Eusebius; Ναυάτος, Socrates) by Greek writers, and also in the verses of Damasus and Prudentius, on account of the metre.

BIOGRAPHY.—We know little of his life. St. Cornelius in his letter to Fabius of Antioch relates that Novatian was possessed by Satan for a season, apparently while a catechumen; for the exorcists attended him, and he fell into a sickness from which instant death was expected; he was, therefore, given baptism by affusion as he lay on his bed. The rest of the rites were not supplied on his recovery, nor was he confirmed by the bishop. "How then can he have received the Holy Ghost?" asks Cornelius. Novatian was a man of learning and had been trained in literary composition. Cornelius speaks of him sarcastically as "that maker of dogmas, that champion of ecclesiastical learning". His eloquence is mentioned by Cyprian (Ep. lx, 3), and a pope (presumably Fabian) promoted him to the priesthood in spite of the protests (according to Cornelius) of all the clergy and many of the laity that it was uncanonical for one who had received only clinical baptism to be admitted among the clergy. The story told by Eulogius of Alexandria that Novatian was Archdeacon of Rome, and was made a priest by the pope in order to prevent his succeeding to the papacy, contradicts the evidence of Cornelius and supposes a later state of things when the Roman deacons were statesmen rather than ministers. The anonymous work "Ad Novatianum" (xiii) tells us that Novatian, "so long as he was in the one house, that is in Christ's Church, bewailed the sins of his neighbours as if they were his own, bore the burdens of the brethren, as the Apostle exhorts, and strengthened with consolation the backsliding in heavenly faith."

The Church had enjoyed a peace of thirty-eight years when Decius issued his edict of persecution early in 250. Pope St. Fabian was martyred on 20 Jan., and it was impossible to elect a successor. Cornelius, writing in the following year, says of Novatian that, through cowardice and love of his life, he denied that he was a priest in the time of persecution; for he was exhorted by the deacons to come out of the cell, in which he had shut himself up, to assist the brethren as a priest now that they were in danger. But he was angry and departed, saying he no longer wished to be a priest, for he was in love with another philosophy. The meaning of this story is not clear. Did Novatian wish to eschew the active work of the priesthood and give himself to an ascetic life?

At all events, during the persecution he certainly wrote letters in the name of the Roman clergy, which were sent by them to St. Cyprian (Epp. xxx and xxxvi). The letters are concerned with the question of the Lapsi (q. v.), and with the exaggerated claim of the martyrs at Carthage to restore them all without penance. The Roman clergy agree with Cyprian that the matter must be settled with moderation by councils to be held when this should be possible; the election of a new bishop must be awaited; proper severity of discipline must be preserved, such as had always distinguished the Roman Church since the days when her faith was praised by St. Paul (Rom., i, 8), but cruelty to the repentant must be avoided. There is evidently no idea in the minds of the Roman priests that restoration of the lapsed to communion is impossible or improper; but there are severe expressions in the letters. It seems that Novatian got into some trouble during the persecution, since Cornelius says that St. Moses, the martyr (d. 250), seeing the boldness of Novatian, separated him from communion, together with the five priests who had been associated with him.

At the beginning of 251 the persecution relaxed, and St. Cornelius was elected pope in March, "when the chair of Fabian, that is the place of Peter, was vacant", with the consent of nearly all the clergy, of the people, and of the bishops present (Cyprian, Ep. lv, 8–9). Some days later Novatian set himself up as a rival pope. Cornelius tells us Novatian suffered an extraordinary and sudden change; for he had taken a tremendous oath that he would never attempt to become bishop. But now he sent two of his party to summon three bishops from a distant corner of Italy, telling them they must come to Rome in haste, in order that a division might be healed by their mediation and that of other bishops. These simple men were constrained to confer the episcopal order upon him at the tenth hour of the day. One of these returned to the church bewailing and confessing his sin, "and we despatched" says Cornelius, "successors of the other two bishops to the places whence they came, after ordaining them." To ensure the loyalty of his supporters Novatian forced them, when receiving Holy Communion, to swear by the Blood and the Body of Christ that they would not go over to Cornelius.

Cornelius and Novatian sent messengers to the different Churches to announce their respective claims. From St. Cyprian's correspondence we know of the careful investigation made by the Council of Carthage, with the result that Cornelius was supported by the whole African episcopate. St. Dionysius of Alexandria also took his side, and these influential adhesions soon made his position secure. But for a time the whole Church was torn by the question of the rival popes. We have few details. St. Cyprian writes that Novatian "assumed the primacy" (Ep. lxix, 8), and sent out his new apostles to many cities to set new foundations for his new establishment; and, though there were already in all provinces and cities bishops of venerable age, of pure faith, of tried virtue, who had been proscribed in the persecution, he dared to create other false bishops over their heads (Ep. lv, 24) thus claiming the right of substituting bishops by his own authority as Cornelius did in the case just mentioned. There could be no more startling proof of the importance of the Roman See than this sudden revelation of an episode of the third century: the whole Church convulsed by the claim of an antipope; the recognized impossibility of a bishop being a Catholic and legitimate pastor if he is on the side of the wrong pope; the uncontested claim of both rivals to consecrate a new bishop in any place (at all events, in the West) where the existing bishop resisted their authority. Later, in the same way, in a letter to Pope Stephen, St. Cyprian urges him to appoint (so he seems to imply) a new bishop at Arles, where the bishop had become a Novatianist. St. Dionysius of Alexandria wrote to Pope Stephen that all the Churches in the East and beyond, which had been split in two, were now united, and that all their prelates were now rejoicing exceedingly in this unexpected peace—in Antioch, Cæsarea of Palestine, Jerusalem, Tyre, Laodicea of Syria, Tarsus and all the Churches of Cilicia, Cæsarea and all Cappadocia, the Syrias and Arabia (which depended for alms on the Roman Church), Mesopotamia, Pontus and Bithynia, "and all the Churches everywhere", so far did the Roman schism cause its effects to be felt. Meanwhile, before the end of 251, Cornelius had assembled a council of sixty bishops (probably all from Italy or the neighbouring islands), in which Novatian was excommunicated. Other bishops who were not present added their signatures, and the entire list was sent to Antioch and doubtless to all the other principal Churches.

It is not surprising that a man of such talents as Novatian should have been conscious of his superiority to Cornelius, or that he should have found priests to assist his ambitious views. His mainstay was in the confessors yet in prison, Maximus, Urbanus, Nicostratus, and others. Dionysius and Cyprian wrote to remonstrate with them, and they returned to the Church. A prime mover on Novatian's side was the Carthaginian priest Novatus, who had favoured laxity at Carthage out of opposition to his bishop. In St. Cyprian's earlier letters about Novatian (xliv-xlviii, l), there is not a word about any heresy, the whole question being as to the legitimate occupant of the place of Peter. In Ep. li, the words "schismatico immo hæretico furore" refer to the wickedness of opposing the true bishop. The same is true of "hæreticæ pravitatis nocens factio" with Ep. liii. In Ep. liv, Cyprian found it necessary to send his book "De lapsis" to Rome, so that the question of the lapsed was already prominent, but Ep. lv is the earliest in which the "Novatian heresy" as such is argued against. The letters of the Roman confessors (Ep. liii) and Cornelius (xlix, 1) to Cyprian do not mention it, though the latter speaks in general terms of Novatian as a schismatic or a heretic; nor does the pope mention heresy in his abuse of Novatian in the letter to Fabius of Antioch (Eusebius, VI, xliii), from which so much has been quoted above. It is equally clear that the letters sent out by Novatian were not concerned with the *lapsi*, but were "letters full of calumnies and maledictions sent in large numbers, which threw nearly all the Churches into disorder" (Cornelius, Ep. xlix). The first of those sent to Carthage consisted apparently of "bitter accusations" against Cornelius, and St. Cyprian thought it so disgraceful that he did not read it to the council (Ep. xlv, 2). The messengers from Rome to the Carthaginian Council broke out into similar attacks (Ep. xliv). It is necessary to notice this point, because it is so frequently overlooked by historians, who represent the sudden but short-lived disturbance throughout the Catholic Church caused by Novatian's ordination to have been a division between bishops on the subject of his heresy. Yet it is obvious enough that the question could not present itself: "Which is preferable, the doctrine of Cornelius or that of Novatian?" If Novatian were ever so orthodox, the first matter was to examine whether his ordination was legitimate or not, and whether his accusations against Cornelius were false or true. An admirable reply addressed to him by St. Dionysius of Alexandria has been preserved (Eusebius, VI, xlv): "Dionysius to his brother Novatian, greeting. If it was against your will, as you say, that you were led, you will prove it by retiring of your free will. For you ought to have suffered anything rather than divide the Church of God; and to be martyred rather than cause a schism would have been no less glorious than to be martyred rather than commit idolatry, nay in my opinion it would have been a yet greater act; for in the one case one is a martyr for one's own soul alone, in the other for the whole Church". Here again there is no question of heresy.

But yet within a couple of months Novatian was called a heretic, not only by Cyprian but throughout the Church, for his severe views about the restoration of those who had lapsed in the persecution. He held that idolatry was an unpardonable sin, and that the Church had no right to restore to communion any who had fallen into it. They might repent and be admitted to a lifelong penance, but their forgiveness must be left to God; it could not be pronounced in this world. Such harsh sentiments were not altogether a novelty. Tertullian had resisted the forgiveness of adultery by Pope Callistus as an innovation. Hippolytus was equally inclined to severity. In various places and at various times laws were made which punished certain sins either with the deferring of Communion till the hour of death, or even with refusal of Communion in the hour of death. Even St. Cyprian approved the latter course in the case of those who refused to do penance and only repented on their death-bed; but this was because such a repentance seemed of doubtful sincerity. But severity in itself was but cruelty or injustice; there was no heresy until it was denied that the Church has the power to grant absolution in certain cases. This was Novatian's heresy; and St. Cyprian says the Novatians held no longer the Catholic creed and baptismal interrogation, for when they said "Dost thou believe in the remission of sins, and everlasting life, through Holy Church?" they were liars.

WRITINGS.—St. Jerome mentions a number of writings of Novatian, only two of which have come down to us, the "De Cibis Judaicis" and the "De Trinitate". The former is a letter written in retirement during a time of persecution, and was preceded by two other letters on Circumcision and the Sabbath, which are lost. It interprets the unclean animals as signifying different classes of vicious men; and explains that the greater liberty allowed to Christians is not to be a motive for luxury. The book "De Trinitate" is a fine piece of writing. The first eight chapters concern the transcendence and greatness of God, who is above all thought and can be described by no name. Novatian goes on to prove the Divinity of the Son at great length, arguing from both the Old and the New Testaments, and adding that it is an insult to the Father to say that a Father who is God cannot beget a Son who is God. But Novatian falls into the error made by so many early writers of separating the Father from the Son, so that he makes the Father address to the Son the command to create, and the Son obeys; he identifies the Son with the angels who appeared in the Old Testament to Agar, Abraham, etc. "It pertains to the person of Christ that He should be God because He is the Son of God, and that He should be an Angel because He announces the Father's Will" (*paternæ dispositionis annuntiator est*). The Son is "the second Person after the Father", less than the Father in that He is originated by the Father; He is the imitator of all His works, and is always obedient to the Father, and is one with Him "by concord, by love, and by affection".

No wonder such a description should seem to opponents to make two Gods; and consequently, after a chapter on the Holy Ghost (xxix), Novatian returns to the subject in a kind of appendix (xxx-xxxi). Two kinds of heretics, he explains, try to guard the unity of God, the one kind (Sabellians) by identifying the Father with the Son, the other (Ebionites, etc.) by denying that the Son is God; thus is Christ again crucified between two thieves, and is reviled by both. Novatian declares that there is indeed but one God, unbegotten, invisible, immense, immortal; the Word (*Sermo*), His Son, is a substance that proceeds from Him (*substantia prolata*), whose generation no apostle nor angel nor any creature can declare. He is not a second God, because He is eternally *in* the Father, else the Father would not be eternally Father. He proceeded from the Father, when the Father willed (this *syncatabasis* for the purpose of creation is evidently distinguished from the eternal begetting *in* the Father), and remained *with* the Father. If He were also the unbegotten, invisible, incomprehensible, there might indeed be said to be two Gods; but in fact He has from the Father whatever He has, and there is but one origin (*origo, principium*), the Father. "One God is demonstrated, the true and eternal Father, from whom alone this energy of the Godhead is sent forth, being handed on to the Son, and again by communion of substance it is returned to the Father." In this doctrine there is much that is incorrect, yet much that seems meant to express the consubstantiality of the Son, or at least His generation out of the substance of the Father. But it is a very unsatisfactory unity which is attained, and it seems to be suggested that the Son is not immense or invisible, but the image of the Father capable of manifesting Him. Hippolytus is in the same difficulty, and it appears that Novatian borrowed from him as well as from Tertullian and Justin. It would seem that Tertullian and Hippolytus understood somewhat better than did Novatian the traditional Roman doctrine of the consubstantiality of the Son, but that all three were led astray by their acquaintance with the Greek theology, which interpreted of the Son as God Scriptural expressions (especially those of St. Paul) which properly apply to Him as the God-Man. But at least Novatian has the merit of not identifying the Word with the Father, nor Sonship with the prolation of the Word for the purpose of Creation, for He plainly teaches the eternal generation. This is a notable advance on Tertullian.

On the Incarnation Novatian seems to have been orthodox, though he is not explicit. He speaks correctly of the one Person having two substances, the Godhead and Humanity, in the way that is habitual to the most exact Western theologians. But he very often speaks of "the man" assumed by the Divine Person, so that he has been suspected of Nestorianizing. This is unfair, since he is equally liable to the opposite accusation of making "the man" so far from being a distinct personality that He is merely flesh assumed (*caro*, or *substantia carnis et corporis*). But there is no real ground for supposing that Novatian meant to deny an intellectual soul in Christ; he does not think of the point, and is only anxious to assert the reality of our Lord's flesh. The Son of God, he says, joins to Himself the Son of Man, and by this connexion and mingling he makes the Son of Man become Son of God, which He was not by nature. This last sentence has been described as Adoptionism. But the Spanish Adoptionists taught that the Human Nature of Christ as joined to the Godhead is the adopted Son of God. Novatian only means that before its assumption it was not by nature the Son of God; the form of words is bad, but there is not necessarily any heresy in the thought. Newman, though he does not make the best of Novatian, says that he "approaches more nearly to doctrinal precision than any of the writers of the East and West" who preceded him (Tracts theological and ecclesiastical, p. 239).

The two pseudo-Cyprianic works, both by one author, "De Spectaculis" and "De bono pudicitiæ", are attributed to Novatian by Weyman, followed by Demmler, Bardenhewer, Harnack, and others. The pseudo-Cyprianic "De laude martyrii" has been ascribed to Novatian by Harnack, but with less probability. The pseudo-Cyprianic sermon, "Adversus Judæos", is by a close friend or follower of Novatian if not by himself, according to Landgraf, followed by Harnack and Jordan. In 1900 Mgr Batiffol with the help of Dom A. Wilmart published, under the title of "Tractatus Origenis de libris SS. Scripturarum", twenty sermons which he had discovered in two MSS. at Orleans and St. Omer. Weyman, Haussleiter, and Zahn perceived that these curious homilies on the Old Testament were written in Latin and are not translations from the Greek. They attributed them to Novatian with so much confidence that a disciple of Zahn's, H. Jordan, has written a book on the theology of Novatian, grounded principally on these sermons. It was, however, pointed out that the theology is of a more developed and later character than that of Novatian. Funk showed that the mention of *competentes* (candidates for baptism) implies the fourth century. Dom Morin suggested Gregorius Bæticus of Illiberis (Elvira), but withdrew this when it seemed clear that the author had used Gaudentius of Brescia and Rufinus's translation of Origen on Genesis. But these resemblances must be resolved in the sense that the "Tractatus" are the originals, for finally Dom Wilmart showed that Gregory of Elvira is their true author, by a comparison especially with the five homilies of Gregory on the Canticle of Canticles (in Heine's "Bibliotheca Anecdotorum", Leipzig, 1848).

THE NOVATIANIST SECT.—The followers of Novatian named themselves καθαροί, or Puritans, and affected to call the Catholic Church the *Apostaticum*, *Synedrium*, or *Capitolinum*. They were found in every province, and in some places were very numerous. Our chief information about them is from the "History" of Socrates, who is very favourable to them, and tells us much about their bishops, especially those of Constantinople. The chief works written against them are those of St. Cyprian, the anonymous "Ad Novatianum" (attributed by Harnack to Sixtus II, 257–8), writings of St. Pacian of Barcelona and St. Ambrose (De pænitentia), "Contra Novatianum", a work of the fourth century among the works of St. Augustine, the "Heresies" of Epiphanius and Philastrius, and the "Quæstiones" of Ambrosiaster. In the East they are mentioned especially by Athanasius, Basil, Gregory of Nazianzus, Chrysostom. Eulogius of Alexandria, not long before 600, wrote six books against them. Refutations by Reticius of Autun and Eusebius of Emesa are lost.

Novatian had refused absolution to idolaters; his followers extended this doctrine to all "mortal sins" (idolatry, murder, and adultery, or fornication). Most of them forbade second marriage, and they made much use of Tertullian's works; indeed, in Phrygia they combined with the Montanists. A few of them did not rebaptize converts from other persuasions. Theodoret says that they did not use confirmation (which Novatian himself had never received). Eulogius complained that they would not venerate martyrs, but he probably refers to Catholic martyrs. They always had a successor of Novatian at Rome, and everywhere they were governed by bishops. Their bishops at Constantinople were most estimable persons, according to Socrates, who has much to relate about them. They conformed to the Church in almost everything, including monasticism in the fourth century. Their bishop at Constantinople was invited by Constantine to the Council of Nicæa. He approved the decrees, though he would not consent to union. On account of the *homoousion* the Novatians were persecuted like the Catholics by Constantius. In Paphlagonia the Novatianist peasants attacked and slew the soldiers sent by the emperor to enforce conformity to the official semi-Arianism. Constantine the Great, who at first treated them as schismatics, not heretics, later ordered the closing of their churches and cemeteries. After the death of Constantius they were protected by Julian, but the Arian Valens persecuted them once more. Honorius included them in a law against heretics in 412, and St. Innocent I closed some of their churches in Rome. St. Celestine expelled them from Rome, as St. Cyril had from Alexandria. Earlier St. Chrysostom had shut up their churches at Ephesus, but at Constantinople they were tolerated, and their bishops there are said by Socrates to have been highly respected. The work of Eulogius shows that there were still Novatians in Alexandria about 600. In Phrygia (about 374) some of them became Quartodecimans, and were called *Protopaschitæ;* they included some converted Jews. Theodosius made a stringent law against this sect, which was imported to Constantinople about 391 by a certain Sabbatius, whose adherents were called *Sabbatiani*.

See the histories of CEILLIER, TILLEMONT, etc.; recent histories, as BRIGHT, GWATKIN, BIGG, DUCHESNE; the histories of dogma by DORNER, HARNACK, LOOFS, SEEBERG, BETHUNE-BAKER, and SCHWANE, TIXERONT, etc.; also FAUSSET (below). Particular studies: HEFELE in *Kirchenlex.* (1895), s. v. *Novatianisches Schisma;* STOKES in *Dict. Christ. Biog.*, s. vv. *Novatianism* and *Novatianus;* HARNACK in *Realencycl. für prot. Theol.*, s. v. *Novatian*. The two works *De Trinitate* and *De cibis* first printed by GANGNEIUS, *Tertullian* (Paris, 1545), and included in subsequent editions of Tertullian; first edited as Novatian's by WELCHMAN (Oxford, 1724); the edition of JACKSON (London, 1728) is reprinted in GALLANDI, *Bibl. Vet. Patr.*, III (Venice, 1767), and *P. L.*, III. The best ed. of *De Trinitate*, with introd. and notes, is by FAUSSET (Cambridge, 1909); it is denied to be Novatian's by HAGEMANN, *Die römische Kirche* (Freiburg, 1864), and is considered a Latin transl. from Hippolytus by QUARRY in *Hermathena*, XXIII (1897). Best ed. of *De cibis Judaicis* by LANDGRAF AND WEYMAN in *Archiv für lat. Lexikogr. u. Gramm.*, XI, ii (1898); see WEYMAN, *Novatian u. Seneka über den Frühtrunk* in *Philologus*, LII (1893). On *De spectaculis* and *De bono pud.* see WOLFFLIN in *Archiv für lat. Lexikogr. u. Gr.*, VIII, i (1892, for Cyprianic authorship); WEYMAN in *Hist. Jahrbuch*, XIII–XIV (1892); HAUSSLEITER in *Theol. Literaturblatt* (16 Sept., 1892; 12 Oct., 1894); DEMMLER in *Theol. Quartalschr.*, LXXXVI (1894), reprinted as *Ueber den Verfasser der . . . Traktat De bono pud. u. De Spect.* (Tübingen, 1894); and see also LANDGRAF AND WEYMAN's ed. of *De cibis* (above). On *De laude martyrii*, see HARNACK, *Eine bisher nicht erkannte Schrift Novatians vom Jahre 249–50* in *Texte und Unters.*, XIII, 4b (Leipzig, 1895). On Adv. *Judæos*, see LANDGRAF, *Ueber den pseudocypr. Traktat adv. Jud.* in *Archiv für lat. Lexikogr. u. Gr.*, XI, i (1898); HARNACK, *Zur Schrift Pseudocyprians Adv. Jud.* in *Texte und Unt.*, XX, new series, V, iii (1900); BATIFFOL AND WILMART, *Tractatus Origenis de libris SS. Scripturarum* (Paris, 1900); for Novatian's authorship, WEYMAN in *Archiv für lat. Lexik.*, XI (1900), 467, 545; IDEM in *Hist. Jahrb.*, XXI (1900), 212; ZAHN in *Neue kirchl. Zeitschr.*, XI (1900), 248; HAUSSLEITER in *Theol. Literaturblatt* (1900), nn. 14–16; IDEM in *Neue kirchl. Zeitschr.*, XIII (1902); JORDAN, *Die Theologie der neuentdeckten Predigten Novatians* (Leipzig, 1902); against Novatian auth., FUNK in *Theol. Quart.*, LXXXII (1900); MORIN in *Revue d'hist. eccl.*, I (1900), 267; IDEM in *Revue Bénédictine*, XIX (1902), 225; BUTLER in *Journal of Theol. Studies*, III (1901), 113, 254; IDEM in *Zeitschr. für N. T. Wiss.*, IV (1903), 79; DE BRUYNE in *Revue Bénéd.* (1907). For Gregory of Elvira, see MORIN in *Rev. d'hist. et de litt. relig.*, V (1901), 145; KUNSTLE in *Lit. Rundschau* (1900), 169; especially WILMART's elaborate proof in *Bulletin de Litt. ecclésiastique de Toulouse*, viii–ix (Oct.-Nov., 1906), which is summarized by LEJAY in *Rev. Bénéd.*, XXV (1908), 435; BUTLER in *Journ. Theol. Stud.*, X (1909), 450.

JOHN CHAPMAN.

Novatus, SAINT, who is mentioned on 20 June with his brother, the martyr Timotheus, was the son of St. Pudens and Claudia Rufina, and the brother of Sts. Pudentiana and Praxedes. His paternal grandfather was Quintus Cornelius Pudens, the Roman senator, who with his wife, Priscilla, was among St. Peter's earliest converts in Rome and in whose house the Apostle dwelt while in that city. A portion of the superstructure of the modern church of St. Pudentiana (Via Urbana) is thought to be part of the senatorial palace or of the baths built by Novatus.

Novena (from *novem*, nine), a nine days' private or public devotion in the Catholic Church to obtain special graces. The octave has more of the festal character: to the novena belongs that of hopeful mourning, of yearning, of prayer. "The number nine in Holy Writ is indicative of suffering and grief" (St. Jerome, in Ezech., vii, 24;—P. L., XXV, 238, cf. XXV, 1473). The novena is permitted and even recommended by ecclesiastical authority, but still has no proper and fully set place in the liturgy of the Church. It has, however, more and more been prized and utilized by the faithful. Four kinds of novenas can be distinguished: novenas of mourning, of preparation, of prayer, and the indulgenced novenas, though this distinction is not exclusive.

The Jews had no nine days' religious celebration or nine days' mourning or feast on the ninth day after the death or burial of relatives and friends. They held the number seven more sacred than any other. On the contrary, we find among the ancient Romans an official nine days' religious celebration whose origin is related in Livy (I, xxxi). After a shower of stones on the Alban Mount, an official sacrifice, whether because of a warning from above or of the augurs' advice, was held on nine days to appease the gods and avert evil. From then on the same novena of sacrifices was made whenever the like wonder was announced (cf. Livy, XXI, lxii; XXV, vii; XXVI, xxiii etc.).

Besides this custom, there also existed among the

Greeks and Romans that of a nine days' mourning, with a special feast on the ninth day after death or burial. This, however, was rather of a private or family character (cf. Homer, Iliad, XXIV, 664, 784; Virgil, Æneid, V, 64; Tacitus, Annals, VI, v.). The Romans also celebrated their *parentalia novendialia*, a yearly novena (13 to 22 Feb.) of commemoration of all the departed members of their families (cf. Mommsen, "Corp. Inscript. Latin.", I, 386 sq.). The celebration ended on the ninth day with a sacrifice and a joyful banquet. There is a reference to these customs in the laws of the Emperor Justinian ("Corp. Jur. Civil. Justinian.", II, Turin, 1757, 696, tit. xix, "De sepulchro violato"), where creditors are forbidden to trouble the heirs of their debtor for nine days after his death. St. Augustine (P. L., XXXIV, 596) warns Christians not to imitate the pagan custom, as there is no example of it in Holy Writ. Later on, the same was done by the Pseudo-Alcuin (P. L., CI, 1278), invoking the authority of St. Augustine, and still more sharply by John Beleth (P. L., CCII, 160) in the twelfth century. Even Durandus in his "Rationale" (Naples, 1478), writing on the Office of the Dead, remarks that "some did not approve this, to avoid the appearance of aping pagan customs".

Nevertheless, in Christian mortuary celebrations, one finds that of the ninth day with those of the third and seventh. The "Constitutiones Apostolicæ" (VIII, xlii; P. G., I, 1147) already speak of it. The custom existed specially in the East, but is found also among the Franks and Anglo-Saxons. Even if it was connected with an earlier practice of the pagans, it nevertheless had in itself no vestige of superstition. A nine days' mourning with daily Mass was a distinction, naturally, which could be shared by none but the higher classes. Princes and the rich ordered such a celebration for themselves in their wills; even in the wills of popes and cardinals such orders are found. Already in the Middle Ages the novena of Masses for popes and cardinals was customary. Later on, the mortuary celebration for cardinals became constantly more simple, until finally it was regulated and fixed by the Constitution "Præcipuum" of Benedict XIV (23 Nov., 1741). For deceased sovereign pontiffs the nine days' mourning was retained, and so came to be called simply the "Pope's Novena" (cf. Mabillon, "Museum Italicum", II, Paris, 1689, 530 sqq., "Ordo Roman. XV"; P. L., LXXVIII, 1353; Const. "In eligendis" of Pius IV, 9 Oct., 1562). The usage still continues and consists chiefly in a novena of Masses for the departed. A rescript of the Sacred Congregation of Rites (22 Apr., 1633) informs us that such novenas of mourning, *officia novendialia ex testamento*, were generally known and allowed in the churches of religious (Decr. Auth. S. R. C., 604). They are no longer in common use, though they have never been forbidden, and indeed, on the contrary, *novendiales precum et Missarum devotiones pro defunctis* were approved by Gregory XVI (11 July, 1853) and indulgenced for a confraternity *agonizantium* in France (Rescr. Auth. S. C. Indulg., 382).

Besides the novena for the dead, we find in the earlier part of the Middle Ages the novena of preparation, but at first only before Christmas and only in Spain and France. This had its origin in the nine months Our Lord was in His Blessed Mother's womb from the Incarnation to the Nativity. In Spain the Annunciation was transferred for the whole country by the tenth Council of Toledo in 656 (Cap. i; Mansi, "Coll. Conc.", XI, 34) to 18 Dec., as the most fitting feast preparatory to Christmas. With this it appears that a real novena of preparation for Christmas was immediately connected for the whole of Spain. At any rate, in a question sent from the Azores (Insulæ Angrenses) to the Sacred Congregation of Rites, an appeal was made to the "most ancient custom" of celebrating, just before Christmas, nine votive Masses of Our Lady. And this usage, because of the people who took part in the celebration, was permitted to continue (28 Sept., 1658; Decr. Auth., 1093). A French *Ordinarium* (P. L., CXLVII, 123) prescribes that the preparation for Christmas on the ninth day should begin with the O anthems and that each day, at the Magnificat, the altar and the choir should be incensed. The Ordinarium of Nantes and the Antiphonary of St. Martin of Tours, in place of the seven common O anthems, have nine for the nine days before Christmas, and these were sung with special solemnity (Martène, "De Antiq. Eccles. Ritib.", III, Venice, 1783, 30). In Italy the novena seems to have spread only in the seventeenth century. Still, the "Praxis cæremoniarum seu sacrorum Romanæ Ecclesiæ Rituum accurata tractatio" of the Theatine Piscara Castaldo, a book approved in 1525 by the author's father general (Naples, 1645, p. 386 sqq.), gives complete directions for the celebration of the Christmas novena with Exposition of the Blessed Sacrament. The author remarks that this novena in commemoration of Our Lord's nine months in the womb was solemnly celebrated in very many places in Italy. And in the beginning of the eighteenth century the Christmas novena held such a distinguished position that the Sacred Congregation of Rites (7 July, 1718), in a special case, allowed for it alone the solemn celebration with Exposition of the Blessed Sacrament (Decr. Auth., 2250).

But before this, at least in Sicily, the custom had sprung up among religious of preparing for the feast of their founder with a novena of Masses, and these *Missæ novendiales votivæ* were also (2 Sept., 1690) declared permissible (Decr. Auth., 1843). In general, in the seventeenth century, numerous novenas were held especially in the churches of religious and to the Saints of the various orders (cf. Prola, "De novendialibus supplicationibus", Romae 1724, *passim*). Two hundred years later, on application from Sicily for Exposition of the Blessed Sacrament in the celebration of novenas, special permission was granted (Decr. Auth., 3728), and in the decrees on the *Missæ votivæ* of 30 June, 1896, there is really question of the *Missæ votivæ novendiales B. M. V.* (Decr. Auth., 3922 V, n. 3). At least in this way, then, the novena is recognized even in the Liturgy.

At the same time as the *novena of preparation*, the proper *novena of prayer* arose, among the faithful, it would seem, who in their need turned to the saints with a novena, especially to recover health. The original home of this novena must have been France, Belgium, and the neighbourhood of the Lower Rhine. Specially noteworthy up to the year 1000 are the novenas to St. Hubert, St. Marcolf, and St. Mommolus. St. Mommolus (or Mummolus) was considered the special patron for head and brain diseases: the novenas to him were made especially in the Holy Cross Monastery of Bordeaux, where the saint was buried (Mabillon, "Act. Sanct. O. S. B.", II, Venice, 1733, 645 sqq.; "Acta SS.", August, II, 351 sqq.; Du Cange, "Glossarium", s. v. "Novena"). St. Marcolf procured for the kings of France the power to cure scrofula by a touch of their hand. For this purpose, shortly after their coronation and anointing at Reims, the kings had to go in person on pilgrimage to the tomb of St. Marcolf at Corbeny and make a novena there. Those who were to be healed had to make a similar novena. But the best known is the novena to St. Hubert, which continues even to our day. This is made against madness by people bitten by a mad dog or wolf (Acta SS., November, I, 871 sqq.).

The last-named novena was attacked in later times, particularly by the Jansenists, and was rejected as superstitious (cf. "Acta SS.", loc. cit., where the attack is met and the novena justified). Before this, Gerson, in the fourteenth century, had given warning against the superstitious abuse of this novena. But he does not reject novenas in general and we see from his works that in his time they were already widespread (Opera, Paris, 1606, II, 328; III, 386, 389). But notwithstanding Gerson's warning, novenas were from that time on ever more and more in favour with the faithful, to which the many, even miraculous, effects of the novenas contributed not a little. Benedict XIV (De canonizat. sanct., lib. IV, p. II, c. xiii, n. 12) tells of a number of such miracles adduced in the processes of canonization. Catholics know from their own experience that the novena is no pagan, superstitious custom, but one of the best means to obtain signal heavenly graces through the intercession of Our Lady and all the saints. The *novena of prayer* is thus a kind of prayer which includes in it, so to speak, as a pledge of being heard, confidence and perseverance, two most important qualities of efficacious prayer. Even if the employment of the number nine in Christianity were connected with a similar use in paganism, the use would still in no way be blameable or at all superstitious. Not, of course, that every single variation or addition made in whatever private novena must be justified or defended. The holiest custom can be abused, but the use of the number nine can not only be justified but even interpreted in the best sense.

The number ten is the highest, the *numerus maximus*, simply the *most perfect*, which is fitting for God; the number nine, which is lacking of ten, is the number of imperfection, which is fitting for mortal kind. In some such way the Pythagoreans, Philo the Jew, the Fathers of the Church, and the monks of the Middle Ages, philosophized on the meaning of the number nine. For this reason it was adapted for use where man's imperfection turned in prayer to God (cf. Jerome, loc. cit.; Athenagoras, "Legat. pro Christian.", P. G., VI, 902; Pseudo-Ambrosius, P. L., XVII, 10 sq., 633; Rabanus Maurus, P. L., CIX, 948 sq., CXI, 491; Angelomus Monach., In lib. Reg. IV, P. L., CXV, 346; Philo the Jew, "Lucubrationes", Basle, 1554, p. 283).

In the novena of mourning and the Mass on the ninth day it was remembered in the Middle Ages that Christ gave up the ghost in prayer at the ninth hour, as in the penitential books (cf. Schmitz, "Die Bussbücher und die Bussdisciplin", II, 1898, 539, 570, 673), or remarked that, by means of Holy Mass on the ninth day, the departed were to be raised to the ranks of the nine choirs of angels (cf. Beleth, loc. cit.; Durandus, loc. cit.). For the origin of the novena of prayer we can point to the fact that the ninth hour in the Synagogue, like None in the Christian Church, was a special hour of prayer from the beginning, so that it was reckoned among the "apostolic hours" (cf. Acts, iii, 1; x, 30; Tertullian, "De jejuniis", c. x, P. L., II, 966; cf. "De oratione", c. xxv, I, 1133). The Church, too, has in the Breviary, has for centuries invoked the Almighty in nine Psalms and honoured Him in nine Lessons, while from ancient times the Kyrie has been heard nine times in every Mass (cf. Durandus, "Rationale, De nona"; Bona, "Opera", Venice, 1764; "De divina psalmodia", p. 401).

As has been said, the simplest explanation of the Christmas novena are the nine months of Christ in the womb. But for every novena of preparation, as also for every novena of prayer, not only the best explanation but also the best model and example was given by Christ Himself to the Church in the first Pentecost novena. He Himself expressly exhorted the Apostles to make this preparation. And when the young Church had faithfully persevered for nine full days in it, the Holy Ghost came as the precious fruit of this first Christian novena for the feast of the establishment and foundation of the Church. If one keeps this is mind and remembers besides that novenas in the course of time have brought so many, even miraculous, answers to prayer, and that finally Christ Himself in the revelation to Blessed Margaret Mary Alacoque recommended the special celebration of nine successive first Fridays of the month (cf. Vermeersch, "Pratique et doctrine de la dévotion au Sacré Cœur de Jésus", Tournai, 1906, 555 sqq.), one must wonder that the Church waited so long before positively approving and recommending novenas rather than that she finally took this step (cf. "Collection de précis historiques", Brussels, 1859, "Des neuvaines", 157 sqq.).

Not until the nineteenth century did the Church formally recommend novenas by the concession of Indulgences. This brings us to the last kind of novenas, those which are indulgenced. Apparently Alexander VII in the middle of the seventeenth century granted Indulgences to a novena in honour of St. Francis Xavier made in Lisbon (cf. Prola, op. cit., p. 79). The first novena indulgenced in the city of Rome, and even there for only one church, was the novena in preparation for the feast of St. Joseph in the church of St. Ignatius. This was done by the Briefs of Clement XI, 10 Feb., and 4 March, 1713 (cf. Prola, loc. cit.; Benedict XIV, "De canoniz.", loc. cit.). The Franciscans, who used before this to have a novena for the feast of the Immaculate Conception (cf. Decr. Auth. S. R. C., 2472) received special Indulgences for it on 10 Apr., 1764 (Resc. Auth. S. C. Indulg., 215). Not until later, especially from the beginning of the nineteenth century, were various novenas enriched with Indulgences in common for the whole Church. They number in all thirty-two, intended for the most part as novenas of preparation for definite feasts.

They are in detail as follows: one in honour of the Most Holy Trinity, which may be made either prior to the feast of the Holy Trinity (first Sunday after Pentecost) or at any other time of the year; two to the Holy Ghost, one to be made prior to the feast of Pentecost for the reconciliation of non-Catholics (this is also made publicly in all parochial churches), one at any time of the year; two novenas to the Infant Jesus, one to be made before the feast of Christmas and the other at any time during the year; three to the Sacred Heart, one prior to the feast of the Sacred Heart (the Friday after the octave of Corpus Christi), one at any time during the year, and the third that of the nine first Fridays, which is based on the promise made to Blessed Margaret Mary by the Sacred Heart assuring the grace of final perseverance and the reception of the Sacraments before death to all who should receive Holy Communion on the first Friday of every month for nine consecutive months; it is customary to offer this novena in reparation for the sins of all mankind; eleven novenas in honour of the Blessed Virgin, viz., in honour of the Immaculate Conception, the Nativity of Mary, her Presentation at the Temple, the Annunciation, the Visitation, the Maternity of Mary, her Purification, her Seven Dolours, the Assumption, the Holy Heart of Mary, and the Holy Rosary; one novena each in honour of the Archangels Michael, Gabriel, and Raphael, and one in honour of the Guardian Angel, two to St. Joseph, one consisting of the recitation of prayers in honour of the seven sorrows and seven joys of the foster-father of Christ, prior to the feast of St. Joseph (19 March) and one at any time during the year; one novena each in honour of St. Francis of Assisi, at any time during the year, St. Vincent de Paul, St. Paul of the Cross, St. Stanislas Kotska, prior to his feast (13 November), St. Francis Xavier, and one for the Holy Souls.

The novena in honour of St. Francis Xavier, known as the "Novena of Grace", originated as follows: in 1633 Father Mastrilli, S.J., was at the point of death as the result of an accident, when St. Francis Xavier, to whom he had great devotion, appeared to him and urged him to devote himself to the missions of the

Indies. Father Mastrilli then made a vow before his provincial that he would go to the Indies if God spared his life, and in another apparition (3 Jan., 1634) St. Francis Xavier exacted of him a renewal of this promise, foretold his martyrdom, and restored him to health so completely that on that same night Father Mastrilli was in a condition to write an account of his cure, and the next morning to celebrate Mass at the altar of the saint and to resume his community life. He soon set out for the Japanese missions where he was martyred, 17 October, 1637. The renown of the miracle quickly spread through Italy, and inspired with confidence in the power and goodness of St. Francis Xavier, the faithful implored his assistance in a novena with such success that it came to be called the "novena of grace". This novena is now made publicly in many countries from 4 to 12 March, the latter being the date of the canonization of St. Francis Xavier together with St. Ignatius. The conditions include a visit to a Jesuit church or chapel. The indulgence may be gained on any day of the novena, and those who are prevented by illness or another legitimate cause from communicating during the novena may gain the indulgence by doing so as soon as possible. All of these novenas without exception are to be made, in private or in public, with pious exercises and the reception of the Sacraments, and for these usually a daily partial Indulgence can be gained and a plenary Indulgence at the end of the novena. The Indulgences and the conditions for gaining them are accurately given in detail in the authentic "Raccolta" and in the works on Indulgences by Beringer and Hilgers, which have appeared in various languages. The indulgenced novenas, to a certain extent official, have but contributed to increase the confidence of the faithful in novenas. Hence, even the private novena of prayer flourishes in our day. Through the novena to Our Lady of Lourdes, through that to St. Anthony of Padua or some other saint, the faithful seek and find help and relief. The history of novenas is not yet written, but it is doubtless a good part of the history of childlike veneration of Our Lady and all the saints, of lively confidence in God, and especially of the spirit of prayer in the Catholic Church.

JOSEPH HILGERS

Novice.—I. DEFINITION AND REQUIREMENTS.— The word *novice*, which among the Romans meant a newly acquired slave, and which is now used to denote an inexperienced person, is the canonical Latin name of those who, having been regularly admitted into a religious order and ordinarily already confirmed in their higher vocation by a certain period of probation as postulants, are prepared by a series of exercises and tests for the religious profession. In Greek, the novice was called ἀρχάριος, a beginner. The religious life, recommended by Jesus Christ is encouraged by the Church and any person is allowed to become a novice who is not prevented by some positive legal impediment. No minimum or maximum age is fixed by canon law for admission into the novitiate. Those, however, who have not arrived at puberty cannot enter without the consent of their parents or guardians; and canon law ("Si quis", I; "De regularibus", III, 31) grants to parents one year to compel the return of a child who has entered without their consent. As the Council of Trent fixes at sixteen years the earliest age for the profession which follows the novitiate, we may conclude that the novice must have completed his fifteenth year if the religious order requires one year of novitiate; or, his fourteenth, if the two years be required, and this opinion is confirmed in respect to Regulars, properly so-called, by the decree of the Sacred Congregation of Religious dated 16 May, 1675, and for nuns by that of the Sacred Congregation of Bishops and Regulars dated 28 May, 1689. According to the rules of procedure, published by the latter congregation, 28 June, 1901, no person may be admitted into a new congregation under the age of fifteen years without special permission of the Holy See. The constitution of Clement VIII, "Cum ad Regularem", of 19 March, 1603, requires the age of nineteen full years for the reception of lay-brothers, but this constitution has not been everywhere carried into effect. Canon law distinctly gives to clerics the right to enter religion (cf. Clerici, unic., c. XIX, i; Alienum, I eodem, q. 2; Benedict XIV, C. "Ex quo dilectus", 14 January, 1747; the reply of the Sacred Congregation of Bishops and Regulars of 20 December, 1859; Nilles, "De libertate clericorum religionem ingrediendi"). Even those who have obtained a burse for study, or who have been maintained at the expense of the seminary retain this right, although it is admitted that the founder of a burse, or the donor of money for educational purposes may impose certain reasonable conditions for the use of his gifts, and may stipulate for instance that the cleric shall undertake to serve the diocese for a certain number of years, or not to enter into religion without the consent of the Holy See. Although the consent of the bishop is not canonically required, the cleric is recommended to inform him of his intention to enter a religious order, and a similar notification is required of any cleric or priest occupying any office or benefice. The bishop in fact must be in a position to fill the vacancy. For the entry into religion of a diocesan bishop nominated or confirmed by the Holy See, the consent of the pope is required. This does not apply to a bishop who has lawfully resigned his see, but some authors consider that it does apply to titular bishops.

However general may be the freedom to enter a religious order, no person is allowed to do this to the detriment of another's right. Thus a married man, at least after the consummation of marriage, cannot enter into religion, unless his wife has by her misconduct given him the right to refuse cohabitation forever, or unless she consents to his entrance, and agrees to make a vow of chastity or to enter into religion herself, in conformity with canonical rules. The liberty of a married woman is similarly limited ("Præterea", 1; "Cum sis", 4; "Ad Apostolicam", 13; "Significavit", 18; "De conversione conjugatorum", III, 32). Parents may not enter into religion without making suitable provision for the education and future of their children; nor children who are under the obligation of maintaining their parents, if their religious profession would prevent them from aiding their parents in any grave necessity. Debtors also are forbidden, at least those who may be expected to be able to pay their debts within a reasonable time (this is a disputed point but we give the most commonly accepted opinion, which is that of St. Alphonsus, "Moral Theology", bk. IV, 5, n. 71). Moreover, a positive order of Sixtus V (Cum de omnibus, 1587), modified to a certain extent by Clement VIII (In Suprema, 1602), forbids the profession of persons involved in debts by their own fault. Canon law also excludes persons branded with infamy and those connected with any criminal proceeding, also those under an obligation to render accounts of a complicated nature. (C. Clement VIII, "In Suprema", 1602.) An illegitimate child is not necessarily excluded, but he cannot be received into any order in which his father is professed (C. Gregory XIV, "Circumspecta", 15 March, 1591).

The canonical regulations spoken of above, concern those religious orders in which solemn vows are taken. Religious congregations are governed generally by the natural law and their own approved constitutions. According to the "Normæ" (Regulations) of 1901, the Holy See imposes the following disabilities, and reserves to itself the right of dispensation: illegitimacy, not removed by legitimation; age, below fifteen and above thirty years; vows binding a person to another order; marriage; debts or liability to render accounts; and for nuns, widowhood. More recently, the decree "Ecclesia Christi" of 7 September, 1909, with which must be read the declarations of 4 January and 5 April, 1910, renders invalid, without the permission of the Holy See, the admission of any person who has been expelled from a college for immorality or other grave fault, or of a person who has been dismissed for any cause whatever from another religious order, a seminary, or any institution for the training of ecclesiastics or religious. A person who has obtained a dispensation from his vows cannot enter into any order but the one which he left. This decree applies both to religious orders, and to congregations with simple vows, at least to those which are not diocesan, and its effect has been extended by the order of 4 January, 1910, to religious communities of women. Only formal expulsion renders admission invalid, but the fact of leaving college or other institution under circumstances which would make it equivalent to expulsion makes it illicit, and the Holy See requires superiors to make such inquiries as are necessary to prevent the admission of undesirable persons. Another decree of 7 September, 1910, "In articulo", while not rendering the reception invalid, forbids the admission of a young man who presents himself in order to become a religious cleric, unless he has gone through a course of at least four years of classical studies. (For these decrees and their explanation see "De religiosis et missionariis", vol. V).

Before the taking of the habit, exact information must be secured to make sure of the qualities and good intentions of the candidates. These precautions are happy substitutions for the rather rude test that had to be undergone in former times (see POSTULANT). Besides being dictated by the natural law, they have been sanctioned for the orders of men by a Constitution of Sixtus V, "Cum de omnibus", 1587, and by another Constitution, "Cum ad regularem", promulgated by Clement VIII, March, 1603, and confirmed by Urban VIII. (The ordinances of Clement VIII concern Italy and the adjacent islands only.) In the celebrated Decree "Romani Pontifices" (25 January, 1848), Pius IX laid a strict injunction on all superiors of orders and congregations of men to admit no one to the habit without testimonial letters from the ordinary of the diocese in which the candidate was born and of the dioceses in which he has lived for more than a year from the age of fifteen. This year is explained in a later declaration to mean twelve successive months spent in the same diocese. In these letters, the ordinaries ought, in as far as they can, to bear witness to the candidate's birth, age, conduct, reputation, and all other qualities that affect his entry into religion. The obligation of exacting such letters is imposed under penalty of censure, but it does not entail nullity. Their receipt does not dispense superiors from making their own inquiries.

II. JURIDICAL CONDITION.—By the fact of his entrance into an approved congregation, the novice becomes an ecclesiastical person. If he is a novice in a religious order, he becomes a regular in the widest sense of the word; as such he is not bound by any vow, but he is protected by the ecclesiastical immunities, and shares in the indulgences and privileges of his order, gaining a plenary indulgence on the day of his admission, at least into an order properly so called. The prelate or superior may exercise in regard to his novices all his powers of absolution in reserved cases, and of dispensations from rules and precepts of the Church. Novices benefit also by any exemption attached to the order to which they belong. The jurisdiction communicated by the superior of the congregation suffices to absolve them. It follows apparently that a confessor approved only by the ordinary of the place could not give them valid absolution, though this point is disputed. According to the common law of regulars, the priest who is master of novices is their only ordinary confessor. The novice is bound to obey the superior who has jurisdiction over him, and power as head of the house. He is bound by any private vows he may have taken, but these may be indirectly annulled by the superior in so far as they are contrary to the rules of the order or the exercises of the novitiate. The training of the novices is entrusted to an experienced religious, ordinarily distinct from the local superior. The latter, though obliged to respect the prerogatives of the novice-master, remains the real immediate superior of the novices, and outside that part of the house which is called the novitiate, the direction of the entire community belongs exclusively to him. By canon law, the novice retains full and entire liberty to leave his order and incurs no pecuniary responsibility by the mere fact of leaving it. Vows of devotion do not change the juridical condition of the novice, and they cease to bind if he is legally expelled. As soon as one has made up his mind to leave, it becomes his duty to inform the superior; and if he fails to do so, he becomes liable to reimburse the order for any unnecessary expense it may incur on his behalf after his decision. This is only natural justice. The order is obliged to restore to him his personal property and anything he may have brought with him. As the order is not bound to the novice by any contract, it may dismiss him. According to the regulations of 28 June, 1901, in new congregations governed by simple vows, the dismissal of a novice must be approved by the superior-general and his council. Dismissal without sufficient cause would be an offence against charity and equity, and a superior guilty of such an offence would fail in his duty to his order.

Although the reception of a novice should be gratuitous, the Council of Trent (c. 16, Sess. 25, "De regularibus") permits the order to stipulate for the payment of his expenses while in the novitiate. In order to ensure the complete liberty of the novice, the same council forbids him to make any renunciation of his property or any important gift, and annuls such renunciation if made. Parents also, to whose property the novice had a right of succession, are debarred from making any considerable donation. By common law, however, a novice may legally renounce his property within the two months immediately preceding his profession, and this renunciation should also be authorized by the bishop or his vicar-general. This formality of authorization is not always insisted upon in practice. The renunciation may extend to property of which he is already possessed, or to such as must necessarily descend to him by right of inheritance; but not seemingly to such as he has only an expectation of receiving. He is free to make over his property to his family, his order, or any pious work, or even to provide for services and Masses after his death. Although the renunciation takes effect only from the date of his profession, and becomes null and void if that profession does not take place, it is not revocable at the pleasure of the novice before his profession, unless he has reserved to himself the right to change the disposition of his property. If no renunciation has been made at the time of solemn profession, canon law assigns the property either to the monastery or to the natural heirs of the religious. Common law requires that the solemn profession shall be preceded by a period of simple vows; before making these vows, the novice is bound to declare to whom he commits the administration of his patrimony, and how he wishes the income to be employed, and the consent of the Holy See is generally required for any change in this arrangement. The religious is entitled to provide for the administration of any additional property which may come to him after his simple profession, and for the disposal of the income of such property. The law of the Council of Trent does not concern congregations which are governed by simple vows; but in these the power of a novice to alienate or retain his property is provided for by their constitutions. Generally speaking, the novice is bound, before taking his vows, to declare how he wishes his property to be administered, and the income expended. According to the Regulations of 1901, he may, even after making his vows, be authorized by the superior-general to modify these dispositions. The renunciation of property, though not made null and void, is forbidden to the novice. The Holy See does not approve that any obligation should be imposed upon the novice to give even the income of his property to his order; he remains free to apply it to any reasonable purpose. Solemn profession vacates all ecclesiastical benefices of which the novice was possessed; the perpetual vows of congregations governed by simple vows vacate residential benefices; that is to say, benefices which require residence are vacated by the simple profession, which prepares the way for solemn profession, or by the temporary vows which precede perpetual vows.

III. EXERCISES.—Except in the case of some special privilege of the religious order (as with the Society of Jesus) or some unavoidable obstacle, the novice should wear a religious habit, though not necessarily the special habit of novices. It is the duty of the novice, under the guidance of the novice-master, to form himself spiritually, to learn the rules and customs of his order, and to try himself in the difficulties of the religious life. The rule ordinarily prescribes that at the outset of his religious career he shall pass some days in spiritual exercises, and make a general confession of the sins of his whole life. By the Constitution "Cum ad regularem" of 19 March, 1603, renewed under Urban VIII in the Decree "Sacra Congregatio" of 1624, Clement VIII laid down, for novitiates approved by the Holy See, some very wise rules in which he directed that there should be a certain amount of recreation, both in the house and out of doors; and he insisted on the separation of the novices from older religious. For a long time, studies, properly so called, were forbidden, at least during the first year of novitiate; but a recent decree dated 27 August, 1910, while maintaining the principle that one year of the novitiate should be devoted especially to the formation of the religious character, recommends certain studies to exercise the mental faculties of the novices, and enable their superiors to form an opinion of their talents and capacities without involving any excessive application, such as the study of the mother-tongue, Latin and Greek, repetition of work previously done, reading the works of the Fathers, etc., in short, studies appropriate to the purpose of the order. Novices, therefore, are bound to give up one hour regularly to private study on all days except feast-days, and also to receive lessons limited to one hour each, not oftener than three times a week. The manner in which the novices apply themselves to these studies is to be taken into account when the question arises of their being admitted to profession (see the decree annotated in Vermeersch, "Periodica de religiosis et missionariis", vol. V, 1910, n. 442, pp. 195, 197). According to the practice of the older orders the novice receives a religious name, differing from his baptismal name.

IV. DURATION.—For all religious orders, the Council of Trent prescribes a full year in the novitiate, under penalty of nullity of profession. In those orders which have a distinctive habit, the novitiate commences with the assumption of the habit; in those which have no habit, it commences from the time when the novice is received into the house lawfully assigned for the purpose by competent authority. This year must be continuous without interruption. It is interrupted whenever the bond between the order and the novice is broken by voluntary departure or legal dismissal; and also when, independently of the wish of either superior or novice, the latter is compelled to live for any considerable time in the world. A dismissal is considered to take effect when once the novice has crossed the threshold of the house; in case of a voluntary departure, a novice who has left the house, but has kept his religious habit and who returns after one or two days' absence, is considered as having given way to a temporary desire for change, not sufficient to cause him to lose the benefit of the time already spent in the novitiate. An interruption makes it necessary that the novitiate should begin afresh as if nothing had previously been done, and it differs in this respect from suspension, which is, so to speak, an interval between two effective periods of novitiate. The time which passes during the suspension does not count, only the time passed before the suspension being added to that which follows. The novitiate is suspended when a novice is withdrawn for a certain time from the superior's direction, but without changing his condition. This would happen in the case of a temporary mental aberration, or an expulsion for some reason shown afterwards to be unfounded, and therefore annulled. It is generally held that if a novice quits his order after having finished his novitiate, and is subsequently readmitted, he has not to begin his novitiate afresh, unless it appears that there has been some serious change in his dispositions. The law of the Council of Trent does not strictly apply to congregations governed by simple vows, but the constitutions of these congregations ordinarily require a year of novitiate at least, and the "Normæ" (Regulations) of 1901 make a complete and continuous year of the novitiate one of the conditions of a valid profession.

The practice of the Holy See has been of late years to interpret this continuity much more strictly than was formerly the case. Some persons consider that one whole day passed outside the novitiate, even for some good reason, and with the permission of superior, is sufficient to render ineffective the whole of the previous probation, but this is too rigorous an interpretation of the rule. To avoid all danger of offending against canon law, superiors will do wisely not to grant permission to pass the night out of the novitiate, except for a very good reason and for a very short time. By the Constitutions of Clement VIII, "Regularis disciplinæ" of 12 March, 1596, and of Innocent XII, "Sanctissimus" of 20 June, 1699, the novitiate house must be approved by the Holy See, and the novitiate cannot be validly passed elsewhere. These directions refer to Italy and the adjacent islands, and do not apply to all religious orders. Nevertheless some authors consider them to be of universal application. The rules of congregations governed by simple vows approved by the Holy See ordinarily reserve to the Holy See the approbation of the novitiate house. Pius IX, in an Encyclical letter of the Sacred Congregation of Bishops and Regulars dated 22 April, 1851, required that in all novitiates there should be a common life; pocket-money and the separate use of chattels of whatever kind (peculium) was forbidden. One part of the novitiate house should be reserved for the novices, and strictly separated from the rest of the dwelling. The novitiate cannot validly be commenced except in the house lawfully set apart for the purpose. Some authors strictly require that the novices shall never be lodged elsewhere; but, although in the orders whose novitiate is bound to be approved by the Holy See, residence in this house is rigorously insisted upon, it does not seem possible that a few days' absence should lessen the value of the probation.

V. HISTORY.—The institution of a time of probation, in order to prepare the candidate who has already been admitted to the religious life for his profession, goes back to very ancient times. According to Mgr Ladeuze (Le cénobitisme Pachomien, p 282), in spite of the testimony of the MS. life of St. Pachomius (MS. 381, "Patrologia", IV, Paris), the novitiate did not exist in the monastery of St. Pachomius as a general institution; but from the fifth century at least it has been the rule for the Coptic monks to pass through a novitiate of three years. (See the "Coptic Ordinal" in the Bodleian Library of Oxford; Evetts in "Revue de l'Orient chrétien", II, 1906, pp. 65, 140.) This term of three years was required also in Persia in the sixth century (Labouret, "Le Christianisme en Perse", p. 80). Justinian, in approving this, says that he borrowed it from the rules of the saints, "Sancimus ergo, sacras sequentes regulas" (Novella V, "de monachis", c. 2, preface and § I). Many Western orders, notably that of St. Benedict, were content with one year. St. Gregory the Great in his letter to Fortunatus, Bishop of Naples (bk. X, Letter 24, in Migne, "P. L.", LXXVII, col. 1082-7) required two years. Many orders of canons left the time to the discretion of the abbot. Common law did not prescribe any term of novitiate and this omission led to the frequent shortening, and occasionally to the entire abolition of the preparatory probation. Innocent III ["C. Apostolicum", 16, "de regularibus" (III, 31)] directs that the novitiate shall be dispensed with only in exceptional circumstances, and forbids the Mendicant Orders to make their profession within one year. Finally the Council of Trent (Sess. XXV, c. xv, "de regularibus") makes a year's novitiate an indispensable condition of valid profession. In the East, since the fourth or fifth century, the novices of Palestine, Egypt, and Tabenna have been accustomed to give up their secular dress, and put on the habit given them by the community. This habit is distinguished from that of the professed by the absence of the *cuculla* or cowl. Those of St. Basil kept their habits. This practice, sanctioned by Justinian (Novella, V, c. 2), was also that of St. Benedict and the Benedictines, but the contrary use has for a long time past prevailed. (See PROFESSION; POSTULANT; NUNS.)

Classical authors: ST. THOMAS, *Summa theologica*, II-II, Q. clxxx, a. 2-7 and Q. clxxxix; PASSERINI, *De hominum statibus*, III, *commenting on St. Thomas, l. c.*; SUAREZ, *De Religione*, tract. VII, bk. IV-VI; LAYMANN, *Theologia moralis, De statu religioso*, c. vi; SCHMALZGRUEBER in bk. III Decr., XXXI, XXXII; in bk. IV, t. VI, n. 38-42; SCHMIER, *Jurisprudentia canonico-civilis*, bk. III, t. I, pt. I, c. iii, s. 2; PELLIZARIUS, *Manuale Regularium*, tr. 2; ROTARIUS, *Theol. mor. Regularium*, t. I, bk. I, II; MARTÈNE, *De antiquis monachorum ritibus*; IDEM,*Commentarius in reg. S. Benedicti;* THOMASSINI, *Vetus et Nova Ecclesiæ disciplina*, t. I, bk. III, etc. More recent writers—ANGELUS A SS. CORDE, *Manuale juris communis regularium et specialis Carmelitorum discalceatorum*, t. I (Ghent, 1899); BACHOFEN, *Compendium juris regularium* (New York, 1903); BOUIX, *De iure regularium*, t. I (Paris, 1857); BATTANDIER, *Guide canonique pour les constitutions des instituts à vœux simples* (4th ed., Paris, 1908); BASTIEN, *Directoire canonique à l'usage des congrégations à vœux simples* (2nd ed., Maredsous, 1911); HEIMBUCHER, *Die Orden und Congregationen der katholischen Kirche* (Paderborn, 1907); LADEUZE, *Etude sur le cénobitisme Pakhomien pendant le IVe siècle et la première moitié du Ve* (Louvain, 1898); NILLES, *De libertate clericorum religionem ingrediendi* (Innsbruck, 1886); PIAT, *Prælectiones iuris regularis*, t. I (Tournai, 1898); SCHIEWIETZ, *Vorgesch. des Mönchtums oder das Ascetentum der die ersten christlichen Jahrhunderten; Das egyptische Mönchtum im vierten Jahrhundert* in *Archiv für Kirchenrecht* (Mainz), LXXVIII, sq. (separately published, 1904); TAUNTON, *The Law of the Church* (London, 1906); VERMEERSCH, *De religiosis institutis et personis*, I (2nd ed., Bruges, 1907); IDEM, *Supplementa et Monumenta*, II (4th ed., Bruges, 1910); IDEM in *Periodica de Religiosis et Missionariis* (Bruges, 1905); WERNZ, *Jus decretalium*, III (Roma, 1901).

A. VERMEERSCH.

Noyon. See BEAUVAIS, DIOCESE OF.

Nubia, in North-eastern Africa, extending from Sennar south to beyond Khartoum and including the Egyptian Sudan. The southern section includes Sennar with Dschesireh-el Dschesire (Island of Islands), the ancient Meroe; the western, Bahr el Abiad, Kordofan, and Darfur; the eastern, Tarka; the central, Dongola; and the northern, Nubia proper. The various tribes belong to the Ethiopian or Berber family, intermixed with Arabians; in the south negroes preponderate. Nubia embraces 335,597 square miles and contains 1,000,000 inhabitants; Dongola, Berber, Khartoum, Fashoda, Sennar, Fassuglo, 75,042 square miles with 2,500,000 inhabitants; Taka, 7766 square miles with 1,000,000 inhabitants; Kordofan, 35,069 square miles with 300,000 inhabitants; Darfur, 106,070 square miles with 4,000,000 inhabitants; Shegga, 85,017 square miles with 1,400,000 inhabitants. The chief cities are: Khartoum, at the junction of the White and Blue Niles, founded in 1823 and the starting-point of all scientific and missionary expeditions, destroyed in 1885 by the Mahdi, rebuilt in 1898; Omdurman, on the Abiad, founded by the Mahdi; Sennar, capital of Southern Nubia; Kassala, capital of Taka. On the Nile are Berber, Abu-Hammed, Old Dongola, and New Dongola, capital of central Nubia; in Nubia proper, Derr, Wadi Halfa, and Assuan; in Kordofan, El-Obeid; in Darfur, El Fasho. Formerly the port of Nubia was Suakin on the Red Sea; from 1906 it has been Port Sudan. Nubia is administered by the Viceroy of Egypt.

HISTORY.—Nubia is said to be derived from the Egyptian *Nub* (gold), as the Egyptians obtained most of their gold there. In the Bible it is called Cush. Egypt sought repeatedly to extend its southern boundaries, and during the eighteenth dynasty reached Wadi Halfa. A temple was built at Napata (near the Fourth Cataract) by Amenophis III, and Rameses II waged successful war with the Ethiopians. After this there arose in Napata near the sacred mountain Gebel Barkal an independent theocratic state; the remains of many of its temples are still to be seen. During the twenty-third dynasty the Nubians shook off the Egyptian yoke, and even conquered Egypt (750 B. C.); three Nubian kings ruled the united territory (732-668). Psametich I (664-10) drove out the Nubians, and Meroe replaced Napata, which maintained its sovereignty over Nubia until destroyed by the native king Ergamenes during the reign of Ptolemy Philadelphus (285-47). During Roman rule, the Nubians attempted to gain the Thebaid, but Petronius in 25 B. C. conquered Napata and forced Queen Candace to make a treaty of peace. In the third century after Christ marauding incursions of Nubian tribes called the Blemmyer forced Diocletian to summon the Nobatæ from El Charge in the Nile valley as confederates of the empire. Nevertheless Prima, Phœnicon, Chiris, Taphis, and Talmis yielded. In the fourth and fifth centuries the Thebaid was so often devastated that Emperor Marcian was forced to conclude an unfavourable peace in 451. Christianity, brought probably by the hermits and monks of the Thebaid, began to spread through the country. The various accounts of this event are confusing; Pliny and Mela give the name of Ethiopia to all the countries in this region, including Abyssinia, while ecclesiastical writers speak of an Ethiopian Church, but give no account of the conversion of individual lands. Christianity was not yet well established, when about the middle of the sixth century under the protection of the empress Theodora, the Alexandrian priest Julian introduced Monophysitism. Its adherents called themselves Copts. The Nobatæan kings Silko and Eirpanomos accepted Christianity in this form, and the Monophysite patriarch Theodosius, Bishop Theodore of Philæ, and Longinus, Julian's successor, put the new doctrine on a firm basis. In 580 Longinus baptized the King of the Alodæ. The final victory of the Monophysites was secured by their union with the Arabs, soon to be masters of Egypt.

In 640 Amr Ben el-Asi'S, the commander-in-chief of the Arabs, conquered Egypt and ended Byzantine supremacy. The Melchite (Catholic) patriarch, George of Alexandria, fled to Constantinople and his see remained vacant for over a hundred years. The Copts secured peace only by becoming confederates of the enemy, and in return received nearly all the Catholic churches; their patriarch alone exercised jurisdiction over the entire territory. According to the Arabian Makrizi, as related by Ibn Selim, when the Nubians requested bishops they received from Alexandria Monophysites, and in this way became and remained Jacobites or Copts. In the following centuries numerous churches and monasteries were built even in Upper Nubia and Sennar, the ruins of which yet remain. Other documents show that Nubia was divided into three provinces with seventeen bishops: Maracu with the suffragan Dioceses of Korta, Ibrim, Bucoras, Dunkala, Sai, Termus, and Suenkur; Albadia with Borra, Gagara, Martin, Arodias, Banazi, and Menkesa; Niexamitis with Soper, Coucharim, Takchi, and Amankul. Yet Christianity was in continual danger from the Mohammedans. Nubia succeeded in freeing itself from the control of Egypt, which became an independent Mohammedan kingdom in 969, but in 1173 Saladin's brother Schems Eddawalah Turanschah advanced from Yemen, destroyed the churches, and carried off the bishop and 70,000 Nubians. At the same time Northern Nubia was conquered. In 1275 the Mameluke sultan Djahn Beibars sent an army from Egypt into Nubia. Dongola was conquered, the Christian king David was obliged to flee, and the churches were plundered. The inhabitants escaped forcible conversion to Mohammedanism only by payment of a head-tax. Nubia was divided into petty states, chief of which was Sennar, founded in 1484 by the negro Funji. For some time Sennar ruled Shendi, Berber, and Dongola. In the eighteenth century the King of Sennar obtained for a time Kordofan also. From the Middle Ages there is little information as to the position of Christianity; Islam became supreme, partly by force, partly by the amalgamation of the native with the Arabian tribes.

In 1821 Sennar and the dependent provinces submitted to Mohammed Ali, the founder of modern Egypt. The commanding position of the capital, Khartoum, led the Holy See to hope that the conversion of Central Africa could be effected from Nubia. On 26 December, 1845, the Propaganda erected a vicariate, confirmed by Gregory XVI, 3 April, 1846. The Austrian imperial family contributed funds and the mission was under the protection of the Austrian consulate at Khartoum. Missionary work was begun by the Jesuits Ryllo (d. 1848) and Knoblecher (d. 1858), who pushed forward as far as 4° 10' north of the equator, Kirchner, and several secular priests (among whom were Haller, d. 1854, and Gerbl, d. 1857). They founded stations at Heiligenkreuz on the Abiad (1855), and at Santa Maria in Gondokoro (1851). In 1861 the missions were transferred to the Franciscans. Father Daniel Comboni (d. at Khartoum, 1881) founded an institute at Verona for the training of missionaries to labour among the negroes of Soudan. The Pious Mothers of the Negro Country (*Pie Madri della Nigrizia*), founded in 1867, devoted itself to conducting schools for girls and dispensaries. The Mahdi, Mohammed Ahmed, in 1880 conquered Kordofan, in 1883 vanquished the Egyptian army, and on 26 January, 1885, destroyed Khartoum. A number of priests and sisters were held for years in captivity; the name of Christian seemed obliterated. After the overthrow of his successor, Caliph Abdullah, by the English under Lord Kitchener, 2 September, 1898, the mission was re-established. In 1895 a mission had been opened at Assuan. In 1899 Mgr Roveggio with Fathers Weiler and Huber established a station at Omdurman, and in 1900 founded the mission near the Shilluk and re-established the station at Khartoum. Under his successor, Geyer, stations were opened in 1904 at Halfaya, Lul, Atiko, Kayango; in 1905 at Mbili among the Djur, at Wau in Bahr el Ghazal, and the mission at Suakin, opened in 1885, was resumed. The Sons of the Sacred Cross, as the Missionaries of Verona had been called from 1887, founded a station at Port Sudan.

Starting from Khartoum the missionary territory is divided into a northern and a southern district. The majority of the population in the north is Mohammedan, and the chief task of the missionaries is pastoral work among the scattered Christian communities. In 1908 Khartoum had 69,344 inhabitants, Omdurman 57,985, among them about 2307 Europeans, of whom about 1000 are Catholics. Khartoum is served by 2 fathers, 1 brother, and 4 sisters; the schools contain 42 boys and 75 girls. In Omdurman there are 300 Catholics, 3 fathers, 1 brother, and 5 sisters; 44 boys and 45 girls attend the school. There is also a school for girls at Halfaya. At Assuan there are 2 fathers, 1 brother, and 4 sisters; 34 boys and 54 girls are taught in the schools. There are 500 Catholics among the workmen. At Port Sudan the Catholics number between 200 and 300. There are Catholics also at Halfa, Abu-Hammed, Dongola, Argo, Meraui, Berber, Atbara, Damer, Shendi, Kassala, Duen, El-Obeid, Bara, and Nahud. The southern missions among the heathen negroes have already advanced beyond the boundaries of Nubia. The statistics for 1907 for the northern and southern missions were: 11 stations, 30 priests, 23 brothers, 41 sisters, 2407 Catholics, 492 boys and girls in the mission-schools.

RENAUDOT, *Liturgiarum orientalium collectio* (2 vols., Paris, 1716); LE QUIEN, *Oriens christianus*, II (Paris, 1740), 659–62; QUATREMÈRE, *Mémoires géographiques et historiques sur l'Egypte*, II (Paris, 1811), 1–161; BURCKHARDT, *Travels in Nubia* (London, 1819); NIEBUHR, *Inscriptiones Nubienses* (Rome, 1820); GAU, *Antiquités de la Nubie* (Paris, 1821–2); ROSELLINI, *I monumenti dell'Egitto e della Nubia* (Pisa, 1832–44); CHAMPOLLION, *Monuments de l'Egypte et de la Nubie* (2 vols., Paris, 1844); MAKRIZI, *Gesch. der Copten*, tr. WÜSTENFELD (Göttingen, 1845); LANE-POOLE, *Hist. of Egypt in the Middle Ages* (London, 1901); BUTLER, *The Arab Conquest of Egypt* (Oxford, 1902); KUMM, *Nubien von Assuan bis Dongola* (Gotha, 1903); COOK, *Handbook for Egypt and the Sudan* (London, 1905); GEYER in *Katholische Missionen* (Freiburg, 1908).

OTTO HARTIG.

Nueva Cáceres, DIOCESE OF (NOVA CACERES), created in 1595 by Clement VIII; it is one of the four suffragan sees of the Archdiocese of Manila, Philippine Islands. It comprises the provinces of Camarines Sur, Camarines Norte, Albay, and Tayabas in the southern part of Luzon, the islands Ticao, Masbate, Burias, and Cantanduanes, also numerous smaller islands off the coast of Southern Luzon. It includes a territory of 13,632 square miles, and has a population of nearly 600,000. The cathedral and episcopal residence are situated in the town of Nueva Cáceres, the capital of Camarines Sur. The territory now included in the diocese was first visited by Augustinian Friars, who had accompanied the famous Legaspi-Urdaneta expedition of 1565. When the missionaries began their labours, they found the natives given over to gross idolatries and superstitions (adoration of the sun, moon, and stars, ancestral worship), and to the propitiation of a multitude of deities by strange sacrifices; nor did they seem to have any idea of a supreme being. So fruitful, however, was the apostolic zeal of the missionaries that, within a few years, many thousands of converts were made in Albay, in Camarines Sur, and in Masbate. Assisted by heroic Catholic laymen, they gathered the natives into villages or reductions, where they instructed them in the truths of religion and taught them the advantages of a settled civilized life. The Augustinians had begun the spiritual conquest of the diocese, but, being few in number, they were unable to attend to so extensive a territory. In 1578 the Franciscans were called to assist them. The arrival of the latter gave a new impulse to the work of evangelization. Missions and reductions were multiplied in Albay, in Camarines Sur, and in Masbate; and new foundations were made in the Province of Tayabas. The ranks of the missionaries were strengthened from time to time by workers from Spain and Mexico; as early as 1595 the Church had made so much progress in these parts that Clement VIII created the Diocese of Nueva Cáceres, taking the name from the town of Nueva Cáceres founded in Camarines Sur in 1579 by Francisco de Sande, second Governor-General of the Philippine Islands. The first bishop was Francisco de Ortega, an Augustinian friar who had laboured for several years in the Province of Manila. He took possession of his diocese in 1600. The present bishop (Rt. Rev. John B. McGinley, con. 1910) is his twenty-seventh successor.

From the beginning until 1890, the greater number of parishes and missions were cared for by the Franciscans and the Augustinians. Although the latter had resigned during the first years in favour of the Franciscans, they returned to the diocese some years later and converted to the faith the whole of Camarines Norte. Each parish had as its parish priest a friar, assisted, according to the importance and population of the district, by one or more native secular priests. Only in later years were the latter placed in full charge of important parishes. As late as 1897, out of a total of 90 parishes, 43 were in charge of friars. The bishops were also generally chosen from the various religious orders, though on several occasions members of the secular clergy held the see, the most noted being (1723) the saintly Bishop de Molina, a native of Iloilo, whose name is still held in veneration. The Lazarists came in 1870, under Bishop Gainza, and were placed in charge of the diocesan seminary then in process of construction. The same prelate introduced the Sisters of Charity and placed them in charge of the academy and normal school which he had founded. In 1886 the Capuchins arrived and were given several missions. In 1898, on account of the revolution against Spanish rule and the feeling against the friars, most of these religious were withdrawn from their parishes and missions, and secular clergy placed in charge. The present (1908) statistics of the diocese are as follows: 168 priests, of whom 25 are regulars; the religious who are not priests number 12 (sisters 9, brothers 3); 122 parishes with resident priests; without resident priests, 6; parochial schools 180, with 46,000 children in attendance (24,000 boys and 22,000 girls); one hospital; one academy for girls, with 200 in attendance; a diocesan seminary, preparatory and theological, with 60 students; a college for secular students attached to the seminary, with 500 students. The total population of the diocese is nearly 600,000, of which number less than 1000 are non-Catholic.

El Archipiélago Filipino (Washington, 1900); *Crónicas de la Apostólica Provincia de Franciscanos Descalzos* (Manila, 1738); DE ZUÑIGA, *Historia de las Islas Philipinas* (Sampoloc, 1803); DE COMYN, *Estado de las Filipinas* (Madrid, 1820); BLUMENTRITT, *Diccionario Mitológico de Filipinas* (Manila, 1895); DE VIGO, *Historia de Filipinas* (Manila, 1876); *Guia Oficial de Filipinas* (Manila, 1897); DE HUERTA, *Estado de la Provincia de San Gregorio en las Islas Filipinas* (Binondo, 1865).

JOS. J. DALY.

Nueva Pamplona, DIOCESE OF (NEO-PAMPILONENSIS), in Colombia, South America, founded in 1549 and a see erected by Gregory XVI on 25 September, 1835. The city contains 15,000 inhabitants and is the capital of the province of the same name in the Department Norte de Satander; the diocese is suffragan of Bogotá, with a population of 325,000, all Catholics except about one hundred dissenters, mostly foreigners. The first bishop, José Jorge Torres Estans, a native of Cartagena, ruled from 30 August, 1837, to 17 April, 1853, when he died at the age of 81, an exile in San Antonio del Fáchira, Venezuela. His successor, José Luis Niño, named vicar Apostolic, was consecrated in October, 1856, and also died an exile in San Antonio del Fáchira, 12 February, 1864. The third bishop, Bonifacio Antonio Toscano, governed from 13 October, 1865, to his retirement in 1873. He convoked the first diocesan synod, and assisted at the Provincial Council of New Granada in 1868 and at the Vatican Council. Indalecio Barreto succeeded him 3 December, 1874, and died 19 March, 1875, at La Vega near Cucuta. The Bishop of Panamá, Ignacio Antonio Parra, his successor, ruled from 8 June, 1876, until his death, 21 February, 1908. Bishop Parra had been exiled by the Liberal government from 1877 to 1878 on account of his efforts to preserve the liberty of the Church. The present incumbent, Evaristo Blanco, was transferred from the Diocese of Socorro, 15 August, 1909.

The diocese has 52 parishes, 75 priests, a seminary, a normal school for women, 10 secondary schools for boys and 13 for girls, 180 primary schools with an average attendance of 10,500, 12 charity hospitals, 4 orphanages for girls, 3 for boys, 2 homes for the aged, 1 convent of Poor Clares, 9 convents of the Sisters of the Presentation, 4 of Bethlehemites, 3 of Little Sisters of the Poor. The Jesuits, Eudists, and Christian Brothers maintain schools. At present the Catholic element is actively promoting good journalism and workingmen's societies, in order to counteract socialism and establish a Christian ideal of society.

ANTONIO JOSÉ URIBE.

Nueva Segovia, DIOCESE OF (NOVÆ SEGOBIÆ), in the Philippines, so called from Segovia, a town in Spain. The town of Nueva, or New, Segovia was in the Province of Cagayan, and was founded in 1581. Manila was the only diocese of the Philippine Islands until 14 Aug., 1595, when Clement VIII created three others, namely Cebú, Nueva Cáceres, and Nueva Segovia. The latter see was established at Nueva Segovia. About the middle of the eighteenth century, the see was transferred to Vigan, where it has since remained. The town of Nueva Segovia declined, was merged with a neighbouring town called Lalloc, and its name preserved only by the diocese. Leo XIII (Const. "Quæ mari Sinico") created four new dioceses in the Philippines, among them Tuguegarao, the territory of which was taken from Nueva Segovia, and comprises the Provinces of Cagayan, Isabela, Nueva Vizcaya, and two groups of small islands. The territory retained by the Diocese of Nueva Segovia embraces the Provinces of Ilocos Norte, Ilocos Sur, Union, Pangasinan, five towns in the province of Tarlac, the sub-province of Abra, and also a large part of what is called the Mountain province; all this territory lies between 15° and 19° N. lat. and is located in the large island of Luzon.

The population of the Diocese of Nueva Segovia is about one million, consisting principally of the Ilocanos and Pangasinanes tribes, besides mountaineers who are nearly all Igorrotes. The Ilocanos and Pangasinanes live, mostly, in the plain between the mountains on the east and the China Sea on the west. They were all converted by the Spaniards, and, up to the present time have, generally speaking, remained faithful to the Catholic Church. Since the American occupation, a few Protestant sects have established themselves here, and have drawn a few of the ignorant class away from the Church. The fidelity of the Catholics was severely tested by the schism of 1902, started by Rev. Gregorio Aglipay, an excommunicated priest. He was born in this diocese, was a high military officer during the rising of the natives against the American sovereignty, and found much sympathy, especially in this part of the islands. He pretended to champion the rights of the native clergy, though the movement was political. He drew with him twenty-one priests and a large number of lay people. He and his movement have been discredited, and the people, in large numbers, have returned to the Church. Only a small part of the Igorrotes has been converted. The Spanish missionaries were evangelizing them until 1898, when the insurrection against the United States broke out, and the missionaries had to flee. Belgian and German priests have taken the place of the Spaniards in the missionary field, and gradually are reclaiming the people from their pagan and especially from their bloodthirsty customs.

There is at Vigan a seminary-college under Spanish Jesuit Fathers, with four hundred collegians and twenty seminarists; there is also a girls' college founded by the last Spanish bishop, Monsignor Hevia Campomanes, who had to flee in 1898. It is in charge of the Sisters of St. Paul of Chartres. The Dominican Fathers have a boys' college in Dagupan, Province of Pangasinan, and the Dominican Sisters have a girls' college in Lingayen, the capital of the same province. In 1910 a parochial school and college, under Belgian sisters, was opened at Tagudin, a town of the Mountain Province, with an attendance of 305 girls, who receive manual as well as intellectual training. A similar institution is projected for the sub-province of Abra, and will be entrusted to German sisters. Gradually parochial schools are being organized, but in many cases it has been found extremely difficult to sustain the expense. The Spanish government supported religion in all its works; but since the separation of Church and State the people, unaccustomed to contribute directly to the support of religion, find the maintenance of ecclesiastical institutions a difficult undertaking. At least Sunday schools are possible, and gradually they are coming into vogue. In Vigan, out of a population of 16,000, about 2000 go to Sunday school. There are not and never were almshouses or asylums of any kind. The people are very charitable towards the poor and afflicted, who have the custom of going at stated times in a body to the homes of the well-to-do, where they receive some gifts and where they then publicly recite the rosary for the spiritual good of their benefactors. Up to 1903 nearly all the bishops of Nueva Segovia were Spaniards. In that year Right Reverend D. J. Dougherty, D.D., an American, was appointed. He was transferred to the Diocese of Jaro, Philippine Islands, and Right Reverend J. J. Carroll, D.D., the present (1910) incumbent, like the former bishop an American, succeeded him.

JAMES J. CARROLL.

Nugent, FRANCIS, priest of the Franciscan Capuchin Order, founder of the Irish and the Rhenish Provinces of said order; b. in 1569 at Brettoville, near Armagh, Ireland, according to some; according to others, at Moyrath, County Meath; d. at Charleville, France, in 1635. His father was Sir Thomas Nugent of Moyrath, and his mother was the Lady Mary, daughter of Lord Devlin. At an early age he was sent to France to receive an education which the Penal Laws denied him at home. Before the age of twenty he obtained the degree of doctor at the Universities of Paris and Louvain, and occupied chairs in these two centres of learning, prior to his entrance into religion. He acquired a profound knowledge of Greek and Hebrew, and could speak a number of European languages fluently. In 1589 he joined the Capuchin Flandro-Belgian Province, taking the name of Francis. In due course he was professed and ordained priest. Towards the close of 1594, or the beginning of 1595, he was sent to France to guide the destinies of the French provinces then being formed, and established communities at Metz and Charleville. Meanwhile he continued to deliver lectures in philosophy and theology at Paris. In 1596 he went as custos-general of France to the general chapter at Rome, and was appointed commissary general of the Capuchins at Venice. Three years later, being again in the Eternal City, he took part in a public disputation in theology at which Clement VIII himself presided. Father Francis maintained his thesis with skill and eloquence, and was enthusiastically awarded the palm of victory.

At the general chapter of 1599 he was relieved of the provincialate and returned to Belgium, where he remained about eleven years. In 1610, at the earnest request of John Zwickhard, Archbishop of Mainz, seven friars of this province were sent to establish the order in the Rhine country, and Father Francis was appointed their commissary general. He founded a convent at Paderborn in 1612, and two years later communities were settled at Essen, Münster, and Aachen. He also established the Confraternity of the Passion at Cologne, and amongst its first protectors were his two great friends Mgr Albergatti, the papal nuncio, and Frederick of Hohenzollern, the dean of the cathedral. In 1615 he began a monastery at Mainz, and Pope Paul V nominated him vicar Apostolic and commissary general, with full power to establish the order in Ireland. That country was then passing through a period of terrible persecution, but the Capuchins braved every danger, mingled with the people, and ministered to their spiritual needs. Meanwhile, in 1618, the monastery of Charleville, in Upper Champagne, became a training-school for friars intended for the Irish mission, and facilities for the same purpose were offered by the Flandro-Belgian Province. A fresh band of workers was soon sent to Ireland, and Father Nugent was thus enabled to found the first monastery in Dublin in 1624. The Archbishop of Dublin, Dr. Fleming, in 1629 addressed to the Irish clergy a letter commending the Capuchin Fathers, specially mentioning "their learning, prudence, and earnestness". Two years later Father Nugent founded a monastery at Slanc, in the diocese of his friend, Dr. Dease, who had previously borne public testimony to the merits of the Capuchins. Owing to failing health, he retired in 1631 to Charleville. He is generally credited with having procured the foundation at Lille of a college for the free education of poor youths from Ulster and Meath for the Irish clergy. He died at Charleville on the Feast of the Ascension, 1635. Rinuccini described him as "a man of most ardent zeal and most exemplary piety", and the annalists of the order state that he refused the Archbishopric of Armagh offered him by Pius V, who styled him "the support of the Church and the light of the orthodox faith". He wrote several works, of which the principal are: "Tractatus De Hibernia", "Cursus philosophicus et theologicus", "De Meditatione et Conscientiæ examine", "Paradisus contemplantium", "Super regula Minorum, Expositio Copiosa".

COGAN, *The Diocese of Meath Ancient and Modern*, III (Dublin, 1870), 648; *Bullarium Ordinis F.F. Minorum. S.P. Francisci*, IV, V; NICHOLAS, *Bibliothèque de Troyes* and *Fran. Cap. Mon.* (MS., 1643) (Dublin); *Franciscan Annals* (1886), Nos. 111, 114, 116; BELLESHEIM, *Geschichte der Katholischen Kirche in Irland*, II (Mainz, 1890), 362–63; PELLEGRINO, *Annali Capuccini*, I (Milan, 1884), 155–160; ROCCO DA CESINALE, *Storia delle Missioni dei Capuccini*, I (Paris, 1867), 375–380, 403 sq.

FATHER AUGUSTINE.

Nugent, JAMES, philanthropist, temperance advocate and social reformer, b. 3 March, 1822, at Liverpool; d. 27 June, 1905, at Formby, near Liverpool. Educated at Ushaw, 1838–43, and the English College, Rome, 1843–6, he was ordained at St. Nicholas's, Liverpool, on 30 August, 1846. After being stationed at Blackburn and Wigan, he was sent to Liverpool 1 January, 1849. In 1851 he introduced the teaching Sisters of Notre Dame, now directing an English Catholic training college for teachers at Mount Pleasant. In 1853 he opened the Catholic Institute, in which Dr. Newman delivered in October, 1853, his lectures on the Turks. In 1863 he was appointed chaplain of Walton Prison, and held the office twenty-two years. In 1865 he established the Refuge for Homeless Boys, which from 1865 to 1905 trained 2000 boys. In 1867 he founded "The Northern Press", which in March, 1872, became the "Catholic Times". On 29 February, 1872, he organized for the spread of temperance the League of the Cross. This he considered his greatest work. In 1870 he began a series of visits to America. After retiring from the chaplaincy of Walton Prison in 1885, he devoted nearly two years to parochial work and inaugurated the new mission of Blundellsands, which he resigned in 1887. To prevent drunkenness he instituted a series of Saturday night free concerts, which gradually became a civic institution and in 1891 established in Bevington Bush a Refuge for Fallen Women and a Night Shelter for homeless women which (1891–1905) received 2300 poor women. In 1892 Leo XIII appointed him a domestic prelate. In memory of his golden jubilee as a priest he purchased for Temperance meetings and concerts, the Jubilee Hall in Burlington St. The citizens of Liverpool on 5 May, 1897, presented to him at an enormous public meeting his own portrait now in the Liverpool Art Gallery and over £1300 with which he began the House of Providence, West Dingle, for young unmarried mothers with their first babies; 200 such cases were sheltered from 1897–1905. In 1904 at the age of eighty-two, he visited America with Abbot Gasquet but taken ill at St. Paul, Minnesota, he hurried home to die. On 8 December, 1906, there was erected near St. George's Hall, a bronze statue commemorating him as: Apostle of Temperance, Protector of the Orphan Child, Consoler of the Prisoner, Reformer of the Criminal, Saviour of Fallen Womanhood, Friend of all in Poverty and Affliction, An Eye to the Blind, a Foot to the Lame, the Father of the Poor.

Catholic Times, Liverpool Daily Post, Catholic Family Annual, files; *London Catholic Weekly* (29 June, 1906).

JAMES HUGHES.

Numbers, the name of the fourth book of the Pentateuch (q. v.).

Numbers, USE OF, IN THE CHURCH.—No attentive reader of the Old Testament can fail to notice that a certain sacredness seems to attach to particular numbers, for example, seven, forty, twelve, etc. It is not merely the frequent recurrence of these numbers, but their ritual or ceremonial use which is so significant. Take, for example, the swearing of Abraham (Gen., xxi, 28 sqq.) after setting apart (for sacrifice) seven ewe lambs, especially when we remember the etymological connexion of the word nishba (נשבע) to take an oath, with sheba (שבע) seven. Traces of the same mystical employment of numbers lie much upon the surface of the New Testament also, particularly in the Apocalypse. Even so early a writer as St. Irenæus (Hær., V, xxx) does not hesitate to explain the number of the beast 666 (Apoc., xiii, 18) by the word ΛΑΤΕΙΝΟΣ since the numerical value of its constituent letters yields the same total (30+1+330+5+10+50+70+200=666); while sober critics of our own day are inclined to solve the mystery upon the same principles by simply substituting for Latinus the words Nero Cæsar written in Hebrew characters which give the same result. Of the ultimate origin of the mystical significance attached to numbers something will be said under SYMBOLISM. Suffice it to note here that although the Fathers repeatedly condemned the magical use of numbers which had descended from Babylonian sources to the Pythagoreans and Gnostics of their times, and although they denounced any system of philosophy which rested upon an exclusively numerical basis, still they almost unanimously regarded the numbers of Holy Writ as full of mystical meaning, and they considered the interpretation of these mystical meanings as an important branch of exegesis. To illustrate the caution with which they proceeded it will be sufficient to refer to one or two notable examples. St. Irenæus (Hær., I, viii, 5 and 12, and II, xxxiv, 4) discusses at length the Gnostic numerical interpretation of the holy name *Jesus* as the equivalent of 888, and he claims that by writing the name in Hebrew characters an entirely different interpretation is necessitated. Again St. Ambrose commenting upon the days of creation and the Sabbath remarks: "The number seven is good, but we do not explain it after the doctrine of Pythagoras and the other philosophers, but rather according to the manifestation and division of the grace of the Spirit; for the prophet Isaias has enumerated the principal gifts of the Holy Spirit as seven" (Letter to Horontianus). Similarly St. Augustine, replying to Tichonius the Donatist, observes that "if Tichonius had said that these mystical rules open out some of the hidden recesses of the law, instead of saying that they reveal all the mysteries of the law, he would have spoken truth" (De Doctrina Christiana, III, xlii,). Many passages from St. Chrysostom and other Fathers might be cited as displaying the same caution and showing the reluctance of the great Christian teachers of the early centuries to push this recognition of the mystical significance of numbers to extremes.

On the other hand there can be no doubt that influenced mainly by Biblical precedents, but also in part by the prevalence of this philosophy of numbers all around them, the Fathers down to the time of Bede and even later gave much attention to the sacredness and mystical significance not only of certain numerals in themselves but also of the numerical totals given by the constituent letters with which words were written. A conspicuous example is supplied by one of the earliest of Christian documents not included in the canon of Scripture, i. e., the so-called Epistle of Barnabas, which Lightfoot is inclined to place as early as A. D. 70–79. This document appeals to Gen., xiv, 14, and xvii, 23, as mystically pointing to the name and self-oblation of the coming Messias. "Learn, therefore", says the writer, "that Abraham who first appointed circumcision, looked forward in spirit unto Jesus when he circumcised, having received the ordinances of three letters. For the Scriptures saith 'And Abraham circumcised of his household eighteen males and three hundred'. What then was the knowledge given unto him? Understand ye that He saith 'the eighteen' first, and then after an interval 'three hundred'. In the eighteen I stands for 10, H for 8. Here thou hast Jesus (ΙΗΣΟΥΣ). And because the cross in the T was to have grace, he saith also 'three hundred'. So he revealeth Jesus in two letters and in the remaining one the cross" (Ep. Barnabas, ix). It will, of course, be understood that the numerical value of the Greek letters ι and η, the first letters of the Holy Name, is 10 and 8=18, while T, which stands for the form of the cross, represents 300. At a period, then, when the Church was forming her liturgy and when Christian teachers so readily saw mystical meanings underlying everything which had to do with numbers, it can hardly be doubted that a symbolical purpose must constantly have guided the repetition of acts and prayers in the ceremonial of the Holy Sacrifice and indeed in all public worship. Even in the formulæ of the prayers themselves we meet unmistakable traces of this kind of symbolism. In the Gregorian Sacramentary (Muratori, "Liturgia Romana Vetus", II, 364) we find a form of Benediction in some codices (it is contained also in the Leofric Missal), assigned to the Circumcision or Octave of the Nativity, which concludes with the following words: "Quo sic in senarii numeri perfectione in hoc sæculo vivatis, et in septenario inter beatorum spirituum agmina requiescatis quatenus in octavo resurrectione renovati; jubilæi remissione ditati, ad gaudia sine fine mansura perveniatis. Amen".

We are fairly justified then when we read of the threefold, five-fold, and seven-fold litanies, of the number of the repetitions of Kyrie eleison and Christe eleison, of the number of the crosses made over the *oblata* in the canon of the Mass, of the number of the unctions used in administering the last sacraments, or the prayers in the coronation of a king (in the ancient form in the so-called Egbert Pontifical these prayers have been carefully numbered), of the intervals assigned for the saying of Masses for the dead, of the number of the lessons or the prophecies read at certain seasons of the year, or of the absolutions pronounced over the remains of bishops and prelates, or again of the number of subdeacons that accompany the pope and of the acolytes who bear candles before him—we are justified, we say, in assigning some mystical meaning to all those things, which may not perhaps have been very closely conceived by those who instituted these ceremonies, but which nevertheless had an influence in determining their choice why the ceremony should be performed in this particular way and not otherwise. (For explanation of the mystical significance commonly attached to the use of numbers see SYMBOLISM.)

HERBERT THURSTON.

Numismatics (from the Greek νόμισμα, "legal currency") is the science of coins and of medals. Every coin or medal being a product of the cultural, economic, and political conditions under which it originated, this science is divided according to the various civilized communities of mankind. It is not only a distinct science, but also, in its respective parts, a branch of all those sciences which are concerned with the history of nations and of their culture—classical archæology, history in its narrower sense, Orientalism, etc. Practically, only ancient, modern, and possibly Oriental numismatics are of importance. Furthermore, a distinction should be made between numismatography, which is chiefly descriptive, and numismatology, which views the coin from its artistic, economic, and cultural side.

The dependence of theoretical numismatics on the pursuit of coin-collecting is clearly seen in the history of the science. The earliest publications of any importance were written to meet the needs of collectors (e. g., the various cabinets of Taler, Groschen, and ducats, and the *Münzbelustibungen*, or "coin-pastimes"), whereas the foundations for a scientific treatment of ancient numismatics were not supplied until 1790, by Eckhel, and for modern not until the nineteenth century by Mader, Grote, and Lelewel. (It is worth remembering that St. Thomas Aquinas, in "De regimine principis", II, xiii, xiv, treated the subject of money and coinage, and this work was for many years the authority among canonists.) The oldest collection of coins of which we have certain knowledge dates back to the fifteenth century, and was made by Petrarch; his example found numerous imitators. Hubert Goltz, in 1556–60, visited the various collections of Europe, of which there are said to have been 950. In comparison with private collections, which are as a rule scattered after the death of their owners, the collections of rulers, states, or museums, possess paramount importance, and furnish the most reliable basis for numismatic investigations. As early as 1756 Francis I of Austria in two works of great beauty, "Monnoyes en or" and "Monnoyes en argent", made known the treasures of his collection; and in recent years the great catalogues, especially those of the British Museum, have become the most important sources of information in this science. The needs of both collectors and theoretical students have called into being a large number of numismatic societies, as well as about 100 technical periodicals, in large part published by these societies. From the meetings of the German Society of Numismatics, held from year to year in different cities, there have developed international congresses: Brussels, 1892; Paris, 1900 (Records and Transactions, published by Comte de Castellane and A. Blanchet); Rome, 1903; (Atti del congresso internazionale di scienze storiche, 6 vols.); Brussels, 1910.

I. COINS.—Coins may be defined as pieces of metal that serve as legal tender. The term includes ordinary currency, commemorative or presentation pieces stamped by public authority in accordance with the established standard, etc., but not paper money or private coinage. To the last class we refer the English tokens which were largely circulated as a result of the insufficient supply of fractional coin about the year 1800; furthermore, the pieces called *mereaux*, issued, especially by church corporations, as vouchers for money, and afterwards for value in general, like *jetons*, or counters, and *Rechnungspfennige*. When each individual is no longer able to wrest from the earth his own subsistence, the necessity arises for sharing labour and distributing its products. This is at first effected by barter of commodities, which requires a universally available medium of exchange usually found in cattle (in Homer the equipment of Menelaus is valued at 9 steers; that of Glacus, at 100). Besides cattle, primitive men have used hides, pelts, cloth, etc., for this purpose. Soon, however, it becomes necessary to find a measure of value that can be employed universally, and for this gold, silver, and copper have been used from very early times; in comparatively recent years after experimentation with many other metals, nickel has been added to these. The first stage of metallic money is reached with the weighing out of pieces of metal of any shape; but, as only the gross weight can be determined by this procedure, and not the degree of fineness (a very essential factor in the case of the precious metals), the necessity arises of certifying fineness by the stamp of public authority, and this stamp makes the lump of metal a coin. The employment of only one of the metals mentioned soon proves insufficient: it is impossible to put into circulation gold coins of sufficiently small denomination or, using the base metal, to issue coins of sufficiently high values. It is necessary, therefore, to make use of two or three metals at the same time. This may be done either by employing the one precious metal as a measure of value and the other, together with copper, only as a commodity or subsidiary coin, or else by using both metals concurrently as measures of value at a ratio fixed by law (bimetallism), a course however, which has frequently caused difficulties on account of the fluctuations in the rate of exchange of the two precious metals.

In form, coins are usually circular, sometimes oval, and quadrangular; these last are particularly common in emergency coinage, and in Sweden had grown to an immense size and great weight. There are also found, especially in the Far East, coins of the most eccentric shapes. In addition to the device and inscription coins frequently bear what are called mint marks or mint-masters' marks which deserve special mention. Mint-masters and die-sinkers have in many cases been accustomed to distinguish their works by means of certain marks or letters; and the mints distinguish their respective coins either by letters, indicating the place of issue by conventional and arbitrary marks, or by some other means—sometimes scarcely perceptible to the uninitiated—such as the placing of a dot beneath a particular letter of the inscription. In this way the various issues of coins, otherwise alike, are kept distinct.

The science of numismatics is materially advanced by finds of coins in large quantities: in addition to a knowledge of previously unknown types, such discoveries afford an instructive insight into the actual circulation of coins at given periods and the extent to which certain coinages were current beyond the confines of their own states, and help us to assign undated varieties, especially those of the Middle Ages, to some particular mint-master or precise period. In the study of the science, as well as in the classification of coins, it is the practice to follow, chronologically, three great eras: the ancient, medieval, and modern; geographically, the different political divisions of the respective times. For the Greek coins, Eckhel has adopted an exemplary system which is still in use. Beginning at the Pillars of Hercules, he takes up the countries of the world, as known to the ancients, in the order of their positions around the Mediterranean: first those of Europe, then Asia as far as India, and lastly Africa from Egypt back to the Straits of Gibraltar.

TYPICAL COINS OF TWENTY-FIVE CENTURIES

1. ÆGINETAN, SILVER. 2. POSIDONIAN, SILVER. 3. SYRACUSAN, SILVER. 4. JEWISH SHEKEL OF SILVER.
5. ROMAN AS, BRONZE. 6. DENARIUS WITH THE DIOSCURI, SILVER. 7. GOLD COIN OF AUGUSTUS.
8. BRONZE COIN OF HADRIAN.
9. DENIER OF CHARLEMAGNE. 10. TOURNOIS. 11. PRAGUE GROSCHEN. 12. AUGUSTALIS OF FREDERIC II.
13. GOLD FLORIN, TIME OF AMADEUS OF SAVOY. 14. VENETIAN SEQUIN.
15. SALZBURG RUBENTALER. 16. SILVER BRACTEATE (GERMAN). 17. CHAISE D'OR. 18. NOBLE.
19. DOUBLE SEQUIN OF LEO X, GOLD.
20. GOLD ZODIAC PIECE. 21. SIAMESE TIHUL. 22. MARIATERESIENTALER.

A. *Greek Coins.*—The term *Greek* is always understood in ancient numismatics to include all coins except those of Roman origin and the Italian *æs grave*. The monetary unit is the talent of 60 minæ (neither the talent nor the mina being represented by any coin), or 6000 drachmæ, each being equal to 6 obols. The various currencies are in most cases based upon the Persian system of weights. The Persians had two different standards of weight for the precious metals: for gold, the Eubœan; for silver, the Babylonian. The gold daric, the common gold coin, corresponding to the Greek silver didrachm, weighed 8.385 grammes (about $129\frac{1}{3}$ grains); the silver daric (shekel), 5.57 grammes (nearly 87 grains). As the value of silver to that of gold was, in antiquity, as 1 to 10, the gold daric is the equivalent of 15 silver darics. Other standards of coinage were the Phocæan, the Æginetan, the Attic, the Corinthian, the Ptolemaic, and the cistophoric standard of Asia Minor; some of these, however, may be derived from the Persian standard. By the substitution of the lighter Attic standard for the old Æginetan Solon brought about the partial abolition of debt. The most abundantly coined pieces were the tetradrachm (25–33mm. in diameter) and the didrachm; pieces of eight, ten, and twelve drachmæ are exceptional, and a forty-drachma piece is a rarity. In the downward scale the division extends to the quarter-obolus ($=\frac{1}{24}$ drachma). In Greek Asia Minor coins made of a mixture of gold and silver (electrum) were used. In Greece the silver coinage greatly predominated; copper coins do not antedate 400 B. C., while gold was but rarely minted. The coinage of the Persians, on the other hand, was very rich in gold, and it was their example that influenced Philip II of Macedon and Alexander the Great. With a few exceptions the highest degree of fineness was aimed at, the gold daric being 97 per cent fine.

In the early times the coining was done with a single die: the reverse of the blank metal was held fast by a peg, generally square, in the anvil, and so received its impress in the form of a quadrangular depression (incuse square); in time this square came to be adorned with lines, figures, and inscriptions. In Southern Italy two dies that fitted into each other were employed, so that the coins present the same design in relief on the obverse and depressed on the reverse (*nummi incusi*). The inscriptions are in different languages, according to nationalities. Bilingual inscriptions—e. g., Greek-Latin—and inscriptions in which the language and type do not correspond—e. g., Greek in Cypriote characters, also occur; and even the Greek characters undergo numerous changes in form in the course of time. The right of coinage being a privilege of sovereignty, the inscriptions first mention the name of the sovereign power under whose authority the coin was struck; in Greece, until the time of Alexander the Great, this was the community. The names of the officials who had charge of the coinage are also found; and later coins also show the year, frequently reckoned from the Seleucid era, 312 B. C. The oldest coins had their origin on the Ægean coasts, perhaps in Lydia, as Herodotus tells us, or at Ægina, to whose king, Pheidon, the Parian chronicle ascribes them, possibly earlier than 600 B. C. Various islands of the same sea furnish coins bearing designs not very dissimilar to these. The coins of Southern Italy are of not much later date, as is proved by the fact that specimens are extant from the city of Sybaris, which was destroyed in 510 B. C. The early coins of Greece proper and Asia Minor are thick pieces of metal, resembling flattened bullets, and, naturally, bear the simplest devices, plants and animals, which soon become typical of particular localities; these are succeeded by the heads and figures of deities and men, sometimes united in groups. About 400 B. C. the Greek art of die-cutting reached its fullest development, attaining a degree of excellence unequalled by any later race: Syracuse holds the first place; after it in order come Arcadia, Thebes, Olynthus, etc.

Of the non-Hellenic peoples whose coins are included in the Greek series, the most important for us are the Jews. At first they made use of foreign coins, but, as one of the results of the national rising under the Machabees against the Syrians, the high priest, Simon, received from Antiochus VII (139–38 B. C.) the right of coinage. Simon minted copper and silver. To him is ascribed the "Shekel Israel": obverse legend (Shekel Israel) and a cup or chalice above which is a date (1–5, reckoning from the conferring of the right of coinage); reverse, legend (Jerusalem the Holy) and a lily-stalk with three buds. The rest of the Machabees—John Hydranus, Judas Aristobulus, Alexander Jannæus, Mattathias Antigonus, and so on—coined copper exclusively with inscriptions in old Hebrew or in Hebrew and Greek. After these came the copper coins of the Idumæan prince Herod and his successors. In the time of Christ Roman coins were also in circulation. This is proved by the story of the tribute money. "And they offered him [Christ] a penny. And Jesus saith to them: Whose image and inscription is this? They say to him: Cæsar's" (Matt., xxii, 19–21). It was only during the two revolts of the Jews against the Romans in A. D. 66–70 and 132–135, that silver was again coined under Eleazar and Simon and Bar-Cochba respectively. On the Bactrian coins of the first century after Christ there occurs the name Gondophares, or some similar name, supposed to be identical with that of one of the three Magi, Caspar.

B. *Roman Coins.*—In Italy the earliest medium of exchange was copper, which had to be weighed at each transaction (*æs rude*). At first it was used in pieces of irregular form, later in clumsy bars. The credit of having first provided a legal tender is ascribed to Servius Tullius, who is said to have had the bars stamped with definite figures, mostly cattle (*primus signavit æs; æs signatum*). The introduction of true coins with marks indicating their value and the emblems of the city belongs to a much later date. The monetary unit was the as of 12 ounces (10.527 oz. Troy), equal to a Roman pound (*libra*—hence, libral standard); usually, however, the weight of an as was only 10 ounces (about $8\frac{3}{4}$ oz. Troy). The divisions of the as (the *semis* $=\frac{1}{2}$, *triens* $=\frac{1}{3}$, *quadrans* $=\frac{1}{4}$, *sextans* $=\frac{1}{6}$, and *uncia* $=\frac{1}{12}$), in order that they might be more readily distinguished, were marked on one side with as many balls as they contained ounces. On the one side was the representation of the prow of a ship, the characteristic device of the city of Rome, on the other, the head of a divinity, which varied with the denomination of the coin. The coins were round, in high, but somewhat clumsy, relief, and cast; some were minted in Campania.

From 268 B. C. the weight of the as steadily decreased; the libral standard became first a triental, then an uncial, and finally even a semiuncial standard—$\frac{1}{24}$ of the original weight. While this reduction of the standard facilitated the manufacture of coins of larger values (*dupondius, tripondius, decussis*, equal to 2, 3, and 10 asses respectively), it resulted in giving to copper coins a current value far above their intrinsic worth and furthered the introduction of stamped, instead of cast, coins. According to Livy the first silver coins were minted in 268 B. C., this first silver piece was the *denarius*, equal to 10 asses. It was followed by the minor denominations, the *quinarius* ($\frac{1}{2}$ *denarius*) and *sestertius* ($\frac{1}{4}$ *denarius*). Besides these the *victoriatus* ($\frac{3}{4}$ *denarius*) was coined for the use of some of the provinces as a commercial currency. The denarius, weighing at first $\frac{1}{72}$ of a pound was reduced in 217 B. C. to $\frac{1}{84}$, the silver used being almost pure. The obverse shows the *dea Roma;* the reverse, the two Dioscuri; of these stamps the former more particularly remained in use for many years. The mint was managed by a commission (*tresviri ære argento auro flando feriundo*), the members of which soon placed upon the coins their names or initials, and later glorified the members of their families and their deeds (family or consular coins). Even at that time, but much more frequently in the imperial period, there were denarii of base metal which were often thinly coated with silver (*denarii subævati*). It rarely happened that gold was coined.

Cæsar marks the transition to the imperial coinage: in 44 B.C. the Senate ordered the issue of coins bearing his portrait. Even Brutus followed this example, and with Augustus begins the uninterrupted series of portrait coins. While Cæsar had already claimed the right of coining gold and silver, Augustus claimed this right for himself alone and left to the Senate only the coinage of copper; and these copper coins are characterized by the letters S.C. (*senatus consulto*). Aurelian (270–76) took even this privilege from the Senate. Beginning with the empire we find a copious coinage of gold. The principal coin is the *aureus*, weighing about 123½ grains; its obverse bears the name, title and portrait of the emperor; its reverse, historical representations in rich variety, buildings, favourite divinities of the emperor, and personifications of the virtues that adorned, or should have adorned, him; the members of his family are also represented. In this respect the series of Trajan and Hadrian are especially rich. With Nero begins the debasement of the coinage, particularly of the silver; and this continued until Constantine again established some degree of order. He introduced a new gold coin, the *solidus*, equal to $\frac{1}{72}$ of a pound (about 70 grains), which for centuries remained an important factor in the development of the monetary system.

Special mention should be made of the medals, peculiarly large and carefully executed works of the mint, issued in commemoration of some event. They were made of gold, silver, or copper, and in the precious metal, generally coined in conformity with the legal standard. There are also specimens made of copper surrounded by a circle of yellowish metal (*médailles des deux cuivres*). The term *contorniate* is applied to a large circular copper coin with a raised rim, used principally in connexion with the circensian games.

The coins of the Roman emperors of the East, which are designated as Byzantine, belong, chronologically at least, to the Middle Ages, but, judged by the standard observed in their coinage and, in the beginning, also by the character of the coins themselves, the entire series is closely connected with the issues of the Roman Empire. Copper was coined abundantly, silver rarely, but the greatest importance attached to the gold coinage. For many years gold was coined only at Byzantium, and these gold pieces served as a model, not only for the gold coinage of the West, which was not resumed until the thirteenth century, but also for that of Islam. Artistic merit is entirely lacking in the Byzantine coins: their type is rigid and monotonous. In place of the former wealth and variety of devices on the reverse, we find religious symbols, the monogram of Christ, and saints. The coinage of John VIII, the last of the emperors but one, about the middle of the fifteenth century, was the last of the Byzantine series.

C. *Medieval Coins.*—The new states that arose within the territorial limits of the old Roman Empire at first made use of the Roman coins, of which a sufficiently large number were in existence. The rare autonomous issues of the period of the racial migration are very closely connected with the Roman series; only the Merovingians, in France, made themselves to some extent independent. Very soon, however, a general decline began in all matters connected with coinage; the coins steadily become coarser, gold currency disappeared, copper was coined only exceptionally; small silver coins were the only medium of payment. Charlemagne restored some kind of order; claiming the right of coining as a royal prerogative, to be exercised by the king alone, he suppressed all private coinage, which at that time had assumed disastrous proportions. He furthermore enjoined greater care in minting and made regulations on this point which became the standard for the greater part of Europe, and which, in their essential features, are operative in England to the present day. The basis was the talent, or pound, of silver (about 11⅘ oz. Troy); it was divided into 20 shillings (pound and shillings being both merely money of account) each equal to 12 pence (*deniers*). The penny therefore weighed 23½ grains. The most common designs on the Carlovingian coins are the representation of the cross and a church adorned with columns, surrounded by the legend *christiana religio*.

The peculiar economic conditions of the Middle Ages gave rise to the issue of silver coins of constantly diminishing weight and fineness, so that they steadily became more and more worthless and, as a result of the general rise in values, could no longer be used as currency. In this way a process began which was repeated several times during the Middle Ages: as a result of the depreciation of the older small coins, new coins, larger and more valuable, were struck in some city whence they made their way triumphantly through the whole of Europe. In course of time these in turn became depreciated and were replaced by a new issue. In the thirteenth century the shilling (equal to 12 pence) was first coined at Tours; in contradistinction to the *denier*, which at that time had become very thin, it was called *nummus grossus*

SILVER GROSCHEN—GEORGE OF SAXONY, 1537—BY FLÖTNER

(thick coin), and, from the name of the place where it was first coined, *grossus turonensis*, or *gros tournois*. One side has a cross with the name of the king and a legend, most commonly *Benedictum sit nomen domini;* the other, a church. The *tournois* spread rapidly through France and along the Rhine, and led to the minting of a similar coin at Prague (the *grossus pragensis*, or *Prager Groschen*), which in its turn was imitated in many countries. After the Merovingian period the only gold coins minted were the *Augustales* of the emperor Frederick II. These were copies of the earlier Roman coin and were struck in Sicily. A regular gold coinage does not begin until about 1250, in the Republic of Florence. These coins bear, on the one side, St. John the Baptist, and, on the other, a lily, the emblem of Florence. From this device (*flos lilii*), or from the name of the city, they received the name *florin*. Their weight was a little more than 540 grains. A few decades later the Doge of Venice, Giovanni Dandolo, began the minting of a gold coin which bears the representation of the doge kneeling before St. Mark and the effigy of Christ with the legend: *Sit tibi Christe datus quem tu regis iste ducatus*. The last word of this legend gave the coin its name, *ducato* (ducat); in Venice it was also called *zecchino* (sequin) from *la zecca*, "the mint". The type of the florin and the name of the ducat soon became current throughout the world.

The transition to modern times is marked by the introduction of still larger silver coins. Of these, besides the Italian *testone* and the French *franc*, the German *Taler* was the most important. In 1485 the Archduke Sigismund of the Tyrol caused the issue of a new silver coin weighing 2 *Loth*, and of a fineness of 15 *Loth;* its value at the rate of exchange of that time corresponded to that of the gold gulden and it was therefore called *Guldengroschen.* The example of the Tyrol was soon followed by many nobles who had the right of coining; the *Joachimstaler* (shortened to *Taler*), made in the mint of the counts of Schlick, at Joachimstal, originated the name of *Taler* (Dollar), which has been retained to the present day. Among the most interesting of the coins of this kind are the *Rubentaler*, coined by Leonard of Keutschach, Archbishop of Salzburg, and named from his armorial bearings, a turnip (Rübe); these are counted among the rarest and most frequently counterfeited coins of the Middle Ages.

The monetary systems of the German Empire during the Middle Ages are of the greatest interest with respect not only to the number of its types of coin, but also the peculiarity of its evolution. Charlemagne, it is true, had established uniformity of coinage and had caused the right of coining to be acknowledged as exclusively belonging to the sovereign; but his weaker successors were gradually compelled to yield this, as well as most of the other royal prerogatives, to the feudatory lords, whose power continued to increase as that of the paramount government weakened. Among these feudatories were, not only all archbishops and bishops, but also the leading abbots and abbesses within the empire. The evolution was gradual. At first permission was granted to hold a fair (*mercatus*), levy a tax (*telonium*), and erect a mint (*moneta*) at some place belonging to one of the feudatories. At first the mint may have been only an exchange, the profits of which, however, in the Middle Ages were often very considerable, and accrued to the lord. Then he was permitted to have coins struck bearing his portrait, but had to maintain the uniform standard. At length these feudatory lords obtained the privilege of coining without any restrictions. When this was done uniformity in the currency of the empire was at an end, a great diversity in the coinage was rendered possible, and the right of coining, instead of being a prerogative of the emperor, became a privilege of every feudatory. These sought to exploit this privilege as a productive source of income by constantly debasing and changing the coinage, thereby causing serious losses to those of their subjects who were engaged in trade. The cities, therefore, which had not yet obtained the right of coinage, endeavoured to gain some control over the system, either by obtaining for themselves the right of coining or by farming mints, or by inducing the owners of mints to exercise their privileges in a more reasonable manner.

Of the German medieval coins, the "bracteates" (Lat. *bractea*, "a thin sheet of metal") deserve special mention. They were not personal ornaments, like the Scandinavian bracteates of earlier times, but genuine coins. As the *denier* had become thinner and thinner in the course of the eleventh century, it was replaced, early in the twelfth century, in some parts of Germany, by very thin but rather large silver coins, made with one die, showing the same design, in relief on one side and depressed on the other. These coins, especially in the beginning, were carefully executed and not without artistic merit. The city of Halle in Swabia (Wurtemberg) issued a small fractional coin which had a wide circulation, and was called *Heller* from the place of its origin. In some respects the evolution of French coinage resembles that of German: here too we find, in the tenth century, coinages of lay and ecclesiastical barons (the archbishops of Vienne, Arles, Reims, etc. in particular), characterized by a fixed type (*type immobilisé*) which is maintained unaltered for a long period. But by the close of the Middle Ages this coinage is confined to a very few powerful feudatories and in comparison with the royal coinage, is no longer of importance. From France we have the *chaise d'or*, a gold coin that was also largely minted in other countries; it represents the king seated upon a Gothic throne. In England sterlings and nobles were struck, both of them often counterfeited. Coins of the archbishops of Canterbury and York are extant. In Italy, because of its numerous political divisions, we find a diversity of coinages similar to that of Germany. The scarcity of coins of ecclesiastical mints is noticeable: with the exception of some isolated examples and the series of Aquileja, Trent, and Trieste, we have only the papal coinages, which, following chiefly the Byzantine model, begin with Adrian I, but do not become important until Clement V (the first of whose coins, however, were struck at Avignon). While eastern Europe was for the most part under the influence of Byzantine, the Crusaders nevertheless brought Western types into the states founded by them in the

SILVER GROSCHEN—MAURICE OF SAXONY, 1544—BY REINHARD
The obverse shows a symbolical representation of the Holy Trinity

Orient. Mohammedan coinage appears only about the year 700; these coins, because the Koran forbids pictorial representations, bear only texts from the Koran and, generally, precise statements concerning the ruler, the mint-master, and the date of coinage.

D. *Modern Coins.*—With the beginning of modern times, partly as the result of the discovery of America and the exploitation of its silver deposits, large silver pieces appear everywhere in great numbers. As a natural consequence of this, we find greater care bestowed upon the execution of the work, more legible characters in the inscriptions, and increased attention to the pictorial representations (portraits and coats-of-arms). Several of the Renaissance issues, particularly the papal coins, are reckoned among the foremost works of art of that time. In the course of the last few centuries, countries which had not come under the influence of the civilization of the Middle Ages enter into numismatic relations with the others, e. g., Russia and the Far East, China having coins of the most extraordinary shapes, some perforated, some in the form of tuning-forks, sabres, etc.; Siam, lumps of twisted silver wire.

While during the earlier centuries the monetary systems of the older civilized countries of Europe generally developed along the lines established in the course of the Middle Ages, the great political and economic revolutions of the nineteenth century brought into being new forces which had their effect on the monetary systems. While the changed relations of the German-speaking peoples resulted in a variation of their currencies (the mark in Germany, krone in Austria, gulden in Holland, and franc in Switzerland), the unification of Italy, on the other hand, resulted in a uniform Italian monetary system (lira). But ecomomic conditions have produced even more lasting results than political. On the 23rd of December, 1865, France, Italy, Belgium, and Switzerland formed the Latin Union, which was joined in 1868 by Greece, agreeing upon a uniform regulation of the coinage of these states on the basis of the French monetary system. This system has now been adopted by a large number of states, which have not themselves joined the Latin monetary Union—Rumania, Bulgaria, Servia, Finland, Spain, and, at least nominally, many of the Central and South American republics, which were formerly Spanish colonies, and furthermore a number of smaller European states. Austria-Hungary and Russia are also approximating to this system. Another monetary union was formed in 1873 and includes Sweden, Denmark, and Norway, the monetary union being the Scandinavian krone. The Portuguese monetary system is still in force in Brazil, its former colony. Even without any formal convention, a coin may gain currency in foreign lands. Thus the Mexican dollar, which in name and value is an offshoot of the German monetary system, is current coin on the farther shore of the Pacific Ocean, in the maritime provinces of China, in Japan, Siam, and part of the Malay Archipelago; it influences Central America and even many of the African maritime provinces. The Indian rupee, too, has gained currency on the shore of the ocean opposite the land of its origin, on the coasts of East Africa, Southern Arabia, and the Malay peninsula. A good example of the crossing of economic and political interests is furnished by Canada, where the English sovereign is legal tender, although Canadian currency follows the standard of the United States. While the coins now in circulation in Austria and Hungary are valid as currency in Liechtenstein and Montenegro and vice versa, an Austrian coin long since put out of circulation in Austria itself, known as the Maria-Teresien taler, and bearing the date 1780, is even now the most important commercial currency in Central Africa, the Sudan, Tripoli, and Arabia. The high degree of perfection which had been attained during the last decades in the technique of coining gave rise, on the one hand, to a number of experiments with coinage (coins made of aluminum, Russian coins of platinum, Belgian pierced coins, English coins of two metals) most of which, however, had no decisive success. On the other hand, it became possible to pay greater attention to the artistic side of coining, as is evidenced by the latest issues of the French and Italian mints.

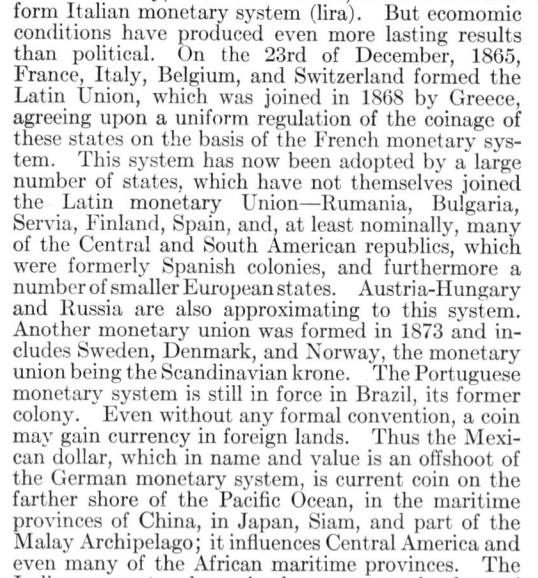

II. MEDALS.—The term *medal* (*medallia* in Florence = $\frac{1}{2}$ denier) is applied to pieces of metal, usually circular, which, though issued by a mint, are not intended as a medium of payment. Their material, form, mode of manufacture, and history prove that they were originally coins, though altered conditions and needs, both artistic and cultural, have made them independent. Their purpose is to commemorate important events in the history of a nation, so much so that attempts have been made to write histories based upon and illustrated by the series of medals of some individual or of a whole country. Occasions for the issue of medals are found in an accession to the throne, a declaration of war, the conclusion of a peace, or an alliance, the completion of a public building; it has also been very extensively used by sovereigns for presentation to persons whom they wished to honour, and in such cases was often a veritable gem of the goldsmith's art. On the other hand, a medal has often been presented by subjects to their sovereign on such occasions as his marriage, in token of homage. But as an expression of the culture of a people the private medal possesses much greater interest, and in this field the German medal of the Renaissance and the following centuries furnishes the most numerous examples. Portrait medals played the part now taken by photography. Medals stamped with coats-of-arms also serve to represent private individuals, and are sometimes put to practical use as tokens, buttons for liveries, etc. They are used to commemorate betrothals, or marriages, silver or golden weddings, births and baptisms, and there are a large number of sponsors' christening gifts in the shape of coins or medals (*Patenpfennige*) made expressly for the purpose and inscribed with the names of the infant and the godparent, the place and date of baptism, and generally a pious maxim. These *Patenpfennige* were often put into rich settings to be worn as ornaments, and were handed down as heirlooms from generation to generation. Not only the entrance into life but also death is recorded in medals; and many such pieces contain detailed biographical notices.

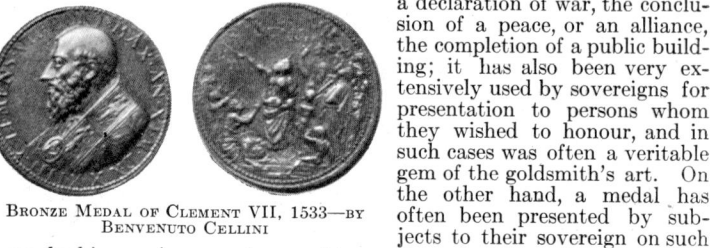

Very often the medal serves a religious purpose; in Kremnitz and especially in Joachimstal extensive series of such religious coinages were struck. Typological representations found great favour, the one side showing the Old-Testament type, the other the New-Testament antitype. The Reformation produced many medals embellished with Biblical phrases. A favourite subject on religious medals was the head of Christ: the city of Vienna has for centuries used medals bearing this design as public marks of distinction. At Easter medals with the Paschal Lamb, at Christmas others with the Infant Jesus, were given as presents. Of the saints, St. George was most frequently represented, on the *Georgstaler* and *Georgsducat*, and a superstition prevailed that the wearing of a medal with the image of St. George was a protection against wounds. A similar superstition was

BRONZE MEDAL OF CLEMENT VII, 1533—BY BENVENUTO CELLINI

connected with the representation of St. Roch and St. Sebastian or of St. Rosalia, as also of the cross with the brazen serpent, as a protection against the plague. There is also an interminable series of wholly superstitious amulets, astrological and alchemistic coinages which profess to be the product of an alchemistic transmutation from a base into a precious metal. The imperial coin-cabinet at Vienna contains one of these pieces, probably the largest medal in existence, weighing about 15½ lbs. avoirdupois; and adorned with the portraits of forty ancestors of the Emperor Leopold I, in whose presence the transmutation is supposed to have taken place. Thus the numerous and manifold purposes for which the medal has been employed faithfully reflect the cultural conditions which led to its coinage and are a source of information that has not yet been fully appreciated.

True medals were unknown to antiquity; their functions were in many respects—particularly as memo-bracteate perpetuates the memory of a pilgrimage of Duke Boleslav III to the tomb of St. Adalbert in Gnesen. A denier of Ladislaus I of Bohemia shows the repulsive head of Satan with a descriptive legend on one side, and on the other a church. Luschin was able to account for this device as follows: after a succession of serious elemental disturbances in Bohemia there came, in the midst of a terrible hurricane, a meteoric shower, during which many persons declared they beheld Satan in human form near the castle; this denier was then struck, bearing on either side the head of Satan and the Church of God. Such coins as these in some measure serve the purpose of commemorative medals.

The first true medal appeared in Italy towards the close of the fourteenth century. Francesco II Carrara, Lord of Padua, had two medals struck, in imitation of the ancient Roman medallions: one, in memory of his father, Francesco I, recalls the later medal-

BRONZE MEDAL OF LEONELLO D'ESTE, 1444—BY VITTORE PISANO
The reverse shows Cupid holding a music scroll and a lion singing

rials of important events—performed by coins. In contrast with the monotonous and generally inartistic coins of the present day, the coins of antiquity, and more particularly those of Greece, were masterpieces of the die-engraver, who was not compelled to seek other opportunities to display his skill. Among the Romans conditions were analogous, with the exception that the medallions of the emperors approximate somewhat to the character of our medals, although they are, as a rule, duplicates of the legal monetary unit; the tokens (*tesseræ*), struck for the games, and the contorniates are even more closely related to the medal. The few gold issues of the Emperor Louis the Pious (814–40) also resemble medals, and in the further course of the Middle Ages we meet with a large number of coins which were evidently intended to commemorate some event in history, although their devices are often very difficult to explain; there is many a puzzle here still awaiting solution. As the symbol of Henry the Lion, the powerful Duke of Bavaria and Saxony, the lion plays an important role on his coins. But his adversary, Otho of Wittelsbach, who, when Henry the Lion had been outlawed, received the Duchy of Bavaria, employed this symbol also and issued deniers which picture him in pursuit of a lion or with the severed head of a lion in his hand. Coins are also very frequently used to commemorate enfeoffments, and these bear a representation of the liege lord from whom the kneeling vassal receives the gonfalon. A Polish lions of Commodus and Septimius Severus; the other, commemorating the capture of Padua in 1390, has a portrait of Francesco II analogous to that of the Emperor Vitellius on his sesterces. The reverse in each case bears the punning device of the Carrara family, a cart (*carro*). These medals are struck in bronze and silver. To the same period belong the medal-like trial-pieces made by the Sesto family of Venice, a family of die-cutters. These, too, were stamped; but the development of the medal in the next period was not due to stamped pieces. Even before the middle of the fifteenth century Italian art suddenly reaches the climax in this department with the cast medal. Vittore Pisano, a painter (b. about 1380, in the Province of Verona; d. 1455 or 1456) is the oldest and most important of the medallists. Like those of his followers, his works are cast from wax models or models cut in iron, a process which frequently makes it necessary for the pieces to be afterwards chiselled. He signs his work *opus Pisani pictoris*. The medals are, for the most part, of large size, and are coated with an artificial patina. On the obverse they present expressive portraits, generally in profile; on the reverse, beautiful and ingenious allegories: thus of Leonello d'Este, a lion singing from a sheet of music held by Cupid; or of Alfonso of Naples, an eagle that generously gives up the slain deer to the vultures. Even though it can be proved that Pisano made use of certain prototypes which in turn were possibly derived from seals, his fame as the real creator of the medallic art is not materially diminished by that fact. Both in composition and in execution he has hardly been equalled, as, for instance, in his representations of the nobler animals, the lion, eagle, horse.

Pisano travelled through the whole of Italy, and portrayed the prominent princes and influential men of his time; he made the medallic art so popular that thenceforth artists, in all the important art centres of Italy, engaged in the manufacture of medals. Such were Matteo de' Pasti, an admirable artist at the court of Rimini; the Venetians Giovanni Boldu and Gentile Bellini, the latter of whom made a portrait-medal for the sultan Mehemet; the Mantuan Sperandio, the most prolific medallist of the fifteenth century, and many others. At this time, too, the stamped medal returns to prominence. In Rome Benvenuto Cellini and, after him, Caradosso, and especially the masters of the papal mint are deserving of mention. The imitations of the bronze coinages of the Roman emperors by Cavino are truly admirable. Finally, at a somewhat later period, Italian medallists are found in the service of foreign princes: Jacopo da Trezzo in the Netherlands, the two Abondio in Germany. The Italian medal exerts the most powerful influence upon the development of the older French productions. The Italian Laurana in the latter half of the fifteenth century struck the first French medals, and the works of the next period clearly show Italian characteristics. Not until the seventeenth century did a new style appear, in which the drapery especially is admirably reproduced; the most prominent artists were Jean Richier, at Metz, and, later, Guillaume Dupré and Jean Warin.

SILVER MEDAL—MODERN AUSTRIAN—BY SCHAFF

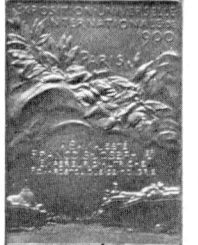

GOLD RECTANGULAR MEDAL, PARIS EXPOSITION, 1900—BY ROTY

In Germany, the earliest large silver pieces were coined at Hall in the Tyrol, under the influence of Italian coinages; and to Gian Marco Cavallo, who was invited to Hall as engraver to the mint, these coins owe their important position in the history of art and their demonstrable influence upon many of the medals of Germany. These, the oldest specimens of the German medallic art, being at the same time coins, were stamped; but, like the Italian, the German medal does not reach its highest perfection in stamped, but in cast pieces. A considerable number of models made of boxwood, of Kehlheim stone, and, later, of wax are still extant. These portraits in wood or stone were at first regarded as final, and only by degrees did they come to be used as models for casting in metal. These cast medals, which made their appearance at the art-centres of Germany (in the beginning of the sixteenth century, Augsburg and Nuremberg) likewise owe their origin to the Italian medal. But only their origin; the further development of the German medal follows entirely original and independent lines until it reaches a degree of excellence, on a level with the Italian. It is true that the Germans fail to produce the magnificent designs with their wealth of figures that we find on the reverse of Italian medals; instead, we find, more commonly, excellent representations of coats of arms. The great strength of the German medal lies in the loving care bestowed upon the execution of the accurate portrait on the obverse; and this accords with the purpose of the medal, which was much more widely distributed among the prominent families of the middle classes than was the case in Italy.

The German medal reaches its prime soon after the year 1500, considerably later than the Italian: among the oldest examples that have come down to us are those of Albrecht Dürer. Many of the artists give us no clue at all to their identity or sign themselves by marks or symbols that are often difficult to interpret. It has now become possible, however, to assign definitely a long series of very valuable medals to Peter Flötner, a master of Nuremberg, who must therefore be considered as one of the foremost of all medallists; he is closely followed by Matthes Gebel. Other noteworthy medallists of this period are Hans Daucher, most of whose work was done for the Court of the Palatinate; Hans Schwarz of Nuremberg, "the best counterfeiter in wood", who executed a large number of works for the members of the Diet of Augsburg of 1518; Jacob Stampfer, in Switzerland; Friedrich Hagenauer, one of the most popular artists; Joachim Deschler, who finally settled in Austria, where, especially in the mints of Vienna, Kremnitz, and Joachimstal, a large number of medals were struck at this period, not all of them, however, to the advantage of the medallic art; Hans Reinhard, from whom we have a number of very carefully chiselled pieces, and Tobias Wolf, both in Saxony. By the end of the sixteenth century the German medal has clearly passed its zenith and becomes dependent upon foreign, and, at first, especially Italian works. In the Netherlands the art attained a high degree of perfection. The great names here are Stephanus Hollandicus and, somewhat later, Konrad Bloc, both of the second half of the sixteenth century, and Peter van Abeele of the seventeenth century. In England the medallists are for the most part foreigners; of the native artists, who do not appear until very late, the most deserving of mention are Th. Simon and William and L. C. Lyon. Caspar and Simon Passe on the other hand attain great artistic skill in the production of very carefully engraved small, thin silver pieces. The other states are of less importance; they employed for the most part foreign artists.

The high artistic level which the medal attained in Italy and Germany at the beginning of the modern

SILVER MEDAL—MODERN FRENCH—BY DUPUIS

age could not be maintained permanently. For while excellent pieces of work were produced here and there, medals as well as coins, as works of art, deteriorated more and more. Not until after the middle of the nineteenth century did the art receive a fresh impetus and that first in France. Considering merely its external manifestations, it is possible even to fix the exact date of the beginning of this movement. On 2 May, 1868, the chemist Dumas, president of the

Comité Consultatif des Graveurs of the Paris mint delivered an address pointing out the defects which prevented the artistic development of the medal, and, as president of the mint, appealing for their amendment. He particularly mentioned the bad taste of the lettering, the polish, the high rim etc. If this address dealt rather with the outer form, a new view of the true purpose of the medal had already been gradually created. Following the productions of Oudines, Paul Dubois, Chapus, above all Herbert Ponscarmes (the first to oppose the polishing of medals) and later Degeorges, Chaplains, and Daniel Dupris, Oscar Roty, by far the most distinguished of the French medallists, won distinction. He excels not only as a portraitist, but more particularly in the composition of the reverse: his fine allegories (e. g., on the medal for merit in connexion with the education of girls—the Republic teaching maidens, the future mothers of men) recall the artists of the *Quattrocento*, which he carefully studied, but did not, as a rule, directly imitate. Just as the execution of the medal is preceded by long and careful deliberation as to how the fundamental idea is to be worked out (Ponscarmes seems to have led the way in this) so the execution itself receives to the very last moment the most careful attention. Only the artist's hand must touch his work. The French medal has thus attained great results, even when judged merely on its technical merits.

Independently of the French movement, a medallic revival has begun in Austria. Anton Scharff brought about a restoration of the medallic style and an emancipation from the rigid conventional forms; working side by side with him are Josef Thautenheym, the elder, Stefan Schwartz, a master of the technique of the chiselled medal, and Franz Xaver Pawlik. Recently Rudolf Marschall has won a high reputation as a portraitist, and received the commission to execute medals for both Leo XIII and Pius X. The French and Viennese medals have called forth in other countries an activity which has already resulted in many beautiful specimens of medallic art.

Gold Medal of Leo XIII by Rudolf Marschall

General Numismatics: Dannenberg, *Grundzüge der Münzkunde* (Leipzig, 1892); Halke, *Einleitung in das Studium der Numismatik* (Berlin, 1889); v. Sallet, *Münzen und Medaillen* (Berlin, 1898); Babelon, *Notice sur la monnaie* (Paris, 1898); Ambrosoli, *Manuale di Numismatica* (Milan, 1895); Lane-Poole, *Coins and Medals* (London, 1894); E. and F. Gnecchi, *Guida numismatica universale* (Milan, 1903); Hirsch, *Bibliotheca numismatica omnium gentium* (Nuremberg, 1760); Lipsius, *Biblioteca numaria* (Leipzig, 1801); Leitzmann, *Biblioteca numaria* (1800–66). On Abbreviations: Schmid, *Clavis numismatica* (Dresden, 1840); Rentzmann, *Numismatisches Legenden Lexikon des Mittelalters und der Neuzeit* (2 parts, Berlin, 1865–66, supplement, 1878); Schlickeisen, *Erklärung der Abkürzungen auf Münzen*, 3rd ed. by Pallmann (Berlin, 1896); Cappelli, *Lexicon abbreviaturarum* (Leipzig, 1901). Dictionaries: de Basinghen, *Traité des monnaies* (Paris, 1764); Schmieder, *Handwörterbuch der gesammten Münzkunde* (Halle and Berlin, 1811, 1815); Ambrosoli, *Vocabolarietto dei numismatici in sette lingue* (Milan, 1897). Periodicals: *Historische Münzbelustigungen* (1729–50); *Numismatische Zeitung* (Weissensee, 1834–73); *Blätter für Münzfreunde* (Leipzig, 1865—); *Numismatischer Anzeiger* (Hanover, 1868—); *Zeitschrift für Numismatik* (Berlin, 1874—); *Numismatisches Literaturblatt* (Berlin, 1880—); *Berliner Münzblätter* (1880—); *Frankfurter Münzblätter*, now *Frankfurter Münzzeitung* (1901—); *Zeitschrift und Monatsblatt der numismatischen Gesellschaft in Wien* (1870—); *Zeitschrift und Mitteilungen der österr. Gesellschaft zur Förderung der Münz- und Medaillenkunde* (1890—); *Mitteilungen der bayrischen numismatischen Gesellschaft* (1872—); *Revue numismatique* (Paris, 1856—), formerly *Revue de la numismatique française* (Blois, 1835–56); *Yearbook of the Société française de numismatique* (1866—); *Bulletin international de numismatique* (Paris, 1902—); *Revue belge numismatique* (Tirlemont, then Brussels, 1842—); *Bulletin mensuel de numismatique et d'archéologie* (Brussels, then Paris, 1881—); *Revue suisse de numismatique; Numismatic Chronicle* (London); *Rivista italiana di numismatica* (Milan); *Gazzetta numismatica* (Rome); *Journal international d'archéologie numismatique* (Athens).

Ancient Coins: Eckhel, *Doctrina nummorum veterum* (Vienna, 1792–98); Mionnet, *Description des médailles antiques grecques et romaines* (6 vols. and supplement, Paris, 1806–13; 9 vols., 1819–37); Head, *Historia numorum. A Manual of Greek Numismatics* (Oxford, 1887); *A Catalogue of Greek Coins in the British Museum* (London, 1878—); Barthélemy, *Nouveau manuel de numismatique ancienne* (Paris, 1890); Imhoof-Blumer, *Monnaies grecques* (Paris, 1883); Madden, *Coins of the Jews*, Vol. III of *Numismata Orientalia* (London, 1886); Saulcy, *Recherches sur la numismatique judaïque* (Paris, 1854); Babelon, *Description historique et chronologique des monnaies de la république romaine vulgairement appelées monnaies consulaires* (Paris, 1885–86); Cohen, *Description générale des monnaies de la république romaine* (Paris, 1857); Sabatier, *Description générale des médaillons contorniates*; Mommsen, *Geschichte des römischen Münzwesens* (Berlin, 1860); Lenormant, *La monnaie dans l'antiquité* (Paris, 1878–79); Cohen, *Description historique des monnaies frappées sous l'empire romain communément appelées médailles impériales* (Paris, 1859–68; 2d ed., 1888–92); Stevenson, *A Dictionary of Roman Coins* (London, 1889); Sabatier, *Description générale des monnaies byzantines* (Paris, 1862).

Medieval and Modern Coins: Lelewel, *Numismatique du moyen-âge* (Paris, 1835); Blanchet, *Nouveau manuel de numismatique du moyen-âge et moderne* (Paris, 1890); Engel-Serrure, *Numismatique du moyen-âge* (Paris, 1891–1905); Idem, *Traité de la numismatique moderne contemporaine* (Paris, 1897–99); Grueber, *Handbook of the Coins of Great Britain and Ireland* (London, 1898).

Medals: Armand, *Les médailleurs italiens des quinzième et seizième siècles* (Paris, 1883–87); Friedlander, *Die italienischen Schaumünzen des 15ten Jahrhunderts* (Berlin, 1880–82); Heiss, *Les médailleurs de la renaissance* (Paris, 1882—); Keary, *A Guide to the Italian Medals* (London, 1882); Fabriczy, *Medaillen der italienischen Renaissance* (Strasburg, 1903); Poey d'Avant, *Trésor de numismatique et de glyptique* (Paris, 1839—); Mazerolle, *Les médailles françaises du 15. siècle au moitié du 17.* (Paris, 1902); Domanig, *Die deutsche Medaille in kunst- und kulturhistorischer Hinsicht nach dem Bestande der Medaillensammlung des ah. Kaiserhauses* (Vienna, 1907); Erman, *Die deutsche Medaille des 16. und 17. Jahrhunderts* (Berlin, 1884) (reprinted from *Zeitschrift für Numismatik*, XII (1885); Simonis, *L'art de médaillier en Belgique* (Jemeppe, 1904); *Medallic Illustrations of the History of Great Britain and Ireland* (published by the British Museum, London, 1904—); Lichtwark, *Die Wiederweckung der Medaille* (Dresden, 1895); Dompierre de Chaufetie, *Les médailles et plaquettes modernes* (Haarleben, 1898—); Marx, *Les médailleurs français contemporains* (Paris); Marx, *Les médailles modernes en France et à l'étranger* (Paris, 1901); Loehr, *Wiener Medailleure* (Vienna, 1899; supplement, 1902).

Aug. v. Loehr.

Nunc Dimittis (The Canticle of Simeon), found in St. Luke's Gospel (ii, 29 32), is the last in historical sequence of the three great Canticles of the New Testament, the other two being the Magnificat (Canticle of Mary) and the Benedictus (Canticle of Zachary). All three are styled, by way of eminence, the "Evangelical Canticles" (see Canticle). The title is formed from the opening words in the Latin Vulgate, "Nunc dimittis servum tuum, Domine" etc. ("Now thou dost dismiss thy servant, O Lord" etc.). The circumstances under which Simeon uttered his song-petition, thanksgiving, and prophecy are narrated by St. Luke (ii, 21–35) (see Candlemas). The words following those quoted above, "according to thy word in peace", are explained by v. 26: "And he had received an answer from the Holy Ghost, that he should not see death, before he had seen the Christ of the Lord." Brief though the Canticle is, it abounds in Old-Testament allusions. Thus, in the following verses, "Because my eyes have seen thy salvation" alludes to Isaias, lii, 10, rendered afterwards by St. Luke (iii, 6), "And all flesh shall see the salvation of God". Verse 31, "Which thou hast prepared before the face of all peoples" accords with the Psalmist (xcvii, 2); and verse 32, "A light to the revelation of the Gentiles, and the glory of thy people Israel", recalls Isaias, xlii, 6.

The text of the Nunc Dimittis is given in full in the brief evening prayer found in the Apostolic Constitutions (Book VII, xlviii) (P. G., I, 1057). In the Roman Office, the canticle is assigned to Complin. If St. Benedict did not originate this canonical Hour, he gave to it its liturgical character; but he nevertheless did not include the Canticle, which was afterwards incorporated into the richer Complin Service of the Roman Rite, where it is preceded by the beautiful responsory, "In manus tuas, Domine, commendo spiritum meum" (Into thy hands, O Lord, I commend my spirit) etc., with the Antiphon following, "Salva nos, Domine, vigilantes, custodi nos dormientes" (O Lord, keep us waking, guard us sleeping) etc.—all this harmonizing exquisitely with the spirit of the Nunc Dimittis and with the general character of the closing Hour of the Office. In the blessing of the candles on the feast of the Purification of the Blessed Virgin, the Canticle, of course, receives great prominence both in its text and in the references to Simeon in the preceding prayers. Its last verse, "Lumen ad revelationem" etc., forms the Antiphon which not only precedes and follows the Canticle, but also precedes every verse of it and the Gloria Patri and Sicut erat of the concluding doxology. The symbolism of the Canticle and of its Antiphon is further emphasized by the lighted candles of Candlemas. The complete Canticle also forms the Tract in the Mass of the feast, when the 2 February follows Septuagesima.

For a fuller explanation of the Nunc Dimittis, the following commentaries (in English) may be consulted: CORNELIUS A LAPIDE, *St. Luke's Gospel*, tr. MOSSMAN (London, 1892), 113–116; MCEVILLY, *An Exposition of the Gospel of St. Luke* (New York, 1888), 61, 62; BREEN, *A Harmonized Exposition of the Four Gospels*, I (Rochester, N. Y., 1899), 209–16; MARBACH, *Carmina Scripturarum* (Strasburg, 1907), 438–40 (gives detailed references to the use of its verses in Mass and Office); *The Office of Compline, in Latin and English, according to the Roman Rite, with full Gregorian Notation* (Rome, 1907); SQUIRE in GROVE, *Dict. of Music and Musicians*, gives s. v. *Nunc Dimittis*, an explanation of its use in Anglican Evensong; HUSENBETH, *The Missal for the Use of the Laity* (London, 1903), 562–66, for the prayers and canticles on the feast of the Purification

H. T. HENRY.

Nuncio, an ordinary and permanent representative of the pope, vested with both political and ecclesiastical powers, accredited to the court of a sovereign or assigned to a definite territory with the duty of safeguarding the interests of the Holy See. The special character of a nuncio, as distinguished from other papal envoys (such as legates, collectors), consists in this: that his office is specifically defined and limited to a definite district (his nunciature), wherein he must reside; his mission is general, embracing all the interests of the Holy See; his office is permanent, requiring the appointment of a successor when one incumbent is recalled, and his mission includes both diplomatic and ecclesiastical powers. Nuncios, in the strict sense of the word, first appear in the sixteenth century. The office, however, was not created at any definite moment or by any one papal ordinance, but gradually developed under the influence of various historical factors into the form in which we find it in the sixteenth century. The first permanent representatives of the Holy See at secular courts were the *apocrisarii* (q. v.; see also LEGATE) at the Byzantine Court. In the Middle Ages the popes sent, for the settlement of important ecclesiastical or political matters, legates (*legati a latere*, q. v.) with definite instructions and at times with ordinary jurisdiction. The officials, sent from the thirteenth century for the purpose of collecting taxes either for the Roman Court or for the crusades, were called *nuntii, nuntii apostolici*. During the fourteenth and fifteenth centuries this title was given also to papal envoys entrusted with certain other affairs of an ecclesiastical or diplomatic nature.

Frequently they were given the right of granting certain privileges, favours, and benefices. During the Great Western Schism and the period of the reform councils (fifteenth century), such embassies were more frequently resorted to by the Holy See. Then were also gradually established permanent diplomatic representation at the various courts. With previous forms of papal representation as a precedent and modelled upon the permanent diplomatic legations of temporal sovereigns, there finally arose in the sixteenth century the permanent nunciatures of the Holy See.

The exact date of the establishment of many of the nunciatures is not easy to determine, as it is impossible to fix exactly in all cases when an earlier type of papal envoy was replaced by a nuncio proper, and especially as in the beginning we find interruptions in the succession of envoys who, owing to their powers and their office, must be regarded as real nuncios. The necessity of resisting Protestantism was a special factor in the increase of the nunciatures. After the Council of Trent they became the chief agents of the popes in their efforts to check the spread of heresy and to carry out true reform. The fact that in 1537 the papal correspondence with foreign powers, previously carried on by the pope's private secretary, was handed over by Paul III to the vice-chancellor, Cardinal Alexander Farnese, was the chief element within the curia which led to the permanence of nunciatures. Thereby the political correspondence of the Holy See lost its somewhat private character, and was entrusted to the secretariate of state, with which the nuncios were henceforth to be in constant communication. The popes also employed extraordinary envoys for special purposes. Angelo Leonini, sent to Venice by Alexander VI in 1500, is commonly regarded as the first nuncio, as we understand the term to-day. In Spain the collector-general of the papal exchequer, Giovanni Ruffo dei Teodoli, was also given diplomatic powers: he resided in the country, and discharged these two offices from 1506 to 1518 or 1519. As his successors were appointed collectors-general with fiscal, and political representatives with diplomatic powers, so that from thenceforth the Spanish nunciature may be regarded as permanent. The beginning of a papal nunciature in Germany dates from 1511 when Julius II sent Lorenzo Campeggio to the Imperial Court. His mission was ratified in 1513 by Leo X, and from 1530 a nuncio was permanently accredited. The nuncios often accompanied Emperor Charles V, even when he resided outside the empire. Another German nunciature was established in 1524, when Lorenzo Pimpinella was sent to the court of King Ferdinand of Austria. The first real nuncio in France was Leone Ludovico di Canossa (1514–17). The French nunciature continued from the Council of Trent to the Revolution.

After the Council of Trent a number of new nunciatures were erected. In Italy diplomatic representatives were appointed for Piedmont, Milan, Tuscany (Florence), and for Naples, where the nunciature underwent the same development as in Spain. The *nuntius* entrusted with the duty of collecting the papal taxes received also diplomatic powers, and was recognized in this capacity by Philip II in 1569. Portugal and Poland likewise received permanent nuncios shortly after the Council of Trent. To foster Catholic revival new nunciatures were erected in the southern parts of the German Empire. Thus, in 1573, Bartolomeo Portia was made nuncio of Salzburg, Tyrol, and Bavaria, although no further successor was appointed after 1538. In 1580 Germanico Malaspina was appointed first nuncio of Styria, but this nunciature was discontinued in 1621. Bishop Bonhomini arrived in Switzerland in 1579, and up to 1581 with great zeal and success introduced ecclesiastical reforms. In 1586 Giovanni Battista Santorio succeeded him, whereupon the Swiss nunciature became permanent.

In Cologne a nunciature was erected in 1584 for northwestern Germany and the Rhine, but in 1596 the Netherlands was detached from the Nunciature of Cologne and received its own nuncio, who was to reside in Brussels (Nunciature of Flanders). The jurisdiction of the Nunciature of Flanders extended also to the English missions. Thus, toward the end of the sixteenth century, nunciatures were fully developed.

A dispute concerning the rights of the pope in the erecting of nunciatures and the competency of the nuncios themselves arose in 1785, when Pius VI determined to establish a new nunciature in Munich at the request of Charles Theodore, Elector of Bavaria. The elector desired the appointment of a special nuncio, because princes subject to the emperor alone were bishops of Bavarian dioceses, but did not reside in Bavaria, thus greatly impeding the exercise of ecclesiastical administration. The three spiritual electors (the Archbishops of Cologne, Mainz, and Trier) protested on the ground that thereby their metropolitan rights would be violated. The pope, however, appointed Zoglio, titular Archbishop of Athens, as nuncio, and to him Charles Theodore ordered his clergy to have recourse in future in all ecclesiastical matters within his jurisdiction. The three electors, imbued with Febronianism (q. v.), formed a coalition with the Archbishop of Salzburg, hoping to recover their pretended primitive metropolitan rights by ignoring the nuncio and by giving decisions and granting dispensations on their own authority, even in cases canonically reserved to the pope. As Rome refused to support them, they appealed to Joseph II, who, in accordance with his principles, heartily approved of their efforts, pledged them his full support, declared that he would never allow the jurisdiction of the bishops of the empire to be curtailed, and that consequently he would recognize the nuncios only in their political character. At the Congress of Ems (q. v.), the three elector archbishops passed resolutions embodying their contentions. Despite this protest, Pacca and Zoglio continued to exercise their spiritual jurisdiction in Cologne and Munich respectively, received appeals from the decisions of ecclesiastical courts, and granted dispensations in cases reserved to the pope. On the other hand the four archbishops arbitrarily extended their own authority, granting dispensations from solemn religious vows as well as from matrimonial impediments, and erecting ecclesiastical tribunals of third instance. The emperor brought the controversy before the Imperial Diet of Ratisbon in 1788, but without definite results. The archbishops, opposed both by the cathedral chapters and the suffragan bishops, renewed communications with the pope, who on 14 Nov., 1789, issued an extensive document giving a detailed exposition of the rights of the Holy See and those of its envoys (Ss. D. N. Pii pp. VI. Responsio ad Metropolitanos Moguntino, Treviren., Colonien. et Salisburgen., supre Nuntiaturis apostolicis, Rome, 1789). Frederick William II, King of Prussia, also recognized the jurisdiction of the Nuncio of Cologne in the territory of Cleves, and in Mainz his ambassadors opposed the pretentions of the emperor. The French revolution ended the dispute. Owing to the political development of Italy in the nineteenth century, the papal nunciatures disappeared completely. With the dissolution of the Holy Roman Empire the Imperial German nunciature became the Austrian nunciature, when Francis II assumed the title of Emperor of Austria. The partition of Poland ended the nunciature there. The first state outside of Europe to receive a papal representative was Brazil. At first an internuncio was assigned to that country, but of late years a nuncio has resided there.

At present there are four papal nunciatures of the first class, four of the second, two internunciatures, and several delegations. The nunciatures of the first class are: (1) Vienna; (2) Paris, where the nunciature was re-established after the Revolution, after Cardinal Caprara had first been sent thither as *legatus a latere* by Pius VII. Since the rupture of diplomatic relations between France and the Holy See in 1904, this office has had no incumbent; (3) Madrid, which, since the Council of Trent, has been the permanent residence of the papal nuncio for Spain. It has a special tribunal, the Rota, which serves only as a court of appeals from the diocesan and metropolitan courts, but cannot handle any cases of first instance. Litigants are free to appeal from its decisions to the sovereign pontiff; (4) Lisbon, which had at first a nunciature only of the second class. It included a special court for ecclesiastical matters, but this was abolished in the beginning of the nineteenth century. From the second half of the sixteenth century Portugal always had a nuncio, although disputes arose at different times. The nunciatures of the second class are: (1) the Swiss nunciature which, in the eighteenth century, comprised the Dioceses of Constance, Basle, Ciore, Sion, and Lausanne. Since the religious troubles of 1873 there has been no incumbent; (2) since the beginning of the nineteenth century the only nunciature in Germany has been that of Munich (the last nuncio of Cologne was Annibale della Genga, later on Pope Leo XII); (3) Brussels, the residence of the Nuncio of Belgium as successor of the former Nuncio of Flanders. During the time of the French occupation this position was vacant. It was only in 1829 that Coppacini was sent to Brussels as internuncio; in 1841, it was again raised to a nunciature. Fornari, the first nuncio, was succeeded in 1843 by Gioacchino Pecci, afterwards Leo XIII. In 1880 the Liberal Ministry severed all diplomatic relations with the Holy See; the old status was restored, when in 1885 the Catholic party regained power; (4) Brazil. In 1807 Lorenzo Caleppi, the Nuncio of Portugal, followed John VI in his flight to Brazil. In 1829 a special internuncio, Felice Ostini, was appointed for Brazil; this marks the beginning of diplomatic relations between the Holy See and the other states of South America. In 1902 the papal Internuncio of Brazil was raised to the dignity of nuncio.

The internunciatures are: (1) the Internunciature of Holland and Luxemburg. Since the separation of these countries, the internuncio receives distinct credential letters for the two governments. From the time of the Peace Conference at the Hague Holland has only a chargé d'affaires; (2) the Internunciature of Argentina, Uruguay, and Paraguay, which was erected in 1900. There had been accredited to these countries a papal delegate since 1847, and an internuncio, Mgr Barili, had been sent in 1851 to what was then New Granada. The Apostolic delegates form a lower rank of papal representatives of diplomatic and ecclesiastical character. There are five Apostolic Delegations in South and Central America: (1) Chile, (2) Columbia, (3) Costa-Rica, (4) Ecuador, Bolivia, and Peru, (5) San Domingo, Haiti and Venezuela, all erected during the nineteenth century. Owing to repeated religious troubles these delegations have often been vacant. Costa-Rica has been without a delegate for a considerable period. It is necessary to distinguish these Apostolic delegations of a diplomatic character from those which are merely ecclesiastical.

The powers to papal nuncios correspond to the twofold character of their mission. As the diplomatic representatives of the pope, they treat with the sovereigns or head of republics to whom they are accredited. With their mission they are given special credentials as well as special instructions, whether of a public or of a private nature. They also receive a secret code and enjoy the same privileges as ambassadors. Their appearances in public are regulated in conformity with general diplomatic customs. They also have certain distinctions, especially that of being ex-officio dean of the entire diplomatic body, within their nunciature, and therefore on public occasions take precedence of all diplomatic representatives. Internuncio and delegates enjoy a similar right of precedence over all other diplomatic representatives of equal rank. This privilege of papal envoys was expressly recognized by the Congress of Vienna in 1815 and is universally observed. Nuncios enjoy the title of "Excellency" and the same special honours as ambassadors. In addition to their diplomatic position nuncios have an ecclesiastical mission, and possess ordinary ecclesiastical jurisdiction. The latter point is especially stated in the "Responsio" of Pius VI to the Rhenish archbishops, and was reaffirmed by Pius IX in a letter to Archbishop Darboy of Paris in 1863, as also in a declaration of the Cardinal Secretary of State Jacobini addressed to Spain, 15 April, 1885. The ample ecclesiastical faculties, granted in the Middle Ages to the legates *a latere* and other papal envoys, had led to abuses; the Council of Trent, therefore, enacted that papal envoys (legati a latere, nuncii, gubernatores ecclesiastici, aut alii quarumcumque facultatum vigore) were not to impede bishops or to disturb their ordinary jurisdiction nor to proceed against ecclesiastical persons until the bishop had first been applied to and had shown himself negligent (Sess. XXIV., cap. xx de ref.).

Apart from the special faculties in conferring ecclesiastical benefices and in granting spiritual favours, the nuncios had the power of instituting proceedings and giving decisions in cases of ecclesiastical administration and discipline reserved to the pope. The nunciatures had special courts, principally for cases of appeal. To-day such a court is attached only to the Nunciature of Spain. In all other points nuncios enjoy essentially the same rights in ecclesiastical matters. They are the representatives of the pope, and as such are the organs through which he exercises his ordinary and immediate supreme jurisdiction. It is their special duty to supervise ecclesiastical administration, and on this they report to the cardinal secretary of state; they grant dispensations in cases reserved to the pope, carry on the process of information for the nomination of new bishops, give permission for reading forbidden books, and enjoy the privilege of granting minor indulgences. In special cases they are delegated for the settlement of important ecclesiastical affairs. In virtue of their position certain ecclesiastical honours are due to them as laid down in the "Cæremoniale Episcoporum". Pius X introduced a change in the practice hitherto followed with regard to nuncios, so that now they hold their position longer than formerly, and a nuncio of the first class, after his recall, is not regularly raised to the cardinalate.

PIEPER, *Zur Entstehungsgesch. der ständigen Nuntiaturen* (Freiburg, 1894); BIAUDET, *Les nonciatures apostoliques permanentes jusqu'en 1648* in Annales Academiæ Scientiarum Fennicæ (Helsinski, 1910); RICHARD, *Origines des nonciatures permanentes* in *Revue d'hist. ecclés.*, VII (1906), 52–70, 217–238; IDEM, *Origines de la nonciature de France* in *Revue des quest. histor.*, LXXVIII (1905), 103 sqq.; MEISTER, *Die Nuntiatur von Neapel im 16. Jahrh.* in *Histor. Jahrb.*, XIV (1893), 70–82; IDEM, *Zur spanischen Nuntiatur im 16. u. 17. Jahrh.* in *Röm. Quartalsch.*, VII (1893), 447–81; FRIEDENSBURG, *Anfänge der Nuntiatur in Deutschland* in *Nuntiaturber. aus Deutschland* I, part I, xxxviii, sqq.; PIEPER, *Die päpstl. Legaten u. Nuntien in Deutschland, Frankreich u. Spanien seit der Mitte des 16. Jahrh.*, I (Münster, 1897); MAERE, *Les origines de la nonciature de Flandre* in *Revue d'histoire ecclés.*, VII (1906), 565–84, 805–25); DE HINOYOSA, *Los despachos de la Diplomacia pontificia en España*, I (Madrid, 1896); BAUMGARTEN, *Der Papst, die Regierung u. Verwaltung der hl. Kirche in Rom* (München, 1904), 447 sqq.

NUNCIATURE REPORTS, the official reports concerning their entire field of work sent by the papal nuncios and legates (or their representatives) to the pope or the cardinal secretary of state. The contents of these dispatches are in accordance with the commission received by the legate or nuncio. The reports of the nuncios filling permanent nunciatures, on whom rested the protection of all the interests of the papacy within their special territory, relate to all the more important ecclesiastical or political questions which had any connexion whatever with their commission. The objects of the reports are: (1) to give the most exact information possible concerning all political and ecclesiastical occurrences which might be of importance to the pope or the cardinal secretary of state; (2) to give exact information concerning the action the nuncios have taken with respect to such occurrences; (3) to send news concerning the princes to whose courts they are accredited, and concerning the persons who are in personal contact with the princes, or appear at court on account of political matters, or in any way have a share in ecclesiastical and political affairs. In doing this attention is naturally paid both to the instructions that had been given to the nuncio before he left for his post, and to the letters regularly received from the office of the papal secretary of state, from the pope, or from other officials. Taken in a wider sense, nunciature reports also include those letters of the nuncios concerning the affairs of their nunciatures, addressed to cardinals or others having high official rank in the Curia. From the first half of the sixteenth century, when the bureau of the papal secretary of state was fully developed and the permanent nunciatures received their ultimate organization, the reports of the nuncios were sent regularly (from the middle of the sixteenth century, often weekly). They were written sometimes in Latin, sometimes in Italian. If important matters were treated, especially those concerning which negotiations needed to be carried on in the most secret manner possible, the nuncio employed the cipher given him before going to this position.

Although the individual dispatches vary greatly in worth, yet, as a whole, the nunciature reports form a very important source from the sixteenth century (especially during the sixteenth and seventeenth centuries) both for the history of the Church and for political history. Only a very small proportion either of the reports made by papal legates in the second half of the fifteenth century or in the early years of the sixteenth century have been preserved. From the second decade of the sixteenth century a much greater number survive, and from the middle of this century the reports of individual nuncios frequently exist in unbroken sequence. Most of the manuscript reports are in the Vatican archives, and are classified in sixteen series, according to the nunciatures. The classification does not agree, however, with the present arrangement of the nunciatures, the series given being as follows: Spain, Portugal, France, Belgium, England, Germany (the imperial nunciature), Cologne, Bavaria, Switzerland, Poland, Savoy, Genoa, Venice, Florence, Naples, and Malta. Individual reports are also in other divisions of the archives. The nunciature reports brought together in the archives of the Vatican show serious gaps, especially for the sixteenth century. The reason is that the diplomatic correspondence of the Curia in that era was not systematically brought together and preserved in a papal archive, but was frequently purloined by the copyists, cardinal favourites, and their secretaries, just as the letters dispatched from Rome were retained by the nuncios and their heirs, and thus became dispersed to some extent in family archives. For example, the greater part of the nunciature reports pertaining to the reign of Paul III (1534–49) are now in the state archives of Naples, to which they came along with the archives of the Farnese family. Other collections of reports are to be found in various Italian archives. The reports preserved are either the original drafts made by the nuncios themselves, or the original letters drawn up in accordance with these, or copies of the original letters. As regards the reports written in cipher, a key can generally be found.

On account of the great historical importance of the reports an effort has been made, since the opening of the Vatican archives for general research, to publish them together with supplementary documents (especially the instructions and letters sent to the nuncios). Heretofore more has been done, in the way of publication, for the German nunciatures than for the others. H. Lämmer published a series of nunciature reports from Germany as early as 1860 in his "Monumenta Vaticana historiam ecclesiasticam sæculi XVI illustrantia"; upon the opening of the Vatican archives, the assistant archivist, Father Balan, brought out further material pertaining to the same subject in his work "Monumenta reformationis Lutheranæ" (Ratisbon, 1883-4). Father Dittrich treats the reports sent by the nuncio Giovanni Morone from the Diet of Ratisbon (1541) in the "Historisches Jahrbuch der Görresgesellschaft", IV (1883), 395-472, 618-73, and, as a complement to this, edited the "Nuntiaturberichte Morones vom deutschen Königshofe" for the years 1539-40 in "Quellen und Forschungen aus dem Gebiete der Geschichte", I (Paderborn, 1892). In the mean time three historical institutes at Rome (the Prussian, the Austrian, and that of the Görresgesellschaft) divided among them the publication of all the nunciature reports sent from the German Empire for the period of the sixteenth and the first half of the seventeenth centuries. These societies have already published a large number of volumes: the first division, extending to 1559, is being published by the Prussian Institute; there have appeared so far vols. I-IV, VIII-X, and XII, comprising the nunciatures of Vergerio, Morone, Migganelli, Varallo, Poggio, Bertano, and Camiani, the legations of Farnese, Cervini, Campegio, Aleander, and Sfondrato (Gotha-Berlin, 1892—). The second division covering the period 1560-72, was undertaken by the Austrian Institute; up to the present vols. I and III, containing the reports of the nuncios Hosius and Belfino, have appeared (Vienna, 1897-1903). A third division, covering the years 1572-85, was also assigned to the Prussian institute which has already issued this series (Berlin, 1892—): vol. I, containing the struggle over Cologne; vol. II, containing the Diets of Ratisbon (1576) and of Augsburg (1582); vols. III-V, containing the nunciature of Bartolomæus of Portia. At this point begin the publications of the Institute of the Görresgesellschaft, which has so far edited in four volumes the reports of the nuncios Bonomi (Bonhomini), Santono, Frangipani, Malaspina, and Sega, and the nunciature correspondence of Caspar Gropper (Paderborn, 1895—). The period assigned to this institute covers 1585-1605. With 1606 begins another period (the fourth division), assigned to the Prussian Institute and covering the seventeenth century. Of this division two volumes have been published containing the reports of the nuncio Paletto (Berlin, 1895—). In this way the material concerning the German nunciatures for the period from the beginning of the sixteenth to the middle of the seventeenth century, that is for the age of the Reformation, will be available at a not far distant date.

Professors Reinhard and Steffens of Fribourg undertook the editing of the nunciature reports for Switzerland and began with Nuncio Bonomi (Bonhomini), of whose reports one volume has been issued (Solothurn, 1907); the introductory volume completed by Steffens after Reinhard's death has since appeared (Solothurn, 1910). As regard other countries the reports of the nuncio Andrea da Burgo, who was in Hungary during the years 1524-6, have been issued in the "Monumenta Vaticana Hungariæ", second series, vol. I: "Relationes oratorum pontificiorum" (Budapest, 1884). For France the publication of the nunciature reports has been begun in the "Archives de l'histoire religieuse de France"; of this Fraikin undertook the nunciatures during the pontificate of Clement VII and has issued so far vol. I (Paris, 1906), covering the years 1525-7, and including the nunciatures of Capino da Capo and Roberto Acciainolo, and the legation of Cardinal Salviati. Ancel, meanwhile, began the nunciatures during the reign of Paul IV, and edited (vol. I, pt. i) the dispatches of Sebastiano Gualterio and Cesare Brancato (1554-7). The general reports of Ottavio Mirto Frangipani and Fabio della Lionessa, the nuncios in Flanders (1605 and 1634), have been published by Cauchie in the "Analectes pour servir à l'histoire ecclésiastique de la Belgique" (Louvain). The publication of the dispatches of the papal nunciature in Spain has been commenced by Hinojosa, "Los Despachos de la Diplomacia Pontificia en España", I (Madrid, 1896). So far no comprehensive publication of this kind has been undertaken for Italy, although individual reports have been published. Tolomei has treated the Venetian nunciature during the pontificate of Clement VII, "La nunziatura di Venezia nel pontificato di Clemente VII" (Turin, 1892), and Curasi has edited the dispatches that have been preserved of the legation of Giacomo Gherardi, "Dispacci e letere di Giac. Gherardi, nunzio pontificio a Firenze e Milano, 11 settembre, 1487-10 ottobre, 1490", in "Studi e Testi", fasc. xxi (Rome, 1909). Besides these comprehensive publications various historians in treating the sixteenth and seventeenth centuries in their works have made use of and published individual dispatches of this kind.

See the introductions to the different publications of the nunciature reports and the bibliography of the article NUNCIO.

J. P. KIRSCH.

Nunez (NONIUS), PEDRO, mathematician and astronomer, b. at Alcacer-do-Sol, 1492; d. at Coimbra, 1577. He studied ancient languages, philosophy, and medicine at Lisbon and mathematics at Salamanca. In 1519 he went as inspector-general of customs to Goa, India, returning to become in 1529 royal cosmographer. After lecturing for three years at Lisbon, a professorship of higher mathematics was established for him at the University of Coimbra, which he held from 1544 to 1562. His utterances on science plunged him into discussions with foreign savants, particularly the French mathematician, Oronce Fine. Having been tutor in the reigning family, he was enabled to spend his last years in ease.

To mathematics, astronomy, and navigation, Nunez made important contributions. He devised a method for obtaining the highest common divisor of two algebraic expressions. In his "De crepusculis" he announced a new and accurate solution of the astronomical problem of minimum twilight and suggested an instrument for the measurement of angles. The *nonius*, never in common use, consisted essentially of forty-six concentric circles divided into quadrants by two diameters at right angles to each other, each quadrantal arc being divided into equal parts, the number of parts diminishing from ninety for the outermost arc to forty-five for the innermost. If one side of any angle is made to coincide with one of the radii, the vertex of the angle falling at the centre of the circles, the other side of the angle will fall on or near some point of division of one of the arcs. If then a is the number of parts intercepted and n is the whole number of parts in the relevant arc, the magnitude of the angle will be $90 \times \frac{a}{n}$ degrees. In "De arte navigandi" he announced his discovery and analysis of the curve of double curvature called the *rumbus*, better known as *loxodrome*, which is the line traced by a ship cutting the meridians at a constant angle. His collected works were published under the title "Petri Nonii Opera" (Basle, 1592). Among them are: "Tratado da sphera com a theorica do sol e da lua e o primeiro livro da geographia de Claudio Ptolomeo Alexandrino" (Lisbon, 1537); "De crepusculis liber unus" (Lisbon, 1542); "De arte atque ratione navigandi" (Coimbra, 1546); "De erratis Orontii Finei" (Coimbra, 1546); "Annotatio in extrema verba capitis de climatibis" (Cologne, 1566); "Livro de algebra em arithmetica e geometria" (Antwerp, 1567); "Annotações á Mechanica de Aristoteles e ás theoricas dos planetas de Purbachio com a arte de Navegar" (Coimbra, 1578).

MONTUCLA, *Histoire des math.* (Paris, 1799, 1802); NAVARRETE, *Recherches sur les progrès de l'astronomie et des sciences nautiques en Espagne*, Fr. tr. DE MOFRAS (Paris, 1839); STOCKLER, *Ensaio historico sobre a origem e progressos das mathematicas em Portugal.*

PAUL H. LINEHAN.

Nuns. I. ORIGIN AND HISTORY.—The institution of nuns and sisters, who devote themselves in various religious orders to the practice of a life of perfection, dates from the first ages of the Church, and women may claim with a certain pride that they were the first to embrace the religious state for its own sake, without regard to missionary work and ecclesiastical functions proper to men. St. Paul speaks of widows, who were called to certain kinds of church work (I Tim., v, 9), and of virgins (I Cor., vii), whom he praises for their continence and their devotion to the things of the Lord. In the earliest times Christian women directed their fervour, some towards the service of the sanctuary, others to the attainment of perfection. The virgins were remarkable for their perfect and perpetual chastity which the Catholic Apologists have extolled as a contrast to pagan corruption (St. Justin, "Apol.", I, c. 15; Migne, "P. G.", VI, 350; St. Ambrose, "De Virginibus", Bk I, c. 4; Migne, "P. L.", XVI, 193). Many also practised poverty. From the earliest times they were called the spouses of Christ, according to St. Athanasius, the custom of the Church ("Apol. ad Constant.", sec. 33; Migne, "P. G.", XXV, 639). St. Cyprian describes a virgin who had broken her vows as an adulteress ("Ep. 62", Migne, "P. L.", IV, 370). Tertullian distinguishes between those virgins who took the veil publicly in the assembly of the faithful, and others known to God alone; the veil seems to have been simply that of married women. Virgins vowed to the service of God, at first continued to live with their families, but as early as the end of the third century there were community houses known as παρθενῶνες; and certainly at the beginning of the same century the virgins formed a special class in the Church, receiving Holy Communion before the laity. The office of Good Friday in which the virgins are mentioned after the porters, and the Litany of the Saints, in which they are invoked with the widows, show traces of this classification. They were sometimes admitted among the deaconesses for the baptism of adult women and to exercise the functions which St. Paul had reserved for widows of sixty years.

When the persecutions of the third century drove many into the desert, the solitary life produced many heroines; and when the monks began to live in monasteries, there were also communities of women. St. Pachomius (292-346) built a convent in which a number of religious women lived with his sister. St. Jerome made famous the monastery of St. Paula at Bethlehem. St. Augustine addressed to the nuns a letter of direction from which subsequently his rule was taken. There were monasteries of virgins or nuns at Rome, throughout Italy, Gaul, Spain, and the West. The great founders or reformers of monastic or more generally religious life, saw their rules adopted by women. The nuns of Egypt and Syria cut their hair, a practice not introduced until later into the West. Monasteries of women were generally situated at a distance from those of men; St. Pachomius insisted on this separation, also St. Benedict. There were, however, common houses, one wing being set apart for women and the other for men, more frequently adjoining houses for the two sexes. Justinian abolished these double houses in the East, placed an old man to look after the temporal affairs of the convent, and appointed a priest and a deacon who were to perform their duties, but not to hold any other communication with the nuns. In the West, such double houses existed among the hospitallers even in the twelfth century. In the eighth and ninth centuries a number of clergy of the principal churches of the West, without being bound by religious profession, chose to live in community and to observe a fixed rule of life. This canonical life was led also by women, who retired from the world, took vows of chastity, dressed modestly in black, but were not bound to give of their property. Continence and a certain religious profession were required of married women whose husbands were in Sacred Orders, or even received episcopal consecration.

Hence in the ninth century the list of women vowed to the service of God included these various classes: virgins, whose solemn consecration was reserved to the bishop, nuns bound by religious profession, canonesses living in common without religious profession, deaconesses engaged in the service of the church, and wives or widows of men in Sacred Orders. The nuns sometimes occupied a special house; the enclosure strictly kept in the East, was not considered indispensable in the West. Other monasteries allowed the nuns to go in and out. In Gaul and Spain the novitiate lasted one year for the cloistered nuns and three years for the others. In early times the nuns gave Christian education to orphans, young girls brought by their parents, and especially girls intending to embrace a religious life. Besides those who took the veil of virgins of their own accord, or decided to embrace the religious life, there were others offered by their parents before they were old enough to be consulted. In the West under the discipline in force for several centuries, these oblates were considered as bound for life by the offering made by their parents. The profession itself might be expressed or implied. One who put on the religious habit, and lived for some time among the professed, was herself considered as professed. Besides the taking of the veil and simple profession there was also a solemn consecration of virginity which took place much later, at twenty-five years. In the thirteenth century, the Mendicant Orders appeared characterized by a more rigorous poverty, which excluded not only private property, but also the possession of certain kinds of property in common. Under the direction of St. Francis of Assisi, St. Clare founded in 1212 the Second Order of Franciscans. St. Dominic had given a constitution to nuns, even before instituting his Friars Preachers, approved 22 December, 1216. The Carmelites and the Hermits of St. Augustine also had corresponding orders of women; and the same was the case with the Clerks Regular dating from the sixteenth century, except the Society of Jesus.

From the time of the Mendicant Orders, founded specially for preaching and missionary work, there was a great difference between the orders of men and women, arising from the strict enclosure to which women were subjected. This rigorous enclosure usual in the East, was imposed on all nuns in the West, first by bishops and particular councils, and afterwards by the Holy See. Boniface VIII (1294–1309) by his constitution "Periculoso", inserted in Canon Law [c. un, De statu regularium, in VI° (III, 16)] made it an inviolable law for all professed nuns; and the Council of Trent (Sess. XXV, De Reg. et Mon., c. v) confirmed that constitution. Hence it was impossible for religious to undertake works of charity incompatible with the enclosure. The education of young girls alone was permitted to them, and that under somewhat inconvenient conditions. It was also impossible for them to organize on the lines of the Mendicant Orders, that is to say to have a superior general over several houses and members attached to a province rather than to a monastery. The difficulty was sometimes avoided by having tertiary sisters, bound only by simple vows, and dispensed from the enclosure. The Breviary commemorates the services rendered the Order of Mercy by St. Mary of Cervellione. St. Pius V took more radical measures by his constitution "Circa pastoralis", of 25 May, 1566. Not only did he insist on the observance of the constitution of Boniface VIII, and the decree of the Council of Trent, but compelled the tertiaries to accept the obligation of solemn vows with the pontifical enclosure. For nearly three centuries the Holy See refused all approbation to convents bound by simple vows, and Urban VIII by his constitution "Pastoralis" of 31 May, 1631 abolished an English teaching congregation, founded by Mary Ward in 1609, which had simple vows and a superior general.

This strictness led to the foundation of pious associations called secular because they had no perpetual vows, and leading a common life intended for their own personal sanctification and the practice of charity, e. g. the Daughters of Charity, founded by St. Vincent de Paul. The constitution of St. Pius V was not always strictly observed; communities existed approved by bishops, and soon tolerated by the Holy See, new ones were formed with the sanctions of the diocesan ordinaries. So great were the services rendered by these new communities to the poor, the sick, the young, and even the missions, that the Holy See expressly confirmed several constitutions, but for a long time refused to approve the congregations themselves, and the formula of commendation or ratification contained this restriction *citra tamen approbationem conservatorii* (without approbation of the congregation). As political difficulties rendered less easy the observance of solemn vows, especially for women, the Holy See from the end of the eighteenth century declined to approve any new congregations with solemn vows, and even suppressed in certain countries, Belgium and France, all solemn professions in the old orders of women. The constitution of Benedict XVI, "Quamvis justo" of 30 April, 1749, on the subject of the Congregation of English Virgins was the prelude to the legislation of Leo XIII, who by his constitution "Conditæ" of 8 December, 1900, laid down the laws common to congregations with simple vows, dividing these into two great classes, congregations under diocesan authority, subject to the bishops, and those under pontifical law.

II. Various Kinds of Nuns. — (1) As regards their *object* they may be purely contemplative, seeking personal perfection by close union with God; such are most of the strictly enclosed congregations, as Premonstratensian Canonesses, Carmelites, Poor Clares, Collettines, Redemptoristines; or they may combine this with the practice of works of charity, foreign missions, like the White Sisters of Cardinal Lavigerie, and certain Franciscan Tertiaries; the education of young girls, like the Ursulines and Visitandines; the care of the sick, orphans, lunatics, and aged persons, like many of the congregations called Hospitallers, Sisters of Charity, Daughters of St. Vincent de Paul, and Little Sisters of the Poor. When the works of mercy are corporal, and above all carried on outside the convent, the congregations are called active. Teaching communities are classed rather among those leading a mixed life, devoting themselves to works which in themselves require union with God and contemplation. The constitution "Conditæ" of Leo XIII (8 December, 1900) charges bishops not to permit sisters to open houses as hotels for the entertainment of strangers of both sexes, and to be extremely careful in authorizing congregations which live on alms, or nurse sick persons at their homes, or maintain infirmaries for the reception of infirm persons of both sexes, or sick priests. The Holy See, by its Regulations (Normæ) of 28 June, 1901, declares that it does not approve of congregations whose object is to render certain services in seminaries or colleges for male pupils, or to teach children or young people of both sexes; and it disapproves their undertaking the direct care of young infants, or of lying-in women. These services should be given only in exceptional circumstances. (2) As regards their *origin*, congregations are either connected with a first order or congregation of men, as in the case of most of the older congregations, Carmelites, Poor Clares, Dominicans, Reformed Cistercians of La Trappe, Redemptoristines etc., or are founded independently, like the Ursulines, Visitandines, and recent institution. In the regulations of 28 June, 1901, Art. 19, 52, the Holy See no longer approves of double foundations, which establish a certain subordination of the sisters to similar congregations of men. (3) As regards their *juridical condition*, we distinguish (a) nuns properly so-called, having solemn vows with papal enclosure, whose houses are monasteries; (b) nuns belonging to the old approved orders with solemn vows, but taking only simple vows by special dispensation of the Holy See; (c) sisters with simple vows dependent on the Holy See; (d) sisters under diocesan government. The house of sisters under simple vows, and the congregations themselves are canonically called *conservatoria*. These do not always fulfil all the essential conditions of the religious state. Those which do are more correctly called religious congregations than the others, which are called *piæ congregationes, piæ societates* (pious congregations or pious socities.) Nuns of the Latin Church only are considered here.

III. Nuns Properly So Called.—Nuns properly so-called have solemn vows with a strict enclosure, regulated by pontifical law which prevents the religious from going out (except in very rare cases, approved by the regular superior and the bishop), and also the entrance of strangers, even females, under pain of excommunication. Even admission to the grated parlour is not free, and interviews with regulars are subject to stringent rules. Though some mitigations have been introduced partly by local usage, partly (in the case of certain convents in America) by express concession of the Holy See. The building should be so arranged that the inner courts and gardens cannot be overlooked from outside, and the windows should not open on the public road. By the fact of their enclosure, these monasteries are independent of one another. At the head of the community is a superior often called the abbess, appointed for life by the chapter, at least outside Italy, for in Italy, and especially in the two Sicilies, the constitution "Exposcit debitum" (1 January, 1583) of Gregory XIII requires that they should be re-elected every three years (see "Periodica de Religiosis", n. 420, vol. 4, 158). The election must be confirmed by the prelate to whom the monastery is subject, the pope, the bishop, or the regular prelate. The bishop presides over the ballot, except in the case of nuns subject to regulars, and he has always the right to be present at the election. The president collects the votes at the grating. Without having jurisdiction, the abbess exercises authority over all in the house, and commands in virtue of their vows. Monasteries not exempt are subject to the jurisdiction of the bishop; exempt monasteries are placed, some under the immediate authority of the Holy See, others under that of a regular First Order. In the absence of any other formal direction, the Holy See is understood to delegate to the bishop the annual visitation of monasteries immediately subject to the pope, to the exclusion of other superiors. This visitation is made by the regular prelate in the case of monasteries dependent on a First Order; but the bishop has in all cases authority to insist on the maintenance of the enclosure, and to control the temporal administration; he also approves the confessors.

The erection of a monastery requires the consent of the bishop, and (at least in practice nowadays) of the Apostolic See. The bishop, by himself, or in consultation with the regular superior, determines the number of nuns who can be received according to the amount of their ordinary revenues. The recent Council of Bishops of Latin America, at Rome in 1899, required that the number should not be less than twelve. It is sometimes permitted to receive a certain number of supernumeraries who pay a double dowry, never less than four hundred crowns, and remain supernumeraries all their lives. According to the decree of 23 May, 1659, candidates must be at least fifteen years old. The decree "Sanctissimus" of 4 January, 1910, annuls the admission to the novitiate or to any vows, if granted without the consent of the Holy See, of pupils expelled for any grave reason from a secular school, or for any reason whatever from any institution preparatory to the religious life, or of former novices or professed sisters expelled from their convents. Professed sisters dispensed from their vows cannot, without the consent of the Holy See, enter any congregation, but the one they have quitted (see NOVICE; POSTULANT; "Periodica de Religiosis", n. 368, vol. 5, 98). The admission is made by the chapter, but, before the clothing, and also before the solemn profession, it is the duty of the bishop, by himself or (if he is prevented) by his vicar-general or some person delegated by either of them, to inquire into the question of the candidate's religious vocation, and especially as to her freedom of choice. The candidate must provide a dowry of at least two hundred crowns unless the founder consents to accept a smaller sum. With certain exceptions, the dowry of choir sisters cannot be dispensed with; it must be paid before the clothing, and invested in some safe and profitable manner. On solemn profession, it becomes the property of the convent, which has, however, no right of alienation; it is returned as a matter of equity to a religious who enters another order, or to one who returns to the world and is in want.

After the novitiate the religious cannot at first, according to the decree "Perpensis" of 3 May, 1902, take any but simple vows whether perpetual or for a year only, if it is customary to take annual vows. The admission to vows is made by the chapter, with the consent of the regular superior or the bishop. Some writers hold that the bishop is bound, before this profession, to make a fresh inquiry into the vocation of the novice, and this inquiry does not dispense from that which the Council of Trent prescribes before solemn profession (see the answer of 19 January, 1909; "Periodica de Religiosis", n. 317, vol. 4, 341). This period of simple vows ordinarily lasts for three years, but the bishop or the regular prelate may prolong it in the case of nuns who are under twenty-five years. During this period, the religious keeps her property, but makes over the administration of it to any one she may choose. She is bound to the rules and the choir, but not to the private recitation of the Divine Office; she can take part in chapters, except in those in which others are admitted to vows; she cannot be elected superior, mother-vicaress, mistress of novices, assistant, counsellor, or treasurer. She participates in all the indulgences and spiritual privileges of those who have taken their solemn vows; and although the solemnly professed take precedence, once the solemn profession is made, the seniority is regulated by the date of simple profession, without regard to any delay in proceeding to solemn profession. The dispensation of vows and dismissal of nuns are reserved to the Holy See. The outward solemnity of profession takes place at the first simple profession; the other takes place without any solemnity. Only the prelate or the ordinary can admit to the latter, but a consultative chapter is held, whose decision is announced by the superior. Solemn profession carries with it the inability to possess property (except in case of a papal indult such as that enjoyed by Belgium and perhaps also Holland), annuls a marriage previously contracted but not consummated, and creates a diriment impediment to any subsequent marriage. Nuns are generally obliged to recite the Divine Office, like religious orders of men; but the Visitandines and some monasteries of Ursulines recite only the Little Office of the Blessed Virgin, even in choir. The obligation of this office, even choral, does not bind under pain of mortal sin, as the Holy See has declared for the Ursulines; whether it can be omitted without venial sin depends apparently on the constitutions.

The bishop appoints the ordinary confessor, also the extraordinary or additional confessors of monasteries subject to him, and approves the confessor nominated by the regular prelate of a monastery subject to a First Order. The approbation for one monastery is not valid for another. As a rule there should be only one ordinary confessor, who should be changed every three years. Since the Council of Trent (Sess. XXV De Reg., c. x), a confessor extraordinary should visit the monastery two or three times a year. Benedict XIV, by his Bull "Pastoralis" of 5 August, 1748, insisted on the appointment of a confessor extraordinary, and also on the provision of facilities for sick nuns. More recently, the decree "Quem ad modum" of 17 October, 1890, ordains that, without asking for any reason, a superior shall allow her subjects to confess to any priest among those authorized by the bishops, as often as they think it necessary for their spiritual necessities. Besides the ordinary or extraordinary confessors, there are additional confessors, of whom the bishop must appoint a sufficient number. The ordinary confessor cannot be a religious except for monasteries of the same order as himself; and in that case the extraordinary confessor cannot belong to the same order. The same decree gives to confessors the exclusive right of regulating the communions of the nuns, who have the privilege of communicating daily since the decree "Sacra Tridentina" of 20 December, 1905 (see "Periodica de Religiosis", n 110, vol. 2, 66), and it forbids superiors to interfere unasked in cases of conscience. The subjects are free to open their minds to their superiors but the latter must not, directly or indirectly, demand or invite such confidence.

IV. NUNS OF THE OLD ORDERS WITHOUT SOLEMN VOWS.—Since the French Revolution, various answers of the Holy See have gradually made it clear that neither in Belgium nor in France are there any longer monasteries of women subject to papal enclosure, or bound by solemn vows. (Cf. for France the reply of the Penitentiary of 23 December, 1835; for Belgium the declaration of the Apostolic visitor Corselis of 1836; Bizzarri, "Collectanea, 1st ed., p. 504, note; Bouix, "De regularibus", vol. 2, 123 sq.). After long deliberation, the Sacred Congregation of Bishops and Regulars decided (cf. letter of 2 September, 1864, to the Archbishop of Baltimore) that in the United States nuns were under simple vows only, except the Visitandines of Georgetown, Mobile, Kaskaskia, St. Louis, and Baltimore, who made solemn profession by virtue of special rescripts. It added that without special indult the vows should be simple in all convents erected in the future. Since then the monastery of Kaskaskia has been suppressed. The Holy See permitted the erection of a monastery of Visitandines with solemn vows at Springfield (Missouri). According to the same letter, the Visitandines with solemn vows must pass five years of simple profession before proceeding to solemn profession (Bizzarri, "Collectanea", 1st ed., 778–91). Except in the case of a pontifical indult placing them in subjection to a first order these nuns are bound by the following rules: (a) The bishop has full jurisdiction over them; he may dispense from all constitutions not reserved to the Holy See, and from particular impediments to admission, but may not modify the constitutions. The vows are reserved to the Holy See, but the French bishops have received power to dispense from all vows except that of chastity. The bishop presides and confirms all elections, and has the right to require an account of the temporal administration. (b) The superior retains such power as is adapted to the vows and the necessities of community life. (c) The obligation of the Divine Office is such as imposed by the rule; the enclosure is of episcopal law. (d) The vow of poverty does not prevent the possession of property. As a rule, dispositions of property "inter vivos" and by will cannot be licitly made without the consent of the superior or the bishop. Unless forbidden by the bishop, the superior may permit the execution of such instruments as are necessary for the purpose. (e) Indulgences and spiritual privileges (among which may be reckoned the use of a special calendar) remain intact. (f) In principle, the prelate of the First Order is without authority over the nuns.

V. RELIGIOUS CONGREGATIONS AND PIOUS SOCIETIES UNDER PONTIFICAL AUTHORITY. (a) *Congregations.*—Since the constitution "Conditæ" of 8 December, 1900, and the Regulations of 28 June, 1901, we possess precise rules by which to distinguish the congregations governed by pontifical law. Before formally approving a congregation and its constitutions, the Holy See is accustomed to give its commendation first to the intentions of the founders and the purpose of the foundation, and then to the congregation itself. The second decree of commendation has the effect of bringing the congregation into the number of those which are governed by pontifical law, and especially by the second part of the constitution "Conditæ". Bizzarri in his "Collectanea" gives a list of congregations so commended up to 1864 (1st ed, 861 sqq.). This approbation is not usually granted until the congregation has existed for some time under the authority of the bishop. The congregations are constituted on the model of the newer religious orders, that is to say they group several houses, each governed by a local superior, under the indirect authority of a superior general; many, but not all, are divided into provinces. Many form communities of tertiaries, who as such have a share in the spiritual privileges of the order to which they are affiliated. Except in the case of a special privilege, like that which places the Daughters of Charity under the Superior General of the Priests of the Mission (see decree of 25 May, 1888) the Holy See no longer permits a bishop, or the delegate of a bishop, or the superior general of a congregation of men to be superior over a congregation of sisters. Before the regulations of 1901 the rules of new congregations differed in many respects. The details of internal government which follow apply to newly established congregations rather than to the older ones, like the Ladies of the Sacred Heart.

The government of the congregations is vested in the general chapter, and in the superior general assisted by a council with certain rights reserved to the bishops, under protection and supreme direction of the Sacred Congregation of Religious. This is the only competent Congregation since the reform of the Roman Curia by the constitution "Sapienti" of 29 June, 1908. The general chapter includes in all cases the superior general, her counsellors, the secretary general, the treasurer general, and if the congregation is divided into provinces, the provincial superiors, and two delegates from each province, elected by the provincial chapter. If there are no provinces, the general chapter includes (besides those mentioned above) all superiors of houses containing more than twelve nuns, accompanied by one religious under perpetual vows elected by all the professed sisters (including those under temporary vows) of such houses. The less important houses are grouped among themselves for this election, or annexed to a principal house. This chapter ordinarily meets every six or twelve years, being summoned by the superior general or mother vicaress; but an extraordinary meeting may be called on the occurrence of a vacancy in the office of superior, or for any other grave reason approved by the Holy See. The general chapter elects by an absolute majority of votes in secret ballot the superior general, the counsellors or assistants general, the secretary general, and the treasurer general, and deliberates on important matters affecting the congregation. In many cases especially when there is a question of modifying the constitutions, the permission and confirmation of the Holy See are required. The capitular decrees remain in force till the next chapter. The bishop as delegate of the Holy See, presides over the elections in person or by his representative. After the ballot he declares the election valid, and announces the result. The provincial chapter, composed of the provincial, the superiors of houses containing at least twelve nuns, and a delegate from each principal house (as above) has no other office, according to common law, but to depute two sisters to the general chapter.

The superior general is elected for six or twelve years; in the former case she may be re-elected, but for a third consecutive term of six years, or a second of twelve years, she must receive two-thirds of the votes, and the consent of the Holy See. She may not resign her office except with the consent of the Sacred Congregation, which has the power to depose her. The house in which she resides is considered the motherhouse, and the permission of the Holy See is necessary for a change of residence. She governs the congregation according to the approved constitutions, and is bound to make a visitation every three years either personally or by a deputy, to exercise a general control over the temporal administration, and to submit to the Sacred Congregation an official report countersigned by the ordinary of the principal house. (See the instruction accompanying the decree of 16 July, 1906, "Periodica de Religiosis", n. 134, vol. 2, 128 sqq.). The superior general nominates to the different non-elective offices, and decides the place of residence of all her subjects. The counsellors general assist the superior general with their advice, and in many matters the consent of the majority is required. Two of them must live with the superior general, and the rest must be accessible. According to the regulations of 1901, the approval of the general council is required for the erection and suppression of houses, the erection and transfer of novitiates, the erection of new provinces, the principal nominations, the retention of a local superior for longer than the usual term of office, the dismissal of a sister or novice, the deposition of a superior, mistress of novices or counsellor, the provisional appointment of a counsellor deceased or deprived of office, the nomination of a visitor not a member of the council, the choice of a meeting place of the general chapter, the change of residence of the superior general, the execution of all contracts, the auditing of accounts, all pecuniary engagements, the sale or mortgage of immovable property, and the sale of movable property of great value. For an election there must be a full meeting of the council, and provision must be made to replace any members who are prevented from attending. In case of a tie, the superior has a casting vote.

The secretary general keeps the minutes of proceedings, and has charge of the archives. The treasurer general administers the property of the whole congregation. The provinces and the houses have also their own property. The Holy See insists that the safes containing valuables shall have three locks, the keys of which shall be kept by the superior, the treasurer, and the oldest of the counsellors. In her administration the treasurer must be guided by the complicated rules of the recent instruction "Inter ea" of 30 July, 1909, which refer especially to pecuniary engagements. The consent of the Holy See is required before any liability can be incurred exceeding ten thousand francs, and in case of smaller liabilities than this but still of any considerable amount, the superiors must take the advice of their councils. A council should at once be appointed if there is none already existing (cf. "Periodica de Religiosis", n. 331, vol. 5, 11 sqq). The bishop must test the vocation of postulants before they take the veil, and before profession; he presides over chapters of election, permits or forbids collections from door to door; is responsible for the observance of partial enclosure, such as is compatible with the objects of the congregation. No house can be established without his consent. To him also belongs the supreme spiritual direction of the communities, and the nomination of the chaplain and confessors. The Holy See reserves to itself the vows, even temporary ones. The dismissal of a professed sister under perpetual vows must be ratified by the Holy See. The dismissal of a novice or of a professed sister under temporary vows is within the power of the general council, if justified by grave reasons; but this dismissal does not relieve from vows for which recourse must be had to the Holy See. The Holy See alone can authorize the suppression of houses, the erection or transfer of a novitiate, the erection of a province, the transfer of a mother-house, and any important alienations of property, and borrowings above a certain sum.

The Holy See permits, though it does not make obligatory, the division of a community into choir sisters or teaching sisters, and lay sisters. Though not opposed to the formation of associations which help the work of the congregation and have a share in its merits, it forbids the establishment of new third orders. A period of temporary vows should precede the taking of perpetual vows. Such is the general law. At the expiration of the term, temporary vows must be renewed. The vow of poverty does not generally forbid the acquisition and retention of rights over property, but only its free use and disposal. A dowry is generally required, of which the community receives the income only, until the death of the sister, and the fruits of their labours belong entirely to the congregation. The vow of chastity creates only a prohibitory impediment to marriage. The bishops generally regulate the confessions of the religious under simple vows, by the same rules as those of nuns in strict enclosure; but in public churches sisters may go to any approved confessor. In all that concerns communions and direction of conscience, the decrees "Quem ad modum" and "Sacra Tridentina" apply to these congregations as well as to monasteries of nuns. These religious congregations have not generally any obligation of choir, but recite the Little Office of the Blessed Virgin and other prayers. They are bound to make a daily meditation of at least half an hour in the morning, sometimes of another half hour in the evening, and an annual retreat of eight days.

(b) *Pious societies* which can only be called congregations by a wide extension of the word, are those which have no perpetual vows, such as the Daughters of Charity, who are free for one day in each year, or those which, if they have perpetual vows, have no outward sign by which they can be recognized: this single fact is sufficient to deprive them of the character of religious congregations (see answer of 11 August, 1889, "De Religiosis Institutis", vol. 2, n. 13).

VI. DIOCESAN CONGREGATIONS.—For a long time the bishops had great latitude in approving new congregations, and gave canonical existence to various charitable institutions. In order to avoid an excessive increase in their number, Pius X by his *Motu Proprio* "Dei Providentis" of 16 July, 1906, required the previous authorization of the Sacred Congregation before the bishop could establish, or allow to be established any new diocesan institution; and the Sacred Congregation refuses to authorize any new creation except after approval of the title, habit, object, and work of the proposed community, and forbids that any substantial change should be made without its authority.

Notwithstanding that pontifical intervention, the congregation remains diocesan. The bishop approves the constitutions only in so far as they are in accordance with the rules approved by the Holy See. As it remains diocesan we may conclude that the Roman disciplinary decrees do not affect it unless this is clearly stated. Diocesan congregations have the bishop as their first superior. It is his duty to control admissions, authorize dismissals, and dispense from vows, except that one reserved to the Holy See, the absolute and perpetual vow of chastity. He must be careful not to infringe the rights acquired by the community. Not only does he preside over elections but he confirms or annuls them, and may in case of necessity depose the superior, and make provision for filling the vacancy. These congregations are sometimes composed of houses independent of one another; this is frequently the case with Sisters Hospitallers, and sometimes several houses and local superiors are grouped under one superior general. Some of the congregations are confined to one diocese, while others extend to several dioceses: in the latter case, each diocesan ordinary has under him the houses in his dioceses with power to authorize or suppress them. The congregation itself depends on the concurrence of the bishops in whose dioceses any houses are situated; and this concurrence is necessary for its suppression. Such is the common law of the constitution "Conditæ". Before it can spread into another diocese, a diocesan congregation must have the consent of the bishop to whom it is subject, and often by agreement among bishops a real superiority is reserved to the bishop of the diocese of origin. As to the laws by which they are governed, a great number of congregations, especially those devoted to the care of the sick in hospitals, follow the rule of St. Augustine and have special constitutions; others have only constitutions peculiar to themselves; others again form communities of tertiaries. The curious institution of Beguines (q. v.) still flourishes in a few cities of Belgium.

Historical: BESSE, *Les Moines d'Orient antérieurs au concile de Chalchédoine (451)* (Paris, 1900); *Le Monachisme Africain*, IV-VI, 5 (Paris, s. d.); BUTLER, *The Lausiac Hist. of Palladius* (Cambridge, 1898); DE BUCK-TINNEBROECK, *Examen Historicum et canonicum libri R. D. Verhoeven, De Regularium et Sæcularium iuribus et officiis*, I (Ghent, 1847); DUCHESNE, *Les origines du culte chrétien* (Paris); FUNK, *Lehrbuch der Kirchengesch.* (Paderborn, (1898); GASQUET, *Saggio storico della Costituzione monastica* (Rome, 1896); HEIMBUCHER, *Die Orden und Kongregationen der Katholischen Kirche* (3 vol., Paderborn, 1896-1908); HÉLYOT, *Hist. des ordres monastiques, religieux et militaires* (8 vol., Paris, 1714-19); LADEUZE, *Etude sur le cénobitisme Pakhomien pendant le IVe siècle et la première moitié du Ve* (Louvain, 1898); MARIN, *Les Moines de Constantinople depuis la fondation de la ville jusqu'à la mort de Photius* (Paris, 1897), (cf. Pargoire *infra*); MARTÈNE, *Commentarius in regulam S.P. Benedicti, De antiquis monachorum ritibus*; PARGOIRE, *Les débuts du monachisme à Constantinople* in *Revue des questions historiques* (vol. 65, 1899); SCHIEWIETZ, *Das morgenländische Mönchtum* (Mainz, 1904); SPREITZENHOFEZ, *Die Entwicklung des alten Mönchtums in Italien von seiner ersten Anfängen bis zum Auftreten des hl. Benedict* (Vienna, 1894); THOMASSIN, *Vetus et nova Ecclesiæ disciplina*, I, 1, 3; WILPERT, *Die Gottgeweihten Jungfrauen in der ersten Jahrhunderten der Kirche* (Freiburg im Br., 1892); *Doctrinal*, besides the general works of the classical authors: BASTIEN, *Directoire canonique à l'usage des Congrégations à vœux simples* (Maredsous, 1911); BATTANDIER, *Guide canonique pour les Constitutions des Instituts à vœux simples* (4th ed., Paris, 1908); BOUIX, *Tractatus de iure regularium* (2 vols., Paris, 1856); PELLIZARIUS, *Tractatus de Monialibus* (1761); PIAT, *Prælectiones iuris Regularium* (2 vol., Tournai, 1898); ROTARIUS, *Theologia moralis regularum*, 3 vols.; TAMBURINI, *De iure abbatissarum et aliarum Monialium*; VERMEERSCH in *De Religiosis Institutis et Personis* 2 vols. (1st vol., 2nd ed., 1907; 2nd vol., 4th ed., 1910); *De Religiosis et Missionariis Periodica, ab anno 1905.*

A. VERMEERSCH.

Nuoro. See GALTELLI-NUORO, DIOCESE OF.

Nuptial Blessing. See MASS, NUPTIAL.

Nuremberg (NÜRNBERG), second largest city in Bavaria, situated in a plain on both sides of the river Pegnitz. Of uncertain origin, it is first mentioned as Noremberc in a document issued by Emperor Henry III at a diet held in the town. The palace was reconstructed as a fortified castle between 1025 and 1050.

The population increased when Henry IV transferred (1062) from Fürth to Nuremberg the right to hold a fair and to coin money. The cult of its patron St. Sebald, also helped its development. In times of war the emperors often found refuge in the town, for which Henry V granted it freedom from custom duties (1112). King Lothair (1112-1137) claimed Nuremberg as part of his empire, while the Hohenstaufen brothers, Conrad and Frederick, claimed it as part of their inheritance under the Salic law. In 1130 the city surrendered to the emperor and the Guelph Henry. The latter possessed it until 1138, when it reverted to the empire. Conrad III liked to visit the flourishing city, and made it an asylum for the then persecuted Jews. Several diets took place in Nuremberg under Frederick Barbarossa, who built a splendid new imperial castle adjoining the old castle of the burggraves (*Burggrafen*). From the end of the eleventh century the city was independent of the burggraves, who, in the early times, in their capacity as imperial officials, exercised jurisdiction in all judicial and military matters and appropriated two-thirds of all moneys collected in criminal and civil cases. When the burggraves (at first descendants of the house of Raabs in Lower Austria, and, when it became extinct in 1190, the house of Zollern) endeavoured to extend their private possessions at the expense of the empire, the emperors of the twelfth century took over the administration of the imperial possessions belonging to the *burg*, and installed a castellan or overseer in the imperial castle. This castellan not only administered the imperial lands surrounding Nuremberg, but levied taxes and constituted the highest judicial court in matters relating to poaching and forestry; he also was the appointed protector of the various ecclesiastical establishments, churches, and monasteries, even of the Bishopric of Bamberg. The privileges of this castellanship were transferred to the city during the last years of the fourteenth, and the first years of the fifteenth centuries. The strained relations between the burggraves and the castellan finally broke into out open enmity, which greatly influenced the history of the city.

In 1219 Nuremberg became a free imperial city, when Frederick II presented it with a most important charter, freeing it from all authority excepting that of the emperor himself. The administration was entrusted to a council, presided over, since the middle of the thirteenth century, by the *Reichsschultheiss*. The "Schöffenkollegium", who assisted this official in his judicial work, also sat in the council. The council became more and more independent, and in 1320 was invested by Louis the Bavarian with supreme jurisdiction. This conflicted with the rights of the *Schultheiss* (usually a knight), whose appointment, however, rested with the council after 1396. This accumulation of rights and privileges made the power of the council equal to that of the sovereign or territorial lords, while the acquisition of the imperial forest near Nuremberg had furnished a basis for future development. Until the middle of the thirteenth century, the *Kleine* (little) or reigning council consisted of thirteen magistrates and thirteen councillors; towards the end of the century were added eight members of the practically unimportant *Grosse* (great) council, and, since 1370, eight representatives of the artisans' associations. The members of the council were chosen by the people usually from the wealthier class; this custom led to the establishment of a circle of "eligibles", to which the artisan class was strongly opposed as being politically an illegal element. With the increasing importance of handicraft a spirit of independence developed among the artisans, and they determined to have a voice in the government of the city. In 1349 the members of the trade unions unsuccessfully rebelled against the patricians. Their unions were then dissolved, and the oligarchic element remained in power while Nuremberg was a free city.

Ecclesiastically speaking, Nuremberg belonged first to the Bishopric of Eichstätt, and from 1015 to that of Bamberg. In place of the oldest chapel in Nuremberg, the *Peterskapelle*, a church was consecrated in 1070 to St. Sebaldus; this was replaced by a new edifice in the thirteenth century. The second church in importance was the *Lorenzkirche*, built about 1278. There also arose the Gothic St. Jacob's Church (twelfth century), which was transferred to the Teutonic Knights in 1209; the Scots Abbey (1140); the monasteries and chapels of the Franciscans, 1227 (thirteenth century), the Augustinians (1218); the Dominicans (1248); the Carmelites (1255); the Carthusians (1382); the Order of Mary Magdalene (*Reuerinnen*) incorporated with the Poor Clares in 1279, and the cloister of St. Catherine, a society of nurses. The hospital of the Holy Ghost was founded 1334-39. At the beginning of the fourteenth century Nuremberg had become wonderfully developed. Charles IV conferred upon it the right to conclude alliances independently, thereby placing it upon a politically equal footing with the princes of the empire. The city protected itself from hostile attacks by a wall and successfully defended its extensive trade against the barons. Frequent fights took place with the burggraves without, however, inflicting lasting damage upon the city. After the castle had been destroyed by fire in 1420 during a feud between Count Frederick (since 1417 Margrave of Brandenburg) and the Duke of Bavaria-Ingolstadt, the ruins and the forest belonging to the castle were purchased by the city (1427), which thereby became master of all that lay within its boundaries. The imperial castle had been ceded to the city by Emperor Sigismund in 1422, on condition that the imperial suite of rooms should be reserved for the emperor. Through these and other acquisitions the city accumulated considerable territory. In 1431 the population was about 22,800 including 7146 persons qualified to bear arms, 381 secular and regular priests; 744 Jews and non-citizens. The Hussite wars, the plague of 1437, the fights with the burggraves (then also margraves of Brandenburg, Anspach, and Bayreuth, reduced it to 20,800 in 1450.

At the beginning of the sixteenth century the war of

CASTLE OF NUREMBERG

succession in Landshut brought new possessions to Nuremberg (the ally of Duke Albert of Bavaria-Munich), so that it possessed more (25 sq. miles) than any imperial free city; it was called the Empire's Treasure Box on account of its political importance, its industrial power, and superior culture. It had now reached the pinnacle of its splendour. As an indication of its importance as an art and science centre during the fourteenth, fifteenth and sixteenth centuries, it records such names as Peter Vischer, Adam Krafft, Veit Stoss, Michael Wohlgemuth, Albert Dürer, Hans Sachs, Conrad Celtes, Willibald and Charitas Pirkheimer,

MAIN PORTAL, ST. SEBALDUS, NUREMBERG

Johann Müller (Regiomontanus), Hartmann Schedel, Martin Behaim and others.

In 1521 Luther's creed was preached by some of the clergy, among whom was Andrew Osiander, preacher at St. Lornzkirche; there was also a distinct leaning towards the new teaching among the members of the council. They prohibited processions, passion plays during the Easter tide, and other celebrations. After 1524 the possessions of the monasteries and clerical institutions were confiscated; in 1525 the council accepted Luther's religion; the Dominicans, Carmelites and Minorites were forbidden to preach or to hear confessions; a preacher was placed over convents and the reception of any more novices forbidden. About the middle of the sixteenth century the city had become almost Protestant; only the members of the Teutonic Knights remained faithful; they suffered many restrictions and the loss of their church. After the Diet of Augsburg, 1529, when most of the Protestant estates of the empire formed the League of Smalkald, Nuremberg did not join. The Diet of Nuremberg, 1532, gave religious freedom at least for a time: Protestants were allowed to continue the innovations already introduced by them and all processes begun against them in the Imperial Chamber, on account of these innovations, were suspended, pending the settlement of the whole religious question by a great council to be called within the year. The aid against the Turks which the emperor and king desired was granted. By consent of the Lutherans the followers of Zwingli were exempted from the provisions of this peace. During this period Nuremberg remained as neutral as possible, so as not to quarrel with the emperor and yet to retain its whole creed of the Gospel; it therefore accepted the interim regulation. During the revolution of the princes against Charles V, in 1552, Nuremberg endeavoured to purchase its neutrality by the payment of 100,000 gulden; but Maigrave Albert Alcibiades, one of the leaders of the revolt, attacked the city without declaring war and forced it to conclude a disadvantageous peace. At the Religious Peace of Augsburg the possessions of the Protestants were confirmed by the emperor, their religious privileges extended and their independence from the jurisdiction of the Bishop of Bamberg affirmed while the secularizing of the possessions of the monasteries was approved.

The unsettled state of affairs in the first half of the sixteenth century, the revolution in commerce and trade due to the discovery of America and the circumnavigation of Africa, and the difficulties in trade caused by the territorial sovereigns, were responsible for the decline of the importance and affluence of the city. During the Thirty Years' War it did not always succeed in preserving its policy of neutrality. Frequent quartering of Imperial, Swedish and League soldiers, war-contributions, demands for arms, semicompulsory presents to commanders of the warring armies and the cessation of trade, caused irreparable damage to the city. The population, which in 1620 had been over 45,000, sank to 25,000.

After the religious war Nuremberg remained aloof from the quarrels and affairs of the world at large; but contributions were demanded for the Austrian War of Succession and the Seven Years' War, the former amounting to six and a half million guldens. Restrictions of imports and exports deprived the city of many markets for its manufactures, especially in Austria, Prussia and Bavaria, and the eastern and northern countries of Europe. The Bavarian elector, Charles Theodore, appropriated part of the land which had been obtained in the war of succession in Landshut and which ever since had been claimed by Bavaria; Prussia also claimed part of the territory of Nuremberg. Realizing its weakness, the city asked to be incorporated in the Kingdom of Prussia, but Frederick William II refused the request, fearing to offend Austria, Russia, and France. At the imperial diet in 1803 the independence of Nuremberg was affirmed. But on the signing of the *Rheinbund* (Rhenish Federation) 12 July, 1806, the city was handed over to Bavaria 8 Sept. Its population was then 25,200 and its public debt twelve and a half million guldens. After the fall of Napoleon its trade and commerce revived; the skill of its inhabitants together with its favourable situation soon rendered the city prosperous, particularly after its public debt had been acknowledged as a part of the Bavarian national debt. Incorporated in a Catholic country the city was compelled to refrain from further discrimination against the Catholics, who had been excluded from the rights of citizenship. Catholic services had been celebrated in the city by the priests of the order of the Teutonic Knights, often under great difficulties. Their possessions having been confiscated by the Bavarian government in 1806, they were given the *Frauenkirche* on the Market in 1809; in 1810 the first Catholic parish was established, which in 1818 numbered 1010 souls.

In 1817 the city was included in the department *Rezatkreis* (later Mittelfranken). The establishment of railways and the joining of Bavaria to the German Customs Union (Zollverein), commerce and industry opened the way to great prosperity. In 1852 there were 53,638 inhabitants, 46,441 Protestants and 6616 Catholics. Since that time it has become the most important industrial city of Bavaria and one of the most prosperous towns of southern Germany. In 1905 its population, including several incorporated suburbs, was 291,351—86,943 Catholics, 196,913 Protestants, 3738 Jews and 3766 members of other creeds; the present population is estimated at 340,000.

Nuremberg belongs to the Archdiocese of Bamberg and possesses notable churches. For want of means the building of churches could not keep pace with the growth of the community; this condition rendered difficult the work of ministry. The Catholic churches at present accommodate barely 8000 people, while the Catholics in the city number over 90,000. The most beautiful church is the Liebfrauenkirche (Church of Our Dear Lady), built 1315–61 in Gothic style; it is one of the greatest ornaments of the city (Essenwein, "Die Liebfrauenkirche in Nürnberg", Nuremberg, 1881). Other churches are, the St. Elisabethenkirche, a mighty edifice, in antique style, begun in 1784, secularized in 1806, purchased by the Catholics in 1885 (Schrötter, "Die Kirche der heiligen Elisabeth in Nürnberg", Nuremberg, 1903); the St. Klarakirche, a Gothic structure, built in 1339, turned over to the Catholics in 1857; the Herz-Jesu-kirche, a basilica in early Gothic style, erected 1898–1902; the Walpurgiskapelle in the castle, dating from the thirteenth century; the temporary structures: St. Joseph (1897–8); St. Anthony (1899–1900); St. Karl Borromäus (1903–4); and a new church at present being erected.

ROTH, *Gesch. des Nürnbergschen Handels* (4 vols., Leipzig, 1800–2); MARX, *Gesch. der Reichsstadt N.* (Nürnberg, 1856); GHILLANY, *N. hist. u. topog. nach den ältesten vorhandenen Quellen u. Urkunden* (Munich, 1863); *Chroniken der deutschen Städte*, I–III, X, XI (Leipzig, 1862–74); HEROLD, *Alt-N. in seinen Gottesdiensten* (Gütersloh, 1890); ROTH, *Die Einführung der Reformation in N.* (Würzburg, 1885); MUMMENHOFF, *Alt-N.* (Bamberg, 1890); IDEM, *Die Burg zu N.* (Nürnberg, 1892); IDEM, *N. Ursprung u. Alter in den Darstellungen der Geschichtschreiber u. im Lichte der Gesch.* (Nürnberg, 1908); *Kulturgeschichtl. Bilder aus N's Vergangenheit* (14 parts, Nürnberg, 1894–1902); ROESEL, *Alt-N.* (Nürnberg, 1895); REICKE, *Gesch. der Reichsstadt N.* (Nürnberg, 1896); RÉE, *N.* (Leipzig, 1900), dealing with the hist. of art; VON SCHUH, *Die Stadt N's im Jubiläumsjahr 1906* (Nürnberg, 1906); MEYER, *Gesch. der Burggrafschaft N. u. der spätern Markgrafschaften Ansbach u. Bayreuth* (Tübingen, 1908); SCHRÖTTER, *Gesch. der Stadt N.* (Nürnberg, 1909); WEISS, *Gesch. der Stadt N. bis zum Uebergang der Reichsstadt an das Königreich Bayern 1806* (Nürnberg, 1909); *Die kathol. Kirchen in N.* (Nürnberg, 1909); *Mitteil. des Vereins für die Gesch. der Stadt N.* (18 vols., Nürnberg, 1879–1909).

JOSEPH LINS.

Nusco, DIOCESE OF (NUSCANA), in the province of Avellino, Italy, suffragan of Salerno, dates from the eleventh century. Among its bishops were Guido (1004); St. Amatus (1167), author of a history of the Normans in Apulia and Calabria; Roger (1198), who restored the cathedral; Cardinal Pietro Paolo Parisio (1538), who presided at the Council of Trent; Francesco Arcudio (1639), a Theatine; Fulgenzio Arminio Monforte (1669), an Augustinian. In 1820 Montemartino was united to Nusco. St. John, a Benedictine (1084), was first Bishop of Montemartino; forty of his successors are known. Nusco has 19 parishes, with 38,300 inhabitants, and 4 religious houses.

CAPPELLETTI, *Le Chiese d'Italia*, XX.

U. BENIGNI.

Nussbaum, JOHANN NEPOMUK VON, German surgeon, b. at Munich 2 Sept., 1829; d. there 31 Oct., 1890. He made his studies in the University of Munich where he was a pupil of Thiersch and later the clinical assistant of Von Rothmund. He received his doctor's degree in 1853, the subject of his dissertation being "Ueber Cornea Artificialis". The following four years he spent in foreign travel, studying surgery under Nélaton, Chassaignac, and Maisonneuve in Paris, Langenbeck in Berlin, and Textor in Würzburg. In 1857 he became a *Privat-docent* (with a thesis on the treatment of various conditions of the cornea). In 1860 he was appointed professor of surgery at the University of Munich which office he held for nearly thirty years. His lectures were noted for their practical character. He studied under Spencer Wells in England which enabled him to greatly aid the development of pelvic surgery. Later he learned antisepsis from Lister and was instrumental in introducing it into the surgical clinics of Germany. His best-known work, "Leitfaden zur antiseptischen Wundbehandlung" (Hints for the antiseptic treatment of wounds), went through five editions and was translated into a number of foreign languages. Altogether his publications number almost 100, the best known of which deal with ovariotomy, the transplantation of bone, radical operation for hernia, and phases of the treatment of cancer. During the war of 1871 Nussbaum was consultant surgeon-general to the Bavarian troops. Throughout his life he was a Catholic and died pronouncing the words "Praised be Jesus Christ".

PAGEL, *Biograph. Dict. der hervorrag. Aerzte des 19. Jahrh.* (Berlin, 1901); IDEM, *Biograph. Lex. der hervorrag. Aerzte* (Berlin); KNELLER, *Das Christentum und die Vertreter der neueren Naturwissenschaft* (Freiburg, 1904).

JAMES J. WALSH.

Nutter, JOHN, VENERABLE. See HAYDOCK, GEORGE, VENERABLE.

Nutter, ROBERT, VENERABLE, English martyr; b. at Burnley, Lancashire, c. 1550; executed at Lancaster, 26 July, 1600. He entered Brasenose College, Oxford in 1564 or 1565, and, with his brother John, also a martyr (see HAYDOCK, GEORGE), became a student of the English College, Reims. Having been ordained priest, 21 Dec., 1581, he returned to England. On 2 Feb., 1583–4 he was committed to the Tower, where he remained in the pit forty-seven days, wearing irons for forty-three days, and twice subjected to the tortures of "the scavenger's daughter". On 10 November, 1584, he was again consigned to the pit, where he remained until, on 21 Jan., 1584–5, he, with twenty other priests and one layman, was shipped aboard the "Mary Martin" of Colchester, at Tower Wharf. Landing at Boulogne, 2 Feb., he revisited Reims in July, but, on 30 November, was again committed to prison in London, this time to Newgate, under the *alias* of Rowley. In 1587 he was removed to the Marshalsea, and thence, in 1589–90, was sent to Wisbech Castle, Cambridgeshire. There, in 1597, he signed a petition to Father Garnet in favour of having a Jesuit superior; but, on 8 Nov., 1598, he and his fellow martyr, Venerable Edward Thwing, with others, besought the pope to institute an archpriest.

VENERABLE EDWARD THWING was the second son of Thomas Thwing, of Heworth, near York, and Jane (née Kellet, of York), his wife. He was at the English College, Reims, 12 July to 12 August, 1583; and 20 July, 1585, to 2 Sept., 1587, having spent the interval with the Jesuits at Pont-à-Mousson. On 2 Sept., 1587 he set out for Rome, returning to become a reader in Greek and Hebrew, and a professor of rhetoric and logic. He was ordained priest at Laon in the following December. On 4 Nov., 1592, he went to Spa suffering from ulcer in the knee. He returned to the English College, which had in the meantime been transferred from Reims to Douai, and went on the mission in 1597. He seems to have been immediately arrested and sent to Wisbech, whence he and Nutter escaped to Lancashire, were arrested, May, 1600, tried at the next assizes and condemned for being priests. Both suffered on the same day.

Catholic Record Society Publications (London, privately printed 1905—), I, 110, II, 248, 252, 256, 270, 273, 277, 279, 282; III, 16, 156, 384, 385, 388; CHALLONER, *Memoirs of Missionary Priests*, I, 120–21; KNOX, *First and Second Diaries of the English College, Douai*, passim; GILLOW, *Bibl. Dict. Eng. Cath.*, V, 203; WAINEWRIGHT, *Ven. John Nutter* in *Catholic Truth Society's penny biographies*; HOLLINSHED, *Chronicles*, IV (London, 1807–8), 554–7; FOSTER, *Glover's Visitation of Yorks* (London, privately printed 1875), 230; *Oxford Historical Society Publications*, LV (Oxford, 1910), 33.

JOHN B. WAINEWRIGHT.

Nuyens, WILHELMUS, historian, b. 18 August, 1823, at Avenhorn in Holland; d. 10 December, 1894, at Westwoud near Horn. Having completed his Humanistic studies in Enkhuizen, he studied medicine at Utrecht, 1842, received the degree of M.D. in 1848, and began practising in Westwoud. He devoted some of his spare time to literature and history, and he published, in 1856, a volume of poems entitled: "De laatste Dochter der Hohenstaufen", on subjects chiefly from the Middle Ages. Then came a series of historical works, first among which was "Het Katholicismus in betrekking met de beschaving van Europa" (Amsterdam, 1856–1857, in 2 volumes), a history of the influence of Catholicism upon the culture and civilization of European nations. In several pamphlets and in that voluminous work, "Geschiedenis der Regering van Pius IX" (Amsterdam, 1862–63), he treated the Roman question of 1859. His chief work, "Geschiedenis der nederlandsche Beroerten in de XVI. eeuw" (Amsterdam, 1865–70, in 8 parts), a history of the revolutionary wars of the Netherlands from 1559 to 1598, discloses no new sources, but examines facts with sagacity and impartiality, and arranges them with skill, thereby showing to the Catholics what rights they were entitled to in the State. New editions appeared in 1886 and 1904. Somewhat as a sequel he wrote: "Geschiedenis der kerkelijke en politieke geschillen in de republiek der zeven vereenigde provincien (1598–1625)" (Amsterdam, 1886–87 in two parts). Intended for popular reading are: "Algemeen Geschiedenis des nederlandschen Volks-van de vroegste tijden tot op onze dagen" (Amsterdam, 1871–82, in 20 parts; new edition, 1896–98, in 24 parts); "Geschiedenis van het nederlandsche Volk van 1815 tot op onze dagen" (Amsterdam, 1883–86, in 4 parts; 2nd edition 1898); and the widely read: "Vaderlandsche Geschiedenis voor de jeugd" (Amsterdam, 1870; 25th edition, 1905, by G. F. I. Douwes). He published a number of pamphlets and articles in periodicals on topics of the times, especially in "Onze Wachter", edited by him from 1871 to 1874 in collaboration with Schaepmann. He was an energetic defender of the rights and the privileges of Catholics, and one of the first to champion the freedom of the Catholic Church in the Netherlands. Catholics erected a monument to him in the church at Westwoud and set aside the surplus of the money contributed as a perpetual fund, called "Nuyensfund", to aid the work of Catholic historians of the Netherlands.

GÖRRIS, *Dr. W. J. F. Nuyens, beschouwd in het licht van zijn tijd* (Nimwegen, 1908). PATRICIUS SCHLAGER.

Nyassa, VICARIATE APOSTOLIC OF, in Central Africa, bounded north by the Anglo-German frontier, east by Lake Nyassa, south by the Anglo-Portuguese frontier, west by a line running northward past Lake Bangwelo. It is under the care of the White Fathers and was founded by Father Lechaptois in June, 1889, at Mponda, Nyassaland. This region passing under British control, the missionaries moved to Mambwe between Nyassa and Tanganika in 1891, but, finding the region desolated by the slave-hunters, they proceeded to Ubemba, a high plateau to the west where the Congo rises. In December, 1894, Fr. Van Oost settled at Kaiambi in Panda, with permission of the chief Mkaca, but was expelled by Mkaca's suzerain, Kiti-Mkulu. Fr. Dupont, however, succeeded in founding a permanent station there in July, 1895. The natives are well-built and warlike; they are being taught agriculture by the fathers. On 13 February, 1897, the mission was made a vicariate Apostolic, Fr. Joseph Dupont (b. at Gesté, Maine et Loire, France, in 1855) being appointed superior and consecrated titular Bishop of Tibaris. When King Momamba was dying in 1898, he asked Mgr Dupont to become king; the bishop accepted the post temporarily to prevent the customary hecatomb following the sovereign's death. In 1904 the south-eastern part of the vicariate was formed into the Prefecture Apostolic of Shiré. The population is about 1,000,000, speaking Kibemba and Kinyassa; catechumens, 30,000; baptized, 2000; missionary priests, 50; Missionary Sisters of Our Lady of Africa, 8; catechists, 127; churches, 9; chapels, 25; stations, 6 in Ubemba and 3 in Angoniland; schools, 34; orphanages, 4.

PIOLET, *Les Missions françaises*, V (Paris), 422–26; DUFF, *Nyassaland under the Foreign Office* (London, 1906):

A. A. MACERLEAN.

Nyitra. See NEUTRA, DIOCESE OF.

Nyssa, a titular see in Cappadocia Prima, suffragan of Cæsarea. It is mentioned by Ptolemy (V, vii, viii), in the "Itinerarium Antonini" in the "Synedemus" of Hierocles (699), and the Greek "Notitiæ episcopatuum", but its history and exact location are unknown. It should be sought on the south bank of the Kizil Irmak (ancient Halys), ten miles above Kessik Keupru (Ramsay, "Asia Minor", 287, 305). Texier ("Asie Mineure", Paris, 1862, 588) wrongly identifies it with Nev Sheir. Hamilton (Researches, II, 265) speaks of a modern village called Nirse, or Nissa, but the maps show no place of this name. Le Quien (Oriens Christ., I, 391) names ten bishops of Nyssa. The last qualified as metropolitan in the sixteenth century, is certainly only a titular bishop. To the list may be added Joannicius, who lived in 1370 (Miklosich and Müller, "Acta patriarchatus Constantinopolitani", Vienna, 1860, I, 537). About this time Nyssa must have disappeared; but its name still recalls the memory of the glorious Doctor, St. Gregory.

S. PÉTRIDÈS.

O

Oakeley, FREDERICK, b. 5 Sept., 1802, at Shrewsbury; d. 30 Jan., 1880, at Islington, the youngest son of Sir Charles Oakeley, Bart, he graduated at Christchurch in 1824, and three years later was elected Fellow of Balliol, where he afterwards became the close friend of W. G. Ward, with whom he joined the Tractarian party. In 1839 he became incumbent of Margaret Chapel, the predecessor of the well-known All Saints, Margaret Street, London, soon noted for its high church services; he was a frequent visitor to Oxford, and stood by Ward at the time of his condemnation in 1845. He defended Tract XC and in consequence his bishop suspended him. He retired to Newman's community at Littlemore, and a few weeks later followed him into the Catholic Church. After a short course of theology at St. Edmund's College, he was ordained by Dr. Wiseman in 1847. The next thirty-three years were spent as a canon of the Westminster chapter and missionary rector of St. John's, Islington. Short-sighted, small of stature, lame, he exercised a wide influence by his personality, his writings, and the charm of his conversation. His chief works are: Before his conversion: "Aristotelian and Platonic Ethics" (Oxford, 1837); "Whitehall Sermons" (Oxford, 1837–9) "The Subject of Tract XC examined" (London, 1841); "Homilies" (London, 1842); "Life of St. Augustine" (Newman's series, Toovey, 1844). After his conversion: "Practical Sermons" (London, 1848); "The Order and Ceremonial of the Mass" (London, 1848); "The Catholic Florist" (London, 1851); "The Church of the Bible" (London, 1857); "Lyra Liturgica" (London, 1865); "Historical Notes on the Tractarian Movement" (London, 1865); "The Priest on the Mission" (London, 1871).

Dict. of Nat. Biog., s. v.; *Bibl. Dict. Eng. Cath.,* s. v.; WARD, *Oxford Movement; The Catholic Revival* (London, 1889 and 1893); MOZLEY, *Reminiscences* (1882); BROWNE, *Annals of Tractarian Movement;* Obituary notices in *Tablet, Weekly Register.*

BERNARD WARD.

O Antiphons (Roman Breviary: *Antiphonæ majores,* "greater antiphons"), the seven antiphons to the Magnificat in the ferial Office of the seven days preceeding the vigil of Christmas; so called because all begin with the interjection "O". Their opening words are: (1) "O Sapientia", (2) "O Adonai", (3) "O Radix Jesse", (4) "O Clavis David", (5) "O Oriens", (6) "O Rex Gentium", (7) "O Emmanuel". Addressed to Christ under one or other of His Scriptural titles, they conclude with a distinct petition to the coming Lord (e. g.: "O Wisdom . . .' come and teach us the way of prudence"; "O Adonai . . . come and redeem us by thy outstretched arm"; "O Key of David . . . come and lead from prison the captive sitting in darkness and in the shadow of death" etc.). Couched in a poetic and Scriptural phraseology they constitute a notable feature of the Advent Offices. These seven antiphons are found in the Roman Breviary; but other medieval Breviaries added (1) "O virgo virginum quomodo fiet" etc., still retained in the Roman Breviary as the proper antiphon to the Magnificat in the second Vespers of the feast Expectatio Partus B.M.V. (18 December), the prayer of this feast being followed by the antiphon "O Adonai" as a commemoration of the ferial office of 18 December; (2) "O Gabriel, nuntius cœlorum", subsequently replaced, almost universally, by the thirteenth-century antiphon, "O Thoma Didyme", for the feast of the Apostle St. Thomas (21 December). Some medieval churches had twelve greater antiphons, adding to the above (1) "O Rex Pacifice", (2) "O Mundi Domina", (3) "O Hierusalem", addressed respectively to Our Lord, Our Lady, and Jerusalem. Guéranger gives the Latin text of all of these (except the "O Mundi Domina"), with vernacular prose translation ("Liturgical Year", Advent, Dublin, 1870, 508–531), besides much devotional and some historical comment. The Parisian Rite added two antiphons ("O sancte sanctorum" and "O pastor Israel") to the seven of the Roman Rite and began the recitation of the nine on the 15th of December. Prose renderings of the Roman Breviary O's will be found in the Marquess of Bute's translation of the Roman Breviary (winter volume). Guéranger remarks that the antiphons were appropriately assigned to the Vesper Hour because the Saviour came in the evening hour of the world (*vergente mundi vespere,* as the Church sings) and that they were attached to the Magnificat to honour her through whom He came. By exception to the rule for ferial days, the seven antiphons are sung in full both before and after the canticle. "In some Churches it was formerly the practice to sing them thrice: that is, before the Canticle, before the Gloria Patri, and after the Sicut erat" (Guéranger). There are several translations into English verse, both by Catholics and non-Catholics, the most recent being that in Dom Gregory Ould's "Book of Hymns" (Edinburgh, 1910, no. 5) by W. Rooke-Ley, in seven quatrains together with a refrain-quatrain giving a translation of the versicle and response ("Rorate", etc). The seven antiphons have been found in MSS. of the eleventh century. A paraphrase of some of these is found in the hymn "Veni, veni, Emmanuel" given by Daniel in his "Thesaurus Hymnologicus" (II, 336) and translated by Neale in his "Medieval Hymns and Sequences" (3rd ed., London, p. 171) and others, and used in various hymn-books (Latin text in "The Roman Hymnal", New York, 1884, 139). Neale supposed the hymn to be of the twelfth century, but it has not been traced back further than the first decade of the eighteenth century. For first lines of translations, see "Julian's Dict. of Hymnol." (2nd ed., London, 1907, 74, i; 1551, i; 1721, i). For the Scriptural sources of the antiphons, see John, Marquess of Bute, "Roman Breviary", Winter, 203, also Marbach's "Carmina Scripturarum" etc. (Strasburg, 1907) under "O" in the *Index Alphabeticus.*

THURSTON, *The Great Antiphons, Heralds of Christmas* in *The Month* (Dec., 1905), 616–631, gives liturgical uses, literary illustrations, and peculiar customs relating to the antiphons; questions the view of CABROL, *L'Avent Liturgique* in *Revue Bénédictine* 1905), n. 4, that they do not antedate the ninth century, gives much illustration (notably from *The Christ of Cynewulf* written circa 800) to show that they "are much older", and knows "no valid reason for regarding them as posterior to the rest of the Roman Antiphonary or to the time of Pope Gregory himself"; CABROL in *Dict. d'archéologie et liturgie chrétienne,* s. v. *Avent,* repeats (col. 3229) his view, but in a foot-note refers the reader to THURSTON'S article in *The Month;* BAYLEY, *Greater Antiphons of Advent* in *Pax* (an Anglican periodical, 6 Dec., 1905), 231–239; STALEY, *O Sapientia* in *Church Times* (13 Dec., 1907), p. 812; WITHERBY, *O Sapientia, Seven Sermons on the Ancient Antiphons for Advent* (London, 1906).

H. T. HENRY.

Oates's Plot, a term conventionally used to designate a "Popish Plot" which, during the reign of Charles II of England, Titus Oates pretended to have discovered. Oates was b. at Oakham, Rutlandshire, in 1649. His father, Samuel Oates, is said to have been a ribbon-weaver in Norfolk who, having taken a degree at Cambridge, afterwards became a minister of the Established Church.

Titus Oates began his career at Merchant Taylors' School in 1665, when he was sixteen. He was expelled two years later and went to a school at Sedlescombe, near Hastings, whence he passed to Cambridge in 1667, being entered as a sizar in Gonville and Caius College, whence he afterwards migrated to St. John's. His reputation at Caius, according to a fellow student, was that of "the most illiterate dunce, incapable of improvement"; at St. John's, Dr. Watson wrote of him: "He was a great dunce, ran into debt, and, being sent away for want of money, never took a degree". "Removing from there", says Echard, "he slipped into Orders", and was preferred to the vicarage of Bobbing in Kent, on 7 March, 1673. At this time or earlier, according to the evidence of Sir Denis Ashburnham at Father Ireland's trial, "he did swear the Peace against a man" and was forsworn, but they did not proceed upon the indictment. Next year he left Bobbing, with a licence for non-residence and a reputation for dishonesty, to act as curate to his father at Hastings. There father and son conspired to bring against Wm. Parker, the schoolmaster, an abominable charge so manifestly trumped up that Samuel was ejected from his living, while Titus, charged with perjury, was sent to prison at Dover to await trial. Having broken jail and escaped to London, unpursued, he next procured an appointment as chaplain on board a king's ship sailing for Tangier, but within twelve months was expelled from the Navy.

In August, 1676, he was frequenting a club which met at the Pheasant Inn, in Fuller's Rents, and there, for the first time, he met Catholics. His admittance into the Duke of Norfolk's household, as Protestant chaplain, followed almost immediately. On Ash Wednesday, 1677, he was received into the Catholic Church. The Jesuit Father Hutchinson (*alias* Berry) was persuaded to welcome him as a repentant prodigal and Father Strange, the provincial, to give him a trial in the English College at Valladolid. Five months later, Oates was expelled from the Spanish college and, on 30 Oct., 1677, was sent back to London. In spite of his disgrace, the Jesuit provincial was persuaded to give him a second trial, and on 10 Dec. he was admitted into the seminary at St. Omers. He remained there as "a younger student" till 23 June, 1678. After being expelled from St. Omer's also, he met Tonge, probably an old acquaintance, and conceived and concocted the story of the "Popish Plot".

Israel Tonge was, as Echard describes him, "a city divine, a man of letters, and of a prolifick head, fill'd with all the Romish plots and conspiracies since the Reformation". There is some evidence and considerable likelihood that he not only suggested the idea of the plot to Oates by his talk, but actually co-operated in its invention. At Stafford's trial Oates declared that he never was but a sham Catholic. If this be true, we may accept Echard's assertion as probable: that Tonge "persuaded him [Oates] to insinuate himself among the Papists and get particular acquaintance with them". Moreover, it is credibly reported that, at a great supper given in the city by Alderman Wilcox in honour of Oates, when Tonge was present, the latter's jealousy led to a verbal quarrel between the two informers, and Tonge plainly told Oates that "he knew nothing of the plot, but what he learned from him". Tonge may or may not have helped Oates in the manufacture of his wares; but he undoubtedly enabled him to bring them to market and dispose of them to advantage. With the help of Kirkby, a man associated with the royal laboratory, he succeeded in bringing the plot before the careless and sceptical notice of King Charles.

Oates' depositions, as they may be read in his "True and Exact Narrative of the Horrid Plot and Conspiracy of the Popish Party against the Life of His Sacred Majesty, the Government and the Protestant Religion, etc., published by the Order of the Right Honorable the Lords Spiritual and Temporal in Parliament assembled", are in themselves clumsy, puerile, ill-written, disjointed libels, hardly worth notice but for the frenzied anger they aroused. The chief items tell of a design to assassinate the king, or rather a complication of plots to do away with "48" or "the Black Bastard"—His Majesty's supposed designations among the Catholic conspirators. Pickering, a Benedictine lay brother, and Grove (Honest William), a Jesuit servant, are told off to shoot him with "jointed carabines" and silver bullets, in consideration of £1,500 to be paid to Grove and 30,000 Masses to be said for Pickering's soul. To make more certain of the business, the king is to be poisoned by Sir George Wakeman, the queen's physician, at a cost of £15,000. Furthermore he is to be stabbed by Anderton and Coniers, Benedictine monks. All these methods failing, there are in the background four Irish ruffians, hired by Dr. Fogarthy, who "were to mind the King's Postures at Winsdor" and have one pound down and £80 afterwards in full discharge of their expenses. There is some frivolous talk of other assassinations—of the removal of the Prince of Orange, the Duke of Ormonde, Herbert, Lord Bishop of Hereford and some lesser fry. And Oates himself is offered and actually accepts £50 to do away with the terrible Dr. Tonge, "who had basely put out the Jesuits' morals in English".

Summing up the plot with the help of someone more scholarly than himself, Oates makes the following declaration: "The General Design of the Pope, Society of Jesus, and their Confederates in this Plot, is, the Reformation, that is, (in their sense) the Reduction of Great Britain and Ireland, and all His Majesties Dominions by the Sword (all other wayes and means being judged by them ineffectual) to the Romish Religion and Obedience. To effect this design; 1. The Pope hath entitled himself to the Kingdomes of *England* and *Ireland*. 2. Sent his Legate, the Bishop of *Cassal* in *Italy* into *Ireland* to declare his Title, and take possession of that Kingdom. 3. He hath appointed Cardinal *Howard* his Legat for *England* to the same purpose. 4. He hath given Commission to the General of the Jesuites, and by him to *White*, their Provincial in *England*, to issue, and they have issued out, and given Commissions to Captain Generals, Lieutenant Generals, etc., namely, the General of the Jesuites hath sent Commissions from *Rome* to *Langhorn* their Advocate General for the Superior Officers: And *White* hath given Commissions here in *England* to Colonels, and inferior Officers. 5. He hath by a Consult of the Jesuits of this Province Assembled at *London*, condemned His Majesty, and ordered Him to be assassinated, etc. 6. He hath Ordered, That in case the Duke of *York* will not accept these Crowns as forfeited by his Brother unto the Pope, as of his Gift, and settle such Prelates and Dignitaries in the Church, and such Officers in Commands and places Civil, Naval and Military, as he hath commissioned as above, extirpate the Protestant Religion, and in order thereunto *ex post facto*, consent to the assassination of the King his Brother, Massacre of His Protestant Subjects, firing of his Towns, etc., by pardoning the Assassins, Murderers and Incendiaries, that then he be also poysoned or destroyed, after they have for some time abused His Name and Title to strengthen their Plot, weakened and divided the Kingdoms of England, Scotland, and Ireland thereby in Civil Wars and Rebellions as in His Father's Time, to make way for the French to seize these Kingdoms, and totally ruine their Infantry and Naval Force."

Besides this Papal, there appears also another French plot, or correspondence (an afterthought, suggested to Oates by the discovery of Coleman's letters), carried on by Sir Ellis Layton, Mr. Coleman and others. Under ordinary circumstances so flimsy a fabric would have been brought to the ground by the first breath of criticism. But it was taken up by the Whig Party and made into what Echard calls "a political contrivance". Shaftesbury, their leader, used it for all its worth. It was quite commonly called "the Shaftesbury Plot". Whether, as some believe, he had a hand in constructing the plot or not, very much of the blame of its consequences must rest upon the use he made of it. Chiefly by the influence and machinations of Shaftesbury and his party, Parliament was incited to declare that "there hath been and still is a damnable and hellish Plot, contrived and carry'd on by popish recusants, for the assassinating and murdering the King and for subverting the government and rooting out and destroying the Protestant Religion." Many who, with Elliot, thought Oates's stories of the "*40,000 Black-bills*, the Army of *Spanish Pilgrims* and *Military commissions* from General *D'Oliva* (S.J.) so monstrously ridiculous that they offer an intolerable affront to the understanding of any man who has but a very indifferent account of the affairs of *Europe*", nevertheless thought also that, "because His majesty and council have declar'd there is a *Popish*-Plot, therefore they have reason to believe one."

Oates had now become the most popular man in the country and acclaimed himself as "the Saviour of the Nation". He assumed the title of "Doctor", professing to have received the degree at Salamanca, a city it is certain he never visited; put on episcopal attire; was lodged at Whitehall; went about with a bodyguard; was received by the primate; sat at table with peers; and, though snubbed by the King, was solemnly thanked by Parliament, which granted him a salary of £12 a week for diet and maintenance, occasional gifts of £50 or so, and drafts on the Treasury to meet his bills. Yet, Oates would have forsworn himself to little purpose but for the mysterious death of Sir Edmund Berry Godfrey, the magistrate before whom Oates's depositions had been sworn. The Whig Party put the blame of this crime—if murder it was—upon the Catholics. Godfrey had been a friend to Catholics rather than an enemy, and had made use of the information received from Oates to do them a service: no good could come to them, and no harm to their enemies, by robbing the magistrate of the copy of Oates's deposition which he retained. Moreover, both his pockets and his house were undisturbed by the supposed assassins. Nevertheless the unanimous verdict was murder, the murder of a good Protestant and a magistrate who had to do with the plot. "The capital and the whole nation", says Macaulay, "went mad with hatred and fear. The penal laws, which had begun to lose something of their edge, were sharpened anew. Everywhere justices were busied in searching houses and seizing papers. All the gaols were filled with Papists. London had the aspect of a city in a state of siege. The train bands were under arms all night. Preparations were made for barricading the great thoroughfares. Patrols marched up and down the streets. Cannon were planted round Whitehall. No citizen thought himself safe unless he carried under his coat a small flail loaded with lead to brain the Popish assassins." For awhile, every word that Oates said was believed. The courts of law, before which the arrested Catholics were brought, were blind and deaf to his shufflings and contradictions and lies. Other disreputable witnesses were picked up in the gutter or prisons and encouraged to come forward, and were paid handsomely for bringing additional perjuries to corroborate those of their chief. The lord chief justice on the Bench would listen to nothing which discredited the king's witnesses; and although, in trials where the prisoners were denied counsel, he himself should, by ancient custom, have looked to their interests, he exerted the full authority of the Court to bring about their condemnation. Sixteen innocent men were executed in direct connexion with the Plot, and eight others were brought to the scaffold as priests in the persecution of Catholics which followed from it. The names of those executed for the plot are: in 1678 Edward Coleman (Dec. 3); in 1679, John Grove, William Ireland, S.J. (Jan. 24), Robert Green, Lawrence Hill (Feb. 21), Henry Berry (Feb. 28), Thomas Pickering, O.S.B. (May 14), Richard Langhorn (June 14), John Gavan, S.J., William Harcourt, S.J., Anthony Turner, S.J., Thomas Whitebread, S.J., John Fenwick, S.J. (June 20); in 1680, Thomas Thwing (Oct. 23), William Howard, Viscount Stafford (Dec. 29); in 1681, Oliver Plunket, Archbishop of Armagh (July 1). Those executed as priests were: in 1679, William Plessington (July 19), Philip Evans, John Lloyd (July 22), Nicholas Postgate (Aug. 7), Charles Mahony (Aug. 12), John Wall (Francis Johnson), O.S.F., John Kemble (Aug. 22), Charles Baker (David Lewis), S.J. (Aug. 27).

It remains to be said about "the Popish Plot" that, since the day when its inventor was discredited, no historian of any consequence has professed to believe in it. A few vaguely assert that there must have been a plot of some sort. But no particle of evidence has ever been discovered to corroborate Oates's pretended revelations. A contemporary Protestant historian says: "After the coolest and strictest examinations, and after a full length of time, the government could find very little foundation to support so vast a fabrick, besides down-right swearing and assurance: not a gun, sword or dagger; not a flask of powder or a dark lanthorn, to effect this villany; and excepting Coleman's writings, not one scrap of an original letter or commission, among the great numbers alleged, to uphold the reputation of the discoveries." Since then the public and private archives of Europe have been liberally thrown open to students, and the most of them diligently examined; yet, as Mr. Marks, also a Protestant, wrote a few years ago: "Through all the troublous times when belief in the Popish Plot raged, one searches in vain for one act of violence on the part of Catholics. After the lapse of two hundred years, no single document has come to light establishing in any one particular any single article of the eighty-one."

In January, 1679, Oates, whose reputation was already declining, together with his partner, Bedloe, laid an indictment before the Privy Council in thirteen articles, against Chief Justice Scroggs, because of the part he took in the acquittal of Wakeman, Marshall, Rumley, and Corker; and in the same year, the Rev. Adam Elliot was fined £200 for saying that "Oates was a perjur'd Rogue, and the Jesuits who suffered, justly died Martyrs." But in August, 1681, Israel Backhouse, master of Wolverhampton Grammar School, when charged with a similar libel was acquitted. In the same year, Oates was thrust out of Whitehall, and next year (Jan., 1682) Elliot prosecuted him successfully for perjury. In April, 1682, his pension was reduced to £2 a week. In June of that year he was afraid to come forward as a witness against Kearney, one of the four supposed Irish ruffians denounced by him in his depositions. Then, while King Charles was still living, he vainly presented petitions to the king and to Sir Leoline Jenkins against the plain speaking of Sir Roger L'Estrange, and two months later (10 May), he was himself committed to prison for calling the Duke of York a traitor. On 18 June, he was fined by Judge Jeffreys £100,000 for *scandalum magnatum*. Then, in May, 1680, he was tried for perjury, and condemned to be whipped, degraded, and pilloried, and imprisoned for life. Jeffreys said of him: "He has deserved more punishment than the laws of the land can inflict."

When William of Orange came to the throne, Oates left prison and entered an unsuccessful appeal in the

House of Lords against his sentence. Later, he obtained a royal pardon and a pension, which was withdrawn in 1693 at the instance of Queen Mary, whose father, James II, he had scandalously attacked. After Mary's death, he was granted from the Treasury £500 to pay his debts and £300 per annum during the lifetime of himself and his wife. In 1690 he was taken up by the Baptists, only to be again expelled the ministry, this time for "a discreditable intrigue for wringing a legacy from a devotee". In 1691 he attempted another fraudulent plot, but it came to nothing. He died in Axe Yard, on 12 July, 1705.

Besides the "Narrative of the Horrid Plot and Conspiracy of the Popish Party" (London, 1679), Oates wrote "The Cabinet of Jesuits' secrets opened" (said to be translated from the Italian), "issued and completed by a gentleman of Quality" (London, 1679), "The Pope's Warehouse; or the Merchandise of the Whore of Rome" (London, 1679), dedicated to the Earl of Shaftesbury, "The Witch of Endor; or the witchcrafts of the Roman Jezebel, in which you have an account of the Exorcisms or conjurations of the Papists", etc. (London, 1679); "Εἰκὼν Βασιλική, or the Picture of the late King James drawn to the Life" (Part I, London, 1696; Parts II, III, and IV, 1697).

POLLOCK, *The Popish Plot* (London, 1903); MARKS, *Who Killed Sir Edmund Berry Godfrey?* (London, 1905); *State Trials*; SECCOMBE in *Dict. Nat. Biog.*, s. v.; COBBETT, *Parliamentary History*, IV; CHARLES DODD, *Church History of England*, III (London, 1737); SALMON, *Examination of Burnet's History*, II (London, 1724); ELLIOT, *A Modest Vindication of Titus Oates* (London, 1682); FOLEY, *Records S. J.*, V (London, 1879); MACAULAY, LINGARD, HUME, *History of England*. CUTHBERT ALMOND.

Oaths.—I. NOTION AND DIVISIONS.—An oath is an invocation to God to witness the truth of a statement. It may be express and direct, as when one swears by God Himself; or implicit and tacit, as when we swear by creatures, since they bear a special relation to the Creator and manifest His majesty and the supreme Truth in a special way: for instance, if one swear by heaven, the throne of God (Matt., v, 34), by the Holy Cross, or by the Gospels. Imprecatory oaths are also tacit (see below). To have an oath in *foro interno*, there must be the intention, at least virtual, of invoking the testimony of God, and a word or sign by which the intention is manifested. Oaths may be: (1) assertory—or affirmative—if we call God to witness the assertion of a past or present fact; promissory, if we call Him to witness a resolution which we bind ourselves to execute, or a vow made to Him, or an agreement entered into with our neighbour, or a vow made to God in favour of a third party; every promissory oath includes of necessity an assertory oath (see below). A promissory oath accompanied by a threat against a third party is said to be comminatory; (2) contestatory—or simple—if there is a mere invocation of the Divine testimony; imprecatory—or execratory—as in the formula "So help me God"; if at the same time we call upon God as a judge and avenger of perjury, offering Him our property and especially our life and eternal salvation, or those of our friends, as a pledge of our sincerity. Thus the expression: "Upon my soul", often used without any intention of swearing, may be either contestatory—the soul being in a special manner the image of God—or execratory—if we wish to call down upon our soul Divine punishment, either temporal or eternal, in case we be wanting in sincerity; (3) private, if used between private individuals; public, if exacted by public authorities; public oaths are divided into: (a) doctrinal, by which one declares that he holds a given doctrine, or promises to be faithful, to teach, and to defend a given doctrine in the future; (b) political, which have as their object the exercise of any authority whatsoever, or submission to such an authority or laws; (c) judicial, which are taken in courts of justice either by the parties to the suit or the witnesses thereof.

II. LAWFULNESS AND CONDITIONS.—An oath is licit, and an act of virtue, under certain conditions. It is, in effect, an act of homage rendered by the creature to the wisdom and omnipotence of the Creator—it is therefore an act of the virtue of religion; moreover, it is an excellent way of affording men security in their mutual intercourse. It is justified in the Old and New Testament; the faithful and the Church from Apostolic times to the present day have employed oaths; and canonical legislation and doctrinal decrees have affirmed their lawfulness. Improper use is often made of oaths, and the habit of swearing may easily lead to abuses and even to perjury. In counselling men "not to swear at all" (Matt., v, 34) Christ meant, as the Fathers and ecclesiastical writers explain, to be so truthful that men could believe them without need of oath to confirm what they say. He did not forbid the use of oaths under proper conditions, when necessary to satisfy others of our truthfulness. These conditions are (Jer., iv, 2): (1) Judgment, or careful and reverent consideration of the necessity or utility of the oath; for it would be showing a want of the respect due to God, to invoke Him as witness in trivial matters; on the other hand, it would be wrong to require a grave or extreme necessity. To swear without a sufficient reason, being an idle use of God's name, is venial sin; (2) truth, for what we affirm should be in conformity with the truth. Consequently in case of an assertory oath, our affirmation must be truthful, and in a promissory oath we must have the intention of doing what we are promising. To swear falsely constitutes the sin of perjury, always mortal in its nature: for it is an insult to the Divine Truth to call God in witness to a lie; besides, such an act is likely to do injury to the common good; see the propositions condemned by Innocent XI, prop. xxiv; (3) justice requiring: (a) in the case of an assertory oath, that it be lawful to make the affirmation which one wishes to corroborate; failure to observe this condition is a venial sin, as when boasting of some evil deed one should swear to it; it is a grievous sin, if one employs an oath as the means and instrument of sin, at least of mortal sin, for example, to make a person believe a grave detraction; (b) in the case of a promissory oath, justice requires that one be able to assume licitly the obligation of doing the thing promised. It is a mortal sin to promise an oath to do a grievously illicit thing; and it is, in the opinion of St. Alphonsus Liguori, a mortal sin to swear to do a thing which is illicit though not grievously so.

III. OBLIGATION ARISING FROM A PROMISSORY OATH.—In a promissory oath, we call on God not only as a witness of our desire to fulfil the promise we make, but also as a guarantee and pledge for its future execution; for at the proper moment He will require us, under pain of sin against the virtue of religion, to do what we have promised in His presence; whence it follows that it is a sin against religion not to perform, when we can, what we promised under oath: a mortal sin if the matter is grave; a venial sin (according to the more common and more probable opinion), if the matter is not grave. Certain conditions are requisite before a promissory oath entails the obligation of fulfilling it, notably the intention of swearing and of binding oneself, full deliberation, the lawfulness of making the promise, as well as the lawfulness and possibility of executing it, etc. Several causes may put an end to this obligation: intrinsic causes, such as a notable change occurring after the taking of the oath, the cessation of the final cause of the oath; or extrinsic causes, such as annulment, dispensation, commutation, or relaxation granted by a competent authority, a release, express or tacit, either by the person in whose favour the obligation was undertaken, or by a competent authority to whom the beneficiary is subject.

See general works on moral theology, especially: ST. THOMAS AQUINAS, *Sum. Theol.*, II-II, Q. lxxxix, Q. xcviii; ST. ALPHONSUS

LIGUORI, *Theol. mor.*, lib. IV, tract. II, cap. ii; NOLDIN, *Theol. Mor.*, II (7th ed.), nn. 243 sqq.; LEHMKUHL, *Theol. mor.*, I (2nd ed.), nn. 552 sqq.; GOEPFERT, *Der Eid* (Mainz, 1883); SLATER, *A Manual of Moral Theology*, I (New York, 1909), 240 sqq.

A. VANDER HEEREN.

Oath, MISSOURI TEST. See TEST OATH, MISSOURI.

Oaths, ENGLISH POST-REFORMATION. The English Reformation having been imposed by the Crown, it was natural that submission to the essential points of its formularies should have been exacted with some solemnity, by oath, test, or formal declaration, and that these should change with the varying moods of those who dominated in the State.

I.—OATH OF ROYAL SUPREMACY.—This oath was imposed in March 1534 (26 Henry VIII, c. 1). The title "Supreme Head" had first been introduced by Henry VIII into a decree of convocation, 11 February, 1531; and had been strenuously resisted by the clergy. Though it did not as yet have any religious significance, and might be a matter of compliment only, it might, they feared, receive another interpretation later. But acting under the advice of Fisher, Warham, and others, whose orthodoxy is above suspicion, they submitted after adding the conditional phrase, "quantum per legem Dei licet". Two years later a change had taken place, which had previously seemed inconceivable. The king had actually broken with the pope, and Parliament had enacted that the king should be "taken, accepted and reputed the only supreme head on Earth of the church of England" by every one of his subjects. But no formula for the oath was laid down in the Act, and great differences seem to have prevailed in practice. Many long "acknowledgments of supremacy" are extant (Camm, "English Martyrs", I, 401) but it would seem that most people were only asked to swear to the Succession, that is to the king's marriage with Anne Boleyn, which the pope condemned, and which therefore involved the supremacy, though the form of the Oath of Succession preserved in *The Lords' Journals*, refers to the supremacy with insidious lightness. We do not know what was its form, when Fisher and More refused to sign it. They were ready to accept the succession of Anne Boleyn's children, but refused the supremacy (Bridgett, *infra* 264–86).

The Act of Supremacy was repealed by Queen Mary (1 Ph. and M. c. 8) and revived by Elizabeth (1 Eliz. c. 1). The formula then adopted ran: "I, A. B., do utterly testify and declare in my conscience, that the Queen's Highness is the only supreme Governor of the Realm . . . as well in all Spiritual or Ecclesiastical things or causes as Temporal, &c. &c. &c. So help me God." This was not to be proposed at once to every one; but was to be taken by the clergy, and by all holding office under the Crown; by others, when asked. This moderation in exacting the oath helped to prevent an outcry against it, and enabled the Government to deal with the recalcitrant in detail. Many years elapsed, for instance, before it was imposed on the graduates of the universities. The last laws passed by Elizabeth against Catholics (1592–3) enjoined a new test for Recusants (35 Eliz. c. 2). It comprised (1) A confession of "grievous offence against God in contemning her Majesty's Government"; (2) Royal Supremacy; (3) A clause against dispensations and dissimulations, perhaps the first of its sort in oaths of this class. The success of Elizabeth's "settlement of religion", had been really due to her alliance with the party afterwards called Puritans, and they were not in love with the supremacy, or unaware that it was unpopular and tyrannical.

In order to excuse their persecutions they therefore preferred (especially after the excommunication of the queen) to make an informal test by asking the suspected person whether he would fight against the pope, if he sent an army to restore Catholicism. The Catholics called this the "bloody question". There was no law to enforce an answer, there was no specific penalty for refusal. But those who refused to answer, were decried as traitors; and then proceeded against to the uttermost by other persecuting laws. Those who in their answers showed any loyalty to the Holy See were in the same plight, a mark for persecution till they bent or broke. But those who answered disrespectfully, were treated less cruelly.

Towards the end of Elizabeth's reign, a split began in the Catholic ranks on this subject. Some of the priests who had joined in the well-known Appeal against the archpriest Blackwell had afterwards presented to Elizabeth a "Protestation of Allegiance" (Tierney-Dodd, *infra*, iii, Ap. 188). Declarations of loyalty there had been before in plenty: those made by the martyrs being often extraordinarily touching. But the signatories of 1603, perhaps stimulated by Cisalpine ideas, for the Protestation was drawn up in Paris, besides protesting their loyalty, went on to withhold from the pope any possible exercise of the deposing power. Before this Catholic loyalists had only denied the validity of the deposition pronounced by Pius V. Several reasons seemed to justify this Protestation, at the time it was made (see BISHOP, WILLIAM), though unfortunate developments followed later.

II.—OATH OF ALLEGIANCE of James I (1606) also called the OATH OF OBEDIENCE. After the Gunpowder Plot (q. v.) a systematic effort was made to persecute Catholics at every turn from the cradle to the grave, by penalizing Catholic baptisms, marriages, burials, as well as education, acquisition of property, &c. An attempt was also made to divide and disgrace Catholics in the matter of allegiance. It was known, from the "Protestation", that there were differences of opinion on the subject of the pope's deposing power, and an oath of allegiance was drafted to make capital out of those differences (for the authorship of the formula, see Thurston *infra*, and Tierney-Dodd, iv, 71). The more important clauses are the following:—"I, A. B., do truly and sincerely acknowledge, &c. that our sovereign lord, King James, is lawful and rightful King &c. and that the pope neither of himself nor by any authority of Church or See of Rome, or by any other means with any other, has any power to depose the king &c., or to authorize any foreign prince to invade him &c., or to give licence to any to bear arms, raise tumults, &c. &c. Also I do swear that notwithstanding any sentence of excommunication or deprivation I will bear allegiance and true faith to his Majesty &c. &c. And I do further swear that I do from my heart abhor, destest, and abjure, as impious and heretical this damnable doctrine and position,—that princes which be excommunicated by the pope may be deposed or murdered by their subjects or by any other whatsoever. And I do believe that the pope has no power to absolve me from this oath. I do swear according to the plain and common sense, and understanding of the same words &c. &c. &c." (3 James I, c. 4). This oath was proclaimed law on 22 June, 1606.

Objections.—On 22 September following the pope condemned the formula, "It cannot be taken, as it contains many things evidently contrary to faith and salvation." It was prudent of the pope, not to attempt to enumerate the objectionable points, for this would have increased the tension, and it is even now difficult to specify them, partly because of the ambiguity of the terms used; partly because of the deceitful interpretation put upon them by the English authorities. For James now hypocritically asserted that his oath was not meant to encroach upon anyone's conscientious convictions. Hereupon minimizers began to maintain that the words of the oath might be interpreted by the intention of the law-giver, that the oath might therefore be taken. But it is necessary here to advert to the Church's doctrine concerning veracity in oaths. These we believe to be addressed to God himself and to be accepted in the precise sense of the words pronounced. If King James had made his subjects swear specifically "in the sense by him explained", the oath might perhaps have been endured, but when he made them "swear according to the plain and common sense, and understanding of the same words", to what was injurious to Catholic consciences, this could not be tolerated. Of the many objections raised against the oath the following are perhaps the chief.

A.—*Objectionable Words.*—The most objectionable words were those in which the deposing power was sworn to be "impious, heretical and damnable." In previous centuries generations and generations of loyal subjects, and numberless patriots and lawyers, and doctors and saints of the Church (with exceptions, of course, but upon the whole in a large majority) had considered that this power was a valuable safeguard for liberty both religious and civil. In later days some people might think it out of date, inapplicable, extinct, perhaps even a mistake. But to call God to witness that one execrated it as "impious, heretical and damnable", was what no God-fearing adherent of the old Faith, who knew what he said and to whom he spoke, could conscientiously do. Indeed anyone who carefully weighs the terms of this oath, will see that the rights of the pontiff are so unreservedly denied, that no room whatsoever is left for the assertion of ecclesiastical liberties. This shows the affinities of the oath with Gallicanism (q. v.), which was acquiring such vogue upon the continent in those days. The Sorbonne, on 30 June, 1681, very shortly before approving the Gallican articles, censored the English oath, and found in it very little to object to (Butler, I, 351). The words here under discussion also evidently presume that he who takes the oath believes in the "Divine right of kings".

B.—*The Deposing Power.*—While all Catholics would condemn the extreme statements just mentioned, as to the deposing power, there were also many at that time, and they of the highest name, who considered any denial of that power as illicit. Two or three generations only had passed since the discipline of papal deposition for extreme cases of misgovernment had been generally accepted. In some parts of Europe it was still the law. Many, and Paul V with his medieval ideals was among them, had not yet perceived that this discipline would never be in vogue again, even in Catholic countries. This explains why Bellarmine, Persons, and several other early opponents of the oath went further in their condemnation of it than later theologians would have done. At the same time it is a mistake to suppose that Catholic resistance to the oath was chiefly or solely due to belief in the deposing power. This statement, however, is often made by Protestants (e. g., Hallam) and also by the Catholic writers, like Preston and others who wrote in defence of the oath, or who had Gallican leanings, such as Charles Butler and Canon Tierney (Butler, I, 359, 396; IV, 120, &c.; Tierney-Dodd, IV, 78 n., 81 n.). We have seen on the contrary that there were from the first English Catholic Non-jurors who explicitly rejected the deposing power. Doctor William Bishop, for instance, did this, but still underwent imprisonment for refusing the oath; and he was afterwards made a bishop by the Holy See.

C.—*Fraudulent Object of the Oath.*—It was always known that the loyalty of the Catholic body was unimpeachable. The reign of Charles I and the fall of the Stuarts showed that is was really far stronger than that of any other religious body. The Oath of Allegiance was designed to obscure this. As a man's repute for veracity may be impaired by prolonged examination on the subject of mental reservation and the like, and by exacting oaths about truthfulness, so these elaborate protests against the deposing power were intended to throw doubt upon the loyalty of Catholics, and so to divide and disgrace them, and this it actually did. Like all religious tests imposed by enemies it was something, not to amend, but to avoid altogether.

D.—*The Dishonour to the Holy See.*—This oath and all those of a similar character amount to a statement beforehand of "the conditions under which the Holy See will be disobeyed", and Rome has ever considered such proposals as dishonourable to herself, just as a nation would consider it a disgrace to lay down beforehand the terms under which her soldiers were to capitulate.

E.—*The Controversy.*—The archpriest Blackwell, then head of the English clergy, had at first disapproved of the oath, then allowed it, then after the pope's Brief disallowed it again, and finally being arrested and thrown into prison, took the oath, relying on James's statement that no encroachment on conscience was intended, and recommended the faithful to do the like. The pope at once issued a new Brief (23 August, 1607), repeating his prohibition, and on 28 Sept., 1607, Cardinal Bellarmine wrote to Blackwell exhorting him to obey the Brief at any cost. As this also proved ineffectual a new archpriest, George Birkhead, or Birkett, was appointed 1–10 Feb., 1608, and Blackwell was informed that his faculties would be taken away if he did not retract in two months. This, however, he still refused to do, and, much to King James's satisfaction, continued to defend his opinion for three years before he was finally suspended. Blackwell's example, as may be imagined, had but too great an influence, and he found successors in his unfortunate apostolate for many a year afterwards.

Meantime James had himself undertaken to answer the missives sent to Blackwell. This he did anonymously in a tract with the quaint title, "Triplici nodo, triplex cuneus" ("A triple wedge for a triple knot", i. e., for two Briefs and the Cardinal's letter). This was answered by Bellarmine, also anonymously, "Responsio ad librum: Triplici nodo, triplex cuneus" (1608). James now dropped his anonymity, and reprinted his tract with a "Premonition to Christian Princes", and an appendix on his adversaries' supposed mistakes (Jan., 1609). Upon this, Bellarmine published, now also using his own name, his "Apologia pro responsione ad librum Jacobi I" (1609). James opposed to this a treatise by a learned Scottish Catholic, W. Barclay, "De potestate papæ" (1609). Barclay was a decided Gallican, and Bellarmine's answer, "Tractatus de potestate summi pontificis in rebus temporalibus" (1610), gave such offence to the gallicanizing party in France, that it was publicly burnt in Paris by a Decree of 26 Nov., 1610. A similar fate befell Father Suarez's answer to James through an *arrêt* of 26 June, 1614; but this decree was eventually withdrawn at the request of the pope. At every stage of the contest between the two champions a host of minor combatants joined the fray. Here it must suffice to enumerate the chief names. On the Catholic side, Cardinal Duperron, Leonard Lessius, Jacob Gretser, Thomas Fitzherbert, Martin Becan, Gaspar Scioppi, Robert Persons, Adolph Schulckenius (who according to Sommervogel is an independent writer, not a pseudonym for Bellarmine, as has been asserted), N. Coeffeteau, A. Eudæmon Joannes. On the other side Bishop Lancelot Andrewes, William Barlow, Robert Burhill, Pierre du Moulin, and especially the Benedictine Roger Widdrington, *vere* Preston. Most of the Protestant books written in Latin, together with all the publications of Preston and Barclay, were put upon the Roman Index.

F.—*Subsequent History.*—Some ideas of the pressure caused by the oath may be gathered from the Acts of the Venerable martyrs, Drury, Atkinson, Almond, Thulis, Arrowsmith, Herst, Gervase, Thomas

Garnett, Gavan, and Heath; the last two have left writings against it. Another illustration will be found in the history of the first Lord Baltimore, whose attempt to settle in Virginia, where the oath had been introduced in 1609, was defeated by it. The second Lord Baltimore, on the other hand, ordered his adventurers to take the oath, but whether he insisted on this is uncertain (Hughes, "Soc. of Jesus in N. America", pp. 260–1, 451 and *passim*). King Charles I generally recognized that Catholics could not conscientiously take the Oath of Supremacy, and frequently exerted his prerogative to help them to avoid it. On the other hand his theory of the Divine right of kings induced him to favour the Oath of Allegiance, and he was irritated with the Catholics who refused it or argued against it. Urban VIII is said to have condemned the oath again in 1626 (Reusch, 327), and the controversy continued. Preston still wrote in its defence; so also, at King Charles's order, did Sir William Howard (1634); this was probably the future martyr (q. v.). Their most important opponent was Father Edward Courtney (*vere* Leedes; cf. Gillow, "Bibl. Dict.", s. v. Leedes, Edward), who was therefore imprisoned by Charles. The matter is frequently mentioned in the dispatches and the "Relatione" of Panzani (q. v.), the papal agent to Queen Henrietta Maria (Maziere Brady, "Catholic Hierarchy", Rome, 1883, p. 88).

III. OATH OF ABJURATION UNDER THE COMMONWEALTH, 1643.—When the Puritan party had gained the upper hand during the civil wars, the exaction of the Oaths of Supremacy and Allegiance fell into desuetude, and they were repealed by the Act of February, 1650, and their place taken by an "engagement of allegiance" to the Commonwealth. But the lot of the Catholics was not only not ameliorated thereby; it was made far worse by the enactment of an "Oath of Abjuration". This was passed 19 August, 1643, and afterwards, in 1656, reissued in an even more objectionable form. Everyone was to be "adjudged a Papist" who refused this oath, and the consequent penalties began with the confiscation of two thirds of the recusant's goods, and went on to deprive him of almost every civic right. Monstrous as the enactments were, their barbarity caused some shame among the more high-minded, and in practice they were sparingly enforced. They checked the gallicanizing party among the English Catholics, which had at first been ready to offer forms of submission similar to the old oath of Allegiance, which is stated (Reusch, 335) to have been condemned anew about this time by Innocent X. The chief writer on the Catholic side was the lawyer Austin, who generally used the pseudonym Birchley.

IV. THE TEST OATH, 1672, 1678, also known as the DECLARATION or ATTESTATION OATH.—The first Parliament after the Restoration revived the Oaths of Supremacy and Allegiance, which were taken on 14 July, 1660. The Catholics in England being at first in some favour at Court, managed, as a rule, to escape taking it. In Ireland the old controversy was revived through an address to the Crown, called "The Irish Remonstrance", which emphasized the principles of the condemned Oath of Allegiance. It had been drawn up by a Capuchin friar (who afterwards left the order), called Peter Walsh (Valesius), who published many books in its defence, which publications were eventually placed upon the Index. (Maziere Brady, "Catholic Hierarchy", Rome, 1888, p. 126.) After the conversion of James, then Duke of York, the jealousy of the Protestant party increased, and in 1672 a Test Act was carried by Shaftesbury, which compelled all holders of office under the Crown to make a short "Declaration against Transubstantiation", viz., to swear that "there is not any transubstantiation in the sacrament of the Lord's Supper, . . . at or after the consecration thereof by any person whatsoever" (25 Chas. II, c. 2). This test was effective: James resigned his post of Lord High Admiral. But when the country and the Parliament had gone mad over Oates's plot, 1678, a much longer and more insulting test was devised, which added a further clause that "The invocation of the virgin Mary, or any Saint and the Sacrifice of the Mass . . . are superstitious and idolatrous . . and that I make this declaration without any evasion, equivocation, or mental reservation whatsoever, and without any dispensation already granted me by the pope, &c., &c. (30 Chas. II, ii. 1). In modern times, the formula has become notorious (as we shall see) under the title of "the King's Declaration". At the time it was appointed for office holders and the members of both Houses, except the Duke of York. On the death of Charles, James II succeeded, and he would no doubt have gladly abolished the anti-Catholic oaths altogether. But he never had the opportunity of bringing the project before Parliament. Of the Oaths of Supremacy and Allegiance we hear less in this reign, but the Test was the subject of constant discussion, for its form and scope had been expressly intended to hamper a reform such as James was instituting. He freed himself, however, more or less from it by the Dispensing Power, especially after the declaration of the judges, June, 1686, that it was contrary to the principles of the constitution to prevent the Crown from using the services of any of its subjects when they were needed. But the Revolution of 1688 quickly brought the Test back into greater vogue than ever. The first Parliament summoned after the triumph of William of Orange added a clause to the Bill of Rights, which was then passed, by which the Sovereign was himself to take the Declaration (1 W. & M., sess. 2, c. 2.). While the Test was obligatory on holders of every sort of office, there was little need to insist on the old Oaths of Supremacy and Allegiance. They were therefore cut down to a line or two, and joined with the oath of fidelity to King William (1 W. & M., sess. 1, c. 8). By this unworthy device no Catholic could ever be admitted to accept the new regime, without renouncing his faith. This law marks the consummation of English anti-Catholic legislation.

V. THE IRISH OATH OF 1774 TO EMANCIPATION, 1829.—For ninety years there seemed no hope of obtaining legislative relief from the pressure of the penal laws, and the first relaxations were due to external pressure. In 1770 General Burgoyne had proposed to free Catholic soldiers from the obligations of the Test, but in vain. In 1771, however, it was necessary to pacify Canada, and the Quebec Act was passed, the first measure of toleration for Catholics sanctioned by Parliament since the days of Queen Mary Tudor. Soon after began the war of American Independence, the difficulties of which gradually awakened English statesmen to the need of reconciling Catholics. The Irish Government took the first step by undoing William III's wicked work of joining the profession of fidelity to the sovereign with the rejection of papal authority. In 1774 an oath was proposed of allegiance to King George (§ 1) and rejection of the Pretender (§ 2), but without prejudice to the pope's spiritual authority, or to any dogma of the Faith. The alleged malpractice of "no faith with heretics" was renounced (§ 3), so was the deposing power (§ 4), but without the objectionable words, "impious, damnable and heretical." The "temporal and civil jurisdiction of the pope, direct and indirect within the realm" was also abjured (§ 5), and the promise was given that no dispensation from this oath should be considered valid (§ 6). This Irish Oath, of 1774, was accepted by the legislative authorities as proof of loyalty, and it was freely taken, though several clauses were infelicitously worded, though no advantage accrued from so doing. In 1778 however, the first Relief Bill, also called Sir George Savile's Act, to relieve the English

Catholics from the worst consequences of the penal laws, came before the English Parliament, and in it was embodied the Irish Oath (18 George III, c. 60). This Act was passed with little difficulty, and the oath was taken without remonstrance by the clergy of all schools.

The relief given by the Bill of 1778 was so imperfect that further legislation was soon called for, and now the disadvantages of the system of tests were acutely felt. A committee of lay Catholics, with Gallican proclivities, who afterwards characteristically called themselves the Cisalpine Club were negotiating with the Government (see BUTLER, CHARLES). To them it was represented that if more concessions were required more assurances should be given. They were accordingly presented with a long "Protest", which not only rejected the alleged malpractices, already disowned by the Irish Oath, but declaimed against them and others of the same kind in strong but untheological language. It reintroduced, for instance, the objectionable terms "impious, heretical and damnable" of James's Oath of Allegiance. That complications might have ensued from signing such a document was not difficult to foresee. Nevertheless, the committee insisted (1) that words would be understood in a broad popular way, and (2) that, to obtain the Relief Act, it must be signed instantly. To prevent such a misfortune, it was freely signed by laity and clergy, and by the four vicars Apostolic, but two of these recalled their names. When, however, the signatures had been obtained, the new Relief Bill was brought forward by Government, with an oath annexed founded on the Protest (hence called the "Protestation Oath"), which excluded from relief those who would not swear to it, and accept the name of "Protesting Catholic Dissenters". A crisis had arisen for the Catholic Church in England; but with the crisis came the man. It was John Milner (q. v.), then only a country priest, to whose energy and address the dissipation of this danger was chiefly due. The Second Relief Act, therefore, passed (1791) without changing the previous oath, or the name of Catholics. Though the Emancipation Bill was eventually carried without any tests, this was not foreseen at first. The Catholic Committee continued its endeavours for disarming Protestant prejudices, but their proposals (like the Veto) too often savoured of Gallicanism. So too did the oath annexed to the bill proposed in 1813, which from its length was styled the "Theological Oath". Eventually, owing to the growing influence exercised by Daniel O'Connell and the Irish, Catholic Emancipation was fully, if tardily, granted without any tests at all in 1829.

VI. REPEAL OF THE STATUTORY OATHS AGAINST CATHOLICITY, 1867–1910.—The Relief Bills, hitherto mentioned, were generally measures of relief only, leaving the old statutes, oaths, and tests still upon the Statute Book, and some of the chief officers of State had still to take them. The actual repeal of the disused tests and oaths of William III have only taken place in quite recent times. In 1867 the Declaration was repealed (30, 31 Vict., c. 75). After this, the only person bound to pronounce the oath was the king himself at the commencement of his reign. In 1871 the Promissory Oaths Bill removed all the old Oaths of Allegiance (34, 35 Vict., c. 48). In 1891 the first attempt was made by Lord Herries in the House of Lords to get rid of the king's Declaration, but the amendments offered by Government were so insignificant that the Catholics themselves voted against their being proposed at all. In 1901 strong resolutions were passed against its retention by the Canadian House of Commons, as also by its hierarchy, and these were emphasized by similar petitions from the hierarchies of Australia, and the Catholics of the English colonies. In 1904, 1905, and 1908 bills or motions to the same effect were introduced by Lord Braye, Lord Grey, Lord Llandaff, the Duke of Norfolk, and Mr. Redmond, but without the desired effect. After the death of King Edward VII, however, King George V is believed to have urged the Government to bring in a repealing Act. This was done and public opinion, after some wavering, finally declared itself strongly on the side of the Bill, which was carried through both Houses by large majorities, and received Royal Assent on 3 August, 1910, thus removing the last anti-Catholic oath or declaration from the English Constitution.

GENERAL.—See the articles BELLARMINE; BUTLER, CHARLES; CHALLONER; ENGLAND SINCE THE REFORMATION; FISHER, JOHN; MILNER; POYNTER. For the full texts of the Acts of Parliament see *The Statutes at Large* (London, 1762—); SCOBELL, *Collection of Acts, 1640–1656* (London, 1657–58); *Statutes at Large (Ireland)* (Dublin, 1765—). For the debates in the parliament, see HANSARD, *Parliamentary Debates; Journals of the House of Lords*, and *Journals of the House of Commons*; COBBETT, *Parliamentary Hist. of England* (London, 1806); BUTLER, *Mem. of English Catholics* (London, 1819), Catholic, but with Gallican proclivities; FLANAGAN, *Hist. of the Church in England* (London, 1857); GILLOW, *Bibl. Dict.; Dict. Nat. Biog.*
PARTICULAR OATHS.—I.—BRIDGETT, *Life of B. John Fisher* (London, 1888); GAIRDNER, *Lollardy and the Reformation in England* (London, 1908); CAMM, *Lives of English Martyrs* (London, 1904). II.—TIERNEY, *Dodd's Church History of England*, IV (London, 1851); REUSCH, *Index der verbotenen Bücher* (Bonn, 1883); SOMMERVOGEL, *Bibl. de la C. de Jésus* (Paris, 1890); DE LA SERVIÈRE, *De Jacobo I. cum Card. R. Bellarmino disputante* (Paris, 1900). III.—BIRCHLEY (vere AUSTIN), *The Catholique's Plea* (London, 1659); IDEM, *Reflections on the Oaths of Supremacy and Allegiance* (London, 1661); PUGH, *Blacklo's Cabal* (s. l., 1680). IV.—THURSTON, *Titus Oates's Test* (London, 1909); IDEM in *The Tablet* (London, 13 August, 1910), 292. V.—MILNER, *Supplementary Memoirs of English Catholics* (London, 1820); BURTON, *Life and Times of Bishop Challoner* (London, 1909); WARD, *Dawn of the Catholic Revival* (London, 1909); LINGARD, *The Catholic Oath* in *The Catholic Miscellany* (1832, 1833), III, 368; IV, 100. VI.—LORD LLANDAFF (MATTHEWS), *The Papal Declaration* in *Report of the Ninth Eucharistic Congress held at Westminster, 1908*, 50; BRIDGETT, *The Religious Test Acts* in *The Month* (London, May, 1895), 58; IDEM, *The English Coronation Oath* in *The Month* (London, March, 1896), 305; GERARD, *The Royal Declaration* in *The Month* (London, May, 1901), 449.

J. H. POLLEN.

Oaxaca (or ANTEQUERA), ARCHDIOCESE OF, situated in the southern part of the Republic of Mexico, bounded on the north by the Bishopric of Huajuapam and the Archbishopric of Puebla, on the east by the Bishopric of Vera Cruz, on the west by that of Tehuantepec, and on the south by the Pacific Ocean. When the conquest of New Spain was accomplished, Hernán Cortés sought the aid of the powerful Tlaxcaltecas, who had established a republic and were at war with the Aztec Emperor Moctezuma. Out of gratitude to the Tlaxcaltecas, the first bishopric that was founded on the American continent was called Tlaxcala, that of Mexico was second, and later that of Guatemala. Oaxaca, the fourth in the order of succession, was established, under the name of Antequera, by Paul III, 21 July, 1535, the first bishop, the Right Rev. Juan López de Zárate, having been preconized that same year. From then to the present day only thirty bishops have governed the diocese, the last being the Most Rev. Eulogio G. Gillow, preconized 23 May, 1887. On 23 June, 1891, Antequera was raised to the rank of an archbishopric by Leo XIII, and has, at the present time as suffragan dioceses, Chiapas, Yucatan, Tabasco, Tehuantepec, and Campeche.

Prior to the Conquest the religion of the entire extensive region now comprised in the Archbishopric of Antequera, or Oaxaca, was idolatry in various forms, according to the different races that populated this district, the Mixteca, Zapoteca, Mixe, anthinanteca predominating, although twenty-two entirely different dialects are known among them. The famous ruins of Mitla indicate that the most venerable priest of the entire American continent resided there, one who was greatly venerated not only by the different villages of the ancient Anahuac, but by others; as those of Peru. We know from history that when the conquerors landed in Vera Cruz, Moctezuma consulted the High-Priest Achiutla, who announced to him that the oracle had predicted the end of his empire. Abjectly crushed, the Emperor yielded to the Spaniards. The kings of Zaachila and Tehuantepec received baptism and submitted to the mild yoke of the Church. After the conquest of Moctezuma's empire the Spaniards who penetrated to Tenochtitlán were amazed to see the wealth that Moctezuma had accumulated, and in all probability knew that a great part of the gold came from Oaxaca. This would explain why from the first they turned their footsteps towards Oaxaca, where the first Mass was celebrated on 25 Nov., 1521, feast of St. Catherine, martyr. Beginning then development was very rapid, as much perhaps from the fact that Cortés was created Marquis of Valle de Oaxaca, in recognition of his distinguished services, as because of the rich mineral resources of the country, whose importance was such that it ranked next to the City of Mexico itself. Missionaries of the different religious orders were introduced: Franciscans, Dominicans, Augustinians, Jesuits, Friars of the Order of Mercy, Carmelites, Brothers of St. John, Bethlehemites, and Oratorians. All these congregations built handsome churches in the capital of Oaxaca, which are still in existence, with their convents and subordinate houses annexed. The Dominicans laboured most zealously for the conversion of the natives by means of missions and parochial work. Four Bishops of Oaxaca have been drawn from that order, while four other orders have each contributed one.

The archbishopric at the present time comprises besides the metropolitan chapter, which is composed of the dean, archdeacon, and chanter, a theological censor, a canon penitentiary, and six other canons. There is a master of ceremonies, a priest sacristan of the main cathedral, and four choir chaplains. The ecclesiastical government consists of a vicar-general, a secretary of the Executive Council, and two assistants. The duties of the *Provisorato* are discharged by the provisor, fiscal promoter, defender of the Holy Office, and diocesan attorney. There is also a Commission of Rites, composed of four ecclesiastics, one of Christian Doctrine under the charge of six ecclesiastics, and a School Board made up of three clergymen and two laymen.

There are 3 parishes in the city each with its respective church, and 19 other churches, that of St. Dominic being notable for the beauty of its architecture and the richness of its ornamentation. The cathedral, which has a nave and four aisles, is remarkable for the exquisite style and ornateness of its decorations, the beauty of its altars, sacred vessels, and vestments, the present bishop having devoted great thought and expenditure to improvements of this kind, which increase the dignity of the service. There exist in the archdiocese 25 *foranias* (deaneries) which comprise 132 parishes and 223 priests.

Only within recent years have there been any Protestants in Oaxaca; these hold their services in private houses. It is not easy to give exactly the number of Catholics belonging to the archbishopric, because they are chiefly natives who live in the rural districts and surrounding mountains, but the population is estimated in 1910 at 1,041,035. The State does not sanction the existence of religious communities of men or women. Since they must carry on their various works without attracting public notice, it is difficult to give statistics either of their number, or of the institutions under their care. So, too, while the parochial schools are steadily increasing it is almost impossible to give their exact number. In the city of Oaxaca (in 1910 pop. 37,469) there is a seminary divided into three sections: ordained students (*clericales*), seminarians (*seminaristas*), and preparatory students (*apostolicos*), of whom 102 are interns, under the charge of 6 Paulist Fathers, 6 assistant professors, and 3 coadjutor brothers. The College of the Holy Ghost, established to train the sons of the best families for various careers, has 70 boarders and 250 day scholars under the direction of 8 ecclesiastics and several professors. There are 3 select academies for young women, with an attendance of 600; 6 free schools for boys, with 1600 pupils, and 4 for girls, with 700. Among the charitable institutions under Catholic control are a day nursery accommodating 80 children under the care of 5 nurses, a charity hospital with 24 beds, 12 for men and 12 for women, and a home for the poor with about 90 inmates.

GILLOW, *Apuntes Históricos* (Mexico, 1889); BATTANDIER, *Ann. Pontif.* (Paris, 1906).

EULOGIO G. GILLOW.

Obadiah. See ABDIAS.

Obazine, MONASTERY OF, Diocese of Tulle, founded by St. Stephen of Obazine about 1134. After his ordination St. Stephen, with another priest, Pierre, began the eremitical life. They attracted a number of followers and with the sanction of Eustorge, Bishop of Tulle, built a monastery on a site granted them by the Viscount Archambault.

Before 1142 they had no established rule; however, in this year, St. Stephen was clothed with the regular habit. He had Cistercian monks train his followers in their mode of life, and affiliated his abbey to Citeaux (1147). The number increasing, several foundations were made. Among the most illustrious abbots of Obazine were François d'Escobleau (d. 1628), Archbishop of Bordeaux, and Charles de la Roche-Aymon (d. 1777), Cardinal Archbishop of Rennes. The monastery was confiscated by the Government during the Revolution (1791). The abbatial church, partly restored, now serves as a parish church.

LE NAIN, *Hist. de Citeaux* (Paris, 1696–7); GUIBERT, *Notice sur le Cartulaire d'Obazine* (Tulle, 1890); *Vie de S. Etienne d'Obazine* (Tulle, 1881); *Gallia christ.*, II; MANRIQUE, *Annales cisterc.* (Lyons, 1642); JANAUSCHEK, *Origines cisterc.* (Vienna, 1877); HENRIQUEZ, *Menologium cisterc.* (Antwerp, 1630).

EDMOND OBRECHT.

Obba, titular see in Byzacena, northern Africa, of unknown history, although mentioned by Polybius (XIV, vi, under the name of Abba), and Titus Livius (XXX, vii). Situated on the highway from Carthage to Theveste (Tebessa), seven miles from Lares (Lorbeus) and sixteen from Althiburus (Henshir Medina), it is the modern Ebba. Three bishops are known, Paul, present at the Council of Carthage in 225, probably the Paul mentioned in the Martyrology for 19 January; Felicissimus, a Donatist, present at the conference at Carthage in 411; and Valerianus, at the Council of Constantinople, 553.

TOULOTTE, *Géog. de l'Afrique chrétienne: Proconsulaire* (Rennes and Paris, 1892), 225.

S. PÉTRIDÈS.

Obedience (Lat. *obœdire*, "to hearken to", hence "to obey") is the complying with a command or precept. It is here regarded not as a transitory and isolated act but rather as a virtue or principle of righteous conduct. It is then said to be the moral habit by which one carries out the order of his superior with the precise intent of fulfilling the injunction. St. Thomas Aquinas considers the obligation of obedience as an obvious consequence of the subordination established in the world by the natural and positive law. The idea that subjection of any sort of one man to another is incompatible with human freedom—a notion that had vogue in the religious and political teachings of the post-Reformation period—he refutes by showing that it is at variance with the constituted nature of things, and the positive prescriptions of Almighty God. It is worthy of note that whilst it is possible to discern a general aspect of obedience in some acts of all the virtues, in so far as obedience stands for the execution of anything that is of precept, it is contemplated in this article as a definitely special virtue.

The element that differentiates it adequately from other good habits is found in the last part of the definition already given. Stress is put upon the fact that one not only does what is actually enjoined but does it with a mind to formally fall in with the will of the commander. It is in other words the homage rendered to authority which ranks it as a distinct virtue. Among the virtues obedience holds an exalted place but not the highest. That distinction belongs to the virtues of faith, hope, and charity (q. v.) which unite us immediately with Almighty God. Amongst the moral virtues obedience enjoys a primacy of honour. The reason is that the greater or lesser excellence of a moral virtue is determined by the greater or lesser value of the object which it qualifies one to put aside in order to give oneself to God. Now amongst our various possessions, whether goods of the body, or goods of the soul, it is clear that the human will is the most intimately personal and most cherished of all. So it happens that obedience, which makes a man yield up the most dearly prized stronghold of the individual soul in order to do the good pleasure of his Creator, is accounted the greatest of the moral virtues. As to whom we are to obey, there can be no doubt that first we are bound to offer an unreserved service to Almighty God in all His commands. No real difficulty against this truth can be gathered from putting in juxtaposition the unchangeableness of the natural law and an order, such as that given to Abraham to slay his son Isaac. The conclusive answer is that the absolute sovereignty of God over life and death made it right in that particular instance to undertake the killing of an innocent human being at His direction. On the other hand the obligation of obedience to superiors under God admits of limitations. We are not bound to obey a superior in a matter which does not fall within the limits of his preceptive power. Thus for instance parents, although entitled beyond question to the submission of their children until they become of age, have no right to command them to marry. Neither can a superior claim our obedience in contravention of the dispositions of a higher authority. Hence, notably, we cannot heed the behests of any human power no matter how venerable or undisputed as against the ordinances of God. All authority to which we bow has its source in Him and cannot validly be used against Him. It is this recognition of the authority of God vicariously exercised through a human agent that confers upon the act of obedience its special merit. No hard and fast rule can be set down for determining the degree of guilt of the sin of disobedience. Regarded formally as a deliberate scorning of the authority itself, it would involve a divorce between the soul and the supernatural principle of charity which is tantamount to a grievous sin. As a matter of fact many other things have to be taken account of, as the greater or less advertence in the act, the relatively important or trifling character of the thing imposed, the manner of enjoining, the right of the person who commands. For such reasons the sin will frequently be esteemed venial.

RICKABY, *Aquinas Ethicus* (London, 1896); ST. THOMAS AQUINAS, *Summa Theologica* (Turin, 1885); TAPPARELLI, *Dritto Naturale* (Rome, 1900); SPIRAGO, *The Catechism Explained* (New York, 1899).

JOSEPH F. DELANY.

Obedience, RELIGIOUS, is that general submission which religious vow to God, and voluntarily promise to their superiors, in order to be directed by them in the ways of perfection according to the purpose and constitutions of their order. It consists, according to Lessius (De Justitia, II, xlvi, 37), in a man's allowing himself to be governed throughout his life by another for the sake of God. It is composed of three elements: (a) the sacrifice offered to God of his own independence in the generality of his actions, at least of such as are exterior; (b) the motive, namely, personal perfection, and, as a rule, also the performance of spiritual or corporal works of mercy and charity; (c) the express or implied contract with an order (formerly also with a person), which accepts the obligation to lead him to the end for which he accepts its laws and direction. Religious obedience, therefore, does not involve that extinction of all individuality, so often alleged against convents and the Church; nor is it unlimited, for it is not possible either physically or morally that a man should give himself up absolutely to the guidance of another. The choice of a superior, the object of obedience, the authority of the hierarchical Church, all exclude the idea of arbitrary rule.

I.—*The Canonical Rule of Obedience.*—A.—The Superiors.—By Divine law, religious persons are subject to the hierarchy of the Church; first to the pope, then to the bishops, unless exempted by the pope from episcopal jurisdiction. This hierarchy was instituted by Christ in order to direct the faithful not only in the way of salvation, but also in Christian perfection. The vow of obedience in the institutes approved by the Holy See is held more and more to be made equally to the pope, who communicates his authority to the Roman congregations entrusted with the direction of religious orders. The superiors of the different orders, when they are clerics and exempt from episcopal jurisdiction, similarly receive a part of this authority; and every one who is placed at the head of a community is invested with the domestic authority necessary for its good government; the vow by which the religious offers to God the obedience which he promises to his superiors confirms and defines this authority. But the right to demand obedience in virtue of the vow does not necessarily belong to all superiors; it is ordinarily reserved to the head of the community; and in order to enforce the obligation, it is necessary that the superior should make known his intention to bind the conscience; in certain orders such expressions as "I will", "I command", have not such binding force. The instructions of the Holy See require that the power of binding the conscience by command shall be employed with the utmost prudence and discretion.

B.—*The limits of the obligation.*—The commands of superiors do not extend to what concerns the inward motion of the will. Such at least is the teaching of St. Thomas (II-II, Q. cvi, a. 5, and Q. clxxxvi, a. 2). Obedience is not vowed absolutely, and without limit, but according to the rule of each order, for a superior cannot command anything foreign to, or outside, his rule (except in so far as he may grant dispensations from the rule). No appeal lies from his order, that is to say, the obligation of obedience is not suspended by any appeal to higher authority; but the inferior has always the right of extra-judicial recourse to a higher authority in the order or to the Holy See.

II.—*The Moral Significance.*—The religious is bound morally to obey on all occasions when he is bound canonically, and whenever his disobedience would offend against the law of charity, as for instance by bringing discord into the community. By reason of the vow of obedience and of the religious profession a deliberate act of obedience and submission adds the merit of an act of the virtue of religion to the other merits of the act. This extends even to the obedience of counsel which goes beyond matters of regular observance, and is also limited by the prescriptions of higher laws, whether human or Divine.

III.—*The Evangelical Foundation.*—The evangelical foundation of religious obedience is first of all found in the perfect accord of that obedience with the spirit of the Gospel. Freedom from ambition which leads a man to choose a position of inferiority, implies a spirit of humility which esteems others as superior, and willingly yields them the first place; the sacrifice of his own independence and his own will presupposes in a high degree that spirit of self-denial and mortification which keeps the passions under proper restraint;

the readiness to accept a common rule and direction manifests a spirit of union and concord which generously adapts itself to the desires and tastes of others; eagerness to do the will of God in all things is a mark of the charity towards God which led Christ to say "I do always the things which please my Father" (John, vii, 29). And since the Church has invested superiors with her authority, religious obedience is supported by all those texts which recommend submission to lawful powers, and especially by the following: "He that heareth you, heareth me" (Luke, x, 16).

Philosophically religious obedience is justified (a) by the experience of the mistakes and illusions to which a man relying on his own unaided opinions is liable. The religious proposes to rule his whole life by devotion to God and his neighbour; how shall he best realize this ideal? By regulating all his actions by his own judgment, or by choosing a prudent and enlightened guide who will give his advice without any consideration of himself? Is it not clear that the latter alternative shows a resolution more sincere, more generous, and at the same time more likely to lead to a successful issue? This obedience is justified also (b) by the help of example and counsel afforded by community life and the acceptance of a rule of conduct, the holiness of which is vouched for by the Church; (c) lastly, since the object of religious orders is not only the perfection of their members, but also the performance of spiritual and corporal works of mercy, they need a union of efforts which can only be assured by religious obedience, just as military obedience is indispensable for success in the operations of war.

Religious obedience never reduces a man to a state of passive inertness, it does not prevent the use of any faculty he may possess, but sanctifies the use of all. It does not forbid any initiative, but subjects it to a prudent control in order to preserve it from indiscretion and keep it in the line of true charity. A member of a religious order has often been compared to a dead body, but in truth nothing is killed by the religious vow but vanity and self-love and all their fatal opposition to the Divine will. If superiors and subjects have sometimes failed to understand the practice of religious obedience, if direction has sometimes been indiscreet, these are accidental imperfections from which no human institution is free. The unbounded zeal of men like St. Francis Xavier and other saints who loved their rule, the prominent part which religious have taken in the mission field, and their successes therein, the savage war which the enemies of the Faith have at all times waged against the religious orders; all these things furnish the most eloquent testimony to the happy influence of religious obedience in developing the activity which it sanctifies. The expression "blind obedience" signifies not an unreasoning or unreasonable submission to authority, but a keen appreciation of the rights of authority, the reasonableness of submission, and blindness only to such selfish or worldly considerations as would lessen regard for authority.

At present, religious have taken a far greater part than formerly in civil and public life, personally fulfilling all the conditions required of citizens, in order to exercise their right of voting and other functions compatible with their profession. Obedience does not interfere with the proper exercise of such rights. No political system rejects the votes of persons in dependent positions, but all freely permit the use of any legitimate influence which corrects to some extent the vicious tendency of equalitarianism: the influence of religious superiors is limited to safeguarding the higher interests of religion. As to the functions to be fulfilled, the superior, by the very fact of permitting his subjects to undertake them, grants all the liberty that is required for their honourable fulfilment.

Historically.—Though St. Paul and the other early hermits were not in a position to practise religious obedience, it was already manifested in the docility with which their imitators placed themselves under the guidance of some older man. St. Cyprian, in his letter "De habitu virginum", shows us that at Rome the virgins followed the direction of the older women. Obedience was then looked upon as a sort of education, from which those were dispensed who were considered perfect and ripe for a solitary life. This idea is found also in the first chapter of the Rule of St. Benedict. St. Pachomius (A. D. 292–346) understanding the importance of obedience in community life made it the foundation of the religious life of the cenobites, preaching by his own example, and inculcating upon all superiors the necessity of a scrupulous observance of the rules of which they were the guardians. The monks (cf. Cassian, "Institutions") thus saw in perfect obedience an excellent application of their universal spirit of self-renunciation. Later, St. Bernard insisted on the complete suppression of self-will, i. e., of that will which sets itself in opposition to the designs of God and to all that is commanded or desired for the good of the community. The obedience of the Eastern monks was imperfect and defective by reason of the facility with which they changed from one superior or monastery to another. St. Benedict, in consequence, advancing a step farther, introduced a new rule binding his monks by a vow of stability. A certain choice of rules still existed, which seemed likely to be hurtful to the common life, for some monasteries had various sets of rules, each set having its own observants. The reforms in the Order of St. Benedict brought into existence monastic congregations known by the identity of their observances, and these were the forerunners of the mendicant orders with their rules which have become canonical laws. St. Thomas thus had before him all the material necessary to enable him to treat fully of the subject of religious obedience in his "Summa Theologica", in which he makes it clear that the vow of obedience is the chief of the vows of religion.

St. Thomas, *Summa Theologica*, II-II, QQ. 104 et 186; Idem, *Opusc. de perfect. vitæ spirit.*, c. x, xii; Idem, *Summa contra Gentiles;* see also the *Commentaries* of Cajetan and Billuart in the portion of the *Summa Theol.* cited above; Bellarmine, *Controv. de monachis*, 1, 2, c. xxi; Suarez, *De religione*, tr. 7, X, and tr. 10, IV, c. xiii-xv; De Valentia, In II-II, disp. 10, q. 4, *De statu relig.*, punctum 1 and 2; Elliot, *Life of Father Hecker* (New York, 1896; French tr. by Klein); Maignen, *Le P. Hecker est-il un saint?* (Paris, 1898); Ladeuze, *Etude sur le cénobitisme Pakhomien pendant le IVe siècle et la première moitié du cinquième* (Louvain, 1898); Schiewietz, *Das morgenland. Mönchtum* (Mainz, 1894); Harnack, *Das Mönchtum, seine Ideale und seine Gesch.*

A. Vermeersch.

Obedientiaries, a name commonly used in medieval times for the lesser officials of a monastery who were appointed by will of the superior. In some cases the word is used to include all those who held office beneath the abbot, but more frequently the prior and sub-prior are excluded from those signified by it. To the obedientiaries were assigned the various duties pertaining to their different offices and they possessed considerable power in their own departments. There was always a right of appeal to the abbot or superior, but in practice most details were settled by the "customary" of the monastery. The list that follows gives the usual titles of the obedientiaries, but in some monasteries other names were used and other official positions may be found: thus, for example, to this day, in the great Swiss monastery of Einsiedeln the name "dean" is given to the official who is called prior in all other Benedictine houses.

(1) The "cantor", or "precentor", usually assisted by the "sub-cantor", or "succentor" (see Cantor). (2) The sacrist, or sacristan, who had charge of the monastic church and of all things necessary for the services. He had, as a rule, several assistants: (a) the subsacrist, also known as the secretary, the "matricularius", or the master of work; (b) the treasurer; (c) the "revestiarius". (3) The cellarer,

or bursar, who acted as chief purveyor of all foodstuffs to the monastery and as general steward. In recent times the name procurator is often found used for this official. He had as assistants: (a) the subcellarer; (b) the "granatorius". Chapter xxxi of St. Benedict's Rule tells "What kind of man the Cellarer ought to be"; in practice this position is the most responsible one after that of abbot or superior. (4) The refectorian, who had charge of the frater, or refectory and its furniture, including such things as crockery, cloths, dishes, spoons, forks, etc. (5) The kitchener, who presided over the cookery department, not only for the community but for all guests, dependants, etc. (6) The novice master (see NOVICE), whose assistant was sometimes called the "zelator". (7) The infirmarian, besides looking after the sick brethren, was also responsible for the quarterly "blood letting" of the monks, a custom almost universal in medieval monasteries. (8) The guest-master, whose duties are dealt with in chapter liii of St. Benedict's Rule. (9) The almoner. (10) The chamberlain, or "vestiarius".

Besides these officials who were appointed more or less permanently, there were certain others appointed for a week at a time to carry out various duties. These positions were usually filled in turn by all below the rank of sub-prior, though very busy officials, e. g., the cellarer, might be excused. The chief of these was the hebdomadarian, or priest for the week. It was his duty to sing the conventual mass on all days during the week, to intone the "Deus in adjutorium" at the beginning of each of the canonical hours, to bless holy water, etc. The antiphoner was also appointed for a week at a time. It was his duty to read or sing the invitatory at Matins, to give out the first antiphon at the Psalms, and also the versicles, responsoria after the lessons etc. The weekly reader and servers in the kitchen and refectory entered upon their duties on Sunday when, in company with the servers of the previous week, they had to ask and receive a special blessing in choir as directed in chapters xxxv and xxxviii of St. Benedict's Rule. Nowadays the tendency is towards a simplification in the details of monastic life and consequently to a reduction in the number of officials in a monastery, but all the more important offices named above exist to-day in every monastery though the name obedientiaries has quite dropped out of everyday use.

GASQUET, *English Monastic Life* (London, 1904), 58–110; *Customary of . . . St. Augustine's, Canterbury, and St. Peter's, Westminster*, ed. THOMPSON (London, 1902); *The Ancren Riwle*, ed. MORTON (London, 1853); FEASEY, *Monasticism* (London, 1898), 175–252. See bibliography appended to MONASTICISM, WESTERN, and also to the articles on the various monastic orders.

G. ROGER HUDLESTON.

Oberammergau. See PASSION PLAYS.

Oblate Sisters of Providence, a congregation of negro nuns founded at Baltimore, Md., by the Rev. Jacques Hector Nicholas Joubert de la Muraille, for the education of coloured children. Father Joubert belonged to a noble French family forced by the Revolution to take refuge in San Domingo. Alone of his family, he escaped from a massacre and went to Baltimore, entering St. Mary's Seminary. After his ordination he was given charge of the coloured Catholics of St. Mary's chapel. Finding he was making no headway as the sermons were not remembered and there were no schools where the children could be taught, he formed the idea of founding a religious community for the purpose of educating these children. In this he was encouraged by his two friends, Fathers Babade and Tessier. He was introduced to four coloured women, who kept a small private school, and lived a retired life with the forlorn hope of consecrating their lives to God. Father Joubert made known to them his plans and they offered to be at his service. With the approval of the Archbishop of Baltimore a novitiate was begun and on 2 July, 1829, the first four sisters, Miss Elisabeth Lange of Santiago, Cuba, Miss Mary Rosine Boegues of San Domingo, Miss Mary Frances Balas of San Domingo, Miss Mary Theresa Duchemin of Baltimore made their vows. Sister Mary Elisabeth was chosen superior, and Rev. Father Joubert was appointed director. Gregory XVI approved the order 2 October, 1831 under the title of Oblate Sisters of Providence. At present the sisters conduct schools and orphanages at Baltimore, Washington, Leavenworth, St. Louis, Normandy (Mo.), and 4 houses in Cuba, 2 in Havana, 1 in Santa Clara, 1 in Cardenas. The mother-house and novitiate is at Baltimore. There were 130 sisters, 9 novices, and 7 postulants in 1910.

HEIMBUCHER, *Die Orden u. Kong. d. kath. Kirche*, III (Paderborn, 1908), 573; *Catholic Directory* (1910).

MAGDALEN GRATIN.

Oblates of Mary Immaculate.—I. NAME AND ORIGIN.—The first members of this society, founded in 1816, were known as "Missionaries of Provence". They received the title of "Missionary Oblates of Mary Immaculate" and approbation as a congregation under simple vows in a Brief of Leo XII dated 17 February, 1826. The founder, Charles Joseph Eugène de Mazenod (b. at Aix, 1 August, 1782), left France at an early age on account of the Revolution, and remained four years at Venice, one at Naples, and three at Palermo, before returning to Paris, where he entered St. Sulpice in 1808. He was ordained priest at Amiens on 21 December, 1811. In 1818 he had gathered a small community around him, and made his religious profession at the church of the Mission, Aix, with MM. Mounier, Tempier, Mye, and Moreau as fellow-priests, and MM. Dupuy, Courtès, and Suzanne as scholastic students. He became Vicar-General of Marseilles in 1823, titular Bishop of Icosia and coadjutor in 1834, and Bishop of Marseilles in 1837. In 1856 he was named senator and member of the Legion of Honour by Napoleon III, and died in 1861, having been superior-general of his congregation from 1816 to that date.

II. MEMBERS AND ORGANIZATION.—The congregation consists of priests and lay-brothers, leading a common life. The latter act as temporal coadjutors, farm or workshop instructors in industrial and reformatory schools, and teachers and catechists on the foreign missions. The central and supreme authority of the society is two-fold: (1) intermittent and extraordinary, as vested in the general chapter meeting once in six years, and composed of the general administrators, provincials, vicars of missions, and delegates from each province or vicariate; (2) ordinary, as vested in the superior-general elected for life by the general chapter, and assisted by a council of four assistants and a bursar-general, named for a term of years, renewable by the same authority. The general administration was situated at Marseilles until 1861, when it was transferred to Paris; the persecutions of 1902 obliged its removal to Liège in 1903, whence it was transferred to Rome in 1905. The congregation is officially represented at the Holy See by a procurator-general named by the central administration; this authority also elects the chaplain-general of the Holy Family Sisters of Bordeaux, founded by Abbé de Noailles, and by him confided to the spiritual direction of the Oblate Fathers. Until 1851 all Oblate houses were directly dependent on the central administration. The general chapter held in that year divided its dependencies into provinces and missionary vicariates, each having its own provincial or vicar aided by a council of four consultors and a bursar. At the head of each regularly constituted house is placed a local superior aided by two assessors and a bursar, all named by the provincial administration. The educational establishments also possess a special council of professors and directors.

III. RECRUITING is made by means of juniorates, novitiates, and scholasticates. (a) *Juniorates or Apostolic Schools.*—The first establishment of this description was founded in 1841 by the Oblates of Notre Dame des Lumières near Avignon, and their example, soon followed by the Jesuit Fathers at Avignon, became widely adopted in France. The congregation has at present thirteen juniorates situated: at Ottawa, Buffalo, San Antonio (Texas), St. Boniface (Manitoba) and Strathcona (Alberta) in the new world; St. Charles (Holland), Waereghem (Belgium), Sancta Maria a Vico and Naples (Italy), Urmieta (Spain), and Belcamp Hall (Ireland) in Europe; Colombo and Jaffna in the Island of Ceylon. (b) *Novitiates* are fed from the juniorates, and also from colleges, seminaries, and gymnasia. They are at present thirteen in number and situated at Lachine (Canada), Tewksbury (Massachusetts), San Antonio (Texas), St. Charles (Manitoba), St. Gerlach, Hünfeld, and Maria Engelport (Germany), Niewenhove (Belgium), Le Bestin (Luxemburg), St. Pierre d'Aoste (Italy), Urmieta (Spain), Stillorgan (Ireland), and Colombo (Ceylon). (c) *Scholasticates* receive novices who have been admitted to temporal vows at the end of a year's probation. The first scholasticate of the congregation was dedicated to the Sacred Heart at Montolivet, Marseilles, in 1857; it was transferred to Autun in 1861, to Dublin in 1880, to St. Francis (Holland) in 1889, and to Liège in 1891. The ten establishments at present occupied are situated at Ottawa, Tewksbury, San Antonio, Rome, Liège, Hünfeld, Stillorgan, Turin, and Colombo (2).

IV. ENDS AND MEANS. — The congregation was formed to repair the havoc caused by the French Revolution, and its very existence so soon afterwards was a sign of religious revival. Its multiple ends may thus be divided: (a) *Primary*: (1) To revive the spirit of faith among rural and industrial populations by means of missions and retreats, in which devotion to the Sacred Heart and to Mary Immaculate is recommended as a supernatural means of regeneration. "He hath sent me to preach the Gospel to the poor", has been adopted as the device of the congregation. (2) Care of young men's societies, Catholic clubs, etc. (3) Formation of clergy in seminaries. (b) *Secondary or Derived.*—To adapt itself to the different circumstances arising from its rapid development in new countries, the congregation has necessarily extended its sphere of action to parochial organization, to the direction of industrial or reformatory schools, of establishments of secondary education in its principal centres, and of higher institutions of learning, such as the University of Ottawa (see OTTAWA, UNIVERSITY OF).

V. PROMINENT MEMBERS, PAST AND PRESENT.—(a) *Superior Generals*: Mgr de Mazenod (1816); Very Rev. J. Fabre (1861); L. Soullier (1893); C. Augier (1898); A. Lavillardière (1906); Mgr A. Dontenwill (1908). (b) *Oblate Bishops*: (1) Deceased: de Mazenod, Bishop of Marseilles; Guibert (1802–86), Cardinal Archbishop of Paris; Semeria (1813–68), Vicar Apostolic of Jaffna; Guigues (1805–74), first Bishop of Ottawa; Allard (1806–89), first Vicar Apostolic of Natal; Faraud (1823–90), first Vicar Apostolic of Athabaska-Mackenzie; D'Herbomez (1822–90), first Vicar Apostolic of British Columbia; Bonjean (1823–92), first Archbishop of Colombo; Taché (1823–94), first Archbishop of St. Boniface; Baläin (1828–1905), Archbishop of Auch; Mélizan (1844–1905), Archbishop of Colombo; Grandin (1829–1902), first Bishop of St. Albert; Clut (1832–1903), Auxiliary Bishop of Athabaska-Mackenzie; Jolivet (1826–1903), Vicar Apostolic of Natal; Durieu, (1830–99), first Bishop of New Westminster; Anthony Gaughren (1849–1901), Vicar Apostolic of Orange River Colony; (2) Living: Dontenwill, Augustin, titular Archbishop of Ptolemais, and actual superior general; Langevin, Archbishop of St. Boniface (consecrated 1895); Coudert, Archbishop of Colombo (1898); Grouard, Vicar Apostolic of Athabaska (1891); Pascal, Bishop of Prince Albert (1891); Joulain, Bishop of Jaffna (1893); Legal, Bishop of St. Albert (1897); Breynat, Vicar Apostolic of Mackenzie (1902); Matthew Gaughren, Vicar Apostolic of Orange River Colony (1902); Delalle, Vicar Apostolic of Natal (1904); Miller, Vicar Apostolic of Transvaal (1904); Joussard, Coadjutor of Athabaska (1909); Cenez, Vicar Apostolic of Basutoland (1909); Fallon, Bishop of London, Ontario (1910); Charlebois, first Vicar Apostolic of Keewatin, Canada (1910).

VI. PRINCIPAL UNDERTAKINGS.—(a) *General*. (1) In canonically constituted countries a parish church or public chapel is attached to each establishment of Oblates. The parishes are all provided with schools, while many have colleges or academies and a hospital. Several of the parochial residences (e. g., Buffalo, Montreal, Quebec, etc.) serve as centres for missionaries who assist the parochial clergy by giving retreats or missions and taking temporary charge of parishes. (2) In new or missionary countries, the posts are considered as fixed residences from which the missionaries radiate to surrounding fields of action (e. g., Edmonton and Calgary, Alberta). Each of these centres possesses fully equipped schools, whilst many have convents, boarding schools, and hospitals. Instruction is given in English, French, or native tongues by religious communities or by the fathers and brothers themselves. Indigenous mission work is carried on by the periodical recurrence of missions or retreats, and the regular instructions of catechists. The printing press is much used, and the congregation has published complete dictionaries and other works in the native idioms among which it labours.

(b) *Special.*—(1) Canada.—Until recent years the evangelization of the Canadian West and of British Columbia was the almost exclusive work of the Oblate Fathers, as that of the extreme north still is. Cathedrals, churches, and colleges were built by them, and often handed over to secular clergy or to other religious communities (as in the case of the St. Boniface College, which is at present flourishing under the direction of the Society of Jesus). The Archiepiscopal See of St. Boniface since 1853, and the episcopal Sees of St. Albert, Prince Albert, with the Vicariates of Athabaska and Mackenzie since their foundation, have been, and are still occupied by Oblates. That of New Westminster ceased to be so in 1908. The Diocese of Ottawa had an Oblate as first bishop, and owes the foundation of most of its parishes and institutions to members of the congregation, who have also founded a number of the centres in the new Vicariates of Temiskaming and the Gulf of St. Lawrence, as well as in the Diocese of Chicoutimi. Among the recent labours of the Oblates in the West a special mention must be given to the religious organization of Germans, Poles, and Ruthenians. The new Vicariate of Keewatin (1910) is entrusted to an Oblate bishop, whose missionaries are devoted to the regeneration of nomadic Indian tribes. (2) South Africa.—The Oblates have founded and occupy the four vicariates Apostolic of Natal, Orange River, Basutoland and Transvaal, as also the Prefecture Apostolic of Cimbebasia. Its members served as military chaplains on both sides during the Boer war. (3) Asia.—The immense Dioceses of Colombo and Jaffna, with their flourishing colleges and missions, are the achievement of the enterprising zeal of Oblate Fathers under Mgr Bonjean, O.M.I. (4) Western Australia. A missionary vicariate was founded from the British Province in 1894, and is actively engaged in parochial and reformatory work.

VII. ESTABLISHMENTS OF EDUCATION AND FORMATION.—(a) *For the Congregation*. (1) Scholasticates affording a course of two years in philosophy and social science (three years in Rome), and of four years in theology and sacred sciences according to the spirit and method of St. Thomas. The Roman scholastics follow the programme of the Gregorian University, and graduate in philosophy, theology, canon law, and Scripture. The scholastics at Ottawa graduate in philosophy and theology at the university, of which they form an integral part. (2) Novitiates giving religious formation with adapted studies. (3) Juniorates providing a complete classical course preparatory to the sacred sciences. The Ottawa juniorists make their course at the neighbouring university, and graduate in the Faculty of Arts. (b) *Higher Education.* (3), British Columbia (3), and Australia (1). There are also about fifteen Indian boarding-schools in the Canadian West. (5) Reformatory schools at Glencree and Philipstown and Maggona in Ceylon.

VIII. CELEBRATED SANCTUARIES AND PILGRIMAGES.—(a) *Of the Sacred Heart.*—(1) The Basilica of the National Vow at Paris, a world centre of adoration and reparation, was directed by Oblate Fathers from 1876 until the expulsions of 1902. (2) The construction of a similar basilica for Belgium was entrusted to them by Leopold II in Jan., 1903. (3) The parishes

STATISTICS

		Houses	Scholasticates	Juniorates	Noviciates	Seminaries and Colleges	University	Industrial and Reformatory Schools	Bishops	Priests	Lay Brothers
General Administration, Rome		..	..	..	..	..	..	..	1	6	..
EUROPE	Central Province { France, Italy, Spain }	10	1	3	2	2	..	..	..	107	40
	Northern " { France, Belgium, Jersey }	9	1	2	3	..	..	..	..	101	57
	British " { England, Ireland, Scotland, Wales }	12	1	1	1	..	..	..	2	57	37
	German "	5	1	1	3	..	..	..	..	84	95
	Belgian "	3	..	1	1	..	..	..	..	37	23
NORTH AMERICA	London (Ontario), Diocese of	..	..	..	..	..	..	..	1	..	..
	Canadian Province { Quebec, Ontario }	11	1	1	1	1	1	..	..	130	45
	United States—First Prov. (North)	8	1	1	1	1	..	..	..	50	20
	" " —Second " (South)	10	1	1	1	2	..	..	..	54	12
	Manitoban Province	21	..	1	1	..	..	3	1	76	17
	Alberta-Saskatchewan, Vicariate of (Dioceses of St. Albert and Prince Albert)	42	..	1	..	..	..	3	2	96	33
	Athabaska, Vicariate Apostolic of	10	..	..	..	..	..	1	1	24	22
	Mackenzie, " "	9	..	..	..	..	..	..	1	19	12
	British Columbia, Vicariate Apostolic of	8	..	..	..	1	..	3	..	35	11
	Keewatin, Vicariate Apostolic of	9	..	..	..	..	..	..	..	8	..
	Yukon, Prefecture Apostolic of	5	..	..	..	..	..	..	1	12	6
ASIA	Vicariate of Missions of Ceylon { Archd. of Colombo, Diocese of Jaffna }	71	1	2	1	4	..	3	2	178	12
AFRICA	Natal, Vicariate Apostolic of	18	..	..	..	1	..	..	1	35	4
	Kimberley " "	10	..	..	..	..	..	..	1	18	3
	Basutoland " "	9	..	..	..	..	..	..	1	22	7
	Transvaal " "	10	..	..	..	..	..	..	1	20	1
	Cimbebasia " "	9	..	..	..	..	..	..	..	20	17
OCEANIA	Vicariate of Missions: Australia	2	..	..	..	..	..	..	..	6	4
	Total	301	8	15	15	12	1	15	14	1195	478

cation.—(1) Concerning the Ottawa University see the special article. (2) Grand Seminaries.—Until the persecution of 1902 the congregation was in charge of these establishments at Marseilles, Frejus, Ajaccio, and Romans. It is at present entrusted with those of Ajaccio, Ottawa (in connexion with the university), San Antonio, Colombo, and Jaffna. The two last-named are occupied in the formation of a native clergy and have already provided over forty priests. (c) Secondary education: (1) classical colleges with a course in English are provided at Buffalo, St. Albert (Alberta), San Antonio, St. Louis (British Columbia), St. Charles (Natal). Two important institutions at Colombo are affiliated to the University of Cambridge; most of the professors have been in residence there, and prepare their pupils for the London matriculation and Cambridge Local examinations. (2) Preparatory seminaries are established at St. Albert, San Antonio, Ceylon (2), and New Westminster. (3) Normal schools for lay teachers are conducted at Jaffna and Ceylon. (4) Industrial schools with full instruction in farming and craftsmanship by lay brothers and assistants in Manitoba (3), Alberta-Saskatchewan of St. Sauveur, Quebec, and St. Joseph's, Lowell, are important centres of Sacred Heart devotion in the New World. (b) *To the Blessed Virgin.*—Until the expulsions of 1902 the Oblates directed the ancient pilgrimage shrines of Notre Dame des Lumières, Avinon; N. D. de l'Osier, Grenoble; N. D. de Bon Secours, Viviers; N. D. de la Garde (Marseilles); N. D. de Talence and N. D. d'Arcachon, Bordeaux; N. D. de Sion, Nancy; and the national pilgrimage of N. D. de Pontmain near Laval, erected after the Franco-Prussian war. During several years they revived the ancient glories of N. D. du Laus, Gap; N. D. de Clery, Orleans; N. D. de la Rovère, Mentone. In England they have the restored pre-Reformation shrine of Our Lady of Grace at Tower Hill, London, and in Canada the shrines of Our Lady of the Rosary at Cap de la Madeleine, Quebec, and Our Lady of Lourdes at Ville Marie and Duck Lake, Saskatoon. In Ceylon they have the national pilgrimage to Our Lady of Madhu. (c) *To various Saints.*—The ancient sanctuary of St. Martin of Tours was re-excavated and revived by Oblate Fathers under Cardinal Guibert in 1862 (see "Life of Léon Papin Dupont", London, 1882).

Ceylon possesses votive churches to St. Anne at Colombo and St. Anthony at Kochchikadai, and the Canadian West that of St. Anne at Lake St. Anne, which is largely frequented by Indians and half-breeds, as well as white people.

IX. FOUNDATION OF RELIGIOUS COMMUNITIES.— Sisters of the Holy Names of Jesus and Mary (Longeuil, 1843); Grey Nuns of Ottawa, separated from the Montreal community by Bishop Guigues in 1845; Oblate Sisters of the Sacred Heart and Mary Immaculate founded at St. Boniface by Archbishop Langevin (1905); and a community of over 300 native sisters, and one of teaching brothers of St. Joseph in Ceylon.

X. APOSTOLATE OF THE PRESS.—(a) *Periodicals on the Work of the Congregation:* "Missions des O. M. I.", printed at Rome for the congregation only; "Petites annales des O. M. I." (Liège); "Maria Immaculata" (German), Hünfeld, New Brunswick; the "Missionary Record", started in 1891, was discontinued in 1903. (b) *General Newspapers, etc.:* the "North West Review" (Winnipeg), "Western Catholic" (Vancouver), "Patriote de l'Ouest" (Duck Lake, Saskatoon), "Ami du Foyer" (St. Boniface), "Die West Canada" (German), "Gazeta Katolika" (Polish), and a recently established Ruthenian journal (Winnipeg), "Kitchiwa Mateh Sacred Heart Review in Cris" (Sacred Heart P. O. Alta), "Cennad Llydewig, Messenger of the Catholic Church in Welsh-English" (Llaanrwst, North Wales); "Ceylon Catholic Messenger", separate editions in English and Cingalese, and the "Jaffna Guardian" in English-Tamil; Parochial Bulletins at St. Joseph's, Lowell, Mattawa (Ontario), and St. Peter's, Montreal.

In connexion with the table given on page 186, the following points may be mentioned: (1) the "houses" are parochial establishments or missionary centres, not mission posts; (2) the table is calculated according to the provinces or vicariates of the congregation, which are not always coterminous with ecclesiastical divisions; (3) the figures given for France represent the state of affairs before 1902. Since that date a large number of religious remain in France, though isolated. Several establishments have been transferred to Belgium, Italy, and Spain; (4) scholastics, novices, and juniorists are not included.

I. FOUNDATION AND DEVELOPMENT.—RAMBERT, *Vie de Mgr de Mazenod* (2 vols., Tours, 1883); RICARD, *Mgr de Mazenod* (Paris, 1892); COOKE, *Sketches of the Life of Mgr de Mazenod and Oblate Missionary Labours* (2 vols., London, 1879); BAFFIE, *Bishop de Mazenod; His Inner Life and Virtues*, tr. DAWSON (London, 1909); *Missions des O. M. I. Petites annales; Missionary Record; Missions Catholiques* (7 vols., Paris), passim.

II. AMERICA AND CANADA.—MORICE, *Hist. of the Cath. Church in Western Canada* (2 vols., Toronto, 1910); TACHÉ, *A Page of the Hist. of the Schools in Manitoba* (St. Boniface, 1893); IDEM, *Vingt années (1845–65) de Missions dans le N. O. de l'Amérique* (Montreal, 1866); MORICE, *Au Pays de l'ours noir* (Paris, 1897); DESROSIERS AND FOURNET, *La Race Française en Amerique* (Montreal, 1910), vii; PARIZOT, *Reminiscences of a Texas Missionary* (San Antonio, 1899).

See also the following articles: BASUTOLAND; BLOOD INDIANS; BRITISH COLUMBIA; COLOMBO; JAFFNA; MISSIONS, CATHOLIC INDIAN, OF CANADA; CANADA.

F. BLANCHIN.

Oblates of St. Ambrose and St. Charles. See AMBROSIANS.

Oblates of Saint Francis de Sales, a congregation of priests founded originally by Saint Francis de Sales at the request of Saint Jane de Chantal. The establishment at Thonon was a preparatory step toward carrying out his design, the accomplishment of which was prevented by his death. With Saint Jane Frances de Chantal's encouragement and assistance, Raymond Bonal of Adge, in France, carried out his plan but this congregation died out at the beginning of the eighteenth century. Two hundred years later it was revived by Ven. Mother Marie de Sales Chappuis, who died in the odour of sanctity, 7 October, 1875, and Abbé Louis Alexander Alphonse Brisson, a professor in the Seminary of Troyes. In 1869 Father Brisson began Saint Bernard's College, near Troyes. In September, 1871, Father Gilbert (d. 10 November, 1909) joined him, and Mgr Ravinet, Bishop of Troyes, received them and four companions into the novitiate. The Holy See approved temporarily their constitutions, 21 Dec., 1875. The first vows were made 27 August, 1876. The definitive approbation of their constitution was given on 8 December, 1897. The members of the institute are of two ranks, clerics and lay-brothers. The postulate lasts from six to nine months; the novitiate from one year to eighteen months. For the first three years the vows are annual, after that perpetual. The institute is governed by a superior general elected for life, and five counsellors general elected at each general chapter, which takes place every ten years. The congregation gradually developed in France. It numbered seven colleges and five other educational houses when the Government closed them all, 31 July, 1903. The founder retired to Plancy where he died 2 February, 1908.

PÈRE BRISSON
Founder and First General of the Oblates of St. Francis de Sales

The mother-house was transferred to Rome, and the congregation divided into three provinces, Latin, German, and English. The first comprises France, Belgium, Italy, Greece, and South America; the second Austria, the German Empire and the southern half of its South-west African colony; the third, England, United States, and the north-western part of Cape Colony. Each province is administered by a provincial, appointed by the superior general and his council for ten years. He is assisted by three counsellors elected at each provincial chapter, which meets every ten years, at an interval of five years between the regular general chapters.

The Latin province has a scholasticate at Albano. In 1909 the church of Sts. Celsus and Julian in Rome was given to the Oblates. The novitiate for the Latin and German provinces is in Giove (Umbria). The Ecole Commerciale Ste Croix, in Naxos (Greece), has about fifty pupils, and the College St. Paul at Piræus (Athens) about two hundred. Four Fathers, stationed in Montevideo (Uruguay) are occupied with mission work. They have a flourishing Young Men's Association. In Brazil, three Fathers have the district of Don Pedrito do Sul (11,000 square miles with a Catholic population of 20,000). The headquarters of the Uruguay-Brazil mission is at Montevideo, Uruguay. One Oblate is stationed in Ecuador, where before the Revolution of 1897 the congregation had charge of the diocesan seminary of Riobamba, several colleges, and parishes. In 1909 a school for the congregation was opened at Dampicourt, Belgium. The German province has a preparatory school of about forty students in Schmieding (Upper Austria). They have charge of St. Anne's (French) church in Vienna, also the church of Our Lady of Dolours in Kaasgraben, Vienna, which is served by six Oblates. At Artstetten, the Archduke Francis Ferdinand gave them charge of the parish (1907) and assisted them to build a school. With the consent of the German Government, Cardinal Fischer gave them the church of Marienburg in 1910. Several Fathers are engaged in mission work. The English province founded its novitiate in Wilmington, Delaware, 23 September, 1903, and transferred it to Childs, Md. (1907). A scholasticate is attached. The Fathers in Wilmington conduct a high school for boys, and are chaplains of several religious communities, the county alms-house, the state insane hospital, the Ferris Industrial School for boys, and the county and state prison. In 1910 the parish of St. Francis de Sales, Salisbury, Md. (1209 square miles with a population of 70,000), was confided to the Oblates.

In Walmer (Kent, England) they have a boarding school for boys, the chaplaincy of the Visitation Convent and Academy of Roselands, and a small parish in Faversham. To this province belongs the Vicariate Apostolic of the Orange River. (For the Vicariate Apostolic of the Orange River and the Apostolic Prefecture of Great Namaqualand, see ORANGE RIVER, VICARIATE APOSTOLIC OF THE.)

HAMMON, *Vie de St. François de Sales* (1909), I, 428 seq., 487; II, 164, 275; *Œuvres de Ste de Chantal*, ed. PLON, IV, 593; VII, 602; *Catholic World*, LXXIV, 234–245; *Echo of the Oblates of St. Francis de Sales*, I, 6–8, 145–51.

J. J. ISENRING.

Oblates of Saint Frances of Rome. See FRANCES OF ROME, SAINT; OBLATI.

Oblati, Oblatæ, Oblates, is a word used to describe any persons, not professed monks or friars, who have been offered to God, or have dedicated themselves to His service, in holy religion. It has had various particular uses at different periods in the history of the Church. The children vowed and given by their parents to the monastic life, in houses under the Rule of St. Benedict, were commonly known by the name during the century and a half when the custom was in vogue, and the councils of the Church treated them as monks—that is, until the Council of Toledo (656) forbade their acceptance before the age of ten and granted them free permission to leave the monastery, if they wished, when they reached the age of puberty. At a later date the word "oblate" was used to describe such lay men or women as were pensioned off by royal and other patrons upon monasteries or benefices, where they lived as in an almshouse or hospital. In the eleventh century, it is on record that Abbot William of Hirschau or Hirsau, in the old Diocese of Spires, introduced lay brethren into the monastery. They were of two kinds: the *fratres barbati* or *conversi*, who took vows but were not claustral or enclosed monks, and the *oblati*, workmen or servants who voluntarily subjected themselves, whilst in the service of the monastery, to religious obedience and observance. Afterwards, the different status of the lay brother in the several orders of monks, and the ever-varying regulations concerning him introduced by the many reforms, destroyed the distinction between the *conversus* and the *oblatus*. The Cassinese Benedictines, for instance, at first carefully differentiated between *conversi*, *commissi*, and *oblati*; the nature of the vows and the forms of the habits were in each case specifically distinct. The *conversus*, the lay brother properly so called, made solemn vows like the choir monks, and wore the scapular; the *commissus* made simple vows, and was dressed like a monk, but without the scapular; the *oblatus* made a vow of obedience to the abbot, gave himself and his goods to the monastery, and wore a sober secular dress. But, in 1625, we find the *conversus* reduced below the status of the *commissus*, inasmuch as he was permitted only to make simple vows and that for a year at a time; he was in fact undistinguishable, except by his dress, from the *oblatus* of a former century. Then, in the later Middle Ages, *oblatus*, *confrater*, and *donatus* became interchangeable titles, given to any one who, for his generosity or special service to the monastery, received the privilege of lay membership, with a share in the prayers and good works of the brethren.

Canonically, only two distinctions were ever of any consequence: first, that between those who entered religion "per modum professionis" and "per modum simplicis conversionis", the former being *monachi* and the latter *oblati*; secondly, that between the oblate who was "mortuus mundo" (that is, who had given himself and his goods to religion without reservation), and the oblate who retained some control over his person and his possessions—the former only (*plene oblatus*) was accounted a *persona ecclesiastica*, with enjoyment of ecclesiastical privileges and immunity (Benedict XIV, "De Synodo Dioce.", VI).

CONGREGATIONS OF OBLATES. WOMEN.—(1) The first society or congregation of oblates was that founded in the fifteenth century by St. Frances of Rome, to which the name of Collatines has been given— apparently by mistake. St. Frances, wife of Lorenzo Ponzani, gathered around her (in 1425, according to Baillet) a number of widows and girls, who formed themselves into a society or confraternity. In 1433, as their own annals witness, she settled them in a house called Tor de' Specchi, at the foot of the Capitol, giving them the Rule of St. Benedict and some constitutions drawn up under her own direction, and putting them under the guidance of the Olivetan monks of S. Maria Nuova. In the same year she asked confirmation of her society from Eugenius IV, who commissioned Gaspare, Bishop of Cosenza, to report to him on the matter, and some days later granted the request, with permission to make a beginning of observance in the house near S. Maria Nuova, while she was seeking a more commodious habitation near S. Andrea in Vinci. They have never quitted their first establishment, but have greatly enlarged and beautified it. The object of the foundation was not unlike that of the Benedictine Canonesses in France—to furnish a place of pious seclusion for ladies of noble birth, where they would not be required to mix socially with any but those of their own class, might retain and inherit property, leave when it suited them, marry if they should wish, and, at the same time, would have the shelter of a convent enclosure, the protection of the habit of a nun, and the spiritual advantages of a life of religious observance. They made an oblation of themselves to God instead of binding themselves by the usual profession and vows. Hence the name of *oblates*. The observance has always been sufficiently strict and edifying, though it is permitted to each sister to have a maid waiting on her in the convent and a lackey to do her commissions outside. They have a year's probation, and make their oblation, in which they promise obedience to the mother president, upon the tomb of St. Frances of Rome. There are two grades amongst them: the "Most Excellent", who must be princesses by birth, and the "Most Illustrious", those of inferior nobility. Their first president was Agnes de Lellis, who resigned in favour of St. Frances when the latter became a widow. After her death, the Olivetan general, Blessed Geronimo di Mirabello, broke off the connexion between the oblates and the Olivetans. The convent and treasures of the sacristy have escaped appropriation by the Italian government, because the inmates are not, in the strict sense, nuns.

(2) Differing little from the Oblates of St. Frances in their ecclesiastical status, but unlike in every other respect are the *Donne Convertite della Maddalena*, under the Rule of St. Augustine, a congregation of fallen women. They had more than one house in Rome. Without any previous noviceship, they promise obedience and make oblation of themselves to the monastery of St. Mary Magdalene and St. Lucy. At Orvieto there are similar houses of oblate penitents under the Rule of Mount Carmel.

(3) *The Congregation of Philippines* (so named

after St. Philip Neri, their protector), founded by Rutilio Brandi, had the care of 100 poor girls, whom they brought up until they either married or embraced religion. These oblates began religious observance at S. Lucia della Chiavica, were transferred to Monte Citorio, and, when the convent there was pulled down by Innocent XII in 1693, returned to S. Lucia. They adopted the Augustinian Rule.

(4) *The Daughters of the Seven Dolours of the Blessed Virgin*, a development out of some confraternities of the same name, founded by St. Philip Benizzi, established a house at Rome in 1652. Their object was to take in infirm women who would not be received in other congregations. They followed the Augustinian Rule and promised stability, *conversio morum*, and obedience according to the constitutions.

CONGREGATIONS OF OBLATES. MEN.—(1) Earliest in origin of the societies or congregations of priests known as oblates is that of St. Charles Borromeo. It is an institute of regular clerks, founded by the saint in 1578 for the better administration of his diocese and to enable the more spiritual-minded of his clergy to lead a more detached and unworldly life. They live, whenever and wherever it is possible, in common. They make a simple vow of obedience to their bishop and, by doing so, bind themselves to exceptional service and declare their willingness to undertake labours for the salvation of souls which are not usually classed among the duties of a parish priest. From their constitution it is evident that their usefulness and development, and even existence, depend on the bishop and the interest he takes in them. At present, they are nowhere a large or important body, and perhaps do not meet with the encouragement they deserve.

(2) The greatest and best-known congregation of oblate priests, that of Mary Immaculate (O.M.I.), is dealt with in a special article. Connected with the institute and under its direction are the Oblate Sisters of the Holy Family.

(3) The Oblates of Mary, not to be confounded with those of Mary Immaculate or with the Marists, are a society of Piedmontese priests founded in 1845. They have houses at Turin, Novara, and Pinerolo, and send missionaries to Burma, Ava, and Pegu in the East Indies.

(4) By a decree of Pope Leo XIII, dated 17 June, 1898, the *Oblati seculares* O.S.B.—that is, those who have received the privilege of the scapular, and, for their friendliness and good offices, have been admitted as *confratres* of any Benedictine monastery or congregation—are now granted all the indulgences, graces, and privileges conceded to those of any other congregations, more particularly the Cassinese. The pope further states that, since Benedictine Oblates cannot, at the same time, be tertiaries of the Franciscan or any other order, it is "congruous" that they should have peculiar privileges. He, therefore, grants them the plenary indulgence on the day of clothing and the chief feasts of oblates etc.; twice a year the blessing in the encyclical letters of Pope Benedict XIV; the general absolution which tertiaries are able to receive on certain days during confession, with the plenary indulgence annexed to it (*adhibita formula pro Tertiariis præscripta*); the special plenary indulgence at the hour of death (observetur ritus et formula a constitutione P. P. Bened. XIV "Pia Mater"); an indulgence of seven years and seven quarantines every time they hear Mass *corde saltem contriti*—in a word, all and each of the privileges and favours granted to the lay tertiaries of St. Francis and of other orders.

HÉLYOT, *Hist. des ordres mon.;* MIGNE, *Dict. des ord. rel.;* GOSCHLER, *Dict. encycl. de la théol. cath.*, s. v. *Oblats;* CALMET, *Comment. in Reg. S. P. Benedicti;* HEIMBUCHER, *Die Orden u. Kongreg. der kath. Kirche* (Paderborn, 1907-8).

J. C. ALMOND.

Oblation. See HOST (CANONICO-LITURGICAL).

Obligation, a term derived from the Roman civil law, defined in the "Institutes" of Justinian as a "legal bond which by a legal necessity binds us to do something according to the laws of our State" (III, 13). It was a relation by which two persons were bound together (*obligati*) by a bond which the law recognized and enforced. Originally both parties were considered to be under the obligation to each other; subsequently the term was restricted to one of the parties, who was said to be under an obligation to do something in favour of another, and consequently that other had a correlative right to enforce the fulfilment of the obligation. The transference of the term from the sphere of law to that of ethics was easy and natural. In ethics it acquired a wider meaning and was used as a synonym for duty. It thus became the centre of some of the fundamental problems of ethics. The question of the source of moral obligation is perhaps the chief of these problems, and it is certainly not one of the easiest or least important. We all acknowledge that we are in general under an obligation not to commit murder, but when we ask for the ground of the obligation, we get almost as many different answers as there are systems of ethics.

The prevailing Catholic doctrine may be explained in the following terms. By moral obligation we understand some sort of necessity, imposed on the will, of doing what is good and avoiding what is evil. The necessity, of which there is question here, is not the physical coercion exercised on man by an external and stronger physical force. If two strong men seize me by the arms and drag me whither I would not go, I act under necessity or compulsion, but this is not the necessity of moral obligation. The will, which is the seat of moral obligation, is incapable of being physically coerced in that manner. It cannot be forced to will what it does not will. It is indeed possible to conceive that the will is necessitated to action by the antecedent conditions. The doctrine of those who deny free will is easily intelligible although we deny that it is true. The will is indeed necessitated by its own nature to tend towards the good in general; we cannot wish for what is evil unless it presents itself to us under the appearance of good. We also necessarily wish for happiness, and if we found ourselves in presence of some object which fully satisfied all our desires, and contained in itself nothing to repel us, we should be necessitated to love it. But in this life there is no such object which can fully satisfy all our desires and thus make us completely happy. Health, friends, fame, wealth, pleasures, singly or all combined, are incapable of filling the void in our hearts. Though in their measure desirable, all earthly goods are limited, and man's capacity for good is unlimited. All earthly goods are defective; we recognize their defects and the evil which the pursuit or possession of them entails. Considered with their defects, they repel as well as attract us; our wills therefore are not necessitated by them. In the presence of any earthly good our wills are free, at least after the first involuntary tendency to what attracts them; they are not necessitated to full and deliberate action.

The necessity, then, which constitutes the essence of moral obligation must be of the kind which an end that must be attained lays upon us of adopting the necessary means towards obtaining that end. If I am bound to cross the ocean and I am unable to fly, I must go on board ship. That is the only means at my disposal for attaining the end which I am bound to obtain. Moral obligation is a necessity of this kind. It is the necessity that I am under, of employing the necessary means towards the obtaining of an end which is also necessary. The necessity, then, which moral obligation lays upon us is the necessity, not of the determinism of nature, nor of the physical coercion of an external and stronger force, but it is of the same general character as the necessity that we are under of employing the necessary means in order to attain an end which must be obtained. There is, however, a special quality in the necessity of moral obligation which is peculiar to itself. We all appreciate this when we say that children are "obliged" to obey their parents, that they "ought" to obey them, that it is their "duty" to do so. We do not simply mean by those assertions that obedience to parents is a necessary means towards their own education, and for securing the peace, harmony, and affection, which should reign in the home. We do not simply mean that the happiness of parents and children depends upon such obedience. Although society at large is much concerned that children should be trained in respect and deference towards lawful authority, yet even the demands of society do not explain what we mean when we affirm that children are obliged to obey their parents. There is a peremptoriness, a sacredness, a universality about the obligation of duty, which can only be explained by calling to mind what man is, what is his origin, and what is his destiny. Man is a creature, made by God his Creator, with Whom he is destined to live for all eternity. That is the end of man's life and of his every action, imposed on him by his Maker, who in making man ordered every fibre of his nature to the end for which he was made. That doctrine explains the peremptoriness, the sacredness, the universality of moral obligation, made known to us, as it is, by the dictates of conscience. The doctrine has seldom been put in clearer or more beautiful language than by Cardinal Newman in his Letter to the Duke of Norfolk (p. 55):—

"The Supreme Being is of a certain character, which, expressed in human language, we call ethical. He has the attributes of justice, truth, wisdom, sanctity. benevolence and mercy, as eternal characteristics in His Nature, the very Law of His being, identical with Himself; and next, when He became Creator, He implanted this Law, which is Himself, in the intelligence of all His rational creatures. The divine Law then is the rule of ethical truth, the standard of right and wrong, a sovereign, irreversible, absolute authority in the presence of men and Angels. 'The eternal law,' says St. Augustine, 'is the Divine Reason or Will of God, commanding the observance, forbidding the disturbance, of the natural order of things.' 'The natural law,' says St. Thomas, 'is an impression of the Divine Light in us, a participation of the eternal law in the rational creature.' This law, as apprehended in the minds of individual men, is called 'conscience'; and though it may suffer refraction in passing into the intellectual medium of each, it is not thereby so affected as to lose its character of being the Divine Law, but still has, as such, the prerogative of commanding obedience. 'The Divine Law,' says Cardinal Gousset, 'is the supreme rule of actions; our thoughts, desires, words, acts, all that man is, is subject to the domain of the law of God; and this law is the rule of our conduct by means of our conscience. Hence it is never lawful to go against our conscience; as the Fourth Lateran Council says, 'Quidquid fit contra conscientiam, aedificat ad gehennam.' . . . The rule and measure of duty is not utility, nor expedience, nor the happiness of the greatest number, nor State convenience, nor fitness, order, and the *pulchrum*. Conscience is not a long-sighted selfishness, nor a desire to be consistent with oneself; but it is a messenger from Him who both in nature and in grace, speaks to us behind a veil, and teaches and rules us by His representatives. Conscience is the aboriginal Vicar of Christ, a prophet in its informations, a monarch in its peremptoriness, a priest in its blessings and anathemas, and even though the eternal priesthood throughout the Church could cease to be, in it the sacerdotal principle would remain and would have a sway."

An injustice would be done to the foregoing doctrine if it were classed with Mysticism, innate ideas, and Intuitionism. On the contrary, it is in the strictest sense rational. It asserts that we can know God, our Creator and Lord, that we can know ourselves and the bonds that bind us to God and to our fellow-men. We can know the actions which it is right and becoming that such a being as man should perform. We can and do know that God, Whom as our Creator and Lord we are bound to obey, commands us to do what is right and forbids us to do what is wrong. That is the eternal law, the Divine reason, or the Divine will, which is the source of all moral obligation. Moral precepts are the commands of God, but they are also the behests of right reason, inasmuch as they are merely the rules of right conduct by which a being such as man is should be guided.

An objection is sometimes urged against the method of analysing moral obligation which we have followed. It is said that moral obligation cannot be explained as a moral necessity of adopting the necessary means to the end of moral action, for it may be asked what is the moral obligation of the end itself. The Utilitarians, for example, maintained that the end of human action should be the greatest happiness of the greatest number. But a man may well ask, why he should be bound to direct his actions towards securing the greatest happiness of the greatest number. It is plain what answer should be given to such a question on the principles laid down above. God is our Creator and Lord, and as such and because He is good, He has every right to our obedience and service. We need not go beyond the preceptive will of God in our analysis; it is obligatory upon us from the very nature of God and our relation to Him. The rules of morality are then moral laws, imposing on us an obligation derived from the will of God, our Creator. That obligation is the moral necessity that we are under of conforming our actions to the demands of our rational nature and to the end for which we exist. If we do what is not conformable to our rational nature and to our end, we violate the moral law and do wrong. The effect on ourselves of such an action is twofold according to Catholic theology. A bad action does not merely subject us to a penalty assigned to wrongdoing, the sanction of the moral law. Besides this *reatus poenae*, there is also the *reatus culpae* in every moral transgression. The sinner has committed an offence against God, something which displeases Him, and which puts an end to the friendship which should exist between the Creator and creature. This state of enmity is accompanied, in the supernatural order to which we have been raised, by the privation of God's grace, and of the rights and privileges annexed to it. This is by far the most important of the effects produced on the soul by sin, the liability to punishment is merely a secondary consequence of it. This shows how far from the truth we should be if we attempted to explain moral obligations by mere liability to punishment which wrongdoing entails in this world or in the next.

The sense of moral obligation is an attribute of man's rational nature, and so we find it wherever we find man. However, in the early history of ethical speculation the notion is not prominent. Before philosophers began to inquire into the meaning and origin of moral obligation, they busied themselves about what is the good, and what the end of human activity. This was the question which occupied the philosophers of ancient Greece. What is the highest good for man? In what does man's happiness consist? Is it pleasure, or virtue practised for its own sake or for the gratification and self-esteem that it brings to the virtuous man? With the exception of the Stoics, the Greek philosophers did not much discuss the question of duty and moral obligation. They thought that, of course, when a man knew where his highest good lay, he could not but pursue it. Vice was really ignorance, and all that was necessary to subdue it was a training in philosophy. But the first principle of the Stoics was: "life according to nature". That was the "becoming", the "proper" thing, whether it brought pleasure or pain, which the Stoic philosopher indeed reckoned of no importance, and affected to despise. This philosophy appealed powerfully to the native sternness of the Roman character, and it was considerably influenced and developed by the ideas of Roman jurisprudence. Thus the treatise of Panætius, a Stoic of the second century before Christ, "On the Things That Are Becoming", was paraphrased by Cicero in the next century, and became his well-known treatise "On Duties". Cicero remarks, and the remark is significant, that Panætius had not given a definition of what duty is. According to Cicero it has reference to the end of good actions, and is expressed in precepts to which the conduct of life can be conformed in all its particulars (De officiis, I, iii). The working out of the doctrine concerning the law of nature is due to a large extent to the Roman lawyers, and Costa Rosetti, a recent Austrian writer on ethics, could find no words more suited to sum up the common Catholic teaching on the point than a passage from Cicero's "De republica" (III, xxii). We cannot do better than give a translation of the passage here, as it will show clearly how fully the doctrine of a law of nature imposing a moral obligation on man had been developed before it was adopted by the Fathers (Lactantius, "De div. inst.", VI, viii):

"Right reason is a true law, agreeing with nature, infused into all men, unchanging, eternal, which summons to duty by its commands, deters from wrong by forbidding it, and which nevertheless neither commands and forbids the good in vain, nor prevails with the bad by commanding and forbidding them. It is not permitted to abrogate this law, nor is it allowed to derogate from it in anything, nor is it possible to abrogate it wholly. We can neither be released from this law by popular vote, nor should another be sought for to gloss and interpret it. It is not one thing at Rome, another at Athens; one thing now, and another afterwards; but one, eternal, and immutable law will govern all men for ever, and there will be one, the common master and ruler of all, God. He it was that proposed and carried this law, and whoever does not yield obedience to it will revolt against himself, and by offering an affront to the nature of man he will thereby suffer the greatest penalties, even if he avoids other supposed sanctions."

The Stoic indeed understood this doctrine in a pantheistic sense. His god was the universal reason of the world, of which a particle was bestowed on man at his birth. It only needed the Christian doctrine of a personal God, the Creator and Lord of all things, Who in many ways manifests His law to man, but more especially through and in the voice of conscience, to turn it into the Catholic doctrine of moral obligation which has been analysed above. In the teaching of Christ, right conduct is summed up in the observance of the commandments. Those commandments constitute the law of God, which He came not to destroy but to fulfil. He required their observance under the most terrible sanctions. St. Paul, of course, only preached the doctrine of his Master. The legalism which he rejected was the ceremonial and the merely outward observance of the Pharisees, not the internal and the external observance of the moral law. Although the Gentile had not the moral law written on tablets of stone, yet he had it written on the fleshy tablets of his heart, and his conscience bore witness to it, as did that of the Jew (Rom., ii, 14). This is the doctrine still taught in the Catholic Church. It derives straight from Christ and His Apostles, though it is often expressed in the language of Stoicism, interpreted according to the exigences of Christian doctrine. Since the Reformation it has been the fashion with many to reject it as legalism in favour of what is called Christian liberty. Christian liberty, however, interpreted by private judgment, developed into various systems of so-called independent morality.

Thomas Hobbes (1588–1679) is justly regarded as one of the chief pioneers of modern thought. According to Hobbes, man in the state of nature seeks nothing but his own selfish pleasure, but such individualism naturally leads to an internecine war in which every man's hand is against his neighbour. In pure self-interest and for self-preservation men entered into a compact by which they agreed to surrender part of their natural freedom to an absolute ruler in order to preserve the rest. The State determines what is just and unjust, right and wrong; and the strong arm of the law provides the ultimate sanction for right conduct. The same fundamental principles form the groundwork of the empirical philosophy of Locke and a long train of followers down to the present day. Some of these followers indeed denied that all the motives that influence man's conduct are selfish; they insist on the existence of sympathetic and social feelings in men, but whether selfish or social, all are rooted in a sensist philosophy. The lineal descent of these views may be traced from Hobbes and Locke, through Hume, Paley, Bentham, the two Mills, and Bain, to H. Spencer and the Evolutionists of our own day. This sensist philosophy, of course, has had its opponents. Cudworth and the Cambridge Platonists strove to defend the essential and eternal distinction of good and evil by reviving Platonism. Butler insisted on the claims of conscience, while the Scotch school, Price, Reid, and Dugald Stewart, postulated a moral sense analogous to the sense of beauty, which infallibly indicates the right course of conduct. In Germany, Kant formulated his ethical system to counteract the scepticism of Hume. Moral obligation, according to him, is derived from the categorical imperative of the autonomous reason. Kant's philosophy, through Fichte and Schelling, gave birth to the pantheism of Hegel. A small but influential school of English Hegelians, represented by such men as T. H. Green, Bradley, Wallace, Bosanquet, and others, regard conscience as the voice of man's true self, and man's true self as ideally one with God. English philosophic thought is thus divided into the schools of Materialism and Pantheism, much as Epicureanism and Stoicism divided the ancient world. Pragmatism, a product of American thought, may without injustice be compared to the scepticism of the Athenian Academy. Each and all of these systems contain grave errors about the nature of man and about his position in the world, and so it is no wonder that they fail to account for moral obligation. (See DETERMINISM; DUALISM; DUTY; ETHICS; FATALISM; FREE WILL; HEDONISM; KANT, PHILOSOPHY OF; LAW; PANTHEISM; POSITIVISM.)

OBLIGATIONS, PROFESSIONAL.—The office of a judge, inasmuch as he is appointed by public authority to administer justice according to the laws, demands in the first place competent knowledge of the laws which are to be administered. Not less important in a judge is a lofty sense of justice and an upright character which cannot be deflected from the path of duty by either fear or favour. The judge, too, must employ at least ordinary diligence in the conduct of the cases that come before him, so that as far as possible a just sentence may be arrived at. He must not transgress the limits of his authority, and he must observe the rules of procedure laid down for his guidance. These obligations of a judge follow from the nature of his office, and he binds himself implicitly to fulfil them when he accepts that office. Judges also usually take an oath by which they expressly bind themselves to administer justice uprightly, without fear or favour. Selling justice for bribes is rightly regarded as a heinous offence in a judge, and besides being liable to severe punishment, it involves the obligation of making restitution, as there is no just title to retain the price of justice. Natural equity requires that all should be presumed to be innocent who have not been proved to be guilty of crime, and so a judge must give those who are accused the benefit of the doubt, when the crime imputed to them cannot be clearly proved. In civil actions he is bound to give sentence according to the merits of the case, and so in default of certainty of right, he must decide in favour of the party who has the better claim. What has been said of judges is applicable in due measure to magistrates, referees, arbitrators, and jurymen, all of whom are invested with some of the functions of a judge.

Advocates and lawyers are persons skilled in the law who for payment undertake the legal business of clients. They are obliged to have the knowledge and skill which are required for the due discharge of their office, and which they implicitly profess to have when they offer their services to the public. They must also employ at least ordinary diligence and care in the conduct of the business entrusted to them. They must keep faith with their clients and use only just means to obtain the objects which they desire. As they act for and in the name of their clients, they must not undertake a cause which is clearly unjust, otherwise they will be guilty of co-operating in injustice, and will be bound to make restitution for all the unjust damage which they cause to others. However, previous certainty of the justice of a cause is not necessary in order that a lawyer may rightly undertake it; it will be sufficient if the justice of the cause to be undertaken is at least probable, for then it may be hoped that the truth will be made clear in the course of the trial. As soon as an advocate is satisfied that his client has no case, he should inform him of the fact, and should not proceed further with the case. An advocate may always undertake the defence of a criminal, whether he be guilty or not, for even if his defence of a real culprit is successful, no great harm will usually be done by a guilty man escaping the punishment which he deserves. To justify a criminal accusation of another there must be morally certain evidence of his guilt, as otherwise there will be danger of doing serious and unjust harm to the reputation of one's neighbour.

From the Decree of the Holy Office, 19 Dec., 1860, in answer to the Bishop of Southwark, it is clear that in England an advocate may undertake a case where there is question of judicial separation between husband and wife. Even in an action for divorce in a civil court he may defend the action against the plaintiff. If the marriage has already been pronounced null and void by competent ecclesiastical authority, a Catholic advocate may impugn its validity in the civil courts. Moreover, for just reason, as, for example, to obtain a variation in the marriage settlement, or to prevent the necessity of having to maintain a bastard child, a Catholic lawyer may petition for a divorce in the civil court, not with the intention of enabling his client to marry again while his spouse is still living, but with a view to obtaining the civil effects of divorce in the civil tribunal. This opinion at any rate is defended as probable by many good theologians. The reason is because marriage is neither contracted nor dissolved before the civil authority; in the formalities prescribed for marriage by civil law there is only question of the civil authority taking cognizance of who are married, and of the civil effects which flow therefrom.

In canon law excommunicated and infamous persons, accomplices, and others are debarred from prosecuting criminals, but as a general rule any one who has full use of his senses may prosecute according to American and English law. Nobody should undertake a prosecution when greater evil than good would follow from it, or when there is not moral certainty as to the guilt of the accused. However, it may be done for the sake of the public good, and there may be an obligation to do it, as when one's office compels one to undertake the task, or the defence of the innocent or the public good requires it, or a precept of obedience commands it. Thus by ecclesiastical law heretics and priests guilty of solicitation in the sacred tribunal are to be denounced to the ordinary.

The defendant in a criminal trial is not himself subjected to examination, according to English law, unless he offers himself voluntarily to give evidence, and then he may be examined like a witness. In canon law the accused is examined, and the question arises whether he is bound to tell the truth against himself. He is bound to tell the truth if he is interrogated according to law; canon law prescribes that when there is *semiplena probatio* of the crime and this is made clear to the defendant he should be interrogated.

The defendant may in self-defence make known the secret crime of a witness against him, if it really conduces to his defence; but, of course, he may never impute false crimes to anybody. A criminal may not defend himself against lawful arrest, for that would be to resist lawful authority, but he is not compelled to deliver himself up to justice, and it is not a sin to escape from justice if he can do so without violence. The law prescribes that he shall be kept in durance, not that he shall voluntarily remain in custody. A criminal lawfully condemned to death is not obliged to save his life by escape or other means if he can do so; he should submit to the execution of the sentence passed upon him, and may do so meritoriously.

Charity or obedience may impose an obligation to give evidence in a court of justice. If serious harm can be prevented by offering one's self as a witness, there will as a rule be an obligation to do so, and obedience imposes the obligation when one is summoned by lawful authority. A witness is bound by his oath and by the obedience due to lawful authority to tell the truth in answer to the questions lawfully put to him. He is not bound to incriminate himself, nor, of course, may the seal of confession ever be broken.

The canon law laid it down that the testimony of two witnesses of unsuspected character was necessary and sufficient evidence of any fact alleged in a court of justice. The testimony of a solitary witness was not usually sufficient or admissible evidence of a crime, and in keeping with this the theologians decided that a solitary witness should not declare what he knew of a crime, inasmuch as he was not lawfully interrogated. English law, however, with most modern systems, admits the testimony of one witness, if credible, as sufficient evidence of a fact, and so as a rule there will be an obligation on such a one of answering according to his knowledge when questioned lawfully in a court of justice.

A doctor who holds himself out as ready to undertake the care of the sick must have competent knowledge of his profession and must exercise his office at least with ordinary care and diligence; otherwise he will sin against justice and charity in exposing himself to the risk of seriously injuring his neighbour. Unless he is bound by some special agreement he is not ordinarily obliged to undertake any particular case, for there are usually others who are willing and able to give the necessary assistance to the sick. Even in time of pestilence he will not commit sin if he leave the neighbourhood, unless he is bound to remain by some special contract.

He should not make exorbitant charges for his services, nor multiply visits uselessly and thus increase his fees, nor call in other doctors without necessity. On the other hand, even at serious inconvenience, he should visit a patient whose case he has undertaken when called as far as is reasonable, and he should be ready to call in other doctors for consultation when necessary or when he is asked to do so. He is sometimes bound by the general law of charity to give his assistance gratis to the poor.

He may not neglect safer remedies in order to try those which are less safe, but there is nothing to prevent him from prescribing what will probably do good if it is certain that it will not do harm. In a desperate case, with the consent of the sick person and of his relations, he may make use of what will probably do good though it may also probably do harm, provided that there is nothing better to be done in the circumstances. It is altogether wrong to make experiments with doubtful remedies or operations on living human beings; *fiat experimentum in corpore vili.*

When the patient is in danger of death, the doctor is bound out of charity to warn him or those who attend on him, that he may make all necessary preparations for death. (See ABORTION; ANÆSTHESIA; CRANIOTOMY; HYPNOTISM.)

Teachers hold the place of parents with regard to those committed to their charge for the purpose of instruction. They are bound in justice to exercise due care and diligence in the discharge of their office. They must have the knowledge and skill which that office demands.

CRONIN, *The Science of Ethics* (London, 1909); MEYER, *Institutiones Juris naturalis* (Freiburg, 1885); SIDGWICK, *The Methods of Ethics* (London, 1890); BALLERINI-PALMIERI, *Opus morale* (Prato, 1892), tr. iii, 14; viii, 527; HUNTER, *Roman Law* (London, 1885); SLATER, *A Manual of Moral Theology*, I (New York, 1908); see BISHOP; CELIBACY; CLERICS; PRIESTHOOD; RELIGIOUS; VOWS.

T. SLATER.

O'Braein, TIGHERNACH, Irish annalist and Abbot of Roscommon and Clonmacnoise, d. 1088. Little is known of his personal history except that he must have been born in the early part of the eleventh century and that he came of a Connaught family. His "Annals" (among the earliest of Irish annals) are of the greatest value to the historian of Ireland because of the author's attempt to synchronize Irish events with those of the rest of Europe from the earliest times to his own day. His learning is shown by his quotations, among others, from the works of the Venerable Bede, Josephus, Eusebius, and Orosius, not to speak of the Vulgate. But his sources for the Irish portions of the "Annals" are not now discoverable because of the loss of the Irish manuscripts from which he drew his information. Only fragments of Tighernach's "Annals" are now extant; these are in a vellum of the twelfth century and one of the fourteenth century in the Bodleian Library, Oxford, and in a fourteenth-century MS. in Trinity College Library (Dublin). These fragments were published by Dr. O'Conor in his "Rerum Hibernicarum Scriptores" (1825), but O'Conor's text is full of errors. They have recently been published and translated by Whitley Stokes in the "Revue Celtique" (vols. XVI, XVII, XVIII). Two pages in facsimile are given in Gilbert's "National Manuscripts of Ireland", part I.

O'CURRY, *Lectures on the Manuscript Materials of Ancient Irish History* (Dublin, 1873), 57.

JOSEPH DUNN.

Obregonians (or POOR INFIRMARIANS), a small congregation of men, who professed the Rule of the Third Order of St. Francis, founded by Bernardino Obregón (b. 5 May, 1540, at Las Huelgas near Burgos, Spain; d. 6 Aug., 1599). Of a noble family Obregón was an officer in the Spanish army, but retired and dedicated himself to the service of the sick in the hospitals of Madrid. Others became associated with him in hospital service and in 1567 by consent of the papal nuncio at Madrid the new congregation was founded. To the three ordinary vows was added that of free hospitality. The congregation did not found hospitals but served in those already existing. It spread in Spain and its dependencies, in Belgium and the Indies. Obregón went to Lisbon, 1592, and there founded an asylum for orphan boys; returning to Spain he assisted King Philip II in his last illness (1598). Paul V, 1609, allowed the Obregonians to

XI.—13

wear over the grey habit of the Third Order of St. Francis a black cross on the left side of the breast, to distinguish them from similar congregations. Since the French Revolution they have entirely disappeared.

DE HERRERA Y MALDONADO, *Vida y Virtudes del . . . Bernardino de Obregón* (Madrid, 1634); DE GUBERNATIS, *Orbis Seraphicus*, II (Lyons, 1685), 940; RATZINGER, *Gesch. der kirchlichen Armenpflege* (2 ed., Freiburg, 1884), 509.

LIVARIUS OLIGER.

Obreption (Lat. *ob* and *repere*, "to creep over"), a canonical term applied to a species of fraud by which an ecclesiastical rescript is obtained. Dispensations or graces are not granted unless there be some motive for requesting them, and the law of the Church requires that the true and just causes that lie behind the motive be stated in every prayer for such dispensation or grace. When the petition contains a statement about facts or circumstances that are suppositious or, at least, modified if they really exist, the resulting rescript is said to be vitiated by obreption. If, on the other hand, silence had been observed concerning something that essentially changed the state of the case, it is called subreption. Rescripts obtained by obreption or subreption are null and void when the motive cause of the rescript is affected by them. If it is only the impelling cause, and the substance of the petition is not affected, or if the false statement was made through ignorance, the rescript is not vitiated. As requests for rescripts must come through a person in ecclesiastical authority, it is his duty to inform himself of the truth or falsity of the causes alleged in the petitions, and in case they are granted, to see that the conditions of the rescript are fulfilled.

TAUNTON, *The Law of the Church* (London, 1906); LAURENTIUS, *Institutiones Juris Ecclesiastici* (Freiburg, 1903).

WILLIAM H. FANNING.

O'Brien, TERENCE ALBERT, b. at Limerick, 1600; d. there, 31 October, 1651. He joined the Dominicans, receiving the name Albert at Limerick, where his uncle, Maurice O'Brien, was then prior. In 1622 he studied at Toledo and after eight years returned to Limerick, to become twice prior there and once at Lorrha, and in 1643 provincial of his order in Ireland. His services to the Catholic Confederation were highly valued by the Supreme Council. At Rome he received the degree of Master in Theology, and on his return made a visitation of two houses of his province at Lisbon, where it was reported that Urban VIII was about to appoint him coadjutor to the Bishop of Emly. He was again named for the coadjutorship by the Supreme Council at the end of 1645, and recommended by the nuncio Rinuccini. Subsequently, at the petition of many bishops, Rinuccini wrote (17 March, 1646) that Burgat, Vicar-General of Emly, was a suitable person for the coadjutorship. In August he renewed his recommendation of Father Terence O'Brien, who was named coadjutor with the right of succession, in March, 1647, and eight months later was consecrated by Rinuccini. Throughout the ensuing troubles he adhered to the nuncio. He signed the declaration against Inchiquin's truce in 1648, and the declaration against Ormond in 1650. When Limerick was besieged in 1651, he urged a stubborn resistance and so embittered the Ormondists and the Parliamentarians, that in the capitulation he was excluded from quarter and protection. The day after the surrender, he with Major General Purcell and Father Wolf were discovered in the pest-house, brought before a court martial and ordered for execution, which took place on the following day.

MEEHAN, *Memoirs of the Irish Hierarchy in the Seventeenth Century* (6th ed., Dublin, about 1888); O'REILLY, *Memorials of those who suffered for the Catholic Faith* (London, 1868); MURPHY, *Our Martyrs* (Dublin, 1896); DE BURGO, *Hibernia Dominicana* (Cologne, 1762); WALSH in *Irish Eccl. Rec.*, Feb., 1894.

O'Bruadair, DAVID, an Irish poet, b. about 1625, most probably in the barony of Barrymore, Co. Cork, but according to many authorities in that of Connello, Co. Limerick; d. January, 1698. He was well educated in the Irish, Latin, and English languages. His historical poems show the influence of Geoffrey Keating, his favourite Irish author. He wrote elegies on the deaths of many historically prominent members of the leading Munster families, especially the Bourkes of Cahirmoyle, the Fitzgeralds of Claonghlais, and the Barrys of Co. Cork, who later befriended him in his poverty. All his poems, whether historical, social, or elegiac, are marked by a freshness rare in the seventeenth century and they furnish many interesting details about the life and manners of his time. Two of his epithalamia, a form of composition rare in Irish literature, have been preserved. They were written to celebrate the marriages of the sisters, Una and Eleanor Bourke of Cahirmoyle. His satires when directed against the Cromwellian Planters or the Duke of Ormonde and his flatterers are bitter, but lighter and more humorous when treating themes of local interest, as in the case of his witty proverbial "Guagan Gliog", or his mock-heroic defence of the smiths of Co. Limerick. His religious poems exhibit great beauty and depth of feeling, especially the poem on the Passion of Christ. Others like those on the schismatical movement of the Remonstrants (1666–70) and on the Oates Plot (1678–82) are polemical and contain details not found elsewhere.

His political poems treating the events of Irish history from the Cromwellian Plantation (1652) to the end of the War of the Revolution (1691) reveal his great political foresight and independent views. His "Suim Purgadora bhfear n-Eireann" summarizes the history of Ireland from 1641 to 1684, and a series of poems commemorates the exciting events of the reign of James II (1685–91). Being written from a national and Catholic standpoint, these poems, owing to the dearth of Irish documents relating to that period, are invaluable for the light which they throw upon the sentiments of the Irish nobles and people during that half-century of war, confiscation, and persecution. Despite his enthusiasm for the national cause, O'Bruadair is no mere eulogizer, and in "An Longbhriscadh" (The Shipwreck, 1691), he criticizes the army and its leaders severely. He warmly defended the conduct of Sarsfield in the negotiations preceding the close of the war (1691). His views upon this subject, when compared with those of Colonel O'Kelly in his "Macariæ Excidium", enable us to appreciate better the divergence of opinions in Irish military circles in regard to the acceptance of the terms offered. O'Bruadair was a master of the art of versification, and wrote with ease and grace in the most varied and complicated syllabic and assonantal metres. His style is vigorous, his language classical, and his vocabulary extensive; but a fondness for archaic expressions prevented most of his poems from being popular in the succeeding centuries. He is copious in illustration, careful to avoid repetition, and never sacrifices reason to rhythm. Though he was an expert scribe and an industrious copyist of ancient historical MSS., the only existing manuscript in his handwriting seems to be H. 1. 18 fol. 4 to 14 in the library of Trinity College, Dublin. It contains three of his latest poems (1693–4), some genealogical matter taken from "Leabhar Iris Ui Mhaoilchonaire" and the "Rental" of Baron Bourke of Castleconnell, Co. Limerick. Most of his poems are preserved in three early manuscripts: 23 M. 25–23 M. 34, by Eoghan O Caoimh (1702), and 23 L. 37, by Seaghan Stac (1706–9), both in the Library of the Royal Irish Academy, Dublin, and Add. 29614, by Seaghan na Raithineach (1725), in the British Museum. Others are to be found in various MSS. in the above-mentioned libraries and in those of Trinity College, Dublin, Maynooth, while a few are preserved in MSS. in private hands. A complete collection of his writings with translation, of which the first volume has appeared (1910), is in course of publication by the present writer for the Irish Texts Society, London.

O'GRADY, *Catalogue of Irish MSS. in British Museum*, 517, etc., contains many extracts from the poems; O'REILLY, *Irish Writers* in *Transactions of the Iberno-Celtic Society for 1820*, I (Dublin, 1820), i, p. cxcvi; HYDE, *Literary History of Ireland* (London, 1899), 592–4; HULL, *Text Book of Irish Literature*, II (Dublin and London, 1908), 188–97.

JOHN MACERLEAN.

Observants. See FRIARS MINOR, ORDER OF.

Obsession. See POSSESSION, DEMONIACAL.

O'Callaghan, EDMUND BAILEY, physician, publicist, and historian, b. at Mallow, Cork, 29 Feb., 1797; d. at New York, 29 May, 1880. His eldest brother Theodore held a commission in the English army; the others, Eugene and David, became priests and were distinguished for their learning. On completing his education in Ireland, Edmund went to Paris (1820) to study medicine. In 1830 he settled in Montreal and besides the practice of medicine, took an active part in the National Patriotic movement and in 1834 became editor of its organ the "Vindicator". Elected to the Provincial Parliament in 1836 he held a conspicuous position in debate for popular rights, took a leading part in the unsuccessful insurrection of 1837, was attainted of treason, fled to the United States, remained nearly a year the guest of Chancellor Walworth in Saratoga, and in 1838 resumed the practice of medicine in Albany, where he edited the "Northern Light", an industrial journal.

The anti-rent agitation of the time led him to study the land-rights of the Patroons. Attracted by the rich but neglected old Dutch records in the possession of the State, he mastered the Dutch language and in 1846 published the first volume of "History of New Netherland", the first real history of New York State. The result of its publication was the official commission of J. R. Brodhead by the New York State Legislature to search the archives of London, Paris, and The Hague, and to make copies of documents bearing on New York colonial history. These documents were published in eleven quarto volumes (1855–61) under the editorship of O'Callaghan and are a monument of care and ability. In 1848 he was made keeper of the historical MSS. of New York State, and in this capacity served for twenty-two years. He was the first to call public attention to the value of the Jesuit Relations, and read a paper before the New York Historical Society, giving description of their purpose and scope. James Lenox began to collect the scattered copies and the Lenox Library in New York, contains the only complete set or series of printed Jesuit Relations. The Thwaites edition in seventy-three volumes was based on the Lenox set of the French, Latin, and Italian texts. O'Callaghan dedicated to Lenox his "List of the editions of the Holy Scripture and parts thereof Printed in America Previous to 1860". An edition of this work with annotations by Lenox is in the Lenox Library, New York.

In 1870 O'Callaghan went to New York and assumed the task of editing its municipal records, but through difficulties about financial resources they were never published. Though highly esteemed for his medical learning, O'Callaghan's great claim on the gratitude of posterity is his historical work. The clearness of his style with accuracy of detail gave authority to his writings, which contain a mine of original information about New York colonial history.

Published works: "History of New Netherland" (New York, 1846–9); "Jesuit Relations" (New York, 1847); "Documentary History of New York" (Albany, 1849–51); "Documents relating to the Colonial History of New York" (Albany, 1855–61); "Remonstrance of New Netherland from original Dutch MSS." (Albany, 1856); "Commissary Wilson's Orderly Book" (Albany, 1857); "Catalogue of Historical papers and parchments in New York State Library" (Albany, 1849); "Orderly Book of Lieut. Gen. John Burgoyne" (Albany, 1860); "Wolley's two years' Journal in New York" (New York, 1860); "Names of persons for whom marriage licenses were issued previous to 1784" (Albany, 1860); "Journal of the Legislation Council of the State of New York, 1691–1775" (Albany, 1860); the companion work: "Minutes of the Execution Council of the State of New York", begun by the state historian Mr. Paltsits in 1910; "Origin of the Legislation Assemblies of the State of New York" (Albany, 1861); "A list of the Editions of Holy Scripture and the parts thereof printed in America previous to 1860" (Albany, 1861); "A Brief and True Narrative of hostile conduct of the barbarous natives towards the Dutch nation", tr. from original Dutch MSS. (Albany, 1863); "Calendar of the Land Papers" (Albany, 1864); "The Register of New Netherland 1626–74" (Albany, 1865); "Calendar of Dutch, English, and Revolutionary MSS. in the office of the Secretary of State" (Albany, 1865–68); "New York Colonial Tracts", 4 vols.: (1) "Journal of Sloop Mary"; (2) "Geo. Clarke's voyage to America"; (3) "Voyages of Slavers"; (4) "Isaac Bobin's letters 1718–30" (Albany, 1866–72); "Laws and Ordinances of New Netherland 1638–74" (Albany, 1868); Index to vols. 1, 2, 3 of transl. of Dutch MSS. (Albany, 1870); "Copie de Trois] Lettres écrites en années par le Rev. P. C. Lallemant" (Albany, 1870); "Relation de ce qui s'est passé en la Nouvelle France en l'année 1626" (Albany, 1870); "Lettre du Rev. P. Lallemant 22 Nov., 1629" (Albany, 1870); "Lettre du Père Charles Lallemant 1627" (Albany, 1870); "De Regione et moribus Canadensium, auctore Josepho Juvencio" (Albany, 1871); "Canadicæ Missionis Relatio 1611–13" (Albany, 1871); "Missio Canadensis, epistola ex Portu-regali in Acadia a R. P. Petro Biardo" (Albany, 1870); "Relatio Rerum Gestacum in Novo-Francica missione annis 1613–4" (Albany, 1871); "Records of New Amsterdam 1653–74", tr. by O'Callaghan were published by Berthold Fernon (New York, 1897).

O'CALLAGHAN, *A Collection of MSS. and Letters in the Library of Congress, Washington, D. C.*, 2 vols. of documents and 9 vols. of correspondence; SHEA in *Magazine of American History*, V, 77; WALSH in *Records of Amer. Cathol. Hist. Soc.* (March, 1905); *Bibl. Bull.*, no. 26 (Albany, 1901); *Report* of BRODHEAD as agent to procure and transcribe documents in Europe relative to Colonial History of New York; *New York State Senate Doc.*, no. 47.

JOHN T. DRISCOLL.

O'Carolan, TORLOGH (Irish, TOIRDHEALBHACH O CEARBHALLÁIN), usually spoken of as the "last of the Irish bards", b. in the County Meath, Ireland, in 1670; d. at Ballyfarnon, 1737. He early became blind from an attack of small-pox. Descended from an ancient family, he achieved renown as a harper. His advent marks the passing of the old Gaelic distinction between the bard and the harper. Celebrated as poet, composer, and harper, he composed probably over two hundred poems, many of them of a lively, Pindaric nature, and mostly addressed to his patrons or fair ladies belonging to the old county families, where he loved to visit and where he was always a welcome guest. His poems are full of curious turns and twists of metre to suit his airs, to which they are admirably wed, and very few are in regular stanzas. There are a few exceptions, as his celebrated "Ode to Whiskey", one of the finest Bacchanalian songs in any language, and his more famous but immeasurably inferior "Receipt for Drinking". His harp is preserved in the hall of the O'Conor Don at Clonalis, Roscommon. Hardiman printed twenty-four of his poems in his "Irish Minstrelsy", and the present writer has collected about twelve more, which seem to be all that survive of his literary output. Moore utilized many of his "planxties" for his "Melodies", as in "The Young May Moon", "O Banquet Not", "Oh, the Sight Entrancing". No complete and accurate collection of his airs has been made, though many of them were introduced into ballad operas. The following note in Irish in the writing of his friend and patron Charles O'Conor occurs in one of the Stowe MSS: "Saturday the XXV day of March, 1738, Toirrdealbhach O Cerbhalláin, the intellectual sage and prime musician of all Ireland died to-day, in the 68th year of his age. The mercy of God may his soul find, for he was a moral and a pious man."

WALKER, *Irish Bards* (Dublin, 1786); O'REILLY, *Irish Writers* (Dublin, 1820); GOLDSMITH, *Essays;* HARDIMAN, *Irish Minstrelsy*, I (London, 1831)—this volume contains a portrait of Carolan "from an original painting"; GRATTAN-FLOOD, *A History of Irish Music* (Dublin, 1905), xxi; O'CAROLAN, *Collection* (Dublin, 1747—Grattan-Flood says he has traced five other editions between the years 1780 and 1804); O'NEILL, *Irish Folk Music* (Chicago, 1910).

DOUGLAS HYDE.

Occasionalism (Latin *occasio*) is the metaphysical theory which maintains that finite things have no efficient causality of their own, but that whatever happens in the world is caused by God, creatures being merely the *occasions* of the Divine activity. The occasion is that which by its presence brings about the action of the efficient cause. This it can do as final cause by alluring the efficient cause to act, or as secondary efficient cause by impelling the primary cause to do what would otherwise be left undone. Occasionalism was foreshadowed in Greek philosophy in the doctrine of the Stoics who regarded God as pervading nature and determining the actions of all beings through the fundamental instinct of self-preservation. It appeared openly in the Arabian thought of the Middle Ages (cf. Stein, II, 193–245 *infra*); but its full development is found only in modern philosophy, as an outgrowth of the Cartesian doctrine of the relation between body and mind. According to Descartes the essence of the soul is thought, and the essence of the body extension. Body and soul therefore have nothing in common. How then do they interact? Descartes himself tried to solve this problem by attributing to the soul the power of directing the movements of the body. But this idea conflicted with the doctrine involved in his denial of any immediate interaction between body and mind. The first step toward a solution was taken by Johannes Clauberg (1625–65). According to him all the phenomena of the outside world are modes of motion and are caused by God. When therefore the mind seems to have acted upon the outside world, it is a pure delusion. The soul, however, can cause its own mental processes, which have nothing in common with matter and its modes of action. Matter, on the other hand, cannot act upon mind. The presence of certain changes in the bodily organism is the occasion whereupon the soul produces the corresponding ideas at this particular time rather than any other. To the soul Clauberg also attributes the power of influencing by means of the will the movements of the body. The Occasionalism of Clauberg is different from that of later members of the school; with him the soul is the cause which is occasioned to act—with the others it is God.

Louis de la Forge (Tractatus de mente humana, 1666) is regarded by some as the real father of Occasionalism. His starting-point was the problem of the relation between energy and matter. Following the Cartesian method, he argued that what cannot be clearly and distinctly conceived cannot be held as true. We can form no clear idea of the attraction exerted by one body on another at a distance nor of the energy that moves a body from one place to another. Such an energy must be something totally different from matter, which is absolutely inert; the union between matter and energy is inconceivable. Matter then, cannot be the cause of the physical phenomena; these must be produced by God, the first, universal, and total cause of all motion. In his theory of the union between body and soul, de la Forge approached the later Leibnizian doctrine of a pre-established harmony. God must have willed and brought about the union between body and soul, therefore He willed to do all that is necessary to perfect this union. The union between body and mind involves the appearance of thoughts in consciousness at the presence of bodily activities and the sequence of bodily movements to carry out the ideas of the mind. God willing the union between body and mind willed also to produce, as first and universal cause, the thoughts that should correspond to the organic movements of sensation, and the movements which follow upon the presence of some conscious processes. But there are other movements for which the soul itself is responsible as efficient cause, and these are the effects of the spontaneous activity of our free will.

The Occasionalism of Arnold Geulincx (1624–1669) is ethical rather than cosmological in its inception. The first tract of his "Ethics" (Land's ed. of the *Opera*, The Hague, 1891–93) is a study of what he termed the cardinal virtues. These are not prudence, temperance, justice, and fortitude. Virtue according to Geulincx is the love of God and of Reason (III, 16–17; 29). The cardinal virtues are the properties of virtue which immediately flow from its very essence and have nothing to do with anything external. These properties are diligence, obedience, justice, humility (III, 17). The division which Geulincx makes of humility is one of fundamental importance in his philosophy. It divides his view of the world into two parts—one, the understanding of our relation to the world, and the other, the concept of our relation to God. Humility consists in the knowledge of self and the forsaking of self. I find in myself nothing that is my own but *to know and to will*. I therefore must be conscious of all that I do, and that of which I am not conscious is not the product of my own causality. Hence the universal principle of causality—*quod nescis quo modo fiat, non facis*—if you do not know how a thing is done then you do not do it. Since then, the movements of my body take place without my knowing how the nervous impulse passes to the muscles and there causes them to contract I do not cause my own bodily actions. "I am therefore a mere spectator of this machine. In it I form naught and renew naught, I neither make anything here nor destroy it. Everything is the work of someone else" (III, 33). This one is the Deity who sees and knows all things. The second part of Geulincx's philosophy is connected with Occasionalism as the effect with the cause. Its guiding principle is: Where you can do nothing there also you should desire nothing (III, 222). This leads to a mysticism and asceticism which however must not be taken too seriously for it is tempered by the obligation of caring for the body and propagating the species.

Nicolas Malebranche (q. v.) developed Occasionalism to its uttermost limit, approaching so near to Pantheism that he himself remarked that the difference between himself and Spinoza was that he taught that the universe was in God and that Spinoza said that God was in the universe. Starting out with the Cartesian doctrine, that the essence of the soul is thought and that of matter is extension, he sought to prove that creatures have no causality of their own. Experience seems to tell us that one body acts upon another, but all that we know is that the movement of one body follows upon that of another. We have no experience of one body causing the movement of another. Therefore, says Malebranche, one body cannot act upon another. By a similar argument he attempts to prove that body cannot act upon mind. Since experience can tell us only that a sensation follows upon the stimulus, therefore the stimulus is not the cause of the sensation. He uses the argument of Geulincx to prove that mind cannot act upon body. Not only is there no interaction between body and mind, and between one body and another, but there is no causality within the mind itself: Our sensations, for example, are not caused by bodies, and are independent of ourselves. Therefore they must be produced by some higher being. Our ideas cannot be created by the mind. Neither can they be copied from a present object, for one would have first to perceive the object in order to copy it, after which the production of an idea would be superfluous. Our ideas cannot be all possessed as complete products from the beginning, because it is a fact that the mind goes through a process of gradual development. Nor can the mind possess a faculty that produces by a sufficient causality its own ideas, because it would have to produce also the ideas of extended bodies and extension is excluded from the essence of the mind and therefore from the scope of its causal efficiency. If then there is no way of accounting for ideas and sensations either by the efficiency of the mind itself or by that of the outside world they must be produced by God, the infinite, omnipresent, universal Cause. God knows all things because He produced all things. Therefore the ideas of all things are in God, and on account of His most intimate union with our souls the spirit can see what is in God.

Among the Occasionalists is also mentioned R. H. Lotze (1817–81). His Occasionalism is really only a statement that we are ignorant of any interaction between body and mind, or between one material thing and another. He is not an Occasionalist in the metaphysical sense of the word. In estimating the value of the Occasionalistic position we must realize that it sprang from a twofold problem, the interaction of body and mind and the relation of body, mind, and world to God, the first cause of all. The success of the Occasionalist answer to the first difficulty was dependent upon the fate of the Cartesian philosophy. If man is composed of two absolutely distinct substances that have nothing in common, then the conclusion of the Occasionalists is logically necessary and there is no interaction between body and mind. What appears to be such must be due to the efficient causality of some external being. This difficulty was not felt so keenly in Scholastic philosophy because of the doctrine of matter and form, which explains the relation of body and soul as that of two incomplete but complementary substances. Very soon, too, it began to lose its hold upon modern thought. For Cartesianism led, on the one hand, to a Monistic Spiritualism and, on the other, to Materialism. In either case the very foundations of Occasionalism were undermined. In its attempt to solve the second difficulty, Occasionalism did not meet with any particular success. From its doctrine of the relation between body and soul it argued to what must be the relation between God and the creature in general. The superstructure could not stand without the foundation.

St. Thomas, *Summa*, I, Q. cv, a. 5; Kayserling, *Die Idee der Kausalität in den Lehren der Occasionalisten* (Heidelberg, 1896); Müller, *Johannes Clauberg und seine Stellung im Cartesianismus mit besonderer Berücksichtigung seines Verhältnisses zu der occasionalistischen Theorie* (Jena, 1891); Pfleiderer, *Arnold Geulincx als Hauptvertreter der okkasionalistischen Metaphysik und Ethik* (Tübingen, 1882); Idem, *Leibnitz und Geulincx* (Tübingen, 1884); Samtleben, *Geulincx ein Vorgänger Spinozas* (Halle, 1885); Seyfarth, *Louis de la Forge und seine Stellung im Occasionalismus* (Jena, 1887); Stein, *Zur Genesis des Occasionalismus* in *Archiv für Gesch. der Phil.*, I (1888), 53–61; Idem, *Antike und mittelalterliche Vorläufer des Occasionalismus* in *Arch. f. Gesch. d. Phil.*, II (1889, 193–245); Tuch, *Lotzes Stellung zum Occasionalismus* (Hamburg, 1897); see also bibliography under Malebranche.

Thomas V. Moore.

Occasions of Sin are external circumstances whether of things or persons which either because of their special nature or because of the frailty common to humanity or peculiar to some individual, incite or entice one to sin. It is important to remember that there is a wide difference between the cause and the occasion of sin. The cause of sin in the last analysis is the perverse human will and is intrinsic to the human composite. The occasion is something extrinsic and, given the freedom of the will, cannot, properly speaking, stand in causal relation to the act or vicious habit which we call sin. There can be no doubt that in general the same obligation which binds us to refrain from sin requires us to shun its occasion. *Qui tenetur ad finem, tenetur ad media* (he who is bound to reach a certain end is bound to employ the means to attain it). Theologians distinguish between the proximate and the remote occasion. They are not altogether at one as to the precise value to be attributed to the terms. De Lugo defines proximate occasion (De pœnit., disp. 14, n. 149) as one in which men of like calibre for the most part fall into mortal sin, or one in which experience points to the same result from the special weakness of a particular person. The remote occasion lacks these elements. All theologians are agreed that there is no obligation to avoid the remote occasions of sin both because this would, practically speaking, be impossible and because they do not involve serious danger of sin. As to the proximate occasion, it may be of the sort that is described as necessary, that is, such as a person cannot abandon or get rid of. Whether this impossibility be physical or moral does not matter for the determination of the principles hereinafter to be laid down. Or it may be voluntary, that is within the competency of one to remove. Moralists distinguish between a proximate occasion which is continuous and one which, whilst it is unquestionably proximate, yet confronts a person only at intervals. It is certain that one who is in the presence of a proximate occasion at once voluntary and continuous is bound to remove it. A refusal on the part of a penitent to do so would make it imperative for the confessor to deny absolution. It is not always necessary for the confessor to await the actual performance of this duty before giving absolution; he may be content with a sincere promise, which is the minimum to be required. Theologians agree that one is not obliged to shun the proximate but necessary occasions. *Nemo tenetur ad impossibile* (no one is bound to do what is impossible). There is no question here of freely casting oneself into the danger of sin. The assumption is that stress of unavoidable circumstances has imposed this unhappy situation. All that can then be required is the employment of such means as will make the peril of sin remote. The difficulty is to determine when a proximate occasion is to be regarded as not physically (that is plain enough) but morally necessary. Much has been written by theologians in the attempt to find a rule for the measurement of this moral necessity and a formula for its expression, but not successfully. It seems to be quite clear that a proximate occasion may be deemed necessary when it cannot be given up without grave scandal or loss of good name or without notable temporal or spiritual damage.

SLATER, *Moral Theology* (New York, 1908); BALLERINI, *Opus Theologicum Morale* (Prato, 1900); GÉNICOT, *Theologiæ Moralis Institutiones* (Louvain, 1898).

JOSEPH F. DELANY.

Occleve (OR HOCCLEVE), THOMAS; little is known of his life beyond what is mentioned in his poems. He was b. about 1368; d. in 1450. The place of his birth and education is unknown. When about nineteen he became a clerk in the Privy-Seal Office, a position which he held for at least twenty-four years. It is recorded in the Patent Rolls (1399) that he received a pension of £10 a year. In his poem "La Male Règle", written in 1406, he confesses to having lived a life of pleasure and even of dissipation, but his marriage in 1411 seems to have caused a change in his career, and his poem "De Regimine Principum", written soon afterwards, bears witness to his reform. In 1424 he was granted a pension of £20 a year for life. His name and reputation have come down to us linked with those of Lydgate; the two poets were followers and enthusiastic admirers of Chaucer. It is most probable that Occleve knew Chaucer personally, as he has left three passages of verse about him, and, in the MS. of the "De Regimine", a portrait of Chaucer (the only one we possess), which he says he had painted "to put other men in remembrance of his person". He was a true Chaucerian as far as love and admiration could make him, but he was unable to imitate worthily his master's skill in poetry. Occleve has left us a body of verse which has its own interest, but none of which, as poetry, can be placed much above mediocrity. Nevertheless, there are many things which give pleasure. There is his devoted love to Our Lady, which causes some of the poems he wrote in her honour (especially "The Moder of God") to be among his best efforts. There is his admiration of Chaucer, already spoken of, and there is also sound morality, and a good deal of "the social sense" in the matter of his poems. Though he had no humour, he could tell a story well, and in several poems he enlists our sympathy by the frank recognition of his weakness both as man and poet.

His work consists of: a long poem, "De Regimine Principum" (the Government of Princes), addressed to Prince Henry, afterwards Henry V; it is written in the seven-line stanza and contains much varied matter, religious, moral, social, and political; two verse stories from the "Gesta Romanorum"; three other poems of some length, largely autobiographical, "La Male Règle", "A Complaint", and "A Dialogue"; "Ars sciendi mori" (the Art of learning to die) a specimen of his work at its best, most of it in the seven-line stanza, but with an ending in prose; many other poems, chiefly Ballades, and mostly short, with the exception of "Cupid's Letter" and the interesting expostulation with Sir John Oldcastle concerning his heresy, "O Oldcastle, alas what ailed thee To slip into the snare of heresie?". All the above poems are contained in the Early English Text Society's edition of Occleve's works (London, 1892–7).

FURNIVALL in *Dict. Nat. Biog.*, IX (reissued, London, 1908); IDEM in *Preface to E. Eng. Text Socy. Edition of Works* (Lond., 1892–7); SAINTSBURY in *Camb. Hist. of Eng. Literature*, II (Cambridge, 1908).

K. M. WARREN.

Occult Art, Occultism.—Under this general term are included various practices to which special articles of the Encyclopedia are devoted: ANIMISM; ASTROLOGY; DIVINATION; FETISHISM. The present article deals with the form of Occultism known as "Magic". The English word *magic* is derived through the Latin, Greek, Persian, Assyrian from the Sumerian or Turanian word *imga* or *emga* ("deep", "profound"), a designation for the Proto-Chaldean priests or wizards. *Magi* became a standard term for the later Zoroastrian, or Persian, priesthood through whom Eastern occult arts were made known to the Greeks; hence μάγος (as also the kindred words μαγικός, μαγεία), a magician or a person endowed with secret knowledge and power like a Persian *magus*. In a restricted sense magic is understood to be an interference with the usual course of physical nature by apparently inadequate means (recitation of formularies, gestures, mixing of incongruous elements, and other mysterious actions), the knowledge of which is obtained through secret communication with the force underlying the universe (God, the Devil, the soul of the world, etc.); it is the attempt to work miracles not by the power of God, gratuitously communicated to man, but by the use of hidden forces beyond man's control. Its advocates, despairing to move the Deity by supplication, seek the desired result by evoking powers ordinarily reserved to the Deity. It is a corruption of religion, not a preliminary stage of it as Rationalists maintain, and it appears as an accompaniment of decadent rather than of rising civilization. There is nothing to show that in Babylon, Greece, and Rome the use of magic decreased as these nations progressed; on the contrary, it increased as they declined. It is not true that "religion is the despair of magic"; in reality, magic is but a disease of religion.

The disease has been widespread; but if one land may be designated as the home of magic it is Chaldea, or Southern Babylonia. The earliest written records of magic are found in the cuneiform incantation inscriptions which Assyrian scribes in 800 B. C. copied from Babylonian originals. Although the earliest religious tablets refer to divination and in the latest Chaldean period astrology proper absorbed the energy of the Babylonian hierarchy, medicinal magic and nature magic were largely practised. The Baru-priest as the diviner seems to have held the foremost rank, but hardly inferior was the Ashipu-priest, the priest of incantations, who recited the magical formularies of the "Shurpu", "Maklu", and "Utukku". "Shurpu" (burning) was a spell to remove a curse due to legal uncleanness; "Maklu" (consuming) was a counter-spell against wizards and witches; "Utukki limmuti" (evil spirits) was a series of sixteen formulæ against ghosts and demons. The "Asaski marsuti" was a series of twelve formulæ against fevers and sickness. In this case the evil influence was first transferred to a wax figure representing the patient or an animal carcass, and the formulæ were recited over the substitute. Ti'i tablets, nine in number, give recipes against headache. The "Labartu" incantations repeated over little figures were supposed to drive away the ogres and witches from children. All these formulæ pronounced over the figures were accompanied by an elaborate ritual, e. g., "A table thou shalt place behind the censer which is before the Sun-God (Statue of Shamash), thou shalt place thereon 4 jugs of sesame wine, thou shalt set thereon 3×12 loaves of wheat, thou shalt add a mixture of honey and butter and sprinkle with salt: a table thou shalt place behind the censer which is before the Storm-God (Statue of Adad) and behind the censer which is before Merodach".

The magicians mentioned above were authorized and practised "white", or benevolent, magic; the "Kashshapi", or unauthorized practitioners, employed "black" magic against mankind. That the latter had preternatural powers to do harm no one doubted; hence the severe punishment meted out to them. The Code of Hammurabi (c. 2000 B. C.) appointed the ordeal by water for one who was accused of being a sorcerer and for his accuser. If the accused was drowned, his property went to the accuser; if he was saved, the accuser was put to death and his property went to the accused. This of course took place only if the accusation could not be satisfactorily proven otherwise. The principal god invoked in Chaldean Magic were Ea, source of all wisdom, and Marduk (Merodach) his son, who had inherited his father's knowledge. A curiously naïve scene was supposed to be enacted before the application of a medicinal spell: Marduk went to Ea's house and said: "Father, headache from the underworld hath gone forth. The patient does not know the reason; whereby may he be relieved?" Ea answered: "O Marduk, my son, what can I add to thy knowledge? What I know thou knowest also. Go, my son Marduk"; and then follows the prescription. This tale was regularly repeated before use of the recipe.

Without suggesting the dependence of one national system of magic upon another, the similarity of some ideas and practices in the magic of all peoples must be noted. All rely on the power of words, the utterance of a hidden name, or the mere existence of the name on an amulet or stone. Magic was supposed to be the triumph of intellect over matter, the word being the key to the mysteries of the physical world: utter the name of a malignant influence and its power is undone; utter the name of a benevolent deity and force goes out to destroy the adversary. The repeated naming of Gibel-Nusku and his attributes destroyed the evil influence in the wax figure representing the person concerned. The force of the Gnostic IAΩ was notorious. In Egyptian magic a mere agglomeration of vowels or of meaningless syllables was supposed to work good or evil. Their barbarous sounds were the object of ridicule to the man of common sense. In many cases they were of Jewish, or Babylonian, or Aramaic origin and because unintelligible to Egyptians, the words were generally corrupted beyond recognition. Thus on a demotic papyrus is found the prescription: "in time of storm and danger of shipwreck cry Anuk Adonai (אנוא־דני) and the disaster will be averted"; on a Greek papyrus the name of the Assyrian Ereskihal is found as Ερεσγιχαλ. So potent is a name that if an inscribed amulet be washed and the water drunk, or the charm written on papyrus be soaked in water and this taken, or if the word be written on hard-boiled eggs without shell and these eaten, preternatural powers come into play. Another prevalent idea in magic is that of substitution: the person or thing to be affected by the spell is replaced by his image, or, like the "ushabtiu" figures in Egyptian tombs, images replace the protective powers invoked, or lastly some part (hair, nail-parings, garments, etc.) take the place of the whole person. The almost universal "magic circle" is only a mimic wall against the wicked spirits outside and goes back to Chaldean magic under the name of *usurtu*, made with a sprinkling of lime and flour. If the medical wizard or the Indian sorcerer surrounds himself or others with a rampart of little stones, this is again but the make-believe of a wall.

After Babylonia Egypt was foremost in magic; the medieval practice of alchemy shows by its name its Egyptian origin. Coptic exorcisms against all sorts of diseases abound amongst the papyri pertaining to magic, and magic claims a great part of ancient Egyptian literature. Unlike Babylonian magic, however, it seems to have retained to the last its medicinal and preventive character; it rarely indulged in astrology or prediction. Egyptian legend spoke of a magician Teta who worked miracles before Khufu (Cheops) (c. 3800 B. C.), and Greek tradition tells of Nectanebus, last native King of Egypt (358 B. C.), as the greatest of magicians.

That the Jews were prone to magic is evidenced by the strict laws against it and the warnings of the Prophets (Exod., xxii, 18; Deut., xviii, 10; Is., iii, 18, 20; lvii, 3; Mich., v, 11; cf. IV Kings, xxi, 6). Nevertheless, Jewish magic flourished, especially just before the birth of Christ, as appears from the Book of Enoch, the Testament of the Twelve Patriarchs, and the Testament of Solomon. Origen testifies that in his day to adjure demons was looked upon as specifically "Jewish", that these adjurations had to be made in Hebrew and from Solomon's books (In Math., xxvi, 63, P. G., XIII, 1757). The frequency of Jewish magic is also corroborated by Talmudic lore.

The Aryan races of Asia seem somewhat less addicted to magic than the Semitic or Turanian races. The Medes and the Persians, in the earlier and purer period of their Avesta religion, or Zoroastrianism, seem to have a horror of magic. When the Persians, after their conquest of the Chaldean Empire, finally absorbed Chaldean characteristics, the *magi* had become more or less scientific astronomers rather than sorcerers. The Indians, likewise, to judge from the Rigveda, were originally free from this superstition. In the Yajurveda, however, their liturgical functions are practically magic performances; and the Atharvaveda contains little else than magical recitations against every ill and for every happening. The Sutras, finally, especially those of the Grihya and Sautra ritual, show how the higher aspects of religion had been overgrown by magical ceremonies. Against this degeneration the Vedanta makes a vigorous stand and attempts to bring the Indian mind back to earlier simplicity and purity. Buddhism, which at first disregarded magic, fell a prey to the universal contagion, especially in China and Tibet.

The Aryans of Europe, Greeks, Romans, Teutons, Celts, were never so deeply infected as the Asiatics. The Romans were too self-reliant and practical to be terrified by magic. Their practice of divination and auguries seems to have been borrowed from the Etruscans and the Marsi; the latter were considered experts in magic even during the empire (Verg., "Æn.", VII, 750, sqq.; Pliny, VII, ii; XXI, xiii). The Dii Aurunci, to avert calamities, used magical power, but they were not native Roman deities. The Romans were conscious of their common sense in these matters and felt themselves superior to the Greeks. In the first century of our era Oriental magic invaded the Roman Empire. Pliny in his "Natural History" (77 A. D.) in the opening chapters of Bk. XXX, gives the most important extant discussion on magic by any ancient writer, only to brand all magic as imposture. None the less his book is a storehouse of magic recipes, e. g.: "Wear as an amulet the carcass of a frog minus the claws and wrapped in a piece of russet-coloured cloth and it will cure fever" (Bk. XXXII, xxxviii). Such advice argues at least a belief in medicinal magic. But among the Romans it may be said that magic was condemned in every age by many of the best spirits of their day: Tacitus, Favorinus, Sextus Empiricus, and Cicero who even demurred against divination. Officially by many laws of the empire against "malefici" and "mathematici" magic was forbidden under Augustus, Tiberius, Claudius, and even Caracalla; unofficially, however, even the emperors sometimes dabbled in magic. Nero is said to have studied it; but failing to work miracles, he abandoned it in disgust. Soon after the magicians found an imperial supporter in Otho, and tolerance under Vespasian, Hadrian, and M. Aurelius, and even financial aid under Alexander Severus.

The Greeks regarded Thessaly and Thrace as the countries especially addicted to magic. The goddess Hecate, who was thought to preside over magical functions, was originally a foreign deity and was probably introduced into Greek mythology by Hesiod. She is not mentioned in the Iliad or Odyssey though magic was rife in Homeric times. The great mythical sorceress of the Odyssey is Circe, famous for the well-known trick of changing men into beasts (Od., X-XII). In later times the foremost magician was Medea, priestess of Hecate; but the gruesome tales told of her express the Greek horror for, as well as belief in, black magic. Curse formulæ or magic spells against the lives of one's enemies seem to have found no mightier name than Hermes Chthonios. As earth-god he was a manifestation of the world-soul and controlled nature's powers. In Egypt he was identified with Thoth, the god of hidden wisdom, became the keeper of magic secrets and gave his name to Trismegistic literature. Greece, moreover, welcomed and honoured foreign magicians. Apuleius, by education an Athenian, in his "Golden Ass" (c. 150 A. D.), satirized the frauds of contemporary wonder-workers but praised the genuine *magi* from Persia. When accused of magic, he defended himself in his "Apology" which shows clearly the public attitude towards magic in his day. He quoted Plato and Aristotle who gave credence to true magic. St. Hippolytus of Rome (A Refutation of All Heresies, Bk. IV) gives a sketch of the wizardry practised in the Greek-speaking world.

Teutons and Celts also had their magic, though less is known of it. The magical element in the First Edda and in the Beowulf is simple and closely connected with nature phenomena. Woden (Wodan) who invented the runes, was the god for healing and good charms, Loki was a malignant spirit who harassed mankind and with the witch Thöck caused the death of Baldur (Balder). The magic of the mistletoe seems to be an heirloom from earliest Teutonic times. The magic of the Celts seems to have been in the hands of the druids, who, though perhaps mainly diviners, appear also as magicians in Celtic heroic literature. As they wrote nothing, little is known of their magical lore. For modern magic amongst uncivilized races consult especially Skeat's "Malay Magic" (London, 1900).

Magic as a practice finds no place in Christianity, though the belief in the reality of magical powers has been held by Christians and individual Christians have been given to the practice. Two main reasons account for the belief: first, ignorance of physical laws. When the boundary between the physically possible and impossible was uncertain, some individuals were supposed to have gained almost limitless control over nature. Their souls were attuned to the symphony of the universe; they knew the mystery of numbers and in consequence their powers exceeded the common understanding. This, however, was natural magic. But, secondly, belief in the frequency of diabolical interference with the forces of nature led easily to belief in real magic. The early Christians were emphatically warned against the practice of it in the "Didache" (v, 1) and the letter of Barnabas (xx, 1). In fact it was condemned as a heinous crime. The danger, however, came not only from the pagan world but also from the pseudo-Christian Gnostics. Although Simon Magus and Elymas, that "child of the devil", (Acts, xiii, 6 sqq.) served as deterrent examples for all Christians, it took centuries to eradicate the propensity to magic. St. Gregory the Great, St. Augustine, St. Chrysostom, and St. Ephraem inveighed against it. A more rational view of religion and nature had hardly gained ground, when the Germanic nations entered the Church and brought with them the inclination for magic inherited from centuries of paganism. No wonder that during the Middle Ages wizardry was secretly practised in many places notwithstanding innumerable decrees of the Church on the subject. Belief in the frequency of magic finally led to stringent measures taken against witchcraft (q. v.).

Catholic theology defines magic as the art of performing actions beyond the power of man with the aid of powers other than the Divine, and condemns it and any attempt at it as a grievous sin against the virtue of religion, because all magical performances, if undertaken seriously, are based on the expectation of interference by demons or lost souls. Even if undertaken out of curiosity the performance of a magical ceremony is sinful as it either proves a lack of faith or is a vain superstition. The Catholic Church admits in principle the possibility of interference in the course of nature by spirits other than God, whether good or evil, but never without God's permission. As to the frequency of such interference especially by malignant agencies at the request of man, she observes the utmost reserve.

R. CAMPBELL THOMPSON, *Semitic Magic* (London, 1908); THORNDYKE, *The Place of Magic in the intellectual history of Europe* in *Stud. Hist. Econom. of Columbia University*, XXIV (New York, 1905); BUDGE, *Egyptian Magic* (London, 1899); SCHERMAN, *Griechische Zauberpapyri* (Leipzig, 1909); KIESEWETTER, *Gesch. des neuren Okkultismus* (Leipzig, 1891); WIEDEMANN, *Magic und Zauberei im alten Egypten* (Leipzig, 1905); LANG, *Magic and Religion* (London, 1910); HABERT, *La religion des peuples non civilisés* (Paris, 1907); IDEM, *La Magie* (Paris, 1908); ABT, *Die Apologie des Apulejus u. d. antike Zauberei* (1908); WEINEL, *Die Wirkung des Geistes . . . bis auf Irenäus* (Freiburg, 1899); DU PREL, *Magie als Naturwissenschaft* (2 vols., 1899); MATHERS, *The Book of Sacred Magic* (1458), reprinted (London, 1898); FRASER, *The Golden Bough: a Study in Magic and Religion* (3 vols., London, 1900). This last-mentioned work is indeed a storehouse of curious information, but is to be used with the utmost caution, as it is vitiated by the author's prejudices. Readers are warned against the following works, which are either books on conjuring or productions of the RATIONALIST PRESS AGENCY: CONYBEARE, *Myth, Magic and Morals*; EVANS, *The Old and New Magic*; A. THOMPSON, *Magic and Mystery*.

J. P. ARENDZEN.

Occurrence (in Liturgy).—I. Definition.—Occurrence is the coinciding or occurring of two liturgical offices on one and the same day; concurrence is the succession of two offices, so that the second vespers of one occur at the same time as the first vespers of the other. The chief causes of occurrence are: (1) the variableness of the feast and cycle of Easter, while the other feasts are fixed; (2) the annual change of the Dominical Letter, whereby Sunday falls successively on different dates of the same month (see Calendar; Dominical Letter). Occurrence may be *accidental* or *perpetual*. (1) The calendar gives as a fixed feast for 28 May the feast of St. Augustine of Canterbury; on the other hand on 28 May, 1891, the table of movable feasts marked that day as the feast of Corpus Christi; thus on 28 May, 1891, these two offices fell on the same day—that is there was an occurrence. But as this coincidence was due to a variable cause, and did not happen the following years, the occurrence was *accidental*. (2) The patronal feast of churches is celebrated with an octave; in the case of a church having St. Martin (11 November) as its patron, the octave day (18 November) falls on a fixed feast marked in the Calendar: "Dedication, etc . . ."; consequently, there is in such a church each year a coinciding of two offices on 18 November; this occurrence is said to be *perpetual*.

II. Rules to be Observed.—In case of an occurrence two questions arise: (1) Which office is to have the preference? (2) What is to be done concerning the less favoured office? (1) The two offices must be compared from the point of view of dignity and of necessity, taken either separately or together. As to dignity, Christmas, the Assumption, etc., prevail over the feasts of saints; as to necessity, the first Sunday of Advent being privileged prevails (if it falls on 30 November) over the Office of St. Andrew the Apostle; *a fortiori*, an office favoured by both conditions will be preferred. (2) As to the less favoured office, it is treated differently according as the recurrence is perpetual or accidental. If perpetual, the authority of the Holy See should intervene to operate a change that will be effectual each year; the mention of the feast is maintained on the day on which it falls, but the office is changed to the first free day (a day not occupied by another office, double or semi-double); liturgists call this change *mutatio* (not *translatio*). When the occurrence is accidental, the compiler of the diocesan ordo, with the approval of the ordinary, decides, in conformity with the rubrics, what is to be done for the year. Either the office in question is transferable, in which the regulations of title X, "De translatione", are to be followed; or else it is not transferable, when it must be seen if it is to be omitted completely, or if a commemoration of it may be made on the day in question. The whole matter is provided for in the general rubrics of the Breviary.

To give an instance of concurrence, the ecclesiastical calendar marks the feast of St. Anthony of Padua on 13 June, and that of St. Basil on 14 June; these two feasts being of double rite have first and second Vespers; on the evening of 13 June, therefore, the second Vespers of St. Anthony and the first Vespers of St. Basil happen at the same time, and there is said to be a concurrence of the two offices.

Gavanti, *Thesaurus sacr. rit. cum additionibus Merati* (3 vols., Venice, 1769); Guyetus, *Heortologia* (Urbini, 1657); Menghini, *Elementa juris liturg.* (Rome, 1907); Van der Stappen, *Tractatus de offic. div.* (Mechlin, 1898)

Fernand Cabrol.

Oceania, Vicariate Apostolic of Central.—The whole of Oceania had at first been entrusted by the Propaganda to the Society of the Sacred Hearts of Jesus and Mary (1825); but the territory proving too large, the western portion was afterwards formed into a vicariate Apostolic and given to the Society of Mary (1836), Mgr Pompallier being appointed vicar Apostolic of Western Oceania. In 1842, the Propaganda created the vicariate Apostolic of Central Oceania, comprising New Caledonia, the Tonga, Samoa, and Fiji Islands. By a further subdivision, the vicariate included only the Tonga, the Wallis Islands, Futuna, and Niué. The Tonga Islands extend from 15° to 22° S. lat. and from 173° to 176° W. long. Niué is three hundred miles to the east. The Wallis Islands lie in 13° S. lat. and 178° W. long.; Futuna, in 40° 14′ S. lat. and 179° 33′ W. long. These archipelagos are divided among several more or less constitutional monarchies; the Kingdoms of Tonga, Niué, Wallis, and the two Kingdoms of Futuna. Tonga and Niué are under British protectorate, Wallis and Futuna, under French. Freedom of worship is theoretically recognized everywhere except in Niué, which is exclusively Protestant. Wallis and Futuna are entirely Catholic. In Tonga there are Catholics, Methodists belonging to the Sydney conference, independent Methodists forming a national Church, some Anglicans, Adventists, and Mormons. The total population is 34,000, with 9200 Catholics. There are 35 churches; 21 European and 1 native Marist priests, and 3 native secular priests; 28 schools with 2039 children; 2 colleges; 1 seminary. The establishments for girls are under the care of 52 Sisters of the Third Order of Mary. The boys' schools are conducted by native lay teachers; the colleges and the seminary by priests. The islands are divided into districts, with resident missionaries who assemble every month for an ecclesiastical conference. There are annual retreats for the priests, for the sisters, and for the catechists, besides general retreats for the faithful about every two years. In each village there is a sodality of men (*Kan Apositolo*) and another of women (*Fakafeao*). The yearly number of baptisms averages 310; of marriages, 105. Mgr Bataillon was the first vicar Apostolic, succeeded by Mgr Lamaze, at whose death (1906) succeeded his coadjutor, Mgr Amand Olier, S.M., the present (1910) vicar Apostolic. The vicariate has given to the Church the proto-martyr of Oceania, Bl. P. Chanel.

Mangeret, *Mgr Bataillon et les missions de l'Océanie Centrale* (Lyons, 1884); Monfat, *Les Tonga* (Lyons, 1893); Hervier, *Les Missions Maristes en Océanie* (Paris, 1902); Nicolet, *Le Martyr de Futuna* (Boston, 1907); *Proceedings of the First Australasian Catholic Congress* (Sydney, 1900); Soane Malia, *Chez les Méridionaux du Pacifique* (Lyons and Paris, 1910).

Joseph Blanc.

Ochrida. See Achrida.

O'Clery, Michael. See Four Masters, Annals of the.

O'Clery, Peregrine. See Four Masters, Annals of the.

O'Connell, Daniel, b. at Carhen, near Cahirciveen, Co. Kerry, Ireland, 1775; d. at Genoa, 1847. The O'Connells, once great in Kerry, had suffered severely by the penal laws, and the family at Carhen was not rich. An uncle, Maurice O'Connell of Darrynane, resident in France, bore the expense of educating Daniel and his brother Maurice. In 1791 they were sent to the Irish College at Liège, but, Daniel being beyond the prescribed age for admission, they proceeded to St. Omer's in France, and after a year went to Douai. Daniel gave evidence of industry and ability at St. Omer's, but at Douai his stay was short, for, owing to the French Revolution, the two O'Connells returned home (1793). In 1794 Daniel became a law student at Lincoln's Inn and in 1798 was called to the Irish Bar. The era of penal legislation in Ireland had ceased, and already a serious breach had been made in the penal code. By a series of remedial measures, ending with the Catholic Relief Act of 1793, Catholics were placed in many respects on a level with other denominations, but were still excluded from Parliament, from the inner bar, and from the higher civil and military offices; and the recall of Fitzwilliam

(1795) and the events following showed that no further concessions would be given. O'Connell could not see why Catholics who paid taxes and were obedient to the law should not have a share in the spending of the taxes and in the making of the laws. He detested violence as a weapon of reform, respected religion and the rights of property, and therefore hated the French Revolution as he did the Rebellion of 1798. The Union he abhorred because it destroyed Ireland's separate nationality; and he has recorded his anger at hearing the ringing of the bells of St. Patrick's cathedral when the Act of Union was passed, and his resolution to do something to undo it. He believed that moderation was the true character of patriotism, and that the rights of Ireland could be won by peaceful agitation, but he had no faith in the efficacy of agitation such as had been carried on by the Catholic body. Leaders like Lords Trimlestown and Fingal attracted no enthusiasm, and the Catholic Committee, controlled by such men and meeting together to present petitions and make periodic professions of loyalty, were simply ploughing the sands. The support of the masses should be enlisted, there should be organization and vigour, and the Catholics should demand concession not as a favour but as a right. O'Connell was the leader for such a movement; a man strong in body and mind, a great orator, debater, and lawyer, a master of sarcasm and invective; a man who could wring truth from a reluctant witness, or curb the insolence of a partisan judge, or melt a jury by his moving appeal. Addressing an audience of coreligionists he was unequalled. The people felt proud of such a leader, and were ready to follow wherever he led.

O'Connell's first appearance on a public platform was in Dublin (1800), when he denounced the contemplated Union, and declared that the Catholics wanted no such Union, and that if a Union were to be the alternative to the re-enactment of the penal laws they would prefer the penal laws. In the subsequent years he regularly attended the meetings of the Catholic Committee and infused more vigour and energy into its proceedings, and by 1810 he had become the most trusted and powerful of the Catholic leaders. In 1810 he sent out a circular from Dublin inviting the people to form local committees in correspondence with the central committee. The Government, afraid of having a national organization to deal with, proclaimed all such local committee meetings, under the Convention Act of 1793; but the magistrates in many cases refused to carry out the proclamations, and when the Dublin committee met, some of the leaders were arrested and prosecuted. But O'Connell successfully defended the first of the accused, Mr. Sheridan.

From 1812 to 1817 the Irish Government was little else than a long-sustained duel between O'Connell and the new chief secretary, Sir Robert Peel. Both were able and determined, and between them began a personal enmity which ended only with their lives. Peel championed privilege and ascendency and attacked the Catholic leaders. O'Connell retorted by calling him "Orange Peel". O'Connell turned the Catholic Committee into the Catholic Board, but Peel proclaimed the Board as he had proclaimed the Committee; and while O'Connell continued to agitate, Peel continued to pass acts and enforce them. Meantime one noted event happened which further endeared O'Connell to the people. The Dublin Corporation had always been reactionary and bigoted, always the champion of Protestant ascendancy. O'Connell in a public speech in 1815 called it a "beggarly corporation". The aldermen and councillors were enraged and, finding that O'Connell would not apologize, one of their number, D'Esterre, sent him a challenge. D'Esterre was a noted duellist and the hope was that if O'Connell attempted to fight there would be an end to his career. To the surprise of all O'Connell met D'Esterre and shot him dead. He bitterly regretted the deed, and to the end of his days he never missed an opportunity of assisting the D'Esterre family. With all his popularity, the Catholic cause was not advancing. The question of the veto was being agitated, and in consequence there was division and weakness in the Catholic ranks. O'Connell, though a fervent Catholic, opposed the veto, and declared that while willing to have his religion from Rome he must have his politics from home. In 1821 there was a gleam of hope, when the new King George IV visited Ireland. As Prince of Wales he had been the friend of the Liberal leaders, and as such it was expected that he would favour Liberal measures. But he left Ireland without saying a word in favour of Emancipation.

At last O'Connell determined to rouse the masses in earnest and, in conjunction with a young lawyer, Mr. Sheil, he founded, in 1823, the Catholic Association. The declared object was to win Emancipation "by legal and constitutional means", and in order to evade the Convention Act the Association assumed no delegated or representative character. It was a club, its members meeting weekly and paying an annual subscription. O'Connell worked unceasingly to spread the organization, and though progress was slow success came at last; and by 1825 a vast organization had spread over the land, exercising all the powers of government. In each district, usually under the presidency of the clergy, there was a branch of the Catholic Association, where local grievances were ventilated, and subscriptions received and sent to Dublin to the central association, whence came advice in difficulties and speakers for local meetings. In 1825 the Government, alarmed at the power of an organization which was a serious rival to the executive, passed a bill suppressing it. But O'Connell, experienced in defeating Acts of Parliament, changed the name to the New Catholic Association, and the work of agitation went on. As much as five hundred pounds a week was subscribed, and in 1826 the Association felt strong enough to put up a candidate for Waterford, who succeeded against all the territorial influence of the Beresfords; similar victories were won in Monaghan,

O'CONNELL MONUMENT
Glasnevin Cemetery, Dublin

Westmeath, and Louth. In 1828 came the Clare election when O'Connell himself was nominated. It was known that he could not as a Catholic take the Parliamentary oath; but if he, the representative of 6,000,000, were driven from the doors of Parliament solely because of his creed, the effect on public opinion would be great. O'Connell was elected, and when he presented himself in Parliament he refused to take the oath offered him. The crisis had come. The Catholic millions, organized and defiant, would have Emancipation; the Orangemen would have no concession; and Ireland, in the end of 1828, was on the brink of civil war. To avoid this calamity Peel and Wellington struck their colours, and in 1829 the Catholic Relief Act was passed.

Henceforth O'Connell was the Uncrowned King of Ireland. To recompense him for his services and to secure these services for the future in Parliament, he was induced to abandon the practice of his profession and to accept instead the O'Connell Tribute, which from the voluntary subscriptions of the people brought him an income of £1600 a year. His first care was for Repeal, but his appeals for Protestant co-operation were not responded to, and the associations he formed to agitate the question were all proclaimed. In this respect the Whigs, whom he supported in 1832, were no better than the Tories. He denounced them as "base, brutal and bloody"; yet in 1835 he entered into an alliance with them by accepting the Lichfield House Compact, and he kept them in office till 1841. During these years Drummond effected reforms in the Irish executive, and measures affecting tithes, poor law, and municipal reform were passed. But Repeal was left in abeyance till Peel returned to power, and then O'Connell established the Repeal Association. Its progress was slow until in 1842 it got the support of the Nation newspaper. In one year it advanced with giant strides, and in 1843 O'Connell held a series of meetings, some of them attended by hundreds of thousands.

The last of these meetings was to be held at Clontarf in October. Peel proclaimed the meeting and prosecuted O'Connell, and in 1844 he was convicted and imprisoned. On appeal to the House of Lords the judgment of the Irish court was reversed and O'Connell was set free. His health had suffered, and henceforth there was a lack of energy and vigour in his movements, a shifting from Repeal to Federalism and back again to Repeal. He also quarrelled with the Young Irelanders. Then came the awful calamity of the famine. O'Connell's last appearance in Parliament was in 1847 when he pathetically asked that his people be saved from perishing. He was then seriously ill. The doctors ordered him to a warmer climate. He felt that he was dying and wished to die at Rome, but got no further than Genoa. In accordance with his wish his heart was brought to Rome and his body to Ireland. His funeral was of enormous dimensions, and since his death a splendid statue has been erected to his memory in Dublin and a round tower placed over his remains in Glasnevin.

O'Connell was married to his cousin Mary O'Connell and had three daughters and four sons, all the latter being at one time or other in Parliament.

JOHN O'CONNELL, third son of the above; b. at Dublin, 24 December, 1810; d. at Kingstown, Co. Dublin, 24 May, 1858. He was returned M.P. for Youghal (1832), Athlone (1837), and Kilkenny (1841–47). As a politician he was not tactful, and, came in conflict with the Young Ireland party. As a writer his "Repeal Dictionary" (1845) showed much literary and polemical power. In 1846 he published a selection of his father's speeches, prefaced by a memoir. His "Recollections and Experiences during a Parliamentary Career from 1833 to 1848" was issued in two volumes (1849). As a Whig, and also a captain in the militia, he fell into disfavour with his Limerick constituents. He retired from politics 1857, and accepted a lucrative Government appointment.

FITZPATRICK, *O'Connell's Correspondence* (London, 1888); HOUSTON, *O'Connell's Journal* (London, 1906); DUNLOP, *O'Connell* (New York, 1900); MCDONAGH, *Life of O'Connell* (London, 1903); O'NEILL DAUNT, *Personal Recollections of O'Connell* (London, 1848); CUSACK, *Life and Times of O'Connell* (London, 1872); CLONCURRY, *Personal Recollections* (Dublin, 1849); DUFFY, *Young Ireland* (London, 1896); MITCHEL, *History of Ireland* (London, 1869); FITZPATRICK, *Dr. Doyle* (Dublin, 1880); LECKY, *Leaders of Public Opinion* (London, 1871); NEMOURS GODRE, *O'Connell, sa vie, son œuvre* (Paris, 1900); SHAW LEFEVRE, *Peel and O'Connell* (London, 1887); JOHN O'CONNELL, *Recollections* (London, 1849); MADDEN, *Ireland and its Rulers* (London, 1844); COLCHESTER, *Diary* (London, 1861); WYSE, *History of the Catholic Association* (London, 1829); D'ALTON, *History of Ireland* (London, 1910).

E. A. D'ALTON.

O'Connell, DENNIS JOSEPH. See SAN FRANCISCO, ARCHDIOCESE OF.

O'Connell, WILLIAM H. See BOSTON, ARCHDIOCESE OF.

O'Connor, JOHN JOSEPH. See NEWARK, DIOCESE OF.

O'Connor, PATRICK JOSEPH. See ARMIDALE, DIOCESE OF.

O'Connor, RICHARD A. See PETERBOROUGH, DIOCESE OF.

O'Conor, CHARLES, b. in the city of New York, 22 January, 1804; d. at Nantucket, Mass., 12 May, 1884. His father, Thomas O'Conor, who came to New York from Ireland in 1801, was "one of the active rebels of 1798", a devoted Catholic and patriot, less proud of the kingly rule of his family than of the adherence of the O'Conors to their ancient faith and patriotic principles. He married (1803) a daughter of Hugh O'Connor, a fellow countryman, but not a kinsman, who had come to the United States with his family in or about 1790. Of this marriage Charles O'Conor was born.

In 1824, in his native city, he was admitted to the practice of the law. In 1827 he was successful as counsel in the case of a contested election for trustees of St. Peter's Church in New York. From the year 1828 his rise in his profession was continuous. As early as 1840 an interested observer of men and events, Philip Hone, refers in his diary to "an able speech" by this "distinguished member of the New York bar" (Tuckerman, "The Diary of Philip Hone", New York, 1889, II, 37). In 1843 by the case of Stewart against Lispenard, his professional standing became most securely established. At the June term in this year of the highest court of the State twenty cases were argued. Of these he argued four. In 1846 he had reached "the front ranks of the profession, not only in the City and State of New York, but in the United States" (Clinton, "Extraordinary Cases", New York, I, 1). Doubtless, to his repute as a jurist should be attributed his nomination by all political parties for the New York State Constitutional Convention of that year. Subsequent to his very early manhood, office-holding could not have attracted him. He once wrote that if elected to office he would accept only, if impelled by "a sense of duty such as might impel the conscripted militia-man" (see "U. S. Catholic Historical Magazine", New York, 1891–92, IV, 402, and his response to tender in 1872 of the presidential nomination, ibidem, 399). Concerning voting for public officers he expressed himself in a similar manner, such voting being, he contended, "the performance of a duty" and no more a personal right than payment of taxes or submitting to military service, although termed "somewhat inaptly" a franchise (see "Address before the New York Historical Society", New York, 1877). During the convention "it was the wonder of his colleagues, how in addition to the faithful work performed in committee he could get time for the research that was needed to equip him for the great speeches with which he adorned the debates" (Alex-

DANIEL O'CONNELL

ander, "A Political History of the State of New York", New York, 1906, II, 112). His views, however, were not those of the majority. First of a minority of only six members he voted against approving a new State Constitution of which after it had been in force many years, he stated that it "gave life, vigor and permanency to the trade of politics, with all its attendant malpractice" (see Address, *supra*).

Notable among cases previous to 1843 in which he was counsel was Jack *v.* Martin, 12 Wendell 311, and 14 Wendell 507; and during the twenty years following 1843 the Mason will case as well as the Parish will case (see Delafield *v.* Parish, 25 New York Court of Appeals Reports, 9). Probably, the most sensational of his cases during the latter period was the action for divorce brought against the celebrated actor, Edwin Forrest, O'Conor's vindication of the character of his client, Mrs. Forrest, eliciting great professional and popular applause (see Clinton, op. cit., 71, 73, U. S. Catholic Historical Magazine, supra, 428). When in 1865 after the overthrow of the Southern Confederacy, Jefferson Davis was indicted for treason, O'Conor became his counsel. Among O'Conor's later cases, the trials concerning property formerly of Stephen Jumel (see, for narrative of one of these, Clinton, op. cit., c. XXIX) displayed, as had the Forrest divorce case, his ability in the capacity of trial lawyer and crossexaminer, while one of the cases in which his learning concerning the law of trusts appeared was the case of Manice against Manice, 43 New York Court of Appeals Reports, 303. In 1871, he commenced with enthusiasm as counsel for the State of New York proceedings against William M. Tweed and others, accused of frauds upon the City of New York, declaring that for his professional services he would accept no compensation. In the autumn of 1875 and while these proceedings were uncompleted, he was prostrated by an illness which seemed mortal, and the cardinal archbishop administered the sacraments. Slowly, however, he regained some measure of strength, and, on 7 February, 1876, roused by a newspaper report, he left his bedroom to appear in court, "unexpected and ghost-like" (according to an eyewitness), that he might save from disaster the prosecution of the cause of the State against Tweed (see Breen, "Thirty Years of New York Politics", New York, 1899, 545–52). In 1877 he appeared as counsel before the Electoral Commission at the City of Washington. His last years were passed on the Island of Nantucket, where, in 1880, he took up his abode, seeking "quiet and a more genial climate". But even here he was occasionally induced to participate in the labours of his beloved profession.

When he passed away, many seemed to concur in opinion with Tilden that O'Conor "was the greatest jurist among all the English-speaking race" (Bigelow, "Letters and literary memorials of Samuel J. Tilden", II, 643).

United States Catholic Historical Magazine, IV (New York, 1891–2), 225, 396; FINOTTI, *Bibliographia Catholica Americana* (New York, 1872), 209, 216; LEWIS, *Great American Lawyers*, V (Philadelphia, 1908), 83; COUDERT, *Addresses*, etc. (New York and London, 1905), 198; VEEDER, *Legal Masterpieces* (St. Paul, 1903), 11, 820; HILL, *Decisive Battles of the Law* (New York and London), 212, 221, 226–7; JOHNSON, *Reports of cases decided by Chief Justice Chase* (New York, 1876), 1, 106.

CHARLES W. SLOANE.

O'Conor, CHARLES, often called "the Venerable", b. at Belanagare, Co. Roscommon, 1710; d. 1791, was descended from an ancient and princely Catholic family. Cultured, educated, an Irish scholar, O'Conor was almost the only Irishman of his time who studied the records of his country, and who did what he could to preserve the Irish manuscripts. He scanned these with a calculating and mathematical mind, continually figuring up and noting upon the margins the dates of kings, princes, prelates, foundations etc., and pointing out conflicting dates. He was the only Irishman with whom Samuel Johnson corresponded with reference to Irish literature. Irish was his native language, so that he was one of the last great Irishmen who continued the unbroken traditions of their race. His private diaries and note-books in which he jotted down household affairs, expenses etc. (now preserved by his direct descendant the O'Conor Don H. M. L. at Clonalis) were written largely in classic Irish. His best known work is his "Dissertations on the History of Ireland" published in 1753 which led to his correspondence with Dr. Johnson, who urged him to write an account of pre-Norman Ireland. His collection of Irish manuscripts passed to his grandson, the younger Charles, and later formed the renowned Stowe Collection in the possession of the Duke of Buckingham, whose librarian the younger Charles became. This collection, including the famous Stowe Missal and the original of the first part of the "Annals of the Four Masters," was for years inaccessible to Irish scholars, but has now been deposited in the Royal Irish Academy. A man of affairs, he was one of the founders of the Roman Catholic Committee in 1757, and with Dr. Curry, may be looked upon as the real lay leaders and representatives of the Irish Catholics during the middle of the eighteenth century. Charles O'Conor (grandson of the above), wrote the "Memoirs of the Life and Writings of the late Charles O'Conor of Belanagare". This is a very rare book, the author having suppressed it, and destroyed the manuscript of the second volume when ready for press. Its destruction was a great loss to the Irish history of the period. The present O'Conor Don possesses many of his letters; others are in the Gilbert Library now acquired by the Corporation of Dublin.

O'CURRY, *Manuscript Materials* (Dublin, 1878), p. 115; O'CONOR DON, *The O'Conors of Connaught* (Dublin, 1891); WEBB, *Compendium of Irish Biography* (Dublin, 1870).

DOUGLAS HYDE.

Octavarium Romanum, a liturgical book, which may be considered as an appendix to the Roman Breviary, but which has not the official position of the other Roman liturgical books. The first mention of this book dates from Sixtus V. In order to introduce a greater variety in the selection of lessons, he ordered the compilation of an Octavarium to comprise the lessons proper to each day of the octaves. The plan was not executed during his pontificate (1585–90). When the question of correcting the Breviary was raised anew under Clement VIII (1592–1605), the projected Octavarium was again spoken of. The consultors, the most distinguished of whom was Baronius, were in favour of the suggested compilation. Gavanti, who was also a consultor, undertook the work, but his book did not appear till 1628. Its title, which is descriptive, is "Octavarium Romanum, Lectiones II et III Nocturni complectens, recitandas infra octavas Festorum, præsertim patronorum locorum et titularium Ecclesiarum quæ cum octavis celebrari debent, juxta rubricas Breviarii Romani, a Sacra Rituum Congregatione ad usum totius orbis ecclesiarum approbatum" (Antwerp, 1628). In addition to the letter of approbation, the Brief of Urban VIII, and the dedication, the book includes a few pages on the origin, cause, and rites of octaves. The body of the work consists of a collection of readings, or lessons, for the feasts of the Holy Trinity, the Transfiguration, the Holy Cross, several feasts of Our Lady (Conception, Purification, Visitation, Our Lady of the Snows), the feasts of St. Michael, the Apostles, Saints Mary Magdalene, Martha, John, Athanasius, Monica, Nereus and Achilleus, the Seven Brothers, Apollinarius, the feast of the Beheading of St. John the Baptist, of Sts. Gregory Thaumaturgus, Basil, Francis, Clement etc. Then follow the lessons for the commons. They are drawn from the writings of the Fathers, and are varied and well-selected. Numerous editions have appeared since then, with occasional variations. One of the most recent is by Pustet (Ratisbon, 1883). The reading of the Octavarium is not obligatory.

ZACCARIA, *Onomasticon*, 62; IDEM, *Bibliotheca Ritualis*, I, 134; BERGEL, *Die Emendation des römischen Breviers unter Klemens VIII* in *Zeitschrift für kathol. Theol.*, VIII (Innsbruck, 1884), 296, 300 sq.; BÄUMER-BIRON, *Histoire du Bréviaire*, II (Paris, 1905), 252, 273 sq. See also OCTAVE.

FERNAND CABROL.

Octave.—I. ORIGIN.—It is the number seven, not eight, that plays the principal rôle in Jewish heortology, and dominates the cycle of the year. Every seventh day is a sabbath; the seventh month is sacred; the seventh year is a sabbatical year. The jubilee year was brought about by the number seven multiplied by seven; the feast of the Azymes lasted seven days, like the paschal feast; the feast of Pentecost was seven times seven days after the Pasch; the feast of the Tabernacles lasted seven days, the days of convocation numbered seven (Willis, "Worship of the Old Covenant", 190–1; "Dict. of the Bible", s. v. Feast and Fasts, I, 859). However, the octave day, without having the symbolic importance of the seventh day, had also its rôle. The eighth day was the day of circumcision (Gen., xxi, 4; Lev., xii, 3; Luke, i, 59; Acts, vii, 8 etc.). The feast of the Tabernacles, which as we have said lasted seven days, was followed on the eighth by a solemnity which may be considered as an octave (Lev., xxiii, 36, 39; Num., xxix, 35; II Esd., viii, 18); the eighth day was the day of certain sacrifices (Lev., xiv, 10, 23; xv, 14, 29; Num., vi, 10). It was on the eighth day, too, that the feast of the dedication of the Temple under Solomon, and of its purifications under Ezechias concluded (II Par., vii, 9; xxix, 17). The ogdoad of the Egyptians and similar numerical phantasies among other peoples had no influence on Christian liturgy. Gavanti's opinion that the custom of celebrating the octave of feasts dates back to the days of the Apostles is devoid of proof (Thesaurus sacr. rit., 31 sq.). At first the Christian feasts have no octaves. Sunday, which may in a sense be considered the first Christian feast, falls on the seventh day; the feasts of Easter and Pentecost, which are, with Sunday, the most ancient, form as it were only a single feast of fifty days. The feast of Christmas, which too is very old, had originally no octave.

In the fourth century, when the primitive idea of the fifty days' feast of the paschal time began to grow dim, Easter and Pentecost were given octaves. Possibly at first this was only a baptismal custom, the neophytes remaining in a kind of joyful retreat from Easter or Pentecost till the following Sunday. Moreover, the Sunday which, after the feasts of Easter and Pentecost, fell on the eighth day, came as a natural conclusion of the seven feast days after these two festivals. The octave, therefore, would have in a certain sense developed of its own accord. If this be so, we may say, contrary to the common opinion that Christians borrowed the idea of the octave from the Jews, this custom grew spontaneously on Christian soil. However, it must be said that the first Christian octave known to history is the dedication of the Churches of Tyre and Jerusalem, under Constantine, and that these solemnities, in imitation of the dedication of the Jewish Temple, lasted eight days (Eusebius, "De vita Constant"., III, xxx sq.; Sozomen, "Hist. eccl.", II, xxvi). This feast may possibly have influenced the adoption of the octave by the Christians. From the fourth century onwards the celebration of octaves is mentioned more frequently. It occurs in the Apostolic Constitutions, the sermons of the Fathers, the Councils ("Const. Apost.", VIII, xxxiii; V, xx; Augustine, "De div. temp.", i; "Ep.", lv, 32, 33 etc.; "Peregrinatio Etheriæ", ed. Gamurrini, p. 100; cf. Cabrol, "Etude sur La Peregrinatio", Paris, 1895, pp. 116–7; "Concil. Matisc. II", ii; "Concil. in Trullo", lvi).

II. CELEBRATION OF OCTAVES IN ANCIENT AND MODERN TIMES.—The liturgy of the octave assumed its present form slowly. In the first period, that is from the fourth to the sixth and even seventh century, little thought seems to have been given to varying the liturgical formulæ during the eight days. The sacramentaries of Gelasius and St. Gregory make no mention of the intervening days; on the octave day the office of the feast is repeated. The *dies octava* is indeed made more prominent by the liturgy. The Sunday following Easter (i. e. Sunday *in albis*) and the octave day of Christmas (now the Circumcision) are treated very early as feast days by the liturgy. Certain octaves were considered as privileged days, on which work was forbidden. The courts and theatres were closed ("Cod. Theod.", XV, tit. v de spect. leg. 5; IX, de quæst. leg. 7; "Conc. Mog.", 813, c. xxxvi). After Easter, Pentecost, and Christmas had received octaves, the tendency was to have an octave for all the solemn feasts. Etheria speaks of the feast of the Dedication (cf. Cabrol, op. cit., pp. 128–9). Theodemar, a contemporary of Charlemagne, speaks only of the octaves of Christmas and the Epiphany, but it must not be concluded that he was ignorant of those of Easter and Pentecost, which were more celebrated.

The practice of having octaves for the feasts of the saints does not seem to be older than the eighth century, and even then it was peculiar to the Latins. From the ninth century it becomes more frequent. The capitularies of Charlemagne speak of the octaves of Christmas, the Epiphany, and Easter. Amalarius, after mentioning the four octaves of Christmas, the Epiphany, Easter, and Pentecost, tells us that it was customary in his time to celebrate the octaves of the feasts of Sts. Peter and Paul and other saints, "quorum festivitas apud nos clarior habetur, . . . et quorum consuetudo diversarum ecclesiarum octavas celebrat" (De eccl. offic., IV, xxxvi). In the thirteenth century this custom extends to many other feasts, under the influence of the Franciscans, who then exerted a preponderating influence on the formation of the modern Breviary (Bäumer-Biron, "Hist. du Breviaire", II, 31, 71, 199). The Franciscan feasts of Sts. Francis, Clare, Anthony of Padua, Bernadine etc., had their octaves. At the time of the reformation of the Breviary (Breviary of St. Pius V, 1568) the question of regulating the octaves was considered. Two kinds of octaves were distinguished, those of feasts of our Lord, and those of saints and the dedication. In the first category are further distinguished principal feasts—those of Easter and Pentecost, which had specially privileged octaves, and those of Christmas, the Epiphany, and Corpus Christi, which were privileged (the Ascension octave was not privileged). Octaves, which exclude all or practically all occuring and transferred feasts, are called privileged. The octaves of saints were treated almost like that of the Ascension. This classification entailed the application of a certain number of rubrics, the details of which can be found in Bäumer-Biron, op. cit., II, 199–200. For the changes introduced under Leo XIII, cf. ibid., 462, and also the rubrics of the Breviary. Under OCTAVARIUM ROMANUM there is an account of Gavanti's attempt to provide a more varied office for the octaves.

The Greeks also to a certain extent admitted the celebration of octaves into their liturgy. However, we must be careful not to confuse, as is too often done, the apodosis of the Greeks with the octave. Although having the same origin as the Latin octave, the apodosis differs from the octave in this, that it occurs sometimes on the eighth, and sometimes on the fifth, the fourth, or the ninth (see Pétridès in "Dict. d'archéol. et de liturgie chrét.", s. v. Apodosis).

AMALARIUS, *De eccles. officiis*, IV, xxxvi; *Micrologus*, xliv, in

P. L., CLI, 1010; ZACCARIA, *Onomasticon*, 61; IDEM, *Bibliotheca ritualis*, II, 414; DRESSER, *De festis diebus christianorum et ethnicorum* (Würzburg, 1588); GRANCOLAS, *Commentarius hist. in brev. rom.* (Venice, 1734), 137; HOSPINIAN, *Festa Christianorum hoc est de origine, progressu, cæremoniis et ritibus* (Zurich, 1593), 26; HITTORP, *De div. cath. eccl. officiis et mysteriis* (Paris, 1610), 486 sq.; GAVANTI, *Thesaurus sacror. rituum cum adnot. merati*, II, 31 sq.; GUYETUS, *Heortologia* (Urbino, 1728), 113 sq.; PITTONUS, *Tractatus de octavis festorum quæ in ecclesia universali celebrantur* (Venice, 1739); MARTÈNE, *De antiq. eccles. rit.* (ed. 1788), III, xxv, n. 1, pp. 182 sqq.; BÄUMER-BIRON, *Hist. du Bréviaire*, II (Paris, 1893), 199 etc; DUCHESNE, *Christian Worship, Its Origin etc.* (London, 1904), 287.

FERNAND CABROL.

O'Cullenan, GELASIUS (GLAISNE), Cistercian, Abbot of Boyle, Ireland, b. probably near Assaroe Abbey, Ballyshannon, Co. Donegal; martyred, 21 Nov., 1580. Three of his brothers were Cistercian abbots, and a fourth Bishop of Raphoe. Gelasius, the eldest, studied at Salamanca University, went thence to Paris where he took his doctorate at the Sorbonne, made his monastic profession, and was created Abbot of Boyle, Co. Roscommon. This abbey had been confiscated and granted to Cusack, Sheriff of Meath; but the Irish regulars continued to appoint superiors to their suppressed houses. The young abbot went immediately to Ireland and is said to have obtained restoration of his abbey. He was, however, seized at Dublin by the Government and imprisoned with Eugene O'Mulkeeran, Abbot of Holy Trinity at Lough Key. Refusing to conform, they were tortured and finally hanged outside Dublin, 21 November, 1580. O'Cullenan's body was spared mutilation through his friends' intercession. His clothes were divided as a martyr's relics among the Catholics.

HARTRY, *Triumphalia Monasterii S. Crucis*, ed. MURPHY (Dublin, 1895); O'REILLY, *Memorials of those who suffered for the Catholic Faith* (London, 1868); MURPHY, *Our Martyrs* (Dublin, 1896).

O'Curry, EUGENE (EOGHAN O COMHRAIDHE), Irish scholar, b. at Dunaha near Carrigaholt, Co. Clare, 1796; d. 1862. His father, a farmer of modest means, was an Irish scholar, a good singer, and well-informed as to the traditions of his people. His son Eugene, or Owen, grew up amid perfect Irish surroundings, and soon learned to read the Irish MSS. which were still common among the people. After the fall of Napoleon (1815), there followed a period of much agricultural distress in Ireland, and the O'Curry farm was broken up. In 1834 Eugene joined the number of men engaged upon the topographical and historical part of the Ordnance Survey of Ireland, Petrie, Wakeman, Clarence Mangan the poet, and last but not least John O'Donovan (q. v.). In search of information concerning Irish places O'Curry visited the British Museum (where he catalogued the Irish MSS. for the authorities), the Bodleian Library at Oxford, the Library of Trinity College, the Royal Irish Academy, and other places. But the Government, afraid, it is said, of the national memories that the work was evoking, abandoned the survey three or four years later and dissolved the staff. The great collection of materials, upwards of 400 quarto volumes of letters and documents bearing upon the topography, social history, language, antiquities, and genealogies of the districts surveyed, was stowed away.

After this O'Curry earned his livelihood by reading, copying, and working on the MSS. in Trinity College and the Royal Irish Academy. The first Archæological Society was founded in 1840, relying chiefly upon the assistance of O'Curry and O'Donovan. In 1853 O'Curry joined the council of the Celtic Society and published for them two Irish texts, the "Battle of Moyleana," and the "Courtship of Momera", with excellent translation and notes. In 1855 he was appointed professor of Irish history and archæology in the recently founded Catholic University of Ireland, whose first rector was John Henry (afterwards Cardinal) Newman. His lectures, published at the expense of the university (1860) under the title of "The Manuscript Materials of Ancient Irish History", proved an invaluable mine of information upon the ancient MSS. of Ireland and their contents—annals, genealogies, histories, epics, historical tales, saints' lives, and other ancient matters ecclesiastical and civil. "O'Curry", writes D'Arbois De Jubainville (L'Epopée celtique en Irlande, p. xvi), "is the first man who studied at their sources the epics of Ireland." His book was a revelation, and opened up an entirely new world to European scholars. It was followed by a series of thirty-eight lectures "on the Manners and Customs of the Ancient Irish", published later (1873) under the editorship of Dr. W. K. Sullivan.

O'Curry, a self-taught man and with little or no classical knowledge, was one of Ireland's most energetic workers. Scarcely an Irish book was to be found which he did not read and scarcely a rare manuscript existed in private hands of which he did not make a copy. In this way he gained an outlook over the field of Irish literature, so full and so far-reaching that though strides have been made in scientific scholarship since his day, no one has come ever near him since in his all-round knowledge of the literature of Ireland. He transcribed accurately Duald MacFirbis's book on Irish genealogies, the Book of Lismore, and scores of others. The last work he was engaged on was the Brehon Laws (q. v.); of these he transcribed eight large volumes, and made a preliminary translation in thirteen volumes. O'Curry was severely tried by government officials who took upon themselves, in crass ignorance and in defiance of all rules of scholarship, to dictate to the master how the translation and compilation of the Brehon Laws were to be carried on. O'Curry has left a fully written posthumous statement of the incredible treatment to which he and O'Donovan were subjected, and his account of how he was the first scholar since the death of the great antiquarian, Duald MacFirbis (murdered in 1670), who was able to penetrate and get a grip of the long forgotten language of the ancient law tracts, is one of the most curious things in literature. Many men, such as Todd, Petrie, Graves, Reeves, were deeply indebted to O'Curry, for with a rare generosity he freely communicated the treasures of his knowledge to all who asked him.

WEBB, *Compendium of Irish Biog.* (Dublin, 1878); *Memoir* in *Irish Monthly Magazine* (April, 1874). Cf. also: *Lectures on the Manuscript Materials of Ancient Irish History* (re-issue, Dublin, 1878); *On the Manners and Customs of the Ancient Irish* (3 vols. Dublin, 1873); *The Battle of Magh Leana etc.* (Dublin, 1855).

DOUGLAS HYDE.

O'Daly, DANIEL, diplomatist and historian, b. in Kerry, Ireland, 1595; d. at Lisbon, 30 June, 1662. On his mother's side he belonged to the Desmond branch of the Geraldines, of which branch his paternal ancestors were the hereditary chroniclers or bards. He became a Dominican in Tralee, Co. Kerry; took his vows in Lugo, studied at Burgos, gained his doctorate of theology in Bordeaux, and returned as priest to Tralee. In 1627 he was sent to teach theology in the newly established College for Irish Dominicans at Louvain. In 1629 he went to Madrid on business connected with this college and, seeing that Philip IV of Spain favoured the project, he, assisted by three of his Irish brethren, established, in Lisbon, the Irish Dominican College of which he became the first rector. He conceived the project of erecting, near Lisbon, a convent of Irish Dominican nuns, to serve as a refuge in time of persecution. Philip granted permission to do so on condition that he should raise a body of Irish soldiers for Spanish service in the Low Countries. O'Daly set sail for Limerick and got the men. On his return to Madrid (1639), Belem on the Tagus, four miles below the city, was selected as a site and, with the assistance of the Countess of Atalaya, the convent of Our Lady of Bom Successo was built. The king had such confidence in him that he made him envoy to Charles I of England, to the exiled Charles II, and to Pope Innocent X (1650). The Queen of Portugal also sent him as envoy to Pope Alexander VIII.

In the year 1655 he was sent as envoy from John IV of Portugal to Anne of Austria and Louis XIV to conclude a treaty between Portugal and France. Here as elsewhere, success attended him; but while negotiations abroad and matters of government at home afforded opportunities of serving the House of Braganza, he would not accept any honour in return. His acquaintances praise his straightforwardness, honesty, tact, and disinterestedness. He refused the Archbishopric of Braga and the Primacy of Goa and the Bishopric of Coimbra; nor would he accept the titles of Privy Councillor or Queen's Confessor, though he held both offices. In 1665 he published "Initium, Incrementum, et Exitus Familiæ Geraldinorum, Desmoniæ Comitum, Palatinorum Kyerriæ in Hibernia, ac Persecutionis Hæreticorum Descriptio" etc., his work on the Earls of Desmond, for which he availed himself of the traditional knowledge of his ancestors. In the first part he describes the origin of the Munster Geraldines, their varying fortunes, and their end in the heroic struggle for faith and fatherland. It is our chief authority on this subject. The second part treats of the cruelties inflicted on the Irish Catholics, and of the martyrdom of twenty Dominicans, many of whom had been with him in Lisbon. The work was translated into French by Abbé Joubert (1697), and into English by the Rev. C. P. Meehan, Dublin (2nd edition annotated, 1878.) During these years his chief concern was to put his college on a firm basis and to make it render the greatest possible service to Ireland. Bom Successo became too small for the number of students. In 1659 he laid the first stone of a larger building which was called Corpo Santo. To provide funds for these houses he consented to become Bishop of Coimbra and, in consequence, President of the Privy Council; but before the papal Bull arrived he died. His remains reposed in the cloister of Corpo Santo until the earthquake of 1755; the inscription on his tomb recorded that he was "In variis Regum legationibus felix, . . . Vir Prudentia, Litteris, and Religione conspicuus.' (Successful in embassies for kings . . . A man distinguished for prudence, knowledge, and virtue.) A few years after the catastrophe, on the same spot, with the same name and object, a new college and church arose, which, with Bom Successo, keep O'Daly's memory fresh in Lisbon to the present day.

MS. preserved in Bom Successo; *Letter of O'Daly* published by MEEHAN (1878); BARON (who knew O'Daly), *Libri quinque apologetici* (Paris, 1666); ECHARD, *Script. Ord. Præd.* (Paris, 1719–21); *Hibernia Dominicana* contains much additiona. information; MEEHAN, *Introduction to his translation;* BELLESHEIM, *Gesch. der kath. Kirche in Ireland*, II, III (for an original letter cf. III, 756); O'CONNELL, *Dominic O'Daly in Faith and Fatherland* (Dublin, 1888).

REGINALD WALSH.

O'Daly, DONOGH MÓR (in Irish DONNCHADH MÓR O DÁLAIGH), a celebrated Irish poet, d. 1244. About thirty of his poems are extant, amounting to four or five thousand lines, nearly all religious. O'Reilly styles him Abbot of Boyle (Irish Writers, p. LXXXVIII) as does O'Curry (Manners and Customs, III, p. 301); he was certainly buried in the abbey there, but it cannot be proved that he was an ecclesiastic. The religious cast of his poetry would naturally account for his having been accepted as one. According to O'Donovan (Four Masters, ad an. 1244) he was the head of the O'Dalys of Finnyvara of Burren in Clare, where the ruins of his house are still pointed out. He has often been called the Irish Ovid, for the smoothness of his verse. He was the second of six brothers, the third of whom, Muireadhach "Albanach" or "the Scotchman", was also a poet. The present writer has heard some of O'Daly's verse from the mouths of the peasantry. Only two or three of his pieces have been published, but Professor Tomás O'Máille of Galway is now preparing them for the press.

O'REILLY, *Catalogue of Irish Writers* (Dublin, 1820), p. LXXXVIII; HYDE, *History of Irish Literature*, p. 466–8; IDEM, *Religious Songs of Connacht*, Vol. I; O'CURRY, *Manners and Customs of the Ancient Irish*, III (Dublin), 301. For an account of his brother see *The Tribes of Ireland*, ed. O'DONOVAN (Dublin, 1852), p. 5.

DOUGLAS HYDE.

Oddfellows. See SOCIETIES, SECRET.

O'Dea, EDWARD JOHN. See SEATTLE, DIOCESE OF.

Odescalchi, BENEDETTO. See INNOCENT XI, POPE.

Odescalchi, CARLO, cardinal, prince, archbishop, and Jesuit, b. at Rome, 5 March, 1786; d. at Modena, 17 August, 1841. His father, Duke of Sirmien, Prince of the Roman empire, was a man of culture and attended personally to Carlo's education. He early manifested a religious vocation. Ordained priest, he said his first Mass 1 Jan., 1809. He won the confidence of many souls, among others, a young cleric afterwards Pius IX, and later he ordained priest Gioacchino Pecci, eventually Leo XIII. Odescalchi was in the suite of Pius VII during the perilous times that preceded the pope's captivity, and after his release, he was rapidly promoted, and sent twice on special missions to Vienna. In 1823 he was created cardinal and immediately afterwards Archbishop of Ferrara, but he remained with the pope who was then dying. He devoted himself to his see with apostolic energy, until he resigned (1826). Returning to Rome he was made Bishop of Sabina, prefect of several congregations, and became protector and promoter of many good works. He was in the conclaves for the elections of Leo XII, Pius VIII, and Gregory XVI. Cardinal Wiseman testifies to the general confidence reposed in his virtue and high principle on these occasions. When the Society of Jesus was restored by Pius VII (1814), Odescalchi had resolved to join it, and a cell had been prepared for him at Sant' Andrea. But the pope would not then allow him to enter, nor would Gregory permit it (1837), a commission of four cardinals, appointed to consider the question, having reported in the negative. Finally, permission to resign the cardinalitial dignity having been given in full consistory (1839), Odescalchi entered the novitiate at Verona, and after a short probation was devoting himself to various ministries when he died. As a youth he had published the not unimportant "Memorie istorico-critiche dell' Academia de' Lincei" (Rome, 1806) and as Bishop of Sabina his "Massime sacerdotali" (Rome, 1834).

BERLENDIS, *Memorie edificanti del P. C. Odescalchi* (Rome, 1842——), Eng. tr. ed. FABER (London, 1849); ANGELINI-ROTA, *Storia del R. P. C. Odescalchi* (Rome, 1850).

J. H. POLLEN.

O Deus Ego Amo Te, the first line of two Latin lyrics sometimes attributed to St. Francis Xavier, but of uncertain date and authorship. The one whose first stanza runs:—

O Deus ego amo te,
Nam prior tu amasti me;
En libertate privo me
Ut sponte vinctus sequar te,

has four additional stanzas in similar rhythm, the last three being apparently a paraphrase of part of a prayer in the "Contemplatio ad amorem spiritualem in nobis excitandum" of St. Ignatius Loyola's Spiritual Exercises: "Take, O Lord, my entire liberty . . whatever I have or possess you have bestowed on me; back to thee I give it all, and to the rule of thy will deliver it absolutely. Give me only thy love and thy grace and I am rich enough; nor do I ask anything more." The hymn (probably first printed in the "Symphonia Sirenum", Cologne, 1695) received in Zabuesnig's "Katholische Kirchengesänge" (Augsburg, 1822), the title of "The Desire of St. Ignatius". Father Caswall's beautiful version appeared in his "Masque of

Mary" etc. (1858), and in his "Hymns and Poems" (1873); also in various Catholic hymnbooks (e. g. "Roman Hymnal", New York, 1884; Tozer's "Catholic Church Hymnal", New York, 1905; and in Ould's "The Book of Hymns", Edinburgh, 1910). The hymn was translated by J. Keble, J. W. Hewett, E. C. Benedict, H. M. Macgill, S. W. Duffield.

The first stanza of the companion hymn is:—

O Deus ego amo te,
Nec amo te ut salves me,
Aut quia non amantes te
Æterno punis igne.

There are four additional stanzas in irregular rhythm, while a variant form adds as a final line: "Et solum quia Deus es" (thus given in Moorsom's "A Historical Companion to Hymns Ancient and Modern", 2nd ed., Cambridge, 1903, p. 176). The hymn has been appropriately styled the "love-sigh" of St. Francis Xavier (Schlosser, "Die Kirche in ihren Liedern", 2nd ed., Freiburg, 1863, I, 445, who devotes sixteen pages to a discussion of its authorship, translations etc.), who, it is fairly certain, composed the original Spanish sonnet "No me mueve, mi Dios, para quererte"—on which the various Latin versions are based, about the year 1546. There is not, however, sufficient reason for crediting to him any Latin version. The form given above appeared in the "Cœleste Palmetum" (Cologne, 1696). An earlier Latin version by Joannes Nadasi is in his "Pretiosæ occupationes morientium" (Rome, 1657), beginning: "Non me movet, Domine, ad amandum te". Nadasi again translated it in 1665. F. X. Drobitka ("Hymnus Francisci Faludi", Budapest, 1899) gives these versions, and one by Petrus Possinus in 1667. In 1668 J. Scheffler gave, in his "Heilige Seelenlust", a German translation—"Ich liebe Gott, und zwar umsonst"—of a version beginning "Amo Deum, sed libere". The form of the hymn indicated above has been translated into English verse about twenty-five times, is found in Catholic and non-Catholic hymn-books, and is evidently highly prized by non-Catholics. Thus, the Rev. Dr. Duffield, a Presbyterian, speaks of both hymns in glowing terms, in his "Latin Hymn Writers and Their Hymns" (New York, 1889): "From the higher critical standpoint, then, these hymns are not unacceptable as Xavier's own work. They feel as if they belonged to his age and to his life. They are transfused and shot through by a personal sense of absorption into divine love, which has fused and crystallized them in its fiercest heat" (p. 300). The Scriptural text for both hymns might well be II Cor., v, 14, 15, or perhaps better still I John, iv, 19—"Let us therefore love God, because God hath first loved us". The text of both hymns is given in Daniel's "Thesaurus Hymnologicus", II, 335; of the second hymn, with notes, in March's "Latin Hymns", 190, 307 etc.

H. T. HENRY.

O'Devany, CORNELIUS (CONCHOBHAR O'DUIBHEANNAIGH), Bishop of Down and Connor, Ireland, b. about 1532; d. at Dublin, 11 February, 1612 (N. S.). He was a Franciscan of Donegal Convent, and while in Rome in 1582 was appointed Bishop of Down and Connor, and consecrated 2 February, 1583. In 1588 he was committed to Dublin Castle. Failing to convict him of any crime punishable with death, Lord Deputy Fitzwilliam sought authority from Burghley to "be rid of such an obstinate enemy to God and so rank a traitor to her Majesty as no doubt he is". He lay in prison until November, 1590, being then released ostensibly on his own petition but doubtless through policy. He was protected by O'Neill until 1607, and escaped arrest until the middle of 1611, when, almost eighty years old, he was taken while administering confirmation and again committed to Dublin Castle. On 28 January, 1612, he was tried for high treason, found guilty by the majority of a packed jury, and sentenced to die on 1 February (O. S.). He was drawn on a cart from the Castle to the gallows beyond the river; the whole route was crowded with Catholics lamenting and begging his blessing. Protestant clergymen pestered him with ministrations and urged him to confess he died for treason. "Pray let me be", he answered, "the viceroy's messenger to me, here present, could tell that I might have life and revenue for going once to that temple", pointing to a tower opposite. He kissed the gallows before mounting, and then proceeding to exhort the Catholics to constancy, he was thrown off, cut down alive, and quartered. With him suffered Patrick O'Loughran, a priest arrested at Cork. The people, despite the guards, carried off the halter, his clothes, and even fragments of his body and chips of the gallows. They prayed all night by the remains, an infirm man was reported cured by touching them, and Mass after Mass was said there from midnight until day. Such was the concourse that the viceroy ordered the members to be buried on the spot, but next night the Catholics exhumed them and interred them in St. James's Churchyard. A list of martyrs compiled by Dr. O'Devany was used by Rothe in his "Analecta".

O'LAVERTY, *Diocese of Down and Connor*, V (Dublin, 1895); ROTHE, *Analecta Nova et Mira*, ed. MORAN (Dublin, 1884); O'REILLY, *Memorials of those who suffered for the Catholic Faith* (London, 1868); MURPHY, *Our Martyrs* (Dublin, 1896).

Odilia, SAINT, patroness of Alsace, b. at the end of the seventh century; d. about 720. According to a trustworthy statement, apparently taken from an earlier life, she was the daughter of the Frankish lord Adalrich (Aticus, Etik) and his wife Bereswinda, who had large estates in Alsace. She founded the convent of Hohenburg (Odilienberg) in Alsace, to which Charlemagne granted immunity, confirmed 9 March, 837, by Louis the Pious who endowed the foundation (Böhmer-Mühlbacher, "Regesta Imperii", I, 866, 933). A tenth-century "Vita" has been preserved, written at the close of the century. According to this narrative she was born blind, miraculously receiving her sight at baptism. A shorter text, probably independent of this, is contained in a manuscript of the early eleventh century. Internal evidences point to an original eighth-century biography. A further "Vita", that J. Vignier claimed to have discovered, has been proved to be a forgery by this historian. Her feast is celebrated 13 December; her grave is in a chapel near the convent church on the Odilienberg. She is represented with a book on which lie two eyes.

PFISTER, *La vie de Ste Odile* in *Anal. Boll.*, XIII (1894), 5–32; SEPET, *Observations sur la légende de Ste Odile* in *Bibliothèque de l'école des Chartes*, LXIII (1902), 517–36; HAVET, *Vignier: Vie de Ste Odile* in *Œuvres de Julien Havet*, I (Paris, 1896), 72–8; POTTHAST, *Bibliotheca historica medii ævi*, II, 1497 sq., *Bibliotheca hagiographica latina*, ed. BOLL., II, 906 sq.; PFISTER, *Le duché mérovingien d'Alsace et la vie de Ste Odile* (Paris and Nancy, 1892); WINTERER, *Hist. de Ste Odile ou l'Alsace chrétienne au VIIe et VIIIe siècles* (5th ed. Gebweiler, 1895); WELSCHINGER, *Ste Odile* in *Les Saints* (Paris, 1901); WEHRMEISTER, *Die hl. Odilia, ihre Legende u. ihre Verehrung* (Augsburg, 1902).

J. P. KIRSCH.

Odilienberg. See HOHENBURG.

Odilo, SAINT, fifth Abbot of Cluny (q. v.), b. c. 962; d. 31 December, 1048. He was descended from the nobility of Auvergne. He early became a cleric in the seminary of St. Julien in Brioude. In 991 he entered Cluny and before the end of his year of probation was made coadjutor to Abbot Mayeul, and shortly before the latter's death (994) was made abbot and received Holy orders. The rapid development of the monastery under him was due chiefly to his gentleness and charity, his activity and talent for organizing. He was a man of prayer and penance, zealous for the observance of the Divine Office, and the monastic spirit. He encouraged learning in his monasteries, and had the monk Radolphus Glaber write a history of the time. He erected a magnificent monastery building, and furthered the reform of the Benedictine monasteries. Under Alphonse VI it spread into Spain. The rule of St. Benedict was substituted in Cluny for the domestic rule of Isidore. By bringing the reformed or newly founded monasteries of Spain into permanent dependence on the mother-house, Odilo prepared the way for the union of monasteries, which Hugo established for maintaining order and discipline. The number of monasteries increased from thirty-seven to sixty-five, of which five were newly established and twenty-three had followed the reform movement. Some of the monasteries reformed by Cluny, reformed others; thus the Abbey of St. Vannes in Lorraine reformed many on the Franco-German borderland. On account of his services in the reform Odilo was called by Fulbert of Chartres the "Archangel of the Monks", and through his relations with the popes, rulers, and prominent bishops of the time Cluny monasticism was promoted. He journeyed nine times to Italy, and took part in several synods there. John XIX and Benedict IX both offered him the Archbishopric of Lyons but he declined. From 998 he gained influence with the Emperor Otto III. He was on terms of intimacy with Henry II when the latter, on political grounds, sought to impair the spiritual independence of the German monasteries. For Germany the Cluny policy had no permanent success, as the monks there were more inclined to individualism. Between 1027 and 1046 the relations between the Cluniac monks and the emperor remained unchanged. In 1046 Odilo was present at the coronation of Henry III in Rome. Robert II of France allied himself with the Reform party.

The conclusion of the Peace of God (Treuga Dei), for which Odilo had worked from 1041, was of great economic importance. During the great famines of that time (particularly 1028–33), he also exercised his active charity and saved thousands from death.

He established All Souls' Day (2 Nov.) in Cluny and its monasteries (probably not in 998 but after 1030), and it was soon adopted in the whole church. Of his writings we have but a few short and unimportant ones: a life of the holy Empress St. Adelaide (q. v.) to whom he was closely related; a short biography of his predecessor Mayeul; sermons on feasts of the ecclesiastical year; some hymns and prayers; and a few letters from his extensive correspondence.

Odilo and his confrères interested themselves in the church reform which began about that time. They followed no definite ecclesiastico-political programme, but directed their attacks principally against individual offences such as simony, marriage of the clergy, and the uncanonical marriage of the laity. The Holy See could depend above all on the religious of Cluny when it sought to raise itself from its humiliating position and undertook the reform of the Church.

He died while on a visitation to the monastery of Souvigny where he was buried and soon venerated as a saint. In 1063 Peter Damien undertook the process of his canonization, and wrote a short life, an abstract from the work of Jotsald, one of Odilo's monks who accompanied him on his travels. In 1793 the relics together with those of Mayeul were burned by the revolutionaries "on the altar of the fatherland". The feast of St. Odilo was formerly 2 January, in Cluny, now it is celebrated on 19 January, and in Switzerland on 6 February.

RINGHOLZ, *Der hl. Abt. Odilo, in seinem Leben und Wirken* (Brünn, 1885); IDEM, *Kirchenlexikon* s. v.; SACKUR, *Die Cluniacenser bis zur Mitte des 11 Jahrhunderts*, I, II (Halle, 1892–94); JARDET, *Saint Odilon, Abbé de Cluny* (Lyons, 1898).

KLEMENS LÖFFLER.

Odin, JOHN MARY, Lazarist missionary, first Bishop of Galveston and second Archbishop of New Orleans, b. 25 Feb., 1801, at Hauteville, Ambierle, France; d. there 25 May, 1870. The seventh of ten children, like most country boys he worked on his father's farm. His piety and love for the poor being looked on as a sign of priestly vocation, he was sent when nine years of age to study Latin under his uncle, curé of Nosilly, whose death soon ended this desultory teaching. After two years at home, he studied the classics at Roanne and Verriere and was a brilliant student of philosophy at L'Argentière and Alix. He was prompt to answer Bishop Dubourg's appeal for volunteers for the Louisiana mission. Reaching New Orleans in June, 1822, he was sent to the seminary of the Lazarists, The Barrens, 80 miles from St. Louis, Mo., to complete his theological studies. There he joined the Lazarists. (Clarke in his lives of deceased bishops of the U. S. erroneously states that he entered at an early age in Paris.) He was ordained priest 4 May, 1824, and to parish duties were added those of teaching. In vacation he preached to the Indians on the Arkansas River, for whose conversion he was most eager. In 1825 he was at times in charge of the seminary, college, and parish. He also gave missions to non-Catholics and to the Indians, until, his health failing, it was decided to send him abroad, where he could also gather recruits and funds for the missions. Accompanying Bishop Rosati to the second Council of Baltimore as theologian, he was commissioned by the council to bring its decrees to Rome for approval. Two years were spent abroad in the interest of "his poor America". Pastoral work, chiefly at Cape Girardeau, where he opened a school (1838), and missions occupied the next five years. Sent to Texas in 1840 as vice-prefect by his provincial visitor, Father Timon, whom the Holy See had made prefect Apostolic of the new republic, he began the hardest kind of labour among Catholics, many of whom had fallen away amid the disorders accompanying the change of government, and among non-catholics and the fierce Comanche Indians. His gentleness and self-sacrifice wrought wonders. His great work was early recognized and he was nominated to the coadjutorship of Detroit but declined. A year later he was named titular Bishop of Claudiopolis and Vicar Apostolic of Texas. He was consecrated 6 March, 1842. He had already succeeded with Father Timon's help in having the Republic recognize the Church's right to the possessions that were hers under the Mexican government. In 1845 he went to Europe and secured many recruits for his mission. In 1847 Texas was made a diocese and Bishop Odin's see was fixed at Galveston. On the death of Archbishop Blanc of New Orleans, he was promoted to that see 15 February, 1861. Neither his age nor infirmities kept him from a vigilant care of his flock. War had wrought havoc during his time in Texas, the civil war scourged his archdiocese now. His influence was extraordinary among the Catholic soldiers. Pius IX wrote to him in the South, as to Archbishop Hughes in the North, to use their influence for peace. His Apostolic labours were interrupted only by journeys to Europe in the interest of his archdiocese. Despite greatly impaired health he went to the Vatican Council. At Rome he grew so ill that he was granted leave to return to Heauteville where he died.

BONY, *Vie de Mgr Jean-Marie Odin* (Paris, 1896), translated in part in *Annals Cong. Miss.*, II, III (Emmitsburg, 1895–6); CLARKE, *Lives of deceased Bishops of U. S.*, II (New York, 1872), 203–40; DEUTCHER, *Life and Times of Rt. Rev. John Timon*, I (Buffalo, 1870); SHEA, *History of the Catholic Church in the United States*, IV, 1892.

B. RANDOLPH.

Odington, WALTER, English Benedictine, also known as WALTER OF EVESHAM, by some writers confounded with WALTER OF EYNSHAM, who lived about fifty years earlier, d. not earlier than 1330. During the first part of his religious life he was stationed at Evesham and later removed to Oxford, where he was engaged in astronomical and mathematical work as early as 1316. He wrote chiefly on scientific subjects; his most valuable work "De Speculatione Musices" was first published in complete form in Coussemaker's

"Scriptores"; other works are in manuscript only. This treatise, written at Evesham and therefore certainly before 1316, according to Riemann before 1300, is a remarkable work in which the author gathered together practically all the knowledge of the theory of music possessed at his time and added some theoretical considerations of his own. A discussion of his work is given by Riemann, who claims for him the distinction of having, before the close of the thirteenth century, established on theoretical grounds the consonance of minor and major thirds. Davey enumerates the following works: "De Speculatione Musices"; "Ycocedron", a treatise on alchemy; "Declaratio motus octavæ spheræ"; "Tractatus de multiplicatione specierum in visu secundum omnem modum"; "Ars metrica Walteri de Evesham"; "Liber quintus geometriæ per numeros loco quantitatum"; "Calendar for Evesham Abbey".

DAVEY, *History of English Music* (London, 1895); IDEM in *Dict. Nat. Biog.*, s. v. *Walter of Evesham*; COUSSEMAKER, *Scriptorum de Musica Medii Ævi nova series*, I (Paris, 1864); RIEMANN, *Geschichte der Musiktheorie* (Leipzig, 1898).

EDWARD C. PHILLIPS.

Odo, SAINT, second Abbot of Cluny, b. 878 or 879, probably near Le Mans; d. 18 November, 942. He spent several years at the court of William, Duke of Aquitaine, and afterwards entered the Abbey of St. Martin at Tours. About 909, he became a monk, priest, and superior of the abbey school in Baume, whose Abbot, Bl. Berno, was transferred to Cluny in 910. He became Abbot of Baume in 924, and Berno's successor at Cluny in 927. Authorized by a privilege of John XI in 931, he reformed the monasteries in Aquitaine, northern France, and Italy. The privilege empowered him to unite several abbeys under his supervision and to receive at Cluny monks from abbeys not yet reformed; the greater number of the reformed monasteries, however, remained independent, and several became centres of reform. Between 936 and 942 he visited Italy several times, founding in Rome the monastery of Our Lady on the Aventine and reforming several convents, e. g. Subiaco and Monte Cassino. He was sometimes entrusted with important political missions, e. g., when peace was arranged between King Hugo of Italy and Alberic of Rome. Among his writings are: a biography of St. Gerald of Aurillac, three books of *Collationes* (moral essays, severe and forceful), a few sermons, an epic poem on the Redemption (Occupatio) in seven books (ed. Swoboda, 1900), and twelve choral antiphons in honour of St. Martin.

SACKUR, *Die Cluniacenser*, I (Halle, 1892), 43–120; ZEISIGER, *Leben und Wirken des Abtes Odo von Cluni*, Programm d. Gymnasiums Sorau 1892; DU BOURG, *Saint Odon* (Paris, 1905).

KLEMENS LÖFFLER.

Odo (ODA), SAINT, Archbishop of Canterbury, d. 2 June, 959 (not in 958, recent researches showing that he was living on 17 May, 959). According to the nearly contemporary account of him in the anonymous "Life of St. Oswald" (op. cit. inf.) his father, a Dane, did not strive to serve God, even endeavouring to hinder his son's constant presence at the church. Later writers represent Odo's parents as pagans and the boy himself as becoming a Christian despite his father's anger. Odo was adopted by Æthelhelm, a nobleman, who regarded him with paternal affection and educated him for the service of God. After his ordination he accompanied Æthelhelm to Rome and on the way cured him when he fell ill, by blessing a cup of wine and causing him to drink therefrom. On his return, according to the same writer, he was made bishop of a city in the province of Wilton, so that he has been described as Bishop of Wilton, his consecration being placed in 920. There is no evidence for this date, and if he was consecrated by Archbishop Wulfhelm, as is stated, it could not have been before 923. There is a further difficulty as to his diocese, erroneously called Wilton. In 927 he was Bishop of Ramsbury, which being in Wiltshire might, loosely speaking, be described as the Diocese of Wilton. But Eadmer states that he was appointed Bishop of Sherborne, and there is an extant document (Cart^m Sax^m 666) which lends some support to this statement. If it be true, he must have filled the See of Sherborne between Æthelbald and Sigehelm. As the latter was bishop in 925 this only allows two years for a possible episcopate of Odo. At the court of Athelstan (925–940) he was highly esteemed, and the king chose him to accompany abroad his nephew Lewis, whom the Frankish nobles had recently elected as their king. In 937 he accompanied Athelstan to the battle of Brunanburh, where the incident occurred of his miraculous restoration, at a critical moment, of the king's lost sword. The story, given by Eadmer, is not mentioned by the earlier anonymous writer. When Archbishop Wulfhelm died in 942, King Eadmund wished Odo to succeed, but he refused, because he was not a monk as previous archbishops had been. Finally he accepted the election, but only after he had obtained the Benedictine habit from the Abbey of Fleury. One of his first acts as archbishop was to repair his cathedral at Canterbury, and it is recorded that during the three years that the works were in progress no storm of rain or wind made itself felt within the precincts. The constitutions which he published as archbishop (Mansi, "Concil.", XVIII; Migne, P. L., CXXXIII) relate to the immunities of the Church (cap. i), the respective duties of secular princes, bishops, priests, clerics, monks (ii–vi), the prohibition of unlawful marriages, the preservation of concord, the practice of fasting and almsdeeds, and the payment of tithes (vii–x). A synodal letter to his suffragan bishops, and an introduction to the life of St. Wilfred, written by him, have also been preserved. Throughout the reign of Eadred (946–955) he supported St. Dunstan, whom he consecrated as Bishop of Worcester, prophetically hailing him as future Archbishop of Canterbury. On the death of Eadred he crowned Eadwig as king. Shortly after the archbishop insisted on Eadwig dissolving his incestuous connexion with Ælfgifu and obtained her banishment. In 959 during the reign of Eadgar, whom he had consecrated king, realizing the approach of death, he sent for his nephew, St. Oswald, afterwards Archbishop of York, but died before his arrival. He was succeeded by the simoniacal Ælfsige who insulted his memory, and whose speedy death was regarded by the people as a judgment of God. The next archbishop, St. Dunstan, held St. Odo in special veneration, would never pass his tomb without stopping to pray there, and first gave him the title of "the Good". The story which represents Odo as having in early manhood followed the profession of arms is only found in later writers, such as William of Malmesbury. Even if it is true that Odo served Edward the Elder under arms, there is no reason to suppose, with the writer in the "Dictionary of National Biography", that he did so after he became a cleric. God bore witness to his sanctity by miracles during his life and after his death.

EADMER, *Vita Sancti Odonis* (the earliest extant life) in WHARTON, *Anglia Sacra*, II, 78–87, and in MABILLON, *Acta SS. O.S.B.*, 1685, and in the *Acta SS.* of the BOLLANDISTS who attribute it to Osbern (July, II), but this is corrected in their *Bibliotheca Hagiographica Latina* (Brussels, 1901), where the ascription to Eadmer is accepted. Contemporary notices will be found in the *Vita S. Oswaldi* in *Historians of the Church of York* (Rolls Series, 1879–94); *Anglo-Saxon Chronicle*, ann. 958, 961 (R. S., 1861); STUBBS, *Memorials of St. Dunstan* (R. S., 1874); GERVASE OF CANTERBURY, *Historical Works* (R. S., 1879–80); WILLIAM OF MALMESBURY, *De Gestis Pontificum Anglorum* (R. S., 1870), and *De Gestis Regum Anglorum* (R. S., 1887–89); WHARTON, *Anglia Sacra* (London, 1691); CHALLONER, *Britannia Sancta* (London, 1745), 4 July; KEMBLE, *Codex Diplomaticus ævi Saxonici* (London, 1839–48); HARDY, *Descriptive Catalogue* (London, 1862–71); HOOK, *Lives of the Archbishops of Canterbury* (London, 1860–84); STANTON, *Menology* (London, 1892), 2 June; BIRCH, *Cartularium Saxonicum* (London, 1885–93); SEARLE, *Anglo-Saxon Bishops, Kings and Nobles* (Cambridge, 1899); CAPGRAVE, *Nova Legenda Angliæ*, ed. HORSTMAN (Oxford, 1901).

EDWIN BURTON.

Odo, Bishop of Bayeux and Count of Kent, b. in Normandy previous to 1037; d. at Palermo, February, 1097. The son of Herluin de Conteville and Herleva de Falaise, previously by Duke Robert the mother of William the Bastard, from whom Odo about 7 October, 1049, received the Diocese of Bayeux. He was present at the assembly of Lillebonne in 1066 at which William's expedition to England was decided upon; he built, at his expense at Port-en-Bassin, fifty or a hundred vessels, accompanied the soldiers, exhorted them on the eve of the battle of Hastings, in which he himself fought. William gave him the castle of Dover and the Earldom of Kent, and three months later when he returned to Normandy he left as his viceroys Odo and William FitzOsbern. Both were merciless in stifling the insurrection of the Saxons. On his return to England in December, 1067, William made Odo a sort of viceroy; he gave him domains in the county of Kent, and several churches and abbeys. Lanfranc, Archbishop of Canterbury, protested successfully at the synod of 1072 against the spoliation of which he was the object; but Odo retained what he had taken from the Abbeys of Ramsey and Evesham. In 1080 he traversed Northumberland with an army, avenging the murder of Bishop Walcher of Durham; he multiplied his cruelties and was called the Great Tamer of the English.

He had the ambition to became pope. A soothsayer had foretold that the successor of Gregory VII should be called Odo. The latter first tried to seduce by his munificence the notables of Rome, where he built a palace; then with Hugh, Count of Chester, and a number of knights he set out for Rome. William met him at Wight, brought him before his barons, and reproached him with his exactions; as the barons refused to arrest the bishop, he declared that as count he would arrest him himself, and he brought him prisoner to Rouen. He refused to release him, despite the protests of Gregory VII. On his death-bed he granted this request reluctantly; for he feared that after his death this "wicked man would make trouble everywhere". Odo, according to Ordericus Vitalis, immediately plotted against the new king, William Rufus, his nephew; but in 1088, being besieged in Rochester, he was forced to accept as a grace the right to leave the town and depart from England. He established his credit in Normandy by the manner in which he assured to his nephew, Robert Courte Heuse, the possession of the city of Le Mans and defended his power against the house of Talvas. According to Ordericus Vitalis, in 1093 he blessed the incestuous union of Philip I of France, with Bertrada, Countess of Anjou, and obtained as a reward the revenues of the Church of Mantes. Urban II, at Dijon, absolved Odo. In 1095 he was present at the Council of Clermont at which the first Crusade was preached; he set out in September, 1096, but died at Palermo. Gilbert, Bishop of Evereux, and Count Roger of Sicily erected a tomb to him in the cathedral.

Despite the eulogies of William of Poitiers it may be said, without approving the severe judgment of Ordericus Vitalis, that the life of this prelate was scarcely that of a churchman. He even had a son, called John. Nevertheless his presence at the synods of Rouen of 1055, 1061, and 1063 is proved; on 14 July, 1077 he consecrated the cathedral of Bayeux; on 13 September, 1077, he assisted at the dedication of the Church of St. Stephen in Caen, and on 23 October, at that of Notre Dame du Bec. He was zealous in obtaining relics. He educated, at his expense, a number of young men who became distinguished prelates, and was liberal in his gifts to the Abbey of St. Augustine at Canterbury. It has been asserted that he placed in the cathedral the famous Bayeux tapestry, but a detailed study of this tapestry has led Marignan to conclude that it was composed according to the description and information contained in the "Roman du Rou" of Robert Wace, and that it was executed in the last thirty years of the twelfth century.

WHARTON, *Anglia Sacra*, I (London, 1691), 334–39; *Gallia Christiana nova*, XI (1759), 353–60; ORDERICUS VITALIS, *Hist. eccles.*, ed. LEPRÉVOST (5 vols., Paris, 1838–55); FREEMAN, *History of the Norman Conquest* (6 vols., Oxford, 1878–79); IDEM, *Reign of William Rufus* (2 vols., Oxford, 1882); FOWKE, *The Bayeux Tapestry* (London, 1898); MARIGNAN, *La Tapisserie de Bayeux* (Paris, 1902); KINGSFORD in *Dict. Nat. Biog.*, s. v.; see also Bibliography of William the Conqueror, ibid.

GEORGES GOYAU.

O'Donaghue, DENIS. See INDIANAPOLIS, DIOCESE OF.

O'Donnell, EDMUND, the first Jesuit executed by the English government; b. at Limerick in 1542, executed at Cork, 16 March, 1575. His family had held the highest civic offices in Limerick since the thirteenth century, and he was closely related to Father David Woulfe, Pope Pius IV's legate in Ireland. He entered the Society of Jesus at Rome, 11 September, 1561, but, developing symptoms of phthisis, was removed to Flanders. In 1564 he returned to Limerick and taught, with a secular priest and a layman, in the school which Woulfe established with connivance of the civic authorities. The school was dispersed in October, 1565, by soldiers sent by Sir Thomas Cusack, and, for a short time, they taught at Kilmallock. In a few months they returned to Limerick, and were not molested again until 1568, when Brady, Protestant Bishop of Meath, visited the city as royal commissioner and made diligent search for them. O'Donnell was ordered to quit the country under pain of death and withdrew to Lisbon, where he was again a student in 1572. Venturing back to Limerick in 1574 he was apprehended soon after landing, and thrown into prison. Rejecting all inducements to embrace Protestantism he was removed to Cork, tried for returning after banishment, denying the royal supremacy, and carrying letters for James Fitzmaurice. He was found guilty, and sentenced to be hanged, drawn and quartered.

He has been called McDonnell, MacDonald, Donnelly, and MacDonough and Donagh. Father Edmund Hogan, S.J., Historiographer of the Irish province, found him recorded as Edmundus Daniell in the Society's archives, and so the name usually appears in Limerick records, though also Dannel and O'Dannel. Copinger and Bruodin give the name as O'Donell (O'Donellus). The archives and a contemporary letter from Fitzmaurice confirm Bruodin's positive assertion that he suffered in 1575, not in 1580 as generally stated.

MURPHY, *Our Martyrs* (Dublin, 1896); HOGAN, *Distinguished Irishmen of the Sixteenth Century* (London, 1895); ROTHE, *Analecta Nova et Mira*, ed. MORAN (Dublin, 1884); HOGAN, *Ibernia Ignatiana* (Dublin, 1880).

O'Donnell, PATRICK. See RAPHOE, DIOCESE OF.

O'Donovan, JOHN, Irish historian and antiquarian, b. at Atateemore, County Kilkenny, Ireland, 1806; d. at Dublin, 9 Dec., 1861. Coming to Dublin in 1823, he was sent to a "Latin School" to prepare for entrance to Maynooth, but later, finding he had no vocation for the priesthood, turned his attention to the study of Irish. O'Donovan himself states that, at the age of nine years, he commenced the study of Irish and Latin, and that in 1819 he could "transcribe Irish pretty well". In Dublin he was soon employed by James Hardiman, antiquarian and historian, to transcribe Irish manuscripts, and through him he was introduced to the Royal Irish Academy circle. Here he met Petrie, and the foundation of a lasting friendship was laid. Petrie's accurate antiquarian sense was supplemented by O'Donovan's knowledge of the native tongue and his ever-growing store of oral and written tradition. Aided by Sir Samuel Ferguson, they helped to destroy the influence of the fanciful theories which then held the field, championed by

Betham and Vallancey. An early example of O'Donovan's historical method is to be found in his edition and translation of the Charter of Newry (Dublin Penny Journal, 22 Sept., 1832). From this on he shared with his brother-in-law, Eugene O'Curry, an undisputed position as supreme authority on the Irish language and Irish antiquities. He may be said to have been the mainstay of the archæological societies and journals of his day—the Kilkenny Archæological society, the Ulster Journal of Archæology, and the Celtic Society. The foundation by the Government of the Ordnance Survey Department of Ireland gave O'Donovan his chance. In Petrie's house, 21 Great Charles Street, the antiquarian section had its offices, and here O'Donovan had as colleagues, among others, Petrie, O'Curry, Mangan, and Wakeman. From the preparation of lists of names of townlands and places, O'Donovan was soon sent by Larcom, the head of the Ordnance Survey, to work "in the field".

From the various places throughout Ireland which he visited, he despatched in the form of letters to Larcom accounts of antiquities and traditions which, collected in 103 volumes and at present deposited in the Royal Irish Academy, Dublin, are popularly known as "O'Donovan's Letters". They are not heavy with mere erudition, but are enlivened with flashes of humorous anecdote and many a merry "quip and crank and jest". He was engaged on the Survey from 1830 to 1842. In 1836 he commenced the catalogue of Irish MSS. in Trinity College; and to aid him in his work of editing and translating MSS., Todd sought a grant in aid from Government. It was refused, and was followed up by the suppression in 1842 of the archæological section of the Ordnance Survey. Private effort had, therefore, to be relied upon, and, with the assistance of the members of the Archæological Society and the Celtic Society, O'Donovan was able to publish his well-known editions of Irish texts with his invaluable introductions and notes. From 1842 till his death in 1861 no year passed without some noteworthy edition of an Irish text appearing from his hands. A complete bibliography of his works was published by Henry Dixon (Dublin). We can only refer to two of his works with which his name is popularly connected—his "Irish Grammar" and his edition and translation of the Annals of the Four Masters. His grammar was published in 1845, and at once elicited the praise of Grimm, on whose recommendation he was elected in 1856 a corresponding member of the Royal Academy of Berlin, an honour which he shared with Zeuss whose epoch-making "Grammatica Celtica" appeared in that year. He was then appointed Professor of Celtic in Queen's College, Belfast. In 1848 appeared the first part of his edition of the Annals of the Four Masters (q. v)., which won for him the Cunningham Gold Medal of the Royal Irish Academy and the LL.D. degree of Trinity College, Dublin. The edition was completed in 1851, and the Government bestowed on him a pension of £50 a year. O'Donovan had decided to go to America, but the establishment of the Brehon Law Commission helped to retain his services for Ireland. He continued his work on the Brehon Law Tracts till his death in Dublin from rheumatic fever, the tendency to which was due to exposure on the outdoor work of the Ordnance Survey.

Besides his works (especially his edition of the Four Masters and MS. Letters in R. I. Academy) consult: *Memoir* by SIR J. GILBERT (London, 1862); LADY FERGUSON, *Life of Bishop Reeves* (London, 1893); LADY GILBERT, *Life of Sir John Gilbert* (London, 1905); WEBB, *Compendium of Irish Biog.* (Dublin, 1878); *Journal of Librarians' Association*, II, n. i. (Dublin); MACSWEENEY, *Centenary Address*; CARRIGAN, *Hist. and Antiq. of the Diocese of Ossory* (Dublin, 1905).

PATRICK M. MACSWEENEY.

Odo of Cambrai, BLESSED, bishop and confessor, called also ODOARDUS, b. at Orleans, 1050; d. at Anchin, 19 June, 1113. In 1087 he was invited by the canons of Tournai to teach in that city, and there soon won a great reputation. He became a Benedictine monk (1095) in St. Martin's, Tournai, of which he became abbot later. In 1105 he was chosen Bishop of Cambrai, and was consecrated during a synod at Reims. For some time after he was unable to obtain possession of his see owing to his refusal to receive investiture at the hands of the Emperor Henry IV, but the latter's son Henry restored the See of Cambrai to Odo in 1106. He laboured diligently for his diocese, but in 1110 he was exiled on the ground that he had never received the cross and ring from the emperor. Odo retired to the monastery of Anchin, where he died without regaining possession of his diocese. Many of his works are lost; those extant will be found in Migne, CLX (P. L.).

ACTA SS., III June (Venice, 1743), 910; MABILLON, *Annales* O. S. B., IV (Paris, 1669), col. 623; ZIEGELBAUER, *Hist. rei literariæ* O. S. B., III (Augsburg, 1754), 126; LE GLAY, *Hist. ecclés. du diocèse de Cambrai* (Paris, 1849); BAUNARD, *Le b. Odon de Tournai* (Orleans, 1862); MARTÈNE, *Thes. nov. anecdot.*, V (Paris, 1717), 853–8; LABIS, *Le b. Odon évêque de Cambrai* in *Revue catholique*, II (Louvain, 1856), 445–60; 519–26; 574–85.

G. ROGER HUDLESTON.

Odo of Canterbury, Abbot of Battle, d. 1200, known as Odo Cantianus or of Kent. A monk of Christ Church, he became subprior in 1163 and was sent by Thomas à Becket to Pope Alexander as his representative to attend an appeal, fixed for 18 Oct., 1163, against the Archbishop of York who, in spite of the remonstrances of St. Thomas and the pope, still continued to carry the cross in the southern province. In 1166 Christ Church appealed against the archbishop and Odo applied to Richard of Ilchester for help (Foliot, Ep. 422, in Migne). In 1167 he became prior with William as subprior. Until the murder of St. Thomas he seems to have wavered in his allegiance between king and archbishop, but then took a decided stand in favour of ecclesiastical authority. On 1 Sept., 1172, in a meeting the monks of Christ Church put forward Odo as worthy of the archbishopric. The king however procrastinated, and no result followed a second meeting at Windsor (6 Oct.). Odo with other monks followed Henry to Normandy and urged that a monk should be chosen as archbishop (Mat. Becket., IV, 181). After protracted negotiations the choice fell upon Richard, Prior of Dover, formerly a monk of Canterbury, in whose behalf Odo wrote to Alexander III (Migne, CC., 1396). In 1173 occurred a great fire at Christ Church and Odo went to the Council of Woodstock on 1 July, 1175, to obtain a renewal of the charters on the model of those at Battle Abbey. St. Martin de Bello had been without an abbot for four years and the monks who attended the council caused Odo to be chosen. He was elected on 10 July. His blessing took place on 28 Sept., at the hands of Archbishop Richard at Malling. On the death of Richard (1184) the monks of Christ Church again put Odo forward for the archbishopric, but Henry again refused, fearing no doubt that he would be too inflexible for his purpose. Baldwin who was appointed quarrelled with the monks, a dispute which lasted till 1188 and occasioned a correspondence between Odo and Urban III (Epp. Cantuar., no. 280). Odo died on 20 Jan., 1200, and was buried in the lower part of the church at Battle. Leland speaks of him as a most erudite man and a great friend of Thomas à Becket and John of Salisbury who describes him as an ardent lover of books. He was a great theologian and preached in French, English, and Latin, and was noted for his humility and modesty. There is some uncertainty as to his writings, owing to a confusion with Odo of Cheriton and Odo of Murimund, but a list of thirteen works, chiefly writings on the Old Testament and sermons, can be ascribed to him. He was venerated at Battle as a saint and in the relic list at Canterbury Cathedral is mentioned "a tooth of the Ven. Odo Abb. of Battle" (Dart. Ap. XLVII).

Materials for History of Thomas Becket (Rolls Series, London, 1875), Index; I, 542; VI, 331; KINGSFORD in *Dict. of Nat. Biog.*, s. v., for list of his writings; LELAND, *Collectanea*, ed. HEARNE, IV (London, 1774), 68; IDEM, *Comment. de Script. Brit.*, 210–12; WRIGHT, *Biog. Brit. Anglo-Norman* (London, 1846), 224–6; HARDY, *Descriptive Catalogue* (1865); *Chronicon de Bello* (London, 1851).

S. ANSELM PARKER.

Odo of Cheriton, preacher and fabulist, d. 1247. He visited Paris, and it was probably there that he gained the degree of Master. Bale mentions a tradition that he was a Cistercian or a Præmonstratensian; but he can hardly have taken vows if, as seems most likely, he was the Master Odo of Cheriton mentioned in Kentish and London records from 1211 to 1247, the son of William of Cheriton, lord of the manor of Delce in Rochester. In 1211–12 William was debited with a fine to the crown, for Odo to have the *custodia* of Cheriton church, near Folkestone. In 1233 Odo inherited his father's estates in Delce, Cheriton, and elsewhere. A charter of 1235–6 (Brit. Mus., Harl. Ch. 49 B 45), by which he quitclaimed the rent of a shop in London, has his seal attached, bearing the figure of a monk seated at a desk, with a star above him (St. Odo of Cluny?).

Like Jacques de Vitry, he introduced *exempla* freely into his sermons; his best known work, a collection of moralized fables and anecdotes, sometimes entitled "Parabolæ" from the opening words of the prologue (*Aperiam in parabolis os meum*), was evidently designed for preachers. Though partly composed of commonly known adaptations and extracts, it shows originality, and the moralizations are full of pungent denunciations of the prevalent vices of clergy and laity. The "Parabolæ" exist in numerous manuscripts, and have been printed by Hervieux (Fabulistes Latins, IV, 173–255); a thirteenth century French version is extant, also an early Spanish translation. Some of the contents reappear, along with many other *exempla*, in his sermons on the Sunday Gospels, completed in 1219, extant in several manuscripts; an abridgment of which, prepared by M. Makerel, was printed by J. Badius Ascensius in 1520. The only other extant works, certainly authentic, are "Tractatus de Poenitentia", "Tractatus de Passione", and "Sermones de Sanctis"; but the "Speculum Laicorum" also cites him as authority for many other *exempla*. Hauréau's contention (Journal des Savants, 1896, 111–123), that the fabulist was a distinct person from the author of the sermons and treatises, is not supported.

HERVIEUX, *Fabulistes Latins*, IV, *Eudes de Cheriton et ses Dérivés* (Paris, 1896); HERBERT, *Catalogue of Romances*, III, 31–78, 371–405.

J. A. HERBERT.

Odo of Glanfeuil (Saint-Maur-sur-Loire), abbot, ninth-century hagiographer. He entered Glanfeuil not later than 856 and became its abbot in 861. In 864 he issued a "Life of St. Maurus", a revision, he claimed, of a "Life" originally written by Faustus of Montecassino, which makes St. Maurus the founder and first abbot of Glanfeuil, and is the chief source for the legendary sojourn of that saint in France. It is so anachronistic that it is generally believed to have been composed by Odo himself, though Mabillon and a few modern writers ascribe it to Faustus [Mabillon in "Annales O.S.B.", I, 629–54, and in "Acta SS. Ord. S. Ben.", I, 259 sq.; Adlhoch in "Studien und Mitteilungen aus dem Benediktiner und Cistercienser Orden", XXVI and XXVII (Brünn, 1905 and 1906); Plaine, ibid., XVI (1905); Huillier, "Etude critique des Actes de S. Maur de Glanfeuil" (Paris, 1903); Halphen in "Revue historique" LXXXVIII (Paris, 1905), 287–95]. The "Life" is printed in "Acta SS.", January, II, 321–332. Another work of Odo, "Miracula S. Mauri, sive restauratio monasterii Glannafoliensis", has some historical value. The author narrates how he fled with the relics of St. Maurus from the Normans in 862 and how the relics were finally transferred to the monastery of St-Maur-des-Fossés near Paris in 868. It is printed in "Acta SS,", January, II, 334–42. In 868 Odo became also Abbot of St-Maur-des-Fossés.

Besides the references mentioned above see LANDREAU, *Les Vicissitudes de l'abbaye de Saint Maur aux VIIIe et IXe siècles* (Angers, 1905), 44–58; ADLHOCH in *Studien und Mitteilungen aus dem Benediktiner und Cistercienser Orden*, XXVII (Brünn, 1906), 575–91; BIHLMEYER in *Kirchliches Handlex.*, II (Munich, 1909), 1192–3.

MICHAEL OTT.

Odoric of Pordenone. See PORDENONE, ODORIC OF.

O'Dugan, JOHN (SEÁGHAN "MOR" O DUBHAGÁIN), d. in Roscommon, 1372. His family were for several centuries hereditary historians to the O'Kellys of Ui Máine. His most important work is a compilation of verse, giving the names of the various tribes and territories of the Irish, and the various chiefs before the coming of the Normans. He devotes 152 lines to Meath, 354 to Ulster, 328 to Connacht, and only 56 to Leinster, leaving it evidently unfinished at his death. His contemporary, Giolla-na-naomh O Huidhrin (Heerin), completed it. This work throws more light upon ancient Irish names and territories than any other similar work. In his monumental "Cambrensis Eversus", Dr. Lynch (q. v.) says that he could not find "any better source than this remarkable poem" concerning the chief Irish families before the coming of the English. His précis of it occupies pages 235–79 of the first volume of Father Matthew Kelly's edition. O'Dugan was the author of several other extant poems, all more or less in the nature of a *memoria technica*, valuable chiefly for their facts about the kings of Ireland and of the provinces. He also composed several rules for determining moveable feasts, etc.

Topographical Poems of John O'Dubhagain and Giolla na Naomh O'Huidhrin, with translations, notes, and introductory dissertations by O'DONOVAN (Dublin, 1862); O'REILLY, *Catalogue of Irish Writers* (Dublin, 1820); WEBB, *Compendium of Irish Biogr.* (Dublin, 1878); *Cambrensis Eversus*, tr. KELLY, I (Dublin, 1848).

DOUGLAS HYDE.

O'Duignan, PEREGRINE. See FOUR MASTERS, ANNALS OF THE.

O'Dwyer, EDWARD THOMAS. See LIMERICK, DIOCESE OF.

O'Dwyer, JOSEPH, physician, inventor of intubation; b. at Cleveland, 1841; d. in New York, January 7, 1898. He was educated in the public schools of London, Ontario, and studied medicine in the office of Dr. Anderson. After two years of apprenticeship he entered the College of Physicians (New York) from which he was graduated in 1865. He won first place in the competitive examination for resident physicians of the Charity, now the City, Hospital of New York City on Blackwell's Island. Twice during his service he contracted cholera. After the completion of his service he took up private practice. Four years later (1872) he was appointed to the staff of the New York Foundling Asylum.

The deaths of many children by suffocation when diptheria brought about closure of the larynx proved too sad a sight for him, so he tried to find something to keep the larynx open. He used a wire spring and experimented with a small bivalve speculum but to no purpose. The inflamed mucous membrane and false membrane forced themselves into the interstices and the difficulty of breathing returned. Besides, the pressure produced ulceration. Finally he tried a tube. The use of a tube for intubation had often been attempted but unsuccessfully. O'Dwyer succeeded in devising the form of tube that would remain and then ingeniously fashioned instruments for the placing and displacing of the tube. After a dozen years of diligent study this method of relieving difficulty of breathing proved successful. Most of his medical colleagues were sure that O'Dwyer's scheme was visionary. Before his death it was universally acknowledged that he had made the most important practical discovery of his generation. His tubes and the accompanying instruments for intubation and extubation, with his methods for the care of these patients, have since come to be employed everywhere throughout the medical world. The tubes are also of great value in stenosis of the larynx due to various other diseases, such as syphilis, and to strictures of the larynx, especially consequent on burns or scalds.

Afterwards O'Dwyer devoted himself to the study of pneumonia, but late in December 1897 he developed symptoms of a brain lesion, probably of infectious origin, which proved fatal. He was a fervent Catholic. His work at the Foundling Hospital helped greatly to make that institution one of the best of its kind.

NORTHROP, *Joseph O'Dwyer; Medical Record* (New York, 1904); WALSH, *Makers of Modern Medicine* (New York, 1907).

JAMES J. WALSH.

Œcolampadius, JOHANN, Protestant theologian, organizer of Protestantism at Basle, b. at Weinsberg, Swabia, in 1482; d. at Basle, 24 November, 1531. His family name was Heussgen or Hussgen, not Husschyn (Hausschein), as the hellenized form Œcolampadius was later rendered. Having received a preliminary classical training at Weinsberg and Heilbronn, he began the study of law at Bologna, but left for Heidelberg in 1499 to take up theology and literature. He was specially interested in the works of the mystics, without obtaining, however, a thorough foundation in Scholastic theology. After his ordination he held a small benefice at Weinsberg, where he delivered his sermons on the Seven Last Words. At Stuttgart (1512) he extended his knowledge of Greek, and at Tübingen became friendly with Melanchthon; returning to Heidelberg, he studied Hebrew under a Jewish convert, and became acquainted with Brenz and Capito. A little later he was appointed preacher at the cathedral of Basle (1515), where he joined the circle of Erasmus. In 1515 he was made a bachelor, in 1516 licentiate, and on 9 September, 1518, a doctor of theology. He had already resigned as preacher at Basle and returned to Weinsberg. In December, 1518, he became cathedral preacher at Augsburg, where he joined the Humanists who sympathized with Luther. He corresponded with Luther and Melanchthon, and directed against Eck the anonymous pamphlet "Canonici indocti Lutherani" (Augsburg, 1519). Œcolampadius, however, far from having taken a definite stand, was engaged in translating the ascetical writings of St. Gregory of Nazianzus from Greek into Latin.

Suddenly he entered the Brigittine monastery at Altomünster (23 April, 1520). He first thought of devoting himself to study in this retreat, but was soon again entangled in controversy, when, at the request of Bernhard Adelmann, he wrote his opinion of Luther, which was very favourable, and sent it in confidence to Adelmann at Augsburg. The latter, however, forwarded it to Capito at Basle and he, without asking the author's permission, published it (Œcolampadii iudicium de doctore Martino Luthero). This was followed by other uncatholic writings, e. g. one against the doctrine of the Church on confession (Augsburg, 1521) and a sermon on the Holy Eucharist (Augsburg, 1521) dealing with transubstantiation as a question of no importance and repudiating the sacrificial character of the Eucharist; these publications finally rendered his position in the monastery untenable. He left in February, 1522, supplied by the community with money for his journey. Through the influence of Franz von Sickingen he became chaplain in the castle on the Ebernburg. In November of the same year he removed to Basle. He publicly defended Luther's doctrine of justification by faith alone (30 August, 1523). The following February he advocated the marriage of priests and used his pulpit to disseminate the new teachings. The progress of Protestantism became much more marked in Basle after the Council had appointed him pastor of St. Martin's (February, 1525), on condition that he should introduce no innovations into Divine service without special authorization of the council, which included Catholics as well as Reformers, and was still cautious; the spread of the new teachings was partially counteracted by the bishop and the university, which, for the greater part, was still Catholic in its tendency.

After Karlstadt's writings had been proscribed by the Basle Council, Œcolampadius, in August, 1525, issued his "De genuina verborum Domini: Hoc est corpus meum, iuxta vetustissimos auctores expositione liber", in which he declared openly for Zwingli's doctrine of the Last Supper, construing as metaphorical the words of institution. The distinction between his explanation and Zwingli's was merely formal, Œcolampadius, instead of *est* interpreted the word *corpus* figuratively (corpus—*figura corporis*). Accordingly the Last Supper was to him merely an external symbol, which the faithful should receive, less for their own sakes than for the sake of their neighbours, as a token of brotherhood and a means of edification. This monograph was confiscated at Basle, and attacked by Brenz on behalf of the Lutheran theologians of Swabia in his "Syngramma Suevicum" (1525), which Œcolampadius answered with his "Antisyngramma ad ecclesiastes Suevos" (1526). Although Œcolampadius had continued to say Mass until 1525, in November of that year he conducted the first "reformed" celebration of the Lord's Supper with a liturgy compiled by himself. In 1526 he arranged an order of Divine service under the title "Form und Gestalt, wie der Kindertauf, des Herrn Nachtmahl und der Kranken Heimsuchung jezt zu Basel von etlichen Predikanten gehalten werden". In May, 1526, he took part in the disputation at Baden, but in Zwingli's absence he was unable to cope successfully with Eck. In May, 1527, the Council of Basle requested the Catholic and Protestant preachers of the city to give in writing their views concerning the Mass. The Catholic belief was presented by Augustin Marius, the Protestant by Œcolampadius. The Council as yet placed no general proscription on the Mass, but allowed each of the clergy to retain or set it aside. In consequence the Mass was abolished in the churches under Protestant preachers and the singing of psalms in German introduced. Monasteries were suppressed towards the end of 1527. The ancient Faith was, however, tolerated for a time in the churches under Catholic control.

After the disputation at Bern in January, 1528, in which Œcolampadius and Zwingli were chief speakers on the Protestant side, the Protestants of Basle threw caution to the winds; at Easter, 1528, and later, several churches were despoiled of their statues and pictures. In December, 1528, at the instance of Œcolampadius, the Protestants petitioned the Council to suppress Catholic worship, but, as the Council was too slow in deciding, the Protestantizing of Basle was completed by means of an insurrection. The Protestants expelled the Catholic members of the Council. The churches previously in the hands of the Catholics, including the cathedral, were seized and pillaged. Œcolampadius, who had married in 1528, became pastor of the cathedral and *antistes* over all the Protestant clergy of Basle, and took the leading part in compiling the Reformation ordinance promulgated by the Council (1 April, 1529). Against those who refused to participate in the Protestant celebration of the Lord's Supper, compulsory measures were enacted which broke down the last remnant of opposition from the Catholics. In contrast to Zwingli, Œcolampadius strove, but with only partial success, to secure for the representatives of the Church a greater share in its management. In October, 1529, Œcolampadius joined in the vain attempt at Marburg to close the sacramental dispute between the Lutherans and the Reformed. In 1531, with Bucer and Blarer, he introduced Protestantism by force into Ulm, Biberach, and Memmingen. He was also concerned in the affairs of the Waldenses, and was largely responsible for their having joined forces with the Reformed at this time.

Œcolampadius was a man of splendid, though misdirected, natural gifts. Among the fathers and leaders of Protestantism he had not, either as theologian or man of action, the importance or forceful personality of Luther, Calvin, and Zwingli, but his name stands among the first of their supporters. As a theologian, after the full development of his religious opinions, he belonged to the party of Zwingli, though remaining independent on some important points. The opinion that he was more tolerant than the other Protestant leaders does not accord with facts, though true on the whole as regards his relations to Protestants of other beliefs. The profound differences which had already appeared among the adherents of the new religion, due particularly to variations in opinion concerning the Lord's Supper, were painful to Œcolampadius; but in contrast to Luther's uncompromising attitude, he strove without surrendering his own views to restore harmony through reciprocal toleration. Towards the Catholic religion, however, he bore the same hatred and intolerance as the other Protestant leaders. Likewise in justifying religious war, he shares Zwingli's standpoint. If his first movements at Basle were more cautious than those of others elsewhere, it was not through greater mildness, but rather out of regard for conditions which he could not change at a single stroke. As soon, however, as he had won over the secular authority, he did not rest until Catholic worship was suppressed, and those who at first resisted were either banished or forced to apostatize.

CAPITO, *Johannis Œcolampadii et Huldrichi Zwinglii epist. libri quatuor* (Basle, 1536), with a biography of Œcolampadius; HESS, *Lebensgesch. Dr. Joh. Œcolampad's* (Zurich, 1793); HERZOG, *Das Leben Joh. Œcolampad's* (Basle, 1843); HAGENBACH, *Œcolampad's Leben und ausgewählte Schriften* (Elberfeld, 1859) in *Leben und ausgewählte Schriften der Väter und Begründer der reformierten Kirche*, II; FEHLEISEN, *Joh. Œcolampadius. Sein Leben und Wirken* (Weinsberg, 1882); BURCKHARDT-BIEDERMANN, *Ueber Œcolampad's Person und Wirksamkeit* in *Theologische Zeitschr. aus der Schweiz*, X (1893), 27–40, 81–92; HERZOG in *Realencyk. für prot. Theol. und Kirche*, 2nd ed., X, 708–24; WAGENMANN in *Allgem. deutsche Biog.*, s. v.; MAYER in *Kirchenlex.*, s. v. For the Augsburg period cf. THURNHOFER, *Bernhard Adelmann von Adelmannsfelden* (Freiburg, 1900), especially pp. 62 sqq. and 115–26; for his controversy with Ambrosius Pelargus and Augustinus Marius on the Mass cf. PAULUS, *Ambrosius Pelargus* in *Hist. polit. Blät.*, CX (1892), 2–12; IDEM in PAULUS, *Die deutschen Dominikaner im Kampfe gegen Luther* (Freiburg, 1903), 191–98.

FRIEDRICH LAUCHERT.

Œconomus, EPISCOPAL (Gr. οἰκονόμος from οἶκος a house, and νέμειν, to distribute, to administer), one who is charged with the care of a house, an administrator. In canon law this term designates the individual who is appointed to take charge of the temporal goods of the Church in a diocese; it is used also of the person in charge of the property of a monastery. This office originated in the Eastern Church and dates back to the fourth century: a law of Honorius and Arcadius in 398 speaks of it as if it were then widespread (Cod. Theodos., IX, tit. 45, lex. 3). The Council of Chalcedon (451) ordered an œconomus to be appointed in every diocese, to take charge of ecclesiastical property under episcopal authority (canon xxvi in Mansi, VII, 367). They were established in the Eastern Church and have continued down to the present day in the schismatical Greek Church (Silbernagl, "Verfassung und gegenwärtiger Bestand sämtlicher Kirchen des Orients", 2nd ed., Ratisbon, 1904, 37). The increase of church property after the Edict of Milan (313) and the multiplication of episcopal duties rendered this office very useful. In the West, we meet with the œconomus in Spain (Council of Seville, 619, can. ix), in Sardinia, and perhaps in Sicily, at the end of the sixth century (Jaffé-Wattenbach, "Regesta Pontificum Romanorum", Leipzig, 1881, I, nn. 1282, 1915). But as a general rule the Western bishops contented themselves with the aid of a confidential assistant, a *vicedominus*, who looked after the temporalities and ranked next to the bishop. The establishment of a domain in connexion with each church made the task of administering the ecclesiastical property much lighter. The office of *vicedominus* was modified by the influence of the feudal system, and by the fact that the bishops became temporal sovereigns. The Council of Trent ordered the chapters of cathedral churches to establish, in addition to a capitulary vicar, one or more œconomi to administer the temporal property of the diocese during an episcopal vacancy (Sess. XXIV, De Reformatione, c. xvi). At the present time, the bishop is not obliged to appoint an œconomus, though he is not hindered from so doing. The Second Plenary Council of Baltimore (c. lxxv) advises bishops to select one from among the ecclesiastics or even the laity, who is skilled in the civil law of the country.

LOENING, *Gesch. des deutschen Kirchenrechts* (Strasburg, 1878), I, 235; II, 342; STUTZ, *Gesch. des kirchl. Benefizialwesens*, I (Berlin, 1895), 9 sq.; SENN, *L'institution des Vidamies en France* (Paris, 1907); LESNE, *Hist. de la propriété ecclés. en France*, I. *Epoque Romaine et Mérovingienne* (Paris, 1910).

A. VAN HOVE.

Œcumenical Council. See COUNCILS, GENERAL.

Œcumenius (οἰκουμένιος), Bishop of Trikka (now Trikkala) in Thessaly about 990 (according to Cave, op. cit. infra, p. 112). He is the reputed author of commentaries on books of the New Testament. A manuscript of the tenth or eleventh century containing a commentary on the Apocalypse attributes it to him. The work consists of a prologue and then a slightly modified version of the commentary of Andrew of Cæsarea (sixth cent.). Manuscripts of the eleventh century contain commentaries on the Acts and on the Catholic and Pauline epistles, attributed since the sixteenth century to Œcumenius. Those on the Acts and Catholic Epistles are identical with the commentaries of Theophylactus of Achrida (eleventh cent.); the Pauline commentaries are a different work, though they too contain many parallel passages to Theophylactus. The first manuscripts, however, are older than Theophylactus, so that it cannot be merely a false attribution of his work. It would seem then that Œcumenius copied Andrew of Cæsarea and was himself copied by Theophylactus. The situation is however, further complicated by the fact that among the authors quoted in these works the name of Œcumenius himself occurs repeatedly. The question then of Œcumenius's authorship is in all cases very difficult. Bardenhewer (Kirchenlex., IX, 1905, coll. 706–10) is doubtful about it; Ehrhard (in Krumbacher's "Byzant. Litt.", 132) says: "The name Œcumenius represents in the present state of investigation a riddle that can be solved only by thorough critical study of the manuscripts in connexion with the whole question of the Catenæ." The commentary on St. Paul's Epistles is a compromise between the usual kind of commentary and a catena. Most explanations are given without reference and are therefore presumably those of the author; but there are also long excerpts from earlier writers, Clement of Alexandria, Eusebius, Chrysostom, Cyril of Alexandria etc., especially from Photius. It is among these that Œcumenius himself is quoted. The Commentary on the Apocalypse was first edited by Cramer: "Catenæ in Nov. Test.", VIII (Oxford, 1840), 497–582; the other three (on Acts, Cath. Ep., and St. Paul) by Donatus (Verona, 1532). Morellus (Paris, 1631) re-edited these with a Latin translation; his edition is reproduced in P. G., CXVIII–CIX.

FABRICIUS-HARLES, *Bibl. græca*, VIII (Hamburg, 1802), 692–5; CAVE, *Scriptorum eccles. hist. liter.*, II (Basle, 1745), 112; KRUMBACHER, *Byzantin. Litteraturgesch.* (2nd ed., Munich, 1897), 131–3.

ADRIAN FORTESCUE.

OENGUS

Oengus, SAINT. See AENGUS, SAINT.

Oertel, JOHN JAMES MAXIMILIAN, journalist, b. at Ansbach, Bavaria, 27 April, 1811; d. at Jamaica, New York, 21 August, 1882. Born a Lutheran, he was sent to the Lutheran University of Erlangen where he studied theology and five years later was ordained a minister. After his ordination he accepted a call to care for his countrymen in the United States, and arrived in New York in October, 1837. The unorthodox opinions of the New York Lutherans displeased him, and he left for Missouri early in 1839. Things were no better there, so he returned to New York. Denominational dissensions weakened his faith, and in 1840 he became a Catholic. An account of his conversion in pamphlet form published 25 March, 1850, had quite a vogue in the controversial literature of the day. After his conversion he taught German at St. John's College, Fordham; later he edited in Cincinnati the "Wahrheitsfreund", a German Catholic weekly, and in 1846 he left for Baltimore where he founded the weekly "Kirchenzeitung", which, under his editorial direction, was the most prominent German Catholic publication in the United States. In 1851, he moved the paper to New York. In 1869 he published "Altes und Neues". In 1875 Pius IX made him a Knight of St. Gregory in recognition of his service to the Church and Catholic literature.

U. S. CATH. HIST. SOC., *Hist. Records and Studies*, IV, parts I and II (New York, Oct., 1906); SHEA, *The Cath. Church in the U. S.* (New York, 1856); *Catholic News* (New York, 18 April, 1908).

THOMAS F. MEEHAN.

Oettingen (ALTÖTTING, OETINGA), during the Carlovingian period a royal palace near the confluence of the Isen and the Inn in Upper Bavaria, near which King Karlmann erected a Benedictine monastery in 876, with Werinolf as first abbot, and also built the abbey church in honour of the Apostle St. Philip. In 907 King Louis the Child, gave the abbey *in commendam* to Bishop Burchard of Passau (903–915), probably identical with Burchard, second and last abbot. In 910 the Hungarians ransacked and burnt the church and abbey. In 1228 Duke Louis I of Bavaria rebuilt them and put them in charge of twelve Augustinian Canons and a provost. The Augustinians remained until the secularization of the Bavarian monasteries in 1803. Under their care was also the Liebfrauen-Kapelle with its miraculous image of Our Lady, dating from the end of the thirteenth or the beginning of the fourteenth century. The pilgrims became so numerous that to aid the Augustinian Canons the Jesuits erected a house in 1591 and remained until the suppression of their order in 1773. Franciscans settled there from 1653 to 1803; from 1803 to 1844 the Capuchins and some secular priests, from 1844 to 1873 the Redemptorists had charge, and since 1872 the Capuchins. About 300,000 pilgrims come annually. Since the middle of the seventeenth century the hearts of the deceased Bavarian princes are preserved in the Liebfrauen-Kapelle.

MAIER, *Gedenkblätter und Culturbilder aus der Geschichte von Altötting* (Augsburg, 1885); KRAUTHAHN, *Geschichte der uralten Wallfahrt in Altötting* (9th ed., Altötting, 1893).

MICHAEL OTT.

Offa, King of Mercia, d. 29 July, 796. He was one of the leading figures of Saxon history, as appears from the real facts stripped of all legend. He obtained the throne of Mercia in 757, after the murder of his cousin, King Æthelbald, by Beornraed. After spending fourteen years in consolidating and ordering his territories he engaged in conquests which made him the most powerful king in England. After a successful campaign against the Hestingi, he defeated the men of Kent at Otford (775); the West Saxons at Bensington in Oxfordshire (779); and finally the Welsh, depriving the last-named of a large part of Powys, including the town of Pengwern. To repress the raids of the Welsh he built Offa's dyke, roughly indicating for the first time what has remained the boundary between England and Wales. Offa was now supreme south of the Humber, with the result that England was divided into three political divisions, Northumbria, Mercia, and Wessex. His next step was to complete the independence of Mercia by inducing the pope to erect a Mercian archbishopric, so as to free Mercia from the jurisdiction of the Archbishop of Canterbury. Hadrian I sent two legates, George and Theophylactus, to England to arrange for the transfer of five suffragan sees of Canterbury (viz. Worcester, Leicester, Lindsay, Elmham, and Dunwich) to the new Archbishopric of Lichfield, of which Higbert was first archbishop. This was effected at the Synod of Celchyth (787), at which Offa granted the pope a yearly sum equal to one mancus a day for the relief of the poor and for lights to be kept burning before St. Peter's tomb. At the same time he associated his son Ecgferth with him in the kingship. He preserved friendly relations with Charlemagne, who undertook to protect the English pilgrims and merchants who passed through his territories. Many charters granting lands to various monasteries are extant, and, though some are forgeries, enough are genuine documents to show that he was a liberal benefactor to the Church. The laws of Offa are not extant, but were embodied by Alfred in his later code. The chief stain on his character is the execution of Æthelbert, King of the East Angles. In all other respects he showed himself a great Christian king and an able and enlightened ruler.

Anglo-Saxon Chronicle, which misdates his death by two years; most of the chief medieval historians, WILLIAM OF MALMESBURY, MATTHEW PARIS etc., and later standard works, LINGARD etc.; MACKENZIE, *Essay on the life and institutions of Offa* (London, 1840); THORPE, *Ancient Laws and Institutes* (London, 1840); KEMBLE, *Codex Diplomaticus ævi Saxonici* (London, 1839–48); JAFFÉ, *Bibl. rerum Germanarum*, IV: *Monumenta Carolina* (Berlin, 1864–73); HADDAN AND STUBBS, *Councils and Ecclesiastical Documents*, III and V (Oxford, 1869–1878); GREEN, *Making of England* (London, 1885); BIRCH, *Cartularium Saxonicum* (London, 1885–93); SEARLE, *Anglo-Saxon Bishops, Kings, and Nobles* (Cambridge, 1899); HUGHES, *On Offa's Dyke* in *Archæologia* (1893), III, 465 sqq.

EDWIN BURTON.

Offerings (OBLATIONS).—I. The word *oblation*, from the supine of the Latin verb *offero* ("to offer"), is etymologically akin to *offering*, but is, unlike the latter, almost exclusively restricted to matters religious. In the English Bibles "oblation", "offering", "gift", "sacrifice" are used indiscriminately for anything presented to God in worship, or for the service of the Temple or priest. This indiscriminate rendering arises from the fact that these words do not purport to render always the same Hebrew expressions. The latter, moreover, are not distinctly specific in their meaning. In this article oblations will be considered in the narrow sense the term has tended to assume of vegetable or lifeless things offered to God, in contradistinction to "bloody sacrifices".

Oblations of this kind, like sacrifices, were found in all ancient Semitic religions—in fact are a world-wide and ever-existing institution. Various theories have been proposed to explain how offerings came to be a part of worship. Unfortunately very many modern scholars assume that mankind began in the savage state. According to one theory, the god being considered the first owner of the land, it was inferred he had a claim to a tribute from the increase of the soil: this is the *tribute* theory. It relies on the fact that the offering of first-fruits is one of the earliest forms of oblations found among ancient peoples. The assumption that primitive men conceived deity under low anthropomorphic forms is the source whence have sprung the *gift* theory, the *table-bond* theory, and the *communion* theory. According to the first of these systems, the god is approached through presents which the worshipper counts on to insure favour (Δῶρα θεοὺς πείθει, δῶρ᾽ αἰδοίους βασιλῆας). That such a misconception of the divinity was prevalent at certain epochs and among certain peoples cannot be gainsaid (Cic., "De Leg.", ii, 16); however, in view of the idea of the sacredness of the bond created by the sharing in a common meal—an idea that still holds sway among Semitic nomads (and nomadic life undoubtedly preceded agricultural life)—the *gift* theory has been mostly superseded by the *table-bond* theory. A bond is entered into between the god and the worshipper when they, as it were, sit at the same table, man furnishing the meal, and the god granting in return the assurance of his protection. The *communion* theory (its chief advocate is W. R. Smith) is based on the totemistic conception of the origin of worship, its essence consisting in that the life of the god, infused into the totem, is assimilated by the worshipper in the sacred repast. This theory would account for animal sacrifices and oblations of such vegetables as were considered totems; but it fails manifestly to explain the many and various oblations custom imposed or sanctioned.

As far as positive information is concerned, the origin of oblations, according to Genesis, may be traced back to Cain's offerings of the fruits of the earth. Some critics would brush aside the statement as the fancy of a Judean writer of the seventh century B. C.; yet the passage expresses the writer's belief that sacrifices and oblations were offered by the very first men. It emphasizes, moreover, the idea that oblation is an act of worship natural to an agricultural population, just as the slaying of a victim is to be expected in the worship of a pastoral people; and it seems to set forth the belief that bloody sacrifices are more pleasing to God than mere oblations—a belief seemingly inspired by the superiority the nomad has ever claimed in the East over the husbandman. At all events it cannot be denied that there is at the root of all oblations the idea that God has a claim upon man, his possessions, and the fruits of his labours, and is pleased at receiving an acknowledgment of His sovereignty.

Whether exterior worship, especially sacrifice, was in the beginning, as W. R. Smith affirms, an affair, not of the individual, but of the tribe or clan, is questionable. As far back as documents go, side by side with public oblations, are others made by individuals in their own name and out of private devotion.

The things thus made over to the deity were among Semitic peoples most varied in nature and value. Offering the first yield of the year's crop was extensively practised, local usage specifying what should be offered. The premices of the corn crop (wheat, barley, sometimes lentils) were generally reserved to the deity; so also among certain tribes the first milk and butter of the year. Sometimes fruits (not only first-fruits, but other fruit-oblations) were offered in their natural state. At Carthage the fruit-offering consisted of a choice branch bearing fruit; possibly such was the form of certain fruit-offerings in Israel. Oblations might also consist of fruit prepared as for ordinary use, in compressed cakes, cooked if necessary, or made in the form of jelly (*debash*; the latter preparation was excluded from the altar in Israel). All cereal oblations, whether of first-fruits or otherwise, among the Hebrews and apparently among the Phœnicians, were mingled with oil and salt before being placed on the altar. As sacrifices were frequently the occasion of social gatherings and of religious meals, the custom was introduced of offering with the victim whatever concomitants (bread, wine, etc.) were necessary. Yet nowhere do we find water offered up as an oblation or used for libations; only the ritual of late Judaism for the Feast of Tabernacles commanded that on each of the seven days of the celebration water drawn from the Fountain of Siloam (D. V., Sellum) should be brought into the Temple amidst the blare of trumpets and solemnly poured out upon the altar. Other articles of food were used for libations, such, for instance, as milk among the Phœnicians, as among nomadic Arabs it is to this very day. Libations of wine were frequent, at least in countries where wine was not too expensive; among the Hebrews, as in Greece and Rome, wine was added to holocausts as well as to victims whose flesh the worshippers partook of, and was then poured out at the base of the altar.

Analogous to offering liquid food to be poured out as a libation was the custom of anointing sacred objects or hallowed places. The history of the patriarchs bears witness to its primitive usage, and the accounts of travellers certify to its existence to-day among many Semitic populations. In this case, oil is generally used; occasionally more precious ointments, but as these largely contain oil, the difference is accidental. Among nomads where oil is scarce, butter is used, being spread on sacred stones, tombs, or on the door-posts or the lintels of venerated shrines. In some places oil is offered by way of fuel for lamps to be kept burning before the tomb of some renowned *wely* or in some sanctuary. Also it has always been a general custom in the East to offer, either together with, or apart from, sacrifices and oblations, spices to be burned at the place of the sacrifice or of the sacrificial meal, or upon a revered tomb, or at any place sacred to the tribe or individual. Among the Arabs it is hardly justifiable to pay religious homage at the tomb of some sainted *wely* or at certain sanctuaries without bringing an offering, however insignificant. If nothing better is at hand, the worshipper will leave on the spot a strip from his garment, a horse-shoe nail, even a pebble from the road.

Tithes (q. v.) appear to be more an impost than an oblation proper, and suppose a settled population; hence they have no place in the religion of nomads, ancient or modern.

Besides the oblations mentioned above (usually articles of food), the votive offerings made among early Semites on very special occasions deserve mention. One of the most characteristic is the offering of one's hair, common also among other ancient peoples. This offering was a personal one, and aimed to create or emphasize the relation between the worshipper and his god; it was usually in connexion with special vows. From this hair-offering we should distinguish the shaving of the head as a kind of purification prescribed in certain cases (Lev., xiv, 9). Owing undoubtedly to the superstitious practice of ancient peoples, associating mourning with a hair-offering, the Pentateuchal legislation enacted on this subject prohibitions (Lev., xix, 27; xxi, 5; Deut., xiv, 1), which, however, were not always observed. The only hair-offering legally recognized among the Hebrews was that connected with the vow of the Nazarite (Num., vi), and likely the writer of the Canticle of Debbora had some such vow in view when he speaks (Judges, v, 2), according to the probable sense of the Hebrew, of men offering their hair and vowing themselves to battle, i. e. vowing not to cut their hair until they should come back in triumph; this vow (still frequent in the East) implied that they should conquer or die. Also in Num., xxxi, 28, we read of a share of the spoils of battle being set aside as an offering to the sanctuary. Although the narrative here concerns a special occurrence, and nothing intimates that this spoil-offering should be held as a precedent, yet it is very likely that it begat at least a pious custom. We see, indeed, in Israel and neighbouring peoples, choice spoils hung up in sanctuaries. It may suffice to recall the trophies heaped up by the Assyrian and Babylonian rulers; also the Ark of the Covenant set up as an offering in the temple of Dagon by the Philistines; and in Israel itself, the arms of Goliath offered by David to the temple of Nob.

II. OBLATIONS AMONG THE JEWS.—Oblations in the Jewish religion were the object of minute regulations in the Law. Some were offered with bloody sacrifices (cf. Num., viii, 8; xv, 4–10), as the offering of meal, oil, and incense that accompanied the daily holocaust. A handful of this meal-offering mingled with oil was burned on the altar together with incense, and the remainder was allotted to the priests, to be eaten unleavened within the Temple precincts (Lev., vi, 14–18; Num., vi, 14–16). In peace-offerings, together with the victim, loaves, wafers, and cakes of flour kneaded with oil, and loaves of leavened bread were presented to the Temple (the loaves of leavened bread were not to be put or burned upon the altar); one cake, one wafer, and one loaf of each kind was the share of the officiating priest (Lev., vii, 11–14; ii, 11). Among the regulations for the sacrifice of thanksgiving to be offered by lepers on their recovery was one that the cleansed, if they had the means, should add to the victims three-tenths of an ephah (the ephah of the second Temple contained about three pecks, dry measure, the old measure being possibly twice as large) of meal tempered with oil; if they were poor, one tenth of an ephah was sufficient (Lev., xiv, 10, 21). Finally the sacrifice of the Nazarite included a basketful of unleavened bread tempered with oil and cakes of like kind, together with the ordinary libations.

For public oblations separate from sacrifices see FIRST-FRUITS; LOAVES OF PROPOSITION; TITHES. Moreover, every day the High Priest presented at the altar in his own name and that of the other priests an oblation of one tenth of an ephah (half in the morning and half in the evening) of meal kneaded with oil, to be burned on the altar (Lev., vi, 19–23; cf. Jos., "Ant. Jud.", III, x, 7). A certain number of private oblations were prescribed by Law. The priest, on entering upon his ministry, offered an oblation, the same in kind and quantity as the daily oblation of the High Priest (Lev., vi, 20, 21). A man obliged to a sin-offering, and too poor to provide a victim, was allowed to present an oblation of one tenth of an ephah of flour without the accompaniments of oil and incense (Lev., v, 1–4, 11, 12). A woman accused of adultery was subjected to a trial during which an offering of one tenth of an ephah of barley-flour without oil or incense was made, a part being burned on the altar. Finally oblations might be made in fulfilment of a vow; but then the matter was left to the choice of the vower. The regulations of the Pentateuchal Law concerning oblations were scrutinized and commented upon by Jewish doctors who took up every possible difficulty likely to occur, for instance, on the nature, origin, preparation, and cooking of the flour to be used, its buying and measuring, the mode of presenting, receiving, and offering the oblation, its division and the attributing of each of the parts (see the forty-second treatise of the Mishna: "Menahoth"). Of these commentaries we will single out only those concerned with the rite to be observed in offering the oblations, because they are the only somewhat reliable explanation of difficult expressions occasionally met with in Holy Writ (D. V.: "to elevate", "to separate", Lev., vii, 34; x, 15, etc.). When an Israelite presented an oblation, the priest went to meet him at the gate of the priests' court; he put his hands under the hands of the offerer, who held oblation, and drew the offerer's hands and the oblation first backwards, then forwards (this was the *thenūphah*, improperly rendered "the separation"), again upwards and downwards (*therūmah*, "the elevation"). These rites were not observed in the oblations by women or Gentiles. The first-fruits offered at the Pasch and the "oblation of jealousy" (on the occasion of an accusation of adultery) were moved about in the manner described, then brought to the south-west corner of the altar; the first-fruits offered at the Pentecost and the *log* (2/5 of a pint) of oil presented by the leper were subject to the *thenūphah* and the *therūmah*, but not brought to the altar; the sin-offering, the oblations of the priests, and the freewill oblations were only brought directly to the altar; lastly the loaves of proposition were neither "separated" and "elevated" nor brought to the altar.

III. OBLATIONS AMONG CHRISTIANS.—Like many Jewish customs, that of offering to the Temple the matter of the sacrifices and other oblations was adapted by the early Christian communities to the new order of things. First in importance among these Christian oblations is that of the matter of the Eucharistic sacrifice. Not only the laity, but the whole clergy, bishops, and pope himself included, had to make this offering. These oblations were collected by the officiating bishop assisted by priests and deacons at the beginning of the "Missa Fidelium", after the dismissal of the non-communicants. This collection, at first performed in silence, was, towards the beginning of the fifth century, made amidst the singing of a Psalm, known in Rome as the "Offertorium", at Milan as the "Offerenda", and in Greek churches as the "Cherubikon" (our Offertory is a remnant of the old "Offertorium", curtailed by reason of the actual gathering of the oblations falling into disuse). Part of the oblations was destined for consecration and communion (cf. the French word *oublie* applied to the matter of the Eucharist). The subdeacon in charge of this part is called in certain "Ordines Romani" the "oblationarius". Another part was destined for the poor, and the remainder for the clergy. So important was this offering held, that the word *oblatio* came to designate the whole liturgical service. Apart from this liturgical oblation, which has been preserved, at least partly, in the liturgy of Milan and in some churches of France, new fruits were at given seasons presented at Mass for blessing, a custom somewhat analogous to the first-fruit offerings in the Old Law; this usage is still in vigour in parts of Germany where, at Easter, eggs are solemnly blessed; but, contrary to Hebrew customs, the Christians usually retained the full disposition of these articles of food. Very early offerings were made over to the Church for the support of the poor and of the clergy. St. Paul emphasized the right of ministers of the Gospel to live by the Gospel (I Cor., ix, 13–14), and he never tired of reminding the churches founded by him of their duty to supply the wants of poorer communities. How, within the limits of each community, the poor were cared for we catch a glimpse of in the records of the early Church of Jerusalem (institution of the deacons); that in certain Churches, as the Church of Rome, the oblations for the poor reached a fair amount, we know from the prominence of the deacons, an illustration of which we have in the history of St. Lawrence, and in the fact that the pope was usually chosen from among their order. In time of persecution, manual offerings were sufficient to support the clergy and the poor; but when peace had come, Christians felt it a duty to insure this support by means of foundations. Such donations multiplied, and the word "oblations" (usually in the plural number) came to mean in Canon Law any property, real or personal, made over to the Church.

EDERSHEIM, *The Temple and its services* (London, 1874); JASTROW, *The Religion of Babylonia and Assyria* (Boston, 1898); SMITH, *The Religion of the Semites* (London, 1907); WELLHAUSEN, *Prolegomena to the History of Israel*, Eng. tr., BLACK AND MENZIES (Edinburgh, 1885); IDEM, *Reste arabischen Heidenthums* (Berlin, 1897); IKEN, *Antiquitates Hebraicæ* (Bremen, 1741); RELAND, *Antiquitates Sacræ* (Utrecht, 1741); SPENCER, *De Legibus Hebræorum ritualibus* (Cambridge, 1727); BERGIER in *Dict. de Théologie* (Lille, n. d.), s. vv. *Oblations, Offrandes*; CABROL, *Le Livre de la prière antique* (Paris, 1903); DHORME, *Coutumes des Arabes au pays de Moab* (Paris, 1908); IDEM, *La religion assyro-babylonienne* (Paris, 1910); DUCHESNE, *Les origines du culte chrétien* (Paris, 1898); ERMONI, *La religion de l'Egypte ancienne* (Paris, 1909); LAGRANGE, *Etudes sur les religions sémitiques* (Paris, 1903); BÄHR, *Symbolik des mosaischen Cultus* (Heidelberg, 1837); BENZIGER, *Hebr. Archäologie* (Freiburg, 1895); NOWACK, *Lehrbuch der hebr. Archäologie*, II (Freiburg, 1894). CHARLES L. SOUVAY.

Offertory (OFFERTORIUM), the rite by which the bread and wine are presented (offered) to God before they are consecrated and the prayers and chant that accompany it.

I. History. — The idea of this preparatory hallowing of the matter of the sacrifice by offering it to God is very old and forms an important element of every Christian liturgy. In the earliest period we have no evidence of anything but the bringing up of the bread and wine as they are wanted, before the Consecration prayer. Justin Martyr says: "Then bread and a cup of water and wine are brought to the president of the brethren" (I Apol., lxv, cf. lxvii). But soon the placing of the offering on the altar was accompanied by a prayer that God should accept these gifts, sanctify them, change them into the Body and Blood of his Son, and give us in return the grace of Communion. The Liturgy of "Apost. Const.", VIII, says: "The deacons bring the gifts to the bishop at the altar . . . the bishop having prayed silently with the priests" . . . (xii, 3–4). This silent prayer is undoubtedly an Offertory prayer. But a later modification in the East brought about one of the characteristic differences between Eastern and Roman liturgies. All Eastern (and the old Gallican) rites prepare the gift before the Liturgy begins. This ceremony (προσκομιδή) is especially elaborate in the Byzantine and its derived rites. It takes place on the credence table. The bread and wine are arranged, divided, incensed; and many prayers are said over them involving the idea of an offertory. The gifts are left there and are brought to the altar in solemn procession at the beginning of the Liturgy of the Faithful. This leaves no room for another offertory then. However, when they are placed on the altar prayers are said by the celebrant and a litany by the deacon which repeat the offertory idea. Rome alone has kept the older custom of one offertory and of preparing the gifts when they are wanted at the beginning of the Mass of the Faithful. Originally at this moment the people brought up bread and wine which were received by the deacons and placed by them on the altar. Traces of the custom remain at a papal Mass and at Milan. The office of the *vecchioni* in Milan cathedral, often quoted as an Ambrosian peculiarity, is really a Roman addition that spoils the order of the old Milanese rite. Originally the only Roman Offertory prayers were the secrets. The Gregorian Sacramentary contains only the rubric: "deinde offertorium, et dicitur oratio super oblata" (P. L., LXXVIII, 25). The *Oratio super oblata* is the Secret. All the old secrets express the offertory idea clearly. They were said silently by the celebrant (hence their name) and so are not introduced by *Oremus*. This corresponds to the oldest custom mentioned in the "Apost. Const."; its reason is that meanwhile the people sang a psalm (the Offertory chant). In the Middle Ages, as the public presentation of the gifts by the people had disappeared, there seemed to be a void at this moment which was filled by our present Offertory prayers (Thalhofer, op. cit. below, II, 161). For a long time these prayers were considered a private devotion of the priest, like the preparation at the foot of the altar. They are a Northern (late Gallican) addition, not part of the old Roman Rite, and were at first not written in missals. Micrologus says: "The Roman order appointed no prayer after the Offertory before the Secret" (cxi, P. L., CLI, 984). He mentions the later Offertory prayers as a "Gallican order" and says that they occur "not from any law but as an ecclesiastical custom". The medieval Offertory prayers vary considerably. They were established at Rome by the fourteenth century (Ordo Rom. XIV., 53, P. L., LXXVIII, 1165). The present Roman prayers were compiled from various sources, Gallican or Mozarabic. The prayer "Suscipe sancte pater" occurs in Charles the Bald's (875–877) prayer book; "Deus qui humanæ substantiæ" is modified from a Christmas Collect in the Gregorian Sacramentary (P. L., LXXVIII, 32); "Offerimus tibi Domine" and "Veni sanctificator" (fragment of an old Epiklesis, Hoppe, "Die Epiklesis", Schaffhausen, 1864, p. 272) are Mozarabic (P. L., LXXXV, 112). Before Pius V's Missal these prayers were often preceded by the title "Canon minor" or "Secretella" (as amplifications of the Secret). The Missal of Pius V (1570) printed them in the Ordinary. Since then the prayers that we know form part of the Roman Mass. The ideas expressed in them are obvious. Only it may be noted that two expressions: "hanc immaculatam hostiam" and "calicem salutaris" dramatically anticipate the moment of consecration, as does the Byzantine Cherubikon.

While the Offertory is made the people (choir) sing a verse (the *Offertorium* in the sense of a text to be sung) that forms part of the Proper of the Mass. No such chant is mentioned in "Apost. Const.", VIII, but it may no doubt be supposed as the reason why the celebrant there too prays silently. It is referred to by St. Augustine (Retract., II, xi, P. L., XXXII, 63). The Offertorium was once a whole psalm with an antiphon. By the time of the Gregorian Antiphonary the psalm has been reduced to a few verses only, which are always given in that book (e.g., P. L., LXXVIII, 641). So also the Second Roman Ordo: "Canitur offertorium cum versibus" (ib., 972). Durandus notes with disapproval that in his time the verses of the psalm are left out (Rationale, IV, 26). Now only the antiphon is sung, except at requiems. It is taken from the psalter, or other book of the Bible, or is often not a Biblical text. It refers in some way to the feast or occasion of the Mass, never to the offering of bread and wine. Only the requiem has preserved a longer offertory with one verse and the repetition of the last part of the antiphon (the text is not Biblical).

II. Present Use.—At high Mass, as soon as the celebrant has chanted the *Oremus* followed by no prayer, the choir sings the Offertory. When they have finished there remains an interval till the Preface which may (when the organ is permitted) be filled by music of the organ or at any time by singing some approved hymn or chant. Meanwhile the celebrant first says the Offertory chant. The corporal has been spread on the altar during the creed. The subdeacon brings the empty chalice and the paten with the bread from the credence table to the altar. The deacon hands the paten and bread to the celebrant. He takes it and holding it up says the prayer: "suscipe sancte Pater". At the end he makes a sign of the cross with the paten over the altar and slips the bread from it on to the corporal. Soon after the paten is given to the subdeacon's charge till it is wanted again for the fraction. The deacon pours wine into the chalice, the subdeacon water, which is first blessed by the celebrant with the form: "Deus qui humanæ substantiæ". The deacon hands the chalice to the celebrant, who, holding it up, says the prayer: "Offerimus tibi Domine". The deacon also lays his right hand on the foot of the chalice and says this prayer with the celebrant—a relic of the old idea that the chalice is in his care. The celebrant makes the sign of the cross with the chalice and stands it behind the bread on the corporal. The deacon covers it with the pall. The celebrant, bowing down, his hands joined and resting on the altar, says the prayer: "In spiritu humilitatis"; rising he says the "Veni sanctificator" making the sign of the cross over all the *oblata* at the word *benedic*. Then follows the incensing of the altar and the Lavabo (q. v.). The use of incense at this point is medieval and not originally Roman (remnant of the incense at the Gallican procession of the *oblata?*). Micrologus notes that the Roman order uses incense at the Gospel, not at the Offertory; but he admits that in his time (eleventh century) the *oblata* are incensed by nearly everyone (De Eccl. Observ., IX). Finally, after the Lavabo the celebrant at the middle of the altar, looking up and then bowing down, says the prayer "Suscipe sancta Trinitas" which sums up the Offertory idea. The *Orate fratres* and secrets follow.

At low Mass, the parts of the deacon and subdeacon are taken partly by the server and partly by the celebrant himself. There is no incense. At requiems the water is not blessed, and the subdeacon does not hold the paten. The Dominicans still prepare the offering before Mass begins. This is one of their Gallican peculiarities and so goes back to the Eastern Proskomide. The Milanese and Mozarabic Missals have adopted the Roman Offertory. The accompanying chant is called *Sacrificium* at Toledo.

DURANDUS, *Rationale divinorum officiorum*, IV, 26–32; DUCHESNE, *Origines du culte chrétien* (Paris, 2nd ed., 1898), 165–167; 194–199; THALHOFER, *Handbuch der katholischen Liturgik*, II (Freiburg, 1890); GIHR, *Das heilige Messopfer* (Freiburg, 1897), 458–508; Eng. tr. (St. Louis, 1908), 494–551; RIETSCHEL, *Lehrbuch der Liturgik*, I (Berlin, 1900), 376–378.

ADRIAN FORTESCUE.

Offertory, COLLECTIONS AT. See OFFERINGS.

Office, DIVINE.—I. THE EXPRESSION "DIVINE OFFICE", signifying etymologically a duty accomplished for God, or in virtue of a Divine precept, means, in ecclesiastical language, certain prayers to be recited at fixed hours of the day or night by priests, religious, or clerics and, in general, by all those obliged by their vocation to fulfil this duty. The Divine Office comprises only the recitation of certain prayers in the Breviary, and does not include the Mass and other liturgical ceremonies. "Canonical Hours", "Breviary", "Diurnal and Nocturnal Office", "Ecclesiastical Office", "Cursus ecclesiasticus", or simply "cursus" are synonyms of "Divine Office". "Cursus" is the form used by Gregory writing: "exsurgente abbate cum monachis ad celebrandum cursum" (De glor. martyr., xv). "Agenda", "agenda mortuorum", "agenda missarum", "solemnitas", "missa" were also used. The Greeks employ "synaxis" and "canon" in this sense. The expression "officium divinum" is used in the same sense by the Council of Aix-la-Chapelle (800), the IV Lateran (1215), and Vienne (1311); but it is also used to signify any office of the Church. Thus Walafrid Strabo, Pseudo-Alcuin, Rupert de Tuy entitle their works on liturgical ceremonies "De officiis divinis". Hittorp, in the sixteenth century, entitled his collection of medieval liturgical works "De Catholicæ Ecclesiæ divinis officiis ac ministeriis" (Cologne, 1568). The usage in France of the expression "saint-office" as synonymous with "office divin" is not correct. "Saint-office" signifies a Roman congregation, the functions of which are well known, and the words should not be used to replace the name "Divine Office", which is much more suitable and has been used from ancient times. In the articles BREVIARY; HOURS, CANONICAL; MATINS; PRIME; TERCE; SEXT; NONE; VESPERS, the reader will find treated the special questions concerning the meaning and history of each of the hours, the obligation of reciting these prayers, the history of the formation of the Breviary etc. We deal here only with the general questions that have not been dwelt on in those articles.

II. PRIMITIVE FORM OF THE OFFICE.—The custom of reciting prayers at certain hours of the day or night goes back to the Jews, from whom Christians have borrowed it. In the Psalms we find expressions like: "I will meditate on thee in the morning"; "I rose at midnight to give praise to thee"; "Evening and morning, and at noon I will speak and declare: and he shall hear my voice"; "Seven times a day I have given praise to thee"; etc. (Cf. "Jewish Encyclopedia", X, 164–171, s. v. "Prayer"). The Apostles observed the Jewish custom of praying at midnight, terce, sext, none (Acts, x, 3, 9; xvi, 25; etc.). The Christian prayer of that time consisted of almost the same elements as the Jewish: recital or chanting of psalms, reading of the Old Testament, to which was soon added reading of the Gospels, Acts, and Epistles, and at times canticles composed or improvised by the assistants. "Gloria in excelsis" and the "Te decet laus" are apparently vestiges of these primitive inspirations. At present the elements composing the Divine Office seem more numerous, but they are derived, by gradual changes, from the primitive elements. As appears from the texts of Acts cited above, the first Christians preserved the custom of going to the Temple at the hour of prayer. But they had also their reunions or *synaxes* in private houses for the celebration of the Eucharist and for sermons and exhortations. But the Eucharistic synaxis soon entailed other prayers; the custom of going to the Temple disappeared; and the abuses of the Judaizing party forced the Christians to separate more distinctly from the Jews and their practices and worship. Thenceforth the Christian liturgy rarely borrowed from Judaism.

III. THE DEVELOPMENT OF THE DIVINE OFFICE was probably in the following manner: The celebration of the Eucharist was preceded by the recital of the psalms and the reading of the Old and New Testaments. This was called the Mass of the Catechumens, which has been preserved almost in its original form. Probably this part of the Mass was the first form of the Divine Office, and, in the beginning, the vigils and the Eucharistic Synaxis were one. When the Eucharistic service was not celebrated, the prayer was limited to the recital or chanting of the psalms and the reading of the Scriptures. The vigils thus separated from the Mass became an independent office. During the first period the only office celebrated in public was the Eucharistic Synaxis with vigils preceding it, but forming with it one whole. In this hypothesis the Mass of the Catechumens would be the original kernel of the whole Divine Office. The Eucharistic Synaxis beginning at eventide did not terminate till dawn. The vigils, independently of the Eucharistic service, were divided naturally into three parts; the beginning of the vigils, or the evening Office; the vigils properly so called, and the end of the vigils or the matutinal Office. For when the vigils were as yet the only Office and were celebrated but rarely, they were continued during the greater part of the night. Thus the Office which we have called the Office of evening or Vespers, that of midnight, and that of the morning, called Matins first and then Lauds, were originally but one Office. If this hypothesis be rejected, it must be admitted that at first there was only one public office, Vigils. The service of eventide, Vespers, and that of the morning, Matins or Lauds, were gradually separated from it. During the day, Terce, Sext, and None, customary hours of private prayers both with the Jews and the early Christians, became later ecclesiastical Hours, just like Vespers or Lauds. Complin appears as a repetition of Vespers, first in the fourth century (see COMPLIN). Prime is the only hour the precise origin and date of which are known—at the end of the fourth century (see PRIME).

At all events, during the course of the fifth century, the Office was composed, as to-day, of a nocturnal Office, viz. Vigils—afterwards Matins—and the seven Offices of the day, Lauds, Prime, Terce, Sext, None, Vespers, and Complin. In the "Apostolic Constitutions" we read: "Precationes facite mane, hora tertia, sexta, nona, et vespere atque galli cantu" (VIII, iv). Such were the hours as they then existed. There are omitted only Prime and Complin, which originated not earlier than the end of the fourth century, and the use of which spread only gradually. The elements of which these hours are composed were at first few in number, identical with those of the Mass of the Catechumens, psalms recited or chanted uninterruptedly (tract) or by two choirs (antiphons) or by a cantor alternating with the choir (responses and versicles); lessons (readings from the Old and New Testaments, the origin of the capitula), and prayers (see BREVIARY).

This development of the Divine Office, as far as concerns the Roman liturgy, was completed at the close of the sixth century. Later changes are not in essential points but rather concern additions, as the antiphons to Our Lady at the end of certain offices, matters of the calendar, and optional offices, like those of Saturday (see LITTLE OFFICE OF OUR LADY), or of the dead (see OFFICE OF THE DEAD), and the celebration of new feasts etc. The influence of St. Gregory the Great on the formation and fixation of the Roman Antiphonary, an influence that has been questioned, now appears certain (see "Dict. d'archéol. et de liturgie", s. v. "Antiphonaire").

While allowing a certain liberty as to the exterior form of the office (e. g. the liberty enjoyed by the monks of Egypt and later by St. Benedict in the constitution of the Benedictine Office), the Church insisted from ancient times on its right to supervise the orthodoxy of the liturgical formulæ. The Council of Milevis (416) forbade any liturgical formula not approved by a council or by a competent authority (cf. Labbe, II, 1540). The Councils of Vannes (461), Agde (506), Epaon (517), Braga (563), Toledo (especially the fourth council) promulgated similar decrees for Gaul and Spain. In the fifth and sixth centuries several facts (see CANON OF THE MASS) made known to us the rights claimed by the popes in liturgical matters. The same fact is established by the correspondence of St. Gregory I. Under his successors the Roman liturgy tends gradually to replace the others, and this is additional proof of the right of the Church to control the liturgy (a thesis well established by Dom Guéranger in his "Institutions Liturgiques", Paris, 1883, and in his letter to the Archbishop of Reims on liturgical law, op. cit., III, 453 sq.). From the eleventh century, under St. Gregory VII and his successors, this influence gradually increases (Bäumer–Biron, "Hist. du Bréviaire", especially II, 8, 22 sqq.). From the Council of Trent the reformation of the liturgical books enters a new phase. Rome becomes, under Popes Pius IV, St. Pius V, Gregory XIII, Sixtus V, Gregory XIV, Urban VIII and his successors, Benedict XIV, the scene of a laborious undertaking—the reformation and correction of the Divine Office, resulting in the modern custom, with all the rubrics and rules for the recitation of the Divine Office and its obligation, and with the reformation of the liturgical books, corrected in accordance with the decisions of the Council of Trent and solemnly approved by the popes (Bäumer-Biron, "Hist. du Bréviaire").

BONA, *De divina Psalmodia*, ii, par. 1; THOMASSIN, *De vet. eccl. disc.*, Part I, II, lxxi–lxxviii; GRANCOLAS, *Traité de la messe et de l'office divin* (Paris, 1713); MACHIETTA, *Commentarius historico-theologicus de divino officio* (Venice, 1739); PIANACCI, *Del offizio divino, trattato historico-critico-morale* (Rome, 1770); *De divini officii nominibus et definitione, antiquitate et excellentia* in ZACCARIA, *Disciplina populi Dei in N. T.*, 1782, I, 116 sq.; MORONI, *Dizionario di erudizione storico ecclesiastica*, LXXXII, 279 sqq.; BÄUMER-BIRON, *Histoire du bréviaire* (Paris, 1905), passim; CABROL, *Dict. d'archéol. et de liturgie*, s. vv. *Antiphonaire, Bréviaire;* GAVANTI, *Compendio delle cerimonie ecclesiastiche*, the part devoted to the rubrics of the Breviary, sections on the obligation, omission, and in general all the questions concerning the recitation of the Office; ROSKOVÁNY, *De cælibatu et Breviario* (Budapest, 1861); BATIFFOL, *Origine de l'obligation personnelle des clercs à la récitation de l'office canonique* in *Le canoniste contemporain*, XVII (1894), 9–15; IDEM, *Histoire du bréviaire romain* (Paris, 1893).

FERNAND CABROL.

Office of the Dead.—I. COMPOSITION OF THE OFFICE.—This office, as it now exists in the Roman Liturgy, is composed of First Vespers, Mass, Matins, and Lauds. The Vespers comprise psalms, cxiv, cxix, cxx, cxxix, cxxxvii, with the Magnificat and the *preces*. The Matins, composed like those of feast days, have three nocturns, each consisting of three psalms and three lessons; the Lauds, as usual, have three psalms (Ps. lxii and lxvi united are counted as one) and a canticle (that of Ezechias), the three psalms Laudate, and the Benedictus. We shall speak presently of the Mass. The office differs in important points from the other offices of the Roman Liturgy. It has not the Little Hours, the Second Vespers, or the Complin. In this respect it resembles the ancient vigils, which began at eventide (First Vespers), continued during the night (Matins), and ended at the dawn (Lauds); Mass followed and terminated the vigil of the feast. The absence of the introduction, "Deus in adjutorium", of the hymns, absolution, blessings, and of the doxology in the psalms also recall ancient times, when these additions had not yet been made. The psalms are chosen not in their serial order, as in the Sunday Office or the Roman ferial Office, but because certain verses, which serve as antiphons, seem to allude to the state of the dead. The use of some of these psalms in the funeral service is of high antiquity, as appears from passages in St. Augustine and other writers of the fourth and fifth centuries. The lessons from Job, so suitable for the Office of the Dead, were also read in very early days at funeral services. The responses, too, deserve notice, especially the response "Libera me, Domine, de viis inferni qui portas æreas confregisti et visitasti inferum et dedisti eis lumen . . . qui erant in poenis . . . advenisti redemptor noster" etc. This is one of the few texts in the Roman Liturgy alluding to Christ's descent into hell. It is also a very ancient composition (see Cabrol, "La descente du Christ aux enfers" in "Rassegna Gregor.", May and June, 1909).

The "Libera me de morte æterna", which is found more complete in the ancient MSS., dates also from an early period (see Cabrol in "Dict. d'archéol. et de liturgie", s. v. Absoute). Mgr Batiffol remarks that it is not of Roman origin, but it is very ancient (Hist. du brév., 148). The distinctive character of the Mass, its various epistles, its tract, its offertory in the form of a prayer, the communion (like the offertory) with versicles, according to the ancient custom, and the sequence, "Dies Iræ" (q. v.; concerning its author see also BURIAL), it is impossible to dwell upon here. The omission of the Alleluia, and the kiss of peace is also characteristic of this mass. There was a time when the Alleluia was one of the chants customary at funeral services (see Dict. d'archéol. et de liturgie, s. v. Alleluia, I, 1235). Later it was looked upon exclusively as a song of joy, and was omitted on days of penance (e. g. Lent and ember week), sometimes in Advent, and at all funeral ceremonies. It is replaced to-day by a tract. A treatise of the eighth-ninth century published by Muratori (Liturg. Rom. vet., II, 391) shows that the Alleluia was then suppressed. The omission of the kiss of peace at the Mass is probably due to the fact that that ceremony preceded the distribution of the Eucharist to the faithful and was a preparation for it, so, as communion is not given at the Mass for the Dead, the kiss of peace was suppressed.

Not to speak of the variety of ceremonies of the Mozarabic, Ambrosian, or Oriental liturgies, even in countries where the Roman liturgy prevailed, there were many variations. The lessons, the responses, and other formulæ were borrowed from various sources; certain Churches included in this office the Second Vespers and Complin; in other places, instead of the lessons of our Roman Ritual, they read St. Augustine, Proverbs, Ecclesiastes, Ecclesiasticus, Osee, Isaiah, Daniel etc. The responses varied likewise; many examples may be found in Martène and the writers cited below in the bibliography. It is fortunate that the Roman Church preserved carefully and without notable change this office, which, like that of Holy Week, has retained for us in its archaic forms the memory and the atmosphere of a very ancient liturgy. The Mozarabic Liturgy possesses a very rich funeral ritual. Dom Férotin in his "Liber Ordinum" (pp. 107 sqq.) has published a ritual (probably the oldest extant), dating back possibly to the seventh century. He has also published a large number of votive masses of the dead.

For the Ambrosian Liturgy see Magistretti, "Manuale Ambrosianum", I (Milan, 1905), 67; for the Greek Ritual, see Burial, pp. 77–8.

II. HISTORY.—The Office of the Dead has been attributed at times to St. Isidore, to St. Augustine, to St. Ambrose, and even to Origen. There is no foundation for these assertions. In its present form, while it has some very ancient characteristics, it cannot be older than the seventh or even eighth century. Its authorship is discussed at length in the dissertation of Horatius de Turre, mentioned in the bibliography. Some writers attribute it to Amalarius, others to Alcuin (see Batiffol, "Hist. du Brév.", 181–92; and for the opposing view, Bäumer-Biron, "Hist. de Brév.", II, 37). These opinions are more probable, but are not as yet very solidly established. Amalarius speaks of the Office of the Dead, but seems to imply that it existed before his time ("De Eccles. officiis", IV, xlii, in P. L., CV, 1238). He alludes to the "Agenda Mortuorum" contained in a sacramentary, but nothing leads us to believe that he was its author. Alcuin is also known for his activity in liturgical matters, and we owe certain liturgical compositions to him; but there is no reason for considering him the author of this office (see Cabrol in "Dict. d'archéol. et de liturgie", s. v. Alcuin). In the Gregorian Antiphonary we do find a mass and an office *in agenda mortuorum*, but it is admitted that this part is an addition; a fortiori this applies to the Gelasian. The Maurist editors of St. Gregory are inclined to attribute their composition to Albinus and Etienne of Liège (Microl., lx). But if it is impossible to trace the office and the mass in their actual form beyond the ninth or eighth century, it is notwithstanding certain that the prayers and a service for the dead existed long before that time. We find them in the fifth, fourth, and even in the third and second century. Pseudo-Dionysius, Sts. Gregory of Nyssa, Jerome, and Augustine, Tertullian, and the inscriptions in the catacombs afford a proof of this (see Burial, III, 76; PRAYERS FOR THE DEAD; Cabrol, "La prière pour les morts" in "Rev. d'apologétique", 15 Sept., 1909, pp. 881–93).

III. PRACTICE AND OBLIGATION.—The Office of the Dead was composed originally to satisfy private devotion to the dead, and at first had no official character. Even in the eleventh, twelfth, and thirteenth centuries, it was recited chiefly by the religious orders (the Cluniacs, Cistercians, Carthusians), like the Office of Our Lady (see Guyet, loc. cit., 465). Later it was prescribed for all clerics and became obligatory whenever a ferial office was celebrated. It has even been said that it was to remove the obligation of reciting it that the feasts of double and semi-double rite were multiplied, for it could be omitted on such days (Bäumer-Biron, op. cit., II, 198). The reformed Breviary of St. Pius V assigned the recitation of the Office of the Dead to the first free day in the month, the Mondays of Advent and Lent, to some vigils, and ember days. Even then it was not obligatory, for the Bull "Quod a nobis" of the same pope merely recommends it earnestly, like the Office of Our Lady and the Penitential Psalms, without imposing it as a duty (Van der Stappen, "Sacra Liturgia", I, Malines, 1898, p. 115). At the present time, it is obligatory on the clergy only on the feast of All Souls and in certain mortuary services. Some religious orders (Carthusians, Cistercians etc.) have preserved the custom of reciting it in choir on the days assigned by the Bull "Quod a nobis".

Apostolic Constitutions, VI, xxx; VIII, xl; Ps.-DIONYS., *De hierarch. eccl.*, vii, n. 2; AMALARIUS in *P. L.*, CV, 1239 (*De eccles. officiis*, III, xlix; IV, xlii); DURANDUS, *Rationale*, VII, xxxv; BELETH, *Rationale* in *P. L.*, CII, 156, 161; RAOUL DE TONGRES, *De observantia canonum*, prop. xx; PITTONUS, *Tractatus de octavis festorum* (1739), I (towards end), *Brevis tract. de commem. omnium fidel. defunct.*; HORATIUS A TURRE, *De mortuorum officio dissertatio postuma* in *Collectio Calogiera, Raccolta d'opuscoli*, XXVII (Venice, 1742), 409–429; GAVANTI, *Thesaur. rituum*, II, 175 sqq.; MARTÈNE, *De antiq. ecclesiæritibus*, II (1788), 366–411; THOMASSIN, *De disciplina eccles.*, I-II, lxxxvi, 9; ZACCARIA, *Bibl. ritualis*, II, 417–8; IDEM, *Onomasticon*, I, 110, s. v. *Defuncti*; BONA, *Rerum liturg.*, I, xvii, §§6–7; HITTORP, *De div. cathol. eccles. officiis*, 1329; GUYET, *Heortologia*, 462–73 (on the rubrics to be observed in the office of the dead); CATALANUS, *Rituale Romanum*, I (1757), 408, 416 etc.; CERIANAI, *Circa obligationem officii defunctorum*; BÄUMER-BIRON, *Hist. du Brév.*, II, 30, 37, 131 etc.; BATIFFOL, *Hist. du Brév.*, 181–92; PLAINE, *La piété envers les morts* in *Rev. du clergé français*, IV (1895), 365 sqq.; *La fête des morts, ibid.*, VIII (1896), 432 sqq.; *La messe des morts, ibid.*, XVI (1898), 196; EBNER, *Quellen u. Forschungen zur Gesch. des Missale Romanum*, 44, 53 etc.; THALHOFER, *Handbuch der kathol. Liturgik*, II (Freiburg, 1893), 502–08; KEFERLOHER, *Das Todtenofficium der röm. Kirche* (Munich, 1873); HOEYNEK, *Officium defunctorum* (Kempten, 1892); IDEM, *Zur Gesch des Officium defunctorum* in *Katholik*, II (1893), 329. See also the literature of the article BURIAL and other articles cited above, CEMETERY, CREMATION etc.

FERNAND CABROL.

Official. See VICAR-GENERAL.

O'Fihely, MAURICE, Archbishop of Tuam, b. about 1460; d. at Galway, 1513. He was, according to Dr. Lynch, a native of Clonfert in Galway, but, according to Ware and Anthony à Wood, a native of Baltimore in Cork. He is sometimes called Maurice a Portu, Baltimore being situated on the sea coast. Part of his education was received at the University of Oxford, where he joined the Franciscans. Later he studied at Padua, where he obtained the degree of Doctor of Divinity. After his ordination he was appointed professor of philosophy in the University of Padua. He was a student of the works of Duns Scotus, and wrote a commentary on them (published at Venice about 1514). O'Fihely acted for some time as corrector of proofs to two well-known publishers at Venice, Scott and Locatelli—in the early days a task usually entrusted to very learned men. O'Fihely was acknowledged one of the most learned men of his time, so learned that his contemporaries called him *Flos Mundi* (Flower of the World). In addition, his piety and administrative capacity were recognized at Rome, and in 1506 he was appointed Archbishop of Tuam. He was consecrated at Rome by Julius II. He did not return to Ireland till 1513, meantime attending as Archbishop of Tuam the first two sessions of the Lateran Council (1512). On leaving for Ireland to take formal possession of his see, he procured from the pope an indulgence for all those who would be present at his first Mass in Tuam. He was destined not to reach Tuam, for he fell ill in Galway, and died there in the Franciscan convent.

Harris's Ware (Dublin, 1764); WOOD, *Athenæ Oxonienses* (London, 1691); BURKE, *Archbishops of Tuam* (Dublin, 1882).

E. A. D'ALTON.

O Filii et Filiæ, the first line of a hymn celebrating the mystery of Easter. As commonly found in hymnals to-day, it comprises twelve stanzas of the form:

O filii et filiæ,
Rex cælestis, Rex gloriæ,
Morte surrexit hodie.
    Alleluia.

It was written by Jean Tisserand, O.F.M. (d. 1494), an eloquent preacher, and originally comprised but nine stanzas (those commencing with "Discipulis adstantibus", "Postquam audivit Didymus", "Beati qui non viderunt" being early additions to the hymn). "L'aleluya du jour de Pasques" is a trope on the versicle and response (closing Lauds and Vespers) which it prettily enshrines in the last two stanzas:

In hoc festo sanctissimo
Sit laus et jubilatio:
BENEDICAMUS DOMINO.—Alleluia.
De quibus nos humillimas,
Devotas atque debitas
DEO dicamus *GRATIAS.*—Alleluia.

The hymn is still very popular in France, whence it has spread to other countries. Guéranger's *Liturgical Year* (Paschal Time, Part I, tr., Dublin, 1871, pp. 190–192) entitles it "The Joyful Canticle" and gives Latin text with English prose translation, with a triple Alleluia preceding and following the hymn. As given in hymnals, however, this triple Alleluia is sung also between the stanzas (see "The Roman Hymnal", New York, 1884, p. 200). In Lalanne, "Recueil d'anciens et de nouveaux cantiques notés" (Paris, 1886, p. 223) greater particularity is indicated in the distribution of the stanzas and of the Alleluias. The triple Alleluia is sung by one voice, is repeated by the choir, and the solo takes up the first stanza with its Alleluia. The choir than sings the triple Alleluia, the second stanza with its Alleluia, and repeats the triple Alleluia. The alternation of solo and chorus thus continues, until the last stanza with its Alleluia, followed by the triple Alleluia, is sung by one voice. "It is scarcely possible for any one, not acquainted with the melody, to imagine the jubilant effect of the triumphant Alleluia attached to apparently less important circumstances of the Resurrection: e. g., St. Peter's being outstripped by St. John. It seems to speak of the majesty of that event, the smallest portions of which are worthy to be so chronicled" (Neale, "Medieval Hymns and Sequences", 3rd ed., p. 163). The rhythm of the hymn is that of number and not of accent or of classical quantity. The melody to which it is sung can scarcely be divorced from the modern lilt of triple time. As a result, there is to English ears a very frequent conflict between the accent of the Latin words and the real, however unintentional, stress of the melody; e. g.: Et Máriá Magdálená, Sed Jóannes Apostolús, Ad sépulchrúm venít priús, etc. A number of hymnals give the melody in plain-song notation, and (theoretically, at least) this would permit the accented syllables of the Latin text to receive an appropriate stress of the voice. Commonly, however, the hymnals adopt the modern triple time (e. g., the "Nord-Sterns Führers zur Seeligkeit", 1671; the "Roman Hymnal", 1884; "Hymns Ancient and Modern", rev. ed.). Perhaps it was this conflict of stress and word-accent that led Neale to speak of the "rude simplicity" of the poem and to ascribe the hymn to the twelfth century in the Contents-page of his volume (although the note prefixed to his own translation assigns the hymn to the thirteenth century). Migne, "Dict. de Liturgie" (s. v. Pâques, 959) also declares it to be very ancient. It is only very recently that its authorship has been discovered, the "Dict. of Hymnology" (2nd ed., 1907) tracing it back only to the year 1650, although Shipley ("Annus Sanctus", London, 1884, p. xxiii) found it in a Roman Processional of the sixteenth century.

The hymn is assigned in the various French *Paroissiens* to the Benediction of the Blessed Sacrament, on Easter Sunday. There are several translations into English verse by non-Catholics. The Catholic translations comprise one by an anonymous author in the "Evening Office", 1748 ("Young men and maids, rejoice and sing"), Father Caswall's "Ye sons and daughters of the Lord" and Charles Kent's "O maids and striplings, hear love's story", all three being given in Shipley, "Annus Sanctus". The Latin texts vary both in the arrangement and the wording of the stanzas; and the plain-song and modernized settings also vary not a little.

GASTOUÉ, *L'O filii, ses origines, son auteur* in *Tribune de Saint-Gervais*, April, 1907, pp. 82–90, discusses the origin, authorship, text, melody; *Hymns Ancient and Modern, historical edition* (London, 1909,) No. 146, Latin and English cento, comment.; MARCH, *Latin Hymns with English Notes* (New York, 1875) gives (p. 206) the Latin text with the same arrangement of stanzas as found in OULD, *The Book of Hymns* (Edinburgh, 1910), 33, and in the *Liber Usualis* (No. 700, Tournai, 1908), 67; a different arrangement is followed by *The Roman Hymnal* (p. 201); GUÉRANGER, *Liturgical Year, Paschal Time*, part I (Dublin, 1871), 190; *Offices de l'Église* (Reims-Cambrai ed., Paris, 1887), 202; LALANNE, *Recueil* (Paris, 1886), 223; *Les principaux chants liturgiques conformes au chant publié par Pierre Valfray en 1669* in modern notation (Paris, 1875), 114; the *Paroissien Noté* (Quebec, 1903), 128, contains another arrangement. Where the same arrangement of stanzas is found, the texts have different readings; the works cited exhibit many variations in melody.

H. T. HENRY.

Ogdensburg (OGDENSBURGDENSIS), DIOCESE OF, comprises the northern towns of Herkimer and Hamilton counties, with the counties of Lewis, Jefferson, St. Lawrence, Franklin, Clinton, and Essex in New York. On the north and east it is bounded by Canada and Vermont and by Lake Ontario on the west. It covers 12,036 sq. miles, to a great extent occupied by the wooded wilderness of the Adirondack Mountains which, however, of late is rapidly opening up for summer resorts and tuberculosis sanatoria. The soil is mostly rocky and sandy and it supports but a relatively small population which is decreasing in the rural districts, but slowly increasing in industrial and iron mining centres.

The territory was formerly the scene of frequent bloody conflicts between the Iroquois and the Hurons and Algonquins, and also between the French and the British. In 1749 the Sulpician, Francis Picquet, established on the banks of the St. Lawrence, where Ogdensburg now is located, the Fort of the Presentation, to protect the Christian Mohawks, who were, however, scattered by the English ten years later. There is still a reservation called St. Regis, partly in Canada (with about 2000 Indians), partly in the State of New York (with about 1200), where the descendants of the former savage tribes of the country, Christianized in the seventeenth century and still nearly all Catholics, worship together and sing the choral part of the Divine services in Iroquois. The first white settlers were Protestants from New England. It was only towards 1790 that Acadian Catholic immigrants occupied lands around Corbeau, now Cooperville, near Lake Champlain, where they were occasionally visited by missionaries from Fort La Prairie, Canada. In 1818, a colony of French and German Catholics was brought to Jefferson County by Count Leray de Chaumont, who built for them, and also for an Irish settlement, several Catholic churches. At the same time Irish and French Canadian immigrants began to arrive and soon there arose Catholic missions in various parts of the future diocese which still belonged to New York.

The first congregations were formed at Ogdensburg in 1827 by Father Salmon, at Carthage by Father Patrick Kelly, at Cooperville in 1818 by Father Mignault, at Plattsburg in 1828 by Father Patrick McGilligan, at Hogansburg in 1836 by Rev. John McNulty. Bishops Dubois, Hughes, and McCloskey visited these parishes and others that were arising in the lumbering and mining districts of the region. After the Papineau rebellion in Canada (1838) many Canadian Catholics settled on American soil, and soon after the famine brought thousands of Irish emigrants into the territory. Bishop Hughes erected in 1838 a theological seminary at Lafargeville near Clayton; but it was transferred in 1840 to Fordham near New York. The Catholic Summer School of America, commenced at New London in 1892, was in 1893 definitely located at Plattsburg and has met with great success. It is a place of learning and recreation for thousands of Catholics of the surrounding country. Attendance at its courses procures teaching diplomas in the State of New York.

The diocese was separated from the Diocese of Albany on 15 February, 1872. The first bishop was the Rt. Rev. Edgar P. Wadhams, b. 1817 at Lewis, Essex County. He was a convert from the Episcopalian Church, in which he had been a deacon. He was rector of the cathedral and Vicar-General of Albany, when called to organize Northern New York into a new diocese. He was consecrated at Albany on 5 May, 1872, by Archbishop, later Cardinal, McCloskey. Bishop Wadhams increased the number of parishes and priests and introduced several religious communities; he founded Catholic schools and erected an orphan asylum, a hospital, and an aged people's home. At his death, 5 December, 1891, the churches and chapels had increased from 65 to 125; priests from 42 to 81; nuns from 23 to 129 and Catholic schools from 7 to 20; the Catholic population had risen from 50,000 to 65,000.

Bishop Wadhams attended the New York Provincial Council of 1883 and the Plenary Council of Baltimore of 1884, and held three diocesan synods. His remains are buried in the crypt of St. Mary's Cathedral which he had enlarged and embellished.

Henry Gabriels, born at Wannegem-Lede, Belgium, on 6 October, 1838, graduated at Louvain as a priest of the Diocese of Ghent and was invited with three other Belgian priests to teach in the newly-founded provincial seminary of Troy, New York. He was appointed professor of dogma and afterwards was professor of church history until 1891. He was consecrated at Albany on 5 May, 1892 by Archbishop Corrigan. The new bishop developed the work begun by his predecessor. He strengthened the Catholic schools although some of the smaller ones had to be closed; he introduced four new religious communities. Bishop Gabriels has made two visits ad Limina, besides other trips to Rome. The former elements of the Catholic population, Irish, French and German, must for permanency rely on their own fecundity. There are a reasonable number of conversions annually, but a new immigration of Poles, Italians, Hungarians, Greeks, Maronites, and others, largely threatens to modify the Catholic body. Yet till now none are numerous enough to form separate congregations except the Poles who are building a church in Mineville.

Statistics:—Religious Communities: Men: Oblates of Mary Immaculate, 5 priests, 2 brothers; Friars Minor, 3 priests, 2 brothers; Fathers of the Sacred Heart of Issoudun, 6 priests; Augustinians, 2 priests; Brothers of Christian Instruction (Lamennais), 12 brothers. Women: Gray Nuns of the Cross, 6 houses; Sisters of Mercy, 7; Sisters of St. Joseph, 4; Sisters of St. Francis, 1; Sisters of the Holy Cross, 2; Ursulines, 1; Daughters of the Holy Ghost, 1; Daughters of Charity of the Sacred Heart of Jesus, 1. Priests, secular, 119; regular, 16; churches, 150; parishes, 8; stations, 79; chapels, 21; brothers, 19; nuns, 240; ecclesiastical students, 20; academies, 13; parochial schools, 15; orphanages, 2; hospitals, 6; home for aged poor, 1; baptisms in 1909: infants, 3617; adults, 302; marriages, 862; Catholic population over 92,000.

SHEA, *History of Cath. Church in United States* (New York, 1894——); WALWORTH, *Reminiscences of Bishop Wadhams* (New York, 1893); SMITH, *Hist. of Dioc. of Ogdensburg* (New York, 1885); *Illus. Hist. of Cath. Church in America*, ed. BEGNI (New York, 1910); CURTIS, *St. Lawrence County* (Syracuse, 1894.)

H. GABRIELS.

Oggione (OGGIONE), MARCO D', Milanese painter, b. at Oggionno near Milan about 1470; d. probably in Milan, 1549. This painter was one of the chief pupils of Leonardo da Vinci, whose works he repeatedly copied. He was a hard-working artist, but his paintings are wanting in vivacity of feeling and purity of drawing, while, in his composition, it has been well said "intensity of colour does duty for intensity of sentiment." He copied the "Last Supper" repeatedly, and one of his best copies is in the possession of the Royal Academy of Arts in England. Of the details of his life we know nothing—not even the date of his important series of frescoes painted for the church of Santa Maria della Pace. His two most notable pictures—one in the Brera (representing St. Michael), and the other in the private gallery of the Bonomi family (representing the Madonna)—are signed Marcus. Others of his works are to be seen at Berlin, Paris, St. Petersburg, and Turin, the one in Russia being a clever copy of the "Last Supper" by Leonardo. Lanzi gives 1530 as the date of his death, but various writers in Milan say it took place in 1540, and the latest accepted date is the one which we give as 1549. He cannot be regarded as an important artist, or even as a very great copyist, but in his pictures the sky and mountains and the distant landscapes are always worthy of consideration, and in these we probably get the painter's best original work.

LANZI, *Storia Pittorica* (Bassano, 1509); AGOSTINO SANTA GOSTINI, *Descrizione delle Pitture di Milano* (Milan, 1671).

GEORGE CHARLES WILLIAMSON.

Ogilvie, JOHN, VENERABLE. eldest son of Walter Ogilvie, of Drum, near Keith, Scotland, b. 1580; d. 10 March, 1615. Educated as a Calvinist, he was received into the Church at Louvain by Father Cornelius a Lapide. Becoming a Jesuit at the age of seventeen he was ordained priest in 1613, and at his own request was sent on the perilous Scottish mission. He landed in Scotland in November, 1613, and during nine months reconciled many with the Church in Edinburgh and Glasgow. He was betrayed in the latter city, but, during a long imprisonment, no tortures could force him to name any Catholics. Though his legs were cruelly crushed, and he was kept awake for nine nights by being continually pricked with needles, scarcely a sigh escaped him. Under searching examinations, his patience, courage, and gaiety won the admiration of his very judges—especially of the Protestant Archbishop Spottiswood—but he was condemned as a traitor and hanged at Glasgow. The customary beheading and quartering were omitted owing to undisguised popular sympathy, and his body was hurriedly buried in the churchyard of Glasgow cathedral. He was declared venerable in the seventeenth century.

JOHN OGILVIE

Authentic account of Imprisonment and Martyrdom of Fr. John Ogilvie, S.J., translated from a Latin pamphlet (Douai, 1615; London, 1877); FORBES-LEITH, *Narratives of Scottish Catholics* (Edinburgh, 1885); A LAPIDE, *Comment. in Isaiam*, c. l, v. 7.

MICHAEL BARRETT.

Ogliastra (OLEASTRENSIS), DIOCESE OF, in the Province of Cagliari, Sardinia. It was formerly under the Archbishop of Cagliari, but Leo XII, at the petition of King Charles Felix, by a bull of 11 November, 1824, erected Ogliastra into a diocese, suffragan of Cagliari, with the Capuchin Serafino Carchero for its first prelate. In the Middle Ages, after the expulsion of the Saracens (1050), Ogliastra was one of the five native *giudicature*, or independent districts, and had for its first lords the Sismondi. Tortoli the episcopal seat is a small city of about 2000 inhabitants, which belongs to the district of Lanusei. The diocese has 29 parishes, 54,500 inhabitants, 53 churches, chapels, and oratories, 46 secular priests, two schools one of which is directed by the Salesians; the present bishop Mgr Emanuele Virgilio, who succeeded Mgr Guiseppe Paderi on 15 April, 1910, was previously Vicar-General of the Diocese of Vanosa.

CAPPELLETTI, *Le chiese d'Italia*, XIV. U. BENIGNI.

O Gloriosa Virginum. See QUEM TERRA, PONTUS, SIDERA.

O'Gorman, THOMAS. See SIOUX FALLS, DIOCESE OF.

O'Growney, EUGENE, priest, patriot, and scholar, b. 25 August, 1863, at Ballyfallon, County Meath; d. at Los Angeles, 18 Oct., 1899. Neither parent spoke Irish and it was little used where he was born; in fact, he was ignorant of the existence of a language of Ireland until a student at St. Finian's seminary at Navan. His interest in the language begun there continued at Maynooth, where from his entrance in 1882 he devoted himself to the study of the Irish language, antiquities, and history. His holidays he spent in the Irish-speaking parts of the country where he acquired his knowledge of the spoken language. Ordained in 1888, in 1891 he was appointed professor of Irish at Maynooth, and at about the same time became editor of the "Gaelic Journal". At the instance of the Archbishop of Dublin he began his series of "Simple Lessons in Irish", first published in the "Weekly Freeman", which have done more than any other book in the last two centuries to familiarize thousands of Irish with the language of their ancestors. He was one of the founders of the Gaelic League, organized in Dublin in 1893 "for the purpose of keeping the Irish language spoken in Ireland", and later became its vice-president, which position he held until his death. In 1894, failing health sent him to Arizona and California, where he died. Some years after, with the aid of the Irish in the United States, his body was brought back to Ireland and buried at Maynooth. An earnest and tireless worker, his services to the Gaelic League outweigh those of all his fellow-workers to the present day, not that his scholarship was above criticism, but because he came at the moment when a man of his kind was needed.

The memorials of Father O'Growney have been collected by O'FARRELLY, *Leabhar an Athar Eoghan* (*The O'Growney Memorial Volume*), (Dublin, 1904).

JOSEPH DUNN.

O'Hagan, JOHN, lawyer and man of letters, b. at Newry, County Down, Ireland, 19 March, 1822; d. near Dublin, 10 November, 1890. He was educated in the day-school of the Jesuit Fathers, Dublin, and in Trinity College, graduating in 1842. Though he made many friendships in Trinity, he was always an earnest advocate of Catholic university education. In this spirit he contributed to the "Dublin Review" (1847) an article which the Catholic Truth Society of Ireland has reprinted under the title "Trinity College No Place for Catholics". Later he contributed to the same Review a criticism of Thomas Carlyle's system of thought, which Carlyle tells in his Diary "gave him food for reflection for several days". In 1842 he was called to the Bar and joined the Munster Circuit. In 1861 he was appointed a Commissioner of National Education, and in 1865 he became Q.C. The same year he married Frances, daughter of the first Lord O'Hagan. After Gladstone had passed his Irish Land Act, he chose Mr. O'Hagan as the first judicial head of the Irish Land Commission, making him for this purpose a judge of Her Majesty's High Court of Justice. This elevation was a tribute not only to his legal attainments and judicial standing but to the place he held in the esteem of his countrymen. He was an earnest Catholic, as is shown in many of his writings, such as "The Children's Ballad Rosary". In his earliest manhood his poems, "Dear Land", "Ourselves Alone", etc., were among the most effective features of "The Nation" in its brilliant youth; in his last years he published the first English translation of "La Chanson de Roland", recognized as a success by the "Edinburg Review" and all the critical journals. Longfellow wrote to him: "The work seems to me admirably well done."

The Irish Monthly, XVIII; DUFFY, *Four Years of Irish History*.

MATTHEW RUSSELL.

O'Hagan, THOMAS, first Baron of Tullyhogue, b. at Belfast, 29 May, 1812; d. 1 February, 1885. Called to the Irish Bar in 1836, he resided at Newry, and married Miss Teeling in 1836. Inclined to journalism, he proved a brilliant editor of the "Newry Examiner" from 1838 to 1841. At the Bar he achieved distinction for his defence of Charles Gavan Duffy, in 1842. Admitted to the inner Bar in 1849, and made a bencher of King's Inn in 1859, in 1860 he was appointed Solicitor General for Ireland, and, in the following year Attorney General, being also called to the Irish Privy Council. He sat as M.P. for Tralee from 1863 to 1865, when he became Justice of the Common Pleas. In 1868 he was made Lord Chancellor of Ireland, the first Catholic in the office since Chancellor Fitton under James II. Created Baron of Tullyhogue in 1870, two years later he married Miss Alice Mary Townley. His chancellorship expired with the Gladstone Ministry in 1874. In 1880 he was re-appointed Lord Chancellor by Gladstone, but resigned in November, 1881. A year later he was made a Knight of St. Patrick. He published: "Selected Essays and Speeches".

Dict. of Nat. Biog. (new ed., London, 1908-9); files of contemporary newspapers.

W. H. GRATTAN-FLOOD.

O'Hanlon, JOHN, b. at Stradbally, Queen's Co., Ireland, 1821; d. at Sandymount, Dublin, 1905. He entered Carlow College to study for the priesthood, but accompanied his parents to the United States where, completing his studies, he was ordained in 1847, obtaining a mission in the Diocese of St. Louis. In 1853 he returned to Ireland, was affiliated to the Archdiocese of Dublin and appointed curate in the parish of Sts. Michael and John in the city, one of his fellow curates being the well-known historical scholar, Father Meehan. In 1880 he took charge of the parish of Sandymount and a few years later was made a member of the metropolitan chapter. Always interested in Irish history, especially in Irish ecclesiastical history, while in America he wrote an "Abridgment of the History of Ireland" and an "Irish Emigrant's Guide to the United States", besides publishing in the "Boston Pilot" a series of learned papers on St. Malachy, Archbishop of Armagh. After his return to Dublin, he published biographies of St. Laurence O'Toole, St. Dympna, and St. Aengus the Culdee, a "Catechism of Irish History", "Devotions for Confession and Holy Communion", and "Irish American History of the United States", edited Monk Mason's "History of the Irish Parliament", and collected materials for a history of Queen's Co. His greatest work was his "Lives of the Irish Saints" (Dublin, 1875—), begun in 1846 and finished shortly before his death. Dr. Walsh, Archbishop of Dublin, described him as a man who worked so hard at his pastoral duties that men wondered how he could have found time to write anything, and who wrote so much that men wondered how he could have done any missionary work. He never spared himself and was never dismayed by any difficulty; when, in 1898, the MS. of his Irish American History was destroyed, he cheerfully rewrote the volume, an example of courage for a man nearing four score.

Freeman's Journal (16 May, 1905); O'LEARY in *Journal of County Kildare Archæol. Soc.* (July, 1905).

E. A. D'ALTON.

O'Hara, THEODORE, b. in Danville, Kentucky, U.S.A., 11 February, 1822; d. in Guerryton, Alabama, 6 June, 1867. The son of Kane O'Hara, an Irish political exile, who became a prominent educator in Kentucky, O'Hara graduated from St. Joseph's College, Bardstown, Kentucky, studied law, and in the Mexican War attained the brevet rank of major, after which he made several filibustering expeditions to Cuba and Central America. He edited various newspapers and was successfully entrusted by the Government with some diplomatic missions. During the

Civil War he served as a staff-officer with Generals Johnson and Breckenridge. He wrote little of special merit besides the two poems, "The Bivouac of the Dead" and "A Dirge for the Brave Old Pioneer". The former was written when the State of Kentucky brought back the remains of her sons who had fallen in the Mexican War to the cemetery at Frankfort. The last four lines of the opening stanza are inscribed over the entrance to the National Cemetery at Arlington, Virginia.

CONNOLLY, *Household Library of Ireland's Poets* (New York, 1887); *Irish American Almanac* (New York, 1879); WEBB, *The Centenary of Catholicity in Kentucky* (Louisville, 1884).

THOMAS F. MEEHAN.

O'Hely, PATRICK, Bishop of Mayo, Ireland; d. at Kilmallock, September, 1579. He was a native of Connaught, and joined the Franciscans at an early age. Four years after his profession he was sent to the University of Alcalá, where he surpassed his contemporaries in sacred studies. Summoned to Rome, he was promoted in 1576 to the See of Mayo, now merged in that of Tuam. Gregory XIII empowered him to officiate in adjoining dioceses, if no Catholic bishop were at hand, and supplied him generously with money. At Paris he took part in public disputations at the university, amazing his hearers by his mastery of patristic and controversial theology, as well as of Scotist philosophy. In autumn, 1579, he sailed from Brittany and arrived off the coast of Kerry after James Fitzmaurice had landed at Smerwick from Portugal with the remnant of Stukeley's expedition. All Munster was then in arms. The House of Desmond was divided, and the politic earl had withdrawn from the scene of action. The bishop and his companion, Conn O'Rourke, a Franciscan priest, son of Brian, Lord of Breifne, came ashore near Askeaton, and sought hospitality at the castle where, in the earl's absence, his countess entertained them. Next day they departed for Limerick; but the countess, probably so instructed, for the earl claimed the merit afterwards, gave information to the Mayor of Limerick, who three days later seized the two ecclesiastics and sent them to Kilmallock where Lord Justice Drury then was with an army. As president of Munster, Drury had recently perpetrated infamous barbarities. In one year he executed four hundred persons "by justice and martial law". Some he sentenced "by natural law, for that he found no law to try them by in the realm". At first he offered to secure O'Hely his see if he would acknowledge the royal supremacy and disclose his business. The bishop replied that he could not barter his faith for life or honours; his business was to do a bishop's part in advancing religion and saving souls. To questions about the plans of the pope and the King of Spain for invading Ireland he made no answer, and thereupon was delivered to torture. As he still remained silent, he and O'Rourke were sent to instant execution by martial law. The execution took place outside one of the gates of Kilmallock.

BOURCHIER, *De Martyrio Fratrum Ord. Min.* (Ingolstadt, 1583); GONZAGA, *De Origine Seraphicæ Religionis* (Rome, 1587); O'REILLY, *Memorials of those who suffered for the Catholic Faith* (London, 1868); BRADY, *Episcopal Succession in Great Britain and Ireland*, II (Rome, 1876); MURPHY, *Our Martyrs* (Dublin, 1896); MORAN, *Spicilegium Ossor.* (Dublin, 1874).

O'Herlahy (O' HIARLAITHE), THOMAS, Bishop of Ross, Ireland, d. 1579. Consecrated about 1560, he was one of three Irish bishops attending the Council of Trent. He incurred such persecution through enforcing its decrees that he fled with his chaplain to a little island, but was betrayed to Perrot, President of Munster, who sent him in chains to the Tower of London. Simultaneously with Primate Creagh, he was confined until released after about three years and seven months on the security of Cormac MacCarthy, Lord of Muskery. Intending to retire to Belgium, ill-health contracted in prison induced him to return to Ireland. He was apprehended at Dublin, but released on exhibiting his discharge, and proceeded to Muskery under MacCarthy's protection. Disliking the lavishness of that nobleman's house, he withdrew to a small farm and lived in great austerity. Relieving distress to the utmost of his power he made a visitation of his diocese yearly, and on great festivals officiated and preached in a neighbouring church. Thus, though afflicted with dropsy, he lived until his sixtieth (or seventieth) year, dying exhausted by labours and sufferings. He was buried in Kilcrea Friary, Co. Cork.

ROTHE, *Analecta Nova et Mira*, ed. MORAN (Dublin, 1884); MORAN, *Spicilegium Ossor.*, I (Dublin, 1874); O'REILLY, *Memorials of those who suffered for the Catholic Faith* (London, 1868).

O'Higgins, AMBROSE BERNARD, b. in County Meath, Ireland, in 1720; d. at Lima, 18 March, 1810. An uncle, a priest in Spain, placed him at school in Cadiz. From there he went to South America landing at Buenos Aires, and thence to Lima, where for a time he was a pedlar. Later he became a contractor for opening new roads, and finally joined the Spanish army in the engineer corps. His talent and energy was soon recognized, and secured for him a series of rapid promotions with a patent of nobility as Count of Ballenar, and later, 26 May, 1788, as Marquis of Orsorno, with the Governor-Generalship of Chile. The following eight years he spent in developing the resources of the country, his enlightened policy accomplishing much for Spanish interest. In 1796 he was appointed Viceroy of Peru, the highest rank in the Spanish colonial service, reaching Lima with that commission on June sixth of that year. His vice-royalty ended with his death. BERNARD O'HIGGINS, his only son, b. at Chillan, 20 August, 1776; d. at Lima, 24 October, 1842. At the age of fifteen his father sent him to a Catholic school in England. At his father's death he returned to Chile where he joined the revolutionists as a colonel of militia against the domination of Spain. His bravery brought him higher rank, and the battle of Chacabuco, 12 February, 1817, which broke the power of Spain in Chile, was mainly won by his gallant impetuosity. This victory led to the capture of the capitol and he was proclaimed by its citizens Dictator of Chile. He gave ample evidence of executive ability during an administration of six years, but a fickle populace deposed him from office in February, 1823, and drove him into exile in Peru. His ashes were brought back by the Chilian Government and interred with great pomp in 1869, and in 1872 his equestrian statue was inaugurated at Santiago amid national rejoicing. His son Demetrio, a wealthy and patriotic Chilian *ranchero*, died in 1869.

THOMAS F. MEEHAN.

Ohio, the seventeenth state of the American Union, admitted on 19 Feb., 1803. It is bounded on the north by Michigan and Lake Erie, on the east by Pennsylvania and West Virginia, on the south by West Virginia and Kentucky, and on the west by Indiana. Its greatest breadth is 215 miles, and its greatest length (north to south) 210 miles; its area is 41,060 square miles. The surface is an undulating plain 450–1550 feet above sea-level. The population (1910) is 4,767,121. The agricultural output in 1908 was valued at $198,502,260; the mineral output at $134,499,335; the value of dairy products was $15,484,849; and the total value of industries $960,811,857. The railroad mileage is 9274 miles, besides 4450 miles of electric railway. Ohio profits commercially by the Ohio River in the south, connecting with the Mississippi, and by Lake Erie on the north. There are also four canals, the Miami and Erie, the Ohio, the Hocking, and the Walhonding.

CIVIL HISTORY.—Ohio was discovered by La Salle about 1670 and formal possession of the territory including the state was taken by the French in 1671. A controversy between France and England was settled by the Treaty of Paris (1763), by which Great Britain obtained all the French dominion in the north, and west as far as the Mississippi River. In 1787 an organization known as the Ohio Company of Associates was formed in New England by a number of those who had served in the American Revolutionary War and under their negotiations a purchase of a large tract of land in the territory northwest of the Ohio River was made from the Government. This was the first public sale of land by the United States. Marietta, the first settlement, was founded on 7 April, 1787.

In connexion with this sale was passed the famous ordinance of 1788 guaranteeing forever civil and religious liberty, the system of common schools, trial by jury, and the right of inheritance.

In 1788 Cincinnati was founded, and thenceforth settlements in the southern portion of the state multiplied rapidly. In 1791 the settlers were harassed by various Indian tribes, who were effectually checked by the victory of General Anthony Wayne at Fallen Timbers on the Maumee River (1794). In the succeeding year the treaty of peace was concluded by which the Indians ceded a great portion of the territory now embraced in the state.

Seal of Ohio

About this time Chillicothe was made the capital of the territory and a capitol building erected. In 1802 a constitution was adopted by the eastern division of the territory north-west of the Ohio River, designated by the name "Ohio" and next year the territory was admitted to statehood. From the date of the first settlement down to the year 1842 the nationality of the principal immigration was German. Between 1842 and 1860 the population of Ohio increased very rapidly owing to the great influx of immigrants from both Ireland and Germany. Since 1870 the Slavonic race has been the predominating factor in immigration. In the Civil War, seventy regiments responded to the first call for troops although the state quota was only thirteen. Troops from Ohio were largely responsible for the saving of West Virginia to the Union. A number of the most celebrated officers of the Union Army, as Grant, Sherman, McDowell, Rosecrans, Sheridan, Garfield, were natives of the state. In national elections Ohio was carried by the Democratic Party from 1803 down to 1836. In that year and ever since, with the exception of the years 1848 and 1852 when it cast its electoral vote for Cass and Pierce, it has been Republican.

Catholic History.—The first Catholic settlement in Ohio was founded among Huron Indian tribes near Sandusky by Father De la Richardie in 1751. The principal periods of Catholic immigration are from 1822 to 1842, from 1842 to 1865, and from 1865 to the present day. In the first period the German race predominated; in the second, the Irish and German races, with a majority of Irish immigrants; and in the third, members of the Slavonic race. Ohio has one archdiocese and two dioceses. The Archdiocese of Cincinnati (diocese, 19 June, 1821; archdiocese, 19 June, 1850) includes the counties south of the northern line of Mercer, Auglaize, Hardin Counties and west of the eastern line of Marion, Union, Madison Counties and the Scioto River to the Ohio River. The Diocese of Cleveland (erected 23 April, 1847) includes that part of the state north of the southern limits of Columbiana, Stark, Wayne, Ashland, Richland, Crawford, Wyandot, Hancock, Allen, and Van Wert Counties. The Diocese of Columbus (erected 3 March, 1868) comprises that portion of the state south of 40' 41" and between the Ohio River on the east and the Scioto River on the west, with Franklin, Delaware, and Morrow Counties. The Catholic population is 557,650, including 298 negroes. Among the prominent Catholics may be mentioned General Philip H. Sheridan, General W. S. Rosecrans, General Don Carlos Buell, Generals Hugh and Charles Ewing, Honorable Bellamy Storer, Rubin R. Springer, Colonel Mack Groarty, Doctor Bonner, Frank Herd, and J. A. McGahan, the liberator of Bulgaria.

Besides the Catholics the principal religious denominations are the Methodists numbering 355,444; the Presbyterians, 138,768; and the Lutherans, 132,439.

Education and Charity.—Besides the Ohio State University, founded in 1870, and attended in 1909 by 3012 students under a faculty of 224 members, Ohio has numerous colleges and universities, as Antioch College, Baldwin College, Buchtel College, Case School of Science, Cedarville College, Defiance College, Dennison University, Franklin University, Miami University, Ohio University, Marietta College. The total number is thirty-six. According to the last report of the state commissioner of common schools, the number of public school buildings in Ohio is 10,723, with 24,188 teachers, 656,783 pupils. The expenditure for education during the year 1908–1909 was $25,011,361. By constitutional provision the principal of funds, entrusted to the State for educational and religious purposes, is not to be diminished, and the income is to be applied solely to the objects of the original grant. The General Assembly is empowered to create and maintain an efficient system of common schools in the state. All children between the ages of eight and fourteen years shall attend either a public, private, or parochial school for the full session, of not less than twenty-four weeks each year, unless prohibited by some disability. The course of instruction must extend to reading, spelling, writing, English grammar, geography, and arithmetic. The employment of any child under sixteen years of age during the school session shall be a misdemeanor, punishable by fine, unless the employer shall have first exacted from the child an age and schooling certificate from the proper authorities, showing that the child has successfully completed the studies above enumerated, and if the child is between fourteen and sixteen, that he is able to read and write legibly the English language. If a child be absolutely compelled to work, such relief shall be granted out of the contingent funds of the school district in which he resides as will enable child to attend school in accordance with the requirements of the statute.

The general supervision of all public charitable institutions of the state is vested in a state board of charities. Direct control of each separate state benevolent association is vested in an individual board of trustees. The following charitable institutions are provided for by statute in Ohio: Institution for Deaf and Dumb; Ohio State School for the Blind; Institution for Feeble Minded; Ohio Soldiers and Sailors Home; Ohio Soldiers and Sailors Orphans Home; asylums for the insane at Cleveland, Columbus, Dayton, Athens, Toledo, Massillon, Cincinnati, Lima; Ohio Hospital for Epileptics; Boys' Industrial School; Girls' Industrial Home; homes for the friendless in the various counties; Ohio State Sanitarium for Consumptives; Ohio Institution for Deformed and Crippled Children; hospitals in the various cities; county and city infirmaries and children's homes. All private and public benevolent or charitable institutions shall be open at all times to the inspection of the county commissioners of the various counties or the board of health of the township or municipality.

LEGISLATION ON RELIGIOUS MATTERS.—It is provided in the Bill of Rights, in the Constitution of Ohio, that no person shall be compelled to support any religion or form of worship against his consent; no preference shall be given to any religion by law; no interference with the rights of conscience shall be permitted; no religious qualifications shall be required for the holding of office, and suitable laws shall be enacted to protect every religious denomination in the peaceable enjoyment of its own mode of worship. The arrest of any person for civil purposes on Sunday is prohibited by statute, also hunting, fishing, shooting, theatrical, dramatic, or athletic performances; common labour or keeping open one's place of business, or requiring any employee to labour on Sunday; the sale of intoxicating liquors is prohibited on that day.

The prohibition of common labour does not apply to those who conscientiously observe and abstain from labour on Saturday. The basis of the observance of Sunday is not religious; it is a municipal or police regulation. As to oaths, a person may be sworn in any form deemed by him binding on his conscience. Belief in the existence of God seems to be a prerequisite, but not a belief in a future state of reward or punishment.

Oath includes affirmation, which may be substituted. An oath is not regarded as having its foundation in Christianity. Profane cursing or swearing by the name of God, Jesus Christ, or the Holy Ghost is a misdemeanor. No use of prayer is provided for in the legislative sessions. There is no recognition of religious holidays as such. New Year's Day and Christmas Day are secular holidays and holidays for business purposes. Under the head of privileged communication a confession made to a clergyman or priest in his professional character, in the course of discipline enjoined by his Church, shall be held sacred.

Corporations not for profit, which include churches, may be formed by five persons, a majority of whom are citizens of Ohio, who acknowledge in due form the articles of incorporation containing name of corporation, place where same is to be located, and purpose for which formed. Any person subscribing to the articles of incorporation as set forth in the records of the corporation may become a member thereby. Under the constitution of Ohio houses used exclusively for public worship and institutions for purely charitable purposes are exempt from taxation. The term *house* includes also the grounds attached thereto and all such buildings necessary for the proper use and enjoyment of such houses. Thus grounds contiguous to churches, schools and priests' houses used in connexion therewith or for ornamental or recreation purposes, fall within this classification. Buildings belonging to the Roman Catholic Church and occupied by the bishops, priests, etc., are considered to come within the constitutional phrase "institutions of purely public charity". It has been held that the residence of a minister, or parsonage, is not exempt, because in addition to being used for purposes of public worship, it is also a place of private residence. Public schools are especially exempt from taxation, and private schools established by private donations for public or semi-public purposes are exempt as coming within the purview of the constitutional provision. With reference to institutions of purely public charity, while church and school property are exempt from all ordinary state, county, and city taxes, such property is subject to special assessments for improvements. Priests and clergymen are exempt from jury duty, but, apparently, not from military duty. Members of religious denominations prohibited by articles of faith from serving are absolutely exempt from military duty.

A male of eighteen years and a female of sixteen years may contract marriage, but consent of the parents or guardian must be obtained if the male is under twenty-one or female under eighteen.

Marriage of first cousins is prohibited. Marriage may be solemnized by a lawfully ordained minister of any religious society, a justice of the peace in his county, or a mayor of an incorporated village in the county where the village lies. A clergyman wishing to perform the ceremony must obtain a licence from the probate court of one of the counties of the state.

The bans of marriage must be published in the presence of the congregation in a place of public worship in the county where the female resides, on two different days previous to the ceremony. The first publication to be at least ten days prior thereto, or the publication of bans may be dispensed with upon the securing of a licence from the probate court of the county where the female resides. Persons applying for a licence are compelled to answer under oath questions touching the age, name, residence, place of birth, etc., of the two parties concerned. Solemnizing marriage without a licence or without the publication of bans is penalized, and any person attempting to perform the ceremony without a certificate from the probate court is guilty of a misdemeanor. The marriage of persons under the statutory age is voidable, but becomes irrevocable by cohabitation or other acts of ratification after the age limit is reached. Common-law marriage, by the weight of authority, is not recognized in Ohio. Grounds for divorce are: previous existing marriage; wilful absence for three years; adultery; impotency; extreme cruelty; fraudulent contract; gross neglect; habitual drunkenness for three years; imprisonment in penitentiary (but suit must be filed while party is in prison); foreign divorce not releasing party in Ohio. The person applying must be a *bona fide* resident of the county where suit is filed and must have been a resident of the state for a year previous to the commencing of the suit. Service on the defendant may be either personal or by publication. A divorce does not affect the legitimacy of the children.

A yearly tax of $1000 is assessed against every person engaged in the trafficking in spirituous, vinous, malt, or other intoxicating liquors. Local option laws provide for the suppressing of the sale of liquor in townships or municipalities where a majority of the electors of the district vote in favour of closing the saloons. The statutes provide for a jail in each county; for a house of refuge for incorrigible or vicious infants; for workhouses for persons convicted of minor offences; for an Ohio State Reformatory for criminals between the ages of sixteen and thirty; and the Ohio State Penitentiary for persons convicted of a felony. Every will, except nuncupative wills, shall be in writing, either handwritten or typewritten, and signed by the testator or by some other person in his presence and by his expressed direction, and shall be attested and subscribed in the presence of the testator by at least two competent witnesses who saw him sign or heard him acknowledge it. Generally speaking, any mark made at the end of the will by the testator with testamentary intent constitutes a good signing. A spoliated or destroyed will may be proven, and its directions carried out, where it was destroyed or lost subsequent to the death of the testator or to his becoming incapable of making a will by reason of insanity. A verbal will made in the last sickness is valid in respect to personal property if reduced to writing and subscribed by proper number of witnesses within ten days after the speaking of the testamentary words. A devisee under a will may be a witness thereto, but a devise to him fails unless the will can be proven without his testimony. Any bequest for charitable purposes made within one year of the testator's death is void if any issue of the testator is living. The word *issue* here used means of the blood of the deceased. The Ohio courts have held, however, that a bequest to a Roman Catholic priest "for the saying of Masses for the repose of my soul and the soul of my husband" is not within the statute and is good although made within less than a year of the testator's death. Municipal corporations are organized by statute to maintain public cemeteries and burial-grounds, and are empowered to appropriate property for cemetery purposes. The cost of lots in such cemeteries is limited to such an amount as will reimburse the corporation for its outlay. Private associations incorporated for cemetery purposes may by statute purchase, appropriate, or otherwise become holders of title of land for cemetery purposes. Burial-lots are exempt from taxation, execution, attachment, or any other claim, lien, or process if used exclusively for burial-purposes, but cemeteries owned by associations are not exempt from assessments for local improvements. Land appropriated for private or individual burying-grounds is not exempt from taxation, execution, etc., if it exceeds $50 in value.

Constitution, State of Ohio; BATES, *Annotated Ohio Statute with Supplement; Ohio State Reports; Ohio Circuit Court Reports; 100, 101 Ohio Laws; Biographical Annals of Ohio* (1908); *Reports of state executive departments; Statesman's Year-Book,* (1910); RYAN, *History of Ohio* (1888); HOUCK, *History of Catholicity in Northern Ohio* (Cleveland, 1902); *Catholic Directory* (1910).

JOHN A. DEASY.

Ohler, ALOYS KARL, educationist, b. at Mainz, 2 January, 1817; d. there, 24 August, 1889. He attended the gymnasium at Mainz, studied theology at Giessen, and was ordained at Mainz on 14 August, 1839. His first charge was that of chaplain at Seligenstadt. Like his colleague, Moufang, he was one of the founders and teachers of the Progymnasium of that city. He became spiritual director of St. Rochus Hospital at Mainz in 1845, and pastor at Abenheim near Worms in 1847. On 21 June, 1852, he was appointed director of the Hessian Catholic teachers' training college at Bensheim. During the fifteen years of his administration, encouraged by Bishop von Ketteler, Ohler laboured to infuse a better spirit into the Catholic teaching body of Hesse. On 8 April, 1867, he was made a canon of the cathedral chapter of Mainz, given charge of educational matters, and appointed lecturer in pedagogy and catechetics at the episcopal seminary—a position he held until the seminary was closed during the *Kulturkampf* in 1878. Ohler's chief work is "Lehrbuch der Erziehung und des Unterrichtes" (Mainz, 1861; 10th ed., 1884). The fundamental idea of the work is that the education of Catholic youth should be conducted on Catholic principles, Church and school co-operating harmoniously to this end. The work was intended for the use of the clergy as well as for teachers. Ohler adapted from the Italian: "Cajetanus Maria von Bergamo, Ermahnungen im Beichtstuhle" (5th ed., Mainz, 1886), "Johannes Baptista Lambruschini, Der geistliche Führer" (Mainz, 1848; 12th ed., 1872), and an abridged edition of the latter, "Der kleine geistliche Führer" (1851; 6th ed., 1861).

SELBST, *Aloys Karl Ohler, Ein Lebensbild* in *Kathol. Schulkunde,* I (Heiligenstadt, 1892), nn. x, xi, pp. 126–7, 135–8, with portrait; PFÜLF, *Bischof von Ketteler* (Mainz, 1899), I, 341–3; II, 121 sq.; 326.

FRIEDRICH LAUCHERT.

O'Hurley, DERMOD, Archbishop of Cashel, Ireland, d. 19–29 June, 1584. His father, William O'Hurley of Lickadoon, near Limerick, a man of substance and standing, holding land under the Earl of Desmond, secured him a liberal education on the continent. He took his doctorate *in utroque jure,* taught first at Louvain and then at Reims, and afterwards went to Rome. Appointed Archbishop of Cashel by Gregory XIII, he was consecrated on 11 September, 1581, *per saltum,* not having previously taken priesthood. Two years later he landed at Drogheda, stayed a short time with the Baron of Slane, and proceeded for his diocese, expecting protection from the Earl of Ormonde. Loftus, Protestant Archbishop of Dublin, and Sir Henry Wallop, then lords justices, having secret information, so intimidated Lord Slane that he hastened to Munster and brought back his guest. The archbishop was committed to Dublin Castle in October, 1583, while the justices, dreading Ormonde's resentment and his influence with Queen Elizabeth, obtained authority to use torture, hoping that he would inform against the Earl of Kildare and Lord Delvin. Still apprehensive, they suggested as Dublin was unprovided with a rack, that their prisoner could be better schooled in the Tower of London. Walsingham replied by bidding them toast his feet in hot boots over a fire. The barbarous suggestion was adopted, and early in March, 1584, the archbishop's legs were thrust into boots filled with oil and salt, beneath which a fire was kindled. Some groans of agony were wrung from the victim, and he cried aloud, "Jesus, son of David, have mercy on me!", but rejected every proposal to abandon his religion. Ultimately he swooned away, and fearing his death, the torturers removed him; as the boots were pulled off, the flesh was stripped from his bones. In this condition he was returned to prison, and the Justices again sought instructions from England, reporting what had been done, and intimating the lawyer's opinion that no charge of treason could be sustained in Irish law against Dr. O'Hurley. Walsingham, having consulted the queen, wrote back her approval of the torture, and her authority to dispatch the archbishop by martial law. He was secretly taken out at dawn, and hanged with a withe on the gibbet near St. Stephen's Green, 19–29 June, 1584. His body was buried by some friends in St. Kevin's churchyard.

ROTH, *Analecta Nova et Mira,* ed. MORAN (Dublin, 1884); MORAN, *Spicilegium Ossor.,* I (Dublin, 1874); O'REILLY, *Memorials of Sufferers for the Catholic Faith* (London, 1868); MURPHY, *Our Martyrs* (Dublin, 1896).

CHARLES MCNEILL.

O'Hussey, MAELBRIGHTE (Irish, MAOL BRIGHDE UA HEODHUSA; Latin, BRIGIDUS HOSSÆUS), known also as GIOLLA-BRIGID and as BONAVENTURA HUSSEY, a Franciscan Friar, b. in the Diocese of Clogher, Ulster. Little is known of his life. The first definite information about him dates from 1 November, 1607, on which day he became one of the original members of the Irish Franciscans at their college of St. Anthony at Louvain. It seems, however, that he had previously been at Douai. At Louvain, he lectured first in philosophy and afterwards in theology. His fame rests upon his profound knowledge of the history and language of Ireland, for which, according to the chronicles of his order, he was even in his own time held in high esteem. As far as we know, his works were all written in Irish, and one of his writings, "A Christian Catechism" (Louvain, 1608), was the first book printed on the Continent in the Irish character. The book must have met with considerable success, for we find that it was several times reprinted and revised. Among his other works are to be mentioned: a metrical abridgment in 240 verses of the Christian Catechism, a poem for a friend who had fallen into heresy, a poem on the author entering the Order of St. Francis, and three or four poems preserved in manuscript in the British Museum and the Royal Irish Academy. A letter in Irish from him to Father Nugent, the superior of the Irish Jesuits, is printed in Rev. E. Hogan's "Hibernia Ignatiana" (p. 167). O'Hussey remained as guardian of the college at Louvain until his death in 1614.

Irish Ecclesiastical Record, VII (1870), 41; MORAN, *Spicilegium Ossoriense,* III, 52; WADDING, *Scriptores ordinis minorum,* 56; WARE-HARRIS, *Writers of Ireland,* 102; O'REILLY, *Irish Writers,* 168.

JOSEPH DUNN.

Oil of Saints (MANNA OIL OF SAINTS), an oily substance, which is said to have flowed, or still flows, from the relics or burial places of certain saints; sometimes the oil in the lamps that burn before their shrines; also the water that flows from the wells near their burial places; or the oil and the water which have in some way come in contact with their relics. These oils are or have been used by the faithful, with the belief that they will cure bodily and spiritual ailments, not through any intrinsic power of their own, but through the intercession of the saints with whom the oils have some connexion. In the days of St. Paulinus of Nola (d. 431) the custom prevailed of pouring oil over the relics or reliquaries of martyrs and then gathering it in vases, sponges, or pieces of cloth. This oil, *oleum martyris*, was distributed among the faithful as a remedy against sickness ["Paulini Nolani Carmen", XVIII, lines 38–40 and "Carmen", XXI, lines 590–600, in "Corpus Script. Eccl. Latinorum" (Vienna, 1866 sq.), XXX, 98, 177]. According to the testimony of Paulinus of Périgueux (wrote about 470) in Gaul this custom was extended also to the relics of saints that did not die as martyrs, especially to the relics of St. Martin of Tours ("Paulini Petricordiæ Carmen de vita S. Martini", V, 101 sq. in "Corpus Script. Eccl. Lat.", XVI, 111). In their accounts of miracles, wrought through the application of oils of saints, the early ecclesiastical writers do not always state just what kind of oils of saints is meant. Thus St. Augustine ("De Civitate Dei", XXII) mentions that a dead man was brought to life by the agency of the oil of St. Stephen.

At present the most famous of the oils of saints is *The Oil of St. Walburga* (*Walburgis oleum*). It flows from the stone slab and the surrounding metal plate on which rest the relics of St. Walburga in her church in Eichstädt in Bavaria. The fluid is caught in a silver cup, placed beneath the slab for that purpose, and is distributed among the faithful in small phials by the Sisters of St. Benedict, to whom the church belongs. A chemical analysis has shown that the fluid contains nothing but the ingredients of water. Though the origin of the fluid is probably due to natural causes, the fact that it came in contact with the relics of the saint justifies the practice of using it as a remedy against diseases of the body and the soul. Mention of the oil of St. Walburga is made as early as the ninth century by her biographer Wolfhard of Herrieden ("Acta SS.", Feb., III, 562–3 and "Mon. Germ. Script.", XV, 535 sq.).

The Oil of St. Menas. Thousands of little flasks with the inscription: ΕΥΛΟΓΙΑ ΤΟΥ ΑΓΙΟΥ ΜΗΝΑ (Remembrance of St. Menas), or the like have recently (1905–8) been excavated by C. M. Kaufmann at Baumma (Karm Abum) in the desert of Mareotis, in the northern part of the Libyan desert. The present Bumma is the burial place of the Libyan martyr Menas, which during the fifth and perhaps the sixth century was one of the most famous pilgrimage places in the Christian world. The flasks of St. Menas were well known for a long time to archæologists, and had been found not only in Africa, but also in Spain, Italy, Dalmatia, France, and Russia, whither they had been brought by pilgrims from the shrine of Menas. Until the discoveries of Kaufmann, however, the flasks were supposed to have contained oil from the lamps that burned at the sepulchre of Menas. From various inscriptions on the flasks that were excavated by Kaufmann, it is certain that at least some, if not all, of them contained water from a holy well near the shrine of St. Menas, and were given as remembrances to the pilgrims. The so-called oil of St. Menas was therefore in reality, water from his holy well, which was used as a remedy against bodily and spiritual ailments.

The Oil of St. Nicholas of Myra is the fluid which emanates from his relics at Bari in Italy, whither they were brought in 1087. It is said to have also flowed from his relics when they were still in Myra. (See NICHOLAS OF MYRA, SAINT.)

St. Gregory of Tours, "De Gloria martyrum", xxx, P. L., LXXI, 730) testifies that a certain substance like flour emanated from the sepulchre of John the Evangelist. The same Gregory writes (*ibid.*, xxxi) that from the sepulchre of the Apostle St. Andrew at Patræ emanated manna in the form of flour and fragrant oil.

Following is a list of other saints from whose relics or sepulchres oil is said to have flowed at certain times: St. Antipas, Bishop of Pergamum, martyred under Emperor Domitian ("Acta SS.", April, II, 4); St. Babolenus, Abbot of St-Maur-des-Fossés near Paris, d. in the seventh century ("Acta SS.", June, VII, 160); St. Candida the Younger, of Naples, d. 586 ("Acta SS.", Sept., II, 230); St. Demetrius of Thessalonica, martyred in 306 or 290 ("Acta SS.", Oct., IV, 73–8); St. Eligius, Bishop of Noyon, d. 660 or soon after (Surius, "De probatis sanctorum historiis", VI, 678); St. Euthymius the Great, abbot in Palestine, d. 473 ("Acta SS.", Jan., II, 687); St. Fantinus, confessor, at Tauriano in Calabria, d. under Constantine the Great ("Acta SS.", July, V, 556); St. Felix of Nola, priest, died about 260 ("Acta SS.", Jan., II, 223); St. Franca, Cistercian abbess, d. 1218 ("Acta SS.", April, III, 393–4); St. Glyceria, martyred during the reign of Antoninus Pius ("Acta SS.", May, III, 191); Bl. Gundecar, Bishop of Eichstädt, d. 1075 ("Acta SS.", August, I, 184); St. Humilitas, first abbess of the Vallombrosian Nuns, d. 1310 ("Acta SS.", May, V, 211); St. John the Almsgiver, Patriarch of Alexandria, d. 620 or 616 ("Acta SS.", Jan., III, 130–1); St. John of Beverley, Bishop of York, d. 721 ("Acta SS.", May, II, 192); St. Luke the Younger, surnamed Thaumaturgos, a hermit in Greece, d. 945–6 ("Acta SS.", Feb., II, 99); St. Paphnutius, bishop and martyr in Greece, d. probably in the fourth century ("Acta SS.", April, II, 620); St. Paul, Bishop of Verdun, d. 648 ("Acta SS.", Feb., II, 174); St. Perpetuus, Bishop of Tongres-Utrecht, d. 630 (Acta SS., Nov., II, 295); St. Peter González, Dominican, d. 1246 ("Acta SS.", April, II, 393); St. Peter Thaumaturgus, Bishop of Argos, d. about 890 ("Acta SS.", May, I, 432); St. Rolendis, virgin, at Gerpinnes in Belgium, d. in the seventh or eighth century ("Acta SS.", May, III, 243); St. Reverianus, Bishop of Autun, and Companions, martyred about 273 ("Acta SS.", June, I, 40–1); St. Sabinus, Bishop of Canosa, d. about 566 ("Acta SS.", Feb., II, 329); St. Sigolena, Abbess of Troclar, d. about 700 ("Acta SS.", July, V, 636); St. Tillo Paulus, a Benedictine monk at Solignac in Gaul, d. 703 ("Acta SS.", Jan., I, 380); St. Venerius, hermit on the Island of Palamaria in the gulf of Genoa, d. in the seventh century ("Acta SS.", Sept., IV, 118); St. William, Archbishop of York, d. 1154 ("Acta SS.", June, II, 140); and a few others.

Besides the references above, see the articles: WALBURGA; MENAS, etc.

MICHAEL OTT.

Oils, HOLY. See HOLY OILS.

Ointment in Scripture.—That the use of oily, fragrant materials to anoint the body is a custom going back to remote antiquity is evidenced by the Old Testament as well as other early literatures. Likewise the ceremonial and sacred use of oil and ointment was of early origin among the Hebrews, and, of course, was much elaborated in the prescriptions of the later ritual. The particularly rich unguent known as the "holy oil of unction" is frequently referred to in the "priestly" sections of the Pentateuch and in Paralipomenon. Its composition is minutely prescribed in Exodus, xxx, 23, 24. Besides the regular basis of olive oil, the other ingredients mentioned are chosen myrrh, cinnamon, calamus, and cassia, all of which are to be used in stated quantities. The making or the use of this holy oil by unauthorized persons was prohibited under pain of sacrilege. In many of the references to ointment in Scripture perfumed oil is meant, and it may have in some cases consisted of oil only. Oil and ointment however, are distinguished in Luke, vii, 46: "My head with oil thou didst not anoint; but she with ointment hath anointed my feet." Identical or similar preparations, in which myrrh was an important ingredient, were used in anointing the dead body as well as the living subject (Luke, xxiii, 56). Ointment of spikenard, a very costly unguent, is mentioned in Mark, xiv, 3, "an alabaster box of ointment of precious spikenard" (cf. John, xii, 3). So prized were these unguents that they were kept in pots of alabaster, and among the Egyptians they were said to retain their fragrance even for centuries. For the oil spoken of by St. James, v, 14, see EXTREME UNCTION.

WILKINSON, *Manners and Customs of the Ancient Egyptians*, I (Boston, 1883), 426; LESÊTRE in VIGOUROUX, *Dict. de la Bible*, s. v. *Onction*.
JAMES F. DRISCOLL.

Ojeda, ALONSO DE, explorer; b. at Cuenca, Spain, about 1466; d. on the island of Santo Domingo, about 1508. He came of an impoverished noble family, but had the good fortune to start his career in the household of the Dukes of Medina Sidonia. He early gained the patronage of Juan Rodríguez de Fonseca, Bishop of Burgos and later Patriarch of the Indies, who made it possible for Ojeda to accompany Columbus in his second voyage to the New World. Ojeda distinguished himself there by his daring in battle with the natives, towards whom, however, he was unduly harsh and vindictive. He returned to Spain in 1496. After three years he again journeyed to the New World with three vessels on his own account, accompanied by the cosmographer Juan de La Cosa and Amerigo Vespucci. In a little over three weeks he sighted the mainland near the mouth of the Orinoco, and after landing on Trinidad and at other places, discovered a harbour which he called Venezuela (little Venice), from its resemblance to the bay of Venice. After some further exploration, he made his way to the island of Hispaniola, where he was not received cordially, because it was thought that he was infringing upon the exploring privileges of Columbus. On his return to Spain in 1500, he took with him many captives whom he sold as slaves. Having still influential friends at home, he was able to fit out a new expedition, which left Cadiz in 1502 and made a landing on the American continent at a place which he named Santa Cruz. There he established a colony which did not last long because of the improvidence of his companions and their extreme cruelty toward the Indians. Chafing under his leadership, these companions turned against him and sent him back a prisoner to Spain, accusing him of having appropriated the royal revenues. He was tried and sentenced to pay a heavy fine. Upon his appeal, however, he was acquitted of all culpability, but was now reduced to poverty.

In some way or other he made his way back to Hispaniola, where his former associate Cosa also was. There he conceived the idea of establishing colonies on the mainland between Cabo de Vela and the Golfo de Uraba, and after some time spent in petitioning the Government, finally the two comrades obtained the necessary permission. He went back to Spain and organized his third and last expedition, only after great effort. Among the persons who embarked in his four vessels was Pizarro, the future conqueror of Peru. Cortes, who was later to dominate Mexico, would have been among the soldiers of fortune engaged in this adventure, had not a sudden illness prevented him from sailing. When he reached his destination, Ojeda found the natives very hostile; they attacked his force and slew every man except Ojeda and one other. The two escaped to the shore, where they were succoured by those whom he had left in charge of the ships. Not yet despairing, he founded a new colony at San Sebastian. It soon became necessary for him to proceed to Hispaniola to obtain supplies for the settlement, in charge of which he left Pizarro. He was shipwrecked on the way, and only after suffering great privations did he finally reach Santo Domingo, where he died.

PIZARRO Y ORELLANA, *Var. ilust. d. Nuevo-Mundo* (1639).
J. D. M. FORD.

Okeghem, JEAN D', also called OKEKEM, OKENGHEM, OKEGNAN, OCKENHEIM, contrapuntist, founder and head of the second Netherland school (1450–1550), b. about 1430, presumably at Termonde, in East Flanders; d. 1495. After serving as a choir boy at the cathedral of Antwerp (1443–4), he is said to have become the pupil of Gilles Binchois and Guillaume Dufay. He entered Holy orders, and in 1453 assumed the post of chief chanter at the Court of Charles VII of France, where he became choir-master. At the expense of the king, he visited Flanders and Spain, but most of his time was spent in Tours where he acted, by royal appointment, as treasurer of the church of St. Martin until his death. At first he followed his predecessors and teachers in his manner writing, but eventually introduced the principle of free imitation in the various voices of his compositions. Previously the strict canon was the ideal contrapuntal form, but he introduced the practice of allowing every new voice to enter freely on any interval and at any distance from the initial note of the original theme. The innovation was epoch making and of the greatest consequence in the development of the a cappella style. The new principle inaugurated an unprecedented era of activity with Okeghem's disciples, chief among whom were Josquin Desprèz, Pierre de la Rue, Antoine Brumel, Jean Ghiselin, Antoine and Robert de Fevin, Jean Mouton, Jacob Obrecht, etc.

Numerous fragments of his works are contained in the histories of music by Forkel, Burney, Kiesewetter, and Ambrose, while in the Proske Library of the Ratisbon cathedral are preserved his "Missa cujusvis toni" for four voices and a collection of "Cantiones sacræ" for four voices. His contemporary, Guillaume Crétin, wrote a poem on the death of Okeghem, in which he mentions that Okeghem produced the greatest masterpiece of his time—a motet in canon form for thirty-six real voices. While the belief in the existence of such a monster production was kept alive by tradition, it was feared that it had been lost. In his "Quellenlexikon", Robert Eitner expresses the opinion, shared by Michel Brenet, that the supposedly lost work is contained in a volume "Tomus III psalmorum", printed in Nuremberg in the sixteenth century by Johannes Petreius. Hugo Riemann reproduces the work in his "Handbuch der Musikgeschichte", I, ii. While the composition requires thirty-six voices, more than eighteen are never active simultaneously. The only words used are "Deo gratias" and there are no modulations from one key into another—probably to maintain as much clearness as is possible under the circumstances. Riemann doubts whether the composition was intended to be performed by vocalists; he thinks that it was to be played on instruments or perhaps to serve as an exhibition of the master's surpassing skill.

BARBURE, *Jan van Okeghem* (Antwerp, 1868); THOMAN, *Déploration de G. Crétin sur le trépas de Jean Okeghem, musicien* (Paris, 1864); BRENET, *Jean de Okeghem* (Paris, 1893); DE MARCY, *Jean Okeghem* (Paris, 1895).

JOSEPH OTTEN.

Oklahoma.—I. GEOGRAPHY.—Oklahoma, the forty-sixth state to be admitted to the Union, is bounded on the north by Colorado and Kansas, on the east by Arkansas and Missouri, on the south by the Red River separating it from Texas, and on the west by Texas and New Mexico. It includes what was formerly Oklahoma Territory and Indian Territory, lying in the south central division of the United States between 33° and 37° North lat. and between 94° and 103° West long. Its extreme length from north to south is about 210 miles, and from east to west about 450 miles. Its has an area of 73,910 square miles. Oklahoma is bountifully blessed with streams, although, exactly speaking, there is not a navigable stream in the state. The rivers flow from the north-west to the south-east. With the exception of the mountain districts the entire surface of the state is just rolling enough to render its scenery beautiful. The climate is delightful. Escaping as it does the extremes of heat and cold, it is fitted for agricultural purposes even during the winter season. An irregular chain of knobs or buttes, entering Oklahoma from Missouri and Arkansas on the east, extends through the southern part of the state to the western boundary, in a manner connecting the Ozark range with the eastern plateau of the Rocky Mountains. The groups, as they range westward across the state, are the Kiamichi, Arbuckle, and Wichita Mountains and the Antelope Hills. The highest mountain, 2600 feet above sea-level, is the Sugar Loaf peak. II. POPULATION.—The report of the government census bureau relative to the special census of Oklahoma, taken in 1907, shows that the State had in that year a total population of 1,414,177, of whom 733,062 lived in what was prior to statehood called the Indian Territory. There were 1,226,930 whites; 112,160 negroes; 75,012 Indians. Since 1907 the influx of people has been enormous. The white people in Oklahoma represent every nationality, having come from every state in the union and from every country since the opening in 1889.

III. INDUSTRIES.—The value of the agricultural output for 1907 was $231,512,903. The principal crops are cotton, corn, and wheat, the production in 1908 being as follows: cotton 492,272 bales; corn 95,-230,442 bushels; wheat 17,017,887 bushels. In that year Oklahoma ranked sixth in cotton production, eighth in corn, thirteenth in wheat, and first in petroleum products. The oil fields of Oklahoma are now the largest and most productive in the world, there being produced in 1908, 50,455,628 barrels. In 1909 the production of natural gas amounted to 54,000,-000,000 cubic feet. Coal has been mined extensively for a number of years; the production in 1909 was 3,-092,240 tons, the number of men employed in this one industry being 14,580. Gold, lead, zinc, asphalt, gypsum, and other minerals are mined in paying quantities. Oklahoma has deposits of Portland cement-stone that are said to be inexhaustible. There are two large cement mills in the state, each operating with a capacity of 5000 barrels per day. In 1908 there were 5,695.36 miles of railway in the state, exclusive of yard tracks and sidings; the total taxable valuation of same amounted to $174,649,682. During the year beginning 1 July, 1907, and ending 30 June, 1908, there were built in Oklahoma 107.89 miles of railroad. There are thirteen railroad companies operating in the state.

IV. EDUCATION.—The State University, located at Norman, was founded in 1892 by an act of the legislature of the Territory of Oklahoma. The value of the university lands is estimated at $3,670,000. For 1908–9 the number of teachers in the institution was 84; enrollment was 790. Other state institutions are three normal schools, located at Edmond, Alva, and Weatherford; the Agricultural and Mechanical College at Stillwater; the university preparatory school at Tonkawa; a school for the deaf at Sulpher; an institute for the blind at Wagoner; the Whitaker Orphans' Home in Pryor Creek; five district agricultural schools, one in each judicial district of the state. There were about 10,000 teachers employed in the public schools of the state, 1908–9, the enrolment of students being about 400,000; the total appropriation for educational purposes during this time was about $500,000.

V. HISTORY.—In 1540 Francisco Vasque de Coronado, commanding 300 Spaniards, crossed with Indian guides the Great Plains region to the eastward and northward from Mexico. In the course of their journey these Spaniards were the first white men to set foot on the soil of Oklahoma. Coronado traversed the western part of what is now Oklahoma, while at the same time de Soto discovered and partially explored the eastern portion of the state. In 1611 a Spanish expedition was sent east to the Wichita Mountains. From that time on until 1629, Padre Juan de Sales and other Spanish missionaries laboured among the tribes of that region. La Salle in 1682 took possession of the territory, of which the State of Oklahoma is now a part, in the name of Louis XIV, and in honour of that monarch named it Louisiana. Prior to the Louisiana Purchase, Bienville, accompanied by Washington Irving, had visited and related the wonderful beauty of the region now known as Oklahoma. In 1816 the Government conceived the project of dividing the region now embraced in the state into Indian reservations. This plan was carried out, but at the close of the Civil War the Seminoles, Creeks, Chickasaws, and Choctaws were induced to transfer back to the Government 14,000,000 acres of this land at 15 to 30 cents per acre. Of these lands the Oklahoma that was opened to settlement in 1889, by proclamation of the President of the United States, embraced 1,392,611 acres ceded by the Creeks, and 495,094 acres ceded by the Seminoles in 1866. The lands so ceded were the western portions of their reservations, including Oklahoma ("the home of the red man"). The Government's object in obtaining the lands was to "colonize friendly Indians and freedom thereon". Captain David L. Payne and his "boomers" declared the territory was thus public land and open to the squatter-settlement. Payne and his followers made several attempts to settle on Oklahoma soil, but the United States troops drove out the colonists. Much credit is due Payne and his followers for their many attempts at colonization; for they caused the lands of Oklahoma to be opened for white settlement. Finally in 1888 the Springer Bill, which provided for the opening of Oklahoma to settlement, although defeated in the senate, opened the way to partial success, and in Congress it was attached as a rider to the Indian Appropriation Bill, and was thus carried. On 2 March, 1889, the Bill opening Oklahoma was signed by President Cleveland; and on 22 March, President Harrison issued the proclamation that the land would be opened to settlement at 12 o'clock noon, 22 April, 1889. The day previous to the opening it was estimated that ten thousand people were at Arkansas City awaiting the signal. Large numbers were also at Hunnewell, Caldwell, and other points along the south line of Kansas. Fifteen trains carried people into the territory from Arkansas City that morning. On foot, horseback, in wagons, and carriages people entered the promised land all along the Kansas border. Other thousands entered Oklahoma from the south, crossing the South Canadian at Purcell. The town of Lexington was perhaps the first village established. Two million acres of land were thrown open to settlement and on that eventful day cities and towns and a new commonwealth were created in a wilderness within twenty-four hours. On 6 June, 1890, Congress created the Territory of Oklahoma with six original counties. Nineteen other counties were from time to time created prior to statehood by the various acts of Congress which provided for the opening of different Indian reservations within the

SEAL OF OKLAHOMA

territory. On 16 September, 1893, the Cherokee Strip was opened for settlement. This was a strip of land extending from the Cherokee Nation west to "No Man's Land" and Texas, being about 58 miles wide and containing an area of 6,014,293 acres. This had once been guaranteed to the Cherokee Indians as a perpetual hunting outlet to the western border of the United States. The last great opening in Oklahoma occurred in December, 1906, when 505,000 acres of land, which had been reserved from the Comanche and Apache lands for pasturage, were sold in tracts of 160 acres to the highest bidders by the Government. In this wise 2500 farms were opened to white settlement.

Oklahoma and Indian Territories became a state on 16 November, 1907. On 20 November, 1906, pursuant to the enabling act passed by Congress, the constitutional convention assembled at Guthrie and closed its labours on 6 July, 1907. The constitution was adopted by a vote of the people on 17 September, 1907, and at the same election the officers of the new state were elected. The inauguration was held in Guthrie on 16 November, 1907.

VI. CONSTITUTION, LAWS ETC.—When the Congress of the United States passed what is known as the enabling act, enabling the people of Oklahoma and of Indian Territory to form a constitution and be admitted to the Union, it was provided in said act: "That perfect toleration of religious sentiment shall be secured and that no inhabitant of the State shall ever be molested in person or property on account of his or her mode of religious worship and that polygamous or plural marriages are forever prohibited". The Constitution of the State provides for the freedom of worship in the same language as quoted above but provides further: "No religious test shall be required for the exercise of civil or political rights". Under the statute law of Oklahoma it is a misdemeanour for any one to attempt, by means of threats or violence, to compel any person to adopt, practise, or profess any particular form of religious belief. It is also a crime under the law for any person to wilfully prevent, by threats or violence, another person from performing any lawful act enjoined upon or recommended to such person by the religion which he professes. Every person who wilfully disturbs, interrupts, or disquiets any assemblage of people met for religious worship, by uttering profane discourse, or making unnecessary noise within or near the place of meeting, or obstructing the free passage to such place of religious meeting, is guilty of a misdemeanour. The laws of Oklahoma provide that: "The first day of the week being by very general consent set apart for rest and religious uses, the law makes a crime to be done on that day certain acts deemed useless and serious interruptions of the repose and religious liberty of the community"; and the following are the acts forbidden on Sunday: servile labour; public sports; trades, manufacturing and mechanical employments; public traffic; serving process, unless authorized by law so to do.

Oaths can be administered only by certain judicial officers and their clerks authorized by law, and persons conscientiously opposed to swearing are allowed merely to affirm but are amenable to the penalties of perjury. Oaths can be taken only when authorized by law. Under the state law blasphemy consists in wantonly uttering or publishing words, casting contumelious reproach or profane ridicule upon God, Jesus Christ, the Holy Ghost, the Holy Scriptures, or the Christian or any other religion. Blasphemy is a misdemeanour. Profane swearing as defined by the state law is: "Any use of the name of God, or Jesus Christ, or the Holy Ghost either in imprecating divine vengeance upon the utterer or any other person, or in light, trifling or irreverent speech." It is punishable by fine, for each offence. It is customary to convene the Legislature of the State with prayer, but the law makes no provision for it. Every Sunday and Christmas are legal holidays. There is no statute law regarding the seal of confession, nor has there ever been a decision of the Supreme Court regarding it. Churches may be incorporated under the laws of Oklahoma and the greatest latitude is given such corporations. They may own or hold as much real property as is necessary for the objects of the association, may sell or mortgage property, and the title to any property held by any bishop in trust for the use and benefit of such congregation shall be vested in his successor or successors in office. The law provides for a fee of $2.00 to the Secretary of State for incorporating any religious corporation. All the property and mortgages on property used exclusively for religious or charitable purposes are exempt from taxation. The clergy are exempt from jury and military service under the laws of the state.

Any unmarried male of the age of twenty-one or upwards and any unmarried female of the age of eighteen or upwards, if not related by blood nearer than second cousins, are capable of contracting and consenting to marriage. The contracting parties are required to secure a licence after filing an application sworn to before the county judge by a person legally competent to make and take oath. The marriage ceremony may be solemnized by any judge, justice of the peace, or any priest or clergyman. The minister is required to make the proper indorsement on the licence and transmit same to the county judge. All Indian marriages, under Indian customs, prior to 1897 have been declared legal and all Indian divorces among Indians, according to their customs, prior to that year have been declared legal. Since 1897 Indians have had to comply with the laws of the state regarding marriage and divorce. Prior to 1893 the law required a residence of only ninety days in order to file petition for a divorce. The state laws now require a residence of one year prior to filing petition and there are ten grounds or causes upon which a divorce may be granted, such as abandonment, extreme cruelty, drunkenness, adultery, impotency, gross neglect of duty etc. A judgment of divorce is final and conclusive and operates as a dissolution of the marriage contract as to both husband and wife. Neither party to the divorce can marry within six months from the date of the decree.

Prior to statehood the sale of liquor in the Indian Territory was prohibited by United States law. Oklahoma Territory was not governed by that law and liquor was sold in all parts of Oklahoma. The enabling act that Congress passed provided for state-wide prohibition and the constitutional convention made provision for a prohibitory clause which was voted upon by the people of the state, but voted upon separately from the constitution. The prohibition clause carried, and since statehood Oklahoma has been a prohibition state. The new state has begun to construct modern buildings for its prisons and reformatories, and has passed many laws for regulation of same. A law that was enacted and included in the constitution provided for the office of commissioner of charities and corrections, and since statehood the office has been filled by a Catholic woman.

The laws regarding wills and testaments in this state differ very little from the general statutory provisions of other states. Property can be devised practically any way that the testator desires; there is no bar to charitable bequests and the law requires that the property be distributed according to the intention of the party making the bequest. Cemetery corporations may hold real property, not exceeding eight acres, for the sole purpose of a burial ground and are given all the powers necessary to carry out the purposes of the corporation, and any cemetery organized or controlled by any fraternal organization or congregation shall be controlled and managed as provided by their rules and by-laws. All the property so held is wholly exempt from taxation, assessments, lien, attachment, and sale upon execution.

VII. DIOCESE OF OKLAHOMA.—What is now the Diocese of Oklahoma was formerly the Vicariate Apostolic of Indian Territory. The diocese comprises the entire State of Oklahoma. Prior to the opening of Oklahoma in 1889 there were only a few missions and scarcely any churches. At the present time (1910) there are within the state 53 churches with resident priests and 71 missions with churches, 300 stations attended occasionally and 12 chapels, 60 secular priests and 34 Benedictines, 14 of whom are in the missions. The Benedictine Fathers were the first missionaries and they established themselves at Sacred Heart Abbey in Pottawatomie County in 1880. The first prefect-Apostolic was the Rt. Rev. Isidore Robot, O.S.B., his appointment dating from 1877. Catholicism in Oklahoma owes much to his persevering efforts. A native of France, he introduced the Benedictine order in the Indian country, choosing the home of the Pottawatomie Indians as the centre of his missionary labours. At this time a few Catholics other than the Pottawatomie and Osage Indians were scattered over this vast country. Soon after Robot's appointment as prefect Apostolic he had the foundations of Sacred Heart College and St. Mary's Academy well established, the latter under the care of the Sisters of Mercy. These institutions have grown and prospered. Father M. Bernard Murphy was the first American to join the Benedictine order and from 1877 was the constant companion and co-worker of Father Robot until the latter's death. Father Robot fulfilled his charge well and laid a solid foundation upon which others were to build as the great state developed. He died 15 February, 1887, and his humble grave is in the little Campo Santo at Sacred Heart Abbey. Well did he say: "Going, I went forth weeping, sowing the word of God; coming, they will come rejoicing, bearing the sheaves."

The second prefect Apostolic was Rt. Rev. Ignatius Jean, O.S.B., whose appointment followed immediately after the death of Father Robot. Father Jean resigned in April, 1890. From the coming of Father Robot, Oklahoma and Indian Territories had been a prefecture Apostolic, but by the Bull of 29 May, 1891, it was erected into a vicariate Apostolic. The Right Rev. Bishop Meerschaert was the first vicar Apostolic of Indian Territory, being consecrated in Natchez, Miss. On 23 August, 1905, by a brief of Pius X the vicariate was erected into the Diocese of Oklahoma with the see in Oklahoma City. Prior to this time the see had been in Guthrie. The Right Reverend Bishop Theophile Meerschaert, the first Bishop of Oklahoma, was born at Roussignies, Belgium. He studied at the American College, Louvain, Belgium, finishing his course there. Coming to America in 1872 he laboured in the Diocese of Natchez, Miss., until 1891. By his example and his labours he has endeared himself to his own flock, and also to fair-minded non-Catholics. When his administration began, his labours were difficult and perplexing; he was compelled to travel long distances and weary miles on horseback, railroad facilities being very meagre and accommodations poor. In those days Mass was celebrated many times in dugouts, no house being available, and churches were very few and only in the larger towns. Development has come with the multitudes of people who have come to this new country to make homes, bringing with them the best ideas of the old states from which they came. The labours of the bishop have been manifold on account of the great influx of people, but the Church has kept pace with all the other developments under his guidance and perseverance, until at the present time (1910) there are within the diocese about 32,000 Catholics and 86 priests (22 from Belgium, 12 from Holland, 15 from France, 12 from Germany, 3 from Ireland, 1 from Canada, 1 Indian, and 20 American priests). The majority of these priests were educated at Louvain, Strasburg, or Rome. There are two parishes for non-English speaking Catholics in the diocese, one Polish at Harrah and one German at Okarche. The parochial schools are conducted by both Brothers and Sisters, some few by lay-teachers. The Brothers of the Sacred Heart and the Christian Brothers have schools within the diocese. The sisterhoods within the diocese are: Sisters of Mercy (mother-house in Oklahoma City), Sisters of Divine Providence (mother-house in San Antonio, Texas), Sisters of St. Francis, Sisters of St. Benedict, and Sisters of the Precious Blood. There are thirty-six schools for white children, fifteen for Indians, two for coloured children; thirty-six parishes with schools; one industrial school; two colleges for boys: St. Joseph's College at Muskogee, under the direction of Brothers of the Sacred Heart, and the College of the Sacred Heart under the direction of the Benedictine Fathers. There are eight academies for young ladies, the principal ones being Mt. St. Mary's Academy at Oklahoma City conducted by the Sisters of Mercy and the academy at Guthrie conducted by the Benedictine Sisters. There is one seminary for students of the Benedictine order. There are in the diocese 14 Benedictine Brothers, 5 Christian Brothers, 8 Brothers of the Sacred Heart, and 234 Sisters in the various congregations. The novitiates are: Sisters of Mercy at Oklahoma City, Benedictine Sisters at Guthrie, and Benedictine Fathers at Sacred Heart. St. Anthony's Hospital at Oklahoma City is conducted by the Sisters of St. Francis.

Oklahoma City, the metropolis, with a population of about 65,000 (1910) has one church, St. Joseph's Cathedral, the pastor of which, Rev. B. Mutsaers, D.D., has two assistants: Rev. John Gruenewald and Rev. Victor Van Durme. Muskogee has a population of 25,000 and one church, Rev. Jos. Van Hulse pastor; Enid has a population of 20,000 and one church, Very Rev. Gustave Dupreitere, vicar-general, pastor. Other cities having one church and a resident priest are Shawnee, Tulsa, El Reno, Guthrie, Chickasha, and McAlester. There are three churches and two schools for negroes, the latter attended by 120 children.

Most of the Indians within the diocese are Baptists and Methodists. Some of the Pottawatomies are Catholics, among the Choctaws there are a great many, and the Osage tribe in the northern part of the state is entirely Catholic. The spiritual interests of the Osage Indians are attended to by Rev. Edward Van Waesberghe at Pawhuska. There are Indian Mission Schools at Purcell, Anadarko, Chickasha, Antlers, Pawhuska, Gray Horse, Quawpaw, Ardmore, Muskogee, and Vinita. 1590 Indian pupils attend these mission schools. These schools are supported by money coming from Rev. Mother Katherine Drexel, the Indian Bureau at Washington, D. C., and from Catholic residents of the state. Much credit is due Rev. Isidore Ricklin, O.S.B., of Anadarko, Rev. Edw. Van Waesberghe of Pawhuska, Rev. Hubert Van Rechem, and Rev. F. S. Teyssier of Antlers, all of whom have laboured many years in the Indian Missions.

In regard to the immigrants the Italians, Bohemians, Germans, Syrians, Mexicans, and French form settlements; but the people of other nationalities assimilate because they are not numerous enough to form settlements and for the further reason that by assimilation they can learn the English language more rapidly. From the time of the opening of Oklahoma in 1889 many Catholics have moved into this diocese. At the present time (1910) there is a good class of Catholics in the diocese and many practical Catholics are constantly coming from all parts of the world. There are retreats for clergy every two years and ecclesiastical conferences are called every four months. In

1908 there were baptisms, white children 1248, adults 327, Indians 172, negroes 9; marriages 290; confirmations 1185. The Catholic population of the diocese on 31 Dec., 1908, numbered about 33,472, of which 29,613 were whites, 3463 Indians, 396 negroes.

HILL, *A History of the State of Oklahoma* (Chicago, 1908); ROCK, *History of Oklahoma* (Wichita, 1890); TINDALL, *Makers of Oklahoma* (Guthrie, 1905); THOBURN AND HOLCOMB, *A History of Oklahoma* (San Francisco, 1908); *The Oklahoman Annual Almanac, and Industrial Record* (Oklahoma City, 1909).

MONT F. HIGHLEY.

Olaf Haraldson, SAINT, martyr and King of Norway (1015–30), b. 995; d. 29 July, 1030. He was a son of King Harald Grenske of Norway. According to Snorre, he was baptized in 998 in Norway, but more probably about 1010 in Rouen, France, by Archbishop Robert. In his early youth he went as a viking to England, where he partook in many battles and became earnestly interested in Christianity. After many difficulties he was elected King of Norway, and made it his object to extirpate heathenism and make the Christian religion the basis of his kingdom. He is the great Norwegian legislator for the Church, and, like his ancestor (Olaf Trygvesson), made frequent severe attacks on the old faith and customs, demolishing the temples and building Christian churches in their place. He brought many bishops and priests from England, as King Saint Cnut later did to Denmark. Some few are known by name (Grimkel, Sigfrid, Rudolf, Bernhard). He seems on the whole to have taken the Anglo-Saxon conditions as a model for the ecclesiastical organization of his kingdom. But at last the exasperation against him got so strong that the mighty clans rose in rebellion against him and applied to King Cnut of Denmark and England for help. This was willingly given, whereupon Olaf was expelled and Cnut elected King of Norway. It must be remembered that the resentment against Olaf was due not alone to his Christianity, but also in a high degree to his unflinching struggle against the old constitution of shires and for the unity of Norway. He is thus regarded by the Norwegians of our days as the great champion of national independence, and Catholic and Protestant alike may find in Saint Olaf their great ideal.

After two years' exile he returned to Norway with an army and met his rebellious subjects at Stiklestad, where the celebrated battle took place 29 July, 1030. Neither King Cnut nor the Danes took part at that battle. King Olaf fought with great courage, but was mortally wounded and fell on the battlefield, praying "God help me". Many miraculous occurrences are related in connexion with his death and his disinterment a year later, after belief in his sanctity had spread widely. His friends, Bishop Grimkel and Earl Einar Tambeskjelver, laid the corpse in a coffin and set it on the high-altar in the church of St. Clement in Nidaros (now Trondhjem). Olaf has since been held as a saint, not only by the people of Norway, but also by Rome. His cult spread widely in the Middle Ages, not only in Norway, but also in Denmark and Sweden; even in London, there is in Hart Street a St. Olave's Church, long dedicated to the canonized King of Norway. In 1856 a fine St. Olave's Church was erected in Christiania, the capital of Norway, where a large relic of St. Olaf (a donation from the Danish Royal Museum) is preserved and venerated. The arms of Norway are a lion with the battle-axe of St. Olaf in the forepaws.

STORM, *Snorre Sturlason's Olav den Helliges Saga*; MUNCH, *Det norske Folks Historie*; SARS, *Udsigt over den norske Historie*; DAAE, *Norges Helgener*; OVERLAND, *Illustreret Norges Historie* (not reliable); VICARY, *Olav the King and Olav King and Martyr* (London, 1887).

NIELS HANSEN.

Oláh (OLAHUS), NICOLAUS, Archbishop of Gran and Primate of Hungary, a distinguished prelate, b. 10 January, 1493, at Nagyszeben (Hermanstadt); d. at Nagyszombat, 15 Jan., 1568. His father, Stephen, a brother-in-law of John Hunyadi, was of Wallachian descent; his mother was Barbara Huszár (also known as Csaszar). His autobiographical notes and correspondence throw light on his life. After having studied at the Chapter School of Várad from 1505 to 1512, he became a page at the court of Wladislaw II, but shortly afterwards chose an ecclesiastical career, and was ordained a priest in 1516 or 1518. While acting as secretary to Georg Szatmáry, Bishop of Fünfkirchen, he was appointed a canon of that chapter, later of Gran, and 1522 became Archdeacon of Komorn. In 1526 he was made secretary to King Louis II; but was transferred to the service of Queen Maria. After the battle of Mohács, Oláh attached himself to the party of King Ferdinand I, but retained his position with the queen-dowager. In 1527 he was appointed "custos" or head of the Chapter of Stuhlweissenburg, and accompanied the queen-dowager in 1530 to the imperial diet at Augsburg. When in 1531 she became Stadtholder of the Netherlands, he went with her to Belgium, where he remained (with a brief interruption in 1539) until his return to Hungary in 1542. In the following year he was made by Ferdinand I royal chancellor and Bishop of Agram. In 1548 he became Bishop of Erlau, and in 1553 Archbishop of Gran. As such he crowned Maximilian King of Hungary, and performed the solemn obsequies (1563) over Ferdinand I. As Archbishop of Gran, Oláh's first care was to put order into the finances and property of the archdiocese. He had the "Jus Piseti" again enforced, i. e. the right of supervision over the mint at Körmöczbánya, for which surveillance the archdiocese enjoyed a large revenue. At his own expense, he redeemed the hypothecated provostship of Turócz, also the encumbered possessions of the Diocese of Neutra. Oláh likewise, as Archbishop of Gran, exercised a supervision over the Diocese of Erlau, and (with the consent of the Holy See) administered the Archdiocese of Kalocsa, vacant for 20 years. After the capture of Gran by the Turks, the archiepiscopal residence was at Nagyszombat or Pozsony.

Oláh was particularly active in the Counter-Reformation (q. v.); even before his elevation to the Archbishopric of Gran, he had been a very zealous opponent of the new Protestant teachings. As Primate of Hungary he threw himself with renewed energy into the great conflict, aiming especially at the purity of Catholic Faith, the restoration of ecclesiastical discipline, the reformation of the clergy, and the establishment of new schools. The mountain cities of Upper Hungary, in which the doctrines of the Reformation had made considerable progress, attracted his particular attention. He organized a visitation of the archdiocese, which he in great part conducted in person, besides convoking, with a similar intention, a number of diocesan synods. The first of these synods was held in 1560 at Nagyszombat; at its close he promulgated a code of dogmatic and moral instructions, intended for the clergy, published during that and the following year. In 1561 a provincial synod was held, likewise at Nagyszombat, to discuss the participation of the bishops of Hungary in the Council of Trent, shortly before re-convened. While it is not certain that Oláh took part in that council, or that he promulgated in Hungary its decrees of 1562 and 1564, it is known that he followed its deliberations with close attention and practically adopted in Hungary some of its decisions. In 1563 Oláh submitted to the council a lengthy memorial, in which he urged the importance of dealing with the critical situation of the Hungarian Church and describing in strong language the efforts he had made to overcome the demoralization that had seized on the clergy. It was particularly through school-reform and the proper instruction of youth that he hoped to offset the progress of the Reformation. He restored the cathedral school at Gran, which had fallen into decay when that city was captured by the Turks; he transferred it, however, to his archiepiscopal city of Nagyszombat and confided it to the Jesuits, whom he invited to Hungary in 1561, and who, by their preaching and spiritual ministrations, profoundly influenced the religious life of the nation. Among the publications initiated by him were the "Breviarium Ecclesiæ Strigoniensis" (1558), and the "Ordo et Ritus Ecclesiæ Strigoniensis" (1560). The revival of the custom of ringing the Angelus was due to him. As chancellor and confidant of Ferdinand I, Oláh possessed much political influence, which he exercised in the special interest of the Catholic religion. In 1562 he acted as royal Stadtholder. He was a diligent writer; his works ("Hungaria et Attila"; "Genesis filiorum Regis Ferdinandi"; "Ephemerides", and "Brevis descriptio vitæ Benedicti Zerchsky") were edited by Kovachich, in Vol. I of the "Scriptores minores".

HERGENRÖTHER, *Histoire de l'église*, V, 394 (tr. BELET); FORGÁCH, *De statu reipublicæ hungaricæ Ferdinando, Johanne, Maximiliano regibus Commentarii* in *Mon. Hung. Historica: Scriptores*, XVI (Pesth, 1866); BÉL, *Adparatus ad Historiam Hungariæ* (Posen, 1735); DANKÓ in *Kirchenlex.*, s. v.

A. ÁLDÁSY.

Olba, a titular see in Isauria, suffragan of Seleucia. It was a city of Cetis in Cilicia Aspera, later forming part of Isauria; it had a temple of Zeus, whose priests were once kings of the country, and became a Roman colony. Strabo (XIV, 5, 10) and Ptolemy (V, 8, 6) call it Olbasa; a coin of Diocæsarea, Olbos; Hierocles (Synecdemus, 709), Olbe; Basil of Seleucia (Mirac. S. Theclæ, 2, 8) and the Greek "Notitiæ episcopatuum", Olba. The primitive name must have been Ourba or Orba, found in Theophanes the Chronographer, hence Ourbanopolis in "Acta S. Bartholomei". Its ruins, north of Selefkeh in the vilayet of Adana, are called Oura. Le Quien (Oriens christ., II, 1031) gives four bishops between the fourth and seventh centuries; but the "Notitiæ episcopat." mentions the see until the thirteenth century.

SMITH, *Dict. Greek and Roman Geog.* s. v. *Obasa*; RAMSAY, *Asia Minor*, 22, 336, 364–75. See MÜLLER's notes to *Ptolemy*, ed. DIDOT, II, 898.

S. PÉTRIDÈS.

Oldcastle, SIR JOHN. See LOLLARDS.

Old Catholics, the sect organized in German-speaking countries to combat the dogma of Papal Infallibility. Filled with ideas of ecclesiastical Liberalism and rejecting the Christian spirit of submission to the teachings of the Church, nearly 1400 Germans issued, in September, 1870, a declaration in which they repudiated the dogma of Infallibility "as an innovation contrary to the traditional faith of the Church". They were encouraged by large numbers of scholars, politicians, and statesmen, and were acclaimed by the Liberal press of the whole world. The break with the Church began with this declaration, which was put forth notwithstanding the fact that the majority of the German bishops issued, at Fulda on 30 August, a common pastoral letter in support of the dogma. It was not until 10 April, 1871, that Bishop Hefele of Rottenburg issued a letter concerning the dogma to his clergy. By the end of 1870 all the Austrian and Swiss bishops had done the same.

The movement against the dogma was carried on with such energy that the first Old Catholic Congress was able to meet at Munich, 22–24 September, 1871. Before this, however, the Archbishop of Munich had excommunicated Döllinger on 17 April, 1871, and later also Friedrich. The congress was attended by over 300 delegates from Germany, Austria, and Switzerland, besides friends from Holland, France, Spain, Brazil, Ireland, and representatives of the Anglican Church, with German and American Protestants. The moving spirit in this and all later assemblies for organization was Johann Friedrich von Schulte, the professor of dogma at Prague. Von Schulte summed up the results of the congress as follows: Adherence to the ancient Catholic faith; maintenance of the rights of Catholics as such; rejection of the new dogmas; adherence to the constitution of the ancient Church with repudiation of every dogma of faith not in harmony with the actual consciousness of the Church; reform of the Church with constitutional participation of the laity; preparation of the way for the reunion of the Christian confessions; reform of the training and position of the clergy; adherence to the State against the attacks of Ultramontanism; rejection of the Society of Jesus; solemn assertion of the claims of Catholics as such to the real property of the Church and to the title to it. A resolution was also passed on the forming of parish communities, which Döllinger vehemently opposed and voted against. The second congress, held at Cologne, 20–22 September, 1872, was attended by 350 Old Catholic delegates, besides one Jansenist and three Anglican bishops, Russian clergy, and English and other Protestant ministers. The election of a bishop was decided on, and among the most important resolutions passed were those pertaining to the organization of the pastorate and parishes. This was followed by steps to obtain recognition of the Old Catholics by various governments; the general feeling of that time made it easy to obtain this recognition from Prussia, Baden, and Hesse. Professor Reinkens of Bonn was elected bishop, 4 June, 1873, and was consecrated at Rotterdam by the Jansenist Bishop of Deventer, Heydekamp, 11 August, 1873. Having been officially recognized as "Catholic Bishop" by Prussia, 19 September, and having taken the oath of allegiance, 7 October, 1873, he selected Bonn as his place of residence. The bishop and his diocese were granted by Prussia an annual sum of 4800 Marks ($1200). Pius IX excommunicated Reinkens by name, 9 November, 1873; previous to which, in the spring of 1872, the Archbishop of Cologne had been obliged to excommunicate Hilgers, Langen, Reusch, and Knoodt, professors of theology at Bonn. The same fate had also overtaken several professors at Braunsberg and Breslau. The fiction brought forward by Friedrich von Schulte that the Old Catholics are the true Catholics was accepted by several governments in Germany and Switzerland, and many Catholic churches were transferred to the sect. This was done notwithstanding the fact that a decree of the Inquisition, dated 17 September, 1871, and a Brief of 12 March, 1873, had again shown that the Old Catholics had no connexion with the Catholic Church; represented, therefore, a religious society entirely separate from the Church; and consequently could assert no legal claims whatever to the funds or buildings for worship of the Catholic Church.

The development of the internal organization of the sect occupied the congresses held at Freiburg in the Breisgau, 1874; at Breslau, 1876; Baden-Baden, 1880; and Krefeld, 1884; as well as the ordinary synods. The synodal constitution, adopted at the urgency of von Schulte, seems likely to lead to the ruin of the sect. It has resulted in unlimited arbitrariness and a radical break with all the disciplinary ordinances of Catholicism. Especially far-reaching was the abolition of celibacy, called forth by the lack of priests. After the repeal of this law a number of priests who were tired of celibacy, none of whom were of much intellectual importance, took refuge among the Old Catholics. The statute of 14 June, 1878, for the maintenance of discipline among the Old Catholic clergy has merely theoretical value. A bishop's fund, a pension fund, and a supplementary fund for the incomes of parish priests have been formed, thanks to the aid given by governments and private persons. In the autumn of 1877 Bishop Reinkens founded a residential seminary for theological students, which, on 17 January, 1894, was recognized by royal cabinet order as a juridical person with an endowment of 110,000

Marks ($27,500). A house of studies for gymnasial students called the Paulinum was founded 20 April, 1898, and a residence for the bishop was bought. Besides other periodical publications there is an official church paper. These statements, which refer mainly to Germany, may also be applied in part to the few communities founded in Austria, which, however, have never reached any importance. In Switzerland the clergy, notwithstanding the very pernicious agitation, acquitted themselves well, so that only three priests apostatized. The Protestant cantons, above all Berne, Basle, and Geneva, did everything possible to promote the movement. An Old Catholic theological faculty, in which two radical Protestants lectured, was founded at the University of Berne. At the same time all the Swiss Old Catholic communities organized themselves into a "Christian Catholic National Church" in 1875; in the next year Dr. Herzog was elected bishop and consecrated by Dr. Reinkens. Berne was chosen as his place of residence. As in Germany so in Switzerland confession was done away with, celibacy abolished, and the use of the vernacular prescribed for the service of the altar. Attempts to extend Old Catholicism to other countries failed completely. That lately an apostate English priest named Arnold Mathew, who for a time was a Unitarian, married, then united with another suspended London priest named O'Halloran, and was consecrated by the Jansenist Archbishop of Utrecht, is not a matter of any importance. Mathew calls himself an Old Catholic bishop, but has practically no following. Some of the few persons who attend his church in London do so ignorantly in the belief that the church is genuinely Catholic.

The very radical liturgical, disciplinary, and constitutional ordinances adopted in the first fifteen years gradually convinced even the most friendly government officials that the fiction of the Catholicism of the Old Catholics was no longer tenable. The damage, however, had been done, the legal recognition remained unchanged, and the grant from the budget could not easily be dropped. In Germany, although there was no essential change in this particular, yet the political necessity which led to a *modus vivendi* in the *Kulturkampf* chilled the interest of statesmen in Old Catholics, particularly as the latter had not been able to fulfil their promise of nationalizing the Church in Germany. The utter failure of this attempt was due to the solidarity of the violently persecuted Catholics. In many cases entire families returned to the Church after the first excitement had passed, and the winning power of the Old Catholic movement declined throughout Germany in the same degree as that in which the *Kulturkampf* powerfully stimulated genuine Catholic feeling. The number of Old Catholics sank rapidly and steadily; to conceal this the leaders of the movement made use of a singular device. Up to then Old Catholics had called themselves such, both for the police registry and for the census. They were now directed by their leaders to cease this and to call themselves simply Catholics. The rapid decline of the sect has thus been successfully concealed, so that it is not possible at the present day to give fairly exact statistics. The designation of themselves as Catholics by the Old Catholics is all the stranger as in essential doctrines and worship they hardly differ from a liberal form of Protestantism. However, the prescribed concealment of membership in the Old Catholic body had this much good in it, that many who had long been secretly estranged from the sect were able to return to the Church without attracting attention. On account of these circumstances only Old Catholic statistics of some years back can be given. In 1878 there were in the German empire: 122 congregations, including 44 in Baden, 36 in Prussia, 34 in Bavaria, and about 52,000 members; in 1890 there were only about 30,000 Old Catholics, on account of a decided decline in Bavaria. In 1877 there were in Switzerland about 73,000; in 1890 only about 25,000. In Austria at the most flourishing period there were perhaps at the most 10,000 adherents, to-day there are probably not more than 4000. It may be said that the total number of Old Catholics in the whole of Europe is not much above 40,000.

It seems strange that a movement carried on with so much intellectual vigour and one receiving such large support from the State should from bad management have gone to pieces thus rapidly and completely, especially as it was aided to large degree in Germany and Switzerland by a violent attack upon Catholics. The reason is mainly the predominant influence of the laity under whose control the ecclesiastics were placed by the synodal constitution. The abrogation of compulsory celibacy showed the utter instability and lack of moral foundation of the sect. Döllinger repeatedly but vainly uttered warnings against all these destructive measures. In general he held back from any active participation in the congresses and synods. This reserve frequently irritated the leaders of the movement, but Döllinger never let himself be persuaded to screen with his name things which he considered in the highest degree pernicious. He never, however, became reconciled to the Church, notwithstanding the many efforts made by the Archbishop of Munich. All things considered, Old Catholicism has practically ceased to exist. It is no longer of any public importance.

For accounts of the movements and tendencies that led up to Old Catholicism see DÖLLINGER; GÜNTHER; HERMES; INFALLIBILITY; LAMENNAIS; SYLLABUS; VATICAN COUNCIL.

FRIEDBERG, *Aktenstücke die altkatholische Bewegung betreffend* (Tübingen, 1876); VON SCHULTE, *Der Altkatholizismus, Geschichte seiner Entwicklung, innere Gestaltung und rechtlichen Stellung in Deutschland* (Giessen, 1887); IDEM, *Lebenerinnerungen. Mein Wirken als Rechtslehrer, mein Anteil an der Politik in Kirche und Staat* (Giessen, 1908); VERING, *Kirchenrecht* (3rd ed., 1893), gives a good summary based on the original authorities. Besides the statements in the statistical year-books there is a good account of Old Catholicism in MACCAFFREY, *History of the Catholic Church in the Nineteenth Century, 1789–1909*, I (Dublin and Waterford, 1909); MARSHALL, *Döllinger and the Old Catholics* in *Amer. Cath. Quart. Review* (Philadelphia, 1890), 267 sqq.; cf. also files of the London *Tablet* and *Dublin Review* (1870–71); BRÜCK-KISSLING, *Geschichte der katholischen Kirche im neunzehnten Jahrhundert* (Münster, 1908); MAJUNKE, *Geschichte des Kulturkampfes in Preussen-Deutschland* (Paderborn, 1882); GRANDERATH-KIRCH, *Geschichte des Vatikanischen Konzils* (Freiburg, 1903–06); cf. also FRIEDRICH, *Geschichte des Vatikanischen Konzils* (Bonn, 1877–87); in addition, the very full polemical literature of 1868–72 concerning the council and the question of Infallibility should be examined. The most important writings are briefly mentioned in the works just mentioned. The two biographies, from opposing points of view, of Döllinger by FRIEDRICH (Munich, 1891–1901) and MICHAEL (Innsbruck, 1892) contain much valuable material.

PAUL MARIA BAUMGARTEN.

Old Chapter, THE.—The origin of the body, formerly known as the Old Chapter, dates from 1623, when after a period of more than half a century during which there was no episcopal government in England, Dr. William Bishop was at length created vicar Apostolic. He survived less than a year; but during that period he organized a regular form of ecclesiastical government, by means of archdeacons and rural deans, throughout the country which continued in force with little change down to the re-establishment of the hierarchy in 1850. An integral part of his scheme was the creation of a chapter consisting of twenty-four canons with Rev. John Colleton as dean. The ecclesiastical status of the chapter has always been a matter of dispute. A chapter without a diocese is an anomaly, unknown in canon law, and Rome always refrained from any positive act of recognition. On the other hand, she equally refrained from any censure, although it was known that the chapter was claiming and exercising large functions. They therefore argued that the chapter existed "sciente et tacente sede apostolica" (with the knowledge and silent consent of the pope) and that this was sufficient to give it a canonical status. When Dr. Bishop died they sent a list of names from which his successor might be chosen, and the Holy See accepted their action choosing the first name—Dr. Richard Smith. Three years later he had to leave the country, and spent the rest of his life in Paris. After his death the chapter assumed the right to rule the country in the vacancy of the episcopal office, and for thirty years all faculties were issued by the dean who claimed the verbal approval of Alexander VII.

When James II ascended the throne, and England was divided into four districts or vicariates, the position of the chapter became still more anomalous. Dr. Leyburn, the first vicar Apostolic of that reign, was required to take an oath not to recognize the chapter, and a decree was issued in general terms suspending all jurisdiction of chapters of regulars and seculars so long as there were vicars Apostolic in England; but doubt was felt whether this was meant to apply to the Old Chapter, for the very reason that its position was anomalous. In practice, however, they submitted, and ceased to exercise any acts of jurisdiction; but they continued their existence. The vicars Apostolic themselves were usually members.

When the hierarchy was re-established in 1850, a chapter was erected in each diocese, and whatever claims to jurisdiction the Old Chapter had, from that time, ceased. Not wishing to dissolve, however, they reconstituted themselves as the "Old Brotherhood of the Secular Clergy", the dean of the chapter becoming president of the brotherhood. Under this title they have continued to the present day. They meet twice a year and distribute their funds to various charities.

Sergeant, *Transactions of English Secular Clergy* (1706), reprinted by William Turnbull, as *An Account of the Chapter* (1853); Kirk, *History of the Chapter* (MS.); Dodd, *Church History of England*, ed. Tierney; Ward, *Catholic London a Century ago* (1905); Burton, *Life of Challoner* (1910); Ward, *Dawn of the Catholic Revival* (1909). See also Kirk's *Biographies*, edited by Pollen and Burton (1909), containing a list of capitulars (p. 273); most of the proceedings of the chapter during the eighteenth century can be found scattered among the biographies.

BERNARD WARD.

Oldcorne, EDWARD, VENERABLE, martyr, b. 1561; d. 1606. His father was a Protestant, and his mother a Catholic. He was educated as a doctor, but later decided to enter the priesthood, went to the English College at Reims, then to Rome, where, after ordination, in 1587, he became a Jesuit. Next year he returned to England in company with Father John Gerard (q. v.), and worked, chiefly in Worcester, until he was arrested with Father Henry Garnet (q. v.) and taken to the Tower. No evidence connecting him with the Gunpowder Plot (q. v.) could be obtained, and he was executed for his priesthood only. Two letters of his are at Stonyhurst (Ang., III, 1; VII, 60); the second, written from prison, overflows with zeal and charity. His last combat took place on 7 April, at Red Hill, Worcester. With him suffered his faithful servant, the Ven. Ralph Ashby, who is traditionally believed to have been a Jesuit lay-brother. Oldcorne's picture, painted after his death for the Gesù, is extant, and a number of his relics.

EDWARD OLDCORNE

Foley, *Records S.J.*, IV, 202; Morris, *John Gerard*, x; Gillow, *Bibl. Dict. Eng. Cath.*, s. v.

J. H. POLLEN.

Oldenburg, a grand duchy, one of the twenty-six federated states of the German Empire. It consists of three widely separated parts: the duchy of Oldenburg; the principality of Lübeck, situated between Holstein and Mecklenburg; and the principality of Birkenfeld, in Rhenish Prussia. The duchy is bounded by the North Sea, and by Hanover. It has an area of 2571 sq. miles and (1 Dec., 1905) 438,856 inhabitants. Oldenburg has 2134 sq. miles and 353,789 inhabitants; Lübeck, 217 sq. miles and 38,583 inhabitants; and Birkenfeld, 202 sq. miles and 46,484 inhabitants.

There were in 1905, in Oldenburg: Catholics, 86,-865; Protestants, 264,805; other Christians, 1163; Jews, 956; in Lübeck: Catholics, 485; Protestants, 38,-064; other Christians, 11; Jews, 23; in Birkenfeld: Catholics, 8717; Protestants, 37,047; other Christians, 177; Jews, 543. In the entire grand duchy: 96,067 Catholics, 399,916 Protestants, 1351 other Christians, 1522 Jews. The percentage of Catholics among the total population is now 21.9; in 1871 it was 22.4. The cause of this lies in the emigration of a part of the agricultural population to the industrial districts of the neighbouring provinces.

The capital is Oldenburg. In that part of the country facing the North Sea, the population is of Frisian descent; further inland it is Low Saxon. The chief rivers are the Weser and the Hunte. Of great importance to the country are the numerous canals. The chief industries are agriculture, cattle raising, horse-breeding, peat-cutting, and fishing. The country's industrial establishments include brick factories, briquette manufacture, shipbuilding, metal and iron works, distilleries of alcohol from rye and potatoes. The most important articles of commerce are cattle, grain, lumber, etc.

The country takes its name from the castle of Oldenburg, erected about the middle of the twelfth century. The founder of the reigning house was Egilmar, who is first mentioned in a document dated 1088. His territory, of which the Duke of Saxony was the liege lord, was situated between the country of the Saxons and the Frisians. The wars with the latter lasted for several centuries, and it was not until 1234 that one of their tribes (the Stedingians) succumbed to the Oldenburg attacks in the battle of Altenesch. The Archbishop of Bremen was in these wars an ally of the counts of Oldenburg. When the famous Saxon duke, Henry the Lion, was forced to flee and the old Dukedom of Saxony was partitioned by Frederick Barbarossa in 1181, the counts of Oldenburg obtained the rights of princes of the Empire, but took little part in its development and progress. Of great importance later on was the marriage which Count Dietrich the Fortunate (d. 1440), concluded with Heilwig of Schauenburg (Schaumburg). Two sons issued from this marriage, Christian and Gerhard the Valiant. Through the influence of his uncle, Duke Adolf VIII of Schleswig, Heilwig's eldest son, Christian, became King of Denmark in 1448, King of Norway in 1450, and King of Sweden in 1457. This last royal crown Christian lost again in 1471. He became, after the death of Duke Adolf, Duke of Schleswig and Count of Holstein. Christian became the ancestor of the House of Holstein-Oldenburg, branches of which are reigning to-day in Denmark, Greece, Norway, Russia, and Oldenburg.

The ancestral lands of Oldenburg were turned over by Christian in 1458 to his brother Gerhard the Valiant. The Emperor Charles V gave Oldenburg as a fief to Count Anton I in 1531. The main line became extinct with the death of Count Anton Günther (1603-67). After lengthy quarrels over the succession, Christian V of Denmark became ruler of Oldenburg in 1676. In 1773, however, the Danish King Christian VII surrendered Oldenburg to the Grand Duke Paul of Russia, in consideration of the latter's renunciation of the sovereignty of Schleswig-Holstein. Grand Duke Paul transferred the country, which was raised to a dukedom in 1777, to his cousin Frederick Augustus. The latter, who although a Protestant, was Prince-Bishop of Lübeck since 1750, added the territory of the former Catholic Bishopric of Lübeck to Oldenburg. Because William, the son of Frederick Augustus, was insane, Peter, first cousin of Frederick Augustus, succeeded the latter in the administration of the dukedom. The succeeding rulers of the country are descended from this Peter. When Napoleon in 1810 united the entire German North Sea districts with his empire, he decided to indemnify the Duke of Oldenburg for his loss by giving him other districts in Thuringia. But because the duke refused those districts, Napoleon punished him by taking possession of all Oldenburg in 1811 and by embodying it in the Departments of Wesermündung and Oberems. The battle of Leipzig in 1813 brought liberty to Oldenburg. Peter again grasped the reins of government. The resolutions of the Vienna Congress raised Oldenburg to the dignity of a grand duchy and enlarged it by adding to it a part of the French Department of the Saar, the old Wittelsbach Principality of Birkenfeld. After the establishment of the German Federation in 1815, Oldenburg became a member of it. In the war between Prussia and Austria in 1866 Oldenburg added its troops to the Prussian army of the Main; later on it joined the North German Federation and in 1871 the German Empire as an independent state. The reigning grand duke since 1900 is Frederick Augustus (b. 16 Nov., 1852).

The larger part of the country was Christianized by the Bishop of Bremen, and especially through the efforts of St. Willebaldus, who was consecrated first Bishop of Bremen in 787. Until the introduction of the Lutheran confession in 1529 by Count Anton I, this district was united with the Archbishopric of Bremen. The reformation here destroyed almost all Catholic life. The southern parts of the duchy, which consist to-day of the administrative districts of Cloppenburg and Vechta, were outlying missions of the Osnabrück Diocese, attended from the monasteries of the Benedictines at Visbeck and Meppen, which had been established by Charlemagne. These parts, the pastoral care of which chiefly devolved on the Benedictine Abbey of Corvey, were subject to the Prince-Bishop of Münster from 1252 until 1803 under the name of "Niederstift" and, therefore, remained Catholic during the Reformation period. The spiritual jurisdiction over the Niederstift was exercised by the Bishop of Osnabrück and not by the Bishop of Münster. In 1688 the jurisdiction of Osnabrück was transferred to Münster. These districts were ceded to Oldenburg in the conference of the federal deputies in 1803. In the papal Bull "De salute animarum", 16 July, 1821, in regard to the establishment and limitation of the Prussian bishoprics, all Oldenburg was transferred to the Prussian bishopric of Münster; however, there were very few Catholics in the northern part of the country.

The principality of Lübeck is a part of the Vicariate Apostolic of the Northern Missions. The Principality of Birkenfeld belongs to the Bishopric of Trier. The plan of Grand Duke Paul to have a separate bishopric for Oldenburg failed on account of financial difficulties. The relations between Church and State were adjusted by the convention of 5 Jan., 1830. The Apostolic delegate to these deliberations was the Prince-Bishop of Ermland, Joseph of Hohenzollern. The supreme guidance of the Catholics of Oldenburg was entrusted to the substitute (*Offizial*) of the Bishop of Münster, who resided in Vechta. The resolutions of the convention became laws by order of the grand ducal cabinet of 5 April, 1831, under the title "Fundamentalstatut der katholischen Kirche in Oldenburg". Simultaneously there was published "Normativ zur Wahrung der landesherrlichen Majestätsrechte circa sacra" (Regulations for the maintenance of the ducal rights *circa sacra*), of which no notice had been given to the ecclesiastical authorities.

These regulations created "a commission for the defence of State rights against the Catholic Church", which exists to this day, and which is composed of two higher State officials, one of whom usually is a Catholic and the other a Protestant. The work of the commission includes all negotiations between the government and the Bishop of Münster, particularly those relating to the appointment of the *Offizial*, his assessors and his secretary as well as the two deacons; furthermore all negotiations between the government and the *Offizial*, such as those relating to the appointment of priests, the establishment of parishes and of ecclesiastical benefices. The commission furthermore must approve every sale or mortgage of church property. The regulations further decreed that all papal and episcopal edicts must be approved by the grand duke before their publication in Oldenburg, and that they shall not be valid without such an approval. On account of this one-sided unjust measure a long controversy arose between the government and the Bishop of Münster. The position of *Offizial* at Vechta was vacant from 1846 to 1853. In 1852 Oldenburg received a constitution. This led to an amelioration in the relations between Church and State, the ducal *placet* was abolished and every religious community or sect was permitted to conduct its affairs independently and without interference; church property was distinctly guaranteed. But as the approval of the government was required for the appointment of the clergy and clerical officials, the conflict continued.

The negotiations, begun in Dec., 1852, between the Bishop of Münster and the government, dragged along almost twenty years. During this conflict the bishop and the *Offizial* did not appoint any parish priests; only temporary pastors were placed in charge of the parishes in which vacancies occurred. In 1868 an agreement was reached according to which the bishops filled clerical vacancies after an understanding in each case with the Government, and they further agreed that the decrees of the Church should be communicated to the Government simultaneously with their publication. Several minor points in dispute were settled in 1872. The Catholics of Oldenburg were not affected by the severe trials of the *Kulturkampf*. Grand Duke Peter openly disapproved of the persecutions and of the severity with which the Church was treated in Prussia.

The Oldenburg part of the Diocese of Münster consists to-day of two deaconries, Cloppenburg and Vechta. The Deaconry of Cloppenburg numbers 38,678 Catholics, 6952 Protestants and 28 Hebrews; the 18 parishes of the *Aemter* Cloppenburg and Friesoythe also belong to it. The Deaconry of Vechta numbers 53,308 Catholics, 264,169 Protestants, 987 Jews; it includes the other 18 parishes of the country. The necessary funds for the payment of clerical expenses were partly taken from the income of several so-called commanderies in the *Amt* Friesoythe which formerly belonged to the Order of Malta. The State sequestrated these and other clerical possessions in the beginning of the nineteenth century, but agreed to turn over the annual income to the Catholic Church, which it has done to this day. Including these revenues the State pays annually about 22,000 Marks for the use of the Catholic Church. In 1910 the Church obtained the right of levying church-taxes. The State does not forbid the foundation of religious houses.

The Dominicans have a boarding college at Vechta, and the Franciscans a house in Mühlen, near Steinfeld. Of female congregations there are 7 houses belonging to the sisters of the third order of St. Francis; 4 houses of the Sisters of Charity; 7 houses of the Sisters of Our Lady; 1 house of the Poor Franciscan nuns of the Sacred Hearts of Jesus and Mary; 1 house of the Grey Nuns of St. Elizabeth; in all there are 20 houses of female congregations. The sisters nurse the sick, or teach in their own schools. Until 1855 the Catholic schools were under church control.

The law of 1855 secularized the entire educational system including the secondary schools. The Catholic educational system and the Protestant system are each under a separate school board. The episcopal "Offizial" is president of the Catholic Church board which controls the Catholic "Gymnasium" at Vechta, the high school at Cloppenburg, the seminary for public school teachers at Vechta, and all Catholic public schools. On 4 Feb., 1910, a new educational law went into effect. It does away with the hitherto existing clerical superintendence of public schools. Only the religious instruction is supervised by the clergyman, who is a member of the school board. If there are more than twenty-five Catholic children in a community which has only a Lutheran school, a separate Catholic school must be established by the parish, should the parents request it.

The ancient Diocese of Oldenburg has no connexion with the country of Oldenburg, or with its principal city. The country of Oldenburg was never subject to the ecclesiastical jursidiction of the Diocese of Oldenburg. The Bishopric of Oldenburg was founded by the German Emperor Otto I about 950, and comprised the present territory of Holstein. The small town of Oldenburg (also called Aldenburg in the Middle Ages), near the coast of the Baltic Sea, which is still in existence, was the ancient seat of the bishop. The Diocese of Oldenburg was suffragan to the Archdiocese of Bremen; during the great revolt of the Slavic peoples in 1066, it ceased to exist, but was re-established in 1149 as the See of St. Vicelin, a missionary among the Slavs. As early as 1163, the seat of the bishopric was transferred to Lübeck, the famous Hanse city, by the Saxon Duke Henry the Lion.

VON HALEM, *Geschichte von Oldenburg* (3 vols., Oldenburg, 1794–96); RUNDE, *Oldenburger Chronik*. (3rd ed., Oldenburg, 1863); NIEMANN, *Das oldenburgische Münsterland in seiner geschichtlichen Entwicklung* (2 vols., Oldenburg, 1889–91); SCHAUENBURG, *Hundert Jahre oldenburgischer Kirchengeschichte 1573–1667* (3 vols., Oldenburg, 1895–1900), Protestant; WILLOH, *Geschichte der Kath. Pfarreien im Herzogtum Oldenburg* (5 vols., Cologne, 1898–99); PLEITNER, *Oldenburg im 19. Jahrhundert* (2 vols., Oldenburg, 1899–1900); IDEM, *Oldenburgisches Quellenbuch* (Oldenburg, 1903); SELLO, *Alt-Oldenburg* (Oldenburg, 1903).

HERMAN SACHER.

Old Hall (ST. EDMUND'S COLLEGE), near Ware, Hertfordshire, England, founded in 1793 after the fall of the English College, Douai, during the French revolution, to carry on for the south of England the same work of training priests for the English mission, and of affording a Catholic education to lay students. It was the seminary for the "London District" until 1850, when it became the joint property of the Sees of Westminster and Southwark. For many years past it has belonged exclusively to the Archbishops of Westminster. The foundation took place on 16 November, 1793, the feast of St. Edmund, Archbishop of Canterbury, when Bishop Douglass reassembled at Old Hall four of the Douai students, and as he states in his diary "commenced studies or established the new college there, a substitute for Douai." He chose Old Hall for this purpose because there was already existing there a Catholic school belonging to the vicars Apostolic, founded in 1749 at Standon Lordship in the same county and removed in 1769 to Old Hall, purchased by Bishop Talbot. A timely legacy of ten thousand pounds from John Sone, a Catholic, enabled Bishop Douglass to build a college, blessed by him on 29 September, 1799. A chapel and refectory were added in 1805 by his successor, Bishop Poynter, who succeeded Dr. Stapleton as president in 1801. The college prospered, particularly under the rule of Thomas Griffiths (1818–34), afterwards Vicar Apostolic of London. He built a larger chapel, designed in the Gothic style by Augustus Welby Pugin and remarkable for the beautiful rood-screen, but he did not live to see the opening of it in 1853 when it was consecrated by Cardinal Wiseman, whose attempts to place the college under the direction of the Oblates of St. Charles led to serious troubles. Connected with these was the appointment of Dr. Herbert Vaughan (Cardinal Archbishop of Westminster) as vice-president of the college (1855–61). After the death of Cardinal Wiseman, Archbishop Manning decided to remove the theological students to London, and from 1869 the college was conducted simply as a school for boys; but in 1905 Archbishop Bourne decided to send back the theological students. There is now accommodation for 250 students; the college grounds cover 400 acres. The chapel contains a relic of St. Edmund, and the museum many interesting relics of the English College, Douai, and of the penal days. Two ecclesiastical councils have been held at the college, the synod of the vicars Apostolic in 1803 and the Fourth Provincial Council of Westminster in 1873.

B. WARD, *Hist. of St. Edmund's College, Old Hall* (London, 1893); IDEM, *Historical Account of St. Edmund's College Chapel* (London, 1903); DOYLE, *A Brief Outline of the Hist. of Old Hall* (London, 1891); *Sermons preached in St. Edmund's College Chapel on various occasions* (London, 1904); BURTON, *Catalogue of Early-printed Books in the Libraries at Old Hall* (Ware, 1902); B. WARD, *Menology of St. Edmund's College, Old Hall* (London, 1909); W. WARD, *Life and Times of Cardinal Wiseman* (London, 1897); PURCELL, *Life of Cardinal Manning* (London, 1896); COX, *Life of Cardinal Vaughan* (London, 1910); B. WARD, *The Dawn of the Catholic Revival* (London, 1909); *The Edmundian* (1893–).

EDWIN BURTON.

Oldham, HUGH, Bishop of Exeter, b. in Lancashire, either at Crumpsell or Oldham; d. 25 June, 1519. Having spent a short time at Oxford, he entered Queen's College, Cambridge. After his ordination he became chaplain to the Countess of Richmond and soon obtained many benefices, being appointed Dean of Wimborne and Archdeacon of Exeter. He also held prebends in the cathedrals of London, Lincoln, and York, and was rector of St. Mildred's, Bread Street, London. Henry VII honoured him by appointing him as one of those who laid the foundation stone of his chapel in 1503. In the following year he was appointed Bishop of Exeter by a Bull of 27 Nov., 1504. Though not a learned man, he encouraged learning and in 1515 founded and endowed Manchester Grammar School. Through his influence over his friend Bishop Foxe of Winchester, Corpus Christi College, Oxford, was founded for the secular clergy, instead of for the Winchester monks. He added six thousand marks to Foxe's foundation, where his portrait is still honoured as that of a benefactor. From 1510 to 1513 he with other bishops was engaged in resisting what they considered the undue claims of Archbishop Warham with regard to the probate courts, and in the end won a considerable measure of success. Less fortunate was his litigation with the Abbot of Tavistock concerning their respective jurisdictions, during which he is said to have incurred excommunication. Before the dispute was ended, he died, so that his burial had to be postponed until absolution was procured from Rome.

FOWLER, *Hist. of Corpus Christi College* (Oxford, 1893); COOPER, *Athenæ Cantabrigienses* (Cambridge, 1858–61); GODWIN, *Catalogue of the Bishops of England with their lives* (London, 1601); FOWLER in *Dict. Nat. Biog.*, s. v.

EDWIN BURTON.

Oldoini, AUGUSTINO, historian and bibliographer, b. 6 Jan., 1612; d. at Perugia, 23 March, 1683. He came from La Spezzia, and entered the Society of Jesus 4 February, 1628. At the end of his novitiate he made the usual study of the humanities, philosophy and theology. For some time he taught classics at Perugia, and was then professor of moral philosophy in the theological school. His first work, "Alcune difficoltà principali della grammatica" (Ancona, 1637), dealing with Latin grammar, was written while he was engaged in teaching the humanities. He devoted his later years to the study of history and bibliography. He prepared a new annotated edition of the "History of the Popes" by Alphonsus Ciacconius, up to Clement IX (1667–9), "Vitæ et res gestæ Pontificum Romanorum et S.R.E. Cardinalium Alphonsi Ciacconi, O. P." (4 vols., Rome, 1670–77). In connexion with this he also published the following: "Necrologium Pontificum ac Pseudo-Pontificum Romanorum" (Rome, 1671); "Clementes titulo sanctitatis vel morum sanctimonia illustres" (Perugia, 1675); "Athenæum Romanum, in quo Summorum Pontificum ac Pseudo-Pontificum necnon S.R.E. Cardinalium et Pseudo-Cardinalium scripta publice exponuntur" (Perugia, 1670). J. Meuschen published an excerpt from Oldoini's "Catalogus eorum qui de Romanis Pontificibus scripserunt", in his work, "Ceremonialia electionis Pontificum Romanorum" (Frankfort, 1731). Oldoini also published "Athenæum Augustum, in quo Perusinorum scripta publice exponuntur" (Perugia, 1680), and "Athenæum Ligusticum seu Syllabus Scriptorum Ligurum necnon Sarzanensium ac Cyrnensium reipublicæ Genuensis subditorum" (Perugia, 1680).

SOMMERVOGEL, *Bibliothèque de la C. de J.*, V (Brussels and Paris, 1894), 1880–81.

J. P. KIRSCH.

Old Testament. See TESTAMENT, THE OLD.

O'Leary, ARTHUR, Franciscan, preacher, polemical writer, b. at Faniobbus, Iveleary, Co. Cork, Ireland, 1729; d. in London, 8 Jan., 1802. Educated with the Franciscans of St. Malo, where he was ordained and acted as prison chaplain till 1771, he returned to Cork to engage in missionary work. Soon famous as a preacher, writer, and controversialist he published tracts characterized by learning, religious feeling, toleration, and steadfast allegiance to the Crown; but his zeal against religious bigotry led him to make rash admissions, and to expose himself unconsciously to the danger of heterodoxy. Among his writings are: "A Defence of the Divinity of Christ and the Immortality of the Soul"; "Loyalty asserted, or the Test Oath Vindicated"; "An Address to the Roman Catholics concerning the apprehended invasion of the French"; "Essay on toleration": "A reply to John Wesley". A brilliant wit, an honorary member of the famous "Monks of the screw", he was commonly called the Catholic Swift of Ireland. He is charged by Froude with having received secret-service money from the Government, but more impartial historians consider the charge unproven. From 1789 till his death he was chaplain to the Spanish embassy in London, and his society was courted by Burke, Sheridan, Fox, Fitzwilliam, and other leading men of Liberal views.

ENGLAND, *Life of Rev. Arthur O'Leary* (Cork, 1822); BUCKLEY, *Life of Rev. Arthur O'Leary* (Dublin, 1868); FROUDE, *The English in Ireland in the eighteenth century; Life and times of Henry Grattan* (London, 1832–46); *Dictionary of British and American Authors* (Philadelphia, 1859–71); *Historical and Archeological Journal* (Cork, Sept., 1892).

E. O'LEARY.

Olenus, a titular see and suffragan of Patras, in Achaia Quarta, one of the twelve primitive cities of Achaia, on the left bank of the Peirus near Dyme. It is mentioned as early as 280 B. C. Shortly after, its inhabitants retired to the villages of Peirai, Euryteiai, and Dyme. At the time of Strabo (VIII, vii, 4), who locates it forty stadia from Dyme and eighty from Patras, it was in ruins. It must have regained its population, for Honorius III in 1217 appointed its first bishop there. From the occupation of the Morea by the Franks, the Church of Olenus had been governed by the Archdeacon John, chaplain of Villehardouin. The Latin Diocese of Olenus was substituted for the ancient Greek See of Elos, and covered the same territory. In the beginning the Latins formed two dioceses, that of Olenus and that of Andravilla, the residence of the princes of Morea (Fabre, "Le Liber censuum de l'Eglise romaine", Paris, 1905, II, 8); moreover it had only one bishop, that of Olenus, who usually lived at Andravilla or Andravida (Hopf, "Geschichte Griechenlands" in Allg. Encyclop., LXXXV, 235; Buchon, Recherches historiques, I, xxxix). Eubel thinks the same in giving the long list of the Bishops of Olenus and Andravilla in "Hierarchia catholica medii ævi", I, 89, 393; II, 99; III, 280. The Greek See of Olenus was established (Gerland, "Neue Quellen zur Geschichte des lateinischen Erzbistums Patras", Leipzig, 1903, 104) shortly after 1340 with that of Kernitza, at the same time Patras had lost all its suffragans. This diocese is first found in a "Notitia Episcopatuum" of Constantinople after 1453 (Gelzer, "Ungedruckte . . . Texte der Notitiæ episcopatuum", 634). To-day Olenus occupies the site of Tsukaleika on the sea, about seven miles from Patras on the way from Olympia. Andravilla, the ancient residence of the bishops of Olenus, about 38 miles from Patras in the same direction, has 2700 inhabitants. The Church of St. Sophia, the ancient cathedral of the Latins, may be seen still, also the church of St. James, belonging to the Templars, in which were interred Geoffroy I, Geoffroy II, and Guillaume of Villehardouin, whose tombs have been restored.

LE QUIEN, *Oriens christianus*, III.

S. VAILHÉ.

Olesnicki, ZBIGNIEW (SBIGNEUS), a Polish cardinal and statesman, b. in Poland, 1389; d. at Sandomir, 1 April, 1455. At the age of twenty he was secretary to King Jagello, and fought with him in the battle of Grünwald on 14 July, 1410. A favourite with the king, he took part in the management of the country's most important affairs. His influence with the king greatly aided him in opposing the Hussites, who had gained royal favour. On 9 July, 1423, he was appointed to the episcopal see of Cracow, and in 1433 was sent by the king as legate to the council of Basle, where he endeavoured to be on friendly terms with both parties. On 18 December, 1439, he was created cardinal priest with the titular church of St. Prisca, by Eugene IV. The opinion that he accepted the same dignity from the antipope Felix V and adhered to him for some time has recently been attacked by P. M. Baumgarten: "Die beiden ersten Kardinals Konsistorien des Gegenpapstes Felix V" in "Römische Quartalschrift", XXII (Rome, 1908), 153. As cardinal, his influence in Poland was second only to that of the king, and, during the frequent absence of Casimir IV in Lithuania, he transacted the affairs of the State. Being a man of great learning, he advanced the study of arts and letters in every possible way, and the flourishing condition of the University of Cracow during his episcopacy is due chiefly to his efforts. To repress the spread of Hussitism he called John Capistran and the Minorites to Cracow.

CARDELLA, *Memorie storiche de' cardinali della s. romana chiesa*, III (Rome, 1792, 81–4; DZIEDUSZYCKI, *Zbigniew Olesnicki* (2 vols., Cracow, 1853–4), in Polish; ZEGARSKI, *Polen u. das Basler Konzil* (Posen, 1910).

MICHAEL OTT.

Olier, JEAN-JACQUES, founder of the seminary and Society of St-Sulpice, b. at Paris, 20 Sept., 1608; d. there, 2 April, 1657. At Lyons, where his father had become administrator of justice, he made a thorough classical course under the Jesuits (1617–25); he was encouraged to become a priest by St. Francis de Sales, who predicted his sanctity and great services to the Church. He studied philosophy at the college of Harcourt, scholastic theology and patristics at the Sorbonne. He preached during this period, in virtue of a benefice with which his father had provided him, adopting the ambitious style of the day; he also frequented fashionable society, causing anxiety to those interested in his spiritual welfare. His success in defending theses in Latin and Greek led him to go to Rome for the purpose of learning Hebrew so as to gain éclat by defending theses in that language at the Sorbonne. His eyesight failing, he made a pilgrimage to Loreto, where he not only obtained a cure, but also a complete conversion to God. For a time he meditated the Carthusian life, visiting monasteries in Southern Italy; the news of his father's death (1631) recalled him to Paris. Refusing a court chaplaincy, with the prospect of high honours, he began to gather the beggars and the poor and catechize them in his home; at Paris he collected the poor and the outcast on the streets for instruction, a practice at first derided but soon widely imitated and productive of much good. Under St. Vincent de Paul's guidance, he assisted his missionaries in Paris and the provinces, prepared for the priesthood, and was ordained 21 May, 1633. He became a leader in the revival of religion in France, associating himself with the followers first of St. Vincent and then of Père de Condren, Superior of the Oratory, under whose direction he passed, though he continued to retain St. Vincent as his friend and advisor. To de Condren, more even, it appears, than to St. Vincent, Olier owed the deepest spiritual influence and many of his leading ideas. The work de Condren had most at heart was the foundation of seminaries after the model laid down at the Council of Trent. The hope of religion lay in the formation of a new clergy through the seminaries. The attempts in France to carry out the designs of the council having failed, de Condren, unable to succeed through the medium of the Oratory, gathered a few young ecclesiastics around him for that purpose, Olier among them. The missions in which he employed them were meant to impress on their minds the religious needs of the country; his ulterior purpose was not disclosed till shortly before his death in 1640.

A first attempt to found a seminary at Chartres failed. On 29 Dec., 1641, Olier and two others, de Foix and du Ferrier, entered upon a community life at Vaugirard, a suburb of Paris. Others soon joined them, and before long there were eight seminarians, who followed with the priests the same rule of life and were instructed in ecclesiastical sciences, M. Olier teaching Holy Scripture. The pastor of Vaugirard profited by the presence of the priests to take an extended vacation, during which time they reformed his parish. Impressed by the fame of this reform, the curé of St-Sulpice, disheartened by the deplorable state of his parish, offered it in exchange for some of M. Olier's benefices. In August, 1641, M. Olier took charge of St-Sulpice. His aims were to reform the parish, establish a seminary, and Christianize the Sorbonne, then very worldly, through the piety and holiness of the seminarians who should attend its courses. The parish embraced the whole Faubourg-St-Germain, with a population as numerous and varied as a large city. It was commonly reputed the largest and most vicious parish, not only in the French capital, but in all Christendom. The enormity of the evils had killed all hope of reformation. Father Olier organized his priests in community life. Those who found the life too strict separated from the work. The parish was divided into eight districts, each under the charge of a head priest and associates, whose duty it was to know individually all the souls under their care, with their spiritual and corporal needs, especially the poor, the uninstructed, the vicious, and those bound in irregular unions. Thirteen catechetical centres were established, for the instruction not only of children but of many adults who were almost equally ignorant of religion. Special instructions were provided for every class of persons, for the beggars, the poor, domestic servants, lackeys, midwives, workingmen, the aged etc. Instructions and debates on Catholic doctrine were organized for the benefit of Calvinists, hundreds of whom were converted. A vigorous campaign was waged against immoral and heretical literature and obscene pictures; leaflets, holy pictures, and prayer books were distributed to those who could not or would not come to church, and a bookstore was opened at the church to supply good literature. The poor were cared for according to methods of relief inspired by the practical genius of St. Vincent de Paul. During the five or six years of the Fronde, the terrible civil war that reduced Paris to widespread misery, and often to the verge of famine, M. Olier supported hundreds of families and provided many with clothing and shelter. None were refused. His rules of relief, adopted in other parishes, became the accepted methods and are still followed at St-Sulpice. Orphans, very numerous during the war, were placed in good parishes, and a house of refuge established for orphan girls. A home was open to shelter and reform the many women rescued from evil lives, and another for young girls exposed to danger. Many free schools for poor girls were founded by Father Olier, and he laboured also at the reform of the teachers in boys' schools, not however, with great success. He perceived that the reform of boys' schools could be accomplished only through a new congregation; which in fact came about after his death through Saint John Baptist de la Salle, a pupil of St-Sulpice, who founded his first school in Father Olier's parish. Free legal aid was provided for the poor. He gathered under one roof the sisters of many communities, who had been driven out of their convents in the country and fled to Paris for refuge, and cared for them till the close of the war. In fine, there was no misery among the people, spiritual or corporal, for which the pastor did not seek a remedy.

His work for the rich and high-placed was no less thorough and remarkable. He led the movement against duelling, formed a society for its suppression, and enlisted the active aid of military men of renown, including the marshals of France and some famous duellists. He converted many of noble and royal blood, both men and women. He combated the idea that Christian perfection was only for priests and religious, and inspired many to the practices of a devout life, including daily meditation, spiritual reading and other exercises of piety, and to a more exact fulfilment of their duties at court and at home. His influence was powerful with the Queen Regent, Anne of Austria, to whom he spoke with great plainness, yet with great respect, denouncing her prime minister, Cardinal Mazarin, as responsible for simoniacal and sacrilegious nominations to the episcopate. He persuaded the rich— royalty, nobles, and others—to a great generosity, without which his unbounded charities would have been impossible. The foundation of the present church of St-Sulpice was laid by him. At times as many as sixty or even eighty priests were ministering together in the parish, of whom the most illustrious, a little after Olier's time, was Fénelon, later Archbishop of Cambrai. This was one of the best effects of Olier's work, for it sent trained, enlightened zealous priests into all parts of France. From being the most vicious in France, the parish became one of the most devout, and it has remained such to this day. Olier was always the missionary. His outlook was worldwide; his zeal led to the foundation of the Sulpician missions at Montreal and enabled him to effect the conversion of the English King, Charles II, to the Catholic faith, though not to perseverance in a Christian life.

The second great work of Olier was the establishment of the seminary of St-Sulpice. By his parish, which he intended to serve as a model to the parochial clergy, as well as by his seminary, he hoped to help give France a worthy secular priesthood, through which alone, he felt, the revival of religion could come.

The seminary was at first installed in the presbytery, but very soon (1 Oct., 1642) removed to a little house in the vicinity, M. de Foix being placed in charge by Father Olier. The beginnings were in great poverty, which lasted many years, for Olier would never allow any revenues from the parish to be expended except on parish needs. From the start he designed to make it a national seminary and regarded as providential the fact that the parish of St-Sulpice and its seminary depended directly on the Holy See. In the course of two years students came to it from about twenty dioceses of France. Some attended the courses at the Sorbonne, others followed those given in the seminary. His seminarians were initiated into parochial work, being employed very fruitfully in teaching catechism. At the Sorbonne their piety, it appears, had a very marked influence. The seminary, fulfilling the hopes of Father Olier, not only sent apostolic priests into all parts of France, but became the model according to which seminaries were founded throughout the kingdom. Its rules, approved by the General Assembly of the Clergy in 1651, were adopted in many new establishments. Within a few years, Father Olier, at the earnest solicitation of the bishops, sent priests to found seminaries in a few dioceses, the first at Nantes in 1648. It was not his intention to establish a congregation to conduct a number of seminaries in France, but merely to lend priests for the foundation of a seminary to any bishop and to recall them after their work was well established. The repeated requests of bishops, considered by him as indications of God's will, caused him to modify his plan, and to accept a few seminaries permanently. The society which formed around him at St-Sulpice was not erected into a religious congregation; it continued as a community of secular priests, following a common life but bound by no special vows, whose aim it should be to live perfectly the life of secular priests. He wished it to remain a small company, decreeing that it should never consist of more than seventy-two members, besides the superior and his twelve assistants. This regulation remained in force till circumstances induced Father Emery to abolish the limitation.

Father Olier's arduous labours brought on a stroke of apoplexy in February, 1652. He resigned his cure into the hands of M. de Bretonvilliers and on regaining sufficient strength visited watering-places in search of health, by command of his physicians, and made many pilgrimages. On his return to Paris, his old energy and enthusiasm reasserted themselves, especially in his warfare against Jansenism. A second stroke, at Péray in September, 1653, rendered him thenceforth a paralytic. His last years were full of intense suffering, both bodily and mental, which he bore with the utmost sweetness and resignation. They were years of prayer, but indeed the whole life of this servant of God, despite his immense external activity, was a prayer; and his principal devotion was to the inner life of Christ. His visions and his mysticism caused the Jansenists to ridicule him as a visionary; but they, as well as all others, acknowledged his sanctity and the singular purity of his intentions. His numerous ascetical writings show him a profound master of spiritual doctrine, and well deserve a close study. His great friend, St. Vincent de Paul, who was with him at his death, considered him a saint; and Father Faber, in his "Growth in Holiness" (Baltimore ed., p. 376) says of him: "Of all the uncanonized servants of God whose lives I have read, he most resembles a canonized Saint." (See SAINT-SULPICE, SOCIETY OF.)

FAILLON, Vie de M. Olier (3 vols., 4th ed., Paris, 1873), the chief printed source of later works; LETOURNEAU, Le Ministère pastoral de J. J. Olier (Paris, 1905); IDEM, La Mission de J. J. Olier (Paris, 1906); DE FRUGES, J. J. Olier (Paris, 1904); THOMPSON, Life of Jean Jacques Olier (London); LEAR, The Revival of Priestly Life in France (London, 1894); BERTRAND, Bibliothèque Sulpicienne (Paris, 1900), contains a complete list of Olier's published and unpublished writings. MIGNE has edited his writings in one volume (Paris, —). A few chapters of a new life of Olier, by MONNIER, were published in the *Bulletin Trimestriel des anciens élèves de S. Sulpice* (Paris, 1910). They suffice to show that this new biography, by its critical acumen, complete knowledge and literary qualities, will supplant all hitherto published.

JOHN F. FENLON.

Olinda, DIOCESE OF, in the north-east of Brazil, suffragan of San Salvador de Bahia. Erected into a vicariate Apostolic by Paul V (15 July, 1614), who annexed to it the Prefecture Apostolic of São Luiz do Maranhão, Olinda was created a bishopric by Innocent XI on 22 November, 1676 (Constitution "Ad Sacram"). Its most distinguished prelate was Thomas of the Incarnation (1774–85), author of "Historia ecclesiæ Lusitaniæ" (Coimbra, 1759). From its original territory Leo XIII erected the Sees of Parahyba (1892) and Alagōas (1900). It is now coextensive with the State of Pernambuco, lying between 7° and 10° 40' S. latitude, and 34° 35' and 42° 10' W. longitude, having an area of 49,575 square miles. The maritime regions are low, fertile, and well settled: the hinterland forms a plateau 500 to 700 feet high, is arid, and sparsely populated. The episcopal city was originally Olinda, founded by Duarte Coelho Pereira in 1534. It was held by the Dutch from 1630 till 1654, who established, a few miles south, a new capital, Moritzstadt, now known as Recife, or Pernambuco, an important seaport having a population of 190,000. The episcopal residence has been transferred thither, to the section called Bōa Vista. Pernambuco has a university, five hospitals (one in charge of the Sisters of Mercy), a college, and many churches, the first being dedicated to Nossa Senhora da Conceicão. Outside the city are the pilgrimages of Nossa Senhora dos Prazeres and Nossa Senhora de Monte. A Benedictine abbey founded at Olinda in 1595, was re-established on 15 August, 1885, from Beuron in Hohenzollern, and is in personal union with the abbey founded at Parahyba in 1903. The present Bishop of Olinda, Mgr Luiz Raymundo da Silva Britto (b. at São Bento do Peri, 24 Aug., 1840; ordained, 19 July, 1864; elected, 18 Feb., 1901), succeeded Mgr Manuel dos Santos Pereira (b. 1827; consecrated, 1893). The diocese contains 81 parishes, 365 filial churches and chapels, 88 secular and 22 regular priests; the population is 1,178,000, all Catholics, except about 4000 Protestants.

GALANTI, *Historia do Brazil* (São Paulo, 1896); TOLLENARE, *Notas Dominicaes* (Recife, 1906); DIAS, *O Brazil Actual* (Rio de Janeiro, 1905).

A. A. MACERLEAN.

Oliva, a suppressed Cistercian abbey near Danzig in Pomerania, founded with the assistance of the dukes of Pomerania some time between 1170–78. After the extinction of the dukes of Pomerania in 1295, Oliva became part of Poland. From 1309–1466 it was under the sovereignty of the Teutonic Order; from 1466–1772 it again formed part of Poland; from 1772–1807 it belonged to Prussia; from 1807–14 to the free city Danzig. In 1831 it was suppressed; the abbey church, a three-naved brick structure in the Romanesque and Gothic style, became the Catholic parish church of the town of Oliva; and nearly all the other buildings were torn down.

In 1224 and in 1234 the abbey was burnt down and its monks killed by the heathen Prussians; in 1350 it was destroyed by fire; in 1433 it was pillaged and partly torn down by the Hussites; in 1577 it was pillaged and almost entirely destroyed by the Protestant soldiers of Danzig, in 1626 and in 1656 it was pillaged by the Swedes. The monks of Oliva have been powerful factors in the Christianization of north-eastern Germany. The dukes of Pomerania and the Teutonic Order liberally rewarded them with large tracts of land.

When Oliva came under the sovereignty of Poland in 1466, it refused to join the Polish province of Cistercians, because most of its monks were Germans.

When about 1500 it asserted its exemptness from the jurisdiction of the bishop of Leslau, the Holy See decided in its favour. Its discipline suffered severely from 1538–1736, because by a degree of the Diet of Petricow only noblemen could be elected abbots, and especially because from 1557–1736 these abbots were appointed by the Polish kings. An impetus to reform was given by Abbot Edmund of Castiglione, who was sent as visitor. He joined Oliva to the Polish Province, and in 1580 drew up new statutes for the two provinces. But under the Prussian rule the king assumed the right of appointing the abbots and a new period of decline began which continued until the suppression.

Fontes Olivenses, ed. HIRSCH in *Script. rerum Prussicarum*, I (Leipzig, 1861) and V (1874), and by KETRZYNSKI in *Mon. Pol. hist.*, VI (Krakow, 1983); HIRSCH, *Das Kloster Oliva* (Danzig, 1850); KRETSCHMER, *Geschichte und Beschreibung der Klöster in Pomerellen:* Part I: *Die Cistercienser Abtei Oliva* (Danzig, 1847); KEMPER, *Die Inschriften des Klosters Oliva* (Neustadt in Westpreussen, 1893).

MICHAEL OTT.

Oliva, GIAN PAOLO, b. at Genoa, 4 October, 1600; d. at Rome, at Sant' Andrea Quirinale, 26 November, 1681. In 1616, he entered the Society of Jesus, in which he excelled by rare intellectual powers, learning, and sanctity. A famous pulpit orator, he was Apostolic Preacher of the Palace under Innocent X, Alexander VII, Clement IX, and Clement X. In 1661, during the critical period of the Provost General Father Goswin Nickel, the general congregation elected him vicar-general with the right of succession. His chief aim was to remove all causes of dissension and of personal friction between his institute and other religious orders, towards which he showed himself most reverent and yielding. He extended and increased the missions, creating new ones outside of Europe, especially in Japan. His book of forty-odd sermons for Lent, and his work of six folio volumes, "In Selecta Scripturæ Loca Ethicæ Commentationes", printed at Lyons, evince his scholarship and piety. He took a keen interest in the events of his time. Remembering what had happened to Cardinal Palavicino, Oliva printed one thousand of his letters, in order that they might not be printed by others and be misconstrued.

OLIVA, *Lettera ai pp. della Compagnia-Lettere*, II (Rome, 1666, 1681); PATRIGNANI, *Menologio di pie memorie ecc.*, IV (Venice, 1730), 189–91; *Journal des Savans*, X (Amsterdam, 1683), 57; CRÉTINEAU-JOLY, *Hist. religieuse, politique etc. de la C. de Jésus*, IV (Paris, 1845), 94–7.

LUIGI TACCHI VENTURI.

Olivaint, PIERRE, was b. in Paris, 22 Feb., 1816. His father, a man of repute, but an unbeliever and imbittered by reverses of fortune and career, died in 1835 without having returned to the faith. He was survived by his wife, also without religion, and three children. At twenty Pierre left home, and the College of Charlemagne, where he had made a brilliant course of studies, imbued him with the doctrines of Voltaire. His heart, however, had remained remarkably pure, and he writes at this time: "I desire, if by any possibility I should become a priest, to be a missionary, and if I am a missionary to be a martyr." In 1836 Pierre entered the Normal School, and, where so many lose their faith, conversion awaited him. Led away at first by Buchez's neo-Catholicism, then won by the sermons of Lacordaire, he made his profession of faith to Father de Ravignan (1837), and from that time became an apostle. At the Normal School he formed a Catholic group which by its piety and charity soon attracted attention and respect. The Conferences of St. Vincent de Paul attracted at that time the élite of the schools, and Olivaint with twelve of his companions established them in the parish of Saint Médard. By the ardour of their charity and faith these heroic youths symbolized the religious renaissance in France. In 1836, Olivaint heard that Lacordaire was going to restore the Dominican Order in France. Several of his friends had already decided to follow the great orator. He wished to follow him also, but was detained by the duty of supporting his mother. After a year of professorship at Grenoble, he returned to Paris, and occupied the chair of history at Bourbon College; in 1841 he accepted a position as tutor to the young George de la Rochefoucaud.

In 1842 Olivaint won the junior fellowship in a history competition. His lecture was on Gregory VII, and M. Saint-Marc Girardin closed the Assembly with these words: "We have just heard virtue, pleading the cause of virtue". At this time war was declared against the Jesuits. Quinet and Michelet changed their lectures into impassioned declarations against the society. On 2 May, 1845, M. Thiers was to conduct before the Assembly an interpellation against these religious. Olivaint saw that it was his duty to be present. "I hesitated", he said to Louis Veuillot, "I hesitate no longer. M. Thiers shows me my duty. I must follow it. I enter today." And the day of the proposed interpellation he entered the novitiate of Laval. This sacrifice was hard for Madame Olivaint who as yet had not been converted by the virtues of her son. After a year's fervent novitiate he was made professor of history at the College of Brugelette, in Belgium. On 3 May, 1847, he made his first vows, and on the completion of theological studies received Holy orders. In the meanwhile the Law of 1850 had established, in France, the right of controlling education. Pierre Olivaint was summoned to Paris, where he remained. On 3 April, 1852, Pierre arrived at the College of Vaugirard of which the Jesuits had accepted charge. He was to spend thirteen years here, first as professor and prefect of studies, then as rector. A model teacher, he trained the heart as well as the mind, and by his exhaustless energy, added to the direction of his college, many works of zeal, among others "L'Œuvre de l'Enfant Jésus pour la première communion des jeunes filles pauvres", and "L'Œuvre de Saint François-Xavier", for the workmen of the parish of Vaugirard.

After twenty-five years devoted to teaching, Father Olivaint was named Superior of the House in Paris (1865). He accepted this burden with courage, and displayed an unbounded zeal. An indefatigable preacher and director, he exercised by his sanctity an irresistible influence over all. His mother yielded to him and under his direction, Madame Olivaint prepared by a life of prayer for a very holy death. In the meantime the spirit of revolt agitated Paris, and spread throughout France. The religious renaissance of the nineteenth century, in which Pierre Olivaint had been an example, called forth a retaliation of evil. In January, 1870, Father Olivaint wrote "Persecution is upon us; it will be terrible: we will pass through torrents of blood." On the desertion of Rome by the emperor had followed the disaster of the French troops. The investment of Paris was planned, and to those who urged him to fly Father Olivaint replied that his was the post of danger. The most formidable danger impending was the commune, now mistress of Paris. "Let us be generous and ready for sacrifice", said Father Olivaint. "France must have the blood of the pure to raise her again; which one of us, indeed, is worthy to offer his life, and what a joy should we be chosen." He was chosen. On 4 April, 1871, the *fédérés* arrested Mgr Darboy and several others. On the fifth, they took possession of the house on the Rue de Sèvres and Father Olivaint quietly gave himself up. On 24 May, Mgr Darboy and five other prisoners were executed; on the twenty-sixth, fifty-two victims, Father Olivaint marching at their head, were dragged through Paris and massacred in the Rue Haxo. The day after this expiation the commune was overthrown. The remains of Father Olivaint and the four priests who fell with him (Fathers

Ducoudray, Caubert, Clerc, et de Bengy) were placed in a chapel in the Rue de Sèvres, where the pious faithful still continue to invoke them, and numberless graces have been attributed to their intercession.

CLAIR, *Pierre Olivaint prêtre de la C. de J.* (Paris, 1878); DE PONLEVOY, *Actes de la captivité et de la mort des PP. Olivaint, Ducoudray etc.* (Paris, 1878); OLIVAINT, *Journal de ses retraites annuelles* (2 vols., Paris, 1872).

PIERRE SUAU.

Oliver, GEORGE, b. at Newington in Surrey in 1781; d. at Exeter in 1861. After studying for some years at the Sedgley Park School, he entered Stonyhurst in 1796, went through the full training, and taught "humanities" for five years. Having been ordained priest in 1806, he was sent the following year to the mission formerly belonging to the Jesuits at Exeter, where he spent the remainder of his life. He was not, however, himself a Jesuit; for during his Stonyhurst days the Society had no canonical existence in England, and although the members of the community kept the rule of St. Ignatius so far as was compatible with their circumstances, in the hope of a future restoration of the Society, they continued to rank as secular priests. When the restoration of the Society took place, Oliver did not join it, but lived and died a secular priest. As a student of archæology he acquired considerable fame, and although some of his conclusions are not accepted at the present day, yet considering the limited sources of knowledge which were available when he lived, his researches show both industry and judgment. Most of his work had a local bearing. He became a well-known authority on the history and antiquities of Devonshire, about which he wrote several standard works.

The one which is best known to Catholics in general is his Collections containing numerous biographical notices of Catholics, both clergy and laity, in the West of England. On the re-establishment of the hierarchy, when the Plymouth Chapter was erected (1852), Oliver was nominated as provost. He had already retired from active work, but continued to reside in his old house until his death. Among his works are: "The Monasteries of Devon" (1820); "History of Exeter" (1821); "Ecclesiastical Antiquities of Devon" (1828, 2nd edition, much changed, 1839); "Collections S.J." (1838); "A View of Devonshire in 1630" (1845); "Monasticon Diœcesis Exoniensis" (1846); "Collections illustrating the history of the Catholic Religion" etc. (1857); "Lives of the Bishops of Exeter" (1861); numerous pamphlets and smaller works. See Brushfield's Bibliography of his works, of which the frontispiece is a portrait of George Oliver.

FOLEY, *Records S. J.*; HUSENBETH, *Hist. of Sedgley Park* (London, 1856); IDEM, *Life of Milner* (Winchester, 1839); obituary notices in *The Tablet, Gentleman's Magazine*, etc.

BERNARD WARD.

Olivet, MOUNT (Lat. *Mons olivertus*), occurring also in the English Bibles as the Mount of Olives (*Mons Olivarum*), is the name applied to "the hill that is over against Jerusalem" (III Kings, xi, 7), that is, "on the east side of the city" (Ezech., xi, 23), beyond the torrent Cedron (II Kings, xv, 23, 30), "a sabbath day's journey" from the city (Acts, i, 12). The passages of the books of the Kings show the high antiquity of the name, undoubtedly suggested by the groves of olive trees which flourished there, traces of which still remain. In the Middle Ages it was called by Arabic writers: Ṭūr ez-Zeitūn, Ṭūr Zeitâ, or Jebel Ṭūr Zeitūn, of which the modern name, Jebel et-Ṭūr, appears to be an abbreviation. Mt. Olivet is not so much a hill as a range of hills separated by low depressions. The range includes, from N. to S., the Rās el-Mushārîf (Scopus; 2686 ft. above the sea-level), Rās el-Madbāse (2690 ft.) and Ras et-Ṭelā ᶜah (2663 ft.); south of the latter, between the old and the new road from Jerusalem to Jericho, is the Jebel eṭ-Ṭūr, or Mt. Olivet proper, rising in three summits called by Christians, respectively: the Men of Galilee (Karem eṣ-Ṣāyyād, "the vineyard of the hunter", 2732 ft.), the Ascension (on which the village Kafr eṭ-Ṭūr is built), and the Prophets, a spur of the preceding owing its name to the old rock-tombs known as the Tombs of the Prophets; south-west of the new road to Jericho, the range terminates in the Jebel Baṭn el-Hāwā, called by Christians the Mount of Offence, tradition locating there Solomon's idolatrous shrines (IV Kings, xxiii, 13).

Mt. Olivet has been the scene of many famous events of Biblical history. In David's time there was there a holy place dedicated to Yahweh; its exact location is not known; but it was near the road to the Jordan, possibly on the summit of the Karem eṣ-Ṣāyyād (II Kings, xv, 32). The site of the village of Bahurim (II Kings, iii, 16) lay no doubt on the same road. We have already mentioned the tradition pointing to the Jebel Baṭn el-Hāwā as the place where Solomon erected his idolatrous shrines destroyed by Josias (III Kings, xi, 7; IV Kings, xxiii, 13); this identification is supported by the Targum which suggests in IV Kings, xxiii, 13, the reading הר המשחה, "Mount of Oil", a good synonym of Mt. Olivet, instead of the traditional הר המשחית, "Mount of Offence", found nowhere else. Accordingly the idolatrous sanctuaries were on the south side of Mt. Olivet proper. Finally we learn from the Jewish rabbis that the Mount of Oil was the traditional place for sacrificing the red heifer (Num., xix.; cf. Maimon., "Treat. of the red heifer", iii, 1). But to Christians especially is Mt. Olivet a most hallowed place, because it was, during the last days of Our Lord's public life, the preferred resort of the Saviour. In connexion therewith several spots are singled out in the Gospels: Bethania, the home of Lazarus and of Simon the Leper (Mark, xiv, 3; Matt., xxvi, 6); Bethphage, whence started the triumphal procession to Jerusalem (Matt., xxi, 1), identified with some probability by Federlin with the ruins called Habalat el-Amîrā or Kehf Abū Lāyān; the site of the Franciscan Chapel of Bethphage, about 1 mile west of El-Azāriyeh, is not well chosen; the place where the fig-tree cursed by our Lord stood (Matt., xxi, 18–22; Mark, xi, 12–14; 20–21); the spot where Jesus wept over Jerusalem (Luke, xix, 41); the site where He prophesied the destruction of the Temple, the ruin of the city and the end of the world (Matt., xxiv, 1 sqq.); the Garden of Gethsemani; lastly the place where the Lord imparted His farewell blessing to the Apostles and ascended into heaven (Luke, xxiv, 50–51). All these spots the piety of Christian ages has, with more or less success, endeavoured to locate and to consecrate by erecting sanctuaries thereon.

THOMSON, *The Land and the Book*, I (London, 1881), 415 sqq.; WARREN, *Mount of Olives* in HASTINGS, *Dict. of the Bible*, s. v.; FEDERLIN, *Quelques localités anciennes situées sur la Montagne des Oliviers* in *La Terre Sainte*, 15 Jan., 1901, pp. 21 sqq.; HEIDET in VIGOUROUX, *Dict. de la Bible*, s. v. *Oliviers (Mont des)*; LIEVIN DE HAMME, *Guide-indicateur de la Terre Sainte* (Jerusalem, 1887); NEUBAUER, *La géographie du Talmud* (Paris, 1868).

CHARLES L. SOUVAY.

Olivetans, a branch of the white monks of the Benedictine Order, founded in 1319. It owed its origin to the ascetic fervour of Giovanni Tolomei (St. Bernard Ptolomei), a gentleman of Siena and professor of philosophy. He is said to have vowed himself to religion in gratitude for the recovery of his eyesight through the intercession of the Blessed Virgin. In fulfilment of this vow he left his home (1313) and went into the wilderness, to forsake the world and give himself to God. Two companions of his, Ambrogio Piccolomini and Patricio Patrici, Sienese senators, accompanied him. They settled on a bit of land belonging to Tolomei. It was a mountain top, exactly suited to the eremitical life. Here they devoted themselves to austerities. Apparently they were somewhat aggressive in their asceticism; for, six years later, they were accused of heresy and summoned to give an explanation of their innovations before John XXII at Avignon. The two disciples— Tolomei remained behind—obeyed the mandate and succeeded in gaining the good-will of the Holy Father, who, however, in order to bring them into line with other monks, bade them go to Guido di Pietromala, Bishop of Arezzo, and ask him to give them a Rule which had the approbation of the Church. The bishop remembered that once, in a vision or dream, Our Lady had put into his hands the Rule of St. Benedict and bade him give white habits to some persons who knelt before her. He did not doubt that these monks were the Sienese hermits commended to his care by the pope. Wherefore, he clothed the three of them with white habits and gave them the Benedictine Rule and placed them under the protection of the Blessed Virgin. Tolomei took the name of Bernard and their olive-clothed mountain hermitage was renamed "Monte Oliveto", in memory of Christ's agony and as a perpetual reminder to themselves of the life of sacrifice and expiatory penance they had undertaken.

Evidently, in what he did, the good bishop had before his mind the history of St. Romuald—there is even a repetition of the well-known "Vision of St. Romuald" in the story—and hoped, through the enthusiasm of Bernard and his monks, to witness another wide-spread monastic revival, like that which spread from the Hermitage of Camaldoli. He was not disappointed. Through the generosity of a merchant a monastery was erected at Siena; he himself built another at Arezzo; a third sprang up at Florence; and within a very few years there were establishments at Camprena, Volterra, San Geminiano, Eugubio, Foligno, and Rome. Before St. Bernard's death from the plague in 1348—he had quitted his monastery to devote himself to the care of those stricken with the disease and died a martyr of charity—the new congregation was already in great repute, as well for the number of its houses and monks as for the saintliness of its members and the rigour of its observance. Yet it never succeeded in planting itself successfully on the other side of the Alps.

St. Bernard Ptolomei's idea of monastic reform was that which had inspired every founder of an order or congregation since the days of St. Benedict—a return to the primitive life of solitude and austerity. Severe corporal mortifications were ordained by rule and inflicted in public. The usual ecclesisatical and conventual fasts were largely increased and the daily food was bread and water. The monks slept on a straw mattress without bed-coverings, and did not lie down after the midnight Office, but continued in prayer until Prime. They wore wooden sandals and habits of the coarsest stuff. They were also fanatical total abstainers; not only was St. Benedict's kindly concession of a *hemina* of wine rejected, but the vineyards were rooted up and the wine-presses and vessels destroyed. Attention has been called to this last particular, chiefly to contrast with it a provision of the later constitutions, in which the monks are told to keep the best wine for themselves and sell the inferior product ("Meliora vina pro monachorum usu serventur, pejora vendantur") and, should they have to buy wine, to purchase only the better quality ("si vinum emendum erit, emetur illud quod melius erit"). Truly, relaxation was inevitable. It was never reasonable that the heroic austerities of St. Bernard and his companions should be made the rule, then and always, for every monk of the order. But the mandate concerning the quality of the wine chiefly aimed to remove any excuse for differential treatment of the monks in meat and drink. Where everything on the table was of exceptional quality, there could be no reason why anyone should be especially provided for. It was always the custom for each one to dilute the wine given him.

Though the foundation of the Olivetans was not professedly an introduction of constitutional reform among the Benedictines, it had that result. They were a new creation and hence, as we may say, up-to-date. They had a superior general, like the friars, and officials of the order distinct from those of the abbey. They set an example of adaptation to present needs by the frequent modification of their constitutions at the general chapters, and by the short term of office enjoyed by the superiors. In 1408 Gregory XII gave them the extinct monastery of St. Justina at Padua, which they occupied until the institution there of the famous Benedictine reform. This great movement, out of which the present Cassinese Congregation resulted, may, therefore, in a very literal sense, be described as having followed in the footsteps of the Olivetans. At the present date, the Order of Our Lady of Mount Olivet numbers only 10 monasteries and 122 brethren.

HÉLYOT, *Hist. des ordres monast.*; MIGNE, *Dict. des ordres relig.*; LANCELOTTO, *Hist. Olivetanæ*; BONANNI, *Catalog. ord. relig.*; CUMMINS, *The Olivetan Constitutions* in *Ampleforth Journal* (Dec., 1896).

J. C. ALMOND.

Olivi, PIERRE JEAN (PETRUS JOHANNIS), Spiritual Franciscan and theological author, b. at Sérignan, Diocese of Béziers, 1248–9; d. at Narbonne, 14 March, 1298. At twelve he entered the Friars Minor at Béziers, and later took the baccalaureate at Paris. Returning to his native province, he soon distinguished himself by his strict observance of the rule and his theological knowledge. When Nicholas III prepared his Decretal "Exiit" (1279), Olivi, then at Rome, was asked to express his opinion with regard to Franciscan poverty (*usus pauper*). Unfortunately there was then in the convents of Provence a controversy about the stricter or laxer observance of the rule. Olivi soon became the principal spokesman of the rigorists, and met with strong opposition on the part of the community. At the General Chapter of Strasburg (1282) he was accused of heresy, and henceforward almost every general chapter concerned itself with him. His doctrine was examined by seven friars, graduates of the University of Paris (see Anal. Franc., III, 374–75), and censured in thirty-four propositions, whereupon his writings were confiscated (1283). Olivi cleverly defended himself in several responses (1283–85), and finally the General Chapter of Montpellier (1287) decided in his favour. The new general, Matthew of Aquasparta, sent him as lector in theology to the convent of Sta. Croce, Florence, whence Matthew's successor, Raymond Gaufredi, sent him as lector to Montpellier. At the General Chapter of Paris (1292) Olivi again gave explanations, which were apparently satisfactory. He spent his last years in the convent of Narbonne, and died, surrounded by his friends, after an earnest profession of his Catholic Faith (published by Wadding ad a. 1297, n. 33).

Peace, however, was not obtained by his death. His friends, friars and seculars, showed an exaggerated veneration for their leader, and honoured his tomb as that of a saint; on the other hand the General Chapter of Lyons (1299) ordered his writings to be collected and burnt as heretical. The General Council of Vienne (1312), in the Decretal "Fidei catholicæ fundamento" (Bull. Franc., V, 86), established the Catholic doctrine against three points of Olivi's teaching, without mentioning the author; these points referred to: (1) the moment Our Lord's body was transfixed by the lance, (2) the manner in which the soul is united to the body, (3) the baptism of infants. In 1318 the friars went so far as to destroy Olivi's tomb, and in the next year two further steps were taken against him: his writings were absolutely forbidden by the General Chapter of Marseilles, and a special commission of theologians examined Olivi's "Postilla in Apocalypsim" and marked out sixty sentences, chiefly joachimistical extravagances (see JOACHIM OF FLORA. For text see Baluzius-Mansi, "Miscellanea", II, Lucca, 1761, 258-70; cf. also Denifle, "Chartularium Universitatis Parisiensis", II, i, Paris, 1891, 238-9). It was only in 1326 that those sentences were really condemned by John XXII, when the fact that Louis the Bavarian used Olivi's writings in his famous Appeal of Sachsenhausen (1324) had again drawn attention to the author. Olivi's fate was a hard one, but was partly deserved through his theological incorrectness. Still Father Ehrle, the most competent judge on this point, considers (Archiv, III, 440) that Olivi was not the impious heretic he is painted in some writings of the Middle Ages, and states (ibid., 448) that the denunciation of his theological doctrine was rather a tactical measure of the adversaries of the severe principles of poverty and reform professed by Olivi. For the rest, Olivi follows in many points the doctrine of St. Bonaventure. The numerous but for the most part unedited works of Olivi are appropriately divided by Ehrle into three classes: (1) Speculative Works, of which the chief is his "Quæstiones" (philosophical and theological), printed partly in an extremely rare edition (Venice, 1509), which contains also his defences against the Paris theologians of 1283-85 which were reprinted by Du Plessis d'Argentré, "Collectio judiciorum", I (Paris, 1724), 226-34; Commentary on the Book of Sentences; "De Sacramentis" etc. (2) Exegetical Works: Five small treatises on principles of introduction, printed under St. Bonaventure's name by Bonelli, "Suppl. ad. op. S. Bonaventuræ" (Trent, 1772-3), I, 23-49, 282-347, 348-74; II, 1038-52, 1053-1113. In the same work (I, 52-281) is printed Olivi's "Postilla in Cant. Canticorum". (See S. Bonav. opera., VI, Quaracchi, 1893, Prolegomena, vi-ix.) The other *postillæ* are: Super Genesim, Job, Psalterium, Proverbia, Ecclesiasten, Lamentationes Jeremiæ, Ezechielem, Prophetas minores, on the Four Gospels, Ep. ad Romanos [see Denifle, "Die Abendl. Schriftausleger bis Luther . . . . (Rom., i, 17) und justificatio" (Mainz, 1905), 156 sq.], ad Corinthios, in epistolas Canonicas, in Apocalypsim; (3) Works on observance of Franciscan Rule (see FRANCIS, RULE OF SAINT).

EHRLE, *Petrus Johannis Olivi, sein Leben u. seine Schriften* in *Archiv für Litt. u Kirchengesch. d. Mittelalters*, III (Berlin, 1887), 409-552; IDEM, *Die Vorgesch. d. Concils von Vienne, ibid.*, II, 353-416; DANOU, *Hist. litt. de la France*, XXI (Paris, 1847), 41-55; FÉRET, *La faculté de théol. de Paris. Moyen Age*, II (Paris, 1895), 99-105; III, 117-25; RENÉ DE NANTES, *Hist. des Spirituels* (Paris, 1909), 267-342; OLIGER, *Descriptio Codicis Capistranensis aliquot opuscula Fr. Petri Johannis Olivi continentis* in *Archivum Francisc. Histor.*, I (Quaracchi, 1908), 617-22; ZIGLIARA, *De mente Concilii Viennensis in definiendo dogmate unionis animæ humanæ cum corpore* (Rome, 1878); WADDING, *Scriptores* (Rome, 1806), 193; SBARALEA, *Suppl. ad Script.*, 595-7.

LIVARIUS OLIGER.

Olivier de la Marche, chronicler and poet, b. 1426, at the Chateau de la Marche, in Franche-Comté; d. at Brussels, 1501. He was knighted by Count de Charolais, later Charles the Bold (1465). Two years later Count de Charolais became ruler of Burgundy and Flanders, and made Olivier bailiff of Amont (now a department of the Haute-Saône) and captain of his guards. Taken prisoner at the battle of Nancy, where the duke lost his life (1477), he regained his liberty by paying a ransom, and rejoined Marie, daughter of Duke Charles and heiress of Burgundy, who made him her *maître d'hôtel*.

As a writer he is best known by his "Mémoirs", which cover the years from 1435-92, first printed at Lyons in 1562. Another edition, by Beaune and d'Arbaumont, was made for the Société de l'Histoire de France (1883-88). The work is singular and important for a knowledge of the period. The author is sincere, but his style contains many *Wallonne* expressions and, as in his other writings, he introduces too many descriptions of fêtes and tournaments. Most of his works are in verse. Among these are: "Le Chevalier Délibéré", a poem which some think is his own biography, others that it is an allegorical life of Charles the Bold; "Le Parement et le Triomphe des Dames d'Honneur", a work in prose and verse, of which each of the twenty-six chapters is named from some articles of ladies' attire; and "La Source d'Honneur pour maintenir la corporelle élégance des Dames". Among his prose works are: "Traité et Avis de quelques gentilhommes sur les duels et gages de bataille", and "Traité de la Manière de célébrer la noble fête de la Toison d'or".

STEIN, *Olivier de la Marche* (Brussels, 1888).

GEORGES BERTRIN.

Ollé-Laprune, LÉON, French Catholic philosopher, b. in 1839; d. at Paris, 19 Feb., 1898. Under the influence of the philosopher Caro and of Père Gratry's book "Les Sources", Ollé-Laprune, after exceptionally brilliant studies at the Ecole Normale Supérieure (1858 to 1861), devoted himself to philosophy. His life was spent in teaching a philosophy illuminated by the light of Catholic faith, first in the *lycées* and then in the Ecole Normale Supérieure from 1875. As Ozanam had been a Catholic professor of history and foreign literature in the university, Ollé-Laprune's aim was to be a Catholic professor of philosophy there. Père de Règnon, the Jesuit theologian, wrote to him: "I am glad to think that God wills in our time to revive the lay apostolate, as in the times of Justin and Athenagoras; it is you especially who give me these thoughts." The Government of the Third Republic was now and then urged by a certain section of the press to punish the "clericalism" of Ollé-Laprune, but the repute of his philosophical teaching protected him. For one year only (1881-82), after organizing a manifestation in favour of the expelled congregations, he was suspended from his chair by Jules Ferry, and the first to sign the protest addressed by his students to the minister on behalf of their professor was the future socialist deputy Jean Jaurès, then a student at the Ecole Normale Supérieure.

Ollé-Laprune's first important work was "La philosophie de Malebranche" (1870). Ten years later to obtain the doctorate he defended before the Sorbonne a thesis on moral certitude. As against the exaggerations of Cartesian rationalism and Positivistic determinism he investigated the part of the will and the heart in the phenomenon of belief. This work resembles in many respects Newman's "Grammar of Assent"; but Ollé-Laprune must not, any more than the English cardinal, be held responsible for subsequent tendencies which have sought to diminish the share of the intelligence in the act of faith and to separate completely the domain of belief from that of knowledge. In his "Essai sur la morale d'Aristote" (1881) Ollé-Laprune defended the "Eudæmonism" of the Greek philosopher against the Kantian theories; and in "La philosophie et le temps présent" (1890) he vindicated, against Deistic spiritualism, the right of the Christian thinker to go beyond the data of "natural religion" and illuminate philosophy by the data of revealed religion. One of his most influential works was the "Prix de la vie" (1894), wherein he shows why life is worth living. The advice given by Leo XIII to the Catholics of France found in Ollé-Laprune an active champion. His brochure "Ce qu'on va chercher à Rome" (1895) was one of the best commentaries on the papal policy. The Academy of Moral and Political Sciences elected him a member of the philosophical section in 1897 to succeed Vacherot. His articles and conferences attest his growing influence in Catholic circles. He became a leader of Christian activity, consulted and heard by all until his premature death when he was about to finish a book on Jouffroy (Paris, 1899). Many of his articles have been collected by Goyau under the title "La Vitalité chrétienne" (1901). Here will also be found a series of his unedited meditations, which by a noteworthy coincidence bore the future motto of Pius X, "Omnia instaurare in Christo". Professor Delbos of the University of Paris published in 1907 the course which Ollé-Laprune had given on reason and rationalism (La raison et le rationalisme). Some months after his death Mr. William P. Coyne called him with justice "the greatest Catholic layman who has appeared in France since Ozanam" ("New Ireland Review", June, 1899, p. 195).

BAZAILLAS, *La crise de la croyance* (Paris, 1901); BLONDEL, *Léon Ollé-Laprune* (Paris, 1900); GOYAU, Preface to *La Vitalité chrétienne*; DELBOS, Preface to *La raison et le rationalisme*; ROURE in *Etudes religieuses* (20 October, 1898); BOUTROUX, *Notice sur M. Ollé-Laprune*, read before the Académie des Sciences morales (Paris, 1900).

GEORGES GOYAU.

Olmütz, ARCHDIOCESE OF (OLOMUCENSIS), in Moravia. It is probable that Christianity penetrated into Moravia as early as the fourth century, but the invasions of the Huns and Avars destroyed these beginnings. Towards the end of the eighth century the Northern Slavs immigrated into this region. Their leader, Rastislav, asked for Christian missionaries, not from the Franks, but from the Greek emperor, Michael III, who sent the brothers Cyril and Methodius, born in Thessalonica but speaking the Slavic tongue and educated in Constantinople. Cyril, known as "the Philosopher", had been a missionary among the Chazars, and had discovered near the Inkermann the body of Clement I, whose transfer to Rome through Bulgaria and Pannonia is marked to this day by three Moravian and eighteen Bohemian churches dedicated to St. Clement. The preaching of the missionary brothers was successful. Cyril invented the Glagolitic alphabet and translated the Bible into Slavic. What is to-day called "Cyrillic" (Glagolitic) script owes its origin to his pupil Clement, Bishop of Welica. German ecclesiastics became jealous of the success of the two Slavic apostles and accused them at Rome, but Adrian II gave them permission to use the Slavic language for religious services. Cyril died in a Roman monastery, while Methodius became Archbishop of Pannonia and Moravia. Despite his high ecclesiastical dignity he was insulted at a Synod of Salzburg and kept a prisoner for two and a half years. He laboured faithfully and successfully in Moravia under the reign of Swatopluk, justified himself repeatedly when accused before John VIII, and died 6 April, 885, at Velehrad on the March.

The Moravian kingdom soon (906) fell before the onslaught of the Hungarians, and the name Moravia for a long time disappears from history. In the report sent by Pilgrim of Passau to Benedict VIII, it is mentioned as part of the Diocese of Passau. When in 973 the See of Prague was established, it included Moravia, Silesia (with Cracow), and the Lausitz. In 1048 Duke Bretislav Achilles founded the first Moravian monastery, Raigern. The medieval concept of a kingdom called for several episcopal sees under a metropolitan. Therefore, when Bretislav's successor, Vratislav II, coveted the royal crown, he created the necessary conditions, and in 1063 Olmütz became a bishopric. The emperor gained a new vassal, and the Archbishop of Mainz another suffragan. The Bishop of Prague, as an indemnity for the loss of tithes in Moravia, received twelve fiefs in Bohemia, and annually the sum of one hundred marks silver from the ducal treasury. The first Moravian bishop was John I (1063-85), a monk of Brevnow. At the same time the Cathedral of Sts. Peter and Paul received a chapter with a dean at its head. John had to suffer a great deal from Bishop Jaromir (Gebhard) of Prague, the unpriestly brother of Duke Vratislav. Jaromir personally attacked and maltreated Bishop John in the latter's episcopal palace. Alexander II thereupon sent a legate Rudolphus, who convoked a synod at Prague which Jaromir ignored. For this insubordination he was deposed. Gregory VII summoned both bishops to Rome. At the Easter Synod of 1074 Jaromir expressed his regret for maltreating John, but declined to give up the fief of Bodovin, whereupon the pope asked Vratislav to expel Jaromir, by force if necessary.

Among the bishops of Olmütz, during the later Middle Ages the following are prominent: Heinrich (called Zdik after his birthplace) transferred his see to the church of St. Wenceslaus, which had been twenty-four years in construction, and at Easter, 1138, took the Premonstratensian habit in the church of the Holy Sepulchre at Jerusalem. Bishop Kaiim, in 1193, while ordaining priests and deacons at Prague, forgot the imposition of hands. His successor, Engelbert, corrected this omission two years later; but the Cardinal-Deacon Petrus declared the ordination null and void, and caused it to be repeated in its entirety in

THE CATHEDRAL, OLMÜTZ

1197. When the legate attempted to enforce a strict observance of the laws relating to celibacy, he was expelled from the country; the laws of the Church, however, were henceforth more strictly observed. During the time that Moravia was joined to Bohemia, the Duke of Bohemia appointed the Bishop of Olmütz. In 1182 Moravia became independent, and thereafter the margraves of Moravia exercised the right of appointment. Premysl Ottokar I, in 1207, granted to the Church of Olmütz freedom from taxes and to the chapter the right of electing the bishop. Innocent III confirmed this grant. After the death of Ottokar II, Rudolph of Hapsburg appointed Bishop Bruno regent in Moravia. Charles IV, in 1343, made Prague the metropolitan see for Leitomischl and Olmütz. The bishopric, as a vassal principality of the Bohemian crown, was the peer of the margravate of Moravia, and from 1365 its prince-bishop was Count of the Bohemian Chapel, i. e. first court chaplain who was to accompany the monarch on his frequent travels. In 1380 the cathedral and the residence of the prince-bishop were both destroyed by fire. During this period the following orders were established: the Premonstratensians (Hradisch, Klosterbrück); Cistercians (Velehrad); the Franciscans and the Dominicans during the lives of their founders; the Teutonic Knights. On the other hand there arose the sects of the Albigenses, Flagellants, Waldensians (Apostolic Brethren, Brethren of the Holy Ghost), Hussites (Bohemian Brethren, Grubenheimer, Picardians). Thus it happened that Protestantism found a well-prepared field. Lutheranism was preached by Speratus at Iglau; Hubmaier and Huter were Baptists. Exiled from Switzerland and Germany, the Anabaptists came in droves into Moravia; Lœlius Socinus, on his homeward journey from Poland to Turin, successfully sowed the seed of Socinianism. Bishop Dubravsky (Dubravius), famous as an author and historian, encouraged the disheartened Catholics (1553). The thirty-three volumes of his history of Bohemia, his five books on fish-raising (piscatology), and the work entitled "Ueber das heilige Messopfer" justify his reputation.

The Reform movement was finally arrested by the Jesuits. Three of them reached Olmütz in 1566 and rapidly acquired influence and power. Bishop Prusinovsky granted them a convent and turned over to them the schools as well as the projected university. At a synod strict orders and regulations were adopted. His fourth successor, Pavlovsky, accomplished wonders in carrying out the decrees of the Council of Trent. Rudolph II conferred upon him the title of duke and prince and made him a member of the royal chapel. The canons whom he gathered at Olmütz were distinguished for learning and virtue. The most important bishop of this see during the Reformation period was Cardinal Franz Dietrichstein (d. 1636), son of Adam, major-domo of the imperial household. He governed the see for thirty-seven years, and accomplished extraordinary things both as statesman and ecclesiastic. His work, of course, met with considerable opposition. He was imprisoned at Brünn, and the See of Olmütz was abolished. Johannes Sarkander, parish priest of Holleschau, became a martyr for the secrecy of the confessional at Olmütz, 17 March, 1620, and in 1860 he was canonized. Better days soon appeared. The title of prince was conferred on both the cardinal and his brother, whose descendants were to inherit the title. Amos Comenius (Komenzky), the last "senior" of the Bohemian Brethren, fled to Poland. Pre-eminent as a pedagogue his influence was felt later on in the intellectual life of his country. Dietrichstein was succeeded by Archduke Leopold Wilhelm, son of Ferdinand II, and by Charles Joseph, son of Ferdinand III. In 1663 Charles Joseph was elected Bishop of Breslau and Olmütz, with a dispensation from Alexander VII, as he was scarcely fourteen years of age; but died the following year. In 1693 Charles, son of Duke Charles of Lorraine, at the age of twenty-three, became sub-deacon and exercised the administrative power in temporal affairs; four years later he obtained the spiritual administration. The dissolution of the Society of Jesus in 1773 affected three hundred and sixty-eight professors in nine colleges of Moravia. In the same year Clement XIV withdrew from the chapter the right of electing its bishop; it was restored, however, by Pius VI.

Maria Theresa, in 1777, raised Olmütz to the dignity of an archbishopric, and subordinated to it the newly-founded See of Brünn. The archdiocese was divided into eight archpresbyterates and fifty-two deaneries. When the toleration edict of Joseph II appeared in 1781, whole districts forsook the Church. The inhabitants since the Counter-Reformation had been Protestants in secret. The emperor therefore ordered those desirous of renouncing the Catholic belief to make known in person their intention to the Commission on Religion. When Emperor Joseph began the dissolution of the monasteries, there were in Moravia and Silesia two thousand monks in eighty-three houses. From the sale of this ecclesiastical property, the so-called "Religion Fund", many parishes were established, three in Olmütz alone. In the rural parts the parishes were not to be more than four miles apart. The parish priests received a stipend of four hundred florins, a local chaplain three hundred florins, and an assistant two hundred florins. The third Archbishop of Olmütz was Archduke Rudolph, brother of Emperor Francis. Cardinal Maximilian Joseph, Freiherr von Somerau-Beckh, had, in 1848, as adviser and assistant, the brilliant chancellor Kutschker. On 2 December of the same year, in the throne room of the prince-archbishop's residence, Francis Joseph assumed the imperial sceptre. While the Austrian Parliament sat at Kremsier, Olmütz was the political capital of Austria. Eighty years old, Somerau-Beckh attended the great assembly of bishops in Vienna in 1849. Here he proposed by legal enactment to abolish the rule requiring every member of the Olmütz chapter to be of noble birth, because this rule was contrary to the spirit of Christianity and the laws of the Church, and an injustice to the untitled clergy of the diocese. The Olmütz chapter for a long time opposed this proposition both at Rome and at the imperial court, but without success. The two last prince-bishops have also been commoners. Cardinal Fürstenberg rebuilt in splendid Gothic style the cathedral with its three towers, carefully preserving the individuality of the old church. The Concordat of Vienna (1448) provided that if any high dignitary of the Church resigned or died while in Rome, the pope should have the right to fill the vacancy thus caused. This he did, when Archbishop Theodor Kohn resigned his office in Rome on account of his great age, and the Bishop of Brünn, Francis Sal. Bauer was appointed archbishop.

At the present (1910) Moravia has two and one half million inhabitants of whom over ninety-five per cent are Catholics, less than three per cent Protestants, and nearly two per cent Hebrews. In the Archdiocese of Olmütz there are 1,785,000 Catholics; 1,507 priests; 220 male and 1,547 female inmates of religious houses. The episcopal city has a population of 22,000.

WOLNY, *Topographie Mährens* (2 vols., Brünn, 1836–42); *Kirchl. Topographie Mährens* (9 vols., Brünn, 1855–63), index, 1866; DUDIK, *Geschichte Mährens* (until 1358) in 12 vols. (Brünn, 1860–88); MÜLLER, *Geschichte der kön. Hauptstadt Olmütz* (Vienna, 1882); TITTEL, *Historia archidiœcesis Olomucensis ejusque Præsulum* (Olmütz, 1889), MSS.; D'ELVERT, *Zur Geschichte des Erzbistums Olmütz* (Brünn, 1895), bibliography, pp. 305–12.

C. WOLFSGRUBER.

O'Loghlen, MICHAEL, b. at Ennis, Co. Clare, Ireland, in 1789; d. 1846. Educated at Ennis Academy, and Trinity College, Dublin, he was called to the Irish Bar in 1811. By force of ability he won a position as a brilliant pleader. His first real success was as a substitute for O'Connell on the day of the memorable duel between O'Connell and D'Esterre (1815); from 1820 to 1830 many cases came from O'Connell through whose influence O'Loghlen was appointed solicitor general for Ireland in 1834, the first Catholic since James II. He was also elected M.P. for Dungarvan, and when Perrin was elevated to the Bench in 1835, he was made attorney general. A year later he succeeded Sir William Cusack Smith as baron of the exchequer—the first Catholic judge for almost one hundred and fifty years. Finally, in 1837, on the death of Sir William MacMahon he was given the Irish mastership of the rolls, which he held till his death. As master of the rolls he effected many legal reforms.

O'FLANAGAN, *Recollections of the Irish Bar* (Dublin, 1870).

W. H. GRATTAN-FLOOD.

Olympias, SAINT, b. 360–5; d. 25 July, 408, probably at Nicomedia. This pious, charitable, and wealthy disciple of St. John Chrysostom came from an illustrous family in Constantinople. Her father (called by the sources Secundus or Selencus) was a "Count" of the empire; one of her ancestors, Ablabius, filled in 331 the consular office, and was also prætorian prefect of the East. As Olympias was not thirty years of age in 390, she cannot have been born before 361. Her parents died when she was quite young, and left her an immense fortune. In 384 or 385 she married Nebridius, Prefect of Constantinople. St. Gregory Nazianzus, who had left Constantinople in 381, was invited to the wedding, but wrote a letter excusing his absence (Ep. cxciii, in P. G., XXXVII, 315), and sent the bride a poem (P. G., loc. cit., 1542 sqq.). Within a short time Nebridius died, and Olympias was left a childless widow. She steadfastly rejected all new proposals of marriage, determining to devote herself to the service of God and to works of charity. Nectarius, Bishop of Constantinople (381–97), consecrated her deaconess. On the death of her husband the emperor had appointed the urban prefect administrator of her property, but in 391 (after the war against Maximus) restored her the administration of her large fortune. She built beside the principal church of Constantinople a convent, into which three relatives and a large number of maidens withdrew with her to consecrate themselves to the service of God. When St. John Chrysostom became Bishop of Constantinople (398), he acted as spiritual guide of Olympias and her companions, and, as many undeserving approached the kind-hearted deaconess for support, he advised her as to the proper manner of utilizing her vast fortune in the service of the poor (Sozomen, "Hist. eccl.", VIII, ix; P. G., LXVII, 1540). Olympias resigned herself wholly to Chrysostom's direction, and placed at his disposal ample sums for religious and charitable objects. Even to the most distant regions of the empire extended her benefactions to churches and the poor.

When Chrysostom was exiled, Olympias supported him in every possible way, and remained a faithful disciple, refusing to enter into communion with his unlawfully appointed successor. Chrysostom encouraged and guided her through his letters, of which seventeen are extant (P. G., LII, 549 sqq.): these are a beautiful memorial of the noble-hearted, spiritual daughter of the great bishop. Olympias was also exiled, and died a few months after Chrysostom. After her death she was venerated as a saint. A biography dating from the second half of the fifth century, which gives particulars concerning her from the "Historia Lausiaca" of Palladius and from the "Dialogus de vita Joh. Chrysostomi", proves the great veneration she enjoyed. During the riot of Constantinople in 532 the convent of St. Olympias and the adjacent church were destroyed. Emperor Justinian had it rebuilt, and the prioress, Sergia, transferred thither the remains of the foundress from the ruined church of St. Thomas in Brokhthes, where she had been buried. We possess an account of this translation by Sergia herself. The feast of St. Olympias is celebrated in the Greek Church on 24 July, and in the Roman Church on 17 December.

Vita S. Olympiadis et narratio Sergiæ de eiusdem translatione in Anal. Bolland. (1896), 400 sqq., (1897), 44 sqq.; BOUSQUET, Vie d'Olympias la diaconesse in Revue de l'Orient chrét. (1900), 225 sqq.; IDEM, Récit de Sergia sur Olympias, ibid. (1907), 255 sqq.; PALLADIUS, Hist. Lausiaca, LVI, ed. BUTLER (Cambridge, 1904); Synaxarium Constantinopol., ed. DELAHAYE, Propylæum ad Acta SS., November (Brussels, 1902), 841–2; MEURISSE, Hist. d'Olympias, diaconesse de Constantinople (Metz, 1670); VENABLES in Dict. Christ. Biog., s. v. See also the bibliography of JOHN CHRYSOSTOM, SAINT.

J. P. KIRSCH.

Olympus, a titular see of Lycia in Asia Minor. It was one of the chief cities of the "Corpus Lyciacum", and was captured from the pirate, Zenicetas, by Servilius Isauricus who transported to Rome the statues and treasure he had stolen. Its ruins (a theatre, temples, and porticoes) are located south of the vilayet of Koniah, at Delik-Tash (Pierced Stone), so-called because of a large rock forming a natural arch. The town was built near Mount Olympus or Phœnicus, which gave forth constant fiery eruptions throughout antiquity; the ancients called it Chimæra and depicted it as a monster which had been vanquished by Bellerophon. Several ancient authors knew that this was only a natural phenomenon. (The Turks call it Yanar Tash—Burning Stone.) Several "Notitiæ Episcopatuum" mention Olympus among the suffragan sees of Myra until the thirteenth century. Only four bishops are known, one of whom was St. Methodius (q. v.).

LEAKE, Asia Minor (London, 1824), 189; FELLOWS, Lycia (London, 1847), 212 sq.; SPRATT AND FORBES, Travels in Lycia, I (London, 1846), 192; SMITH, Dict. Greek and Rom. Geog., s. v.; LE QUIEN, Oriens Christ., I, 975.

S. PÉTRIDÈS.

Omaha, DIOCESE OF (OMAHENSIS), embraces all that part of the State of Nebraska north of the southern shore of the South Platte River. Area, 52,996 sq. miles.

Early Missionaries.—The first missionaries in Nebraska were priests of the Society of Jesus, who, from about 1838, occasionally visited the native Indians, many of whom received baptism. In 1851 the Holy See cut off from the Diocese of St. Louis all the country north from the south line of Kansas to Canada, and west from the Missouri River to the Rocky Mountains, and erected it into the Vicariate of the Rocky Mountains, with Rt. Rev. John B. Miège, S.J., as first vicar Apostolic (see LEAVENWORTH). On 6 January, 1857, this vicariate was again divided, and a new vicariate called the Vicariate of Nebraska was erected, Bishop Miège being authorized to govern it until the appointment of a resident vicar Apostolic of Nebraska.

The first resident vicar Apostolic was the Right Rev. James Miles O'Gorman, D.D., b. near Nenagh, Co. Tipperary, Ireland, 1804, took the Trappist habit at Mount Melleray, Co. Waterford, 1 Nov., 1839, and was ordained priest, 1843. He was one of the band who came to Dubuque, Iowa, in 1849 to establish New Melleray (see CISTERCIANS). In 1859 he was appointed Vicar Apostolic of Nebraska, and on 8 May of the same year was consecrated titular Bishop of Raphanea by Archbishop Kenrick of St. Louis. The vicariate at this time embraced the present State of Nebraska, the Dakotas west of the Missouri River, Wyoming, and Montana east of the Rocky Mountains. On his arrival at Omaha, Bishop O'Gorman found in his vast jurisdiction a Catholic population of some three hundred families of white settlers living along the river counties, and a few thousand Indians, chiefly in Montana. There were in the entire territory, two seculars, and one Jesuit priest in Montana in charge of the native tribes.

During the fifteen years of his episcopate Bishop O'Gorman laboured to provide for the needs of his scattered flock. He placed priests in the more important centres of population, and in the sixties, priests of the vicariate ministered to the Catholics of Western Iowa. During his administration the Sisters of Mercy were established at Omaha, the Benedictines in Nebraska City, and the Sisters of Charity in Helena, Montana. At his death (4 July, 1874) his jurisdiction contained 19 priests, 20 churches, and a Catholic population of 11,722.

The second vicar Apostolic was the Right Rev. James O'Connor, D.D., b. at Queenstown, Ireland, 10 Sept., 1823. At the age of fifteen he came to America. He was educated at St. Charles's Seminary, Philadelphia, and in the Propaganda College, Rome, where he was ordained priest in 1848. The following year he was appointed rector of St. Michael's Seminary, Pittsburgh, and in 1862 rector of St. Charles's Seminary, Overbrook, Pennsylvania. In 1872 he was appointed pastor of St. Dominic's Church,

Holmesburg, Pennsylvania. In 1876 he was appointed Vicar Apostolic of Nebraska, and on 20 August of the same year he was consecrated titular Bishop of Dibona by Bishop Ryan of St. Louis. During his episcopate the vicariate developed with wonderful rapidity. The construction of the Union Pacific Railway in 1867, and more especially the extension of the Burlington Railway in the seventies and eighties, opened up Nebraska to colonists, and white settlers began to pour in from the Eastern states. It became the duty of the new vicar to provide for the growing needs of the faithful, and the yearly statistics of the vicariate show how successful were his labours. In 1880 the Dakotas were erected into a vicariate, and on 7 April, 1887, Montana was cut off.

Diocese of Omaha.—On 2 October, 1885, the vicariate was erected into the Diocese of Omaha, and Bishop O'Connor was appointed its first bishop. The new diocese embraced the present States of Nebraska and Wyoming. On 2 August, 1887, the Dioceses of Cheyenne and Lincoln were erected, leaving Omaha its present boundaries. Through the generosity of the Creighton family, Bishop O'Connor was enabled to erect a Catholic free day college in the city of Omaha. On its completion in 1879, the bishop, who held the property in trust, deeded over the institution to the Jesuit Fathers, who are since in charge and hold the property as trustees (see CREIGHTON UNIVERSITY). Bishop O'Connor also introduced into his jurisdiction the Franciscan Fathers, the Poor Clares, the Religious of the Sacred Heart, the Benedictines, and the Sisters of Providence. A most important work in the bishop's life was the foundation, in conjunction with Miss Catherine Drexel, of the Sisters of the Blessed Sacrament, in 1889 (see BLESSED SACRAMENT, SISTERS OF THE; also "Indian Sentinel", 1907). Bishop O'Connor also helped to establish a Catholic colony in Greeley Co., and (1889) the Cath. Mutual Relief Soc. of America.

The present bishop is the Right Rev. Richard Scannell, D.D., b. in the parish of Cloyne, Co. Cork, Ireland, 12 May, 1845. Having completed his classical studies in a private school at Midleton, in 1866 he entered All Hallows College, Dublin, where he was ordained priest 26 Feb., 1871. In the same year he came to the Diocese of Nashville and was appointed assistant at the cathedral. In 1878 he became rector of St. Columba's Church, East Nashville, and in 1879 rector of the cathedral. From 1880 to 1883 he was administrator of the diocese, *sede vacante.* In 1885 he organized St. Joseph's parish in West Nashville and built its church. The following year he was appointed vicar-general, and on 30 Nov., 1887, was consecrated first Bishop of Concordia by Archbishop Feehan.

On 30 January, 1891, he was transferred to Omaha. During his administration the diocese shows the same wonderful growth that characterized this territory in the time of his predecessors. Parishes, parochial schools, and academies have more than doubled in number. The diocesan priests have increased from 58 to 144, and the religious from 23 to 37. The old frame churches are fast being replaced by structures of brick and stone, and a fine cathedral of the Spanish style of architecture is in process of erection. The Creighton Memorial St. Joseph's Hospital, costing over half a million dollars, has been erected, and a new hospital—St. Catherine's—has just been opened, a home of the Good Shepherd has been established, and Creighton University has been many times enlarged. Bishop Scannell introduced the following orders: (men) the Third Order Regular of St. Francis, who conduct a flourishing college; (women) the Sisters of St. Joseph, of the Presentation, of the Resurrection, of St. Benedict, of the Blessed Sacrament, of the Good Shepherd, the Dominicans, Felicians, Ursulines, and Franciscans.

Pioneer Priests.—Fathers Kelly, Daxacher, Hartig, Ryan, Cannon, Powers, Erlach, Curtis, Hayes, Byrne, Groenebaum, Uhing, Lechleitner. The following filled the office of vicar-general or administrator:—Very Rev. Fathers Kelly, Curtis, Byrne, Choka, and Rt. Rev. Mgr Colaneri, the present vicar-general and chancellor.

Statistics.—Priests, secular 144, regular 37; parishes, 117; university, 1, students 856; college, 1, students 150; academies for young ladies, 10, pupils 1127; parochial schools, 77, pupils 479; orphan asylum, 1, orphans 145; Good Shepherd Home, 1, inmates 210; religious orders of men, 3, members 77; religious orders of women, 17, members 427; hospitals, 5; Catholic population (1910), 85,319. (For early explorations see CORONADO.)

MORTON, *History of Nebraska* (Lincoln, 1906); SAVAGE AND BELL, *History of Omaha* (New York and Chicago, 1894); *The Western Historical Co. Hist. of Nebraska* (Chicago, 1882); SHEA, *Hist. of the Catholic Church in the United States* (New York); PALLADINO, *Indian and White in the North-west* (Baltimore, 1894); PERKINS, *Hist. of the Trappist Abbey of New Melleray* (Iowa City, 1892); DOWLING, *Creighton University Reminiscences* (Omaha, 1903).

JAMES AHERNE.

Ombus, titular see and suffragan of Ptolemais in Thebais Secunda. The city is located by Ptolemy (IV, v, 32) in the nomos of Thebes. It is mentioned by the "Itinerarium Antonini" (165); Juvenal (XV, 35); the "Notitia dignitatum"; Hierocles (Synecdemus) etc. As late as the Ptolemaic epoch it was only a small garrison town built on a high plateau to protect the lower course of the Nile. It became afterwards the capital of the nomos Ombitos, then of the southern province of Egypt instead of Elephantine (see in "Ptolemæi Geographia", ed. Müller, I, 725, note 4, the epigraphic texts relating to this nome). Ombus was situated 30 miles north of Syene. Its history is unknown. Le Quien ("Oriens christ.", II, 613) mentions two of its bishops: Silvanus and Verres, contemporaries of the patriarch Theophilus. Another is noted in an inscription of the seventh century (Lefebvre, "Recueil des inscriptions grecques chrétiennes d'Egypte", Cairo, 1907, n. 561). The city was discovered in the ruins of Kom Ombo. A temple of the Ptolemaic epoch could be seen there but it was destroyed in 1893; it had replaced a sanctuary of the epoch of Thothmes III.

SMITH, *Dictionary of Greek and Roman Geography*, II, 491; HAMILTON, *Ægyptiaca*, 34; CHAMPOLLION, *L'Egypte sous les Pharaons*, II, 167–69; AMÉLINEAU, *La géographie de l'Egypte à l'époque copte* (Paris, 1893), 287.

S. VAILHÉ.

O'Meara, KATHLEEN, novelist and biographer, b. in Dublin, 1839; d. in Paris, 10 Nov., 1888; daughter of Dennis O'Meara of Tipperary, and grand-daughter of Barry Edward O'Meara, surgeon in the British navy and medical attendant to Napoleon at St. Helena. When about five years old, she accompanied her parents to Paris, which she made her home. She visited the United States in the early eighties. In 1867 she published, over the pen-name of Grace Ramsey, her first novel, "A Woman's Trials" (London, 1867). This did not meet with success, which came to her only later in life, after hard work. Mindful of her early struggles, she was ever ready with encouragement to young writers. Of her six novels, "Narka, a Story of Russian Life" is probably the best. Great social problems, such as poverty and suffering, are handled in a large-hearted sympathetic way. The problem is stated in an unobtrusive manner and the solution offered in the old yet new method of Christian charity. Throughout them all there runs a wholesome spirit, remarkable for purity of tone and delicacy of feeling.

Her best work, however, is in biography, for which, it has been said, she had a genius. "The Bells of the Sanctuary" (1st, 2nd, and 3rd series) contain a number of delightful sketches of noted Catholic men and women. "Madame Mohl, her Salon and her Friends, a Study of Social Life in Paris" (London, 1885; another edition, Boston, 1886) presents with a nice sense of discrimination a delightful picture of that unique institution, the Parisian Salon, introducing the men and women who were leaders in the social, literary, and political world. "Thomas Grant, First Bishop of Southwark" (London, 1874) besides doing justice to a noble character that was much misunderstood, gives within a brief compass a clear straightforward account of the restoration of the Catholic hierarchy in England. "Frederick Ozanam, Professor at the Sorbonne, His Life and Works" (Edinburgh, 1876) is a deeply interesting narrative and is proof of the author's genius for biography. Had she written nothing else, this would entitle her to distinction. No better book can be placed in the hands of a young man to quicken his sympathies and bring out the good that is in him. Her last work "The Venerable Jean Baptiste Vianney, Curé d'Ars" (London, 1891) was not published till after her death. She was Paris correspondent of "The Tablet", and a frequent contributor to American magazines, such as the "Atlantic Monthly" and the "Ave Maria".

Ave Maria (March, 1889); *Irish Monthly* (October, 1889); *Tablet* (London, 17 Nov., 1888); *Times* (London, 13 and 14 Nov., 1888).

MATTHEW J. FLAHERTY.

Omer, SAINT, b. of a distinguished family towards the close of the sixth or the beginning of the seventh century, at Guldendal, Switzerland; d. c. 670. After the death of his mother, he, with his father, entered the monastery of Luxeuil in the Diocese of Besançon, probably about 615. Under the direction of Saint Eustachius, Omer studied the Scriptures, in which he acquired remarkable proficiency. When King Dagobert requested the appointment of a bishop for the important city of Terouenne, the capital of the ancient territory of the Morini in Belgic Gaul, he was appointed and consecrated in 637.

Though the Morini had received the Faith from Saints Fuscian and Victoricus, and later Antimund and Adelbert, nearly every vestige of Christianity had disappeared. When Saint Omer entered upon his episcopal duties the Abbot of Luxeuil sent to his assistance several monks, among whom are mentioned Saints Bertin, Mommolin, and Ebertran, and Saint Omer had the satisfaction of seeing the true religion firmly established in a short time. About 654 he founded the Abbey of Saint Peter (now Saint Bertin's) in Sithiu, soon to equal if not surpass the old monastery of Luxeuil for the number of learned and zealous men educated there. Several years later he erected the church of Our Lady of Sithiu, with a small monastery adjoining, which he turned over to the monks of Saint Bertin. The exact date of his death is unknown, but he is believed to have died about the year 670. The place of his burial is uncertain; most probably he was laid to rest in the church of Our Lady which is now the cathedral of Saint Omer's. His feast is celebrated on 9 September—when and by whom he was raised to the altar cannot be ascertained.

BOLLANDISTS, *Acta S. S.*, September, III; BUTLER, *Lives of the Saints*, III (Baltimore), 437–9.

FRANCIS J. O'BOYLE.

Omer, COLLEGE OF SAINT. See SAINT OMER'S COLLEGE.

Omission (Lat. *omittere*, to lay aside, to pass over) is here taken to be the failure to do something which one can and ought to do. If this happens advertently and freely a sin is committed. Moralists took pains formerly to show that the inaction implied in an omission was quite compatible with a breach of the moral law, for it is not merely because a person here and now does nothing that he offends, but because he neglects to act under circumstances in which he can and ought to act. The degree of guilt incurred by an omission is measured like that attaching to sins of commission, by the dignity of the virtue and the magnitude of the precept to which the omission is opposed as well as the amount of deliberation. In general, according to St. Thomas, the sin of omission consisting as it does in a leaving out of good is less grievous than a sin of commission which involves a positive taking up with evil. There are, of course, cases in which on account of the special subject matter and circumstances it may happen that an omission is more heinous. It may be asked at what time one incurs the guilt of a sin of omission in case he fails to do something which he is unable to do by reason of a cause for which he is entirely responsible. For instance, if a person fails to perform a duty in the morning as a result of becoming inebriated the previous night. The guilt is not incurred at the time the duty should be performed because while intoxicated he is incapable of moral guilt. The answer seems to be that he becomes responsible for the omission when having sufficiently foreseen that his neglect will follow upon his intoxication he does nevertheless surrender himself to his craving for liquor.

RICKABY, *Aquinas Ethicus* (London, 1896); BOUQUILLON, *Theologia moralis fundamentalis* (Bruges, 1903); ST. THOMAS AQUINAS, *Summa Theologica* (Turin, 1885).

JOSEPH F. DELANY.

Omnipotence (Latin *omnipotentia*, from *omnia* and *potens*, able to do all things) is the power of God to effect whatever is not intrinsically impossible. These last words of the definition do not imply any imperfection, since a power that extends to every possibility must be perfect. The universality of the object of the Divine power is not merely relative but absolute, so that the true nature of omnipotence is not clearly expressed by saying that God can do all things that are possible to Him; it requires the further statement that all things are possible to God. The intrinsically impossible is the self-contradictory, and its mutually exclusive elements could result only in nothingness. "Hence", says St. Thomas (Summa I, Q. xxv, a. 3), "it is more exact to say that the intrinsically impossible is incapable of production, than to say that God cannot produce it." To include the contradictory within the range of omnipotence, as does the Calvinist Vorstius, is to acknowledge the absurd as an object of the Divine intellect, and nothingness as an object of the Divine will and power. "God can do all things the accomplishment of which is a manifestation of power", says Hugh of St. Victor, "and He is almighty because He cannot be powerless" (De sacram., I, ii, 22).

As intrinsically impossible must be classed: (1) Any action on the part of God which would be out of harmony with His nature and attributes. (a) It is impossible for God to sin.—Man's power of preferring evil to good is a sign not of strength, but of infirmity, since it involves the liability to be overcome by unworthy motives; not the exercise but the restraint of that power adds to the freedom and vigour of the will. "To sin", says St. Thomas, "is to be capable of failure in one's actions, which is incompatible with omnipotence" (Summa, I, Q. xxv, a. 3). (b) The decrees of God cannot be reversed.—From eternity the production of creatures, their successive changes, and the manner in which these would occur were determined by God's free will. If these decrees were not irrevocable, it would follow either that God's wisdom was variable or that His decisions sprang from caprice. Hence theologians distinguish between the *absolute* and the *ordinary*, or *regulated*, power of God (*potentia absoluta; potentia ordinaria*). The absolute power of God extends to all that is not intrinsically impossible, while the ordinary power is regulated by the Divine decrees. Thus by His absolute power God could preserve man from death; but in the present order this is impossible, since He has decreed otherwise. (c) The creation of an absolutely best creature or of an absolutely greatest number of creatures is impossible, because the Divine power is inexhaustible.— It is sometimes objected that this aspect of omnipotence involves the contradiction that God cannot do all that He can do; but the argument is sophistical; it is no contradiction to assert that God can realize whatever is possible, but that no number of actualized possibilities exhausts His power. (2) Another class of intrinsic impossibilities includes all that would simultaneously connote mutually repellent elements, e. g. a square circle, an infinite creature, etc. God cannot effect the non-existence of actual events of the past, for it is contradictory that the same thing that has happened should also not have happened.

Omnipotence is perfect power, free from all mere potentiality. Hence, although God does not bring into external being all that He is able to accomplish, His power must not be understood as passing through successive stages before its effect is accomplished. The activity of God is simple and eternal, without evolution or change. The transition from possibility to actuality or from act to potentiality, occurs only in creatures. When it is said that God *can* or *could* do a thing, the terms are not to be understood in the sense in which they are applied to created causes, but as conveying the idea of a Being possessed of infinite unchangeable power, the range of Whose activity is limited only by His sovereign Will. "Power", says St. Thomas, "is not attributed to God as a thing really different from His Knowledge and Will, but as something expressed by a different concept, since power means that which executes the command of the will and the advice of the intellect. These three (viz., intellect, will, power), coincide with one another in God" (Summa, I, Q. xxv, a. 1, ad 4). Omnipotence is all-sufficient power. The adaptation of means to ends in the universe does not argue, as J. S. Mill would have it, that the power of the designer is limited, but only that God has willed to manifest His glory by a world so constituted rather than by another. Indeed the production of secondary causes, capable of accomplishing certain effects, requires greater power than the direct accomplishment of these same effects. On the other hand even though no creature existed, God's power would not be barren, for creatures are not an end to God.

The omnipotence of God is a dogma of Catholic faith, contained in all the creeds and defined by various councils (cf. Denziger-Bannwart, "Enchiridion", 428, 1790). In the Old Testament there are more than seventy passages in which God is called *Shaddai*, i. e., omnipotent. The Scriptures represent this attribute as infinite power (Job, xlii, 2; Mark, x, 27; Luke, i, 37; Matt., xix, 26, etc.) which God alone possesses (Tob., xiii, 4; Ecclus., i, 8; etc.). The Greek and Latin Fathers unanimously teach the doctrine of Divine omnipotence. Origen testifies to this belief when he infers the amplitude of Divine providence from God's omnipotence: "Just as we hold that God is incorporeal and *omnipotent* and invisible, so likewise do we confess as a certain and immovable dogma that His providence extends to all things" (Genesis, Hom. 3). St. Augustine defends omnipotence against the Manichæans, who taught that God is unable to overcome evil (Hæres, xlvi and Enchir., c. 100); and he speaks of this dogma as a truth recognized even by pagans, and which no reasonable person can question (Serm. 240, de temp., c. ii). Reason itself proves the omnipotence of God. "Since every agent produces an effect similar to itself", says St. Thomas (Summa, I, Q. xxv, a. 3), "to every active power there must correspond as proper object, a category of possibilities proportioned to the cause possessing that power, e. g. the power of heating has for its proper object that which can be heated. Now Divine Being, which is the basis of Divine power, is infinite, not being limited to any category of being but containing within itself the perfection of all being. Consequently all that can be considered as being is contained among the absolute possibilities with respect to which God is omnipotent." (See CREATION; GOD; INFINITE; MIRACLES.)

The question of omnipotence is discussed by philosophers in works on natural theology and by theologians in the treatise on One God (De Deo Uno). See especially ST. THOMAS, *Summa*, I, Q. xxv; IDEM, *Contra Gentes*, II, vii sq.; SUAREZ, *De Deo*, I₁₁, ix; HURTER, *Compendium theologiæ dogmaticæ*, II (Innsbruck, 1885), 79 sq.; POHLE, *Lehrbuch der Dogmatik*, I (Paderborn, 1908), 143 sq.

J. A. McHUGH.

Omodeo, GIOVANNI ANTONIO. See AMADEO.

O'Molloy, FRANCIS. See MOLLOY, FRANCIS.

O'Mulconry, FARFASSA. See FOUR MASTERS, ANNALS OF THE.

Oneida Community. See COMMUNISM.

O'Neill, HENRY. See DROMORE, DIOCESE OF.

O'Neill, HUGH, Earl of Tyrone, b. 1540; d. at Rome, 1616; was the youngest son of Mathew, of questionable parentage, but recognized as heir by Conn, first Earl of Tyrone. As such he was ennobled with the title of Baron of Dungannon. Shane O'Neill contested this arrangement and in the petty wars which followed both Mathew and his eldest son lost their lives. In 1562 Hugh, the youngest son, became Baron of Dungannon. His early years were spent partly in Ireland and partly at the English court, where he learned English ways and became more like an English noble than an Irish chief. He did not object even to go to the Protestant church though he was bred as a Catholic and died one. Camden describes him as a man "whose industry was great, his mind large and fit for the weightiest businesses . . . he had much knowledge in military affairs and a profound, dissembling heart, so as many deemed him born either for the great good or ill of his country". In his early years he interfered but little in the quarrels and contests of the Irish chiefs, and had no share in the final overthrow of Shane O'Neill, but in 1574, he aided the Earl of Essex to lay waste the territory of O'Neill of Clanaboy, and in 1580 helped the Earl of Ormonde to crush the Geraldines. In 1585 he sat as a peer in Perrot's Parliament, assenting to the attainting of the Earl of Desmond and the confiscation of his lands; in the following year he accompanied Perrot to Ulster to put down the Antrim Scots. His loyalty to England was gratefully recognized both by viceroy and queen who confirmed him in the title of Earl of Tyrone and in possession of all the lands held by his grandfather. On his side, O'Neill undertook to provide for the sons of Shane O'Neill, to lay no "cess" (tax) on the Ulster chiefs, and to build an English fort in Tyrone. His position soon became difficult, and he went to London where he justified himself, undertaking at the same time to renounce forever the name of O'Neill, to make Tyrone shireground, with English law and English officials, and to have in it neither nuns nor priests.

At the Irish Council his enemies were the viceroy and Marshal Bagnal, whose sister he had married; but the queen censured Bagnal and recalled Fitzwilliam, appointing in his place Sir William Russell. This was in 1594, when O'Donnell, Maguire, and MacMahon were already in open rebellion. The same year O'Neill's brother joined the rebels, which caused O'Neill himself to be suspected, and when he appeared in Dublin he was charged by Bagnal with favouring the rebels, with being in league with the pope and the King of Spain, and with having assumed the title of The O'Neill. Though these charges could not be proved, the queen ordered him detained; but secretly warned, he hurriedly left Dublin and the next year broke out into rebellion, proving the most formidable

Irish rebel with whom England had ever been called upon to deal, cool, wary, far-seeing, laying his plans with care, never moved by passion, never boasting, and as skilful in the council chamber as on the battlefield. He had been allowed to have a certain number of soldiers in the queen's pay and these he changed frequently, thus training to arms a large number of his clansmen at the queen's expense. Pretending he required it for roofing, he had purchased large quantities of lead, which he cast into bullets. He continued to be friendly with the Ulster chiefs. Thus he took the field not altogether unprepared, and had no difficulty in capturing Portmore on the Blackwater, and defeating the English at Clontibret, thus preventing the relief of Monaghan. He protested, however, his loyalty to England and entered into negotiations demanding for the Catholics of Ulster freedom to practise their religion, and security in their lands. These conditions being refused, the war was successfully renewed in 1597. In the next year Bagnal, sent with five thousand men to relieve Portmore, was defeated at the mouth of the Yellow Ford by O'Neill, O'Donnell, and Maguire. The Earl of Essex was no more successful.

The next viceroy was Lord Mountjoy, with Sir George Carew as President of Munster. Both were able and unscrupulous men, and so well did Carew succeed that in six months the power of the Munster rebels was broken. Mountjoy overran Leinster, and his lieutenant, Dowcra, established himself at Derry, while O'Neill, kept busy by repeated attacks from the south, was only able to hold his own in Tyrone. In 1601 came the long-expected Spaniards, under D'Aguilla; they were besieged in Kinsale by Carew and Mountjoy, in turn besieged by O'Neill and O'Donnell. Between the Irish and the Spanish the English fared ill, and O'Neill's advice was to be patient; but O'Donnell would not be restrained and insisted on attacking the English. The result was the disastrous battle of Kinsale. Still with wonderful skill and resource O'Neill held out, and when he surrendered in 1603 it was on condition of being pardoned and secured in all his honours and estates. James I, confirming this arrangement, received both O'Neill and O'Donnell with great favour. But O'Neill's enemies so dogged his footsteps with spies, and persecuted his religion that he was at last driven, with O'Donnell and Maguire, to leave Ireland (1607). Arriving at Havre they proceeded to Flanders and thence to Rome, where they were received by the pope. Attainted by the Irish Parliament, his lands confiscated and planted, O'Neill died at Rome, and was buried in the Franciscan church of San Pietro on the Janiculum.

Carew Papers; HAMILTON, Atkinson's, Russell's, and Prendergast's Calendars of State Papers; FYNES MORYSON, Itinerary (Dublin, 1735); Pacata Hibernia (London, 1896); Annals of the Four Masters (Dublin, 1851); MEEHAN, Earls of Tyrone and Tyrconnell (Dublin, 1886); MITCHEL, Life of Hugh O'Neill (Dublin, 1846); BAGWELL, Ireland under the Tudors (London, 1885); GARDINER, History of England (London, 1883); D'ALTON, History of Ireland (London, 1910).

E. A. D'ALTON.

O'Neill, OWEN ROE, b. 1582; d. near Cavan, 6 Nov., 1649, the son of Art O'Neill and nephew of Hugh, the great Earl of Tyrone. He was too young to take part in the long war in which his uncle was engaged, and when peace came in 1603 Owen went abroad and took service with the archdukes in Flanders. By 1606 he had reached the rank of captain and was then residing at Brussels. When Richelieu determined to interfere in the Thirty Years War, O'Neill was already colonel, and for skill, and courage, and resource stood deservedly high among Spanish commanders. He was, therefore, selected to defend Arras against the French in 1640; and though he had but 1500 men and was assailed by a force which from 30,000 was subsequently increased to three times that number, he stubbornly held his ground for nearly two months. His conduct extorted the admiration of the French commander who captured the place and who told O'Neill that he had surpassed the French in everything but fortune. Meantime important events had taken place in Ireland. The flight of the earls, the plantation of Ulster, the persecution of the Catholics, and the tyranny of Strafford proved that Irish Catholics had no security either in their religion or their lands. O'Neill was informed of all these events by the Irish leaders at home, and was equally determined as they that, as peaceful measures were unavailing, there should be a recourse to arms. He was not, however, able to be in Ireland when the rebellion broke out in 1641, nor did he come till the summer of 1642, when he landed on the coast of Donegal bringing with him a good supply of arms and ammunition and 200 Irish officers, who like himself had acquired experience in foreign wars. O'Neill was at once appointed commander-in-chief of the rebel forces in Ulster. At that date the prospects were not bright. Dublin Castle had not been taken, nor Drogheda, Dundalk had not been held, and Sir Phelim O'Neill had but 1500 untrained men, while there were 12,000 English and Scotch soldiers in Ulster. While waiting to get a trained army together Owen Roe wanted to avoid meeting the enemy, nor did he fight except at Clones, where he was beaten, and at Portlester in Meath, where he defeated Lord Moore. Then, in 1643, came the cessation with Ormonde. The Puritans ignored both Ormonde and the cessation, and continued active in the several provinces. This compelled O'Neill to be vigilant and prepared, and in 1646 he fought the battle of Benburb with General Monroe. The latter was superior in numbers, and he had artillery which O'Neill lacked; but the Irishmen had the advantage of position, and won a great victory. Monroe fled to Lisburn without hat or cloak leaving more than 3000 of his men dead on the field, and arms, stores, colours, and provisions fell into O'Neill's hands. The fruits of this splendid victory were frittered away by futile negotiations with Ormonde and by divisions among the Catholics. O'Neill, backed by the nuncio, Rinuccini, wanted to cease negotiating, and to fight both the Puritans and the Royalists; but the Pale Catholics were more in agreement with Ormonde than with O'Neill, and in spite of the fact that he was the only Catholic general who had been almost uniformly successful, they went so far as to declare him a rebel. Nor would Ormonde, even in 1649, make any terms with him until Cromwell had captured Drogheda. Then Ormonde made terms on the basis of freedom of religion and restoration of lands. At the critical moment when O'Neill's services would have been invaluable against Cromwell he took suddenly ill and died. The story that he was poisoned may be dismissed, for there is no evidence to sustain it.

GILBERT, History of Irish Affairs (Dublin, 1882); RINUCCINI, Letters (Dublin, 1873); MURPHY, Cromwell in Ireland (Dublin, 1897); MAHAFFY, Calendars; CARTE, Ormond (London, 1735); TAYLOR, Owen Roe O'Neill (Dublin, 1896); D'ALTON, History of Ireland (London, 1910).

E. A. D'ALTON.

Onias ('Oνίας), name of several Jewish pontiffs of the third and second centuries before Christ. I.—ONIAS I, son and successor of the high-priest Jaddua, who, according to Josephus (Antiq., XI, viii, 7) received Alexander the Great in Jerusalem. Succeeding his father soon after the death of Alexander (Josephus, ibid.), he held office for twenty-three years (323–300 B. C.). In I Mach., xii, 7, he is said to have received a friendly letter from Arius, ruler of the Spartans. The letter is mentioned by Josephus (Antiq., XII, iv, 10), who gives its contents with certain modifications of the form in Machabees (xii, 20–23). During Onias's pontificate Palestine was the scene of continual conflicts between the forces of Egypt and Syria, who several times alternated as masters of the country. During this period also, and because of unsettled conditions at home, many Jews left Palestine for the newly founded city of Alexandria.

II.—ONIAS II, son of Simon the Just. He is not mentioned in the Bible, but Josephus says (Antiq., XII, iv, 1–6) that, though a high-priest, he was a man "of little soul and a great lover of money." He refused to pay the customary tribute of twenty talents of silver to Ptolemy Euergetes, who then threatened to occupy the Jewish territory, a calamity which was averted by the tactful activity of Joseph, a nephew of Onias, who went to Ptolemy and purchased immunity from invasion.

III.—ONIAS III, son and successor (198 B. C.) of Simon II, and grandson of Onias II. Josephus erroneously attributes to him the correspondence with Arius of Sparta (see above, ONIAS I). He is mentioned in II Mach., xv, 12, as a good and virtuous man, modest and gentle in his manner. During his pontificate Seleucus Philopator, King of Syria, sent his minister, Heliodorus, to Jerusalem with a view to obtain possession of the alleged treasures of the Temple (II Mach., iii).

IV.—ONIAS, also called Menelaus. Mention is made in II Mach., iv, of Menelaus, brother of Simon, who became the unjust accuser of Onias III, and later a venal usurper of the priesthood. According to Josephus, on the other hand, he originally bore the name Onias, changed for political reasons into one more characteristically Greek (Antiq., XII, v, 1).

V.—ONIAS IV, son of Onias III, too young to succeed his father in the priesthood, which was usurped successively by Jason and Menelaus (see above) and later by Alcimus. In the meantime Onias withdrew into Egypt, where he obtained from Ptolemy Philometor a tract of land near Heliopolis, on which (about 160 B. C.) he erected a sort of temple. Here a regular Temple worship was inaugurated in defiance of the Law, but the innovation was doubtless justified in the mind of Onias by the scandalous conditions at the home sanctuary, and by the great number of Jews resident in Egypt. The project was censured by the authorities in Jerusalem (Mishna, Menachoth xiii, 10) and it was blamed by Josephus (Bell. Jud., VII, x, 3). Nevertheless, the worship was maintained until after A. D. 70, when it was abolished by Lupus, prefect of Alexandria (Josephus, "Bell. Jud.", VII, x, 4).

VI.—ONIAS, a pious Jew of Jerusalem in the days of the high-priest Hyrcanus, i. e. about the middle of the first century B. C. (see Mishna, Thaanith iii, 8, and Josephus Antiq., XIV, ii, 1).

JAMES F. DRISCOLL.

Ontario, the most populous and wealthy province of Canada, has an area of 140,000,000 acres, exclusive of the Great Lakes, of which approximately 24,700,000 acres have been sold, 115,300,000 remaining vested in the Crown. It is bounded on the south and south-west by Lakes Ontario, Erie, Huron, and Superior, with their connecting waters, and Minnesota: on the north-east by Quebec, and the Ottawa River; on the north by James Bay; on the north-west by Keewatin; and on the west by Manitoba. It is probable that a large part of Keewatin will soon be added to the province. Old Ontario (lying between the Ottawa River, the St. Lawrence River, and Lakes Ontario, Erie, and Huron) is well settled and cultivated: New Ontario, lying north and west, is sparsely inhabited.

CLIMATE.—Moderate near the Great Lakes, subject to extremes of heat and cold in the north and north-west, the climate is everywhere healthful, the extremes being of short duration and easily endured owing to the dryness of the atmosphere inland.

HISTORICAL INCIDENTS.—Held by France up to 1763, Quebec, including Ontario, was then ceded to Great Britain. Visited by Champlain in 1615, explored by French missionaries and voyageurs, it had been the scene of frightful Indian wars, and massacres, and of the martyrdom in 1649 of the Jesuits, Brébeuf and Lalemant. Except for missionaries and their entourage, trappers, soldiers in some isolated posts, and a few settlers on the Detroit and Ottawa Rivers, and near the Georgian Bay, Ontario in 1763 was an uninhabited wilderness roamed over by Ojibways and remnants of the Hurons and Algonquins. After the American War of Independence many colonial adherents of the British Crown crossed to Upper Canada. In 1786 some 4487 of them were settled on the St. Lawrence and Lake Ontario. For twenty years immigration from the United States was extensive. With accessions from Ireland, Scotland, and England, it brought the population in 1806 up to 70,000. This was the nucleus of the Province of Ontario. In 1791 Upper Canada (Ontario) was separated from Quebec and given its own governor and legislature, which first met in 1792 at Newark, now Niagara-on-the-Lake. The laws of England were then introduced. In 1797 the capital was moved to York (Toronto). In 1812 Upper Canada sustained the brunt of the war between Great Britain and the United States and was the scene of several noted battles, Queenston Heights, Lundy's Lane, etc. In 1837 abuses by the dominant party and irresponsible executives provoked a rebellion in Upper and Lower Canada, which resulted in their union and the establishment of responsible government in 1841. In 1866 Fenian raids from the United States were successfully repelled. Difficulties of administration due largely to racial differences led to confederation in 1867, Upper Canada becoming a distinct province under the name of Ontario. Subsequent growth has been rapid; population has nearly doubled; known wealth has increased many fold; and development of industries and resources has been enormous.

POPULATION.—The last census (1901) gives the population as 2,182,947. Municipal assessment returns for 1909 place it at 2,289,438, of which 1,049,240 was rural, 515,078 dwelt in towns and villages, and 725,120 in cities. The Ontario Department of Agriculture considers that the actual population exceeds these figures by 10 per cent. On this basis the population in 1909 is estimated at 2,518,362.

CITIES.—The principal cities, with their estimated populations are: Toronto, the provincial capital, 360,000; Ottawa, the capital of Canada, 90,000; Hamilton, 77,250; London, 55,000; Brantford, 22,750; Kingston, 21,000; Fort William, 20,000.

AGRICULTURE.—In 1909 the value of farms, implements, and live stock was $1,241,019,109; field crops were worth $167,966,577, hay and clover, oats, wheat, barley, corn, potatoes, peas, and mixed grains being the principal items; dairy produce was officially estimated at $31,000,000; live stock on hand was valued at $184,747,900, sold or slaughtered at $64,464,923. Peaches and grapes, grown chiefly in the south-west, are a large industry. The average yearly value of the apple crop for the years 1901–05 was $8,671,275. In 1910 the Government Agricultural College at Guelph had 975 students; the Macdonald Institute for farmers' daughters, 411. The Government maintains experimental farms and liberally aids agricultural institutes. 24,000,000 acres are now under cultivation.

MINING.—The province is rich in minerals of various kinds. The figures given are for 1908, when mining products realized $39,232,814. The most important nickel deposits in America are in the Sudbury district, producing 18,636 tons, about 80 per cent of the world's output. Iron occurs in various places (principally hæmatite at Michipicoten on Lake Superior) yielding 231,453 tons. The output of gold bullion is 3246 oz. Important gold fields are being opened up at Porcupine. The fame of the silver mines of the Cobalt district is world-wide. Average ores carry from 2000 to 4000 oz. to the ton; 955 tons of silver yielded $15,436,994. Petroleum and natural gas are important products of the southwest. Portland cement brings $3,144,000. Arsenic, cobalt, copper, corundum, graphite, gypsum, marble, mica, salt, and silver are also found.

FORESTS.—The forest area is estimated at 102,000 sq. miles. The Department of Forests and Mines estimates that there is still standing on unlicensed Crown lands 13,500,000,000 feet of red and white pine, and 300,000,000 cords of spruce, jack-pine, and poplar, suitable for pulp-wood; and on licensed lands, 7,000,000 feet of timber. The output for 1910 was 605,000,000 feet b. m. of pine: of other woods 95,000,000 feet; of square timber 308,000 cubic feet; of pulp-wood, 138,000 cords; of cord-wood, 40,000 cords; and of railway ties, 3,800,000 pcs. The province has an enlightened system of reforestation.

Forest Reserves cover 17,860 sq. miles, containing it is estimated, 7,000,000,000 feet of pine. There are two large provincial parks, Rondeau in the south-west, and Algonquin in the north-west of old Ontario.

MANUFACTURES.—The manufacturing output of Ontario is greater than that of any other Canadian province. For 1905 (the last return available) its value was $361,372,741. It is now considerably greater.

FISHERIES.—The value of the commercial fisheries in 1908 was $2,100,079. The opportunities for sport are excellent, the trout-fishing in the Nepigon being exceptionally fine. Northern Ontario is much resorted to by sportsmen in the hunting season.

WATERS.—In addition to the Great Lakes there are countless inland lakes of much beauty and utility, the largest, Lakes Nepigon, Nipissing, Simcoe, and the Lake of the Woods. Innumerable rivers and watercourses furnish abundant natural power, little of it developed. A hydro-electric government commission with municipal co-operation, supplies electric power from Niagara Falls throughout the south-west. This commission is charged with the development and supplying of power in other parts of the province.

TOURIST RESORTS.—Niagara Falls, the Thousand Islands in the St. Lawrence, the Thirty Thousand Islands in the Georgian Bay, the Muskoka Lakes, and the Lake of the Woods are famous.

RAILWAYS AND CANALS.—Ontario is covered by a network of railways, principally operated by the Grand Trunk, the Canadian Pacific, and the Canadian Northern. Now traversed by one transcontinental railway, it will shortly be crossed by two others. The mileage in 1909 was 8229. The St. Lawrence Canals, the Welland Canal, overcoming the fall of 326 feet in the Niagara River, and the great lock at Sault Sainte Marie permit of navigation from Montreal to the head of Lake Superior, about 1400 miles. The Rideau and the Trent Valley canals are also works of importance. All canals are free.

CONSTITUTION AND GOVERNMENT.—The constitution of the province is found in the British North America Act, 1867 (Imperial). Although its legislative powers are confined to enumerated subjects, the constitution being "similar in principle to that of the United Kingdom", legislative jurisdiction over the matter assigned to it, except education, is restricted only by the limitation, that provincial enactments must not clash with Imperial statutes made applicable to the province, or with legislation of the Parliament of Canada within the field assigned to it.

Legislature.—The legislature consists of a lieutenant-governor, appointed and paid by the Government of Canada, and a single chamber of 106 members elected for four years. The party system prevails. The franchise is on a manhood suffrage basis. Ontario has 86 members in the Dominion House of Commons, consisting of 221 members, and 24 in the Senate, of which the membership is 87.

Executive.—The executive is directly responsible to the Legislative Assembly, in which it must always command a majority. It consists at present of a prime minister and ten colleagues. The ministers holding portfolios are: the president of the council (at present the prime minister), the attorney-general, the secretary and registrar, the treasurer, the minister of lands, forests, and mines, the minister of agriculture, the minister of public works, and the minister of education.

Judiciary.—The Constitutional Act assigns to the province "the constitution, maintenance, and organization of the provincial courts", civil and criminal, and to the Dominion the appointment and remuneration of judges. Judges of the superior courts are appointed for life. Those of the county and district courts must retire at the age of eighty. The province appoints surrogate court judges, police magistrates, and justices of the peace. The Supreme Court of Judicature comprises the Court of Appeal, with five judges, and the High Court, with twelve judges. The county and district judges have limited powers as local judges of the High Court. In the Division Courts (small debt) they try claims, ascertained by signature up to $200, upon contract up to $100, and other personal claims up to $60. In the County and District courts they have jurisdiction, speaking generally, in actions upon contract up to $800, in other personal actions up to $500, and in actions respecting rights of property, where the value of the property affected does not exceed $500. Unless the defendant disputes jurisdiction, these courts may deal with any civil case whatever the amount involved. The jurisdiction of the High Court is unlimited. In important cases an appeal lies from the provincial court of appeal to the Supreme Court of Canada, or to the Judicial Committee of the Imperial Privy Council.

Officials.—Sheriffs, court officers, Division Court bailiffs, etc., are appointed by the provincial government.

Municipal System.—The municipal system is based on American models. Municipal government is carried on by councils and presiding officers elected by popular vote. In large urban centres, Boards of Control elected by the municipalities at large have extensive powers. The councils appoint the administrative officers.

RELIGION.—There is no State church. Legally all religions are on a footing of equality. Legislation, however, is based on the fundamental principles of Christian morality. Sessions of the House of Assembly open with prayers read by the Speaker. Blasphemous libels, the obstruction of, or offering violence to, officiating clergymen, and disturbance of meetings for religious worship are criminal offences. Sunday is strictly observed.

Exemptions.—Places of worship and lands used in connexion therewith, churchyards and burying-grounds, and buildings and grounds of educational and charitable institutions are exempt from taxation. Clergymen are exempt from jury duty and military service.

Incorporation.—Religious organizations can readily obtain incorporation, with liberal powers of acquiring and holding real estate. Land may be given for "charitable uses", by deed made more than six months before the grantor's death, or by will, but must be sold within two years, unless the High Court, being satisfied that it is required for actual occupation for the purpose of the charity, sanctions its retention. All Catholic church property is vested in the bishop of the diocese who is a statutory corporation sole.

Catholicism.—In 1763 the few French settlers were Catholics. Immigration from the United States after 1783 was almost exclusively Protestant. Some Scotch Catholics settled in Glengarry, and a considerable number of Irish Catholics, principally after the War of 1812 and particularly from 1847 to 1851, in various parts of Ontario. The See of Kingston, established in 1826, included the entire province. Rt. Rev. Alex. Macdonell was the first bishop. Kingston became an archdiocese in 1889. The Diocese of Toronto, erected in 1841, became an archdiocese in 1870. The Diocese of Ottawa, erected in 1847, became an archdiocese in 1886. The Province has now seven suffragan sees, Hamilton, London, Pembroke, Temiskaming (Vicariate), Peterborough, Alexandria, and Sault Sainte Marie. Portions of Ottawa, Pembroke, and Temiskaming are in Quebec; the other dioceses are wholly in Ontario. Diocesan priests number 383; priests of religious orders, 244 (1910).

The Catholic population in 1871 was 274,162; in 1881, 321,162; in 1891, 358,300; in 1901, 390,304; and in 1910 (est.), 450,000. Of these, 190,000 (est.), residing chiefly in Eastern Ontario, Essex, Nipissing, and Algoma, are French Canadians: the remainder principally of Irish descent. The Apostolic Delegate to Canada resides at Ottawa. The headquarters of the Catholic Church Extension Society of Canada (canonically established) are at Toronto. Catholic charitable institutions are numerous, and receive a fair share of government and municipal aid. As a minority, Catholics have reason to be satisfied with their status and recent treatment.

EDUCATION.—At Confederation the British North America Act conferred on the province power to deal with education, saving rights and privileges, with respect to denominational schools then enjoyed. During the union of Protestant Upper Canada (Ontario) and Catholic Lower Canada (Quebec), from 1841 to 1867, provision was made for denominational schools for the religious minority in each province. The Ontario Separate Schools law, fundamentally as it stands to-day, was enacted in 1863. The rights then conferred on the Catholic minority are therefore constitutional.

Expenditure.—The educational system is administered by the Department of Education. Out of $8,891,004.68 revenue, the Government in 1910 expended on education, exclusive of money spent through the Department of Agriculture, $2,220,796.75. In 1909 (1910 returns incomplete) $8,782,302.51 was raised by local taxation for primary and secondary education.

System.—The system embraces free primary education in public and separate schools; intermediate education in high schools, partly free; and university training at slight cost to the student. Every person between the ages of five and twenty-one years may, every child between eight and fourteen, unless lawfully excused, must, attend a public or separate school. The courses of study and textbooks are controlled by the Department, which sanctions for separate schools only books approved by the Catholic authorities. Subject to departmental regulations, primary schools are managed by trustees locally elected, there being distinct boards for public and separate schools. Every teacher must hold a certificate of qualification from a provincial normal school. With its own taxes the municipality collects for each board the amount it requires for its purposes. For public schools, attended in 1910 by 401,268 pupils, government aid was $731,160.99 and local taxation (1909) $6,565,987.90. For separate schools, attended in 1910 by 55,034 pupils, government aid was $53,033.63 and local taxation (1909) $764,779.56. Where Catholics are the majority they sometimes use and control public schools; in some localities they are too few to support a separate school. The separate school attendance is therefore substantially less than the number of Catholic school children.

High Schools.—For High Schools attended in 1910, by 33,101 pupils, government aid was $157,383.03, and local taxation (1909) $1,451,535.05. There is no legal provision for separate high schools. On its Normal College (Hamilton) and two normal schools at Toronto and Ottawa the Government spent in 1910, $208,524.11, training 1198 students.

Separate Schools Law.—Catholic separate schools are easily established. Their supporters are legally exempt from public school taxation. They elect their own trustees, who determine their rate of school taxation. Catholic teachers are employed and Catholic religious training is given. Separate school inspectors are speciallly appointed by the Government. Many of the teachers are Christian Brothers and Sisters of teaching orders, all holding government certificates. At the government examinations (1910) for entrance to high schools, in Toronto the percentage of public school candidates who passed was 54.59; that of separate school candidates was 57.81.

Universities.—The University of Toronto is supported by the Government. In 1910 it had 4000 students. The revenue from succession duties, in 1910, $519,999.27, is devoted to it; it also received $15,000 for the faculty of education. With it is affiliated St. Michael's College, Toronto, conducted by the Basilian Fathers, the students of which in 1910 numbered over 250. The university is unsectarian. Catholic students take lectures in philosophy and history at St. Michael's. There are also: the Western University, London; Queen's (Presbyterian), Kingston; and McMaster (Baptist), Toronto. Victoria College (Methodist), Wycliffe (Anglican), Knox (Presbyterian), Trinity (Anglican), all at Toronto, are affiliated with the University of Toronto. Queen's University receives $42,000 from the Government for a school of mining, and $10,500 for its faculty of education.

The Catholic University of Ottawa, conducted by the Oblate Fathers, with complete French and English courses and, in 1910, 547 students, receives no government aid. It holds a charter from the Papal Court as well as from the province.

There are other Catholic colleges: Regiopolis at Kingston, conducted by secular priests; St. Jerome's, at Berlin, by Fathers of the Resurrection, and Assumption, at Sandwich, by Basilians. In nearly every city and town there is a good convent school. In Toronto a Catholic Seminary for ecclesiastical education, capable of accommodating, at first 110, and later 310 students, the gift of Mr. Eugene O'Keefe, Private Chamberlain to His Holiness, is in course of construction. Ottawa has a diocesan seminary.

MARRIAGE AND DIVORCE.—By the British North America Act, marriage and divorce are assigned to the Dominion Parliament, while the solemnization of marriage is made a subject of provincial jurisdiction. *Marriage.*—Under the Ontario Marriage Act, marriage may be solemnized by "the ministers and clergymen of every church and religious denomination, duly ordained or appointed". Special provisions are made for the Congregations of God or of Christ, the Salvation Army, the Farringdon Independent Church, the Brethren, and the Society of Friends. There is no provision for purely civil marriage. The person solemnizing marriage must be "a resident of Canada". The marriage must be preceded by publication of banns, or authorized by a licence, or certificate of the Provincial Secretary, issued by a local issuer appointed by the Government. Unless necessary to prevent illegitimacy, the marriage of any person under fourteen is prohibited. To obtain a licence for the marriage of a person under eighteen, not a widower or widow, consent of the father if resident in Ontario, and if not, of the mother if so resident, or of the guardian (if any), is required. Marriage within any degree of consanguinity closer than that of first cousins is prohibited. But by statute of Canada, marriage with a sister of a deceased wife or with a daughter of a deceased wife's sister is legalized; yet marriage with a daughter of a deceased wife's brother, with a brother of a deceased husband, and with a deceased husband's nephew remains illegal. The validity of marriage depends on the *lex loci contractus*.

Divorce.—There is no Divorce Court. Divorce can be obtained only by Act of the Dominion Parliament, and adultery is the sole ground on which it is granted. In 1907 Parliament granted 3 divorces for Ontario; in 1908, 8; in 1909, 8; and in 1910, 14. Ontario courts recognize a foreign divorce only where it is valid according to the law of the state in which it is obtained, and the husband had at the time a *bona fide* domicile, as understood in English law, in such state. Subject to a saving provision in favour of a person who, in good faith and on reasonable grounds, believes his or her spouse to be dead, and of a person whose spouse has been continually absent for seven years and who has not known such spouse to be alive at any time during that period, any married person, not validly divorced, who goes through a second form of marriage in Canada commits bigamy: any such person who, being a British subject resident in Canada, goes through such ceremony elsewhere, if he left Canada with intent to do so, also commits bigamy under Canadian law.

Nullity.—The Ontario High Court has jurisdiction to adjudge marriage void, and it has special statutory power to declare a marriage null, if the plaintiff was under the age of eighteen when married, and the ceremony was without the consent required by law, and was not necessary to prevent illegitimacy. The action must be brought before the plaintiff attains the age of nineteen, and it must be proved in open court and after notice to the attorney-general (who is authorized to intervene) that there has not been cohabitation after the ceremony.

FRASER, *History of Ontario* (Toronto, 1907); KINGSFORD, *History of Canada* (Toronto and London, 1887—); DAWSON, *North America* (London, 1897); *Canada Year Book* (Ottawa, 1909); *Ontario Government Reports on Agriculture, Industries, Mining, Forests, Municipal Statistics* (1909–1910); *Heaton's Annual* (Toronto, 1910); *Canadian Catholic Directory* (Toronto, 1910); *The Official Catholic Directory* (Milwaukee and New York, 1910); ANGLIN, *Catholic Education in Canada in its Relation to the Civil Authority* (Columbus, Ohio, 1910); *Statutes of Canada; Statutes of Ontario*.

FRANK A. ANGLIN.

Ontologism (from ὤν, ὄν, ὄντος, being, and λόγος, science), an ideological system which maintains that God and Divine ideas are the first object of our intelligence and the intuition of God the first act of our intellectual knowledge. *Exposition.*—Malebranche (q. v.) developed his theory of "la vision en Dieu" in different works, particularly "Recherche de la vérité", III, under the influence of Platonic and Cartesian philosophies, and of a misunderstanding of St. Augustine's and St. Thomas's principles on the origin and source of our ideas. It is also in large part the consequence of his theory of occasional causes (see OCCASIONALISM). Our true knowledge of things, he says, is the knowledge we have of them in their ideas. The ideas of things are present to our mind, endowed with the essential characteristics of universality, necessity, and eternity, and are not the result of intellectual elaboration or representations of things as they are, but the archetypes which concrete and temporal things realize. Ideas have their source and real existence in God; they are the Divine essence itself, considered as the infinite model of all things. "God is the locus of our ideas, as space is the locus of bodies." God is then always really present to our mind; we see all things, even material and concrete things, in Him, Who contains and manifests to our intelligence their nature and existence. Vincenzo Gioberti (1801–52) developed his Ontologism in "Introduzione allo studio della filosofia" (1840), I, iii; II, i. Our first act of intellectual knowledge is the intuitive judgment "ens creat existentias" (Being creates existences). By that act, he says, our mind apprehends directly and immediately in an intuitive synthesis (a) being, not simply in general nor merely as ideal, but as necessary and real, viz., God; (b) existences or contingent beings; (c) the relation which unites being and existences, viz., the creative act. In this judgment being is the subject, existences the predicate, the creative act the copula. Our first intellectual perception is, therefore, an intuition of God, the first intelligible, as creating existences. This intuition is finite and is obtained by means of expressions or words (*la parola*). Thus the *primum philosophicum* includes both the *primum ontologicum* and the *primum psychologicum*, and the *ordo sciendi* is identified with the *ordo rerum*. This formula was accepted and defended by Orestes A. Brownson. (Cf. Brownson's Works, Detroit, 1882; I, "The Existence of God", 267 sq.; "Schools of Philosophy, 296 sq.; "Primitive Elements of Thought", 418 sq. etc.)

Ontologism was advocated, under a more moderate form, by some Catholic philosophers of the nineteenth century. Maintaining against Malebranche that concrete material things are perceived by our senses, they asserted that our universal ideas endowed with the characteristics of necessity and eternity, and our notion of the infinite cannot exist except in God; and they cannot therefore be known except by an intuition of God present to our mind and perceived by our intelligence not in His essence as such, but in His essence as the archetype of all things. Such is the Ontologism taught by C. Ubaghs, professor at Louvain, in "Essai d'idéologie ontologique" (Louvain, 1860); by Abbé L. Branchereau in "Prælectiones Philosophicæ"; by Abbé F. Hugonin in "Ontologie ou études des lois de la pensée" (Paris, 1856–7); by Abbé J. Fabre in "Défense de l'ontologisme"; by Carlo Vercellone, etc. We find also the fundamental principles of Ontologism in Rosmini's philosophy, although there have been many attempts to defend him against this accusation (cf. G. Morando, "Esame critico delle XL proposizione rosminiane condannate dalla S.R.U. inquisizione", Milan, 1905). According to Rosmini, the form of all our thoughts is being in its ideality (*l'essere ideale, l'essere iniziale*). The idea of being is innate in us and we perceive it by intuition. Altogether indetermined, it is neither God nor creature; it is an appurtenance of God, it is something of the Word ("Teosophia", I, n. 490; II, n. 848; cf. "Rosminianarum propositionum trutina theologica", Rome, 1892). At the origin and basis of every system of Ontologism, there are two principal reasons: (1) we have an idea of the infinite and this cannot be obtained through abstraction from finite beings, since it is not contained in them; it must, therefore, be innate in our mind and perceived through intuition; (2) our concepts and fundamental judgments are endowed with the characteristics of universality, eternity, and necessity, e. g., our concept of man is applicable to an indefinite number of individual men; our principle of identity "whatever is, is", is true in itself, necessarily and always. Now such concepts and judgments cannot be obtained from any consideration of finite things which are particular, contingent, and temporal. Gioberti insists also on the fact that God being alone intelligible by Himself, we cannot have any intellectual knowledge of finite things independently of the knowledge of God; that our knowledge to be truly scientific must follow the ontological, or real, order and therefore must begin with the knowledge of God, the first being and source of all existing beings. Ontologists appeal to the authority of the Fathers, especially St. Augustine and St. Thomas.

Refutation.—From the philosophical point of view, the immediate intuition of God and of His Divine ideas, as held by Ontologists, is above the natural power of man's intelligence. We are not conscious, even by reflection, of the presence of God in our mind; and, if we did have such an intuition we would find in it (as St. Thomas rightly remarks) the full satisfaction of all our aspirations, since we would know God in His essence (for the distinction between God in His essence and God as containing the ideas of things, as advanced by Ontologists, is arbitrary and cannot be more than logical); error or doubt concerning God would be impossible. (Cf. St. Thom. in Lib. Boetii de Trinitate,

Q. I, a. 3; de Veritate, Q. XVIII, a. 1.) Again, all our intellectual thoughts, even those concerning God, are accompanied by sensuous images; they are made of elements which may be applied to creatures as well as to God Himself; only in our idea of God and of His attributes, these elements are divested of the characteristics of imperfection and limit which they have in creatures, and assume the highest possible degree of perfection. In a word, our idea of God is not direct and proper; it is analogical (cf. GOD; ANALOGY). This shows that God is not known by intuition.

The reasons advanced by Ontologists rest on confusion and false assumptions. The human mind has an idea of the infinite; but this idea may be and in fact is, obtained from the notion of the finite, by the successive processes of abstraction, elimination, and transcendence. The notion of the finite is the notion of being having a certain perfection in a limited degree. By eliminating the element of limitation and conceiving the positive perfection as realized in its highest possible degree, we arrive at the notion of the infinite. We form in this way, a negativo-positive concept, as the Schoolmen say, of the infinite. It is true also that our ideas have the characteristics of necessity, universality, and eternity; but these are essentially different from the attributes of God. God exists necessarily, viz., He is absolutely, and cannot not exist; our ideas are necessary in the sense that, when an object is conceived in its essence, independently of the concrete beings in which it is realized, it is a subject of necessary relations: man, if he exists, is necessarily a rational being. God is absolutely universal in the sense that He eminently possesses the actual fulness of all perfections; our ideas are universal in the sense that they are applicable to an indefinite number of concrete beings. God is eternal in the sense that He exists by Himself and always identical with Himself; our ideas are eternal in the sense that in their state of abstraction they are not determined by any special place in space or moment in time.

It is true that God alone is perfectly intelligible in Himself, since He alone has in Himself the reason of His existence; finite beings are intelligible in the very measure in which they exist. Having an existence distinct from that of God, they have also an intelligibility distinct from Him. And it is precisely because they are dependent in their existence that we conclude to the existence of God, the first intelligible. The assumption that the order of knowledge must follow the order of things, holds of absolute and perfect knowledge, not of all knowledge. It is sufficient for true knowledge that it affirm as real that which is truly real; the order of knowledge may be different from the order of reality. The confusion of certain Ontologists regarding the notion of being opens the way to Pantheism (q. v.). Neither St. Augustine nor St. Thomas favours Ontologism. It is through a misunderstanding of their theories and of their expression that the Ontologist appeals to them. (Cf. St. August., "De civitate Dei", lib. X, XI; "De utilitate credendi", lib. 83, cap. XVI, Q. xlv, etc.; St. Thomas, "Summa Theol.", I, Q. ii, a. 11; Q. lxxxiv-lxxxviii; "Qq. disp.", de Veritate", Q. xvi, a. l; Q. xi, "De magistro", a. 3, etc.)

The Condemnation of Ontologism by the Church.—The Council of Vienna (1311–12) had already condemned the doctrine of the Begards who maintained that we can see God by our natural intelligence. On 18 September, 1861, seven propositions of the Ontologists, concerning the immediate and the innate knowledge of God, being, and the relation of finite things to God, were declared by the Holy Office *tuto tradi non posse* (cf. Denzinger-Bannwart, nn. 1659–65). The same congregation, in 1862, pronounced the same censure against fifteen propositions by Abbé Branchereau, subjected to its examination, two of which (xii and xiii) asserted the existence of an innate and direct perception of ideas, and the intuition of God by the human mind. In the Vatican Council, Cardinals Pecci and Sforza presented a *postulatum* for an explicit condemnation of Ontologism. On 14 December, 1887, the Holy Office reproved, condemned, and proscribed forty propositions extracted from the works of Rosmini, in which the principles of Ontologism are contained (cf. Denzinger-Bannwart, nn. 1891–1930).

LIBERATORE, *Trattato della conoscenza intellettuale* (Rome, 1855); ZIGLIARA, *Della Luce intellettuale e dell' Ontologismo* (Rome, 1874); LEPIDI, *Examen philosophico-theologicum de Ontologismo*; KLEUTGEN, *Die Philosophie der Vorzeit* (Innsbruck, 1878); MERCIER, *La Psychologie*, III (Louvain, 1899), i, 2–3; BOEDDER, *Natural Theology*, I (London, 1902), i.

GEORGE M. SAUVAGE.

Ontology (ὤν, ὄντος, being, and λόγος, science, the science or philosophy of being).—I. DEFINITION.—Though the term is used in this literal meaning by Clauberg (1625–1665) (Opp., p. 281), its special application to the first department of metaphysics was made by Christian von Wolff (1679–1754) (Philos. nat., sec. 73). Prior to this time "the science of being" had retained the titles given it by its founder Aristotle: "first philosophy", "theology", "wisdom". The term "metaphysics" (q. v.) was given a wider extension by Wolff, who divided "real philosophy" into general metaphysics, which he called ontology, and special, under which he included cosmology, psychology, and theodicy. This programme has been adopted with little variation by most Catholic philosophers. The subject-matter of ontology is usually arranged thus: (1) The objective concept of being in its widest range, as embracing the actual and potential, is first analyzed, the problems concerned with essence (nature) and existence, "act" and "potency" are discussed, and the primary principles—contradiction, identity, etc.—are shown to emerge from the concept of entity. (2) The properties coextensive with being—unity, truth, and goodness, and their immediately associated concepts, order and beauty—are next explained. (3) The fundamental divisions of being into the finite and the infinite, the contingent and the necessary, etc., and the subdivisions of the finite into the categories (q. v.) substance and its accidents (quantity, quality, etc.) follow in turn—the objective—reality of substance, the meaning of personality, the relation of accidents (q. v.) to substance being the most prominent topics. (4) The concluding portion of ontology is usually devoted to the concept of cause and its primary divisions—efficient and final, material and formal—the objectivity and analytical character of the principle of causality receiving most attention.

Ontology is not a subjective science as Kant describes it (Üb. d. Fortschr. d. Met., 98) nor "an inferential Psychology", as Hamilton regards it (Metaphysics, Lect. VII); nor yet a knowledge of the absolute (theology); nor of some ultimate reality, whether conceived as matter or as spirit, which Monists suppose to underlie and produce individual real beings and their manifestations. Ontology is a fundamental interpretation of the ultimate constituents of the world of experience. All these constituents—individuals with their attributes—have factors or aspects in common. The atom and the molecule of matter, the plant, the animal, man, and God agree in this that each is a being, has a characteristic essence, an individual unity, truth, goodness, is a substance and (God excepted) has accidents, and is or may be a cause. All these common attributes demand definition and explanation—definition not of their mere names, but analysis of the real object which the mind abstracts and reflectively considers. Ontology is therefore the fundamental science since it studies the basal constituents and the principles presupposed by the special sciences. All the other parts of philosophy, cosmology, psychology, theodicy, ethics, even logic, rest on the foundation laid by ontology. The physical sciences—physics, chemistry, biology, mathematics likewise, presuppose the same foundations. Nevertheless ontology is dependent in the order of analysis, though not in the order of synthesis, on these departments of knowledge; it starts from their data and uses their information in clarifying their presuppositions and principles. Ontology is accused of dealing with the merely abstract. But all science is of the abstract, the universal, not of the concrete and individual. The physical sciences abstract the various phenomena from their individual subjects; the mathematical sciences abstract the quantity—number and dimensions—from its setting. Ontology finally abstracts what is left—the essence, existence, substance, causality, etc. It is idle to say that of these ultimate abstractions we can have no distinct knowledge. The very negation of their knowableness shows that the mind has some knowledge of that which it attempts to deny. Ontology simply endeavours to make that rudimentary knowledge more distinct and complete. There is a thoroughly developed ontology in every course of Catholic philosophy; and to its ontology that philosophy owes its definiteness and stability, while the lack of an ontology in other systems explains their vagueness and instability.

II. HISTORY.—It was Aristotle who first constructed a well-defined and developed ontology. In his "Metaphysics" he analyses the simplest elements to which the mind reduces the world of reality. The medieval philosophers make his writings the groundwork of their commentaries in which they not only expand and illustrate the thought, but often correct and enrich it in the light of Revelation. Notable instances are St. Thomas Aquinas and Suarez (1548–1617). The "Disputationes Metaphysicæ" of the latter is the most thorough work on ontology in any language. The Aristotelean writings and the Scholastic commentaries are its groundwork and largely its substance; but it amplifies, and enriches both. The work of Father Harper mentioned below attempts to render it available for English readers. The author's untimely death, however, left the attempt far from its prospected ending. The movement of the mind towards the physical sciences—which was largely stimulated and accelerated by Bacon—carried philosophy away from the more abstract truth. Locke, Hume, and their followers denied the reality of the object of ontology. We can know nothing, they held, of the essence of things; substance is a mental figment, accidents are subjective aspects of an unknowable noumenon; cause is a name for a sequence of phenomena. These negations have been emphasized by Comte, Huxley, and Spencer.

On the other hand the subjective and psychological tendencies of Descartes and his followers dimmed yet more the vision for metaphysical truth. Primary notions and principles were held to be either forms innate in the mind or results of its development, but which do not express objective reality. Kant, analysing the structure of the cognitive faculties—perception, judgment, reasoning—discovers in them innate forms that present to reflection aspects of phenomena which appear to be the objective realities, being, substance, cause, etc., but which in truth are only subjective views evoked by sensory stimuli. The subject matter of ontology is thus reduced to the types which the mind, until checked by criticism, projects into the external world. Between these two extremes of Empiricism and Idealism the traditional philosophy retains the convictions of common sense and the subtle analysis of the Scholastics. Being, essence, truth, substance, accident, cause, and the rest, are words expressing ideas but standing for realities. These realities are objective aspects of the individuals that strike the senses and the intellect. They exist concretely outside of the mind, not, of course, abstractly as they are within. They are the ultimate elementary notes or forms which the mind intuitively discerns, abstracts, and reflectively analyses in its endeavour to comprehend fundamentally any object. In this reflective analysis it must employ whatever information it can obtain from empirical psychology. Until recently this latter auxiliary has been insufficiently recognized by the philosophers. The works, however, of Maher and Walker mentioned below manifest a just appreciation of the importance of psychology's co-operation in the study of ontology.

CATHOLIC: HARPER, *The Metaphysics of the School* (London, 1879–84); DE WULF, *Scholasticism Old and New*, tr. COFFEY (Dublin, 1907); PERRIER, *The revival of Scholastic Philosophy in the Nineteenth Century* (New York, 1909) (full bibliography); RICKABY, *General Metaphysics* (London, 1898); WALKER, *Theories of Knowledge* (London, 1910); MAHER,, *Psychology* (London, 1903); BALMES, *Fundamental Philosophy* (tr., New York, 1864); TURNER, *History of Philosophy* (Boston, 1903); MERCIER, *Ontologie* (Louvain, 1905); DOMET DE VORGES, *Abrégé de métaphysique* (Paris, 1906); DE REGNON, *Métaphysique des causes* (Paris, 1906); GUTBERLET, *Allgemeine Metaphysik* (Münster, 1897); URRABURU, *Institutiones philosophiæ* (Valladolid, 1891); BLANC, *Dictionnaire de philosophie* (Paris, 1906).

NON-CATHOLIC: MCCOSH, *First and Fundamental Truths* (New York, 1894); IDEM, *The Intuitions of the Mind* (New York, 1880); LADD, *Knowledge, Life and Reality* (New York, 1909); TAYLOR, *Elements of Metaphysics* (London, 1903); WINDELBAND, *History of Philosophy* (tr., New York, 1901); BALDWIN, *Dictionary of Philosophy and Psychology* (New York, 1902); EISLER, *Wörterbuch der philos. Begriffe* (Berlin, 1904).

F. P. SIEGFRIED.

Oostacker, SHRINE OF, a miraculous shrine of the Blessed Virgin, and place of pilgrimage from Belgium, Holland, and Northern France. It takes its name from a little hamlet two miles from Ghent in the Province of East Flanders, Belgium. Its origin as a centre of pilgrimage is comparatively recent, dating from 1873. In 1871 the Marquise de Calonne de Courtebourne had built in the park of her estate at Oostacker an aquarium in the form of an artificial cave or grotto. One day, while on a visit to the park, M. l'abbé Moreels, the parish priest, suggested that a statue of Our Lady of Lourdes be placed among the rocks. For two years the grotto remained simply an aquarium, but gradually the members of the family formed the habit of stopping there to recite a Hail Mary. Soon it was decided to bless the statue publicly. The ceremony took place on 23 June, 1873, and was attended by nearly all the inhabitants of the village. The pious Flemish peasants asked permission of the owner to come frequently to the park to give vent to their devotion. Accordingly, access was allowed them on Sunday afternoon. At that time the world was ringing with the fame of Lourdes, and the shrine at Oostacker soon became popular; marvellous graces and wonderful cures were reported. Before long Sunday afternoon no longer sufficed to receive the throngs of pilgrims, and the park was thrown open to the public by the generous owner. Then a large Gothic church was built, the corner-stone being laid on 22 May, 1875, by Mgr Bracq. A priest's house followed, and the marchioness in memory of her son, a deceased Jesuit, confided shrine, church, and house to the Society of Jesus. The fathers took possession on 8 April, 1877, and on 11 September of the same year the Apostolic nuncio, Seraphino Vannutelli, consecrated the church. That part of the estate, in which the grotto was, was now definitively given over to the service of Our Lady, a long avenue being built from the road to the shrine and a Way of the Cross erected. Fully 60,000 pilgrims come annually from Belgium, Holland, and Northern France, in about 450 organized pilgrimages.

PONCELET, *La Compagnie de Jésus en Belgique* (Brussels, 1907); *Pélerinages célèbres aux sanctuaires de Notre Dame* (Paris, 1901); SCHIERLINCK, *Lourdes en Flandre* (Ghent, 1874).

J. WILFRID PARSONS.

Ophir, in the Bible, designates a people and a country.

The people, for whom a Semitic descent is claimed, is mentioned in Gen., x, 29, with the other "sons of Jectan", whose dwelling "was from Messa as we go on as far as Sephar, a mountain in the east" (Gen., x, 30).

The place Ophir was that from which the Bible

represents Solomon's fleet bringing gold, silver, thyine (probably santal) wood, precious stones, ivory, apes, and peacocks (III Kings, ix, 26-28; x, 11, 22; II Par., viii, 17-18; ix, 10). Its location has been sought where the articles mentioned are native productions; still, while Ophir is repeatedly spoken of as a gold-producing region (Job, xxii, 24; xxviii, 16; Ps. xliv, 10; Is., xiii, 12), it does not follow that the other articles came from there; whether they were natural products, or only bought and sold there, or even purchased by the merchantmen at intervening ports, cannot be gathered from the text, as it states merely that they were fetched to Asiongaber. The Bible does not give the geographical position of Ophir; it only says that the voyage out from Asiongaber and back lasted three years (III Kings, x, 22). Scholars have been guided in their several identifications of the site by the importance they attach to this or that particular indication in the sacred text—especially the products brought to Solomon—also by resemblances, real or fanciful, between the Hebrew names of Ophir and of the articles mentioned in connexion therewith and names used in various countries and languages. The Greek translators of the Bible, by rendering the Hebrew *Ophir* into *Sophir*, the Coptic name for India, would locate the Biblical El Dorado in India, according to some in the land of the Abhira, east of the delta of the Indus, according to others, on the coast of Malabar or at Ceylon, and according to others still in the Malay Peninsula. The opinion that it was situated on the southern or south-eastern coast of Arabia has many advocates, who contend from the text of Gen., x, 29, 30, that Ophir must be located between Saba and Hevilath. Another opinion says it was not in Asia, but either on the south-eastern coast of Africa (Sofala) or inland in Mashonaland.

HALL AND NEAL, *The Ancient Ruins of Rhodesia* (London, 1902); CORY, *The Rise of South Africa* (London, 1909); LOW, *Maritime Discovery*, I (London, 1881); PEYRON, *Lexicon Linguæ Copticæ* (Turin, 1835); HUET, *Commentaires sur les navigations de Salomon* in BRUZEN DE LA MARTINIÈRE, *Traités géographiques et historiques pour faciliter l'intelligence de l'Ecriture Sainte*, II (The Hague, 1730); QUATREMÈRE, *Mémoire sur le pays d'Ophir* in *Mémoires de l'Académie des Inscriptions*, XV (Paris, 1842); VIGOUROUX, *La Bible et les découvertes modernes*, III (6th ed., Paris, 1896); VIVIEN DE SAINT-MARTIN, *Histoire de la géographie et des découvertes géographiques* (Paris, 1875); GESENIUS, *Ophir* in ERSCH AND GRUBER, *Encyklopädie der Wissenschaften* (1833); GLASER, *Skizze der Geschichte und Geographie Arabiens*, II (1890); GUTHE, *Kurzes Bibelwörterbuch* (Tübingen, 1903); HERZFELD, *Handelsgeschichte der Juden der Alterthums* (1879); LASSEN, *Indische Alterthumskunde*, I (1866); LIEBLEIN, *Handel und Schiffahrt auf dem rothen Meer in alten Zeiten* (Leipzig, 1886); MAUCH, *Reisende in Ost-Afrika* (1871); MERENSKY, *Beiträge zur Kenntniss Sud-Afrikas* (1875); MÜLLER, *Asien und Europa nach altägyptischen Denkmälern* (1893); PETERS, *Das goldene Ophir Salomons* (Munich, 1895); SOETBEER, *Das Goldland Ophir* (1880).

CHARLES L. SOUVAY.

Ophites. See GNOSTICISM.

Opinions, THEOLOGICAL. See THEOLOGY.

Oporto, DIOCESE OF (PORTUCALENSIS), in Portugal; comprising 26 civil *concelhos* of the districts of Oporto and Aveiro; probably founded in the middle of the sixth century. At the third Council of Toledo (589) the Arian usurper Argiovito was deposed in favour of Constancio the rightful bishop. In 610 Bishop Argeberto assisted at a council at Toledo, summoned by King Gundemar to sanction the metropolitan claims of Toledo. Bishop Ansiulfo was present at the Sixth Council of Toledo (638) and Bishop Flavio at the Tenth (656). Bishop Froarico attended the Third Council of Braga (675) and the Twelfth, Thirteenth, and Fifteenth Councils of Toledo (681, 683, and 688), and his successor Felix appeared at the Sixteenth Council (693). No other bishop is recorded under the Visigothic monarchy. After the Arab invasion Justus seems to have been the first bishop. Comado was probably elected in 872, when King Affonso III won back the city. The names of only four other prelates have been preserved: Froarengo (906), Hermogio (912), Ordonho, and Diogo. Oporto fell again into Moorish hands, and on its recovery, Hugo became bishop (1114–1134–6). He secured exemption from the Archbishop of Braga. He greatly enlarged his diocese and the cathedral patrimony increased by the donations he secured; thus, in 1120, he received from D. Theresa jurisdiction over the City of Oporto with all the rents and dues thereof. John Peculiar was promoted to Braga (1138), his nephew, Pedro Rabaldis, succeeding at Oporto. Next came D. Pedro Pitões (1145 to 1152 or 1155), D. Pedro Senior (d. 1172), and D. Fernão Martins (d. 1185). Martinho Pires instituted a chapter, was promoted to Braga, 1189 or 1190. Martinho Rodrigues ruled from 1191 to 1235. He quarrelled with the chapter over their

WAY OF THE CROSS, CATHEDRAL, OPORTO
The building, in Gothic style, dates from 1385—the mural decorations date from the XVIII century

share of the rents of the see. Later on, fresh disagreements arose in which King Sancho intervened against the bishop, who was deprived of his goods and had to flee, but was restored by the king when Innocent III espoused the bishop's cause. Another quarrel soon arose between prelate and king, and the bishop was imprisoned; but he escaped and fled to Rome, and in 1209 the king, feeling the approach of death, made peace with him. His successor, Pedro Salvadores, figured prominently in the questions between the clergy and King Sancho II, who refused to ecclesiastics the right of purchasing or inheriting land. Portugal fell into anarchy, in which the clergy's rights were violated and their persons outraged, though they themselves were not guiltless. Finally, Pope Innocent IV committed the reform of abuses to Affonso, brother of Sancho, who lost his crown.

Under Bishop Julian (1247–60) the jurisdiction difficulty became aggravated. A settlement was effected at the Cortes of Leiria (1254), which the bishop refused to ratify, but he had to give way. When King Affonso III determined (1265) that all rights and properties usurped during the disorders of Sancho's reign should revert to the Crown, nearly all the bishops, including the Bishop of Oporto, then D.

Vicente, protested; and seven went to Rome for relief, leaving Portugal under an interdict. When the king was dying, in 1278, he promised restitution. Vicente (d. 1296) was one of the negotiators of the Concordat of 1289 and the supplementary Accord of Eleven Articles. He was succeeded by Sancho Pires, who ruled until 1300. Geraldo Domingues resigned in 1308 to act as counsellor of the King's daughter Constança, future Queen of Castile. Tredulo was bishop for two and a half years. The Minorite Frei Estevan was succeeded in 1313 by his nephew Fernando Ramires. Both uncle and nephew quarrelled with King Denis and left the realm. Owing to the hostility of the citizens, Bishop Gomes lived mostly outside his diocese. When Pedro Affonso became bishop in 1343, he had a quarrel over jurisdiction and, like his predecessor, departed, leaving the diocese under interdict. Six years later he returned, but again the monarch began to encroach, and it was not until 1354 that the bishop secured recognition of his rights. His successor was Affonso Pires. Egidio is probably the bishop represented in the old Chronicles as being threatened with scourging by King Pedro for having lived in sin with a citizen's wife. The accusation was probably groundless, but Egidio left the city, which for twelve years had no bishop. In 1373 or 1375 John succeeded and supported the lawful popes in the Great Schism, and the Master of Aviz against Spanish claims.

Other bishops were: John de Zambuja, or Estevans; and Gil, who in 1406 sold the episcopal rights over Oporto to the Crown for an annual money payment, reduced in the reign of D. Manuel to 120 silver marks; Fernando da Guerra, who in 1425 was created Archbishop of Braga; Vasco.—Antão Martins de Chavis, who succeeded Vasco in 1430, was sent by the pope to Constantinople to induce the Greek emperor to attend the Council of Basle. He succeeded, and as a reward was made cardinal. He died in 1447. Succeeding incumbents were: Durando; Gonçalves de Obidos; Luis Pires (1454–64), a negotiator of the Concordat of 1455 and a reforming prelate; John de Azevedo (1465–1494), a benefactor of the cathedral and chapter, as was his successor Diego de Sousa, afterwards Archbishop of Braga and executor of King Manuel. The see was then held by two brothers in succession, Diego da Costa (1505–7) and D. Pedro da Costa (1511–39), who restored the bishop's palace and enriched the capitular revenues from his own purse; Belchior Beliago; and the Carmelite Frei Balthazar Limpo (1538–52), the fiftieth bishop. He held a diocesan synod in 1540.

In the time of Rodrigo Pinheiro, a learned humanist, Oporto was visited by St. Francis Borgia and the Jesuits established themselves in the city. Ayres da Sylva, ex-rector of Coimbra University, after ruling four years, fell in the battle of Alcacer in 1578 with King Sebastian. Simão Pereyra was followed by the Franciscan Frei Marcos de Lisboa, chronicler of his order. He added to the cathedral and convoked a diocesan synod in 1585. In 1591 another ex-rector of Coimbra, Heironymo de Menezes, became bishop; he was succeeded by the Benedictine Frei Gonçalo de Moraes, a zealous defender of the rights of the Church. He built a new sacristy and chancel in the cathedral. In 1618 Bishop Rodrigo da Cunha, author of the history of the Bishops of Oporto, was appointed. His "Catalogo" describes the state of the cathedral and enumerates the parishes of the diocese with their population and income in 1623 and is the earliest account we possess. His successor was Frei John de Valladares, transferred from the See of Miranda. Gaspar do Rego da Fonseca, who held the see four years (1635–39). King Philip III named Francisco Pereira Pinto, but the revolution in 1640 prevented his taking possession, so that the see was considered vacant until 1671, being ruled by administrators appointed by the chapter. In 1641 John IV chose D. Sebastião Cesar de Menezes as bishop, but the pope, influenced by Spain, would neither recognize the new King of Portugal nor confirm his nominations. Next came Frei Pedro de Menezes; Nicolau Monteiro took possession in 1671, Fernando Correia de Lacerda, in 1673, who was succeeded by João de Sousa. Frei José Saldanha (1697–1708), famed for his austerity, never relinquished his Franciscan habit, a contrast to his successor Thomas de Almeida, who in 1716 became the first Patriarch of Lisbon. The see remained vacant until 1739, and, though Frei John Maria was then elected, he never obtained confirmation. In the same year Frei José Maria da Fonseca, formerly Commissary General of the Franciscans, became bishop. Several European States selected him as arbiter of their differences. He contributed to the canonization of a number of saints. He founded and restored many convents and hospitals.

Next in order were: Frei Antonio de Tavora (d. 1766), Frei Aleixo de Miranda Henriques, Frei John Raphael de Mendonça (1771–3), and Lourenço Correia de Sá Benevides (1796–8). Frei Antonio de Castro became Patriarch of Lisbon in 1814, being followed at Oporto by John Avellar. Frei Manuel de Santa Ignez, though elected, never obtained confirmation, but some years after his death, relations between Portugal and the Holy See were re-established by a concordat and Jeronymo da Costa Rebello became bishop in 1843. From 1854 to 1859 the see was held by Antonio da Fonseca Moniz; on his death it remained vacant until 1862, when John Castro e Moura, who had been a missionary in China, was appointed (d. 1868). The see was again vacant until the confirmation of Americo Ferreira dos Santos Silva in 1871. This prelate was obliged to combat the growing Liberalism of his flock and the Protestant propaganda in Oporto. A popular lawyer named Mesquita started a campaign against him, because the bishop refused to dismiss some priests, reputed reactionary, who served the Aguardente Chapel; getting himself elected judge of the Brotherhood of the Temple, he provoked a great platform agitation with the result that the chapel was secularized and became a school under the patronage of the Marquis of Pombal Association. In 1879 Americo was created cardinal and on his death the present (1911) Bishop, Antonio Barroso, an ex-missionary, was transferred from the See of Mylapore to that of Oporto.

The Diocese of Oporto is suffragan to Braga. It has 479 parishes, 1120 priests, a Catholic population of 650,000, and 500 Protestants.

CERQUEIRA PINTO, *Cataloga dos Bispos do Porto composto pelo Illmo D. Rodrigo da Cunha* (Oporto, 1742); FORTUNATO DE ALMEIDA, *Historia da Igreja em Portugal*, I (Coimbra, 1910); BRUNO, *Portuenses illustres*, III (Oporto, 1908).

EDGAR PRESTAGE.

Oppenordt (OPPENORD), Gilles-Marie, b. in Paris, 1672; d. there, 1742; a celebrated rococo artist, known as "the French Borromini". As a boy he was sent to Rome as a royal pensioner, where, for eight years he studied, principally under Bernini and Borromini. The way had been paved in France for this style, for in the latter days of Louis XIV a change had appeared in the architectural productions of the Baroque style. The endowment of the Renaissance was adapted to the taste of Louis XV's time. It was called the Style of the Regency, the *salon et boudoir* style. Oppenordt, in connexion with Robert de Cotte, developed the voluptuous *rocaille* border and shell ornamentation founded on the Italian Grotesque. The high altar of St. Germain des Prés and that of Saint-Sulpice (1704) gained for him the favour of the regent. He was entrusted with the restoration and decoration of the Château Villers Cotterets, for the reception of the king after his anointing at Reims. In the Palais Royal and the Hotel du Grand Prieur de France he proved himself an elegant decorator. In 1721 the continuation of the work on Saint-Sulpice was transferred to him. He had already (in 1710) built the chapel of St. John the Baptist in the cathedral of Amiens and earlier the Dominican novitiate church in Paris. He possessed unusual talent as a draughtsman. In his "Dessins, couronnements et amortissements convenables pour dessus de porte" etc., Huquières gives many of Oppenordt's designs.

OPPENORD, *L'Art décoratif du 18e siècle* (Paris, 1888); GUILMARD, *Les maîtres ornemanistes* (Paris, 1881); DESTAILLEUR, *Recueil d'estampes* (Paris, 1863—); IDEM, *Notices sur quelques artistes français* (Paris, 1863); LANCE, *Dictionnaire des architectes français* (Paris, 1873).

G. GIETMANN.

Oppido Mamertina, DIOCESE OF (OPPIDENSIS), suffragan of Reggio Calabria, Italy, famous for its prolonged resistance to Roger (eleventh century). Bishop Stefano (1295) is the first prelate of whom there is mention. In 1472 the see was united to that of Gerace, under Bishop Athanasius Calceofilo, by whom the Greek Rite was abolished, although it remained in use in a few towns. In 1536 Oppido became again an independent see, under Bishop Pietro Andrea Ripanti; among other bishops were Antonio Cesconi (1609) and Giovanni Battista Montani (1632), who restored the cathedral and the episcopal palace; Bisanzio Fili (1696), who founded the seminary; Michele Caputo (1852), who was transferred to the See of Ariano, where it is suspected that he poisoned King Ferdinand II; eventually, he apostatized. Oppido has 19 parishes, with 28,000 inhabitants.

CAPPELLETTI, *Le Chiese d'Italia*, vol. XXI.

U. BENIGNI.

Optatus, SAINT, Bishop of Milevis, in Numidia, in the fourth century. He was a convert, as we gather from St. Augustine: "Do we not see with how great a booty of gold and silver and garments Cyprian, *doctor suavissimus*, came forth out of Egypt, and likewise Lactantius, Victorinus, Optatus, Hilary?" (De Doctrina Christ., xl). Optatus probably had been a pagan rhetorician. His work against the Donatists is an answer to Parmenian, the successor of Donatus in the See of Carthage. St. Jerome (De viris ill., cx) tells us it was in six books and was written under Valens and Valentinian (364–75). We now possess seven books, and the list of popes is carried as far as Siricius (384–98). Similarly the Donatist succession of antipopes is given (II, iv), as Victor, Bonifatius, Encolpius, Macrobius, Lucianus, Claudianus (the date of the last is about 380), though a few sentences earlier Macrobius is mentioned as the actual bishop. The plan of the work is laid down in Book I, and is completed in six books. It seems, then, that the seventh book, which St. Jerome did not know in 392, was an appendix to a new edition in which St. Optatus made additions to the two episcopal lists. The date of the original work is fixed by the statement in I, xiii, that sixty years and more had passed since the persecution of Diocletian (303–5). Photinus (d. 376) is apparently regarded as still alive; Julian is dead (363). Thus the first books were published about 366–70, and the second edition about 385–90.

St. Optatus deals with the entire controversy between Catholics and Donatists (see DONATISTS). He distinguishes between schismatics and heretics. The former have rejected unity, but they have true doctrine and true sacraments, hence Parmenian should not have threatened them (and consequently his own party) with eternal damnation. This mild doctrine is a great contrast to the severity of many of the Fathers against schism. It seems to be motived by the notion that all who have faith will be saved, though after long torments,—a view which St. Augustine has frequently to combat. Donatists and Catholics were agreed as to the necessary unity of the Church. The question was, where is this One Church? Optatus argues that it cannot be only in a corner of Africa; it must be the *catholica* (the word is used as a substantive) which is throughout the world. Parmenian had enumerated six *dotes*, or properties, of the Church, of which Optatus accepts five, and argues that the first, the episcopal chair, *cathedra*, belongs to the Catholics, and therefore they have all the others. The whole schism had arisen through the quarrel as to the episcopal succession at Carthage, and it might have been expected that Optatus would claim this property of *cathedra* by pointing out the legitimacy of the Catholic succession at Carthage. But he does not. He replies: "We must examine who sat first in the chair, and where. . . . You cannot deny that you know that in the city of Rome upon Peter first the chair of bishop was conferred, in which sat the head of all the Apostles, Peter, whence also he was called Cephas, in which one chair unity should be preserved by all, lest the other Apostles should each stand up for his own chair, so that now he should be a schismatic and a sinner who should against this one chair set up another. Therefore in the one chair, which is the first of the *dotes* Peter first sat, to whom succeeded Linus." An incorrect list of popes follows, ending with, "and to Damasus Siricius, who is to-day our colleague, with whom the whole world with us agrees by the communication of commendatory letters in the fellowship of one communion. Tell us the origin of your chair, you who wish to claim the holy Church for yourselves". Optatus then mocks at the recent succession of Donatist antipopes at Rome.

Optatus argues, especially in book V, against the doctrine which the Donatists had inherited from St. Cyprian that baptism by those outside the Church cannot be valid, and he anticipates St. Augustine's argument that the faith of the baptizer does not matter, since it is God who confers the grace. His statement of the objective efficacy of the sacraments *ex opere operato* is well known: "Sacramenta per se esse sancta, non per homines" (V, iv). Thus in baptism there must be the Holy Trinity, the believer and the minister, and their importance is in this order, the third being the least important. In rebuking the sacrileges of the Donatists, he says: "What is so profane as to break, scrape, remove the altars of God, on which you yourselves had once offered, on which both the prayers of the people and the members of Christ have been borne, where God Almighty has been invoked, where the Holy Ghost has been asked for and has come down, from which by many has been received the pledge of eternal salvation and the safeguard of faith and the hope of resurrection? . . . For what is an altar but the seat of the Body and Blood of Christ?" In book VII a notable argument for unity is added: St. Peter sinned most grievously and denied his Master, yet he retained the keys, and for the sake of unity and charity the Apostles did not separate from his fellowship. Thus Optatus defends the willingness of the Catholics to receive back the Donatists to unity without difficulty, for there must be always sinners in the Church, and the cockle is mixed with the wheat; but charity covers a multitude of sins.

The style of St. Optatus is vigorous and animated. He aims at terseness and effect, rather than at flowing periods, and this in spite of the gentleness and charity which is so admirable in his polemics against his "brethren", as he insists on calling the Donatist bishops. He uses Cyprian a great deal, though he refutes that saint's mistaken opinion about baptism, and does not copy his easy style. His descriptions of events are admirable and vivid. It is strange that Dupin should have called him *minus nitidus ac politus*, for both in the words he employs and in their order he almost incurs the blame of preciosity. He is as strict as Cyprian as to the metrical cadences at the close of every sentence. He was evidently a man of good taste as well as of high culture, and he has left us in his one work a monument of convincing dialectic, of elegant literary form, and of Christian charity. But the general marshalling of his arguments is not so good as is the development of each by itself. His allegorical interpretations are far-fetched; but those of Parmenian were evidently yet more extravagant. An appendix contained an important dossier of documents which had apparently been collected by some Catholic controversialist between 330 and 347 (see DONATISTS). This collection was already mutilated when it was copied by the scribe of the only MS. which has preserved it, and that MS. is incomplete, so that we have to deplore the loss of a great part of this first-rate material for the early history of Donatism. We can tell what has been lost by the citations made by Optatus himself and by Augustine.

St. Optatus has apparently never received any ecclesiastical cultus; but his name was inserted in the Roman Martyrology on the fourth of June, though it is quite unknown to all the ancient Martyrologies and calendars. The *editio princeps* was by Cochlæus (Mainz, 1549). More MSS. were used by Balduinus (Paris, 1563 and 1569), whose text was frequently reprinted in the seventeenth century. Dupin's edition includes a history of the Donatists and a geography of Africa (Paris, 1700—); it is reprinted in Gallandi and in Migne (P. L., XI). The best edition is that of Ziwsa (C.S.E.L., XXVI, Vienna, 1893), with description of the MSS.

TILLEMONT, *Mémoires*, VI; DUPIN's preface; PHILLOTT in *Dict. Christ. Biog.*, s. v.; BARDENHEWER in *Kirchenlex.*, s. v.; HARNACK in *Realencyk.*, s v.; PAUCKER and RÖNSCH on the Latin of Optatus in *Zeitschr. für die Oester. Gymnas.*, XXXV, 1884; on the appended documents, VÖLTER, SEECK, DUCHESNE (see DONATISTS).

JOHN CHAPMAN.

Optimism (Latin *optimus*, best) may be understood as a metaphysical theory, or as an emotional disposition. The term became current in the early part of the eighteenth century to designate the Leibnizian doctrine that this is the best of all possible worlds. The antithesis of optimism is pessimism (q. v.). Between these extremes there are all shades of opinion, so that it is at times hard to classify philosophers. Those, however, are to be classed as optimists who maintain that the world is on the whole good and beautiful, and that man can attain to a state of true happiness and perfection either in this world or in the next, and those who do not are pessimists. The term optimism as thus extended would also include "meliorism", a word first used in print by Sully to designate the theory of those who hold that things are, indeed, bad, but that they can be better, and that it is in our power to increase the happiness and welfare of mankind.

As an emotional disposition optimism is the tendency to look upon the bright and hopeful side of life, whereas pessimism gives a dark colouring to every event and closes the vistas of hope. The emotional disposition is one that depends upon internal organic conditions rather than external good fortune. To what extent the emotional disposition has influenced the opinion of philosophers cannot be decided off-hand. It has no doubt been a factor, but not always the only or even the decisive factor. A list of optimists will show that in general the greater minds have taken the hopeful view of life. As optimists are to be reckoned: Plato, Aristotle, the Stoics, St. Augustine, St. Thomas and the Scholastics, Leibniz, Kant, Fichte, Hegel (sought to unite optimism and pessimism), Lotze, Wundt.

It has been held by some that the Old Testament is optimistic, and the New Testament pessimistic. The evidence brought forward for this theory is found mainly in the passages of the Old Testament which point to the rewards of the present life, and those in the New which call attention to the transitoriness of all human joys. This view is too narrow, and is not correct. Optimism as a philosophical term means that the universe as a whole is good and that man's ultimate destiny is one of happiness. The Old Testament is optimistic because of such passages as the following: "And God saw all things that he had made, and they were very good" (Gen., i, 31). Even in Eccl. we read, "He hath made all things good in their time" (iii, 11). The New Testament is optimistic because it shows that the sufferings of this life are not worthy to be compared to the glory that is to come. If optimism and pessimism are to be taken as emotional dispositions, either one or the other may exist in the ascetic or the profligate. It cannot be argued that the doctrine of Our Lord was pessimistic because He taught asceticism and celibacy. For as a rule ascetics and celibates have been and are, as a matter of fact, disposed to look upon the bright side of life. They surely believe that it is better to live than not to live, that the world which God has made is good and beautiful, and that man's destiny is eternal bliss.

As typical metaphysical exponents of optimism one may mention the extreme position of Leibniz, and the more moderate doctrine of St. Thomas Aquinas.

Leibniz looked upon the series of possible worlds as actually infinite. This entire series must have passed as it were, through the mind of the All-Good and Omniscient God. In spite of the fact that the series is infinite, He must have seen that one of its members was supremely perfect. Each one of these series strives to be realized in proportion to its perfection. Under such circumstances, it is impossible that a less perfect world should come into being. Since, furthermore, the wisdom and goodness of God are infinite, it is necessary that the world that proceeds from His intellect and will should be the best possible one that under any circumstances can exist. Only one such world is possible, and therefore God chooses the best. The very fact of the world's existence makes it metaphysically certain that it is the very best possible. [See Leibniz, IX, 137, subsection, (4) Optimism.] This argument might seem convincing, if one overlooks the fact of the evil in the world. The world as it is, Leibniz maintained, with all its evil, is better than a world without any evil. For the physical evil of the universe only serves to set off by contrast the beauty and glory of the good. As to moral evil, it is a negation and therefore cannot be looked upon as a real object of the Divine Will. Its presence, therefore, does not conflict with the holiness of the Divine decrees by which the world was ordained. Furthermore, since a morally evil being is only a less perfect creature, the absolutely perfect series of beings in order to contain all possible perfection, must, by necessity, contain the less as well as the more perfect. For if the series contained no beings lacking in moral perfection, it would be a shortened series, and therefore lacking in the types of less perfect beings.

Against the extreme optimism of Leibniz, one might say that God is not necessitated to choose the best of all possible worlds, because this is in itself an impossibility. Whatever exists besides God, is finite. Between the finite and the infinite there is always a field of indefinite extent. And since the finite cannot become infinite, simply because the created can never be uncreated, it therefore follows that whatever exists, besides God, is, and always will be, limited. If so, no matter what may exist, something better could be conceived and brought into being by God. An absolutely best possible world would, therefore, seem to be a contradiction in terms and impossible even by the Omnipotence of God, who can bring into being all and only that which is intrinsically possible. If, then, one should take the words "doing the best possible" as meaning creating something than which nothing better is possible, no world could be the best possible. But there is another sense in which the words may be taken. Though one is not making the best thing that can be made, he still may be doing what he does in the best possible manner. In this sense, according to St. Thomas, God has made this world *relatively* the best possible. "When it is said that God can do anything better than He does it, this is true if the words 'anything better' stand for a noun. No matter what you may point out, God can make something that is better. . . . If, however, the words are used adverbially, and designate the mode of operation, God cannot do better than He does, for He cannot work with greater wisdom and goodness" (I, Q. xxv, a. 5, ad 1um). It is just this distinction which Leibniz failed to make, and was thereby led to his extreme position. According to St. Thomas, God was free to make a less or more perfect world. He made the world that would best fit the purposes of creation, and wrought it in the best possible manner.

Against this optimism may be urged the same objections from the presence of physical and moral evil which troubled Leibniz. But there are several considerations that reduce their force. (1) We see only in part. We cannot criticize the Divine plan intelligently until we see its full development, which indeed will only be in eternity. (2) The physical evils and sufferings of this life are not worthy to be compared with the glory that is to come. Should one object that it would be better to have glory both in this world and the next, one might answer that this is not certainly true. Only by the endurance of suffering and sorrow do we attain to the true strength and glory of our manhood. That which we acquire by the sweat of our brow is earned and truly our own. That which comes to us by inheritance is but loaned and possessed by us for a time, till we can hand it on to another. What is true of the individual is true of the human race as a whole. It seems to be the Divine plan that it should work its way on, from little beginnings, with great toil and suffering, to its final goal of perfection. When all things are fulfilled in eternity man can then look back upon something as his own. Perhaps this will then seem to us much more beautiful and glorious than if God had allowed us to remain forever in a garden of paradise, happy indeed, but lifting nothing with the strength He gave us. (See also in this connexion the article EVIL.)

ST. THOMAS, I, Q. xix, a. 9; I, Q. xxv, aa. 5 and 6; ENGLER, *Darstellung und Kritik des leibnitzsischen Optimismus* (Jena, 1883); GUTTMACHER, *Optimism and Pessimism in the O. and N. Testaments* (Baltimore, 1903); KELLER, *Optimism* (New York, 1903); KOPPEHL, *Die Verwandtschaft Leibnitzens mit Thomas v. Aquino in der Lehre vom Bösen* (Jena, 1892); VON PRANTL, *Ueber die Berechtigung des Optimismus* (Munich, 1879); SULLY, *Pessimism* (New York, 1891); WILLARETH, *Die Lehre vom Uebel bei Leibniz, seiner Schule in Deutschland, und bei Kant. Diss.* (Strasburg, 1898).

For an extensive bibliography see BALDWIN, *Dict. of Philosophy and Psychology*, III, Part ii, 903–907

THOMAS V. MOORE.

Option, RIGHT OF.—In canon law an option is a way of obtaining a benefice or a title, by the choice of the new titulary himself. Many chapters enjoyed this right formerly and it is still the privilege of some: the canon, who has held his office for the longest time, may, in conformity with the statutory regulation, resign the prebend he enjoys to accept another that has become vacant. A second right of option existed in France before 1789: by virtue of a custom a prebendary, who was appointed to and had entered into possession of a benefice incompatible with one he already held, was entitled to select whichever of the two he preferred, when, according to the common law, he had already lost the incompatible benefice which he had previously held. The right of option still exists with regard to cardinalitial titles (see CARDINAL).

SCHNEIDER, *Die bischöflichen Domkapitel* (Mayence, 1885); VAN ESPEN, *Jus ecclesiasticum universum* (Cologne, 1778), part II, s. III, tit. 3, c. 4, t. I, 691; HINSCHIUS, *System des katholischen Kirchenrechts*, II (Berlin, 1878), 615, 701.

A. VAN HOVE.

O'Queely, MALACHIAS (Maolsheachlainn O Cadhla), Archbishop of Tuam, Ireland, b. in Thomond, date unknown; d. at Ballipodare, 27 October, 1645 (N.S.). He studied in Paris at the College of Navarre. Having administered Killaloe as vicar Apostolic, he was consecrated Archbishop of Tuam at Galway, 11 October, 1631. His subjects, who received him unwillingly, soon learned to admire him. He held a provincial synod at Galway in 1632 to promulgate the Tridentine decrees and correct abuses, and his unremitting labours in Tuam provoked a complaint from the Protestant archbishop in 1641. Dr. O'Queely attended the national synod of 1643, by which the Catholic Confederation was organized, and at the first meeting of the General Assembly he was elected to the Supreme Council, being afterwards appointed President of Connaught. He undertook to recover Sligo from the Scottish Covenanters in 1645, but the Scots surprised his camp at Ballysodare, 17–27 October, 1645. Everyone abandoned him but his secretary, Father Thaddeus O'Connell, and another priest. The archbishop was cut down with his companions, and the victors discovered in his carriage a draft of the secret treaty between King Charles and the Confederates, which the English Parliament published to prejudice both parties. His body was redeemed for £30 and buried with solemn ceremonies at Tuam. He wrote an account of the Aran Islands, printed in Colgan's "Acta Sanctorum".

MEEHAN, *Irish Hierarchy in the 17th Century* (16th edit., Dublin, about 1888); MURPHY, *Our Martyrs* (Dublin, 1896).

Oracle (*oraculum; orare*, to speak), a Divine communication given at a special place through specially appointed persons, also the place itself. This form of divination (q. v.) was found among various peoples of the ancient world.

I. BABYLON AND ASSYRIA.—Extremely ancient texts present the oracle-priest [*bârû*, 'he who sees': *bîra barû*, 'to see a sight'; hence, to give an oracle, divine the future. Cf. הרא of Samuel, I Sam., ix, 9; I Chr., ix, 22 etc.; of Hanani, II Chr., xvi, 7, 10; cf. Is., xxviii, 7; xxx, 10] alongside of the *âshipu* (whose rôle is incantation, conjuration) as officer of one of the two main divisions of the sacerdotal caste. He is the special servant of Shamash and Adad; his office is hereditary (cf. the "sons of Aaron", "of Zadok"); blemish of person or pedigree (cf. Lev., xxi, 23) disqualifies him; he forms part of a college. Lengthy initiation, elaborate ritual, prepare him for the reception, or exercise, of the *bârûtu*. He rises before dawn, bathes, anoints himself with perfumed oil, puts on sacred vestments [cf. Ex., xxx, 17, 23; Lev., xvi, 4. Lagrange, "Études sur les religions sémitiques" (Paris, 1905), 236, n. 1; and "Rev. Bibl.", VIII (1899), 473; also Ancessi, "L'Égypte et Moïse", pt. i (1875); Les vêtements du Grand-Prêtre, c. iii, plate 3. Is the blood-red, jewelled Babylonian scapular the analogate to the Hebrew ephod and pectoral?]. After a preliminary sacrifice (usually of a lamb: but this, as those of expiation and thanksgiving, we cannot, in our limits, detail), he escorts the inquirer to the presence of the gods, and sits on the seat of judgment; Shamash and Adad, the great gods of oracle, lords of decision, come to him and give him an unfailing answer [*têrtu*, presage: Divine teaching. Probably not connected with תורה. There is no likely borrowing or adaptation of Babylonian oracle-words by the Hebrews (Lagrange, op. cit., 234, n. 8)]. All the customary modes of divination (interpretation of dreams, of stars, monstrosities, of signs in oil, the liver etc.) culminated in oracles; but an enormous literature of precedents and principles left little initiative to a *bârû* whose memory was good. We may add a characteristic example of oracle style (about 680 B. C.).

O Shamash, great lord, to my demand in thy faithful favour, deign to answer! Between this day, the 3rd day of this month, the month of Arû, until the 11th day of the month of Abû of this year, within these hundred days and these hundred nights . . . within this fixed space of time will Kashtariti with his troops, or the troops of the Cimmerians . . . or all other enemy, succeed in their designs? By assault, by force . . . by starvation, by the names of the god and goddess, by parley and amicable conference, or by any other method and stratagem of siege, shall they take the town of Kishassu? shall they enter the walls of this town of Kishassu? . . . shall it fall into their hands? Thy great godhead knoweth it. Is the taking of this town of Kishassu, by whatsoever enemy it be, from this day unto the [last] day appointed, ordained and decreed by the order and mandate of thy great godhead, O Shamash, great Lord? Shall we see it? Shall we hear it? etc. Observe the preoccupation of leaving the god no avenue of elusion—every possible contingency is named.

Among the nomad Arabs the priest is primarily a giver of oracles (by means of arrow-shafts, cf. Ezech., xxi, 21), though named *Kâhin* the Hebrew כֹּהֵן. But since in Hebrew, Phœnician, Aramaic, and Ethiopian *Kôhen* means priest, and cannot be etymologically connected with "divination", we must conclude (Lagrange, op. cit., 218) that the Arabian oracle-monger is a degenerate priest, not (Wellhausen) that all Semitic priests were aboriginally oracle-mongers.

II. THE HEBREWS.—Oracles were vouchsafed to the Hebrews by means of the Urim and Thummim, which are to be connected with the Ephod. The אֵפוֹד (see EPHOD) was (i) a linen dress worn in ritual circumstances (by priests, I Sam., xxii, 18, the child Samuel, ibid., ii, 18; David, II Sam., vi, 14); (ii) 'the' ephod, described in Exod., xxviii, peculiar to the high-priest; over it was worn the pectoral containing Urim and Thummim; (iii) an idolatrous, oracular image, connected with the Teraphim (also oracular); that which Gideon erected weighed 1700 sikels of gold (Judges, viii, 27; xvii, 5; xviii, 14, 20; Osee, iii, 4 etc.). But why was this image called an ephod (a dress)? In Isaias, xxx, 22, עִפוּי the silver overlaying of idols, is parallel to אֲפֻדָּה, their golden sheath. If then the Israelites were already familiar with an oracle operating in close connexion with a jewelled ephod, it will have been easy to transfer this name to a richly plated oracular image. See van Hoonacker, "Sacerdoce lévitique" (Louvain, 1899), 372.

The law directs (Num., xxvii, 18) that the leader of the people shall stand before the priest, and proffer his request: the priest shall "inquire for him by the judgment of Urim and Thummim before Yahweh". The priest alone [for the Aḥi-jah of I Sam., xiv, 3, 18, is the Aḥi-melek of xxi, 1; xxii, 9, with the Divine name corrected] carries the ephod before Israel, and inquires on behalf of the chief alone (for Ahimelek, I Sam., xxii, 13–15, *denies* having inquired for David while Saul still is king: see van Hoonacker, op. cit., 376). Thus history would agree with the Law as to the unity of the oracle, and its exclusive use by priest and prince.

Josephus thought the אוּרִים וְתֻמִּים were stones of changing lustre. The meaning of the names is unknown. Though they seem to have been used for sacred lots, and though I Sam., xiv, 37 sqq. (especially in LXX) makes it fairly clear that they gave answer by Yes and No (in I Sam., xxiii, 2, 4, 11, 12; xxx, 8, the long phrasing is priestly commentary), and though I Sam., xiv, 42 (if indeed this still refers to the oracle and not to a private ordeal offered by Saul to, and rejected by, the people) by using the word הַפִּילוּ βάλλετε, "throw (between me and Jonathan)", suggests a casting of lots, yet the U and T were not mere pebbles (e. g., black and white), for besides answering Yes and No, they could refuse answer altogether. This happened when the inquirer was ritually unclean (so Saul, in the person of his son, I Sam., xiv, 37; cf. the exclusion from the new-moon meal, ibid., xx, 26; sexual intercourse precludes from eating sacred bread, ibid., xxi, 4).—Observe the lack, in Yahweh's oracle, of the magical element, and extreme complication, which disfigure those quoted in I. Notice, too, how Hebrew priest and prince alike submit unquestioningly to the Divine communication. The prince does not dare to seek to cajole or terrify the priest; nor the priest to distort or invent the answer. Finally, when once the era of the great prophets opens, it is through them God manifests His will; the use of the ephod ceases; the Urim and Thummim are silent and ultimately lost.

III. GREECE AND ROME.—["Oraculum: quod inest in his deorum oratio", Cic., "Top.", xx, "Voluntas divina hominis ore enuntiata", Senec., "Controv.", I. prf. Μαντεῖον: √MA as in μαίνομαι, *mens*. The μάντις was the mouthpiece, the προφήτης, the interpreter of the oracle (so already Plato, "Tim.", lxxii, B). χρηστήριον: χράω, "furnish what is needful"; hence (active), to give (middle), to consult an oracle].

Oracles in the familiar sense flourished best in Greek or hellenized areas, though even here the ecstatic element probably came, as a rule, from the East. The local element, however (for Hellenic oracles essentially localize divination), and the practice of interpreting divine voices as heard in wind, or tree, or water (φήμη θεῶν; ὄσσα, ὀμφὴ Διός—Zeus was πανομφαῖος cf. the Italian *fauni, karmentes*) were rooted in Greek or pre-Greek religion. An enormous history lies behind the oracles of "classical" times. Thus at Delphi the stratification of cults shows us, undermost, the prehistoric, chthonian worship of the pre-Achæans: Gaia (followed by, or identical with, "Themis"?) and the impersonal nymphs are the earliest tenants of the famous chasm and the spring Kassotis. Dionysos, from orgiast Thrace, or, as was then held, from the mystic East, invaded the shrine, importing, or at least accentuating, elements of enthusiasm and religious delirium; for the immense development and Orphic reformation of his cult, in the seventh century, can but have modified, not introduced, his worship. Apollo, disembarking with the Achæans on the Krisean shore, strives to oust him, and, though but sharing the year's worship and the temple with his predecessors, eclipses what he cannot destroy. Echoes of this savage fight, this stubborn resistance of the dim, old-fashioned worship to the brilliant new-comer, reach us in hymn and drama, are glossed by the devout Æschylus (Eumen. prol.), and accentuated by the rationalist Euripides (Ion etc.); vase paintings picture the ultimate reconciliation. For, in the end, a compromise is effected: the priestess still sits by the cleft, drinks of the spring, still utters the frantic inarticulate cries of ecstasy; but the prophets of the rhythmic Apollo discipline her ravings into hexameters, and thus the will of Zeus, through the inspiration of Apollo, is uttered by the pythoness to all Greece.

Apollo was the cause at once of the glory and the downfall of Delphi. Partly in reaction against him, partly in imitation of him, other oracles were restored or created. In our brief limits we cannot describe or even enumerate these. We may mention the extremely ancient oracle of Dodona, where the spirit of Zeus (ὁ τοῦ Διὸς σημαίνει—the oracles began) spoke to the priestesses in the oak, the echoing bronze, the waterfall; the underground Trophonius oracle in Lebadæa, with its violent and extraordinary ritual (Paus., IX, 39, 11: Plut., "Gen. Socr.", 22); and the incubation oracles of Asklepios, where the sleeping sick awaited the epiphany of the hero, and miraculous cure. Thousands of votive models of healed wounds and straightened limbs are unearthed in these shrines; and at Dodona, leaden tablets inquire after a vanished blanket, whether it be lost or stolen; or by prayer to what god or hero faction-rent Corcyra may find peace. Other especially famous oracles were those of Apollo at Abæ, Delos, Patara, Claros; of Poseidon at Onchestos; of Zeus at Olympia; of Amphiraos at Thebes and Oropos; about a hundred of Asklepios are known. Most were established by a source, many near a mephitic chasm or grotto. Usually the clients would stand in a large vestibule, or *chresmographion*, from which they could see the *naos* or shrine, with the god's statue. In the centre, usually at a lower level, was the adyton, where the spring, chasm, tripod, and laurel bushes were seen. Here the prophetess received the divine inspiration. Nearly all the oracles were administered by a group of officials, originally, no doubt, members of some privileged family. At Delphi, the saints (ὅσιοι); at Miletus, the Branchidai and Euangelidai, etc. These usually elected the staff of resident priests, the schools of prophets (at the oracle of Zeus Ammon, e. g., under an arch-prophet), and even, at times, the pythoness. At Delphi, the priests elected her from the neighbourhood: she was to be over fifty (so, on account of a scandalous incident), and quite ignorant. Her guidance was not to be too positive!

In its best days, the Delphic oracle exercised an enormous influence: its staff was international and highly expert; gold flowed in unceasing streams into its treasury, free access to it was guaranteed to pilgrims even in time of war. In constitutional and colonial history, in social and religious crises, in things artistic as in matters of finance, its intervention was constant and final. Had it realized its own position, its work of unification, whether as regards religion or politics in Hellas, might have been unlimited. Like all human things, it but half-saw its ideal (human as that ideal could at best have been) and but half-realized what it saw. Easily corrupted by the gold and prayers of kings, the centre of Asiatic and African, no less than of European intrigues, it became an end to itself. At the time of the Persian War, it sacrificed Athens and imperilled all Western civilization. It was responsible for more than one war. It drained the colonies of their revenues. It gradually set against itself the indignant rivalries of the local cults of Greece. No moral or religious instruction can be accredited to it. Thus, while formidable enemies were ranged against it at home, the conquests of Alexander dimmed national glories, and opened the gates to far more fascinating cults. The prophecies based upon the rigid data of astrology supplanted the Pythian ravings; Plutarch relates the decay and silencing of the oracles (De defect. orac.). In Rome diviners and astrologers, always suspected, had long found legislation active against them. The Sibylline books, huge records of oracles ceaselessly interpolated by each new philosophy, by Jewish and even Christian apocalyptic prophecy, had been famous by the side of indigenous oracles, the *carmina Marciana*, for example: yet as early as 213 B. C. the Senate began its confiscations; Augustus made an *auto-da-fé* of over 2000 volumes; Tiberius, more scrupulous, expurgated the rest. Constant enactments proved vain against the riot of superstition in which the empire was collapsing; the sanest emperors were themselves adepts; Marcus Aurelius consulted the miserable charlatan Alexander, with his snake-oracle at Abonoteichos. Christianity alone could conquer the old homes of revelation. Constantine stripped Delphi and Dodona, and closed Ægæ and Aphaka; Julian tried to re-awake the stammering, failing voices; but under Theodosius the repression is complete, and henceforward the oracles are dumb. (See DIVINATION.)

BABYLON AND ASSYRIA: JASTROW, *Die Religion Babyloniens u. Assyriens*. (Giessen, 1906), xix, and in HASTINGS, *Dict. of the Bible*, extra vol. (London, 1904), 556–63; KNUDTZON, *Assyrische Gebete a. d. Sonnengott* (Leipzig, 1893); DHORME, *Choix de textes* (Paris, 1907), xxxvi, 382; *Relig. assyro.-babylonienne* (Paris, 1910), 203, 291 etc.
THE HEBREWS: DHORME, *Les livres de Samuel* (Paris, 1910); LAGRANGE. *Le livre des Juges* (Paris, 1903) *ad locc.*; HASTINGS, *Dict. of the Bible*, extra vol. (London, 1904), 641a, 662b etc.
GREECE AND ROME; cf. especially BOUCHÉ-LECLERCQ, *Hist. de la divination dans l'antiquité* (Paris, 1879–82), and DAREMBERG AND SAGLIO, s. v. *Divination*; MONCEAU, *ibid.*, s. v. *Oraculum*; COUGNY, *Anthol. græc.*, append. (Paris, 1890), 464–533 for relics of verse oracles; BOISSIER, *Fin du paganisme*, II. On Sibylline literature: WOLFF, *De novissima oraculorum ætate* (Berlin, 1854); *Porphyrii de Philosophia ex oraculis haurienda librorum reliquiæ* (Berlin, 1856); HENCLESS, *Oracula græca* (Halle, 1877); ROUSE, *Greek Votive Offerings* (Cambridge, 1902); FARNELL, *Cults of the Greek States*, IV, 181 sqq., 1907; MYERS in *Hellenica* (London, 1880), 426–92.

C. C. MARTINDALE.

Oran, DIOCESE OF (ORANENSIS), in Algiers, separated from the Archdiocese of Algiers, 25 July, 1866, to which it is suffragan. In the early centuries there were no less than 123 dioceses in Cæsarean and Tingitan Mauretania. Tlemcen (in the present diocese) was an important see. Victor, Bishop of Tlemcen, assisted at the Council of Carthage (411); Honoratus (484) was exiled by King Huneric for denying Arianism. Though the Arabs (708) destroyed many churches, according to Abou-Obed-el-Bekrii in his "Roads and Empires", there were in 963, churches and Christians at Tlemcen. Until 1254 Christian troops were in the service of the Moorish kings of Tlemcen; from a Bull of Nicholas IV (1290) it is evident that a bishop of Morocco, legate of the Holy See, had jurisdiction over this region, ravaged by a violent persecution in the second half of the thirteenth century.

Oran, probably of Moorish origin, was taken by the Spanish in 1509. The expedition which Comte d'Alcaudette, captain general from 1534 to 1558, led against Tlemcen (1543) was in fact a crusade. The Spaniards ruled until 1708, and again from 1732 to 1792. The Bey having sought the protection of France, the French occupied Oran (10 December, 1830).

The pilgrimage of Notre-Dame du Salut at Santa Cruz near Oran was founded in 1849. Before the Associations Law of 1901 the diocese had Jesuits; Lazarists; and several orders of teaching Brothers, one native to the diocese, namely the Brothers of Our Lady of the Annunciation, with their mother-house at Misserghin. The Trinitarian Sisters, with their mother-house at Valence (Drôme) are numerous. The diocese in 1901 contained 273,527 Europeans, excluding the French army; in 1905 there were 5 canonical parishes; 77 succursal parishes, 13 curacies remunerated by the State; 14 auxiliary priests.

MORCELLI, *Africa Christiana* (Brescia, 1816); BARGÈS, *Tlemcen, ancienne capitale du royaume de ce nom* (Paris, 1859); DE PRATS, *L'Eglise Africaine* (Tours, 1894); RUFF, *La domination espagnole à Oran sous le gouvernement du comte d'Alcaudette, 1535–1558* (Paris, 1900).

GEORGES GOYAU.

Orange, COUNCILS OF.—Two councils were held at Orange (Arausio), a town in the present department of Vaucluse in southern France. The first met on 8 November, 441, in the church called "Ecclesia Justinianensis" or "Justianensis". The council is designated either by the name of the church, "synodus Justinianensis", or by that of the episcopal city, "Arausicana Ia" (first of Orange). St. Hilary of Arles presided, as the diocese formed part of his metropolitan district. Among the other sixteen bishops present was St. Eucherius who, as Metropolitan of Lyons, signed the acts in the name of all his suffragans. The council, as appears from its twenty-ninth canon, was held in obedience to an ordinance of the Synod of Riez (439) prescribing semi-annual provincial synods. The thirty canons which it issued have occasioned considerable controversy. Their subject-matter was: the administration of the sacraments (canons i-iv, xii-xvii), the right of sanctuary (v-vi), mutual episcopal relations (viii-xi), catechumens (xviii-xx), bishops (xxi, xxx), the marriage of clerics (xxii-xxv), deaconesses (xxvi), widowhood and virginity (xxvii-xxviii), the holding of councils (xxix). To these genuine canons Gratian and others added unauthentic ordinances printed in the "Corpus Juris canonici" and reproduced by Mansi in his collection of councils (VI, 441–3).

Much more important was the second council (held on 3 July, 529), the first in Gaul to publish a decision in matters of faith. The occasion was the dedication of a church built at Orange by Liberius, the pretorian prefect of Narbonensian Gaul. It was attended by fourteen bishops with St. Cæsarius of Arles as president, and its deliberations bore on the current errors concerning the doctrine of grace and free will, i. e. Semipelagianism. Cæsarius had informed Felix IV (III) of the pernicious activity of the Semipelagians in Gaul and had applied to him for support. The pope, in response, sent him a series of "Capitula", i. e. propositions or decrees drawn almost in their entirety from the works of St. Augustine and the "Sententiæ" of St. Prosper of Aquitaine. These "Capitula" became the basis of the twenty-five issued by the Synod of Orange, and these in turn were freely used by the Council of Trent in its condemnation of Luther. The acts of the Synod of Orange contain, after a preamble: (a) eight canons or anathematisms; (b) seventeen merely declaratory propositions (both of these classes are known as "Capitula"); (c) a sort of demonstration of the defined doctrine against the objections of the Semipelagians. The subjects of the "Capitula" are thus logically grouped by Portalić in "Dict. Théol. Cath." (I, 2526). (1) Causes of the necessity of grace. They are: (a) original sin which cannot be wiped out without it (can. ii); (b) the weakness of the will resulting from the fall of man (i); (c) the very condition of creature (xix). (2) Operation of grace before justification. It precedes every effort conducive to salvation. From it proceed: (a) prayer (can. iii); (b) the desire of justification (iv); (c) the inception of faith (v); (d) every effort towards faith (vi); (e) every salutary act (vii); (f) every preparation to justification (viii, xii); (g) all merit (xviii). (3) Operation of grace in initial justification or baptism. It restores (xiii), justifies (xiv), improves (xv), confers the justice of Christ (xxviii). (4) Work of grace after justification in the just. It is necessary for good actions (ix); perseverance (x); the taking of vows (xi); Christian fortitude (xvii); the life of Christ within us (xxiv); the love of God (xxv). (5) Universal necessity of grace. This need of grace to do good and avoid evil is expressed in propositions ix, xx, and the variously interpreted proposition xxii. In the demonstration which follows the "Capitula" the fathers also reject the doctrine of predestination to evil and declare salvation within the reach of all baptized. The acts of the council, which were signed by the bishops, the pretorian prefect Liberius and seven other distinguished laymen, were forwarded to Rome and approved by Boniface II on 25 January, 531 (see BONIFACE II). They consequently enjoy œcumenical authority and are printed in Denzinger's "Enchiridion Symbolorum" (10th ed., nos. 174–200).

MANSI, *Concilia*, VI, 433–52; VIII, 711–34; MAASSEN, *Concilia ævi merovingici* (Hanover, 1893), 44–54; HEFELE-LECLERCQ, *Histoire des conciles*, II, i, 430–54; II, ii, 1085–1108 (Paris, 1908). The acts of both councils and abundant bibliographical details will be found in the latter work. HEFELE, tr., III, 159–64; IV, 152 sq.; WOODS, *Canons of the Second Council of Orange, A.D. 529* (London, 1882). N. A. WEBER.

Orange Free State, one of the four provinces of the Union of South Africa, lies between 29° 30′ and 30° 40′ S. lat., and between 24° 20′ and 30° E. long. The Orange and Vaal rivers which separate it from the Cape Province and the Transvaal form respectively its southern and northern boundaries; Natal and Basutoland bound it on the east, and the northern portions of the Cape Province on the west. Its name is derived from the Orange River which flows along its southern frontier for over 200 miles. It has an area of 50,392 square miles and a population, according to the census of 1904, of 387,315; of these only 142,679 are whites, the remainder belonging to the coloured races—mostly Kafirs and Hottentots. The climate is excellent. With a mean altitude of from four to five thousand feet above sea level and an average yearly rainfall of only twenty-two inches, it is a country well suited to persons suffering from pulmonary troubles, the air being dry and invigorating and the nights always cool. Being an immense grassy plateau and almost treeless, its scenery is uninteresting (even depressing) except on the eastern border where the vast Drakensburg mountain range comes into view. It is mainly a pastoral country, though a portion of it alongside Basutoland contains some of the finest corn lands in Africa. The exports, valued in 1908–09 at 17,800,000 dollars, are principally diamonds, wool, ostrich feathers, and maize; its imports in the same period amounted to 15,000,000 dollars.

The white inhabitants are mostly the descendants of the *Voortrekkers* (or emigrant Dutch farmers) from the old Cape Colony, who in 1836 and subsequent years crossed the Orange River in thousands and settled on territories peopled by various Bantu tribes until their virtual extermination by Moselekatze and his hordes of Matabile warriors—a short time previously. The "Great Trek", as the migration of these farmers came to be called, brought about an anomalous political situation. Rather than live under British rule in the Colony, they had abandoned their homes and sought independence in "the wilderness". But the British Government, whilst always claiming them as its subjects and forbidding them to molest the neighbouring native tribes, refused to annex the territory to which they had fled. Such a state of things manifestly could not long endure, and so in 1848 the country between the Orange and Vaal Rivers was officially proclaimed British territory under the title of the "Orange River Sovereignty". The emigrant Boers, headed by a farmer named Andreas Pretorius, struggled to retain their independence but were defeated at the battle of Boomplaats by the English general, Sir Harry Smith, in August, 1848. The British Government, finding the newly annexed territory of little value and desiring in view of European complications and the enormous cost of Kafir wars to limit its responsibilities in South Africa, soon determined to retrocede their country to the Boers; thus, at a convention held in Bloemfontein on 23 February, 1854, Sir George Clark in the name of Queen Victoria renounced British dominion over the Orange River Sovereignty. The Boers thereupon set up a Republic, which, under the name of the Orange Free State, enjoyed a period of peace and prosperity that lasted up to the Anglo-Boer War of 1899–1902. In that struggle the Free Staters, having joined the Transvaallers, shared in their defeat, and their country was annexed to the British Empire under the title of the Orange River Colony. For some years the new colony was administered by a governor and a lieutenant-governor assisted by an executive and a legislative council, but in June, 1907, responsible government was conferred on it with a legislative council of eleven, and a legislative assembly of thirty-eight members.

Since 31 May, 1910, under the title of "The Orange Free State Province of the Union of South Africa", it forms part (together with the Transvaal, Natal, and the Cape of Good Hope) of a self-governing dominion of the British Empire, the first parliament of which was opened at Cape Town on 4 November, 1910. In that parliament the Orange Free State Province is represented by sixteen senators—one-fourth of the entire number—and by seventeen members of the House of Assembly (out of a total of 121). English and Dutch are the official languages. The former is spoken mostly in the towns and the latter—or rather a dialect of it known as the *Afrikansche Taal*—in the country districts. The religion of the great majority of the white inhabitants is Calvinism (Dutch Reformed). Those of English origin belong to the different dominations usually found in the British colonies and in the United States of America. The Orange Free State contains a good number of neat little towns with populations varying from one to eight thousand. Bloemfontein, capital of the province, so called from a spring (fontein) on the farm of Jan Bloem, an early German settler, is a spacious, clean, and well-built city of 33,000 inhabitants, and the seat of the provincial council as well as the legal and judicial centre of the entire Union. It is distant 400 miles from East London, the nearest seaport, and 290 miles from Pretoria, the executive capital. Other important towns are Kroonstad, Harrismith, Jagersfontein, and Smithfield, in each of which there is a Catholic church. The total number of Catholics in the Orange Free State is about 2000, mostly of European origin or descent. The province forms part of the Vicariate of Kimberley (q. v.), which is in the Cape Province, and in which the vicar Apostolic resides. The present (1910) vicar Apostolic is the Right Reverend Matthew Gaughren, O.M.I., titular Bishop of Tentyra. Catholics enjoy absolute freedom of worship, but receive no government aid for their clergy or schools. The Roman Dutch Law, which is administered in the courts, is favourable to Catholics on such points as tenure of ecclesiastical property, marriage, wills, and charitable bequests. The clergy are not liable to serve on juries or as burghers "on command", nor are churches taxed. Flourishing convent schools and academies are directed by the Sisters of the Holy Family at Bloemfontein and Jagersfontein, and by the Sisters of Notre Dame (of Namur) at Kroonstad.

WILMOT, *Hist. of our own times in South Africa* (London, 1897–9); THEAL, *Hist. of S. A. since 1795* (London, 1908); DEHERAIN, *L'expansion des Boers au XIXe siècle* (Paris, 1905); *Hist. of S. A. to the Jameson Raid* (Oxford, 1899); CANA, *S. A. from the Great Trek to the Union* (London, 1909); BRYCE, *Impressions of S. A.* (London, 1899); CAPPON, *Britain's Title to S. A.* (London, 1901); BROWN, *Guide to S. A.* (London, 1909–10); *Catholic Directory of S. A.* (Cape Town, 1910).

H. MACSHERRY.

Orange River, VICARIATE APOSTOLIC OF, and the PREFECTURE APOSTOLIC OF GREAT NAMAQUALAND, in South Africa. The vicariate was erected in 1897 after having been a prefecture Apostolic since July, 1885. It comprises the whole of Little Namaqualand (beginning on the northern line of Clan William County in Cape Colony, i. e. 30° 35′ S. lat.); extends to the Atlantic Ocean on the west, and to the Orange River on the north. It further includes Bushmanland, the districts of Kenhardt, Van Rhyns, Dorp, and Frazerburg on the east, and beyond the Orange River, the district of Gordonia in Bechuanaland. The prefecture, detached from the vicariate in July, 1909, is bounded on the west by the Atlantic Ocean. It extends from the Orange River as far as Damaraland (23° 20′ S. lat.), and comprises the city of Rehboth and its district. The eastern boundary line is 20° E. long.

GREAT NAMAQUALAND.—For thirty or forty, or in certain districts even a hundred miles inland, this district is only a sandy desert, which extends on the eastern side to the great Kalahari desert. The central portion depends for its fertility almost exclusively on thunder-storms, without which it would be nearly destitute of water. The vicariate is but little better in this respect. When, however, a sufficiently long rain waters these forlorn regions, the richest pastures spring up in an incredibly short time. The very air then becomes saturated to such a degree with the odour of vegetation that many suffer from headache. Swarms of locusts devour the exuberant produce, unless some powerful east wind carries them into the sea. The "aristocracy" in Great Namaqualand consists of German immigrants, and, in the other parts of the mission, of English, Irish, and Boer settlers, while the Hottentots form the bulk of the scanty population in the two Namaqualands. They are not negroes. Their skin is like that of whites much browned by jaundice, and their build more like that of the Egyptians as seen on ancient monuments; or again, resembling that of the Chinese, only exceeding them or any other race on earth in their ugliness, especially when burdened with years. Unselfish hospitality appears to be their only natural virtue. They love music. Their habit of imitating is such as to rouse either a smile or exasperation; a crowd of Hottentots at Holy Mass, when receiving the priest's blessing, all repeated the sign of the Cross over him! The late Max Müller, nevertheless, vouched for their ancestors having been a cultured race. Although they have in their language a word signifying Deity, it took a long time to make them understand spiritual doctrines other than that of the existence of the devil. They are extremely disinclined to any form of labour or exertion. To induce them, for example, to navigate, the missionaries built a boat by which to cross the Orange River. For weeks, neither encouraging words nor exhibitions of safe sailing appeared to make any impression on them. One missionary relates that, among his Hottentot catechumens, there was one who never could learn how to make the sign of the Cross, nor the answers of the catechism, nor any prayer except these words of the Pater Noster: "Our Father, give us this day our daily bread." The missionaries have shown here what an uplifting influence the Catholic Church exercises over the most forlorn nations, since the younger generation, trained by the missionaries as far as circumstances allowed, are considerably more intelligent and susceptible of culture than their elders.

BUSHMANLAND.—In this territory are found the Bushmen (or Bojesmen), a tribe kindred to the Hottentots. They are short in stature, and generally malicious and intractable. Intellectually and morally they are not on a higher level than the Hottentots, but, as far as they have been accessible to the missionaries, they have improved in both respects.

BECHUANALAND.—The Bechuanas belong to the Kafir race. Many of them show some skill in iron and copper working and in mining, also in tanning hides. Very different from the Hottentots, many of them present a pleasing appearance, and some are handsome.

MISSIONS.—When the Oblates of St. Francis de Sales arrived in Little Namaqualand, to which the mission was then confined, they found not one hundred Catholics. In 1903, without any change of population, they counted 2735. There were six stations with churches and resident priests, five other stations regularly attended, 125 conversions during the year, and 98 children were baptized; 122 confirmations, 25 marriages; 3 hospitals and homes for the aged, 8 schools, 3 orphanages, 82 orphans, 8 missionary priests, 3 catechists; 15 missionary sisters aided the mission. Some fifty places are now visited by the priests to attend to the spiritual and temporal wants of the people. In several places, all Catholic adults receive Holy Communion on the first Friday of every month and the great feasts of the year. Sella is the residence of the vicar Apostolic, and Hierachalis that of the prefect Apostolic. These results are most encouraging, when the great difficulties confronting the missionaries are considered. In 1909 the approximate statistics for the two missions were: 1 bishop; 14 priests; 3 catechists; 22 missionary sisters; 480 children in Catholic schools; 175 baptisms of children, 315 of adults. In Little Namaqualand the natives understand Dutch or English; but in Great Namaqualand, besides German, the extremely difficult language of the Hottentots has to be mastered.

For reports and statistics of the missions, consult the following periodicals: *Annales salésiennes* (Paris), an illustrated monthly; *Licht* (Vienna); *Echo of the Oblates of Saint Francis de Sales* (Childs, Maryland). Cf. also *Missiones Catholicæ* (Rome, 1907); *Statesman's Year Book* (London).

J. J. ISENRING.

Orans (ORANTE).—Among the subjects depicted in the art of the Roman catacombs one of those most numerously represented is that of a female figure with extended arms known as the Orans, or one who prays. The custom of praying in antiquity with outstretched, raised arms was common to both Jews and Gentiles; indeed the iconographic type of the Orans was itself strongly influenced by classic representations (see Leclercq, "Manuel d'arch. chrét.", I, 155). But the meaning of the Orans of Christian art is quite different from that of its prototypes. Numerous Biblical figures, for instance, depicted in the catacombs—Noah, Abraham, Isaac, the Three Children in the Fiery Furnace, Daniel in the lions' den—are pictured asking the Lord to deliver the soul of the person on whose tombs they are depicted as He once delivered the particular personage represented. But besides these Biblical Orans figures there exist in the catacombs many ideal figures (153 in all) in the ancient attitude of prayer, which, according to Wilpert, are to be regarded as symbols of the deceased's soul in heaven, praying for its friends on earth. This symbolic meaning accounts for the fact that the great majority of the figures of this order are female, even when depicted on the tombs of men. One of the most convincing proofs that the Orans was regarded as a symbol of the soul is an ancient lead medal in the Vatican Museum showing the martyr, St. Lawrence, under torture, while his soul, in the form of a female Orans, is just leaving the body (see Kraus, "Gesch. der christl. Kunst.", I, 126, fig. 56). An arcosolium in the Ostrianum cemetery represents an Orans with a petition for her intercession: *Victoriæ Virgini* . . . *Pete*. . . . The Acts of St. Cecilia speaks of souls leaving the body in the form of virgins: "Vidit egredientes animas eorum de corporibus, quasi virgines de thalamo", and so also the Acts of Sts. Peter and Marcellinus.

Very probably the medieval representations of a diminutive body, figure of the soul, issuing from the mouths of the dying, to be received by angels or demons, were reminiscences of the Orans as a symbol of the soul. The earlier Orantes were depicted in the simplest garb, and without any striking individual traits, but in the fourth century the figures become richly adorned, and of marked individuality—an indication of the approach of historic art. One of the most remarkable figures of the Orans cycle, dating from the early fourth century, is interpreted by Wilpert as the Blessed Virgin interceding for the friends of the deceased. Directly in front of Mary is a boy, not in the Orans attitude and supposed to be the Divine Child, while to the right and left are monograms of Christ.

LOWRIE, *Monuments of the Early Church* (New York, 1901); KRAUS, *Geschichte der christl. Kunst.* (Freiburg, 1895); WILPERT, *Ein Cyklus christologischer Gemälde* (Freiburg, 1891); NORTHCOTE AND BROWNLOW, *Roma Sotterranea* (London, 1879).

MAURICE M. HASSETT.

Orate Fratres, the exhortation ("Pray brethren that my sacrifice and yours be acceptable to God the Father almighty") addressed by the celebrant to the people before the Secrets in the Roman Mass. It is answered: "May the Lord receive the sacrifice from thy hands to the praise and glory of his name, and for our benefit also and for that of all his holy Church."

THE BLESSED VIRGIN AS AN ORANTE
Fourth Century fresco in the Cœmeterium Ostrianum

The celebrant adds: "Amen". The form is merely an expansion of the usual *Oremus* before any prayer. It is a medieval amplification. The Jacobite rite has an almost identical form before the Anaphora (Brightman, "Eastern Liturgies", Oxford, 1896, 83); the Nestorian celebrant says: "My brethren, pray for me" (ib., 274). Such invitations, often made by the deacon, are common in the Eastern rites. The Gallican rite had a similar one (Duchesne, "Christian Worship", London, 1904, 109). The Mozarabic invitation at this place is: "Help me brethren by your prayers and pray to God for me" (P. L., LXXXV, 537). The medieval derived rites had similar formulæ (e. g. "Missale Sarum", Burntisland, 1861–3, 596). Many of the old Roman Secrets (really Offertory prayers) contain the same ideas. Durandus knows the *Orate Fratres* in a slightly different form ("Rationale", IV, 32). A proof that it is not an integral part of the old Roman Mass is that it is always said, not sung, aloud (as also are the prayers at the foot of the altar, the last Gospel etc.). The celebrant after the "Suscipe Sancta Trinitas" kisses the altar, turns to the people and says: *Orate fratres*, extending and joining his hands. Turning back he finishes the sentence inaudibly. At high Mass the deacon or subdeacon, at low Mass the server, answers. The rubric of the Missal is: "The server or people around answer, if not the priest himself." In this last case he naturally changes the word *tuis* to *meis*.

Gihr, *The Holy Sacrifice of the Mass* (3rd ed., St. Louis, 1908), 547-50.

ADRIAN FORTESCUE.

Oratorians. See ORATORY OF SAINT PHILIP NERI.

Oratorio, as at present understood, is a musical composition for solo voices, chorus, orchestra, and organ, to a religious text generally taken from Holy Scripture. The dramatic element contained in the text depends for its expression on the music alone.

The tradition that the oratorio originated in St. Philip Neri's oratory has recently been attacked, notably by the historian and critic E. Schelle, in "Neue Zeitschrift für Musik" (Leipzig, 1864). The chief point he makes is that the oratories of San Girolamo and Santa Maria in Vallicella, at Rome, were unsuitable for the performance of sacred dramas. In refutation, it suffices to recall the established fact that Emiglio del Cavaglieri's *rapprasentazione sacra*, "Anima e corpo", had its first performance in the Vallicella (Chiesa Nuova) in 1600, five years after the death of St. Philip. Although the name *oratorio* was not applied to the new form until sixty years later (Andrea Bontempi, 1624-1705), there is an unbroken tradition connecting the exercises established by St. Philip with the period when the new art-form received its definite character. While in the sixteenth century liturgical polyphonic music reached its highest development, secular music boasted only one *ensemble* or choral form, the madrigal. The spirit of the Renaissance, that is the revolt against the domination of the arts by the spirit of the Church, led to the restoration of Greek monody, and gradually perfected compositions for one or more voices and instruments which ultimately culminated in the opera.

St. Philip, realizing the great power of music, provided in the rule for his congregation, "that his fathers together with the faithful, should rouse themselves to the contemplation of heavenly things by means of musical harmony". He seized upon the good in the new trend and made it the foundation of a new form upon which he, perhaps unconsciously, put a stamp retained ever since. He practically created a style midway between liturgical and secular music. His love of simplicity caused him to oppose and counteract the prevailing artificial semi-pagan, literary, and oratorical style which had its musical counterpart in the display of contrapuntal skill for its own sake practised to so great an extent at that time. He drew to himself masters like Giovanni Annimuccia and Pier Luigi da Palestrina, formed them spiritually, and bade them set to music, in simple and clear style, for three or four voices, short poems in the vernacular, generally written by himself, and called "Laudi spirituali". Many of these were preserved by F. Soto di Langa, a musician and a disciple of the saint. Their performance alternated with spiritual reading, prayer, and a sermon by one of the fathers, by a layman, or even by a boy. From these exercises, which attracted enormous crowds, and obtained great renown throughout Italy, it was but a step to the *Commedia harmonica* "Amfiparnasso", by Orazio Vecchi (1550-1605), a dialogue in madrigal form between two choirs (first performed at Modena in 1594), and the *rapprasentazione sacra* "Anima e corpo", by Cavaglieri. The latter consisted of short phrases for a single voice, more varied in form than the *recitativo secco*, but not yet sufficiently developed to have a distinct melodic physiognomy, accompanied by instruments, and choral numbers, or madrigals. Similar productions multiplied rapidly. Wherever the Oratorians established themselves they cultivated this form to attract the young people. The municipal library of Hamburg contains a collection, gathered by Chrysander, of twenty-two different texts which originated with the disciples of St. Philip during the second half of the seventeenth century. Even more active in the creation and propagation of these musico-dramatic productions throughout this period were the Jesuits, who, especially in Germany, used these musical plays in their schools and colleges everywhere. Up to the latter part of the seventeenth century the burden of the texts for these compositions was either a legend, the history of a conversion, the life of a saint, or the passion of a martyr.

Among those who cultivated, or helped in developing, the oratorio in Italy were Benedetto Ferrari (1597-1681), "Samsone"; Agostino Agazzari (1578-1640), *dramma pastorale*, "Eumelio"; Loreto Vitorii (1588-1670) "La pellegrina costante", "Sant' Ignazio Loyola". Giacomo Carissimi (1604-74), through whom the oratorio made a notable advance, was the first master to turn to Holy Scripture for his texts. His works, with Latin or Italian texts, many of which have been preserved (see CARISSIMI) together with those of his contemporaries, show practically the same construction as is followed in the present time: recitatives, arias, duets, and terzettos, alternating with single and double choruses and instrumental numbers. The *historicus* or narrator (in some scores designated by the word *testo*, "text") has replaced scenic display and dramatic action. Carissimi's orchestration exhibits a resourcefulness and charm before unknown. His oratorio "Jephtha" (in an arrangement by Dr. Immanuel Faisst) was performed successfully at Leipzig as recently as 1873. After him, the greatest Italian master was Alessandro Scarlatti (1659-1725) a pupil of Francesco Provenzale and Carissimi. Chief among his works are "I dolori di Maria" and "Il Sacrificio d'Abramo".

About this time the leadership passed to Germany, where Heinrich Schütz (1585-1672) had previously prepared the soil by his compositions known as "Passion music" and other works resembling the Italian oratorio. Others who had received their formation in Italy, but whose activity was chiefly confined to Germany, and who transplanted the oratorio thither, were Ignatius Jacob Holzbauer (1711-83), "Bethulia liberata"; Johann Adolphe Hasse (1699-1783), "La Conversione di S. Agostino" etc.; Antonio Caldara (1670-1736); Nicolo Jomelli (1714-1774); Marc-Antoine Charpentier (1634-1704), a pupil of Carissimi and a gifted composer, wrote, besides a large number of works for the church, several oratorios in the style of his master which had great vogue in France. His "Reniement de St. Pierre" has recently been revived with great success in Paris, and has since been published. In the hands of Johann Mattheson (1681-1764), the oratorio becomes identified with Protestant worship in Germany. Contemporary with George Frederick Händel (1685-1759) he wrote twenty-four oratorios, intended to be divided into two parts by a sermon, the whole constituting a religious service. His texts were mostly taken from Scripture. Biblical events are brought into conjunction and contrasted with contemporary happenings, and a moral is drawn. Others who cultivated the oratorio form, particularly in Protestant Germany, were George Philip Telemann (1681-1767), Constantine Bellermann (1696-1758), and Dietrich Buxtehude (1637-1707).

Through Händel the oratorio attained a position in musical art more important than at any previous period in its history and never surpassed since. In his hands it became the expression of the sturdy Saxon faith unaffected by the spirit of doubt latent in the religious revolt of the sixteenth century. Formed in Germany and Italy, he united in a pre-eminent degree the highest creative gifts. The most productive period of his life was spent in England, and, after having cultivated the opera for a number of years, he finally turned to the oratorio, producing a series of works ("The Messiah", "Israel in Egypt", "Saul", "Jephtha", "Belshazar", "Samson" etc.) unrivalled for heroic grandeur and brilliancy. It may be said that they express the national religious ideal of a Protestant Christian people more adequately than does their form of worship. This undoubtedly accounts for the interest taken in oratorio performances by the people in England and in Protestant Germany. Joseph Haydn (1732–1809) produced two of the greatest oratorios which we possess: "The Creation" and "The Seasons". While composed to secular texts, they breathe the most tender piety and joy through an inexhaustible wealth of lyric and lofty music. A third oratorio, "Ritorno di Tobia", on a Biblical text, has not the same importance, nor does Mozart (1756–91), in his only oratorio, "Davidde penitente", attain the artistic level of most of his productions. Ludwig van Beethoven (1770–1827) wrote one oratorio, "The Mount of Olives", which shows him at his best.

Felix Mendelssohn-Bartholdy (1809–47), in "Elijah" and "St. Paul", returns to the early Protestant feature of letting the supposed congregation or audience participate in the performance by singing the chorales or church hymns, the texts of which consist of reflections and meditations on what has preceded. From this period the oratorio begins to be cultivated almost exclusively by Catholics. Franz Liszt (1811–86), with his "Christus" and "Legende der Heiligen Elizabeth", opens up a new and distinctly Catholic era. France, which, since the days of Charpentier, had practically neglected the oratorio, probably on account of the opera appealing more strongly to French taste and temperament, and because of the lack of amateur singers has, within the last thirty years, furnished a number of remarkable works. Charles-François Gounod (1818–93) with his "Redemption", and "Mors et Vita", gave a renewed impetus to the cultivation of the oratorio. The "Samson and Delilah" of Camille Saint-Saëns (1835–) may be performed either as an oratorio or as an opera; as opera it has attained the greater favour. Jules Massenet (1842–) has essayed the form with his "Eve" and "Mary Magdalen", but his style is entirely too sensational and melodramatic to carry the text. Gabriel Pierné's (1863–) "Children's Crusade" and the smaller work, "The Children at Bethlehem", have both obtained great popularity in Europe and America.

Italy's sole representative of any note in more than two hundred years is Don Lorenzo Perosi (1872–), with his trilogy "The Passion of Our Lord according to St. Mark", "The Transfiguration of Christ", and "The Resurrection of Lazarus", a "Christmas Oratorio", "Leo the Great", and "The Last Judgment". Belgium and England have produced the three most remarkable exponents of the oratorio within the last fifty years. César Auguste Franck's (1822–90) oratorios, "Ruth", "Rebecca", "Redemption", and, above all, his "Beatitudes", rank among the greatest of modern works of the kind. Edward William Elgar (1857–) has become famous by his "Dream of Gerontius" and his "Apostles". But Edgar Tinel (1854–) is probably the most gifted among the modern Catholics who have reclaimed the oratorio from non-Catholic supremacy. His world-famous "St. Francis of Assisi" is perhaps more remarkable for the spiritual heights it reveals than for its dramatic power. Other works of his which have attracted attention are "Godoleva" and "St. Catherine". It is a happy omen that all these authors, in the fore-front of present-day composers, command the highest creative and constructive skill which enables them to turn into Catholic channels all the modern conquests in means of expression. The Catholic Oratorio Society of New York was founded in 1904 to promote the knowledge and reproduction of oratorios that best exemplify the religious ideal.

CAPECELATRO, tr. POPE, *The Life of St. Philip Neri* (London, 1894); KRETZSCHMAR, *Führer durch den Concertsaal*, II (Leipzig, 1899); REIMANN, *Geschichte der Musiktheorie* (Leipzig, 1898); SPITTA, *Die Passionsmusiken von Sebastian Bach und Heinrich Schütz* (Hamburg, 1893); *Jahrbuch der Musikbibliothek Peters für 1903* (Leipzig, 1904).

JOSEPH OTTEN.

Oratory (Lat. *oratorium*, from *orare*, to pray), as a general term, signifies a place of prayer, but technically it means a structure other than a parish church, set aside by ecclesiastical authority for prayer and the celebration of Mass. Oratories seem to have originated from the chapels erected over the tombs of the early martyrs where the faithful resorted to pray, and also from the necessity of having a place of worship for the people in country districts when churches proper were restricted to cathedral cities. We also find early mention of private oratories for the celebration of Mass by bishops, and later of oratories attached to convents and to the residences of nobles. In the Eastern Church, where the parochial organization is neither so complete nor so rigid as in the West, private oratories were so numerous as to constitute an abuse. In the Latin Church oratories are classed as (1) public, (2) semipublic, and (3) private.

(1) PUBLIC ORATORIES are canonically erected by the bishop and are perpetually dedicated to the Divine service. They must have an entrance and exit from the public road. Priests who celebrate Mass in public oratories must conform to the office proper to those oratories, whether secular or regular. If, however, the calendar of an oratory permits a votive Mass to be said, the visiting priest may celebrate in conformity with his own diocesan or regular calendar.

(2) SEMIPUBLIC ORATORIES are those which, though erected in a private building, are destined for the use of a community. Such are the oratories of seminaries, pious congregations, colleges, hospitals, prisons, and such institutions. If, however, there be several oratories in one house, it is only the one in which the Blessed Sacrament is preserved that has the privileges of a semipublic oratory. All semipublic oratories (which class technically includes the private chapel of a bishop) are on the same footing as public oratories in regard to the celebration of Mass. The calendar of feasts to be observed in them (unless they belong to a regular order having its proper calendar) is that of the diocese. In oratories belonging to nuns, the feasts of their community are to be celebrated in accordance with the decrees or indults they have received from the Holy See. Regulars visiting a semipublic oratory cannot celebrate the feasts of saints of their own order unless the calendar proper to the oratory prescribes the same or permits of a votive Mass. Public and semipublic oratories are ordinarily under the control of the bishop. The Congregation of Rites declared (23 Jan., 1899): "In these (oratories), as, by the authority of the ordinary, the holy sacrifice of the Mass can be offered, so also all those present thereat can satisfy thereby the precept which obliges the faithful to hear Mass on prescribed days." The same decree also gives an authoritative definition of the three species of oratories.

(3) PRIVATE ORATORIES are those erected in private houses for the convenience of some person or family by an indult of the Holy See. They can be erected only by permission of the pope. Oratories in private houses date from Apostolic times when the Sacred Mysteries could not be publicly celebrated owing to the persecutions. Even after the peace of Constantine, the custom continued to prevail. Kings and nobles especially had such oratories erected in their palaces. As early as the reign of Emperor Justinian, we find regulations concerning private oratories as distinguished from public churches, and prohibitions against saying Mass in private houses (Novel., lviii and cxxxi). Permissions to celebrate were granted, however, freely in the West by popes and councils. The latest decree regulating private oratories is that of the Sacred Con-

gregation of the Discipline of the Sacraments of 7 Feb., 1909. According to this, private oratories are conceded by the Holy See only on account of bodily infirmity, or difficulty of access to a public church or as a reward for services done to the Holy See or to the Catholic cause. The grant of a private oratory may be temporary or for the life of the grantee, according to the nature of the cause that is adduced. In either case, the simple concession of an oratory implies that only one Mass a day may be celebrated, that the precept of the Church concerning the hearing of Mass on prescribed days (certain special festivals generally specified in the indult excluded) may be there satisfied only by the grantees, and that the determination of the place, city, and diocese where the oratory is to be erected is approved. The rescript will be forwarded to the ordinary. The decree then recites the various extensions of the before-mentioned privileges that may be conceded to grantees:

(a) *As to the satisfaction of the precept of hearing Mass:* This is usually conceded by the indult only to the following: relatives of the grantee living under the same roof, dependants of the family, and guests or those who share his table. The others living in the house may not satisfy the precept except it be a funeral Mass or on account of the distance of the public church. If the oratory be a rural one, those employed on the estate may there hear Mass, but in that case the grantee must provide for a catechetical instruction and an explanation of the Gospel. The same holds for a private oratory in a camp or castle or a widespread domain. In very peculiar circumstances (to be judged by the ordinary) all others may also hear Mass in a private oratory while the conditions prevail.

(b) *As to hearing Mass in the absence of the grantees:* This is allowed in the presence of one of the relatives living under the same roof, but the concession is to be understood of a temporary absence of the grantees and that the relative be expressly determined. The same is extended to the principal one among the familiars, rural servants, or dependants.

(c) *As to the number of Masses:* If the grantees are two priests who are brothers, both may celebrate Mass. A thanksgiving Mass is also allowed if the ordinary recommends it. Priests who are guests may say Mass in the oratory of the house where they are staying if they have commendatory letters from the ordinary, provided they are infirm or the church is distant. Several Masses may also be said during the last agony or at the death or anniversary of one of the grantees and likewise on the feast of his patron saint.

(d) *As to greater festivals:* By an extension of privileges, Mass may be allowed in private oratories on all days except on the feast of the local patron, the Assumption, Christmas, and Easter. Sometimes the concession may extend to the first three feasts, but very rarely to Easter, and then only on the urgent recommendation of the ordinary, exception being made for grantees who are infirm priests.

(e) *As to concessions:* Sometimes a grantee may have the rights of a private oratory in two dioceses, but then both ordinaries must give testimonial letters. In case the oratory is situated in a place where the parish priest has to say two Masses on the same day, a priest from some other place may say Mass in the oratory but he may not say another Mass in addition. An oratory near a sick-room is also allowed occasionally during sickness. This decree likewise allows ordinaries (for ten cases only) to grant a private oratory to poor priests who are aged and infirm. It will be noted that this legislation is a very liberal extension of the provisions formerly governing private oratories.

TAUNTON, *Law of the Church* (London, 1906), s. v. *Oratory;* FERRARIS, *Bibliotheca canonica* (Rome, 1889), s. v *Oratorium; Analecta Eccles.* (Rome, April, 1910).

WILLIAM H. W. FANNING.

Oratory of Saint Philip Neri, THE.—Under this head are included the Italian, Spanish, English, and other communities, which follow the rule of St. Philip Neri. The revolt of the sixteenth century, though apparently threatening in its spread and strength the very life of the Church, evoked a marvellous display of its Divine fecundity. That century saw the origin of the Society of Jesus, founded by St. Ignatius Loyola; the Theatines, by St. Cajetan; the Barnabites, by St. A. M. Zaccaria; the Brothers Hospitallers, by St. John of God; the Oratory of St. Philip. The foundation of the last was laid at S. Girolamo, Rome, where his disciples gathered for spiritual instruction. Gradually these conferences took definite shape, and St. Philip, now a priest, constructed an oratory over the aisle of S. Girolamo, where they might be held; from this probably the congregation was named. In 1564 he took charge of the church of the Florentines, where his disciples who were priests said Mass and preached four sermons daily, interspersed by hymns and popular devotions. Eleven years' work at St. John's proved to the growing community the necessity of having a church of their own and of living under a definite rule. They obtained from the pope the church of S. Maria in Vallicella, rebuilt and now known as the Chiesa Nuova, where the congregation was erected by Gregory XIII, 15 July, 1575. The new community was to be a congregation of secular priests living under obedience, but bound by no vows. So particular was St. Philip on this point that he ruled, that even if the majority wished to bind themselves by vows, the minority who did not were to possess the property of the community. "Habeant possideant", were St. Philip's words. Another characteristic of the institute was the fact that each house was independent, and when it was represented to him, that while one house might have but a handful of members and another a surplus, both would benefit by a transference of subjects from the more numerous community, he replied, "Let each house live by its own vitality, or perish of its own decrepitude." His motive probably was to exclude the possibility of any community lingering in a state of decay.

The rule, an embodiment of St. Philip's mode of governing, was not drawn up till seventeen years after his death, and was finally approved by Paul V in 1612. The provost is elected for three years by a majority of all the decennial Fathers, i. e., those who have been ten years in the congregation. To assist him in the government of the congregation four deputies are elected. All matters of grave importance are decided by the general congregation, only the decennial Fathers voting. Admission to the congregation is also by election, and the candidate must be "natus ad institutum", between the ages of eighteen and forty, and possessed of sufficient income to maintain himself. The novitiate lasts three years, and was probably thus extended to test thoroughly the vocation to an institute not bound by vows. At the conclusion of the three years, the novice if approved becomes a triennial Father and a member of the congregation, but he has no elective vote till his ten years are completed, when by election he becomes a decennial. Expulsion is effected by a majority of two-thirds of the voters. No member is allowed to take any ecclesiastical dignity. Regulations for the clothing, mode of life in the community, and for the refectory are also laid down. The object of the institute is threefold: prayer, preaching, and the sacraments. "Prayer" includes special care in carrying out the liturgical Offices, the Fathers being present in choir at the principal feasts, as well as assisting at the daily popular devotions. The "Sacraments" imply their frequent reception, which had fallen into disuse at the foundation of the Oratory. For this purpose one of the Fathers is to sit daily in the confessional, and all are to be present in their confessionals on the eve of feasts. The mode of direction as taught by St. Philip is to be gentle rather than severe, and abuses are to be attacked indirectly. "Once let a little love find entrance to their hearts," said St. Philip, "and the rest will follow."

"Preaching" included, as has been said, four sermons in succession daily, an almost impossible strain upon the hearers as it would now appear, but the discourses at the Oratory had an attraction of their own. Savonarola had already compared the inability of the preachers of his day to awaken dead souls with their subtle arguments and rhetorical periods, to the impotent efforts of the flute-players to revivify by their mournful music the corpse of Jairus's daughter, and Bembo in St. Philip's day reiterated this reproach. "What can I hear in sermons", he says, "but Doctor Subtilis striving with Doctor Angelicus, and Aristotle coming in as a third to decide the quarrel." The sermons at the Oratory were free from these defects. They were simple and familiar discourses; the first an exposition on some point of the spiritual reading which preceded them and therefore impromptu; the next would be on some text of Holy Scripture; the third on ecclesiastical history, and the fourth on the lives of the saints. Each sermon lasted half an hour, when a bell was rung and the preacher at once ceased speaking. The music, though popular, was of a high order. Palestrina, a penitent of the saint, composed many of the Laudi which were sung. Their excellence excited the admiration of foreigners. John Evelyn in his diary, 8 November, 1644, speaks of himself as ravished with the entertainment of the sermon by a boy and the musical services at the Roman Oratory. Animuccia, choir master at St. Peter's, attended constantly to lead the singing. In close connexion with the Oratory is the Brotherhood of the Little Oratory, a confraternity of clerics and laymen, first formed from the disciples of St. Philip who assembled in his room for mental prayer and Mass on Sundays, visited in turn a hospital daily, and took the discipline at the exercises of the Passion on Friday. They made together the pilgrimage of the seven churches, especially at carnival time, and their devout and recollected demeanour converted many.

The "exercises", as the Oratory services were called, aroused bitter opposition. The preachers were denounced as teaching extravagant and unsound doctrine, the processions were forbidden, and St. Philip himself was suspended from preaching. He submitted at once and forbade any action being taken in his favour. At length Paul IV, having made due investigation, sent for him and bade him go on with his good work. Baronius says of these exercises that they seemed to recall the simplicity of the Apostolic times; Bacci testifies to the holiness of many under St. Philip's care. Among the most celebrated members were Baronius, author of the "Ecclesiastical Annals", and the "Martyrology", to prepare him for which work St. Philip obliged him to preach the history of the Church for thirty years in the Oratory; Bozio Tommaso, author of many learned works; B. Giovenale Ancina, Superior of the Oratory at Naples, and later Bishop of Saluzzo, a close friend of St. Francis de Sales; B. Antonio Grassi of the Oratory of Fermo; B. Sebastian Valfré, the "Apostle of Turin", and founder of the Oratory there. The Oratory Library of S. Maria in Vallicella is celebrated for the number and quality of its contents, among them the well-known Codex Vallicensis. Up to 1800 the Oratory continued to spread through Italy, Sicily, Spain, Portugal, Poland, and other European countries; in South America, Brazil, India, Ceylon, the founder of which was the celebrated missioner Giuseppe de Vaz. Under Napoleon I the Oratory was in various places despoiled and suppressed, but the congregation recovered and, after a second suppression in 1869, again revived; many of its houses still exist.

ORATORIANS, ENGLISH.—The Oratory was founded in England by Cardinal Newman in 1847. Converted in 1845, he went to Rome in 1846 and with the advice of Pius IX selected the Oratory of St. Philip Neri as best adapted for his future work. After a short novitiate at Santa Croce he returned in 1847 with a Brief from Pius IX for founding the Oratory. He established himself at Maryvale, Old Oscott, where in 1848 he was joined by Father Faber and his Wilfridian community. After a temporary sojourn at St. Wilfrid's, Staffordshire, and Alcester St., Birmingham, the community found a permanent home at Edgbaston, a suburb of that town, in 1854. The institute of the English congregation is substantially that of the Roman. The Fathers live under St. Philip's Rule and carry out his work. In compliance with a widely expressed wish of English Catholics, Cardinal Newman founded at Edgbaston a still flourishing higher class school for boys. A Brotherhood of the Little Oratory is also attached to the community and the exercises are a focus of spiritual life. Among the best known writers of the English Oratory are, besides its illustrious head, Father Caswell, a poet, Father Ignatius Ryder, a controversialist and essayist, and Father Pope. A Newman memorial church in the classical style was opened in 1910. The library contains among many valuable works Cardinal Newman's series of the Fathers.

The London Oratory.—In 1849 Cardinal Newman sent a detachment of his community to found a house in London. Premises were secured at 24 and 25 King William St., Strand, a chapel was speedily arranged, and on 31 May, Cardinal Wiseman assisted pontifically and preached at the high Mass; Father Newman delivered at Vespers the sermon on the "Prospects of the Catholic Missioner", now published in his "Discourses to Mixed Congregations". The Catholic Directory of 1849 shows that the Oratory at King William St. was the first public church served by a religious community to be opened in the diocese. The exercises of the Oratory, accompanied as they were with hymns composed by Father Faber and the Roman devotions and processions, then strange to England, seemed to many a hazardous innovation. Time proved the popularity of the exercises, and Father Faber's preaching attracted large crowds. His spiritual works published year by year increased the interest in his Oratory, while the lives of the saints edited by him, forty-two in number, in spite of their literary defects, did a great work in setting forth the highest examples of Christian holiness. The community removed to their present site in South Kensington in 1854, and in 1884 their new church was opened in the presence of the bishops of England. Among the writers of the London Oratory may be named, after Father Faber, Father Dalgairns (q. v.); Father Stanton, "Menology of England and Wales" (London, 1887); Father Hutchison, "Loreto and Nazareth" (London, 1863); Father Knox, "The Douai Diary" (London, 1878), and "Life of Cardinal Allen" (London, 1882); Father Philpin de Rivière, "The Holy Places", and other works; Father John Bowden, "Life of Fr. Faber" (London, 1869); Father Morris, "Life of St. Patrick"; and Father Antrobus, translator of Pastor's "Popes" (vols. I–VI, St. Louis, 1902) and the "Pregi dell' Oratorio".

WOODHEAD, *The Institutions of the Oratory* (Oxford, 1687); GALLONIO, *Vita Beati Philippi Nerii* (Rome, 1600, tr. into Italian, Rome, 1601); BACCI, *Vita del B. Filippo Neri* (Rome, 1622, frequently reprinted; tr. into English, 2 vols., 1847; new ed., with illustrations, notes, etc., by ANTROBUS, 2 vols., London, 1902); IDEM, *Vita con l'aggiunta d'una notitia d'alcuni suoi compagni per G. Ricci* (O.P.), tr. into English, *The Companions of St. Philip* (London, 1848); SONZONIO, *Vita del Santo Patr., Filippo Neri* (Venice, 1727; 2nd ed., Padua, 1733); CAPECELATRO, *La Vita di S. Filippo Neri* (2 vols., Naples, 1879; tr. into English by POPE, 2 vols., London, 1882); IDEM, *Card. Newman e la religione Cattolica in Inghilterra* (2 vols., Naples, 1859); FABER, *The Spirit and Genius of St. Philip* (London, 1850); IDEM, *The School of St. Philip*, tr. from Italian (London, 1850); *Pregi della Congr. dell' Oratorio* (Venice, 1825; tr. into English by ANTROBUS, London, 1881); MARCIANO, *Memorie Historiche della Congr. dell' Oratorio* (5 vols. fol., Naples, 1693–1702); *Centenario di S. Filippo Neri in*

Periodico Mensuale (Rome, 1894–5); see also works cited in prefaces to translation of Bacci, ed., ANTROBUS (London, 1902).

H. BOWDEN.

ORATORY, FRENCH CONGREGATION OF THE, founded at Paris at the beginning of the seventeenth century by Cardinal Pierre de Bérulle (q. v.), who, in Bossuet's words, "made glisten in the Church of France the purest and most sublime lights of the Christian priesthood and the ecclesiastical life". It was precisely to work more effectively towards the rehabilitation of the ecclesiastical life that Cardinal de Bérulle founded (in 1611) the new congregation, which he named after that of St. Philip Neri, adopting also in part the rules and constitutions of the latter. To meet the special needs of the Church in France at the period, however, and because of the tendency toward centralization which "especially from this period forms one of the dominant characteristics of the French national spirit" (Perraud), he made one very important modification; whereas in the Italian congregation the houses were independent of one another, de Bérulle placed the government of all the houses in the hands of the superior-general. On 10 May, 1613, Paul III issued a Bull approving the new institute, which now made great progress. During the lifetime of its founder, more than fifty houses were either established or united to the Oratory; subsequently there were more than twice this number, divided into four provinces. As St. Philip had wished, so also the French Oratory was solely for priests; the members were bound by no vows except those of the priesthood, and had for sole aim the perfect fulfilment of their priestly functions. The Congregation of the Oratory is not a teaching order; Oratorians have directed many colleges, notably de Juilly; but neither this nor instruction in seminaries was ever the sole object of the congregation, though it was the first to organize seminaries in France according to the ordinances of the Council of Trent. The congregations of M. Bourdoise, St. Nicolas du Chardonnet, Saint-Sulpice, and Saint-Lazare were all inspired by the ideas of Cardinal de Bérulle. The definite aim and characteristic of the French Oratory is in the words of Cardinal Perraud "the pursuit of sacerdotal perfection".

The supreme authority of the congregation is vested in the superior-general (elected for life) and in the general assemblies convoked regularly every three years—or extraordinarily immediately on the resignation or death of a general. These assemblies are composed of members who have been seven years in the congregation and three in the priesthood; the number of members is one out of every twelve Oratorians thus qualified, and they are elected by all Oratorian priests three years in the congregation. The general assemblies appoint all the officers—a superior general (if necessary), his three assistants, the visitors, the procurator general, and the secretary general. They also examine and decide upon all questions of any importance concerning the congregation in general; the general and his assistants, in the interval between the assemblies, exercise only ordinary administration. The founder, who died at the altar in 1629, was succeeded by Father Charles de Condren, who, like Father de Bérulle, was imbued with the spirit of the Oratorians from his youth. Even during his life, Saint Jeanne de Chantal wrote of him that "it would seem that Father de Condren was capable of teaching the angels"; St. Vincent de Paul was wont to say that "there had never been a man like him". Father de Condren governed the Oratory most wisely, completing its organization according to the intentions of its founder. Among his works must be specially remembered the part he played in the institution of Saint-Sulpice, whose founder, the saintly and celebrated Olier (q. v.), was under his direction. He died in 1641; his remains, recovered by the present writer in 1884, are now preserved in the choir of the chapel of the college of Juilly. The succeeding generals were: François Bourgoing (q. v.; 1641–62); François Senault (1662–72), a celebrated preacher; Abel-Louis de Sainte-Marthe, who resigned in 1696, only to die the following year. During his generalship the congregation was greatly disturbed by the troubles of Jansenism (see A. M. P. Ingold, "Le pretendu jansénisme du P. de Ste-Marthe", Paris, 1882). There was the same disturbance under his successor, Father Pierre d'Arérez de la Tour (1696–1733), who began by appealing against the Bull "Unigenitus", with the Archbishop of Paris and a large part of the French clergy. Later, however, having a better knowledge of the facts, he revoked his appeal, and also obtained the submission of Cardinal de Noailles—which shows that his difficulty was not a doctrinal one, but arose rather from considerations of discipline and opportuneness. Many Oratorians have been caluminated on this point by prejudiced or ignorant historians, as the present writer has endeavoured to prove in several publications. Father d'Arérez de la Tour was one of the most esteemed spiritual directors of his time. The seventh general was Father Thomas de la Valette (1733–72); the eighth, Father Louis de Muly (1773–9); the ninth, Father Sauvé Moisset (1779–90).

On the death of this last, at the height of the French Revolution, the congregation was unable to meet in a general assembly to elect a successor, and was soon engulfed in the revolutionary storm, which overwhelmed the Church in France; but, in dying, the Oratory again attested to its faithful attachment to the Chair of Peter. If some of the Oratorians at this time supported Constitutionalism, the great majority remained faithful to the Catholic Faith, and a certain number among them paid for their fidelity by their lives (cf. Ingold, "L'Oratoire et la Révolution", Paris, 1885).

It was only in 1852 that the French Congregation of the Oratory was restored by Father Gratry (q. v.) and Father Pététot, the latter, who was earlier pastor of Saint-Roch de Paris, becoming first superior-general of the revived institute. In 1884 he resigned and was replaced by Father (later Cardinal) Perraud. Father Pététot died in 1887. Father Perraud's successor, Father Marius Nouvelle, still governs the congregation, which, greatly weakened by the persecution which reigns in France, numbers only a few members, residing for the most part in Paris.

The French Oratory at various stages in its history has given a large number of distinguished subjects to the Church; preachers like Lejeune (q. v.), Massillon (q. v.), and Mascaron; philosophers like Malebranche, (q. v.); theologians like Thomassin (q. v.), Morin (q. v.); exegetes like Houbigant (q. v.), Richard Simon, Duguet. One must note, however, that the last two were forced to leave the congregation where they had been trained—the former on account of the rashness of his exegesis, the latter in consequence of his Jansenistic tendencies.

Naturally, the Oratory of France exercised little direct influence in foreign countries, except through its houses, St. Louis-des-Français in Rome, Madrid, and Lisbon. In connexion with England, Father de Bérulle's mission with twelve of his confrères at the court of Henrietta of France (1625), wife of the unfortunate Charles I, must be remembered. Among the Oratorians were Father Harlay de Sancy, Father de Balfour, the latter of an old English family, and Father Robert Philips, a Scotchman and theologian of great merit, who entered the Oratory in 1617 after having been tortured for the Faith in his own country. When Protestant intolerance forced the other Oratorians to leave England, Father Philips remained as confessor to the queen, and in 1644 returned with her to France, where he died in 1647. Later other English ecclesiastics joined the Oratory. Among the best known are: Father William Chalmers of Aberdeen (d. about 1660), who entered the Oratory in 1627, author of "Disputationes philosophicæ" (1630) and an edition of various patristic works (1634). After leaving the Oratory in 1637, he published several other works, including "A Brief History of the Church in Scotland" (1643). Father John Whyte, of Loughill in Ireland, entered the Oratory in 1647 and died a member in 1678. He was also a noted theologian and published "Theoremata ex universa theologia" (1670). A still more distinguished member about this period was Father Stephen Gough of Sussex. At first chaplain to the Anglican Archbishop of Canterbury and doctor at Oxford, he was converted to Catholicism by the Oratorians of the court of Henrietta of France, whom we mentioned above, and in 1652 entered the Oratory of Paris, at the age of twenty-seven. The general of the Oratory, Father Bourgoing, stationed him at Notre-Dame-des-Vertus, near Paris, at the head of a seminary for English Catholic priests which he had founded, and for which the English clergy thanked the Oratory in a beautiful letter of congratulation. From 1661 Father Gough lived in Paris as almoner of the Queen of England. He died of apoplexy in 1682, without publishing the commentary on the Epistles of St. Paul with immediate reference to the Protestant controversy, which he had been preparing for many years. In contrast to this illustrious convert is Father Levassor of Orléans, who entered the Oratory in 1667. A man of ability, but, according to Batterel, "too fond of sport and good cheer", he ended by leaving the Oratory and apostatizing, and died in England in 1718, a canon in the Established Church.

PERRAUD, *L'Oratoire de France* (1865); BATTEREL, *Mémoires domestiques*; INGOLD, *Bibliographie oratorienne*.

A. M. P. INGOLD.

Orbellis, NICOLAS D', Franciscan theologian and philosopher, Scotist; b. about 1400; d. at Rome, 1475. He seems to have entered the monastery of the Observantines, founded in 1407, one of the first in France. He appears to have been professor of theology and philosophy in the University of Angers, where he enjoyed great reputation as an expounder of the teaching of John Duns Scotus. After 1465 he wrote his chief work, a commentary on the Four Books of Sentences. He was interred in the church of the Ara Cœli on the Capitoline. His chief works are: "Expositio in IV Sententiarum Libros", a compilation based on the teachings of John Duns Scotus, published first at Rouen without date or place (s. l. et a.) and then at Rouen without the year (s. a.); at Paris, twice in 1488, again in 1499, 1511, and 1517; at Lyons, 1503; at Hagenau, 1503; Venice, 1507; "Expositio in XII Libros Metaphysicæ Aristotelis secundum viam Scoti" (Bologna, 1485; Paris, 1505); "Ex-

THE LAST JUDGMENT
Andrea Orcagna, Campo Santo, Pisa

positio Logicæ secundum Doctrinam Doctoris Subtilis Scoti" (Parma, 1482; Basle, 1494; Venice, 1507); "Logicæ Summula", with passages from Francis of Mayron, Antonio Andrea, Bonetus, and Scotus (Venice, 1489 and 1500). "Compendium Mathematicum" appeared without place or date (about 1485) (Bologna, 1485); "De Scientia Mathematica, Physica" etc. (Basle, 1494 and 1503).

WADDING, *Annales O. Min.*, XIII (Rome, 1735), 166; XIV, 125; XV, 319; WADDING, *Scriptores O. Min.* (Rome, 1650), 268; *ibid.* (1806), 182 sq.; *ibid.* (1906), 179 sq.; SBARALEA, *Supplement. ad Script. O. Min.* (Rome, 1806), 561-2; GLASSBERGER, *Chronica Observ.* in *Analecta Franciscana*, II (Quaracchi, 1887), 460; OUDINUS, *Scriptores ecclesiast.*, III (Leipzig, 1722), 2546-7; PORT, *Dict. de Maine-et-Loire*, III (Paris, 1878), 35; HAIN, *Repertor. bibliogr.*, 12041ss.; COPPINGER, *Supplem.*, 12043ss.

MICHAEL BIHL.

Orcagna (the conventional name in art history of ANDREA DI CIONE, also called ARCAGNUOLO or ARCANGIO); b. at Florence, early in the fourteenth century; d. there, 1368. The son of a goldsmith, he became architect, sculptor, mosaist, painter, and poet. His brothers, Nardo, Jacopo, and Matteo, were also architects, sculptors, and painters: Nardo, the eldest, painted the famous fresco of "The Last Judgment", still to be seen in the Strozzi chapel in S. Maria Novella, a composition inspired by the "Divina Commedia", and comprising the Judgment, Paradise, and Hell as its three parts. This fresco has been erroneously attributed to Andrea, who became the most famous of the Cioni, but Lorenzo Ghiberti testifies to its being the work of Nardo. In the same way, the "Triumph of Death" and "The Last Judgment" in the Campo Santo of Pisa, owing to their similarity to the S. Maria Novella fresco, used to be attributed to Nardo and Andrea di Cione. Both these brothers were registered in the Florentine Guild of Painters in 1357. In that year Andrea (Orcagna) collaborated with Francesco di Talento on plans for the enlargement of S. Maria del Fiore. In 1358 he executed mosaics for the façade of the cathedral of Orvieto. Vasari makes Andrea Pisano his master in the art of sculpture, but this honour is more probably due to Neri di Fieravante, his sponsor when he matriculated in the Guild of "masters of stone and wood", in 1352.

According to Vasari, the Brotherhood of Orsammichele took the offerings made to the Blessed Virgin during the plague of 1348 and used them to build around her image an elaborately ornamented marble tabernacle. Orcagna was entrusted with this work, which he completed in 1359. For brilliancy and richness of architecture as well as of decoration, Burckhardt regards this tabernacle as the most perfect work of its kind in Italian Gothic. The mysteries of the life of the Blessed Virgin are represented in bas-relief with a series of allegorical figures of the Virtues. The Announcement of Mary's Death and the Assumption are especially worthy of note. This tabernacle of Orsammichele is Orcagna's only authentic sculptural work, but his manner is discernible in the "Annunciation" of Santa Croce and in the bas-reliefs of the Campanile of S. Maria del Fiore which represent the Virtues and Liberal Arts.

The chief paintings of Orcagna which have survived are: a St. Matthew, painted, in collaboration with his brother Jacopo, for S. Maria Novella, now in the Uffizi; a "Virgin with Angels", in the Somzée collection at Brussels; a "Vision of St. Bernard", in the Academy of Florence; a "Coronation of the Virgin", executed for San Pier Maggiore, Florence, now in the National Gallery, London. In 1357 Tommaso di Rossello Strozzi commissioned Orcagna to paint an altar-piece for the same chapel in which Nardo had painted the frescoes. This re-table is divided into five parts: in the centre Christ is enthroned, a pyramidal crown on his brow, two little angels at his feet, playing music; at Christ's right hand is the Blessed Virgin, presenting St. Thomas Aquinas to Him; at His left hand is the Precursor who indicates Christ to a kneeling St. Peter. In the last two compartments are seen, on one side St. Lawrence and St. Paul, on the other St. Michael and St. Catherine. Orcagna was commissioned in the following year to paint the life of the Blessed Virgin on the walls of the choir of S. Maria Novella. These paintings were ruined by damp, owing to a leaking roof, but were restored by Ghirlandajo who drew his inspiration from the happy "inventions of Orcagna" (Vasari).

Vasari, *Le vite de' più eccellenti pittori*, ed. Milanesi, I (Florence, 1878), 593, with the editor's *Commentario alla vita di A. Orcagna*, ibid., 615; Baldinucci, *Vita dell' Orcagna in Notizie dei professori del disegno*, II (Florence, 1768); Crowe and Cavalcaselle, *A New History of Painting in Italy*, II (London, 1865); Burckhardt and Bode, *Le Cicerone*, II, 328; Fr. tr. Gérard (Paris, 1892); Bryan, *Dict. Painters and Engravers*, I (London, 1903); Suida, *Florentinische Maler um die Witte des XIV Jahrhunderts* (Strasburg, 1905); Venturi, *Storia dell' arte italiana*, IV, 637; V, 767 (Milan, 1906–07).

Gaston Sortais.

Orcistus, titular see in Galatia Secunda. It is only mentioned in Peutinger's "Table". An inscription of 331 fixes the site at Alikel Yaila, also called Alekian, in the vilayet of Angora. It was then a station at the intersection of four roads and formed part of the "Diocese of Asia"; consequently it must have belonged to Phrygia. In 451 it was in Galatia Secunda or Salutaris, probably from the formation of that province about 386–95. The name comes from a tribe called Orci, which dwelt in the plains on the eastern frontier of Phrygia. Only three bishops are known: Domnus, at Ephesus (451); Longinus, at Chalcedon (451); and Segermas, at Constantinople (692). But the see is mentioned by the "Notitiæ episcopatuum" until the thirteenth century among the suffragans of Pessinus.

Leake, *Asia Minor*, 71; Hamilton, *Researches in Asia Minor*, I, 446; Ramsay, *Asia Minor*, 228; Le Quien, *Oriens Christ.*, I, 493.

S. Pétridès.

Ordeals (*Iudicium Dei;* Anglo-Saxon, *ordâl;* Ger. *Urteil*) were a means of obtaining evidence by trials, through which, by the direct interposition of God, the guilt or innocence of an accused person was firmly established, in the event that the truth could not be proved by ordinary means. These trials owed their existence to the firm belief that an omniscient and just God would not permit an innocent person to be regarded as guilty and punished in consequence, but that He would intervene, by a miracle if necessary, to proclaim the truth. The ordeals were either imposed by the presiding judge, or chosen by the contesting parties themselves. It was expected that God, approving the act imposed or permitted by an authorized judge, would give a distinct manifestation of the truth to reveal the guilt or innocence of the accused. It was believed from these premises that an equitable judgment must surely result. Ordeals are of two kinds: those undergone only by the accused, and those taken part in by both parties to the action. It was the common opinion that the decision of God was made known in the result of the test, either immediately or after a short time. Ordeals were resorted to when the contesting parties were unable to bring forward further evidence, for according to the ancient German law, the production of evidence was not arranged for by the court itself, but was left to the contestants.

Ordeals were known and practised by various peoples of antiquity, and are still to be met with to-day among uncivilized tribes. The Code of Hammurabi prescribes their use for the ancient Babylonians. The person accused of a certain crime was subjected to the test of cold water, which consisted in the person's plunging into a river; if the river bore him away his guilt was established; if he remained quiet and uninjured in the water, his innocence was believed to have been proved (Winkler, "Die Gesetze Hammurabis", Leipzig, 1902, 10). Among the Jews existed the test of the Water of Jealousy, conducted by the priests, in which the woman accused of adultery must consume the draught in their presence, after having offered certain sacrifices, and the effects of which established the woman's guilt or innocence (Num., v, 12–31). Among the Indians are to be found likewise various kinds of ordeals, particularly that of the red-hot iron. This test of holding a red-hot iron was also known among the Greeks. The Romans, however, with their highly-developed system of dispensing justice, did not employ this means of obtaining proof. Ordeals found their chief development among the Germanic peoples, in Germany itself as well as in those kingdoms which came into existence, after the migration of the nations, in the old Roman Provinces of Gaul, Italy, and Britain. They were an essential part of the judicial system of the Germanic races in pagan times, were preserved and developed after the conversion of these peoples to Christianity, became widespread and were in constant use.

The Christian missionaries did not in general combat this practice. They opposed only the duel, and endeavoured to minimize the barbarity attendant upon the practice of ordeals. By prayer and religious ceremonies, by the hearing of holy Mass and the reception of holy communion before the ordeal, the missionaries sought to give to it a distinctly religious character. The liturgical prayers and ceremonies are to be found in Franz, "Die kirchlichen Benediktionen im Mittelalter" (Freiburg im Br., 1909), II, 364 sqq.; the celebration of Mass on the occasion of the ordeal, in Franz, "Die Messe in deutschen Mittelalter" (Freiburg im Br., 1902), 213 sqq. This attitude of the clergy in regard to ordeals may be explained if one takes into consideration the religious ideas of the times, as well as the close connexion which existed between ordeals and the Germanic judicial system.

The principal means of testing the accuser as well as the accused in the Germanic judicial practice was the Oath of the Co-jurors. It being often difficult to find jurors who were properly qualified, perjury frequently resulted, and the oath could be rejected by the opposing party. In such cases, the ordeal was brought forward as a substitute in determining the truth, the guilt, or the innocence. This mode of procedure was tolerated by the Church in Germanic countries in the early Middle Ages. A thoroughgoing opposition to ordeals would have had little prospect of success. The only bishop to take measures against the practice of ordeals during the conversion to Christianity of the Germanic races was St. Avitus of Vienne (d. about 518). Later, Agobard of Lyons (d. 840) attacked the judicial duel and other ordeals in two writings ("Liber adversus legem Grundobadi and Liber contra iudicium Dei", in Migne, P. L., CIV, 125 sqq., 254 sqq.). On the other hand, shortly afterwards, Archbishop Hincmar of Reims, at the time of the matrimonial disagreement between King Lothair and Theutberga, declared himself to be of the opinion that ordeals were permissible, in support of which he must assuredly have brought forward noteworthy arguments ("De divortio Lotharii regis et Tetbergæ", in Migne, P. L., CXXV, 659-80; cf. also Hincmar's "Epistola ad Hildegarium episcopum", ibid., 161 sqq.). The universal opinion among the peoples of the Frankish kingdom favoured the authorization of ordeals, and the same may be said of Britain. In 809 in the Capitulary of Aachen, Charlemagne declared: "that all should believe in the ordeal without the shadow of a doubt" (Mon. Germ. Hist., Capitularia, I, 150). In the Byzantine Empire also, we encounter in the later Middle Ages the practice of ordeals, introduced from the countries of the West.

The ordeals, strictly speaking, of the Germanic countries are the following:

(1) *The duel*, called *judicium Dei* in the Book of Laws of the Burgundian King Gundobad (c. 500). (Mon. Germ. Hist., Leges, III, 537.) The outcome of the judicial duel was looked upon as the judgment of God. Only freemen were qualified to take part, and women and ecclesiastics were permitted to appoint substitutes. The duel originated in the pagan times of the Germanic peoples. In certain individual nations were to be found various usages and regulations regarding the manner in which the duel was to be conducted. The Church combatted the judicial duel; Nicholas I declared it to be an infringement of the law of God and of the laws of the Church ("Epist. ad Carolum Calvum", in Migne, P. L., CXIX, 1144), and several later popes spoke against it. Ecclesiastics were forbidden to take part in a duel either personally, or through a substitute. Only English books of ritual of the later Middle Ages contain a formula for the blessing of the shield and the sword for use in the judicial duel; otherwise, no medieval Ritual contains prayers for these ordeals, a proof that they were not looked upon favourably by the Church.

(2) *The cross*, in which both parties, the accuser and the accused, stood before a cross with arms outstretched in the form of a cross. Whoever first let fall his arms was defeated. The earliest information we possess regarding this form of ordeal dates from the eighth century. It was destined to replace the duel, and was prescribed by various capitularies of the ninth century, especially for disputes with ecclesiastics.

(3) *The hot iron*, employed in various ways, not only in courts of law, where the accused in ancient times to prove his innocence must pass through fire or place his hand in the flames, but also to prove the authenticity of relics, and to reveal the truth in other ways. The judicial test by fire, as an ordeal, was ordinarily conducted in the following manner: the accused must walk a certain distance (nine feet, among the Anglo-Saxons) bearing a bar of red-hot iron in his hands, or he must pass barefooted over red-hot ploughshares (usually nine). If he remained uninjured, his innocence was considered established. Medieval ecclesiastical Rituals of various dioceses contain prayers and ceremonies for use before the undergoing of the test. The accused was also obliged to prepare himself beforehand by confession and fasting.

(4) *Hot water*, or the cauldron. The accused must draw a stone with his naked arm from the bottom of a vessel filled with hot water, after which the arm was bound up and the bandage sealed; three days later it was removed, and, according to the condition of his arm, the accused was considered innocent or guilty. The religious ceremonies for this ordeal were similar to those used for the ordeal of the hot iron.

(5) *Cold water*, in use at an early date among the Germanic races, and which continued to be practised notwithstanding the prohibition of the Emperor Louis the Pious in 829. The accused, with hands and feet bound, was cast into the water; if he sank, he was considered guilty; if however he floated upon the water, his innocence was believed to be established. For this test also, the accused prepared himself by fasting, confession, and communion, and by assisting at Mass.

(6) *The blessed morsel* (*iudicium offæ*, Anglo-Saxon *corsnaed*, *nedbread*), which consisted in the consuming by the accused of a piece of bread and a piece of cheese in the church before the altar, the morsels being blessed with special prayers. If he was able to swallow them, his innocence was established, but if not, he was considered guilty. This test was in use principally among the Anglo-Saxons. It is not mentioned in the ancient Germanic codes of the Continent.

(7) *The suspended loaf*.—A loaf of bread was baked by a deacon from meal and blessed water, through which a stick of wood was passed. The suspected person then appeared with two witnesses, between whom the bread was suspended, which, if it turned in a circle, was supposed to be a proof of guilt.

(8) *The Psalter*, which consisted in clamping into the Book of Psalms a stick of wood with a knob attached, and then placing the whole in an opening made in another piece of wood, so that the book could turn. The guilt of the accused was established if the Psalter turned from west to east, and his innocence, if it turned in a contrary direction.

(9) *The Examen in mensuris*.—Though forms of prayer in connexion with its use have been handed down to us, they do not give us a clear idea of how this test was conducted. It would seem to have been practised but seldom. It appears to have been an ordeal decided by lot, or by the measuring of the accused by a stick of a determined length.

(10) *Bleeding*, to discover a murderer. The person suspected of the murder was forced to look upon the body or the wounds of the victim. If the wounds then began to bleed afresh, the guilt was supposed to have been proved.

In addition to these forms of genuine ordeals, two other kinds are frequently considered, which, however, do not exactly correspond to the idea of a judgment of God, as in their case there is no question of a direct establishment of a fact by the interposition of God. The first of these is the oath, which is but a means of establishing the truth, accompanied by a solemn calling upon God, but which is not in any sense a judgment of God. Another example is furnished by the belief that the perjured would, sooner or later, be overtaken by death, which was God's punishment for perjury, but this was not a judicial ordeal. The same is true of the Eucharistic test. The firm belief existed that if anyone to prove his innocence should receive Holy Communion, he would, if guilty, be punished by God with instant death. Here also it is question of Divine chastisement; the judgment however not taking place by means of a judicial process. When at the Synod of Worms in 868 it was ordered that the bishops and priests should clear themselves of suspicion by the celebration of Mass, and the monks by the reception of Holy Communion, this was in reality of the same significance as the oath of purgation, by which those under shadow of suspicion swore to their innocence.

The ecclesiastical authorities of the Frankish and Anglo-Saxon kingdoms, as we have remarked above, were very broad-minded in their acceptance of the greater number of species of ordeals; several councils publishing regulations concerning them [cf. Hefele, "Konziliengeschichte," 2 ed., III, 611, 614, 623, 690, 732; IV, 555; Synod of Tribur (895), IV, 672; Synod of Seligenstadt (1022)]. Ordeals were practised in Britain, France, and Germany in connexion with legal processes before civil as well as ecclesiastical tribunals up to and during the thirteenth and fourteenth centuries. From then on they were gradually discontinued.

The tribunals of Rome never made use of ordeals. The popes were always opposed to them, and began, at an early date, to take measures for their suppression. It is true that in the beginning no general decree was published regarding them; however, in individual cases concerning ordeals brought to Rome, the popes always pronounced against the practice, and designated it as unlawful. This course was followed by Nicholas I when, in 867, he prohibited the duel by which King Lothair sought to decide his matrimonial dispute with Theutberga. The latter had previously, through one of her servants, submitted to the test of hot water to prove her innocence, and indeed with favourable results. Upon the inquiry of the Archbishop of Mainz as to whether or not the tests of the hot water and the glowing iron could lawfully be made use of in the case of parents who were accused of having smothered their sleeping child, Stephen V (885-891) forbade these ordeals (Decr. C. 20, C. II, qu. 5). Alexander II (1061-73) likewise condemned these tests, and Alexander III (1159-81) prohibited the bishop and the clergy of the Diocese of Upsala from countenancing a duel or other ordeal imposed by law, as such a practice was disapproved of by the Catholic Church. Before long definite condemnations were published by the popes, as for example, that of Celestine III (1191-98) regarding the duel. At the Council of the Lateran in 1215, Innocent III promulgated a general decree against ordeals, which prohibited anyone from receiving the blessing of the Church before submitting to the test of the hot water or to that of the glowing iron, and confirming the validity of the previous prohibition against the duel (Can. xviii; in Hefele, l. c., V, 687).

Various accounts in regard to the co-operation of the popes in the practice of ordeals in Frankish times which are contained in apocryphal writings have no historic value. From the twelfth century, a thorough and widespread opposition to ordeals, as a result of the stand taken by the popes, began to manifest itself generally, and whereas, at an earlier date, no one was found to support Agobard of Lyons in his opposition to these tests, which was without result, the writings of Peter Cantor (d. 1197) against the proceedings of the civil courts with regard to ordeals (in his "Verbum abbreviatum", Migne, P. L., CCV, 226 sqq.) had a far greater success. In "Tristan", Gottfried of Strasburg sets forth his disapproval of ordeals.

As a result of the General Council of 1215, several synods of the thirteenth and fourteenth centuries published prohibitions in this connexion. A synod held at Valladolid in 1322 declares in Can. xxvii: "The tests of fire and water are forbidden; whoever participates in them is *ipso facto* excommunicated" (Hefele, "Konziliengesch.", VI, 616). The Emperor Frederick II also prohibited the duel and other ordeals in the Constitution of Melfi, 1231 (Michael, "Geschichte des deutschen Volkes", I, 318). Nevertheless, there are to be found in Germanic code books as late as the thirteenth century, regulations for their use. However, a clearer recognition of the false ground for belief in ordeals, a more highly-developed judicial system, the fact that the innocent must be victims of the ordeal, the prohibitions of the popes and the synods, the refusal of the ecclesiastical authorities to co-operate in the carrying out of the sentence—all these causes worked together to bring about, during the course of the fourteenth and fifteenth centuries, the gradual discontinuance of the practice. The ancient test of the cold water was resuscitated in the sixteenth and seventeenth centuries in the ducking of so-called witches, consequent upon the trials for witchcraft.

ZEUMER, *Formulæ Merovingici et Karolini ævi* in *Mon. Germ. Hist.: Legum*, sec. V (Hanover, 1882); FRANZ, *Die kirchlichen Benediktionen im Mittelalter*, II (Freiburg im Br., 1909), 307-98; PHILLIPS, *Ueber die Ordalien bei den Germanen* (Munich, 1847); PFALZ, *Die germanischen Gottesurteile* in *Bericht über die Realschule* (Leipzig, 1865); DAHN, *Studien zur Geschichte der germanischen Gottesurteile* (Berlin, 1880); PATTETA, *Le Ordalie. Studio di storia del diritto* (Turin, 1890); DE SMEDT, *Les origines du duel judiciaire* in *Etudes religieuses*, LXIII, 1894, 337 sqq.; IDEM, *Le duel judiciaire et l'Eglise, ibid.*, LXIV, 1895, 49 sqq.; VACANDARD, *L'Eglise et les ordalies* in *Etudes de critique et d'histoire religieuse* (Paris, 1905), 19 sqq.

J. P. KIRSCH.

Order, SUPERNATURAL. See SUPERNATURAL ORDER.

Ordericus Vitalis, historian, b. 1075; d. about 1143. He was the son of an English mother and a French priest who came over to England with the Normans and received a church at Shrewsbury. At the age of ten he was sent over by his father to St. Evroult in southern Normandy and remained for the rest of his life a monk of that abbey. He must have travelled occasionally: we have evidence of his presence at Cambrai, for instance, and at Cluny, and he went three or four times to England: still he passed most of his days at home. He considered himself, however, an Englishman, "Vitalis Angligena", and was always full of interest in English affairs. His history was intended at first to be a chronicle of his abbey but it developed into a general "Historia Ecclesiastica" in 13 books. Books I and II are an abridged chronicle from the Christian era to 1143; books III-V describe the Norman Conquests of South Italy and England; book VI gives the history of his abbey. Books VII-XIII consist of his universal history from 751 to 1141, book IX being devoted to the first Crusade. The work begins to have real historical importance from about the date of the Norman Conquest, but Ordericus is discriminating throughout in his choice of authorities. Chronologically it is ill-arranged and very inaccurate; it is often pedantic in form. The author has, however, a wide interest and a keen sense of detail and picturesque incident. He was a very well-read man, but he united to his learning a taste seldom so frankly admitted for popular stories and songs. He was a man of observation and he attempted to give the outward appearance of the characters he described. He was fair-minded, anxious to give two sides of a question and to be moderate in his judgments. In spite, therefore, of its clumsy arrangements and chronological errors the "Historia Ecclesiastica" gives a very vivid picture of the times and is of great historical value. A competent authority has declared it the best French history of the twelfth century. Ordericus was also something of a poet and there are manuscripts of his collected Latin poems. The best text of the "Historia Ecclesiastica" is that edited by Le Prévost for the "Société de l'histoire de France" (5 vols., 1838–55). The fifth volume contains a valuable introduction by L. Delisle. There is also a text in Migne, vol. CLXXXVIII. A French translation was published in Guizot's "Collection des mémoires" and an English translation in Bohn's "Antiquarian Library" (4 vols., 1853-5).

MOLINIER, *Les sources de l'histoire de France*, II, 219; FREEMAN, *Norman Conquest*, IV, 495-500.

F. F. URQUHART.

Orders, ANGLICAN. See ANGLICAN ORDERS.

Orders, HOLY.—Order is the appropriate disposition of things equal and unequal, by giving each its proper place (St. Aug., " De civ. Dei," XIX, xiii). Order primarily means a relation. It is used to designate that on which the relation is founded and thus generally means rank (St. Thom., "Suppl.", Q. xxxiv, a. 2, ad 4um). In this sense it was applied to clergy and laity (St. Jer., "In Isaiam", XIX, 18; St. Greg. the Great, "Moral.", XXXII, xx). The meaning was restricted later to the hierarchy as a whole or to the various ranks of the clergy. Tertullian and some early writers had already used the word in that sense, but generally with a qualifying adjective (Tert., "De exhort. cast.", vii, ordo sacerdotalis, ordo ecclesiasticus; St. Greg. of Tours, "Vit. patr.", X, i, ordo clericorum). Order is used to signify not only the particular rank or general status of the clergy, but also the outward action by which they are raised to that status, and thus stands for ordination. It also indicates what differentiates laity from clergy or the various ranks of the clergy, and thus means spiritual power. The Sacrament of Order is the sacrament by which grace and spiritual power for the discharge of ecclesiastical offices are conferred.

Christ founded His Church as a supernatural society, the Kingdom of God. In this society there must be the power of ruling; and also the principles by which the members are to attain their supernatural end, viz., supernatural truth, which is held by faith, and supernatural grace by which man is formally elevated to the supernatural order. Thus, besides the power of jurisdiction, the Church has the power of teaching (*magisterium*) and the power of conferring grace (power of order). This power of order was committed by our Lord to His Apostles, who were to continue His work and to be His earthly representatives. The Apostles received their power from Christ: "as the Father hath sent me, I also send you"(John, xx, 21). Christ possessed fullness of power in virtue of His priesthood—of His office as Redeemer and Mediator. He merited the grace which freed man from the bondage of sin, which grace is applied to man mediately by the Sacrifice of the Eucharist and immediately by the sacraments. He gave His Apostles the power to offer the Sacrifice (Luke, xxii, 19), and dispense the sacraments (Matt., xxviii, 18; John, xx, 22, 23); thus making them priests. It is true that every Christian receives sanctifying grace which confers on him a priesthood. Even as Israel under the Old dispensation was to God "a priestly kingdom" (Exod., xix, 4–6), thus under the New, all Christians are "a kingly priesthood" (I Pet., ii, 9); but now as then the special and sacramental priesthood strengthens and perfects the universal priesthood (cf. II Cor., iii, 3, 6; Rom., xv, 16).

SACRAMENT OF ORDER.—From Scripture we learn that the Apostles appointed others by an external rite (imposition of hands), conferring inward grace. The fact that grace is ascribed immediately to the external rite, shows that Christ must have thus ordained. The fact that χειροντονεῖν, χειροτονία, which meant electing by show of hands, had acquired the technical meaning of ordination by imposition of hands before the middle of the third century, shows that appointment to the various orders was made by that external rite. We read of the deacons, how the Apostles "praying, imposed hands upon them" (Acts, vi, 6). In II Tim., i, 6 St. Paul reminds Timothy that he was made a bishop by the imposition of St. Paul's hands (cf. I Tim., iv, 4), and Timothy is exhorted to appoint presbyters by the same rite (I Tim., v, 22; cf. Acts, xiii, 3; xiv, 22). In Clem., "Hom.", III, lxxii, we read of the appointment of Zachæus as bishop by the imposition of Peter's hands. The word is used in its technical meaning by Clement of Alexandria ("Strom.", VI, xiii, cvi; cf. "Const. Apost.", II, viii, 36). "A priest lays on hands, but does not ordain" (χειροθετεῖ οὐ χειροτονεῖ) "Didasc. Syr.", IV; III, 10, 11, 20; Cornelius, "Ad Fabianum" in Euseb., "Hist. Eccl.", VI, xliii.

Grace was attached to this external sign and conferred by it. "I admonish thee, that thou stir up the grace of God which is in thee, through (διά) the imposition of my hands" (II Tim., i, 6). The context clearly shows that there is question here of a grace which enables Timothy to rightly discharge the office imposed upon him, for St. Paul continues "God hath not given us the spirit of fear: but of power, and of love, and of sobriety." This grace is something permanent, as appears from the words "that thou *stir up* the grace which is in thee"; we reach the same conclusion from I Tim., iv, 14, where St. Paul says, "Neglect not the grace that is in thee, which was given thee by prophecy, with (μετά) imposition of hands of the priesthood." This text shows that when St. Paul ordained Timothy, the presbyters also laid their hands upon him, even as now the presbyters who assist at ordination lay their hands on the candidate. St. Paul here exhorts Timothy to teach and command, to be an example to all. To neglect this would be to neglect the grace which is in him. This grace therefore enables him to teach and command, to discharge his office rightly. The grace then is not a charismatic gift, but a gift of the Holy Spirit for the rightful discharge of official duties. The Sacrament of Order has ever been recognized in the Church as such. This is attested by the belief in a special priesthood (cf. St. John Chrys., "De sacerdotio"; St. Greg. of Nyss., "Oratio in baptism. Christi"), which requires a special ordination. St. Augustine, speaking about baptism and order, says, "Each is a sacrament, and each is given by a certain consecration, . . . If both are sacraments, which no one doubts, how is the one not lost (by defection from the Church) and the other lost?" (Contra. Epist. Parmen., ii, 28–30). The Council of Trent says, "Whereas, by the testimony of Scripture, by Apostolic tradition, and by the unanimous consent of the Fathers, it is clear that grace is conferred by sacred ordination, which is performed by words and outward signs, no one ought to doubt that Order is truly and properly one of the Seven Sacraments of Holy Church" (Sess. XXIII, c. iii, can. 3).

NUMBER OF ORDERS.—The Council of Trent (Sess. XXIII, can. 2) defined that, besides the priesthood, there are in the Church other orders, both major and minor (q. v.). Though nothing has been defined with regard to the number of orders it is usually given as seven: priests, deacons, subdeacons, acolytes, exorcists, readers, and doorkeepers. The priesthood is thus counted as including bishops; if the latter be numbered separately we have eight; and if we add first tonsure, which was at one time regarded as an order, we have nine. We meet with different numberings in different Churches, and it would seem that mystical reasons influenced them to some extent (Martène, "De antiq. eccl. rit.", I, viii, l, 1; Denzinger, "Rit. orient.",

II, 155). The "Statuta ecclesiæ antiqua" enumerate nine orders, adding psalmists and counting bishops and priests separately. Others enumerate eight orders, thus, e. g. the author of "De divin. offic.", 33, and St. Dunstan's and the Jumièges pontificals (Martène I, viii, 11), the latter not counting bishops, and adding cantor. Innocent III, "De sacro alt. minister.", I, i, counts six orders, as do also the Irish canons, where acolytes were unknown. Besides the psalmista or cantor, several other functionaries seem to have been recognized as holding orders, e. g., *fossarii (fossores)* grave-diggers, *hermeneutæ* (interpreters), *custodes martyrum* etc. Some consider them to have been real orders (Morin, "Comm. de sacris eccl. ordin.", III, Ex. 11, 7); but it is more probable that they were merely offices, generally committed to clerics (Benedict XIV, "De syn. dioc.", VIII, ix, 7, 8). In the East there is considerable variety of tradition regarding the number of orders. The Greek Church acknowledges five, bishops, priests, deacons, subdeacons, and readers. The same number is found in St. John Damascene (Dial. contra manichæos, iii); in the ancient Greek Church acolytes, exorcists, and doorkeepers were probably considered only as offices. (cf. Denzinger, "Rit. orient.", I, 116).

In the Latin Church a distinction is made between major and minor orders (q. v.). In the East the subdiaconate is regarded as a minor order, and it includes three of the other minor orders (porter, exorcist, acolyte). In the Latin Church the priesthood, diaconate, and subdiaconate (q. v.) are the major, or sacred, orders, so-called because they have immediate reference to what is consecrated (St. Thom., "Suppl.", Q. xxxvii, a. 3). The hierarchical orders strictly so-called are of divine origin (Conc. Trid., Sess. XXIII, can. 6). We have seen that our Lord instituted a ministry in the persons of His Apostles, who received fullness of authority and power. One of the first exercises of this Apostolic power was the appointment of others to help and succeed them. The Apostles did not confine their labours to any particular Church, but, following the Divine command to make disciples of all men, they were the missionaries of the first generation. Others also are mentioned in Holy Scripture as exercising an itinerant ministry, such as those who are in a wider sense called Apostles (Rom., xvi, 7), or prophets, teachers, and evangelists (Eph., iv, 11). Side by side with this itinerant ministry provision is made for the ordinary ministrations by the appointment of local ministers, to whom the duties of the ministry passed entirely when the itinerant ministers disappeared (see DEACON).

Besides deacons others were appointed to the ministry, who are called πρεσβύτεροι and ἐπίσκοποι. There is no record of their institution, but the names occur casually. Though some have explained the appointment of the seventy-two disciples in Luke x, as the institution of the presbyterate, it is generally agreed that they had only a temporary appointment. We find presbyters in the Mother Church at Jerusalem, receiving the gifts of the brethren of Antioch. They appear in close connexion with the Apostles, and the Apostles and presbyters sent forth the decree which freed the gentile converts from the burden of the Mosaic law (Acts, xv, 23). In St. James (v, 14, 15) they appear as performing ritual actions, and from St. Peter we learn that they are shepherds of the flock (I Pet. v, 2). The bishops hold a position of authority (Phil., i; I Tim., iii, 2; Tit., i, 7;) and have been appointed shepherds by the Holy Ghost (Acts, xx, 28). That the ministry of both was local appears from Acts, xiv, 23, where we read that Paul and Barnabas appointed presbyters in the various Churches which they founded during their first missionary journey. It is shown also by the fact that they had to shepherd the flock, *wherein* they have been appointed, the presbyters have to shepherd the flock, that is *amongst them* (I Pet., v, 2). Titus is left in Crete that he might appoint presbyters in every city (κατὰ πόλιν, Tit., i, 5; cf. Chrys., "Ad Tit., homil.", II, i).

We cannot argue from the difference of names to the difference of official position, because the names are to some extent interchangeable (Acts, xx, 17, 28; Tit., i, 6, 7). The New Testament does not clearly show the distinction between presbyters and bishops, and we must examine its evidence in the light of later times. Towards the end of the second century there is a universal and unquestioned tradition, that bishops and their superior authority date from Apostolic times (see HIERARCHY OF THE EARLY CHURCH). It throws much light on the New-Testament evidence and we find that what appears distinctly at the time of Ignatius can be traced through the pastoral epistles of St. Paul, to the very beginning of the history of the Mother Church at Jerusalem, where St. James, the brother of the Lord, appears to occupy the position of bishop (Acts, xii, 17; xv, 13; xxi, 18; Gal., ii, 9); Timothy and Titus possess full episcopal authority, and were ever thus recognized in tradition (cf. Tit., i, 5; I Tim., v, 19 and 22). No doubt there is much obscurity in the New Testament, but this is accounted for by many reasons. The monuments of tradition never give us the life of the Church in all its fullness, and we cannot expect this fullness, with regard to the internal organization of the Church existing in Apostolic times, from the cursory references in the occasional writings of the New Testament. The position of bishops would necessarily be much less prominent than in later times. The supreme authority of the Apostles, the great number of charismatically gifted persons, the fact that various Churches were ruled by Apostolic delegates who exercised episcopal authority under Apostolic direction, would prevent that special prominence. The union between bishops and presbyters was close, and the names remained interchangeable long after the distinction between presbyters and bishops was commonly recognized, e. g., in Iren., "Adv. hæres.", IV, xxvi, 2. Hence it would seem that already, in the New Testament, we find, obscurely no doubt, the same ministry which appeared so distinctly afterwards.

Which of the Orders are Sacramental?—All agree that there is but one Sacrament of Order, i. e., the totality of the power conferred by the sacrament is contained in the supreme order, whilst the others contain only part thereof (St. Thomas, "Supplem.", Q. xxxvii, a. i, ad 2um). The sacramental character of the priesthood has never been denied by anyone who admitted the Sacrament of Order, and, though not explicitly defined, it follows immediately from the statements of the Council of Trent. Thus (Sess. XXIII, can. 2), "If any one saith that besides the priesthood there are not in the Catholic Church other orders, both major and minor, by which as by certain steps, advance is made to the priesthood, let him be anathema." In the fourth chapter of the same session, after declaring that the Sacrament of Order imprints a character "which can neither be effaced nor taken away; the holy synod with reason condemns the opinion of those who assert that priests of the New Testament have only a temporary power". The priesthood is therefore a sacrament.

With regard to the episcopate the Council of Trent defines that bishops belong to the divinely instituted hierarchy, that they are superior to priests, and that they have the power of confirming and ordaining which is proper to them (Sess. XXIII, c. iv, can. 6, 7). The superiority of bishops is abundantly attested in Tradition, and we have seen above that the distinction between priests and bishops is of Apostolic origin. Most of the older scholastics were of opinion that the episcopate is not a sacrament; this opinion finds able defenders even now (e. g., Billot, "De sacramentis", II), though the majority of theologians hold it is certain that a bishop's ordination is a sacrament. With regard to the sacramental character of the other orders see DEACONS; MINOR ORDERS; SUBDEACONS.

Matter and Form.—In the question of the matter and form of this sacrament we must distinguish between the three higher orders and the subdiaconate and minor orders. The Church having instituted the latter, also determines their matter and form. With regard to the former, the received opinion maintains that the imposition of hands is the sole matter. This has been undoubtedly used from the beginning; to it, exclusively and directly, the conferring of grace is ascribed by St. Paul and many Fathers and councils. The Latin Church used it exclusively for nine or ten centuries, and the Greek Church to this day knows no other matter. Many scholastic theologians have held that the tradition of the instruments was the sole matter even for the strictly hierarchical orders, but this position has long been universally abandoned. Other scholastics held that both imposition of hands and the tradition of the instruments constitute the matter of the sacrament; this opinion still finds defenders. Appeal is made to the Decree of Eugene IV to the Armenians, but the pope spoke "of the integrating and accessory matter and form, which he wished Armenians to add to the imposition of hands, long since in use amongst them, that they might thus conform to the usage of the Latin Church, and more firmly adhere to it, by uniformity of rites" (Bened., XIV, "De syn. dioc.", VIII, x, 8). The real foundation of the latter opinion is the power of the Church with regard to the sacrament. Christ, it is argued, instituted the Sacrament of Order by instituting that in the Church there should be an external rite, which would of its own nature signify and confer the priestly power and corresponding grace. As Christ did not ordain His Apostles by imposition of hands, it would seem that He left to the Church the power of determining by which particular rite the power and grace should be conferred. The Church's determination of the particular rite would be the fulfilling of a condition required in order that the Divine institution should take effect. The Church determined the simple imposition of hands for the East and added, in the course of time, the tradition of the instruments for the West—changing its symbolical language according as circumstances of place or time required.

The question of the form of the sacrament naturally depends on that of the matter. If the tradition of the instruments be taken as the total or partial matter, the words which accompany it will be taken as the form. If the simple imposition of hands be considered the sole matter, the words which belong to it are the form. The form which accompanies the imposition of hands contains the words "Accipe spiritum sanctum", which in the ordination of priests, however, are found with the second imposition of hands, towards the end of the Mass, but these words are not found in the old rituals nor in the Greek Euchology. Thus the form is not contained in these words, but in the longer prayers accompanying the former imposition of hands, substantially the same from the beginning. All that we have said about the matter and form is speculative; in practice, whatever has been prescribed by the Church must be followed, and the Church in this, as in other sacraments, insists that anything omitted should be supplied.

Effect of the Sacrament.—The first effect of the sacrament is an increase of sanctifying grace. With this, there is the sacramental grace which makes the recipient a fit and holy minister in the discharge of his office. As the duties of God's ministers are manifold and onerous, it is in perfect accord with the rulings of God's Providence to confer a special grace on His ministers. The dispensation of sacraments requires grace, and the rightful discharge of sacred offices presupposes a special degree of spiritual excellence. The external sacramental sign or the power of the order can be received and may exist without this grace. Grace is required for the worthy, not the valid, exercise of the power, which is immediately and inseparably connected with the priestly character. The principal effect of the sacrament is the character (q. v.), a spiritual and indelible mark impressed upon the soul, by which the recipient is distinguished from others, designated as a minister of Christ, and deputed and empowered to perform certain offices of Divine worship (Summa, III, Q. lxiii, a. 2). The sacramental character of order distinguishes the ordained from the laity. It gives the recipient in the diaconate, e. g., the power to minister officially, in the priesthood, the power to offer the Sacrifice and dispense the sacraments, in the episcopate the power to ordain new priests and to confirm the faithful. The Council of Trent defined the existence of a character (Sess. VII, can. 9). Its existence is shown especially by the fact that ordination like baptism, if ever valid, can never be repeated. Though there have been controversies with regard to the conditions of the validity of ordination, and different views were held at different times in reference to them, "it has always been admitted that a valid ordination cannot be repeated. Reordinations do not suppose the negation of the inamissible character of Order—they presuppose an anterior ordination which was null. There can be no doubt that mistakes were made regarding the nullity of the first ordination, but this error of fact leaves the doctrine of the interability of ordination untouched" (Saltet, "Les Réordinations", 392).

Minister.—The ordinary minister of the sacrament is the bishop, who alone has this power in virtue of his ordination. Holy Scripture attributed the power to the Apostles and their successors (Acts, vi, 6; xvi, 22; I Tim., v, 22; II Tim., i, 6; Tit., i, 5), and the Fathers and councils ascribe the power to the bishop exclusively. Con. Nic. I, can. 4, Apost. Const. VIII, 28 "A bishop lays on hands, ordains . . . a presbyter lays on hands, but does not ordain." A council held at Alexandria (340) declared the orders conferred by Caluthus, a presbyter, null and void (Athanas., "Apol. contra Arianos", ii). For the custom said to have existed in the Church of Alexandria see EGYPT. Nor can objection be raised from the fact that *chorepiscopi* are known to have ordained priests, as there can be no doubt that some *chorepiscopi* were in bishops' orders (Gillman, "Das Institut der Chorbischöfe im Orient," Munich, 1903; Hefele-Leclercq, "Conciles", II, 1197–1237). No one but a bishop can give any orders now without a delegation from the pope, but a simple priest may be thus authorized to confer minor orders and the subdiaconate. It is generally denied that priests can confer priests' orders, and history, certainly, records no instance of the exercise of such extraordinary ministry. The diaconate cannot be conferred by a simple priest, according to the majority of theologians. This is sometimes questioned, as Innocent VIII is said to have granted the privilege to Cistercian abbots (1489), but the genuineness of the concession is very doubtful. For lawful ordination the bishop must be a Catholic, in communion with the Holy See, free from censures, and must observe the laws prescribed for ordination. He cannot lawfully ordain any except his own subjects without authorization (see below).

Subject.—Every baptized male can validly receive ordination. Though in former times there were several semi-clerical ranks of women in the Church (see DEACONESSES), they were not admitted to orders properly so called and had no spiritual power. The first requisite for lawful ordination is a Divine vocation; by which is understood the action of God, whereby He selects some to be His special ministers, endowing them with the spiritual, mental, moral, and physical qualities required for the fitting discharge of their order and inspiring them with a sincere desire to enter the ecclesiastical state for God's honour and their own sanctification. The reality of this Divine call is manifested in general by sanctity of life, right faith, knowledge corresponding to the proper exercise of the order to which one is raised, absence of physical defects, the age required by the canons (see IRREGULARITY). Sometimes this call was manifested in an extraordinary manner (Acts, i, 15; xiii, 2); in general, however, the "calling" was made according to the laws of the Church founded on the example of the Apostles. Though clergy and laity had a voice in the election of the candidates, the ultimate and definite determination rested with the bishops. The election of the candidates by clergy and laity was in the nature of a testimony of fitness, the bishop had to personally ascertain the candidates' qualifications. A public inquiry was held regarding their faith and moral character and the electors were consulted. Only such as were personally known to the electing congregation, i. e., members of the same Church, were chosen.

A specified age was required, and, though there was some diversity in different places, in general, for deacons the age was twenty-five or thirty, for priests thirty or thirty-five, for bishops thirty-five or forty or even fifty (Apost. Const., II, i). Nor was physical age deemed sufficient, but there were prescribed specified periods of time, during which the ordained should remain in a particular degree. The different degrees were considered not merely as steps preparatory to the priesthood, but as real church offices. In the beginning no such periods, called interstices, were appointed, though the tendency to orderly promotion is attested already in the pastoral Epistles (I Tim., iii, 3, 16). The first rules were apparently made in the fourth century. They seem to have been enforced by Siricius (385) and somewhat modified by Zosimus (418), who decreed that the office of reader or exorcist should last till the candidate was twenty, or for five years in case of those baptized as adults; four years were to be spent as acolyte or subdeacon, five years as deacon. This was modified by Pope Gelasius (492), according to whom a layman who had been a monk might be ordained priest after one year, thus allowing three months to elapse between each ordination, and a layman who had not been a monk might be ordained priest after eighteen months. At present the minor orders are generally conferred together on one day.

The bishops, who are the ministers of the sacrament ex officio, must inquire about the birth, person, age, title, faith, and moral character of the candidate. They must examine whether he is born of Catholic parents, and is spiritually, intellectually, morally, and physically fit for the exercise of the ministry. The age required by the canons is for subdeacons twenty-one, for deacons twenty-two, and for priests twenty-four years completed. The pope may dispense from any irregularity and the bishops generally receive some power of dispensation also with regard to age, not usually for subdeacons and deacons, but for priests. Bishops can generally dispense for one year, whilst the pope gives dispensation for over a year; a dispensation for more than eighteen months is but very rarely granted. For admission to minor orders, the testimony from the parish priest or from the master of the school where the candidate was educated—generally, therefore, the superior of the seminary—is required. For major orders further inquiries must be made. The names of the candidate must be published in the place of his birth and of his domicile and the result of such inquiries are to be forwarded to the bishop. No bishop may ordain those not belonging to his diocese by reason of birth, domicile, benefice, or *familiaritas*, without dimissorial letters from the candidate's bishop. Testimonial letters are also required from all the bishops in whose dioceses the candidate has resided for over six months, after the age of seven. Transgression of this rule is punished by suspension *latæ sententiæ* against the ordaining bishop. In recent years several decisions insist on the strict interpretation of these rules. Subdeacons and deacons should pass one full year in these orders and they may then proceed to receive the priesthood. This is laid down by the Council of Trent (Sess. XXIII, c. xi.), which did not prescribe the time for minor orders. The bishop generally has the power to dispense from these interstices, but it is absolutely forbidden, unless a special indult be obtained, to receive two major orders or the minor orders and the subdiaconate in one day.

For the subdiaconate and the higher orders there is, moreover, required a title, i. e., the right to receive maintenance from a determined source. Again, the candidate must observe the interstices, or times required to elapse between the reception of various orders; he must also have received confirmation and the lower orders preceding the one to which he is raised. This last requirement does not affect the validity of the order conferred, as every order gives a distinct and independent power. One exception is made by the majority of theologians and canonists, who are of opinion that episcopal consecration requires the previous reception of priest's orders for its validity. Others, however, maintain that episcopal power includes full priestly power, which is thus conferred by episcopal consecration. They appeal to history and bring forward cases of bishops who were consecrated without having previously received priest's orders, and though most of the cases are somewhat doubtful and can be explained on other grounds, it seems impossible to reject them all. It is further to be remembered that scholastic theologians mostly required the previous reception of priest's orders for valid episcopal consecration, because they did not consider episcopacy an order, a view which is now generally abandoned.

Obligations.—For obligations attached to holy Orders see BREVIARY; CELIBACY OF THE CLERGY.

Ceremonies of Ordination.—From the beginning the diaconate, priesthood, and episcopate were conferred with special rites and ceremonies. Though in the course of time there was considerable development and diversity in different parts of the Church, the imposition of hands and prayer were always and universally employed and date from Apostolic times (Acts, vi, 6; xiii, 3; I Tim., iv, 14; II Tim., i, 6). In the early Roman Church these sacred orders were conferred amid a great concourse of clergy and people at a solemn station. The candidates, who had been previously presented to the people, were summoned by name at the beginning of the solemn Mass. They were placed in a conspicuous position, and anyone objecting to a candidate was called upon to state his objections without fear. Silence was regarded as approval. Shortly before the Gospel, after the candidates were presented to the pope, the entire congregation was invited to prayer. All prostrating, the litanies were recited, the pope then imposed his hands upon the head of each candidate and recited the Collect with a prayer of consecration corresponding to the order conferred. The Gallican Rite was somewhat more elaborate. Besides the ceremonies used in the Roman Church, the people approving the candidates by acclamation, the hands of the deacon and the head and hands of priests and bishops were anointed with the sign of the Cross. After the seventh century the tradition of the instruments of office was added, alb and stole to the deacon, stole and planeta to the priest, ring and staff to the bishop. In the Eastern Church, after the presentation of the candidate to the congregation and their shout of approval, "He is worthy", the bishop imposed his hands upon the candidate and said the consecrating prayer.

We now give a short description of the ordination rite for priests as found in the present Roman Pontifical. All the candidates should present themselves in the church with tonsure and in clerical dress, carrying the vestments of the order to which they are to be raised, and lighted candles. They are all summoned by name, each candidate answering "*Adsum*". When a general ordination takes place the tonsure is given after the Introit or Kyrie, the minor orders after the Gloria, subdiaconate after the Collect, the diaconate after the Epistle, priesthood after Alleluia and Tract. After the Tract of the Mass the archdeacon summons all who are to receive the priesthood. The candidates, vested in amice, alb, girdle, stole, and maniple, with folded chasuble on left arm and a candle in their right hand, go forward and kneel around the bishop. The latter inquires of the archdeacon, who is here the representative of the Church as it were, whether the candidates are worthy to be admitted to the priesthood. The archdeacon answers in the affirmative and his testimony represents the testimony of fitness given in ancient times by the clergy and people. The bishop, then charging the congregation and insisting upon the reasons why "the Fathers decreed that the people also should be consulted", asks that, if anyone has anything to say to the prejudice of the candidates, he should come forward and state it.

The bishop then instructs and admonishes the candidates as to the duties of their new office. He kneels down in front of the altar; the *ordinandi* lay themselves prostrate on the carpet, and the Litany of the Saints is chanted or recited. On the conclusion of the Litany, all arise, the candidates come forward, and kneel in pairs before the bishop while he lays both hands on the head of each candidate in silence. The same is done by all priests who are present. Whilst bishop and priests keep their right hands extended, the former alone recites a prayer, inviting all to pray to God for a blessing on the candidates. After this follows the Collect and then the bishop says the Preface, towards the end of which occurs the prayer, "Grant, we beseech Thee etc." The bishop then with appropriate formulæ crosses the stole over the breast of each one and vests him with the chasuble. This is arranged to hang down in front but is folded behind. Though there is no mention of the stole in many of the most ancient Pontificals, there can be no doubt of its antiquity. The vesting with the chasuble is also very ancient and found already in Mabillon "Ord. VIII and IX." Afterwards the bishop recites a prayer calling down God's blessing on the newly-ordained. He then intones the "Veni Creator", and whilst it is being sung by the choir he anoints the hands of each with the oil of catechumens.

In England the head also was anointed in ancient times. The anointing of the hands, which in ancient times was done with chrism, or oil and chrism, was not used by the Roman Church, said Nicholas I (A. D. 864), though it is generally found in all ancient ordinals. It probably became a general practice in the ninth century and seems to have been derived from the British Church (Haddan and Stubbs, "Councils and Eccl. Documents", I, 141). The bishop then hands to each the chalice, containing wine and water, with a paten and a host upon it. This rite, with its corresponding formula, which as Hugo of St. Victor says ("Sacr.", III, xii), signifies the power which has already been received, is not found in the oldest rituals and probably dates back not earlier than the ninth or tenth century. When the bishop has finished the Offertory of the Mass, he seats himself before the middle of the altar and each of those ordained make an offering to him of a lighted candle. The newly-ordained priests then repeat the Mass with him, all saying the words of consecration simultaneously. Before the Communion the bishop gives the kiss of peace to one of the newly-ordained. After the Communion the priests again approach the bishop and say the Apostles' Creed. The bishop laying his hands upon each says: "Receive ye the Holy Ghost, whose sins you shall forgive they are forgiven them; and whose sins you shall retain, they are retained." This imposition of hands was introduced in the thirteenth century. The chasuble is then folded, the newly-ordained make a promise of obedience and having received the kiss of peace, return to their place.

Time and Place.—During the first centuries ordination took place whenever demanded by the needs of the Church. The Roman pontiffs generally ordained in December (Amalarius, "De offic.", II, i). Pope Gelasius (494) decreed that the ordination of priests and deacons should be held at fixed times and days, viz., on the fasts of the fourth, seventh, and tenth months, also on the fasts of the beginning and midweek (Passion Sunday) of Lent and on (holy) Saturday about sunset (Epist. ad ep. Luc., xi). This but confirmed what Leo the Great laid down, for he seems to speak of ordination on Ember Saturdays as an Apostolic tradition (Serm. 2, de jejun. Pentec.) The ordination may take place either after sunset on the Saturday or early on Sunday morning. The ordination to major orders took place before the Gospel.

Minor orders might be given at any day or hour. They were generally given after holy communion. At present minor orders may be given on Sundays and days of obligation (suppressed included) in the morning. For the sacred orders, a privilege to ordain on other days than those appointed by the canons, provided the ordination takes place on Sunday or day of obligation (suppressed days included), is very commonly given. Though it was always the rule that ordinations should take place in public, in time of persecution they were sometimes held in private buildings. The place of ordinations is the church. Minor orders may be conferred in any place, but it is understood that they are given in the church. The Pontifical directs that ordinations to sacred orders must be held publicly in the cathedral church in presence of the cathedral chapter, or if they be held in some other place, the clergy should be present and the principal church, as far as possible, must be made use of (cf. Conc. Trid., Sess. XXIII, c. vii). (See SUBDEACON, DEACONS, HIERARCHY, MINOR ORDERS, ALIMENTATION).

The subject of ORDER is treated in its various aspects in the general works on Dogmatic Theology (Church and Sacraments). BILLOT; PESCH, *De Sacr.*, pars II (Freiburg, 1909); TANQUEREY; HURTER; WILHELM AND SCANNELL, *A Manual of Catholic Theology*, II (London, 1908), 494–509; EINIG; TEPL; TOURNELY; SASSE; PALMIERI, *De Romano Pontifice;* PETAVIUS, *De Ecclesia;* HIBRARCH in *Dogm.*, III; DE AUGUSTINIS, HALTZCLAU in *Wirceburgenses.* In Moral Theology and Canon Law, LEHMKUHL; NOLDIN, *De Sacr.* (Innsbruck, 1906); AERTNYS; GENICOT; BALLERINI-PALMIERI; LAURENTIUS; DEVOTI; CRAISSON; LOMBARDI; EINIG in *Kirchenlex.*, s. v. *Ordo;* FUNK in KRAUS, *Real-Encyklopädie*, s. v. *Ordo;* HATCH in *Dictionary of Christian antiquities*, s. v. *Orders, Holy.* Special: HALLIER, *De Sacris Electionibus et Ordinationibus* (Paris, 1636), and in MIGNE, *Theol. Cursus*, XXIV; MORIN, *Comment. historico-dogmaticus de sacris ecclesiæ ordinationibus* (Paris, 1655); MARTÈNE, *De Antiquis Ecclesiæ Ritibus* (Venice, 1733); BENEDICT XIV, *De Synod. Diœcesana* (Louvain, 1763); WITASSE, *De Sacramento Ordinis* (Paris, 1717); DENZINGER, *Ritus Orientalium* (Würzburg, 1863); GASPARRI, *Tractatus Canonicus de Sacra Ordinatione* (Paris, 1894); BRUDERS, *Die Verfassung der Kirche* (Mainz, 1904), 365; WORDSWORTH, *The Ministry of Grace* (London, 1901); IDEM, *Ordination Problems* (London, 1909); WHITHAM, *Holy Orders* in *Oxford Library of Practical Theology* (London, 1903); MOBERLEY, *Ministerial Priesthood* (London, 1897); SANDAY, *Conception of Priesthood* (London, 1898); IDEM, *Priesthood and Sacrifice, a Report* (London, 1900); HARNACK, tr. OWEN, *Sources of the Apostolic Canons* (London, 1895); SEMERIA, *Dogma, Gerarchia e Culto* (Rome, 1902); DUCHESNE, *Christian Worship* (London, 1903); SALTET, *Les Réordinations* (Paris, 1907); MERTENS, *Hierarchie in de eerste seuwen des Christendoms* (Amsterdam, 1908); GORE, *Orders and Unity* (London, 1909). For St. Jerome's opinions see SANDERS, *Etudes sur St. Jérome* (Brussels, 1903), and the bibliography on *Hierarchy, ibid.*, pp. 335–44.

H. AHAUS.

Orders, MENDICANT. See MENDICANT FRIARS.
Orders, MILITARY. See MILITARY ORDERS.
Orders, MINOR. See MINOR ORDERS.
Orders, RELIGIOUS. See RELIGIOUS ORDERS.
Orders of Merit. See DECORATIONS, PONTIFICAL.

Ordinariate (from ORDINARY, q. v.).—This term is used in speaking collectively of all the various organs through which an ordinary, and especially a bishop, exercises the different forms of his authority. This word, which is employed particularly in Germany, does not occur in strict canonical language; but it is exactly equivalent to what canonists call the *curia*. Just as the pope is officially responsible for all that is done in his name and by his authority in the different branches of the Roman Curia (congregations of cardinals, tribunals, offices), so, too, an ordinary and especially a bishop bears the official responsibility of whatever is done, in his name and with his authority, by the persons or committees composing his curia, who are the organs of his administration (vicar-general, official, judges, secretaries, councils of various kinds). Whatever may be the exact form of this administration in each diocese, it is still the diocesan administration and the ordinariate. (See BISHOP; DIOCESAN CHANCERY; OFFICIAL; VICAR-GENERAL; VICAR CAPITULAR.)

A. BOUDINHON.

Ordinary (Lat. *ordinarius*, i. e., *judex*), in ecclesiastical language, denotes any person possessing or exercising ordinary jurisdiction, i. e., jurisdiction connected permanently or at least in a stable way with an office, whether this connexion arises from Divine law, as in the case of popes and bishops, or from positive church law, as in the case mentioned below. Ordinary jurisdiction is contrasted with delegated jurisdiction, a temporary communication of power made by a superior to an inferior; thus we speak of a delegated judge and an ordinary judge. A person may be an ordinary within his own sphere, and at the same time have delegated powers for certain acts or the exercise of special authority. The jurisdiction which constitutes an ordinary is real and full jurisdiction in the external forum, comprising the power of legislating, adjudicating, and governing. Jurisdiction in the internal forum, being partial and exercised only in private matters, does not constitute an ordinary. Parish priests, therefore, are not ordinaries, though they have jurisdiction in the internal forum, for they have not jurisdiction in the external forum, being incapable of legislating and acting as judges; their administration is the exercise of paternal authority rather than of jurisdiction properly so called.

There are various classes of ordinaries. First, they are divided into those having territorial jurisdiction and those who have not. As a rule ordinary jurisdiction is territorial as well as personal, as in the case of the pope and the bishops; but ordinary jurisdiction may be restricted to certain persons, exempt from the local authority. Such for instance is the jurisdiction of regular prelates, abbots, generals, and provincials of religious orders making solemn vows; they can legislate, adjudicate, and govern; consequently they are ordinaries; but their jurisdiction concerns individuals, not localities; they are not, like the others, called local ordinaries, *ordinarii locorum*. Superiors of congregations and institutes bound by simple vows are not ordinaries, though they may enjoy a greater or less degree of administrative exemption. The jurisdiction of local ordinaries arises from Divine law or ecclesiastical law. The pope is the ordinary of the entire church and all the faithful; he has ordinary and immediate jurisdiction over all (Conc. Vatic., Const. "Pastor æternus", c. iii). Bishops are the pastors and ordinary judges in their dioceses, appointed to govern their churches by the Holy Ghost (Acts, xx, 28). Certain bishops have, by ecclesiastical law, a mediate ordinary power over other bishops and dioceses; these are the metropolitans, primates, and patriarchs. In a lower rank, there is another class of ordinaries, viz., prelates who exercise jurisdiction in the external forum over a given territory, which is not a diocese, either in their own name, as in the case of prelates or abbots *nullius* or in the name of the pope, like vicars and prefects Apostolic until the erection of their territories into complete dioceses.

Local ordinaries being unable personally to perform all acts of their jurisdiction may and even ought to communicate it permanently to certain persons, without, however, divesting themselves of their authority; if the duties of these persons are specified and determined by law, they also are ordinaries, but in a restricted and inferior sense. This is vicarial jurisdiction, delegated as to its source, but ordinary as to its exercise, and which would be more accurately termed quasi-ordinary. In this sense vicars-general and diocesan officials are ordinaries; so also, in regard to the pope, the heads of the various organs of the Curia are ordinaries for the whole Church; the cardinal vicar for the Diocese of Rome and his district; the *legate a latere*, for the country to which he is sent. Finally, there are ordinaries with an interimary and transitory title during the vacancy of sees. Thus when the Holy See is vacant, the ordinaries are the College of Cardinals and the cardinal camerlengo; when a diocese, the chapter and also the vicar capitular, and in general the interimary administrator; so, too, the vicar, for religious orders. These persons possess and exercise exterior jurisdiction, although with certain restrictions, and this in virtue of their office; they are therefore ordinaries.

In practice, the determination of the persons included under the term ordinary is of importance in the case of indults and the execution of rescripts issued from Rome. Since the decrees of the Holy Office dated 20 February, 1888, and 20 April, 1898, indults and most of the rescripts, instead of being addressed to the bishop, are addressed to the ordinary; and it has been declared that the term ordinary comprises bishops, Apostolic administrators, vicars, prelates or prefects with separate territorial jurisdiction, and their officials or vicars-general; and also, during the vacancy of a see, the vicar capitular or lawful administrator. Thus the powers are handed on, without intermission or renewal, from one ordinary to his successor. (See JURISDICTION.)

See the canonical writers on the titles *De officio judicis ordinarii*, 1. I, tit. 31, and *De officio ordinarii*, 1. I, tit. 16, in VI; SÄGMÜLLER, *Lehrbuch des kathol. Kirchenrechts* (Freiburg, 1909), §60, 87 sq.

A. BOUDINHON.

Ordination. See ORDERS, HOLY.

Ordines Romani.—The word *Ordo* commonly meant, in the Middle Ages, a ritual book containing directions for liturgical functions, but not including the text of the prayers etc., recited by the celebrant or his asssistants. These prayers were contained in separate books, e. g., the Sacramentary, Antiphonary, Psalter, but the Ordo concerned itself with the ceremonial pure and simple. Sometimes the title "Ordo" was given to the directions for a single function, sometimes to a collection which dealt in one document with a number of quite different functions e. g., the rite of baptism, the consecration of a church, extreme unction, etc. Amalarius (early ninth century) speaks of the writings "quæ continent per diversos libellos Ordinem Romanum" (P. L., CV, 1295). Speaking generally, the word *Ordo* in this sense gave place after the twelfth century to "Cæremoniale", "Ordinarium" and similar terms, but was retained in other senses, especially to denote the brief conspectus of the daily Office and Mass as adapted to the local calendar (see DIRECTORIES).

A considerable number of Ordines are preserved among our manuscripts from the eighth to the twelfth century. The first printed in modern times was the so-called "Ordo Romanus Vulgatus", which after an edition published by George Cassander at Cologne (in 1561) was reprinted by Hittorp in his "De divinis catholicæ ecclesiæ officiis" (Cologne, 1568) and is hence often known as the Ordo Romanus of Hittorp. This is not a pure Roman document of early date. Already in the seventeenth century G. M. Tomasi rightly characterized it as a "farrago diversorum rituum secundum varias consuetudines", and declared that its heterogeneous elements could only be disentangled by careful study of the earlier Ordines. At present it is regarded as the work of a compiler in Gaul in the second half of the tenth century, the precise date being still disputed (cf. Mönchemeyer, "Amalar von Metz", 140 and 214; Bäumer in "Katholik", 1889, I, 626). Moreover, this conflated Ordo Romanus of Hittorp which is largely derived from the first, second, third, and sixth of the Ordines of Mabillon, mentioned below, is only one among a number of analogous compilations. Similar documents of about the same period have been published by other scholars; e. g., by Martène ("Thes. nov. anec.", V, 101—this is a valuable monastic Ordo of comparatively early date), by Muratori ("Lit. Rom. Vet.", II, 391), by Gattico ("Acta cæremon.", I, 226), and by Gerbert ("Mon. Vet. lit. alem.", II, 1 sqq.). In view of its composite character, the Ordo Vulgatus is of no great liturgical importance, though it sometimes fills a gap in our knowledge upon points not elsewhere minutely treated. It deals primarily with pontifical high Mass, but it also describes the rite of the consecration of the pope and of a bishop, the dedication of churches, the blessing of bells, the coronation of the emperor and of a king, the blessing of a knight, that is of a soldier (*militis*) dedicated to the service of the Church, the benediction of a bride, and the ceremonies to be observed in the opening of a general or provincial council. It should be noticed, moreover, that in these miscellaneous offices we do not find the characteristic features of an ordo in its technical sense. In the later portions of the Ordo Romanus of Hittorp not only are the details of the ceremonial indicated in their due sequence, but, as in a modern Pontifical, the text of the prayers, blessings etc., to be recited by the celebrant, is given in full.

Much more valuable to the liturgical student is the series of fifteen consuetudinaries, first printed by Mabillon in his "Museum Italicum" (1689), to which the term *Ordines Romani* is commonly applied. They are not indeed all of them pure and homogeneous documents, neither do they represent an unadulterated Roman tradition, nor are they all, strictly speaking, Ordines in the sense defined above. But in default of better material, and while we are waiting for more profound critical investigation to sort out our earliest documents and assign to them their proper date and provenance, Mabillon's Ordines constitute the most reliable source of information regarding the early liturgical usages of the Roman Church. Covering the whole period from the sixth to the fifteenth century, they may be said, taken collectively, to have some pretensions to completeness.

ORDO I.—The first of these Ordines Romani, describing the ceremonies of a solemn Mass celebrated by the pope himself or his deputy, is the most valuable, as it is also one of the most ancient. Modern opinion inclines to the belief that the early part of it (numbers 1–21) really represents in substance the usages of a stational Mass in the time of Pope Gregory the Great (Kösters, "Studien zu Mabillons röm. Ord.", 6; cf. Grisar, "Analecta Romana", I, 193), but there are also, undoubtedly, in our present text adjustments and additions which must be attributed to the end of the seventh century (Atchley, "Ord. Rom. Primus", 7, favours a later date, but in this he only follows Probst). The fact that Amalarius, who seems to have had a copy of this Ordo before him, did not find its description of paschal ceremonies in agreement with the actual Roman practice of his day, as expounded to him by Archdeacon Theodore in 832, need not lead us, with Mönchemeyer ("Amalar", 141), to the conclusion that the ceremonial never represented the official Roman use, and that it was merely an outline serving as a model for similar ceremonies in the Frankish dominions. On the contrary, so far as regards numbers 1–21, every detail attaches itself in the closest way to the pontifical ceremonies of Rome. An introduction portions out the liturgical service among the clerics of the seven regions. Then the procession to the stational church and the arrival and reception there are minutely described. This is followed with an account of the vesting, the Introit, the Kyries, the Collects, and all the early part of the Mass. Very full details are also given of the manner of the reception of the offerings of bread and wine from the clergy and people, and to this succeeds a description of the Canon, the Kiss of Peace, the Communion, and the rest of the Mass. The account ends with number 21.

This is the section which Grisar has proved, with all reasonable probability, to belong to the time of Gregory the Great ("Analecta Romana", 195–213). In one or two points the evidence of early date must impress even the casual reader. Such is the bringing of the holy Eucharist to the pontiff when the procession moves towards the altar-steps before the beginning of Mass. It is thus described in n. 8: "But before they arrive at the altar . . . two acolytes approach holding open pixes containing the Holy Things [*tenentes capsas cum sanctis patentes*]; and the subdeacon attendant taking them and keeping his hand in the aperture of the pix shows the Holy Things to the pontiff or to the deacon who goes before him. Then the pontiff or the deacon salutes the Holy Things with bowed head." Nothing of this appears in the account of Amalarius, who could hardly have failed to record it if it had been in existence in his time. Quite in accordance with such an inference, this bringing of the Eucharist to the pontiff has, in the second Ordo Romanus, admittedly of later date, been replaced by a sort of visit of the pontiff to the Blessed Sacrament in the church, a practice observed in pontifical Masses to this day. Again we may note that the first Ordo contains no mention of the Credo, which was certainly in use in Rome, according to Walafrid Strabo, about the year 800. Again the word *cardinales*, in accordance with the usage of St. Gregory's own letters, is not applied to the bishops, priests, and deacons attached to the papal service, but in the later chapters of the same Ordo, we do find reference to *presbyteri cardinales* (n. 48). All these, with other indications of early date, are pointed out by Grisar. It is not easy to prove that the second portion of the first Ordo, nn. 22–51, was all originally one document. On the contrary, nn. 22 and 48–51 seem to be closely connected, while all the intervening numbers (23–47), giving an account of the services in Lent and the last three days of Holy Week and showing, in several details, signs of a later origin, are clearly continuous and independent of the rest. The fact that Pope Hadrian and Charlemagne are mentioned in this section, as also that the Mass of the Presanctified (contrary to the Einsiedeln Ordo of the seventh century published by De Rossi in "Inscrip. Christ.", II, i, 34) was celebrated by the pontiff on Good Friday after the veneration of the Cross, prove that this section can hardly be older than the ninth century. Finally the chapters published by Mabillon from another manuscript as an appendix to Ordo I under a separate numeration have clearly no immediate connexion with what goes before. They simply provide another series of directions for Lent and the last days of Holy Week, sometimes coinciding even verbally with the rubrics given in nn. 23–47 and sometimes differing in various particulars. This appendix is generally assumed to be later in date than the second section of the Ordo.

ORDO II.—The second Ordo Romanus printed by Mabillon describes again a solemn pontifical Mass and is clearly based upon the first portion of Ordo I, sometimes quoting, or epitomizing, but elsewhere developing and adapting the directions of the earlier document. It contains some ritual features which are certainly not of Roman but of Gallican origin (for example the recitation of the Creed in the Mass, which some, in spite of Walafrid Strabo, consider not to have been known in Rome before the eleventh century, as also the giving of a pontifical blessing after the "Pax Domini"). It is generally accepted that this Ordo II belongs to the time of the general introduction of the Roman Liturgy into Gaul in the days of Charlemagne, i. e. about the beginning of the ninth century. This Ordo, as well as Ordo I and probably another now lost, was known to Amalarius, who in his "Ecloga" has annotated it with a view to the spiritual edification of his readers.

ORDO III AND ORDO IV contain yet another series of directions for a solemn Mass celebrated by the pope. That of Ordo IV is only a fragment, but both III and IV are generally considered older than the eleventh century. Mabillon considered Ordo III to be distinctly of later date than II and the fact that the stational church in III is called "Monasterium", a designation which does not seem to have come into use before the ninth century, lends support to this view. It is also confirmed by the fact that this Ordo III was apparently unknown to Amalarius. On the other hand III has clearly been extensively used in the compilation of the Ordo Romanus Vulgatus, which, as already stated, probably took shape in the second half of the tenth century. That the fragmentary Ordo IV is of later date than any of those previously mentioned has been inferred by Mabillon from the fact that the pope is here described as communicating at the altar and not at his throne, as in the preceding rituals. Still, the manuscript in which it is found cannot be later than the first half of the eleventh century (Ebner, "Quellen", 133).

ORDO V AND ORDO VI are again entirely consecrated to the celebration of a pontifical high Mass. Ordo V goes into details as to the vestments worn by the pope, and separately as to the vestments worn by a Roman bishop and the lesser clergy. It is specifically a Roman document and throughout assumes that the pope is pontificating. The pope here communicates at his throne and the Credo is sung after the gospel. But though Berno of Reichenau affirms that this last custom only began at Rome in 1014, the fact that Walafrid Strabo describes it as sung at Rome about the year 800 (P. L., CXIV, 947) renders this a very unsatisfactory test of date. On the other hand, the sixth Ordo is not directly connected with Rome, but like Ordo II it describes the ceremonies of a pontifical Mass adapted from the papal function for use elsewhere. In the opinion of Kösters, (Studien, 17) it probably belongs to the first half of the tenth century, since it was used by the compiler of the Ordo Vulgatus. It has been copied by a later twelfth century hand upon a blank page of the English "Benedictional of Archbishop Robert", and is there described as a "ritual drawn up by the ancient Fathers of the West".

ORDO VII is probably the most ancient of all Mabillon's Ordines and is assigned by Probst, Kösters, and others to the sixth century. The whole document deals with the ceremonies of Christian initiation, i. e. the catechumenate with its Lenten scrutinies (see BAPTISM), the rite of the consecration of the baptismal water, the baptism itself, and finally confirmation. The Ordo is closely related to the Gelasian Sacramentary, and the prayers, given in full in the Gelasianum, are here for the most part only indicated by their beginnings. Like the Gelasianum, the Ordo speaks throughout of *infantes* as if they alone were likely to be subjects for baptism, and the whole ceremony is modified to suit the case of infants in arms. When the catechumens are called upon to recite the Nicene Creed, it is directed that one of the acolytes shall take up one of the children upon his left arm, lay his right hand upon the child's head and recite the Creed in Greek, while another acolyte, holding another child, subsequently recites the Creed in Latin. None the less, the ceremonial of the scrutinies was originally designed for adult catechumens who were capable of understanding the Gospels and of learning and reciting the Creed for themselves. On the other hand, if the Ordo VII consistently regards the catechumens as *infantes*, this cannot be interpreted as a proof of relatively late date, for we find that already at the beginning of the sixth century the *vir illustris*, Senarius, asks of John, deacon of Rome, "quare tertio ante Pascha scrutinentur infantes" (why the infants have to undergo the scrutinies three times before Easter, Migne, P. L., LIX, 401). Seeing that the Gelasian Sacramentary also seems to know only of three scrutinies, it is possible that Ordo VII which requires seven scrutines may be of even older date than the sixth century, for it is hardly likely that when there was question of none but infant catechumens, the number of scrutinies should have been increased from three to seven. The whole tendency must have been in the direction of simplification. It may be noticed that Mabillon's Ordo VII is incorporated entire in an instruction on baptism by Jesse, Bishop of Amiens, c. 812.

ORDO VIII is concerned with the subject of ordinations and falls naturally into two divisions. The first part deals with the ordination of acolytes, subdeacons, deacons, and priests, the second with the ceremonial of the consecration of a bishop. Although the first part is extremely concise, and the second, more particularly in regard to the *quatuor capitula* (four forms of crime held to be a bar to ordination), is relatively developed, there seems no sufficient reason for questioning the essential unity of the whole document. In spite of certain expressions, notably the "ancilla dei sacrata quæ a Francis nonnata dicitur", which may easily be an interpolation or a gloss, and of references to the Ember seasons, to the *nomenclator*, and the schola (i. e. the choir—which last seems to suggest an age posterior to Gregory the Great) certain critics, notably Kösters (Studien, 21-23), make no difficulty in assigning the document to the early part of the sixth century. It is certainly noteworthy that though there is no mention in Ordo VIII of exorcists or any cleric lower than the grade of acolyte, the usages described closely agree with the language of the letter of Johannes Diaconus to Senarius at the beginning of the sixth century (Migne, P. L., LIX, 405). The function of the acolytes "portandi Sacramenta", here as in Ordo I, is recognized by assigning to them little bags (*sacculi*) as their distinctive attribute, instead of the candlestick of a later date, while the delivery of the chalice is emphasized as the significant act in the consecration of a subdeacon. When Bishop John Wordsworth (Ministry of Grace, 180) assumes that the delivery of the chalice is a Gallican ceremony and that it was introduced into the Roman Church in the seventh century at the earliest, he has clearly forgotten the explicit language of the latter to Senarius: "hic apud nos ordo est ut accepto sacratissimo calice in quo consuevit pontifex dominici sanguinis immolare mysterium subdiaconus iam dicatur". Again both Kösters and Grisar (Geschichte Roms, 765) regard the testing of the candidate for ordination by the *quatuor capitula*, requiring him to swear his innocence of certain unnatural crimes, as an indication which points to an age when many adult pagans still entered the Church as converts and were likely to be promoted to orders.

ORDO IX is entitled "De gradibus Romanæ ecclesiæ" and deals briefly with the ordination of deacons and priests, with the consecration of a bishop somewhat more fully, and finally with the consecration and coronation of a pope, while an appendix with a separate heading treats of the ember days. The date and composition of this document has recently been investigated by Dr. Kösters in a very able chapter of his "Studien". His conclusions are, that the substance of the Ordo was drawn up in the time of Pope Constantine I (708–15), and underwent some revision under Pope Stephen III (752–7). However, the most startling part of Dr. Kösters' discussion is his demonstration that the section describing the coronation of the pope, which incidentally introduces the name of Leo, belongs not to the period of Pope Leo III (c. 800), as has hitherto been supposed, but to that of Saint Leo IX (1044), and that in fact the papal *regnum*, or crown, which this Ordo describes as "made of white cloth in the form of a helmet", was for the first time worn by that pontiff. The statement made in this Ordo that the new pope should be a priest or deacon ordained by his predecessor and that he ought not to be a bishop (*nam episcopus esse non poterit*) is particularly interesting in view of the fact that Cardinal Deusdedit in the eleventh century, who comments on the text of this document, had apparently before him no clause to this effect. It is probably an interpolation of about that period. Other points of interest are the mention of *diaconissæ* and *presbiterissæ*, and the ceremony of holding the book of the Gospels over the pope at his ordination (*tenet evangelium super caput vel cervicem eius*). We hear of this last ceremony earlier in the East (cf. Apostolic Constitutions, VIII, iv) and in Gaul, and it is now part of the rite of consecration of every bishop, but it appears late at Rome. The appendix on the ember days, attached to this Ordo in the Saint-Gall Manuscript, had probably no original connexion with it and may be assumed to be not Roman.

ORDO X is a relatively long and very miscellaneous document and has no real claim to be included in the series of Ordines. It is, strictly speaking, a primitive form of Pontifical, though it is Roman in origin, and it is difficult to persuade oneself that it has not resulted from the fusion of at least two separate elements. The description of the Holy Week ceremonies which occupies nn. 1–24 may be described as a Cæremoniale pure and simple, and so is the burial service for the Roman clergy in nn. 36–40, the Roman character of both being unmistakable, but the intervening sections 26–35, which consist of an Ordo for administering the Sacrament of Penance, and for visiting, anointing, and giving Viaticum to the sick, form a service-book complete in itself, including not merely the incipits but the entire text of the prayers to be said by the priest, like any modern Ritual. Thalhofer (Liturgik, I, 48) has sought to draw a presumption of late date from the form of absolution in n. 29, which is indicative and not precative, *absolvimus te vice beati Petri* etc.; but substantially the same formula occurs with an interpolated Anglo-Saxon translation in the Egbert Pontifical of the tenth century. Neither are the reasons convincing, upon which Kösters bases his conclusion that the document as a whole is posterior to the year 1200. We must probably be content to leave the question of date unsettled.

ORDO XI has a tolerably full account of the papal ceremonial as it extended through the whole ecclesiastical year. This description is particularly valuable, inasmuch as it includes not only the functions of great solemnities but also the everyday usages and a considerable amount of detail regarding the Divine Office. It has lately been shown by Dr. Kösters that what we now possess in Ordo XI is only a fragment of a much larger work compiled by Benedict, Canon of St. Peter's, which was primarily a treatise upon the dignity of the Roman pontiff and upon the cardinals and various officials of the Roman Court, and which from the nature of its contents was called "Liber Politicus". This title has left a trace of itself in the heading of the manuscript used by Mabillon, where by a strange perversion it appears as "liber pollicitus". The treatise seems to have been completed just before the year 1143.

ORDO XII likewise contains a somewhat minute description of the papal ceremonial in ecclesiastical and quasi-ecclesiastical functions throughout the year, much space being occupied by a detailed record of the regulations followed in the distribution of the bounties called *presbyteria*. This Ordo is avowedly extracted from the "Liber Censuum", a treatise compiled towards the end of the twelfth century by Cardinal Cencius de Sabellis, afterwards Pope Honorius III (1216–1227). But here again Kösters has shown that the last two sections, dealing with the election and consecration of the pope and with the crowning of the emperor, can be traced back to the "Politicus" of Benedict. Various miscellaneous matters, concerning, e. g., the duties and dues of certain minor officials, the oath taken by senators to the pope, etc., also find a place in this collection.

ORDO XIII is one of the few Ordines which we possess, at least substantially, in the form in which it was first written. This is admittedly an official treatise drawn up by command of Pope Gregory X, shortly after the publication of the Constitution "Ubi periculum", issued in 1274 to regulate the procedure of the cardinals assembled in conclave for a papal election. The earliest portion of the document (nn. 1–12) is in fact concerned with the choice, consecration, and coronation of a new pope, provision being made for the case of his being a bishop, priest, or deacon. The treatise seems to presuppose an acquaintance with Ordo XI and Ordo XII and it is probably in consequence of this that the directions for the ordinary ceremonial are very concise. This Ordo marks the transition stage to a different type of liturgical document, much more developed and distinctively framed with a view to the part played by the Roman pontiff and his great retinue of ecclesiastical officials. Up to Ordo XIII we may say that the Ordines Romani are represented at the present day by the "Pontificale" and the "Cæremoniale Episcoporum" (q. v.), which are liturgical text-books common to the whole of Latin Christianity. But the two remaining Ordines, XIV and XV, are represented to-day by the "Cæremoniale Romanum", which constitutes the rubrical code for papal functions in Rome and has no application in the ceremonial of the Catholic Church outside the Eternal City.

ORDO XIV, which in the manuscripts bears the significant title "Ordinarium" instead of Ordo, is a much longer document than any of those hitherto considered. It is in fact the first rough outline of the bulky "Cæremoniale Romanum" which regulates the detail of papal functions at the present day. The history of Ordo XIV has been very carefully worked out by Dr. Kösters in his "Studien". The substance of the document seems to have been the work of Napoleone Orsini and Cardinal Jacopo Gaetani Stefaneschi, the latter having by far the larger share of its composition. By the aid of a manuscript found by Father Ehrle, the librarian of the Vatican, at Avignon, we are able to trace how the work took shape. (See Denifle and Ehrle, "Archiv. f. Lit- und Kirchengeschichte des. M.A.", V, 564 sqq.) It was begun in Rome before the popes left for France, but it was further developed and modified during the first third of the fourteenth century while the papal Court was at Avignon, and we know at any rate that the first nine chapters were quoted, as we now have them, in the conclave which assembled in 1334. But there must have been a revision of the treatise about or after 1389, when the long chapter 45: "Incipit Ordo qualiter Romanus Pontifex apud basilicam beati Petri Apostoli debeat consecrari", with its directions for the "possessio", or taking possession of the Lateran, was drawn up, the ceremony being in abeyance while the popes were at Avignon. Long, however, as the document is, and fully as it may seem to cover the ordinary requirements of papal official life, it may be doubted whether we possess the treatise in its entirety. In the original plan of Stefaneschi we know that the papal obsequies were included, but nothing upon this head is now contained in Ordo XIV, and it is difficult to conceive that this omission can have taken place through an oversight when so many other needs are minutely provided for.

Ordo XV is a fresh attempt to work up the same materials, while supplying at the same time the lacunæ which had hitherto existed. According to Kösters, chapters 1–100 and 143–153 were first drafted in the middle of the fourteenth century and were revised and supplemented by Pietro Amelii down to the year 1400. But the work of revision and modification was further carried on as far as 1435 by Peter, Bishop of Oloyca, while a final editor, who may very possibly have been Peter Kirten, Bishop of Olivna, put a last hand to the work in the second half of the same century. A selection of some of the more noteworthy headings of the 153 chapters of the work will perhaps serve better than anything else to give an idea of the comprehensiveness of this prototype of the Cæremoniale Romanum, which Mabillon prints under the name of Pietro Amelii:—

Advent; Vigil of the Nativity; Entoning of the Antiphons; Matins; Reading of the Lessons; First Mass on Christmas Day; Second Mass; Third Mass; St. Stephen and the following feasts; Epiphany; Blessing of the Candles on 2 Feb. with the Procession; Serving the Pope; Ash Wednesday; What happens when the King receives Ashes; Different occurrences in Lent; The Progresses of the Pope in penitential Seasons; Taking off the Pope's Mitre; Fourth Sunday of Lent which is called Rose Sunday; Blessing of the Palms, followed by detailed instructions for the Holy Week ceremonies, especially regarding the Maundy and the banquet on Maundy Thursday; Cardinal-Priest who serves the Pope on Holy Saturday; Easter and the Communion of the Cardinal Deacons etc.; Short details regarding the other Feasts of the Year; Office for the Dead on All Souls' Day; What is to be Observed when the Pope Sickens; Death of the Pope; Exequies of the Pope; Novendiale; Distributions of Cloth after the Pope's Death; Directions for the Conclave. Meeting a Cardinal who comes to the Roman Court; Canonisations, notably that of St. Bridget (1391).

Ordines Romani Published since Mabillon.— Mabillon's selection by no means exhausted the materials of this nature still available. Documents unknown in his time have since come to light and have been published by scholars who recognized their value. Foremost amongst these is the Einsiedeln Ordo, already alluded to, which was first printed by De Rossi in his "Inscriptiones Christianæ" (II, I, 34) and has since been re-edited by Duchesne in his "Origines du Culte Chrétien" (tr. Christian Worship, 481). This supplies an earlier and more purely Roman account of the ceremonial of the last three days of Holy Week than that contained in Mabillon's Ordo I. Again an extremely important text covering much the same ground as Ordo I but including, besides the pontifical Mass and the Holy Week ceremonial, some account of the ember-day ordinations, the rite of the dedication of a church with relics, and the candle procession on the feast of the Purification, has been published by Mgr Duchesne in the work just named from a ninth-century manuscript of St-Amand. Other documents of less moment have been printed by Gerbert in his "Monumenta vet. lit. alcman." (St. Blasien, 1770), by Martène in his "De antiquis eccles. ritibus", by Kösters as an appendix to his "Studien" and by others.

The *Ordines Romani* of Mabillon were first published in his *Musæum Italicum* (Paris, 1689), with a full introduction and annotations. The whole has been reprinted in Migne, *P. L.*, LXXXVIII, 851 sqq. By far the best discussion of the subject is by Kösters, *Studien zu Mabillons röm Ord.* (Münster, 1905); but see also Kober in *Kirchenlex.*, s. v.; Probst, *Die ältesten römischen Sakramentarien und Ordines* (Münster, 1892), 386 sqq.; Grisar in *Zeitschrift f. kath. Theologie*, 1881, pp. 699 sqq., 1885, pp. 385 sqq., 1886, pp. 727 sqq.; Idem, *Analecta Romana* (Rome, 1899), 198 sqq.; Thalhofer-Ebner, *Liturgik*, I (Freiburg, 1894), 46 sqq.; Mekel in *Theolog. Quartalschrift*, 1862, 60 sqq.; Atchley, *Ordo Romanus Primus* (London, 1905).

Herbert Thurston.

Oregon, one of the Pacific Coast States, seventh in size among the states of the Union. It received its name from the Oregon (now the Columbia) River, which is the state's greatest inland waterway. The ultimate origin of the name is obscure. Oregon is bounded on the north by the State of Washington, on the east by Idaho, on the south by Nevada and California, and on the west by the Pacific Ocean. Its length is 300 miles from north to south; its breadth 396 miles. Its total area is 96,030 sq. miles, including 1470 of water surface. It lies between 42° and 46° 18' N. lat., and between 116° 35' and 124° 35' W. long.

Physical Characteristics.—In the western portion of the state two mountain ranges one hundred miles apart run parallel with the coast line; in the eastern part there stretches out a vast inland plateau. The coast range traverses the state at a distance of about twenty miles from the ocean; it has an average height of 3500 feet, and is densely covered with fir, spruce, and cedar, most of which is valuable for lumber. The Cascade Mountains, a prolongation of the Sierra Nevada, extend through the state from north to south at a distance of about 120 miles from the coast. While the average height of this range is about 6000 feet, it is crowned with a line of extinct volcanoes whose snow-capped peaks reach a height of 9000 feet, Mt. Hood, just east of the city of Portland, attaining an altitude of 11,225 feet.

Seal of Oregon

Division.—The state is divided physically into three sections known as Western, Southern, and Eastern Oregon, differing in temperature, rainfall, and products. The Willamette Valley lies in Western Oregon. It is bounded on the north by the Columbia River, on the east by the Cascades, on the west by the Coast Range, and on the south by the Calapooia Mts. It is the most thickly settled part of the state, and is noted for its beautiful farm homes and equable climate. The valley is about 160 miles long, and has an average width of sixty miles, not including its mountain slopes. It presents one beautiful sweep of valley containing about 5,000,000 acres, all of which is highly fertile. It is drained by the Willamette River, which runs north, receives the waters of many important streams rising in the Cascades and coast range, and discharges into the Columbia River, just north of Portland. Western Oregon also includes the important counties west of the Willamette Valley on the coast. Southern Oregon lies west of the Cascades, between the Willamette Valley and California. It comprises the counties of Douglas, Coos, Curry, Josephine, and Jackson. The principal streams of this section are the Umpqua and Rogue Rivers, which rise in the Cascades, pierce the Coast Range, and empty into the Pacific Ocean. The valleys of these rivers are notable for their abundant and varied fruit production. The mountains in this section are rich in gold, which is extensively mined. The portion of this section west of the coast range is generally heavily timbered with fir, spruce, and cedar. Extensive coal deposits are found, some of which are developed and yield largely. Coos Bay is one of the best harbours on the Oregon Coast. Eastern Oregon embraces all the state east of the Cascade Mountains, forming a parallelogram 275 miles long and 230 miles wide. It is a great inland plateau of an altitude varying between 2000 and 5000 feet. The southern half of this plateau belongs to the Great American Basin, while the northern portion slopes towards the Columbia river valley. In the north-eastern part of the state, between the Snake and Columbia rivers, are the Blue Mountains whose summits are more than 6000 feet high, and whose streams are used for the purpose of irrigation. The Government is reclaiming large tracts by irrigation in this section. Here also is the most valuable and important mineral belt of the state. In the southern portion of Eastern Oregon are several short mountain ranges from 2000 to 3000 feet high which are a continuation of the longitudinal basin-ranges of Nevada. Irrigation is contributing largely towards bringing this section into prominence. The Klamath irrigation project, under the supervision of the United States Government, contains about 200,000 acres and is making rapid progress.

RESOURCES.—All the four great natural resources—viz: forest, fisheries, soil, and minerals—are present in almost inexhaustible supply awaiting development.

Lumber.—Oregon has approximately three hundred billion feet of standing merchantable timber (or nearly one-fifth of the standing merchantable timber in the United States), valued at $3,000,000,000. Timber covers about 57 per cent of the area of the state. Apart from the value of this timber as a source of lumber supply, it serves an important purpose in maintaining a perpetual flow of water in the mountain streams by retarding the melting of snow and holding a continuous supply of moisture in the ground during the summer. The most densely timbered area of the state is west of the Cascade Range, due to the greater rainfall in that section. The average stand of timber on the forested area west of the cascades is 17,700 feet B. M. to the acre. Localities where the stand is 50,000 feet per acre for entire townships are common in the coast counties of Clatsop and Tillamook. Some sections are found where a yield of 150,000 feet to the acre is estimated, many of the trees scaling 40,000 feet or more of commercial lumber. The Douglas fir sometimes attains a height of 300 feet, and five to six feet in thickness. Bridge timbers more than 100 feet in length are obtained from these trees. About 66 per cent of the timber is of this variety, which yields more commercial product to the acre than any other tree in North America. Three per cent of the merchantable timber of Oregon is hardwood, such as ash, oak, maple, and myrtle. There are about ninety-five species that attain to the dignity of trees: of these thirty-eight are coniferous, seventeen deciduous softwoods, and forty hardwoods. At present the lumber industry is one of Oregon's chief sources of revenue. The output of sawed lumber for 1906 was 2,500,000,000 feet valued at $30,000,000. The output of other forest products (piling, poles, shingles, ties, etc.) brought the total forest product from the state for that year to the sum of $60,000,000, which is about the average annual production. Portland is the largest lumber shipping port in the world. The work of preventing destructive forest fires is carried on by the United States Government on its forest reserves, and the state maintains a patrol of 300 men to protect the forests of the state.

Minerals.—There is a great wealth and variety of minerals to be found in Oregon, including gold, silver, copper, iron, asbestos, nickel, platinum, coal, antimony, lead, and clay, salt and alkali deposits, and an inexhaustible supply of building stone (including sandstone, limestone, and volcanic rock). Gold is found to a greater or less extent in seventeen counties, and is the only mineral mined to any notable extent. It is found especially in the Blue Mountains. A large number of quartz mills are operated in Eastern and Southern Oregon, and in these districts placer mines yield largely. There are two pronounced copper zones in the state—one in Baker County, the other in the south-western section. Oregon coals are lignitic, the largest bed uncovered being in the vicinity of Coos Bay. The largest iron beds in the state are in the Willamette Valley. The ore is of limonite variety, showing about fifty per cent of metallic iron.

Fisheries.—Oregon is unequalled by any other state in salmon fisheries and canning. The most notable species of salmon is the Columbia River Royal Chinook. The fish industry in the state produces upwards of $5,000,000 annually. Reckless overfishing threatened to exhaust the supply and to imperil the industry, until the state regulated it by law and provided for it by hatcheries. The state through its department of fisheries operates at the annual expense of $50,000 ten salmon hatcheries, from which nearly 70,000,000 young salmon are liberated annually. Thus the Columbia River is made to produce year after year practically the same supply of salmon. In addition to the canneries, cold storage plants are operated, practically the whole output of which is shipped to European markets.

Agriculture.—Late years have seen a great expansion in all lines of farming. In 1908 the total production of the farms of the State represented a gross value of about one hundred million dollars. Owing to the lack of a large rural population, however, only a fraction of the agricultural lands of the state yield even a respectable revenue. The most thickly settled agricultural sections are the great Willamette Valley in Western Oregon (where nearly everything grown in a temperate climate thrives), and a stretch of nearly five hundred miles of rich bottom land along the Columbia River and the shore line of the coast counties. The great wheat and meat producing section of the state is in Eastern and Central Oregon. The Columbia River Basin in Eastern Oregon is one of the best grain districts in the world. Wasco, Sherman, Gilliam, Morrow, and Umatilla counties produce from ten to fifteen million bushels of wheat annually. The soil is mainly a volcanic ash and silt, very fertile and generally deep. Hood River, among the best-known apple regions in the world, is included in this district. Umatilla County may be taken as typical of this section: its wheat crop averages about 5,000,000 bushels annually, while the alfalfa lands, comprising about 50,000 acres, yield three crops each year, totalling seven tons to the acre. Live stock is also an extensive industry: there are in this county about 350,000 sheep (with fleeces averaging 9½ pounds) and 30,000 cattle. Most of the sheep and a large proportion of the cattle of the state are raised in central Oregon which comprises about twenty million acres. This immense territory has been hitherto without any railroad communication whatever, and is at present devoted to range systems of husbandry. South-eastern Oregon, comprising Klamath and Lake Counties, is a stock and dairy section. On 1 Jan., 1909, the live stock of the state was valued at $54,024,000. The revenue to the state from dairy products was $17,000,000. In Southern Oregon poultry raising has become quite an industry, and this section practically supplies the large cities on the coast.

MEANS OF COMMUNICATION.—Oregon is bounded on three sides by navigable water: the Pacific Ocean on the west, the Columbia River on the north, and the Snake River on the east. Nine inlets on the western coast provide harbour facilities. Of these Coos Bay ranks next in importance to the Columbia harbour. Ocean-going vessels enter the Columbia, and find at Portland the only freshwater port on the Pacific coast. Deep

XI.—19

water navigation now extends 150 miles along the northern boundary of Oregon, and, with the completion of the ship railway above the Cascades, will extend to 250 miles. The Snake River runs along the eastern boundary of the state for 150 miles, and is navigable for a considerably greater distance from where it enters the Columbia. The Willamette River which empties into the Columbia just north of Portland is navigable as far as Eugene, 150 miles from Portland. The region between the coast and the Cascade ranges, and the northern fringe of the state along the Columbia and Snake rivers are well supplied with railroad facilities. The vast area of Eastern Oregon, however, has been hitherto practically without railroad service. This immense territory is finally being opened up (1910) by the construction of railroads by two rival systems through the Deschutes Valley.

EDUCATIONAL SYSTEM.—The State Board of Education is composed of the governor, the secretary of state, and a superintendent of public instruction. In each county there is a superintendent who holds office for two years, and each school district has a board comprising from three to five directors whose term is three years. The state course of study provides for eight grades in the grammar schools and four years in the high schools. The state university at Eugene and the agricultural college at Corvallis complete the state school system. An irreducible fund of $3,500,000 has been secured by the sale of part of the school lands of the state. In 1884 Congress set aside sections 16 and 36 of all the public domain in Oregon for public schools. For many years previous to 1909 there were four state normal schools, which were practically local high schools subsidized by the state. The subsidy was withdrawn by the legislature of that year, and there is now one state normal located at Monmouth. The state university was established in 1872. The agricultural college at Corvallis, which also gives a college course in the liberal arts and sciences, has about one thousand students. There are a large number of denominational colleges and secondary schools in the state. At Salem, the state capital, are located the charitable and penal institutions of the state, viz., the schools for the blind and deaf mutes, the insane asylum, boys' reform school, and the penitentiary.

HISTORY.—*Explorations.*—In 1543 the Spanish navigator Ferrelo explored the Pacific Coast—possibly to the parallel of 42°, the southern boundary of Oregon. Sir Francis Drake in "The Golden Hind" (1543), carried the English colours a few miles farther north than Ferrelo had ventured. The same point was reached by the Spaniard Vizcaino in 1603. In 1774 Juan Perez sailed in the "Santiago" from the harbour of Monterey and explored the north-west coast as far as parallel 55°. The following year the Spanish explored the north-west coast under Heceta, who, on his return, observed the strong currents at the mouth of the Columbia. Nootka Sound was visited and named by the English navigator Cook in 1778. The visit of Cook had important consequences. The natives loaded his ship with sea-otter skins in exchange for the merest trifles. The value of these skins was not suspected, until the ship touched at Asiatic and European ports where they were sold for fabulous prices. The commercial value of the north-west had been discovered. The ships of all nations sought for a profitable fur-trade with the Indians, and the strife for the possession of the territory entered a new phase. Captain Robert Gray of Boston discovered the Columbia River in 1792 and named it after his ship. The country was first explored by the American expedition of Lewis and Clark in 1804–5. Astoria, at the mouth of the Columbia, the first white settlement in Oregon, was founded in 1811 by the American Fur Company under the direction of John Jacob Astor. Two years later the Northwest Company (a Canadian fur company) bought out Astoria, and maintained commercial supremacy until it merged with the great Hudson's Bay Company in 1821.

This latter company dominated Oregon for a quarter of a century. The Oregon country at that time embraced an area of 400,000 sq. miles and extended from the Rocky Mountains on the east to the Pacific Ocean and from the Mexican possessions on the south to the Russian possessions on the north. In 1824 a commanding personality arrived on the Columbia as chief factor of the Hudson's Bay Co., in the Oregon country. This was Dr. John McLoughlin (q. v.), the most heroic figure in Oregon history. Realizing that the great trading post should be at the confluence of the Columbia and Willamette Rivers, McLoughlin transferred the headquarters of the company from Fort George (Astoria) to Fort Vancouver. He refused to sell liquor to the Indians, and bought up the supplies of rival traders to prevent them from selling it. He commanded the absolute obedience and respect of the Indian population, and Fort Vancouver was the haven of rest for all travellers in the Oregon country. Speaking of McLoughlin's place in Oregon history, his biographer, Mr. Frederick V. Holman, a non-Catholic, pays him the following just tribute: "Of all the men whose lives and deeds are essential parts of the history of the Oregon country, Dr. John McLoughlin stands supremely first,—there is no second".

Missionaries.—The first tidings of the Catholic Faith reached the Oregon Indians through the Canadian employees of the various fur-trading companies. The expedition of Astor in 1811 was accompanied by a number of Canadian *voyageurs*, who some years later founded at St. Paul the first white settlement in the Willamette Valley. These settlers applied in 1835 to Bishop Provencher of Red River (St. Boniface, Manitoba) for priests to come among them to bless their marriages with their savage consorts, to baptize their children, and revive the Faith among themselves. It was in answer to this petition that Fathers F. N. Blanchet and Modeste Demers were sent to the Oregon country in 1838. On their arrival the missionaries found a log church already erected on the prairie above St. Paul. Meanwhile another request for missionaries had gone forth. The Indians in the Rocky Mountains had repeated the Macedonian cry to their brethren in the East. In 1831 the Flatheads with their neighbours, the Nez Percés, sent a deputation to St. Louis to ask for priests. They had heard of the black robes through Iroquois Indians, who had settled among them and thus transplanted the seed sown by Father Jogues. It was not until 1840 that Bishop Rosati of St. Louis was able to send a missionary. In that year Father De Smet, S.J., set out on his first trip to the Oregon country where he became the apostle of the Rocky Mountain Indians. A peculiar perversion of the facts concerning the visit of the Indians to St. Louis got abroad in the Protestant religious press and started a remarkable movement towards Oregon. The Methodists sent out Jason and Daniel Lee in 1834, and the Methodist mission was soon reinforced until it was valued in a few years at a quarter of a million dollars and became the dominating factor in Oregon politics. The American Board Mission was founded by Dr. Marcus Whitman, a physician, and Mr. Spalding, a minister. With them was associated W. H. Gray as agent, the author of a "History of Oregon" which was responsible for the spread of a great deal of misinformation concerning the early missionary history of Oregon.

The savage murder of Dr. Whitman in 1847 was a great catastrophe. Dr. Whitman, who was a man of highly respected character, opened his mission among the Cayuse Indians near Fort Walla Walla. His position as physician made him suspected by the

Indians when an epidemic carried off a large number of the tribe. They were accustomed to kill the "medicine man" who failed to cure. Besides the Indians were rendered hostile by the encroachments of the whites. The immediate cause of the massacre seems to have been the story of Jo Lewis, an Indian who had the freedom of the mission and who reported that he overheard a conversation of Whitman and Spalding, in which Whitman said he would kill off the Indians so that the whites could get their land. The massacre took place on 29 Nov., 1847. Dr. and Mrs. Whitman and several others were brutally slain. Spalding was saved only by the prudence of Father Brouillet whose mission was near by. Spalding seems to have been crazed by the outrage. He began to charge the Catholic priests with instigating the massacre. There had been hard feelings before between the missionary forces, but now the embers were fanned into a flame and, in spite of the fact that all serious historians have exonerated the Catholic missions of the slightest complicity in the outrage, Spalding's ravings instilled a prejudice which half a century has been required to obliterate.

Nearly twenty years after Whitman's death Spalding originated a new story of Whitman's services in saving Oregon to the United States, in which the Catholics were again brought into prominence. "History will be searched in vain", says Bourne, "for a more extraordinary growth of fame after death." The story as published in 1865 by Spalding represents that in autumn, 1842, Whitman was aroused by discovering that the Hudson's Bay Co. and the Catholic missionary forces were planning to secure the Oregon Country for England. He immediately set out for Washington to urge the importance of Oregon to the United States and to conduct a band of immigrants across the plains to settle the country with Americans. It is represented further that he found Webster ready to exchange Oregon for some cod fisheries on the shores of Newfoundland and some concessions in settling the boundary of Maine. Whitman, however, had recourse to President Tyler, who promised to delay the negotiations between Webster and Ashburton until Whitman could demonstrate the possibility of leading a band of emigrants to the north-west. Finally, the legend relates that Whitman organized a great band of immigrants and conducted them to Oregon in 1843, thus proving to the authorities at Washington the accessibility of the disputed territory and filling the territory with American home builders. Thus Oregon was saved to the United States. Every detail of this story has now been completely discredited by critical historians. The core of fact consists merely in this, that in 1842 Whitman went east to plead with the authorities of the American Board not to close down the southern section of his mission, and on his return to Oregon in 1843 he happened in with a band of immigrants who had assembled under the leadership of Peter Burnett. The legend is gradually being expunged from school books.

GOVERNMENT AND LEGISLATION.—In 1843 a provisional government with an executive council was organized by the settlers in the Willamette Valley. Two years later a governor was chosen who held office until the Oregon Territory was organized under the U. S. Government on 14 August, 1848. Lane, the first governor of the territory, arrived in 1849. Oregon was admitted as a State 14 Feb., 1859, with its present boundaries. The primary election law is in operation, and there is a provision that the state legislators may obligate themselves with their constituencies under Statement No. 1, to cast their ballot for United States Senator for the candidate receiving the highest popular vote at the primary election. Thus it happened that United States Senator Geo. E. Chamberlain was elected in 1907 representing the minority party in the state legislature. The initiative and referendum obtain, and a large number of measures are brought before the people by petition under the initiative power. The state legislature provides a subsidy for institutions caring for dependent and delinquent minors.

Freedom of Worship is provided for in the Bill of Rights in the Oregon Constitution. By its provisions all persons are secured in their "natural right to worship Almighty God according to the dictates of their own conscience". No law shall in any case control the free exercise and enjoyment of religious opinion. No religious test shall be required as a qualification for any office of trust or profit. No money shall be drawn from the treasury for the benefit of any religious or theological institution, nor shall money be appropriated for the payment of religious services in either houses of the legislative assembly. But by recent enactment the salaries of two chaplains, one a Catholic, the other a non-Catholic, for the State Penitentiary is provided for at the expense of the State. The Constitution further provides that no person shall be rendered incompetent as a witness or juror in consequence of his religious opinions, nor be questioned in any court of justice touching his religious belief to affect the weight of his testimony. Oaths and affirmations shall be such as are most consistent with and most binding upon the consciences of the persons to whom they are administered. No law shall be passed restraining freedom to express opinions, or the right to speak, write, or print freely on any subject, but every person shall be held responsible for the abuse of this right. Persons whose religious tenets or conscientious scruples forbid them to bear arms shall not be compelled to do so in time of peace, but shall pay an equivalent for personal service.

There are many enactments regarding the observance of Sunday. The Sundays of the year as well as Christmas are legal and judicial holidays. No person may keep open a house or room in which liquor is retailed on Sunday,—the penalty being a fine which goes to the school fund of the county in which the offence is committed. In general it is illegal to keep open on Sunday any establishment "for the purpose of labor or traffic", except drug stores, livery stables, butcher and bakery shops, etc.

The seal of the confessional is guarded by the following provision: "A priest or clergyman shall not, without the consent of the person making the confession, be examined as to any confession made to him in his professional character in the course of discipline enjoined by the church to which he belongs."

Persons over eighteen years of age may dispose of goods and chattels by will. "A person of twenty-one years of age and upwards and of sound mind may by last will devise all his estate, real and personal, saving to the widow her dower." The will must be in writing. It must be signed by the testator or by some other person under his direction and in his presence, and also by two or more competent witnesses subscribing their names in presence of the testator.

Divorce.—The following grounds are recognized in Oregon for the dissolution of marriage: (1) Impotency existing at the time of marriage and continuing to the time of suit. (2) Adultery. (3) Conviction of felony. (4) Habitual gross drunkenness contracted since marriage. (5) Willful desertion for one year. (6) Cruel and inhuman treatment or personal indignities rendering life burdensome. (Bellinger and Cotton, "Annotated Codes and Statutes of Oregon.")

CATHOLIC EDUCATION.—One of the earliest cares of Vicar-General Blanchet on arriving in Oregon was the Christian education of the youth committed to his charge. In autumn, 1843, it was decided to open a school for boys at St. Paul. On 17 October in that year, the vicar-general opened St. Joseph's College with solemn blessing and placed Father Langlois in charge. On the opening day thirty boys entered as boarders—all sons of farmers except one, the son of an Indian chief. The first Catholic school for girls in Oregon was opened early in October, 1844, by six Sisters of Notre Dame de Namur who had just arrived from Belgium with Father De Smet. So immediate was the success of the sisters that Father De Smet writing under date of 9 Oct., 1844, says that another foundation was projected at Oregon City. This plan was not realized until 1848. In September of that year four sisters took up their residence and opened a school at the Falls. Meanwhile two events occurred which paralyzed all missionary work for a decade. The first was the Whitman massacre already referred to, which aroused the intensest hostility to the Catholic missionaries. The second was the discovery of gold in California which for the time caused a large emigration of the male population from Oregon. This movement of the population deprived the Archdiocese of all religious, both men and women. In May, 1849, a large brigade composed of Catholic families from St. Paul, St. Louis, and Vancouver started for the California mines. As a consequence St. Joseph's College was permanently closed in June of the same year. The Jesuit Fathers closed the mission of St. Francis Xavier on the Willamette; the Sisters of Notre Dame closed their school at St. Paul in 1852, and the following spring closed the school at Oregon City and left for California. The outlook was very dark. The tide of immigration soon turned again towards Oregon, but found the Church crippled in its educational and missionary forces. A debt had been contracted in building the cathedral and convent at Oregon City. To raise funds Archbishop Blanchet went to South America in September, 1855, and remained there making collections until the end of 1857.

A new era opened for Catholic education in Oregon in Oct., 1859, when twelve Sisters of the Holy Names arrived from Montreal and opened at Portland St. Mary's academy and college, which as the mother-house of the community in the province of Oregon has for half a century played an honourable part in the educational work of the north-west. In August, 1871, a school for boys, called St. Michael's College, was opened with 64 pupils. Its first principal was Father Glorieux, now Bishop of Boise. In 1875 we find the pupils publishing a college paper, "The Archangel". At the invitation of Archbishop Gross, the Christian Brothers took charge of St. Michael's College in 1886. The name was subsequently changed to that of Blanchet Institute in honour of the first archbishop. This school has since been superseded by the modern and ample structure of the Christian Brothers' Business College. In 1882 the Benedictine Fathers, at the invitation of Archbishop Seghers, established their community first at Gervais, and two years later at Mt. Angel. A college for young men at Mt. Angel was opened in 1888. The destruction of the monastery by fire in 1892 was the occasion of building the magnificent monastery and college in its present commanding position. While Mt. Angel's theological department is intended primarily for the education of young men for the order, it has been the Alma Mater of a number of the priests of the archdiocese. In 1904 the priory was raised to the dignity of an abbey. At Mt. Angel, too, has been located since 1883 an academy for girls conducted by the Benedictine Sisters, and the mother-house of the community in Oregon. Columbia University was opened at Portland by Archbishop Christie in 1901. The following year it was placed in charge of the Holy Cross Fathers, under whose direction the institution has experienced a gratifying development and has come to occupy a large place in the Catholic life of the metropolis. St. Mary's Institute near Beaverton, an academy for girls, is the mother-house of the Sisters of St. Mary. This congregation was founded by Archbishop Gross in 1886. The Dominican Sisters (San Jose, California), the Sisters of the Immaculate Heart of Mary (Scranton, Penn.), the Sisters of Mercy, and the Sisters of St. Francis (Milwaukee) conduct a number of excellent schools in the archdiocese. About nine-tenths of the parishes of the archdiocese are provided with Catholic schools. An annual Catholic Teachers' Institute has been held under the auspices of the Catholic Educational Association of Oregon since 1905. These summer meetings have become very popular, and are attended by all the teachers in the Catholic schools of the archdiocese. Prominent educators from various sections of the country are invited to address the institute. The meetings serve also to promote interchange of ideas and good fellowship between the teaching communities and contribute notably to the uniform educational progress of the schools.

CHARITABLE INSTITUTIONS.—The archdiocese is well equipped with institutions of charity. St. Vincent's Hospital, conducted by the Sisters of Charity of Providence, was established in Portland in 1874. It will accommodate about 350 patients. The same community conducts a hospital at Astoria. The Sisters of Mercy have charge of hospitals at Albany, North Bend, and Roseburg. The Sisters of the Good Shepherd have conducted a home for wayward girls in Portland since 1902. The judges of the juvenile court have repeatedly commended the work of these sisters in the highest terms. The archdiocese has three homes for dependent children. St. Agnes' Baby Home, conducted by the Sisters of Mercy at Park Place near Oregon City, was established in 1902; it receives orphans and foundlings under the age of four years, and cares constantly for about ninety babies. St. Mary's Home for Boys is situated near Beaverton and is in charge of the Sisters of St. Mary. Here too is the location of the Levi Anderson Industrial school for boys. Occupying a commanding site on the Willamette near Oswego is the magnificent new home for orphan girls under the care of the Sisters of the Holy Names. Since 1901 the Sisters of Mercy have conducted in Portland a home for the aged, where more than a hundred old people of either sex find a home in their declining years. St. Vincent de Paul's and women's charitable societies (e. g. St. Ann and Ladies' Aid) are well equipped to relieve the needy. Fraternal societies (e. g. the Knights of Columbus, Ancient Order of Hibernians, and Catholic Order of Foresters, all of which are flourishing) aid materially in the relief of the poor. The Catholic Women's League of Portland was organized in the interests of young women wage-earners, especially for that very large class who have come west to find positions and are without home ties. The proportion of Catholics to the entire population of Oregon has never been very great, perhaps not more than one-tenth, though recent immigration has tended to increase the percentage. Catholics have, however, been well represented in public life and in professional and business pursuits. In early Oregon history Dr. McLoughlin and Chief Justice Peter Burnett were distinguished converts. The latter, who subsequently became first governor of California, is the author of "Reminiscences of an old Pioneer" and "The Path which led a Protestant Lawyer to the Catholic Church". General Lane, the first Governor of Oregon, was also received into the Church. Among the most distinguished citizens of the state to-day are ex-United States Senator John M. Gearin and General D. W. Burke.

Transactions of the O. Pioneer Association (Salem, 1874–87); *Quarterly of the O. Hist. Society* (Portland, 1900—); *The Oregonian* (Portland, 1850—), files; *The Catholic Sentinel* (Portland, 1870—), files; BANCROFT, *Hist. of the Northwest Coast* (San Francisco, 1884); IDEM, *Hist. of O.* (San Francisco, 1886–88); SCHAFER, *Hist. of the Pacific Northwest* (New York, 1905); HOLMAN, *Dr. John McLoughlin* (Cleveland, 1907); BOURNE, *Essays in Historical Criticism* (New York, 1901), containing a critical examination of the Whitman Legend; MARSHALL, *History vs. the Whitman Saved Oregon Story* (Chicago, 1904); O'HARA, *Dr. John McLoughlin* in

Catholic Univ. Bulletin, XIV, n. 2; IDEM, *De Smet in the Oregon Country* in *Quarterly of O. Hist. Soc.* (September, 1909); CHITTENDEN AND RICHARDSON, *De Smet's Life and Travels*; DE BAETS, *Mgr Seghers* (Paris, 1896); BROUILLET, *Authentic Account of the Murder of Dr. Whitman* (2nd ed., Portland, 1869); SNOWDEN, *Hist. of Washington*, I-II (New York, 1909); SISTER OF THE HOLY NAMES, *Gleanings of Fifty Years* (Portland, 1909).

EDWIN V. O'HARA.

Oregon City, ARCHDIOCESE OF (OREGONOPOLITAN), includes that part of the State of Oregon west of the Cascade Mountains, being bounded on the east by the counties of Wasco, Crook, and Klamath. It comprises an area of 21,398 square miles. By an indult of the Holy See dated 28 Feb., 1836, the Oregon Country north of the American line was annexed to the vicariate Apostolic of Mgr Provencher of Red River. By letters of 17 April, 1838, Rev. F. N. Blanchet was appointed vicar-general to the Archbishop of Quebec and assigned to the Oregon mission. The vicar-general established his first mission at St. Paul on the Willamette, and on 6 Jan., 1839, dedicated at that place the first Catholic church in Oregon. The church had been constructed three years earlier by the Canadian settlers who had anticipated the coming of a missionary among them.

As the line of demarcation between British and American territory was still undecided, and missionary priests had been sent into the country both from Canada and from the United States (De Smet had come from St. Louis), Oregon became a joint mission depending upon the Bishops of Quebec and Baltimore. At the suggestion of these bishops, the mission was erected into a vicariate Apostolic by a brief of 1 Dec., 1843. On 24 July, 1846, the vicariate was transformed into a province comprising the Archdiocese of Oregon City and the Dioceses of Walla Walla and Vancouver's Island. With the transfer of the See of Walla Walla to Nesqually (1848), the northern boundary of the Archdiocese of Oregon City was fixed at the Columbia River and the 46° lat. This territory was diminished by the erection of the Vicariate of Idaho (1868) and finally received its present limits by the erection of the Diocese of Baker City (1903).

Bishops: (1) François Norbert Blanchet (q. v.), b. 3 Sept., 1795, consecrated 25 July, 1845. There were in the diocese in 1845 ten priests, thirteen Sisters of Notre-Dame, and two educational institutions. The first priest ordained in Oregon was Father Jayol, the ceremony being performed by Archbishop Blanchet at St. Paul, 19 Sept., 1847. On 30 Nov., the archbishop consecrated at St. Paul, Bishop Demers of Vancouver's Island. He convened the First Provincial Council of Oregon City, 28 Feb., 1848. On 21 Dec., Archbishop Blanchet left St. Paul and took up his residence at Oregon City. In 1852 the first church in the City of Portland was dedicated under the title of the Immaculate Conception. It became the pro-cathedral when Archbishop Blanchet moved to Portland in 1862. (2) Charles John Seghers, b. 26 Dec., 1839, at Ghent, successor to the pioneer Bishop Demers of Vancouver's Island, was transferred to Oregon City, 10 Dec., 1878, and became coadjutor to Archbishop Blanchet who at once retired from active life. Archbishop Seghers is remembered for his heroic devotion to the Indian missions of Alaska (q. v.), which led him to resign the See of Oregon City in 1884. (3) William H. Gross (consecrated Bishop of Savannah, 1873) was promoted to the archiepiscopal See of Oregon City, 1 Feb., 1885, and invested with the pallium in Portland by His Eminence Cardinal Gibbons 9 Oct. On his death 14 Nov., 1898, he was succeeded by the present archbishop. (4) Most Rev. Alexander Christie (consecrated Bishop of Vancouver's Island, 29 June, 1898) was promoted to the archiepiscopal See of Oregon City, 12 Feb., 1899. Statistics for 1909: diocesan priests, 50; priests of rel. orders, 40; colleges, 3; secondary schools, 12; elementary schools, 35; pupils, 5500.

BLANCHET, *Historical Sketches* (Portland, 1870); *The Catholic Sentinel* (Portland, 1870–1910), files; *Catholic Directory; Diocesan Archives*.

EDWIN V. O'HARA.

O'Reilly, BERNARD, historian, b. 29 Sept., 1820, in County Mayo, Ireland; d. in New York, U. S. A., 26 April, 1907. In early life he emigrated to Canada, where in 1836 he entered Laval University. He was ordained priest in Quebec, 12 Sept., 1843, and ministered in several parishes of that diocese. He was one of the heroic priests who attended the plague-stricken Irish emigrants in the typhus-sheds along the St. Lawrence after the "black '47". Later he entered the Society of Jesus and was attached to St. John's College, Fordham, New York. When the Civil War broke out he went as a chaplain in the Irish Brigade and served with the Army of the Potomac during a large part of its campaigns. He then withdrew from the Jesuits and devoted himself to literature, becoming one of the editorial staff of the "New American Cyclopedia" to which he contributed articles on Catholic topics. At the conclusion of this work he travelled extensively in Europe, sending for several years an interesting series of letters to the New York "Sun". He lived for a long period in Rome where Pope Leo XIII, besides appointing him a prothonotary Apostolic in 1887, gave him the special materials for his "Life of Leo XIII" (New York, 1887). Among the many books he published these were notable: "Life of Pius IX" (1877); "Mirror of True Womanhood" (1876); "True Men" (1878); "Key of Heaven" (1878); "The Two Brides" (1879); "Life of John MacHale, Archbishop of Tuam" (1890). On his return to New York from Europe he was made chaplain at the convent of Mount St. Vincent, where he spent the rest of his days. On the occasion of his sacerdotal jubilee he was given a signed testimonial of appreciation of his fellow priests and friends.

Catholic News (New York, May, 1907); *Ave Maria* (Notre Dame, Indiana), files; *Nat. Cyclo. of Am. Biog.*, s. v.

THOMAS F. MEEHAN.

O'Reilly, CHARLES JOSEPH. See BAKER CITY, DIOCESE OF.

O'Reilly, EDMUND, Archbishop of Armagh, b. at Dublin, 1616; d. at Saumur, France, 1669, was educated in Dublin and ordained there in 1629. After ordination he studied at Louvain, where he held the position of prefect of the college of Irish Secular Ecclesiastics. In 1640 he returned to Dublin and was appointed vicar-general. In 1642 the Archbishop of Dublin, Dr. Fleming, having been appointed on the Supreme Council of the Confederate Catholics, transferred his residence to Kilkenny and until 1648 O'Reilly administered the Archdiocese of Dublin. With the triumph of the Puritans he was imprisoned, and in 1653, ordered to quit the kingdom, he took refuge at the Irish College of Lisle where he was notified of his appointment to the See of Armagh, and shortly after consecrated at Brussels. Ireland was then a dangerous place for ecclesiastics, and not until 1658 did he attempt to visit his diocese; even then he could proceed no farther than London. Ordered to quit the kingdom, he returned to France, but in the following year went to Ireland, this time directly from France, and for the next two years exercised his ministry. Accused of favouring the Puritans and of being an enemy of the Stuarts, he was ordered by the pope to quit Ireland. At Rome he was able to vindicate himself, but he was not allowed to return to Ireland by the English authorities until 1665, and then only in the hope that he would favour the Remonstrance of Peter Walsh. O'Reilly, like the great majority of the Irish bishops and priests, rejected it, nor could the entreaties of Walsh or the threats of Ormond change him. In consequence he was imprisoned by Ormond, and when released, driven from the kingdom. He spent the remaining years of his life in France, chiefly concerned with the care of the Irish colleges there.

STUART, *Historical Memoirs of Armagh*, ed. COLEMAN (Dublin, 1900); RENEHAN, *Irish Archbishops* (Dublin, 1861); D'ALTON, *Archbishops of Dublin* (Dublin, 1838); BRADY, *Episcopal Succession in Ireland and England* (Rome, 1876).

E. A. D'ALTON.

O'Reilly, EDMUND, theologian, b. in London, 30 April, 1811; d. at Dublin, 10 November, 1878. Educated at Clongowes and Maynooth, he made his theological studies at Rome, where after seven years in the Roman College he gained the decree of Doctor of Divinity by a "public act" *de universa theologia*. After his ordination in 1838 he taught theology for thirteen years at Maynooth into which he was mainly instrumental in introducing the Roman spirit and tradition, after which he entered the Jesuit novitiate at Naples. He taught theology for some years at St. Beuno's College in North Wales till he was appointed Professor of Theology under Newman in the Catholic University of Ireland. During the remainder of his life he resided at Milltown Park near Dublin as rector of a House of Spiritual Exercises; and he was Provincial of Ireland 1863-70. Constantly consulted on theological questions by the bishops and priests of Ireland, Cardinal Newman in his famous "Letter to the Duke of Norfolk" calls him "a great authority" and "one of the first theologians of the day". Dr. W. G. Ward, editor of "The Dublin Review", said: "It is a great loss to the Church that so distinguished a theologian as Father O'Reilly has published so little". Dr. Ward wrote of his chief work, "The Relations of the Church to Society", "Whatever is written by so able and so solidly learned a theologian, one so docile to the Church and so fixed in the ancient theological paths, cannot but be of signal benefit to the Catholic reader in these anxious and perilous times."

Freeman's Journal (Dublin, November, 1878); *Irish Monthly*, VI, 695.

MATTHEW RUSSELL.

O'Reilly, HUGH, Archbishop of Armagh, head of the Confederates of Kilkenny, b. 1580; d. on Trinity Island in Lough Erne. He first conceived the idea of forming this national movement into a regular organization. He convened a provincial synod at Kells early in March, 1642, in which the bishops declared the war undertaken by the Irish people for their king, religion, and country to be just and lawful. The following May (1642) he convened a national synod, consisting of prelates and civil lords, at Kilkenny. After having ratified their former declaration, they framed an oath of association to be taken by all their adherents, binding them to maintain the fundamental laws of Ireland, the free exercise of religion, and true allegiance to Charles I. Orders were issued to levy men and raise money; to establish a mint and an official printing press; to take the duty off such foreign imports as wheat and corn, lead, iron, arms and ammunition; the bishops and clergy should pay a certain sum for national purposes out of the ecclesiastical revenues that had come back into their possession; and agents should be sent to Catholic courts to solicit aid. They gave letters of credit and chartered some light vessels that were to fly the Confederate colours and protect the coast, and they drafted a remonstrance to the king declaring their loyalty and protesting against the acts of tyranny, injustice, and intolerance of the Puritan lord justices and Parliament of Dublin in confiscating Catholic lands and putting a ban on Catholic school-teachers. The assembly lasted until 9 January, agreeing to meet 20 May following. The seal of the Confederation bore in its centre a large cross rising out of a flaming heart, above were the wings of a dove, on the left a harp, and on the right a crown; the legend read: PRO DEO, REGE, ET PATRIA, HIBERNI UNANIMES.

Wherever the primate's partisans commanded, the Protestant bishops, ministers, and people were safe, and were even protected in the exercise of their own religious worship. Archbishop O'Reilly was, throughout the war and the terrible years that followed it, the soul and guide of the national party; he did his utmost to restrain the violence of the people, who would have wreaked vengeance on their persecutors had they been left to their own instincts at that crisis. He urged Sir Phelim O'Neile and Lord Iveagh to keep the armed multitudes in check and prevent the massacre and pillage of Protestants. Such salutary restraint produced the most happy results, for even the rudest of the northern chieftains respected him too much to violate his lessons of forbearance and charity. When the great chieftain, Owen Roe, was dying, he had himself taken to Ballinacorgy Castle, the residence of his brother-in-law Philip O'Reilly, where he was attended by Archbishop O'Reilly. Local tradition gives the ruined Abbey of the Holy Trinity, on an island a few miles from Ballinacorgy Castle, as his last resting-place. In the same locality Archbishop O'Reilly was buried. The primate's signature is still to be seen in most of the manifestoes of the Confederation of Kilkenny as "Hugo Armacanus".

D'ALTON, *History of Ireland*, III (Dublin, 1910); GILBERT, *Hist. of the Irish Confederation and the War in Ireland, 1640-41* (7 vols., Dublin, 1882-91).

SISTER M. STANISLAUS AUSTIN.

O'Reilly, JOHN. See ADELAIDE, ARCHDIOCESE OF.

O'Reilly, JOHN BOYLE, poet, novelist, and editor, b. at Douth Castle, Drogheda, Ireland, 24 June, 1844; d. at Hull, Massachusetts, 10 August, 1890; second son of William David O'Reilly and Eliza Boyle. He attended the National School, conducted by his father, and was employed successively as printer on the "Drogheda Argus", and on the staff of "The Guardian", Preston, England; he afterwards became a trooper in the Tenth Hussars. Entering actively into the Fenian movement, believing in his inexperience that Ireland's grievances could be redressed only by physical force, he was betrayed to the authorities and duly court-martialled. On account of his extreme youth, his life sentence was commuted to twenty years' penal servitude in Australia. Later study of his country's cause made him before long an earnest advocate of constitutional agitation as the only way to Irish Home Rule. In 1869, O'Reilly escaped from Australia, with the assistance of the captain of a whaling barque from New Bedford, Massachusetts. In 1870, he became editor of "The Pilot", Boston, and from 1876 until his death in 1890 he was also part proprietor, being associated with Archbishop Williams of Boston. His books include four volumes of poems: "Songs of the Southern Seas", "Songs, Legends, and Ballads", "The Statues in the Block", and "In Bohemia"; a novel, "Moondyne", based on his Australian experiences; his collaboration in another novel, "The King's Men", and "Athletics and Manly Sport". A sincere Catholic, his great influence, used lavishly in forwarding the interests of younger Catholics destined to special careers, and in lifting up the lowly without regard to any claim but their need, was for twenty years a valuable factor in Catholic progress in America. He was married in 1872 to Mary Murphy, in Boston, who died in 1897. Their four daughters survive them.

ROCHE, *Life of John Boyle O'Reilly* (New York, 1891); CONWAY, *Watchwords from John Boyle O'Reilly* (Boston, 1891).

KATHERINE E. CONWAY.

O'Reilly, MYLES WILLIAM PATRICK, soldier, publicist, *littérateur*, b. near Balbriggan, Co. Dublin, Ireland, 13 March, 1825; d. at Dublin, 6 Feb., 1880. In 1841 he entered Ushaw College (England), and graduated a B.A. of London University. From 1845 to 1847 he studied in Rome, and then returned to Ireland to assist the famine-stricken peasants. In 1851 he was associated with Newman and Archbishop Leahy to report on the projected Catholic University, and, in 1854 he became captain of the Louth Rifles. He married Miss Ida Jerningham, 3 Aug., 1859. Some months later he offered his services to Pius IX, against Garibaldi. Having formed an Irish Brigade, he was appointed major, under General Pimodan, and fought gallantly in every engagement until the surrender of Spoleto, 18 Sept., 1860. From 1862 to 1876 he represented County Longford in the British Parliament, and was one of those who signed the requisition for the famous Home Rule Conference under Isaac Butt. He ably supported Catholic interests, and assisted in the movement to obtain Catholic chaplains for the army. He wrote "Sufferings for the Faith in Ireland" (London, 1868). He also contributed to the "Dublin Review" and other periodicals, writing especially in defence of the Holy See and of Catholic educational matters. After the death of his wife in 1876, he accepted the position of Assistant Commissioner of Intermediate Education for Ireland in April, 1879, which he filled until his death. He was interred at Philipstown, not far from his family residence in Co. Louth.

O'CLERY, *The Making of Italy* (London, 1898); Contemporary newspapers; CONRY, *The Irish Brigade in Italy* (Dublin, 1907); GOGARTY, *MS. Memoir* (1910).

W. H. GRATTAN-FLOOD.

O'Reilly, PETER J. See PEORIA, DIOCESE OF.

Oremus, invitation to pray, said before collects and other short prayers and occuring continually in the Roman Rite. It is used as a single ejaculation in the East (e. g., Nestorian Rite, Brightman, "Eastern Liturgies", Oxford, 1896, 255, etc.; Jacobite, ib., 75, 80, etc.), or the imperative: "Pray" (Coptic, ib., 162), "Stand for prayer" (ib., 158); most commonly, however with a further determination, "Let us pray to the Lord" (τοῦ κυρίου δεηθῶμεν, throughout the Byzantine Rite), and so on. Mgr Duchesne thinks that the Gallican collects were also introduced by the word *Oremus* ("Origines du Culte", Paris, 1898, 103). It is not so in the Mozarabic Rite, where the celebrant uses the word only twice, before the *Agios* (P. L., LXXXV, 113) and *Pater Noster* (ib., 118). *Oremus* is said (or sung) in the Roman Rite before all separate collects in the Mass, Office, or on other occasions (but several collects may be joined with one *Oremus*), before Post-Communions; in the same way, alone, with no prayer following, before the offertory; also before the introduction to the Pater noster and before other short prayers (e. g., *Aufer a nobis*) in the form of collects. It appears that the *Oremus* did not originally apply to the prayer (collect) that now follows it. It is thought that it was once an invitation to private prayer, very likely with further direction as to the object, as now on Good Friday (*Oremus pro ecclesia sancta Dei*, etc.). The deacon then said: *Flectamus genua*, and all knelt in silent prayer. After a time the people were told to stand up (*Levate*), and finally the celebrant collected all the petitions in one short sentence said aloud (see COLLECT). Of all this our *Oremus* followed at once by the collect would be a fragment.

GIHR, *The Holy Sacrifice of the Mass* (St. Louis, 1908), 368, 416, 497.

ADRIAN FORTESCUE.

Orense, DIOCESE OF (AURIENSIS), suffragan of Compostela, includes nearly all of the civil Province of Orense, and part of those of Lugo and Zamora, being bounded on the north by Pontevedra, Lugo, and Leon; on the east by Leon and Zamora; on the south by Portugal; on the west by Portugal and Pontevedra. Its capital, Orense (pop., 14,168), is a very ancient city on the banks of the Miño (Minho), famous since classical antiquity for its hot springs. The See of Orense dates from a remote period, certainly before the fifth century. The First Council of Braga (561) created four dioceses, the bishops of which afterwards signed the acts of the Second Council of Braga below the Bishop of Orense—an indication that they were of junior standing. Moreover, the signatures of the Bishops of Tuy and Astorga, two very ancient Churches, come after that of the Bishop of Orense. According to Idacius, two bishops, Pastor and Siagrius, were consecrated in the convent of Lugo in 433, and one of them (it is not known which) was a Bishop of Orense.

In 464, the Suevians, who had invaded Galicia, embraced Arianism, and only in the time of King Chararic (560) were they reconciled to Catholicism. St. Gregory of Tours tells us that the Galicians embraced the Faith with remarkable fervour. The conversion and instruction of both king and people appear to have been completed by St. Martin of Dumium. The names of the bishops of Orense are unknown until 571, when the diocese was governed by Witimir, a man of noble Suevian lineage, who assisted at the Second Council of Braga. He was an intimate friend of St. Martin of Braga, who dedicated to him as his "most dear father in Christ", his treatise "De ira". In 716 Orense was destroyed by Abdelaziz, son of Muza. In 832 Alfonso II combined the two Dioceses of Orense and Lugo: Orense, nevertheless, appears to have retained its titular bishops, for a charter of Alfonso the Chaste is witnessed by Maydo, Bishop of Orense. When Alfonso III (866–910) had reconquered Orense, he gave it to Bishop Sebastian, who had been Bishop of Arcabica in Celtiberia and was succeeded by Censeric (844), Sumna (886), and Egila (899), who took part in the consecration of the church of Santiago and in the Council of Oviedo. In the episcopacy of Ansurius (915–22) the holy abbot Franquila (906) erected the Benedictine monastery of S. Esteban de Ribas del Sil (St. Stephen on the Sil), where Ansurius himself and eight of his successors died in the odour of sanctity.

At the end of the tenth century the diocese was laid waste, first by the Northmen (970) and then by Almanzor, after which it was committed to the care of the Bishop of Lugo until 1071, when, after a vacancy of seventy years, Sancho II appointed Ederonio to the see. Ederonio rebuilt the old cathedral called S. Maria la Madre (1084–89). The most famous bishop of this period was Diego Velasco, whom his epitaph calls "light of the Church and glory of his country". He assisted at a council of Palencia and three councils of Santiago, and, with the assent of Doña Urraca and her son Alfonso, granted privileges (*fueros*) to Orense. He ruled for thirty years and was succeeded by Martin (1132–56) and Pedro Seguín. The latter was confessor to Ferdinand II, who granted him the lordship of Orense. Bishop Lorenzo was the jurist whom Tudense called the "pattern of the law" (*regla del derecho*); he rebuilt the cathedral and the bishop's palace, and constructed the famous bridge of Orense, with its principal arch spanning more than 130 feet. He assisted at the Council of Lyons in 1245. Vañez de Novoa quarrelled with the Franciscans, while he was precentor, and burned their convent, which had sheltered one of his enemies, but, having become bishop, he rebuilt it magnificently. Vasco Perez Mariño (1333–43) was distinguished for his devotion to the "Holy Christ of Orense", which he caused to be transferred from Finisterre to Orense and built for it a beautiful chapel, modified in subsequent periods. Other distinguished occupants of this see were Cardinal Juan de Torquemada, a Dominican, who assisted at the Councils of Constance and Basle; Diego de Fonseca (1471–84), who repaired the cathedral; Cardinals Antoniotto Pallavicino and Pedro de Isvalles, and the inquisitor general Fernando Valdés. Francisco Blanco founded the Hospital of S. Roque, assisted at the Council of Trent, founded the Jesuit colleges at Malaga and Compostela, and endowed that at Monterey. The zealous Juan Muñoz de la Cueva, a Trinitarian, wrote "Historical Notes on the Cathedral Church of Orense" (Madrid, 1727). Pedro Quevedo y Quintana (d. 1818), having been president of the Regency in 1810, was exiled by the Cortes of Cadiz; he founded the conciliar seminary of Orense in 1802.

The original cathedral was dedicated to the Mother of God, and is still known as Santa Maria la Madre. The Suevian king Chararic (see above) built (550) another, more sumptuous, church in honour of St. Martin of Tours and made it the cathedral, as it is to this day. Both churches, having suffered severely from time and the invasions of Arabs and Northmen, have been repeatedly restored. The later cathedral is Romanesque, with features of Gothic transition: its oldest portions date from the thirteenth century, and its latest from the early sixteenth; the façade has been rebuilt in modern times. The high altar has a silver tabernacle, given by Bishop Miguel Ares, and statues of Our Lady and St. Martin. In two side altars are the relics of St. Euphemia and her companions in martyrdom, Sts. Facundus and Primitivus. The plan of the church is a Latin cross, with three naves, the tower standing apart. The choir stalls are the work of Diego de Solis and Juan de Anges (late sixteenth century). Of the cloisters only a small portion remains, a perfect gem of ogival work. The church of St. Francis and the Trinity should also be mentioned; it was founded probably about the middle of the twelfth century as a hospice for pilgrims.

The famous men of the diocese include Padre Feijóo, a polygrapher who exploded many superstitions; Antonio de Remesar, the historian of Chiapa and Guatemala; Gregorio Hernandez, the sculptor; Castellar Ferrer, the historian of Galicia; St. Francis Blanco, a martyr of Japan.

PELAYO, *Heterodoxos españoles*, I (Madrid, 1879); MADOZ, *Dicc. geográfico-estadístico-histórico de España* (Madrid, 1848); FLOREZ, *Esp. Sagrada* (Madrid, 1789); DE LA FUENTE, *Hist. ecl. de Esp.* (Barcelona, 1855)

RAMÓN RUIZ AMADO.

Oresme, NICOLE, philosopher, economist, mathematician, and physicist, one of the principal founders of modern science; b. in Normandy, in the Diocese of Bayeux; d. at Lisieux, 11 July, 1382. In 1348 he was a student of theology in Paris; in 1356 grand master of the Collège de Navarre; in 1362, already master of theology, canon of Rouen; dean of the chapter, 28 March, 1364. On 3 August, 1377, he became Bishop of Lisieux. There is a tradition that he was tutor to the dauphin, afterwards Charles V, but this is irreconcilable with the dates of Oresme's life. Charles seems to have had the highest esteem for his character and talents, often followed his counsel, and made him write many works in French for the purpose of developing a taste for learning in the kingdom. At Charles's instance, too, Oresme pronounced a discourse before the papal Court at Avignon, denouncing the ecclesiastical disorders of the time. Several of the French and Latin works attributed to him are apocryphal or doubtful. Of his authentic writings, a Christological treatise, "De communicatione idiomatum in Christo", was commonly used as early as the fifteenth century by the theological Faculty of Paris.

But Oresme is best known as an economist, mathematician, and physicist. His economic views are contained in a Commentary on the Ethics of Aristotle, of which the French version is dated 1370; a commentary on the Politics and the Economics of Aristotle, French edition, 1371; and a "Treatise on Coins". These three works were written in both Latin and French; all three, especially the last, stamp their author as the precursor of the science of political economy, and reveal his mastery of the French language. The French Commentary on the Ethics of Aristotle was printed in Paris in 1488; that on the Politics and the Economics, in 1489. The treatise on coins, "De origine, natura, jure et mutationibus monetarum", was printed in Paris early in the sixteenth century, also at Lyons in 1675, as an appendix to the "De re monetaria" of Marquardus Freherus, and is included in the "Sacra bibliotheca sanctorum Patrum" of Margaronus de la Bigne IX, (Paris, 1859), p. 159, and in the "Acta publica monetaria" of David Thomas de Hagelstein (Augsburg, 1642). The "Traictié de la première invention des monnoies", in French, was printed at Bruges in 1477.

His most important contributions to mathematics are contained in "Tractatus de figuratione potentiarum et mensurarum difformitatum", still in manuscript. An abridgment of this work printed as "Tractatus de latitudinibus formarum" (1482, 1486, 1505, 1515), has heretofore been the only source for the study of his mathematical ideas. In a quality, or accidental form, such as heat, the Scholastics distinguished the *intensio* (the degree of heat at each point) and the *extensio* (e. g., the length of the heated rod): these two terms were often replaced by *latitudo* and *longitudo*, and from the time of St. Thomas until far on in the fourteenth century, there was lively debate on the *latitudo formæ*. For the sake of lucidity, Oresme conceived the idea of employing what we should now call rectangular co-ordinates: in modern terminology, a length proportionate to the *longitudo* was the abscissa at a given point, and a perpendicular at that point, proportionate to the *latitudo*, was the ordinate. He shows that a geometrical property of such a figure could be regarded as corresponding to a property of the form itself only when this property remains constant while the units measuring the *longitudo* and *latitudo* vary. Hence he defines *latitudo uniformis* as that which is represented by a line parallel to the longitude, and any other *latitudo* is *difformis;* the *latitudo uniformiter difformis* is represented by a right line inclined to the axis of the longitude. He proves that this definition is equivalent to an algebraical relation in which the longitudes and latitudes of any three points would figure: i. e., he gives the equation of the right line, and thus forestalls Descartes in the invention of analytical geometry. This doctrine he extends to figures of three dimensions.

Besides the longitude and latitude of a form, he considers the *mensura*, or *quantitas*, of the form, proportional to the area of the figure representing it. He proves this theorem: A form *uniformiter difformis* has the same quantity as a form *uniformis* of the same longitude and having as latitude the mean between the two extreme limits of the first. He then shows that his method of figuring the latitude of forms is applicable to the movement of a point, on condition that the time is taken as longitude and the speed as latitude; quantity is, then, the space covered in a given time. In virtue of this transposition, the theorem of the latitude *uniformiter difformis* became the law of the space traversed in case of uniformly varied motion: Oresme's demonstration is exactly the same as that which Galileo was to render celebrated in the seventeenth century. Moreover, this law was never forgotten during the interval between Oresme and Galileo: it was taught at Oxford by William Heytesbury and his followers, then, at Paris and in Italy, by all the followers of that school. In the middle of the sixteenth century, long before Galileo, the Dominican Dominic Soto applied the law to the uniformly acclerated falling of heavy bodies and to the uniformly decreasing ascension of projectiles.

Oresme's physical teachings are set forth in two French works, the "Traité de la sphère", twice printed in Paris (first edition without date; second, 1508), and the "Traité du ciel et du monde", written in 1377 at the request of King Charles V, but never printed. In most of the essential problems of statics and dynamics, Oresme follows the opinions advocated in Paris by his predecessor, Jean Buridan de Béthune, and his contemporary, Albert de Saxe (see SAXE, ALBERT DE). In opposition to the Aristotelean theory of weight, according to which the natural location of heavy bodies is the centre of the world, and that of light bodies the concavity of the moon's orb, he proposes the following: The elements tend to dispose themselves in such manner that, from the centre to the periphery their specific weight diminishes by degrees. He thinks that a similar rule may exist in worlds other than this. This is the doctrine later substituted for the Aristotelean by Copernicus and his followers, such as Giordano Bruno. The latter argued in a manner so similar to Oresme's that it would seem he had read the "Traité du ciel et du monde". But Oresme had a much stronger claim to be regarded as the precursor of Copernicus when one considers what he says of the diurnal motion of the earth, to which he devotes the gloss following chapters xxiv and xxv of the "Traité du ciel et du monde". He begins by establishing that no experiment can decide whether the heavens move from east to west or the earth from west to east; for sensible experience can never establish more than relative motion. He then shows that the reasons proposed by the physics of Aristotle against the movement of the earth are not valid; he points out, in particular, the principle of the solution of the difficulty drawn from the movement of projectiles. Next he solves the objections based on texts of Holy Scripture; in interpreting these passages he lays down rules universally followed by Catholic exegetists of the present day. Finally, he adduces the argument of simplicity for the theory that the earth moves, and not the heavens, and the whole of his argument in favour of the earth's motion is both more explicit and much clearer than that given by Copernicus.

MEUNIER, *Essai sur la vie et les ouvrages de Nicole Oresme* (Paris, 1857); WOLOWSKI ed., *Traictié de la première invention des monnoies de Nicole Oresme, textes français et latin d'après les manuscrits de la Bibliothèque Impériale, et Traité de la monnoie de Copernic, texte latin et traduction française* (Paris, 1864); JOURDAIN, *Mémoire sur les commencements de l'Economie politique dans les écoles du Moyen-Age* in *Mémoires de l'Académie des Inscriptions et Belles-Lettres*, XXVIII, pt. II (1874); CURTZE, *Der Algorismus proportionum des Nicolaus Oresme* in *Zeitschr. für Mathematik u. Physik*, XIII, Supplementary (Leipzig, 1868), 65–79; IDEM, *Der Tractatus de Latitudinibus Formarum des Nicolaus Oresme* (Ibid., 1868), 92–97; IDEM, *Die mathematischen Schriften des Nicole Oresme* (Berlin, 1870); SUTER, *Eine bis jetzt unbekannte Schrift des Nic. Oresme* in *Zeitschr. für Mathematik und Physik*, XXVII, Hist.-litter. Abtheilung (Leipzig, 1882), 121–25; CANTOR, *Vorlesungen über die Gesch. der Mathematik*, II (2nd ed., Leipzig, 1900), 128–36; DUHEM, *Un précurseur français de Copernic: Nicole Oresme (1377)* in *Revue générale des Sciences* (Paris, 15 Nov., 1909); IDEM, *Dominique Soto et la Scolastique parisienne* in *Bulletin hispanique* (Bordeaux, 1910–11).

PIERRE DUHEM.

Organ (Greek ὄργανον, "an instrument"), a musical instrument which consists of one or several sets of pipes, each pipe giving only one tone, and which is blown and played by mechanical means. I. ORIGIN AND DEVELOPMENT.—As far as the sounding material is concerned, the organ has its prototype in the syrinx, or Pan's pipe, a little instrument consisting of several pipes of differing length tied together in a row. The application of the mechanism is credited to Ctesibius, a mechanician who lived in Alexandria about 300 B. C. According to descriptions by Vitruvius (who is now generally believed to have written about A. D. 60) and Heron (somewhat later than Vitruvius), the organ of Ctesibius was an instrument of such perfection as was not attained again until the eighteenth century. The blowing apparatus designed by Ctesibius consisted of two parts, just as in the modern organ; the first serving to compress the air (the "feeders"); the second, to store the compressed air, the "wind", and keep it at a uniform pressure (the "reservoir"). For the first purpose Ctesibius used air-pumps fitted with handles for convenient working. The second, the most interesting part of his invention, was constructed as follows: a bell-shaped vessel was placed in a bronze basin, mouth downwards, supported a couple of inches above the bottom of the basin by a few blocks. Into the basin water was then poured until it rose some distance above the mouth of the bell. Tubes connecting with the air-pumps, as well as others connecting with the pipes of the organ, were fitted into the top of the bell. When, therefore, the air-pumps were worked, the air inside the bell was compressed and pushed out some of the water below. The level of the water consequently rose and kept the air inside compressed. Any wind taken from the bell to supply the pipes would naturally have a tendency to raise the level of the water in the bell and to lower that outside. But if the supply from the air-pumps was kept slightly in excess of the demand by the pipes, so that some of the air would always escape through the water in bubbles, a very even pressure would be maintained. This is what was actually done, and the bubbling of the water, sometimes described as "boiling", was always prominent in the accounts given of the instrument.

Over the basin there was placed a flat box containing a number of channels corresponding to the number of rows of pipes. Vitruvius speaks of organs having four, six, or eight rows of pipes, with as many channels. Each channel was supplied with wind from the bell by a connecting tube, a cock being inserted in each tube to cut off the wind at will. Over the box containing the channels an upper-board was placed, on the lower side of which small grooves were cut transversely to the channels. In the grooves close-fitting "sliders" were inserted, which could be moved in and out. At the intersections of channels and grooves, holes were cut vertically through the upper board and, correspondingly, through the top covering of the channels. The pipes, then, stood over the holes of the upper-board, each row, representing a scale-like progression, standing over its own channel, and all the pipes belonging to the same key, standing over the same groove. The sliders also were perforated, their holes corresponding to those in the upper board and the roof of the channels. When, therefore, the slider was so placed that its holes were in line with the lower and upper holes, the wind could pass through the three holes into the pipe above; but if the slider was drawn out a little, its solid portions would cut off the connexion between the holes in the roof of the channels and those in the upper-board, and no wind could pass. There was thus a double control of the pipes. By means of the cocks, wind could be admitted to any one of the channels, and thus supply all the pipes standing over that channel, but only those pipes would get the wind whose slide was in the proper position. Again, by means of the slide, wind could be admitted to all the pipes standing in a transverse row, but only those pipes would be blown to whose channels wind had been admitted by the cocks. This double control is still a leading principle in modern organ-building, and a row of pipes, differing in pitch, but having the same quality of tone, is called a stop, because its wind supply can be stopped by one action. It is not quite certain what the stops in the ancient organ meant. It is very unlikely that different stops produced different qualities of tone, as in the modern organ. Most probably they represented different "modes". For the convenient management of the slides each was provided with an angular lever, so that on pressing down one arm of the lever, the slide was pushed in; the lever being released, the slide was pulled out again by a spring.

This organ, called *hydraulus*, or *organum hydraulicum*, from the water used in the blowing apparatus, enjoyed great popularity. Writers like Cicero are loud in its praise. Even emperors took pride in playing it. It was used to heighten the pleasures of banquets and was associated particularly with the theatre and the circus. Numerous representations, particularly on coins called contorniates, also testify to its general repute. At an early period we meet organs in which the air pumps were replaced by bellows. Whether in these organs the water apparatus was dispensed with, is not quite certain. It would be strange, however, if this important means of regulating the wind pressure had been discontinued while the hydraulus was still in vogue. About the sixth century organ-building seems to have gone down in Western Europe, while it was continued in the Eastern Empire. It was a great event when, in 757, the Emperor Constantine V Coprony- mus made a present of an organ to King Pepin. In 826 a Venetian priest named Georgius erected an organ at Aachen, possibly following the directions left by Vitruvius. Shortly afterwards organ-building seems to have flourished in Germany, for we are told (Baluze, "Misc.", V, 480) that Pope John VIII (872- 80) asked Anno, Bishop of Freising, to send him a good organ and an organist. By this time the hydraulic apparatus for equalizing the wind-pressure had cer- tainly been abandoned, presumably because in north- ern climates the water might freeze in winter time. The wind, therefore, was supplied to the pipes directly from the bellows. To get anything like a regular flow of wind, it was necessary to have a number of bellows worked by several men. Thus, an organ in Winches- ter cathedral, built in 951, and containing 400 pipes, had twenty-six bellows, which it took seventy men to blow. These seventy men evidently worked in relays. In all probability one man would work one bellows, but the work was so exhausting that each man could con- tinue only for a short time. The bellows were pressed down either by means of a handle or by the blower standing on them. It seems that the device of weight- ing the bellows—so that the blower had merely to raise the upper board and leave the weights to press it down again—was discovered only in the beginning of the sixteenth century.

Another point in which the medieval organ was inferior to the hydraulus, was the absence of stops. There were, indeed, several rows of pipes, but they could not be stopped. All the pipes belonging to one key sounded always together, when that key was de- pressed. Thus the Winchester organ had ten pipes to each key. What the difference between these various pipes was, we do not know; but it appears that at an early date pipes were introduced to re-enforce the over- tones of the principal tone, giving the octave, twelfth, and their duplicates in still higher octaves. Then, to counterbalance these high-pitched pipes, others were added giving the lower octave, and even the second lower octave. In the absence of a stop action, variety of tone quality was of course unattainable, except by having different organs to play alternately. Even the Winchester organ had two key-boards, representing practically two organs (some authorities think there were three). From a contemporary description we learn that there were two organists (or three according to some), each managing his own "alphabet". The term *alphabet* is explained by the fact that the alpha- betical name of the note was attached to each slide. The modern name *key* refers to the same fact, though, according to Zarlino ("Istitutioni armoniche", 1558), in a roundabout manner: he says that the letters of the alphabet placed at the beginning of the Guidonian staff (see NEUM, p. 772, col. 2) were called keys (*claves, clefs*) because they unlocked the secrets of the staff, and that, hence, the same name was ap- plied to the levers of instruments like the organ inscribed with the same alphabetical letters.

While, in the Winchester organ, the two key-boards belonged to one organ, we know that there used to be also entirely separate organs in the same building. The smallest of these were called "portatives", be- cause they could be carried about. These were known in France in the tenth century (Viollet-le-Duc, "In- struments de musique", p. 298). A larger kind was called "positive", because it was stationary, but it, again, seems to have been distinguished from a still larger instrument known simply as the organ. Later on, when in reality several organs were combined in the same instrument, one of the softer divisions was called "positive". This name is still retained on the Conti- nent, while in English-speaking countries it has been changed to "choir organ". There was still another in- strument of the organ kind called a "regal". Its peculiarity was that, instead of pipes, it had reeds, fastened at one end and free to vibrate at the other. It was therefore the precursor of our modern harmo- nium. In the fourteenth century organs were con- structed with different key-boards placed one above the other, each controlling its own division of the or- gan. Soon afterwards couplers were designed, that is, mechanical appliances by which a key depressed in one key-board (or manual) would simultaneously pull down a corresponding key in another. The invention of a special key-board to be played by the feet, and hence called "pedals", is also placed in the fourteenth century. Sometimes the pedal keys merely pulled down manual keys by means of a chord; sometimes they were provided with their own rows of pipes, as in some fourteenth-century Swedish organs described by C. F. Hennerberg in a paper read at the International Musical Congress at Vienna, in 1909 ("Bericht", 91 sqq., Vienna and Leipzig, 1909).

It seems that stops were not reinvented until the fifteenth century. The form then used for a stop ac- tion was that of a "spring-box". About the four- teenth century, it appears, the slider for the key action had been discontinued, and channels (grooves) had been used, as in the ancient hydraulus, but running transversely, each under a row of pipes belonging to the same key. Into these grooves wind was admitted through a slit covered by a valve (pallet), the valve being pulled down and opened by the key action, and closed again by a spring. Such an arrangement is found in some remnants of the fourteenth century Swedish organs (see Hennerberg, l. c.). In these grooves, then, about the fifteenth century, secondary spring valves were inserted, one under each hole lead- ing to a pipe. From each of these secondary valves a string led to one of a number of rods running longi- tudinally under the sound-board, one for each set of pipes corresponding to a stop. By depressing this rod, all the secondary valves belonging to the corre- sponding stop would be opened, and wind could enter the pipes as soon as it was admitted into the grooves by the key action. Later on it was found more con- venient to push these valves down than to pull them. Little rods were made to pass through the top of the sound-board and to rest on the front end of the valves. These rods could be depressed, so as to open the valves, by the stop-rod running over the sound-board. From these secondary valves the whole arrangement re- ceived the name *spring-box*.

The spring-box solved the problem in principle, but had the drawback of necessitating frequent repairs. Hence, from the sixteenth century onwards, organ- builders began to use sliders for the stop action. Thus the double control of the pipes by means of channel and slide was again used as in the hydraulus, but with exchanged functions, the channel now serving for the key action and the slider for the stop action. In modern times some builders have returned to the an- cient method of using the channel longitudinally, for the stops (*Kegellade* and similar contrivances; pneu- matic sound-boards). Mention should also be made of attempts to do away with the channels altogether, to have all the pipes supplied directly from a universal wind-chest, and to bring about the double control of key and stop action by the mechanism alone. Each pipe hole is then provided with a special valve, and key and stop mechanism are so arranged that only their combined action will open the valve. Shortly after the stop-action had been reinvented, builders began to design varieties of stops. The earlier pipes had been all of our open diapason kind, which in principle is the same as the toy-whistle. These were now made in different "scales" (*scale* being the ratio of diameter to length). Also, the form of a cone, upright or inverted, replaced the cylindrical form. Stopped pipes—that is, pipes closed at the top—were added, and reeds—pipes with a "beating" reed and a body like the "flue" pipes—were introduced. Thus, by the sixteenth century all the main types now used had been invented.

The keys in the early medieval organs were not, it seems, levers, as in the ancient organ and modern instruments, but simply the projecting ends of the slides, being, presumably, furnished with some simple device making it convenient for the fingers to push in or pull out the slides. The invention of key-levers is generally placed in the twelfth century. These were for a long time placed exactly opposite their sliders. When, therefore, larger pipes began to be placed on the sound-board, the distances between the centres of the keys had to be widened. Thus we are told that organs had keys from three to five inches wide. This inconvenience was overcome by the invention of the roller-board, which is placed in the fourteenth century. The rollers are rods placed longitudinally under the sound-board and pivoted. From each two short arms project horizontally, one being placed over a key, the other under the corresponding slider or valve. Thus the length of the key-board became independent of the length of the sound-board. Consequently we learn that in the fifteenth century the keys were so reduced in size that a hand could span the interval of a fifth, and in the beginning of the sixteenth the key-board had about the size it has at present.

The number of keys in the early organs was small: only about one or two octaves of natural keys with at most the addition of *b* flat. Slowly the number of keys was increased, and in the fourteenth century we hear of key-boards having thirty-one keys. In the same century chromatic notes other than *b* flat began to be added. Then the question of tuning became troublesome. Various systems were devised, and it was not till the eighteenth century, through the powerful influence of J. S. Bach, that equal temperament was adopted. This consists in tuning in fifths and octaves, making each fifth slightly flat so that the 12th fifth will give a perfect octave. About the beginning of the sixteenth century the lower limit of the key-boards began to be fixed on the Continent at C, the *c* that lies below the lowest tone of the average bass voice and requires an open pipe of about 8 feet in length. In England organ key-boards were generally carried down to the G or F below that C, and only about the middle of the nineteenth century the continental usage prevailed also here. The total compass of the manuals now varies from four and a half to five octaves, that of the pedals from two octaves and three notes to two octaves and six notes (C—d' of C—f'). In 1712 it occurred to a London organ-builder named Jordan to place one manual department of the organ in a box fitted with shutters which could be opened or closed by a foot-worked lever, a kind of *crescendo* and *decrescendo* being thus obtained. This device, which received the name of *swell*, soon became popular in England, while in Germany it found favour only quite recently.

As we have seen, all through the Middle Ages the blowing apparatus consisted of bellows which delivered the wind directly to the sound-board. It was only in the eighteenth century that two sets of bellows were employed, one to supply the wind, the other to store it and keep it at even pressure. Thus, after an interval of about a thousand years, the blowing apparatus regained the perfection it had possessed in the hydraulus during the preceding thousand years. In 1762 a clock-maker named Cummings invented a square, weighted bellows, serving as a reservoir, and supplied by other bellows called "feeders". The feeders are generally worked by levers operated either by hand or foot. In quite recent times machinery has been applied to supersede the human blower, hydraulic, or gas, or oil engines, or electromotors being used. The difficulty of regulating the supply is easily overcome in the case of hydraulic engines, which can be made to go slowly or fast as required. But it is serious in the case of the other engines. Gas and oil engines must always go at the same speed, and even with electromotors a control of their speed is awkward. Hence, nowadays, bellows serving as feeders are frequently superseded by centrifugal fans, which can go at their full speed without delivering wind. It is sufficient, therefore, to fit an automatic valve to the reservoir, which will close when the reservoir is full. There is this drawback in the fans: that to produce a pressure as required in modern organs, they must go at a high speed which is apt to produce a disturbing noise. To obviate this difficulty several fans are arranged in series, the first raising the wind only to a slight pressure and so delivering it to a second fan, which delivers it at an increased pressure to the next, and so on, until the requisite pressure is attained by a practically noiseless process.

A genuine revolution in the building of organs was brought about by the invention of the pneumatic lever. Up to the twelfth century, it appears, the "touch" (or key-resistance) was light, so that the organs could be played with the fingers (see an article by Schubiger in "Monatshefte für Musikgeschichte", I, No. 9). Later on, possibly with the change to the groove and pallet system, it became heavy, so that the keys had to be pushed down by the fists. With improvement in the mechanism a lighter touch was secured again, so that playing with the fingers became possible after the fifteenth century. Still, a difficulty was always felt. In large organs the valve which admits the wind to the key channels (the pallet) must be of considerable size, if all the pipes are to get sufficient wind. Consequently, the wind-pressure which has to be overcome in opening the valve becomes so great that it taxes the power of the organist's fingers unduly. This difficulty is increased when couplers are used, as the finger then has to open two or more valves at the same time. To overcome this difficulty, Barker, an Englishman, in 1832, thought of using the power of the wind itself as an intermediate agent, and he induced the French organ-builder Cavaillé-Coll to adopt his idea in an organ erected in 1841. The device consists in this: that the key, by opening a small valve, admits the wind into a bellows which acts as motor and pulls down the pallet. Once this appliance was thoroughly appreciated, the way was opened to dispense altogether with the mechanism that connects the key with the pallet (or the draw-stop knob with the slider), and to put in its stead tubular-pneumatic or electro-pneumatic action. In the former the key opens a very small valve which admits the wind into a tube of small diameter; the wind, travelling through the tube in the form of a compression wave, opens, at the far end, another small valve controlling the motor bellows that opens the pallet. In the electro-pneumatic action the key makes an electric contact, causing the electric current to energize, at the organ end, an electro-magnet which, by its armature, causes a flow of wind and thus operates on a pneumatic lever.

With these inventions all the restrictions in organ-building, as to number of stops, pressure of wind, distances etc., were removed. Also means of control could easily be multiplied. Couplers were increased in number, and besides those connecting a key of one manual with the corresponding key of another, octave and sub-octave couplers were added, both on the same manual and between different manuals. In the matter of a stop-control, combination pedals—that is foot-worked levers drawing a whole set of stops at a time—

had been in use before the pneumatic lever. They were now often replaced by small pistons placed conveniently for the hands. These pistons are sometimes so designed as not to interfere with the arrangement of stops worked by hand; sometimes they are made "adjustable"—that is, so contrived as to draw any combination of stops which the player may previously arrange. Attempts have also been made to have individual stops playable from several manuals. This is a great advantage, but, on the other hand, it implies inaccessible mechanism. Casson's "Octave-duplication" avoids this objection, while, by making a whole manual playable in octave pitch, it considerably increases the variety of tone obtainable from a given number of stops.

A special difficulty in organ-playing is the manipulation of the pedal stops. On the manuals quick changes of strength and quality can be obtained by passing from one key-board to another. But, as only one pedal key-board is feasible, similar changes on the pedals can only be made by change of stops. Hence special facilities are here particularly desirable. Casson's invention, in 1889, of "pedal helps"—little levers, or pistons, one for each manual, which make the pedal stops adjust themselves automatically to all changes of stops on the corresponding manual—is the most satisfactory solution of this difficulty.

II. FAMOUS ORGAN BUILDERS.—Ctesibius, the inventor of the hydraulus, and the Venetian Georgius, who built the first organ north of the Alps, have already been mentioned. It is interesting to find a pope among the organ-builders of history: Sylvester II (999–1003), who seems to have built a hydraulic organ (Pretorius, "Syntagma Musicum", II, 92). We may also record here the first instructions on organ-building since the time of Vitruvius and Heron, contained in a work, "Diversarum artium schedula", by Theophilus, a monk, who seems to have written before 1100 (Degering, "Die Orgel", p. 65). After this names are scarce until the thirteenth century. Then we hear in Germany of a large organ in Cologne cathedral, built, probably, by one Johann, while the builders of famous organs in Erfurt Cathedral (1225) and in St. Peter's near Erfurt (1226) are not known. A Master Guncelin of Frankfort built a large organ for Strasburg cathedral in 1292, and a Master Raspo, also of Frankfort, probably built one for Basle cathedral in 1303. The famous organ at Halberstadt, with four keyboards, was built between 1359 and 1361 by Nicholas Faber, a priest. Of the fifteenth century we will mention only Steffan of Breslau, who built a new organ for Erfurt cathedral in 1483. In the sixteenth century Gregorius Vogel was famous for the beauty and variety of tone of his stops. In the seventeenth and eighteenth centuries the Silbermann family were renowned. The first of them to take up organ-building was Andreas Silbermann (1678–1733); his brother Gottfried (1683–1753), the most famous organ-builder in the family, was also one of the first to build pianofortes. Three sons of Andreas continued the work of their father and uncle: Johann Andreas (1712–83), Johann Daniel (1717–1766), and Johann Heinrich (1727–1799), the last two building mainly pianofortes. In a third generation we meet Johann Josias (d. 1786), a son of Johann Andreas, and Johann Friedrich (1762–1817), a son of Johann Heinrich. In the nineteenth century we may mention Moser, who, about 1830, built a large organ for Freiburg in Switzerland, where they imitate thunder-storms; Schulze of Paulinzelle, Ladegast of Weissenfels, Walcker of Ludwigsburg, Mauracher of Graz, Sauer of Frankfort-on-the-Oder, Weigle of Stuttgart, Stahlhuth of Aachen.

In England we hear in the fourteenth century of John the Organer and of Walter the Organer, who was also a clock-maker. From the fifteenth and sixteenth centuries the names of a large number of organ-builders are transmitted to us, showing organ-building was in a flourishing condition, but the Puritans destroyed most organs, and organ-builders almost disappeared. When organ-building was taken up again, in 1660, there was a scarcity of competent builders, and Bernard Schmidt, with his two nephews Gerard and Bernard, came over from Germany. Bernard the elder was commonly known as Father Smith, to distinguish him from his nephew. At the same time John Harris, a son of Thomas Harris of Salisbury, who had been working in France, returned to England. His son, Renatus, became the principal rival of Father Smith. In the following century another German, John Snetzler (1710–c. 1800) settled in England and became famous for the quality of his organ pipes. His business eventually became that of W. Hill and Son, London. In the nineteenth century the most prominent builder was Henry Willis (1821–1901), who designed several ingenious forms of pneumatic actions and brought the intonations of reeds to great perfection. Mention should also be made of R. Hope-Jones of Birkenhead, whose electro-pneumatic action marked a great step forward.

In Italy the Antegnati family were prominent during the fifteenth and sixteenth centuries. Bartolomeo Antegnati built an organ in 1486 for Brescia cathedral, where he was organist. He had three sons: Giovan Francesco, Giov. Giacomo, and Giov. Battista. Francesco is also known as a maker of harpsichords. G. Giacomo was the organist of Milan cathedral and built for Brescia cathedral a choir organ which was famous in its time. Graziado, a son of G. Battista, built a new large organ for Brescia in 1580. His son Costanzo (b. 1557) was an organist and a composer of renown. In the preface to a collection of *ricercari* (1608) he gives a list of 135 organs built by members of his family (cf. Damiano Muoni, "Elgi Antegnati", Milan, 1883). Vincenzo Columbi built a fine organ for St. John Lateran in 1549. In France we hear of an organ in the Abbey of Fécamp in the twelfth century. In the eighteenth century a well-known organ-builder was Joh. Nicolaus le Ferre, who, in 1761, built an organ of 51 stops in Paris. More famous is Don Bedos de Celles (1714–97), who also wrote an important book, "L'art du facteur d'orgues" (Paris, 1766–78). In the nineteenth century a renowned firm was that of Daublaine & Co., founded 1838; in 1845 it became Ducrocquet & Co. and sent an organ to the London Exhibition of 1851; in 1855 it changed its name again to Merklin, Schütze & Co. and erected some of the earliest electro-pneumatic organs. The most famous builder of modern times, however, was Aristide Cavaillé-Col (1811–99), a descendant of an old organ-building family, mentioned above in connexion with Barker's invention of the pneumatic lever; he was also highly esteemed for the intonation of his reeds.

In America the first organ erected was imported from Europe in 1713 for Queen's Chapel, Boston. It was followed by several others, likewise imported. In 1745 Edward Broomfield of Boston built the first organ in America. More famous was W. M. Goodrich, who began business in the same city in 1800. The best known of American organ builders is Hilborne L. Roosevelt of New York, who, with his son Frank, effected many bold improvements in organ building. In 1894 John Turnell Austin patented his "universal air-chest", an air-chest large enough to admit a man for repairs and containing all the mechanism, as well as the magazine for storing the wind and keeping it at equal pressure (Mathews, "A Handbook of the Organ").

III. THE ORGAN IN CHURCH SERVICE.—In the early centuries the objection of the Church to instrumental music applied also to the organ, which is not surprising, if we remember the association of the hydraulus with theatre and circus. According to Platina ("De vitis Pontificum", Cologne, 1593), Pope Vitalian (657–72) introduced the organ into the church service. This, however, is very doubtful. At all events, a strong objection to the organ in church service remained pretty general down to the twelfth century, which may be accounted for partly by the imperfection of tone in organs of that time. But from the twelfth century on, the organ became the privileged church instrument, the majesty and unimpassioned character of its tone making it a particularly suitable means for adding solemnity to Divine worship.

According to the present legislation organ music is allowed on all joyful occasions, both for purely instrumental pieces (voluntaries) and as accompaniment. The organ alone may even take the place of the voices in alternate verses at Mass or in the Office, provided the text so treated be recited by someone in an audible voice while the organ is played. Only the Credo is excepted from this treatment, and in any case the first verse of each chant and all the verses at which any liturgical action takes place—such as the "Te ergo quæsumus", the "Tantum ergo", the "Gloria Patri" —should be sung.

With some exceptions, the organ is not to be played during Advent and Lent. It may be played on the Third Sunday in Advent (Gaudete) and the Fourth in Lent (Lætare) at Mass and Vespers, on Holy Thursday at the Gloria, and on Holy Saturday at and, according to general usage, after the Gloria. Moreover, it may be played, even in Advent and Lent, on solemn feasts of the saints and on the occasion of any joyful celebration—as e. g. the Communion of children [S. R. C., 11 May, 1878, 3448 (5728)]. Moreover, by a kind of indult, it would seem, the organ is admitted, even in Lent and Advent, to support the singing of the choir, but in this case it must cease with the singing. This permission, however, does not extend to the last three days of Holy Week (S. R. C., 20 March, 1903, 4009). At Offices of the Dead organ music is excluded; at a Requiem Mass, however, it may be used for the accompaniment of the choir, as above.

It is appropriate to play the organ at the beginning and end of Mass, especially when a bishop solemnly enters or leaves the church. If the organ is played during the Elevation, it should be in softer tones; but it would seem that absolute silence is most fitting for this august moment. The same may be said about the act of Benediction with the Blessed Sacrament. It should be observed that the legislation of the Church concerns itself only with liturgical services. It takes no account of such things as singing at low Mass or popular devotions. But it is fitting, of course, to observe on such occasions the directions given for liturgical services.

IV. Organ-Playing.—In ancient times and in the early Middle Ages organ-playing was, of course, confined to rendering a melody on the organ. But it is not improbable that the earliest attempts at polyphonic music, from about the ninth century on, were made with the organ, seeing that these attempts received the name of *organum*. From the thirteenth century some compositions have come down to us under that name without any text, and probably intended for the organ. In the fourteenth century we hear of a celebrated organ-player, the blind musician Francesco Landino of Florence, and in the fifteenth of another Florentine player, Squarcialupi. At this time Konrad Paumann flourished in Germany, some of whose organ compositions are extant, showing the feature which distinguishes organ, like all instrumental music, from vocal music, namely the diminution or figuration, ornamentation, of the melodies. With Paumann this figuration is as yet confined to the melody proper, the top part. With Claudio Merulo (1533–1604) we find the figuration extended to the accompanying parts also. More mature work was produced by Giovanni Gabrieli (1557–1612) in his "Canzone e Sonate" (1597 and 1615). Further development of a true instrumental style was brought about by Samuel Scheidt (1587–1654). Then follow a series of illustrious composers for the organ, of whom we may mention Girolamo Frescobaldi (1583–1644), Johann Jacob Froberger (died 1667), Dietrich Buxtehude (died 1707), and Johann Sebastian Bach (1685–1750), at whose hands organ composition reached its highest point.

After Bach the general development of music, being in the direction of more individual expression and constantly varying emotion, was not favourable to organ composition. Accordingly, none of the best men turned their attention to the organ, Mendelssohn's compositions for the instrument being a notable exception. In modern times a large number of composers have written respectable music for the organ, among whom we may mention the French Guilmant and Widor and the German Rheinberger and Reger. But none of them, with the possible exception of Reger, can be counted as first-class composers. The scarcity of really good modern organ compositions has led organists to the extended use of arrangements. If these arrangements are made with due regard to the nature of the organ, they cannot be altogether objected to. But it is clear that they do not represent the ideal of organ music. As the characteristic beauty of organ tone lies in its even continuation, *legato* playing must be the normal for the organ even more than for other instruments. While, therefore, *staccato* playing cannot absolutely be excluded, and an occasional use of it is even desirable for the sake of variety, still the modern tendency to play everything *staccato* or *mezzo-legato* is open to great objections. The alternation and contrast of tone-colours afforded by the variety of stops and the presence of several manuals is a legitimate and valuable device. But too much variety is inartistic, and, in particular, an excessive use of solo stops is alien to the true organ style.

A word may be added about the local position of the organ in the church. The considerations determining this question are threefold: the proximity of the organ to the singers, the acoustical effect, and the architectural fitness. The combination of these three claims in existing churches frequently causes considerable difficulty. Hence it is desirable that in planning new churches architects should be required to provide ample room for an organ.

There is no good history of the organ. On the ancient organ a good book is Degering, *Die Orgel* (Münster, 1905); cf. Maclean, *The Principle of the Hydraulic Organ* in *Quarterly Mag. of the International Musical Society*, pt. 2 (Leipzig, 1905), and *Schlesinger, Researches into the Origin of the Organs of the Ancients, ibid.*, pt. 2 (Leipzig, 1901). On the later history, Williams, *The Story of the Organ* (London, 1903) is fairly reliable. The historical part of Hopkins and Rimbault, *The Organ, Its History and Construction* (London, 1877), though out of date, is still useful. Further works are: Ritter, *Zur Geschichte des Orgelspiels im 14. bis 18. Jahrhundert* (Leipzig, 1884); Wangemann, *Geschichte der Orgel* (Leipzig, 1887); Grégoire, *Histoire de l'orgue* (Antwerp, 1865); Hinton, *Story of the Electric Organ* (London, 1909); Bewerunge, *Die Röhrenpneumatik* in *Kirchenmusikalisches Jahrbuch* (Ratisbon, 1905); Buhle, *Die musikalischen Instrumente in den Miniaturen des frühen Mittelalters*: I. *Die Blasinstrumente* (Leipzig, 1903); Viollet-le-Duc, *Dictionnaire raisonné du mobilier français de l'époque Carolingienne à la Renaissance*: II. *Instruments de musique* (Paris, 1874).

On the construction of the organ the principal works are: Audsley, *The Art of Organ-Building* (2 vols., 4°, New York and London, 1905); Robertson, *A Practical Treatise on Organ-Building* (London, 1897); Töpfer-Allihn, *Die Theorie und Praxis des Orgelbaues* (Weimar, 1888); Hill, *Organ Cases and Organs of the Middle Ages and Renaissance* (2 vols., folio, London, 1883, 1891); Wedgwood, *Dictionary of Organ Stops* (London, 1905); Matthews, *A Handbook of the Organ* (London, 1897) (treats also of organ-playing); Dienel, *Die moderne Orgel* (Berlin, 1891); Schweitzer, *Deutsche u. französische Orgelbaukunst und Orgelkunst* (Leipzig, 1906); Casson, *The Modern Organ* (Denbigh, 1883); Idem, *The Pedal Organ* (London, 1905); Idem, *Modern Pneumatic Organ Mechanism* (London, 1908); Swanton, *Lecture on Organ Blowing* (London, 1905); *International Rules for Organ Building*, issued by the Third Congress of the International Musical Society (Leipzig, 1909).

The ecclesiastical legislation on organ-playing is contained in the *Cæremoniale Episcoporum* and in *Decrees of the S. Congregation of Rites*. The latter, as far as they concern the subject, are conveniently put together in Auer, *Die Entscheidungen der h. Riten-Kongregation in Bezug auf Kirchenmusik* (Ratisbon and New York, 1901).

H. Bewerunge.

Organic Articles. See ARTICLES, THE ORGANIC.

Oria, DIOCESE OF (URITANA), in the Province of Lecce, Apulia, Italy, suffragan of Taranto. In the Middle Ages, Oria was a principality that passed to the Borromei; St. Charles sold it for 40,000 crowns, which he distributed among the poor. Oria was besieged by Manfred in 1266. When Brindisi was destroyed by the Saracens in the ninth century, its bishops established their see at Oria and called themselves Bishops of Brindisi and Oria, even after their return to their former capital. It would appear that Oria, in early times, had bishops of its own, because there is a record on a slab in the cathedral, dating from the eighth or ninth century, in which there is mention of a Bishop Theodosius, not one of the bishops of Brindisi. In 979 Bishop Andrew was slain by Porphyrius. In 924 and 977 Oria was sacked by the Mohammedans. The town was erected into an episcopal see in 1591; its first bishop was Vincent Tufo. The diocese has 15 parishes, 120,000 inhabitants, 9 religious houses of men, and 11 of women.

CAPPELLETTI, *Le Chiese d' Italia*, XXI.

U. BENIGNI.

Oriani, BARNABA, Italian Barnabite and astronomer, b. at Carignano, near Milan, 17 July, 1752; d. at Milan, 12 November, 1832. After receiving an elementary education in his native town, he studied at the College of San Alessandro, Milan, where he was educated and supported by the Barnabites. He later joined the Barnabites, and, after studying the humanities, physical and mathematical sciences, philosophy, and theology, was ordained priest at the age of twenty-three. Specially interested in astronomy, he was shortly after his ordination (1776) appointed on the staff of the Observatory of Brera in Milan. He became assistant astronomer in 1778, and director in 1802. In 1778 he began to publish the dissertations on astronomical subjects which form an important part of the original memoirs appearing in the "Effemeridi di Milano" during the next fifty-two years. His work soon attracted considerable attention, and in 1785 a notable memoir containing his calculation of the orbit of Uranus and a table of elements for that planet won for him a prominent place among the astronomers of his time. He was admitted to membership in numerous learned societies, and offered the position of professor of astronomy at Palermo, which, however, he did not accept. In the following year he travelled throughout Europe at the expense of the state, visiting the chief observatories. When Napoleon set up the republic in Lombardy, Oriani refused absolutely to swear hatred towards monarchy; the new government modified the oath of allegiance in his regard, retained him in his position at the observatory, and made him president of the commission appointed to regulate the new system of weights and measures. When the republic was transformed into the Napoleonic kingdom, Oriani received the decorations of the Iron Crown and of the Legion of Honour, was made count and senator of the kingdom, and was appointed in company with De Cesaris, to measure the arc of the meridian between the zeniths of Rimini and Rome. He was a devoted friend of the Theatine monk Piazzi, the discoverer of Ceres, and for thirty-seven years cooperated with him in many ways in his astronomical labours. Besides his constant contributions to the "Effemeridi di Milano", he published a series of important memoirs on spherical trigonometry (Memorie dell' Istituto Italiano, 1806–10) and the "Istruzione suelle misure e sui pesi" (Milan, 1831).

GABBA in TIPALDO, *Italiani Illustri*, III (Venice, 1836), 473–81; POGGENDORFF, *Handwörterbuch zur Gesch. der exacten Wissenschaften*, II (Leipzig, 1863); CACCIATORE AND SCHIAPPARELLI, *Correspondenza Astronomica fra Giuseppe Piazzi e Barnaba Oriani* (Milan, 1874), introduction.

EDWARD C. PHILLIPS.

Oriental Church. See EASTERN CHURCHES.

Oriental Study and Research.—In the broadest sense of the term, Oriental study comprises the scientific investigation and discussion of all topics—linguistics, archæology, ethnology, etc.—connected with the East, in particular, the discovery and interpretation of Eastern literary and archæological remains. So vast is the subject that it has of a necessity been divided into many departments, each of which in turn embraces various specialized branches. Thus the study of the language, customs, philosophy, and religion of China and the Far East is in itself a vast though relatively little-explored field of scientific investigation, while the study of Sanskrit, together with the classic lore of the ancient Hindus, which has cast so much light on our knowledge of the European languages and peoples, forms another great division of Oriental research.

From the religious point of view, however, the greatest and most valuable results have been achieved by the study of the group of languages generally termed Semitic, and through archæological research in the so-called Bible Lands—Assyria and Babylonia, Syria and Palestine, Arabia and the Valley of the Nile. Not only have these studies and explorations cast a great deal of light on the Old-Testament writings but they have, moreover, revealed with considerable precision and detail the well-nigh forgotten history of empires and civilizations that had flourished for many centuries and passed away even before Greece or Rome had acquired any great political or literary importance. The earliest efforts of European scholars in the field of Oriental research were naturally connected with the scientific study of Hebrew, the language of the Old Testament. To say nothing of the work done by the rabbis of the medieval period under the influence of Arabic culture in the Jewish colonies of Spain and northern Africa, we find prior to the Reformation the names of Johann Reuchlin (1455–1522) and the Dominican Santes Pagninus (1471–1541), pioneers who prepared the way for such scholars as the famous Johann Buxtorf (1564–1629) and his son (1599–1664), both successively professors at Basle, and others of the same period. For ulterior developments in the study of Hebrew see article HEBREW LANGUAGE AND LITERATURE.

In connexion with the impetus given to Biblical Oriental studies in the sixteenth century, mention should be made of the Complutensian Polyglot published under the direction of Cardinal Ximenes (1436–1517). It was the first printed edition of the Scriptures in the original text accompanied by the principal ancient versions, and antedated by more than a century the London Polyglot of Brian Walton. This great work, which is dedicated to Pope Leo X, comprises six folio volumes, the last being devoted to a Hebrew lexicon and other scientific apparatus. It was begun in 1502 and finished in 1517, though not published until 1522. In its preparation the cardinal was aided by several Greek and Oriental scholars, among whom were the celebrated Stunica (D. López de Zúñiga), Vergara, and three Jewish converts. The zeal for Hebrew naturally led to the study of other Semitic languages (Syriac, Arabic, Ethiopic, etc.), which were eagerly taken up not only as a means of obtaining a more comprehensive knowledge of Hebrew through the newly-introduced methods of comparative philology, but also on account of the literary treasures they contained, which had hitherto remained practically unknown to European scholars. In this broader field the greatest credit is due to the illustrious Maronite family of the Assemani (q. v.). (For the work done by scholars in the study of Syriac see SYRIAC LANGUAGE AND LITERATURE.)

The first European scholar who turned his attention to Ethiopic was Potken of Cologne, about 1513. A grammar and dictionary were published by Jacob Wemmers, a Carmelite of Antwerp, in 1638; and in

1661 appeared the first edition of the great Lexicon by Job Ludolf, who in the edition of 1702 prefixed a "Dissertatio de Harmonia Linguæ Æth. cum. cet. Orient." Ludolf was also the author of a commentary on Ethiopic history. Later scholars who have attained eminence in this branch are Dillmann, who among other works published several books of the Ethiopic version of the Old Testament: Octateuch (Leipzig, 1853), the four Books of Kings (Leipzig, 1861-71), the Book of Enoch (1851), and the "Book of the Jubilees" (1859); R. Lawrence, who published the "Ascensio Isaiæ" (Oxford, 1819), and the "Apocalypse of Ezra" (1820); Hupfeldt, "Exercitationes Æthiopicæ" (1825); Ewald "Ueber des Æthiop. Buch's Henokh Entstehung" (1854) etc. (See article ETHIOPIA.—*Language and Literature.*)

In the field of Arabic the greatest honour is due to Baron Sylvestre de Sacy (1758–1838), a scholar of marvellous erudition and versatility, equally proficient in the other Semitic languages as well as in Greek, Latin, and the modern European tongues. He may be said to have laid the foundations of Arabic grammar. Among his works are a "Chrestomathie arabe" (3 vols., Paris, 1806); "Grammaire arabe" (2 vols., 1810) etc. In Germany, George W. Freytag (1788–1861) became a great authority on Arabic. His greatest work is the "Lexicon Arabico-Latinum" (1830–37). Among the great number of more recent scholars may be mentioned Brockelmann, "Geschichte der Arabischen Literatur" (2 vols., Berlin, 1899–1902); Hartwig Derenbourg, C. Caspari, Theo. Noeldeke etc. In this connexion it may be noted that an important school of Arabic studies has been instituted by the Jesuit Fathers in Beirut, Syria. As regards the study of Armenian, modern scholarship owes not a little to the scientific and literary labours of the Mechitarists (q. v.), a religious community of Armenians established at Venice since 1716. From this institution, which is equipped with excellent printing facilities, have been issued numerous publications of Armenian texts, as well as translations of the same into various European languages. The latter half of the nineteenth century was marked by a great revival of interest in Oriental studies, owing to the magnificent and unexpected results of archæological exploration in the Bible Lands, particularly in Assyria, Babylonia, and Egypt. The account of the discovery and deciphering of the historic remains unearthed in these countries is of fascinating interest, and records one of the greatest scientific triumphs in the annals of Western scholarship. Of this great movement, which has resulted in the production of hundreds of volumes, only the briefest account can be given here.

Assyro-Babylonian Research.—Though preceded by the tentative work of Rich in 1811 and 1820, systematic explorations in Assyria may be said to have been inaugurated in 1843 by Paul-Emile Botta (French vice-consul residing at Mosul), at Kuyunjik (site of ancient Ninive), and at Khorsabad. These were interrupted the following year, but were resumed by Victor Place, Botta's successor, in 1851 and continued till 1855, all at the expense of the French Government, which also published the results in monumental form. Henry Austen Layard also began excavations in 1845 at the Mounds of Nimrud, near Mosul, and his work was continued on this and other sites until 1847. In 1849 he began another exploring expedition which lasted three years. It was under the auspices of the British Museum and was remarkably successful. Layard also deserves great credit for the graphic and scholarly manner in which he presented his discoveries to the public, and for having aroused interest by connecting them with the Bible story. In the mean time another expedition sent out by the French Government, under the direction of Fulgence Fresnel, was exploring Babylonia, but unfortunately the material results of the excavations were lost through the sinking of a raft on the Tigris (1851). In 1852 the Assyrian Exploration Fund was organized in England, and, under the direction of Sir Henry Rawlinson, Loftus, and Taylor, excavations were carred on in various parts of Babylonia, and by Hormuzd Rassam at Kuyunjik. Less attention was being now paid to the identification of ancient sites, and more to the inscribed clay tablets which were discovered in great quantities; and Rassam, without knowing it, unearthed at Ninive a portion of the famous library of Assurbanipal (688–26 B. C.).

From the time that cuneiform inscriptions and tablets began to be brought from the East, European scholars had applied themselves to the extremely difficult task of deciphering and translating them, but without success until George Grotefend (1775–1853), professor at the lyceum of Hanover, found a key and partially deciphered a few inscriptions. The chief credit, however, for the great achievement which at last gave access to the vast treasures of the cuneiform writings belongs to Sir Henry Rawlinson. Between the years 1835 and 1839 he succeeded in copying the great inscription of Darius at Behistun in Persia. This inscription was chiselled in three columns on the face of a mountain cliff more than three hundred feet above the ground, and it was copied only after strenuous labour and with serious risk of life. Rawlinson assumed as a working hypothesis that the first column was old Persian written in cuneiform characters, and the assumption was justified when the decipherment of this column was published in 1846. This furnished a key to the third column, which proved to be Babylonian (the most important for students of Assyriology), and the contents of this column, after much painstaking labour, were published in 1851. The second column, called the Median or Susian text, was not deciphered intil 1890. Over and above this splendid achievement, Rawlinson rendered invaluable service to the science of Assyriology by editing the Cuneiform Inscriptions of Western Asia published by the British Museum. Between 1855 and 1872 little was done by way of excavation, but in the latter year George Smith, a young employee in the British Museum, discovered some tablets containing fragments of a Flood legend strikingly similar in some respects to the Biblical narrative. The interest aroused by the publication of these fragments determined a new era of excavation. Between 1872 and 1875 Smith was three times sent to Assyria in the hope of finding more fragments bearing on Biblical accounts. In this he was unsuccessful, and, unfortunately for the cause of Assyriology, he died prematurely while on his third expedition in 1876.

The exploration work for the British Museum was continued by Hormuzd Rassam, who, besides other valuable treasures found in various parts of Babylonia, unearthed in the expedition of 1887–82 the great bronze doors with the inscriptions of Shalmaneser II (859–26 B. C.). About the same time M. de Sarzec, French consul at Bassorah in Southern Babylonia, excavated the very ancient Telloh statues which were acquired by the French Government for the Museum of the Louvre. The work of de Sarzec was continued until his death in 1903, and resulted in the discovery of an enormous quantity of clay tablets, bronze and silver figures, vases, etc. The French expedition to Susa, under the direction of M. J. de Morgan (1897–1902), was one of the most important in the history of Assyriology, for it resulted in the finding of the Hammurabi Code of Laws. This great code, which illustrates in many respects the Pentateuchal Law, was first translated by Father Scheil, the eminent Dominican scholar who was the Assyriologist of the expedition ("Textes Elamitiques-Sémitiques", Paris, 1902), and later into German by Dr. Hugo Winckler of Berlin, into English by Dr. Johns and into Italian by Rev. Dr. Francesco Mari. (See articles by Dr.

Gabriel Oussani in the "New York Review", "The Code of Hammurabi", Aug.-Sept., 1905; "The Code of Hammurabi and the Mosaic Legislation", Dec., 1905-Jan., 1906.) In 1884 the first American expedition was sent to Babylonia under the auspices of the Archæological Institute of America, and under the direction of W. H. Ward. In 1888 the Babylonian Exploration Fund, organized in Philadelphia, was sent out under the direction of Dr. John Peters in the interests of the University of Pennsylvania. The site chosen was Nippur, and the work of excavation was continued at intervals mainly on this site until 1900. These expeditions resulted in the recovery of more than 40,000 inscriptions, clay tablets, stone monuments etc. The vast amount of material brought to light by the excavations in Assyria and Babylonia powerfully stimulated the ardour of students of Assyriology both in Europe and America. The limits of the present article will allow but the mention of a few distinguished names.

In Germany.—Eberhard Scrader (1836) has been called the father of German Assyriology. Successively professor at Zurich, Giessen, Jena, and Berlin (1875), he has written many works on the subject, among which: "Die Assyrisch-Babylonisch Keilinschriften" (1872, tr. "The Cuneiform Inscriptions and the Old Testament", 1885–9); "Keilinschriften und Geschichtsforschung" (1878); "Zur Frage nach dem Ursprung der Altbabylonischer Kultur" (1884). Other German scholars of note are Hugo Winckler (Alttestamentliche Untersuchen, Leipzig, 1892, etc.); Friederich Delitsch (Grammar, Lexicon etc.), J. Jeremias, B. G. Niebuhr, F. Hommel, F. Kaulen (Assyrien und Babylonien nach dem neuesten Entdeckungen, Freiburg, 1899, etc.), C. P. Tiele, Mürdter, Brunnow, Peiser etc. *In France.*—F. Lenormant (Etudes cunéiformes, 5 parts, Paris, 1878–80); J. Menant (Ninive et Babylon, Paris, 1887); Halévy (Documents religieux de l'Assyrie et de la Babylonie, Paris, 1882); V. Scheil, O. P. (Textes Elamites, 3 vols., Paris, 1901–04); Rev. F. Martin (Textes religieux Assyriens et Babyloniens, Paris, 1900); F. Thureau-Dangin (Recherches sur l'Origine de l'écriture cunéiforme, Paris, 1893), oppert, Loisy, Fossey etc. *In England.*—Sir H. Rawlinson (Cuneiform Inscriptions of Western Asia, 5 vols., 1861–1884, etc.); A. H. Sayce (Higher Criticism and the Monuments, London, 1894, etc.); L. W. King (Letters and Inscriptions of Hammurabi . . . and other Kings of the First Dynasty of Babylon, London, 1898–1900); C. W. Johns, T. G. Pinches, J. A. Craig etc. *In America.*—Besides the scholars already referred to may be mentioned R. W. Rogers (History of Babylonia and Assyria, I, New York, 1900); H. V. Hilprecht (Explorations in Bible Lands during the Nineteenth Century, New York, 1903); Paul Haupt (numerous publications); R. F. Harper, M. Jastrow, C. Johnston, J. D. Lyon, J. D. Prince etc.

Egyptian Research.—Modern Oriental research in the Valley of the Nile began in 1798 with the Egyptian campaign of Napoleon, who with characteristic foresight invited M. Gaspard Monge (1746–1818) with a corps of savants and artists to join the expedition. The results of their observations were published at the expense of the French Government (1809–13) in several folio volumes under the title: "Description de l'Egypte", but the numerous specimens collected by these scientists fell into the hands of the English after the naval battle of Aboukir and formed later the nucleus of the Egyptian department of the British Museum. The mysterious hieroglyphic characters which they exhibited were soon made the object of intense study both in England and France and the famous Rosetta Stone which bears a trilingual inscription (in Greek, in the Egyptian demotic script, and in the hieroglyphic writing) furnished a key to the meaning of the latter, which was discovered almost simultaneously in France by J. François Champollion (1791–1832), and in England by Thomas Young (1773–1827). Thus the Rosetta inscription (embodying a part of a decree of Ptolemy V Epiphanes, 205–181 B. C.) stands in the same relation to the discoveries bearing on the literature and civilization of ancient Egypt as does the Behistun inscription with regard to the antique treasures discovered in Assyria and Babylonia. Champollion's discovery aroused a great interest in Egyptian inscriptions and in 1828 the French scholar was sent to Egypt together with Rosellini at the head of a Franco-Italian expedition which proved most fruitful in scientific results. A German expedition under the direction of Lepsius was sent out in 1840 to study Egyptian monuments in relation to Bible history, and in addition to explorations made in Egypt and Ethiopia a visit was made to the Sinaitic peninsula. In 1850 Auguste Mariette, a French savant, made the remarkable discovery of the tombs of the sacred Apis bulls at Memphis together with thousands of memorial inscriptions. In 1857 he was appointed director of the museum of antiquities newly established in Cairo, and at the same time he received from the khedive the exclusive right of excavating in Egyptian territory for scientific purposes—a right which he exercised until his death in 1880. The results of his explorations were enormous and the science of Egyptology probably owes more to Mariette than to any other scholar. He was succeeded by another eminent French scholar, G. Maspero, and the explorations still remaining in the hands of the French were carried on systematically and with steady success; but under the new administration permission was given to representatives of other nations to conduct excavations and, with certain restrictions, to export the results of their findings. The Egyptian Exploration fund was organized in England in 1883, and after excavations in the Delta on the site of the Biblical city of Pithom and of the Greek city of Naukratis, the work of the society was transferred in 1896 to Upper Egypt. At that time also the excavations were placed under the direction of W. Flinders Petrie who has achieved astonishing results, especially in reconstructing in accordance with the testimony of the monuments the account of ancient Egyptian history, which he has carried back to a period antedating the reign of the formerly-supposed mythical king Menes, founder of the first Egyptian dynasty. Independent expeditions were also fitted out by Swiss, Germans, and Americans, and the Orient Gesellschaft organized in 1899 has conducted systematic explorations at various points in the Orient. Among the almost incredible number of objects brought to light by the Egyptian explorers, and which besides filling the new and enlarged museum of Cairo built in 1902, go to make up numerous and important collections in Europe and America, may be mentioned the many papyrus documents (e. g. the Logia of Jesus, various apocalypses, heretical gospels, etc.), which throw light on early Christian history and on the period immediately preceding it. The abundance and historic importance of the treasures found in the land of the Pharaohs caused a great number of European scholars to devote their attention to the study of Egyptology. In addition to the names already referred to the following are taken at random from a list of scholars far too numerous to be even mentioned in the present article. G. Perrot and C. Chippiez (History of Art in Ancient Egypt, 2 vols., London, 1883); P. Renouf (Translation of the Book of the Dead, parts i-iv, London, 1893–95, completed by E. Naville, 1907); E. A. W. Budge (The Mummy: Chapters on Egyptian Funeral Archeology, Cambridge, 1873; The Book of the Dead, 3 vols., London, 1898); W. Max Müller (Asien und Europa nach altägyptischen Denkmälern, Leipzig, 1893); J. de Morgan (Recherches sur les origines de l'Egypte, Paris, 1895–96); J. M. Broderick and A. Morton (Concise Dictionary of Egyptian Archeology, London, 1901); J. P. Mahaffy (The Empire of the Ptolemies, London, 1895); H. Wallis, J. Capart, H. Schneider, J. H. Breasted, A. Wiedemann, M. C. Strack, P. Pierret, K. Piehl, A. Ermann etc. Connected with Egyptology is the study of Coptic, the language of the descendants of the ancient Egyptians. The extant Coptic literature is almost exclusively Christian, and except for liturgical purposes, it fell into disuse after the Moslem supremacy in Egypt in the seventh century. Among the scholars who have made a specialty of this branch of Oriental studies may be mentioned E. Renaudet (eighteenth century), E. M. Quatremère (Recherches critiques et historiques sur la langue et la littérature de l'Égypte, Paris, 1808); A. J. Butler (Ancient Coptic Churches of Egypt, Oxford, 1884), B. T. Evetts, E. Amélineau, E. C. Butler, W. E. Crum, and H. Hyvernat, professor of Oriental languages and archæology at the Catholic University in Washington, who has published in monumental form the text and translation of the "Acts of the Martyrs of the Coptic Church".

Explorations in Syria and Palestine.—Explorations in the Bible lands proper were taken up later than those in Assyria and Egypt and thus far they have been less fruitful in archæological results. The first work, chiefly topographical, was undertaken by Dr. Edward Robinson of New York in 1838 and again in 1852. The results of his investigations appeared in "Biblical Researches", 3 vols., Berlin and Boston, 1841 (3rd edition, 1867), but he is better known through the publication of his popular work entitled "The Land and the Book". In 1847 the American Government commissioned Lieutenant Lynch of the U. S. Navy to explore the Valley of the Jordan and the Dead Sea. In 1865 the Palestine Exploration Fund was organized in England, and among other important results of its activities has been an accurate survey and mapping out of the territory west of the Jordan. From 1867 to 1870 the Fund conducted excavations at Jerusalem under the direction of Sir Charles Warren. They proved valuable in connexion with the identification of the ancient Temple and other sites, but little was found in the line of archeological remains. In 1887 a German Palestine Exploration Fund was organized, and beginning in 1884 it carried out under the direction of Dr. Schumacher a careful survey of the territory east of the Jordan. The most important archæological discoveries in Palestine are the inscription of Mesha, King of Moab (ninth century B. C.) found at Dibon by the German missionary Klein in 1868, the Hebrew inscription, probably of the time of Ezechias, found in the Siloam tunnel beneath the hill of Ophel, and the Greek inscription discovered by Clermont-Ganneau. In this connexion mention should be made of the still more important finding by natives in Egypt (1887) of the famous Tel el-Amarna tablets (q. v.), or letters written in cuneiform characters and proving that about 1400 B. C., prior to the Hebrew conquest, Palestine was already permeated by the Assyro-Babylonian civilization and culture. Further excavations in Palestine have been conducted at various points by W. Flinders Petrie, the Egyptian explorer, (1889) and by the American savant F. J. Bliss (1890-1900). Of still greater importance for Oriental studies bearing on the Bible has been the establishment (1893) by the Dominican Fathers at Jerusalem of a school of Biblical studies under the direction of F. M. Lagrange, O. P. This institute, which has for its object a theoretical and practical training in Oriental subjects pertaining to Holy Scripture, numbers among its staff of instructors such scholars as Father Scheil and Father Vincent who with their co-workers publish the scholarly "Revue biblique internationale". Similar schools were later founded at Jerusalem by the Americans (1900) and by the Germans (1903).

Besides the works already mentioned, see CONDAMIN, *Babylone et la Bible* in *Dict. apologét. de la foi cathol.* (Paris, 1909); HILPRECHT, *Explorations in Bible Lands during the Nineteenth Century* (Philadelphia, 1903); PETERS in the *Encyclopedia Americana*, s. v. *Oriental Research*; JASTROW, *Religion of Assyria and Babylonia* (Boston, 1898); OUSSANI, *The Bible and the Ancient East* in the *New York Review* (Nov.-Dec., 1906); IDEM, *The Code of Hammurabi* (loc. cit., Aug.-Sept., 1905); DUNCAN, *The Exploration of Egypt and the Old Testament* (New York, 1908); ERMONI, *La bible et l'archéologie syrienne* (Paris, 1904); IDEM, *La bible et l'égyptologie* (Paris, 1905); ROGERS, *History of Babylonia and Assyria* (New York, 1900); MASPERO, *Dawn of Civilization* (1894); IDEM, *The Struggle of the Nations* (New York, 1897); PATON, *Early History of Syria and Palestine* (New York, 1901); PINCHES, *The Old Testament in the Light of the History of Assyria and Babylonia* (London, 1902).

JAMES F. DRISCOLL.

Orientation of Churches.—According to Tertullian the Christians of his time were, by some who concerned themselves with their form of worship, believed to be votaries of the sun. This supposition, he adds, doubtless arose from the Christian practice of turning to the east when praying (Apol., c. xvi). Speaking of churches the same writer tells us that the homes "of our dove", as he terms them, are always in "high and open places, facing the light" (Adv. Val., c. iii), and the Apostolic Constitutions (third to fifth century) prescribe that church edifices should be erected with their "heads" towards the East (Const. Apost., II, 7).

The practice of praying while turned towards the rising sun is older than Christianity, but the Christians in adopting it were influenced by reasons peculiar to themselves. The principal of these reasons, according to St. Gregory of Nyssa, was that the Orient contained man's original home, the earthly paradise. St. Thomas Aquinas, speaking for the Middle Ages, adds to this reason several others, as for example, that Our Lord lived His earthly life in the East, and that from the East He shall come to judge mankind (II-II, Q. lxxxiv, a. 3). Thus from the earliest period the custom of locating the apse and altar in the eastern extremity of the church was the rule. Yet the great Roman Basilicas of the Lateran, St. Peter's, St. Paul's (originally), St. Lorenzo's, as well as the Basilica of the Resurrection in Jerusalem and the basilicas of Tyre and Antioch, reversed this rule by placing the apse in the western extremity. The reasons for this mode of orientation can only be conjectured. Some writers explain it by the fact that in the fourth century the celebrant at Mass faced the people, and, therefore in a church with a western apse, looked towards the East when officiating at the altar. Others conjecture that the peculiar orientation of the basilicas mentioned, erected by Constantine the Great or under his influence, may have been a reminiscence of the former predilection of this emperor for sun-worship. In the Orient the eastern apse was the rule, and thence it made its way to the West through the reconstructed Basilica of St. Paul's, the Basilica of S. Pietro in Vincoli, and the celebrated basilica of Ravenna. From the eighth century the propriety of the eastern apse was universally admitted, though, of course strict adherence to this architectural canon, owing to the direction of city streets, was not always possible.

KRAUS, *Gesch. d. christ. Kunst*, I (Freiburg, 1895); *Realencyklopädie d. christ. Altertümer*, s. v. *Orientirung* (Freiburg, 1886); LOWRIE, *Monuments of the Early Church* (New York, 1901); ENLART, *Manuel d'archéologie française*, I (Paris, 1902).

MAURICE M. HASSETT.

Orientius, Christian Latin poet of the fifth century. He wrote an elegiac poem (*Commonitorium*) of 1036 verses (divided into two books) describing the way to heaven, with warnings against its hindrances. He was a Gaul (II, 184), who had been converted after a life of sin (I, 405 sq.), was evidently an experienced pastor, and wrote at a time when his country was being devastated by the invasion of savages. All this points to his identification with Orientius, Bishop of Augusta Ausciorum (Auch), who as a very old man was sent by Theodoric I, King of the Goths, as ambassador to the Roman generals Ætius and Litorius in 439 ("Vita S. Orientii" in "Acta SS.", I May, 61). The *Commonitorium* quotes classical poets—Virgil, Ovid, Catullus—and is perhaps influenced by Prudentius. It exists in only one MS. (Cod. Ashburnham. sæc. X), and is followed by some shorter anonymous poems not by Orientius, and by two prayers in verse attributed to him. The first complete edition was published by Martène, "Veterum Scriptorum Monumenta", I (Rouen, 1700); then by Gallandi, "Bibliotheca veterum Patrum", X (Venice, 1774), 185–96, reprinted in "P. L.", LXI, 977–1006. The best modern edition is by Ellis in the "Corpus Scriptorum Eccl. Latinorum", XVI (Vienna, 1888): "Poetæ Christiani minores", I, 191–261.

MANITIUS, *Gesch. d. Litt. d. Mittelalters im Abendlande*, I (Leipzig, 1889), 410–4; FESSLER-JUNGMANN, *Institutiones Patrologiæ*, II, ii (Innsbruck, 1896), 374–6.

ADRIAN FORTESCUE.

Oriflamme.—In verses 3093–5 of the "Chanson de Roland" (eleventh century) the oriflamme is mentioned as a royal banner, called at first "Romaine" afterwards "Montjoie". According to the legend it was given to Charlemagne by the pope, but no historical text affords us any information with regard to this oriflamme, which is perhaps fabulous. As Eudes, who became king in 888, was Abbot of St. Martin, the banner of the church of St. Martin of Tours was the earliest military standard of the Frankish monarchy. It was a plain blue, a colour then assigned in the liturgy to saints who were, like St. Martin, confessors and pontiffs. The azure ground strewn with gold fleur-de-lis remained the symbol of royalty until the fourteenth century, when the white standard of Jeanne d'Arc wrought marvels, and by degrees the custom was introduced of depicting the fleur-de-lis on white ground. But from the time of Louis VI (1108–37) the banner of St. Martin was replaced as ensign of war by the oriflamme of the Abbey of St. Denis, which floated about the tomb of St. Denis and was said to have been given to the abbey by Dagobert. It is supposed without any certainty that this was a piece of fiery red silk or *sendal* the field of which was covered with flames and stars of gold. The standard-bearer carried it either at the end of a staff or suspended from his neck. Until the twelfth century the standard-bearer was the Comte de Vexin, who, as "vowed" to St. Denis, was the temporal defender of the abbey. Louis VI the Fat, having acquired Vexin, became standard-bearer; as soon as war began, Louis VI received Communion at St. Denis and took the standard from the tomb of the saint to carry it to the combat. "Montjoie Saint Denis", cried the men-at-arms, even as in England they cried "Montjoie Notre Dame" or "Montjoie Saint George". The word *Montjoie* (from *Mons gaudii* or *Mons Jovis*) designates the heaps of stones along the roadside which served as mile-stones or as sign-posts, and which sometimes became the meeting-places for warriors; it was applied to the oriflamme the sight of which was to guide the soldiers in the *mêlée*. The descriptions of the oriflamme which have reached us in Guillaume le Breton (thirteenth cent.), in the "Chronicle of Flanders" (fourteenth cent.), in the "Registra Delphinalia" (1456), and in the inventory of the treasury of St. Denis (1536), show that to the primitive oriflamme there succeeded in the course of centuries newer oriflammes which little resembled one another. At the battles of Poitiers (1356) and Agincourt (1415) the oriflamme fell into the hands of the English; it would seem that after the Hundred Years' War it was no longer borne on the battle-field.

GALLAND, *Des anciennes enseignes et étendards de France* (Paris, 1782); DUPRÉ, *Revue des sociétés savantes*, I (1875), 153–5; BAUDOIN, *Montjoie St. Denis* in *Revue des Pyrénées*, XIV (1902).

GEORGES GOYAU.

Origen and Origenism.—I. *Life and Work of Origen.*—A. BIOGRAPHY.—Origen, most modest of writers, hardly ever alludes to himself in his own works; but Eusebius has devoted to him almost the entire sixth book of "Ecclesiastical History". Eusebius was thoroughly acquainted with the life of his hero; he had collected a hundred of his letters; in collaboration with the martyr Pamphilus he had composed the "Apology for Origen"; he dwelt at Cæsarea where Origen's library was preserved, and where his memory still lingered; if at times he may be thought somewhat partial, he is undoubtedly well informed. We find some details also in the "Farewell Address" of St. Gregory Thaumaturgus to his master, in the controversies of St. Jerome and Rufinus, in St. Epiphanius (Hæres., LXIV), and in Photius (Biblioth. Cod. 118).

(1) *Origen at Alexandria (185–232)*.—Born in 185, Origen was barely seventeen when a bloody persecution of the Church of Alexandria broke out. His father Leonides, who admired his precocious genius and was charmed with his virtuous life, had given him an excellent literary education. When Leonides was cast into prison, Origen would fain have shared his lot, but being unable to carry out his resolution, as his mother had hidden his clothes, he wrote an ardent, enthusiastic letter to his father exhorting him to persevere courageously. When Leonides had won the martyr's crown and his fortune had been confiscated by the imperial authorities, the heroic child laboured to support himself, his mother, and his six younger brothers. This he successfully accomplished by becoming a teacher, selling his manuscripts, and by the generous aid of a certain rich lady, who admired his talents. He assumed, of his own accord, the direction of the catechetical school, on the withdrawal of Clement, and in the following year was confirmed in his office by the patriarch Demetrius (Eusebius, "Hist. eccl.", VI, ii; St. Jerome, "De viris illust.", liv). Origen's school, which was frequented by pagans, soon became a nursery of neophytes, confessors, and martyrs. Among the latter were Plutarch, Serenus Heraclides, Heron, another Serenus, and a female catechumen, Herais (Eusebius, "Hist. eccl.", VI, iv). He accompanied them to the scene of their victories encouraging them by his exhortations. There is nothing more touching than the picture Eusebius has drawn of Origen's youth, so studious, disinterested, austere and pure, ardent and zealous even to indiscretion (VI, iii and vi). Thrust thus at so early an age into the teacher's chair, he recognized the necessity of completing his education. Frequenting the philosophic schools, especially that of Ammonius Saccas, he devoted himself to a study of the philosophers, particularly Plato and the Stoics. In this he was but following the example of his predecessors Pantenus and Clement, and of Heracles, who was to succeed him. Afterwards when the latter shared his labours in the catechetical school, he learned Hebrew, and communicated frequently with certain Jews who helped him to solve his difficulties.

The course of his work at Alexandria was interrupted by five journeys. About 213, under Pope Zephyrinus and the emperor Caracalla, he desired "to see the very ancient Church of Rome", but he did not remain there long (Eusebius, "Hist. eccl.", VI, xiv). Shortly afterwards he was invited to Arabia by the governor who was desirous of meeting him (VI, xix). It was probably in 215 or 216 when the persecution of Caracalla was raging in Egypt that he visited Palestine, where Theoctistus of Cæsarea and Alexander of Jerusalem, invited him to preach though he was still a layman. Towards 218, it would appear, the empress Mammæa, mother of Alexander Severus, brought him to Antioch (VI, xxi). Finally, at a much later period, under Pontian of Rome and Zebinus of Antioch (Eusebius, VI, xxiii), he journeyed into Greece, passing through Cæsarea where Theoctistus, Bishop of that city, assisted by Alexander, Bishop of Jerusalem, raised him to the priesthood. Demetrius, although he had given letters of recommendation to Origen, was very much offended by this ordination, which had taken place without his knowledge and, as he thought, in derogation of his rights. If Eusebius (VI, viii) is to be believed, he was envious of the increasing influence of his catechist. So, on his return to Alexandria, Origen soon perceived that his bishop was rather unfriendly towards him. He yielded to the storm and quitted Egypt (231). The details of this affair were recorded by Eusebius in the lost second book of the "Apology for Origen"; according to Photius, who had read the work, two councils were held at Alexandria, one of which pronounced a decree of banishment against Origen while the other deposed him from the priesthood (Biblioth. cod. 118). St. Jerome declares expressly that he was not condemned on a point of doctrine.

(2) *Origen at Cæsarea (232)*.—Expelled from Alexandria, Origen fixed his abode at Cæsarea in Palestine (232), with his protector and friend Theoctistus, founded a new school there, and resumed his "Commentary on St. John" at the point where it had been interrupted. He was soon surrounded by pupils. The most distinguished of these, without doubt, was St. Gregory Thaumaturgus who, with his brother Apollodorus, attended Origen's lectures for five years and delivered on leaving him a celebrated "Farewell Address". During the persecution of Maximinus (235–37) Origen visited his friend, St. Firmilian, Bishop of Cæsarea in Cappadocia, who made him remain for a long period. On this occasion he was hospitably entertained by a Christian lady of Cæsarea, named Juliana, who had inherited the writings of Symmachus, the translator of the Old Testament (Palladius, "Hist. Laus.", 147). The years following were devoted almost uninterruptedly to the composition of the "Commentaries". Mention is made only of a few excursions to the Holy Places, a journey to Athens (Eusebius, VI, xxxii), and two voyages to Arabia, one of which was undertaken for the conversion of Beryllus, a Patripassian (Eusebius, VI, xxxiii; St. Jerome, "De viris ill.", lx), the other to refute certain heretics who denied the Resurrection (Eusebius, "Hist. eccl.", VI, xxxvii). Age did not diminish his activities. He was over sixty when he wrote his "Contra Celsum" and his "Commentary on St. Matthew". The persecution of Decius (250) prevented him from continuing these works. Origen was imprisoned and barbarously tortured, but his courage was unshaken and from his prison he wrote letters breathing the spirit of the martyrs (Eusebius, "Hist. eccl.", VI, xxxix). He was still alive on the death of Decius (251), but only lingering on, and he died, probably, from the results of the sufferings endured during the persecution (253 or 254), at the age of sixty-nine (Eusebius, "Hist. eccl.", VII, i). His last days were spent at Tyr, though his reason for retiring thither is unknown. He was buried with honour as a confessor of the Faith. For a long time his sepulchre, behind the high-altar of the cathedral of Tyr, was visited by pilgrims. To-day, as nothing remains of this cathedral except a mass of ruins, the exact location of his tomb is unknown.

B. WORKS.—Very few authors were as fertile as Origen. St. Epiphanius estimates at six thousand the number of his writings, counting separately, without doubt, the different books of a single work, his homilies, letters, and his smallest treatises (Hæres., LXIV, lxiii). This figure, repeated by many ecclesiastical writers, seems greatly exaggerated. St. Jerome assures us that the list of Origen's writings drawn up by St. Pamphilus did not contain even two thousand titles (Contra Rufin., II, xxii; III, xxiii); but this list was evidently incomplete. Eusebius ("Hist. eccl.", VI, xxxii) had inserted it in his biography of St. Pamphilus and St. Jerome inserted it in a letter to Paula, the interesting part of which, discovered in the last century, was published by Klostermann among others (Sitzungsber. der . . . Akad. der Wiss. zu Berlin, 1897, pp. 855–70).

(1) *Exegetical Writings*.—Origen had devoted three kinds of works to the explanation of the Holy Scriptures: commentaries, homilies, and scholia (St. Jerome, "Prologus interpret. homiliar. Orig. in Ezechiel"). The commentaries (τόμοι libri, volumina) were a continuous and well-developed interpretation of the inspired text. An idea of their magnitude may be formed from the fact that the words of St. John: "In the beginning was the Word", furnished material for a whole roll. There remain in Greek only eight books of the "Commentary on St. Matthew", and nine books of the "Commentary on St. John"; in Latin an anonymous translation of the "Commentary on St. Matthew" beginning with chapter xvi, three books and a half of the "Commentary on the Canticle of Canticles" translated by Rufinus, and an abridgment of the "Commentary on the Epistles to the Romans" by the same translator. The homilies (ὁμιλίαι, homiliæ, tractatus) were familiar discourses on texts of Scripture, often extemporary and recorded as well as possible by stenographers. The list is long and undoubtedly must have been longer if it be true that Origen, as St. Pamphilus declares in his "Apology", preached almost every day. There remain in Greek twenty-one (twenty on Jeremias and the celebrated homily on the witch of Endor); in Latin, one hundred and eighteen translated by Rufinus, seventy-eight translated by St. Jerome and some others of more or less doubtful authenticity, preserved in a collection of homilies. The twenty "Tractatus Origenis" recently discovered are not the work of Origen, though use has been made of his writings. Origen has been called the father of the homily; it was he who contributed most to popularize this species of literature in which are to be found so many instructive details on the customs of the primitive Church, its institutions, discipline, liturgy, and sacraments. The scholia (σχόλια, excerpta, commaticum interpretandi genus) were exegetical, philological, or historical notes, on words or passages of the Bible, like the annotations of the Alexandria grammarians on the profane writers. Except some few short fragments all of these have perished.

(2) *Other Writings*.—We now possess only two of Origen's letters: one addressed to St. Gregory Thaumaturgus on the reading of Holy Scripture, the other to Julius Africanus on the Greek additions to the Book of Daniel. Two *opuscula* have been preserved entire in the original form; an excellent treatise "On Prayer" and an "Exhortation to Martyrdom", sent by Origen to his friend Ambrose, then a prisoner for the Faith. Finally two large works have escaped the ravages of time: the "Contra Celsum" in the original text, and the "De principiis" in a Latin translation by Rufinus and in the citations of the "Philocalia" which might equal in contents one-sixth of the whole work. In the eight books of the "Contra Celsum" Origen follows his adversary point by point, refuting in detail each of his false imputations. It is a model of reasoning, erudition, and honest polemic. The "De principiis", composed at Alexandria, and which, it seems, got into the hands of the public before its completion, treated successively in its four books, allowing for numerous digressions, of: (a) God and the Trinity, (b) the world and its relation to God, (c) man and his free will, (d) Scripture, its inspiration and interpretation. Many other works of Origen have been entirely lost: for instance, the treatise in two books "On the Resurrection", a treatise "On Free Will", and ten books of "Miscellaneous Writings" (Στρωματεῖς). For Origen's critical work see HEXAPLA. For his writings see Westcott in "Dict. of Christ. Biog.", s. v.; Preuschen in Harnack, "Die Ueberlieferung und

Bestand der altchristl. Litteratur" (Leipzig, 1893), 333–90; Bardenhewer, "Geschichte der altkirchl. Literatur." (Freiburg), II, 68–149; Prat in Vigouroux, "Dict. de la Bible", s. v.

C. POSTHUMOUS INFLUENCE OF ORIGEN.—During his lifetime Origen by his writings, teaching, and intercourse exercised very great influence. St. Firmilian of Cæsarea in Cappadocia, who regarded himself as his disciple, made him remain with him for a long period to profit by his learning (Eusebius, "Hist. eccl.", VI, xxvi; Palladius, "Hist. Laus.", 147). St. Alexander of Jerusalem his fellow-pupil at the catechetical school was his intimate faithful friend (Eusebius, VI, xiv), as was Theoctistus of Cæsarea in Palestine, who ordained him (Photius, cod. 118). Beryllus of Bostra, whom he had won back from heresy, was deeply attached to him (Eusebius, VI, xxxiii; St. Jerome, "De viris ill.", lx). St. Anatolus of Laodicea sang his praises in his "Carmen Paschale" (P. G., X, 210). The learned Julius Africanus consulted him, Origen's reply being extant (P. G., XI, 41–85). St. Hippolytus highly appreciated his talents (St. Jerome, "De viris ill.", lxi). St. Dionysius, his pupil and successor in the catechetical school, when Patriarch of Alexandria, dedicated to him his treatise "On the Persecution" (Eusebius, VI, xlvi), and on learning of his death wrote a letter filled with his praises (Photius, cod. 232). St. Gregory Thaumaturgus, who had been his pupil for five years at Cæsarea, before leaving addressed to him his celebrated "Farewell Address" (P. G., X, 1049–1104), an enthusiastic panegyric. There is no proof that Heracles, his disciple, colleague, and successor in the catechetical school, before being raised to the Patriarchate of Alexandria, wavered in his sworn friendship. Origen's name was so highly esteemed that when there was question of putting an end to a schism or rooting out a heresy, appeal was made to it.

After his death his reputation continued to spread. St. Pamphilus, martyred in 307, composed with Eusebius an "Apology for Origen" in six books, the first alone of which has been preserved in a Latin translation by Rufinus (P. G., XVII, 541–616). Origen had at that time many other apologists whose names are unknown to us (Photius, cod. 117 and 118). The directors of the catechetical school continued to walk in his footsteps. Theognostus, in his "Hypotyposes", followed him even too closely, according to Photius (cod. 106), though his action was approved by St. Athanasius. Pierius was called by St. Jerome "Origenes junior" (De viris ill., lxxvi). Didymus the Blind composed a work to explain and justify the teaching of the "De principiis" (St. Jerome, "Adv. Rufin.", I, vi). St. Athanasius does not hesitate to cite him with praise (Epist. IV ad Serapion., 9 and 10) and points out that he must be interpreted generously (De decretis Nic., 27).

Nor was the admiration for the great Alexandrian less outside of Egypt. St. Gregory of Nazianzus gave significant expression to his opinion (Suidas, "Lexicon", ed. Bernhardy, II, 1274: Ὠριγένης ἡ πάντων ἡμῶν ἀχόνη). In collaboration with St. Basil, he had published, under the title "Philocalia", a volume of selections from the master. In his "Panegyric on St. Gregory Thaumaturgus", St. Gregory of Nyssa called Origen the prince of Christian learning in the third century (P. G., XLVI, 905). At Cæsarea in Palestine the admiration of the learned for Origen became a passion. St. Pamphilus wrote his "Apology", Euzoius had his writings transcribed on parchment (St. Jerome, "De viris ill.", xciii). Eusebius catalogued them carefully and drew upon them largely. Nor were the Latins less enthusiastic than the Greeks. According to St. Jerome, the principal Latin imitators of Origen are St. Eusebius of Verceil, St. Hilary of Poitiers, and St. Ambrose of Milan; St. Victorinus of Pettau had set them the example (St. Jerome, "Adv. Rufin.", I, ii; "Ad Augustin. Epist.", cxii, 20). Origen's writings were so much drawn upon that the solitary of Bethlehem called it plagiarism, *furta Latinrum*. However, excepting Rufinus, who is practically only a translator, St. Jerome is perhaps the Latin writer who is most indebted to Origen. Before the Origenist controversies he willingly admitted this, and even afterwards, he did not entirely repudiate it; cf. the prologues to his translations of Origen (Homilies on St. Luke, Jeremias, and Ezechiel, the Canticle of Canticles), and also the prefaces to his own "Commentaries" (on Micheas, the Epistles to the Galatians, and to the Ephesians etc.).

Amidst these expressions of admiration and praise, a few discordant voices were heard. St. Methodius, bishop and martyr (311), had written several works against Origen, amongst others a treatise "On the Resurrection", of which St. Epiphanius cites a long extract (Hæres., LXVI, xii–lxii). St. Eustathius of Antioch, who died in exile about 337, criticized his allegorism (P. G., XVIII, 613–673). St. Alexander of Alexandria, martyred in 311, also attacked him, if we are to credit Leontius of Byzantium and the emperor Justinian. But his chief adversaries were the heretics, Sabellians, Arians, Pelagians, Nestorians, Apollinarists. On this subject see Prat, "Origène", 199–200.

II. ORIGENISM.—By this term is understood not so much Origen's theology and the body of his teachings, as a certain number of doctrines, rightly or wrongly attributed to him, and which by their novelty or their danger called forth at an early period a refutation from orthodox writers. They are chiefly: A.—Allegorism in the interpretation of Scripture; B.—Subordination of the Divine Persons; C.—The theory of successive trials and a final restoration. Before examining how far Origen is responsible for these theories, a word must be said of the directive principle of his theology.

The Church and the Rule of Faith.—In the preface to the "De principiis" Origen laid down a rule thus formulated in the translation of Rufinus: "Illa sola credenda est veritas quæ in nullo ab ecclesiastica et apostolica discordat traditione". The same norm is expressed almost in equivalent terms in many other passages, e. g., "non debemus credere nisi quemadmodum per successionem Ecclesiæ Dei tradiderunt nobis" (In Matt., ser. 46, Migne, XIII, 1667). In accordance with those principles Origen constantly appeals to ecclesiastical preaching, ecclesiastical teaching, and the ecclesiastical rule of faith (κανών). He accepts only four canonical Gospels because tradition does not receive more; he admits the necessity of the baptism of infants because it is in accordance with the practice of the Church founded on Apostolic tradition; he warns the interpreter of the Holy Scriptures, not to rely on his own judgment, but "on the rule of the Church instituted by Christ". For, he adds, we have only two lights to guide us here below, Christ and the Church; the Church reflects faithfully the light received from Christ, as the moon reflects the rays of the sun. The distinctive mark of the Catholic is to belong to the Church, to depend on the Church outside of which there is no salvation; on the contrary, he who leaves the Church walks in darkness, he is a heretic. It is through the principle of authority that Origen is wont to unmask and combat doctrinal errors. It is the principle of authority, too, that he invokes when he enumerates the dogmas of faith. A man animated with such sentiments may have made mistakes, because he is human, but his disposition of mind is essentially Catholic and he does not deserve to be ranked among the promoters of heresy.

A. *Scriptural Allegorism.*—The principal passages on the inspiration, meaning, and interpretation of the Scriptures are preserved in Greek in the first fifteen chapters of the "Philocalia". According to Origen, Scripture is inspired because it is the word and work of God. But, far from being an inert instrument, the inspired author has full possession of his faculties, he is conscious of what he is writing: he is physically free to deliver his message or not; he is not seized by a passing delirium like the pagan oracles, for bodily disorder, disturbance of the senses, momentary loss of reason are but so many proofs of the action of the evil spirit. Since Scripture is from God, it ought to have the distinctive characteristics of the Divine works: truth, unity, and fullness. The word of God cannot possibly be untrue; hence no errors or contradictions can be admitted in Scripture (In Joan., X, iii). The author of the Scriptures being one, the Bible is less a collection of books than one and the same book (Philoc., V, iv–vii), a perfect harmonious instrument (Philoc., VI, i–ii). But the most Divine note of Scripture is its fullness: "There is not in the Holy Books the smallest passage (χεραία) but reflects the wisdom of God" (Philoc., I, xxviii, cf. X, i). True there are imperfections in the Bible: antilogies, repetitions, want of continuity; but these imperfections become perfections by leading us to the allegory and the spiritual meaning (Philoc., X, i–ii).

At one time Origen, starting from the Platonic trichotomy, distinguishes the *body*, the *soul*, and the *spirit* of Holy Scripture; at another, following a more rational terminology, he distinguishes only between the letter and the spirit. In reality, the *soul*, or the *psychic* signification, or *moral* meaning (that is the *moral parts* of Scripture, and the *moral applications* of the other parts) plays only a very secondary rôle, and we can confine ourselves to the antithesis: *letter* (or *body*) and *spirit*. Unfortunately this antithesis is not free from equivocation. Origen does not understand by letter (or body) what we mean to-day by the literal sense, but the grammatical sense, the proper as opposed to the figurative meaning. Just so he does not attach to the words spiritual meaning the same signification as we do: for him they mean the spiritual sense properly so called (the meaning added to the literal sense by the express wish of God attaching a special signification to the fact related or the manner of relating them), or the figurative as contrasted with the proper sense, or the accommodative sense, often an arbitrary invention of the interpreter, or even the literal sense when it is treating of things spiritual. If this terminology is kept in mind there is nothing absurd in the principle he repeats so often: "Such a passage of the Scripture has no corporal meaning." As examples Origen cites the anthropomorphisms, metaphors, and symbols which ought indeed to be understood figuratively.

Though he warns us that these passages are the exceptions, it must be confessed that he allows too many cases in which the Scripture is not to be understood according to the letter; but, remembering his terminology, his principle is unimpeachable. The two great rules of interpretation laid down by the Alexandria catechist, taken by themselves and independently of erroneous applications, are proof against criticism. They may be formulated thus: (1) Scripture must be interpreted in a manner worthy of God, the author of Scripture. (2) The corporal sense or the letter of Scripture must not be adopted, when it would entail anything impossible, absurd, or unworthy of God. The abuse arises from the application of these rules. Origen has recourse too easily to allegorism to explain purely apparent antilogies or antinomies. He considers that certain narratives or ordinances of the Bible would be unworthy of God if they had to be taken according to the letter, or if they were to be taken *solely* according to the letter. He justifies the allegorism by the fact that otherwise certain accounts or certain precepts now abrogated would be useless and profitless for the reader: a fact which appears to him contrary to the providence of the Divine inspirer and the dignity of Holy Writ. It will thus be seen that though the criticisms directed against his allegorical method by St. Epiphanius and St. Methodius were not groundless, yet many of the complaints arise from a misunderstanding. Cf. Zöllig, "Die Inspirationslehre des Origenes" (Freiburg, 1902).

B. *Subordination of the Divine Persons.*—The three Persons of the Trinity are distinguished from all creatures by the three following characteristics: absolute immateriality, omniscience, and substantial sanctity. As is well known many ancient ecclesiastical writers attributed to created spirits an aerial or ethereal envelope without which they could not act. Though he does not venture to decide categorically, Origen inclines to this view, but, as soon as there is question of the Divine Persons, he is perfectly sure that they have no body and are not in a body; and this characteristic belongs to the Trinity alone (De princip., IV, 27; I, vi, 4; II, ii, 2; II, iv, 3 etc.). Again the knowledge of every creature, being essentially limited, is always imperfect and capable of being increased. But it would be repugnant for the Divine Persons to pass from the state of ignorance to knowledge. How could the Son, who is the Wisdom of the Father, be ignorant of anything ("In Joan.", 1, 27; "Contra Cels.", VI, xvii). Nor can we admit ignorance in the Spirit who "searcheth the deep things of God" (De princip., I, iii, 4; iv, 35). Finally, holiness is accidental in every creature, whereas it is essential, and therefore immutable, in the Trinity. Origen incessantly recalls this principle which separates the Trinity from all created spirits by an impassable abyss ("De princip.", I, v, 4; I, vi, 2; I, vii, 3; "In Num. hom.", XI, 8 etc.). As substantial holiness is the exclusive privilege of the Trinity so also is it the only source of all created holiness. Sin is forgiven only by the simultaneous concurrence of the Father, the Son, and the Holy Ghost; no one is sanctified at baptism save through their common action; the soul in which the Holy Ghost indwells possesses likewise the Son and the Father. In a word the three Persons of the Trinity are indivisible in their being, their presence, and their operation.

Along with these perfectly orthodox texts there are some which must be interpreted with diligence, remembering as we ought that the language of theology was not yet fixed and that Origen was often the first to face these difficult problems. It will then appear that the subordination of the Divine Persons, so much urged against Origen, generally consists in differences of appropriation (the Father creator, the Son redeemer, the Spirit sanctifier) which seem to attribute to the Persons an unequal sphere of action, or in the liturgical practice of praying the Father *through* the Son in the Holy Ghost, or in the theory so widespread in the Greek Church of the first five centuries, that the Father has a pre-eminence of rank (τάξις) over the two other Persons, inasmuch as in mentioning them He ordinarily has the first place, and of dignity (ἀξίωμα), because He represents the whole Divinity, of which He is the principle (ἀρχή), the origin (αἴτιος), and the source (πηγή). That is why St. Athanasius defends Origen's orthodoxy concerning the Trinity and why St. Basil and St. Gregory of Nazianzus replied to the heretics who claimed the support of his authority that they misunderstood him.

C. *The Origin and Destiny of Rational Beings.*— Here we encounter an unfortunate amalgam of philosophy and theology. The system that results is not coherent, for Origen, frankly recognizing the contradiction of the incompatible elements that he is trying to unify, recoils from the consequences, protests against the logical conclusions, and oftentimes corrects by orthodox professions of faith the heterodoxy of his speculations. It must be said that almost all the texts about to be treated of, are contained in the "De principiis", where the author treads on most dangerous ground. The system may be reduced to a few hypotheses, the error and danger of which were not recognized by Origen.

(1) *Eternity of the Creation*—Whatever exists outside of God was created by Him: the Alexandrian catechist always defended this thesis most energetically against the pagan philosophers who admitted an uncreated matter ("De princip.", II, i, 5; "In Genes.", I, 12, in Migne, XII, 48–49). But he believes that God created from eternity, for "it is absurd", he says, "to imagine the nature of God inactive, or His goodness inefficacious, or His dominion without subjects" (De princip., III, v, 3). Consequently he is forced to admit a double infinite series of worlds before and after the present world. (2) *Original Equality of the Created Spirits.*—In the beginning all intellectual natures were created equal and alike, as God had no motive for creating them otherwise" (De princip., II, ix, 6). Their present differences arise solely from their different use of the gift of free will. The spirits created good and happy grew tired of their happiness (op. cit., I, iii, 8), and, through carelessness, fell, some more some less (I, vi, 2). Hence the hierarchy of the angels; hence also the four categories of created intellects: angels, stars (supposing, as is probable, that they are animated, "De princip.", I, vii, 3), men, and demons. But their rôles may be one day changed; for what free will has done, free will can undo, and the Trinity alone is essentially immutable in good.

(3) *Essence and raison d'être of Matter.*—Matter exists only for the spiritual; if the spiritual did not need it, matter would not exist, for its finality is not in itself. But it seems to Origen—though he does not venture to declare so expressly—that created spirits even the most perfect cannot do without an extremely diluted and subtle matter which serves them as a vehicle and means of action (De princip., II, ii, 1; I, vi, 4 etc.). Matter was, therefore, created simultaneously with the spiritual, although the spiritual is logically prior; and matter will never cease to be because the spiritual, however perfect, will always need it. But matter which is susceptible of indefinite transformations is adapted to the varying condition of the spirits. "When intended for the more imperfect spirits, it becomes solidified, thickens, and forms the bodies of this visible world. If it is serving higher intelligences, it shines with the brightness of the celestial bodies and serves as a garb for the angels of God, and the children of the Resurrection" (op. cit., II, ii, 2).

(4) *Universality of the Redemption and the Final Restoration.*—Certain Scriptural texts, e. g., I Cor., xv, 25–28, seem to extend to all rational beings the benefit of the Redemption, and Origen allows himself to be led also by the philosophical principle which he enunciates several times, without ever proving it, that the end is always like the beginning: "We think that the goodness of God, through the mediation of Christ, will bring all creatures to one and the same end" (De princip., I, vi, 1–3). The universal restoration (ἀποκατάστασις) follows necessarily from these principles.

On the least reflection, it will be seen that these hypotheses, starting from contrary points of view, are irreconcilable: for the theory of a final restoration is diametrically opposed to the theory of successive indefinite trials. It would be easy to find in the writings of Origen a mass of texts contradicting these principles and destroying the resulting conclusions. He affirms, for instance, that the charity of the elect in heaven does not fail; in their case "the freedom of the will will be bound so that sin will be impossible" (In Roman., V, 10). So, too, the reprobate will always be fixed in evil, less from inability to free themselves from it, than because they wish to be evil (De princip., I, viii, 4), for malice has become natural to them, it is as a second nature in them (In Joann., xx, 19). Origen grew angry when accused of teaching the eternal salvation of the devil. But the hypotheses which he lays down here and there are none the less worthy of censure. What can be said in his defence, if it be not with St. Athanasius (De decretis Nic., 27), that we must not seek to find his real opinion in the works in which he discusses the arguments for and against doctrine as an intellectual exercise or amusement; or, with St. Jerome (Ad Pammach. Epist., XLVIII, 12), that it is one thing to dogmatize and another to enunciate hypothetical opinions which will be cleared up by discussion?

III. ORIGENIST CONTROVERSIES.—The discussions concerning Origen and his teaching are of a very singular and very complex character. They break out unexpectedly, at long intervals, and assume an immense importance quite unforeseen in their humble beginnings. They are complicated by so many personal disputes and so many questions foreign to the fundamental subject in controversy that a brief and rapid *exposé* of the polemics is difficult and well-nigh impossible. Finally they abate so suddenly that one is forced to conclude that the controversy was superficial and that Origen's orthodoxy was not the sole point in dispute.

A.—*First Origenist Crisis.*—It broke out in the deserts of Egypt, raged in Palestine, and ended at Constantinople with the condemnation of St. Chrysostom (392–404). During the second half of the fourth century the monks of Nitria professed an exaggerated enthusiasm for Origen, whilst the neighbouring brethren of Sceta, as a result of an unwarranted reaction and an excessive fear of allegorism, fell into Anthropomorphism. These doctrinal discussions gradually invaded the monasteries of Palestine, which were under the care of St. Epiphanius, Bishop of Salamis, who, convinced of the dangers of Origenism, had combatted it in his works and was determined to prevent its spread and to extirpate it completely. Having gone to Jerusalem in 394, he preached vehemently against Origen's errors, in presence of the bishop of that city, John, who was deemed an Origenist. John in turn spoke against Anthropomorphism, directing his discourse so clearly against Epiphanius that no one could be mistaken. Another incident soon helped to embitter the dispute. Epiphanius had raised Paulinian, brother of St. Jerome, to the priesthood in a place subject to the See of Jerusalem. John complained bitterly of this violation of his rights, and the reply of Epiphanius was not of a nature to appease him.

Two new combatants now enter the lists. From the time when Jerome and Rufinus settled, one at Bethlehem and the other on Mt. Olivet, they had lived in brotherly friendship. Both admired, imitated, and translated Origen, and were on most amicable terms with their bishop, when in 392 Aterbius, a monk of Sceta, came to Jerusalem and accused them both of Origenism. St. Jerome, very sensitive on the question of orthodoxy, was much hurt by the insinuation of Aterbius and two years later sided with St. Epiphanius, whose reply to John of Jerusalem he translated into Latin. Rufinus learnt, it is not known how, of this translation, which was not intended for the public, and Jerome suspected him of having obtained it by fraud. A reconciliation was effected sometime later, but it was not lasting. In 397 Rufinus, then at Rome, had translated Origen's "De principiis" into Latin, and in his preface followed the example of St. Jerome, whose dithyrambic eulogy addressed to the Alexandrian catechist he remembered. The solitary of Bethlehem, grievously hurt at this action, wrote to his friends to refute the perfidious implications of Rufinus, denounced Origen's errors to Pope Anastasius, tried to win the Patriarch of Alexandria over to the anti-Origenist cause, and began a discussion with Rufinus, marked with great bitterness on both sides.

Until 400 Theophilus of Alexandria was an acknowledged Origenist. His confident was Isidore, a former monk of Nitria, and his friends, "the Tall Brothers", the accredited leaders of the Origenist party. He had supported John of Jerusalem against St. Epiphanius, whose Anthropomorphism he denounced to Pope Siricius. Suddenly he changed his views, exactly why was never known. It is said that the monks of Sceta, displeased with his paschal letter of 399, forcibly invaded his episcopal residence and threatened him with death if he did not chant the palinody. What is certain is that he had quarrelled with St. Isidore over money matters and with "the Tall Brothers", who blamed his avarice and his worldliness. As Isidore and "the Tall Brothers" had retired to Constantinople, where Chrysostom extended his hospitality to them and interceded for them, without, however, admitting them to communion till the censures pronounced against them had been raised, the irascible Patriarch of Alexandria determined on this plan: to suppress Origenism everywhere, and under this pretext ruin Chrysostom, whom he hated and envied. For four years he was mercilessly active: he condemned Origen's books at the Council of Alexandria (400), with an armed band he expelled the monks from Nitria, he wrote to the bishops of Cyprus and Palestine to win them over to his anti-Origenist crusade, issued paschal letters in 401, 402, and 404 against Origen's doctrine, and sent a missive to Pope Anastasius asking for the condemnation of Origenism. He was successful beyond his hopes; the bishops of Cyprus accepted his invitation. Those of Palestine, assembled at Jerusalem, condemned the errors pointed out to them, adding that they were not taught amongst them. Anastasius, while declaring that Origen was entirely unknown to him, condemned the propositions extracted from his books. St. Jerome undertook to translate into Latin the various elucubrations of the patriarch, even his virulent diatribe against Chrysostom. St. Epiphanius, preceding Theophilus to Constantinople, treated St. Chrysostom as temerarious, and almost heretical, until the day the truth began to dawn on him, and suspecting that he might have been deceived, he suddenly left Constantinople and died at sea before arriving at Salamis.

It is well known how Theophilus, having been called by the emperor to explain his conduct towards Isidore and "the Tall Brothers", cleverly succeeded by his machinations in changing the rôles. Instead of being the accused, he became the accuser, and summoned Chrysostom to appear before the conciliabule of the Oak (ad Quercum), at which Chrysostom was condemned. As soon as the vengeance of Theophilus was satiated nothing more was heard of Origenism. The Patriarch of Alexandria began to read Origen, pretending that he could cull the roses from among the thorns. He became reconciled with "the Tall Brothers" without asking them to retract. Hardly had the personal quarrels abated when the spectre of Origenism vanished (cf. Dale, "Origenistic Controversies" in "Dict. of Christ. Biog.", IV, 146–151).

B. *Second Origenistic Crisis.*—This new phrase, quite as intricate and confusing as the former, has been partially elucidated by Prof. Dickamp, upon whose learned study, "Die origenistischen Streitigkeiten in sechsten Jahrhundert" (Münster, 1899), we draw. In 514 certain heterodox doctrines of a very singular character had already spread among the monks of Jerusalem and its environs. Possibly the seeds of the dispute may have been sown by Stephen Bar-Sudaili, a troublesome monk expelled from Edessa, who joined to an Origenism of his own brand certain clearly pantheistic views. Plotting and intriguing continued for about thirty years, the monks suspected of Origenism being in turn expelled from their monasteries, then readmitted, only to be driven out anew. Their leaders and protectors were Nonnus, who till his death in 547 kept the party together, Theodore Askidas and Domitian who had won the favour of the emperor and were named bishops, one to the See of Ancyra in Galatia, the other to that of Cæsarea in Cappadocia, though they continued to reside at court (537). In these circumstances a report against Origenism was addressed to Justinian, by whom and on what occasion it is not known, for the two accounts that have come down to us are at variance (Cyrillus of Scythopolis, "Vita Sabæ"; and Liberatus, "Breviarium", xxiii). At all events, the emperor then wrote his "Liber adversus Origenem", containing in addition to an *exposé* of the reasons for condemning it twenty-four censurable texts taken from the "De principiis", and lastly ten propositions to be anathematized. Justinian ordered the patriarch Mennas to call together all the bishops present in Constantinople and make them subscribe to these anathemas. This was the local synod (σύνοδος ἐνδημοῦσα) of 543. A copy of the imperial edict had been addressed to the other patriarchs, including Pope Vigilius, and all gave their adhesion to it. In the case of Vigilius especially we have the testimony of Liberatus (Breviar., xxiii) and Cassiodorus (Institutiones, 1).

It had been expected that Domitian and Theodore Askidas, by their refusal to condemn Origenism, would fall into disfavour at Court; but they signed whatever they were asked to sign and remained more powerful than ever. Askidas even took revenge by persuading the emperor to have Theodore of Mopsuestia, who was deemed the sworn enemy of Origen, condemned (Liberatus, "Breviar.", xxiv; Facundas of Hermianus, "Defensio trium capitul.", I, ii; Evagrius, "Hist.", IV, xxxviii). Justinian's new edict, which is not extant, resulted in the assembling of the fifth œcumenical council, in which Theodore of Mopsuestia, Ibas, and Theodoretus were condemned (553).

Were Origen and Origenism anathematized? Many learned writers believe so; an equal number deny that they were condemned; most modern authorities are either undecided or reply with reservations. Relying on the most recent studies on the question it may be held that: (1) It is certain that the fifth general council was convoked exclusively to deal with the affair of the Three Chapters (q. v.), and that neither Origen nor Origenism were the cause of it. (2) It is certain that the council opened on 5 May, 553, in spite of the protestations of Pope Vigilius, who though at Constantinople refused to attend it, and that in the eight conciliary sessions (from 5 May to 2 June), the Acts of which we possess, only the question of the Three Chapters is treated.

(3) Finally it is certain that only the Acts concerning the affair of the Three Chapters were submitted to the pope for his approval, which was given on 8 December, 553, and 23 February, 554. (4) It is a fact that Popes Vigilius, Pelagius I (556–61), Pelagius II (579–90), Gregory the Great (590–604), in treating of the fifth council deal only with the Three Chapters, make no mention of Origenism, and speak as if they did not know of its condemnation. (5) It must be admitted that before the opening of the council, which had been delayed by the resistance of the pope, the bishops already assembled at Constantinople had to consider, by order of the emperor, a form of Origenism that had practically nothing in common with Origen, but which was held, we know, by one of the Origenist parties in Palestine. The arguments in corroboration of this hypothesis may be found in Dickamp (op. cit., 66–141). (6) The bishops certainly subscribed to the fifteen anathemas proposed by the emperor (ibid., 90–96); an admitted Origenist, Theodore of Scythopolis, was forced to retract (ibid., 125–129); but there is no proof that the approbation of the pope, who was at that time protesting against the convocation of the council, was asked. (7) It is easy to understand how this extra-conciliary sentence was

mistaken at a later period for a decree of the actual œcumenical council.

Besides the works cited in the body of the article, the following may be consulted: on the life, works, and theology of Origen: HUET, *Origeniana* in *P. G.*, XVII; REDEPENNING, *Origenes* (Bonn, 1841–6).

On the recent works concerning Origen, see EHRHARD, *Die altchristliche Litteratur und ihre Erforschung von 1884–1900* (Freiburg, 1900), 320–51.

On Origen's doctrine: BIGG, *The Christian Platonists of Alexandria* (Oxford, 1886); FAIRWEATHER, *Origen and Greek Patristic Theology* (Edinburgh, 1901); FREPPEL, *Origène* (Paris, 1868); DENIS, *La philosophie d'Origène* (Paris, 1884); CAPITAINE, *De Origenis ethica* (Münster, 1898); PRAT, *Origène, le théologien et l'exégète* (Paris, 1907).

The best edition of Origen's works is the one in course of publication by the Academy of Sciences of Berlin; the following works have appeared: *De martyrio, Contra Celsum, De oratione* by KÖTSCHAU (2 vols., Leipzig, 1899); *Twenty Homilies on Jeremias, Homily on the Witch of Endor*, and *Fragments* by KLOSTERMANN (Leipzig, 1901); *Commentary on St. John* (nine books and fragments) by PREUSCHEN (Leipzig, 1903). For the still unedited texts of the Philocalia there is the excellent edition of Robinson (Cambridge, 1893). There is an English translation of the *De principiis* and the *Contra Celsum* by CROMBIE in *Ante-Nicene Christian Library*, Edinburgh, X (1869) and XXIII (1872); a translation of the *Commentaries on St. Matthew and on St. John* by MENZIES in the supplementary vol. (1897) of the same collection.

F. PRAT.

Original Sin.—I. Meaning; II. Principal Adversaries; III. Original Sin in Scripture; IV. Original Sin in Tradition; V. Original Sin in face of the Objections of Human Reason; VI. Nature of Original Sin; VII. How Voluntary.

I. MEANING.—Original sin may be taken to mean: (1) the sin that Adam committed; (2) a consequence of this first sin, the hereditary stain with which we are born on account of our origin or descent from Adam. From the earliest times the latter sense of the word was more common, as may be seen by St. Augustine's statement: "the deliberate sin of the First man is the cause of original sin" (De nupt. et concup., II, xxvi, 43). It is the hereditary stain that is dealt with here. As to the sin of Adam we have not to examine the circumstances in which it was committed nor to make the exegesis of the third chapter of Genesis.

II. PRINCIPAL ADVERSARIES.—Theodorus of Mopsuestia opened this controversy by denying that the sin of Adam was the origin of death. (See the "Excerpta Theodori", by Marius Mercator; cf. Smith, "A Dictionary of Christian Biography", IV, 942.) Celestius, a friend of Pelagius, was the first in the West to hold these propositions, borrowed from Theodorus: "Adam was to die in every hypothesis, whether he sinned or did not sin. His sin injured himself only and not the human race" (Mercator, "Liber Subnotationum", preface). This, the first position held by the Pelagians, was also the first point condemned at Carthage (Denzinger, "Enchiridion", no 101—old no. 65). Against this fundamental error Catholics cited especially Rom., v, 12, where Adam is shown as transmitting death with sin. After some time the Pelagians admitted the transmission of death—this being more easily understood as we see that parents transmit to their children hereditary diseases — but they still violently attacked the transmission of sin (St. Augustine, "Contra duas epist. Pelag.", IV, iv, 6). And when St. Paul speaks of the transmission of sin they understood by this the transmission of death. This was their second position, condemned by the Council of Orange [Denz., n. 175 (145)], and again later on with the first by the Council of Trent [Sess. V, can. ii; Denz., n. 789 (671)]. To take the word *sin* to mean death was an evident falsification of the text, so the Pelagians soon abandoned the interpretation and admitted that Adam caused sin in us. They did not, however, understand by sin the hereditary stain contracted at our birth, but the sin that adults commit in imitation of Adam. This was their third position, to which is opposed the definition of Trent that sin is transmitted to all by generation (*propagatione*), not by imitation [Denz., n. 790 (672)]. Moreover, in the following canon are cited the words of the Council of Carthage, in which there is question of a sin contracted by generation and effaced by regeneration [Denz., n. 102 (66)]. The leaders of the Reformation admitted the dogma of original sin, but at present there are many Protestants imbued with Socinian doctrines whose theory is a revival of Pelagianism.

III. ORIGINAL SIN IN SCRIPTURE.—The classical text is Rom., v, 12 sqq. In the preceding part the Apostle treats of justification by Jesus Christ, and to put in evidence the fact of His being the one Saviour, he contrasts with this Divine Head of mankind the human head who caused its ruin. The question of original sin, therefore, comes in only incidentally. St. Paul supposes the idea that the faithful have of it from his oral instructions, and he speaks of it to make them understand the work of Redemption. This explains the brevity of the development and the obscurity of some verses. We shall now show what, in the text, is opposed to the three Pelagian positions:

(1) The sin of Adam has injured the human race at least in the sense that it has introduced death— "Wherefore as by one man sin entered into this world and by sin death; and so death passed upon all men". Here there is question of physical death. First, the literal meaning of the word ought to be presumed unless there be some reason to the contrary. Second, there is an allusion in this verse to a passage in the Book of Wisdom in which, as may be seen from the context, there is question of physical death, Wis., ii, 24: "But by the envy of the devil death came into the world". Cf. Gen., ii, 17; iii, 3, 19; and another parallel passage in St. Paul himself, I Cor., xv, 21: "For by a man came death and by a man the resurrection of the dead". Here there can be question only of physical death, since it is opposed to corporal resurrection, which is the subject of the whole chapter.

(2) Adam by his fault transmitted to us not only death but also sin—"for as by the disobedience of one man many [i. e., all men] were made sinners" (Rom., v, 19). How then could the Pelagians, and at a later period Zwingli, say that St. Paul speaks only of the transmission of physical death? If according to them we must read *death* where the Apostle wrote *sin*, we should also read that the disobedience of Adam has made us *mortal* where the Apostle writes that it has made us *sinners*. But the word *sinner* has never meant *mortal*, nor has sin ever meant *death*. Also in verse 12, which corresponds to verse 19, we see that by one man two things have been brought on all men, sin and death, the one being the consequence of the other and therefore not identical with it.

(3) Since Adam transmits death to his children by way of generation when he begets them mortal, it is by generation also that he transmits to them sin, for the Apostle presents these two effects as produced at the same time and by the same causality. The explanation of the Pelagians differs from that of St. Paul. According to them the child who receives mortality at his birth receives sin from Adam only at a later period when he knows the sin of the first man and is inclined to imitate it. The causality of Adam as regards mortality would, therefore, be completely different from his causality as regards sin. Moreover, this supposed influence of the bad example of Adam is almost chimerical; even the faithful when they sin do not sin on account of Adam's bad example, *a fortiori* infidels who are completely ignorant of the history of the first man. And yet all men are, by the influence of Adam, sinners and condemned (Rom., v, 18, 19). The influence of Adam cannot, therefore, be the influence of his bad example which we imitate (Augustine, "Contra Julian.", VI, xxiv, 75).

On this account, several recent Protestants have thus modified the Pelagian explanation: "Even without being aware of it all men imitate Adam inasmuch as they merit death as the punishment of their own sins just as Adam merited it as the punishment for his sin." This is going farther and farther from the text of St. Paul. Adam would be no more than the term of a comparison, he would no longer have any influence or causality as regards original sin or death. Moreover, the Apostle did not affirm that all men, in imitation of Adam, are mortal on account of their actual sins; since children who die before coming to the use of reason have never committed such sins; but he expressly affirms the contrary in the fourteenth verse: "But death reigned", not only over those who imitated Adam, but "even over them also who have not sinned after the similitude of the transgression of Adam." Adam's sin, therefore, is the sole cause of death for the entire human race. Moreover, we can discern no natural connexion between any sin and death. In order that a determined sin entail death there is need of a positive law, but before the Law of Moses there was no positive law of God appointing death as a punishment except the law given to Adam (Gen., ii, 17). It is, therefore, his disobedience only that could have merited and brought it into the world (Rom., v, 13, 14). These Protestant writers lay much stress on the last words of the twelfth verse. We know that several of the Latin Fathers understood the words, "in whom all have sinned", to mean, all have sinned in Adam. This interpretation would be an extra proof of the thesis of original sin, but it is not necessary. Modern exegesis, as well as the Greek Fathers, prefers to translate "and so death passed upon all men *because* all have sinned". We accept this second translation which shows us death as an effect of sin. But of what sin? "The personal sins of each one", answer our adversaries, "this is the natural sense of the words 'all have sinned.'" It would be the natural sense if the context was not absolutely opposed to it. The words "all have sinned" of the twelfth verse, which are obscure on account of their brevity, are thus developed in the nineteenth verse: "for as by the disobedience of one man many were made sinners". There is no question here of personal sins, differing in species and number, committed by each one during his life, but of one first sin which was enough to transmit equally to all men a state of sin and the title of sinners. Similarly in the twelfth verse the words "All have sinned" must mean, "all have participated in the sin of Adam", "all have contracted its stain". This interpretation too removes the seeming contradiction between the twelfth verse, "all have sinned", and the fourteenth, "who have not sinned", for in the former there is question of original sin, in the latter of personal sin. Those who say that in both cases there is question of personal sin are unable to reconcile these two verses.

IV. ORIGINAL SIN IN TRADITION.—On account of a superficial resemblance between the doctrine of original sin and the Manichæan theory of our nature being evil, the Pelagians accused the Catholics and St. Augustine of Manichæism. For the accusation and its answer see "Contra duas epist. Pelag.", I, II, 4; V, 10; III, IX, 25; IV, III. In our own times this charge has been reiterated by several critics and historians of dogma who have been influenced by the fact that before his conversion St. Augustine was a Manichæan. They do not identify Manichæism with the doctrine of original sin, but they say that St. Augustine, with the remains of his former Manichæan prejudices, created the doctrine of original sin unknown before his time. It is not true that the doctrine of original sin does not appear in the works of the pre-Augustinian Fathers. On the contrary, their testimony is found in special works on the subject. Nor can it be said, as Harnack maintains, that St. Augustine himself acknowledges the absence of this doctrine in the writings of the Fathers. St. Augustine invokes the testimony of eleven Fathers, Greek as well as Latin (Contra Jul., II, x, 33). Baseless also is the assertion that before St. Augustine this doctrine was unknown to the Jews and to the Christians; as we have already shown, it was taught by St. Paul. It is found in the fourth Book of Esdras, a work written by a Jew in the first century after Christ and widely read by the Christians. This book represents Adam as the author of the fall of the human race (vii, 48), as having transmitted to all his posterity the permanent infirmity, the malignity, the bad seed of sin (iii, 21, 22; iv, 30). Protestants themselves admit the doctrine of original sin in this book and others of the same period (see Sanday, "The International Critical Commentary: Romans", 134, 137; Hastings, "A Dictionary of the Bible", I, 841). It is therefore impossible to make St. Augustine, who is of a much later date, the inventor of original sin.

That this doctrine existed in Christian tradition before St. Augustine's time is shown by the practice of the Church in the baptism of children. The Pelagians held that baptism was given to children, not to remit their sin, but to make them better, to give them supernatural life, to make them adoptive sons of God, and heirs to the Kingdom of Heaven (see St. Augustine, "De peccat. meritis", I, xviii). The Catholics answered by citing the Nicene Creed, "Confiteor unum baptisma in remissionem peccatorum". They reproached the Pelagians with introducing two baptisms, one for adults to remit sins, the other for children with no such purpose. Catholics argued, too, from the ceremonies of baptism, which suppose the child to be under the power of evil, i. e., exorcisms, abjuration of Satan made by the sponsor in the name of the child [Aug., loc. cit., xxxiv, 63; Denz., n. 140 (96)].

V. ORIGINAL SIN IN FACE OF THE OBJECTIONS OF REASON.—We do not pretend to prove the existence of original sin by arguments from reason only. St. Thomas makes use of a philosophical proof which proves the existence rather of some kind of decadence than of sin, and he considers his proof as probable only, *satis probabiliter probari potest* (Contra Gent., IV, lii). Many Protestants and Jansenists and some Catholics hold the doctrine of original sin to be necessary in philosophy, and the only means of solving the problem of the existence of evil. This is exaggerated and impossible to prove. It suffices to show that human reason has no serious objection against this doctrine which is founded on Revelation. The objections of Rationalists usually spring from a false concept of our dogma. They attack either the transmission of a *sin* or the idea of an injury inflicted on his race by the first man, of a decadence of the human race. Here we shall answer only the second category of objections, the others will be considered under a later head (VII).

(1) The law of progress is opposed to the hypothesis of a decadence. Yes, if the progress was necessarily continuous, but history proves the contrary. The line representing progress has its ups and downs, there are periods of decadence and of retrogression, and such was the period, Revelation tells us, that followed the first sin. The human race, however, began to rise again little by little, for neither intelligence nor free will had been destroyed by original sin and, consequently, there still remained the possibility of material progress, whilst in the spiritual order God did not abandon man, to whom He had promised redemption. This theory of decadence has no connexion with our Revelation. The Bible, on the contrary, shows us even spiritual progress in the people it treats of; the vocation of Abraham, the law of Moses, the mission of the Prophets, the coming of the Messias, a revelation which becomes clearer and clearer, ending in the Gospel, its diffusion amongst all nations, its fruits of holiness, and the progress of the Church.

(2) It is unjust, says another objection, that from the sin of one man should result the decadence of the whole human race. This would have weight if we took this decadence in the same sense that Luther took it, i. e. human reason incapable of understanding even

moral truths, free will destroyed, the very substance of man changed into evil. But according to Catholic theology man has not lost his natural faculties: by the sin of Adam he has been deprived only of the Divine gifts to which his nature had no strict right, the complete mastery of his passions, exemption from death, sanctifying grace, the vision of God in the next life. The Creator, whose gifts were not due to the human race, had the right to bestow them on such conditions as He wished and to make their conservation depend on the fidelity of the head of the family. A prince can confer a hereditary dignity on condition that the recipient remains loyal, and that, in case of his rebelling, this dignity shall be taken from him and, in consequence, from his descendants. It is not, however, intelligible that the prince, on account of a fault committed by a father, should order the hands and feet of all the descendants of the guilty man to be cut off immediately after their birth. This comparison represents the doctrine of Luther which we in no way defend. The doctrine of the Church supposes no sensible or afflictive punishment in the next world for children who die with nothing but original sin on their souls, but only the privation of the sight of God [Denz., n. 1526 (1389)].

VI. NATURE OF ORIGINAL SIN.—This is a difficult point and many systems have been invented to explain it: it will suffice to give the theological explanation now commonly received. Original sin is the privation of sanctifying grace in consequence of the sin of Adam. This solution, which is that of St. Thomas, goes back to St. Anselm and even to the traditions of the early Church, as we see by the declaration of the Second Council of Orange (A. D. 529): one man has transmitted to the whole human race not only the death of the body, which is the punishment of sin, but even sin itself, *which is the death of the soul* [Denz., n. 175 (145)]. As death is the privation of the principle of life, the death of the soul is the privation of sanctifying grace which according to all theologians is the principle of supernatural life. Therefore, if original sin is "the death of the soul", it is the privation of sanctifying grace.

The Council of Trent, although it did not make this solution obligatory by a definition, regarded it with favour and authorized its use (cf. Pallavicini, "Istoria del Concilio di Trento", vii-ix). Original sin is described not only as the death of the soul (Sess. V, can. ii), but as a "privation of justice that each child contracts at its conception" (Sess. VI, cap. iii). But the council calls "justice" what we call sanctifying grace (Sess. VI), and as each child should have had personally his own justice so now after the fall he suffers his own privation of justice. We may add an argument based on the principle of St. Augustine already cited, "the deliberate sin of the first man is the cause of original sin". This principle is developed by St. Anselm: "the sin of Adam was one thing but the sin of children at their birth is quite another, the former was the cause, the latter is the effect" (De conceptu virginali, xxvi). In a child original sin is distinct from the fault of Adam, it is one of its effects. But which of these effects is it? We shall examine the several effects of Adam's fault and reject those which cannot be original sin:—

(1) Death and Suffering.—These are purely physical evils and cannot be called sin. Moreover St. Paul, and after him the councils, regarded death and original sin as two distinct things transmitted by Adam.

(2) Concupiscence.—This rebellion of the lower appetite transmitted to us by Adam is an occasion of sin and in that sense comes nearer to moral evil. However, the occasion of a fault is not necessarily a fault, and whilst original sin is effaced by baptism concupiscence still remains in the person baptized; therefore original sin and concupiscence cannot be one and the same thing, as was held by the early Protestants (see Council of Trent, Sess. V, can. v).

(3) The absence of sanctifying grace in the new-born child is also an effect of the first sin, for Adam, having received holiness and justice from God, lost it not only for himself but also for us (loc. cit., can. ii). If he has lost it for us we were to have received it from him at our birth with the other prerogatives of our race. Therefore the absence of sanctifying grace in a child is a real privation, it is the want of something that should have been in him according to the Divine plan. If this favour is not merely something physical but is something in the moral order, if it is holiness, its privation may be called a sin. But sanctifying grace is holiness and is so called by the Council of Trent, because holiness consists in union with God, and grace unites us intimately with God. Moral goodness consists in this that our action is according to the moral law, but grace is a deification, as the Fathers say, a perfect conformity with God who is the first rule of all morality. (See GRACE.) Sanctifying grace therefore enters into the moral order, not as an act that passes but as a permanent tendency which exists even when the subject who possesses it does not act; it is a turning towards God, *conversio ad Deum*. Consequently the privation of this grace, even without any other act, would be a stain, a moral deformity, a turning away from God, *aversio a Deo*, and this character is not found in any other effect of the fault of Adam. This privation, therefore, is the hereditary stain.

VII. How VOLUNTARY.—"There can be no sin that is not voluntary, the learned and the ignorant admit this evident truth", writes St. Augustine (De vera relig., xiv, 27). The Church has condemned the opposite solution given by Baius [prop. xlvi, xlvii, in Denz., n. 1046 (926)]. Original sin is not an act but, as already explained, a state, a permanent privation, and this can be voluntary indirectly—just as a drunken man is deprived of his reason and incapable of using his liberty, yet it is by his free fault that he is in this state and hence his drunkenness, his privation of reason is voluntary and can be imputed to him. But how can original sin be even indirectly voluntary for a child that has never used its personal free will? Certain Protestants hold that the child on coming to the use of reason will consent to its original sin; but in reality no one ever thought of giving this consent. Besides, even before the use of reason, sin is already in the soul, according to the data of Tradition regarding the baptism of children and the sin contracted by generation. Some theosophists and spiritists admit the pre-existence of souls that have sinned in a former life which they now forget; but apart from the absurdity of this metempsychosis, it contradicts the doctrine of original sin, it substitutes a number of particular sins for the one sin of a common father transmitting sin and death to all (cf. Rom., v, 12 sqq.). The whole Christian religion, says St. Augustine, may be summed up in the intervention of two men, the one to ruin us, the other to save us (De pecc. orig., xxiv). The right solution is to be sought in the free will of Adam in his sin, and this free will was ours: "we were all in Adam", says St. Ambrose, cited by St. Augustine (Opus imperf., IV, civ). St. Basil attributes to us the act of the first man: "Because *we* did not fast (when Adam ate the forbidden fruit) we have been turned out of the garden of Paradise" (Hom. i de jejun., iv). Earlier still is the testimony of St. Irenæus; "In the person of the first Adam we offend God, disobeying His precept" (Hæres., V, xvi, 3).

St. Thomas thus explains this moral unity of our will with the will of Adam. "An individual can be considered either as an individual or as part of a whole, a member of a society. . . . Considered in the second way an act can be his although he has not done it himself, nor has it been done by his free will but by the rest of the society or by its head, the nation being considered as doing what the prince does. For a society is considered as a single man of whom the individuals are the different members (St. Paul, I Cor., xii). Thus the multitude of men who receive their human nature from Adam is to be considered as a single community or rather as a single body. . . . If the man, whose privation of original justice is due to Adam, is considered as a private person, this privation is not his 'fault', for a fault is essentially voluntary. If, however, we consider him as a member of the family of Adam, as if all men were only one man, then his privation partakes of the nature of sin on account of its voluntary origin, which is the actual sin of Adam" (De Malo, iv, 1). It is this law of solidarity, admitted by common sentiment, which attributes to children a part of the shame resulting from the father's crime. It is not a personal crime, objected the Pelagians. "No", answered St. Augustine, "but it is paternal crime" (Op. imperf., I, cxlviii). Being a distinct person I am not strictly responsible for the crime of another, the act is not mine. Yet, as a member of the human family, I am supposed to have acted with its head who represented it with regard to the conservation or the loss of grace. I am, therefore, responsible for my privation of grace, taking responsibility in the largest sense of the word. This, however, is enough to make the state of privation of grace in a certain degree voluntary, and, therefore, "without absurdity it may be said to be voluntary" (St. Augustine, "Retract.", I, xiii).

Thus the principal difficulties of non-believers against the transmission of sin are answered. "Free will is essentially incommunicable." Physically, yes; morally, no; the will of the father being considered as that of his children. "It is unjust to make us responsible for an act committed before our birth." Strictly responsible, yes; responsible in a wide sense of the word, no; the crime of a father brands his yet unborn children with shame, and entails upon them a share of his own responsibility. "Your dogma makes us strictly responsible for the fault of Adam." That is a misconception of our doctrine. Our dogma does not attribute to the children of Adam any properly so-called responsibility for the act of their father, nor do we say that original sin is voluntary in the strict sense of the word. It is true that, considered as "a moral deformity", "a separation from God", as "the death of the soul", original sin is a real sin which deprives the soul of sanctifying grace. It has the same claim to be a sin as has habitual sin, which is the state in which an adult is placed by a grave and personal fault, the "stain" which St. Thomas defines as "the privation of grace" (I–II, Q. cix. a. 7; III, Q. lxxxvii, a. 2, ad 3um), and it is from this point of view that baptism, putting an end to the privation of grace, "takes away all that is really and properly sin", for concupiscence which remains "is not really and properly sin", although its transmission was equally voluntary (Council of Trent, Sess. V, can. v.). Considered precisely as voluntary, original sin is only the shadow of sin properly so-called. According to St. Thomas (In II Sent., dist. xxv, Q. i, a. 2, ad 2um), it is not called "sin" in the same sense, but only in an analogous sense.

Several theologians of the seventeenth and eighteenth centuries, neglecting the importance of the privation of grace in the explanation of original sin, and explaining it only by the participation we are supposed to have in the act of Adam, exaggerate this participation. They exaggerate the idea of voluntary in original sin, thinking that it is the only way to explain how it is a sin properly so called. Their opinion, differing from that of St. Thomas, gave rise to un-called-for and insoluble difficulties. At present it is altogether abandoned.

For the Scriptural proof: MacEvilly, *An Exposition of the Epistles of St. Paul*, I (4th ed., New York, 1891); 45; Cornely, *Commentarius in epist. ad Romanos* (Paris, 1896), 269; Corluy, *Spicilegium dogmatico-biblicum*, I (Ghent, 1884), 228; Prat, *La Théologie de S. Paul*, I (Paris, 1908), 292.—For the doctrine of St. Augustine: Augustine, *Anti-Pelagian Works* (London, 1880); Schwane, *Dogmengeschichte*, II (2nd ed., Freiburg im Br., 1894); Portalié in *Dict. de théol. cath.*, s. v. Augustin.—For the theological explanation: St. Thomas, II–II, QQ. clxiii, clxiv; De Rubeis, *De peccato originali* (Würzburg, 1857); Scheeben, *Dogmatik*, II (Freiburg im Br., 1880), clxxxvi; Möhler, *Symbolism* (London, 1894); Le Bachelet, *Le péché originel* (Paris, 1900); Lahousse, *De Deo Creante* (Bruges, 1904); Pesch, *Prælectiones de Deo Creante* (3rd ed., Freiburg im Breisgau, 1908). —For the rationalistic view: Tennant, *The Sources of the doctrines of the Fall and Original Sin* (Cambridge, 1903).

S. Harent.

Orihuela, Diocese of (Oriolensis, Oriolana), comprises all the civil Province of Alicante except the two townships (*pueblos*) of Caudete (Albacete) and Ayora (Valencia). The city of Orihuela, with its suburbs, has a population of 24,364. The episcopal see was in ancient times at Bigastro or the place known as Cehegín. Jaime the Conqueror recovered Orihuela from the Moors in 1265, giving it to his son-in-law Alfonso X, the Wise, of Castile, and restoring the church, which came under the jurisdiction of the See of Cartagena. When Orihuela was lost to the Castilian crown, in 1304, Martin of Aragon petitioned the pope to give it a bishop of its own. The first concession was made by the antipope Benedict XIII (Luna), who made the church of El Salvador a collegiate church. On the petition of Alfonso V, Martin V instituted a vicariate-general, independent of Murcia and Cartagena, for the portion of the diocese lying within the Kingdom of Aragon. No bishop was appointed until 1437, when it was given as its first, a scion of the House of Corella, who never took possession. Eugenius IV suppressed the new diocese; Julius II accorded to the church of Orihuela the rank of cathedral (1510), but subject to the Bishop of Cartagena. Peace was secured only when Philip II, in the Cortes of Monzón (1563), decided to separate the church of Orihuela from Cartagena, and obtained from Pius IV, in 1564, the creation of a new bishopric.

The first bishop was a native of Burgos, Gregorio Gallo y Andrada, confessor to Queen Isabel of Valois. Among his successors, José Esteban added to the cathedral the chapter of St. Stephen, where he is buried. Juan Elias Gómez de Terán built at his own expense (1743) the conciliar seminary of La Purísima Concepción, the Seminary of St. Miguel, and the House of Mercy. He also caused to be erected the Chapel of the Holy Communion, the chapter house, and the *archivium*. This bishop lies buried in the church of La Misericordia at Alicante. José de Rada y Aguirre was confessor to Ferdinand VI. José Tormo enlarged the seminary, rebuilt much of the episcopal palace, erected episcopal residences at Cox and Elche, and the Chapel of the Holy Communion in the great church of the latter city. Several works of public utility are due to him, such as the aqueduct of Elche, the bridge of Rojales, and a wall protecting the cultivated lands of Orihuela against inundation. Another occupant of this see was Cardinal Despuig (1791). Francisco Antonio Cebrián y Valda (1797) ruled the diocese eighteen years, afterwards becoming Patriarch of the Indies. The episcopate of Felix Herrero Valverde was long and fruitful; he improved the cathedral and other churches, laboured to repair the damage done by the earthquake of 1829, and suffered a long exile in Italy after the death of Ferdinand VII.

Conspicuous among the buildings of Orihuela is the Seminary of St. Miguel, situated upon a rocky eminence. Founded in 1743, it possesses a good library, a hall of exercises (*salón de actos*) built by Bishop Pedro María Cubero (1859), and the general *archivium* of the diocese. It is divided into two colleges: that of the Apostolic Missionaries, founded by Bishop Terán, and the episcopal college. The most notable of the churches is the Cathedral of the Transfiguration (El Salvador): its style is a simple ogival of the fourteenth century. The principal door—the "Door of the Chains"—is Gothic; that of the Annunciation is Plateresque. The great chapel, of beautiful ogival work, was demolished in 1827 to enlarge the enclosure. The grille of the choir and the high altar have been considered the finest in the kingdom (Viciana): they are Renaissance of the sixteenth century. The vast episcopal palace, separated from the cathedral by a street, was built in 1733 by Bishop José Flores Osirio, on the left bank of the River Segura. It contains a magnificent staircase. The principal churches are Sta Justa y Rufina and the Apóstol Santiago (St. James the Apostle), both restored Gothic. The former is said to have been a parish church in the time of the Goths, but it was reconstructed between 1319 and 1348. That of Santiago is a fine Gothic structure, and bears the device of the Catholic Sovereigns: TANTO MONTA; and the arms of Charles V. The great chapel was built between 1554 and 1609, and the tabernacle, of rare marbles, is eighteenth-century work.

Orihuela had many monasteries and convents— Augustinian, Franciscan, Carmelite, Mercedarian, Dominican, Trinitarian, Alcantarine, Capuchin, and of the Hospitallers of St. John of God. Those of the Franciscans and the Capuchins are still extant, as also of the Salesian and Augustinian Sisters and the Clarissas. But the principal edifice of Orihuela is that of its university, otherwise called the Patriarchal College of Preachers, founded by the prelate Fernando de Loaces, a native of Orihuela, who spent 80,000 ducats ($800,000) on it and gave it to the Dominicans. At first this institution was occupied only with ecclesiastical studies, for members of the order, but it afterwards obtained faculties for the conferring of scientific degrees, with privileges equal to those of the most celebrated universities, and the titles of Illustrious, Royal, and Pontifical (1640). It was suppressed in 1824. The building, having been declared an historical monument, was given to the Jesuits, who now carry on in it a college and boarding-school. In the same building the public archives and library are housed, the latter consisting largely of books taken from the suppressed convents. The sarcophagus of the founder is in the chancel of the magnificent church. A statue of St. Thomas stands above the principal door, and above it a colossal Minerva.

By the Concordat of 1851, the See of Orihuela is to be transferred to Alicante, a city with two excellent churches: that of S. Nicolás and the older church of Sta. María, formerly a mosque. It was destroyed by fire and entirely rebuilt in the ogival style. The collegiate church founded by Alfonso X, the Wise, was made a collegiate church by Clement VIII (1600), and, by the terms of the Concordat, is destined to be the cathedral of Alicante. Also celebrated is the sanctuary of the Holy Face at Alicante, originally occupied by Hieronymites, but now by the Poor Clares. The linen cloth bearing the imprint of the Holy Face was brought from Rome by Mossén Mena of Alicante and is an object of great veneration in that part of the country. Elcha, famous for its palm-trees, has a noteworthy church dedicated to the Assumption, on which feast it still holds a dramatic representation of medieval character. Orihuela has a hospital, a Casa de Misericordia for the poor and orphans (1734), and a foundling asylum founded by Charles III in 1764.

RUFINO GEA, *Páginas de la Historia de Orihuela: El pleito del obispado de 1383–1564* (Orihuela, 1900); MOLLÁ, *Crónica del obispado de Orihuela* (Alicante, 1900); LLORENTE, *España, sus monumentos y artes: Valencia*, II (Barcelona, 1889); DE LA FUENTE, *Historia de las Universidades de España* (Madrid, 1885); IDEM, *Historia eclesiástica de España* (Barcelona, 1855).

RAMÓN RUIZ AMADO.

Oriol, JOSEPH, SAINT, priest, "Thaumaturgus of Barcelona", b. at Barcelona, 23 November, 1650; d. there, 23 March, 1702. He studied in the University of Barcelona, receiving the degree of Doctor of Theology, 1 August, 1674. Ordained priest, 30 May, 1676, he visited Rome in 1686 and was granted a benefice in the church of Nuestra Señora del Pino, in Barcelona. His priestly life was remarkable for a spirit of penance, profound humility, and prudence in directing souls. Impelled by a desire of martyrdom, he went to Rome in April, 1698, to offer himself for the foreign missions, but, falling sick at Marseilles, he returned to Barcelona. God bestowed upon him prophetic and miraculous power. The dying, the blind, the deaf and dumb, the lame, and the paralytic, were instantly cured by him. He was beatified by Pius VII, 5 September, 1806, and canonized by Pius X, 20 May, 1909. His feast occurs on 23 March.

SALOTTI, *Vita di San Giuseppe Oriol* (Rome, 1909); MASDEU, *Vida del Beato Josef Oriol* (Italian and Spanish, 1806; new Spanish ed., Barcelona, 1886); BALLESTER, *Vida de San José Oriol* (Barcelona, 1909); EULARIA ANZIZU, *Vida de St. Joseph Oriol* (in Catalan, Barcelona, 1909; Spanish tr., Barcelona, 1910).

CHARLES J. MULLALY.

Oristano, DIOCESE OF (ARBORENSIS), in Sardinia. Oristano was the capital of the *giudicatura* (independent district) of Arborea, given to the House of Sardi, after the expulsion of the Saracens, and was subject to Pisa. It was the last city to surrender to the Aragonese (1478), against whom it was valiantly defended by Mariano. Bishops of Arborea are mentioned for the first time in the letters of Gregory VII. The bishop Tragadorio (1195) built the cathedral; Friar Guido Cattano (1312) took part in the Franciscan controversy on the poverty of Jesus Christ; Jacopo Serra (1492) was Vicar of Rome and became a cardinal; Girolamo Barberani (1565) had several disputes with the Dominicans and Pius V; Antonio Canopolo (1588) founded the seminary, rebuilt by Luigi Emanuele del Carretto (1756), and contributed also to other works of public utility. In 1503 there was united to the See of Oristano that of Santa Giusta, where SS. Justa, Justina, and Ænedina martyred under Hadrian(?), are venerated. Bishops of Santa Giusta are known from the year 1119. The diocese is a suffragan of Cagliari; it has 74 parishes, with 97,000 inhabitants, 3 religious houses of men, and 7 of women, 3 schools for boys, and 2 for girls.

CAPPELLETTI, *Le Chiese d'Italia*, V.

U. BENIGNI.

Orkneys, a group of islands situated between 58° 41' and 59° 24' N. lat. and 2° 22' and 3° 25' W. long., and lying to the north of Scotland, from which they are separated by Pentland Firth. They include Holme and Klippen, the most important, however, being Pomona or Mainland. The total area is over three hundred and seventy-five square miles and the population (of Norse descent), almost exclusively Calvinist and English speaking, numbers 30,000. These islands, for the most part level (the greatest altitude being 1541 feet, on Hoy), rocky, barren, treeless, partly covered by swampland, produce only barley, oats, potatoes, and beets. Stock raising is an important industry, the yearly production being 30,000 cattle, 40,000 sheep, 5000 pigs, and 6000 horses of a small but sturdy breed. The hunting of birds, seal, and whales, and the deep-sea fisheries (herring, cod, and lobsters) furnish the inhabitants with further means of sustenance. Excellent trout are to be caught in the numerous fiords and small lakes. Mining for iron, tin, and silver is also carried on successfully. The exportation of down and woven stuffs, (shawls, etc.) forms a lucrative source of income. Politically, the Orkneys form, with the Shetlands, a county, the capital being Kirkwall (a town of 5000 inhabitants), important as a trading centre, with a good harbour.

HISTORY.—Among the ancients the Ὀρκάδες νῆσοι, also called *Orcades insulæ*, are the Orkneys, mentioned by Pliny, Mela, and Tacitus. Julius Agricola, as commander of the troops garrisoned in Britain, in A. D. 69, had the coast of England explored by his ships of war, and took back more trustworthy information concerning these mythical territories, which he brought under the sceptre of Rome for the time being. Nothing is known of the inhabitants at that time, but they were probably Celts. About 872 the rulers of the separate islands were forced to submit to the rule of Harold Haarfager, King of Norway, who also subjugated the Hebrides, Isle of Man, and Ireland. Later Eric Blodsee sought refuge on the Orkneys from his victorious adversaries. From these islands also Olaf Trygvesson undertook the conquest of his ancestral kingdom (995), and Harold Hardrada set forth on his last campaign against England (1066). Thence also Olaf Kyrre returned to his native land (1067) and Hakon IV began his military expedition against Scotland (1263). In 1271 Magnus IV of Norway ceded to King Alexander III of Scotland all Scottish islands "with the exception of the Orkneys", in return for a yearly tribute, a condition which was renewed in later documents. Instead of being under the direct government of the monarchs of Norway, the Orkneys were now ruled by *jarls*, appointed by them from the houses of Strathearn and Sinclair. After the marriage of James III of Scotland to the daughter of Christian I, King of the united countries, the latter mortgaged the Orkneys to Scotland as security for his daughter's dowry (6 Sept., 1468), which he had not paid, and later attempts at redemption proved fruitless. Thus it was that Scottish ways and the English language gradually found access into the Orkneys and then became predominant. But many Norse customs and many Scandinavian forms of expression still persist, as though the nation preserved a certain attachment for the mother-country, with which tradition says it will be one day reunited.

RELIGIOUS HISTORY.—Although the monks from Iona were active in the Orkneys at a very early period, the exact date when the Gospel was first preached and the nationality of the first missionaries are unknown. The early Christian communities probably succumbed during the disturbances of the migratory movements, and the later Norse settlers were pagans. Christianity first attained predominance, however, under Olaf Trygvesson. About the middle of the eleventh century Kirkwall (*Kirkevaag*) was made the seat of a diocese (*diœcesis Orcadensis*), in connexion with which a cathedral chapter was later established, and the Shetland Islands were assigned it as an archidiaconate. The prelates (at first prevailingly Norse, and later of Scotch extraction) were suffragans of the Archbishop of Lund, were later under Trondhjem (Nidaros), and after 1472 under St. Andrews. Practically nothing is known as to their names and the dates of their episcopates, and the documentary sources show important discrepancies. Some bishops received academic honours, which would indicate that they were not ignorant men for their times. This is especially true of the last Catholic bishop, Robert Reid (d. 14 Sept., 1558), who is described as "vir omni literatura cultus et in rebus gerendis peritissimus", and who in 1540 brought to completion the magnificent cathedral of St. Magnus, which had been begun by his predecessors. His successor, Adam Bothwell, died (23 Aug., 1593) an apostate. At this time the last sparks of Catholicism were extinguished on the Orkneys under the fury of Calvinistic fanaticism which had been raging for decades, laying waste churches and employing both craft and force to draw the inhabitants from the faith of their fathers.

HISTORY OF ART.—Burial chambers and stone circles (at Stenness on Mainland) testify to the primitive artistic sense of the original Celtic inhabitants. The earliest traces of the Norse occupation are to be found on Sandey,—burial mounds such as those in Scandinavia and great stone walls as ramparts about the houses of warriors. The settlements were copies, on a more modest scale, of the native places of the founders, Osko, Nidaros etc. No secular buildings of the Middle Ages have survived. Only the ruins of the episcopal residence at Kirkwall, where King Hakon IV died (15 December, 1263), are to be seen. The first Christian temple at Birgsay has completely disappeared. Of two churches at Deer Ness and Broch of Birsay on Mainland (remarkable for their double towers between nave and choir) only sketches are extant. It is over a hundred years since the first disappeared, but considerable ruins of the second are still to be seen. There are also traces of the church of St. Magnus at Egilsay and of the round apsidal church on Orphir. The great monumental, architectural work of the whole archipelago, however, is the cathedral of St. Magnus at Kirkwall (*Kirkevaag*), which is surpassed but slightly by the celebrated cathedral of Trondhjem. It was begun in 1137 by St. Ragnvald (canonized 1192), prince (*jarl*) and crusader, and represents the artistic ideas of generations. Laid out originally according to Norman-Roman style, it seems to have been strongly influenced by the Gothic, and shows a harmonious combination of the two elements. The central nave is supported by twenty-eight columns of surpassing beauty. Above the intersection of the nave and transept rises an imposing square tower, the dome of which was unfortunately ruined by fire in the seventeenth century and was replaced by another which is too low. Doors made of stones of many colours fitted together open into the interior of the temple. Since the introduction of Calvinism altars, statues of the saints, and sacred vessels have disappeared; even the relics of the founder were scattered to the winds. The burial sites of the *jarls* have likewise been forgotten.

MELA, *De situ orbis*, III, vi; PLINY, *Hist. nat.*, IV, xxx; TACITUS, *Agricola*, x; STYFFE, *Skandinavien under unionstiden* (2nd ed., Stockholm, 1880); TUDOR, *Orkneys and Shetlands Geology, Flora, etc.* (London, 1883); WALLACE, *Description of the Isles of Orkney* (London, 1884); FEA, *Present State of the Orkney Islands* (London, 1885); STORM, *Hist. top. skrifter om Norgeog norske Landsdale* (Christiania, 1895); DIETRICHSON, *Vorefæders verk* (Christiania, Copenhagen, 1906); WALSH, *Hist. of the Cath. Church in Scotland* (Glasgow, 1874); LYON, *Hist. of St. Andrews* (2 vols., Edinburgh, 1843); KEYSER, *Den norske kirkes historie under Katolicismen* (2 vols. Christiania, 1856–58) GAMS, *Series episc.* (Ratisbon, 1873); EUBEL, *Hierarchia catholica medii ævi* (2 vols., Ratisbon, 1898–1901).

PIUS WITTMANN.

Orlandini, NICCOLÒ, b. at Florence, 1554; d. 1606 at Rome, 17 May. He entered the Jesuit novitiate 7 Nov., 1572; became rector of the Jesuit college at Nola; was master of novices at Naples for five years; and finally appointed secretary of the general Acquaviva, who in 1558 detailed him to write the history of the Jesuit Order. This work comprises only the generalate of St. Ignatius. It was edited by Sacchini, and appeared under the title "Historiæ Societatis Jesu prima pars" (Rome, 1614, 1615, 1621; Antwerp, 1620; Cologne, 1620). It is written in the form of annals, and is based chiefly on a life written by the saint's secretary, de Polanco. Ranke, "Hist. of the Popes", III (London, 1903), 328, says of Orlandini: "In his style of writing, as well as in the business of life, he was exceedingly careful, accurate, and wary". The history was continued by Sacchini, Possinus, Jouvancy, and Cordara. The sixth and last part, reaching to 1633, was published at Rome in 1758. Other works are: "Annuæ litteræ Societatis Jesu, anni 1583–85" (Rome, 1585–86–88); "Vita Petri Fabri" (Lyons, 1617); the same under the title "Forma sacerdotis Apostolici, expressa in exemplo Petri Fabri" (Dillingen, 1647); and "Tractatus seu Commentarii in Summarium Constitutionum et in regulas communes", ed. Soero (Roehampton, 1876). His "Vita Petri Fabri" has been translated into French (Bordeaux, 1617) and Italian (Rome, 1629).

SOMMERVOGEL, *Bibliothèque de la C. de J.*, V (Brussels and Paris, 1894), 1934–35; SACCHINI in introduction to *Historiæ Societatis Jesu prima pars*, mentioned above.

MICHAEL OTT.

Orlandus de Lassus. See LASSUS.

Orléans, Councils of.—Six national councils were held at Orléans in the Merovingian period. I.—At the first, convoked by Clovis (July, 511), thirty-three bishops assisted and passed thirty-one decrees on the duties and obligations of individuals, the right of sanctuary, and ecclesiastical discipline. These decrees, equally applicable to Franks and Romans, first established equality between conquerors and conquered. The council claimed the right of sanctuary in favour of churches and episcopal residences; it stipulated that ecclesiastics need not produce the culprit, if the pursuer would not swear on the Gospels to do him no injury. It settled the conditions of freedom for a slave upon whom Holy orders had been conferred; ruled that freemen should not be ordained without the king's consent, or authorization of the judge; determined the immunities of ecclesiastics and church property and committed to the bishops the welfare of the sick and the poor; settled the relations of monks with their abbots and of abbots with the bishops. The practice of divination was forbidden. Clovis approved the decrees of the council, which thus appears as the first treaty between the Frankish State and the Church. II.—The second national council held under Childebert (June, 533), attended by twenty-five bishops, decreed that, conformably to the earnest desire of Pope Hormisdas, annual provincial councils should be held; further, that marriage could not be dissolved by will of the contracting parties for infirmities consequent on the contract; forbade the marriage of Christians and Jews; and excommunicated those who partook of flesh offered in sacrifice to idols. III.—The third national council (May, 538), attended by thirteen bishops, determined impediments of marriage; pronounced excommunication against ecclesiastics in the higher orders who lived incontinently; decreed that the archbishops should be elected by the bishops of the province, with the consent of the clergy and the citizens; the bishops by the archbishop, the clergy, and the people of the city. IV.—The fourth national council (541) assembled thirty-eight bishops and maintained the date fixed by Pope Victor for Easter, contrary to Justinian's ordinances, and ordered those who had or wished to have a parish church on their lands to take the necessary measures for the dignity of Divine worship. Finally it perfected the measures taken by the Council of 511 relative to the emancipation of slaves: slaves emancipated by bishops were to retain their freedom after the death of their emancipators, even though other acts of their administration were recalled; it authorized the official ransom of Christians who had fallen into the power of the Jews but had invoked the right of sanctuary to recover their freedom; it declared that Jews who exhorted Christian slaves to become Jews in order to be set free should be forbidden to own such slaves. V.—The fifth national council (October, 549) assembled nine archbishops and forty-one bishops. After defending Mark, Bishop of Orléans, from attacks made on him, it pronounced an anathema against the errors of Nestorius and Eutyches, it prohibited simony, prescribed that elections of bishops take place in all freedom, with consent of the clergy, the people, and the king, and that no bishop be consecrated until it had been one year in the clergy. It censured all who attempted to subject to any servitude whatsoever slaves emancipated within the Church, and those who dared take, retain, or dispose of church property. It threatened with excommunication all who embezzled or appropriated funds given by King Childebert for the foundation of the hospital of Lyons, and it placed lepers under the special charge of each bishop. VI.—The sixth national council, held under Clovis II about 638 or 639 at the request of Sts. Eloi and Ouen, condemned and expelled from the kingdom a Greek partisan of Monothelitism, at the request of Salvius, Bishop of Valence. VII.—The seventh national council, held in 1022 under Bishop Odolric, proceeded against the Manichæans and their few adherents in the city. In September, 1478, Louis XI held at Orléans a fruitless assembly of the clergy and the nobility to discuss the Crusade, the necessity for a general council, and the re-establishment of the "pragmatic sanction".

Duchateau, *Hist. du diocèse d'Orléans* (Orléans, 1892); Hefele, *Hist. des Conciles*, new French tr. Leclercq (Paris, 1907 sqq.).

Georges Goyau.

Orléans, Diocese of (Aurelianum), comprises the Department of Loiret, suffragan of Paris since 1622, previously of Sens. After the Revolution it was re-established by the Concordat of 1802, when it included the Departments of Loiret and Loir et Cher, but in 1822 Loir et Cher was included in the new Diocese of Blois. The present Diocese of Orléans differs considerably from that of the old regime; it has lost the arrondissement of Romorantin which has passed to the Diocese of Blois and the canton of Janville, now in the Diocese of Chartres. It includes the arrondissement of Montargis, formerly subject to Sens, the arrondissement of Gien, once in the Diocese of Auxerre, and the canton de Châtillon sur Loire, once belonging to Bourges. To Gerbert, Abbot of St. Pierre le Vif at Sens (1046–79), is due a detailed narrative according to which Saints Savinianus and Potentianus were sent to Sens by St. Peter with St. Altinus; the latter, it was said, came to Orléans as its first bishop. Before the ninth century there is no historical trace in the Diocese of Sens of this Apostolic mission of St. Altinus, nor in the Diocese of Orléans before the end of the fifteenth. Diclopitus is the first authentic bishop; he figures among the bishops of Gaul who (about 344) ratified the absolution of St. Athanasius. Other bishops of the early period are: St. Euvertius, about 355 to 385, according to M. Cuissard; St. Aignan (Anianus) (385–453), who invoked the aid of the "patrician" Ætius against the invasion of Attila, and forced the Huns to raise the siege of Orléans; St. Prosper (453–63); St. Monitor (about 472); St. Flou (Flosculus), d. in 490; St. Eucherius (717–43), native of Orléans and a monk of Jumièges, who protested against the depredations of Waifre, a companion of Charles Martel, and was exiled to Cologne by this prince, then to Liège, and died at the monastery of St. Trond.

Of the eighth-century bishops, Theodulfus was notable. It is not known when he began to govern, but it is certain that he was already bishop in 798, when Charlemagne sent him into Narbonne and Provence as *missus dominicus*. Under Louis le Débonnaire he was accused of aiding the rebellious King of Italy, was deposed and imprisoned four years in a monastery at Angers, but was released when Louis came to Angers in 821. The "Capitularies" which Theodulfus addressed to the clergy of Orléans are considered a most important monument of Catholic tradition on the duties of priests and the faithful. His Ritual, his Penitential, his treatise on baptism, confirmation, and the Eucharist, his edition of the Bible, a work of fine penmanship preserved in the Puy cathedral, reveal him as one of the foremost men of his time (see P. L., CV, 187). His fame rests chiefly on his devotion to the spread of learning. The Abbey of Ferrières was then becoming under Alcuin a centre of learning. Theodulfus opened the Abbey of Fleury to the young noblemen sent thither by Charlemagne, invited the clergy to establish free schools in the country districts, and quoted for them, "These that are learned shall shine as the brightness of the firmament: and they that instruct many to justice, as stars to all eternity" (Dan., xii, 3). One monument of his time still survives in the diocese, the apse of the church of Germigny modelled after the imperial chapel, and yet retaining its unique mosaic decoration. Other noteworthy bishops are: Jonas (821–43), who wrote a treatise against the Iconoclasts, also a treatise on the Christian life and a book on the duties of kings (for these texts see P. L., CVI, 117); St. Thierry II (1016–21); Blessed Philip Berruyer (1234–6); Blessed Roger le Fort (1321–8); Cardinal Jean de Longueville (1521–33), who received Queen Eleanor, sister of Charles V, in the cathedral of Orléans, and King Francis I in the church of St. Aignan of Orléans; Cardinal Antoine Sanguin (1534–52), who received Charles V at Orléans in 1539; Bernier (1802–6); Fayer (1843–9), member of the Constituent Assembly of 1848; Dupanloup (1849–78). For the Abbeys of Fleury and Ferrières see FLEURY and FERRIÈRES.

After his victory over the Alamanni, Clovis was bent on the sack of Verdun, but the archpriest there obtained mercy for his fellow-citizens. To St. Euspicius and his nephew St. Mesmin (Maximinus), Clovis also gave the domain of Micy, near Orléans at the confluence of the Loire and the Loiret, for a monastery (508). When Euspicius died, St. Maximinus became abbot, and during his rule the religious life flourished there notably, and the monastery counted many saints. From Micy monastic life spread. St. Liphardus and St. Urbicius founded the Abbey of Meung-sur-Loire; St. Lyé (Lætus) died a recluse in the forest of Orléans; St. Viatre (Viator) in Sologne; St. Doulchard in the forest of Ambly near Bourges. St. Leonard introduced the monastic life into the territory of Limoges; St. Almir, St. Ulphacius, and St. Bomer in the vicinity of Montmirail; St. Avitus (d. about 527) in the district of Chartres; St. Calais (d. before 536) and St. Leonard of Vendœuvre (d. about 570) in the valley of the Sarthe; St. Fraimbault and St. Constantine in the Javron forest, and the aforesaid St. Bomer (d. about 560) in the Passais near Laval; St. Leonard of Dunois; St. Alva and St. Ernier in Perche; St. Laumer (d. about 590) became Abbot of Corbion. St. Lubin (Leobinus), a monk of Micy, became Bishop of Chartres from 544–56. Finally Ay (Agilus), Viscount of Orléans (d. after 587), a protector of Micy, was also a saint. The monks of Micy contributed much to the civilization of the Orléans region; they cleared and drained the lands and taught the semi-barbarous inhabitants the worth and dignity of agricultural work. Early in the eighth century, Theodulfus restored the Abbey of Micy and at his request St. Benedict of Aniane sent fourteen monks and visited the abbey himself. The last abbot of Micy, Chapt de Rastignac, was one of the victims of the "September Massacres", at Paris, 1792, in the prison of L'Abbaye.

The schools of Orléans early acquired great prestige; in the sixth century Gontran, King of Burgundy, had his son Gondebaud educated there. After Theodulfus had developed and improved the schools, Charlemagne, and later Hugh Capet, sent thither their eldest sons as pupils. These institutions were at the height of their fame from the eleventh century to the middle of the thirteenth. Their influence spread as far as Italy and England whence students came to them. Among the medieval rhetorical treatises which have come down to us under the title of "Ars" or "Summa Dictaminis" four, at least, were written or re-edited by Orléans professors. In 1230, when for a time the doctors of the University of Paris were scattered, a number of the teachers and disciples took refuge in Orléans; when Boniface VIII, in 1298, promulgated the sixth book of the Decretals, he appointed the doctors of Bologna and the doctors of Orléans to comment upon it. St. Yves (1253–1303) studied civil law at Orléans, and Clement V also studied there law and letters; by a Bull published at Lyons, 27 January, 1306, he endowed the Orléans institutes with the title and privileges of a University. Twelve of his successors granted the new university many privileges. In the fourteenth century it had as many as five thousand students from France, Germany, Lorraine, Burgundy, Champagne, Picardy, Normandy, Touraine, Guyan, Scotland. Among those who studied or lectured there are quoted: in the fourteenth century, Cardinal Pierre Bertrandi; in the fifteenth, John Reuchlin; in the sixteenth, Calvin and Théodore de Bèze, the Protestant Anne Dubourg, the publicist François Hotmann, the jurisconsult Pierre de l'Etoile; in the seventeenth, Molière (perhaps in 1640), and the savant Du Cange; in the eighteenth, the jurisconsult Pothier.

Among the notable saints of the diocese are: St. Baudilus, a Nîmes martyr (third or fourth century); the deacon St. Lucanus, martyr, patron of Loigny (fifth century); the anchorite St. Donatus (fifth century); St. May, abbot of Val Benoît (fifth century); St. Mesme, virgin and (perhaps) martyr, sister of St. Mesmin (sixth century); St. Felicule, patroness of

CATHEDRAL, ORLÉANS

Gien (sixth century); St. Sigismund, King of Burgundy, who, by order of the Merovingian, Clodomir, and despite the entreaties of St. Avitus, was thrown (524) into a well with his wife and children; St. Gontran, King of Orléans and Burgundy (561–93), a confessor; St. Loup (Lupus), Archbishop of Sens, born near Orléans, and his mother St. Agia (first half of the seventh century); St. Gregory, former Bishop of Nicopolis, in Bulgaria, who died a recluse at Pithiviers (1004 or 1007); St. Rose, Abbess of Ervauville (d. 1130); Blessed Odo of Orléans, Bishop of Cambrai (1105–13); the leper St. Alpaix, died in 1211 at Cudot where she was visited by Alix of Champagne, widow of Louis VII; St. Guillaume (d. 1209), Abbot of Fontainejean and subsequently Archbishop of Bourges; the Dominicans, Blessed Reginald, dean of the collegiate church of St. Aignan, Orléans (d. 1220); the Englishman St. Richard, who studied theology at Orléans in 1236, Bishop of Chichester in 1244, a friend of St. Edmund of Canterbury; St. Maurus, called to France by St. Innocent, Bishop of Mans, and sent thither by St. Benedict, resided at Orléans with four companions in 542; St. Radegonde, on her way from Noyon to Poitiers in 544, and St. Columbanus, exiled from Luxeuil at the close of the sixth century, both visited Orléans. Charlemagne had the church of St. Aignan rebuilt and reconstructed the monastery of St. Pierre le Puellier. In the cathedral of Orléans on 31 December, 987, Hugh

Capet had his son Robert (b. at Orléans) crowned king. Innocent II and St. Bernard visited Fleury and Orléans in 1130.

The people of Orléans were so impressed by the preaching of Blessed Robert of Arbrissel in 1113 that he was invited to found the monastery of La Madeleine, which he re-visited in 1117 with St. Bernard of Thiron. The charitable deeds of St. Louis at Puiseaux, Châteauneuf-sur-Loire, and Orléans, where he was present at the translation of the relics of St. Aignan (26 October, 1259), and where he frequently went to care for the poor of the Hôtel Dieu, are well known. Pierre de Beaufort, Archdeacon of Sully and canon of Orléans, as Gregory XI (1371–8), was the last pope

SOUTH SIDE, CATHEDRAL, ORLÉANS

that France gave to the Church; he created Cardinal Jean de la Tour d'Auvergne, Abbot of St. Benoît-sur-Loire. Blessed Jeanne de Valois was Duchess of Orléans and after her separation from Louis XII (1498) she established, early in the sixteenth century, the monastery of L'Annonciade at Châteauneuf-sur-Loire. Etienne Dolet (1509–46), a printer, philologian, and pamphleteer, executed at Paris and looked upon by some as a "martyr of the Renaissance", was a native of Orléans. Cardinal Odet de Coligny, who joined the Reformation about 1560, was Abbot of St. Euvertius, of Fontainejean, Ferrières, and St. Benoît. Admiral Coligny (1519–72) (see SAINT BARTHOLOMEW'S DAY) was born at Châtillon-sur-Loing in the present diocese. At the beginning of the religious wars Orléans was disputed between the Guises and the followers of the Protestant Condé. In the vicinity of Orléans Duke Francis of Guise was assassinated 3 February, 1562.

The Calvinist, Jacques Bongars, councillor of Henry IV, who collected and edited the chronicles of the Crusades in his "Gesta Dei per Francos", was born at Orléans in 1554. The Jesuit, Denis Petav (Petavius), a renowned scholar and theologian, was born at Orléans in 1583. St. Francis of Sales came to Orléans in 1618 and 1619. Venerable Mother Françoise de la Croix (1591–1657), a pupil of St. Vincent de Paul, who founded the congregation of Augustinian Sisters of Charity of Notre Dame, was born at Petay in the diocese. The Miramion family, to which Marie Bonneau is celebrated in the annals of charity under the name of Mme de Miramion (1629–96), belonged by marriage, were from Orléans. St. Jane de Chantal was superior of the Orléans convent of the Visitation in 1627. Mme Guyon, celebrated in the annals of Quietism (q. v.), was born at Montargis in 1648. France was saved from English domination through the deliverance of Orléans by Joan of Arc (8 May, 1429). On 21 July, 1455, her rehabilitation was publicly proclaimed at Orléans in a solemn procession, and before her death in November, 1458, Isabel Romée, the mother of Joan of Arc, saw a monument erected in honour of her daughter, at Tournelles, near the Orléans bridge. The monument, destroyed by the Huguenots in 1567, was set up again in 1569 when the Catholics were once more masters of the city. Until 1792, and again from 1802 to 1830, finally from 1842 to the present day, a great religious feast, celebrated 8 May of every year at Orléans in honour of Joan of Arc, attracted multitudes (see JOAN OF ARC). The Church of Orléans was the last in France to take up again the Roman liturgy (1874). The Sainte Croix cathedral, perhaps built and consecrated by St. Euvertius in the fourth century, was destroyed by fire in 999 and rebuilt from 1278 to 1329; the Protestants pillaged and destroyed it from 1562 to 1567; the Bourbon kings restored it in the seventeenth century.

The principal pilgrimages of the diocese are: Our Lady of Bethlehem, at Ferrières (q. v.); Our Lady of Miracles at Orléans, dating back to the seventh century (Joan of Arc visited its sanctuary 8 May, 1429); Our Lady of Cléry, dating from the thirteenth century, visited by Philip the Fair, Philip VI, and especially by Louis XI, who wore in his hat a leaden image of Notre Dame de Cléry and who wished to have his tomb in this sanctuary where Dunois, one of the heroes of the Hundred Years' war was also interred. Prior to the Associations Law of 1901 the Diocese of Orléans counted Franciscans, Benedictines, Missionary Priests of the Society of Mary, Lazarists, Missionaries of the Sacred Heart, and several orders of teaching Brothers. Among the congregations of women which originated in this diocese must be mentioned: the Calvary Benedictines, a teaching and nursing order founded in 1617 by Princess Antoinette d'Orléans-Longueville, and the Capuchin Leclerc du Tremblay known as Père Joseph; the Sisters of St. Aignan, a teaching order founded in 1853 by Bishop Dupanloup, with mother-house in Orléans. At the beginning of the twentieth century the religious congregations of this diocese conducted: 1 crèche; 77 infant schools; 2 institutions for the deaf and dumb; 10 orphanages; 2 houses for penitent women, 12 religious houses for the care of the sick in their own homes; 2 houses of retreat; 27 hospitals or asylums; 1 poor house. In 1905 (last year of the Concordat) the diocese had 371,019 inhabitants; 41 pastorates; 293 succursal parishes; 23 vicariates subventioned by the State.

Gallia Christiana, VIII (1744), 1408–1513; *Instrumenta*, 479–546; DUCHESNE, *Fastes Épiscopaux*, 453–60; CUISSARD, *Les premiers évêques d'Orléans* (Orléans, 1887); DUCHATEAU, *Hist. du diocèse d'Orléans* (ibid., 1888); BIMBENET, *Hist. de la ville d'Orléans* (3 vols., ibid., 1884–7); BAUNARD, *Vie des saints et personages illustres de l'église d'Orléans* (3 vols., ibid., 1862–3); COCHARD, *Les saints de l'église d'Orléans* (ibid., 1879); CUISSARD, *Théodulfe, évêque d'Orléans, sa vie et ses œuvres* (ibid., 1892); SÉJOURNÉ, *Les reliques de St. Aignan, évêque d'Orléans* (ibid., 1905); CUISSARD; DELISLE, *Les chanoines et dignitaires de la cathédrale d'Orléans* (ibid., 1900); DELISLE, *Les écoles d'Orléans au douzième et au treizième siècles* (Paris, 1869); BIMBENET, *Hist. de l'université d'Orléans* (Orléans, 1853); FOURNIER, *Les statuts et privilèges des Universités françaises*, I (Paris, 1890); JAROSSAY, *Hist. d'un monastère orléanais, Micy St. Mesmin, son influence religieuse et sociale* (Orléans, 1901).

GEORGES GOYAU.

Orley, BARENT VAN (BERNARD), painter, b. at Brussels, about 1491; d. there 6 January, 1542. He studied under Raphael in 1509. He returned to Brussels and was commissioned in 1515 to paint an altar-piece for the Confraternity of the Holy Cross at Furnes. In 1518 he was appointed official painter to Margaret of

Austria, Regent of the Netherlands, and two years afterwards entertained Dürer in his house for some time, during which Dürer painted Orley's portrait, now in the Dresden Museum. In 1530, Margaret of Austria having died, Orley received the official appointment from her successor, Mary of Hungary. Orley was a Catholic, but assisted at various Lutheran meetings held in his father's house. He and his brother were arrested, with several other painters, and sentenced to pay fines, and to do public penance in the church of St. Gudule (Brussels). The artist had seven children by his first wife, Agnes Segheres, and two by his second wife, Catherine Hellincx.

He painted in oil and in tempera, and made a great many designs for glass windows. Some of the finest windows in St. Gudule's are from his drawings. He was an engraver and an able craftsman. With Michael Cocxie he superintended the manufacture of the tapestries for the Vatican designed from Raphael's cartoons for Leo X. Three pieces of tapestry from his own drawings are at Hampton Court, the Louvre, and the Caserta Palace at Naples. Many of his pictures derive their extreme brilliance from being painted on a ground of gold-leaf. A tradition that he visited England lacks definite proof. The eight portraits of the first Regent of the Netherlands, and four of the second, he is said to have painted, have not yet been found. His works occasionally bear the family motto "Elx sijne tijt" (Every man his day).

FETIS, *Musée Royal de Belgique* (Brussels, 1865); and see the writings of VAN MANDER, MICHIELS, SIRET, and OPHEMERT.

GEORGE CHARLES WILLIAMSON.

Orme, PHILIBERT DE L', architect, b. about 1512; d. 1570. His style, classical and of the more severe Italian type, later developed characteristics showing greater personal independence. He has also importance as an author on subjects in his particular line, and is our chief source of information on his own works and the events of his life, although his writings are not devoid of exaggerations. While still a youth he went to Rome; he would probably have remained there in the service of Paul III, had not Cardinal du Bellay and others urged him to go to France. Soon after his return to his native city of Lyons (1536) he gave evidence of his originality as an artist in the invention of the *trompe* vaulting, so popular with the French, i. e. arches with double curves supporting weight imposed on them from the side and in the artistic stone carving, which gives them their charm. He was obliged to leave the portal of St. Nizier at Lyons incomplete in order to build the château of St. Maur-les-Fossés at Paris for Bellay, which he later had to enlarge. According to his own statements, he introduced in this important innovations, e. g. in the construction of columns. In 1538 he prevented the occupation of Brest by the English. Francis I now deputed him to make a semi-annual inspection of the fortifications on the coast of Brittany, and review and provide for the vessels stationed there, and appointed him commandant of fortifications. In 1547 Orme began work on the king's tomb. Under Henry II he was promoted until he finally became supervisor of all royal buildings. In this capacity he directed the work on the châteaux of Fontainebleau, St-Germain-en-Laye, Madrid etc., and had at the same time to investigate the character of the service which had been rendered Francis I in connexion with these undertakings.

While in his fifties he built the château of Anet and Meudon. The former, in which he was allowed complete liberty, is of special importance for the study of his style; the disposition of the columns shows the pure classic style. An unfortunate arrangement of some water-piping in the second building, in itself a very important piece of work, brought on him the mockery of his jealous rivals. Although he was a layman, the king and queen granted him various abbeys, the revenues from which made him a wealthy man. He experienced for a time the disfavour of the court, and in 1559 was superseded by Primaticcio as supervisor of royal buildings. In 1564 he was commissioned by the regent to build the Tuileries. According to his plan, of which he himself gives a detailed description and appreciation, the whole was to be in the form of a quadrangle, with four corner pavilions, enclosing a large central court and four smaller courts, an entrance being provided on each of the two longer sides of the rectangle. Only the garden façade was completed. The central pavilion with the cupola is especially beautiful. In this the master took liberties which, despite his admiration for the classic, he proclaimed as theoretical. He wrote that he had never found columns or ornamentation exhibiting like proportions or even similar arrangement of columns, and that the limitations of the architect came less from the prescribed measurements than from the stipulations made with regard to the building. This accounts for the "French column", among other things in the Tuileries, with its Ionic capital, but consisting of many fluted drums, separated by ornamental bands. Above all, Orme's works are not devoid of curious attempts at originality. In the last years he wished to work out his compositions according to "Biblical laws and sacred numbers".

As an author, Orme would have taken his place beside Vitruvius and Alberti had he completed his work on "Architecture". In two of the nine books of the first volume he deals in a masterly manner with stone-carving and the construction of the vault. A new edition of his work was issued by C. Nizet in 1894. Another work he entitled "Nouvelles inventions pour bien bâtir et à petits frais", as he describes in this his device for constructing roofs of great span by bolting together planks (instead of using single heavy beams). This was republished at Rouen in 1648 with his "Architecture". Of interest in itself, and also as illustrating his activity, is a memoir in which he defends himself against the attacks of his adversaries. This was incorporated by Berty in the "Grands architectes français de la Renaissance" (Paris, 1860).

PALUSTRE, *La Renaissance en France* (Paris, 1879); VON GEYMÜLLER, *Die Baukunst der Renaissance in Frankreich* (Stuttgart, 1896 and 1901); DESTAILLEUR, *Notices sur quelques artistes français* (Paris, 1863).

G. GIETMANN.

Ormuzd and Ahriman. See AHRIMAN.

Oroomiah. See URUMIAH, DIOCESE OF.

Oropus, titular see, suffragan of Anazarbus in Cilicia Secunda. It never really depended on Anazarbus but on Seleucia in Isauria, as is evident from the Greek text of the "Notitiæ Episcopatuum" of Antioch in the sixth and tenth centuries ("Echos d'Orient", 1907, X, 95, 145), where the city figures as Oropa or Oroba, and from the Latin translation where it is called Oropus ("Itinera Hierosolymitana", Geneva, 1880, I, 334). Oropus is no other than Olba, suffragan of Seleucia, annexed with the Province of Isauria to the Patriarchate of Constantinople in the eighth century, and is mentioned in the "Notitiæ" of Leo the Wise and of Constantine Porphyrogenitus. (See OLBA.)

S. VAILHÉ.

O'Rorke, PATRICK HENRY, soldier, b. in County Cavan, Ireland, 25 March, 1837; killed at the battle of Gettysburg, Penn., U. S. A., July, 1863. He was a year old when his parents emigrated to the United States. They settled in Rochester, N. Y., where he attended the public schools, and in 1853 went to work as a marble-cutter. Shortly after he was appointed a cadet in the U. S. Military Academy at West Point, graduating with highest honours in June, 1861. Commissioned as a lieutenant in the regular army, he distinguished himself in the Civil War as a staff-officer in the engineer corps, was made colonel of the 140th regiment of New York Volunteers, with which command he participated in the battles of Fredericksburg and Chancellorsville. At Gettysburg while leading his men in defence of Little Round Top, in the very crisis of the battle he caught up the colours, and, mounting a rock to urge on his men, was struck and fell dead. The Comte de Paris in his "Histoire de la guerre civile en Amérique" (VI, iv, 379) says this was one of the most striking and dramatic episodes of the battle. His widow became a Religious of the Sacred Heart and one of the successful educators in their New York convents.

CULLUM, *Biog. Register of Officers and Graduates of the U. S. Military Academy* (Boston, 1891); O'HANLON, *Irish American History of the U. S.*, II (New York, 1906), 500; FITZGERALD, *Ireland and Her People*, II (Chicago, 1910); *Nat. Cyclopedia Am. Biog.*, s. v.

THOMAS F. MEEHAN.

Orosius, PAULUS, historian and Christian apologist; b. probably at Bracara, now Braga, in Portugal, between 380 and 390, the dates of birth and death not being precisely known. His first name has been known only since the eighth century. Having early consecrated himself to the service of God, he was ordained, and went to Africa in 413 or 414. The reason for his leaving his native country is not known; he tells us only that he left his fatherland "sine voluntate, sine necessitate, sine consensu" (Commonitorium, i). He repaired to St. Augustine, at Hippo, to question him as to certain points of doctrine, concerning the soul and its origin, attacked by the Priscillianists. In 414 he prepared for St. Augustine a "Commonitorium de errore Priscillianistarum et Origenistarum" (P. L., XXXI, 1211–16; also, ed. Schepss, in "Priscilliani quæ supersunt", in "Corpus script. eccl. lat.", Vienna, 1889, XVIII, 149 sqq.) to which St. Augustine replied with his "Ad Orosium contra Priscillianistas et Origenistas". In order to become better acquainted with these questions concerning the soul and its origin, Orosius, with a hearty recommendation from St. Augustine (Epist. clxvi), went to Palestine, to St. Jerome. Pelagius was then trying to spread his false doctrines in Palestine, and Orosius aided St. Jerome and others in their struggle against this heresy. In 415 Bishop John of Jerusalem, who was inclined to the teaching of Origen and influenced by Pelagius, summoned the presbyters of his church to a council at Jerusalem. At this council Orosius sharply attacked the teachings of Pelagius. But, as Pelagius declared that he believed it impossible for man to become perfect and avoid sin without God's assistance, John did not condemn him, but decided that his opponents should state their arguments before Pope Innocent. In consequence of his opposition to Pelagius, Orosius was drawn into dissensions with Bishop John, who accused him of having maintained that it is not possible for man to avoid sin, even with God's grace. In answer to this charge, Orosius wrote his "Liber apologeticus contra Pelagium de Arbitrii libertate" (P. L., XXXI, 1173–1212, and ed. Zangemeister, "Orosii opera" in "Corpus script. eccl. lat.", V, Vienna, 1882), in which he gives a detailed account of the Council of 415 at Jerusalem, and a clear, correct treatment of the two principal questions against Pelagius: the capability of man's free will, and Christian perfection in doing God's will here on earth.

In the spring of 416 Orosius left Palestine, to return to Augustine in Africa, and thence home. He brought a letter from St. Jerome (Epist. cxxxiv) to St. Augustine, as well as writings of the two Gallic bishops, Hero and Lazarus, who were in Palestine struggling against Pelagianism (cf. St. Augustine, Epist. clxxv). He also brought from Jerusalem the then recently discovered relics of the Protomartyr Stephen and a Latin letter from Lucian, who had discovered them (Gennadius, "De Viris Illustr.", xxxi, xlvi, xlvii, ed. Czapla, Münster, 1898, 87–89, 104). After a short stay with Augustine at Hippo, Orosius began his journey home, but, on reaching Minorca, and hearing of the wars and devastations of the Vandals in Spain, he returned to Africa. The relics of St. Stephen, which he left in Minorca, became the object of a great veneration, which spread into Gaul and Spain. On the conversion of Jews through these relics, cf. Severus, "De virtutibus ad conversionem Judæorum in Minoricensi Insula factis", P. L., XLI, 821–32. Orosius went back to Africa and at St. Augustine's suggestion wrote the first Christian Universal History: "Historiarum adversus paganos libri septem" (P. L., XXXI, 663–1174; ed. Zangemeister, in "Corpus script. eccl. lat.", V, Vienna, 1882), thought to be a supplement to the "Civitas Dei", especially the third book, in which St. Augustine proves that the Roman Empire suffered as many calamities before as after Christianity was received, combating the pagan argument, that the abandonment of their deities had led to calamity. St. Augustine wished to have this proof developed in a special work through the whole period of human history, and this Orosius did, reviewing the history of all the known peoples of antiquity, with the fundamental idea that God determines the destinies of nations. According to his view, two chief empires had governed the world: Babylon in the East, and Rome in the West. Rome received the heritage of Babylon through the intermediate Macedonian and Carthaginian Empires. Thus he holds that there were four great empires in history—a view widely accepted in the Middle Ages. The first book briefly describes the globe, and traces its history from the Deluge to the founding of Rome; the second gives the history of Rome to the sack of the city by the Gauls, that of Persia to Cyrus, and of Greece to the Battle of Cunaxa; the third deals chiefly with the Macedonian Empire under Alexander and his successors, as well as the contemporary Roman history; the fourth brings the history of Rome to the destruction of Carthage; the last three books treat Roman history alone, from the destruction of Carthage to the author's own time. The work, completed in 418, shows signs of haste. Besides Holy Scripture and the chronicle of Eusebius revised by St. Jerome, Livy, Eutropius, Cæsar, Suetonius, Florus, and Justin are used as sources. In pursuance of the apologetic aim, all the calamities suffered by the various peoples are described. Though superficial and fragmentary, the work is valuable; it contains contemporary information on the period after A. D. 378. It was used largely during the Middle Ages as a compendium, and nearly 200 manuscript copies are still extant. Alfred the Great translated it into Anglo-Saxon (ed. H. Sweet, London, 1843).

DE MOERNER, *De Orosii vita eiusque historiarum libris 7 adv. paganos* (Berlin, 1844); MÉJEAN, *Paul Orose et son apologétique contre les païens* (Strasburg, 1882); EBERT, *Allg. Geschichte der Literatur des Mittelalters im Abendland*, I (Leipzig, 1889), 337–44; BARDENHEWER, *Patrology*, tr. SHAHAN (St. Louis, 1908); POTTHAST, *Bibl. historica medii ævi*, II (Berlin, 1896), 882–3.

J. P. KIRSCH.

Orphans and Orphanages.—The death of one or both parents makes the child of the very poor a ward of the community. The obligation of support is imposed upon parents or grandparents by nearly every system of laws; but there is no such obligation upon any other relative. Natural sympathy, however, and willingness to bear a distributed burden for the common good, rather than to enforce an individual one, contribute to the acceptance of the care of orphans as a public duty. In Biblical times the fatherless, the stranger, and the widow shared the excess fruits of the harvest (Deut., xxiv, 21). The people were told God "is the father of orphans" (Ps. lxvii, 6) and

His bounty was to be shared with them. Luxury and paganism introduced more selfish considerations. Neglect of the destitute orphan is only to be expected in a world where the unwelcome infant is exposed to any fate. The Romans apparently did not provide for widows and orphans. The Athenians viewed the duty as economic and patriotic, and ordained that children of citizens killed in war were to be educated up to eighteen years of age by the State. Plato (Laws, 927) says:—"Orphans should be placed under the care of public guardians. Men should have a fear of the loneliness of orphans and of the souls of their departed parents. A man should love the unfortunate orphan of whom he is guardian as if he were his own child. He should be as careful and as diligent in the management of the orphan's property as of his own or even more careful still."

When Christianity began to affect Roman life, the best fruit of the new order was charity, and special solicitude was manifested towards the orphan. Antoninus Pius had established relief agencies for children. The Christians founded hospitals, and children's asylums were established in the East. St. Ephraem, St. Basil, and St. John Chrysostom built a great number of hospitals. Those for the sick were known as *nosocomia*, those for poor children were known as *euphotrophia*, and those for orphans, *orphanotrophia*. Justinian released from other civic duties those who undertook the care of orphans. In the Apostolic Constitutions, "Orphans as well as widows are always commended to Christian love. The bishop is to have them brought up at the expense of the Church and to take care that the girls be given, when of marriageable age, to Christian husbands, and that the boys should learn some art or handicraft and then be provided with tools and placed in a condition to earn their own living, so that they may be no longer than necessary a burden to the Church" (Apost. Const., IV, ii, tr. Uhlhorn, p. 185). St. Augustine says: "The bishop protects the orphans that they may not be oppressed by strangers after the death of the parents." Also epistles 252–255: "Your piety knows what care the Church and the bishops should take for the protection of all men but especially of orphan children." The rise of monastic institutions following upon this period was accelerated by the fruit of charitable work for the poor, chief amongst which was the care of children. During the Middle Ages the monasteries preserved to modern times the notion of the duty of the Church to care for its orphans. They were the shelters where the orphans were taught learning and trade avocations. The laity also were exhorted to perform their share of this charge.

No one figure stands out so prominently in the history of the care of orphans as that of St. Vincent de Paul (1576–1660). To this work he attracted the gentlemen of the court, noble ladies, and simple peasants. In his distracted country he found the orphan the most appealing victim, and he met the situation with the skill of a general. No distinction was observed between foundlings and orphans in the beginning of his work with the Association of Charity; nor was there any distinction as to the condition of the children that were aided, other than that they were orphans, or abandoned, or the children of the poor. Seventeen years or more after that he established amongst noble women the "Ladies of Charity". When the war between France and Austria had made orphans the most acute sufferers, St. Vincent de Paul secured as many as possible from the provinces, and had them cared for in Paris by Mlle le Gras and the Sisters of Charity then fully established. Three towns alone furnished no less than 1000 orphans under the age of seven years. The Sisters of Charity spread over the world, and ever since have been looked to for the protection of the orphan, or have been the inspiration for other orders seeking to perform the same work.

When the Revolution broke out in France there were 426 houses of benevolence conducted in that country by the Sisters of Charity, and of these a large majority cared for orphans. They were suppressed, but many were reopened by Napoleon.

In more modern times a similar enlistment of women to serve the orphan has been observed all over Europe. In England, Ireland, and Scotland fifty-one houses of Sisters of Charity had been established between 1855 and 1898; and in all, except in a few hospitals, the work of an orphanage is conducted to a greater or less extent. On the American Continent, however, the first orphan asylum antedated St. Vincent de Paul's influence by a century, and was due not to French but to Spanish inspiration. This was an orphanage for girls, which was established in 1548 in Mexico by a Spanish order and was called La Caridad (Steelman, "Charities for Children in Mexico"). The first orphanage in the territory now comprised in the United States was that of the Ursulines, founded in New Orleans in 1727 under the auspices of Louis XV.

Whenever in Europe, following the religious changes of the sixteenth and seventeenth centuries, the care of orphans was not committed to ecclesiastical oversight, it was considered to be a public duty. Under the English poor law it was the duty of the parish to support the indigent so that none should die. It is probable that destitute orphans were cared for under this principle, but apprenticing and indenturing were the only solutions of the difficulties arising from the presence of orphans or dependent children. In later years, if children were too young or too numerous for this they were kept in the workhouse, one of the provisions being as follows: "Children under seven are placed in such of the wards appropriated to female paupers as may be deemed expedient." The so-called orphanage movement began in England in 1758 by the establishment of the Orphan Working Home. In the next century the exposures, principally by Charles Dickens, of the evils bred by the workhouse and the indenturing system led to many reforms. Numerous private asylums were founded in the reign of Queen Victoria under royal patronage, and with considerable official oversight and solicitude. In Colonial America the influence of the English poor law was felt, with the same absence of distinction as to child and adult, and as to care of the child. All paupers were the charges of the towns or counties. Almshouses were established, and later, in most States of the Union, orphan children were cared for in these. Indenturing was practised as often as possible. In New York State children were removed from almshouses following the passage of a law directing this in 1875. It provided that all children over three years of age, not defective in mind or body, be removed from poorhouses and be placed in families or orphan asylums. It has since been amended by reducing the age to two years and not excepting the defectives. The first orphan asylum in New York City, a Protestant institution, now located at Hastings-on-Hudson, N. Y., was established in 1806 largely through the efforts of Mrs. Alexander Hamilton. The first Catholic orphan asylum in New York City was founded in 1817 by the Sisters of Charity in Prince Street, and is now maintained in two large buildings at Kingsbridge, N. Y.

Of the seventy-seven charities for children, mostly orphanages, established in America before the middle of the nineteenth century as listed by Folks, twenty-one were Catholic and all of these were orphanages. One of the most interesting of the others is Girard College, founded by the merchant prince of Philadelphia, Stephen Girard, with an endowment of $6,000,000 which has since increased nearly fivefold. By the terms of Girard's will no minister of the Gospel is permitted to cross the threshold. Neither the educational results nor the philanthropy to orphan boys seem to be adequate to the fortune involved. An interesting asylum in New York City is the Leake and Watts Asylum founded in 1831 to provide "a free home for well-behaved full orphans of respectable parentage in destitute circumstances, physically and mentally sound, between the ages of three and twelve years, who are entrusted to the care of the trustees until fifteen years of age. Disorderly and ungovernable children are not admitted." The Hebrew orphan asylums of New York City are large and well managed, caring for about 3000 children. In the Catholic institutions of the Archdiocese of New York the orphans and half-orphans number about 8000. In the Diocese of Brooklyn they number close to 3600. In all the large cities of America, Catholic orphanages are found. It is probable that they would number close to 300 and the orphan inmates close to 50,000.

The upkeep and management of these large institutions call for the solution of many complex problems of varying components. They must provide plenty without wastefulness, clothe adequately without cheapness or painful uniformity, educate in letters and handicraft without overwork, and provide amusement without laxity, as well as discipline without repression. Buildings must be safe and have adequate sanitary details conducive to health. A thorough medical oversight of inmates, individually and collectively, completes a programme of requirements which bear very heavily and continuously on the management. Always and everywhere it has been considered an honour to take part in such works and in the oversight of them. Naturally the feature about orphan asylums most often remarked by visitors not accustomed to the situation is the radical difference from domestic life in the surroundings of the children. This has led some to propose changes in the institutional scheme, by which buildings of reduced size but adequate number shall be substituted for one or two large ones; that a matron or house-mother be employed to supervise each, and that each also shall have its own outfit and details for domestic management. Some would recommend that such charges be put in the joint care of a man and his wife, that the home-like provision of the children may be provided for. These and similar features comprise what is known as the "Cottage System". It fails in many points to present the hoped-for advantages. The fixed charges and salary list are so extensively increased that the burden would be in most cases unbearable. Some few institutions have made efforts in this direction, resulting in sudden and heavy increases in expenditures. Adopted on a modest scale, the "Cottage System" offers some advantages to Catholic religious communities operating orphanages, and its success would seem to be a question of wisely planned management and skillful architecture, controlled by conservative authority over the proposed, new, and regularly recurrent expenditures. Perhaps the real difficulty is that it does not improve the situation of the child in the matter of accustoming it to the natural life of the outside world.

Over against this institutional method of caring for destitute children, resulting in what is called the orphanage, but not necessarily opposed to it, are those methods which seek to put the child earlier under the influences of family life. This is done by boarding-out and by placing-out. The former is a system in which the overseer of the poor or similar officer confides the child to some family, as a boarder, and pays regularly for its care up to the age of self-support. Success and prevention of wrong in this system can only be obtained at great expense and by rigorous watchfulness. It originated in the English poor law and was designed to provide a means by which children could be removed from the poorhouse; it is much in vogue still throughout the United States. The weakness seems to lie in the danger of profit-seeking amongst people who offer to care for children for money. More permanent good for the child is obtained by the second method—placing-out in free homes. This is sometimes called indenturing in the cases of older children and sometimes adoption. The former has almost disappeared in the United States, except as a form observed by some overseers of the poor and some child-caring agencies. Real apprenticing or "binding-out" has passed away. Adoption is not a legal act unless confirmed by the proper procedure in a court of record. Advantage in placing-out appears to lie in the full absorption of the child into a vacancy in a household, where affection can be expected to develop, and where the conditions surrounding the child during all of its maturing years will be those entirely normal to any similar family group in the community. Nearly all the States which have laws bearing upon this practice have recognized religious rights, and have provided that where practicable such children must be placed in homes of their own religious faith. Placing-out can only be practised where an ample number of excellent homes can be obtained. By specializing in the work it becomes possible to place even large numbers of orphans and to surround them with a strong and enlightened protection. The good results most often are mutual, the foster-parents gaining as much by their charity as the child.

When the New York Catholic Protectory was taken over in 1863 from the St. Vincent de Paul Society which had organized it, Archbishop Hughes impressed upon the managers how placing-out should be conducted: "Let one or two gentlemen be employed, the one to keep office during the absence of the other, but one or the other to go abroad through the interior of the country, with good letters to make the acquaintance of the bishop of a diocese and the priest of a parish as well as such Catholic mechanics and farmers as might be disposed to receive one or other of the children who will come under your charge, and in this way let the children be in their house of protection just as short as possible. Their lot is, and is to be in one sense, a sufficiently hard one under any circumstances, but the sooner they know what it is to be, the better they will be prepared for encountering its trials and difficulties" (Letter to B. Silliman Ives, 19 June, 1863). The St. Vincent de Paul Society of New York City had for years assisted in performing such a work as this, and in 1898 established a special agency for it, known as the Catholic Home Bureau. It acts with the co-operation between the committing authorities and the institutions housing orphans and other destitute children. About two hundred and fifty children are placed by it each year in good Catholic families. Subsequent visitation of the children is practised with great care. In 1909 a similar bureau was started in Washington and another in Baltimore. In many cities of the Union, Catholic agents are employed by the local children's aid societies to perform this work for the protection of Catholic children.

Placing-out was the practice in early Christian days. The widows and deaconesses of the early church took orphans into their homes as Fabiola did in Rome. Some believe that the terms *widow* and *orphan* are so often found joined in ancient Christian literature because of this custom. It was the general practice at the time of the first persecutions. Uhlhorn (Christian Charity in the Ancient Church, p. 185) says: "It would also often happen that individual members of the Church would receive orphans, especially those whose parents had perished in a persecution." Thus was Origen adopted, after Leonidas, his father, had suffered martyrdom, by a pious woman in Alexandria (Eusebius, "Hist. Eccl.", VI, ii). Again the child of the female martyr, Felicitas, found a mother; and Eusebius tells us of Severus, a Palestinian composer, who especially interested himself in the orphans and widows of those who had fallen. In the Apostolic Constitutions members of the Church are urgently exhorted to such acts. "If any Christian, whether boy or girl, be left an orphan, it is well if one of the brethren, who has no child, receives and keeps him in a child's place. They who do so perform a good work by becoming fathers to the orphans and will be rewarded by God for this service". The taking of an orphan to rear, and giving it a place in a new family circle has always been an honoured custom amongst good people in all times. In simple communities it is the sole solution of a distressing problem. When in modern times a war or an extraordinary disaster created an embarrassment by reason of the number to be cared for, the organized asylum has been a blessing. The same must be said of the asylums caring for the army of orphans found in the large cities, particularly since they serve as shelters during the period of observation, and in the case of handicapped children during a longer period.

UHLHORN, *Christian Charity in the Ancient Church* (Edinburgh, 1883); BAART, *Orphans and Orphan Asylums* (Buffalo, 1885); L'ALLEMAND, *Hist. des enfants abandonnés* (Paris, 1885); BOUGAUD, *History of St. Vincent de Paul* (London, 1899); FOLKS, *The Care of Destitute, Neglected and Delinquent Children* (New York, 1907); BALUFFI, *The Charity of the Church a Proof of her Divinity* (Dublin, 1885); DEVAS, *Studies of Family Life* (London, 1886); STEELMAN, *Charities for Children in Mexico* (Chicago, 1907).

CHARLES F. MCKENNA.

Orsi, GIUSEPPE AGOSTINO, cardinal, theologian, and ecclesiastical historian, b. at Florence, 9 May, 1692, of an aristocratic Florentine family; d. at Rome, 12 June, 1761. He studied grammar and rhetoric under the Jesuits, and entered the Dominican Order at Fiesole, 21 February, 1708. At his profession he received the name of Giuseppe Agostino, having been called in secular life Agostino Francesco. His studies included not only theology, in which he gave particular attention to the Fathers and the great Scholastics, but also the classical and Italian literatures. Having been master of studies for some time at the convent of San Marco at Florence, he was called to Rome in 1732 as professor of theology at the college of St. Thomas, where he was also made prior. He held this position two years, when he became the theologian of Cardinal Neri Corsini, nephew of Pope Clement XII. In 1738 he was appointed secretary of the Congregation of the Index. In 1749 Benedict XIV made him "Magister Sacri Palatii", or papal theologian, and on 24 September, 1759, Clement XIII created him cardinal of the Title of San Sisto. In this position Orsi was an active member of several Congregations until his death. He was buried in his church of San Sisto.

Orsi's literary activity covered especially dogmatics, apologetics, and church history. His most important works are the following: "Dissertatio historica qua ostenditur catholicam ecclesiam tribus prioribus sæculis capitalium criminum reis pacem et absolutionem neutiquam negasse" (Milan, 1730); "Dissertatio apologetica pro SS. Perpetuæ, Felicitatis et sociorum martyrum orthodoxia adversus Basnagium" (Florence, 1728); "Dell' origine del dominio e della sovranità temporale de' Romani Pontefici" (Rome, 1742); and "Storia ecclesiastica"—this, his chief work (20 vols., Rome, 1747–61), brought the narrative only to the close of the sixth century; the twenty-first volume, which Orsi had begun, was finished by his former pupil Gio. Bottari (Rome, 1762). The work was afterwards brought up to the year 1587 by the Dominican Fil. Becchetti (new ed. in 42 vols., Venice, 1822; in 50 vols., Rome, 1838). It has been translated into foreign languages. Other writings of Orsi are: "Dissertazione dommatica e morale contra l'uso materiale della parola" (Rome, 1727); "Dimostrazione teologica" (Milan, 1729), in defence of the preceeding work on truthfulness (the question of *restrictio mentalis*); "Dissertatio theologica de invocatione Spiritus Sancti in liturgiis Græcorum et Orientalium" (Milan, 1731); "Dissertationes duæ de baptismo in nomine Jesu Christi et de chrismate confirmationis" (Milan, 1733)

—this was defended by Orsi, in the "Vindiciæ dissertationis de baptismo in nomine Jesu Christi" (Florence, 1735), against the attacks of the doctors of Paris; "De concordia gratiæ et liberi arbitrii" (Rome, 1734); "De irreformabili Romani Pontificis in definiendis fidei controversiis judicio" (Rome, 1739); "De Romani Pontificis in Synodos œcumenicos eorumque canones potestate" (Rome, 1740). The last two are directed against Gallicanism.

BOTTARI, *Vita del card. Orsi*, in vol. XXI of the *Storia ecclesiastica;* FABRONI, *Vitæ Italorum illustrium*, XI, 1–37; HURTER, *Nomenclator* (3d ed.), IV, 1505 sqq.

J. P. KIRSCH.

Orsini, one of the most ancient and distinguished families of the Roman nobility, whose members often played an important rôle in the history of Italy, particularly in that of Rome and of the Papal States. The Roman or principal line of the family, from which branched off a series of collateral lines as time went on, may be traced back into the early Middle Ages, and a legendary ancestry goes back even as far as early Roman times. The Roman line, as well as its branches, had large possessions in Italy and were the rulers of numerous and important dominions, fortified towns, and strongholds. In Rome, the Orsini were the hereditary enemies of the equally distinguished Colonna (q. v.): in the great medieval conflict between papacy and empire, the latter were for the most part on the side of the emperor and the leaders of the Ghibelline party, while the Orsini were ordinarily champions of the papacy and leaders of the Guelph party. The Orsini gave three popes to the Church—Celestine III (q. v.), Nicholas III (q. v.), and Benedict XIII (q. v.)—as well as many cardinals and numerous bishops and prelates. Other members of the family distinguished themselves in political history as warriors or statesmen, and others again won renown in the fields of art and science. The wars between the Orsini and Colonna form an important part of the medieval history of Rome and of Central Italy. Forming as they did a part of the conflicts waged by the emperors in Italy, they influenced in a very prominent manner the general historical development of that time.

Among the cardinals of the Orsini family who were distinguished in the history of the Church, as well as in ecclesiastico-political history, the following are especially worthy of mention:—

(1) MATTEO ROSSO ORSINI, nephew of Cardinal Gaetano Orsini (later Pope Nicholas III), created a cardinal by Urban IV in December, 1262; d. 4 Sept., 1305 (according to some authorities, 1306). As legate for the provinces of the Patrimony of Peter and of the Marches, he fought against Peter de Vico, who, in the name of Manfred, invaded the papal territory with German mercenaries. Soon after the elevation of his uncle, Nicholas III, to the papal throne (1277), he was named by this pope archpriest of the Vatican Basilica, rector of the great Hospital of the Holy Ghost in Vatican territory, and cardinal protector of the Franciscan Order. After the death of Nicholas III (1280), the cardinals assembled in Viterbo for the election of his successor, but, owing to party dissensions, many months passed before a decision was reached. The party which inclined towards the French, and which had the support of Charles of Anjou, King of Naples, himself present in Viterbo, wished to elect an exponent of the policy of France, and chose as their candidate the French Cardinal Simon. However, the two cardinals Orsini, Matteo Rosso and Giordano, the latter a brother of the deceased pope, Nicholas III, energetically opposed this choice. As neither party could command the necessary majority, no election resulted. In February, 1281, the French party resolved to have recourse to a bold stroke. At the instigation of the marshal of the conclave, Annibaldi, who was at variance with the Orsini, citizens from Viterbo suddenly attacked the anti-French cardinals, and took

prisoners the two Orsini, carrying them away from the Conclave and holding them in custody. The candidate of the French party was now elected pope under the name of Martin IV (22 February, 1281), whereupon Giordano was released, and afterwards Matteo Rosso. The instigator of the attack was excommunicated and the city of Viterbo placed under an interdict. When the news of the capture of the two Cardinals Orsini was received in Rome, great confusion ensued. Their relatives were driven from the city by the adherents of the Annibaldi, but were later recalled by Martin IV, with whom the Cardinals Orsini had become reconciled. During the conflict between Boniface VIII and Philip the Fair of France, it was Cardinal Matteo who, having remained faithful to the persecuted pontiff, brought Boniface back to Rome after the attack of Anagni (1303). Cardinal Matteo attended the numerous conclaves held between 1254 and 1305, there being no less than thirteen. He died in Perugia in 1305 or 1306. His body was later transferred to Rome, where it lies in the Orsini Chapel in St. Peter's.

(2) NAPOLEONE ORSINI, son of Rinaldo, a brother of Pope Nicholas III, b. 1263; d. at Avignon, 24 March, 1342. In his youth he embraced the ecclesiastical state, was appointed papal chaplain by Honorius IV (1285-7), was created Cardinal Deacon of S. Adriano by Nicholas IV in May, 1288, and later, under Clement V was named archpriest of St. Peter's. Commissioned by Pope Boniface VIII, he brought Orvieto back to its submission to the Holy See, shortly after which the pope named him legate for Umbria, Spoleto, and the March of Ancona. In this capacity he left the Curia on 27 May, 1300, returning, however, on 28 May, 1301. During this time he had to combat various enemies of the Roman Church, and recovered the city of Gubbio for the pope. He was entrusted with his second papal legation by Clement V. Leaving Avignon, which was at that time the residence of the Curia, he set out on 8 March, 1306, for the Papal States with the commission to make peace between the parties which were everywhere at variance, and to bring back the various states of the Roman Church to their allegiance to the pope. This mission occupied more than three years, terminating on 12 June, 1309. Cardinal Napoleone played an important part during the political disturbances of the time. At first an opponent of the Colonna and their ambitions, he later became a promoter of French policy and entered into close relations with the French rulers. At the elections of Clement V and John XXII he exercised a decisive influence, but subsequently became an enemy of the latter. He upheld the Franciscan Spirituals, and espoused the cause of King Louis of Bavaria against the pope. A cardinal for fifty-four years, he took part in the election of seven popes (Celestine V to Clement VI), on at least three of whom he placed the tiara. He is also known as an author, having written a biography of St. Clare of Montefalco.

(3) GIAN GAETANO ORSINI, prothonotary Apostolic, raised to the cardinalate by Pope John XXII in December, 1316; d. 1339 (or, according to some sources, 27 August, 1335). In 1326 he was sent to Italy as papal legate for certain lands belonging to the Papal States, and remained there until 1334. He endeavoured, though with little success, to bring back several rebellious states and vassals to their allegiance to the Apostolic See, excommunicated the obstinate Castruccio of Lucca and Bishop Guido Tarlato of Arezzo, as both supported the Visconti of Milan in their conflict against the pope, and, after the coronation of King Louis the Bavarian in Rome in 1327, placed that city under an interdict. After the departure of the excommunicated emperor, the legate entered Rome with the army of King Robert of Naples, whereupon the people once more agreed to recognize the suzerainty of the pope. John XXII, however, refused to sanction the war undertaken by the cardinal legate against the Colonna, and ordered him to return to Tuscany. In November, 1328, he opened a campaign against the cities of Corneto and Viterbo, which submitted to the pope in the following year. The years between 1334 and his death he passed in Avignon.

(4) MATTEO ORSINI, d. probably on 18 August, 1340. He entered the Dominican Order, completed the full course of theology, obtained the Degree of Master, and taught theology at Paris, Florence, and Rome. He won great distinction by his zeal for the spread of the order, and was appointed provincial of the Roman province in 1322. In this capacity he became a member of the embassy deputed by the Romans to invite John XXII to transfer his residence to the Eternal City. On 20 October, 1326, the pope named him Bishop of Girgenti (Sicily), but shortly after (15 June, 1327) transferred him to the archiepiscopal See of Liponto (Manfredonia, Southern Italy), made him Cardinal-Priest of S. Giovanni e Paolo on 18 December, 1327, and Cardinal-Bishop of Sabina on 18 December, 1338. He continued in various ways to promote the welfare of the Dominican Order, richly endowing the Convent of St. Dominic in Bologna.

(5) GIACOMO ORSINI, created cardinal-deacon by Gregory XI on 30 May, 1371, d. at Vicovaro or at Tagliacozzo, 1379. He was distinguished for his knowledge of the law. Appointed papal legate in Siena in 1376, he was a strong supporter of Gregory XI. In the Conclave of 1378, he espoused the cause of Urban VI, but later attached himself to the antipope Clement VII.

(6) PONCELLO ORSINI, Bishop of Aversa (Southern Italy) from 19 June, 1370, d. 2 February, 1395. He was created cardinal-priest with the title of St. Clement at the great consistory convoked by Urban VI on 28 September, 1378. He became papal legate, and at first worked zealously for the interests of Urban VI after the outbreak of the schism. Later, however, repelled by the impetuous procedure of the pope, he secretly left the Curia and took up his abode upon his own possessions. At the Conclave of 1389, he was a candidate for the papacy. The new pope, Boniface IX, appointed him to important ecclesiastical offices, and he exercised great influence upon the Curia until his death.

(7) TOMMASO, of the line of the Counts of Manupello, raised to the cardinalate (1381) by Urban VI; d. 10 July, 1390. He was sent by the pope as legate to the Patrimony and the Marches, where Prince Rinaldo Orsini of Aquila and Tagliacozzo had seized the cities of Urbino and Spoleto in addition to other territory. The legate declared war against him and won back for the pope the cities of Narni, Ameli, Terni, and later also Viterbo. His conduct towards the Papal Vicar of Viterbo, brought upon himself the disfavour of the pope, who imprisoned him in the fortress of Amelia, but later granted him his liberty. On the occasion of the conspiracy of several of the cardinals against Urban, Cardinal Orsini remained loyal to the pope. His relations were intimate with Urban's successor, Boniface IX, during whose pontificate he died.

(8) GIORDANO ORSINI, a very distinguished personality in the College of Cardinals in the first three decades of the fifteenth century, d. at Petricoli, 29 July, 1438. After a thorough and comprehensive training, he became Auditor of the Rota, and in February, 1400, was raised by Boniface IX to the Archiepiscopal See of Naples. On 12 June, 1405, Innocent VII made him a member of the College of Cardinals, at first with the title of St. Martino of Monti, and later with that of S. Lorenzo in Damaso. In 1412 he was appointed Cardinal-Bishop of Albano, and in 1431 Cardinal-Bishop of Sabina. He participated in the election of Gregory XII (1406), but later, with several other cardinals, renounced allegiance to the pope,

against whom he published a tract. He assisted at the Council of Pisa, and took part in the election of the Pisan pope, Alexander V (1409), and of his successor John XXIII (Balthasar Cossa). The latter sent him as envoy to Spain, later appointing him papal legate to the Marches, in which position he was equally distinguished for his ability and prudence. He assisted zealously at the Council of Constance, and took part in the election of Martin V (1417). He was sent by this pope as legate to England and France, in company with Cardinal Filastre, to make peace between the two countries. He was also selected for the difficult embassy to Bohemia and the neighbouring countries (1426), where he was to combat the Hussite heresy. On this occasion he took with him as his secretary the future cardinal, Nicholas of Cusa. Upon his return, the pope entrusted to him another difficult task, namely the visitation and reform of the churches and ecclesiastical institutions of Rome. In the Conclave of 1431 Eugene IV was elected pope. A close friendship existed between him and Giordano, and the latter supported him loyally and energetically during all the trying conditions of the time. With two other cardinals, Giordano was commissioned to proceed against the usurpers of ecclesiastical possessions in Italy, after which he was delegated by the pope to attend the Council of Basle (q. v.), where he exerted every effort to uphold the rights of the pope against the schismatic element in the council. We are indebted to him for a diary of this council. Later, as papal legate, he journeyed with Cardinal Conti to Siena to meet Emperor Sigismund on his way to Rome to receive the imperial crown. A man of wide culture, Giordano took an active part in the literary life of his time. Numerous and valuable manuscripts were the result of his journeyings as legate, and these he willed to St. Peter's in Rome (cf. the catalogue of manuscripts in Cancellieri, "De secretariis basilicæ Vaticanæ", II, Rome, 1786, pp. 906–14). An Augustinian monastery was founded by him in Bracciano. He died dean of the College of Cardinals, and was buried in St. Peter's in a chapel founded and richly endowed by him.

(9) LATINO ORSINI, likewise of the Roman branch of the family and the owner of rich possessions, b. 1411; d. 11 August, 1477. He entered the ranks of the Roman clergy as a youth, became subdeacon, and as early as 10 March, 1438, was raised to the Episcopal See of Conza in Southern Italy. Transferred from this see to that of Trani (Southern Italy) on 8 June, 1439, he remained archbishop of the latter after his elevation to the cardinalate by Nicholas V on 20 December, 1448. On 4 December, 1454, the Archbishopric of Bari was conferred upon him, which made it possible for him to take up his residence in Rome, the See of Trani being given to his brother, John Orsini, Abbot of Farfa. Paul II appointed him legate for the Marches. Sixtus IV, for whose election in 1471 Cardinal Latino had worked energetically, named him *camerlengo* of the College of Cardinals, granted him in 1472 the Archdiocese of Taranto, which he governed by proxy, and, in addition, placed him at the head of the government of the Papal States. He was also appointed commander-in-chief of the papal fleet in the war against the Turks, and, acting for the pope, crowned Ferdinand King of Naples. He founded in Rome the monastery of S. Salvatore in Lauro, which he richly endowed and in which he established the canons regular, donating to it also numerous manuscripts. In the last years of his life he became deeply religious, though he had been worldly in his youth, leaving a natural son named Paul, whom, with the consent of the pope, he made the heir of his vast possessions.

(10) GIAMBATTISTA ORSINI, nephew of Latino, d. 22 Feb., 1503. He entered the service of the Curia at an early age, became cameral cleric, canon of St. Peter's, and was elevated to the cardinalate by Sixtus IV in 1483. Innocent VIII conferred upon him in 1491 the Archiepiscopal See of Taranto, which he governed by proxy, and, as papal legate for Romagna, the Marches, and Bologna, he was entrusted with the administration of these provinces of the Ecclesiastical States. In the Conclave of 1492, the election of Alexander VI was almost entirely due to him. However, Cardinal Giambattista, together with the head of the House of Orsini, the Duke of Bracciano, having espoused the cause of the Florentines and the French in the Italian wars, was taken prisoner in the Vatican at the command of the pope and thrown into the dungeon of the Castel Sant' Angelo, where he died. The report was current that he had been poisoned by Alexander VI.

Other cardinals of the family of Orsini who are worthy of mention because of the active part taken by them either as administrators of the papal states or as legates in other lands are the following:

(11) FLAVIO ORSINI, flourished in the sixteenth century, d. 16 May, 1581. He was created a cardinal in 1565, having been a bishop since 1560, first of the See of Muro and later that of Spoleto. In 1572 he was sent by Gregory XIII as legate to Charles IX of France, principally to support this monarch in his conflict with the Huguenots.

(12) ALESSANDRO ORSINI, belonging to the ducal family of Bracciano, b. 1592; d. 22 August, 1626. He was brought up at the court of the Grand Duke Ferdinand I of Tuscany, and in 1615 created a cardinal by Paul V. As Legate to Ravenna under Gregory XV, he distinguished himself in 1621 by his great charity on the occasion of the outbreak of a malignant pestilence. Upon his return to Rome, he devoted himself to religion and to the practice of an austere asceticism. He even begged permission of the pope to resign the cardinalate and to enter the Jesuit Order, but this was refused. Nevertheless, the pious cardinal always remained closely united to the Jesuits. He was a patron of Galileo.

(13) VIRGINIO ORSINI, likewise of the ducal family of Bracciano, b. 1615; d. 21 August, 1676. He renounced his birthright in his youth, entered the military order of the Knights of Malta, and more than once distinguished himself in the war against the Turks by his reckless bravery. In December, 1641, Urban VIII raised him to the dignity of cardinal, and appointed him Protector of the Polish as well as of the Portuguese Orient. He was commissioned to direct the building of the new fortifications with which Urban VIII enclosed the Leonine City and a quarter of Trastevere, and which are still in existence. In 1675 he became Cardinal Bishop of Frascati, but died the next year, leaving behind him a reputation of a pious, gentle, and benevolent prince of the Church.

In addition to the members of the Orsini family who were prominent as cardinals in the history of the Roman Church, others have gained a place in political history as statesmen, warriors, or patrons of the arts and sciences.

(1) ORSO DI BOBONE, nephew of Pope Celestine III (1191–8) and the first Orsini to hold a conspicuous place in Rome. Under the protection of his uncle, the pope, he was destined to have the principal part in laying the foundation of the dominion, power, and prestige of the Roman Orsini. His grandchild, (2) MATTEO ROSSO ORSINI, was made senator of Rome by Pope Gregory IX in 1241. In this capacity he took a decided stand against the ventures of Emperor Frederick II in Italy. He was a patron of religious undertakings, a personal friend of St. Francis of Assisi, and a member of that saint's Third Order. While one of the sons of Matteo Rosso, Gian Gaetano, ascended the papal throne as Nicholas III, another, (3) RINALDO, continued the activities of his father in the political field, exerting himself to the utmost to prevent the

alliance of Rome with the Hohenstaufen Konradin. A son of this Rinaldo, (4) MATTEO ORSINI, was twice senator in Rome. His wise and energetic uncle, Nicholas III (q. v.), to show that papal rule was once more dominant in Rome, deprived King Charles of Anjou of the senatorial dignity, and in 1278 published the decree that thenceforth no foreign emperor or king could become senator, a Roman being alone eligible for the dignity, and then only with the consent of the pope and for one year. The power of the Orsini was in general much strengthened by this capable pope of their race.

In the course of the fourteenth and fifteenth centuries, the following were particularly famous as military leaders in the numberless internal wars of Italy; (5) PAOLO ORSINI, who in the beginning of the fifteenth century fought as *condottiere* in the service of several popes, was taken prisoner by Ladislas of Naples, again set at liberty, and fell in battle against Braccio da Montone before Perugia on 5 July, 1416. (6) VIRGINIO ORSINI, Lord of Bracciano, was leader of the forces of Sixtus IV (1471-84) in the war against Ferrara, and victor at the battle of Campo Morto against the Neapolitans (1482). Later, however, he entered the service of Naples to oppose King Charles VIII of France (1483-98); in 1494, however, he took the side of the latter, and was imprisoned on this account. He died on 18 January, 1497, in prison at Naples. (7) NICCOLO ORSINI, Count of Petigliano, was, at this time, in the service of the Anjous, military leader in the war against Naples, Sixtus IV, Siena, Florence, and Venice. Later, however, he went over with his army to the Venetian standard, and became general-in-chief of the Venetian Republic in the war against the League of Cambrai. He captured Padua, but was defeated in 1509, and died in the following year. Of the members of the Orsini family who flourished during the sixteenth century (8) PAOLO GIORDANO ORSINI is also worthy of mention. Born in 1541, he was created a duke, with the title of Bracciano, by Pope Pius IV (1560). Under Paul IV, he was general of the papal troops in the war against the Turks (1566). His first wife, Isabella Medici, being murdered, he took as his second wife Vittoria Accorambuni, widow of the murdered Francesco Peretti, a nephew of Sixtus V. Accused of murdering the latter, Paolo Giordano was obliged to leave Rome. He died at Salo in 1585. (9) FULVIO ORSINI was distinguished as a humanist, historian, and archæologist, b. on 11 December, 1529; d. in Rome, 18 May, 1600. He was the natural son probably of Maerbale Orsini of the line of Mugnano. Cast off by his father at the age of nine, he found a refuge among the choir boys of St. John Lateran, and a protector in Canon Gentile Delfini. He applied himself energetically to the study of the ancient languages, published a new edition of Arnobius (Rome, 1583) and of the Septuagint (Rome, 1587), and wrote works dealing with the history of Rome—"Familiæ Romanæ ex antiquis numismatibus" (Rome, 1577), "Fragmenta historicorum" (Antwerp, 1595), etc. He brought together a large collection of antiquities, and built up a costly library of manuscripts and books, which later became part of the Vatican library (cf. de Nolhac, "La bibliothèque de Fulvio Orsini", Paris, 1887).

A woman of the Orsini family likewise played an important political rôle in the seventeenth century: MARIE ANNE, *née* de la Trémoille, b. 1642. Her first husband was Talleyrand, Prince de Chalais, after whose death she married Flavio Orsini, Duke of Bracciano, who remained loyal to Pope Innocent XI in his difficulties with Louis XIV of France. Marie Anne used her influence with the Curia in the interests of France and of Louis XIV, and in 1701, after the death of her husband, went to Madrid as mistress of the robes to Queen Marie-Louise, who, together with her husband Philip V of Spain, was completely under her influence. She did much to strengthen the throne of these rulers, but, nevertheless, in 1714 when Philip married Elizabeth Farnese, she was dismissed with ingratitude and returned to Rome, where she died on 5 December, 1722 (see Hill, "The Princess Orsini", London, 1899).

The ancient family of the Roman Orsini is extinct. The present princes of the family in Rome descend from the Neapolitan line, which may be traced back to Francesco Orsini, Count of Trani and Conversano. In 1463 they became Dukes of Gravina, later (1724) princes of the Empire and Roman princes. The head of the family always enjoys the dignity of assistant at the papal throne. The present head is Filippo Orsini-Gravina-Sarzina, b. 10 December, 1842. Several noble families outside of Italy trace back their descent to the ancient Italian Orsini, as for example the Juvenels des Ursins in France and the Rosenbergs in Austria and Germany.

SANSOVINO, *Hist. di casa Orsini e degli uomini illustri della medesima* (Venice, 1505); INCHOFF, *Genealogiæ familiæ Ursinæ* (Amsterdam, 1710); CIACONIUS, *Vitæ et res gestæ Summorum Pontif. Roman. et S. R. E. Cardinalium* (4 vols., Rome, 1677), continued by GUARNACCI (2 vols., Rome, 1751); HUYSKENS, *Kardinal Napoleo Orsini* (part 1, Marburg, 1902); IDEM, *Das Kapitel von St. Peter unter dem Einfluss der Orsini (1276–1342)* in *Histor. Jahrb.*, XXVII (1906), 266–90; STERNFELD, *Der Kardinal Johann Gaetan Orsini* (Berlin, 1905); FINKE, *Aus den Tagen Bonifaz VIII* (Münster, 1902), 96 sqq. (regarding Cardinal Matteo Rosso Orsini); SOUCHON, *Die Papstwahlen von Bonifaz VIII bis Urban VI* (Brunswick, 1888); GREGOROVIUS, *Gesch. der Stadt Rom im Mittelalter* (5th ed., Stuttgart, 1903); REUMONT, *Gesch. der Stadt Rom* (3 vols., Berlin, 1867–70); PASTOR, *Gesch. der Päpste* (4th ed., Freiburg, 1901—); MORONI, *Dizionario di erudizione storico-ecclesiastica*, s. v. *Orsini*.

J. P. KIRSCH.

Orsisius ('Ἀρσίσιος, Oresiesis - Heru - sa Ast), an Egyptian monk of the fourth century, was a disciple of Pachomius on the island Tabenna in the Nile. When Pachomius died (348), Orsisius was chosen as his successor; but he resigned in favour of Theodore. It was not till Theodore's death (c. 380) that Orsisius, advised by St. Athanasius, accepted the office of hegumen. Theodore and Orsisius are said to have helped Pachomius in the composition of his rule; Gennadius (De. vir. ill., IX) mentions another work: "Oresiesis the monk, a colleague of Pachomius and Theodore and a man perfectly learned in the Scriptures, composed a Divinely savoured book containing instruction for all monastic discipline, in which nearly the whole Old and New Testaments are explained in short dissertations in as far as they affect monks; and shortly before his death he gave this book to his brethren as his testament." This is supposed to be the work: "Doctrina de institutione monachorum" translated by St. Jerome into Latin (P. L., CIII, 453 sq., and P. G., XL., 870–894). Migne prints after it (P. G., XL., 895 sq.) another work attributed to the same author: "De sex cogitationibus sanctorum", which, however, is probably by a later Oresius.

CAVE, *Scriptorum eccl. historia literaria*, I (Basle, 1741), 209; CEILLIER, *Histoire générale des auteurs sacrés*, IV (Paris, 1860), 235 sq.

ADRIAN FORTESCUE.

Orte. See CIVITÀ CASTELLANA, ORTE AND GALLESE, DIOCESE OF.

Ortelius (OERTEL), ABRAHAM, cartographer, geographer, and archæologist, b. in Antwerp, 4 April, 1527; d. there, 28 June, 1598. His family came from Augsburg, wherefore Ortelius frequently referred to himself as "Belgo-Germanus". The death of his father in 1535, who had been a wealthy merchant, seems to have placed the family in difficulties, for Ortelius began to trade or peddle geographical charts and maps while still a mere youth. When twenty years of age he joined a guild as a colourer of charts. By purchasing as valuable maps as possible, mounting them on canvas, colouring, and re-selling them, he managed to assist in supporting the family, as may be gleaned from a contemporary letter. This trading in maps was probably one of the chief reasons for his unusually extended trips to Germany, England, Italy, and particularly for his annual visits to the great fair at Leipzig. Meanwhile he did not confine himself entirely to trafficking in charts. Five years before Mercator published his famous *Carta Navigatoria* (1569) appeared Ortelius's great eight-leaved map of the world. As the only extant copy of this great map is that in the library of the University of Basle (cf. Bernoulli, "Ein Karteninkunabelnband", Basle, 1905, p. 5) it is still almost entirely unknown. No copy has yet been found of Ortelius's great map of Asia, but in his chief work, which assures him for all time a place of honour in the history of cartography, we find not only his own map of Asia on a smaller scale, but also a number of maps of other cartographers, who otherwise are completely unknown. This work is the "Theatrum orbis terrarum", which appeared in 1570; it was the first great modern atlas, and contained seventy copper engravings on fifty-three double-folio pages. Ortelius has combined in this work in a systematic manner all recent maps of the world and separate countries, of which he had heard during his long activity as trader and collector. Where several maps of one country were available, he chose the most modern and most reliable copy. When the name of the author was mentioned on the map, Ortelius did not change a line or a name then, but, when the author's name was not given, he resolutely made such changes as appeared to him necessary. He conscientiously gave credit to the author of maps which were published on a reduced scale by himself. Considering geography as an eye of history (*historiæ oculus*), he usually added the ancient historical names of countries and cities to the modern ones.

ABRAHAM ORTELIUS

To the atlas he appended a geographical dictionary which contained both the ancient and modern names. More important for us than this dictionary is the appended catalogue of maps (*Catalogus auctorum tabularum geographicarum*), in which appear the names and works of ninety-nine cartographers who lived before 1570. As concerning many of these cartographers we have no other knowledge than that contained in this catalogue, and as Ortelius utilized but forty-six of the maps mentioned by him, this little list is to-day one of the most important sources for a history of cartography. Later on this "Theatrum" was enlarged and improved. In 1593 there were 137, in 1612 no less than 166 maps, while the list of authors reached 183 for the time up to 1595; antiquated maps were replaced by more modern ones, or changed according to the more accurate reports forwarded for the most part by missionaries, and it soon appeared not only in the Latin language, but also in Dutch, High German, Italian, and French translations. Very numerous were the smaller editions and extracts in the various languages. As late as 1697 there appeared in Venice a "Teatro del Mondo di Abramo Ortelio". As the "Theatrum" had been dedicated to the Spanish king Philip II by Ortelius, the latter was given the title of a Royal Geographer (*geographus regius*). His contemporaries honoured him as the "Ptolemy of his century".

Separate from his atlas Ortelius published in 1587 the "Thesaurus geographicus", which possesses to this day considerable value as a dictionary of old geography. In the form of a letter to his friend Gerhard Mercator, Ortelius published in 1575 his "Itinerarium per nonnullas Galliæ Belgicæ partes", which contains much valuable information as to the old geography of Belgium, but which is chiefly valuable on account of its philologico-archæological importance. One of the fruits of his restless activity as a collector of archæological specimens was his pamphlet: "Deorum, Dearumque Capita e veteribus numismatibus" (1575), which contained a number of reproductions from his widely admired archæological collection. In his "Aurei seculi imago sive Germanorum veterum mores, ritus et religio delineata et commentariis ex utriusque linguæ scriptoribus descripta", he gives a short commentary to the works of ancient writers on Germany, illustrated with ten engravings. Despite the great honour freely accorded to Ortelius, he remained humble and modest. "Until his very end he was", as F. Ratzel says, "a good Catholic and had particularly many friends among the Jesuits". True to his motto, "Contemno et orno [mundum], mente, manu", Ortelius, unmarried and earnest, remained above the petty squabbles which so often disturb scientific circles. "Quietis cultor sine lite, uxore, prole" is written on his tombstone in the Præmonstratensian abbey at Antwerp. This epitaph was written by Justus Lipsius.

Theatrum orbis terrarum, especially the introduction to the first posthumous edition; RATZEL in *Allg. deutsche Biogr.*, XXIV, 428–33; HESSELS, *Ecclesiæ Londinæ-Batavæ Archivum*, I: *Abrahami Ortelii (Geographi Antverpensis) et virorum eruditorum ad eundum . . . epistulæ* (Cambridge, 1887); TIELE, *Het Kaartboek van Abraham Ortelius* in *Biblogr. Adversaria*, III ('s Gravenhage, 1876–7), 83–121; OBERHAMMER in *Sitzungsber. d. philos.-philolog. u. hist. Kl. d. k. bay. Akad. d. Wiss.*, II (1899), 438–45.

JOSEPH FISCHER.

Orthodox Church, the technical name for the body of Christians who use the Byzantine Rite in various languages and are in union with the Patriarch of Constantinople but in schism with the Pope of Rome. The epithet *Orthodox* (ὀρθόδοξος), meaning "right believer", is, naturally, claimed by people of every religion. It is almost exactly a Greek form of the official title of the chief enemies of the Greeks, i. e. the Moslems (*mu'min, fidelis*). The Monophysite Armenians call themselves *ughapar*, meaning exactly the same thing. How "Orthodox" became the proper name of the Eastern Church it is difficult to say. It was used at first, long before the schism of Photius, especially in the East, not with any idea of opposition against the West, but rather as the antithesis to the Eastern heretics—Nestorians and Monophysites. Gradually, although of course both East and West always claimed both names, "Catholic" became the most common name for the original Church in the West, "Orthodox" in the East. It would be very difficult to find the right name for this Church. "Eastern" is too vague, the Nestorians and Monophysites are Eastern Churches; "Schismatic" has the same disadvantage. "Greek" is really the least expressive of all. The Greek Church is only one, and a very small one, of the sixteen Churches that make up this vast communion. The millions of Russians, Bulgars, Rumanians, Arabs, and so on who belong to it are Greek in no sense at all. According to their common custom one may add the word "Eastern" to the title and speak of the Orthodox Eastern Church (ἡ ὀρθόδοξος ἀνατολικὴ ἐκκλησία). The Orthodox, then, are the Christians in the East of Europe, in Egypt and Asia, who accept the Councils of Ephesus and Chalcedon (are therefore neither Nestorians nor Monophysites), but who, as the result of the schisms of Photius (ninth cent.) and Cerularius (eleventh cent.), are not in communion with the Catholic Church. There is no common authority obeyed by all, or rather it is only the authority of "Christ and the seven Œcumenical Synods" (from Nicæa I, in 325, to Nicæa II, in 787). These sixteen Churches are: (1) The four Eastern patriarchates—Constantinople, Alexandria, Antioch, Jerusalem—and the Church of Cyprus, independent since the Council of Ephesus. (2) Since the great schism eleven new churches have been added, all but one formed at the expense of the once vast Patriarchate of Constantinople. They are the six national Churches of Russia, Greece, Servia, Montenegro, Rumania, and Bulgaria, four independent Churches in the Austro-Hungarian Monarchy, namely Carlovitz, Hermannstadt, Czernovitz, Bosnia-Herzegovina, and lastly the Church of Mount Sinai, consisting of one monastery separated from Jerusalem. One of these Churches, that of Bulgaria, is in schism with Constantinople since 1872. The total number of Orthodox Christians in the world is estimated variously as 95 to 100 millions. (See EASTERN CHURCHES; GREEK CHURCH; CONSTANTINOPLE, *Heresy and Schism;* RUSSIA.)

ADRIAN FORTESCUE.

Orthodoxy, ὀρθοδοξία, signifies right belief or purity of faith. Right belief is not merely subjective, as resting on personal knowledge and convictions, but is in accordance with the teaching and direction of an absolute extrinsic authority. This authority is the Church founded by Christ, and guided by the Holy Ghost. He, therefore, is orthodox, whose faith coincides with the teachings of the Catholic Church. As divine revelation forms the deposit of faith entrusted to the Church for man's salvation, it also, with the truths clearly deduced from it, forms the object and content of orthodoxy. Although the term *orthodox* or *orthodoxy* does not occur in the Scriptures, its meaning is repeatedly insisted on. Thus Christ proclaims the necessity of faith unto salvation (Mark, xvi, 16). St. Paul, emphasizing the same injunction in terms more specific, teaches "one Lord, one faith, one baptism" (Eph., iv, 5, 6). Again, when directing Titus in his ministerial labours, he admonishes him to speak in accord with "sound doctrine" (Tit., ii, 1). And not only does St. Paul lay stress on the soundness of the doctrine to be preached, but he also directs attention to the form in which it must be delivered: "Hold the form of sound words which thou hast heard of me in faith" (II Tim., i, 13). Consistent with the teachings and method of Christ and the Apostles, the Fathers point out the necessity of preserving pure and undefiled the deposit of revelation. "Neither in the confusion of paganism", says St. Augustine, "nor in the defilement of heresy, nor in the lethargy of schism, nor yet in the blindness of Judaism is religion to be sought; but among those alone who are called Catholic Christians, or the *orthodox*, that is, the custodians of sound doctrine and followers of right teaching" (De Vera Relig., cap. v). Fulgentius writes: "I rejoice that with no taint of perfidy you are solicitous for the true faith, without which no conversion is of any avail, nor can at all exist" (De Vera Fide ad Petrum, Proleg). The Church, likewise, in its zeal for purity of faith and teaching, has rigorously adhered to the example set by the Apostles and early Fathers. This is manifest in its whole history, but especially in such champions of the faith as Athanasius, in councils, condemnations of heresy, and its definitions of revealed truth. That orthodox faith is requisite for salvation is a defined doctrine of the Church. "Whosoever wishes to be saved", declares the Athanasian Creed, "must first of all hold *integral* and *inviolate* the Catholic faith, without which he shall surely be eternally lost". Numerous Councils and papal decisions have reiterated this dogma (cf. Council of Florence, Denz., 714; Prof. of Faith of Pius IV, Denz., 1000; condemnation of Indifferentism and Latitudinarianism in the Syll. of Pius IX, Denz., 1715, 1718; Council of the Vatican, "De Fide", can. vi, Denz., 1815; condemnation of the Modernistic position regarding the nature and origin of dogma, Encyc. "Pascendi Dominici Gregis", 1907, Denz., 2079). While truth must be intolerant of error (II Cor., vi, 14, 15), the Church does not deny the possibility of salvation of those earnest and sincere persons outside her fold who live and die in invincible ignorance of the true faith (cf. Council of the Vatican, Sess. III, cap. iii, Denz., 1794; S. Aug., Ep. xliii ad Galerium). (See CHURCH; FAITH; FAITH, PROTESTANT CONFESSIONS OF; HERESY; INDIFFERENTISM.)

ST. THOMAS, *Summa Theol.*, II-II, *De fide*, QQ. i–vii; RUSSO, *The True Religion and Its Dogmas* (Boston, 1886); RICARDS, *Catholic Christianity and Modern Unbelief* (New York, 1884).

CHARLES J. CALLAN.

Orthodoxy, FEAST (or SUNDAY) OF, the first Sunday of the Great Forty days (Lent) in the Byzantine Calendar (sixth Sunday before Easter), kept in memory of the final defeat of Iconoclasm and the restoration of the holy icons to the churches on 19 February (which was the first Sunday of Lent), 842 (see ICONOCLASM). A perpetual feast on the anniversary of that day was ordained by the Synod of Constantinople, and is one of the great feasts of the year among Orthodox and Byzantine Uniats. The name "Orthodoxy" has gradually affected the character of the feast. Originally commemorating only the defeat of Iconoclasm, the word was gradually understood in a more general sense as opposition to all heterodoxy. In this way, though its first occasion is not forgotten, the feast has become one in honour of the true Faith in general. This is shown by its special service. After the Orthros and before the holy Liturgy a procession is made with crosses and pictures to some destined spot (often merely round the church). Meanwhile a Canon, attributed to St. Theodore of Studium, is sung. Arrived at the place, the Synodikon is read. This Synodikon begins with the memory of certain saints, confessors, and heroes of the faith, to each of whose names the people cry out: "Eternal Memory!" (αἰωνία ἡ μνήμη) three times. Then follows a long list of heretics of all kinds, to each of which the answer is: "Anathema" once or thrice. The heretics comprise all the old offenders of any reputation, Arians, Nestorians, Monophysites, Monothelites, Iconoclasts, and so on. Then comes again "Eternal Memory" to certain pious emperors, from Constantine on. There is inevitably considerable difference between the Orthodox and Uniat lists. The Orthodox acclaim Photius, Cerularius, other anti-Roman patriarchs and many schismatical emperors. They curse Honorius among the Monothelites, the opponents of Hesychasm. The Uniat Synodikon is purged of these names. In Russia politics have their place in the Synodikon; the emperor and his family are acclaimed; all are cursed who deny the divine right of the Russian monarchy and all who "dare to stir up insurrection and rebellion against it". The text of the Canon, Synodikon, etc., and the rubrics will be found in either Triodion, Orthodox or Uniat.

ALLATIUS, *De dominicis et hebdomadis Græcorum*, xv, appendix to *De ecclesiæ occid. et orient. perpetuo consensu* (Cologne, 1648); NILLES, *Kalendarium manuale* (2nd ed., Innsbruck, 1897), 101–18.

ADRIAN FORTESCUE.

Orthosias, a titular see of Phœnicia Prima, suffragan of Tyre. The city is mentioned for the first time in I Mach., xv, 37, as a Phœnician port (D. V., Orthosias); Pliny (Hist. Nat., V, xvii) places it between Tripoli, on the south, and the River Eleutherus, on the north; Strabo (Geographia, XVI, ii, 12, 15), near the Eleutherus; Peutinger's "Table", agreeing with Hierocles, George of Cyprus, and others, indicates it between Tripoli and Antaradus. Le Quien (Oriens Christ., II, 825) mentions four bishops, beginning with Phosphorus in the fifth century. Two Latin titulars of the fourteenth century appear in Eubel, "Hierarchia cath. medii ævi", I, 396. In the "Not.

Episcop." of Antioch for the sixth century ("Echos d'Orient", X, 145) Orthosias is suffragan of Tyre, while in that of the tenth century (op. cit., X, 97) it is confounded with Antaradus or Tortosa. The discovery on the banks of the Eleutherus of Orthosian coins, dating from Antoninus Pius and bearing figures of Astarte, led to the identification of the site of Orthosias near the River El-Barid at a spot marked by ruins, called Bordj Hakmon el-Yehoudi.

BEURLIER in VIGOUROUX, *Dict. de la Bible*, s. v.; SMITH, *Dict. of Greek and Roman Geography*, II, 407.

S. VAILHÉ.

Ortolano Ferrarese, painter of the Ferrara School, b. in Ferrara, about 1490; d. about 1525. His real name was Giovanni Battista Benvenuti, and he was called L'Ortolano because his father, Francisco, was a gardener. Of his career little is known, save that he was a diligent student of the works of Raphael and Bagnacavallo in 1512-13 at Bologna. His masterpiece, a picture of rich colour and fine draughtsmanship, representing Saint Sebastian, Saint Roch, and Saint Demetrius, is in the National Gallery, London. It was brought from the church of Bondeno near Ferrara in 1844, and purchased by the gallery in 1861. In the cathedral at Ferrara are other works attributed to him, which later critics have given to Garofalo, but in some of the smaller churches of Ferrara, those of San Niccolò, the Servi, and San Lorenzo, there are pictures which may be readily accepted as his. His work so resembles that of Garofalo that there is a never-ceasing controversy between the critics who accept the respective claims of each, and nearly as much dispute has arisen over his works as over those of Giorgione. There is a fine picture usually accepted as his, in the possession of Lord Wimborne in England, and this shows very strongly the influence upon the painter of Lorenzo Costa. Two of his paintings are in the gallery at Ferrara, and others at Naples and Berlin, while there are several similar works in private possession in Ferrara.

LANZI, *Storia Pittorica* (Bassano, 1509); LADERCHI, *Pittura Ferrarese* (Ferrara, 1611); IDEM, *Guida di Ferrara* (Ferrara, 1525).

GEORGE CHARLES WILLIAMSON.

Ortona. See LANCIANO AND ORTONA, ARCHDIOCESE OF.

Ortwin. See GRATIUS (VAN GRAES), ORTWIN.

Orval (AUREA VALLIS, GUELDENTHAL), formerly a Cistercian abbey in Belgian Luxemburg, Diocese of Trier. It was founded in 1071 by Benedictines from Calabria, who left in 1110 to be succeeded by Canons Regular. These were replaced in 1132 by Cistercians from the newly founded monastery of Tre Fontane. Their first abbot Constantine had been a disciple of St. Bernard of Clairvaux, dying in the repute of holiness after fourteen years. Owing to the industry and frugality of the monks, and the competent management of the abbots, Orval became exceptionally rich. In 1750 it owned no less than 300 towns, villages, and manors, and had an annual income of 1,200,000 livres. In proportion to its riches was its charity towards the poor. Under the leadership of able and pious abbots its discipline was always in a flourishing condition, with the exception of a short period towards the end of the sixteenth and the beginning of the seventeenth century, when the storms of the Reformation raged in the Netherlands. Abbot Bernard de Montgaillard (1605-28), who was famous for piety and learning, restored the decaying discipline by drawing up new statutes for the monastery. After a short interruption during the Thirty Years' War, the reform which Bernard had introduced was zealously carried out by the succeeding abbots, especially by Carl von Benzeradt (1668-1707), who also founded the abbey of Düsselthal in 1707. The doctrines of Jansenius were espoused by a few monks early in the eighteenth century, but, happily, those that were imbued with them had to leave the monastery in 1725. The abbey and its church fell a prey to the ravages of the French Revolution in 1793. In the literary field the monks of Orval did not distinguish themselves in any special manner. The only noteworthy writer was Gilles d'Orval, who lived in the first half of the thirteenth century. He wrote the continuation, to the year 1251, of the "Gesta Pontificum Leodiensium", which had been written up to the year 1048 by Heriger of Lobbes and Anselm of Liège (Mon. Germ. Script., XXV, 1-129).

TILLIÈRE, *Hist. de l'abbaye d'Orval* (2nd ed., Namur, 1907); JEANTIN, *Chroniques histor. sur l'abbaye d'Orval* (Nancy, 1850); MARX, *Gesch. des Erzstiftes Trier*, II, i (Trier, 1860), 568-79; SCHORN, *Eiflia sacra*, II (Bonn, 1889), 297-308.

MICHAEL OTT.

Orvieto, DIOCESE OF (URBEVETANA), in Central Italy. The city stands on a rugged mass of tufa, near the rivers Paglia and Chiana, the swamps of which were drained by Sixtus V. Some believe this town to be the ancient Hebanum or Oropitum; others, e. g. Müller and Gamurrini, hold that it was the primitive port (therefore *Urbs vetus*, or old city) of the Etruscan city of Volsinii, destroyed by the Romans at an uncertain date, and rebuilt on the site of the present Bolsena which gives its name to the largest lake of the Italian peninsula. In the country around Orvieto there are many Etruscan tombs. The name of Urbs Vetus appears for the first time in Procopius, corrupted into Urbebentum; it is also found in the writings of St. Gregory the Great.

During the Gothic War, Orvieto was defended by the Goths for a long time. Later, it fell into the hands of the Lombards (606). From the latter end of the tenth century the city was governed by consuls, who, however, took the oath of fealty to the bishop; but from 1201 it governed itself through a *podestà* (in that year, the Bishop Richard) and a captain of the people. On account of its position, Orvieto was often chosen by the popes as a place of refuge and Adrian IV fortified it. A "Studium Generale" was granted to the city by Gregory XI in 1337. In the middle of the thirteenth century, bitter feuds arose between the Filipeschi and the Monaldeschi families, and were not quelled until the city came under the rule of Ermanno Monaldeschi, whom Cardinal Albornoz reduced to obedience to the Holy See. One of the first convents of the Dominican Order was built at Orvieto (1220); and in 1288 there was founded in the town a monastery of Armenian monks. In 1199 the martyrdom of St. Pietro Parenzo took place at Orvieto; he was a Roman whom Innocent III had sent to govern that city with a view to suppressing the Patarian movement that Ermanno of Parma and Gottardo of Marsi had roused in the town.

The cathedral of Orvieto is one of the most beautiful churches in Italy; it was begun in 1285, and is of the Gothic style, with three naves; its tripartite façade was a conception of Lorenzo Maitani, and is embellished in its lower portion with scenes from the Old and New Testaments, and in its upper part with mosaics and statues of the Blessed Virgin, the Prophets, and the Apostles. The walls in the interior of the edifice are built of layers of Travertine marble and of basalt; the choir is adorned with frescoes, illustrating the life of the Blessed Virgin; they are by Ugolino di Prete Ilario, Peter di Puccio, and Anthony of Viterbo; the stalls of the choir are of inlaid work. The chapel on the right, called Our Lady of San Brizio, was painted by the Blessed Angelico of Fiesole ("Christ Glorified", "Last Judgment", and "The Prophets", done in 1447) and by Luca Signorelli ("Fall of Antichrist", "Resurrection of the Dead", "Damned and Blessed", etc.); Michelangelo took inspiration from these paintings for his "Last Judgment" of the Sistine Chapel; there is, also by Signorelli, the "Burial of

Jesus", and there are several sculptures by Scalza (1572), among them the group of the Pietà, chiselled from a single block of marble. The chapel on the opposite side, called "of the Corporal", contains the large reliquary in which is preserved the corporal of the miracle of Bolsena (see below). This receptacle was made by order of Bishop Bertrand dei Monaldeschi, by the Sienese Ugolino di Mæstro Vieri (1337); it is of silver, adorned with enamellings that represent the Passion of Jesus and the miracle; the frescoes of the walls, by Ugolino (1357-64), also represent the miracle. In the palace of the popes, built by Boniface VIII, is the civic museum, which contains Etruscan antiquities and works of art that are, for the greater part, from the cathedral. Among the other notable churches of Orvieto are San Giovenale, which contains remnants of ancient frescoes, and San Andrea, which has a dodecagon tower; in 1220 Pierre d'Artois was consecrated King of Jerusalem by Honorius III in this church.

The first known Bishop of Orvieto was John (about 590), and in 591 appears a Bishop Candidus; among its other prelates were Constantino Medici, O.P., sent by Alexander IV in 1255 to Greece, where he died; Francesco Monaldeschi (1280), who did much for the construction of the cathedral. In 1528 Clement VII sought refuge at Orvieto, and while there ordered the construction of the "Pozzo di San Patrizio" (the well of St. Patrick), by Sangallo. Bishop Sebastiano Vanzi (1562) distinguished himself at the Council of Trent and built the seminary, which was enlarged afterwards by Cardinal Fausto Polo (1645) and by Giacomo Silvestri, the latter of whom gave to it the college and other property of the Jesuits (1773); Cardinal Paolo Antamori (1780) caused the history of the cathedral of Orvieto to be written by Guglielmo della Valle; and lastly G. B. Lambruschini (1807).

With the See of Orvieto has been united from time immemorial that of Bolsena (the ancient Volsinii), of the ruins of which there are still the remnants of the temple of Nortia, of the "Thermæ", or hot baths, of Sejanus, of the mausoleum of L. Canuelius, etc. According to Pliny, 2000 statues were taken to Rome from Volsinii, when the latter was destroyed in 254 B. C. In the Middle Ages, Bolsena had much to suffer from the neighbouring lords (Vico, Bisenzo, Cerbara, etc.), and from the Orvietans, who claimed dominion over it; while, in 1377, the town was sacked by the adventurer Hawkwood (Acuto). On the Island of Martana, in the lake near by, Amalasunta, daughter of Theodoricus and wife of Theodatus, was strangled. To this island, in the sixth century, was transferred the body of St. Christina, a virgin and martyr of Bolsena (297?), but it was later returned to the city; the church of this saint contains a reclining statue of her by Luca della Robbia; annexed to the church is an ancient Christian cemetery, and ancient Christian inscriptions are numerous at Bolsena. Three bishops of Volsinii are known: Gaudentius (499), Candidus (601), who, it appears, is not the Bishop of Orvieto of that name, and Agnellus (680).

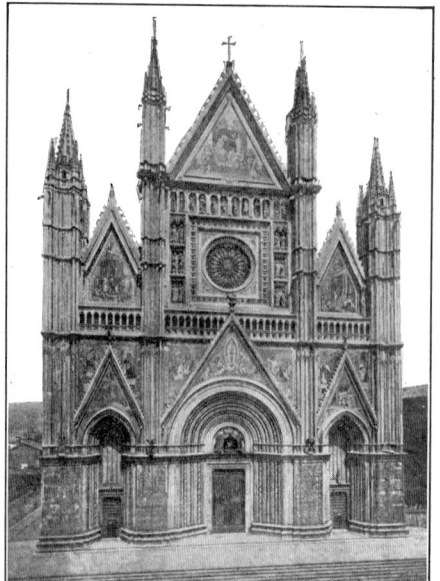

PAPAL PALACE, ORVIETO
Erected by Pope Boniface VIII (1294-1303)

The Miracle of Bolsena is not supported by strong historical evidence, and its tradition is not altogether consistent; for in the first place Urban IV makes no mention of it in the Bull by which he established the feast of Corpus Christi, although the miracle is said to have taken place in his day and to have determined him in his purpose of establishing that feast; likewise, the two biographers of Pope Urban impugn the truth of this tradition by their silence, i. e. Muratori, "Rerum Italicarum scriptores", III, pt. I, 400 sq.; and especially Thiericus Vallicoloris, who, in his life of the pope in Latin verse, describes in detail all the acts of the pontiff during the latter's stay at Orvieto, referring elsewhere also to the devotion of Urban in celebrating the Mass, and to the institution of the Feast of Corpus Christi, without at any time making allusion to the miracle at Bolsena. The latter is related in the inscription on a slab of red marble in the church of St. Christina, and is of later date than the canonization of St. Thomas Aquinas (1328). The oldest historical record of the miracle is contained in the enamel "histories" that adorn the front of the reliquary (1337-39). It is to be noted that in the narratives of the miracle cited by Fumi (Il Santuario, 73) the reliquary only is called "tabernaculum D.N.J.C.", or "tab . . . pro D.N.J.C." or, again, "tabernacolo del Corpo di Xpo."

CATHEDRAL, ORVIETO
Designed by Lorenzo Maitani (1275-1330)

In 1344 Clement VI, referring to this matter in a Brief, uses only the words "propter miraculum aliquod" (Pennazzi, 367); Gregory XI, in a Brief of 25 June, 1337, gives a short account of the miracle; and abundant reference to it is found later on (1435), in the sermons of the Dominican preacher Leonardo Mattei of Udine ("In festo Corp. Christi", xiv, ed.

Venice, 1652, 59) and by St. Antoninus of Florence ("Chronica", III, 19, xiii, 1), the latter, however, does not say (as the local legend recites) that the priest doubted the Real Presence of Christ in the Holy Eucharist, but, merely that a few drops from the chalice fell upon the corporal. For the rest, a similar legend of the "blood-stained corporal" is quite frequent in the legendaries of even earlier date than the fourteenth century, and coincides with the great Eucharistic polemics of the ninth to the twelfth centuries. The reddish spots on the corporal of Bolsena, upon close observation, show the profile of a face of the type by which the Saviour is traditionally represented.

FUMI, *Codice diplom. della città di Orvieto* (Florence, 1884); *Orvieto, note storiche* (Città di Castello, 1891); *Il duomo di Orvieto* (Rome, 1891); *Il Santuario del SS. Corporale nel duomo di Orvieto* (Rome, 1896); CAPPELLETTI, *Le Chiese d'Italia*, V; ADAMI, *Storia di Volseno* (3 vols., 1737); PENNAZZI, *Storia dell' Ostia e del Corporale, etc.* (Montefiascone, 1731).

U. BENIGNI.

Ory, MATTHIEU, inquisitor and theologian, b. at La Caune, 1492; d. at Paris, 1557. Entering the Dominican Order at the age of eighteen, he studied in the convent of St-Jacques, Paris, and at the Sorbonne, obtaining the licentiate in theology, 6 February, 1527. His reputation for learning and eloquence led to his appointment as grand inquisitor for France (1534), an office which he held until his death. Compelled to pronounce upon false accusations made against Saint Ignatius Loyola and "The Spiritual Exercises", he detected the fraud of the calumniators. Instead of condemning the saint, he praised and assisted him, and kept for himself a copy of the Exercises. He was indefatigable in preaching the Word of God, held several offices in his order, and combated false doctrines and evil-doing. Some writers erroneously call Ory a Spaniard and write his name Ortiz. The only fully authenticated printed work of Ory is his "Alexipharmacum" (Paris, 1544; Venice, 1551–58). In the second part he uses against the heretics five words of St. Paul, viz. grace, justification, sin, liberty, law (no exclusive reference to I Cor., xiv, 19). Other works attributed to him are: "Opusculum de imaginibus", and "Septem scholæ contra hæreticos", but Echard does not assign the places or dates of their publication.

QUÉTIF AND ECHARD, *Scriptores Ord. Præd.*, II (Paris, 1721), 162; SIXTUS SENENSIS, *Bibliotheca Sancta* (Venice, 1566; Lyons, 1591); ORLANDINI, *Historiæ Societatis Jesu pars prima, sive Ignatius* (Rome, 1615); THOMPSON, *Saint Ignatius Loyola* (London, 1910), 65; in the alphabetical index to this work Ory is called Ortiz. See IGNATIUS LOYOLA.

D. J. KENNEDY.

Osage Indians. See SIOUX.

Osaka, DIOCESE OF (OSACHENSIS). Osaka (*Oye*, great river; *saka*, cliff), one of the three municipal prefectures (*ken*) of Japan, is situated on both banks of the Yodo River and along the eastern shore of Osaka Bay. The second city in Japan in population, it far outstrips all other cities of the empire in wealth, commerce, and industries. The name Osaka apparently dates only from about 1492; previously the town was called *Naniwa* ("dashing waves", still used in poetry). According to our earliest information concerning the town, not undoubtedly genuine, it received its original name from Jinmu, first Emperor of Japan, who landed there about 660 B. C. In A. D. 313 Emperor Nintoku made it his capital. Various subsequent emperors (e. g. Kotoku in 645 and Shomu in 724) also resided there, but it was only after it had become in the sixteenth century a great Buddhist religious centre that the wealth and importance of the city began rapidly to increase. Fortified in 1534, it was the chief stronghold of the Buddhists during the bloody persecution to which they were subjected under Nebunaga. All efforts to dislodge them failed until, in obedience to the order of the emperor, they yielded up possession of the town in 1580. The true founder of the modern prosperity and importance of Osaka was undoubtedly Hideyoshi (see JAPAN). Recognizing that the strategic position of the town would enable him to dominate the *daimyos* of the south and west, he determined to make Osaka his capital, and built on the site of the great Buddhist monastery the Castle of Osaka—an admirable example of old Japanese architecture. The palace which he built within this castle has been placed by some authorities among the most glorious the world has ever seen; it was deliberately burned by the Tokugawa party in 1868, before they retreated to Yedo (now Tokio). Hideyoshi devoted himself sedulously to the improvement of the town, laying out new streets and causing the wealthy merchants of Fushumi and Sakai to immigrate thither. Situated in the middle of the richest agricultural district of Japan, the growth of Osaka has been unceasing during the last three centuries, although its commercial supremacy was for a time imperilled when the seat of government was transferred from Kioto to Yedo (1868). In 1871 a mint was established in Osaka, its manage-

CASTLE, OSAKA, JAPAN

ment being entrusted to European officials. The port was opened to foreign trade in 1868, but, as the harbour was poor and unsuitable for large vessels, Kobé (20 miles west) attracted most of the foreign commerce especially after the establishment of railway connexion between the cities in 1873. At present, however, an extensive scheme of improvement to render the harbour capable of accomodating the largest vessels is being executed, and, on its completion, Osaka will take first place in foreign, as in internal commerce. Judging from the rapid growth of its population (821,235 in 1898; 1,226,590 in 1908), Osaka should be in the near future the real metropolis of Japan. Intersected by a myriad of canals, the city is often called the "Venice of the East", while its numerous industries, among which cotton-spinning occupies a leading position, has won it the title of the "Manchester of Japan".

The diocese embraces the territory stretching from Lake Biwa and the confines of the imperial provinces of Jetchidzen, Mino, and Owari to the western shores of the island of Nippon, together with the adjacent islands (except Shikoku) belonging to this territory. While it was St. Francis Xavier's intention to proceed directly to Miako (the modern Kioto), then the religious and political capital of Japan, it was not until 1559 that Christianity was first preached in the territory by Father Gaspar Vilela, S.J., founder of the Church in Miako. After converting about one hundred natives and fifteen bonzes, a plot against his life necessitated his temporary withdrawal, and the civil war, which for some years devastated the capital, afforded little opportunity for cultivating further the seeds of Christianity. Peace being restored, Christianity began again to make headway, and in September, 1564, we find five churches erected in the neighbourhood of the capital. By 1574 the number of faithful included many in the shogun's palace and even one of his brothers-in-law. Between 1577 and 1579 the converts in the Miako region were estimated at between 9000 and 10,000. In 1582 the central provinces contained 25,000 faithful, ministered to by five fathers and nine brothers of the Jesuit Order. When Hideyoshi determined to transfer the seat of government from Kioto to Osaka, Father Organtino, S.J., in accordance with the advice of Justus Ukondono, a Christian noble, petitioned the Taiko for a site for a church. His request was granted and the first church in Osaka was opened at Christmas, 1583. By 1585 the number of nobles baptized at Osaka was sixty-five. On the issue of the Taiko's edict banishing the missionaries and closing the churches (see JAPAN), there were in the eighteen leagues between Miako and Sakai twenty churches and 35,000 faithful. Though no European met with martyrdom during the first persecution, the sufferings of the Christians were terrible; fifty churches and eight residences of the Jesuits in the central provinces were burned, although the churches in Osaka, Miako, and Sakai were spared. Henceforth until the Taiko's death the ministry had to be carried on secretly. In 1593 the Franciscan embassy from the Philippines arrived, and erected the Church of Our Lady of Portiuncula and a hospital for lepers in Miaho. In the next year Franciscans established the Convent of Bethlehem in Osaka. (Concerning the persecution following the San Felipe incident see JAPAN; NAGASAKI, DIOCESE OF.) From Hideyoshi's death (1598) to 1613, the Church in Japan enjoyed comparative peace. At the court of Hideyori, the successor of Hideyoshi, were numerous Christians, several of whom commanded his troops during the bombardment of Osaka (1615). A list of the Christians in Miaho, Fushumi, Osaka, and Sakai having been drawn up in 1613, a decree was published at Miaho on 11 Feb., 1614, ordering all to depart within five days. For details of the persecution, for which this decree was the signal and which within twenty-five years annihilated the Church in Japan, consult Deplace, "La Catholicisme au Japon", II (Mechlin, 1909). The first church in Osaka after the reopening of Japan to foreigners was erected by Father Cousin (now Bishop of Nagasaki) in 1869. The agnosticism of the Japanese and the general laxity of morals constitute formidable obstacles to the growth of Christianity. The mission is entrusted to the Paris Society of Foreign Missions. It was erected into a diocese on 16 March, 1888, the present bishop being Mgr Jules Chatron (elected 23 July, 1896). According to the latest statistics the diocese counts: 27 missionaries (3 native), 4 Marianite Brothers, 37 catechists, 16 sisters, 34 stations, 32 churches, 24 oratories, 4 schools with 419 pupils, 1 high-school with 100 pupils, 5 orphanages with 228 inmates, 32 hospitals, 3711 Christians.

For bibliography, see JAPAN and NAGASAKI.

THOMAS KENNEDY.

O Salutaris Hostia (O SAVING HOST), the first line of the penultimate stanza of the hymn, "Verbum supernum prodiens", composed by St. Thomas Aquinas for the Hour of Lauds in the Office of the Feast of Corpus Christi. This stanza and the final stanza, or doxology (*Uni trinoque domino*), have been selected to form a separate hymn for Benediction of the Most Blessed Sacrament. Usually, and most appropriately, it is begun either when the door of the tabernacle is opened or when the monstrance is being placed on the throne of exposition. In England the singing of the "O Salutaris" is enjoined in the "Ritus servandus", the code of procedure approved by a former synod of the Province of Westminster (see BENEDICTION OF THE BLESSED SACRAMENT). But the use of the hymn, not being prescribed in the rubrics, is not of universal obligation. It is, however, very generally used, although any other appropriate text is permissible, such as the "Adoro Te devote", the "Pange, lingua", the antiphon "O sacrum convivium" etc. While it is not forbidden to sing vernacular hymns at Benediction the "O Salutaris", being a liturgical text, cannot be sung in the vernacular (S.R.C., 27 Feb., 1882, Leavenworth. Cf. "Am. Eccl., Rev.", April, 1895, 341). The hymn is often chosen as a motet for solemn Mass, and may thus be used after the proper Offertory for the day has been sung or recited. An indefensible, but, fortunately, very rare, custom, perhaps inaugurated by Pierre de la Rue, the profound contrapuntal composer of the fifteenth century, was that of replacing the "Benedictus" at Mass by the "O Salutaris". Gounod imitated his example in his first "Mass of the Orphéonistes", but in his second mass of that name gives both the "Benedictus" and the "O Salutaris", as Rossini in his posthumous "Messe Solennelle" and Prince Poniatowski in his "Mass in F". The plain-song melody in the eighth mode is beautiful, and forms the theme of de la Rue's musical *tour de force* in the Mass of that title. The modern settings have been very numerous, although not always serviceable, inasmuch as many are too theatrical for church use; others are entirely for solo use, and still others probably violate the prescription of the Motu Proprio of 22 November, 1903, requiring that in hymns the traditional form be preserved. There are about twenty-five poetical versions of the hymn in English.

H. T. HENRY.

Osbald, King of Northumbria, d. 799. Symeon of Durham (Historia Regum) tells us that when Ecfwald, a pious and just king, took up the reins of government in Northumbria on the expulsion of Ethelred, Osbald with another eorlderman named Athelheard collected a force early in 780 at Seletune (probably Silton in the North Riding of Yorkshire), and set fire to the house of Bearn, whom Huntingdon and Wendover call the king's justiciary. In 793 the deacon Alcuin addressed an affectionate but forcible letter to King Ethelred, Osbald, and Osberct, whom he calls most dear friends and children, urging them to flee from vices which lead to destruction and practise virtues by which we ascend to heaven. He points out the terrible lesson to be learnt from the iniquities and consequent destruction of former rulers. When King Ethelbert, who had been liberated from exile and reigned seven years, was murdered on 19 April, 796, at Corbe or Corebrygge (Corbridge), Osbald the "patrician" was chosen by some of the nobles of his nation as king, but, after a reign of only twenty-seven days, deserted by all the royal following and the nobles, he fled and took refuge with a few others on the island of Lindisfarne. Eardulf was then recalled from exile and crowned in May at St. Peter's, York, and reigned for the next ten years. Probably, when at Lindisfarne, Osbald received the letter sent to him in 796 by Alcuin. In this the latter states that for more than two years he had endeavoured to persuade Osbald to assume the monastic habit and fulfil the vow he had taken; but now he had gained a still worse reputation and more unhappy events had befallen him. He suspects him further of the murder of Ethelred, besides shedding the blood of nobles and people alike. He urges him not to add sin to sin by attempting his restoration to power. It would be more to his shame to lose his soul than to desert his impious comrades. Rather he should endeavour to the utmost to gain the reward not only of his own conversion, but that of others who are in exile with him. Finally he begs him frequently to have his letter read to him. Alcuin's advice bore fruit and Osbald with some brethren sailed from Lindisfarne to the land and king of the Picts. He became an abbot and, on his death, was buried in the church at York.

Symeon of Durham's Historia Regum, Surtees Soc., LI (1868), pp. 25, 37, 211, 219 (also in the Rolls Series); Alcuin's Letters in P. L., C–CI, nn. xi and lxi and notes; Monumenta Alcuin, ed. JAFFÉ (Berlin, 1864), 184–195, 305.

S. ANSELM PARKER.

Osbaldeston, EDWARD, VENERABLE, English martyr, b. about 1560; hanged, drawn, and quartered at York, 16 November, 1594. Son of Thomas Osbaldeston, and nephew of Edward Osbaldeston, of Osbaldeston Hall, Blackburn, Lancashire, he went to the English College of Douai, then at Reims, where he was ordained deacon in December, 1583, and priest 21 September, 1585. He was sent on the mission 27 April, 1589, and was apprehended at night through the instrumentality of an apostate priest named Thomas Clark at an inn at Tollerton, Yorkshire, upon St. Jerome's day, 30 September, 1594. He had said his first Mass on the feast day of St. Jerome, and in consequence had a great devotion to the saint. The day following his arrest he was taken to York, where he was tried at the next assizes and attainted of high treason for being a priest. Bishop Challoner prints the greater part of a letter addressed by the martyr to his fellow-prisoners in York Castle, the full text of which is still extant, and which reveals the great humility and serene trust in God with which he anticipated his death.

CHALLONER, Memoirs of Missionary Priests, I, no. 106; KNOX, First and Second Douay Diaries (London, 1878); Catholic Record Society's Publications, IV (London, 1907); Bibl. Dict. Eng. Cath., V.

JOHN B. WAINEWRIGHT.

Osbern, hagiographer, sometimes confused with Osbert de Clare alias Osbern de Westminister, b. at Canterbury and brought up by Godric, who was dean from 1058–80. He became a monk, and later, prior of Christ Church, and was ordained by Archbishop Lanfranc. He died probably between 1088 and 1093. He was very skilful in music and is said to have written two treatises "De re musica" and "De vocum consonantiis" (Fétis, "Biog. Music.", Paris, 1870, VI, 383). But he is known best as a translator of saints' lives from the Anglo-Saxon and as an original writer. William of Malmesbury (Gesta Regum, II, 166) praises the elegance of his style. Works: 1. "Vita S. Alphegi et de translatione S. Alphegi", written at Lanfranc's command, about 1080 when there arose some dispute concerning Alphege's sanctity; it is printed in "Acta SS.", April, II, 631; in Mabillon, "Acta SS. O.S.B.", sæc. vi, 104; in P. L., CXLIX, 375; in Wharton, "Anglia Sacra", II, 122; see "Gesta Pontificum", in Rolls Series, 1870, p. 33. 2. "Vita S. Dunstani" and "Liber Miraculorum Sancti Dunstani", written in 1070; printed in Mabillon op. cit., sæc. v, 644–84; in "Acta SS.", May, IV, 359; in P. L., CXXXVII, 407; and in Stubbs, "Memorials of St. Dunstan". The life given in Mabillon, op. cit. (p. 684), is probably the work of Eadmer. 3. "Vita S. Odonis archiepiscopi Cantuariensis". From William of Malmesbury's "Gesta Pontif.", in Rolls Series 1870, p. 24, we learn that Osbern wrote Odo's life, but the work has perished; the life in P. L., CXXXIII, 831 and Mabillon, op. cit., sæc. v, 287 is not his. Wharton, in his "Anglia Sacra" (London, 1691), 75–87 published a life of St. Bregwin which was wrongly attributed to Osbern.

STUBBS, Memorials of S. Dunstan in Rolls Series: introduction and life; HARDY, Descrip. Catal. of British History (1865); WRIGHT, Biog. Brit. Lit. Anglo-Norman (London, 1846); 26; KINGSFORD in Dict. Nat. Biog. (London, 1909), s. v.; CEILLIER, Auteurs sacrés (Paris, 1858), s. v.

S. ANSELM PARKER.

Oscott (ST. MARY'S COLLEGE).—In 1793, a number of the Catholic nobility and gentry of England formed a committee for the establishment of a school for the education of their sons and the clergy in an English atmosphere. The buildings at Oscott, intended for the bishop's residence, were accepted for the projected institution by agreement with Bishop Thomas Talbot, Vicar Apostolic of the Midland District. Oscott (anciently Auscot) is a hamlet in the Perry Barr township, in the parish of Handsworth, about four miles north of Birmingham, and at the extreme south of Staffordshire. A mission had been founded there at the close of the seventeenth century by Andrew Bromwich, a confessor of the faith.

Dr. John Bew, sometime president of St. Gregory's College, Paris, was nominated president in February, 1794. The first three boys entered in May, and the establishment was formally opened in November as a college for boys and ecclesiastics under the joint management of a committee of laymen and the bishop of the district. Structural additions were made, and the total number of boys rose to thirty-five. The outlook was gloomy, and when in 1808, the college with its liabilities was offered to Bishop Milner, he accepted it not without reluctance. Thus ended the "Old Government". The "New Government", under Milner's strenuous guidance, with Thomas Potts as president (1808–15) and Thomas Walsh (afterwards bishop of the district) as spiritual director, speedily changed the aspect of affairs. Milner invigorated the discipline, and improved the studies and liturgical observances. Important additions were made to the building, and the chapel of the Sacred Heart, the first on English soil, was opened in 1820. Francis Quick, a convert, held the office of president from 1816 to 1818. On the death of Bishop Milner in 1826, the president, Thomas Walsh (1818–1826) became Vicar Apostolic of the Midland District, and Henry Weedall became president (1825–40). Under the direction of the pious and courteous Weedall, the man who more than any other created the spirit of Oscott, the institution progressed till the buildings were no longer able to accommodate the number of pupils. Plans of a new college, on the lines of Wadham College, Oxford, were prepared by Joseph Potter, the cathedral architect of Lichfield. A rich and providential bequest, together with the gifts of the clergy and faithful, supplied the means; and in less than three years a stately Gothic pile arose on an eminence two miles from the old college. The new edifice is situated at the extreme north of Warwickshire, some six miles from the centre of Birmingham, and was built on a piece of ground overgrown with heather and gorse at the edge of the Sutton Coldfield common. The name of Oscott has been transferred to the new site, previously associated with the name of Jordan's Grave. Bishop Wiseman succeeded Weedall in 1840. His reputation as a scholar and his knowledge of men and affairs made his appointment in the early days of the Oxford Movement most opportune. During the forties and onwards, Oscott afforded the incoming clergymen from the Establishment a welcome, a home, and a place of study. In those years we meet with the names of Le Page Renouf, St. George Mivart, John Brande Morris, H. M. Walker, T. Wilkinson, D. H. Haigh, C. Cholmondely, E. Estcourt, B. Smith etc. Augustus Welby Pugin, himself a convert, taught and worked at Oscott. The saintly Passionist Father Dominic was received there when he came over from Italy to convert England in November, 1840. Father Ignatius Spencer resided and exercised a fruitful apostolate in the college from 1839 to 1846. Cardinal Newman referred gratefully to the fact that just after he had been received into the Church by Father Dominic at Littlemore, he "at once found himself welcomed and housed at Oscott." In February, 1846, Newman and his community removed to Old Oscott at the suggestion of Bishop Wiseman. Newman called the old college "Maryvale", a name which it still bears. There they remained till 1849.

Henry F. C. Logan was president from 1847 to 1848, John Moore from 1848 to 1853, and Mgr Weedall from 1853 to 1859. The first Provincial Synod of the restored hierarchy of Westminster took place at Oscott in the summer of 1852, on which occasion Dr. Newman preached the sermon entitled "The Second Spring". The second and third Provincial Synods were likewise held there in 1855 and 1859. After the presidency of George Morgan (1859–60) a distinguished period in the life of the college opened in the autumn of 1860, with the appointment of James Spencer Northcote. A scholar, a gentleman, an ideal educator, brought up amid the culture of Oxford, and since his conversion in 1846 saturated with the spirit of ancient Christian Rome, he was eminently the man for the time. He developed the scholastic work of the college, and brought it into line with the non-Catholic public schools. In 1863 Cardinal Wiseman and Mgr. Manning took part in the celebration of the silver jubilee of the new college. After Northcote's retirement in 1877 on account of ill health, John Hawksford (1877–80), Edward Acton (1880–4), and Mgr. J. H. Souter (1885–9) carried on and expanded the tradition they had inherited. But a new fashion, the memory doubtless of the Fitzgerald v. Northcote trial, and of the two outbreaks of sickness in the sixties, and the opening of the Oratory School at Edgbaston (May, 1859) under the direction of Dr. Newman, told against them. The roll of students declined steadily, and notwithstanding the enthusiastic celebration of the golden jubilee of the new college in 1888, the venerable institution was closed in July, 1889, to be opened in the September following as the ecclesiastical seminary for the Diocese of Birmingham.

The high prestige which St. Mary's College enjoyed for so long a time is due to the number of distinguished families of England, Ireland, and other countries, whose sons were educated within its walls, and to the solid piety and fine courteous tone by which Oscotians were recognised. Oscott counts among its *alumni* one cardinal and twenty bishops, many members of Parliament, and others distinguished in the diplomatic and military services.

In accord with the movement promoted by the early provincial synods of Westminster, Bishop Ullathorne established in 1873 the Birmingham diocesan seminary at Olton, a few miles south of Birmingham. He placed the Rev. Edward Ilsley (now bishop of the diocese) over it as rector, while he himself personally directed its spirit. The institution flourished, though the number of students averaged but twenty. Meanwhile Oscott maintained its own school of philosophers and theologians. Oscott, like Olton, suffered from financial strain. With a bold stroke Bishop Ilsley closed Oscott as a mixed college, sold the seminary buildings and estate, and gathered all his seminarists and teaching staff into the one greater seminary of St. Mary's, Oscott. The new institution began with thirty-six students in September, 1889, under the rectorship of the bishop. Subjects from other dioceses arrived, and in a year or two a maximum of eighty-six was reached. This success, combined with the advantages of a central position, a splendid site, commodious buildings, a beautiful chapel, and a rich library, led in 1897 to the conversion of Oscott, on the urgent initiative of Cardinal Vaughan, into a central seminary for seven of the midland and southern dioceses of England, with Mgr. H. Parkinson as rector. The institution did its work well and progressively until the death of Cardinal Vaughan, when a new policy of concentration of diocesan resources commended itself to the ecclesiastical authorities, and the dissolution of the central seminary followed in 1909. From that date Oscott has continued its earlier work as the diocesan seminary, though admitting, as had been its custom, subjects from other dioceses. In the Birmingham seminary the lectures in theology and philosophy have invariably been given in Latin, and the usual scholastic discussions have supplemented the lectures. The course has been gradually improved by the extension of philosophy to three years, by the addition of two years of physical science in connexion with philosophy. Ascetical theology has been taught regularly since 1873. Hebrew, Greek, Elocution, the history of philosophy and of religion, and also social science take their proper places in the curriculum. "Recreative" lectures by outsiders are frequently given, and the "Exchange" lectures, delivered alternately at Stonyhurst and at Oscott by the professors of each institution, have provided fruitful opportunities of intercourse.

The interior aspect of the college is like a glimpse of the old Catholic world. The windows of the cloisters and refectory are blazoned with the armorial bearings of ancient Catholic families. The walls are adorned with 260 oil paintings of religious subjects, mainly the gift of John, sixteenth Earl of Shrewsbury. Its libraries of 30,000 volumes include the "Harvington" library, dating back to the middle of the eighteenth century, the "Marini" library, purchased in Rome for the college in 1839 at the cost of £4,000, a valuable collection of early printed books, early books on the English Martyrs, the "Kirk" collection, MSS. and pamphlets, and the "Forbes" collection of Oriental and other memoirs, consisting in all of sixty large folio volumes. Among the numerous treasures of ecclesiastical art may be mentioned the collection of embroidery of the fifteenth, sixteenth, and seventeenth centuries, the silver-gilt monstrance by an Antwerp artist of 1547, valued at £2,000, and the massive bronze lectern (early sixteenth century) from St. Peter's Louvain, which is an artistic achievement of the highest excellence.

THE OSCOTIAN, 1825–28, new series, 1881–88, third series, 1900; HUSENBETH, *The History of Sedgley Park School* (London, 1856); IDEM, *Life of Mgr. Weedall* (London, 1860); IDEM, *Life of Milner* (Dublin, 1862); GREANEY, *The Buildings, Museum etc., of St. Mary's College, Oscott* (Birmingham, 1899); IDEM, *A Catalogue of the Works of Art and Antiquity of St. Mary's College* (Birmingham, 1880); PARKINSON, *St. Mary's College, Oscott* in *The Catholic University Bulletin* (March and April, 1909); WARD, *The Life and Times of Cardinal Wiseman* (London, 1897).

HENRY PARKINSON.

Osee.—NAME AND COUNTRY : Osee (Hêshêá'—Salvation), son of Beeri, was one of the Minor Prophets, and a subject of the Ephraimite Kingdom which he calls "the land", whose king is for him "our king", and the localities of which are familiar to him, while he speaks of Juda but seldom and does not even make mention of Jerusalem.

TIME OF HIS MINISTRY:—According to the title of the book, Osee prophesied during the reign of Jeroboam II in Israel, and in the time of Ozias, Joatham, Achaz, and Ezechias, kings of Juda, hence from about 750 to 725 B. C. The title, however, is not quite satisfactory and does not seem to be the original one, or, at least, to have been preserved in its primitive form. None of the historical allusions with which the prophecy is filled appears to be connected with any event later than the reign of Manahem (*circa* 745–735); there is nothing concerning the Syro-Ephraimite war against Juda, nor the terrible intervention of Tiglath-Pileser III (734–733). The era of the Prophet, therefore, if it is to be judged from his writings, ought to be placed about 750–735; he was perhaps contemporaneous with the closing years of Amos and certainly with the first appearance of Isaias. The reign of Jeroboam II was marked by great and glorious external prosperity; but this prosperity contributed to make the political and religious decadence more rapid. Political dissolution was approaching. Zachary, son of Jeroboam, was assassinated after a reign of six months. His murderer, Sellum, retained the sceptre but one month, and was put to death by Manahem, who occupied the throne for ten years, 745–735. Israel was hastening to its ruin, which was to be completed by the taking of Samaria by Sargon (722).

THE BOOK OF OSEE:—It always occupies the first place among the twelve minor prophets, most probably on account of its length. In point of time Amos preceded it. The book is divided into two distinct parts: cc. i–iii, and cc. iv–xiv. (a) In the first part, Osee relates how, by order of Jahve, he wedded Gomer, a "wife of fornications", daughter of Debelaim, in order to have of her "children of fornications":—symbols, on the one hand, of Israel, the unfaithful spouse who gave to Baal the homage due to Jahve alone; and, on the other, figures of the children of Israel, who in the eyes of Jahve, are but adulterous children. The outraged husband incites the children against their guilty mother, whom he prepares to punish: while for the children themselves is reserved a fate in keeping with their origin. The first is named Jezrahel—the reigning dynasty is about to expiate the blood shed by its ancestor Jehu in the valley of Jezrahel. The second is a daughter, Lô-Ruhamah, "disgraced" Jahve will be gracious no more to his people. The third is called Lô-Ammî, "not my people"—Jahve will no longer recognize the children of Israel as his people. However, mercy will have the last word. Osee is commanded to receive Gomer again and to prepare her, by a temporary retirement, to renew conjugal intercourse—Israel was to prepare herself in captivity to resume with Jahve the relationship of husband and wife.

Is the marriage of Osee historical or purely allegorical? The hypothesis most in favour at present says that the marriage is historical, and the grounds for it are, (1) the obvious sense of the narrative; (2) the absence of any symbolical sense in the words Gomer and Debelaim; (3) that the second child is a daughter. It appears to us, however, with Davidson (Hastings, "Dict. of the Bible", II, 421 sqq.) and Van Hoonacker, that the first reason is not convincing. A careful reading of cc. i–iii discloses the fact that the action is extremely rapid, that the events are related merely in order to express a doctrine, and, moreover, they appear to take place within the single time requisite to one or two speeches. And yet, if these events are real, a large part of the Prophet's life must have been spent in these unsavoury circumstances. And again, the names of the children appear to have been bestowed just at the time that their meaning was explained to the people. This is especially the case with regard to the last child: "Call his name, Not my people: for you are not my people. . . ." Another reason for doubting this hypothesis is that it is difficult to suppose that God ordered His Prophet to take an unfaithful wife merely with a view to her being unfaithful and bearing him adulterous children. And how are we to explain the fact that the prophet retained her notwithstanding her adultery till after the birth of the third child, and again received her after she had been in the possession of another? That the second child was a daughter may be explained by dramatic instinct, or by some other sufficiently plausible motive. There remain the names Gomer and Debelaim. Van Hoonacker proposes as possible translations: consummation (imminent ruin), doomed to terrible scourges; or, top (of perversity), addicted to the cakes of figs (oblations offered to Baal). Nestle also translates *Bath Debelaim* by daughter of the cakes of figs, but in the sense of a woman to be obtained at a small price (Zeitsch. für alttest. Wissenschaft, XXIX, 233 seq.). These are but conjectures; the obscurity may be due to our ignorance. Certain it is at least that the allegorical meaning, adopted by St. Jerome, satisfies critical exigencies and is more in conformity with the moral sense. The doctrinal meaning is identical in either case and that is the only consideration of real importance.

(b) The second part of the book is the practical and detailed application of the first. Van Hoonacker divides it into three sections, each of which terminated with a promise of salvation (iv–vii, 1a . . . vii, 1b . . . xi . . . xii–xiv). We may accept this division if we also admit his ingenious interpretation of vi, 11—viii, 1a:—And yet Juda, I shall graft on thee a branch (of Ephraim) when I shall re-establish my people; when I shall heal Israel. In the first section he speaks almost exclusively of religious and moral corruption. The princes and especially the priests are chiefly responsible for this and it is on them that the punishment will principally fall; and as he speaks simply of the "house of the king" it would appear that the dynasty of Jehu still occupied the throne. It is different in the following chapters. In vii, 1a–viii, the political and social disorders are especially emphasized. At home there are conspiracies, regicides, anarchy, while abroad alliances with foreign powers are sought. No doubt Menahem was already reigning. And yet the religious disorders remained the principal object of the prophet's reprobation. And in spite of all, mercy ever retains its prerogatives. Jahve will gather together again some day His scattered children. In the last section it is felt that the final catastrophe is close at hand; and, nevertheless, once again, love remains victorious. The book ends with a touching exhortation to the people to turn to God who on His part promises the most tempting blessings. An epiphonema reminds at last every one that the good and the wicked shall receive the retribution each has merited.

STYLE AND TEXT.—St. Jerome has described in a few words the style of our Prophet: "Osee commaticus est, et quasi per sententias loquens." (P. L., XXVIII, 1015.) An intense emotion overpowers the Prophet at the sight of his dying country. He manifests this grief in short broken phrases with little logical sequence, but in which is revealed a tender and afflicted heart. Unfortunately the notorious obscurity of the Prophet hides many details from our view; this obscurity is due also to many allusions which we cannot grasp, and to the imperfect condition of the text. The question has been raised as to whether we possess it at least in its substantial integrity. Some critics claim to have discovered two main series of interpolations; the first, of small extent, consists of texts relative to Juda; the second, which is of far greater importance, consists of the Messianic passages which, it is said, lie outside the range of the prophet's vision. It is possible to detect several probable glosses in the first series: the second assertion is purely arbitrary. The Messianic texts have all the characteristics of Osee's style; they are closely connected with the context and are entirely in accordance with his general doctrines.

TEACHING.—It is fundamentally the same as that of Amos:—the same strict Monotheism, the same ethical conception which paves the way for the *Beati pauperes* and the worship which must be in spirit and in truth. Only Osee lays much more stress on the idolatry which perhaps had been increased in the interval and was in any case better known to the Ephraimite Prophet than to his Judean predecessor. And Amos had in return a much more extended historical and geographical horizon. Osee sees but the dying Israel. His characteristic point of view is the bond between Jahve and Israel. Jahve is the spouse of Israel, the bride of Jahve,—a profoundly philosophical and mystical image which appears here for the first time and which we find again in Jeremias, Ezechiel, Canticle of Canticles, Apocalypse, etc.

(a) *The Ancient Alliance.*—Jahve has taken to Himself His spouse by redeeming her out of the bondage of Egypt. He has united Himself to her on Sinai. The bride owed fidelity and exclusive love, trust, and obedience to the spouse; but alas! how has she observed the conjugal compact? Fidelity.—She has prostituted herself to the Baals and Astartes, degrading herself to the level of the infamous practices of the Canaanite high places. She has worshipped the calf of Samaria and has given herself up to every superstition. No doubt she has also paid homage to Jahve, but a homage wholly external and carnal instead of the adoration which must be above all things internal and which He Himself exacts: "With their flocks, and with their herds they shall go to seek the Lord, and shall not find him . . ." (v, 6). "For I desired mercy and not sacrifice: and the knowledge of God more than holocausts" (vi, 6). Trust has failed in like manner. Costly alliances were sought with other nations as though the protection of the spouse were not sufficient: —"Ephraim hath given gifts to his lovers (viii, 9). He hath made a covenant with the Assyrians, and carried oil into Egypt" (Vulg., xii, 1). The very favours which she has received from Jahve in her ingratitude she ascribes to false gods. She said: "I will go after my lovers, that gave me my bread, and my water, my wool, and my flax" (Vulg., ii, 5). Obedience:—All the laws which govern the pact of union have been violated: "Shall I write to him [Ephraim] my manifold laws, which have been accounted as foreign" (viii, 12). It is a question here at least primarily of the Mosaic legislation. Osee and Amos in spite of contrary opinion knew at least in substance the contents of the Pentateuch. Anarchy is therefore rife in politics and religion: "They have reigned but not by me: they have been princes, and I knew not: of their silver, and their gold they have made idols to themselves" (viii, 4).

The root of all these evils is the absence of "knowledge of God" (iv–v) for which the priest especially and the princes are to blame, an absence of theoretical knowledge no doubt, but primarily of the practical knowledge which has love for its object. It is the absence of this practical knowledge chiefly that Osee laments. The Prophet employs yet another symbol for the bond of union. He sets forth in some exquisite lines the symbol of the chosen son. Jahve has given birth to Israel by redeeming it out of the bondage of Egypt. He has borne it in his arms, has guided its first feeble steps and sustained it with bonds of love; he has reared and nourished it (xi, 1 sq.) and the only return made by Ephraim is apostasy. Such is the history of the covenant. The day of retribution is at hand; it has even dawned in anarchy, civil war, and every kind of scourge. The consummation is imminent. It would seem that repentance itself would be unable to ward it off. As later Jeremias, so now Osee announces to his people with indescribable emotion the final ruin: Jezrahel "Disgraced", "Not my people." The children of Israel are about to go into exile, there they "shall sit many days without king, and without prince, and without sacrifice, and without altar, and without ephod and without teraphim" (iii, 4). National authority shall come to an end and public national religion will be no more.

(b) *The New Covenant.*—Yet the love of Jahve will change even this evil into a remedy. The unworldly princes, now separated from the people, will no longer draw them into sin. The disappearance of the external national religion will cause the idolatrous sacrifices, symbols, and oracles to disappear at the same time. And the road will be open to salvation; it will come "at the end of days". Jahve cannot abandon forever His chosen son. At the very thought of it He is filled with compassion and his heart is stirred within him. Accordingly after having been the lion which roars against his guilty people He will roar against their enemies, and His children will come at the sound of His voice from all the lands of their exile (xi, 10 sq.). It will be, as it were, a new exodus from Egypt. Juda will be reinstated and a remnant of the tribe of Ephraim shall be joined with him (vi, 11—vii, 1a). "The children of Israel shall return and shall seek the Lord their God, and David their king" (iii, 5). The new alliance shall never be broken: it shall be contracted in justice and in righteousness, in kindness and in love, in fidelity and knowledge of God. There shall be reconciliation with nature and peace among men and with God. Prosperity and unlimited extension of the people of God shall come to pass, and the children of this new kingdom shall be called the sons of the living God. Great shall be the day of Jezrahel (the day when "God will sow"); (ch. ii), ch. i, 1–3 (Vulg., i, 10—ii, 1) ought likely to be set at the end of ch. ii. Cf. Condamin in "Revue biblique", 1902, 386 sqq. This is an admirable sketch of the Church which Christ is to found seven and a half centuries later. The doctrine of Osee, like that of Amos, manifests a transcendence which his historical and religious surroundings cannot explain. *Digitus Dei est hic.*

Among Catholic commentaries cf. especially VAN HOONACKER, *Les douze petits prophètes* (Paris, 1908). Among Protestant works HARPER, *A Critical and Exegetical Commentary on Amos and Hosea* (Edinburgh, 1905), a commentary of Liberal tendencies.

JEAN CALÈS.

Osimo, DIOCESE OF (AUXIMANA), in the Province of Ascoli Piceno, Italy. Osimo was contained in the territory of the Donation of Pepin. In the conflicts between the popes and the Swabian emperors, it was Ghibelline; but remained faithful when in 1375, at the instigation of the Florentines, nearly all the cities of the Pontifical States rebelled against the Holy See. Among other rulers it had Pandolfo Malatesta (1416); Francesco Sforza (1435); and finally, Buccolino, who surrendered the city to the Holy See in 1494. Remnants of the Roman walls and baths still exist; the cathedral is of the eighth century, restored and enlarged by Bishop Gentilis (1205); the baptistery of the church of St. John the Baptist is notable; the communal palace possesses a collection of inscriptions; the Collegio Campana had among its students Leo XII and Pius VIII. Saints Florentius, Sisinnius, and Diocletius were martyrs of Osimo; the city venerates as its first bishop St. Leopardus, of unknown era; the first bishop of certain date is Fortunatus (649). Among its prelates were Vitalianus (743), and Gentilis (1177). Gregory IX transferred the see to Ricanati in 1240 to punish Osimo for its felony, but Bishop Rinaldo persuaded Urban IV to restore the see to Osimo, and the first bishop thereafter was St. Benvenuto Scotivoli (d. 1283), who was succeeded by Berardo Berardi, afterwards cardinal; C. Giovanni Uguccione (1320), who died in prison, for which reason the see was again suppressed, the bishops residing at Cingoli; Urban VI restored the diocese, and among its subsequent bishops were Antonino Ugolino Sinibaldi (1498); Cardinal Antonio M. Galli (1591); and the Dominican Cardinal Galamini (1620). Under

CATHEDRAL, OSIMO (XIII CENTURY)

Bishop Agostino Pipia, Benedict XIII re-established the Diocese of Cingoli, uniting it to that of Osimo.

Cingoli, an ancient city of Piceno, is frequently named in connexion with the war between Cæsar and Pompey; its cathedral of Santa Maria is of the seventeenth century; the Gothic church of Sant' Esuperanzio is a notable temple. The first known bishop of this see was Theodosius (495) succeeded by Julianus, who accompanied Pope Vigilius to Constantinople in 544; between the dates of Theodosius and Julianus is placed the incumbency of St. Esuperantius, whose history is legendary. No other bishops of Cingoli are known. The Diocese of Osimo is subject directly to the Holy See; it has 34 parishes, with 49,200 inhabitants, 2 religious houses of men, and 4 of women, 2 schools for boys and 2 for girls.

CAPPELLETTI, *Le Chiese d'Italia*, VII; MARTORELLI, *Memorie storiche della città di Osimo* (Venice, 1705); COMPAGNONI, *Memorie della Chiesa e dei vescovi di Osimo* (Rome, 1782).

U. BENIGNI.

Osius. See HOSIUS OF CORDOVA.

Osma, DIOCESE OF (OXOMENSIS), borders Burgos and Logroño on the north, Soria and Saragossa on the east, Soria and Guadalajara on the south, and Segovia on the west; and includes the civil provinces of Soria and Burgos, with a small portion of Segovia. It is the ancient Uxama and has 1250 inhabitants. Burgo de Osma, the episcopal see, has 3000. The origin of the diocese is obscure: some refer it to St. James the Apostle, others to the reign of Constantine the Great. Flórez alleges it only as "probable" that it existed in the first centuries, when bishops, to escape persecution, used to establish their sees in obscure places; hence it might have been selected rather than Clunia, the capital of a judicial district. John, Bishop of Osma, signed the acts of the Synod of Toledo, in 597; Gregory signed at the synod of 610; Gila signed the acts of the fourth and fifth Councils of Toledo, and sent as his delegate to the eighth, Godescalchus, who afterwards succeeded him, and signed the eleventh; Severian signed at the twelfth, and Sonna at the thirteenth and sixteenth. After the Arab invasion the bishops of Osma continued, as titulars, in Asturias: a letter against Adoptionism, addressed to Elipandus, Archbishop of Toledo, is signed by Eterius, Bishop of Osma, and Beatus, a priest. The "Chronicon Albedense" mentions Felmirus, Bishop of Osma, in the time of Alfonso III (821).

The succession was then lost until Fernán Gonzalez, Count of Castile, conquered Osma, placing in its see Silo, a monk of Arlanza. The place was again lost, and the see with it; but eventually Alfonso VI called in the Cluniacs, under Bernardo Salvitá (later Archbishop of Toledo), and made Pierre de Vituris, a French monk, Bishop of Osma. Then began protracted boundary disputes with the Bishops of Oca and of Burgos, compromised at the Council of Husillos, in Palencia, in 1088; others followed with the Bishops of Sigüenza and of Tarazona, to whose jurisdiction Alfonso the Fighter assigned the territory taken from Castile, finally settled in the time of Alfonso VII, at a council at Burgos, where Cardinal Guido was present as papal legate. After Vituris, the see was occupied by Pedro, formerly archdeacon of Toledo, canonized as St. Peter of Osma. Finding the old church in ruins he chose as the site for a new one El Espinar. His successor, the Frenchman, Raymond Salvitá, continued the boundary controversy and the building of the church, and, having been transferred to the See of Toledo, was succeeded by Beltrán (1128). To provide for the building of his church, Bishop Beltrán obtained a commutation of the Vow of Santiago for a visit and alms to Osma; he also founded the Confraternity of the True Cross, the brethren of which bound themselves to leave legacies for the building of the cathedral.

Bishop Diego de Acebes accompanied St. Dominic against the Albigenses. In 1232 Bishop Juan Dominguez, finding the cathedral again too small, rebuilt it, with the exception of some cloister chapels, still to be seen, spared out of respect for the memory of St. Peter of Osma. It is in the transition style from Romanesque to ogival, with later improvements and additions. Pedro Gonzalez, Cardinal de Mendoza, Bishop of Osma in 1478, built the marble pulpit. Bishop Pedro Acosta, who had previously occupied the See of Oporto, brought with him the Italian Giovanni di Juni, who (1540) embellished the re-table of the high altar with figures of St. Peter of Osma and St. Dominic, and also designed the university. Bishop Acosta founded (1557), in Aranda de Duero, the "Sancti Spiritus" convent of the Dominicans, and the chapel of the Santo Cristo del Milagro, originally designed as a chapel of St. Dominic de Guzmán. The organ on the right is the gift of Bishop Martin Carrillo in 1641, that on the left, of the chapter in 1765. The chapel of the Cristo del Milagro contains an altar and re-table, with an inscription giving the traditional legend, built by Bishop Andrés de Soto. With the assistance of Bishop García de Loaisa, Melendez de Gumiel, Dean of Osma, built the chapel of St. Peter, now the chief patron of the diocese. The chapel of Our Lady of the Thorn-bush, planned by Bishop Pedro Arastegui, corresponds to the Santo Christo. In 1506, Bishop Alonso Enriquez, rebuilt the cloisters. Between 1736 and 1744 Pedro Agustín de la Cuadra built the new tower adjoining the west wall in the Barocque style. Joaquín de Electa, confessor to Charles III, built a chapel for Juan de Palafox, Bishop of Osma, completed in 1781. The frescoes are by Mariano Maella.

The bishops of Osma were formerly lords of the city. At the petition of Bishop John II, Alfonso VIII issued a warrant confirming the lordship to the cathedral chapter, and left instructions that the lordship of Osma, with its castle, should be given to Bishop Mendo (1210–25) in recompense for his services at the battle of Las Navas de Tolosa (1212). King John I granted the castle of Osma to Bishop Pedro González de Frias, Bishop Pedro de Montoya surrounded Burgo with a wall, in 1456. Bishop Pedro Alvarez de Acosta founded the university at his own expense, and in 1578, adjacent to the cathedral, the consistorial buildings, prison, and public granary. Bishop Sebastian Perez (1582–83) transferred the seminary from the college of the university to the Casas del Cortijo (Farm Buildings), and Fernando de Acebedo (1610–15) began the Seminary of S. Domingo de Guzmán, which Bishop Joaquín Eleta reconstructed in 1783 after plans made by the engineer Sebastini. Sebastian de Arévalo rebuilt the Hospital of S. Agustín, founded in 1468 by Pedro de Montoya.

Soria, the capital, disputes with Osma the right to the episcopal see. There is the church of S. Pedro, restored by Alfonso I of Aragon, in 1108, and made collegiate in 1152 by John II, Bishop of Osma. Over the altar of the retro-choir is an "Entombment of Christ", by Titian. It was rebuilt by Bishop Acosta. Near Soria are the Romanesque ruins of the monastery of S. Juan de Duero and the hermitage of St. Saturius, patron of the city. The convent of La Merced at Soria once had for its superior the dramatist Gabriel Tellez (Tirso de Molina), to whom are due the building and painting of the sacristy of Nuestra Señora de la Merced.

CORVALÁN, *Descripción histórica del Obispado de Osma* (Madrid, 1788); DE QUIRÓS, *Vida de S. Pedro de Osma*; FLÓREZ, *España sagrada*, VII (Madrid, 1789); RABAL, *España, sus monumentos . . . Soria* (Barcelona, 1889); DE LA FUENTE, *Historia de las Universidades de España*, II (Madrid, 1885); *Biografía eclesiástica* (Madrid, 1848–68).

RAMÓN RUIZ AMADO.

Osmund, SAINT, Bishop of Salisbury, d. 1099; his feast is kept on 4 Dec. Osmund held an exalted position in Normandy, his native land, and according to a late fifteenth-century document was the son of Henry, Count of Séez, and Isabella, daughter of Robert, Duke of Normandy, who was the father of William the Conqueror (Sarum Charters, 373). With his uncle, the king, he came over to England, proved a trusty counsellor, and was made chancellor of the realm. The same document calls him Earl of Dorset. He was employed in many civil transactions and was engaged as one of the chief commissioners for drawing up the Domesday Book. He became Bishop of Sarum, virtually William's choice, by authority of Gregory VII and was consecrated by Lanfranc in 1078. This diocese comprised the Counties of Dorsetshire, Wiltshire, and Berkshire, for in 1058 the old Bishoprics of Sherborne and Ramsbury had been united under Bishop Hermann and the see transferred to Old Sarum. This is described as a fortress rather than a city, placed on a high hill, surrounded by a massive wall ("Gest. Pontif", 183) and Peter le Blois refers to the Castle and Church as "the ark of God shut up in the temple of Baal". In 1086 Osmund was present at the Great Gemôt held at Old Sarum when the Domesday Book was accepted and the great landowners swore fealty to the sovereign (see Freeman, "Norman Conquest"). He died in the night of 3 Dec., 1099, and was succeeded, after the see had been vacant for eight years, by Roger, a crafty and time-serving statesman. His remains were buried at Old Sarum, translated to New Salisbury on 23 July, 1457, and deposited in the Lady Chapel where his sumptuous shrine was destroyed under Henry VIII. A flat slab with the simple inscription MXCIX has lain in various parts of the cathedral. In 1644 it was in the middle of the Lady Chapel. It is now under the eastern-most arch on the south side.

Osmund's work was threefold:—(1) The building of the cathedral at Old Sarum, which was consecrated on 5 Apr., 1092. Five days afterwards a thunderstorm entirely destroyed the roof and greatly damaged the whole fabric. (2) The constitution of a cathedral body. This was framed on the usual Norman model, with dean, precentor, chancellor, and treasurer, whose duties were exactly defined, some thirty-two canons, a subdean, and succentor. All save the last two were bound to residence. These canons were "secular", each living in his own house. Their duties were to be special companions and advisers of the bishop, to carry out with fitting solemnity the full round of liturgical services and to do missionary work in the surrounding districts. There was formed a school for clergy of which the chancellor was the head. The cathedral was thoroughly constituted "the Mother Church" of the diocese, "a city set on a hill". Osmund's canons were renowned for their musical talent and their zeal for learning, and had great influence on the foundation of other cathedral bodies. (3) The formation of the "Sarum Use". In St. Osmund's day there were many other "Uses" (those of York, Hereford, Bangor, and Lincoln remained) and other customs peculiar to local churches, and the number was increased by the influx of Normans under William. Osmund invented or introduced little himself, though the Sarum rite had some peculiarities distinct from that of other churches. He made selections of the practices he saw round him and arranged the offices and services. Intended primarily for his own diocese, the Ordinal of Osmund, regulating the Divine Office, Mass, and Calendar, was used, within a hundred years, almost throughout England, Wales, and Ireland, and was introduced into Scotland about 1250. The unifying influence of the Norman Conquest made its spread more easy. It held general approval until in Mary's reign so many clergy obtained particular licences from Cardinal Pole to say the Roman Breviary that this became universally received. The "Register of St. Osmund" is a collection of documents without any chronological arrangement, gathered together after his time, divided roughly into two parts: the "Consuetudinary" (Rolls Series, 1–185, and in Rock, vol. III, 1–110), styled "De Officiis Ecclesiasticis", and a series of documents and charters, all more or less bearing on the construction of the cathedral at Old Sarum, the foundation of the cathedral body, the treasures belonging to it, and the history of dependent churches. The existing "Consuetudinary" was taken from an older copy, re-arranged with additions and modifications and ready probably when Richard Poore consecrated the cathedral at New Salisbury in 1225. A copy, almost verbatim the same as this, was taken from the older book for the use of St. Patrick's, Dublin, which was erected into a cathedral and modelled on the church at Sarum by Henry de Loundres who was bishop from 1213–28. This is given by Todd in the British Magazine (vols. xxx and xxxi).

William of Malmesbury in summing up Osmund's character says he was "so eminent for chastity that common fame would itself blush to speak otherwise than truthfully concerning his virtue. Stern he might appear to penitents, but not more severe to them than to himself. Free from ambition, he neither imprudently wasted his own substance, nor sought the wealth of others" (Gest. Pontif., 184). He gathered together a good library for his canons and even as a bishop did not disdain to transcribe and bind books himself. At one time Osmund thought Archbishop Anselm too unyielding and needlessly scrupulous in the dispute concerning investitures and in 1095 at the Council of Rockingham favoured the king. But after the Lateran Council in 1099, he boldly sided with the archbishop and the beautiful anecdote is related, showing his simple sincerity, how when Anselm was on his way to Windsor, Osmund knelt before him and received his forgiveness. He had a great reverence for St. Aldhelm who 300 years before as Bishop of Sherborne had been Osmund's predecessor. He officiated at the saint's translation to a more fitting shrine at Malmesbury and helped Lanfranc to obtain his canonization. Abbot Warin gave him a bone of the left arm of St. Aldhelm which he kept at Sarum where miracles were wrought. In 1228 the Bishop of Sarum and the canons applied to Gregory IX for Osmund's canonization but not until some 200 years afterwards on 1 Jan., 1457, was the Bull issued by Callistus III. In 1472 a special indulgence was granted by Sixtus IV for a visit to his cathedral on his festival and a convocation held in S. Paul's in 1481 fixed 4 Dec. as the day to commemorate him.

Acta SS., Jan., I; ROCK, *Church of Our Fathers* (London, 1853); JONES, *Register of St. Osmund* (Rolls Series, 1883 and 1884), with long and good introductions to each vol.; *Sarum Charters and Documents* (Rolls Series, London, 1891); MALMESBURY, *Gesta Pontif.* (Rolls Series), 95, 183–4, 424–429; IDEM, *Gesta Regum;* BUTLER, *Lives*, s. v. (London, 1833); EADMER, *Hist. Novorum*, I and II, in *P. L.*, CLIX; CEILLIER, *Auteurs sacrés*, s. v. (Paris, 1863). For the saint's canonization see WILKINS, *Concilia* (London, 1737), I, 561; III, 432, 613; BEKYNTON, *Correspondence*, I, 117 (Rolls Series).

S. ANSELM BARKER.

Osnabrück, DIOCESE OF (OSNABRUGENSIS), directly subject to the Holy See, comprises, in the Prussian Province of Hanover, the civil districts of Osnabrück and Aurich (excepting Wilhelmshaven) and that part of Hanover situated on the west of the Weser. In 1910 it numbered 12 deaneries, 108 parishes, 153 pastoral stations, 271 secular and 12 regular priests, 204,500 Catholics. As Apostolic administrator, the bishop is Vicar Apostolic of the Northern Missions of Germany and Prefect-Apostolic of Schleswig-Holstein (see GERMANY, VICARIATE APOSTOLIC OF NORTHERN). According to the Bull "Impensa Romanorum" (26 March, 1824), he is elected by the chapter of the cathedral, composed of a dean, six canons, and four vicars, elected in turn by the bishop and by the chapter. Among the higher educational institutions of the diocese is the Gymnasium Carolinum, founded by Charlemagne; similar schools are at Meppen, Papenburg, and Osnabrück. The only religious communities of men are the Capuchin convent at Klemenswerth and the Apostolic School of the Marists at Meppen. The religious orders of women include Benedictines, Borromeans, Franciscans, Ursulines, and others.

The Romanesque cathedral of Sts. Crispin and Crispinian was built at the beginning of the twelfth century, and replaced the wooden church erected by Charlemagne. Later it took on Gothic embellishments, and in time became a treasury of precious objects of medieval art. Other fine churches are St. John's, Osnabrück, with three naves, Transition style (1256-1592), the Sacred Heart church (1897-1901), and the churches in Iburg, Lingen, Meppen, Kloster-Oesede, Bissendorf, Norden, Salzbergen, and others.

HISTORY.—The foundation of the diocese is veiled in obscurity, for lack of authentic documents. Osnabrück is certainly the oldest see founded by Charlemagne in Saxony. The first bishop was St. Wiho (785-804); the second bishop, Meginhard, or Meingoz (804-33), was the real organizer of the see. The temporal possessions of the see, originally quite limited, grew in time, and its bishops exercised an extensive civil jurisdiction within the territory covered by their rights of immunity (q. v.). The temporal protectorate (Advocatia, Vogtei) exercised over so many medieval dioceses by laymen became after the twelfth century hereditary in the Amelung family, from whom it passed to Henry the Lion. After Henry's overthrow it fell to Count Simon of Tecklenburg and to his descendants, though the source of many conflicts with the bishops. In 1236 the Count of Tecklenburg was forced to renounce all jurisdiction over the town of Osnabrück, and the lands of the see, the chapter, and the parish churches. On the other hand, the bishop and chapter, from the thirteenth century on, spread their jurisdiction over many convents, churches, and hamlets. Scarcely any other German see freed itself so thoroughly from civil jurisdiction within its territory. The royal prerogatives were transferred little by little to the bishop, e. g., the holding of fairs and markets, rights of toll and coinage, forest and hunting rights, mining royalties, fortresses, etc., so that the bishop by the early part of the thirteenth century was the real governor of the civil territory of Osnabrück.

Among the prominent medieval bishops are Drogo (952-68); Conrad of Veltberg (1002); the learned Thietmar or Detmar (1003-22); Benno II (1067-88); Johann I (1001-10), who built the actual cathedral in place of the wooden one destroyed by fire in the time of his predecessor; Diethard I (1119-37) was the first bishop elected by the free choice of the cathedral clergy; Philip II (1141-73) ended the conflicts between his see and the Abbeys of Corvey and Hersfeld; Arnold (1137-1191) died a crusader before Akkon. In the time of Engelbert of Isenburg (1239-50), Bruno of Isenburg, and Conrad II of Rietberg (1269-97) the new orders of Franciscans, Dominicans, and Augustinians were received with favour. In the fourteenth and fifteenth centuries the power of the bishops waned before the increasing influence of the chapter, of the military servants (or knights) of the diocese, and of the town of Osnabrück. The latter sought to free itself from the bishop's sovereignty, but never became a free city of the empire. The see was almost continually engaged in warlike troubles and difficulties and had also to defend itself against the Bishops of Minden and Münster. From the fourteenth century on we meet many auxiliary bishops of Osnabrück, made necessary by the civil duties that absorbed the attention of the ordinary.

The successor of Bishop Conrad IV of Rietberg (1488-1508) was Eric of Brunswick (1508-32), simultaneously Bishop of Münster and Paderborn. He opposed the Reformers strongly and successfully. Franz of Waldeck (1533-53), also Bishop of Minden, acted, on the contrary, a very doubtful part. He offered little resistance to Lutheranism in Münster, though he vigorously opposed the Anabaptists; after 1543 he allowed in Osnabrück an evangelical service. But the chapter and the Dominicans opposed a German service that dispensed with all the characteristics of the Mass. In 1548 Bishop Franz promised to suppress the Reformation in Osnabrück, and to execute the Augsburg "Interim", but fulfilled his promise very indifferently; on his death-bed he received Lutheran communions. His successor, John IV of Hoya (1553-74), was more Catholic, but was succeeded by three bishops of a Protestant temper: Henry III of Saxony (1574-85), Bernhard of Waldeck (1585-91), and Philip Sigismund (1591-1623). Under them the Reformation overran nearly the whole diocese.

In 1624 Cardinal Eitel Frederick of Hohenzollern became Bishop of Osnabrück, and called in the Jesuits. But he had scarcely begun his work when he died, and left to his successor, Francis of Wartenberg (1625-61), the task of executing the Counter-Reformation (q. v.). The city-council was purified of anti-Catholic elements, and the former Augustinian convent was turned over to the Jesuits. The Edict of Restitution was executed successfully by him, and in 1631 he founded a university at Osnabrück. But in 1633 Osnabrück was captured by the Swedes, the university was discontinued, Catholic religious exercises suppressed, and the see (1633-51) administered by the conquerors. By the Peace of Westphalia, the bishop succeeded in preventing the secularization of the see, as contemplated by the Swedes. Nevertheless, it was stipulated that henceforth a Catholic and a Protestant bishop (of the Augsburg Confession) would alternately hold the see. During the rule of the Protestant bishop, always chosen from the House of Brunswick-Lüneburg, the spiritual government of the Catholics was committed to the Archbishop of Cologne. Wartenberg was made cardinal in 1660, and was succeeded by the Protestant married "bishop", Ernest Augustus (1661-98), who transferred the residence to Hanover. He was succeeded by the Catholic bishop, Prince Charles Joseph of Lorraine, Bishop of Olmütz, later Archbishop of Trier (1698-

1715). The Protestant Bishop Ernest Augustus (1715-21) was succeeded by Clemens August of Bavaria, Elector of Cologne (1721-61). The last bishop, Prince Frederick of England (1761-1803), later Duke of York, was, until his majority (1783), under the guardianship of his father, George III of England.

In 1803 the see, the chapter, the convents, and the Catholic charitable institutions were finally secularized. The territory of the see passed to Prussia in 1806, to the Kingdom of Westphalia in 1807, to France in 1810, and again to Hanover in 1814. Klemens von Gruben, titular Bishop of Paros, was made vicar Apostolic, and as such cared for the spiritual interests of the Catholic population. Under Leo XII the Bull "Impensa Romanorum Pontificum" (26 March, 1824) re-established the See of Osnabrück as an exempt see, i. e., immediately subject to Rome. This Bull, recognized by the civil authority, promised that, for the present, the Bishop of Hildesheim would be also Bishop of Osnabrück, but had to be represented at Osnabrück by a vicar-general and an auxiliary bishop, and this lasted for thirty years. Klemens von Gruben was succeeded by the auxiliary bishop Karl Anton von Lüpke, also administrator of the North German Missions. After his death new negotiations led to the endowment of an independent see. Pius IX, with the consent of King George V of Hanover, appointed Paulus Melchers of Münster, bishop, 3 August, 1857. In 1866 the territory of the diocese passed, with Hanover, to Prussia; Melchers became Archbishop of Cologne, and was succeeded in 1866 by Johannes Heinrich Beckmann (1866-78), who was succeeded by Bernard Höting (1882-98) after a vacancy of four years owing to the Kulturkampf (q. v.). The present bishop (1911), Hubert Voss, was appointed 12 April, 1899.

MÖSER, *Osnabrückische Geschichte* (Osnabrück, 1768), also in MÖSER's collected works, vols. VI-VIII (Berlin, 1843); SANDHOFF, *Antistitum Osnabrugensis ecclesiæ regesta* (2 parts, Münster, 1785); F. E. STÜVE, *Beschreibung und Geschichte des Hochstifts und des Fürstentums Osnabrück* (Osnabrück, 1789); C. STÜVE, *Gesch. des Hochstifts Osnabrück* (Jena and Osnabrück, 1853, 1872, 1882), three pts.; MEURER, *Das Bistum Osnabrück* (Münster, 1856); MÖLLER, *Gesch. der Weihbischöfe von Osnabrück* (Lingen, 1887); *Osnabrücker Urkundenbuch*, ed. by PHILLIPS AND BÄR (4 vols., Osnabrück, 1892-1902); JOSTES, *Die Kaiser- und Königsurkunden des Osnabrücker Landes* (Münster, 1899); *Osnabrücker Geschichtsquellen* (Osnabrück, 1891—); SOPP, *Die Entwicklung der Landesherrlichkeit im Fürstentum Osnabrück* (Idstein, 1902); HOFFMEYER, *Gesch. der Stadt und des Regierungsbezirks Osnabrück* (Osnabrück, 1904); JAEGER, *Die Schola Carolina Osnabrugensis* (Osnabrück, 1904); numerous papers in *Zeitschrift für vaterländische Gesch. und Altertumskunde* (Münster 1838—); and in *Mitteilungen des Vereins für Geschichte und Landeskunde von Osnabrück* (33 vols., Osnabrück, to 1909); *Elenchus cleri diœceseos Osnabrugensis pro 1910* (Osnabrück, 1910); WÜRM, *Führer von Osnabrück* (2nd ed., 1906).

JOSEPH LINS.

O sola magnarum urbium. See QUICUMQUE CHRISTUM QUÆRITIS.

Osrhoene. See ABGAR; EDESSA.

Ossat, ARNAUD D', French cardinal, diplomat, and writer, b. at Larroque-Magnoac (Gascony), 20 July, 1537; d. at Rome, 13 March, 1604, was the son of a blacksmith. He was sent to the College of Auch as tutor to the sons of a nobleman, then to Paris, where he became the pupil and friend of the famous Ramus, whom he defended in two pamphlets against Charpentier, rector of the university. He next studied law at Bourges under Cujas and became an advocate before the Parliament of Paris, while acting as tutor to Jean de la Barrière, the future reformer of the Feuillants. In 1572 he joined the household of Paul de Foix, Archbishop-elect of Toulouse, whom he accompanied on various embassies and finally to Rome. De Foix dying in 1584, d'Ossat remained at Rome, supervising the French embassy for a year, and then becoming secretary successively to Louis d'Este and Joyeuse, two cardinal protectors of the interests of France. In 1588 he refused the post of minister of foreign affairs to Henry III. Driven from Rome by the rupture of diplomatic relations after the murder of Cardinal de Guise (1588), he returned after the death of Henry III (1589) as the private agent of his widow, Louise de Vaudemont. He used his position to support the cause of Henry IV, whose conversion he prepared the pope to accept. As agent for that prince, co-operating with du Perron, he negotiated the reconciliation with the pope, which took place 19 Sept., 1595. This was the greatest act of d'Ossat's diplomatic career, assuring as it did the definitive triumph of Henry IV over the League, and the restoration of peace and prosperity to France after more than thirty years of civil war. D'Ossat was appointed Bishop of Rennes (1596), cardinal (1589), and finally Bishop of Bayeux. Remaining at Rome without any well-defined office, he was charged with occasional missions to Venice and Florence (1598), or managed the French embassy in the absence of the ambassador, and was always the enlightened and devoted representative of French interests. All the ambassadors of Henry IV had orders to make known to him the business with which they were charged and to be guided by his advice. Villeroy, the minister for foreign affairs, himself consulted him on all matters in anyway connected with Rome. Ossat, through his influence and talents, secured for Henry IV the pope's aid and, when necessary, induced the Holy See to accept, at least, without public protest, such measures as the expulsion of the Jesuits, the non-publication of the Council of Trent, the Edict of Nantes, the Franco-Turkish and Franco-English alliances, the annulment of Henry IV's marriage with Margaret of Valois, and the conclusion of that between the Duc de Bar and Catherine de Bourbon, Henry's sister and a stubborn Calvinist. At the same time d'Ossat used his influence at Rome for the benefit of the historian de Thou, the philosopher Montaigne, and the savant Peiresc. Clement VIII showed his esteem of Ossat by commanding that the cardinal's family should attend his obsequies with all the assistants at the pontifical throne. D'Ossat was buried in the church of St. Louis of the French, where his tomb is still to be seen. Bentivoglio, in his "Mémoires", says of him that never was a man more worthy of the hat because of his religious zeal, the integrity of his morals, and the eminence of his learning.

In the course of his diplomatic career d'Ossat wrote many letters and memoranda. Garnier de Mauléon edited some of them in 1614, when they were printed for the first time; several editions, largely augmented, afterwards appeared, the best being that of Amelot de la Haussaie, in 1708, which contains nearly 400 letters. Since then twenty-one letters have been published by Tamizey de Larroque, and eleven by the writer of this article. These letters formerly served as models for diplomats, owing not only to the importance of the questions which they treat, but especially to the talent for exposition which d'Ossat displays in them. The French Academy inscribed Ossat among the "dead authors who have written our French language most purely". Wiquefort in his "Mémoires sur les ambassadeurs" finds in them "the clearest and most enlightened judgment ever displayed by any minister", and Lord Chesterfield wrote to his son that the "simplicity and clearness of Cardinal d'Ossat's letters show how business letters should be written". Besides these letters his published works are: "Arnaldi Ossati in disputationem Jacobi Carpentarii de methodo" (4º, Paris, 1564) and "Arnaldi Ossati additio ad expositionem de methodo" (Paris, 1564).

D'ARCONVILLE, *Vie du cardinal d'Ossat* (Paris, 1771); DEGERT, *Le cardinal d'Ossat, évêque de Rennes et de Bayeux (1537–1604)* (Paris, 1894).

ANTOINE DEGERT.

Ossory, DIOCESE OF (OSSORIENSIS), in the Province of Leinster, Ireland, is bounded on the south by the Suir, on the east by the Barrow, on the west by Tipperary and King's County, and on the north by Queen's County. It has an area of 600,000 acres, and corresponds geographically with the ancient Kingdom of Ossory, whose first king, Aengus Osrithe, flourished in the second century of the Christian era. His successors extended their boundaries to include part of Tipperary. In the fifth century the neighbouring tribe of the Deisi, aided by the Corca-Laighde, conquered South Ossory, and for over a century the Corca-Laighde chiefs ruled in place of the dispossessed Ossory chiefs. Early in the seventh century the ancient chiefs recovered much of their lost possessions, the foreigners were overcome, and the descendants of Aengus ruled once more. One of the greatest was Carroll, prominent in the ninth century and distinguished in the Danish wars.

Ossory had been Christianized long before this. St. Kieran, its apostle, now the patron of the diocese, was born about the fourth century at a place now known as St. Kieran's Strand, near Cape Clear, and was probably converted to the Faith by foreign traders. According to the tradition, he went to Rome and was there ordained priest and bishop. Having met St. Patrick, St. Kieran received from him a bell with the charge to return to Ireland and found a monastery on the spot where the bell should first sound. When the saint had passed beyond Ossory, and was descending the western slopes of Slieve Bloom, the bell at length sounded; and here St. Kieran established the monastery of Seir-Kieran, the centre from which Ossory was evangelized. St. Patrick also visited Ossory and preached and founded churches there. There is some difficulty in accepting the story of St. Kieran having preached before St. Patrick, since the former is said to have flourished in the sixth century. It is, however, certain that St. Kieran laboured in Ossory. In the centuries following the newly-converted kingdom was ruled from Seir-Kieran by the abbots. They had other monasteries subject to them, and probably other bishops, and perhaps were not always bishops themselves, though at Seir-Kieran, as at Iona, there was always a bishop. Their jurisdiction was tribal rather than territorial, and hence the diocese was enlarged or contracted as the fortunes of the Ossory chiefs rose or fell. At the synod of Rathbreasail (1118) the limits of the diocese were permanently fixed substantially as they have since remained. At the same time the see was transferred from Seir-Kieran to Aghaboe (see CANICE, SAINT), but at the end of the twelfth century it was transferred to Kilkenny, where it has since remained. It is probable that St. Canice founded a monastery at Kilkenny, and not unlikely that the beginnings of a town soon appeared there, to become more important when the bishops changed from Aghaboe. Kilkenny also became the residence of Marshall, Earl of Pembroke, Strongbow's heir and descendant, by whom Kilkenny Castle was built. Before the fourteenth century Marshall's inheritance passed to the Butlers, and under them Kilkenny became great. It was made up of an Irish and an English town, each with a charter, and each, until 1800, returning two members to the Irish Parliament. The united towns were incorporated by a charter from Elizabeth, and by a further charter from James I, as a free city, with a mayor. The city still returns a member to the Imperial Parliament. The Butlers, ennobled as Earls and Dukes of Ormonde, have always interested themselves in its welfare. These powerful nobles were sometimes charged with the government of Ireland; not infrequently Kilkenny was the residence of the viceroy and saw a Parliament sitting within its walls, and there the Statute of Kilkenny was passed (1367). The Ormondes were always favourable to Anglo-Norman development at Kilkenny, and after the beginning of the thirteenth century no Irishman was appointed to the See of Ossory. In the reign of Bishop Hugh De Rous (1202–15) the cathedral of St. Canice was built. Two subsequent bishops, De Mapilton (1251–60) and Thomas Barry (1427–60), filled the office of treasurer of Ireland, while another, Richard De Northalis (1387–95), acted as the King's ambassador abroad. At the Reformation, though the Earls of Ormonde were among the first to conform, Ossory clung to the Faith; and when John Bale was appointed bishop by Edward VI, and endeavoured to Protestantize the people, he was roughly handled and driven from Kilkenny, leaving Ossory in peace. The peace ended with the death of Mary, and in Elizabeth's reign the see was vacant for seventeen years. From 1602 to 1618 Ossory was again without a bishop, and when Dr. Rothe was appointed (1620) there was not a

ST. MARY'S CATHEDRAL, KILKENNY

RUINS OF CISTERCIAN ABBEY AT JERPOINT
Diocese of Ossory, Co. Kilkenny, Ireland

Catholic bishop in Ireland. In the rebellion of 1641 Kilkenny was the centre of national resistance and the headquarters of the Catholic Confederation. The part played by Dr. Rothe was prominent and patriotic; but his best efforts were unavailing, for Ormonde was able to foment divisions, the Anglo-Irish and the old Irish would not blend for the common good, and the want of vigour in Catholic counsels prepared the way for Ormonde's treachery and Cromwell's victories. While the Cromwellians held Kilkenny, Rothe died there (1650), and for twenty years following Ossory was governed by vicars. During the few periods of toleration in the reign of Charles II a feeble revival of religion took place. In 1678 the bishop reported to Rome, that in many cases one priest was in charge of five or six parishes; that the few remaining Franciscans, Dominicans, Jesuits, and Capuchins ministered by stealth and in ruined churches; and that the Carmelites, Cistercians, and Canons Regular of St. Augustine had completely disappeared.

In the penal times Ossory suffered much, but its faith survived, and when toleration came it was ruled by an exceptional man, De Burgo (1759-86). Equally capable was his successor, Troy (1777-86), subsequently Archbishop of Dublin. To understand his praise of George III, his friendship with the viceroy and with Luttrell, son of the infamous Lord Carhampton, we must make allowance for the times in which he lived. He acted from no personal motive, but for the good of the Church, for he was zealous in propagating the Faith and enforcing discipline. He was among the first of the Irish bishops to take advantage of the relaxation of the penal laws and set up a college for his diocese by the purchase of Burrell's Hall, Kilkenny. Two of its first staff became his successors, Dr. Dunne (1787-89) and Dr. Lanigan (1789-1812). Under the latter the college at Burrell's Hall was transferred to more suitable premises and its curriculum extended. It was not until the episcopate of Dr. Kinsella that a diocesan college worthy of Ossory was founded. In 1836 the foundation stone of St. Kieran's College, Kilkenny, was laid and two years later the college was opened for students. Dr. Kinsella also aided his priests to build several parochial churches. He laid the foundation stone of the Cathedral of St. Mary in 1843, though the exterior was not finished until 1857, nor solemnly consecrated until 1899. Dr. Walsh (1846-72) succeeded Dr. Kinsella, and was succeeded by Dr. Moran, now (1911) Cardinal Archbishop of Sydney. Dr. Moran was succeeded, in 1884, by Dr. Brownrigg, a native of Carlow. Educated at Maynooth, Dr. Brownrigg displayed unusual ability, was ordained priest in 1861, and was subsequently professor at St. Peter's College, Wexford, and superior of the House of Missions at Enniscorthy.

No diocese in Ireland is more interesting than Ossory for historical and antiquarian remains. There are the relics of old churches associated with the lives and acts of the early Irish saints, such as those of Seir-Kieran and Aghaboe. There are round towers, Norman castles, and holy wells, raths and mounds, ancient forts, cromlechs, and pillar stones. In the parish of Danesfort is Burnchurch castle, in Durrow the castle of Cullahill. There are the ruins of Kells Priory and of Inistioge, the Dominican priory of Rosebercon, and the Cistercian abbey of Jerpoint. Kilkenny Castle is an interesting relic of history, and near by are the remains of the Franciscan abbey, the Black Abbey, and St. John's priory. The number of distinguished men connected with the diocese is large. Clyn and Grace, the annalists, were both of Kilkenny. Rothe was not only a public man, but an author of eminence. De Burgo's work on the Irish Dominicans is still an essential book for Irish historians. Other famous men are: James Butler, Archbishop of Cashel, author of "Butler's Catechism"; Dr. Minogue, Bishop of Sacramento; Dr. Ireland, Archbishop of St. Paul's; Dr. O'Reilly, Archbishop of Adelaide; Dr. John O'Donovan; Dr. Kelly, for many years professor of ecclesiastical history at Maynooth; Dr. O'Hanlon, theological professor in the same college; Dr. MacDonald, his successor; and Dr. Carrigan, whose "History of Ossory" is the most complete history of any Irish diocese. In 1910 the diocese contained: 41 parishes; 36 parish priests; 5 administrators; 58 curates; 11 regulars (a total of 119 priests); 96 churches; 1 college; 4 houses of regulars; 15 convents; 4 houses of Christian Brothers. In 1901 the Catholic population was 83,519; the non-Catholic, 6029.

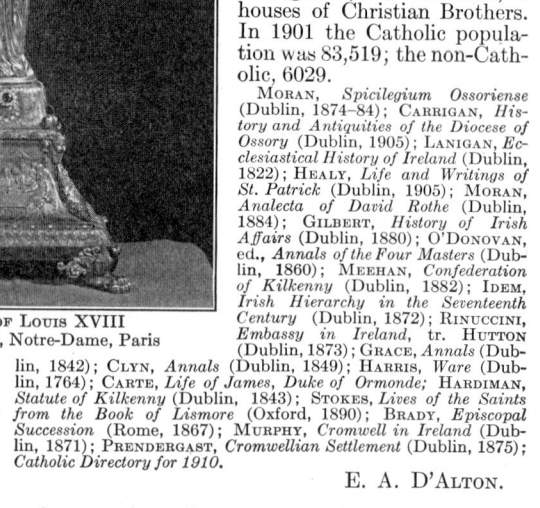

MORAN, *Spicilegium Ossoriense* (Dublin, 1874-84); CARRIGAN, *History and Antiquities of the Diocese of Ossory* (Dublin, 1905); LANIGAN, *Ecclesiastical History of Ireland* (Dublin, 1822); HEALY, *Life and Writings of St. Patrick* (Dublin, 1905); MORAN, *Analecta of David Rothe* (Dublin, 1884); GILBERT, *History of Irish Affairs* (Dublin, 1880); O'DONOVAN, ed., *Annals of the Four Masters* (Dublin, 1860); MEEHAN, *Confederation of Kilkenny* (Dublin, 1882); IDEM, *Irish Hierarchy in the Seventeenth Century* (Dublin, 1872); RINUCCINI, *Embassy in Ireland*, tr. HUTTON (Dublin, 1873); GRACE, *Annals* (Dublin, 1842); CLYN, *Annals* (Dublin, 1849); HARRIS, *Ware* (Dublin, 1764); CARTE, *Life of James, Duke of Ormonde*; HARDIMAN, *Statute of Kilkenny* (Dublin, 1843); STOKES, *Lives of the Saints from the Book of Lismore* (Oxford, 1890); BRADY, *Episcopal Succession* (Rome, 1867); MURPHY, *Cromwell in Ireland* (Dublin, 1871); PRENDERGAST, *Cromwellian Settlement* (Dublin, 1875); *Catholic Directory for 1910*.

E. A. D'ALTON.

OSTENSORIUM OF LOUIS XVIII
Cathedral Treasure, Notre-Dame, Paris

Ostensorium (from *ostendere*, "to show") means, in accordance with its etymology, a vessel designed for the more convenient exhibition of some object of piety. Both the name *ostensorium* and the kindred word *monstrance* (*monstrantia*, from *monstrare*) were originally applied to all kinds of vessels of goldsmith's or silversmith's work in which glass, crystal, etc. were so employed as to allow the contents to be readily distinguished, whether the object thus honoured were the Sacred Host itself or only the relic of some saint. Modern usage, at any rate so far as the English language is concerned, has limited both terms to vessels intended for the exposition of the Blessed Sacrament, and it is in this sense only that we use *ostensorium* here.

It is plain that the introduction of ostensoria must have been posterior to the period at which the practice of exposing the Blessed Sacrament or carrying it in procession first became familiar in the Church. This (as may be seen from the articles BENEDICTION OF THE BLESSED SACRAMENT, CORPUS CHRISTI, and EXPOSITION OF THE BLESSED SACRAMENT) cannot be assigned to an earlier date than the thirteenth century. At the same time, Lanfranc's constitutions for the monks of Christ Church, Canterbury (c. 1070), direct that in the Palm Sunday procession two priests vested in albs should carry a portable shrine (feretrum) "in which also the Body of the Lord ought to be deposited". Although there is here no suggestion that the Host should be exposed to view, but rather the contrary, still we find that this English custom led, in at least one instance, to the construction of an elaborately decorated shrine for the carrying of the Blessed Sacrament on this special occasion. Simon, Abbot of St. Albans (1166–83), presented to the abbey a costly ark-shaped vessel adorned with enamels representing scenes of the Passion, which was to be used on Palm Sunday "that the faithful might see with what honour the most holy Body of Christ should be treated which at this season offered itself to be scourged, crucified and buried" ("Gesta Abbatum", Rolls Series, I, 191–92). That this, however, was in any proper sense an ostensorium in which the Host was exposed to view is not stated and cannot be assumed. At the same time it is highly probable that such ostensoria in the strict sense began to be constructed in the thirteenth century, and there are some vessels still in existence—for example, an octagonal monstrance at Bari, bearing the words "Hic Corpus Domini"—which may very well belong to that date.

A large number of medieval ostensoria have been figured by Cahier and Martin (Mélanges Archéologiques, I and VII) and by other authorities, and though it is often difficult to distinguish between simple reliquaries and vessels intended for the exposition of the Blessed Sacrament, a certain line of development may be traced in the evolution of these latter. Father Cahier suggests with some probability (Mélanges, VII, 271) that while at first the ciborium itself was employed for carrying the Blessed Sacrament in processions, etc., the sides of the cup of the ciborium were at first prolonged by a cylinder of crystal or glass, and the ordinary cover superimposed. Such a vessel might have served for either purpose, viz., either for giving Communion or for carrying the Host visibly in procession. Soon, however, the practice of exposition became sufficiently common to seem to require an ostensorium for that express object, and for this the upright cylindrical vessel of crystal was at first retained, often with supports of an architectural character and with tabernacle work, niches, and statues. In the central cylinder a large Host was placed, being kept upright by being held in a lunette (q. v.) constructed for the purpose. Many medieval monstrances of this type are still in existence. Soon, however, it became clear that the ostensorium could be better adapted to the object of drawing all eyes to the Sacred Host itself by making the transparent portion of the vessel just of the size required, and surrounded, like the sun, with rays. Monstrances of this shape, dating from the fifteenth century, are also not uncommon, and for several hundred years past this has been by far the commonest form in practical use.

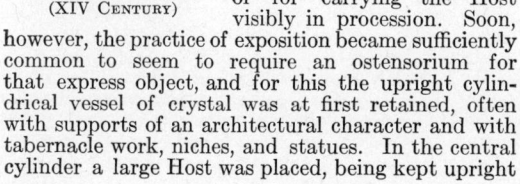

OSTENSORIUM—GERMAN GOLDSMITH'S WORK (XIV CENTURY)

Of course the adoption of ostensoria for processions of the Blessed Sacrament was a gradual process, and, if we may trust the miniatures found in the liturgical books of the Middle Ages, the Sacred Host was often carried on such occasions in a closed ciborium. An early example of a special vessel constructed for this purpose is a gift made by Archbishop Robert Courtney, an Englishman by birth, who died in 1324, to his cathedral church of Reims. He bequeathed with other ornaments "a golden cross set with precious stones and having a crystal in the middle, in which is placed the Body of Christ, and is carried in procession upon the feast of the most holy Sacrament." In a curious instance mentioned by Bergner (Handbuch d. Kirch. Kunstaltertümer in Deutschland, 356) a casket constructed in 1205 at Augsburg, to hold a miraculous Host from which blood had trickled, had an aperture bored in it more than a century later to allow the Host to be seen. Very probably a similar plan was sometimes adopted with vessels which are more strictly Eucharistic. Early medieval inventories often allow us to form an idea of the rapid extension of the use of monstrances. In the inventories of the thirteenth century they are seldom or never mentioned, but in the fifteenth century they have become a feature in all larger churches. Thus at St. Paul's, London, in 1245 and 1298 we find no mention of anything like an ostensorium, but in 1402 we have record of the "cross of crystal to put the Body of Christ in and to carry it upon the feast of Corpus Christi and at Easter". At Durham we hear of "a goodly shrine ordained to be carried on Corpus Christi day in procession, and called 'Corpus Christi Shrine', all finely gilded, a goodly thing to behold, and on the height of the said shrine was a four-square box all of crystal wherein was enclosed the Holy Sacrament of the Altar, and it was carried the same day with iiij priests" (Rites of Durham, c. lvi). But in the greater English churches a preference seems to have been shown, connected no doubt with the ceremonial of the Easter sepulchre, for a form of monstrance which reproduced the figure of Our Lord, the Sacred Host being inserted behind a

BRASS OSTENSORIUM (XV CENTURY) Basilica of St. Ambrose, Milan crystal door in the breast. This, at any rate, was the case, i. e. in the Lincoln, Salisbury, and other famous cathedrals. These statues, however, for the exposition of the Blessed Eucharist seem to have been of comparatively late date. On the continent, and more particularly in Spain, a fashion seems to have been introduced in the sixteenth century of constructing ostensoria of enormous size, standing six, seven, or even ten, feet in height, and weighing many hundreds of pounds. Of course it was necessary that in such cases the shrine in which the Blessed Sacrament was more immediately contained should be detachable, so that it could be used for giving benediction. The great monstrance of the cathedral of Toledo, which is more than twelve feet high, and the construction of which occupied in all more than 100 years, is adorned with 260 statuettes, one of the largest of which is said to be made of the gold brought by Columbus from the New World.

In the language of the older liturgical manuals, the ostensorium is not infrequently called *tabernaculum*, and it is under that name that a special blessing is provided for it in the "Pontificale Romanum". Several other designations are also in use, of which the commonest is perhaps *custodia*, though this is also specially applied to the sort of transparent pyx in which the Sacred Host is immediately secured. In Scotland, before the Reformation, an ostensorium was commonly called a "eucharist", in England a "monstre" or "monstral". The orb and rays of a monstrance should at least be of silver or silver gilt, and it is recommended that it should be surmounted by a cross.

An excellent chapter in CORBLET, *Histoire du Sacrement de l'Eucharistie*, II (Paris, 1882), gives a general account with a description of many famous ostensoria. SCHROD in *Kirchenlexikon*, s. v. *Monstranz*; RAIBLE, *Der Tabernakel einst und jetzt* (Freiburg, 1908); THURSTON, *Benediction of the Blessed Sacrament* in *The Month* (July, 1901); OTTE, *Handbuch der kirchlichen Kunst-Archäologie*, I (Leipzig, 1883), 208–10; MARTIN AND CAHIER, *Mélanges archéologiques*, I, VII (Paris, 1847–75); REUSSENS, *Archéologie chrétienne*, II, 334 sqq.; BARBIER DE MONTAULT, *Les ostensoires du XIVᵉ siècle en Limousin* in the *Congrès Archéolog. de France*, 1879, 555–590. See also articles too numerous to specify in detail in the *Revue de l'Art Chrétien* and the *Zeitschrift für christliche Kunst*, where many excellent reproductions of medieval monstrances will be found. HERBERT THURSTON.

Ostia and Velletri, SUBURBICARIAN DIOCESE OF (OSTIENSIS ET VELITERNENSIS), near Rome, central Italy. Ostia, now a small borough, was the ancient port of Rome, the first Roman colony founded by Ancus Marcius, chiefly to exploit the salt deposits. Prior to Imperial times, it had no harbour, the mouth of the Tiber affording the only shelter for shipping; the Emperor Claudius, therefore, built an artificial harbour at Ostia, and Trajan afterwards built a basin there, and enlarged the canal by which the harbour communicated with the Tiber. Here a new city sprang up, called Portus Romanus, which was embellished by Marcus Aurelius and other emperors, and connected with Rome by a new way, the Via Portuensis, along the right bank of the Tiber. With the decay of the Empire, Ostia and Portus decayed, and in the tenth century the basin of Portus had become a marsh. Between 827 and 844 Gregory IV restored the city, fortified it against the Saracens, and gave it the name of Gregoriopolis.

Leo IV defeated the Saracen fleet at Ostia in 847, and stretched a chain across the Tiber. Ostia was afterwards fortified by Cardinal Ugolino (Gregory IX), by Cardinal Giuliano della Rovere (Julius II), and by Paul III, while Paul V, in 1612, reopened the basin north of the Tiber. Excavations at Ostia were begun under Pius VII; they disclosed the forum, a theatre, three temples, the sanctuaries of Mithra and of the Magna Mater, the emporium, and a great many inscriptions.

Not counting St. Cyriacus, martyr, and Maximus the bishop who, according to the Acts of St. Laurence, consecrated Pope Dionysius in 269, the first Bishop of Ostia was Maximus, A. D. 313. We know from St. Augustine that the Bishop of Ostia sometimes consecrated the pope. St. Monica (q. v.) died at Ostia, and was buried in the church of St. Aurea, though her body was transferred, later, to Rome. The great hospital which St. Gallicanus built at Ostia was a noted establishment. As early as 707, the Bishop of Ostia resided at Rome, holding the office of *bibliothecarius sanctæ ecclesiæ*. The popes later on employed them in the administration of the Universal Church, especially in legations. They were among the bishops who took turns in exercising the pontifical functions during vacancies of the Holy See, and who became known as *episcopi cardinales*, or "cardinal bishops". Among the Bishops of Ostia were Georgius, who in 755 accompanied Stephen III to France; Donatus, who was sent by Nicholas I to Constantinople in 866 to deal with the case of Photius, but was stopped at the Byzantine frontier. In 869 this Donatus was head of the legation to the Council of Constantinople and to Bulgaria. Others were: Blessed Gregory (1037); St. Peter Damian (1058); Gerard of Châtillon (1072) and Otho of Châtillon (Urban II) (1077), who served as legates on various occasions, and were both imprisoned by Henry IV; Leo Marsicanus, also called Ostiensis (1101), the chronicler; Lambert Faganini (1117) (Honorius II); Alberic (1135), legate in the Holy Land, where he presided over the Council of Jerusalem, and also in England and France. Hugo (1150) was the first to bear the double title of Ostia and Velletri.

Velletri (Velitræ) is an ancient city of the Volscians, which, in 494 B. C., became a Latin colony, but revolted in 393, and was among the first of Rome's enemies in the Latin War, for which reason, in 338, the walls of the town were destroyed, while its inhabitants were taken to Rome to people the Trastevere, their lands being distributed among colonists. Velletri was the home of the family of Augustus. In its later history, the battle of Velletri (1744) is famous. The cemetery near the Villa Borgia shows the great antiquity of Christianity in this region. The first known Bishop of Velletri was Adeodatus (about 464); Joannes, in 592, was entrusted by Gregory the Great with the care of the Diocese of Tres Tabernæ (Three Taverns), now Cisterna (see ALBANO). From the eighth century, Velletri again had bishops of its own; of whom the last recorded was Joannes (868). Another see, united with Velletri, is that of Norma (Norba); its territory is a deserted, malarial country; only one of its bishops, who lived in the tenth century, is known. Other bishops of Velletri, before the union of the sees, were Gaudiosus (Gaudericus), one of the legates to the Council of Constantinople (869), and Joannes, who, in 1058, usurped the pontifical Throne, under the name of Benedict X.

Among the successors of Hugo in the united sees were Ubaldo Allucingoli (Lucius III); Ugolino de' Conti, 1206 (Gregory IX); Rinaldo de' Conti (Alexander IV); Petrus a Tarantasia, O.P., 1272 (Innocent V); Latino Malabranca Orsini (1278), a great statesman and diplomat; Nicolò Boccasino, O.P. (Benedict XI); Nicolò da Prato, the pacifier of Tuscany (1304). During the Avignon period, all the bishops of Ostia were Frenchmen, residing at Avignon or serving as legates; the most famous of them was Pierre d'Etain (1373), who persuaded Urban V to go to Rome. During the schism, each of the rival popes appointed a Bishop of Ostia. Among the legitimate bishops may be mentioned William of Estouteville (1461), who built the episcopal palace; Giuliano della Rovere (Julius II); Alessandro Farnese, 1524 (Paul III); Gian Pietro Carafa, 1534 (Paul IV); Alessandro Farnese (1580), who restored the cathedral; Antonio M. Sauli (1623), founder of a Basilian monastery; Domenico Ginnasio (1683), who restored the cathedral and founded a hospital at Ostia; Bartholommeo Pacca (q. v.); Louis Micara (1844).

The united dioceses have 16 parishes, with 34,000 inhabitants, 5 religious houses of men and 5 of nuns, 1 educational establishment for male students, and 3 for girls.

CAPPELLETTI, *Le Chiese d' Italia*, I; BORGIA, *Istoria della Chiesa e città di Velletri* (Nocera, 1723).

U. BENIGNI.

Ostiarius. See PORTER.

Ostiensis. See HENRY OF SEGUSIO, BLESSED.

Ostiensis, surname of LEO MARSICANUS, Benedictine chronicler, b. about 1045; d. 22 May, 1115, 1116, or 1117. He belonged to an old noble family, and at the age of fourteen entered Monte Cassino, where his talents soon won him the regard of Abbot Desiderius, later Pope Victor III. Desiderius entrusted his education to the future Cardinal Aldemar. On the completion of his studies, Ostiensis became librarian and archivist of the monastery, and, as such, his main task was to settle, in accordance with the existing documents, all disputes concerning landed property in which the monastery became involved. Abbot Oderisius, who succeeded Desiderius, urged Ostiensis to write a history of the monastery, but, on account of his numerous duties, he was unable to give himself entirely to the work. Paschal II created him Cardinal Bishop of Ostia. In the conflict between the pope and Henry V, Ostiensis vigorously defended the papacy. His unfinished chronicle, originally called "Legenda sancti Benedicti longa", treats the period between 529 and 1075; Petrus Diaconus continued it to 1139. Trustworthy and impartial, the chronicle is a valuable mine of information for the history of Lower Italy, but as the documents on which the narrative rests are still extant, it has no special importance for our knowledge of the time. It was first edited under the title, "Chronica sacri monasterii Casinensis auctore Leone cardinali episcopo Ostiensi", by Abbot Angelus de Nuce (Paris, 1668); then by Wattenbach in "Monumenta Germaniæ: Scriptores", VII, 574–727, and Migne in "P. L.", CLXXIII, 479–763. Ostiensis has left several lesser works: "Narratio de consecratione ecclesiarum a Desiderio et Oderisio in Monte Casino ædificatarum" (P. L., CLXXIII, 997–1002), and "Vita sancti Mennatis eremitæ et confessoris" (edited in part, P. L., CLXXIII, 989–92).

GATTULA, *Hist. abbatiæ Casinensis* (Venice, 1733); 879; POTTHAST, *Bibl. hist. medii ævi*, I (Berlin, 1896), 718; WATTENBACH, *Deutschlands Geschichtsquellen*, II (Berlin, 1894), 236–8.

PATRICIUS SCHLAGER.

Ostracine, titular see and suffragan of Pelusium in Augustamnica prima. Pliny (Hist. naturalis, V, xiv) places the town sixty-five miles from Pelusium. Ptolemy (IV, v, 6) locates it in Cassiotis, between Mount Cassius and Rhinocolura. We learn from Josephus ("Bellum Jud.", IV, xi, 5) that Vespasian stopped there with his army on the way from Egypt into Palestine; the city then had no ramparts. It received its water from the Delta by a canal. A Roman garrison was stationed there. Hierocles, George of Cyprus, and other geographers always mention it as in Augustamnica. Le Quien (Oriens christianus, II, 545) speaks of three bishops, Theoctistus, Serapion, and Abraham, who lived in the fourth and fifth centuries. There is at present in this region, near the sea, a small town called Straki, which probably replaced Ostracine.

AMÉLINEAU, *La Géographie de l'Egypte à l'époque copte* (Paris, 1893), 288.

S. VAILHÉ.

Ostraka, CHRISTIAN, inscriptions on clay, wood, metal, and other hard materials. Like papyri, they are valuable especially as the literary sources for early Christianity. They are found chiefly in Oriental countries, especially Egypt. The greatest number are pieces of clay or scraps of pots inscribed with colours or ink. The oldest Christian ostraka, like the papyri, are Greek and date from the fifth century. Next come the Coptic and Arabian ostraka. Some of the texts not yet deciphered include several Nubian ostraka in a language spoken in the old Christian negro-kingdoms in the vicinity of Aloa on the Blue Nile. In these inscriptions Greek letters are used, with some other signs. As to contents, ostraka are either profane or ecclesiastical. Potsherds were often used for correspondence in place of the less durable papyrus; occasionally the recipient wrote the answer on the back of the potsherd. Ostraka were also used for mercantile purposes, as bills, receipts, etc. C. M. Kaufmann and J. C. Ewald Falls, while excavating the town of Menas in the Libyan desert, discovered ostraka of this class—the oldest Christian potsherds in the Greek language (fifth century)—and H. J. Bell and F. G. Kenyon of the British Museum deciphered them. They refer to the vine-culture of the sanctuaries of Menas and represent, for the most part, short vouchers for money or provisions. The currency is based upon gold solidi issued by Constantine; the date is reckoned by the year of indiction. Of historical interest is the assistance given to invalid workmen, the employment of the lower clergy, the manner of provisioning the workmen, and especially the statements about the harvest periods in the Libyan district. The series of Coptic ostraka which deals with the clergy and the monasteries in the Nile valley is particularly extensive. We find references to all phases of administration and popular life.

The ecclesiastical ostraka, in a narrow sense, contain Biblical citations from the New Testament, prayers, extracts from the *synaxaria* (lives of the saints), and are partly of a liturgic character. Greek, which was then the language of the Church, is much used, with the Coptic. Among the samples published by W. E. Crum, the best judge of Coptic dialects, there is a local confession of faith from the sixth century, besides the Preface and Sanctus of the Mass, prayers from the Liturgy of St. Basil and of St. Mark, a part of the didascalia of Schenûte of Athribis, a Greek confession, and an excommunication, also in Greek. Particularly remarkable are those ostraka which contain liturgical songs. They represent our present song-books for which purpose rolls of papyrus were less suited than the more durable potsherds; in some cases wooden books were used. Among the pieces translated by Crum we find petitions for ordination in which the petitioner promises to learn by heart one of the Gospels, and a reference to an ancient abstinence movement, against which is directed a decree that the consecration-wine should be pure or at least three-fourths pure.

A complete collection of Greek, Coptic, and Arabic ostraka from the beginnings of the Christian epoch does not exist. The most important may be found in WILKEN, *Griechische Ostraka aus Aegypten und Nubien* (2 vols., Leipzig, 1899); CRUM, *Coptic Ostraka from the Collections of the Egypt Exploration Fund, the Cairo Museum and others* (London, 1902).

CARL MARIA KAUFMANN.

Ostrogoths, one of the two chief tribes of the Goths, a Germanic people. Their traditions relate that the Goths originally lived on both sides of the Baltic Sea, in Scandinavia and on the Continent. Their oldest habitations recorded in history were situated on the right bank of the Vistula. They left these, all or in part, about the middle of the second century, and settled near the Black Sea, between the Don and Danube. Thence they emerged frequently to attack and pillage the cities of Greece and Asia Minor, and fought continuously with the Romans and the neighbouring Germanic tribes. The emperor Decius fell in battle with them in 251. Crossing the Danube into Thracia in 269 they were defeated by Claudius; Aurelian drove them back across the Danube and gave them Dacia. We now find the Ostrogoths east of the River Dniester, and the Visigoths to the west. During the reign of Constantine they again attempted to cross the Danube but were repulsed. During the years 350–75 the Goths were united under the leadership of Ermanaric, the Ostrogoth. In 375 they were conquered by the Huns. Some escaped into the Crimea, where they retained their language up to the sixteenth century; the mass of the people, however, remained in their own lands and paid tribute to the Huns; but were otherwise fairly independent and elected their own kings. When the empire of the Huns collapsed after the death of Attila (453), the Ostrogoths regained independence. Their old lands between Don and Danube, however, they had to surrender to the Huns, while they obtained Pannonia from the Romans. Theodoric, the Amaling, who was their king from 474 or 475, fought with the Byzantine emperor Zeno at various times, although he obtained peaceful relations during most of his reign. He endeavoured to secure permanent domiciles for his people. In 488 he started for Italy, aided and abetted by Zeno. Theodoric defeated Odoacer, who reigned as king in Italy, and founded in 493 the great Ostrogothic Empire, which included Italy, Sicily, Dalmatia, Upper Rhætia, and later on Provence, with the capital Ravenna, and which stood under Byzantine suzerainty. Theodoric dreamed of an amalgamation of the Teutons and the Romans, of a Germanic state, in which the Ostrogoths were to dominate. He succeeded in establishing law and order in his lands; Roman art and literature flourished. He was tolerant towards the Catholic Church and did not interfere in dogmatic matters. He remained as neutral as possible towards the pope, though he exercised a preponderant influence in the affairs of the papacy. He and his people were Arians and Theodoric considered himself as protector and chief representative of the sect. His successor did not possess the necessary vigour and ability to continue this work. His daughter Amalasvintha succeeded him in 526, first as regent for her son Athalaric, and after the latter's death, in 534, as queen. She was assassinated by her cousin Theodahad, the rightful heir to the throne. The Byzantine emperor Justinian now made himself her avenger and declared war upon the Ostrogoths. His general Belisarius captured Naples in 536. In place of the incompetent Theodahad the Goths chose Witiches as king, but he also proved to be an incapable general. Belisarius succeeded in entering Ravenna in 539 and in taking Witiches prisoner. After his recall in 540, the Goths reconquered Italy under their new king Totila. In 544 Belisarius appeared once more and the war was continued with varying success. In 551 Narses became commander-in-chief in place of Belisarius, and in the following year he defeated Totila at Taginæ in the Apennines. Totila was killed in the battle. The survivors of the Ostrogoths chose Teja as their king, but were practically annihilated in the battle near Mount Vesuvius in 553, after a desperate struggle in which Teja was killed. Their last fortress fell in 555, after which the Ostrogoths disappear. The few survivors mingled with other peoples and nations; some were romanized in Italy, and others wandered north where they disappeared among the various Germanic tribes. Italy became a Byzantine province.

BRADLEY, *The Goths* (London, 1898); DAHN, *Die Könige der Germanen*, II–IV (Würzburg, 1861–66); MANSO, *Geschichte des ostgotischen Reichs in Italien* (Breslau, 1824); HODGKIN, *Italy and her invaders*, III, IV (London, 1885); HARTMANN, *Das italienische Königreich* (Gotha, 1897); WIETERSHEIM, *Geschichte der Völkerwanderung*, I, II (Leipzig, 1880, 81).

KLEMENS LÖFFLER.

Ostuni. See BRINDISI, DIOCESE OF.

O'Sullivan Beare, PHILIP, b. in Ireland, c. 1590; d. in Spain, 1660, son of Dermot O'Sullivan and nephew of Donal O'Sullivan Beare, Lord of Dunboy. He was sent to Spain in 1602, and was educated at Compostella by Vendamma, a Spaniard, and Father Synnott, an Irish Jesuit. He served in the Spanish army. In 1621 he published his "Catholic History of Ireland", a work not always reliable, but valuable for the Irish wars of the author's own day. He also wrote a "Life of St. Patrick", a confutation of Gerald Barry and a reply to Usher's attack on his "History".

MAGEE, *Irish Writers of the Seventeenth Century* (Dublin, 1846); O'SULLIVAN, *Catholic History of Ireland*, ed. KELLY (Dublin, 1850); O'SULLIVAN, *History of Ireland*, tr. BYRNE (London, 1904).

E. A. D'ALTON.

Oswald, SAINT, Archbishop of York, d. on 29 February, 992. Of Danish parentage, Oswald was brought up by his uncle Odo, Archbishop of Canterbury, and instructed by Fridegode. For some time he was dean of the house of the secular canons at Winchester, but led by the desire of a stricter life he entered the Benedictine Monastery of Fleury, where Odo himself had received the monastic habit. He was ordained there and in 959 returned to England betaking himself to his kinsman Oskytel, then Archbishop of York. He took an active part in ecclesiastical affairs at York until St. Dunstan procured his appointment to the See of Worcester. He was consecrated by St. Dunstan in 962. Oswald was an ardent supporter of Dunstan in his efforts to purify the Church from abuses, and aided by King Edgar he carried out his policy of replacing by communities the canons who held monastic possessions. Edgar gave the monasteries of St. Albans, Ely, and Benfleet to Oswald, who established monks at Westbury (983), Pershore (984), at Winchelcumbe (985), and at Worcester, and re-established Ripon. But his most famous foundation was that of Ramsey in Huntingdonshire, the church of which was dedicated in 974, and again after an accident in 991. In 972 by the joint action of St. Dunstan and Edgar, Oswald was made Archbishop of York and journeyed to Rome to receive the pallium from John XIII. He retained, however, with the sanction of the pope, jurisdiction over the Diocese of Worcester where he frequently resided in order to foster his monastic reforms (Eadmer, 203). On Edgar's death in 975, his work, hitherto so successful, received a severe check at the hands of Elfhere, King of Mercia, who broke up many communities. Ramsey, however, was spared, owing to the powerful patronage of Ethelwin, Earl of East Anglia. Whilst Archbishop of York, Oswald collected from the ruins of Ripon the relics of the saints, some of which were conveyed to Worcester. He died in the act of washing the feet of the poor, as was his daily custom during Lent, and was buried in the Church of St. Mary at Worcester. Oswald used a gentler policy than his colleague Ethelwold and always refrained from violent measures. He greatly valued and promoted learning amongst the clergy and induced many scholars to come from Fleury. He wrote two treatises and some synodal decrees. His feast is celebrated on 28 February.

Historians of York in *Rolls Series*, 3 vols.; see *Introductions* by RAINE. The anonymous and contemporary life of the monk of Ramsey, I, 399–475, and EADMER, *Life and Miracles*, II, 1–59 (also in *P. L.*, CLIX) are the best authorities; the lives by SENATUS and two others in vol. II are of little value; *Acta SS.*, Feb., III, 752; *Acta O.S.B.* (Venice, 1733), sæc. v, 728; WRIGHT, *Biog. Lit.*, I (London, 1846), 462; TYNEMOUTH and CAPGRAVE, ed. HORSTMAN, II (Oxford, 1901), 252; HUNT, *Hist of the English Church from 597–1066* (London, 1899); IDEM in *Dict. of Nat. Biog.*, s. v.; LINGARD, *Anglo-Saxon Church* (London, 1845).

S. ANSELM PARKER.

Oswald, SAINT, king and martyr; b., probably, 605; d. 5 Aug., 642; the second of seven brothers, sons of Ethelfrid, who was grandson of Ida, founder of the Kingdom of Northumbria in 547. Oswald's mother was Acha, daughter of Ella or Alla, who, after Ida's death, had seized Deira and thus separated it from the Northern Bernicia. The years of Oswald's youth were spent at home, as long as his father reigned, but when, in 617, Ethelfrid was slain in battle by Redwald, King of the East Angles, Oswald with his brothers fled for protection from Edwin, their uncle, Acha's brother, to the land of the Scots and were cared for at Columba's Monastery at Hii, or Iona. There they remained until Edwin's death in the battle of Heathfield (633). Eanfrid, his elder brother, then returned to accept the Kingdom of Deira, whilst Osric, cousin of Edwin, received Bernicia. The kingdom was thus again divided and both parts relapsed into paganism. In the following year Osric was slain in battle, and Eanfrid treacherously murdered by the British king, Cadwalla. Oswald thereupon came down from the North, and in 635 a small but resolute band gathered round him near the Roman Wall at a spot seven miles north of Hexham, afterwards known as Hevenfelt, or Heaven's Field. Here, encouraged by a vision and promise of victory from St. Columba, who shrouded with his mantle all his camp, Oswald set up a cross of wood as his standard—the first Christian symbol ever raised in Bernicia—and gave battle to the Britons, who were led, probably, by Cadwalla. The Britons were completely routed, and thenceforth could only act on the defensive.

Oswald's victory reunited the Northumbrian Kingdom not only because he delivered it from the humiliating yoke of the Mercians and Britons, but also because on his father's side he was a descendant of Ida of Bernicia and on his mother's of the royal house of Ella of Deira. Thus united, Northumbria could not fail to become the chief power in a confederation against Penda of Mercia and the Britons of Wales. Oswald was thoroughly grounded in the principles of the Christian religion, and, though but twelve nobles with whom he returned from exile were Christians, far from abandoning his faith, his first care was to spread it among the Bernicians, thus confirming the political union effected by Edwin with a religious union unknown before. Edwin, it is true, had himself received the Faith in 627, through the influence of his wife Ethelburga, sister of the Kentish King, who had brought St. Paulinus to the North, but his example was followed only by the people of Deira. Oswald, brought up in Columba's monastery at Iona, naturally looked to the North for missionaries. The first preacher who set forth soon returned, having found the Northumbrian people too barbarous and stubborn. Then Aidan was sent, "a man of singular meekness, piety and moderation", who established his episcopal see at Lindisfarne, in 635. Oswald's zealous co-operation with the monk-bishop soon filled the land with churches and monasteries, and the church at York, begun by Edwin, was completed. Moreover, his wonderful humility in the midst of success, his charity, and his piety soon had their effect in turning his subjects from Woden to Christ. We are told that the king in his Court acted as the interpreter of the Irish missionaries who knew not the tongue of his thanes.

It was Oswald's work to add to the warlike glory of his father Ethelfrid and the wise administration of his uncle Edwin the moral power of Christianity, and to build up a great kingdom. Edwin had gathered the whole English race into one political body and was overlord of every English kingdom save that of Kent. The Venerable Bede (III, 6) says that Oswald had a greater dominion than any of his ancestors, and that "he brought under his sway all the nations and provinces of Britain, which are divided into four languages, namely the Britons, the Picts, the Scots, and the English". He had great power in the North-West, as far south as Chester and Lancashire, and was probably owned as overlord by the Welsh Kingdom of Strath Clyde, as well as by the Picts and the Scots of Dalriada. In the East he was supreme in Lindsey, and the words of Bede seem to imply that he was overlord of Mercia, which was still ruled by Penda; but this could have been scarcely more than nominal. The West Saxons in the South, influenced by the fear of Penda, readily acknowledged Oswald, their allegiance being strengthened, in 635, by the conversion of King Cynegils, of Wessex, at whose baptism Oswald stood sponsor, and whose daughter he married. Both sovereigns then established Bishop Birinus at Dorchester.

This vast supremacy, extending from north to south, and broken only by Penda's kingdom in Mid-Britain and that of the East Angles, led Adamnan of Hii to call Oswald "The Emperor of the whole of Britain". Christianity seemed to be forming a network round the pagan Penda of Mercia. The kingdom of the East Angles, which was still Christian, but acknowledged Penda as overlord, was necessary to Oswald to maintain the connexion between his dominions in the north and the south. War was therefore inevitable. At the battle of Maserfeld, said to be seven miles from Shrewsbury, "on the border of Wales, near Offa's dyke", Oswald was slain on 5 Aug., 642, and thus perished "the most powerful and most Christian King" in the eighth year of his reign and in the flower of his age. His last words were for the spiritual welfare of his soldiers, whence the proverb: "God have mercy on their souls, as said Oswald when he fell." His body was mutilated by Penda, and his limbs set up on stakes, where they remained a full year, until they were taken away by Oswy and given to the monks at Bardney in Lindsey. In the tenth century some of the bones were carried off by Ethelred and Ethelfleda of Mercia to St. Peter's, Gloucester. His head was taken from the battlefield to the church of St. Peter in the royal fortress at Bamborough, and was afterwards translated to Lindisfarne, where, for fear of the Danes, it was placed in 875 in the coffin of St. Cuthbert which found its resting-place at Durham in 998. It was in the coffin at the translation of St. Cuthbert in 1104, and was thought to be there when the tomb was opened in 1828. His arm and hand (or hands) were taken to Bamborough and perhaps afterwards removed to Peterborough, and were still incorrupt in the time of Symeon of Durham, early in the twelfth century. Reginald gives an account of his personal appearance: arms of great length and power, eyes bright blue, hair yellow, face long and beard thin, and his small lips wearing a kindly smile.

BEDE, *History;* REGINALD, *Life* (printed by the Surtees Soc., and all portions not containing matter taken from Bede in *R. S.* among works of Sym. of Durham); SYM. OF DURHAM, *Hist. Dunelm.;* IDEM, *Hist. Regum* in *R. S.* and *Surtees Soc. Publications;* ADAMNAN, *Life of S. Columba,* ed. and tr. by FOWLER (Oxford, 1894); ALCUIN, *Carmen* in *Historians of York,* in *R. S.;* WILLIAM OF MALMESBURY, *Gesta Pontif;* IDEM, *Gesta Regum* in *R. S.; Miscell. Biogr.* in *Surtees Soc. Publications.* For account of his relics see also RAINE, *St. Cuthbert;* IDEM, *Opening of S. Cuthbert's Tomb* (Durham, 1828); WALL, *Shrines of British Saints: Oswald and Cuthbert* (London, 1905).—RAINE in *Dict. of Christ. Biogr.,* s. v.; BUTLER, *Lives,* Aug. 5; GREEN, *Making of England* (London, 1897), vi; BELLESHEIM, *Cath. Ch. of Scotland,* tr. HUNTER-BLAIR, I (Edinburgh, 1887); MONTALEMBERT, *Moines d'Occident,* tr. (London, 1896); SKENE, *Celtic Scotland,* I (Edinburgh, 1876); HUNT, *History of the English Church from 597–1066* (London, 1899).

S. ANSELM PARKER.

Oswin, SAINT, king, and martyr, murdered at Gilling, near Richmond, Yorkshire, England, on 20 August, 651, son of Osric, King of Deira in Britain. On the murder of his father by Cadwalla in 634, Oswin still quite young was carried away for safety into Wessex, but returned on the death of his kinsman St. Oswald, in 642, either because Oswy had bestowed upon him Deira, one portion of the Kingdom of Northumbria, himself ruling Bernicia, or, as is more probable, because the people of Deira chose him for king in preference to Oswy. Under his sway of seven years, peace, order, and happiness reigned throughout the kingdom. But in the relations between Oswy and Oswin there was apparent peace only, the former was employing every subtlety to bring about his rival's death. At length Oswy declared an open warfare, and Oswin, unable to meet the superior forces of his adversary, disbanded his army, either from worldly prudence (Bede) or heroic virtue (monk of Tynemouth), and made his way for greater security to Hunwald an eorldorman upon whom he had lately conferred the fief of Gilling. Hunwald promised to conceal him but treacherously betrayed him to Ethelwin, one of Oswy's officers, and he was murdered. He was buried at Gilling and soon afterwards transferred to Tynemouth, though another account says he was buried at Tynemouth. The anonymous monk of St. Albans, who in the reign of King Stephen was resident at Tynemouth, and there wrote the saint's life, says that his memory was forgotten during the Danish troubles, but in 1065 his burial-place was made known by an apparition to a monk named Edmund, and his relics were translated on 11 March, 1100, and again on 20 August, 1103. At the dissolution of the monasteries under Henry VIII there was still a shrine containing the body and vestments of St. Oswin. A portion of his body was preserved as a relic at Durham (cf. Smith, "Bede", III, xiv). Eanfleda, Oswy's queen, daughter of St. Edwin, prevailed upon him to found in reparation a monastery at Gilling, some remains of which still exist, though it was destroyed by the Danes. Bede in his "History" (III, xiv) gives a description of his character and features: "most generous to all men and above all things humble; tall of stature and of graceful bearing, with pleasant manner and engaging address". There is now preserved in the British Museum (Cotton MS. Galba A. 5.) a psalter which until the fire of 1731 bore the inscription "Liber Oswini Regis."

TYNEMOUTH AND CAPGRAVE, *Nova Legenda Angliæ*, ed. HORSTMAN, II (Oxford, 1901), 268; *Acta SS.*, Aug., IV, 63; *Surtees Soc. Publ.: Miscellanea Biographica*, VIII, 1–59, and Introd. (London, 1834); *Lives of English Saints*, ed. NEWMAN (London, 1900); RAINE in *Dict. of Christ. Biog.*, s. v.; and BUTLER, *Lives of the Saints*, III (Baltimore), 287–88.

S. ANSELM PARKER.

Otfried of Weissenburg, the oldest German poet known by name, author of the "Evangelienbuch", a rhymed version of the Gospels, flourished in the ninth century, but the exact dates of his life are unknown. He was probably born at or near Weissenburg in Alsace, where he also seems to have received his earliest education. Later on he studied at Fulda under the famous Rabanus Maurus, who was abbot there after 822 and presided over the monastic school. After completing his studies, Otfried returned to Weissenburg and entered the well-known Benedictine abbey there, becoming prefect of the abbey-school. He was notary there in 851. At Weissenburg he began his great poem, the "Liber evangeliorum theotisce conscriptus", the completion of which occupied the greater part of his life. It was dedicated to King Louis the German and to Bishop Salomo of Constance, to both of whom rhymed epistles are addressed in the Franconian dialect. The poet also addressed an epistle in Latin prose to Bishop Liutbert of Mainz to gain official approbation for his work. Hence the poem must have been finished some time between 863, when Liutbert became archbishop, and 871, when Salomo died. In the letter to Liutbert, Otfried tells us that he undertook to write the poem at the request of some of the brethren and of a venerable lady, whose name is not mentioned, for the express purpose of supplanting the worldly poetry that found such favour with the people. He furthermore wished to make known the story of the Gospels to those who did not know Latin. The poem itself is in strophic form and contains some 15,000 lines. It is divided into five books, with reference to the five senses, which are to be purified and sanctified by the reading of the sacred story. The first book narrates the Nativity of Christ; the second and third, His Teachings and Miracles; the fourth, the Passion; the fifth, the Resurrection, Ascension, and Last Judgment. Between the narrative portions chapters are inserted superscribed "Moraliter", "Spiritaliter", "Mystice", in which the events narrated are interpreted allegorically and symbolically.

While Otfried bases his work chiefly on the Vulgate, he also makes use of the writings of Rabanus, Bede, and Alcuin, as well as those of St. Jerome, St. Augustine, and others. In fact he is more of a theologian than a poet, though some passages show undeniable poetic talent. Still, the poem is far inferior to the "Heliand" (q. v.), and never became really popular. Particularly noteworthy is the opening chapter of the first book, where the author explains his reasons for writing in German, and not in Latin. This passage glows with a noble patriotism; the Franks are praised with sincere enthusiasm and are favourably compared with the Greeks and Romans. In form, Otfried's poem marks an epoch in German literature: it is the first poem to employ rhyme instead of the old Germanic alliteration, though the rhyme is still very imperfect, being often mere assonance, with frequent traces of alliteration. Three almost complete manuscripts of the work are preserved, at Vienna, Heidelberg, and Munich; fragments of a fourth are found at Berlin, Wolfenbüttel, and Bonn. The Vienna codex is the best. Otfried was noticed as early as 1495 by the Abbot of Tritheim, and passages from his poem appeared in print as early as 1531, in the "Libri tres rerum Germanicarum" of Beatus Rhenanus. An edition then appeared at Basle, 1571, with a preface by Mathias Flacius, of Illyria. Graff, who published an edition at Königsberg, 1831, called the poem "Krist", but that name is now obsolete. Modern editions are those of Kelle (3 vols., Ratisbon, 1856–81), Piper (Paderborn, 1878, and Freiburg, 1882–84), and Erdmann in Zacher's "Germanistische Handbibliothek", V (Halle, 1882). Modern German versions have been made by Rapp (Stuttgart, 1858) and Kelle (1870).

See introductions to the editions of KELLE, PIPER, and ERDMANN. Also, LACHMANN, *Otfrid* in *Kleinere Schriften*, I (Berlin, 1876), 449–60; SCHÖNBACH, *Otfridstudien* in *Zeitschrift für deutsches Altertum*, 38–40; SCHÜTZE, *Beiträge zur Poetik Otfrids* (Kiel, 1887); MARTIN in *Allgemeine Deutsche Biographie*, XXIV, 529 sq.; PLUMHOFF, *Beiträge zu den Quellen Otfrids* (Kiel, 1898).

ARTHUR F. J. REMY.

Othlo (OTLOH), a Benedictine monk of St. Emmeran's, Ratisbon, b. 1013 in the Diocese of Freising; d. 1072. Having made his studies at Tegernsee and Hersfeld, he was called to Würzburg by Bishop Meginhard on account of his skill in writing. He entered the Benedictine Order, 1032, at St. Emmeran's in Ratisbon, was appointed dean, 1055, and entrusted with the care of the monastic school. To escape the oppressions of Bishop Otto he fled to Fulda in 1062 where he remained until 1067, when, after a short stay at Amorbach, he returned to Ratisbon and employed his time in literary work. In his early days he had a great relish for the Classics, especially for Lucan, but later he thought them not suited for religious, and tried to replace the heathen authors by writings of his own which served for education and edification. Othlo is praised as modest and pious; he was opposed to dialectics, not out of lack of education but because he wished to be untrammelled by set words and forms. He is accused of having originated the legend of the transfer of the relics of St. Denis the Areopagite to Ratisbon, and also of having forged many letters of exemption for his abbey (Lechner in "Neues Archiv", XXV, 627, and "Zeitschr. für kath. Theol.", XXXI, 18). Among his writings are: "Dialogus de suis tentationibus, varia fortuna et scriptis", which marked the beginning of autobiography in the Middle Ages (Mabillon, "Anal. nov.", IV, 107); Life of St. Wolfgang of Ratisbon ("Acta SS.", Nov., II, 1, 565); Life of St. Boniface, compiled from the letters of the saint found at Fulda; Life of St. Alto (partly in "Acta SS.", Feb., II, 359 and entire in "Mon. Ger. hist.: Scriptores", XV, 2, 843); Life of St. Magnus ("Acta SS.", Sept., II, 701).

In Pez ("Thesaurus", III, 143–613) are found: "Dialogus de tribus quæstionibus", treating of the symbolism of the number three; "De promissionis bonorum et malorum causis"; "De cursu spirituali"; "De translatione s. Dionysii e Francia in Germaniam", a fragment; "De miraculo quod nuper accidit cuidam laico"; "De admonitione clericorum et laicorum"; "De spirituali doctrina", in hexameters; "Liber Proverbiorum"; "Sermo in natali apostolorum"; "Liber visionum tum suarum tum aliorum". His collected works are found in Migne (P. L., CXLVI, 27–434).

ESSER in *Kirchenlex.*, s. v.; *Allg. d. Biographie;* WATTENBACH, *Geschichtsquellen*, II, 65; MICHAEL, *Gesch. des deutsch. Volkes*, III (Freiburg, 1903), 19; HAUCK, *Kirchengesch. deutschl.*, III, 968, IV, 80, 94.

FRANCIS MERSHMAN.

Othmar (AUDOMAR), SAINT, d. 16 Nov., 759, on the island of Werd in the Rhine, near Eschnez, Switzerland. He was of Alemannic descent, received his education in Rhætia, was ordained priest, and for a time presided over a church of St. Florinus in Rhætia. This church was probably identical with the one of St. Peter at Remüs, where St. Florinus had laboured as a priest and was buried. In 720 Waltram of Thurgau appointed Othmar superior over the cell of St. Gall. He united into a monastery the monks that lived about the cell of St. Gall, according to the rule of St. Columban, and became their first abbot. He added a hospital and a school; during his abbacy the Rule of St. Columban was replaced by that of St. Benedict. When Karlmann renounced his throne in 747, he visited Othmar at St. Gall and gave him a letter to his brother Pepin, recommending Othmar and his monastery to the king's liberality. Othmar personally brought the letter to Pepin, and was kindly received. When the Counts Warin and Ruodhart unjustly tried to gain possession of some property belonging to St. Gall, Othmar fearlessly resisted their demands. Hereupon they captured him while he was on a journey to Constance, and held him prisoner, first at the castle of Bodmann, then on the island of Werd in the Rhine. At the latter place he died, after an imprisonment of six months, and was buried. In 769 his body was transferred to the monastery of St. Gall and in 867 he was solemnly entombed in the new church of St. Othmar at St. Gall. His cult began to spread soon after his death, and now he is, next to St. Maurice and St. Gall, the most popular saint in Switzerland. His feast is celebrated on 16 November. He is represented in art as a Benedictine abbot, generally holding a little barrel in his hand, an allusion to the alleged miracle, that a barrel of St. Othmar never became empty, no matter how much he took from it to give to the poor.

P. L., CXIV, 1029–42; *Mon. Germ. Hist.: Script.*, II, 41–47. To this life was added by ISO OF ST. GALL: *De miraculis S. Othmari, libri duo*, in *P. L.*, CXXI, 779–96, and *Mon. Germ. Hist.: Script.*, II, 47–54; BURGENER, *Helvetia Sancta*, II (Einsiedeln and New York, 1860), 147–51.

MICHAEL OTT.

Otho, MARCUS SALVIUS, Roman emperor, successor, after Galba, of Nero, b. in Rome, of an ancient Etruscan family settled at Ferentinum, 28 April, A. D. 32; d. at Brixellum on the Po, 15 April, 69. He led a profligate life at the court of Nero. As husband of the courtesan Poppæa Sabina he was sent for appearance's sake to Lusitania as governor. When Sulpicius Galba was proclaimed emperor, Otho returned to Rome with him. In contrast to the miserly Galba, he sought to win the affection of the troops by generosity. On 15 January, 69, five days after Galba had appointed Lucius Calpurnius Piso co-emperor and successor, twenty-three soldiers proclaimed Otho emperor upon the open street. As Galba hurried to take measures against this procedure, he and his escort encountered his opponents at the Forum; there was a struggle, and Galba was murdered. Otho was now sole ruler; the senate confirmed his authority. The statues of Nero were again set up by Otho who also set aside an immense sum of money for the completion of Nero's Golden House (*Aurea Domus*). Meantime Aulus Vitellius, legate under Galba to southern Germany, was proclaimed emperor at Cologne. Alienus Cæcina, who had been punished by Galba for his outrageous extortion, persuaded the legions of northern Germany to agree to this choice; their example was followed by the troops in Britain. In a short time a third of the standing army had renounced the emperor at Rome. In the winter of 69 these troops advanced into the plain of the River Po, stimulated by anticipation of the wealth of Italy and Rome, and strengthened by the presence of German and Belgian auxiliaries. On the march they learned that Galba was dead and Otho was his successor. At first Vitellius entered into negotiations with the new ruler at Rome. Compromise failing, both made ready for the decisive struggle. Otho vainly sought to force the citizens of Rome to take energetic measures for security. To expiate any wrong done he recalled the innocent persons who had been banished by Nero's reign, and caused Nero's evil adviser, Sophonius Tigellinus, to be put to death. Finally he placed the republic in the care of the Senate and started for upper Italy on 14 March, with the main part of his guard, that had been collected in Rome, and two legions of soldiers belonging to the navy, while seven legions were advancing from Dalmatia, Pannonia, and Mœsia. A fleet near Narbonensis was to check the hostile troops from Gaul, that would advance from the south. After some favourable preliminary skirmishes near Placentia and Cremona Otho gave the command for a pitched battle before a junction had been effected with the legions from Mœsia. While the emperor himself remained far from the struggle at Brixellum on the right bank of the Po, his soldiers were defeated in battle near Cremona, and large numbers of them killed (14 April). The next day the remnant of his army was obliged to surrender. On receiving news of the defeat, Otho killed himself. His body was burned, as he had directed, on the spot where he had so ingloriously ended. Vitellius was recognized as emperor by the Senate.

SCHILLER, *Geschichte der römischen Kaiserzeit*, I (Gotha, 1883); VON DOMASZEWSKI, *Geschichte der römischen Kaiser*, II (Leipzig, 1909).

KARL HOEBER.

O'Toole, LAWRENCE. See LAWRENCE O'TOOLE, SAINT.

Otranto, ARCHDIOCESE OF (HYDRUNTINA).—Otranto is a city of the Province of Lecce, Apulia, Southern Italy, situated in a fertile region, and once famous for its breed of horses. It was an ancient Greek colony, which, in the wars of Pyrrhus and of Hannibal, was against Rome. As it is the nearest port to the eastern coast of the Adriatic Sea, it was more important than Brindisi, under the Roman emperors. In the eighth century, it was for some time in the possession of Arichis, Duke of Benevento (758–87). Having come again under Byzantine rule, it was among the last cities of Apulia to surrender to Robert Guiscard (1068), and then became part of the Principality of Taranto. In the Middle Ages the Jews had a school there. In 1480 there occurred the sack of Otranto by the Turks, in which 12,000 men are said to have perished—among them, Bishop Stephen Pendinelli, who was sawn to death; the "valley of the martyrs" still recalls that dreadful event. On other occasions, as in 1537, the Turks landed at Otranto, but they were repulsed. In 1804, the city was obliged to harbour a French garrison that was established there to watch the movements of the English fleet; and in 1810, Napoleon gave Otranto in fief to Fouché.

The cathedral of Otranto is a work of Count Roger I (1088), and was adorned later (about 1163), by Bishop Jonathas, with a mosaic floor; the same Count Roger also founded a Basilian monastery here, which, under Abbot Nicetas, became a place of study; its library was nearly all bought by Bessarion. The first known bishop of this see was Petrus, to whom St. Gregory the Great refers in 596; and there is record of his two successors; they were Sabinus (599) and Petrus (601); Bishop Marcus (about 870) is believed to be the author of the office for Holy Saturday; Petrus (958) was raised to the dignity of metropolitan by Polyeuctus, Patriarch of Constantinople (956-70), with the obligation to establish the Greek Rite throughout the province. The Latin Rite was introduced again after the Norman conquest, but the Greek Rite remained in use in several towns of the archdiocese and of its suffragans, until the sixteenth century. Bishop Jacob IV (1378), also Patriarch of Jerusalem, had a part in the schism of the West, for which reason he was imprisoned by Charles of Anjou, and compelled to abjure publicly; after that, however, he betook himself to Avignon; Peter Anthony of Capua (1536) distinguished himself at the Council of Trent; Francis M. dall'Aste (1596) was author of "Memorabilia Hydruntinæ Ecclesiæ".

In 1818 Castro, formerly a suffragan of Otranto, was united to it. Castro's bishops are known from 1137; among them was John Parisi, killed in 1296 by Canon Hector, of Otranto.

The suffragans of Otranto are Gallipoli, Lecce, and Ugento; the archdiocese has 56 parishes, 100,200 inhabitants, 4 religious houses of men, 11 of women, 2 schools for boys, and 9 for girls.

CAPPELLETTI, *Le Chiese d'Italia;* XXI.

U. BENIGNI.

Ottawa, ARCHDIOCESE OF (OTTAWIENSIS), in Canada, originally comprised the Ottawa Valley, traversed by the river of the same name. The northern portion of this diocese was, in 1882, made the Vicariate Apostolic of Pontiac, and then became the Diocese of Pembroke, itself dismembered in 1908 to form the Vicariate Apostolic of Temiskamingue. Ottawa still has an area of 10,000 square miles, extends into the Counties of Carleton, Russell, Prescott, and Lanark of the Province of Ontario, and into those of Wright, Labelle, Argenteuil, Terrebonne, and Montcalm of the Province of Quebec. The Dominion official census of 1901 gave the population of the archdiocese as 158,000 Catholics, 128,000 of whom are French-speaking and 30,000 English-speaking. A few hundreds more speak other languages.

Ottawa, metropolitan see and capital of the Dominion, was founded in 1827 simultaneously with the opening of works on the Rideau Canal, and took its first name of Bytown from Colonel By, a British officer and engineer, who had charge of the construction of the canal. With its water power and admirable position at the foot of the Chaudière Falls and at the mouth of two rivers, Bytown soon came to the front as a centre of industry. In 1848 its prospects were such that Rome raised the thriving little town to the rank of an episcopal see. In 1854 Bytown was granted city incorporation, and took the name of Ottawa. When the Canadian Confederation was definitively established in 1867, Ottawa was chosen as capital, and has been ever since the residence of the governor-general and the headquarters of Canadian federal politics.

Joseph-Eugène-Bruno Guigues, first Bishop of Ottawa (1848-74) gave his incipient diocese a solid organization; churches and schools were built, and the college, seminary, and hospital soon followed. Gifted with keen foresight, Bishop Guigues formed a diocese with the slender resources at his disposal. At his death the Catholic population of the diocese had increased from 32,000 to 93,000, and the number of priests from 15 to 80.

Joseph-Thomas Duhamel, second bishop and first Archbishop of Ottawa, whose episcopate of thirty-four years brought the diocese to its present prosperous state, will figure in the ecclesiastical history of Canada, as a prudent, saintly, and indefatigable worker. A country parish-priest before ascending the episcopal throne, he continued to lead the laborious life of an ordinary priest. His episcopal visitation was his only holiday. On these occasions he would preach several times in the day, preside at the usual ceremonies of the visitation, and investigate carefully the administration of the parish. Though stricken with angina pectoris two years before his death, he remained at his post and died in one of his country parishes while making his visitation, 5 June, 1908. He had been made an archbishop in 1886.

Archbishop Gauthier has been translated from the See of Kingston, Ontario to Ottawa, 6 Sept., 1910.

The Catholic University is Ottawa's foremost seat of learning (see OTTAWA, UNIVERSITY OF). Higher education for young ladies is in the hands of the Grey Nuns of the Cross and of the Sisters of the Congregation of Notre Dame (q. v.). Each of these communities has a large institute receiving hundreds of boarders and day pupils. The elementary schools are established in conformity with the Separate School Laws of Ontario and the Public School Laws of Quebec. Catholic elementary schools are, therefore, maintained by government taxation. Catholic ratepayers have nothing to pay for other elementary schools. The Catholic schools are efficient and well equipped. In the mind of Archbishop Duhamel, Ottawa, situated on the borders of two great provinces and possessing government libraries and museums, was destined to be an educational centre. Hence the numerous houses of studies established by religious orders in the capital.

Orders of Men: Oblates of Mary Immaculate, with five parishes, the university, a scholasticate, and juniorate; Dominicans with parish and scholasticate; the Capuchins, with parish and juniorate; Fathers of the Company of Mary, with five parishes, scholasticate, and juniorate; Regular Canons of the Immaculate Conception, with five parishes and college; Redemptorists, with house of studies; Fathers of the Holy Ghost, with agricultural college.

The most important charitable institutions are (1) four orphanages directed by the Sisters of Wisdom, the Grey Nuns, and the Sisters of Providence; (2) three homes for the aged, directed by the Grey Nuns and the Sisters of Providence; (3) one house of correction for girls, under charge of the Sisters of Charity; (4) one Misericordia Refuge for fallen women; (5) three hospitals conducted by the Grey Nuns of the Cross. The Ottawa General Hospital, the largest of the three, was founded in 1845 and has been enlarged at different times. The Youville Training School for Nurses is attached; (6) St. George's Home, the Canadian headquarters of the Catholic Emigration Society of England. The Sisters of Charity of St. Paul receive there the emigrant Catholic children and distribute them in Canadian families.

The Cathedral of the Immaculate Conception, usually called the Basilica, since it has received the title of minor basilica, is a vast Gothic structure with twin towers two hundred feet high, and a seating capacity of 2000. The parishes of St. Joseph, the Sacred Heart, St. John the Baptist, and St. Bridget have also beautiful churches.

ALEXIS, *Histoire de la Province ecclésiastique d'Ottawa* (Ottawa, 1897).

F. X. BRUNET.

Ottawa, UNIVERSITY OF, conducted by the Oblates of Mary Immaculate, founded in 1848. It was incorporated in 1849 under the title of the "College of Bytown," thus taking the original name of the city chosen in 1866 as the capital of the Dominion of Canada, and now known as Ottawa. The title in question was changed in 1861 to that of the "College of Ottawa", and the power of granting degrees was conferred on the institution by civil charter in 1866. The university thus began its complete secular existence with the confederation of the Canadian Provinces, and has grown with the growth of the Dominion. Pope Leo XIII, by Brief of 5 February, 1889, raised the College and the State University of Ottawa to the rank of a Catholic University. The Brief expresses the will of the Holy See that the Archbishop of Ottawa shall be *ex officio* Apostolic chancellor of the university, and that he and the "other bishops of the [ecclesiastical] provinces of Ottawa and Toronto who shall affiliate their seminaries and colleges and other similar institutions with the aforesaid university, do watch over the preservation of a correct and sound doctrine in the same." It may be added that the institution has also been of late years placed among the number of Colonial and Indian universities, whose students are entitled to certain privileges accorded by a statute of the University of Oxford, passed in 1887.

Situated in the capital of the Dominion, and in a district which is largely French in population, the University of Ottawa offers parallel courses in English and French. It is left to the choice of parents and students to take the classical course in one or other of the two languages. The university is governed by a chancellor, rector, vice-rector, senate, and council of administration. The faculties so far organized are those of: (1) theology, (2) law, this being an examining body only, according to certain provisions and regulations made, in this regard, by the provincial legislature of Ontario, (3) philosophy, and (4) arts. Other departments are the collegiate course and the commercial course, the former leading to matriculation which admits to the arts course in Canadian universities and to technical schools. The course in arts, after matriculation, covers four years. In theology a course of four years is provided, and embraces all the branches of ecclesiastical science usually taught in Catholic seminaries. The university has, in a separate building known as the Science Hall, well-equipped physical, chemical, and mineralogical laboratories, also a natural history museum and excellent numismatic and conchological collections.

On 2 December, 1903, fire totally destroyed the main building, a structure covering the greater part of a block 400 feet by 200. The library of the university, consisting of over 30,000 volumes, was wholly destroyed, but has been replaced, in great part, largely by donations.

The teaching staff consists of fifty professors and instructors. The number of students in 1909-10 was 591; of these 350 were in residence in the Theological Building, or Scholasticate of the Oblate Fathers, the Collegiate Building or Juniorate, and the New Arts Building. Students whose homes are not in Ottawa are required to live in the University buildings. Private rooms are provided. The University Calendar gives a long list of graduates and alumni, including names of men prominent in every walk of Canadian life.

The Science Hall, completed in 1901, and the New Arts Building erected to replace the building destroyed in 1903, are fire-proof structures and are among the best-equipped college buildings in Canada. The University owns ten acres of property in the city.

Like other seats of learning in Canada, the university lately began to offer the advantages of an extra-mural course to those who desire to pursue collegiate studies, but who are unable to attend its lectures. Extra-mural students are allowed to do the work of the arts course, and to present themselves for examinations. Before being registered, candidates for a degree must pass the matriculation, or an examination accepted by the senate as equivalent. Students are to attend the university for the latter part of the course, if at all possible.

The "Calendar" and "Annuaire", published annually by the university, give detailed information in regard to courses of study, conditions of admission, examinations, and fees in all departments. The "University of Ottawa Review", issued monthly and forming an annual volume of from four to five hundred pages, is the organ of the students.

FRANCIS W. GREY.

Otto, SAINT, Bishop of Bamberg, b. about 1060; d. 30 June, 1139. He belonged to the noble, though not wealthy, family of Mistelbach in Swabia, not to the Counts of Andechs. He was ordained priest, but where he was educated is not known. While still young he joined the household of Duke Wladislaw of Poland; in 1090 he entered the service of Emperor Henry IV, and about 1101 was made chancellor. In 1102 the emperor appointed and invested him as Bishop of Bamberg. In the conflict of investitures (q. v.) he sided chiefly in political matters with Henry IV, although he avoided taking sides openly. He refused to be consecrated by a schismatic bishop. Through ambassadors he declared his loyalty to the Holy See. In 1105 he joined the party of Henry V, went to Rome, and there on 13 May, 1106, was consecrated bishop. He never became a partisan. In 1110-11 he accompanied Henry on his journey to Rome, but, like other noble characters, he disapproved of the disgraceful treatment of Pope Paschal. This is clear from the fact that he received the pallium from the pope on 15 April, 1111. When the war broke out again, he did not desert Henry V, and in consequence was suspended by the papal party at the Synod in Fritzlar in 1118. At the Congress of Würzburg in 1121 he strove hard for peace, which was concluded in 1122 at Worms. Meanwhile he had devoted himself entirely to his diocese and as bishop had led a model, simple, and even a poor life. He increased the possesssions of the Church by new acquisitions, recovered alienated dependencies, completed the cathedral, improved the cathedral school, built castles and churches. In particular he favoured the monks, and founded over twenty monasteries in the Dioceses of Bamberg, Würzburg, Ratisbon, Passau, Eichstätt, Halberstadt and Aquileia. He reformed other monasteries. Thus he merited the name of "Father of the Monks".

His greatest service was his missionary work among the Pomeranians. In the Peace with Poland in 1120 the latter had engaged to adopt Christianity. Attempts to convert them through Polish priests and through an Italian Bishop, Bernard, proved futile. Duke Boleslaus III then appealed to Otto, and it is due to Otto that the undertaking partook of a German character. Through an understanding with the pope, who appointed him legate, the emperor and the princes, he started in May, 1124, and travelled through Prague, Breslau, Posen, and Gnesen in East Pomerania, was received by the duke with great respect, and won over the people through his quiet yet firm attitude, his magnificent appearance, generous donations, and gentle, inspiring sermons. He converted Pyritz, Kammin, Stettin, Julin, and in nine places established eleven churches; 22,165 persons were baptized. In 1125 he returned to Bamberg. As heathen customs began to assert themselves again, he once more journeyed to Pomerania through Magdeburg and Havelberg about the year 1128. In the Diet of Usedom he gained over through his inspiring discourses all the nobles of the land to Christendom. He then converted new communities, and led back those who had fallen away. Even after his return (in the same year) he was in constant communication with the Pomeranians and sent them priests from Bam-

XI.—23

berg. His wish to consecrate a bishop for Pomerania was not fulfilled, as the Archbishops of Magdeburg and Gnesen claimed the metropolitan rights. Only in 1140 was his former companion Adalbert confirmed as Bishop of Julin. In 1188 the bishopric was removed to Hammin and made directly subject to the Holy See. In Bamberg he once more gave himself up to his duties as bishop and prince and performed them with great zeal. He kept out of all political turmoil. In the papal schism of 1130-31 he tried to remain neutral. The active, pious, clever bishop was greatly esteemed by the other princes and by Emperor Lothair. He was buried in the monastery of St. Michael in Bamberg. Bishop Embrice of Würzburg delivered the funeral oration and applied to Otto the words of Jeremias: "The Lord called thy name, a plentiful olive tree, fair, fruitful, and beautiful." On his mission journey he is reported to have worked many miracles. Many happened also at his tomb. In 1189 Otto was canonized by Clement III. His feast is kept on 30 September, partly also on 30 June; in Pomerania on 1 October.

LOOSHORN, *Geschichte des Bistums Bamberg*, II (Munich, 1888), 1-368; JURITSCH, *Geschichte des Bischofs Otto I von Bamberg* (Gotha, 1889); WIESENER, *Geschichte der christlichen Kirche in Pommern* (Berlin, 1889); HAUCK, *Kirchengeschichte Deutschlands*, III (Leipzig, 1903), 571-87.

KLEMENS LÖFFLER.

Otto I, THE GREAT, Roman emperor and German king, b. in 912; d. at Memleben, 7 May, 973; son of Henry I and his consort Mathilda. In 929 he married Edith, daughter of King Athelstan of England. He succeeded Henry as king in 936. His coronation at Aachen showed that the Carlovingian traditions of empire were still in force. Otto projected a strong central power, which was opposed by the German spirit of individualism. Otto's brother Henry headed those great insurrectionary movements which Otto was first obliged to suppress. The new Duke of Bavaria, Eberhard, refused to pay homage to the king. Otto subdued Bavaria and bestowed the ducal throne upon Arnulf's brother Berthold. This attitude towards the ducal, by the royal, power, now for the first time openly assumed, roused strong opposition. The Franks, ancient rivals of the Saxons, resented this absorption of power. The Frankish Duke Eberhard formed an alliance with Otto's half-brother, Thankmar, and with other disaffected nobles. Otto's younger brother Henry and the unruly Duke Eiselbert of Lorraine raised the banner of insurrection. Agitation was stirred up on the Rhine and in the royal Palatinate on the Saale. The affair first took a decisive turn when Dukes Eberhard and Giselbert fell in the battle of Andernach. The victory did not, however, result in absolute power. An internecine agitation in Franconia between the lesser nobles and the duchy favoured the king. Henry now became reconciled with his royal brother, but his insincerity was manifest when, shortly after, he conspired with the Archbishop of Mainz and the seditious border nobles to assassinate Otto. The plot was discovered. In 941 there was a final reconciliation. The monarchic principle had triumphed over the particularism of the nobles, and the way was paved for a reorganization of the constitution. Otto made good use of his success.

OTTO I, THE GREAT
From a print in the British Museum

The hereditary duchies were filled by men closely connected with the royal house. Franconia was held by Otto in his own possession; Lorraine fell to Conrad the Red, his son-in-law; his brother Henry received Bavaria, having meanwhile married Judith, daughter of the Bavarian duke; while Swabia was bestowed upon his son Ludolph. The power of these dukes was substantially reduced. Otto was manifestly endeavouring to restore their ancient official character to the duchies. This belittling of their political position suited his design to make his kingdom more and more the sole exponent of the imperial idea. It would have been a significant step in the right direction could he have made it an hereditary monarchy, and he worked energetically towards this object.

The apparently united realm now reverted to Charlemagne's policies in the regions where he had paved the way. The Southern races promoted the work of Germanizing and Christianizing in the adjacent Slav states, and by degrees German influence spread to the Oder and throughout Bohemia. The ancient idea of universal empire now possessed Otto's mind. He endeavoured to extend his suzerainty over France, Burgundy, and Italy, and welcomed the quarrel between Hugo of France and Ludwig IV, each of whom had married one of his sisters. King and dukes in France balanced the scales of power which Otto could grasp at any time as supreme arbitrator. With similar intent he turned the private quarrels of the reigning house of Burgundy to account. Conrad of Burgundy now appeared as Otto's protégé. More significant was the attitude he was about to assume towards the complicated situation in Italy. The spiritual and moral debasement in the Italian Peninsula was shocking, even in Rome. The names of Theodora and Marozia recall an unutterably sad chapter of church history. The disorder in the capital of Christendom was only a symptom of the conditions throughout Italy. Upper Italy witnessed the wars of Berengarius of Friuli, crowned emperor by Marozia's son, John X, against Rudolph II of Upper Burgundy. After the assassination of Berengarius in 924, the strife was renewed between this Rudolph and Hugo of Lower Burgundy. Hugo finally became sole ruler in Italy and assumed the imperial throne. But his supremacy was shortly after overthrown by Berengarius of Ivrea, against whom, also, there appeared a growing opposition in favour of Adelaide, the daughter of Rudolph II of Upper Burgundy, to suppress which Berengarius obtained forcible possession of the princess. All these disorders had been studied by Otto. Convinced of the significance of the ancient ideas of empire, he wished to subject Italy to his authority, basing his right upon his royal rank. In 951 he came to Italy, released Adelaide and married her, whilst Berengarius swore allegiance to him. Under the influence of the Roman Alberich, the son of Marozia, Pope Agapetus refused the imperial crown to the German king. But even without the coronation, the universality of his rule was apparent. He stood *de facto* at the head of the West. The royal power was now in need of the strongest support. New and dangerous insurrections demonstrated the lack of internal solidarity. Particularism once more raised its head. Otto's son Ludolph was the spirit of the new uprising. He demanded a share in the government and was especially irritated by the influence of Otto's Burgundian consort. The particularist element assembled in Ludolph's camp. It fermented throughout almost the entire duchy and broke out openly in many parts. The danger was more threatening than it had been in the first insurrection. In 954 the Magyars once more thronged into the empire. Owing to this crisis, the necessity for a strong, central power was generally recognized, and the insurrection died out. It was definitively terminated at the Imperial Diet of Auerstadt, where it was announced that Conrad and

Ludolph had forfeited their duchies. Meanwhile the Magyar hordes surrounded Augsburg. Bishop Ulrich heroically defended the threatened city. In the great battle on the Lechfelde in 955, the Hungarian army was completely routed by Otto, who had advanced to the defence of the city. By this victory he freed Germany finally from the Hungarian peril. It marked a crisis in the history of the Magyar race, which now became independent and founded an empire with definite boundaries. It also caused Otto to realize that his great object of preventing the participation of power with the duchies was not attainable by force or through the prestige of his kingly rank. He at once endeavoured to obtain a strong support from the German Church throughout the empire.

The Ottonian system, a close alliance of the German realm with the Church, was begun. Charlemagne, too, had carried out the great conception of unity of Church and State, but the ecclesiastical idea had given a religious colouring to Frankish statemanship, whilst Otto planned a State Church, with the spiritual hierarchy a mere branch of the interior government of the realm. In order to solve this problem Otto was first constrained to permeate the Church with new spiritual and moral life and also free himself from the dominion of the lay aristocracy. His own deeply religious nature was his best guarantee. Some part of the spirit of ascetic piety which distinguished his mother, Mathilda, was found also in the son; and his brother Bruno, later Archbishop of Cologne, as the clever representative of ecclesiastical views, also exercised a great influence upon the king's religious dispositions. The close union of Church and State had an equally salutary effect upon both of the powers concerned. By granting the Church such royal domains as were not in use, the State could devote its revenues to military purposes. For the united realms this situation was likewise rich in blessings, since under the protection of the bishops, commerce and trade were developed on the great ecclesiastical estates, and the lower classes received from the Church protection against the nobles. The kingdom everywhere retained supremacy over the Church: the king could nominate bishops and abbots; the bishops were subject to the royal tribunals; and synods could only be called with the royal approval. The German court became the centre of religious and spiritual life. In the so-called Ottonian renaissance, however, women were chiefly concerned, led by the women of the royal family: Mathilda, Gerberga, Judith, Adelaide, and Theophano. Quedlinburg, founded by Otto in 936, was an influential centre of culture. But this Ottonian system depended upon one premise: if it were to benefit the State, the king must control the Church. As a matter of fact, the supreme authority over the German Church was the pope. Yet Otto's policy of imperialism was rooted in the recognition of the above premise. The conquest of Italy should result in the subjection of the highest ecclesiastical authority to German royalty. Otto was consequently obliged to make this campaign; and the much discussed question of the motive dictating the imperial policy is resolved. The unworthy John XII was at that time reigning in Rome. He was the son of Alberich, the Tyrant of Rome, whose covetous glances were directed towards the Exarchate and the Pentapolis. A rival in these aspirations rose in the person of Berengarius who endeavoured to extend his rule over Rome. Otto complied with the pope's request for aid, which exactly suited his projected church policy. He had previously caused his son Otto, a minor, to be elected and anointed king at the Diet of Worms in 961. He left his brother Bruno, and his natural son, Wilhelm, regents in Germany, and journeyed over the Brenner and thus to Rome, where he was crowned emperor on 2 Feb., 962. On this occasion the so-called Ottonian privilege was conferred, whose genuineness has been frequently, though unjustly, attacked. In its first part this privilege recalls the Pactum Illudovici of 817. It confirms the grants which the Church received from the Carlovingians and their successors. The second part goes back to the Constitution of Lothair (824), according to which the consecration of kings should not be permitted before swearing allegiance to the German ruler. When Otto marched against Berengarius, Pope John entered into treasonable relations with the emperor's enemies; whereupon Otto returned to Rome and forced the Romans to take an oath never to elect a pope without his own or his son's approval. John was deposed and a layman, Leo VIII, placed upon the papal throne. Then Berengarius was defeated in his turn and carried a prisoner to Bamberg. Once more Rome, always in a state of unrest, rose in arms. The exiled pope, John, forced his supplanter to flee. But John died in 964, and the Romans elected a new pope, Benedict V. The emperor energetically restored order and Leo was reinstated in his position. It was already apparent that the emperor really controlled the papacy which occupied the position of a mere link in the German constitution. The Ottonian system was of the greatest significance to Germany in her position towards the secular powers. How greatly the German King was strengthened through the close alliance between Church and State and how it enhanced the prestige of the empire, is evident from the progress that Teutonism and Christianity were making in Slav territory. Otto chose Magdeburg, for which he had a special attachment, as the local centre of this new civilization, and raised it to an archbishopric.

Recurring disorders now recalled him to Rome. The pope whom he had chosen, John XIII, found antagonists in the Roman nobility. The emperor performed his duties as protector of the Church with stern justice and punished the turbulent nobles. John XIII then crowned his son, Otto, emperor. As a logical consequence of his imperial policy, he now openly avowed his intention of acquiring Lower Italy. His supremacy would be absolutely safeguarded if he succeeded in gaining possession of the southern part of the peninsula. Otto, however, finally abandoned the war in the south. His son's prospect of obtaining a Byzantine princess for his bride turned the scale against it. The old German axiom of legitimacy, which was once more honoured in this marriage, was destined later on to revenge itself bitterly.

Otto was buried at Magdeburg. His contemporaries compared his tremendous physical strength to that of a lion. He was a Saxon through and through. In his youth he had learned all the arts of the profession of arms. Though subject to violent fits of temper, and conscious of his power and genius, he prayed as devoutly as a child. A shrewd calculator, always convincing and always toiling, he correctly estimated the importance of diplomatic negotiations. He was a keen observer and possessed a fine knowledge of human nature which always enabled him to select the proper persons for important offices in the government.

KÖPKE AND DÖNNIGES, *Jahrbücher des deutschen Reiches unter Otto dem Grossen* (Berlin, 1838); KÖPKE AND DÜMMLER, *Kaiser Otto der Grosse* (Leipzig, 1876); FICKER, *Das deutsche Kaiserreich in seinen universellen und nationalen Beziehungen* (Innsbruck, 1861); VON SYBEL, *Die deutsche Nation und das Kaiserreich* (Düsseldorf, 1862); SACKUR, *Die Quellen für den ersten Römerzug Ottos I* in *Strassburger Festschrift zur 46. Versammlung deutscher Philologen* (Strasburg, 1901); SICKEL, *Das Privilegium Otto I fur die römische Kirche vom Jahre 962* (Innsbruck, 1883); MENKEL, *Ottos I Beziehungen zu den deutschen Erzbischofen seiner Zeit und die Leistungen der letzteren für Staat, Kirche und Kultur* (Program, Magdeburg, 1900); MITTAG, *Erzbischof Friedrich von Mainz und die Politik Ottos des Grossen* (Halle, 1895).

F. KAMPERS.

Otto II, King of the Germans and Emperor of Rome, son of Otto I and Adelaide, b. 955; d. in Rome, 7 Dec., 983. In 961 he was elected king at Worms, and was crowned at Aix, 26 May. Frail in body, he possessed an intrepid and arbitrary spirit. With him began that extravagant policy of imperialism, which aimed at restoring the world boundaries of the ancients, and to encompass the Ancient Sea (the Mediterranean). Germany and Italy were to wield the balance of power. Reacting against this imperialistic policy was the revived strength of particularism. The conflict with the ducal House of Bavaria gave a dangerous aspect to affairs. In Bavaria (with Otto's approval) the duchess dowager Judith acted as regent for her son Henry. Upon coming of age he was given the Duchy of Bavaria in fee by Otto II, who, at the same time, invested Ludolph's son Otto with Swabia on the death of Duke Burchard, ignoring the latter's widow, Hedwig, a daughter of Judith. Henry, named the "Quarrelsome", supported by Abraham of Friesing, Boleslaw of Bohemia, and Mesislav of Poland, opposed this. The war finally ended by Judith being immured in a cloister and Henry declared to have forfeited his duchy. Ludolph's son Otto received the vacant ducal throne. The Eastmark was separated from Bavaria and given in fee to Luitpold of Babenberg, who laid the foundation of the future renown of his family. In 978 Lothair, who aspired to the acquisition of Western Germany, invaded Lorraine, and pillaged Aix where Otto narrowly escaped capture. But Lothair did not advance further. In Dortmund a war of reprisal was at once decided upon; with 60,000 men, Otto marched upon Paris, which he failed to take. Lothair, however, was obliged to come to terms, and in 980 the two kings met near Sedan, where Otto obtained an agreement securing the former boundaries.

In Rome, Crescentius, a son of Theodora, headed a disorderly factional government and sought to settle the affairs of the Holy See by coercion. Otto crossed the Alps and freed the papacy. While in Rome his mind became imbued with dreams of ancient imperialism; he would give his imperialistic policy a firm foundation by bringing all Italy under subjection. In Southern Italy the Byzantines and Saracens united against the German pretensions, and in 982 the war with these ancient powers commenced. Tarentum fell into the hands of the German king, but 15 July, 982, he was defeated near Capo Colonne, not far from Cotrone. This battle resulted in the surrender of Apulia and Calabria and destroyed the prestige of the imperial authority throughout Italy. The effect spread to the people of the North and the turbulent Slavs on the East, and shortly after the Danes and Wends rose up in arms. But Otto was victorious. The Christian mission, under the leadership of pilgrims of Passau, had made great progress in the territory of the Magyars. Then came the defeat in Calabria, whereupon all of Slavonia, particularly the heathen part, revolted against German sovereignty. The promising beginnings of German and Christian culture east of the Elbe, inaugurated by Otto, were destroyed. In Bohemia the ecclesiastical organization was thoroughly established, but the emperor was unable to support the bishop whom he had placed there. On the Havel and the Spree Christianity was almost annihilated. Affairs were in equally bad condition among the Wends. The reign of Otto II has been justly called the period of martyrdom for the German Church. The missions which had been organized by Otto I were, with few exceptions, destroyed. Otto II now renewed the despotic policy towards the Saxonian border nobles and incited open discontent. In 983 he held an Imperial Diet where his son was elected king as Otto III and where the assembled nobles pledged their support. He departed with high hopes for Southern Italy. Fortune seemed to favour the imperial leader, who expected to wipe out the disgrace suffered in the south. He chose a new pope, Peter of Pavia (John XIV). While in Rome he was stricken with malaria and was buried in St. Peter's. At the time of his death the relations of the empire towards the papacy were still undefined. He had been unable to maintain his political ascendency in Rome. His imperialistic policy had placed the restraints of progressive and pacific Christianity and Germanization on the borders; and he, pursuing fanciful dreams, believed that he might dare to transfer the goal of his policy to the south.

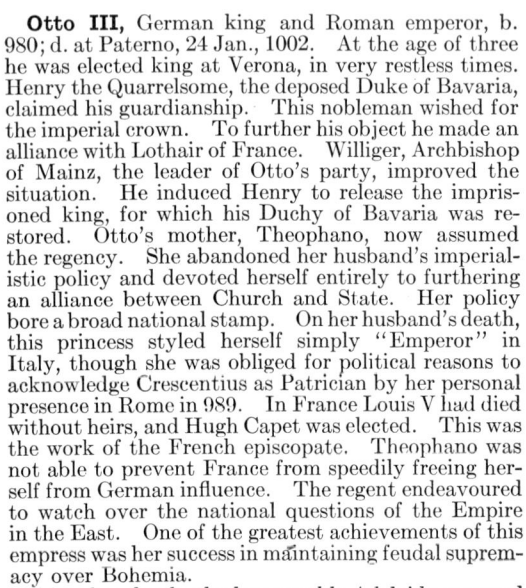

TOMB OF OTTO II
Vatican Crypts, St. Peter's, Rome

GIESEBRECHT, *Jahrbücher des deutschen Reiches unter Otto II* (Berlin, 1840); UHLER, *Jahrbücher des deutschen reiches unter Otto II u. Otto III* (Leipzig, 1902); DETMER, *Otto II bis zum Tode seines Vaters* (Leipzig, 1878); MÜLLER-MANN, *Die auswärtige Politik Kaiser Ottos II* (Basle, 1898); MOLTMANN, *Theophano, die Gemahlin Ottos II in ihrer Bedeutung fur die Politik Otto I u. Otto II* (Göttingen, 1873).

F. KAMPERS.

Otto III, German king and Roman emperor, b. 980; d. at Paterno, 24 Jan., 1002. At the age of three he was elected king at Verona, in very restless times. Henry the Quarrelsome, the deposed Duke of Bavaria, claimed his guardianship. This nobleman wished for the imperial crown. To further his object he made an alliance with Lothair of France. Williger, Archbishop of Mainz, the leader of Otto's party, improved the situation. He induced Henry to release the imprisoned king, for which his Duchy of Bavaria was restored. Otto's mother, Theophano, now assumed the regency. She abandoned her husband's imperialistic policy and devoted herself entirely to furthering an alliance between Church and State. Her policy bore a broad national stamp. On her husband's death, this princess styled herself simply "Emperor" in Italy, though she was obliged for political reasons to acknowledge Crescentius as Patrician by her personal presence in Rome in 989. In France Louis V had died without heirs, and Hugh Capet was elected. This was the work of the French episcopate. Theophano was not able to prevent France from speedily freeing herself from German influence. The regent endeavoured to watch over the national questions of the Empire in the East. One of the greatest achievements of this empress was her success in maintaining feudal supremacy over Bohemia.

After her death, the less capable Adelaide assumed the regency. Unlike her predecessor, hers was not a nature fitted to rule; the Slavs rose on the eastern border, and the Normans were with difficulty held in check. She died in 999. The influence of these two women upon the education of the young king (who assumed the government in 994) was not slight. But two men exercised even greater influence on him: Johannes Nonentula, a protégé of Theophano, and Bernward of Hildesheim. The austere Bernward awakened in him inclinations to fanciful enthusiasm which coloured his dreams of empire.

Supported by the spiritual princes of the Empire, he marched into Italy. Here he behaved as though the Roman see were a metropolitan bishopric under the Empire. He it was who presided at synods and dared to revoke papal decisions, and who selected the popes. Like Charlemagne, he was convinced of the spiritual character of his imperial dignity, and deduced from this the necessity of setting the empire over the papacy. He raised a German, Bruno, to the Chair of Peter under the name of Gregory V. The new pope crowned Otto emperor 21 May, 996, but he did not act counter to the ancient claims of the Curia, and he emphasized the duties and rights of the popes.

Otto returned to Germany in 996. It was of the greatest consequence that in Bruno the papal throne contained a man who encouraged the ideas of the reform party for purification and spiritualization within the Church, and a consequent exaltation of the papacy. Harmonizing with this reform party was the ascetic movement within the Church, whose principal exponent was a native of Southern Italy called Nilus. Among his pupils was the Bohemian, Adalbert, second Bishop of Prague, who was at that time in Rome devoting himself entirely to mystical and ascetic enthusiasm. In 996 Otto met this remarkable man whom he succeeded in sending back to his see. As he scrupled returning to Bohemia, he went as missionary to the Prussian country, where he was put to death in 999. The emperor was affected by the grotesque piety of this man, and it had aroused ascetic inclinations in him also. Still another person obtained great influence over him: the learned Frenchman, Gerbert, who came to the Imperial court in 997.

In Rome, meanwhile, Crescentius had set up an antipope named John XVI and forced Gregory V to flee. In 998 Otto went to Rome, where he pronounced severe judgment upon those who had rebelled against his decisions. Gregory died in 999, and the emperor raised his friend Gerbert to the papacy as Sylvester II. He too, followed the ancient path of the Curia, and advocated papal supremacy over all Christendom. How was this consistent and energetic policy of the Curia to affect the youthful emperor's dreams of a fusion of the ideal state with the ideal church in an Augustan Theocracy? The interference with Italian affairs was now to react bitterly upon Germany. In 1000 Otto made a pilgrimage to the tomb of his friend Adelbert at Gnesen, where he erected an archbishopric destined to promote the emancipation of the Eastern Slavonians. He practised mortifications at the tomb of an ascetic, and thrilled with the highest ideas of his imperial dignity, he afterwards caused the tomb of Charlemagne at Aix to be opened. Before long his dreams of empire faded away. Everywhere there was fermentation throughout Italy. Otto, lingering in Rome, found himself, with the pope, obliged to abandon the city. In Germany the princes united in a national opposition to the imperialism of this capricious sovereign. He had few supporters in his plan to reconquer the Eternal City. Only by recourse to arms could his body be brought to Aix, where recently his tomb has been discovered in the cathedral.

WILMANS, *Jahrbücher des Deutschen Reiches unter Ottos III* (Berlin, 1840); BENTZINGER, *Das Leben der Kaiserin Adelheid, Gemahlin Ottos I., während der Regierung Ottos III* (Breslau Dissertation, 1883); OTTO, *Papst Gregor V* (Münster Dissertation, 1881); LUX, *Papst Silvester II Einfluss auf die Politik Kaiser Ottos III* (Breslau, 1898); VOIGT, *Adalbert von Prag* (Berlin, 1898); SCHULTTESS, *Papst Silvester II als Lehrer und Staatsmann* (Hamburg, 1891); ZHARSKI, *Die Slavenkriege zur Zeit Ottos III und die Pilgerfahrt nach Gnesen* (Lemberg, 1882).

F. KAMPERS.

Otto IV, German king and Roman emperor, b. at Argentau (Dept. of Orne), c. 1182; d. 19 May, 1218; son of Henry the Lion and of his wife Mathilda, daughter of King Henry II of England and sister of Richard Cœur de Lion. In the latter, by whom he was made Earl of March, Otto found a constant support. This connexion of the Guelphs with England encouraged Adolf of Cologne, upon the death of Henry VI and the election of Philip of Swabia by the Hohenstaufens, to proclaim Otto king, which took place in Cologne, on 9 June, 1198. The next aim of Otto was to obtain the confirmation of his position as head of the kingdom. The power of the Hohenstaufens was, however, too great. Otto and his followers hoped that Pope Innocent III, who was hostile to the Hohenstaufens, would espouse Otto's cause in the contest for the German throne. Innocent awaited developments. To him the individual was of little importance, his chief solicitude being for the recognition of his right to decide contested elections to the German throne, and, in consequence, his suzerainty over kingdom and empire. The year 1200 was favourable to Philip. He, however, made the mistake of taking possession of the episcopal See of Mainz in defiance of canonical regulations, whereupon Innocent declared for Otto. The year 1201 marked the beginning of energetic action on the part of the Curia in Otto's behalf. While the papal legate, Guido of Palestrina, constantly gained new friends to Otto's cause, the "sweet youth" (*süsse junge Mann*), as Walther von der Vogelweide calls Philip, remained inactive, protesting the while at the attitude of the pope. When, in 1203, Thuringia and Bohemia also deserted him, Philip's affairs were nearly hopeless. Otto had made the broadest concessions to the Holy See, wishing "to become King of the Romans through the favour of God and the pope". He confirmed the papacy in its secular possessions, relinquished the property of Mathilda of Tuscany, and even guaranteed to the pope the revenues of Sicily. He resigned all claims to dominion in Italy, promising to treat with the Romans and with the cities of Italy only in concurrence with the pope. The purpose of Innocent to become the overlord of Italy was thus all but accomplished. The moral results of this great contest for the throne were unfortunate. Princes and bishops shamelessly changed their party allegiance.

In 1204 the scale turned in Philip's favour. This was due to the fact that the whole north-western part of the kingdom became involved in the war for the succession in Holland, and could therefore manifest but little interest in the affairs of the Guelphs. The year 1205 saw a general desertion from Otto's cause, his dominion being finally limited to the city of Cologne and his possessions in Brunswick. The Archbishop of Cologne, Adolf, had also gone over to Philip's standard, upon which sentence of excommunication had been pronounced against him. The Diocese of Cologne was then subjected to all the confusion of a schism. In addition the city of Cologne finally fell into the hands of the Hohenstaufens. Without further delay, the pope withdrew his support from the apparently lost cause of the Guelphs, and began negotiations with the Hohenstaufens, in which he was joined by the other cities of Italy. After mutual concessions, the pope promised to acknowledge Philip and to crown him emperor. When about to deal the last crushing blow to the Guelphs, Philip was murdered by the Count Palatine Otto von Wittelsbach at Bamberg, on 21 June, 1208. The princes now rallied round Otto, who had shown his recognition of their right of election by coming forward once more as a candidate for the crown. Otto's next step was to take as his wife the daughter of his murdered enemy, which was an added incentive to the Hohenstaufens to yield themselves to his sway.

On 11 November, 1208, he was once more elected, this time at Frankfort, which event was followed by a period of mutual understanding and a short term of peace for the kingdom. To ensure the support of the pope, Otto drew up a charter at Speyer on 22 March, 1209, in which he renewed the concessions previously made, and added others. He now promised not to prevent appeals regarding ecclesiastical affairs being made to the Holy See. Of the greatest significance was his act acknowledging the exclusive right of election of the cathedral chapter. In 1209 Otto journeyed to Rome to receive the imperial crown. On this occasion he did not come as a humble petitioner, but as German king to order the affairs of Italy and to bring about the re-establishment of its relations with his kingdom. As soon as the coronation was an accomplished fact (4 Oct., 1209), it was apparent that he intended to make the policy of the Hohenstaufens his own. His first step was to lay claim to Sicily. The pope, who must have feared a re-establishment of the dominion of Henry VI in lower Italy, excommunicated Otto on 18 October, 1210, and determined to place the young Hohenstaufen, Frederick II, upon the throne. The latter secured the support of France, and thus succeeded once more in winning the German princes to his cause. On the death of Otto's wife, a Hohenstaufen princess, the Hohenstaufen party completely abandoned his standard for that of Frederick. The renewed conflict between the Guelphs and the Hohenstaufens was not decided in Germany, but abroad. Conditions in the kingdom were so changed that foreign arms were destined to decide the contest for the German crown. So crushing was the defeat inflicted upon the Guelph and English forces by Philip Augustus at Bouvines (27 July, 1214), that Otto's cause was lost. Although he endeavoured in 1217 and 1218 to make a further effort to secure the throne, he met with no great success. Absolved from his excommunication, he died on 19 May, 1218, and was buried at St. Blasien in Brunswick.

LANGERFELDT, *Kaiser Otto IV der Welfe* (Hanover, 1872); WINKELMANN, *Philipp von Schwaben und Otto IV von Braunschweig* (2 vols., Leipzig, 1873–78); HURTER, *Geschichte Papst Innocenz III und seiner Zeitgenossen* (4 vols., Hamburg, 1834–72); GROTEFEND, *Zur Charakteristik Philipps von Schwaben und Ottos IV von Braunschweig* (Jena, 1886); SCHWEMER, *Innocenz III und die deutsche Kirche während des Thronstreites von 1198–1208* (Strasburg, 1882); LUCHAIRE, *Innocent III* (1904).

F. KAMPERS.

Ottobeuren (OTTOBURA, MONASTERIUM OTTOBURANUM), formerly a Benedictine abbey, now a priory, near Memmingen in the Bavarian Allgäu. It was founded in 764 by Blessed Toto, and dedicated to St. Alexander, the martyr. Of its early history little is known beyond the fact that Toto, its first abbot, died about 815 and that St. Ulric was its abbot in 972. In the eleventh century its discipline was on the decline, till Abbot Adalhalm (1082–94) introduced the reform of Hirsau. The same abbot began to restore the decaying buildings, which were completed, with the addition of a convent for noble ladies, by his successor, Abbot Rupert I (1102–45). Under the rule of the latter the newly founded abbey of Marienberg was recruited with monks from Ottobeuren. His successor, Abbot Isengrim (1145–80), wrote "Annales minores" (Mon. Germ. Hist.: Script., XVII, 315 sq.) and "Annales majores" (ibid., 312 sq.). In 1153, and again in 1217, it was consumed by fire. In the fourteenth and fifteenth centuries it declined so completely that at the accession of Abbot Johann Schedler (1416–43) only six or eight monks were left, and its annual revenues did not exceed 46 silver marks. Under Abbot Leonard Wiedemann (1508–46) it again began to flourish: he erected a printing establishment and a common house of studies for the Suabian Benedictines. The latter, however, was soon closed, owing to the ravages of the Thirty Years' War.

The most flourishing period in the history of Ottobeuren began with the accession of Abbot Rupert Ness (1710–40) and lasted until its secularization in 1802. From 1711–1725 Abbot Rupert erected the present monastery, the architectural grandeur of which has merited for it the name of "the Suabian Escorial". In 1737 he also began the building of the present church, completed by his successor, Anselm Erb, in 1766. In the zenith of its glory Ottobeuren fell a prey to the greediness of the Bavarian Government (see Schleglmann, "Geschichte der Säkularisation im rechtsrheinischen Bayern", III, Ratisbon, 1906, 611–54). In 1834 King Louis I of Bavaria restored it as a Benedictine priory, dependent on the abbey of St. Stephen at Augsburg. At present (1910) the community consists of five fathers, sixteen lay brothers, and one lay novice, who have under their charge the parish of Ottobeuren, a district school, and an industrial school for poor boys. Noteworthy among monks of Ottobeuren are: Nicolas Ellenbog, humanist, d. 1543; Jacob Molitor, the learned and saintly prior, d. 1675; Albert Krey, the hagiographer, d. 1713; Fr. Schmier, canonist, d. 1728; Augustine Bayrhamer, d. 1782, and Maurus Feyerabend, d. 1818, historians; the learned Abbot Honoratus Goehl (1767–1802), who was a promoter of true church music, and founded two schools; Ulric Schiegg, the mathematician and astronomer, d. 1810.

LINDNER, *Album Ottoburanum* in *Zeitschrift des hist. Vereins für Schwaben und Neuburg*, XXXI (Augsburg, 1905); IDEM, *Die Schriftsteller des Benediktiner-Ordens in Bayern*, II (Ratisbon, 1880), 69–113; FEYERABEND, *Des ehemaligen Reichsstiftes Ottenbeuren Benediktinerordens in Schwaben sämmtliche Jahrbücher* (Ottobeuren, 1813–6); BERNHARD, *Beschreibung des Klosters und der Kirche zu Ottobeuren* (Ottobeuren, 1883); AUFLEGER, *Die Klosterkirche in Ottobeuren* (Munich, 1892–4); BAUMANN, *Geschichte des Allgäus* (Kempten, 1880–95).

MICHAEL OTT.

Ottoboni, PIETRO. See ALEXANDER VIII.

Otto of Freising, bishop and historian, b. between 1111 and 1114, d. at Morimond, Champagne, France, 22 September, 1158. He was the son of St. Leopold of Austria, and Agnes, daughter of Henry IV. Through his mother's first marriage with the Hohenstaufen Frederick I, Duke of Swabia, he was half-brother of Conrad III and uncle of Emperor Frederick Barbarossa. Like his younger brothers, he was early destined for the priesthood, and when scarcely more than a child he was made provost of the chapter of canons at Klosterneuburg, near Vienna, founded in 1114. For his education he was sent to the University of Paris, the centre of learning, philosophical, theological, and classical. On his journey home he and fifteen other noblemen entered the Cistercian Order at Morimond. It is not known what led him to take this sudden step. Within three years he was elected abbot of the monastery, but shortly afterwards, probably in the same year (1137 or 1138), was called to Freising as bishop, though he did not lay aside the habit of his order. As bishop he displayed a highly beneficent activity by founding and reforming monasteries, and zealously furthering scientific studies by introducing Aristotelean philosophy and scholastic disputations on the model of the University of Paris. As a result the school at Freising flourished anew. He removed many of the abuses that had crept in, in consequence of the investiture strife, and demanded back the properties of which the Church had been robbed. In every way he raised the prestige of the Church in Freising as against the nobility, and after bitter struggles freed it from the burdensome bailiwick of the Wittelsbach counts palatine. As prince of the German Empire and closely connected with the Hohenstaufen family, he possessed great influence, and used his high standing to adjust differences within the empire. He was especially active in bringing about a reconciliation between Frederick and Henry the Lion, and in restoring peace between the emperor and the pope. In 1147 he accompanied Conrad III on his unsuccessful crusade to the Holy Land. The part of the army entrusted to Otto was completely annihilated, and he himself returned home after undergoing the severest privations and facing the greatest dangers. Otto was to have accompanied Emperor Frederick on his march into Italy in 1158, but remained behind on account of ill-health. He went to France to attend the general chapter of his order, and died while revisiting the monastery of Morimond.

In addition to a short fragment of a history of Hildebrand (edited by Goldast, "Apologia pro Henrico IV", Hanover, 1611, 18 sqq.), two historical works by Otto of Freising are extant, the so-called "Chronicle" (Chronicon seu rerum ab initio mundi ad sua usque tempora 1146 libri VIII) and the "History of Emperor Frederick" (Gesta Friderici I imperatoris usque ad 1156 libri II). The "Chronicle", dedicated to the cleric Isingrim (perhaps Abbot of Ottobeuren), is a universal history in eight books based in the main on the great medieval chronicles, especially on Ekkehard, but also on the church histories of Rufinus and Orosius. Otto's work, however, is by no means a chronicle in the sense of its predecessors. He himself did not call it a chronicle, but gave it the title of "De duabus civitatibus", since, as he asserted, he did not wish merely to enumerate the different events but to combine, as in a tragedy, a picture of the evil which abounded in his time. For this purpose he adheres closely to St. Augustine's teaching of two states, especially as elaborated in the "De Civitate Dei", though he also used the ideas of Orosius concerning the misery of the world. Although the doctrine of the two states as it appears in Otto's historical work can be variously interpreted, he undoubtedly wished to represent the conflict between the *civitas Dei* (City of God) and the *civitas diaboli* (City of the Devil), between the children of God and the *cives Babyloniæ mundique amatores* (citizens of Babylon and lovers of the world). Evidently his belief is, that after Christ the conflict between the mundane state of Babel and the Divine state of Israel changed into a conflict between Christianity and paganism or heresy. After the complete victory of Christianity, however, he treats almost exclusively of the *civitas Dei*, which then merges into the Church. Nevertheless, he is compelled to represent it in its earthly admixture as a *corpus admixtum*, in which the chosen ones must live and act side by side with the outcasts. Guided by these views, he gives a narrative in the first seven books extending from the creation of the world to the year 1146, while the eighth book depicts the Antichrist, the Second Coming, the Resurrection of the Dead, the Last Judgment, the end of the mundane state, and the beginning of the Divine state. Thus, through a unifying conception, he succeeded in representing the entire range of history as a connected whole, by which he became, if not the first, certainly the most important representative of the medieval philosophy of history. The work, which was spread in many manuscripts, was first published in 1515 in Strasburg (*ex ædibus M. Schureri*). Wilmans issued a critical edition of it in "Monumenta Germ. Scriptores", XX (Hanover, 1868), pp. 115–301, and a German translation of the sixth and seventh books was published in Leipzig (1881, 1894).

Otto began his second historical work, "Gesta Friderici", almost ten years after the completion of his "Chronicle". But he could not finish it, and at his death entrusted the continuation of it to his chaplain Rahewin. Of course he had command of excellent, reliable sources, and therefore could reproduce verbatim a number of extremely important documents. Although a unifying thought is not so apparent in this work, it is not difficult to perceive that Otto here desired to prove that happiness in this world depends upon the harmonious co-operation of Church and State. Throughout the "Gesta" he endeavours to show that a happy state of peace followed the termination of the conflicts between the emperor and the pope at Frederick's accession to the throne. And even though the feeling for the world's misery (the so-called pessimism of Otto, or rather of the Middle Ages—cf. Hauck, "Kirchengeschichte", IV, 479 sqq.), which dominates his "Chronicle", crops up repeatedly, a spirit of "cheerful buoyancy" pervades the entire work, and the dramatis personæ are depicted more freely and with greater self-confidence. In the first book he describes the events from the beginning of the disputes between the empire and the papacy under Henry IV to the death of Conrad III. In the second he relates the history of the years of peace (1152–6). The "Gesta Friderici", therefore, is an extremely important work, despite the fact that the author himself could not give it the final polish. It is notable both as to form and content, though it cannot be expected to fulfil all the requirements of modern standards. The first edition was published at Strasburg in 1515; Wilmans published a critical edition of it in "Monumenta Germ. Scriptores", XX (Hanover, 1868), pp. 347–415, and a German translation of it appeared in Leipzig (1883, 1894).

POTTHAST, *Bibl. hist. med. ævi*, II (Berlin, 1896), 885–7, contains many bibliographical references; WATTENBACH, *Deutschlands Geschichtsquellen im Mittelalter*, II (Berlin, 1894), 271–9; BERNHEIM, *Der Charakter Ottos und seiner Werke* in *Mitteil. des Instituts für österr. Geschichtsforschung*, VI (1885), 1–51; HASHAGEN, *Otto von Freising als Geschichtsphilosoph und Kirchenpolitiker* (Leipzig, 1900); HAUCK, *Kirchengesch. Deutschlands*, IV (Leipzig, 1903), 476–85; SCHMIDLIN, *Die geschichtsphilos. und kirchenpolit. Weltanschauung Ottos von Freising* (Freiburg, 1906).

PATRICIUS SCHLAGER.

Otto of Passau.—All we know of him is in the preface of his work, in which he calls himself a member of the Franciscan Order, at one time lector of theology at Basle, and says that he finished his writing on 2 (1) Feb., 1386, dedicating it to all the "friends of God", both clerical and lay, male and female, and begs for their prayers. According to Sbaralea ("Suppl. Script. Franciscani ordinis", Rome, 1806, 571) he was a native of Flanders and belonged to the Franciscan province of Cologne. His book bears the title "Die vierundzwanzig alten oder der guldin Tron der minnenden seelen". He introduces the twenty-four ancients of Apoc., iv, 4, and makes them utter sentences of wisdom by which men can obtain the golden throne in eternal life. The sentences are taken from Holy Scripture, the Fathers, Scholastics, and from those heathen authors, "whom the Church does not condemn". He thus enumerates 104 "masters", among whom are also some of the mystics, as Hugo and Richard of St. Victor. He generally gives accurate quotation of his sources though he also draws from some not specified, e. g., St. Elizabeth of Schönau. He tries to remain on strictly Catholic ground, but sometimes loses himself in dogmatical intricacies and quibbles. To be plain and intelligible he frequently uses trivial expressions. He writes on the nature of God and of man, on their mutual relation, on the requisites for perfection: contrition, confession, and penance; on internal and external life, purity of motives, shunning idleness, love of God and of the neighbour, the necessity of faith, and the grace of God. He speaks of the Scriptures as the storehouse of Divine wisdom and urges the faithful to read them. In speaking of contemplative life he insists that none can reach it without spending time in the active service of God and man. The term "friends of God" he explains according to John, xv, 15, and speaks of prayer, humility, obedience, spiritual life, virtues and vices, and shows Christ as the model of all virtues. The longest chapters, eleven and twelve, he devotes to the Holy Eucharist and to the Blessed Virgin. The last chapters treat of death and the future life. The number of manuscript copies of the book (about forty) bears evidence of the estimation in which it was held. It found its way to all "friends of God" in the south of

Germany, along the Lower Rhine and in the Netherlands. It first appeared in print in 1470, probably by Pfister in Bamberg. A modernized edition, "Die Krone der Aeltesten", was made in 1835 at Landshut as a tenth volume of "Leitstern auf der Bahn des Heils".

Allg. deutsche Biogr., XXIV, 741, and XXV, 794; HURTER, *Nomenclator*, II (1906), 725.

FRANCIS MERSHMAN.

Otto of St. Blasien, chronicler, b. about the middle of the twelfth century; d. 23 July, 1223, at St. Blasien in the Black Forest, Baden. Nothing is known of the events of his life. It is probable that in his later days he became abbot of the renowned Benedictine monastery of St. Blasien. He is known as the writer who continued the chronicles of Otto of Freising, like whom he possessed a great talent for presenting a clear survey of events. His language was lofty, and followed the model of the ancient classics. Like many of his contemporaries, he liked to apply the fixed formulas of Justinian to the German emperors, probably on the assumption, then widespread, that the Holy Roman Empire was only the continuation of the Roman Empire of the Cæsars. His chronicles, written in the form of annals, "Ad librum VII chronici Ottonis Frisingensis episcopi continuatæ historiæ appendix sive Continuatio Sanblasiana", embrace the period from 1146 to 1209, that is, the period from Conrad III to the murder of Philip of Swabia. Since he was distant in time from the facts he narrates, his accounts are wholly objective, even though he makes no concealment of his prejudice in favour of the Hohenstaufen, who in 1218 received the bailiwick of St. Blasien from the dukes of Zähringen. Yet, even after Otto IV of Wittelsbach was recognized as German emperor, he writes of him in the same objective way as of his predecessors. Nevertheless, without any apparent cause, the narrative breaks off at the coronation of Otto IV. Perhaps the chronicler shrank from describing the bloody party conflicts of the times. His chief sources were the "Gesta Friderici" and perhaps Alsatian chronicles. On the whole his statements may be trusted. It is only when he has to resort to oral reports that he becomes unreliable; this is especially the case in his chronology, though he is not to be reproached with intentional misrepresentation of facts for this reason. His chronicles were published by R. Wilmans in "Mon. Germ. Hist.: Script." (XX, pp. 304–34); they were translated into German by Horst Kohl in "Geschichtschreiber der deutschen Vorzeit" (12 century, vol. VIII, Leipzig, 1881, 2nd ed., 1894).

POTTHAST, *Bibl. hist. medii ævi*, II (Berlin, 1896), 884 sq.; THOMÆ, *Die Chronik d. Otto von St. B. kritisch untersucht* (Leipzig, 1877); WATTENBACH, *Deutschlands Geschichtsquellen*, II (Berlin, 1894), 284 sq.

PATRICIUS SCHLAGER.

Ouen, ST. (OWEN; DADON, Lat. *Audœnus*), Archbishop of Rouen, b. at Sancy, near Soissons about 609; d. at Clichy-la-Garenne, near Paris, 24 Aug., 683. His father, Autharius, and his mother, Aiga, belonged to the Gallo-Roman race. Shortly after Ouen's birth they came to Ussy-sur-Marne, where he spent his childhood, with which tradition connects a series of marvellous events. Being afterwards sent to the Abbey of St. Médard he received an education which caused him to be welcomed at the court of Clothaire II a short time previous to the death of that prince. The latter's successor, Dagobert I, made him his referendary or chancellor and profited greatly by his talents and learning. He charged him with important missions and, it is believed, with compiling the Salic Law. St. Ouen found at the royal court Eloi (Eligius), another holy person, whose life was very similar to his own, and with whom he was united in close friendship. Both of them, despite the disorders of the Frankish king, served him faithfully. But when Dagobert was dead they considered themselves released from all secular duties, and leaving the court they devoted themselves in seclusion to the theological studies which attracted them.

St. Ouen, who in 634 founded the Abbey of Rabais, was ordained priest by Dieudonné, Bishop of Mâcon. Some time later his virtues and great ability marked him out for the archiepiscopal See of Rouen, left vacant by the death of St. Romain. Elected in 639 he was consecrated at Rouen, 21 May, 640, with his friend St. Eloi, who became Bishop of Moyon. The Diocese of Rouen, in which there were still barbarian districts from which paganism had not disappeared, was transformed under the administration of St. Ouen who caused the worship of false gods to cease, founded numerous monasteries, and developed theological studies. Occasionally the statesman reappeared in St. Ouen. For instance he upheld Ebroin the mayor of the palace in his strife against the aristocracy. After Ebroin's death, at the invitation of Thierry I he went to Cologne and succeeded in restoring peace between Neustria and Austrasia. Shortly after he was attacked by the illness to which he succumbed. His body, which was brought to Rouen and interred in the Abbey of St. Pierre which henceforth assumed his name, was translated several times, in 842, 918, and finally in 1860. St. Ouen, who survived St. Eloi, wrote the life of his friend. This biography, which is one of the most authentic historical monuments of the seventh century, contains a store of valuable information regarding the moral and religious situation of that time. It was published for the first time by Dom Luc d'Achery in vol. V of his "Spicilegium".

CEILLIER, *Hist. gén. des aut. sacr. et ecclés.*, XVII (Paris, 1750), 687–89; CHERUEL in *Rev. de Rouen*, II (1836), 251–64, I; (1837), 21–36; *Hist. Litt. de la France* (Paris, 1735–8), III, 623–28; IV, 74; LANOVIUS; *SS. Franciæ cancell.* (1634), 24–79; PETIT, *Histoire de S. Ouen* (Rouen, s. d.); REICH, *Ueber Audoens Lebensbeschreib d. heilig. Eligius* (Halle, 1872); VACANDARD, *L'enfance de S. Ouen* in *Prec. trav. acad. Rouen* (Rouen, 1896–97), 129–53; IDEM, *S. Ouen avant son épiscopat* in *Revue des questions historiques*, XIX (Paris, 1898), 5–50.

LÉON CLUGNET.

Our Father. See LORD'S PRAYER.

Our Lady, Help of Christians, FEAST OF.—The invocation *Auxilium Christianorum* (Help of Christians) originated in the sixteenth century. In 1576 Bernardino Cirillo, archpriest of Loreto, published at Macerreta two litanies of the Bl. Virgin, which, he contended, were used at Loreto: one a form which is entirely different from our present text, and another form ("Aliæ litaniæ B. M. V.") identical with the litany of Loreto, approved by Clement VIII in 1601, and now used throughout the entire Church. This second form contains the invocation *Auxilium Christianorum*. Possibly the warriors, who returning from Lepanto (7 Oct., 1571) visited the sanctuary of Loreto, saluted the Holy Virgin there for the first time with this new title; it is more probable, however, that it is only a variation of the older invocation *Advocata Christianorum*, found in a litany of 1524. Torsellini (1597) and the Roman Breviary (24 May, Appendix) say that Pius V inserted the invocation in the litany of Loreto after the battle of Lepanto; but the form of the litany in which it is first found was unknown at Rome at the time of Pius V (see LITANY OF LORETO; Schuetz, "Gesch. des Rosenkranzgebetes", Paderborn, 1909, 243 sq.).

The feast of Our Lady, Help of Christians, was instituted by Pius VII. By order of Napoleon, Pius VII was arrested, 5 July, 1808, and detained a prisoner for three years at Savona, and then at Fontainebleau. In January, 1814, after the battle of Leipzig, he was brought back to Savona and set free, 17 March, on the eve of the feast of Our Lady of Mercy, the Patroness of Savona. The journey to Rome was a veritable triumphal march. The pontiff, attributing the victory of the Church after so much agony and distress to the Blessed Virgin, visited many of her sanctuaries on the way and crowned her images (e. g. the "Madonna del Monte" at Cesena, "della Misericordia" at Treja, "della Colonne" and "della Tempestà" at Tolentino). The people crowded the streets to catch a glimpse of the venerable pontiff who had so bravely withstood the threats of Napoleon. He entered Rome, 24 May, 1814, and was enthusiastically welcomed (McCaffrey, "History of the Catholic Church in the Nineteenth Cent.", 1909, I, 52). To commemorate his own sufferings and those of the Church during his exile he extended the feast of the Seven Dolours of Mary (third Sunday in September) to the universal Church, 18 Sept., 1814. When Napoleon left Elba and returned to Paris, Murat was about to march through the Papal States from Naples; Pius VII fled to Savona (22 March, 1815), where he crowned the image of our Lady of Mercy, 10 May, 1815. After the Congress of Vienna and the battle of Waterloo he returned to Rome, 7 July, 1815. To give thanks to God and Our Lady he (15 Sept., 1815) instituted for the Papal States the feast of Our Lady, Help of Christians, to be celebrated, 24 May, the anniversary of his first return. The Dioceses of Tuscany adopted it, 12 Feb., 1816; it has spread nearly over the entire Latin Church, but is not contained in the universal calendar. The hymns of the Office were composed by Brandimarte (Chevalier, "Repert. Hymnolog.", II, 495). This feast is the patronal feast of Australasia, a double of the first class with an octave (Ordo Australasiæ, 1888), and in accordance with a vow (1891) is celebrated with great splendour in the churches of the Fathers of the Foreign Missions of Paris. It has attained special celebrity since the Ven. Dom Bosco, founder of the Salesian Congregation, 9 June, 1868, dedicated to Our Lady, Help of Christians, the mother church of his congregation at Turin. The Salesian Fathers have carried the devotion to their numerous establishments.

HOLWECK, *Fasti Mariani* (Freiburg, 1892); GUÉRANGER, *Liturgical year*, 24 May. F. G. HOLWECK.

Our Lady of Good Counsel, FEAST OF.—Records dating from the reign of Paul II (1464–71) relate that the picture of Our Lady, at first called " La Madonna del Paradiso" and now better known as "Madonna del Buon Consiglio", appeared at Genazzano, a town about twenty-five miles southeast of Rome, on St. Mark's Day, 25 April, 1467, in the old church of Santa Maria, which had been under the care of Augustinians since 1356. The venerated icon itself, which is drawn on a thin scale of wall-plaster little thicker than a visiting-card, was observed to hang suspended in the air without the slightest apparent support; thus early tradition, which furthermore tells how one might have passed a thread around the image without touching it. At once devotion to Our Lady in Santa Maria sprang up; pilgrim-bands began to resort thither; while miracles in ever-increasing numbers, of which a register was opened two days after the event, were wrought, as they still continue to be, at the shrine. In July following, Pope Paul deputed two bishops to investigate the alleged wonder-working image. Their report, however, is not known to be extant. The cult of Our Lady increased. In 1630 Urban VIII himself went to Genazzano on a pilgrimage, as did Pius IX in 1864. On 17 Nov., 1682, Innocent XI had the picture crowned with gold by the Vatican Basilica. In 1727 Benedict XIII granted the clergy of Genazzano an Office and Mass of Our Lady for 25 April, anniversary of the apparition, elsewhere the feast being kept a day later so as not to conflict with that of St. Mark the Evangelist. On 2 July, 1753, Benedict XIV approved of the Pious Union of Our Lady of Good Counsel for the faithful at large, and was himself enrolled therein as its pioneer member; Pius IX was a member, and also Leo XIII. On 18 Dec., 1779, Pius VI, while re-approving the cult of Our Lady, granted all Augustinians an Office with hymns, lessons, prayer, and Mass proper of double-major rite; with a plenary indulgence also for the faithful, to which Pius VIII added another for visitors to the shrine. On 18 Dec., 1884, Leo XIII approved of a new Office and Mass of second-class rite for all Augustinians, while on 17 March, 1903, he elevated the church of Santa Maria—one of the four parish churches at Genazzano—to the rank of minor basilica; and, on 22 April following, authorized the insertion in the Litany of Loreto of the invocation "Mater Boni Consilii" to follow that of "Mater Admirabilis". The same pontiff, ten years earlier (21 Dec., 1893) had sanctioned the use of the White Scapular of Our Lady of Good Counsel for the faithful. In the United States there are many churches and institutions in honour of Our Lady of Good Counsel.

NORTHCOTE, *Celebrated Sanctuaries* (Philadelphia, 1868); DILLON, *The Virgin Mother of Good Counsel* (Rome, 1884); BENNETT, *Our Lady of Good Counsel in Genazzano* (New York, 1888); GOUGH, *Our Lady of Good Counsel* (London, 1894); VANUTELLI, *Cenni Storici . . . di Genazzano* (Roma, 1839); BUONANNO, *Della Immagine di Maria SSa. . . . memorie storiche* (Naples, 1874); PIFFERI, *Relazione . . . del Santuario* (Roma, 1903); DE ORGIO, *Istoriche notizie della prodigiosa Apparizione* (n. p. n. d.).

THOMAS C. MIDDLETON.

Our Lady of the Fields, BROTHERS OF, a Canadian congregation founded in 1902 at St-Damien de Buckland in the Diocese of Quebec by Rev. M. J.-O. Brousseau. Its object is to train orphans in industrial and agricultural pursuits, and the arts of colonization. The Sisters of Notre Dame of Perpetual Help, also founded by Rev. M. J.-O. Brousseau in 1892, care for the orphans up to the age of twelve years: they are then confided to the care of the Brothers for the purposes above indicated. The mother-house is at St-Damien, Bellechasse Co., Lac Vert, P. Q., Canada. There are at present six brothers and four novices.

Our Lady of the Snow, FEAST OF ("Dedicatio Sanctæ Mariæ ad Nives"), a feast celebrated on 5 August to commemorate the dedication of the church of Santa Maria Maggiore on the Esquiline Hill in Rome. The church was originally built by Pope Liberius (352–366) and was called after him "Basilica Liberii" or "Liberiana". It was restored by Pope Sixtus III (432–440) and dedicated to Our Lady. From that time on it was known as "Basilica S. Mariæ" or "Mariæ Majoris"; since the seventh century it was known also as "Maria ad Præsepe". The appellation "ad Nives" (of the snow) originated a few hundred years later, as did also the legend which gave this name to the church. The legend runs thus: During the pontificate of Liberius, the Roman patrician John and his wife, who were without heirs, made a vow to donate their possessions to Our Lady. They prayed her that she might make known to them in what manner they were to dispose of their property in her honour. On 5 August, during the night, snow fell on the summit of the Esquiline Hill and, in obedience to a vision which they had the same night, they built a basilica, in honour of Our Lady, on the spot which was covered with snow. From the fact that no mention whatever is made of this alleged miracle until a few hundred years later, not even by Sixtus III in his eight-lined dedicatory inscription [edited by de Rossi, "Inscript. christ.", II, i (Rome, 1888), 71; Grisar (who has failed to authenticate the alleged miracle), "Analecta Romana", I (Rome, 1900), 77; Duchesne, "Liber Pontificalis", I (Paris, 1886), 235; Marucchi, "Eléments d'archéologie chrétienne", III (Paris and Rome, 1902), 155, etc.] it would seem that the legend has no historical basis. Originally the feast was celebrated only at Sta Maria Maggiore; in the fourteenth century it was extended to all the churches of Rome and finally it was made a universal feast by Pius V.

Clement VIII raised it from a feast of double rite to double major. The Mass is the common one for feasts of the Blessed Virgin; the Office is also the common one of the Bl. Virgin, with the exception of the second Nocturn, which is an account of the alleged miracle. The congregation, which Benedict XIV instituted for the reform of the Breviary in 1741, proposed that the reading of the legend be struck from the Office and that the feast should again receive its original name, "Dedicatio Sanctæ Mariæ".

Analecta Juris Pontificii, XXIV (Rome, 1885), 915; HOLWECK, *Fasti Mariani* (Freiburg, 1892), 164–6.

MICHAEL OTT.

Overbeck, FRIEDRICH, convert and painter of religious subjects, b. at Lübeck, 3 July, 1789; d. at Rome, 12 November, 1869. Overbeck is one of the most fascinating figures in the realm of modern Christian art. He was the soul of that romantic school of painters who, under the name of "Nazarites", exerted great influence on the formation of the German religious art of the nineteenth century. When eighteen years old, Overbeck became a pupil at the Academy of Fine Arts at Vienna. After he had attained proficiency he quickly withdrew from the compulsion and formalism of the academy, and went with three friends to Italy and above all to Rome as the great centre for the exercise of art. In 1810 he made his home in the monastery of the Irish Franciscans at Rome, San Isidoro, which was then unoccupied. He was the first to recognize that the tradition of ecclesiastical art had been completely suspended by the Reformation and the iconoclastic outbreaks, and that later the stifling overgrowth of Humansim is introduced elements into it, which had cast a mythological garb over the Catholic ideal of art. His work was, by the power of genius, to throw a bridge over the period of stagnation and depression that had lasted for three centuries. Overbeck lived to see the complete success of his titanic labours. At Rome the father of the "Nazarites", as perhaps he may now be called, was joined by the later masters, Cornelius, Schadow, and Philip Veit, and these men united together into a school. It was Overbeck's art and studies that brought him back to the Church, and the mystical power of his piety alone empowered him to produce his lofty creations. The series of frescoes of the history of Joseph in Egypt in the house called Casa Bartholdi, those illustrating Tasso's "Jerusalem Delivered" in the villa of Prince Massimo, and above all that wonderful composition "The Miracle of Roses" in the Portiuncula chapel at Assisi, astonished the world by modern technic, completely independent grasp of the subject, and most of all by proper relation of the painting to the dominating sister art of architecture. Overbeck was not able personally to develop the ideal he had formed, the adornment of northern, especially German churches with frescoes, but his school, largely as represented by Eduard von Steinle, has partially carried out his wishes.

FRIEDRICH OVERBECK

The influence of Overbeck's spirit was by no means limited to Germany. France, particularly, understood the graphic speech of this new religious art; Belgium, Poland, and Spain followed in the footsteps of the master at Rome. The reputation of the new leader of art was spread throughout all classes of society, largely by his smaller works, especially by his Biblical cartoons. His oil paintings are conspicuous for their qualities but are not numerous; the most noted of them, "The Triumph of Religion in the Arts", is the chief ornament of the Städel Gallery at Frankfort. If the work produced by Overbeck appears meagre, when contrasted with the amount put forth by artists who came after him, the reason is to be found in the subtility of his manner, owing to which he could execute masterly work, even in old age, as the wonderful cartoons of the "Seven Sacraments", and the sketches for the decoration of the cathedral of Diakovár, which were only used in part. Hostility to the art of Overbeck and his followers, the "Nazarite" school, did not fail to appear during Overbeck's lifetime, nor is it lacking now. Some say that the "Nazarites", most of all Overbeck, Veit, Führich, and Steinle, have introduced Italian art into Northern Europe, and have made German ecclesiastical art, which was stern and austere, shallow and insipidly sweet. Of the same opinion as these "orthodox" artists are the "moderns", who assert that the "Nazarite" canons of art are outstripped and antiquated. To these men, style, the canons, and dogmas of art are superfluous, stereotyped, and out-of-date. Overbeck and his companions have been justified by their extraordinary success as far as regards ecclesiastical art, which must always be a religious art. Their influence may be recognized also in the closely related art of architecture, at least as far as the Germanic people are concerned.

RAISING OF LAZARUS
Friedrich Overbeck, Karlsruhe

HOWITT, *Friedrich Overbeck, sein Leben und Schaffen*, ed. by BINDER (Freiburg, 1886); ATKINSON, *J. F. Overbeck: a memoir* (London, 1882).

C. M. KAUFMANN.

Overberg, BERNHARD HEINRICH, German ecclesiastic and educator, b. 1 May, 1754; d. 9 November, 1826. Of poor parents in the peasant community of Höckel, near Osnabrück, he became a pedlar like his father. At fifteen a priest prepared him for college, and he studied with the Franciscans in Rheine. Later (1774) he studied in Münster, and was ordained priest in 1779. As curate in Everswinkel, he did such good work in teaching religion that the vicar-general, Freiherr von Fürstenberg (q. v.), offered him the position of director of the normal school, which he was about to found in Münster. Thenceforth he was Fürstenberg's right hand in the reorganization and reformation of the schools. In 1783 he settled in Münster, where his first duty was to conduct a course of practical and theoretical study for schoolteachers during the autumn vacation. This institution was known as the *Normalschule*. The village schools at that time were very poor; in Prussia a number of discharged non-commissioned officers made a pretence of teaching, while in Westphalia, mere day labourers wielded the "stick". Of "method" there was little, except scolding and beating; Overberg had had personal experience of that in his own childhood. Not even reading—much less writing and arithmetic—was taught to all. Overberg, therefore, stood before a gigantic problem. He solved it, as Fürstenberg says, "earnestly and yet mildly, without ambition, without egotism, without any deception or deceit, untiring and with a persistency that feared no obstacles." His aim was to educate and instruct teachers and to improve their wretched material circumstances. All the teachers were to take part in the course at public expense. The course closed with an examination, and those who passed it obtained an increase in salary. As Overberg considered it best to separate the sexes in his schools, he instructed a number of women teachers who eagerly accepted the work. He really created the profession of female lay-teacher. At first, Overberg himself instructed the teachers, giving five lessons daily between 21 August to November, and teaching method as well as the various school subjects. Later he employed an assistant teacher. Soon his normal school was attended by young people who wished to become teachers. This normal school, therefore, became what is now known in Germany as a *Seminary*, and had more than 100 pupils (at first 20-30). Besides teaching in this school he gave instruction in the catechism for twenty-seven years in the Ursuline convent without remuneration. Every Sunday he recapitulated all that he had lectured upon during the week in a public lecture which was attended by people of all classes, especially by students of theology. In this work he showed not only his inborn faculty of teaching, but also his child-like faith and simplicity.

In 1789, Princess Gallitzin chose him as her confessor. He influenced her entire activity, and met in her company the most important men of the times. By his tactful kindness he brought about the conversion of Count Friedrich Leopold von Stolberg. Overberg was the chief author of the Münster school ordinance, formulated on 2 Sept., 1801. He remained director of the normal school even when he became regent of the ecclesiastical seminary in 1809, before which he had been for some time synodal examiner and member of the *Landschulkommission*. In 1816 he was made a consistorial and school counsellor, in 1823, honorary rector of the cathedral, and in 1826, shortly before his death, *Oberconsistorialrat*. Overberg was quite familiar with the pedagogical theories and achievements of his time, and utilized many of them. He was especially well acquainted with Rochow, Felbiger (q. v.), and Francke. But his own system is, on the whole, unique; for everywhere he allows for the demands of life. He lays emphasis upon the importance of habit, the power of example, and the telling of stories. As the main support of all education and discipline he considers religion. Ideal thoughts and practical everyday considerations are well combined in his work. His basic idea is to lead man toward his eternal goal, but he lays emphasis upon the necessity of caring for the temporary conditions of life, of cultivating prudence, and doing away with stupidity and superstition. His instruction is catechetic, and he mentions as its advantages the training of reason, the formation of clear impressions and ideas, and practice in the expression of one's own opinions: "children should be trained to think by questioning them, and should be guided in their method of thinking in such a way that they will find out for themselves the things which we want to teach them". Overberg's writings contain much that is interesting to teachers even to-day. The most important of them are: "Anweisung zum zweckmässigen Schulunterricht" (1793); newly edited by Gansen (5th ed., 1908); "Biblische Geschichte" (1799), which has appeared in over thirty editions and is still used as a house book; "Christkatholisches Religionsbuch" (1804); "Katechismus der christlichen Lehre" (1804), used in the Diocese of Münster until 1887 and in Osnabrück until 1900; and "Sechs Bücher vom Priesterstande" (posthumous, 1858).

REINERMANN, *Bernh. O. in seinem Leben u. Wirken* (Münster, 1829); KRABBE, *Leben O.* (Münster, 1831; 3rd ed., 1864); REUSCH in *Allg. deutsche Biogr.*, XXV (Leipzig, 1887), 14–17; KNECHT in *Kirchenlex.* s. v.; ZÖCKLER in *Realencykl. für prot. Theol.*, s. v. *Overberg u. der Gallitzinsche Kreis*.

KLEMENS LÖFFLER.

Oviedo, DIOCESE OF (OVETENSIS), comprises the civil province of the same name (the ancient Kingdom of Asturias), besides certain rural deaneries in the provinces of Lugo, León, Zamora, and Santander. Its capital, the city of Oviedo, has a population of 42,716. The ancient capital of the Asturias country was Astorga (Asturica); Oviedo was founded by King Fruela I (756–68). In 760 Abbot Fromistanus and his nephew Maximus built a monastery there and dedicated a church to St. Vincent the Martyr; Fruela had houses built and the basilica of S. Salvador. His son, Alfonso II, the Chaste, made Oviedo his capital and restored the Church of S. Salvador. The same king founded the See of Oviedo, in 805, combining with it the ancient See of Britonia. A number of bishops, expelled from their sees by the Saracens, were gathered at Oviedo, where they held two councils. It was there proposed to make Oviedo a metropolitan see, and such it was from 869 until the ancient archdioceses of the Peninsula were restored, when the pope declared Oviedo exempt (1105); the Concordat of 1851 made it suffragan to Santiago.

The Cathedral of S. Salvador was restored in the twelfth century by Archbishop Pelayo, the chronicler. Bishop Fernando Alfonso (1296–1301) undertook another restoration of the chapter-house, and his successor, Fernando Alvarez (1302–1321), began the cloister. At the end of the thirteenth century Gutierre de Toledo began the new Gothic basilica, the principal chapel bearing his arms, though it was completed by his successor Guillén. Diego Ramirez de Guzmán (1421–41) built the two chapels of the south transept (now replaced by the sacristy), the old entrance to the church, and the gallery of the cloister adjoining the chapter-house. Alonzo de Palenzuela (1470–85) completed the other part of the transept. Juan Arias (1487–97) left his cognizance, the fleur-de-lys and four scallops, on the nave. Juan Daza (1497–1503) erected the grille of the choir; Valerano (1508–12) added the stained-glass windows. Diego de Muros, founder of the great college at Salamanca known as the Oviedo, had the crestings of the porch wrought by Pedro de Bunyeres and Juan de Cerecedo, while Giralte and Valmaseda completed the carving of the precious retable in the time of Francisco de Mendoza (1525–28). Cristóbal de Rojas (1546–56) affixed his coat-of-arms to the completed tower, with its octagonal pyramid, one of the marvels of Gothic architecture. The chief feature of the cathedral is the "Camara Santa", with its venerable relics. Bishop Pelayo relates that a coffer made by the disciples of the Apostles, and containing the most precious relics of the Holy City, was taken from Jerusalem to Africa, and after several translations was finally deposited at Oviedo by Alfonso II. In the sixteenth century, Bishop Cristóbal de Sandoval y Rojas wished to open it, but could not, being overcome with religious fear. Many other relics are to be seen.

The most famous sanctuary of the diocese is at Covadonga (*Cova longa*), dedicated to the Blessed Virgin, by whose help the Spaniards, in 718, overcame the Arabs commanded by Alkaman. The old building was consumed by fire 17 October, 1777. The Canons Regular of St. Augustine, who had charge of it, had been driven by lack of revenues to live scattered about in various parishes, when Philip IV compelled them to return to community life, increasing their endowment, and building houses for them beside the monastery. Urban VII made an order that the abbot should be a dignitary of the cathedral of Oviedo. Charles III wished to rebuild the chapel sumptuously, but never went beyond beginning the work. In recent times it has been completely restored by Bishop Sanz y Fores. Also noteworthy are the two monasteries of S. Vicente and S. Pelayo at Oviedo. West of the city is the Gothic convent of S. Francisco, now used as a hospital. The church of the convent of S. Domingo is of the so-called Modern Gothic style; that of Sta Clara has a lofty tower; S. Isidro, formerly a Jesuit church, has a splendid façade in ashlar stone. In the environs of Oviedo and on the slope of Monte Naranco are the famous churches of Sta María and S. Miguel, two art treasures of the ninth century and worthy of endless study. The conciliar seminary of Oviedo was founded in 1851 by Bishop Ignacio Diaz Caneja; it consists of a great seminary in Oviedo, and a little seminary at Valdedios de Villaviciosa, an old Cistercian monastery. Besides the Provincial Institute of Secondary Education of Oviedo, there is another, founded by Jovellanos, at Gijon.

Other bishops worthy of mention are: Bishop Serrano, venerated as a saint: Rodrigo, counsellor to Ferdinand II of León; the Tuscan Fredolo, the pope's envoy to Alfonso the Wise; Rodrigo Sanchez, who executed important commissions for popes and kings of Spain; Fernando de Valdés, founder of the University of Oviedo, afterwards Archbishop of Seville and inquisitor general; Jerónimo de Velasco, one of the fathers of the Council of Trent, and founder of the Hospital of Santiago at Oviedo; Alonso Antonio de San Martín, said to have been a natural son of Philip IV. The University of Oviedo celebrated its tercentenary in September, 1908. Its building is severe and simple, in Doric order of the seventeenth century; the library is very extensive, and there is a good museum of natural history and meteorological observatory. This university is now considered the least important in Spain, having but one faculty, that of civil law. Of recent years it has been falling under the influence of the Spanish Krausists. This sect, founded by Sanz del Rio, imported from Germany the Pantheistic doctrines of Kraus, and seeks to extend its activities by conferences and courses outside of the university, even in the Latin American republics. Among the distinguished men of the diocese may be mentioned: the Alvarez of Asturias, who were famous in the Middle Ages; Ruy Pérez de Avilés, celebrated in connexion with the conquest of Seville; Gutierre Bernaldode Quirós, the hero of Aljubarrota; Pedro Méndez, the conqueror of Florida; in modern times, the Jansenist Jovellanos, the Regalist Campomanes, the Liberal Argüelles Florez Estrada, Pidal, Posada Herrera; Cardinals Cienfuegos Sierra, Cienfuegos Jovellanos, Inguanzo, and many notable prelates.

Risco, continuator of Florez, *España Sagrada* (Madrid, 1789), XXXVII–XXXIX; Cuadrado, *España, sus monumentos y rates: Asturias y León* (Barcelona, 1885); *Guía eclesiástica de España para 1888* (Madrid); *Diccionario geográfico y estadístico de Madoz*, XII (Madrid, 1849); de la Fuente, *Historia eclesiástica de España* (Barcelona, 1855).

Ramón Ruiz Amado.

Owen, Nicholas, a Jesuit lay-brother, martyred in 1606. There is no record of his parentage, birthplace, date of birth, or entrance into religion. Probably a carpenter or builder by trade, he entered the Society of Jesus before 1580, and had previously been the trusty servant of the missionary fathers. More (1586–1661) associates him with the first English lay-brothers. He was imprisoned on the death of Bl. Edmund Campion for openly declaring that martyr's innocence, but afterwards served Fathers Henry Garnett and John Gerard for eighteen years, was captured again with the latter, escaped from the Tower, and is said to have contrived the escape of Father Gerard. He was finally arrested at Hindlip Hall, Worcestershire, while impersonating Father Garnett. "It is incredible", writes Cecil, "how great was the joy caused by his arrest . . . knowing the great skill of Owen in constructing hiding places, and the innumerable quantity of dark holes which he had schemed for hiding priests all through England." Not only the Secretary of State but Waade, the Keeper of the Tower, appreciated the importance of the disclosures which Owen might be forced to make. After being committed to the Marshalsea and thence removed to the Tower, he was submitted to most terrible "examinations" on the Topcliffe rack, with both arms held fast in iron rings and body hanging, and later on with heavy weights attached to his feet, and at last died under torture. It was given out that he had committed suicide, a calumny refuted by Father Gerard in his narrative. As to the day of his death, a letter of Father Garnett's shows that he was still alive on 3 March; the "Menology" of the province puts his martyrdom as late as 12 Nov. He was of singularly innocent life and wonderful prudence, and his skill in devising hiding-places saved the lives of many of the missionary fathers.

Foley, *Records of English Jesuits* (London, 1875–82), IV, 245; VII, 561; More, *Hist. Prov. Anglicanæ* (St. Omers, 1660), 322; Nash, *Mansions of England* (London, 1906); Taunton, *Hist. of Jesuits in England* (London, 1901); *Bibl. Dict. Eng., Cath. s. v.*; Pollard in *Dict. Nat. Biog.* (London, 1909), s. v.

S. Anselm Parker.

Oxenford, John, dramatist, critic, translator, and song-writer, b. in London, 12 Aug., 1812; d. there 21 Feb., 1877. Mostly self-educated, for a time he was under the tuition of a brilliant and erratic scholar, S. T. Friend. His master recognizing his faculty for philosophy and his versatility wished to divert him from the dramatic career towards which he seemed inclined. In 1837 he was articled to a solicitor and is said to have spent some time in the London office of a relative and to have written on commerce and finance. He early read the literature of Germany, Italy, France, and Spain, and was always "a devourer of books". From the German he translated, amongst other things, Fischer's "Francis Bacon" (London, 1857); Goethe's "Autobiography" (London, 1888); Eckermann's "Conversations with Goethe" (London, 1904), the two last translations having almost become English classics and finding a place in Bohn's well-known series. From the French he translated Molière's "Tartuffe"; from the Italian Boyardo's "Orlando Innamorato" (in part), and from the Spanish a play of Calderon. But Oxenford's chief interest lay in the drama. Between 1835, when his first play was written, and his death he was producing dramatic work. Sixty-eight plays, at least, are attributed to him. Several have been translated into German, French, and Dutch. He also wrote librettos for operas etc. For the last twenty years of his life he was, in addition, dramatic critic to the "Times". He frequently contributed to newspapers and magazines, among others the "Athenæum". In April, 1853, he wrote for the "Westminster Review" an essay on Schopenhauer's philosophy which is said to have founded the fame of that philosopher both in England and abroad. In late life Oxenford's health weakened. He died of

CHURCH OF SANTA MARIA DE NARANCO, OVIEDO
NINTH CENTURY

heart failure in 1877. Eighteen months earlier he had been received into the Church.

An appreciative sketch of his life appeared in the "Times" of 23 Feb., 1877. The writer extols his originality and scholarship: "As an appreciator of others, and as a quick discoverer of anything new likely to exercise a future influence on thought he had few equals". The value of Oxenford's criticism, however, is somewhat lowered by a too great leniency, proceeding from his natural kindliness. In private life he was much beloved. His conversational powers were remarkable; and he possessed an "unsurpassed sweetness of character and self-forgetting nobleness and childlikeness".

Athenæum, II (London, 1877), 258; *Annual Register*, II (London, 1877); *Catholic Standard and Weekly Register* (7 April, 1877).

K. M. WARREN.

Oxenham, HENRY NUTCOMBE, English controversialist and poet, b. at Harrow, 15 Nov., 1829; d. at Kensington, 23 March, 1888; was the son of the Rev. William Oxenham, second master of Harrow. He was educated at Harrow School and Balliol College, Oxford, taking his degree in 1850. After receiving Anglican orders, he became curate first at Worminghall, in Buckinghamshire, then at St. Bartholomew's, Cripplegate. While at the latter place, he was received into the Church by Monsignor (afterwards Cardinal) Manning. For a time he contemplated becoming a priest, for which purpose he entered St. Edmund's College, Old Hall, but after receiving minor orders, he left: it is said that his reason was that he believed in the validity of Anglican orders, and considered himself already a priest. He continued to dress as an ecclesiastic and in this anomalous position he spent the remainder of his life. His ambition was to work for the reunion of the Anglican with the Catholic Church, with which end in view, he published a sympathetic article, in answer to Pusey's "Eirenicon", in the shape of a letter to his friend and fellow-convert, Father Lockhart. After the Vatican Council his position became still more anomalous, for his unwillingness to accept the doctrine of Papal Infallibility was known. Though influenced by the action of Dr. Döllinger, with whom he was on intimate terms, he never outwardly severed his connexion with the Catholic Church, and before his death received all the sacraments at the hands of Father Lockhart.

His published works include: "The Sentence of Kaires and Poems" (3rd ed., London, 1871); Translation of Döllinger's "First Age of Christianity" (London, 1866, 2 vols: two subsequent editions) and "Lectures on Reunion" (London, 1872); "Catholic Eschatology" (1876; new edition, enlarged, 1878); "Memoir of Lieut. Rudolph de Lisle, R. N." (London, 1886); numerous pamphlets and articles, especially in "The Saturday Review", over the initials X. Y. Z.

RIGG in *Dict. of Nat. Biog.*; GILLOW, *Bibl. Dict. of Eng. Cath.*; obituary notices in *The Saturday Review*, *The Athenæum*, *The Manchester Guardian*, etc. BERNARD WARD.

Oxford, one of the most ancient cities in England, grew up under the shadow of a convent, said to have been founded by St. Frideswide as early as the eighth century. Its authentic history begins in 912, when it was occupied by Edward the Elder, King of the West Saxons. It was strongly fortified against the Danes, and again after the Norman Conquest, and the massive keep of the castle, the tower of St. Michael's Church (at the north gate), and a large portion of the city walls still remain to attest the importance of the city in the eleventh century. West of the town rose the splendid castle, and, in the meadows beneath, the no less splendid Augustinian Abbey of Oseney: in the fields to the north the last of the Norman kings built the stately palace of Beaumont; the great church of St. Frideswide was erected by the canons-regular who succeeded the nuns of St. Frideswide; and many fine churches were built by the piety of the Norman earls. Oxford received a charter from King Henry II, granting its citizens the same privileges and exemptions as those enjoyed by the capital of the kingdom; and various important religious houses were founded in or near the city. A grandson of King John established Rewley Abbey (of which a single arch now remains) for the Cistercian Order; and friars of various orders (Dominicans, Franciscans, Carmelites, Augustinians, and Trinitarians), all had houses at Oxford of varying importance. Parliaments were often held in the city during the thirteenth century, but this period also saw the beginning of the long struggle between the town and the growing university which ended in the subjugation of the former, and the extinction for centuries of the civic importance of Oxford. The accession of thousands of students of course brought it material prosperity, but it was never, apart from the university, again prominent in history until the seventeenth century, when it became the headquarters of the Royalist party, and again the meeting-place of Parliament. The city of Oxford showed its Hanoverian sympathies long before the university, and feeling between them ran high in consequence. The area and population of the city remained almost stationary until about 1830, but since then it has grown rapidly. The population is now (1910) about 50,000; the municipal life of the city is vigorous and flourishing, and its relations with the university are more intimate and cordial than they have ever been during their long history.

Oxford is the cathedral city of the Anglican Diocese of Oxford, erected by Henry VIII. Formerly included in the vast Diocese of Lincoln, it is now part of the Catholic Diocese of Birmingham. The handsome Catholic church of St. Aloysius (served by the Jesuits) was opened in 1875; the Catholic population numbers about 1200, besides about 100 resident members of the university; and there are convents of the following orders—St. Ursula's, Daughters of the Cross, Sisters of Nazareth, Sisters of the M. Holy Sacrament, and Sisters of the Holy Child. The Franciscan Capuchin fathers have a church and college in the suburb of Cowley, as well as a small house of studies in Oxford; and the Benedictines and Jesuits have halls, with private chapels, within the university.

PARKER, *Early History of Oxford* (Oxford, 1885); WOOD, *Survey of the Antiquities of the City of Oxford* (1889–99); GREEN AND ROBERTSON, *Studies in Oxford History* (Oxf., 1901); TURNER, *Records of City of Oxford* (Oxf., 1880); and the publications of the OXFORD HISTORICAL SOCIETY (Oxford, various dates).

D. O. HUNTER-BLAIR.

Oxford, UNIVERSITY OF.—I. ORIGIN AND HISTORY. —The most extraordinary myths have at various times prevailed as to the fabulous antiquity of Oxford as a seat of learning. It is sufficient to mention that the fifteenth century chronicler Rous assigns its origin to the time when "Samuel the servant of God was judge in Judæa"; while a writer of Edward III's reign asserts that the university was founded by "certain philosophers when the warlike Trojans, under the leadership of Brutus, triumphantly seized on the Islands of Albion". A much more long-lived fiction— one, indeed, which, first heard of in the middle of the fourteenth century, persisted down to the nineteenth —was that King Alfred, well-known as a patron of education, was the real founder of Oxford University. The truth is that it is quite impossible to assign even an approximate date to the development of the schools which in Saxon times were grouped round the monastic foundation of St. Frideswide (on the site of what is now Christ Church) into the corporate institution later known as Oxford University. Well-known scholars were, we know, lecturing in Oxford on theology and canon law before the middle of the twelfth century, but these were probably private teachers attached to St. Frideswide's monastery. It is not until the end of Henry II's reign, that is about 1180, that we know, chiefly on the authority of Giraldus Cambrensis, that a large body of scholars was in residence at Oxford, though not probably yet living under any organized constitution.

Half a century later Oxford was famous throughout Europe as a home of science and learning; popes and kings were among its patrons and benefactors; the students are said to have been numbered by thousands; and the climax of its reputation was reached when, during the fifty years between 1220 and 1270, the newly-founded orders of friars—Dominican, Franciscan, Carmelite, and Austin—successively settled at Oxford, and threw all their enthusiasm into the work of teaching. Kindled by their zeal, the older monastic orders, encouraged by a decree of the Lateran Council of 1215, began to found conventual schools at Oxford for their own members. The colleges of Worcester, Trinity, Christ Church, and St. John's are all the immediate successors of these Benedictine or Cistercian houses of study. Up to this time the secular students had lived as best they might in scattered lodgings hired from the townsmen; of discipline there was absolutely none, and riots and disorders between "town and gown" were of continual occurrence. The stimulus of the presence of so many scholars living under conventual discipline incited Walter de Merton, in 1264, to found a residential college, properly organized and supervised, for secular students. Merton College (to the model of which two institutions of somewhat earlier date, University and Balliol, soon conformed themselves) was thus the prototype of the self-contained and autonomous colleges which, grouped together, make up the University of Oxford as it exists to-day. The succeeding half-century saw the foundation of ten additional colleges: two more were founded during the Catholic revival under Queen Mary; and three in the reigns of Elizabeth and James I. Between 1625 and 1911—that is, for nearly three centuries, there have been only three more added to the list, namely Worcester (1714), Keble (1870), and Hertford (1874), the first and last being, however, revivals rather than new foundations.

The institution of "non-collegiate" students (i. e. those unattached to any college or hall) dates from 1868; one "public hall" (St. Edmund's) survives, of several founded in very early times; and there are several "private halls", under licensed masters who are allowed to take a limited number of students. As a corporate body, the university dates only from the reign of Queen Elizabeth, when, under the influence of the chancellor, Robert Dudley, Earl of Leicester, an Act of Parliament was passed in 1571, incorporating the "chancellor, masters and scholars" of Oxford. In the same reign were imposed upon the university the Royal Supremacy and the Thirty-nine Articles, subscription to which was required from every student above the age of sixteen; and from that date, for a period of three centuries, the university, formerly opened to all Christendom, was narrowed into an exclusively Anglican institution and became, as it has ever since remained, in spite of subsequent legislation abolishing religious tests, the chosen home and favourite arena of Anglican controversy, theology, and polemics. Keble, however, is now the only college whose members must be Anglicans by creed, although a certain number of scholarships in other colleges are restricted to adherents of the English Church. Attendance at the college chapels is no longer compulsory; and there is no kind of religious test required for admission to any college (except Keble) or for graduating in Arts, Science, or Civil Law. Only the faculty of Divinity (including the degrees of bachelor and doctor) remains closed by statute to all except professing Anglicans; and the examiners in the theological school, which is open to students of any creed or none, are all required to be clergymen of the Church of England.

II. CONSTITUTION AND GOVERNMENT.—Taken as a whole, the university consists of about 14,500 members, graduate and undergraduate, having their names on the registers of the university as well as of the twenty-six separate societies (colleges, halls, public and private, and the non-collegiate body) which together form the corporation of the university. Of the above number about 3800 are undergraduates, of whom the great majority are reading for the degree of B.A., and about a thousand are graduates, either tutors, fellows of colleges, officials of the university, or M.A.'s unofficially resident within its precincts. About 4800 members of the university are thus actually living in Oxford, the remainder being those who, while keeping their names "on the books", reside in other parts of the kingdom. All masters of arts remaining on the registers are *ipso facto* members of "Convocation", the legislative and administrative body through which the university acts; and those actually residing in Oxford for a fixed period in each year form the smaller body called "Congregation", by which all measures must be passed previous to their coming before "Convocation". Legislation in every case, however, must be initiated by the "Hebdomadal Council", consisting of the vice-chancellor, proctors, and eighteen members elected by "Congregation".

The executive officers of the university comprise the chancellor, a nobleman of high rank, as a rule non-resident, who delegates his authority to the vice-chancellor, the head of one of the colleges, and the two proctors, who are elected by the several colleges in turn, and assist the vice-chancellor in the enforcement of discipline, as well as in the general supervision of all university affairs, including the administration of its property and the control of its finances. The peculiar feature of the constitution of Oxford (as of Cambridge), when compared with that of every other university in the world, is that the authority of the vice-chancellor and proctors, that is of the central university body, while nominally extending to every resident member of the university, is not as a matter of fact exercised within the college walls, each college being, while a constituent part of the university, autonomous and self-governing, and claiming entire responsibility for the order and well-being of its own members.

III. THE COLLEGIATE SYSTEM.—According to the combined university and college system which prevails at Oxford, each college is an organized corporation under its own head, and enjoying the fullest powers of managing its own property and governing its own members. Each college is regulated not only by the general statutes of the university, but by its own separate code of statutes, drawn up at its foundation (as a rule centuries ago) and added to or amended since as found expedient. Every college is absolutely its own judge as to the requirements for admission to its membership, the result being that in no two colleges is the standard of necessary knowledge, or the mental equipment with which a youth enters on his university career, identical or even necessarily similar. The mere fact of a man having matriculated at certain colleges stamps him as possessed of more than average attainments, while at others the required standard may be so low as to afford no guarantee whatever that their members are in any real sense educated at all.

The twenty-one colleges and four halls, and the delegacy of non-collegiate students—that is of students not affiliated to any college or hall—have all the same privileges as to receiving undergraduate members; and no one can be matriculated, i. e. admitted to membership of the university by the central authority, until he has been accepted by one of the above-mentioned societies. The colleges provide a certain number of sets of rooms within their own walls for students, the remainder living in licensed lodgings in the city. Meals are served either in the college halls or in the students' rooms; and attached to every college is a chapel where daily service is held during term according to the forms of the Church of England.

IV. TUITION, EXAMINATIONS, AND DEGREES.—The university provides 130 professors, lecturers, and readers to give instructions in the several faculties of theology (9), law (8), medicine (17), natural science, including mathematics (27), and arts, including ancient and modern languages, geography, music, fine arts etc. (69). The chief burden of tuition, however, does not fall on this large body of highly-equipped teachers, whose lectures are in many cases very sparsely attended, but on the college tutors, whose lectures, formerly confined to members of their own colleges, are now practically open to the whole university. The extension of, and great improvement in, the tuition afforded by the college tutors has led to the practical disappearance at Oxford, at least in work for honours, of the private tutor or "coach", who formerly largely supplemented the official college teaching. What is noteworthy at Oxford is the trouble taken by tutors in the work of individual instruction, which, while involving a great, and sometimes disproportionate, expenditure of time and talent, has done much to establish and consolidate the personal relations between tutor and pupil which is a distinctly beneficial feature of the Oxford system.

Examinations.—For students aspiring to the B.A. degree are prescribed two strictly-defined compulsory examinations, and two so-called public examinations, in which candidates may choose from a wide range of alternative subjects. *Responsions*, generally passed before matriculation, includes Latin, Greek, and mathematics, all of a pretty elementary kind. The second compulsory examination, that in Holy Scripture (for which a book of Plato may be substituted), includes the Greek text of two of the Gospels. In the two "public examinations", i. e. Moderations and the Final Schools, either a "pass" or "honours" may be aimed at. The passman must first satisfy the examiners in Moderations (i. e. classics combined with logic or mathematics), and then for his Final School may choose between various subjects, such as classics, mathematics, natural science, and modern languages. The "honour-man", if aiming at "greats", has, as a rule, first a searching examination in classics, and then a final examination in ancient history and philosophy; the successful candidates in both these examinations being divided into four classes. A first class in "Greats" (or *literæ humaniores*) is still reckoned the highest honour attainable in the Oxford curriculum; but the student has seven other Final Honour Schools open to him, those of modern history (which now attracts the largest number of candidates), mathematics, jurisprudence, theology, English literature, Oriental studies, and natural science.

Degrees.—A student who has passed the examinations requisite for the B.A. degree, can further qualify himself for the degree of (a) Bachelor of Medicine and Surgery, by passing two examinations in medical and surgical subjects; (b) Bachelor of Civil Law, by passing an examination in general jurisprudence, Roman, English, or international law; (c) Bachelor of Theology (if in orders of the Church of England) by presenting two dissertations on a theological subject. For what are known as "research degrees" (Bachelor of Letters, or Science) two years of residence are required, followed by an examination, or the submission of a dissertation showing original work. Candidates for the degree of Bachelor of Music are exempted from residence, and need only have passed the examination of Responsions. Bachelors of Arts can present themselves for the degree of Master at the end of a stated period, without further examination; but the Bachelor of Medicine must pass an examination or submit a dissertation before obtaining the degrees of M.D. or Master of Surgery: and there is a similar qualification required for proceeding to the degrees of Doctor of Divinity, of Civil Law, of Music, and of Letters or Science. There is now no religious test in the case of any degrees excepting those of theology; but all candidates for masters' or doctors' degrees have to promise faithful observance of the statutes and customs of the university. Honorary degrees in all the faculties may be granted to distinguished persons, without examination, by decree of Convocation.

Diplomas in certain subjects, as health, education, geography, and political economy, are granted by Convocation after a certain period of study and an examinational test. These diplomas are obtainable by women students, who are not eligible for any degrees, although they may, and do, enter for the same examination as men. The halls of women students are

MAGDALEN COLLEGE, OXFORD

entirely extra-collegiate; but women receive on examination certificates testifying to the class gained by them in such honour-examinations as they choose to undergo.

V. EXPENSE OF THE UNIVERSITY COURSE.—It is difficult to fix this even approximately, so much depends on a student's tastes, habits, and recreations, and also on the question whether the sum named is to include his expenses for the whole year, or only for the six months of the university terms. £120 a year ought to cover the actual fees and cost of board and other necessary charges, which are pretty much the same at all the colleges; and if another £100 or £120 be added for the supplementary expenses of college life, and vacation expenses as well, we arrive at what is probably the average annual sum expended. A man with expensive tastes or hobbies may of course spend double or treble that amount, whereas members of some of the smaller colleges may do very well on much less; while the emoluments of the numerous college and university scholarships and exhibitions lessen the expenses of those who hold them by a corresponding amount. The Rhodes Scholarships, open to Colonial and American students, are of the annual value of £300 each; but it is to be considered that their holders have as a rule to make this sum suffice for all their wants, in vacation as well as in term-time.

VI. UNIVERSITY AND COLLEGE BUILDINGS.—The chief university buildings are grouped round the quadrangle of the Bodleian Library, founded in 1602 by Sir Thomas Bodley, and first housed in the room (built in 1480) known as Duke Humphrey's Library. Since 1610 the Bodleian has received by right a copy of every book published in the kingdom, and it now contains more than 500,000 books and nearly 40,000 manuscripts. In the galleries is an interesting collection of historical portraits. West of the Bodleian is the beautiful fifteenth-century Divinity School, with its elaborate roof, and further west again the Convocation House, built in 1639. Close by are the the Sheldonian Theatre, built by Wren in 1669, where the annual Commemoration is held, and honorary degrees are conferred; the Old Clarendon Printing-house, built in 1713 out of the profits of Lord Clarendon's "History of the Rebellion"; the old Ashmolean Building, and the Indian Institute, built in 1882 for the benefit of Indian students in the university. South of the Bodleian rises the imposing dome of the Radcliffe Library, founded in 1749 by Dr. William Radcliffe for books on medicine and science, but now used as a reading room for the Bodleian. The Examination Schools (1876–82), a fine Jacobean pile which cost £100,000, are in High Street; and the chief other university buildings are the New Museum (1855–60), an ugly building in early French Gothic, containing splendid collections of natural science and anthropology, as well as a fine science library; the Taylor Buildings and University Galleries, a stately classical edifice containing the Arundel and Pomfret Marbles, a priceless collection of drawings by Raphael, Michelangelo, Turner, and other masters, and many valuable paintings; the Ashmolean Museum, behind the galleries, containing one of the most complete archæological collections in England; the new Clarendon Press (1830), and the Observatory, founded in 1772 by the Radcliffe trustees.

Taking the different colleges in alphabetical order, we have: *All Souls*, founded by Archbishop Chichele in 1437, in memory of those who fell in the French wars. Its features are the absence of undergraduate members, the magnificent reredos in the chapel, re-discovered and restored in 1872, after being lost sight of for three centuries, and the splendid library, especially of works on law.

Balliol, founded by Devorgilla, widow of John Balliol, about 1262, and distinguished for the brilliant scholarship of its members, and the liberality and tolerance of its views. The buildings are mostly modern and of little interest; in the fine hall (1877) is a striking portrait of Cardinal Manning (a scholar here 1827–30). Opposite the Master of Balliol's house a cross in the roadway marks the spot where Cranmer, Ridley, and Latimer were burned in 1555 and 1556; and the so-called Martyrs' Memorial (by Gilbert Scott, 1841), opposite the west front of the college, commemorates the same event; it was erected chiefly as a protest against the Tractarian movement headed by Newman.

Brasenose, founded in 1509 by Bishop Smyth of Lincoln and Sir Richard Sutton, as an amplification of the much older Brasenose Hall, a knocker on the door of which, in the shape of a nose, is the origin of the curious name. In the chapel, a singular mixture of classical and Gothic design, are preserved two pre-Reformation chalices. A magnificent new south front in High Street (by Jackson) was completed in 1910.

Christ Church, the largest and wealthiest college in Oxford, founded as "Cardinal College" by Thomas Wolsey in 1525, on the site of St. Frideswide's suppressed priory, and re-established by Henry VIII as Christ Church in 1546. Wolsey built the hall and kitchen (1529), the finest in England, and began the great ("Tom") quadrangle, which was finished in 1668. The old monastic church, dating from 1120, serves both as the college chapel and as the cathedral of the Anglican Diocese of Oxford, erected by Henry VIII; in Catholic times Oxford formed part of the immense Diocese of Lincoln. Peckwater Quad was built 1705–60, and Canterbury Quad (on the site of Canterbury Hall, a Benedictine foundation), in 1770. The hall and library contain many valuable portraits and other paintings.

Corpus Christi, founded in 1516 by Bishop Richard Foxe of Winchester, and dedicated to Sts. Peter, Andrew, Cuthbert, and Swithin, patrons of the four sees, (Exeter, Bath, Durham, and Winchester), which he had held in turn. The buildings, though not extensive, are of great interest, mostly coeval with the founder; and the college possesses some valuable old plate. Angels bearing the Sacred Host are depicted in an oriel window over the great gateway. Corpus Christi has always maintained a high reputation for sound classical learning.

Exeter, founded in 1314 by Bishop de Stapledon of Exeter. Most of the buildings are modern; the chapel (1857) being an elaborate copy by Gilbert Scott of the Sainte Chapelle at Paris. There is a charming little garden. Exeter has of recent years been more frequented by Catholic students than any other college.

Hertford, revived in 1874, having been originally founded in 1740 but dissolved in 1818 and occupied by Magdalen Hall. A handsome new chapel by Jackson was opened in 1909.

Jesus, frequented almost exclusively by Welsh students, was founded by Queen Elizabeth in 1571; and more than half the scholarships and exhibitions are restricted to persons of Welsh birth or education. Sir John Rhys, the eminent Celtic scholar, is the present principal. The buildings are modern, or much restored.

Keble, founded by subscription in 1870 in memory of John Keble, and now the only college whose members must, by the terms of its charter, all be members of the Anglican Church. It is governed by a warden and council (there are no fellows), and one of its principles is supposed to be special economy and sobriety of living. The buildings of variegated brick are quite foreign to the prevailing architecture of Oxford, but the chapel is spacious and sumptuously decorated.

Lincoln, founded by Bishop Richard Fleming and Thomas Rotherham, both of Lincoln, in honour of the B.V.M. and All Saints, specially to educate divines to preach against the Wycliffian heresies. The buildings

OXFORD

BALLIOL COLLEGE AND THE MARTYRS' MEMORIAL
CHRIST CHURCH, SHOWING TOM TOWER

SHELDONIAN THEATRE
BRASENOSE COLLEGE

are of little interest, but the chapel contains some very good seventeenth-century Italian stained glass.

Magdalen, perhaps the most beautiful college in Oxford, if not in Christendom, was founded in 1458 by Bishop Waynflete of Winchester. The chapel, hall, cloisters, tower, and other buildings, all erected in the founder's lifetime, are of unique beauty and interest. The extensive and charming grounds include the famous "Addison's Walk", and a deer-park with fine timber. The musical services in the chapel are famous throughout England. Magdalen possesses much landed property, and is one of the wealthiest colleges in the university.

Merton, founded in 1264 by Walter de Merton, in Surrey, and transferred to Oxford in 1274, was the first organized college, and the prototype of all succeeding ones. The library (1349) is the oldest in England, and the so-called "Mob" quad is of the same date. The chapel, of exquisite Decorated Gothic, contains some beautiful old stained glass. Merton was specially intended by its founder for the education of the secular clergy.

New, founded in 1379 on a magnificent scale by Bishop William de Wykeham, of Winchester (founder also of Winchester College). The splendid chapel, with its elaborate reredos, was restored in 1879; the ante-chapel windows contain the original pre-Reformation glass, and there are many fine brasses. Other features of the college are the picturesque cloisters (used during the Civil War as a depot for military stores), the great hall, with its rich panelling, the valuable collection of old plate, and the lovely gardens, enclosed on three sides by the ancient city walls. New College vies with Magdalen in the excellence of its chapel choir.

Oriel, founded by Edward II in 1326 on the suggestion of his almoner, Adam de Brome; but none of the buildings are older than the seventeenth century. The college is identified with the rise of the Oxford Movement, led by Newman, who was a fellow here from 1822 to 1845. There are two portraits of him (by Ross and Richmond respectively) in the college common-room.

Pembroke, second of the four colleges of Protestant foundation, erected in 1624 out of the ancient Broadgates Hall, and chiefly notable for the membership of Dr. Samuel Johnson, of whom there is a fine portrait and various relics.

Queen's, founded in 1340 by Robert de Eglesfield, chaplain to Queen Philippa, in honour of whom it was named. The buildings are mostly late seventeenth-century; there is some good Dutch glass in the chapel, and a very valuable library, chiefly historical. The hall is hung with (mostly fictitious) portraits of English kings, queens, and princes.

St. John's, formerly St. Bernard's, a house of studies for Cistercian monks, was refounded in 1555 by Sir John White, in honour of St. John the Baptist. The chapel, hall, and other parts of the outer quad belong to the monastic foundation; the inner quad, with its beautiful garden front, was built by Archbishop Laud, president of the college 1611–21. The gardens are among the most beautiful in Oxford.

Trinity, originally Durham College, a house of studies for the Durham Benedictines, was refounded by Sir Thomas Pope in 1554. The old monastic library, and other fragments of the buildings of Durham, remain; the chapel, with its fine wood-carving by Grinling Gibbons, is from designs by Wren. Newman became a scholar of Trinity in 1819; he was elected an honorary fellow in 1878, and visited the college as cardinal in 1880. A fine portrait of him, by Ouless, hangs in the hall.

University, which ranks as the oldest college, though its connexion with King Alfred, said to have founded it in 872, is absolutely legendary. It was really founded by Archdeacon William of Durham in 1249, and acquired its present site a century later. None of the buildings are more than two hundred years old. Frederick William Faber, the famous Oratorian, was a member of this college, which was much identified with the Catholic revival in James II's reign.

Wadham, founded in 1610 by Dorothy Wadham, in completion of her husband's designs; it occupies the site of a house of Austin Friars, who probably laid out the beautiful garden. Wadham is interesting as a fine specimen of Jacobean work, and as the only college whose buildings remain practically as left by their founder.

Worcester, established in 1283, under the name of Gloucester College, as a house of studies for Benedictines from Gloucester and other great English abbeys, survived as Gloucester Hall for a century and a half after the Reformation, and was re-founded and endowed by Sir Thomas Cookes, under its present name, in 1714. There still remain the ancient lodgings used by the students of the several abbeys, overlooking the finely-timbered grounds and lake. The interior decoration of the eighteenth-century chapel is very sumptuous.

The only survivor of the once numerous "public halls" is "St. Edmund's", founded in the thirteenth century in honour of St. Edmund Rich, Archbishop of Canterbury, canonized by Innocent III in 1247. The buildings are all of the seventeenth century. This hall is closely connected with Queen's College, the provost of which appoints the principal.

VII. CATHOLICS AT THE UNIVERSITY.—Besides the colleges and single public hall, there are at present three "private halls" conducted by licensed masters (i. e. M.A.'s authorized and approved by the Vice-Chancellor) and receiving a limited number of undergraduate students. Two of these halls are in Catholic hands, one (Pope's Hall) founded for students belonging to the Society of Jesus, and the other (Parker's Hall) established by Ampleforth Abbey, in Yorkshire, for Benedictine students belonging to that monastery. Good work is done in both of these institutions, the members of which, for the most part, are preparing to take part in tuition at the English Jesuit and Benedictine colleges; and many of their members have obtained the highest academical honours in the various university examinations. The Franciscan Capuchin Fathers have recently (1910) opened a small house of studies for junior members of their Order; they have at present the status of non-collegiate students. The lay Catholics who enter the university as undergraduates have no college or hall of their own under Catholic direction, but become members of any one of the colleges which they desire to join, or of the non-collegiate body which, since 1868, has been authorized to receive students who are not members of any college or hall.

Catholics are, of course, exempt from attending the college chapels, and they have a central chapel of their own, with a resident chaplain appointed by the Universities Catholic Board (of which one of the English bishops is chairman), who says Mass daily for the Catholic students. The Board also appoints every term a special preacher or lecturer, who gives, by the special injunction of the Holy See, weekly conferences to the students on some historical, theological, or philosophical subject. There are two or three resident Catholic fellows and tutors in the university; but the general tone and spirit of the instruction given in the lecture-rooms, though not on the whole anti-Catholic, may be described as generally non-religious. The mission church of St. Aloysius is served by several Jesuit fathers, and good preachers are often heard there; and several religious communities have recently been established in the city. The number of Catholic members of the University, graduate and undergraduate, resident in Oxford does not exceed a hundred.

RASHDALL, *The Universities of Europe in the Middle Ages* (Oxford, 1895), II, good bibliography; AYLIFFE, *Ancient and Present State of the University of Oxford* (2 vols., London, 1714); *Oxford Univ. Commission, Minutes of Evidence*, etc. (London, 1881); BOASE, *Register of the University of Oxford* (Oxford, 1885); LYTE, *Hist. of the University of Oxford* (London, 1886); CLARK, *The Colleges of Oxford* (London, 1891); *Oxford College Histories* (London, s. d.); FOSTER, *Alumni Oxonienses 1715–1886* (London, 1887); HURST, *Oxford Topography* (Oxford, 1899); *Publications of the Oxford Historical Society* (Oxford, s. d.); *Statuta et Decreta Univ. Oxon.* (Oxford, 1909); *Oxford University Calendar* (Oxford, 1910–11); GOLDIE, *A Bygone Oxford* in *The Month* (Sept., 1880); CAMM, *The University of Oxford and the Reformation* in *The Month* (July and August, 1907).

D. O. HUNTER-BLAIR.

Oxford Movement, THE (1833–1845), may be looked upon in two distinct lights. "The conception which lay at its base", according to the Royal Commission on Ecclesiastical Discipline, 1906, "was that of the Holy Catholic Church as a visible body upon earth, bound together by a spiritual but absolute unity, though divided . . . into national and other sections. This conception drew with it the sense of ecclesiastical continuity, of the intimate and unbroken connexion between the primitive Church and the Church of England, and of the importance of the Fathers as guides and teachers . . . It also tended to emphasize points of communion between those different branches of the Church, which recognize the doctrine or fact of Apostolic Succession" (Report, p. 54). That is the point of view maintained in the "Tracts for the Times" from 1833 to 1841, which gave its familiar name to the "Tractarian" Movement. They originated and ended with J. H. Newman.

But a second, very unlike, account of the matter was put forward by Newman himself in his "Lectures on Anglican Difficulties" of 1850. There he considers that the drift or tendency of this remarkable change was not towards a party in the Establishment, or even towards the first place in it, but away from national divisions altogether. It was meant ultimately to absorb "the various English denominations and parties" into the Roman Church, whence their ancestors had come out at the Reformation. And as Newman had been leader in the Anglican phase of the movement, so he opened the way towards Rome, submitted to it in 1845, and made popular the reasoning on which thousands followed his example. There seems no other instance adducible from history of a religious thinker who has moulded on permanent lines the institution which he quitted, while assigning causes for its abandonment. But this result was in some measure a consequence of the "anomalous and singular position", as Dean Church allows, held by the English Establishment, since it was legally set up under Elizabeth (Acts of Supremacy and Uniformity, 8 May, 1559)

Lord Chatham brought out these anomalies in a famous epigram. "We have", he remarked, "a Popish Liturgy, Calvinistic articles, and an Arminian clergy." Such differences were visible from the first. "It is historically certain", says J. A. Froude, "that Elizabeth and her ministers intentionally framed the Church formulas so as to enable every one to use them who would disclaim allegiance to the Pope." When the Armada was scattered and broken, many adherents of the old faith appear to have conformed; and their impetus accounts for the rise of a High Anglican party, whose chief representative was Launcelot Andrewes, Bishop of Winchester (1555-1626). The Anglo-Catholic school was continued by Laud, and triumphed after the Restoration. In 1662 it expelled from the Church, Baxter and the Presbyterians. But from the Revolution in 1688 it steadily declined. The non-juring bishops were wholly in its tradition, which, through obscure by-ways, was handed on from his father to John Keble and so to Hurrell Froude and Newman.

However, the Laudian or Carolinian divines must not be supposed to have ever succeeded in driving out their Calvinistic rivals, so powerful when the Thirty-Nine Articles were drawn up, and known from Shakespeare's time as Puritans (see Malvolio in "Twelfth Night"). Andrewes himself, though taking St. Augustine and St. Thomas for his masters, did not admit the sacerdotal doctrine of the Eucharist. At every period Baptismal Regeneration, Apostolic Succession, and the Real Presence were open questions, not decided one way or another by "the stammering lips of ambiguous Formularies". If there was a High Church in power, and if what the Arminians held, as it was wittily said, were all the best livings in England, yet Calvin's theology, whether a little softened by Archbishop Whitgift or according to the text of the "Institutes", never did involve deprivation. It was sheltered by the Articles, as Catholic tradition was by the Prayer Book; and the balance was kept between contending schools of opinion by means of the Royal Supremacy.

Suggested by Thomas Cromwell, asserted in Parliamentary legislation under Henry VIII (1534), this prime article of Anglicanism made the king supreme head of the English Church on earth, and his tribunal the last court of appeal in all cases, spiritual no less than secular. It has been said of Henry, and is equally true of Edward VI, that he claimed the whole power of the keys. Elizabeth, while relinquishing the title of Head and the administration of holy rites, certainly retained and exercised full jurisdiction over "all persons and all causes" within the realm. She extinguished the ancient hierarchy "without any proceeding in any spiritual court", as Macaulay observes, and she appointed the new one. She "tuned the pulpit", admonished archbishops, and even supplied by her own legal authority defects in the process of episcopal consecration. The Prayer Book itself is an Act of Parliament. "The supreme tribunal of appeal, in ecclesiastical causes, from 1559 to 1832", we are told, "was that created by 25 Hen. VIII, c. 19, which gave an appeal from the Church Courts to the King in Chancery for lack of justice" (Dodd, Hist. Canon Law, 232). These powers were exercised by the court of delegates; in 1832 they were transferred to the judicial committee of the privy council, whose members may all be laymen; and, if bishops, they do not sit by virtue of their episcopal office but as the king's advisers. Contrast will drive the matter home. The constituent form of the Catholic Church is the pope's universal jurisdiction (see FLORENCE, COUNCIL OF; VATICAN COUNCIL). But the constituent form of the English Church, as established by Parliament, is the universal jurisdiction of the Crown. In either case there is no appeal from the papal or the royal decision. When Elizabeth broke with the Catholic bishops who would not acknowledge her spiritual headship, and when William III deprived Sancroft and his suffragans who refused the oath of allegiance, a test was applied, dogmatic in 1559, perhaps not less so in 1690, which proves that no cause of exemption can be pleaded against the king when he acts as supreme governor of the Church.

Such is the doctrine often called Erastian, from Erastus, a Swiss theologian (1524-83), who denied to the clergy all power of excommunication. In England the course of events had run on before Erastus could publish its philosophy. Politicians like Burghley and Walsingham acted on no theory, but drew their inspiration from Henry VIII. The abstract statement of a view which identifies the Church with the nation and subjects both equally to the king, may be found in Hooker, "The Laws of Ecclesiastical Polity" (1594-97). It was vigorously asserted by Selden and the lawyers at all times. During the critical years of the nineteenth century, Arnold, Stanley, and Kingsley were its best known defenders among clergymen. Stanley declared that the Church of England "is by the very conditions of its being neither

High nor Low, but Broad" ("Ed. Rev.", July, 1850). In coarser but equally practical terms men said, "The Church was grafted upon the State, and the State would remain master." No ruling, in fact, of bishop or convocation need be regarded by Anglicans, lay or clerical, unless it implies, at all events tacitly, the consent of the Crown, i. e., of Parliament.

So long as the State excluded Dissenters and Catholics from its offices, the system, in spite of the Great Rebellion, nay after the more truly disastrous Revolution of 1688, worked as well as could be expected. But in 1828 the Test Act was repealed; next year Catholic Emancipation passed into law. In 1830 the French drove out their Bourbon dynasty; Belgium threw off the yoke of Holland. In 1832 came the Reform Bill, which Tories construed into an attack on the Church. What would the Royal Supremacy mean if Parliament was no longer to be exclusively Anglican? Lord Grey told the bishops to set their house in order; ten Irish bishoprics were suppressed. Arnold wrote in 1832, "The Church, as it now stands, no human power can save." Whateley thought it difficult to "preserve the Establishment from utter overthrow". Alexander Knox, a far-seeing Irish writer, said, "The old High Church race is worn out." The "Clapham sect" of Evangelicals, who came down from Calvin, and the "Clapton sect", otherwise called High and Dry, who had no theology at all, divided "serious" people among them. Bishops were great persons who amassed wealth for their families, and who had attained to place and influence by servile offices or by editing Greek plays. In the presence of threatened revolution they sat helpless and bewildered. From them neither counsel nor aid was to be expected by earnest churchmen. Arnold would have brought in Dissenters by a "comprehension" which sacrificed dogma to individual judgment. Whateley protested against "that double usurpation, the interference of the Church in temporals, of the State in spirituals". A notable preacher and organizer, Dr. Hook, "first gave body and force to Church theology, not to be mistaken or ignored". But it was from Oxford, "the home of lost causes", always Cavalier at heart, still "debating its eternal Church question as in the days of Henry IV", that salvation came.

Oriel, once illustrated by Raleigh and Butler, was now the most distinguished college in the university. For some thirty years it had welcomed original thinkers, and among its fellows were, or had been, Copleston, Whateley, Hawkins, Davison, Keble, Arnold, Pusey, and Hurrell Froude. "This knot of Oriel men", says Pattison, "was distinctly the product of the French Revolution". Those among them who indulged in "free inquiry" were termed "Noetics"; they "called everything in question; they appealed to first principles, and disallowed authority in intellectual matters." The university, which Pattison describes as "a close clerical corporation", where all alike had sworn to the Prayer Book and Articles, had thus in its bosom a seed of "Liberalism", and was menaced by changes analogous to the greater revolutions in the State itself. Reaction came, as was to be expected, in the very college that had witnessed the provocation. Oxford, of all places, would surely be the last to accept French and democratic ideas.

John Keble (1792-1865) was the leading fellow of Oriel. As a mere boy, he had carried off the highest honours of the university. In 1823 he became his father's curate at Fairford, and in 1827 he published "The Christian Year", a cycle of poems or meditations in verse, refined, soothing, and akin to George Herbert's "The Temple", by their spiritual depth and devout attachment to the English Church. They have gone through innumerable editions. Keble, though a scholarly mind, had no grasp of metaphysics. An ingrained conservative, he took over the doctrines, and lived on the recollection of the Laudian school.

Without ambition, he was inflexible, never open to development, but gentle, shrewd, and saintly. His convictions needed an Aaron to make them widely effective; and he found a voice in his pupil, the "bright and beautiful" Froude, whose short life (1802-36) counts for much in the Oxford Movement. Froude was the connecting link between Keble and Newman. His friendship, at the moment when Newman's Evangelical prejudices were fading and his inclination towards Liberalism had received a sharp check by "illness and bereavement", proved to be the one thing needful to a temper which always leaned on its associates, and which absorbed ideas with the vivacity of genius. So the fusion came about. Elsewhere (see NEWMAN, JOHN HENRY) is related the story of those earlier years in which, from various sources, the future Tractarian leader gained his knowledge of certain Catholic truths, one by one. But their living unity and paramount authority were borne in upon him by discussions with Froude, whose teacher was Keble. Froude, says Newman, "professed openly his admiration for the Church of Rome, and his hatred of the Reformers. He delighted in the notion of an hierarchical system, of sacerdotal power, and of full ecclesiastical liberty. He felt scorn of the maxim, 'the Bible and the Bible only is the religion of Protestants'; and he gloried in accepting tradition as a main instrument of religious teaching. He had a high severe idea of the intrinsic excellence of virginity. . . He delighted in thinking of the saints. . . He embraced the principle of penance and mortification. He had a deep devotion to the Real Presence in which he had a firm faith. He was powerfully drawn to the Medieval Church, but not to the Primitive." ("Apol.", p. 24.)

These, remarkably enough, are characteristics of the latter phases of the Movement, known as Ritualism, rather than of its beginning. Yet Newman's friendship with Froude goes back to 1826; they became very intimate after the rejection of Peel by the university in 1829; and the Roman tendencies, of which mention is made above, cannot but have told powerfully on the leader, when his hopes for Anglicanism were shattered by the misfortunes of "Tract 90". Keble, on the other hand, had "a great dislike of Rome", as well as of "Dissent and Methodism". The first years of the revival were disfigured by a strong anti-Roman polemic, which Froude, on his death-bed, condemned as so much "cursing and swearing". But Newman had been as a youth "most firmly convinced that the Pope was the Antichrist predicted by Daniel, St. Paul, and St. John." His imagination was stained by the effects of this doctrine as late as the year 1843. In consequence, his language towards the ancient Church only just fell short of the vituperation lavished on it by the Puritans themselves. The movement, therefore, started, not on Roman ground, but in a panic provoked by the alliance of O'Connell with the Whigs, of Dissenters with Benthamites, intent on destroying all religious establishments. How could they be resisted? Newman answers in his opening tract, addressed to the clergy by one of themselves, a fellow-presbyter. "I fear", he tells them, "we have neglected the real ground on which our authority is built, our Apostolical descent." And he made his appeal to the ordination service—in other words, to the Prayer Book and the sacramental system, of which the clergy were the Divinely appointed ministers.

The first three tracts are dated 9 Sept., 1833. Newman and Froude, after their voyage to the Mediterranean in Dec., 1832, had returned in the midst of an agitation in which they were speedily caught up. Keble's sermon—in itself not very striking—on "National Apostasy", had marked 14 July, 1833, as the birthday of a "second Reformation". At Hadleigh, H. J. Rose and three other clergymen had met in conference, 25–29 July, and were endeavouring to start a society of Church defence, with machinery and safeguards, as befitted responsible persons. But Newman would not be swamped by committees. "Luther", he wrote, "was an individual". He proposed to be an Apostolical Luther. He was not now tutor of Oriel. Hawkins had turned him out of office—a curious acknowledgement of the vote by which he had made Hawkins provost instead of Keble. But he was Vicar of St. Mary's—a parish dependent on Oriel, and the university church. His pulpit was one of the most famous in England. He knew the secret of journalism, and had at his command a stern eloquence, barbed by convictions, which his reading of the Fathers and the Anglican folios daily strengthened. He felt supreme confidence in his position. But he was not well read in the history of the Anglican origins or of the Royal Supremacy. His Church was an ideal; never, certainly, since the legislation of Henry and Elizabeth had the English Establishment enjoyed the freedom he sought. It had issued articles of faith imposed by political expediency; it had tolerated among its communicants Lutherans, Calvinists, Erastians, and in the persons of high dignitaries like Bishop Hoadley even Socinians. It had never been self-governing in the past any more than it was now. If the "idea or first principle" of the movement was "ecclesiastical liberty", it must be pronounced a failure; for the Royal Supremacy as understood by lawyers and lamented over by High Church divines is still intact.

On that side, therefore, not a shadow of victory appears. Anyone may believe the doctrines peculiar to Tractarian theology, and any one may reject them, without incurring penalties in the Church Establishment. They are opinions, not dogmas, not the exclusive teaching that alone constitutes a creed. Fresh from Aristotle's "Ethics", where virtue is said to lie in a mean, the Oriel scholar termed his position the Via Media; it was the golden mean which avoided papal corruptions and Protestant heresies. But did it exist anywhere except in books? Was it not "as a doctrine, wanting in simplicity, hard to master, indeterminate in its provisons, and without a substantive existence in any age or country"? Newman did not deny that "it still remains to be tried whether what is called Anglo-Catholicism, the religion of Andrewes, Laud, Hammond, Butler, and Wilson, is capable of being professed, acted on, and maintained . . . or whether it be a mere modification or transition-state of Romanism or of popular Protestantism." The Via Media was an experiment. Perhaps the Established Church "never represented a doctrine at all . . . never had had an intellectual basis"; perhaps it has "been but a name, or a department of State" (Proph. Office, Introd.). To this second conclusion the author finally came; but not until during eight years he had made trial of his "middle way" and had won to it a crowd of disciples. The Tractarian Movement succeeded after his time in planting among the varieties of Anglican religious life a Catholic party. It failed altogether in making of the Establishment a Catholic Church.

Palmer, of Worcester College, and his clerical associates presented an address in 1834, signed with 10,000 names, to the Archbishop of Canterbury, defending the imperilled interests. Joshua Watson, a leading layman, brought up one more emphatic, to which 230,000 heads of families gave their adhesion. But of these collective efforts no lasting result came, although they frightened the Government and damped its revolutionary zeal. Mr. Rose, a man of high character and distinction, had started the "British Magazine" as a Church organ; the conference at Hadleigh was due to him; and he seemed to be marked out as chief over "nobodies" like Froude and Newman. His friends objected to the "Tracts" which were the doing of these free lances. Newman, however, would not give way. His language about the Reformation offended Mr. Rose, who held it to be a "deliverance"; and while Froude was eager to dissolve the union of Church and State, which he considered to be the parent or the tool of "Liberalism" in doctrine, he called Rose a "conservative". Between minds thus drawing in opposite directions any real fellowship was not likely to endure. Rose may be termed an auxiliary in the first stage of Church defence; he never was a Tractarian; and he died in 1839. His ally, William Palmer, long survived him. Palmer, an Irish Protestant, learned and pompous, had printed his "Origines Liturgicæ" in 1832, a volume now obsolete, but the best book for that period on the Offices of the Church of England. His later "Treatise on the Church", of 1838, was purely Anglican and therefore anti-Roman; it so far won the respect of Father Perrone, S.J., that he replied to it.

Palmer was no Tractarian either, as his "Narrative of Events", published in 1843, sufficiently proves. The difference may be sharply stated. Genuine Anglicans identified the Catholic Church once for all with the local body of which they were members, and interpreted the phenomena whether of medieval or reformed Christianity on this principle; they were Englishmen first and Catholics after. Not so with Newman, who tells us, "I felt affection for my own Church, but not tenderness . . . if Liberalism once got a footing within her, it was sure of the victory in the event. I saw that Reformation principles were powerless to rescue her. As to leaving her, the thought never crossed my imagination; still I ever kept before me that there was something greater than the Established Church, and that was the Church Catholic and Apostolic, set up from the beginning, of which she was but the local presence and the organ." These divergent views went at last asunder in 1845.

"The new Tracts", says Dean Church, "were received with surprise, dismay, ridicule, and indignation. But they also at once called forth a response of eager sympathy from numbers." An active propaganda was started all over the country. Bishops were perplexed at so bold a restatement of the Apostolic Succession, in which they hardly believed. Newman affirmed the principle of dogma; a visible Church with sacraments and rites as the channels of invisible grace; a Divinely ordained episcopal system as inculcated by the Epistles of St. Ignatius. But the Erastian or Liberal did not set store by dogma; and the Evangelical found no grace *ex opere operato* in the sacraments. Episcopacy to both of them was but a convenient form of Church government, and the Church itself a voluntary association. Now the English bishops, who were appointed by Erastians ("an infidel government" is Keble's expression), dreaded the power of Evangelicals. At no time could they dare to support the "Tracts". Moreover, to quote Newman, "All the world was astounded at what Froude and I were saying; men said that it was sheer Popery." There were searchings of heart in England, the like of which had not been felt since the non-jurors went out. Catholics had been emancipated; and "those that sat in the reformers' seats were traducing the Reformation". To add to the confusion, the Liberalizing attack on the university had now begun. In 1834 Dr. Hampden wrote and sent to Newman his pamphlet, in which he recommended the abolition of tests for Dissenters, or, technically, of subscription to the Articles by undergraduates. On what grounds? Because, he said, religion was one thing, theological opinion another. The Trinitarian and Unitarian doctrines were merely opinions, and the spirit of the English Church was not the spirit of dogma. Hampden did little more than repeat the well-known arguments of Locke and Chillingworth; but he was breaking open the gates of Oxford to unbelief, as Newman foresaw, and the latter answered wrathfully that Hampden's views made shipwreck of the Christian faith. "Since that time", says the "Apologia", "Phaethon has got into the chariot of the sun; we, alas, can only look on, and watch him down the steep of heaven." In Mark Pattison's phrase, "the University has been secularized." The Noetics of Oriel were followed by the Broad Churchmen of Balliol, and these by the agnostics of a more recent period. From Whateley and Arnold, through the stormy days of "Tract 90" and Ward's "degradation", we come down to the Royal Commission of 1854, which created modern Oxford. Subscription to the Articles was done away; fellowships ceased to be what some one has styled "clerical preserves"; there was an "outbreak of infidelity", says Pattison with a sneer, and names like Arthur Clough, Matthew Arnold, J. A. Froude, Jowett, and Max Müller triumphantly declare that the Liberals had conquered.

Newman lost the university, but he held it entranced for years by his visible greatness, by his preaching, and by his friendships. The sermons, of which eight volumes are extant, afforded a severe yet most persuasive commentary upon tracts and treatises, in themselves always of large outlook and of nervous though formal style. These, annotated after 1870 from the Catholic point of view, were reprinted in "Via Media", "Historical Sketches", "Discussions and Arguments", and two volumes of "Essays" (see popular edition of his Works, 1895). Keble republished Hooker as if an Anglo-Catholic Aquinas (finished 1836); and from the chair of poetry were delivered his graceful Latin "Prælections", deeply imbued with the same religious colouring. Hurrell Froude attempted a sketch of his own hero, St. Thomas à Becket, pattern of all anti-Erastians. Bowden compiled the life of Pope Gregory VII, evidently for the like motive. Nor were poetical manifestos wanting. To the "Lyra Apostolica" we may attribute a strong influence over many who could not grasp the subtle reasoning which filled Newman's "Prophetic Office". Concerning the verses from his pen, A. J. Froude observes that, in spite of their somewhat rude form, "they had pierced into the heart and mind and there remained". "Lead, Kindly Light", he adds, "is perhaps the most popular hymn in the language." Here, indeed, "were thoughts like no other man's thoughts, and emotions like no other man's emotions". To the "Lyra" Keble and others also contributed poems. And High Anglican stories began to appear in print.

But inspiration needed a constant power behind it, if the tracts were not to be a flash in the pan. It was given in 1834 and 1835 by the accession to the movement of E. B. Pusey, Canon of Christ Church and Hebrew professor. Pusey had enormous erudition, gained in part at German universities; he was of high social standing (always impressive to Englishmen), and revered as a saint for his devout life, his munificence, his gravity. Though a "dull and tedious preacher", most confused and unrhetorical, the weight of his learning was felt. He took the place that Mr. Rose could not have occupied long. At once the world out of doors looked up to him as official head of the movement. It came to be known as "Puseyism" at home and abroad. University wits had jested about "Newmaniacs" and likened the Vicar of St. Mary's to the conforming Jew, Neander; but "Puseyite" was a serious term even in rebuke. The Tractarian leader showed a deference to this "great man" which was always touching; yet they agreed less than Pusey understood. Towards Rome itself the latter felt no drawing; Newman's fierceness betrayed the impatience of a thwarted affection. "O that thy creed were sound, thou Church of Rome!" he exclaimed in the bitterness of his heart. Pusey, always mild, had none of that "hysterical passion". Neither did he regard the judgment of bishops as decisive, nor was he troubled by them if they ran counter to the Fathers' teaching, so intimately known to this unwearied student.

He was "a man of large designs", confident in his position, "haunted by no intellectual perplexities". He welcomed responsibility, a little too much sometimes; and now he gave the tracts a more important character. His own in 1835 on Holy Baptism was an elaborate treatise, which led to others on a similar model. In 1836 he advertised his great project for a translation or "library" of the Fathers, which was executed mainly in conjunction with the pious and eccentric Charles Marriot. The republication of Anglican divines, from Andrewes onwards, likewise owed its in--ception to Pusey. The *instauratio magna* of theology and devotion, intended to be purely Catholic, thus made a beginning. It has taken on it since the largest dimensions, and become not only learned but popular; Anglican experts have treated the liturgy, church history, books for guidance in the spiritual life, hymnology, architecture, and ritual with a copious knowledge and remarkable success. Of these enterprises Dr. Pusey was the source and for many years the standard.

In 1836 Hurrell Froude, returning from Barbadoes in the last stage of weakness, died at his father's house in Devonshire. His "Remains", of which we shall speak presently, were published in 1837. Newman's dearest friend was taken from him just as a fresh scene opened, with alarums and excursions to be repeated during half a century—legal "persecutions", acts of reprisals, fallings away on the right hand and the left. Froude died on 28 Feb., 1836. In May Dr. Hampden —who had been appointed, thanks to Whateley, Regius Professor of Divinity on 7 Feb.—was censured by the heads of houses, the governing board of the university, for the unsound doctrine taught in his "Bampton Lectures". All the Oxford residents at this time, except a handful, were incensed by what they considered the perils to faith which Dr. Hampden's freethought was provoking. But it was Newman who, by his "Elucidations", pointed the charge, and gave to less learned combatants an excuse for condemning what they had not read. Nemesis lay in wait on his threshold. The Evangelicals who trooped into Convocation to vote against Hampden "avowed their desire that the next time they were brought up to Oxford, it might be to put down the Popery of the Movement".

At this date even Pusey celebrated the Reformers as "the founders of our Church"; and that largely fabulous account of the past which Newman calls "the Protestant tradition" was believed on all sides. Imagine, then, how shocked and alarmed were old-fashioned parsons of every type when Froude's letters and diaries upset "with amazing audacity" these "popular and conventional estimates"; when the Reformation was described as "a limb badly set", its apologist Jewel flung aside as "an irreverent Dissenter", its reasoning against the Catholic mysteries denounced as the fruit of a proud spirit which would make short work of Christianity itself. Froude, in his graphic correspondence, appeared to be the *enfant terrible* who had no reserves and no respect for "idols" whether of the market-place or the theatre. Friends were pained, foes exultant; "sermons and newspapers", says Dean Church, "drew attention to Froude's extravagances with horror and disgust". The editors, Keble no less than Newman, had miscalculated the effect, which was widely irritating and which increased the suspicion their own writings had excited of some deep-laid plot in favour of Rome (Letter to Faussett, June, 1835). To be at once imprudent and insidious might seem beyond man's power; but such was the reputation Tractarians bore from that day. Froude's outspoken judgments, however, marked the turning of the tide in ecclesiastical history. "The divines of the Reformation", continues Dean Church, "never can be again, with their confused Calvinism, with their shifting opinions, their extravagant deference to the foreign oracles of Geneva and Zurich, their subserviency to bad men in power, the heroes and saints of Churchmen." Since

Cobbet's indictment of the Reformation no language had so stirred the rage of "general ignorance", long content to take its legends on trust. Froude's "Remains" were a challenge to it in one way, as the "Library of the Fathers" was in another, and yet again the ponderous "Catenas" of High Church authorities, to which by and by the "Parker Society" answered with its sixty-six volumes, mostly unreadable, of the Cranmer, Bullinger, and Zurich pattern. The Reformation theology was doomed. What the "Anglican regiment" has accomplished, J. A. Froude proclaims, "is the destruction of the Evangelical party in the Church of England".

When Samson pulled down the temple of the Philistines, he was buried in its ruins. Newman did not shrink from that sacrifice; he was ready to strike and be stricken. Though Hampden's condemnation would never have been carried by the Tractarians alone, they gave it a force and an edge in the very spirit of Laud. To put down false teachers by authority, to visit them with penalties of censure and deprivation, they held was the duty of the Church and of the State as God's minister. They would have repealed Catholic Emancipation. They resisted the grant to the College of Maynooth. They had saved the Prayer Book from amendments, and frightened politicians, who would have distributed the spoils of the Church among more or less "Liberal" schemes. By the year 1838 they had won their place in Oxford; the "Times" was coming over to their side; Bampton Lectures were beginning to talk of Catholic tradition as the practical rule of faith; and Evangelicals, infuriated if not dismayed, were put on their defence. Whateley from Dublin, Hawkins, Faussett, Hampden, Golightly, in Oxford, were calling up a motley array, united on one point only, that Tractarians must be handled as the emissaries of Rome. Dr. Arnold in the "Edinburgh" launched an invective against the "Oxford Malignants", accusing them of "moral dishonesty". Newman's former friend, Whateley, shrieked over "this rapidly increasing pestilence", and transfixed its leaders with epithets; they were "veiled prophets"; their religion was "Thuggee"; they were working out "infidel designs". Lord Morpeth in the House of Commons trampled on "a sect of damnable and detestable heretics lately sprung up at Oxford", and mentioned Newman by name. From every quarter of the compass a storm was blowing up; but it moved round a thunder cloud called "Rome".

"Just at this time, June, 1838", says Newman, "was the zenith of the Tract Movement." A change of fortune began with his bishop's charge, animadverting lightly on its Roman tendencies, to which the answer came at once from Newman, that if it was desired he would suppress the tracts. It was not asked of him; but he had written to Bowden the significant words, "I do not see how the bishop can materially alter his charge or how I can bear any blow whatever". Some of his friends objected to publishing the tract on the Roman Breviary; for it was not then realized how much the Anglican Prayer Book owes to Catholic, i. e. to Latin and papal sources. Newman impatiently rejoined that they must have confidence in him. To Keble he disclosed his idea of giving up the tracts, the "British Critic", and St. Mary's. For while preaching high Anglican doctrine, he said, "one cannot stop still. Shrewd minds anticipate conclusions, oblige one to say yes or no." He collected in January, 1839, "all the strong things" which he and others had flung out against the Church of Rome, and made of them "advertisements" to the Puseyite publications. By way of protest on the Low Church side, bishops, clergy, and laity united in the Martyrs' Memorial to Cranmer and Latimer, set up near the spot where they suffered, in front of Balliol College. But the tracts were selling faster than the printers could meet the demand. In July, Newman, taking up again his always projected and never issued edition of Dionysius of Alexandria, plunged into the record of the Monophysites and the Council of Chalcedon. In September he wrote to F. Rogers, "I have had the first real hit from Romanism"; an allusion to Wiseman's telling article on the Donatist schism in the "Dublin" for August. Walking with H. Wilberforce in the New Forest he made to him the "astounding confidence" that doubt was upon him, thanks to "the position of St. Leo in the Monophysite controversy, and the principle 'Securus judicat orbis terrarum' in that of the Donatists." A vista had opened to the end of which he did not see. His mind was never settled again in Anglicanism. "He has told the story . . . with so keen a feeling of its tragic and pathetic character", as Dean Church truly says, "that it will never cease to be read where the English language is spoken." It was the story of a deliverance. But still Samson paid for it with all he held dear.

Parallels from antiquity might affect a student like Newman. To the many, inside or beyond Oxford, they meant nothing. The live question always was, how to combat Rome, which appeared at the end of every vista as the goal of Tractarian reasoning. The "shrewd minds" which now harried and drove on their leader did not take to any "middle way"; these men cut into the movement at right angles and sang loudly *Tendimus in Latium*, they were pilgrims to St. Peter's shrine. J. B. Morris, Dalgairns, Oakeley, Macmullen (converts in the sequel), came round Newman while his older associates had not advanced. But the captain of the band was W. G. Ward, lecturer at Balliol, a friend of Stanley's and for a time attracted by Arnold, then suddenly changed for good by the sermons at St. Mary's, with his one sole article of faith, *Credo in Newmannum*. Ward, a strange, joyous, provoking figure, pervading the university with his logic and his jokes, was the *enfant terrible* of this critical time, as Froude had been previously. They differed in a hundred ways; but both certainly urged Newman forward at a pace he would not have chosen. Froude "did not seem to be afraid of inferences"; Ward revelled in them. It was Froude who first taught Newman "to look with admiration towards the Church of Rome". Ward, of all men the least inclined to compromise, did not care one jot for the Church of England, except in so far as it could be proved Catholic, by which he understood, as Protestants and Liberals did before him, the doctrine and discipline of the papal communion. He had "the intellect of an archangel", as he said ingenuously; his acuteness and audacity were a continual challenge to Newman, who partly resented but still more yielded to them; and so the problem took a formidable shape:—how much of "infused Catholicism" would the Establishment bear. It was "like proving cannon". The crucial test was applied in "Tract 90", which came out on 27 February, 1841.

Once more, as in the case of Froude's "Remains", Newman miscalculated. He had drifted so far that he lost sight of the ever-enduring Protestantism which, to this day, is the bulwark of the national feeling against Rome. He thought his peace-offering would not cause offence. But Ward prophesied, and his instinct proved true, that it would "be hotly received". A lively epistle from Church (afterwards Dean of St. Paul's) to F. Rogers at Naples shows the storm raging early in March. What "Tract 90" affirmed was that the Thirty-Nine Articles might be signed in a Catholic, though not in a Roman sense; that they did not condemn the Council of Trent, which in 1562, the date of their publication, was not ended; and that a distinction must be drawn between the corruptions of popular religion and the formal decrees approved by the Holy See. It is now admitted, in the language of J. A. Froude, that "Newman was only claiming a position for himself and his friends which had been purposely left open when the constitution of the Anglican

Church was framed". But he appeared to be an innovator and, in that excited season, a traitor. The Philistines held him bound by his own cords; Erastians or Evangelicals, they well knew that his bishop would not shield him from attack. Four leading tutors, egged on by the fanatical Golightly, and including A. C. Tait, afterwards Archbishop of Canterbury, demanded the writer's name and charged him with dangerous tendencies. The hebdomadal board now retorted on Newman the "persecution" dealt out to Hampden. They would not wait even twelve hours for his defence. They resolved on 15 March, that "modes of interpretation such as are suggested in the said Tract, evading rather than explaining the sense of the Thirty-nine Articles, and reconciling subscription to them with the adoption of errors, which they were designed to counteract, defeat the object, and are inconsistent with the due observance of the above mentioned Statutes."

This anathema was posted up on every buttery hatch, or public board, of the colleges, as a warning to undergraduates. Newman acknowledged his authorship in a touching letter, perhaps too humble; and a war of pamphlets broke out. Keble, Palmer, and Pusey stood up for the tract, though Pusey could not bring himself to approve of its method unconditionally. But Ward, with great effect, hurled back the charge of "insincerity" on those who made it. How could Whateley and Hampden use the services for baptism, visitation of the sick, or ordination, all dead against their acknowledged principles? But neither did Ward follow Newman. Later on, he described the articles as "patient of a Catholic but ambitious of a Protestant meaning". Whatever their logic, their rhetoric was undoubtedly Protestant. For himself, in subscribing them, he renounced no Roman doctrine. This, like all Ward's proceedings, was pouring oil on fire. Newman had made the mistake of handling an explosive matter without precaution, in the dry legal fashion of an advocate, instead of using his incomparable gift of language to persuade and convince. His refinements were pilloried as "Jesuitism", and his motive was declared to be treason. An "immense commotion" followed. The "Apologia" describes it, "In every part of the country, and every class of society, through every organ and opportunity of opinion, in newspapers, in periodicals, at meetings, in pulpits, at dinner-tables, in coffee-rooms, in railway-carriages, I was denounced as a traitor who had laid his train, and was detected in the very act of firing it against the time-honoured Establishment." His place in the movement was gone.

He would not withdraw the tract; he reiterated its arguments in a Letter to Dr. Jelf; but at his bishop's request he brought the series to an end, addressing him in a strikingly beautiful pamphlet, which severed his own connexion with the party he had led. He retired to Littlemore; and there, he says, "between July and November I received three blows that broke me". First, in translating St. Athanasius, he came on the Via Media once more; but it was that of the heretical Semi-Arians. Second, the bishops, contrary to an "understanding" given him, began to charge violently, as of set purpose, against "Tract 90", which they accused of Romanizing and dishonesty. Last came the unholy alliance between England and Prussia by which an Anglican Bishop was appointed at Jerusalem over a flock comprising, it would appear, not only Lutherans but Druses and other heretics. The "Confession of Augsburg" was to be their standard. Now, "if England could be in Palestine, Rome might be in England." The Anglican Church might have the Apostolical Succession; so had the Monophysites; but such acts led Newman to suspect that since the sixteenth century it had never been a Church at all.

Now then he was a "pure Protestant", held back from Rome simply by its apparent errors and idolatries. Or were these but developments, after all, of the primitive type and really true to it? He had converted Ward by saying that "the Church of the Fathers might be corrupted into Popery, never into Protestantism". Did not living institutions undergo changes by a law of their being that realized their nature more perfectly? and was the Roman Church an instance? At Littlemore the great book was to be composed "On the Development of Christian Doctrine", which viewed this problem in the light of history and philosophy. Newman resigned St. Mary's in Sept., 1843. He waited two years in lay communion before submitting to Rome, and fought every step of the journey. Meanwhile the movement went on. Its "acknowledged leader" according to Dean Stanley was now W. G. Ward. On pure Anglicans a strong influence was exerted by J. B. Mozley, Newman's brother-in-law. Keble, who was at odds with his bishop, vacated the chair of poetry; and the Tractarian candidate, Isaac Williams, was defeated in Jan., 1842. Williams had innocently roused slumbering animosities by his "Tract 80", on "Reserve in communicating religious knowledge", a warning, as ever since, Low Church partisans have maintained, that the Establishment was to be secretly indoctrinated with "Romish errors". The heads of houses now proposed to repeal their censure of 1836 on Hampden, though he withdrew not a line of his Bampton Lectures. It was too much. Convocation threw out the measure by a majority of three to two. Hampden, by way of revenge, turned the formal examination of a Puseyite, Macmullen of Corpus, for the B.D. into a demand for assent to propositions which, as he well knew, Macmullen could not sign. The vice-chancellor backed up Hampden; but the Delegates reversed that iniquitous judgment and gave the candidate his degree. The spirit of faction was mounting high. Young men's testimonials for orders were refused by their colleges. A statute was brought up in Feb., 1844, to place the granting of all divinity degrees under a board in conjunction with the vice-chancellor, which would mean the exclusion from them of Tractarians. This, indeed, was rejected by 341 votes to 21. But Newman had said a year earlier, that the authorities were bent on exerting their "more than military power" to put down Catholicism. R. W. Church calls them "an irresponsible and incompetent oligarchy". Their chiefs were such as Hawkins, Symons, and Cardwell, bitterly opposed to the movement all through. As Newman had retired, they struck at Pusey; and by a scandalous inquisition of "the six doctors" they suspended him, without hearing a word of his defence, from preaching for two years, 2 June, 1843. His crime consisted in a moderate Anglican sermon on the Holy Eucharist.

Espionage, delation, quarrels between heads and tutors, rejection of Puseyites standing for fellowships, and a heated suspicion as though a second Popish Plot were in the air, made of this time at Oxford a drama which Dean Church likens to the Greek faction-fights described by Thucydides. The situation could not last. A crisis might have been avoided by good sense on the part of the bishops outside, and the ruling powers within the university. It was precipitated by W. G. Ward. Ejected from his lectureship at Balliol, he wrote violent articles between 1841 and 1843 in the "British Critic", no longer in Newman's hands. His conversation was a combat; his words of scorn for Anglican doctrines and dignitaries flew round the colleges. In 1843 Palmer of Worcester in his dreary "Narrative of Events" objected strongly to Ward's "Romanizing" tendencies. The "British Critic" just then came to an end. Ward began a pamphlet in reply; it swelled to 600 pages, and in the summer of 1844 burst on an irritated public as "The Ideal of a Christian Church."

Its method was simple. The writer identified all

that was Roman with all that was Catholic; and proceeded to apply this test to the Church of England, which could ill bear it. Rome satisfied the conditions of what a Church ought to be; the Establishment shamefully neglected its duties as a "guardian of morality" and a "teacher of orthodoxy". It ignored the supernatural; it allowed ethics to be thrown overboard by its doctrine of justification without works; it had no real Saints because it neither commended nor practised the counsels of perfection; it was a schismatic body which ought humbly to sue for pardon at the feet of the true Bride of Christ. To evade the spirit of the Articles while subscribing them, where necessary, in a "non-natural" sense, was the only alternative Ward could allow to breaking with Anglicanism altogether. Unlike Newman, who aimed at reconciling differences, and to whom the Lutheran formula was but "a paradox or a truism", Ward repudiated the "solifidian" view as an outrage on the Divine sanctity; it was "a type of Antichrist", and in sound reason no better than Atheism. So his "relentless and dissolving logic" made any Via Media between Catholics and Protestants impossible. The very heart of the Elizabethan compromise he plucked out. His language was diffuse, his style heavy, his manner to the last degree provoking. But whereas "Tract 90" did not really state, and made no attempt to resolve, the question at issue, Ward's "Ideal" swept away ambiguous terms and hollow reconcilements; it contrasted, however clumsily, the types of saintliness which were in dispute; it claimed for the Catholic standard not toleration but supremacy; and it put the Church of England on its knees before Rome.

How could Oxford or the clergy endure such a lesson? So complete a change of attitude on the part of Englishmen, haughtily erect on the ruins of the old religion, was not to be dreamt of. This, then, was what "Tract 90" had in view with its subtleties and subterfuges—a second Cardinal Pole absolving the nation as it lay in the dust, penitent. The result, says Dean Stanley, was "the greatest explosion of theological apprehension and animosity" known to his time. Not even the tract had excited a more immediate or a more powerful sensation. Ward's challenge must be taken up. He claimed, as a priest in the Church of England, to hold (though not as yet to teach) the "whole cycle of Roman doctrine". Newman had never done so; even in 1844 he was not fully acquiescent on all the points he had once controverted. He would never have written the "Ideal"; much of it to him read like a theory. But in Oxford the authorities, who were acting as if with synodical powers, submitted to Convocation in Dec., 1844, three measures: (1) to condemn Ward's book; (2) to degrade the author by taking away his university degrees; and (3) to compel under pain of expulsion, every one who subscribed the Articles to declare that he held them in the sense in which "they were both first published and were now imposed by the university".

Had the penalty on Ward, vindictive and childish as it now appears, stood alone, few would have minded it. Even Newman wrote in Jan., 1845, to J. B. Mozley, "Before the Test was sure of rejection, Ward had no claims on anyone". But over that "Test" a wild shriek arose. Liberals would be affected by it as surely as Tractarians. Tait, one of the "Four Tutors", Maurice, the broadest of Broad Churchmen, Professor Donkin, most intellectual of writers belonging to the same school, came forward to resist the imposition and to shield "Tract 90", on the principle of "Latitude." Stanley and another obtained counsel's opinion from a future lord chancellor that the Test was illegal. On 23 Jan., they published his conclusion, and that very day the proposal was withdrawn. But on 25 Jan., the date in 1841 of "Tract 90" itself, a formal censure on the tract, to be brought up in the approaching Convocation, was recommended to voters by a circular emanating from Faussett and Ellerton. This anathema received between four and five hundred signatures in private, but was kept behind the scenes until 4 Feb. The hebdomadal board, in a frenzy of excitement, adopted it amid protests from the Puseyites and from Liberals of Stanley's type. Stanley's words during the tumult made a famous hit. In a broadside he exclaimed, "The wheel is come full circle. The victors of 1836 are the victims of 1845. The victims of 1845 are the victors of 1836. The assailants are the assailed. The assailed are the assailants. The condemned are the condemners. The condemners are the condemned. The wheel is come full circle. How soon may it come round again?" A comment on this "fugitive prophecy" was to be afforded in the Gorham case, in that of "Essays and Reviews", in the dispute over Colenso, and in the long and vexatious lawsuits arising out of Ritualism. The endeavour was made to break every school of doctrine in succession on this wheel, but always at length in vain.

Convocation met in a snowstorm on 13 Feb., 1845. It was the last day of the Oxford Movement. Ward asked to defend himself in English before the vast assembly which crowded into the Sheldonian Theatre. He spoke with vigour and ability, declaring "twenty times over" that he held all the articles of the Roman Church. Amid cries and counter-cries the votes were taken. The first, which condemned his "Ideal", was carried by 777 to 386. The second, which deprived him of university standing, by 569 to 511. When the vice-chancellor put the third, which was to annihilate Newman and "Tract 90", the proctors rose, and in a voice that rang like a trumpet Mr. Guillemard of Trinity, the senior, uttered their "Non placet". This was fatal to the decree, and in the event to that oligarchy which had long ruled over Oxford. Newman gave no sign. But his reticence boded nothing good to the Anglican cause. The University repudiated his followers and they broke into detachments, the many lingering behind with Keble or Pusey; others, and among them Mark Pattison, a tragic instance, lapsing into various forms of modern unbelief; while the genuine Roman group, Faber, Dalgairns, Oakeley, Northcote, Seager, Morris, and a long stream of successors, became Catholics. They left the Liberal party to triumph in Oxford and to remould the University. If 13 Feb., 1845, was the "Dies Iræ" of Tractarian hopes, it saw the final discomfiture of the Evangelicals. Henceforth, all parties in the National Church were compelled to "revise the very foundations of their religion". Dogma had taken refuge in Rome.

In April, 1845, the country was excited by Sir R. Peel's proposals for the larger endowment of Maynooth (see Macaulay's admirable speech on the occasion). In June, Sir H. Jenner Fust, Dean of Arches, condemned Oakeley of Margaret Street chapel for holding the like doctrines with Ward, who was already married and early in September was received into the Church. Newman resigned his Oriel fellowship, held since 1822, at the beginning of October. He did not wait to finish the "Development"; but on the feast of St. Denys, 9 Oct., made his profession of the Catholic Faith to Father Dominic at Littlemore. The Church of England "reeled under the shock". Deep silence, as of stupor, followed the clamours and long agonies of the past twelve years. The Via Media swerved aside, becoming less theoretical and less learned, always wavering between the old Anglican and the new Roman road, but gradually drawing nearer to the Roman. Its headquarters were in London, Leeds, and Brighton, no longer in Oxford.

But an "aftermath" of disputes, and of conversions in the year 1851, remains to be noticed. On 15 Nov., 1847, the Prime Minister, Lord John Russell, nominated to the See of Hereford the "stormy petrel" of those controversies, Dr. Hampden. He did so "to strengthen the Protestant character of our

Church, threatened of late by many defections to the Church of Rome". The "Times" expressed amazement; Archbishop Howley and thirteen other bishops remonstrated; but Dr. Pusey was "the leader and oracle of Hampden's opponents." At Oxford the Heads of Houses were mostly in favour of the nominee, though lying under censure since 1836. An attempt was made to object at Bow Church when the election was to be confirmed; but the Archbishop had no freedom, and by *congé d'élire* and exercise of the Royal Supremacy a notoriously unsound teacher became Bishop of Hereford. It was the case of Hoadley in a modern form.

Almost at the same date (2 Nov., 1847) the Rev. G. C. Gorham, "an aged Calvinist", was presented to the living of Brampton Speke in Devonshire. "Henry of Exeter", the bishop, holding High Anglican views, examined him at length on the subject of baptismal regeneration, and finding that he did not believe in it, refused to induct Mr. Gorham. The case went to the Court of Arches—a spiritual court—where Sir H. Jenner Fust decided against the appellant, 2 Aug., 1849. Mr. Gorham carried a further appeal to the judicial committee, the lay royal tribunal, which reversed the decision of the spiritual court below. Dr. Philpotts, the Bishop of Exeter, refused to institute; and the dean of arches was compelled to do so instead. The bishop tried every other court in vain; for a while he broke off communion, so far as he dared, with Canterbury. As Liberalism had won at Hereford, so Calvinism won at Brampton Speke.

These decisions of the Crown in Council affected matters of doctrine most intimately. Newman's lectures on "Anglican Difficulties" were drawn forth by the Gorham judgment. But Pusey, Keble, Gladstone, and Anglo-Catholics at large were dumbfounded. Manning, Archdeacon of Chichester, had neither written tracts nor joined in Newman's proceedings. He did not scruple to take part with the general public though in measured terms, against "Tract 90". He had gone so far as to preach an out-and-out Protestant sermon in St. Mary's on Guy Fawkes' day, 1843. In 1845 he "attacked the Romanizing party so fiercely as to call forth a remonstrance from Pusey". And then came a change. He read Newman's "Development", had a serious illness, travelled in Italy, spent a season in Rome, and lost his Anglican defences. The Gorham judgment was a demonstration that lawyers could override spiritual authority, and that the English Church neither held nor condemned baptismal regeneration. This gave him the finishing stroke. In the summer of 1850, a solemn declaration, calling on the Church to repudiate the erroneous doctrine thus implied, was signed by Manning, Pusey, Keble, and other leading High Anglicans; but with no result, save only that a secession followed on the part of those who could not imagine Christ's Church as tolerating heresy. On 6 April, 1851, Manning and J. R. Hope Scott came over. Allies, a scholar of repute, had submitted in 1849, distinctly on the question now agitated of the royal headship. Maskell, Dodsworth, Badeley, the two Wilberforces, did in like manner. Pusey cried out for freedom from the State; Keble took a non-juring position, "if the Church of England were to fail, it should be found in my parish". Gladstone would not sign the declaration; and he lived to write against the Vatican decrees.

Surveying the movement as a whole, we perceive that it was part of the general Christian uprising which the French Revolution called forth. It had many features in common with German Romanticism; and, like the policy of a Free Church eloquently advocated by Lamennais, it made war on the old servitude to the State and looked for support to the people. Against free-thought, speculative and anarchic, it pleaded for Christianity as a sacred fact, a revelation from on high, and a present supernatural power. Its especial task was to restore the idea of the Church, and the dignity of the sacraments, above all, of the Holy Eucharist. In the Laudian tradition, though fearfully weakened, it sought a fulcrum and a precedent for these happier changes.

Joseph de Maistre, in the year 1816, had called attention to the English Church, designating it as a middle term between Catholic unity and Protestant dissent; with an augury of its future as perhaps one day serving towards the reunion of Christendom. Alexander Knox foretold a like destiny, but the Establishment must be purged by suffering. Bishop Horsley, too, had anticipated such a time in remarkable words. But the most striking prophecy was uttered by an aged clergyman, Mr. Sikes of Guilsborough, who predicted that, whereas "the Holy Catholic Church" had long been a dropped article of the Creed, it would by and by seem to swallow up the rest, and there would be an outcry of "Popery" from one end of the country to another (Newman's "Correspondence", II, 484). When the tracts began, Phillips de Lisle saw in them an assurance that England would return to the Holy See. And J. A. Froude sums it all up in these words, "Newman has been the voice of the intellectual reaction of Europe", he says, "which was alarmed by an era of revolutions, and is looking for safety in the forsaken beliefs of ages which it had been tempted to despise."

Later witnesses, Cardinal Vaughan or W. E. Gladstone, affirm that the Church of England is transformed. Catholic beliefs, devotions, rites, and institutions flourish within it. But its law of public worship is too narrow for its religious life, and the machinery for discipline has broken down (Royal Commission on Discipline, concluding words). The condemnation of Anglican Orders by Pope Leo XIII in the Bull "Apostolicæ Curæ", 13 Sept., 1896, shuts out the hope entertained by some of what was termed "corporate reunion", even if it had ever been possible, which Newman did not believe. But he never doubted that the movement of 1833 was a work of Providence; or that its leaders, long after his own departure from them, were "leavening the various English denominations and parties (far beyond their own range) with principles and sentiments tending towards their ultimate absorption into the Catholic Church".

Lives of Newman, Manning, Faber, Pusey, Ward, Wiseman, include contemporary letters. Besides works under these names see: CHURCH, *Hist. of the O. M.* (1891); OVERTON, *The Anglican Revival* (1897); PALMER, *Narrative of Events* (1843–1883); M. PATTISON, *Memoirs* (1885); T. W. ALLIES, *A Life's Decision;* BLATCHFORD, *Letters;* BURGON, *Lives of twelve Good Men;* A. J. FROUDE in *Short Studies,* Vols. III and IV, *Revival of Romanism;* H. FROUDE, *Remains* (1837); GLADSTONE, *Letters on Religious Subjects,* ed. LATHBURY (1910); GUINEY, *Hurrell Froude* (1907); *Hampden's Life,* by his daughter; A. KNOX, *Remains* (1837); STEPHENS, *Life of Hook; Life of Keble,* by J. T. COLERIDGE, also by LOCK; J. B. MOZLEY, *Letters,* ed. A. MOZLEY; OAKELEY, *Notes on the T. M.;* J. R. HOPE-SCOTT, *Reminiscences* (includes correspondence); STANLEY, *Life of Arnold;* IDEM, *Essays on Church and State;* PROTHERO, *Life of Stanley;* WHATELEY, *Tracts; Life of Whateley,* by his daughter; BLANCO WHITE, *Autobiography* (1845); *Life of Bishop Wilberforce,* by his son; ISAAC WILLIAMS, *Autobiography;* also, *Ecclesiastical Courts Commission, 1883,* summary of report by HOLLAND; *Commission on Eccles. Discipline, Evidence and Report.*

WILLIAM BARRY.

Oxyrynchus, titular archdiocese of Heptanomos in Egypt. It was the capital of the district of its name, the nineteenth of Upper Egypt, whose god was Sit, incarnated in a sacred fish of the Nile, the Mormyrus. Thence comes its Greek name, for in Egyptian it is called Pemdje. It has been mentioned by Strabo, Pliny, Ptolemy, etc. Its inhabitants early embraced Christianity, and at the end of the fourth century ("Vitæ Patrum" of Rufinus of Aquileia) it possessed neither pagan nor heretic. It had then twelve churches, and its monastic huts exceeded in number its ordinary dwellings. Surrounding the city were many convents to which reference is made in Palladius, the "Apophthegmata Patrum", Johannes

Moschus, etc. In 1897, in 1903 and the years following, Grenfel and Hunt found papyri containing fourteen sentences or fragments of sentences (λόγια) attributed to Jesus and which seem to belong to the first half of the second century, also fragments of Gospels, now lost, besides Christian documents of the third century, etc. A letter, recently discovered, written by Peter the martyr, Bishop of Alexandria, in 312, gives an interesting picture of this Church at that time. Le Quien (Oriens christianus, II, 577–590) mentions 7 metropolitans of this city, nearly all Meletians or Monophysistes. In the Middle Ages under the dynasty of the Mamelukes, it was the leading city of a province. To-day under the name of Behneseh, it is entirely dismantled. Mounds of débris alone make it possible to recognize its circuit.

GRENFEL AND HUNT, *The Oxyrynchus Papyri*, in the publications of the EGYPT EXPLORATION FUND (London); WESSELY, *Les plus anciens monuments du christianisme écrits sur papyrus* (Paris, 1906); SCHMIDT, *Fragmente einer Schrift des Märtyerbischofs Petrus von Alexandrien* (Leipzig, 1901).

S. VAILHÉ.

Ozanam, ANTOINE-FRÉDÉRIC, great grand-nephew of Jacques Ozanam, b. at Milan, 23 April, 1813; d. at Marseilles, 8 Sept., 1853. His father, settled at first in Lyons as a merchant, after reverses of fortune decided to go to Milan. Later he returned to Lyons and became a physician. At eighteen Frédéric, in defence of the Faith, wrote "Réflexions sur la doctrine de Saint-Simon". Later he studied law in Paris, and lived for eighteen months with the illustrious physician Ampère. He formed an intimate friendship with the latter's son, Jean-Jacques Ampère, well known later for his works on literature and history. Meanwhile he became a prey of doubt. "God", he said, "gave me the grace to be born in the Faith. Later the confusion of an unbelieving world surrounded me. I knew all the horror of the doubts that torment the soul. It was then that the instructions of a priest and philosopher (Abbé Noirot) saved me. I believed thenceforth with an assured faith, and touched by so rare a goodness, I promised God to devote my life to the services of the truth which had given me peace". Rarely was a promise more faithfully fulfilled.

In 1836 he left Paris, where he had known Châteaubriand, Ballanche, Montalembert, and Lacordaire, and was appointed to the bench at Lyons, but two years later returned to Paris to submit his thesis on Dante for his doctorate in letters. His defence was a triumph. "Monsieur Ozanam", Cousin said to the candidate, "there is no one more eloquent than you have just proved yourself." He was given the chair of commercial law, just created at Lyons. The following year he competed for admission to the Faculties at Paris, and was appointed to substitute for one of the judges of the Sorbonne, Fauriel, philosopher and professor of foreign literature. At the same time he taught at Stanislas College, where he had been called by Abbé Gratry. On Fauriel's death in 1844, the Faculty unanimously elected Ozanam his successor. Like his friend Lacordaire he believed that a Christian democracy was the end towards which Providence was leading the world, and after the Revolution of 1848 aided him by his writings in the "Ere Nouvelle". In 1846 he visited Italy to regain his strength, undermined by a fever. On his return he published "Etudes germaniques" (1847); "Poètes franciscains en Italie au XIIIe siècle"; finally, in 1849, the greatest of his works: "La civilisation chrétienne chez les Francs". The Academy of Inscriptions awarded him the "Grand Prix Gobert" for two successive years. In 1852 he made a short journey to Spain an account of which is found in the posthumous work: "Un pélerinage au pays du Cid". In the beginning of the next year, his doctors again sent him to Italy, but he returned to Marseilles to die. When the priest exhorted him to have confidence in God, he replied "Oh why should I fear God, whom I love so much?" Complying with his desire the Government allowed him to be interred in the crypt of the "Carmes".

A brilliant apologist, impressed by the benefits of the Christian religion, he desired that they should be made known to all who might read his works or hear his words. To him the Gospel had renewed or revivified all the germs of good to be found in the ancient and in the barbarian world. In his many miscellaneous studies he endeavored to develop this idea, but was unable to fully realize his plan. In the two volumes of the "Etudes germaniques" he did for one nation what he desired to do for all. He also published, with the same view, a valuable collection of hitherto unpublished material: "Documents inédits pour servir à l'histoire de l'Italie, depuis le VIIIe siècle jusqu'au XIIe" (Paris, 1850). Ozanam was untiring in energy, had a rare gift for precision and historical insight, and at the same time a naturalness in his verse and a spontaneous, pleasing eloquence, all the more charming because of his frankness. "Those, who wish no religion introduced into a scientific work," he wrote, "accuse me of a lack of independence. But I pride myself on such an accusation. . . . I do not aspire to an independence, the result of which is to love and to believe nothing." His daily life was animated by an apostolic zeal. He was one of those who signed the petition addressed to the Archbishop of Paris to obtain a large body of religious teachers for the Catholic school children, whose faith was endangered by the current unbelief. As a result of this petition Monseigneur de Quélen created the famous "Conférences de Notre Dame", which Lacordaire (q. v.) inaugurated in 1835. When but twenty, Ozanam with seven companions had laid the foundations of the Society of St. Vincent de Paul, in order, as he said to "insure my faith by works of charity". During his life he was an active member and a zealous propagator of the society (see SAINT VINCENT DE PAUL, SOCIETY OF). With all his zeal, he was, however, tolerant. His strong, sincere books exhibit a brilliant and animated style, enthusiasm and erudition, eloquence and exactness, and are yet very useful introductions to the subjects of which they treat.

Œuvres complètes d'A. F. Ozanam (2nd ed., in 11 vols., Paris, 1862); LACORDAIRE, *Frédéric Ozanam*, in the V vol. of the complete edition of his works; O'MEARA, *F. Ozanam* (London, 1879); C.-A. OZANAM (a brother of Frédéric), *Vie de Frédéric Ozanam* (2nd ed., 1882); HUIT, *Frédéric Ozanam* (1888); BAUDRILLART, *L'apologétique de Frédéric Ozanam* in *Revue pratique d'apologétique* (15 May, 1909).

GEORGES BERTRIN.

Ozanam, JACQUES, French mathematician, b. at Bouligneux (Ain), 1640; d. in Paris, 3 April, 1717. He came of a rich family which had renounced the Jewish for the Catholic religion. From the same family sprang the better known Antoine-Frédéric Ozanam (q. v.). Though he began the study of theology to please his father, he was more strongly attracted to mathematics, which he mastered without the aid of a teacher. At the age of fifteen he produced a mathematical treatise. Upon the death of his father, he gave up theology after four years of study and began, at Lyons, to give free private instruction in mathematics. Later, as the family property passed entirely to his elder brother, he was reluctantly driven to accept fees for his lessons. In 1670, he published trigonometric and logarithmic tables more accurate than the then existing ones of Ulacq, Pitiscus, and Briggs. An act of kindness in lending money to two strangers secured for him the notice of M. d'Aguesseau, father of the chancellor, and an invitation to settle in Paris. There he enjoyed prosperity and contentment for many years. He married, had a large family, and derived an ample income from teaching mathematics to private pupils, chiefly foreigners. His mathematical publications were numerous and well received. The manuscript entitled "Les six livres de l'Arithmétique de

Diophante augmentés et reduits à la spécieuse" received the praise of Leibnitz. "Récréations", translated later into English and well known to-day, was published in 1694. He was elected member of the Academy of Sciences in 1701. The death of his wife plunged him into deepest sorrow, and the loss of his foreign pupils through the War of the Spanish Succession, reduced him to poverty.

Ozanam was honoured more abroad than at home. He was devout, charitable, courageous, and of simple faith. As a young man he had overcome a passion for gaming. He was wont to say that it was for the doctors of the Sorbonne to dispute, for the pope to decide, and for a mathematician to go to heaven in a perpendicular line. Among his chief works are: "Table des sinus, tangentes, et sécantes" (Lyons, 1670); "Méthode générale pour tracer des cadrans" (Paris, 1673); "Géométrie pratique" (Paris, 1684); "Traité des lignes du premier genre" (Paris, 1687); "De l'usage du compas" (Paris, 1688); "Dictionnaire mathématique" (Paris, 1691); "Cours de mathématiques" (Paris, 1693, 5 vols., tr. into English, London, 1712); "Traité de la fortification" (Paris, 1694); "Récréations mathématiques et physiques" (Paris, 1694, 2 vols., revised by Montucla, Paris, 1778, 4 vols., tr. by Hutton, London, 1803, 4 vols., revised by Riddle, London, 1844); "Nouvelle Trigonométrie" (Paris, 1698); "Méthode facile pour arpenter" (Paris, 1699); "Nouveaux Eléments d'Algèbre" (Amsterdam, 1702); "La Géographie et Cosmographie" (Paris, 1711); "La Perspective" (Paris, 1711).

Fontenelle, *Eloge d'Ozanam* in *Œuvres*, I, 401–408 (Paris, 1825) or in *Mém. de l'Acad. des sc. de Paris* (*Hist.*), ann. 1717.

PAUL H. LINEHAN.

Ozias עֲזִיָּה, עֲזַרְיָה, i. e., "Yahweh is my strength", name of six Israelites mentioned in the Bible. (1) Ozias, King of Juda (809–759 B. C.), son and successor of Amazias. On the latter's death he was chosen king though he was only sixteen years of age (IV Kings, xiv, 21, where, as in ch. xv also, the name Azarias appears instead of Ozias, probably through a copyist's error; cf. II Par., xxvi, 1). His long reign of fifty-two years is described as pleasing to God, though he incurs the reproach of having tolerated the "high places". This stricture is omitted by the chronicler, who, however, relates that Ozias was stricken with leprosy for having presumed to usurp the priestly function of burning incense in the Temple. Ozias is mentioned among the lineal ancestors of the Saviour (Matt., i, 8, 9). (2) Ozias, son of Uriel, and father of Saul of the branch of Caath (I Par., vi, 24). (3) Ozias, whose son Jonathan was custodian of the treasures possessed by King David outside of Jerusalem (I Par., xxvii, 25). (4) Ozias, son of Harim, one of the priests who having taken "strange wives", were forced to give them up during the reform of Esdras (I Esdr., x, 21). (5) Ozias, son of Misha, of the tribe of Simeon, a ruler of Bethulia (Judith, vii, 12). (6) Ozias, one of the ancestors of Judith, of the tribe of Ruben (Judith, viii, 1).

Lesêtre in Vigouroux, *Dict. de la Bible*, s. v.

JAMES F. DRISCOLL.

P

Pacandus, titular see, recorded under "Pacanden." among the titular sees in the official list of the Curia Romana as late as 1884, when it was suppressed as never having existed as a residential see. Its present titular is Mgr Léon Livinhac, superior general of the White Fathers. The name of "Pacanden." owes its origin, without doubt, to the See of Acanda in Lycia, whose bishop, Panætius, signed in 458 the letter of the bishops of Lycia to Emperor Leo, and which is mentioned in the "Notitiæ Episcopatuum" from the seventh to the thirteenth century among the suffragans of Myra. Its exact site is unknown.

LE QUIEN, *Oriens christianus*, I, 985; PÉTRIDÈS, *Acanda* in *Dict. d'hist. et de géog. eccl.*, I, 253.

S. PÉTRIDÈS.

Pacca, BARTOLOMMEO, cardinal, scholar, and statesman, b. at Benevento, 27 Dec., 1756; d. at Rome, 19 Feb., 1844; son of Orazio Pacca, Marchese di Matrice, and Crispina Malaspina. He was educated by the Jesuits at Naples, by the Somaschans in the Clementine College at Rome, and at the Accademia de' Nobili Ecclesiastici. In 1785 Pius VI appointed him nuncio at Cologne, the centre of anti-Roman agitation. He was consecrated titular Archbishop of Damiata and arrived at Cologne in June, 1786. The Archbishop of Cologne, Archduke Maximilian of Austria, who had written a courteous letter to Pacca at Rome, told him he would not be recognized unless he formally promised not to exercise any act of jurisdiction in the archdiocese. The same attitude was taken by the Archbishops of Trier and Mainz. Hostility to Rome, incited chiefly by the work of Febronius (see FEBRONIANISM) was then at a high pitch on account of the establishment of the new nunciature of Munich. The other bishops, however, and the magistrates of Cologne received Pacca with all due respect. Even Prussia made no difficulty, and its monarch, in recognition of his friendly attitude, was accorded at Rome the title of king, against which Clement XI (1701) had protested when the emperor would have granted it. On his journey through his dominions on the Rhine Frederick William received the nuncio with great honour.

BARTOLOMMEO PACCA

Pacca's position with respect to the three ecclesiastical electors was difficult. When the Archbishop of Cologne, in 1786, opened the University of Bonn, that of Cologne being still loyal to the Holy See, the discourses given were a declaration of war against the Holy See. At Cologne, too, an attempt was made to support Febronian propositions, but was frustrated by the nuncio, against whom innumerable pamphlets were directed. But Pacca induced some prominent German writers to uphold the rights of the Holy See. He soon had a dispute with the Elector of Cologne. Conformably to the Punctuation of Ems, agreed on by the three archbishop electors and the Archbishop of Salzburg in 1786, the Archbishop of Cologne protested against a matrimonial dispensation given by the nuncio in virtue of his faculties, and went so far as to grant dispensations not contained in his quinquennial faculties, instructing the pastors to have no further recourse to the nuncio for similar dispensations. The nuncio, in accordance with instructions from Rome, directed a circular to all the pastors in his jurisdiction apprising them of the invalidity of such dispensations. The four archbishops thereupon appealed to Joseph II to entirely abolish the jurisdiction of the nuncios, and the emperor referred the matter to the Diet of Ratisbon, where it was quashed. Pacca also opposed freedom of worship for the Protestants of Cologne, but so tactfully that his intervention was not apparent, and did not offend the King of Prussia. In 1790 he went on a secret mission to the Diet of Frankfort to safeguard the interests of the Holy See, and prevented the adoption of a new concordat.

When the French invaded the Rhine Provinces, he was ordered to leave Cologne, but he had the satisfaction of being finally recognized as nuncio by the Archbishop of Trier. In 1794 he was appointed nuncio in Portugal, but accomplished nothing of importance there. Of both nunciatures, he wrote memoirs, containing observations on the character of the countries and their governments. While still at Lisbon, he was created cardinal of the title of S. Silvestro in Capite (23 February, 1801), and assigned to various congregations. In 1808 French troops were stationed in Rome. Yielding to the insistence of Napoleon, Pius VII sacrificed Cardinal Consalvi, his faithful secretary of State, and the pro-secretaries, Casoni, Doria, and Gabrielli. The last-named was surprised in his apartments by the soldiers, placed under arrest, and ordered to leave papal territory. Two days later (18 June, 1808) the pope appointed Pacca pro-secretary.

In his new position Pacca carefully avoided everything that might provoke the emperor's anger, even ignoring the excesses of the French soldiery in and about Rome. But in August he felt obliged to publish in every province a decree forbidding subjects of the Holy See to enlist in the new "Civic Guard" (see NAPOLEON I) and, in general, under any foreign command. The "Civic Guard" was a hotbed of turbulence that might easily produce a rebellion in the Pontifical States. But Miollis, the French commandant, was furious, and threatened Pacca with dismissal from Rome. The pro-secretary replied that he took orders from the pope alone. Realizing that the annexation of Rome was inevitable, Pacca took precautions to prevent a sudden attack on the Quirinal; at the same time advising calm and quiet. The Bull of excommunication against Napoleon had been prepared in 1806, to be published in the event of annexation. On 10 June, 1809, when the change of government actually took place, the Bull was promulgated; on 6 July, the Quirinal was attacked, the pope arrested and taken to France and thence to Savona. Pacca was among those who accompanied him. As far as Florence, he tried to cheer Pius VII; at Florence he was torn from the pontiff's side, much to his sorrow, and saw him again only at Rivoli and Grenoble. From Grenoble he was conducted (6 Aug., 1809) to Fenestrelle, where he was confined with great severity, and could hardly find opportunities for confession and communion. Later, however, this restriction was removed. During this period the captive minister found time to write those records which formed the substance of his "Memorie storiche del ministero" etc.

Finally, on 30 January, 1813, he was told that in view of the concordat concluded between the pope and Napoleon at Fontainebleau (25 January) he was free to join the pope. Napoleon had long objected to his liberation, declaring: "Pacca is my enemy". At Fontainebleau he and the other liberated cardinals insisted that Pius VII should retract the last concordat and refuse further negotiations until he was back in Rome with full freedom. Pacca also suggested the re-establishment of the Society of Jesus, although both the pope and he himself had been educated in prejudices against the society. When Pius VII was conducted to Savona the second time, Pacca was deported to Uzès (January, 1814), leaving that place on 22 April. He joined the pope at Sinigaglia whence he accompanied him to Rome. Appointed cardinal camerlengo in the same year, he exerted himself to re-establish the religious orders from the foundations not already sold.

During the absence of Consalvi at the Congress of Vienna, Pacca again became pro-secretary of State, the restoration of the pontifical Government thus devolving on him. He was reproved by Consalvi, from Vienna, for his severity towards the supporters of the Napoleonic regime, and vainly tried to justify his conduct. When Murat, King of Naples, sent his troops through the Pontifical States to meet the Austrians, Pacca advised Pius VII to seek temporary refuge at Genoa, fearing that Murat would attempt to ravage the domains of the Holy See. During the pope's absence, the provisional Government caused the arrest of Cardinal Maury on a charge of having secret intelligence with Murat, and his trial was continued even after the pope's return. But Consalvi, immediately on his arrival, stopped the proceedings. The rest of Pacca's life was occupied in the affairs of the different congregations to which he was assigned, and in the administration of the suburbicarian sees. Leo XII appointed him pro-datary, he was the first to hold the post of cardinal legate of Velletri, and he was active against the Carbonari.

Cardinal Pacca's house was frequented by the most illustrious scientists, men of letters, and artists, both Roman and foreign. He had excavations made at Ostia at his own expense, and with the objects discovered formed a small museum in his vineyard on the Via Aurelia (Casino of Pius V).

Acute observations on politics and the philosophy of history are found in his "Memorie storiche della nunziatura di Colonia"; "Dei grandi meriti verso la Chiesa Cattolica del clero dell' Università e de' Magistrati di Colonia nel secolo XVI"; "Notizie sul Portogallo e sulla nunziatura di Lisbona"; "Memorie storiche per servire alla storia ecclesiastica del secolo XIX" (1809–14); "Notizie storiche intorno alla vita e gli scritti di Mons. Franc. Pacca, arcivescovo di Benevento (1752–75)". (See also CONSALVI; PIUS VII.)

Diario di Roma (1844), n. 39; *Album di Roma* (1844), n. 16; RINIERI, *Corrispondenza inedita de' cardinali Consalvi e Pacca nel tempo del Congresso di Vienna* in *Diplomazia pontificia*, V (Turin, 1903); WISEMAN, *Recollections of the Last Four Popes* (London, 1858).

U. BENIGNI.

Paccanarists. See SACRED HEART OF JESUS, SOCIETY OF.

Pace, PETER. See GOZO, DIOCESE OF.

Pachomius, SAINT, d. about 346. The main facts of his life will be found in MONASTICISM. II. *Eastern Monasticism before Chalcedon*. Having spent some time with Palemon, he went to a deserted village named Tabennisi, not necessarily with the intention of remaining there permanently. A hermit would often withdraw for a time to some more remote spot in the desert, and afterwards return to his old abode. But Pachomius never returned; a vision bade him stay and erect a monastery; "very many eager to embrace the monastic life will come hither to thee". Although from the first Pachomius seems to have realized his mission to substitute the cenobitical for the eremitical life, some time elapsed before he could realize his idea. First his elder brother joined him, then others, but all were bent upon pursuing the eremitical life with some modifications proposed by Pachomius (e. g., meals in common). Soon, however, disciples came who were able to enter into his plans. In his treatment of these earliest recruits Pachomius displayed great wisdom. He realized that men, acquainted only with the eremitical life, might speedily become disgusted, if the distracting cares of the cenobitical life were thrust too abruptly upon them. He therefore allowed them to devote their whole time to spiritual exercises, undertaking himself all the burdensome work which community life entails. The monastery at Tabennisi, though several times enlarged, soon became too small and a second was founded at Pabau (Faou). A monastery at Chenoboskion (Schenisit) next joined the order, and, before Pachomius died, there were nine monasteries of his order for men, and two for women.

How did Pachomius get his idea of the cenobitical life? Weingarten (Der Ursprung des Mönchthums, Gotha, 1877) held that Pachomius was once a pagan monk, on the ground that Pachomius after his baptism took up his abode in a building which old people said had once been a temple of Serapis. In 1898 Ladeuze (Le Cénobitisme pakhomien, 156) declared this theory rejected by Catholics and Protestants alike. In 1903 Preuschen published a monograph (Mönchthum und Serapiskult, Giessen, 1903), which his reviewer in the "Theologische Literaturzeitung" (1904, col. 79), and Abbot Butler in the "Journal of Theological Studies" (V, 152) hoped would put an end to this theory. Preuschen showed that the supposed monks of Serapis were not monks in any sense whatever. They were dwellers in the temple who practised "incubation", i. e. sleeping in the temple to obtain oracular dreams. But theories of this kind die hard. Mr. Flinders Petrie in his "Egypt in Israel" (published by the Soc. for the Prop. of Christ. Knowl., 1911) proclaims Pachomius simply a monk of Serapis. Another theory is that Pachomius's relations with the hermits became strained, and that he recoiled from their extreme austerities. This theory also topples over when confronted with facts. Pachomius's relations were always affectionate with the old hermit Palemon, who helped him to build his monastery. There was never any rivalry between the hermits and the cenobites. Pachomius wished his monks to emulate the austerities of the hermits; he drew up a rule which made things easier for the less proficient, but did not check the most extreme asceticism in the more proficient. Common meals were provided, but those who wished to absent themselves from them were encouraged to do so, and bread, salt, and water were placed in their cells. It seems that Pachomius found the solitude of the eremitical life a bar to vocations, and held the cenobitical life to be in itself the higher (Ladeuze, op. cit., 168) The main features of Pachomius's rule are described in the article already referred to, but a few words may be said about the rule supposed to have been dictated by an angel (Palladius, "Hist. Lausiaca", ed. Butler, pp. 88 sqq.), of which use is often made in describing a Pachomian monastery. According to Ladeuze (263 sqq.), all accounts of this rule go back to Palladius; and in some most important points it can be shown that it was never followed by either Pachomius or his monks. It is unnecessary to discuss the charges brought by Amélineau on the flimsiest grounds against the morality of the Pachomian monks. They have been amply refuted by Ladeuze and Schiwietz (cf. also Leipoldt, "Schneute von Atripe", 147).

In addition to the bibliography already given (Eastern Monasticism before Chalcedon) consult CABROL, *Dict. d'archéol. chrét.*, s. v. *Cénobitisme;* BOUSQUET AND NAU, *Hist. de S. Pacomus* in *Ascetica . . . patrologia orient.*, IV (Paris, 1908).

F. J. BACCHUS.

Pachtler, GEORGE MICHAEL, controversial and educational writer, b. at Mergentheim, Würtemberg, 14 Sept., 1825; d. at Exaten, Holland, 12 Aug., 1889. He studied in the University of Tübingen and was ordained priest in 1848; he then took a course of philology in the University of Munich and became professor in the Gymnasium at Ellwangen. In 1856 Father Pachtler entered the Society of Jesus and some years later was appointed professor in the Jesuit College of Feldkirch, Austria. His educational labours were interrupted twice, when he acted as military chaplain to the Tyrolese troops during the Italian campaign (1866), and to German volunteers in the papal army (1869-70). After the expulsion of the Society of Jesus from the German Empire (1872), Pachtler lived mostly in Holland and Austria, devoting himself to literary work. He was the first editor of the "Stimmen aus Maria-Laach", published by the German Jesuits, one of the leading Catholic periodicals in Germany. He was an able and fertile writer on questions of the day: the Vatican Council, the Roman question, the labour movement, Freemasonry, and Liberalism.

Among his works are: "Acta et Decreta Sacrosancti et Œcumenici Concilii Vaticani" (1871), "Die Internationale Arbeiterverbindung" (1871), "Der Götze der Humanität oder das Positive der Freimaurerei" (1875), "Der stille Krieg gegen Thron und Altar, oder das Negative der Freimaurerei" (1873), "Der Europäische Militarismus" (1876), "Die Geistige Knechtung der Völker durch das Schulmonopol des modernen Staates" (1876), "Das göttliche Recht der Familie und der Kirche auf die Schule" (1879). His book on the reform of higher education: "Die Reform unserer Gymnasien" (1883), attracted the attention of the foremost German educationists, and he was invited to become a contributor to the "Monumenta Germaniæ Pædagogica", published in Berlin under the editorship of Karl Kehrbach. He contributed four volumes (II, V, IX, and XVI of the series, 1887-94), the last being edited by Father Duhr, S.J., after the author's death. Pachtler's volumes form the standard work on the educational system of the Jesuits; it is entitled: "Ratio Studiorum et Institutiones Scholasticæ Societatis Jesu, per Germaniam olim Vigentes". The work contains the official documents of the society which have reference to education, parts of the constitutions, decrees of the legislative assemblies of the order, ordinances of generals, reports of official visitations, the various revisions of the "Ratio Studiorum", schedules of study, disciplinary regulations, directions for the training of teachers, and treatises of private individuals which explain the practical working of the system. Much of the material had never been published. Through the publication of these valuable documents, certain erroneous conceptions entertained by many concerning the Jesuit system of education, its aims, and methods, have forever been removed. Although the work deals particularly with the Jesuit schools in Germany, Austria, Switzerland, and the Netherlands, it contains much that is of general interest, and constitutes the most important source of information on the educational labours of the Society of Jesus.

Stimmen aus Maria-Laach, XXXVII (1889); *Monumenta Germaniæ Pædagogica*, XVI, introduction.

ROBERT SCHWICKERATH.

Pacianus, SAINT. See BARCELONA, DIOCESE OF.

Pacificus, a disciple of St. Francis of Assisi, b. probably near Ascoli, Italy, in the second half of the twelfth century; d. probably at Lens, France, c. 1234. Local authors identify him with a certain William of Lisciano. Before becoming a Friar Minor he had been poet laureate at the Court of Frederick II of Sicily. When St. Francis, towards 1212, preached at San Severino, in the Marches, the poet saw two resplendent swords crossed on the saint's breast. Deeply impressed by this vision, he asked to be received into the new order, and St. Francis gladly complied, giving him the name of Pacificus. In 1217 he was sent to France, where he is said to have been the founder and first provincial of the Friars Minor. In the Spring of 1226 Pacificus witnessed the holy "Stigmata of St. Francis" (II Cel., II, 99). When the saint composed the "Canticle of the Sun" he wished to summon Brother Pacificus and send him with other friars through the world, preaching the praises of God (Spec. Perfect., c. 100). The last certain date in the life of Brother Pacificus is that of the Bull "Magna sicut", 12 April, 1227 (Bull. Franc., I, 33-34; Raynaldus, ad an. 1227, 64, 65), in which Gregory IX recommends the Poor Clares of Siena to his care. Later authors who say he died at Suffiano, in the Marches, confounded him with another friar of the same name. According to Gonzaga, he was sent by Brother Elias back to France, where he died. Pacificus was long credited with having put the songs of St. Francis into verse. But for the simple construction of the "Canticle of the Sun", the saint needed no help, whilst the other two do not belong to him at all. Some Italian verses said to have been composed by Pacificus are given by Italian authors.

THOMS A CELANO, *Vitæ S. Francisci* (Rome, 1906); *Speculum perfectionis*, ed. SABATIER (Paris, 1898); ST. BONAVENTURE, *Leg. duæ* (Quaracchi, 1898), iv; *Analecta Franciscana*, III (Quaracchi, 1897), 7-8; 10; IV (Quaracchi, 1906), 285-86; THOMAS TUSCUS, *Gesta Imperatorum et Pontificum* in *Mon. Germ. Hist.: Script.*, XXII (Hanover, 1872), 492; GONZAGA, *De origine Seraph. Religionis* (Rome, 1587); WADDING, *Annales Minorum*, ad an. 1212, 39-42; *Acta SS.*, Jul., III, 170-74; LANCETTI, *Memorie intorno ai poeti laureati* (Milan, 1839), 82-86; COSMO, *Frate Pacifico, Rex Versuum* in *Giornale storico della letteratura Italiana*, XXXVIII (Turin, 1901), 1-40; MARIOTTI, *I primordi gloriosi dell' Ordine minoritico nelle Marche* (Castelplanio, 1903), 124.

LIVARIUS OLIGER.

Pacificus of Ceredano (CERANO), also known as PACIFICUS OF NOVARA (NOVARIENSIS), BLESSED, b. 1420 at Cerano, in the Diocese of Novara in Lombardy, supposedly of the much respected family of Ramati; d. 14 June, 1482. He entered the Franciscan Order of Observants at Novara in 1445. After his ordination, he was employed in preaching, in which field the Italian Observants of that time were especially prominent. Pacificus also had a share in the preaching of the crusade against the Turks undertaken by his order. The general chapter of the Observants, held in Ferrara, 15 May, 1481, sent him as commissioner to Sardinia to administer and inspect the Franciscan monasteries in that country, where he died. According to his wish, his body was brought to Cerano and buried in the church attached to the Franciscan monastery. His head was given to the parish church of that place. He was at once honoured as a saint, and, in 1745, Benedict XIV approved his veneration for the Franciscan Order and the Diocese of Novara. His feast is celebrated on 5 June. Bl. Pacificus is famous as the author of a dissertation, written in Italian and named after him the "Summa Pacifica", which treats of the proper method of hearing confessions. It was first printed at Milan in 1479 under the title: "Somma Pacifica o sia Trattato della Scienza di confessare" (Hain, "Repert. typogr.", n. 12259; Copinger, "A Supplement to Hain", n. 12259; II, 4573-5). The work was also published in Latin at Venice (1501 and 1513).

WADDING, *Annales Ord. Min.*, XIV (Rome, 1735), 165, 266, 326; (1650), 271; (1806), 184; (1906), 181; SBARALEA, *Supplem. ad Script. O. M.* (Rome, 1806), 571; (Anonymous) *Vita del B. Pacifico da Cerano* (Novara, 1878); BASILIO DA NEIRONE, *Sul. b. Pacifico da Cerano* (Genoa, 1882); CAZZOLA, *Il b. Pacifico Ramati* (Novara, 1882); *Acta SS.*, Jun., I, 802-3 (2nd ed., 789-90); JEILER in *Kirchenlex.*, s. v.

MICHAEL BIHL.

Pacificus of San Severino, SAINT, b. at San Severino, in the March of Ancona, 1 March, 1653; d. there 24 Sept., 1721; the son of Antonio M. Divini and Mariangela Bruni. His parents died soon after his confirmation when three years old; he suffered many hardships until in December, 1670, he took the Franciscan habit in the Order of the Reformati, at Forano, in the March of Ancona, and was ordained on 4 June, 1678, subsequently becoming Lector or Professor of Philosophy (1680–83) for the younger members of the order, after which, for five or six years, he laboured as a missionary among the people of the surrounding country. He then suffered lameness, deafness, and blindness for nearly twenty-nine years. Unable to give missions, he cultivated more the contemplative life. He bore his ills with angelic patience, worked several miracles, and was favoured by God with ecstasies. Though a constant sufferer, he held the post of guardian in the monastery of Maria delle Grazie in San Severino (1692–3), where he died. His cause for beatification was begun in 1740; he was beatified by Pius VI, 4 August, 1786, and solemnly canonized by Gregory IX, 26 May, 1839. His feast is celebrated on 24 September.

MELCHIORRI, *Vita di S. Pacifico da San Severino* (Rome, 1839), compiled from the Acts of Canonization; SDERCI DA GAJOLE, *Vita di S. Pacifico da Sanseverino* (Prato, 1898); DIOTALLEVI, *Vita di S. Pacifico Divini dei Minori da Sanseverino* (Quaracchi, 1910).

MICHAEL BIHL.

Pacioli (PACIUOLO), LUCAS, mathematician, b. at Borgo San Sepolco, Tuscany, towards the middle of the fifteenth century; died probably soon after 1509. Little is known concerning his life. He became a Franciscan friar and was successively professor of mathematics at Perugia, Rome, Naples, Pisa, and Venice. With Leonardo da Vinci, he was in Milan at the court of Louis the Moor, until the invasion of the French. The last years of his life were spent in Florence and Venice. His scientific writings, though poor in style, were the basis for the works of the sixteenth-century mathematicians, including Cardan and Tartaglia. In his first work, "Summa de Arithmetica, Geometria, Proportioni, et Proportionalita", Venice, 1494, he drew freely upon the writings of Leonardo da Pisa (Fibonacci) on the theory of numbers. Indeed he has thus preserved fragments of some of the lost works of that mathematician. The application of algebra to geometry, and the treatment, for the first time, of double-entry book-keeping and of the theory of probability also help to make this treatise noteworthy. The "Divina Proportioni" (Venice, 1509), was written with some co-operation on the part of Leonardo da Vinci. It is of interest chiefly for some theorems on the inscription of polyhedrons in polyhedrons and for the use of letters to indicate numerical quantities. His edition of Euclid was published in 1509 in Venice.

CHASLES, *Aperçu historique sur l'Origine et le Développement des Méthodes en Géométrie* (3rd ed., Paris, 1889); LIBRI, *Histoire des Sciences Mathématiques en Italie*, III (2nd ed., Halle, 1865).

PAUL H. LINEHAN.

Pactum Calixtinum. See CALLISTUS II, POPE; CONCORDAT.

Paderborn, DIOCESE OF (PADERBORNENSIS), suffragan of Cologne, includes: the District of Minden, Westphalia, except the parish of Lette; the District of Arnsberg, Westphalia, except a few parishes; Prussian Saxony; five districts in the Rhine Province; the Principality of Lippe; the Principality of Waldeck; the Duchy of Gotha; the Principalities of Schwarzburg-Rudolstadt and Schwarzburg-Sondershausen; and the Vicariate Apostolic of Anhalt (see GERMANY, map). The diocese is divided into 53 deaneries. There are 547 parishes (20 missionary, 266 succursal); 1403 secular and 93 regular priests; 1,508,000 Catholics, and 5,250,000 non-Catholics. The part of the diocese in Thuringia is also divided among three other ecclesiastical administrative districts: the episcopal commissaries of Magdeburg and Heiligenstadt, and the "Ecclesiastical Court" (*Geistliches Gericht*) of Erfurt.

The cathedral chapter has the right to elect the bishop; it consists of a provost, a dean, 8 capitular and 4 honorary canons; 6 cathedral vicars are stationed at the cathedral. The diocesan institutions are: the seminary for priests, the diocesan institute of philosophy and theology with 8 professors, the theological college (*Collegium Leoninum*), the seminary for boys (*Collegium Liborianum*) at Paderborn, the seminary for boys (*Collegium Bonifatianum*) at Heiligenstadt, and the orphans' home of Lippe at Paderborn. Under religious direction also are the boys' colleges of Warburg, Attendorn, and Brilon.

The orders existing in the diocese are: Franciscans, 8 monasteries, 69 fathers, 21 clerics, 68 brothers; Dominicans, 1 monastery, 5 fathers, 4 brothers; Redemptorists, 1 monastery, 8 fathers, 7 brothers; Missionaries of the Sacred Heart of Jesus, 1 community, 11 fathers, 51 clerics, 21 brothers; Brothers of Charity, 4 monasteries, 82 brothers. The female orders and congregations, which have 256 institutions with 3320 sisters, include: the Benedictine Sisters of Perpetual Adoration, 2 priorates; Canonesses of St. Augustine, 1 convent; Poor School Sisters of Notre Dame, 3 institutions; Ursulines, 3 houses; Sisters of Christian Charity; Daughters of the Blessed Virgin Mary of the Immaculate Conception, mother-house at Paderborn and 15 institutions; Sisters of Charity of the Christian Schools, mother-house at Heiligenstadt, and 6 institutions; Sisters of St. Vincent de Paul, mother-house at Paderborn and 99 houses; Poor Franciscan Sisters of Perpetual Adoration, mother-house at Olpe, 39 institutions; Franciscan Sisters of the Sacred Hearts of Jesus and Mary, mother-house at Salzkotten, 23 houses; Grey Sisters of St. Elizabeth from Breslau, provincial house at Halle, 20 institutions; Sisters of Charity of St. Vincent, from Fulda, 5 houses; Poor Sisters of St. Francis, from Aachen, 4 institutions; Sisters of Charity of St. Francis, from Münster, 3 convents; Sisters of St. Francis, from Thuine, near Freren, 5 institutions; Poor Franciscan Sisters, from Waldbreitach, 2 institutions; Poor Servants of Jesus Christ, from Dernbach, 18 institutions; Sisters of Clement, from Münster, 3 houses; Sisters of Charity of St. Elizabeth, from Essen, 1 house; Sisters of the Holy Cross from Strasburg, 2 institutions; Daughters of Christian Charity of St. Vincent from Cologne-Nippes, 1 house; Sisters of Our Lady from Mülhausen (Rhineland), 1 institution.

The city of Paderborn is the headquarters of the Boniface Association (q. v.); among others are the Society of St. Vincent, the Society of St. Elizabeth, the Mothers' Society, the Young Men's Society, the Young Women's Sodalities, the Society of Catholic Germany, etc. The Catholic institutions include 120 institutions for the protection of children; 50 orphan asylums; 100 schools for handicrafts and domestic science; 135 sanatoria and hospitals; 65 stations for visiting nurses; and 300 religious homes for the poor. Among the newspapers are: the "Westfälisches Volksblatt", the "Sonntagsblatt Leo", the "Bonifatiusblatt", and the scientific magazine, "Theologie und Glaube". The most important churches are: the cathedral at Paderborn, which in its present form dates from the twelfth and fourteenth centuries; a church with three naves of equal height in the style of the Romanesque and Transition periods; the Romanesque cathedral of St. Patroclus at Soest, built in 954; the cathedral at Erfurt, dates back to 1153; and the Gothic cathedral at Minden, built between the eleventh and the fifteenth centuries.

The first church at Paderborn was founded in 777, when Charlemagne held a diet there. It is certain that Paderborn was a bishopric in 805 or 806; the bishop was Hathumar, a Saxon (d. 815). Before this Paderborn was under the Diocese of Würzburg. The Diocese of Paderborn then included the larger part of Lippe, Waldeck, and nearly half of the former Countship of Ravensberg.

St. Badurad (815-62) completed the cathedral, encouraged the building of the cathedral school, and the establishment of several monasteries. He received from Louis the Pious special protection for his diocese, which was benefited financially, in that henceforward it received all the court fees. When the bishops received the countship is unknown, but this was confirmed to Bishop Liuthard (862-86) in 881 by King Louis. Otto II bestowed the right to a free election of bishops upon Bishop Folkmar in 974 (d. 981). In 1000 the cathedral was burnt; Rethgar (d. 1009) began a new cathedral, completed by his successor, Meinwerk. The latter established the Benedictine Monastery of Abdinghof at Paderborn, founded a diocesan college at Busdorf, and improved the cathedral school. During the Strife of Investitures, Poppo (1076-83) was first an adherent of the emperor, later of the pope. Heinrich I, Count of Assel, elected bishop under the protection of the opposing King Hermann, in 1090 was exiled by the Emperor Henry IV, and fled to Magdeburg, where in 1102 he was elected archbishop. The See of Paderborn was occupied by Heinrich II, Count of Werl-Arnsberg, who had had himself installed in 1084 at Rome as bishop by Henry IV, and who had helped in the expulsion of Heinrich I. He received the papal sanction in 1106. Bernhard II, Lord of Oesede (1127-60), restored the cathedral (burnt in 1133).

Siegfried (1178-80) lived to see the downfall of Henry the Lion, Duke of Saxony. The rights which the old dukedom had exercised over Paderborn were transferred to the Archbishop of Cologne. The claims of the archbishops of Cologne were settled in the thirteenth century, almost wholly in favour of Paderborn. Under Bernhard II of Ibbenbüren (1198-1204) the bailiwick over the diocese, which since the middle of the eleventh century had been held as a fief by the Counts of Arnsberg, returned to the bishops. This was an important advance in the development of the bishops' position as temporal sovereigns. From this time on the bishops did not grant the bailiwick as a fief, but managed it themselves, and had themselves represented in the government by one of their clergy. They strove successfully to obtain the bailiwicks over the abbeys and monasteries situated in their diocese. During the reign of Bernhard IV (1228-47) the Minorites settled in the diocese. Under him the community life of the cathedral canons ceased completely, and the canons, twenty-four in number, shared with the bishop the property, archdiaconates, and obediences (1231).

Simon I, Lord of Lippe (1247-77), was engaged in struggles with Cologne; Otto von Rietberg had also to contend with Cologne; in 1281, when only bishop-elect, he received the regalia from Rudolph of Habsburg, and full judicial power (except penal judicature); henceforward the bishops were actual sovereigns, though not over the whole of their diocese.

Bernhard V of Lippe (1321-41) had to acknowledge the city of Paderborn as free from his judicial supremacy. Heinrich III Spiegel zum Desenberg (1361-80), also Abbot of Corvey, left his spiritual functions to a suffragan; in 1371 he rebuilt the Burg Neuhaus at Paderborn. Simon II, Count of Sternberg (1380-89), involved the bishopric in feuds with the nobility, who after his death devastated the country. Wilhelm Heinrich von Berg, elected 1399, sought to remedy the evils which had crept in during the foregoing feuds, but when in 1414 he interested himself in the vacancy in the Archbishopric of Cologne, the cathedral chapter in his absence chose Dietrich von Mörs (1415-63). The wars of Dietrich, also Archbishop of Cologne, brought heavy debts upon the bishopric; during the feuds of the bishop with the City of Soest (1444-49) Paderborn was devastated. The reign of Simon III of Lippe (1463-89) was occupied with the correction of Church discipline. Hermann I, Landgrave of Hesse (1495-1508), was an excellent ruler.

Under Erich, Duke of Brunswick-Grubenhagen (1502-32), the Reformation obtained a foothold in the diocese, although the bishop remained loyal to the Church. Hermann von Wied (1532-47), also Archbishop of Cologne, sought to introduce the new teaching at Paderborn as well as Cologne, but he was opposed by all classes. The countships of Lippe, Waldeck, and Pyrmont, the part of the diocese in the Countship of Ravensberg, and most of the parishes on the right bank of the Weser became Protestant. After the removal of Hermann von Wied, Paderborn had three active Catholic bishops: Rembert von Kerrsenbrock (1547-68), Johann II von Hoya (1568-1574) published the Tridentine Decrees, and Salentin, Count of Isenburg (1574-77), also Archbishop of Cologne. Heinrich IV, Duke of Saxe-Lauenburg (1577-85), was a Lutheran; he permitted the adoption of the Augsburg Confession by his subjects. Apostasy from the Church made such advances that in the city of Paderborn only the cathedral and the Monastery of Abdinghof remained faithful. To save the Catholic cause, the cathedral chapter summoned the Jesuits to Paderborn in 1580. Theodor von Fürstenberg (1585-1618) restored the practice of the Catholic religion, built a gymnasium for the Jesuits, and founded the University of Paderborn in 1614.

Ferdinand I of Bavaria (1618-50) was not able to save the bishopric from the horrors of the Thirty Years' War. Theodor Adolf von der Reck (1650-91) tried to repair the damages of the war. Ferdinand II von Fürstenberg (1661-83), poet, historian, scholar, and promoter of the arts and sciences, founded the "Ferdinandea", for the support of thirteen missionaries for the northern Vicariate. Hermann Werner (1683-1704) and his nephew Franz Arnold (1704-18) were admirable prelates. Under Klemens August of Bavaria (1719-61), the Seven Years' War wrought great damage. Wilhelm Anton von der Asseburg (1763-82) founded a seminary for priests in 1777. Franz Egon von Fürstenberg (1789-1825) lived to see the secularization of nearly all the chapters and monasteries in his diocese. The territory of the diocese went to Prussia, the bishop became a prince of the empire;

Church at Halberstadt

BASILICA OF S. ANTONIO, COMMONLY CALLED THE SANTO, PADUA

but his spiritual jurisdiction was untouched. He saw the enlargement of his diocese, resulting from the Bull "De Salute Animarum", 16 July, 1821, which extended Paderborn, and placed it under Cologne.

Friedrich Klemens von Ledebur-Wicheln (1826–41) divided the diocese into deaneries. Konrad Martin (1856–79) held a diocesan synod in 1867, and took part in the Vatican Council. In the Kulturkampf he stood firmly for the freedom of the Church, suffered many penalties, and died an exile in Belgium. Franz Kaspar Drobe (1882–91) revived the institutions for the education of priests. Hubertus Simar (1891–1900) rebuilt the theological seminary in 1895 and became Archbishop of Cologne in 1900; Wilhelm Schneider (1900–1909) was a philosopher and theologian; Karl Joseph Schulte, formerly Professor of Apologetics and Canon Law in Paderborn, was elected in 1909, and consecrated 19 March, 1910.

FÜRSTENBERG, *Monumenta Paderbornensia* (Paderborn, 1672; 4th ed., Lemgo, 1754); SCHATEN, *Annales Paderbornenses* (3 vols., 2nd ed., Münster, 1774–75); BESSEN, *Geschichte des Bistums Paderborn* (2 vols., Paderborn, 1820); GIEFERS, *Die Anfänge des Bistums Paderborn* (Paderborn, 1860); EVELT, *Die Weihbischöfe von Paderborn* (Paderborn, 1869, 1879); LÖHER, *Geschichte des Kampfes um Paderborn 1597–1604* (Berlin, 1874); WILMANS AND FINKE, *Die Urkunden des Bistums Paderborn* (Münster, 1874–94); *Westfälisches Urkundenbuch*, IV; HOLSCHER, *Die ältere Diözese Paderborn* (Paderborn, 1886); RICHTER, *Geschichte der Paderborner Jesuiten* (Paderborn, 1892), I; IDEM, *Geschichte der Stadt Paderborn*, I, II (Paderborn, 1899–1903); IDEM, *Studien und Quellen zur Geschichte Paderborns*, I (Paderborn, 1893); IDEM, *Preussen und die Paderborner Klöster und Stifter 1802–1806* (Paderborn, 1905); TREISEN, *Die Universität Paderborn* (Paderborn, 1898); TENCKHOFF, *Die Bischöfe von Paderborn von Hatsumar bis Rethar* (Paderborn, 1900); SCHULTZ, *Beiträge zur Geschichte der Landeshoheit im Bistum Paderborn* (Münster, 1903); LIESE, *Die katholischen Wohltätigkeitsanstalten und sozialen Vereine in der Diözese Paderborn* (Freiburg, 1906); FREISEN, *Staat und katholische Kirche in den deutschen Bundesstaaten Lippe, Waldeck-Pyrmont, Anhalt usw.* (2 vols., Stuttgart, 1906); LEINEWEBER, *Die Paderborne Fürstbischöfe in der Zeit der Glaubensneuerung* (Münster, 1908); HENSE, *Führer durch Paderborn* (Paderborn, 1910); *Zeitschrift für vaterländische Geschichte und Altertumskunde*, section *Paderborn* (Münster, 1839—); *Schematismus des Bistums Paderborn* (Paderborn, 1909; supplement, 1911).

JOSEPH LINS.

Padilla, JUAN DE, Friar Minor, protomartyr of the United States of America, member of the Andalusian province, came to Mexico probably in 1528, joining the province of the Holy Gospel. During 1529–1531 he, with an unnamed friar, accompanied Nuño de Guzmán to Nueva Galicia and Culiacán, and prevented the oppression of the natives while acting as military chaplain. From 1531 to 1540 he made missionary tours among the Indians of Tlamatzolán, Tuchpán, Tzapotitlán, Totlamán, Amula, Caulán, Xicotlán, Avalos or Zaolán, Amacuccán, Atoyac, Tzacoalco, and Colima. He founded the convent of Tzapotlán, becoming its first superior, and erected another at Tuchpán, making it the headquarters for the missionary friars. He established the monastery of Tulantcingo, governing it until 1540, when he resigned to follow Fr. Marcos de Niza, the discoverer of Arizona and New Mexico, with Francisco Vásquez de Coronado, on the memorable march to the fabled Seven Cities, and thus reached the Upper Rio Grande near the present Bernalillo about the end of 1540. He also accompanied Coronado in his search for Quivira, probably as far as central Kansas. When the disappointed general and his army in 1542 abandoned New Mexico, Fr. de Padilla, Fr. Juan de la Cruz, Brother Luis de Ubeda or Escalona, resolved to stay behind to evangelize the Indians. A Portuguese soldier, Andres da Campo, two Mexican tertiaries, Lucas and Sebastian, two other Mexican Indians, and a half-breed boy also remained with the zealous friars.

After working with success among the Tíguez on the Rio Grande for some time, Fr. de Padilla's zeal urged him to afford other tribes an opportunity of knowing and serving Christ. Accompanied by Da Campo, Lucas, Sebastian, and the two Mexican Indians, he set out for the north-east. When the little party reached the plains, they encountered a band of savages, who attacked them and slew Fr. de Padilla as he calmly knelt in prayer. The savages threw the body into a pit. The date and locality of his martyrdom are uncertain, Fr. Vetancurt in his Menologio assigning 30 November, 1544. Some believe he perished in eastern Colorado, or western Kansas, but this is conjecture. The story, believed in New Mexico, that his body was discovered by Pueblo Indians, brought to Isleta, interred beneath the sanctuary of the church, and that it rises and falls at stated periods is a myth. The remains of the Franciscan buried there are doubtless those of Fr. Juan José de Padilla, who died a peaceful death there two centuries later. Fr. de la Cruz and Brother de Ubeda were likewise put to death at the instigation of Indian sorcerers at the missions on the Rio Grande.

MENDIETA, *Historia eclesiástica indiana* (reprint, Mexico, 1870); TELLO, *Crónica de la Santa Provincia de Xalisco* (reprint, Guadalajara, 1891); MOTA PADILLA, *Historia de la Conquista de la Nueva Galicia* (Mexico, 1870); VETANCURT, *Menologio Franciscano* (Mexico, 1697); TORQUEMADA, *Monarquía indiana* (Madrid, 1723); BEAUMONT, *Crónica de la prov. de Michoacan* (reprint, Mexico, 1874); *Fourteenth Ann. Rept. of the Bur. of Ethnol.* (Washington); SHEA, *The Catholic Church in Colonial Days* (New York, 1886); BANDELIER, *American Catholic Quarterly Review* (Philadelphia, July, 1890); LUMMIS, *Spanish Pioneers* (Chicago, 1893); BANCROFT, *History of New Mexico and Arizona* (San Francisco, 1889); DEFOURI, *The Martyrs of New Mexico* (Las Vegas, 1893); ENGELHARDT, *The Franciscans in Arizona* (Harbor Springs, 1899).

ZEPHYRIN ENGELHARDT.

Padroado, THE. See GOA, ARCHDIOCESE OF; PROTECTORATE OF MISSIONS.

Padua, DIOCESE OF (PATAVINA), Northern Italy. The city is situated on a fertile plain, and is surrounded and traversed by the Bachiglione River. Its streets are almost all flanked with colonnades. The most splendid of its churches is "il Santo", that is, the basilica of St. Anthony of Padua, begun in 1232; its style is mixed Romanesque and Byzantine, irrespective of later modifications; it has seven cupolas, and is divided into three naves. On the high altar is a crucifix in bronze by Donatello, the author also of the bronze bas-reliefs on the walls of the apse; the bronze candelabra are by Andrea Riccio; the chapel, called "Capella del Santo" (1500–33), is filled with ex-voto offerings, and contains nine bas-reliefs by Lombardi, representing miracles of the saint; the chapel of the relics and that of San Felice are also full of works of art. The paintings in this church are by Mantegna, Paolo Veronese, and Tiepolo, while the frescoes are by Giotto and Altichiero da Zevia. The Church of Santa Giustina, rebuilt in 1502, is crowned by eight cupolas, and has fourteen side chapels; there are paintings by Paolo Veronese, Luca Giordano, and Parodio. Beside this church is a famous monastery of the Benedictines, which dates from the ninth century; in the fifteenth century a reform of the order began in this convent of Santa Giustina, now used as barracks. The cathedral was destroyed by an earthquake in 1117, and was rebuilt by Michelangelo, who, however, finished only the choir and the sacristy. The church, called "degli Eremitani" (1264 and 1309), contains frescoes by Mantegna. The seminary was founded by Bishop Federico Cornaro in 1577, and was greatly enlarged by Blessed Cardinal Gregorio Barberigo in 1671; connected with it are a printing press and a rich library.

Among the secular buildings are the Palazzo della Ragione, dating from 1166, restored in 1218, 1420, and 1756; the Loggia del Consiglio (the palace of the "Capitano"); and the university (1493), by Palladio or Sansovino; annexed to it are a library, with 2500 MSS., an anatomical amphitheatre, founded in 1594 by Fabrizio d'Acquapendente, a museum of natural history, a large collection of ancient physical instruments, a collection of petrified objects, a botanical garden (1545, the first in Europe), and an observatory, erected on a tower of the castle of Ezzelino. Among the public monuments are: the equestrian statue of

Gattamelata by Donatello on the piazza del Santo; the statue of Petrarch; and the tomb of Antenor, the legendary founder of the city.

Padua (*Patavium*) was the chief city of the Veneti, who were continually at war with the Gauls; the Veneti, therefore, were naturally friends of Rome. In 302 B. C. Cleonymus, King of Sparta, sailed up the Po with a part of his fleet; but the Patavians drove him back with severe loss. The city long enjoyed independence, and obtained Roman citizenship only in 49 B. C. Under the first emperors, Padua was one of the most heavily-taxed cities. It had a flourishing wool industry, and its people were famous for their orderly conduct. Latin literature also flourished among them (Livy, Ascanius Pedanius, Thrasea Pætus). With the growth of Aquileia the importance of Padua waned; it was destroyed in 408 by Alaric, in 452 by Attila, and in 601 by Agilulfus, King of the Lombards. In the tenth century it was harassed by the Hungarians, especially in 903. In 1087, with the consent of Henry IV, Padua made itself a free commune; and in the time of Barbarossa it was among the first cities to establish the Lombard League. It was at war with Venice in 1110 and 1214; with Vicenza in 1140, 1188, and 1201; and with the Ezzelini. Ezzelino IV succeeded in obtaining the sovereignty in 1237. For eighteen years he exercised a most inhuman tyranny; among his victims was the prior of Santa Giustina, Arnaldus, who died after an imprisonment of eight years. In 1256 an army of crusaders, sent by Alexander IV, captured the city, which Ezzelino attempted in vain to recapture.

The city once more flourished; but internal discord developed anew, and wars with neighbours began again, with the result that Padua, following the example of other cities, offered the lordship to Jacopo Carrara in 1318. In 1320, however, Padua was compelled to receive an imperial vicar; and the attempt of Marsilio I of Carrara, son of Jacopo (1328), to rid himself of that functionary, turned only to the advantage of the Scaligeri (Alberto and Mastino), which family were driven from Padua in 1337 by Marsilio, succeeded by Ubertino. The latter greatly increased the territory of the state, and was succeeded by Marsilio II Papafava, and by Jacopo II (1345) a protector of letters and of the arts, assassinated in 1350 by Gulielmo, natural son of Giacomo I. Francesco I, captain of the league against the Visconti, succeeded, but was unsuccessful against Venice and was compelled to accept a humiliating peace; in 1378 he assisted the Genoese in the war of Chioggia. He was more successful, however, against the Scaligeri, from whom he took Feltre, Belluno, Treviso, and Ceneda (1384). His son Francesco Novello (1388) voluntarily submitted to the Visconti of Milan; but was imprisoned, together with his father, who had withdrawn from the government. Francesco Novello escaped from prison, and in 1390 reconquered Padua; and in 1403 he waged war against the Visconti and took Brescia and Verona. In 1404 he made an attempt against Vicenza that brought upon him a war with Venice. After a long siege, father and son went to Venice, to obtain favourable conditions of peace, were detained and put to death (1405); the rule of the Carrara thus came to an end, and Padua fell to Venice. In 1509 the Emperor Maximilian I took the city from the Venetians; the Venetians having retaken it, the town was besieged again by the imperialists, who had already taken a bastion, when the explosion of a mine drove them back; thenceforth Padua followed the fortunes of Venice.

Padua is the birthplace of: the poetess Isabella Andreini; another poetess Gaspera Stampa; the jurist Jacopo Zabarella, his son Cardinal Francesco Zabarella, and his nephew Bartolommeo; Ottonello Descalzo; the man of letters Cesarotti; the naturalist Donati; the mechanician Giacomo dell' Orologio; the painters Francesco Squarcione (Paduan school), Stefano dall' Arzere; G. B. Bissoni; Campagnola, Girolamo Padovano; Mantegna; Alessio Varotari (Il Padovanino); the female painter Domenica Scanferla; the sculptor Tiziano Aspetti; Blessed Pellegrino Manzoni (d. 1267); Blessed Compagno (d. 1264), and of Blessed Cardinal Bonaventura da Padova (d. 1385).

Padua gave a number of martyrs to the Church: St. Giustina, Virgin; St. Daniel; and the Bishop Maximus. The first bishop is said to have been St. Prosdocimus, who cannot have governed the diocese earlier than the beginning of the third century, when the See of Milan was created, even if Crispinus, at the Council of Sardica in 347, was the twelfth Bishop of Padua. After the destruction of the city by Attila, the bishops resided on the island of Melamocco, and took part in the schism of The Three Chapters; Tricidius (620) returned to Padua, which had again grown up. Among the other bishops were Gauslinus, who, in 964, found the relics of the third bishop St. Fidentius; Blessed Bernardo Maltraverso (1031); Pietro (1096), deposed by the Council of Guastalla; St. Bellino Bertaldo, killed in 1147 by Tommaso Capodivacca; Gerardo Marostica (1169), a pacifier. On account of the tyranny of Ezzelino IV, the see was vacant from 1239; Pagano della Torre (1302) built the episcopal palace; Ildebrandino (1319), Pontifical legate on various occasions; Pileo da Prata (1359), founder of the Collegio Pratense; Pietro Barba (1448), Pope Paul II; Fantino Dandolo (1449), formerly a high functionary of Venice; Jacopo Zeno (1460), the biographer of his uncle Carlo, who commanded in the war against Genoa; Nicolò Ormanetto (1570); Giorgio Cornaro (1697) held important charges under the republic; Carlo Rezzonico (1743), Pope Clement XIII; Francesco Scipione Doni dall' Orologio (1807). The provincial Synod of 1350 was important.

The diocese is suffragan of Venice; it has 321 parishes, 570,200 inhabitants, 1 Catholic daily paper, and 1 weekly Catholic publication.

CAPPELLETTI, *Le Chiese d'Italia*, X; IDEM, *Storia di Padua* (2 vols., 1875–76); DALL' OROLOGIO, *Dissert. sopra l'istoria di Padova* (9 vols., Padua, 1802–1813); SARTORI, *Guida stor. delle Chiese di Padova* (Padua, 1884); VERCI, *Storia degli Ecelini* (Bassano, 1779); CITADELLA, *Storia della dominazione carrarese in Padova* (2 vols., Padua, 1842); VOLKMANN, *Padua als Kunststatte* (Leipzig, 1904).

U. BENIGNI.

UNIVERSITY OF PADUA dates, according to some anonymous chronicles (Muratori, "Rer. Ital. Script.", VIII, 371, 421, 459, 736), from 1222, when a part of the Studium of Bologna, including professors and students, withdrew to Padua. The opinion that Frederick II transferred the Studium of Bologna to Padua in 1241 is groundless. But even before this emigration there were professors of law at Padua, as Gerardus Pomadellus (c. 1165), afterwards Bishop of Padua; furthermore, his predecessor, Bishop Carzo, was called *sacrorum canonum doctor*. The contract proposed by the commune of Vercelli to the Rectors of the students of Padua in 1228 shows that besides both laws and dialectics, medicine and grammar were taught there. The students were divided into four nationalities: French, Italian, German, and Provençal. This contract stipulated that all or part of the university (14 professors and sufficient students to occupy 500 houses) should be transferred to Vercelli for at least eight years. The university, however, was not suspended on that account, as is evident from the Life of St. Antonio. But the tyranny of Ezzelino (1237-56) caused its decadence. From 1260 it revived under the commune which established the rights of the professors and students, and the salaries (300 lire for legists and 200 for canonists); the examinations were held before the bishop, who also granted the teachers' licences. In 1274 Padua had the decrees of the Council of Lyons, equal with the Universities of Paris and Bologna. In 1282, on account of certain communal laws against the clergy and the university, Nicholas IV threatened to deprive Padua of its Studium, but the commune relented, and the Studium acquired great renown, rivalling Bologna, especially in jurisprudence. From the beginning of the fourteenth century the school of medicine was also famous. The professors in this faculty introduced Averroism in philosophy. The theological faculty was instituted by Urban V in 1363. In the same year the Collegium Tornacense was founded, the first of its kind in Padua. There were other institutes from 1390, as the college of St. Marco for six medical students, the college of Cardinal Pileo (1420) for twenty (afterwards twelve) students.

The professors of this first period included the jurisconsults, Alberto Galeotto, Guido Suzzara, Jacopo d'Arena, Riccardo Malombra, Albrado Ponte, Rolando Piazzola, Jacopo Belvisio, Bartol Saliceti, and the celebrated Baldo; the canonists, Ruffino and Jacopo da Piacenza, Lapoda Castiglionchio, and the canonist and theologian, Francesco Zabarella, afterwards cardinal; in medicine, Bruno da Longoburgo, Pietro d'Albano, Dino del Garbo, Jacopo and Giovanni Dondi (also excellent mechanicians), Marcilio, Giovanni and Guglielmo Santa Sofia, Jacopo da Forlè, and Biagio Pelacani. Philosophy was often taught, as elsewhere, by professors of medicine, mostly averroists, like Petrus Aponensis and Mundinus. The most distinguished philosophers who were not physicians were Pier Paolo Vergerio (1349-1414), afterwards Bishop of Capo d'Istria, a learned humanist and student of antiquity; the Franciscan, Antonio Trombetta, a famous Scotist. From the fifteenth century there were in theology and metaphysics two courses, one Thomistic, with professors preferably Dominican, and the other Scotist, with professors chiefly from the Friars Minor. Famous in the beginning of the sixteenth century were the controversies between the averroist philosopher, Achillini, and the Alexandrist, Pietro Pomponazzi (q. v.). The doctrines of the latter (who had gone to Bologna), especially on the soul were opposed, among others, by Agostino Nifo, another professor of philosophy at Padua. The humanist Girolamo Fracastoro taught philosophy there.

Among the professors of letters were: Rolandino, historian of Padua (thirteenth century), and Giovanni da Ravenna, friend of Petrarch; the humanists Gosparino Barzizi, Francisco Filelfo, Vittorino da Feltre, a distinguished pedagogical writer and educator, Lauro Quirino; the Greeks Demetrio Chalcocondylas, Alessandro Zenos, Nicolas Leonicos, Marino Becichem, Romolo Amasacus, and Nicolo Caliachius; Giovanni Fascolus, Francesco Robortellos, the historian Sigonius, the great French Latinist Marc. Ant. Muretus, Justus Lipsius, and the great Latin lexicographers of the eighteenth century, Jacopus Faciolatus, and Egidio Forcellini. Astronomy, or astrology, was taught already in the fourteenth century. The most noted professors were, in the fifteenth century, Georg Pearbach, and his disciple Johann Müller, called Regiomontanus; in the sixteenth century, Giovanni Battista Capuano and Galileo Galilei, who also taught mechanics and other physical sciences. Chief among the theologians was the French Dominican Hyacinthe Serry (1698), who introduced there the new method of basing theology more on Scriptural and patristic arguments than on philosophical speculations, in which he encountered much opposition from the Conventual Fra Nicola Buico. Among the jurisconsults, after the closing of the university (1509-17), were the canonist Menochius, Alciatus, Lancelotti, and Pancirolo, famous also for his knowledge of Roman antiquities.

A characteristic of the University of Padua, even in the eighteenth century, was its internationalism, as seen from the list of professors about Facciolati; it was attended especially by Germans. When Venice passed under Austrian domination (1814) the university was transformed, like that of Pavia. At present it has the ordinary four faculties, besides a school of applied engineering and a school of pharmacy and obstetrics. Various astronomical institutes, bacteriological, physiological, hygienic, and pathological; chemical, physical, and geodetic laboratories; an anthropological museum; a botanical garden; and an astronomical observatory complete the equipment of the university. It has 128 chairs, 68 professors, 20 paid, and 107 private, tutors. In 1906, there was established near the university an institution for the education of Catholic young men. University education in Italy is strictly governmental, and without it all professional possibilities are closed to young men. At some seats of learning, Catholic Clubs were started to help them against the peril to their faith and morals, but they failed. The small Pensionata, situated in the neighbourhood of Padua, between the Basilica and the church of Sta. Juliana, was transformed into a large establishment. The students attend a weekly conference which treats of points of faith affecting modern conditions of life and science.

COLLE, *Storia scientifico letteraria dello Studio di Padova* (Padua, 1824); FACCIOLATUS, *Fasti gymnasii Patavini* (Padua, 1757); FAVARO, *Lo Studio di Padova e la Republica Veneta* (Venice, 1889); *Cenni storici sulla R. Università di Padova* (Padua, 1873).

U. BENIGNI.

Paganism, in the broadest sense, includes all religions other than the true one revealed by God, and, in a narrower sense, all except Christianity, Judaism, and Mohammedanism. The term is also used as the equivalent of Polytheism (q. v.). It is derived from the Latin *pagus*, whence *pagani* (i. e. those who live in the country), a name given to the country folk who remained heathen after the cities had become Christian. Various forms of Paganism are described in special articles (e. g. Brahminism, Buddhism, Mithraism); the present article deals only with certain aspects of Paganism in general which will be helpful in studying its details and in judging its value.

I. CLAIMS OF PAGANISM TO THE NAME OF RELIGION. INFLUENCE ON PUBLIC AND PRIVATE LIFE.—Historians of religion usually assume that religions developed upwards from some common germ which they call Totemism, Animism, Solar or Astral Myth, Nature Worship in general or Agrarian in particular, or some other name implying a systematic interpretation of the facts. We do not propose to discuss, theologically, philosophically, or even historically, the underlying unity, or universal originating cause, of all religions, if any such there be. History as a matter of fact presents us in each case with a religion already existing, and in a more or less complicated form. Somewhere or other, some one of the human elements offered as universal, necessary, and sufficient germ of the developed religion, can, of course, be found. But we would point out that, in the long run, this element was not rarely a cause of degeneration, not progress; of lower forms of cult and creed, not pure Monotheism. Thus it is almost certain that Totemism went for much in the formation of the Egyptian religion. The animal-standards of the tribes, gradually and partially anthropomorphized, created the jackal-, ibis-, hawk-headed gods familiar to us. But there is no real trace of the evolution from Zoolatry to Polytheism, and thence to Monotheism. The monotheistic records are more sublime, more definite in the earlier dynasties. Atum, the object of a superb worship, has no animal equivalent. Even the repression of popular follies by a learned official caste failed to check the tendency towards gross and unparalleled Zoolatry, which was food for Roman ridicule and Greek bewilderment, and stirred the author of Wisdom (xi, 16) to indignation (Loret, "L'Egypte au temps du totemisme", Paris, 1906; Cappart in "Rev. d'hist. relig.", LI, 1905, p. 192; Clement Alex., "Pæd.", III, ii, 4; Diodorus Siculus, I, lxxxiv; Juvenal, "Satires", xv).

Animism also entered largely into the religions of the Semites. Hence, we are taught, came Polydæmonism, Polytheism, Monotheism. This is not correct. Polydæmonism is undoubtedly a system born of belief in spirits, be these the souls of the dead or the hidden forces of nature. It "never exists alone and is not a 'religious' sentiment at all": it is not a degenerate form of Polytheism any more than its undeveloped antecedent. Animism, which is really a naïve philosophy, played an immense part in the formation of mythologies, and, combined with an already conscious monotheistic belief, undoubtedly gave rise to the complex forms of both Polydæmonism and Polytheism. And these, in every Semitic nation save among the Hebrews, defeated even such efforts as were made (e. g. in Babylon and Assyria) to reconstitute or achieve that Monotheism of which Animism is offered as the embryo. These facts are clearly indicated and summed up in Lagrange's "Etudes sur les Religions sémitiques" (2nd ed., Paris, 1904).

Nature Worship generally, and Agrarian in particular, were unable to fulfil the promise they appeared to make. The latter was to a large extent responsible for the Tammuz cult of Babylon, with which the worships of Adonis and Attis, and even of Dionysus, are so unmistakably allied. Much might have been hoped from these religions with their yearly festival of the dying and rising god, and his sorrowful sister or spouse: yet it was precisely in these cults that the worst perversions existed. Ishtar, Astarte, and Cybele had their male and female prostitutes, their Galli: Josiah had to cleanse the temple of Yahweh of their booths (cf. the *Qedishim* and *Kelabim*, Deut., xxiii, 17; II Kings, xxiii, 7; cf. I Kings, xiv, 24; xv, 12), and even in the Greek world, where prostitution was not else regarded as religious, Eryx and Corinth at least were contaminated by Semitic influence, which Greece could not correct. "Although the story of Aphrodite's love", says Dr. Farnell, "is human in tone and very winning, yet there are no moral or spiritual ideas in the worship at all, no conception of a resurrection that might stir human hopes. Adonis personifies merely the life of the fields and gardens that passes away and blooms again. All that Hellenism could do for this Eastern god was to invest him with the grace of idyllic poetry" ("Cults of the Greek States", II, 649, 1896–1909; cf. Lagrange, op. cit., 220, 444 etc.)

Mithraism (q. v.) is usually regarded as a rival to nascent Christianity; but Nature Worship ruined its hopes of perpetuity. "Mithra remained", says S. Dill, "inextricably linked with the nature-worship of the past." This connexion cleft between it and purer faiths "an impassable gulf" which meant its "inevitable defeat" ("Roman Soc. from Nero to Aurel.", London, 1904, pp. 622 sqq.), and, "in place of a divine life instinct with human sympathy, it had only to offer the cold symbolism of a cosmic legend" (ibid.). Its very adaptability, M. Cumont reminds us, "prevented it from shaking itself free from the gross or ridiculous superstitions which complicated its ritual and theology; it was involved, in spite of its austerity, in a questionable alliance with the orgiastic cult of the mistress of Attis, and was obliged to drag behind it all the weight of a chimerical or hateful past. The triumph of Roman Mazdeism would not only have ensured the perpetuity of all the aberrations of pagan mysticism, but of the erroneous physical science on which its dogma rested." We have here an indication why religions, into which the astral element entered largely, were intrinsically doomed. The divine stars that ruled life were themselves subject to absolute law. Hence relentless Fatalism or final Scepticism for those sufficiently educated to see the logical results of their mechanical interpretation of the universe; hence the discrediting of myth, the abandonment of cult, as mendacious and useless; hence the silencing of oracle, ecstasy, and prayer; but, for the vulgar, a riot of superstition, the door new opened to magic which should coerce the stars, the cult of hell, and honour for its ministers—things all descending into the Satanism and witchcraft of not unrecent days. Even the supreme and solar cult reached, not Monotheism, but a splendid Pantheism. A sublime philosophy, a gorgeous ritual, the support of the earthly Monocracy which mirrored that of heaven, a liturgy of incomparable solemnity and passionate mysticism, a symbolism so pure and high as to cause endless confusion in the troubled mind of the dying Roman Empire between Sun-worship and the adorers of the Sun of Righteousness—all this failed to counteract the aboriginal lie which left God still linked essentially to creation. (See F. Cumont, "Les religions orientales dans le paganisme romain", 2nd ed., Paris, 1909, especially cc. v, vii-viii; "Le mysticisme astral", Brussels, 1909, invaluable for references and bibliography; "Textes et Monuments . . . relatifs aux Mystères de Mithra", I, 1899, II, 1896; "Théol. solaire du paganisme rom.", Paris, 1909.) We do not hint that these elements which have been assigned as the origin of an upward revolution have always, or only, been a cause of degeneration: it is important to note, however, that they have been at times a germ of death as truly as of life.

II. SOCIAL ASPECT.—Christianity first and alone of religions has preached, as one of its central doctrines, the value of the individual soul. What natural religion already, but ineffectually implied, Christianity asserted, reinforced, and transmuted. The same human nature is responsible at once for the admirable kindnesses of the pagan, and for the deplorable cruelties of Christian men, or groups, or epochs; the pagan religions did little, if anything, to preserve or develop the former, Christianity waged ceaseless battle against the latter. As for woman, the promiscuity which is the surest sign of her degradation never existed as a general or stable characteristic of primitive folk. In China and Japan, Buddhism and Confucianism depressed, not succoured her; in ancient Egypt, her position was far higher than in late; it was high too among the Teutons. Even in historic Greece as in Rome, divorce was difficult and disgraceful, and marriage was hedged about with an elaborate legislation and the sanctions of religion. The glimpses we have of ancient matriarchates speak much for the older, honourable position of women; their peculiar festivals (as in Greece, of the Thesmophoria and Arrephoria; in Rome, of the *Bona Dea*) and certain worships, as of the local Κόραι or of Isis, kept their sex within the sphere of religion. As long, however, as their intrinsic value before God was not realized, the brute strength of the male inevitably asserted itself against their weakness; even Plato and Aristotle regarded them more as living instruments than as human souls; in high tragedy (an Alcestis, an Antigone) or history (a Clœlia, a Camilla), there is no figure which can at all compare, for religious and moral influence, with a Sara, a Rachel, an Esther, or a Deborah. It is love for mother, rather than for wife, that Paganism acknowledges (see J. Donaldson, "Woman in anc. Greece and Rome, etc. . . . among the early Christians", London, 1907; C. S. Devas, "Studies of Family Life", London, 1886; Daremberg and Saglio, "Gynæceum", etc.).

Essentially connected with the fate of women is that of children. Their charm, pathos, possibilities had touched the pagan (Homer, Euripides, Vergil, Horace, Statius), even the claim of their innocence to respect (Juvenal). Yet too often they were considered merely as toys or the destined support of their parents, or as the hope of the State. With Christianity, each becomes a soul, infinitely precious for God's sake and its own. Each has its heavenly guardian, and for each death is better than loss of innocence. Education, in the fullest sense, was created by Christianity. The elaborate schemes of Aristotle and Plato are subordinated to state interest. Though based upon "sacred" books, education in ancient times, when organized, found these highly mythological, as in Greece or Rome, or rationalized, as in Confucian spheres of influence. Both Greeks and Romans attached great importance to a complete education, supported it with state patronage (the Ptolemies), state initiative and direction (the Antonines), and conceived for it high ideals (the "turning of the soul's eye towards the light", Plato, "Republic", 515 b); yet, failing to appreciate the value of the individual soul, they made education in fact merely utilitarian, the formation of a citizen being barely more complete than under the narrow and rigid systems of Sparta and Crete. The restriction, in classical Greece, of education among women to the *Hetairai* is a fact significant of false ideal and disastrous in results (J. B. Mahaffy, "Old Gk. Educ.", London, 1881; S. S. Laurie, "Historical Survey of Pre-Christian Educ.", London, 1900; L. Grasberger, "Erziehung u. Unterricht im klass. Alterum", Würzburg, 1864–81; G. Boissier, "L'instruct. publique dans l'empire romain." in "Rev. de Deux Mondes", March, 1884; J. P. Rossignol, "De l'educ. des hommes et des femmes chez les anciens", Paris, 1888).

Error in education was conditioned, we saw, by error of political ideal. No doubt, all the older polities were sanctioned directly by religion. The local god and the local ruler were, for the Semites, each a *melek* (king), a *baal* (proprietor), and their attributes and qualification almost fused. Or, the ruling dynasty descended remotely, or immediately, from a god or hero, making the king divine; so the Mikado, the Ionian and Doric overlords. Especially the Orient went this way, most notably Egypt. The Chinese emperor alone might pray to the Sublime Ruler whose son he was. Rome deifies herself and her governors, and the emperor-cult dominates army and province, and welds together aristocracy and the masses (J. G. Frazer, "Early Hist. of the Kingship", London, 1905; Maspero, "Comment Alex. devint Dieu en Egypte"; Cumont, "Textes et Monuments de Mithra", I, p. ii, c. iii; J. Toutain, "Cultes paiens dans l'emp. rom.", I, Paris, 1907). It is hard to judge of the practical effects; obviously autocracy profited, the development of obedience, loyalty, courage in the governed (Rome; Japan) being undoubted. Yet the system reposed upon a lie. The scandals of the court, the familiarities of the camp, the inevitable accidents of human life, dulled the halo of the god-king. Far more stable were the organizations resulting from the subtle polities devised by Greek experiment and speculation, and embodied in Roman law. Aristotle's political philosophy, almost designed—as Plato's frankly was— for the city state, was carried on through the Stoic vision of the City of Zeus, of world-empire, into the concrete majesty of Rome, which was itself to pass, when confronted in Christianity with that individual conscience it would not recognize, into the *Civitas Dei* of an Augustine. Aristotle and Plato survived in Aquinas, the Stoic vision in Dante; Gregory VII reproduced, in his age and manner, the effective work of an Augustus. And of it all the soul was that Kingdom, Hebrew-born, which, spiritualized by Christ and preached by Paul, has been a far mightier force for civilization than ever was the πόλις of the Greeks. As long as the ultimate source of authority, the inalienable rights of conscience, and the equality of all in a Divine sonship were unrealized, no true solution of the antinomy of state and individual, such as Paul could offer (Rom., xiii etc.) was possible. [Cf. E. Barker, "Polit. Thought of Plato and Aristotle", London, 1906, esp. pp. 237–50, 281–91, 119–61, 497–515; G. Murray, "Rise of the Gk. Epic.", Cambridge, 1907; P. Allard, "Ten Lectures on the Martyrs", tr. (London, 1907); Idem, "Les Persécutions" (Paris, 1885–90); Sir W. Ramsay's books on St. Paul, esp. "Pauline Studies" (London, 1906); "Paul the Traveller" (1897); "Ancient King Worship", C. C. Lattey, S.J., English C.T.S.]

In these systems, the weakest necessarily went to the wall. Even the good Greek legislation on behalf of orphans, wards, the aged, parents, and the like; even the admirable instinct of αἰδώς which shielded the defenceless, the suppliant, the stranger, the "stricken of God and afflicted", could not (e. g.) stop the exposition of sickly or deformed infants (defended even by Plato), or render poverty not ridiculous, suffering not merely ugly, death not defiling. Yet the sober religion of the Avesta preaches charity and hospitality, and these, the latter especially, were recognized Greek virtues. In proportion as travel widened minds, and ideals became cosmopolitan, the barbarian became a brother; under the Antonines charity became official and organized. Always, in the Greek world, the temples of Æsculapius were hospices for the sick. Yet all this is as different in motive, and therefore in practical effect, from the "mutual ministry of love" obligatory within the great family of God's children, as is the counterpart of Christian self-sacrifice, Buddhist Altruism. (Cf. L. de la V. Poussin, "Bouddhisme", Paris, 1909, especially pp. 7–8, where he quotes Oldenberg, "Buddhismus u. christliche Liebe" in "Deutsche Rundschau", 1908, and "Orientalischen Relig.", pp. 58, 266 sqq., 275 sqq.) In slavery, of course, a chasm is cleft between Paganism and Christianity. By proclaiming the rights of conscience and the brotherhood of men, Christianity did for the slave what could never have been accomplished by demanding the instant and universal abolition of slavery, thereby risking the dislocation of society. In Christ, a new relation of master to man springs up (I Cor., vii, 21; I Tim., vi, 2): the Epistle to Philemon becomes possible. Yet while it is true that in many ways the slave's lot might be miserable (the *ergastulum*), and inhuman (the Roman slave might technically not marry), and immoral (Petronius: "nil turpe quod dominus jubet"), yet here too, human nature has risen above its own philosophies, laws, and conventions. Kindness increases steadily: even Cato was kind; social motives (Horace), philosophical considerations (Seneca), sheer legislation (already under Augustus), devotion (at Delphi, slaves are manumitted to Apollo; contrast the beautiful Christian emancipation in Ennodius, P. L., LXIII, 257; sentiment, and even law protected the slaves' tomb or *loculus*) answered the promptings of gentle hearts. The *contubernium* became parallel to marriage; nationality never of itself meant slavery; education could make friends of master and man ("loco filii habitus", says one inscription); Seneca generalizes: "homo res sacra homini; servi, humiles amici." But not all the sense of the "dignity of man", taught by the Roman comedians and philosophers, could supply even the emancipating principles, far less the force, of Christian equality in the service of God and the fellowship of Christ (H. A. Wallon, "Hist. de l'Esclavage de l'Antiq.", Paris, 1847; Bocckh, "Staatshaushaltung d. Athener.", I, 13; C. S. Devas, "Key en." (1906), 143–150 and c. v; P. Allard, "Les Esclaves chrét.", Paris, 1876; G. Boissier, "Relig. romaine", II, Paris, 1892).

III. ART AND RITUAL.—*Omnia plena deo:* the nearer God is realized to be, the richer the efflorescence of religious art and ritual; and the purer the concept of His nature, the nobler the sense-worship that greets it. Hence the world's grandest art has grown round Christ's Real Presence, though Christ said no word of art. Thus, heresy has always been iconoclastic; the distant God of Puritanism, the disincarnate Allah of Islam must be worshipped, but not in beauty. To Hindus, gods were near, but vile; and their art went mad. To the Greeks, save to a smaller band of mystics, whose enthusiasm annihilated external beauty in the effort after spiritual loveliness, all comeliness was bodily; hence the splendid soulless statues of gods (though for a few choice perceptions—Pausanias, Plutarch—the Olympian Zeus had "expression", and conveyed divine significance); hence their treatment of the inanimate beauty of Nature was far less successful and profound than was that of the austere Hebrew, to whom, in his struggle against nature worship and idolatry, plastic art was forbidden, but whose nature-psalms rise higher than anything in Greek literature. The pure new spirit breathing in the art of the Catacombs disguises from us, at first, that its categories are all pagan—though in human models little was directly borrowed, the Orpheus, Hercules, Aristeas type are given to Christ; strange symbols (the disguised cross, the dolphin speared on trident) occur sporadically; "pagan" sarcophagi were doubtless bought direct from pagan warehouses; most startlingly is the difference felt in the spiritual treatment by early Christian Art of the nude (E. Müntz, "Etudes s. l'hist. de la peinture et de l'iconographie chrétienne", Paris, 1886; A. Pératé, "L'archéologie chrét.", Paris, 1892; Wilpert, "Roma Sotteranea: le pitture, etc.", Rome, 1903).

Christian ritual developed when, in the third century, the Church left the Catacombs. Many forms of self-expression must needs be identical, in varying times, places, cults, as long as human nature is the same. Water, oil, light, incense, singing, procession, prostration, decoration of altars, vestments of priests, are naturally at the service of universal religious instinct. Little enough, however, was directly borrowed by the Church—nothing, without being "baptized", as was the Pantheon. In all these things, the spirit is the essential: the Church assimilates to herself what she takes, or, if she cannot adapt, she rejects it (cf. Augustine, Epp., xlvii, 3, in P. L., XXXIII, 185; "Contra Faust.", XX, xxiii, ibid., XLII, 387; Jerome, "Epp.", cix, ibid., XXII, 907). Even pagan feasts may be "baptized": certainly our processions of 25 April are the Robigalia; the Rogation days may replace the Ambarualia; the date of Christmas Day may be due to the same instinct which placed on 25 Dec., the Natalis Invicti of the solar cult. But there is little of this; our wonder is, that there is not far more [see Kellner, "Heortologie" (Freiburg, 1906). See CHRISTMAS; EPIPHANY. Also Thurston, "Influence of Paganism on the Christian Calendar" in "Month" (1907), pp. 225 sqq.; Duchesne, "Orig. du Culte chrétien", tr. (London, 1910) passim; Braun, "Die priestlichen Gewänder" (Freiburg, 1897); Idem, "Die pontificalen Gewänder" (Freiburg, 1898); Rouse, "Greek Votive Offerings" (Cambridge, 1902), esp. c. v]. The cult of saints and relics is based on natural instinct and sanctioned by the lives, death, and tombs (in the first instance) of martyrs, and by the dogma of the Communion of Saints; it is not developed from definite instances of hero-worship as a general rule, though often a local martyr-cult was purposely instituted to defeat (e. g.) an oracle tenacious of pagan life (P. G., L, 551; P. L., LXXI, 831; Newman, "Essay on Development, etc.", II, cc. ix, xii., etc.; Anrich, "Anfang des Heiligenkults, etc.", Tübingen, 1904; especially Delehaye, "Légendes hagiographiques," Brussels, 1906). Augustine and Jerome (Ep. cii, 8, in P. L., XXXIII, 377; "C. Vigil.", vii, ibid., XXXIII, 361) mark wise tolerance:

Duchesne ["Hist. ancienne de l'église", I (Rome, 1908), 640; cf. Sozomen, "Hist. eccl." VII, xx, in P. G., LXVII, 1480] reminds us of the occasional necessary repression: Gregory, writing for Augustine of Canterbury, fixes the Church's principle and practice (Bede, "Hist. eccl.", I, xxx, xxxii, in P. L., XCV, 70, 72). Reciprocal influence there may to some small extent have been; it must have been slight, and quite possibly felt upon the pagan side not least. All know how Julian tried to remodel a pagan hierarchy on the Christian (P. Allard, "Julien l'Apostat", Paris, 1900).

IV. MORALITY, ASCESIS, MYSTICISM.—For an appreciation of pagan religions in themselves, and for an estimate of their pragmatic value in life, it should be noted that, in proportion as a pagan religion caught glimpses of high spiritual flights, of ecstacy, penance, otherworldliness, the "heroic", it opened the gates of all sorts of moral cataclysms. A *frugi religio* was that of Numa: the old Roman in his worship was *cautissimus et castissimus*. For him, Servus says, religion and fear (=awe) went close together. *Pietas* was a species of justice (filial, no doubt), but never *superstitio*. The ordinary man "put the whole of religion *in doing things*", veiling his head in presence of the modest, featureless *numina*, who filled his world and (as their adjective-names show—*Vaticanus, Argentarius, Domiduca*) presided over each sub-section of his life. Later the Roman virtues, *Fides, Castitas, Virtus* (manliness), were canonized, but religion was already becoming stereotyped, and therefore doomed to crumble, though to the end the volatile Greeks (παῖδες ἀεί) marvelled at its stability, dignity, and decency. So too the high abstractions of the Gâthâs (Moral Law, Good Spirit, Prudent Piety etc., the Amesha-spentas of the Avesta to be—Obedience, Silent Submission, and the rest), especially the enormous value set by Persian ethic upon Truth (a virtue dear to Old Rome), witness to lives of sober, quiet citizenship, generous, laborious, unimaginative, just to God and man. Exactly opposite, and disastrous, were the tendencies of the idealistic Hindu, losing himself in dreams of Pantheism, self-annihilation, and divine union. Especially the worship of Vishnu (god of divine grace and devotion), of Krishna (the god so strangely assimilated by modern tendency to Christ), and of Siva (whence Saktism and Tantrism) ran riot into a helpless licence, which must modify, one feels, the whole national destiny. We cannot pass conventional judgments on these aberrations. It is easily conceded that pagans constantly lived better than their creed, or, anyhow, than their myth; blind terrors, faulty premisses, warped traditions originated, preserved, or distorted customs pardonable when we know their history: astounding contradictions coexist (the ritual murders and prostitution of Assyria, together with the high moral sense revealed in the self-examination of the second Shurpu tablet; the sanctified incest and gross myth of Egypt, with the superb negative Confession of the Book of the Dead). Even in Greece, the terrifying survivals of the old clithonic cults, the unmoral influence (for the most part) of the Olympian deities, the unexacting and far more popular cult of local or favourite hero (Herakles, Asklepios), are subordinate to the essential instincts of αἰδώς, θέμις, νέμεσις (so well analysed by G. Murray, op. cit.), with their taboos and categorical imperatives, reflected back, as by necessity, to the expressed will of God. The religion of the ordinary man is perfectly and finally expressed in Plato's sketch of Cephalus (Republic, init.), whose instincts and traditions had carried him, at life's close, to a goal practically identical with that achieved by the philosophers at the end of their laborious inquiry.

All asceticism is, however, founded on a certain Dualism. In Persia, beyond all others dualist, the fight between Light and Darkness was noble and fruitful till it ran out into Manichæism and its debased allies. Certainly, from the East came much of the mystic Dualism, enjoining penance, focusing attention beyond the grave, preconizing purity of all sorts (even that abstention from thought which leads to ecstacy), which inspired Orphism, Pythagoreanism etc., and transfused the Mysteries. Till Plato, these notions achieved no high literary success. Æschylus preaches a sublime gospel: his austere series—Wealth, Self-sufficiency, Insolence, God-sent Infatuation, Ruin —has echoes of Hebrew prophecy and anticipates the "Exercises"; yet even his stern δράσαντι παθεῖν is calmed into the παθεῖν μάθος—a true wisdom, repose, reconciliation. Even in this life Sophocles sees high laws living eternally in serene heaven, a joy for men of obedience. Euripides, in the chaos of his scepticism, lives in angry bewilderment, not knowing where to place his ideal, since Aphrodite and Artemis and the other world-forces are, for him, essentially at war. It is in Plato, far better than in the nihilist asceticisms of the East, that the note—not even yet quite true— of asceticism is struck. The body is our tomb (σῶμα, σῆμα); we must strip ourselves of the leaden weights, the earthy incrustations of life: the true life is an exercise in death, a ὁμοίωσις τῷ θεῷ, as far as may be; like the swans we sing when dying, "going away to God", whose servants we are; "death dawns", and we owe sacrifice to the Healer-hero for the cure of life's fitful fever; "I have flown away", (the Orphic magic tablets will cry) "from the sorrowful weary wheel" of existences.

Directly after Plato, the schools are coloured by his thought, if not its immediate heirs. Stoic and Epicurean really aimed at one thing when they preached their ἀπάθεια and ἀταραξία, respectively Ἀνέχου καὶ ἀπέχου: be the αὐτάρχης, master of your self and fate. In Roman days of imperial persecution, this Stoicism, "touched with emotion", passed into the beautiful, though ill-founded religion of Seneca: all philosophy became practical, an *ars vivendi*: Life is our *ingens negotium*, yet not to be despaired of. Heaven is not proud: *ascendentibus di manum porrigent*. Ἄνω φρονεῖν, St. Paul was even then enjoining (Col., iii, 1, 2), echoing Plato's φρονεῖν ἀθάνατα καὶ θεῖα (Tim., 90 c), his τῆς ἄνω ὁδοῦ ἀεὶ ἑξόμεθα (Rep., 621 c.), his "life must be a flight" ἀπὸ τῶν ἐνθένδε ἐκεῖσε (529 A), and Aristotle's doctrine that a man must ἀθανατεῖν ἐφ' ὅσον ἐνδέχεται (Eth. N., X, vii), written so long ago. The more acute expressions of this mystical asceticism were much occupied with the future life and much fostered or provoked by the developed *Mysteries*. Impossible as it seems to find a race which believed in the extinction of the soul by death, survival was often a vague and dismal affair, prolonged in cavernous darkness, dust, and unconsciousness. So Babylon, Assyria, the Hebrews, earlier Greece. Odysseus must make the witless ghosts drink the hot blood before they can think and speak. At best, they depend on human attendance and even companionship; hence certain offerings and human sacrifice on the grave. Or they can, on fixed days, return, harry the living, seek food and blood. Hence expulsion-ceremonies, the Anthesteria, Lemuria, and the like. Kindlier creeds, however, are created, and, at the *Cara Cognatio*, the souls are welcomed to the places set for them, as for the gods, at the hearth and table, and the family is reconstituted in affection. Hopes and intuitions gather into a full and steady light, even before the inscriptions of the catacombs show that death was by now scarcely reason for tears at all. The "surer bark of a divine doctrine", for which the anxious lad in the "Phædo" had sighed, had been given to carry souls to that "further shore" to which Vergil saw them reaching yearning hands.

But the *Mysteries* had already fostered, though not created, the conviction of immortality. They gave no revelations, no new and secret doctrine, but powerfully and vividly impressed certain notions (one of them, immortality) upon the imagination. Gradually, however, it was thought that initiation ensured a happy after-life, and atoned for sins that else had been punished, if not in this life, in some place of expiation (Plato, "Rep.", 366; cf. Pindar, Sophocles, Plutarch). These mysteries usually began with the selection of *initiandi*, their preliminary "baptism", fasting, and (Samothrace) confession. After many sacrifices the Mysteries proper were celebrated, including nearly always a mimetic dance, or "tableaux", showing heaven, hell, purgatory; the soul's destiny; the gods [so in the Isis mysteries. Appuleius (Metamorphoses) tells us his thrilling and profoundly religious experiences]. There was often seen the "passion" of the god (Osiris): the rape and return of Kore and the sorrows of Demeter (Eleusis), the sacred marriage (Here at Cnossus), or divine births (Zeus: Brimos), or renowned incidents of the local myth. There was also the "exhibition" of symbolical objects—statues usually kept veiled, mysterious fruits or emblems (Dionysus), an ear of corn (upheld when Brimos was born). Finally there was usually the meal of mystic foods—grains of all sorts at Eleusis, bread and water in the cult of Mithra, wine (Dionysus), milk and honey (Attis), raw bull's flesh in the Orphic Dionysus-zagreus cult. Sacred formulæ were certainly imparted, of magical value.

There is not much reason to think these mysteries had a directly moral influence on their adepts; but their popularity and impressiveness were enormous, and indirectly reinforced whatever aspiration and belief they found to work on. Naturally, it has been sought to trace a close connexion between these rites and Christianity (Anrich, Pfleiderer). This is inadmissible. Not only was Christianity ruthlessly exclusive, but its apologists (Justin, Tertullian, Clement) inveigh loudest against the mysteries and the myths they enshrine. Moreover, the origin of the Christian rites is historically certain from our documents. Christian baptism (essentially unique) is alien to the repeated dippings of the *initiandi*, even to the Taurobolium, that bath of bull's blood, whence the dipped emerged *renatus in æternum*. The totemistic origin and meaning of the sacred meal (which was not a sacrifice) wherein worshippers communicated in the god and with one another (Robertson Smith, Frazer) is too obscure to be discussed here (cf. Lagrange, "Etudes, etc.", pp. 257, etc.). The sacred fish of Atergatis have nothing to do with the origin of the Eucharist, nor, even probably, with the Ichthys anagram of the catacombs. (See Fr. J. Dölger: IXΘΤΣ, das Fischsymbol, etc., Rome, 1910. The anagram does indeed represent Ἰησοῦς Χριστὸς Θεοῦ Υἱὸς Σωτήρ, the usual *order* of the third and fourth words being inverted owing to the familiar formula of the imperial cult; the propagation of the symbol was often facilitated owing to the popular Syrian fish-cult.) That the terminology of the mysteries was largely transported into Christian use (Paul, Ignatius, Origen, Clement etc.), is certain; that liturgy (especially of baptism), organization (of the catechumenate), *disciplina arcani* were affected by them, is highly probable. Always the Church has forcefully moulded words, and even concepts (σωτήρ, ἐπιφανής, βαπτισμός, φωτισμός, τελέτης, λόγος) to suit her own dogma and its expression. But it were contrary to all likelihood, as well as to positive fact, to suppose that the adogmatic, mythic, codeless practices and traditions of Paganism could subdue the rigid ethic and creed of Christianity. [Consult Cumont, opp. cit.; Anrich, "Das antike Mysterienwesen, etc." (Göttingen, 1894); O. Pfleiderer, "Das Christenbild, etc." (Berlin, 1903), tr. (London, 1905). Especially Cabrol, "Orig. liturgiques" (Paris, 1906); Duchesne, "Christian Worship", *passim;* Blötzer in "Stimmen aus Maria Laach", LXXI, (1906), LXXII, (1907); G. Boissier, "Fin du Paganisme" (Paris, 1907), especially 1, 117 sqq.; "Religion Romaine", *passim;* Sir S. Dill, op. cit.; C. A. Lobeck, "Aglaophamus" (1829); E. Rohde, "Psyche" (Tübingen, 1907); J. Reville, "Relig. à Rome, s. l. Sevères" (Paris, 1886); J. E. Harrison, "Prolegomena" (Cambridge, 1908), especially the appendix; L. R. Farnell, op. cit., and the lexicons.]

As strange historical phenomena, we note therefore the coexistence of the highest with the lowest; the sublime tendency, the *exiguum clinamen*, and the terrific catastrophe: human nature buffeted by the craving for divine union, prayer, and purity, and by the sense of sin, the need of penance, and helplessness of its own powers. Hence, savagery and blood attend the communion-feasts, grotesque myths accompany the loftiest ideals, sensual reaction follows flagellation and fasting. And we admire how, in the Hebrew nation alone, the teleological ascent was constant; sobriety meant no lowered aim; passion implied no frenzy. In the strong grasp of the Christian discipline alone, the further antimony of self-abnegation and self realization was practically and spiritually solved, though theoretically no adequate expression may ever be discovered for that solution. As historical problems remain certain connexions yet to be more accurately defined between the "dress" of Christian dogma and rite (whether liturgical, or of formula, or of philosophic category) and the circumambient religions. As historical certainty stands out the impassable gulf, in essence and origin, between the moral and religious systems of contemporary Paganism, especially of the Mysteries, and the Christian dogma and rite, formed on Palestinian soil with extraordinary rapidity, and rigidly exclusive of infection from alien sources. [Cf. L. Friedländer, "Roman Life and Manners, etc." (1909–10), espec. III, 84–313; O. Seeck, "Gesch. des Unterganges der antiken Welt", I (Berlin, 1910), II (1901), III (1909), and appendices, B. Allo, "L'Evangile en face du syncrétisme païen" (Paris, 1910).]

V. RELIGIOUS PHILOSOPHY.—This, we suppose, is the highest form of human reaction upon the religious datum of which the soul finds itself in possession, or at least may provide it with the purest, if not the most imperative, mode of worship. From this point of view the older rationalizing cosmogonies (as of Greece) are of little interest to us, save in so far as they witness already to that distinction between Zeus, supreme, and Fate, to which he yet is subject, an earlier unconscious attempt, perhaps, to reconcile the antinomies easily seized by true religious instinct in the popular traditions as to the gods. The mythological cosmogonies of Babylon and Assyria will, however, be of surpassing interest to the "comparative" student of Semitic religions. Noteworthy is the curve of Greek tendency —starting in Ionia, monistic, static, and anti-religious; grown dynamic in Heraclitus, whose Fire will pass, as Logos, into the Stoic system; transferred after the Persian wars to Attica, and profoundly dualized in Plato and Aristotle, whose concepts, however, of World-soul and of the Immanent Nature-force were powerful for all time. Through the Stoics, expressed in terms borrowed consistently from the exquisite Egyptian mythology, of Thot, of Osiris, and of Isis, this elaborate system of converging currents is synthesized in Plutarch, while from Plutarch's sources Philo had drawn the philosophy in which he strove to see the doctrines of Moses, and in terms of which he struggled to express the Hebrew books.

Thus was it that the Logos, in theory, impersonal, immanent, blindly evolving in the world, became (transfigured on the one hand by pagan myth, and by too close contact, on the other, with the Angel of Yahweh and the ideals of the Alexandrian sapiential literature) so near to personification, that John could take the expression, mould it to his dogma, cut short all perilous speculation among Christians, and assert once and for all that the Word was made flesh and was Jesus Christ. Yet many of the earlier apologists were to make great trouble with their use of Platonic formulæ, and with the Logos. Two principles emerge as governing Greek thought—God must have the first place, οὐ γὰρ πάρεργον δεῖ ποιεῖσθαι τὸν θεόν,—and yet the nearer we approach Him, the less can we express Him, θεὸν εὑρεῖν τὲ ἔργον, εὑρόντα δὲ ἐκφέρειν ἐν πολλοῖς ἀδύνατον (Pythagoras, Plato). To how many answers tentatively given does Euripides's sad prayer witness: "O Thou that upholdest earth, and on earth hast Thy Throne, whoe'er Thou be, hard to guess, hard to know —Zeus, be Thou law of nature, or human thought of man, to Thee I pray: for Thou, moving in silent path, in justice guidest all things mortal." To the immanent, supreme Force, consciously exacting service, or, at least, blindly imposing obedience, Greek philosophy almost inevitably came, and, in spite of itself and its sceptical and mechanical premises, amounted to a religion. In the mouth of Epictetus God is still sung triumphantly—"What can I do, I, a lame old man, save sing God's praises, and call on all men to join me in my song?"—till the Stoic current died out in Aurelius, stunned to acquiescence, no more enthusiastically uniting himself to the great law of God in the world.

But into neo-Platonism, coloured with Persian, Jewish, and even Christian language, the movement passed; already, in the "Isis and Osiris" of Plutarch, a pure mysticism and sublimity of emotion barely to be surpassed had been achieved; in the "Metamorphoses" of Apuleius the syncretistic cult of the Egyptian goddess expresses itself in terms of tenderness and majesty that would fit the highest worship, and, in the concluding prayer of the Apuleian Hermes, an ecstatic adoration of God is manifested in language and thought never equalled, still less surpassed, save in the inspired writers of the Church. But all these efforts of pagan religious philosophy, committed nearly always to a rigid Dualism, entangled accordingly in mechanical and magic practices, tricked out in false mythology, risking and losing psychical balance by the use of a nihilist asceticism of sense and thought, died into the miserable systems of Gnosticism, Manichæism, and the later neo-Platonism; and the current of true life, renewed and redirected by Paul and John, passed into the writings of Augustine. [Consult Zeller, "Phil. der Griechen" (Leipzig, 1879), tr. (London, 1881); Idem, "Grundriss, etc." (4th ed., Leipzig, 1908), tr. (London, 1892); Gomperz, "Gr. Denken" (Leipzig, 1903), tr. (London, 1901); cf. Flinders Petrie, "Personal Relig. in Egypt before Christianity" (New York, 1909), unsatisfactory; J. Adam, "Religious Teachers of Greece" (Edinburgh, 1908); Dill, op. cit.; Idem, "Roman Society in the last century of the Western Empire", especially valuable as a picture of the tenacity of the dying pagan cult and thought; Spence, "Early Christianity and Paganism" (London, 1904); L. Habert, "Doctr. Relig. d. Philosophes Grecs" (Paris, 1909); L. Campbell, "Religion in Greek Literature" (London, 1898); E. Caird, "Evolution of Theology in Greek Philosophies" (Glasgow, 1904), "Evolution of Religion" (Glasgow, 1907); H. Pinard in "Revue Apologétique" (1909); J. Lebreton, "Origines du Dogme de la Trinité", I (Paris, 1910), where the summits reached by Greek and Hellenized Jewish religious endeavour are appreciated. On the general question: de Broglie, "Problèmes et Conclusions de l'hist. des Religions", Paris, 1889.]

VI. RELATIONS BETWEEN PAGANISM AND REVELATION.—Ethnology and the comparative history of pagan religions do not impose upon us as an hypothesis that primitive Revelation which Faith ascertains to us. As a hypothesis it would, however, solve many a problem; it was the easier therefore for the Traditionalist of a century ago to detect its traces everywhere, and for Bishop Huet ("Demonstr. evangelica", Paris, 1690, pp. 68, 153, etc.), following Aristobulus, Philo, Josephus, Justin, Tertullian, and many another disciple of the Alexandrians, to see in all pagan law and ritual an immense pillage of Jewish tradition, and, in all the gods, Moses. The opposite school has, in all ages, fallen into worse follies. Celsus saw in Judaism an "Egyptian heresy", and in Christianity a Jewish heresy, on an equality with the cults of Antinous, Trophonius etc. (C. Cels., III, xxi); Calvin (Instit., IV, x, 12) and Middleton (A letter from Rome, etc., 1729) saw an exact conformity between popery and paganism. Dupuis and Creuze herald the modern race of comparative religionists, who deduce Christianity from pagan rites, or assign to both systems a common source in the human spirit. Far wiser in their generation were those ancient Fathers, who, not always seeing in pagan analogies the trickery of devils (Justin in P. G., VI, 364, 408, 660; Tertullian in P. L., I, 519, 660; II, 66; Firmicus Maternus, ibid., XII, 1026, 1030), disentangle, with a true historic and religious sense, the reasons for which God permitted, or directed, the Chosen People to retain or adapt the rites of their pagan ancestry or environment, or at least, reproaching them with this, recognize the facts (Justin, loc. cit., VI, 517; Tertullian, P. L., II, 333; Jerome, ibid., XXV, 194, XXIV, 733, XXII, 677, is striking; Eusebius, P. G., XXII, 521; especially Chrysostom, ibid., LVII, 66, and Gregory of Nazianzus, ibid., XXXVI, 161, who are remarkable. Cf. St. Thomas, I-II, Q. cii, a. 2). The relation of the Hebrew code and ritual to those of pagan systems need not be discussed here: the facts, and, a fortiori, the comparison and construction of the facts, are not yet satisfactorily determined: the admirable work of the Dominican school (especially the "Religions semitiques" of M. J. Lagrange; cf. F. Prat, S.J., "Le Code de Sinai", Paris, 1904) is preparing the way for more adequate considerations than are at present possible.

Whether Paganism made straight a path for Christianity may be considered from two points of view. Speaking from the standpoint of pure history, no one will deny that much in the antecedent or environing aspirations and ideals formed a præparatio evangelica of high value. "Christo jam tum venienti", sang Prudentius, "crede, parata via est". The pagan world "saw the road", Augustine could say, from its hilltop. "Et ipse Pileatus Christianus est", said the priest of Attis; while, of Heraclitus and the old philosophers, Justin avers that they were Christians before Christ. Indeed, in their panegyric of the Platonic philosophy, the earlier Apologists go far beyond anything we should wish to say, and indeed made difficulties for their successors. Attention is nowadays directed, not only to the ideas of the Divine nature, the logos-philosophies, popular at the Christian era, but especially to those oriental cults, which, flooding down upon the shrivelled, officialized, and dying worship of the Roman or Hellenic-Roman world, fertilized within it whatever potentialities it yet contained of purity, prayer, emotional religion, other-worldliness generally. A whole new religious language was evolved, betokening a new tendency, ideal, and attitude; here too Christianity did not disdain to use, to transcend, and to transform.

Theologically, moreover, we know that God from the very outset destined man to a supernatural union with Himself. "Pure nature", historically, has never existed. The soul is naturaliter Christiana. The truest man is the Christian. Thus the "human spirit" we have so often mentioned, is no human spirit left to itself, but solicited by, yielding to a resisting grace. Better than Aristotle guessed, mankind ἔχει τι θεῖον. For Christus cogitabatur. Ἀεὶ πονεῖ τὸ ζῶον, said the same philosopher: and all creation groans and travails together until the full redemption; "all nations of men" were by God "made of one blood for to dwell on all the face of the earth . . . that they should seek the Lord, if haply they might grope after Him and find Him." They failed, alas, though they had the ἐπίγνῶσις of God (Rom., i, 32; cf. i, 19): the higher they went, the more terribly they fell: but, alongside of the tragic first chapter of Paul's Epistle, is the second, and we dare not forget that the elect people, the Eldest Son, the heir of oracles and law, fell equally or worse, and made the name of God to be blasphemed among the Gentiles it contemned (Rom., ii, 24). Yet for all that, God used the Jews in his plan, and none will dare to say He did not use the Gentiles. They reveal themselves in history as made for God, and restless till they rest in him. History shows us their effort, and their failure; we thank God for the one, and dare not scorn the other. God's revelation has been in many fragments and in many modes; and to the pagan king, whose right hand He had holden, He declared: "For Jacob my servant's sake, and Israel my chosen, I have called thee by thy name: I have surnamed thee, though thou, thou hast not known Me: I am Yahweh, and there is none else; beside Me there is no God: (yet) will I guide thee, though Me thou hast not known" (Is., xlv, 4 sq.). For still Cyrus worshipped at the shrine of Ahura.

C. C. MARTINDALE.

Pagano, MARIO, jurisconsult and man of letters, b. in Brienza, Province of Salerno, 8 Dec., 1748; d. at Naples, 29 Oct., 1799. At twenty he became special lecturer in moral philosophy at the University of Naples, at the same time practising law. He published various works on criminal jurisprudence, e. g., "Considerazioni sulla procedura criminale". He became professor of law in 1787. He likewise published in 1792 some political essays on barbarian peoples, and the origin and decadence of civilized society and of nations, revealing the idea of Vico. As early as 1768 he had written a political review of the entire Roman legislation, which was much applauded. In this is discerned the influence of Montesquieu and in general of the philosophy then in vogue. The novelty, and in part the audacity, of these theories created some enemies, and, although he enjoyed the favour of the Court, he was imprisoned. His writings, accused of irreligion, were subjected to theological examinations, which resulted in his favour. When in 1799 the French established the republic at Naples, Pagano was one of the most active. He wrote the constitution, built up on the remains of the French Constitution of 1793. On the restoration of the monarchy, Pagano was on the side of those republicans who made the last resistance at the Castel Nuovo. Contrary to the agreement of capitulation, he was imprisoned and condemned. In prison he composed æsthetic discourses and produced a number of lyric and dramatic compositions, of which only two were printed, the tragedy "Gerbino", and the melodrama "Agamemnon".

GIUSTINIANI, *Memorie degli scrittori legali del regno di Napoli* (Naples, 1787–88); MASSA, *Elogio di Pagano*.

U. BENIGNI.

Page, ANTHONY, VENERABLE, English martyr, b. at Harrow-on-the-Hill, Middlesex, 1571; d. at York, 20 or 30 April, 1593. He was of gentle birth and matriculated at Oxford from Christ Church, 23 November, 1581, being described as "scholaris Mri-Wodson". He entered the English College, Reims, 30 September, 1584, and received minor orders, April, 1585. He was ordained deacon at Laon, 22 September, 1590, and priest at Reims, 21 September, 1591. Dr. Anthony Champney, who was his contemporary at Reims, in his MS. (q. v.) history of the reign of Elizabeth, as quoted by Bishop Challoner, describes him, as being of wonderful meekness, of a virginal modesty and purity, and of more than common learning and piety, and as having endeared himself to all by his singular candour of mind and sweetness of behaviour. He was condemned for being a priest, under 27 Eliz., c. 2., and was hanged, disembowelled, and quartered.

CHALLONER, *Missionary Priests*, I, no. 98; CLARK, *Register of Oxford University*, II (Oxford, 1887–9), 105; KNOX, *Douay Diaries* (London, 1878), 202, 205, 234, 241.

JOHN B. WAINEWRIGHT.

Page, FRANCIS, VENERABLE. See TICHBORNE, THOMAS, VENERABLE.

Pagi, ANTOINE, and his nephew FRANÇOIS, two French ecclesiastical historians. ANTOINE, b. 31 March, 1624, at Rognes in the Department of Bouches-du-Rhone; d. 5 June, 1699 at Aix. After studying with the Jesuits at Aix, he entered the monastery of the Conventual Franciscans at Arles, and made solemn profession on 31 January, 1641. For some time he devoted himself to preaching, but at the age of twenty-nine years he was elected provincial, an office which he held four times. He devoted his spare time to the study of history. Discerning numerous chronological errors, and frequently misstatements of facts in the "Annales ecclesiastici" of Baronius, he made it his life-work to correct them and otherwise elucidate the valuable work. Pagi's first volume was printed during his lifetime (Paris, 1689); the remaining three volumes, reaching till the year 1198, the last year in the work of Baronius, were completed in manuscript shortly before his death. The whole work was edited in four volumes by his nephew François Pagi: "Critica historico-chronologica in universos annales ecclesiasticos em. et rev. Cæsaris Card. Baronii" (Geneva, 1705; second ed., 1727). Mansi embodied it in his edition of the "Annales" of Baronius (Lucca, 1736–59). Though, on the whole, the "Critica" manifests great care and an unusual knowledge of history, it is not entirely free of errors. His other works are: "Dissertatio hypatica seu de consulibus cæsareis" (Lyons, 1682), printed also in "Apparatus in Annales ecclesiasticos" (Lucca, 1740), pp. 1–136; "Dissertatio de die et anno mortis S. Martini ep. turonensis", and a few minor treatises in defense of his "Dissertatio hypatica", in which he had set down various rules for determining the consulship of the Roman emperors, and which had been attacked by Cardinal Noris and others. He also edited: "D. Antonii Paduani O. Min. sermones hactenus inediti" (Avignon, 1685).

FRANÇOIS, b. 7 September, 1654, at Lambesc in Provence; d. 21 January, 1721, at Orange. After studying with the Oratorians at Toulon, he became a Conventual Franciscan, was three times provincial, and assisted his uncle in the correction of the "Annales" of Baronius. Besides editing the "Critica" of his uncle he wrote a history of the popes up to the year 1447: "Breviarium historico-chronologico-criticum illustriora Pontificum romanorum gesta, conciliorum generalium acta . . . complectens" (4 vols., Antwerp, 1717–27). The history was continued in two volumes by his nephew, Antoine Pagi, the Younger (Antwerp, 1748–53).

Mémoires de Trévoux (Trévoux, 1711), 1512–39, 1903-31; (1712) 273–291; (1717), 1939–67; *Apparatus in Annales Baronii*, p. xvii; *Bibliothèque ancienne et moderne*, VII, 119–200; XXVIII, 211–228; *Journal des Savants*, LXII, 189-198; LXV, 274–280.

MICHAEL OTT.

Pagnani, CLEMENT. See KANDY, DIOCESE OF.

Pagnino, SANTES (or XANTES), Dominican, b. 1470 at Lucca, Tuscany; d. 24 Aug., 1541, at Lyons, one of the leading philologists and Biblicists of his day. At sixteen he took the religious habit at Fiesole, where he studied under the direction of Savonarola and other eminent professors. In acquiring the Oriental languages, then cultivated at Florence, he displayed unwonted quicksightedness, ease, and penetration. His genius, industry, and erudition won him influential friends, among them the Cardinals de' Medici, subsequently Leo X and Clement VII. As a sacred orator his zeal and eloquence kept abreast with his erudition and were as fruitful. Summoned to Rome by Leo X, he taught at the recently opened free school for Oriental languages until his patron's death (1521). He then

THE EMPRESS THEODORA AND HER SUITE

MOSAIC IN S. VITALE, RAVENNA. (VI CENTURY)

spent three years at Avignon and the last seven years of his life at Lyons. Here he was instrumental in establishing a hospital for the plague-stricken, and, by his zeal and eloquence, diverted an irruption of Waldensianism and Lutheranism from the city, receiving in acknowledgement the much coveted rights and privileges of citizenship. The epitaph, originally adorning his tomb in the Dominican church at Lyons, fixes the date of his death beyond dispute. The merit of his "Veteris et Novi Testamenti nova translatio" (Lyons, 1527) lies in its literal adherence to the Hebrew, which won for it the preference of contemporary rabbis and induced Leo X to assume the expenses of publication. After the pontiff's death these devolved on the author's relatives and friends. Several editions of it, as well as of the monumental "Thesaurus linguæ sanctæ" (Lyons, 1529), were brought out by Protestants as well as Catholics. Among other productions, all of which treat of Sacred Scripture, Greek, or Hebrew, were "Isagoges seu introductionis ad sacras literas liber unus" (Lyons, 1528, etc.), and "Catena argentea in Pentateuchum" in six volumes (Lyons, 1536).

See VERSIONS OF THE BIBLE; QUÉTIF-ECHARD, *Scriptores O. P.*, II (Paris, 1721); TOURON, *Hist. des hommes illustres de l'ordre de St. Dominique*, IV (Paris, 1747); TIRABOSCHI, *Storia della letter. ital.*, VII (Venice, 1451); MANDONNET, s. v. *Dominicains*, and VIGOUROUX, *Dict. de la Bible*, s. v. (Paris, 1910).

THOS. À K. REILLY.

Painting, RELIGIOUS.—Painting has always been associated with the life of the Church. From the time of the Catacombs it has been used in ecclesiastical ornamentation, and for centuries after Constantine religious art was the only form of living art in the Christian world. Its fecundity has been wonderful, and even now, although much diminished, is still important. Until the Renaissance the Church exercised a veritable monopoly over this sphere. Profane painting in Europe dates only from the last three centuries, and it took the lead only in the last century. It may therefore be said that throughout the Christian Era the history of painting has been that of religious painting.

It would be absurd to seek to place the Church in contradiction to the Gospel on this point, as did the Iconoclasts in the eighth century and the Protestants in the sixteenth. The doctrine of the Church has been clearly enunciated by Molanus in his "Historia SS. Imaginum" (Louvain, 1568; the best edition is that of Paquot, Louvain, 1771; an ample bibliography is found on pp. 212-24). It is truly remarkable that such a magnificent development of artistic thought should proceed from a purely spiritual doctrine preached by humble Galilean fishermen who were ignorant of art and filled with the horror of idolatry characteristic of the Semitic races. Far from reproaching the Church with infidelity to the teachings of her Founder, we should rather acknowledge her wisdom in rejecting no natural form of human activity, and thus furthering the work of civilization.

The very fact that the Church permitted painting obliged her to assign it a definite object and to prescribe certain rules; art never seemed to her an end in itself; as soon as she adopted it she made it a means of instruction and edification. "The picture", says the Patriarch Nicephorus, "conceals the strength of the Gospel under a coarser, but more expressive form." "The picture is to the illiterate", says Pope St. Gregory, "what the written word is to the educated." In like manner St. Basil: "What speech presents to the ear painting portrays by a mute imitation." And Peter Comestor says, in a famous text: "The paintings of the churches are in place of books to the uneducated" (*quasi libri laicorum*). "We are, by the grace of God, those who manifest to the faithful the miracles wrought by faith"—thus the painters of Siena express themselves in the statutes of their guild (1355). The same ideas are contained in the "Treatise on Painting" of Cennino Cennini, and in France in the "Livre des Métiers" of the Parisian Etienne Boileau (1254). In 1513, at the height of the Renaissance, Albrecht Dürer wrote: "The art of painting is used in the service of the Church to depict the sufferings of Christ and of many other models; it also preserves the countenances of men after their death." Almost the same definition is given by Pacheco, father-in-law of Velasquez, in his "Arte de la Pintura", printed at Seville in 1649.

The constant doctrine of the Church was defined at the Second Council of Nicæa (787), and is summed up in the often quoted formula: "The composition of the image is not the invention of the painters, but the result of the legislation and approved tradition of the Church" (Labbe, "Concil.", VII, "Synod. Nicæna", II, Actio VI, 831, 832). It would be impossible to define more clearly the importance of art in the life of the Church, and at the same time its subordinate position. Thence, obviously, results one of the chief characteristics of religious painting, its conservative instinct and its tendency to hieratic formalism. Art being regarded as didactic, necessarily partook of the severe nature of dogma. The slightest error bordered on heresy. To alter anything in the garments of the saints or of the Blessed Virgin, to depict the former shod or the latter barefooted, to confuse the piety of the simple by innovations and individual whims, were all serious matters. The Christian artist was surrounded by a strict network of prohibitions and prescriptions. From this resulted the artistic danger of soulless, mechanical repetition, which religious painting did not always escape. The responsibility for this, however, must not be ascribed to the Church, but rather to human slothfulness of mind, for, as a matter of fact, there is an element of mobility in art as it is understood by the Church. Religious art may be called a realistic art. Its appeal to the emotions by the representation of facts obliges it to be more and more exactly imitative, and it must adopt the progressive stages of technic to express all the phases of human feeling. Even the most immobile of the great Christian schools, the Byzantine, has only an apparent immobility; more intimate knowledge inspires increasing admiration for its vitality and elasticity. The innovating and creative faculty has never been denied to the religious painters. In the twelfth century Guillaume Durand, the famous Bishop of Mende, wrote in his "Rationale" (I, 3): "The various histories as well of the New as of the Old Testament are depicted according to the inclination of the painters. For to painters as to poets a license has ever been conceded to dare whatever they pleased."

I. THE CATACOMBS.—The monuments of religious painting for the first four centuries are to be sought only at Rome (see CATACOMBS, ROMAN; ECCLESIASTICAL ART, ORIGIN). But this peculiar art must not be taken as typical of what was in vogue elsewhere. It is a great mistake to look in the Roman cemeteries for the origin or the cradle of Christian painting: as has been conclusively proved by the learned researches of Strzygowski and Ajnalof, an art, which seems to have been fully developed by the end of the fifth century, grew up in Syria, Egypt, or Asia Minor, and completely supplanted that of the Catacombs. The latter did not survive the very special conditions under which it arose, and was but an isolated and local school without development or future, but none the less valuable, venerable, and pleasing.

II. BYZANTINE PAINTING.—A. *The New Iconography*.—By the edict of 313 Christianity was recognized as the official religion of the Empire. The Church left its hiding-places and breathed freely, and the period of the basilicas began. A profound transformation of religious painting was the result of this triumph. The time had come to display the insignia of Christ's victory with the same material splendour which the State attached to the imperial majesty of Cæsar. The Good Shepherd of the Catacombs and the pastoral scenes gradually disappeared; the last traces of them are found in the rotunda of St. Constantia and in the mausoleum of Galla Placidia at Ravenna (c. 450). In the magnificent mosaic of S. Pudenziana at Rome (before 410), the Cross, which stands in mid-heaven above a Senate of Apostles wearing the laticlave, is already a symbol of triumph. Christ appears as a celestial *imperator* invested with awe-inspiring glory. "The arches of the world", writes Eusebius, "are His throne, the earth is His footstool. The celestial armies are His guard."— Thus formidably is the God of the Gospel portrayed on the porch of the ancient Vatican.

Rome still preserves the oldest remains of the new art, but the East has claims to priority. Such recent discoveries as those of M. Clédat in the necropolis of El Bagaout (fourth century) and in the convent of Baouit (sixth century), the excavations of M. Gayet in the tombs of Antinoe and the funeral portraits unearthed at Fayum form an accumulation of evidence which leaves no doubt on this point. To these may be added the famous miniatures of Cosmas Indicopleustes and of the "Roll of Josue" (preserved at the Vatican), the originals of which date from the sixth century, or those of the Mesopotamian Evangeliary, illustrated in 586 by the monk Rabula (Laurentian Library, Florence), and, although of somewhat later date, the paintings of the Evangeliaries of Etschmiadzin (Armenian, dated 989) and Rossano, reproduced from obviously earlier models, either Alexandrian or Syriac. These paintings are chiefly narrative and historical in character. The Church, having conquered paganism, must now face the task of supplying its place. And the Church quickly recognized in her own experience with paganism the efficacy of images as means of instruction. This is testified by a letter (end of the fourth century) from St. Nilus to the prefect Olympiodorus, who had built a church and wished to know if it were fitting that he should adorn it only with scenes of the chase and angling, with foliage, etc., having in view only the pleasure of the eye. St. Nilus replied that this was mere childish nonsense, that the fitting thing in the sanctuary was the image of the Cross, and on the walls scenes from the Old Testament and the Gospel, so that those who, being unable to read the Scriptures, might by these pictures be reminded of the beautiful deeds of the followers of the true God, and thereby impelled to do in like manner. Obviously, the holy anchorite here recommended genuine historical compositions. The Church, replacing the vast pagan repertory of legend and fable, created for the imagination a new basis, likewise derived from the past. At that date the best apology for the Church was the story of its life and its genealogy, and this was perseveringly set forth during the early centuries after Constantine. This historical tendency is clearly evident at St. Mary Major's in the forty mosaics, executed in the time of Pope Sixtus III (432–40), which relate the lives of the Patriarchs Abraham, Isaac, Jacob, Moses, and Josue. Christ's victory and His glorious Advent also find expression in the "triumphal arches" of St. Paul's Without the Walls (under Leo I, 440–61) and of the Lateran (under Hilary I, 461–68).

But Rome, conquered by the hordes of Alaric, had fallen from her political rank, and henceforth the evolution of Byzantine painting must be followed at Ravenna and Constantinople.

B. *Monumental Painting to the Iconoclastic Controversy.*—Representing deeds rather than ideals, events rather than symbols, the Byzantine School endowed Christianity with a complete system of representation of all types, some of which are still used, and once for all formulated the essential traits of the great scenes of religious history. (See BYZANTINE ART.)

In its early period Byzantine painting was strictly realistic. The mosaics, e. g., on either side of the choir of S. Vitale at Ravenna, show the Court of Justinian and Theodora—sickly, dissolute figures; the men, coarse; the women, bleached and bedizened, overladen with jewels and dressed in the extreme of luxury—unforgettable personifications of a corrupt and dazzling life. This care for documentary exactitude was applied also to the past: historic characters were treated as contemporary. The Christians of the first three centuries had been obliged to content themselves with conventional types, without individual character, for their figures of Christ; but here Byzantine art raised new questions. The Christological disputes of the time necessitated new dogmatic definitions. In painting a certain school, appealing to a text of Isaias, maintained that Christ was hideous. In answer to these, appeal was made, in the fourth century, to the so-called "Letter of Lentulus to the Senate". Christ, according to this document, had blue eyes and light hair falling smooth to His ears, then in curls over his shoulders. One recognizes here the desire to give to the figure of the Saviour a certain majestic beauty embodied in the stereotyped traits of a portrait which leaves no room for the play of fancy.

The same process of determination went on at the same time for the principal characters of sacred history, for the Blessed Virgin, the Patriarchs, and the Apostles, and each of these pictorial types acquired the force of a law. The Council of 692, for example, decreed that Christ should be represented as the Lamb. This scrupulosity extends to accessories and embellishments: at San Vitale, Ravenna, the "Hospitality of Abraham" has for its setting a vast verdant landscape; at San Apollinare Nuovo, the city of Classis and the palace of Theodoric are accurately represented. In Gospel scenes veritable reproductions of Jerusalem were aimed at. The care for exact representation was, at the same time, counteracted by the passion for grandeur and splendour of effect which dominated all Byzantine painting. The latter tendency arose partly from the exigencies of decorative work and the inexorable laws governing monumental style. Decoration implies work intended to be viewed from a distance, and therefore simple in outline and colossal in scale, reduced to absolute essentials strikingly displayed on a wall-surface. Hence certain conventions, the result of optical laws: few gestures, little action, no agitation or confusion. The countenances have an impassive and fixed expression, as the tragic actor, in the Greek theatre, assumed mask and cothurnus, and chanted the solemn lines to a slow recitative.

This theatrical and imposing style was, however, less artificial than might be supposed. It naturally ascribed to the personages of the sacred drama the ceremonious dignity of the Byzantine world, modelling the past on the present. One of the most marked effects of these ideas is the repugnance to representing suffering and death. At San Apollinare Nuovo, in the portrayal of the Passion, not Christ, but his executioner, carries His Cross. The artist reverently omits the scene on Calvary, and indeed Christian art for a long time observed the same reticence (cf. Bréhier, "Origines du Crucifix", Paris, 1904). But on the other hand there is the taste for noble composition, the love of symmetry, the striving after grandiose and solemn effects. From these same ideals of pomp and grandeur resulted a type of expression in harmony with them, monumental painting in the more solid, more luxurious style of mosaic. This was already an ancient art, well known to the Alexandrians, practised also by the Romans, who used it chiefly for the pavements of their villas. But it was reserved for the Byzantines, who applied it to mural decoration, to discover its true resources. (See MOSAICS.)

C. *From the Iconoclast Controversy to the School of Mount Athos.*—The Iconoclast controversy (725–850) arrested the development of this powerful school at its height. The movement originated in Islam as a fierce outburst of the Semitic idealism of the desert. The Iconoclast emperors were by no means barbarians, but enlightened princes, dilettanti in their way, very often devotees and theologians; such in particular were Leo the Isaurian and Theophilus. These emperors prided themselves on being worshippers "in spirit and in truth", and proscribed art only in its "idolatrous", or religious, applications. Feminine devotion in the end triumphed over these scruples. Meanwhile there had been wide devastation; the convents had suffered especially; and when the veneration of images was re-established, nearly all the churches had lost their ornaments, the mosaics had been torn down, and the frescoes whitewashed. As often happens, however, the Church came out of the conflict more vigorous than ever. A new Byzantine School, very different from the first, and a second golden age were to commence. The first Byzantine School was an historical one, the second was wholly liturgical and didactic. Each decorative element assumed a symbolical value. Christ the king, surrounded by the celestial hierarchy, looks down from the vaults; in the sanctuary, behind the altar, reigns the Virgin, seated, holding the Child in her lap as a figure of the Church, the "living throne of the Almighty"; the rest of the apse presents the precursors of Christ, the bishops, doctors, and two great Eucharistic scenes, the "Communion of the Apostles" and the "Divine Liturgy"; on the walls are developed the lives of the saints and martyrs and that of Christ. In the story of the Gospel the order of time is broken and from the mass of miracles a few great scenes are detached which the Church celebrates at the twelve principal feasts. Two essential ideas are brought into prominence: the Redemption and the Resurrection—the scene of Calvary and the Descent into Limbo. In the narthex, the Life of the Virgin assumes a novel importance, while the Old Testament, on the contrary, tends to disappear.

Four important monuments in the East mark the apogee of the new style; these are: St. Luke in Phocis, the Nea Moni of Chios, the beautiful church of Daphni near Athens, and, in Russia, that of St. Sophia at Kiev. All four date from the tenth century, but show none of the perfection of detail and precision of execution which make the mosaics of S. Vitale a finished type of painting; but the decorative effect is beyond compare. Nothing in the art of painting can surpass these churches encased in golden shells and peopled by a host of gaunt, colossal figures. At this date most of the Gospel compositions were virtually stamped with a *Ne varietur;* for each of them a group of artistic geniuses had provided a permanent type.

A more important fact is that at this time the Byzantine style conquered the West and became truly universal. At about the same time the West was undergoing a singular upheaval: the old feudalism was separating itself from the soil and setting itself in motion. For two centuries the exodus of the Crusades was to continue, marking the beginning of a new civilization for Europe. Byzantine colonies appeared in Italy, notably those of Venice, in the North, and of Sicily, in the South, forming hotbeds of Byzantism at the two ends of the Peninsula. Within thirty years (1063–95) Venice accomplished the marvel of St. Mark's which she was to go on decorating and perfecting for three centuries (the narthex is of the thirteenth century, the baptistry of the fourteenth century). In the neighbourhood of Venice there are examples at Torcello, Murano, and Trieste, while the twelfth century witnesses in Sicily, under the Norman princes, the appearance of four incomparable churches: that of Martorana (1143), that of Cefalù (1148), the palace church at Palermo (c. 1160), and the Cathedral of Monreale (c. 1180). Of all these masterpieces St. Mark's is the best known, but only from the Pantocrator in the apse at Cefalù is it possible to realize to what beauties of nobility and melancholy, and to what majesty of style, the art attained.

For the sake of completeness, mention must be made of the numerous icons, the various types of the Madonna (Panagia, Nicopœia, Hodegetria), of the miniature paintings in manuscripts (which were important for the diffusion of motives), of enamels such as those in the Pala d'Oro of St. Mark's, and of the small portable mosaic pictures, like the valuable diptych preserved at the Opera del Duomo, at Florence. The task of the Byzantine School was accomplished, but it did not at once disappear. In the fourteenth century it produced the fine mosaic cycle of Kahrie-djami and at the beginning of the fifteenth century, within the solitude of Athos, shut in by the Mussulman world, it continued to produce and covered all Eastern Europe with countless paintings of the school of Panselinos. With the twelfth century, however, it had fulfilled its purpose, and the further development of religious painting was in the West.

III. RELIGIOUS PAINTING IN THE WEST, TO THE CINQUE CENTO.—A. *North of the Alps.*—Through the medium of the monks and the Crusades all Europe was rendered fruitful by the Byzantine School. From the Byzantine a Western art was to develop, in which the loss in external luxury was gradually supplied by pliancy and power of expression. A distinction must here be made between the art of the countries north of the Alps, and that of the southern countries. Little need be said of the former: the Romanesque churches seem to have been very rich in paintings, but most of them are lost, and in the Gothic churches, which soon after began to be erected, there was little room for mural painting; stained glass took its place. But the personality of the artist was scarcely felt in this art, and as to drawing and subjects, stained glass is scarcely more than a reflexion of miniature painting. Its study, therefore, has but a purely iconographic interest. It began in France with the windows of St-Denis (1140–44), and the school of St-Denis spread throughout the North, to Chartres (c. 1145), York, Le Mans (c. 1155), Angers, and Poitiers. During the following century the school of Notre-Dame-de-Paris played the same part.

The iconography of these windows is essentially symbolic, and the allegorical spirit of the Middle Ages is nowhere more apparent. It was an old Christian idea that each person and fact of the Old Testament was an image prefiguring a person of the New. This idea only expanded with full wealth of detail in the Gothic art of the thirteenth and fourteenth centuries. With wonderful subtlety of interpretation the attempt was made to discover the most unforeseen, and sometimes the oldest, relations. Books such as those of Rabanus Maurus, or the "Speculum ecclesiæ" of Honorius of Autun, or the "Glossa ordinaria" of Walafrid Strabo, must be read to obtain an idea of the spirit in which the Middle Age read its Bible and pictured it. In the "Bestiaries", too, which supplied material for this art, there is a fantastic natural history, a singular menagerie, each curiosity of which conceals some pious allegory. The material universe was transformed into a sort of vast psychomachia, an immense system of metaphors. No other school ever equalled this astounding idealism.

B. *In Italy.*—(1) Giotto and the Giottesques.—After the fall of Rome and the Empire, Italy was for centuries in a most miserable condition. In the sixth and seventh centuries the Iconoclast reaction sent in the direction of Rome a host of Orientals, principally monks, who were the chief victims of the persecution. It it probably to these Greeks that we owe the frescoes, doubtless dating from the seventh century, which were discovered, in 1898, at Sta Maria Antiqua.

Under the influence of the great Abbot Desiderius, the school of Monte Cassino assumed the leadership in an artistic movement which was to extend as far as Cluny. Some eleventh-century monuments, such as the church of S. Angelo in Formis, have preserved frescoes which attest the importance of this Benedictine school; but its traces are to be found chiefly in miniatures, and especially in volumes of a particular kind, such as the "Exultet-rolls" (see EXULTET). This style spread throughout Italy in the twelfth century, but soon declined. In the churches and museums of Tuscany are to be found a great number of icons, madonnas and crucifixes, such as the miraculous Christ preserved at St. Clare of Assisi, and which is said to have spoken to St. Francis. These works show to what a depth of barbarism the Byzantine school had fallen about 1200. Nevertheless, it was still capable of producing beautiful work. The Madonna of Guido of Siena, for instance, preserved in the Public Palace, and dated 1221 (not 1281, as according to Milanesi), proclaims a veritable renewal of the ancient formula, tempered by the grave and gentle Siennese mysticism. This is still more obvious in the works of the great Duccio (see DUCCIO DI BUONINSEGNA), the Rucellai Madonna (1285) or the "Madonna Maesta" (1311).

Such was the persistency of the Byzantine movement at Siena, but a movement in another direction issued from Rome in the middle of the thirteenth century. Recent excavations have brought to light at S. Maria in Trastevere a cycle of very important frescoes of which Ghiberti, in his "Commentary", gives Pietro Cavallini as the author. The chief scene represents the Last Judgment. It is impossible to praise excessively the beauty of this composition, the nobility of the draperies, the majesty of the types. Ancient art undoubtedly exercised a powerful influence on Cavallini, as on his contemporary, the sculptor Nicholas of Pisa. In the thirteenth century a revival took place at Rome which foreshadowed the Renaissance of a later age. Unhappily, few of its monuments remain, but the mosaics of S. Maria in Trastevere, that of St. Mary Major, by Jacopo Torriti (1296), and the Genesis frescoes of St. Paul Without the Walls, known through drawings in a MS. at the Vatican, reveal the importance of this ancient Roman school. The same compositions are also found in the upper church at Assisi, which was to be the cradle of Italian painting. It is now proved that these scenes were the work of Cavallini and his school. There is nothing to prove that Cimabue did not work here, but he would have done so only as a pupil of the Roman school (see CIMABUE).

This is also true of the great Giotto in his earliest dated works: the Navicella of St. Peter's (1298), the Stefaneschi retable and the Jubilee fresco painted in 1300 at St. John Lateran. It was otherwise with his second sojourn in Rome, for his early Assisi frescoes, the 28 scenes of the "Life of St. Francis" (c. 1293) are wholly in the Roman manner. At Rome, therefore, in the thirteenth century was created the *giottesco* style, the *dolce stil nuovo* which was to charm Italy for a hundred years. (See GIOTTO DI BONDONE.) Giotto instilled into the painting of age the wonderful poetry of Franciscan Christianity. St. Francis has been called the Father of Italian art, and the saying is true if taken with a certain elasticity of meaning. Both he and St. Dominic rejuvenated and reanimated the Church. The history of religious art down to the Reformation and the Council of Trent could only be accurately written in the light of this great historic fact. All that Byzantine and early medieval art had represented as dogmas assumed the stirring character of life. To say that art became secularized would be to risk miscomprehension, but in truth, from being intellectual and theological, it became democratic and popular. Faith became visualized. The whole effort of the painters, as well as of the people, was to imagine as vividly as possible the life and sufferings of Christ. A multitude of dramatic elements developed in Christianity, and originated a sort of rudimentary theatre. (See ITALY, ITALIAN LITERATURE; JACOPONE DA TODI.)

All these characteristics began to show themselves in painting also. At Padua, in 1306, Giotto outlined the earliest and best formulated of his school in the "Life of the Virgin", closely linked with the history of the Passion. The painter retained only the pathetic elements of Christianity. A number of new scenes appeared, while the old ones were enriched with countless new features. The picture is filled with figures, gestures are softened, expression grows tender and human. "Giotto", says Vasari, "was the first to put more kindness into his figures". During three centuries of development some scenes, such as the Nativity and the Epiphany, continued to grow in movement, expression, and picturesque effect. Symbolism and didactic intent are absent: painting ceases to have any object but to represent life. The teaching of Christ, the parables, and the sacraments disappear, to be replaced by scenes of sorrow and the drama of Calvary, every moment of which is minutely treated in detail. What primitive Christian art avoided with a sort of modesty or fear now became its chosen and persistent subject. The striking feature of these pictures is a wholly new impression of familiarity and warmth.

After the great frescoes of the Life of St. Francis at Assisi a host of local saints and contemporary *beati* were honoured in like manner. In painting these contemporary lives, the artists had to create traditions; therefore they painted what they saw—faces, costumes, assemblages of people. They became realists and observers, and these same tendencies appeared in their paintings of the Gospel. There was little need of invention: the theatre and its representations, the processions, and the *tableaux vivants* assisted their imagination (cf. Male, "Renouvellement de l'art par les mystères" in "Gazette des Beaux-Arts", Feb.-May, 1904). The following are some "Passions" of the Giottesque school, in chronological order: in the lower church of Assisi, by Pietro Lorenzetti (c. 1325); by Gerini, at S. Croce, Florence; by a Sienese master in the Neapolitan church of Donna Regina, or that by Andrea da Firenze (c. 1350) at the Spanish chapel; lastly the splendid frescoes of Altichiero and Avanzi in the chapel of the Santo of Padua (1370).

But all this realism was never an end in itself: its object was to reach the emotions; and it made manifest the character of humanity in Christianity. Hence the many paintings of the Blessed Virgin, in which art incessantly sang to her the tenderest hymns of love. The Panagia of the Byzantines, the Virgin of the Middle Ages, Throne of God, Queen of Heaven, gave place to the Mother, the most beautiful, the sweetest, and the tenderest of women. After St. Bernard—*il suo fedele Bernardo*—St. Francis of Assisi, and St. Bonaventure, devotion to the Madonna became one of the chief Christian devotions. Schools competed as to which should paint the holiest and most exquisite Virgins, and none were more charming than those of Siena—*Sena vetus civitas Virginis*.

The Madonnas of Simone di Martino, of the two Lorenzetti, of Lippo Memmi, and their successors, began the incomparable poem to which Raphael, Van Dyck, or Murillo added perfect strophes, without, however, obliterating the memory of their ancient predecessors.

The same inspiration is evident in the paintings which represent the moral, didactic, or philosophic painting of that time, such as the frescoes of "Good and Evil Government" at Siena by the Lorenzetti (c.

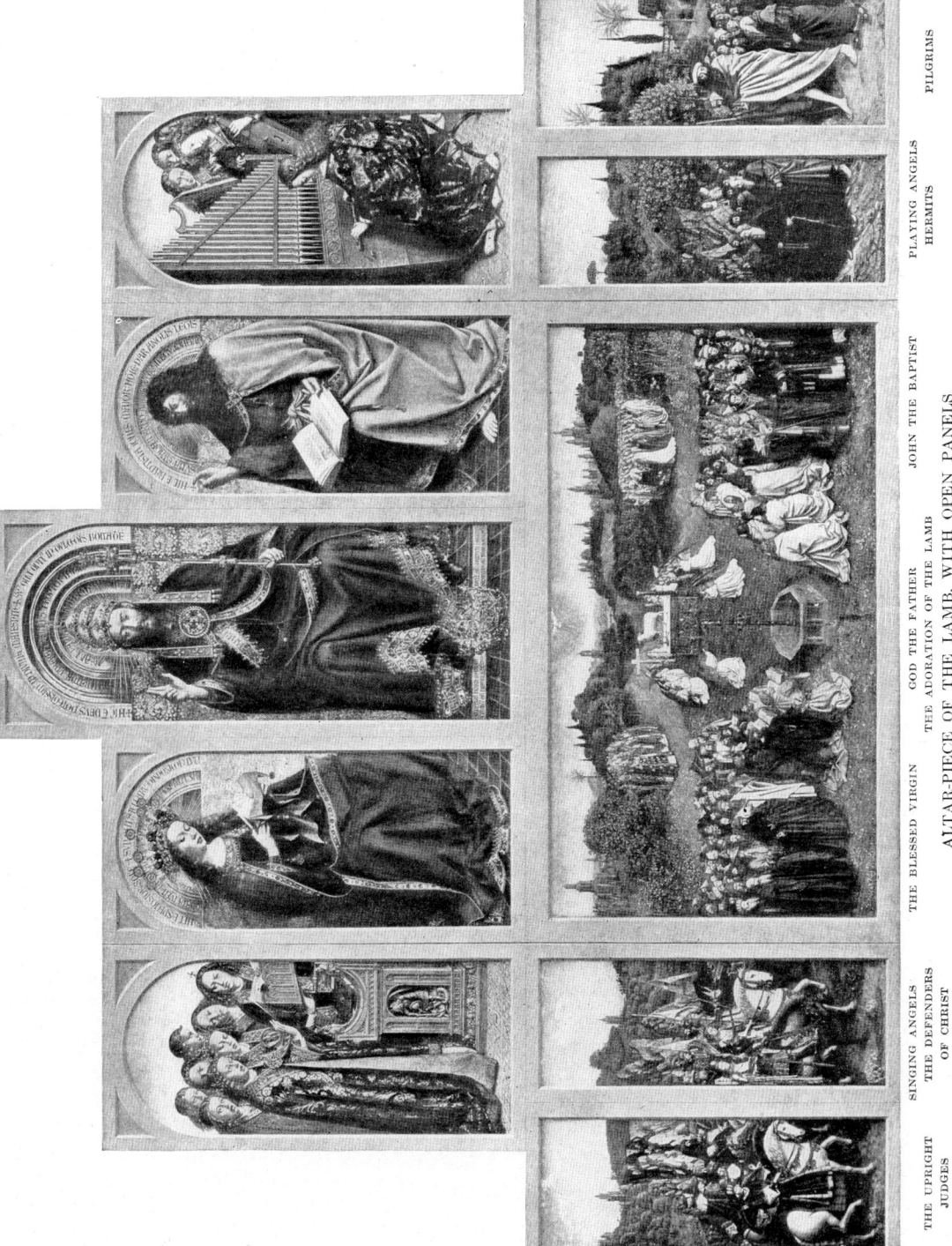

THE UPRIGHT SINGING ANGELS THE BLESSED VIRGIN GOD THE FATHER JOHN THE BAPTIST PLAYING ANGELS PILGRIMS
JUDGES THE DEFENDERS THE ADORATION OF THE LAMB HERMITS
 OF CHRIST ALTAR-PIECE OF THE LAMB, WITH OPEN PANELS
HUBERT AND JAN VAN EYCK, GHENT
(THE TWO MISSING PANELS ARE PRESERVED AT BRUSSELS)

1340), those of the Church militant and the Church teaching in the Spanish Chapel (c. 1355), or those of the "Anchorites" and the "Triumph of Death" in the Campo Santo of Pisa (c. 1370), all showing the same popular and practical character. Such pictures have the force of a sermon; there is no strictly artistic intention, but an obvious intention to instruct and impress. This is also made clear by the celebrated allegories of the Franciscan Virtues, in the lower church of Assisi (c. 1335), and in the frequent repetition of the Last Judgment (by Giotto at Padua and the Florence Signoria; by Orcagna at S. Maria Novella, etc.). This theme of death and the Judgment was evidently a favourite one with the Mendicants: at Assisi and Padua are two frescoes representing a Friar Minor indicating a skeleton beside him. And hence the "Triumph of Death" at Pisa and the terrible "Dance of Death" of northern Europe.

This popular art required popular modes of expression. Cavallini and Giotto still made mosaics, and Cimabue is best known to us as a mosaicist. But this slow and expensive method was unsuited to a democratic, sentimental, and impassioned art, while fresco, which had never been abandoned, even during the Byzantine period, offered to the new ideas a more plastic and animated mode of expression. With less material opulence, the latter process was rapid, cheap, and apt at reproducing the undulations of life, expressing at once the exactness of nature and the emotion of the artist. Thereby a new element entered into the execution itself, an individual element of sentiment and spontaneity only limited by the conditions of mural painting and the exigencies of an art always somewhat oratorical. Inebriated, as it were, with this new liberty, the Giottesque painters covered Italy with innumerable paintings. Indeed, this school, as a whole, despite grave faults, constitutes the richest and freest fund of religious painting.

(2) *Masaccio and His Age.*—But it must be acknowledged that the Giottesques formed a popular school which was too often satisfied with worthless improvisation. The task of imbuing painting with artistic feeling was that of the two great painters, Masolino (q. v.) and Masaccio (q. v.), the latter especially, in his frescoes in the Carmelite chapel at Florence (1426) sounding the keynote of the future. Nevertheless, despite their seriousness of conception and aim, the religious element of these frescoes is scarcely to be taken into account. There are evidences of great progress in the art, the nobility of ideas, the elevation of style, the seriousness and grandeur of the work, but the gain of Christian feeling and piety is less manifest. But Masaccio's powerful naturalness was for a time in harmony with the mystic sense, and religious art then yielded perhaps its most exquisite flowers. The works of Gentile da Fabriano, such as the "Adoration of the Magi" (1423; Academy of Florence), those of Pisaniello, such as the "Legend of St. George" (c. 1425; St. Anastasia, Verona), and in a lesser degree those of the Milanese Stefano da Zevio breathe the inimitable grace of a pure and holy joy, which is still more charmingly apparent in the works of the Camaldolese Lorenzo Monaco, and especially in those of the Dominican Fra Giovanni da Fiesole, whose genius won for him the surname of Angelico (q. v.).

Angelico's disciples did not reach his level, but a youthful charm distinguishes the spiritual paintings of Benozzo Gozzoli, whose "Adoration of the Magi" in the Riccardi chapel is one of the most perfect works of the Renaissance, while his "Genesis" frescoes in the Campo Santo of Pisa (1469–85) will always be loved for their exquisite figures amid rich landscapes. But perhaps this pious joy never inspired anything more lovable than the works of the old Umbrian masters, Ottaviano Nelli, Allegretto Nuzi, Domenico Bonfigli, and Boccati da Camerino. The early Renaissance was a fortunate period, in which the simplicity of the soul was not marred by the discovery of nature and art. Even the poor Carmelite Fra Filippo Lippi, unwilling monk as he was, whose restless life was far from exemplary, was animated by true and delicate piety. His "Nativity" (Berlin), his "Madonna" (Uffizi), and his "Adoration of the Holy Child" (c. 1465; Louvre) recall Angelico.

C. *The Fifteenth Century in the North.*—What Masaccio's frescoes were for fifteenth-century Italy, that and much more was the retable of the Van Eycks for the rest of Europe. This colossal work was begun in 1420, completed and set up in 1432. Throughout the fifteenth century the art of the schools of the North retained the allegorical and symbolical character which marks this great work. Such books as the "Speculum humanæ salvationis" or the "Biblia pauperum" dominated iconography and furnished artists with their favourite subjects. But, with all this, in Flanders naturalism was unrestrained, that of the Van Eycks making even Masaccio's seem vague and abstract. A portion of the change accomplished by them is foreshadowed in the works of the Limbourgs (see LIMBOURG, POL DE). To the revolution which they effected in the manner of beholding corresponds another in the manner of painting. The whole fifteenth century spoke of the "invention of the Van Eycks": it is hard to say in what this consisted, but if they did not, as was believed, discover oil-painting, they certainly invented new processes and a new style. (See EYCK, HUBERT AND JAN VAN.) Undoubtedly this realism lacked taste and charm. The types were common, vulgar, and middle-class, and these faults were even exaggerated by the disciples of the school—Jean Daret, Ouwater, Dirck Bouts, Van der Goes, and Petrus Cristus. The school's photographic impassibility, on the other hand, was suddenly offset by the equally exaggerated and somewhat contorted passion of the Brabançon Van der Weyden, at once a realist and a mystic. Such as it was, this robust school conquered Europe in a few years, even Italy feeling its powerful influence. In France, Simon Marmion, Nicolas Fremont, and Jean Fouquet were little more than somewhat refined and gallicized Flemings. In Spain it suffices to mention Luis Dalmaù and in Portugal, Nuño Gonçalez, both being pure Flemish.

German painting, on the other hand, while it owed much to the neighbouring Flemish school, remained much more original in spirit. In it is found the deep and tender sentiment lacking in the school of the Low Countries, a popular mysticism derived, not from books, but from the interior treasures of the soul. The school which produced (c. 1380) the *Clarenaltar* of Cologne and (c. 1400) the delightful little "Paradise" of Frankfort obviously possessed but mediocre gifts; its sense of form was often defective, but even the piety of Angelico did not speak a purer language. A superior plastic education produced the work of Stephan Lochner, the fine *Dombild* (1430), the "Madonna of the Violet", and the marvellously sweet "Madonna of the Rose Garden". From this school was descended the most famous of the Northern mystics, the tender and graceful Memling (q. v.). In his work a new aristocracy, that of sentiment, transfigures the Flemish opulence. The same moral delicacy and familiarity with Divine things sweeten and spiritualize the works of Gerard David, and especially of Quentin Massys, who became a painter through love. At the end of the fifteenth century there was no German town or province which had not its local school. For a long time only two of these were known or regarded: that of Cologne, with its anonymous masters, the Master of the Passion of Lyversberg, the Master of the Death of Mary, the Master of the Holy Family (*Heiligensippe*), and, most powerful of all, the Master of the *Bartholomäusaltar;* and the school of Nuremberg, with its two famous painters, Wohlgemuth and Pleydenwurff. But in reality no corner of Franconia, Suabia, Alsace, or the Tyrol remained sterile. It was a popular art, localized, sentimental, and extremely incorrect, often coarse in form, but refined in soul even to affectation, and which in its pious imagery expressed better than any other certain ideas of sympathy and tenderness. There is nothing more thrilling than the Passion of Hans Multescher nor more appealing than the altarpiece of St. Wolfgang by the Tyrolese Michel Pacher. Elsewhere in Germany there were other admirable stylists, such as Hans Baldung and Conrad Witz at Fribourg and Basle, foreshadowing the perfection of Holbein.

But the great Albrecht Dürer was to express all that was most intimate in Germanic religion, and beautiful as were his pictures he expressed the deepest meanings in his prints. This more direct and less expensive art, produced for the masses, satisfied the German demands for popularity and individuality. To this Dürer's genius was wholly devoted, and art does not possess more moving masterpieces than the "Apocalypse" series (1498), the "Life of the Blessed Virgin" (1506), the "Little Passion" (1509), and the "Great Passion" (1510). But side by side with this contemplative, intimate, and noble spiritual art was a second tendency, no less thoughtful, but impassioned, violent, dramatic, and which went to extremes in the search for expression and the mania for the pathetic. It was inspired by the mystery plays. All technical progress and perfection of realization were utilized to express emotion. It began with Van der Weyden, Memling did not escape it in his Munich picture of the "Seven Sorrows of the Blessed Virgin", Massys painted bloodbesprinkled Holy Faces and Magdalens with reddened and streaming eyes, Dürer's "Passions" terrify by their intensity of sorrow, but the most tragic of all was Mathias Grünewald, whose terrible "Crucifixions" at Colmar and Stuttgart are like the nightmare of a barbarian visionary. This love of the horrible became a *genre*. Infernal fantasies, the dreams of an unhealthy imagination, haunt the thoughts of Jerome Bosch, while, on the other hand, idyllic insipidity and childishness appear in the "Holy Family" and "Flight into Egypt" of Cranach and Patenier. At this juncture came the Reformation, which destroyed painting in Germany.

IV. THE CINQUE CENTO AND THE LATER SCHOOLS.— A. *Tuscany, Umbria, and Rome.*—The two tendencies observed in the North, naturalism and pathos, developed also in contemporary Italy. Protestant criticism has greatly exaggerated the irreligion of the Renaissance. Undoubtedly some painters, absorbed by problems of expression and the study of atmosphere, models, and perspective, neglected religious emotions. At Florence especially there were a number of artists who saw in their craft only a question of form. Form, as a matter of fact, owes much of its progress to the studies of Castagno, Paolo Uccello, the Pollaiuoli, Andrea Verrocchio, and Baldovinetti, but their learning, importance, and great services cannot conceal the poverty of their art and the narrowness of their ideas; they were professors and useful pedagogues, but neither poets nor true artists. On the other hand the Renaissance was the period when the love of ideas, so unnatural to Italian thought, manifested itself by most important works. The decoration of the Sistine Chapel (c. 1480) at the command of a Franciscan pope, is perhaps the most clearly symbolical assemblage of Italian art. On the walls the life of Moses is portrayed parallel with that of Christ. Thirty years later Michelangelo depicted on the ceiling the Delivery of Israel, the Prophets, the Sibyls, and the Ancestors of Christ. The Appartamento Borgia was decorated by Pinturicchio with didactic frescoes in imitation of the Spanish chapel; Filippino Lippi represented at the Minerva the "Triumph of St. Thomas Aquinas"; while Perugino at the Cambio of Perugia and Raphael in his *stanze* produced the masterpieces of the painting of ideas.

It would be vain to deny that the spirit of the Renaissance possessed irreligious tendencies. Certainly such a work as that of Ghirlandajo in the choir of S. Maria Novella is singularly secular in tone. Even in more serious works, such as Leonardo's wonderful "Last Supper" at Milan, it is readily seen that despite its sublime beauty it was not intended merely to edify. However, these matters must be treated with reserve, owing to the delicate nature of questions of religious sincerity. We can hardly assert that the Dominicans for whom these works were executed were poorer judges than we, nor is it clear by what right we connect religious meaning with certain archaic forms. In this the Church has judged with more delicacy, never having restricted a sentiment to certain forms, but having left it free to create that most fitting to it and to speak to each age the language which will be best understood. The fact is that at no period was religious activity so fruitful; no other has bequeathed to us so many altar-pieces, oratory pictures, Madonnas and saints. It was the age of countless pictures for pious confraternities, and it is quite probable that the artist, who was so often a member of the confraternity, infused something of his heart into his work. At Siena especially such charming painters as Vecchietta or Benvenuto di Giovanni were no less remarkable for their piety than their talents. Perugino, it is true, has been called an Atheist, but of this we have no certainty, nor do we know Vasari's authority for the statement. On the other hand we note in him (before he lapsed into mechanical production) a reaction against dryness and intellectualism. (See PERUGINO.) Botticelli and Filippino Lippi show a tendency to the nervous pathos of Roger van der Weyden and Quentin Massys. An extremely ascetic and terrifying spirit distinguishes Luca Signorelli.

More worthy of study are the works of Crivelli and Cosimo Tura at Verona and Ferrara, showing a love for depicting suffering which borders on caricature. At Bologna, on the other hand, the productions of Costa and Francia are marked by a more temperate religious emotion, while a group of Milanese painters including Foppa and Borgognone upheld, even amid Leonardo's influence, the mystical traditions of the ancient school. The appearance of new *motifs* based on devotion to the Precious Blood, to the Holy Family, the maternity of the Blessed Virgin, etc., indicated the continuous enriching of religious life and the constant activity of Christian piety. Undoubtedly when Leonardo painted the "St. Anne" of the Louvre, and Raphael his "Madonna of the Goldfinch", they did not aim at portraying ascetic mortification, but rather a serene confidence in the beauty and nobility of life. It is difficult to stamp this optimism as an error.

B. *Venice and the Schools of Northern Italy.*—The Venetian school has been greatly misjudged from a religious standpoint. Because the Venetians could paint better than any others, and because they set great value on the charm of colouring, they have been charged with paganism and immorality. Quite the contrary is true. Two very different traditions are evident in Venetian painting: the first that of the popular painters employed by the confraternities, the guilds, and the *scuole;* the other that of the official painters in the service of the State, the patricians, and the convents. The former school, which was that of Lazzaro Bastiani Carpaccio, Cima da Conegliano, and Diana, filled the parishes of Venice and the Islands with brilliant and delightfully ingenuous works. Nothing could be more charming than Carpaccio's paintings, such as his Legend of St. Ursula or the oratory pictures in San Giorgio de' Schiavoni. The second and more scholarly school, proceeding from the Vivarini and the great Paduan master, Andrea Mantegna, is chiefly represented by the three Bellini, the last of whom, Giovanni, is not only one of the most beautiful of painters, but also one of the most elevated and recollected. The works of Giorgione are no less poetically inspired, and his heads of Christ are marvels of emotion. It may be questioned how Titian can be charged with irreligion in his "Assumption", his Pesaro Madonna, his "Martyrdom of St. Lawrence", his frescoes in the Santo of Padua, or his "Death of St. Peter Martyr". In his "Bacchanal" of Madrid and the "Flora" of the Uffizi we encounter the same problem presented by Raphael, which then faced all cultured minds. We can scarcely accuse of religious insincerity the author of the "Entombment" and "Crowning with Thorns" of the Louvre, who after so many joyous pictures painted as his last testament and farewell to life the funereal "Pietà" of the Accademia of Venice. The same is true of the other great Venetians, Palma, Veronese, Bonifazio, Tintoretto, and the divine Correggio.

But the Church was obliged by harsh criticism to be vigilant with regard to humanistic extremes. At Florence the work of Fra Bartolommeo or Andrea del Sarto, at Ferrara that of Garofalo, at Brescia that of Moretto or Romanino, at Vercelli that of Gaudenzio Ferrari, at Venice itself that of Lorenzo Lotto, are so many heralds of a "counter-reformation", which became definite about 1550, at the time of the Council of Trent, and which derived its origin from Venice. A significant circumstance was the action of the Inquisition against Veronese for having introduced fanciful figures into his religious pictures. The painter was acquitted, but the art of the Renaissance had received a blow from which it never recovered. It was the period when the pope ordered Daniele di Volterra (Ricciarelli) to clothe decently the too audacious nakedness of his "Last Judgment", when the learned Molanus (Meulen) wrote his work on images, when St. Charles Borromeo and his cousin the cardinal, with their circle of zealous associates, preached a return to an enlightened, serious religion, purified of popular medieval superstitions and recovered from the dangerous compromise with the external forms of pagan naturalism (cf. J. A. Symond's "Renaissance in Italy: The Catholic Reaction", I, i–iv). After having exercised great toleration the Church was about to take vigorously in hand the direction of ideas. Tintoretto's last works at the Scuola di S. Rocco display a system of symbols as abstract as a stained-glass window of the thirteenth century; painting once more became the handmaid of theology. From Venice itself came the last Byzantine, the strange Greco, the pupil of Titian and Veronese, whose emaciated, sickly, dried-up style is a protest against the whole luxuriant ideal of the Renaissance, and who became the founder of Spanish painting.

C. *The Baroque School.*—The most striking trait of the new school was its unity of style and method. In the fifteenth and even in the sixteenth century there was an endless number of little schools, each town having its own, but in the seventeenth century painting once more became international. A single manner of seeing and thinking predominated and there was no essential difference between a Flemish and an Italian or Spanish picture. More than one social or political reason may be advanced for this, e. g., the political supremacy of Spain and the establishment of the Viceroyalty of Naples, or the cosmopolitanism of the painters. But the only good reason was the existence of a general organization, a universal institute which forced a common direction on all ideas. But the time has gone by when the word *baroque* was used to disparage two centuries of art, as the word *Gothic* thinly disguised a condemnation. What science is to the modern world the idea of beauty was to sixteenth-century Italy. Thus the lost Grecian ideal was restored through Florence and Venice, but the cultivation of the form without thought for its import was what dried up and poisoned the school which issued from Raphael and especially from Michelangelo, the art of Giulio Romano, Zuccheri, Vasari, and Giuseppino. Before the end of the century a strong reaction set in against this corrupt and empty art. In 1582 the Carracci founded their academy at Bologna, and at Rome, about the same time, the independent and eccentric Caravaggio scandalized the public by brutal painting roughly borrowed from the lowest reality. In his "Death of the Blessed Virgin" (c. 1605) now at the Louvre he did not hesitate to copy a drowned woman. Nevertheless Caravaggio did much to turn art once more in the direction of nature and truth. His "Entombment", at the Vatican, is one of the important works of modern painting and the manifestation of a new art.

Thus, of its own volition, art inclined to return to naturalism while religion endeavoured to hold it back. St. Ignatius in his "Spiritual Exercises" indicates the share of sentiment and imagination in the psychology of belief, laying great stress on the "composition of place" and the use of the senses as aids to the imagination with the object of arousing an emotion. It will readily be seen what assistance painting would be to such a system, and that is why the Jesuits restored to art all the importance which the Protestants had taken from it. Naturalism was the necessary result of this spirit, and in this Jesuit art merely resumed the constant tradition of Christianity. Nor was this all; the picture should inspire emotion, and the corollary of naturalism was pathos. By more than one characteristic the Catholic school of the seventeenth century recalls the great Franciscan school of the fourteenth. A curious fact is the recurrence of popularity of Franciscan legend. The "Vision of St. Francis", the "Stigmata", the "Vision of St. Anthony of Padua", the "Last Communion of St. Francis of Assisi" are the titles of masterpieces in the schools of Antwerp, Bologna, Naples, and Seville. A still more significant circumstance was that the Renaissance, like the ancient Byzantine art, had avoided all portrayal of the sufferings of Christ: Raphael, Titian, or Michelangelo never painted a Crucifixion, though among the masterpieces of Rubens were an "Ascent of Calvary", an "Erection of the Cross", a "Piercing with the Lance", and a "Descent from the Cross". The Renaissance had also lost the taste for and the sense of narrative; but the art of the seventeenth century presents numerous examples of this ability restored, such as the "Life of St. Cecilia" at S. Luigi di Francesi and the "Life of St. Nilus" at Grottaferrata, by Domenichino; the Lives of St. Thomas and St. Peter Nolasco by Zurbaran, etc. The Gospel and the "Legenda aurea" were restored to honour. If the Renaissance had been a retrogression or an eclipse of Christian sentiment, Baroque art was a real resurrection.

V. MODERN RELIGIOUS PAINTING.—Great religious painting ends with Tiepolo; his Spanish imitators, Bayeù and Goya, produced charming works, but did nothing new. Save for a few somewhat touching works of Lesueur the classic French school was wholly lacking in religious originality. Philippe de Champagne was a Fleming, a good painter whose talent Jansenism almost destroyed. New theories and the spirit of the eighteenth century struck a fatal blow against the painting of the Church. To the admirers of extreme antiquity such as Winckelmann and Lessing, and their disciple, Diderot, Christianity was an inferior religion which had diffused an unworthy system of æsthetics throughout the world. European painting was dominated by a sort of artistic Jacobinism. David and his school produced no religious painting; under the Empire the only "Christ" worthy of mention is that of the gentle Prud'hon. However, a curious reaction followed this arid fanaticism; the

Middle Ages began to be understood. Even under the Directory and in David's studio there was a small body calling themselves the "Primitifs". Chateaubriand's "Genius of Christianity" was published on the same day as the Concordat of 1802. At Rome a little circle of German artists, weary of Goethe's Hellenic rationalism, returned to mysticism, discovered St. Francis of Assisi, and by painting reopened the sources of the moral life. Unfortunately these "Nazarenes", Overbeck, Steinle, and the rest, had but a poor artistic sense. A Frenchman, Jean Dominique Ingres, had better success and endowed with life his "Bestowal of the Keys" (1820), his "Vow of Louis XIII" (1824), his "St. Symphorian" (1834), and some of his Virgins.

Other painters also treated religious subjects: the Protestant Ary Scheffer, Paul Delaroche, even Decamps. But the only one who succeeds in arousing emotion is Paul Delacroix, whose "Christ on Mt. Olivet" (1827), "Descent from the Cross" (1834), "Good Samaritan" at Mantua, "Christ Stilling the Tempest", and especially his Chapel of the Angels in the church of St. Sulpice, are examples of immortal passion and poetry. With Flandrin's frescoes may be mentioned those of Victor Mottoz at St. Germain l'Auxerrois, of Chassériau at St. Roch, and especially the splendid scenes from the "Legend of St. Genevieve" (1878–98) by Puvis de Chavannes in the old Pantheon. Henner and Léon Bonnat have painted famous Christs; Ernest Hébert has painted Virgins such as that of "The Deliverance" (1872) which are real masterpieces. Some of Bouguereau's are also worthy of mention.

But in France, as elsewhere, religious painting properly so called tends to disappear. The attempts of some sincere painters in England and Germany have had but few imitators. Despite rare merits, the Pre-Raphaelite school has left only studied works in which scholarship supersedes sentiment. This is especially true of Burne-Jones and Rossetti, whose style too often shows affectation and artifice. James Tissot, with his scrupulous Orientalism, has failed to capture the true Evangelical perfume. The best work of this school has been produced by Holman Hunt in his "Scapegoat" and "Shadow of the Cross", which display singular refinement, somewhat hardened by emphasis, but new, impressive, and original. The German Gebhardt does not approach these masterpieces in his "Last Supper" of the Berlin Museum. A recent Franciscan Pre-Raphaelitism in France has produced the prints of Charles Marie Dulac and some charming decorations of Maurice Denis, such as his "Assumption" in the church of Vésinet.

The reason for this impoverishment of religious art must not be sought in a diminution of the Christian sentiment. It is due primarily to the fact that religious art has become an industry and concurrence is no longer possible between the artists and the dealers, but the chief reason lies in the very evolution of religious ideas, which now seek a new form. This has been shown by the painter John La Farge ("Higher Life in Art," 1908). Much of the religious sentiment of the nineteenth century has been expressed in landscape painting. To the angelic soul of Corot painting was always a prayer, and the same is true of our greatest Christian painter, Millet, whose peasants naturally assume the appearance of Biblical characters, as of the paintings of the same class by Léon Lhermitte ("Pilgrims of Emmaus", 1894, Boston Museum; "Among the Lowly", 1905, New York Museum), those of Lérolle, Fritz von Uhde, and especially of Eugène Carrière.

Such are the outlines of religious painting during the past 900 years. Ancient Christianity expressed every sentiment and ignored no shade of human nature. And if religious painting now seems uncertain in Europe, in view of the great movement incessantly impelling from East to West and in consideration of the wonderful development of the Church in the New World, who knows what future still awaits it in America?

GENERAL: SEROUX D'AGINCOURT, *Hist. de l'art par les monuments* (Paris, 1892), 6 vols. in fol.; WINTER AND DEHIO, *Kuntsgeschichte in Bildern* (5 vols., Leipzig, 1899–1900); REINACH, *Répertoire de peintures antérieures au XVIIIe s.* (3 vols., Paris, 1905–10); KRAUS, *Geschichte der christlichen Kunst* (Freib. im Breisg., 1895–1900); WOERMANN AND WOLTMANN, *Geschichte de Malerei* (Leipzig, 1879–88); MICHEL, *Histoire de l'art depuis les premiers temps chrétiens jusqu'à nos jours* (Paris, 1895); VENTURI, *Storia dell' Arte Italiana* (Milan, 1901); BURCKHARDT, *Le Cicerone* (Paris, 1892); LOWRIE, *Christian Art and Archæology* (New York, 1901); GRADMANN, *Geschichte der christlichen Kunst* (Stuttgart, 1902); MUTHER, *History of Painting from the Fourth to the Eighteenth Century* (New York, 1907).

SPECIAL: First period.—DE ROSSI, *Roma Sotterranea* (Rome, 1864–67); PÉRATÉ, *L'archéologie chrétienne* (Paris, 1892); SCHULTZE, *Archæologie de altchristlichen Kunst* (Munich, 1895); MARUCCHI, *Le catacombe romane* (Rome, 1903); IDEM, *Elementa d'archéologie chrétienne* (Paris, 1899–1902); WILPERT, *Die Katacombengemälde* (Freiburg, 1892).

Second period.—DIEHL, *Manuel d'art byzantin* (Paris, 1910); STRZYGOWSKI, *Orient oder Rom* (Leipzig, 1902); IDEM, *Kleinasien* (Leipzig, 1903); KONDAKOFF, *Histoire de l'art byzantin considéré principalement dans les miniatures*, French tr. (Paris, 1886–91); AINALOW, *Origines hellénistiques de l'art byzantin* (St. Petersburg, 1900); SCHULTZ AND BARNSLEY, *The monastery of St. Luke of Stiris in Phocis* (London, 1902); MILLET, *Le monastère de Daphni* (Paris, 1899); DIDRON, *Manuel de la peinture* (Paris, 1845).

Third period.—KRAUS, BURCKHARDT, MICHEL, etc., opp. cit. above; MALE, *L'art religieux en France au XIIIe siècle* (2nd ed., Paris, 1902); IDEM, *L'art religieux en France à la fin du moyen âge* (Paris, 1908); DIDRON, *Iconographie chrétienne* (Paris, 1843); DIDRON AND CAHIER, *Les Vitraux de Bourges* (Paris, 1846); MÜNTZ, *Les Précurseurs de la Renaissance* (Paris, 1882; Italian ed., Florence, 1902); MÜNTZ, *Histoire de l'art pendant la Renaissance* (Paris, 1889–95); WÖLFFLIN, *Die Klassische Kunst, Einführung in die Italienische Renaissance* (Munich, 1901); CROWE AND CAVALCASELLE, *Geschichte der Italienischen Malerei* (Leipzig, 1869–76; English ed., London, 1903); THODE, *Franz von Assisi und die Anglänge der Kunst in Italien* (Berlin, 1903; French tr., 1909); L. DOUGLAS, *History of Siena* (London, 1902); IDEM, *Fra Angelico* (London, 1902); JANITSCHEK, *Geschichte der deutschen Malerei* (Berlin, 1890); RÉAU, *Les Primitifs allemands* (Paris, 1910); BOUCHOT, *Les Primitifs français* (Paris, 1904); SAMFERE Y MIGUEL, *Quattrocentistas catalañas* (Barcelona, 1907); BERTAUX, *L'Exposition de Saragosse* (1911); CROWE AND CAVALCASELLE, *Les anciens peintres flamands* (Brussels, 1862–63); DEHAISNES, *De l'art chrétien en Flandre* (Douai, 1860); WEALE, *The Early Painters of the Netherlands* in *Burlington Magazine* (1903); IDEM, *Hans Memlinc* (London, 1902); BERENSON, *Lorenzo Lotto* (London, 1902); COSSIO, *El Greco* (Madrid, 1908); BROUSSOLLE, *L'art religieux pendant la Renaissance* (Paris, 1908).

Fourth period.—EBE, *Die Spätrenaissance* (Berlin, 1886); GURLITT, *Geschichte des Barockstiles* (Stuttgart, 1887–89); FRASCHETTI, *Il Bernini* (Milan, 1900); BOEHM, *Guido Reni* (Bielefeld, 1910); FUSTI, *Murillo* (Leipzig, 1892); FROMENTIN, *Les Maîtres d'autrefois* (Paris, 1876); BODE, *Studien zur geschichte der holländischen Malerei* (Brunschurg, 1883); VENTURI, *Tiepolo*, French tr. (Paris, 1911).

Fifth period.—DELABORDE, *Hippolyte Flandrin* (Paris, 1872); IDEM, *Ingres* (Paris, 1867); ROLLAND, *J. L. Millet* (London, 1903); STEINLE, *Briefwechsel* (Fribourg, 1898); DE LA SIZERAUNE, *La peinture anglaise contemporaine* (3rd ed., Paris, 1903); IDEM, *Ruskin et la religion de la Beauté* (5th ed., 1903); IDEM, *Le miroir de la vie* (Paris, 1902); W. H. HUNT, *The Preraphaelite Brotherhood* (London, 1906); SÉAILLES, *Eugène Carrière* (Paris, 1911).

LOUIS GILLET.

Pakawá Indians, also written Pacoá, one of a group of cognate tribes, hence designated the Pakawán (formerly Coahuiltecan) stock, formerly ranging on the upper waters of the San Antonio and Nueces rivers, in Southern Texas, and extending to or beyond the Rio Grande. The group comprised at least fifty small tribes—few of which contained more than two or three hundred souls—the principal being the Pakawá, Payaya, Sanipao, Tilijae, Pamaque, and Xarame. They are notable for their connexion with the famous San Antonio missions and for the record which Father García has left of their language, which appears to have been used over a considerable area for intertribal communication. Almost nothing is known of the ethnology of the Pakawán tribes, which were of low culture, without agriculture or fixed habitation, but roving from place to place, subsisting upon game and the wild fruits of the mesquite, pecan, and cactus, dwelling under temporary shelters of brushwood and grass thatch, and with very little tribal cohesion or organization. While their neighbours, the Tónkawa and other tribes of eastern Texas were notorious cannibals, this was probably not true of the Pakawá who,

AMONG THE LOWLY

LÉON LHERMITTE, 1905, METROPOLITAN MUSEUM, NEW YORK

while inconstant, seem to have been of unwarlike and generally friendly disposition.

The first civilized men to encounter the Pakawán tribes were the shipwrecked Cabeza de Vaca and his three companions, survivors of the Narváez expedition, who spent seven years (1529–1536) wandering over the Texas plains before finally reaching Mexico. It is possible also that the Pakawá were represented among the neophytes whom the Franciscan Father Andrés de Olmos drew out of Texas and established under the name of Olives in a Tamaulijas mission in 1544. The earliest known missionary effort among the Pakawán tribes is that of the Franciscan Damian Massanet (or Manzanet), the father of the Texas missions, who in 1691 stopped at the village of the Payaya tribe, near the present San Antonio, set up a cross and altar and said Mass in the presence of the tribe, explaining the meaning of the ceremony, afterwards distributing rosaries and gaining the good will of the chief by the gift of a horse. Throughout their history the Spanish Texas missions were in charge of Franciscans, directed from the Colleges of Zacatecas and Querétaro in Mexico. In 1718 was established the Spanish *presidio*, or garrison post, which later grew into the city of San Antonio. In the same year the mission of San Francisco Solano, founded in 1700 on the Rio Grande, was removed by Fr. Antonio de Olivares to the neighbourhood of the new post and renamed San Antonio de Valero, famous later as the Alamo. The principal tribe represented was the Xarame. Other establishments followed until in 1731 there were within a few miles of San Antonio five missions, occupied almost exclusively by Indians of Pakawán stock, viz:

(1) San Antonio de Valero (later, the Alamo)—1718—on San Antonio river, opposite the city. In 1762 it had 275 neophytes. (2) San José y San Miguel de Aguayo—1720—six miles below San Antonio. This was the principal and most flourishing of the Texas missions, and residence of the superior, with what was said to be the finest church in New Spain. In 1762 it had 350 neophytes, and 1500 yoke of work oxen. (3) Purísima Concepción de Acuña (originally a Caddo mission in east Texas), removed 1731 to San Antonio river just below the city. In 1762 it had 207 neophytes. (4) San Juan Capistrano (originally the Caddo mission of San José in east Texas), removed 1731 to San Antonio river about seven miles below the city. In 1762 it had 203 neophytes, with 5000 horses, cattle, and sheep. (5) San Francisco de la Espada (originally a Caddo mission in east Texas), removed 1731 to San Antonio river, nine miles below the city. The chief tribes represented were the Pacao, Pajalat, and Pitalac, numbering together about 1000 souls. In 1762 it had 207 neophytes with some 6000 cattle, horses, sheep, and goats. It was here that Father García wrote his "Manual". The ruins are locally known as the "fourth mission".

The missions probably reached their zenith about 1740. In that or the preceding year an epidemic disease wasted the Texas tribes, and about the same time the jealousies of the San Antonio settlers and the increasingly frequent raids of the wild Lipán and Comanche checked further development. In 1762 an official report showed 1242 neophytes, although the missions were already on the decline. In 1778 smallpox ravaged the whole Texas area, practically exterminating several small tribes. In 1793 the report showed fewer than 300 neophytes remaining in the five missions, and in the next year they were formally dissolved by official Spanish order, provision being made for securing a portion of lands to the few surviving Indians. Some of the monks remained and continued their ministrations for at least ten years longer. In 1801 another smallpox visitation practically completed the destruction of the tribes. In 1886 Dr. Albert Gatschet, of the Bureau of Ethnology, could find only 28 representatives of the stock, all on the Mexican side of the Rio Grande in the neighbourhood of Camargo. Excepting for a short vocabulary collected by him, our only knowledge of the language is derived from Fr. Bartholomé García's "Manual para administrar los santos sacramentos, etc." (1760), written in Pakawá for the San Antonio missions and published in 1760.

BANCROFT, *Hist. of the North Mexican States and Texas* (San Francisco, 1886–9); BOLTON in HODGE, *Handbook Am. Inds.* (*Bur. Am. Ethn. Bulletin*), Texas tribal and mission articles (2 pts., Washington, 1907–10); GARRISON, *Texas* (Boston, 1903); PILLING, *Proofsheets of a Bibliography of the Languages of the N. Am. Inds.* (Bur. Ethnology, Washington, 1885), for García title; SHEA, *Hist. of the Catholic Church in the United States* (New York, 1886).

JAMES MOONEY.

Palæography (παλαιά, "ancient", γραφή, "writing"), the art of deciphering ancient writing in manuscripts or diplomas. It is distinguished from epigraphy, which provides rules for reading carved inscriptions, and from diplomatics, which studies the intrinsic character of written documents, while palæography concerns itself only with written characters and the classification of documents by their external characters.

During the Renaissance period the reading of manuscripts, necessary to the printing of classic authors, became widespread, but it was only in the seventeenth century that scholars thought of reducing their observations to a system and formulating rules for the reading of manuscripts and diplomas. As early as 1681, in the first edition of his "De re diplomatica", Mabillon devoted a study (I, xi) to the various kinds of Latin writing, and gave specimens of these in the plates accompanying his book. It was on this model that Montfaucon, after having worked on the editions of the Greek Fathers, published his "Palæographia Græca" (Paris, 1708), simultaneously creating the word and the thing. From that time, thanks to the labours of Villoison, Natalis de Wailly, Léopold Delisle, and Henri Omont in France, of Thompson in England, of Gardthausen in Germany, palæography has become the basis of all study of historical, religious, or literary texts. There are as many branches of palæography as there are different kinds of writings, but the science of Oriental written characters is as yet hardly formed. In general students have had to be content with determining the place of each character in the succession of such characters. (See Ph. Berger, "Histoire de l'écriture dans l'antiquité", Paris, 1892.) In 1819, however, Kopp, in his "Palæographia Critica", laid the foundations for Oriental palæography, while devoting himself exclusively to Semitic languages. The province of palæology, therefore, more particularly consists of Greek and Latin characters, together with all those derived therefrom (Gothic alphabets, Slavic, etc.).

I. GREEK PALÆOGRAPHY covers two periods: A. Antiquity (till the fourth century after Christ); B. the Byzantine Period (from the fourth century to modern times).

A. *Antiquity.*—This period is much better known to-day, owing to the numerous discoveries of papyri which have been made in Egypt (see MANUSCRIPTS). The differences between the various modes of writing are not so marked as in Latin documents. Besides, the material employed influenced the form of the letters: papyrus does not lend itself as well as parchment to rounded forms. The chief systems of characters used on papyrus are: (1) The Capital, employed somewhat rarely, and chiefly known through inscriptions. On the papyri it is already mixed with uncial forms. One of the most ancient documents of this writing is the papyrus called the "Invocation of Artemis" (Library of Vienna, third century B. C.). The words are not separated from one another, and the uncial form of the lunar *sigma* C is found. The greater number of the other letters—A, E, P, Π, etc.—have the same form as in the inscriptions.

(2) *The Uncial.*—The term is borrowed by analogy from Latin palæology. A passage from St. Jerome ("In Job", ed. D. Valarsii, ix, 100) proves that capital writing was formerly designated uncial. The term is now conventionally applied to rounded forms as distinguished from the square forms of the capital. It does not appear to have been definitively formed until the Hellenistic period, and then chiefly at Alexandria. The most characteristic uncial letters are: ᴀ ᴀ, Δ Δ, Ɛ Ɛ, ᴍ ᴍ, ⵎ ⵣ, C, ω ω. The first four of these letters have similar forms in the Latin alphabet. On the papyri thus composed (Papyrus of Chrysippus in the Louvre, end of third century B. C.; fragment of Euripides on parchment at Berlin, 100 B. C.; papyrus of the Constitution of Athens in British Museum, first century after Christ), the abbreviations are few, the words are not separated, and punctuation is rare. The accents and breathings perfected by the grammarians of Alexandria appear by degrees. (3) *The Cursive*, directly derived from the capital, the forms of which it retained for a long time. The letters are joined by ligatures which allowed the writer to write flowingly without raising his *calamus* after each letter. This writing is chiefly used on administrative papyri for accounts, census, contracts, letters, reports, etc.; it is found, however, in copies of literary works and a part of the Constitution of Athens, cited above, is written in cursive writing. In this writing the α takes the minuscule form, the B retains its capital form or takes the simplified appearance of *u*; the H has the form of ƥ; from the Roman period only dates ᴍ, ᴍ the prolongation of the first stroke of the ᴍ, ᴍ. The majuscule cursive, which is that of the ancient papyri, is distinguished from the minuscule cursive, used on the papyri of the sixth and seventh centuries.

B. *Byzantine Period.*—The history of Greek writing in the Middle Ages is more or less parallel with that of Latin. Until the ninth century uncials predominated. (Manuscripts in epigraphical capitals were not found in the East as in the West.) In the ninth century there arose in the Eastern, as in the Carlovingian, Empire a minuscule which became the customary script of manuscripts, but which always retained its traditional forms more faithfully than did the Latin character. The uncial is the chief script of parchment MSS. from the fourth to the ninth century. Dated MSS. written at this period are rare, and no more than its beginning and ending can be determined. According to the rules laid down by Montfaucon and Gardthausen, a manuscript is ancient in proportion as its characters resemble those of inscriptions. The most ancient MSS. have disconnected letters and abbreviations; they incline to rounded or almost square forms; the letters are nearly always of an equal height; the strokes are slightly marked; as a general thing, the simplest forms are the most ancient. The position of the initials is also an indication: not much larger than other letters on the papyri, they begin to spread over the margin in the fourth century, and soon acquire great importance; they are at first black, but are later embellished with colours. Such is the character of the ancient uncial, one of the most important specimens of which is furnished by the fourth-century "Codex Sinaiticus" (q. v.). The same is true of the "Dioscorides" of Vienna, written about A. D. 506, in which is found the abbreviation ℸ for *ov*.

The new uncial, on the other hand, appeared only at the end of the seventh and during the eighth century. To the square and round letters succeeded elongated characters terminating in a point; right angles were replaced by sharp corners; circles became pointed and tapering ovals. The origins of this style have been mistakenly sought in the ancient papyri (see Gardthausen, "Byz. Zeit.", XI, 112): examples of it may, indeed, be found in marginal glosses of the sixth- and seventh-century Syriac MSS. preserved in London, but this is all. The style appears fully formed chiefly in the MSS. of the ninth and tenth centuries. Through all these MSS. is traced the growing use of breathings and accents. Ligatures and abbreviations become more frequent. Beginning with the tenth century, dated uncial MSS. multiply. Script, hitherto sloping, becomes almost perpendicular. In Cod. Vat. 354 (dated 949) reappear the round, full forms, which increased in number in the eleventh and twelfth centuries. In the Evangelary of Harlei 5589 (dated 995) the B assumes the appearance of a Slavic letter Б Б, the Δ and the Θ are ornamented with little points, we meet with ligatures and abbreviations, ȣ, ᴅ for τοῦ and τά etc. Soon, especially in religious books, round letters returned to favour. There then arose a liturgical uncial with ornamented letters (eleventh and twelfth cent.). The papyri of the Byzantine period (sixth and seventh centuries) show the minuscule cursive, distinguished from the majuscule cursive by the greater ease with which the letters are joined by means of ligatures, and by more frequent abbreviations. This script, which is characteristic of papyri, is found only exceptionally in parchment MSS.: traces of it are found in the ninth-century Codex Bezæ in the possession of the University of Cambridge (see Codex Bezæ).

Minuscule character appears suddenly in Greek MSS. of the ninth century, at the very time when it was taking root in the West as a consequence of the Carlovingian reform. As in the West, it was destined to supplant all others. It has been thought, not without probability, that St. Theodore the Studite (759–826), who attached such importance to the copying of MSS., was instrumental in this reform. The cursive minuscule may have furnished the elements for this character; it appears, however, chiefly as the continuation of the small uncial, which increases in refinement in the MSS. of the eighth century. Thence arose the idea of combining the advantages of the uncial with that of the cursive, and the new writing quickly spread through all the monastic studios of the Greek world. Definitively adopted for the copying of MSS. and engrossing of diplomas, it never underwent such radical changes as did the Carlovingian. Its development may, however, be divided into three stages: (1) Ancient Minuscule (ninth to end of tenth century), connected with the cursive of the papyri, but with the letters more carefully separated, in spite of the ligatures. (2) Middle Minuscule (from middle of tenth to end of eleventh century) shows a revival of the uncial and the cursive. The MSS. of this period evidence particular care; except for the ascenders, or uprights, which go beyond the line, the letters are of an almost equal height; the words are generally separated and the abbreviations, still limited, follow precise rules. (3) The New Minuscule (twelfth century to modern times) acquires an increasingly obscure appearance because of the growth of abbreviations and ligatures. Besides, the employment of paper, which was partly substituted for parchment, contributed to make it assume a more cursive character. One of the most characteristic letters is the B, which is found under the cursive form 𝒰 until the twelfth century and then resumes its normal shape.

The three alphabets (Gardthausen, op. cit. infra in bibliography, tables 5, 6, 9) are:

α υ γ δ ϵ ʒ h θ ɩ υ ʌ μ μ 3 ο ϖ ρ σ τ υ φ χ † ω
α υ γ δ ϵ ʒ υ θ ɩ κ ʌ μ ρ ʒ ο ϖ ρ σ τ υ φ χ † ω
α β γ δ ϵ ζ н θ ɩ κ λ μ μ ρ ʒ ο ϖ ρ σ τ υ φ χ ψ ω

The first printers adopted this minuscule character for their type. Until the eighteenth century books printed in Greek retained a part of the ligatures and a large number of the abbreviations of the minuscule of the MSS. It was also adopted by imperial or episcopal chanceries for copying diplomas.

Abbreviations.—In Greek handwriting two sorts of abbreviations are to be distinguished. (1) Those of religious MSS. are the most ancient, being found in uncial MSS. and transmitted by tradition to the minuscule. The abbreviation is effected by the suppression of vowels and indicated by a bar. The nouns thus abbreviated were those having a religious character.

$\overline{\Theta \Sigma}$ Θεός $\overline{\Theta KO\Sigma}$ Θεοτόκος $\overline{IH\Lambda}$ Ἰσραήλ
$\overline{I C}$ Ἰησοῦς $\overline{I\Lambda HM}$ Ἱερουσαλήμ $\overline{I\omega}$ Ἰωάννης
$\overline{XC}$ Χριστός $\overline{CTPOC}$ σταυρός

(2) In minuscule MSS. abbreviations are made by interrupting the word and cutting off the last letter with a transverse line. For the reader's assistance the scribe retained the characteristic consonance of the last syllable. These abbreviations, tables of which will be found in the works of Montfaucon and Gardthausen, are by far the most numerous and increase from the beginning of the thirteenth century. Examples:—

ἀδ/ (ἀδελφός), αὐγ/ (αὔγουστος), γ/ (γίνεται), εἰκ/ (εἰκόνος), εἰρ/ (εἰρήνη).

Abbreviations by superscribed letters are also found:—

ἐπ (ἐπί), ἀπ (ἀπό), αντ (ἀντί).

Among the abbreviated endings may be cited:—

u (ης), θ (θαι), (μων), (ναι), (ον), (ος), (ου)

Some conventional signs (found tabulated in Gardthausen, op. cit., p. 259) are veritable hieroglyphics; they are used chiefly in astrological or chemical treatises. The moon is designated by a crescent, the sea by three undulating lines, etc. (see Wiedmann, "Byzantinische Zeitschrift", XIX, 144). Lastly, the Greeks, like the Latins, knew a tachygraphical character in which syllables were represented by signs. Several of these tachygraphical signs, indicating endings, parts of the verb "to be", etc., are transferred to the minuscule, and some recur in Latin handwriting.

(εἶναι) (καί) (ἤν)
(ἐστίν) (οὐ) (ὅτι)
(εἰσί) (τῆς) (σιν)
(αἶς) (ὡς) (των)
(ἀπό) (δέ)
(ἐν)

Numerals.—In Greek MSS. numerals are expressed by letters of the alphabet followed by an accent. Three archaic letters are made use of. From 1000 the same letters are used with accents written beneath. Arabic numerals reached the Greeks through the West, and do not appear in MSS. before the fifteenth century. Dates, according to the era of the Creation of the World, are written in letters.

ς (sti) = 6
ϟ (koppa) = 90
ϡ (sampi) = 900

National and Provincial Writings.—Owing to the unity of culture which prevailed throughout the territory subject to the Greek Church, there is no marked difference between the MSS. copied at Constantinople and those which originated in the provinces. Mgr Batiffol considers the minuscule in the MSS. of Southern Italy (Abbey of Rossano) as but slightly different from that of Constantinople; but his conclusions have been opposed by Gardthausen (Byzant. Zeit., XV, 236); who sees here simply the difference between the work of disciples and that of masters. The same scholar has studied, at Sinai, Greek MSS. copied in Armenia or Georgia in the thirteenth century, and has found their writing the same as that of Constantinople. In the West the national writings, as they are called, disappeared before the Carlovingian minuscule, and in the East the influence of the Greek Church was such as to prevent the formation of provincial handwriting. In the West, where the monks sometimes copied Greek MSS. and edited bilingual glosses (see Miller, "Glossaire Gréco-latine de Laon", notices and extracts from MSS., 29, 2), the Greek writing is frequently awkward or irregular, but, far from seeking to modify its forms, the copyists sought, on the contrary, to scrupulously transcribe the characters which the MSS. copied by the Greeks offered as models.

It was quite otherwise with alphabets derived from the Greek and applied to foreign languages. Created under the influence of the Greek Church, but adapted to a vocabulary very different from the Greek, they became truly national writings. Such is the character adopted by the Copts, which resembles Greek writing, and is merely a transformation of the fourth-century uncial. It was also from the Greek uncial that Ulfilas, Bishop of the Goths, borrowed, in the fourth century, the characters of which he made use to translate the Bible into the Gothic language (Socrates, "Hist. Eccles", IV, xxxiii, 6), but he was also indebted to the Latin alphabet; moreover, traces are found in this ancient Gothic writing of the runes in use before that time. So, about 400, St. Mesrop, also desiring to translate the Bible, created the national alphabet of the Armenians by a mixture of the Greek uncial and cursive. The Georgian character, a still nearer neighbour to the Greek, has the same origin. Finally, the missionaries sent by the Greek Church among the Slavic people, especially Sts. Cyril and Methodius, created the Slavonic alphabet, from which the writings of all the Slavonic peoples are derived. This was about 855. The Glagolitic alphabet (glagol, "word"), which Slavic legend attributes to the invention of St. Jerome, is probably due to some disciple of St. Cyril, who composed it with the aid of Slavic runes and the Cyrillic alphabet (Leger's hypothesis —"Cyrille et Méthode", Paris, 1868), unless it is simply an adapted Greek minuscule (Gardthausen, "Palæog.", 109). The most ancient MS. in Cyrillic characters is the Gospel of Ostromir, dated 1057, but there was discovered at Prespa (Bulgaria), in 1888, an inscription in this writing in the name of the Tsar Samuel, dated 993 (Bulletin of the Russian Archæological Institute of Constantinople, III, 1899).

LATIN PALÆOGRAPHY.—The Latin alphabet is derived, according to the most widely accepted opinion, from the Greek alphabets of Southern Italy. Its letters are composed of the following elements, the nomenclature of which it is important to know: (1) Of vertical lines called ascenders when they extend above the line, and tails when they are prolonged below it; (2) horizontal lines, called bars or crosses; (3) convex lines, designated under the name of paunches or curls. Thus B is formed of an ascender and a double paunch, H is formed of two ascenders and a cross, etc.

The history of Latin writing and its derivatives is divided into five periods: A. Antiquity; B. Barbarian Period; C. Carlovingian Reform; D. Gothic Period; E. Sixteenth-Century Reform and Modern Writing. On two occasions there has been a systematic reform in Latin writing intended to restore it to its primitive purity: under Charlemagne, and in the sixteenth century.

A. *Antiquity.*—In the most ancient MSS. (fourth and fifth centuries) there are four kinds of writing. (1) The Capital is composed of large and regular letters written between two parallel lines, beyond which they seldom extended. It seems to have been the oldest in use among the Romans, who made use of it almost exclusively for inscriptions. The epigraphical, or elegant, capital, similar to the ordinary majuscule of our printed books, was used in MSS., but there exist only rare specimens of it. Such is the Virgil of the Vatican (Lat. 3256), which may be attributed to the beginning of the fourth century; other MSS. of Virgil of the same period are in the Vatican (Lat. 3255) and at St. Gall. The only difficulty in reading these MSS. lies in the fact that the words are not separated. The letters differ but little from those of our printed books. The A ordinarily appears under one of two forms: Λ and Λ. The character V designates both U and V; in the same manner I is used for both I and J. This beautiful writing seems to have been reserved for MSS. *de luxe* and for the most revered works, such as Virgil or the Bible. The rustic capital, much used from the end of antiquity, is less graceful; its characters are more slender and less regular; their extremities are no longer flattened by the small graceful bar which adorns the epigraphical capital. Such is the writing of the Prudentius of Paris (Bib. Nat., Lat. 8084), in which is found the signature of the consul Mavortius (527). All these MSS. lack punctuation, and in those where it occurs it was added later.

(2) The Uncial is a transformed capital writing in which the ascenders are curved and the angles rounded. At first this expression, derived from the Latin *uncia*, "one-twelfth", was applied to the capital writing itself. Examples occur in the Latin inscriptions of Africa, but it is above all the writing used in MSS. The letters most modified are: A, D, E, G, H, M, Q, T, V, which became respectively:

a, ɔ, ϵ, ϛ, h, ɱ, q, τ, u

An example of a MS. in uncials is furnished in the collection of Acts of the Council of Aquileia (381), transcribed shortly after this date (Paris, Bib. Nat., Lat. 8907); others are the Livy of the Bibliothèque Nationale (Lat. 5720) and several MSS. of the sixth and seventh centuries.

(3) The Half-Uncial, a combination of uncial and minuscule letters. The letters E, V, H retain the uncial form; the D has sometimes the uncial form, sometimes the minuscule; the N is in capital. Characteristic letters are: a, ʒ, ɼ (respectively, a, g, r). The most ancient specimen is the Verona palimpsest, written in 486, containing the consular annals from 439 to 486.

(4) Minuscule (*scriptura minuta*) presents simplified forms similar to the modern characters of ordinary or italic print, within more restricted limits than the capital and the uncial. It was used from the imperial period for accounts, business letters, etc. The best known MSS. are not prior to the sixth century (Latin MS. 12097, Bib. Nat., Paris); the greater number date only from the seventh century. Even in the Roman period ligatures were numerous. The most characteristic forms are those of a, b, d, e, f, g, i, l, m, n, r, a, b, d, e, f, ʒ, ɩ, l, m, n, r, ſ and s, respectively.

(5) The Cursive includes all rapidly traced writing. The size of the letters is smaller, their shape is simplified, and they are joined together. From this resulted occasional serious deformations of the alphabet. Before the sixth century it was a modification of the capital; from this time forth it borrowed its characters chiefly from the minuscule. The most ancient known specimens are the papyrus fragments of Herculaneum (W. Scott, "Fragmenta Herculanensia", Oxford, 1865), which date from A. D. 53 and A. D. 79; the wax tablets of the gold mines of Vorotspak (Transylvania), written between A. D. 131 and A. D. 167 (Corpus Inscript. Latinar., III, 2); the Egyptian papyri of the fourth century (Karabaček, "Mitteilungen aus der Sammlung der Papyrus Erzherzog Rainer", Vienna, 1886); the fragments of sixth-century imperial rescripts found in Egypt, which are distinguished by large irregular letters, joined, without any separation of words (Thompson, "Handbook of Palæog.", 211–13). This writing was much employed in legal documents down to the seventh century, and it is found in the papyrus charters of Ravenna (end of sixth century); on the other hand, it was but little used in the copying of MSS., and serves only for glosses and marginal notes.

(6) The Tironian Notes.—The Romans were acquainted with a still more rapid system of writing, used to take down speeches or notes. These were the Tironian notes, the invention of which is attributed to Tullius Tiro, a freedman of Cicero (Suetonius, "De Viris illust. reliq.", 135), or to the poet Ennius. According to Plutarch (Cato Jun. 23) Cicero had formed tachygraphs for taking down his speeches. These notes were not arbitrary signs, like those of modern stenography, but mutilated letters reduced to a straight or curved line and linked together. Sometimes a single letter indicated a whole word (e. g., P for *primus*). The chanceries of the Middle Ages doubtless made much use of these notes.

There is no punctuation in the most ancient MSS. But according to the Greek grammarians, whose doctrine is reproduced by Isidore of Seville, a single sign, the point, was employed: placed above, it indicated a long pause (*disjunctio*, or *periodus*, whence our word *period*); placed below, a short pause (*subdistinctio*, *comma*); in the middle, a pause of medium length (*distinctio media*, colon). In the greater number of MSS. the point above or *periodus*, and the point below, or *comma*, were used exclusively.

B. *Barbarian Period (Fifth to Eighth Century).*—After the Germanic invasions there developed in Europe a series of writings called national, which were all derived from the Roman cursive, but assumed distinctive forms in the various countries. Such was, in France, the Merovingian minuscule, characterized by lack of proportion, irregularity, and the number of ligatures. The writing is upright, slightly inclined to the left, the MSS. are not ruled, and the lines sometimes encroach on one another. The phrases are separated by points and begin with a majuscule letter in capital or uncial; the abbreviations are few. According to the Corbie MS. of Gregory of Tours (Paris, Bib. Nat., Lat. 17665), the a has the form of a double c *cc* and is sometimes superscribed *ɔ̨ᴜd* when it is joined to the following letter *ɫ* (*apud*); the c is surmounted by an appendix in the form of a crosier; the e is often looped and resembles an 8: , true, also, of the o: *orsniccm* (*toronicam*), the l affects cursive forms, ; the r and s are distinguished with difficulty; and t is included in a great many ligatures which change its form; the i, without a dot, often goes above the line. The writings of royal diplomas, thirty-seven of which are preserved in the Bib. Nat., Paris, differs only from the minuscule of MSS. in that the higher and more slender characters are connected by tradition with the cursive of the imperial acts of the fifth century. The first line and the royal signature are in more elongated characters; at the beginning of the document is the chrismon, or monogram of Christ, formed of the Greek letters X and P interlaced, which replaces the invocation in use in the imperial diplomas. Tironian notes also accompany the signatures on twenty-seven diplomas; they represent the names of persons—referendaries or notaries—who assisted in the preparation and expediting of the document. The reading of these, undertaken by Jules Havet (d. 1893) and completed by Jusselin (Biblioth. Ecole des Chartes, 1907, 482), has furnished valuable information on the organization of the royal chancery. Tironian notes are also employed for the correction of MSS. and for marginal notes.

Lombardic writing, which developed in Italy during this period, until the ninth century, bore a great resemblance to the Merovingian minuscule; it was also introduced into some Frankish monasteries in the eighth century. From the ninth century it assumed, in Southern Italy, a more original character and long survived the Carlovingian reform. In the twelfth century it reached its apogee in the scriptorium of Monte Cassino; it became regular, and was characterized by the thickness of the strokes which contrasted with the slender portions of the letters. In the twelfth century this writing acquired more and more angular shapes. It persisted in Southern Italy until the end of the thirteenth century. Its use in diplomas was abolished by Frederick II as early as 1231. Until the beginning of the twelfth century the pontifical chancery made use of a similar handwriting called *littera beneventana*, characterized by letters with long ascenders and by exceptional shapes—e. g., the a in the form of the Greek ω, the E and J with a loop like that of the O. The Visigothic handwriting (*littera toletana, mozarabica*) was employed in Spain from the eighth to the twelfth century. It combined with the Roman cursive some elements of the uncial and is generally illegible. According to Rodrigo of Toledo (De rebus Hispaniæ, VI, 29) a Council of Toledo in 1080 decreed—doubtless under the influence of the Cluniac monks—that it should be replaced by the French minuscule.

Irish writing (*scriptura scottica*), unlike the others, did not proceed from the Roman cursive. It is found under two forms: (1) A half-uncial, somewhat large and regular, with rounded outlines (seventh-century Evangeliarium of Trinity College, Dublin, called the "Book of Kells"; Maesyck Evangeliarium, Belgium, eighth century). The words are separated, the ligatures numerous, the initials often encircled with red dots, and the abbreviations rather frequent. Some conventional signs also occur: (*ejus*), (*enim*), (*est*), (*autem*). This writing was chiefly used for the transcription of liturgical books. (2) A pointed minuscule, bearing no relation to the Roman cursive, and also derived from the half-uncial. This writing acquired still more angular forms in the eleventh century, and throughout the Middle Ages remained the national writing of Ireland. The Irish MSS. are remarkable for the fantastic and rich decoration of their initials (see MANUSCRIPTS, ILLUMINATED).

The Anglo-Saxon writing is derived from both the Irish writing and the Roman script of the MSS. which the missionaries brought to the island. As in Ireland, it is sometimes round, broad, and squat (especially in the seventh and eighth centuries), sometimes angular, with long and pointed ascenders. The liturgical MSS. differ from those of Ireland in the frequent use of gold in the initials. The Evangeliary of Lindisfarne (Book of Durham), transcribed about 700 (London, Brit. Museum), is one of the most beautiful examples of round writing. Anglo-Saxon writing disappeared after the Norman Conquest, but the Carlovingian minuscule which succeeded it was formed partly under the influence of the Irish and Anglo-Saxon monks who had been brought to the Continent.

C. *Carlovingian Reform.*—The reform of writing undertaken in the monasteries on Charlemagne's initiative was inspired by the desire for correct and easily legible texts of the Sacred Books. Models were sought in the ancient MSS., and Servatus Lupus, Abbot of Ferrières, persuaded Eginhard that the royal scribe Bertcaudus should take as a model the ancient capital ("Lettres", ed. Desdevises du Dezert, Paris, 1888, pp. 60, 61). The monastery of St. Martin of Tours, of which Alcuin was abbot (796–804), may be considered the chief centre of this reform and produced the most beautiful manuscripts of this period—e. g., the Evangeliary of Lothair, the Bible of Charles the Bald, the Sacramentary of Autun, the book of St. Martin of Quedlinburg. These MSS. served as models for the monastic scriptoria throughout the empire, and by degrees the Carlovingian writing conquered all the West. In these MSS. are found the various kinds of ancient writing: the epigraphic capital, the rustic capital, the uncial, the half-uncial, and the minuscule. With few exceptions, the capital was little used except for titles, initials, and copies of inscriptions. The MSS. of St. Martin of Tours show a partiality for a beautiful half-uncial, but the most important reform was the creation of the minuscule, which became, except for titles, initials, and the first lines of chapters, the writing used in the greater number of MSS. This minuscule prevailed throughout Europe in the twelfth century, and in the sixteenth century, when another reform of writing was inaugurated, the Italian copyists and typographers again used it as a model. M. L. Delisle (Mém. Acad. des Inscript., XXXII) has shown that the half-uncial and the cursive uncial, employed in the sixth and seventh centuries for the annotation of MSS., may be traced as elements in the Carlovingian minuscule. Among its chief characteristics are: A sometimes open *cc*, sometimes closed, and derived from the uncial a; the ascenders b, d, l, h of the b, d, l, and h broadened at the top; the g retains its semi-uncial form; the i no longer goes above the line. The MSS. hence forth well ordered present a clear and pleasing appearance. The words are nearly always well separated from one another; ligatures are rare, but that of the & (for *and*) has been retained. Sentences begin with majuscules and are separated by points (weak punctuation) or semi-colons (strong punctuation). At first, abbreviations were few, but they increased in the tenth century. One of the most beautiful specimens of this minuscule is furnished by the MS. Lat. 1451, in Bib. Nat., Paris, transcribed in 796, and containing a collection of conciliar canons and a catalogue of the popes.

In documents of the imperial chancery the reform of writing was at first less pronounced, and the scribes retained the elongated writing of the Merovingian period; it became, however, clearer, more regular, and less encumbered with ligatures, while care was taken in the separation of the words. In the time of Louis the Pious, on the other hand, the minuscule of MSS. began to be seen in official documents, and soon it supplanted writing. At the same time it followed some ancient traditions: it is generally more ornamented than the writing of MSS., the space between the lines is greater, the ascenders of the d, i, and l are usually lengthened, the first line of a diploma is always in slender and elongated characters.

Such is the system of writing which, thanks to its simplicity and clearness, spread throughout the West, and everywhere, except in Ireland, took the place of the national writings of the barbarian period. In the tenth century it was, however, less regular, and it became more slender in the eleventh century. The MSS. and official documents are generally very carefully executed, the words are well separated, and abbreviations are not yet very numerous. Beginning with Clement IV (1046–48), the pontifical Chancery substitutes this writing for the *littera beneventana;* however, until Paschal II (1099–1118), the two systems were employed simultaneously. It was only in the latter pontificate period that the Carlovingian became the exclusive writing of the pontifical notaries, as it remained until the sixteenth century.

D. *Gothic Period (twelfth to sixteenth century).*— Gothic writing arose from the transformations of the Carlovingian minuscule, much as Gothic architecture is derived from Romanesque. The transition was at first imperceptible, and most of the MSS. of the first thirty years of the thirteenth century do not differ from those of the preceding epoch. It is only noticeable that the letters thicken and assume a more robust appearance, and that abbreviations are more frequent. Soon changes are introduced: the regularity is more pronounced, curves are replaced by angles, the lower extremities of certain strokes are provided with more or less fine lines in the shape of hooks, which turn up to the right to join the next stroke; the upper curves of the letters m and n are replaced by angles. Among the most ancient examples is a MS. copied at St. Martin of Tournai in 1105 (Paris, Bib. Nat., Lat. Nouv. 2195, reproduced in Prou, "Palæography", pl. VII, 1), and a charter of the Abbey of Anchin near Lille (between 1115–20; Flammermont, "Album paléog. du nord de la France", pl. IV). On the mortuary roll of Bl. Vitalis, Abbot of Savigny (d. 1122), are found, among signatures collected in France and England, specimens of the new writing mingled with the Carlovingian minuscule. Diplomatic writing follows ancient tradition until the thirteenth century, and retains the elongated ascenders, which sometimes end in a more or less curled stroke. Nevertheless, as early as about 1130 the influence of Gothic writing was felt in the charters of the North, some of which are even written in the characters used in MSS. Among the most beautiful charters of this period may be mentioned those of the papal Chancery; in the twelfth century their writing had become simple, elegant, and clear.

At the end of the twelfth and during the thirteenth century the change in handwriting was more pronounced. MSS. and charters in the vulgar tongue are more and more numerous. Writing ceases to be a monastic art; it no longer possesses its former beautiful uniformity, and takes an individual character from the scribe. Abbreviations multiply; side by side with the elegantly shaped Gothic minuscule appears in official documents (registers, minutes, etc.) a smaller, more cursive writing, pointed and ligatured. The tendency during this period is to diminish the size and to thicken the letters. In luxuriously executed liturgical books, however, large thick letters, termed "letters of form", are used. This sort of letters persisted until the sixteenth century and served as a model for the earliest type used in printing. Finally, the diplomatic writing used in charters disappears in the first part of the thirteenth century, but the writing of books takes on a cursive character. In the fourteenth century the writing of ordinary books becomes more and more slender, angular, and compressed. The "letter of form" is reserved for inscriptions, for copying the Bible and liturgical books. The same characters appear in official documents where cursive writing becomes more and more frequent, not only in minutes and registers, but even in certified copies (*expéditions solennelles*). It is evident that the scribes wrote more frequently and freed themselves from the ancient traditions. This transformation became still more pronounced in the fifteenth century, when Gothic writing took on a national character in the various countries of Europe. The writing of charters then became finer and more cursive, the letters are less carefully formed and all joined together. At last printing, which spread through the West about 1450, fixed the characters then in use. The majuscule letters, called capitals, used to begin sentences or proper names, are always borrowed from uncial or capital writing. Cursive writing was much employed, even for the copying of books. Moreover, according to the temperament of individual scribes, gradual transitions occur between the "letter of form" and the cursive. Such, e. g., is MS. 9242 of the Library of Brussels (Chronicle of Jacques de Guise), dated 1446.

Abbreviations.—One of the chief difficulties in reading documents of the twelfth to the sixteenth century is the frequency of abbreviations. This was carried to such an excess in official documents that some princes—e. g., Philip the Fair, by his ordinance of July, 1304 (Ordonnances des Roys de France, I, 417)— vainly endeavoured to restrain their use. Abbreviations continued to multiply until the fifteenth century and they are found not only in manuscripts but also in the greater number of printed books previous to 1520. Happily, these abbreviations were not arbitrarily conceived: their use followed determined rules. Besides, each branch of learning had special abbreviations for its technical terms. In writing the vernaculars—English, French, German, etc.—abbreviations were less numerous, and they followed the same rules as Latin abbreviations. These rules are reduced to a few essential principles.

(1) Abbreviation, by a sigla, or single letter, represents the whole word of which it is the initial. The sigla is doubled to indicate the plural (D. N. for *Dominus Noster;* DD. NN. for *Domini Nostri;* FF. for *Fratres*). In the pontifical charters of the thirteenth century occur: *a. s. (apostolica scripta); e. m. (eumdem modum); f. u. (fraternitati vestræ).* Siglas, which were frequently used in inscriptions, were less common in manuscripts and charters. Of rather frequent occurrence are: *e (est),* S. *(signum,* "seal"), SS. *(subscripsi), i. (id est).*

(2) Abbreviation by interior contraction consists in suppressing one letter or more in the interior of a word, the suppression being indicated by a horizontal line above the word. (a) Suppression of vowels (the oldest used): D̄n̄s (*Dominus*) s̄c̄s (*sanctus*), ēp̄s, ēp̄c (*episcopus*), s̄p̄s (*spiritus*). (b) Suppression of a single vowel: ap̄d̄ (*apud*), f̄cit (*fecit*), ūl (*vel*). (c) Retention of only the initial and final letters: p̄r (*pater*), m̄r (*martyr*), h̄c (*hoc*). (d) Contraction of the last syllable, especially the termination *unt:* fuer̄t (*fuerunt*) ātr (*aliter*), orāo (*oratio*); of the termination *ation* in French: obligāon (*obligation*). In Latin and French the final letters are always retained in substantives, adjectives, and adverbs.

(3) A small letter placed above a word indicates the suppression of one or several letters. A vowel written over another vowel indicates the initial letter and the termination. The consonants *m, r, t* placed above the line are used to indicate the terminations *um, ur, it.*

(4) Abbreviation by suspension consists in leaving the word unfinished; the omission being indicated by a stroke, which cuts through any ascender that may be in its way: ān (*ante*) **sot** (*solidos*), parisiēn (*parisiensis*), amār (*amarunt*); in French, lieuten (*lieutenant*). The syllable *ram* and the genitive plural terminations, *orum, arum,* are abbreviated by the suppression of the last two letters; in this case the foot of the r is

given a transverse bar: *cor* (*coram*) *antecessor* (*antecessorum*).

(5) Abbreviations by special signs.—The sign most widely used is a small horizontal bar, sometimes waved, placed above the word, which indicates an abbreviation by contraction or suspension: n̄ra (*nostra*). In the thirteenth century the bar has the forms: ⌒ ⌐ ⌒. The signs, ⌐ - ; ⌒, represent sometimes the termination *us*, especially in ablative plurals in *bus;* sometimes the terminations *que, et,* and the final *m* of the accusative. Other signs have a more determined value: ⌐ for *r;* ⌐ ⌐ for *ur, os, us,* and in the North of France ⌐ all terminations in *s* and, exceptionally, in *et.* The origin of this sign is a Tironian note; it arises from the joining of *u* with *s.* The following are abbreviations of the verb *esse* and others of the most widely used signs:

Esse ēē, =, ≈, ⌐, ⌐

Est ⌐, ÷ and in fifteenth century ⌐, ⌐, ⌐

Et ⌐, ⌐, ⌐, ⌐, ⌐, ⌐, &

Per ⌐, ⌐

Pro ⌐, ⌐

Præ ⌐, ⌐, ⌐

Obiit, obitus, Θ, ⌐

(6) Letters enclosed in larger letters, found chiefly in inscriptions on titles of MSS.

(7) Monograms.—The letters of a single word combined in a single figure. This custom must have been borrowed from the Greek chanceries in the Carlovingian period. The best known are those of Charlemagne (*Karolus*) and Clotaire (*Hlotarius*):—

Dictionaries of abbreviations will be found in special works (see bibliography). From ancient times siglas were so numerous that, under Nero, the grammarian Valerius Probus compiled a lexicon of them, of which only the juridical section has survived (ed. Mommsen, "Grammatici latini", IV, 265). At the end of the fifteenth century lexicons of the same kind were compiled in Italy; one of these published at Brescia in 1534 has been reproduced (Bib. de l'Ecole des Chartes, 1902, pp. 8, 9).

Numerals.—Roman numerals never ceased to be used, and with two exceptions they were placed between two points.

.IIII. represents IV
ω " VI—in Merovingian MSS.
∞ " M
$_s$ " ½
X^s " 10½

Numbers were indicated by the multipliers—IIII^{xx} = 80, V^{xx} = 100. Roman numerals were nearly always written in minuscules. The termination indicates a cardinal or ordinal adjective: ⌐^{o}, *millesimo.* The Arabic figures, of Hindu origin, employed as early as the tenth century by Gerbert, appear in mathematical treatises in the twelfth century and are hardly found in other works before the fifteenth century. In the fifteenth century the forms of the 1 (⌐), 2, 3, +, 9, 6, 7, 8, 9 nine digits are:

Tironian notes and tachygraphy.—Tironian notes continued to be used in diplomas or for glosses of MSS. until the twelfth century. Latin MS. 1597 (Bib. Nat., Paris) contains some tenth-century exercises from the Tironian manual (see Bib. Ec. des Chartes, 1906, 270). Pope Sylvester II also used for his letters a North-Italian tachygraphical system, in which each syllable is represented by a sign of its own (see J. Havet "Séances de l'Académie des Inscriptions", 1887). In the Middle Ages various secret codes were used for writing (cryptography). These mostly consisted in suppressing vowels and supplying their places with groups of points. Sometimes the consonants, while retaining their own value, also represent the preceding vowel in alphabetical order (b=a, f=e, k=i, p=o).

Chief Difficulties in Reading Medieval Documents.—First to be reckoned with are errors of transcription, which occur not only in authors' MSS., but even in diplomas. Examples of two words joined in one also occur, of which the most frequent cases are: the joining of the possessive adjective to the substantive (e. g., *virisui* for *viri sui*), the personal pronoun to the verb (e. g., *tueris* for *tu eris*), of the preposition to its complement (*invitasua* for *in vita sua*), of the conjunction to the following word (*sitalis* for *si talis*). Another difficulty arises from the arbitrary division of words between two lines. It is now admitted that division can only be made at the end of a syllable, and there is a custom of placing a hyphen at the end of the line to indicate that the word is divided: in the Middle Ages the same syllable was unhesitatingly divided between two lines, and the hyphen, introduced in the fifteenth century, never became universal. Finally, before beginning the study of documents it is necessary to have some ideas of the orthography of the languages in which the texts are written. Not only had the vulgar tongues (English, French, German, Provençal, etc.) forms which have now disappeared, but the orthography of Latin itself was very different from ours. Not to mention letters improperly added to words, and Germanic breathings (especially in the Merovingian period), it must be remembered that the termination of the genitive feminine singular is always in *e* (*rose* for *rosæ*). During the greater part of this period, also, the diphthongal vowels *ae* are written separate.

Sixteenth Century Reform and Modern Writings.—One consequence of the Renaissance was a progressive abandonment of Gothic for the writing of books. The Italian typographers created the modern Latin character on the model of the Carlovingian minuscule. This reform was adopted in Latin countries; in England Latin characters were introduced as early as 1467 and by degrees supplanted the Gothic character or "black letter". On the other hand, this character persisted in German-speaking countries, which have not even yet entirely abandoned it. Books copied by hand became more and more rare. In legal documents and correspondence writing assumed a more individual character; abbreviations were left to the fancy of each writer—a licence which sometimes increases the difficulty of deciphering. At the beginning of the eighteenth century writing tended to become more regular and by the end of that century attained great perfection. The thoroughly individual character of nineteenth-century writing renders all palæographical study of it hopeless.

ORIENTAL.—ROSNY, *Archives paléographiques de l'Orient et de l'Amérique*, I (Paris, 1869–71) (notices on Turkish, Sanskrit, Chinese, Japanese, Siamese, Ligurian, Cuneiform, American, Oceanian writing); SILVESTRE, *Paléographie universelle* (Paris, 1839–41); MOELLER, *Orientalische Paläographie* (Eisleben, 1844); BURBELL, *Elements of South Indian Palæography* (London, 1878); MORITZ, *Arabic Palæography* (Cairo, 1905); PALÆOGRAPHICAL SOCIETY, ed. WRIGHT, *Oriental Series* (London, 1875), 83.

GREEK.—MONTFAUCON, *Palæographia Græca* (Paris, 1708); JORET, *La paléographie grecque de Villoison*, in *Revue de philologie* (1908), 175–80; GARDTHAUSEN, *Griechische Paläographie* (Leipzig, 1879) (still the only complete handbook); THOMPSON, *Handbook of Greek and Latin Palæography* (London, 1894); OMONT, *Fac-similé de manuscrits grecs datés de la Bibliothèque Nationale du IXe au XIVe siècle* (Paris, 1891); IDEM, *Fac-similé des plus anciens manuscrits grecs en onciales et en minuscule de la Biblioth. Nat. VIe–XIe siècle* (Paris, 1892); HENRY, *History of Writing* (London, 1907) (portfolios); KENYON, *The Palæography of Greek Papyri*

(Oxford, 1899); WESSELY, *Studien zur Paläographie und Papyrusforschung* (Leipzig, 1901—); GARDTHAUSEN, *Geschichte der griechischen Tachygraphie im Alterthum* in *Archiv für Stenographie* (1905); HOHLWEIN, *La papyrologie grecque* (Louvain, 1905).
    LATIN.—MABILLON, *De re diplomatica*, I (Paris, 1601); DUCANGE, *Glossarium mediæ et infimæ latinitatis: Scriptura;* NATALIS DE WAILLY, *Eléments de paléographie* (Paris, 1838); CHASSANT, *Paléographie des chartes et des manuscrits du XIe au XVIIe siècle* (Paris, 1876); *Dict. des abbréviations latines et françaises* (Paris, 1876); PROU, *Manuel de paléographie latine du VIe au XVIIIe siècle* (Paris, 1890; new ed., 1910); REUSENS, *Eléments de paléographie* (Louvain, 1899); BLASS, *Lateinische Paläographie;* MÜLLER, *Handbuch der klassischen Altertumswissenschaft*, I (1892); GROEBER, *Grundriss der romanischen Philologie*, I (1888), 157–196; *Die schriftlichen Quellen;* PAUL, *Grundriss der germanischen Philologie*, I (1901), 263–82; MEISTER, *Grundriss der Geschichtswissenschaft*, I (1906), 21–171; BRETHOLZ, *Lateinische Paläographie;* STEFFENS, *Paläographie latine* (Trier and Paris, 1908); MUÑOZ Y RIVERO, *Manual de paleografía diplomática española* (Madrid, 1890); *Chrestomathia paleographica* (Madrid, 1890); THOMPSON (see above, under GREEK); FRIEDRICH, *Ucebnà Kniha paleographie latinské* (Prague, 1898); DELISLE, *Mélanges de paléographie et de bibliographie* (Paris, 1880); *Mémoires sur l'école calligraphique de Tours* in *Mém. Acad. Inscript.*, XXXII, I (1885); CHAMPOLLION, *Paléographie des classiques latins* (Paris, 1837); BOND, THOMPSON, AND WARNER, *Occidental Series of the Palæographical Soc.* (London, 1873–83); CHATELAIN, *Paléographie des classiques latins* (Paris, 1884–97); *Album paléographique de la Société de l'Ecole des Chartes* (Paris, 1887); BOURMONT, *Lecture et transcription des vieilles écritures: Manuel de paléographie des XVIe, XVIIe, XVIIIe siècles* (Caen, 1881); GILBERT, *Facsimiles of National Manuscripts of Ireland* (Dublin and London, 1874–84); SANDERS, *Facsimiles of National Manuscripts of England* (Southampton, 1865–68); IDEM, *Facsimiles of Anglo-Saxon Manuscripts* (Southampton, 1878–84); MUSÉE DES ARCHIVES NATIONALES, *Documents originaux de l'histoire de France* (Paris, 1872); MUSÉE DES ARCHIVES DÉPARTEMENTALES, *Recueil de fac-similés* (Paris, 1878); FLAMMERMONT, *Album paléographique du nord de la France* (Lille, 1896); PROU, *Recueil de fac-similés d'écritures du XIIe au XVIIe siècle* (Paris, 1904); KOENNECKE, *Bilderatlas der deutschen national Litteratur* (Marburg, 1894) (numerous facsimiles); DE VRIES, *Album palæographicum* (Leyden, 1909); BOND AND THOMPSON in *Palæographical Society's Publications* (London, 1874–94) (455 plates). Reorganized as The New Palæographical Society, the same Society has published, since 1903, various specimens of Greek and Latin writing (7th fasc., 1909).

LOUIS BRÉHIER.

Palæologus, HOUSE OF. See BYZANTINE EMPIRE.

Palæontology (λόγος τῶν παλαιῶν ὄντων), or the science of fossils, deals with extinct or primeval animals and plants. It treats of their characteristics, classification, life and habits, geographical distribution, and succession. It embraces also whatever deductions may be drawn from these investigations for the history of the organisms and of the earth. Palæontology, therefore, is closely connected with geology, botany, zoology, comparative anatomy, and embryology, or ontogeny, which at the same time serve it as auxiliary sciences. The science of fossils is divided into palæophytology (φυτόν, plant), also called phytopalæontology, or palæobotany (βοτάνη, herb), treating of fossil plants, and palæozoology (ζῷον, animal), treating of extinct animals.

Historical Summary.—Even in antiquity fossil marine animals attracted the attention of a number of philosophers who, in some measure, explained them correctly, drawing the conclusion that at one time there had been a different distribution of sea and land. The earliest of these philosophers was Xenophanes of Colophon, the founder of the Eleatic school of philosophy (600 B. C.). After him came Strabo, Seneca etc.; the earliest Christian observers were Tertullian of Carthage (160-230), and Eusebius of Cæsarea (about 270-339). In the Middle Ages little attention was paid to fossils, which were generally regarded as products of a creative force of the earth (*vis plastica*, or *virtus formativa*), though a few men like Albertus Magnus, and later Leonardo da Vinci (1452-1519) held correct views on the subject. In the sixteenth century the first engravings of fossils were published by the Swiss physician Conrad Gessner. It was not until a century later, however, that a few scholars, particularly the Englishmen, Robert Hooke, John Ray, and John Woodward, vigorously maintained the organic origin of fossils. The opinion was still universal that fossils represented life destroyed by the flood, a theory championed especially by Scheuchzer. William Smith (1769-1839) was the first to recognize the value of fossils for the historical investigation of the strata of the earth, his theory being introduced into France by Alexander Brongniart (1770-1847), who, with Cuvier (1769-1832), was the first to apply the principles of botany, zoology, and comparative anatomy to palæontology, whereby the latter became a science. The designation "palæontology", however, was first given it by a pupil of Cuvier, Ducrotay de Blainville, and the zoologist Fischer of Waldheim. Since then about one hundred thousand species of extinct organisms have been described. Cuvier and his successors, as d'Orbigny, Agassiz, d'Archiac, and Barrande, however, maintained the catastrophic theory, that is, the doctrine that at the end of each geologic period the entire fauna was destroyed, and replaced by a new order of life. Darwin's "The Origin of Species by Means of Natural Selection" (1859) proved a turning-point for these theories, for since that time the theory of descent was also applied to palæontology, and to-day is generally accepted. We may especially mention the works on this subject by Kowalewsky, Rütimeyer, Gaudry, Cope, W. Waagen, Neumayr, and Zittel.

The geological and palæontological collections of universities serve for the study of palæontology and instruction in this science, as do also similar collections in museums of natural history. The national geological collections and geological societies have the same object. There are only two purely palæontological societies, the Swiss and the London; their object being the publication of palæontological works. Palæozoology is cultivated almost exclusively by geologists; it is only in exceptional cases that zoologists occupy themselves with this science, while phytopalæontology is carried on mainly by botanists.

The object of palæontological study is petrefactions (from πέτρος, stone, and *facere*, to make), or fossils (*fossilis*, what is buried). Fossils are those remains or traces of plants and animals which before the beginning of the present geological era found their way into the strata of the earth and have been preserved there. Most of the species thus found are extinct, but the more recent the strata the greater the number of extant species it contains. As implied by the word petrefaction, most palæontological remains have been transformed into stone, but leaves and bones completely incrusted in limestone, and therefore petrified, have been found which belong to the present geological era and are, therefore, not considered fossils, whereas the skeletons of the mammoth and rhinoceros frozen in the ice of Siberia, or the insects preserved in amber are. The fossilization of the remains of plants and animals could take place only under very unusual conditions, for in the normal process of decay only the hard parts of the bodies of animals at the most, as bones, teeth, shells of molluscs, etc., are preserved. Even these hard parts gradually disappear by disintegration through atmospheric influences. One very important process of preservation for primeval organisms is carbonization, which affects plants particularly; it takes place under water, air being excluded. Most frequently, however, organic remains are completely penetrated by solutions of mineral matter and are thus in the literal sense mineralized or petrified. Generally the petrifying substance is carbonate of lime, but silicious earth, and more rarely brown clay iron-ore, red iron-ore, zinc-spar, sulphide of zinc, black lead-ore etc., also contribute to produce fossils. The mineralization does not always destroy the original structure of the tissue, especially in case of silicatization. But there are still other means of preserving as fossils the remains of ancient organisms. Not infrequently such remains are covered by mineral waters with an envelope, the organic body itself was afterwards dissolved, leaving only an impression. On the other hand molluscs, echinoderms, corals, etc., have their hollow chambers filled with a mineral substance and afterwards the outer shell is chemically removed, so that only a cast of the inside or a hard kernel remains. Finally, the tracks of birds and reptiles, and traces of the trails of crustacea and worms which have been preserved as impressions are counted as fossils. These are often found with the remains of molluscs, as the well-known impressions of medusæ in the lithographic slate of Bavaria.

The study of palæontological objects is often attended with great difficulties as for the most part the remains found are incomplete and their correct interpretation requires careful comparison with living organisms. Palæontology, therefore, makes use of the methods of zoology and botany, but its task is a far more difficult one. In the fossils of animals all the fleshy parts are lacking, and even the hard parts are often enough only very imperfectly represented, and preserved in fragments. The blossoms of plants are completely wanting, while leaves, fruit, stem, and root are hardly ever found together. Consequently, palæontologists have given special attention to the study of the comparative anatomy of the hard parts of organisms, and thus discovered important organic laws; among these should be especially mentioned Cuvier's "law of correlation". By this is meant the mutual dependence of the different parts of an organism, which enables us, e. g., from the teeth alone, to decide whether an animal was carnivorous or herbivorous etc. Furthermore, by the aid of palæontology the material of the biological sciences was enlarged to an astonishing degree, and many gaps therein were filled. The problems of the development theory received much light from the same source. Finally palæogeography is wholly dependent on this science, as the fossils indicate where there were continents and oceans, where the animal life of the coast developed, where coral reefs grew, where lakes containing fresh water organisms existed, where the primeval tropical forests flourished, and where the tundras of the cold regions extended. This not only enables us to fill the outlines of ancient continents and oceans, but also furnishes the means of determining the geographical distribution of plants and animals, and the climatic conditions during the different geological eras.

Of special importance is the historical side of palæontology. As has already been said, William Smith was the first to recognize the importance of fossils for the historical investigation of the earth's strata. Before his day they were regarded as proofs of the Flood. The greater part of the surface of the earth consists of varying stratified rocks that have been deposited by the ocean, by brackish, and by fresh water. Geology studies the individual strata and infers their age from their succession. This can easily be done in a limited district, but if two districts somewhat distant from each other are compared, then it will prove impossible by geology alone to establish that the two strata are of the same age, for at the same time in one place limestone may have been deposited, in another sandstone, and in a third clay. Again, strata of an epoch which appear in one place may be wanting in another. In such cases the geologist may receive great assistance from palæontology. For the stratified portion of the earth generally contains fossils which are found more or less frequently, which are so distributed that each group of strata corresponds to a definite collection of species that lived when these strata were deposited. In such a case palæontology determines the chronological succession of the several fauna and flora and studies the mutual relations of the organic remains found at the different localities. By this means the contemporaneousness of the various strata may be recognized or the parallelism of the several strata established. In doing this, however, many obstacles have been overcome with considerable difficulty. Most strata have been deposited by the sea. At the same time, however, deposits were formed by lakes; on land forests grew and land animals lived, in warm seas there were luxuriant growths of coral. Naturally each of these regions produced organisms utterly different; consequently some lucky discovery such as that of shells which found their way into deposits of plants, or that of the bone of a mammal imbedded in the sea-sand is required, in order to be able to decide whether the deposits are contemporaneous. From what has been said it is clear that all fossils are not equally important and useful in determining the age of strata. Thus, all remains of land and fresh-water organisms are of less importance, because most strata were deposited by the ocean. Even the marine fossils are not all equally important. The most important are those combining the most rapid changes in character with the most extensive geographical distribution.

The most important task of palæontology is the investigation of the history of the development of life, for it is the only science which furnishes means and in the fossils offers documents to elucidate this problem. Only in this way is it possible to learn whether the past and present organisms form a continuous whole, or whether the fauna and flora of the various periods in the earth's history were destroyed by catastrophes and were replaced by a new creation. There are two fundamental characteristics of all organisms: heredity and variation. It is, at the same time, interesting to prove that the conception of mutation and with it of the evolution of living beings is older than the knowledge of its capacity of persistence. Aristotle believed that eels sprang from mud, Theophrastus accepted the belief that the tubers of a number of plants were formed from the earth, and even Goethe maintained the opinion that plant-lice were developed from parts of the plants. With Linnæus began the perception of the great importance in physical law of the capacity of persistence in organisms, which makes it possible for the naturalist to organize the whole of the great kingdom of living beings into genera and species. Darwin was as the opponent of Linnæus, in that he once more brought the capacity for mutation of all organisms into the focus of natural philosophy.

According to the theory of the evolutionist all life issued from several cells, or according to some from a single cell. Of this cell, of course, no fossilized traces can have been preserved. Yet according to this theory we should expect the most ancient strata to be filled with the remains of animals and plants of the lowest type capable of preservation. This, however, is not the case. In the Cambrian, the oldest stratified formation, which has yielded somewhat abundant fossils, all families of the animal kirgdom are found, with exception of the vertebrates; all plants are likewise missing. These two groups first appear in the Silurian formation. The organisms found in the Cambrian formation are not the lowest of their kind, the brachiopods, for instance, and the trilobites are as highly-organized as the present representatives of their species. In the same manner, vertebrates are represented in the Silurian formation by the trunk-fish or *ostraciidæ*, and the oldest known plants are the *algæ* and the highly-organized ferns. Consequently the lowest classes are not the earliest. When by the discovery of older remains the limits of life were traced further back, here also remains of higher organisms were found, so that even here we are very far removed from the beginnings of life. In attempting to find traces of the simplest organisms the *Eozoon canadense* played a great rôle until it was seen that in the remains in question crystals of olivin or chrysolite, that had been converted into serpentine, had produced the illusion of an organic structure. Great importance was also attached to the appearance of graphite in the earliest of strata, until Weinschenk proved, at least for many of them, that they owed their existence to volcanic action. Equally inconclusive are the earliest limestones, now that we know that these are still being produced chemically in the ocean. In short, palæontology tells us nothing about the origin of life; the whole series of organisms, from the simplest protoplasmic masses to the differentiated forms found in the Cambrian rocks is missing.

If we survey the fossils so far known in historical order, the following facts are ascertained: The earliest or primary period of the earth is the era of the *Pteridophyta*, the ferns, horsetails, and club-mosses; in the Triassic and Jurassic periods the gymnosperms prevail, and beginning with the cretaceous period the angiosperms. The history of the animal kingdom is similar. Of the *articulata*, only the crustacea appear in the earliest formations, insects and spiders are not found until the Upper Carboniferous. The first vertebrates are found in the Upper Silurian, these are some trunk-fish or ostraciidæ, which reached their most flourishing period in the Upper Devonian. The first vertebrates living on land appear in the Carboniferous period; these were amphibians represented by the stegocephala, and the first reptiles. The Triassic also yields the first small mammals, which, however, do not become important until the Old Tertiary period, while true birds are already known in the Jurassic. Man, who appears in the Quaternary, concludes the series. Thus, starting from geological antiquity, the fossils of which still in part seem strange to us, although in almost all cases they can be inserted without difficulty in the existing orders and classes of the animal and vegetable kingdoms, there is found a progressive approximation to the organisms now existing which is completed by the gradual and unbroken succession of beings more and more highly differentiated.

At the first glance this seems to be a brilliant confirmation of the theory of development, but when more closely examined it is seen that the guiding-thread, which should lead from one point to another, is continually broken and the loose ends cannot readily be connected. Vertebrates first appear in the Silurian and angiosperms in the cretaceous, but there are no organisms leading up to these groups. Thus we are met by the broad fact that both vertebrates and flowering plants with covered seed appear without intermediate links. The same thing is true of each one of the classes in the animal and vegetable kingdoms. We see them, indeed, appear one after another in time, but we always miss the intervening links which would indicate genetic relations among the several orders. It is true that at times animal remains are found which, it is believed, may rightly be claimed as the missing links. The best known of these is probably the aboriginal bird, the archæopteryx, which ranks midway between reptile and bird. Its plumage, its bird-like foot, and the closed capsule of its skull characterize it as a bird, while the structure of the vertebræ, the teeth, and the long, lizard-like tail point to the reptiles. Since, however, it has been found that these reptile-like peculiarities also appear in embryonic birds, there is no longer any doubt that the species under consideration are real birds, the highly-differentiated last link of an extinct class of birds. In the same way the opinion that the theromorpha, a kind of reptile, are the aboriginal form of vertebrates, has not proved tenable. At the same time we now and then find in the record of successive geological strata forms that may be regarded as the common starting-point of two or of several orders. We know, for instance, the connecting links between the four-branched and six-branched corals, or between the ganoids, and the teleosts (bony fish), also between the two great groups of carnivorous and insectivorous marsupials on the one side and the herbivorous marsupials on the other. At the base of the placental mammalia are found forms which unite the characteristics of hoofed animals, beasts of prey, and insectivorous animals. Such collective types as they are called, however, are very rare, whereas according to the theory of descent they should be found in large numbers.

In the smallest classified case of minute systematic units it is true palæontological series of descent may be recognized, for here individual species by imperceptible mutations lead to new species. The best known line of descent of this kind is probably the ancestral tree of the horse, published long ago by Huxley; but this very case illustrates the difficulties of such problems, for just now it is very doubtful if some of the links should be inserted in the series. Moreover, such proofs always contain hypothetical elements. Besides, connecting links are often lacking; or parts separately found, such as teeth or bones, are the only means of completing a line of ancestral descent. A special obstacle to the recognition of true relationship is the phenomenon called convergence. By convergence is meant the fact that, in consequence of similar conditions of life, uniformity of organs or even of the entire structure can be developed by animals far apart in systematic classification. Thus, for example, a mollusc of the cretaceous period, a brachiopod of the Carboniferous, and a coral of the Devonian externally are much alike. Or, again, in Mesozoic times the *reptilia* prevailed in water, air, and on land. There existed in this period beasts of prey, along with herbivorous and insectivorous animals, *cheiroptera* in the air, and fish-like *carnivora* in the ocean. In the latest geological periods the mammals took the lead, and placental mammals took possession of all three elements. Alongside of these there existed carnivorous, insectivorous, and rodent marsupials.

If we study the fossils of successive strata we will notice along with the forms which are gradually changed, numerous new forms unconnected with previously-existing forms. There is, therefore, a gap which cannot be filled up by means of small, inappreciable changes, as the Darwinian theory of descent demands, because there is not time enough for numerous intermediate members of the series. Häckel, therefore, assumes a process of change which he calls metakinesis, by this he understands "an almost violent and always far-reaching change in the forms, which certainly cannot take place in the adult form of the organism, but only in its earlier younger stages when the individual organs are not yet histologically specialized and therefore possess a more or less independent plasticity". In the shortest space of time such metakinetic processes can completely change the appearance of the entire fauna and flora, and in the history of life periods of relative constancy alternate with those of violent change and new formation. Under these conditions the individual genera act very differently. Many genera of the brachiopods, the foraminifera, the echinoderms, gasteropods, as well as the mollusca, the cephalopods, and the crustacea extend almost without change from geological antiquity up into the present time. Other genera, on the contrary, have only a life of very brief duration. In these latter is perceived, at times, a very gradual remodelling by mutations, mutations which being separated into fragments by a violent metakinetic break-up, afterwards give rise to a large number of species; thus the vital energy of the genera is soon exhausted. This phenomenon brings us, therefore, face to face with a new problem, commonly called the "extinction of species".

One circumstance must, however, still be pointed out, namely that the variability of the form groups does not appear to be unlimited in all directions, but that this variability in different families frequently moves independently in the same direction. For instance, there was a tendency toward bilateral symmetry in the animal kingdom at a fairly early period, and individual echinoderms attained it; but it was not general until the era of the worms. One family of worms already had gills, yet it was only upon the appearance of the *molluscoidea* that such organs for breathing were always present. In the same manner the crocodiles, alone of the reptilia, have a heart divided into two ante-chambers and two main chambers, a form of heart which is found, once more, without exception among birds and mammals. This agreement among various groups, however, cannot be based upon a close relationship, but, strictly speaking, comes also under the conception of convergence.

If we survey extinct organisms, there are without doubt many important considerations which tell for the theory of development. However, the theory of development in its extreme, monistic sense, signifies that all life, both animal and plant, springs from a single root. For this many proofs are still lacking, even if we set aside the fact that the oldest organisms of every family (except the vertebrates and plants) are highly organized, inasmuch as their oldest progenitors may have been made unrecognizable by the metamorphosis of the earliest rocks and thus withdrawn from our observation; and even if the enormous length of time required for the development of forms so highly specialized as the trilobite, does not seem to be sufficiently represented in the eozoic sediments. But in the later formations also the entire family of vertebrates appear without any preparation; among the plants to name only a few, the flowering cretaceous angiosperms appear without any precursors, and the Older Tertiary brings without warning us, all ten orders of the mammalia; even among these ten orders a closer relationship can be conjectured in only a few cases. In the pedigree of organic beings, therefore, we meet with chasms which cannot be bridged over even with the help of Häckel's metakinesis. In view of this fact it is hardly possible any longer to maintain the opinion that all life has sprung from a single root (monophyletic). It appears much more probable that the different genera of animals and plants originate in various roots (polyphyletic). The advocates of the monophyletic theory, it is true, declare that the experience of animal breeders and florists shows that new variations appear for the first time in few examples only, and that in view of the fragmentary character of palæontological records these first examples may have perished. If we were to accept this explanation we should deceive ourselves as to the difficulties of the problem of development. For in every case a whole series of intermediate links is missing, and it would, therefore, be strange that none of these should have been transmitted to us. It would be still more startling if the transition-links had regularly perished in all the larger units of classification.

We infer therefore that the facts presented to us by the known fossils compel us to accept a polyphyletic descent. It is, therefore, interesting that zoologists like E. von Beer, Fleischmann, and Th. Boveri, and a number of botanists like A. von Kerner, who work in a different field, have also gradually adopted a polyphyletic line of descent.

Finally, if we examine more closely the individual groups of forms, we see their mutual relations in a new and peculiar light. For the studies in question show that the extinct animals and plants, while differing more or less in structure from those now living, did not fall below them in the perfection of their organization, that, on the contrary, in many cases indeed, a decline is manifested. All the great orders begin at once with highly differentiated forms, so that, with Koken, we can only speak of a "modification of limited systematic divisions".

Development may, therefore, take place without progress in organizations, for all forms which have been classified as belonging to the same genus or the same family stand upon the same level of organization. The difference consists essentially in a strong differentiation and specialization of peculiarities, which are subject now to an increase and again to a decrease. By means of this metamorphosis new species, new genera, and even new families may easily arise. This may exemplify for us progressive development, which, however, should be strictly distinguished from ascending development. The new forms produced to-day in the breeding of animals or in floriculture, belong entirely to the domain of progressive evolution. Hitherto unquestioned proofs of ascending development have been lacking in palæontology, nor does experiment supply the deficiency. We may therefore say that the organisms of the geological ages are connected by descent, and that there is good reason for accepting progressive development in the several lines of descent down to the present time. But if we go beyond this and set up a divergent line of descent for the whole world of organisms, or seek to trace all organisms back to a single cell, we abandon the foundation of fact. If, therefore, we infer that a general development cannot be established by the facts, we are still within the lines of the theory of descent, for the essential conception of this theory is that the systematic species of zoology and botany are not rigid and unchangeable, but have developed from ancestors unlike themselves, and may likewise develop into differently formed descendants. It is the business of the theory of development to investigate the facts and causes which underlie the series of organic forms, at the head of which stand existing species. Consequently, it is no essential part of its aim to prove that development is ascending or that it supposes a single original progenitor.

One of the questions involved in this problem is that of the descent of man, which will be touched on here because it has aroused the greatest interest. We may begin by stating that palæontology has, indeed, made known to us an older race of men with very beetling brows and an almost total absence of chin, but that up to now no ape-like progenitors of men have been discovered. Wherever fossil remains of man have been found—and hitherto they have been found only in the Quaternary period, for all reports of Tertiary man have so far been proved unreliable—man always appears as a true man. So far only a relatively small number of remains of Quaternary man are known (e. g. the skulls of Spy, Neandertal, and Krapina, and the lower jaws of Schipka, La Naulette, and Ochos). There is, moreover, the *Pithecanthropus erectus*, parts of the skeleton of which were found by the Dutch military surgeon Eugen Dubois in 1891 on the island of Java. Since its discovery it has been industriously brought forward by certain supporters of the theory of development as the long-sought missing link between ape and man. At present, however, it is agreed that this *Pithecanthropus* is only a large gibbon, an ape, although there is no doubt that, as regards the size of brain, he should be placed between the largest man-ape now known and man. One more fact must be emphasized. Volz and Elbert have lately investigated the locality in Java where the *Pithecanthropus* was found, and they have proved incontestably that the strata in which these remains were discovered belong to the Quaternary period, that therefore the *Pithecanthropus erectus* was a contemporary of man and could not be his ancestor.

When we look at Häckel's "Stammbaum der Primaten" (Descent of the Primates), the pedigree seems somewhat fuller. In this work the ancestors of man are arranged in the following order: *Archiprimas*, from which are descended the *Pachylemures*, including the *Lemuravidæ*, from which in turn the *necrolemures* are descended; and these are the direct ancestors of the apes. Starting with the ape the descent is continued as follows: *Archipithecus*, the primeval ape: *Prothylobates*, the primeval gibbon; *Pithecanthropus alalus*, the speechless man-ape; *Homo stupidus*, the stupid man; and finally *Homo sapiens*. It will not be uninteresting to examine this line of descent a little more closely. Both the *Pachylemures* and the *Necrolemures* are conceived quite indefinitely. The specially indicated forms: *Archiprimas, Archipithecus, Prothylobates, Pithecanthropus alalus*, are pure inventions, not even the smallest bone belonging to them is known, in fact there is nothing to them but their imposing names. Nevertheless, as Klaatsch asserts, it cannot be doubted that there are a sufficient number of facts to lead every thinking man to the inexorable conclusion that man has sprung from the same source of life as the animal kingdom. The only question is: whether, from the similarity of two beings in structure and function of body, in spite of what we know of the phenomena of convergence, we not only may, but, as Klaatsch says, logically must, infer their genetic connexion in the sense of a blood relationship or of descent from the same basic form? Klaatsch answers this question in the affirmative, but we rather agree with Kathariner, whose answer is: "At this point our views diverge, and all the more as it is impossible to reach a completely satisfactory conclusion on the origin of mankind if we base it solely on morphology and ignore man's spiritual side. A discussion of this question based on palæontological data is fruitless, as the decision is too greatly influenced by the conception which men have of creation as a whole and of its need of a first cause, of their views on the theory of cognition, and of other subjective considerations." Consequently, neither palæontology nor morphology can say anything positive concerning the physical origin of man.

When we review the facts of palæontology, we recognize that this science, while offering probable arguments for a progressive evolution of the organic world, can only to a limited degree—even with the aid of fossil fauna and flora—explain the process of development, and that certain phenomena, such as the complete disappearance of entire large groups, cannot at present be satisfactorily explained. The question of the efficient causes of the changes in the organic world has already begotten many theories, to decide the merits of which palæontology sometimes assists us. Darwin's theory has exceedingly few adherents among palæontologists. On the other hand, Lamarck's teaching, developed by Cope as neo-Lamarckism, meets with continually increasing acceptance. It teaches that the development of organisms rests mainly on hereditary changes, produced by the use or non-use of the organs, as well as by correlation and direct transforming influences, while selection has only a slight, if any, importance. Nevertheless, we must confess, with Diener, that "in our attempts to explain the changes of the present forms of life, which are the results of purely mechanical causes still acting before our eyes, we constantly meet with the action of factors, which we cannot directly understand with the aid of physical science alone. The knowledge of the phenomena of adaptation is a matter of experience, but the explanation, how such an adaptation of the cell-groups of a complicated body is possible, belongs to the domain of metaphysics. Whether we speak of new creations, in the sense of A. d'Orbigny, or of the modification of the fauna, in both cases we formulate biological phenomena which are not clear to us in their nature, and the explanation of which by a mechanical method does not satisfy our need of causality."

KNORR AND WALCH, *Sammlung von Merkwürdigkeiten der Natur* (Nuremberg, 1755–71); CUVIER, *Ossements fossiles* (12 vols., Paris, 1834–37); BRONN-RÖMER, *Lethæa geognostica* (6 vols. and atlas, 1851–56); GOLDFUSS, *Petrefacta Germaniæ* (3 vols., 1826–44 and 1862), and ed. GIEBEL (1866); QUENSTEDT, *Deutschlands Petrefaktenkunde* (7 vols. and atlas, 1849–84); IDEM, *Handbuch der Petrefaktenkunde* (1885); UNGER, *Urwelt* (3d ed., 1864); ZITTEL, *Handbuch der Palæontologie* (5 vols., Munich, 1876–93); IDEM, ed. BROILI, *Grundzüge der Paläontologie* (Munich, 1910); STEINMANN AND DÖDERLEIN, *Elemente der Paläontologie* (1890); FRECH, *Lethæa geognostica* (1876—); GAUDRY, *Les Enchainments du monde animal* (Paris, 1878–1890); IDEM, *Paléontologie philosophique* (Paris, 1896); COPE, *Evolution of the Vertebrata* (Chicago, 1884); IDEM, *The Primary Factors of Organic Evolution* (Chicago, 1896); STEINMANN, *Einführung in die Paläontologie* (Leipzig, 1907); NICHOLSON AND LYDEKKER, *Manual of Palæontology* (London, 1889); ZITTEL AND EASTMANN, *Textbook of Palæontology* (2 vols., London, 1900–02); SCHIMPER, *Traité de paléontologie végétale* (3 vols. with atlas, Paris, 1869–74); SAPORTA, *Monde des plantes avant l'app. de l'homme* (Paris, 1878); SEWARD, *Fossil Plants* (2 vols., Cambridge, 1898—); POTONIÉ, *Lehrbuch der Phytopaläontologie* (Leipzig, 1910); ZEILLER, *Elém. de paléobot.* (Paris, 1900); ZITTEL, *Geschichte der Paläontologie* (Munich, 1899); SCOTT, *Stud. in Foss. Bot.* (London, 1900); NEUMAYR, *Erdgeschichte* (2 vols., Leipzig, 1889); ed. UHLIG (Leipzig, 1895); IDEM, *Die Stämme des Tierreiches* (Vienna, 1889); KOKEN, *Die Vorwelt und ihre Entwicklungsgeschichte* (Leipzig, 1893); IDEM, *Paläontologie und Descendenzlehre* (Jena, 1902); DÉPÉRET, *Les transformations du monde animal* (Paris, 1907); German tr. WEGENER, *Die Umbildung der Erde und des Lebens* (Stuttgart, 1909); WALTHER, *Geschichte der Erde und des Lebens* (Leipzig, 1908); WAAGEN, *Unsere Erde* (Munich, 1909); DIENER, *Paläontologie und Abstammungslehre* (Leipzig, 1910); GÜRICH, *Leitfossilien* (Berlin, 1908—); STROMER VON REICHENBACH, *Lehrbuch der Paläozoologie* (Leipzig, 1909—).

Periodicals.—*Palæontolographica* (Stuttgart, from 1846); *Publications of the Palæontolographical Society of London* (from 1847); *Neues Jahrbuch für Mineralogie und Palæontologie* (Stuttgart, 1830—); *Beiträge zur Geologie und Paläontologie Oesterreichs Ungarns und des Orients* (Vienna, from 1882); *Transactions of the Swiss Palæontological Society* (Basle, from 1874); *Mém. de la Soc. Géol. de France*, Section of Palæontology (Paris, 1890—); *Abhandlungen der k.k. geolog. Reichsanstalt* (Vienna, from 1852); *Palæontolographia Italica* (Pisa, 1895—); *Palæontologia Indica* (Calcutta, 1861—).

LUKAS WAAGEN.

Palafox y Mendoza, JUAN DE, Bishop of La Puebla de los Angeles in Mexico, b. at Fitero in Navarre, 24 June, 1600; d. at Osma in Spain, 1 October, 1659. He was a son of Jaime de Palafox y Mendoza, Marquess of Ariza. After studying at the University of Salamanca he was appointed member of the Council of War and of the Indies at the Court of Madrid. In 1629 he renounced this dignity and was ordained priest. He accompanied Princess Mary as almoner to Germany and upon his return was consecrated Bishop of Puebla de los Angeles, 27 December, 1639, and appointed "visitador general" of Mexico. He arrived there, June, 1640. He soon came in conflict with the Franciscans, Dominicans, and Augustinians, whose many exemptions and privileges he looked upon as encroachments on his episcopal jurisdiction. In May, 1642, he received secret advice from Madrid to take temporary charge of the Government in place of the viceroy, Villena, who had been accused of financial mismanagement and of secret sympathy with the Portuguese rebels in New Spain. At the same time he was appointed Archbishop of Mexico. From 10 June to 23 November, 1642, he was acting viceroy, but would not accept the dignity of archbishop. During his viceroyalty of five months he corrected many financial abuses, framed new statutes for the University of Mexico, and, to root out idolatry among the aborigines, destroyed many Aztec idols and other pagan antiquities collected by preceding viceroys.

In 1647 began his conflict with the Jesuits. The reason of the strife was the numerous exemptions and privileges which the Jesuit missionaries had enjoyed in Mexico since the beginning of the seventeenth century and which, in the opinion of Palafox, undermined his episcopal authority. In a letter to Innocent X, dated 25 May, 1647, he denounced the use which the Jesuits were making of their privileges and asked the pope for redress. The pope answered with a brief, dated 14 May, 1648, in which he sustains the bishop in all disputed points of jurisdiction, but exhorts him to be more kind and lenient towards the Jesuits. A second letter to Pope Innocent X, dated 8 January, 1649, more acrimonious than the first, is often attributed to Palafox, but was probably forged by enemies of the Jesuits, as it is disavowed by Palafox in a defence of his actions which he addressed to Philip IV of Spain in 1652. In May, 1649, Palafox left for Spain. On 27 May, 1653, Pope Innocent X issued a new brief, in which he confirmed his previous decision in favour of Palafox. The bishop was transferred to the Diocese of Osma in Spain on 24 November, 1653. He spent the remainder of his life labouring with his usual zeal for the spiritual welfare of his flock, which honoured and reverenced him as a saint.

The process of his canonization was introduced in 1726 under Benedict XIII and was continued during the pontificates of Benedict XIV, Clement XIII, Clement XIV, and Pius VI. At the last session which was held on 28 February, 1777, twenty-six out of forty-one votes favoured his beatification, but Pius VI suspended the final decision. His literary productions, consisting chiefly of ascetical, pastoral, and historical treatises in Spanish, were published in fifteen volumes (Madrid, 1762).

Istoria della vita del venerabile monsignore Don Giovanni di Palafox e Mendoza, vescovo d'Angelopoli e poi d'Osma, I, II (Florence, 1773); ROSENDE, *Vida y virtudes de D. Juan de Palafox y Mendoza* (Madrid, 1666); DINOUART, *Vie de Jean de Palafox* (Cologne, 1767), anti-jesuitical; BANCROFT, *History of Mexico*, III (San Francisco, 1883), 98–134; EGUREN, *Palafox y los Jesuitas* (Madrid, 1878).

MICHAEL OTT.

Palamas, GREGORY. See HESYCHASM.

Palasor (or PALLISER), THOMAS, VENERABLE, English martyr, b. at Ellerton-upon-Swale, parish of Catterick, North Riding of Yorkshire; d. at Durham, 9 August, 1600. He arrived at Reims 24 July, 1592, whence he set out for Valladolid 24 August, 1592. There he was ordained priest in 1596. He was arrested in the house of John Norton, of Ravensworth, near Lamesley, County Durham, who seems to have been the second son of Richard Norton, of Norton Conyers, attainted for his share in the Rebellion of 1569. Norton and his wife (if the above identification be correct, she was his second wife, Margaret, daughter of Christopher Redshaw of Owston) were arrested at the same time, and with them John Talbot, one of the Talbots of Thornton-le-Street, North Riding of Yorkshire. All four were tried at Durham and condemned to death, Palasor for being a priest, and the others for assisting him. Another gentleman was condemned at the same time but saved his life by conforming, as they might have done. Mrs. Norton, being supposed to be with child, was reprieved. The others suffered together. Bishop Challoner tells how an attempt to poison Palasor and his companions made by the gaoler's wife resulted in the conversion of her maid-servant Mary Day.

CHALLONER, *Missionary Priests*, I, no. 122; FOSTER, *Glover's Visitation of Yorkshire* (privately printed, London, 1875), 244, 245, 577; KNOX, *Douay Diaries* (London, 1878), 246, 247; *Bibl. Dict. Eng. Cath.*, V, 198, 237.

JOHN B. WAINEWRIGHT.

Palatinate, RHENISH (Ger. *Rheinpfalz*), a former German electorate. It derives its name from the title of a royal official in the old German Empire, the palsgrave (*Pfalzgraf*) or count palatine. In the Carlovingian period the count palatine was merely the representative of the king in the high court of justice. Otto the Great in 937 appointed a count palatine for Bavaria—and subsequently for other duchies also—who also had supervision of the crown lands situated in the duchy, as well as of the imperial revenues payable there, and had to see that the duke did not extend his powers at the king's expense. The palsgrave of Lorraine, who had his seat at Aachen, was later esteemed the foremost in rank. In 1155, after the death of the palsgrave Hermann of Stahleck, Frederick Barbarossa transferred the countship to his half-brother Conrad (1155–95), who united the lands belonging to the office with his own possessions on the central Rhine, the inheritance of the Salic kings. He made his residence at Heidelberg, where he built a strong castle. Thus the palatinate of Lorraine advanced up the Rhine and became the palatinate "of the Rhine". Neither the lands of the palatinate, nor those which Conrad had inherited, formed a compact whole; but by further acquisitions which Conrad made, the foundation was laid for the principality to which the name Palatinate has clung. Conrad's daughter Agnes married Henry the Lion's son, the Guelph Henry the Long, who became palsgrave (1195–1211); in 1211 he resigned it to his son Henry the Younger, who d. childless (1214). The dignity passed to the Duke of Bavaria, Louis of Kelheim of the House of Wittelsbach; Louis's son, Otto the Illustrious, married Henry the Long's daughter, who also bore the name Agnes. In this way the Rhenish estates of the Hohenstaufen came to the House of Wittelsbach, in whose hands part of them remain to the present day.

Otto the Illustrious acquired in addition, one-half of the county of Katzenellenbogen; Louis II the Severe (1253–96) received from the last Hohenstaufen, Conradin, the latter's estates in the Nordgau, in the present Upper Palatinate (*Oberpfalz*, in Bavaria), as pledge. In the thirteenth century the dignity of palsgrave was raised from its original ministerial character to complete independence, and the count palatine, largely in consequence of the union with Bavaria, became one of the powerful territorial magnates, subsequently the foremost of the secular princes of the empire. The union with Bavaria was dissolved by Emperor Louis the Bavarian, who after 1319 governed the Palatinate also; in the family compact of Pavia, 1329, he divided the possessions of the Wittelsbachs so that he himself retained the old Bavarian lands, while he left to his nephews Rudolf and Rupprecht the Rhenish Palatinate and the Upper Palatinate. This division existed until 1777. The electoral dignity, according to the compact, was to be exercised alternately by Bavaria and the Palatinate; but this provision was altered in the "Golden Bull" of Charles IV, to the effect that the electoral office was attached to the Palatinate alone, which on that account has since been called the electoral Palatinate; in return the Palatinate had to relinquish the northern part of the Upper Palatinate to Charles. Of the nephews of Louis the Bavarian, Rudolf reigned until 1352, Rupprecht until 1390. Rupprecht was one of the foremost champions of the interests of the princes as opposed to the cities, and by his victory over the league of Rhenish cities at Alzei in 1388 again restored the princes' authority on the central Rhine. He founded the University of Heidelberg in 1386. His nephew Rupprecht II (1390–98) regained from King Wenzel part of the Upper Palatinate; the rest was won by Rupprecht III (1398–1410), who in 1400 was elected King of Germany.

By the "Golden Bull" the division of a territory, to which the electoral dignity was attached, was forbidden; this provision was evaded by selecting special estates for the establishment of younger sons. Several lines were thus formed in the Palatinate after the death of Rupprecht III: the old electoral line; the line of Stephen, which in 1459 split into Simmern and Zweibrücken; the line of Neumarkt, extinct in 1448, and the line of Mosbach, extinct in 1499, whereupon the lands belonging to these two lines reverted to the electoral house. In the electoral line Rupprecht III was succeeded by his son Louis III (1410–36), one of the leading personalities at the Council of Constance; the deposed John XXIII was held in custody by him for three years at the Castle of Eichelsheim; his men carried out the execution of John Hus. He laid the foundation of the famous Palatine Library. Louis IV (1437–49) was succeeded by his brother Frederick the Victorious (1449–75), who governed for his nephew Philip, but wore the electoral cap himself. His reign is almost wholly taken up with wars, in which he was nearly always victorious. He is entitled to special credit for his services to the University of Heidelberg. From his marriage with Klara Tött (or Dett) of Augsburg the family of the princes Löwenstein is descended. After him his nephew Philip the Sincere (1475–1508) reigned alone. The Renaissance was zealously fostered; Heidelberg Castle, in which Johann Dahlberg, Rudolf Agricola, Johannes Reuchlin, Konrad Celtes and others were hospitably received, became the rallying point of the champions of a reform in literature and science, while the university remained unaffected. After the death of George the Rich of Bavaria-Landshut, he claimed for his second son Rupprecht, who had married George's daughter, the lands of Lower Bavaria; this led to a conflict with Albrecht, Duke of Upper Bavaria, who found in his brother-in-law, Emperor Maximilian, a powerful helper. For the Palatinate little was gained by the war, which lasted until 1505: only the city of Neuburg on the Danube with its environs was ceded to the sons of Rupprecht, who had fallen in battle, as the "New Palatinate", while the rest was given to Upper Bavaria.

In the electoral Palatinate Louis V the Peaceable (1508–44) succeeded, a man of conservative views, who personally kept aloof from, and regretted the Reformation, but did nothing to withstand it. He added a number of buildings, the last of the Gothic period, to Heidelberg Castle. His brother Frederick II (1544–56), who for a time belonged to the Smalkaldic League, was more ready to give ear to innovations, but in many respects still wavered. Otto Henry, a son of that Rupprecht who had laid claim to Lower Bavaria, succeeded to the electoral dignity; the "New Palatinate", which he now held, was given by him to his relatives of the line of Zweibrücken. Otto Henry (1556–59) enforced the Lutheran Reformation in his lands resolutely and indiscriminately, and aided the new humanistic movement to victory in the University of Heidelberg. He added to Heidelberg Castle the building named for him, the *Ottheinrichsbau*, the most brilliant creation of the Renaissance on German soil. The electoral dignity and the lands passed to Frederick III (1559–76) of the Palatinate-Simmern line, a family who zealously championed Protestantism. Frederick's son John Casimir fought in France for the Protestant cause; his younger brother Christopher in the Netherlands, where he fell, 1574, on the Mooker Heath; John Casimir's son in 1654, as Charles X, ascended the Swedish throne, which the house of Palatinate-Zweibrücken occupied until 1751.

From 1545 to 1685 the ruling family of the Palatinate changed its creed no less than nine times. Frederick III was a zealous Calvinist; he made the Palatinate Calvinistic, caused the drawing-up, in 1562, of the Heidelberg Catechism, and sheltered French Huguenots. His son Louis VI (1576–83) brought about a Lutheran reaction; John Casimir, regent from 1573–92 for Louis's son Frederick IV, restored Calvinism. Frederick IV (1592–1610) attained the leadership of German Protestantism; he was the founder of the Evangelical Union, 1608. Frederick V (1610–23), the husband of the British Princess Elizabeth (daughter of James I), was a man of boundless self-confidence and ambition, and when he took the crown of Bohemia, offered him by the insurgents, the Thirty Years' War broke out. The battle at Weissen Berg, near Prague (1620), cost Frederick not only the "Winter Kingdom" but also his electoral Palatinate, which together with the electoral dignity and the Upper Palatinate was transferred in 1623 to Maximilian of Bavaria. The entire burden of the war rested for decades upon the Palatinate; the famous library of Heidelberg was presented to the pope by Tilly, who had captured the city in 1622. At the Peace of Westphalia Frederick's son, Charles Frederick (1648–80), received back the Rhenish Palatinate undiminished, but had to give up the Upper Palatinate and be content with a newly-created electoral vote. In spite of his diminished resources, he raised the country materially and intellectually to a highly-flourishing condition. In contrast with his predecessors he permitted the three great creeds of Germany to exist side by side, and received colonists from all lands without questioning them as to their religion. Church and schools found in him a zealous patron: the University of Heidelberg, deserted since 1630, was again opened by him in 1652, and renowned scholars such as Pufendorf were appointed to the professorships. In the wars between Germany and France he remained loyal to the emperor; as a consequence his lands suffered severely from the devastation of the French soldiers in the Wars for Reunion. With his incompetent son, Charles Louis (1680–88), the Palatinate-Simmern line became extinct.

With Philip William (1685–90) the government passed to the Catholic line of Palatinate-Neuburg, which by marriage (1614) had come into possession of Jülich-Berg, and in 1624 into that of Ravensberg. The allodial lands of the family, however, were claimed by Louis XIV for his brother the Duke of Orléans, who was wedded to the sister of Charles Louis, Elizabeth Charlotte. When his claims were rejected Louis in revenge undertook a number of sanguinary expeditions into the Palatinate, particularly in 1688–89, and transformed it into a veritable desert. Heidelberg with its castle, Mannheim, Sinsheim, Bretten, Bruchsal, Durlach, Pforzheim, Baden, Rastatt, and others, as well as numerous villages were given to the flames. Peace was not restored until 1697, at Ryswick. The son of Philip William, the ostentatious John William (1690–1716), resided at Düsseldorf; during the War of the Spanish Succession, he, for a short time, again obtained for his family the Upper Palatinate. His brother Charles Philip (1716–42), in consequence of friction with the Protestants of Heidelberg, transferred his residence to Mannheim (1720), where he erected a magnificent palace in the French style.

With him the Palatinate-Neuburg line ended; historians averse to Catholicism have painted the religious policy of these three Catholic electors in the blackest colours. In reality, if they gave Catholicism the opportunity to expand without hindrance, and reintroduced the Catholic Divine service in many places, they did nothing more than Protestant princes have at all times done in favour of Protestantism in their dominions, and, in accordance with the principle then in force, *Cuius regio, eius est religio*, they were just as much justified as Protestant rulers. The occupation of the Palatinate by the French (1688–89) was also to the advantage of the Catholics, as the French gave them complete or joint possession of a number of churches, and the title to the property thus obtained by the Catholics in many places was upheld by the Peace of Ryswick. As the non-Catholics considered these conditions and the introduction of simultaneous services in many churches a great hardship and made complaint to Brandenburg, the leading Protestant power, who threatened reprisals, complete religious liberty was proclaimed for the three chief creeds (Catholics, Lutherans, and Reformed), in the declaration of 1705; the joint use of the churches was replaced (1706) by the division of the churches into a Catholic and a non-Catholic part. From 1686 Jesuit professors were appointed at Heidelberg; after their suppression Lazarists took their places.

Charles Theodore (1742–99), of the Palatinate-Sulzbach line, succeeded; he promoted the arts and sciences at great expense, so that his reign was later regarded as the Golden Age in the Palatinate. In 1777 Charles Theodore inherited Bavaria; the Palatinate electorate thereupon became extinct. Mannheim was given up, and Munich became the seat of the court. In 1794 the French entered the Palatinate and took possession of Mannheim, which they were compelled to surrender to the imperial troops under General Wurmser in 1795, after a prolonged siege. The armistice of 1796 practically decided the cession to France of that portion of the Palatinate lying on

CATHEDRAL, PALENCIA, AND CHOIR SCREEN

the left bank of the Rhine, which was actually carried out by the Peace of Luneville in 1801. The successor of Charles Theodore, Max Joseph (1799–1803) of the Palatinate-Zweibrücken line, afterwards King of Bavaria, in August, 1801, formally renounced all claim to the left bank of the Rhine, for which he was to receive indemnity in the form of secularized church lands. The Palatinate on the right bank of the Rhine by the decision of the deputation of the estates, 1803, was taken from Bavaria and divided between Baden and Hesse, so that the greater part fell to Baden. After the yoke of Napoleon had been thrown off, the Palatinate on the left bank of the Rhine together with the territory of the former Bishopric of Speyer (so far as this lay to the left of the Rhine) with somewhat modified boundaries was restored to Bavaria, 1815, and at the present time forms the administrative District of Pfalz (Palatinate), which in 1905 had 885,833 inhabitants (391,200 Catholics, 479,694 Protestants, and 9606 Jews). The part of the former electoral Palatinate situated on the right bank of the Rhine, however, in spite of the protest of Bavaria, was retained by Baden and Hesse and the Congress of Aachen recognized, 1818, the right of succession of the Baden-Hochberg line, descended from the second marriage of the Margrave of Baden, Charles Frederick, with a woman below him in rank, to that part which had been added to Baden, although Louis of Bavaria laid claim to these parts of Baden and maintained this claim until 1827. The name Palatinate has since then been confirmed to that administrative district of Bavaria, which in ecclesiastical affairs forms the Bishopric of Speyer. (See GERMANY, map; SPEYER.)

MAYS, *Pfälzische Bibliographie* (Heidelberg, 1886); HÄBERLE, *Pfälzische Bibliographie* (3 vols., Munich, 1909–11); IDEM, *Pfälzische Heimatkunde* (1910); HÄUSSER, *Geschichte der rhenischen Pfalz* (2 vols., Heidelberg, 1844–45); PFAFF, *Geschichte des Pfalzgrafenamtes* (Halle, 1847); SCHMITZ, *Geschichte der lothringischen Pfalzgrafen* (Bonn, 1878); KOCH AND WILLE, *Regesten der Pfalzgrafen am Rhein* (Innsbruck, 1884); GÜMBEL, *Die Geschichte der protestantischen Kirche der Pfalz* (Kaiserslautern, 1885); GLASSCHRÖDER, *Urkunden zur pfälzischen Kirchengeschichte im Mittelalter* (Munich and Freising, 1903); ROTT, *Friedrich II von der Pfalz und die Reformation* (Heidelberg, 1904); LOSSEN, *Staat und Kirche in der Pfalz im Ausgang des Mittelalters* (Münster, 1907); BERINGER, *Kurpfälzische Kunst und Kultur* (Freiburg, 1907); *Neues Archiv für Geschichte der Stadt Heidelberg und der Pfalz* (Heidelberg, 18—); *Mitteilungen des Historischen Vereins der Pfalz* (Speyer, 1870—); *Zeitschrift für Geschichte des Oberrheins* (Karlsruhe, 1850—).

JOSEPH LINS.

Palatini (Lat. *palatium*, "palace"), the designation, primarily, of certain high officials of the papal court. In the early Middle Ages the *judices palatini* were the highest administrative officers of the papal household; with the growth of the temporal power of the popes they acquired great importance. These *judices palatini* were (1) the *primicerius notariorum* and (2) *secundicerius notariorum*, the two superintendents of the papal *notarii*, who superintended the preparation of official documents, conducted judicial investigations, and also exercised jurisdiction in legal matters voluntarily submitted by the interested parties to the papal court; they were the highest officers of the papal Chancery and of the Archives in the Lateran Palace. Other *palatini* were: (3) the *nomenculator*, or *adminiculator* (originally perhaps two distinct officials), who took charge of, and decided upon, petitions to the pope. (The nomenculator was superseded in the course of the ninth century by the *protoscriniarius*, or superintendent of the Roman public schools for scribes.) (4) The *arcarius* and (5) *saccellarius* were the highest financial officers, custodians of the treasures of the Lateran Palace, who had charge of the receipt and payment of moneys. (6) The *primicerius* and (7) *secundicerius defensorum*, being superintendents of the *defensores*, who aided and protected widows, orphans, captives, and other needy persons, had the supervision of charitable institutions.

These various offices developed from the end of the fourth century, with the formation of the papal household. Their functions covered the whole central administration of the papacy, both at Rome and in the outlying possessions (*patrimonia*) of the Roman Church. The *judices palatini* were also employed as papal envoys; they also had definite duties in the solemn processions and other great church ceremonies at which the pope was present in person. Their authority continued down to the middle of the eleventh century, when the reform of the papal administration, inaugurated after the troubles of the tenth century, placed the cardinals in that position at the Roman curia, which the *judices palatini* had previously occupied, and the latter gradually disappeared. In later times the designation *palatini* has been borne (1) by certain cardinals, whose position brings them into constant relations with the pope, and who formerly resided in the papal palace, and (2) by the highest prelates of the pope's personal suite. Until very recent times the *cardinales palatini* were: the cardinal-prodatary, the cardinal secretary of State, the cardinal secretary of Briefs, and the cardinal secretary of Memorials. Pius X has abolished the two last-mentioned positions; the holders of the other two are still called *cardinales palatini*, or "palatine cardinals", but only the cardinal secretary of State actually lives in the Vatican. The *prœlati palatini* are: the majordomo (*maggiordomo*), the high chamberlain (*maestro di camera*), the auditor of the pope (*uditore santissimo*), and the pope's theologian (*maestro del sacro palazzo*). The last-named is always a Dominican.

In the times of the Frankish kings and of the German emperors there were *comites palatini*, counts palatine, who originally presided in the High Court of Justice of a palatinate as representatives of the Crown. In Germany the counts palatine were entrusted, after Otto I (936–73), with the supervision of the imperial lands and revenues, and were also imperial judges. The Court officials bearing this title, introduced by Charles IV (1346–78), had various powers, partly judicial, partly administrative.

GALLETTI, *Del Primicerio di S. Sede Apostolica e di altri uffiziali maggiori del sacro Palazzo Lateranense* (Rome, 1776); KELLER, *Die sieben römischen Pfalzrichter im byzantinischen Zeitalter* in STUTZ, *Kirchenrechtliche Abhandlungen*, XII (Stuttgart, 1904); *Die katholische Kirche unserer Zeit und ihre Diener*, I: *Rom, das Oberhaupt, die Einrichtung und Verwaltung der Gesammtkirche* (Berlin, 1899), 276 sqq.; SCHROEDER, *Lehrbuch der deutschen Rechtsgeschichte* (Leipzig, 1907).

J. P. KIRSCH.

Palawan, PREFECTURE APOSTOLIC OF, in the Philippine Islands, comprises Palawan, Cuyo, Culion, Twahig, and Calamines Islands. It was separated from the Diocese of Jaro (q. v.) on 11 April, 1910, and confided to the Augustinians. The first prefect Apostolic is Mgr. Fernando Hermand y d'Arenas, who resides at Puerto Princesa. The Jesuits and Sisters of St. Paul have houses on Culion where a leper settlement under government control has been established.

Catholic Directory (Milwaukee, 1911).

Palencia, DIOCESE OF (PALENTINA), comprises the civil provinces of Palencia, Santander, Valladolid, Burgos, and Leon. Palencia, the capital of the province of that name, has a population of 15,050. Flórez dates the origin of the diocese from the first centuries. Its bishop may have been among those assembled in the third century to depose Basilides, Bishop of Astorga. According to Idatius the city of Palencia was almost destroyed (457) in the wars between the Suevi and the Visigoths. The Priscillianistic heresy originated in Galicia, and spread over the Tierra de Campos. It was strongly opposed by St. Toribius, Bishop of Astorga. Maurila, an Arian bishop placed by Leovigild in Palencia, abjured that heresy when King Recared (587) was converted, and in 589 he assisted at the

Third Council of Toledo. Conantius, the biographer of St. Ildephonsus, assisted at the synod held in Toledo in 610, and at the fourth, fifth, and sixth Toledan Councils. He composed many new ecclesiastical melodies and a book of prayers from the Psalms. He ruled the see for more than thirty years, and had for pupil St. Fructuosus of Braga.

To defend his new country, Alfonso I devastated the Campos Góticos (Gothic Fields), i. e. the Tierra de Campos, as far as the Duero. The Arabian authors only once cite Palencia in the division of the provinces previous to the Ommiad dynasty. In the Council of Oviedo (811) we find Abundantius, Bishop of Palencia, but he was apparently only a titular bishop. Froila, Count of Villafruela, succeeded in restoring the see in 921, but the true restorer was Sancho the Elder, of Navarre and Castile. The first prelate of the restored see (1035) is said to have been Bernardo, who was given command over the city and its lands, with the various castles and abbeys. Bernardo was born in France or Navarre, and devoted himself to the construction of the original cathedral built over the crypt of St. Antoninus (Antolin). It was rebuilt three centuries later. Its principal treasure was the relics of St. Antoninus, formerly venerated in Aquitania. Alfonso VI conferred many privileges on Bernardo's successor, Raimundo. Pedro, a native of Agen (France) and one of the noted men brought in by Bishop Bernardo of Toledo, succeeded Bishop Raimundo. For his fidelity to Queen Urraca, he was imprisoned by Alfonso I of Aragon. In 1113 a provincial council was held in Palencia by Archbishop Bernardo to quell the disorders of the epoch. On the liberation of Pedro, another council was held in Palencia during the Lent of 1129, at which Raimundo, Archbishop of Toledo, and the celebrated Archbishop of Santiago, Diego Gelmírez, assisted. The long and beneficent administration of Pedro was succeeded by that of Pedro II, who died in Almeria and was succeeded by Raimundo II. Bishop Tello took part in the battle of Las Navas de Tolosa in 1212, where the Palencians won the right to emblazon the cross over their castle.

At the beginning of the fifteenth century Bishop Sancho de Rojas valiantly fought the Moors of Antequera, and in the Treaty of Caspe aided the Infante Ferdinand to secure the crown of Aragon. St. Vincent Ferrer preached in Palencia, converting thousands of Jews, with whose synagogue he founded the hospital of S. Salvador, later connected with that of S. Antolin. Among the succeeding bishops of Palencia, who, as feudal lords, were members of the noblest families, we may mention Rodrigo de Velasco (d. 1435); Rodrigo Sanchez de Arévalo, author of a history of Spain in Latin (1466); the bishops Mendoza (1472–1485) and Fonseca (1505–1514) who decorated the new cathedral; Pedro de Castilla (1440–1461); Fray Alonso de Burgos (1485–1499); La Gasca (1550–1561), and Zapata (1569–1577).

THE UNIVERSITY OF PALENCIA was founded by Alfonso VIII at the request of Bishop Tello Téllez de Meneses and was the first university of Spain. It was the model upon which was patterned the University of Salamanca. Study began to flourish in Palencia and men notable for their virtue and science came from its schools, among them St. Julian of Cuenca, St. Dominic, and St. Peter González Telmo; hence the adage: "En Palencia armas y ciencia" (In Palencia arms and science). The university was founded about 1212, shortly after the aforesaid victory of "Las Navas" (others say in 1208), and the king summoned from France and Italy noted teachers of various arts and sciences, retaining them in Palencia on large salaries. The death of the founder in 1214, the minority of Henry I, and the growth of its fortunate rival, Salamanca, caused the decay of Palencia, many of whose professors and students went to Salamanca, whence the erroneous belief of a transfer of the university to the latter place. In 1243 Archbishop Rodrigo records that in spite of unpropitious events, study continued in Palencia and that the cardinal legate, Juan de Abbeville, in a Council of Valladolid (1228) had endeavoured to revive it. Bishop Fernando obtained from Urban IV (14 May, 1263) a Bull granting to the professors and students of Palencia all the privileges of the University of Paris. But lack of financial support and the proximity of the prosperous University of Salamanca made a revival of Palencia impossible, and it died out before the end of the thirteenth century, probably in 1264, at which time the university was definitely transferred to Valladolid. It was Bishop Tello who also established convents of the Dominicans and Franciscans; the former was famous for the striking conversion of St. Peter González Telmo.

SECTION OF THE CHOIR, CATHEDRAL, PALENCIA

Among the most celebrated natives of the province are the first Marquis of Santillana, Bishop Inigo López de Mendoza, the immortal Berruguete, and Doña María de Padilla.

Palencia is famous for the great Benedictine monastery of S. Zoilo, a *rococo* monument, the work of Juan de Badajoz. Mention has already been made of the hospital of S. Barnabé and S. Antolin. The conciliar seminary was founded in 1584 by Bishop Alvaro de Mendoza.

PEDRO FERNÁNDEZ DEL PULGAR, *Historia secular y eclesiástica de la ciudad de Palencia;* FLÓREZ, *España Sagrada*, VIII (3rd ed., Madrid, 1869); VILLALBA, *Crónica general de España: Crónica de la Provincia de Palencia* (Madrid, 1867); VICENTE DE LA FUENTE, *Historia de las universidades de España,* I (Madrid, 1884); CUADRADO, *España, sus monumentos y artes: Palencia* (Barcelona, 1885).
RAMÓN RUIZ AMADO.

Paleopolis (PALÆOPOLIS), a titular see of Asia Minor, suffragan of Ephesus. The history of this city is unknown. In the sixth century it is mentioned by Hierocles (Synecdemus, 660, 4). It is found in the "Notitiæ Episcopatuum", as late as the thirteenth century, among the suffragan sees of Ephesus. It is now the town of Baliambol in the vilayet of Smyrna. Le Quien (Oriens christianus, I, 729) mentions seven bishops of this city known by their presence at the councils: Rhodon at Ephesus, 431; Basilicus at Chalcedon, 451; Eusebius at Constantinople, 536; George at Constantinople, 692; Gregory at Nicæa, 787; Peter at Constantinople, 869; Julian at Constantinople, 879.

S. PÉTRIDÈS.

Paleotti, GABRIELE, Cardinal, Archbishop of Bologna, b. at Bologna, 4 October, 1522; d. at Rome, 22 July, 1597. Having acquired, in 1546, the title of Doctor of Civil and Canon Law, he was appointed to teach civil law. In 1549 he became canon of the cathedral, but did not become a priest until later. He gave up teaching in 1555, and although he had many times refused the episcopal dignity, he became in 1556 auditor of the Rota. Pius IV sent him to the Council of Trent where he played an important rôle. His "Diarium", or journal, on the proceedings of the council, forms one of the most important documents for its history. The complete text will be published in the third volume of the "Concilium Tridentinum. Diariorum, Actorum, Epistularum, tractatuum nova collectio, edidit Societas Goerresiana" (Freiburg; see Vol. I, ed. S. Merkle, p. XXXVI, Freiburg, 1901). A résumé was published by Mendham (London, 1842) and Theiner ("Acta Concilii Tridentini", Agram, 1874, II, 523–580). After the council Paleotti became one of the commission of cardinals and prelates that served as a basis of the Congregation of the Council. On 12 March, 1565, he became cardinal, and on 13 January, 1567, was made Bishop of Bologna; he was also the first archbishop, for in 1582 this see became an archdiocese. His biographers never cease praising his zeal in introducing the Tridentine reforms in his diocese, comparing his activity at Bologna to that of Saint Charles Borromeo at Milan. The latter held him in high esteem. In 1589 Paleotti became Cardinal-Bishop of Albano and in 1591 of Sabina. There also he distinguished himself by his zeal for reform. At the conclave in 1590 which elected Gregory XIV, he obtained the votes of an important minority. His principal works are: "De nothis spuriisque filiis liber" (Bologna, 1850; Frankfort, 1573; The Hague, 1655); "De sacris et profanis imaginibus libri V" (Bologna, 1582; Ingoldstadt, 1594); "Episcopale Bononiensis civitatis" (Bologna, 1580), and "Archiepiscopale Bononiensis civitatis" (Rome, 1594), remarkable works dealing with the good administration of a diocese; "De sacris consistorii consultationibus" (Ingoldstadt, 1594; Rome, 1596); "De bono senectutis" (Rome, 1595).

BRUNI, *Vita Gabrielis Palæoti* in MARTÈNE ET DURAND, *Veterum scriptorum et monumentorum amplissima collectio*, VI (Paris, 1729), 1387 sq.; LEDESMA, *De vita et rebus gestis Gabrielis Palæoti* (Bologna, 1647); FANTUZZI, *Notizie degli scrittori Bolognesi*, VI (Bologna, 1781–94), 242–259; SCHULTE, *Die Geschichte der Quellen und Literatur des canonischen Rechts*, III (Stuttgart, 1880), 453–454; MERKLE, *Kardinal Paleottis litterarischer Nachlass* in *Römische Quartalschrift*, XI (Rome, 1897), 333–429.

A. VAN HOVE.

Palermo, ARCHDIOCESE OF (PANORMITANA), in Sicily. The city is built on an inlet of the Mediterranean and is partly surrounded, to the south, by a semicircle of mountains and hills, of which the highest are Catalfano to the east, and Montepellegrino to the west. Among the churches are the Duomo, built in 1170 by the Archbishop Gualtiero Offamiglio on the site of an ancient basilica which had been changed into a mosque during the Saracen domination. The walls are decorated with frescoes and mosaics of the twelfth and thirteenth centuries. In the first chapel on the right are six tombs of kings and queens of Sicily. Other objects of interest in the cathedral are sculptures by Gagini and by Villareale; an Assumption by Velasquez, and other paintings by well-known masters; the crypt with 21 tombs of archbishops of Palermo, and the *tabularium*, or archives with interesting Latin, Greek, and Arabic documents. S. Domenico (1300), restored in 1414 and in 1640 is the largest and one of the most beautiful churches of Palermo; it contains the tombs of many famous Sicilians, also paintings by Anemolo, Fondulli, Paladino, and Vito d'Anna, as well as sculptures by Gagini. In the Olivella (1598) there is a beautiful Madonna, said to be by Raphael or by Lorenzo di Credi. S. Giorgio dei Genovesi, which represents the most beautiful architecture of the sixteenth century in Palermo, has paintings by Palma Vecchio, Giordano, Paladino, and others. La Badia Nuova has paintings by Morrealese. by whom also are the frescoes in the vault of the church. At S. Giuseppe there are two admirable crucifixes, one in ivory, and the other in bronze, works of Fra Umile da Petralia, and also paintings by Tancredi, Morrealese and Giuseppe Velasquez. L'Annunziata, called la Martorana, was built by George of Antioch, an admiral of King Roger (twelfth century); it is famous for its mosaics and for a painting, the Ascension, by Anemolo. At Santa Maria di Gesù there are paintings of the thirteenth century. Other monumental churches are S. Antonio (1220); S. Matteo (seventeenth century), which has the "Sposalizio" by Novelli; S. Eulalia dei Catalani; Santa Maria la Nuova (1339), which has a fine portico; the church and the seminary "dei greci", dating, respectively, from 1540 and 1734; S. Cita, connected with the military hospital, which has a Madonna by C. Maratta; the church of the Cancelliere (1171), built by Matteo d'Aielo, chancellor of King William the Good; S. Caterina; S. Cataldo, which is in the Greco-Norman style; Santa Maria degli Angeli; S. Giacomo in Mazara (Norman); the parish church "dell'Albergheria", which has a fine belfry; S. Giovanni dell'Origlione; the Badia della Magione, of the Teutonic Order, which has a Pietà by Gagini; S. Giacomo la Marina (1336); S. Anna la Misericordia (statutes by Gagini).

Among the secular buildings is the Palazzo Reale, built on the site of the Saracen fortress by the Norman kings. It was a mass of halls, of silk and of wool factories, churches, chapels, and towers; of the latter, only one remains, that of S. Ninfa, which, since 1791, has been the seat of the astronomical observatory. It was from this observatory that Ceres, the first of the asteroids to be observed, was discovered by the Theatine Padre Piazzi (1801). The Palazzo dei Tribunali was the property of the Chiaramonte family, but was confiscated and served as the seat of the Inquisition. The university has a magnificent portico, and contains the Museo Nazionale and also a picture gallery with a Pietà by Spagnoletto, a Holy Family by Rubens, a Madonna with angels by Ruzzolone, etc. Other buildings are the Sopraintendenza agli Archivi di Stato; the Palazzo Firenze (1578), formerly the custom-house, now used for banks and other institutions; the tower of Palitelli, which dates from the Saracen period; the former college of the Jesuits, which contains a library (now national) of 120,000 volumes and 1269 MSS.; the private palaces Aiutamicristo, Campofranco (collection of paintings), Trabia (art collection and library), Forcella, Butera, and others. There are, moreover, a conservatory of music, several educational institutes, and two other public libraries, one of the commune, and the other of the Oratorio di S. Filippo Neri. Outside the city, are the cave of St. Rosalia, where her relics were found, which has been transformed into a church; S. Giovanni dei lebbrosi; S. Spirito, where the first episode of the famous Sicilian Vespers took place; I Cappuccini, with its well-known catacombs; the ancient convent of Baida on the slopes of Mt. Aguzzo.

Palermo is a city of Phœnician origin, the name of which means "surrounded by rocky cliffs". In time, it came under the rule of the Carthaginians. In 254, however, the Romans took possession of Palermo. Palermo retained its form of government, but under Augustus became a colony; and the Greek language, which under the Carthaginians was the predominant tongue of the city, little by little ceded its place to the Latin. The Saracens obtained possession of Palermo for a time in 820, but in 835 their rule was established permanently. In 1063, the Pisans made an unsuccessful attempt to take Palermo. Finally, Roger, abetted by the treason of the Christian soldiers in

Palermo, took the city in 1071, and made it the capital of his Sicilian possessions. Under Roger II, it became the capital of the Two Sicilies, and so remained, until the conquest by Charles of Anjou. Under the Normans the arts and letters (Greek, Arabic, and Latin) flourished at Palermo, and the Mohammedan religion was tolerated, the kings being only too zealous imitators of the customs of the caliphs. The famous Sicilian Vespers (31 March, 1282) were the signal of revolt against the Angevin domination, in favour of Peter, King of Aragon, who was hailed as legitimate heir of the rights of Conradin; and in the new Kingdom of Sicily, Palermo again became a capital. At the death of Martin I (1409) Sicily was united with the Kingdom of Aragon, and at Palermo was governed by its own viceroys, independent of those of Naples after the conquest of the latter state by the Aragonese. In fact, the customs of Sicily, and especially of the nobility, were left unchanged under Spanish rule, which was therefore peaceful, although the conduct of the troops of Diego Veru, returning from Tripoli in 1511, caused a sort of Second Vespers, soon suppressed, however, by the viceroy Moncada. There was another more serious revolt, contemporaneous with that of Masaniello at Naples; it took place in 1647, and was caused by a famine. The new governor, Cardinal Trivulzio, combining severity and clemency, re-established order. From 1713 to 1720, Sicily was again separated from the Kingdom of Naples, and Vittorio Amedeo of Savoy was crowned at Palermo. Afterwards, the island followed the fortunes of Naples, under the Bourbons. In 1798, the royal family was driven by the Revolution to seek refuge in Sicily, and again by the French occupation in 1806. The suppression of Sicilian autonomy was the cause of several revolutionary movements at Palermo. In that of 1820-21, a governing commission was created, with Cardinal Gravina at its head; on this occasion peace was re-established with Austrian aid. In 1848 a provisional government was established that offered the crown of Sicily to Ferdinand of Savoy, who, however, did not accept it. General Filangieri retook Palermo fourteen months later; and finally, Garibaldi overthrew the Bourbon government, and substituted for it, not the autonomy of Sicily, but the annexation of the island to the Kingdom of Italy. A last movement in favour of independence was made in 1866, but was quelled in its beginning.

Christianity was preached at an early date in Palermo. According to Prædestinatus (I, 6), its bishop, Theodorus, together with the Bishop of Lilybæum, condemned the heresy of Heracleon, Theodorus being a contemporary of Pope St. Alexander (second decade of the eleventh century); his predecessor, it is said, was St. Philippus. The bishop, St. Mamilianas, who is said to have suffered martyrdom under Diocletian, and whose relics are preserved in the cathedral, may be identical with St. Mamilianus, whom the Vandals relegated to the island of Monte Cristo in 450. Other martyrs under Diocletian were Claudius, Sabinus, and Maximus. Among the bishops were Gratianus, 503, Victor who died in 603, and Joannes, 603 (St. Gregory the Great was in correspondence with the two last named); Felix, 649, and Theodorus, 787. During the Saracen domination there appears to have been no bishop of Palermo; it was in that period (828) that SS. Philaretus and Oliva suffered martyrdom. In 1049, Leo IX sent to Sicily, as archbishop, the Humbertus who, later, became Cardinal Bishop of Silva Candida; but the Normans, then enemies of the pope, prevented the archbishop from landing. In 1065, Bishop Nicodemus was appointed. Other bishops were Alcherius (1083); Gualterius (1113), the first to bear the title of archbishop, although the pallium had been sent to Joannes (603); Stephanus (1166), compelled by his enemies to resign; Gualtiero Offamiglio (of the Mill), an Englishman, who died in 1191; Bartolomeo (1201), brother of the preceding, who was sent into exile; Gualtiero da Polena, who was appointed in 1201 by Innocent III and transferred to Catania, Parisius being installed in his stead; Berardo di Castaca (1214-52), a great diplomat and a mediator between the popes and Frederick II; Licio de Colle (1296), a benefactor of the cathedral; Bartolomeo da Antiochia (1305); Francesco da Antiochia (1311); Giovanni Orsini (1320); Matteo Orsini (1371); Nicolò d'Agrigento, O. Min. (1383); Lodovico Bonnito (1387) and Giliforte Riccobono (1397), both persecuted by the Chiaramonte faction; Nicolò da Tudisco (1434-1445), a great canonist (Panormitanus) and one of the pillars of the Council of Basle, who became a cardinal of the antipope, Felix V; Simone Beccatelli (1445), a generous restorer of the cathedral and of other churches; Nicolò Puxades (1466), who caused the stalls of the choir of the cathedral to be adorned with inlaid work; Giovanni Borghi (1467), who had been a famous physician; Filippo (1474), who was a nephew of King Ferdinand, and died under the walls of Granada in 1488; Cardinal Pietro, Count of Foix, O. Min. (1485); Cardinal Tommaso de Vio, O.P. (Caietanus), who was elected in 1519, but not recognized by Charles V, the pope not recognizing Giovanni Carandolet, the king's candidate; Ottaviano Preconi, O. Min. (1562), zealous for the decoration of the churches; Cesare Marulli (1578), who founded the seminary; Cardinal Giannetto Doria (1609-42), who was for a time viceroy and reformed the nuns, and distinguished himself for his charity during the famine of 1624; Martín de Leon y Cardenas (1650), who donated the beautiful tabernacle of the cathedral; Pietro Martinez Rubio (1656), who was noted for his charity and obtained the use of the mitre for his canons; Cardinal Domenico Pignatelli (1802); Cardinal Pietro Gravina (1816); Cardinal Gaetano M. Trigona e Parisi (1832); Cardinal Ferdinando M. Pignatelli (1839), who had been a general of the Theatines; Cardinal Geremia Celesia (1871-1904).

Cefalù, Mazzara, and Trapani, are the suffragans of Palermo; the archdiocese has 50 parishes, with 444,982 inhabitants, 18 religious houses of men and 24 of women, 12 educational establishments for male students and 27 for girls, and 1 Catholic daily paper.

PIRRI, *Sicilia sacra* (Palermo, 1735); CAPPELLETTI, *Le chiese d'Italia*, XXI; MONGITORE, *Palermo santificato* (Palermo, 2d ed., 1888); DI GIOVANNI, *Topografia antica di Palermo* (Palermo, 1899); DI BARTOLO, *Monografia sulla cattedrale di Palermo* (Palermo, 1903); *Annuario dell' archidiocesi di Palermo* (1906).

U. BENIGNI.

UNIVERSITY OF PALERMO—The Convent of St. Dominic of Palermo may be considered the nucleus of the future University of Palermo. In this convent instruction was given in theology and philosophy, not only for the Dominicans; but also for the public. In 1469 Father Tommaso Schifaldo gave lessons there in Latin literature. A theological lecturer, Father Salvo Cassetta, had so large a following that he lectured in the public square; he was also well versed in mathematics. In 1553 the commune wished to have a medical school and called upon the famous Gianfilippo Ingrassia. His lectures too were delivered at the Convent of St. Dominic. In 1555 the commune also engaged Dominican professors of philosophy, including the historian Fazello. The chair of jurisprudence was founded in 1556, and the first professor was Geo. Ant. de Contovo. At the end of the sixteenth century nothing more was heard of the Dominican School. From 1591, philosophy and theology were taught in the Jesuit College (founded in 1550). In 1599 the number of chairs was increased. The college had the right of conferring degrees in these two sciences. The courses of the Jesuits were well attended.

CATHEDRAL, PALERMO
RECONSTRUCTED—1169 TO 1185

In 1632 the Jesuit Pietro Salerno, gave his patrimony to the university which was about to be established in the college of the order. The royal concession was obtained and furthermore a contention arose between the rector of the college and the archbishop, each of whom desired to be chancellor; this controversy hindered the formation of the university itself, that is, of the two other faculties, law and medicine. Courses in medicine were given until 1621 in the Spedale Grande (Academy of Anatomy) through the initiative of Dr. Baldassare Grassia. On the failure of this, another similar course began in 1645, in the house of Camillini, which course continued, supplemented by instruction in mathematics. On the suppression of the Jesuits, their college was entrusted to secular priests. In 1777 the Senate of Palermo began to erect a complete university, which was established 1779 with three chairs in theology, four in law, six in medicine, seven in philosophy and the natural sciences. The great professors were Spedalieri in philosophy, Cari in law, Sergio in political economy, Father Bernardino d'Ugria and the Benedictine Eutichio Barone in the natural sciences, Maronglia in mathematics. In 1780 new chairs were added, and in the following year the university acquired the right of conferring degrees. In 1805 it was enacted that the rectors should be taken from the Theatine Order which furnished many renowned professors, e. g., the astronomer Piazzi (1786). When the Jesuit Order was re-established, the academy had to change its place; but it was also in that year (1805) that the said academy took the name of university. Among the professors we may mention: Scina, Gorgone, Amari, Ugdulene, and the late Canizarro (1826–1910).

The university has the usual four faculties of jurisprudence, medicine, letters, and philosophy and sciences, besides a practical school for engineers and a school of pharmacy. It has also a botanical garden, a cabinet of physics, including chemistry, mineralogy, geology, physiology, and anatomy, an astronomical observatory, various clinics and an archæological museum. The number of students in 1909 was 1535; regular professors, 68; special professors, 111. It supports 84 chairs, and more than 123 teachers.

SAMPOLO, *La R. Accademia degli Studi di Palermo* (Palermo, 1888); AUBE, *Sur l'instruction publique en Sicile et particulièrement sur l' Université de Palermo* (Paris, 1872).

U. BENIGNI.

Palestine. See GEOGRAPHY, BIBLICAL.

Palestrina, DIOCESE OF (PRÆNESTINENSIS); the town of Palestrina, in the province of Rome, central Italy, is the ancient Præneste, situated on the Via Labicana, the origin of which was attributed by the ancients to Ulysses, or to another fabulous personage. It is first mentioned in history as an ally of Rome against the Latins, in 499 B. C. From 373 to 370, however, it was in continual war against Rome or her allies, and was defeated by Cincinnatus; in 354 and in 338 it lost portions of its territory. Thenceforth it was always an ally of Rome, but disdained Roman citizenship until 90 B. C. In 82, having received Marius, it was taken and sacked by Sulla; later, under Tiberius, it became a *municipium*. It was a summer resort of the Romans, who ridiculed the language and the rough manners of its inhabitants. The modern town is built on the ruins of the famous temple of Fortuna Primigenia. From the eleventh century, it was a fief of the Colonna, and a refuge in their rebellions against the popes; consequently, it was several times destroyed, as in 1297, by order of Boniface VIII, and in 1436, by Giovanni Vitelleschi, at the command of Eugenius IV. It was rebuilt in 1447, sacked in 1527, and occupied by the Duke of Alba, in 1556. In 1630, it was sold to the Barberini. The town contains remnants of cyclopean walls and of the aforesaid great temple of Fortune. The cathedral has fine paintings and frescoes. In the Church of St. Rosalia (1677) there is an admirable Pietà, carved in the solid rock. Palestrina is the birthplace of the archæologist Andrea Fulvio and of the prince of sacred music, Giovanni Pierluigi da Palestrina. The oldest Christian record of this city relates to the martyrdom of St. Agapitus, patron of the cathedral, which took place under Aurelian; this basilica was restored and enriched with costly gifts by Leo III. Secundus, Bishop of Palestrina, was at the Council of Rome (313), and the names of several other of its bishops in ancient times are known. From the sixth century there was a flourishing monastery on the site of Castel S. Pietro, overlooking the city. After the seventh century, the Bishop of Palestrina was one of the hebdomadary prelates for the services of the Lateran basilica, and was, therefore, a cardinal; he is the fourth, in order, of the cardinal-bishops.

Among the prelates of this see may be mentioned Gregory, who in 757 consecrated the antipope Constantine; Andreas, legate of Adrian I to King Desiderius, in 772; Petrus (996), the first to bear the title of cardinal; Uberto (1073), legate of Gregory VII to Henry IV; Conon (1111), who embellished the crypt of St. Agapitus; S. Stefano (1122), a Cistercian monk, praised by St. Bernard and John of Salisbury for his piety; Guarino Guarini (1144), a Regular Canon of St. Augustine, famous for his virtues; Manfredo (1166) who persuaded Barbarossa to become reconciled with Alexander III; Paolo Scolari (1181), later Clement III; Blessed Guido de Pare (1196), a Cistercian; Jacopo Pecoraria (1231); Stefano III (1244), previously Archbishop of Gran; Girolamo d'Ascoli (1278), a Franciscan, later Nicholas IV; Pietro d'Anablay (1306), Grand Chancellor of France; Simon de Langham (1376), an Englishman. During the schism, the popes of Avignon, also, appointed cardinal-bishops of Palestrina. Thereafter, as a result of the custom that gave to cardinal-bishops the option of selecting another suburbicarian see, the rule of the prelates of Palestrina was of short duration. Among those who followed were Hugues de Lusignan (1431), a brother of the King of Cyprus; Guglielmo Brissonette (1507), deposed by Julius II for attending the conciliabule of Pisa; Lorenzo Campeggio (1535); Gianvicenzo Carafa (1539); Giovanni M. del Monte (1543), later Julius III; Louis de Bourbon (1550); Federico Cesi (1557); Giovanni Morone (1562); Cristoforo Madruzzi (1564); Gian Antonio Serbelloni (1578); Marcantonio Colonna (1587); Alessandro Medici (1602), later Leo XI; Guido Bentivoglio (1641); Alfonso de la Queva (1644); Antonio Barberini (1661), who founded the seminary; Paluzzo Altieri (1691); Girolamo Spinola (1775); Aurelio Rovarella (1809), who died an exile in France, in 1812; Diego Caracciolo (1814); Giuseppe Spina (1820); Castruccio Castracani degli Antelminelli (1844). The sanctuary of Our Lady of Good Counsel of Genazzano is in this diocese; here, also, are the ancient see of Gabii, ten bishops of which, between the fifth and the ninth centuries, are known, and that of Subaugusta, four bishops of which are known between 465 and 502. The diocese has 24 parishes, 45,700 inhabitants, 10 religious houses of men, 14 of women, and 3 girls' schools.

CAPPELLETTI, *Le Chiese d'Italia*, I; MORONI, *Dizionario*, s. v.; MARUCCHI, *Guida archeol. dell' antica Prœneste* (Rome, 1885); CECCONI, *Storia di Palestrina* (Ascoli, 1756).

U. BENIGNI.

Palestrina, GIOVANNI PIERLUIGI DA, the greatest composer of liturgical music of all time, b. at Palestrina (ancient Præneste) in 1514 or 1515, according to Baini, Riemann, and others, according to Haberl, in 1526; d. at Rome, 2 February, 1594. His early history is practically unknown. Giusseppi Ottavia Pittoni (1657–1743), in "Notizie dei maestri di cappella si di Roma che altramontani, 1500–1700", a manuscript in the Vatican, relates that young Pierluigi sang in the streets of Rome while offering for sale the products of his parents' farm and that he was heard on such an occasion by the choir-master of Santa Maria Maggiore, who, impressed by the boy's beautiful voice and pronounced musical talent, educated him musically. As to the identity of the choir-master, tradition gives no clue. Some hold that Palestrina was taught by Jacques Arcadelt (1514–60), choir-master and composer in Rome from 1539 to 1549. The opinion, so long held, that Claude Goudimel (1505–72) was his principal teacher has now been definitively abandoned. As far as is known, he began his active musical life as organist and choir-master in his native city in 1544; his reputation increasing, in 1551 he was called to Rome, entrusted with the direction and musical formation of the choir-boys at St. Peter's, and within the same year was advanced to the post of choir-master. In 1554 he dedicated to Julius III (1549–55) his first compositions, a volume of masses for four voices, and was rewarded with the appointment as a member of the papal chapel in contravention of the rules governing that body. The pope had set aside the rule requiring those who held membership in the papal choir to be in Holy orders, and also used his authority to exempt him from the usually severe entrance examination. These circumstances and the further fact that his voice was much inferior to those of the other singers, aroused the opposition and antagonism of his fellow-members. The papal singers did not appreciate the object of the pope, which was to secure for the gifted young man the necessary leisure to compose.

In the course of the same year, Palestrina published a volume of madrigals. The texts of some of these the composer himself in later years considered too free. In the dedication of his setting of the Canticle of Canticles to Gregory XIII, he expresses not only regret but repentance, for having caused scandal by this publication. Marcellus II, as cardinal, had protected and admired Palestrina, but died after a reign of only twenty-one days. Paul IV, shortly after his accession, re-inforced the former rules for the government of the papal choir. Besides Palestrina, there were two other lay married members in the choir. All were dismissed with a small pension, in spite of the understanding that these singers were engaged for life. The worry and hardship caused by the dismissal brought on a severe illness; restored, the composer took charge, 1 October, 1555, of the choir at St. John Lateran, where he remained until February, 1561. During this period he wrote, besides Lamentations and Magnificats, the famous "Improperia". Their performance by the papal choir on Good Friday was ordered by Paul IV, and they have remained in its repertoire for Holy Week ever since. This production greatly increased Palestrina's fame. In 1561 he asked the chapter of St. John Lateran for an increase in salary, in view of his growing needs and the expense of publishing his works. Refused, he accepted a similar post at Santa Maria Maggiore, which he held until 1571. It is not known at what period of his career Palestrina came under the influence of St. Philip Neri, but there is every reason to believe it was in early youth. As the saint's penitent and spiritual disciple, he gained that insight into the spirit of the liturgy, which enabled him to set it forth in polyphonic music as it had never before been done. It was his spiritual formation even more than his artistic maturity, which fitted him for the providential part he played in the reform of church music.

The task of hastening the reforms decreed by the Council of Trent was entrusted by Pius IV to a commission of eight cardinals. A committee of two of these, St. Charles Borromeo and Vitellozo Vitelli, was appointed to consider certain improvements in the discipline and administration of the papal choir, and to this end they associated to themselves eight of the choir members. Cardinal Vitelli caused the singers to perform certain compositions in his presence, in order to determine what measures could be taken for the preservation of the integrity and distinct declamation of the text in compositions in which the voices were interwoven. St. Charles, as chancellor of his uncle, Pius IV, was the patron of Palestrina, increasing his pension in 1565. He celebrated a solemn Mass in presence of the pontiff on 19 June, 1565, at which Palestrina's great "Missa Papæ Marcelli" was sung. These historical data are the only discoverable basis for the legends, so long repeated by historians, concerning the trial before the cardinals and pope of the cause of polyphonic music, and its vindication by Palestrina, in the composition and performance of three masses, the "Missa Papæ Marcelli" among them. Haberl's studies of the archives conclusively demolished these fictions, but their continued repetition for nearly two hundred years emphasizes the fact of Palestrina's activity, inspired by St. Philip and encouraged by St. Charles, in the reform of church music, an activity which embraced his entire career and antedated by some years the disciplinary measures of the church authorities.

GIOVANNI PIERLUIGI DA PALESTRINA
After an original in the musical archives of the Vatican Museum

The foundation of his reform is the two principles legitimately deduced from the only references to church music in the Tridentine decrees: (1) the elimination of all themes reminiscent of, or resembling, secular music; (2) the rejection of musical forms and elaborations tending to mutilate or obscure the liturgical text. Pius IV created for Palestrina the office of "Composer to the Papal Chapel" with an increased salary. In this office he had only one successor, Felice Anerio. When in 1571 Giovanni Annimuccia, choirmaster at St. Peter's, died, Palestrina became his successor, thus being connected with the papal choir and St. Peter's at the same time. An attempt of his jealous and intriguing colleagues in the papal chapel to have him dismissed by Pius V was unsuccessful. During this year he wrote a number of motets and *laudi spirituali* for the Oratory of St. Philip Neri. Besides the duties of choirmaster at St. Peter's, composer to the papal chapel, director of music at St. Philip's Oratory, he also taught at the school of music of Giovanni Maria Nanini. In addition, Gregory XIII commissioned him to prepare a new version of the Gregorian chant. His exact share in this edition, afterwards published under the name of "editio Medicæa" because printed in a press belonging to Cardinal de' Medici, and what was prepared by his pupil Giovanni Guidetti, Felice

Anerio, and Francesco Suriano, has long been a matter of controversy. The undertaking was not particularly congenial to Palestrina and kept him from original production, his real field of activity. His wife's death in 1580 affected him profoundly. His sorrow found expression in two compositions, Psalm cxxxvi, "By the waters of Babylon", and a motet on the words "O Lord, when Thou shalt come to judge the world, how shall I stand before the face of Thy anger, my sins frighten me, woe to me, O Lord". With these he intended to close his creative activity, but with the appointment in 1581 as director of music to Prince Buoncompagni, nephew of Gregory XIII, he began perhaps the most brilliant period of his long life.

Besides sacred madrigals, motets, psalms, hymns in honour of the Blessed Virgin, and masses, he produced the work which brought him the title of "Prince of Music", twenty-nine motets on words from the "Canticle of Canticles". According to his own statement, Palestrina intended to reproduce in his composition the Divine love expressed in the Canticle, so that his own heart might be touched by a spark thereof. For the enthronement of Sixtus V, he wrote a five-part motet and mass on the theme to the text "Tu es pastor ovium", followed a few months later by one of his greatest productions, the mass "Assumpta est Maria". Sixtus had intended to appoint him director of the papal choir, but the refusal of the singers to be directed by a layman, prevented the execution of his plan. During the last years of his life Palestrina wrote his great "Lamentations", settings of the liturgical hymns, a collection of motets, the well-known "Stabat Mater" for double chorus, litanies in honour of the Blessed Virgin Mary, and the offertories for the ecclesiastical year. His complete works, in thirty-three volumes, edited by Theodore de Witt, Franz Espagne, Franz Commer, and from the tenth volume on, by Haberl, are published by Breitkopf and Hartel; Mgr Haberl presented the last volume of the completed edition to Pius X on Easter Monday, 1908. Palestrina's significance lies not so much in his unprecedented gifts of mind and heart, his creative and constructive powers, as in the fact that he made them the medium for the expression in tones of the state of his own soul, which, trained and formed by St. Philip, was attuned to and felt with the Church. His creations will for all time stand forth as the musical embodiment of the spirit of the counter-reformation, the triumphant Church.

BAINI, *Memorie storico-critiche della vita e delle opere di Giovanni Pierluigi da Palestrina* (Rome, 1828); BÄUMKER, *Palestrina* (Freiburg, 1877); *Kirchenmusikalisches Jahrbuch* (Ratisbon, 1886); FELIX, *Palestrina et la musique sacrée* (Paris, 1897); CAPECELATRO, *Life of St. Philip Neri* (London, 1894); HABERL, *Bausteine für Musikgesch* (Leipzig, 1888).

JOSEPH OTTEN.

Paley, FREDERICK APTHORP, classical scholar, b. at Easingwold near York, 14 Jan., 1815; d. at Bournemouth, 9 Dec., 1888, son of the Rev. Edmund Paley and grandson of William Paley who wrote "Evidences of Christianity". He was educated at Shrewsbury School and St. John's College, Cambridge, where he taught and continued to study for eight years after his B. A. degree (1838). His studies were mainly classical; but, despite an incapacity for mathematics, he was interested in mechanics and in natural science, and was an enthusiastic ecclesiological antiquary. In 1846, being well known as a Cambridge sympathizer with the Oxford Movement, he was expelled from residence in St. John's College, on suspicion of having influenced one of his pupils to become a Catholic. He was himself received into the Church in this year. For the next fourteen years he supported himself as a private tutor in several Catholic families successively (Talbot, Throckmorton, Kenelm Digby) and by his pen. From 1860, when Tests began to be relaxed, he again lived at Cambridge until 1874: from 1874 to 1877 he was professor of classical literature at the abortive Catholic University College at Kensington. From 1877 till his death he continued to write assiduously. But the interruption of his university career, the want of a settled competence, and his banishment from the place, the society, and the learned facilities which might best have improved his talents and industry, had the effect of rendering nearly all his voluminous production ephemeral. His many classical editions, which had a great and not undeserved vogue and influence in their day, became soon obsolete and marked no decisive epoch in classical philology. Yet his work on Euripides and Æschylus in particular may still be consulted with profit, at least as a monument of protest against the Victorian mock-archaic convention in translations from Greek poetry; and it is easy to underrate now the merits of work which met a great demand for school and college use, and itself did much to evoke the more scientific scholarship which has superseded it.

His works number more than fifty volumes, besides numerous magazine articles and reviews contributed to the "American Catholic Quarterly", "Edinburgh Review", "Journal of Philology" etc. The first of his classical publications, and the one which established his reputation as a scholar, was the text of Æschylus (1844–7); during the next forty years he edited with the commentaries, Propertius (1853); Ovid's "Fasti" (1854); Æschylus (1855); Euripides (1857); Hesiod (1861); Theocritus (1863); Homer's "Iliad" (1866); Martial (1868); Pindar (transl. with notes) 1868; Aristophanes' "Peace" (1873); Plato's "Philebus" (1873); "Private Orations of Demosthenes" (1874); Plato's "Thætetus" (1875); Aristophanes' "Acharnians" (1876); "Medicean Scholia of Æschylus" (1878); Aristophanes' "Frogs" (1878); Sophocles (1880). To these must be added many critical inquiries, especially on the Homeric question; and most of his Commentaries ran through three or four editions, of which Marindin remarks that "every new edition was practically a new work". He found leisure to issue books on architecture; his "Manual of Gothic Mouldings", first published in 1845, went into a fifth edition in 1891.

Dict. Nat. Biog., s. v.

J. S. PHILLIMORE.

Pall, a heavy, black cloth, spread over the coffin in the church at a funeral, or over the catafalque at other services for the dead. In the centre of it there is generally a white or red cross. It must always be black, but its material and ornamentation may vary. Symbols of death, such as skulls, cross-bones etc., forbidden on the altar and ministers' vestments, are allowed on palls. The pall is in universal use, though not prescribed. Where, however, there is no catafalque or bier, absolution may not be given except a black cloth be extended on the floor of the sanctuary (S. R. C., 3535, 5).

CASTALDUS, lib. II, s. 9, c. v; DE HERDT, *Sac. Liturg. Praxis*, III, n. 248.

ANDREW B. MEEHAN.

Pall (CHALICE COVER). See ALTAR, sub-title ALTAR-LINENS; CHALICE.

Palladio, ANDREA, Italian architect, b. at Vicenza, 1508; d. at Venice, 19 Aug., 1580. There is a tradition that he was the son of a poor carpenter, with no surname of his own, and that the famous humanistic poet, Gian Giorgio Trissino, became his patron and gave him the name of Palladio, in fanciful allusion to Pallas, the Greek goddess of wisdom. After a brief apprenticeship as sculptor he travelled and studied the remains of classical architecture, endeavouring to determine its principles by the aid of Vitruvius's writings. The results of these studies appear in the buildings which he constructed, of which the earliest known is the Palazzo Godi at Lonedo (1540). The execution of his design for the rebuilding of the basilica in his native town was commenced in 1549. The colonnades of this basilica are his most famous work. His Arco di Trionfo, also at Vicenza, is even now the best modern imitation of a Roman triumphal arch. A fine sense of proportion, combined with scholarly refinement and fertility of invention, characterizes the palaces of Vicenza, where Palladio had a free hand. He was a favourite of society in and about Vicenza, and was therefore a most prolific designer of villas. Few of these were ever completed, many have been changed or dismantled, and nearly all have lost the environment of gardens and accessories which were a necessary part of the composition. All are, however, stately, spacious and airy, effective in mass, dignified in detail, and free from affectation. Two standard types are the Villa Capra, in the environs of Vicenza, and the Villa Giacomelli at Treviso.

Only three sacred buildings are surely his work, the small chapel near the last-named villa, and the churches of San Giorgio (1565) and Il Redentore (begun, 1576, finished after his death) at Venice. These two churches are cruciform, with aisles, crossing-domes, and apsidal terminations to choirs and transepts. The interiors are cold, powerful, and spacious; the exteriors are frankly structural, of inferior materials, with semi-circular, lead-covered domes, and with no ornamentation except in the façades.

Palladio may be taken as the representative of a wholesome reaction against the decadent tendencies of his age, and may be said to have fixed good architectural style for many succeeding centuries. Although in France a more meretricious taste prevailed, represented by Lescaut and by De l'Orme in England, through Inigo Jones, Palladio became so much the controlling spirit that the English style of the seventeenth century is now known as "Palladian". Naturally, the Georgian architecture of the United States develops directly from Palladio through the later masters who followed Inigo Jones. Palladio's writings, particularly "Le Antichità di Roma" and the "Quattro Libri dell' Architettura", did more than anything else to spread his influence over Europe: many editions were published in Italy between 1554 and 1642. They were widely translated, and in England Inigo Jones acted as editor and commentator.

SCAMOZZI, *L'Architecture Universale* (1694); GUALDO, *Vita di Andrea Palladio* (1749); TEMANZA, *Vita di Andrea Palladio* (1762–1778); MILIZIA, *Memorie degli Architetti* (1781); tr. CRECY, *Lives of Celebrated Architects* (London, 1826); MAGRINI, *Dell' Architettura in Vicenza* (1845); BURCHKHARDT, *Die Renaissance in Italien* (1867); BARICHELLA, *Andrea Palladio e la sua Scuola* (1880); GOODYEAR, *Renaissance and Modern Art* (New York, 1894); FLETCHER, *Andrea Palladio* (London, 1902).

RALPH ADAMS CRAM.

ANDREA PALLADIO

Palladius, SAINT, first bishop sent by Pope Celestine to Ireland (431). The chronicle of the contemporary St. Prosper of Aquitaine presents two important entries relating to Palladius. Under date of 429 it has "Agricola, a Pelagian, son of Severianus, a Pelagian bishop, corrupted the churches of Britain by the insinuation of his doctrine; but at the instance of the Deacon Palladius (*ad actionem Palladii Diaconi*) Pope Celestine sends Germanus, Bishop of Auxerre, as his representative to root out heresy and direct the Britons to the Catholic Faith". Again under date of 431, in the consulship of Bassus and Antiochus: "Palladius was consecrated by Pope Celestine and sent to the Scots believing in Christ, as their first bishop" (Ad Scotos in Christum credentes, ordinatur a Papa Celestino Palladius et primus episcopus mittitur). In his work against Cassian, St. Prosper compendiates both entries: "Wherefore the Pontiff Celestine of venerable memory, to whom the Lord gave many gifts of His grace for safeguarding the Catholic Church, knowing that for those who are already condemned, the remedy to be applied is not a further judicial inquiry but only repentance, gave instructions for Celestius, who asked for a further hearing in a matter already settled, to be driven from the borders of all Italy . . . with no less jealous care he delivered Britain from the same disease, when he drove even from that hidden recess of the ocean some enemies of Grace who were settling in their native soil; and by ordaining a bishop for the Irish (*Scotis*), whilst he laboured to keep the Roman Island Catholic, he made also the barbarous Island Christian." The words in the second entry of the chronicle "to the Scots believing in Christ" can only have the meaning that when the chronicle was being written in 447, the Irish had become a Christian people.

Some writers with Dr. Todd regard Palladius as deacon of St. Germanus, but it appears more probable that he held the high rank of Deacon of Rome; it can hardly be supposed that a Deacon of Auxerre would exercise such influence in Rome as that assigned to Palladius, and it is in accordance with St. Prosper's usage to indicate the Roman deacon by the simple title *diaconus*. Thus in the chronicle we have frequent entries such as "Hilarius Diaconus", "Ioannes Diaconus", "Leo Diaconus", which invariably refer to the deacons of Rome. The seventh century life of St. Patrick by Muircu Maccumacthenus in the "Book of Armagh" expressly styles Palladius "Archidiaconus Papæ Cœlestini urbis Romæ Episcopi", repeated in several of the other lives of St. Patrick. Ussher registers the tradition long current in England that Palladius was born in Britain and that he had combated the Pelagian heresy there. The Bollandists are also of the opinion that he was "a Briton by birth". The Palladii, however, were reckoned among the noblest families of France and several of them held high rank about this time in the Church of Gaul. These conflicting opinions may perhaps be reconciled. Under Julian the Apostate there was a Palladius holding prominent rank in the army of Gaul, who, for his fearless profession of the Faith, was exiled into Britain. We may easily suppose that the scion of such a privileged Gallo-British family would attain the position of Deacon of Rome, would take much interest in the British Church, and, would by his familiarity with the Celtic language, be qualified to undertake the mission of first bishop to the Irish. Palladius is honoured in the Scottish calendar on 6 July. The Aberdeen Breviary describes him as "pontificem et fidei Catholicæ apostolum pariter et doctorem". In some ancient records he is styled a martyr, probably because of the hardships endured during his missionary career in Ireland.

Palladius landed in the territory of the Hy-Garchon, on the strand where the town of Wicklow now stands, then occupied by the tribe of Cualann who have left their name on the beautiful valley of Glencullen, seven miles distant from the spot where Palladius landed. The chieftain of the district had no welcome for the missionaries. However some of the tribe appear to have extended a better measure of kindness to them and at least three churches were in after times assigned as the result of Palladius's mission. The Life of St. Patrick, already referred to, records the failure of the mission: "Palladius was ordained and sent to convert this island lying under wintry cold, but God hindered him, for no man can receive anything from earth unless it be given to him from heaven; and neither did those fierce and cruel men receive his doctrine readily, nor did he himself wish to spend time in a strange land, but returned to him who sent him. On his return hence, however, having crossed the first sea and commenced his land journey, he died in the territory of the Britons." In the Scholia on St. Fiacc's Hymn in the ancient "Liber Hymnorum" it is stated that in the country of the Hy-Garchon, Palladius "founded some churches: *Teach-na-Roman*, or the House of the Romans, *Kill-Fine*, and others. Nevertheless he was not well received, but was forced to go round the coast of Ireland towards the north, until driven by a tempest he reached the extreme part of Modhaidh towards the south, where he founded the church of Fordun, and *Pledi* is his name there." The *Vita Secunda*, life of St. Patrick, in Colgan's collection, adds further interesting details: "The most blessed Pope Celestine ordained Bishop the Archdeacon of the Roman Church, named Palladius, and sent him into the Island of Hibernia, after having committed to him the relics of Blessed Peter and Paul and other Saints, and having also given him the volumes of the Old and New Testaments. Palladius, entering the land of the Irish, arrived at the territory of the men of Leinster where Nathi Mac Garrchon was chief, who was opposed to him. Others, however, whom the Divine mercy had disposed towards the worship of God, having been baptized in the name of the sacred Trinity, the blessed Palladius built three Churches in the same district; one, which is called *Cellfine*, in which even to the present day, he left his books which he had received from St. Celestine and the box of relics of the blessed Peter and Paul and other Saints, and the tablets on which he used to write, which in the Irish language are called from his name Pallere, that is, the burden of Palladius, and are held in veneration. Another, *Tech-na-Roman*, and the third *Domnach Ardec*, in which are buried the holy men of the companions of Palladius, Sylvester and Salonius, who are honoured there. After a short time Palladius died in the plain of Girgin in a place which is called Fordun. But others say that he was crowned with martyrdom there." Another ancient document, known as the *Vita Quinta* in Colgan's work, repeats the particulars here given relating to the foundation of three churches, and adds: "But St. Palladius, seeing that he could not do much good there, wishing to return to Rome, migrated to the Lord in the region of the Picts. Others, however, say that he was crowned with martyrdom in Ireland."

The three churches have been identified. *Teach-na-Roman* is Tigroney, where are the ruins of an old church in the parish of Castle Mac Adam in the county of Wicklow. *Kill-Fine* was supposed by Father Shearman to be the same as Killeen Cormac, a remarkable old churchyard, three miles south-west of Dunlavin, but more probably situated in the parish of Glendalough, in the townland which the Ordnance Survey has named Lara-West, but which is still called Killfinn by the people. The third church *Domnach Ardec* is Donard which gives its name to a parish and village in the west of the County Wicklow in the barony of Lower Talbotstown. This parish, as Father Shearman writes, retains "some vestiges of its ancient importance; the sites of primeval Christian churches, large and well-preserved Raths and Tumuli, Cromlechs, Ogham Pillars, ancient ecclesiastical Cashels, Pagan Cathairs on the surrounding hills, with many other evidences of a civilized and numerous population". The modern critical Scottish historians, Bishop Forbes, Skene, and others, confess that in regard to the connexion of St. Palladius with Scotland, the Irish documents are the only reliable sources. The traditions set forth in Fordun's chronicle and later writings are regarded as purely mythical. One assigns to Palladius an apostolate in Scotland of twenty-three years; another makes him the tutor of St. Servanus, contemporary of St. Adamnan and Brude, King of the Picts (A. D. 697–706), all of which is irreconcilable with the Irish narratives and with the date of the saint's mission from St. Celestine. A German theory has found favour with some writers in recent times, to the effect that the Bishop Palladius referred to in the second entry by Prosper as sent to Ireland by Celestine was none other than St. Patrick. This theory viewed independently of the ancient historical narratives would have much to commend it. It would merely imply that the Bishop Palladius of the second entry in the chronicle was distinct from the Deacon Palladius of the first entry, and that the scanty records connected with Palladius's mission to Ireland were to be referred to St. Patrick. But this theory is inconsistent with the unbroken series of testimonies in the ancient lives of St. Patrick and cannot easily be reconciled with the traditions of the Scottish Church.

SHEARMAN, *Loca Patriciana* (Dublin, 1879); STOKES, *Vita Tripartita* in Rolls Series (London, 1888); FORBES, *Kalendars of Scottish MSS.* (Edinburgh, 1872); SKENE, *Celtic Scotland*, II (Edinburgh, 1886); BELLESHEIM, *Hist. of the C. Church in Scotland*, tr. HUNTER-BLAIR, I (Edinburgh and London, 1887). See also lives of St. Patrick by HEALY, TODD, BURY, etc.

PATRICK FRANCIS CARDINAL MORAN.

Palladius (Παλλάδιος), b. in Galatia, 368; d. probably before 431. The identity of the author of the "Historia Lausiaca", of the Palladius who wrote a life of St. John Chrysostom, and of the Bishop of Helenopolis, long disputed, has been vindicated of late years (Preuschen, Butler, op. cit.) and is now generally accepted. A disciple of Evagrius of Pontus (q. v.) and an admirer of Origen, he became, when twenty years of age, a monk on the Mount of Olives under a certain priest, Innocent. After three years he went to Egypt to study the life of the famous Egyptian monks (see MONASTICISM), but later, falling into ill-health, wandered from one colony of monks to another, and made the acquaintance of Didymus the Blind (d. 395) who had known St. Anthony. In the Nitrian desert, then inhabited by thousands of monks living partly in communities and partly as isolated hermits, he met Evagrius. For nine years he stayed among these monks, observing their life and hearing the traditions of their founders, Anthony, Paul, Pachomius, Pambo, etc.; he also visited the monks and nuns of the Thebaid and Scete, so that he saw all the chief monastic colonies of Egypt. On the death of Evagrius (399), Palladius set out for his own country (Asia Minor) by Alexandria and Palestine. At Bethlehem he met St. Jerome, whose great knowledge, he declares, was marred by "envy and jealousy" (Hist. Laus., l, Of Possidonius). The great opponent of Origen was naturally not sympathetic to his visitor. At Jerusalem Palladius saw Rufinus of Aquileia and Melania. In Bithynia he was ordained bishop (ibid., xlix, Of John of Lycus). St. John Chrysostom ordained him for the See of Helenopolis, but Bardenhewer thinks that Palladius of Helenopolis mentioned by Socrates, "Hist. Eccl.", VII, xxxvi (Freiburg, 1894, p. 354), is another person. From this time he becomes a zealous adherent of his patriarch, whose troubles in 403 he shared. He was imprisoned for eleven months in a dark cell (Hist. Laus., loc. cit.). Later he lived for a time in Palestine near Jericho under a famous hermit, Elpidius of Cappadocia (Hist. Laus., lx, Of Elpidius). In 405 he went to Rome to plead the cause of Chrysostom with Innocent I (401–17) and Emperor Honorius (395–423). He came back to Constantinople as a member of the mission sent by Honorius to Arcadius (395–408) in favour of the banished patriarch. But there he and his colleagues were imprisoned and then banished, Palladius being sent to Syene in Upper Egypt. Later he went to Antinoe and was in Ancyra after 412. In 417 he changed his Diocese of Helenopolis for Aspuna in Galatia (Socrates, loc. cit.). In 420 he wrote his "Historia Lausiaca" (Butler, "The Lausiac History", I, 179 sq.). After that he disappears; but he died apparently before 431, in which year a certain Eusebius was Bishop of Aspuna.

His chief work is the "Historica Lausiaca", a history of the monks of Egypt and Palestine in the form of anecdotes and short biographies. Its name comes from the dedication to Lausos, a chamberlain of Theodosius II (408–50) Ἡ πρὸς Λαῦσον ἱστορία and then shortly, Λαυσιακόν or Λαυσαϊκόν. Difficulties about the text are examined in great part solved by Dom Cuthbert Butler (see below). The chief difficulty is that Palladius repeats nearly all the contents of Rufinus, "Historia monachorum" (written from a Greek source between 404 and 410). The text, as it is in Migne, evidently depends on Rufinus's source. There are also many variant texts. The book was popular among monks all over the East, who appear to have added to it considerably in transcribing it. The first edition was a Latin version by Gentianus Hervetus (Paris, 1555), reprinted by H. Rosweyde ("Vitæ patrum", VIII, Paris, 1628). A shorter Greek text was published by J. Meursius (Leyden, 1616), and a longer one by Fronton Leduc ("Auctarium bibliothecæ Patrum", IV, Paris, 1624), and a still more complete one by J. Cotelerius ("Monumenta eccl. græcæ", III, Paris, 1686; reprinted in P. G., XXXIV, 995–1260). This longer version contains the text of Rufinus. Butler, Preuschen, and others think that the shorter text (of Meursius) is Palladius's authentic work, the longer version being interpolated. Amélineau (op. cit.) holds that the longer text is all Palladius's work, and that the first thirty-seven chapters (about the monks of Lower Egypt) are mainly an account of what the author saw and heard, though even here he has also used documents. But he thinks the second part (about Upper Egypt) is merely a compilation from a Coptic or Greek document which Rufinus also used; so that Palladius's visit to Upper Egypt must be a literary fiction. (See also Fessler-Jungmann, op. cit.) But the shorter text itself exists in various forms. A Syrian monk, Anan-Isho, living in the sixth-seventh centuries in Mesopotamia, translated the "Lausiac History" into Syriac with further interpolations ("Paradisus Patrum", ed. Bedjan, "Acta martyrum et sanctorum", VII, Paris, 1897; tr. E. A. Wallis Budge, "The Paradise of the Fathers", 2 vols., London, 1907). At one time the "Lausiac History" was considered a compilation of imaginary legends (see Weingarten, "Der Ursprung des Mönchtums", Gotha, 1877, and others). Later research has very considerably rehabilitated Palladius; the chief authorities now (Butler, Preuschen) consider the "Lausiac History" to be in the main a serious historical document as well as an invaluable picture of the lives and ideas of the earliest Christian monks (cf. Preuschen, op. cit., 210).

Palladius's object is not so much to save material for history as to provide spiritual reading; at the same time the author has a controversial purpose as an Origenist. Rosweyde in his edition adds to the "Lausiac History" an alphabetic list of "Sayings of the Fathers" (Ἀποφθέγματα τῶν πατέρων, in the "Vitæ Patrum", V–VI). These are later and consist partly of old traditions of Egyptian monks, partly of apocryphal additions (Butler, "The Lausiac History", I, 208–15). Under the name of Palladius there is also a life of St. John Chrysostom (Dialogue with Theodore, deacon of the Roman Church, about the life and manners of John Chrysostom). It was first edited in Greek with a Latin translation by E. Bigot (Paris, 1680); it is included in de Montfaucon's edition of Chrysostom (XIII, Paris, 1718–38), and in P. G. (XLVII, 5–82). There are difficulties about the identification of its author with that of the "Lausiac History" and the Bishop of Helenopolis, so that all possible combinations have been suggested, including that of three separate persons. The chief of these difficulties is that the biographer distinguishes himself from the bishop (c. iii, "P. G.", loc. cit., 13). Bardenhewer ("Patrologie", 354) and Fessler-Jungmann ("Institutiones Patrologiæ", II, i, 209–10) identify the author of the "Lausiac History" and the biographer, but distinguish from them the bishop. It is, however, now very common to identify the bishop and the Lausiac author (Dr. Wallis Budge, "The Paradise of the Fathers", p. xxi), so that we come to the identity of all three as supposed in this article. Preuschen explains the difficulty in the Dialogue as a literary fiction (Palladius u. Rufinus, 246).

The best modern edition of the *Lausiac History* is DOM CUTHBERT BUTLER, *Palladius, The Lausiac History*; I. *A critical discussion*; II. *The Greek text in Texts and Studies*, VI (Cambridge, 1898, 1904); PREUSCHEN, *Palladius u. Rufinus, ein Beitrag zur Quellenkunde des ältesten Mönchtums* (Giessen, 1897); AMÉLINEAU, *De hist. Lausiaca* (Paris, 1887); HURTER, *Nomenclator*, I (Innsbruck, 1903), 322; FESSLER-JUNGMANN, *Institutiones Patrologiæ*, ii, i (Innsbruck, 1892), 209–12.

ADRIAN FORTESCUE.

Pallavicino, PIETRO SFORZA, cardinal, b. 28 Nov., 1607; d. 5 June, 1667. Descended from the line of Parma of the ancient and noble house of the Marchese, Pallavicini, the first-born of his family, he renounced the right of primogeniture and resolved to enter the priesthood. He obtained the doctorate in philosophy in 1625, theology in 1628 (the theses, printed in the years mentioned, being extant). Pope Urban VIII (1623–44) appointed him *referendarius utriusque signaturæ* and member of several congregations. He was highly esteemed in the literary circles of Rome. When his friend Giovanni Ciampoli, the secretary of briefs, fell into disfavour, Pallavicino's standing at the papal court was also seriously affected. He was sent in 1632 as *governatore* to Jesi, Orvieto, and Camerino, where he remained for a considerable time. In spite of his father's opposition, he entered the Society of Jesus on 21 June, 1637. After the two years' novitiate he became, 1639, professor of philosophy at the Collegium Romanum. In 1643, when John de Lugo was made cardinal, Pallavicino became his successor in the chair of theology, a position he occupied until 1651. At the same time he was frequently employed by Innocent X in matters of importance. In this way he became a member of the commission appointed to examine the writings of Jansenius. He was furthermore commissioned to examine the writings of M. de Barcos, two of which were condemned in 1647.

Before his entrance into the Jesuit order he had published orations and poems. Of his great poem "I fasti sacri", which was to have been completed in fourteen cantos, he had published one part (Rome, 1636); but upon his entrance into the novitiate he gave up its further publication. His first considerable literary work as Jesuit was a tragedy, "Ermenegildo martire" (Rome, 1644). In the same year there appeared "Del bene libri quattro" (Rome 1644 and often reprinted). He began editing the works of his former friend Giovanni Ciampoli; of these the "Rime" appeared in Rome (1648) and the "Prose" (1667 and 1676). In rebuttal of the numerous accusations raised against the Society of Jesus, Pallavicino composed a circumstantial refutation, "Vindicationes Societatis Jesu, quibus multorum accusationes in eius institutum, leges, gymnasia, mores refelluntur" (Rome, 1649). In the same year he began the publication of his great dogmatic work in conjunction with his theological lectures, "Assertiones theologicæ". The complete work treats the entire field of dogma in nine books. The first five books appeared in three volumes (Rome, 1649), the remaining four books are included in volumes IV–VIII (Rome, 1650–1652). Immediately after this he began the publication of disputations on the second part of the "Summa theologica" of St. Thomas, "R. P. Sfortiæ Pallavicini . . . Disputationum in Iam IIæ d. Thomæ tomus I" (Lyons, 1653). However, only this first volume of the work appeared, for in the meantime Pallavicino had been directed by the pope to write a refutation of Sarpi's History of the Council of Trent.

The odious and hostile account of the Council of Trent by Sarpi had appeared as early as 1619 under a fictitious name ("Historia del Concilio Tridentino, nella quale si scoprono tutti gli artifici della corte di Roma . . . di Pietro Soave Pollano", London, 1619). Several Catholic scholars had already begun to collect the material for a refutation of this work, but none had been able to finish the gigantic undertaking. Felix Contelorio and the Jesuit, Ter. Alciati, in particular had collected a rich mass of material. The latter, moreover, had already begun with the compilation, when he died suddenly in 1651. Pallavicino by order of the pope was now to take up the work anew. Accordingly he resigned his professorship at the Collegium Romanum, to devote himself exclusively to this prodigious task. He utilized all the available material previously gathered by Contelorio and Alciati, and added much that was new from Roman and non-Roman archives. The reports of the council in the secret archives of the Vatican were at his unrestricted disposal (cf. Ehses, in "Römische Quartalschrift", 1902, p. 296 sqq.). He was thus able to bring out the work as early as 1656 and 1657 in two folio volumes under the title, "Istoria del Concilio di Trento, scritta dal P. Sforza Pallavicino, della Comp. di Giesù ove insieme rifiutasi con auterevoli testimonianze un Istoria falsa divolgata nello stesso argomento sotto nome di Petro Soave Polano" (first part, Rome, 1656; second part, Rome, 1657). The author himself was able to bring out a new edition in three volumes (Rome, 1664). With the assistance of his secretary Cataloni, he made an abridgement in which the polemical portions are omitted (Rome, 1666). Until within very recent years Pallavicino's History of the Council of Trent was the principal work on this important ecclesiastical assembly. Reprints of it have appeared frequently, and Antonio Zaccaria published an annotated edition (Rome, 1733, 4 vols.), which has been reprinted three times. The work was also translated into Latin by a Jesuit, Giattini (Antwerp, 1670); into German by Klitsche (Augsburg, 1835–1837); into French (Migne series, Paris, 1844–1845); and into Spanish. Pallavicino's work is more copious, more conscientious, and more in accordance with the truth than that of his adversary Sarpi. But it is an apologetic treatise, and for that reason not free from partiality as it is not without errors [cf. "Concilium Tridentinum, Diariorum pars prima", ed. Seb. Merkle (Freiburg im Breisgau, 1901), p. xiii]. In any case, however, Pallavicino did not purposely falsify the history of the council, and he has reported much that proves his frankness and objectivity in the recital.

Pallavicino received due recognition from his friend, Alexander VII (1655–67). On 19 April, 1657, he was created cardinal *in petto;* on 10 Nov., 1659, his elevation to the cardinalate was published. Nevertheless he continued his simple, pious way of living. The pope often consulted him in matters of importance. He attended to his diverse tasks with the greatest conscientiousness. His income was in a large measure employed in supporting scientific endeavours. His own work in literature was likewise continued, as is proved by the new edition of his History of the Council of Trent and the edition of the "Prose" of Ciampoli. A work of ascetic character, "Arte della perfezione cristiana, divisa in tre libri", appeared in 1665 (Rome). Several of his works were not printed until later; others are still in manuscript. After becoming cardinal, Pallavicino continued loyal to the Jesuit Order and was its protector and patron. He died during the vacancy of the Holy See in 1667.

In the year after his death his former secretary, Giambattista Galli Pavarelli, published a collection of his letters, "Lettere dettate dal card. Sforza Pallavicino" (Rome, 1668). Other collections appeared in Bologna (1669), in Venice (1825), in Rome (4 vols., 1848). An opinion which he had written on the question whether it was most appropriate that the pope live in Rome at St. Peter's, was printed together with a discussion of the same question by Lucas Holstenius, in Rome (1676). Larger collections of various works of Pallavicino were brought out as late as the nineteenth century. The following editions of his "Opera" are to be noted as the most important: Rome, 1834 (in 2 volumes); Rome, 1844–48 (in 33 volumes); and a collection of other works in five volumes published at the same time by Ottavio Gilgi.

AFFÒ, *Biography of Pallavicino* in *Raccolta di opuscoli scientifici e letteraij di autori italiani*, V (Ferrara, 1780), 1–64 [this account is printed with additions in the ed. of the *Istoria del Concilio* by ZACCARIA (Faenza, 1792)]; SOMMERVOGEL, *Bibliothèque de la Compagnie de Jésus*, VI, Bibliography (new edition, Brussels, 1895), 120–143; HURTER, *Nomenclator literarius*, IV (Innsbruck, 1910), 192; GIORDANI, *Opera inedita del P. S. Pallavicino* in *Vita di Aless.* VII, I (Prato, 1839), 3 sqq.

J. P. KIRSCH.

Pallium.—*Form and Use of the Modern Pallium.*—The modern pallium is a circular band about two inches wide, worn about the neck, breast, and shoulders, and having two pendants, one hanging down in front and one behind. The pendants are about two inches wide and twelve inches long, and are weighted with small pieces of lead covered with black silk. The remainder of the pallium is made of white wool, part of which is supplied by two lambs presented annually as a tax by the Lateran Canons Regular to the Chapter of St. John on the feast of St. Agnes, solemnly blessed on the high altar of that church after the pontifical Mass, and then offered to the pope. The ornamentation of the pallium consists of six small black crosses—one each on the breast and back, one on each shoulder, and one on each pendant. The crosses on the breast, back, and left shoulder are provided with a loop for the reception of a gold pin set with a precious stone. The pallium is worn over the chasuble.

The use of the pallium is reserved to the pope and archbishops, but the latter may not use it until, on petition, they have received the permission of the Holy See. Bishops sometimes receive the pallium as a mark of special favour, but it does not increase their powers or jurisdiction, nor give them precedence. The pope may use the pallium at any time. Others, even archbishops, may use it only in their respective dioceses, and there only on the days and occasions designated in the "Pontificale" (Christmas, the Circumcision, and other specified great feasts; during the conferring of Holy orders, the consecration of abbots, etc.), unless its use is extended by a special privilege. Worn by the pope, the pallium symbolizes the *plenitudo pontificalis officii* (i. e. the plenitude of pontifical office); worn by archbishops, it typifies their participation in the supreme pastoral power of the pope, who concedes it to them for their proper church provinces. An archbishop, therefore, who has not received the pallium, may not exercise any of his functions as metropolitan, nor any metropolitan prerogatives whatever; he is even forbidden to perform any episcopal act until invested with the pallium. Similarly, after his resignation, he may not use the pallium; should he be transferred to another archdiocese, he must again petition the Holy Father for the pallium. In the case of bishops, its use is purely ornamental. The new palliums are solemnly blessed after the Second Vespers on the feast of Sts.

Peter and Paul, and are then kept in a special silver-gilt casket near the *Confessio Petri* until required. The pallium is conferred in Rome by a cardinal-deacon, and outside of Rome by a bishop; in both cases the ceremony takes place after the celebration of Mass and the administration of the oath of allegiance.

History and Antiquity.—It is impossible to indicate exactly when the pallium was first introduced. According to the "Liber Pontificalis", it was first used in the first half of the fourth century. This book relates, in the life of Pope Marcus (d. 336), that he conferred the right of wearing the pallium on the Bishop of Ostia, because the consecration of the pope appertained to him. At any rate, the wearing of the pallium was usual in the fifth century; this is indicated by the above-mentioned reference contained in the life of St. Marcus, which dates from the beginning of the sixth century, as well as by the conferring of the pallium on St. Cæsarius of Arles by Pope Symmachus in 513. Besides, in numerous other references of the sixth century, the pallium is mentioned as a long-customary vestment. It seems that, from the beginning, the pope alone had the absolute right of wearing the pallium. Its use by others was tolerated only in virtue of the permission of the pope. We hear of the pallium being conferred on others, as a mark of distinction, as early as the sixth century. The honour was usually conferred on metropolitans, especially those nominated vicars by the pope, but it was sometimes conferred on simple bishops (e. g. on Syagrius of Autun, Donus of Messina, and John of Syracuse by Pope Gregory the Great). The use of the pallium among metropolitans did not become general until the ninth century, when the obligation was laid upon all metropolitans of forwarding a petition for the pallium accompanied by a solemn profession of faith, all consecrations being forbidden them before the reception of the pallium. The object of this rule was to bring the metropolitans into more intimate connexion with the seat of unity and the source of all metropolitan prerogatives, the Holy See, to counteract the aspirations of various autonomy-seeking metropolitans, which were incompatible with the Constitution of the Church, and to counteract the evil influences arising therefrom: the rule was intended, not to kill, but to revivify metropolitan jurisdiction. The oath of allegiance which the recipient of the pallium takes to-day originated, apparently, in the eleventh century. It is met with during the reign of Paschal II (1099–1118), and replaced the profession of faith. It is certain that a tribute was paid for the reception of the pallium as early as the sixth century. This was abrogated by Pope Gregory the Great in the Roman Synod of 595, but was reintroduced later as partial maintenance of the Holy See. These pallium contributions have often been, since the Middle Ages, the subject of embittered controversies, the attitude of many critics being indefensibly extreme and unjustifiable.

Character and Significance.—As early as the sixth century the pallium was considered a liturgical vestment to be used only in the church, and indeed only during Mass, unless a special privilege determined otherwise. This is proved conclusively by the correspondence between Gregory the Great and John of Ravenna concerning the use of the pallium. The rules regulating the original use of the pallium cannot be determined with certainty, but its use, even before the sixth century, seems to have had a definite liturgical character. From early times more or less extensive restrictions limited the use of the pallium to certain days. Its indiscriminate use, permitted to Hincmar of Reims by Leo IV (851) and to Bruno of Cologne by Agapetus II (954), was contrary to general custom. In the tenth and eleventh centuries, just as to-day, the general rule was to limit the use of the pallium to a few festivals and some other extraordinary occasions. The symbolic character now attached to the pallium dates back to the time when it was made an obligation for all metropolitans to petition the Holy See for permission to use it. The evolution of this character was complete about the end of the eleventh century; thenceforth the pallium is always designated in the papal Bulls as the symbol of *plenitudo pontificalis officii*. In the sixth century the pallium was the symbol of the papal office and the papal power, and for this reason Pope Felix transmitted his pallium to his archdeacon, when, contrary to custom, he nominated him his successor. On the other hand, when used by metropolitans, the pallium originally signified simply union with the Apostolic See, and was the symbol of the ornaments of virtue which should adorn the life of the wearer.

Formal Development.—There is a decided difference between the form of the modern pallium and that in vogue in early Christian times, as portrayed in the Ravenna mosaics. The pallium of the sixth century was a long, moderately wide, white band, ornamented at its extremity with a black or red cross, and finished off with tassels; it was draped around the neck, shoulders, and breast in such a manner that it formed a V in front, and the ends hung down from the left shoulder, one in front and one behind (see illustration). In the eighth century it became customary to let the ends fall down, one in the middle of the breast and the other in the middle of the back, and to fasten them there with pins, the pallium thus becoming Y-shaped. A further development took place during the ninth century (according to pictorial representations, at first outside of Rome where ancient traditions were not maintained so strictly): the band, which had hitherto been kept in place by the pins, was sewed Y-shaped, without, however, being cut. The present

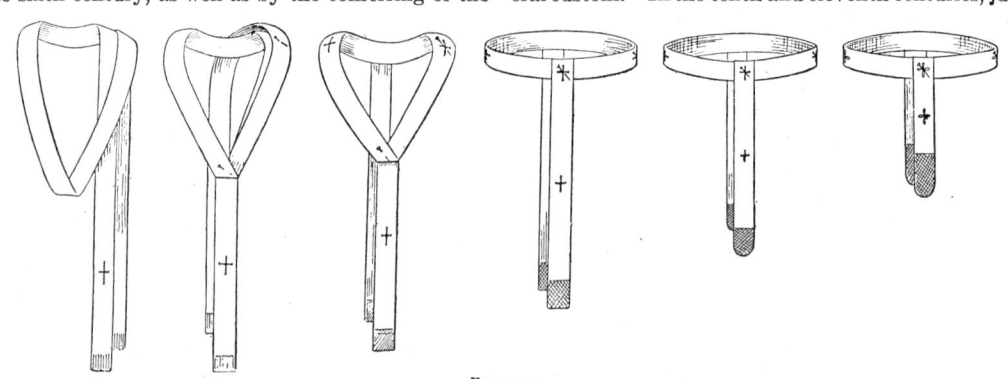

PALLIUM
Showing development

circular form originated in the tenth or eleventh century. Two excellent early examples of this form, belonging respectively to Archbishop St. Heribert (1021) and Archbishop St. Anno (d. 1075), are preserved in Siegburg, Archdiocese of Cologne. The two vertical bands of the circular pallium were very long until the fifteenth century, but were later repeatedly shortened until they now have a length of only about twelve inches. The illustration indicates the historical development of the pallium. At first the only decorations on the pallium were two crosses near the extremities. This is proved by the mosaics at Ravenna and Rome. It appears that the ornamentation of the pallium with a greater number of crosses did not become customary until the ninth century, when small crosses were sewed on the pallium, especially over the shoulders. There was, however, during the Middle Ages no definite rule regulating the number of crosses, nor was there any precept determining their colour. They were generally dark, but sometimes red. The pins, which at first served to keep the pallium in place, were retained as ornaments even after the pallium was sewed in the proper shape, although they no longer had any practical object. That the insertion of small leaden weights in the vertical ends of the pallium was usual as early as the thirteenth century is proved by the discovery in 1605 of the pallium enveloping the body of Boniface VIII, and by the fragments of the pallium found in the tomb of Clement IV.

Origin.—There are many different opinions concerning the origin of the pallium. Some trace it to an investiture by Constantine the Great (or one of his successors); others consider it an imitation of the Hebrew ephod, the humeral garment of the high priest. Others again declare that its origin is traceable to a mantle of St. Peter, which was symbolical of his office as supreme pastor. A fourth hypothesis finds its origin in a liturgical mantle, which, they assert, was used by the early popes, and which in the course of time was folded in the shape of a band; a fifth says its origin dates from the custom of folding the ordinary mantle-pallium, an outer garment in use in imperial times; a sixth declares that it was introduced immediately as a papal liturgical garment, which, however, was not at first a narrow strip of cloth, but, as the name suggests, a broad, oblong, and folded cloth. Concerning these various hypotheses see Braun, "Die liturgische Gewandung im Occident und Orient," sect. iv, ch. iii, n. 8, where these hypotheses are exhaustively examined and appraised. To trace it to an investiture of the emperor, to the ephod of the Jewish high-priest, or to a fabled mantle of St Peter, is entirely inadmissible. The correct view may well be that the pallium was introduced as a liturgical badge of the pope, and it does not seem improbable that it was adopted in imitation of its counterpart, the pontifical omophorion, already in vogue in the Eastern Church.

OMOPHORION.—The omophorion of the Greek Rite —we may here pass over the other Oriental rites— corresponds to the Latin pallium, with the difference that in the Greek Rite its use is a privilege not only of archbishops, but of all bishops. It differs in form from the Roman pallium. It is not a circular garment for the shoulders, with short pendants before and behind, but is, like the original Roman pallium, a broad band, ornamented with crosses and draped loosely over the neck, shoulders, and breast. The only change in the omophorion has been the augmentation of its width. We find distinct testimony to the existence of the omophorion as a liturgical vestment of the bishop in Isidore of Pelusium about 400. It was then made of wool and was symbolical of the duties of bishops as shepherds of their flocks. In the miniatures of an Alexandrian "Chronicle of the World", written probably during the fifth century, we already find pictorial representation of the omophorion. In later times we meet the same representation on the renowned ivory tablet of Trier, depicting the translation of some relics. Among the pictures dating from the seventh and eighth centuries, in which we find the omophorion, are the lately discovered frescoes in S. Maria Antiqua in the Roman Forum. The representation in these frescoes is essentially the same as its present form. Concerning the origin of the omophorion similar theories have been put forth as in the case of the pallium. Attempts have been made to prove that the omophorion was simply an evolution of the ordinary mantle or pallium, but it was most probably derived from the civil omophorion, a shoulder garment or shawl in general use. We must suppose either that the bishops introduced directly by a positive precept as a liturgical pontifical badge a humeral cloth resembling the ordinary omophorion and called by that name, or that the civil omophorion was at first used by the bishops as a mere ornament without any special significance, but in the course of time gradually developed into a distinctively episcopal ornament, and finally assumed the character of an episcopal badge of office.

RUINART, *Ouvrages posthumes*, II (Paris, 1724); MARRIOTT, *Vestiarium christ.* (London, 1868); BOCK, *Hist. of Liturg. Vestments*, II (Bonn, 1866); GARRUCCI, *Storia della arte christ.*, I (Prato, 1872); DUCHESNE, *Origine du culte chrét.* (Paris, 1903); WILPERT, *Un capitolo della storia del vestiario* (Rome, 1898–99); GRISAR, *Das röm. Pallium* in *Festschr. zum 1100-jährigen Jubiläum d. deutchen Campo Santo zu Rom* (Freiburg, 1897); THURSTON, *The Pallium* (London, 1892); ROHAULT DE FLEURY, *La messe*, VIII (Paris, 1889); BRAUN, *Die pontif. Gewänder des Abendlandes* (Freiburg, 1898); IDEM, *Die liturg. Gewandung im Occident u. Orient* (Freiburg, 1907).

JOSEPH BRAUN.

Pallium (ANTIPENDIUM). See ALTAR, sub-title ALTAR-FRONTAL.

Pallotti, VINCENT MARY, VENERABLE, founder of the Pious Society of Missions (q. v.), b. at Rome, 21 April, 1798; d. there, 22 Jan., 1850. He lies buried in the church of San Salvatore in Onda. He was descended from the noble families of the Pallotti of Norcia and the De Rossi of Rome. His early studies were made at the Pious Schools of San Pantaleone, whence he passed to the Roman College. At the age of sixteen, he resolved to become a secular priest, and on 16 May, 1820, he was ordained. He celebrated his first Mass in the church of the Gesù in Frascati. On 25 July he became a Doctor of Theology, and was soon made a substitute professor of theology in the Roman Archigymnasium. He gave promise of being a distinguished theologian, but decided to dedicate himself entirely to pastoral work.

Rome had in him a second Philip Neri. Hearing confessions and preaching were his constant occupations. From morning until night he could be seen hurrying along the streets of Rome to assist at the bedside of the sick in the hospitals, to bring aid and comfort to the poor in their miserable dwellings, or to preach to the unfortunates in prison. Once he went so far as to disguise himself as an old woman in order to reach the bedside of a dying young man, who had a pistol under his pillow ready to kill the first priest who should approach him. During the cholera plague in 1837, Pallotti constantly endangered his life in ministering to the stricken. After a day spent in apostolic labour he was accustomed to pass almost the whole night in prayer, disciplining himself even to blood, and sleeping for a few hours on a chair or on the bare floor. The most distinguished representatives of the Roman aristocracy, bishops, cardinals, and even Popes Gregory XVI and Pius IX honoured him, but the only advantage he took of their friendship was to advocate the claims of the poor. Even as a young man, he often returned home barefooted, after having given away half his clothing in alms; and more than once was he known to have given away his bed to the needy. Leo XIII, who spoke from his personal observations, said he would not hesitate to consider him a saint. Shortly after his death the preparatory examinations for his beatification began; in 1887 he was declared Venerable.

It was Venerable Pallotti who started in 1836 the special observance at Rome of the Octave of the Epiphany. Since then the celebration has been faithfully maintained. Pallotti's chief desire was to make this observance a means of uniting the dissenting Oriental Churches with Rome.

MELLIA, *Vincent Pallotti* (London); there is a biography in Italian by ORLANDI (Rome), and in German by the PALLOTTINI FATHERS (Limburg).
JOHN VOGEL.

Palma Vecchio (JACOPO NIGRETI), b. at Serinalta near Bergamo, about 1480; d. at Venice, 30 July, 1528. Like Giorgione and Lotto, he studied under Giovanni Bellini, from whom he drew the inspiration for his altar-pieces, introducing, however, more freedom of arrangement. His works are strong and broad rather than graceful. Imitating Giorgione, Palma treated sacred subjects as "tableaux de genre", wherein the sometimes exuberant strength, animation, and limpid, transparent colouring deserve admiration while they lack religious sentiment. Among these productions are: the "Madonna with St. George and St. Lucy", painted for San Stefano, Vicenza; "Saint Peter with six saints" (Accademia of Venice); "Adoration of the Shepherds" (Louvre); "Meeting of Jacob and Rachel" (Dresden Museum). His favourite subjects were the so-called "Holy Conversations", i. e., the Holy Family or the Madonna surrounded by saints. Examples are to be seen at Rome, in the Colonna and Borghese Galleries, at Florence, in the Uffizi and Pitti Palaces, at Dresden, Munich, and Vienna. One of his most beautiful "conversations" is that of the Holy Family with St. John Baptist and St. Lucy, in the Accademia of Venice. His master-piece is the altar-piece in Santa Maria Formosa, Venice. It is a triptych representing St. Barbara between St. Anthony the Hermit and St. Sebastian. Palma was also a remarkable portrait painter, excelling especially in portraits of women, most of whom were court ladies. Worthy of note are: the "Bella", in the collection of Baron Alphonse de Rothschild; the "Violante", in the museum of Vienna; the "Three Sisters", in the museum of Dresden. His portraits of men are also excellent, especially that of an unknown man (museum of Berlin), and Palma himself (Pinacothek, Munich). He received the surname Vecchio to distinguish him from his nephew, Jacopo Palma Giovane (1544–1628).

SAINT BARBARA
Palma Vecchio, Santa Maria Formosa, Venice

VASARI, *Le vite de' più eccellenti pittori*, ed. MILANESI, V (Florence, 1880), 243–96; BLANC, *Hist. des peintres de toutes les Ecoles: Ecole vénitienne* (Paris, 1865–77); MÜNTZ, *Hist. de l'art pendant la Renaissance*, III (Paris, 1895), 612–14; BRYAN, *Dict. painters and engravers*, IV (London, 1904); PÉRATÉ, *Palma Vecchio* in *Hist. gén. de l'art*, ed. MICHEL, IV (Paris, 1909), 437–40.
GASTON SORTAIS.

Palmas, LAS. See CANARY ISLANDS, THE.

Palmer, WILLIAM, b. at Mixbury, Oxfordshire, 12 July, 1811; d. at Rome, 4 April, 1879; the elder brother of Roundell Palmer, afterwards Lord Chancellor of England and first Earl of Selborne. He himself was educated at Rugby and Oxford (Magdalen College), where he proceeded M.A. in 1833, being then in deacon's orders of the Church of England. He was, successively, tutor at Durham University (1834–37), classical examiner at Oxford 1837–39, and tutor at Magdalen College (1838–43). In 1840 he visited Russia to obtain, if possible, official recognition of the Anglican Church as a branch of the Catholic Church; but after a year's fruitless labour his claim to communion was rejected by the Metropolitan of Moscow. A second attempt in 1842 only resulted in the express rejection by the Russian Church of Anglican claims to Catholicism. After the Gorham Judgment in 1852 he contemplated joining the Russian Church, but was deterred by the necessity for rebaptism. He spent some time in Egypt and then went to Rome, where he was received into the Church, 28 Feb., 1855, and where he spent the rest of his life. His works, which show a wide acquaintance with both Anglican and Eastern theology, were mainly concerned with his efforts to obtain intercommunion between these bodies. Chief among these were: "Harmony of Anglican Doctrine with the Doctrine of the Eastern Church" (Aberdeen, 1846; Greek version, Athens, 1851); "An appeal to the Scottish Bishops and Clergy" (Edinburgh, 1849); and "Dissertations on subjects relating to the Orthodox or Eastern Catholic Communion" (London, 1853). After he became a Catholic he devoted himself to archæology and wrote: "An Introduction to Early Christian Symbolism" (London, 1859); and "Egyptian Chronicles, with a harmony of sacred and Egyptian Chronology" (London, 1861). He also wrote a Latin commentary on the Book of Daniel (Rome, 1874), and a number of minor works. After his death his friend Cardinal Newman edited his "Notes of a Visit to the Russian Church" (London, 1882).

Rugby School Registers, 1675–1874 (London, 1881–6); BLOXAM, *Magdalen College Registers* (London, 1853–85); NEALE, *Life of Patrick Torry, D.D.* (London, 1856), vi; WORDSWORTH, *Annals of my Life, 1847–1856* (London, 1893); LIDDON, *Life of Pusey* (London, 1893–4); BROWNE, *Annals of the Tractarian Movement* (London, 1856); MOZLEY, *Reminiscences* (London, 1882).
EDWIN BURTON.

Palmerston. See NORTHERN TERRITORY, PREFECTURE APOSTOLIC OF THE.

Palmieri, DOMENICO, theologian, b. at Piacenza, Italy, 4 July, 1829; d. in Rome, 29 May, 1909. He studied in his native city, where he was ordained priest in 1852. On 6 June, 1852, he entered the Society of Jesus, where he completed his studies. He taught in several places, first rhetoric, then philosophy, theology, and the Sacred Scriptures. In these courses, especially during the sixteen years that he was professor in the Roman College, he acquired fame as a philosopher. In this field he published: "Animadversiones in recens opus de Monte Concilii Viennensis" (Rome, 1878); a more interesting work is his "Institutiones Philosophicæ" (3 vols., Rome, 1874–76). In this he followed the scholastic method; but the doctrines in many points differ from those common to the Peripatetic philosophers. As regards the composition of bodies he admits the dynamic theory, and considers the first elements of bodies to be formally simple, endowed with an attractive and repulsive force, but which he says are virtually extended. On the other hand he does not admit the real accidents, and to explain the permanence of the Eucharistic Species, he has recourse to the phenomena of ether, which persist by Divine operation, the substance of bread and wine ceasing to exist. He held a conception altogether his own of the life of plants, and assigned simple souls to animals, which expire with their death. As regards the origin of the idea, he was true to the scholastic principles in admitting that the intellectual apprehension has its origin in the apprehension of the senses; but to his last day would not admit the necessity of the intelligible species. His works have a very forcible quality of argument, which obliges one to recognize the thinker, even when at variance with his mode of thought.

In Scriptural study also he made his mark. Having taught the Holy Scriptures from 1880–87, and Oriental languages to the scholastics of his society in Maestricht, he published "Commentarius in epistolam ad Galatas" (Gulpen, 1886); and "De veritate historica libri Judith aliisque ss. Scripturarum locis specimen criticum exegeticum" (Gulpen, 1886). Many others of his minor works can be placed under this head. When Loisy's book, "L'Evangile et l'Eglise", appeared, he was one of the first to give alarm to the Catholic party, and to show, in a treatise in the form of letters, the errors contained in this author's works. He examined more minutely another work of Loisy's, "Autour d'un Petit Livre", in his "Esame di un opuscolo che gira intorno ad un piccolo libro". To this demonstration he joins a more complete one of certain of the favourite errors of the new school, that is to say, not demonstrating the Divinity of Our Lord from the Synoptics. He does the same with another book entitled "Se e come i sinottici ci danno Gesù Cristo per Dio" (Prato, 1903). Only the first part of this book, concerning the Gospel of St. Matthew, was published; but these books contain nevertheless a valid defence of Catholic truth.

Palmieri's reputation, however, rests principally on his theology in the Roman College: (a) "Tractatus de Romano Pontifice cum prolegomeno de Ecclesia" (3rd ed., Prato, 1902); (b) "Tractatus de Pœnitentia" (2nd ed., Prato, 1896); (c) "Tractatus de Matrimonio Christiano" (2nd ed., Prato, 1897); (d) "Tractatus de Gratia Divina Actuali" (Gulpen, 1885); (e) "Tractatus Theologicus de Novissimis" (Prato, 1908); (f) "Tractatus de Creatione et de Præcipuis Creaturis" (Prato, 1910); (g) "Tractatus de Ordine Supernaturali et de Lapsu Angelorum" (Prato, 1910); (h) "Tractatus de Peccato Originali et de Immaculato Beatæ Virginis Deiparæ Conceptu" (Prato, 1904).

The last three treatises here noted, taken together, form a new edition in many parts perfected and rearranged from his former treatise on God the Creator, printed first in Rome, 1878. The third part was published before the other two, because the author wished with it to render homage to the Immaculate Conception on the fiftieth anniversary of the proclamation of the dogma. In his treatise on creation and the special creatures, a posthumous work, but of which he left the manuscript completed and prepared, we have to note the change made by him regarding the union of the soul with the body, because while he first asserted that the union was only natural and not substantial, now that it is defined doctrine that the human nature consists entirely in the synthesis of two elements, that is to say, of the body and of the reasoning soul, he admits that this union is substantial, although he asserts that it is not yet sufficiently determined how one nature can result from these two elements.

The originality of his theological works consists principally in the method which he followed, which amounts to an exhaustive demonstration of the existence of the dogma, and in its scholastic exposition and defence, so that his treatises are almost complete from the positive, scholastic, and polemic viewpoints. Father Antonio Ballerini left at his death a valuable collection of studies in moral theology. It was in the form of a commentary on the "Medulla" of Busenbaum, but not complete. Palmieri undertook the task of putting in order this work and made many additions of his own. To the acumen shown in his theological works he here adds evidence of a sound practical judgment, hereby proving himself a great moralist. For this reason, on the election of Cardinal Steinhuber, he was appointed to succeed him as theologian of the S. Pœnitentiaria, in which capacity his work was greatly appreciated by Leo XIII and Pius X. These labours were followed by a commentary on the Divine Comedy of Dante Allighieri, a work undertaken by him at the suggestion of his mother, Giuseppina Rocci Palmieri, a lady of high ideals and culture. To this he brought all the profundity of his philosophy and theology, and produced a work wonderful to all those who, knowing these sciences, are able to appreciate the profound thought which is revealed, especially in a most learned introduction and in the scientific observations appended to the individual cantos.
BENEDETTO OJETTI.

Palmieri, LUIGI, physicist and meteorologist, b. at Faicchio, Benevento, Italy, 22 April, 1807; d. in Naples, 9 Sept., 1896. He first studied at the seminary of Caiazzo, then took up mathematics and the natural sciences in Naples, getting his degree in architecture from the University of Naples. He taught successively in the secondary schools of Salerno, Campobasso, and Avellino, until in 1845 he became professor of physics at the Royal Naval School at Naples. In 1847 he was called to the chair of physics at the university. He began his connection with the meteorological observatory on Mount Vesuvius in 1848 and became its director in 1854, after the death of Melloni. The chair of meteorological and terrestrial physics was created especially for him at the university. He filled it in 1860 together with the position of director of the physical observatory of Naples.

Member of the Royal Society of Naples (Academy of Sciences) since 1861, he became a member of the Academy of the Lincei (Florence) in 1871. Among other honours were the following: Member of the Superior Council of Meteorology, Senator of the Kingdom, Grand Commander of the Order of the Crown of Italy, Commander of the Order of Rosa del Brazile, etc. His work is chiefly connected with the observation of the eruptions on Mount Vesuvius and with the study of earthquakes and meteorological phenomena in general. He watched all the volcanic disturbances at the observatory and nearly lost his life there during the eruption of 1872. He was very successful in the invention and improvement of delicate apparatus. He modified the Peltier electrometer and used it for his investigation of atmospheric electricity during forty years. His seismometer for the detection and measurement of ground vibration was so sensitive that he was able to detect very slight movements and to predict the eruption of the volcano. A modification of the Morse telegraph, an anemometer, and a pluviometer were also among his inventions. His tribute to Galluppi has often been applied to himself: "The

Catholic religion was the guide of his studies during life, and, supported by its inexpressible consolation, he left this earth to live forever in heaven."

Reports of his observation and studies at the volcano were published in the "Aunali dell' osservatorio Vesuviano" (1869-73). Numerous memoirs also appeared in the "Rendiconto dell' accademia delle scienze fisiche e matematiche di Napoli", and in the "Atti della R. Acc., Napoli". Among his larger works were the following: "Incendio Vesuviano del 26 Aprile 1872" (Naples, 1872; Ger. tr., Berlin, 1872); "Il Vesuvio e la sua storia" (Milan, 1880); "Nuove lezioni di fisica sperimentale e di fisica terrestre" (Naples, 1883); "Die Atmosphärische Elektrizität" (tr., Vienna, 1884); "Les lois et les origines de l'électricité" (tr., Paris, 1885).

Pop. Sc. Miscellany, L (New York, 1896), 430; *Civiltà Cattolica*, series 16, XI (Rome, 1897), 470; VILLARI in *Rendiconto dell' Acc. Napoli*, XXXV (Naples, 1896), 236.

WILLIAM FOX.

Palm in Christian Symbolism.—In pre-Christian times the palm was regarded as a symbol of victory (Aulus Gellius, "Noct. Att.", III, vi). It was adopted by the early Christians, and became a symbol of the victory of the faithful over the enemies of the soul. The palm, says Origen (In Joan., XXXI), is the symbol of victory in that war waged by the spirit against the flesh. In this sense it was especially applicable to martyrs, the victors *par excellence* over the spiritual foes of mankind; hence the frequent occurrence in the Acts of the martyrs of such expressions as "he received the palm of martyrdom." On 10 April, 1688 it was decided by the Congregation of Rites that the palm when found depicted on catacomb tombs was to be regarded as a proof that a martyr had been interred there. Subsequently this opinion was acknowledged by Mabillon, Muratori, Benedict XIV and others to be untenable; further investigation showed that the palm was represented not only on tombs of the post-persecution era, but even on pagan tombs. The general significance of the palm on early Christian monuments is slightly modified according to its association with other symbols (e. g., with the monogram of Christ, the Fish, the Good Shepherd). On some later monuments the palm was represented merely as an ornament separating two scenes.

KRAUS, *Real-Encyklopädie* (Freiburg, 1882-86), s. v.; IDEM, *Gesch. der christl. Kunsts*, I (Freiburg, 1896); TYRWHITT in *Dict. of Christ. Antiquities* (London, 1875-80), s. v.

MAURICE M. HASSETT.

Palms, SYNOD OF. See SYMMACHUS, SAINT, POPE.

Palm Sunday, the sixth and last Sunday of Lent and beginning of Holy Week, a Sunday of the highest rank, not even a commemoration of any kind being permitted in the Mass. In common law it fixes the commencement of Easter duty. The Roman Missal marks the station at St. John Lateran (see STATIONS) and before September, 1870, the pope performed the ceremonies there. The Greeks celebrate the day with great solemnity; they call it κυριακὴ or ἑορτὴ τῶν βαΐων or ἑορτὴ βαϊοφόρος or also Lazarus Sunday, because on the day before they have the feast of the resuscitation of Lazarus. The emperors used to distribute branches of palm and small presents among their nobles and domestics. The Latin liturgical books call it Dominica in Palmis, Dominica or Dies Palmarum. From the cry of the people during the procession the day has received the name Dominica Hosanna or simply Hosanna (Ozanna). Because every great feast was in some way a remembrance of the resurrection of Christ and was in consequence called *Pascha*, we find the names *Pascha floridum*, in French *Pâques fleuries*, in Spanish *Pascua florida*, and it was from this day of 1512 that our State of Florida received its name (Nilles, II, 205). From the custom of also blessing flowers and entwining them among the palms arose the terms *Dominica florida* and *dies floridus*. Flower-Sunday was well known in England, in Germany as *Blumensonntag* or *Blumentag*, as also among the Serbs, Croats, and Ruthenians, in the Glagolite Breviary and Missal, and among the Armenians. The latter celebrate another Palm Sunday on the seventh Sunday after Easter to commemorate the "Ingressus Domini in cœlum juxta visionem Gregorii Illuminatoris" called *Secundus floricultus* or *Secunda palmarum dominica* (Nilles, II, 519). Since this Sunday is the beginning of Holy Week, during which sinners were reconciled, it was called *Dominica indulgentiœ*, *competentium*, and *capitilavium* from the practice of washing and shaving of the head as a bodily preparation for baptism. During the early centuries of the Church this sacrament was conferred solemnly only in the night of Holy Saturday, the text of the creed had been made known to the catechumens on the preceding Palm Sunday. This practice was followed in Spain (Isidore, "De off. eccl.", I, 27), in Gaul (P. L., LXXII, 265), and in Milan (Ambrose, Ep. xx). In England the day was called Olive or Branch Sunday, Sallow or Willow, Yew or Blossom Sunday, or Sunday of the Willow Boughs. Since the celebration recalled the solemn entry of Christ into Jerusalem people made use of many quaint and realistic representations; thus, a figure of Christ seated on an ass, carved out of wood, was carried in the procession and even brought into the church. Such figures may still be seen in the museums of Basle, Zurich, Munich, and Nürnberg (Kellner, 50).

In some places in Germany and France it was customary to strew flowers and green boughs about the cross in the churchyard. After the Passion had been recited at Mass blessed palms were brought and this cross (in consequence sometimes called the Palm cross) was wreathed and decked with them to symbolize Christ's victory. In Lower Bavaria boys went about the streets singing the "Pueri Hebræorum" and other carols, whence they received the name of Pueribuben ("Theologisch-praktische Quartalschrift", 1892, 81). Sometimes an uncovered crucifix, or the gospel-book, and often the Blessed Sacrament, was carried in procession. In many parts of England a large and beautiful tent was prepared in the churchyard. Two priests accompanied by lights brought the Blessed Sacrament in a beautiful cup or pyx hung in a shrine of open work to this tent. A long-drawn procession with palms and flowers came out of the church and made four stations at the Laics' cemetery north of the church, at the south side, at the west door, and before the church-yard cross, which was then uncovered. At each of these stations Gospels were sung. After the singing of the first Gospel the shrine with the Blessed Sacrament was borne forward. On meeting, all prostrated and kissed the ground. The procession then continued. The door of the church was opened, the priests held up on high the shrine with the Blessed Sacrament, so that all who went in had to go under this shrine, and thus the procession came back into the church. The introduction of the Blessed Sacrament into the Palm Sunday procession is generally ascribed to Bl. Lanfranc who ordered the ceremony for his Abbey of Bec.

Liturgical writers differ in assigning a time for the introduction of the benediction of palms and of the procession. Martène, "De antiq. eccl. discipl.", xx, 288, finds no mention of them before the eighth or ninth century. Peliccia, "Christian. eccl. politia", II, 308, is of the same opinion and mentions Amularius, "De div. off.", I, x, as the first to speak of them. Binterim, V, i, 173, on the authority of Severus, Patriarch of Antioch, and of Josue Stylites, states that Peter, Bishop of Edessa, about 397 ordered the benediction of the palms for all the churches of Mesopotamia. The ceremonies had their origin most probably in Jerusalem. In the "Peregrinatio Sylviæ", undertaken between 378 and 394, they are thus described: On the Lord's Day which begins the Paschal, or Great, Week, after all the customary exercises from cock-crow till morn had taken place in the Anastasia and at the Cross, they went to the greater church behind the Cross on Golgotha, called the Martyrium, and here the ordinary Sunday services were held. At the seventh hour (one o'clock p. m.) all proceeded to the Mount of Olives, Eleona, the cave in which Our Lord used to teach, and for two hours hymns, anthems, and lessons were recited. About the hour of None (three o'clock p. m.) all went, singing hymns, to the Imbomon, whence Our Lord ascended into heaven. Here two hours more were spent in devotional exercises, until about 5 o'clock, when the passage from the Gospel relating how the children carrying branches and palms met the Lord, saying "Blessed is He that cometh in the Name of the Lord" is read. At these words all went back to the city, repeating "Blessed is He that cometh in the Name of the Lord." All the children bore branches of palm or olive. The faithful passed through the city to the Anastasia, and there recited Vespers. Then after a prayer in the church of the Holy Cross all returned to their homes.

In the three oldest Roman Sacramentaries no mention is found of either the benediction of the palms or the procession. The earliest notice is in the "Gregorianum" used in France in the ninth and tenth centuries. In it is found among the prayers of the day one that pronounces a blessing on the bearers of the palms but not on the palms. The name *Dominica in palmis, De passione Domini* occurs in the "Gelasianum", but only as a superscription and Probst ("Sacramentarien und Ordines", Münster, 1892, 202) is probably correct in suspecting the first part to be an addition, and the *De passione Domini* the original inscription. It seems certain that the bearing of palms during services was the earlier practice, then came the procession, and later the benediction of the palms.

The principal ceremonies of the day are the benediction of the palms, the procession, the Mass, and during it the singing of the Passion. The blessing of the palms follows a ritual similar to that of Mass. On the altar branches of palms are placed between the candlesticks instead of flowers ordinarily used. The palms to be blessed are on a table at the Epistle side or in cathedral churches between the throne and the altar. The bishop performs the ceremony from the throne, the priest at the Epistle side of the altar. An antiphon "Hosanna to the Son of David" is followed by a prayer. The Epistle is read from Exodus xv, 27–xvi, 7, narrating the murmuring of the children of Israel in the desert of Sin, and sighing for the fleshpots of Egypt, and gives the promise of the manna to be sent as food from heaven. The Gradual contains the prophetic words uttered by the high-priest Caiphas, "That it was expedient that one man should die for the people"; and another the prayer of Christ in the Garden of Olives that the chalice might pass; also his admonition to the disciples to watch and pray. The Gospel, taken from St. Matthew, xvi, 1–9, describes the triumphant entry of Christ into Jerusalem when the populace cut boughs from the trees and strewed them as He passed, crying, Hosanna to the Son of David; blessed is he that cometh in the name of the Lord. (In private Masses this Gospel is read at the end of Mass instead of that of St. John.) Then follow an oration, a preface, the Sanctus, and Benedictus.

In the five prayers which are then said the bishop or priest asks God to bless the branches of palm or olive, that they may be a protection to all places into which they may be brought, that the right hand of God may expel all adversity, bless and protect all who dwell in them, who have been redeemed by our Lord Jesus Christ. The prayers make reference to the dove bringing back the olive branch to Noah's ark and to the multitude greeting Our Lord; they say that the branches of palms signify victory over the prince of death and the olive the advent of spiritual unction through Christ. The officiating clergyman sprinkles the palms with holy water, incenses them, and, after another prayer, distributes them. During the distribution the choir sings the "Pueri Hebræorum". The Hebrew children spread their garments in the way, and cried out saying, "Hosanna to the Son of David; Blessed is he that cometh in the name of the Lord." Then follows the procession, of the clergy and of the people, carrying the blessed palms, the choir in the mean time singing the antiphons "Cum appropinquaret", "Cum audisset", and others. All march out of the church. On the return of the procession two or four chanters enter the church, close the door and sing the hymn "Gloria, laus", which is repeated by those outside. At the end of the hymn the subdeacon knocks at the door with the staff of the cross, the door is opened, and all enter singing "Ingrediente Domino". Mass is celebrated, the principal feature of which is the singing of the Passion according to St. Matthew, during which all hold the palms in their hands.

Palm branches have been used by all nations as an emblem of joy and victory over enemies; in Christianity as a sign of victory over the flesh and the world according to Ps. xci, 13, "Justus ut palma florebit"; hence especially associated with the memory of the martyrs. The palms blessed on Palm Sunday were used in the procession of the day, then taken home by the faithful and used as a sacramental. They were preserved in prominent places in the house, in the barns, and in the fields, and thrown into the fire during storms. On the Lower Rhine the custom exists of decorating the grave with blessed palms. From the blessed palms the ashes are procured for Ash Wednesday. In places where palms cannot be found, branches of olive, box elder, spruce or other trees are used and the "Cæremoniale episcoporum", II, xxi, 2, suggests that in such cases at least little flowers or crosses made of palm be attached to the olive boughs. In Rome olive branches are distributed to the people, while the clergy carry palms frequently dried and twisted into various shapes. In parts of Bavaria large swamp willows, with their catkins, and ornamented with flowers and ribbons, were used.

Rock, *The Church of Our Fathers* (London, 1904); Duchesne, *Christian Worship* (London, 1904), 247; *American Ecclesiastical Review* (1908), 361; *Kirchenlexicon*; Kellner, *Heortology* (tr. London, 1908); Kraus, *Realencyklopädie*; Nilles, *Kalendarium Manuale* (Innsbruck, 1897).

Francis Mershman.

Palmyra, titular metropolitan see in Phœnicia Secunda. Solomon (III Kings, ix, 18) built Palmira (A. V. Tadmor) in the wilderness, but it is not certain that this means Palmyra, the Greek name of Tadmor, and the reference may be to Thamar (Ezech., xlvii, 19).

For a long time it was a market for the Romans and Parthians, as it was situated on the route of the caravans. The city had a Greek constitution, made use of the era of the Seleucides, the Macedonian calendar, and a Semitic alphabet; the language was a dialect of Aramaic. Hadrian visited it in 129 and thenceforth the town was called Hadriana Palmyra. Its prosperity and monuments date from this period. The Romans used it as a starting-point for their expeditions against the Parthians. Septimius Severus and Alexander Severus sojourned there. In 258 Septimius Odænath, the descendant of a local dynasty, was Prince of Palmyra. He proclaimed himself king in 260, and in 264 received the title of emperor. After his death (267) his inheritance passed under the regency of Zenobia. She established an empire with the assistance of her ministers Longinus and Paul of Samosata, Bishop of Antioch, conquered Egypt and a part of Asia Minor. In 272 the Emperor Aurelian sacked Palmyra and carried off Zenobia a prisoner. Diocletian established a camp there where the first Illyrian Legion afterwards sojourned. Justinian restored it in the sixth century (Procopius, "De Ædificiis", xi). In 745 it suffered from the wars of the Ommiads and Abbassids, in 1089 underwent an earthquake, and then fell completely into oblivion.

The date of the introduction of Christianity into Palmyra is unknown. In 325 its bishop, Marinus, assisted at the Council of Nicæa; another, John, signed at Chalcedon in 451 as suffragan of Damascus; another John was expelled as a Monophysite in 518 (Le Quien, "Oriens christ.", II, 845). The diocese first depended on Tyre in Phœnicia, then on Damascus in Lebanon Phœnicia, as is shown by the Antioch "Notitia episcopatuum" of the sixth century ("Echos d'Orient", X, 145; "Hieroclis Synecdemus", ed. Burckhardt, 40); George of Cyprus, "Descriptio orbis romani", ed. Gelzer, 50). After 761 Palmyra was a suffragan of Emesa (Echos d'Orient, X, 96). The ruins of Palmyra (now Toudmour) are among the most beautiful in the world.

WOOD AND DAWKINS, *Les ruines de Palmyre autrement dite Tadmor* (Paris, 1819); SELLER, *Antiquities of Palmyra* (London, 1696); SAINT-MARTIN, *Histoire de Palmyre* (Paris, 1823); WRIGHT, *Palmyra and Zenobia* (London, 1896); LITTMANN, *Semitic Inscriptions* (New York, 1904); VOGÜÉ, *Syrie centrale. Inscriptions sémitiques* (Paris, 1868); WADDINGTON, *Explication des inscriptions grecques et latines de Grèce et d'Asie Mineure*, n. 2571-2626; DOUBLE, *Les Césars de Palmyre* (Paris, 1877); VON SALLET, *Die Fürsten von Palmyra* (Berlin, 1866); MORITZ, *Zur antiken Topographie der Palmyrene* (Berlin, 1899); MARQUARDT, *Organisation de l'empire romain* (Paris, 1892), II, 360-62; HORNS, *Essai sur le règne de l'empereur Aurélien* (Paris, 1904); *Revue biblique*, I, 633-38; II, 117, 627-30; VI, 592-97; XI, 94-98; 608-618; XII, 77-80.

S. VAILHÉ.

PALMYRA

Palou, FRANCISCO, Friar Minor, b. at Palma, Island of Majorca, about 1722; d. in 1789 or 1790. He entered the Franciscan order at his native place. In 1740 he began the study of philosophy under the illustrious Father Junipero Serra. With the latter he volunteered for the American Indian missions, and joined the missionary College of San Fernando de Mexico early in 1740. With his friend he was also in the same year assigned to the Indian missions of the Sierra Gorda, north of Querétaro, and laboured there until 1759 when with Father Serra he was recalled in order to work among the Indians in the San Sabás region, Texas. For some reason the college failed to accept those missions. Father Palou was therefore employed in the City of Mexico until 1767 when with Father Serra and fourteen other Franciscan friars he was sent to Lower California. In April, 1768, on reaching Loreto, he was given charge of Mission San Francisco Javier. In the following year, when Father Serra proceeded to establish the missions of Upper California, Father Palou succeeded him in the office of *presidente* or superior of the lower missions. While at the head of the friars in Lower California, he demonstrated his eminent fitness for the position in a protracted struggle with the hostile Governor, Phelipe Barri, whom he held at bay, and whose schemes against the missionaries and Indians he defeated while in the territory. When in 1773 the Franciscans turned the peninsula missions over to the Dominican Fathers, Father Palou joined his brethren in Upper California and acted as superior until the return from Mexico of Father Serra in 1774. In November of that year he accompanied Captain Rivera's exploring expedition to the Bay of San Francisco, and on 4 December, planted the cross on Point Lobos in view of the Golden Gate and Pacific Ocean, the first priest to reach that point. In June, 1776, he accompanied Lieutenant Moraga to the same bay, and on June 28, offered up the first holy Mass on the spot later under the Mission Dolores (q. v.) or San Francisco, which Father Palou founded a few weeks after. He remained in charge until July, 1784, when he was called to Mission San Carlos in order to administer the last sacraments to his fatherly friend and superior, Father Junipero Serra. When the latter had passed away on 28 August, 1784, Father Palou became acting *presidente* of the missions. Age, ill-health, and the necessity of having an experienced advocate near the vice-regal court to defend the rights of the Indians and their spiritual guides against the assumptions of the governor, induced Father Palou to retire to the College of San Fernando in September, 1785. In July of the following year he was elected guardian of the college, and held this office until his death. While in charge of Mission San Francisco he compiled his "Noticias" in four volumes. It is the standard history of the California missions from 1767 to 1784. At San Carlos Mission he wrote the Life of Father Serra which contains the history of the first nine missions, San Diego to San Buenaventura.

PALOU, *Noticias de la Antigua y Nueva California*, I-IV (San Francisco, 1875); PALOU, *Relación Histórica de la Vida del Ven. P. Fr. Junipero Serra* (Mexico, 1787); *Santa Barbara Mission Archives*; *California Archives* (San Francisco); *Archbishop's Archives* (San Francisco); ENGELHARDT, *Franciscans in California* (Harbor Springs, Mich., 1897); IDEM, *Missions and Missionaries of California*, I (San Francisco, 1908); II (San Francisco, 1911); BANCROFT, *History of California*, I (San Francisco, 1886).

ZEPHYRIN ENGELHARDT.

Paltus, a titular see and suffragan of Seleucia Pieria in Syria Prima. The town was founded by a colony from Arvad or Aradus (Arrianus, Anab. II, xiii, 17). It is located in Syria by Pliny (Hist. Natur., V, xviii) and Ptolemy (V, xiv, 2); Strabo (XV, iii, 2; XVI, ii, 12) places it near the river Badan. When the province of Theodorias was made by Justinian, Paltus became a part of it (Georgii Cyprii Descriptio orbis romani, ed. Gelzer, 45). From the sixth century according to the "Notitia episcopatuum" of Anastasius [Echos d'Orient, X, (1907), 144] it was an autocephalous archdiocese and depended on Antioch; in the tenth century it still existed and its precise limits are known [Echos d'Orient, X (1907), 97]. Le Quien (Oriens christ., II, 799) mentions five of its bishops: Cymatius, friend of St. Athanasius, and Patricius, his successor; Severus (381); Sabbas at the Council of Chalcedon (451); finally John exiled by the Monophysites and reinstated by Emperor Justin I (518). The ruins of Paltus may be seen at Belde at the south of Nahr es-Sin or Nahr el-Melek, the ancient Badan.

S. VAILHÉ.

Paludanus, PETER (PETRUS DE PALUDE), theologian and archbishop, b. in the County of Bresse, Savoy, about 1275; d. at Paris, 1342. He entered the Dominican Order at Lyons, completed his theological studies at the University of Paris, and was made a

Doctor and Master of Theology in 1314. Wishing to devote his life to teaching and writing, he avoided all offices of honour in the order, except those pertaining to the direction of studies. Twice, however, he was sent as definitor from the Province of France to the General Chapter. John XXII, wishing to organize a Crusade, sent him in 1318 as legate to the Court of Flanders, in the hope of establishing peace between the prince and the King of France. The mission was not successful, and his associates made charges to the pope against the legate, who, however, easily cleared himself. He was also a member of the commission appointed by John XXII to examine the writings of Petrus Olivi, whose books contained some errors of the Fraticelli (Denzinger, 484-91, interesting account in Touron). About this time he wrote "De causa immediata ecclesiasticæ potestatis" (Paris, 1506) against John of Poilly, whose errors were condemned 25 July, 1321 (Denzinger, 491, 495). In 1329 the pope called him to Avignon, and consecrated him Patriarch of Jerusalem. The same year he journeyed into Egypt, to negotiate with the sultan for the deliverance of the Holy Land. The sultan was immovable. The accounts which the patriarch gave of the miserable condition of the Holy Land led to the announcement of another Crusade, but owing to apathy, and dissensions among the Christian princes, the project failed. Peter resumed his studies, composing at this time his commentaries on the Sentences of Peter Lombard, in which he combats Durandus. About 1332 he was appointed by the King of France to preside over the deliberations of a body of prelates and theologians whom Philip had convoked at Versailles to discuss the charge made against John XXII, of asserting that the souls of the just will not be admitted to the beatific vision until after the general judgment. The patriarch and his associates manifested consummate prudence in dealing with this matter. In a letter to the king they declared (1) their entire submission to the pope's authority, and their filial devotion to his person; (2) their belief, based on the testimony of trustworthy witnesses, that John XXII had not held, much less taught, the opinion attributed to him, but at the most, had mentioned it (*recitando*) and examined it; (3) that since the death of Christ the souls of the just with no faults to expiate immediately after death, and the souls of other just persons after complete purgation, are admitted to the beatific vision, which will endure forever. This doctrine was defined by Benedict XII, 29 Jan., 1336 (Denzinger, 530). Besides the works mentioned, Paludanus wrote commentaries on all the books of the Bible, and "Concordantiæ ad Summam S. Thomæ" (Salamanca, 1552).

Du Boulay, *Cat. illustr. academ. Hist. Univ. Parisi*, IV, 984 (Paris, 1673); Quétif-Echard, *Script. Ord. Præd.*, I, 603 (Paris, 1719); Touron, *Hist. des hommes illustres de l'Ordre de S. Dom.*, II (Paris, 1745), 223; Sixtus Senensis, *Bibliot. Sancta*, lib. IV (Venice, 1566, Lyons, 1591); see Benedict XII; Durandus; Fraticelli; John XXII.

D. J. Kennedy.

Pamelius (Jacques de Joigny de Pamele), Belgian theologian, b. at Bruges, Flanders, 13 May, 1536; d. at Mons in Hainaut, 19 September, 1587. He was educated at the Cistercian Abbey of Boneffe in the Province of Namur; studied philosophy at Louvain, and on 27 March, 1553, he was promoted *magister artium*. For the next nine years he studied theology under the direction of Ruard Tapper and Josse Ravestein and after receiving the baccalaureate he followed the course of the Sorbonne. On 19 June, 1561, he was made a canon of St-Donatien at Bruges, and was ordained priest probably 21 February, 1562. He visited all the libraries of the Low Countries to procure manuscripts and unedited works, and devoted himself to the publication of rare texts, beginning with the "Micrologus de ecclesiasticis observationibus" (Antwerp, 1565), a valuable liturgical commentary on the Roman "Ordo" which dates probably from the beginning of the twelfth century. From 1568 to 1571, Pamelius was dean of the *chrétienté* of Bruges. He was appointed (1570) a member of the commission for the examination of books by Remi Drieux, Bishop of Bruges, and aided in the publication of the "Index expurgatorius" of 1571. In 1574 he replaced George de Vrieze as scholar of the chapter of St-Donatien and shared in the installation of the college of the Jesuits at Bruges in 1575. The protection which Pamelius extended to the victims of Calvinistic violence at Bruges drew upon him the hatred of the heretics and he was obliged to withdraw to Douai. In 1581 the chapter of St-Omer promoted him to the dignity of the Archdiaconate of Flanders. After the death of Bishop Jean Six (11 Oct., 1586), Philip II appointed Pamelius his successor in the See of St-Omer, but Pamelius died before receiving his bulls of confirmation. Besides the "Micrologus", he wrote "Liturgica latinorum" (Cologne, 1571); "De religionibus diversis non admittendis . . . relatio" (Antwerp, 1589); a catalogue of ancient commentaries on the Bible (Antwerp, 1566); and he edited the works of St. Cyprian (Antwerp, 1566), Tertullian (Paris, 1584), and Rhabanus Maurus (Cologne, 1527).

Eulogy by Taelbomius (Antwerp, 1589); *Gratulationes et mox tumuli D. Jacobo Pamelio ab Ant. Hoio, Brug. et Fred. Jamotio medico* (Douai, 1587); De Schrevel, *Pamele (Jacques de Joigny de)* in *Biographie nationale . . . de Belgique*, XVI (1901), 528–542.

L. Van der Essen.

Pamiers, Diocese of (Apamæa), comprising the Department of Ariège, and suffragan of Toulouse. The territory forming it was united to the Archbishopric of Toulouse on the occasion of the Concordat of 1801; the Concordat of 1817 re-established at Pamiers a diocese which existed only in September, 1823, uniting the ancient Dioceses of Pamiers and Couserans, the larger portion of the former Dioceses of Mirepoix and Rieux and a deanery of the former Diocese of Alet (See Carcassonne). A decree of the Holy See 11 March, 1910, re-established the titles of the former Sees of Couserans and Mirepoix.

A.—*Diocese of Pamiers*. The traditions of the diocese mention as its first Apostle of Christianity, St. Antoninus, born at Fredelacum near Pamiers, an apostle of the Rouergue, martyred in his native country (date uncertain). The Abbey of St. Antonin was founded near Fredelacum about 960; in 1034 it passed under the jurisdiction of the Bishops of Girone and was annexed in 1060 to the Congregation of Cluny. A castle built on the site of the abbey by Roger II, Count of Foix (1070–1125), was called *Appamia;* hence the name of Pamiers which passed to the neighbouring small town. Boniface VIII created a see at Pamiers by the Bull "Romanus Pontifex" 23 July, 1295, and made it a suffragan of Narbonne. He named Bernard Saisset Abbot of St. Antonin, and by a decree 18 April, 1296, settled the boundaries of the new diocese dismembered from that of Toulouse. The opposition of Hughes Mascaron, Bishop of Toulouse, and the conflict between Saisset and Roger Bernard III, Count of Foix, prevented Saisset from taking immediate possession of his diocese; Abbé Vidal has proven that it is not true, as had long been thought, that St. Louis of Anjou, who became Bishop of Toulouse at the death of Mascaron, had been appointed provisional administrator of the Diocese of Pamiers. Saisset took possession of his see on 19 April, 1297; having sided with Boniface VIII (1301), he was imprisoned by order of Philip the Fair.

After careful investigation, Clement V, 3 August, 1308, complied with certain demands of Toulouse concerning the decree of Boniface VIII, and the Diocese of Pamiers remained, but with poorer resources than those assigned it by Boniface VIII. However, when John XXII raised Toulouse to an archbishopric, 22 Feb., 1318, he also extended the Diocese of Pamiers which he made suffragan of Toulouse. Saisset's successor was Jacques Fournier (1317–26), subsequently pope under the name of Benedict XII (q. v.). Vidal discovered in the Vatican Library the record of the procedure of the Inquisition tribunal created at Pamiers, by Jacques Fournier in 1318, for the extirpation of the remnants of Albigensianism in the Foix region; this document is most important for the history of the Inquisition, representing as it does, and perhaps in this instance only, that particular tribunal in which the monastic inquisitor and the diocesan bishop had almost equal power, as decreed in 1312 by the Council of Vienna. In this new regime the traditional procedure of the Inquisition was made milder by temporizing with the accused who persisted in error, by granting defendants a fair amount of liberty, and by improving the prison regime. Among the noteworthy bishops of Pamiers were Cardinal Arnaud de Villemur (1348–50); Cardinal Amanieu d'Albret (1502–06); John of Barbançon (1550–55), who became a Calvinist; Robert of Pellevé (1557–79), during whose episcopate the religious wars gave rise to cruel strife: protestants destroyed every church in Pamiers, among them the magnificent cathedral of Notre-Dame du Camp, and three times they demolished the episcopal palace of the Mas Saint-Antonin. Henry of Sponde (1626–42), Spondanus, who summarized and continued the Ecclesiastical Annals of his friend Baronius; the Jansenist François Etienne de Caulet (1644–1680).

B.—*See of Couserans or Conserans.*—According to St. Gregory of Tours, the first bishop was St. Valier (Valerius) before the sixth century. Bishop Glycerius was present at the Council of Agde in 506. According to Mgr Duchesne he should be identified with a certain Licerius (St. Lizier) whom the "Gallia Christiana" places lower in the list of bishops; he was patron saint of St-Lizier, the episcopal residence of the bishops of Couserans, suffragans of Auch. The historian Bishop Pierre de Marca (1643–52) president of the Parliament of Navarre, was subsequently Bishop of Toulouse and Archbishop of Paris.

C.—*See of Rieux*, erected by John XXII in 1317, as suffragan to the archiepiscopal See of Toulouse. Among its bishops were: Cardinal de Rabastens (1317–21); Cardinal de St-Martial (1359–72).

D.—*See of Mirepoix*, erected by John XXII in 1317 as suffragan of the Archbishop of Toulouse. Among its bishops were Jacques Fournier (1326–1327); David Béthon, Cardinal de Balfour (1537–46); Innocent, Cardinal de Monti (1553–1555); Jean Suavius, Cardinal de Mirepoix (1555–60); the academician Boyer, preceptor to the Dauphin, father of Louis XVI (1730–1736).

The Diocese of Pamiers specially honours St. Gerontius, martyr (date unknown) who gave his name to the city of St-Girons. The Council of Pamiers in 1212 drew up forty-nine articles concerning the police of the States of Simon de Montfort, and of the other seigneurs to whom had been given the lands of the defeated Albigensian noblemen (See ALBIGENSES). In a council held at Foix in 1226, Cardinal de Saint-Ange, Honorius III's legate, absolved Bernard, Count of Foix, who had become a follower of the Albigenses, of the crime of heresy. The celebrated Guy de Levis who had the title of "Maréchal de la foi et des croisés", received in acknowledgement of his conduct in the Albigensian war, the city of Mirepoix which remained the property of the house of Levis until the revolution. Aside from the pilgrimage of St. Antonin at Pamiers, the chief pilgrimage centres are: Notre-Dame d'Ax les Thermes; Notre-Dame du Camp at Pamiers; Notre-Dame de Celles at Celles; Notre-Dame de l'Isard in the valley of Aran; Notre-Dame du Marsan at St-Lizier, pilgrimage centre dating back to the tenth century; Notre-Dame de Sabart, established after a victory won by Charlemagne over the Saracens; Notre-Dame du Val d'Amour, at Belesta; Notre-Dame de Vals; Notre-Dame de Varilhes. Pilgrims are also attracted to St-Martin of Oydes by the relics of St. Anastasius, by St. Anthony's at Lezat, and by the miraculous fountain of Eycheil, which according to tradition, gushed forth after St. Lizier had been praying to St. John the Baptist. Prior to the enforcement of the Law of 1901, the Diocese of Pamiers had Dominicans, Carmelite monks and teaching Brothers. At the beginning of the twentieth century, the religious congregations of the diocese had charge of 19 day nurseries, 2 orphanages for girls, 4 industrial rooms, 2 sheltering houses, 10 hospitals, 1 insane asylum, 2 houses of nuns for the care of the sick in their own homes. In 1905 (last year of the period covered by the Concordat) the Diocese of Pamiers had a population of 210,527, with 22 parishes, 321 mission churches, 20 vicariates subventioned by the State.

Gallia Christiana, nova (1715), I, 1123–44, *instr.*, 185–7; *nova* (1785), XIII, 150–79, 186–99, 267–84, *instr.*, 87–180, 221–46; DUCHESNE, *Fastes Episcopaux*, II, 99–100; VIDAL, *Les origines de la province ecclésiastique de Toulouse* (Annales du Midi, XV, 1903); VIDAL, *Le tribunal d'inquisition de Pamiers* (Toulouse, 1906); FONS, *Evêques de Pamiers* in *Mémoires de l'Académie des Sciences de Toulouse* (1873); BLAZY, *Nos anciens évêques* (Foix, 1902); LAFONT DE SENTENAC, *Armorial des évêques de Pamiers* (Foix, 1902); LAHONDÈS, *Annales de Pamiers* (Toulouse, 1882); HAROT, *Armorial des évêques de Rieux* (Toulouse, 1908; BARRIÈRE-FLAVY, *Pouillé du diocèse de Rieux* (Foix, 1896); DOUAIS, *Documents pontificaux sur l'évêché de Couserans* (1425–1619) in *Revue de Gascogne* (1888); ROBERT, *L'ancien Diocèse de Mirepoix* (Foix, 1908); CHEVALIER, *Topo-bibl.* 1952, 2237–2238, 2554.

GEORGES GOYAU.

Pammachius, SAINT, Roman senator, d. about 409. In youth he frequented the schools of rhetoric with St. Jerome. In 385 he married Paulina, second daughter of St. Paula. He was probably among the *viri genere optimi religione præclari*, who in 390 denounced Jovinian to Pope St. Siricius (Ambrose, Ep. xli). When he attacked St. Jerome's book against Jovinian for prudential reasons, Jerome wrote him two letters (Epp. xlviii–ix, ed. Vallarsi) thanking him; the first, vindicating the book, was probably intended for publication. On Paulina's death in 397, Pammachius became a monk, that is, put on a religious habit and gave himself up to works of charity (Jerome, Ep. lxvi; Paulinus of Nola, Ep. xiii). In 399 Pammachius and Oceanus wrote to St. Jerome asking him to translate Origen's "De Principiis", and repudiate the insinuation of Rufinus that St. Jerome was of one mind with himself with regard to Origen. St. Jerome replied the following year (Epp. lxxxiii–iv). In 401 Pammachius was thanked by St. Augustine (Ep. lviii) for a letter he wrote to the people of Numidia, where he owned property, exhorting them to abandon the Donatist schism. Many of St. Jerome's commentaries on Scripture were dedicated to Pammachius. After his wife's death Pammachius built in conjunction with St. Fabiola (Jerome, Epp. lxvi, lxxvii), a hospice at Porto, at the mouth of the Tiber, for poor strangers. The site has been excavated, and the excavations have disclosed the plan and the arrangement of this only building of its kind. Rooms and halls for the sick and poor were grouped around it (Frothingham, "The Monuments of Christian Rome," p. 49). The church of SS. John and Paul was founded either by Pammachius or his father. It was anciently known first as the Titulus Bizantis, and then as the Titulus Pammachii. The feast of Pammachius is kept on 30 August.

CEILLIER, *Hist. des auteurs eccles.*, X, 99 sqq.; TILLEMONT, *Mémoires*, vol. X, p. 567; GRISAR, *Storia di Roma*, I, 73; LANCIANI, *Pagan and Christian Rome*, 158–9; MARUCCHI, *Eléments d'Archéol. chrét.*, 203.

F. J. BACCHUS.

Pamphilus of Cæsarea, SAINT, martyred 309. Eusebius's life of Pamphilus is lost, but from his "Martyrs of Palestine" we learn that Pamphilus belonged to a noble family of Beirut (in Phœnicia), where he received a good education, and that he quitted his native land after selling all his property and giving the proceeds to the poor. He attached himself to the "perfect men". From Photius (cod. 118), who took his information from Pamphilus's "Apology for Origen", we learn that he went to Alexandria where his teacher was Pierius, then the head of the famous Catechetical School. He eventually settled in Cæsarea where he was ordained priest, collected his famous library, and established a school for theological study (Eusebius, "Hist. eccl.", VII, xxxii, 25). He devoted himself chiefly to producing accurate copies of the Holy Scriptures. Testimonies to his zeal and care in this work are to be found in the colophons of Biblical MSS. (for examples see EUSEBIUS OF CÆSAREA). St. Jerome (De Vir. Ill., lxxv) says that Pamphilus "transcribed the greater part of the works of Origen with his own hand", and that "these are still preserved in the library of Cæsarea." He himself was a possessor of "twenty-five volumes of commentaries of Origen", copied out by Pamphilus, which he looked upon as a most precious relic of the martyr. Eusebius (Hist. eccl., VI, xxxii) speaks of the catalogue of the library contained in his life of Pamphilus. A passage from the lost life, quoted by St. Jerome (Adv. Rufin., I, ix), describes how Pamphilus supplied poor scholars with the necessaries of life, and, not merely lent, but gave them copies of the Scriptures, of which he kept a large supply. He likewise bestowed copies on women devoted to study. The great treasure of the library at Cæsarea was Origen's own copy of the Hexapla, probably the only complete copy ever made. It was consulted by St. Jerome ("In Psalmos comm.", ed. Morin, pp. 5, 21; "In Epist. ad. Tit."). The library was certainly in existence in the sixth century, but probably did not long survive the capture of Cæsarea by the Saracens in 638 (Swete, "Introd. to O. T. in Greek", 74–5).

The Diocletian persecution began in 303. In 306 a young man named Apphianus—a disciple of Pamphilus "while no one was aware; he even concealed it from us who were even in the same house" (Eusebius, "Martyrs of Palestine")—interrupted the governor in the act of offering sacrifice, and paid for his boldness with a terrible martyrdom. His brother Ædesius, also a disciple of Pamphilus, suffered martyrdom about the same time at Alexandria under similar circumstances (ibid.). Pamphilus's turn came in November, 307. He was brought before the governor and, on refusing to sacrifice, was cruelly tortured, and then relegated to prison. In prison he continued copying and correcting MSS. (see EUSEBIUS OF CÆSAREA). He also composed, in collaboration with Eusebius, an "Apology for Origen" in five books (Eusebius afterwards added a sixth). Pamphilus and other members of his household, men "in the full vigour of mind and body", were without further torture sentenced to be beheaded in Feb., 309. While sentence was being given a youth named Porphyrius—"the slave of Pamphilus", "the beloved disciple of Pamphilus", who "had been instructed in literature and writing"—demanded the bodies of the confessors for burial. He was cruelly tortured and put to death, the news of his martyrdom being brought to Pamphilus before his own execution.

Of the "Apology for Origen" only the first book is extant, and that in a Latin version made by Rufinus. It begins with describing the extravagant bitterness of the feeling against Origen. He was a man of deep humility, of great authority in the Church of his day, and honoured with the priesthood. He was above all things anxious to keep to the rule of faith that had come down from the Apostles. The soundness of his doctrine concerning the Trinity and the Incarnation is then vindicated by copious extracts from his writings. Then nine charges against his teaching are confronted with passages from his works. St. Jerome stated in his "De Viris illustribus" that there were two apologies—one by Pamphilus and another by Eusebius. He discovered his mistake when Rufinus's translation appeared in the height of the Origenistic controversy, and rushed to the conclusion that Eusebius was the sole author. He charged Rufinus, among other things, with palming off under the name of the martyr what was really the work of the heterodox Eusebius, and with suppressing unorthodox passages. As to the first accusation there is abundant evidence that the "Apology" was the joint work of Pamphilus and Eusebius. Against the second may be set the negative testimony of Photius who had read the original; "Photius, who was severe to excess towards the slightest semblance of Arianism, remarked no such taint in the Apology of Origen which he had read in Greek" (Ceillier). The Canons of the alleged Council of the Apostles at Antioch were ascribed by their compiler (late fourth century) to Pamphilus (Harnack, "Spread of Christianity", I, 86–101). The ascription to Pamphilus, by Gennadius, of a treatise "Contra mathematicos" was a blunder due to a misunderstanding of Rufinus's preface to the "Apology". A Summary of the Acts of the Apostles among the writings associated with Euthalius bears in its inscription the name of Pamphilus (P. G., LXXXIX, 619 sqq.).

BARDENHEWER, *Gesch. der altkirch Lit.*, II, 242 sqq.; HARNACK, *Altchrist Lit.*, 543 sqq.; CEILLIER, *Hist. des aut.*, III, 435 sqq.; TILLEMONT, *Hist. ecclés.*, V, 418 sqq.; ROUTH, *Reliq. sac.*, III, 258 sqq.; RUFINUS's *Translation of the Apology for Origen* will be found in editions of the works of Origen.

F. J. BACCHUS.

Pamplona, DIOCESE OF (PAMPILONENSIS), comprises almost all of Navarre and part of Guipuzçoa. This diocese is said to date from Apostolic times. It is matter of tradition in the churches of Pamplona, Toledo, and Toulouse (France), that St. Saturninus, disciple of St. Peter, sent from Toulouse the priest Honestus to preach to the inhabitants of Navarre, and later came in person. Finding that Honestus had already made many converts, Saturninus left him in Pamplona. Honestus was the teacher of St. Firminus (son of the senator Firmus), first Bishop of Pamplona. Firminus went later into France, where he was martyred at Amiens. There is no note of any other Bishop of Pamplona until 589, when Liliolus signed as such in the Third Council of Toledo. During the seventh century other bishops are known as signatories of various councils of Toledo. It was not known with certainty whether the Arabs succeeded in establishing themselves in Pamplona (Ferreras affirms and Moret denies it); at all events, there is no record of a Bishop of Pamplona from the Saracen invasion until the reign of Opilanus (829). The old cathedral had meanwhile fallen into ruins, and the bishops now took refuge in the monastery of San Salvador of Leyre (founded in the eighth century). Inigo Arista recovered Pamplona in 848 or 849, and restored the monastery, converting it into a stronghold. This was for a long time the episcopal court and see, and hither Arista had transferred the bodies of the holy virgins Nunilona and Alodia, martyred at Huesca in the time of Abd-er-Rahman II.

It was the wish of Sancho the Elder to introduce into Leyre the Cluniac reform, but the bishops and abbots (e. g. in the Council of Pamplona of 1023) resisted until 1090, during the reign of Sancho Ramirez. In the said council they resolved to restore the See of Pamplona, and decreed that all the bishops of Pamplona should be thereafter of the monastery of Leyre like Sancho I, who then occupied the see. In 1025 the monks of Leyre were affiliated with the canons of Pamplona, and Juan II took the title of Bishop of Pamplona and Leyre, and signed in a number of decrees "Joannes, ecclesiæ Navarrensium rector". Until the reign of Sancho Ramirez (1076-94) Leyre remained the seat of the bishops of Pamplona. The monastery held under its jurisdiction fifty-eight towns and seventy-two religious houses, and was besides the mausoleum of the Kings of Navarre. Theobald I brought Cistercian monks to Leyre, but at the end of the same century the monks of Cluny returned and occupied it for some time. The monastery is now in ruins, and its church serves as that of a rural parish. The see having been re-established in Pamplona, King Sancho Ramirez (1076-94) procured the appointment as Bishop of Pedro de Roda, monk of St. Pons de Tomières, who built the new cathedral and established a chapter of canons under the Rule of St. Augustine. The bishops of Pamplona, as such, presided over the ecclesiastical order and the three estates that made up the Cortes of Navarre. The cathedral of Santa Maria held the seigniory of the city, and its canons enjoyed the privileges of the royal family. Bishop Sancho de Larrosa consecrated the cathedral, completed in 1124. His predecessor, Guillermo Gastón, had accompanied King Alfonso to the conquest of Saragossa, and there founded the Church of "St. Michael of the Navarrese".

In the Cathedral of Pamplona is venerated the ancient statue of "St. Mary, the White Virgin" (*Santa María la Blanca, Santa María de la Sede* or *del Sagrario*), which was preserved in Leyre from very ancient times until the eleventh century. There is also a reliquary containing a thorn from Our Saviour's crown, given by St. Louis to Theobald II; likewise the heads of the virgins Nunilona and Alodia, whose bodies were in Leyre. Bishop Pedro de Artajona—known as Pedro of Paris, because it was there he had received his education—obtained from Celestine III (1191) the confirmation of all the privileges of the Church of Pamplona, and procured besides from the Bishop of Amiens a few relics of St. Firmin, whose feast was from this time (1186) celebrated with the same solemnity as the feasts of the Apostles. In 1197 Sancho the Strong ceded his palace to Bishop Garcia. The sovereigns, Donna Juana and Philip of Evreux, recovered it, leaving it in turn to Bishop Arnaldo de Barbazán; their son, Carlos the Bad, returned it to Bishop Miguel Sanchez de Asiain, and later to Bishop Bernardo Folcant. Since the union of Navarre and Castille, it had been occupied by the viceroys, and is to-day the headquarters of the Captaincy-General. The bishops resided later in the "Casa del Condestable" (House of the Constable, i. e., of the Duke of Alba) until Bishop Melchor Angel Gutierrez Vallejo commenced the new palace, completed by Francisco III Ignacio Añoa y Busto. In 1317 Jimeno III, Garcia being bishop, Pamplona, formerly a suffragan of Tarragona, became a suffragan of Saragossa. Carlos III the Noble reconstructed the cathedral, and gave it for twelve years the fortieth part of the royal revenues from Navarre. Bishop Martin de Zavala, partisan of the antipope Pedro de Luna, aided in the erection. In 1400 Emperor Manuel Palæologus gave to the Church of Pamplona a particle of the wood of the True Cross and another of the reputed blue vestment of Our Lord; these relics are preserved in the cathedral. Toward the end of the eighteenth century Bishop Sancho de Oteyza completed the façade.

The parish church of St. Saturnioro is a very old structure and has but one nave; not far from this is pointed out the well where the saint baptized his first converts. The parish church of St. Lorenzo was renovated in the eighteenth century, and enlarged by the erection of the Chapel of St. Firminus on the spot where tradition says he was born. The basilica of St. Ignatius of Loyola was erected in the place where that saint was wounded when fighting against the French. In 1601 Viceroy Juan de Cardona had an arch erected with an inscription, and later Count de Santisteban urged the Jesuits to raise the basilica, which was opened on 10 October, 1694. Former Dominican and Carmelite convents have been converted into barracks and hospitals, and the convent of St. Francis into schools. The sanctuaries of Ignatius Loyola and Francis Xavier belong to this diocese. That of Loyola contains the old house of St. Ignatius enshrined in a monument constructed by Fontana under the auspices of Queen Mariana of Austria, mother of Carlos II (1689-1738). The sanctuary of St. Francis Xavier, home of the Apostle of the Indies, has been restored by the generosity of the Dukes of Villahermosa (1896-1901). The collegiate church of our Lady of Roncesvalles was founded at the beginning of the ninth century as a hospice for travellers on their way to Compostela or from Spain to Rome and Jerusalem. There are two seminaries in Pamplona, a *conciliar* and an *episcopal*. There was also a university, first incorporated with that of Saragossa and in 1745 with that of Alcalá. It was founded in 1608 by resolution of the Cortes of Navarre in the Dominican College of the Rosary, approved by Philip III in 1619, and established by Gregory XV in 1621. Urban VIII in 1623 and Philip IV in 1630 confirmed it. In this university the well-known moralist, Francisco Larraga, was a professor. It boasts of other famous scholars—jurists like Martin de Azpilcueta, historians like the Jesuit Moret, missionaries like Calatayud, and bishops like the Benedictine Prudencio de Sandoval, historian of Charles V.

MORET, *Anales del Reino de Navarra* (Tolosa, 1890); MELIDA, *Album de Javier* (Madrid, 1901); DE LA FUENTE, *Historia de las Universidades de España*, II (Madrid, 1885); PEREZ, *La santa Casa de Loyola* (Bilbao, 1891); DE MADRAZO, *España, sus monumentos y artes : Navarra y Logrono* (Barcelona, 1886).

RAMÓN RUIZ AMADO.

Panama, REPUBLIC AND DIOCESE OF, in Central America, occupies the Isthmus of Panama, or Darien, which extends east and west between the Caribbean Sea, on the north, and the Pacific Ocean, on the south. The republic is bounded on the east by the Republic of Colombia, and on the west by that of Costa Rica. Its extreme length is about 480 miles; its width varies from 37 to 110 miles; it has an area of 31,500 square miles and a population estimated at about 420,000. Most of the inhabitants are of mixed Aboriginal, Spanish, and Negro blood; the canal works, however, have attracted many North American whites and some 40,-000 negroes, chiefly from the British West Indies. The country is rich in natural resources. Although only about one-fourth of the soil is under cultivation, the value of bananas exported from Panama annually exceeds $600,000 United States money; coffee, cocoa, and rubber are produced in abundance, besides vegetable drugs (sarsaparilla, etc.), cabinet woods, and coco-nuts. It is said that coal is the only common mineral not found in the soil of the republic. Cattle-rearing is carried on to a certain extent. Other minor industries are pearl-fishing (in the Gulf of Panama) and the collection of turtle-shells for exportation.

Panama, until then a state of the Republic of Colombia, became an independent republic on 4 November, 1903. The Government of the United States, having resolved to construct an inter-oceanic canal from Colon, on the Caribbean Coast, to the City of Panama, on the Pacific, concluded an important treaty (signed, 18 Nov., 1903; ratified, 23 Feb., 1904) with the newly constituted Republic of Panama. By this treaty the United States acquired "the use in perpetuity" of a tract five miles wide on each side of the route marked out for the canal (the Canal Zone), with the control of all this territory for police, judicial, sanitary, and other purposes; to provide for the defence of the canal, both the Caribbean and Pacific coast lines of the Canal Zone were also ceded to the United States; lastly, while the Cities of Colon and Panama remained integral parts of the territory of the republic, jurisdiction in those two cities in all matters of sanitation and quarantine is granted to the United States. The Con-

MAP OF PANAMA CANAL and the CANAL ZONE.

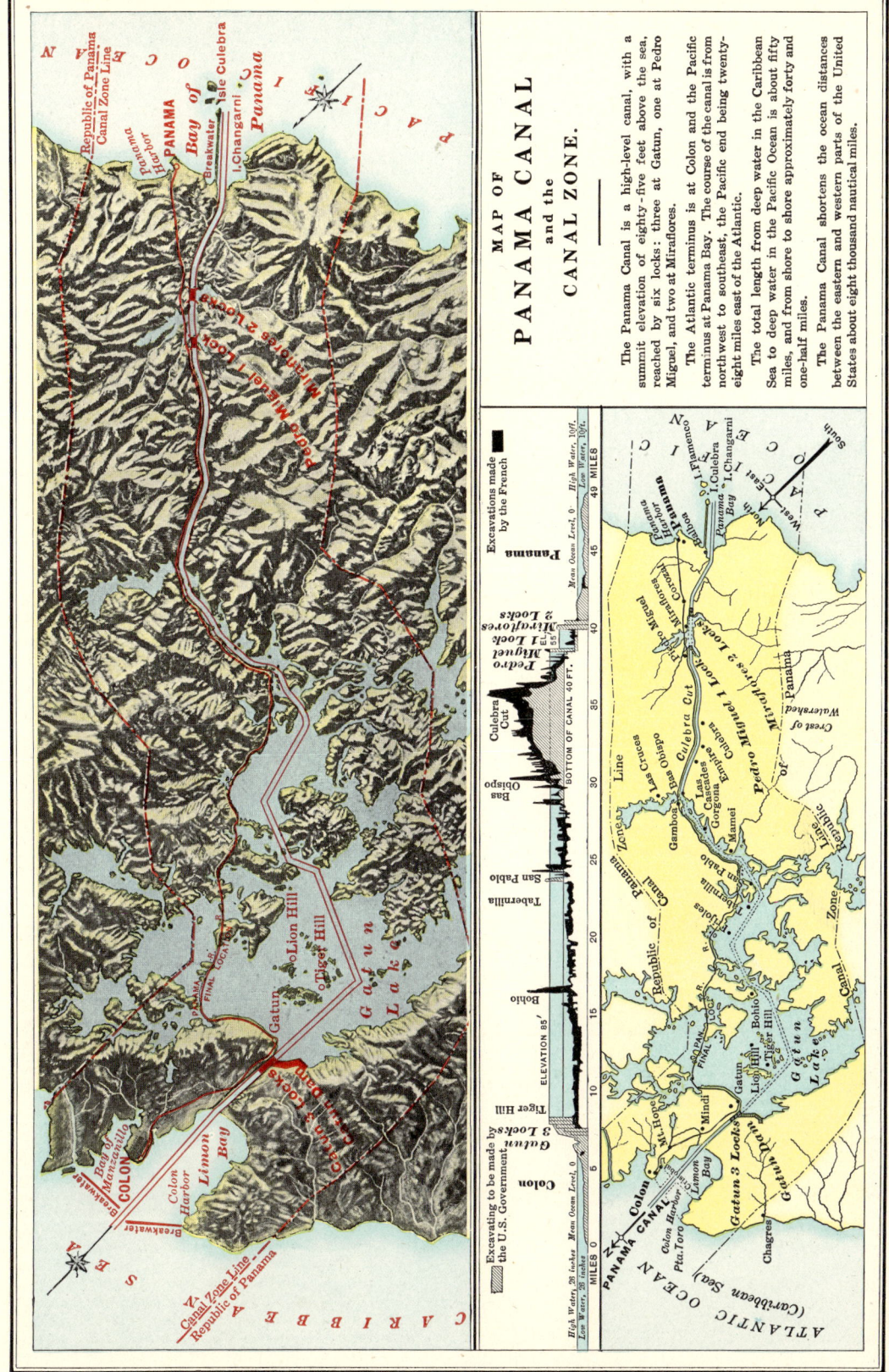

The Panama Canal is a high-level canal, with a summit elevation of eighty-five feet above the sea, reached by six locks: three at Gatun, one at Pedro Miguel, and two at Miraflores.

The Atlantic terminus is at Colon and the Pacific terminus at Panama Bay. The course of the canal is from northwest to southeast, the Pacific end being twenty-eight miles east of the Atlantic.

The total length from deep water in the Caribbean Sea to deep water in the Pacific Ocean is about fifty miles, and from shore to shore approximately forty and one-half miles.

The Panama Canal shortens the ocean distances between the eastern and western parts of the United States about eight thousand nautical miles.

stitution of Panama provides for a National Legislature (*Assamblea*, or Chamber of Deputies) elected by the people on the basis of one deputy to every 10,000 inhabitants, to meet on 1 September of every alternate year; a president elected for a term of four years, and two vice-presidents. The president is assisted by a Cabinet of five members. José Domingo de Obaldia, elected president in 1908, to succeed Manuel Amador Guerrero, died during his term of office (1 March, 1910) and was succeeded by Vice-President C. A. Mendoza.

RELIGIOUS CONDITIONS.—The secession of the Isthmus of Panama, comprising the Department and Diocese of Panama (see below), from the Republic of Colombia took place when the Constitutional Government of that republic had a Catholic representation, and, after three years of civil war, the enemies of religion seemed, politically, vanquished. None of the promoters of the independence of Panama seemed to contemplate any religious change. But in order to rally to the Separatist movement the forces of the Liberal doctrinaires, so as to win over the great mass of the population to the cause of independence, the leaders had to make terms with them. Besides, some of the chief promoters of the cause, being anxious to adopt every North-American idea and custom, and not merely those which seemed likely to be beneficial, conceived certain erroneous notions: thus they assumed as an axiomatic truth that separation of Church and State was the only means of uniting those of different creeds for the common purpose of self-government and progress. In spite of the protestations which Manuel Amador Guerrero, who led the way to independence, had made to the bishop—to the effect that the political transformation would lead to no change in the relations of Panama with the Holy See, and that the missions should receive all possible support—when the Constituent Assembly began to elaborate the constitution of the new nation, it was barely admitted that a great part of the inhabitants were Catholics. The intercourse with the Holy See, which existed in accordance with the terms of the Colombian Concordat of 1887, was not recognized. The obligation of paying to the Diocese of Panama a fixed sum in compensation, or restitution, for the church property previously confiscated by the Colombian Government, and now in possession of many citizens of Panama, was repudiated. The appropriation for the Conciliar Seminary and the missions might be considered some equivalent, although the title of the Church, in strict justice, to receive these contributions as the State's creditor, was ignored. Since it was voted, this appropriation has been religiously complied with, in spite of the efforts of certain individuals to curtail, withhold, or divert it.

The National Legislatures (*Assambleas*), successors of the Constituent Assembly, have continued to yield to the Liberal majority, which has manifested anti-Catholic tendencies. The cemeteries have been laicized (Law 29 of 1909), in virtual derogation of the restitution made by the Republic of Colombia years before and confirmed in the above-mentioned concordat with the Holy See. This concordat had been recognized as a law by the Colombian Republic, and it was specially declared to be still in force—at least so far as concerned this point—by the new-born nation of Panama. The cemeteries were left at the free disposal of the municipalities. Fortunately, these bodies, representing the village communities, are, as a rule, composed of Christian men. There is also a tendency to secularize education, not merely by submitting it entirely to state control or supervision, but by introducing teachers and doctrines hostile to religion. Indeed, some of the functionaries in this branch of the public service have not waited for legal measures, but have attempted to impose their views on the school system and on the pupils.

The Diocese of Panama (*Panamanensis*) was erected by Leo X in 1520 (Annuaire Pont.) or in 1515, or by Clement VII, in 1534 (Moroni, "Diz. di Erud. Storico-Eccl."). It was at first suffragan of Lima, but is now of Cartagena. Its territory coincides with that of the republic. The present incumbent of the see (1911), Mgr F. X. Junguito, S.J., was b. at Bogota, 3 Dec., 1841, and was appointed bishop, 15 April, 1901. The bishop, residing in the City of Panama, is assisted by his vicar-general, the priest of the most populous parish, his secretary, the priest of the parish of the Sagrario, and two other secular priests, who, with the assistance of a residence of the Jesuit Fathers (seven priests), one of the Lazarists (five priests), and one of the Discalced Augustinians (three priests and two lay brothers), labour to supply the spiritual needs of the 30,000 inhabitants, at least two-thirds of whom are Catholics. The community of Christian Brothers, from whom the present government took away the normal school, to incorporate it in the discredited Instituto, conducts in Panama a primary school recognized by the State, and an independent college which is now in jeopardy, being non-official. The same congregation has similar schools at Colon and in each of the six most important centres of population. The Daughters of Charity of St. Vincent of Paul have, at Panama, a primary school for girls, with 400 pupils, a pension and orphanage of the Holy Family, independent of the State, a government asylum, and another institution which is supported by the ecclesiastical authority. It will be easy for them to open the benevolent institutions which are eagerly solicited of them at two or three other places.

The religious interests of the Catholics who are employed at the Canal Zone are cared for at Ancon, Balboa, Culebra, Empire, Gorgona, Gatun, Cristobal, and Colon by priests specially qualified for the work by their knowledge of several languages. The Lazarists are to establish a residence at Gorgona, to give more attention to the natives, who avoid places where the Americans are numerous, under the belief that the Northern strangers look down upon them. By this means priests are provided for every Catholic in the Canal Zone, though there are not enough to work the parishes properly. The Salesian Fathers of Dom Bosco have lately come to Panama to care for a parish in a quarter of the city which is filled with workingmen, as it contains the principal railroad station. In this neighbourhood they have opened an orphan asylum which, with astonishing rapidity, is preparing the way for a school of arts and manufactures destined to educate good Christian workingmen. The Salesians number three priests and two brothers who act as masters or managers of the work. They formerly had the direction of the School of Arts and Crafts (Escuela de Artes y Oficios) established by the Government, and everything went prosperously until their anti-clerical opponents forced them to resign.

For Bibliography see COLOMBIA, REPUBLIC OF. Also, WALDO, *The Panama Canal Work and the Workers* (New York, 1907); RODRIGUEZ, *The Panama Canal* (London, 1907); MACMAHON, *A Glimpse of Panama Old and New* in *Cath. World*, LXXIII (1901), 653 sqq.

F. X. JUNGUITO.

Pancratius, SAINT. See NEREUS, ACHILLEUS, DOMITILLA, AND PANCRATIUS, SAINTS.

Pandects (PANDECTÆ, or DIGESTA).—This part of Justinian's compilation was his most important contribution to jurisprudence (see JUSTINIAN I). The language of d'Aguesseau, applied by him to pre-Napoleonic Continental law, has equal application to the Common Law System. The reasons underlying legal institutions are either historical or logical; and every logical rule of law is capable of illumination from the law of the Pandects. There is no other standard of comparative jurisprudence. D'Aguesseau pithily observes: "Justice has fully unveiled her mysteries only to the Roman jurists. They are the safest interpreters of our own laws: they lend their spirit to our usages, their reason to our customs; and, by the principles they give us, serve as our guides even when we walk in paths that were unknown to them." Of the Pandects, Prost de Royer says: "It is an immense edifice, without distribution, without proportion, without ensemble. The pediments have disappeared, the columns are broken, the statues are mutilated: it is no longer imposing by its grandeur, by the beauty of its parts, by the richness of its details. After so many centuries, the digging goes on, as our artists still go to seek rules and models among the ruins of Palmyra, of Athens and of Rome."

Hastily compiled by Tribonian and his associates (in a scant three years) from the writings of thirty-nine eminent jurisconsults, the Pandects leave much to be desired in arrangement and abound in repetitions and antinomies. The arrangement, which follows that of the Perpetual Edict, is historical or traditional, rather than scientific. The adjective, or remedial, element dominates the classification. Although more rights were actually defined or capable of definition in the Roman legal system than is even now possible in the Common Law System, no classification based upon rights was evolved. The thing classified was an actual system of law, and the only principles of arrangement were those of tradition and convenience. Neither the jurists nor the compilers were concerned with theoretical jurisprudence. The materials of the Digest were not written into a continuous text. The fragments give the name of the jurist and the book from which they are taken. This method was designed to perpetuate the fame of the jurists and we thus enjoy a certain familiarity with them, although their writings for the greater part have perished. There are four hundred and thirty-two "titles" contained in the fifty books of the Digest. The whole is divided into seven parts: the first, called πρῶτα, has four books (I-IV); the second, "De judiciis", seven books (V-XI); the third, "De rebus", eight books (XII-XIX); the fourth, "Umbilicus", eight books (XX-XXVII); the fifth, "De testamentis", nine books (XXVIII-XXXVI); the sixth, with a great variety of matters, eight books (XXXVII-XLIV); the seventh part, six books (XLV-L). The sixth and seventh parts seem to have had no special designation. This division into seven parts was never of practical importance.

The later, or occidental, arbitrary division adopted by the glossators during the Middle Ages was probably due to the order of time in which the materials became available for the production of a complete vulgate text. The division was as follows: "Digestum vetus" (bk. I-XXIV, tit. 2); the "Infortiatum" (bk. XXIV, tit. 3,—XXXV, tit. 2, §82); the "Tres partes" (bk. XXXV, tit. 2, §83—XXXVIII); the "Digestum novum" (bk. XXXIX-L). The vulgate MSS. are in three *volumina* (the "Infortiatum" with the "Tres partes"). The first printed editions follow this valueless division, and it was abandoned only in the seventeenth century. The celebrated fragment from Gaius (a facsimile of which, as it appears in the Florentine MS., is shown in the accompanying illustration): "Omne jus quo utimur pertinet vel ad personas vel ad res vel ad actiones" (Every right which we enjoy concerns either persons, or things or actions) is not an Aristotelean division of law, was not so regarded by Gaius himself, and was given no importance as a canon of classification by the compilers of the Digest.

The Florentine MS.—The rediscovery of the Pisan, or Florentine, MS. of the Pandects has been regarded as the critical secular event for modern civilization by those who associate the revival of Roman law with the legend of Amalfi. Charlemagne, who destroyed the Lombard monarchy (c. 800), was unable to find a copy of the works of Justinian. Yves de Chartres, three centuries later, mentions fragments, and shortly after his death the legendary narrative begins. Pothier accepts it and relates the circumstances in which the "complete copy of the Pandects emerged from the shadows of the tomb as by a miracle of Divine Providence". During the siege of Amalfi (about 1136 or 1137), the Emperor Lothair II, sustaining the cause of Innocent II against Roger, Count of Sicily, champion of the anti-pope Pietro Pierleone (see ANACLETUS II), recovered the priceless MS. and gave it to the Pisans as a reward for their great service in furnishing him a fleet. A Pisan historian claims to have seen the original deed of gift. The MS. was long treasured at Pisa, but at last fell into the hands of the victorious Florentines, who carried it away in triumph in the early fifteenth century. It was preserved with great veneration in the ducal palace at Florence, as an original written in the time of Justinian and by him sent to Amalfi. About the time of the fabled finding at Amalfi, a copy of the Code and a second copy of the Pandects were unearthed at Ravenna.

The sacking of Amalfi (according to the tradition) led to the founding, by Irnerius of the first and most famous school, that of Bologna, and was the beginning of the revival. Sigonius gave his authority to the story, and it was generally credited until 1726, when Grandi, a Pisan professor, seriously questioned it. The revival of the study of Roman law was well under way at Ravenna and at Bologna long before the alleged sacking of Amalfi and the immediate school of Irnerius had reached its zenith before the year 1118. It is an established fact that there was a very ancient MS. at Pisa, that this MS. was brought to Florence in 1406 or 1411, and that it is still in existence. It is however a copy, not an original, and probably dates from about one hundred years after Justinian. Odofredus (d. 1265) says it was brought to Pisa from Constantinople; according to Bartolus (d. 1357), it had always been at Pisa. That it ever was at Amalfi is improbable, and the legend is supported only by Pisan chronicles. Laferrière maintains that the story is true. Savigny and Ortolan reject it. Ortolan argues that if Irnerius and the early glossators became acquainted with it only as the result of the sacking of Amalfi, they would not have passed over so momentous an event in silence.

The Vulgate.—By comparison of earlier MSS. then extant with each other and with the MS. at Pisa, the glossators reconstructed the generally received text of Bologna, known as the Vulgate.

Pandekten.—In the sixteenth century the Roman law was received in Germany and became the positive common law. The law of the Pandekten in the special sense is Roman law, as a body of actual law, modern Roman law "modified by the Canon law, the customary law of Italy and Germany, and by the statute of the German Empire". The Pandekten, as part of the legal curriculum, give the altered Roman law. The pure private law of Rome, the Roman law of the sixth century, is generally designated *Institutionen*. The Pandekten, in the special sense, since the adoption of the new German Civil Code, are no longer of legal efficacy in Germany.

For modern texts of the Pandects, for translations into vernacular languages, and general references, see LAW, ROMAN and bibliography to that article: ORTOLAN, POTHIER, SOHM, HOLLAND AND SHADWELL, MÜHLENBRUCH, and other authorities there cited.

JOSEPH I. KELLY.

Pandulph, papal legate and Bishop of Norwich, d. at Rome, 16 Sept., 1226. He is commonly but erroneously called Cardinal Pandulph, owing to his being confused with Cardinal Pandulph Masca of Pisa (created cardinal, 1182; d. 1201). The identification involves the supposition that the legate lived more than a hundred years after his ordination as subdeacon. A Roman by birth, Pandulph first came into notice as a clerk in the court of Innocent III, where he was one of the subdeacons attached to the papal household. In 1211 Innocent sent him to England to induce the king to receive Langton as Archbishop of Canterbury, and thus to relieve England from the interdict which weighed so heavily on all classes. His interview with the king at Northampton elicited only threats from the king to hang the archbishop if he landed in England. Pandulph joined Langton and the exiled English bishops in Flanders and then returned to Rome. The whole account of this mission is rejected by some writers as resting solely on the authority of the annalist of Burton; but his account, confirmed by allusions in Matthew Paris and other writers, may be accepted as true. In 1213 Pandulph was again sent as papal envoy to England, as the king seemed prepared to submit, and on 15 May took place in Dover Castle the historic interview at which King John surrendered his crown into Pandulph's hands and received it back as a fief of the Holy See. The king also paid to Pandulph the sum of £8000 as an instalment of the compensation due for damage done to the Church during the interdict, the sum being delivered to the exiled bishops. Pandulph now stopped the threatened French invasion. When the papal legate, Cardinal Nicholas of Tusculum, arrived in England, Pandulph naturally fell into a secondary position, but he continued active, collecting money to compensate sufferers from the interdict and mediating between the king and the Welsh. In 1214 he was sent to Rome to counter-check the English bishops who were appealing against the legate; in this he failed, for the legate was recalled, and Pandulph again returned to England where he remained through the struggle for Magna Charta, in which his name occurs as one of those by whose counsel the Charter was granted. The king, anxious to retain his support, procured his election as Bishop of Norwich, though he did not yet receive consecration. When Innocent's Bull arrived annulling Magna Charta, Pandulph excommunicated the barons who would not receive it, and suspended Langton himself on his setting out to appeal to the pope in person. Again superseded by the advent of the papal legate, Pandulph, on the death of John, apparently returned to Rome where he held the positions of papal notary and chamberlain. On 12 Sept., 1218, he was sent to England as papal legate. As Henry III was a minor and the ministers who governed after the death of the regent Pembroke were disunited, the position of the legate as representing the pope, who was now suzerain of England, was very powerful. From 1219 to 1221 Pandulph practically acted as ruler of England. His administration was successful; the revenue was increased, the country prosperous, truces were made with France and Scotland, Jewish usurers suppressed, and justice was firmly administered. But he encountered the opposition of Cardinal Langton, who considered the exercise of legatine power prejudicial to the rights of Canterbury, and of Hubert de Burgh, who opposed the legate's action in the government of Poitou. During a visit to Rome, Langton procured the withdrawal of the legate, and on 19 July, 1221, Pandulph publicly resigned his function as legate at Westminster. He had hitherto at the pope's desire postponed his consecration as Bishop of Norwich to avoid coming under the archbishop's jurisdiction, but, as this reason now no longer held good, he was consecrated bishop by the pope himself on his return to Rome (29 May, 1222). He spent the rest of his life there engaged in diplomatic affairs, but after his death his body was brought back to England and buried in Norwich cathedral.

MATTHEW PARIS, *Hist. Major*, especially SHIRLEY's introduction, Rolls Series (1872–83); *Annals of Burton*, giving documents of John's submission and reconciliation in *Annales Monastici*, I, Rolls Series (1869); *Annals of Thomas Wykes (Osney) of Margam, Waverley, Worcester, Dunstable* and *Tewkesbury* in *Annales Monastici*, Rolls Series (1869); *Epistolæ Innocentii III* in P. L., CCXVI-VII; BLISS, *Calendar of Papal Letters*, I (London, 1893); SHIRLEY, *Royal Letters of the Reign of Henry III*, Rolls Series (1862–6); STUBBS, *Registrum Sacrum Anglicanum*, where he is confused with Masca (2nd ed., Oxford, 1897); IDEM, *Constitutional History* (Oxford, 1875–8); IDEM, *Select Charters* (Oxford, 1895); TOUT in *Dict. Nat. Biog.*, s. v. *Pandulf*; GASQUET, *Henry III and the Church* (London, 1905).

EDWIN BURTON.

Paneas. See CÆSAREA PHILIPPI.

Panemotichus, a titular see of Pamphylia Secunda, suffragan of Perge. Panemotichus coined money during the Roman epoch (Head, "Historia numorum", 591). A Bishop Faustus assisted at the Council of Nicæa, 325, when the city belonged to Isauria. Later it was part of Pamphylia Secunda. Another bishop, Cratinus, may have assisted at the Council of Chalcedon, 451. Hierius signed the provincial letter to Leo the Wise, 458. Helladius assisted at a Council of Constantinople in 536. (Le Quien, I, 1031). There is record of no other bishop and the see is not mentioned in the "Notitiæ Episcopatuum". The city is spoken of by Hierocles in the sixth century (Synecdemus, 681, 3) and in the tenth by Constantine Porphyrogenitus ("De thematibus", ed. Bonn, III, 38). Radet ("Les villes de la Pisidie", 4, reprinted from "Revue Archéologique", Paris, 1893) identifies it with the ruins of Badem Aghatch, south of Ghirme, in the vilayet of Koniah.

S. PÉTRIDÈS.

Pange Lingua Gloriosi, the opening words of two hymns celebrating respectively the Passion and the Blessed Sacrament. The former, in unrhymed verse, is generally credited to St. Venantius Fortunatus (6 cent.), and the latter, in rhymed accentual rhythm, was composed by St. Thomas Aquinas (13 cent.).

I. THE HYMN OF FORTUNATUS.—The hymn has been ascribed to Claudianus Mamertus (5 cent.) by Gerbert in his "Musica sacra", Bähr in his "Die christl. Dichter," and many others. Pimont, who cites many other authorities in his support, is especially urgent in his ascription of the hymn to Mamertus, answers at great length the critics of the ascription in his Note sur l'auteur du Pange . . . prælium certaminis (Hymnes du brév. rom. III, 70–76), so that it seems hardly correct to say with Mearns (Dict. of Hymnol., 2nd ed., 880), that "it has been sometimes, apparently without reason, ascribed to Claudianus Mamertus." Excluding the closing stanza or doxology, the hymn comprises ten stanzas, which appear in the MSS. and in some editions of the "Roman Missal" in the form:

Pange lingua gloriosi prœlium certaminis
Et super crucis tropæo dic triumphum nobilem,
Qualiter Redemptor orbis immolatus vicerit.

The stanza is thus seen to comprise three tetrameter trochaic catalectic verses. In the "Roman Breviary" the hymn is assigned to Passion Sunday and the ferial Offices following it down to and including Wednesday in Holy Week, and also to the feasts of the Finding of the Holy Cross, the Exaltation of the Holy Cross, the Crown of Thorns, the Five Wounds. In this breviary use, the hymn is divided into two, the first five stanzas being said at Matins, the second five (beginning with the words "Lustra sex qui jam peregit") at Lauds; and each line is divided into two, forming a stanza of six lines, e. g.:

> Pange lingua gloriosi
> Lauream certaminis,
> Et super crucis trophæo
> Dic triumphum nobilem:
> Qualiter Redemptor orbis
> Immolatus vicerit.

The whole hymn is sung during the ceremony of the Adoration of the Cross on Good Friday, immediately after the *Improperia* or "Reproaches", but in a peculiar manner, the hymn being preceded by the eighth stanza (*Crux fidelis*) while the stanzas are followed alternately by the first four and the last two lines of the (divided) eighth stanza.

It will have been noticed that in the six-lined stanza quoted above, "lauream" is substituted for the "prœlium" of the three-lined stanza. The correctors of the Breviary under Urban VIII apparently saw a pleonasm in the expression "prœlium certaminis". Their substitution of "lauream" has not commended itself to hymnologists, who declare that no pleonasm is involved, since "prœlium" refers to the battle and "certamen" to the occasion or cause of it; so that "prœlium certaminis" means the battle for the souls of men (see Kayser, "Beiträge zur Gesch. und Erklärung der ältesten Kirchenhym.", Paderborn, 1881, p. 417). He very aptly instances St. Cyprian (Ep. ad Ant., 4): "Prælium gloriosi certaminis in persecutione ferveret", and adds that "certamen" reveals the importance and length of the strife and renders salient the master thought of the whole poem. In the hands of the correctors the hymn suffered many emendations in the interest of classical exactness of phrase and metre. The corrected form is that found to-day in the Roman Breviary. The older form, with various manuscript readings, will be found in March (Latin Hymns, 64; with grammatical and other notes, 252), Pimont (Les Hymnes etc., III, 47–70, with a note on the authorship, 70–76), etc. The Commission on Plain Chant established by order of Pius X in many cases restored older forms of the liturgical texts. In the Gradual (the Antiphonary has not appeared as yet) the older form of the "Pange lingua" is now given, so that it can be compared with the form still used in our Breviary. For the variant readings of MSS. see "Analecta Hymnica" (Leipzig, 1907), 71–73. Dreves ascribes the hymn to Fortunatus. See also the "Hymnarium Sarisburiense" (London, 1851), 84.

It will be of interest to give here some specimens of Catholic translations of some stanzas of the hymn.

i

Sing loud the conflict, O my tongue,
  The victory that repaired our loss;
Exalt the triumph of thy song
  To the bright trophy of the cross;
Tell how the Lord laid down his life
  To conquer in the glorious strife.
                                    (J. T. Aylward, O. P.)

ii

Eating of the Tree forbidden,
  Man had sunk in Satan's snare,
When his pitying Creator
  Did this second Tree prepare;
Destined, many ages later,
  That first evil to repair.
                                    (Father Caswall.)

v

Thus God made Man an Infant lies,
  And in the manger weeping cries;
His sacred limbs by Mary bound,
  The poorest tattered rags surround;
And God's incarnate feet and hands
  Are closely bound with swathing-bands.
                                    (Divine Office, 1763.)

vi

Soon the sweetest blossom wasting,
  Droops its head and withered lies;
Early thus to Calvary hasting,
  On the cross the Saviour dies;
Freely death for all men tasting,
  There behold our sacrifice.
                                    (R. Campbell.)

ix

Bend, O noble Tree, thy branches;
  Let thy fibres yielding be,
Let the rigid strength be softened
  Which in birth was given thee,
That the limbs of my dear Jesus
  May be stretched most tenderly.
                                    (Amer. Eccl. Rev., 8191.)

The selected stanzas do not exhaust the examples of Catholic versions, but offer some variety in metre and in rhyming schemes. They represent neither the best nor the worst work of their authors in the translation of this hymn. In the preface to his "Annus Sanctus" Orby Shipley declared that "the love of Catholics for their hymns is no recent . . . fancy . . . and that the results achieved are not less wide in extent, not less worthy in merit than attempts of Protestant translators, facts overlooked even by Catholic translators." His thought is worthy of much consideration in view of the fact that the English version in the Marquess of Bute's translation of the Roman Breviary (I, 409), in the (Baltimore) "Manual of Prayers" (614), and Tozer's "Catholic Church Hymnal" (p. 48), was the work of an Anglican, Dr. Neale.

It may well be doubted if any translator has expressed better in English verse the strength and nobility of the original Latin than did the unknown Catholic author of the version found in the Divine Office of 1763 (given in stanza v above). Daniel gives the following stanza (Thes. Hymnol., I, 168):

> Quando judex orbis alto vectus axe veneris,
> Et crucis tuæ tropæum inter astra fulserit,
> O sis anxius asylum et salutis aurora.

which Neale translates (Medieval Hymns, 3rd ed., p. 5) and thinks ancient though not original; but Daniel's source is the "Corolla Hymnorum" (Cologne, 1806). The text reads "salutis anchora". Daniel also gives (IV, 68) four stanzas which Mone thought might be of the seventh century; but they would add nothing to the beauty or neat perfection of the hymn. For first lines, authors, dates of translation, etc., see Julian, "Dict. of Hymnol.", 880–881, 1685. For Latin text and translation with comment, see "Amer. Eccles. Review", March, 1891, 187–194, and "H. A. and M., Historical Edition" (London, 1909, No. 107).

II. THE HYMN OF ST. THOMAS AQUINAS.—Composed by the saint (see LAUDA SION) for the Office of Corpus Christi (see CORPUS CHRISTI, FEAST OF). Including the last stanza (which borrows the words "Genitori Genitoque"—"Procedenti ab utroque, Compar" from the first two strophes of the second sequence of Adam of St. Victor for Pentecost) the hymn comprises six stanzas appearing in the MSS.

Pange, lingua, gloriosi corporis mysterium,
Sanguinisque pretiosi quem in mundi pretium
Fructus ventris generosi Rex effudit gentium.

Written in accentual rhythm, it imitates the triumphant march of the hymn of Fortunatus, and like it is divided in the Roman Breviary into stanzas of six lines whose alternating triple rhyming is declared by Pimont to be a new feature in medieval hymnody. In the Roman Breviary the hymn is assigned to both Vespers, but of old the Church of Salisbury placed it in Matins, that of Toulouse in First Vespers only, that of Saint-Germain-des-Prés at Second Vespers only, and that of Strasburg at Compline. It is sung in the procession to the repository on Holy Thursday and also in the procession of Corpus Christi and in that of the Forty Hours' Adoration.

With respect to the metre, M. de Marcellus, quoted in Migne's "Littérature", remarks that the hymn is composed in the long trochaic verses such as are found in Catullus, Seneca, Sophocles, and Euripides. In addition to the felicitous rhythm chosen by St. Thomas, critics recognize its poetical and hymnodal values (thus Neale: "This hymn contests the second place among those of the Western Church with the Vexilla Regis, the Stabat Mater, the Jesu dulcis memoria, the Ad Regias Agni Dapes, the Ad Supernam, and one or two others . . .") and "its peculiar qualities, its logical neatness, dogmatic precision, and force of almost argumentative statement" (Duffield, "Latin Hymns", 269), in which qualities "it excels all these mentioned" by Neale.

The translations have not been many nor felicitous. *Generosi* in the first stanza is not "generous" (as in Neale's version) but "noble" (as in Caswall's). But, as Neale truly says, "the great crux of the translator is the fourth verse" (i e, "Verbum caro panem verum, etc."), so full is it of verbal and real antitheses. To illustrate the question of translation we select from the specimen versions the fourth stanza, since its very peculiar condensation of thought and phrase, dogmatic precision and illuminating antitheses, have made it "a bow of Ulysses to translators". Its text is:

Verbum caro panem verum
Verbo carnem efficit;
Fitque sanguis Christi merum;
Et si sensus deficit,
Ad firmandum cor sincerum
Sola fides sufficit.

A literal translation would be: "The Word–(made)–Flesh makes by (His) word true bread into flesh; and wine becomes Christ's blood; and if the (unassisted) intellect fails (to recognize all this), faith alone suffices to assure the pure heart". *Sensus* (singular) is taken here to indicate the inner sense, as distinguished from *sensuum* (plural) of the following stanza, where the word directly refers to the external senses. Perhaps the word has the same implication in both stanzas. "Sincere" (in its modern meaning) may be a better word than "pure". Taking first the old versions found in books of Catholic devotion, we find in the "Primer" of 1604:

The word now being flesh become,
So very bread flesh by the word,
And wine the blood of Christ is made,
Though our sense it not afford,
But this in heart sincere to fix
Faith sufficeth to accord.

It is not in the rhythm of the Latin, and contains but three monosyllabic rhymes instead of the six double rhymes of the Latin. The "Primer" of 1619 makes an advance to six monosyllabic rhymes; and the "Primer" of 1685 arranges the rhymes in couplets. The "Primer" of 1706 retains the rhythm and the rhymic scheme, but is somewhat more flowing and less heavy:

The Word made flesh for love of man,
With words of bread made flesh again;
Turned wine to blood unseen of sense,
By virtue of omnipotence;
And here the faithful rest secure,
Whilst God can vouch and faith ensure.

A distinct advance in rhythmic and rhymic correspondence was made in more recent times by Catholic writers like Wackerbarth, Father Caswall, and Judge D. J. Donahoe.

At the incarnate Word's high bidding
Bread to very flesh doth turn,
Wine becometh Christ's blood-shedding;
And if sense cannot discern,
Guileless spirits never dreading
May from faith sufficient learn.
(Wackerbarth, 1842)

Word made flesh, the bread of nature
By his word to flesh he turns;
Wine into his blood he changes:—
What though sense no change discerns?
Only be the heart in earnest,
Faith her lesson quickly learns.
(Caswall, 1849)

Neale criticises the version of Wackerbarth: "Here the antithesis is utterly lost, by the substitution of Incarnate for made flesh, and bidding for word, to say nothing of Blood-shedding for Blood"; and declares that Caswall "has given, as from his freedom of rhyme might be expected, the best version". He remarks, however, that Caswall has not given the "panem verum" of St. Thomas.

By his word the bread he breaketh
To his very flesh he turns;
In the chalice which he taketh,
Man the cleansing blood discerns,—
Faith to loving bosoms maketh
Clear the mystic truth she learns.
(D. J. Donahoe, 1908)

Some of the more recent translations take little account of the nice discriminations of antithesis pointed out by Dr. Neale, who when he attempted in his day a new version, modestly wrote that it "claims no other merit than an attempt to unite the best portions of the four best translations with which I am acquainted—Mr. Wackerbarth's, Dr. Pusey's, that of the Leeds book, and Mr. Caswall's". His version is:

Word made Flesh, by Word He maketh
Very bread his flesh to be;
Man in wine Christ's Blood partaketh,
And if senses fail to see,
Faith alone the true heart waketh
To behold the mystery.

The present writer rendered the stanza in the "Amer. Eccles. Review" (March, 1890), 208, as follows:

Into Flesh the true bread turneth
By His word, the Word made Flesh;
Wine to Blood: while sense discerneth
Nought beyond the sense's mesh,
Faith an awful mystery learneth,
And must teach the soul afresh.

Neale's version is given in the Marquess of Bute's "Roman Breviary". The Anglican hymnal, "Hymns Ancient and Modern", declares its version "based on tr. from Latin by E. Caswall"; but, as Julian points out, most of it is based on Neale, four of whose stanzas it rewrites, while a fifth is rewritten from Caswall (i. e. the third stanza), and the fourth stanza is by the compilers. The arrangement found in the Anglican hymnal is taken bodily into the (Baltimore) "Manual of Prayers"—a rather infelicitous procedure, as the fourth stanza is not faithful to the original (Neale, "Medieval Hymns and Sequences," 181). The last stanza and the doxology form a special hymn (see TANTUM ERGO) prescribed for Benediction of the Most Blessed Sacrament. The Vatican edition of the Graduale gives its plain-song melody in two forms, both of great beauty.

JULIAN, *Dict. of Hymnol.*, 2nd ed., s. v., 878 and 1685, for first lines of translations; HENRY in *Amer. Cath. Quarterly Review* (April, 1893), 288–292, for difficulties of translation; IDEM in *Amer. Eccles. Review* (March, 1890), 206–213, for text, verse-translation, comment, and notes; PIMONT, *Hymnes du bréviaire romain*, III (Paris, 1884), 164–176. A list of hymns beginning with the words "Pange lingua" is given in the *Analecta Hymnica*, IV, 70; IV, 257; and indexes *passim*.

H. T. HENRY.

Panigarola, FRANCESCO, preacher and controversialist, Bishop of Asti, b. at Milan, 6 Feb., 1548; d. at Asti, 31 May, 1594. As a student of law at Pavia and Bologna he led a dissipated life, until, moved by grace, he entered the Order of Friars Minor at Florence, 15 March, 1567. At the age of twenty-three he was sent to Rome, where his sermons attracted much attention. Pius V had him sent to Paris where for two years he studied the Fathers and the Councils, Greek and Hebrew. Returning to Italy he preached during thirteen years in the principal towns. He converted many Calvinists in France and Savoy; at Naples there was collected, through one of his sermons, enough money to build a hospital for incurables. He also assisted in the construction of the Italian church of Antwerp, and of the Franciscan buildings at Genoa, Venice, Milan, and Turin. In 1579 Panigarola attended, as custos of his province, the general chapter at Paris. Finally in 1586 Sixtus V appointed him titular Bishop and Coadjutor of Ferrara, whence in 1587 he was transferred to the See of Asti. Shortly after he was sent to France as assistant to the Papal Legate, Cardinal Henry Cajetan. When Henry IV had renounced Calvinism, the bishop returned to Asti.

Melchiorri (Annales Min. cont. XXIII ad a. 1594, n. 76–81) gives the most complete catalogue of Panigarola's works. The most important are: "Il Compendio degli Annali ecclesiastici del Padre Cesare Baronio", Rome, 1590; 2nd ed., Venice, 1593, comprises only the first volume of Baronius. "B. Petri Apostolorum Principis Gesta . . . in rapsodiæ, quam catenam appellant, speciem disposita", Asti, 1591. "Lettioni sopra dogmi, dette Calviniche", Venice, 1584. This work, translated into Latin (Milan, 1594), was attacked by Giacomo Picenino in "Apologia per i Riformatori e per la Religione Riformata contro le Invettive di F. Panigarola e P. Segneri", Coira, 1706. "Il Predicatore di F. Francesco Panigarola . . . overo Parafrase, comento e discorsi intorno al libro dell' Elocutione di Demetrio Falereo . . .", Venice, 1609. He also wrote commentaries (Psalms, Jeremias etc.) and many collections of sermons, published in Italian and Latin.

WADDING, *Scriptores Ord. Min.* (Rome, 1806), 87–89 (Rome, 1906), 88–90; SBARALEA, *Supplementum ad Script.* (Rome, 1806), 176–78, (Rome, 1908), 292–94; RODULPHIUS TOSSINIANENSIS, *Historiarum Seraphicæ Religionis libri tres* (Venice, 1586), fol. 317; UGHELLI, *Italia Sacra*, IV (2nd ed., Venice, 1719), 401–02; BOATTERI, *Serie cronologico-storica de' Vescovi della Chiesa d'Asti* (Asti, 1807), 110–14; TIRABOSCHI, *Storia della Letteratura italiana*, VII (Rome, 1785), iii, 424–29; VII (Rome, 1784), i, 366; MELCHIORRI, *Annales Minorum Wadd. cont.*, XXIII (Ancona, 1859), 157–64, ad an. 1594, n. 57–84; MARCELLINO DA CIVEZZA, *Storia Universale delle Missioni Francescane*, VII (Prato, 1883), i, 436–49.

LIVARIUS OLIGER.

Panis Angelicus. See SACRIS SOLEMNIIS.

Pannartz, ARNOLD, and SWEINHEIM, KONRAD, printers; Pannartz d. about 1476, Sweinheim in 1477. Pannartz was perhaps a native of Prague, and Sweinheim of Eltville near Mainz. Zedler believes (Gutenberg-Forschungen, 1901) that Sweinheim worked at Eltville with Gutenberg in 1461–64. Whether Pannartz had been connected with Sweinheim in Germany is not known. It is certain that the two brought Gutenberg's invention to Italy.

The Benedictine monastery of Subiaco was the cradle of Italian printing. Probably Cardinal Giovanni of Turrecremata, who was Abbot *in commendam* of Subiaco, summoned the two printers there. They came in 1464. The first book that they printed at Subiaco was a Donatus; it has not, however, been preserved. The first book printed in Italy that is still extant was a Cicero, "De oratore" (now in the Buchgewerbehaus at Leipzig), issued in September, 1465. It was followed by Lactantius, "De divinis institutionibus", in October, 1465, and Augustine's "De civitate Dei" (1467). These four impressions from Subiaco are of particular importance, because they abandon the Gothic type of the early German books. In Italy Roman characters were demanded. Pannartz and Sweinheim, however, did not produce a pure but only a "half Roman" type.

In 1467 the two printers left Subiaco and settled at Rome, where the brothers Pietro and Francesco de' Massimi placed a house at their disposal. Their proof and manuscript reader was Giovan de' Bussi, since 1469 Bishop of Aleria. The works they printed are given in two lists of their publications, issued in 1470 and 1472. Up to 1472 they had published twenty-eight theological and classical volumes, viz. the Bible, Lactantius, Cyprian, Augustine, Jerome, Leo the Great, Thomas Aquinas, Cicero, Apuleius, Gellius, Virgil, Livy, Strabo, Pliny, Quintilian, Suetonius, Ovid etc., in editions varying from 275 to 300 copies each, in all 12,475 volumes. But the printers shared the fate of their master, Gutenberg; they could not sell their books, and fell into want. In 1472 they applied to Sixtus IV for Church benefices. From this we know that both were ecclesiastics: Pannartz of Cologne and Sweinheim of Mainz. The pope had a reversion drawn up for them, a proof of his great interest in printing. In 1474 Sweinheim was made a canon at St. Victor at Mainz. It is not known whether Pannartz also obtained a benefice. Perhaps the pope also aided them; at any rate they printed eighteen more works in 1472 and 1473. After this they separated. Pannartz printed by himself twelve further volumes. Sweinheim took up engraving on metal and executed the fine maps for the "Cosmography" of Ptolemy, the first work of this kind, but died before he had finished his task.

BURGER, *The Printers and Publishers of the XV Century* (London, 1902), 523, 524, 605, 606; FUMAGALLI, *Dictionnaire géogr. d'Italie pour servir à l'histoire de l'imprimerie dans ce pays* (Florence, 1905), 331–37, 405–09; LÖFFLER, *Sweinheim und Pannartz* in *Zeitschrift für Bücherfreunde*, IX (Bielefeld, 1905), 311–17; IDEM, *Die ersten deutschen Drucker in Italien* in *Historisch-politische Blätter*, CXLIII (Munich 1909), 13–27.

KLEMENS LÖFFLER.

Pannonhalma. See MARTINSBERG.

Pano Indians, a former important mission tribe on the middle Ucayali River, Peru, being the principal of a group of twenty or more closely cognate tribes constituting the Panoan linguistic stock, and holding most of the territory of the Huallaga, Ucayali, and Javarí Rivers in north-eastern Peru, with outlying tribes on the Juruá, Puruó, Beni, and upper waters of the Madeira in extreme western Brazil and northern Bolivia. Among the most important of these beside the Pano, are the Cashibo, Conibo, Mayoruna (q. v.), Remo, Sensi, Setebo, and Shipibo, all of whom, excepting the Cashibo who are still cannibal savages, were at one time in part connected with the famous Jesuit missions of the "Province of Mainas" (see MAINAS), of which the central headquarters was at first San Francisco de Borja and later the Pano town of Laguna.

The primitive culture of the Pano and cognate tribes was very similar, and was intermediate between that of the Quichua tribes of Peru and the wandering savages of the Amazon forests. They were sedentary and agricultural. Their villages, always close to the water, consisted of large communal structures of oval shape, and sometimes more than 120 feet in length, built of canes and thatched with palm leaves, with two or more fire-places inside, and raised platforms for beds along the walls. The furniture consisted chiefly of clay pots of various sizes and purposes, manufactured by the women, a wooden trough for holding the chicha liquor, with the weapons and fishing gear of the men. They cultivated corn, bananas, yuca, and a native cotton which they wove into girdles and simple fabrics. They had also bed coverings made from the inner bark of trees softened by beating. Besides the cultivated plants, they subsisted largely upon fish, wild game, and the oil procured from turtle eggs, which were gathered in great quantities during the laying season in late summer. The oil or "butter" was obtained by breaking up the eggs in a trough, pouring water over the mass, and skimming off the grease which rose to the top after the sun's rays had warmed it. This turtle oil formed a considerable article of commerce with the tribes of the upper Amazon as well as of the Orinoco.

Their weapons for war and hunting were the bow, the knife, the blow-gun with poisoned arrows, the lance, and the wooden club, armed with deer-horn spikes and ornamented with feathers. The most prized possession was the dug-out canoe, from thirty to forty feet long, and sometimes requiring months for completion. The men cleared the ground of trees, with the help of their neighbours, but the cultivation was by the women. Men and women went nearly naked, but painted in various colours, with the hair flowing loosely either full length or cut off about the shoulders. They stained their teeth a dark blue with a vegetable dye. The women wore nose pendants, necklaces of various trinkets, and bracelets and anklets of lizard skin. In general both sexes were of medium size but well formed. Their mentality was of a low order and they could seldom count beyond four. There was practically no government or chiefship, every man acting for himself except as common interest brought them together. They paid special reverence to the sun, fire, and the new moon, and were in great dread of evil spirits. Some of the tribes had a genesis hero who was said to have struck his foot upon the ground and called them forth out of the earth. In accord with a widespread Indian custom, one of a pair of twins was always killed at birth, as also all deformed children, considered the direct offspring of evil spirits. The dead were buried in large jars in the earth floor of the house. In the case of the warrior, his canoe was used as a coffin, all his small belongings being buried with him. There seems to have been no fear of the presence of the dead. Their ceremonies consisted of a few simple dances to the sound of the drum and Pandean pipes, and invariably ended in a drinking orgy. They had few traditions, but sometimes kept a record of events by means of pictographs painted upon bark cloth. Girls were betrothed in childhood, and married with somewhat elaborate ceremony when very young.

In 1666 the Jesuit, Father Lorenzo Lucero, afterward killed by the savages, established the mission of Santiago de la Laguna, at the present Laguna, on the east bank of the Huallaga, near its mouth in northeastern Peru. Here he gathered a number of Indians of various tribes, Pano and Setebo of cognate stock, Cocama and others of Tupian stock. In a short time the settlement contained 4000 souls, ranking among the most important missions of the Mainan province. Smallpox visitations and Portuguese slave raids (see MAMELUCO) within the next century greatly reduced it, but on the expulsion of the Jesuits in 1768 it still contained 1600 Christian Indians, ranking first among the 33 existing Jesuit missions of the upper Amazon and its branches. The missionary then in charge was Father Adam Vidman, a Bavarian. With the other missions it was turned over to the care of the Franciscans, under whom it continued until the establishment of the republican government in Peru in 1821, when the missionaries were again scattered, most of the missions abandoned and the others, being left without support, rapidly declined, the Indians rejoining their wild kinsmen of the forest and relapsing into their original barbarism. The Laguna mission continued, but in 1830, in consequence of dissensions between the Cocama and the Pano, the former removed to the towns of Nauta and Parinari on the Marañon, while the Pano joined the mission of Sarayacú on the lower Ucayali, founded by the Franciscan Father Girbal in 1791. Lieutenant Smyth has given us an interesting account of this mission as he found it in 1835, having then a mixed population of 2000 Pano, Conibo, Setebo, Shipibo, and Sensi, all using the Pano language, which was the dominant one along the lower Ucayali. While the Indians had accepted Christianity, taken on some of the customs of civilization, and showed the greatest devotion to their padre, they were still greatly given to child-murder and to their besetting sin of drunkenness from chicha, in spite of every effort of the missionary. It must be remembered in explanation that the whole country was a tropical wilderness, without a single white inhabitant other than the padre himself, who laboured without salary or government recognition, and that the mission Indians were in constant communication with their wild kinsmen of the woods. Of the Indians, Smyth says: "Their manners are frank and natural, and show without any disguise their affection or dislike, their pleasure or anger. They have an easy, courteous air, and seem to consider themselves on a perfect equality with everybody, showing no deference to anyone but the Padre, to whom they pay the greatest respect". Sarayacú still exists, though no longer a mission town, but the Pano name and language are gradually yielding to the Quichua influence from beyond the mountains. (See also PIRO INDIANS; SARAYACÚ MISSION.)

For the tribes and missions of the upper Amazon region during the Jesuit period: CHANTRE Y HERRERA, *Historia de las Missiones de la Compañia de Jesus en el Marañon Español* (Madrid, 1901); for more recent conditions: SMYTH AND LOWE, *Journey from Lima to Para* (London, 1836). Consult also RODRIGUEZ, *El Marañon y Amazonas* (Madrid, 1684); HERNDON, *Exploration of the Valley of the Amazon* (Washington, 1853); BRINTON, *American Race* (New York, 1891); MARKHAM, *Tribes in the Valley of the Amazon* in *Jour. Anth. Inst.*, XXIV (London, 1895); RECLUS, *South America: the Andes Regions* (New York, 1894).

JAMES MOONEY.

Panopolis, a titular see, suffragan of Antinoe in Thebais Prima; the ancient Apu or Khimmin which the Greeks made Khemmis and Panopolis, capital of the Panopolitan "nomos" or district; one of the most important towns of Upper Egypt made famous by the god Mîn. Herodotus (II, 91) speaks of its temple. Strabo (XVII, i, 41) says the population was composed of weavers and stone-cutters. As bishops, LeQuien mentions (Oriens christianus, II, 601–4) Arius, friend of Saint Pachomius, who had built three convents there; Sabinus, at Ephesus in 431; St. Menas, venerated 11 February; and some other Jacobites. Recent excavations have disclosed a necropolis, numerous tapestries, similar to Gobelin work, important for the history of tapestry from the second to the ninth century; numerous Christian manuscripts, among them fragments of the Book of Henoch, of the Gospel, and of the Apocalypse according to Peter, and the Acts of the Council of Ephesus; and numerous Christian inscriptions (see AKHMÎN).

BOURIANT in *Mémoires publiés par la Mission archéologique française du Caire* (Paris); GERSPACH, *Les tapisseries coptes* (Paris, 1890); FÖRRER, *Die Gräber-und Textilfunde von Akhmîn-Panopolis* (Strasburg, 1891); MASPÉRO, *Mélanges de mythologie et d'archéologie égyptiennes*, I, 214; AMÉLINEAU, *La géographie de l'Egypte à l'époque copte* (Paris, 1893), 18–22; LEFEBVRE, *Recueil des inscriptions grecques chrétiennes d'Egypte* (Cairo, 1907), 46–66; LECLERCQ in CABROL, *Dict. d'archéologie chrét.* (q. v. *Akhmîn*).

S. VAILHÉ.

Panormia. See CANONS, COLLECTIONS OF ANCIENT; IVO OF CHARTRES, SAINT.

Panormitanus. See NICOLÒ DE' TUDESCHI.

Panpsychism (Greek πᾶν, all; ψυχή, soul) is a philosophical theory which holds that everything in the universe, the inorganic world as well as the organic, has some degree of consciousness. It is closely related to the theory of hylozoism, which teaches that all matter is endowed with life. As synonymous with hylozoism must be regarded the word *panbiotism*, which was coined by Paul Carus to distinguish his theory from the panpsychism of Häckel ("Monist", 1892–93, III, 234–57). Between panpsychism and hylozoism there is no sharp distinction, because the ancient hylozoists not only regarded the spirits of the material universe and plant world as alive, but also as more or less conscious. The Renaissance witnessed a revival of the ancient hylozoism. The Italian philosophers of nature and the alchemists speculated about the spirits that were present in all things and the "feelings" and "strivings" of the "principles" of nature. The monadism of Leibniz is evidently panpsychistic. All things are made up of monads. Every monad is conscious and mirrors intellectually in itself the entire universe. One monad differs from another only in the clearness with which this mental representation is expressed.

Apart from these early movements there is the modern school of panpsychism, during the development of which the word itself was coined. It began with Fechner (1801–87) and received a new impetus from Darwinian philosophy in England and metaphysical speculation in America.

The panpsychism of Fechner and later German writers is most closely connected with the Renaissance revival of hylozoism. Both Fechner and Lotze have much in common with the mystical speculations of Paracelsus and van Helmont. To Fechner everything is animated; the earth is truly our mother, and a living mother at that. The panpsychism of Lotze (1817–81) arises as a dreamy speculation, rather than a coldly-reasoned conclusion. "Has one half of creation, that which we comprise under the name of the material world, no function whatever save that of serving the other half, the realm of mind, and are we not justified in longing to find the lustre of sense in that also whence we always derive it?" (Microcosmos, I, Book III, ch. iv, p. 353.) By making the atom unextended Lotze thought that he had removed the last objection to his panpsychism. Of a similar type is the panpsychism of Paulsen, and not far removed are the speculations of Häckel on the pleasures and pains of the elements. With G. Heymans panpsychism appears as a reasoned conclusion from a metaphysical consideration of the relation between body and mind.

In England panpsychism was advocated by William Kingdon Clifford as early as January, 1878 (Mind, III, 57–67). He arrived at the theory as a corollary from the doctrine of evolution. Consciousness exists in man; man is evolved from inorganic matter; therefore inorganic matter has in it the elements of consciousness. This conclusion was then extended to the assertion that "the universe consists entirely of mind stuff". As his forerunners in this conception Clifford mentioned Kant and Häckel — and especially Wundt — of whom he wrote: "the first statement of the doctrine in its true connexion that I know of is by Wundt" (Lectures and Essays, II, 73).

In America as early as 1885, Dr. Morton Prince advocated the theory of panpsychism, though not under that name. He looked upon his theory as a vindication of materialism, arguing that if matter is psychical in its nature and mind is to be interpreted as the resultant of these mental forces of nature, such an interpretation must be materialistic; for "as long as anything is the resultant of the forces of nature it belongs to materialism" (The Nature of Mind, 152). His panpsychism was in reality an illegitimate conversion of the proposition: "all conscious processes are physical changes" to "all physical changes are conscious processes". This inference was supplemented by hints at the evolutionary argument of Clifford. While the panpsychism of Clifford and Prince was more or less empirical, that of Prof. C. A. Strong is more pronouncedly metaphysical; it deals with the problem of interaction between body and mind. Prof. Strong proposes to solve it by eliminating the essential distinction between body and soul, in holding that matter itself is psychical rather than physical in its nature. His work, "Why the Mind Has a Body" (New York, 1903) called forth a lively discussion of this theory.

The first article of the eighteenth question in the first part of the "Summa Theologica" of St. Thomas is entitled: "Is every thing in nature alive?" It is a discussion of the theory of hylozoism and tells us also the position of the great scholastic on the question of panpsychism. St. Thomas decides that the test of life is to be sought in the possession of those characteristics that are proper to beings which are most evidently alive. These characteristics he embraces under what he terms the power of spontaneous movement. By this he does not mean the mere capability of moving about from place to place, but any spontaneous tendency towards any kind of change (*quæcumque se agunt ad motum vel operationem aliquam*). As examples of such motion he mentions the tendency of a thing from a less to a more perfect state (growth), and the sensations and understanding which constitute the activity of animals that have already acquired their full development. The question then becomes one of fact. Are there any things in nature that do not manifest the power of spontaneous movement, i. e. growth or the activity of sensory and intellectual life? Yes. There are things which have no spontaneous activity of their own and do not move except by an impulse from without, and these things are lifeless or dead. We may see analogies in them to living things, but they can never be said to live, except we are speaking poetically and by way of metaphor. St. Thomas therefore rejects hylozoism and panpsychism.

The only serious arguments in favor of panpsychism are: the evolutionary one put forward by Clifford, and the metaphysical reasoning of Prof. Strong. But until there is evidence to show that the chemical elements manifest some kind of mental process, we have no right to say that they do, no matter how much it would aid any theory of evolution, or how easy it might make our metaphysical explanation of the relation between body and mind.

St. Thomas Aquinas, *Summa Theologica*, I, Q. xiii, a. 1; Bawden, *The Meaning of the Psychical* in *Philos. Review*, XIII (1904), 298–319; Carus, *Panpsychism and Panbiotism* in *The Monist*, III (1892–93), 234–57; Clifford, *Lectures and Essays*, II; *Body and Mind* in *Fortnightly Review* (Dec., 1874); Idem, *On the Nature of Things-in-Themselves* in *Mind* (Jan., 1878); Fechner, *Zend Avesta* (3rd ed., 2 vols., Leipzig, 1906); Flournoy, *Sur le panpsychisme* in *Archives de psychologie*, IV (1904–05), 129–44; Häckel, *The Riddle of the Universe* (London, 1900); *Our Monism* in *The Monist*, II (1891–92), 481–86; Heymans, *Zur Parallelismusfrage* in *Zeitschrift für Psychologie*, XVII (1898), 62–105; Lotze, *Microcosmus*, tr. Hamilton and Jones, I (Edinburgh, 1881), bk. III, iv; Paulsen, *Introduction to Philosophy*, tr. Thilly (New York, 1895), bk. I, i, § 5, 87–111; Prince, *The Nature of Mind and the Human Automatism* (Philadelphia, 1885); *The Identification of Mind and Matter* in *Philos. Review*, XIII (1904), 444–51; Strong, *Why the Mind Has a Body* (New York, 1903); Idem, *Quelques considérations sur le panpsychisme* in *Arch. de psychol.*, IV (1904–5), 145–54.

Thomas V. Moore.

Pantænus, head of the Catechetical School of Alexandria about 180 (Eusebius, "Hist. eccl.", V, x), still alive in 193 (Eusebius, "Chron." Abr., 2210). As he was succeeded by Clement who left Alexandria about 203, the probable date of his death would be about 200. He was trained in the Stoic philosophy; as a Christian missionary, he reached India (probably South Arabia), and found there Christians possessing the Gospel of St. Matthew in Hebrew, which they had received from St. Bartholomew. All this is given by

Eusebius as what was "said" (Hist. eccl., V, xi). Eusebius continues: "In his 'Hypotyposes' he [Clement] speaks of Pantænus by name as his teacher. It seems to me that he alludes to the same person also in his 'Stromata'." In the passage of the "Stromata" (I, i), which Eusebius proceeds to quote, Clement enumerates his principal teachers, giving their nationality but not their names. The last, with whom Eusebius would identify Pantænus, was "a Hebrew of Palestine, greater than all the others [in ability], whom having hunted out in his concealment in Egypt, I found rest." These teachers "preserving the true tradition of the blessed doctrine from the Holy Apostles Peter and James, John and Paul . . . came, by God's will, even to us" etc. Against Eusebius's conjecture it may be suggested that a Hebrew of Palestine was not likely to be trained in Stoic philosophy. In its favour are the facts that the teacher was met in Egypt, and that Pantænus endeavoured to press the Greek philosophers into the service of Christianity. It may well be that a mind like Clement's "found rest" in this feature of his teaching.

Eusebius (VI, xiii) says again that Clement in his "Hypotyposes" mentioned Pantænus, and further adds that he gave "his opinions and traditions". The inference commonly drawn from this statement is that, in the extant fragments of the "Hypotyposes" where he quotes "the elders", Clement had Pantænus in mind; and one opinion or tradition in particular, assigned to "the blessed elder" (Eusebius, "Hist. eccl.", VI, xiv), is unhesitatingly ascribed to Pantænus. But this is incautious, for we cannot be sure that Clement would have reckoned Pantænus among the elders; and if he did so, there were other elders whom he had known (Hist. eccl., VI, xiii). Origen, defending his use of Greek philosophers, appeals to the example of Pantænus, "who benefited many before our time by his thorough preparation in such things" (Hist. eccl., VI, xix). That Pantænus anticipated Clement and Origen in the study of Greek philosophy, as an aid to theology, is the most important fact we know concerning him. Photius (cod. 118) states, in his account of the "Apology for Origen" by Pamphilus and Eusebius (see PAMPHILUS OF CÆSAREA, SAINT), that they said Pantænus had been a hearer of men who had seen the Apostles, nay, even had heard them himself. The second statement may have been a conjecture based upon the identification of Pantænus with one of the teachers described in "Stromata", I, i, and a too literal interpretation of what is said about these teachers deriving their doctrine direct from the Apostles. The first statement may well have been made by Clement; it explains why he should mention Pantænus in his "Hypotyposes", a book apparently made up of traditions received from the elders. Pantænus is quoted (a) in the "Eclogæ ex Prophetis" (Migne, "Clem. Alex.", II, 723) and (b) in the "Scholia in Greg. Theolog." of St. Maximus Confessor. But these quotations may have been taken from the "Hypotyposes". The last named in his prologue to "Dionys. Areop." (ed. Corder, p. 36) speaks casually of his writings, but he merely seems to assume he must have written. A conjecture has been hazarded by Lightfoot (Apost. Fathers, 488), and followed up by Batiffol ("L'église naissante", 3rd ed., 213 sqq.), that Pantænus was the writer of the concluding chapters of the "Epistle to Diognetus" (see DIOGNETUS). The chief, though not the only ground for this suggestion, is that Anastasius Sinaita in two passages (ed. Migne, pp. 860, 892) singles out Pantænus with two or three other early Fathers as interpreting the six days of Creation and the Garden of Eden as figuring Christ and the Church—a line of thought pursued in the fragment.

BARDENHEWER, *Gesch. der altkirch. Lit.*, II, 13 sqq.; HARNACK, *Altchrist. Lit.*, 291 sqq.; TILLEMONT, *Hist. ecclés.*, III, 170 sqq.; CEILLIER, *Hist. des aut.*, II, 237 sqq.; ROUTH, *Reliq. sac.*, I, 237 sqq.

F. J. BACCHUS.

Pantaleon, SAINT, martyr, d. about 305. According to legend he was the son of a rich pagan, Eustorgius of Nicomedia, and had been instructed in Christianity by his Christian mother, Eubula. Afterwards he became estranged from Christianity. He studied medicine and became physician to the Emperor Maximianus. He was won back to Christianity by the priest Hermolaus. Upon the death of his father he came into possession of a large fortune. Envious colleagues denounced him to the emperor during the Diocletian persecution. The emperor wished to save him and sought to persuade him to apostasy. Pantaleon, however, openly confessed his faith, and as proof that Christ is the true God, he healed a paralytic. Notwithstanding this, he was condemned to death by the emperor, who regarded the miracle as an exhibition of magic. According to legend, Pantaleon's flesh was first burned with torches; upon this Christ appeared to all in the form of Hermolaus to strengthen and heal Pantaleon. The torches were extinguished. After this, when a bath of liquid lead was prepared, Christ in the same form stepped into the cauldron with him, the fire went out and the lead became cold. He was now thrown into the sea, but the stone with which he was loaded floated. He was thrown to the wild beasts, but these fawned upon him and could not be forced away until he had blessed them. He was bound on the wheel, but the ropes snapped, and the wheel broke. An attempt was made to behead him, but the sword bent, and the executioners were converted. Pantaleon implored heaven to forgive them, for which reason he also received the name of Panteleemon (the all-compassionate). It was not until he himself desired it that it was possible to behead him.

The lives containing these legendary features are all late in date and valueless. Yet the fact of the martyrdom itself seems to be proved by a veneration for which there is early testimony, among others from Theodoret (Græcarum affectionum curatio, Sermo VIII, "De martyribus", in Migne, P. G., LXXXIII, 1033), Procopius of Cæsarea (De ædificiis Justiniani, I, ix; V, ix), and the "Martyrologium Hieronymianum" (Acta SS., Nov., II, 1, 97). Pantaleon is venerated in the East as a great martyr and wonderworker. In the Middle Ages he came to be regarded as the patron saint of physicians and midwives, and became one of the fourteen guardian martyrs. From early times a phial containing some of his blood has been preserved at Constantinople. On the feast day of the saint the blood is said to become fluid and to bubble. Relics of the saint are to be found at St. Denis at Paris; his head is venerated at Lyons. His feast day is 27 July, also 28 July, and 18 February.

Acta SS., July, VI, 397–425; *Biblioth. hagiogr. græca* (2nd ed., Brussels, 1909), 196–97; *Biblioth. hag. lat.*, II (Brussels, 1900–01), 929–32 GÜNTER *Legendenstudien* (Cologne, 1906), 22, passim.

KLEMENS LÖFFLER.

Pantheism (πᾶν, all; θεός, god), the view according to which God and the world are one. The name *pantheist* was introduced by John Toland (1670–1722) in his "Socinianism truly Stated" (1705), while *pantheism* was first used by his opponent Fay in "Defensio Religionis" (1709). Toland published his "Pantheisticon" in 1732. The doctrine itself goes back to the early Indian philosophy; it appears during the course of history in a great variety of forms, and it enters into or draws support from so many other systems that, as Professor Flint says ("Antitheistic Theories", 334), "there is probably no pure pantheism". Taken in the strictest sense, i. e. as identifying God and the world, Pantheism is simply Atheism. In any of its forms it involves Monism (q. v.), but the latter is not necessarily pantheistic. Emanationism (q. v.) may easily take on a pantheistic meaning and, as pointed out in the Encyclical, "Pascendi dominici gregis", the same is true of the modern doctrine of immanence (q. v.).

VARIETIES.—These agree in the fundamental doctrine that beneath the apparent diversity and multiplicity of things in the universe there is one only being absolutely necessary, eternal, and infinite. Two questions then arise: What is the nature of this being? How are the manifold appearances to be explained? The principal answers are incorporated in such different earlier systems as Brahminism, Stoicism, Neo-Platonism, and Gnosticism, and in the later systems of Scotus Eriugena and Giordano Bruno (qq. v.).

Spinoza's pantheism was realistic: the one being of the world had an objective character. But the systems that developed during the nineteenth century went to the extreme of idealism. They are properly grouped under the designation of "transcendental pantheism", as their starting-point is found in Kant's critical philosophy. Kant (q. v.) had distinguished in knowledge the matter which comes through sensation from the outer world, and the forms, which are purely subjective and yet are the more important factors. Furthermore, he had declared that we know the appearances (*phenomena*) of things but not the things-in-themselves (*noumena*). And he had made the ideas of the soul, the world, and God merely immanent, so that any attempt to demonstrate their objective value must end in contradiction. This subjectivism paved the way for the pantheistic theories of Fichte, Schelling, and Hegel.

Fichte set back into the mind all the elements of knowledge, i. e. matter as well as form; phenomena and indeed the whole of reality are products of the thinking Ego—not the individual mind but the absolute or universal self-consciousness. Through the three-fold process of thesis, antithesis, and synthesis, the Ego posits the non-Ego not only theoretically but also for practical purposes, i. e. for effort and struggle, which are necessary in order to attain the highest good. In the same way the Ego, free in itself, posits other free agents by whose existence its own freedom is limited. Hence the law of right and all morality; but hence also the Divine being. The living, active, moral order of the world, says Fichte, is itself God; we need no other God, and can conceive of no other. The idea of God as a distinct substance is impossible and contradictory. Such, at any rate, is the earlier form of his doctrine, though in his later theorizing he emphasizes more and more the concepts of the Absolute as embracing all individuals within itself.

According to Schelling, the Absolute is the "identity of all differences"—object and subject, nature and mind, the real order and the ideal; and the knowledge of this identity is obtained by an intellectual intuition which, abstracting from every individual thinker and every possible object of thought, contemplates the absolute reason. Out of this original unity all things evolve in opposite directions: nature as the negative pole, mind or spirit as the positive pole of a vast magnet, the universe. Within this totality each thing, like the particle of a magnet, has its nature or form determined according as it manifests subjectivity or objectivity in greater degree. History is but the gradual self-revelation of the Absolute; when its final period will come to pass we know not; but when it does come, then God will be.

The system of Hegel (q. v.) has been called "logical pantheism", as it is constructed on the "dialectical" method; and "panlogismus", since it describes the entire world-process as the evolution of the Idea. Starting from the most abstract of notions, i. e. pure being, the Absolute developes first the various categories; then it externalizes itself, and Nature is the result; finally it returns upon itself, regains unity and self-consciousness, becomes the individual spirit of man. The Absolute, therefore, is Mind; but it attains its fulness only by a process of evolution or "becoming", the stages of which form the history of the universe.

These idealistic constructions were followed by a reaction due largely to the development of the natural sciences. But these in turn offer, apparently, new support to the central positions of pantheism, or at any rate they point, it is claimed, to that very unity and that gradual unfolding which pantheism has all along asserted. The principle of the conservation of energy through ceaseless transformations, and the doctrine of evolution applied to all things and all phenomena, are readily interpreted by the pantheist in favour of his own system. Even where the ultimate reality is said to be unknowable, as in Herbert Spencer's "Synthetic Philosophy", it is still one and the same being that manifests itself alike in evolving matter and in the consciousness that evolves out of lower material forms. Nor is it surprising that writers like the late Professor Paulsen should see in pantheism the final outcome of all speculation and the definitive expression which the human mind has found for the totality of things ("Einleitung in die Philosophie", Berlin, 1882, 242).

His statement, in fact, may well serve as a summary of the pantheistic doctrine: (1) Reality is a unitary being; individual things have no absolute independence; they have existence in the All-One, the *ens realissimum et perfectissimum* of which they are the more or less independent members; (2) The All-One manifests itself to us, so far as it has any manifestations, in the two sides of reality—nature and history; (3) The universal interaction that goes on in the physical world is the showing forth of the inner æsthetic teleological necessity with which the All-One unfolds his essential being in a multitude of harmonious modifications, a cosmos of concrete ideas (monads, entelechies). This internal necessity is at the same time absolute freedom or self-realization (op. cit., 239–40).

CATHOLIC DOCTRINE.—The Church has repeatedly condemned the errors of pantheism. Among the propositions censured in the Syllabus of Pius IX is that which declares: "There is no supreme, all-wise and all-provident Divine Being distinct from the universe; God is one with nature and therefore subject to change; He becomes God in man and the world; all things are God and have His substance; God is identical with the world, spirit with matter, necessity with freedom, truth with falsity, good with evil, justice with injustice" (Denzinger-Bannwart, "Ench.", 1701). And the Vatican Council anathematizes those who assert that the substance or essence of God and of all things is one and the same, or that all things evolve from God's essence (ibid., 1803 sqq.).

CRITICISM.—To our perception the world presents a multitude of beings each of which has qualities, activities, and existence of its own; each is an individual thing. Radical differences mark off living things from those that are lifeless; the conscious from the unconscious; human thought and volition from the activities of lower animals. And among human beings each personality appears as a self, which cannot by any effort become completely one with other selves. On the other hand, any adequate account of the world other than downright materialism includes the concept of some original Being which, whether it be called First Cause, or Absolute, or God, is in its nature and existence really distinct from the world. Only such a Being can satisfy the demands of human thought, either as the source of the moral order or as the object of religious worship. If, then, pantheism not only merges the separate existences of the world in one existence, but also identifies this one with the Divine Being, some cogent reason or motive must be alleged in justification of such a procedure. Pantheists indeed bring forward various arguments in support of their several positions, and in reply to criticism aimed at the details of their system; but what lies back of their reasoning and what has prompted the construction of all pantheistic theories, both old and new, is the craving for unity. The mind, they insist, cannot accept dualism or pluralism as the final account of reality. By an irresistible tendency, it seeks to substitute for the apparent multiplicity and diversity of things a unitary ground or source; and, once this is determined, to explain all things as somehow derived though not really separated from it.

That such is in fact the ideal of many philosophers cannot be denied; nor is it needful to challenge the statement that reason does aim at unification on some basis or other. But this very aim and all endeavours in view of it must likewise be kept within reasonable bounds: a theoretical unity obtained at too great a sacrifice is no unity at all, but merely an abstraction that quickly falls to pieces. Hence for an estimate of pantheism two questions must be considered: (1) at what cost does it identify God and the world; and (2) is the identification really accomplished or only attempted? The answer to (1) is furnished by a review of the leading concepts which enter into the pantheistic system.

God.—It has often been claimed that pantheism by teaching us to see God in everything gives us an exalted idea of His wisdom, goodness, and power, while it imparts to the visible world a deeper meaning. In point of fact, however, it makes void the attributes which belong essentially to the Divine nature. For the pantheist God is not a personal Being. He is not an intelligent Cause of the world, designing, creating, and governing it in accordance with the free determination of His wisdom. If consciousness is ascribed to Him as the one Substance, extension is also said to be His attribute (Spinoza), or He attains to self-consciousness only through a process of evolution (Hegel). But this very process implies that God is not from eternity perfect: He is forever changing, advancing from one degree of perfection to another, and helpless to determine in what direction the advance shall take place. Indeed, there is no warrant for saying that He "advances" or becomes more "perfect"; at most we can say that He, or rather It, is constantly passing into other forms. Thus God is not only impersonal, but also changeable and finite—which is equivalent to saying that He is not God.

It is true that some pantheists, e. g. Paulsen (op. cit.), while frankly denying the personality of God, pretend to exalt His being by asserting that He is "supra-personal". If this means that God in Himself is infinitely beyond any idea that we can form of Him, the statement is correct; but if it means that our idea of Him is radically false and not merely inadequate, that consequently we have no right to speak of infinite intelligence and will, the statement is simply a makeshift which pantheism borrows from agnosticism. Even then the term "supra-personal" is not consistently applied to what Paulsen calls the All-One; for this, if at all related to personality, should be described as infra-personal.

Once the Divine personality is removed, it is evidently a misnomer to speak of God as just or holy, or in any sense a moral Being. Since God, in the pantheistic view, acts out of sheer necessity, i. e. cannot act otherwise, His action is no more good than it is evil. To say, with Fichte, that God is the moral order, is an open contradiction; no such order exists where nothing is free, nor could God, a non-moral Being, have established a moral order either for Himself or for other beings. If, on the other hand, it be maintained that the moral order does exist, that it is postulated by our human judgments, the plight of pantheism is no better; for in that case all the actions of men, their crimes as well as their good deeds, must be imputed to God. Thus the Divine Being not only loses the attribute of absolute holiness, but even falls below the level of those men in whom moral goodness triumphs over evil.

Man.—No such claim, however, can be made in behalf of the moral order by a consistent pantheist. For him, human personality is a mere illusion: what we call the individual man is only one of the countless fragments that make up the Divine Being; and since the All is impersonal no single part of it can validly claim personality. Futhermore, since each human action is inevitably determined, the consciousness of freedom is simply another illusion, due, as Spinoza says, to our ignorance of the causes that compel us to act. Hence our ideas of what "ought to be" are purely subjective, and our concept of a moral order, with its distinctions of right and wrong, has no foundation in reality. The so-called "dictates of conscience" are doubtless interesting phenomena of mind which the psychologist may investigate and explain, but they have no binding force whatever; they are just as illusory as the ideas of virtue and duty, of injustice to the fellow-man and of sin against God. But again, since these dictates, like all our ideas, are produced in us by God, it follows that He is the source of our illusions regarding morality—a consequence which certainly does not enhance His holiness or His knowledge.

It is not, however, clear that the term *illusion* is justified; for this supposes a distinction between truth and error—a distinction which has no meaning for the genuine pantheist; all our judgments being the utterance of the One that thinks in us, it is impossible to discriminate the true from the false. He who rejects pantheism is no further from the truth than he who defends it; each but expresses a thought of the Absolute whose large tolerance harbours all contradictions. Logically, too, it would follow that no heed should be taken as to veracity of statement, since all statements are equally warranted. The pantheist who is careful to speak in accordance with his thought simply refrains from putting his philosophy into practice. But it is none the less significant that Spinoza's chief work was his "Ethics", and that, according to one modern view, ethics has only to describe what men do, not to prescribe what they ought to do.

Religion.—In forming its conception of God, pantheism eliminates every characteristic that religion presupposes. An impersonal being, whatever attributes it may have, cannot be an object of worship. An infinite substance or a self-evolving energy may excite fear; but it repels faith and love. Even the beneficent forms of its manifestation call forth no gratitude, since these result from it by a rigorous necessity. For the same reason, prayer of any sort is useless, atonement is vain, and merit impossible. The supernatural of course disappears entirely when God and the world are identified.

Recent advocates of pantheism have sought to obviate these difficulties and to show that, apart from particular dogmas, the religious life and spirit are safeguarded in their theory. But in this attempt they divest religion of its essentials, reducing it to mere feeling. Not action, they allege, but humility and trustfulness constitute religion. This, however, is an arbitrary procedure; by the same method it could be shown that religion is nothing more than existing or breathing. The pantheist quite overlooks the fact that religion means obedience to Divine law; and of this obedience there can be no question in a system which denies the freedom of man's will. According to pantheism there is just as little "rational service" in the so-called religious life as there is in the behaviour of any physical agent. And if men still distinguish between actions that are religious and those that are not, the distinction is but another illusion.

Immortality.—Belief in a future life is not only an incentive to effort and a source of encouragement; for the Christian at least it implies a sanction of Divine law, a prospect of retribution. But this sanction is of no meaning or efficacy unless the soul survive as an individual. If, as pantheism teaches, immortality is absorption into the being of God, it can matter little what sort of life one leads here. There is no ground for discriminating between the lot of the righteous and that of the wicked, when all alike are merged in the Absolute. And if by some further process of evolution such a discrimination should come to pass, it can signify nothing, either as reward or as punishment, once personal consciousness has ceased. That perfect union with God which pantheism seems to promise, is no powerful inspiration to right living when one considers how far from holy must be a God who continually takes up into Himself the worst of humanity along with the best—if indeed one may continue to think in terms that involve a distinction between evil and good.

It is therefore quite plain that in endeavouring to unify all things, pantheism sacrifices too much. If God, freedom, morality, and religion must all be reduced to the One and its inevitable processes, there arises the question whether the craving for unity may not be the source of illusions more fatal than any of those which pantheism claims to dispel. But in fact no such unification is attained. The pantheist uses his power of abstraction to set aside all differences, and then declares that the differences are not really there. Yet even for him they *seem* to be there, and so from the very outset he is dealing with appearance and reality; and these two he never fuses into one. He simply hurries on to assert that the reality is Divine and that all the apparent things are manifestations of the infinite; but he does not explain why each manifestation should be finite or why the various manifestations should be interpreted in so many different and conflicting ways by human minds, each of which is a part of one and the same God. He makes the Absolute pass onward from unconsciousness to consciousness but does not show why there should be these two stages in evolution, or why evolution, which certainly means becoming "other", should take place at all.

It might be noted, too, that pantheism fails to unify subject and object, and that in spite of its efforts the world of existence remains distinct from the world of thought. But such objections have little weight with the thorough-going pantheist who follows Hegel, and is willing for the sake of "unity" to declare that Being and Nothing are identical.

There is nevertheless a fundamental unity which Christian philosophy has always recognized, and which has God for its centre. Not as the universal being, nor as the formal constituent principle of things, but as their efficient cause operating in and through each, and as the final cause for which things exist, God in a very true sense is the source of all thought and reality (see St. Thomas, "Contra Gentes", I). His omnipresence and action, far from eliminating secondary causes, preserve each in the natural order of its efficiency—physical agents under the determination of physical law and human personality in the exercise of intelligence and freedom, the foundation of the moral order. The straining after unity in the pantheistic sense is without warrant; the only intelligible unity is that which God himself has established, a unity of purpose which is manifest alike in the processes of the material universe and in the free volition of man, and which moves on to its fulfilment in the union of the created spirit with the infinite Person, the author of the moral order and the object of religious worship.

PLUMTRE, *General Sketch of the Hist. of Pantheism* (London, 1881); JUNDT, *Hist. du Panth. populaire au moyen âge* (Paris, 1875); SAISSET, *Essai de philos. religieuse* (Paris, 1859), tr., *Modern Pantheism* (Edinburgh, 1863); MARET, *Essai sur le Panthéisme* (Paris, 1839); HARRIS, *Pantheism in Journal of Spec. Philos.*, IX (1875); *ibid.*, XIX (1885); WEISSENBERG, *Theismus u. Pantheismus* (Vienna, 1880); DE SAN, *Inst. Metaphysicæ Specialis*, I (Louvain, 1881); HONTHEIM, *Inst. Theod.* (Freiburg, 1893); FLINT, *Anti-Theistic Theories* (5th ed., Edinburgh, 1894); DE WULF, *Quelques formes contemp. du Panthéisme* in Rev. Néo-scol., IV (1897); GERARD, *The Old Riddle and the Newest Answer* (London, 1904); UHLMANN, *Die Persönlichkeit Gottes u. ihre modernen Gegner* (Freiburg, 1906); PAULSEN, *Der moderne Pantheismus u. die christl. Weltansch.* (Halle, 1906); WOLF, *Moderner P. u. christl. Theismus* (Stuttgart, 1906); see bibliog. under GOD; MONISM.

EDWARD A. PACE.

Panvinio, ONOFRIO, historian and archæologist, b. at Verona, 23 February, 1530; d. at Palermo, 7 April, 1568. At eleven he entered the Augustinian Hermits. After graduating in Rome as bachelor of arts in 1553, he instructed the young men of his order there for one year, and then taught theology in the monastery of his order at Florence. In 1557 he obtained the degree of doctor of theology, visited various libraries in Italy, making historical researches, and went to Germany in 1559. Refusing the episcopal dignity, he accepted the office of corrector and reviser of the books of the Vatican Library in 1556. He died while accompanying his friend and protector Cardinal Farnese to the Synod of Monreale. He was recognized as one of the greatest church historians and archæologists of his time. Paul Manutius called him "antiquitatis helluo", and Scaliger styled him "pater omnis historiæ".

He is the author of numerous historical, theological, archæological, and liturgical works, some of which are posthumous publications, others are still preserved in manuscript in the Vatican Library. Of his printed works the following are the most important: "Fasti et triumphi Romanorum a Romulo usque ad Carolum V" (Venice, 1557); a revised edition of Sigonio's "Fasti consulares" (Venice, 1558); "De comitiis imperatoriis" (Basle, 1558); "De republica Romana" (Venice, 1558); "Epitome Romanorum pontificum" (Venice, 1557); a revised edition of Platina's "De vitis pontificum" (Venice); "XXVII Pontif. Max. elogia et imagines" (Rome, 1568); "De sibyllis et carminibus sibyllinis" (Venice, 1567); "Chronicon ecclesiasticum a C. Julii Cæsaris tempore usque ad imp. Maximilianum II" (Cologne, 1568); "De episcopatibus, titulis, et diaconiis cardinalium" (Venice, 1567); "De ritu sepeliendi mortuos apud veteres Christianos" (Cologne, 1568); "De præcipuis Urbis Romæ basilicis" (Rome, 1570, Cologne, 1584); "De primatu Petri et apostolicæ sedis potestate" (Verona, 1589); "Libri X de varia Romanorum pontificum creatione" (Venice, 1591); "De bibliotheca pontificia vaticana" (Tarragona, 1587); "Augustiniani ordinis chronicon" (Rome, 1550).

PERINI, *Onofrio Panvinio e le sue opere* (Rome, 1899); ORLANDO, *Onofrio Panvinio* (Palermo, 1883); OSSINGER, *Bibliotheca Augustiniana historica, critica, et chronologica* (Ingolstadt and Augsburg, 1768), 656–62; TIRABOSCHI, *Storia della Letteratura Italiana*, VII (Modena, 1792), iii, 825–31. A life of Panvinio by Professor SCHROERS of Bonn is in preparation.

MICHAEL OTT.

Panzani, GREGORIO, Bishop of Mileto, d. early in 1662. He was a secular priest of Arezzo, having left the Congregation of the Oratory on account of ill-health, when in 1634 he was chosen by Cardinal Barberini for the important and delicate task of a secret agency in London. He is described by the writer of his memoirs as a man "of experienced virtue, of singular address, of polite learning and in all respects well qualified for the business". His commission was to gain first-hand information as to the state of English Catholics, then much divided on the question of the oath of allegiance and the appointment of a vicar Apostolic, to settle the differences that had arisen on these points between the seculars and regulars, and to establish informal relations with the Government. Panzani himself realized that the appointment of a bishop was necessary, and he resented the efforts of the Jesuits to hinder this. Though he was successful in reconciling the seculars with the Benedictines and other religious, the Jesuits were left out of the settlement, and Panzani's subsequent efforts to bring them in were fruitless. He had repeated interviews with Windebank and Cottington, the secretaries of state, enjoyed the confidence of the queen, and was admitted to secret audience with the king. He was also in communication with the Anglican Bishop of Chichester on the subject of corporate reunion. He was recalled in 1634 when a scheme of reciprocal agency was established between the pope and the king. Returning to Rome he was made a canon of S. Lorenzo in Damaso, and obtained a judicial position in the civil courts. On 13 Aug., 1640, he was elected Bishop of Mileto, in the Province of Catanzaro. An account of his English mission was written in Italian by someone who had access to his papers, and a copy of this was used by Dodd, who, however, thought it imprudent to publish these memoirs in full. But in 1793 the Rev. Joseph Berington published a translation of them with an historical introduction and supplement. Their authenticity was immediately called in question by Father Charles Plowden, S.J. (op. cit. inf.), who regarded them as a forgery by Dodd. The subsequent researches by Tierney, however, conclusively proved that the "Memoirs" were genuine. The original manuscript, then in the possession of Cardinal Gualterio, was purchased by the British Museum in 1854 (Add. MSS. 15389).

BERINGTON, *Memoirs of Gregorio Panzani, giving an account of his agency in England in the years 1634, 1635 and 1636* (Birmingham, 1793); PLOWDEN, *Remarks on a book entitled 'Memoirs of Gregorio Panzani'* (Liège, 1794); ANON., *The Pope's Nuncio or Negotiation of Signor Panzani* (London, 1643); PRYNNE, *The Popish Royal Favourite* (London, 1643); N. D., *Vindiciæ Caroli Regis* (s. l., 1654); DODD, *Church Hist.* (Brussels vere Wolverhampton, 1737–42); FLANAGAN, *Hist. of the Church in England* (London, 1857); GILLOW, *Bibl. Dict. Eng. Cath.*, s. vv. *Berington, Joseph*, and *Plowden, C.*

EDWIN BURTON.

Paoli, ANGELO, VENERABLE, b. at Argigliano, Tuscany, 1 Sept., 1642; d. at Rome, 17 January, 1720. The son of Angelo Paoli and Santa Morelli, he was particularly distinguished for his charity towards the poor. As a young man he spent the greater part of his leisure time in teaching Catholic doctrine to the poor children of Argigliano. At eighteen, he was admitted to the novitiate of the Calced Carmelites at Siena. After making his vows he spent six years at his studies, was ordained priest, and appointed to the community at Pisa, where he made rapid progress in perfection. He was subsequently transferred to Cupoli, Monte Catino, and Fivizzano. Specially devoted to the Passion, he caused wooden crosses to be erected on the hills around Fivizzano (and afterwards in the Coliseum at Rome) to bring the sacred tragedy more vividly before the minds of the inhabitants. In 1687, he was called to Rome and stationed at the Convent of St. Martin. The remaining years of his life were divided between the care of the sick poor in the city hospitals and the office of Master of Novices. He was called by the citizens "the father of the poor". Many miracles were wrought by him both before and after his death. His virtues were declared by Pius VI in 1781 to be heroic, and the general chapter of the order held at Rome, 1908, included his name among those Carmelite servants of God, the cause of whose beatification was to be at once introduced.

Analecta ordinis Carmelitarum, fasc. I-XII.

HENRY ANTHONY LAPPIN.

Paolo Veronese. See CALIARI, PAOLO.

Papacy.—This term is employed in an ecclesiastical and in an historical signification. In the former of these uses it denotes the ecclesiastical system in which the pope as successor of St. Peter and Vicar of Jesus Christ governs the Catholic Church as its supreme head. In the latter, it signifies the papal influence viewed as a political force in history. (See APOSTOLIC SEE; APOSTOLIC SUCCESSION; CHURCH; PAPAL ARBITRATION; POPE; UNITY.)

G. H. JOYCE.

Pápago Indians, an important tribe of Shoshonean linguistic stock, speaking a dialect of the Pima language and resembling that tribe in all essentials of culture and characteristics. Their territory, which they shared with the closely cognate and afterward incorporated Sobaipuri, comprised the valleys of the San Pedro and Santa Cruz rivers, southern tributaries of the Gila, in south-eastern Arizona, together with most of the Rio del Altar, in the State of Sonora, northern Mexico. The name by which they are commonly known is a derivation from the proper form, Papah-óotam, as given by their missionary, Father Kino, signifying "bean people", whence the Spanish, *Frijoleros*, and has no reference to "baptized", as has sometimes been asserted. The Pápago were and are a semi-sedentary and agricultural people, occupying numerous scattered villages of houses, usually dome-shaped and grass-thatched but frequently with flat roofs covered with earth. They practise irrigation and cultivate corn, beans, and cotton, besides making use of the desert food plants, particularly mesquite beans and the fruit of the saguaro or giant cactus (*Cereus giganteus, Pitahaya*). From the lagoons they collect salt, which they formerly traded to other tribes. Their women are expert basket-makers, but their pottery does not rank so high. In their aboriginal condition the men went naked excepting for the G-string, while the women wore only a short skirt. What remains of their primitive myths and ceremonies accords nearly with those of the Pima. In temperament they were noted for their industry and friendly disposition towards the whites, while carrying on ceaseless warfare with their hereditary enemies, the predatory Apache.

Owing to the isolation due to their desert environment the Pápago remained practically unknown for nearly a century and a half after the more eastern and southern tribes had come under Spanish dominion. Their connected history begins in 1687, when the noted German Jesuit missionary and explorer, Father Eusebio Francisco Kino (properly Kühn) founded the mission of Nuestra Señora de los Dolores, about the eastern head streams of the Rio del Altar and not far from the present Cucurpe, Sonora. From this headquarters station until his death in 1711 he repeatedly traversed the country of the Pápago, Pima, and Sobaipuri from the Altar to the distant Gila, for some years alone, but later aided by other Jesuit workers, notably Fathers Campos and Januske. Other missions and *visitas* were established on both sides of the line, the most important within the limits of Arizona being San Xavier del Bac, originally a Sobaipuri village of about 800 souls. It was first visited by Father Kino in 1692, but the church was not begun until 1699.

In 1695 the arbitrary cruelty of a local Spanish commandant provoked a rising among the southern Pima and their allies, who attacked and plundered the missions on the Sonora side, excepting Dolores where Father Kino was stationed, and killing Father Saeta at Caborca with the usual savage cruelties. The insurrection was soon put down by the energetic measures of Governor Jironza, and through the intercession of the missionaries a general pardon was accorded to the revolted tribes. In 1751 a more serious rebellion broke out, again involving the three tribes, in whose territory there were now eight missions, served by nine Jesuit priests. Of these missions two only were within the present limits of Arizona, viz., San Xavier del Bac, already noted, and San Miguel de Guevavi, founded in 1732 near to the present Nogales. For a period of more than twenty years after Father Kino's death in 1711 the scarcity of workers had compelled a withdrawal from the northern missions, with the result that many of the Indians had relapsed into their original heathenism. The return of the missionaries was followed a few years later by an influx of Spanish miners and garrison troops, leading to trouble with the natives, which culminated in November, 1751, in a massacre of Spaniards and a general attack upon missions and settlements alike. Nearly 120 whites lost their lives, including Fathers Zello and Ruhn, and the missions were again abandoned until peace was restored in

1752. They never fully recovered from this blow, and were already on the decline when the Jesuit order was expelled from Mexico in 1767 and the missions were turned over to the Franciscans, among whom, in this region, the most noted was Father Francisco Garcés, first Franciscan missionary at San Xavier del Bac and author of a journal of exploration among the tribes of the Lower Colorado River.

San Xavier had dwindled from 830 souls in 1697 to 270 in 1772, while the other missions had declined in proportion, their former tenants, whose numbers were constantly diminishing by neglect and Apache raids, having scattered over the desert. In 1828 the revolutionary Government of Mexico confiscated the missions, and for many years even San Xavier was left without attention, except for occasional visits by a secular priest from Sonora. In 1864 a Catholic school was once more re-established in connexion with the ancient church, and continues in successful operation. The Pápago, including most of the descendants of the Sobaipuri, number now altogether about 5500 souls, of whom all but about 1000 are in Arizona, the rest being in Sonora, Mexico. Those in Arizona are on two reservations at Gila Bend and San Xavier, established in 1874 and 1882, or scattered in villages throughout Pima County. They are farmers, stock raisers, and general labourers, practically all civilized and Catholic. See KINO; PIMA.

BANCROFT, *Hist. North Mex. States and Texas* (San Francisco, 1886); IDEM, *Hist. of Arizona and New Mex.* (San Francisco, 1889); COUES (ed.), *Garcés Diary* (New York, 1900); ORTEGA, *Apost. afanes de la C. de J.* (Barcelona, 1754), repub. as *Hist. del Nayarit* (Mexico, 1887); ORTEGA (?), *Rudo ensayo . . . descripcion geographica de . . . Sonora, ca. 1762* (St. Augustine, 1863), tr. Guiteras in *Am. Cath. Hist. Soc. Records*, V (Philadelphia, 1894); COMMISSIONER OF INDIAN AFFAIRS, annual reports (Washington); *Bur. Cath. Ind. Miss.*, annual reports of director (Washington).

JAMES MOONEY.

Papal Arbitration, an institution almost coeval with the papacy itself. The principle of arbitration presupposes that the individuals or groups of individuals submitting to arbitrament are united in some common bond. As soon therefore as this common bond has come prominently before public opinion, there necessarily results a tendency to settle disputes by reference to it. Thus the growth of law, i. e. the gradual evolution from private revenge or *vendetta* to the judgment of some public authority, can in the history of any known nation or tribe be traced parallel with the awakening feeling of social solidarity. It was just because men began to realize, however rudely, that they were not single units but members of a society, that they understood how every tort or wrong-doing disturbed not merely the individual directly affected, but the whole body of which he was a member. It was this recognition of the social disadvantages of disorder that led to compromise, to mutual pledges, to trials by combat, to ordeals, and eventually to the regulations of courts of law. This is most patently manifest among the Northern nations in the primitive history of the jury system.

Now this same principle was bound to operate internationally whenever the various groupings of Europe realized their solidarity. The same undoubted advance would be made when men became conscious that the theory into which law had developed as an adjudication between individuals by the society, was applicable also in matters of international dispute. But this consciousness required to be preceded by the recognition of two principles: (1) that nations were moral persons (2) that they were united in some common organism. The first principle was too abstract in its nature to be professed explicitly at once (Figgis, "From Gerson to Grotius", vi, 177). The second would be very quickly recognized if only some concrete symbol of it could become evident to public opinion. This concrete symbol was fortunately at hand, and the result was arbitration. For the medieval papacy directing the conscience of Europe, legislating for the newly-converted peoples, drawing to itself the representatives of each national episcopate, constituting a sacred shrine for royal pilgrimages, could not fail to impress on the Christian nations a sense of their common faith. It was the papacy which therefore at one and the same time, by treating each nation as a separate unit, expressed in a primate with his suffragan bishops, and yet by legislating identically in matters of faith and morals for all the nations, expounded the double thesis of nationalism and internationalism. It was a standing concrete expression of the two principles aforesaid, viz. that the nations were separate individuals, yet members of a Christian brotherhood, moral persons yet subject to the common law of Christendom. Hence, owing to the circumstances of Western politics, papal arbitration was a necessary consequence of the very idea of the papacy. In treating of papal arbitration, three points must be set out: (A) the principles on which the popes claimed the right to arbitrate, i. e. the papal theory of the relationship between the Holy See and the temporal powers; (B) the most important cases of historical arbitration by the popes; (C) the future opportunity for this arbitration.

A. *The Papal Theory.*—It is evident that before the conversion of Constantine there could have been little question of the relations between Church and State. The Church was undeniably conscious of her independence, but up to that date Christianity had practically none but spiritual duties to perform. The Apostolic writings preach submission to authority and do not at all raise the problem of the adjustment of the relationship between pope and Cæsar. The conversion of Constantine therefore opened up a large field of speculation. This begins indeed from the assembling of the General Council of Nicæa (325). Here, according to Rufinus (H. E., I, ii, in P. L., XXI, 470), the emperor himself laid the basis of all development in this direction. He declared that God had given to the priests (i. e. to the whole ecclesiastical corporation) power to judge even emperors (*et ideo nos a vobis recte judicamur*).

Hosius of Cordova, who had been president of that council, in his defence of Athanasius has the same thought, noting that God had given to Constantine the empire and to the priesthood He had confided the Church (quoted by St. Athanasius, "History of the Arians", xliv, in P. G., XXV, 717). This entire separation of the two powers, ecclesiastical and lay, is generally laid down with very definite clearness by the earlier writers (Lucifer of Cagliari, "Pro Athanasio", in P. L., XIII, 826; St. Optatus, "De Schismate Donatistarum", III, iii, in P. L., XI, 999). Not that any slight is put upon the imperial dignity, for to the prince first of all is applied the title which subsequently becomes proper to the popes alone. He is called *Vicarius Dei* (Ambrosiaster, "Quæstiones Veteris et Novi Testamenti XCI", in P. L., XXV, 2284; Sedulius Scotus, "De Rectoribus Christianis", 19 in P. L., CXII, 329). Yet he has no jurisdiction over the spiritual functions of his subjects, "for who", says St. Ambrose (Ep., XXI, 4, ad Valentinum, II, in P. L., XVI, 1046), "would venture to deny that in matters of faith, it is the bishops who sit in judgment over emperors, and not the emperors who sit in judgment over bishops?"; and the two popes who first have any prominent teaching on the matter, Felix III (483) and Gelasius I (492), use precisely the same language, describing the Church and the State as two parallel powers, entirely separate.

"The emperor", says Gelasius in an epigram (Ep. XV, 95, ad Episcopos Orientales, in P. L., LIX), "is the Church's son, not sovereign" (*Filius est non præsul ecclesiæ*). This pope has fortunately left us two complete treatises on this question. In his Fourth Tractate and his Eighth Letter (P. L., LIX, 41), he formulates his views, which completely agree with this idea of two different orders, separate, yet in so far interdependent that they both work towards the same purpose, i. e. the salvation of the souls of men. The next step is marked by the forcible and clear doctrine of St. Gregory the Great (590). His relations with the emperors are too well-known to need re-statement. It will be sufficient to note that, in his own words, he would go as far as possible to accept every law and statute of the imperial throne. "If what he does is according to the canons, we will follow him; if it be contrary to the canons, then so far as may be without sin, we will bear with him" (Epist., Lib. XI, 47, in P. L., LXXVII, 1167). Indeed, when in actual fact the Emperor Maurice prohibited public officials from entering monasteries, Gregory promulgated the decree, though at the same time warning Maurice that it by no means agreed with the declared will of the Divine Omnipotence. By thus acting he said he had performed his duty of obeying the civil power and yet had kept his faith with God by declaring the matter of that obedience unlawful (Lib. III, 65, in P. L., LXXVII, 663).

A last example of the papal doctrine of this period may be taken from the writings of this same pope. Maurice had given judgment in some matter, contrary to the sacred laws and canons. The Bishop of Nicopolis, who as Metropolitan of Corcyra happened to be concerned in the affair, appealed to the pope against the imperial rescript. Gregory wrote admitting the bishop's interpretation to be correct and adhering to it, yet declared that he could not dare publicly to censure the emperor lest he should seem in any way to oppose or despise the civil power. (Lib. XIV, 8, in P. L., LXXXII, 1311). His whole idea appears to have been that the prince represented God. Every action therefore of the public authority (whether it tended to the sacred ends for which Government was founded, or was apparently destructive of ecclesiastical liberties) was equally to be respected or at least not publicly to be flouted. This curious position taken up by the popes, of excessive subservience to the civil rulers, was due to a threefold cause:

(a) The need of correcting a certain anarchical spirit noted by the Apostles (I Pet., ii, 15, 16; Gal., v, 1; II Cor., iii, 17; I Thess., iv, 10, 11, v, 4).

(b) The relation in which the protected Church stood to the first Christian emperor, represented by the words of St. Optatus, "De Schismate Donatistarum", III, iii: "Non enim respublica est in Ecclesia, sed Ecclesia in republica est . . . Super Imperatorem non sit nisi solus Deus" (The state is not in the Church, but the Church is in the state . . . Let God alone be above the emperor).

(c) The influence of the Biblical language as regards the theocratic kingship of Israel.

The teaching of the papacy that civil authority was held independently of any ecclesiastical gift was continued even in the days of Charlemagne, whose father owed so much of his power to papal influence (Decretals, I, 6, 34). Yet even the new line of Cæsars claimed to hold their power of God. Their titles run "Gratia Dei Rex" or "Per misericordiam Dei rex" etc. (cf. Coronation of Charlemagne in "Journal of Theological Studies", April and July, 1901). Thus through the ninth and tenth centuries the separation-theory of Pope Gelasius was generally taught and admitted. Both pope and emperor claimed to hold their power direct from God. He is the sole source of all authority. A new theory, however, was developing. While admitting that civil rulers are of God, the good by God's direct appointment, the wicked by God's permission for the chastisement and correction of the people's sin (Hincmar, "Ep. xv ad Karolum regem", in P. L., CXXVI, 98), some writers partially broach the idea that without justice the king is no king at all, but a tyrant (Mon. Germ. Hist.: Epp., IV, "Epistolæ Variæ Karoli Magni Script.", 7 etc.), for he must govern according to the laws which in turn depend on the consent of the people (Hincmar, "De Ordine Palatii", 8, in M. G. H.: Leg., sect. II, vol. II).

Thus the compact-theory of a mutually binding engagement between sovereign and subjects enters the full stream of European political thought. It is perpetuated in the Old English Coronation oaths (Stubbs, "Select Charters", Oxford, 1900, 64 etc.). The use made of this theory by the popes will appear shortly. So far then the papal political ideals sketched out two authorities, independent, separate; the one supreme in temporal matters, the other in spiritual. Then in the tenth century, the point was raised, at first in a perfectly academic way, as to the relative importance of these two spheres of Government, as to which took precedence of the other. At first, the result of the controversy left things more or less as they had been. The one side asserted that the priesthood was the higher, because, while it was true that the priests had to render obedience to kings in temporal matters and the kings to priests in spiritual matters, yet on the priests rested the further burden of responsibility of seeing that the king performed his temporal duties in a fitting way, i. e. that the king's actions were matters of duty, therefore matters of conscience, and therefore matters that lay under the spiritual jurisdiction of the Church.

These arguments may be briefly summarized thus: (a) that both powers lay within the physical pale of the Church; (b) that the priest was responsible for seeing that the king did his duty; (c) that the priest consecrated the king and not vice versa. The others ("Tractatus Eboracensis", in M. G. H.: Libelli de Lite, III, 662 sq.) replied by asserting that the emperor had no less to see that the Church affairs were properly conducted (as much later Sigismund at Council of Constance; Lodge, "Close of Middle Ages", London, 1904, 212). Thus Leo III and Leo IV had submitted practically to the interference of Charlemagne (800) and Louis II (853); and the concrete example of the Synod of Ponthiou (853), summoned by the pope and commanded by the emperor, was a standing example of this general responsibility of each for the other (M. G. H.: Leg., II, vol. II, no. 279). It is interesting however to recall a distinction thrown out almost at hazard by a twelfth-century canonist (Rufinus, "Summa Decretorum", D. xxi. c. 1). Commenting on a supposed letter of Nicholas II to the people of Milan, he distinguishes the papal right to interfere in temporal matters by conceding to him not a *jus administrationis* but a *jus jurisdictionis*, i. e. the right of consecrating, etc.

The advent (1073) of Gregory VII to the papal chair greatly affected the policy of the Holy See (Tout, "Empire and Papacy", London, 1909, 126; Gosselin, "Power of the Pope in the Middle Ages"). But it is not so much his actions as his theories which are here under consideration. He took over the old patristic teaching that all rule and government had its origin in the fall of Adam, that original sin caused the necessity for one man to have command over another. Consequently he had hard things to say of the imperial position. Moreover he claimed more power than his predecessors. Both he and the emperor took extreme views of their respective offices. The pope wished to put himself at the head of the temporal rule, exercising the power described in Jeremias i, 10. The emperor spoke of his traditional right of appointing and deposing popes. Neither can be taken as representing the general sentiment of their time. The story of Canossa with its legendary details is no more representative of public opinion in the eleventh century than is the dramatic surrender of Pascal II in the twelfth. Hildebrand, despite his high courage and noble character, does not really continue the teaching of his predecessors.

Eventually, the Concordat of Worms (23 Sept., 1122) took up and handed down the average medieval political practice, without satisfying the extreme representatives of papal or imperial claims. Gregory, however, developed the contractual idea of the Coronation oath. This he declared to be, as were all other oaths, under the Church's dominion, and consequently could be annulled by papal authority, thus releasing subjects from obedience to their sovereign (Decretum, causa xv, Q. 6, c. 2; Stephen of Tournai, "Summa Decretorum", causa xv, Q. 6, c. 2. Auctorit. iii). The next great papal ruler, Innocent III (1198–1216), did not take the same attitude toward temporal power, though in personal exercise of authority he exceeded Gregory. He says explicitly: "We do not exercise any temporal jurisdiction except indirectly" (Epistolæ, IV, 17, 13). He interfered, it is true, to annul the election of Philip of Suabia and to confirm Otto in the imperial dignity, but he was at pains to point out that his legate was only a *denunciator*, or declarer of worthiness, not a *cognitor* or elector. The pope could not override the electoral system of the empire, he could only judge, confirm, and, in divided elections only, decide on the candidate (Decretals, 1, 6, 34; Carlyle, "History of Mediæval Political Thought", II, 217; Barry, "Papal Monarchy", XVIII, 292).

Again in the dispute between the French and English Kings, Innocent III distinctly declares that he makes no claim to settle matters of fiefs (*non enim intendimus judicare de feudo cujus ad ipsum spectat judicium*, Decretals, ii, I, 13). Nor had he any intention of diminishing the royal authority. His whole justification rests on three grounds: (a) the English king had appealed to him against his brother-king on the Gospel principle, for it was a matter of sin, i. e. against peace; (b) Philip had himself appealed earlier against Richard I; (c) A treaty had been made, confirmed by oaths, then broken. This therefore lay within the pope's jurisdiction. On another occasion, he even went so far as to order the Bishop of Vercelli to declare null and void any letters produced from the Holy See dealing with matters that belonged to the secular courts of Vercelli, as he would only interfere on appeal, especially since the imperial dignity was at the moment vacant (Decretals, ii, 2, 10; cf. Alexander III's action in a similar case, Decretals, ii, 2, 6). Even excommunication was in his hands no arbitrary power, for, if it were applied unjustly or even unreasonably, he protested that it would be null and void (Decretals, v, 39, 28). He retained of course in his own hands the right to decide whether a particular matter came within the cognizance of the spiritual courts or not (Ibid., iv, 17, 13).

After Innocent's death, the attitude of Gregory VII was revived by Boniface VIII (1294–1303) and John XXII (1316–34). Though some twenty years separate their reigns, these two pontiffs held practically the same attitude towards temporal rulers and gave rise to a large polemical literature, which is practically continuous for some fifty years (see Scholz and Riezler, *infra*, bibliography). It seemed to those times that either pope or emperor must be supreme. The writers who defend the lay side are of many shades of feeling: Pierre du Bois (Wailly, "Summaria Brevis", 1849, "Mémoires de l'Académie des Inscriptions" etc., 435–94); Marsilius of Padua (Poole, "Illustrations of the History of Mediæval Thought", 276 *et passim*); William of Ockham (ibid. 260); John Wycliff (De civili dominio, 1 cap., 17 fol., 40, c, ibid. 284). Not merely do they protest against papal interference, but, as a counterblast, endeavour to make the king or emperor—according as they defend Philip the Fair, Edward I, or Louis of Bavaria—take the most important place in the working of the Church's internal organism (cf. Baldus de Ubaldis, 1327–1400, in his "Consilia", 228, n. 7: *Imperator est dominus totius mundi et Deus in terra*, i. e. the emperor is lord of the whole world and God on earth).

Certain defenders of the Holy See are no less vehement. They rightly forbid Cæsar to meddle with matters within the spiritual sphere of life; but, not content with this, they endeavour to put the emperor directly under the pope. Augustinus Triumphus (De potestate ecclesiastica XXXVIII, 1, 224), and Ægidius Colonna (De ecclesiastica potestate, II, 4) assert that all temporal rule comes ultimately from the pope, that he alone has the supreme plenitude of power, and that none can be absolved from his high jurisdiction. While these high claims, the inheritance of ages of universal faith when the popes were really the saviours of popular liberties, were being thus set forth, the power of the civil authority had *de facto* enormously increased. The theorizing of Marsilius of Padua, Ockham, and others led to the doctrine of unrestrained royal absolutism (Poole, loc. cit., 259). The German princes with their territorializing ideals, the French kings with their strong and efficient monarchy, and the English Tudor sovereigns no longer brooked interference from Rome even in purely spiritual matters. The phrase of the Treaty of Westphalia (1648) *cujus regio ejus religio*, i. e. the religion of the prince is the religion of the land, sums up the secular reply to the ecclesiastical order.

After the Reformation had served, even in countries like France and Spain which did not adopt the new religion, the purpose of fettering conscience even more than before, the State had in actual practice put the Church under its heel. The State continued to claim, because it exercised, the power to interfere and rule in all matters, whether spiritual or temporal. The Church claimed, though it no longer freely exercised, the right to independence, nay supremacy, in all matters affecting religion, and to be in some way the fountain of all temporal dominion (St. Thomas, "Quodlibet", 12, Q. xiii, a. 19, ad 2um: *Reges sunt vasalli Ecclesiæ*). Suarez and later theologians certainly moderate the vehemence of Augustinus Triumphus and his companions. It is true of course that the post-tridentine writers expound what has been called "the indirect power" of the pope in civil affairs, while they curb in various ways the growing civil absolutism of the times. The name of sovereignty was withdrawn, but its substitute was suzerainty, which meant little less than the other (Figgis, "From Gerson to Grotius", VI, 181). Hence the undeniable tendency of Catholic theologians to repeat in clear language the cases in which rulers may lawfully be put to death. Hence also their unqualified defence of popular rights. Says Filmer ("Patriarcha", I, i, 2, 1880) concerning the power of the people to deprive or correct the sovereign: "Cardinal Bellarmine and Calvin both look asquint this way".

No doubt in this long controversy both ecclesiastical and secular writers went too often to extremes. It is in the rights that each allows the other, that we must look for the more workable hypothesis. Thus when the lay writers describe the spiritual rule of the Papacy (Dante, "De Monarchia"; Ockham, "Octo Questiones", q. 1, c. 6, ad 2), they depict almost literally the position of a Leo XIII or a Pius X, prophesying the greatness of such an office. And when the ecclesiastico-political writers sketch their theory of a state (Nicolas of Cusa, "Concordantia Catholica"; Schardius, "Syntagma"), directing, ordering, educating the free lives of free citizens, they are no less prophets of a desirable order. Moreover Pius IX expressly declared that, for their execution in the temporal sphere, the ecclesiastical ideals depended no less than the lay ideals on the consent and custom of the people, in the absence of which the papacy no longer claims to exercise power and rights, that public law and common consent once accorded to the Supreme Judge of Christendom for the common welfare (Discorso agli Accademici di Religione Catholica, 20 July, 1871).

It appears, therefore, that in the past all papal attempts to end wars and decide between contending rights of disputing sovereigns, were really in the nature of *arbitration*. Popes like Innocent III never claimed to be the sources of temporal rule, or that whatever they did for the peace of Europe was done by them as supreme temporal rulers; but only on the invitation or acceptance of the princes interested. Even popes like Gregory VII, Boniface VIII, and others, who exercised most fully their spiritual prerogatives, were unable to act efficiently as peacemakers, until they were called in by those at war.

B. *Historical Cases of Papal Arbitration*.—The various interpositions of Innocent III to allay the differences in European diplomacy, such as it then was, have been already alluded to. It will be better to pass at once to later historical examples.

(1) The popes made frequent efforts to negotiate between the Kings of France and England during the Hundred Years' War, but the most famous attempt is that of Boniface VIII in 1297. It came just after the controversy between Philip the Fair and the pope concerning the Bull "Clericis laicos". Eventually Boniface gave up many of his earlier demands, partly through pressure from the French king, partly because he found that he had gone too far, partly in the interests of European peace. The more fully to achieve the latter purpose, he offered to arbitrate in the quarrel that had been further complicated by the alliance formed between the Flemish and the English. The Cardinal of Albano and Præneste was sent to Creil on 20 April, 1297. But the temper of French thought is expressed in the protest of King Philip that he would submit to arbitration, as did Edward I and the Count of Flanders, but that he looked for nothing more than arbitration, not for recourse to the pope as to a higher feudal court. He laid down three propositions and completed them by a practical conclusion: (a) The government of France belonged solely to the king; (b) the king recognized no temporal superior; (c) he submitted his temporal affairs to no man living. Therefore he came to the Roman Court for arbitration, not as to Boniface VIII the supreme sovereign pontiff, but as to the lawyer Benedetto Gaetani. The terms of the arbitrament are not of present interest; this only should be noted, that Boniface placated the French king by deciding largely in his favour, to the disgust of the Count of Flanders, but issued his award in a Bull (Lavisse, "Hist. de France" (Paris, 1901).

(2) One of the first public acts of Alexander VI was to effect a settlement between Spain and Portugal. These two nations had been foremost in undertaking voyages of discovery in the East and West. The result was, that as each expedition on landing annexed the new-found territories to its own home government, there was continual friction between the rival nations. In the interests of peace, Alexander VI offered to arbitrate between the two countries. He issued his Bull "Inter Cætera," 14 May, 1493, fixing the line at meridian of 100 leagues west of the Azores and Cape Verde Islands—assumed to be practically of the same longitude—Spain to have the western, Portugal the eastern division. The following year (7 June) by the treaty of Tordesillas the imaginary line was moved to 370 leagues west of Cape Verde. To this the pope as arbitrator assented, and thus averted war between the two countries ("Civiltà Cattolica", 1865, I, 665–80; Winsor, "History of America", 1886, I, 13, 592; "Cambridge Modern History", I, 23–24).

(3) More curious examples are found in the invitation given to Leo X and later to Clement VII to arbitrate between Russia and Poland over Lithuania (Rombaud, "History of Russia", London, 1885).

The success of this led to Gregory XIII being asked to settle the difference between Bathory of Poland and Ivan the Terrible. Gregory between 1572 and 1583 sent to Moscow the Jesuit Antonio Possevino (q. v.), who arranged peace between them. Ivan ceded Polotsk and all Livonia to the Poles ("Revue des Questions Historiques," Jan., 1885).

(4) Perhaps the best-remembered case is that of 1885, when war was averted between Germany and Spain by the arbitration of Leo XIII. It was over the question of the Caroline Islands, which though discovered by Spain had been practically abandoned for many years. England and Germany had presented a joint note to Spain, refusing to acknowledge her sovereignty over the Caroline and Palao group of islands. German colonists had been established there. But the climax was reached when on 25 August, 1885, both Spanish and German war vessels planted the flags of their respective countries and took solemn possession of Yap. On 24 September, Bismarck, out of compliment to Spain and to propitiate the pope (Busch, "Life of Bismarck", 469–70, London, 1899), referred the matter to Leo XIII. The pope gave his award on 22 October, succeeding perfectly in adjusting the conflicting claims of Spanish sovereignty and German interests. Finally the whole matter was amicably accepted and signed at the Vatican by both powers on 17 December of the same year (O'Reilly, "Life of Leo XIII", xxxiii, 537–54).

(5) Lastly, in 1897, the same pontiff arbitrated between Hayti and San Domingo. But the terms of his arbitration do not appear to have been published (Darby, "Proved Practicability of International Arbitration", London, 1904, 19). For the celebrated case of Adrian IV and his gift of Ireland to Henry II, see ADRIAN IV.

C. *Future*.—The increasing movement of arbitration, growing stronger with each fresh exercise of it, together with the fact that owing to the action of Italy the popes have been excluded from the Hague Conference, makes the thought suggest itself of how far the papacy is situated to-day to act as a general arbitrator: (1) It has ceased to hold any territorial dominion and can therefore stand forward as an impartial judge unlikely to be affected by temporal interests. (2) It has interests in too many lands to be likely to favour any one country at the expense of others. (3) It is wholly international, and adaptable, because alive, to the various environments of temperament, customs, laws, languages, political constitutions, social organizations, in which it finds itself. The clergy of each country are national in the sense of being patriotic; not in the sense of being separated in matters of faith from Catholics elsewhere. (4) It is ruled by a pontiff, ordinarily indeed Italian; but his group of advisers is a privy council drawn from every continent, race, and nation. So detached has he been, that it is precisely three Italian popes who have refused to acknowledge the Italian spoliation of the Patrimony of St. Peter. (5) As the greatest Christian force in the modern world its whole influence must be heavily thrown into the scale of peace. (6) It has about it a halo of past usefulness, touched about with the mellow hue of time. It has seemed to men so different as Leibniz (Opera, V, 65), Voltaire (Essais, II, ix), Ancillon (Tableau des Revolutions, I, 79, 106, Berlin, 1803), to have been set in a position not to dictate to, but to arbitrate for, the world. And because it has gone back to the older, simpler, more spiritual theories of Gelasius I, Gregory I, and Innocent III it has now opportunities which were denied it, so long as it claimed the more showy rights of Gregory VII, Boniface VIII, and John XXII. Just as under Pius II the Church created the idea of a European Congress (Boulting, "Æneas Sylvius," 279, 350–51, London, 1908), so it is to be hoped that under her presidency the practice of arbitration by a permanent tribunal may be made more universal, more practicable, and of greater sanction.

NEGRO, *Bismarck, il Papa et l'Arbitrato Internacionale* (Asti, 1882); POOLE, *Illustrations of Mediæval Political Thought* (London, 1884); MURPHY, *Chair of Peter* (London, 1885); LÓPEZ, *Derecho y Arbitraje internacional* (Paris, 1891); RICHET, *Les Guerres et la paix* (Paris, 1899); GIERKE, *Das deutsche Genossenschaftsrecht*, III, tr. MAITLAND, *Political Theories of the Middle Age* (Cambridge, 1900); OLIPHANT, *Rome and Reform* (London, 1902); BARRY, *Papal Monarchy* (London, 1902); CARLYLE, *History of Mediæval Political Thought in the West*, I (London and Edinburgh, 1903), II (London and Edinburgh, 1909); BARRY in *Dublin Review* (Oct., 1907), 221–43; FIGGIS, *Political Theories from Gerson to Grotius* (Cambridge, 1907); GOSSELIN, *The Power of the Pope in the Middle Ages* (New York, 1852); SCHOLTZ, *Die Publizistik zur Zeit Philipps des Schönen* (Stuttgart, 1903); RIEZLER, *Die literarischen Wiedersacher der Päpste zur Zeit Ludwigs des Bayers* (Leipzig, 1874); HERGENRÖTHER, *Church and State*, etc. tr. (London, 1872).

BEDE JARRETT.

Papal Chancery. See ROMAN CURIA.

Papal Elections.—The method of electing the pope has varied considerably at different periods of the history of the Church. As to the earliest ages, Ferraris (op. cit. *infra*) says that St. Peter himself constituted a senate for the Roman Church, consisting of twenty-four priests and deacons. These were the councillors of the Bishop of Rome and the electors of his successors. This statement is drawn from a canon in the "Corpus Juris Canonici" (can. "Si Petrus", caus. 8, Q. 1). Historians and canonists, however, generally hold that the Roman bishopric was filled on its vacancy in the same manner as other bishoprics, that is, the election of the new pope was made by the neighbouring bishops and the clergy and faithful of Rome. Nevertheless, some maintain that the naming of the successor of St. Peter was restricted to the Roman clergy, and that the people were admitted to a part in the elections only after the time of Sylvester I (fourth century). After Constantine had given peace to the Church, the Christian Roman emperors often took part in the institution of a new pope and at times their influence was very marked. From the fourth century onwards, therefore, a new force had to be reckoned with. The occasion for the interference of the Roman emperors and later of the kings of Italy was afforded by disputed elections to the papal chair. The most noted of the earlier instance was at the election of Boniface I (418). This gave occasion to the decree (c. 8, dist. 79) that when an election was disputed a new candidate should be chosen.

The interference of the secular power was always distasteful to the Roman clergy, as shown by their unwillingness to observe decrees on the subject made even by popes, as in the case of Simplicius and others. The example of the Roman emperors was followed by the barbarian kings of Italy, of whom the first to interfere was Theodoric the Ostrogoth, at the election of Symmachus in 498. On the recovery of their influence in the Italian peninsula, the Eastern emperors required that the choice of the electors for a new pope must be made known to the Exarch of Ravenna, who in turn forwarded it to Constantinople, and until the emperor's confirmation was received, the candidate was not to be acknowledged as Bishop of Rome. This resulted in long vacancies of the Holy See. The custom lasted until the pontificate of Benedict II (684–85). A similar claim was put forward by the Western emperors in the Middle Ages, and some demanded it owing to a concession made by Adrian I to Charlemagne. This pretended concession is now recognized as spurious. As to the so-called confirmation of papal elections by the secular power, Ferraris (loc. cit. *infra*) notes that it must not be so understood as to imply that the new pope received the papal power from the emperor. This would be heretical, for the elected candidate receives his power from Christ.

The confirmation of the emperor, then, was only to ensure that the canons of the Church should be carried out without hindrance from factious and seditious dissenters. It must be admitted that the Holy Roman emperors sometimes made use of their overwhelming power unscrupulously, and more than once candidates were elected to the papacy by direct imperial nomination. Otto III is credited with the nomination of Gregory V and Sylvester II, and Henry III with the effectual naming of Clement II, Damasus II, Leo IX, and Victor II. But it is obvious that such nomination is not real election, for the acceptance of the legal electors was necessary to ratify the choice, though undoubtedly they would naturally be swayed by circumstances to give effect to the imperial preference. It has sometimes been said that in the earlier ages popes have appointed their successors in the pontificate. Thus, St. Peter is said to have so chosen Clement I. The authority on which the statement rests is now generally acknowledged to be apocryphal. Boniface II chose Vigilius for his successor in 531, but later repented and publicly withdrew the nomination. Baronius (H. E., ann. 1085, 1087) states that Gregory VII in 1085 elected Victor III as his successor; that Victor in like manner chose Urban II in 1086, and Urban elected Paschal II in 1099. It is to be noted that the canon "Si Transitus" in the "Corpus Juris" (can. "Si Trans.", 10, dist. 70) seems to imply the right of the pope to nominate his successor, since its opening words are: "If the death of the pope take place so unexpectedly that he cannot make a decree concerning the election of his successor, etc." However, these so-called elections were never more than nominations, for none of the persons thus named ever presumed to declare themselves popes before the ratification of the legal electors had been obtained.

It is certain at present, that, according to ecclesiastical law (c. "Episcopo", 3; c. "Plerique", 5; can. "Moyses", 6, caus. 8, Q. 1), the pope cannot elect his successor. It is commonly held also that he is prohibited from doing so by Divine law, though the contrary has also been held by canonists. As to the gradual restrictions and determinations governing the mode of election of the pontiffs, we note that in 606 Boniface III decreed that the electors should not meet until the third day after the pope's burial. In 769 a decree was framed in a synod of the Lateran, that the Roman clergy were to choose as pope only a priest or deacon, and forbade the laity to take any part in the election. The newly-elected was, however, to receive the homage of the laity before he was conducted to the Lateran basilica. This decree caused widespread discontent among the influential laymen, and Nicholas I in a Roman Synod held in 862 restored the right of suffrage to the Roman nobles. John IX in 898 confirmed the custom of having the consecration of the new pontiff take place in the presence of the imperial ambassadors. In 963, the Emperor Otto I endeavoured to bind the Romans by oath not to elect anyone as pope until he had been nominated by the emperor.

An epoch-making decree in the matter of papal elections is that of Nicholas II in 1059. According to this constitution, the cardinal bishops are first to meet and discuss the candidates for the papacy, and select the names of the most worthy. They are then to summon the other cardinals and, together with them, proceed to an election. Finally, the assent of the rest of the clergy and the laity to the result of the suffrage is to be sought. The choice is to be made from the Roman clergy, unless a fit candidate cannot be found among them. In the election regard is to be had for the rights of the Holy Roman emperor, who in turn is to be requested to show similar respect for the Apostolic See. In case the election cannot be held in Rome, it can validly be held elsewhere. What the imperial rights are is not explicitly stated in the decree, but it seems plain from contemporary evidence that they require the results of the election to be forwarded to the emperor by letter or messenger, in order that he may assure himself of the validity of the election. Gregory VII (1073), however, was the last pope who asked for imperial confirmation. It will be seen that the decree of Pope Nicholas reserves the actual election to the cardinals, but requires the assent (*laudatio*) of the lower clergy and laity.

The Tenth Œcumenical Synod (Lateran) in 1139 restricted, however, the entire choice to the cardinals, and in 1179, another Lateran Council under Alexander III made the rule that the pope is to be chosen by a two-thirds majority of the electors who are present. This last decree did not state what was to be done in case such a majority could not be obtained. When the cardinals found themselves face to face with this contingency on the death of Clement IV in 1268, they commissioned six cardinals as plenipotentiaries to decide on a candidate. The vacancy of the Holy See had lasted for two years and nine months. To prevent a recurrence of this evil, the Second Council of Lyons under Gregory X (1274) decreed that ten days after the pope's decease, the cardinals should assemble in the palace in the city in which the pope died, and there hold their electoral meetings, entirely shut out from all outside influences. If they did not come to an agreement on a candidate in three days, their victuals were to be lessened, and after a further delay of five days, the food supply was to be still further restricted. This is the origin of conclaves.

The decretal of Gregory X on this subject is called "Ubi periculum majus". For the later regulations governing papal elections see CONCLAVE. According to certain ancient canons (can. "Oportet", 3; can. "Nullus", 4, dist. 79), only cardinals should be chosen pope. However, Alexander III decreed (cap. "Licet", 6, "De elect.") that "he, without any exception, is to be acknowledged as pontiff of the Universal Church who has been elected by two-thirds of the cardinals." As late as 1378, Urban VI was chosen, though not a cardinal (consult, however, Constitut. 50 of Sixtus V, "Postquam", § 2). A layman may also be elected pope, as was Celestine V (1294). Even the election of a married man would not be invalid (c. "Qui uxorem", 19, caus. 33, Q. 5). Of course, the election of a heretic, schismatic, or female would be null and void. Immediately on the canonical election of a candidate and his acceptance, he is true pope and can exercise full and absolute jurisdiction over the whole Church. A papal election, therefore, needs no confirmation, as the pontiff has no superior on earth.

FERRARIS, *Bibliotheca Canonica*, VI (Rome, 1890), s. v. *Papa*, art. 1; SÄGMÜLLER, *Lehrbuch des Kirchenrechts* (Freiburg, 1903); WERNZ, *Jus Decretalium*, II (Rome, 1899); SMITH, *Elements of Ecclesiastical Law*, I (New York, 1895).

WILLIAM H. W. FANNING.

Papal Letters. See LETTERS, ECCLESIASTICAL.

Papal States. See STATES OF THE CHURCH.

Papebroch, DANIEL VON. See BOLLANDISTS, THE.

Paphnutius.—I. The most celebrated personage of this name was bishop of a city in the Upper Thebaid in the early fourth century, and one of the most interesting members of the Council of Nicæa (325). He suffered mutilation of the left knee and the loss of his right eye for the Faith under the Emperor Maximinus (308–13), and was subsequently condemned to the mines. At Nicæa he was greatly honoured by Constantine the Great, who, according to Socrates (H. E., I, 11), used often to send for the good old confessor and kiss the place whence the eye had been torn out. He took a prominent, perhaps a decisive, part in the debate at the First Œcumenical Council on the subject of the celibacy of the clergy. It seems that most of the bishops present were disposed to follow the precedent of the Council of Elvira (can. xxxiii) prohibiting conjugal relations to those bishops, priests, deacons, and, according to Sozomen, sub-deacons, who were married before ordination. Paphnutius earnestly entreated his fellow-bishops not to impose this obligation on the orders of the clergy concerned. He proposed, in accordance "with the ancient tradition of the Church", that only those who were celibates at the time of ordination should continue to observe continence, but, on the other hand, that "none should be separated from her, to whom, while yet unordained, he had been united". The great veneration in which he was held, and the well known fact that he had himself observed the strictest chastity all his life, gave weight to his proposal, which was unanimously adopted. The council left it to the discretion of the married clergy to continue or discontinue their marital relations. Paphnutius was present at the Synod of Tyre (335).

II. PAPHNUTIUS, surnamed (on account of his love of solitude) THE BUFFALO, an anchorite and priest of the Scetic desert in Egypt in the fourth century. When Cassian (Coll., IV, 1) visited him in 395, the Abbot Paphnutius was in his ninetieth year. He never left his cell save to attend church on Saturdays and Sundays, five miles away. When in his paschal letter of the year 399, the Patriarch Theophilus of Alexandria condemned anthropomorphism, Paphnutius was the only monastic ruler in the Egyptian desert who caused the document to be read.

III. PAPHNUTIUS, deacon of the church of Boou, in Egypt, suffered martyrdom in the persecution of Diocletian, under the Prefect Culcianus.

HEFELE-LECLERCQ, *Histoire des conciles*, I, i (Paris, 1907).

MAURICE M. HASSETT.

Paphos, titular see, suffragan of Salamis in Cyprus. There were two towns of this name, Old Paphos which owed its renown to the Phœnician goddess Astarte, as represented by a sacred stone or bætylus, and now identified with Kouklia, on the right bank of the Diorizo; and New Paphos, located at the village of Baffo, over nine miles distant from the former. The latter was the see. Under the Romans it was the metropolis of the island. In 15 B. C. it received the surname of Augusta, and was later called Sebaste Claudia Flavia Paphos. The proconsul Sergius Paulus resided there when Paul and Barnabas, after having confounded the magician Elymas, converted the governor to Christianity (Acts, xiii, 6 sqq.). The first known bishop, Cyril, assisted in 325 at the Council of Nicæa; for the other Greek titulars see Le Quien, "Oriens christianus" (II, 1059–62); Hackett, "A History of the Orthodox Church of Cyprus" (London, 1901, p. 314). Among them were Theodore (seventh century), the biographer of St. Spiridion, St. Nicholas, and St. Macarius, otherwise unknown. The list of Latin bishops from 1215 to 1597 has been compiled by Le Quien (op. cit., III, 1215–20); Du Cange "Les familles d'outre-mer" (Paris, 1869, pp. 865–68); Eubel, "Hierarchia cathol. med. ævi" (I, 407; II, 234; III, 287); Hackett (op. cit., 564–68). The last residential bishop, Francesco Contarini, who in 1563 had assisted at the Council of Trent, was slain in 1570 during the siege of the town by the Turks. During the Frankish occupation the Greek see was one of the four which the Latins supported in 1222, but the bishop was compelled to reside at Arsinoe or Chrysochou. It still exists. Baffo is a miserable village, the larger portion of its population living at Ktima half a league away. In the Middle Ages the Latin Diocese of Paphos was dependent on the Archdiocese of Nicosia.

CESNOLA, *Cyprus, its ancient cities, tombs and temples* (London, 1877), 210–13; *Journal of Hellenic Studies*, IX, 158–271; PERROT AND CHIPIEZ, *Hist. de l'art dans l'antiquité*, III (Paris), 264–275.

S. VAILHÉ.

Papias, SAINT, Bishop of Hierapolis (close to Laodicea and Colossæ in the valley of the Lycus in Phrygia) and Apostolic Father, called by St. Irenæus "a hearer of John, and companion of Polycarp, a man of old time". He wrote a work in five books, λογίων κυριακῶν ἐξήγησις, of which all but some fragments is lost. We learn something of the contents from the preface, part of which has been preserved by Eusebius (III, xxix): "I will not hesitate to add also for you to my interpretations what I formerly learned with care from the Presbyters and have carefully stored in memory, giving assurance of its truth. For I did not take pleasure as the many do in those who speak much, but in those who teach what is true, nor in those who relate foreign precepts, but in those who relate the precepts which were given by the Lord to the faith and came down from the Truth itself. And also if any follower of the Presbyters happened to come, I would inquire for the sayings of the Presbyters, what Andrew said, or what Peter said, or what Philip or what Thomas or James or what John or Matthew or any other of the Lord's disciples, and for the things which Aristion and the Presbyter John, the disciples of the Lord, were saying. For I considered that I should not get so much advantage from matter in books as from the voice which yet lives and remains." From this we learn that Papias's book consisted mainly of "interpretations"—it was a kind of commentary on the "Logia of the Lord". The word *logia*, meaning "oracles", is frequently at the present day taken to refer to sayings, as opposed to narratives of Our Lord's actions (so Zahn and many others). But Lightfoot showed long ago (Essays on Supernatural Religion, 171–7) that this view is untenable. Philo used the word for any part of the inspired writings of the Old Testament, whether speech or narrative. St. Paul, Irenæus, Clement, Origen, even Photius, have no other usage. St. Irenæus speaks of corrupting the oracles of the Lord just as Dionysius of Corinth speaks of corrupting the Scriptures of the Lord. Λόγια κυριακά in Papias, in Irenæus, in Photius, means "the divine oracles" of the Old or New Testament or both. Besides these "interpretations", Papias added oral traditions of two kinds: some he had himself heard from the Presbyters, παρὰ τῶν πρεσβυτέρων; others he had at second hand from disciples of the Presbyters who happened to visit him at Hierapolis. The Presbyters related what the "disciples of the Lord"—Peter, Andrew etc.—used to say in old days. Other informants of Papias's visitors were still living, "Aristion and John the Presbyter, the disciples of the Lord", as is shown by the present tense, λέγουσιν. We naturally assume that Papias counted them also among the direct informants whom he had mentioned before, for as they lived at Ephesus and Smyrna, not far off, he would surely know them personally. However, many eminent critics—Zahn and Lightfoot, and among Catholics, Funk, Bardenhewer, Michiels, Gutjahr, Batiffol, Lepin—identify the Presbyters with Andrew, Peter etc., thus making them Apostles, for they understand "what Andrew and Peter and the rest said" as epexegetic of "the words of the Presbyters". This is impossible, for Papias had just spoken of what he learned directly from the Presbyters, ὅσα ποτὲ παρὰ τῶν πρεσβυτέρων καλῶς ἔμαθον, yet it is admitted that he could not have known many apostles. Again, he seems to distinguish the sayings of the disciples of the Lord, Aristion and John, from those of the Presbyters, as though the latter were not disciples of the Lord. Lastly, Irenæus and Eusebius, who had the work of Papias before them, understand the Presbyters to be not Apostles, but disciples of disciples of the Lord, or even disciples of disciples of Apostles. The same meaning is given to the word by Clement of Alexandria. We are therefore obliged to make "what Andrew and Peter and the rest said" not co-ordinate with but subordinate to "the sayings of the Presbyters", thus: "I would inquire for the sayings of the Presbyters, what (they related that) Andrew and Peter and the rest said, and for the things Aristion and John were saying". Eusebius has caused a further difficulty by pointing out that two Johns are mentioned, one being distinguished by the epithet presbyter from the other who is obviously the Apostle. The historian adds that Dionysius of Alexandria said he heard there were two tombs of John at Ephesus. This view has been adopted by practically all liberal critics and by such conservatives as Lightfoot and Westcott. But Zahn and most Catholic writers agree that Dionysius was mistaken about the tomb, and that Eusebius's interpretation of Papias's words is incorrect. For he says that Papias frequently cited John the Presbyter; yet it is certain that Irenæus, who had a great veneration for the work of Papias, took him to mean John the Apostle; and Irenæus had personal knowledge of Asiatic tradition and could not have been ignorant of the existence of John the presbyter, if there ever was such a person in Asia. Again, Irenæus tells us that the Apostle lived at Ephesus until the time of Trajan, that he wrote the Apocalypse in the last days of Domitian. Irenæus had heard Polycarp relate his reminiscences of the Apostle. Justin, who was at Ephesus about 130–5, asserts that the Apostle was the author of the Apocalypse (and therefore the head of the Asiatic Churches). But if the Apostle lived at Ephesus at so late a date, (and it cannot be doubted with any show of reason), he would naturally be the most important of Papias's witnesses. Yet if Eusebius is right, it would seem that John the Presbyter was his chief informant, and that he had no sayings of the Apostle to relate. Again, "the Presbyter" who wrote I and II John has the name of John in all MSS., and is identified with the Apostle by Irenæus and Clement, and is certainly (by internal evidence) the writer of the fourth Gospel, which is attributed to the Apostle by Irenæus and all tradition. Again, Polycrates of Ephesus, in recounting the men who were the glories of Asia, has no mention of John the presbyter, but of "John, who lay upon the Lord's breast", undoubtedly meaning the Apostle. The second John at Ephesus is an unlucky conjecture of Eusebius.

A fragment is, however, attributed to Papias which states that "John the theologian and James his brother were killed by the Jews". It is not possible that Papias should really have said this, otherwise Eusebius must have quoted it and Irenæus could not have been ignorant of it. There is certainly some error in the quotation. Either something has been omitted, or St. John Baptist was meant. That St. John is mentioned twice in the list of Papias's authorities is explained by the distinction between his earlier sayings which the Presbyters could repeat and the last utterances of his old age which were reported by visitors from Ephesus. The most important fragment of Papias is that in which he gives an account of St. Mark from the words of the Presbyter, obviously St. John. It is a defence of St. Mark, attesting the perfect accuracy with which he wrote down the teachings of St. Peter, but admitting that he did not give a correct order. It is interesting to note that (as Dr. Abbott has shown) the fourth Gospel inserts or refers to every incident given in St. Mark which St. Luke has passed over. The prologue of St. Luke is manifestly cited in the fragment, so that Papias and the Presbyter knew that Gospel, which was presumably preferred to that of Mark in the Pauline Church of Ephesus; hence the need of the rehabilitation of Mark by "the Presbyter", who speaks with authority as one who knew the facts of the life of Christ as well as Peter himself. The famous statement of Papias that St. Matthew wrote his *logia* (that is, his canonical work) in Hebrew, and each interpreted (translated) it as he was able, seems to imply that when Papias wrote an accepted version was current—our present St. Matthew. His knowledge of St. John's Gospel is proved not merely by his mention of aloes, but by a citation of John xiv, 2, which occurs in the curious prophecy of a miraculous vintage in the millenium which he attributed to Our Lord (Irenæus,

V, xxxvi). The reference in his preface to our Lord as "the Truth" also implies a knowledge of the fourth Gospel. He cited I John and I Peter according to Eusebius, and he evidently built largely upon the Apocalypse, from which he drew his chiliastic views. It was formerly customary among liberal critics to assume (for no proof was possible) that Papias ignored St. Paul. It is now recognized that a bishop who lived a few miles from Colossæ cannot be suspected of opposition to St. Paul merely on the ground that the few lines of his writings which remain do not contain any quotation from the Apostle. It is highly probable that Papias had a New Testament containing the Four Gospels, the Acts, the chief Epistles of St. Paul, the Apocalypse and Epistles of St. John, and I Peter.

Eusebius says that Papias frequently cited traditions of John and narrations of Aristion. He had also received information from the daughters of Philip, one of whom was buried like her father at Hierapolis, and had apparently been known to Papias. He related the raising to life of the mother of Manaïmos (probably not the same as Manaen the foster-brother of Herod); also the drinking of poison without harm by Justus Barsabas: he may have related this in connexion with Mark, xvi, 18, as it is the only one of the miracles promised in that passage by our Lord which is not exemplified in Acts. It would be interesting if we could be sure that Papias mentioned this last section of Mark, since an Armenian MS. attributes it to Aristion. Eusebius says Papias "published a story of a woman accused of many sins before the Lord, which is contained in the Gospel according to the Hebrews". This appears to refer to the *pericope adulteræ*, John, viii.

The cause of the loss of this precious work of an Apostolic Father was the chiliastic view which he taught, like St. Justin and St. Irenæus. He supported this by "strange parables of the Saviour and teachings of His, and other mythical matters", says Eusebius. We can judge of these by the account of the wonderful vine above referred to. His method of exegesis may perhaps be estimated to some extent by a comparison of the chiliastic portion of St. Irenæus's fifth book with the original ending of Victorinus's commentary on the Apocalypse, as published by Haussleiter (Theologisches Litteraturblatt, 26 April, 1895); for both passages are evidently based on Papias, and contain the same quotations from the Old Testament. Eusebius was an opponent of chiliastic speculations, and he remarks: "Papias was a man of very small mind, if we may judge by his own words". It would seem that the fragment of Victorinus of Pettau "De fabrica mundi" is partly based on Papias. In it we have perhaps the very words to which Eusebius is referring: "Nunc igitur de inenarrabili gloria Dei in providentia videas memorari; tamen *ut mens parva poterit*, conabor ostendere". This passage probably preserves the substance of what Papias said, according to the testimony of Anastasius of Mount Sinai, as to the mystical application to Christ and the Church of the seven days of creation. A wild and extraordinary legend about Judas Iscariot is attributed to Papias by a catena. It is probable that whenever St. Irenæus quotes "the Presbyters" or "the Presbyters who had seen John", he is citing the work of Papias. Where he attributes to these followers of John the assertion that our Lord sanctified all the ages of man, he is probably quoting Papias; but it does not follow that Papias had inferred that our Lord reached the age of fifty, as Irenæus concludes, nor need we be too certain that Papias explicitly cited the Presbyters in the passage in question. His real statement is possibly preserved in a sentence of "De fabrica mundi", which implies only that our Lord reached the perfect age (between 30 and 40) after which decline begins.

Of Papias's life nothing is known. If Polycarp was born in 69, his "comrade" may have been born a few years earlier. The fragment which makes him state that those who were raised to life by Christ lived on until the age of Hadrian cannot be used to determine his date, for it is clearly made up from the quite credible statement of Quadratus (Eusebius, iv, 3) that some of those cured by our Lord lived until his own time and the fact that Quadratus wrote under Hadrian; the name of Papias has been substituted by the egregious excerptor. The work of Papias was evidently written in his old age, say between the years 115 and 140.

The literature on Papias is of overwhelming quantity. Every introduction to the New Testament, every book on the Fourth Gospel mentions him. The best discussion in English is LIGHTFOOT'S *Essays on Supernatural Religion*, reprinted from the *Contemporary Review* (London, 1889); on the preface see especially ZAHN, *Forschungen*, VI (1900); on the two Johns, DRUMMOND, EZRA ABBOTT, CAMERLYNCK, and others on the Gospel of St. John; for the view that the Apostle was not at Ephesus but only the presbyter, HARNACK, *Gesch. der altchr. Litt.*, II (1897), and (making the presbyter the beloved disciple) DELFF, *Gesch. d. Rabbi Jesus* (Leipzig, 1889); IDEM, *Das vierte Evang. wiederhergestellt*; IDEM, *Neue Beiträge zur Kritik und Erklärung des vierten Ev.* (both at Husum, 1890); SANDAY, *The Criticism of the Fourth Gospel* (Oxford, 1905); BOUSSET, *Offenbarung d. Joh.* (Leipzig, 1896); also ZAHN, *loc. cit.*; STANTON, *The Gospels as Hist. Documents*, I (1903); CHAPMAN, *John the Presbyter* (Oxford, 1911); on the supposed martyrdom of St. John, DE BOOR, *Neue Fragmente des Papias* in *Texte u. Unters.*, V, II (1888); DELFF, *loc. cit.*; CHAPMAN, *loc. cit.*; SCHWARTZ, *Ueber den Tod der Söhne Zebedæi* (in favour of the martyrdom, Berlin, 1904); against are: ARMITAGE ROBINSON, *The Historical Character of St. John's Gospel* (London, 1908); BERNARD in *Irish Church Quarterly* (Jan., 1908); EDWIN ABBOTT, *Notes on New Testament Criticism* (London, 1906); for a general account of Papias, see BARDENHEWER, *Gesch. der altkirchl. Litt.*, I (Freiburg, 1902), who gives sufficient references to older books and articles; more in RICHARDSON's *Synopsis* (Buffalo, 1887). On St. John in Irenæus, CHAPMAN, *Papias on the Age of our Lord* in *Journal of Theol. Studies*, IX (Oct., 1907), 33; GUTJAHR, *Die Glaubwürdigkeit des irendischen Zeugnisses* (Graz, 1904); LEWIS, *The Irenæus testimony to the Fourth Gospel* (Chicago, 1908); on the Chiliasm of Papias, ATZBERGER, *Gesch. der christl. Eschatologie* (Freiburg, 1896); GRY, *Le millénarisme* (Paris, 1904; New York, 1899).

JOHN CHAPMAN.

Papiensis, BERNARDUS, Italian canonist of the thirteenth century; d. 18 Sept., 1213. He was born at Pavia, studied law and theology at Bologna, was provost of the cathedral of Pavia until 1191, Bishop of Faenza until 1198, and then Bishop of Pavia until his death. He is renowned for his "Breviarium extravagantium" (later called "Compilatio prima antiqua"), a collection of canonical texts comprising ancient canons not inserted in the "Decretum" of Gratian and also later documents. The work was compiled between 1187 and 1191, and was edited by Friedberg ("Quinque compilationes antiquæ", Leipzig, 1882). Papiensis is the author of a "Summa" on his own compilation, which he wrote while Bishop of Faenza; it was edited by Laspeyres, as were also other works of the same author: "Summa de matrimonio", "Summa de electione", "Casus decretalium", and a gloss on his "Breviarium extravagantium" ("Bernardi Papiensis Summa decretalium", Ratisbon, 1861). He is also the author of a "Vita sancti Lanfranci" (Acta SS., IV Jun., 620 sqq.), a "Commentarius in Ecclesiasticum", and a "Commentarius in Canticum Canticorum".

SCHULTE, *Die Gesch. der Quellen u. Lit. des canon. Rechts*, I (Stuttgart, 1875), 175–82; LAURIN, *Introd. in Corp. Jur. Canon.* (Freiburg, 1889), 20, 97–105; SCHNEIDER, *Die Lehre von den Kirchenrechtsquellen* (Ratisbon, 1892), 126–29.

A. VAN HOVE.

Papini, NICHOLAS, historian, b. at San Giovanni Valdarno, between Florence and Arezzo, about 1751; d. at Terni, Umbria, 16 Dec., 1834. Having entered the Order of the Conventuals he taught Italian literature at Modena, was secretary of the Provincial of Tuscany, *custos* of the Sacred Convent of Assisi, 1800(?)–1803, a short time guardian of Dodici Apostoli at Rome, and finally named Minister General of the Conventuals 1803–09. Later on he lived at Assisi and Terni, where he is buried. His printed works are "L'Etruria Francescana o vero raccolta di notizie storiche interessanti l'Ordine de FF. Minori Conventuali di S. Francesco in Toscana", I, Siena, 1797; "Notizie sicure della morte, sepoltura, canonizzazione e traslazione di S. Francesco d'Assisi e del ritrovamento del di lui corpo", 2nd ed., Foligno, 1824; "Storia del Perdono d'Assisi con documenti e osservazioni", Florence, 1824; "La Storia di S. Francesco di Assisi, opera critica," 2 vols., Foligno, 1827.

ROBINSON, *A Short Introduction to Franciscan Literature* (New York, 1907), 19, 44; EUBEL, *Sbaraleas und Papinis literarischer Nachlass* in *Historisches Jahrbuch*, X (1889), 67–9; *Manuale dei Novizii e Professi Chierici e Laici Minori Conventuali* (Rome, 1897), 278, 342; LANZI, *Note e ricordi sulla Chiesa di S. Francesco in Terni* in *Miscellanea Francescana*, IX (1902), 6–7.

LIVARIUS OLIGER.

Para. See BELEM DO PARA, ARCHDIOCESE OF.

Parables.—The word parable (Heb. מָשָׁל, mâshâl; Syr. mathla, Gr. παραβολή) signifies in general a comparison, or a parallel, by which one thing is used to illustrate another. It is a likeness taken from the sphere of real, or sensible, or earthly incidents, in order to convey an ideal, or spiritual, or heavenly meaning. As uttering one thing and signifying something else, it is in the nature of a riddle (Heb. khidah, Gr. αἴνιγμα or πρόβλημα), and has therefore a light and a dark side,—"dark sayings", Wis., viii, 8; Ecclus., xxxix, 3;—it is intended to stir curiosity and calls for intelligence in the listener, "He that hath ears to hear, let him hear" Matt., xiii, 9. Its Greek designation (from παραβάλλειν, to throw beside or against) indicates a deliberate "making up" of a story in which some lesson is at once given and concealed. As taking simple or common objects to cast light on ethics and religion, it has been well said of the parable that "truth embodied in a tale shall enter in at lowly doors." It abounds in lively speaking figures, and stands midway between the literalism of mere prose and the abstractions of philosophy. What the Hebrew מָשָׁל is derived from we do not know. If connected with Assyrian mashalu, Arab. matala, etc., the root meaning is "likeness". But it will be a likeness which contains a judgment, and so includes the "maxim", or general proposition bearing on conduct (Greek "gnomic wisdom"), of which the Book of Proverbs (Meshalim) is the chief inspired example. In classic Latin, the Greek word is translated *collatio* (Cicero, "De invent.", i–xxx), *imago* (Seneca, "Ep. lix."), *similitudo* (Quintil., "Inst.", v, 7–8). Observe that παραβολή does not occur in St. John's Gospel, nor παροιμία (proverb) in the Synoptics.

Likeness and abstraction enter into the idea of language, but may be contrasted as body and spirit, standing as they do in a relation at once of help and opposition. Wisdom for the practice of life has among all nations taken a figurative shape, passing from myth or fable into the contracted sayings we term proverbs, and arriving in the Greek schools of philosophy at ethical systems. But system, or technical metaphysics, does not appeal to the Semite; and our Sacred Books were never written with a view to it. If, however, system be not made the vehicle of teaching, what shall a prophet employ as its equivalent? The image or comparison remains. It is primitive, interesting, and easily remembered; and its various applications give it a continual freshness. The story came into use long before the system, and will survive when systems are forgotten. Its affinity, as a form of Divine speech, with the "Sacrament" (μυστήριον) as a form of Divine action, may profitably be kept in mind. Neither can we overlook the points of resemblance which exist between parables and miracles, both exhibiting through outward shows the presence of a supernatural doctrine and agency.

Hence we may speak of the irony which must always be possible in devices adapted to human weakness of understanding, where heavenly secrets are concerned. Bacon has said excellently well, "parables are serviceable as a mask and veil, and also for elucidation and illustration" (De sap. vet.). Of Scripture parables we conclude that they illustrate and edify by revealing some Divine principle, with immediate reference to the hearers addressed, but with more remote and recondite applications in the whole Christian economy to which they belong. Thus we find two lines of interpretation, the first dealing with Our Lord's parables as and when they were spoken—let this be termed critical exegesis; and the second bringing out their significance in the history of the Church, or ecclesiastical exegesis. Both are connected and may be traced to the same root in Revelation; yet they are distinct, somewhat after the fashion of the literal and mystical sense in Scripture generally. We cannot lose either out of sight. The parables of the New Testament refuse to be handled like Æsop's fables; they were intended from the first to shadow forth the "mysteries of the Kingdom of Heaven", and their double purpose may be read in St. Matthew, xiii, 10–18, where it is attributed to Christ Himself.

Modern critics (Jülicher and Loisy) who deny this, affirm that the Evangelists have deflected the parables from their original meaning in the interest of edification, suiting them to the circumstances of the primitive Church. In making such accusations these critics, following the example of Strauss, not only reject the witness of the Gospel writers, but do violence to its text. They overlook the profoundly supernatural and prophetic idea on which all Scripture moves as its vital form,—an idea certified to us by the usage of our Lord when quoting the Old Testament, and admitted equally by the Evangelists and St. Paul. That they run counter to Catholic tradition is manifest. Moreover, parables thus detached from a Christological significance would hang in the air and could claim no place in the teaching of the Son of God. A valid exegesis will therefore be prepared to discover in them all not only the relevance which they had for the multitude or the Pharisees but their truth, *sub specie sacramenti*, for "the Kingdom", i. e., for Christ's Church. And on this method the Fathers have expounded them without distinction of school, but especially among Westerns, St. Ambrose, St. Augustine, and St. Gregory the Great, as their commentaries prove.

Of the proverb not an ill definition might be that it is a closed or contracted parable: and of the parable that it is an expanded proverb. An instance, hovering on the verge of both, occurs Matt., xi, 17: "We have piped to you, and you have not danced; we have lamented, and you have not mourned." The words were taken from some child's game, but they are applied to St. John the Baptist and to Our Lord, with a gnomic moral, "Wisdom is justified by her children." In a *myth* or *allegory*, fictitious persons, gods and men, are introduced; and the significance lies within the story, as in Apuleius, "Eros and Psyche". But a parable looks at life as it is lived, deals in no personifications, and requires to be interpreted from without. Fable is marked by giving speech and thought to irrational or inanimate objects; parable as our Lord employs it never does so. *Examples* or "histories with a moral" have at least a core of reality—the instances occurring in Scripture and allowed by critics are such as Esther, Susanna, Tobias; but a parable need not quote individual persons, and except in the doubtful case of Lazarus, we shall not light upon instances of this kind among the stories told in the Gospels. A *type* consists in the significance given by prophecy to a person or his acts; e. g., to Isaac as the lamb of sacrifice, and the symbolical deeds of Ezechiel or Jeremias. But the parable brings in no types directly or in its immediate sense, and no determined persons. *Metaphor* (Lat. *translatio*) is a vague term, which might be applied to any short parabolic saying but does not fit the narrative of an action, such as we mean by a parable in the New Testament. The Socratic myth which adorns the "Gorgias", "Phædo", and "Republic", is confessedly a fable, whereas in our synoptic Gospels whatever illustrations we meet are chosen from daily occurrences.

The Hebrew genius, unlike that of the Hellenes, was not given to myth-making; it abhorred the personifications of nature to which we are indebted for gods of the elements, for Nereids and Hamadryads; it seldom pursued an allegory to any length; and its "realism" in treating of landscape and visible phenomena strikes most forcibly on the modern imagination. Theism was the breath of its nostrils; and where for a moment it indulges a turn for ancient folk-lore (as in Is., xiii, 21) it is far removed from the wild Pantheon of Greek nature-worship. In the parables we never come across enchanted stones or talking beasts or trees with magical virtues; the world which they describe is the world of every day; not even miracles break in upon its established order. When we consider what Oriental fancy has made of the universe, and how it is depicted in cosmogonies like that of Hesiod, the contrast becomes indescribably great. It is in the world which all men know that Christ finds exemplified the laws of human ethics, and the correspondences on which His kingdom shall be carried to its Divine consummation. Seen with purged eyes nature is already the kingdom of God.

No language is more concrete in its presentation of laws and principles, or more vividly figured, than that which the Old Testament affords. But of parables strictly taken it has only a few. Jotham's apologue of the trees choosing a king (Judges, ix, 8–15) is more properly a fable; so is the scornful tale of the thistle and the cedar in Lebanon which Joas of Israel sent by messengers to Amasias, King of Juda (IV Kings, xiv, 8–10). Nathan's rebuke to David is couched in the form of a parable (II Kings, xii, 1–4;) so the wise woman of Thecua (ibid., xiv, 4); so the Prophet to Achab (III Kings, xx, 39); and the song of the vineyard (Is., v, 1–8). It has been suggested that chapters i–iii of Osee must be construed as a parable, and do not contain a real history. The denunciation of woe on Jerusalem in Ezech., xxiv, 3–5, is expressly named a *mashal*, and may be compared with the Gospel similitude of the leaven. But our Lord, unlike the Prophets, does not act, or describe Himself as acting, any of the stories which He narrates. Hence we need not take into account the Old-Testament passages, Is., xx, 2–4; Jer., xxv, 15; Ezech., iii, 24–26, etc.

That the character of Christ's teaching to the multitude was mainly parabolic is clear from Matt., xiii, 34, and Mark, iv, 33. Perhaps we should ascribe to the same cause an element of the startling and paradoxical, e. g., in His Sermon on the Mount, which, taken literally, has been misunderstood by simple or again by fanatical minds. Moreover, that such a form of instruction was familiar to the Jews of this period cannot be doubted. The sayings of Hillel and Shammai still extant, the visions of the Book of Enoch, the typical values which we observe as attaching to the stories of Judith and Tobias, the Apocalypse and the extensive literature of which it is the flower, all betoken a demand for something esoteric in the popular religious preaching, and show how abundantly it was satisfied. But if, as mystical writers hold, the highest degree of heavenly knowledge is a clear intuition, without veils or symbols dimming its light, we see in our Lord exactly this pure comprehension. He is never Himself drawn as a visionary. The parables are not for Him but for the crowd. When He speaks of His relation to the Father it is in direct terms, without metaphor. It follows that the scope of these exquisite little moralities ought to be measured by the audience whom they were designed to benefit. In other words they form part of the "Economy" whereby truth is dispensed to men as they are able to bear it (Mark, iv, 33; John, xvi, 12). Since, however, it is the Lord that speaks, we must reverently construe His sayings in the light of the whole Revelation which furnishes their ground and context. The "real sense of Scripture", as Newman points out in accord with all the Catholic Fathers, is "the scope of the Divine intelligence", or the scheme of Incarnation and Redemption.

Subject to this Law, the New-Testament parables have each a definite meaning, to be ascertained from the explanation, where Christ deigns to give one, as in the sower; and when none such is forthcoming, from the occasion, introduction, and appended moral. Interpreters have differed importantly on the question whether everything in the parable is of its essence (the "kernel") or anything is mere machinery and accident (the "husk"). There is an obvious negative rule. We must not pass over as unmeaning any detail without which the lesson would cease to be enforced. But shall we insist on a correspondence at all points, so that we may translate the whole into spiritual values, or may we neglect whatever does not seem to compose a feature of the moral to be drawn? St. John Chrysostom (In Matt., lxiv) and the School of Antioch, who were literalists, prefer the latter method; they are sober in exposition, not imaginative or mystic; and Tertullian has expressions to the like purpose (De Pudic., ix); St. Augustine, who holds of Origen and the Alexandrians, abounds in the larger sense; yet he allows that "in prophetic narrations details are told us which have no significance" (De Civ. Dei, XVI, ii). St. Jerome in his earlier writings follows Origen; but his temper was not that of a mystic and with age he becomes increasingly literal. Among modern commentators the same difference of handling appears.

In a problem which is literary as well as exegetical, we must guard against applying a hard and fast rule where taste and insight are required. Each of the parables will need to be dealt with as if it were a poem; and fulness of meaning, refinement of thought, slight but suggestive hints and touches, characteristic of human genius, will not be wanting to the method of the Divine Teacher. In the highest criticism, as Goethe warns us, we cannot divide as with an axe the inward from the outward. Where all is living, the metaphor of kernel and husk may be often misapplied. The meaning lies implicit in the whole and its parts; here as in every vital product the ruling spirit is one, the elements take their virtue from it and separately are of no account. As we move away from the central idea we lose the assurance that we are not pursuing our own fancies; and the substitution of a mechanical yet extravagant dogmatism for the Gospel truth has led Gnostics and Manichæans, or latter-day visionaries like Swedenborg, into a wilderness of delusions where the severe and tender beauty of the parables can no longer be discerned. They are literary creations, not merely hieratic devices; and as awakening the mind to spiritual principles their intent is fulfilled when it muses on the deep things of God, the laws of life, the mission of Christ, of which it is thus made intimately aware.

St. Thomas and all Catholic doctors maintain that articles of faith ought to be deduced only from the literal sense of Scripture whenever it is quoted in proof of them; but the literal sense is often the prophetic, which itself as a Divine truth may well be applicable to an entire series of events or line of typical characters. The Angel of the Schools declares after St. Jerome that "spiritual interpretation should follow the order of history". St. Jerome himself exclaims, "never can a parable and the dubious interpretations of riddles avail for the establishment of dogmas" (Summa, I–I, Q. x; St. Jerome, In Matt., xiii, 33). From a parable alone, therefore, we do not argue categorically; we take it in illustration of Christian verities proved elsewhere. It was this canon of good sense which the Gnostics, especially Valentinus, disregarded to their own hurt, and so fell into the confusion of ideas miscalled by them revelation. Irenæus constantly opposes church tradition or the rule of faith, to these dreamers (II, xvi, against the Marcosians; II, xxvii, xxviii, against Valentinus). Tertullian in like manner,

"Heretics draw the parables whither they will, not whither they ought", and "Valentinus did not make up Scriptures to suit his teaching, but forced his teaching on the Scriptures." (See De Pudic., viii, ix; De Præscript., viii; and compare St. Anselm, "Cur Deus homo", I, iv.)

We learn what the parables signify, on this showing, from "the school of Christ"; we interpret them on the lines of "apostolic and ecclesiastical tradition" (Tert., "Scorp.", xii; Vinc. Lcrin., xxvii; Conc. Trid., Sess. IV). The "analogy of faith" determines how far we may go in applying them to life and history. With Salmeron it is allowed to distinguish in them a "root", the occasion and immediate purpose, a "rind", the sensible imagery or incidents, and a "marrow", the Christian truth, thus conveyed. Another way would be to consider each parable as it relates to Christ himself, to the Church as His spiritual body, to the individual as putting on Christ. These are not different, still less contrary elucidations; they flow out of that great central dogma, "The Word was made flesh". In dealing on such a system with any part of Holy Writ we keep within Catholic bounds; we explain the "Verbum scriptum" by the "Verbum incarnatum". To the same principle we can reduce the "four senses", often reckoned as derivable from the sacred text. These medieval refinements are but an effort to establish on the letter, faithfully understood, implications which in all the works of genius, other than scientific, are more or less contained. The governing sense remains, and is always the standard of reference.

There are no parables in St. John's Gospel. In the Synoptics Mark has only one peculiar to himself, the seed growing secretly (iv, 26); he has three which are common to Matthew and Luke, the sower, mustard seed, and wicked husbandman. Two more are found in the same Gospels, the leaven and the lost sheep. Of the rest eighteen belong to the third and ten to the first Evangelist. Thus we reckon thirty-three in all; but some have raised the number even to sixty, by including proverbial expressions. An external but instructive division parts them into three groups; those delivered about the Lake of Galilee (Matt., xiii); those on the way up to Jerusalem (Luke, x-xviii); those uttered during the final stage of Our Lord's life, given in either Gospel; or parables of the kingdom, the Christian's rule; the judgment on Israel and mankind. In various ways commentators follow this arrangement, while indicating more elaborate distinctions. Westcott refers us to parables drawn from the material world, as the sower; from the relations of men to that world, as the fig tree and lost sheep: from the dealings of men with one another, as the prodigal son; and with God, as the hidden treasure. It is clear that we might assign examples from one of these classes to a different heading without violence. A further suggestion, not unreal, brings out the Messianic aspect of the parables in St. Matthew, and the more individual or ethical of those in St. Luke. Again the later chapters of St. Matthew and the third Gospel tend to enlarge and give more in detail; perhaps at the beginning of our Lord's ministry these illustrations were briefer than they afterwards became. We can surely not imagine that Christ never repeated or varied His parables, as any human teacher would under various circumstances. The same story may well be recorded in different shapes and with a moral adapted to the situation, as, e. g., the talents and the pounds, or the king's son's marriage and the unworthy wedding guest. Nor ought we to expect in the reporters a stereotyped accuracy, of which the New Testament nowhere shows itself to be solicitious. Though we have received the parables only in the form of literature, they were in fact spoken, not written—and spoken in Aramaic, while handed down to us in Hellenistic Greek.

Although, according to most non-Catholic writers, Sts. Matthew and Luke are founded upon St. Mark, it is natural to begin our exposition of the parables in the first Gospel, which has a group of seven consecutively (xiii, 3–57). The sower with its explanation, introduces them; the draw net completes their teaching; and we cannot refuse to see in the number seven (cf. St. John's Gospel) an idea of selected fitness which invites us to search out the principle involved. Men favourable to what is known as an "historic and prophetic" system of exegesis, have applied the seven parables to seven ages of the Church. This conception is not foreign to Scripture, nor unfamiliar in patristic writings, but it can scarcely be pressed in detail. We are not qualified to say how the facts of church history correspond, except in their general features, with anything in these parables; neither have we the means of guessing at what stage of the Divine Economy we stand. It may be enough to remark that the sower denotes the preaching of the Gospel; the tares or cockle, how it meets with hindrances; the mustard seed and the leaven, its noiseless yet victorious growth. From the hidden treasure and the pearl of price we learn that those who are called must give up all to possess the kingdom. Finally, the draw net pictures God's judgment on His Church, and the everlasting separation of good and bad.

From all this it appears that St. Matthew has brought the parables together for a purpose (cf. Maldonatus, I, 443) and he distinguishes between the "multitude", to whom the first four were chiefly addressed, and the "disciples", who were privileged to know their prophetic significance. They illustrate the Sermon on the Mount, which ends with a twofold comparison, the house on the rock typifying Christ's Church, and the house on the sand opposed to it. Nothing can be clearer, if we believe the Synoptics, than that our Lord so taught as to enlighten the elect and to leave obstinate sinners (above all, the Pharisees) in their darkness (Matt., xiii, 11–15; Mark, iv, 11–12; Luke, viii, 10). Observe the quotation from Isaias (Matt., xiii, 14; Is., vi, 9, according to the Septuagint) intimating a judicial blindness, due to Israel's backslidings and manifest in the public troubles of the nation while the evangelists were writing. Unbelievers or "Modernists", reluctant to perceive in the man Christ Jesus any supernatural powers, look upon such sayings as prophecies after the event. But the parable of the sower contains in itself a warning like that of Isaias, and was certainly spoken by Christ. It opens the series of His Messianic teachings, even as that of the wicked husbandman concludes them. From first to last the rejection of the Jews, all except a holy "remnant", is contemplated. Moreover, since the Prophets had constantly taken up this attitude, denouncing the corrupt priesthood and disparaging legalism, why should we dream that language of similar import and contents was not heard from the lips of Jesus? And if anywhere, would it not be found in His parabolic delineations of the New Law? There is no solid reason why the double edge of these moralities should be ascribed to a mere "tendency" in the recorders, or to an edifying afterthought of primitive Christians. If the "allegory", i. e., the application to history, be intended by all three evangelists (which we grant), that intention lay at the root of the parable when it was delivered. Christ is "the Sower", and the seed could not escape the divers fortunes which befell it on the soil of Judaism. Even from the modernist point of view our Saviour was the last and greatest of the Prophets. How then could He avoid speaking as they did of a catastrophe which was to bring in the reign of Messias? Or how shall we suppose that He stood alone in this respect, isolated from the seers who went before Him and the disciples who came after Him? It is certain that, for the Evangelists, "He that hath ears to hear let him hear" did not signify merely a "call to attention"; we may compare it to the classic formulæ, Eleusinian and other, which it resembles, as carrying with it an intimation of some Divine mystery. The more an esoteric meaning is put upon the Gospels as their original scope, so much the more will it be evident that our Lord Himself made use of it.

Dismissing the minute conjectural criticism which would leave us hardly more than a bare outline to go upon, and not regarding verbal differences, we can treat the parables as coming direct from our Lord. They teach a lesson at once ethical and dogmatic, with implications of prophecy reaching to the consummation of all things. Their analogy to the sacraments, of which our Lord's Incarnation is the source and pattern, must never be left out of view. Modern objections proceed from a narrow "enlightened" conception as of the "reasonable man", teaching general truths in the abstract, and attaching no importance to the examples by which he enforces them. But the Evangelists, like the Catholic Church, have considered that the Son of God, instructing His disciples for all time, would commit to them heavenly mysteries, "things hidden from the foundation of the world" (Matt., xiii, 35). So perfectly does this correspondence with history apply to the tares, the good samaritan, the "watching" parables, to Dives and Lazarus (whether a real incident or otherwise), and to the wicked husbandmen, that it cannot be set aside. In consequence, certain critics have denied that Christ spoke some of these "allegories", but the grounds which they allege would entitle them to reject the others; that conclusion they dare not face (cf. Loisy, "Ev. synopt.", II, 318).

All orthodox writers take the sower (Matt., xiii, 3–8; Mark, iv, 3–8; Luke, viii, 5–8.) as a model both of narrative and interpretation, warranted by the Divine Master Himself. The general likeness between teaching and sowing is found in Seneca, "Ep. lxxiii"; and Prudentius, the Christian poet, has thrown the parable into verse, "Contra Symmachum", II, 1022. Salmeron comes near the method suggested above by which we get most profit from these symbols, when he declares that Christ is "the Sower and the Seed". We are immediately reminded of the Greek Fathers who call our Redeemer the seed sown in our hearts, Λόγος σπερματικός, who comes forth from God that He may be the principle of righteousness in man (Justin, "Apol.", II, xiii; Athan., "Orat.," ii, 79; Cyril Alex., "In Joan.", 75; and see Newman, "Tracts", 150–177). I Pet., i, 1–23, reads like an echo of this parable. Note that our Lord does not use personifications, but refers good and evil alike to persons; it is the "wicked one" who plucks away the seed, not a vague impersonal mischief. The rocky bottom, the burning wind and scorching sun, tell us of Palestinian scenery. We find "thorny cares" in Catullus (lxiv, lxxii) and in Ovid (Metamorp., XIII, 5, 483). Theologians warn us not to imagine that the "good and perfect heart" of the receiver is by nature such; for that would be the heresy of Pelagius; but we may quote the axiom of the Schools, "To him that doeth what he can God will not deny His grace". St. Cyprian and St. Augustine (Ep. lxix; Serm. lxxiii) point out that free will acceptance is the teaching of the Gospel; and so Irenæus against the Gnostic forerunners of Lutheranism (V, xxxix).

The tares or cockle (Matt., xiii, 24–30 alone). Whatever be meant by ζιζάνια the word, found only here in the Greek Scripture, is originally semite (Arab. zuwan). In the Vulgate it is retained and in popular French Wyclif renders it "darnel or cockle", and curiously enough the name of his followers, the Lollards, has been derived from a Latin equivalent, "lolium." In the Reims New Testament we have "cockle", for which compare Job, xxxi, 40: "Let thistles grow instead of wheat, and cockle instead of barley." It is pretty well determined that the plant in question is "lolium temulentum," or bearded darnel; and the mischievous practice of "oversowing" has been detected among Easterns, if not elsewhere. The late weeding of the fields is in "substantial agreement with Oriental custom", at a time when good and evil plants can be fully distinguished. Christ calls Himself the "Son of Man"; He is the sower, good men are the seed; the field is indifferently the Church or the world, i. e., the visible Kingdom in which all kinds are mingled, to be sorted out in the day of His coming. He explains and fits in detail the lesson to the incidents (Matt., xiii, 36–43), with an adaptation so clear to the primitive age of Christianity that Loisy, Jülicher, and other modern critics, refuse to consider the parable authentic. They suppose it to be drawn out of some brief comparison in the original lost "source" of Mark. These random guessings have no scientific value. Historically, the moral which recommends sufferance of disorders among Christians when a greater evil would follow on trying to put them down, has been enforced by the Church authorities against Novatus, and its theory developed in St. Augustine's long disputes with those hard African Puritans, the Donatists. St. Augustine, recognizing in Our Lord's words as in the spiritual life a principle of growth which demands patience, by means of it reconciles the imperfect militant state of His disciples now with St. Paul's vision of a "glorious church, not having spot or wrinkle" (Eph., v, 27). Such is the large Catholic philosophy, illustrated by the Roman Church from early times, despite men like Tertullian; from the medieval condemnation of the Cathari; and from the later resistance to Calvin, who would have brought in a kind of Stoic republic or "Kingdom of the Saints", with its inevitable consequences, hypocrisy and self-righteous pharisaism. Yet Calvin, who separated from the Catholic communion on this and the like motives, calls it a dangerous temptation to suppose that "there is no Church wherever perfect purity is not apparent." (Cf. St. Augustine, "In Psalm. 99"; "Contra Crescon.", III, xxxiv; St. Jerome, "Adv. Lucifer"; and Tertull. in his orthodox period, "Apol.", xli: "God does not hasten that sifting out, which is a condition of judgment, until the world's end.")

If in the tares we perceive a stage of Christ's teaching more advanced than in the sower, we may take the mustard seed as announcing the outward manifest triumph of His Kingdom, while the leaven discloses to us the secret of its inward working (Matt., xiii, 31–2; Mark, iv, 30–32; Luke, xiii, 18–9, for the first; Matt., xiii 33; Luke, xiii, 20–21, for the second). Strange difficulties have been started by Westerns who had never set eyes on the luxuriant growth of the mustard plant in its native home, and who demur to the letter which calls it "the least of all seeds." But in the Koran (Sura xxxi) this proverbial estimate is implied; and it is an elementary rule of sound Scripture criticism not to look for scientific precision in such popular examples, or in discourses which aim at something more important than mere knowledge. The tree, salvadora persica, is said to be rare. Obviously, the point of comparison is directed to the humble beginnings and extraordinary development of Christ's Kingdom. Wellhausen believes that for the Evangelists the parable was an allegory typifying the Church's rapid growth; Loisy would infer that, if so, it was not delivered by our Lord in its actual form. But here are three distinct yet cognate stories, the mustard seed, the leaven, the seed growing secretly, occurring in the Synoptics, contemplating a lapse of time, and more applicable to after-ages than to the brief period during which Christ was preaching,— shall we say that He uttered none of them? And if we allow these prophetic anticipations at all, does not the traditional view explain them best? (Wellh.,

"Matt.", 70; Loisy, "Ev. syn.", III, 770-3.) It has been questioned whether in the leaven we should recognize a good influence, answering to the texts, "you are the salt of the earth, the light of the world" (Matt., v, 13-14), or the evil to be "purged out" according to St. Paul (I Cor., v, 6-8). Better to take it as the "good seed", with consequent applications, as St. Ignatius does (Ad Magnes., x), and St. Gregory Naz. (Orat., xxxvi, 90). By the "three measures" were understood in the Gnostic system the "earthly", "carnal", and "spiritual" classes among Christians (Iren., I, viii). Trench admirably describes these two parables as setting before us the "mystery of regeneration" in the world and the heart of man. For the "leaven of the Pharisees", consult authors on Matt., xvi, 6.

The hidden treasure (Matt., xiii, 44); the pearl of price (ibid., 45). With Origen we may term these "similitudes"; in one the object is found as if by accident (Is., lxv, 1; Rom., x, 20: "I was found by them that did not seek me"); in the other a man seeks and buys it deliberately. Under such figures would be signified the calling of the Gentiles and the spiritual strivings of those who, with Simeon, waited "for the consolation of Israel". There is surely an allusion to the joy of martyrdom in the first (Matt., x, 37). The concealed treasure is a widespread Eastern idea (Job, iii, 21; Prov., ii, 4); pearls or rubies, which may be represented by the same Hebrew word (Job, xxviii, 18; Prov., iii, 15, etc.) will mean the "jewel" of faith, our Lord Himself, or everlasting life; and Christians must make the great surrender if they would gain it. No keeping back is possible, so far as the spirit is concerned; a man must give the whole world for his "soul", which is worth more, hence he rejoices. Here, as elsewhere, the comparison does not imply any judgment on the morality of the persons taken by way of figures; the casuistry of "treasure trove", the possible overreaching in business, belong to the "rind" not the "marrow" of the story and yield no lesson. St. Jerome understands Holy Writ to be the treasure; St. Augustine, "the two Testaments of the Law", but Christ never identifies the "Kingdom" with Scripture. A strange interpretation, not warranted by the context, looks on the Saviour as at once seeker and finder.

The draw net (Matt., xiii, 47-50) completes the sevenfold teaching in the first Gospel. The order was chosen by St. Matthew; and if we accept the mystic signification of the number "seven", i. e., "perfection", we shall perceive in this parable not a repetition, as Maldonatus held, of the tares, but its crown. In the tares separation of good and bad is put off; here it is accomplished. St. Augustine composed a kind of ballad for the people against the Donatist schismatics which expresses the doctrine clearly, "seculi finis est littus, tunc est tempus separare" (see Enarr. in Ps., lxiv, 6). The net is a sweeping net, Lat. *verriculum*, or a seine, which of necessity captures all sorts, and requires to be hauled on shore and the division made. For the Jews, in particular, the clean must be taken and the unclean cast away. Since it is distinctly stated that within the net are both good and bad, this implies a visible and a mixed congregation until the Lord comes with His angels to judgment (Matt., xiii, 41; Apoc., xiv, 18). The Evangelist, Loisy observes, has understood this parable, like the others quoted, allegorically, and Christ is the Fisher of men. Clement of Alexandria perhaps wrote the well-known Orphic hymn which contains a similar appellation. The "fiery furnace", the "tears and the gnashing of teeth", going beyond the figures in the story, belong to its meaning and to Christian dogma. In the conclusion "every scribe" (xiii, 52) points to the duty which Our Lord's Apostles will hand on to the Church of bringing forth to believers the hidden spiritual sense of tradition, "the new and the old". Specifically, this does not serve as a distinction of the Testaments; but we may compare, "I came not to destroy but to fulfil", and "not one jot, or one tittle" (Matt., v, 17-18). Modernist critics attribute the whole idea of a Christian "scribe" to St. Matthew and not to our Lord. The expression "instructed" is literally, "having been made a disciple", $\mu\alpha\theta\eta\tau\epsilon\upsilon\theta\epsilon$ίς, and is of rare occurrence (Matt in loco; xxvii, 57; xxviii, 19; Acts, xiv, 21). It answers to the Hebrew "Sons of the prophets" and is thoroughly Oriental (IV Kings, ii, 3, etc.)

The unmerciful servant, or "serve nequam" (Matt., xviii, 21-35), might be summed up in two words, "Forgiven, forgive". This chapter xviii resumes the parabolic teaching; Christ sets the little child in the midst of His disciples as an example of humility, and tells the story of the Good Shepherd (verses 11-13) which St. John's Gospel repeats in the first person. Undoubtedly, Christ said "I am the Good Shepherd", as He says here, "The Son of man is come to save that which was lost" (11). St. Peter's question, "How oft shall my brother sin against me and I forgive him?" brings out the very spirit of Jewish legalism, in which the Apostle was yet bound, while it provokes a statement of the Christian ideal. Contrast, frequently employed to heighten the effect of our Lord's teaching, is here visible in the attitude taken up by Peter and corrected by His Master. "Until seventy times seven times", the perfection of the perfect, signifies of course not a number but a principle, "Be not overcome by evil, but overcome evil by good" (Rom., xii, 21). That is the "secret of Jesus" and constitutes His revelation. St. Jerome read a curious variant, plainly a gloss, in the "Gospel according to the Hebrews" (Loisy, II, 93). The proverbial number is perhaps taken from Lamech's song of revenge (Gen., iv, 24); where however the A. V. reads "seventy and sevenfold". This parable is the first in which God appears and acts like a king, though of course the title is frequent in the Old Testament. As regards the persons, observe that Our Lord does not give them names, which makes the story-telling more difficult. The "wicked servant" may be a satrap, and his enormous debt would be the tribute of his Government. That he and his were sold into slavery would seem natural to an Eastern, then or later. "Ten thousand talents" may refer to the Ten Commandments. "A hundred pence" owed by his "fellow servant" graphically depicts the situation as between man and man compared with human offences towards God. The "prison" in which torture is to wring from the culprit all he possesses, represents what has ever taken place under the tyrannies of Asia, down to recent times (compare Burke's charges against Warren Hastings in reference to similar acts). "Till he paid" might signify "never", according to a possible sense of "donec", and was taken so by St. John Chrysostom. Later theologians construe it more mildly and adapt the words to a prison where spiritual debts may be redeemed, i. e., to purgatory (Matt., v, 25-26, closely corresponds). The moral has been happily termed "Christ's law of retaliation", announced by Him aforetime in the Sermon on the Mount (Matt., v, 38-48), and the Lord's Prayer makes it a condition of our own forgiveness.

The labourers in the vineyard (Matt., xx, 1-16) has become celebrated in modern economical discussions by its pregnant phrase "To this last." Calderon, the Spanish poet, renders its meaning well, "To thy neighbour as to thee". But among parables it is one of the hardest to work out, and is variously expounded. In the main it is an answer to all Pharisees and Pelagians who demand eternal life as a recompense due to their works, and who murmur when "sinners" or the less worthy are accepted, though coming late to the Divine call. It might seasonably introduce the Epistle to the Romans, which proceeds on identical lines and teaches the same lesson. Yet no one has denied its authorship to Christ. (Cf. Romans, iii, 24–27; iv, 1; ix, 20, esp. "O man, who art thou that repliest against God?") The attitude of Christ towards publicans and sinners which gave offence to the Pharisees (Mark, ii, 16; Luke, v, 30), affords the clearest comment on the parable as a whole. Some critics reject the last sentence, "Many are called", as an interpolation from the parable of the marriage feast. Early mystical views understand the labourers to be Israel and the heathen; Irenæus, Origen, Hilary adapt the different hours to stages of the Old Covenant. St. Jerome compares the prodigal son, for which this may be St. Matthew's equivalent lesson. Note the "evil eye" and other references to it (Deut., xv, 9; II Kings, xviii, 9; Prov., xxiii, 6).

The two sons (Matt., xxi, 28–32) begins in this Gospel a series of denunciations addressed to the Pharisees. Its drift is plain. These "hypocrites" profess to keep God's law and break it; hence their scorn of the Baptist's preaching; whereas "publicans and harlots" were converted; therefore they shall go into the Kingdom before the others. But if it be accommodated to Jews and Gentiles, who is the elder son, who the younger? From the text no reply can be drawn and commentators are not agreed. In some MSS. the order is reversed, but without foundation. (See Luke, vii, 29–30, 37–50.)

The wicked husbandmen (Matt., xxi, 33–45; Mark, xii, 1–12; Luke, xx, 9–19). This remarkable challenge to the "chief priests and Pharisees", occurring in all the Synoptics, and foretelling how God's vineyard shall be transferred from its present keepers, reminds us of the good samaritan and the prodigal son, with which it harmonizes, though severe in its tone as they are not. However, its extreme clearness of application in detail has led the modernist critics to deny that Our Lord spoke it. They call it an allegory, not a parable. The "vineyard of the Lord of Hosts" is in Is., v, 1–7, and the prophecy in both cases analogous. That Jesus foresaw His rejection by the "chief priests" cannot be doubtful. That He contemplated the entrance into God's Kingdom of many Gentiles is apparent from Luke, xiii, 29, as from parables already quoted. This, indeed, was boldly pictured in the Old Testament (Is., ii, 1–4; xix, 20–25; Mich., iv, 1–7). In the first Gospel our Lord addresses the Pharisees; in the third He speaks to the "people". The "tower" is Mount Sion with its temple; the "servants" are the Prophets; when the "beloved son" is murdered we may think of Naboth dying for his vineyard and the crucifixion comes into sight. Christ is the "heir of all things" (Heb., i, 2). We must grant to Loisy that the anticipation of vengeance is an apocalypse in brief, while upholding the genuineness of the larger view in Matt., xxiv, which his school would attribute to a period after the fall of Jerusalem. For the "stone which the builders rejected" and which "is become the head of the corner", see Ps., cxvii (Hebrew cxviii), 22, 23, and Acts, iv, 11. The reading is from the Septuagint, not the Hebrew.

The marriage of the king's son, or less accurately, the wedding garment (Matt., xxii, 1–14). If, like Maldonatus and Theophylact, we identify this with the great supper in St. Luke (xiv, 16), we must allow that the differences observable are due to the inspired reporters who had in view "not history but doctrine". Or we might hold that the discourse had been varied to meet another occasion. Read St. Augustine, "De consensu evang.", II, lxxii, who is for distinguishing them. The Lucan story would be earlier; the present, spoken in wrath when all hope of Christ's acceptance by clergy or scribes is at an end, reveals the mood of severe sadness which overshadowed our Lord's last days. Naturally the mythical school (Strauss and even Keim, with recent Modernists) discovers in the violence of the invited guests and their punishment an apologetic tendency, due to the editors of the original tale. "These additions", says Loisy, "were made after the taking of Jerusalem by Titus; and the writer had never heard Jesus, but was manipulating a text already settled" (Ev. synopt., II, 326). That the reign of the Messias, following on the rejection of Israel, was always meant in this story, is incontestable. Catholic faith would of course allow that the "servants" maltreated were, in our Lord's mind, such as St. John Baptist, the Apostles, the first martyrs. The feast, in our commentaries, may well be the Incarnation; the wedding garment is sanctifying grace, "put ye on the Lord Jesus" (Rom., xiii, 14). Thus Iren., IV, xxxvi; Tert., "De resurrect. carnis", xxvii, etc.

The ten virgins (only in Matt., xxv, 1–13) may be considered as first of several parables declaring that the advent of the Kingdom will be unexpected. These are all comments on the text, "of that day and hour no one knoweth, no not the angels of heaven, but the Father alone" (Matt., xxiv, 36). It is a "watching" parable, and is not in praise of virginity as such, though applied by the Fathers, as St. Gregory Martyr, to the duties of the virgin-state. St. Augustine writes, "souls that have the Catholic faith and appear to have good works" (Serm. xciii, 2); St. Jerome, "they boast the knowledge of God and are untainted with idolatry". There seems to be a reminiscence of this parable in Luke, xii, 36, wrought into the admonition to men "that wait for their Lord". Wellhausen's idea that St. Matthew composed it from St. Luke is untenable. In the East it is usual that the bride should be conveyed with honour to the bridegroom's house; but there might be exceptions, as here. Mystically, Christ is the bridegroom, His parousia the event, and the preparation by faith shining out in Christian deeds is imaged in the burning lamps or torches. For the "closed door" see Luke, xiii, 25. The conclusion, "Vigilate", is a direct lesson and no part of the story. St. Methodius wrote the "Banquet of the Ten Virgins", a rude mystery play in Greek.

The talents (Matt., xxv, 14–30) and the pounds or the minæ (Luke, xix, 11–27). Whether we shall identify or divide these two celebrated apologues can scarcely be determined. St. Mark (xiii, 34–36) blends his brief allusion with a text from the ten virgins. The circumstances in the first and third Gospels differ; but the warning is much the same. Commentators note that here the active life is extolled, as in the virgins a heedful contemplation. No argument for the lawfulness of usury can be drawn from verse 27. The "servant" was a bondslave; all that he had or acquired would be his master's property. "To him that hath shall be given" is one of the "hard sayings" which, while disclosing a law of life, seems not to harmonize with Christian kindness. Yet the analogy of God's dealings—not "mere" benevolence, but "wise and just" recognition of moral effort—is hereby maintained. If our Lord, as tradition tells, said, "Be ye good money changers" (cf. I Thess., v, 21), the same principle is commended. Ethically, all that we have is a trust of which we must give account. For the diversity of talents, note St. Paul, I Cor., xii, 4, and the reconciliation of that diversity in "the same spirit". Both parables relate to Christ's second coming. Hence Loisy and others attribute to the Evangelists, and especially to St. Luke, an enlargement, founded on later history, perhaps taken from Josephus, and intended to explain the delay of the Parousia (Ev. synopt., II, 464–80). Not accepting these premises, we put aside the conclusion. Maldonatus (I, 493), who treats the stories as variants, observes, "it is no new thing that our Evangelists should appear to differ in circumstances of time and place, since they consider only the general outline (*summam rei gestæ*), not the order or the time. Where else we find them seeming to disagree, they wish to explain not Christ's words but the drift of the parable as a whole".

Leaving St. Matthew, we note the one short story

peculiar to St. Mark, of the seed growing secretly (iv, 26–29). We have already assigned it to the group of the mustard tree and the leaven. Its point is conveyed in the Horatian line, "Crescit occulto velut arbor ævo" (Odes, I, xii, 36). The husbandman who "knows not how" the harvest springs cannot be the Almighty, but is the human sower of the word. For homiletic purposes we may combine this parable with its cognate, "unless the grain of wheat die" (John, xii, 24) which applies it to Christ Himself and His Divine influence.

In St. Luke the two debtors (vii, 41–43) is spoken by our Lord to Simon "the leper" (Mark, xiv, 2–9) on occasion of Mary Magdalene's conversion, with its touching circumstances. At least since St. Gregory the Great, Catholic writers have so understood the history. The double saying "Many sins are forgiven her, for she loved much", and "to whom less is forgiven, he loveth less", has a perfectly clear human sense, in accordance with facts. We cannot deduce from such almost proverbial expressions a theory of justification. The lesson concerns gratitude for mercies received, with a strong emphasis on the hard arrogance of the Pharisee over against the lowly and tender bearing of the "woman who was a sinner". Thus, in effect, St. Augustine (Serm. xcix, 4). The contrast between dead faith and faith animated by love—which Maldonatus would introduce—is not directly meant. And we need not suppose the latter portion of the story artificial or pieced together by St. Luke from other Gospel fragments. With the problem of the four narratives (Matt., xxvi; Mark, xiv; Luke, vii; John, xii) the present article is not concerned.

The good samaritan (Luke, x, 37) is certainly authentic; it can be explained mystically in detail, and is therefore as much an "allegory" as a parable. If it was spoken by our Lord so was the wicked husbandmen. It does not exactly reply to the question "Who is thy neighbour?" but propounds and answers a larger one, "Whom in distress should I like to be neighbour to me?" and gives an everlasting instance of the golden rule. At the same time it breaks down the fences of legalism, triumphs over national hatreds, and lifts the despised Samaritan to a place of honour. In the deeper sense we discern that Christ is the Good Samaritan, human nature the man fallen among robbers, i. e., under Satan's yoke; neither law nor Prophets can help; and the Saviour alone bears the charge of healing our spiritual wounds. The inn is Christ's Church; the oil and wine are His sacraments. He will come again and will make all good. The Fathers, Sts. Ambrose, Augustine, Jerome, are agreed in this general interpretation. Mere philanthropy will not satisfy the Gospel idea; we must add, "the charity of Christ presseth us" (II Cor., v, 14).

The friend at midnight (Luke, xi, 5–8) and the unjust judge (Luke, xviii, 1–8) need no explanation. With a certain strength of language both dwell on the power of continued prayer. Importunity wins, "the kingdom of heaven suffereth violence, and the violent bear it away" (Matt., xi, 12). Dante has beautifully expressed the Divine law which these parables teach (Paradiso, xx, 94–100).

The rich fool (Luke, xii, 16–21) and Dives and Lazarus (xvi, 19–31) raise the question whether we should interpret them as true histories or as instructive fictions. Both are directed against the chief enemy of the Gospel, riches loved and sought after. The rich fool ("Nabal", as in I Kings, xxv) was uttered on occasion of a dispute concerning property and Christ answers "Man, who hath appointed me judge, or divider, over you?" Not injustice, but covetousness, "the root of all evil", is here reprehended. Read St. Cyprian, "De opere et eleemosyna", 13.

The story of Lazarus, which completes this lesson by contrast, appears to have no concealed meaning, and would therefore not fulfil the definition of a parable. Catholics, with Irenæus, Ambrose, Augustine, and the church liturgy, regard it as a narrative. The modern school rejects this view, allows that our Lord may have spoken the first half of the recital (Luke, xvi, 19–26) but considers the rest to be an allegory which condemns the Jews for not accepting the witness of Moses and the Prophets to Jesus as the Messias. In any case our Lord's resurrection furnishes an implied reference. "Abraham's bosom" for the middle state after death is adopted by the Fathers generally; it receives illustration from IV Mach., xiii, 17. For a recent Jewish exposition of the parable see Geiger in "Judische Zeitschr. für Wissenschaft", VII, 200. St. Augustine (De Gen. ad Litt., viii, 7) doubts whether we can take literally the description of the other world. On the relation, supposed by rationalizing critics, of this Lazarus to St. John's Gospel, x, see JOHN, GOSPEL OF SAINT; LAZARUS.

Passing over the barren fig tree (Luke, xiii, 6–9) which gave a plain warning to Israel; and just referring to the lost sheep (Matt., xviii, 12–14; Luke, xv, 3–7) and the lost groat or drachma (Luke, xv, 8–10), none of which need detain us, we come to the great supper (Luke, xiv, 15–24). That this parable concerns the calling of the Gentiles is admitted and is important, as bearing on the universal commission, Matt., xxviii, 19. "Compel them to enter", like the strong sayings quoted above (importunate widow etc.), must be taken in the spirit of Christianity, which compels by moral suasion, not by the sword (Matt., xxvi, 52).

The prodigal son (Luke, xv, 11–32), so called from verse 13, has a deep ethical meaning, but likewise a dogmatic, in which the two sons are the Israelite, staying at home in his father's house, and the Gentile who has wandered away. As the message of pardon it deserves to be called the very heart of Christ's gospel. We have justified these parallel lines of interpretation, for ethics and revelation, which were both visible to the Evangelist. Tertullian's narrow use of the story is uncritical. St. John Chrysostom and the Church always have applied it to Christian, i. e., baptized penitents. The "first [or best] robe" is naturally assumed by theologians to be "original justice", and the feast of reconciliation is our Lord's atoning sacrifice. Those who grant a strong Pauline influence in St. Luke's Gospel ought not to deny it here. The "jealousy of good men" towards returned prodigals, which has exercised commentators, is true to life; and it counted for much in the dissensions that finally clove asunder the Church of Israel from the Church of Christ (I Thess., ii, 14–16). The joy over a sinner's conversion unites this parable with those of the lost sheep and the lost drachma.

The unjust steward (Luke, xvi, 1–9) is, beyond question, the hardest of all our Lord's parables, if we may argue from the number and variety of meanings set upon it. Verses 10–13 are no part of the narration but a discourse to which it gives rise. The connecting link between them is the difficult expression "mammon [more correctly 'Mamon'] of iniquity"; and we may suppose with Bengel that Christ was speaking to those of His followers, like Levi, who had been farmers of the taxes, i. e., "publicans". In the contrast between the "children of this world" and the "children of light" we find a clue to the general lesson. Mark the resemblance to St. John's Gospel in the opposition thus brought out. There are two generations or kinds of men—the worldling and the Christian; but of these one behaves with a perfect understanding of the order to which he belongs; the other often acts foolishly, does not put his talent to interest. How shall he proceed in the least Christian of all occupations, which is the handling of money? He must get good out of its evil, turn it to account for everlasting life, and this by almsgiving, "yet that which remaineth, give alms; and behold, all things are clean unto you" (Luke, xi, 41). The strong conclusion follows, which lies implicit in all this, "You cannot serve God and mammon" (Luke, xvi, 13).

Much unwisdom has been shown by commentators who were perplexed that our Lord should derive a moral from conduct, evidently supposed unjust, on the steward's part; we answer, a just man's dealings would not have afforded the contrast which points the lesson, viz., that Christians should make use of opportunities, but innocently, as well as the man of business who lets slip no chance. Some critics have gone farther and connect the hidden meaning with Shakespeare's "soul of good in things evil", but we may leave that aside. Catholic preachers dwell on the special duty of helping the poor, considered as in some sense keepers of the gates of Heaven, "everlasting tents". St. Paul's "faithful dispenser" (I Cor., iv, 2) may be quoted here. The "measures" written down are enormous, beyond a private estate, which favours the notion of "publicani". The Revised Version transforms "bill" happily into "bond". It may be doubted which is "the lord" that commended the unjust steward. Whether we apply it to Christ or the rich man we shall obtain a satisfactory sense. "In their generation" should be "for their generation", as the Greek text proves. St. Ambrose, with an eye to the dreadful scandals of history, sees in the steward a wicked ruler in the Church. Tertullian (De Fuga) and, long afterwards, Salmeron apply all to the Jewish people and to the Gentiles, who were indeed debtors to the law, but who should have been treated indulgently and not repelled. Lastly, there seems no ground for the widespread belief that "mammon" was the Phoenician Plutus, or god of riches; the word signifies "money".

St. Luke (xvii, 7–10) gives a short apologue of the unprofitable servants, which may be reckoned as a parable, but which needs no explanation beyond St. Paul's phrase "not of works, but of Him that calleth" (Rom., ix, 11—A. V.). This will be true equally as regards Jews and Christians, in whose merits God crowns His own gifts.

The lesson is driven home by contrast, once more, between the pharisee and the publican (Luke, xviii, 9–14), disclosing the true economy of grace. On the one hand it is permissible to understand this with Hugo of St. Victor and others as typifying the rejection of legal and carnal Judaism; on the other, we may expand its teaching to the universal principle in St. John (iv, 23–24) when our Lord transcends the distinction of Jew and heathen, Israelite and Samaritan, in favour of a spiritual Church or kingdom, open to all. St. Augustine says (Enarr. in Ps. lxxiv), "The Jewish people boasted of their merits, the Gentiles confessed their sins". It is asked whether those "who trusted in themselves that they were righteous and despised others" were in fact the pharisees or some of the disciples. From the context we cannot decide. But it would not be impossible if, at this period, our Saviour spoke directly to the pharisees, whom He condemned (at no time for their good works, but) for their boasting and their disdain of the multitude who knew not the law (cf. Matt., xxiii, 12, 23; John, vii, 49). The pharisee's attitude, "standing", was not peculiar to him; it has ever been the customary mode of prayer among Easterns. He says "I fast twice in a week", not "twice on the Sabbath". "Tithes of all that I possess" means "all that comes to me" as revenue. This man's confession acknowledged no sin, but abounds in praise of himself—a form not yet extinct where Christians approach the sacred tribunal. One might say, "He does penance; he does not repent". The publican is of course a Jew, Zacchæus or any other; he cannot plead merit; but he has a "broken heart" which God will accept. "Be merciful to me" is well rendered from the Greek by the Vulgate, "Be propitious", a sacrificial and significant word. "Went down to his house justified rather than the other" is a Hebrew way of saying that one was and the other was not justified, as St. Augustine teaches. The expression is St. Paul's, δικαιοῦσθαι; but we are not required to examine here the idea of justification under the Old Law. Mystically, the exaltation and abasement indicated would refer to the coming of the Kingdom and the Last Judgment.

It remains to observe, generally, that a "double sense" has always been attached by the Fathers to our Lord's miracles, and to the Gospel history as a whole. They looked upon the facts as reported much in the light of sacraments, or Divine events, which could not but have a perpetual significance for the Church and on that account were recorded. This was the method of *mystical* interpretation, according to which every incident becomes a parable. But the most famous school of German critics in the nineteenth century turned that method round, seeing in the parabolic intention of the Evangelists a force which converted sayings into incidents, which made of doctrines allegories, and of illustrations miracles, so that little or nothing authentic would have been handed down to us from the life of Christ. Such is the secret of the *mythical* procedure, as exemplified in modern dealing with the multiplication of the loaves, our Lord's walking on the sea, the resurrection of the widow's son at Naim, and many other Gospel episodes (Loisy, "Ev. synopt.", passim).

Parable, in this view, has created seeming history; and not only the Johannine document but the synoptic narratives must be construed as made up from supposed prophetic references, by adaptation and quotation of Old-Testament passages. It is for the Catholic apologist to prove in detail that, however deep and far-reaching the significance attributed by the Evangelists to the facts which they relate, those facts cannot simply be resolved into myth and legend. Nature also is a parable; but it is real. "The blue zenith", says Emerson admirably, "is the point in which romance and reality meet". And again, "Nature is the vehicle of thought", the "symbol of spirit"; words and things are "emblematic". If this be so, there is a justification for the Hebrew and Christian philosophy, which sees in the world below us analogies of the highest truths, and in the Word made flesh at once the surest of facts and the most profound of symbols.

The various commentaries on the Gospels, in courses of Scripture, such as: VAN STEENKISTE, *Comment. in Evangel. secundum Matthæum* (Bruges, 1880–2); MACEVILLY, *Exposition of the Gospels* (Dublin, 1877); SCHANZ, *Commentar über das Evangel. d. h. Lucas* (Tübingen, 1883); MAAS, *Comment. of Gospel of St. Matthew* (New York, 1898); ROSE, *Evangile selon s. Matthieu* (Paris, 1904); KNABENBAUER (1894); LIAGRE (1889); FILLION (1883). Mystical exegesis in ORIGEN, AMBROSE, AUGUSTINE, GREGORY M.; literal in CHRYSOST., THEOPHYLACTUS, JEROME.

From the sixteenth century: special writers among early Protestants, CALVIN; later, VITRINGA, *Schriftmässige Erklärung* (Frankfort, 1717); among Catholics, MALDONATUS, *In IV evang.* (Pont à Mousson, 1597; latest ed., Barcelona, 1881–2); SALMERÓN, *Sermones in Parabolas* (Antwerp, 1600). Modern Protestant writers: —GRESWELL (London, 1839); TRENCH (London, 1841; last ed., 1906); BRUCE, *Parabolic Teaching of Christ* (Edinburgh, 1882). Critical.—WEISS, *Mark and Matthew* (1872); JÜLICHER (1888–99), these in German; followed by LOISY, *Les évangiles synoptiques* (Paris, 1907–8). For Jewish parables, LAUTERBACH in *Jewish Encyc.* And see lives of Christ by MAAS, FOUARD, DIDON.

WILLIAM BARRY.

Parabolani, παράβολοι, παραβαλάνοι the members of a brotherhood who in the Early Church voluntarily undertook the care of the sick and the burial of the dead. It has been asserted, though without sufficient proof, that the brotherhood was first organized during the great plague in Alexandria in the episcopate of Dionysius the Great (second half of third century). They received their name from the fact that they risked their lives (παραβάλλεσθαι τὴν ζωήν) in exposing themselves to contagious diseases. In addition to performing works of mercy they constituted a bodyguard for the bishop. Their number was never large. The Codex Theodosianus of 416 (xvi, 2, 42) restricted the enrolment in Alexandria to 500. A new law two years later increased the number to 600. In Constantinople the number was reduced according to the Codex Justinianus (I, 2, 4) from 1100 to 950. The Parabolani are not mentioned after Justinian's time. Though they were chosen by the bishop and always remained under his control, the Codex Theodosianus placed them under the supervision of the *Præfectus Augustalis*. They had neither orders nor vows, but they were enumerated among the clergy and enjoyed clerical privileges and immunities. Their presence at public gatherings or in the theatres was forbidden by law. At times they took a very active part in ecclesiastical controversies, as at the Robber Synod of Ephesus.

BINTERIM, *Denkwürdigkeiten der chriskath. Kirche*, VI, 3, 30; BINGHAM, *Antiquities*, II, 37.

PATRICK J. HEALY.

Paracelsus, THEOPHRASTUS, celebrated physician and reformer of therapeutics, b. at the Sihlbrücke, near Einsiedeln, in the Canton of Schwyz, 10 Nov., 1493; d. at Salzburg, 24 Sept., 1541. He is known also as Theophrastus von Hohenheim, Eremita (of Einsiedeln), and Theophrastus Bombastus von Hohenheim. It is now established that the family originally came from Würtemberg, where the noble family of Bombastus was in possession of the ancestral castle of Hohenheim near Stuttgart until 1409, Paracelsus is the Latin form in common use among the German scholars of the time. Wilhelm Bombast von Hohenheim, physician to the monastery of Einsiedeln and father of Theophrastus, changed the family residence to Villach in Carinthia (c. 1502), where at the time of his death (8 Sept., 1534), he was city physician.

Paracelsus mentions the following as his earliest teachers, his father, Eberhard Paumgartner, Bishop of Lavant, Matthæus von Scheidt, Bishop of Seckau, and Matthæus Schacht, Bishop of Freising. He was initiated into the mysteries of alchemy by Joannes Trithemius (1462-1516), Abbot of Sponheim, and a prolonged interval spent in the laboratories of Sigmund Fugger at Schwaz made him familiar with metallurgy. All his life restless and eager for travel, he attended the most important universities of Germany, France, and Italy, and, in 1526, went to Strasburg, where, already a doctor, he joined the guild of surgeons. The same year he was appointed, probably through the influence of Joannes Œcolampadius, the theologian, and Joannes Frobenius, the publisher, to the office of city physician of Basle, with which was connected the privilege of lecturing at the university.

His teaching, as well as his opposition to the prevailing Galeno-Arabic system, the burning of Avicenna's writings in a public square, the polemical tone of his discourses, which, contrary to all custom, were delivered in German, his dissensions with the faculty, attacks on the greed of apothecaries, and to a certain extent, also, his success as a practitioner—all drew upon him the hatred of those in authority. In February he fled from Basle to Colmar. A typical vagrant, his subsequent life was spent in continual wandering, surrounded by a troop of adventurers, with the reputation of a charlatan, but all the while observing all things with remarkable zeal, and busied with the composition of his numerous works. In 1529 we find him at Nuremberg, soon afterwards at Beritzhausen and Amberg, in 1531 at St. Gall, later at Innsbruck, in 1534 at Sterzing and Meran, in 1535 at Bad Pfäffers, Augsburg, 1537 at Vienna, Presburg, and Villach, and finally at Salzburg, where he died a natural death and, in accordance with his wish, was buried in the cemetery of St. Sebastian. The present tomb in the porch of St. Sebastian's Church, was erected by some unknown person in 1752. According to recent research the portrait on the monument is that of the father of Paracelsus. Paracelsus did not join the ranks of the Reformers, evincing, rather, an aversion to any form of religion. The clause in his will, however, giving directions for a requiem Mass would indicate that before his death he regarded himself as a member of the Church.

Paracelsus is a phenomenon in the history of medicine, a genius tardily recognized, who in his impetuosity sought to overturn the old order of things, thereby rousing bitter antagonists. He sought to substitute something better for what seemed to him antiquated and erroneous in therapeutics, thus falling into the mistake of other violent reformers, who, during the process of rebuilding, underestimate the work of their contemporaries. He was not in touch with the humanist movement or with the study of anatomy then zealously pursued, the most prominent factors in reorganization; leaving out of consideration his great services to special departments, he stands alone and misunderstood. His influence was felt specially in Wittenberg, but only in a few schools of Germany, while he was entirely discounted throughout Italy.

THEOPHRASTUS PARACELSUS

He sought the cause of pathological changes, not in the cardinal humours, blood, phlegm, yellow and black gall (humoral pathology), but in the entities, which he divided into *ens astrorum* (cosmic influences differing with climate and country), *ens veneni* (toxic matter originating in the food), the cause of contagious diseases, *ens naturale et spirituale* (defective physical or mental constitution), and *ens deale* (an affliction sent by Providence). The diseases known as tartaric, especially gout and lithiasas, are caused by the deposit of determinate toxins (tartar), are discovered chiefly by the urine test, and are cured by means of alkalies. Like the followers of Hippocrates he prescribes the observation of nature and dietetic directions, but attaches too great a value to experience (empiricism). In nature all substances have two kinds of influences, helpful (*essentia*) and harmful (*venena*), which are separated by means of alchemy. It requires experience to recognize essences as such and to employ them at the proper moment. His aim was to discover a specific remedy (*arcanum*) for every disease.

It was precisely here, however, that he fell into error, since not infrequently he drew a conclusion as to the availability of certain remedies from purely external signs, e. g., when he taught that the pricking of thistles cures internal inflammation. This untrustworthy "doctrine of signatures" was at a later date developed farther by Rademacher, and to a certain extent also by Hahnemann. Although the theories of Paracelsus as contrasted with the Galeno-Arabic system indicate no advance, inasmuch as they ignore entirely the study of anatomy, still his reputation as a reformer of therapeutics is justified in that he broke new paths in the science. He may be taken as the founder of the modern materia medica, and pioneer of scientific chemistry, since before his time medical science received no assistance from alchemy. To

Paracelsus is due the use of mercury for syphilis as well as a number of other metallic remedies, probably a result of his studies in Schwaz, and partly his acquaintance with the quicksilver works in Idria. He was the first to point out the value of mineral waters, especially the Pfäffer water, even attempting to produce it by artificial means. He recognized the tincture of gallnut as a reagent for the iron properties of mineral water. He showed a particular preference for native herbs, from which he obtained "essences" and "tinctures", the use of which was to replace the curious composite medicines so popular at the time. Regarding him from an ethical standpoint, his noble ideals of the medical profession, his love for the poor, and his piety deserve to be exalted. The perusal of his writings disproves the accusation of drunkenness which had so often been made against him by his enemies.

For the most part Paracelsus dictated his works, in many cases bequeathing the manuscript to friends with the request to have it printed. His name, being well known, was often misappropriated, so that later it became necessary to draw a fixed line between authentic and unauthentic writings. The former are characterized by a simple, direct, intelligible style. Cf. Schubert-Sudhoff, "Paracelsusforschungen" (Frankfort on the Main, 1887-89); Sudhoff, "Bibliographia Paracelsica" (Berlin, 1894); Idem, "Versuch einer Kritik der Echtheit der Paracelsischen Schriften" (Berlin, 1894-99). The best of the collective editions, which, however, includes some unauthentic works, is that of Huser (Basle, 1589-91, 10 vols.; Frankfort, 1603, 3 vols.; Strasburg, 1616). A detailed list of the authentic and unauthentic writings is to be found in Albr. von Haller, "Bibliotheca medicinæ practicæ", II (Basle, 1777), 2-12. Among his most important writings may be mentioned: "Opus Paramirum" I, II, re-edited by Dr. Franz Strunz (Jena, 1904), which contains the system of Paracelsus; "Drei Bücher von den Franzosen" (syphilis and venereal diseases); "Grosse Wundarznei, über das Bad Pfäffers, über die Pest in Sterzing".

FERGUSON, *Bibliographia Paracelsica* (Glasgow, 1877); *The Hermetic and Alchemical Writings of Aureolus Philippus Theophrastus Bombast*; ed. WAITE (London, 1894); HARTMANN, *The Life of Paracelsus and the Substance of his Teachings* (London, 1886); MOOK, *Theophrastus Paracelsus* (Würzburg, 1876); ABERLE, *Grabdenkmal, Schädel und Abbildungen des Theophrastus Paracelsus* (Salzburg, 1891); STRUNZ, *Theophrastus Paracelsus sein Leben und Persönlichkeit* (Leipzig, 1903).

LEOPOLD SENFELDER.

Paraclete, Comforter (L. *Consolator;* Gr. παράκλητος), an appellation of the Holy Ghost. The Greek word which, as a designation of the Holy Ghost at least, occurs only in St. John (xiv, 16, 26; xv, 26; xvi, 7), has been variously translated "advocate", "intercessor", "teacher", "helper", "comforter". This last rendering, though at variance with the passive form of the Greek, is justified by Hellenistic usage, a number of ancient versions, patristic and liturgical authority, and the evident needs of the Johannine context. According to St. John the mission of the Paraclete is to abide with the disciples after Jesus has withdrawn His visible presence from them; to inwardly bring home to them the teaching externally given by Christ and thus to stand as a witness to the doctrine and work of the Saviour. There is no reason for limiting to the Apostles themselves the comforting influence of the Paraclete as promised in the Gospel (Matt., x, 19; Mark, xiii, 11; Luke, xii, 11, xxi, 14) and described in Acts, ii. In the above declaration of Christ, Cardinal Manning rightly sees a new dispensation, that of the Spirit of God, the Sanctifier. The Paraclete comforts the Church by guaranteeing her inerrancy and fostering her sanctity (see CHURCH). He comforts each individual soul in many ways. Says St. Bernard (Parvi Sermones): "De Spiritu Sancto testatur Scriptura quia procedit, spirat, inhabitat, replet, glorificat. Procedendo prædestinat; spirando vocat quos prædestinavit; inhabitando justificat quos vocavit; replendo accumulat meritis quos justificavit; glorificando ditat prœmiis quos accumulavit meritis". Every salutary condition, power, and action, in fact the whole range of our salvation, comes within the Comforter's mission. Its extraordinary effects are styled gifts, fruits, beatitudes. Its ordinary working is sanctification with all it entails, habitual grace, infused virtues, adoption, and the right to the celestial inheritance. "The charity of God", says St. Paul (Rom., v, 5), "is poured forth in our hearts by the Holy Ghost who is given to us." In that passage the Paraclete is both the giver and the gift; the giver of grace (*donum creatum*) and the gift of the Father and the Son (*donum increatum*). St. Paul teaches repeatedly that the Holy Ghost dwells in us (Rom., viii, 9, 11; I Cor., iii, 16).

That indwelling of the Paraclete in the justified soul is not to be understood as though it were the exclusive work of the third Person nor as though it constituted the *formalis causa* of our justification. The soul, inwardly renovated by habitual grace, becomes the habitation of the three Persons of the Blessed Trinity (John, xiv, 23), yet that indwelling is rightly appropriated to the third Person who is the Spirit of Love. As to the mode and explanation of the Holy Ghost's inhabitation in the soul of the just, Catholic theologians are not agreed. St. Thomas (I, Q. XLIII, a. 3) proposes the rather vague and unsatisfactory simile "sicut cognitum in cognoscente et amatum in amante". To Oberdöffer it is an ever acting force, maintaining and unfolding habitual grace in us. Verani takes it to be merely objective presence, in the sense that the justified soul is the object of a special solicitude and choice love from the Paraclete. Forget, and in this he pretends to bring out the true thought of St. Thomas, suggests a sort of mystical and quasi-experimental union of the soul with the Paraclete, differing in degree but not in kind from the intuitive vision and beatific love of the elect. In so difficult a matter, we can only revert to the words of St. Paul (Rom., viii, 15): "You have received the spirit of adoption of sons whereby we cry: Abba (Father)." The mission of the Paraclete detracts nothing from the mission of Christ. In heaven Christ remains our παράκλητος or advocate (I John, ii, 1). In this world, He is with us even to the consummation of the world (Matt., xxviii, 20), but He is with us through His Spirit of whom He says: "I will send Him to you. He shall glorify me; because He shall receive of mine, and shall shew it to you" (John, xvi, 7, 14). See HOLY GHOST.

VERANI, *Theol. Specul. De Trinitate*, XV, iii (Munich, 1700); GAUME, *Traité de l'Esprit-Saint*, II (Paris, s.d.), 7; OBERDÖRFFER, *De inhabitatione Spiritus Sancti* (Tournai, 1890); FORGET, *De l'habitation du St-Esprit* (Paris, 1898); BELLEVUE, *L'Œuvre du Saint-Esprit* (Paris, 1902); MANNING, *The Internal Mission of the Holy Ghost* (London, 1875); DEVINE, *A Manual of Ascetical Theology* (London, 1902); WILHELM AND SCANNELL, *A Manual of Catholic Theology* (London and New York, 1906); see also KITTO, CHEYNE, HASTINGS, VIGOUROUX; commentators on St. John, CORNELIUS À LAPIDE, FILLION, CALMES, etc.

J. F. SOLLIER.

Paradise. See TERRESTRIAL PARADISE.

Para du Phanjas, FRANÇOIS, writer, b. at the Castle of Phanja Champsaur, Basses-Alpes, 1724; d. at Paris, 1797. After his admission into the Society of Jesus in 1740 he taught mathematics and physics and later philosophy at Besançon. Many of his pupils became distinguished in the sciences and in apologetics. He was esteemed both for his learning and for his conciliatory disposition. On the suppression of the Society, the Archbishop of Paris and the Princess Adelaide granted him a pension. In 1791 he took the oath to the new authorities, but retracted it as soon as the pope had spoken. Amongst his works are: "Théorie des êtres sensibles" (5 vols., Paris, 1772; 4 vols., Paris,

1788); this work is both an encyclopedia of physics and a philosophy of the sciences; "Principes du calcul" (1st ed., Paris, 1773; 2nd ed., 1783); "Théorie des nouvelles découvertes en physique et en chimie"; "Théorie des êtres insensibles" (3 vols., Paris, 1779). Para's eclecticism is not always too happy. He sides with Clarke in the latter's discussion with Leibniz as to the nature of absolute space. He keeps too close to Condillac's theory of the origin of ideas, and is deeply influenced by Malebranche's occasionalism. His works, "Les principes de la saine philosophie conciliés avec ceux de la philosophie, ou la philosophie de la religion", and "Tableau historique et philosophique de la religion", proved very useful to the apologists of the succeeding generation. The general treatment is marked by ingenuity in answering objections and the judicious use of his erudition.

SOMMERVOGEL, *Bibl. de la C. de J.*, VI, 192; QUÉRARD, *La France littéraire*; ROCHAS, *Biographie du Dauphiné*, II, 213; CHÉRIAS, *Aperçu sur les illustrations gapençaises* (1849); FELLER, *Journal* (1780), 507–23.

P. SCHEUER.

Parætonium, a titular see of Lybia Secunda or Inferior (i. e. Marmarica), suffragan of Darnis. This city, which some claim should be called Ammonia, owed its celebrity to its port, whence Alexander visited the oracle of Amun (Ammon). Mark Antony stopped there before Actium. Justinian fortified it to protect Egypt on the west. It has since disappeared and the port is partially covered with sand; the site, long called by the Arabs, Baretoun, to-day bears the name Mirsa Berek, in the vilayet of Benghazi (Tripolitana). Mention is made of three bishops: Titus, present at the Council of Nicæa, 325; Siras, an Arian; and his successor Gaius, who assisted at the Council of Alexandria, 362 (Le Quien, "Oriens christ." II, 631).

SMITH, *Dictionary of Greek and Roman Geog.*, s. v.; PACHO, *Voyage dans la Marmarique* (Paris, 1829), 28.

S. PÉTRIDÈS.

Paraguay, one of the inland republics of South America, separated from Spain and constituted as an independent state in 1811.

Etymology.—Historians disagree as to the true origin of the word "Paraguay", one of the most common versions being that it is a corruption of the term "Payagua", the name of an Indian tribe, and "i", the Guaraní for water or river, thus "Paragua-i", or "river of the Payaguas". Another version, which is accepted as more correct, is that which construes the word as meaning "crowned river", from "Paragua" (palm-crown) and "i" (water or river).

Geography.—The Republic of Paraguay, with an area of about 196,000 square miles, occupies the central part of South America, bounded by Brazil to the north and east, by the Argentine Republic to the south-east and south-west, and by Bolivia to the west and north-west. It lies between 22° 4′ and 27° 30′ S. lat., and 54° 32′ and 61° 20′ W. long. The Paraguay River divides its territory into two great regions, viz.: the Oriental, which is Paraguay proper, and the Occidental, commonly known as the Chaco.

Population.—The population of Paraguay is composed of Indians, white Europeans, a very small number of negroes, and the offspring of the mixture of the various races, among whom the Spanish-Indian predominates. According to the last census (1908) the total number of inhabitants is 805,000, of which nearly 700,000 are Catholics. Most of the Indian tribes which are still uncivilized are scattered throughout the immense territory of the Chaco, the principal ones being the Guaranís, the Payaguas, and the Agaces.

Languages.—The official and predominating language is Spanish, and of the Indian dialects the one most in use is Guaraní.

History.—Originally, Paraguay comprised the entire basin of the River Plate, and it was discovered in 1525 by Sebastian Cabot during his explorations along the Upper Paraná and Paraguay Rivers. He was followed by Juan de Ayolas and Domingo Martinez de Irala (1536–38). It was during the first administration of the latter (1538–42) that Christianity was first preached, by the Franciscan Fathers, who, as in almost every instance, were the priests accompanying the first conquerors. In 1542 Irala was superseded by Alvar Nuñez Cabeza de Vaca, famous for his explorations in North America, who had been appointed governor of the River Plate, and received among other instructions from the king that of "propagating the Christian religion with the greatest zeal". This task was, however, beset with many difficulties. In the first place the priests, although picked and of high moral character, were few in number; then they had to preach through interpreters; and worst of all, the cruel treatment of the Indians by the soldiers was itself sufficient to engender in the hearts of the natives a keen antipathy towards the religion that their new masters professed. Furthermore, the corrupt morals of the conquerors, their insatiable thirst for riches, their quarrels in the struggle for power, and their own discords and controversies could not but render their religion suspicious to the Indians. The new governor was well aware of all this; so his first official act upon reaching Asunción (11 March, 1542) was to call the missionaries together to convey to them the wishes of his sovereign, impressing upon them the kindness with which the Indians should be treated as the necessary means of facilitating their conversion; he made them responsible for the success of the undertaking. He then convoked the Indians of the surrounding country and exhorted them to receive the Faith. The administration of Alvar Nuñez was characterized by his wisdom, tact, and spirit of justice, no less than by his courage, energy, and perseverance. He succeeded in subduing the Indians, tribe after tribe, mainly through a policy of conciliation, and by force when necessary. It was thus that the march of Christianity in Paraguay was greatly facilitated during his short régime (1542–44). His achievements, however, only served to increase the jealousies of Martinez de Irala, who, never forgetting his relegation to a subordinate post, finally succeeded in turning most of the officers and soldiers against the governor. As a result of this rebellion, Nuñez was made a prisoner and sent to Spain, where he was acquitted after a trial that lasted eight years.

Irala was then left in full command of the province (1542) until his death in 1557. His second administration was noted for the many improvements he introduced, such as the establishment of schools, the construction of the Cathedral of Asunción and other public buildings, the promotion of local industries, etc. He was succeeded by Gonzalo de Mendoza, upon whose death (1559) Francisco Ortiz de Vergara was made governor, ruling until 1565, when he was deposed. Juan Ortiz de Zarate was then appointed, but, having sailed for Spain immediately thereafter in order to obtain the confirmation of the king, Felipe de Cáceres was left in charge of the government. Although Zarate secured the confirmation, he did not assume command, for he died in the same year. Juan de Garay then took the reins of government, and upon his assassination by the Indians in 1580, he was followed by Alonso de Vera y Aragon, who resigned in 1587 leaving Juan Torres de Vera in command.

Torres de Vera was still governing the province when S. Francis Solanus, a Spanish Franciscan missionary, made his celebrated journey through the Chaco to Paraguay, coming from Peru. In the course of that expedition he preached to the natives in their own tongues and converted thousands and thousands of them (1588–89). When Torres de Vera resigned his post, Hernando Arias de Saavedra, a native of Asunción, was elected governor, ruling until 1593, when Diego Valdes de Banda was appointed in his stead. Upon the death of the latter, Hernandarias. as he is also known, again took command in 1601. It was during this second administration of Arias (1601–09) that the Jesuits obtained official recognition for the first time in Paraguay, by virtue of an order from Philip III (1608), approving the plan submitted by Governor Arias for the establishment of missions by the disciples of Loyola. This marked the beginning of the flourishing period of the Church in Paraguay, as well as that of the welfare and advancement of the natives, just as the expulsion of the Jesuit Fathers in 1767, by order of Charles III, marked the decadence of the Faith among the Indians of the Chaco and their falling back into their former state of barbarism.

Paraguay was then nominally under the jurisdiction of the Viceroy of Peru, but in 1776 the Viceroyalty of La Plata was created, including Paraguay.

Finally, when in 1811 Paraguay declared its independence of Spain, the foundations of the Church were firmly established, as was the case in the other Latin-American countries.

After its emancipation, the country was ruled, more or less despotically, by José Gaspar Rodriguez de Francia, as dictator (1811–40); Carlos Antonio Lopez (1841–62); Marshal Francisco Solano Lopez, a son of the former, during whose rule (1862–70) was fought one of the bloodiest wars in the history of South America, between Paraguay on one side, and Brazil, Argentina, and Uruguay on the other. The results of this struggle, provoked by the political ambitions of Lopez, were most disastrous for Paraguay. It began on 24 Nov., 1864, and lasted until 1 March, 1870, on which date the Paraguayan president was killed in the battle of Cerro Cora. At the close of the war, Paraguay was in a state of desolation, with its population decimated, its agriculture destroyed, and its treasury completely exhausted. After the peace was signed, a constitution was promulgated (1870), under whose shadow the republic has recuperated within the comparatively short term of forty years, having now entered upon an era of prosperity, peace, and stability of government.

Relations between the Church and State.—Under the constitution in force, promulgated 25 Nov., 1870, the religion of the nation is the Roman Catholic, and the chief prelate must be a Paraguayan. Congress, however, has no power to forbid the free exercise of any other religion within the territory of the Republic (article 3).

By authority of paragraph 7, article 2, of the constitution, the president exercises the rights of national patronage vested in the republic, and nominates the bishop of the diocese, said nomination to be made upon presentation of three names by the legislative senate, with the advice and consent of the ecclesiastical senate or, in default thereof, of the national clergy assembled. It is further provided by the constitution (par. 8, art. 102) that the president may grant or refuse, with the advice of congress, the acceptance of the decrees of the councils and of the Bulls, Briefs, or Rescripts of the Supreme Pontiff.

The Minister of Justice, Worship, and Public Instruction is charged with the inspection of all branches of Divine worship in so far as the national patronage over the Church is concerned; it is also his duty to negotiate with the Apostolic Delegates in behalf of the executive. The fiscal budget assigns the sum of $2,259 for the salaries of the bishop, vicar-general, and secretary of the diocese.

The Diocese.—The Diocese of Paraguay (*Paraguayensis*) was created under a Bull issued by Paul III on 1 July, 1547, eleven years after the foundation of Asuncion by Juan de Ayolas, 15 Aug., 1536, and is therefore the oldest see of the River Plate. The first bishop was Father Pedro de La Torre, a Franciscan, who arrived at Asuncion on the eve of Palm Sunday, 1555, during the second administration of Martinez de Irala. Directly dependent upon Rome, its jurisdiction extends over the whole territory of the republic, which is divided into 102 parishes, 6 of them being located in the capital. The present Cathedral of Asunción was formally dedicated on 27 Oct., 1845.

Laws Affecting the Church.—As above stated, the constitution provides that worship shall be free within the territory of the republic. The incorporation of churches and tenure of church property in Paraguay are governed under laws similar to those in force in the Argentine Republic, and the same may be said as to wills and testaments, charitable bequests, marriage, divorce, etc., the Argentine Civil Code having been adopted as a law of the country under an act of congress dated 19 Aug., 1876. All Catholic marriages are *ipso facto* valid for the purposes of the civil law, and by an act of 27 Sept., 1887, marriages performed under other rites should be recorded in the civil register in order that they may have legal force.

Under the Paraguayan law the clergy are exempt from military and jury service, and all accessories of Divine worship are admitted free of duty when imported at the instance of the bishop.

Law for the Conversion of the Indian Tribes.—On 6 Sept., 1909, a law was enacted providing for the conversion of Indians to Christianity and civilization. By virtue of this law, the President of the Republic is authorized to grant public lands to individuals or companies organized for the purpose of converting the said tribes, in parcels not exceeding 7,500 hectares (about 18,750 acres) each, on which the *concessionaire* shall establish a reduction with the necessary churches, houses, schools, etc. Several English Episcopalian missions have been established in the Chaco under this law.

Education.—By law of 22 July, 1909, and in accordance with the Constitution (Art. 8) primary instruction is compulsory in the republic for all children between 5 and 14 years of age. At the beginning of 1909 there were in Paraguay 344 primary schools, attended by 40,605 pupils, and employing 756 teachers. These figures do not include the private schools, which had during the same year an attendance of from 2,000 to 3,000 pupils. The course of primary instruction covers a period of six years. Secondary instruction is given in five national colleges, one of which is in the capital, and the others in Villa Concepción, Villa Rica, Villa Encarnación, and Villa del Pilar. There are also two normal schools for the preparation of teachers. Higher education is provided for in the University of Asunción, which offers a six-years' course in law, social sciences, and medicine. Further courses in pharmacy and other branches have recently been added. There is besides a school of agriculture and a military academy.

Conciliar Seminary.—For the education of young men in the ecclesiastical career there is at Asunción an excellent institution known as the "Seminario Conciliar", founded in 1881 upon the initiative of Ana Escate, who personally collected the funds necessary for its establishment. During the thirty years of its existence sixty priests have graduated therefrom, one of them being the present Bishop of Paraguay, Monsignor Juan Sinforiano Bogarin.

WASHBURN, *History of Paraguay* (Boston, 1871); FUNES, *Ensayo de la Historia Civil del Paraguay*, Buenos Ayres y Tucuman (Buenos Aires, 1816); BOUGARDE, *Paraguay*, tr. (New York, 1892); MASTERMAN, *Seven Eventful Years in Paraguay* (London, 1870); GRAHAM, *A Vanished Arcadia* (New York, 1901); BANCO AGRICOLA DEL PARAGUAY, *Paraguay* (Asunción, 1910); BUTLER, *Paraguay* (Philadelphia, 1901); YUBERO, *Guia General del Paraguay* (Asunción, 1910); *Bulletin of the Pan-American Union* (August, 1910).

JULIAN MORENO-LACALLE.

Paraguay, REDUCTIONS OF. See REDUCTIONS OF PARAGUAY.

Parahyba, Diocese of (Parahybenesis), in the State of Parahyba, Brazil, suffragan of Bahia, founded 27 July, 1892, having been separated from the Diocese of Olinda (q. v.). It is coterminous with the State of Parahyba, one of the smallest in Brazil, bordering on the Atlantic Ocean, and is bounded, north by the State of Rio Grande do Norte, south by Pernambuco, and west by Ceará. It has an area of 28,850 square miles. The episcopal city, which is also the state capital, dates from a Portuguese settlement of 1579. It is situated partly on an elevated plateau and partly on the surrounding plain, the latter (and newer) section along the Parahyba comprising, with its port of Cobadello, the business quarter. Sugar, cacao, rice, and tobacco are some of the products of this coast region, while the slopes back of the town are heavily forested. The chief ecclesiastical buildings of the city are the cathedral, Notre Dame dos Neves (Our Lady of the Snows), and the former Jesuit College, now occupied by the State offices. The first and present (1911) bishop of the diocese, Mgr de Miranda Henriques, is a native of Parahyba. Born 30 August, 1855, he studied at the Pio-Latino American College at Rome and received there the degree of Doctor of Canon Law. Ordained priest 18 September, 1880, he was made canon of Bahia 14 August, 1885, and appointed bishop 2 January, 1894. He was consecrated on 7 January, 1894, and assumed his duties the following March. The diocese numbers (1911) 735,572 Catholics; 1000 Protestants; 48 parishes; 52 secular, 10 regular priests; 1 college.

United States of Brazil (issued by the Bureau of American Republics, Washington, 1901); Galanti, *Compendio de Hist. do Brazil* (4 vols., São Paulo, 1896); *Annuaire pontifi. cath.*

K. Crofton.

Paralipomenon, The Books of (Παραλειπομένων, α′, β′; Libri Paralipomenon), two books of the Bible containing a summary of sacred history from Adam to the end of the Captivity. The title Paralipomenon, books "of things passed over", which, from the Septuagint, passed into the old Latin Bible and thence into the Vulgate, is commonly taken to imply that they supplement the narrative of the Books of Kings (otherwise known as I–II Sam. and I–II Kings); but this explanation is hardly supported by the contents of the books, and does not account for the present participle. The view of St. Jerome, who considers Paralipomenon as equivalent to "epitome of the Old Testament", is probably the true one. The title would accordingly denote that many things are passed over in these books. The Hebrew title is *Dîbhĕrê Hâyyāmîm*, "the acts of the days" or "annals". In the printed Hebrew and the Protestant Bibles they are entitled "Books of Chronicles".

Unity and Places in the Canon.—The two books are really one work, and are treated as one in the Hebrew MSS. and in the Massoretic summary appended to the second book. The division was first made in the Septuagint for the sake of convenience, and thence was adopted into the Latin Bibles. The Hebrew text was first divided in Bomberg's edition of the rabbinical Bible (Venice, 1516-7). Moreover, there is a probability that Paralipomenon originally formed part of a larger work which included the two Books of Esdras (Esdras Nehemias). For not only is there similarity of diction and style, of spirit and method, but I Esdras begins where II Par. ends, the decree of Cyrus being repeated and completed.

It should be remarked, however, that these facts can be explained by simple community of authorship. In the Septuagint and Vulgate, as well as in the Protestant bibles, the Books of Paralipomenon are placed immediately after the Books of Kings. In the printed editions of the Hebrew Bible they stand at the end of the third division, or *Kĕthûbhîm*.

Contents.—The first part of I Par. (i–ix), which is a sort of introduction to the rest of the work, contains a series of genealogical and statistical lists, interspersed with short historical notes. It comprises: (1) the genealogy of the patriarchs from Adam to Jacob (i); (2) the genealogy of the twelve tribes (ii–viii); (3) a list of the families of Juda, Benjamin, and Levi dwelling in Jerusalem after the Exile, with the genealogy of the family of Saul repeated (ix). The second part of I Par. contains the history of the reign of David preceded by the account of the death of Saul (x–xxix). II Par. comprises the reign of Solomon (i–ix), and the reigns of the kings of Juda (x–xxxvi, 21). Part of the edict of Cyrus allowing the Jews to return and to rebuild the temple is added as a conclusion (xxxvi, 22–23). The historical part of Paralipomenon thus covers the same period as the last three Books of Kings. Hence naturally much of the matter is the same in both; often, indeed, the two narratives not only agree in the facts they relate, but describe them almost in the same words. The Books of Paralipomenon also agree with the Books of Kings in plan and general arrangement. But side by side with these agreements there are many differences. The Books of Paralipomenon narrate some events more briefly, or present them in a different manner, and omit others altogether (e. g., the adultery of David, the violation of Thamar, the murder of Amnon, and the rebellion of Absalom), while they dwell more on facts regarding the temple, its worship and its ministers, furnishing much information on these subjects which is not found in the other books. Moreover, they ignore the northern kingdom except where the history of Juda requires mention of it.

Object.—On comparing Paralipomenon with the Books of Kings we are forced to the conclusion that the writer's purpose was not to supplement the omissions of these latter books. The objects of his interest are the temple and its worship, and he intends primarily to write the religious history of Juda with the temple as its centre, and, as intimately connected with it, the history of the house of David. This clearly appears when we consider what he mentions and what he omits. Of Saul he narrates only his death as an introduction to the reign of David. In the history of David's reign he gives a full account of the translation of the ark to Mount Sion, of the preparations for the building of the temple, and of the levitical families and their offices; the wars and the other events of the reign he either tells briefly, or passes over altogether. Solomon's reign is almost reduced to the account of the building and the dedication of the temple. After the disruption of the kingdom the apostate tribes are hardly mentioned, while the reigns of the pious kings, Asa, Josaphat, Joas, Ezechias, and Josias, who brought about a revival of religion and showed great zeal for the temple and its worship, are specially dwelt on. Again, the additions to the narrative of the Books of Kings in most cases refer to the temple, its worship and its ministers. Nor is the decree of Cyrus allowing the rebuilding of the temple without significance. The same purpose may be noted in the genealogical section, where the tribes of Juda and Levi are given special prominence and have their genealogies continued beyond the Exile. The author, however, writes his history with a practical object in view. He wishes to urge the people to a faithful and exact adherence to the worship of God in the restored temple, and to impress upon them that thus only will the community deserve God's blessings and protection. Hence he places before them the example of the past, especially of the pious kings who were distinguished for their zeal in building the temple or in promoting the splendour of its worship. Hence, too, he takes every occasion to show that the kings, and with them the people, prospered or were delivered from great calamities because of their attachment to God's worship, or experienced misfortune because of their unfaithfulness. The frequent mention of the Levites and of their offices was probably intended to induce them to value their calling and to carry out faithfully their duties.

AUTHOR AND TIME OF COMPOSITION.—The Books of Paralipomenon were undoubtedly written after the Restoration. For the genealogy of the house of David is carried beyond Zorobabel (I Par., iii, 19–24), and the very decree of Cyrus allowing the return is cited. Moreover, the value of the sums collected by David for the building of the temple is expressed in darics (I Par., xxix, 7, Heb.), which were not current in Palestine till the time of the Persian domination. The peculiarities of style and diction also point to a time later than the Captivity. The older writers generally attributed the authorship to Esdras. Most modern non-Catholic scholars attribute the work to an unknown writer and place its date between 300 and 250 B. C. The main reasons for this late date are that the descendants of Zorobabel are given to the sixth (in the Septuagint and the Vulgate to the eleventh) generation, and that in II Esdras (xii, 10, 11, 22) the list of the high-priests extends to Jeddoa, who, according to Josephus, held the pontificate in the time of Alexander the Great. These lists, however, show signs of having been brought up to date by a later hand and cannot, therefore, be considered as decisive. On the other hand, a writer living in Greek times would not be likely to express the value of ancient money in darics. Moreover, a work written for the purpose mentioned above would be more in place in the time immediately following the Restoration, while the position and character of Esdras would point him out as its author. Hence most Catholic authors still adhere to Esdrine authorship, and place the time of composition at the end of the fifth or at the beginning of the fourth century B. C.

HISTORICAL VALUE.—The reliability of the Books of Paralipomenon as a historical work has been severely attacked by such critics as de Wette, Wellhausen etc. The author is accused of exaggeration, of misrepresenting facts, and even of appealing to imaginary documents. This harsh judgment has been considerably mitigated by more recent writers of the same school, who, while admitting errors, absolve the author of intentional misrepresentation. The objections urged against the books cannot be examined here in detail; a few general remarks in vindication of their truthfulness must suffice. In the first place, the books have suffered at the hands of copyists; textual errors in names and in numbers, which latter originally were only indicated by letters, are especially numerous. Gross exaggerations, such as the slaying of 7000 charioteers (I Par., xix, 18) as against 700 in II Kings (x, 18) and the impossibly large armies mentioned in II Par. (xiii, 3), are plainly to be attributed to this cause. In the next place, if the sections common to Paralipomenon and the Books of Kings are compared, substantial agreement is found to exist between them. If the author, then, reproduces his sources with substantial accuracy in the cases where his statements can be controlled by comparing them with those of another writer who has used the same documents, there is no reason to suspect that he acted differently in the case of other sources. His custom of referring his readers to the documents from which he has drawn his information should leave no doubt on the subject. In the third place, the omission of the facts not to the credit of the pious kings (e. g. the adultery of David) is due to the object which the author has in view, and proves no more against his truthfulness than the omission of the history of the northern tribes. He did not intend to write a full history of the kings of Juda, but a history for the purpose of edification. Hence, in speaking of the kings whom he proposes as models, he naturally omits details which are not edifying. Such a presentation, while one-sided, is no more untruthful than a panegyric in which the foibles of the subject are passed over. The picture is correct as far as it goes, only it is not complete.

GIGOT, *Special Introd.*, I (New York, 1901), 291 sqq.; DRIVER, *Liter. of the O. T.* (Edinburgh, 1909), 516 sqq.; CURTIS AND MADDEN, *Comm. on the Books of Chronicles* (Edinburgh, 1910); CORNELY, *Introd.*, II (Paris, 1897); i, 311 sqq.; HUMMELAUER, *Comm. in Lib. I Par.* (Paris, 1905); KAULEN, *Einleitung* (3rd ed., Freiburg, 1890), 240 sqq.; MOVERS, *Kritische Untersuchungen über die bibl. Chronik* (Bonn, 1834); KEIL, *Apologetischer Versuch über die B. der Chronik* (Berlin, 1834); NAGL, *Die nachdavidische Königsgesch. Israels* (Vienna, 1905); MANGENOT in VIGOUROUX, *Dict. de la Bible*, s. v. *Paralipomènes, Les deux livres des*; KLOSTERMANN in *Realencyclop. für prot. Theol.*, s. v. *Chronik, Die Bücher der*.

F. BECHTEL.

Parallelism, the balance of verse with verse, an essential and characteristic feature in Hebrew poetry. Either by repetition or by antithesis or by some other device, thought is set over against thought, form balances form, in such wise as to bring the meaning home to one strikingly and agreeably. In the hymns of the Assyrians and Babylonians parallelism is fundamental and essential. Schrader takes it for granted that the Hebrews got this poetic principle from them (Jahrbuch für Protestant. Theologie, i, 121); a common Semitic source, in days long before the migration of Abraham, is a likelier hypothesis. The Syriac, Vulgate, and other ancient versions, recognized and to a certain extent reproduced the balance of verse with verse in the Bible. Not until the sixteenth century did Hebraists speak of it as a poetical principle, essential to the Hebrews. It was then that Rabbi Azaria de Rossi, in his work מאור עינים "The Light of the Eyes", first divided various poetic portions of the Bible into verses that brought out the fact of parallelism and of a fixed number of recurrent accents. Schöttgen ("Horæ Hebraicæ et Talmudicæ", Dissertatio vi, Dresden, 1733, vol. I, p. 1252), though erring in that he calls it absurd to speak of iambs and hexameters in Hebrew poetry, deserves the credit of having first drawn up the canons of parallelism, which he calls exergasia (ἐξεργασία, the working up of a subject, Polybius, X, xlv, 6). According to these canons Biblical prose differs from Biblical poetry solely in that the poet works up a subject by reiteration of the same idea either in the same or in different words, by omission of either the subject or the predicate, by antithesis of contrary thoughts etc. Bishop Lowth (De Sacra Poesi Hebræorum, 1753; Isaiah, 1778) based his investigations upon the studies of Schöttgen and coined the term parallelism. He distinguished three kinds of parallelism: the synonymous, the antithetical, and the synthetic. His conclusions have been generally accepted.

I. *Synonymous Parallelism.*—The very same thought is repeated, at times in the very same words. The following examples, being close translations of the original text, will better illustrate Hebrew parallelism than does our Douai version which (in regard to the Psalms) has reached us through the medium of a Latin translation of the Septuagint Greek:

(a) Up have the rivers lifted, Jahweh,
Up have the rivers lifted their voices,
Up the rivers lift their breakers.
Ps., xcii, 3 (Hebrew, xciii).

(b) Yea, in the night is Ar-Moab put down,
set at naught;
Yea, in the night is Kir-Moab put down,
set at naught.
Is., xv, 2.

II. *Antithetical Parallelism.*—The thought of the first line is expressed by an antithesis in the second; or is counterbalanced by a contrast in the second. This parallelism is very common in the Book of Proverbs:

(a) The tongue of the wise adorneth knowledge,
The mouth of the fool blurteth out folly.
Prov., xv, 2.

(b) Soundness of heart is the life of the flesh,
Envy is the rot of the bones.
Prov., xiv, 30.

III. *Synthetic Parallelism.*—The theme is worked up by the building of thought upon similar thought:
(a) Mightier than the voices of many waters,
   Mightier than the breakers of the ocean
   In the high place is Jahweh.
         Ps., xcii, 4 (Hebrew, xciii).
(b) Know ye that Jahweh he is the Lord,
   He hath made us; his we are;
   His folk are we, yea, the flock of His pasture.
         Ps., xcix, 1 (Hebrew, c).

IV. *Introverted Parallelism* (named by Jebb, in "Sacred Literature", sec. 4). The thought veers from the main theme and then returns thereto.
   Only in God be still, my soul.
      From Him is my life;
   Only He is my rock, my salvation,
      My fortress. I totter not.

   How long will ye set upon a man,—
      Will ye dash upon him, all of you?
   Only to thrust me from my height they plan,
      As from a toppling wall.
   They love the lie; they bless with the lips;
      And in their hearts they curse.
   Only in God be still, my soul.
      From Him is my life;
   Only He is my rock, my salvation,
      My fortress. I totter not.
         Ps. lxi, 2–7 (Hebrew, lxii).

V. *Stair-like Parallelism.*—The thought is repeated, in pretty much the same words, and is developed still further:
   Jahweh shall guard thee from all evil,
   Jahweh shall guard thy soul;
   Jahweh shall guard thy coming and thy going
      From now for ever more.
         Ps. cxx, 7–8 (Hebrew, cxxi).

VI. *Emblematic Parallelism.*—The building up of a thought by use of simile:
   Jahweh, my God, early I seek Thee;
   My soul doth faim for Thee;
   My flesh doth faint for Thee;
   Like a land of drought it thirsts for Thee.
         Ps. lxii, 2, 3 (Hebrew, lxiii).

Parallelism may be seen in distichs or tristichs. In fact, scholars are now coming round to the theory that the principle of balance and counterbalance is far more comprehensive in Hebrew poetry than are the above-named parallelisms. Each individual line is a unit of sense, and combines with other such units to form larger units of sense. Recent scholars, like Zenner, have found an almost endless variety of balance and counterbalance of words with words; of lines with lines, either of the same strophe or of an antistrophe; of strophe with antistrophe or with another strophe etc. In fact, this wider application of the principle of parallelism or balance in the study of Hebrew poetry has enabled modern scholars to go far in their efforts to reconstruct the metres of the sacred writers.

SCHLÖGL, *De re metrica veterum Hebræorum* (Vienna, 1890); DÖLLER, *Rhythmus, Metrik und Strophik in der Biblisch-Hebräischen Poesie* (Paderborn, 1899); GRIMME, *Grundzüge der Hebräischen Akzent- und Vocallehre* (Fribourg, 1896); ZENNER, *Die Chorgesänge im Buch der Psalmen* (Freiburg im Br., 1896); ZENNER AND WIESMANN, *Die Psalmen nach dem Urtext* (Münster, 1906); KAUTZSCH, *Die Poesie und die poetischen Bücher des Alten Testaments* (Leipzig, 1902); BRIGGS, *Psalms* (New York, 1906); BICKELL, *Metrices bibl. reg. exempl. illustrat.* (Innsbruck, 1882), *Carmina V. T. metrice* (Innsbruck, 1882); GIETMANN, *De re metrica Hebræorum* (Freiburg im Br., 1880).

WALTER DRUM.

Parallelism, PSYCHO-PHYSICAL, a doctrine which states that the relation between mental processes, on the one hand, and physical, physiological, or cerebral processes on the other, is one merely of invariable concomitance: each psychical change or psychical state, each *psychosis*, involves a corresponding neural change or neural state, *neurosis*, and vice versa. It denies the possibility of interaction between body and mind. At most there can be a certain point-for-point correlation such that, given any process in the nervous system, a definite mental process is its invariable accompaniment; and, given any particular process in consciousness, a corresponding brain-state or neurosis will invariably be present.

The fundamental principles of Psycho-physical Parallelism are based (1) upon the fact that all psychical processes presuppose as their condition *sine qua non* processes of a physical character in the nervous organism; (2) upon the principle of the conservation of energy; and (3) upon the assumption that mind and matter are so utterly unlike and so utterly opposed in character that interaction between them is impossible.

The psychological data upon which the theory rests we may in general grant. The modern science of psychophysics (q. v.) aided by cerebral anatomy, cerebral physiology, and pathology, proves fairly conclusively that (1) sensation and perception are conditioned by nervous processes in the brain and in the peripheral end-organs of sense, depending in part at least upon external stimuli; (2) that memory and imagination likewise presuppose, and are conditioned by, cerebral connexions and cerebral activity; and (3) that this is also to some extent the case with regard to intellectual operations and rational volition.

We have so far little more than an experimental verification of two Scholastic principles: (1) that sensation is an act of the composite organism, and (2) that intellectual activity is conditioned by phantasmata, and indirectly by nervous processes. In truth the data scarcely warrant us in going further than this. But the parallelist goes further. He asserts that intellectual operations have an exact physiological counterpart, which is more than he can prove. An *image* has doubtless its counterpart, physiologically in the brain and physically in the outside world. The association of ideas is conditioned by, and in a sense is the psychical parallel of, the simultaneous or successive activity of different parts of the brain, between which there is a physical and functional connexion; and without such association of ideas intellectual operations are impossible—so long, that is, as soul and body are united in one being. But that intellectual operations proper—judgment, logical inference, general concepts, vast and far-reaching as they are in their significance, should have an exact counterpart in the activity of brain-cells and their neuronic connexions, is a hypothesis which the known facts of psycho-physics fail to bear out, and which is also inconceivable. How, for instance, can a general concept, referring as it does to objective reality and embracing schematically in a single act many diverse notes, bear any resemblance to the disturbance of nervous equilibrium that accompanies it, a disturbance which has no unity at all except that it occurs in different parts of the same brain more or less simultaneously? Or, how can cerebral processes of a peculiarly unstable and almost haphazard type be, as they are alleged to be, the physiological counterpart of processes of reasoning, rigid, exact, logical, necessary?

The assertion that all psychical processes have a physiological "parallel" is unwarranted, and scarcely less unwarranted is the assertion that all physiological processes have a psychical "parallel". This latter point can be established only by appeal to the fiction of "subliminal" or "subconscious" consciousness. The existence of a "threshold of consciousness", or, in other words, of a limit of intensity which must be exceeded by the stimulus, as also by the nervous impulse which results, before the latter can affect our consciousness, has been experimentally proved, and this fact cannot be accounted for by the parallelist except on the assumption that there are states of consciousness of which we are wholly unconscious.

The second line of argument advanced in favour of Parallelism is as follows: The principle of the conservation of energy supposes, we are told, that the universe is a closed mechanical system in which events, whether past or future, are calculable with the utmost precision, given the knowledge of any one stage in the development of that universe and the laws according to which that development takes place. Such a system will brook no interference whatsoever from without. Hence interaction between mind and matter is impossible, and parallelism is the only other alternative.

This conclusion is quite illegitimate. Energy, as understood in the law which states that its sum is invariable, is strictly a *non-directed* quantity. Hence, even though this law is applicable to the lower phenomena of animal life, as the experiments of Atwater and Hubner show, it by no means disproves the influence of consciousness and will, for mind could still *direct* material energy and the law remain intact. This is admitted by Fechner, Mach, Boltzmann, Höfler, and von Hartmann, the latter being a determinist. (Cf. ENERGY, THE LAW OF THE CONSERVATION OF.)

Moreover, were the absolute independence of the physical world indeed a fact, the existence of consciousness would become an insoluble mystery, and the existence of a parallelism between it and the physical world a manifest contradiction. If there be no interaction between mind and matter, consciousness ceases to be an instrument whereby we modify our physical environment to suit our needs. Purposive striving, deliberation, choice, volition, are thus rendered wholly unnecessary and irrelevant, and the belief that we can really do something to change things in the outside world and so promote both our comfort and that of our neighbour is a hopeless delusion. The practical utility of physical science also becomes illusory, for our bodies, which alone can give it effect, are declared to be merely automata with the working of which consciousness has nothing to do. Parallelism is useless here, if interaction be abolished; nay, more, is incompatible with that very independence on account of which its existence is affirmed. Absolute independence and universal concomitance are contradictory. If there is concomitance, directly or indirectly, as Mill said, there must be causal connexion.

That such a causal connexion between mind and matter really exists the consciousness of activity, purpose, will, and responsibility, directly testifies; and in the face of this testimony to hark back to the Cartesian doctrine of radical opposition between body and soul, extension and thought, is futile and contrary to experience.

Variations and developments of parallelism may in general be classed under two heads; conscious automatism—the theory of Huxley that the human body is a mere machine of which consciousness is the "collateral product", a shadow or epiphenomenon which symbolically indicates, though it in no wise influences, the mechanical processes which underlie it; and the "Dual-aspect Theory" which maintains that psychical and physical phenomena between which there is a point-for-point correspondence all along the line, are but different aspects or expressions of the same common substance. Huxley's view emphasizes the material at the expense of mental, curiously oblivious of the fact that all we know of the physical universe and all the theories that we are able to formulate about it, originate in, and belong to, consciousness. The dual-aspect view improves upon this, by giving to consciousness a value at any rate equal to that of mechanical movement. It is in fact a form of Monism (q. v.) akin to that of Spinoza and involves most of the difficulties to which that system leads. But from our point of view its chief error lies in its assertion that parallelism is the only relation which holds between the physical and the psychical, a relation which can be proved to hold so far as sensation and perception are concerned, but which, if further generalized to the exclusion of interaction, inevitably leads to contradiction.

Expository: BAWDEN, *The Functional View of the Relation between the Psychical and the Physical* in *Philos. Review*, XI, 1902, 474–84; CLIFFORD, *Lectures and Essays*, II (London, 1886), 31–70; ERHARDT, *Die Wechselwirkung zwischen Leib und Seele* (Leipzig, 1897); FLECHSIG, *Gehirn und Seele* (Leipzig, 1896); HUXLEY, *Collected Essays* (London, 1893–94); MACH, *Analysis of the Sensations* (tr. Chicago, 1897); REIFF, *Der moderne psychophysische Parallelismus* (Basle, 1901); RICKERT, *Psychophysische Kausalität und psychophysischer Parallelismus* (Tübingen, 1900); STOUT, *Manual of Psychology* (London, 1904), iii.

Critical: G. W. BALFOUR, *Psychical Research and Current Doctrines of Mind and Body* in *Hibbert Journal*, VIII (April, 1910), 3; BUSSE, *Geist und Körper, Leib und Seele* (Leipzig, 1903); DRISCOLL, *The Soul* (New York, 1898); GARDAIR, *Corps et Ame* (Paris, 1892); GUTBERLET, *Der Kampf um die Seele* (Mainz, 1899); HÖFLER, *Die Metaphysischen Theorien von der Beziehung zwischen Leib und Seele* (Vienna and Prague, 1897); JAMES, *Principles of Psychology* (2 vols., London, 1890); JODL, *Lehrbuch der Psychologie* (Stuttgart, 1896); LADD, *Philosophy of Mind* (London and New York, 1895); LOTZE, *Metaphysic*, III (tr. Oxford, 1887), 5; MASCI, *Il Materialismo psicofisico e la Dottrina del Parallelismo in Psicologia* (Naples, 1901); MERCIER, *Les Origines de la Psychologie contemporaine* (Louvain and Paris, 1908); PESCH, *Seele und Leib als zwei Bestandteile der einen Menschensubstanz* (Fulda, 1901); VILLA, *Contemporary Psychology* (London and New York, 1903); WARD, *Naturalism and Agnosticism* (2 Vols., London, 1906); WUNDT, *Ueber psychische Causalität und das Princip des psychophysischen Parallelismus* in *Philosophische Studien*, X (Leipzig, 1894); *Human and Animal Psychology* (tr. London, 1907).

LESLIE J. WALKER.

Paralus, a titular see, suffragan of Cabasa in Ægyptus Secunda. One of the seven mouths of the Nile, Sebennys or Paralus ("Georgii Cyprii Descriptio orbis romani", ed. Gelzer, 39) was situated there. The see is mentioned during the Arab regime in the Coptic "Notitia episcopatuum" (Rougé, "Géographie ancienne de la Basse Egypte", 38, 153). Its bishop, Athanasius, assisted at the Council of Ephesus, 431 (Mansi, IV, 1128, 1160, 1220; V, 590; VI, 874); another, Pasmeius, was present at the Robber Council of Ephesus, 449, and at the Council of Chalcedon, 451 (Mansi, VI, 572, 612, 859, 925; VII, 52). Le Quien (Oriens christ., II, 571) mentions two other Jacobite bishops. The site is now called Burlos or Burollos, the promontory Ras Burlos, the ancient lake of Sebennys Baheret-Burlos.

CHAMPOLLION, *L'Egypte sous les Pharaons*, II, 360; GELZER, *Georgii Cyprii Descriptio orbis romani*, 127.

S. VAILHÉ.

Paraná, DIOCESE OF (PARANENSIS), suffragan of Buenos Aires, in Argentine until recently, comprised two civil provinces, Entre Rios and Corrientes, and the civil Government of Misiones (see Map of South America in Vol. III). This territory belonged to the Diocese of Buenos Aires until 1854, when it became a separate pro-vicariate Apostolic, to be erected into a diocese by the Bull of Pius IX dated 13 June, 1859. The area of Entre Rios is 28,754 sq. miles; Corrientes, 32,545 sq. miles; Misiones, 8571 sq. miles. The respective populations are: Entre Rios, 408,000; Corrientes, 322,000; Misiones, 44,000. Thus the diocese has a total area of 69,870 sq. miles and a population of 774,000. The Diocese of Corrientes has recently been erected.

The first Bishop of Paraná, José Gabriel Segura y Cuvas, b. at Catamarca, Argentine Republic, 1802; d. 13 October, 1862, took possession of the see 3 June, 1860. His successor, José María Gelabert y Crespo, b. in 1820; d. 23 November, 1897, took possession of the see 23 August, 1865, and was succeeded by Rosendo de la Lastra y Gordillo (d. 3 July, 1909). The present bishop (1911), Abel Bazan y Bustos, b. at La Rioja, 28 August, 1867, was preconized 7 February, 1910, consecrated 8 May, and took possession of the see 15 May, of the same year. The Province of Entre Rios is divided into sixteen parishes and ten chaplaincies (*capellanías vicarias*); Corrientes, forming one vicariate forain, twenty parishes; Misiones, one parish and three chaplaincies. The cathedral has a chapter of ten canons, including the five dignitaries. The "Guia Eclesiastica de Argentina" for 1910 gives the total number of clergy (parish priests and chaplains) for the diocese as 96; no mention, however, is here made of priests belonging to religious institutes engaged in educational work in the diocese. The conciliar seminary (Calle Urquiza, Paraná), under the direction of a rector, vice-rector, and five professors, has an aggregate of forty-three students in all its departments. The Benedictine Fathers have an agricultural school at Victoria, and the Capuchins conduct a college for boys at Concordia, both in Entre Rios. There are nine parochial schools in Entre Rios and one in Corrientes. Educational institutions for girls and charitable institutions of various kinds are conducted by the Daughters of the Immaculate Conception, the Religious of the Perpetual Adoration (*Adoratrices*), Servants of the Holy Spirit, Sisters of St. Francis, of St. Joseph (Lyons), and of the Garden, Vincentian Sisters, Belgian Tertiaries, Sisters of the Poor of St. Catherine of Siena, Carmelites (Tarragona), Mercedarians, and Tertiaries of Charity and of Carmel. Pious and charitable societies well represented in the diocese are the Acción Católica, the Apostleship of Prayer, the Confraternities (both for men and for women) of St. Vincent of Paul, Association for the Propagation of the Faith, Confraternities of Our Lady of Perpetual Succour and of Carmel, Daughters of Mary, and the peculiarly national Society of Our Lady of Itatí.

The Diocese of Corrientes also embraces Misiones. Rev. Luis A. Niella has been appointed bishop by the pope.

La Diócesis del Paraná en el quincuagésimo aniversario de su erección canónica (compiled under the direction of the Diocesan Jubilee Commission, Buenos Aires, 1909); *Guia Eclesiástica de Argentina* (Buenos Aires, 1910).

CLAUDIO POYET.

Parasceve (Gr. παρασκευή) seems to have supplanted the older term προσάββατον, used in the translation of Judith, viii, 6, and in the title—not to be found in Hebrew—of Ps. xcii (xciii). It became, among Hellenistic Jews, the name for Friday, and was adopted by Greek ecclesiastical writers after the writing of "The teaching of the Twelve Apostles". Apparently it was first applied by the Jews to the afternoon of Friday, then to the whole day, its etymology pointing to the "preparations" to be made for the Sabbath, as indicated in the King James Bible, where the Greek word is translated by "Day of Preparation". That the regulations of the Law might be minutely observed, it was made imperative to have on the Parasceve three meals of the choicest food laid ready before sunset (the Sabbath beginning on Friday night); it was forbidden to undertake in the afternoon of the sixth day any business which might extend to the Sabbath; Augustus relieved the Jews from certain legal duties from the ninth hour (Josephus, "Antiq. Jud.", XVI, vi, 2).

Parasceve seems to have been applied also to the eve of certain festival days of a sabbatic character. Foremost among these was the first day of the unleavened bread, Nisan 15. We learn from the Mishna (Pesach., iv, 1, 5) that the Parasceve of the Pasch, whatever day of the week it fell on, was kept even more religiously than the ordinary Friday, in Judæa work ceasing at noon, and in Galilee the whole day being free. In the schools the only question discussed regarding this particular Parasceve was when should the rest commence: Shammai said from the very beginning of the day (evening of Nisan 13); Hillel said only from after sunrise (morning of Nisan 14).

The use of the word Parasceve in the Gospels raises the question concerning the actual day of Our Lord's crucifixion. All the Evangelists state that Jesus died on the day of the Parasceve (Matt., xxvii, 62; Mark, xv, 42; Luke, xxiii, 54; John, xix, 14, 31), and there can be no doubt from Luke, xxiii, 54–56 and John, xix, 31, that this was Friday. But on what day of the month of Nisan did that particular Friday fall? St. John distinctly points to Nisan 14, while the Synoptists, by implying that the Last Supper was the Paschal meal, convey the impression that Jesus was crucified on Nisan 15. But this is hardly reconcilable with the following facts: When Judas left the table, the disciples imagined he was going to buy the things which were needed for the feast (John, xiii, 29)—a purchase which was impossible if the feast had begun; after the Supper, Our Lord and his disciples left the city, as also did the men detailed to arrest Him —this, on Nisan 15, would have been contrary to Ex., xii, 22; the next morning the Jews had not yet eaten the Passover; moreover, during that day the Council convened; Simon was apparently coming from work (Luke, xxiii, 26); Jesus and the two robbers were executed and were taken down from the crosses; Joseph of Arimathea bought fine linen (Mark, xv, 46), and Nicodemus brought "a mixture of myrrh and aloes about an hundred pound weight" (John, xix, 39) for the burial; lastly the women prepared spices for the embalming of the Saviour's body (Luke, xxiii, 55)—all things which would have been a desecration on Nisan 15. Most commentators, whether they think the Last Supper to have been the Paschal meal or an anticipation thereof, hold that Christ, as St. John states, was crucified on the Parasceve of the Pasch, Friday, Nisan 14.

Lives of Christ by DIDON, FOUARD, LE CAMUS etc.; PLUMMER, *The Gospel according to St. John*, appendix A (Cambridge, 1905); WESTCOTT, *Introduction to the Study of the Gospels*, note on *The Day of the Crucifixion* (New York, 1875), 335–42; PATRIZI, *De Evangeliis*, III, diss. L (Rome, 1852–53); CALMES, *L'Evangile selon Saint-Jean* (Paris, 1904); STAPFER, *La Palestine au temps de Jésus-Christ* (Paris, s. d.).

CHARLES L. SOUVAY.

Paray-le-Monial, a town of five thousand inhabitants in the Department of Sâone-Loire, Diocese of Autun, France. It is indisputable that Paray

CHAPEL OF THE VISITATION, PARAY-LE-MONIAL

(*Paredum; Parodium*) existed before the monks who gave it its surname of Le Monial, for when Count Lambert of Chalon, together with his wife Adelaide and his friend Mayeul de Cluny, founded there in 973 the celebrated Benedictine priory, the borough had already been constituted, with its *ædiles* and communal privileges. At that time an ancient temple was dedicated to the Mother of God (Charter of Paray). The Cluny monks were, 999–1789, lords of the town.

Protestantism made many proselytes here; but in 1618 the Jesuits were summoned, and after a century there remained only a few Protestant families, who have long since disappeared. In order to complete the work, Père Paul de Barry, the author of "Pensez-y-bien", in 1678 brought thither the Visitandines.

Paray-le-Monial has become a much-frequented place of pilgrimage since 1873, as many as 100,000 pilgrims arriving yearly from all parts of Europe and America. The most venerated spot is the Chapel of the Visitation, where most of the apparitions to Blessed Margaret Mary Alacoque (q. v.) took place. Next comes the Basilica of the Sacred Heart, in charge of secular chaplains, formerly the church of the monks, which is one of the most beautiful monuments of Cluniac architecture (tenth or eleventh century). The Hotel de Ville, in Renaissance style, the façade of which is adorned with a large statue of the Blessed Virgin, is also one of the historical monuments. Pilgrimage is also made to the *Hieron* or temple-palace, erected by a layman in honour of the Eucharistic King, where there is a very curious collection of pictures and objects of art bearing on the Holy Eucharist. Despite the difficulties of the present religious situation in France, Paray still possesses a number of communities or monasteries which justify its surname. Moreover, with this town are connected the associations the object of which is the cult of the Sacred Heart, such as the Apostleship of Prayer, the Archconfraternity of the Holy Hour (established at Paray itself in 1829 by Père Robert Debrosse), and the Communion of Reparation, organized in 1854 by Père Victor Drevon. The latter maintains its headquarters at Paray.

From a secular point of view the town is unimportant, but its religious glory is abundant. It is more than enough for its honour that it should be, as Leo XIII said in his Brief of Coronation of Notre Dame de Romay (25 July, 1896), "*Cœlo gratissimum oppidum*", "a town very dear to heaven".

CHEVALIER, *Cartulaire du Paray-le-Monial* (Paris, 1890); SACKUR, *Cluniazenser*, I (1892), 241 sq.; II (1894), 40-92.

JOSEPH ZELLE.

Pardies, IGNACE-GASTON, French scientist, b. at Pau, 5 Sept., 1636; d. of fever contracted whilst ministering to the prisoners of Bicêtre, near Paris, 22 April, 1673. He entered the Society of Jesus 17 Nov., 1652 and for a time taught classical literature; during this period he composed a number of short Latin works, in prose and verse, which are praised for their delicacy of thought and style. After his ordination he taught philosophy and mathematics at the College of Louis-le-Grand in Paris. His early death cut short a life of unusual activity in the sciences. His earliest work is the "Horologium Thaumanticum Duplex" (Paris, 1662), in which is described an instrument he had invented for constructing various kinds of sun-dials. Three years later appeared his "Dissertatio de Motu et Natura Cometarum", published separately in Latin and in French (Bordeaux, 1665). His "Discours du mouvement local" (Paris, 1670), "La Statique" (Paris, 1673), and the manuscript "Traité complet d'Optique", in which he followed the undulatory theory, form part of a general work on physics which he had planned. He opposed Newton's theory of refraction and his letters together with Newton's replies (which so satisfied Pardies that he withdrew his objections) are found in the "Philosophical Transactions" for 1672 and 1673. His "Discours de la Connaissance des Bestes" (Paris, 1672) combatted Descartes's theories on the subject so feebly that many looked on it as a covert defence rather than a refutation, an impression which Pardies himself afterwards endeavoured to destroy. His "Elémens de Géométrie" (Paris, 1671) was translated into Latin and English. He left in manuscript a work entitled "Art de la Guerre" and a celestial atlas comprising six charts, published after his death (Paris, 1673-74). His collected mathematical and physical works were published in French (The Hague, 1691) and in Latin (Amsterdam, 1694).

SOMMERVOGEL, *Bibl. de la C. de J.* (Brussels, 1895).

EDWARD C. PHILLIPS.

Pardons of Brittany.—Pardon, from the Latin *perdonare*,—assimilated in form to *donum*, a gift, middle English, to the old French *perdun* and *pardun*, and modern French *pardonner*—signifies in Brittany the feast of the patron saint of a church or chapel, at which an indulgence is granted. Hence the origin of the word "Pardon" as used in Brittany. The Pardons do not extend farther east in Brittany than Guingamp, the date of whose celebration occurs on the first Sunday in July. There are five distinct kinds of Pardons in Brittany: St. Yves at Tréguier—the Pardon of the poor; Our Lady of Rumengol—the Pardon of the singers; St. Jean-du-Doigt—the Pardon of fire; St. Ronan—the Pardon of the mountain; and St. Anne de la Palude—the Pardon of the sea. The Pardons begin in March and end in October, but the majority of them are between Easter and Michaelmas. Two Breton Pardons, to which very large pilgrimages are annually made, are that of St. Jean-du-Doigt near

ARRIVAL OF THE PARDON OF STE-ANNE DE FOUESNANT
Alfred Guillon, Luxembourg Gallery

Morlaix, and that of Ste-Anne d'Auray in Morbihan. The former occurs on 24 June, and that of Ste Anne d'Auray on 24 July, the anniversary of the finding of the statue of Ste Anne by the peasant Nicolazic. The latter is regarded as the most famous pilgrimage in all Brittany, and attracts pilgrims from Tréguier, Léonnais, Cornouaille, and especially from Morbihan. Each diocese and parish is known by its costume.

To these Breton Pardons come pilgrims from every side, clad in their best costumes which are only to be seen there and at a wedding. It is a pilgrimage of devotion and piety. The greater part of the day is spent in prayer and the Pardon begins with early Mass at 4 A.M. Its observance, however, has actually commenced earlier, for the preceding evening is devoted to confession, and the rosary is generally recited by the pilgrims, the whole way to the place of the Pardon. After the religious service, the great procession takes place around the church. This is the most picturesque part of the Pardon and may be regarded as its *mise en scène*. At Ste-Anne d'Auray, this procession is especially striking and impressive. In the procession join all those whom the intercession of Ste Anne has saved from peril and danger. The sailors are there with fragments of the vessel, upon which they escaped in the shipwreck; the lame are there carrying on their shoulders the crutches, for which they have no longer need; and those rescued from fire are also in the procession, carrying the rope or ladder, by means of which they escaped from the flames. The Pardon in Brittany has practically remained unchanged for over two hundred years. It is not a pretext for feasting or revel, but a reverent and religious gathering where young and old commune with God and His saints in prayer. There is indeed a social side to the Breton Pardon, but it is purely incidental. Its true import is religious.

WELD, *A Vacation in Brittany* (London, 1856); BARING-GOULD, *A Book of Brittany*, V (London, 1901); GOSTLING, *The Bretons at Home*, II and III (Chicago, 1909); LE BRAZ, *Au Pays des Pardons*, translated by GOSTLING (New York, 1906); SOUVESTRE, *En Bretagne*, III and V (Paris, 1891).

THOMAS O'HAGAN.

Paré, AMBROISE, French surgeon, b. at Bourg-Hersent, near Laval, department of Maine, 1517; d. 20 Dec., 1590. He was apprenticed to a barber at an early age, became barber-surgeon at the Hôtel-Dieu, Paris, surgeon in the army of Francis I (1536-38), re-enlisted on the reopening of hostilities (1542-44), and in 1545 began the study of anatomy at Paris, under François-Jacques Dubois (Sylvius). He was appointed field-surgeon by Marshal Rohan, and (1552) became surgeon to King Henry II, in 1554 member of the Collège de St-Cosme, exempt from taxation, and in 1563, after the siege of Rouen, first surgeon and chamberlain to King Charles IX. A Catholic throughout his life, Tal has given documentary refutation of the legend that Paré was a Huguenot and was spared during the Massacre of St. Bartholomew's Day (1572) by direct command of the king. On account of his humanitarian activity he was held in special regard among soldiers. His motto, as inscribed above his chair in the Collège de St-Cosme, read: "Je le pansay et Dieu le guarist." A monument was erected to him at Laval.

AMBROISE PARÉ

Paré's pioneer work was chiefly in the department of military surgery. His importance in the development of modern surgery may be compared with that of his contemporary, Andreas Vesalius, in the development of modern anatomy. The chief services rendered by Paré are a reform in the treatment of gunshot wounds, and the revival of the practice of ligating arteries after amputation. From the time of Giovanni Vigo (c. 1460-1520), surgeon-in-ordinary to Pope Julius II, gunshot wounds were classified as contused, burned, and poisoned, and the last-named, on the supposition that all gunshot wounds were poisoned by powder, were cauterized with red-hot iron or hot oil. On one occasion, after a battle, Paré, not having sufficient oil, applied ointment and bandaged the wounds, and observed that the healing process proceeded more favourably under this treatment. His observations, published in 1545, gave the impetus to a rational reform of the whole system of dealing with wounds, and did away with the theory of poisoned gunshot wounds, despite the fact that the Italians, Alfonso Ferri (1552), and Giovanni Francesco Rota (1555), obstinately defended the old view. Vascular ligation, which had been practised by the Alexandrians, was revived by Paré at amputations in the form of ligating the artery, though thereby the nerves were bruised. This discovery, which he published in 1552, he speaks of as an inspiration which came to him through Divine grace. In cases of strangulated hernia of the groin he performed the operation known as herniotomy, while heretofore physicians feared to operate in such cases, leaving the patient to die miserably. In obstetrics we owe to him the revival of foot-presentation, but he was always averse to the Cæsarean operation (*sectio cæsarea*). In all departments of surgery we find Paré an independent observer and thinker; but his advanced notions encountered much opposition on the part of the Paris faculty of medicine. Thus at the time of his enrolment in the faculty of the Collège de St-Cosme, in 1554, the faculty made his ignorance of Latin a ground of objection against him. Nor could it ever forgive him for rendering ludicrous supposed panaceas, the so-called *arcana* (*mumia, ceratum humanum, unicornu*).

The best edition of PARÉ's works, which also contains biographical notices, is that of MALGAIGNE, *Œuvres d'Ambroise Paré* (3 vols., Paris, 1840-41); they were also edited by LE PAULMIER, *Ambroise Paré d'après de nouveaux documents* (Paris, 1885). Earlier editions are: *Œuvres de M. Ambr. Paré* (Paris, 1575, eleven editions to 1685; Latin, Paris, 1582; tr., London, 1578; Dutch, 1604; German, 1601). The more important editions of the single treatises are: *Cinq livres de chirurgie* (Paris, 1572), his masterpiece; *La méthode de traicter les playes faictes par hacquebutes et aultres bastons à feu: et de celles qui sont faictes par fleches, flecdardz et semblables: aussi des combustions specialement faictes par la pouldre à canon* (Paris, 1545, 1552; tr. 1617); *La méthode curative des playes et fractures de la teste humaine* (Paris, 1561); *Briefve collection de l'administration anatomique* (Paris, 1550, 1561), at one time a very highly esteemed anatomical work; *Discours de la mumie, des venins, de la licorne et de la peste* (Paris, 1532); *Réplique à la response faicte contre son discours de la licorne* (Paris, 1584). See TEELING in *The Month* (March, 1903).

LEOPOLD SENFELDER.

Pareja, FRANCISCO, missionary, probably b. at Auñon in the Diocese of Toledo, Spain, date unknown; d. in Mexico, 25 January, 1628. He was sent to Florida with eleven other Franciscans, and arrived at St. Augustine in 1593 or early in 1594. He laboured as a missionary among the savages of the peninsula, notably at San Juan on the coast, and then became guardian of the monastery of the Immaculate Conception, at St. Augustine. He is also styled "custos", and must have held the office before 1613, when the custody was elevated to the rank of a province under the patronage of St. Helena. Subsequently, he joined the province of the Holy Gospel in Mexico. Father Pareja is noted for having published the first books in the language of an Indian tribe within the United States, the Timuquanan, and may for that purpose have gone to Mexico. His various works are: "Catecismo en lengua castellana y timuquana" (Mexico, 1612); "Catecismo y breve exposición de la doctrina cristiana" (Mexico, 1612); "Confesionario en lengua castellana y timuquana" (Mexico, 1613); "Gramatica de la lengua timuquana de Florida" (Mexico, 1614); "Catecismo de la doctrina cristiana en lengua timuquana" (Mexico, 1617); "Catecismo y examen para los que comulgan, en lengua castellana y timuquana" (Mexico, 1627).

BARCIA, *Ensayo Cronológico* (Madrid, 1723); VETANCURT, *Menologio* (Mexico, 1697); TORQUEMADA, *Monarquía Indiana* (Madrid, 1723); SHEA, *Catholic Church in Colonial Days* (New York, 1886); IDEM, *Catholic Missions* (New York, 1854); PILLING, *North American Linguistics* (Washington, 1884); SABIN, *Dictionary of Books Relating to America*, V (New York, 1884).

ZEPHRYIN ENGELHARDT.

Parents (Lat. *parere*, to beget).—I. DUTIES OF PARENTS TOWARDS THEIR CHILDREN.—In the old pagan world, with due allowance for the operation of the natural law, love and reverence were replaced by authority and fear. The Roman jurisprudence during a time at least exaggerated the paternal power to the point of ownership, but it did not emphasize any duties that he had to perform. His dominion over his children was not less complete than that over his slaves. He possessed an undisputed right of life and death; he might sell them into slavery and dispose of any property they had acquired. Compatible with this general idea, abortion, infanticide, and exposition were widespread. The laws seemed to contemplate these crimes as venial offences and to have been largely inoperative in such cases.

In consequence the filial observance implied in the ancient *pietas* could not always be translated as affection. This earlier condition was modified by decrees of the later emperors. Alexander Severus distinguished the right of a father to put an adult child to death, whilst Diocletian made it illegal for fathers to sell their children.

Under Christianity parents were not merely the repositories of rights and duties whose affirmation nature demanded, but they were to be regarded as the representatives of God Himself, from whom "all paternity is named", and found in this capacity the way to mingle love and reverence, as well as the strongest motive for a cheerful obedience on the part of the children.

The first duty of parents towards their children is to love them. Nature inculcates this clearly, and it is customary to describe parents who lack this affection as unnatural. Here the offence is against a distinct virtue which the theologians call *pietas*, concerned with the demeanour reciprocally of parents and children. Hence the circumstance of this close relationship must be made known in confession when there is question of sins of this sort. In the case of serious damage done by parents to their children, besides the sin against justice there is contracted the quite different malice derived from this propinquity. This virtue, interpreting the precept of the natural law, also requires parents diligently to care for the proper rearing of their children, that is, to provide for their bodily, mental, and spiritual well-being. This is so even in the supposition that the children are illegitimate. Parents are guilty of grievous sin who treat their children with such cruelty as to indicate that their conduct is inspired by hatred, or who, with full intent, curse them or exhibit a notable and unreasonable preference for one child rather than another. Parents are bound to support their children in a manner commensurate with their social condition until these latter can support themselves. The mother is bound to do nothing to prejudice the life or proper development of her unborn infant, and after birth she must under pain of venial sin nurse it herself unless there is some adequate excuse.

A father who is idle or unthrifty so that his family is left without fitting maintenance is guilty of grievous sin. Parents must see that their children obtain at least an elementary education. They are bound with special emphasis to watch over the spiritual welfare of their children, to afford them good example, and to correct the erring. The teaching of the Church is that the right and duty to educate their own offspring abides natively and primarily with the parents. It is their most important task; indeed understood in its full sense it is ranked by no obligation. In so far as it means instruction in the more elementary branches of human knowledge it is in most cases identical with the obligation of bestowing care in the selection of a school for the children.

Hence, in general, parents may not with a safe conscience send their children to non-Catholic schools, whether these be sectarian or secularist. This statement admits of exception in the instance where there are grave reasons for permitting Catholic children to frequent these schools, and where such dangers as may exist for their faith or morals are by fitting means either neutralized or rendered remote. The judge in such cases, both of the sufficiency of the reasons alleged as well as of the kind of measure to be employed to encounter successfully whatever risks there are, is, in the United States, the bishop of each diocese. The attendance at non-Catholic schools by Catholic children is something which, for weighty motives and with due safeguards, can be tolerated, not approved. In any case parents must carefully provide for the child's religious instruction.

As to higher education, parents have a clear duty to see that the faith of their children is not imperilled by their going to non-Catholic universities and colleges. In the lack of positive legislation before parents can assent to their children attending non-Catholic universities or colleges there must be a commensurately grave cause, and such dangers as may threaten faith or morals are to be rendered remote by suitable remedies. The last-named requirement is obviously the more important. Failure to fall in with the first, provided that means had been taken faithfully to comply with the second, would not oblige the confessor to refuse absolution to such parents. There is an undoubted and under ordinary circumstances inalienable authority to be exercised by parents. The extent of this is a matter to be determined by positive law. In the instances in which it becomes necessary to decide upon one of the parents rather than the other as custodian of the children, the rule of legal preference in the United States is that the children are confided to the charge of the father. There is, however, a growing disposition to favour the mother. Parents have the right to administer chastisement to delinquent children. Their omission to punish suitably may be a serious offense before God.

II. DUTIES OF CHILDREN TOWARDS PARENTS.—Children have a threefold obligation of love, reverence, and obedience toward their parents. This is enjoined by the virtue which St. Thomas calls *pietas*, and for which the nearest English equivalent phrase is "dutiful observance". As religion makes it obligatory for us to worship God, so there is a virtue distinct from all the others which inculcates the attitude we ought to hold towards parents, in so far as they in a secondary sense are the principles of our being and of its regulation. The violation of this obligation therefore is reputed a grievous sin unless the smallness of the matter involved make the offence a venial one. Of the obligations referred to, love and reverence are in force during the parents' lifetime. Obedience ceases when the children pass from under the parental authority. The duty of love of parents, strongly intimated to the conscience by the natural law, is expressly emphasized by the positive law of God. The Fourth Commandment, "Honour thy father and thy mother", is universally interpreted to mean not only respect and submission, but also the entertaining and manifestation of affection they deserve at the hands of their children.

Those children are guilty of grievous sin who habitually exhibit towards their parents a heartless demeanour, or who fail to succour them in serious need, either bodily or spiritual, or who neglect to carry out the provisions of their last will and testament in so far as the amount devised will permit. It is not merely the external bearing which has to be governed. The inward sentiment of affection must be deep-seated. The Christian concept of parents as being the delegates of God carries with it the inference that they are to be treated with peculiar respect. Children incur the guilt of grievous sin who strike their parents, or even raise their hands to do so, or who give them well-founded reason for great sorrow. The same is to be said of those who put their parents in a violent rage, who curse them or revile them, or refuse to recognize them.

Besides the parental relationship and dignity account is to be taken of their authority. Children, so long as they remain under its yoke, are bound to obey. This does not mean, according to the teaching of St.

Thomas (II–II, Q. civ, a. 2, ad 1um), that they must intend to do what is commanded precisely because it is enjoined; it is enough that they be minded to do what is prescribed. This obligation covers all those matters and those only which make for the proper rearing of the offspring. Parents have no power to order their children to do what is sinful, nor can they impose upon them against their will any particular calling in life. Theologians find their criterion for determining the grievousness of the sin of disobedience by scrutinizing the command given as well as the matter with which it is concerned. They say that the offence is then to be rated as mortal when the communication of the parental will takes the form of a real precept given in earnest and not merely a counsel or exhortation. They further require that this behest should have to do with something important.

There is no hard and fast rule to gauge the gravity of the matter in which an infraction of the duty of obedience will become a mortal sin. Moralists declare that this valuation must be made by the good sense of thoughtful persons. They add that in general when an act of disobedience is calculated to work serious harm to the parents, or interfere seriously with domestic discipline, or put in jeopardy the temporal or spiritual welfare of the children themselves, it is to be accounted a mortal sin. When the thing for whose performance or omission the parent's command is issued is already binding under pain of grievous sin, either by the natural or positive law, the setting at naught of the parental injunction does not involve a distinct sin of disobedience requiring a separate accusation in confession. The reason is that the motive of the command is assumed to remain the same in both cases. An example in point would be the defiance of an order given by a parent to a child to assist at Mass on Sunday, something which the latter is already bound to do.

Children are released from parental control when they attain their majority, or are legally emancipated. In the United States this latter may be done either by a written instrument or by means of certain facts which the statutes construe as sufficiently manifesting the consent of the parents.

SLATER, *Manual of Moral Theology* (New York, 1908); LECKY, *History of European Morals* (New York, 1910); SPIRAGO, *The Catechism Explained* (New York, 1899); DEVAS, *Key to the World's Progress* (London, 1906); D'ANNIBALE, *Summula Theologiæ Moralis* (Rome, 1908); BALLERINI, *Opus Theologicum Morale* (Prato, 1899); ST. THOMAS, *Summa Theologica*.

JOSEPH F. DELANY.

Parenzo-Pola (PARENTINA-POLENSIS), DIOCESE OF.—The little town of Parenzo is picturesquely situated on a promontory extending into a creek of the Adriatic. At the head of this promontory, close to the water, rises the cathedral, the pride of Parenzo. Built by the first bishop, Euphrasius, in the time of Justinian, under whom Byzantine architecture first reached the shores of the Adriatic, it is the best preserved monument of that epoch in Austria. Moreover, archæologists have proved that it bears witness to the antiquity of Christianity in Parenzo, as it is the most recent of three churches, the second of which belongs to the time of Constantine the Great, while the oldest antedates that epoch. Parenzo was a separate diocese from the time of Euphrasius until in 1827 it was united with Pola, whose first bishop, Venerius, died about 520. At present Parenzo-Pola is under the jurisdiction of Görz and numbers 132,000 Catholics, including 135 secular priests, one monastery with 21 monks, and 6 (or 8) convents containing 132 nuns.

Codice diplomatico Istriano, 3 vols. appearing as supplement to KANDLER's *L'Istria* (1846); CAPPELLETTI, *Le chiese d'Italia* (Venice, 1844–71); KANDLER, *Fasti sacri e profane de Trieste e dell' Istria* (Triest, 1849).

C. WOLFSGRUBER.

Parini, GIUSEPPE, Italian poet, b. at Bosisio, 23 May, 1729; d. at Milan, 15 Aug., 1799. Parini was early taken to Milan. He was an apt pupil and showed that he possessed marked ability for teaching, which was to be the work of the greater part of his life. His poetic talent also evinced itself at an early date and secured his entrance into several of the *Accademie*, especially into the "Arcadia". Taking Holy orders in 1754, he served as tutor in several noble families and gained that knowledge of fashionable life which he was to put to good use in his "Giorno". From 1773 on he was professor of fine arts in the Brera at Milan. When the Cisalpine Republic was established with its capital at Milan, Bonaparte made him a member of the municipal government; this position he lost on account of his liberal utterances. The latter part of his life was passed in rather straitened circumstances. The poetical fame of Parini depends upon his "Odi" and the "Giorno", particularly upon the latter. The "Odi" (1st ed., Milan, 1791) are in the conventional manner of the eighteenth century Arcadian compositions; some of them deal with matters of moral and social speculation. The "Giorno", upon which he had begun to work about 1760, is a satire upon the life of the young man of fashion of the time. In the four parts of it—the "Mattino", the "Mezzogiorno", the "Vespro", and the "Notte"—he passes in review the futile daily occupations of a typical society beau, all the while ridiculing the effeminate and corrupt customs of the youth of the age. The interest of the composition is diversified by the introduction of pleasing episodes. The verse form is that of unrhymed decasyllables. Some occasional verses, a cantata ("La figlia di Jefte"), a dramatic work ("Ascanio in Alba"), and a few minor compositions in prose constitute the rest of his literary productions.

See the biography by REINA prefixed to PARINI's *Opere* (Milan, 1881–4); CANTÙ, *Giorno* (Milan, 1854); CARDUCCI, *Storia del Giorno di Giuseppe Parini* (Bologna, 1892); SALVERAGLIO, *Odi* (Bologna, 1882).

J. D. M. FORD.

Paris, ARCHDIOCESE OF (PARISIENSIS), comprises the Department of the Seine. It was re-established by the Concordat of 1802 with much narrower limits than it had prior to the Revolution, when, besides the city of Paris and its suburbs, it comprised the archdeanery of Josas (including the deaneries of Châteaufort and Montlhéry) and the archdeanery of Brie (including the deaneries of Lagny and Vieux-Corbeil). The deanery of Champeaux, enclosed within the territory of the Diocese of Sens, was also dependent on the Archdiocese of Paris, which had then 492 parishes. The Concordat gave to the dioceses of Versailles and Meaux the archdeaneries of Josas and Brie, which had nearly 350 parishes, and reduced the Archdiocese of Paris to 42 urban and 76 suburban parishes. According to the Concordat it had eight suffragans: Amiens, Arras, Cambrai, Orléans, Meaux, Soissons, Troyes, and Versailles. The re-establishment under the Restoration of the Archdioceses of Reims and Sens removed the Dioceses of Troyes, Amiens, and Soissons from the jurisdiction of Paris, but the Dioceses of Blois and Chartres, created in 1882, were attached to the Province of Paris. In 1841 Cambrai, having become a metropolitan see, ceased to be a suffragan of Paris, Arras being made its suffragan.

THE ROMAN LUTETIA.—The Gaul Camulogenus burnt Lutetia in 52 B. C., while defending against Cæsar the tribe of the *Parisii*, whose capital it was. The Romans erected a new city on the left slope of Mt. Lucotilius (later Mont Ste-Geneviève). That the Romanization of Paris was very quickly accomplished is proved: (1) by the altar (discovered in 1710 under the choir of Notre-Dame) raised to Jupiter under

Tiberius by the *Nautæ Parisiaci*, on which are represented several deities borrowed from the Roman pantheon; (2) by the remains of a pedestal (found in 1871 on the site of the old Hôtel-Dieu), which doubtless supported a statue of Germanicus, and on which is represented *Janus Quadrifrons*, the Roman symbol of peace. At the end of the third century Lutetia was destroyed by the barbarians, but an important military camp was at once installed in this district. Cæsar Julian, later emperor and known as Julian the Apostate, defended Lutetia against fresh invasions from the north over the road from Senlis to Orléans. There, in 360, he was proclaimed Augustus by his soldiers, and Valentian I also sojourned there. The ruins found in the garden of the Musée de Cluny have, since the twelfth century, been regarded as the ruins of the *Thermæ*, but in 1903-04 other *thermæ* were discovered a little distance away, which must be either those of the palace of Julian the Apostate, or, according to M. Julian, those of the communal house of the *Nautæ Parisiaci*. Ruins have also been discovered of an arena capable of holding from 8000 to 9000 persons.

BEGINNINGS OF CHRISTIANITY AT PARIS.—Paris was a Christian centre at an early date, its first apostles being St. Denis and his companions, Sts. Rusticus and Eleutherius. Until the Revolution the ancient tradition of the Parisian Church commemorated the seven stations of St. Denis, the stages of his apostolate and martyrdom: (1) the ancient monastery of Notre-Dame-des-Champs of which the crypt, it was said, had been dedicated to the Blessed Virgin by St. Denis on his arrival in Paris; (2) the Church of St-Etienne-des-Grès (now disappeared), which stood on the site of an oratory erected by St. Denis to St. Stephen; (3) the Church of St-Benoît (disappeared), where St. Denis had erected an oratory to the Trinity (*Deus Benedictus*); (4) the chapel of St-Denis-du-Pas near Notre-Dame (disappeared), on the site of the tribunal of the prefect Sicinnius, who tried St. Denis; (5) the Church of St-Denis-de-la-Châtre, the crypt of which was regarded as the saint's cell (now vanished); (6) Montmartre, where, according to the chronicle written in 836 by Abbot Hilduin, St. Denis was executed; (7) the basilica of St-Denis (see below). The memorials of the saint's activity in Paris have thus survived, but even the date of his apostolate is a matter of controversy. The legend stating St. Denis came to Gaul in the time of St. Clement, dates only from the end of the eighth century. It is found in the "Passio Dionisii", written about 800, and in the "Gesta Dagoberti", written at the Abbey of St-Denis at the beginning of the ninth century. Still later than the formation of this legend Abbot Hilduin identified St. Denis of Paris with Denis the Areopagite (see DIONYSIUS THE PSEUDO-AREOPAGITE), but this identification is no longer admitted, and history is inclined to accept the opinion of St. Gregory of Tours, who declares St. Denis one of the seven bishops sent by Pope Fabian about 250. It is certain that the Christian community of Paris was of some importance in the third century. Recent discoveries seem to prove that the catacombs of the Gobelins and of St. Marcellus on the left bank were the oldest necropolis of Paris; here have been found nearly 500 tombs, of which the oldest date from the end of the third century. Doubtless in this quarter was situated the church spoken of by St. Gregory of Tours as the oldest in the city; here was the sarcophagus of the virgin Crescentia, granted that our hypothesis agrees with a legend referring to this region the foundation of the chapel under the patronage of Pope St. Clement, in which Bishop St. Marcellus was buried in the fifth century. This bishop, who was a native of Paris, governed the Church of Paris about 430; he is celebrated in popular tradition for his victory over a dragon, and his life was written by Fortunatus.

MEROVINGIAN PARIS.—Paris was preserved from the invasion of Attila through the prayers and activity of St. Genevieve (q. v.), who prevailed on the Parisians not to abandon their city. Clovis, King of the Franks, was received there in 497 after his conversion to Christianity, and made it his capital. The coming of the Franks brought about its great religious development. At the summit of the hill on the left bank Clovis founded, in honour of the Apostles Peter and Paul, a basilica to which the tomb of St. Genevieve drew numbers of the faithful, and in which St. Clotilde, who died at Tours, was buried. On the right bank were built as early as the fifth century two churches consecrated to St. Martin of Tours—one near the present Notre-Dame, the other further in the country, in the place where the Church of St-Martin-des-Champs now stands. Childebert (d. 558), son of Clovis, having become King of Paris in 511, added to the religious prestige of the city. After his campaign in Spain, he made peace with the inhabitants of Saragossa on condition that they would deliver to him the sacred vessels and the stole of St. Vincent, and on his return, at the instance of St. Germain (q. v.), built a church in honour of St. Vincent, which later took the name of Germain himself. The present church of St-Germain-des-Prés still preserves some columns from the triforium, which must date from the first building. After the death of Caribert, son of Clotaire I (567), Paris was not divided among the other sons of Clotaire, but formed a sort of municipal republic under the direction of St. Germain. Owing to this exceptional situation Paris escaped almost entirely the consequences of the civil wars with which the sons of Clotaire, and later Fredegunde and Brunhilde, disturbed Merovingian France. Mgr Duchesne concedes a certain authority to an ancient catalogue of the bishops of Paris, preserved in a sacramentary dating from the end of the ninth or the beginning of the tenth century. After St. Germain other bishops of the Merovingian period were: St. Céran (Ceraunus, 606-21), who collected and compiled the Acts of the Martyrs, and during whose episcopate a council of seventy-nine bishops (the first national council of France) was held at the basilica of Sts. Peter and Paul; St. Landry (650-6), who founded under the patronage of St.

CHURCH OF THE MADELEINE, PARIS

Christopher the first charity hospital (*Hôtel-Dieu*) of Paris, and who caused the monk Marculf to compile, under the name of "Recueil de Formules", the first French and Parisian code, which is a real monument of the legislation of the seventh century; St. Agilbert (666–80), who was the brother of St. Theodechilde, first Abbess of Jouarre, and who had, during his youth in England, instructed in Christianity the King of the Saxons; St. Hugues (722–30), nephew of Charles Martel, previously Archbishop of Rouen and Abbot of Fontenelle.

PARIS UNDER THE CARLOVINGIANS.—The Carlovingian period opened with the episcopate of Déodefroi (757–75), who received Pope Stephen at Paris. Special mention must be made of Æneas (appointed bishop in 853 or 858; d. 870), who wrote against Photius, under the title "Libellus adversus Græcos", a collection of texts from the Fathers on the Holy Ghost, fasting, and the Roman primacy. As the Carlovingians most frequently resided on the banks of the Meuse or the Rhine, the bishops of Paris greatly increased their political influence, though confronted by counts who represented the absent sovereigns. The bishops were masters of most of the *Ile de la Cité* and of a considerable portion of the right bank, near St-Germain-l'Auxerrois. As early as the ninth century the property of the chapter of Notre-Dame, established (775–95) by Bishop Erchenrade, was distinct from that of the diocese, while the cloister and the residences of the canons were quite independent of the royal power. Notre-Dame and the Abbey of St-Germain-des-Prés were then two great economic powers which sent through the kingdom their agents (*missi negociantes*), charged with making purchases. When the Normans entered Paris in 845 or 846, the body of St. Germain was hurriedly removed. They established themselves in the abbey, but left on payment of 7000 livres, whereupon the saint's body was brought back with great pomp. Another Norman invasion in 850 or 856 again occasioned the removal of St. Germain's body, which was restored in 863. Other alarms came in 865 and 876, but the worst attack took place on 24 Nov., 885, when Paris was defended by its bishop, the celebrated Gozlin, a Benedictine and former Abbot of St-Germain-des-Prés, and by Count Eudes of Paris, later King of France. The siege lasted a year, of which an account in Latin verse was written by the monk Abbo Cernuus. Gozlin died in the breach on 16 April, 886. His nephew Ebles, Abbot of St-Germain, was also among the valiant defenders of the city. The Parisians called upon Emperor Charles the Fat to assist them, and he paid the Normans a ransom, and even gave them permission to ascend the Seine through the city to pillage Burgundy; the Parisians refused to let them pass, however, and the Normans had to drag their boats around the walls. After the deposition of Charles the Fat, Eudes, who had defended Paris against the Normans, became king, and repelled another Norman attack, assisted by Gozlin's successor, Bishop Anscheric (886–91). After the death of Eudes the Parisians recognized his brother Robert, Count of Paris and Duke of France, and then Hugh the Great. Hugh Capet, son of Hugh the Great, prevented Paris from falling into the hands of the troops of Emperor Otto II in 978; in 987 he founded the Capetian dynasty.

PARIS UNDER THE CAPETIANS.—"To form a conception of Paris in the tenth and eleventh centuries", writes M. Marcel Poète, "we must picture to ourselves a network of churches and monasteries surrounded by cultivated farm-lands on the present site of Paris." Take, for example, the monastery of St. Martin-des-Champs, which in 1079 was attached to the Order of Cluny; about this monastery and its hospice was grouped a real agricultural colony, while all trades were practised in the monastic school. The same was true of the monastery of Sts. Barthélemy and Magloire, which was celebrated at the beginning of the Capetian period, and was dependent on the Abbey of Marmoutiers (see TOURS). But a still more famous monastic establishment was the Abbey of St-Germain-des-Prés. Its estates of Issy and of Celle-St-Cloud were vast possessions, and the polyptych (record of the monastic possessions), drawn up at the beginning of the ninth century under the direction of Abbot Irminon, shows how these estates, which extended into Indre and Normandy, were administered and cultivated. The first Capetians generally resided at Paris. Louis the Fat quarrelled with Bishop Etienne de Senlis (1124–42). The bishop placed the royal domain under interdict, whereupon the king confiscated the temporalities of the diocese, but the intervention of the pope and of St. Bernard put an end to the difference, and to seal the reconciliation, the king invited the bishop to the coronation of his son, Louis VII. The episcopal court of Peter Lombard (1157 or 1159 to 1160 or 1164) contributed to the scholarly reputation of the Church of Paris. The University of Paris did not yet exist, but, from the beginning of the twelfth century, the monastic schools of Notre-Dame were already famous, and the teaching of Peter Lombard, known as the Master of the Sentences, added to their lustre. Louis VI declared in a diploma that he had passed "his childhood in the schools of Notre-Dame as in the maternal bosom". At Notre-Dame William of Champeaux (q. v.) had taught dialectics, been a professor, and become an archdeacon, and had Abelard as a disciple before he founded the school of St-Victor in 1108. Until about 1127 the students of Notre-Dame resided within the chapter enclosure. By a command of Alexander III the principle of gratuitous instruction was asserted. In a letter written between 1154 and 1182 Philippe de Harvengt says: "There is at Paris such an assemblage and abundance of clerics that they threatened to outnumber the laity. Happy city, where the Holy Books are so assiduously studied and their mysteries so well expounded, where such diligence reigns among the students, and where there is such a knowledge of Scripture that it may be called the city of letters!" At the same period Peter of Blois says that all who wish the settlement of any question should apply to Paris, where the most tangled knots are untied. In his letter to Archbishop William of Sens (1169), St. Thomas à Becket declares himself ready to submit his difference with the King of England to the judgment of the scholars at Paris.

The long episcopate of Maurice de Sully (1160–96), the son of a simple serf, was marked by the consecration of the Cathedral of Notre-Dame (see below) and the journey to Paris of Pope Alexander III (1163). Hughes de Monceaux, Abbot of St-Germain, requested the pope to consecrate the monastery church. Maurice de Sully, Bishop of Paris, having accompanied the pope to the ceremony, was invited by the abbot to withdraw, and Alexander III declared in a sermon, afterwards confirmed by a Bull, thenceforth the Church of St-Germain-des-Prés was dependent only on the Roman pontiff, and subsequently conferred on the abbot a number of episcopal prerogatives. In time the Abbey of St-Germain became the centre of a bourg, the inhabitants of which were granted municipal freedom by Abbot Hughes de Monceaux about 1170. Eudes de Sully (1197–1208), the successor of Maurice, courageously opposed King Philip II, when he wished to repudiate Ingeburge and wed Agnes de Méran. Philip II was a benefactor of Paris, and the university was founded during his reign (1215). (See PARIS, UNIVERSITY OF.) The thirteenth century, and especially the reign of St. Louis, was a period of great industrial and commercial prosperity for Paris, as is shown by the "Livre des Mestiers" of Etienne Boileau and the invectives of Petrarch. Bishop Guillaume d'Auvergne (1227–49) received from St. Louis the

Crown of Thorns, which was borne in procession to Paris on 18 August, 1239. Under St. Louis the Parliament was permanently established at Paris and the Bishop of Paris declared a *conseiller-né*. Under Philip the Fair occurred at Paris the trial of the Templars (q. v.) which ended (1314) with the execution of Jacques de Molai (q. v.).

PARIS UNDER THE VALOIS.—The troubles of the Hundred Years' War throw into relief the character of Pierre de la Forest, Bishop of Paris (1350–2), later Archbishop of Rouen and cardinal. After the Battle of Poitiers (1356), at which John II was taken prisoner, the dauphin Charles (afterwards Charles V) convoked at Paris the States General of 1356, 1357, and 1358. At these assemblies the provost of merchants, Etienne Marcel, and Robert Le Coq, Bishop of Laon, were the leaders of a violent opposition to the royal party. The result of the assassination of Etienne Marcel was the dauphin's victory. Having become king as Charles V, the latter made himself a magnificent residence at the Hôtel St-Paul, rebuilt the Louvre, and began the construction of the Bastille. During his reign the cardinalitial purple was first given to the bishops of Paris. Etienne de Paris (1363–8) and Aimeri de Maignac (1368–84) received it in turn. The revolt of the Maillotins (1381) and the wars between the Burgundians and Armagnacs during the first twenty years of the fifteenth century filled Paris with blood. After the Treaty of Troyes (1420) Paris received an English garrison. Because of his sympathy with Charles VI, John Courtecuisse, a theologian of Gallican tendencies who became bishop in 1420, was compelled to go into exile at Geneva, where he died in 1423. The attack of Joan of Arc on Paris in 1430 was unsuccessful. The Treaty of Arras between Philip the Good, Duke of Burgundy, and Charles VII, restored Paris under the dominion of the kings of France. Louis XI (q. v.), successor of Charles VII, was much beloved by the citizens of Paris. The poet Jean du Bellay, friend of Francis I and several times ambassador, was Bishop of Paris from 1532 to 1551, and was made cardinal in 1535. With him the Renaissance was established in the diocese, and it was at his persuasion that Francis I founded for the teaching of languages and philology the Collège Royal, which later became the Collège de France (1529). In 1533 du Bellay negotiated between Henry VIII and Clement VII in an attempt to prevent England's break with the Holy See, and, when in 1536 the troops of Charles V threatened Picardy and Champagne, he received from Francis I the title of Lieutenant-General of the Kingdom and placed Paris in a state of defence. Du Bellay was a typical prelate of the Renaissance, and was celebrated for his three books of Latin poetry and his magnificent Latin discourses. For a time he had for his secretary, Rabelais, whom he is said to have inspired to write "Pantagruel". He was disgraced under Henry II, resigned his bishopric in 1551, and went to Rome, where he died. The consequences of the rise of Protestantism and of the wars of religion in regard to Paris are treated under SAINT BARTHOLOMEW'S DAY; LEAGUE, THE; FRANCE.

PARIS UNDER THE BOURBONS.—With Cardinal Pierre de Gondi (d. 1598), who occupied the See of Paris from 1568, began the Gondi dynasty which occupied the see for a century. As ambassador to Pius V, Gregory XIII, and Sixtus V, Pierre de Gondi always opposed the League and favoured the accession of Henry of Navarre. After the episcopate of his nephew Cardinal Henri de Gondi (1598–1622), Paris became an archiepiscopal see, and was given to Jean François de Gondi. As early as 1376 Charles V had sought the erection of Paris to archiepiscopal rank, but, out of regard for the archbishops of Sens, the Holy See had then refused to grant the petition. Louis XIII was more successful, and by a Bull of October, 1622, Paris was made a metropolitan see with Chartres, Meaux, and Orléans as suffragans. Jean François de Gondi did much to further the development of religious congregations (see BÉRULLE, PIERRE DE; ORATORY, FRENCH CONGREGATION OF THE; OLIER, JEAN-JACQUES; ST-SULPICE, SOCIETY OF; VINCENT DE PAUL, SAINT), and, during the civil disturbances of the Fronde, laboured for the relief of the suffering populace, whose tireless benefactor was St. Vincent de Paul. The archbishop's coadjutor was his nephew Jean François Paul de Gondi, Cardinal de Retz (q. v.), who often played the part of a political conspirator. In 1662 the See of Paris was for a very brief period occupied by the Gallican canonist Pierre de Marca, earlier Archbishop of Toulouse. He was succeeded by Hardouin de Péréfixe de Beaumont (1662–71), during whose episcopate began the sharp conflicts evoked by Jansenism. He had been tutor to Louis XIV and was the biographer of Henry IV. Harlay de Champvallon (1671–95) is the subject of a separate article. Louis Antoine de Noailles (1695–1729), made cardinal in 1700, played an important part in the disputes concerning Quietism and Jansenism. After an attempt to reconcile Bossuet and Fénelon he took sides against the latter, successively approved and condemned Quesnel's book, and did not subscribe to the Bull "Unigenitus" until 1728. In the eighteenth century the See of Paris was made illustrious by Christophe de Beaumont (1746–81), earlier Bishop of Bayonne and Archbishop of Vienne, who succeeded in putting an end to the opposition lingering among some of the clergy to the Bull "Unigenitus". The parliamentarians protested against the denial of the sacraments to impenitent Jansenists, and Louis XV, after having at first forbidden the Parliament to concern itself with this question, turned against the archbishop, exiled him, and then endeavoured to secure his resignation by offering him tempting dignities. But it was especially against the *philosophes* that this prelate waged war; pamphlets were written against him, among them the "Lettre de Jean Jacques Rousseau à monseigneur l'archévêque de Paris". Antoine Le Clerc de Juigné (d. 1811), who succeeded Beaumont in 1781, was president of the clergy at the States General of 1789. He

CHURCH OF ST. AUGUSTIN, PARIS

went into exile during the Revolution, and at the Concordat resigned his see at the pope's request.

Paris During the Revolution.—Within the present boundaries of the archdiocese the number of priests forming the active clergy at the time of the Revolution was about 1000, of whom 600 were in Parisian parishes, 150 in those of the suburbs, and 250 were chaplains. There were 921 religious, belonging to 21 religious families divided among 38 convents. Immediately after the adoption of the Civil Constitution of the clergy 8 new parishes were created in Paris and 27 were suppressed. Out of 50 Parisian pastors 26 refused to take the oath; out of 69 first or second curates 36 refused; of the 399 other priests having spiritual powers, 216 refused. On the other hand among the priests who, not exercising parochial duties, were not called upon to swear, 196 declared that they would take the oath and 14 refused. On 13 March, 1791, Gobel (b. 1727), Bishop of Lydda, Coadjutor Bishop of Basle, and a member of the Constitutional Assembly, was elected bishop by 500 votes. Loménie de Brienne, Archbishop of Sens, and Jarente, Bishop of Orléans, though both had accepted the civil constitution of the clergy, refused to give Gobel canonical institution, and he received it from the famous Talleyrand, Bishop of Autun. Gobel surrounded himself with married clerics, such as Louis de Saint Martin, Colombart, and Aubert, and through the Marquis of Spinola, Minister of the Republic of Genoa, endeavoured to obtain from the Holy See a sum of money in exchange for his submission. At the beginning of 1793 he was at the head of about 600 "sworn" priests, about 500 of whom were employed in parishes. On 7 November, 1793, he solemnly declared before the Convention that his subordinates and he renounced the duties of ministers of Catholic worship, whereupon the Convention congratulated him on having "sacrificed the grotesque baubles of superstition". On the same day Notre-Dame was dedicated to the worship of Reason, Citizeness Aubry, a *comédienne*, impersonating that goddess and Gobel presiding at the ceremony. Finally, the Commune of Paris decided that all churches should be closed, and that whosoever requested that they be reopened should be regarded as a suspect. In March, 1794, Gobel was condemned to death as an atheist by the followers of Robespierre, and was executed after lengthy spiritual interviews with the Sulpician Emery and after he had addressed to Abbé Lothringer a letter in which he declared his repentance. In the absence of Juigné, the legitimate bishop, the Catholic faithful continued to obey a council formed of the Abbés de Malaret, Emery, and Espinasse, under the leadership of the former vicar-general, Charles Henri du Valk de Dampierre, who was in hiding. Public worship was restored by the Law of Ventose, Year III, and by the law of 2 Prairial, Year III (30 March, 1795), fifteen churches were reopened. As early as 1796 about fifty places of worship had been reopened in Paris; sixteen or seventeen, of which eleven were parochial churches, were administered by priests who had accepted the Constitution. More than thirty others, of which three were parochial churches, were administered by priests who were in secret obedience to the legitimate archbishop, and the number of Constitutional priests had fallen from 600 to 150.

Paris in the Nineteenth Century.—The Archdiocese of Paris became more and more important in France during the nineteenth century. Jean Baptiste de Belloy, former Bishop of Marseilles, who was appointed archbishop in 1802, was then ninety-three years old. On 18 April, 1802, he presided at Notre-Dame over the ceremony at which the Concordat was solemnly published. Despite his great age he reorganized worship in Paris, and re-established religious life in its forty-two parishes. In a conciliatory spirit he appointed to about twelve of these parishes priests who had taken the oath during the Revolution. He became cardinal in 1803 and died in 1808. The conflict between Napoleon and Pius VII was then at its height. Napoleon attempted to make Fesch accept the See of Paris, while the latter wished to retain that of Lyons. Cardinal Maury (1746–1817), formerly a royalist deputy to the Constitutional Assembly, also ambassador to the Holy See from the Count of Provence, but who went over to the Empire in 1806 and in 1810 became chaplain to King Jerome, was named Archbishop of Paris by Napoleon on 14 Oct., 1810. The chapter at once conferred on him the powers of vicar-capitular, until he should be preconized by the pope, but, when it became known that Pius VII, by a Brief of 5 November, 1810, refused to recognize the nomination, Maury was actively opposed by a section of the chapter and the clergy. The emperor took his revenge by striking at the vicar-capitular, Astros (q. v.). At the fall of Napoleon, despite his zeal in persuading it to adhere to the deposition of the emperor, Maury was deprived of his faculties by the chapter. In agreement with Rome, Louis XVIII named as Archbishop of Paris (1 Aug., 1817) Alexandre Angélique de Talleyrand-Périgord (1736–1821), who, despite the Concordat, chose to retain his title of Archbishop of Reims until 1816 and who was created cardinal on 28 July, 1817. Talleyrand-Périgord did not take possession of his see until Oct., 1819. He divided the diocese into three archdeaneries, which division is still in force.

On the death of Talleyrand-Périgord in 1821, his coadjutor Hyacinthe Louis de Quélen (1778–1840), court chaplain, succeeded him. A member of the Chamber of Peers under the Restoration, Quélen, as president of the commission for the investigation of the school situation, vainly endeavoured to prevent the promulgation of the Martignac ordinances against the Jesuits in June, 1828. His friendly relations with Louis XVIII and Charles X drew upon him in 1830 the hostility of the populace; his palace was twice sacked, and the Monarchy of July regarded him with suspicion, but the devotion he showed during a terrible cholera epidemic won many hearts to him. Assisted by Dupanloup he converted the famous Talleyrand, nephew of his predecessor, on his death-bed in 1838. Quélen died 8 Jan., 1840, and was succeeded by Denis-Auguste Affre, (q. v., 1793–1848), who was slain at the barricades in 1848. Marie-Dominique-Auguste Sibour (1792–1862), formerly Bishop of Digne, succeeded Affre; among the prelates consulted by Pius IX with regard to the opportuneness of defining the Immaculate Conception, he was one of the few who opposed it. He was killed in the church of St-Étienne-du-Mont on 3 Jan., 1857, by a suspended priest. After the short episcopate of Cardinal Morlot (1857–62) the see was occupied from 1862 to 1872 by Georges Darboy (q. v.), who was slain during the Commune. Joseph-Hippolyte Guibert (1802–86), previously Bishop of Viviers and Archbishop of Tours, became Archbishop of Paris on 27 Oct., 1871. His episcopate was made notable by the erection of the basilica of Montmartre (see below), and the creation of the Catholic University, at the head of which he placed Mgr d'Hulst. His successor was François-Marie-Benjamin Richard (1819–1907), former Bishop of Belley, who had been coadjutor of Paris since July, 1875, became cardinal 24 May, 1889, and was active in the defence of the religious congregations. Mgr Léon Amette (b. at Douville, in the Diocese of Evreux, 1850), coadjutor to Cardinal Richard since February, 1906, succeeded him in the See of Paris, on 28 Jan., 1908.

Notre-Dame-de-Paris.—On the site now occupied by the courtyards of Notre-Dame de Paris there was as early as the sixth century a church of Notre-Dame, which had as patrons the Blessed Virgin, St. Stephen, and St. Germain. It was built by Childebert about

528, and on the site of the present sacristy there was also a church dedicated to St. Stephen. The Norman invasions destroyed Notre-Dame, but St-Etienne remained standing, and for a time served as the cathedral. At the end of the ninth century Notre-Dame was rebuilt, and the two churches continued to exist side by side until the eleventh century when St-Etienne fell to ruin. Maurice de Sully resolved to erect a magnificent cathedral on the ruins of St-Etienne and the site of Notre-Dame. Surrounded by twelve cardinals, Alexander III, who sojourned at Paris from 24 March to 25 April, 1163, laid the corner-stone. Henri de Château-Marçay, papal legate, consecrated the high altar in 1182; Hierarchus, Patriarch of Jerusalem, officiated in 1185 in the completed choir; the façade was finished in 1218, the towers in 1235. Jean and Pierre de Chelles completed the work, and, at the beginning of the fourteenth century, the cathedral was as it is now. The following are among the noteworthy events which took place at Notre-Dame: the depositing by St. Louis (10 Aug., 1239) of the Crown of Thorns, a portion of the True Cross, and a nail of the Passion; the obsequies of St. Louis (21 May, 1271); the assembling of the first States-General (10 April, 1302); the coronation of Henry VI of England as King of France (17 Nov., 1431); the coronation of Mary Stuart (4 April, 1560); the funeral oration of the Duc de Mercœur by St. Francis de Sales (27 April, 1602); the vow of Louis XIII, making the Assumption a feast of the kingdom (10 Feb., 1638); the abjuration of the Maréchal de Turenne (23 Oct., 1668); the funeral oration of the Prince de Condé by Bossuet (10 March, 1687).

During the French Revolution, in the period following 1790, the treasury was despoiled of many of its precious objects, which were sent to the mint to be melted down. The Crown of Thorns was taken to the cabinet of antiquities of the Bibliothèque Nationale and thus escaped destruction. The statues of the kings, which adorned the porch, were destroyed in October, 1793, by order of the Paris Commune. The feast of Reason was celebrated in Notre-Dame in November, 1793; in December of the same year Saint-Simon, the future founder of the Saint-Simonian religion, was about to purchase the church and destroy it. From 1798 it contained the offices of the Constitutional clergy, and from 5 March to 28 May, 1798, it was also the meeting-place of the Theophilanthropists. Catholic worship was resumed on 18 April, 1802, and the coronation of Napoleon took place there on 2 December, 1804. By the preface of his novel "Notre Dame de Paris" (1832) Victor Hugo aroused a strong public sentiment in favour of the cathedral. In April, 1844, the Government entrusted Lassus and Viollet le Duc with a complete restoration, which was completed in 1864. On 31 May, 1864, Archbishop Darboy dedicated the restored cathedral. The marriage of Napoleon III (30 January, 1853), the funeral services of President Carnot (1 July, 1894), the obsequies of President Félix Faure (23 Feb., 1899), took place at Notre-Dame. Notre-Dame has been a minor basilica since 27 Feb., 1805. As early as the beginning of the thirteenth century at least two churches were copied entirely from the cathedral of Paris, viz. the collegiate church of Mantes (Seine-et-Oise) and the cathedral of Nicosia in the Island of Cyprus, the bishop of which was a brother of the cantor of Notre-Dame. The *Ile de la Cité*, where Notre-Dame stands, also contains the Sainte-Chapelle, in the Palais de la Justice, one of the most beautiful religious buildings in Paris. It was built (1212–47) under St. Louis by Pierre de Montereau, with the exception of the spire. Its stained-glass windows are admirable. In former times the king, from an ogival baldachin, displayed to the people the relics of the Passion.

PRINCIPAL CHURCHES ON THE RIGHT BANK OF THE SEINE.—The Church of St-Germain-l'Auxerrois was built between the thirteenth and the sixteenth century on the site of a baptistery built by St. Germain, where baptism was administered on fixed dates. At other times the *piscina* was dry, and the catechumens came and seated themselves on the steps while catechetical classes were held. Three tragic recollections are connected with this church. On 24 August, 1572, its bells gave the signal for the Massacre of St. Bartholomew; in 1617, the body of Concini, Maréchal d'Ancre, which had been buried there, was disinterred by the mob and mutilated; on 14 Feb., 1831, the people sacked the church under the pretext that an anniversary Mass was being celebrated for the soul of the Duc de Berry. The Church of St-Eustache, built between 1532 and 1637, was the scene of the First Communion of Louis XIV (1649), the funeral oration of Turenne preached by Fléchier (1676), and Massillon's sermon

THE PANTHEON, PARIS

on the small number of the elect (1704). Massillon preached the Lenten sermons in the church of St-Leu (fourteenth century), and the conspirator Georges Cadoudal hid in its crypt from the police of Bonaparte. In the Church of St-Gervais (early sixteenth-century), where the League was established, Bossuet preached the funeral sermon of Chancellor Michel Le Tellier. Its doorway, of which Louis XIII laid the first stone in 1616, is a very beautiful work of Salomon de Brosse. Blessed Marie de l'Incarnation was baptized at Saint-Merry (1520–1612). In Saint-Louis-en-l'Ile (rebuilt 1664–1726) St. Vincent de Paul presided over the meetings at which the charity bureaux were organized. Charles VI, Charles VII, and Olier were baptized in the Church of St-Paul, destroyed during the Revolution. The Church of St-Louis (seventeenth-century), former chapel of the Jesuit professed house, where Bourdaloue preached the funeral sermon of Condé and where he was buried, was chosen at the Concordat to replace the parish of St-Paul, and took the name of St-Paul-St-Louis. The Madeleine (begun 1764 and finished 1824), of which Napoleon I wished to make a Temple of Glory, had within less than a century two pastors, who were martyred, Le Ber, butchered in 1792, and Deguerry, shot in 1871. The Church of St-Lawrence (fifteenth-century) was often visited by St. Vincent de Paul, who lived in the convent of St-Lazare within the confines of the parish. Here was buried Venerable Madame Le Gras, foundress of the Sisters of Charity. During the Revolution it was given to the Theophilanthropists who made of it the "Temple of Hymen and Fidelity". With regard to Notre-Dame-des-Victoires see below under FAMOUS PILGRIMAGES. St-Denys-de-la-Chapelle (thirteenth-century) stands where St. Genevieve and her companions rested, when they were making a pilgrimage from Paris to the tomb of St. Denis. Bl. Joan of Arc, who had come to besiege Paris, stopped here to pray.

PRINCIPAL CHURCHES ON THE LEFT BANK.—St-Nicholas-du-Chardonnet (1656–1758) is famous for the seminary which Bourdoise founded in the vicinity, for the Forty Hours preached there by St. Francis de Sales, and for the funeral oration of Lamoignon preached there by Fléchier. St-Sulpice (1646–1745) is famous for its pastor Olier (q. v.); in 1793 it was a temple of Victory, under the Directory it was used by the Theophilanthropists, and there Pius VII consecrated the bishops of La Rochelle and Poitiers. To the architectural importance of St-Germain-des-Prés was added in the nineteenth century the attraction of Flandrin's frescoes. St-Médard (fifteenth-sixteenth-century) became celebrated in the eighteenth century owing to the sensation caused by the Jansenists with regard to the wonders wrought at the tomb of the deacon Paris. St-Séverin (fourteenth-fifteenth-century), one of the most remarkable Gothic edifices of Paris, replaced an older church in which Foulques de Neuilly preached the fourth crusade in 1199; St. Vincent de Paul, Bossuet, Massillon, Fléchier, Lacordaire, and Ravignan preached in this church. Originally dedicated to St. Severinus, a Parisian hermit, who was buried there in 555, it was dedicated to St. Severinus of Agaune from the fifteenth to the eighteenth century, and since 1753 has had both these saints as patrons. Ste-Clotilde (1846–61) was made a minor basilica on 19 April, 1897, at the time of the fourteenth centenary of Clovis. St-Lambert-de-Vaugirard had as pastor Olier, who founded the Society of St-Sulpice, and St. John Baptist de la Salle opened his first school in this parish; its name of Vaugirard (*Vallis Gerardi*) recalls the charitable Abbot of St-Germain-des-Prés, Gerard de Moret, who built dwellings for sick religious in the locality. The church of the Sorbonne, where religious services are no longer held, was begun in 1635, Richelieu laying its foundation stone, and completed in 1646. Richelieu's tomb in this church was violated during the Revolution; the cardinal's head, which was taken away on this occasion, was restored to this church in 1866. The chapel of Val-de-Grâce, a very beautiful specimen of the Jesuit style and famous for its cupola wherein Mignard has depicted the glory of the blessed, was built in fulfillment of a vow made by Anne of Austria. Mansart was its first architect, and the corner-stone was laid in 1645 by Louis XIV at the age of seven. Here was buried Henrietta of France, wife of Charles I of England, and here Bossuet preached the Lenten sermons of 1663. It is now the chapel of the Paris military hospital. The chapel of St-Louis-des-Invalides contains the tomb of Napoleon I. In the crypt of the Church of St-Joseph-des-Carmes, built by the Carmelites between 1613 and 1625 and now the church of the Institut Catholique, are the tomb of Ozanam and the remains of the 120 priests massacred in this church on 2 Sept., 1792, after fifteen days of captivity. In this crypt Lacordaire remained attached to a cross for three hours.

PRINCIPAL ABBEYS.—The Benedictine Abbey of St-Germain-des-Prés, the foundation and medieval splendour of which have been described above, was long famous for the fair which it held. During the seventeenth century its important library made it a centre of learning, and Luc d' Achéry, Mabillon, and Montfaucon rendered it illustrious. Abbé Prévost, author of the famous romance "Manon Lescaut", was for a time a Benedictine at St-Germain-des-Prés, where he worked on "Gallia Christiana". John Casimir, first a Jesuit and later King of Poland, died as Abbot of St-Germain-des-Prés in 1672. The abbey prison was the scene of the September massacres in 1792.

The origin of the Abbey of St-Victor was a hermitage, to which William of Champeaux (q. v.) retired in 1108. The abbey was founded by a royal charter in 1113, and had as first abbot Gilduin, confessor of Louis the Fat. The abbey governed the priories of Corbeil, Château-Laudon, Etampes, Mantes, Poissy, Dreux, and even the cathedral of Séez. During the first century it was rendered illustrious by Richard of St-Victor, Hugh of St-Victor, and the liturgical poet, Adam of St-Victor. Grave abuses having crept into the Congregation of the Canons of St. Genevieve, Pope Eugenius III and Suger in 1148 introduced the Canons Regular of St. Augustine from the Abbey of St-Victor. From the thirteenth to the fifteenth century the abbey passed through a period of decadence, and in 1498 two strange monks, John Standonck, rector of the College of Montaigu, and John Monbaer of Windesheim near Zwolle, spent nine months at the abbey to effect its reform. With the sixteenth century began a series of commendatory abbots, one of whom, Antonio Caracciolo, became a Protestant. The canons of St-Victor took a very important part in the League. The first half of the seventeenth century was characterized by a conflict between Jean de Toulouse, prior of St-Victor, and the Genovéfains; a decision of the *official* (28 June, 1645) declared St-Victor autonomous. Jansenism found its way into St-Victor, and was combatted by Simon Gourdan, who was persecuted. In the eighteenth century its library was celebrated, and was open to the public three times a week. The librarian Mulot, who was also grand prior, published a translation of "Daphnis and Chloe". The abbey's end was sad. When the Revolutionary commissaries questioned the twenty-one religious present, only one, aged 81, affirmed his desire to remain; nine did not reply, eleven left the monastery, and the librarian Mulot became a deputy of the Legislative Assembly. The abbey was destroyed in November, 1798.

The early history of the Abbey of Saint-Denis, near Paris, is very obscure. In the second half of the fifth century the clergy of Paris erected at the instance of St. Genevieve in the village of Catulliacus where the saint was buried, a basilica, administered by a community of monks. Pilgrims flocked thither, and, as early as 625, a charter of Clotaire II authorized the abbot to receive a legacy. Nevertheless, tradition regards Dagobert I (628–38) as the real founder. According to Mabillon, Félibien, and M. Léon Levillain, he merely decorated and embellished the already existing basilica; according to Julian Havet, this early basilica stood at the place called Saint-Denis-de-l' Entrée, west of the present church, and between 623 and 625 Dagobert founded the new abbey church, to which the relics were removed in 626. Whatever the solution of this problem, with which scholars have occupied themselves since the seventeenth century, Dagobert was the abbey's signal benefactor: the altar ornaments, the tomb containing the body of St. Denis, the golden cross set with precious stones which stood behind the high altar were the work of the goldsmith, St. Eligius (Eloi), the king's friend. Dagobert himself desired to be buried at Saint-Denis. At the instance of Abbot Fulrad (d. 784) Pepin the Short had the abbey rebuilt, and here on 28 July, 754, Pope Stephen II solemnly administered the royal anointment to Pepin, Queen Bertha, and their two sons, and consecrated an altar. The new edifice was dedicated on 24 Feb., 775, in the presence of Charlemagne. Hilduin, who became abbot in 814, wrote the life of St.

STS. GERMANUS AND LUPUS, ON THEIR WAY TO BRITAIN (A.D. 429), PERCEIVE
THE SIGNS OF FUTURE SANCTITY IN THE CHILD GENEVIÈVE

PUVIS DE CHAVANNES, THE PANTHEON, PARIS

Denis, and identifies him with St. Denis the Areopagite. During the ninth century the Normans several times levied tribute on and pillaged the monastery. During the siege of Paris in 886, the monks sought refuge with Archbishop Foulques of Reims, taking with them the body of St. Denis. After these disasters the abbey was restored and perhaps, as some scholars maintain, entirely rebuilt. St. Gerard, of a noble family of the Low Countries, was a monk at St-Denis previously to founding the Abbey of Broglie in 1030. In 1106 Paschal II visited the abbey, and for a time Abelard was a monk there. Suger, minister of Louis VI and Louis VII, who became Abbot of St-Denis in 1122, wished to erect a sumptuous new church; his architectural work is known to us through two of his writings, the "Book of his Administration" and the "Treatise on the Consecration of the Church of St. Denis". St-Denis then attracted numerous pilgrims, whom Suger describes as crowding to the doors, "squeezed as in a press". By a charter of 15 March, 1125, Suger released from mortmain the people of St-Denis, who in gratitude gave him the money for the reconstruction of the church. The work began doubtless about 1132; the choir was consecrated on 11 June, 1144, in the presence of Louis VII, five archbishops, and fourteen bishops, and the translation of the relics took place the same day. The alliance of the Capetians with the monastery of St. Denis was thenceforth sealed. Odo of Deuil, Suger's successor as abbot, was chaplain to Louis VII during the second crusade, of which he wrote a chronicle. The Abbey of St-Denis was the repository of the royal insignia—the crown, sceptre, *main de justice*, and the garments and ornaments used at the coronation of the kings. For each coronation the abbot brought them to Reims. The oriflamme (q. v.) was also kept there, and thither repaired Bl. Joan of Arc after the coronation of Charles VII at Reims.

The new Church of St-Denis has an extreme importance for the history of medieval architecture. It was the earliest important building in which the pointed arch (*croisée d'ogive*) was used in the chapels of the deambulatory, thus inaugurating this wonderful invention of the Gothic style. The church exercised also a great influence on the development of the industrial arts: the products of the goldsmith's and enameller's art ordered by Suger formed one of the most beautiful treasures of Christianity, some remnants of which are still preserved in the Gallery of Apollo at the Louvre. As regards monumental sculpture M. André Michel, the art historian, writes that "the grand chantry of St-Denis was the decisive studio in the elaboration and, if we may so speak, the proclamation of the new style." In 1231 the religious of St-Denis resolved to reconstruct the basilica, and the chronicler Guillaume de Nangis, a monk at the abbey, says that St. Louis, a friend of their abbot Mathieu de Vendôme, advised them to do so. It may be that portions of the edifice built by Suger had fallen to ruin, or perhaps St. Louis's plan to erect tombs to his predecessors was the origin of the plan. Of Suger's building the western façade, the deambulatory, the chapels of the apse, and the crypt were retained, the remainder being rebuilt. The work was directed by the architect Pierre de Montereau, thanks to whose genius the nave and transept form a glorious example of the splendid Gothic art of the thirteenth century. St-Denis was the historical laboratory of the old French monarchy: the abbot selected a religious who followed the court as historiographer to the king, and, on the death of each king, the history of his reign, after having been submitted to the chapter, was incorporated in the "Grandes Chroniques". Especially important, as historical sources, are the works of the monk Rigord on Philip Augustus and that of Guillaume de Nangis on St. Louis. On the invention of printing the "Grandes Chroniques" were put in order by Jean Chartier, who completed them with the history of Charles VII and published them in 1476, this being the earliest book known to have been printed in Paris.

From 1529 St-Denis had commendatory abbots, the first of whom was Louis Cardinal de Bourbon. The Religious Wars were a disastrous period for the abbey. In 1562 and 1567 tombs were destroyed, the archives ravaged, and the reliquaries of the saints stripped of their plates of gold and silver. Catherine de' Medici planned to erect beside the church a chapel for Henry II and herself; François Primatice, Jean Bullant, and Androuet de Cerceau in turn supervised the work on this great mausoleum, which, owing to the civil disturbances, was never finished and was demolished in 1719. The troubles of the League brought about fresh

Church of St. Etienne du Mont, Paris

pillages. Here on 25 July, 1593, Renaud de Beaune, Archbishop of Bourges, received the abjuration of Henry IV. In 1633 the Benedictines of the Congregation of St. Maur reformed the abbey, and for a time the celebrated Mabillon (1632–1707) was guardian of the treasury. In 1686 Louis XIV transferred the abbatial revenues to the recently founded royal house of St-Cyr. In 1691 the title and dignity of its abbot were suppressed, and thenceforth the abbey was directed by grand priors, dependent on the superior-general of the congregation who resided at the Abbey of St-Germain-des-Prés. These grand priors were of right vicars-general of the archbishops of Paris. In 1706 the monk Félibien (1666–1719) published the history of the abbey. In the eighteenth century the abbey buildings were entirely rebuilt by the monks, and they were about to change completely the Gothic appearance of the church itself when the Revolution broke out. St-Denis was then called *Franciade*, the church became first a temple of Reason, and then a market-house. In August, 1793, the Convention, on the recommendation of Barère, ordered the destruction of the tombs of the kings. Immediately most of the Gothic tombs were destroyed, and between 14 and 25 Oct., 1793, the ashes of the Bourbons were scattered to the winds. In 1795 Alexander Lenoir had all the tombs that had been spared removed to the Museum of French Monuments. Napoleon (20 Feb., 1805) decided that the church should be restored, re-established worship there, and decreed that thenceforth St-Denis should be the burial-place of the emperors. At the Restoration the tombs which had been removed to the Museum of French Monuments were restored to St-Denis, but in such a disorderly fashion that Montalembert, in a discourse of 1847, called the Church of St. Denis "a museum of bric-à-brac". A truly artistic restoration was accomplished finally (1847–79) by Viollet le Duc.

Of the thirty-two Capetian kings from Hugh Capet to Louis XV only three were buried elsewhere than in St-Denis. The series of authentic portraits of the kings of France at St-Denis opens with the sepulchral statue of Philip III the Bold (d. 1285). Until the sixteenth century the royal tombs at St-Denis maintained modest proportions, but in that century the church was filled with works of art. The monument of the Dukes of Orléans, erected by Louis XII, was the work of four Genoese sculptors; that of Louis XII (d. 1515) and Anne of Brittany (d. 1514), is the work of the Juste family, Italian sculptors residing at Tours; the magnificent monument of Francis I and Claude of France is the work of the great architect Philibert Delorme and of the sculptor Pierre Bontemps; that of Henry II and Catherine de' Medici, executed under the direction of Primatice, is admired for the sculptures of Germain Pilon. The only monument representing the art of the seventeenth century is that of Turenne. The episcopal chapter of St-Denis, created by Napoleon I to care for the basilica, was composed of ten canons whose head was the grand almoner. The canons had to be former bishops more than fifty years of age. The Restoration created canons of a second order, who were not chosen from among the bishops, and the grand almoner received the title of *primicier* (dean) of the chapter. The empire and the Restoration claimed that this chapter, which Napoleon had created without taking counsel with Rome, should not be subject to the jurisdiction of the ordinary. This was the cause of conflict until 1846, when the pope issued a Bull placing the chapter of St-Germain under the direct supervision of the Holy See; the primate retained episcopal authority over the church and the house of the Legion of Honour annexed to the church, and the Archbishop of Paris had no spiritual jurisdiction over either of these buildings. The budget for the chapter of St-Denis was suppressed by the State in 1888. The theologian Maret, famous for his writings against the opportuneness of the definition of infallibility, was the last primate.

FAMOUS PILGRIMAGES.—(1) *Tomb of St. Genevieve.*—St. Genevieve is the patroness of Paris, but after the conversion of the church into a Pantheon of France's great men the saint had no church in Paris. Since 1803 her tomb has been at St-Etienne-du-Mont (built 1517–1620), the burial-place of Racine and Pascal. There Pius VII went to pray on 10 January, 1805, and it was the scene of the assassination of Archbishop Sibour on 3 January, 1857. The veneration of St. Genevieve is expressed in two feasts: (1) on her feast proper (3 January) and the following eight days a solemn novena takes place at St-Etienne-du-Mont and at the church of Nanterre, birthplace of St. Genevieve, whither Clotaire II, St. Louis, Blanche of Castile, Louis XIII, and Anne of Austria went to venerate her memory: (2) on 26 November, anniversary of the miracle whereby, in 1130, a procession of the relics of St. Genevieve cured many Parisians of the *mal des ardents* (*Miracle des ardents*).

(2) *Notre-Dame-des-Victoires.*—In consequence of the visions granted to Catherine Labouré (who six months previously had become a member of the Sisters of Charity), M. Aladel, assistant of the Lazarists, with the approval of Mgr de Quélen, had struck the "miraculous medal" of Mary Conceived without Sin, more than 4,000,000 of which were distributed throughout the world within four years. In 1838 Desgenettes, pastor of Notre-Dame-des-Victoires, organized in that church the Association in honour of the Holy and Immaculate Heart of Mary, which Gregory XVI made a confraternity on 24 April, 1838, and the badge of which was the miraculous medal. In virtue of another indult of Gregory XVI (7 Dec., 1838) the Diocese of Paris received the right to transfer to the second Sunday of Advent the solemnity of the feast of the Immaculate Conception. On 10 July, 1894, Leo XIII granted to the Lazarists, and to the dioceses that should request it, the faculty of celebrating yearly on 27 November the manifestation of the Blessed Virgin through the miraculous medal. This feast was first celebrated at Paris in the chapel of Rue du Bac on 25, 26, and 27 November, 1894. On 27 July, 1897, the statue of the Blessed Virgin in this chapel was solemnly crowned in virtue of a Brief of Leo XIII (2 March, 1897). In 1899 the number of Masses celebrated by foreign priests at Notre-Dame-des-Victoires was 3031; the number of Communions, 110,000; intentions 1,305,980, or an average of 3578 per day.

(3) *Montmartre.*—Prior to the ninth century there were two churches on the hill of Montmartre—one, half way up, stood on the traditional site of the martrydom of St. Denis, while the other, on the summit, was said to replace a temple dedicated to Mars. In 1095 these two churches became the property of a monastery occupied first (1095–1134) by the monks of St-Martin-des-Champs, and from 1034 to the Revolution by the Benedictines. The church on the summit was rebuilt in the twelfth century, and consecrated on 21 April, 1147, by Pope Eugenius III with St. Bernard of Clairvaux as deacon, and Peter the Venerable, Abbot of Cluny, as subdeacon. Alexander III visited it in 1162; St. Thomas à Becket in 1170; St. Thomas Aquinas, Bl. Joan of Arc, St. Ignatius, St. Francis Xavier, St. Vincent de Paul, Olier, and Blessed John Eudes prayed there. During the war of 1870–71 MM. Legentil and Rohault de Fleury issued from Poitiers an appeal in behalf of the erection at Paris of a sanctuary to the Sacred Heart to obtain the release of the pope and the salvation of France. On 23 July, 1873, the National Assembly passed a law declaring the construction of this sanctuary a matter of public utility. After a meeting in which seventy architects took part Abadie was charged with its construction, in Byzantine style. Cardinal Guibert laid the corner-stone on 16 June, 1875, and said the first Mass in the crypt on 21 April, 1881. Cardinal Richard blessed the church on 5 June, 1891, and on 17 October 1899, blessed the cross surmounting the main dome.

(4) Pilgrimage to the Church of St. Francis in honour of the famous *Miracle des Billettes* in 1290, when blood flowed from a Host which had been profaned by a Jew and Christ appeared above the receptacle where the Jew had thrown the Host.

(5) Pilgrimage to the chapel of the Picpus in honour of the statue of Notre-Dame-de-Paix which the famous Capuchin Joyeuse, known as Père Ange, gave to his convent (sixteenth century).

(6) Pilgrimage of Notre-Dame-des-Vertus at the church of Aubervilliers (dating from 1336), whither Louis XIII, St. Ignatius, Blessed John Eudes, St. Francis de Sales, St. Vincent de Paul, St. John Baptist de la Salle, and Bossuet went to pray.

(7) Pilgrimage of Notre-Dame-des-Miracles at Saint-Maur, dating from the erection of a chapel of the Blessed Virgin by the Abbot St. Babolein about 640. The future Pope Martin IV, Philip Augustus, St. Louis, Emperor Charles IV of Germany, and Olier prayed there.

(8) Pilgrimage in honour of St. Vincent de Paul to the parish church of Clichy, built by the saint.

SAINTS OF PARIS.—A number of saints are especially connected with the history of the Diocese of Paris: Sts.

Agoard and Aglibert, martyred at Cretil; St. Lucan, martyred at Paris; St. Eugene, who according to the legend was sent by Saint Denis to Spain, founded the Church of Toledo, and was martyred at Deuil; St. Yon, a disciple of St. Denis; St. Lucian, companion of St. Denis, martyred at Beauvais (third century); St. Rieul, founder (c. 300) of the Church of Senlis, visited and encouraged the Christian community of Paris; St. Martin (316–400), Bishop of Tours, while at Paris, cured a leper by embracing him; Sts. Alda (Aude) and Célinie, companions of St. Genevieve; the nun St. Aurea, disciple of St. Genevieve (fifth century); St. Germain (380–448), Bishop of Auxerre, whose name is linked with the history of St. Genevieve; St. Séverin, Abbot of Agaune (d. 508), who was summoned to Paris to cure Clovis of a serious illness; Queen St. Clotilde (d. 545); St. Leonard, a noble of Clovis's court, who became a hermit in Limousin and died about 559; St. Columbanus (540–615), who performed a miracle during his stay in Paris; St. Cloud (d. 560), grandson of St. Clotilde, who was made a monk by St. Séverin; St. Radegund (519–87), wife of Clotaire I; St. Eloi (Eligius, 588–659), founder of the convent of St. Martial, minister of Clotaire II and of Dagobert; St. Bathilde, Queen of France (d. 680); St. Domnolus (sixth century), Abbot of St-Laurent, Paris, prior to becoming Bishop of Le Mans; St. Bertechramnus (Bertrand, 553–623), Archdeacon of Paris, later Bishop of Le Mans; St. Aure, virgin (7th century), first Abbess of St. Martial; St. Merry, Benedictine Abbot (d. 700); St. Ouen (609–86), who was a friend of St. Eligius and died Archbishop of Rouen; St. Sulpice (seventh century), chaplain of Clotaire II, died as Archbishop of Bourges; St. Doctrovée (seventh century), first Abbot of St. Vincent; St Leu, Bishop of Sens (seventh century), who on his way through Paris released a number of prisoners; St. John of Matha (1160–1213), who was a student of the University of Paris, and, while saying his first Mass in the chapel of the Bishop of Paris, had the vision which induced him to found the Trinitarians; St. William, canon of Paris, who died in 1209 as Archbishop of Bourges; Bl. Reginald (1160–1220), professor of canon law at the University of Paris; St. Bonaventure (1221–74), student and afterwards professor at the University of Paris; St. Thomas Aquinas (1227–74), successively student, professor, and preacher at the University of Paris; Bl. Gregory X (pope 1271–6), doctor of the University of Paris; St. Yves (1253–1303), who studied law at the University of Paris; Bl. Innocent V (pope 1276), who succeeded St. Thomas Aquinas as professor of theology at the University of Paris; St. Louis (1215–70), and his sister Bl. Isabelle (1224–70), foundress of the Abbey of Poor Clares of Longchamps, who later called themselves Urbanists because their rule was confirmed by Urban V; Bl. Peter of Luxemburg (1369–87), canon of Paris before becoming Bishop of Metz; Blessed Urban V (pope 1362–70), sometime professor of canon law at the University of Paris; Bl. Jeanne-Marie de Maille (1332–1414), who came to Paris to make known to the king her prophetical visions concerning France; Bl. Jeanne de Valois (1464–1505), daughter of Louis XI and wife of Louis XII, foundress of the Annunciades; St. Ignatius Loyola (1491–1556); St. Francis Xavier (1506–52), who studied at the Collège de St-Barbe and made his vows as a Jesuit at Montmartre; Mme Acarie, venerated as Bl. Marie de l'Incarnation (1565–1618), a Parisian by birth, who, under the protection of the Duchesse de Longueville, established at Paris the Carmelites of the Faubourg St-Jacques; St. Francis de Sales (1567–1622), who was educated at the Collège de Clermont, Paris, and later preached there on two occasions; St. Vincent de Paul (1576–1660), who, having received from Jean-François de Gondi the Collège des Bons Enfants, founded there the Congregation of the Mission; Bl. Louis Grignion de Montfort (seventeenth century), who studied at St-Sulpice and preached several times at Paris.

SPECIAL FEATURES OF ECCLESIASTICAL PARIS.—The feast of the Immaculate Conception was celebrated at Paris as early as the thirteenth century by the students of the English and Norman nations in the Church of St-Séverin, and a confraternity was established there in honour of the Immaculate Conception in the fourteenth century. Even in the last quarter of the twelfth century the poet Adam, canon regular of St-Victor, seems to have accepted this dogma. The University of Paris opposed it until the arrival of Duns Scotus, who came to debate the question with the Dominican doctors at Paris. The belief spread during the fourteenth century, and the Dominican Jean de Montson, having maintained in 1387 that the theory was contrary to faith, was excommunicated. The doctors of the university were among those most eager to hasten at the Council of Basle the investigations preparatory to the definition of the Immaculate Conception, which this council, in the meantime become schismatical, promulgated in 1439. At last, on 9 March, 1497, the university issued a decree obliging all its members to promise on oath to profess and defend the doctrine of the Immaculate Conception, and declaring the contrary opinion false, impious, and erroneous. In 1575 it took issue with the famous Jesuit Maldonatus, who still regarded it as an optional opinion, but it refrained from formally branding as heretics those who did not admit the doctrine, as laid down by Benedict XIV in his treatise, "De festis". The procession in honour of the Assumption was inaugurated at Paris in 1638, when Louis XIII placed his kingdom under the protection of the Blessed Virgin. Devotion to the departed souls is perhaps the most deeply rooted form of Parisian piety. Even in the eighteenth century the *clocheteurs* of the dead traversed the streets at night, ringing their bells and calling:

Réveillez vous, gens qui dormez,
Priez Dieu pour les trépassés.

The Association of Our Lady of Suffrage for the Dead, founded in 1838 at the Church of St. Merry by Archbishop Quélen and raised to an archconfraternity in 1857 by Pius IX, is still flourishing. Several expiatory chapels exist in Paris: (1) in memory of Louis XVI and the members of his family who fell victims to the Terror; (2) in memory of the 1300 persons beheaded at the barrier of the Place du Trône (including the 16 Carmelites of Compiègne) and buried in the

CHURCH OF ST. JACQUES, PARIS

cemetery of Picpus; (3) in memory of the Duc d'Orléans, who was killed in 1842 in a carriage accident; (4) in memory of the victims of the dreadful fire at the Charity Bazar (4 May, 1897).

RELIGIOUS CONGREGATIONS.—Prior to the application of the Law of Associations of 1901, there was a large number of religious congregations in Paris. Among those having their mother-house in the city were: the Assumptionists, who preserved in their chapel a statue of Notre-Dame-de-Salut which, according to tradition, smiled on Duns Scotus in 1304 when he was about to preach on the Immaculate Conception; the Eudists (q. v.); the Missionary Priests of Mercy (founded in 1808 by Père Rauzau), who were the founders of the French parish in New York; the Oblates of Mary Immaculate (founded in 1816 by Eugène de Mazenod), the apostles of Upper and Lower Canada, New Brittany, Oregon, British Columbia, Texas, and Mexico; the Oratorians, founded in 1611 by Pierre de Bérulle (q. v); the Priests of Picpus (founded in 1805 by Abbé Coudrin), the founders of missions in Oceania—four of its members were martyred under the Commune (1871), Pères Radique, Tuffier, Rouchouze, and Tardieu; the Fathers of the Blessed Sacrament, founded by Père Eymard; the Brothers of the Christian Schools (q. v.), founded by St. John Baptist de la Salle; the Marianist Brothers founded at Bordeaux in 1817 for the education of the young; the Nuns of the Assumption, founded in 1839 under the patronage of Archbishop Affre for the education of young girls; the Sisters of Charitable Instruction of the Child Jesus (of St. Maur) for nursing and teaching, which was founded in 1666 by Père Barré, O. Minim., and has missions in Japan, Siam, and Malacca; the Sisters of Mary Help, founded in 1854 for the care of young working-women; the Sisters of Our Lady of Charity of the Refuge (of St. Michael), founded in 1641 by Venerable Eudes to receive voluntary penitents; the Religious of the Mother of God, a teaching order founded by Olier in 1648; the Religious of the Cenacle founded at Paris in 1826; the Religious of the Sacred Heart, founded in the beginning of the nineteenth century by Madame Barat (q. v.); the Sisters of Picpus, a teaching and contemplative order founded at Poitiers and removed to Paris in 1804; the Sisters of Our Lady of Sion, a teaching order founded by Père Ratisbonne.

Prior to 1901 there were also at Paris: Carmelites; Dominicans, several of whom were martyred during the Commune (martyrs of Arcueil); Franciscans; Jesuits, five of whom were martyred during the Commune (viz. Pères Olivaint, Clerc, de Bengy, Ducoudray, and Caubert); Marists; Priests of Mercy; Missionaries of the Sacred Heart; and Redemptorists. Important educational works brought to an end by the law of 1901 were the boarding-schools of the Abbaye aux Bois, Oiseaux, and Roule, conducted by the Canons Regular of St. Augustine, a congregation founded at the end of the sixteenth century by St. Peter Fourier. The same law also terminated the existence of two great Carmelite convents—the one, founded in 1604 in the Faubourg St-Jacques by Marie de l'Incarnation, had witnessed the Lenten preaching of Bossuet in 1661, the vows of Mme de la Vallière in 1675, and the funeral oration of the Princess Palatine in 1685; the other, founded in 1664 and established in the Avenue de Saxe in 1854, possessed a miraculous crucifix, rescued intact from the flames at the capture of Besançon by Louis XIV. Paris still possesses two Visitation monasteries, which date respectively from 1619 and 1626. They were founded by St. Francis de Sales and St. Jane-Frances de Chantal, and in the middle of the nineteenth century one of them had as superior Venerable Marie de Sales Chappuis. The Sisters of Charity, instituted in 1629 by St. Vincent de Paul and Venerable Mme Le Gras (née Louise de Marillac) and having their mother-house at Paris, still have the right to exercise their nursing activity, but are legally bound to discontinue gradually their work as teachers. Among the still existing congregations of women are: the Congregation of Adoration of Reparation, founded in 1848 by Mother Marie-Thérèse of the Heart of Jesus; the Helpers of the Souls in Purgatory, founded in 1856; the Helpers of the Immaculate Conception, founded in 1859 by the Abbé Largentier for the care of the sick in their homes; the Benedictine Sisters of the Blessed Sacrament, founded in 1653 by Catherine de Bar—a second house was founded in 1816 by the Princess Louise de Bourbon-Condé (Mother Marie-Joseph de la Miséricorde).

SEMINARIES.—The Seminary of St-Sulpice, founded by Olier in 1642, had been supplemented since 1814 by the house at Issy, in the suburbs of Paris, reserved for the teaching of philosophy. The Paris seminary was seized by the State in virtue of the recent laws, and the present theological school of the Parisian clergy is located at Issy. The seminary of Foreign Missions was founded in 1663. Twenty-eight houses were confided to it by the Holy See. This seminary belongs to the Society of Foreign Missions and is still authorized by the State, as also is the Seminary of the Holy Ghost, located in the mother-house of the Congregations of the Holy Ghost and the Immaculate Heart of Mary—the former was founded in 1703 by Poullard Desplace, the latter in 1841 by Venerable Francis-Mary-Paul Libermann, and the two were merged in 1848. This seminary provides priests for the evangelization of the negroes in Africa and the colonies. Neither has the State disturbed the Congregations of the Mission of St-Lazarus (Lazarists), founded by St. Vincent de Paul, with its mother-house at Paris. They devote themselves to the evangelization of the poor by means of missions and to the foreign missions. For a long time their chapel held the body of St. Vincent de Paul, now removed to Belgium. The Lazarist Blessed Jean-Gabriel Perboyre, martyred in China, is venerated here. With regard to the Irish College in Paris see IRISH COLLEGES.

OTHER RELIGIONS.—As early as 1512 Lefèvre d'Etaples, at the Collège du Cardinal Lemoine, and Briçonnet, Abbot of St-Germain-des-Prés and shortly afterwards Bishop of Meaux, spread at Paris certain theological ideas which prepared the way for Protestantism. In 1521 Luther's book, "The Babylonian Captivity", was condemned by the Sorbonne. In 1524 Jacques Pavannes (or Pauvert), a disciple of Lefèvre, underwent capital punishment for having attacked the veneration of the Blessed Virgin, purgatory, and holy water; the same penalty was inflicted on Louis de Berquin in 1529. Until 1555 the Protestants of Paris had no pastor, but in that year they assembled at the house of one of their number, named La Ferrière. As he had a child to baptize, the gathering elected as pastor Jean le Maçon, a young man of twenty-two years, who had studied law. He exercised his ministry at Paris until 1562, when he took up his residence as pastor at Angers. The first general synod of the Reformed Church of France was held at Paris from 26 to 28 May, 1558, and drew up a confession of faith—later called the Confession of La Rochelle, because it only received its final form at the eighteenth national synod convened at La Rochelle in 1607. In 1560 a number of Protestants perished at Paris, among them the magistrate Anne du Bourg. It is estimated that the Reformed Church of Paris had 40,000 members in 1564. In 1572 took place the massacre of St. Bartholomew. The Edict of July, 1573, having authorized the Protestants of Paris to assemble at a distance of two leagues from the city, they held their meetings at Noisy le Sec. In 1606 Henry IV permitted them to build a church at Charenton. During the seventeenth century the Reformed Church of Paris was administered by the pastors

Dumoulin, Mestrezat, Durand, and Montigny. At the revocation of the Edict of Nantes (1685) Pastor Claude was compelled to leave Paris; Pastors Malzac, Giraud, and Givry, who endeavoured despite the revocation to maintain a Protestant church at Paris, were imprisoned in 1692. During the eighteenth century the chaplains attached to the embassies of Protestant princes gave spiritual assistance to the Protestants of the city. Marron, chaplain at the Dutch embassy, became pastor in Paris when Louis XVI promulgated the edict of toleration (1787). A decree of 1802 gave over to the Protestant sect the old church of the Visitandines in the Rue St-Antoine (built by Mansart); one of 1811 gave them the church of the Oratorians in the Rue St-Honoré, while the July Monarchy gave them the old Church of Notre-Dame-de-Pentemont, which under the old régime had belonged to the Augustinian Sisters of the Incarnate Word of the Blessed Sacrament. At present the Reformed Church possesses nineteen places of worship in Paris and seventeen in the suburbs; the Lutherans, eleven places of worship in Paris and eight in the suburbs; the Protestant Free Churches, four places of worship; the Baptists, four churches in Paris and one in the suburbs. The American Episcopal, Anglican, Scotch, Congregationalist, and Wesleyan Churches conduct services in English. There are in Paris about 50,000 Jews.

PUBLIC ASSISTANCE AND PUBLIC CHARITY.—Under the old régime, what is now called "Public Assistance" included several distinct departments: (1) that of the Hôtel-Dieu, one of the oldest hospitals in Europe, doubtless founded by the Bishop St. Landry after the epidemic of 651. It was at first directed by the canons of Notre-Dame, and after 1505 by a commission of citizens with whom Louis XIV associated, together with the Archbishop of Paris, several representatives of the Government and of the chief judiciary bodies. This department undertook the administration of the Hospital for Incurables, the Hospital of St. Louis, and that of St. Anne; (2) department of the General Hospital, created by Louis XIV in 1656 for the sick, the aged, children, and beggars, and with which were connected the infirmaries of Pitié, Bicêtre, the Salpêtrière, Vaugirard, the foundling hospital, and that of the Holy Ghost; (3) several independent hospitals, e. g. Cochin Hospital, founded in 1680 by the Abbé Cochin, pastor of St-Jacques, and the Necker Hospital, established in 1779 at the initiative of Mme Necker; (4) the Bureau of Charity, dependent on the parishes; (5) the central Bureau of the Poor (*grand bureau des pauvres*), established under Francis I for the relief of the indigent. It was presided over and directed by the *procureur général* of the Parlement and levied a yearly "alms tax" on all the inhabitants of Paris. It administered the infirmary of Petites Maisons.

The Revolution effected a radical change in this system. The central *Bureau des Pauvres* was at first replaced by forty-eight beneficent committees (*comités de bienfaisance*); these were replaced in 1816 by twelve bureaus of charity, which in 1830 took the name of *bureaux de bienfaisance* and number twenty since 1860. While in the communes of France all the hospital departments are under an administration distinct from that of the bureau of beneficence, at Paris, in virtue of the law of 10 Jan., 1849, the General Administration of Public Assistance directs both the hospitals and the departments for relief at home. At present the Department of Public Assistance directs 31 hospitals, 14 being general hospitals, 7 special, 9 children's hospitals, and 1 insane asylum. At the laicization of the hospitals, the hospital of St. Joseph, conducted by the Sisters of St. Vincent de Paul, was opened in 1884 under the patronage of the Archbishop of Paris; that of Notre-Dame-de-Bon-Secours, in care of the Augustines, was founded by Abbé Carton, pastor of St-Pierre-de-Montrouge and bequeathed by him in 1887 to the Archbishop of Paris. The hospital of Notre-Dame-de-Perpétuel-Secours at Lavallois is conducted by the Dominican Sisters. The St-Jacques, Hahnemann, St-François, and St-Michel hospitals are also in the hands of congregations. The Villepinte Institution, in charge of the Sisters of Marie Auxiliatrice, cares for children and young women suffering from tuberculosis. The Marie-Thérèse infirmary was founded for aged or infirm priests by the wife of Châteaubriand. The Little Sisters of the Poor have nine houses in the diocese. The Brothers of St. John of God maintain a private hospital and an asylum for incurable young men. The Institution of the Ladies of Calvary, founded at Lyons in 1842 by Mme Garnier and established at Paris in 1874, is conducted by widows for the care of the cancerous, and receives into its infirmaries patients whom no other hospital

FONTAINE ST. MICHEL, PARIS

will admit; it also has houses at Lyons, Marseilles, St. Etienne, and Rouen. The Little Sisters of the Assumption, nurses of the poor, who have nine houses in the diocese, stay night and day without pay in the houses of the sick poor. The same is done by the Sisters of Notre-Dame of the Rue Cassini in the homes of poor women in their confinement. Other orders for the care of the sick in their homes are the Franciscan nursing sisters (7 houses) and the Sisters Servants of the Poor (4 houses).

Among the institutions now dependent on the State, the foundation of which was formerly the glory of the Church, must be mentioned that of *Quinze Vingts* for the blind. As early as the eleventh century there was a confraternity for the blind; St. Louis built for it a house and a church, gave it a perpetual revenue, and decreed that the number of the *Quinze Vingts* (300 blind) should be maintained complete. When the king was canonized in 1297 the blind took him as their patron (see EDUCATION OF THE BLIND). The Catholic institutions of Paris for the relief of the poor and the uplifting of the labouring classes are very numerous. For the Society of St. Vincent de Paul see MISSION, CONGREGATION OF PRIESTS OF THE. The Philanthropic Society, founded in 1780 under the protection of Louis XVI, established dispensaries, economical kitchens, night shelters, and settlement houses. The Central Office of Charitable Institutions investigates the condition of workmen and the poor, and conducts employment and restoration bureaux. The Association of Ladies of Charity, established (1629) in the parish of St-Sauveur by St. Vincent de Paul for the visitation of the sick poor and reconstituted in 1840, has given rise to the Society for the Sick Poor, the Society for the Sick Poor in the Suburbs, and the Society for the Visitation of the Poor in the Hospitals. Most parishes have their organizations of charitable women who, under the pastor's supervision, distribute clothing and visit the poor. The *Société de Charité Maternelle*, which dates from 1784, when it was patronized by Marie Antoinette, assists married women in their confinement without regard to creed. In each quarter of Paris women visitors determine the families deserving assistance. In 1898 the society assisted 2797 women and 2853 children. The *Association des Mères de Famille*, founded in 1836 by Mme Badenier, assists at childbirth women who do not meet the conditions required by the *Société de Charité Maternelle* or who are numbered among the disreputable poor. The *Œuvre des Faubourgs*, through a number of women, visits 2000 families and 8000 children in the Paris suburbs. The *Œuvre de la Miséricorde* (Work of Mercy), founded in 1822, assists the disreputable poor. An organization founded in 1841 by Mgr Christophe, later Bishop of Soissons, helps convalescent lunatics. The objects of the *Œuvre de l'Hospitalité du Travail* are to offer a free temporary shelter without distinction of creed or nationality to every homeless woman or girl who has determined to work for an honourable livelihood, to employ its clients at useful tasks, to endeavour to revive the habit of working in those who have lost it, and to assist them in securing honourable employment which will also enable them to provide for the future. This organization, founded in 1881 under the direction of Sister St. Antoine, a member of the Order of Calvary, between 1881 and 1903 gave shelter to 70,240 women. In 1894 Sister St. Antoine annexed to it the *Œuvre du Travail à Domicile pour les Mères de Famille* (Association for procuring home-work for mothers of families) which between 1892 and 1902 assisted 7449 mothers. The *Maison de Travail* for men, founded in 1892 by M. de Laubespin, performs the same service for unemployed and homeless men, and is also in charge of the Sisters of Calvary.

The Catholics of Paris have taken part in the syndicate movement by the creation in 1887 of the syndicate of commercial and industrial employees, by the organization of the *Aiguille* (a professional association of patronesses and women employees and workers on clothing), and by the *Union Centrale*, made up of five professional syndicates of working-girls, business employees, seamstresses, servant girls, and nurses, with "La Ruche syndicale" as their organ. The great Society of St. Nicholas, founded in 1827 by Mgr de Bervanger and Count Victor de Noailles and directed by a staff of Catholic laymen, has four houses (Paris, Issy, Igny, and Buzenval), where it gives a professional education to boys whom it adopts as early as their eighth year. The Society of the Friends of Childhood, founded in 1828, is concerned with the education and apprenticeship of poor boys. The *Ecole commerciale de Francs Bourgeois*, created in 1843 by the Brothers of the Christian Schools, prepares pupils for commercial, industrial, and administrative professions. Numerous homes and restaurants for young working girls have been founded by Catholics. The Charitable Society of St. Francis Regis was founded in 1826 by M. Gassin to facilitate the religious and civil marriage of the poor of the diocese and the legitimatization of their natural children. The day-nurseries, which care for children from 15 days to 3 years of age while their mothers are employed, date from M. Marbeau's foundation in 1844. The Sisters of St. Paul have founded in the parishes of St-Vincent-de-Paul and St-Séverin a society for the relief of mothers who wish their children to remain at home. The *Œuvre de l'Adoption* was founded in 1859 by Abbé Maitrias to gather as many orphans as possible. Out of so many other associations, the following must be mentioned: the Association des Jeunes Economes which, under the direction of the Sisters of St. Vincent de Paul, uses the generous donations of a large number of young women for the apprenticing and employment of poor girls; the Society of St. Anne, founded in 1824; the Society for Abandoned Children, founded in 1803; the Society for the Adoption of Abandoned Little Girls, founded in 1879 (all concerned with finding homes for orphans); the Society of the Child Jesus, which shelters during their convalescence poor girls who have been discharged from hospitals.

There is a recent tendency towards the complete reorganization of Catholic charity in a single quarter by the centralization of all charitable departments for the development and protection of family life. For example the Fresh Air Society for Mothers and Children, founded by Mlle Chaptal in 1901, includes: (1) a department for the investigation of home conditions; (2) one for free consultations for poor mothers and their nursing children; (3) one for assisting mothers whose confinement takes place at home; (4) one for the distribution of tickets for meat, cereal, or farinaceous food for women who have been confined; (6) the fresh air department, which sends a number of the women of the district into the country. The Society of Ste-Rosalie also combines a number of admirable works which perpetuate the memory of the good done in the Faubourg St-Marcel during the July Monarchy by Sister Rosalie Rendu, who worked in collaboration with Vicomte Armand de Mélun. The Working Women's Society of Our Lady of the Rosary was the nucleus of a flourishing parish in a district previously deprived of all religious help. The Union Familiale, founded at Charonne by Mlle Gahéry in 1899, has completely transformed the district; it has established a Fröbelian nursery for the small children, and receives children after school hours; since 1904 it assembles families in a family educational circle; it organizes groups of "little mothers," little girls of ten, who every Thursday take care of 3 or 4 children; it has gardening classes and a department for trousseaux, and since 1900 it has had vacation colonies, known as fresh air societies. The original congregation of the Blind Sisters of St. Paul, founded in 1851 by Abbé Juge and Anne Bergunion, looks after blind young women.

According to the report of the Abbé Fonsagrives to the Diocesan Congress of 1908, the Archdiocese of Paris has 356 Catholic *patronages*, of which 63 are for male pupils of the free schools, 79 for male pupils of the lay schools, 101 for female pupils of the free schools, 113 for female pupils of the lay schools. At that date lay *patronages* were only 245. The Society for the Patronage of Young Working Girls, founded in 1851, receives young girls after their First Communion. The Sisters of the Presentation of Tours conduct the association and society for mutual relief for young business women; the Sisters Servants of Mary and Sisters of the Cross secure situations for servants. The Sisters of St. Vincent de Paul have societies called "patronages internes", which shelter working-girls who are orphans or who live at a distance from their families. The *Œuvre des Petites Préservées et le Vestiaire des Petits Prisonniers*, founded in 1892 by the Comtesse de Biron, looks after the preservation of young girls discharged from prison. The Catholic International Society for the Protection of Young Women, organized at Freiburg in 1897 after the Organization of the Protestant International Union of the Friends of Young Women, in 1905 alone gave shelter to 11,919 young girls in Paris.

There is at present a great renewal in Catholic methods of charity and relief at Paris, the spirit of which is shown in the report concerning Catholic relief societies read (Aug., 1910) at the International Congress of Public and Private Relief held at Copenhagen under the presidency of President Loubet: "The great originality of Catholic relief work in recent years consists in the multiplication of works for social education. This arises more and more from the 'patriarchal' conception of these undertakings. The modern wish and tendency is to give him who suffers a share in his own relief, to give him a collaborative or directing part in the effort which is being made to assist and uplift him. Henceforth the favourite works of charity among Catholics will be those known as preventive. To prevent misery by an hygienic, domestic, professional education is the object of the founders of modern works of relief. They are concerned not only with the strife against the consequences of misery but with that against its production. Without neglecting individual alms, Catholic charity aims especially at social relief; it prefers to precede misery to prevent it, rather than to follow it to relieve it; it prefers to uplift families rather than assist them, to help them when they are stumbling rather than to raise them up when they have fallen; it prefers to help them actively to better working conditions, than to relieve passively the results of these evil conditions. All instruction imparted in organizations for Catholic youth and in the Catholic *patronages* of Paris is impregnated with this apparently new spirit which on closer view is seen to be merely a return to the Christian solidarity of the Middle Ages."

RELIGIOUS RENEWAL OF THE TWENTIETH CENTURY.—In 1905 at the end of the concordatory period the Diocese of Paris had 3,599,870 inhabitants, 38 parishes, 104 *succursales*, 7 vicariates, formerly remunerated by the State. Since the separation of Church and State, the religious character of Paris shows signs of renewal. Statistics of the religious and civil burials from 1883 to 1903, drawn up by the Abbé Raffin, afford a very exact idea of the religious condition of Paris at the end of the nineteenth century. The largest proportion of civil burials, 23 per cent, was reached in 1884. At the end of the nineteenth century the proportion of civil burials had fallen to 18 per cent; from 1901 to 1903, they showed a tendency to rise to 20 per cent. Civil funerals take place chiefly among the poor. For example in 1888 in the five most costly classes of burials the number of civil burials did not exceed 4·5 per cent; on the other hand, the ninth class, which is the cheapest, and the free class show 25 to 30 per cent. At present among the wealthy classes there is a slight increase in the number of civil funerals, and a slight decrease among the working classes, but the fact remains that, despite the gratuitousness of religious assistance in the case of the poor, the average number of 10,000 civil funerals which take place yearly at Paris consists chiefly of funerals of the poor. One reason for this is the insufficiency of religious assistance in the hospitals. Although more than a third of the Parisians die in hospitals, there are only about thirty hospital chaplains, and these the management does not permit to approach the sick unless they are summoned. Another reason lies in the excessive size of suburban parishes and in the difficulty of reaching an immense fluctuating population. At the beginning of the twentieth century Notre-Dame-de-Ménilmontant had 70,000, St-Pierre-de-Montrouge 83,000, Notre-Dame-de-Clignancourt 120,000 inhabitants. For a long time these enormous parishes had no more priests than the smaller ones in the centre of Paris. At St-Ambroise there were 8 to 10 priests for 80,000 souls, while St-Thomas-d'Aquin had 8 priests for 14,000, and St-Sulpice 17 for 38,000 (see the report of M. Thureau Dangin, permanent secretary of the French Academy, concerning the *Œuvre des chapelles de secours*). M. Thureau Dangin calculated in 1905 that Paris, with its 522 pastors or curates, had an average of 37,000 or 38,000 souls to a parish, while at Lyons there was 1 priest for every 3000 souls, at Antwerp 1 for every 500, at New York 1 for every 1500.

The realization of this dearth and its dangers caused the organization of the *Œuvre des Séminaires* as early as 1882 to increase and facilitate vocations, and in 1905 Cardinal Richard pointed out the urgent necessity of the creation of about thirty new parishes or of *chapelles de secours*. At present the diocesan administration is most actively engaged in the organization of these *chapelles de secours*. Every year a

ARC DE TRIOMPHE, PARIS

dignitary of the French Academy or of the Institute presents a report of the progress made, MM. François Coppée, Thureau Dangin, de Mun, d'Haussonville, Georges Picot, and Etienne Lamy having been heard in turn. The Christian Doctrine Society (*Œuvre des Catéchismes*) founded in 1885 by Cardinal Richard was erected into a confraternity by Leo XIII on 30 May, 1893, with which all the catechetical societies of France may be affiliated. This society is formed of voluntary catechists and promoters paying dues. In addition to the multiplication of places of worship, special religious services have been organized for certain classes of persons. For example, the missionary work among young seamstresses (*Midinettes*) has developed greatly between 1908 and 1910; it consists of short instructions between 12.35 and 12.50 p. m., so that the young women may return punctually to work. More than 5000 working girls have profited by these missions. The Society of Diocesan Missions, founded in 1886 by Cardinal Richard, supports from 18 to 20 missionaries, who according to the report of their superior, the Abbé Gibergues, made to the Diocesan Congress of 1908, have brought back to the Church more than 40,000 persons in less than a quarter of a century. Lastly, the Archdiocese of Paris has assumed the direction of the Catholic social movement. In 1910 a social secretariat was organized, as a bureau of information and headquarters for social undertakings, and the archbishop has interested himself actively in the abolition of the night-work of bakers, addressing a letter to the parochial committees to arouse Catholic sentiment in favour of the claims of these workmen, and on 21 December, 1908, presiding at the meeting organized by the *Jeunesse catholique française* for the suppression of this work.

An interesting organization from the social point of view is that of the provincial associations, formed at Paris under Catholic auspices to bring together the immigrants from each province, to assist them to maintain close ties among themselves, and to procure spiritual help in the loneliness of the great city. In 1892 was founded the society *La Bretagne*, and in 1895 the *Union aveyronnaise*. The latter, which had 1600 members in 1908, supports eight sisters who, in 1908 alone, spent 2641 days or nights with sick Aveyronnais. In imitation of this association were founded successively the *Union lozérienne*, the *Association des Dames limousines et creusoises*, the *Union lyonnaise et forésienne*, the *Union pyrénéenne*, the *Alliance catholique savoisienne*, and many others. There is a special society for the Bretons residing at Paris, which provides sermons and lectures in the Breton tongue. All the provincial unions are federated under the presidency of the Catholic economist, M. Henri Joly, a member of the Institut. A list of these associations has been affixed in recent times to the doors of all the churches in Paris. All these undertakings for the development of Christian life in Paris are studied and developed by the Diocesan Committee organized on 1 March, 1905, with a double aim: (1) "to sustain, promote, and unite under the archbishop's authority all movements concerning the religious, moral, social, and even material welfare of the diocese;" (2) "to promote the formation of parochial committees modelled on and connected with itself". It is divided into five commissions, dealing respectively with works of religion and piety, instruction and education, perseverance and patronage, charitable and social works, and with the press and propaganda. At the beginning of 1910 there were 67 parochial committees, nearly half the parishes being already provided with them. Since 1905 diocesan congresses have taken place yearly. That of 1909 was especially concerned with the labour of women, with organizations for instruction of youth, provincial and journalistic organizations. That of 1910 dealt exclusively with liberty of teaching, the formation and recruiting of teachers, and with school books.

CATHOLIC INSTRUCTION IN PARIS IN THE TWENTIETH CENTURY.—The suppression of the teaching congregations and the gradual but rapid closing of the establishments directed by them was a serious blow to the prosperity of the independent schools in the Archdiocese of Paris. In October, 1904, Cardinal Richard instituted a diocesan committee of "free instruction", which exhorted all the male and female teachers in private institutions to form separate diocesan associations. Mutual-aid societies were established in 1909 to provide for the future of these teachers, male and female, and in 1910 the diocese promulgated a regulation fixing the conditions of their promotion and granting certain guarantees for their professional future. On 8 December, 1906, arrangements were made for the supervision of religious instruction in the schools not under the public authorities, and in June, 1908, a board for the direction of secondary and primary diocesan instruction was created. From 1879 to 1910 the expenditure for the foundation and maintenance of the independent schools was $8,000,000, for which appeal was made to the charity of individuals. Their annual support costs about $600,000. Most of the schools are supported by a special committee by means of collections, subscriptions, etc.; some belong to civil societies which rent them to the committees, while others are wholly at the expense of the pastor. At the beginning of 1910 there were in the 162 parishes of Paris and its suburbs 217 independent schools, of which only 36 are still in the hands of congregations, and these also in virtue of the Associations Law are destined after a short time to be under the supervision of lay Catholics. The number of pupils frequenting these schools is estimated to be about 42,000. The "Jeunesse prévoyante du diocèse de Paris", established in 1902, constitutes a flourishing school mutual-aid society. A district union groups together thirty-five associations of former pupils of the independent schools (called *Amicales*), and is a bond among 4500 members. The initiative in domestic economy in Paris was taken by Catholics. Even before the public authorities had made sacrifices for this end, the Comtesse de Diesbach had established (15 June, 1902) a first course in domestic economy, lasting a month. It was succeeded by nine other courses in 1903–05, attended by 110 pupils, 60 of them religious from 14 orders. In 1905 was opened the Normal Institute of Domestic Economy which in its three first years gave to the independent schools 150 teachers of domestic economy. Higher Catholic education at Paris is assured by a number of institutions conducted by ecclesiastics, and by the Bossuet, Fenélon, Gerson, and Massillon schools, which send their pupils to the state *lycées*.

For the Institut Catholique, see PARIS, UNIVERSITY OF.

A. SOURCES.—BARROUX, *Essai de bibliogr. critique des généralités de l'hist. de Paris* (Paris, 1908), essential; POËTE, *Les sources de l'hist. de P. et les historiens de P.* in *Revue Bleue* (18 and 25 Nov., 1905); TOURNEUX, *Bibliogr. de l'hist. de P. pendant la Révolution française* (4 vols., Paris, 1890–1906), especially III; *Bull. de la Soc. de l'hist. de P. et de l'Ile de France (1874—)*; *Bull. du Comité d'hist. et d'archéol. du dioc. de P.* (1883–5); *Bibliothèque d'hist. de P.* (1909—).

B. GENERAL.—LEBEUF, *Hist. de la ville et de tout le dioc. de P.* (15 vols., Paris, 1754–58), new ed. by AUGIER (5 vols.); *Tables* (1 vol., Paris, 1884); BOURNON, *Rectifications et Additions à l'Abbé Lebeuf* (4 fascicles, Paris, 1890–1901); IDEM, *P. hist., monuments, administration* (Paris, 1888); IDEM, *P. Atlas* (Paris, 1900); CAIN, *Promenades dans P., Pierres de P., Coins de P.* (4 vols., Paris, 1905–10); DAVIS, *About P.* (New York, 1895); HARE, *P.* (London, 1896); MEMPES, *P.* (London, 1907); OKEY, *P. and its Story* (London, 1904); FRANKLIN, *La vie privée d'autrefois. Arts et métiers, modes, mœurs, usages des Parisiens du XIIe au XVIIe siècle* (27 vols., Paris, 1887–1902); HARRISON, *Memorable P. Houses with illustrative, critical, and anecdotal notices* (London, 1893).

C. ECCLESIASTICAL.—*Gallia christ.*, VII (1744), 1–219, *Instrumenta*, 1–192; FISQUET, *La France pontificale* (2 vols., Paris, 1864–6); LONGNON, *L'ancien dioc. de P. et ses subdivisions* in *Bull. du Comité d'hist. et d'archéol. du dioc. de P.*, I (1883), pp. 10–19; BERNARD, *Les origines de l'église de P., établissement du christianisme dans les Gaules;saint Denys de P.* (Paris, 1870); CHARTIER, *L'ancien chapitre de Notre-Dame-de-P. et sa maîtrise* (Paris, 1897); JAUNAY, *Hist. des évêques et archevêques de P.* (Paris, 1884); DEPOIN, *Essai sur la chronologie des évêques de P. de 768 à 1138* in *Bull. histor. et philol.* (1906); FÉRET, *L'abbaye de Ste-Geneviève et la congrégation de France* (Paris, 1883); BONNARD, *Hist. de l'abbaye royale de l'ordre des chanoines réguliers de St-Victor* (2 vols., Paris, 1908); BROUILLET, *Les églises paroissiales de P.* (monographs, Lyons, 1897–1904); LONERGAN, *Historic Churches of P.* (London, 1896); MORTET, *Etude histor. et archéol. sur la cathédrale et le palais épiscopal de P. au VIe et XIIe siècle* (Paris, 1888); AUBERT, *La cathédrale N.-D.-de-P.* (Paris, 1909); HIATT, *N.-D.-de-P., a Short History and Description of the Cathedral* (London, 1902); DUPLESSY, *P. religieux* (Paris, 1900); D'AYZAC, *Hist. de l'abbaye de St-Denis en France* (2 vols., Paris, 1860–1); HAVET, *Les origines de St-Denis* (Paris, 1890); PARIS, *Les grandes chroniques de France, selon qu'elles sont conservées en l'église de St-Denis* (6 vols., Paris, 1830–9); VITRY AND BRIÈRE, *L'église abbatiale de St-Denis* (Paris, 1908); LESÊTRE, *L'Immaculée Conception et l'Eglise de Paris* (Paris, 1904); DOUMERGUE, *Paris protestant au XVIe siècle* in *Bull. de la Soc. du protestantisme français* (1896); DOUEN, *La Révocation de l'édit de Nantes à P.* (3 vols., Paris, 1894); DECOPPET, *P. protestant* (Paris, 1876); ROBINET, *Le mouvement religieux à P. pendant la Révolution, 1789–1801* (2 vols., Paris, 1896); DELARC, *L'église de P. pendant la Révolution française, 1789–1801* (3 vols., Paris, 1895–8); GRENTE, *Le culte catholique à P. de la Terreur au Concordat* (Paris, 1903); PISANI, *L'église de P. sous la Révolution* (3 vols., Paris, 1909–10); DE LANZAC DE LABORIE, *P. sous Napoléon*, especially IV (Paris, 1907).

D. CHARITIES.—CHEVALIER, *L'hôtel-Dieu de P. et les Sœurs Augustines (650 à 1810)* (Paris, 1901); BRUNET, *La charité paroissiale à P. au XVIIe siècle d'après les règlements des compagnies de charité* (Caen, 1906); CAHEN, *Le grand bureau des pauvres de P. au milieu du 18e siècle* (Paris, 1904); MAXIME DU CAMP, *La charité privée à P.* (Paris, 1885); IDEM, *P. bienfaisant* (Paris, 1888); DU THIL-

NOTRE-DAME DE PARIS

LEUL, *L'assistance publique à P., ses bienfaiteurs et sa fortune mobilière* (2 vols., Paris, 1904); *P. charitable et prévoyant*, published by the Central Office of Charitable Institutions (3rd ed., Paris, 1904); *Manuel des Œuvres* (new ed., Paris, 1911), supplies the most recent information and a detailed description concerning all French Catholic charitable works, especially those of Paris.

GEORGES GOYAU.

PARIS, UNIVERSITY OF.—*Origin and Early Organization.*—Three schools were especially famous at Paris, the palatine or palace school, the school of Notre-Dame, and that of Sainte-Geneviève. The decline of royalty inevitably brought about the decline of the first. The other two, which were very old, like those of the cathedrals and the abbeys, are only faintly outlined during the early centuries of their existence. The glory of the palatine school doubtless eclipsed theirs, until in the course of time it completely gave way to them. These two centres were much frequented and many of their masters were esteemed for their learning. It is not until the tenth century, however, that we meet with a professor of renown in the school of Ste-Geneviève. This was Hubold, who, not content with the courses at Liège, came to continue his studies at Paris, entered or allied himself with the chapter of Ste-Geneviève, and by his teaching attracted many pupils. Recalled by his bishop to Belgium, he soon profited by a second journey to Paris to give lessons with no less success. As to the school of Notre-Dame, while many of its masters are mentioned simply as having been professors at Paris, in its later history we meet with a number of distinguished names: in the eleventh century, Lambert, disciple of Fulbert of Chartres; Drogo of Paris; Manegold of Germany; Anselm of Laon. These two schools, attracting scholars from every country, produced many illustrious men, among whom were: St. Stanislaus, Bishop of Cracow; Gebbard, Archbishop of Salzburg; St. Stephen, third Abbot of Cîteaux; Robert d'Arbrissel, founder of the Abbey of Fontevrault etc. The honour of having formed similar pupils is indiscriminately ascribed to Notre-Dame and to Ste-Geneviève, as du Molinet has justly remarked (Bibl. Sainte-Geneviève, MS.H. fr. 21, in fol., p. 576). Humanistic instruction comprised grammar, rhetoric, dialectics, arithmetic, geometry, music, and astronomy (*trivium* and *quadrivium*). To the higher instruction belonged dogmatic and moral theology, whose source was the Scriptures and the Fathers, and which was completed by the study of canon law. Three men were to add a new splendour to the schools of Notre-Dame and Ste-Geneviève, namely William of Champeaux, Abelard, and Peter Lombard. A new school arose which rivalled those of Notre-Dame and Ste-Geneviève. It owed its foundation to the same William of Champeaux when he withdrew to the Abbey of St-Victor and it took the name of that abbey. Two men shed special radiance on this school, Hugh and Richard, who added to their own names that of the abbey at which they were religious and professors.

The plan of studies expanded in the schools of Paris as it did elsewhere. The great work of a monk of Bologna, known as the "Decretum Gratiani", brought about a division of the science of theology. Hitherto the discipline of the Church had not been separate from theology properly so-called; they were studied together under the same professor. But this vast collection necessitated a special course, which was naturally undertaken first at Bologna, where Roman law was taught. In France, first Orléans and then Paris erected chairs of canon law, which except at Paris were usually also chairs of civil law. The capital of the kingdom might thus boast of this new professorate, that of the "Decretum Gratiani", to which before the end of the twelfth century were added the Decretals of Gerard (or Girard) La Pucelle, Mathieu d'Angers, and Anselm (or Anselle) of Paris, but civil law was not included. In the course of the twelfth century also medicine began to be publicly taught at Paris. A professor of medicine is mentioned in this city at this time, namely Hugo, "physicus excellens qui quadrivium docuit", and it is to be assumed that this science was included in his teaching.

For the right to teach, two things were necessary, knowledge and appointment. Knowledge was proved by examination, the appointment came from the examiner himself, who was the head of the school, and was known as *scholasticus, capiscol*, and eventually as "chancellor". This was called the licence or faculty to teach. Without this authorization there was danger of the chairs being occupied by ignorant persons, whom John of Salisbury depicts as "children yesterday, masters to-day; yesterday receiving strokes of the ferrule, to-day teaching in a long gown" (Metalogicus, I, xxv *in init.*). The licence had to be granted gratuitously. Without it no one could teach; on the other hand, it could not be refused when the applicant deserved it.

The school of St-Victor, which shared the obligations as well as the immunities of the abbey, conferred the licence in its own right; the school of Notre-Dame depended on the diocese, that of Ste-Geneviève on the abbey or chapter. It was the diocese and the abbey or chapter which through their chancellor gave professorial investiture in their respective territories, i. e. the diocese in the city *intra pontes* and other places subject to the ordinary, the abbey or chapter on the left bank of the river as far as its jurisdiction reached. Consequently, as du Molinet explains, it was incumbent on the chancellor of Notre-Dame and Ste-Geneviève to examine "those who applied to teach in the schools", to "license after study those who sought to be masters and regents" (op. cit., 585). Besides these three centres of learning there were several schools on the "Island" and on the "Mount". "Whoever", says Crevier "had the right to teach might open a school where he pleased, provided it was not in the vicinity of a principal school". Thus a certain Adam, who was of English origin, kept his "near the Petit Pont"; another Adam, Parisian by birth, "taught at the Grand Pont which is called the Pont-au-Change" (Hist. de l'Univers. de Paris, I, 272).

The number of students in the schools of the capital grew constantly, so that eventually the lodgings were insufficient. Among the French students there were princes of the blood, sons of the nobility, and the most distinguished youths of the kingdom. The courses at Paris were considered so necessary as a completion of studies that many foreigners flocked to them. Popes Celestine II and Adrian IV had studied at Paris, Alexander III sent his nephews there, and, under the name of Lothaire, a scion of the noble family of Seigny, who was later to rule the Church as Innocent III, belonged to the student body. Otto of Freisingen, Cardinal Conrad, Archbishop of Mainz, St. Thomas of Canterbury, and John of Salisbury were among the most illustrious sons of Germany and England in the schools of Paris; while Ste-Geneviève became practically the seminary for Denmark. The chroniclers of the time call Paris the city of letters *par excellence*, placing it above Athens, Alexandria, Rome, and other cities: "At that time", we read in the "Chroniques de St-Denis", "there flourished at Paris philosophy and all branches of learning, and there the seven arts were studied and held in such esteem as they never were at Athens, Egypt, Rome, or elsewhere in the world" ("Les gestes de Philippe-Auguste"). Poets said the same thing in their verses, and they compared it to all that was greatest, noblest, and most valuable in the world.

To maintain order among the students and define the relations of the professors, organization was necessary. It had its beginnings, and it developed as circumstances permitted or required. Three features in this organization may be noted: first, the professors formed an association, for according to Matthew Paris,

John of Celles, twenty-first Abbot of St. Albans, England, was admitted as a member of the teaching corps of Paris after he had followed the courses (Vita Joannis I, XXI, abbat. S. Alban). Again, the masters as well as the students were divided according to provinces, for as the same historian states, Henry II, King of England, in his difficulties with St. Thomas of Canterbury, wished to submit his cause to a tribunal composed of professors of Paris, chosen from various provinces (Hist. major, Henry II, to end of 1169). This was probably the germ of that division according to "nations" which was later to play an important part in the university. Lastly, mention must be made of the privileges then enjoyed by the professors and students. In virtue of a decision of Celestine III, they were amenable only to the ecclesiastical courts. Other decisions dispensed them from residence in case they possessed benefices and permitted them to receive their revenues.

These three schools of Notre-Dame, Ste-Geneviève, and St-Victor may be regarded as the triple cradle of the *Universitas scholarium*, which included masters and students; hence the name *University*. Such is the common and more probable opinion. Denifle and some others hold that this honour must be reserved to the school of Notre-Dame (Chartularium Universitatis Parisiensis), but the reasons do not seem convincing. He excludes St-Victor because, at the request of the abbot and the religious of St-Victor, Gregory IX in 1237 authorized them to resume the interrupted teaching of theology. But the university was in large part founded about 1208, as is shown by a Bull of Innocent III. Consequently the schools of St-Victor might well have furnished their contingent towards its formation. Secondly, Denifle excludes the schools of Ste-Geneviève because there had been no interruption in the teaching of the liberal arts. Now this is far from proved, and moreover, it seems incontestable that theology also had never ceased to be taught, which is sufficient for our point. Besides, the rôle of the chancellor of Ste-Geneviève in the university cannot be explained by the new opinion; he continued to give degrees in arts, a function which would have ceased for him when the university was organized if his abbey had no share in its organization. And while the name *Universitas scholarium* is quite intelligible on the basis of the common opinion, it is incompatible with the recent (Denifle's) view, according to which there would have been schools outside the university.

Organization in the Thirteenth Century.—As completing the work of organization the diploma of Philip Augustus and the statutes of Robert de Courçon are worthy of note. The king's diploma was given "for the security of the scholars of Paris", and in virtue of it from the year 1200 the students were subject only to ecclesiastical jurisdiction. Hence the provost and other officers were forbidden to arrest a student for any offence, and if in exceptional cases this was done it was only to hand over the culprit to ecclesiastical authority, for in the event of grave crime royal justice was limited to taking cognizance of the procedure and the verdict. In no case could the king's officers lay hands on the head of the schools or even on a simple regent, this being allowed only in virtue of a mandate proceeding from ecclesiastical authority. The statutes of the Apostolic legate are later by some years, bearing the date 1215. They had for their object the moral or intellectual part of the instruction. They dealt with three principal points, the conditions of the professorate, the matter to be treated, and the granting of the licence. To teach the arts it was necessary to have reached the age of twenty-one, after having studied these arts at least six years, and to take an engagement as professor for at least two years. For a chair in theology the candidate had to be thirty years of age with eight years of theological studies, of which the last three years were at the same time devoted to special courses of lectures in preparation for the mastership. These studies had to be made in the local schools and under the direction of a master, for at Paris one was not regarded as a scholar unless he had a particular master. Lastly, purity of morals was not less requisite than learning. Priscian's "Grammar", Aristotle's "Dialectics", mathematics, astronomy, music, certain books of rhetoric and philosophy were the subjects taught in the arts course; to these might be added the Ethics of the Stagyrite and the fourth book of the Topics. But it was forbidden to read the books of Aristotle on Metaphysics and Physics, or abbreviations of them. The licence was granted, according to custom, gratuitously, without oath or condition. Masters and students were permitted to unite, even by oath, in defence of their rights, when they could not otherwise obtain justice in serious matters. No mention is made either of law or of medicine, probably because these sciences were less prominent.

A denial of justice by the queen brought about in 1229 a suspension of the courses. Appeal was taken to the pope who intervened in the same year by a Bull which began with a eulogy of the university. "Paris", said Gregory IX, "mother of the sciences, is another Cariath-Sepher, city of letters". He compared it to a laboratory in which wisdom tested the metals which she found there, gold and silver to adorn the Spouse of Jesus Christ, iron to fashion the spiritual sword which should smite the inimical powers. He commissioned the Bishops of Le Mans and Senlis and the Archdeacon of Châlons to negotiate with the French Court for the restoration of the university. The year 1230 came to an end without any result, and Gregory IX took the matter directly in hand by a Bull of 1231 addressed to the masters and scholars of Paris. Not content with settling the dispute and giving guarantees for the future, he sanctioned and developed the concessions of Robert de Courçon by empowering the university to frame statutes concerning the discipline of the schools, the method of instruction, the defence of theses, the costume of the professors, and the obsequies of masters and students. What was chiefly important was that the pope recognized in the university or granted it the right, in case justice were denied it, to suspend its courses until it should receive full satisfaction. It must be borne in mind that in the schools of Paris not only was the granting of licence gratuitous but instruction also was free. This was the general rule; however, it was often necessary to depart from it. Thus Pierre Le Mangeur was authorized by the pope to levy a moderate fee for the conferring of the licence. Similar fees were exacted for the first degree in arts and letters, and the scholars were taxed two *sous* weekly, to be deposited in the common fund.

The university was organized as follows: at the head of the teaching body was a rector. The office was elective and of short duration. At first it was limited to four or six weeks. Simon de Brion, legate of the Holy See in France, rightly judging that such frequent changes caused serious inconvenience, decided that the rectorate should last three months, and this rule was observed for three years. Then the term was lengthened to one, two, and sometimes three years. The right of election belonged to the procurators of the four nations. The "Nations" appeared in the second half of the twelfth century; they were mentioned in the Bull of Honorius III in 1222 and in another of Gregory IX in 1231; later they formed a distinct body. In 1249 the four nations existed with their procurators, their rights (more or less well-defined), and their keen rivalries; and in 1254, in the heat of the controversy between the university and the mendicant orders, a letter was addressed to the pope bearing the seals of the four nations. These were the French, English, Normans, and Picards. After the Hundred Years' War the English nation was replaced by the Germanic or German. The four nations constituted the faculty of arts or letters. The expression faculty, though of ancient usage, did not have in the beginning its present meaning; it then indicated a branch of instruction. It is especially in a Bull of Gregory IX that it is used to designate the professional body, and it may have had the same meaning in a university Act of 1221 (cf. "Hist. Universitatis Parisiensis", III, 106).

If the natural division of the schools of Paris into nations arose from the native countries of the students, the classification of knowledge must quite as naturally have introduced the division into faculties. Professors of the same science were brought into closer contact; community of rights and interests cemented the union and made of them distinct groups, which at the same time remained integral parts of the teaching body. Thus the faculties gradually arose and consequently no precise account of their origin can be given. The faculty of medicine would seem to be the last in point of time. But the four faculties were already formally designated in a letter addressed in Feb., 1254, by the university to the prelates of Christendom, wherein mention is made of "theology, jurisprudence, medicine, and rational, natural, and moral philosophy". In the celebrated Bull "Quasi Lignum" (April, 1255), Alexander IV speaks of "the faculties of theology" of other "faculties", namely those of canonists, physicians, and artists. If the masters in theology set the example in this special organization, those in decretals and medicine hastened to follow it. This is proved by the seals which the last-named adopted some years later, as the masters in arts had already done.

The faculties of theology, or canon law, and medicine, were called "superior faculties". The title of "dean" as designating the head of a faculty, was not in use until the second half of the thirteenth century. In this matter the faculties of decretals and medicine seem to have taken the lead, which the faculty of theology followed, for in authentic acts of 1268 we read of the deans of decretals and medicine, while the dean of theology is not mentioned until 1296. It would seem that at first the deans were the oldest masters. The faculty of arts continued to have four procurators of its four nations and its head was the rector. As the faculties became more fully organized, the division into four nations partially disappeared for theology, decretals and medicine, while it continued in arts. Eventually the superior faculties were to include only doctors, leaving the bachelors to the nations. At this period, therefore, the university had two principal degrees, the baccalaureate and the doctorate. It was not until much later that the licentiate, while retaining its early character, became an intermediate degree. Besides, the university numbered among its members beadles and messengers, who also performed the duties of clerks.

The scattered condition of the scholars in Paris often made the question of lodging difficult. Recourse was had to the townsfolk, who exacted high rates while the students demanded lower. Hence arose friction and quarrels, which, as the scholars were very numerous, would have developed into a sort of civil war if a remedy had not been found. The remedy sought was taxation. This right of taxation, included in the regulation of Robert de Courçon, had passed on to the university. It was upheld in the Bull of Gregory IX of 1231, but with an important modification, for its exercise was to be shared with the citizens. These circumstances had long shown the need of new arrangements. The aim was to offer the students a shelter where they would fear neither annoyance from the owners nor the dangers of the world. The result was the foundation of the colleges (*colligere*, to assemble). This measure also furthered the progress of studies by a better employment of time, under the guidance sometimes of resident masters and out of the way of dissipation. These colleges were not usually centres of instruction, but simple boarding-houses for the students, who went from them to the schools. Each had a special object, being established for students of the same nationality or the same science. Four colleges appear in the twelfth century; they became more numerous in the thirteenth, and among them may be mentioned Harcourt and the Sorbonne. Thus the University of Paris, which in general was the type of the other universities, had already assumed the form which it afterwards retained. It was composed of seven groups, the four nations of the faculty of arts, and the three superior faculties of theology, law, and medicine. Ecclesiastical dignities, even abroad, seemed reserved for the masters and students of Paris. This preference became a general rule, and eventually a right, that of eligibility to benefices. Such was the origin and early organization of the University of Paris which might even then, in virtue of their protection, call itself the daughter of kings, but which was in reality the daughter of the Church. St. Louis, in the diploma which he granted to the Carthusians for their establishment near Paris, speaks of this city, where "flow the most abundant waters of wholesome doctrine, so that they become a great river which after refreshing the city itself irrigates the Universal Church". Clement IV uses a no less charming comparison: "the noble and renowned city, the city which is the source of learning and sheds over the world a light which seems an image of the celestial splendour; those who are taught there shine brilliantly, and those who teach there will shine with the stars for all eternity" (cf. du Boulay, "Hist. Univers. Paris", III, 360–71).

Later History.—Abuses crept in; to correct these and to introduce various needed modifications in the work of the university was the purpose of the reform carried out in the fifteenth century by Cardinal d'Estouteville, Apostolic legate in France. As a whole it was less an innovation than a recall to the better observance of the ancient statutes. The reform of 1600, undertaken by the royal government, was of the same character with regard to the three superior faculties. As to the faculty of arts, the study of Greek was added to that of Latin, only the best classical authors were recommended; the French poets and orators were used along with Hesiod, Plato, Demosthenes, Cicero, Virgil, and Sallust. The prohibition to teach civil law was never well observed at Paris. But in 1679 Louis XIV authorized the teaching of civil law in the faculty of decretals. As a logical consequence the name "faculty of law" replaced that of "faculty of decretals". The colleges meantime had multiplied; those of Cardinal Le-Moine and Navarre were founded in the fourteenth century. The Hundred Years' War was fatal to these establishments, but the university set about remedying the injury.

Remarkable for its teaching, the University of Paris played an important part: in the Church, during the Great Schism; in the councils, in dealing with heresies and deplorable divisions; in the State, during national crises; and if under the domination of England it dishonoured itself in the trial of Joan of Arc, it rehabilitated itself by rehabilitating the heroine herself. Proud of its rights and privileges, it fought energetically to maintain them. Hence the long struggle against the mendicant orders on academic as well as on religious grounds. Hence also the conflict, shorter but also memorable, against the Jesuits, who claimed by word and action a share in its teaching. It made liberal use of its right to decide administratively according to occasion and necessity. In some instances it openly endorsed the censures of the faculty of theology and in its own name pronounced condemnation, as in the case of the Flagellants.

Its patriotism was especially manifested on two occasions. During the captivity of King John, when

Paris was given over to factions, the university sought energetically to restore peace; and under Louis XIV, when the Spaniards had crossed the Somme and threatened the capital, it placed two hundred men at the king's disposal and offered the Master of Arts degree gratuitously to scholars who should present certificates of service in the army (Jourdain, "Hist. de l'Univers. de Paris au XVIIe et XVIIIe siècle", 132–34; "Archiv. du ministère de l'instruction publique").

The ancient university was to disappear with ancient France under the Revolution. On 15 Sept., 1793, petitioned by the Department of Paris and several departmental groups, the National Convention decided that independently of the primary schools, already the objects of its solicitude, "there should be established in the Republic three progressive degrees of instruction; the first for the knowledge indispensable to artisans and workmen of all kinds; the second for further knowledge necessary to those intending to embrace the other professions of society; and the third for those branches of instruction the study of which is not within the reach of all men". Measures were to be taken immediately: "For means of execution the department and the municipality of Paris are authorized to consult with the Committee of Public Instruction of the National Convention, in order that these establishments shall be put in action by 1 November next, and consequently colleges now in operation and the faculties of theology, medicine, arts, and law are suppressed throughout the Republic". This was the death-sentence of the university. It was not to be restored after the Revolution had subsided, any more than those of the provinces. All were replaced by a single centre, viz., the University of France. The lapse of a century brought the recognition that the new system was less favourable to study, and it was sought to restore the old system, but without the faculty of theology.

RASHDALL, *Universities of Europe in the Middle Ages*, I (Oxford, 1895); DENIFLE, *Die Universitäten* . . . (Berlin, 1885); DENIFLE AND CHATELAIN, *Chartularium Univ. Paris* (Paris, 1889–97); DU BOULAY, *Hist. Univ. Paris* (Paris, 1665–73); CREVIER, *Hist. de l'Univ. de P.* (Paris, 1761); THUROT, *De l'organisation de l'enseignement dans l'Univ. de P.* (Paris, 1850); JOURDAIN, *Hist. de l'Univ. de P. au 17e et au 18e siècle* (Paris, 1866); RALEIGH, *The Univ. of Paris* (Oxford, 1873); FERET, *La Faculté de théol. et ses docteurs les plus célèbres* (Paris, 1894–1909). See also bibliography under UNIVERSITY.

P. FERET.

Paris, ALEXIS-PAULIN, philologist, b. at Avenay, Marne, France, 25 March, 1800; d. 13 Feb., 1881. Having finished his classical studies at Reims, he was sent by his father to Paris to study law, but devoted most of his time to literature. In 1824 he published "Apologie de l'Ecole Romantique", in which he advocated the imitation of Byron and the study of medieval art. Besides contributing articles to various literary reviews, he translated Byron's complete works (13 vols., Paris, 1827–32). In 1828 he obtained a clerkship in the manuscript department of the King's Library (now known as the Bibliothèque Nationale), and was afterwards promoted to the rank of assistant librarian. He took advantage of his position to pursue his research work on medieval literature, and publish a few old epics, "Berte aux Grans Piés" (Paris, 1831), "Garin le Loherain" (1835), and a collection of popular songs under the title of "Romancero Français" (Paris, 1833). He then turned to historical writings, publishing in 1833 "Mémoire sur la Relation Originale des Voyages de Marco Polo", and from 1836 to 1840, the "Grandes Chroniques de Saint Denis". His most important work as a librarian, was his book on "Les Manuscrits Français de la Bibliothèque du Roi" (Paris, 1836–48), which is not a mere catalogue, but a lengthy dissertation on the authors and contents of the MSS.

In recognition of his achievements, he was elected to the Academy of Inscriptions and Belles-lettres in 1837 and soon after was made a member of the committee entrusted with the task of continuing the "Histoire littéraire de la France", a most valuable publication, begun in the eighteenth century by the Benedictines. In 1853 a chair of medieval literature was created for him in the Collège de France, and for nineteen years he lectured in a most scholarly manner on the origins of the French language, the old French epics or "Chansons de Geste", the novels of the Round Table, and the early French theatre. Medieval literature appealed to him, because he found in it a naïve but strong expression of his religious faith. Busy as he was with the preparation of his lectures, he found time to publish, with dissertations and annotations, such works as "Historiettes de Tallemand des Réaux" (9 vols., Paris, 1860), "Aventures de Maître Renart et d'Ysengrin" (Paris, 1861), "Recueil complet des Poèmes de St-Pavin" (1861), "Romans de la Table Ronde" (1868–77), "Le Livre du Voir Dit", by Guillaume de Machault (1867). He resigned his chair in the Collège de France in 1872.

PARIS, *Paulin Paris et la littérature française du moyen âge* in *Romania*, XI (1882).

LOUIS N. DELAMARRE.

Paris, GASTON-BRUNO-PAULIN, a French philologist, son of Paulin, b. at Avenay (Marne), 9 August, 1839; d. at Cannes, 6 March, 1903. After graduating from the Collège Rollin, Paris, he studied at the Universities of Göttingen and Bonn, where he was a pupil of the celebrated philologist Diez. On his return, while taking courses at the Ecole des Chartes, he studied law and literature at the University of Paris, obtaining the degree of doctor in literature in 1865. He taught for a while French grammar in a private school, and was appointed professor of languages at the Ecole Pratique des Hautes Etudes, and soon after was made director of that section of the school, a position he retained till his death. In 1872, he succeeded his father as professor of medieval literature at the Collège de France and was made director of the college in 1895. A year later, he was elected to the French Academy, taking the seat made vacant by the death of Alexandre Dumas, Jr. For more than thirty years he was regarded as the highest authority in France on philology of the Romance languages. By his vast erudition, his scientific methods, and his patient researches in that new field, he made his name famous throughout Europe. His lectures were attended by enthusiastic crowds gathered from all parts of the world. His salon, where he used to receive every Sunday his friends, pupils, and distinguished foreign scholars, was one of the most celebrated in Paris. Because of his sojourn in Protestant universities and the influence of Renan, he lost for a time his religious faith, but towards the end of his life he returned to the sentiments of his childhood and was buried in the Church. Among his numerous publications, without mentioning his contributions to the "Revue critique" and "Romania", which he founded, the former in 1865, the latter in 1872, the chief to be cited are: "Etude sur le rôle de l'accent latin dans la langue française" (Paris, 1862); "De Pseudo-Turpino" (Paris, 1865), a Latin thesis for the doctorate; "Histoire poétique de Charlemagne" (Paris, 1866); "La vie de saint Alexis" (texts of the eleventh, twelfth, thirteenth, and fourteenth centuries); "Dissertation critique sur le poème latin Ligurius" (Paris, 1873); "Le petit Poucet, la grande Ourse" (Paris, 1875); "Les contes orientaux dans la littérature du moyen âge" (Paris, 1875); "Les miracles de Notre-Dame par Personnages" (Paris, 1877); "Le mystère de la Passion par Arnoul Gréban" (1878); "Deux Rédactions du roman des sept sages de Rome" (Paris, 1879); "Aucassin et Nicolette" (Paris, 1878); "Poètes et Penseurs" (Paris, 1893) etc.

MASSON, *Discours de réception à l'Académie française* (Paris, 1904); *Romania* (April, 1903); TODD, *Gaston Paris* in *Modern*

Languages Association Publications (Baltimore, 1899); ROQUES AND BEDIER, *Bibl. des œuvres de Gaston Paris* (Paris, 1905).

LOUIS N. DELAMARRE.

Paris, MATTHEW, Benedictine monk and chronicler, b. about 1200; d. 1259. There seems no reason to infer from the name by which he was commonly known that this famous English historian was directly connected with Paris either by birth or education. He became a monk at St. Albans on 21 January, 1217, and St. Albans remained his home until his death. We know, however, that on occasion he moved about freely, visiting London and the Court, and one memorable episode of his life took him as visitor with full powers to the Abbey of St. Benet Holm in Norway where he remained nearly a year. Simple monk as he was, Matthew seems always to have been treated as a personage of consideration. In his journey to Norway he was the bearer of letters from St. Louis of France to Haakon IV, inviting the Norwegian king to join the crusade. Haakon subsequently became his personal friend and we have much evidence in Matthew's own writings of the intimate terms upon which he stood with the English king, Henry III, and with his brother Richard, Earl of Cornwall. From them and from the members of their household the chronicler must have derived that wide, if not always quite accurate, acquaintance with the details of foreign contemporary history in which Matthew Paris stands unrivalled among medieval historians. His gifts were not merely those of the student and man of letters. He was famed as an artist and an expert in writing and he probably executed with his own hand many of the telling little drawings which illustrate the margins of his manuscripts.

As an historian Matthew holds the first place among English chroniclers. For his ease of style, range of interest and information, vivid though prolix elaboration of detail, he is much more readable than any of those monastic scholars who wrote either before or after him. His great work, the "Chronica Majora", extends from the creation until 1259, the year of his death. Down to 1235 this is simply an expansion and embellishment of the chronicle of his fellow-monk, Roger of Wendover, but "he re-edited Wendover's work with a patriotic and anti-curialist bias quite alien to the spirit of the earlier writer" (Tout, 451). From 1235 to 1259 Paris is a first-hand authority and by far the most copious source of information we possess. The "Chronica Majora" has been admirably edited, with prefaces and supplements, in seven volumes by Dr. Luard. A compendium of this work from 1067 to 1253 was also prepared by Paris. It is known as the "Historia Minor" and it bears evidence of a certain mitigation of previous judgments which in his later years he deemed over severe. This work has been edited by Sir F. Madden. Other minor works connected especially with St. Albans, and a short "Life of Stephen Langton" (printed by Liebermann in 1870) are also attributed to Paris.

With regard to his trustworthiness as a source of history there seems to be a tendency amongst most English writers, notably for example J. R. Green or Dr. Luard, to glorify him as a sort of national asset and to regard his shortcomings with partisan eyes. There can be no question that Matthew's allegations against the friars and his denunciations of the avarice and tyranical interference of the Roman Court should be received with extreme caution. Lingard perhaps goes too far when, in speaking of his "censorious disposition", he declares, "It may appear invidious to speak harshly of this famous historian, but this I may say, that when I could confront his pages with authentic records or contemporary writers, I have in most instances found the discrepancy between them so great as to give his narrative the appearance of a romance rather than a history" (Lingard, "History", II, 479). But we may rest content with the verdict of a more recent writer, open to no suspicion of religious bias. "Matthew", says Professor Tout, "was a man of strong views, and his sympathies and his prejudices colour every line he wrote. His standpoint is that of a patriotic Englishman, indignant at the alien invasions, at the misgovernment of the King, the greed of the curialists and the Poitevins, and with a professional bias against the mendicant friars" (Polit. Hist. of Eng., III, 452).

The principal sources of information regarding Matthew Paris have all been gathered up in the prefaces of Dr. Luard to his monumental edition of the *Chronica Majora* in the *Rolls Series* (1872–83). On the question of Matthew's caligraphy etc., Luard's views should be compared with Sir F. Madden's preface to the *Historia Minor* in Rolls Series (3 vols., 1866–69) and with Sir T. Duffus-Hardy's preface to his *Catalogue of British History*, vol. III (1871), equipped with many facsimiles. See also *Cambridge History of English Literature*, I (Cambridge, 1907), 178–80; TOUT in *Political History of England*, III (London, 1905), 451–53; GASQUET, *Henry III and the Church* (London, 1905); BERGER, *St. Louis et Innocent IV* (Paris, 1894); IDEM, in his preface to the *Regesta Innocentii Papæ Quarti*.

HERBERT THURSTON.

Parish (L. *parœcia, parochia*, Gk. παροικία, a group of neighbouring dwellings). I. *General Notions*.—A parish is a portion of a diocese under the authority of a priest legitimately appointed to secure in virtue of his office for the faithful dwelling therein, the helps of religion. The faithful are called parishioners, the priest *parochus*, curate, parish priest, pastor (q. v.). To form a parish there must be (1) a certain body of the faithful over whom pastoral authority is exercised; the ordinary manner of determining them is by assigning a territory subject to the exclusive jurisdiction of the parish priest. Uncertainty of parish boundaries may work harm and the Council of Trent (Sess. XXIV, c. xiii, de ref.) orders the boundaries of parishes to be defined. The faithful become parishioners by acquiring a domicile or a quasi-domicile (see DOMICILE) within the territory, or by simply living in it for a month (Decree, "Ne temere", on marriage, 2 August, 1907). Travellers, however, may address themselves to the parish priest of the locality, though without detriment to the rights of their own pastor. The exclusive attribution of a territory to a parish and its pastor is not absolutely necessary; certain parishes coexist with others in the same territory, the respective parishes being distinguished by rite or nationality, e. g. in the Orient or in large American cities. There are even rare instances of parishes formed solely of families, without regard to territory. (2) A special priest, having in virtue of his title a mission and authority to give religious succour to the parishioners, is required. In strict law, the care of souls in a single parish must devolve on several priests, and in fact, such was formerly the case in most chapters (q. v.); but the Council of Trent (Sess. XXIV, c. xiii, de ref.) commands bishops to assign to each parish its own individual rector. If the care of souls is entrusted to a moral body, like a chapter, it must be exercised by a vicar, perpetual as far as possible, who is called the "actual" curate, the chapter remaining the "habitual" curate, without right of interfering in any way in the parochial ministry (Sess. VII, c. vii).

The parish priest may have assistants, but the latter exercise their ministry in dependence on him and in his name. If the priest, even when alone, does not exercise his office in his own name, if he is only the delegate of a higher authority, he is not really a parish priest and his district is not a true parish. That is why there are no real parishes (as there are no real dioceses) but only stations in vicariates Apostolic and missionary countries. The same may occur in dioceses during the provisional period which precedes the erection of certain districts into parishes. But the parish exists, when the priest exercises the ministry in his own name, whether his title be perpetual or he be removable at the will of the bishop. From this results

(3) *parochial law*, 1. e., the reciprocal rights and duties of the parish priest and parishioners. This constitutes the care of souls (*cura animarum*), an essential and constitutive element of a parish, distinguishing a parochial benefice from all others. Finally there is required (4) a suitable church which must have besides the liturgical equipment necessary for Divine worship, a baptismal font (exception is occasionally made in favour of a cathedral or a mother-church; hence in the Middle Ages parish churches were often called baptismal churches), a confessional, and a cemetery. Records of the baptisms, marriages, and burials must be kept, while the entire parish is the object of a *liber status animarum*, prescribed by the Ritual. Finally, the parish has fixed or occasional contributions for Divine service, the building, liturgical furniture, parochial works, and all that implies an administration. Local laws determine the share of the parishioners or their representatives in this administration. The parish must likewise furnish the parish priest with his presbytery or dwelling.

II. *The Parish as a Benefice.*—The canonical legislation relative to parishes is part of the legislation concerning benefices (q. v.). To the care of souls is annexed by common law a benefice, by its purpose distinct from any other. All parishes are benefices, at least in the wide acceptation of the term; according to canon law, every church should have a stable income, especially land revenues, sufficient to insure not only the Divine service but also the support of its clergy. Every parish priest ought to have a fixed beneficial revenue, his *congrua*, the minimum of which is fixed by the Council of Trent (Sess. XXIV, c. xiii, de ref.), at one hundred ducats (about one hundred and forty-two dollars), a sum insufficient to-day; the *congrua* may be replaced by contributions from the public treasury, in certain countries, paid in return for former ecclesiastical property now confiscated. Parishes without fixed incomes are nevertheless benefices in a broad sense of the term, since they insure a living for their parish priests by gifts and offerings, either voluntary or payable on the occasion of certain acts of the curial ministry, according to rates approved by the bishop. Parishes, like other benefices, may be divided into several classes. Most parishes are "free", i. e. the bishop himself selects the incumbent; but others are subject to the right of patronage; the patrons present to the bishop their candidate. Most parishes are independent, but some are united to other ecclesiastical bodies: chapters, dignities (high ecclesiastical offices), monasteries. By common law they are served by the secular clergy and are hence called secular parishes; but some, united to houses of religious orders, are served by religious and are consequently termed regular. Those confided to religious in virtue of a personal title, are not properly speaking regular.

The care of souls places parochial benefices in a special category, and has led to regulations peculiar to them alone. (1) Parishes, to be "free", i. e., freely collated, should be conferred by the bishop within six months like other benefices; but his choice is limited by the concursus (q. v.) ordered by the Council of Trent (Sess. XXIV, c. xviii, de ref.). (2) By common law, a parochial benefice, like other benefices, is perpetual, and the beneficiary irremovable (see IRREMOVABILITY; Decree, "Maxima cura", 20 August, 1910). According to this Decree parish priests who were heretofore removable are now withdrawn from purely administrative transference. Irremovable parish priests may have their faculties withdrawn, without any trial properly so called, when the good of souls demands it. The nine reasons given in the aforesaid Decree as grounds for this withdrawal of faculties relate to corporal or spiritual defects, criminal conduct, serious and prolonged neglect of duty, persistent disobedience; these reasons, however, are not here dealt with as crimes, but solely as obstacles to a useful parochial ministry; hence the parish priest on being removed is to be provided for. This administrative procedure adequately secures the right of initiative necessary for the bishop, and at the same time safeguards the interests of the parish priest. It comprises three stages: the bishop who thinks that a parish priest is no longer working faithfully among his flock, is bound to select as counsellors two of the synodal or pro-synodal examiners, in order of their nomination, and explain the situation to them. If the majority decides to remove the parish priest, the bishop must first officially request him to resign within ten days under threat of pronouncing a decree of removal. The priest may reply to the reasons alleged against him, and his answer is examined by this council; if the reply is deemed unsatisfactory, the bishop issues the decree and notifies the priest. Properly speaking the latter cannot appeal from the decree, but he may present his case to a new council, composed of the bishop and two parish priests as consultors, who examine whether the reasons given for the removal have been proved and whether the formalities demanded by the decree have been observed; a majority vote decides (see Council of Trent, Sess. XXI, c. vi, de ref.).

(3) The same zeal for the welfare of souls inspires special legislation for the erection and division of parishes. The erection of a parish takes place by creation when the district and the faithful assigned to the new parish did not belong previously to any priest. This case is extremely rare, as usually the territory of each diocese is divided into parishes more or less extensive. A parish is created when a centre of religious activity becomes canonically recognized as a parish, as when a vicariate Apostolic is erected into a diocese. The erection of parishes usually takes place by dismemberment or division. While in theory the division of benefices is looked on unfavorably by the law (c. 8 de Præbendis), it is authorized and even necessitated by the welfare of the faithful in the case of parishes. The Council of Trent (Sess. XXI, c. iv, de ref.), referring expressly to the Decree "Ad audientiam" of Alexander III (lib. III, tit. 48, c. 3), desires bishops, if necessary as delegates of the Apostolic See, to establish new parishes, in spite of the parish priest's opposition, wherever distance or difficulty of communication does not allow the faithful to frequent the church. In cities an excessive increase of population necessitates the multiplication of parishes. The Council in such a case desires bishops to oblige the parish priests to have sufficient number of assistants; but if the population is too great for the parish priest "to know his sheep" (Sess. XXI, c. i), the erection of a new parish is obligatory and the Congregation of the Council has several times recognized this as a legitimate reason. The legal formalities for the erection of a new parish further require the request either of the parish priest whose parish is to be divided, or of other interested persons, if there be any such; the consent of the chapter, unless custom has ruled otherwise; finally the guarantee of a sufficient income for the new parish, either by a partition of the property of the dismembered parish or parishes, or at least by the contributions of the inhabitants of the new one. The erection is effected by an episcopal decree. As a rule a special kinship exists between the old and the new parishes; the old being called the "mother" and the new the "filial" parish, the latter being bound to make certain offerings to the former, generally honorary, e. g., the annual gift of a candle. Special "foundations" of the old parish, created for the benefit, not of the clergy, but of the faithful (alms for the poor) are divided pro rata. Finally, the same procedure is observed for the extinction or suppression of a parish, by its union with another, when the number of the faithful has decreased so as no longer to warrant the presence of a parish priest.

III. *History*.—The first Christian communities were founded in cities and the entire Divine service was carried on by the bishop and his clergy; the few faithful outside the cities went to the city or were visited from time to time by clerics from the presbyteries. In the fourth century we find in the villages groups sufficiently large to be served by a resident clergy. Canon 77 of Elvira (about A. D. 300) speaks of a deacon in charge of the people (*diaconus regens plebem*). In the East at a very early period the churches of the cities and of the country districts were organized; the Council of Neocæsarea, about 320 (can. 13), speaks of country priests and bishops of villages, the "chorepiscopi", who had a subordinate clergy. Such churches and their clergy were originally under the direct administration of the bishop; but soon they had their own resources and a distinct administration (Council of Chalcedon, 451, can. 4, 6, 17). The same change took place in the West, but more slowly. In proportion as the country districts were evangelized (fourth to sixth centuries), churches were erected, at first in the *vici* (hamlets or villages), afterwards on church lands or on the property of private individuals, and at least one priest was appointed to each church. The clergy and property depended at first directly on the bishop and the cathedral; the churches did not yet correspond to very definite territorial circumscriptions: the centre was better marked than the boundaries. Such was the church which the councils of the sixth and seventh century call *ecclesia rusticana, parochitana*, often *diœcesis*, and finally *parochia*. By that time most of these churches had become independent: the priest administered the property assigned to him by the bishop, and also the property given directly to the church by the pious faithful; from that moment the priest became a beneficiary and had his title. More plentiful resources required and permitted a more numerous clergy. The devotion of the faithful, especially towards relics, led to the erection of numerous secondary chapels, *oratoria, basilicæ, martyria*, which also had their clergy. But these *tituli minores* were not parishes; they depended on the principal church of the *vicus*, and on the archpriest so often mentioned in the councils of the sixth and seventh centuries, who had authority over his own clergy and those of the oratories.

These secondary churches emphasize the parochial character of the baptismal churches, as the faithful had to receive the sacraments and pay their tithes in the latter. The monasteries in turn ministered to the people grouped around them. From the eighth century parochial centres multiplied on the lands of the churches and the monasteries, and the *villæ* or great estates of the kings and nobles. Then the *villæ* were subdivided and the parish served a certain number of *villæ* or rural districts, and thus the parish church became the centre of the religious and even the civil life of the villages. This condition, established in the eleventh and twelfth centuries, has scarcely varied since, as far as concerns the parochial service. As benefices, however, parishes have undergone many vicissitudes, owing to their union with monasteries or chapters, and on account of the inextricable complications of the feudal order. Parish churches had ordinarily attached to them schools and charitable works, especially for the poor enrolled on the *matricula*, or list of those attached to the Church. In the episcopal and other cities the division into parishes took place much more slowly, the cathedral or the archipresbyteral church being for a long time the only parochial church. However numerous the city churches, all depended on it and, properly speaking, had no flock of their own. At Rome, as early as the fourth century, there was a quasi-parochial service in the "titles" and cemeterial churches (Innocent I to Decentius, c. 5, an. 416). It is only towards the close of the eleventh century that separate urban parishes began; even then there were limitations, e. g. baptism was to be conferred in the cathedral; the territories, moreover, were badly defined. The chapters turned over to the clergy of the churches the parochial ministry, while the corporations (guilds) insisted especially on the granting of parochial rights to the churches which they founded and supported.

All manuals of canon law have a chapter on the parish and the parish priest; the commentators of the Decretals treat the subject in Book III, tit. v, *De præbendis*, and tit. xxix, *De parochis et alienis parochianis;* BOUIX, *De parocho* (Paris, 1867); FERRARIS, *Prompta bibliotheca*, s. v. *Parochia;* SÄGMÜLLER, *Lehrbuch des kath. Kirchenrechts* (Freiburg, 1909), §§ 58, 100; THOMASSIN, P. I. I, ii, c. 21 sq.; IMBART DE LA TOUR, *Les paroisses rurales du IVe au VIe siècle* (Paris, 1900); LESÊTRE, *La Paroisse* (Paris, 1908); TAUNTON, *Law of the Church* (London, 1906), s. v.

A. BOUDINHON.

IN ENGLISH-SPEAKING COUNTRIES.—In the United States and English-speaking lands generally (with the exception of Ireland, Canada, and possibly California), it has not been found advisable as yet to erect canonical parishes. The districts confided to priests having the cure of souls are technically designated as missions or quasi-parishes, though in common parlance the word *parish* is employed. The establishment of canonical parishes in these countries was not found possible, owing either to the devastation wrought in the so-called Reformation period or to the fact that, as new lands were slowly evangelized and settled, circumstances did not allow the establishment of the Church's parochial system as prescribed in her canon law.

A. *The Missions or Quasi-Parishes*. — Certain churches are designated by the bishop which are to be regarded as parish churches (*ad instar parœciarum*). Over these churches are placed priests provided with the necessary faculties. They are designated missionary rectors, or quasi-parish priests, though familiarly referred to as pastors or parish priests. A certain district around each church is then more or less definitely marked out by the bishop, within the limits of which the pastor is to exercise jurisdiction over the faithful and have care of ecclesiastical buildings. Within the limits of such missions or quasi-parishes, the bishop may institute new ecclesiastical divisions when such action becomes advisable. If the parish be held by members of a religious order, the bishop is not thereby constrained to entrust the newly-formed district to regulars. The institution of new quasi-parishes in English-speaking countries proceeds generally along the same lines as those prescribed by Church law for the erection of canonical parishes. Consequently, the bishop can erect a new parish by way of creation, union, or division. If the territory in question has not yet been assigned to any parish church, the institution is said to be by way of creation. There cannot be the slightest doubt that the bishop can proceed to such action in virtue of his powers as ordinary of the diocese. In creating such new parish, he is bound to provide as far as possible for the proper support of the new incumbent. In English-speaking countries there is no necessity of recurring to the civil power for the creation of a new parish. When the bishop establishes new quasi-parishes by way of division, he is not required to observe all the formalities prescribed by law for the dismemberment of canonical parishes. He must, nevertheless, act on the advice of his consultors, and after hearing the opinion of the pastor whose territory is to be divided. It is obvious that a division which would cripple or impoverish the church would not be in the best interests of religion, yet the bishop can proceed to such dismembering even against the will and advice of the pastor. In that case, however, an appeal against the decree of the ordinary can be lodged with the metropolitan or the Holy See. It is to be noted that, while very specific reasons are laid down in canon law according to which a bishop may divide parishes, yet our bishops are not limited to such reasons. Leo XIII lays down explicitly in his Constitution "Romanos Pontifices" that our missions may be divided by the ordinaries for a greater number of reasons and for less important ones than those specified in the common law of the Church.

When a parish committed to regulars is to be divided, the bishop must hear the opinion of the religious superior before taking action. A right of appeal against the dismemberment of the mission is allowed both to seculars and regulars. In case of the former, generally, the appeal is to be made to the metropolitan, as the bishop acts in virtue of his ordinary jurisdiction; in case of the latter, the appeal is to be laid before the Holy See as the bishop is generally using his powers of papal delegation. No appeal, however, can effect a suspension of the bishop's mandate but only subject it to reconsideration by the higher tribunal. It is possible, however, for the ordinary to act as delegate of the Holy See for seculars as well as for regulars, exempt and non-exempt. In that case the appeal must always be made to Rome. Parishes are sometimes formed by way of union, that is, when several parishes are joined together so as to form, either strictly or loosely, one new parish. The united parishes are simply governed by one pastor without any further change in their status (*unio æque principalis*); we have frequently a similar arrangement in English-speaking countries, where two or more churches or missions are served by one priest, though otherwise independent of each other. With us, however, such union is preparatory to a division as soon as the revenues of the churches or the number of priests allows of it. As to union by subjection, the usual form this takes among us is when small mission stations are made (for the most part temporarily) dependent on some parish church. The power possessed by the bishop of disuniting parishes formerly joined together is frequently exercised in these countries in the above mentioned cases. As a right of patronage does not exist in the United States, the making of new parishes is never complicated by the necessity of consulting an ecclesiastical patron. The counsel, which the bishop must take to ensure validity in the formation of new parishes, must be with his diocesan consultors, where such a body is established, or with the cathedral chapter, when the diocese possesses such a body, as in the British Isles. The regulations of ecclesiastical law by which a new parish or church must pay a certain tribute as a sign of dependence and respect to the church from which it was separated (the relation of the *filia* to the *ecclesia matrix*, or mother-church) is generally unknown in missionary countries.

B. *Pastors or Rectors of Churches.*—The rectors of missions are not canonical parish priests, though they have been invested with nearly all the privileges of canonical incumbents by particular synods or decrees of Roman congregations. These rectors are of two kinds, removable and irremovable. The common law of the Church requires that every parish should have an irremovable rector, but in countries where the Church is not canonically established, this is not always feasible, and therefore the Holy See permits the appointment of pastors who are removable at the will of the ordinary (*ad nutum episcopi*). Priests belonging to religious orders, who are in charge of parishes, may be removed either by their superior or by the bishop, without either being constrained to give the reason for his action to the other. On the removal of a regular, his religious superior nominates his successor. It is the expressed desire of the Holy See, that all rectors of parishes should, as far as possible, be endowed with the quality of perpetuity in their pastoral charge and, where this is impossible, that at least a certain number of the rectors of parishes be declared irremovable. The proportion of one out of every ten was determined on as the minimum number in American dioceses. When a certain rectorship has once been declared irremovable, it is not in the power of the ordinary to reduce it to the status of a removable rectorship. This is plain from the Third Council of Baltimore (No. 34), as well as from the general law of the Church, which forbids ecclesiastical superiors to lower the status or condition of churches. When a parish is declared an irremovable rectorship, the appointment of the first rector lies with the bishop after hearing the diocesan consultors. For instituting all other irremovable rectors, it is necessary that a written examination or concursus be held, at which the same questions must be proposed to all the candidates. From among those whom the examiners shall deem worthy after a consideration of their answers and testimonials, the bishop selects one on whom he confers the parish. This rule as to a concursus does not hold, however, in all English-speaking countries. An appeal to a higher tribunal is not stopped by a concursus, for a dissatisfied candidate may lay his complaint before the metropolitan, either on account of the improper judgment of the examiners or of the unreasonable selection made by the ordinary.

No examination is required for the appointment of pastors to removable rectorships. When a rector has once acquired the privilege of permanency, he cannot be removed against his will except for causes laid down by ecclesiastical decrees or in such cases as fall under the new Constitution of Pius X, "Maxima Cura" (20 Aug., 1910). Removable rectors, though they are appointed at the will of the bishop, cannot be removed except for grave cause, if such removal would affect their character or their emoluments, and in case of grievance they may have recourse to the Holy See. The First Synod of Westminster (D. 25) warns priests that the appointment to permanent rectorships rests with the bishop, and that no right of preferment is acquired by serving as assistant priest on a mission or even administering it temporarily. On appointment to a parish, an irremovable rector must make a profession of faith. Whether the same obligation rests on removable rectors is disputed by canonists. The profession of faith is explicitly demanded of all rectors by the First Council of Westminster, but there has been no such pronouncement for the United States. The Decree of Pius X "Sacrorum Antistitum" (1 Sept., 1910) is, of course, binding everywhere. All priests having cure of souls are bound to reside in their parishes, and the statutes of some dioceses require the bishop's consent for one week's absence. As our rectors are not canonical parish priests, they are not bound to offer up the Mass gratuitously for their people on Sundays and holy days of obligation. In Ireland and Canada, however, this obligation rests on parish priests, though dispensations are commonly given from offering this Mass on suppressed holy days.

The duty of instructing the young in catechism is insisted on by the synods of Baltimore, and, especially in places where there are no parochial schools, this instruction is to be carried on by means of Sunday schools. Pastors are obliged to establish parochial schools where possible, and they are exhorted to visit them frequently and see to their efficient management. They are also obliged to preach to their people and give them facility for approaching the sacraments. The Westminster Synod exhorts pastors to provide missions and spiritual retreats for their flocks. As our rectors are quasi-parish priests, they have jurisdiction similar to that of canonical parish priests conferred on them by various councils. As regards the sacraments, baptism should be conferred only in the parish to which the person belongs, and the contrary practice is strictly prohibited (II Balt., No. 227); penance cannot be administered, even to his parishioners, outside the diocese to which the rector belongs, though this would be a prerogative of a canonical parish priest; the Paschal Communion may be made in any public chapel or church, unless there be special legislation against it; Mass may be celebrated twice a day, with episcopal permission, when otherwise a considerable number of persons would be deprived of Mass on Sundays and holy days; matrimony is to be administered by one's own pastor for liceity; and when the contracting parties are of different parishes, it is usual for the bishop to designate the parish of the bride as the proper place for the ceremony. These requirements, however, do not affect the validity of the sacrament. As regards funeral rights of pastors, there is no special legislation for the United States, but the common law of the Church is usually followed. The administration of the Viaticum and extreme unction are rights reserved to the pastor, and these rights may not be infringed without penalty. Rectors of parishes are required to keep registers of baptisms, marriages, confirmations, and interments. They are also exhorted to keep a *liber status animarum* as far as circumstances permit it. In some dioceses, the acceptance of a perpetual foundation for a daily or anniversary Mass is subject to the approval of the ordinary, who is to decide on the adequacy of the endowment.

C. *Rectors and the Parochial Temporalities.*—Pastors are the administrators of the parochial property, but their rights in this regard are subordinated to the episcopal authority, for the ordinary is the supreme administrator and guardian of the ecclesiastical temporalities of his diocese. A financial statement of the condition of the parochial property must consequently be made by the rector to the bishop whenever he requires it. Generally, an annual statement is to be made. Whatever regulations are laid down by the ordinary for the better administration of the temporalities are binding on the pastors. When lay trustees are appointed to assist in the management of the parochial property, the rectors must obtain the episcopal consent for such appointment. In the United States, no outlay exceeding three hundred dollars may be made by the trustees without the bishop's written authorization, if such outlay is for special objects other than the ordinary expenditures. The pastors must see that lay trustees clearly understand that they are in no sense owners of ecclesiastical property and that appropriation of it for their own use entails excommunication. Alienation of all ecclesiastical property, movable and immovable, is unlawful without the permission of the Apostolic See, when such property is of considerable value. In cases involving a sum of not more than five thousand dollars only the bishop's consent is necessary, provided he has the special faculties usually granted to American bishops to that effect. The penalty for unlawful alienation is excommunication *ipso facto*. The pastor should make a careful inventory of all the parochial property, and file one copy in the parish archives and send another to the bishop. In cases where the civil law would vest the title to church property in lay trustees, it may be necessary that the bishop should hold the temporalities in his own name in fee simple. It is very undesirable that the same should be done by the pastors. As the rectors are the immediate custodians of the parochial property, it is their duty to keep it in proper repair. The Westminster Synods lay down clear and detailed rules in regard to the duty of rectors concerning church property.—" Whoever is set over the administration of a mission . . . should keep a day-book of all the receipts and expenses of the mission, both of which should be entered most accurately every day in their proper order. He should also keep a ledger to which he will transfer, every month or three months, all the entries in the other book arranged in order, according to the heads under which each sum received or expended ought to be placed." "Every administrator should keep an open account in some bank in his own name and in the names of two honest persons. Let these know that they are taken only to prevent the money from any peril of loss and that they must not interfere in the administration. If one fail from any cause the two who remain shall take care to have another elected by the bishop to supply the place. The administrator should never keep for longer than ten days on hand more than 20*l*. of money belonging to the mission . . . but he should diligently place it in the bank." "All buildings belonging to a mission should be insured against fire by an annual payment to some society for this purpose." "As soon as any priest enters on his mission let him receive an inventory of all things belonging to the mission from the vicar foran or from some one deputed by the bishop. He is bound to keep the furniture and buildings in good repair, yea, rather to improve them, that he may deliver to his successors as much, at least, as he received himself." "In every mission, the money contributed by the faithful (for seat rents, offertories, house to house collections and special collections) . . . is to be accounted church property and not as gifts given to the priest."—By the Constitution "Romanos Pontifices", regulars administering missions must render an account to the bishop of all money given to them with a view to the mission.

SMITH, *Elements of Ecclesiastical Law*, I (New York, 1895); TAUNTON, *The Law of the Church* (London, 1906), s. vv. *Missions; Rectors; Col. Conc. Lacensis* gives the synods of English-speaking countries.

WILLIAM H. W. FANNING.

Parish Priest. See PASTOR.

Parium, titular see, suffragan of Cyzicus in the Hellespontus. The Acts of the martyr St. Onesiphorus prove that there was a Christian community there before 180. Other saints worthy of mention are: Menignus, martyred under Decius and venerated on 22 November; Theogenes, bishop and martyr, whose feast is observed on 3 January; Basil, bishop and martyr in the ninth century, venerated on 12 April. Le Quien (Oriens christ., I, 787–90) mentions 14 bishops, the last of whom lived in the middle of the fourteenth century. An anonymous Latin bishop is mentioned in 1209 by Innocent III (Le Quien, op. cit., III, 945) and a titular bishop in 1410 by Eubel (Hier. Cathol. med. ævi, I, 410). At first a suffragan of Cyzicus, Parium was an autocephalous archdiocese as early as 640 (Gelzer, "Ungedruckte . . . Texte", 535) and remained so till the end of the thirteenth century. Then the Emperor Andronicus II made it a metropolis under the title of Πήγων καὶ Παρίου. In 1354 Pegæ and Parium were suppressed, the metropolitan receiving in exchange the See of Sozopolis in Thrace (Miklosich and Müller, "Acta patriarchatus Constantinopolitani", I, 109, 111, 132, 300, 330). This was the end of this episcopal see. The ruins of Parium are at the Greek village of Kamares (the vaults), on the small cape Tersana-Bournou in the caza and sandjak of Bigha.

TEXIER, *Asie Mineure* (Paris, 1862), 174; WÄCHTER, *Der Verfall des Griechentums in Kleinasien im XIV Jahrhundert* (Leipzig, 1903), 49.

S. VAILHÉ.

Park, ABBEY OF THE, half a mile south of Louvain, Belgium, founded in 1129 by Duke Godfrey, surnamed "Barbatus", who possessed an immense park near Louvain and had invited the Norbertines to take possession of a small church he had built there. Walter, Abbot of St. Martin's, Laon, brought a colony of his canons and acted as their superior for nearly three years. The canons, now in sufficient number, elected Simon, a canon of Laon, as their abbot. The canons performed the general work of the ministry in the district of Louvain, bringing back those seduced by the errors of Tanchelin (see PREMONSTRATENSIAN CANONS). In 1137 the abbot was able to found the Abbey of Our Lady and SS. Cornelius and

Cyprian at Ninove. Godfrey made the Abbot of the Park and his successors his arch-chaplains. Simon (d. 30 March, 1142) was succeeded by Philip whose learning and holiness may be judged from his correspondence with St. Hildegard (q. v.) in the archives of the Park Abbey. Philip and his successors enlarged the buildings and prepared the land for agriculture. At the time there was living at the abbey a canon, Blessed Rabado, whose devotion to the Passion was attested by miracles. Abbot Gerard van Goetsenhoven (1414–34) had much to do with the erection of the University of Louvain (q. v.), and was also delegated by Duke John to transact state affairs with the King of England and the Duke of Burgundy. Abbot van Tulden (1462–94) was successful in his action against commendatory abbots being imposed on religious houses in Belgium. Abbot van den Berghe (1543–58) managed the contributions levied in support of the Belgian theologians present at the resumed Council of Trent.

The abbey frequently suffered during the wars waged by William of Orange and the Calvinists, but was fortunate to have then at its head men of marked learning, zeal, and discretion, such as Loots (1577–1583), van Vlierden (1583–1601), Druys (1601–1634) (q. v.), Maes (1635–1647), De Pape (1648–1682), van Tuycum (1682–1702). They all favoured higher education at the University of Louvain, and studies were in a flourishing state in the abbey. Under Joseph II, Emperor of Germany, the abbey was confiscated, because Abbot Wauters (d. 23 Nov., 1792) refused to send his religious to the general seminary erected by the emperor at Louvain. A revolution against the emperor's injustices being successful, the religious returned to their abbey. Wauters was succeeded by Melchior Nysmans (1793–1810). Under the French Republic the abbey was confiscated again on 1 Feb., 1797. At the request of the people the church was declared to be a parish church and was thus saved. The abbey was bought by a friendly layman who wished to preserve it for the religious, in better times. One of the canons, in the capacity of parish priest, remained in or near the abbey. When Belgium was made a kingdom and religious freedom restored, the surviving religious resumed the community life and elected Peter Ottoy, then rural dean of Diest, as their superior.

In 1897 the abbey undertook the foundation of a priory in Brazil. It counts at present (Jan., 1911) 48 religious; 8 of these are doing missionary work in Brazil. The canons of the Park Abbey publish the following reviews: (1) "Analectes de l'Ordre de Prémontré" (four times a year); (2) "Revue de l'Ordre de Prémontré et de ses missions" (six times a year); "'T Park's maandschrift" (monthly).

Annales Præm., s.v. Parchum; LIBERT DE PAPE, Summaria chronologia Parchensis (Louvain, 1662); RAYMAEKERS in Recherches historiques sur l'ancienne abbaye de Parc (Louvain, 1858); Revue de l'Ordre de Prémontré and 'T Park's maandschrift (passim), both published at the abbey.

F. M. GEUDENS.

Parkinson, ANTHONY, historian, b. in England, 1667; d. there 30 January, 1728. In 1692 he was appointed professor of philosophy at the Franciscan Convent of Douai; the following year he was approved for preaching and hearing confessions. He came to the missions in England in 1695 and was president of the Franciscans at Warwick 1698–1701, of Birmingham 1701–10, Definitor of the province 1707–10. Parkinson was also nominal guardian of Worcester 1704–7, of Oxford 1710–13, and twice governed the hidden English Province as provincial 1713–6, and 1722–5. As such he assisted at the General Chapter of the Order in Rome, May, 1723. His chief work is the "Collectanea Anglo-Minoritica, or a Collection of the Antiquities of the English Franciscans, or Friars Minors, commonly called Gray Friars", two parts, with an appendix concerning the English Nuns of the Order of St. Clare, London, 1726, in 4°. There are also extant some unedited manuscripts.

THADDEUS, The Franciscans in England 1600–1850 (London, 1898), 113, 282; COOPER in Dict. Nat. Biog., ed. LEE, XLIII (London, 1895), 312.

LIVARIUS OLIGER.

Parlais, a titular see of Pisidia, suffragan of Antioch. As a Roman colony it was called Julia Augusta Parlais, and money was coined under this title (Eckhel, "Historica veterum nummorum", III, 33). Ptolemy (V, 6, 16) calls it Paralais and places it in Lycaonia. Kiepert identifies it with Barla, in the vilayet of Koniah, but Ramsay (Asia Minor, 390 sqq.) believes that it is contained in the ruins known as Uzumla Monastir. The "Notitiæ Episcopatuum" mention the see as late as the thirteenth century under the name Parlaos, Paralaos, and even Parallos. Four bishops are known: Patricius, at the Council of Constantinople, 381; Libanius, at Chalcedon, 451 (in the decrees the see is placed in Lycaonia); George, at Constantinople, 692; Anthimus, at Constantinople, 879. Academius who assisted at the Council of Nicæa, 325, was Bishop of Pappa, not of Parlais as Le Quien claims (Oriens christianus, I, 1057).

S. PÉTRIDÈS.

Parlatore, FILIPPO, Italian botanist, b. at Palermo, 8 Aug., 1816; d. at Florence, 9 Sept., 1877, a devout and faithful Catholic. He studied medicine at Palermo, but practised only for a short time, his chief activity being during the cholera epidemic of 1837. Although at that time he had been an assistant professor of anatomy, a subject on which he had already written (Treatise on the human retina), he soon gave up all other interests to devote his entire attention to botany. He first made a study of the flora of Sicily, publishing in 1838 "Flora panormitana" (Palermo); he also dealt with the Sicilian flora in later works. In 1840 he left home to begin his extended botanical expeditions. He travelled all through Italy, then into Switzerland (where he remained for a time at Geneva with Decandolle), to France (where he was at Paris with Webb, the Englishman) and to England, his longest stay being at Kew. His part in the Third Congress of Italian naturalists held at Florence in 1841 was of significance for him and for the development of botanical studies in Italy. At this congress, in his celebrated memoir "Sulla botanica in Italia", he proposed, among other things, that a general herbarium be established at Florence. This proposal was adopted. Grand Duke Leopold sought his assistance for this herbarium, gave him the post of professor of botany at the museum of natural sciences (a chair which had been vacant for almost thirty years), and made him director of the botanical garden connected with the museum. For more than three decades Parlatore was most active in fulfilling the duties of these positions, one of his principal services being the contribution of "Collections botaniques du musée royale de physique et d'histoire naturelle" (Florence, 1874) to the great collection entitled "Erbario centrale italiano". His own private herbarium is now a part of the central herbarium, containing about 1900–2500 fascicules. In 1849 he made an investigation of the flora of the Mont-Blanc chain of the Alps; in 1851 he explored those of Northern Europe, Lapland, and Finland; the reports of these two expeditions appeared respectively in 1850 and 1854.

He published numerous treatises on botanical subjects,—discussing questions of system, organography, physiology, plant geography, and palæontology—in various periodicals, chiefly in the "Giornale botanico Italiano" (1844—), which he had founded. He also gave considerable attention to the history of botany in Italy. His lifework in botany, however, is "Flora

CATHEDRAL AND BAPTISTERY, PARMA (XII AND XIII CENTURY)

Italiana", of which five volumes appeared between 1848 and 1874; the next five were issued by T. Caruel (to 1894) with the assistance of Parlatore's MS. This work stands in high repute among all botanists. Mention should also be made of "Lezioni di botanica comparata" (Florence, 1843) and "Monographia delle fumarie" (Florence, 1844). To the sixteenth volume of Decandolle's "Prodromus", Parlatore contributed the accounts of the coniferi and gnetaceæ; to Webb's "Histoire naturelle des îles Canaries" (Paris, 1836–50), the accounts of the umbelligeri and graminæ. In 1842 Boissier, the botanist, named a genus of cruciferi "Parlatoria".

SACARDO, *La botanica in Italia*, I, II (Venice, 1895, 1901); HAYNALDO in *Literar. Berichte aus Ungarn*, III (Budapest, 1879).

JOSEPH ROMPEL.

Parma, DIOCESE OF, Central Italy. The city is situated on the river of the same name, an affluent of the Po, flowing through a fertile plain, where grain and vines are cultivated; it also contains many fine pastures; the silk culture is highly developed, as also the cheese, tobacco, and leather industries.

The cathedral was begun in 1060, to replace the ancient one destroyed by fire two years earlier; finished in 1074, it was dedicated in 1106 by Paschal II. It is a fine example of the Lombard style, in the shape of a Latin cross, with three naves; three tiers of galleries, supported by small columns, give a bright aspect to the façade; the cupola, of the sixteenth century, is adorned with frescoes by Correggio, Parmigianino (Girolamo Mazzuola), and other masters; the inlaid work and the carvings of the choir and of the sacristy are by Lendinara and the Consorzialis; there are four statues by Giacomo and Damiano da Gonzate; the ciborium of the high altar, with its beautiful sculptures, is of the fifteenth century; in the crypt is the tomb of the Bishop St. Bernardo, with sculptures by Prospero Clementi. The baptistery is separate, in the shape of an irregular octagon, and was begun in 1196 by the architect and sculptor Benedetto Antelami.

Other churches of note are: San Giovanni Evangelista, formerly of the Benedictines, founded in 981, restored in 1510, façade by Simone Moschino (1604), contains the best paintings of Correggio and Mazzuola; the Steccata (1521), by Zaccagni, on the plan of a Greek cross, with a majestic cupola, containing pictures by Parmigianino and other masters; the Annunziata, in which there are frescoes by Correggio; Santa Maria del Quartiere, the cupola of which was painted by Barnabei; S. Rocco; S. Antonio; S. Sepolcro contains works by Baglioni, Cignaroli, and Mazzola; and the Oratorio di S. Lodovico, formerly the ducal chapel. Among the palaces are: del Giardino (1564), with frescoes by Carracci; della Pilotta (1597), with a museum of antiquities, and a gallery of paintings especially rich in works by Correggio; and the Biblioteca Palatina, containing 303,836 volumes, 4770 manuscripts and 60,000 copper engravings. There are monuments in honour of Correggio and Parmigianino. The university, which dates from 1025, was instituted with pontifical privileges only in 1392, and was developed, more especially, by Duke Ferdinando di Borbone; there are several intermediary schools, besides the episcopal seminary, a seminary for foreign missions, an Accademia of the fine arts, and State archives.

Parma was a city of the Boian Gauls, to which a Roman colony was sent in 183 B. C. In 377, the town suffered so greatly from the barbarians that St. Ambrose numbers it among the ruined cities. The Lombards took the city in 569 or 570, but their chief in 590 placed himself under the exarch Callinicus, who in 601 took possession of Parma, and imprisoned the Duke Godiscalc; the city however soon returned to the Lombards (603). According to the "Vita Hadriani", Parma was comprised in the donation of Pepin to the Holy See; but in reality, it appears to have belonged to the kings of Italy, who, in the tenth century, gave over the government to its bishops, in whose hands it remained until St. Bernardo resigned it in 1106; from which time the city governed itself as a free commune, first under a consul, and then under a podestà. In 1167 it was obliged to join the Lombard League. In the thirteenth century (1199, 1200, 1204), Parma was at war with its neighbour Piacenza; later it aroused the indignation of Innocent III by the robbery of a pontifical legate. In 1218 a peace was established. In the struggle between the popes and Frederick II, Parma was at first on the side of the emperor; but in 1247, the Guelphs obtained possession of the town, which Frederick attempted in vain to take. Uberto Pallavicino, a native of Parma and a Ghibelline, stood out against Ezzelino, and succeeded in becoming podestà of Parma. In the fourteenth century (1303–16) Gilberto da Correggio became lord; after him, Gianquirico Sanvitale and the brothers de' Rossi contended for the lordship; then came John of Bohemia (1331), Mastino della Scala (1335–41), the sons of da Correggio, Obizzo d'Este.

Finally, through purchase, Parma was annexed to the Duchy of Milan, and so remained, except for a time when it was governed by the de' Rossi and by the Terzi (1404–20), until 1499, when Louis XII of France took possession. In 1512 Julius II united Parma to the Pontifical States; it should be said that John of Bohemia had previously held it as a fief of the Holy See; but from 1515 to 1521, the city was again in the hands of the King of France. In 1545, Paul III erected Parma and Piacenza into a duchy, in favour of his son Pierluigi Farnese; then began for Parma an era of splendour, during which Correggio (Allegri), Mazzola, and other famous masters showered treasures of art upon it. Pierluigi, loved by the people and hated by the nobles, fell at Piacenza, 10 Sept., 1547, the victim of a conspiracy directed by Ferrante Gonzaga, imperial Governor of Milan. The garrison of Parma prevented the city from falling into the power of Ferrante, as Piacenza fell; and after long negotiations with the emperor, the son of Pierluigi, Ottavio, was confirmed in the duchy by Julius III in 1550. That prince governed wisely, and a conspiracy against him by Count Landi was happily frustrated.

He was succeeded in 1585 by Alessandro Farnese, who became famous in the wars of Flanders and of France, and who died of a wound at Arras, in 1592. Ranuccio enlarged the state and protected study, founding a college of nobles; his son Odoardo, in 1622, succeeded to the duchy, which was governed during his minority by his mother Margherita and his uncle Cardinal Odoardo, as regents. During this reign there arose the contention with the Barberini for possession of the Duchy of Castro, an ancient fief of the Farnese, and that strife ended in the destruction of Castro, in 1649 under the son of Ranuccio II (1646–94). Duke Francesco, having died without children, was succeded by his brother Antonio (1727–31), who also died without issue; and the succession to the duchy complicated the War of the Spanish Succession. By the treaty of Seville, the duchy was given to Charles of Bourbon, son of Philip V of Spain and Isabella Farnese (daughter of Francesco); and when Charles ascended the throne of Naples, the Peace of Vienna gave Parma to Austria (1736; the battle of Parma, 1734); but the intrigues of Isabella did not cease until the Peace of Aix-la-Chapelle had given the Duchy of Parma and Piacenza, enlarged with that of Guastalla, to her other son Philip (1749). This prince inaugurated a French absolutism in the duchy, especially at the expense of the Church. In 1765 he fell from his horse, was trampled upon, and dogs tore him to pieces. Under Ferdinando (1765–1802) relations with the Holy See grew still more strained; in imitation of the

French court, he first concentrated, and then suppressed the religious houses, and was supported against Rome by the other Bourbon courts. In 1802 the duchy was annexed to the French republic, In 1814 it was given to Marie Louise, wife of Napoleon, against whom a revolution broke out in 1831, but was quickly suppressed by Austrian troops. Marie Louise was succeeded by Carlo Lodovico, Duke of Lucca, against whom a new revolution broke out in 1848, and the city was occupied by the Piedmontese. On the other hand, Carlo II abdicated in favour of his son Carlo III (1849). After the Piedmontese defeat at Novara, the Austrians placed Carlo III on the throne of Parma, but he was stabbed to death in 1854, and in 1859 his son Robert was dethroned, while the annexation of his state to Piedmont was decreed.

The first known Bishop of Parma is Urbanus, a partisan of the antipope Ursicinus, and deposed by Pope Damasus in 378. Other bishops were: Gratiosus (680); Lantpertus (827); Wihbodus (860–77), who bore important charges from Louis II and his successors; Aicardus in 920 restored the cathedral, which had been destroyed by fire; Sigefredus, a former chancellor of King Hugo, accompanied in 937 Hugo's daughter Berta, the promised bride of Constantine Porphyrogenitus; Hucbertus (961), to whom Ratherius di Verona dedicated his "De contemptu canonum"; Cadalous obtained his see through simony, and became the antipope Honorius II, while remaining Bishop of Parma; his successor, Everardo (1073), was a partisan of the anti-pope Clement III, in whose interest Everardo even resorted to arms, but was defeated by the Countess Matilda, near Sorbara (1084); he was succeeded by another schismatic, Wido (1085), in whose place was put (1091) St. Bernardo-degli Uberti, Abbot of Vallombrosa and a cardinal; St. Bernardo, however, in 1104, was dragged violently from the altar, and driven from his see, to which he was not able to return peacefully until 1106; he resigned the temporal power held by the bishops of this diocese and, having opposed the coronation of Conrad (1127) was again obliged to flee from Parma, and died in 1133; Aicardo, a partisan of Barbarossa, and therefore deposed (1167); Obizzo Fieschi, an uncle of Innocent IV; Gratian (1224), professor of law at Bologna; Alberto Sanvitale (1243), and his brother Obizzo (1259), nephews of Innocent IV; Obizzo exerted himself greatly for the reform of morals, favoured the "Milizia di Gesù Cristo", and exposed the sect of the Apostolici, founded by the Parmesan Gherardo Segarelli; Ugolino Rossi (1322) was obliged to flee from Parma, with his father Guglielmo, on account of the latter's political reverses (1334); Gian Antonio da S. Giorgio (1500) a learned cardinal; Alessandro Farnese (1509), became Pope Paul III, he resigned the See of Parma in favour of his nephew, Cardinal Alessandro; Alessandro Sforza (1560), who distinguished himself at the Council of Trent; Ferrante Farnese, (1573) active in the cause of ecclesiastical reform; Camillo Marazzani (1711), who governed the diocese during forty-eight years; Adeodato Turchi (1788), a Capuchin who wrote beautiful pastorals and homilies; Cardinal Francesco Caselli (1804), a former superior of the Servites and a companion of Consalvi during the negotiation of the Concordat with Napoleon; at the national council of Paris in 1811, he defended the rights of the Holy See.

The diocese, a suffragan of Milan, and later of Ravenna and of Bologna (1582), depends immediately on the Holy See since 1815; it has 306 parishes, 232,913 inhabitants, 9 religious houses of men, 18 of women, 3 educational establishments for male students, 5 for girls, 1 bi-weekly periodical (*Ol Giornale del popolo*) and 2 monthly magazines (*L'Eco; Lede e Civiltà*).

Cappelletti, *Le Chiese d'Italia*, XV; Allodi, *Serie cronologica dei vescovi di Parma* (2 vols., Parma, 1854–57); Affó, *Storia della città di Parma* (4 vols., Parma, 1792–95), continued by Pezzana (5 vols., 1837–59); Scarabelli, *Storia dei ducati di Parma, Piacenza, Guastala* (2 vols., Guastala, 1858); Benassi, *Storia di Parma* (4 vols., 1899); *Archivo storico per le provincie parmensi* (Parma, 1892—).

U. Benigni.

Parmenianus. See Donatists.

Parmentier, Andrew. See Bayer, Adèle.

Parmentier, Antoine-Augustin, agriculturist, b. at Montdidier, 17 August, 1737; d. in Paris, 13 Dec., 1813. Left an orphan at an early age, he was compelled before taking a college course to become a pharmacist, in which capacity he joined the army of Hanover in 1757. Taken prisoner several times in the course of this service, he profited by his captivity in Prussia to gain knowledge which he later put to valuable use. He resumed his studies, on his return to Paris in 1774, and was appointed pharmacist at the Hôtel-des-Invalides. At this time, he introduced the use of potatoes as food in France. He also promoted the improved cultivation of maize and chestnuts, and tried to reform the methods of baking. During the Revolution he had charge of the preparation of salted provisions, and manufactured a sea-biscuit. He wrote a number of books on horticultural and agricultural topics, which betray his lack of early education. André Parmentier (1780–1830), who attained distinction as a horticulturist in the United States, was a collateral relative.

Antoine-Augustin Parmentier

Silvestre, *Notice biog. sur Parmentier* (Paris, 1815); Mutel, *Vie de Parmentier* (Paris, 1819); Mouchon, *Notice hist. sur Parmentier* (Lyons, 1843).

Thomas F. Meehan.

Parmigiano, Il (The Parmesan), the current name of Francesco Mazzuola, Mazzola, Mazzuoli, or Mazzoli, Italian painter, b. at Parma, 1504; d. at Casal Maggiore, 1540. He was the son of Filippo Mazzuola, a painter, also known as Filippo dell' Erbette, who died in 1505. Francesco's uncles, Michele and Pierilario, brought him up. With a strong taste for painting, the boy developed a particular enthusiasm for Correggio, the founder of the Parmesan School. His "St. Bernard", painted for the Observantines of Parma, and other early works of his, show him to have been an eager follower of Correggio. At twenty, longing to study the masterpieces of Michelangelo, he set out for Rome, where his precocious talent soon won renown. According to Vasari, it was a saying at Rome, that "the soul of Raphael had passed into the Parmesan's body". Clement VII commissioned him to paint a "Circumcision". But the sack of Rome (1527) checked this bright beginning. Mazzuola fled to Bologna, where he painted many altar-pieces, notably, the "Virgin and Child", "St. John", "St. Margaret and St. Jerome" (now in the Louvre). For San Petronio he executed a "St. Roch". He was in Parma in 1531, since his contract with the Confraternity of the Steccata is dated 10 May of that year. He frescoed the arcade of the choir in that church, where his chiaroscuro, "Moses breaking the Tables of the Law", is one of the masterpieces of his school. Unfortunately, he never finished the Steccata commission. His passion for alchemy not only cost him time, money, and health, but prevented him from keeping his engagements. As he had been paid part in advance, the Steccata Confraternity, weary of waiting, had him prosecuted and condemned to prison in 1537. Released upon promise to finish the work, he again defaulted, and made his escape to Casal Maggiore, where he died. He was buried in the church of the Servites.

Brief as was his career, Il Parmigiano has left a very large number of works: at Bologna (Pinacotheca), "Virgin and Child with Saints", "St. Margaret", "Martha and Mary"; at Florence (Pitti), "La Madonna del Collo Longo", (Uffizi) portrait of himself, and "Holy Family"; at Genoa (Palazzo Rosso), "Marriage of St. Catharine"; at Modena (Museum), "Apollo and Marsyas"; at Naples (Museum), "Annunciation", "Holy Family", "St. Sebastian", "Lucretia", and some portraits; at Parma (Museum), "St. Catherine with Angels", "Madonna with Saints"; (Annunziata) "Baptism of Christ", "St. Bernardino", "Holy Family", "Entry of Christ into Jerusalem", besides the Steccata frescoes, several paintings in San Giovanni Evangelista, and a "History of Diana", in the Villa Sanvitale; at Rome (Barberini Palace), "Marriage of St. Catherine"; (Borghese Palace), portrait of Cesare Borgia (formerly attributed to Raphael and then to Bronzino) and St. Catherine; at Berlin (Museum), "Baptism of Christ"; at Dresden (Museum), "Virgin and Child", "Madonna of the Rose"; in London (National Gallery), "Vision of St. Jerome"; at Madrid (Prado), "Holy Family", "St. Barbara", "Cupid", and two portraits; in Paris (Louvre), two "Holy Families"; at St. Petersburg (Hermitage), "Burial of Christ"; at Vienna (Belvedere) "Cupid with Bow", "St. Catherine", his own portrait, and several others. He also left some engravings, among them seven Holy Families, a Resurrection, "Judith with the Head of Holophernes", and "Sts. Peter and John Healing the Lame Man".

Parmigiano developed the germ of decay latent in Correggio's work. He delighted his contemporaries with ingenious contrasts, elegant mannerisms, and sensual frivolity. His religious pictures are deficient in gravity and sincerity, being, in many cases—like the "Madonna del Collo Longo"— types of false distinction and pretentious affectation. "His St. Catherine (Borghese Palace) declines the compliments of the angels with an air of good breeding which is beyond description" (Burckhardt). These faults are less pronounced in such profane works as the frescoes of the Villa Sanvitale; and in portraiture, where he is inspired by no factitious ideal, they disappear altogether. "The very name of Parmigianino", says Ch. Blanc, "which the Italians like to write in the diminutive form, seems to say that this master has his amiable failings, and is a great master diminished" (grand maître diminué).

VASARI, Le vite de' piu eccellenti pittori, ed. MILANESI, V (Florence, 1880), 217–42; AFFÒ, Vita di Parmigianino (Parma, 1784); LANZI, tr. ROSCOE, History of Painting in Italy, II (London, 1847), 402; BLANC, Histoire des peintres de toutes les Ecoles: Ecole lombarde (Paris, 1865–77); BURCKHARDT AND BODE, Le Cicerone, French tr. GÉRARD, II (Paris, 1892), 718; MÜNTZ, Histoire de l'Art pendant la Renaissance, III (Paris, 1895), 581–82.

GASTON SORTAIS.

GIROLAMO FRANCESCO MARIA MAZZUOLA, CALLED "IL PARMIGIANO"
Portrait by himself, bevelled mirror in front of him

Parnassus, a titular see in Cappadocia Secunda, suffragan of Mocessus. Situated between Ancyra and Archelais, it was formerly important. Another route led to Nyssa. It is mentioned by Polybius (XXV, iv) and the Itineraries; in the sixth century by Hierocles, "Synecdemus" (700, 7). Hamilton places it at Kotch Hissar, near Touz Gheul (ancient Lake Tatta), vilayet of Angora; Ramsay (Asia Minor, 298), north-east of this lake on the left bank of Kizil Irmak (ancient Halys), near Tchikin Aghyl. The see first depended on Cæsarea; under Valens it passed to Cappadocia Secunda; and about 536 was made suffragan of Mocessus. The "Notitiæ Episcopatuum" mention it in the thirteenth century. Le Quien (Oriens christianus, I, 415) mentions nine bishops: Pancratius, at the Arian Council of Philippopolis, 344; Hypsius, replaced by the Arian Eedicius in the time of St. Basil; Olympius, at the Council of Constantinople, 381; Eustathius, at Ephesus, 341, deposed as a Nestorian, retracted, assisted at Constantinople (448) and Chalcedon (451); and signed in 458 the letter of the bishops of Cappadocia Secunda to the Emperor Leo; Pelagius, at Constantinople, 538; Eustathius, at the Council "in Trullo", 692; Stephanus, at Nicæa, 787; and Theognostus, at Constantinople, 869.

S. PÉTRIDÈS.

Parochial Mass.—The parish is established to provide the parishioners with the helps of religion, especially with Mass. The parochial Mass is celebrated for their welfare on all Sundays and holidays of obligation, even when suppressed. The parish priest is not obliged to say it personally; but if he does not, he must offer his own Mass for that intention. Parishioners now fulfil their duty by assisting at Mass in any church; but formerly they had at least to hear a Mass in the parish church (ch. "Vices", 2, "De treuga et pace" in "Extrav. Comm." of Sixtus IV in 1478). This obligation fell into desuetude owing to the privileges granted to the religious orders; the Council of Trent (Sess. XXII, "De observ. et evit. in celebr. miss." and Sess. XXIV, c. iv, de ref.), treats it only as a counsel; and notwithstanding certain provincial and diocesan regulations of the sixteenth and seventeenth centuries, the obligation ceased (Bened. XIV, "De syn.", XI, xiv). The Mass not being strictly conventual, it is not obligatory by common law for it to be sung, but it may be, and frequently this is prescribed by the statutes or custom. It is then preceded by the blessing and aspersion of water on Sundays. Even if not sung, it is celebrated with additional solemnity, with more than two candles on the altar, and two servers (S. Rit. C., 6 Feb., 1858, n. 3065). What is characteristic of it is the instruction, with its special prayers, the announcements made to the congregation, the publication of banns of marriage, and finally the familiar sermon or homily. (See MASS; also PASTOR.)

A. BOUDINHON.

Parochial Schools. See SCHOOLS.

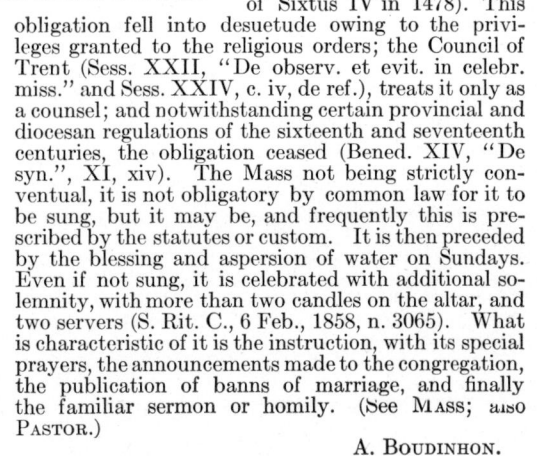

Parœcopolis, a titular see of Macedonia, suffragan of Thessalonica. It is mentioned by Ptolemy (III, 13, 30) as being in Sintice, a part of Macedonia, and by Phlegon "Fragm. histor. gr." ed. Didot, III, 609). Hierocles (Synecdemus, 639, 8) and Constantine Porphyrogenitus (De thematibus, 2) call it Parthicopolis, but the second locates it in Thrace. Stephanus Byzantius calls it Parthenopolis and relates according to Theagenes the legend of its foundation by Geræstus, son of Mygdon, said to have named the city in honour of his two daughters. Pliny (IV, xi) has the same name, but places it in Thrace. Its bishop, Jonas or John, assisted at the Council of Sardica (342 or 343); at the Council of Chalcedon (451) there was present John "Parthicopolis primæ Macedoniæ" (Le Quien, "Oriens christianus", II, 75). This see is not mentioned in any of the Greek "Notitiæ episcopatuum".

S. Pétridès.

Parousia. See Second Advent.

Parrenin, Dominique, b. at Russey, near Besançon, 1 Sept., 1665; d. at Pekin, 29 Sept., 1741. He entered the Jesuit order 1 September, 1685, and in 1697 was sent to China. At Peking (1698) he attracted the attention of K'ang-hi. His varied knowledge, and familiar use of the court languages, Chinese and Tatar-Manchu, gained him the good-will of the emperor. Father Parrenin utilized this favour in the interest of religion and science. While satisfying the extraordinary curiosity of K'ang-hi, especially about physics, medicine, and the history of Europe, he demonstrated how the scientific culture of the West was due to Christianity. Obliged to travel with the emperor, he visited the native Christians. Well liked by important personages at the court and the highest dignitaries of the empire, he led them to look with favour on the spreading of Christianity. In the "Lettres édifiantes," he has written of the admirable examples set by the princes of the Sounou family, whose conversion, begun by Father Suarez, he completed. He rendered the greatest services to religion during the reign of Yong-tching (1723–35), son of K'ang-hi. The new emperor soon made known his aversion for Christianity and only his consideration for the missionaries at Peking, principally for Father Parrenin, prevented the extermination of Christianity in China. This emperor respected the missionaries, not for their scientific knowledge, but for their characters and virtues. He demanded services of more tangible importance, notably at audiences granted to the ambassadors of Russia and Portugal and during the long negotiations, both commercial and political, with the former of the two powers. The Chinese ministers needed the missionaries, not only as conscientious and trusty interpreters, but men capable of dispelling Chinese ignorance of European matters and of inspiring confidence. Parrenin, who had served the Government of K'ang-hi so capably in this dual rôle, was no less serviceable under Yong-tching. He was assisted by his *confrères*, Fathers Mailla and Gaubil. The mission at Peking continued to exist amid most violent persecutions, and became the salvation of the Christians of the provinces: as long as Christianity sustained itself at the capital, its position in the rest of the empire was not hopeless; subaltern persecutors hesitated to apply the edicts in all their rigour against a religion which the emperor tolerated in his capital, and against men whose *confrères* the emperor treated with honour.

Science is indebted to Parrenin for his services in drawing up the great map of China (see Regis, Jean-Baptiste). He roused in K'ang-hi a desire to see his entire domain represented by methods more exact than those of the Chinese cartographers. Father Parrenin had a hand in the preparations for the making of this map in the Provinces of Pechili, Shan-tung, and Liao-tung. He also collaborated on a map of Peking and environs, which the emperor caused to be made in 1700. He translated into the Tatar-Manchu language for K'ang-hi several of the works published in the "Mémoires de l'Académie des Sciences" at Paris. In 1723 Dortous de Mairan, of the Académie des Sciences, and Fréret, perpetual secretary of the Académie des Inscriptions, sent him their "doubts" about the history, chronology, and astronomy of the Chinese. His answers led to other questions, and this scientific correspondence continued until 1740. Father Parrenin's conduct may not have been always above reproach during the agitation caused in the Chinese missions by the famous controversy about the rites (see China; The Question of Rites). But his whole life contradicts the odious character attributed to him by writers who edited with more passion than truth the "Mémoires historiques du Cardinal de Tournon" and the "Ancedotes sur l'Etat de la Religion dans la Chine".

Lettres édifiantes et curieuses. 26e Recueil, Préface et Lettre du P. Chalier (Paris, 1753); Lettre du P. Antoine Gaubil on the death of P. Parrenin, MS. 12225 in the Bibliothèque Nationale, with the letters of Parrenin to Mairan and Fréret (1729–60), unedited; Lettres de M. de Mairan au R. P. Parrenin, contenant diverses questions sur la Chine (Paris, 1759–70); Brucker, La Misssion de Chine de 1722 à 1735 in Revue des questions historiques, XXIX, 491 (1881); Idem, Correspondance scientifique d'un missionaire français à Peking, au XVIIIe Siècle in Revue du Monde catholique, LXXVI, 701 (1883); De Bacher-Sommervogel, Bibliothèque des écrivains de la C. de J., VI, 284–90, IX, 757; Cordier, Bibliotheca Sinica.

Joseph Brucker.

Parsis (Parsees) a small community in India, adherents of the Zoroastrian religion and originally emigrants from Persia. According to the census of 1881 their total number in India was 85,397, to which must be added for sake of completeness about 3,000 scattered about various other countries and also about 8,000 in various parts of Persia—thus bringing up the total of Zoroastrians in the world to something under 100,000. Of the 85,397 in India, 82,091 were by the same census found in the Bombay presidency, and 3,306 scattered over the rest of the country. Of those in the Bombay presidency more than half (48,507) resided in Bombay City, 6,227 in Surat, and 3,088 in Broach; about 10,000 being in Native States, and the rest in other parts, chiefly of Guzerat. The census of 1901 reveals a rise to a total of 94,190 in India, of whom 78,800 are in the Bombay presidency, not inclusive of 8,409 found in Baroda State. In Persia the Zoroastrians (called Iranis to distinguish them from those in India) are chiefly found in Yezd and the twenty-four surrounding villages, where according to figures collected in 1854, there were a thousand families, comprising 6,658 souls—a few merchants, the remainder artisans or agriculturalists. At Kerman there were also about 450; and at Teheran, the capital of Persia, about fifty of the merchant class. They were formerly much more numerous; they now show a constant tendency to decline.

History.—This small community owes its origin to those few Persians who, when Khalif Omar subjugated Persia in A.D. 641, resisted the efforts of the conquerors to impose on them the Moslem faith. Escaping to the coast they found a first refuge in the Island of Ormuz, at the mouth of the Persian Gulf; but having here little permanent chance of safety or sustenance for any large number, they began a series of emigrations across the sea, landing first at Diu on the Kathiawar coast some time about A.D. 700. After remaining here for nineteen years they were led, by an omen in the stars, to cross the Gulf of Cambay. After suffering shipwreck they landed at Sanjan, some twenty-five miles south of Daman on the Guzerat coast, where the local ruler, Jadi Râna, on hearing their pathetic story and an account of their religious beliefs, allowed them to settle on condition that they would learn the language of the country, abstain from the use of arms, dress and conduct their marriages in the Hindu manner etc. A spirit of accommodation to surroundings has characterized the Parsis throughout their history, and accounts at once for many of their usages in dress and manners, and for their subsequent success in industrial arts and trades. They thus became a regular part of the population of Sanjan, adopted the Guzerati language as their vernacular, and erected their first fire temple in A. D. 721. Here they remained for over five centuries of uneventful history, till in 1305 the incursion of the Moslems forced them to take refuge elsewhere. Partly by further emigrations from Persia, and partly by spreading from their centre at Sanjan, they gradually settled in various other localities such as Cambray, Ankleshwar, Variav, Vankaner, Broach, Surat, Thana, Chaul etc., and traces of them are found even as far as Delhi. When in the sixteenth century the Portuguese at Thana brought moral pressure to bear in order to make them Christians, they managed by a subterfuge to escape to Kalyan, only returning in 1774 when Thana had fallen under British rule. The advent of the English to Surat in 1612 opened up new connexions for industry and trade, so that Surat, as well as Broach, soon became two of their chief settlements. Finally, when the government of the East India Company was (in 1668) transferred to Bombay, the Parsis followed and soon began to occupy posts of trust in connexion with Government and public works in Bombay. Gradually certain families acquired wealth and prominence (Sorabji, Modi, Kama, Wadia, Jeejeebhoy, Readymoney, Dadyset, Petit, Patel, Mehta, Allbless, Tata etc.), many of whom are noted for their participation in the public life of the city, and for their various educational, industrial, and charitable enterprises. The Parsis had formerly a domestic tribunal called the Panchayat, which possessed judicial control and the power of excommunication; but for nearly a century back its influence has been curtailed, so that at present it is little more than a trust for the administration of public charitable funds.

The education movement began among the Parsis in 1849. Parsi schools since then have been multiplied, but other schools and colleges are also freely frequented. In 1854 they started the "Persian Zoroastrian Amelioration Fund," which, after long efforts lasting till 1882, succeeded in obtaining for their poor Irani brethren in Persia a remission of the Jazia tax, besides inaugurating schools and charitable institutions among them. Many of these Persians come over to India and set up cheap restaurants, which on that account are familiarly known as "Irani shops."

The Parsis are divided into two sects, the Shehanchais or old, and the Kadmis or new party—not on any point of religion, but merely on a question of chronology (like that of the "old" and "new style" in Europe). The old party follow the Indian, and the new party the Persian way of framing the calendar, which makes a difference of about one month in the observance of their "New Year's day." Among salient peculiarities should be mentioned: worship in fire temples (which contain nothing remarkable except a vase of sandalwood kept perpetually alight); praying on the sea shore to the rising and setting sun; celebration of marriages in public assembly; exposure of their dead to birds of prey, in what are called "towers of silence"; exclusiveness as regards marriage; refusal to incorporate aliens into religious membership; the rule of never uncovering the head; and of never smoking. But they are free from the Hindu trammels of caste, have no religious restrictions about food, are free to travel and take their meals with other races etc. It should be remarked that their "worship" of fire, as explained by themselves, is not open to the charge of idolatry, but is reducible to a *relative* veneration of that element as the highest and purest symbol of the Divinity. The Parsis have remained faithful to their Zoroastrian faith and are proud of their racial purity. And although the colour among many families, chiefly of the lower classes, reveals the effect of mixed marriages, the community as a whole is unmixed, and marriage with outsiders is rare. In very recent times the influence of Western ideas has led to a relaxing of the old religious and social bonds, so that many are now merely nominal believers, while others dabble in theosophy and religious eclecticism, and adopt such habits as smoking, the uncovering of the head, and even marrying European women etc. For an account of their religion see AVESTA.

KARAKA, *History of the Parsis* (London, 1884); HAUG, *Essays on the Parsis* (London, 1878); HARROSSOWITZ, *Zarathushtra and Zarathushtrianism* (Leipzig); *Statesman's Year-Book;* GEIGER, *Civilization of the Eastern Iranians* (London, 1885): DOSABHOY FRAMJER, *The Parsees, their History, Manners, Customs and Religion* (London, 1858).

ERNEST R. HULL.

Particular Examen. See EXAMINATION OF CONSCIENCE.

Partnership, an unincorporated association of two or more persons, known as partners, having for its object the carrying on in common by the partners of some predetermined occupation for profit, such profit, according to the usual definition, to be shared by the several partners. "The terms partnership and partner", remarks Lindley (The Law of Partnership, 7th ed., London, 1905, 10), "are evidently derived from *to part* in the sense of to divide amongst or share", and the use of the word "co-partnership" in the general sense of "co-ownership" is now obsolete (Queen against Robson, English Law Reports, 16 Queen's Bench Division, 140). Lindley, however, suggests that an association might be deemed according to the English Common Law a partnership even though its object were the application of profits to other use than the use of the partners (op. cit., where numerous definitions of partnership are quoted).

The Roman Civil Law treated elaborately of partnership under the name of *Societas* (Pothier, "Pandectæ Justinianeæ", LXVII, Tit. II). And archæologists claim to have ascertained its existence "in a highly developed state" in ancient Babylon (Johns, "Babylonian and Assyrian Laws", New York, 1904, 287, 290, 291).

Partnerships in the Roman Law were included among consensual contracts, those which required no certain form, nor any writing, but which became effectual by simple consent, *qui nudo consensu perficiuntur*, "Pandectæ", *supra*, "The Commentaries of Gaius", III (Cambridge, 1874), 135, 136.

And in like manner by the English Common Law, the basis of the law of the several States of the United States, except Louisiana, as well as the basis of the law of all British possessions, except those acquired from France, Holland, and Spain (Burge, "Commentaries on Colonial and Foreign Laws", new ed., London, 1907, 1, 7, 8), partnership may be formed by verbal agreement, although it is usually evidenced by written articles (see as to Statute of Frauds rendering a written agreement necessary, 116 New York Court of Appeals Reports, 97).

The contract of partnership can be legally entered into only by persons who are competent to contract. Accordingly, a partnership could not be formed at Common Law between husband and wife (Bowker against Bradford, 140 Massachusetts Supreme Court Reports, 521).

The English Law of partnership was itself to a great extent founded on what was known as the "Law Merchant", and thus "on foreign ideas as to matters of trade and the customs of merchants drawn frequently from the Lombard or Jew traders of the Continent", which became "by Statute Law, custom or court decision . . . such a considerable body of the English law as to have a name to itself" (Stimson, "Popular Law-making", New York, 1910, 90.

Profit or gain is the object of the relation; but not necessarily profit or gain to result from buying or selling of goods. Lawyers, for example, may enter into partnership (Kent, "Commentaries on American Law", III, 28). But since the pursuit of gain is essential to the legal notion of partnership, therefore, a "Young Men's Christian Association" defining its object to be "the extension of the kingdom of the Lord Jesus Christ among young men, and the development of their spiritual life and mental powers", has been held to be not such an association as the law deems to be a partnership (Queen against Robson, *supra*). The title of the association, the partnership or firm name, if not prescribed by express agreement, may be acquired by usage.

These expressions "firm" and "partnership" are frequently employed synonymously. Originally, however, the word firm signified "the partners or members of the partnership taken collectively" (Parsons, "A treatise on the Law of partnership", 4th ed., Boston, 1893, 1). In the English Partnership Law of 1890 "partners are called collectively a firm" (Lindley, op. cit., 10); and Parsons (op. cit., 2) remarks that "the business world" regards the firm "as a body which has independent rights against its members as well as against strangers". This distinction sanctioned by the law of Louisiana, and also by the law of those European countries whose jurisprudence is based on the Roman Civil Law, has not always been so clearly recognized by the English Courts (ibid, 3; Lindley, op. cit., 127, 128). According to the Common Law, the property, or stock in trade, of the firm is owned by the partners in joint tenancy, but without the right of survivorship which ownership in joint tenancy usually implies; "and this", remarks Kent, op. cit., III, 36, "according to Lord Coke was part of the law merchant for the advancement and continuance of commerce and trade".

It is of the essence of the contract that each partner shall "engage to bring into the common stock something that is valuable"; but one of the partners may advance funds and another skill (ibid, 24, 25). And the proportions of their respective interests in the firm property are such as they may have agreed (Parsons, op. cit., 138).

In the course of the business of the partnership and within its scope, every partner "is virtually both a principal and an agent" (Cox against Hickman, 8 House of Lords cases, 312, 313). As principal, each partner binds himself, and, as agent, binds the partnership, or more properly, the firm (Parsons, op. cit., 3, Cox against Hickman *supra*). The firm is bound by a sale which one of the partners may effect of partnership property, disposition of the property being the object of the partnership (Parsons, op. cit., 134). And so, purchase of property by a partner binds the firm, if the purchase be made "in the course and within the scope of the regular business of the firm" (ibid, 139).

Death of a partner dissolves the firm, unless the partnership agreement provide to the contrary (ibid, 431, 432, note). In the absence of such a provision the surviving partners have, indeed, a right to the possession and management of the property and business, "but only for the purpose of selling and closing the same" (ibid., 443).

And dissolution of a partnership before the lapse of a period agreed upon for its continuance may result from some event other than the death of a partner. The relation being one of mutual and personal confidence and of "exuberant trust" (Bell, "Principles of the Law of Scotland" 10th ed., Edinburgh, 1899, sec. 358), no partner may introduce, whether voluntarily or involuntarily, a substitute for himself. On assignment by an insolvent partner for benefit of his creditors, the assignee becomes entitled to an accounting, but without becoming a partner. And a like result follows bankruptcy of a partner. (Kent, op. cit., 59). Bankruptcy of the firm works its dissolution, the property vesting in an assignee or other statutory official who cannot carry on the business (ib., 58). So, according to the Common Law, marriage of a female partner dissolved the partnership, "because her capacity to act ceases and she becomes subject to the control of her husband" (ibid, 55).

If at any time dissensions among the partners destroy mutual trust and confidence, there seems to be great doubt, at least, whether the discordant partners ought to be compelled to continue in partnership (Parsons, op. cit., 371, 396, note c).

"The law merchant gave a right for an accounting by the representatives of a deceased partner against the survivor" (Street, "Foundations of legal liability", New York, 1906, II, 334), and whenever the partnership is to be dissolved and its affairs settled, each partner or his legal representative is entitled to "his distributive share after the partnership accounts are settled and the debts paid" (Parsons, op. cit., 231, 508).

LINDLEY, *The Law of Partnership* (7th ed., London, 1905); PARSONS, *A Treatise on the Law of Partnership* (4th ed., Boston, 1893).

CHARLES W. SLOANE.

Paruta, PAOLO, Venetian historian and statesman, b. at Venice, 14 May, 1540; d. there, 6 Dec., 1598. Of a Luccan family, he was devoted from youth to literature and philosophy, also the composition of poetry. He applied himself especially to history and political science, and was at the end of the fifteenth century what Macchiavelli, though in a different way, was at the beginning. He belonged intellectually to the group of recently ennobled men who met at the residence of the Morosini to discuss politics, which party (it may be called the liberal party) came into authority in 1582. Previous to this he occupied positions of secondary importance; in 1562 he accompanied the ambassador Michele Suriano to the Court of Maximilian II, and acted as official historiographer of the Republic, during which office he delivered the funeral oration for those killed at the battle of Lepanto (1572); after the change of government he was made *Savio di Terraferma*, and became a senator; he was *Commisario del Cadore* (1589), Governor of Brescia (1590–92), ambassador to Rome (1592–95), procurator of St. Mark (1596), next in dignity after the doge, and *Provveditore delle Fortezze* (1597).

His chief works are the "Guerra di Cipro" (1570–72) and the "Storia Veneziana", a continuation of Bembo's history, embracing the years 1513 to 1551, works composed at the request of the Government, but written with truth and impartiality, showing especially the connexion between the current events of Venice and the general history of Europe. His "Despatches" from Rome and the "Relazione" written at the end of his diplomatic mission reveal his great political foresight, by his accurate estimate of men and affairs at Rome, and which are equal to those of the greatest Venetian ambassadors. Of his political writings, the "Della perfezione della vita politica" in dialogue form, written between 1572 and 1579, has a somewhat didactic and academic tone, and treats principally of the relative superiority of the active and contemplative life, a problem he decides in favour of the active life on account of its contributing more to the welfare of the Republic. It was supposed, not without reason, to have been written to controvert the ideas contained in Bellarmine's "De officio principis christiani". His "Discorsi politici" were not published till after his death. The first book treats of the greatness and decadence of the Romans; the second of modern governments, especially Venice, being really an apology for the latter's policy. Though Paruta is an independent thinker, Macchiavelli's influence is notable. The policy of Italian equilibrium, which a century later developed into that of European equilibrium, was clearly foreseen by him. In his political views economy is not an important part, and therein he is inferior to his contemporary, the Piedmontese Botero.

FLAMINI, *Il Cinque cento* in *Storia della Letteratura italiana* (Milan, 1894), 458; COMANIO, *Le dottrine politiche di P. Paruta*.

U. BENIGNI.

Pascal, BLAISE, b. at Clermont-Ferrand, 19 June, 1623; d. in Paris, 19 August, 1662. He was the son of Etienne Pascal, advocate at the court of Aids of Clermont, and of Antoinette Bégon. His father, a man of fortune, went with his children (1631) to live in Paris. He taught his son grammar, Latin, Spanish, and mathematics, all according to an original method. In his twelfth year Blaise composed a treatise on the communication of sounds; at sixteen another treatise, on conic sections. In 1639 he went to Rouen with his father, who had been appointed intendant of Normandy, and, to assist his father in his calculations, he invented the arithmetical machine. He repeated Torricelli's vacuum experiments and demonstrated, against Père Noël, the weight of air (cf. Mathieu, "Revue de Paris", 1906; Abel Lefranc, "Revue Bleue", 1906; Strowski, "Pascal", Paris, 1908). He published works on the arithmetical triangle, on wagers and the theory of probabilities, and on the roulette or cycloid.

Meanwhile, in 1646, he had been won over to Jansenism, and induced his family, especially his sister Jacqueline, to follow in the same direction. In 1650, after a sojourn in Auvergne, his family returned to Paris. On the advice of physicians Pascal, who had always been ailing and who now suffered more than ever, relaxed his labours and mingled in society, with such friends as the Duc de Roannez, the Chevalier Méré, the poet Desbarreaux, the actor Miton. This was what has been called the worldly period of his life, during which he must have written the "Discours sur les passions de l'amour", inspired, it is said, by Mlle de Roannez. But the world soon became distasteful to him, and he felt more and more impelled to abandon it. During the night of 23 November, 1654, his doubts were settled by a sort of vision, the evidence of which is in a writing, always subsequently carried in the lining of his coat, and called "Pascal's talisman". After this he practised the most severe asceticism, renounced learning, and became the constant guest of Port Royal. In 1656 he undertook the defence of Jansenism, and published the "Provinciales". This polemical work was nearing completion when Pascal had the joy of seeing his friends, the Duc de Roannez and the jurisconsult Domat, converted to Jansenism, as well as his niece Marguerite Perier, who had been cured of a fistula of the eye by contact with a relic of the Holy Thorn preserved at Port Royal. Thenceforth, although exhausted by illness, Pascal gave himself more and more to God. He multiplied his mortifications, wore a cincture of nails which he drove into his flesh at the slightest thought of vanity, and to be more like Jesus crucified, he left his own house and went to die in that of his brother-in-law. He wrote the "Mystère de Jésus", a sublime memorial of his transports of faith and love, and he laboured to collect the materials for a great apologetic work. He died at the age of thirty-nine, after having received in an ecstasy of joy the Holy Viaticum, for which he had several times asked, crying out as he half rose from his couch: "May God never abandon me!"

Pascal left numerous scientific works, among which must be mentioned "Essai sur les coniques" (1640); "Avis à ceux qui verront la machine arithmétique" (1645); "Récit de la grande expérience de l'équilibre des liqueurs" (1648); "Traité du triangle arithmétique" (1654). He shows himself a determined advocate of the experimental method, in opposition to the mathematical and mechanical method of Descartes. In his "Traité sur la vide", often reprinted with the "Pensées" under the title "De l'autorité en matière de philosophie", Pascal clearly puts the question regarding progress, which he answers, boldly yet prudently, in "L'esprit géometrique", where he luminously distinguishes between the geometrical and the acute mind, and establishes the foundations of the art of persuasion. As to his authorship of the "Discours sur les passions de l'amour", that essay at least contains certain theories familiar to the author of the "Pensées" on the part played by intuition in sentiment and æsthetic, and its style for the most part resembles that of Pascal. The "Entretien avec M. de Saci sur Epictète et Montaigne" gives the key to the "Pensées"; psychology serving as the foundation and criterion of apologetics, various philosophies solving the problem only in one aspect, and Christianity alone affording the complete solution.

But Pascal's two masterpieces are the "Provinciales" and the "Pensées". The occasion of the "Provinciales" was an accident. The Duc de Liancourt, a friend of Port Royal, having been refused absolution by the curé of Saint Sulpice. Antoine Arnauld wrote two letters which were censured by the Sorbonne. He wished to appeal to the public in a pamphlet which he submitted to his friends, but they found it too heavy and theological. He then said to Pascal: "You, who are young, must do something." The next day (23 Jan., 1656) Pascal brought the first "Provinciale". The "Petites lettres" followed to the number of nineteen, the last unfinished, from January, 1656, to March, 1657. Appearing under the pseudonym of Louis de Montalte, they were published at Cologne in 1657 as "Les Provinciales, ou Lettres écrites par Louis de Montalte à un provincial de ses amis et au RR. PP. Jésuites sur le sujet de la morale et de la politique de ces pères". The first four treat the dogmatic question which forms the basis of Jansenism on the agreement between grace and human liberty. Pascal answers it by practically, if not theoretically, denying sufficient grace and liberty. The seventeenth and eighteenth letters take up the same questions, but with noteworthy qualifications. From the fourth to the sixteenth Pascal censures the Jesuit moral code, or rather the casuistry, first, by depicting a *naïf* Jesuit who, through silly vanity, reveals to him the pretended secrets of the Jesuit policy, and then by direct invective against the Jesuits themselves. The most famous are the fourth, on sins of ignorance, and the thirteenth, on homicide.

That Pascal intended this to be a useful work, his whole life bears witness, as do his deathbed declarations. His good faith cannot seriously be doubted, but some of his methods are more questionable. Without ever seriously altering his citations from the casuists, as he has sometimes been wrongfully accused of doing, he arranges them somewhat disingenuously; he simplifies complicated questions excessively, and, in setting forth the solutions of the casuists sometimes lets his own bias interfere. But the gravest reproach against him is, first, that he unjustly blamed the Society of Jesus, attacking it exclusively, and attributing to it a desire to lower the Christian ideal and to soften down the moral code in the interest of its policy; then that he discredited casuistry itself by refusing to recognize its legitimacy or, in certain cases, its necessity, so that not only the Jesuits, but religion itself suffered by this strife, which contributed to hasten the condemnation of certain lax theories by the Church. And, without wishing or even knowing it, Pascal furnished weapons on the one hand to unbelievers and adversaries of the Church and on the other to the partisans of independent morality. As to their literary form, the "Provinciales" are, in point of time, the first prose masterpiece of the French language, in their satirical humour and passionate eloquence.

The "Pensées" are an unfinished work. From his conversion to Jansenism Pascal nourished the project of writing an apology for the Christian Religion which the increasing number of libertines rendered so necessary at that time. He had elaborated the plan, and at intervals during his illness he jotted down notes, fragments, and meditations for his book. In 1670 Port Royal issued an incomplete edition. Condorcet, on the advice of Voltaire, attempted, in 1776, to connect Pascal with the Philosophic party by means of a garbled edition, which was opposed by that of the Abbé Bossuet (1779). After a famous report of Cousin on the MS. of the "Pensées" (1842), Faugère published the first critical edition (1844), followed since then by a host of others, the best of which is undoubtedly that of Michaut (Basle, 1896), which reproduces the original MS. pure and simple. What Pascal's plan was, can never be determined, despite the information furnished by Port Royal and by his sister. It is certain that his method of apologetics must have been at once rigorous and original; no doubt, he had made use of the traditional proofs—notably, the historical argument from prophecies and miracles. But as against adversaries who did not admit historical certainty, it was a stroke of genius to produce a wholly psychological argument, and, by starting from the study of the human soul, to arrive at God. Man is an "incomprehensible monster", says he, "at once sovereign greatness and sovereign misery." Neither dogmatism nor pyrrhonism will solve this enigma: the one explains the greatness of man, the other his misery; but neither explains both. We must listen to God. Christianity alone, through the doctrine of the Fall and that of the Incarnation, gives the key to the mystery. Christianity, therefore, is truth. God being thus apprehended and felt by the heart—which "has its reasons that the mind knows not of", and which, amid the confusion of the other faculties, is never mistaken—it remains for us to go to Him through the will, by making acts of faith even before we have faith.

Another curious argument of Pascal's is that which is known as the argument of the wager. God exists or He does not exist, and we must of necessity lay odds for or against Him.

If I wager *for* { and God is—infinite gain; and God is not—no loss.

If I wager *against* { and God is—infinite loss; and God is not—neither loss nor gain.

In the second case there is an hypothesis wherein I am exposed to the loss of everything. Wisdom, therefore, counsels me to make the wager which insures my winning all or, at worst losing nothing. Innumerable works were devoted to Pascal in the second half of the nineteenth century. Poets, critics, romance-writers, theologians, philosophers have drawn their inspiration from him or made him the subject of discussion. As M. Bourget has said, he is not only one of the princes of style, but he represents the religious soul in its most tragic and terrified aspects. Moreover, the problems which he presents are precisely those which confront us nowadays.

Sainte-Beuve, *Port-Royal*, I, II, III (Paris, 1860); Vinet, *Etudes sur Blaise Pascal* (Paris, 1848); Sully-Prudhomme, *La vraie religion selon Pascal* (Paris, 1909); Brunetière, *Etudes critiques*, ser. 1, 3, 4; *Hist. et littérature*, II (Paris, 1880–1903); Michaut, *Les époques de la pensée de Pascal* (Paris, 1897); Giraud, *Pascal; l'homme, l'œuvre, l'influence* (Paris, 1905); Boutroux in *Coll. des grands écrivains français* (Paris, 1900); Strowski, *Pascal et son temps* (Paris, 1909) (especially important); Taylor, *Pascal's Thoughts on Religion and Philosophy* (London, 1894); Janssens, *La philosophie et l'apologétique de P.* (Louvain, 1896).

J. Lataste.

Pascal Baylon, Saint, b. at Torre-Hermosa, in the Kingdom of Aragon, 24 May, 1540, on the Feast of Pentecost, called in Spain "the Pasch of the Holy Ghost", whence the name of Paschal; d. at Villa Reale, 15 May, 1592, on Whitsunday. His parents, Martin Baylon and Elizabeth Jubera, were virtuous peasants. The child began very early to display signs of that surpassing devotion towards the Holy Eucharist, which forms the salient feature of his character. From his seventh to his twenty-fourth year, he led the life of a shepherd, and during the whole of that period exercised a salutary influence upon his companions. He was then received as a lay-brother amongst the Franciscan friars of the Alcantarine Reform. In the cloister, Paschal's life of contemplation and self-sacrifice fulfilled the promise of his early years. His charity to the poor and afflicted, and his unfailing courtesy were remarkable. On one occasion, in the course of a journey through France, he triumphantly defended the dogma of the Real Presence against the blasphemies of a Calvinist preacher, and in consequence, narrowly escaped death at the hands of a Huguenot mob. Although poorly educated, his counsel was sought for by people of every station in life, and he was on terms of closest friendship with personages of eminent sanctity. Pascal was beatified in 1618, and canonized in 1690. His cultus has flourished particularly in his native land and in Southern Italy, and it was widely diffused in Southern and Central America, through the Spanish Conquests. In his Apostolic letter, *Providentissimus Deus*, Leo XIII declared St. Pascal the especial heavenly protector of all Eucharistic Congresses and Associations. His feast is kept on 17 May. The saint is usually depicted in adoration before a vision of the Host.

Staniforth, *The Saint of the Eucharist* (London, 1908); *Lives and Saints of the three orders of Saint Francis* (London, 1886); Ximenes, *Chronicles* (Valencia, 1600); D'Arta, *Supplement to above work* (Rome, 1672); De Porrentruy, *Saint Paschal Baylon* (Paris, 1899)

Oswald Staniforth.

Pascendi, Dominici Gregis. See Modernism.

Pasch or Passover.—Jews of all classes and ways of thinking look forward to the Passover holidays with the same eagerness as Christians do to Christmastide. It is for them the great event of the year. With the exception of the Temple sacrifices, their manner of observing it differs but little from that which obtained in the time of Christ. Directions for keeping the feast were carefully laid down in the Law (see Exod., xii, xiii, etc.), and carried out with great exactness after the Exile.

The feast of the Passover begins on the fourteenth day of Nisan (a lunar month which roughly corresponds with the latter part of March and the first part of April) and ends with the twenty-first. The Jews now, as in ancient times, make elaborate preparations for the festival. Every house is subjected to a thorough spring cleaning. The Saturday preceding the day of the Pasch (fifteenth) is called a "Great Sabbath", because it is supposed that the tenth day of the month Abib (or Nisan), when the Israelites were to select the Paschal lambs, before their deliverance from Egypt, fell on a Sabbath. On this Sabbath, the day of the following week on which the Passover is to fall is solemnly announced. Some days before the feast, culinary and other utensils to be used during the festival are carefully and legally purified from all contact with leaven, or leavened bread. They are then said to be *kosher*. Special sets of cooking and table utensils are not unfrequently kept in every household. On the evening of the thirteenth, after dark, the head of the house makes the "search for leaven" according to the manner indicated in the Mishna (Tractate "Pesachim", i), which is probably the custom followed by the Jews for at least two thousand years. The search is made by means of a lighted wax candle. A piece of ordinary, or leavened, bread is left in some conspicuous place, generally on a window-sill. The search begins by a prayer containing a reference to the command to put away all leaven during the feast. The place of the piece of bread just mentioned is first marked to indicate the beginning of the search. The whole house is then carefully examined, and all fragments of leaven are carefully collected on a large spoon or scoop by means of a brush or bundle of quills. The search is ended by coming back to the piece of bread with which it began. This, also is collected on the scoop. The latter, with its contents, and the brush are then carefully tied up in a bundle and suspended over a lamp to prevent mice from scattering leaven during the night and necessitating a fresh search. The master of the house then proclaims in Aramaic that all the leaven that is in his house, of which he is unaware, is to him no more than dust. During the forenoon of the next day (fourteenth) all the leaven that remains is burnt, and a similar declaration made. From this time till the evening of the 22nd, when the feast ends, only unleavened bread is allowed. The legal time when the use of leavened bread was prohibited was understood to be noon on the fourteenth Nisan; but the rabbis, in order to run no risks, and to place a hedge around the Law, anticipated this by one or two hours.

On this day, the fourteenth, the first-born son of each family, if he be above thirteen, fasts in memory of the deliverance of the first-born of the Israelites, when the destroying angel passed over Egypt. On the evening of the fourteenth the male members of the family, attired in their best, attend special services in the synagogue. On their return home they find the house lit up and the *Seder*, or Paschal Table, prepared. The head of the family takes his place at the head of the table, where there is an arm-chair prepared for him with cushions or pillows. A similar chair is also ready for the mistress of the house. The meal is called *Seder* by the Ashkenazaic Jews, and *Haggadah* (because of the story of the deliverance recited during it) by the Sephardic Jews. All the members of the Jewish family, including servants, sit round the table. In front of the head of the family is the Seder-dish, which is of such a kind as to allow three unleavened cakes or *matzoth*, each wrapped in a napkin, to be placed in it one above the other. A shank bone of lamb (with a small portion of meat attached) which has been roasted on the coals is placed, together with an egg that has been roasted in hot ashes, on another dish above the three unleavened cakes. The roasted shank represents the paschal lamb, and the roasted egg the *chagigah*, or free-will offerings, made daily in the Temple. Bitter herbs, such as parsley and horseradish, a kind of sop called *charoseth*, consisting of various fruits pounded into a mucilage and mixed with vinegar, and salt water, are arranged in different vessels, sometimes disposed like candelabra above the unleavened bread. The table is also furnished with wine, and cups or glasses for each person, an extra cup being always left for the prophet Elias, whom they expect as the precursor of the Messiah.

When all are seated around the table the first cup of wine is poured out for each. The head of the house rises and thanks God for the fruits of the vine and for the great day which they are about to celebrate. He then sits down and drinks his cup of wine in a reclining posture, leaning on his left arm. The others drink at the same time. In the time of the Temple the poorest Jew was to drink four cups of wine during this joyful meal; and if he happened to be too poor, it was to be supplied out of public funds. Though four cups are prescribed, the quantity is not restricted to that amount. Some water is generally added to the wine. In early days red wine was used; but, on account of the fear of fostering the groundless blood accusations against the Jews, this usage was discontinued. Unfermented raisin wine or Palestinian wine is now generally used. After drinking the first cup the master rises and washes his hands, the others remaining seated, and Edersheim is of opinion that it was at this point of the supper that Christ washed the disciples' feet. After washing his hands, the head of the family sits down, takes a small quantity of bitter herbs, dips them in salt water, and eats them, reclining on his left elbow. Jewish interpreters say that only the first Passover was to be eaten standing, and with circumstances of haste. During the Passovers commemorative of the first they reclined "like a king [or free man] at his ease, and not as slaves"—in this probably following the example of the independent Romans with whom they came into contact. After the head of the family has eaten his portion of bitter herbs, he takes similar portions, dips them in salt water, and hands them round to be eaten by the others. He then takes out the middle unleavened cake, breaks it in two, and hides away one-half under a pillow or cushion, to be distributed and eaten after supper. If this practice existed in the time of Christ, it is not improbable that it was from this portion, called *afikoman*, that the Eucharist was instituted. As soon as this portion is laid aside, the other half is replaced, the dish containing the unleavened cakes is uncovered, and all, standing up, take hold of the dish and solemnly lift it up, chanting slowly in Aramaic: "This is the bread of affliction which our fathers ate in Egypt. . . . This year here, next year in Jerusalem. This year slaves, next year free." The dish is then replaced, and the shank bone, roasted egg, etc. restored to their places above it. All sit down, and the youngest son asks why this night above all other nights they eat bitter herbs, unleavened bread, and in a reclining posture. The head of the house then tells how their fathers were idolaters when God chose Abraham, how they were slaves in Egypt, how God delivered them, etc. God is praised and blessed for His wondrous mercies to their nation, and this first part of the ceremony is brought to a close by their breaking forth with the recitation of the first part of the *Hallel* (Pss., cxiii and cxiv) and drinking the second cup of wine, which is triumphantly held aloft and called the cup of the Haggadah or story of deliverance.

The ceremony so far has been only introductory. The meal proper now begins. First, all wash their hands; the president then recites a blessing over the unleavened cakes, and, after having dipped small fragments of them in salt water, he eats them reclining. He next distributes pieces to the others. He also takes some bitter herbs, dips them in the *charoseth*, and gives them to the others to be eaten. He next makes a kind of sandwich by putting a portion of horse-radish between two pieces of unleavened bread and hands it round, saying that it is in memory of the Temple and of Hillel, who used to wrap together pieces of the paschal lamb, unleavened bread, bitter herbs, and eat them, in fulfilment of the command of Ex., xii, 8. The supper proper is now served, and consists of many courses of dishes loved by Jews, such as soup, fish, etc., prepared in curious ways unknown to Gentiles. At the end of the meal some of the children snatch the *afikoman* that has been hidden away, and it has to be redeemed by presents—a custom probably arising from a mistranslation of the Talmud. It is then divided between all present and eaten. Oesterley and Box think that this is a survival from an earlier time when a part of the paschal lamb was kept to the end and distributed, so as to be the last thing eaten. When the *afikoman* is eaten the third cup is filled; and grace after meals is said, and the third cup drunk in a reclining posture. A cup of wine is now poured out for the prophet Elias, in a dead silence which is maintained for some time, and the door is opened. Imprecations against unbelievers, taken from the Psalms and Lamentations, are then recited. These were introduced only during the Middle Ages. After this the fourth cup is filled and the great *Hallel* (Pss., cxv–cxviii) and a prayer of praise are recited. Before drinking the fourth cup, the Jews of some countries recite five poetical pieces, and then the fourth cup is drunk. At the end a prayer asking God to accept what they have done is added. Among the German and Polish Jews this prayer is followed by popular songs.

The same ceremonies are observed the next evening. According to the Law the fifteenth and twenty-first were to be kept as solemn festivals and days of rest. At present the fifteenth and sixteenth, the twenty-first and twenty-second are whole holidays, a custom introduced among the Jews of the Dispersion to make sure that they fulfilled the precepts of the Law on the proper day. The other days are half-holidays. Special services are held in the synagogues throughout the Passover week. Formerly the date of the Pasch was fixed by actual observation [Schürer, "History of the Jewish People" (Edinburgh, 1902), I, II, Append. 3]. It is now deduced from astronomical calculations.

OESTERLEY AND BOX, *Religion and Worship of the Synagogue* (London, 1907); DEMBITZ, *Jewish Services in the Synagogue and Home* (Philadelphia, 1898); LESÊTRE in VIGOUROUX, *Dict. de la Bible*, s. v. *Paque*; *Jewish Encycl.*; GINSBURG in KITTO, *Cyclop. of Bibl. Lit.*; ABRAHAMS in HASTINGS, *Dict. of the Bible*, s. v. *Passover*; SMITH, *Bibl. Dict.*; ZANGWILL, *Dreamers of the Ghetto* (London); JACOBS, *Jewish Year Book* (London, annual); EDERSHEIM, *Life and Times of Jesus the Messiah*, II (London, 1900), 479.

C. AHERNE.

Paschal I, POPE (817–824), the date of his birth is unknown; he died in April, May, or June, 824. He was the son of a Roman named Bonosus. While still young he joined the Roman clergy and was taken into the papal patriarchate (Lateran Palace) where he was instructed in the Divine Service and the Holy Scripture. Leo III having appointed him superior of the monastery of St. Stephen near the Basilica of St. Peter in the Vatican, he took care of the pilgrims who came to Rome. On the death of Stephen IV (24 January, 817) Paschal was unanimously chosen as his successor. On the following day he was consecrated and enthroned. He entered into relations with Emperor Louis, sending him several ambassadors in rapid succession. In 817 he received from the emperor a document, "Pactum Ludovicianum", confirming the rights and possessions of the Holy See. This document with later amendments is still extant (cf. especially Sickel, "Das Privileg Ottos I für die römische Kirche", Innsbruck, 1883, 50 sqq., 174 sqq.). Paschal remained on friendly terms with the Frankish nobility and sent a special legation with rich gifts to the marriage of King Lothair I, son of Emperor Louis. In spring, 823, Lothair went to Rome and on 5 April he was solemnly crowned emperor by Paschal. Although the pope himself opposed the sovereignty of the Frankish emperors over Rome and Roman territory, high officials in the papal palace, especially Primicerius Theodore and his son-in-law Leo Nomenculator, were at the head of the party which supported the Franks, and advocated the supremacy of the emperor. Shortly after the departure of King Lothair in 823, both these officials were blinded and killed by the pope's servants. Paschal himself was accused of being the originator of this deed, but he cleared himself of suspicion by an oath. The ambassadors sent to Rome by Emperor Louis to investigate the affair could not punish the perpetrators, as the pope declared the murdered officials guilty of treason. Paschal supported new missionary expeditions which went out from the Frankish Empire. He sent a letter of introduction to Bishop Halitgar of Cambria, and appointed Archbishop Ebo of Rheims as papal legate to the pagan countries in Northern Europe.

In 814 under Leo the Armenian, the Iconoclastic controversy broke out with renewed violence in the Byzantine Empire. Theodore of Studium, the great champion of orthodoxy, wrote repeatedly to Pope Paschal, who encouraged him to persevere. At the same time Theodosius of Constantinople, unlawfully made patriarch by Emperor Leo, sent a legation to the pope. The latter, however, remained loyal to the cause of Theodore of Studium, and dispatched legates to Leo to win him from the Iconoclasts, but without success. Numerous monks who had been driven out of Greece by Leo came to Rome where the pope received them kindly, assigning them places in the newly-erected monasteries, such as St. Praxedis, St. Cecilia, Sts. Sergius and Bacchus, near the Lateran Palace. Paschal was very active in completing, restoring, and beautifying churches and monasteries. The basilicas of St. Praxedis, St. Cecilia, and S. Maria in Dominica were completely rebuilt by him. The mosaics, which at that time ornamented the apses of these three churches as well as the chapel of St. Zeno in St. Praxedis, demonstrate to-day the deterioration of this art. In St. Peter's he erected chapels and altars, in which the remains of martyrs from the Roman catacombs, especially those of Sts. Processus and Marinianus, were placed. He also placed the relics of many Roman martyrs in the church of St. Praxedis where their names are still legible. The discovery of the relics of St. Cecilia and companions, and their translation to the new church of St. Cecilia in Trastevere, are well described in "Liber Pontificalis" (cf. Kirsch, "Die hl. Cäcilia in der römischen Kirche des Altertums", Paderborn, 1910). He made great improvements in the choir of the church of S. Maria Maggiore. Paschal was interred in the church of St. Praxedis, and is honoured as a saint on 14 May.

Liber Pontificalis, ed. DUCHESNE, II, 52 sqq.; *Einhardi Annals* in *Mon. Germ. hist.*: Script., I, 124 sqq.; JAFFÉ, *Regesta Rom. Pont.*, 2nd ed., I (Leipzig, 1885), 318 sqq.; SIMSON, *Jahrbücher der deutschen Reiches unter Ludwig dem Frommen* (Leipzig, 1874–76); DUCHESNE, *Les premiers temps de l'Etat pontifical* in *Revue d'hist. et de littér. religeuses*, I (Paris, 1896), 297 sqq.; HARTMANN, *Geschichte Italiens im Mittelalter*, III, pt. i (Gotha, 1908); MARUCCHI, *Basiliques et églises de Rome* (Rome, 1902).

J. P. KIRSCH.

Paschal II, POPE (RAINERIUS), succeeded Urban II, and reigned from 13 Aug., 1099, till he died at Rome, 21 Jan., 1118. Born in central Italy, he was received at an early age as a monk in Cluny. In his twentieth year he was sent on business of the monastery to Rome, and was retained at the papal court by Gregory VII, and made Cardinal-Priest of St. Clement's church. It was in this church that the conclave met after the death of Pope Urban, and Cardinal Rainerius was the unanimous choice of the sacred college. He protested vigorously against his election, maintaining, with some justice, that his monastic training had not fitted him to deal with the weighty problems which confronted the papacy in that troublous age. His protestations were disregarded by his colleagues, and he was consecrated the following day in St. Peter's. Once pope, he betrayed no further hesitation and wielded the sceptre with a firm and prudent grasp. The main lines of his policy had been laid by the master minds of Gregory and Urban, in whose footsteps he faithfully followed, while the unusual length of his pontificate, joined to a great amiability of character, made his reign an important factor in the development of the medieval papal dominion. Urban II had lived to witness the complete success of his wonderful movement for the liberation of the Holy Land and the defence of Christendom. He had died a fortnight after Jerusalem fell into the hands of the crusaders. To continue the work inaugurated by Urban remained the fixed policy of the Holy See for many generations. Paschal laboured vigorously by synods and journeys through Italy and France to keep alive the crusading spirit. Of more vital importance was the Investiture Conflict (see INVESTITURE, CONFLICT OF). It was fortunate that the antipope, Guibert (Clement III), died a few months after the elevation of Paschal. Three other antipopes, Theodoric (1100), Aleric (1102), and Maginulf, who took the name of Sylvester IV (1105), were offered by the imperialistic faction; but the schism was practically ended. Two of these pretendants were sent by Paschal to do penance in monasteries; the third had little or no following. Henry IV, broken by his previous conflicts, had no desire to renew the struggle He obstinately refused to abjure his claim to imperial investitures, and, consequently, was again excommunicated, and died at Liège, 7 Aug., 1106.

His death and the accession of his son were of dubious advantage to the papal cause; for although he had posed as the champion of the Church, he soon showed himself as unwilling as his father had been to relinquish any of the pretensions of the crown. Since the pope continued to denounce and anathematize lay investitures in the synods over which he presided, the chief of which were at Guastalla (1106) and Troyes (1107), and since Henry persisted in bestowing benefices at pleasure, the friendly relations between the two powers soon became strained. Paschal decided to change his proposed journey to Germany, and proceeded to France, where he was received enthusiastically by King Philip (who did penance for his adultery and was reconciled to the Church) and by the French people. Henry resented the discussion of a German question on foreign soil, though the question of Investitures was one of universal interest; and he threatened to cut the knot with his sword, as soon as circumstances permitted his going to Rome to receive the imperial crown. In August, 1110, he crossed the Alps with a well-organized army, and, what emphasized the entrance of a new factor in medieval politics, accompanied by a band of imperialistic lawyers, one of whom, David, was of Celtic origin. Crushing out opposition on his way through the peninsula, Henry sent an embassy to arrange with the pontiff the preliminaries of his coronation. The outcome was embodied in the Concordat of Sutri. Before receiving the imperial crown, Henry was to abjure all claims to investitures, whilst the pope undertook to compel the prelates and abbots of the empire to restore all the temporal rights and privileges which they held from the crown.

When the compact was made public in St. Peter's on the date assigned for the coronation, 12 Feb., 1111, there arose a fierce tumult led by the prelates who by one stroke of the pen had been degraded from the estate of princes of the empire to beggary. The indignation was the more intense, because the rights of the Roman See had been secured from a similar confiscation. After fruitless wrangling and three days of rioting, Henry carried the pope and his cardinals into captivity. Abandoned as he was by everyone, Paschal, after two months of imprisonment, yielded to the king that right of investiture against which so many heroes had contended. Henry's violence rebounded upon himself. All Christendom united in anathematizing him. The voices raised to condemn the faint-heartedness of Paschal were drowned by the universal denunciation of his oppressor. Paschal humbly acknowledged his weakness, but refused to break the promise he had made not to inflict any censure upon Henry for his violence. It was unfortunate for Paschal's memory that he should be so closely associated with the episode of Sutri. As head of the Church, he developed a far-reaching activity. He maintained discipline in every corner of Europe. The greatest champions of religion, men like St. Anselm of Canterbury, looked up to him with reverence. He gave his approval to the new orders of Citeaux and Fontevrauld. On his numerous journeys he brought the papacy into direct contact with the people and dedicated a large number of churches. If it was not given to him to solve the problem of Investitures, he cleared the way for his more fortunate successor.

DUCHESNE, *Lib. Pont.*, II, 296 sqq.; GREGOROVIUS, *The Historians of the City of Rome*; HEFELE, *Concilieng.*, V, ed. VON REUMONT; HERGENRÖTHER, *Kircheng.*, II, 378; ARTAND DE MONTOR, *Hist. of the Popes* (New York, 1867).

JAMES F. LOUGHLIN.

Paschal III (GUIDO OF CREMA), second antipope in the time of Alexander III. He was elected in 1164 to succeed Cardinal Octavian, who, under the name of Victor IV, had warred so many years against Alexander III. To meet the demands of Frederick Barbarossa, he canonized Charlemagne in 1165, but this action was never ratified by the Church (see CHARLEMAGNE). He died in 1168.

Paschal, ALBERT. See PRINCE ALBERT, DIOCESE OF.

Paschal Candle.—The blessing of the "paschal candle", which is a column of wax of exceptional size, usually fixed in a great candlestick specially destined for that purpose, is a notable feature of the service on Holy Saturday. The blessing is performed by the deacon, wearing a white dalmatic. A long Eucharistic prayer, the "Præconium paschale" or "Exultet" (q. v.) is chanted by him, and in the course of this chanting the candle is first ornamented with five grains of incense and then lighted with the newly blessed fire. At a later stage in the service, during the blessing of the font, the same candle is plunged three times into the water with the words: "Descendat in hanc plenitudinem fontis virtus Spiritus Sancti" (May the power of the Holy Spirit come down into the fulness of this fountain). From Holy Saturday until Ascension Day the paschal candle is left with its candlestick in the sanctuary, standing upon the Gospel side of the altar, and it is lighted during high Mass and solemn Vespers on Sundays. It is extinguished after the Gospel on Ascension Day and is then removed.

The results of recent research seem all to point to the necessity of assigning a very high antiquity to the paschal candle. Dom Germain Morin (Revue Bénédictine, Jan., 1891, and Sept., 1892) has successfully vindicated, against Mgr Duchesne and others, the authenticity of the letter of St. Jerome to Presidius, deacon of Placentia (Migne, P. L., XXX, 188), in which the saint replies to a request that he would compose a *carmen cerei*, in other words, a form of blessing like our "Exultet". Clearly this reference to a *carmen cerei* (poem of the candle) must presuppose the existence, in 384, of the candle itself which was to be blessed by the deacon with such a form, and the saint's reply makes it probable that the practice was neither of recent introduction nor peculiar to the church of Placentia. Again St. Augustine (De Civit. Dei, XV, xxii) mentions casually that he had composed a *laus cerei* in verse; and from specimens of similar compositions— all of them, however, bearing a close family resemblance to our "Exultet"—which are found in the works of Ennodius (Opusc., 14 and 81), it appears that there can be no sufficient ground for doubting the correctness of this statement. Moreover, Mgr Mercati has now shown good reason for believing that the existing "Præconium paschale" of the Ambrosian Rite was composed in substance by St. Ambrose himself or else founded upon hymns of which he was the author (see "Studi e Testi", XII, 37–38). There is, therefore, no occasion to refuse to Pope Zosimus (c. 417) the credit of having conceded the use of the paschal candle to the suburbicarian churches of Rome, although the mention of this fact is only found in the second edition of the "Liber Pontificalis". Mgr Duchesne urges that this institution has left no trace in the earliest purely Roman Ordines, such as the Einsiedeln Ordo and that of Saint-Amand; but these speak of two *faculæ* (torches) which were carried to the font before the pope and were plunged into the water as is now done with the paschal candle. The question of size or number does not seem to be very vital. The earliest council which speaks upon the subject, viz., the Fourth of Toledo (A. D. 633, cap. ix), seems to couple together the blessing of the *lucerna* and *cereus* as of equal importance and seems also to connect them both symbolically with some *sacramentum*, i. e. mystery of baptismal illumination and with the Resurrection of Christ. And undoubtedly the paschal candle must have derived its origin from the splendours of the celebration of Easter Eve in the early Christian centuries. As pointed out in the article HOLY WEEK, our present morning service on Holy Saturday can be shown to represent by anticipation a service which in primitive times took place late in the evening, and which culminated in the blessing of the font and the baptism of the catechumens, followed immediately by Mass shortly after midnight on Easter morning. Already in the time of Constantine we are told by Eusebius (De Vita Constantini, IV, xxii) that the emperor "transformed the night of the sacred vigil into the brilliancy of day, by lighting throughout the whole city pillars of wax (κηροῦ κίονας), while burning lamps illuminated every part, so that this mystic vigil was rendered brighter than the brightest daylight". Other Fathers, like St. Gregory Nazianzus and St. Gregory of Nyssa, also give vivid descriptions of the illumination of the Easter vigil. Further, it is certain, from evidence that stretches back as far as Tertullian and Justin Martyr, that upon this Easter eve the catechumens were baptized and that this ceremony of baptism was spoken of as φώτισμος, i. e., illumination. Indeed, it seems highly probable that this is already referred to in Heb., x, 22, where the words "being illuminated" seem to be used in the sense of being baptized (cf. St. Cyril of Jerusalem, Cat. i, n. 15). Whether consciously designed for that purpose or not, the paschal candle typified Jesus Christ, "the true light which enlighteneth every man that cometh into this world", surrounded by His illuminated, i. e. newly baptized disciples, each holding a smaller light. In the virgin wax a later symbolism recognized the most pure flesh which Christ derived from His blessed Mother, in the wick the human soul of Christ, and in the flame the divinity of the Second Person of the Blessed Trinity. Moreover, the five grains of incense set cross-wise in the candle recalled the sacred wounds retained in Christ's glorified body, and the lighting of the candle with new fire itself served as a lively image of the resurrection.

Of the practice of medieval and later times regarding the paschal candle much might be said. We learn on the authority of Bede, speaking of the year 701, that it was usual in Rome to inscribe the date and other particulars of the calendar either upon the candle itself or on a parchment affixed to it. Further, in many Italian basilicas the paschal candlestick was a marble construction which was a permanent adjunct of the ambo or pulpit. Several of these still survive, as in San Lorenzo fuori della mura at Rome. Naturally the medieval tendency was to glorify the paschal candle by making it bigger and bigger. At Durham we are told of a magnificent erection with dragons and shields and seven branches, which was so big that it had to stand in the centre of the choir. The Sarum Processional of 1517 directs that the paschal candle, no doubt that of Salisbury cathedral, is to be thirty-six feet in height, while we learn from Machyn's diary that in 1558, under Queen Mary, three hundred weight of wax was used for the paschal candle of Westminster Abbey. In England these great candles, after they had been used for the last time in blessing the font on Whitsun Eve, were generally melted down and made into tapers to be used gratuitously at the funerals of the poor (see Wilkins, "Concilia", I, 571, and II, 298). At Rome the Agnus Deis (q. v.) were made out of the remains of the paschal candles, and Mgr Duchesne seems to regard these consecrated discs of wax as likely to be even older than the paschal candle itself.

BERLIÈRE in *Messager des Fidèles* (Maredsous, 1888), 107 sqq.; MÜHLBAUER, *Geschichte und Bedeutung der Wachslichter bei den kirch. Funktionen*, 184 sqq.; MORIN in *Revue Bénédictine* (Maredsous, Jan., 1891, and Sept., 1892); IDEM in *Rassegna Gregoriana*, II (Rome, 1903), 193–194; MERCATI in *Studi e Testi*, No. XII (Rome, 1904), 24–43, where is also printed an Hispano-Visigothic formula of the *Præconium Paschale* belonging to the seventh century; CABROL, *Le Livre de la Prière Antique* (Paris, 1902); THURSTON in *The Month* (London), April, 1896; IDEM, *Lent and Holy Week* (London, 1904); MARTÈNE, *De antiquis ecclesiæ ritibus*, IV, xxiv.

HERBERT THURSTON.

Paschal Controversy. See EASTER CONTROVERSY.

Paschal Cycle. See CALENDAR, CHRISTIAN; EASTER.

Paschal Lamb. See LAMB.

Paschal Precept. See COMMANDMENTS OF THE CHURCH.

Paschal Tide.—I. LITURGICAL ASPECT. The fifty days from Easter Sunday to Pentecost are called by the older liturgists "Quinquagesima paschalis" or "Quin. lætitiæ". The octave of Easter which closes after Saturday has its own peculiar Office (see EASTER). Since this octave is part and complement of the Easter Solemnity, Paschal Tide in the liturgical books commences with the First Vespers of Low Sunday and ends before the First Vespers of Trinity Sunday. On Easter Sunday the Armenian Church keeps the Commemoration of All the Faithful Departed and on Saturday of Easter Week the Decollation of St. John. The Greek Church on Friday of Easter Week celebrates the feast of Our Lady, the Living Fountain (shrine at Constantinople).

The Sundays from Easter to Ascension Day, besides being called the First, Second (etc.) Sunday after Easter, have their own peculiar titles. The first is the "Dominica in albis", or Low Sunday (see LOW SUNDAY). In the Dioceses of Portugal and Brazil (also in the province of St. Louis, Mo.) on the Monday after Low Sunday is celebrated the feast of the Joys or Exultation of Mary at the Resurrection of her Son (double of the second class). The Russians, on Tuesday of this week, go in procession to the cemeteries and place Easter eggs on the graves [Maltzew, "Fasten- und Blumen- Triodion" (Berlin, 1899), 791]. In the Latin Church the second Sunday is called from its Gospel the Sunday of the Good Shepherd and from the Introit "Misericordias Domini"; in many dioceses (Seville, Capuchins) it is called the feast of Our Lady, Mother of the Good Shepherd (d. 2nd cl.); at Jerusalem and in the churches of the Franciscans it is called the feast of the Holy Sepulchre of Christ; in the Greek Church it is called ἰὼν Μυροφόρων (Sunday of the women who brought ointments to the sepulchre of Christ); the Armenians celebrate on this Sunday the dedication of the first Christian church on Mount Sion. The third Sunday is called from the Introit "Jubilate" and the Latin Church has assigned to it the feast of the Patronage of St. Joseph (d. 2nd cl.); the Greeks call it the Sunday of the Paralytic, from its Gospel. The Oriental Churches on Wednesday after the third Sunday celebrate with a very solemn Office and an octave the Μεσοπεντεκοστή, the completion of the first half of Paschal Tide; it is the feast of the manifestation of the Messiah, the victory of Christ and the Church over Judaism ["Zeitschrift für katholische Theologie" (1895), 169–177]; the Slav nations in this day have a solemn procession and benediction of their rivers (Nilles, "Kal.", II, 361). The fourth Sunday is called "Cantate"; by the Orientals it is called Sunday of the Samaritan Woman. The fifth Sunday, "Vocem jucunditatis"; in the Orient, Sunday of the Man Born Blind. In the Latin Church follow the Rogation Days (q. v.); in the Greek Church on Tuesday is kept the ἀπόδοσις or conclusion of the feast of Easter. The Greeks sing the Canons of Easter up to this Tuesday in the same manner as during Easter Week, whilst in the Latin Church the specific Easter Office terminates on Saturday following the feast. Thursday is the feast of the Ascension (see ASCENSION). The Friday of this week, in Germany, is called "Witterfreitag"; the fields are blessed against frost and thunderstorms. Sunday within the octave of Ascension is called "Exaudi" from the Introit; in some dioceses it is called Feast of Our Lady, Queen of the Apostles (double major) or of the Cenacle (Charleston and Savannah, first class); in Rome it was called Sunday of the Roses ("Pascha rosarum" or "rosatum"), since in the Pantheon rose-leaves were thrown from the rotunda into the church; in the Greek and Russian Churches it is the feast of the 318 Fathers of the first Nicene Council; the Armenians call it the "second feast of the flowers", a repetition of Palm Sunday. By older liturgists the week before Pentecost is called "Hebdomada expectationis", week of the expectation of the Holy Ghost. On the Vigil of Pentecost the baptismal water is blessed in the Latin Church; in the Oriental Churches this Saturday is the Ψυχοσάββατον (All Souls' Day); on this day the Greeks bless wheat cakes and have processions to the cemeteries. (See WHITSUNDAY.)

Paschal Tide is a season of joy. The colour for the Office *de tempore* is white; the Te Deum and Gloria are recited every day, even in the ferial Office. On Sundays the "Asperges" is replaced by the "Vidi Aquam" which recalls the solemn baptism of Easter eve. There is no feast day from Easter until Ascension. The Armenians during this period do away even with the abstinence on Fridays. Prayers are said standing, not kneeling. Instead of the "Angelus" the "Regina Cœli" is recited. From Easter to Ascension many churches, about the tenth cent., said only one Nocturn at Matins; even some particular churches in the city of Rome adopted this custom from the Teutons (Bäumer, "Gesch. des Breviers", 312). Gregory VII limited this privilege to the week of Easter and of Pentecost. Some dioceses in Germany, however, retained it far into the nineteenth century for 40 days after Easter. In every Nocturn the three psalms are said under one antiphon. The Alleluia appears as an independent antiphon; an Alleluia is also added to all the antiphons, responsories, and versicles, except to the versicles of the *preces* at Prime and Compline. Instead of the "suffragia sanctorum" in the semidouble and ferial Offices a commemoration of the Holy Cross is used. The iambic hymns have a special Easter doxology. The feasts of the holy Apostles and martyrs have their own *commune* from Easter to Pentecost. At Mass the Alleluia is added to the Introit, Offertory, and Communion; in place of the Gradual two Alleluias are sung followed by two verses, each with an Alleluia; there is also a special Preface for Paschal Time.

II. In CANON LAW Paschal Tide is the period during which every member of the faithful who has attained the years of discretion is bound by the positive law of the Church to receive Holy Communion (Easter duty). During the early Middle Ages from the time of the Synod of Agde (508) it was customary to receive Holy Communion at least three times a year, Christmas, Easter, and Pentecost. A positive precept was issued by the IV Lateran Council (1215) and confirmed by the Council of Trent (Sess. XIII, can. ix). According to these decrees the faithful of either sex, after coming to the age of discretion, must receive at least at Easter the Sacrament of the Eucharist (unless by the advice of the parish priest they abstain for a while). Otherwise during life they are to be prevented from entering the church and when dead are to be denied Christian burial. The paschal precept is to be fulfilled in one's parish church. [Taunton, "The Law of the Church" (London and St. Louis, 1906), 391, 474.] Although the precept of the IV Lateran to confess to the parish priest fell into disuse and permission was given to confess anywhere, the precept of receiving Easter Communion in the parish church is still in force where there are canonically-erected parishes. The term Paschal Tide was usually interpreted to mean the two weeks between Palm and Low Sundays (Synod of Avignon, 1337); by St. Antonine of Florence it was restricted to Easter Sunday, Monday, and Tuesday; by Angelo da Chiavasso it was defined as the period from Maundy Thursday to Low Sunday. Eugene IV, 8 July, 1440, authoritatively interpreted it to mean the two weeks between Palm and Low Sundays [G. Allmang, "Kölner Pastoralblatt" (Nov., 1910), 327 sq.]. In later centuries the time has been variously extended: at Naples from Palm Sunday to Ascension; at Palermo from Ash Wednesday to Low Sunday. In Germany, at an early date, the second Sunday after Easter terminated Paschal Tide, for which reason it was called "Predigerkirchweih", because the hard Easter labour was over, or "Buch Sunday", the obstinate sinners putting off the fulfillment of the precept to the last day. In the United States upon petition of the Fathers of the First Provincial Council of Baltimore Paschal Tide was extended by Pius VIII to the period from the first Sunday in Lent to Trinity Sunday (II Plen. Coun. Balt., n. 257); in England it lasts from Ash Wednesday until Low Sunday; in Ireland from Ash Wednesday until the octave of SS. Peter and Paul, 6 July (O'Kane "Rubrics of the Roman Ritual", n. 737; Slater, "Moral Theology", 578, 599); in Canada the duration of the Paschal Tide is the same as in the United States.

Kirchenlex., s. v., *Oesterliche Zeit;* NILLES, *Kal. man.*, II, 337 sqq.; TONDINI, *Calendrier liturgique de la nation arménienne* (Rome, 1906); BAUMSTARK, *Festbrevier und Kirchenjahr der syrischen Jakobiten* (Paderborn, 1910).

F. G. HOLWECK.

Paschasius, SAINT, deacon of the Roman Church about 500; d. after 511. Almost all that is known of Paschasius is related by Gregory the Great in his "Dialogues" (IV, xl). According to Gregory he was a man of extraordinary sanctity, and a father of the poor. Until his death he was a firm adherent of the antipope Laurentius (498–505; d. before 514). This, however, was not the result of malice but of error and ignorance. He died during the reign of Pope Symmachus (498–514), and after his death a demoniac was healed by touching his dalmatic. Long after this, Paschasius appeared to Bishop Germanus of Capua at the hot springs of Angulus (Angelum); he told Germanus that he had to do penance in these baths for his former mistake, and begged the bishop to pray for him. This Germanus did with great zeal, and after some days no longer found him at the springs. Gregory remarks that Paschasius had left books on the Holy Spirit that were correct in all particulars and perfectly intelligible. As a matter of fact two books "De spiritu sancto" are assigned to Paschasius in several manuscripts, and until lately were printed under his name. Engelbrecht, not long ago, denied his authorship of them, assigned them to Bishop Faustus of Riez, and has published them in the works of Faustus. If this is correct, then the work of Paschasius has disappeared. A letter written by him to Eugippius (511) has been preserved. The latter had begged his venerated and dearly loved friend Paschasius, who had great literary skill, to write a biography of St. Severinus from the accounts of the saint which he (Eugippius) had put together in crude and inartistic form. Paschasius, however, replied that the acts and miracles of the saint could not be described better than had been done by Eugippius. The feast of Paschasius is celebrated on 31 May.

MIGNE, *P. L.*, LXII, 9–40, 1167–70; LXXVII, 397–98; ENGELBRECHT, *Studien über die Schriften des Bischofs von Reii Faustus* (Vienna, 1889), 28–46; *Corpus scriptorum ecclesiasticorum latinorum*, XXI (Vienna, 1891); *Paschasii epistola ad Eugippium, ibid.*, IX (1886), ii, 68–70; BERGMANN, *Der handschriftlich bezeugte Nachlass des Faustus von Reji* (Leipzig, 1898), 35–55; *Acta SS.*, May, VII, 438–40; DANIELL in *Dict. Christ. Biog.*, s. v.

KLEMENS LÖFFLER.

Paschasius Radbertus, SAINT, theologian, b. at Soissons, 786; d. in the Monastery of Corbie, c. 860 (the date 865 is improbable). As a child he was exposed, but was taken in and brought up by Benedictine Nuns at Soissons. He entered the Benedictine Order at Corbie under Abbot Adalard, and was for many years instructor of the young monks. In 822 he accompanied Abbot Adalard into Saxony for the purpose of founding the monastery of New Corvey (Westphalia). He saw four abbots, namely Adalard, Wala, Heddo, and Isaac pass to their reward and on the death of Abbot Isaac, Paschasius was made Abbot of Corbie, though only a deacon; through humility he refused to allow himself to be ordained priest. On the occasion of a disagreement he resigned his office after about seven years and was thus enabled to devote himself to study and literature.

He wrote a learned commentary on the Gospel of St. Matthew, "Commentarii in Matt. libri XII"; an exposition of the 44th Psalm, "Expos. in Ps. 44 libri III" and a similar work on Lamentations, "Expos. in Lament. libri V"; and a life of Abbot Adalard (cf. Bolland., 2 Jan.). His biography of the Abbot Wala is a work of greater usefulness as an historical source (cf. Rodenburg, "Die Vita Walæ als historische Quelle", Marburg, 1877). He revised the "Passio Rufini et Valerii". His earliest work in dogmatic theology was a treatise, "De fide, spe et caritate" (first published in Pez, "Thesaur. Anecdot.", I, 2, Augsburg, 1721); he next wrote two books "De Partu Virginis", in which he defended the perpetual virginity of Mary, the Mother of God.

The most important of his works is: "De corpore et sanguine Domini", in Martène, "Vet. scriptor. et monum. amplissima Collectio", t. IX, written in 831 for his pupil Placidus Varinus, Abbot of New Corvey, and for the monks of that monastery, revised by the author and sent in 844 to Emperor Charles the Bald. The emperor commissioned the Benedictine Ratramnus of Corbie to refute certain questionable assertions of Paschasius, and when Rabanus Maurus joined in the discussion (cf. Ep. iii ad Egilem, P. L., CXII, 1513) there occurrred the first controversy on the Eucharist, which continued up to the tenth century and even later, for both the followers of Berengarius of Tours in the eleventh century and the Calvinists in the sixteenth century vigorously assailed the work, because they thought that they had found the real source of doctrinal innovations, especially in regard to the Catholic dogma of Transubstantiation. His primary object herein was to give in accordance with the doctrine of the Fathers of the Church (e. g. Ambrose, Augustine, and Chrysostom), the clearest and most comprehensive explanation of the Real Presence. In carrying out his plan he made the mistake of emphasizing the identity of the Eucharistic Body of Christ with His natural (historical) Body in such exaggerated terms that the difference between the two modes of existence was not sufficiently brought out.

In opposition to his assertion that the Eucharistic Body of Christ is "non alia plane caro, quam quæ nata est de Maria et passa in cruce et resurrexit de sepulchro" (loc. cit.), Ratramnus thought it necessary to insist that the Body of Christ in the Sacred Host—notwithstanding its essential identity with the historical Body—is present by a spiritual mode of existence and consequently as an "invisible substance", and hence that our eyes cannot immediately perceive the Body of Christ in the form of bread. It is difficult to admit that Paschasius really believed what is here inferred: his narration, however, of certain Eucharistic miracles may have given some foundation for the suspicion that he inclined towards a grossly carnal, Capharnaite-like apprehension of the nature of the Eucharist. His opponents also reproached him with having, in direct contradiction to his fundamental viewpoint, simultaneously introduced the notions of a *figura* and of a *veritas*, thus placing side by side without any reconciliation the symbolic and the realistic conceptions of the Eucharist. The accusation seems altogether unwarranted; for by *figure* he understood merely that which appears outwardly to the senses, and by *veritas*, that which Faith teaches us. At bottom his doctrine was as orthodox as that of his opponents. He defended himself with some skill against the attacks of his critics, especially in his "Epistola ad Frudegardum". But a more thorough vindication of St. Paschasius was made by Gerbert, afterwards Pope Sylvester II (d. 1003), who, in a work bearing the same title "De corpore et sanguine Domini", contended that the doctrine of St. Paschasius was correct in every particular. The scientific advantage which accrued to theology from this first controversy on the Eucharist is by no means unimportant. For, through the accurate distinction made between the Eucharistic Body of Christ and its exterior sensible appearances, the way was cleared for a deeper understanding of the Eucharistic species or accidents in distinction from, and in opposition to, the invisible Body of Christ hidden under them. Hence also the difficult notion of Transubstantiation gained much in clearness, distinctness, and precision.

St. Paschasius was first buried in the Church of St. John at Corbie. When numerous miracles took place at his grave under Abbot Fulco, his remains were solemnly removed by order of the pope, 12 July, 1073, and interred in the Church of St. Peter, Corbie. His feast is on 26 April.

The collected *Opera Paschasii* were first published by SIRMOND (Paris, 1618); these were republished with numerous additions in *P.L.*, CXX. His letters are in PERTZ, *Mon. Ger. Hist.: Epist.*, VI, 132 sq.; his poems in PERTZ, *Poet. lat.*, III, 38 sqq., 746 sq.; *Das Epitaphium Arsenii* (pseudonym for WALA), ed. DÜMMLER in *Abhandlungen der Berliner Akademie* (1900); *Vita Paschasii* is given in MABILLON, *Acta SS. O.S.B.*, IV (Lucca, 1735), 2, 122 sq.; and in PERTZ, *Mon. Germ. Hist.: Script.*, XV, 452 sq.; HAUSHERR, *Der hl. Paschasius Radbertus* (Mainz, 1862); SARDEMANN, *Der theol. Lehrgehalt der Schriften des Paschasius* (Marburg, 1877); ERNST, *Die Lehre des Paschasius Radbertus von der Eucharistie mit besonderer Rücksicht der Stellung des Rabanus Maurus und des Ratramnus* (Freiburg, 1896); CHOISY, *Paschase Radbert* (Geneva, 1889); NÄGLE, *Ratramnus und die hl. Eucharistie, zugleich eine dogmatisch-historische Würdigung des ersten Abendmahlstreites* (Vienna, 1903); SCHNITZER, *Berengar von Tours* (Stuttgart, 1892), 127 sq.; BACH, *Dogmengeschichte des Mittelalters*, I (Vienna, 1873); EBERT, *Allgemeine Geschichte der Literatur des Mittelalters*, II (Leipzig, 1880), 230 sq.; GÖTZ, *Die heutige Abendmahlsfrage in ihrer geschichtlichen Entwickelung* (2nd ed., Leipzig, 1908).

J. POHLE.

Passaglia, CARLO, b. at Lucca, 9 May, 1812; d. at Turin, 12 March, 1887. He entered the Society of Jesus in 1827; when scarcely thirty years old, he was teaching at the Sapienza, and was prefect of studies at the German College. In 1845 he took the solemn vows and became professor of dogmatic theology at the Gregorian University. In 1850 he took a leading part in preparing the definition of the dogma of the Immaculate Conception, on which he wrote three large volumes. He showed in his works a rare knowledge of the theological literature of all times. His historico-linguistic method met with criticism. It was said that "he substituted grammar for dogma". His chief works are: an edition of the "Enchiridion" of St.

Augustine, with copious notes (Naples, 1847); "De prærogativis b. Petri" (Rome, 1850); "Conferences" given at the Gesù and published in "Civiltà Cattolica" (1851); "Commentariorum theologicorum partes 3" (1 vol., Rome, 1850–51); "De ecclesia Christi" (3 vols., Ratisbon, 1853—incomplete); "De æternitate pœnarum" (Ratisbon, 1854).

The trouble between Passaglia and his superiors grew steadily more serious; he finally left the Society in 1859. Pius IX gave him a chair at the Sapienza. Then he came in contact with the physician Pantaleoni, Cavour's agent; Cavour summoned him to Turin for a personal interview (February, 1861). Afterwards, at Rome, he held several conferences with Cardinal Santucci, and, persuaded that the ground was ready, he wrote "Pro causa italica" (1861), which was placed on the Index. Passaglia fled to Turin, where he held the chair of moral philosophy until his death. Ignorant of the world and men, he believed that the opponents of temporal power were guided by the best of intentions. He founded the weekly, "Il Medicatore" (1862–66), in which he wrote long articles full of undigested erudition, and to which he welcomed the contribution of any priest with a grievance. From 1863 to 1864 he edited the daily, "La Pace", and in 1867 "Il Gerdil", a weekly theological review. He could not say Mass at Turin, and put off the clerical dress. But as regards dogma, he never swerved from the true Faith; nevertheless he criticized the Syllabus. We have still to mention his book, "Sul divorzio" (1861), and his refutation of Renan (1864). In 1867 the Bishops of Mondovi and Clifton tried to reconcile him with the Church, but he did not retract until a few months before his death.

BIGINELLI, *Biografia del sacerdote C. Passaglia* (Turin, 1887); D'ERCOLE, *C. Passaglia* in *Annunzio dell' Università di Torino* (1887–88).

U. BENIGNI.

Passau, DIOCESE OF (PASSAVIENSIS), in Bavaria, suffragan of Munich-Freising, including within its boundaries one district and one parish in Upper Bavaria and the City of Passau and 10 districts in Lower Bavaria (see GERMANY, *Map*).

HISTORY.—The Diocese of Passau may be considered the successor of the ancient Diocese of Lorch (*Laureacum*). At Lorch, a Roman station and an important stronghold at the junction of the Enns and the Danube, Christianity found a foothold in the third century, during a period of Roman domination, and a Bishop of Lorch certainly existed in the fourth. During the great migrations, Christianity on the Danube was completely rooted out, and the Celtic and Roman population was annihilated or enslaved. In the region between the Lech and the Enns, the wandering Bajuvari were converted to Christianity in the seventh century, while the Avari, to the east, remained pagan. The ecclesiastical organization of Bavaria was brought about by St. Boniface, who, with the support of Duke Odilo, erected the four sees of Freising, Ratisbon, Passau, and Salzburg. He confirmed as incumbent of Passau, Bishop Vivilo, or Vivolus, who had been ordained by Pope Gregory III, and who was for a long time the only bishop in Bavaria. Thenceforth, Vivilo resided permanently at Passau, on the site of the old Roman colony of Batavis. Here was a church, the founder of which is not known, dedicated to St. Stephen. To Bishop Vivilo's diocese was annexed the ancient Lorch, which meanwhile had become a small and unimportant place. By the duke's generosity, a cathedral was soon erected near the Church of St. Stephen, and here the bishop lived in common with his clergy. The boundaries of the diocese extended westwards to the Isar, and eastwards to the Enns. In ecclesiastical affairs Passau was probably, from the beginning, suffragan to Salzburg. Through the favour of Dukes Odilo and Tassilo, the bishopric received many costly gifts, and several monasteries arose—e. g. Niederalteich, Niebernburg, Mattsee, Kremsmünster —which were richly endowed. Under Bishop Waltreich (774–804), after the conquest of the Avari, who had assisted the rebellious Duke Tassilo, the district between the Enns and the Raab was added to the diocese, which thus included the whole eastern part (Ostmark) of Southern Bavaria and part of what is now Hungary. The first missionaries to the pagan Hungarians went out from Passau, and in 866 the Church sent missionaries to Bulgaria.

Passau, the outermost eastern bulwark of the Germans, suffered most from the incursions of the Hungarians. At that time many churches and monasteries were destroyed. When, after the victory of Lech, the Germans pressed forward and regained the old Ostmark, Bishop Adalbert (946–971) hoped to extend his spiritual jurisdiction over Hungary. His successor Piligrim (971–91), who worked zealously and successfully for the Christianization of Pannonia, aspired to free Passau from the metropolitan authority of Salzburg, but was completely frustrated in this, as well as in his attempt to assert the metropolitan claims which Passau was supposed to have inherited from Lorch, and to include all Hungary in his diocese. By founding many monasteries in his diocese he prepared the way for the princely power of later bishops. It is undoubtedly to his credit that he built many new churches and restored others from ruins. His successor, Christian (991–1002) received in 999 from Otto III the market privilege and the rights of coinage, taxation, and higher and lower jurisdiction. Henry II granted him a large part of the North Forest. Henceforward, indeed, the bishops ruled as princes of the empire, although the title was used for the first time only in a document in 1193. Under Berengar (1013–45) the whole district east of the Viennese forest as far as Letha and March was placed under the jurisdiction of Passau. During his time the cathedral chapter made its appearance, but there is little information concerning its beginning as a distinct corporation with the right of electing a bishop. This right was much hampered by the exercise of imperial influence.

At the beginning of the Conflict of Investures, St. Altmann (q. v.) occupied the see (1065–91) and was one of the few German bishops who adhered to Gregory VII. Ulrich I, Count of Höfft (1092–1121), who was for a time driven from his see by Henry IV, furthered the monastic reforms and the Crusades. Reginmar (1121–38), Reginhert, Count of Hegenau (1136–47) who took part in the crusade of Conrad III, and Conrad of Austria (1149–64), a brother of Bishop Otto of Freising, were all much interested in the foundation of new monasteries and the reform for those already existing. Ulrich, Count of Andechs (1215–21), was formally recognized as a prince of the empire at the Reichstag of Nuremberg in 1217. The reforms which were begun by Gebhard von Plaien (1221–32) and Rüdiger von Rodeck (1233–1250) found a zealous promoter in Otto von Lonsdorf (1254–65), one of the greatest bishops of Passau. He took stringent measures against the relaxed monasteries, introduced the Franciscans and Dominicans into his diocese, promoted the arts and sciences, and collected the old documents which had survived the storms of the preceding period, so that to him we owe almost all our knowledge of the early history of Passau. (See Schmidt, "Otto von Lonsdorf, Bischof zu Passau", Würzburg, 1903.) Bishop Peter, formerly Canon of Breslau, contributed much to the greatness of the House of Habsburg by bestowing episcopal fiefs on the sons of King Rudolph. Under Bernhard of Brambach (1285–1313) began the struggles of Passau to become a free imperial city. After an uprising in May, 1298, the bishop granted the burghers, in the municipal ordinance of 1299, privileges in conformity with what was called the Bernhardine Charter. The cathedral having been burned down in 1281, he built a new cathedral which lasted until 1662. Albert III von Winkel (1363-80) was particularly active in the struggle with the burghers and in resisting the robber-knights. The Black Death visited the bishopric under Gottfried II von Weitzenbeck (1342-62). George I von Hohenlohe (1388-1421), who, after 1418, was imperial chancellor, energetically opposed the Hussites. During the time of Ulrich III von Nussdorf (1451-79) the diocese suffered its first great curtailment by the formation of the new Diocese of Vienna (1468). This diocese was afterwards further enlarged at the expense of Passau by Sixtus IV. Towards the close of the fifteenth century the conflict between an Austrian candidate for the see and a Bavarian brought about a state of war in the diocese.

The Reformation was kept out of all the Bavarian part of the diocese, except the Countship of Ortenburg, by the efforts of Ernest of Bavaria who, though never consecrated, ruled the diocese from 1517 to 1541. The new heresy found many adherents, however, in the Austrian portion. Wolfgang I Count of Salm (1540-55) and Urban von Trennbach (1561-98) led the counter-Reformation. Under Wolfgang the Peace of Passau was concluded, in the summer of 1552 (see CHARLES V). The last Bavarian prince-bishop was Urban, who in his struggles during the Reformation received substantial aid for the Austrian part of the diocese from Albert V, Duke of Bavaria, and, after 1576, from Emperor Rudolph II. All the successors of Urban were Austrians. Bishop Leopold I (1598-1625) (also Bishop of Strasburg after 1607) was one of the first to enter the Catholic League of 1609. In the Thirty Years' War he was loyal to his brother, Emperor Ferdinand II. Leopold II Wilhelm (1625-62), son of Ferdinand II, a pious prince and a great benefactor of the City of Passau, especially after the great conflagration of 1662, finally united five bishoprics. Count Wenzelaus von Thun (1664-73) began the new cathedral which was completed thirty years later by Paul Philip of Lamberg. He and his nephew Joseph Dominicus, his mediate successor (1723-62), became cardinals. When Vienna was raised to an archdiocese in 1722, he relinquished the parishes beyond the Viennese Forest, hence was exempted from the metropolitan authority of Salzburg, and obtained the pallium for himself and his successors. Leopold Ernst, Count of Firmian (1763-83), created cardinal in 1772, established an institute of theology at Passau and, after the suppression of the Jesuits, founded a lyceum. Under Joseph, Count of Auersperg (1783-95), Emperor Joseph II took away two-thirds of the diocese to form the two dioceses of Linz and St. Pölten (see LINZ). The last prince-bishop, Leopold von Thun (1796-1826), saw the secularization of the old bishopric in 1803; the City of Passau and the temporalities on the left bank of the Inn and the right bank of the Ilz went to Bavaria, while the territory on the left banks of the Danube and of the Ilz went to the Grand Duchy of Tuscany and afterwards to Austria. On 22 February, 1803, when the Bavarians marched into Passau, the prince-bishop withdrew to his estates in Bohemia, and never revisited his former residence.

By the Concordat of 1818, the diocese was given the boundaries which it still has. After the death of the last prince-bishop, Passau's exemption from metropolitan power ceased, and the diocese became suffragan of Munich-Freising. Bishop Charles Joseph von Riccabona (1826-38) turned his attention to the care of the rising generation of clergy. With the support of King Louis I, he founded a preparatory course and then reopened the lyceum with a faculty of law and of theology. Henry von Hofstätter (1839-75) established a complete theological seminary, and a school for boys. The former of these found a great benefactor in Bishop Franz von Weckert (1875-79); the latter, in Michael von Rampf (1889-1901), who for sixteen years had been vicar-general of the Archdiocese of Munich-Freising. He was followed by Antonius von Thoma (March-October, 1889), who was promoted to the archiepiscopal See of Munich, and succeeded by Antonius von Henle (1901-06), who was transferred to Ratisbon. The present diocesan, Sigismund Felix von Ow-Felldorf, was appointed 11 January, 1906, and consecrated on 24 February, 1906.

ACTUAL CONDITIONS.—The diocese is divided into a city commission and 19 rural deaneries. In 1910 it numbered 222 parishes, and 102 other benefices and *exposituren*, 607 clerics, of whom 219 were parish priests, 49 were engaged at the cathedral and in diocesan educational institutions, and 67 were regulars. The resident Catholic population was 354,200. The cathedral chapter consists of a cathedral provost, a dean, 8 canons, 6 vicars, 1 preacher, and 1 precentor (*Domkapellmeister*). The diocesan institutions are the seminary for clerics, dedicated to St. Stephen, with 95 alumni, and the boys' seminary at Passau; the state institutions are a gymnasium at Passau, 2 homes for priests, 1 home for superannuated priests. There is a state lyceum at Passau with 8 religious professors, where candidates for the priesthood study philosophy and theology. The following orders and congregations were established in the diocese: Benedictine Missionaries of St. Ottilien, a missionary seminary with 9 fathers and 20 brothers; Capuchins, 5 monasteries, 54 fathers, 24 tertiary clerics, and 65 lay brothers; Redemptorists, 1 monastery with 3 fathers and 3 brothers. Female orders: Benedictines, 1 convent, 46 sisters; Cistercians, 1 house, 48 sisters; English Ladies, 3 mother-houses, 30 affiliated institutions, 866 members; Poor School Sisters of Notre Dame, from the mother-house at Munich, 7 institutions, with 35 sisters; Sisters of Charity of St. Vincent de Paul from the mother-house at Munich, 18 houses with 79 sisters; Sisters of the Most Holy Redeemer, from Neiderbronn, Alsace, 2 institutions with 9 sisters; Sisters of the Third Order of St. Francis, from Mallersdorf, Lower Bavaria, 25 institutions with 125 sisters. The English Ladies and the School Sisters devote themselves to the education of girls, while those in most of the remaining institutions of the diocese (the Benedictines and Cistercians being contemplatives) are occupied with the care of the sick. Among the pious organizations of the diocese may be mentioned the Society of St. Vincent de Paul, the Society of St. Elizabeth, the Brotherhood for the Perpetual Adoration of the Blessed Sacrament, the Society of St. Cecilia, the Societies of Catholic Workmen, the Volksverein of Catholic Germany. The most important Catholic periodicals are "Die Donauzeitung" and "Die Theologisch-praktische Monatschrift", both published at Passau.

The cathedral, with the exception of the choir and the transept built in 1407, was rebuilt after the fire of 1662 by the Italians Lorago and Carlone, in the baroque style; its two towers were finished in 1896-98 by Heinr. von Schmidt. From Gothic times date the parish church of the city of Neuötting (1450-80), the cathedral at Altötting (fourteenth and fifteenth centuries) with the tombs of Karlmann and of Tilly, the Herrenkapelle near the cathedral at Passau (1414); Renaissance and Baroque are the former Cistercian church at Aldersbach (1700-34), the Church of the Premonstratensians at Osterhofen (completed in 1740), the parish church at Niederalteich, formerly the church of a Benedictine abbey (1718-26). The diocese contains the most famous place of pilgrimage in all Bavaria: the Chapel of Our Lady at Altötting, which is visited each year by from 200,000 to 300,000 pilgrims. In this chapel the hearts of the Bavarian royal family have been preserved opposite the miraculous picture, since the time of the Elector Maximilian I.

BUCHINGER, *Geschichte des Fürstentums Passau* (Munich, 1816-24); SCHÖLLER, *Geschichte der Bischöfe von Passau* (Passau, 1844); ERHARD, *Geschichte der Stadt Passau* (Passau, 1862, 1864) (the bishops especially are treated in the first volume); SCHRÖDL, *Passavia sacra: Geschichte des Bistums Passau bis zur Säkularisation des Fürstentums Passau* (Passau, 1879); ROTTMAYER, *Statistische Beschreibung des Bistums Passau* (Passau, 1867); RÖHM, *Das historische Alter der Diözese Passau* (Passau, 1880); *Die bischöflichen Seminarien der Diözese Passau* (1893); HEINWIESER, *Die rechtliche Stellung der Stadt Passau bis zur Stadtherrschaft der Bischöfe* (Passau, 1910); *Schematismus für das Jahr 1910* (Passau, 1910); *Verhandlungen des Historischen Vereins für Niederbayern* (Landshut, 1846—). The traditions of the diocese are treated in BITTERAUF, *Necrologia von Fastlinger*. On the Peace of Passau, KÜHNS, *Geschichte des Passauer Vertrags* (Giessen, 1907) and BONWETSCH, *Geschichte des Passauischen Vertrags von 1552* (Göttingen, 1907).

JOSEPH LINS.

Passerat, VENERABLE JOSEPH, b. 30 April, 1772, at Joinville, France; d. 30 October, 1858. The difficulties he had to surmount in following his vocation to the priesthood were great. He was driven from the seminary, imprisoned, and forced to serve in the army from 1788 to 1792. Owing to his lofty stature he was made drum-major, and later quarter-master. At the first opportunity he left the service and entered the Congregation of the Most Holy Redeemer in Warsaw. Bl. Clement M. Hofbauer (q. v.) trained him for the religious life and priesthood, and he in turn trained new-comers. Later with great difficulty owing to the circumstances of the times he established houses outside of Poland. After the death of Bl. Clement, Venerable Passerat succeeded him as vicar-general over all the transalpine communities. While thus engaged (1820-48) he founded houses in the United States, in Bavaria, Prussia, Switzerland, Belgium, France, Portugal, Holland, and England. Difficulties were many in the United States, and in Europe the danger of suppression was imminent, but never wavering, he communicated his confidence in God to his subjects. He used to say: "Console yourselves, we are seed, be it that we are reduced to ten, these like grains of corn reduced to dust under the earth will one day give a rich harvest". The growth of the congregation verified his prediction. He governed his numerous family with zeal, wisdom, and tenderness. When the revolution decreed the destruction of the Redemptorists, he said to his subjects: "Fear not: stand courageously. Let it not be said of us that we have failed to meet martyrdom, but that martyrdom has failed to meet us". On 6 April, 1848, he was driven out of Vienna with his community without the bare necessaries of life. After much hardship he reached Belgium. Worn out with old age and labour he resigned his office and became director of the Redemptoristines at Bruges. The ordinary process for his beatification was begun at Tournai in 1892, and the introduction of the cause of this venerable servant of God was approved by Leo XIII on 13 May, 1901. The Apostolic Process is already completed.

DESURMONT, *Joseph Passerat et sous sa conduite Les Redemptoristes pendant les guerres de l'Empire* (Montreuil-sur-Mer, 1893); GIROUILLE, *Un grand serviteur de Dieu, Le Rev. Père Joseph Passerat* (Montreuil-sur-Mer, 1893). See REDEMPTORISTINES; CLEMENT MARY HOFBAUER, BLESSED.

J. MAGNIER.

Passignano, DOMENICO (known as IL CRESTI, or IL PASSIGNANO, Cresti being his family name), Venetian painter, b. at Passignano, near Florence, in 1558; d. at Florence, 1638. Although a Florentine by birth, he belongs to the Venetian school. He appears to have lived for a while at Florence, and afterwards at Pisa, but going to Venice, he accepted the Venetian traditions which he followed through the rest of his career. Personally, he was a man of charming manners, delightful in conversation. Pope Clement VIII knighted him and gave him many commissions, and Urban VIII added to his honours and emoluments. He returned to Florence, where he was greatly beloved and regarded as the chief member of its Academy, although recognized by all his companions as Venetian in style and out of sympathy with the Florentine methods. He painted with extraordinary facility, and so rapidly as to be nicknamed *Passa Ognuno*. This name has been regarded as a sort of play upon the name of his birthplace, and one author asserts that the name *Passignano* was derived from it; but there appears to be no authority for this. According to the custom of the time, the artist would derive his familiar cognomen from his birthplace.

Passignano's drawing was not particularly correct, but his ideas of composition were ingenious and clever. He regarded Tintoretto's work with very high favour, and many of his own paintings closely resemble those of the great master. But his desire to paint rapidly caused him to use his colours so thinly that many of his important works have for this very reason perished. He was responsible for the street decorations in Florence on the occasion of the marriage of the Grand Duke Ferdinand I with Christina of Lorraine, and the frescoes of the church of San Andrea at Rome were very largely his work. His own portrait is in the Uffizi Gallery at Florence, and the same city contains several of his best works. He is also to be studied in Paris, London, and Vienna.

VASARI (various editions); LANZI, *Storia Pittorica* (Bassano, 1809).

GEORGE CHARLES WILLIAMSON.

Passing Bell. See BELLS.

Passio (PASSIONALE, PASSIONARIUM). See LEGENDS OF THE SAINTS; MARTYRS, ACTS OF THE.

Passionei, DOMENICO, cardinal, theologian, b. at Fossombrone, 2 Dec., 1682; d. 5 July, 1761. Educated in the Clementine College at Rome, later he joined the household of his brother Guido, afterwards secretary of the Sacred College, devoting himself to higher studies at the Sapienza. He was soon made a prelate and in 1706 was sent to Paris to present the nuncio with the red hat, but he there acquired the Jansenistic tendencies which he never entirely eradicated. In 1708 he was sent on a confidential mission to The Hague; in 1712 he was present at Utrecht as official representative of the Holy See and successfully maintained the cause of Ruiswych concerning religion. His efforts were less successful at Baden (1714) and at Turin. He was later sent to Malta as inquisitor (1717-19); he became Secretary of Propaganda, Secretary of Latin Letters, and in 1721 nuncio in Switzerland, where he wrote "Acta Apostolicæ Legationis Helvetiæ 1723-29" (Zurich, 1729; Rome, 1738). He blessed the marriage of Maria Theresa and was instrumental in converting Friedrich Ludwig, Prince of Würtemberg. Later on he was hostile to Austria.

After his return to Rome he became secretary of briefs and cardinal of the title of S. Bernardo. In 1755 he succeeded Quirini as librarian of the Holy Roman Church. Although a member of the Academy of Berlin, he published little. But he carried on a learned correspondence with the most distinguished *literati*. He protected the Jansenists and encouraged them to publish Arnauld's works. His library of 32,000 volumes was open to all; it was acquired by the Augustinians. His character was impetuous and haughty, especially towards the Romans. He was compelled to confirm the decree prohibiting the "Exposition de la doctrine chrétienne" of Masenguy, his protégé, but this so afflicted him as to hasten his death.

GALLETTI, *Memorie per servire alla storia del card. Dom. Passionei* (Rome, 1762); GOUJET, *Eloge hist. du card. Passionei* (The Hague, 1763); letters in *Ouvrages posthumes de Mabillon* (Paris, 1724); *Nova acta historico-ecclesiastica*, IX (Weimar, 1769).

U. BENIGNI.

Passionists.—The full title of the Passionist institute is: THE CONGREGATION OF DISCALCED CLERKS OF THE MOST HOLY CROSS AND PASSION OF OUR LORD JESUS CHRIST.

Foundation.—The founder was St. Paul of the Cross, called in the world Paul Francis Danei. The saint was born 3 Jan., 1694, at Ovada, a small town in the then Republic of Genoa. He spent his youth at Castellazzo, in Lombardy, where his parents had taken up their residence when Paul was only ten years old. This was his father's native place. It is to Castellazzo we have to turn our thoughts for the beginnings of the Passionist Congregation. There Paul received his inspirations concerning the work for which God destined him. There he was clothed by his bishop in the habit of the Passion, and there wrote the Rules of the new institute.

The Rules were written by St. Paul while yet a layman and before he assembled companions to form a community. He narrates, in a statement written in obedience to his confessor, how Our Lord inspired him with the design of founding the congregation, and how he wrote the Rules and Constitutions. "I began", he says, "to write this holy rule on the second of December in the year 1720, and I finished it on the seventh of the same month. And be it known that when I was writing, I went on as quickly as if somebody in a professor's chair were there dictating to me. I felt the words come from my heart" (see "Life of St. Paul of the Cross", II, v, Oratorian Series). In 1725 when on a visit to Rome with his brother John Baptist, his constant companion and co-operator in the foundation of the institute, Paul received from Benedict XIII *vivæ vocis oraculo*, permission to form a congregation according to these Rules. The same pope ordained the two brothers in the Vatican basilica 7 June, 1727. After serving for a time in the hospital of St. Gallicano they left Rome with permission of the Holy Father and went to Mount Argentaro, where they established the first house of the institute. They took up their abode in a small hermitage near the summit of the mount, to which was attached a chapel dedicated to St. Anthony. They were soon joined by three companions, one of whom was a priest, and the observance of community life according to the rules began there and is continued there to the present day. This was the cradle of the congregation, and we may date the foundation of the Passionists from this time.

Formation and Development.—By an Apostolic rescript of 15 May, 1741, Benedict XIV approved the Rules of the institute, whose object, being to awaken in the faithful the memory of the Passion of Christ, commended itself in a special manner to him, and he was heard to say, after signing the rescript, that the Congregation of the Passion had come into the world last, whereas it ought to have been the first. Clement XIV confirmed the Rules and approved the institute by the Bull *Supremi Apostolatus* of 16 Nov., 1769, which concedes to the Passionist Congregation all the favours and privileges granted to other religious orders. The same pope afterwards gave to St. Paul and his companions the Church of Sts. John and Paul in Rome, with the large house annexed to it on Monte Celio, and this remains the mother-house of the congregation to the present day. Before the holy founder's death the Rules and the institute were again solemnly confirmed and approved by a Bull of Pius VI, "Præclara virtutum exempla", 15 Sept., 1775. These two Bulls of Clement XIV and Pius VI gave canonical stability to the institute, and are the basis and authority of its rights and privileges.

After the congregation had been approved by Benedict XIV many associates joined St. Paul, some of whom were priests; and the new disciples gave themselves up to such a life of fervent penance and prayer that upon Mount Argentaro the sanctity of the ancient anchorites was revived. Before the death of the founder twelve houses or "retreats" of the congregation were established throughout Italy and formed into three provinces, fully organized according to the Rules—a general over the entire congregation, a provincial over each province, rectors over the several houses, a novitiate in each province. These superiors were to be elected in provincial chapters held every three years and general chapters every six years.

Distinctive Spirit.—The congregation embraces both the contemplative and the active life, as applied to religious orders. The idea of the founder was to unite in it the solitary life of the Carthusians or Trappists with the active life of the Jesuits or Lazarists. The Passionists are reckoned among the mendicant orders in the Church. They have no endowments, nor are they allowed to possess property either in private or in common, except their houses and a few acres of land attached to each. They therefore depend upon their labours and the voluntary contributions of the faithful.

The end of the congregation, as stated in the Rules, is twofold: first, the sanctification of its members; and secondly, the sanctification of others. This twofold end is to be secured by means of their distinctive

PASSIONIST MONASTERY, BRIGHTON, MASS.

spirit, namely the practice and promotion of devotion to the Passion of Our Lord as the most efficacious means for withdrawing the minds of men from sin and leading them on to Christian perfection. To this end the Passionists at their profession add to the three usual religious vows of poverty, chastity, and obedience, a fourth—to promote to the utmost of their power, especially by such means as their rules point out, a devotion to the Passion of Our Divine Saviour.

Recruiting and Training of Members.—The Passionists have no colleges for the education of seculars, and have no young men or boys under their care, except those who wish to become members of the congregation, and those who are novices and professed students. They depend therefore for their subjects upon the attraction which the spirit and work of the congregation exercise upon youths who come to know them. The congregation admits of two classes of religious: choir brothers and lay brothers. The former, unless priests already, are to give themselves to study for the priesthood. The latter are charged with the domestic duties of the retreat. The conditions for the reception of novices are, besides those common to all religious orders: (1) that they be at least fifteen years of age, and not over twenty-five (from this latter the father general can dispense for any just and sufficient reason); (2) that they show special aptitude for the life of a Passionist; (3) if they are to be received as clerics they must have made due progress in their studies and show the usual signs of vocation to the priesthood. After profession and the completion of their classical and intermediate studies, the students take a seven years' course of ecclesiastical studies under the direction and tuition of professors, or lectors as they are called, in philosophy, theology, Holy Scripture etc., and when they have passed the required examinations they are promoted to Holy orders *sub titulo Paupertatis*.

The vows made in the congregation are *simple*, not *solemn* vows, and they are perpetual, or for life, so that no religious can leave the congregation of his own accord after profession, and no one can be dismissed except for some grave and canonical reason. For the sanctification of its members and the maintenance of the spirit of the congregation in their community life, besides practising the austerities and mortifications prescribed by Rule and familiar only to themselves, the Passionists spend five hours every day in choir chanting the Divine Office or in meditation. They rise at midnight and spend one hour and a half chanting Matins and Lauds. They abstain from flesh meat three days in the week throughout the year, and during the whole of Lent and Advent; but in cold and severe climates, such as the British Isles, a dispensation is usually granted allowing the use of flesh meat two or three times a week during those seasons. They wear only sandals on their feet. Their habit is a coarse woollen tunic. They sleep on straw beds with straw pillows. They spend the time free from choir and other public acts of observance in study and spiritual reading, and, that they may have Our Lord's Sacred Passion continually before their mind, they wear upon their breasts and mantles the badge of the congregation on which are inscribed the words *Jesu XPI Passio* (Passion of Jesus Christ).

Activities or Missionary Labours.—For the spiritual good of others, the second end of their institute, in Catholic countries they do not ordinarily undertake the cure of souls or the duties of parish priests, but endeavour to assist parish priests of the places where their houses are established, especially in the confessional. In non-Catholic countries, and in countries where the population is mixed, that is, made up of Catholics and non-Catholics, the Rule provides for such circumstances, and they may undertake ordinary parochial duties and the cure of souls when requested to do so by the bishops or ordinaries, and this is the case in England, in the United States of America, and in Australia. Otherwise the congregation could not have been established or maintained in these countries. Wherever houses and churches of the congregation exist, the fathers are always ready to preach, to instruct, and to hear the confessions of all persons who may have recourse to them. They also receive into their houses priests or laymen who wish to go through a course of spiritual exercises under their direction.

The principal means, however, employed by the Passionists for the spiritual good of others, is giving missions and retreats, whether to public congregations in towns or country places, or to religious communities, to colleges, seminaries, to the clergy assembled for this purpose, or to particular sodalities or classes of people, and even to non-Catholics, where this can be done, for the purpose of their conversion. In their missions and retreats, in general, they follow the practice of other missioners and accommodate themselves to the exigencies of the locality and of the people; a special feature, however, of their work is that every day they give a meditation or a simple instruction on the Passion of Our Saviour Jesus Christ; in some form or other this subject must invariably be introduced in public missions and private retreats. The Passionists make no particular vow, like that of the Jesuits, to be ready to go on foreign missions among the infidels or wherever the pope may send them, but their Rules enjoin them to be thus ready and at the disposal of the pope or of the Sacred Congregation of Propaganda; and accordingly Passionist bishops and missioners have been engaged in propagating the faith and in watching over the faithful in Rumania and Bulgaria almost since the time of St. Paul of the Cross. At an early period also a few Italian Passionists went to preach the Gospel to the aborigines of Australia, but they had to abandon that mission after many trials and sufferings and the missioners were scattered. Some of them returned to Italy and rejoined their brethren (see Moran, "History of the Catholic Church in Australasia").

In respect to missionary work and labours for the good of souls the Passionists profess to serve everyone, never to refuse their services in any department of Our Lord's Vineyard, whether the place to which they are sent be the meanest and poorest, or the people with whom they have to deal be the most thankless or intractable, and even though they may have to expose their lives by attending to those affected by pestilential diseases.

CHURCH AND MONASTERY OF SS. JOHN AND PAUL, ROME

Growth and Extent. —Before the death of its founder twelve retreats of the institute had been established in different parts of Italy, and between the year of his death (1775) and 1810 several others had been founded, but all in Italy. These were all closed in the general suppression of religious institutes by order of Napoleon. For the Passionists, who had no house outside Italy, this meant total suppression, as the whole of that country was under the tyrant's sway. After the fall of Napoleon and the return of Pius VII to Rome and to his possessions, the religious orders were speedily restored. The first of the orders to attract the pope's attention was the Congregation of the Passion, although it was the smallest of all. They were the first to resume the religious garb and community life in their Retreat of Sts. John and Paul. This event took place on 16 June, 1814. They soon regained their former retreats and new ones were in a short time founded in the Kingdoms of Naples and Sardinia, in Tuscany, and elsewhere.

From the time of the restoration of the congregation under Pius VII it has continued without interruption to increase in numbers and influence. It has branched into many and distant countries outside Italy. At present, retreats of the Congregation exist in England, Scotland, Ireland, Belgium, France (in this country the communities have been disbanded since 1903 by the Republican Government), Spain, United States of America, Argentine Republic, Chile, Mexico, and Australia; and Passionist missioners continue their labours under two Passionist bishops in Bulgaria.

The Anglo-Hibernian Province.—The first foundation in English-speaking countries in the order of time is the Anglo-Hibernian Province of St. Joseph. The Passionists were introduced into England by Father Dominic of the Mother of God (Barberi) who arrived at Oscott College, Birmingham, for this purpose with only one companion, Father Amadeus (7 Oct., 1841). They came in the spirit of Apostles without gold or silver, without scrip or staff or shoes or two coats. They had, however, three ecclesiastical friends who received them kindly and encouraged them in their enterprise by advice and patronage. These were: Dr. Walsh, Bishop of the Midland District; Dr. Wiseman, then his coadjutor bishop; and Father Ignatius Spencer, who joined the congregation in 1847 and laboured as one of its most saintly and devoted sons until his death in 1865. Father Dominic and his companion took possession of Aston Hall, near Stone, Staffordshire, on 17 Feb., 1842, and there established the first community of Passionists in England. At the time of the arrival of the Passionists there were only 560 priests in England and the distressful state of the Church there may be learned from the Catholic Directory of 1840.

The Passionists with Father Dominic at their head soon revived without commotion several Catholic customs and practices which had died out since the Reformation. They were the first to adopt strict community life, to wear their habit in public, to give missions and retreats to the people, and to hold public religious processions. "They gloried in the disgrace of the Cross, were laughed at by Protestants, warned by timid Catholics, but encouraged always by Cardinal Wiseman. Their courage became infectious, so that in a short time almost every order now in England followed their example. There were two or three Fathers of Charity then in England, but they were engaged teaching in colleges until they might become proficient in the language. Father Dominic, after he had given his first mission, wrote to Dr. Gentili and begged him and his companions to start a missionary career. They did so and the memory of their labours is not yet dead" (MS. by Father Pius Devine, 1882). Father Dominic laboured only for seven years in England, during which he founded three houses of the congregation. He died in 1849. For fourteen years after its introduction into England, the progress of the congregation had been slow. In the beginning of 1856 there were only nine native priests and three lay-brothers; the rest, to the number of sixteen or seventeen, were foreigners.

Foundation in Ireland.—It was during this year they secured their first foundation in Ireland, which was the beginning of a new era of progress for the Passionists at home and beyond the seas. Father Vincent Grotti, then acting-provincial, invited and encouraged by Cardinal Cullen, in 1856 purchased the house and property called Mount Argus, near Dublin, where their grand monastery and church now stand. A community was soon formed there. Father Paul Mary (Hon. Reginald Pakenham, son of the Earl of Longford) was the first rector of the retreat, and died there 1 March, 1857. This remarkable scion of a noble house, first an officer in the army, received into the Catholic Church by Cardinal Wiseman at the age of twenty-nine, entered the Congregation of the Passion in 1851, lived for six years an austere and penitential life according to its Rule, and died in the odour of sanctity.

In course of time other houses were founded in England, Ireland, Scotland, and Wales. In 1887 four priests, Fathers Alphonsus O'Neill, Marcellus Wright, Patrick Fagan, Colman Nunan, and Brother Lawrence Carr, at the invitation of Cardinal Moran, went from this province to establish the congregation in Australia. Soon three houses of the institute were founded at Sydney, Goulborn, and Adelaide respectively. All three remain united to the home province. In 1862 a house was founded in Paris (which became afterwards known as St. Joseph's church in the Avenue Hoche) for the benefit of English-speaking Catholics, and it has remained the centre of spiritual ministrations for the purpose for which it was founded to the present time, though secularized in 1903 by the Republican Government.

This province of St. Joseph, including Australia, possesses twelve houses or retreats. It numbers 106 priests, 36 professed students (24 of whom are reading theology), 12 novices, and 27 professed lay-brothers; in all 181 members.

In the United States.—In 1852 Dr. O'Connor, Bishop of Pittsburg, obtained from the general of the Passionists three fathers and a lay-brother to start a branch of the congregation in his diocese. The missionaries were Fathers Anthony, Albinus, and Stanislaus. They were totally ignorant of the English language and, humanly speaking, most unlikely men to succeed in Apostolic labours in America. They were at first housed in the bishop's palace, but a retreat was soon built for them, and these three Passionists soon attracted others to be their companions and, in the space of twenty years, were able to build up a flourishing province. In that period as Father Pius writes; "Five splendid houses of our Congregation graced and beautified the States: a basilica has arisen in Hoboken; Cincinnati, Dunkirk, Baltimore, and Louisville can testify how these poor men increased and multiplied, and how their poor beginnings came to have such splendid results. They have built two extra churches in Pittsburg, and two more in New Jersey. Recently a foundation has been made in the Diocese of Brooklyn at Shelter Island. It will be used as a house of studies for novices and as a summer retreat for the priests. The American Province is more numerous and flourishing than any other in the order at present. Not only have they supplied their own wants, but they have sent offshoots to Mexico, Buenos Ayres, and Chile to be seeds of future provinces which may one day vie with their own" (1882, MS.).

The number of the religious and of the houses of the congregation increased gradually until the province became so extended that the superiors deemed it advisable to form a new province in the States. Accordingly, as a branch from the old and first province, a second was founded, under the title of the Holy Cross, by the authority of the Sacred Congregation of Bishops and Regulars, in 1906. There are therefore at present two Passionist provinces in the United States, namely, the Province of St. Paul of the Cross and that of the Holy Cross. The former comprises 6 retreats, 113 professed priests and students, and 26 lay-brothers; the latter has 5 retreats, 76 priests and students, and 19 lay-brothers.

According to the general catalogue issued in 1905, the whole congregation includes 12 provinces, 94 retreats, and 1387 religious. A retreat of the congregation, dedicated to St. Martha, was founded at Bethany, near Jerusalem, in 1903.

The Congregation of the Passion has never had a regular cardinal protector, as is the case with other religious orders. The sovereign pontiffs have always retained it under their own immediate protection, and have always been ready, according to the spirit and the words of Clement XIV, to assist it by their authority, protection, and favour (letter to the founder, 21 April, 1770), and Pius VII by a special Rescript in 1801 declared the congregation to be under the immediate protection of the pope.

HEIMBUCHER, *Orden u. Kongregationen*, s. v. *Passionisten;* PIUS A SPIRITU SANCTO, *The Life of St. Paul of the Cross* (Dublin, 1868); HÉLYOT-MIGNE, *Dict. des ordres religieux*, IV (Paris, 1859), supplement, 1044 sq.

PASSIONIST NUNS.—In the "Life of St. Paul of the Cross" by Venerable Strambi, we have evidence of his design from the beginning of the Congregation of the Passion to found an institute in which women, consecrated to the service of God, should devote themselves to prayer and meditation on our Lord's Passion. It was not until towards the end of his life that he wrote the rules of the institute which were approved by a Brief of Clement XIV in 1770. St. Paul had as co-operatrix in the foundation of the Passionist nuns, a religious, known as Mother Mary of Jesus Crucified, whose secular name was Faustina Gertrude Costantini. She was born at Corneto, 18 August, 1713. In youth she placed herself under the direction of St. Paul of the Cross, and became a Benedictine in her native city, awaiting the establishment of a Passionist convent. Through the generosity of her relatives, Dominic Costantini, Nicolas his brother, and Lucia his wife, a site was obtained for the first convent of the new institute in Corneto, and a suitable house and chapel were built. On the Feast of the Holy Cross, 1771, Mother Mary of Jesus Crucified, with the permission of Clement XIV, with ten postulants, was clothed in the habit of the Passion and entered the first convent of Passionist nuns, solemnly opened by the vicar capitular of the diocese. St. Paul, detained by illness, was represented by the first consultor general of the order, Father John Mary. Mary of Jesus Crucified became the first mother superior of her order and remained so until her death in 1787. The spirit of the institute and its distinctive character is devotion to the Passion of Christ, to which the sisters bind themselves by vows. Their life is austere, but in no way injurious to health. Postulants seeking admission must have a dowry. Their convents are strictly enclosed. The sisters chant or recite the Divine Office in common and spend the greater part of the day in prayer and other duties of piety. They attend to the domestic work of the convent, and occupy themselves in their cells with needlework, making vestments etc. With the approbation of Pius IX a house was established at Mamers in the Diocese of le Mans, France, in 1872, and continued to flourish until suppressed with other religious communities in 1903 by the Government. There is also a Passionist convent at Lucca whose foundation was predicted by Gemma Galganino, the twentieth-century mystic. On 5 May, 1910, five Passionist nuns from Italy arrived in Pittsburg to make the first foundation of their institute in the United States.

SISTERS OF THE MOST HOLY CROSS AND PASSION.—This second Order of Passionist nuns was founded in England in 1850 when Father Gaudentius, one of the first Passionists who joined Father Dominic in that country, formed a plan of providing a home for factory girls in Lancashire. With the sanction and approbation of Dr. Turner, then Bishop of Salford, and his vicar-general, a house was secured for a convent and home in Manchester in 1851. The first superior was Mother Mary Joseph Paul. The community prospered and rules were drawn up. The sisters took the name of Sisters of the Holy Family and in course of time became aggregated to the Congregation of the Passionists (although immediately subject to the bishop of the diocese) under the name of Sisters of the Most Holy Cross and Passion. The institute under this title and its rules were approved by Pius IX on 2 July, 1876 *per modum experimenti ad decennium* and received its final approbation from Leo XIII, by a Decree dated 21 June, 1887. The institute had its origin chiefly in the lamentable state of female operatives in the large towns of England, who, though constantly exposed to the greatest dangers to faith and morals, had no special guardians or instructors save the clergy. To protect and maintain these women, and, if erring, to help them reform, are the special tasks of the sisters. The Passionist spirit of the institute may be known from their approved rules. "As this congregation is affiliated to and bears the same name as the Congregation of Clerks of the Most Holy Cross and Passion of Jesus Christ . . . let them in a particular manner strive to keep alive in their hearts the memory of Jesus Crucified, and cultivate an ardent and tender devotion to His most holy Passion and Death, so that they may imbibe His spirit, learn His virtues, and faithfully imitate them. Although the Sisters are not bound, as are the above named Clerks, by a special vow, they should, nevertheless, with all eagerness promote the same salutary devotion in the hearts of those whose education they undertake" (Rules, ch. I). The sisters have founded Houses of Refuge and Homes for factory girls; they also teach parochial schools, and have boarding schools for secondary education. They instruct converts and others, visit the sick, and perform all the duties of Sisters of Mercy and Charity. Since their final approbation they have increased rapidly and now have two provinces with 18 convents in England, 3 in Ireland, and 3 in Scotland, 2 training colleges for teachers, and large parochial schools wherever their houses are established, 9 homes for factory girls; the sisters number 430.

A similar Society was established in Chili by the Passionists a few years ago and these are now, by their own request, to be aggregated to the Anglo-Hibernian sisterhood. Another active community of Passionist Sisters was established, and existed in Lourdes until 1903.

A. DEVINE.

Passion Music.—Precisely when, in the development of the liturgy, the history of the Passion of Our Lord ceased, during Holy Week, to be merely read and became a solemn recitation, has not yet been ascertained. As early as the eighth century the deacon of the Mass, in alb, solemnly declaimed, in front of the altar, on a fixed tone, the history of the Passion. The words of our Lord were, however, uttered on the gospel tone, that is, with inflections and cadences. The original simplicity of having the whole allotted to one person gave way in the twelfth century to a division into three parts assigned to three different persons, the priest, or celebrant, the deacon, and the sub-deacon. To the priest were assigned the words of our Lord, the deacon assumed the rôle of the Evangelist, or *chronista*, while the sub-deacon represented the crowd, or *turba*, and the various other persons mentioned in the narrative. The interrelation of the alternating voices, their relative pitch, and the manner of interpreting the part allotted to each have come down to us and may be heard in Holy Week in almost any city church, the only change since the early times being that all three parts are now generally sung by priests. The juxtaposed melodic phrases extend over an ambitus, or compass of the whole of the fifth and two tones of its plagal, or the sixth mode. The evangelist, or *chronista*, moves between the tonic and the dominant, while the *suprema vox*, representing the crowd, etc., moves between the dominant and the upper octave. The tones upon which the words of our Lord are uttered are the lower tetra-chord of the fifth mode with two tones of the sixth. Later the fourth tone of the fifth mode, b, was altered into b flat, to avoid the tritonus between the tonic and the fourth. Throughout the Middle Ages the Passion was the theme most frequently treated in mystery plays and sacred dramas. The indispensable music in these performances was either the plain chant or liturgical melodies or religious folk-songs. It was not until toward the end of the fifteenth century that the whole narrative received harmonic treatment.

Jacobus Hobrecht, or Obrecht (1450–1505), was the first composer, so far as is known, who presented the subject in the form of an extended motet, a departure which laid the foundation for a rich and varied literature of passion music. In Obrecht's composition the three melodic phrases are, in a most ingenious manner, made to serve as *canti fermi*, and, by skilful combining of the various voices and letting them unite, as a rule, only on the utterances of the *turba*, variety is maintained. The work must have become known in a comparatively short time, for it soon found imitators, not only among Catholic composers, of almost every country in Europe, but also at the hands of those in Germany, who joined the Reformation. Besides the choral, or motet, form, of which Obrecht's work has remained the type, another species of setting came into vogue in which the three original chanters were retained, and the chorus participation was mainly confined to the utterances of the *turba*. Both forms were cultivated simultaneously, according to the predilection of the composer, for almost a century and a half. Among the more noted Catholic masters who have left settings of the passion texts must be mentioned Metre Jehan (Jean le Cock, d. before 1543), choir-master at the Court of the Duke of Ferrara, who wrote a work for from two to six voices. Cyprian de Rore (b. 1516), left a setting for two, four, and six voices. Ludovicus Daser (1525-89), Orlandus Lassus's predecessor as choir-master at the ducal Court of Bavaria wrote one for four voices. Lassus himself gave to posterity four different interpretations which are notable for the fact that the master frequently substitutes original melodies for the liturgical ones and sometimes the chorus is employed to give expression to the texts belonging to a single person. The *turba* is always represented by a five part chorus. Probably the most important musical interpretations of this text are the two by Tomas Luis da Vittoria (1540-1613). Vittoria retains the plain-chant melodies for single persons and makes them serve, after the manner of Obrecht, as *canti fermi* in the ensemble. The value of these works is proved by the fact that for more than three hundred years they have formed part of the repertory of the Sistine Chapel choir for Holy Week. Giovanni Matteo Asola (d. 1609), in his three different settings, ignored the traditional custom of employing the chorus for the *turba* only, but used it indiscriminately. The Spanish master, Francisco Guerrero (1527-99), in two works, is quite free in his treatment and replaces the Roman by Mozarabic plain-chant melodies, while William Byrd's creation for soprano, alto, and tenor, still further departs from the accustomed form, not only by limiting his vocal means to the three high voices, but also by substituting for the liturgical melody recitatives of his own invention, all of which gives the composition a character lyric rather than dramatic. Jacobus Gallus, or Jacob Handl (1550-91), wrote three settings, one for four and five voices, one for six, and the third for eight voices in which, in a general way he follows Obrecht's model.

The passion texts seemed to have particular attraction for many of the composers who cast their lot with the Reformation. For a considerable period they adhered in their manner of treatment to the original Catholic model, inasmuch as they used the Latin text and retained the liturgical melodies. Between 1520 and 1550, the Lutheran Johannes Galliculus (Hähnel) produced at Leipzig a work, resembling Obrecht's in many ways, which constitutes the beginning of a long series of works important not only as music, but more particularly on account of the rôle they played in the development of Protestant worship. While Joachimus von Burgk (1540-1610), whose real name was Möller, was the first to discard the Latin text and compose passion music to the German vernacular, it was Johann Walther (1496-1570), Luther's friend, whose four settings, though retaining most of the Catholic form, voiced more than any other works the new spirit. They retained their hold upon German Protestants for more than a hundred years. Bartholomeus Gesius's (1555-1613) two settings, one for five, the other for six voices, are modelled on Obrecht and Galliculus, but Christoforus Demantius (1567-1643) in a six part composition, in addition to adopting the German vernacular, abandons the liturgical for original melodies and shows those chromatic and dramatic elements which find expression with Heinrich Schütz (1585-1672), who, in his epoch-making "Historia der fröhligen und siegreichen Auferstehung unseres Herrn Jesu Christi", for from two to nine voices, abandons the *a cappella* style in which all previous passion music had been written and calls into service stringed instruments and a figured bass to be played on the organ. Johann Sebastiani (1622-83) anticipated Schütz by the employment of a single violin as an accompaniment to the chorales sung by the congregation during the performance, a custom he also originated and which became such a great feature in later Protestant works, but it was Schütz who assigned to the instruments an integral part in the harmonic structure.

With Johann Sebastian Bach (1685-1750) whose monumental work "Passion according to St. Matthew" for soli, eight part chorus, a choir of boys, orchestra, and organ is the creation of a great genius imbued with profound faith, the form reaches its highest development. Only one other similar work by a Protestant writer, Karl Heinrich Graun's (1701-59) "Tod Jesu", has enjoyed as great popularity in Protestant Germany. Schütz's passion music as arranged for performance by Karl Riedel, Bach's "Passion according to St. Matthew", and Graun's "Tod Jesu" continue to be to non-Catholic Germany what Händel's "Messiah" still is to the English-speaking world. While the source resorted to by non-Catholic composers for the last mentioned great works seems to have been exhausted, no similar compositions appearing for more than a century, three Catholics have essayed the form: Joseph Haydn and Théodore Dubois have interpreted "The Seven Last Words on the Cross" and Lorenzo Perosi has set to music the "Passion according to St. Mark", but these compositions partake of the form of the oratorio. Settings in which the utterances of the *turba*, in *falso-bordone* style, alternate with the liturgical melodies are numerous. Among the more noted are those by Caspar Ett (1788-1847), Ignatius Mitterer, Franz Nekes, Emil Nikel, and others.

SPITTA, *Die Passionsmusiken von J. Sebastian Bach und Heinrich Schütz* (Hamburg, 1893); AMBROS, *Gesch. der Musik*, III (Leipzig, 1881); KADE, *Die ältere Passionskomposition bis zum Jahre 1631* (Gütersloh, 1893).

JOSEPH OTTEN.

Passion of Christ, COMMEMORATION OF THE, a feast kept on the Tuesday after Sexagesima. Its object is the devout remembrance and honour of Christ's sufferings for the redemption of mankind. Whilst the feast in honour of the instruments of Christ's Passion —the Holy Cross, Lance, Nails, and Crown of Thorns —called "Arma Christi", originated during the Middle Ages, this commemoration is of more recent origin. It appears for the first time in the Breviary of Meissen (1517) as a *festum simplex* for 15 Nov. The same Breviary has a feast of the Holy Face for 15 Jan., and of the Holy Name for 15 March [Grotefend, "Zeitrechnung" (Hanover, 1892), II, 118 sqq.]. These feasts disappeared with the introduction of Lutheranism. As found in the appendix of the Roman Breviary, it was initiated by St. Paul of the Cross (d. 1775). The Office was composed by Thomas Struzzieri, Bishop of Todi, the faithful associate of St. Paul. This Office and the corresponding feast were approved by Pius VI (1775-99) for the Discalced Clerics of the Holy Cross and the Passion of Christ (commonly called Passionists), founded by St. Paul of the Cross. The feast is celebrated by them as a double of the first class with an octave (Nilles, "Kal. man.", II, 69). At the same time Pius VI approved the other Offices and feasts of the Mysteries of Christ's Passion: the feast of the Prayer of Our Lord in the Garden (Tuesday after Septuagesima); the Crown of Thorns (Friday after Ash-Wednesday); the Holy Lance and Nails (Friday after the first Sunday in Lent); and for the following

Fridays: the feasts of the Holy Winding Sheet, the Five Wounds, and the Precious Blood of Christ (cf. appendix to Roman Brev.). These feasts were, at least in part, readily adopted by many dioceses and religious orders. Most of them are found in the *proprium* of Salerno (a. 1798), as also is the feast of the Passion (a double of the first class with an octave). This latter feast is celebrated with an octave in all the dioceses of the former Kingdom of Naples. On 30 Aug., 1809, the privilege of the feast (double major) was granted to the Diocese of Leghorn for the Friday before Passion Sunday. In the old St. Louis Ordo (1824) it was assigned to Friday after Ash-Wednesday, which day it still retains in the Baltimore Ordo. The seven Offices of the Mysteries of the Passion of Christ were adopted by the City of Rome in 1831 (Corresp. de Rome, 1848, p. 30) and since then all the dioceses that have the feast of the Passion of Christ in their calendar keep it on the Tuesday after Sexagesima. By permission of Leo XIII (8 May, 1884) the octave in the calendar of the Passionists is privileged and admits only feasts of the first and second class. By a decree of 5 July, 1883, the votive Office of the Passion of Christ may be said every Friday which is not taken up by a semi-double or a double Office, except during the period from Passion Sunday to Low Sunday and from 18 December to 13 January. The Office composed by Struzzieri is very rich and full of pious sentiment; the hymns, however, are rather modern.

NILLES, *Kal. man.* (2nd ed., Innsbruck, 1897); *Kirchenlex.*, s. v. *Hymnus;* SCHULTE, *Die Hymnen des Breviers* (2nd ed., Paderborn, 1906).

FREDERICK G. HOLWECK.

Passion Offices.—The recitation of these offices, called also Of the Instruments of the Passion, was first granted collectively to the Congregatio Clericorum Passionis D.N.J.C., or the Passionist Fathers, whose special aim is to spread the devotion to the Sacred Passion of Our Lord. Soon other religious communities and dioceses obtained a similar concession. They were granted to the United States 12 December, 1840, on petition of the Fourth Provincial Council of Baltimore. The offices are affixed to the days specified and cannot be transferred. In case of special indult, as in the United States, they may be transferred, but not beyond Lent; they have the rank of a secondary double major and give place to feasts of higher rank and to primary ones of the same rank. The offices are (1) For Tuesday after Septuagesima: Of the Prayer of Our Lord on Mount Olivet; (2) For Tuesday after Sexagesima: Of the Passion; (3) First Friday of Lent: Of the Crown of Thorns, first celebrated on the occasion of the solemn introduction of the sacred crown into Paris, under Louis IX in 1241 and thence spread into Germany and France (Nilles, II, 95); (4) Second Friday: Of the Spear and Nails, permitted by Innocent VI, 13 February, 1353 for Germany and Bohemia at the request of Charles IV (Nilles, II, 122); granted to some places for Friday after Low Sunday; (5) Third Friday: Of the Winding-sheet, first allowed 1606 to the church of Chambéry in Savoy by Julius II, and soon extended to the entire kingdom (Nilles, II, 126); (6) Fourth Friday: Of the Five Holy Wounds; (7) Fifth Friday: Of the Most Precious Blood. Besides these a special second feast of the Precious Blood was granted to the world for the first Sunday of July by Pius IX, 10 August, 1849. Moreover, by Decree of the Sacred Congregation of Rites of 5 July, 1883, Leo XIII permitted the recitation of a votive Office of the Passion for every Friday not impeded according to rules there laid down. The Greeks have no special offices of the Passion, but on the night between Maundy Thursday and Good Friday they hold a very elaborate series of exercises in its honour.

NILLES, *Kalendarium manuale utriusque ecclesiæ,* II (Innsbruck, 1897); MORONI, *Dizionario* (Venice, 1840-61), XXXVII, 91-2, LXVI, 188-95, LXVIII, 91-2; KERKER in *Kirchenlex.*, s. v. *Dornenkrone;* SCHROD, *ibid.,* s. vv. *Lanze, Sindon.*

FRANCIS MERSHMAN.

Passion of Jesus Christ, DEVOTION TO THE.—The sufferings of Our Lord, which culminated in His death upon the cross, seem to have been conceived of as one inseparable whole from a very early period. Even in the Acts of the Apostles (i, 3) St. Luke speaks of those to whom Christ "shewed himself alive after his passion" (μετὰ τὸ παθεῖν αὐτοῦ). In the Vulgate this has been rendered *post passionem suam*, and not only the Reims Testament but the Anglican Authorized and Revised Versions, as well as the medieval English translation attributed to Wyclif, have retained the word "passion" in English. *Passio* also meets us in the same sense in other early writings (e. g. Tertullian, "Adv. Marcion.", IV, 40) and the word was clearly in common use in the middle of the third century, as in Cyprian, Novatian, and Commodian. The last named writes:

"Hoc Deus hortatur, hoc lex, hoc passio Christi
Ut resurrecturos nos credamus in novo sæclo."

St. Paul declared, and we require no further evidence to convince us that he spoke truly, that Christ crucified was "unto the Jews indeed a stumbling-block, and unto the Gentiles foolishness" (I Cor., i, 23). The shock to Pagan feeling, caused by the ignominy of Christ's Passion and the seeming incompatibility of the Divine nature with a felon's death, seems not to have been without its effect upon the thought of Christians themselves. Hence, no doubt, arose that prolific growth of heretical Gnostic or Docetic sects, which denied the reality of the man Jesus Christ or of His sufferings. Hence also came the tendency in the early Christian centuries to depict the countenance of the Saviour as youthful, fair, and radiant, the very antithesis of the *vir dolorum* familiar to a later age (cf. Weis Libersdorf, "Christus- und Apostel-bilder", 31 sq.) and to dwell by preference not upon His sufferings but upon His works of mercifulness, as in the Good Shepherd motive, or upon His works of power, as in the raising of Lazarus or in the resurrection figured by the history of Jonas.

But while the existence of such a tendency to draw a veil over the physical side of the Passion may readily be admitted, it would be easy to exaggerate the effect produced upon Christian feeling in the early centuries by Pagan ways of thought. Harnack goes too far when he declares that the Death and Passion of Christ were regarded by the majority of the Greeks as too sacred a mystery to be made the subject of contemplation or speculation, and when he declares that the feeling of the early Greek Church is accurately represented in the following passage of Goethe: "We draw a veil over the sufferings of Christ, simply because we revere them so deeply. We hold it to be reprehensible presumption to play, and trifle with, and embellish those profound mysteries in which the Divine depths of suffering lie hidden, never to rest until even the noblest seems mean and tasteless" (Harnack, "History of Dogma", tr., III, 306; cf. J. Reil, "Die frühchristlichen Darstellungen der Kreuzigung Christi", 5). On the other hand, while Harnack speaks with caution and restraint, other more popular writers give themselves to reckless generalizations such as may be illustrated by the following passage from Archdeacon Farrar: "The aspect", he says, "in which the early Christians viewed the cross was that of triumph and exultation, never that of moaning and misery. It was the emblem of victory and of rapture, not of blood or of anguish." (See "The Month", May, 1895, 89.) Of course it is true that down to the fifth century the specimens of Christian art that have been preserved to us in the catacombs and elsewhere, exhibit no traces of any sort of representation of the crucifixion. Even the simple cross is rarely found before the time of Constantine (see CROSS), and when the figure of the Divine Victim comes to be indicated, it at first appears most commonly under some symbolical form, e. g. that of a lamb, and there is no attempt as a rule to represent the crucifixion realistically. Again, the Christian literature which has survived, whether Greek or Latin, does not dwell upon the details of the Passion or very frequently fall back upon the motive of our Saviour's sufferings. The tragedy known as "Christus Patiens", which is printed with the works of St. Gregory Nazianzus and was formerly attributed to him, is almost certainly a work of much later date, probably not earlier than the eleventh century (see Krumbacher, "Byz. Lit.", 746).

In spite of all this it would be rash to infer that the Passion was not a favourite subject of contemplation for Christian ascetics. To begin with, the Apostolical writings preserved in the New Testament are far from leaving the sufferings of Christ in the background as a motive of Christian endeavour; take, for instance, the words of St. Peter (I Pet., ii, 19, 21, 23): "For this is thankworthy, if for conscience towards God, a man endure sorrows, suffering wrongfully"; "For unto this are you called: because Christ also suffered for us, leaving you an example that you should follow his steps"; "Who, when he was reviled, did not revile", etc.; or again: "Christ therefore having suffered in the flesh, be you also armed with the same thought" (ibid., iv, 1). So St. Paul (Gal., ii, 19): "with Christ I am nailed to the cross. And I live, now not I; but Christ liveth in me"; and (ibid., v, 24): "they that are Christ's, have crucified their flesh, with the vices and concupiscences" (cf. Col., i, 24); and perhaps most strikingly of all (Gal., vi, 14): "God forbid that I should glory, save in the cross of our Lord Jesus Christ; by whom the world is crucified to me, and I to the world." Seeing the great influence that the New Testament exercised from a very early period upon the leaders of Christian thought, it is impossible to believe that such passages did not leave their mark upon the devotional practice of the West, though it is easy to discover plausible reasons why this spirit should not have displayed itself more conspicuously in literature. It certainly manifested itself in the devotion of the martyrs who died in imitation of their Master, and in the spirit of martyrdom that characterized the early Church.

Further, we do actually find in such an Apostolic Father as St. Ignatius of Antioch, who, though a Syrian by birth, wrote in Greek and was in touch with Greek culture, a very continuous and practical remembrance of the Passion. After expressing in his letter to the Romans (cc. iv, ix) his desire to be martyred, and by enduring many forms of suffering to prove himself the true disciple of Jesus Christ, the saint continues: "Him I seek who dies on our behalf; Him I desire who rose again for our sake. The pangs of a new birth are upon me. Suffer me to receive the pure light. When I am come thither then shall I be a man. Permit me to be an imitator of the Passion of my God. If any man hath Him within himself, let him understand what I desire, and let him have fellow-feeling with me, for he knoweth the things which straiten me." And again he says in his letter to the Smyrnæans (c. iv): "near to the sword, near to God (i. e. Jesus Christ), in company with wild beasts, in company with God. Only let it be in the name of Jesus Christ. So that we may suffer together with Him" (εἰς τὸ συμπαθεῖν αὐτῷ).

Moreover, taking the Syrian Church in general—and rich as it was in the traditions of Jerusalem it was far from being an uninfluential part of Christendom—we do find a pronounced and even emotional form of devotion to the Passion established at an early period. Already in the second century a fragment preserved to us of St. Melito of Sardis speaks as Father Faber might have spoken in modern times. Apostrophising the people of Israel, he says: "Thou slewest thy Lord and He was lifted up upon a tree and a tablet was fixed up to denote who He was that was put to death— And who was this?—Listen while ye tremble:—He on whose account the earth quaked; He that suspended the earth was hanged up; He that fixed the heavens was fixed with nails; He that supported the earth was supported upon a tree; the Lord was exposed to ignominy with a naked body; God put to death; the King of Israel slain by an Israelitish right hand. Ah! the fresh wickedness of the fresh murder! The Lord was exposed with a naked body, He was not deemed worthy even of covering, but in order that He might not be seen, the lights were turned away, and the day became dark because they were slaying God, who was naked upon the tree" (Cureton, "Spicilegium Syriacum", 55).

No doubt the Syrian and Jewish temperament was an emotional temperament, and the tone of their literature may often remind us of the Celtic. But in any case it is certain that a most realistic presentation of Our Lord's sufferings found favour with the Fathers of the Syrian Church apparently from the beginning. It would be easy to make long quotations of this kind from the works of St. Ephraem, St. Isaac of Antioch, and St. James of Sarugh. Zingerle in the "Theologische Quartalschrift" (1870 and 1871) has collected many of the most striking passages from the last two writers. In all this literature we find a rather turgid Oriental imagination embroidering almost every detail of the history of the Passion. Christ's elevation upon the cross is likened by Isaac of Antioch to the action of the stork, which builds its nest upon the treetops to be safe from the insidious approach of the snake; while the crown of thorns suggests to him a wall with which the safe asylum of that nest is surrounded, protecting all the children of God who are gathered in the nest from the talons of the hawk or other winged foes (Zingerle, ibid., 1870, 108). Moreover St. Ephraem, who wrote in the last quarter of the fourth century, is earlier in date and even more copious and realistic in his minute study of the physical details of the Passion. It is difficult to convey in a short quotation any true impression of the effect produced by the long-sustained note of lamentation, in which the orator and poet follows up his theme. In the Hymns on the Passion (Ephraem, "Syri, Hymni et Sermones," ed. Lamy, I) the writer moves like a devout pilgrim from scene to scene, and from object to object, finding everywhere new motives for tenderness and compassion, while the seven "Sermons for Holy Week" might both for their spirit and treatment have been penned by any medieval mystic. "Glory be to Him, how much he suffered!" is an exclamation which bursts from the preacher's lips from time to time. To illustrate the general tone, the following passage from a description of the scourging must suffice:

"After many vehement outcries against Pilate, the all-mighty One was scourged like the meanest criminal. Surely there must have been commotion and horror at the sight. Let the heavens and earth stand awestruck to behold Him who swayeth the rod of fire, Himself smitten with scourges, to behold Him who spread over the earth the veil of the skies and who set fast the foundations of the mountains, who poised the earth over the waters and sent down the blazing lightning-flash, now beaten by infamous wretches over a stone pillar that His own word had created. They, indeed, stretched out His limbs and outraged Him with mockeries. A man whom He had formed wielded the scourge. He who sustains all creatures with His might submitted His back to their stripes; He who is the Father's right arm yielded His own arms to be extended. The pillar of ignominy was embraced by Him who bears up and sustains the heaven and the earth in all their splendour" (Lamy, I, 511 sq.). The same strain is continued over several pages, and amongst other quaint fancies St. Ephraem remarks: "The very column must have quivered as if it were alive, the cold stone must have felt that the Master was bound to it who had given it its being. The column shuddered knowing that the Lord of all creatures was being scourged". And he adds, as a marvel, witnessed even in his own day, that the "column had contracted with fear beneath the Body of Christ".

In the devotional atmosphere represented by such contemplations as these, it is easy to comprehend the scenes of touching emotion depicted by the pilgrim lady of Galicia who visited Jerusalem (if Dr. Meester's protest may be safely neglected) towards the end of the fourth century. At Gethsemane she describes how "that passage of the Gospel is read where the Lord was apprehended, and when this passage has been read there is such a moaning and groaning of all the people, with weeping, that the groans can be heard almost at the city". While during the three hours' ceremony on Good Friday from midday onwards we are told: "At the several lections and prayers there is such emotion displayed and lamentation of all the people as is wonderful to hear. For there is no one, great or small, who does not weep on that day during those three hours, in a way that cannot be imagined, that the Lord should have suffered such things for us" (Peregrinatio Sylviæ in "Itinera Hierosolymitana", ed. Geyer, 87, 89). It is difficult not to suppose that this example of the manner of honouring Our Saviour's Passion, which was traditional in the very scenes of those sufferings, did not produce a notable impression upon Western Europe. The lady from Galicia, whether we call her Sylvia, Ætheria, or Egeria, was but one of the vast crowd of pilgrims who streamed to Jerusalem from all parts of the world. The tone of St. Jerome (see for instance the letters of Paula and Eustochium to Marcella in A. D. 386; P. L., XXII, 491) is similar, and St. Jerome's words penetrated wherever the Latin language was spoken. An early Christian prayer, reproduced by Wessely (Les plus anciens mon. de Chris., 206), shows the same spirit.

We can hardly doubt that soon after the relics of the True Cross had been carried by devout worshippers into all Christian lands (we know the fact not only from the statement of St. Cyril of Jerusalem himself but also from inscriptions found in North Africa only a little later in date) that some ceremonial analogous to our modern "adoration" of the Cross upon Good Friday was introduced, in imitation of the similar veneration paid to the relic of the True Cross at Jerusalem. It was at this time too that the figure of the Crucified began to be depicted in Christian art, though for many centuries any attempt at a realistic presentment of the sufferings of Christ was almost unknown. Even in Gregory of Tours (De Gloria Mart.) a picture of Christ upon the cross seems to be treated as something of a novelty. Still such hymns as the "Pange lingua gloriosi prælium certaminis", and the "Vexilla regis", both by Venantius Fortunatus (c. 570), clearly mark a growing tendency to dwell upon the Passion as a separate object of contemplation. The more or less dramatic recital of the Passion by three deacons representing the "Chronista", "Christus", and "Synagoga", in the Office of Holy Week probably originated at the same period, and not many centuries later we begin to find the narratives of the Passion in the Four Evangelists copied separately into books of devotion. This, for example, is the case in the ninth-century English collection known as "the Book of Cerne". An eighth-century collection of devotions (MS. Harley 2965) contains pages connected with the incidents of the Passion. In the tenth century the Cursus of the Holy Cross was added to the monastic Office (see Bishop, "Origin of the Prymer", p. xxvii, n.).

Still more striking in its revelation of the developments of devotional imagination is the existence of such a vernacular poem as Cynewulf's "Dream of the Rood", in which the tree of the cross is conceived of as telling its own story. A portion of this Anglo-Saxon poem still stands engraved in runic letters upon the celebrated Ruthwell Cross in Dumfriesshire, Scotland. The italicized lines in the following represent portions of the poem which can still be read upon the stone:

I had power all
his foes to fell,
but yet I stood fast.
Then the young hero prepared himself,
That was Almighty God,
Strong and firm of mood,
he mounted the lofty cross
courageously in the sight of many,
when he willed to redeem mankind.
I trembled when the hero embraced me,
yet dared I not bow down to earth,
fall to the bosom of the ground,
but I was compelled to stand fast,
a cross was I reared,
I raised the powerful King
The lord of the heavens,
I dared not fall down.
They pierced me with dark nails,
on me are the wounds visible.

Still it was not until the time of St. Bernard and St. Francis of Assisi that the full developments of Christian devotion to the Passion were reached. It seems highly probable that this was an indirect result of the preaching of the Crusades, and the consequent awakening of the minds of the faithful to a deeper realization of all the sacred memories represented by Calvary and the Holy Sepulchre. When Jerusalem was recaptured by the Saracens in 1187, worthy Abbot Samson of Bury St. Edmunds was so deeply moved that he put on haircloth and renounced flesh meat from that day forth—and this was not a solitary case, as the enthusiasm evoked by the Crusades conclusively shows.

Under any circumstances it is noteworthy that the first recorded instance of stigmata (if we leave out of account the doubtful case of St. Paul) was that of St. Francis of Assisi. Since his time there have been over 320 similar manifestations which have reasonable claims to be considered genuine (Poulain, "Graces of Interior Prayer", tr., 175). Whether we regard these as being wholly supernatural or partly natural in their origin, the comparative frequency of the phenomenon seems to point to a new attitude of Catholic mysticism in regard to the Passion of Christ, which has only established itself since the beginning of the thirteenth century. The testimony of art points to a similar conclusion. It was only at about this same period that realistic and sometimes extravagantly contorted crucifixes met with any general favour. The people, of course, lagged far behind the mystics and the religious orders, but they followed in their wake; and in the fourteenth and fifteenth centuries we have innumerable illustrations of the adoption by the laity of new practices of piety to honour Our Lord's Passion. One of the most fruitful and practical was that type of spiritual pilgrimage to the Holy Places of Jerusalem, which eventually crystallized into what is now known to us as the "Way of the Cross" (q. v.). The "Seven Falls" and the "Seven Bloodsheddings" of Christ may be regarded as variants of this form of devotion. How truly genuine was the piety evoked in an actual pilgrimage to the Holy Land is made very clear, among other documents, by the narrative of the journeys of the Dominican Felix Fabri at the close of the fifteenth century, and the immense labour taken to obtain exact measurements shows how deeply men's hearts were stirred by even a counterfeit pilgrimage. Equally to this period belong both the popularity of the Little Offices of the Cross and "De Passione", which are found in so many of the Horæ, manuscript and printed, and also the introduction of new Masses in honour of the Passion, such for example as those which are now almost universally celebrated upon the Fridays of Lent. Lastly, an inspection of the prayer-books compiled towards the close of the Middle Ages for the use of the laity, such as the "Horæ Beatæ Mariæ Virginis", the "Hortulus Animæ", the "Paradisus Animæ" etc., shows the existence of an immense number of prayers either connected with incidents in the Passion or addressed to Jesus Christ upon the Cross. The best known of these perhaps were the fifteen prayers attributed to St. Bridget, and described most commonly in English as "the Fifteen O's", from the exclamation with which each began.

In modern times a vast literature, and also a hymnology, has grown up relating directly to the Passion of Christ. Many of the innumerable works produced in the sixteenth, seventeenth, and eighteenth centuries have now been completely forgotten, though some books like the medieval "Life of Christ" by the Carthusian Ludolphus of Saxony, the "Sufferings of Christ" by Father Thomas of Jesus, the Carmelite Guevara's "Mount of Calvary", or "the Passion of Our Lord" by Father de La Palma, S.J., are still read. Though such writers as Justus Lipsius and Father Gretser, S.J., at the end of the sixteenth century, and Dom Calmet, O.S.B., in the eighteenth, did much to illustrate the history of the Passion from historical sources, the general tendency of all devotional literature was to ignore such means of information as were provided by archæology and science, and to turn rather to the revelations of the mystics to supplement the Gospel records.

Amongst these, the Revelations of St. Bridget of Sweden, of Maria Agreda, of Marina de Escobar and, in comparatively recent times, of Anne Catherine Emmerich are the most famous. Within the last fifty years, however, there has been a reaction against this procedure, a reaction due probably to the fact that so many of these revelations plainly contradict each other, for example on the question whether the right or left shoulder of Our Lord was wounded by the weight of the cross, or whether Our Saviour was nailed to the cross standing or lying. In the best modern lives of Our Saviour, such as those of Didon, Fouard, and Le Camus, every use is made of subsidiary sources of information, not neglecting even the Talmud. The work of Père Ollivier, "The Passion" (tr., 1905), follows the same course, but in many widely-read devotional works upon this subject, for example: Faber, "The Foot of the Cross"; Gallwey, "The Watches of the Passion"; Coleridge, "Passiontide" etc.; Groenings, "Hist. of the Passion" (Eng. tr); Belser, D'Gesch. d. Leidens d. Hernn; Grimm, "Leidengeschichte Christi", the writers seem to have judged that historical or critical research was inconsistent with the ascetical purpose of their works.

HERBERT THURSTON.

Passion of Jesus Christ in the Four Gospels.—We have in the Gospels four separate accounts of the Passion of Our Lord, each of which supplements the others, so that only from a careful examination and comparison of all can we arrive at a full and clear knowledge of the whole story. The first three Gospels resemble each other very closely in their general plan, so closely indeed that some sort of literary connexion among them may be assumed; but the fourth Gospel, although the writer was evidently familiar at least with the general tenor of the story told by the other three, gives us an independent narrative.

If we begin by marking in any one of the Synoptic Gospels those verses which occur in substance in both of the other two, and then read these verses continously, we shall find that we have in them a brief but a complete narrative of the whole passion story. There are of course very few details, but all the essentials of the story are there. In St. Mark's Gospel the marked verses will be as follows: xiv, 1, 10–14, 16–18, 21–23, 26, 30, 32, 35–6, 41, 43, 45, 47–9, 53–4, 65 to xv, 2, 9, 11–15, 21–2, 26–7, 31–33, 37–9, 41, 43, 46–7. Verbal alterations would be required to make the verses run consecutively. Sometimes the division will not quite coincide with the verse. It is possible that this nucleus, out of which our present accounts seem to have grown, represents more or less exactly some original and more ancient narrative, whether written or merely oral matters little, compiled in the earliest days at Jerusalem. This original narrative, so far as we can judge from what is common to all the three Synoptics, included the betrayal, the preparation of the Paschal Supper, the Last Supper with a brief account of the institution of the Eucharist, the Agony in the Garden, the arrest and taking of Our Lord before Caiphas, with His examination there and condemnation for blasphemy. Then follow Peter's denials, and the taking of Our Lord before Pilate. Next comes Pilate's question: "Art thou the king of the Jews?" and Our Lord's answer, "Thou sayest it", with Pilate's endeavour to set Him free on account of the feast, frustrated by the demand of the people for Barabbas. After this Pilate weakly yields to their insistence and, having scourged Jesus, hands Him over to be crucified. The story of the Crucifixion itself is a short one. It is confined to the casting of lots for the garments, the accusation over the head, the mocking of the chief priests, the supernatural darkness, and the rending of the Temple veil. After the death we have the confession of the centurion, the begging of the body of Jesus from Pilate, and the burial of it, wrapped in a clean linen cloth, in Joseph's new tomb hewn out in the rock close by.

In order to distinguish what is peculiar to each Evangelist we must notice a remarkable series of additional passages which are found both in St. Matthew and St. Mark. There are no similar coincidences between St. Matthew and St. Luke, or between St. Mark and St. Luke. These passages taken as they occur in St. Mark, are as follows: Mark, xiv, 15, 19–20, 24–28, 31, 33–4, 37–40, 42, 44, 46, 50–2, 55–8, 60–4, xv, 3–8, 10, 16–20, 23–4, 29–30, 34–6, 40, 42. They have the character rather of expansions than of additions. Still some of them are of considerable importance, for instance, the mocking of Our Lord by the soldiers in the Prætorium, and the cry from the Cross, "My God, my God, why hast thou forsaken me?" Possibly this series also formed part of an original narrative omitted by St. Luke, who had a wealth of special information on the Passion. Another explanation would be that St. Mark expanded the original narrative, and that his work was then used by St. Matthew.

The passages found in St. Mark alone are quite unimportant. The story of the young man who fled naked has very generally been felt to be a personal reminiscence. Mark alone speaks of the Temple as "made with hands", and he is also the only one to note that the false witnesses were not in agreement one with another. He mentions also that Simon the Cyrenian was "father of Alexander and of Rufus", no doubt because these names were well known to those for whom he was writing. Lastly, he is the only one who records the fact that Pilate asked for proof of the death of Christ. In St. Matthew's Gospel the peculiarities are more numerous and of a more distinctive character. Naturally in his Gospel, written for a Jewish circle of readers, there is insistence on the position of Jesus as the Christ. There are several fresh episodes possessing distinctive and marked characteristics. They include the washing of Pilate's hands, the dream of Pilate's wife, and the resurrection of the saints after the death of Christ, with the earthquake and the rending of the tombs. The special features by which St. Luke's passion narrative is distinguished are very numerous and important. Just as St. Matthew emphasizes the Messianic character, so St. Luke lays stress on the universal love mani-

THE CRUCIFIXION

FROM THE PASSION PLAY OF OBERAMMERGAU

fested by our Lord, and sets forth the Passion as the great act by which the redemption of mankind was accomplished. He is the only one who records the statement of Pilate that he found no cause in Jesus; and also the examination before Herod. He alone tells us of the angel who came to strengthen Jesus in his agony in the garden, and, if the reading is right, of the drops of blood which mingled with the sweat which trickled down upon the ground. To St. Luke again we owe our knowledge of no less than three of the seven words from the Cross: the prayer for His murderers; the episode of the penitent thief; and the last utterance of all, "Father, into thy hands I commend my spirit". Finally it is St. Luke alone who tells us of the effect produced upon the spectators, who so short a time before had been so full of hatred, and how they returned home "striking their breasts".

The traditional character of the Fourth Gospel as having been written at a later date than the other three, and after they had become part of the religious possession of Christians generally, is entirely borne out by a study of the passion. Although almost all the details of the story are new, and the whole is drawn up on a plan owing nothing to the common basis of the Synoptists, yet a knowledge of what they had written is presupposed throughout, and is almost necessary before this later presentment of the Gospel can be fully understood. Most important events, fully related in the earlier Gospels, are altogether omitted in the Fourth, in a way which would be very perplexing had we not thus the key. For instance, there is no mention of the institution of the Holy Eucharist, the agony in the garden, or the trial and condemnation before Caiphas. On the other hand, we have a great number of facts not contained in the Synoptists. For instance, the eagerness of Pilate to release our Lord and his final yielding only to a definite threat from the Jewish leaders; the presence of our Lady at the foot of the Cross, and Jesus' last charge to her and to St. John. Most important of all perhaps, is the piercing of the side by the soldier's spear, and the flowing forth of blood and water. It is St. John alone, again, who tells us of the order to break the legs of all, and that Jesus Christ's legs were not broken, because he was already dead.

There seems at first sight a discrepancy between the narrative of the Fourth Gospel and that of the Synoptists, namely, as to the exact day of the crucifixion, which involves the question whether the Last Supper was or was not, in the strict sense, the Paschal meal. If we had the Synoptists only we should almost certainly decide that it was, for they speak of preparing the Pasch, and give no hint that the meal which they describe was anything else. But St. John seems to labour to show that the Paschal meal itself was not to be eaten till the next day. He points out that the Jews would not enter the court of Pilate, because they feared pollution which might prevent them from eating the Pasch. He is so clear that we can hardly mistake his meaning, and certain passages in the Synoptists seem really to point in the same direction. Joseph, for instance, was able to buy the linen and the spices for the burial, which would not have been possible on the actual feast-day. Moreover, one passage, which at first sight seems strongest in the other direction, has quite another meaning when the reading is corrected. "With desire I have desired", said Jesus to His Apostles, "to eat this pasch with you, before I suffer. For I say to you, that from this time I will not eat it, till it be fulfilled in the kingdom of God" (Luke, xxii, 15). When the hour for it had fully come He would have been already dead, the type would have passed away, and the Kingdom of God would have already come. ARTHUR S. BARNES.

Passion Plays.—The modern drama does not originate in the ancient, but in the religious plays of the Middle Ages, themselves an outcome of the liturgy of the Church. Ecclesiastical worship was thoroughly dramatic, particularly the Holy Mass, with its progressive action, its dialogue between the priests and their ministers at the altar, or, on feast-days, between the officiating priest and his assistants, with the choir of singers, and the people. Often —e. g. at Christmas, Epiphany, and Easter—the text of the Gospel called for a variety of rôles. The celebration of the feasts was as rich and varied as they were numerous; poetry and music, in particular, helped to impress properly on the laity the full significance of the great events commemorated. The Benedictines of St. Gall, in Switzerland, in the tenth century wrote sequences, hymns, litanies, and tropes and set them to music. The tropes—elaborations of parts of the Liturgy, particularly the Introit, fine musical settings—found universal acceptance and remained in use in various forms until the end of the seventeenth century. These tropes were dramatic in construction and, as their musical settings prove, were sung alternately by two choirs of men and boys, or by two half-choirs. The history of the ecclesiastical drama begins with the trope sung as Introit of the Mass on Easter Sunday. It has come down to us in a St. Gall manuscript dating from the time of the monk Tutilo (tenth century).

The conversation held between the holy women and the angels at the sepulchre of our Lord forms the text of this trope, which is comprised in the four sentences: "Quem quæritis in sepulchro, o christicolæ?—Jesum Nazarenum, o cœlicolæ—Non est hic. Surrexit, sicut prædixerat. Ite nuntiate, quia surrexit de sepulchro.—Resurrexi, postquam factus homo, tua jussa paterna peregi."—The first three sentences are found in many liturgical books dating from the tenth to the eighteenth century. The trope, however, did not develop into a dramatic scene, until it was brought into connexion with the Descent from the Cross, widely commemorated in Continental monasteries, but which appears first in a Ritual of English origin, attributed to St. Dunstan (967). In giving directions for public services, the Ritual refers to this custom, particularly as observed at Fleury-sur-Loire and Ghent. On Good Friday, after the morning services, a crucifix swathed in cloth was laid in a sort of grave arranged near the altar, where it remained until Easter morning. On Easter morning, after the third responsory of the Matins, one or two clerics clothed in albs, and carrying palms in their hands, went to the grave and seated themselves there. Thereupon three other priests vested in copes, and carrying censers representing the three holy women, joined them. Upon their arrival the angel asked them: "Whom seek ye?" The women answered; they hear from the angel the message of the Resurrection and were told to go forth and announce it. Then they intoned the antiphon: "Surrexit enim, sicut dixit dominus. Alleluia". The choir finished Matins with the "Te Deum".

This simplest form of liturgical Easter celebration was elaborated in many ways by the addition of Biblical sentences, hymns, and sequences, in particular the "Victimæ paschali", which dates from the first half of the eleventh century; also by the representation of St. Peter and St. John running to the grave, and by the appearance of the Lord, who thenceforth becomes the central figure. The union of these scenes in one concerted action (the dialogue), rendered in poetic form (hymns, sequences) or in prose (Bible texts), and the participation of a choir gave to the Nuremberg Easter celebration of the thirteenth century the character of a short chanted drama. Such celebrations, however, remained parts of the liturgy as late as the eighteenth century. They were inserted between Matins and Lauds, and served for the instruction of the people, whose hearts and minds were more deeply impressed by reproductions of the Resurrection of the Lord, which appealed to the senses, than by a sermon. The Latin text was no obstacle, since the separate parts of the plays were known or were previously explained. The wide diffusion of these liturgical plays, in which priests took the different parts, is proof of their popularity. Lange, to whom we owe some thorough studies on this subject, proves the existence of 224 Latin Easter dramas, of which 159 were found in Germany, 52 in France, and the rest in Italy, Spain, Holland, and England.

The popular taste for dramatic productions was fed by these Easter celebrations. The clergy emphasized more and more the dramatic moments, often merely hinted at in the rude original celebrations, and added new subjects, among them some of a secular nature. They introduced the characters of Pilate, the Jews, and the soldiers guarding the sepulchre, added the figure of an ointment-vender bargaining with the holy women, and other features which did not contribute to the edification or instruction of the people, though they satisfied their love of novelty and amusement. In this way the early Easter celebrations became real dramatic performances, known as the Easter Plays. Since the element of worldly amusement predominated more and more (a development of which Gerhoh of Reichersberg complained as early as the twelfth century), the ecclesiastical authorities began to prohibit the production of Easter Plays in the churches. It became necessary to separate them from church services, because of their length, which increased greatly, particularly after the introduction of the story of the Passion. Fragments of an Easter Play in Latin dating from the thirteenth century are found in the Benedictbeurn Easter Play, also in that of Klosterneuburg, both of which, probably, go back to the same source as the Mystery of Tours, composed as late as the twelfth century, and which, better than any other, offers an insight into the development of the Easter Plays from the Latin Easter celebrations.

When, in course of time, as shown in the Easter Play of Trier, German translations were added to the original texts as sung and spoken, the popularizing of the Easter Play had begun. That of the monastery of Muri, in Switzerland, belongs to this period, and is written entirely in German. But it was only after the popular element had asserted itself strongly in all departments of poetry, in the fourteenth and fifteenth centuries, that the popular German religious drama was developed. This was brought about chiefly by the strolling players who were certainly responsible for the introduction of the servant, of the ointment-vender (named Rubin), whose duty it was to entertain the people with coarse jests (Wolfenbüttel, Innsbruck, Berlin, Vienna, and Mecklenburg Easter Plays, 1464). The Latin Easter Plays, with their solemn texts, were still produced, as well as the German plays, but gradually, being displaced by the latter, the Latin text was confined to the meagre Biblical element of the plays and the player's directions. The clergy still retained the right to direct these productions, even after the plays reflected the spirit and opinions of the times. Popular poetry, gross and worldly, dominated in the plays, particularly susceptible to the influence of the Carnival plays.

The Easter Plays represented in their day the highest development of the secular drama; nevertheless this most important event in the life of the God-Man did not suffice: the people wished to see His whole life, particularly the story of His Passion. Thus a series of dramas originated, which were called Passion Plays, the sufferings of Jesus being their principal subject. Some of them end with the entombment of Christ; in others the Easter Play was added, in order to show the Saviour in His glory; others again close with the Ascension or with the dispersion of the Apostles. But, since the persecution of the Saviour is intelligible only in the light of His work as teacher, this part of the life of Christ was also added, while some authors of these plays went back to the Old Testament for symbolical scenes, which they added to the Passion Plays as "prefigurations"; or the plays begin with the Creation, the sin of Adam and Eve, and the fall of the Angels. Again two short dramas were inserted: the Lament of Mary and the Mary Magdalene Play. The sequence "Planctus ante nescia", which was brought to Germany from France during the latter half of the twelfth century, is the basis for the Lamentations of Mary. This sequence is merely a monologue of Mary at the foot of the Cross; by the introduction of John, the Saviour, and the bystanders as taking part in the lamentations, a dramatic scene was developed which became a part of almost all Passion Plays and has been retained even in their latest survivor. The Magdalene Play represents the seduction of Mary Magdalene by the devil and her sinful life up to her conversion. In Magdalene's sinfulness the people saw a picture of the depraved condition of mankind after the sin of the Garden, from which it could be redeemed only through the sacrifice of Christ. This profound thought, which could not be effaced even by the coarse reproduction of Magdalene's life, explains the presence of this little drama in the Passion Play.

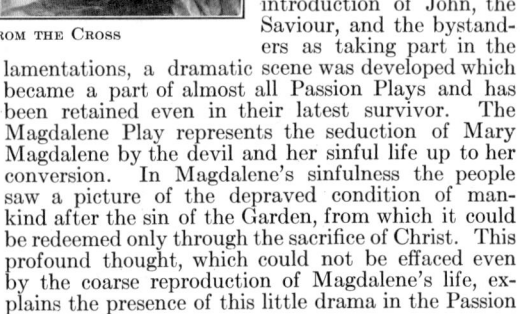

The evolution of the Passion Play was about the same as that of the Easter Play. It originated in the ritual of the Church, which prescribes, among other things, that the Gospel on Good Friday should be sung in parts divided among various persons. Later on, Passion Plays, properly so called, made their appearance, first in Latin, then in German; contents and form were adapted more and more to popular ideas until, in the fifteenth century, the popular religious plays had developed. Thus the Benedictbeurn Passion Play (thirteenth century) is still largely composed of Latin ritual sentences in prose and of church hymns, and, being designed to be sung, resembles an oratorio. Yet even this oldest of the Passion Plays

THE DESCENT FROM THE CROSS

already shows, by the interpolation of free translations of church hymns and of German verses not pertaining to such hymns, as well as by the appearance of the Mother of Jesus and Mary Magdalene in the action, a tendency to break away from the ritual and to adopt a more popular form. From these humble beginnings the Passion Play must have developed very rapidly, since in the fourteenth century we see it at a stage of development which could not have been reached except by repeated practice. From this second period we have the Vienna Passion, the St. Gall Passion, the oldest Frankfort Passion, and the Maestricht Passion. All four Plays, as they are commonly called, are written in rhyme, principally in German. The Vienna Passion embraces the entire history of the Redemption, and begins with the revolt and fall of Lucifer; it is to be regretted that the play as transmitted to us ends with the Last Supper. The oldest Frankfort Passion play, that of Canon Baldemar von Peterwell (1350–80), the production of which required two days, was more profusely elaborated than the other Passion Plays of this period. Of this play only the "Ordo sive Registrum" has come down to us, a long roll of parchment for the use of the director, containing directions and the first words of the dialogues. The plays based on this list of directions lead us to the period in which the Passion Play reached its highest development (1400–1515). During this period the later Frankfort Passion Play (1467), the Alsfelder, and the Friedberger (1514) originated. Connected with this group are the Eger, the Donaueschingen, Augsburg, Freising and Lucerne Passion Plays, in which the whole world drama, beginning with the creation of man and brought down to the coming of the Holy Ghost, is exhibited, and which was produced with great splendour as late as 1583.

Nearly all these Passion Plays have some relation to those coming from the Tyrol, some contributing to, others taking from, that source. These, again, are founded upon the Tyrolese Passion Play which originated during the transition period of the fourteenth to the fifteenth century. Wackernell, with the aid of the plays that have reached us, has reconstructed this period. In the Tyrol the Passion Plays received elaborate cultivation; at Bozen they were presented with great splendour and lasted seven days. Here, too, the innovation of placing the female rôles in the hands of women was introduced, which innovation did not become general until during the seventeenth century. The magnificent productions of the Passion Plays during the fifteenth century are closely connected with the growth and increasing self-confidence of the cities, which found its expression in noble buildings, ecclesiastical and municipal, and in gorgeous public festivals. The artistic sense and the love of art of the citizens had, in co-operation with the clergy, called these plays into being, and the wealth of the citizens provided for magnificent productions of them on the public squares, whither they migrated after expulsion from the churches. The citizens and civil authorities considered it a point of honour to render the production as rich and diversified as possible. Ordinarily the preparations for the play were in the hands of a spiritual brotherhood, the play itself being considered a form of worship. People of the most varied classes took part in the production, and frequently the number of actors was as high as two hundred and even greater. It was undoubtedly no small task to drill the performers, particularly since the stage arrangements were still very primitive.

The stage was a wooden structure, almost as broad as it was long, elevated but slightly above the ground and open on all sides. A house formed the background; a balcony attached to the house represented Heaven. Under the balcony three crosses were erected. Sometimes the stage was divided into three sections by doors. Along the sides of the stage, taken lengthwise, stood the houses required for the production; they were indicated by fenced-in spaces, or by four posts upon which a roof rested. The entrance into hell was pictured by the mouth of a monster, through which the devil and the souls captured or released during the plays passed back and forth. The actors entered in solemn procession, led by musicians or by a *præcursor* (herald), and took their stand at the places appointed them. They remained on the stage all through the performance; they sat on the barriers of their respective divisions, and were permitted to leave their places only to recite their lines. As each actor finished speaking, he returned to his place. The audience stood around the stage or looked on from the windows of neighbouring houses. Occasionally platforms, called "bridges", were erected around the stage in the form of an amphitheatre.

The scenery was as simple as the stage. There were no side scenes, and consequently no stage perspective. Since an illusion of reality could not be had, indications were made to suffice. Thus a cask standing on end represents the mountain on which Christ is tempted by the devil; thunder is imitated by the report of a gun; in order to signify that the devil had entered into him, Judas holds a bird of black plumage before his mouth and makes it flutter. The suicide of Judas is an execution, in which Beelzebub performs the hangman's duty. He precedes the culprit up the ladder, and draws Judas after him by a rope. Judas has a black bird and the intestines of an animal concealed in the front of his clothing, and when Satan tears open the garment the bird flies away, and the intestines fall out, whereupon Judas and his executioner slide down into hell on a rope. A painted picture, representing the soul, is hung from the mouth of each of the two thieves on the cross; the angel takes the soul of the penitent, the devil that of the impenitent thief. Everything is presented in the concrete, just as the imagination of the audience pictures it, and the scenic conditions, resembling those of the antique theatre, demand. All costume, however, is contemporary, historical accuracy being ignored.

The Passion Plays of the fifteenth century, with their peculiar blending of religious, artistic, and popular elements, gave a true picture of German city life of those times. Serious thought and lively humour were highly developed in these plays. When, however, the patricians, in the sixteenth century, withdrew more and more from the plays, these, left to the lower classes, began to lose their serious and (in spite of the comic traits) dignified character. The influence of the Carnival plays (*Fastnachtspiele*) was felt more and more. Master Grobianus with his coarse and obscene jests was even introduced into the Passion Plays. In time the ecclesiastical authorities forbade the production of the plays. Thus the Bishop of Havelberg commanded his clergy, in 1471, to suppress the Passion Plays and legend plays in their parish districts because of the disgraceful and irrelevant farces interspersed through the productions. In a similar manner the Synod of Strasburg (1549) opposed the religious plays, and the year previous (1548), the Parliament of Paris forbade the production of "the Mysteries of the Passion of our Redeemer and other Spiritual Mysteries". One consequence was that the secular plays were separated from the religious, and, as Carnival plays, held the public favour. The Passion Plays came to be presented more rarely, particularly as the Reformation was inimical to them.

School dramas now came into vogue in Catholic and Protestant schools, and frequently enough became the battle-ground of religious controversies. When, in the seventeenth century, the splendidly equipped Jesuit drama arose, the Passion Plays were relegated to out-of-the-way villages and to the monasteries, particularly in Bavaria and Austria. Towards the end of the eighteenth century, during the so-called age of enlightenment, efforts were made in Catholic Germany, particularly in Bavaria and the Tyrol, to destroy even the remnants of the tradition of medieval plays. Public interest in the Passion Play awoke anew during the last decades of the nineteenth century, and since then Brixlegg and Vorderthiersee in the Tyrol, Höritz in southern Bohemia, and above all, Oberammergau in Upper Bavaria attract thousands to their plays. The text of the play of Vorderthiersee (*Gespiel in der Vorderen Thiersee*) dates from the second half of the seventeenth century, is entirely in verse, and comprises in five acts the events recorded in the Gospel, from the Last Supper to the Entombment. A prelude (*Vorgespiel*), on the Good Shepherd, precedes the play. After being repeatedly remodelled, the text received its present classical form from the Austrian Benedictine, P. Weissenhofer. Productions of the play, which came from Bavaria to the Tyrol in the second half of the eighteenth century, were arranged at irregular intervals during the first half of the nineteenth century; since 1855 they have taken place at regular intervals, at Brixlegg every ten years. The Höritz Passion Play, the present text of which is from the pen of Provost Landsteiner, has been produced every five years, since 1893.

The chief survival, however, of former times is the Passion Play of Oberammergau. The first mention we find of it is in 1633, when it is referred to in connexion with a vow made to obtain relief from the Black Death, when the people of Ammergau vowed to produce the play every ten years. As early as 1634 the Passion was enacted (*tragiert*). Since this Passion Play was then well-known, productions must have taken place before that date. The oldest text still in existence was written about 1600 and contains traces of two older dramas, one of which was preserved at St. Ulric, the other at St. Afra, Augsburg. In 1662 a Passion text by the Augsburg Meistersinger, Sebastian Wild, was woven into it, together with parts of the Weilheim Passion Play of Rector Johann Aelbel (c. 1600). About the middle of the eighteenth century the text was revised by the Benedictine Rosner, after the model of the Jesuit drama; in 1780 this bombastic version was again reduced to a simpler form by the Benedictine Knipfelberger. Finally, P. Otmar Weiss and M. Daisenberger gave it its present simple and dignified form, and transcribed the verse into prose. Stage and costuming are adapted to modern requirements. The music is by Rochus Dedler. (See also MIRACLE PLAYS AND MYSTERIES.)

WRIGHT, *English Mysteries* (London, 1838); POLLARD, *English Miracle Plays* (London, 1904); CHAMBERS, *The Mediæval Stage* (Oxford, 1903); TUNISON, *Dramatic Traditions of the Dark Ages* (Cincinnati, 1907); SCHELLING, *Hist. of English Drama* (Boston, 1908); COLLIER, *Hist. of English Dramatic Poetry* (London, 1879); DU MÉRIL, *Theatri liturgici* (Paris, 1849); COUSSEMAKER, *Drames liturgiques du moyen âge* (Rennes, 1860); GRIFFITH, *Origin of Customs of Easter Day* in *Potter's Am. Mag*, X (1878), 306; HAMPSON, *Medii Ævi Kalendarium*(London, 1847); MONE, *Altdeutsche Schauspiele* (Quedlinburg, 1847); IDEM, *Schauspiele des Mittelalters* (Karlsruhe, 1846); DEVRIENT, *Geschichte der deutschen Schauspielkunst*, I (Leipzig, 1848); HOLLAND, *Die Entwicklung des deutschen Schauspieles im Mittelalter und das Ammergauer Passionsspiel* (Munich, 1861); WILKEN, *Geschichte der geistlichen Spiele in Deutschland* (Göttingen, 1872); CALLENBERG, *Das geistliche Schauspiel des Mittelalters in Frankreich* (Mühlhausen, 1875); MILCHSACK, *Die Oster- und Passionsspiele* (Wolfenbüttel, 1880); GAUTIER, *Histoire de la poésie liturgique au moyen âge* (Paris, 1886); LANGE, *Die Lateinischen Osterfeiern* (Munich, 1887); CREIZENACH, *Geschichte des neueren Dramas*, I (Halle, 1893); FRONING, *Das Drama des Mittelalters*, B. d.); WIRTH, *Die Oster- und Passionsspiele bis zum 16 Jahrhundert* (Halle, 1889); WACKERNELL, *Altdeutsche Passionsspiele aus Tirol* (Graz, 1897); WILMOTTE, *Les passions allemands du Rhin dans leurs rapports avec l'ancien théâtre français* (Paris, 1898); TRAUTMANN, *Oberammergau und sein Passionsspiel* (Bamberg, 1890); *Text des Oberammergauer Passionsspieles* (Munich, 1910); HEINZEL, *Abhandlungen zum altdeutschen Drama* (Vienna, 1895); HAUFFEN, *Ueber das Höritzer Passionsspiel* (Prague, 1894); *Text des Höritzer Passionsspieles* (Stuttgart, 1908); *Text des Passionsspieles in Vorderthiersee* (Munich, 1905); WEBER, *Geistliches Schauspiel und christliche Kunst* (Stuttgart, 1894).

ANSELM SALZER.

Passions.—By passions we are to understand here motions of the sensitive appetite in man which tend towards the attainment of some real or apparent good, or the avoidance of some evil. The more intensely the object is desired or abhorred, the more vehement is the passion. St. Paul thus speaks of them: "When we were in the flesh, the passions of sin, which were by the law, did work in our members, to bring forth fruit unto death" (Rom., vii, 5). They are called passions because they cause a transformation of the normal condition of the body and its organs which often appears externally. It may also be noted that there is in man a rational appetite as well as a sensitive appetite. The rational appetite is the will; and its acts of love, joy, and sorrow are only called passions metaphorically, because of their likeness to the acts of the sensitive appetite. They are classified by St. Thomas and the Schoolmen as follows: The sensitive appetite is twofold, concupiscible and irascible, specifically distinct because of their objects. The object of the concupiscible is real or apparent good, and suitable to the sensitive inclination. The object of the irascible appetite is good qualified by some special difficulty in its attainment. The chief passions are eleven in number: Six in the concupiscible appetite—namely, joy or delight, and sadness, desire and aversion or abhorrence, love and hatred—and five in the irascible—hope and despair, courage and fear, and anger.

To explain the passions in their relation to virtue it is necessary to consider them first in the moral order. Some moralists have taught that all passions are good if kept under subjection, and all bad if unrestrained. The truth is that, as regards morality, the passions are indifferent, that is, neither good nor bad in themselves. Only in so far as they are voluntary do they come under the moral law. Their motions may sometimes be antecedent to any act of the will; or they may be so strong as to resist every command of the will. The feelings in connexion with the passions may be lasting, and not always under the control of the will, as for example the feelings of love, sorrow, fear, and anger, as experienced in the sensitive appetite; but they can never be so strong as to force the consent of our free will unless they first run away with our reason.

These involuntary motions of the passions are neither morally good nor morally bad. They become voluntary in two ways: (1) by the command of the will, which can command the inferior powers of the sensitive appetite and excite its emotions; (2) by non-resistance, for the will can resist by refusing its consent to their promptings, and it is bound to resist when their promptings are irrational and inordinate. When voluntary, the passions may increase the intensity of the acts of the will, but they may also lessen their morality by affecting its freedom.

In regard to virtue the passions may be considered in the three stages of the spiritual life: first, its acquisition; secondly, its increase; thirdly, its perfection. When regulated by reason, and subjected to the control of the will, the passions may be considered good and used as means of acquiring and exercising virtue. Christ Himself, in whom there could be no sin nor shadow of imperfection, admitted their influence, for we read that He was sorrowful even unto death (Mark, xiv, 34), that He wept over Jerusalem (Luke, xix, 41), and at the tomb of Lazarus He groaned in the spirit, and troubled Himself (John, xi, 33). St. Paul bids us rejoice with them that rejoice, and weep with them that weep (Rom., xii, 15). The sensitive appetite is given to man by God, and therefore its acts have to be employed in His service. Fear of death, judgment, and hell prompts one to repentance, and to the first efforts in acquiring virtue. Thoughts of the mercy of God produce hope, gratitude, and correspondence. Reflection on the sufferings of Christ moves to sorrow for sin, and to compassion and love for Him in His suffering.

The moral virtues are to regulate the passions and employ them as aids in the progress of spiritual life. A just man at times experiences great joy, great hope and confidence, and other feelings in performing duties of piety, and also great sensible sorrow, as well as sorrow of soul, for his sins, and he is thus confirmed in his justice. He can also merit constantly by restraining and purifying his passions. The saints who have reached the exalted state of perfection, have retained their capacity for all human emotions and their sensibility has remained subject to the ordinary laws; but in them the love of God has controlled the mental images which excite the passions and directed all their emotions to His active service. It has been justly said that the saint dies, and is born again: he dies to an agitated, distracted, and sensual life, by temperance, continency, and austerity, and is born to a new and transformed life. He passes through what St. John calls "the night of the senses", after which his eyes are opened to a clearer light. "The saint will return later on to sensible objects to enjoy them in his own way, but far more intensely than other men" (H. Joly, "Psychology of the Saints", 128). Accordingly we can understand how the passions and the emotions of the sensitive appetite may be directed and devoted to the service of God, and to the acquisition, increase, and perfection of virtue.

All admit that the passions, unless restrained, will carry a man beyond the bounds of duty and honesty, and plunge him into sinful excesses. Unbridled passions cause all the moral ruin and most of the physical and social evils which afflict men. There are two adverse elements in man contending for the mastery, and designated by St. Paul as "the flesh" and "the spirit" (Gal., v, 17). These two are often at variance with each other in inclinations and desires. To establish and preserve harmony in the individual, it is necessary that the spirit rule, and that the flesh be made obedient to it. The spirit must set itself free from the tyranny of the passions in the flesh. It must free itself by the renunciation of all those unlawful things which our lower nature craves, that right order may be established and preserved in the relations of our higher and lower nature. The flesh and its appetites, if allowed, will throw everything into confusion and vitiate our whole nature by sin and its consequences. It is therefore man's duty to control and regulate it by reason and a strong will aided by God's grace.

CRONIN, *The Science of Ethics* (Dublin, 1909); DEVINE, *Manual of Mystical Theology* (London, 1903); JOLY, *Pyschology of the Saints;* MAHER, *Psychology* (London, 1890); ST. JOHN OF THE CROSS, *The Dark Night of the Soul;* SCARAMELLI, *Il Direttorrio Mystico* (Venice, 1765); BILLUART, *Summa Summæ S. Thomæ de Passionibus* (Paris, 1884).

ARTHUR DEVINE.

Passion Sunday, the fifth Sunday of Lent, a Sunday of the first class, not permitting the celebration of any feast, no matter of what rank, but allowing a commemoration of feasts which are not transferred. It is called *Dominica de Passione* in the Roman Missal, and *Dominica Passionis* in the Breviary. Durandus and other liturgical writers speak of it as *Dominica in Passione,* or simply *Passio,* or *Passio Domini.* It is also known as *Judica* Sunday, from the first word of the Introit of Mass; *Isti sunt,* from the beginning of the first response in the Matins; *Octava mediana,* it being the eighth day after *Lætare* Sunday, called sometimes *Mediana,* or Middle of Lent; *Repus,* an abbreviation of *repositus,* i. e. *absconditus,* or hidden from the veiling of the Crosses (Du Cange, "Glossar." s. v. *repositus*). Among the Slavs it is the *Nedéla strastna* (pain, suffering, terrible), *muki* (painful, or sorrowful), *gluha* (deaf or silent), *tiha* (quiet), *smertelna* (relating to death), or also *cerna* (black), which appellation is also found in some parts of Germany as *Schwartzer Sonntag.* Since after this Sunday there are not many more days of the Lenten season the Greek Church admonishes the faithful to special mortifications, and places before them the example of the penitent St. Mary of Egypt.

BUTLER, *Movable Feasts and Fasts* (New York); GUERANGER, *The Liturgical Year, Lent.*

FRANCIS MERSHMAN.

Passiontide, the two weeks between Passion Sunday and Easter. The last week is Holy Week, while the first is called by the Latins "Hebdomas Passionis", by the Greeks "Week of the palms" (from the Sunday following). During this time the monks of the East, who had chosen the desert for a severer mode of life, returned to their monasteries (Cyril of Scythopolis in "Life of St. Euthymius", n. 11). The rubrical prescriptions of the Roman Missal, Breviary, and "Cæremoniale Episcoporum" for this time are: before Vespers of Saturday preceding Passion Sunday the crosses, statues, and pictures of Our Lord and of the saints on the altar and throughout the church, with the sole exception of the crosses and pictures of the Way of the Cross, are to be covered with a violet veil, not translucent, nor in any way ornamented. The crosses remain covered until after the solemn denudation of the principal crucifix on Good Friday. The statues and pictures retain their covering, no matter what feast may occur, until the Gloria in Excelsis of Holy Saturday. According to an answer of the S. R. C. of 14 May, 1878, the practice may be tolerated of keeping the statue of St. Joseph, if outside the sanctuary, uncovered during the month of March, which is dedicated to his honour, even during Passiontide. In the Masses *de tempore* the Psalm Judica is not said; the Gloria Patri is omitted at the Asperges, the Introit, and the Lavabo; only two orations are recited and the Preface is of the Holy Cross. In the Dominical and ferial offices of the Breviary the doxology is omitted in the Invitatorium and in the responses, whether long or short. The crosses are veiled because Christ during this time no longer walked openly among the people, but hid himself. Hence in the papal chapel the veiling formerly took place at the words of the Gospel: "Jesus autem abscondebat se." Another reason is added by Durandus, namely that Christ's divinity was hidden when he arrived at the time of His suffering and death. The images of the saints also are covered because it would seem improper for the servants to appear when the Master himself is hidden (Nilles, "Kal.", II, 188).

In some places the crosses were covered on Ash Wednesday; in others on the first Sunday of Lent. In England it was customary on the first Monday of Lent to cover up all the crucifixes, images of every kind, the reliquaries, and even the cup with the Blessed Sacrament. The cloths used were of white linen or silk and marked with a red cross (Rock, *infra,* IV, 258). The two beautiful hymns of the season, "Vexilla Regis" and "Pange lingua gloriosi", are the work of Venantius Fortunatus (q. v.), Bishop of Poitiers. On the Friday of Passion Week the Church very appropriately honours the Seven Dolours of Our Lady. On Saturday the Greeks commemorate the resuscitation of Lazarus.

ROCK, *The Church of Our Fathers* (London, 1904); NILLES, *Kal. man.* (Innsbruck, 1897).

FRANCIS MERSHMAN.

Passos (or, more fully, SANTOS PASSOS), the Portuguese name locally used to designate certain pious exercises, including representations of the Sacred Passion, practised annually during Lent at Goa and in other Catholic communities in India. The representations of the Passion are made by means of images and figures, although at one period in the past, living beings also took part in them. According to Father

Francisco de Souza, the chronicler of the Society of Jesus in India, their origin was as follows: Father Gaspar Barzeo, S.J., having returned to Goa from his mission to Ormuz in October, 1551, was entrusted with the publication of the first plenary jubilee for India, granted at the request of St. Ignatius and St. Francis Xavier. Father Barzeo preached every day with such good effect that Goa seemed another Ninive converted. In order to keep up this devotion and reformation of manners, Father Barzeo instituted a procession of flagellants, who every Friday assembled in the church, singing the litanies, and listening to a sermon on the words of the Psalmist: "Multa flagella peccatoris". At the end of the sermon there was a period of silence, during which each penitent meditated on his past life. The preacher then spoke for another half-hour on some passage of the Passion of Christ, after which a crucifix was displayed to the people, who shed abundant tears and scourged themselves. From this beginning, the sermons, representations, and processions became a regular custom during Lent. At the close of the Lenten weekly sermon, a representation of some scene from the Passion was displayed on a stage in the church, after which there was a procession.

At first Father Barzeo encountered opposition from the other religious orders, but they afterwards saw the wisdom of following his example. Thus the practice spread through India and the missions in other parts of Asia. In some places these representations are said to have greatly helped forward the work of conversion. But as time went on, many abuses crept in. These abuses were at various times checked by the archbishops and the synods of Goa. At last, after continuing for over two centuries, the processions of flagellants were abolished by Archbishop Francisco d'Assumpçao e Brito, in 1775, penitents being forbidden to scourge themselves. Other subsequent prohibitions were: the taking down of the image from the cross on Palm Sunday; artificial movements of the image in the representations; the carrying of a woman in the procession to represent the Blessed Virgin; Veronica wiping the face of Our Lord; the supper on Maundy Thursday with the figures of the Twelve Apostles; the placing of the Blessed Sacrament in a dark sepulchre on Good Friday; the use, in the scene of the Descent from the Cross, of men wearing long beards, Moorish headgear, etc. to represent Jews; the carrying of the images over flights of steps to represent those of the houses of Caiphas, Pilate, etc.; the sprinkling of red fruit-juice over the images to represent blood; the carrying in the procession of figures of Adam with a hoe or spade, and Eve with a distaff, of the Serpent, of Abraham, Isaac, and others; the representation of the scenes in a temporary structure outside the church.

With the omission of these details, the representations now take place in almost all the churches of Goa, in other parts of India, and in other Asiatic missions. On a stated day (generally Sunday) of each week in Lent, a sermon is preached on some passage of the Passion. A curtain is then raised, and the representation of the same passage is displayed on a movable stage before the high altar, only the image of Christ being shown. The representations are made in the following order: Christ in the Garden of Gethsemani; Christ in prison; the Scourging; the Crowning with Thorns; the Ecce Homo; the Carrying of the Cross; lastly (on Good Friday), the Crucifixion. At the end of each representation there is a procession with singing. On Palm Sunday, the image of Christ carrying the Cross is taken from the stage and borne in procession; and on Good Friday, after the figure is devoutly taken down from the Cross (invariably behind the curtain) it is carried in the procession, the image of the Blessed Virgin also accompanying on both these days. On the last two occasions the procession is always interrupted by a sermon preached from a pulpit erected outside the church.

D'Souza, *Oriente Conquistado;* D'Albuquerque, *Decretos do Arcebispado de Goa; O Oriente Portuguez,* II (1905), nos. 1, 2; *O Anglo-Lusitano* (7 April, 1887).

A. X. D'Souza.

Passover. See Pasch.

Pasteur, Louis, chemist, founder of physio-chemistry, father of bacteriology, inventor of bio-therapeutics; b. at Dole, Jura, France, 27 Dec., 1822; d. near Sèvres, 28 Sept., 1895. His father was a poor tanner who moved to Arbois when his son was but two months old. Pasteur received his early education at the Collège Communal of Arbois, but paid little attention to his books, devoting himself to fishing and sketching. For a time it seemed as though he would become a painter. When science was reached in the course he grew interested. He received his degree at Besançon and then in order to devote himself to science went to Paris to study under Dumas, Balard, and Biot. His father helped him, but he had to support himself partly by his own labours. His first original work was done on crystals. Mitscherlich announced that two tartaric acids, apparently identical in chemical qualities and in crystalline form, acted differently in solution toward polarized light. Refusing to accept this dictum, Pasteur demonstrated that the crystals thought to be similar were different, and explained the seeming inconsistency.

His discovery attracted wide attention. As a result he devoted himself to the study of what he called dissymmetry, pointing out that inorganic substances are not dissymmetrical in their crystallization, while all the products of vegetable and animal life are dissymmetric. He concluded that there was some great biological principle underlying this. As the result of his discovery he was made (1848) professor of physics at the Lycée of Dijon; three months later he became deputy professor of chemistry at the University of Strasburg, and full professor in 1852; in 1854 dean and professor of chemistry at the new University of Lille; in 1856 the English Royal Society conferred on him the Rumford Medal for researches on the polarization of light with hemihedrism of crystals; in 1857 he became director of scientific studies at the Paris Ecole Normal, in 1863 professor of geology and chemistry at the Ecole des Beaux Arts, in 1867 professor of chemistry at the Sorbonne, where he remained till 1889, when he became the Director of the Pasteur Institute, founded in his honour.

His early chemical studies led him to the investigation of fermentation and putrefaction, which he showed were due to living germs of various kinds. From this the demonstration that spontaneous generation does not take place was but a step. He showed that in highly-organized material, if the living germs are all destroyed, and if further access of germs be prevented, even though air may be allowed free access, fermentation or putrefaction does not take place. A piece of cotton wool, or a mere bending of the neck of the flask to keep germs from entering, is sufficient after sterilization to keep organic solutions quite sterile. The study of fermentations led Pasteur to studies in vinegar, wine, and beer. As the result of his successful investigation of ferments he was asked by the Empress Eugénie whether he would not now devote himself to the organization of great manufacturing industries for the benefit of France. He replied that he considered it quite beneath the dignity of a scientist to give up his time to commerce, and while he was willing that others should take advantage of his discoveries he wanted to push on to further scientific work.

This was a fortunate decision. His successful investigations led the French Government to appeal to him to study the silk-worm disease. This had produced such ravages in the silk industry in France that the end of it seemed not far off. Many expedients and

LOUIS PASTEUR IN HIS LABORATORY
PAINTING BY A. EDELFELT

supposed remedies had been tried. Fresh silk-worms had been brought from China on a number of occasions, but they succumbed to the disease, or their progeny became affected by it. Nothing availed and the case seemed hopeless. Pasteur found the silkworm had been suffering from two diseases, *pebrine* and *flacherie*, and that the spread of these diseases could be prevented by careful segregation of healthy worms from those diseased. The announcement seemed too good to be true and was scouted. Pasteur demonstrated its absolute truth and his practical ability by taking charge of the villa of the French Prince Imperial, where the silk industry had been ruined. At the end of the year the sale of cocoons gave a net profit of 26,000,000 francs (over $5,000,000).

Naturally Pasteur proceeded to the study of diseases of animals and human beings. He demonstrated the bacterial cause of anthrax, which had made serious ravages among cattle in France. The organism was distributed by contact, real contagion. Earthworms, he showed, carry it up from the bodies of animals buried in shallow graves to infect grazing animals. He found further that he could by heat reduce the vitality of the anthrax microbe, so that it produced but a mild form of the disease which would protect cattle against the fatal form. Then he discovered the cause of fowl cholera. He cultivated it artificially and after a time his cultures would not produce the disease in fowl, though it served to protect them against injections of virulent cultures which would kill "control" fowl. The discoveries of vaccinating viruses for these two diseases saved France millions of dollars every year.

Pasteur proceeded with the development of bacteriology and its relation to disease. Having studied many cases of child-bed fever at the hospitals, he declared before a medical society that he had seen its cause, and challenged he drew a picture resembling a rosary of what we now know as a streptococcus, or chain coccus. He discovered other coccus (berry) forms of pathological microbes, some of them arranged in bunches like grapes, thence called staphylococci. Finally came his work on rabies. Unable to find the cause of the disease, which has not yet been discovered, he succeeded in making from the dessicated spinal cords of animals dead from the disease a vaccinating virus, which protects human beings bitten by a rabid animal against the development of rabies. This treatment met with great opposition. The Germans talked sneeringly of "a remedy of which we know nothing for a disease of which we know less". With time Pasteur's vindication came. The Russians, who suffered severely from rabies, from the bites of mad wolves on the steppes, found it of great service, and the tsar honoured Pasteur by a personal visit. Next the British in India found it wonder-working. Other countries adopted it. Finally the German Government established Pasteur Institutes, and acclaimed the discovery.

Many honours came to Pasteur. Besides the Rumford and Copley Medals (1856–1874), in 1868 the Austrian Government gave him a prize of 10,000 francs for his work on silk-worms; in 1873 the French Société d'Encouragement, a prize of 12,000 francs; the Russian Society of Rural Economy, a medal (1882); the Albert medal (1882); the Bressa Prize, 5000 francs (Turin Academy, 1888); the French Government, an annual pension of 12,000 francs (1874), increased in 1883 to 25,000 francs, and besides all the degrees of the Legion of Honour orders were conferred on him by Russia, Denmark, Greece, Brazil, Sweden, Turkey, Norway, and Portugal. Oxford gave him a D.C.L., Bonn, an honorary M.D., the English Royal Society, foreign membership, and the French Academy, its membership (1881). He was made Perpetual Secretary of the Academy of Sciences in 1887. There was a magnificent celebration of his jubilee on his seventieth birthday, 27 Dec., 1892, to which contributions were sent from every civilized country and all the great institutions of learning.

Pasteur's faith was as genuine as his science. In his panegyric of Littré, whose *fauteuil* he took, he said: "Happy the man who bears within him a divinity, an ideal of beauty and obeys it; an ideal of art, an ideal of science, an ideal of country, an ideal of the virtues of the Gospel". These words are graven above his tomb in the Institut Pasteur. In his address Pasteur said further "These are the living springs of great thoughts and great actions. Everything grows clear in the reflections from the Infinite". Some of his letters to his children breathe profound simple piety. He declared "The more I know, the more nearly is my faith that of the Breton peasant. Could I but know all I would have the faith of a Breton peasant woman." What he could not above all understand is the failure of scientists to recognize the demonstration of the existence of the Creator that there is in the world around us. He died with his rosary in his hand, after listening to the Life of St. Vincent de Paul which he had asked to have read to him, because he thought that his work like that of St. Vincent would do much to save suffering children.

Pasteur's principal works are: "Etudes sur le Vin", (1866); "Etudes sur le Vinaigre" (1868); "Etudes sur la Maladie des Vers à Soie" (2 vols., 1870); "Quelques Réflexions sur la Science en France" (1871); "Etudes sur la Bière" (1876); "Les Microbes organisés, leur rôle dans la Fermentation, la Putréfaction et la Contagion" (1878); "Discours de Réception de M. L. Pasteur à l'Académie Française" (1882); "Traitement de la Rage" (1886).

VALLERY-RADOT, *Life of Pasteur* (tr. New York, 1902); DUCLAUX, *Pasteur: Histoire d'un esprit* (Paris, 1896); VIRCHOW, *Berl. Klin. Wochenschr.* (1895), 947; FRANKLAND, *Pasteur* (New York, 1900); HERTER, *Influence of Pasteur on Medical Science* (New York, 1904); *Jubilé de M. Pasteur (1822–1892)*, (Paris, 1893); WALSH, *Makers of Modern Medicine* (New York, 1907).

JAMES J. WALSH.

Pasto, DIOCESE OF (PASTENSIS, PASTOPOLITANA), a Colombian see, suffragan of Popayán, from which it was separated by the Bull of Pius IX, "In excelsa militantibus ecclesia", 10 April, 1859. Situated in the State of Cauca, it is bounded on the north by the Dioceses of Garzon and Popayán, and on the south by the Vicariate Apostolic of Napo, Ecuador. The present bishop, Mgr Adolfo Perea, b. 1853 in the Diocese of Popayán, elected 16 December, 1907, succeeded Mgr Ezequiel Moreno, O.S.A. (b. at Alfaro, Tarazona, 9 April, 1838, made titular Bishop of Pinara, 23 October, 1893, transferred to Pasto, 2 December, 1893). The diocese contains 315,640 Catholics, 41,000 pagan Indians, 68 parishes, 90 secular and 23 regular priests, 133 churches or chapels. The town of Pasto, containing about 12,000 inhabitants, is well built and is a busy trade centre between Colombia and Ecuador. It is situated at the eastern base of the volcano La Galera at an altitude of 8650 feet. Founded in 1539, it was captured by Bolivar during the War of Independence in 1822, and suffered severely from an earthquake in 1834. It contains many churches, a seminary, a Jesuit college, and an hospital under the care of the Sisters of Charity. On 23 December, 1904, the Prefecture Apostolic of Caquetá (q. v.) was separated from Pasto.

GROOT, *Hist. eclesiástica y civil de Nueva Granada* (1869); CIEZA DE LEÓN, *Crónica del Perú*, I (Antwerp, 1554); PETRE, *The Republic of Colombia* (London, 1906).

A. A. MACERLEAN.

Pastor.—This term denotes a priest who has the cure of souls (*cura animarum*), that is, who is bound in virtue of his office to promote the spiritual welfare of the faithful by preaching, administering the sacraments, and exercising certain powers of external government, e. g., the right of supervision, giving precepts, imposing light corrections—powers rather paternal in their nature, and differing from those of a bishop, which are legislative, judicial, and coactive. A pastor is properly called a parish-priest (*parochus*) when he exercises the cure of souls in his own name with regard to a determined number of subjects, who are obliged to apply to him for the reception of certain sacraments specified in the law. In this article "parish-priest" is always taken in this strict sense. Pastors (whether parish-priests or not) are either irremovable (*inamovibiles*) or movable (*amovibiles ad nutum*). An irremovable pastor or rector is one whose office gives him the right of perpetuity of tenure; that is, he cannot be removed or transferred except for a canonical reason, viz., a reason laid down in the law, and, in the case of a criminal charge, only after trial. (See IRREMOVABILITY.) A movable pastor or rector is one whose office does not give him this right; but the bishop must have some just and proportionate reason for dismissing or transferring him against his will, and, should the priest believe himself wronged in the matter, he may have recourse to the Holy See, or to its representative where there is one having power in such cases. Moreover, according to some canonists, even movable pastors in case of a criminal charge cannot be absolutely removed from their office without a trial (cf. Pierantonelli, "Praxis Fori Ecclesiastici," tit. iv; Smith, "Elements of Ecclesiastical Law", n. 418.) This, certainly, is the case in the United States of America (Decrees of Propaganda, 28 March, and 20 May, 1887).

The Council of Trent (Sess. XXIV, cap. xiii, de Ref.) shows it to be the mind of the Church that dioceses should, wherever it is possible, be divided into canonical parishes (see PARISH), to be governed by irremovable parish-priests. In places, therefore, where the Tridentine law cannot be fully carried out, bishops adopt measures which fulfil this requirement as nearly as circumstances allow. One such measure was the erection of quasi-parishes, districts with defined limits, ordered for the United States in 1868 (Second Plenary Council of Baltimore, n. 124). Another such was the institution of irremovable rectors (pastors with the right of perpetuity of tenure), ordered for England in 1852 (First Provincial Council of Westminster, Decr. xiii), and for the United States in 1886 (Third Plenary Council of Baltimore, n. 33).

The power to appoint pastors is ordinarily vested in the bishop. Among the candidates possessed of the necessary qualifications the appointment should fall on the one who is best fitted for the office. Moreover, according to the Council of Trent (Sess. XXIV, cap. xviii, de Ref) candidates for the office of parish-priest should (a few cases excepted) pass a competitive examination (*concursus*). This provision of the Council of Trent is sometimes by particular enactments applied in the selection of candidates for the office of irremovable rectors, as happens in the United States (Third Plenary Council of Baltimore, tit. ii, cap. vi).

With regard to the faculties and powers of pastors, those of parish-priests are sufficiently defined by the law, and hence are ordinary, not delegated. Of these faculties some are called rights strictly parochial, because in a parish they belong exclusively to the parish-priest, so that their subjects cannot with regard to them have recourse to another priest, except with his or the bishop's consent. These rights are the following: the right of administering baptism, holy viaticum, and extreme unction in all cases where there is no urgent necessity; the right of administering paschal communion, of proclaiming the banns of marriage, and of blessing marriages. To the parish-priest are also reserved the celebration of funerals (except in certain cases specified in the law), and the imparting of certain blessings, the chief one being blessing of the baptismal font. To pastors, who are not parish-priests, the right of assisting at marriages is given by the law as to parish-priests. The other rights usually are granted to them by the bishops and are defined in the particular laws; such is very commonly the case in the United States, England, and Scotland, with regard to baptism, holy viaticum, extreme unction, and funerals. Mention should be made here of the custom which exists in certain dioceses of the United States, whereby the faithful of one district are permitted to receive such sacraments from the pastor of another district if they rent a pew in his church (Second Plenary Council of Baltimore, nn. 117, 124, 227, and the statutes of several diocesan synods). Rights not strictly parochial are those which belong by law to parish-priests, but not exclusively. Such are the faculties of preaching, celebrating Mass, low or solemn, hearing confessions, administering Holy Communion. Pastors who are not parish-priests receive these faculties from their bishop.

Pastors are naturally entitled to a salary. This is furnished by the revenues of the parochial benefice, should there be one; otherwise, it is taken from the revenues of the church or from the offerings. Such offerings as the faithful contribute of their own accord, without specifying the purpose of their donation, belong to the pastor. This assertion is based on the presumption that these gifts are meant to show the gratitude of the faithful towards the priests who spend their lives in caring for the souls committed to their charge. This presumption, however, ceases wherever custom or law provides that at least a certain portion of these offerings should belong to the church. This is generally the case where churches, not possessing other sources of income, depend entirely on the offerings. An illustration of such laws is to be found in the eighth decree of the Second Provincial Council of Westminster, approved by Leo XIII in the Constitution "Romanos Pontifices" of 8 May, 1881. Accordingly, in countries where this is in force, the usual collections taken up in the churches belong to each mission, in addition to the pew-rents, and it is from these revenues that the salaries of pastors and assistants are ordinarily drawn.

Pastors, besides having rights, have also obligations. They must preach and take care of the religious instruction of the faithful, especially of the young, supply their spiritual needs by the administration of the sacraments, reside in their parish or mission, administer diligently the property entrusted to their care, watch over the moral conduct of their parishioners, and remove, as far as possible, all hindrances to their salvation. Moreover, parish-priests must make a profession of faith and take the oath prescribed by Pius X in his "Motu Proprio", 1 Sept., 1910; they must also offer the Holy Sacrifice on behalf of their flock on Sundays and certain holydays set down in the law. When the number of the faithful entrusted to the care of the pastor is so large that he alone cannot fulfil all the duties incumbent on his office, the bishop has the right to order him to take as many priests to help him as may be necessary. These are called assistants or auxiliary priests, and differ both from coadjutors who are given to pastors for other reasons determined by the law, and from administrators who take charge of a parish during its vacancy, or the absence of its pastor.

Positive law (Council of Trent, Sess. XXI, cap. iv, de Ref.), modified in some countries by custom, reserves to the parish-priest the right to choose his assistants, a choice, however, which is subject to the approval of the bishop, and it is also from the bishop that assistants receive their faculties. The amount of their salary is likewise to be determined by the bishop, and, as to its source, the same rules hold as those already mentioned with regard to pastors. As to their removal, (a) when their nomination belongs by law to the parish-priest, they can be removed either by him or by the bishop, (b) when their nomination belongs to the bishop, he alone can remove them; in any case a reasonable cause is necessary, at least for the lawfulness of the act, and the assistant who believes that he has been wronged may have recourse to higher authorities, as mentioned above with regard to movable pastors. Their office, however, does not cease with the death of the priest or bishop who appointed them, unless this was clearly expressed in the letters of appointment. For the recent legislation regarding the removal of parish-priests, see PARISH, section II, 2.

BAART, *Legal Formulary* (4th ed., New York), nn. 86–113; BOUIX, *De Parocho* (3rd ed., Paris, 1889); FERRARIS, *Bibliotheca Canonica etc.* (Rome, 1885–99); NARDI, *Dei Parrochi* (Pesaro, 1829–60); SANTI, *Prælectiones juris canonici* (New York, 1905); SCHERER, *Handbuch des Kirchenrechts* (Graz, 1886), xcii-iii; SMITH, *Elements of Ecclesiastical Law*, I (9th ed., New York, 1893), nn. 639–70; WERNZ, *Jus Decretalium* (Rome, 1899), tit. xxxix; RAYMUNDI ANTONII EPISCOPI, *Instructio Pastoralis* (5th ed., Freiburg, 1902); AICHNER, *Compendium juris eccl.* (6th ed., Brixen, 1887), 426–41; CRONIN, *The New Matrimonial Legislation* (Rome, 1908).

HECTOR PAPI.

Pastoral Letters. See LETTERS, ECCLESIASTICAL.

Pastoral Staff. See CROSIER.

Pastoral Theology. See THEOLOGY.

Pastoureaux, CRUSADE OF THE, one of the most curious of the popular movements inspired by a desire to deliver the Holy Land. St. Louis, King of France, had gone on the Crusade (1248), leaving the regency to his mother, Blanche of Castile. Defeated at the battle of Mansourah (8 Feb., 1250) and taken prisoner, he regained his freedom by surrendering Damietta, embarked for Saint-Jean d'Acre, and sent his brothers to France to obtain relief. But Blanche of Castile endeavoured in vain to send him reinforcements, neither nobles nor clergy showing good will in this respect. At this juncture the shepherds and labourers rose up, announcing that they would go to the king's rescue. About Easter (16 April), 1251, a mysterious person whose real name is unknown but who was soon called the "Master of Hungary", began to preach the Crusade in the name of the Blessed Virgin to the shepherds in the north of France. He was sixty years of age and aroused wonder by his long beard, his thin face, and his always-closed hand, which held, it was said, the map given to him by the Blessed Virgin. He drew crowds by his eloquence, and distributed the Cross among them without authorization from the Church.

The movement spread rapidly—from Picardy to Flanders, then to Brabant, Hainault, Lorraine, and Burgundy. Soon an army of 30,000 men was formed, carrying a banner on which was depicted the Blessed Virgin appearing to the Master of Hungary. The movement was equally successful in the towns, and the citizens of Amiens furnished provisions to the army. However the Pastoureaux soon showed themselves hostile to the clergy, especially to the Friars Preachers, whom they accused of having induced St. Louis to go to Palestine. Moreover, a host of idlers, robbers, cut-throats, and fallen women joined their ranks, and thenceforth with growing audacity they slew clerics and preached against the bishops and even the pope. Blanche of Castile seems to have imagined that she could send the Pastoureaux to the relief of St. Louis, and summoning the master to her she questioned him and dismissed him with gifts.

Emboldened by this reception the Pastoureaux entered Paris, and the grand-master, wearing a mitre, preached from the pulpit of St. Eustache. Clerics and monks were hunted, slain, and thrown into the Seine, the Bishop of Paris was insulted, and the University of Paris was compelled in its own defence to close the Petit-Pont between the Cité and the left bank of the Seine. The Pastoureaux then left Paris and divided into several armies which spread terror everywhere. At Rouen the archbishop and his clergy were expelled from the cathedral (4 June, 1251). At Orléans a large number of university clerics were killed and thrown into the Loire (11 June). At Tours the Pastoureaux took by storm the convent of the Dominicans and desecrated the churches. The credulous populace regarded them as saints and brought them the sick to be cured. At last Blanche of Castile realized that she had been mistaken and commanded the royal officers to arrest and destroy them. When they reached Bourges the clerics and priests had fled, whereupon they seized the possessions of the Jews, sacked the synagogues, and pillaged the city. An attempt was made to imprison them, but they broke down the gates. A troop of citizens pursued and halted them near Villeneuve-sur-Cher. The Master of Hungary was slain, together with a large number of his followers. Some reached the valley of the Rhône and even Marseilles; others went to Bordeaux, whence they were driven by Simon de Montfort, Earl of Leicester and Governor of Guienne in the name of the King of England, who caused their leader to be thrown into the Gironde.

Another leader went to England and assembled some shepherds who, learning that the Pastoureaux were excommunicated, killed him. Henry II ordered the Lord Warden of the Cinque Ports to take measures to prevent their invasion of his kingdom. Some of them submitted, and after having received the Cross at the hands of clerics set out for the Holy Land. Ecclesiastical chroniclers assert that the Pastoureaux had concluded with the sultan a secret treaty to subject Christianity to Mohammedanism. "It is said that they have resolved first to exterminate the clergy from the face of the earth, then to suppress the religious, and finally to fall upon the knights and nobles in order that the country thus deprived of defence may more easily be delivered up to the errors and incursions of the pagans" (Letter from the Guardian of the Paris Friars Minor to his brethren at Oxford; Chartularium Univ. Parisiensis, Paris, 1889, I, 225). This is obviously a fable, but as a matter of fact this popular movement, sincere and somewhat mystical in origin, soon acquired an anarchistic character.

The same is true of the second movement of the Pastoureaux in 1320 during the reign of Philip V. In the north of France a suspended priest and unfrocked monk preached the Crusade to a band of peasants, thundering against the indifference of the king and the nobles with regard to the deliverance of Palestine. As in 1251, the ignorant mystics were soon joined by ruffians of every description whose object was to profit by their simplicity. Clad in rags and armed with sticks and knives they marched on Paris, liberated the prisoners in the Châtelet, and defied the king, who merely intrenched himself in the palace of the Cité and in the Louvre. From Paris they went to Berry, thence to Saintonge and Aquitaine to the number of 40,000, pillaging as they went. At Verdun-sur-Garonne five hundred Jews imprisoned in a dungeon strangled one another so as not to fall into their hands. They were often aided by the people of the cities and even the middle-class citizens applauded the massacre of the Jews. In reply to the papal excommunication they marched to Avignon, and then resolved to embark like St. Louis at Aigues-Moretes. But the Seneschal of Carcassonne assembled his men at arms, closed the gates of the city against them, and drove them into the neighbouring marshes, where hunger dispersed them. The soldiers then organized hunting parties which resulted in the hanging of thousands of the Pastoureaux, but for a long time a number of their bands continued to lay waste the south of France.

Chroniques de St. Denis in *Hist. de Fr.*, XXI, 115 sq.; BERGER, *Hist. de Blanche de Castille* (Paris, 1895), 392–402; BEMONT, *Simon de Montfort, Comte de Leicester* (Paris, 1884); RÖHRICHT, *Die Pastorellen* in *Zeit. für Kirchengesch.* (1884), 290–96; VIDAL, *L'émeute des Pastoureaux en 1320* in *Annales de St. Louis des Français* (1899), 121–74; LEHUGUEUR, *Hist. de Philippe le Long* (Paris, 1897), 417–21.

LOUIS BRÉHIER.

Patagonia is the name given to the southernmost extremity of South America. Its boundary on the north is about 44° S. lat., and on the south the Straits of Magellan. On the west it extends to the Cordilleras and Chile, and on the east to the South Atlantic. It has an area of about 300,000 square miles. It was discovered by Magellan in 1520, although as early as 1428 a map of the world described by Antonio Galvao showed the Straits of Magellan under the title of the Dragon's Tail. Magellan is supposed to have called the inhabitants "Patagoas" on account of the largeness of their feet. To this day they wear coltskin shoes which project far beyond their toes, which accounts for their size and his mistake.

The surface of the country is very varied. Trackless *pampas* (plains) rise in gently graduated terraces to the lofty ranges of the Andes, between which there is a mighty network of rivers and lagoons. From the south to the Sierra Nevada stretch these pampas in ever-rolling waves of tussock grass, thorn bushes, guanacos, and mirages. On the western rim the Cordilleras rise against the sky, holding in their jagged bosoms glaciers and icy blue lakes. On the flanks of these mountains are to be found thousands of square miles of shaggy, primeval forests, only the bare edges of which have up to the present been explored. On the eastern coast the Chubut, the Deseado, the Southern Chico (which joins the Santa Cruz in a wide estuary before emptying its waters into the South Atlantic), and the Gallegos, are the only really important rivers. In general it may be said that the eastern part of Patagonia is level and treeless, with few bays, whilst the west, really the Chilian seaboard, is everywhere pierced with fiords, and has many headlands covered with dark, thick forests, jutting out into the sea.

The climate in the north of Patagonia is not so severe as in the south. Very little ice is seen there, except in the mountains, and snow seldom remains long on the ground. In the south it is very cold, the ground being covered with snow in winter, and the lakes and rivers choked with ice. For at least six months in the year there are strong gales of wind, and rain is prevalent all over the country. In the south there is practically no summer, whilst in the north there is a mild season which lasts for several months.

The principal settlements are: Gallegos, 3000 inhabitants, on the Gallegos River; Punta Arenas, 11,000 inhabitants; and the smaller Welsh ones at Trelew, Rawson, Gaimon Colhaupi near Lake Musters, and Chubut. The original inhabitants are all descended from the Araucanian race. They are mostly tall and muscular, averaging at least six feet, and are splendidly developed. In the interior are to be found the Pampas Indians and the tribes of the Tehuelches. The latter are very lazy, and amongst those whom the missionaries have not yet evangelized; it is said that wives are still bought and sold. There is the tribe of the Alacalufe in the south, and the warlike Onas who inhabit Tierra del Fuego. The natives are nomadic in their habits, and live principally on the products of the chase. They hunt the pampa fox, the ostrich (*rhea Darwini*), the guanaco or wild llama, and the puma. Some of the tribes, however, are not sufficiently civilized to understand the use of the bow and arrow. They live in *toldos*, or tents made of raw hide. Agriculture is unknown among them. They are ruled by military governors from Chili or Argentina, according to the territory in which they live. These governors reside in the larger settlements, such as Punta Arenas, Gallegos, and Chubut. They are each at the head of a small military force, to be used if necessary in punitive expeditions.

Their religion is the crudest form of Dualism. They believe in a bad spirit called Gualicho, and in an inferior good spirit. The latter is much neglected, whilst the former, with his attendant devils, requires a great deal of propitiation. Their notion of Heaven is a very elementary one, and consists in a kind of happy hunting ground. Their language is guttural and harsh. It is very deficient in words, one sound having frequently to do duty for a large number of ideas. Owing, however, to their intercourse with the whites, many of them have acquired a sufficient knowledge of Spanish to make themselves understood. Ancient remains have been discovered in the country, at about 44° S. lat. Skulls and flint arrow-heads and knives have been found, also the mummy of a female, which has been presented to the Smithsonian Institute. There is no industry to be found in Patagonia, except among the European settlers. They are largely engaged in sheep breeding, and in cattle and horse raising.

The government of the Catholic Church in Patagonia is divided into two parts, northern and southern. The Vicariate of Northern Patagonia was founded in 1883, and canonically approved by Decree on 20 Jan., 1902. Monsignor Giovanni Cagliero, S.C., titular Archbishop of Sebaste, and Apostolic Delegate of Costa Rica, is at its head, with the Very Rev. Father Stefano Pagliere, S.C., as his vicar-general for the missions. The entire vicariate is under the control and direction of the Salesian Congregation. There are now in it about fifty priests and a large number of brothers, engaged in mission work and in the various institutes and schools. In the beginning the pioneer work was done by Monsignor Cagliero, Fathers Fagnano, Costamagna, Rabagliati, and Espinosa, who formed a small band of missionaries, carefully trained under the eye of the founder of the congregation, Don Bosco. So far there has been no synod, the special conditions of the situation rendering it unnecessary. Besides the priests who are sent on the mission from Europe, there are many undergoing training in the institutes and houses established in the vicariate. Each house is a centre from which the natives are visited in their settlements. There are at present nineteen centres, which are situated as follows:—

The Institute of Don Bosco of the Holy Family, the parish church of Our Lady of Mercy, and the subordinate church and Institute of Our Lady of Pity, all in the same settlement of Bahia Blanca; the Mission of the Sacred Heart of Jesus, at Choele-Choel; the parish church of Our Lady Immaculate, at Chosmalal; the church and Institute of St. Lawrence, at Conesa-Sur; the Instituto of St. Peter, at Fortin Mercedes; the parish and Institute of Mary Immaculate, at General Acha; the parish of St. Rose of Toay, at Guardia Pringles; the parish and Institute of Our Lady of Snow, at Junin de los Andes; the parish of Our Lady of Carmel and the Institute of St. Joseph, at Patagones; the parish and Institute of St. Michael, and St. Joseph's School of Agriculture, at Roca; the parish and Institute of Mary Help of Christians, at Victorica; the parish of Our Lady of Mercy, and the Institute of Arts and Trades, dedicated to St. Francis de Sales, at Viedma; the Michael Rua Institute and the Mission of the Sacred Heart of Jesus, at Puerto Madryn, Chubut; the parish and Institute of Our Lady of Sorrows, at Rawson; and St. Dominic's Institute, at Trelew.

The Prefecture of Southern Patagonia was founded in 1883, and received canonical approval by Decree dated 20 Jan., 1902. The prefect Apostolic is Monsignor Fagnano, S.C. This prefecture is also under the control of the Salesian Congregation, all its missions and institutes being in the hands of its members. There are about twenty-four priests engaged in mission and teaching work, and there are also many brothers being prepared for the same field of labour. In this southern part of Patagonia the pioneer work was done by Monsignor Fagnano, with Fathers Beauvoir, Borgatello, and Diamond; the latter afterwards founded the Mission of Our Lady Star of the Sea, at Port Stanley, Falkland Islands, in 1888.

There are at present ten centres, which are situated as follows:—The Mission of Our Lady of Candelaria, at Cabo Peña; the Mission of St. Agnes, at Cabo Santa Ines; the Mission of the Good Shepherd, and that of St. Raphael, on Dawson Island; the parish and Institute of Our Lady of Lujin, Gallegos, on the River Gallegos; the church and Institute of Our Lady Star of the Sea, at Port Stanley, Falkland Islands; the Institute of St. Joseph, at Punta Arenas, and the dependent parish of St. Francis de Sales at Porvenir; the parish and Institute of the Holy Cross, at Santa Cruz; and the Church of Our Lady of Mercy, at Ushaia, Tierra del Fuego.

In both Northern and Southern Patagonia the entire religious and educational work is in the hands of the Salesian Congregation, and the Sisters of Mary Help of Christians. There is no other religious order at present in Patagonia, and no native missionaries. Many Indian youths have been received as students, but so far not one has been raised to the dignity of the priesthood.

The principal work of the Sisters of Mary Help of Christians is the care of children, especially during the winter time. In fact this is the only period of the year when the children can be instructed in the Catholic religion, as during the summer months they are away with their parents on their nomadic excursions. The children in the institutes, which are attached to nearly every one of the Salesian Missions, are fed, clothed, and taught by the nuns. A few of the girls have been admitted into the order, where they are working for their compatriots.

The Sodality of the Children of Mary, among the girls, the Guild of St. Aloysius, among the boys, and the Confraternity of the Sacred Heart among the adults, are in a flourishing condition. Slowly and steadily, as far as it can be done, the Catholic parochial system and life are being introduced and developed among these poor and uncivilized natives.

REID, *Patagonian Antiquities*; PRITCHARD, *Through the Heart of Patagonia* (London, 1902); DARWIN, *Origin of Species* (London, 1888), xi, xii; IDEM, *The Voyage of the Beagle* (London, 1839—); SNOW, *A Two Years' Cruise off . . . Patagonia*; MUSTERS, *At Home with the Patagonians* (London, 1873); CUNNINGHAM, *Natural History of the Strait of Magellan* (Edinburgh, 1878); MOREÑO, *Viage á la Patagonia*; LISTA, *Mis esploraciones . . . en la Patagonia* (Buenos Ayres, 1880); BOVE, *Patagonia, Tierra del Fuego*; ONELLI, *A travers les Andes*; *The Salesian Bulletin*; *Catalogue of the Salesian Congregation* (1910). ERNEST MARSH.

Patara, titular see of Lycia, suffragan of Myra, formerly a large commercial town, opposite Rhodes. Founded perhaps by the Phœnicians, it received later a Dorian colony from Crete; a legend traces its foundation to Patarus, son of Apollo. Renowned for its wealth, it was more so for its temple of Apollo where the oracles of the god were rendered during the winter.

Ptolemy Philadelphus extended it, naming it Arsinoe. On his third missionary journey St. Paul embarked from here for Tyre (Acts, xxi, 1–3). The "Notitiæ Episcopatuum" mention it among the suffragans of Myra as late as the thirteenth century. Le Quien (Oriens christianus, I, 977) names seven bishops: St. Methodius, more probably Bishop of Olympus; Eudemus, at Nicæa, 325; Eutychianus, at Seleucia, 359; Eudemus, at Constantinople, 381; Cyrinus, at Chalcedon, 451, signed the letter of the bishops of Lycia to Emperor Leo, 458; Licinius, at Constantinople, 536; Theodulus, at the Photian Council of Constantinople, 879. Its ruins are still visible near Djelemish, vilayet of Koniah; they consist of the remains of a theatre built by Antoninus Pius, public baths of the time of Vespasian, temples, and tombs. The port is choked with sand.

SMITH, *Dict. of Greek and Roman Geog.*, s. v.; BEAUFORT, *Karamania*, II, 6; FELLOWS, *An account of Discoveries in Lycia* (London, 1841), 222; SPRATT AND FORBES, *Travels in Lycia* (London, 1847), I, 30, II, 189; BENNDORF AND NIEMANN, *Reisen in Lykien und Karien* (Vienna, 1884), I, 114 sq., II, 118; HILL, *Catalogue of the Greek Coins of Lycia*, 25–27. S. PÉTRIDÈS.

Paten.—The eucharistic vessel known as the *paten* is a small shallow plate or disc of precious metal upon which the element of bread is offered to God at the Offertory of the Mass, and upon which the consecrated Host is again placed after the Fraction. The word paten comes from a Latin form *patina* or *patena*, evidently imitated from the Greek πατάνη. It seems from the beginning to have been used to denote a flat open vessel of the nature of a plate or dish. Such vessels in the first centuries were used in the service of the altar, and probably served to collect the offerings of bread made by the faithful and also to distribute the consecrated fragments which, after the loaf had been broken by the celebrant, were brought down to the communicants, who in their own hands received each a portion from the *patina*. It should be noted, however, that Duchesne, arguing from the language of the earliest Ordines Romani (q. v.), believes that at Rome white linen bags were used for this purpose (Duchesne, "Lib. Pont.", I, introduct., p. cxliv). We have, however, positive evidence that silver dishes were in use, which were called *patinæ ministeriales*, and which seem to be closely connected with the *calices ministeriales* in which the consecrated wine was brought to the people. Some of these *patinæ*, as we learn from the inventories of church plate in the "Liber Pontificalis" (I, pp. 202, 271 etc.), weighed twenty or thirty pounds and must have been of large size. In the earliest times the patens, like the chalices, were probably constructed of glass, wood, and copper, as well as of gold and silver; in fact the "Liber Pontificalis" (I, 61 and 139) speaks of glass patens in its notice of Pope Zephyrinus (A. D. 198–217).

When towards the ninth century the zeal of the faithful regarding the frequent reception of Holy Communion very much declined, the system of consecrating the bread offered by the faithful and of distributing Communion from the *patinæ* seems gradually to have changed, and the use of the large and proportionately deep *patinæ ministeriales* fell into abeyance. It was probably about the same time that the custom grew up for the priest himself to use a paten at the altar to contain the sacred Host, and obviate the danger of scattered particles after the Fraction. This paten, however, was of much smaller size and resembled those with which we are now familiar. Some rather doubtful specimens of the old ministerial patens are preserved in modern times. The best authenticated seems to be one discovered in Siberia in 1867 (see de Rossi in "Boll. di Archeol. Crist.", 1871, 153), but this measures less than seven inches in diameter. Another, of gold, of oblong form, was found at Gourdon. There is also what is believed to be a Byzantine paten of alabaster in the treasury of St. Mark's at Venice. Some of these patens are highly decorated, and this is what we should expect from the accounts preserved in the "Liber Pontificalis". In the altar patens of the medieval period we usually find a more marked central depression than is now customary. This well or depression is usually set round with ornamental lobes, seven, ten, or more in number. At the present day hardly any ornament is used or permitted.

The paten, like the bowl of the chalice, must be of gold or silver gilt, and it cannot be used before it has been consecrated with chrism by a bishop. The formula employed speaks of the vessel as blessed "for the administration of the Eucharist of Jesus Christ, that the Body of our Lord may be broken upon it", and also as "the new sepulchre of the Body and Blood of Jesus Christ". In the Oriental liturgies there is placed upon the altar a vessel called the *discus*, analogous to the paten, but it is of considerably larger size.

KRULL in KRAUS, *Realencyclopädie fr. christ. Alt.*; DE FLEURY, *La Messe*, IV (Paris, 1887), 155–67, with the plates thereto belonging, which supply the best available collection of illustrations; OTTE, *Handb. der Kirch. Kunst-Archäologie*, I (Leipzig,

1883), 231; ALDENKIRCHEN, *Drei liturg. Schüsseln d. M.A.* (Bonn, 1883); KAUFMANN, *Handb. d. c. Archäol.* (Paderborn, 1901), 563 sq.; KLEINSCHMIDT in *Theol. Prak. Quartalschrift* (1901), 32, (1902), 289.

HERBERT THURSTON.

Patenson, WILLIAM, VENERABLE, English martyr, b. in Yorkshire or Durham; d. at Tyburn, 22 January, 1591–2. Admitted to the English College, Reims, 1 May, 1584, he was ordained priest September, 1587, and left for the English mission 17 January, 1588–9. On the third Sunday of Advent, 1591, he said Mass in the house of Mr. Lawrence Mompesson at Clerkenwell, and while dining with another priest, James Young, the priest-catchers surprised them. Young found a hiding-place, but Patenson was arrested and condemned at the Old Bailey after Christmas. According to Young, while in prison he converted and reconciled three or four thieves before their death. According to Richard Verstegan, he converted, the night before his martyrdom, six out of seven felons, who occupied the condemned cell with him. On this account he was cut down while still conscious.

POLLEN, *Acts of the English Martyrs* (London, 1891), 115–7; *English Martyrs 1584–1603* (London, 1908), 208, 292; CHALLONER, *Missionary Priests*, I, no. 94; KNOX, *Douay Diaries* (London, 1878), 201, 217, 222.

JOHN B. WAINEWRIGHT.

Pathology, MENTAL.—I. LOCALIZATION OF MENTAL FACULTIES.—In the cerebral cortex—that is, the thin covering which envelopes the entire surface of the brain—are distinguished various areas, connected by long nerve tracts with the organs of sense, the skin, the muscles, and in fact with the entire surface of the body. These connexions constitute what is known as the *Projection System*. There are other areas which are not connected with the outer world, but are related in the closest manner by numerous nerve fibres one with another, and with the areas of the projection system. These constitute the *Association System*. In the former, definite elementary psycho-physiological functions are accurately localized. There are sharply defined centres for the movements of the individual members (the tongue etc.), for the sensations (taste etc.), for hearing, sight etc. In the left cerebral hemisphere (in the right for left-handed persons), there is a specifically human centre, that for speech; destruction of this definite portion of the brain cortex causes a loss of the power of speech and of the understanding of spoken words, even though there be no deafness, paralysis of the tongue, mental disorder, or anything of this order.

The higher and specifically psychical functions, and indeed all psychical processes (attention, mental moods, will, etc.) are localized in the *association* centres, the entire massive frontal lobes serving exclusively as such. Modern attempts to localize the individual mental faculties are as little successful as Gall's endeavours to deduce scientifically defects or developments from the formation of the skull.

The external forms of normal psychical conduct have a normally functionating foundation—a healthy brain cortex; unhealthy changes in this latter disturb the normal psychical processes, that is, they lead to mental disease.

II. CAUSES OF MENTAL DISTURBANCES.—The normal mechanism of the cerebral cortex may be impaired in a variety of ways. Impairment may result from the originally insufficient or defective construction of the entire brain (as in congenital dementia, idiocy), or by the destruction of extensive portions of the normally developed brain by injury, inflammation, softening, malignant new growths etc. In very many cases it is due to the action of poisons, which either temporarily or permanently affect the activities of the sound and well-proportioned elements of the cortex. The number and variety of such active poisons is extremely great; among them are alcohol, morphine, cocaine, hashish, lead, poison products of microscopically small organisms or bacteria (fever deliria), abnormal products of metabolism coming from the gastro-intestinal tract (gastro-intestinal auto-intoxication—hallucinatory confused states), syphilis (in general paresis), poisons from the disturbance of important glandular organs (e. g. disease of the thyroid glands in the dementia of cretinism). In other cases, a disease process of the blood-vessel system affects also the blood vessels of the brain, and thus injures the cerebral cortex (mental diseases due to the calcification of the blood vessels, arterio-scelerotic psychosis).

One and the same poisonous agent (e. g. alcohol) may be taken within definite limits and withstood by one individual, whereas another individual's reaction to the drug may occasion a nervous or mental disease. The personal predisposition plays an important causative factor. This individual constitution (i. e. inferiority, lower capacity for resistance) of the central nervous system is for the most part congenital and hereditary, just as temperament, talent etc. Mental diseases due to alcoholism or nervousness are doubly severe in persons to whom a corresponding taint has been transmitted by their ancestors. In some instances this inferiority may be induced in previously healthy and normally constituted nervous systems by sunstroke, concussion of the brain etc. Injuries to the head, especially those accompanied by concussion of the brain, cause not only an increased disposition to mental disease, but are not infrequently its direct cause. A chronic state of exhaustion produces psychoses, severe and protracted hæmorrhages, weakness due to chronic purulent disease, malignant new growths, etc. Occasionally the mental disturbance bears a direct relation to phases of the female sexual life (menstruation, pregnancy, labour, suckling, change of life).

In some markedly predisposed individuals, very intense bodily pain or continuous physical irritations may occasion attacks of mental disturbance (confused states in migraine, toothache, polypi in the ear, worms in the intestines etc.). In very many instances we are entirely ignorant of any direct cause, and can only interpret the unstable disposition as due to a strong hereditary taint. In many forms of mental disease we know absolutely nothing concerning the causes.

It is striking that psychical factors themselves (worry, care, shock etc.) as sole and direct causes of mental disease play a very minor rôle—a fact in striking contrast to the popular notion. Only in extremely hysterical individuals, i. e. those already disposed to disease, do violent psychical emotions frequently give rise to rapidly-passing attacks of mental disorder. Furthermore, long-continued excitement, trouble, and the like, work only indirectly in the ætiology of the psychoses—e. g. by reducing the power of resistance of the central nervous system, that is, by giving rise to an increased disposition to nervous and mental disease, which itself is transmissible to posterity. Alcoholics make up a third, paretics almost two-thirds of all the mentally diseased. If the teachings of Christianity were to be generally followed, there would very rarely be a paretic, since for the most part syphilis is acquired only from illegitimate intercourse; there would be no alcoholism; and the untold distress caused by mental disturbance would be spared mankind.

With reference to the question whether one may through one's own fault bring on psychoses [as was expressly taught by the Protestant psychiatrist Heinroth (d. 1843)], modern psychiatry teaches as follows: as has been said above, there are many purely bodily causes of mental disease, in connexion with which there can be no question raised as to personal responsibility. In the case of alcoholism the matter is not so simple. While it is certain that the abuse of alcohol is one of the most important causes of mental disease, it is also certain that a great proportion, even the majority, of habitual drinkers are severely burdened by heredity, and start as psychopathic inferiors. They are not degenerate because they drink, but they drink because they are degenerate, and alcoholism merely destroys an already ailing nervous system. The true cause of drunkenness lies primarily in the individual's constitution, and may frequently be traced to the ancestors. The sins of the fathers are visited upon the sons, even to the third and fourth generation. In so far as illegitimate intercourse is a sin, syphilis and its attendant paresis may be regarded as one's own fault. It should not, however, be forgotten that syphilis can be acquired in other ways (e. g. by drinking from an infected glass). One finds the accusations of conscience and self-reproach in wholly irresponsible melancholic patients, and unrepentant criminals often live a long life without developing insanity. In short, the question whether the soul through its passions or burdens can make itself diseased must in general, according to modern experience, be answered negatively, or the possibility of such causative combinations may be acknowledged only with important reservations and the greatest restrictions.

III. VARIETIES OF INSANITY.—The forms that mental disease may assume, according to their symptoms, their course, and their results, are extraordinarily complex. Only those of most importance will be touched upon.

(1) *Melancholia.*—The most important feature here is a primary (*sc.* not induced by external events), sad, and anxious depression, with retardation of the thought processes. The patients feel themselves deeply unhappy, are tired of life, and overwhelm themselves with self-reproaches that they are unable to work, are lazy, stupid, wicked, or unamiable. In many cases the patients themselves can give no reason for their depression; they often cite in explanation long-forgotten sins of youth, all kinds of more or less unimportant occurrences and circumstances, the cares of daily life which are treated as a matter of course in times of health, or the very symptoms of their illness. Because they take no pleasure in anything, in prayer or in the presence of their families, they accuse themselves of impiety and want of affection. In other instances pure delusions arise. The patients accuse themselves of crimes which they have never committed: they have made everybody unhappy, have desecrated the Host, and have given themselves up to the Devil. Many cases of dæmonomania of the Middle Ages and of the times of the Reformation belong to this category, as was clearly recognized by many ecclesiastics. Regino, Abbot of Prüm (892–99), Gregory VII (1074) etc. protested energetically against the execution of witches; the Jesuit Friedrich von Spee (d. 1675), in his "Cautio criminalis", condemned the trying of witches as an institution opposed to humanity, science, and the Catholic Church.

The patients often feel a terrible anxiety, fear a cruel martyrdom; sleep suffers, bodily nutrition fails, and painful centres of pressure are often found in different nerve tracts. The danger of suicide is extremely great. The greater number of all suicides occurs as a result of recognized melancholia; other conditions, such as an intense state of anxiety, may often render such patients dangerous also to others. The self-accusations are uninfluenced by any words of comfort; a hundred times confessed, they return again and again. The severest cases end in a condition of inability to speak or to move (stupor).

(2) *Mania.*—By this we understand a *primary* (i. e. not caused by external influences), happy, elated mood subject to very rapid variations, especially to impulsive, wrathful emotions. Self-consciousness is increased, the flow of ideas is precipitate and rambling; there is over-talkativeness and excessive restlessness. The severest cases end in flighty ideas, confusion, and frenzy. But even the mild cases are disastrous for the patients and for their surroundings. Abnormal sensuality shows itself; individuals of previously high moral standards give themselves up to violent alcoholic excesses, and practise all kinds of sexual crimes. The patients are senselessly lavish, are guilty of deceits and thefts, and, by reason of their irritability, quarrel with their associates, superiors etc., insult them, and disturb the public peace, commit violence, are arrogant, quarrelsome, contentious, and delight in intolerable hair-splitting. Sleep is badly broken, the eyes shine, the play of the countenance is full of expression and vivacious; many patients resemble persons slightly intoxicated. Very frequently maniacal and melancholic states occur with characteristically regular alternations, and repeat themselves in one and the same individual, who during the intervals is mentally normal (circular insanity with lucid intervals).

(3) *General Paresis.*—This disease leads with gradually increasing mental and physical decay to dementia, paralysis, and death. Frequently, in the early stages maniacal states, antecedent to severe dementia, are already observable. The patients are not only distracted and forgetful, but above all irritable, sleepless, brutal, shameless, sensual, lavish, extravagant etc., exactly like true maniacs, only in a still more coarse and unrestrained fashion, because of the simultaneously appearing dementia. Very often one finds the most grotesque and changeable ideas of grandeur (megalomania); the patients believe themselves immeasurably rich, are emperors, opera-singers, even God Himself; they have discovered perpetual motion, know all languages, have thousands of wives, etc. In other cases there are hypochondriacal delusions (the patients complain they are dead, or putrescent, etc.). Not infrequently the delusions are permanent, and the patients simply grow less rational from day to day. On the physical side, one observes most frequently a characteristic difficulty in speech; the speech becomes stuttering, uncertain, and finally an unintelligible babble. The pupils of the eyes lose their circular form, are often unequal (e. g. the right narrow, the left very wide), and do not contract on exposure to light (Argyll-Robertson pupil). Very frequently transitory apoplectic or epileptic attacks occur. In the last stages the patients are quite insane, prostrated, confined to bed, and pass their excretions involuntarily until death intervenes. In the earlier stages, almost at any stage in fact, marked and continued improvement and stationary periods may take place at any moment.

(4) *Juvenile Insanity* (*Dementia præcox*).—This disease process usually sets in after the years of puberty, and gradually leads to a condition of dementia. Quite frequently only the ethical side of the psyche is at first affected. Boys and girls who have been active will suddenly develop a dislike to work, become irritable and headstrong, give themselves up to coarse excesses, go about in bad company, lose every family sense, etc. After a year or more the loss of intelligence becomes unmistakable. At times the initial stages take on a hypochondriacal colouring. Natures previously healthy and full of the joy of life begin to observe themselves with anxiety, go from physician to physician, have recourse to quacks, etc. They found their complaints on all kinds of foolish notions; there must be an animal, or a sore, in their stomachs, etc. Very frequently in the further course of the disease (occasionally at the beginning), hallucinations of hearing and of sight occur. Conditions of confusion, delusions of persecution, of poisoning, of megalomania of varying types occur. Peculiar so-called catatonic states of muscular tension develop, in which the patients remain expressionless and motion-

less in all sorts of positions. Set forms of speech, certain songs and motions are repeated in a stereotyped manner. All of these states can change with great rapidity. Very often a remarkably sudden improvement sets in, leading one to expect a recovery. Little by little a state of incurable dementia becomes established.

(5) *Senile Dementia.*—On a basis of a general breakdown due to old age, there develops increasing dementia, chiefly characterized by a disturbance of memory. In the mild cases the patients remember the occurrences, persons, and names from their early years, but cannot retain in their memory anything recent. In the severe cases the patients live entirely in the past, speak of their parents as still living, think themselves from twenty to thirty years old, do not know where they are, nor what is going on about them. As a result such patients are easily led, are *suggestible;* they do not know, for instance, what they have done in the morning, but declare, on being questioned, that they have been to school. Married women recall only the names of their parents and forget that they have had children. As a result of forgetting many words, their speech also is often very characteristic. Many nouns having escaped them, they help themselves out by frequent repetitions of stop-gap expressions, such as "what-d'ye-call-it", etc., or they use tiresome circumlocutions (e. g. instead of key, they say, "a thing that one opens things with"). The patients are irritable, hypochondriacal, suspicious, believe that their pockets have been picked, or that they have been poisoned. As in general paresis and *dementia præcox,* it is especially important to remember that marked loss of the moral sense may for some time precede the loss of intelligence. Sexual desire especially mounts up again in unhealthy fashion in these old people, and leads with special frequency to immoral attacks upon small children. Very frequently, in the early stages of senile dementia, there may be observed silly, intense ideas of jealousy, whose object is often the aged wife with whom the patient has lived for many decades in the happiest of wedlock. By reason of the disturbance of memory and the above-mentioned suggestibility, these patients often fall victims to unprincipled scoundrels, who swindle them out of their entire fortunes, induce them to make foolish wills, etc.

(6) *Chronic Delusion (Paranoia).*—Certain patients develop ever-increasing fixed delusions with clear consciousness and without any weakening of the intellect. The individual stages of this disorder may usually be distinguished. At first, these patients believe themselves to be under observation, to be pursued by enemies. Everything that is done has a deliberate reference to themselves; people slander them, spy upon them, or watch them. Hallucinations of hearing develop (e. g. mocking, abusive voices). The circle of their persecutors gradually enlarges; it is no longer a definite person (an enemy, a rival, a business competitor, etc.) who is the originator of this persecution and slander, but entire classes or bodies (Freemasons, Jesuits, political parties, the entire Civil Service, the members of the royal household, etc.). As their grandiose ideas develop, the patients believe themselves the victims of widespread intrigues and persecutions, because others are envious of them, or because of their importance. The concrete content of the delusions varies greatly in different cases, but remains fixed in the same individual. One believes himself to be an important inventor; another, a reformer; a third, a legitimate successor to the throne; a fourth, the Messias. In addition to the hallucinations of hearing, different bodily hallucinations develop. The patients feel themselves electrified, penetrated with the röntgen rays, etc. In the initial stages the patients are very often well able to hide their delusional ideas in case of necessity, and to pretend that they no longer believe in them (dissimulation). By reason of the obstinacy of the ideas of persecution, and especially because of their clearness of thought in other respects, these patients may become very dangerous, attacking those about them with violence, taking their revenge by killing, or by well-planned murders of their supposed persecutors.

In many cases the apparent sanity of these patients, and the fanaticism with which they promulgate their ideas, deceive an uncritical following, so that healthy but undiscriminating people share in their delusions (induced insanity). Many cases of so-called psychic epidemics, of perversely abstruse religious sects, belong to this category. In some cases the ideas of persecution are based on real or imaginary legal injustice suffered by the patient, who then believes that all advocates, judges, and administrative authorities are in league against him (*Paranoia querulans,* litigious paranoia). Traces of this are seen in the cases of obstinate litigants, who spend large amounts of money on lawyers to recover absurdly insignificant sums. When their complaints are dismissed everywhere, they commit a crime merely in order to come before a jury and be thus enabled to renew their old suit.

(7) *Alcoholic Mental Disease.*—In addition to what has already been said of alcoholism, it may be added that in chronic drinkers there often arise characteristic, motiveless delusions of jealousy (alcoholic paranoia), which, by reason of the habitual brutality of the drinker, lead to continuous cruelty, and at times to assault and murder of the wife.

Pathological intoxication is another important disease, in which the symptoms of ordinary drunkenness do not appear, but which constitutes a true psychosis. This is usually of short duration; the patients are for the most part unusually violent, are entirely confused, and on recovery have no memory whatever of their mental disturbance. In *delirium tremens,* in addition to the marked tremor, sweating, and absolute sleeplessness, one finds vivid hallucinations of sight (of numberless small animals, mice, vermin, men, fiery devils, etc.), confusion, and feverish activity, during which the patients go about restlessly, working with imaginary tools. In other cases active hallucinations of hearing take place. They hear threatening and abusive voices, which may make the patient so anxious as to lead him to impulsive suicide.

(8) *Epileptic Psychosis.*—Mild but permanent psychical anomalies are observed in very many epileptics. These patients are for the most part extremely sensitive and irritable, and, in contrast with this, may often simultaneously show an exaggeratedly tender and pathetic pietism. Not infrequently one observes characteristic periodic variations in the mood. From time to time the patients themselves feel an incomprehensible internal unrest, anxiety, or sadness; some seek to mitigate this condition by taking strong nerve poisons, at times in excessive doses (many cases of dipsomania belong to this class); others have recourse to debauchery; a third class go off like tramps for days; while a fourth attempt suicide. In other cases we meet with moodiness, which is not sad but irritable and angry, and consequently differs from the regular irritability of the epileptic; it frequently leads to most violent attacks upon those about them. Such conditions may often be traced even to earliest childhood.

In connexion with eclampsia, or even in its place, there often take place characteristic mental disturbances which begin very suddenly (dream or twilight states), last but a short time and pass, usually leaving no trace in the memory. These attacks show themselves outwardly in characteristic impulsive acts—as for instance in aimless wanderings (many cases of military desertion are due to such attacks), or in delirious confused conditions, mostly of a horrifying nature (fire, blood, ghosts, etc.). Such patients are often very dangerous, for in their blind anxiety they assail those about them, no matter who they may be. The cases among the Malays of "running amuck" are of this nature. In other cases of frequent occurrence the patients have visionary, ecstatic deliria; they sing psalms aloud, believe that they see the heavens open, see the Last Judgment, speak with God, etc. (Mohammed was an epileptic). Often the attacks occur only at night (epileptic night-walkers, somnambulists).

(9) *Hysterical Psychosis.*—Many hysterical patients are at the same time permanently abnormal from the psychical point of view; they are egregiously selfish, irritable, and untruthful. Conscious simulation and diseased imagination run into one another so as to be indistinguishable. The mental disturbances of the hysterical show many superficial resemblances to those of the epileptic; the latter however are spontaneous, while the former are due to definite psychical causes, fright, anger, and the like; the sexual life also plays here an important rôle. Visionary ecstatic dreamy conditions occur, whereby an hysterical person can psychically infect hundreds of others (cf. the epidemics of the Middle Ages of flagellants, dancers, etc.; superstitious "miracles" of modern times; speakers of foreign tongues, and the like, where no sharp boundary exists between conscious swindling and pathological suggestibility).

On the physical side one meets with strange paralyses, cramps, blindness, isolated anæsthetic spots [thus explaining the notorious "mark of the devil" in the "Malleus Maleficarum" (1489), met with in ancient witch trials]. All of these symptoms can disappear just as suddenly as they come. The majority of the wonder-cures by charms or similar superstitions are possible only in the case of hysterical persons, in whom the imagination causes both the disease and the cure.

In modern times hysteria plays a large rôle in injuries—traumatic neurosis, "railway spine"—which is a combination of symptoms following a railway collision, or after accidents during employment.

(10) *Imbecility, Weakmindedness.*—The severer forms (idiocy) and also those of moderate severity are easily recognized, even by the layman. The milder forms, however, may be overlooked very readily, since the mechanical accomplishments of memory may be very good, although the judgment (i. e. independent critical thought) is lacking. The weak-minded know only what they have committed to memory, but not the why and wherefore; they cannot draw conclusions, cannot adapt acquired knowledge to suit new and unaccustomed circumstances; they are at a loss when confronted by questions demanding intelligence. The weak-minded child, for instance, can learn a poem by heart, but cannot by himself perceive its significance; he can name the holidays, but does not understand their meaning; he can calculate well (i. e. mechanically) 9+3, but does not understand the question: "I think of a number, add 3 to it, and the answer is 12; what is the number I thought of?" By reason of their inability to think independently, such individuals are blindly led by the authority of others for good or evil. Because of the impossibility of reflecting upon anything exactly, they often commit, not only very foolish, but also dangerous and criminal acts, to free themselves from a momentarily unpleasant situation. Their emotional life is characterized by unreasonableness and irrepressibility. On the physical side one finds deformations of the skull, defects of speech, squint-eyes etc. One of the most important causes is alcoholic excess on the part of the parents; brain disease during childhood or before birth is also sometimes responsible. In many cases the defect involves that side of psychical life which is called the moral or social side, which cannot be acquired by intellectual means but is essentially connected with sentiment. Without moral sensibility, moral conduct is impossible. Hence arises the sad picture of the incorrigible reprobates who cannot be reached by educational influences, who in spite of kindness or sternness, in spite of the best example and breeding at home, are criminally inclined from childhood, and later become lazy vagabonds, prostitutes, or habitual criminals.

These children, when hardly past infancy, are conspicuous for their unusual unruliness, selfishness, and lack of family affection. They show a characteristic malice and cruelty, maltreat animals in the most refined ways, and take a truly diabolical delight in tormenting their brothers, sisters, and comrades. They have a kind of explosive irritability and impulsive sensuousness, shown especially in an uncontrollable appetite for sweets, to satisfy which they have recourse even to theft and violence. They take to drinking when very young, and practise various other forms of immorality. Shamelessness, absolute laziness, and an extreme mendacity always characterize these persons. Their mendacity appears not only in lies told to escape punishment or to obtain something desirable, but also in fantastic romancing (*pseudologia phantastica*). We also usually observe in these patients a variety of bodily malformations and combinations of epilepsy and hysteria. As causes may be mentioned: heredity (especially from alcoholism), infantile brain disease (severe epilepsies), injury to the infantile skull during childbirth, cerebral concussion, etc.

(11) *Compulsory Ideas.*—Even in patients whose intelligence is intact, certain ideas recur over and over again against their will, cannot be banished, and hinder and cross the normal flow of ideas, in spite of the fact that their folly and senselessness are always clearly recognized. The number of these impulsive ideas is very great. For the clergy the knowledge of certain forms is important, especially those that occur fairly frequently among religious persons, and are highly troublesome and painful. Such people, for instance, although they are believers, are forced constantly to brood over such questions as: "Who is God?" "Is there a God?" Others have fancies of the lowest and most obscene character, which annoy them only during prayer, and return with the greater persistency according as the patient is more anxious to dispel them. Such patients require hours to say a simple *Pater noster*, because they believe they have profaned the prayer by a sudden obscene fancy and must therefore begin all over again. The reassuring words of the confessor make little impression, save for the moment. Such sufferers torment themselves and their confessor incessantly by the endless repetition of their religious scruples, notwithstanding the fact that they clearly recognize the disordered compulsion (i. e. the involuntary nature of their ideas). But they cannot help themselves; the thoughts return against their will.

(12) *Menstrual Psychosis.*—A few words may be added about a mental disturbance, which is of importance to jurists and to the clergy. In nervous women a menstrual psychosis occurs, i. e. mental anomalies which appear only at the time of the catamenia (usually a few days earlier) in individuals otherwise healthy. Conditions of confusion, unfounded ideas of jealousy, or excited states with marked excitability or sexual excitement manifest themselves. In women just delivered, excited and confused states occur in which the patient kills the new-born child; afterwards there is complete loss of memory of the deed.

(13) *Impulsive Psychosis.*—By this is meant the occurrence of an irresistible impulse to steal (kleptomania), to burn (pyromania), to wander about (poriomania), the diseased nature of the action being especially recognizable in the complete lack of motive (no need, no satisfaction, etc.). The stolen articles, for instance, will not be used or sold, but carelessly and immediately thrown away after the theft has been committed; the thief often enjoys good social and

XI.—35

material position. Such impulsive inclinations often exist throughout life, but oftener occur at intervals—as for instance during puberty; in women, not infrequently only during menstruation, or during pregnancy. In all these forms, as also in cases of so-called moral insanity, one must be unusually sceptical if one is to avoid favouring the introduction of the most dangerous abuses into the administration of justice.

(14) *Sexual Psychopathy. Anomalies of the Sexual Life.*—The pathological abnormalities of the sexual impulse belong to the most melancholy chapters of psycho-pathology, and the horror that arises from the study of these occurrences can only be mitigated by the knowledge that what is so frequent is not always a disgusting vice and depravity, but often a mental disorder. But, as has been already said, we should be exceedingly cautious in assuming the existence of mental disturbance in cases which naturally lead to criminal prosecution, and where there is of course frequently a tendency to simulation.

IV. FREEDOM OF THE WILL AND RESPONSIBILITY.—In the question of moral responsibility or liability (from the theological or legal standpoint) a further and very important question arises. Mental soundness implies freedom of the will, while mental disease destroys it. In nature, however, there are no rigid, definite boundaries between disease and health, but only gradual transitions. We meet with so-called "border-land" cases between health and disease, a well-recognized example being weakmindedness. While the difference between the two extremes (an animal-like idiot, on the one hand, and, on the other, a Newton, a Pasteur, etc.) is at once palpable to all, where are the sharp boundaries between the moderately serious and mild forms of imbecility, between these latter and the very mildest forms, and finally between these and simple, but in no wise pathological, stupidity? The same may be said of moral imbecility, which passes by insensible gradations from the undoubtedly healthy to the irresponsible, superficial, sensual, and violent individual. The same may be said of menstrual psychosis, which shows its physiological roots in the increased general nervousness of every woman at the menstrual period. In short, in the entire domain of psycho-pathology one often meets with these borderland conditions, and the question of freedom of will cannot be answered by a simple yes or no, but requires a strictly individual weighing of all of the conditions of the concrete act. Not infrequently the psychopathic changes constitute, not indeed a total exculpation, but a mitigating circumstance. Or the matter may be such that one and the same individual, by reason of his mental abnormality, may be completely responsible for one crime, and irresponsible for another. A kleptomaniac, for instance, certainly commits a theft in a condition of irresponsibility; he must be held to answer, however, for another type of crime, for instance, an act of immorality. Even individuals, who are continuously free from characteristic psychopathic traits of a general nervous order, may by a combination of a number of definite external disturbances develop passing conditions of irresponsibility. The so-called *pathological affects* belong to this class. By reason of the simultaneous combination of long-continued depressing influences (trouble, care, etc.), of fatigue, sleeplessness, exhaustion, hunger, digestive disturbances, and pain, a normal emotional activity may reach a pathological or diseased height, accompanied by impulsive violence, and followed by dreamy or incomplete memory.

V. PATHOLOGICAL CHANGES IN THE BRAIN STRUCTURE.—Constant and definite changes in the brain we know to be proved at the present time only in such forms of mental disease as accompany defective states, either of congenital (e. g. idiocy) or acquired origin (e. g. senility, paresis etc.). The weight of the brain remains considerably under normal in these conditions. In contrast to the average of 1360 grammes for males, and 1230 grammes for females (the weight of Gauss's brain was 1492 grammes; of Turgenieff's, 2120 grammes), in full-grown idiots we find weights of 417 to 720 grammes (in one case only 200), and in paretics weights of about 1000 grammes. With the naked eye one can see in paresis, in senile dementia etc., the great diminution and disappearance of the cerebral cortex, adhesions between the cortex and the brain coverings, œdema of the ventricles, scars, shrinkages, softenings, changes in the blood-vessels, etc. In idiots one observes in addition the most various congenital malformations (resemblance to lower animals, or persistence of embryonal stages, etc.), the remains of inflammatory processes, etc. The pathological findings by the microscope of fine changes in the brain cortex (in the ganglion cells, nerve fibres, etc.) are even richer.

In all the other forms of mental disease pathological anatomy has failed to give us any information. Autopsy either reveals no abnormal conditions in the brain, or the changes that are found are either inconstant or have no particular relation to the psychosis, as for example the very fine alterations of the cortical cells, which modern microscopy has proved to exist in acute psychosis, can be induced also by other bodily diseases which cause death. Our knowledge in this field is still very hazy.

MARIE, *Traité international de psychologie pathologique* (Paris, 1910); KRAEPELIN, *Lehrbuch der Psychiatrie* (8th ed., Leipzig, 1909); PILCZ, *Lehrbuch der gerichtlichen Psychiatrie* (Vienna, 1908); BESSMER, *Störungen im Seelenleben* (2nd ed., Freiburg im Br., 1907).

A. PILCZ.

Patmore, COVENTRY, one of the major poets of the nineteenth century, in spite of the small bulk of his verse, b. at Woodford, Essex, 23 July, 1823; d. at Lymington, 26 Nov., 1896. His father was a man of letters, and a writer of ability and fancy, who lived among writers, making one of the company that included Lamb, Hazlitt, Leigh Hunt, "Barry Cornwall", and others of less well-remembered names. Meeting with financial reverses late in life, P. G. Patmore unavoidably left his son, carefully educated but unprepared for any profession, to gain a difficult livelihood. Coventry Patmore married, in his early twenties, Emily Augusta Andrews, daughter of a Nonconformist clergyman who was Ruskin's tutor in Greek before the young student went to the university. Monckton Milnes (later Lord Houghton), meeting Coventry Patmore at Mrs. Proctor's house, and interested by his intellectual face and his evident poverty, recommended him for employment in the British Museum Library, and this it was that made his marriage possible. Coventry Patmore's early poems were published by the zeal of his father, and gained prophecies of future greatness from Leigh Hunt and others. In 1853 was published his first mature work, "Tamerton Church Tower and other Poems", and in 1854 appeared the first part of a more deliberate work, "The Angel in the House", a versified love-story of great simplicity, interspersed with brief meditations,

COVENTRY PATMORE

now grave, now epigrammatically witty, on the profounder significances of love in marriage. The book became quickly famous. In 1862 the poet's wife died, leaving him with six young children. As happy love had been his earlier, the grief of loss became in great measure his later theme; poignantly touching and also most sublime thoughts upon love, death, and immortality are presented under greatly poetic imagery in the odes of "The Unknown Eros". Coventry Patmore became a Catholic in Rome very soon after his first wife's death. His second wife, Marianne Byles, was of the same faith. She was a woman of considerable fortune as well as beauty. Bringing him no children, she died after some twenty years of marriage, and the poet, somewhat late in life, made a third alliance, his wife being Miss Harriet Robson, also a Catholic; she became the mother of one son.

Patmore's prose works are the essays collected under the title "Principle in Art", and "Rod, Root, and Flower". They belong to the latter half of his life. The volume named second is in great part deeply and loftily mystical. During the period of his first marriage Patmore had lived in the intimacy of Ruskin, Browning, Tennyson, Dobell, Millais, Woolner, Rossetti, and Holman Hunt, and was associated with the Pre-Raphaelites, especially in the production of the "Germ", to which he contributed poetry and prose. During his last years he withdrew into the country, and gave his time almost entirely to meditation. His unique lot was to be at first the most popular, and later the least popular of poets. Between the periods of composition occurred long spaces of silence. Yet there was no change in the spirit of the poet. He smiled to see such different estimation wait upon poetry that was as starry and divine in the trivial-seeming and much-read "Angel" as in the "Unknown Eros", hardly opened by the public, and only now beginning to take its place as a great English classic in the minds of students.

ALICE MEYNELL.

Patmos, a small volcanic island in the Ægean Sea, off the coast of Asia Minor, to the south of Samos and west of Miletus, in lat. 37° 20' N. and long. 26° 35' E. Its length is about ten miles, its breadth six miles, and its coast-line thirty-seven miles. The highest point is Hagios Elias (Mt. St. Elias), rising to over 1050 feet. The island was formerly covered with luxuriant palm-groves, which won it the name of *Palmosa;* of these groves there remains but a clump in the valley called "The Saint's Garden". The ancient capital occupied the northern (Ruvali) isthmus. The modern town of Patmos lies in the middle part of the island. Above it towers the battlements of St. John's monastery, founded in 1088 by St. Christobulus. The Island of Patmos is famous in history as the place of St. John's exile: "I, John . . . was in the island, which is called Patmos, for the word of God, and for the testimony of Jesus" (Apoc., i, 9); there according to general belief the Beloved Disciple wrote the Apocalypse, the imagery of which was in part inspired by the scenery of the island. The spot where St. John was favoured with his revelations is pointed out as a cave on the slope of the hill, half way between the shore and the modern town of Patmos.

CLARK, *Travels* (London, 1818); MURRAY, *Handbook to Asia Minor* (London); TOZER, *The Islands of the Ægean* (London, 1890); GUÉRIN, *Description de l'Ile de Patmos* (Paris, 1856); LACROIX, *Les îles de la Grèce* (Paris, 1853); LE CAMUS, *Voyage aux pays bibliques* (Paris, 1890); Ross, *Reisen auf den griechischen Inseln* (Stuttgart, 1840).

CHARLES L. SOUVAY.

Patna. See ALLAHABAD, THE DIOCESE OF.

Patras, metropolitan see in Achaia. It was one of the twelve ancient cities of Achaia, built near Mount Panachaicon (now Voidia), and formed of three small districts, Aroe, Antheia, and Mesatis. After the Dorian invasion Patreus established there a colony from Laconia, and gave his name to the city. In the Peloponnesian War it took sides with Athens, and, in 419 B. C., Alcibiades advised the construction of long walls to connect the town with its harbour. Reverses having reduced it to extreme misery, Augustus restored it after the victory at Actium by a military colony, called Aroe Patrensis, the existence of which till the reign of Gordianus III is attested by coins. It became very prosperous through its commerce and especially through its weaving industry. In the sixth century it suffered from an earthquake (Procopius, "Bell. Goth.", IV, xxv), and afterwards from the ravages of the Slavs. In 807, however, it resisted the attacks of the Slavs and, in return, received the title of metropolitan see from the Emperor Nicephorus I. Patras was dependent on Rome until 733, when it became subject to the Patriarchate of Constantinople. Nothing is known of the beginning of Christianity in the city, unless we accept the tradition that it was evangelized by the Apostle St. Andrew. A celebrated Stylite lived there in the tenth century, to whom St. Luke the Younger went to be trained (P. G., CXI, 451). In 1205 William of Champlitte took possession and installed canons; they in turn elected Anthelme, a monk of Cluny, as archbishop. The territory formed a barony subject to the Aleman family and included in the principality of Morea or Achaia. The Latin archbishops held it from the second half of the thirteenth century till 1408, when they sold it to Venice. In 1429 it again fell into the power of the Greeks, and was taken by the Turks in 1460. Under the Ottoman dominion Patras became the capital of the pashalik of Morea, and underwent severe trials. In 1532 it was captured by Andrea Doria; in 1571, at the time of the Battle of Lepanto, the Greek metropolitan aroused the populace on behalf of the Venetians and was cut to pieces by the Turks. It was burnt by the Spaniards in 1595; pillaged by the Maltese in 1603, and captured by the Venetians on 24 July, 1687, and kept by them for thirty years. In 1770, at the instigation of the Russians, the city revolted, and was sacked by the Turks. On 4 April, 1821, it rose unsuccessfully against the Ottomans, who held it until it was delivered by General Maison on 5 October, 1828. It is now the capital of the nome Achaia, and has 38,000 inhabitants.

The Greek see, first dependent on Corinth, became a metropolitan see in the ninth century. It had four suffragans (Gelzer, "Ungedruckte . . . Texte der Notitiæ episcopatuum", 557); then five about 940 (Gelzer, "Georgii Cyprii Descriptio orbis Romani", 77); after 1453 it had only two, which successively disappeared (Gelzer, op. cit., 634). Its titulars were called Metropolitans of Patras from the ninth century until the Middle Ages, Metropolitans of Old Patras until 1833, Bishops of Achaia until 1852, Archbishops of Patras and Eleia from that time. The list of its titulars has been compiled by Le Quien (Oriens christ., II, 177–82), Gelzer (in Gerland, "Neue Quellen zur Geschichte des lateinischen Erzbistums Patras", Leipzig, 1903), 247–55, Pargoire (in "Echos d'Orient", VII, 103–07). The Latin archdiocese, created in 1205, lasted until 1441, when it became a titular see. It had five suffragans, Andravida, Amyclæ, Modone, Corone, and Cephalonia-Zante; even when Modone and Corone belonged to the Venetians they continued to depend on Patras. The list of Latin titulars has been drawn up by Le Quien (op. cit., III, 1023–32), Eubel (Hierarchia cath. med. ævi, I, 412; II, 236; III, 289), and Gerland (op. cit., 244–46). In 1640 the Jesuits established themselves at Patras, and in 1687 the Franciscans and Carmelites. In the nineteenth century the pope confided the administration of the Peloponnesus to the Bishop of Zante, in 1834 to the Bishop of Syra. Since 1874 the city has formed a part of the Apostolic Delegation of Athens. It contains from 8000 to 10,000 Catholics. The parish work is in charge of secular priests. There is a convent of Sisters of the Immaculate Conception of Ivrea.

SMITH, *Dict. of Greek and Roman Geography*, II, 557; GERLAND, *op. cit.*; THOMOPOULOS, *History of the town of Patras* (Athens, 1888), in Greek.

S. VAILHÉ.

Patriarch, πατριάρχης.—The word *patriarch* as applied to Biblical personages comes from the Septuagint version, where it is used in a broad sense, including religious and civil officials (e. g. I Par., xxiv, 31; xxvii, 22). In the more restricted sense and common usage it is applied to the antediluvian fathers of the human race, and more particularly to the three great progenitors of Israel: Abraham, Isaac, and Jacob. In the New Testament the term is extended also to the sons of Jacob (Acts, vii, 8–9) and to King David (ibid., ii, 29). For an account of these later patriarchs see articles ABRAHAM; ISAAC; JACOB; etc. The earlier patriarchs comprise the antediluvian group, and those who are placed between the Flood and the birth of Abraham. Of the former the Book of Genesis gives a twofold list. The first (Gen., iv, 17–18, passage assigned by critics to the so-called "J" document) starts with Cain and gives as his descendants Henoch, Irad, Maviael, Mathusael, and Lamech. The other list (Gen., v, 3–31, ascribed to the priestly writer, "P") is far more elaborate, and is accompanied by minute chronological indications. It begins with Seth and, strange to say, it ends likewise with Lamech. The intervening names are Enos, Cainan, Malaleel, Jared, Henoch, and Mathusala.

The fact that both lists end with Lamech, who is doubtless the same person, and that some of the names common to both are strikingly similar, makes it probable that the second list is an amplification of the first, embodying material furnished by a divergent tradition. Nor should this seem surprising when we consider the many discrepancies exhibited by the twofold genealogy of the Saviour in the First and Third Gospels. The human personages set forth in these lists occupy a place held by the mythical demi-gods in the story of the prehistoric beginnings of other early nations, and it may well be that the chief value of the inspired account given of them is didactic, destined in the mind of the sacred writer to inculcate the great truth of monotheism which is so distinctive a feature of the Old Testament writings. Be that as it may, the acceptance of this general view helps greatly to simplify another difficult problem connected with the Biblical account of the early patriarchs, viz. their enormous longevity. The earlier account (Gen., iv, 17–18) gives only the names of the patriarchs there mentioned, with the incidental indication that the city built by Cain was called after his son Henoch. The later narrative (Gen., v, 3–31) gives a definite chronology for the whole period. It states the age at which each patriarch begot his first-born son, the number of years he lived after that event, together with the sum total of the years of his life. Nearly all of the antediluvian fathers are represented as living to the age of 900 or thereabouts, Mathusala, the oldest, reaching 969.

These figures have always constituted a most difficult problem for commentators and Bible readers; and those who defend the strict historical character of the passages in question have put forward various explanations, none of which are considered convincing by modern Biblical scholars. Thus it has been conjectured that the years mentioned in this connexion were not of ordinary duration but of one or more months. There is, however, no warrant for this assumption in the Scripture itself, where the word year has a constant signification, and is always clearly distinguished from the minor periods. It has also been suggested that the ages given are not those of individuals, but signify epochs of antediluvian history, and that each is named after its most illustrious representative. The hypothesis may be ingenious, but even a superficial reading of the text suffices to show that such was not the meaning of the sacred writer. Nor does it help the case much to point out a few exceptional instances of persons who in more modern times are alleged to have lived to the age of 150 or even 180. For even admitting these as facts, and that in primitive times men lived longer than at present (an assumption for which we find no warrant in historic times), it is still a long way from 180 to 900.

Another argument to corroborate the historical accuracy of the Biblical account has been deduced from the fact that the legends of many people assert the great longevity of their early ancestors, a circumstance which is said to imply an original tradition to that effect. Thus the first seven Egyptian kings are said to have reigned for a period of 12,300 years, making an average of about 1757 years for each, and Josephus, who is preoccupied with a desire to justify the Biblical narrative, quotes Ephorus and Nicolaus as relating "that the ancients lived a thousand years". He adds, however, "But as to these matters, let every one look upon them as he thinks fit". (Antiq., I, iii, *in fine*). On the other hand, it is maintained that as a matter of fact there is no trustworthy historic or scientific evidence indicating that the average span of human life was greater in primitive than in modern times. In this connexion it is customary to cite Gen., vi, 3, where God is represented as decreeing by way of punishment of the universal corruption which was the occasion of the Flood, that henceforth the days of man "shall be a hundred and twenty years". This is taken as indicating a point at which the physical deterioration of the race resulted in a marked decrease in longevity. But apart from critical considerations bearing on this passage, it is strange to note further on (Gen., xi) that the ages of the subsequent patriarchs were by no means limited to 120 years. Sem lived to the age of 600, Arphaxad 338 (Massoretic Text 408), Sale 433, Heber 464 etc.

The one ground on which the accuracy of all these figures can be defended is the a priori reason that being contained in the Bible, they must of a necessity be historically correct, and this position is maintained by the older commentators generally. Most modern scholars, on the other hand, are agreed in considering the genealogical and chronological lists of Gen., v, and xi, to be mainly artificial, and this view seems to be confirmed, they say, by a comparison of the figures as they stand in the Hebrew original and in the ancient versions. The Vulgate is in agreement with the former (with the exception of Arphaxad), showing that no substantial alteration of the figures has been made in the Hebrew at least since the end of the fourth century A. D.

But when we compare the Massoretic Text with the Samaritan version and the Septuagint, we are confronted by many and strange discrepancies which can hardly be the result of mere accident. Thus for instance, with regard to the antediluvian patriarchs, while the Samaritan version agrees in the main with the Massoretic Text, the age at which Jared begot his first-born is set down as 62 instead of the Hebrew 162. Mathusala, likewise, who according to the Hebrew begot his first-born at the age of 187, was only 67 according to the Samaritan; and though the Hebrew places the same event in the case of Lamech when he was 182, the Samaritan gives him only 53. Similar discrepancies exist between the two texts as regards the total number of years that these patriarchs lived, viz. Jared, Heb. 962, Sam. 847; Mathusala, Heb. 969, Sam. 720; Lamech, Heb. 777, Sam. 653. Comparing the Massoretic Text with the Septuagint, we find that in the latter the birth of the first-born in the case of Adam, Seth, Enos, Cainan, Malaleel, and Henoch was at the respective ages of 230, 205, 190, 170, 165, and 165, as against 130, 105, 90, 70, 65, and 65 as stated in the Hebrew, and the same systematic difference of 100 years in the period before the birth of the first-born appears likewise in the lives of the postdiluvian patriarchs, Arphaxad, Sale, Heber, Phaleg, Reu, and Sarug. For this list, however, the Samaritan agrees with the Septuagint as against the Massoretic Text.

As regards the list of the antediluvians, the Hebrew and Septuagint agree as to the sum total of each patriarch's life, since the Greek version reduces regularly by a hundred years the period between the birth of the first-born and the patriarch's death. These accumulated differences result in a wide divergence when the duration of the entire patriarchal period is considered. Thus the number of years which elapsed from the beginning down to the death of Lamech is, according to the Hebrew, 1651, while the Samaritan gives 1307, and the Septuagint 2227. These are but a few of the peculiarities exhibited by the comparison of these perplexing genealogical lists. That the divergences are for the most part intentional seems to be a necessary inference from their systematic regularity, and the implied manipulation of the figures by the early translators goes far to make probable the more or less artificial character of these primitive chronologies as a whole.

Von Hummelauer, *Comment. in Genesim* (Paris, 1895); Gigot, *Special Introduction to the Study of the Old Testament*, I (New York, 1901), 184 sq.; Vigouroux, *Livres Saints et Critique Rationaliste*, IV (Paris, 1891), 224 sq.; Idem, *Manuel Biblique*, II (Paris, 1880), n. 333; Kaulen in *Kirchenlexikon*, s. v.; see also Chronology, Biblical.   James F. Driscoll.

Patriarch and Patriarchate, names of the highest ecclesiastical dignitaries after the pope, and of the territory they rule.

I. Origin of the Title.—Patriarch (Gr. πατριάρχης; Lat. *patriarcha*) means the father or chief of a race (πατριά, a clan or family). The word occurs in the Septuagint for the chiefs of the tribes (e. g. I Par., xxiv, 31; xxvii, 22, πατριάρχαι τῶν φυλῶν; cf. II Par., xxiii, 20 etc.); in the New Testament (Heb., vii, 4) it is applied to Abraham as a version of his title "father of many nations" (Gen., xvii, 4), to David (Acts, ii, 29), and to the twelve sons of Jacob (Acts, vii, 8–9). This last became the special meaning of the word when used of Scriptural characters. The heads of the tribes were the "Twelve Patriarchs", though the word is used also in a more general sense for the fathers of the Old Law in general, e. g. the invocation in the litany, "All ye holy Patriarchs and Prophets".

Names of Christian dignitaries were in early days taken sometimes from civil life (ἐπίσκοπος, διάκονος), sometimes borrowed from the Jews (πρεσβύτερος). The name patriarch is one of the latter class. Bishops of special dignity were called patriarchs just as deacons were called levites, because their place corresponded by analogy to those in the Old Law. All such titles became technical terms, official titles, only gradually. At first they were used loosely as names of honour without any strict connotation; but in all such cases the reality existed before any special name was used. There were ecclesiastical dignitaries with all the rights and prerogatives of patriarchs in the first three centuries; but the official title does not occur till later. As a Christian title of honour the word patriarch appears first as applied to Pope Leo I in a letter of Theodosius II (408–50; Mansi, VI, 68). The bishops of the Byzantine jurisdiction apply it to their chief, Acacius (471–89; Evagrius, "H. E.", III, 9). But it was still merely an honourable epithet that might be given to any venerable bishop. St. Gregory of Nazianzus says: "the elder bishops, or more rightly, the patriarchs" (Orat., xlii, 23). Socrates says that the Fathers of Constantinople I (381) "set up patriarchs", meaning apparently metropolitans of provinces (H. E., V, viii). As late as the fifth and sixth centuries Celidonius of Besançon and Nicetius of Lyons are still called patriarchs (Acta SS., Feb., III, 742; Gregory of Tours, "Hist. Francorum", V, xx).

Gradually then—certainly from the eighth and ninth centuries—the word becomes an official title, used henceforth only as connoting a definite rank in the hierarchy, that of the chief bishops who ruled over metropolitans as metropolitans over their suffragan bishops, being themselves subject only to the first patriarch at Rome. During these earlier centuries the name appears generally in conjunction with "archbishop", "archbishop and patriarch", as in the Code of Justinian (Gelzer, "Der Streit über den Titel des ökumen. Patriarchen" in "Jahrbuch für protest. Theol.", 1887). The dispute about the title Œcumenical Patriarch in the sixth century (see John the Faster) shows that even then the name was receiving a technical sense. Later medieval and modern developments, schisms, and the creation of titular and so-called "minor" patriarchates have produced the result that a great number of persons now claim the title; but in all cases it connotes the idea of a special rank—the highest, except among Catholics who admit the still higher papacy.

Patriarchate (Gr. πατριαρχεία; Lat. *patriarchatus*) is the derived word meaning a patriarch's office, see, reign, or, most often, the territory he governs. It corresponds to episcopacy, episcopate, and diocese in relation to a bishop.

II. The Three Patriarchs.—The oldest canon law admitted only three bishops as having what later ages called patriarchal rights—the Bishops of Rome, Alexandria, and Antioch. The successor of St. Peter as a matter of course held the highest place and combined in his own person all dignities. He was not only bishop, but metropolitan, primate, and patriarch; Metropolitan of the Roman Province, Primate of Italy, and first of the patriarchs. As soon as a hierarchy was organized among bishops, the chief authority and dignity were retained by the Bishop of Rome. The pope combines the above positions and each of them gives him a special relation to the faithful and the bishops in the territory corresponding. As pope he is visible head of the whole Church; no Christian is outside his papal jurisdiction. As Bishop of Rome he is the diocesan bishop of that diocese only; as metropolitan he governs the Roman Province; as primate he governs the Italian bishops; as patriarch he rules only the West. As patriarch the Roman pontiff has from the beginning ruled all the Western lands where Latin was once the civilized, and is still the liturgical language, where the Roman Rite is now used almost exclusively and the Roman canon law (e. g. celibacy, our rules of fasting and abstinence, etc.) obtains. To Christians in the East he is supreme pontiff, not patriarch. Hence there has always been a closer relation between Western bishops and the pope than between him and their Eastern brethren, just as there is a still closer relation between him and the suburban bishops of the Roman Province of which he is metropolitan. Many laws that we obey are not universal Catholic laws, but those of the Western patriarchate. Before the Council of Nicæa (325) two bishops in the East had the same patriarchal authority over large territories, those of Alexandria and Antioch. It is difficult to say exactly how they obtained this position. The organization of provinces under metropolitans followed, as a matter of obvious convenience, the organization of the empire arranged by Diocletian (Fortescue, "Orthodox Eastern Church", 21–23). In this arrangement the most important cities in the East were Alexandria of Egypt and Antioch of Syria. So the Bishop of Alexandria became the chief of all

Egyptian bishops and metropolitans; the Bishop of Antioch held the same place over Syria and at the same time extended his sway over Asia Minor, Greece, and the rest of the East. Diocletian had divided the empire into four great prefectures. Three of these (Italy, Gaul, and Illyricum) made up the Roman patriarchate, the other, the "East" (Præfectura Orientis) had five (civil) "dioceses"—Thrace, Asia, Pontus, the Diocese of the East, and Egypt. Egypt was the Alexandrine patriarchate. The Antiochene patriarchate embraced the civil "Diocese" of the East. The other three civil divisions of Thrace, Asia, and Pontus would have probably developed into separate patriarchates, but for the rise of Constantinople (ibid., 22–25). Later it became a popular idea to connect all three patriarchates with the Prince of the Apostles. St. Peter had also reigned at Antioch; he had founded the Church of Alexandria by his disciple St. Mark. At any rate the Council of Nicæa in 325 recognizes the supreme place of the bishops of these three cities as an "ancient custom" (can. vi). Rome, Alexandria, and Antioch are the three old patriarchates whose unique position and order were disturbed by later developments.

III. THE FIVE PATRIARCHATES.—When pilgrims began to flock to the Holy City, the Bishop of Jerusalem, the guardian of the sacred shrines, began to be considered as more than a mere suffragan of Cæsarea. The Council of Nicæa (325) gave him an honorary primacy, saving, however, the metropolitical rights of Cæsarea (can. vii). Juvenal of Jerusalem (420–58) succeeded finally, after much dispute, in changing this honorary position into a real patriarchate. The Council of Chalcedon (451) cut away Palestine and Arabia (Sinai) from Antioch and of them formed the Patriarchate of Jerusalem (Sess. VII and VIII). Since that time Jerusalem has always been counted among the patriarchal sees as the smallest and last (ibid., 25–28). But the greatest change, the one that met most opposition, was the rise of Constantinople to patriarchal rank. Because Constantine had made Byzantium "New Rome", its bishop, once the humble suffragan of Heraclea, thought that he should become second only, if not almost equal, to the Bishop of Old Rome. For many centuries the popes opposed this ambition, not because any one thought of disputing their first place, but because they were unwilling to change the old order of the hierarchy. In 381 the Council of Constantinople declared that: "The Bishop of Constantinople shall have the primacy of honour after the Bishop of Rome, because it is New Rome" (can. iii). The popes (Damasus, Gregory the Great) refused to confirm this canon. Nevertheless Constantinople grew by favour of the emperor, whose centralizing policy found a ready help in the authority of his court bishop. Chalcedon (451) established Constantinople as a patriarchate with jurisdiction over Asia Minor and Thrace and gave it the second place after Rome (can. xxviii). Pope Leo I (440–61) refused to admit this canon, which was made in the absence of his legates; for centuries Rome still refused to give the second place to Constantinople. It was not until the Fourth Lateran Council (1215) that the Latin Patriarch of Constantinople was allowed this place; in 1439 the Council of Florence gave it to the Greek patriarch. Nevertheless in the East the emperor's wish was powerful enough to obtain recognition for his patriarch; from Chalcedon we must count Constantinople as practically, if not legally, the second patriarchate (ibid., 28–47). So we have the new order of five patriarchs—Rome, Constantinople, Alexandria, Antioch, Jerusalem—that seemed, to Eastern theologians especially, an essential element of the constitution of the Church [see (ibid., 46–47) the letter of Peter III of Antioch, c. 1054].

IV. FURTHER DEVELOPMENT.—At the time of Cerularius's schism (1054) the great Church of the empire knew practically these five patriarchs only, though "minor" patriarchates had already begun in the West. The Eighth General Council (Constantinople IV, in 869) had solemnly affirmed their position (can. xxi). The schism, and further distinctions that would not have existed but for it, considerably augmented the number of bishops who claimed the title. But before the great schism the earlier Nestorian and Monophysite separations had resulted in the existence of various heretical patriarchs. To be under a patriarch had come to be the normal, apparently necessary, condition for any Church. So it was natural that these heretics when they broke from the Catholic patriarchs should sooner or later set up rivals of their own. But in most cases they have been neither consistent nor logical. Instead of being merely an honourable title for the occupants of the five chief sees, the name patriarch was looked upon as denoting a rank of its own. So there was the idea that one might be patriarch of any place. We shall understand the confusion of this idea if we imagine some sect setting up a Pope of London or New York in opposition to the Pope of Rome. The Nestorians broke away from Antioch in the fifth century. They then called their catholicus (originally a vicar of the Antiochene pontiff), patriarch; though he has never claimed to be Patriarch of Antioch, which alone would have given a reason for his title. Babæus (Bab-Hai, 498–503) is said to be the first who usurped the title, as Patriarch of Seleucia and Ctesiphon (Assemani, "Bibl. Orient.", III, 427). The Copts and Jacobites have been more consistent. During the long Monophysite quarrels (fifth to seventh cent.) there were continually rival or alternate Catholic and Monophysite patriarchs of Alexandria and Antioch. Eventually, since the Moslem conquest of Egypt and Syria, rival lines were formed. So there is a line of Coptic patriarchs of Alexandria and of Jacobite patriarchs of Antioch as rivals to the Melchite ones. But in this case each claims to represent the old line and refuses to recognize its rivals, which is a possible position.

The Armenian Church has made the same mistake as the Nestorians. It has now four so-called patriarchs, of which two bear titles of sees that cannot by any rule of antiquity claim to be patriarchal at all, and the other two have not even the pretence of descent from the old lines. The Armenian Catholicus of Etchmiadzin began to call himself a patriarch on the same basis as the Nestorian primate—simply as head of a large and, after the Monophysite schism (Synod of Duin in 527), independent Church. It is difficult to say at what date he assumed the title. Armenian writers call all their catholici patriarchs, back to St. Gregory the Illuminator (fourth cent.). Silbernagl counts Nerses I (353–73?) first patriarch (Verfassung u. gegenw. Bestand, 216). But a claim to patriarchal rank could hardly have been made at a time when Armenia was still in union with and subject to the See of Cæsarea. The Catholicus's title is not local; he is "Patriarch of all Armenians." In 1461 Mohammed II set up an Armenian Patriarch of Constantinople to balance the Orthodox one. A temporary schism among the Armenians resulted in a Patriarchate of Sis, and in the seventeenth century the Armenian Bishop of Jerusalem began to call himself patriarch. It is clear then how entirely the Armenians ignore what the title really means.

The next multiplication of patriarchs was produced by the Crusades. The crusaders naturally refused to recognize the claims of the old, now schismatical, patriarchal lines, whose representatives moreover in most cases fled; so they set up Latin patriarchs in their place. The first Latin Patriarch of Jerusalem was Dagobert of Pisa (1099–1107); the Orthodox rival (Simon II) had fled to Cyprus in 1099 and died there the same year (for the list of his successors see Le Quien, III, 1241–68). It was not till 1142 that the Orthodox continued their broken line by electing Arsenios II, who like most Orthodox patriarchs at that time lived at Constantinople. At Antioch, too, the crusaders had a scruple against two patriarchs of the same place. They took the city in 1098, but as long as the Orthodox patriarch (John IV) remained there they tried to make him a Catholic instead of appointing a rival. However, when at last he fled to Constantinople they considered the see vacant, and Bernard, Bishop of Arthesia, a Frenchman, was elected to it (the succession in Le Quien, III, 1154–84).

In 1167 Amaury II, King of Jerusalem, captured Alexandria, as did Peter I, King of Cyprus, in 1365. But both times the city was given back to the Moslems at once. Nor were there any Latin inhabitants to justify the establishment of a Latin patriarchate. On the other hand, the Orthodox patriarch, Nicholas I (c. 1210–after 1223; Le Quien, II, 490) was well disposed towards reunion, wrote friendly letters to the pope, and was invited to the Fourth Lateran Council (1215). There was then a special reason for not setting up a Latin rival to him. Eventually a Latin patriarchate was established rather to complete what had been done in other cases than for any practical reason. Giles, Patriarch of Grado, a Dominican, was made first Latin Patriarch of Alexandria by Clement V in 1310. An earlier Latin Athanasius seems to be mythical (Le Quien, III, 1143). For the list of Giles's line see Le Quien (III, 1141–1151). When the Fourth Crusade took Constantinople in 1204, the patriarch John X fled to Nicæa with the emperor, and Thomas Morosini was made Latin patriarch to balance the Latin emperor (Le Quien, III, 793–836). It will be seen then that the crusaders acted from their point of view correctly enough. But the result was for each see double lines that have continued ever since. The Orthodox lines went on; the Latin patriarchs ruled as long as the Latins held those lands. When the crusaders' kingdoms came to an end they went on as titular patriarchs and have been for many centuries dignitaries of the papal court. Only the Latin Patriarch of Jerusalem was sent back in 1847 to be the head of all Latins in Palestine. By that time people were so accustomed to see different patriarchs of the same place ruling each his own "nation" that this seemed a natural proceeding.

The formation of Uniat Churches since the sixteenth century again increased the number of patriarchates. These people could no longer obey the old schismatical lines. On the other hand each group came out of a corresponding schismatical Church; they were accustomed to a chief of their own rite, their own "nation" in the Turkish sense. The only course seemed to be to give to each a Uniat patriarch corresponding to his schismatical rival. Moreover, in many cases the line of Uniat patriarchs comes from a disputed succession among the schismatics, one claimant having submitted to Rome and being therefore deposed by the schismatical majority. The oldest of these Uniat patriarchates is that of the Maronites. In 680 the Patriarch of Antioch, Macarius, was deposed by the Sixth General Council for Monotheletism. The Monotheletes then grouped themselves around the hegumenos of the Maronite monastery, John (d. 707). This begins the separated Maronite (at that time undoubtedly Monothelete) Church. John made himself Patriarch of Antioch for his followers, who wanted a head and were in communion with neither the Jacobites nor the Melchites. At the time of the crusades the Maronites united with Rome (1182 and again in 1216). They are allowed to keep their Patriarch of Antioch as head of their rite; but he in no way represents the old line of St. Peter and St. Ignatius. The next oldest Uniat patriarchate is that of Babylon for the Chaldees (converted Nestorians). It began with the submission of the Nestorian patriarch, John Sulaga (d. 1555). There has been a complicated series of rivalries and schisms since, of which the final curious result is that the present Uniat patriarch represents the old Nestorian line, and his Nestorian rival the originally Catholic line of Sulaga. The title of "Babylon" was not used till Pope Innocent XI conferred it in 1681. The Melchite patriarchate dates from 1724 (Cyril VI, 1724–1759). It began again with a disputed succession to the old patriarchal See of Antioch; the Melchite occupant has quite a good claim to represent the old line. The Uniat Byzantine Sees of Alexandria and Jerusalem are for the present considered as joined to that of Antioch; the Melchite patriarch uses all three titles (see MELCHITES). The Uniat Armenians have a patriarch who resides at Constantinople, but does not take his title from that city. His line began with a disputed election to Sis, one of the secondary Armenian patriarchates, in 1739. He is called Patriarch of Cilicia of the Armenians. In 1781 Ignatius Giarve, Jacobite Bishop of Aleppo, was elected canonically Patriarch of Antioch. He then made his submission to Rome and the heretical bishops deposed him and chose a Monophysite as patriarch. From Giarve the line of Uniat Syrian patriarchs of Antioch descends. Lastly, in 1895, Pope Leo XIII erected a Uniat Coptic Patriarchate of Alexandria for the many Copts who were at that time becoming Catholics. This exhausts the list of Uniat patriarchs. In three cases (the Chaldees, Melchites, and Syrians) the Uniat patriarch has, on purely historical grounds, at least as good a claim as his schismatical rival, if not better, to represent the old succession. On the other hand, the existence of several Catholic patriarchs of the same see, for instance, the Melchite, Jacobite, Maronite, and Latin titulars of Antioch, is a concession to the national feeling of Eastern Christians, or, in the case of the Latin, a relic of the crusades that archæologically can hardly be justified.

It is curious that there is no Uniat Patriarch of Constantinople. There was for a time, however brief, a new patriarchate among the Orthodox. In the sixteenth century the Church of Russia had become a very large and flourishing branch of the Orthodox communion. The Russian Government then thought the time had come to break its dependence on Constantinople. In 1589 the Tsar Feodor I (1581–98) made the Metropolitan See of Moscow into an independent patriarchate. In 1591 the other patriarchs in synod confirmed his arrangement and gave Moscow the fifth place, below Jerusalem. Orthodox theologians were delighted that the sacred pentarchy, the classical order of five patriarchs, was thus restored; they said that God had raised up Moscow to replace fallen Rome. But their joy did not last long. Only ten Russian patriarchs reigned. In 1700 the last of these, Adria, died. Peter the Great did not allow a successor to be elected, and in 1721 replaced the patriarchate by the Holy Directing Synod that now rules the Russian Church. But many Russians who resent the present tyranny of State over Church in their country hope for a restoration of the national patriarchate as the first step towards better things.

There remain only the so-called "minor" patriarchates in the West. At various times certain Western sees, too, have been called patriarchal. But there is a fundamental difference between these and any Eastern patriarchate. Namely, the pope is Patriarch of the West; all Western bishops of whatever rank are subject not only to his papal but also to his patriarchal jurisdiction. But a real patriarch cannot be subject to another patriarch; no patriarch can have another under his patriarchal jurisdiction, just as a diocesan ordinary cannot have another ordinary in his diocese. Eastern patriarchs claim independence of any other patriarch as such; the Catholics obey the pope as pope, the Orthodox recognize the civil headship of Constantinople, the Armenians a certain primacy of honour in their catholicus. But in every case the essence of a patriarch's dignity is that he has no other patriarch over him *as patriarch*. On the other hand, these Western minor patriarchs have never been supposed to be exempt from the Roman patriarchate. They have never had fragments cut away from Rome to make patriarchates for them, as for instance Jerusalem was formed of a fragment detached from Antioch.

Indeed, none of them has ever had any patriarchate at all. It may be said that the origin of the title in the West was an imitation of the East. But legally the situation was totally different. The Western patriarchates have never been more than mere titles conveying no jurisdiction at all. The earliest of them was Aquileia in Illyricum. It was an important city in the first centuries; the see claimed to have been founded by St. Mark. During the rule of the Goths in Italy (fifth to sixth centuries) the Bishop of Aquileia was called patriarch, though the name was certainly not used in any technical sense. It is one more example of the looser meaning by which any venerable bishop might be so called in earlier times. However, the Bishop of Aquileia began to use his complimentary title in a more definite sense. Though Illyricum undoubtedly belonged legally to the Roman Patriarchate, it was long a fruitful source of dispute with the East (Orth. Eastern Church, 44–45); Aquileia on the frontier thought itself entitled to some kind of independence of either Rome or Constantinople. At first the popes resolutely refused to acknowledge this new claim in any form. Then came the quarrel of the Three Chapters.

When, however, Pope Vigilius had yielded to the second Council of Constantinople (553), a number of North Italian bishops went into formal schism, led by Macedonius of Aquileia (539–56). From this time the Bishops of Aquileia call themselves patriarchs, as heads of a schismatical party, till 700. Paulinus of Aquileia (557–71) moved his see to Grado, a small island opposite Aquileia, keeping, however, the old title. This line of bishops in Grado became Catholics about 606; their schismatical suffragans then restored the old see at Aquileia as a schismatical patriarchate. The popes seem to have allowed or tolerated the same title for the Bishops of Aquileia-Grado. The Synod at Aquileia in 700 put an end to the schism finally.

From that time, however, there were two lines of so-called patriarchs, those of Aquileia and of Grado (where the bishop now kept the title of Grado only). Neither had more than metropolitical jurisdiction. Both these titles are now merged in that of the Patriarch of Venice. The See of Venice absorbed Grado in the fifteenth century. The city of Aquileia was overthrown by an earthquake in 1348, but the line of patriarchs continued at Udine. It came thus entirely in the power of the Venetian Republic; the patriarch was always a Venetian. Eventually Benedict XIV, in 1751, changed the title to that of Patriarch of Venice.

The discovery of America added a vast territory to the Church, over which it seemed natural that a patriarch should reign. In 1520 Leo X created a "Patriarchate of the West Indies" among the Spanish clergy. In 1572 Pius V joined this rank to the office of chief chaplain of the Spanish army. But in this case, too, the dignity is purely titular. In 1644 Innocent X gave the patriarch some jurisdiction, but expressly in his quality of chaplain only. He has no income as patriarch and is often also bishop of a Spanish diocese. In 1716 Clement XI, in answer to a petition of King John, who, in return for help in fighting Turks, wanted a patriarch like the King of Spain, erected a titular Patriarchate of Lisbon at the king's chapel. The city was divided between the jurisdiction of the Archbishop of Lisbon and the new patriarch. In 1740 Benedict XIV joined the archbishopric to the patriarchate. The Patriarch of Lisbon has certain privileges of honour that make his court an imitation of that of the pope. His chapter has three orders like those of the College of Cardinals; he himself is always made a cardinal at the first consistory after his preconization and he uses a tiara (without the keys) over his arms, but he has no more than metropolitical jurisdiction over seven suffragans. Lastly, Leo XIII, in 1886, as a counterpoise to the Patriarchate of the West Indies, erected a titular Patriarchate of the East Indies attached to the See of Goa.

At various times other Western bishops have been called patriarchs. In the Middle Ages those of Lyons, Bourges, Canterbury, Toledo, Pisa were occasionally so called. But there was never any legal claim to these merely complimentary titles.

V. EXISTING PATRIARCHS.—We give first a complete list of all persons who now bear the title. A. *Catholics.*—The pope as Patriarch of the West (this is the commonest form; "Patriarch of Rome", or "Latin Patriarch" also occur) rules all Western Europe from Poland to Illyricum (the Balkan Peninsula), Africa west of Egypt, all other lands (America, Australia) colonized from these lands and all Western (Latin) missionaries and dwellers in the East. In other words, his patriarchal jurisdiction extends over all who use the Western (Roman, Ambrosian, Mozarabic) rites, and over the Byzantine Uniats in Italy, Corsica, and Sicily. As patriarch he may hold patriarchal synods and he frequently makes laws (such as ritual laws and our form of clerical celibacy) for the Western patriarchate alone.

The Uniat Catholic patriarchs are as follows: (1) Melchite Patriarch of Antioch, Alexandria, Jerusalem, and all the East, ruling over all Melchites (q. v.); (2) the Syrian Patriarch of Antioch and all the East; (3) the Maronite Patriarch of Antioch and all the East; (4) the Coptic Patriarch of Alexandria; (5) the Patriarch of Cilicia of the Armenians; (6) the Patriarch of Babylon of the Chaldees. These rule over all members of their rite, except that the Armenian has no jurisdiction in Austria or the Crimea, where the Armenian Bishops of Lemberg and Artwin are exempt, being immediately subject to the Holy See.

Of the Latin patriarchs only one has jurisdiction: the Latin Patriarch of Jerusalem (over all Latins in Palestine and Cyprus). All the others are titular, namely: the Latin Patriarchs of Constantinople, Antioch and Jerusalem, ornaments of the papal court at Rome; the "minor" Patriarchs of Venice, Lisbon, the West Indies, the East Indies. It should be noted that the modern Roman lists (e. g. the "Gerarchia Cattolica") ignore the difference between those who have jurisdiction and the titular patriarchs and count all who bear the title of one of the old patriarchates (Constantinople, Alexandria, Antioch, Jerusalem) as major, all others (including Babylon and Cilicia) as minor.

B. *Non-Catholics.*—Non-Catholics who bear the title now are the Orthodox Patriarchs of Constantinople, Alexandria, Antioch, Jerusalem; the Nestorian patriarch at Kuchanis (his title is now "Catholicus and Patriarch of the East"); the Coptic Patriarch of Alexandria; the Jacobite Patriarch of Antioch; four Armenian patriarchs, the "Catholicus and Patriarch of all Armenians" at Etchmiadzin and those of Constantinople, Sis, and Jerusalem. The rights, dignity, and duties of patriarchs form part of the canon law of each Church. They are not the same in all cases. As a general principle it may be said that the fundamental notion is that a patriarch has the same authority over his metropolitans as they have over their suffragan bishops. Moreover, a patriarch is not himself subject to another patriarch, or rather he is not subject to any one's patriarchal jurisdiction. But there is here a difference between Catholics and the others. All Catholics, including patriarchs, obey the supreme (papal) authority of the Roman pontiff; further we must except from our consideration the merely titular patriarchs who have no authority at all. In the case of the Eastern Churches the general principle is that a patriarch is subject to no living authority save that of a possible general council. But here again we must except the Armenians. Their catholicus had for many centuries authority over all his Church very like that of the pope. It is diminished now; but still one can hardly say that the other patriarchs are quite independent of him. He alone may summon national synods. The (Armenian) Patriarch of Constantinople has now usurped most of his rights in the Turkish Empire. One of these two ordains all bishops. The Patriarch of Sis may not even consecrate chrism, but is supplied from Etchmiadzin. A somewhat similar case is that of the Orthodox. Since the Turkish conquest the Œcumenical Patriarch has been the *civil* head of all the Orthodox in the Turkish Empire. He has continually tried and still to a great extent tries to turn his civil headship into supreme ecclesiastical authority, to be in short an Orthodox pope. His attempts are always indignantly rejected by the other patriarchs and the national Churches, but not always successfully. Meanwhile he has kept at least one sign of authority. He alone consecrates chrism for all Orthodox bishops, except for those of Russia and Rumania.

In the East the general principle is that the patriarch ordains all bishops in his own territory. This is a very old sign of authority in those countries. He is elected by his metropolitans or (permanent) synod, ordained, as a rule, by his own suffragans, makes laws, and has certain rights of confirming or deposing his bishops, generally in conjunction with his synod, and may summon patriarchal (temporary) synods. The question of the deposition of patriarchs among the non-Catholics is difficult. Among the Orthodox they have been and are constantly deposed by their metropolitans or synod. They nearly always refuse to acknowledge their deposition and a struggle follows in which Constantinople always tries to interfere. Eventually the Turk settles it, generally in favour of deposition, since he gets a large bribe for the new patriarch's *berat*. The special rights and duties of the patriarchs of the various Eastern Churches are given in Silbernagl (*infra*).

In the Catholic Church since Eugene IV (1431–47) cardinals have precedence over patriarchs. Uniat patriarchs are elected by a synod of all the bishops of the patriarchate and confirmed by the Holy See. They must send a profession of Faith to the pope and receive the pallium from him. Their rights are summed up by a Constitution of Benedict XIV ("Apostolica", 14 Feb., 1742), namely: to summon and preside at patriarchal synods (whose acts must be confirmed at Rome), to ordain all bishops of their territory and consecrate chrism, to send the omophorion to their metropolitans, receive appeals made against the judgments of these, and receive tithes of all episcopal income; in synod they may depose their bishops. They bear their patriarchal cross not only throughout their own territory, but, by a special concession, everywhere except at Rome. All have a permanent representative at Rome. They must visit all their dioceses every third year and may not resign without the pope's consent. The Bull "Reversurus" of Pius IX (1867) made further laws first for the Armenian patriarch; then with modifications it has been extended to other Uniats. The precedence among patriarchs is determined by the rank of their see, according to the old order of the five patriarchates, followed by Cilicia, then Babylon. Between several titulars of the same see but of different rites the order is that of the date of their preconization.

The titular Latin patriarchs have only certain ceremonial prerogatives. The Roman *patriarchia* are five basilicas, one the pope's own cathedral, the others churches at which the other patriarchs officiated if they came to Rome, near which they dwelt. The papal *patriarchium* was originally the "Domus Pudentiana"; since the early Middle Ages it is the Basilica of Saint Saviour at the Lateran (St. John Lateran). The others are, or were, St. Peter for Constantinople, St. Paul Without the Walls for Alexandria, St. Mary Major for Antioch, St. Lawrence for Jerusalem. These are now only titles and memories.

Le Quien, *Oriens christianus* (Paris, 1740); Bingham, *Origines ecclesiasticæ*, I (London, 1708–22), 232 sq.; Lübeck, *Reichseinteilung u. kirchliche Hierarchie des Orients bis zum Ausgang des vierten Jahrhunderts* (Münster, 1900); Hinschius, *System des katholischen Kirchenrechts*, I (1869); Kattenbusch, *Lehrbuch der vergleichenden Konfessionskunde*, I (Freiburg, 1892); Silbernagl, *Verfassung und gegenwärtiger Bestand sämtlicher Kirchen des Orients* (Ratisbon, 1904); Fortescue, *The Orthodox Eastern Church* (London, 1907), i.

Adrian Fortescue.

Patriarchs, Testaments of the Twelve. See Apocrypha, sub-title II.

Patrician Brothers (or Brothers of Saint Patrick).—This Brotherhood was founded by the Right Rev. Dr. Daniel Delaney, Bishop of Kildare and Leighlin, at Tullow, in the County of Carlow, Ireland, on the feast of the Purification of the Blessed Virgin Mary, in 1808, for the religious and literary education of youth and the instruction of the faithful in Christian piety. Catholic Ireland was at this period just emerging from the troubled times of the penal laws. These laws made it treasonable for a Catholic parent to procure for his child a religious and secular education in consonance with his belief, and consequently not only were the young deprived of the means of instruction, but adults also were in a state of enforced ignorance of Christian doctrine and its practices. Bishop Delaney set about the good work of founding the Religious Congregation of the Brothers of Saint Patrick in his diocese, for the purpose of affording his people that education of which they had been so long deprived. He chose from among the catechetical instructors of the Sunday schools seven young men who formed the nucleus of the new order, and under the personal instruction of the bishop, and direction of his successor, the illustrious Dr. Doyle, the congregation was established as a diocesan institution. In succeeding years filiations were established in other dioceses of Ireland, and the Brothers were invited by several Australian and Indian bishops to these distant countries. Several foundations were made, among them those of Sydney, to which archdiocese the Brothers were invited by Cardinal Moran; and that of Madras in India, undertaken at the request of the late prelate of that diocese, Bishop Stephen Fennelly.

In 1885 the Brothers made application to the Holy See for the approval of the congregation, for constituting a central government and for establishing a common novitiate. The request was granted. After taking the opinions of the bishops in whose dioceses the Brothers were labouring, Pope Leo XIII provisionally approved the congregation for five years by a Rescript dated 6 January, 1888, and on 8 September, 1893, issued a decree of final confirmation, highly commending the good work hitherto accomplished by the Brothers, approving of their rules and constitutions, granting them all the facilities and powers necessary for carrying on the duties of their congregation, constituting India and Australia separate provinces, and imparting to the institute the Apostolic Benediction. The houses of the order, which had hitherto been independent and separate communities, were united under a superior general who with four assistants governs the congregation.

A general chapter of the Patrician communities assembles every six years. As a result of the confirmation of the institute the Brothers have been enabled to perfect and extend their congregation in Ireland, and to open new colleges, schools, and orphanages in the above-mentioned foreign countries. The scope of their work, which embraces primary, intermediate, and university education, has been much extended in recent years. The introduction of a scheme of technical and scientific study by the different educational departments has been warmly supported by the Brotherhood; while by their management of orphanages and industrial schools they aid thousands of youths to raise themselves to a higher place in the social scale. Their residential colleges and secondary day-schools equip the students for responsible positions in life. The colleges of the Brothers in India are affiliated to the Allahabad and Calcutta Universities, in which their students have distinguished themselves; while in Australia, notwithstanding that the Brothers receive no State aid, their pupils compete successfully with those of the highly subsidized Government schools for positions in the civil service. On the occasion of the centenary in 1908, His Holiness Pope Pius X bestowed on the order many favours and special indulgences. The superior general and his assistants reside at the mother-house, Tullow, Ireland, where are also the novitiate and house of studies.

JEROME F. BYRNE.

Patrick, SAINT, APOSTLE OF IRELAND, b. at Kilpatrick, near Dumbarton, in Scotland, in the year 387; d. at Saul, Downpatrick, Ireland, 17 March, 493. He had for his parents Calphurnius and Conchessa. The former belonged to a Roman family of high rank and held the office of *decurio* in Gaul or Britain. Conchessa was a near relative of the great patron of Gaul, St. Martin of Tours. Kilpatrick still retains many memorials of Saint Patrick, and frequent pilgrimages continued far into the Middle Ages to perpetuate there the fame of his sanctity and miracles. In his sixteenth year, Patrick was carried off into captivity by Irish marauders and was sold as a slave to a chieftain named Milchu in Dalaradia, a territory of the present county of Antrim in Ireland, where for six years he tended his master's flocks in the valley of the Braid and on the slopes of Slemish, near the modern town of Ballymena. He relates in his "Confessio" that during his captivity while tending the flocks he prayed many times in the day: "the love of God", he added, "and His fear increased in me more and more, and the faith grew in me, and the spirit was roused, so that, in a single day, I have said as many as a hundred prayers, and in the night nearly the same, so that whilst in the woods and on the mountain, even before the dawn, I was roused to prayer and I felt no hurt from it, whether there was snow or ice or rain; nor was there any slothfulness in me, such as I see now, because the spirit was then fervent within me." In the ways of a benign Providence the six years of Patrick's captivity became a remote preparation for his future apostolate. He acquired a perfect knowledge of the Celtic tongue in which he would one day announce the glad tidings of Redemption, and, as his master Milchu was a druidical high priest, he became familiar with all the details of Druidism from whose bondage he was destined to liberate the Irish race.

Admonished by an angel he after six years fled from his cruel master and bent his steps towards the west. He relates in his "Confessio" that he had to travel about 200 miles; and his journey was probably towards Killala Bay and onwards thence to Westport. He found a ship ready to set sail and after some rebuffs was allowed on board. In a few days he was among his friends once more in Britain, but now his heart was set on devoting himself to the service of God in the sacred ministry. We meet with him at St. Martin's monastery at Tours, and again at the island sanctuary of Lérins which was just then acquiring widespread renown for learning and piety; and wherever lessons of heroic perfection in the exercise of Christian life could be acquired, thither the fervent Patrick was sure to bend his steps. No sooner had St. Germain entered on his great mission at Auxerre than Patrick put himself under his guidance, and it was at that great bishop's hands that Ireland's future apostle was a few years later promoted to the priesthood. It is the tradition in the territory of the Morini that Patrick under St. Germain's guidance for some years was engaged in missionary work among them. When Germain commissioned by the Holy See proceeded to Britain to combat the erroneous teachings of Pelagius, he chose Patrick to be one of his missionary companions and thus it was his privilege to be associated with the representative of Rome in the triumphs that ensued over heresy and Paganism, and in the many remarkable events of the expedition, such as the miraculous calming of the tempest at sea, the visit to the relics at St. Alban's shrine, and the Alleluia victory. Amid all these scenes, however, Patrick's thoughts turned towards Ireland, and from time to time he was favoured with visions of the children from Focluth, by the Western sea, who cried out to him: "O holy youth, come back to Erin, and walk once more amongst us."

Pope St. Celestine I (q. v.), who rendered immortal service to the Church by the overthrow of the Pelagian and Nestorian heresies, and by the imperishable wreath of honour decreed to the Blessed Virgin in the General Council of Ephesus, crowned his pontificate by an act of the most far-reaching consequences for the spread of Christianity and civilization, when he entrusted St. Patrick with the mission of gathering the Irish race into the one fold of Christ. Palladius (q. v.) had already received that commission, but terrified by the fierce opposition of a Wicklow chieftain had abandoned the sacred enterprise. It was St. Germain, Bishop of Auxerre, who commended Patrick to the pope. The writer of St. Germain's Life in the ninth century, Heric of Auxerre, thus attests this important fact: "Since the glory of the father shines in the training of the children, of the many sons in Christ whom St. Germain is believed to have had as disciples in religion, let it suffice to make mention here, very briefly, of one most famous, Patrick, the special Apostle of the Irish nation, as the record of his work proves. Subject to that most holy discipleship for 18 years, he drank in no little knowledge in Holy Scripture from the stream of so great a well-spring. Germain sent him, accompanied by Segetius, his priest, to Celestine, Pope of Rome, approved of by whose judgment, supported by whose authority, and strengthened by whose blessing, he went on his way to Ireland." It was only shortly before his death that Celestine gave this mission to Ireland's apostle and on that occasion bestowed on him many relics and other spiritual gifts, and gave him the name "Patercius" or "Patritius", not as an honorary title, but as foreshadowing the fruitfulness and merit of his apostolate whereby he became *pater civium* (the father of his people). Patrick on his return journey from Rome received at Ivrea the tidings of the death of Palladius, and turning aside to the neighbouring city of Turin received episcopal consecration at the hands of its great bishop, St. Maximus, and thence hastened on to Auxerre to make under the guidance of St. Germain due preparations for the Irish mission.

It was probably in the summer months of the year 433, that Patrick and his companions landed at the mouth of the Vantry River close by Wicklow Head. The Druids were at once in arms against him. But Patrick was not disheartened. The intrepid missionary resolved to search out a more friendly territory in which to enter on his mission. First of all, however, he would proceed towards Dalaradia, where he had been a slave, to pay the price of ransom to his former master, and in exchange for the servitude and cruelty endured at his hands to impart to him the blessings and freedom of God's children. He rested for some days at the islands off the Skerries coast, one of which still retains the name of Inis-Patrick, and he probably visited the adjoining mainland, which in olden times was known as Holm Patrick. Tradition fondly points out the impression of St. Patrick's foot upon the hard rock—off the main shore, at the entrance to Skerries harbour. Continuing his course northwards he halted at the mouth of the River Boyne. A number of the natives there gathered around him and heard with joy in their own sweet tongue the glad tidings of Redemption. There too he performed his first miracle on Irish soil to confirm the honour due to the Blessed Virgin, and the Divine birth of our Saviour. Leaving one of his companions to continue the work of instruction so auspiciously begun, he hastened forward to Strangford Lough and there quitting his boat continued his journey over land towards Slemish. He had not proceeded far when a chieftain, named Dichu, appeared on the scene to prevent his further advance. He drew his sword to smite the saint, but his arm became rigid as a statue and continued so until he declared himself obedient to Patrick. Overcome by the saint's meekness and miracles, Dichu asked for instruction and made a gift of a large *sabhall* (barn), in which the sacred mysteries were offered up. This was the first sanctuary dedicated by St. Patrick in Erin. It became in later years a chosen retreat of the saint. A monastery and church were erected there, and the hallowed site retains the name Sabhall (pronounced Saul) to the present day. Continuing his journey towards Slemish, the saint was struck with horror on seeing at a distance the fort of his old master Milchu enveloped in flames. The fame of Patrick's marvellous power of miracles had preceded him. Milchu, in a fit of frenzy, gathered his treasures into his mansion and setting it on fire, cast himself into the flames. An ancient record adds: "His pride could not endure the thought of being vanquished by his former slave".

Returning to Saul, St. Patrick learned from Dichu that the chieftains of Erin had been summoned to celebrate a special feast at Tara by Leoghaire, who was the Ard-Righ, that is, Supreme Monarch of Ireland. This was an opportunity which Patrick would not forego; he would present himself before the assembly, to strike a decisive blow against the Druidism that held the nation captive, and to secure freedom for the glad tidings of Redemption of which he was the herald. As he journeyed on he rested for some days at the house of a chieftain named Secsnen, who with his household joyfully embraced the Faith. The youthful Benen, or Benignus, the son of the chief, was in a special way captivated by the Gospel doctrines and the meekness of Patrick. Whilst the saint slumbered he would gather sweet-scented flowers and scatter them over his bosom, and when Patrick was setting out, continuing his journey towards Tara, Benen clung to his feet declaring that nothing would sever him from him. "Allow him to have his way", said St. Patrick to the chieftain, "he shall be heir to my sacred mission." Thenceforth Benen was the inseparable companion of the saint, and the prophecy was fulfilled, for Benen is named among the "comhards" or successors of St. Patrick in Armagh. It was on 26 March, Easter Sunday in 433, that the eventful assembly was to meet at Tara, and the decree went forth that from the preceding day the fires throughout the kingdom should be extinguished until the signal blaze was kindled at the royal mansion. The chiefs and Brehons came in full numbers and the druids too would muster all their strength to bid defiance to the herald of good tidings and to secure the hold of their superstition on the Celtic race, for their demoniac oracles had announced that the messenger of Christ had come to Erin. St. Patrick arrived at the hill of Slane, at the opposite extremity of the valley from Tara, on Easter Eve, in that year the feast of the Annunciation, and on the summit of the hill kindled the Paschal fire. The druids at once raised their voice. "O King", (they said) "live for ever; this fire, which has been lighted in defiance of the royal edict, will blaze for ever in this land unless it be this very night extinguished." By order of the king and the agency of the druids, repeated attempts were made to extinguish the blessed fire and to punish with death the intruder who had disobeyed the royal command. But the fire was not extinguished and Patrick shielded by the Divine power came unscathed from their snares and assaults. On Easter Day the missionary band having at their head the youth Benignus bearing aloft a copy of the Gospels, and followed by St. Patrick who with mitre and crozier was arrayed in full episcopal attire, proceeded in processional order to Tara. The druids and magicians put forth all their strength and employed all their incantations to maintain their sway over the Irish race, but the prayer and faith of Patrick achieved a glorious triumph. The druids by their incantations overspread the hill and surrounding plain with a cloud of worse than Egyptian darkness. Patrick defied them to remove that cloud,

St. Patrick's Bell
National Museum, Dublin

and when all their efforts were made in vain, at his prayer the sun sent forth its rays and the brightest sunshine lit up the scene. Again by demoniac power the Arch-Druid Lochru, like Simon Magus of old, was lifted up high in the air, but when Patrick knelt in prayer the druid from his flight was dashed to pieces upon a rock. Thus was the final blow given to paganism in the presence of all the assembled chieftains. It was, indeed, a momentous day for the Irish race. Twice Patrick pleaded for the Faith before Leoghaire. The king had given orders that no sign of respect was to be extended to the strangers, but at the first meeting the youthful Erc, a royal page, arose to show him reverence; and at the second, when all the chieftains were assembled, the chief-bard Dubhtach showed the same honour to the saint. Both these heroic men became fervent disciples of the Faith and bright ornaments of the Irish Church. It was on this second solemn occasion that St. Patrick is said to have plucked a shamrock from the sward, to explain by its triple leaf and single stem, in some rough way, to the assembled chieftains, the great doctrine of the Blessed Trinity. On that bright Easter Day, the triumph of religion at Tara was complete. The Ard-Righ granted permission to Patrick to preach the Faith throughout the length and breadth of Erin, and the druidical prophecy like the words of Balaam of old would be fulfilled: the sacred fire now kindled by the saint would never be extinguished.

The beautiful prayer of St. Patrick, popularly known as "St. Patrick's Breast-Plate", is supposed to have been composed by him in preparation for this victory over Paganism. The following is a literal translation from the old Irish text:—

I bind to myself to-day
The strong virtue of the Invocation of the Trinity:
I believe the Trinity in the Unity
The Creator of the Universe.

I bind to myself to-day
The virtue of the Incarnation of Christ with His Baptism,
The virtue of His crucifixion with His burial,
The virtue of His Resurrection with His Ascension,
The virtue of His coming on the Judgment Day.

I bind to myself to-day
The virtue of the love of seraphim,
In the obedience of angels,
In the hope of resurrection unto reward,
In prayers of Patriarchs,
In predictions of Prophets,
In preaching of Apostles,
In faith of Confessors,
In purity of holy Virgins,
In deeds of righteous men.

I bind to myself to-day
The power of Heaven,
The light of the sun,
The brightness of the moon,
The splendour of fire,
The flashing of lightning,
The swiftness of wind,
The depth of sea,
The stability of earth,
The compactness of rocks.

I bind to myself to-day
God's Power to guide me,
God's Might to uphold me,
God's Wisdom to teach me,
God's Eye to watch over me,
God's Ear to hear me,
God's Word to give me speech,
God's Hand to guide me,
God's Way to lie before me,
God's Shield to shelter me,
God's Host to secure me,
Against the snares of demons,
Against the seductions of vices,
Against the lusts of nature,
Against everyone who meditates injury to me,
Whether far or near,
Whether few or with many.

I invoke to-day all these virtues
Against every hostile merciless power
Which may assail my body and my soul,
Against the incantations of false prophets,
Against the black laws of heathenism,
Against the false laws of heresy,
Against the deceits of idolatry,
Against the spells of women, and smiths, and druids,
Against every knowledge that binds the soul of man.

Christ, protect me to-day
Against every poison, against burning,
Against drowning, against death-wound,
That I may receive abundant reward.

Christ with me, Christ before me,
Christ behind me, Christ within me,
Christ beneath me, Christ above me,
Christ at my right, Christ at my left,
Christ in the fort,
Christ in the chariot seat,
Christ in the poop,
Christ in the heart of everyone who thinks of me,
Christ in the mouth of everyone who speaks to me,
Christ in every eye that sees me,
Christ in every ear that hears me.

I bind to myself to-day
The strong virtue of an invocation of the Trinity,
I believe the Trinity in the Unity
The Creator of the Universe.

St. Patrick remained during Easter week at Slane and Tara, unfolding to those around him the lessons of Divine truth. Meanwhile the national games were being celebrated a few miles distant at Taillten (now Telltown) in connexion with the royal feast. St. Patrick proceeding thither solemnly administered Baptism to Conall, brother of the Ard-Righ Leoghaire, on Wednesday, 5 April. Benen and others had already been privately gathered into the fold of Christ, but this was the first public administering of baptism, recognized by royal edict, and hence in the ancient Irish Kalendars to the fifth of April is assigned "the beginning of the Baptism of Erin". This first Christian royal chieftain made a gift to Patrick of a site for a church which to the present day retains the name of Donagh-Patrick. The blessing of heaven was with Conall's family. St. Columba is reckoned among his descendants, and many of the kings of Ireland until the eleventh century were of his race. St. Patrick left some of his companions to carry on the work of evangelization in Meath, thus so auspiciously begun. He would himself visit the other territories. Some of the chieftains who had come to Tara were from Focluth, in the neighbourhood of Killala, in Connaught, and as it was the children of Focluth who in vision had summoned him to return to Ireland, he resolved to accompany those chieftains on their return, that thus the district of Focluth would be among the first to receive the glad tidings of Redemption. It affords a convincing proof of the difficulties that St. Patrick had to overcome, that though full liberty to preach the Faith throughout Erin was granted by the monarch Leoghaire, nevertheless, in order to procure a safe conduct through the intervening territories whilst proceeding towards Connaught he had to pay the price of fifteen slaves. On his way thither, passing through Granard he learned that at Magh-Slecht, not far distant, a vast concourse was engaged in offering worship to the chief idol Crom-Cruach. It was a huge pillar-stone, covered with slabs of gold and silver, with a circle of twelve minor idols around it. He proceeded thither, and with his crosier smote the chief idol that crumbled to dust; the others fell to the ground. At Killala he found the whole people of the territory assembled. At his preaching, the king and his six sons, with 12,000 of the people, became docile to the Faith. He spent seven years visiting every district of Connaught, organizing parishes, forming dioceses, and instructing the chieftains and people. On the occasion of his first visit to Rathcrogan, the royal seat of the kings of Connaught, situated near Tulsk, in the County of Roscommon, a remarkable incident occurred, recorded in many of the authentic narratives of the saint's life. Close by the clear fountain of Clebach, not far from the royal abode, Patrick and his venerable companions had pitched their tents and at early dawn were chanting the praises of the Most High, when the two daughters of the Irish monarch— Ethne, the fair, and Fedelm, the ruddy—came thither, as was their wont, to bathe. Astonished at the vision that presented itself to them, the royal maidens cried out: "Who are ye, and whence do ye come? Are ye phantoms, or fairies, or friendly mortals?" St. Patrick said to them: "It were better you would adore and worship the one true God, whom we announce to you,

than that you would satisfy your curiosity by such vain questions." And then Ethne broke forth into the questions:—
"Who is God?"
"And where is God?"
"Where is His dwelling?"
"Has He sons and daughters?"
"Is He rich in silver and gold?"
"Is He everlasting? is He beautiful?"
"Are His daughters dear and lovely to the men of this world?"
"Is He in the heavens or on earth?"
"In the sea, in rivers, in mountains, in valleys?"
"Make Him known to us. How is He to be seen? How is He to be loved? How is He to be found?"
"Is it in youth or is it in old age that He may be found?"

But St. Patrick, filled with the Holy Ghost, made answer:
"God, whom we announce to you, is the Ruler of all things."
"The God of heaven and earth, of the sea and the rivers."
"The God of the sun, and the moon, and all the stars."
"The God of the high mountains and of the low-lying valleys."
"The God who is above heaven, and in heaven, and under heaven."
"His dwelling is in heaven and earth, and the sea, and all therein."
"He gives breath to all."
"He gives life to all."
"He is over all."
"He upholds all."
"He gives light to the sun."
"He imparts splendour to the moon."
"He has made wells in the dry land, and islands in the ocean."
"He has appointed the stars to serve the greater lights."
"His Son is co-eternal and co-equal with Himself."
"The Son is not younger than the Father."
"And the Father is not older than the Son."
"And the Holy Ghost proceeds from them."
"The Father and the Son and the Holy Ghost are undivided."
"But I desire by Faith to unite you to the Heavenly King, as you are daughters of an earthly king."

The maidens, as if with one voice and one heart, said:
"Teach us most carefully how we may believe in the Heavenly King; show us how we may behold Him face to face, and we will do whatsoever you shall say to us."

And when he had instructed them he said to them:
"Do you believe that by baptism you put off the sin inherited from the first parents."
They answered: "We believe."
"Do you believe in penance after sin?"
"We believe."
"Do you believe in life after death? Do you believe in resurrection on the Day of Judgment?"
"We believe."
"Do you believe in the unity of the Church?"
"We believe."

Then they were baptized, and were clothed in white garments. And they besought that they might behold the face of Christ. And the saint said to them: "You cannot see the face of Christ unless you taste death, and unless you receive the sacrifice." They answered: "Give us the sacrifice, so that we may be able to behold our Spouse." And the ancient narrative adds: "when they received the Eucharist of God, they slept in death, and they were placed upon a couch, arrayed in their white baptismal robes."

In 440 St. Patrick entered on the special work of the conversion of Ulster. Under the following year, the ancient annalists relate a wonderful spread of the Faith throughout that province. In 444 a site for a church was granted at Armagh by Daire, the chieftain of the district. It was in a valley at the foot of a hill, but the saint was not content. He had special designs in his heart for that district, and at length the chieftain told him to select in his territory any site he would deem most suitable for his religious purpose. St. Patrick chose that beautiful hill on which the old cathedral of Armagh stands. As he was marking out the church with his companions, they came upon a doe and fawn, and the saint's companions would kill them for food; but St. Patrick would not allow them to do so, and, taking the fawn upon his shoulders, and followed by the doe, he proceeded to a neighbouring hill, and laid down the fawn, and announced that there, in future times, great glory would be given to the Most High. It was precisely upon that hill thus fixed by St. Patrick that, a few years ago, there was solemnly dedicated the new and beautiful Catholic cathedral of Armagh. A representative of the Holy See presided on the occasion, and hundreds of priests and bishops were gathered there; and, indeed, it might truly be said, the whole Irish race on that occasion offered up that glorious cathedral to the Most High as a tribute of their united faith and piety, and their never-failing love of God. From Ulster St. Patrick probably proceeded to Meath to consolidate the organization of the communities there, and thence he continued his course through Leinster. Two of the saint's most distinguished companions, St. Auxilius and St. Iserninus, had the rich valley of the Liffey assigned to them. The former's name is still retained in the church which he founded at Killossy, while the latter is honoured as first Bishop of Kilcullen. As usual, St. Patrick's primary care was to gather the ruling chieftains into the fold. At Naas, the royal residence in those days, he baptized the two sons of the King of Leinster. Memorials of the saint still abound in the district—the ruins of the ancient church which he founded, his holy well, and the hallowed sites in which the power of God was shown forth in miracles. At Sletty, in the immediate neighbourhood of Carlow, St. Fiacc, son of the chief Brehon, Dubthach, was installed as bishop, and for a considerable time that see continued to be the chief centre of religion for all Leinster. St. Patrick proceeded through Gowran into Ossory; here he erected a church under the invocation of St. Martin, near the present city of Kilkenny, and enriched it with many of the precious relics which he had brought from Rome. It was in Leinster, on the borders of the present counties of Kildare and Queen's, that Odhran, St. Patrick's charioteer, attained the martyr's crown. The chieftain of that district honoured the demon-idol, Crom Cruach, with special worship, and, on hearing of that idol being cast down, vowed to avenge the insult by the death of our apostle. Passing through the territory, Odhran overheard the plot that was being organized for the murder of St. Patrick, and as they were setting out in the chariot to continue their journey, asked the saint, as a favour, to take the reins, and to allow himself, for the day, to hold the place of honour and rest. This was granted, and scarcely had they set out when a well-directed thrust of a lance pierced the heart of the devoted charioteer, who thus, by changing places, saved St. Patrick's life, and won for himself the martyr's crown.

St. Patrick next proceeded to Munster. As usual, his efforts were directed to combat error in the chief centres of authority, knowing well that, in the paths of conversion, the kings and chieftains would soon be followed by their subjects. At "Cashel of the Kings" he was received with great enthusiasm, the chiefs and Brehons and people welcoming him with joyous acclaim. While engaged in the baptism of the royal prince Aengus, son of the King of Munster, the saint, leaning on his crosier, pierced with its sharp point the prince's foot. Aengus bore the pain unmoved. When St. Patrick, at the close of the ceremony, saw the blood flow, and asked him why he had been silent, he replied, with genuine heroism, that he thought it might be part of the ceremony, a penalty for the joyous blessings of the Faith that were imparted. The saint admired his heroism, and, taking the chieftain's shield, inscribed on it a cross with the same point of the crozier, and promised that that shield would be the signal of countless spiritual and temporal triumphs. Our apostle spent a considerable time in the present County of Limerick. The fame of his miracles and sanctity had gone before him, and the inhabitants of Thomond and northern Munster, crossing the Shannon in their frail coracles, hastened to receive his instruction. When giving his blessing to them on the summit of the hill of Finnime, looking out on the rich plains before him, he is said to have prophesied the coming of St. Senanus: "To the green island in the West, at the mouth of the sea [i. e., Inis-Cathaigh, now Scattery Island, at the mouth of the Shannon, near Kilrush], the lamp of the people of God will come; he will be the head of counsel to all this territory." At Sangril (now Singland), in Limerick, and also in the district of Garryowen, the holy wells of the saint are pointed out, and the slab of rock, which served for his bed, and the altar on which every day he offered up the Holy Sacrifice. On the banks of the Suir, and the Blackwater, and the Lee, wherever the saint preached during the seven years he spent in Munster, a hearty welcome awaited him. The ancient Life attests: "After Patrick had founded cells and churches in Munster, and had ordained persons of every grade, and healed the sick, and resuscitated the dead, he bade them farewell, and imparted his blessing to them." The words of this blessing, which is said to have been given from the hills of Tipperary, as registered in the saint's Life, to which I have just referred, are particularly beautiful:—

"A blessing on the Munster people—
Men, youths, and women;
A blessing on the land
That yields them fruit.

"A blessing on every treasure
That shall be produced on their plains,
Without any one being in want of help,
God's blessing be on Munster.

"A blessing be on their peaks,
On their bare flagstones,
A blessing on their glens,
A blessing on their ridges.

"Like the sand of the sea under ships,
Be the number of their hearths;
On slopes, on plains,
On mountains, on hills, a blessing."

St. Patrick continued until his death to visit and watch over the churches which he had founded in all the provinces of Ireland. He comforted the faithful in their difficulties, strengthened them in the Faith and in the practice of virtue, and appointed pastors to continue his work among them. It is recorded in his Life that he consecrated no fewer than 350 bishops. He appointed St. Loman to Trim, which rivalled Armagh itself in its abundant harvest of piety. St. Guasach, son of his former master, Milchu, became Bishop of Granard, while the two daughters of the same pagan chieftain founded close by, at Clonbroney, a convent of pious virgins, and merited the aureola of sanctity. St. Mel, nephew of our apostle, had the charge of Ardagh; St. MacCarthem, who appears to have been particularly beloved by St. Patrick, was made Bishop of Clogher. The narrative in the ancient Life of the saint regarding his visit to the district of Costello, in the County of Mayo, serves to illustrate his manner of dealing with the chieftains. He found, it says, the chief, Ernasc, and his son, Loarn, sitting under a tree, "with whom he remained, together with his twelve companions, for a week, and they received from him the doctrine of salvation with attentive ear and mind. Meanwhile he instructed Loarn in the rudiments of learning and piety." A church was erected there, and, in after years, Loarn was appointed to its charge.

The manifold virtues by which the early saints were distinguished shone forth in all their perfection in the life of St. Patrick. When not engaged in the work of the sacred ministry, his whole time was spent in prayer. Many times in the day he armed himself with the sign of the Cross. He never relaxed his penitential exercises. Clothed in rough hair-shirt, he made the hard rock his bed. His disinterestedness is specially commemorated. Countless converts of high rank would cast their precious ornaments at his feet, but all were restored to them. He had not come to Erin in search of material wealth, but to enrich her with the priceless treasures of the Catholic Faith. From time to time he withdrew from the spiritual duties of his apostolate to devote himself wholly to prayer and penance. One of his chosen places of solitude and retreat was the island of Lough Dergh, which, to our own day, has continued to be a favourite resort of pilgrims, and is known as St. Patrick's Purgatory. Another theatre of his miraculous power and piety and penitential austerities in the west of Ireland merits particular attention. In the far west of Connaught there is a range of tall mountains, which, arrayed in rugged majesty, bid defiance to the waves and storms of the Atlantic. At the head of this range arises a stately cone in solitary grandeur, about 4000 feet in height, facing Crew Bay, and casting its shadow over the adjoining districts of Aghagower and Westport. This mountain was known in pagan times as the Eagle Mountain, but ever since Ireland was enlightened with the light of Faith it is known as Croagh Patrick, i. e. St. Patrick's mountain, and is honoured as the Holy Hill, the Mount Sinai, of Ireland. St. Patrick, in obedience to his guardian angel, made this mountain his hallowed place of retreat. In imitation of the great Jewish legislator on Sinai. he spent forty days on its summit in fasting and prayer, and other penitential exercises. His only shelter from the fury of the elements, the wind and rain, the hail and snow, was a cave, or recess, in the solid rock; and the flagstone on which he rested his weary limbs at night is still pointed out. The whole purpose of his prayer was to obtain special blessings and mercy for the Irish race, whom he evangelized. The demons that made Ireland their battlefield mustered all their strength to tempt the saint and disturb him in his solitude, and turn him away, if possible, from his pious purpose. They gathered around the hill in the form of vast flocks of hideous birds of prey. So dense were their ranks that they seemed to cover the whole mountain, like a cloud, and they so filled the air that Patrick could see neither sky nor earth nor ocean. St. Patrick besought God to scatter the demons, but for a time it would seem as if his prayers and tears were in vain. At length he rang his sweet-sounding bell, symbol of his preaching of the Divine truths. Its sound was heard over the valleys and hills of Erin, everywhere bringing peace and joy. The flocks of demons began to scatter, He flung his bell among them; they took to precipitate flight, and cast themselves into the ocean. So complete was the saint's victory over them that, as the ancient narrative adds, "for seven years no evil thing was to be found in Ireland." The saint, however, would not, as yet, descend from the mountain. He had vanquished the demons, but he would now wrestle with God Himself, like Jacob of old, to secure the spiritual interests of his people. The angel had announced to him that, to reward his fidelity in prayer and penance, as many of his people would be gathered into heaven as would cover the land and sea as far as his vision could reach. Far more ample, however, were the aspirations of the saint, and he resolved to persevere in fasting and prayer until the fullest measure of his petition was granted. Again and again the angel came to comfort him, announcing new concessions; but all these would not suffice. He would not relinquish his post on the mountain, or relax his penance, until all were granted. At length the message came that his prayers were heard: (1) many souls would be freed from the pains of purgatory through his intercession; (2) whoever in a spirit of penance would recite his hymn before death would attain the heavenly reward; (3) barbarian hordes would never obtain sway in his Church; (4) seven years before the Judgment Day, the sea would spread over Ireland to save its people from the temptations and terrors of Antichrist; and (5) greatest blessing of all, Patrick himself would be deputed to judge the whole Irish race on the last day. Such were the extraordinary favours which St. Patrick, with his wrestling with the Most High, his unceasing prayers, his unconquerable love of heavenly things, and his unremitting penitential deeds, obtained for the people whom he evangelized.

It is sometimes supposed that St. Patrick's apostolate in Ireland was an unbroken series of peaceful triumphs, and yet it was quite the reverse. No storm of persecution was, indeed stirred up to assail the infant Church, but the saint himself was subjected to frequent trials at the hands of the druids and of other enemies of the Faith. He tells us in his "Confessio" that no fewer than twelve times he and his companions were seized and carried off as captives, and on one occasion in particular he was loaded with chains, and his death was decreed. But from all these trials and sufferings he was liberated by a benign Providence. It is on account of the many hardships which he endured for the Faith that, in some of the ancient Martyrologies, he is honoured as a martyr. St. Patrick, having now completed his triumph over Paganism, and gathered Ireland into the fold of Christ, prepared for the summons to his reward. St. Brigid came to him with her chosen virgins, bringing the shroud in which he would be enshrined. It is recorded that when St. Patrick and St. Brigid were united in their last prayer, a special vision was shown to him. He saw the whole of Ireland lit up with the brightest rays of Divine Faith. This continued for centuries, and then clouds gathered around the devoted island, and, little by little, the religious glory faded away, until, in the course of centuries, it was only in remotest valleys that some glimmer of its light remained. St. Patrick prayed that that light would never be extinguished, and, as he prayed, the angel came to him and said: "Fear not; your apostolate shall never cease." As he thus prayed, the glimmering light grew in brightness, and ceased not until once more all the hills and valleys of Ireland were lit up in their pristine splendour, and then the angel announced to St. Patrick: "Such shall be the abiding splendour of Divine truth in Ireland." At Saul (Sabhall), St. Patrick received the summons to his reward on 17 March, 493. St. Tassach administered the last sacraments to him. His remains were wrapped in the shroud woven by St. Brigid's own hands. The bishops and clergy and faithful people from all parts crowded around his remains to pay due honour to the Father of their Faith. Some of the ancient Lives record that for several days the light of heaven shone around his bier. His remains were interred at the chieftain's Dun or Fort two miles from Saul, where in after times arose the cathedral of Down.

WRITINGS OF ST. PATRICK.—The "Confessio" and the "Epistola ad Coroticum" are recognized by all modern critical writers as of unquestionable genuineness. The best edition, with text, translation, and critical notes, is by Rev. Dr. White for the Royal Irish Academy, in 1905. The 34 canons of a synod held before the year 460 by St. Patrick, Auxilius, and Isserninus, though rejected by Todd and Haddan, have been placed by Professor Bury beyond the reach of controversy. Another series of 31 ecclesiastical canons entitled "Synodus secunda Patritii", though unquestionably of Irish origin and dating before the close of the seventh century, is generally considered to be of a later date than St. Patrick. Two tracts (in P. L., LIII), entitled "De abusionibus sæculi", and "De tribus habitaculis", were composed by St. Patrick in Irish and translated into Latin at a later period. Passages from them are assigned to St. Patrick in the "Collectio Hibernensis Canonum", which is of unquestionable authority and dates from the year 700 (Wasserschleben, 2nd ed., 1885). This "Collectio Hibernensis" also assigns to St. Patrick the famous synodical decree: "Si quæ quæstiones in hac insula oriantur, ad Sedem Apostolicam referantur." (If any difficulties arise in this island, let them be referred to the Apostolic See). The beautiful prayer, known as "Faeth Fiada", or the "Lorica of St. Patrick" (St. Patrick's Breast-Plate), first edited by Petrie in his "History of Tara", is now universally accepted as genuine. The "Dicta Sancti Patritii", or brief sayings of the saint, preserved in the "Book of Armagh", are accurately edited by Fr. Hogan, S.J., in "Documenta de S. Patritio" (Brussels, 1884). The old Irish text of "The Rule of Patrick" has been edited by O'Keeffe, and the translation by Archbishop Healy in the appendix to his Life of St. Patrick (Dublin, 1905). It is a tract of venerable antiquity, and embodies the teaching of the saint.

The *Trias thaumaturga* (fol., Louvain, 1647) of the Franciscan COLGAN is the most complete collection of the ancient *Lives* of the saint. The Kenmare *Life of St. Patrick* (CUSACK, Dublin, 1869) presents from the pen of HENNESSY the translation of the Irish *Tripartite Life*, with copious notes. WHITLEY STOKES, in the *Rolls Series* (London, 1887), has given the text and translation of the *Vita Tripartita*, together with many original documents from the *Book of Armagh* and other sources. The most noteworthy works of later years are SHEARMAN, *Loca Patriciana* (Dublin, 1879); TODD, *St. Patrick, Apostle of Ireland* (Dublin, 1864); BURY, *Life of St. Patrick* (London, 1905); HEALY, *The Life and Writings of St. Patrick* (Dublin, 1905).

PATRICK FRANCIS CARDINAL MORAN.

Patrimony of Saint Peter. See STATES OF THE CHURCH.

Patripassians. See MONARCHIANS.

Patristics. See FATHERS OF THE CHURCH; PATROLOGY.

Patrizi, FRANCIS XAVIER, Jesuit exegete, b. at Rome, 19 June, 1797; d. there 23 April, 1881. He was the eldest son and heir of the Roman Count Patrizi, entered the Society of Jesus 12 Nov., 1814, was ordained priest in 1824, and soon became professor of Sacred Scripture and Hebrew in the Roman College. The revolution of 1848 caused Patrizi and his fellow professor Perrone to take refuge in England. Here, and afterwards at Louvain, Patrizi taught Scripture to the Jesuit scholastics. When peace was restored at Rome, he again began to lecture in the Roman College. The revolution of 1870 ended his career as a teacher, and he found a home in the German-Hungarian College of Rome, remaining there till death.

He wrote twenty-one Biblical and ascetical works. Of the former the most important are: "De interpretatione scripturarum sacrarum" (2 vols., Rome, 1844); "De consensu utriusque libri Machabæorum" (Rome, 1856); "De Evangeliis" (3 vols., Freiburg im Breisgau, 1853); "In Joannem commentarium" (Rome, 1857); "In Marcum commentarium" (Rome, 1862); "In actus Apostolorum commentarium" (Rome, 1867); "Cento salmi tradotti letteralmente dal testo ebraico e commentati" (Rome, 1875); "De interpretatione oraculorum ad Christum pertinentium" (Rome, 1853); "De immaculata Mariæ origine" (Rome, 1853);

"Delle parole di San Paolo: In quo omnes peccaverunt" (Rome, 1876). His Latin is classic, but only the earnest Biblical student appreciates the immense erudition of his heavily burdened sentences. No one has better stated the rules of sane interpretation and illustrated those rules in practice. His master-work on interpretation has gone through many editions. The Gospel commentaries are meant especially to refute the rationalistic errors of the time.

HURTER in *Kirchenlexikon*, s. v.; SOMMERVOGEL, *Bibliothèque de la C. de J.*, VI, 366–69; *Civiltà Cattolica*, 11th series, VI, 491.

WALTER DRUM.

Patrology, the study of the writings of the Fathers of the Church, has more commonly been known in England as "patristics", or, more commonly still, as "patristic study". Some writers, chiefly in Germany, have distinguished between *patrologia* and *patristica:* Fessler, for instance, defines *patrologia* as the science which provides all that is necessary for the using of the works of the Fathers, dealing, therefore, with their authority, the criteria for judging their genuineness, the difficulties to be met with in them, and the rules for their use. But Fessler's own "Institutiones Patrologiæ" has a larger range, as have similar works entitled Patrologies, of which the most serviceable is that of Bardenhewer (tr. Shahan, Freiburg, 1908). On the other hand, Fessler describes *patristica* as that theological science by which all that concerns faith, morals, or discipline in the writings of the Fathers is collected and sorted. Lastly, the lives and works of the Fathers are described by another science: literary history. These distinctions are not much observed, nor do they seem very necessary; they are nothing else than aspects of patristic study as it forms part of fundamental theology, of positive theology, and of literary history. Another meaning of the word *patrologia* has come to it from the title of the great collections of the complete works of the Fathers published by the Abbé Migne (q. v.), "Patrologia Latina", 221 vols., and "Patrologia Græca", 161 vols.

For bibliography see FATHERS OF THE CHURCH.

JOHN CHAPMAN.

Patronage of Our Lady, FEAST OF THE.—It was first permitted by Decree of the Sacred Congregation of Rites, 6 May, 1679, for all the provinces of Spain, in memory of the victories obtained over the Saracens, heretics, and other enemies from the sixth century to the reign of Philip IV. Benedict XII ordered it to be kept in the Papal States on the third Sunday of November. To other places it is granted, on request, for some Sunday in November, to be designated by the ordinary. The Office is taken entirely from the Common of the Blessed Virgin, and the Mass is the "Salve sancta parens". In many places the feast of the Patronage is held with an additional title of Queen of All Saints, of Mercy, Mother of Graces. The Greeks have no feast of this kind, but the Ruthenians, followed by all the Slavs of the Greek Rite, have a feast, called "Patrocinii sanctissimæ Dominæ" etc., or *Pokrov Bogorodicy*, on 1 October, which, however, would seem to correspond more with our Feast of the Scapular.

NILLES, *Kalendarium Manuale*, II, 532; BENEDICT XIV, *De festis*, II, §§173, 174; MARTINOV, *Précis historiques* (1858), July.

FRANCIS MERSHMAN.

Patronage of St. Joseph, FEAST OF THE. See JOSEPH, SAINT.

Patron and Patronage.—I. By the right of patronage (*ius patronatus*) is understood a determinate sum of rights and obligations entailed upon a definite person, the patron, especially in connexion with the assignment and administration of a benefice; not in virtue of his hierarchical position, but by the legally regulated grant of the Church, out of gratitude towards her benefactor. Inasmuch as the rights of the patron pertain to the spiritual order, the right of patronage is designated in the decretals as *ius spirituali annexum*, and is therefore subject to ecclesiastical legislation and jurisdiction. Since, however, the question of property rights is also involved, a far-reaching influence is wielded to-day by civil laws and civil courts in matters pertaining to patronage.

II. In the Oriental Church the founder of a church was permitted to nominate an administrator for the temporal goods and indicate to the bishop a cleric suitable for appointment (L. 46, C. de episc. I, 3. Nov. LVII, c. 2). In the Western Church the Synod of Orange (441) granted such a right of presentation to a bishop who had built a church in another diocese (c. i, C. XVI, q. 5) and the Synod of Toledo (655) gave a layman this privilege for each church erected by him (c. 32, C. XVI, q. 7). But the founder had no proprietary rights (c. 31, C. XVI, q. 7). In the countries occupied by the Germanic tribes, on the basis of the individual temple and church rights found in their national laws, the builder of a church, the feudal lord, or the administrator possessed full right of disposal over the church founded or possessed by him, as his own church (*ecclesia propria*) and over the ecclesiastics appointed by him, whom he could dismiss at pleasure. To obviate the drawbacks connected with this, the appointment and dismissal of ecclesiastics at least formally was made subject to the consent of the bishop (c. 37, C. XVI, q. 7). In the course of the Conflict of Investitures, however, the private right over churches was abolished, although to the lord of the estate, as patron, was conceded the right as *ius spirituali annexum* of presenting a cleric to the bishop (*ius præsentandi*) on the occasion of a vacancy in the church (c. 13, C. XVI, q. 7; C. 5, 16, *X de iure patronatus*, III, 38).

III. The right of patronage may be: personal (*ius patronatus personale*) or real (*reale*); spiritual (*ecclesiasticum; clericale*), or lay (*laicale*), or mixed (*mixtum*); hereditary (*hæreditarium*), or restricted to the family, or even to a definite person (*familiare; personalissimum*); individual (*singulare*) or shared (*ius comparatronatus*); complete (*plenum*) or diminished (*minus plenum*). A personal right of patronage is peculiar to a person as such, while a real right of patronage belongs to one in possession for the time being of something with which a patronage is connected, provided of course that he is qualified for the possession of the right of patronage. A spiritual patronage is one belonging to the incumbent of an ecclesiastical office, or established by the foundation of a church or a benefice out of ecclesiastical funds, or instituted by a layman and later presented to the Church. Thus the patronages in possession of secularized bishoprics, monasteries, and ecclesiastical foundations are regarded as spiritual. A lay patronage is established when an ecclesiastical office is endowed by anyone out of private means. A patronage is mixed when held in common by the incumbent of an ecclesiastical office and a layman.

IV. Any church benefice, with the exception of the papacy, the cardinalate, the episcopate, and the prelatures of cathedral, collegiate, and monastic churches, may be the object of the right of patronage. All persons and corporate bodies may be subject to the right of patronage. But persons, besides being capable of exercising the right, must be members of the Church. Thus heathens, Jews, heretics, schismatics, and apostates are ineligible for any sort of patronage, even real. Nevertheless in Germany and Austria it has become customary as a result of the Peace of Westphalia, for Protestants to possess the rights of patronage over Catholic, and Catholics over Protestant church offices. In modern concordats Rome has repeatedly granted the right of patronage to Protestant princes. Entirely ineligible for patronage are the *excommunicati vitandi* (the *excommunicati tolerati* are able at least to acquire it), and those who are infamous according to ecclesiastical or civil law. On the other hand, illegitimates, children, minors, and women may acquire patronages.

V. A right of patronage comes into existence or is originally acquired by foundation, privilege, or prescription. Under foundation or *fundatio* in the broader sense is included the granting of the necessary means for the erection and maintenance of a benefice. Thus, granting that a church is necessary to a benefice, three things are requisite: the assignment of land (*fundatio* in the narrow sense), the erection of the church at one's private expense (*ædificatio*), and the granting of the means necessary for the support of the church and beneficiaries (*dotatio*). If the same person fulfils all three requirements, he becomes *ipso jure* patron, unless he waives his claim (c. 25, X de iure patr. III, 38). Whence the saying: *Patronum faciunt dos, ædificatio, fundus*. Different persons performing these three acts become co-patrons. It is an accepted theory that one who is responsible for only one of the three acts mentioned, the other two conditions being fulfilled in any manner whatsoever, becomes a patron. It is possible to become a patron also through the *reædificatio ecclesiæ* and *redotatio beneficii*. A second manner in which a patronage may be acquired is through papal privilege. A third is by prescription.

VI. Derivatively, a patronage may be obtained through inheritance *ex testamento* or *ex intestato*, in which case a patronage may easily become a co-patronage; by presentation, in which a lay patron must have the sanction of the bishop if he desires to transfer his right to another layman, but an ecclesiastic requires the permission of the pope to present it to a layman, or that of the bishop to give it to another ecclesiastic (c. un. Extrav. comm. de rebus eccl. non alien. III, 4). Furthermore an already existing right of patronage may be acquired by exchange, by purchase, or by prescription. In exchange or purchase of a real patronage the price of the object in question may not be raised in consideration of the patronage; the right of patronage being a *ius spirituali annexum*, such a thing would be simony. That the ruler of a country may acquire the right of patronage in any of the three ways mentioned, like any other member of the Church, goes without saying. On the other hand, it would be false to teach, as did the Josephinists and representatives of the "Illuminati", that the sovereign possesses the right of patronage merely by being ruler of the country, or that he receives the patronage of bishoprics, monasteries, and ecclesiastical foundations through secularization. Yet this question is now generally settled in Germany, Austria, etc. by agreement between the civil Governments on the one hand and the pope or bishops on the other.

VII. The rights involved in patronage are: the right of presentation, honorary rights, utilitarian rights, and the *cura beneficii*.

(a) The right of presentation (*ius præsentandi*), the most important privilege of a patron, consists in this, that in case of a vacancy in the benefice, he may propose (*præsentare*) to the ecclesiastical superiors empowered with the right of collation, the name of a suitable person (*persona idonea*), the result being that if the one suggested is available at the time of presentation, the ecclesiastical superior is bound to bestow on him the office in question. Co-patrons with the right of presentation may take turns, or each may present a name for himself, or it may be decided by vote. In the case of juridical persons the presentation may be made according to statute, or by turns, or by decision of the majority. The drawing of lots is excluded.

With regard to the one to be presented, in the case of a benefice involving the cure of souls, the ecclesiastical patron must choose from among the candidates for presentation the one he believes the most suitable, judging from the parish concursus. The lay patron has only to present the name of a candidate who is suitable in his opinion. In case this candidate has not passed the parish concursus, he must undergo an examination before the synodal examiners. In the case of a mixed patronage, the rights of which are exercised in common by an ecclesiastical and a lay patron, the same rule holds as in the case of a lay patronage. Here it is the rule to deal with the mixed patronage, now as a spiritual and again as a lay patronage, according as it is most pleasing to the patrons. If the prerogatives of the mixed patronage are exercised in turn, however, it is considered as a spiritual or a lay patronage, as suits the nature of the case. The patron cannot present his own name. Co-patrons may, however, present one of their own number. If through no fault of the patron, the name of an ineligible person is presented, he is granted a certain time of grace to make a new presentation. If, however, an ineligible person has been knowingly presented, the spiritual patron loses for the time being the right of presentation, but the lay patron, so long as the first interval allowed for presentation has not expired, may make an after-presentation. Thus the presentation of the spiritual patron is treated more after the manner of the episcopal collation. On that account the spiritual patron is not permitted an after-presentation or a variation in choice, which is permitted the lay patron, after which the bishop has the choice between the several names presented (*ius variandi cumulativum*, c. 24, X de iure patr. III, 38).

A presentation may be made by word of mouth or in writing. But under penalty of nullity all expressions are to be avoided which would imply a bestowal of the office (c. 5, X de iure patr. III, 38). A simoniacal presentation would be invalid. The time allowed for presentation is four months to a lay patron, and six to a spiritual patron; six months is stipulated for a mixed patronage when exercised in common, four or six months when turn is taken (c. 22, X de iure patr. III, 38). The interval begins the moment announcement is made of the vacancy. For one who through no fault of his own has been hindered in making a presentation, the time does not expire at the end of the period mentioned. When his candidate has been unjustly rejected by the bishop, the patron may appeal, or make an after presentation.

(b) The honorary rights (*iura honorifica*) of the patron are: precedence in procession, a sitting in the church, prayers and intercessions, ecclesiastical mentions, burial in the church, ecclesiastical mourning, inscriptions, special incensing, the asperges (holy water), ashes, palms, and the Pax.

(c) The utilitarian rights (*iura utilia*) of the patron consist essentially in this: that in so far as he is a descendant of the founder he is entitled to an allowance sufficient for his maintenance from the superfluous funds of the church connected with the patronage, if, through no fault of his own, he has been reduced to such straits as to be unable to support himself, and no one else is under any obligation to assist him (c. 25, X de iure patr. III, 38). To draw any other material advantages from the church connected with the patronage, as so frequently happened in the Middle Ages, it is requisite for this condition to have been made at the time of foundation with the consent of the bishop, or that it be subsequently stipulated (c. 23, X de iure patr. III, 38. C. un. Extrav. comm. de rebus eccl. non alien. III, 4).

(d) The right or important duty (*iura onerosa*) of the patron is, in the first place the *cura beneficii*, the care to preserve unimpaired the status of the benefice and the conscientious discharge of the obligations connected therewith. He must not, however, interfere in the administration of the property of the benefice or the discharge of the spiritual duties on the part of the holder of the benefice. This *cura beneficii* entitles the patron to have a voice in all changes in the benefice

XI.—36

and the property belonging to it. Again, on the patron is incumbent the *defensio* or the *advocatia beneficii* (c. 23, 24, X de iure patr. III, 38). In the present administration of justice, however, this obligation has practically disappeared. Lastly, the patron has the subsidiary duty of building (Trent, Sess. XXI, "de ref.", c. vii).

VIII. The right of patronage lapses *ipso iure* at the suppression of the subject or object. If the church connected with the patronage is threatened with total ruin, or the endowment with a deficit, if those first bound to restore it are not at hand, the bishop is to exhort the patron to rebuild (*reædificandum*) or renew the endowment (*ad redotandum*). His refusal forfeits him the right of patronage, at least for himself personally. Furthermore, the right of patronage is lost upon express or tacit renunciation. And lastly, it lapses in cases of apostasy, heresy, schism, simoniacal alienation, usurpation of the ecclesiastical jurisdiction over the patronal church or appropriation of its goods and revenues, murder or mutilation of an ecclesiastic connected with the church.

HINSCHIUS, *Das Kirchenrecht der Katholiken und Protestanten in Deutschland*, II (Berlin, 1878), 618 sqq.; ZHISHMAN, *Das Stifterrecht in der morgenländischen Kirche* (Vienna, 1888); WAHRMUND, *Das Kirchenpatronatsrecht und seine Entwicklung in Oesterreich* (Vienna, 1894); STUTZ, *Geschichte des kirchlichen Benefizialwesens* (Berlin, 1895); THOMAS, *Le droit de propriété des laïques au moyen âge* (Paris, 1906); PÖSCHL, *Bischofsgut und mensa episcopalis*, I (Bonn, 1898), 32 sqq.

JOHANNES BAPTIST SÄGMÜLLER.

Patron Saints.—A patron is one who has been assigned by a venerable tradition, or chosen by election, as a special intercessor with God and the proper advocate of a particular locality, and is honoured by clergy and people with a special form of religious observance. The term "patron", being wider in its meaning than that of "titular", may be applied to a church, a district, a country, or a corporation. The word "titular" is applied only to the patron of a church or institution. Both the one and the other, according to the legislation now in force, must have the rank of a canonized saint.

PATRONS OF CHURCHES.—*Origin*.—During the first three centuries of the Church's history, the faithful assembled for worship in private houses, in cemeteries, or other retired places. At intervals it had been possible to erect or adapt buildings for the sacred rites of religion. Such buildings, however, were not dedicated to the saints, but were spoken of as the House of God, the House of Prayer, and sometimes as the Temple of God. They were also known as *Kyriaca*, *Dominica*, or *Oratoria*. Larger structures received the name of basilicas, and the term church (*ecclesia*) was constantly employed to designate the place where the faithful assembled to hear the word of God and partake of the sacraments. After peace had been given to the Church by Constantine, sacred edifices were freely erected, the emperor setting the example by the character and magnificence of his own foundations. The Christians had always held in deep reverence the memory of the heroes who had sealed with blood the profession of their faith. The celebration of the solemn rites had long been intimately associated with the places where the bodies of the martyrs reposed, and the choice of sites for the new edifices was naturally determined by the scene of the martyrs' sufferings, or by the spot where their sacred remains lay enshrined. The great basilicas founded by Constantine, or during his lifetime, illustrate this tendency. The churches of St. Peter, St. Paul outside the walls, St. Lawrence in Agro Verano, St. Sebastian, St. Agnes on the Via Nomentana were all cemeterial basilicas, i. e. they were built over the spot where the bodies of each of these saints lay buried. The same practice finds illustration in the churches of SS. Domitilla and Generosa, SS. Nereus and Achilleus, St. Felix at Nola, and others. From this custom of rendering honour to the relics of the martyrs were derived the names of *Memoriæ* (memorial churches), *Martyria*, or *Confessio*, frequently given to churches. The name of "Title" (*Titulus*) has from the earliest times been employed with reference to the name of the saint by which a church is known. The practice of placing the body or some relics of a martyr under the altar of sacrifice has been perpetuated in the Church, but the dedication was early extended to confessors and holy women who were not martyrs. The underlying doctrine of patrons is that of the communion of saints, or the bond of spiritual union existing between God's servants on earth, in heaven, or in purgatory. The saints are thereby regarded as the advocates and intercessors of those who are making their earthly pilgrimage.

Choice of Patrons.—Down to the seventeenth century popular devotion, under the guidance of ecclesiastical authority, chose as the titulars of churches those men or women renowned for their miracles, the saintliness of their lives, or their apostolic ministry in converting a nation to the Gospel. Urban VIII (23 March, 1638) laid down the rules that should guide the faithful in the future selection of patrons of churches, cities, and countries, without, however, interfering with the traditional patrons then venerated (Acta S. Sedis, XI, 292). As during the days of persecution the most illustrious among the Christians were those who had sacrificed their lives for the faith, it was to be expected that during the fourth century the selection of the names of martyrs as titulars would everywhere prevail. But with the progress of the Church in times of comparative peace, with the development of the religious life, and the preaching of the Gospel in the different countries of Europe and Asia, bishops, priests, hermits, and nuns displayed in their lives lofty examples of Christian holiness. Churches, therefore, began to be dedicated in their honour. The choice of a particular patron has depended upon many circumstances. These, as a rule, have been one or other of the following: (1) The possession of the body or some important relic of the saint; (2) his announcement of the Gospel to the nation; (3) his labours or death in the locality; (4) his adoption as the national patron; (5) the special devotion of the founder of the church; (6) the spirit of ecclesiastical devotion at a given time. Leo XIII enumerated (28 Nov., 1897) as characteristic religious movements of our time:—devotion to the Sacred Heart, to Our Lady of the Rosary, to St. Joseph, and to the Blessed Sacrament. It should be clearly understood that a church is, and always has been, dedicated to God: other dedications are annexed on an entirely different plane. Thus a church is dedicated to God in honour (for example) of the Blessed Virgin and the saints. A typical form is the following: "Deo sacrum in honorem deiparæ immaculatæ et SS. Joannis Baptistæ et Evangelistæ." In 1190 a collegiate church in Dublin was dedicated "to God, Our Blessed Lady, and St. Patrick". Sometimes out of several who are mentioned the patron is expressly designated, as in the dedication of a chaplainry in Arngask (Scotland) in 1527, "for the praise, glory, and honour of the indivisible Trinity, the most glorious Virgin and St. Columba, abbot, our patron of the parish". The celestial patronage here considered will be restricted in the first instance to churches and chapels. Patrons in different countries generally present a distinctly national colouring; but the principles which have governed the selection of names will be made apparent by the examination of a few instances. In comparing place with place, the rank or precedence of patrons should be kept in view. A convenient arrangement will be the following: Dedications (1) to God and the Sacred Humanity of Christ or its emblems; (2) to the Mother of God; (3) to the Angels; (4) to the holy personages who introduced the New Law of Christ; (5) to the Apostles and Evangelists; (6) to other saints.

Rome.—Rome is illustrious for churches named after its local martyrs. The most important are the basilicas of St. Peter, of St. Paul Outside the Walls, of St. Lawrence, St. Sebastian, and of St. Agnes in the Via Nomentana. Other churches have received their title from the fact of being constructed in connexion with houses belonging to the martyrs in question: St. Clement's, St. Pudentiana's, St. Alexius's, St. Cecilia's, St. Praxedes's, St. Bartholomew's, Sts. John and Paul, St. Frances's of Rome. Santa Croce recalls St. Helen ; the *Domine quo vadis* chapel refers to the meeting of Our Lord and St. Peter on the Appian Way; San Pietro in Carcere is erected above the Mamertine prison; San Pietro in Montorio adjoins the place of St. Peter's martyrdom; San Pietro in Vincoli contains the actual chains with which St. Peter was bound. St. John Lateran's was first dedicated to Our Saviour, but the title was changed in the twelfth century; St. Gregory on the Cœlian recalls the home of St. Gregory and the site of the church he built in honour of St. Andrew; St. Lorenzo in Damaso recalls its founder, Pope Damasus. There are thirty-four churches dedicated to the Mother of God, distinguished often topographically (as Sta Maria in Via lata, or Sta Maria in Trastevere) and also in other ways (as Sta Maria Maggiore, so called in relation to other Roman churches of Our Lady, Sta Maria della Pace, Sta Maria dell'Anima, etc.). The formal dedications to God consist of Trinità dei Pellegrini, Trinità dei Monti, S. Spirito in Sassia, S. Salvatore in Lauro, S. Salvatore in Thermis, and the Gesu. There are no dedications to the Angels nor (until recently) to St. Joseph, the Sacred Heart, All Saints, or All Souls. In a few instances titulars occur more than once: Lawrence, 6; Peter, 4; Paul, Andrew, Charles, John, Nicholas, 3 each (see ROME).

England.—St. Augustine and his companions brought with them to England the Roman customs and traditions respecting the naming and dedication of churches. Altars were consecrated with the ashes of the martyrs. One of the earliest dedication prayers of the Anglo-Saxon Church runs thus: "Tibi, sancta Dei genitrix, virgo Maria (vel tibi, sancte J. B. Domini, . . . vel martyres Christi, vel confessores Domini) tibi commendamus hanc curam templi hujus, quod consecravimus Domino Deo nostro, ut hic intercessor existas; preces et vota offerentium hic Domino Deo offeras; odoramenta orationum plebis . . . ad patris thronum conferas", etc. (Lingard, "The History and Antiquities of the Anglo-Saxon Church", II, 40). Among the titulars of the Anglo-Saxon period are found: Christ Church (Canterbury), St. Mary's de Comeliis, St. Mary's of Huntingdon, and of Lyming, All Hallows (Lincoln), Peter (to whom the greater part of the Anglo-Saxon churches were dedicated), Peter and Paul (Canterbury), Paul (Jarrow), Andrew (Rochester), Martin (near Canterbury), Pancratius (Canterbury). Accepting the figures of F. A. Foster in her "Studies in Church Dedications", and without drawing a line between pre-Reformation and post-Reformation English churches (not now Catholic), we get the following enumeration of titulars: Christ 373, Holy Cross or Holy Rood 83, Michael, or Michael the Archangel, or St. Michael and the Angels 721 (one in six of the churches, ancient and modern, now attached to the Established Church bears the name of Our Lady or one of her titles, the total being 2162, and the proportion in pre-Reformation times was still larger), John Baptist, 576; Peter, 936; Peter and Paul, 277; Paul, 329; Holy Innocents, 15; Helen, 117; Augustine of Canterbury, 57; Thomas of Canterbury, 70; Nicholas, 397; Lawrence, 228. The Catholic Church in England at the present time has shown the same spirit of conservatism and of independence which is everywhere manifested in the choice of patrons. Among the chief of the 170 dedications to God of the churches and chapels (not counting religious houses, colleges, or institutions), the numbers are: Holy Trinity, 16; Holy Cross, 15; Sacred Heart, 90. Consecrations in honour of the Blessed Virgin maintain their ancient pre-eminence, reaching a total of 374. The simple designation of St. Mary's is the most frequent appellation. The form "Our Lady" occurs usually in combination with other titles. Among the numerous special titles are the following: Immaculate Conception, Our Lady of Sorrows, Help of Christians, Star of the Sea, Assumption, Our Lady of the Rosary. One church only bears the title of the Transfiguration, and one only is distinguished by each of the following titles: Our Lady of Refuge, of England, of Pity, of Paradise, of Reparation, of Reconciliation, Spouse of the Holy Ghost, Most Pure Heart of Mary. The angels are not favoured, Michael standing almost alone, but with 38 dedications. St. John Baptist has 20, while the name of Joseph appears as titular in no fewer than 145 churches. Apostles and Evangelists reach a total of 153: Peter leads the way with 43; the Beloved Disciple counts his 30, Peter and Paul follow with 17. Each of the remaining Apostles has at least 2 churches under his invocation, except Matthias, Barnabas, and Mark, who have but 1. Among the male saints: Anthony of Padua, Charles, Edward, Edmund, George, and Richard have each between 10 and 20; but Patrick, with 46, heads the list; then follow Augustine 22, Benedict 19, Cuthbert 18, and Francis of Assisi 21. A special interest attaches to names which occur but once, for frequently they are dedications to a local saint, as in the instances of Birinus (Dorchester), Dubritius (Treforest), Gwladys (Newport, Mon.), Ia (St. Ives), Neot (Liscard), Oswin (Tynemouth), Prian (Truro), Teilo (Tenby), Simon Stock (Faversham), Frideswide (Abingdon), and Walstan (Cossey). Nothing could have been more appropriate than the saints' names selected in the northern dioceses corresponding with the ancient Northumbria. There we meet with dedications to Aidan, Bede, Bennet, Columba, Cuthbert, Ninian, Hilda, Oswald, etc. Among the female saints Anne, the mother of Our Lady, occupies a position of eminence with 30 churches, Winefrid ranks next with 10, and Catherine follows with 8. The Saxon virgins and widows are honoured in the localities which they hallowed by their saintly lives, thus: Begh (Northumbria); Etheldreda (Ely); Hilda (Whitby); Mildred (Minster); Modwena (Burton-on-Trent); Osberg (Coventry); Wereburg (Chester); Winefrid (Holywell).

Scotland.—Celtic and Medieval.—In the days of the Picts, St. Peter was held in preference, from A. D. 710 when Roman usages were adopted, but Andrew claimed the greater number of dedications from the time his relics had been brought to the coast by St. Regulus. As instances of double titulars, native and foreign, the following may be taken: St. Mary and St. Manchar (Old Aberdeen); St. Mary and St. Boniface; Sts. Mary and Peter; Madrustus and John Baptist; Stephen and Moanus. In pre-Reformation times Holy Trinity occurred less frequently than in England; the Holy Ghost is met with three times; many churches bore the title of Christ (Kilchrist, Kildomine); Holy Blood and Holy Rood are found in several instances. A chapel styled "Teampull-Cro-Naomh" (Temple of the Holy Heart) once stood on the shore at Gauslan in Lews. Numerous churches bore Our Lady's name (Lady Kirk); the Assumption is found as early as 1290, and a church is dedicated to Our Lady of Loreto in 1530. Many churches had St. Michael for patron (Kilmichael). St. Anne is the titular in several places, and an altar to the Three Kings existed in almost every church. St. Joseph is nowhere found as a church titular, though he held the position of joint titular of an altar in 1518. The present day.—The choice of titulars in the Catholic churches of Scotland at the present time displays the same twofold direction that we find elsewhere: the honour of the saints of Scotland and of other lands, and the promptings of modern devotion. The Sacred Heart has 8 dedications, the Holy Rood 3. The Apostles receive the special honour of 39 churches, John being the patron of 13, and Andrew of 7. 77 churches are dedicated to the Blessed Virgin, of which 11 celebrate the Immaculate Conception, 7 bear the title of Star of the Sea; Our Lady of the Waves and Our Lady of Good Aid stand alone. Churches with the titles of modern saints are in a minority, for Patrick takes the lead with 12; Ninian, Scotland's first apostle, has 6; Columba 5; Mungo 4; David 3; and Margaret 2. Many Celtic saints occur but once, as for example, Bean, Brendan, Cadoc, Columbkille, Fillian, Kessog, Kieran, Mirin, and Winning.

Ireland.—The history of the patron saints of Ireland has yet to be written. The country has passed through long periods of trouble and oppression, yet several of the Celtic dedications have been preserved and linger in some districts even to this day. The Catholic church is often known simply by the name of the street in which it is situated, as the Cathedral, Marlborough St., Dublin, or the Jesuit church in Gardiner Street. A similar instance occurs in Dublin with regard to the church dedicated to St. Francis of Assisi, but always styled "Adam and Eve", from the fact that when the building was erected in the seventeenth century, there swung at the end of the alley, in which the chapel was situated, a public-house sign with the full figures of our first parents. The two religious edifices in a town are sometimes called the "Cathedral" and the "Old Chapel". In the days of persecution, when churches and endowments had alike been confiscated, the conditions of Catholic worship recalled the secrecy of the catacombs. During the nineteenth century the old "barns" that had so long served for chapels were replaced by beautiful and spacious churches for which Irish saints were frequently selected as patrons; but as a rule the choice has been determined by the tendencies of modern devotion. There are dedications to the Sacred Heart, to Our Lady under her various titles, and to many of the more recently canonized saints, such as St. Vincent and St. Francis de Sales. Still the people continue to refer to the churches by the names of the streets. In Celtic times many churches were dedicated to Our Lady and called Kilmurray. All the Donaghmore (*Dominica Major*) churches were dedicated to St. Patrick, because they had been founded by him. Other dedications include Bridget (Kilbride), Peter (Kilpedder), Paul (Kilpool), Catherine of Alexandria (Killadreenan, Kilcatherine). The Holy Sepulchre found a place among the oldest dedications. In Dublin or the neighbourhood the titles of Peter, Bride, Martin, Kevin, McTail (St. Michael-le-Pole), Nicholas within and Nicholas without the walls, were to be met with. Then there were churches under the patronage of All Hallows, Macud (Kilmacud), Machonna, Fintan, Brendan (Carrickbrenan), Begnet (St. Bega, Kilbegnet), Gobhain (Kilgobbin), Tiernan (Kilter, Kilternan). Bern's church was so called because founded by a priest of Byrne's clan. The title of Cell-Ingen-Leinin (Church of the five daughters of Leinin, whence the name Killiney) was so called from its founders. New names were introduced by the Normans, as Audven (Dublin), being St. Ouen of Rouen. The colony from Chester, brought over to repeople Dublin which had been decimated by the plague at the end of the twelfth century, erected a church dedicated to their patroness, St. Werburg.

Continental Europe.—With regard to the patrons of churches on the continent of Europe it must suffice to mention that in France alone there are 3000 dedications under the invocation of St. Martin, and then to take a glance at the single diocese of Bruges in Belgium: Bruges is the diocese of an old country that has never lost the faith. Its churches have 95 titulars which are distributed as follows: Holy Trinity 1; Holy Redeemer 2; Sacred Heart 3; Exaltation of the Holy Cross 3; Our Lady (Notre Dame) 24; Immaculate Conception 4; Assumption 6; Nativity 4. Michael holds the patronage of 7 churches, Joseph of 5, and John the Baptist of 16. Seven of the Apostles are honoured with 63 dedications: Peter has 23; Peter's Chains 3; Paul 5; Conversion of Paul 2; Bartholomew 6; James 6; and John only 3. Every town and district of Belgium is hallowed with the traditions of the holy men and women of ancient days, so that the devotion shown to the saints of other countries is not a little remarkable. Out of 57 male saints adopted as titulars Martin has the highest number, namely 20; Nicholas 13; Lawrence 8; Blaise 6. Amand, Apostle of the Flemings, has been chosen patron of 19 churches, Audomar of 8; Bavo, the hermit of Ghent, of 7; Eligius of 10; Medard of 6; and Vaast of 4.

United States.—The fourteen archdioceses of the United States have been examined as affording suitable material for a study of local piety, namely, Baltimore, Boston, Chicago, Cincinnati, Dubuque, Milwaukee, New Orleans, New York, Oregon City, Philadelphia, St. Louis, St. Paul, San Francisco, and Santa Fé. Over this area are found some 300 churches under dedications of the first rank, the principal ones being here enumerated: Most Holy Trinity 27; Holy Ghost 10; Holy Redeemer 11; Sacred Heart 109; Blessed Sacrament (including Corpus Christi 4, Holy Eucharist 1) 14; Holy Name 12; Holy Cross 19. The life of Christ is adequately represented, thus: Incarnation 3; Nativity 9; Epiphany 3; Transfiguration 4; Resurrection 3; Ascension 9. Other titles may be mentioned: Holy Spirit 3; Gesu 2; Atonement, Good Shepherd, Holy Comforter, Holy Saviour, Providence of God, St. Sauveur, and Sacred Hearts of Jesus and Mary 1 each. With the increasing realization of the gifts of the Incarnation which appears in modern devotions, it will excite little wonder that some 500 or more churches are dedicated to the Mother of God under one or other of her many titles, the principal being: St. Mary 148; Immaculate Conception 105; Assumption 36; Holy Rosary 19; Annunciation 12; Visitation 10; Star of the Sea 9; Presentation 6; Nativity 5; Holy Name of Mary 3; Maternity 3; Immaculate Heart of Mary 2; Purification 2; Most Pure Heart of Mary 1. Titles from the Litany of Loreto attract in so far as they represent the more recent expressions of Catholic devotion, thus: Mother of God 2; Mother of Divine Grace 1; Our Lady of Good Counsel 10; Gate of Heaven 1; Help of Christians 13; Queen of the Angels 1; Our Lady of the Angels 6; Our Lady of the Rosary 11. With the foregoing list certain derivative titles may be connected: Our Lady of Consolation 6; of Good Voyage 1; of Grace 3; of Help 2; of Mercy 4; of Perpetual Help 10; of Pity 2; of Prompt Succour 1; of Refuge 1; of Solace 1; of Sorrows 6; of the Lake 5; of the Sacred Heart 3; of the Seven Dolours 5; of the Snow 1; of Victory 8. The following geographical determinations occur: Our Lady of Czentochowa 4; of Guadalupe 8; of Hungary 2; of Loreto 1; of Mount Carmel 22; of Lourdes 14; of Pompeii 4; of Vilna 2. Notre Dame de Bon Port, du Bon Secours, de Chicago, de la Paix, Nuestra Señora de Belen, del Pilar, Sancta Maria Addolorata, and Sancta Maria Incoronata, 1 each, suggest French Spanish, and Italian affiliations.

The list of male saints in the fourteen dioceses comprises 156 names, and the female 41. For the sake of convenience these have been divided into groups. 10 churches are dedicated to All Saints, the Apostles in general have 1; Peter, the Prince of the Apostles, 58; James 26; Andrew 15; Thomas 11; Matthias 5; Philip 5; Barnabas 3; Bartholomew 2; Jude 1; the Evangelists have: John 59; Matthew 13; Mark 9; Luke 6. St. Paul is honoured with 26 dedications; Peter and Paul have 28; Philip and James 3; John and James 1. Michael the Archangel has 57; the Holy Angels 6; the

Guardian Angels 7; Gabriel 7; Raphael 10. In the long list of male saints Joseph heads the list with 183 dedications, followed by Patrick who counts 83, and then in numerical order: John the Baptist and Anthony 43 each; Francis of Assisi and Stephen 23 each; Augustine and Vincent 19 each; Francis de Sales, Francis Xavier, and Lawrence 16 each; Bernard, Ignatius, and Thomas Aquinas 15 each; Aloysius, Charles, and Louis 14 each; Alphonsus and Nicholas 11 each; Leo and Martin 10 each; Dominic 9; Edward 8; Ambrose, Clement, Jerome, and Joachim 7 each; Benedict and Pius 6; Gregory 5; Anselm, Athanasius, Bonaventure, Denis, Hubert, Maurice, Peter Claver, and Philip Neri 3 each; Dionysius, Eloi, Ferdinand, Francis Borgia, Gall, Hyacinth, Isidore, Liborius, Nicholas of Tolentino, Sebastian, Vincent Ferrer, and William 2 each; Albert, Alphonsus Turibius, Anthony the Hermit, Basil, Bride, Canicius, Cyprian, Cyril, David, Donatus, Edmund, Engelbert, Eustachius, Florian, Fidelis, Francis Solano, Frederick, Irenæus, John Baptist de la Salle, John Berchmans, John Capistrano, John Chrysostom, John Francis Regis, John the Martyr, Kyran, Landry, Lazarus, Leander, Leon, Leonard of Port Maurice, Luis Bertrand, Maron, Martin of Tours, Maurus, Nicholas of Myra, Napoleon, Norbert, Raymund, Rock, Theodore, Thomas of Canterbury, Thomas of Villanova, Timothy, Valentine, Viator, Victor, Willebrod, Zephyrin, 1 each.

The female patronesses are 41 in number, those whose names appear more frequently being: Anne 36; Rose 22; the three Catherines 21; Teresa 14; Agnes 13; Cecilia 12; Margaret 10; Elizabeth 9; Monica 8; Genevieve 6; Philomena 5; Clare, Gertrude, and Mary Magdalen 4 each; Agatha, Helen, and Veronica 3 each; Anastasia, Angela, and Lucy 2 each; Barbara, Cunegunde, Elizabeth of Hungary, Eulalia, Frances of Rome, Madeline, Mary Magdalen de Pazzi, Scholastica, Sylvia, Ursula, Victoria, Walburga, 1 each. Among the saints, more than in any other class, the nationality of devotion finds occasion for its manifestation. Celtic centres are shown by such titles as: Brendan 5; Canice 1; Colman 3; Columba 5; Columbanus 2; Columbkille 6; Cronan 1; Finbar 1; Jarlath 1; Kevin 1; Kilian 3; Lawrence O'Toole 3; Malachy 6; Mel 1; Attracta 1; Bridget 11; Ita 1; George, a widely favoured national patron, has 17 churches. Rita of Cascia 3, and Rocco 2, show the Italian; Ludmilla 1, Procopius 1, and Vitus 1, are Bohemian; Stephen with 23 suggests Hungary; Boniface with 21 dedications, and Henry with 8, tell of Germany. Benedict the Moor (New York) is the patron of the church for negroes. The numerous Polish population has adopted distinctive patrons: Adalbert 8; Casimir 10; Cyril and Methodius 8; Josaphat 3; John Cantius 4; John Nepomucene 8; Ladislaus 1; Stanislaus 23; Vojtiechus 1; Wenceslaus 9; Hedwig 6; Salomea 1.

Canada.—In the Dominion of Canada, to a very great extent, the name of a district or village is the same as that of the patron of the church. Obviously the different localities have been named after their respective patrons. The number of titulars is considerable, the names having been assigned on the plan of avoiding repetitions. In the list examined the names of about 400 male, and 100 female, saints are represented, and the entire range of popular devotion is covered. It is a surprise to find that in this long list of provincial divisions no dedications are to be found to the Most Holy Trinity, the Holy Ghost, the Blessed Sacrament. Moreover, only five are to be found which in any way relate to Christ or the mysteries of His life, these being, St. Sauveur, Le Précieux Sang, L'Epiphanie, Sacré Cœur de Jésus, L'Ascension. The Holy Family is represented, also the Angels Guardian, and Our Lady under the various mysteries of her life and many of her most popular titles of devotion, such as: La Conception, La Présentation, L'Annunciation, La Visitation, L'Assomption, Notre Dame de la Mercie, Notre Dame de la Paix, Notre Dame des Anges, Notre Dame des Nièges, Notre Dame de Bon Conseil, Notre Dame du Mont Carmel, Notre Dame du Rosaire, Sacré Cœur de Marie etc. The patrons of churches, outside the class just referred to, have been listed according to the number of churches dedicated to them in the Archdioceses of Halifax, Kingston, Montreal, Ottawa, Quebec, St. Boniface, Toronto, Vancouver, and the Archdiocese of St. John's, Newfoundland, and are as follows: Most Holy Trinity 2; Holy Ghost 1; Sacred Heart 15; Most Holy Redeemer 1; Holy Name of Jesus 2; Infant Jesus 3; Holy Child 1; Holy Family 5; Blessed Sacrament, Transfiguration, Ascension, St. Sauveur, and Gesu 1 each; Holy Cross 4. To Our Lady we find: Immaculate Conception 7, Nativity 5, Presentation 2, Annunciation 4, Visitation 3, Purification 1, Assumption 6, Mary Immaculate 1, Holy Name of Mary 4, St. Mary 9, Notre Dame 4, Notre Dame de la Consolation 1, Notre Dame de la Garde 2, Notre Dame de l'Espérance 2, Sacred Heart of Mary 5, Stella Maris 1, Our Lady Help of Christians 1, of Good Counsel 5, of Grace 4, of la Salette 2, of Loreto 1, of Lourdes 3, of Mercy 3, of Mount Carmel 6, of Peace 1, of Perpetual Succour 5, of Victory 3, of the Angels 2, of the Blessed Sacrament 1, of the Rosary 7, of the Sacred Heart 1, of the Seven Dolours 3, of the Snow 2, of the Wayside 2.

To the saints: Joseph 21; Patrick 20; Anthony 10; Louis 9; James, Michael, Paul, and Peter 8 each; John, John the Baptist, John the Evangelist, and Vincent de Paul 7 each; Francis of Assisi 6; Augustine, Bernard, and Charles 5 each; Edward, Francis de Sales, Francis Xavier 4 each; Ambrose, Charles Borromeo, Gabriel, George, Gerard, Joachim, Luke, Thomas Aquinas, and Viateur 3 each; Alexander, Aloysius, Anastasius, Andrew, Anselm, Columban, Edward the Confessor, Felix, Francis Regis, Germaine, Gregory, Gregory Nazianzus, Gregory the Great, Ignatius, Leon of Westminster, Peter in Chains, Philip Neri, Stephen, and Thomas 2 each; Adrian, Aimé, Alfred, Alphonsus Ligouri, Arsenius, Athanasius, Barnaby, Basil, Benedict, Benjamin, Bernardin of Siena, Bonaventure, Boniface, Bride, Cajetan, Calixtus, Camillus of Lellis, Carthagh, Casimir, Clement, Columbanus, Columbkille, Cosmos, Cuthbert, Cyril and Methodius, Cyprian, Daniel, Denis, Désiré, Donatus, Dominic, Edmund, Eugene, Faustinus, Felix of Valois, Good Thief, Henry, Hugh, Hyacinth, Ignatius Loyola, Irenæus, Isidor, Jerome, John Berchmans, John Cantius, John Chrysostom, John of the Cross, Jovita, Jude, Justin, Kyran, Lawrence, Lawrence O'Toole, Leo, Malachy, Malo, Mark, Martin, Matthew, Narcissus, Nicholas, Odilo, Pascal-Babylon, Peter Celestine Philippe, Raphael, Remigius, Rock, Romuald, Sixtus, Stephen de Lauzon, Turibius, Vitalis, Vitus, Zephyrim, and Zoticus 1 each; Anne 7; Bridget and Philomena 4 each; Helen 3; Agnes, Cecilia, Emily, and Marguerite 2 each; Agatha, Anastasia, Angelica, Catherine, Catherine of Siena, Clare of Tereanville, Clotilde, Cunegundes, Elizabeth, Elizabeth of Hungary, Elizabeth of Portugal, Euphemia, Felicitas, Jeanne de Neuville, Magdalen, Margaret, Monica, Veronica, All Saints, 1 each.

Australia.—This includes the Archdioceses of Sydney, Melbourne, Hobart, Adelaide, Brisbane, and the Archdiocese of Wellington, which comprises all the territory of New Zealand. The patrons of churches are: (1) Trinity 3; Good Shepherd 2; Most Holy Redeemer 3; Sacred Heart 63; St. Saviour 1; Real Presence 1; Holy Name 4; Blessed Sacrament 2; Church of the Reparation 1; Church of the Passion 1; Holy Cross 7. (2) St. Mary 74; Immaculate Conception 21; Nativity 1; Annunciation 1; Assumption 6; Our Lady Help of Christians 2; of Good Counsel 1; of Lourdes 1; of Mercy 1; of Mount Carmel 4; of Perpetual Succour 3; of the Rosary 11; of the Sacred Heart 1; of the Seven

Dolours 3; of the Suburbs 1; of Victories 1; Refuge of Sinners 1; Auxilium Christianorum 1; Blessed Virgin 2; Holy Heart of Mary, Holy Name of Mary, Mary Immaculate, and Queen of Angels 1 each; St. Mary of the Angels 2; Star of the Sea 19. (3) Guardian Angels 4; Holy Angels 2. (4–5) Patrick 85; Joseph 74; Michael 24; Peter 16; Peter and Paul 13; Francis of Assisi and Paul 10 each; John the Evangelist, Columba, Francis Xavier, John, Anthony, and James 8 each; Augustine and Francis de Sales 7 each; Andrew, John the Baptist, Lawrence, Matthew, and Vincent 6 each; Bede, Benedict, Lawrence O'Toole, Malachy, Stephen, and Thomas 4 each; Aidan, Brendan, Colman, and Ignatius 3 each; Aloysius, Bernard, Charles, Columbkille, Edward, Gabriel, George, Gregory, Joachim, Mark, Martin, Raphael, Stanislaus, and Thomas Aquinas 2 each; Alphonsus, Ambrose, Athanasius, Barnabas, Bartholomew, Boniface, Carthagh, Clement, Cleus, Declan, Felix, Fiacre, Finbar, Furseus, Gerard, John and Paul, John Berchmans, John of God, John of the Cross, Joseph and Joachim, Kevin, Kieran, Leo, Leonard, Luke, Maro, Michael and George, Munchin, Nicholas, Nicholas of Myra, Paulinus, Peter Chanel, Philip and James, Pius, Rock, Rupert, Vigilius, William, and the Apostles 1 each. (6) Brigid 19; Anne 7; Canice and Monica 4 each; Agnes 3; Margaret 2; Agatha, Clare, Gertrude, Helen, Ita, Joan of Arc, Rose of Lima, Teresa, Winefred, 1 each. All Saints 6, All Souls 2.

British South Africa.—This includes the Eastern and Western Vicariates, the Vicariates of Natal, Kimberley, Transvaal, Orange River, Basutoland, and the Prefectures Apostolic of Great Namaqualand and Rhodesia. The churches are dedicated as follows: (1) Trinity 1; Sacred Heart 16; St. Saviour 1; Holy Family 2. (2) St. Mary 17; Immaculate Conception 12; Annunciation 1; Assumption 1; Mater Dolorosa 2; Our Lady 1; Our Lady of Good Counsel 3; of Grace 1; of Lourdes 1; of Perpetual Succour 1; of Sorrows 1; of the Rosary 4; of the Sacred Heart 2; Star of the Sea 2. (3) Michael and the Holy Angels 1. (4–5) Joseph 11; Augustine and Patrick 5 each; Francis Xavier and Michael 4 each; Peter, and Peter and Paul 3 each; Charles, Dominic, Francis de Sales, and Ignatius Loyola 2 each; Anthony, Benedict, Boniface, Columba, Francis of Assisi, Gabriel, James, Joachim, John, John the Baptist, Leo, Martin, Matthew, Paul, Peter Claver, Simon and Jude, Thomas, and Triashill 1 each. (6) Anne and Monica 2 each; Agnes and Mechtilda 1 each. All Saints 1.

PATRONS OF COUNTRIES.—An authentic catalogue of patron saints of countries of the world has yet to be made. Some countries appear to have no celestial patron, others have several assigned to them, and it is by no means clear that the distinction between patron and Apostle is invariably taken into account. The following list gives the patrons of some few countries of the world: Austria (Our Lady), Belgium (St. Joseph), Brazil (declared "The Land of the Holy Cross", 3 May, 1500), Borneo (St. Francis Xavier), Canada (St. Anne and St. George), The Congo (Our Lady), Chili (St. James), England (St. George), East Indies (St. Thomas, Apostle), Ecuador (styled "The Republic of the Sacred Heart"), Finland (Henry of Upsal), France (St. Denis), Germany (St. Michael), Holland (St. Willibrord), Hungary (St. Stephen), Ireland (St. Patrick), Italy (various), Lombardy (St. Charles), Mexico (Our Lady of Help, and Our Lady of Guadaloupe), Norway (St. Olaf), Portugal (St. George), Piedmont (St. Maurice), Scotland (St. Andrew), Sweden (St. Bridget), Spain (St. James), South America (St. Rose of Lima), United States of North America (Our Lady under the title of Immaculate Conception), Wales (St. David).

PATRONS OF TRADES AND PROFESSIONS.—The beliefs of a Catholic in an age of Faith prompted him to place not only his churches under the protection of some illustrious servant of God, but the ordinary interests of life, his health, and family, trade, maladies, and perils, his death, his city and country. The whole social life of the Catholic world before the Reformation was animated with the idea of protection from the citizens of heaven. It has been stated that in England there existed 40,000 religious corporations, including ecclesiastical bodies of all kinds, monasteries and convents, military orders, industrial and professional guilds, and charitable institutions, each of which had its patron, its rites, funds, and methods of assistance. Some idea of the vastness of the subject may be gathered from a few examples of the trades under their respective patrons: Anastasia (weavers), Andrew (fishermen), Anne (houseworkers and cabinet-makers), Christopher (porters), Cloud (nailmakers), Cosmas and Damian (doctors), Crispin (shoemakers), Eloi (all workers with the hammer), Hubert (huntsmen), Lydia (dyers), Joseph (carpenters, Mark (notaries), Luke (painters), Nativity (trades for women), Raymund Nonnatus (midwives), Raymund of Pennafort (canonists), Stephen (stonemasons), Vincent Martyr (winegrowers), Vitus (comedians). Conditions of life: foundlings (Holy Innocents), girls (Blandina), boys (Aloysius), singers and scholars (Gregory), philosophers (Catherine), musicians (Cecilia), persons condemned to death (Dismas). There were patrons or protectors in various forms of illness, as for instance: Agatha (diseases of the breast), Apollonia (toothache), Blaise (sore throat), Clare and Lucy (the eyes), Benedict (against poison), Hubert (against the bite of dogs). These patrons with very many others were chosen on account of some real correspondence between the patron and the object of patronage, or by reason of some play on words, or as a matter of individual piety. Thus, while the great special patrons had their clients all over Christendom, other patrons in regard of the same class of objects might vary with different times and places. In order to complete this imperfect and summary sketch of the subject of patrons, a list of the patrons announced by the Holy See within the last few years should here find a place: St. Joseph was declared patron of the universal Church by Pius X on 8 Dec., 1870. Leo XIII during the course of his pontificate announced the following patrons: St. Thomas Aquinas, patron of all universities, colleges, and schools (4 Aug., 1880); St. Vincent, patron of all charitable societies (1 May, 1885); St. Camillus of Lellis, patron of the sick and of those who attend on them (22 June, 1886); the patronal feast of Our Lady of the Congo to be the Assumption (21 July, 1891); St. Bridget, patroness of Sweden (1 Oct., 1891); the Holy Family, the model and help of all Christian families (14 June, 1892); St. Peter Claver, special patron of missions to the negroes (1896); St. Paschal Baylon, patron of Eucharistic congresses and all Eucharistic societies (28 Nov., 1897). On 25 May, 1899, he dedicated the world to the Sacred Heart, as Prince and Lord of all, Catholics and non-Catholics, Christians and non-Christians. Lourdes was dedicated to our Lady of the Rosary (8 Sept., 1901). Pius X declared St. Francis Xavier patron of the Propagation of the Faith (25 Mar., 1904).

The honouring of the saints has in some instances doubtless been the occasion of abuse. Spells and incantations have been intruded in the place of trust and prayer; the prayerful abstinence of a vigil has been exchanged for the rollicksome enjoyment of wakes; reverence may have run incidentally to puerile extravagance; and patrons may have been chosen before their claim to an heroic exercise of Christian virtue had been juridically established. Still it remains true that the manifestation of Christian piety in the honour paid to angels and saints has been singularly free from the taint of human excess and error.

CAHIER, *Caractéristiques des Saints* (Paris, 1867); HUSENBETH, *Emblems of the Saints*, ed. JESSOP (3rd ed., Norwich, 1882); BONA,

Rerum Liturgicarum I, xix; STANTON, *Menology of England and Wales* (London, 1887); LINGARD, *The History and Antiquities of the Anglo-Saxon Church*, II; FORSTER, *Studies in Church Dedications* (3 vols., London, 1899); MACKINLEY, *Ancient Church Dedications in Scotland* (Edinburgh, 1910); DONNELLY, *History of Dublin Parishes* (Dublin); C. T. S. publications; COLEMAN, *Historical Memoirs of the City of Armagh* (Dublin, 1900); SMITH, *English Guilds* (London, 1870); HAZLITT, *The Livery Companies of the City of London* (London, 1892); BESSE, *Les Saints Protecteurs du Travail*, n. 336 in *Science et Religion* (Paris). See also various ecclesiastical Directories in DIRECTORIES, CATHOLIC.

HENRY PARKINSON.

Patti, DIOCESE OF (PACTENSIS), in the Province of Messina (Sicily), on the western shore of the gulf of the same name. The city has a large trade in tunny-fish. In its cathedral is preserved the body of St. Febronia, virgin and martyr. The city was rebuilt by Count Roger, after the Saracens had been driven from Messina (1058); it stands near the site of the ancient Tyndaris, a Lacedæmonian colony that had a very flourishing commerce; the magnificent temple of Mercury in the latter city was despoiled by Verres. In the time of Pliny, however, the sea had encroached greatly upon the shore, and after the foundation of Patti, Tyndaris was almost entirely abandoned; there remains only the church of Santa Maria del Tindaro, with a Franciscan monastery. Three of the bishops of Tyndaris are known: Severinus (501); Eutychius (594), with whose zeal for the conversion of pagans St. Gregory the Great was well pleased; and Theodorus (649).

Patti was destroyed by Frederick of Aragon about 1300, on account of its attachment to the House of Anjou; rebuilt in the sixteenth century, it was sacked by the Turks. Count Ruggiero had founded there a Benedictine abbey, and in 1131, the antipope Anacletus II made Patti an episcopal see, uniting it, however, with the Abbey of Lipari; Eugenius III in 1157 confirmed the action of the antipope, the first legitimate pastor of the see being Gilbertus. In 1399, Lipari and Patti were separated, and the first bishop of the separate see of Patti was Francesco Hermemir. Other bishops were: Francesco Urvio (1518), who in the course of controversies with the *capitano dello spagnuolo* was imprisoned; later he was transferred to the Diocese of Urgel; Bartolomeo Sebastiani (1548), distinguished himself at the Council of Trent, and was Governor of Sicily for three years; Alfonso de los Cameros (1652), the founder of the seminary, restored later by Bishop Galletti (1727); Cardinal Geremia Celesia, later Archbishop of Palermo, Bishop of Patti, 1860–71.

The diocese is a suffragan of Messina; it has 49 parishes, 20,000 inhabitants, 5 religious houses of men, and 15 of sisters, who conduct 4 institutes for girls and several schools.

CAPPELLETTI, *Le Chiese d' Italia*, XXI.   U. BENIGNI.

Paul, SAINT.—I. PRELIMINARY QUESTIONS.—A. *Apocryphal Acts of St. Paul.*—Professor Schmidt has recently published a photographic copy, a transcription, a German translation, and a commentary of a Coptic papyrus composed of about 2000 fragments, which he has classified, juxtaposed, and deciphered at a cost of infinite labour ("Acta Pauli aus der Heidelberger koptischen Papyrushandschrift Nr. 1", Leipzig, 1904, and "Zusätze", etc., Leipzig, 1905). Most critics, whether Catholic (Duchesne, Bardenhewer, Ehrhard etc.), or Protestant (Zahn, Harnack, Corssen etc.), believe that these are real "Acta Pauli", although the text edited by Schmidt, with its very numerous gaps, represents but a small portion of the original work. This discovery modified the generally accepted ideas concerning the origin, contents, and value of these apocryphal Acts, and warrants the conclusion that three ancient compositions which have reached us formed an integral part of the "Acta Pauli" viz. the "Acta Pauli et Theclæ", of which the best edition is that of Lipsius ("Acta Apostolorum apocrypha", Leipzig, 1891, 235–72), a "Martyrium Pauli" preserved in Greek and a fragment of which also exists in Latin (op. cit., 104–17), and a letter from the Corinthians to Paul with the latter's reply, the Armenian text of which was preserved (cf. Zahn, "Gesch. des neutest. Kanons", II, 592–611), and the Latin discovered by Berger in 1891 (cf. Harnack, "Die apokryphen Briefe des Paulus an die Laodicener und Korinther", Bonn, 1905). With great sagacity Zahn anticipated this result with regard to the last two documents, and the manner in which St. Jerome speaks of the περίοδοι Pauli et Theclæ (De viris ill., vii) might have permitted the same surmise with regard to the first.

Another consequence of Schmidt's discovery is no less interesting. Lipsius maintained—and this was hitherto the common opinion—that besides the Catholic "Acts" there formerly existed Gnostic "Acts of Paul", but now everything tends to prove that the latter never existed. In fact Origen quotes the "Acta Pauli" twice as an estimable writing ("In Joann.", xx, 12; "De princip.", II, i, 3); Eusebius (Hist. eccl., III, iii, 5; XXV, 4) places them among the books in dispute, such as the "Shepherd" of Hermas, the "Apocalypse of Peter", the "Epistle of Barnabas", and the "Teaching of the Apostles". The stichometry of the "Codex Claromontanus" (photograph in Vigouroux, "Dict. de la Bible", II, 147) places them after the canonical books. Tertullian and St. Jerome, while pointing out the legendary character of this writing, do not attack its orthodoxy. The precise purpose of St. Paul's correspondence with the Corinthians which formed part of the "Acts", was to oppose the Gnostics, Simon and Cleobius. But there is no reason to admit the existence of heretical "Acts" which have since been hopelessly lost, for all the details given by ancient authors are verified in the "Acts" which have been recovered or tally well with them. The following is the explanation of the confusion: The Manichæans and Priscillianists had circulated a collection of five apocryphal "Acts", four of which were tainted with heresy, and the fifth were the "Acts of Paul". The "Acta Pauli" owing to this unfortunate association are suspected of heterodoxy by the more recent authors such as Philastrius (De hæres., 88) and Photius (Cod., 114). Tertullian (De baptismo, 17) and St. Jerome (De vir. ill., vii) denounce the fabulous character of the apocryphal "Acts" of Paul, and this severe judgment is amply confirmed by the examination of the fragments published by Schmidt. It is a purely imaginative work in which improbability vies with absurdity. The author, who was acquainted with the canonical Acts of the Apostles, locates the scene in the places really visited by St. Paul (Antioch, Iconium, Myra, Perge, Sidon, Tyre, Ephesus, Corinth, Philippi, Rome), but for the rest he gives his fancy free rein. His chronology is absolutely impossible. Of the sixty-five persons he names, very few are known and the part played by these is irreconcilable with the statements of the canonical "Acts". Briefly, if the canonical "Acts" are true the apocryphal "Acts" are false. This, however, does not imply that none of the details have historical foundation, but they must be confirmed by an independent authority.

B. *Chronology.*—If we admit according to the almost unanimous opinion of exegetes that Acts, xv, and Gal., ii, 1–10, relate to the same fact it will be seen that an interval of seventeen years—or at least sixteen, counting incomplete years as accomplished—elapsed between the conversion of Paul and the Apostolic council, for Paul visited Jerusalem three years after his conversion (Gal., i, 18) and returned after fourteen years for the meeting held with regard to legal observances (Gal., ii, 1: Ἔπειτα διὰ δεκατεσσάρων ἐτῶν). It is true that some authors include the three years prior to the first visit in the total of fourteen, but this explanation seems forced. On the other hand, twelve or thirteen years elapsed between the Apostolic council and the end of the captivity, for the captivity lasted nearly five years (more than two years at Cæsarea, Acts, xxiv, 27, six months travelling, including the sojourn at Malta, and two years at Rome, Acts, xxviii, 30); the third mission lasted not less than four years and a half (three of which were spent at Ephesus, Acts, xx, 31, and one between the departure from Ephesus and the arrival at Jerusalem, I Cor., xvi, 8; Acts, xx, 16, and six months at the very least for the journey to Galatia, Acts, xviii, 23); while the second mission lasted not less than three years (eighteen months for Corinth, Acts, xviii, 11, and the remainder for the evangelization of Galatia, Macedonia, and Athens, Acts, xv, 36–xvii, 34). Thus from the conversion to the end of the first captivity we have a total of about twenty-nine years. Now if we could find a fixed point that is a synchronism between a fact in the life of Paul and a certainly dated event in profane history, it would be easy to reconstruct the Pauline chronology. Unfortunately this much wished-for mark has not yet been indicated with certainty, despite the numerous attempts made by scholars, especially in recent times. It is of interest to note even the abortive attempts, because the discovery of an inscription or of a coin may any day transform an approximate date into an absolutely fixed point. These are: the meeting of Paul with Sergius Paulus, Proconsul of Cyprus, about the year 46 (Acts, xiii, 7), the meeting at Corinth with Aquila and Priscilla, who had been expelled from Rome, about 51 (Acts, xviii, 2), the meeting with Gallio, Proconsul of Achaia, about 53 (Acts, xviii, 12), the address of Paul before the Governor Felix and his wife Drusilla about 58 (Acts, xxiv, 24). All these events, as far as they may be assigned approximate dates, agree with the Apostle's general chronology but give no precise results. Three synchronisms, however, appear to afford a firmer basis:—

(1) The occupation of Damascus by the ethnarch of King Aretas and the escape of the Apostle three years after his conversion (II Cor., xi, 32–33; Acts, ix, 23–26).—Damascene coins bearing the effigy of Tiberius to the year 34 are extant, proving that at that time the city belonged to the Romans. It is impossible to assume that Aretas had received it as a gift from Tiberius, for the latter, especially in his last years, was hostile to the King of the Nabatæans whom Vitellius, Governor of Syria, was ordered to attack (Joseph., "Ant.", XVIII, v, 13); neither could Aretas have possessed himself of it by force for, besides the unlikelihood of a direct aggression against the Romans, the expedition of Vitellius was at first directed not against Damascus but against Petra. It has therefore been somewhat plausibly conjectured that Caligula, subject as he was to such whims, had ceded it to him at the time of his accession (16 March, 37). As a matter of fact nothing is known of imperial coins of Damascus dating from either Caligula or Claudius. According to this hypothesis St. Paul's conversion was not prior to 34, nor his escape from Damascus and his first visit to Jerusalem, to 37.

(2) Death of Agrippa, famine in Judea, mission of Paul and Barnabas to Jerusalem to bring thither the alms from the Church of Antioch (Acts, xi, 27–xii, 25).—Agrippa died shortly after the Pasch (Acts, xii, 3, 19), when he was celebrating in Cæsarea solemn festivals in honour of Claudius's recent return from Britain, in the third year of his reign, which had begun in 41 (Josephus, "Ant.", XIX, vii, 2). These combined facts bring us to the year 44, and it is precisely in this year that Orosius (Hist., vii, 6) places the great famine which desolated Judea. Josephus mentions it somewhat later, under the procurator Tiberius Alexander (about 46), but it is well known that the whole of Claudius's reign was characterized by poor harvests (Suet., "Claudius", 18) and a general famine was usually preceded by a more or less prolonged period of scarcity. It is also possible that the relief sent in anticipation of the famine foretold by Agabus (Acts, xi, 28, 29) preceded the appearance of the scourge or coincided with the first symptoms of want. On the other hand, the synchronism between the death of Herod and the mission of Paul can only be approximate, for although the two facts are closely connected in the Acts, the account of the death of Agrippa may be a mere episode intended to shed light on the situation of the Church of Jerusalem about the time of the arrival of the delegates from Antioch. In any case, 45 seems to be the most satisfactory date.

(3) Replacing of Felix by Festus two years after the arrest of Paul (Acts, xxiv, 27).—Until recently chronologists commonly fixed this important event in the year 60–61. Harnack, O. Holtzmann, and McGiffert suggest advancing it four or five years for the following reasons: (1) In his "Chronicon", Eusebius places the arrival of Festus in the second year of Nero (Oct., 55–Oct., 56, or if, as is asserted, Eusebius makes the reigns of the emperors begin with the September after their accession, Sept., 56–Sept., 57). But it must be borne in mind that the chroniclers being always obliged to give definite dates, were likely to guess at them, and it may be that Eusebius for lack of definite information divided into two equal parts the entire duration of the government of Felix and Festus. (2) Josephus states (Ant., XX, viii, 9) that Felix having been recalled to Rome and accused by the Jews to Nero, owed his safety only to his brother Pallas who was then high in favour. But according to Tacitus (Annal., XIII, xiv–xv), Pallas was dismissed shortly before Britannicus celebrated his fourteenth anniversary, that is, in January, 55. These two statements are irreconcilable; for if Pallas was dismissed three months after Nero's accession (13 Oct., 54) he could not have been at the summit of his power when his brother Felix, recalled from Palestine at the command of Nero about the time of Pentecost, arrived at Rome. Possibly Pallas, who after his dismissal retained his wealth and a portion of his influence, since he stipulated that his administration should not be subjected to an investigation, was able to be of assistance to his brother until 62 when Nero, to obtain possession of his goods, had him poisoned.

The advocates of a later date bring forward the following reasons: (1) Two years before the recall of Felix, Paul reminded him that he had been for many years judge over the Jewish nation (Acts, xxiv, 10–27). This can scarcely mean less than six or seven years, and as, according to Josephus who agrees with Tacitus, Felix was named procurator of Judea in 52, the beginning of the captivity would fall in 58 or 59. It is true that the argument loses its strength if it be admitted with several critics that Felix before being procurator had held a subordinate position in Palestine. (2) Josephus (Ant., XX, viii, 5–8) places under Nero everything that pertains to the government of Felix, and although this long series of events does not necessarily require many years it is evident that Josephus regards the government of Felix as coinciding for the most part with the reign of Nero, which began on 13 Oct., 54. In fixing as follows the chief dates in the life of Paul all certain or probable data seem to be satisfactorily taken into account: Conversion, 35; first visit to Jerusalem, 37; sojourn at Tarsus, 37–43; apostolate at Antioch, 43–44; second visit to Jerusalem, 44 or 45; first mission, 45–49; third visit to Jerusalem, 49 or 50; second mission, 50–53; (I and II Thessalonians), 52; fourth visit to Jerusalem, 53; third mission, 53–57; (I and II Corinthians; Galatians), 56; (Romans), 57; fifth visit to Jerusalem, arrest, 57; arrival of Festus, departure for Rome, 59; captivity at Rome, 60–62; (Philemon; Colossians; Ephesians; Philippians), 61; second period of activity, 62–66; (I Timothy; Titus), second arrest, 66; (II Timothy), martyrdom, 67. (See Turner, "Chronology of the N. T." in Hastings, "Dict. of the Bible"; Hönicke, "Die Chronologie des Lebens des Ap. Paulus", Leipzig, 1903.)

II. LIFE AND WORK OF PAUL.—A. *Birth and Education.*—From St. Paul himself we know that he was born at Tarsus in Cilicia (Acts, xxi, 39), of a father who was a Roman citizen (Acts, xxii, 26–28; cf. xvi, 37), of a family in which piety was hereditary (II Tim., i, 3) and which was much attached to Pharisaic traditions and observances (Phil., iii, 5–6). St. Jerome relates, on what ground is not known, that his parents were natives of Gischala, a small town of Galilee, and that they brought him to Tarsus when Gischala was captured by the Romans ("De vir. ill.", v; "In epist. ad Phil.", 23). This last detail is certainly an anachronism, but the Galilean origin of the family is not at all improbable. As he belonged to the tribe of Benjamin he was given at the time of his circumcision the name of Saul, which must have been common in that tribe in memory of the first king of the Jews (Phil., iii, 5). As a Roman citizen he also bore the Latin name of Paul. It was quite usual for the Jews of that time to have two names, one Hebrew, the other Latin or Greek, between which there was often a certain assonance and which were joined together exactly in the manner made use of by St. Luke (Acts, xiii, 9: Σαῦλος ὁ καὶ Παῦλος). See on this point Deissmann, "Bible Studies" (Edinburgh, 1903), 313–17. It was natural that in inaugurating his apostolate among the Gentiles Paul should have adopted his Roman name, especially as the name Saul had a ludicrous meaning in Greek. As every respectable Jew had to teach his son a trade, young Saul learned how to make tents (Acts, xviii, 3) or rather to make the mohair of which tents were made (cf. Lewin, "Life of St. Paul", I, London, 1874, 8–9). He was still very young when sent to Jerusalem to receive his education at the school of Gamaliel (Acts, xxii, 3). Possibly some of his family resided in the holy city; later there is mention of the presence of one of his sisters whose son saved his life (Acts, xxiii, 16). From that time it is absolutely impossible to follow him until he takes an active part in the martyrdom of St. Stephen (Acts, vii, 58–60; xxii, 20). He was then qualified as a young man (νεανίας), but this was a very elastic appellation and might be applied to a man between twenty and forty.

B. *Conversion and early Labours.*—We read in the Acts of the Apostles three accounts of the conversion of St. Paul (ix, 1–19; xxii, 3–21; xxvi, 9–23) presenting some slight differences, which it is not difficult to harmonize and which do not affect the basis of the narrative, which is perfectly identical in substance. See J. Massie, "The Conversion of St. Paul" in "The Expositor", 3rd series, X, 1889, 241–62. Sabatier, agreeing with most independent critics, has well said (L'Apôtre Paul, 1896, 42): "These differences cannot in any way alter the reality of the fact; their bearing on the narrative is extremely remote; they do not deal even with the circumstances accompanying the miracle but with the subjective impressions which the companions of St. Paul received of these circumstances. . . . To base a denial of the historical character of the account upon these differences would seem therefore a violent and arbitrary proceeding." All efforts hitherto made to explain without a miracle the apparition of Jesus to Paul have failed. Naturalistic explanations are reduced to two: either Paul believed that he really saw Christ, but was the victim of an hallucination, or he believed that he saw Him only through a spiritual vision, which tradition, recorded in the Acts of the Apostles, later erroneously materialized. Renan explained everything by hallucination due to disease brought on by a combination of moral causes such as doubt, remorse, fear, and of physical causes such as ophthalmia, fatigue, fever, the sudden transition from the torrid desert to the fresh gardens of Damascus, perhaps a sudden storm accompanied by lightning and thunder. All this combined, according to Renan's theory, to produce a cerebral commotion, a passing delirium which Paul took in good faith for an apparition of the risen Christ.

The other partisans of a natural explanation, while avoiding the word hallucination, eventually fall back on the system of Renan which they merely endeavour to render a little less complicated. Thus Holsten, for whom the vision of Christ is only the conclusion of a series of syllogisms by which Paul persuaded himself that Christ was truly risen. So also Pfleiderer, who however, causes the imagination to play a more influential part: "An excitable, nervous temperament; a soul that had been violently agitated and torn by the most terrible doubts; a most vivid phantasy, occupied with the awful scenes of persecution on the one hand, and on the other by the ideal image of the celestial Christ; in addition the nearness of Damascus with the urgency of a decision, the lonely stillness, the scorching and blinding heat of the desert—in fact everything combined to produce one of those ecstatic states in which the soul believes that it sees those images and conceptions which violently agitate it as if they were phenomena proceeding from the outward world" (Lectures on the influence of the Apostle Paul on the development of Christianity, 1897, 43). We have quoted Pfleiderer's words at length because his "psychological" explanation is considered the best ever devised. It will readily be seen that it is insufficient and as much opposed to the account in the Acts as to the express testimony of St. Paul himself. (1) Paul is certain of having "seen" Christ as did the other Apostles (I Cor., ix, 1); he declares that Christ "appeared" to him (I Cor., xv, 8) as He appeared to Peter, to James, to the Twelve, after His Resurrection. (2) He knows that his conversion is not the fruit of his reasoning or thoughts, but an unforeseen, sudden, startling change, due to all-powerful grace (Gal., i, 12–15; I Cor., xv, 10). (3) He is wrongly credited with doubts, perplexities, fears, remorse, before his conversion. He was halted by Christ when his fury was at its height (Acts, ix, 1–2); it was "through zeal" that he persecuted the Church (Phil., iii, 6), and he obtained mercy because he had acted "ignorantly in unbelief" (I Tim., i, 13). All explanations, psychological or otherwise, are worthless in face of these definite assertions, for all suppose that it was Paul's faith in Christ which engendered the vision, whereas according to the concordant testimony of the Acts and the Epistles it was the actual vision of Christ which engendered faith.

After his conversion, his baptism, and his miraculous cure Paul set about preaching to the Jews (Acts, ix, 19–20). He afterwards withdrew to Arabia—probably to the region south of Damascus (Gal., i, 17), doubtless less to preach than to meditate on the Scriptures. On his return to Damascus the intrigues of the Jews forced him to flee by night (II Cor., xi, 32–33; Acts, ix, 23–25). He went to Jerusalem to see Peter (Gal., i, 18), but remained only fifteen days, for the snares of the Greeks threatened his life. He then left for Tarsus and is lost to sight for five or six years (Acts, ix, 29–30; Gal., i, 21). Barnabas went in search of him and brought him to Antioch where for a year they worked together and their apostolate was most fruitful (Acts, xi, 25–26). Together also they were sent to Jerusalem to carry alms to the brethren on the occasion of the famine predicted by Agabus (Acts, xi, 27–30). They do not seem to have found the Apostles there; these had been scattered by the persecution of Herod.

C. *Apostolic Career of Paul.*—This period of twelve years (45–57) was the most active and fruitful of his life. It comprises three great Apostolic expeditions of which Antioch was in each instance the starting-point and which invariably ended in a visit to Jerusalem.

(1) First mission (Acts, xiii, 1–xiv, 27).—Set apart by command of the Holy Ghost for the special evan-

gelization of the Gentiles, Barnabas and Saul embark for Cyprus, preach in the synagogue of Salamina, cross the island from east to west doubtless following the southern coast, and reach Paphos, the residence of the proconsul Sergius Paulus, where a sudden change takes place. After the conversion of the Roman proconsul, Saul, suddenly become Paul, is invariably mentioned before Barnabas by St. Luke and manifestly assumes the leadership of the mission which Barnabas has hitherto directed. The results of this change are soon evident. Paul, doubtless concluding that Cyprus, the natural dependency of Syria and Cilicia, would embrace the faith of Christ when these two countries should be Christian, chose Asia Minor as the field of his apostolate and sailed for Perge in Pamphylia, eight miles above the mouth of the Cestrus. It was then that John Mark, cousin of Barnabas, dismayed perhaps by the daring projects of the Apostle, abandoned the expedition and returned to Jerusalem, while Paul and Barnabas laboured alone among the rough mountains of Pisidia, which were infested by brigands and crossed by frightful precipices. Their destination was the Roman colony of Antioch, situated a seven days' journey from Perge. Here Paul spoke on the vocation of Israel and the providential sending of the Messias, a discourse which St. Luke reproduces in substance as an example of his preaching in the synagogues (Acts, xiii, 16–41). The sojourn of the two missionaries in Antioch was long enough for the word of the Lord to be published throughout the whole country (Acts, xiii, 49). When by their intrigues the Jews had obtained against them a decree of banishment, they went to Iconium, three or four days distant, where they met with the same persecution from the Jews and the same eager welcome from the Gentiles. The hostility of the Jews forced them to take refuge in the Roman colony of Lystra, eighteen miles distant. Here the Jews from Antioch and Iconium laid snares for Paul and having stoned him left him for dead, but again he succeeded in escaping and this time sought refuge in Derbe, situated about forty miles away on the frontier of the Province of Galatia. Their circuit completed, the missionaries retraced their steps in order to visit their neophytes, ordained priests in each Church founded by them at such great cost, and thus reached Perge where they halted to preach the Gospel, perhaps while awaiting an opportunity to embark for Attalia, a port twelve miles distant. On their return to Antioch in Syria after an absence of at least three years, they were received with transports of joy and thanksgiving, for God had opened the door of faith to the Gentiles.

The problem of the status of the Gentiles in the Church now made itself felt with all its acuteness. Some Judeo-Christians coming down from Jerusalem claimed that the Gentiles must be submitted to circumcision and treated as the Jews treated proselytes. Against this Paul and Barnabas protested and it was decided that a meeting should be held at Jerusalem in order to solve the question. At this assembly Paul and Barnabas represented the community of Antioch. Peter pleaded the freedom of the Gentiles; James upheld him, at the same time demanding that the Gentiles should abstain from certain things which especially shocked the Jews. It was decided, first, that the Gentiles were exempt from the Mosaic law. Secondly, that those of Syria and Cilicia must abstain from things sacrificed to idols, from blood, from things strangled, and from fornication. Thirdly, that this injunction was laid upon them, not in virtue of the Mosaic law, but in the name of the Holy Ghost. This meant the complete triumph of Paul's ideas. The restriction imposed on the Gentile converts of Syria and Cilicia did not concern his Churches, and Titus, his companion, was not compelled to be circumcised, despite the loud protests of the Judaizers (Gal., ii, 3–4). Here it is assumed that Gal., ii, and Acts, xv, relate to the same fact, for the actors are the same, Paul and Barnabas on the one hand, Peter and James on the other; the discussion is the same, the question of the circumcision of the Gentiles; the scenes are the same, Antioch and Jerusalem; the date is the same, about A. D. 50; and the result is the same, Paul's victory over the Judaizers. However, the decision of Jerusalem did not do away with all difficulties. The question did not concern only the Gentiles, and while exempting them from the Mosaic law, it was not declared that it would not have been counted meritorious and more perfect for them to observe it, as the decree seemed to liken them to Jewish proselytes of the second class. Furthermore the Judeo-Christians, not having been included in the verdict, were still free to consider themselves bound to the observance of the law. This was the origin of the dispute which shortly afterwards arose at Antioch between Peter and Paul. The latter taught openly that the law was abolished for the Jews themselves. Peter did not think otherwise, but he considered it wise to avoid giving offence to the Judaizers and to refrain from eating with the Gentiles who did not observe all the prescriptions of the law. As he thus morally influenced the Gentiles to live as the Jews did, Paul demonstrated to him that this dissimulation or opportuneness prepared the way for future misunderstandings and conflicts and even then had regrettable consequences. His manner of relating this incident leaves no room for doubt that Peter was persuaded by his arguments (Gal., ii, 11–20).

(2) Second mission (Acts, xv, 36–xviii, 22).—The beginning of the second mission was marked by a rather sharp discussion concerning Mark, whom St. Paul this time refused to accept as travelling companion. Consequently Barnabas set out with Mark for Cyprus and Paul chose Silas or Silvanus, a Roman citizen like himself, and an influential member of the Church of Jerusalem, and sent by it to Antioch to deliver the decrees of the Apostolic council. The two missionaries first went from Antioch to Tarsus, stopping on the way in order to promulgate the decisions of the Council of Jerusalem; then they went from Tarsus to Derbe, through the Cilician Gates, the defiles of Taurus, and the plains of Lycaonia. The visitation of the Churches founded during his first mission passed without notable incidents except the choice of Timothy, whom the Apostle while in Lystra persuaded to accompany him, and whom he caused to be circumcised in order to facilitate his access to the Jews who were numerous in those places. It was probably at Antioch of Pisidia, although the Acts do not mention that city, that the itinerary of the mission was altered by the intervention of the Holy Ghost. Paul thought to enter the Province of Asia by the valley of Meander which separated it by only three days' journey, but they passed through Phrygia and the country of Galatia, having been forbidden by the Holy Ghost to preach the word of God in Asia (Acts, xvi, 6). These words (τὴν φρυγίαν καὶ Γαλατικὴν χώραν) are variously interpreted, according as we take them to mean the Galatians of the north or of the south (see GALATIANS). Whatever the hypothesis, the missionaries had to travel northwards in that portion of Galatia properly so called of which Pessinonte was the capital, and the only question is as to whether or not they preached there. They did not intend to do so, but as is known the evangelization of the Galatians was due to an accident, namely the illness of Paul (Gal., iv, 13); this fits very well for Galatians in the north. In any case the missionaries having reached the upper part of Mysia (κατὰ Μυσίαν), attempted to enter the rich Province of Bithynia which lay before them, but the Holy Ghost prevented them (Acts, xvi, 7). Therefore, passing through Mysia without stopping to preach (παρελθόντες) they reached Alexandria of Troas, where God's will was again made known to them in the vision of a Macedo-

nian who called them to come and help his country (Acts, xvi, 9–10).

Paul continued to follow on European soil the method of preaching he had employed from the beginning. As far as possible he concentrated his efforts in a metropolis from which the Faith would spread to cities of second rank and to the country districts. Wherever there was a synagogue he first took his stand there and preached to the Jews and proselytes who would consent to listen to him. When the rupture with the Jews was irreparable, which always happened sooner or later, he founded a new Church with his neophytes as a nucleus. He remained in the same city until persecution, generally aroused by the intrigues of the Jews, forced him to retire. There were, however, variations of this plan. At Philippi, where there was no synagogue, the first preaching took place in the uncovered oratory called the *proseuche*, which the Gentiles made a reason for stirring up the persecution. Paul and Silas, charged with disturbing public order, were beaten with rods, imprisoned, and finally expelled. But at Thessalonica and Berea, whither they successively repaired after leaving Philippi, things turned out almost as they had planned. The apostolate of Athens was quite exceptional. Here there was no question of Jews or synagogue, Paul, contrary to his custom, was alone (I Thess., iii, 1), and he delivered before the areopagus a specially framed discourse, a synopsis of which has been preserved by the Acts (xvii, 23–31) as a specimen of its kind. He seems to have left the city of his own accord, without being forced to do so by persecution. The mission to Corinth on the other hand may be considered typical. Paul preached in the synagogue every Sabbath day, and when the violent opposition of the Jews denied him entrance there he withdrew to an adjoining house which was the property of a proselyte named Titus Justus. He carried on his apostolate in this manner for eighteen months, while the Jews vainly stormed against him; he was able to withstand them owing to the impartial, if not actually favourable, attitude of the proconsul, Gallio. Finally he decided to go to Jerusalem in fulfillment of a vow made perhaps in a moment of danger. From Jerusalem, according to his custom, he returned to Antioch. The two Epistles to the Thessalonians were written during the early months of his sojourn at Corinth. For occasion, circumstances, and analysis of these letters see THESSALONIANS.

(3) Third mission (Acts, xviii, 23-xxi, 26).—Paul's destination in his third journey was obviously Ephesus. There Aquila and Priscilla were awaiting him, he had promised the Ephesians to return and evangelize them if it were the will of God (Acts, xviii, 19–21), and the Holy Ghost no longer opposed his entry into Asia. Therefore, after a brief rest at Antioch he went through the countries of Galatia and Phrygia (Acts, xviii, 23) and passing through "the upper regions" of Central Asia he reached Ephesus (xix, 1). His method remained the same. In order to earn his living and not be a burden to the faithful he toiled every day for many hours at making tents, but this did not prevent him from preaching the Gospel. As usual he began with the synagogue where he succeeded in remaining for three months. At the end of this time he taught every day in a class-room placed at his disposal by a certain Tyrannus "from the fifth hour to the tenth" (from eleven in the morning till four in the afternoon), according to the interesting addition of the "Codex Bezæ" (Acts, xix, 9). This lasted two years, so that all the inhabitants of Asia, Jews and Greeks, heard the word of the Lord (Acts, xix, 20).

Naturally there were trials to be endured and obstacles to be overcome. Some of these obstacles arose from the jealousy of the Jews, who vainly endeavoured to imitate Paul's exorcisms, others from the superstition of the pagans, which was especially rife at Ephesus. So effectually did he triumph over it, however, that books of superstition were burned to the value of 50,000 pieces of silver (about $9000). This time the persecution was due to the Gentiles and inspired by a motive of self-interest. The progress of Christianity having ruined the sale of the little facsimiles of the temple of Diana and statuettes of the goddess, which devout pilgrims had been wont to purchase, a certain Demetrius, at the head of the guild of silversmiths, stirred up the crowd against Paul. The scene which then transpired in the theatre is described by St. Luke with memorable vividness and pathos (Acts, xix, 23–40). The Apostle had to yield to the storm. After a stay at Ephesus of two years and a half, perhaps more (Acts, xx, 31: τριετίαν), he departed for Macedonia and thence for Corinth, where he spent the winter. It was his intention in the following spring to go by sea to Jerusalem, doubtless for the Pasch; but learning that the Jews had planned his destruction, he did not wish, by going by sea, to afford them an opportunity to attempt his life. Therefore he returned by way of Macedonia. Numerous disciples divided into two groups, accompanied him or awaited him at Troas. These were Sopater of Berea, Aristarchus and Secundus of Thessalonica, Gaius of Derbe, Timothy, Tychicus and Trophimus of Asia, and finally Luke, the historian of the Acts, who gives us minutely all the stages of this voyage: Philippi, Troas, Assos, Mitylene, Chios, Samos, Miletus, Cos, Rhodes, Patara, Tyre, Ptolemais, Cæsarea, Jerusalem. Three more remarkable facts should be noted in passing. At Troas Paul resuscitated the young Eutychus, who had fallen from a third-story window while Paul was preaching late into the night. At Miletus he pronounced before the ancients of Ephesus the touching farewell discourse which drew many tears (Acts, xx, 18–38). At Cæsarea the Holy Ghost by the mouth of Agabus, predicted his coming arrest, but did not dissuade him from going to Jerusalem.

St. Paul's four great Epistles were written during this third mission: the first to the Corinthians from Ephesus, about the time of the Pasch prior to his departure from that city; the second to the Corinthians from Macedonia, during the summer or autumn of the same year; that to the Romans from Corinth, in the following spring; the date of the Epistle to the Galatians is disputed. On the many questions occasioned by the despatch and the language of these letters, or the situation assumed either on the side of the Apostle or his correspondents, see CORINTHIANS, EPISTLE TO THE; GALATIANS, EPISTLE TO THE; ROMANS, EPISTLE TO THE.

D. *Captivity* (Acts, xxi, 27–xxviii, 31).—Falsely accused by the Jews of having brought Gentiles into the Temple, Paul was ill-treated by the populace and led in chains to the fortress Antonia by the tribune Lysias. The latter having learned that the Jews had conspired treacherously to slay the prisoner sent him under strong escort to Cæsarea, which was the residence of the procurator Felix. Paul had little difficulty in confounding his accusers, but as he refused to purchase his liberty Felix kept him in chains for two years and even left him in prison, in order to please the Jews, until the arrival of his successor, Festus. The new governor wished to send the prisoner to Jerusalem there to be tried in the presence of his accusers; but Paul, who was acquainted with the snares of his enemies, appealed to Cæsar. Thenceforth his cause could be tried only at Rome. This first period of captivity is characterized by five discourses of the Apostle: The first was delivered in Hebrew on the steps of the Antonia before the threatening crowd; herein Paul relates his conversion and vocation to the Apostolate, but he was interrupted by the hostile shouts of the multitude (Acts, xxii, 1–22). In the second, delivered the next day before the Sanhedrin assembled at the command of Lysias, the Apostle skillfully embroiled the Pharisees with the Sadducees and no accusation could be brought. In the third, Paul, answering his accuser Tertullus in the presence of the Governor Felix, makes known the facts which had been distorted and proves his innocence (Acts, xxiv, 10–21). The fourth discourse is merely an explanatory summary of the Christian Faith delivered before Felix and his wife Drusilla (Acts, xxiv, 24–25). The fifth, pronounced before the Governor Festus, King Agrippa, and his wife Berenice, again relates the history of Paul's conversion, and is left unfinished owing to the sarcastic interruptions of the governor and the embarrassed attitude of the king (Acts, xxvi).

The journey of the captive Paul from Cæsarea to Rome is described by St. Luke with an exactness and vividness of colours which leave nothing to be desired. For commentaries see Smith, "Voyage and Shipwreck of St. Paul" (1866); Ramsay, "St. Paul the Traveller and Roman Citizen" (London, 1908). The centurion Julius had shipped Paul and his fellow-prisoners on a merchant vessel on board which Luke and Aristarchus were able to take passage. As the season was advanced the voyage was slow and difficult. They skirted the coasts of Syria, Cilicia, and Pamphylia. At Myra in Lycia the prisoners were transferred to an Alexandrian vessel bound for Italy, but the winds being persistently contrary a place in Crete called Goodhavens was reached with great difficulty and Paul advised that they should spend the winter there, but his advice was not followed, and the vessel driven by the tempest drifted aimlessly for fourteen whole days, being finally wrecked on the coast of Malta. The three months during which navigation was considered most dangerous were spent there, but with the first days of spring all haste was made to resume the voyage. Paul must have reached Rome some time in March. "He remained two whole years in his own hired lodging . . . preaching the kingdom of God, and teaching the things which concern the Lord Jesus Christ, with all confidence, without prohibition" (Acts, xxviii, 30–31). With these words the Acts of the Apostles conclude.

There is no doubt that Paul's trial terminated in a sentence of acquittal, for (1) the report of the Governor Festus was certainly favourable as well as that of the centurion. (2) The Jews seem to have abandoned their charge since their co-religionists in Rome were not informed of it (Acts, xxviii, 21). (3) The course of the proceedings led Paul to hope for a release, of which he sometimes speaks as of a certainty (Phil., i, 25; ii, 24; Philem., 22). (4) The pastorals if they are authentic assume a period of activity for Paul subsequent to his captivity. The same conclusion is drawn from the hypothesis that they are not authentic, for all agree that the author was well acquainted with the life of the Apostle. It is the almost unanimous opinion that the so-called Epistles of the captivity were sent from Rome. Some authors have attempted to prove that St. Paul wrote them during his detention at Cæsarea, but they have found few to agree with them. The Epistles to the Colossians, the Ephesians, and Philemon were despatched together and by the same messenger, Tychicus. It is a matter of controversy whether the Epistle to the Philippians was prior or subsequent to these, and the question has not been answered by decisive arguments (see PHILIPPIANS, EPISTLE TO THE; EPHESIANS, EPISTLE TO THE; COLOSSIANS, EPISTLE TO THE; PHILEMON, EPISTLE TO).

E. *Last Years.*—This period is wrapped in deep obscurity for, lacking the account of the Acts, we have no guide save an often uncertain tradition and the brief references of the Pastoral epistles. Paul had long cherished the desire to go to Spain (Rom., xv, 24, 28) and there is no evidence that he was led to change his plan. When towards the end of his captivity he announces his coming to Philemon (22) and to the Philippians (ii, 23–24), he does not seem to regard this visit as immediate since he promises the Philippians to send them a messenger as soon as he learns the issue of his trial; he therefore plans another journey before his return to the East. Finally, not to mention the later testimony of St. Cyril of Jerusalem, St. Epiphanius, St. Jerome, St. Chrysostom, and Theodoret, the well-known text of St. Clement of Rome, the witness of the "Muratorian Canon", and of the "Acta Pauli" render probable Paul's journey to Spain. In any case he can not have remained there long, for he was in haste to revisit his Churches in the East. He may have returned from Spain through southern Gaul if it was thither, as some Fathers have thought, and not to Galatia, that Crescens was sent later (II Tim., iv, 10). We may readily believe that he afterwards kept the promise made to his friend Philemon and that on this occasion he visited the churches of the valley of Lycus, Laodicea, Colossus, and Hierapolis.

The itinerary now becomes very uncertain, but the following facts seem indicated by the Pastorals: Paul remained in Crete exactly long enough to found there new churches, the care and organization of which he confided to his fellow-worker Titus (Tit., i, 5). He then went to Ephesus, and besought Timothy, who was already there, to remain until his return while he proceeded to Macedonia (I Tim., i, 3). On this occasion he paid his promised visit to the Philippians (Phil., ii, 24), and naturally also saw the Thessalonians. The letter to Titus and the First Epistle to Timothy must date from this period; they seem to have been written about the same time and shortly after the departure from Ephesus. The question is whether they were sent from Macedonia or, which seems more probable, from Corinth. The Apostle instructs Titus to join him at Nicopolis of Epirus where he intends to spend the winter (Titus, iii, 12). In the following spring he must have carried out his plan to return to Asia (I Tim., iii, 14–15). Here occurred the obscure episode of his arrest, which probably took place at Troas; this would explain his having left with Carpus a cloak and books which he needed (II Tim., iv, 13). He was taken from there to Ephesus, capital of the Province of Asia, where he was deserted by all those on whom he thought he could rely (II Tim., i, 15). Being sent to Rome for trial he left Trophimus sick at Miletus, and Erastus, another of his companions, remained at Corinth, for what reason is not known (II Tim., iv, 20). When Paul wrote his Second Epistle to Timothy from Rome he felt that all human hope was lost (iv, 6); he begs his disciple to rejoin him as quickly as possible, for he is alone with Luke. We do not know if Timothy was able to reach Rome before the death of the Apostle.

Ancient tradition makes it possible to establish the following points: (1) Paul suffered martyrdom near Rome at a place called Aquæ Salviæ (now Tre Fontane), somewhat east of the Ostian Way, about two miles from the splendid Basilica of San Paolo fuori le mura which marks his burial place. (2) The martyrdom took place towards the end of the reign of Nero, in the twelfth year (St. Epiphanius), the thirteenth (Euthalius), or the fourteenth (St. Jerome). (3) According to the most common opinion, Paul suffered in the same year and on the same day as Peter; several Latin Fathers contend that it was on the same day but not in the same year; the oldest witness, St. Dionysius the Corinthian, says only κατὰ τὸν αὐτὸν καιρόν, which may be translated "at the same time" or "about the same time". (4) From time immemorial the solemnity of the Apostles Peter and Paul has been celebrated on 29 June, which is the anniversary either of their death or of the translation of their relics. Formerly the pope, after having pontificated in the Basilica of St. Peter, went with his attendants to that of St. Paul, but the

ST. PAUL
RIBERA (SPAGNOLETTO), THE PRADO, MADRID

distance between the two basilicas (about five miles) rendered the double ceremony too exhausting, especially at that season of the year. Thus arose the prevailing custom of transferring to the next day (30 June) the Commemoration of St. Paul. The feast of the Conversion of St. Paul (25 January) is of comparatively recent origin. There is reason for believing that the day was first observed to mark the translation of the relics of St. Paul at Rome, for so it appears in the Hieronymian Martyrology. It is unknown to the Greek Church (Dowden, "The Church Year and Kalendar", Cambridge, 1910, 69; cf. Duchesne, "Origines du culte chrétien", Paris, 1898, 265–72; McClure, "Christian Worship", London, 1903, 277–81).

F. *Physical and Moral Portrait of St. Paul.*—We know from Eusebius (Hist. eccl., VII, 18) that even in his time there existed paintings representing Christ and the Apostles Peter and Paul. Paul's features have been preserved in three ancient monuments: (1) A diptych which dates from not later than the fourth century (Lewin, "The Life and Epistles of St. Paul", 1874, frontispiece of Vol. I and Vol. II, 210). (2) A large medallion found in the cemetery of Domitilla, representing the Apostles Peter and Paul (Op. cit., II, 411). (3) A glass dish in the British Museum, depicting the same Apostles (Farrar, "Life and Work of St. Paul", 1891, 896). We have also the concordant descriptions of the "Acta Pauli et Theclæ", of Pseudo-Lucian in Philopatris, of Malalas (Chronogr., x), and of Nicephorus (Hist. eccl., III, 37). Paul was short of stature; the Pseudo-Chrysostom calls him "the man of three cubits" ($ἄνθρωπος\ τρίπηχυς$); he was broad-shouldered, somewhat bald, with slightly aquiline nose, closely-knit eyebrows, thick, greyish beard, fair complexion, and a pleasing and affable manner. He was afflicted with a malady which is difficult to diagnose (cf. Menzies, "St. Paul's Infirmity" in the "Expository Times", July and Sept., 1904), but despite this painful and humiliating infirmity (II Cor., xii, 7–9; Gal., iv, 13–14) and although his bearing was not impressive (II Cor., x, 10), Paul must undoubtedly have been possessed of great physical strength to have sustained so long such superhuman labours (II Cor., xi, 23–29). Pseudo-Chrysostom, "In princip. apostol. Petrum et Paulum" (in P. G., LIX, 494–95), considers that he died at the age of sixty-eight after having served the Lord for thirty-five years. The moral portrait is more difficult to draw because it is full of contrasts. Its elements will be found: in Lewin, op. cit., II, xi, 410–35 (Paul's Person and Character); in Farrar, Op. cit., Appendix, Excursus I; and especially in Newman, "Sermons preached on Various Occasions", vii, viii.

III. THEOLOGY OF ST. PAUL. — A. *Paul and Christ.*—This question has passed through two distinct phases. According to the principal followers of the Tübingen School, the Apostle had but a vague knowledge of the life and teaching of the historical Christ and even disdained such knowledge as inferior and useless. Their only support is the misinterpreted text: "Et si cognovimus secundum carnem Christum, sed nunc jam novimus" (II Cor., v, 16). The opposition noted in this text is not between the historical and the glorified Christ, but between the Messias such as the unbelieving Jews represented Him, such perhaps as he was preached by certain Judaizers, and the Messias as He manifested Himself in His death and Resurrection, as He had been confessed by the converted Paul. It is neither admissible nor probable that Paul would be uninterested in the life and preaching of Him, Whom he loved passionately, Whom he constantly held up for the imitation of his neophytes, and Whose spirit he boasted of having. It is incredible that he would not question on this subject eyewitnesses, such as Barnabas, Silas, or the future historians of Christ, Sts. Mark and Luke, with whom he was so long associated. Careful examination of this subject has brought out the three following conclusions concerning which there is now general agreement: (1) There are in St. Paul more allusions to the life and teachings of Christ than would be suspected at first sight, and the casual way in which they are made shows that the Apostle knew more on the subject than he had the occasion or the wish to tell. (2) These allusions are more frequent in St. Paul than in all the other writings of the New Testament, except the Gospels. (3) From Apostolic times there existed a *catechesis*, treating among other things the life and teachings of Christ, and as all neophytes were supposed to possess a copy it was not necessary to refer thereto save occasionally and in passing.

The second phase of the question is closely connected with the first. The same theologians, who maintain that Paul was indifferent to the earthly life and teaching of Christ, deliberately exaggerate his originality and influence. According to them Paul was the creator of theology, the founder of the Church, the preacher of asceticism, the defender of the sacraments and of the ecclesiastical system, the opponent of the religion of love and liberty which Christ came to announce to the world. If, to do him honour, he is called the second founder of Christianity, this must be a degenerate and altered Christianity since it was at least partially opposed to the primitive Christianity. Paul is thus made responsible for every antipathy to modern thought in traditional Christianity. This is to a great extent the origin of the "Back to Christ" movement, the strange wanderings of which we are now witnessing. The chief reason for returning to Christ is to escape Paul, the originator of dogma, the theologian of the faith. The cry "Zurück zu Jesu" which has resounded in Germany for thirty years, is inspired by the ulterior motive, "Los von Paulus". The problem is: Was Paul's relation to Christ that of a disciple to his master? or was he absolutely autodidactic, independent alike of the Gospel of Christ and the preaching of the Twelve? It must be admitted that most of the papers published shed little light on the subject. However, the discussions have not been useless, for they have shown that the most characteristic Pauline doctrines, such as justifying faith, the redeeming death of Christ, the universality of salvation, are in accord with the writings of the first Apostles, from which they are derived. Jülicher in particular has pointed out that Paul's Christology, which is more exalted than that of his companions in the apostolate, was never the object of controversy, and that Paul was not conscious of being singular in this respect from the other heralds of the Gospel. Cf. Morgan, "Back to Christ" in "Dict. of Christ and the Gospels", I, 61–67; Sanday, "Paul", loc. cit., II, 886–92; Feine, "Jesus Christus und Paulus" (1902); Goguel, "L'apôtre Paul et Jésus-Christ" (Paris, 1904); Jülicher, "Paulus und Jesus" (1907).

B. *The Root Idea of St. Paul's Theology.*—Several modern authors consider that theodicy is at the base, centre, and summit of Pauline theology. "The apostle's doctrine is *theocentric*, not in reality anthropocentric. What is styled his 'metaphysics' holds for Paul the immediate and sovereign fact of the universe; God, as he conceives Him, is all in all to his reason and heart alike" (Findlay in Hastings, "Dict. of the Bible", III, 718). Stevens begins the exposition of his "Pauline Theology" with a chapter entitled "The doctrine of God". Sabatier (L'apôtre Paul, 1896, 297) also considers that "the last word of Pauline theology is: God all in all", and he makes the idea of God the crown of Paul's theological edifice. But these authors have not reflected that though the idea of God occupies so large a place in the teaching of the Apostle, whose thought is deeply religious like that of all his compatriots, it is not characteristic of him, nor does it distinguish him from his companions in the apostolate nor even from contemporary

Jews. Many modern Protestant theologians, especially among the more or less faithful followers of the Tübingen School, maintain that Paul's doctrine is "anthropocentric", that it starts from his conception of man's inability to fulfil the law of God without the help of grace to such an extent that he is a slave of sin and must wage war against the flesh. But if this be the genesis of Paul's idea it is astonishing that he enunciates it only in one chapter (Rom., vii), the sense of which is controverted, so that if this chapter had not been written, or if it had been lost, we would have no means of recovering the key to his teaching. However, most modern theologians now agree that St. Paul's doctrine is Christocentric, that it is at base a soteriology, not from a subjective standpoint, according to the ancient prejudice of the founders of Protestantism who made justification by faith the quintessence of Paulinism, but from the objective standpoint, embracing in a wide synthesis the person and work of the Redeemer. This may be proved empirically by the statement that everything in St. Paul converges towards Jesus Christ, so much so, that abstracting from Jesus Christ it becomes, whether taken collectively or in detail, absolutely incomprehensible. This is proved also by demonstrating that what Paul calls his Gospel is the salvation of all men through Christ and in Christ. This is the standpoint of the following rapid analysis:

C. *Humanity without Christ.*—The first three chapters of the Epistle to the Romans shows us human nature wholly under the dominion of sin. Neither Gentiles nor Jews had withstood the torrent of evil. The Mosaic Law was a futile barrier because it prescribed good without imparting the strength to do it. The Apostle arrives at this mournful conclusion: "There is no distinction [between Jew and Gentile]: for all have sinned, and do need the glory of God" (Rom., iii, 22–23). He subsequently leads us back to the historical cause of this disorder: "By one man sin entered into this world, and by sin death; and so death passed upon all men, in whom all have sinned" (Rom., v, 12). This man is obviously Adam, the sin which he brought into the world is not only his personal sin, but a predominating sin which entered into all men and left in them the seed of death: "All sinned when Adam sinned; all sinned in and with his sin" (Stevens, "Pauline Theology", 129). It remains to be seen how original sin which is our lot by natural generation, manifests itself outwardly and becomes the source of actual sins. This Paul teaches us in chap. vii, where describing the contest between the Law assisted by reason and human nature weakened by the flesh and the tendency to evil, he represents nature as inevitably vanquished: "For I am delighted with the law of God, according to the inward man: But I see another law in my members fighting against the law of my mind, and captivating me in the law of sin" (Rom., vii, 22–23). This does not mean that the organism, the material substratum, is evil in itself, as some theologians of the Tübingen School have claimed, for the flesh of Christ, which was like unto ours, was exempt from sin, and the Apostle wishes that our bodies, which are destined to rise again, be preserved free from stain. The relation between sin and the flesh is neither inherent nor necessary; it is accidental, determined by an historical fact, and capable of disappearing through the intervention of the Holy Ghost, but it is none the less true that it is not in our power to overcome it unaided and that fallen man had need of a Saviour.

Yet God did not abandon sinful man. He continued to manifest Himself through this visible world (Rom., i, 19–20), through the light of conscience (Rom., ii, 14–15), and finally through His ever active and paternally benevolent Providence (Acts, xiv, 16; xvii, 26). Furthermore, in His untiring mercy, He "will have all men to be saved, and to come to the knowledge of the truth" (I Tim., ii, 4). This will is necessarily subsequent to original sin since it concerns man as he is at present. According to His merciful designs God leads man step by step to salvation. To the Patriarchs, and especially to Abraham, He gave his free and generous promise, confirmed by oath (Rom., iv, 13–20; Gal., iii, 15–18), which anticipated the Gospel. To Moses He gave His Law, the observation of which should be a means of salvation (Rom., vii, 10; x, 5), and which, even when violated, as it was in reality, was no less a guide leading to Christ (Gal., iii, 24) and an instrument of mercy in the hands of God. The Law was a mere interlude until such time as humanity should be ripe for a complete revelation (Gal., iv, 1–7). In fact the Law brought nothing to perfection (Heb., vii, 19); it heightened the offence (Gal., iii, 19; Rom., v, 20), and thus provoked the Divine wrath (Rom., iv, 15). But good will arise from the excess of evil and "the Scripture hath concluded all under sin, that the promise, by the faith of Jesus Christ, might be given to them that believe" (Gal., iii, 22). This would be fulfilled in the "fulness of the time" (Gal. iv, 4; Eph., i, 10), that is, at the time set by God for the execution of His merciful designs, when man's helplessness should have been well manifested. Then "God sent his Son, made of a woman, made under the law: that he might redeem them who were under the law: that we might receive the adoption of sons" (Gal., iv, 4).

D. *The Person of the Redeemer.*—Nearly all statements relating to the person of Jesus Christ bear either directly or indirectly on His rôle as Saviour. With St. Paul Christology is a function of soteriology. However broad these outlines, they show us the faithful image of Christ in His pre-existence, in His historical existence, and in His glorified life (see F. Prat, "Théologie de Saint Paul").

(1) *Christ in His pre-existence.*—(a) Christ is of an order superior to all created beings (Eph., i, 21); He is the Creator and Preserver of the World (Col., i, 16–17); all is by Him, in Him, and for Him (Col., i, 16). (b) Christ is the image of the invisible Father (II Cor., iv, 4; Col., i, 15); He is the Son of God, but unlike other sons is so in an incommunicable manner; He is the Son, the own Son, the well-Beloved, and this He has always been (II Cor., i, 19; Rom., viii, 3, 32; Col., i, 13; Eph., i, 6; etc.). (c) Christ is the object of the doxologies reserved for God (II Tim., iv, 18; Rom., xvi, 27); He is prayed to as the equal of the Father (II Cor., xii, 8–9; Rom., x, 12; I Cor., i, 2); gifts are asked of Him which it is in the power of God alone to grant, namely, grace, mercy, salvation (Rom., i, 7; xvi, 20; I Cor., i, 3; xvi, 23; etc.); before Him every knee shall bow in heaven, on earth, and under the earth (Phil., ii, 10), as every head inclines in adoration of the majesty of the Most High. (d) Christ possesses all the Divine attributes; He is eternal, since He is the "first born of every creature" and exists before all ages (Col., i, 15, 17); He is immutable, since He exists "in the form of God" (Phil., ii, 6); He is omnipotent, since He has the power to bring forth being from nothingness (Col., i, 16); He is immense, since He fills all things with His plenitude (Eph., iv, 10; Col., ii, 10); He is infinite, since "the fulness of the Godhead dwells in Him" (Col., ii, 9). All that is the special property of God belongs of right to Him; the judgment seat of God is the judgment seat of Christ (Rom., xiv, 10; II Cor., v, 10); the Gospel of God is the Gospel of Christ (Rom., i, 1, 9; xv, 16, 19, etc.); the Church of God is the Church of Christ (I Cor., i, 2 and Rom., xvi, 16 sqq.); the Kingdom of God is the Kingdom of Christ (Eph., v, 5), the Spirit of God is the Spirit of Christ (Rom., viii, 9 sqq.). (e) Christ is the one Lord (I Cor., viii, 6); He is identified with Jehovah of the Old Covenant (I Cor., x, 4, 9; Rom., x, 13; cf. I Cor., ii, 16; ix, 21); He is the God who has purchased the church "with his own blood" (Acts, xx, 28); He is our "great

God and Saviour Jesus Christ" (Tit., ii, 13); He is the "God over all things" (Rom., ix, 5), effacing by His infinite transcendency the sum and substance of created things.

(2) *Jesus Christ as Man.*—The other aspect of the figure of Christ is drawn with no less firm a hand. Jesus Christ is the second Adam (Rom., v, 14; I Cor., xv, 45–49); "the mediator of God and men" (I Tim., ii, 5), and as such He must necessarily be man (ἄνθρωπος χριστὸς Ἰησοῦς). So He is the descendant of the Patriarchs (Rom., ix, 5; Gal., iii, 16), He is "of the seed of David, according to the flesh" (Rom., i, 3), "born of a woman" (Gal., iv, 4), like all men; finally, He is known as a man by His appearance, which is exactly similar to that of men (Phil., ii, 7), save for sin, which He did not and could not know (II Cor., v, 21). When St. Paul says that "God sent His Son in the likeness of sinful flesh" (Rom., viii, 3), he does not mean to deny the reality of Christ's flesh, but excludes only sinful flesh.

Nowhere does the Apostle explain how the union of the Divine and the human natures is accomplished in Christ, being content to affirm that He who was "in the form of God" took "the form of a servant" (Phil., ii, 6–7), or he states the Incarnation in this laconic formula: "For in him dwelleth all the fulness of the Godhead corporeally" (Col., ii, 9). What we see clearly is that there is in Christ a single Person to whom are attributed, often in the same sentence, qualities proper to the Divine and the human nature, to the pre-existence, the historical existence, and the glorified life (Col., i, 15–19; Phil., ii, 5–11; etc.). The theological explanation of the mystery has given rise to numerous errors. Denial was made of one of the natures, either the human (Docetism), or the Divine (Arianism), or the two natures were considered to be united in a purely accidental manner so as to produce two persons (Nestorianism), or the two natures were merged into one (Monophysitism), or on pretext of uniting them in one person the heretics mutilated either the human nature (Apollinarianism), or the Divine, according to the strange modern heresy known as Kenosis.

The last-mentioned requires a brief treatment, as it is based on a saying of St. Paul "Being in the form of God . . . emptied himself (ἐκένωσεν ἑαυτόν, hence κένωσις) taking the form of a servant" (Phil., ii, 6–7). Contrary to the common opinion, Luther applied these words not to the Word, but to Christ, the Incarnate Word. Moreover he understood the *communicatio idiomatum* as a real possession by each of the two natures of the attributes of the other. According to this the human nature of Christ would possess the Divine attributes of ubiquity, omniscience, and omnipotence. There are two systems among Lutheran theologians, one asserting that the human nature of Christ was volunatrily stripped of those attributes (κένωσις), the other that they were hidden during His mortal existence (κρύψις). In modern times the doctrine of Kenosis, while still restricted to Luthern theology, has completely changed its opinions. Starting with the philosophical idea that "personality" is identified with "consciousness", it is maintained that where there is only one person there can be only one consciousness; but since the consciousness of Christ was a truly human consciousness, the Divine consciousness must of necessity have ceased to exist or act in Him. According to Thomasius, the theorist of the system, the Son of God was stripped, not after the Incarnation, as Luther asserted, but by the very fact of the Incarnation, and what rendered possible the union of the Logos with the humanity was the faculty possessed by the Divinity to limit itself both as to being and activity. The other partisans of the system express themselves in a similar manner. Gess, for instance, says that in Jesus Christ the Divine *ego* is changed into the human *ego*. When it is objected that God is immutable, that He can neither cease to be, nor limit Himself, nor transform Himself, they reply that this reasoning is on metaphysical hypotheses and concepts without reality. (For the various forms of Kenosis see Bruce, "The Humiliation of Christ", p. 136.)

All these systems are merely variations of Monophysitism. Unconsciously they assume that there is in Christ but a single nature as there is but a single person. According to the Catholic doctrine, on the contrary, the union of the two natures in a single person involves no change in the Divine nature and need involve no physical change of the human nature of Christ. Without doubt Christ is the Son and is morally entitled even as man to the goods of His Father, viz. the immediate vision of God, eternal beatitude, the state of glory. He is temporarily deprived of a portion of these goods in order that he may fulfil His mission as Redeemer. This is the abasement, the annihilation, of which St. Paul speaks, but it is a totally different thing from the Kenosis as described above.

E. *The Objective Redemption as the Work of Christ.*— We have seen that fallen man being unable to arise again unaided, God in His mercy sent His Son to save him. It is an elementary and often repeated doctrine of St. Paul that Jesus Christ saves us through the Cross, that we are "justified by his blood", that "we were reconciled to God by the death of his Son" (Rom., v, 9–10). What endowed the blood of Christ, His death, His Cross, with this redeeming virtue? Paul never answers this question directly, but he shows us the drama of Calvary under three aspects, which there is danger in separating and which are better understood when compared: (a) at one time the death of Christ is a sacrifice intended, like the sacrifice of the Old Law, to expiate sin and propitiate God. Cf. Sanday and Headlam, "Romans", 91–94, "The death of Christ considered as a sacrifice". "It is impossible from this passage (Rom., iii, 25) to get rid of the double idea: (1) of a sacrifice; (2) of a sacrifice which is propitiatory . . . Quite apart from this passage it is not difficult to prove that these two ideas of sacrifice and propitiation lie at the root of the teaching not only of St. Paul but of the New Testament generally." The double danger of this idea is, first, to wish to apply to the sacrifice of Christ all the mode of action, real or supposed, of the imperfect sacrifices of the Old Law; and, second, to believe that God is appeased by a sort of magical effect, in virtue of this sacrifice, whereas on the contrary it was He Who took the initiative of mercy, instituted the sacrifice of Calvary, and endowed it with its expiatory value. (b) At another time the death of Christ is represented as a redemption, the payment of a ransom, as the result of which man was delivered from all his past servitude (I Cor., vi, 20; vii, 23 [τιμῆς ἠγοράσθητε]; Gal., iii, 13; iv, 5 [ἵνα τοὺς ὑπὸ νόμον ἐξαγοράσῃ]; Rom., iii, 24; I Cor., i, 30; Eph., i, 7, 14; Col., i, 14 [ἀπολύτρωσις]; I Tim., ii, 6 [ἀντίλυτρον]; etc.). This idea, correct as it is, may have inconveniences if isolated or exaggerated. By carrying it beyond what was written, some of the Fathers put forth the strange suggestion of a ransom paid by Christ to the demon who held us in bondage. Another mistake is to regard the death of Christ as having a value in itself, independent of Christ Who offered it and God Who accepted it for the remission of our sins.

(c) Often, too, Christ seems to substitute Himself for us in order to undergo in our stead the chastisement for sin. He suffers physical death to save us from the moral death of sin and preserve us from eternal death. This idea of substitution appealed so strongly to Lutheran theologians that they admitted quantitative equality between the sufferings really endured by Christ and the penalties deserved by our sins. They even maintained that Jesus underwent the penalty of loss (of the vision of God) and the malediction of the Father. These are the extravagances which have cast so much discredit on the theory of substitution. It has been rightly said that the transfer of a chastisement from one person to another is an injustice and a contradiction, for the chastisement is inseparable from the fault and an undeserved chastisement is no longer a chastisement. Besides St. Paul never said that Christ died in our stead ($ἀντί$), but only that he died for us ($ὑπέρ$) because of our sins ($περί$).

In reality the three standpoints considered above are but three aspects of the Redemption which, far from excluding one another, should harmonize and combine, modifying if necessary all the other aspects of the problem. In the following text St. Paul assembles these various aspects with several others. We are "justified freely by his grace, through the Redemption, that is in Christ Jesus, whom God hath proposed to be a propitiation, through faith in his blood, to the shewing of his [hidden] justice, for the remission of former sins, through the forbearance of God, for the shewing of his justice in this time; that of himself may be [known as] just, and the justifier of him, who is in the faith of Jesus Christ" (Rom., iii, 24–26). Herein are designated the part of God, of Christ, and of man: (1) God takes the initiative; it is He who offers His Son; He intends to manifest His justice, but is moved thereto by mercy. It is therefore incorrect or more or less inadequate to say that God was angry with the human race and that He was only appeased by the death of His Son. (2) Christ is our Redemption ($ἀπολύτρωσις$), He is the instrument of expiation or propitiation ($ἱλαστήριον$), and is such by His Sacrifice ($ἐν τῷ αὐτοῦ αἵματι$), which does not resemble those of irrational animals; it derives its value from Christ, who offers it for us to His Father through obedience and love (Phil., ii, 8; Gal., ii, 20). (3) Man is not merely passive in the drama of his salvation; he must understand the lesson which God teaches, and appropriate by faith the fruit of the Redemption.

F. *The Subjective Redemption.*—Christ having once died and risen, the Redemption is completed in law and in principle for the whole human race. Each man makes it his own in fact and in act by faith and baptism which, by uniting him with Christ, causes him to participate in His Divine life. Faith, according to St. Paul, is composed of several elements; it is the submission of the intellect to the word of God, the trusting abandonment of the believer to the Saviour Who promises him assistance; it is also an act of obedience by which man accepts the Divine will. Such an act has a moral value, for it "gives glory to God" (Rom., iv, 20) in the measure in which it recognizes its own helplessness. That is why "Abraham believed God, and it was reputed to him unto justice" (Rom., iv, 3; Gal., iii, 6). The spiritual children of Abraham are likewise "justified by faith, without the works of the law" (Rom., iii, 28; cf. Gal., ii, 16). Hence it follows: (1) That justice is granted by God in consideration of faith. (2) That, nevertheless, faith is not equivalent to justice, since man is justified "by grace" (Rom., iv, 6). (3) That the justice freely granted to man becomes his property and is inherent in him. Protestants formerly asserted that the justice of Christ is imputed to us, but now they are generally agreed that this argument is unscriptural and lacks the guaranty of Paul; but some, loth to base justification on a good work ($ἔργον$), deny a moral value to faith and claim that justification is but a forensic judgment of God which alters absolutely nothing in the justified sinner. But this theory is untenable; for: (1) even admitting that "to justify" signifies "to pronounce just", it is absurd to suppose that God really pronounces just anyone who is not already so or who is not rendered so by the declaration itself. (2) Justification is inseparable from sanctification, for the latter is "a justification of life" (Rom., v, 18) and every "just man liveth by faith" (Rom., i, 17; Gal., iii, 11). (3) By faith and baptism we die to the "old man", our former selves; now this is impossible without beginning to live as the new man, who "according to God, is created in justice and holiness" (Rom., vi, 3–5; Eph., iv, 24; I Cor., i, 30; vi, 11). We may, therefore, establish a distinction in definition and concept between justification and sanctification, but we can neither separate them nor regard them as separate.

G. *Moral Doctrine.*—A remarkable characteristic of Paulinism is that it connects morality with the subjective redemption or justification. This is especially striking in chap. **vi** of the Epistle to the Romans. In baptism "our old man is crucified with [Christ] that the body of sin may be destroyed, to the end that we may serve sin no longer" (Rom., vi, 6). Our incorporation with the mystical Christ is not only a transformation and a metamorphosis, but a real creation, the production of a new being, subject to new laws and consequently to new duties. To understand the extent of our obligations it is enough for us to know ourselves as Christians and to reflect on the various relations which result from our supernatural birth: that of sonship to God the Father, of consecration to the Holy Ghost, of mystical identity with our Saviour Jesus Christ, of brotherly union with the other members of Christ. But this is not all. Paul says to the neophytes: "Thanks be to God, that you were the servants of sin, but have obeyed from the heart unto that form of doctrine, into which you have been delivered. . . . But now being made free from sin, and become servants to God, you have your fruit unto sanctification, and the end life everlasting" (Rom., vi, 17, 22). By the act of faith and by baptism, its seal, the Christian freely makes himself the servant of God and the soldier of Christ. God's will, which he accepts in advance in the measure in which it shall be manifested, becomes thenceforth his rule of conduct. Thus Paul's moral code rests on the one hand on the positive will of God made known by Christ, promulgated by the Apostles, and virtually accepted by the neophyte in his first act of faith, and on the other, in baptismal regeneration and the new relations which it produces. All Paul's commands and recommendations are merely applications of these principles.

H. *Eschatology.*—(1) The graphic description of the Pauline *parousia* (I Thess., iv, 16–17; II Thess., i, 7–10) has nearly all its main points in Christ's great eschatological discourse (Matt., xxiv; Mark, xiii, Luke, xxi). A common characteristic of all these passages is the apparent nearness of the *parousia*. Paul does not assert that the coming of the Saviour is at hand. In each of the five epistles, wherein he expresses the desire and the hope to witness in person the return of Christ, he at the same time considers the probability of the contrary hypothesis, proving that he had neither revelation nor certainty on the point. He knows only that the day of the Lord will come unexpectedly, like a thief (I Thess., v, 2–3), and he counsels the neophytes to make themselves ready without neglecting the duties of their state of life (II Thess., iii, 6–12). Although the coming of Christ will be sudden, it will be heralded by three signs: general apostasy (II Thess., ii, 3), the appearance of Antichrist (ii, 3–12), and the conversion of the Jews (Rom., xi, 26). A particular circumstance of St. Paul's preaching is that the just who shall be living at Christ's second advent will pass to glorious immortality without dying [I Thess., iv, 17; I Cor., xv, 51 (Greek text); II Cor., v, 2–5].

(2). Owing to the doubts of the Corinthians Paul treats the resurrection of the just at some length. He does not ignore the resurrection of the sinners, which he affirmed before the Governor Felix (Acts, xxiv, 15), but he does not concern himself with it in his Epistles. When he says that "the dead who are in Christ shall rise first" (πρῶτον, I Thess., iv, 16, Greek) this "first" offsets, not another resurrection of the dead, but the glorious transformation of the living. In like manner "the end" of which he speaks (τὸ τέλος, I Cor., xv, 24) is not the end of the resurrection, but of the present world and the beginning of a new order of things. All the arguments which he advances in behalf of the resurrection may be reduced to three: the mystical union of the Christian with Christ, the presence within us of the Spirit of Holiness, the interior and supernatural conviction of the faithful and the Apostles. It is evident that these arguments deal only with the glorious resurrection of the just. In short, the resurrection of the wicked does not come within his theological horizon. What is the condition of the souls of the just between death and resurrection? These souls enjoy the presence of Christ (II Cor., v, 8); their lot is enviable (Phil., i, 23); hence it is impossible that they should be without life, activity, or consciousness.

(3) The judgment according to St. Paul as according to the Synoptics, is closely connected with the *parousia* and the resurrection. They are the three acts of the same drama which constitute the Day of the Lord (I Cor., i, 8; II Cor., i, 14; Phil., i, 6,10; ii, 16). "For we must all be manifested before the judgment seat of Christ, that every one may receive the proper things of the body, according as he hath done, whether it be good or evil" (II Cor., v, 10). Two conclusions are derived from this text: (1) The judgment shall be universal, neither the good nor the wicked shall escape (Rom., xiv, 10–12), nor even the angels (I Cor., vi, 3); all who are brought to trial must account for the use of their liberty. (2) The judgment shall be according to works: this is a truth frequently reiterated by St. Paul, concerning sinners (II Cor., xi, 15), the just (II Tim., iv, 14), and men in general (Rom., ii, 6–9). Many Protestants marvel at this and claim that in St. Paul this doctrine is a survival of his rabbinical education (Pfleiderer), or that he could not make it harmonize with his doctrine of gratuitous justification (Reuss), or that the reward will be in proportion to the act, as the harvest is in proportion to the sowing, but that it will not be because of or with a view to the act (Weiss). These authors lose sight of the fact that St. Paul distinguishes between two justifications, the first necessarily gratuitous since man was then incapable of meriting it (Rom., iii, 28; Gal., ii, 16), the second in conformity to his works (Rom., ii, 6: κατὰ τὰ ἔργα), since man, when adorned with sanctifying grace, is capable of merit as the sinner is of demerit. Hence the celestial recompense is "a crown of justice which the Lord the just judge will render" (II Tim., iv, 8) to whomsoever has legitimately gained it.

Briefly, St. Paul's eschatology is not so distinctive as it has been made to appear. Perhaps its most original characteristic is the continuity between the present and the future of the just, between grace and glory, between salvation begun and salvation consummated. A large number of terms, redemption, justification, salvation, kingdom, glory and especially life, are common to the two states, or rather to the two phases of the same existence linked by charity which "never falleth away".

Of the innumerable works dealing directly with the life or doctrine of St. Paul the reader is directed only to the following as being most recent, accessible or useful:

BIOGRAPHIES:—LEWIN, *Life and Epistles of St. Paul* (London, 1851); CONYBEARE AND HOWSON, *Life and Epistles of St. Paul* (London, 1851); FARRAR, *Life and Works of St. Paul* (London, 1879); these three works, especially the last, have since passed through numerous editions. FOUARD, *St. Paul, ses missions* (1892), *ses dernières années* (1897), tr. English, GRIFFITH (New York—London, 1894); IVERACH, *St. Paul, his Life and Times* (s. d.); CONE, *Paul, the Man, the Missionary and the Teacher* (New York, 1898).

THEOLOGY:—ADENEY, *The Theology of the N. T.* (New York, 1894); STEVENS, *Theology of the N. T.* (Edinburgh, 1899); *Pauline Theology* (New York, 1906); WEISS, *Lehrbuch der bibl. Theol. des N. T.* (Stuttgart, 1903), also Eng. tr.; BEYSCHLAG, *Neutestam. Theologie* (Halle, 1896); SABATIER, *L'Apôtre Paul* (Paris, 1896), Eng. tr.; HOLTZMANN, *Lehrb. der neutestam. Theologie* (Freiburg, 1897); PFLEIDERER, *Der Paulinismus* (Leipzig, 1890); FEINE, *Theologie des N. T.* (Leipzig, 1910); PRAT, *La théologie de St. Paul* (Paris, 1908–11); there are also numerous other theologies of the N. T. such as those of LUTTERBECK (1852); REUSS (1852); HAHAN (1854); MESSNER (1856); SCHMID (1863); OOSTERZEE (1867), tr. EVANS (1876); IMMER (1877); BAUR (1864); HOLSTEN (1898); BOVON (1893–94); and of St. Paul in particular, USTERI (1831); DAHNE (1835); SCHRADER (1833); and the Catholic LIMAR, *Die theologie des heiligen Paulus* (Freiburg, 1864; 2nd ed., 1883).

SPECIAL QUESTIONS:—CLARKE, *The Ideas of the Apostle Paul translated into their modern equivalents* (Boston, 1884); EVERETT, *The Gospel of Paul* (Boston, 1893); BRUCE, *St. Paul's Conception of Christianity* (Edinburgh, 1894); SOMERVILLE, *St. Paul's Conception of Christ* (Edinburgh, 1897); DU BOSE, *The Gospel according to St. Paul* (London, 1907).

MÉNÉGOZ, *Le péché et la redemption d'après St. Paul* (Paris, 1882); LIPSIUS, *Die paulinische Rechtfertigungslehre* (Leipzig, 1853); TOBAC, *Le problème de la justification dans saint-Paul* (Louvain, 1908).

DICKSON, *St. Paul's use of the terms Flesh and Spirit* (Glasgow, 1883); SIMON, *Die Psychologie des Apostels Paulus* (Göttingen, 1897); SOKOLOWSKI, *Die Begriffe Geist und Leben bei Paulus* (Göttingen, 1903).

ALEXANDER, *The Ethics of St. Paul* (Glasgow, 1910); ERNESTI, *Die Ethik des Apostels Paulus* (Göttingen, 1880); JUNCKER, *Die Ethik des Apostels Paulus* (1904).

KENNEDY, *St. Paul's Conceptions of the Last Things* (London, 1904); KABISCH, *Die Eschatologie des Paulus* (Göttingen, 1893); TICHMANN, *Die paulinischen Vorstellungen von Auferstehung und Gericht* (Leipzig, 1896); TILLMANN, *Die Wiederkunft Christi nach deu paulin Briefen* in *Biblische Studien*, XIV, 1–2.

RAMSAY, *St. Paul the Traveller and the Roman Citizen* (London, 1908); IDEM, *The Church in the Roman Empire*; IDEM, *The Cities of St. Paul*.

F. PRAT.

Paul I, POPE, 757–67, date of birth unknown; d. at Rome, 28 June, 767. He was a brother of Stephen II. They had been educated for the priesthood at the Lateran palace. Stephen entrusted his brother, who approved of the pope's course in respect to King Pepin, with many important ecclesiastical affairs, among others with the restoration to the Roman States of the cities which had been seized by the Lombard Kings Aistulf and Desiderius; these cities Desiderius promised to give up. While Paul was with his dying brother at the Lateran, a party of the Romans gathered in the house of Archdeacon Theophylact in order to secure the latter's succession to the papal see. However, immediately after the burial of Stephen (d. 26 April, 757), Paul was elected by a large majority, and received episcopal consecration on the twenty-ninth of May. Paul continued his predecessor's policy towards the Frankish king, Pepin, and thereby continued the papal supremacy over Rome and the districts of central Italy in opposition to the efforts of the Lombards and the Eastern Empire. Pepin sent a letter to the Roman people, exhorting them to remain steadfast to St. Peter. In the reply sent by the senate and the people of Rome to the Frankish king, the latter was urged to complete the enlargement of the Roman province which he had wrested from the barbarians, and to persevere in the work he had begun. In 758 a daughter was born to Pepin, and the king sent the pope the cloth used at the baptism as a present, renewing in this way the papal sponsorship. Paul returned thanks and informed Pepin of the hostile action of Desiderius, who had failed to deliver the cities of Imola, Osimo, Ancona, and Bologna to Rome, and had also devastated the Pentapolis on his expedition against the rebellious Dukes of Spoleto and Benevento. The two duchies were conquered and annexed by Desiderius (758). At Benevento Desiderius had a conference with the Greek ambassador Georgios, and agreed on a mutual alliance of Byzantines and Lombards in central Italy. On his way home Desiderius came to Rome, and when the pope demanded the return of the aforesaid cities, he refused to comply. He promised to give back Imola, but on condition that the pope should persuade Pepin to send back the Lombard hostages whom the Frankish king had carried off, some time before, at the time of his second victory over the Lombard King Aistulf. If Paul would not do this, Desiderius threatened to go to war with him. The pope was in great straits. He found it difficult even to get the Frankish king informed of his position. He gave two letters to Bishop George of Ostia and the Roman priest Stephen, his ambassadors to Pepin, who made the journey with the Frankish messenger Ruodpertus. In the one letter that was to secure the envoys a safe passage through Lombard territory, he agreed to the demands of Desiderius and begged Pepin to accede to the wishes of the Lombards by making a treaty of peace and returning the hostages. At the same time the envoys were to give the Frankish king a second secret letter, in which the pope communicated to him the latest occurrences, informed him of the agreement of Desiderius with the Byzantines for the conquest of Ravenna, and implored Pepin to come to the aid of the pope, to punish the Lombard king, and to force him to yield the towns retained by him. Towards the close of 759 another envoy was sent to Pepin. Early in 760 two Frankish envoys, Bishop Remidius of Rouen, brother to Pepin, and Duke Antschar, came to Desiderius, who promised to return its patrimony to the Roman Church in April, and also to yield the towns demanded by the pope. But he again refused to carry out his promises, dallied, and even forced his way into Roman territory. Once more Paul implored the Frankish king's help. The position of affairs was made even more threatening by Byzantine action. Georgios had gone from southern Italy to the court of Pepin and had here won over a papal envoy, Marinus. With all his efforts Georgios could not move Pepin. In 760 a report spread through Italy that a large Byzantine fleet was under sail for Rome and the Frankish kingdom. Later it was reported that the Byzantines intended to send an army to Rome and Ravenna. The Archbishop Sergius of Ravenna received a letter from the Byzantine emperor, in which the latter sought to obtain the voluntary submission of the inhabitants of Ravenna. The same attempt was also made in Venice. Sergius sent the letter of the emperor to the pope, and the pope notified Pepin. In case of a war with the Eastern Empire it was important to make sure of the support of the Lombards, consequently Pepin desired to come to an agreement with Desiderius. Thereupon the Lombard king showed more complaisance in the question of the Roman patrimony included in the Lombard territory, and when he visited Rome in 765, the boundary disputes between him and the pope were arranged. The Frankish king now directed Desiderius to aid the pope in recovering the Roman patrimony in the regions in southern Italy under Byzantine rule, and to support the ecclesiastical rights of the pope against the bishops of these districts. Paul's opposition to the schemes of the Emperor Constantine Copronymus had no real political basis. The pope's aim was to defend ecclesiastical orthodoxy regarding the doctrine of the Trinity and the veneration of images against the Eastern emperor. Paul repeatedly dispatched legates and letters in regard to the veneration of images to the emperor at Byzantium. Constantine sent envoys to western Europe who in coming to King Pepin did not disguise their intention to negotiate with him concerning dogmatic questions, also about the submission of the Exarchate of Ravenna to Byzantine suzerainty. Papal legates also came to Pepin in regard to these matters. On their return the legates were able to reassure the pope as to the views of the Frankish ruler, who kept two of the papal envoys, Bishop George and the priest Peter, near him. In 767 a Frankish synod was held at Gentilly, near Paris, at which the Church doctrines concerning the Trinity and the veneration of images were maintained. Paul showed great activity and zeal in encouraging religious life at Rome. He turned his paternal home into a monastery, and near it built the church of San Silvestro in Capite. The founding of this church led to his holding a synod at Rome in 761. To this church and other churches of Rome, Paul transferred the bones of numerous martyrs from the decayed sanctuaries in the catacombs devastated by the Lombards in 756. He transferred the relics of St. Petronilla (q. v.) from the catacomb of St. Domitilla to a chapel in St. Peter's erected by his predecessor for this purpose. The legend of St. Petronilla caused her at that era to be regarded as a daughter of St. Peter, and as such she became the special Roman patroness of the Frankish rulers. Paul also built an oratory of the Blessed Virgin in St. Peter's, and a church in honour of the Apostles on the Via Sacra beyond the Roman Forum. He died near the church of San Paolo fuori le mura, where he had gone during the heat of summer. He was buried in this church, but after three months his body was transferred to St. Peter's. The "Liber Pontificalis" also praises the Christian charity and benevolence of the pope which he united with firmness. Paul is venerated as a saint. His feast is celebrated on the twenty-eighth of June.

Liber Pontificalis, ed. DUCHESNE, I, 463–467; *Liber Carolinus*, ed. *Mon. Germ. Hist.: Epist.*, III, 507 sqq.; KEHR in *Nachrichten der Gesellschaft der Wiss. zu Göttingen* (1896), 103 sqq.; JAFFÉ, *Regesta Rom. Pont.*, I, 277 sqq.; LANGEN, *Geschichte der römischen Kirche*, II (Bonn, 1885), 668 sqq.; HEFELE, *Konziliengeschichte*, 2nd ed., III, 431 sqq., 602; SCHNÜRER, *Die Entstehung des Kirchenstaates* (Cologne, 1894); DUCHESNE, *Les premiers temps de l'Etat pontifical* (2nd ed., Paris, 1904); DE ROSSI, *Insigni scoperte nel cimitero de Domitilla* in *Bull. di archeol. crist.*, ser. II, an. VI (1875), 5 sqq., 45 sqq.; IDEM, *Sepolcro di S. Petronilla nella basilica in via Ardeatina e sua traslazione al Vaticano, ibid.*, ser. III, an. III (1878), 125 sqq.; an. IV (1879), 5 sqq., 139 sqq.; MARUCCHI, *Basiliques et églises de Rome* (2nd ed., Rome, 1909); MANN, *Lives of the Popes* (London, 1902).

J. P. KIRSCH.

Paul II, POPE (PIETRO BARBO), b. at Venice, 1417; elected 30 August, 1464; d. 26 July, 1471; son of Niccolo Barbo and Polixena Condulmer, sister of

ARMS OF PAUL II

Eugene IV. Although he studied for a business career he received an excellent religious education and, at the elevation of his uncle to the papacy, entered the ecclesiastical state. He became Archdeacon of Bologna, Bishop of Cervia and of Vicenza, and in 1440 cardinal-deacon. Noted for his generosity and imposing appearance, the Cardinal of Venice, as he was called, was very influential under Eugene IV, Nicholas V, and Calixtus III, less so under Pius II. He became the latter's successor, and owed his election partly to the dissatisfaction of some of the cardinals with the policy of his predecessor. To this could be traced the oath which Barbo swore to at the conclave, but which he rightfully set aside after election, since it was opposed to the monarchial constitution of the Church. Paul II delighted in display. He intro-

PAUL III AND HIS NEPHEWS, ALESSANDRO AND OTTAVIO FARNESE
TITIAN, NATIONAL MUSEUM, NAPLES

duced splendid carnival festivities, built the palace of S. Marco (now di Venezia), revised the municipal statutes of Rome, organized relief work among the poor, granted pensions to some cardinals, and to all the privilege of wearing the red biretta. His suppression in 1466 of the college of abbreviators aroused much opposition, intensified by a similar measure against the Roman Academy. Platina, a member of both organizations, who had been repeatedly imprisoned, retaliated by writing a calumnious biography of Paul II.

That Paul II was not opposed to Humanistic studies, as such, is evidenced by the fact that he protected universities, encouraged the art of printing, and was himself a collector of works of ancient art. The suppression of the Roman Academy was justified

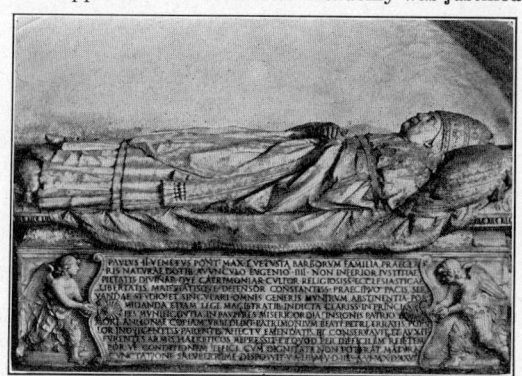

MONUMENT OF PAUL II

by the moral degeneracy and pagan attitude which it fostered. On the other hand the charge of immorality brought against Paul II by Gregory of Heimburg is untenable. The pope punished the Fraticelli in the Papal States, prosecuted heretics in France and Germany, decreed in 1470 the observance of the jubilee every twenty-five years, and made an unsuccessful attempt at uniting Russia with the Church. The Turkish question received his earnest attention, particularly after the fall of Negropont (1470). Financial assistance was granted to Hungary and the Albanian leader Scanderbeg. No general results were obtained, however, owing to the lack of co-operation among the Christian powers; to disturbances in the Papal States, where Paul II suppressed the robber knights of Anguillara, and perhaps chiefly to the conflict between the papacy and King George Podiebrad of Bohemia.

CANENSIUS, *Vita Pauli II* (Rome, 1740); GASPAR VERONENSIS, *De Gestis Pauli II*, partly in MURATORI, *Rer. Ital. Script.*, III, II, 1025-53 (Milan, 1734); CREIGHTON, *History of the Papacy*, new ed., IV (New York, 1903), 3-63, 315-27; PASTOR, *Geschichte der Päpste*, II (4th ed., Freiburg, 1904), 291-447, 757-79; tr. ANTROBUS, IV (London, 1894), 3-194, 475-504.

N. A. WEBER.

Paul III, POPE (ALESSANDRO FARNESE), b. at Rome or Canino, 29 Feb., 1468; elected, 12 Oct., 1534; d. at Rome, 10 Nov., 1549. The Farnese were an ancient Roman family whose possessions clustered about the Lake of Bolsena. Although counted among the Roman aristocrats, they first appear in history associated with Viterbo and Orvieto. Among the witnesses to the Treaty of Venice between Barbarossa and the pope, we find the signature of a Farnese as Rector of Orvieto; a Farnese bishop consecrated the cathedral there. During the interminable feuds which distracted the peninsula, the Farnese were consistently Guelph. The grandfather of the future pontiff was commander-in-chief of the papal troops under Euge-

ARMS OF PAUL III.

nius IV; his oldest son perished in the battle of Fornuovo; the second, Pier Luigi, married Giovannella Gaetani, sister to the Lord of Sermoneta. Among their children were the beautiful Giulia, who married an Orsini, and Alessandro, later Paul III. Alessandro received the best education that his age could offer; first at Rome, where he had Pomponio Leto for a tutor; later at Florence in the palace of Lorenzo the Magnificent, where he formed his friendship with the future Leo X, six years his junior. His contemporaries praise his proficiency in all the learning of the Renaissance, especially in his mastery of classical Latin and Italian. With such advantages of birth and talent, his advancement in the ecclesiastical career was assured and rapid. On 20 Sept., 1493 (Eubel), he was created by Alexander VI cardinal-deacon with the title SS. Cosmas and Damian. He wore the purple for over forty years, passing through the several gradations, until he became Dean of the Sacred College. In accordance with the abuses of his time, he accumulated a number of opulent benefices, and spent his immense revenue with a generosity which won for him the praises of artists and the affection of the Roman populace. His native ability and diplomatic skill, acquired by long experience, made him tower above his colleagues in the Sacred College, even as his Palazzo Farnese excelled in magnificence all the other palaces of Rome. That he continued to grow in favour under pontiffs so different in character as the Borgia, Rovera, and Medici popes is a sufficient proof of his tact.

He had already on two previous occasions, come within measurable distance of the tiara, when the conclave of 1534, almost without the formality of a ballot, proclaimed him successor to Clement VII. It was creditable to his reputation and to the good will of the cardinals, that the factions which divided the Sacred College were concordant in electing him. He was universally recognized as the man of the hour; and the piety and zeal, which had characterized him after he was ordained priest, caused men to overlook the extravagance of his earlier years.

The Roman people rejoiced at the elevation to the tiara of the first citizen of their city since Martin V. Paul III was crowned 3 Nov., and lost no time in setting about the most needed reforms. No one, who has once studied his portrait by Titian, is likely to forget the wonderful expression of countenance of that worn-out, emaciated form. Those piercing little eyes, and that peculiar attitude of one ready to bound or to shrink, tell the story of a veteran diplomat who was not to be deceived or taken off guard. His extreme caution, and the difficulty of binding him down to a definite obligation, drew from Pasquino the facetious remark that the third Paul was a "Vas dilationis." The elevation to the cardinalate of his grandsons, Alessandro Farnese, aged fourteen, and Guido Ascanio Sforza, aged sixteen, displeased the reform party and drew a protest from the emperor; but this was forgiven, when shortly after, he introduced into the Sacred College men of the calibre of Reginald Pole, Contanini, Sadoleto, and Caraffa.

Soon after his elevation, 2 June, 1536, Paul III summoned a general council to meet at Mantua in the following May; but the opposition of the Protestant princes and the refusal of the Duke of Mantua to assume the responsibility of maintaining order frustrated the project. He issued a new bull, convoking a council at Vicenza, 1 May, 1538; the chief obstacle was the renewed enmity of Charles V and Francis I. The aged pontiff induced them to hold a conference with him at Nizza and conclude a ten years' truce. As a token of good will, a granddaughter of Paul was married to a French prince, and the emperor gave his daughter, Margaret, to Ottavio, the son of Pier Luigi, founder of the Farnese dynasty of Parma.

Many causes contributed to delay the opening of

the general council. The extension of power which a re-united Germany would place in the hands of Charles was so intolerable to Francis I, that he, who persecuted heresy in his own realm with such cruelty that the pope appealed to him to mitigate his violence, became the sworn ally of the Smalcaldic League, encouraging them to reject all overtures to reconciliation. Charles himself was in no slight measure to blame; for, notwithstanding his desire for the assembling of a council, he was led into the belief that the religious differences of Germany might be settled by conferences between the two parties. These conferences, like all such attempts to settle differences outside of the normal court of the Church, led to a waste of time, and did far more harm than good. Charles had a false idea of the office of a general council. In his desire to unite all parties, he sought for vague formulæ to which all could subscribe, a relapse into the mistakes of the Byzantine emperors. A council of the Church, on the other hand, must formulate the Faith with such precision that no heretic can subscribe to it. It took some years to convince the emperor and his mediatizing advisors that Catholicism and Protestantism are as opposite as light and darkness. Meanwhile Paul III set about the reform of the papal court with a vigour which paved the way for the disciplinary canons of Trent. He appointed commissions to report abuses of every kind; he reformed the Apostolic Camera, the tribunal of the Rota, the Penitentiaria, and the Chancery. He enhanced the prestige of the papacy by doing single-handed what his predecessors had reserved to the action of a council. In the constantly recurring quarrels between Francis and Charles, Paul III preserved a strict neutrality, notwithstanding that Charles urged him to support the empire and subject Francis to the censures of the Church. Paul's attitude as a patriotic Italian would have been sufficient to prevent him from allowing the emperor to be sole arbiter of Italy. It was as much for the purpose of securing the integrity of the papal dominions, as for the exaltation of his family, that Paul extorted from Charles and his reluctant cardinals the erection of Piacenza and Parma into a duchy for his son, Pier Luigi. A feud arose with Gonzaga, the imperial Governor of Milan, which ended later in the assassination of Pier Luigi and the permanent alienation of Piacenza from the Papal States.

When the Treaty of Crespi (18 Sept., 1544) ended the disastrous wars between Charles and Francis, Paul energetically took up the project of convening a general council. Meanwhile it developed that the emperor had formed a programme of his own, quite at variance in some important points with the pope's. Since the Protestants repudiated a council presided over by the Roman pontiff, Charles was resolved to reduce the princes to obedience by force of arms. To this Paul did not object, and promised to aid him with three hundred thousand ducats and twenty thousand infantry; but he wisely added the proviso, that Charles should enter into no separate treaties with the heretics and make no agreement prejudicial to the Faith or to the rights of the Holy See. Charles now contended that the council should be prorogued, until victory had decided in favour of the Catholics. Furthermore, foreseeing that the struggle with the preachers of heresy would be more stubborn than the conflict with the princes, he urged the pontiff to avoid making dogmas of faith for the present and confine the labours of the council to the enforcement of discipline. To neither of these proposals could the pope agree. Finally, after endless difficulties (13 Dec., 1545) the Council of Trent held its first session. In seven sessions, the last 3 March, 1547, the Fathers intrepidly faced the most important questions of faith and discipline. Without listening to the threats and expostulations of the imperial party, they formulated for all time the Catholic doctrine on the Scriptures, original sin, justification, and the Sacraments. The work of the council was half ended, when the outbreak of the plague in Trent caused an adjournment to Bologna. Pope Paul was not the instigator of the removal of the council; he simply acquiesced in the decision of the Fathers. Fifteen prelates, devoted to the emperor, refused to leave Trent. Charles demanded the return of the council to German territory, but the deliberations of the council continued in Bologna, until finally, 21 April, the pope, in order to avert a schism, prorogued the council indefinitely. The wisdom of the council's energetic action, in establishing thus early the fundamental truths of the Catholic creed, became soon evident, when the emperor and his semi-Protestant advisers inflicted upon Germany their Interim religion, which was despised by both parties. Pope Paul, who had given the emperor essential aid in the Smalcaldic war, resented his dabbling in theology, and their estrangement continued until the death of the pontiff.

Paul's end came rather suddenly. After the assassination of Pier Luigi, he had struggled to retain Piacenza and Parma for the Church and had deprived Ottavio, Pier Luigi's son and Charles's son-in-law, of these duchies. Ottavio, relying on the emperor's benevolence, refused obedience; it broke the old man's heart, when he learned that his favourite grandson, Cardinal Farnese, was a party to the transaction. He fell into a violent fever and died at the Quirinal, at the age of eighty-two. He lies buried in St. Peter's in the tomb designed by Michelangelo and erected by Guglielmo della Porta. Not all the popes repose in monuments corresponding to their importance in the history of the Church; but few will be disposed to contest the right of Farnese to rest directly under Peter's chair. He had his faults; but they injured no one but himself. The fifteen years of his pontificate saw the complete restoration of Catholic faith and piety. He was succeeded by many saintly pontiffs, but not one of them possessed all his commanding virtues. In Rome his name is written all over the city he renovated. The Pauline chapel, Michelangelo's work in the Sistine, the streets of Rome, which he straightened and broadened, the numerous objects of art associated

Paul III
National Museum, Naples
(Attributed to Michelangelo)

with the name of Farnese, all speak eloquently of the remarkable personality of the pontiff who turned the tide in favour of religion. If to this we add the favour accorded by Paul to the new religious orders then appearing, the Capuchins, Barnabites, Theatines, Jesuits, Ursulines, and many others, we are forced to confess that his reign was one of the most fruitful in the annals of the Church.

PANVINIUS, *Pont. Romanorum vitæ*; PALLAVICINI, *Concilio di Trento*; PASTOR, *Gesch. der Päpste*, V; EHSES, *Concilium Tridentinum*, V; VON RANKE, *Hist. of the Popes in the XVI–XVIII Centuries*; ARTAUD DE MONTOR, *Hist. of the Popes* (New York, 1867).

JAMES F. LOUGHLIN.

Paul IV, POPE (GIOVANNI PIETRO CARAFFA), b. near Benevento, 28 June, 1476; elected 23 May, 1555; d. 18 Aug., 1559. The Caraffa were one of the most illustrious of the noble families of Naples, and had given distinguished scions to Church and State. The name of Cardinal Oliviero Caraffa recurs frequently in the history of the papacy during the days of the Renaissance. One of the great cardinal's merits was that of superintending the training of his young relative, Giovanni Pietro, whom he introduced to the papal Court in 1494, and in whose favour he resigned the See of Chieti (in Latin, *Theate*), from which word he was thenceforward known as *Theatinus*. Leo X sent him on an embassy to England and retained him for some years as nuncio in Spain. His residence in Spain served to accentuate that detestation of Spanish rule in his native land which characterized his public policy during his pontificate. From early childhood he led a blameless life; and that longing for asceticism which had prompted him to seek admission into the Dominican and the Camaldolese Orders asserted itself in 1524 when he persuaded Clement VII, though with difficulty, to accept the resignation of his benefices and permit him to enter the congregation of clerics regular founded by St. Cajetan, but popularly named "Theatines", after Caraffa, their first general. The young congregation suffered more than its share during the sack of Rome in 1527, and its few members retired to Venice. But the sharp intellect of Paul III had perceived the importance of the institute in his projected reform of the clergy, and he summoned the Theatines back to Rome. Caraffa was placed by the pontiff on the committee named to outline the project of reform of the papal Court; and on 22 Dec., 1536 he was created cardinal with the title of San Pancrazio. Later he was made Archbishop of Naples; but, owing to the emperor's distrust and fear of him, it was only with difficulty he could maintain his episcopal rights. Although Caraffa was highly educated and surpassed most of his contemporaries in the knowledge of Greek and Hebrew, still he remained throughout medieval in life and thought. His favourite author was St. Thomas Aquinas. The few *opuscula* which he found time to write were Scholastic in character. For the party of Pole, Contarini, and Morone he had the most heartfelt detestation; and his elevation boded them no happiness. Caraffa was the head and front of every effort made by Paul III in the interest of reform. He reorganized the Inquisition in Italy on papal lines and for a generation was the terror of misbelievers. How so austere a person could be chosen pope was a mystery to everyone, especially to himself. "I have never conferred a favour on a human being", he said. It is most likely that the octogenarian would have refused the dignity, were it not that the emperor's agent, Cardinal Mendoza, had pronounced decidedly that Charles would not permit Caraffa to be pope. This was to challenge every principle for which the aged cardinal had stood during his long career. He was elected in spite of the emperor, and for four years held aloft the banner of the independence of Italy. Historians seem to be unjust towards Paul IV. That unbending Italian patriot, born whilst Italy was "a lyre with four strings", Naples, Rome, Florence, and Venice, was certainly justified in using the prestige of the papacy to preserve some relics of liberty for his native country. The Austrian and Spanish Habsburgers treated Paul IV with studied contempt, and thus forced him to enter an alliance with France. Neither in the matter of the succession to the empire nor in the conclusion of the religious peace were the interests of the Holy See consulted in the slightest degree.

Paul IV elevated to the cardinalate his nephew Carlo Caraffa, a man utterly unworthy and without any ecclesiastical training, and enriched other relatives with benefices and estates taken from those who favoured the Spaniards. At the end of the unfortunate war with Philip II the aged pope lost faith in his nephews and banished them from the Court. Still more disastrous were his relations with England, which had been reconciled to Rome by Mary, and Cardinal Pole. Paul IV refused to sanction Pole's settlement in regard to the confiscated goods of the Church, and demanded restitution. Pole himself was relieved by the pontiff of his legatine office and ordered to come to Rome to stand before the Inquisition. Upon the death of Mary and Pole, he rejected Elizabeth's claim to the crown, on the ground that she was of illegitimate birth. His activity was more fruitful in the spiritual concerns of the Church. He could boast that no day passed without seeing a new decree of reform. He made the Inquisition a powerful engine of government, and was no respecter of persons. The great Cardinal Morone was brought before the tribunal on suspicion of heresy and committed to prison. Paul established the hierarchy in the Netherlands and in the Orient.

The pontificate of Paul IV was a great disappointment. He who at the beginning was honoured by a public statue, lived to see it thrown down and mutilated by the hostile populace. He was buried in St. Peter's 19 Aug., 1559, and was later transferred to S. Maria sopra Minerva.

Lives by CARACCIOLI and BROMATO; VON RANKE, *Hist. of the Popes in the XVI–XVIII Centuries*; REUMONT, *Gesch. der Stadt Rom*; ARTAUD DE MONTOR, *History of the Popes* (New York, 1867).

JAMES F. LOUGHLIN.

Paul V, POPE (CAMILLO BORGHESE), b. at Rome, 17 Sept., 1550; elected 16 May, 1605; d. 28 Jan., 1621. Although proud to call himself, as we read on the façade of St. Peter's and on his epitaph, a Roman, Borghese was descended from a noble family of Siena which held important positions in that city, and claimed St. Catherine for a relative. Their removal to Rome was caused by the endless disturbances which made life in Siena unbearable. Camillo was carefully trained in jurisprudence at Perugia and Padua, and became a canonist of marked ability. He rose in the ecclesiastical career steadily, if not rapidly; in 1596 he was made cardinal by Clement VIII, and became Cardinal-Vicar of Rome. He held aloof from all parties and factions, devoting all his spare time to his lawbooks. In consequence, on the death of Leo XI, all eyes were centred on him, and he ascended the papal throne without engagement or obligation of any sort. His legal training was soon visible in all his words and actions. He knew nothing of compromises, and proceeded to rule the Church not from the standpoint of diplomacy but from the decretals. He conceived it his duty to maintain inviolate every right and claim advanced by his predecessors. This made his character at times assume a very stern and uncompromising aspect. His first public act was to send home to their sees the prelates and even the cardinals who were sojourning at Rome upon one or other pretext. The Council of Trent had declared it a grave sin for a bishop to be an absentee. That he was engaged in Rome doing the business of the Holy See made no difference. Paul was soon involved in controversy with various cities of Italy on matters concerning ecclesiastical jurisdiction and the relations between Church and State. The bitterest quarrel was with the proud Republic of Venice, which refused to acknowledge the exemption of the clergy from the jurisdiction of the civil courts and passed two laws obnoxious to the Roman *Curia*, the first forbidding the alienation of real property in favour of the clergy, the second demanding the approval of the civil power for the building of new churches. Paul demanded the repeal of these anti-clerical ordinances, and insisted that two clerics who had been committed to prison should be surrendered to the ecclesiastical court. The dispute became daily more bitter and gradually developed into a broad discussion of the relative position of Church and State. What gave the quarrel a European importance

MONUMENT OF PAUL V

was the ability of the champions who entered the field on either side. For the claims of the Church stood Cardinals Baronius and Bellarmine; the cause of Venice was defended by the Servite Paolo Sarpi, a man of wonderful literary skill and a sworn enemy of the Roman Court. On 17 April, 1606, the pope pronounced sentence of excommunication against the doge, Senate, and Government collectively. He allowed a very short space for submission, after which he imposed an interdict on the city. The clergy had now to take sides for or against the pope. With the exception of the Jesuits, the Theatines, and the Capuchins, who were immediately expelled, the entire body of secular and regular clergy held with the Government and continued to hold services, notwithstanding the interdict. The festival of Corpus Christi was celebrated with unusual splendour, and Sarpi said Mass for the first time in years. The schism lasted about a year; and peace was patched up through the mediation of France and Spain. The Republic refused to repeal the obnoxious laws openly, but promised " to conduct itself with its accustomed piety". With these obscure words the pope was forced to be content; he removed the censures 22 March, 1607. The Theatines and Capuchins were permitted to return; an exception was made against the Jesuits.

The pope watched vigilantly over the interests of the Church in every nation. On 9 July, 1606, he wrote a friendly letter to James I of England to congratulate him on his accession to the throne, and referred with grief to the plot recently made against the life of the monarch. But he prays him not to make the innocent Catholics suffer for the crime of a few. He promises to exhort all the Catholics of the realm to be submissive and loyal to their sovereign in all things not opposed to the honour of God. Unfortunately the oath of allegiance James demanded of his subjects contained clauses to which no Catholic could in conscience subscribe. It was solemnly condemned in two Briefs, 22 Sept., 1606, and 23 Aug., 1607. This condemnation occasioned the bitter dissension between the party of the archpriest George Blackwell and the Catholics who submitted to the decision of the Holy See. In Austria the efforts of the pope were directed to healing the disputes among the Catholics and to giving moral and material aid to the Catholic Union. He survived the battle of Prague, which put an end to the short reign of the Calvinistic "winter-king".

Paul V was no more free from nepotism than the other pontiffs of that century. But if he seemed to show too many favours to his relatives, it must be said that they were capable men of blameless lives, and devoted their large revenues to the embellishment of Rome. Paul had the honour of putting the finishing touches to St. Peter's, which had been building for a century. He enriched the Vatican Library, was fond of art, and encouraged Guido Reni. He canonized St. Charles Borromeo and St. Frances of Rome. He beatified Sts. Ignatius Loyola, Francis Xavier, Philip Neri, Theresa the Carmelite, Louis Bertrand, Thomas of Villanova, and Isidore of Madrid. During his pontificate a large number of new institutes for education and charity added new lustre to religion. His remains were placed in the magnificent Borghese chapel in St. Mary Major's, where his monument is universally admired.

Life, in Latin, by BZOVIO, It. tr. in continuation of PLATINA, *Vite dei Pontefici* (Venice, 1730); see also VON RANKE, *History of the Popes in the Sixteenth, etc., Centuries;* VON REUMONT, *Gesch. der Stadt Rom;* ARTAUD DE MONTOR, *History of the Popes* (New York, 1867).

JAMES F. LOUGHLIN.

Paul, REGULAR CLERICS OF SAINT. See BARNABITES.

Paula, SAINT, b. in Rome, 347; d. at Bethlehem, 404. She belonged to one of the first families of Rome. Left a widow in 379 at the age of 32 she became, through the influence of St. Marcella and her group, the model of Christian widows. In 382 took place her decisive meeting with St. Jerome, who had come to Rome with St. Epiphanius and Paulinus of Antioch. These two bishops inspired her with an invincible desire to follow the monastic life in the East. After their departure from Rome and at the request of Marcella, Jerome gave readings from Holy Scripture before the group of patrician women among whom St. Paula held a position of honour. Paula was an ardent student. She and her daughter Eustochium, studied and mastered Hebrew perfectly. By their studies they aimed not so much to acquire knowledge, as a fuller acquaintance with Christian perfection.

She did not, however, neglect her domestic duties. A devoted mother, she married her daughter, Paulina (d. 395), to the senator Pammachius; Blesilla soon became a widow and died in 384. Of her two other daughters, Rufina died in 386, and Eustochium accompanied her mother to the Orient where she died in 419. Her son Toxotius, at first a pagan, but baptized in 385, married in 389 Læta, daughter of the pagan priest Albinus. Of this marriage was born Paula the Younger, who in 404 rejoined Eustochium in the East and in 420 closed the eyes of St. Jerome. These are the names which recur frequently in the letters of St. Jerome, where they are inseparable from that of Paula.

The death of Blesilla and that of Pope Damasus in 384 completely changed the manner of life of Paula and Jerome. In September, 385, Paula and Eustochium left Rome to follow the monastic life in the East. Jerome, who had preceded them thither by a month, joined them at Antioch. Paula first made in great detail the pilgrimage of all the famous places of the Holy Land, afterward going to Egypt to be edified by the virtues of the anchorites and cenobites, and finally took up her residence at Bethlehem, as did St. Jerome. Then began for Paula, Eustochium, and Jerome their definitive manner of life. The intellectual and spiritual intercourse among these holy persons, begun at Rome, continued and developed. Two monasteries were founded, one for men, the other for women. Paula and Eustochium took a larger share in the exegetical labours of Jerome, and conformed themselves more and more to his direction. An example of their manner of thinking and writing may be seen in the letter they wrote from Bethlehem about 386 to Marcella to persuade her to leave Rome and join them; it is Letter XLVI of the correspondence of Jerome. But God was not sparing of trials to His servants. Their peace was disturbed by constant annoyances, first the controversy concerning Origenism which disturbed their relations with John, Bishop of Jerusalem, and later Paula's need of money, she having been ruined by her generosity. She died in the midst of these trials and good works. The chief and almost the only source of Paula's life is the correspondence of St. Jerome (P. L., XXII). The Life of St. Paula is in Letter CVIII, which, though somewhat rhetorical, is a wonderful production. The other letters which specially concern St. Paula and her family are XXII, XXX, XXXI, XXXIII, XXXVIII, XXXIX, LXVI, CVII.

LAGRANGE, *Histoire de Ste Paule* (2nd ed., Paris, 1868); *Acta SS.*, Jan., III, 327–37; see also *Historia lausiaca*, lxxix, in *P. G.*, XXXIV, 1180; ST. JEROME, *De viris illustribus* in *P. L.*, XXIII, 719; UPTON, *The House on the Aventine* in *Catholic World*, LXVII, 633–643.

LOUIS SALTET.

Pauli, JOHANNES, b. about 1455; d. after 1530 in the monastery at Thann in Alsace. What little is known of his life rests upon unreliable information. Ludwig von Pastor rejects the story that he was of Jewish descent, and baptised at an early age, taking the name of Johannes Pauli from his godfather (see below). Pauli became Master of Arts in Strasburg, entered the Franciscans (the "Barefooted"), and delivered his first sermon in Thann in 1479. Two years later, he was sent to the convent at Oppenheim; in 1504 the conventual monastery at Bern desired him as a guardian; he held the same office in Strasburg 1506–10; in 1516 he is mentioned as preacher in Schlettstadt; later in Villingen in the Black Forest, and finally in Thann. Prompted by his acquaintance with Geiler of Kaisersberg, he published in 1515 "Das Evangelienbuch"; in 1516 "Die Emeis, Buch von der Omeissen"; in 1517 "Die Brösamlin Geilers"; in 1520 "Das Narrenschiff, aus dem Latein ins Deutsch gebracht". His own work, which assured him a lasting place in German literature, is the famous collection of farces and humorous stories "Schimpf (Scherz) und Ernst". This a geniune "folk's book", written in an easy and plain style, filled with humour and pointed satire, intended to instruct while it amused. "He did not desire," as Georg Rollenhagen says in his preface to "Froschmäusler", "to make people laugh without teaching them something; his book was like the old legends and sagas, full of fabulous happenings and incidents, but written so that in them, as in a comedy, there are combined with poetry and imagination the plain, unvarnished, bitter truths of life, worded so as to tell serious things in a jocular manner, with a laugh and a smile." Pauli drew his information from a variety of sources, and his farces became the inspiration of the later German poets, especially for Hans Sachs. He exercised a wide influence upon the culture of the whole century.

VEITH, *Ueber den Barfüsser Johannes Pauli* (Vienna, 1839); OESTERLEY, *Johannes Paulis Schimpf und Ernst* (Stuttgart, 1866); EUBEL, *Gesch. der oberdeutschen Minoritenprovinz* (Wurzburg, 1886); JANSSEN, *Gesch. des deutschen Volkes*, ed. PASTOR, VI (Freiburg, 1901); BOBERTAG, *Deutsche Nationallitteratur* (Kürschner), XXIV; WEIGERT, *Deutsche Volkschwänke des 16. Jahrhunderts* (Kempten, 1909).

NICHOLAS SCHEID.

Paulicians, a dualistic heretical sect, derived originally from Manichæism. The origin of the name *Paulician* is obscure. Gibbon (Decline and Fall, liv), says it means "Disciples of St. Paul" (Photius, op. cit., II, 11; III, 10; VI, 4). Their special veneration for the Apostle, and their habit of renaming their leaders after his disciples lend some colour to this view. On the other hand, the form (Παυλικιᾶνοι, not Παυλιᾶνοι) is curious; and the name seems to have been used only by their opponents, who held that they were followers of Paul of Samosata (Conybeare, op. cit., cv). The birthplace of their founder evidently suggested this; but there is no connexion between their doctrine and his. Photius relates that a certain Manichee woman, named Kallinike, sent her two sons Paul and John to Armenia to propagate this heresy; the name is corrupted from Παυλοιωάννοι (Friedrich, op. cit., I). The existence of such persons is now generally denied. The latest authority, Ter Mkrttschian (Die Pauliciancr, 63), says the name is an Armenian diminutive and means "followers of little Paul", but does not explain who little Paul may be. It occurs first in the Acts of the Armenian Synod of Duin in 719, a canon of which forbids any one to spend the night in the house of "the wicked heretics called Pollikian" (Ter Mkrttschian, 62).

I. DOCTRINE.—The cardinal point of the Paulician heresy is a distinction between the God who made and governs the material world and the God of heaven who created souls, who alone should be adored. They thought all matter bad. It seems therefore obvious to count them as one of the many neo-Manichæan sects, in spite of their own denial and that of modern writers (Ter Mkrttschian, Conybeare, Adeney, loc. cit.; Harnack, "Lehrbuch der Dogmengeschichte", Tübingen, 1909, II, 528). But there is a strong Marcionite element too. They rejected the Old Testament; there was no Incarnation, Christ was an angel sent into the world by God, his real mother was the heavenly Jerusalem. His work consisted only in his teaching; to believe in him saves men from judgment. The true baptism and Eucharist consist in hearing his word, as in John, iv, 10. But many Paulicians, nevertheless, let their children be baptized by the Catholic clergy. They honoured not the Cross, but only the book of the Gospel. They were Iconoclasts, rejecting all pictures. Their Bible was a fragmentary New Testament. They rejected St. Peter's epistles because he had denied Christ. They referred always to the "Gospel and Apostle", apparently only St. Luke and St. Paul; though they quoted other Gospels in controversy.

The whole ecclesiastical hierarchy is bad, as also all Sacraments and ritual. They had a special aversion to monks. Their own organization consisted first of the founders of their sect in various places. These were apostles and prophets. They took new names after people mentioned by St. Paul, thus Constantine called himself Silvanus; apparently they claimed to be these persons come to life again. Under the apostles and prophets were "fellow-workers" (συνέχδημοι) who formed a council, and "notaries" (νοτάριοι), who looked after the holy books and kept order at meetings. Their conventicles were called, not churches, but "prayer-houses" (προσευχαί). They maintained that it was lawful to conceal or even deny their ideas for fear of persecution; many of them lived exteriorly as Catholics. Their ideal was a purely spiritual communion of faithful that should obliterate all distinctions of race. Their enemies accuse them constantly of gross immorality, even at their prayer-meetings. One of their chief leaders, Baanes, seems to have acquired as a recognized surname the epithet "filthy" (ὁ ῥυπρός). They would recognize no other name for themselves than "Christians"; the Catholics were "Romans" (Ῥωμαῖοι), that is, people who obey the Roman emperor, as the Monophysites called their opponents Melchites. Harnack sums them up as "dualistic Puritans and Individualists" and as "an anti-hierarchic Christianity built up on the Gospel, and Apostle, with emphatic rejection of Catholic Christianity" (Dogmengeschichte, II, 528).

Since Gibbon the Paulicians have often been described as a survival of early and pure Christianity, godly folk who clung to the Gospel, rejecting later superstitions, who were grossly calumniated by their opponents. Conybeare (op. cit.) thinks they were a continuation of the Adoptionists. Dr. Adeney calls them "in many respects Protestants before Protestantism" (The Greek and Eastern Churches, 219). This idea accounts for the fact that the sect has met among modern writers with more interest and certainly more sympathy than it deserves.

II. HISTORY.—Constantine of Mananalis, calling himself Silvanus, founded what appears to be the first Paulician community at Kibossa, near Colonia in Armenia. He began to teach about 657. He wrote no books and taught that the New Testament as he presented it (his "Gospel and Apostle") should be the only text used by his followers (Georgios Monachos, ed. Friedrich, 2). The other Paulician Apostles after Constantine were Symeon (called Titus), sent by the emperor Constantine Pogonatus (668–85) to put down the sect, but converted to it; then Gegnesius an Armenian (Timothy); Joseph (Epaphroditus); Zachary, who was rejected by many and called a hireling; Baanes; Sergius (Tychicus). They founded six congregations in Armenia and Pontus, to which they gave the names of Pauline Churches (Kibossa was "Macedonia", and so on).

Constantine-Silvanus, after having preached for twenty-seven years and having spread his sect into the Western part of Asia Minor, was arrested by the Imperial authorities (by Symeon), tried for heresy and stoned to death. In 690 Symeon-Titus himself, having become a Paulician, was also executed with many others. The history of these people is divided between their persecutions and their own quarrels. An Armenian Paul (thought by some to have given his name to the sect) set up a congregation at Episparis in the (Armenian) district Phanaroea (d. c. 715). His two sons Gegnesius-Timothy and Theodore quarrelled about his succession. Gegnesius went to Constantinople in 717 and persuaded the emperor Leo III and the patriarch Germanus I that he was orthodox. Armed with an imperial safe-conduct he came to Mananalis and succeeded in crushing Theodore's opposition. After his death his son Zachary (the "hireling") and his son-in-law, Joseph-Epaphroditus, again quarrelled and formed parties as to which should succeed. Zachary's party went under; many of them were destroyed by the Saracens.

Joseph (d. 775) founded communities all over Asia Minor. Then came Baanes (Vahan; d. 801). Under him the sect decreased in numbers and influence. But a certain Sergius-Tychicus, who made a new schism, reformed and strengthened the movement in his party. The Paulicians were now either Baanites (the old party), or Sergites (the reformed sect). Sergius was a zealous propagator of the heresy; he boasted that he had spread his Gospel "from East to West, from North to South" (Petrus Siculus, "Historia Manichæorum", op. cit., 45). The Sergites meanwhile fought against their rivals and nearly exterminated them. From the Imperial government the Paulicians met with alternate protection and persecution. Constantine IV, and still more Justinian II, persecuted them cruelly. The first Iconoclast emperors (Leo III and his successors) protected them; Conybeare counts these emperors as practically Paulicians themselves (op. cit.). Nicephorus I tolerated them in return for their service as soldiers in Phrygia and Lycaonia. Michael I began to persecute again and his successor Leo V, though an Iconoclast, tried to refute the accusation that he was a Paulician by persecuting them furiously. A great number of them at this time rebelled and fled to the Saracens. Sergius was killed in 835. Theodora, regent for her son Michael III, continued the persecution; hence a second rebellion under one Karbeas, who again led many of his followers across the frontiers.

These Paulicians, now bitter enemies of the empire, were encouraged by the khalifa. They fortified a place called Tephrike, and made it their headquarters. From Tephrike they made continual raids into the empire; so that from this time they form a political power, to be counted among the enemies of Rome. We hear continually of wars against the Saracens, Armenians, and Paulicians. Under Basil I the Paulician army invaded Asia Minor as far as Ephesus, and almost to the coast opposite Constantinople. But they were defeated, and Basil destroyed Tephrike in 871. This eliminated the sect as a military power. Meanwhile other Paulicians, heretics but not rebels, lived in groups throughout the empire. Constantine V had already transferred large numbers of them to Thrace; John I Tzimiskes sent many more to the same part to defend it against the Slavs. They founded a new centre at Philippopolis, from which they terrorized their neighbours. During the ninth and tenth centuries these heretics in Armenia, Asia Minor, and Thrace constantly occupied the attention of the government and the Church. The "Selicians", converted by the Patriarch Methodius I (842–46), were Paulicians. Photius wrote against them and boasts in his Encyclical (866) that he has converted a great number. In Armenia the sect continued in the "Thonraketzi" founded by a certain Smbat in the ninth century. Conybeare attributes to this Smbat a work, "The Key of Truth", which he has edited. It accepts the Old Testament and the Sacraments of Baptism, Penance, and the Eucharist. This work especially has persuaded many writers that the Paulicians were much maligned people. But in any case it represents a very late stage of their history, and it is disputed whether it is really Paulician at all. Constantine IX persuaded or forced many thousands to renounce their errors.

The emperor Alexius Comnenus is credited with having put an end to the heresy. During a residence at Philippopolis he argued with them and converted all, or nearly all, back to the Church (so his daughter: "Alexias", XV, 9). From this time the Paulicians practically disappear from history. But they left traces of their heresy. In Bulgaria the Bogomile sect, which lasted through the Middle Ages and spread to the West in the form of Cathari, Albigenses, and other Manichæan heresies, is a continuation of Paulicianism. In Armenia, too, similar sects, derived from them, continue till our own time.

There were Paulician communities in the part of Armenia occupied by Russia after the war of 1828–29. Conybeare publishes very curious documents of their professions of faith and disputations with the Gregorian bishop about 1837 (Key of Truth, xxiii–xxviii). It is from these disputations and "The Key of Truth" that he draws his picture of the Paulicians as simple, godly folk who had kept an earlier (sc. Adoptionistic) form of Christianity (ibid., introduction).

III. SOURCES.—There are four chief documents:

(1) Photius, Four books against the Paulicians (Διήγησις περὶ τῆς τῶν νεοφάντων μανιχαίων ἀναβλαστήσεως), in P. G., CII, 15–264. (2) Euthymius Zigabenus, in his "Panoplia", XXIV [P. G., CXXX, 1189, sqq., separate edition of the part about the Paulicians, ed. Gieseler (Göttingen, 1841)]. (3) Peter the Abbot, "Concerning the Paulicians and Manichees", ed. Gieseler (Göttingen, 1849), who identifies the author with Petrus Siculus, who wrote a "Historia Manichæorum qui Pauliciani dicuntur", first published by Rader (Ingolstadt, 1604), of which work Gieseler considers "Concerning the Paulicians" to be merely an excerpt. (4) George Monachos, "Chronikon", ed. Muralt (St. Petersburg, 1853).

Of Photius's work only book I contains the history; the rest is a collection of homilies against the heresy. There is interdependence between these four sources. The present state of criticism (due chiefly to Karapet Ter-Mkrttschian) is this:—Photius's account (book I) falls into two parts. Chapters i–xiv are authentic, xv–xxvii a later edition. The original source of all is lost. George Monachos used this. Peter the Monk either copied George or used the original work. Photius may have used Peter (so Ter-Mrkttschian) or perhaps the original. Derived from these are Zigabenus and the spurious part of Photius's book. Bonwetsch (Realencyklopädie für prot. Theol., 3rd ed., Leipzig, 1904, XV, 50) represents (according to Friedrich and as probable only) the order of derivation as: (1) An account contained in a MS. of the tenth century (Cod. Scorial., I, Φ, 1, fol. 164 sqq.), ed. Friedrich in the "Sitzungsbericht der Münchener Akademie", (1896), 70–81; (2) Photius, i–x; (3) George Monachos; (4) Peter the Abbot; (5) Zigabenus; (6) Pseudo-Photius, x–xxvii; (7) Petrus Siculus.

Other sources are the Armenian bishop, John Ozniensis [ed. by Aucher (Venice, 1834), and used by Döllinger and Conybeare], and the "Key of Truth" [Mrkttschian in "Zeitschrift für Kirchengeschichte", 1895, and Conybeare's edition, Armenian and English, with introduction and notes (Oxford, 1898)].

TER-MKRTTSCHIAN, *Die Paulicianer im byzantinischen Kaiserreich und verwandte ketzerische Erscheinungen in Armenien* (Leipzig, 1893); DÖLLINGER, *Beiträge zur Sektengeschichte des Mittelalters*, I (Munich, 1890), 1–31; LOMBARD, *Pauliciens, Bulgares et Bonshommes* (Geneva, 1879); HERGENRÖTHER, *Photius*, III (Ratisbon, 1869), 143–53; GIBBON, *Decline and Fall*, ed. BURY, VI (London, 1898), liv, and appendix 6; ADENEY, *The Greek and Eastern Churches* (Edinburgh, 1908), v.

ADRIAN FORTESCUE.

Pauline Privilege. See DIVORCE.

Paulinus, SAINT, Archbishop of York, d. at Rochester, 10 Oct., 644. He was a Roman monk in St. Andrew's monastery at Rome, and was sent by St. Gregory the Great in 601, with St. Mellitus and others, to help St. Augustine and to carry the pallium to him. He laboured in Kent—with the possible exception of a mission to East Anglia before 616—till 625, when he accompanied Ethelburga (Æthelburh), the sister of King Eadbald of Kent, when she went to the Northumbrian Court to marry King Edwin, then a pagan (see EDWIN, SAINT). Before leaving Kent, he was consecrated bishop by St. Justus, Archbishop of Canterbury. He was successful in converting Edwin and large numbers of his people, the king's baptism taking place on 12 April, 627. With the assistance of St. Edwin, he established his see at York and began to build a stone church there. His apostolic labours in instructing and baptizing the people of the north country were unceasing, and tradition perpetuates his ministry at Yeavering, Catterick Bridge, Dewsbury, Easingwold, Southwell, and elsewhere, while his own name is preserved in the village of Pallingsburn in Northumbria. On the defeat of St. Edwin in 633, Paulinus carried the queen and her children safely to Kent; and, as the heathen reaction under Penda made missionary work impossible in Northumbria, he devoted himself to the Diocese of Rochester, then vacant.

It was after his flight that he received the pallium from Rome (634), sent to him as Archbishop of York. Though Anglican writers have disagreed among themselves as to whether he was justified in leaving his archbishopric, Catholic writers, following St. Bede, have held that he had no choice and was the best judge of what was advisable under the circumstances. St. Bede describes him as tall and thin with a slightly stooping figure; he had black hair and an aquiline nose and was of venerable and awe-inspiring aspect. He was buried in his church at Rochester, and, on the rebuilding of the cathedral, his relics were translated by Archbishop Lanfranc to a silver shrine where they lay till the Reformation. His festival is observed in England on 10 Oct., the anniversary of his death.

BEDE, *Hist. Ecc.*, II, ix, xii–xiv, xvi–xx; *Anglo-Saxon Chronicle*, ann. 601, 625, 633, and 644; *Registrum Roffense* (London, 1769); ALCUIN, *De pontif. eccl. Ebor.* in P. L., CI; CAPGRAVE, *Nova Legenda Angliæ* (Oxford, 1901); *Acta SS.*, V, October; *Bibl. hagiog. lat.* (Brussels, 1901); CHALLONER, *Britannia Sancta* (London, 1745); BUTLER, *Lives of the Saints*, 10 Oct.; KEMBLE, *Codex Diplomaticus ævi Saxonici* (London, 1839–48); HADDAN AND STUBBS, *Ecclesiastical Documents*, I, III (Oxford, 1869–78); BRIGHT, *Chapters of Early Eng. Church Hist.* (Oxford, 1878); RAINE, *Historians of the Church of York*, Rolls Series (London, 1879–94); BIRCH, *Cartularium Saxonicum* (London, 1885–93); RAINE in *Dict. Christ. Biog.*, s. v. *Paulinus* (20); STANTON, *Menology* (London, 1892), 10 Oct.; SEARLE, *Anglo-Saxon Bishops, Kings and Nobles* (Cambridge, 1899); HUNT in *Dict. Nat. Biog.*, s. v.; CABROL, *Angleterre chrétienne avant les Normands* (Paris, 1909).

EDWIN BURTON.

Paulinus, SAINT, BISHOP OF NOLA (PONTIUS MEROPIUS ANICIUS PAULINUS), b. at Bordeaux about 354; d. 22 June, 431. He sprang from a distinguished family of Aquitania and his education was entrusted to the poet Ausonius. He became governor of the Province of Campania, but he soon realized that he could not find in public life the happiness he sought. From 380 to 390 he lived almost entirely in his native land. He married a Spanish lady, a Christian named Therasia. To her, to Bishop Delphinus of Bordeaux and his successor the Presbyter Amandus, and to St. Martin of Tours, who had cured him of some disease of the eye, he owed his conversion. He and his brother were baptized at the same time by Delphinus. When Paulinus lost his only child eight days after birth, and when he was threatened with the charge of having murdered his brother, he and his wife decided to withdraw from the world, and to enter the monastic life. They went to Spain about 390.

At Christmas, 394, or 395, the inhabitants of Barcelona obliged him to be ordained, which was not canonical as he had not previously received the other orders. Having had a special devotion to St. Felix, who was buried at Nola in Campania, he laid out a fine avenue leading to the church containing Felix's tomb, and beside it he erected a hospital. He decided to settle down there with Therasia; and he distributed the largest part of his possessions among the poor. In 395 he removed to Nola, where he led a rigorous, ascetic, and monastic life, at the same time contributing generously to the Church, the aqueduct at Nola, and the construction of basilicas in Nola, Fondi etc. The basilica at Nola counted five naves and had on each side four additions or chapels (*cubicula*), and an apsis arranged in a clover shape. This was connected with the old mortuary chapel of St. Felix by a gallery. The side was richly decorated with marble, silver lamps and lustres, paintings, statuary, and inscriptions. In the apsis was a mosaic which represented the Blessed Trinity, and of which in 1512 some remnants were still found.

About 409 Paulinus was chosen Bishop of Nola. For twenty years he discharged his duties in a most praiseworthy manner. His letters contain numerous Biblical quotations and allusions; everything he performed in the spirit of the Bible and expressed in Biblical language. Gennadius mentions the writings of Paulinus in his continuation of St. Jerome's "De

Viris Illustribus" (xlix). The panegyric on the Emperor Theodisius is unfortunately lost, as are also the "Opus sacramentorum et hymnorum", the "Epistolæ ad Sororem", the "Liber de Pænitentia", the "Liber de Laude Generali Omnium Martyrum", and a poetical treatment of the "De Regibus" of Suetonius which Ausonius mentions. Forty-nine letters to friends have been preserved, as those to Sulpicius Severus, St. Augustine, St. Delphinus, Bishop Victricius of Rouen, Desiderius, Amandus, Pammachius etc. Thirty-three poems are also extant. After 395 he composed annually a very long poem for the feast of St. Felix, in which he principally glorified the life, works, and miracles of his holy patron. Then going further back he brought in various religious and poetic motives. The epic parts are very vivid, the lyrics full of real, unaffected enthusiasm and an ardent appreciation of nature. Thirteen of these festal poems and fragments of the fourteenth have been preserved.

Conspicuous among his other works are the poetic epistles to Ausonius, the nuptial hymn to Julianus, which extols the dignity and sanctity of Christian marriage, and the poem of comfort to the parents of Celsus on the death of their child. Although Paulinus has great versatility and nicety, still he is not entirely free from the mannerisms and ornate culture of his period. All his writings breathe a charming, ideal personality, freed from all terrestrial attachments, ever striving upward. According to Augustine, he also had an exaggerated idea concerning the veneration of saints and relics. His letter xxxii, written to Sulpicius Severus, has received special attention because in it he describes the basilica of Nola, which he built, and gives copious accounts of the existence, construction, and purpose of Christian monuments. From Paulinus too we have information concerning St. Peter's in Rome. During his lifetime Paulinus was looked upon as a saint. His body was first interred in the cathedral of Nola; later, in Benevento; thence it was conveyed by Otto III to S. Bartolomeo all' Isola, in Rome, and finally in compliance with the regulation of Pius X of 18 Sept., 1908 (Acta Apostolicæ Sedis, I, 245 sq.) it was restored to the cathedral of Nola. His feast, 22 June, was raised to the rank of a double.

Sancti Paulini Nolani Epistolæ et Carmina, ed. HARTEL in *Corpus scriptorum ecclesiasticorum latinorum*, XXIX, XXX (Vienna, 1894); BUSE, *Paulin, Bischof von Nola*, I, II (Ratisbon, 1856); LAGRANGE, *Histoire de St. Paulin de Nole* (2nd ed., Paris, 1882); LAFON, *Paulin de Nole* (Montauban, 1885); BAUMGARTNER, *Geschichte der Weltliteratur*, IV (Freiburg, 1900), 143–51; HOLTZINGER, *Die Basilika des Paulinus zu Nola* in *Zeitschrift für bildende Kunst*, XX (Leipzig, 1885), 135-41; AUGUSTI, *Beiträge zur christlichen Kunstgeschichte und Liturgik*, I (Leipzig, 1841), 146–79.

KLEMENS LÖFFLER.

Paulinus II, SAINT, PATRIARCH OF AQUILEIA, b. at Premariacco, near Cividale, Italy, about 730–40; d. 802. Born probably of a Roman family during Longobardic rule in Italy, he was brought up in the patriarchal schools at Cividale. After ordination he became master of the school. He acquired a thorough Latin culture, pagan and Christian. He had also a deep knowledge of jurisprudence, and extensive Scriptural, theological, and patristic training. This learning won him the favour of Charlemagne. After the destruction of the Kingdom of the Longobards in 774, Charles invited Paulinus to France in 776, to be royal master of "grammar". He assisted in restoring civilization in the West.

In 777 Paulinus made his first acquaintance with Petrus of Pisa, Alcuin, Arno, Albrico, Bona, Riculph, Raefgot, Rado, Lullus, Bassinus, Fuldrad, Eginard, Adalard, and Adelbert, the leading men of that age. His devotion to Charlemagne was rewarded by many favours, among them the gift of the property of Waldand, son of Mimo of Lavariano, with a diploma dated from Ivrea, and his appointment by Charles as Patriarch of Aquileia in 787. Paulinus took a prominent part in the important matters of his day. In his relations with the churches of Istria, or with the Patriarch of Grado, the representative of Byzantine interests, he showed the greatest prudence and pastoral zeal. Paulinus obtained diplomas for the free election of the future patriarchs, and other privileges for the Church of Aquileia, viz. the monastery of St. Mary in Organo, the church of St. Laurence of Buia, the hospitals of St. John at Cividale and St. Mary at Verona. He helped in preparing the new Christian legislation, and amongst the "Italic Capitularia" we find some canons of his synods.

In 792 he was present at the Council of Ratisbon, which condemned the heresy of Adoptionism taught by Eliphand and Felix, Bishop of Urgel. In 794 he took a leading part in the national Synod of Frankfort-on-the-Main, where Adoptionism was again condemned, and wrote a book against it, which was sent to Spain in the name of the council. Leaving Frankfort Paulinus paid a visit to Cividale and accompanied Pepin against the Avars. At Salzburg he presided over a synod of bishops, in which were discussed the evangelization of the barbarians, and baptism, as we learn from letters of Charles, Alcuin, Arno, and Paulinus. Returning from the expedition the patriarch once more opposed the Adoptionists at the Synod of Cividale in 796. Paulinus expounded the Catholic doctrine about the Blessed Trinity, especially about the procession of the Holy Ghost from the Father and the Son. At this synod fourteen "canons" on ecclesiastical discipline, and on the sacrament of marriage, were framed and a copy of the Acts was sent to the emperor. Paulinus is said to have assisted at the Council of Altinum, but Hefele has proved that a council was never held there. In 798 he was "Missus Dominicus" of Charlemagne at Pistoia, with Arno and ten other bishops; and afterwards he went to Rome as imperial legate to the pope. The activity of Paulinus as metropolitan is clear from the "Sponsio Episcoporum ad S. Aquileiensem Sedem".

Among his works are: "Libellus Sacrosyllabus contra Elipandum"; "Libri III contra Felicem"; the protocol of the conference with Pepin and the bishops on the Danube, a work very important for the history of that expedition. Paulinus was also a poet, and we still possess some of his poetical productions: "Carmen de regula fidei"; the "rythmus" or elegy for the death of his friend, Duke Heric, killed in battle, 799; another rhythm on the destruction of Aquileia; eight rhythms or hymns to be sung in his own church for Christmas, the Purification, Lent, Easter, St. Mark, Sts. Peter and Paul, the dedication, and "Versus de Lazaro". He died revered as a saint. In MSS. prior to the Martyrology of Usuard his feast is recorded on 11 Jan. In the calendars of saints of the thirteenth, fourteenth and fifteenth centuries, used in the Church of Aquileia and Cividale, his feast has a special rubric. The first appearance of the name St. Paulinus in the Liturgy occurs in the "Litaniæ" of Charles the Bald of the ninth century. It appears also in the "Litaniæ Carolinæ", in the "Litaniæ a S. Patribus constitutæ", and finally in the "Litaniæ" of the Gertrudian MS. of the tenth century. Down to he sixteenth century the feast was celebrated on 11 Jan., during the privileged octave of the Epiphany. The patriarch Francesco Barbaro at the beginning of the seventeenth century translated the feast to 9 Feb. The Church of Cividale keeps his feast on 2 March. After several translations the relics of the saintly patriarch were laid to rest under the altar of the crypt of the basilica of Cividale del Friuli.

Acta SS., Jan., I, 713–18; ALCUIN, *Letters and Poems* in JAFFÉ, *Bibl. Rer. German.*, VI; AMELLI, *Paolo Diacono, Carlomagno e Paolino d'Aquileia* (Monte Cassino, 1899); BÄHR, *Geschichte d. Röm. Litteratur i. Karol. Zeitalter* (Karlsrühe, 1840); BELLONI, *Patriarchi Aquilejesi* in MURATORI, *Rer. Ital. Script.*, XVI, i, 32; BRANDILEONE, *Note ad alcuni canoni* (Cividale, 1900); CALISSE, *San Paolino* in *Riv. Intern.* (Sept., 1900); CARDUCCI, *La risurre-*

zione in A. Manzoni e in S. Paolino, vol. X (Bologna, 1898); Centenario di S. Paolino, numero unico (Cividale, 1906); CEILLIER, Histoire générale des auteurs sacrés (Paris, 1862); DE RUBEIS, Monumenta Eccl. Aquilejensis (Strasburg, 1740); IDEM, Dissertationes variæ eruditionis (Venice, 1762); Diplomata of Charles the Great in P. L.; DÜMMLER, Mon. Germ. Hist.: Poet. Lat. œv. Karol. I, 160-351 (Hanover, 1875-89); ELLERO, S. Paolino Patriarca d'Aquileia (Cividale, 1901); FOSCHIA, S. Paolino (Udine, 1884); GIANNONI, Paulinus II Patriarch von Aquileja (Vienna, 1896); LEICHT, I diplomi imperiali concessi ai Patriarchi d'Aquileja (Udine, 1895); HOEPLI, Miscellanea per il XI Centenario di S. Paolino (Milan, 1905); TAMASSIA, Paolo Diacono (Cividale, 1900); TIRABOSCHI, Storia d. lett. Ital., III (Rome, 1782); WIEGAND, Paulinus von Aquileia.

ALUIGI COSSIO.

Paulinus a S. Bartholomæo (PHILIP WESDIN), missionary and Orientalist, b. at Hoff in Lower Austria, 25 Apr., 1748; d. in Rome, 7 Jan., 1806. Having entered the Carmelite Order, he was sent in 1774 as missionary to India (Malabar) and there was appointed vicar general of his order and Apostolic visitor. Recalled in 1789 to Rome to give an account of the state of that mission, he was charged with the edition of books for the use of missionaries. On account of political troubles he stayed from 1798 to 1800 at Vienna. He returned to Rome as prefect of studies at the Propaganda. Paulinus is the author of many learned books on the East, which were highly valued in their day and have contributed much to the study and knowledge of Indian literature and Indian life. We are indebted to him for the first printed Sanskrit grammar. The following are some of his more important works:

(1) "Systema brahmanicum liturgicum, mythologicum, civile, ex monumentis indicis musei Borgiani Velitris dissertationibus historico-criticis illustratum" (Rome, 1791), translated into German (Gotha, 1797); (2) "Examen historico-criticum codicum indicorum bibliothecæ S. C. de Propaganda" (Rome, 1792); (3) "Musei Borgiani Velitris codices manuscripti avenses, Peguani, Siamici, Malabarici, Indostani . . . illustrati" (Rome, 1793); (4) "Viaggio alle Indie orientali" (Rome, 1796), translated into German by Förster (Berlin, 1798); (5) "Sidharubam, seu Grammatica sanscridamica, cui accedit dissert. hist. crit. in linguam sanscridamicam vulgo Samscret dictam" (Rome, 1799), another edition of which appeared under the title "Vyacaranam" (Rome, 1804); (6) "India orientalis christiana" (Rome, 1794), an important work for the history of missions in India. Other works bear on linguistics and church history.

BARONE, Vita, precursori ed opere di P. Paolino da S. Bartolomeo (Naples, 1888); HEIMBUCHER, Die Orden und Kongregationen der katholischen Kirche, II (2nd ed., Paderborn, 1907), 568-69.

LIVARIUS OLIGER.

Paulinus of Antioch. See MELETIUS OF ANTIOCH.

Paulinus of Pella, Christian poet of the fifth century; b. at Pella in Macedonia, but of a Bordelaise family. He was the son of an official, which explains his birth in Macedonia and his sojourn at Carthage while he was a child. He soon returned to Bordeaux. He was probably the grandson of the poet Ausonius. At the age of eighty-three he composed an account of his life: "Eucharisticon Deo sub ephemeridis meæ textu". His autobiography is a thanksgiving, although illness, loss of property, and dangers from invasion occupy more space in it than do days of happiness. The account is interesting, for it presents a sincere picture of the period, and the expression of exalted sentiments. Unfortunately the style and versification do not always correspond to the sincerity and the height of inspiration. The date is uncertain. The passage which apparently gives it (474 sqq.) is altered but may be between 459 and 465. The very name of the author has not been preserved by the single MS. of the poem. We know it only through Margarin de La Bigne, the author of the "Bibliotheca Patrum" (Paris, 1579, appendix, VIII), who had handled another manuscript giving the name of Paulinus. The "Eucharisticon" was published by W. Brandes in vol. I of "Poetæ Christiani minores" (1888).

TEUFFEL, Gesch. d. röm. Literatur, §474, 4; EBERT, Gesch. d. Literatur des Mittelalters, I (Leipzig, 1889), 405; DUCHESNE, Fast. épis. de l'ancienne Gaule, II (2nd ed., Paris, 1900), pt. II.

PAUL LEJAY.

Paulists.—From the time that the abode and virtues of St. Paul the first hermit (q. v.) were revealed to St. Anthony, various communities of hermits adopted him as patron. The name Paulists, however, was also applied to the members of congregations established under the patronage of St. Paul the Apostle. (See the articles on BARNABITES; MINIMS; PIARISTS; and THEATINES.)

(1) *Hermits of St. Paul of Hungary*, formed in 1250 by Blessed Eusebius of Gran, of two communities, one founded at Patach in 1215 by Bishop Bartholomew of Pecs who united the scattered hermits of his diocese, and the other consisting of his own followers. In 1246 Blessed Eusebius, canon of the cathedral of Gran, resigned his dignities, distributed his goods among the poor, and withdrew to the solitude of Pisilia, a forest near Zante, to lead a life of penance with a few companions. Four years later he is said to have been admonished in a vision to gather into community the other hermits living in the vicinity, for whom he built a monastery and church. In the same year he proposed and obtained affiliation with the Patach community under the rule prescribed by its founder, and was chosen superior. He received the approbation of Ladislaus, Bishop of Pecs, for the new congregation, but the publication of the decrees of the Lateran Council at this time necessitated a journey to Rome to secure the further sanction of the Holy See. In 1263 a new rule was given the congregation by the Bishop of Pecs, which was superseded by still another drawn up by Andrew, Bishop of Agria, after the death of Eusebius (20 Jan., 1270), and this was followed until 1308, when the permission of the Holy See was obtained to adopt the Rule of St. Augustine. The order was accorded many privileges by succeeding pontiffs, among others that of exemption from episcopal jurisdiction, and provisions were made for the pursuit of higher studies in many of the monasteries, one papal regulation ordaining that no member could be raised to any dignity in the order without the degree of Doctor of Divinity, for which a rigid examination was prescribed.

The congregation spread rapidly through Hungary, where alone it soon numbered 170 houses, and it attained an equal degree of prosperity in other countries, being divided into five flourishing provinces: Hungary, Germany (including Croatia), Poland, Istria, and Sweden. In 1381 the body of St. Paul, patron of the order, was transferred from Venice to the monastery of St. Laurence in Hungary, which thereby gained greatly in prestige. Among the other famous houses of the congregation were the historical Polish monastery of Our Lady of Claremont (commonly called Czestochovia), with its miraculous image of Our Lady (according to legend the work of St. Luke and discovered by St. Helena with the True Cross), and the monasteries at Presburg and Neustadt near Vienna. The church of San Stefano Rotondo at Rome was attached to the Hungarian College by Gregory XIII. In 1783 a number of houses in Austria, Bohemia, Styria, etc. were suppressed, and political disturbances in Hungary brought the same fate to most of the Hungarian convents, which had rendered incalculable services to religion and education. The destruction of the annals of these houses left the historical sources very meagre. There are still a few houses of the congregation in Galicia and Russian Poland, and the church connected with the monastery at Kracow may be regarded as a national sanctuary.

Among the members of the congregation to attain prominence were George Martinuzzi, Bishop of Grosswardein and cardinal (murdered 16 Dec., 1551), an important figure in the history of Hungary; Matthias Fuhrmann of Hernals (d. 1773), historian of Austria and editor of the Acts of St. Paul of Thebes; Fortunatus Dürich (1802), and Franz Faustin Prochaska (d. 1809), editors of a Czech translation of the Scriptures. The garb was originally brown, but about 1341 white was adopted, with a cincture, and over the habit a scapular with a hood. In choir a white mantle is worn.

(2) *Hermits of St. Paul of France*, also called Brothers of Death.—There is much discussion as to the origin of this congregation, but it was probably founded about 1620 by Guillaume Callier, whose constitutions for it were approved by Paul V (18 Dec., 1620) and later by Louis XIII (May, 1621). There were two classes of monasteries, those in the cities, obliged to maintain at least twelve members, who visited the poor, the sick, and prisoners, attended those condemned to death, and buried the dead; and the houses outside the city, with which were connected separate cells in which solitaries lived, the whole community assembling weekly for choir and monthly in chapter to confess their sins. Severe fasts and disciplines were prescribed. The name Brothers of Death originated in the fact that the thought of death was constantly before the religious. At their profession the prayers for the dead were recited; their scapular bore the skull; their salutation was *Memento mori*; the death's head was set before them at table and in their cells. This congregation was suppressed by Urban VIII in 1633.

(3) *Hermits of St. Paul of Portugal*.—Among the conflicting accounts of the foundation of this congregation, the most credible seems to be that it was established about 1420 by Mendo Gomez, a nobleman of Simbria, who resigned dearly bought military laurels to retire to a solitude near Setuval, where he built an oratory and gave himself up to prayer and penance, gradually assuming the leadership of a number of other hermits in the vicinity. Later a community of hermits of Sierra de Ossa, the date of whose foundation is also in dispute, being left without a superior, prevailed on Mendo Gomez to unite the two communities, under the patronage of St. Paul, first hermit. At the chapter held after the death of the founder (24 Jan., 1481), constitutions were drawn up, which at a later date were approved, with some alterations, by Gregory XIII (1578), at the request of Cardinal Henry of Portugal, who also obtained for the congregation the privilege of adopting the Rule of St. Augustine. This congregation was later suppressed. Probably the most celebrated member was Antonius a Matre Dei, author of "Apis Libani", a commentary on the Proverbs of Solomon.

(4) *Blind Sisters of St. Paul*, founded at Paris in 1852, by A. F. Villemain (d. 1870), Anne Bergunion (d. 1863), and the Abbé Jugé, to enable blind women to lead a religious life, and to facilitate the training of blind children in useful occupations. A home was established for blind women and girls with defective sight.

(5) *Sisters of St. Paul of Chartres* (also called to St. Maurice) known also as Hospitallers of Chartres, founded in the latter part of the seventeenth century for teaching and the care of the poor and sick. After the Revolution the congregation was revived, was authorized by the Government in 1811, and soon numbered 1200 sisters and over 100 houses in England, Guadeloupe, Martinique, French Guiana, Corea, China, Japan, Further India, the Philippines, etc. In China a novitiate has been established for native subjects, and in Hong-Kong a school for European children, besides various benevolent institutions. In Further India there are thirty institutions, chiefly of a benevolent nature, in addition to a novitiate, which has already admitted a number of native postulants. In the Philippines are schools and a leper hospital.

HEIMBUCHER, *Orden und Kongregationen* (Paderborn, 1907); HÉLYOT, *Ordres religieux* (Paris, 1859), s. v. EGGERER, *Fragmen panis Corvi proto-eremitici* (Vienna, 1663); cont. by BORKOVICH AND BENGER (Presburg, 1743); MALLECHICH, *Quadripartitum regularium s. de privilegiis et iuribus O. s. Pauli* (Vienna, 1708); *Regulæ s. constitutiones monachorum excalceatorum s. Pauli primi eremitæ cong. Lusitanæ* (Lisbon, 1785); NICOLAS DE MARIA, *Chron. da ord. dos Conegos Regrant. de S. Agostino; La congrégation des sœurs aveugles de St Paul pendant son premier demi-siècle* (Paris, 1903).

FLORENCE RUDGE MCGAHAN.

Paulists. See MISSIONARY SOCIETY OF SAINT PAUL THE APOSTLE.

Paul of Burgos (PAUL DE SANTA MARIA; Jewish name, SOLOMON HA-LEVI), a Spanish archbishop, lord chancellor and exegete, b. at Burgos about 1351; d. 29 Aug., 1435. He was the most wealthy and influential Jew of Burgos, a scholar of the first rank in Talmudic and rabbinical literature, and a Rabbi of the Jewish community. The irresistible logic of the Summa of St. Thomas led him to the Faith of Christ. He received Baptism, 21 July, 1390. His brothers Pedro Suarez and Alvar Garcia, together with his daughter and four boys, aged from three to twelve years, were baptized with him. His wife Joanna died a Jewess shortly after. Paul de Santa Maria, as he was called, spent some years at the University of Paris, where he took his degree of doctor in theology. His sincerity, keen insight into human nature, thorough education, and soul-stirring eloquence marked him out as a prominent churchman of the future. In 1405 he became Bishop of Cartagena; in 1415, Archbishop of Burgos. In 1416 King Henry of Castile named him lord chancellor. After the king's death Archbishop Paul was a member of the council which ruled Castile in the name of the regent Doña Catalina, and by the will of the deceased king he was tutor to the heir to the throne—later John II of Castile. The published writings of Archbishop Paul were:—(1) "Dialogus Pauli et Sauli contra Judæos, sive Scrutinium scripturarum" (Mantua, 1475; Mainz, 1478; Paris, 1507, 1535; Burgos, 1591). (2) "Additiones" to the "Postilla" of Nicholas of Lyra (Nuremberg, 1481; 1485; 1487, etc.; Venice, 1481, 1482, etc.). It is chiefly on the latter work that Paul's reputation as an exegete rests. The "Additiones" were originally mere marginal notes written in a volume of the "Postilla" which he sent to his son Alfonso. Their publication aroused Matthias Döring, the provincial of the Saxon Franciscans, to publish his "Replicæ", a bitter rejection of almost half of the 1100 suggestions and additions Paul had made. The converted Jew was superior to Nicholas of Lyra in Hebrew, but not in Biblical interpretations; in fact, Paul erred in not admitting an inspired allegorical meaning of Holy Writ, prejudiced against it, no doubt, by the extravagance of Talmudic allegorical fancies. (3) "De nomine divino quæstiones duodecim" (Utrecht, 1707). These tracts are excerpts from the "Additiones" in regard to Exod., iii, and are joined to the *scholia* of J. Drusius on the correct pronunciation of the name of Jahweh. Archbishop Paul was succeeded in the See of Burgos by his second son, Alfonso.

SANCTOTIS, *Vita d. Pauli episcopi Burgensis;* MARIANA, *Historia general de España,* IV (Barcelona, 1839), 324; ANTONIO, *Biblioth. hispan. vetus,* II (Madrid, 1788), 237.

WALTER DRUM.

Paul of Middelburg, scientist and bishop, b. in 1446 at Middelburg, the ancient capital of the province of Zealand, belonging then to the German Empire, now to Holland; d. in Rome, 13 December, 1534. After finishing his studies in Louvain he received a canonry in his native town, of which he was afterwards deprived. The circumstances of this fact are not known, but in his apologetic letter on the celebration of Easter he calls it a usurpation, and shows great bitterness against his country, calling it "barbara Zelandiæ insula", "vervecum patria", "cerdonum regio", etc. He then taught for a while in Louvain, was invited by the Signoria of Venice to take a chair for sciences in Padua (1480), travelled through Italy, became physician to Francesco Maria della Rovere, Duke of Urbino, and friend to Maximilian, Archduke of Austria, afterwards emperor. By the former he was endowed with the Benedictine Abbey St. Christophorus in Castel Durante (1488), and by the latter he was recommended to Alexander VI for the Bishopric of Fossombrone (Moroni, LXXXV, 314). Being nominated to that see, in 1494, he destroyed some of his former publications; first "Giudizio dell' anno 1480", in which he had censured a number of mathematicians; then a "Practica de pravis Constellationibus", and a defence of that work against the nephew of Paul II (1484); and finally an "Invectiva in superstitiosum Vatem". He chose for himself an astronomical coat of arms, and, in 1497, enlarged and embellished the episcopal palace. Besides some smaller treatises against usurers and against the superstitious fear of a flood in 1524 (Fossombrone, 1523), he wrote important works on the reform of the Calendar, which procured for him invitations by Julius II and Leo X to the Fifth Lateran Council (1512–1518). His "Epistola ad Universitatem Lovaniensem de Paschate recte observando" (1487) was followed by an "Epistola apologetica" (1488), and finally by his principal work "Paulina, de recta Paschæ celebratione" (Fossombrone, 1513). The contents and result of the work are described under the article LILIUS. He died while assisting at the Divine Office in Rome, and was buried in S. Maria dell' Anima. His family name is unknown, but in one place he is called Paolo di Adriano (Moroni, XLIV, 120). Scaliger, who calls him "Omnium sui sæculi mathematicorum . . . facile princeps", was his godson.

SCHMIDLIN, *Gesch. der deutschen Nationalkirche in Rom* (Freiburg, 1906), 349.

J. G. HAGEN.

Paul of Samosata, Bishop of Antioch. Several synods, probably three, were held against him about 264–66. St. Dionysius of Alexandria had desired to attend the first of these, but was prevented by his infirmities. Firmilian of Cæsarea, St. Gregory Thaumaturgus, his brother Athenodorus, and many others, were present. Paul held the civil office of *Procurator ducenarius*, and was protected by Zenobia, the famous Queen of Palmyra. He was a wealthy man, and had many obsequious followers among neighbouring bishops. Many defended his doctrine, and he declared himself orthodox. In the first meetings the bishops were satisfied. At another Paul was condemned, but promised to retract his errors. This he failed to do. A final council was summoned. Firmilian died on the way to it. The principal part was taken by a priest of Antioch, Malchion, who was an accomplished man of letters and head of the school of Greek literature at Antioch. In disputation with Paul he plainly convicted him of heresy, and procured his deposition. A letter written by Malchion in the name of the synod and addressed to Pope Dionysius of Rome, Maximus of Alexandria, and all the bishops and clergy throughout the world, has been preserved by Eusebius in part; a few fragments only remain of the shorthand report of the disputation.

The letter accuses Paul of acquiring great wealth by illicit means, of showing haughtiness and worldliness, of having set up for himself a lofty pulpit in the church, and of insulting those who did not applaud him and wave their handkerchiefs, and so forth. He had caused scandal by admitting women to live in his house, and had permitted the same to his clergy. Paul could not be driven from his see until the emperor Aurelian took possession of Antioch in 272. Even then he refused to vacate the house belonging to the church. An appeal was made to Aurelian, and the pagan emperor, who was at this time favourable to Christians, decided most justly, says Eusebius (vii, 30, 19), that the house should be given up to those to whom the bishops in Italy and the city of Rome should write;—evidently it had been argued before him that the question of legitimacy depended on communion with Rome, to be granted after examination by the pope and his council. Paul was driven out in utter disgrace by the civil power. Of his life no more is known to us. His doctrine was akin to the dynamistic Monarchianism of Theodoltus, and he was nicknamed a follower of Artemas. We can gather these points: the Father, Son, and Holy Ghost are but a single Person ($\pi\rho\delta\sigma\omega\pi\sigma\nu$). The Son or Logos is without hypostasis, being merely the wisdom and science of God, which is in Him as reason is in a man. Before all worlds He was born as Son ($\Lambda\delta\gamma\sigma\varsigma\ \pi\rho\sigma\phi\sigma\rho\iota\kappa\delta\varsigma$) without a virgin; he is without shape and cannot be made visible to men. He worked in the Prophets, especially in Moses (let us remember that Zenobia was a Jewess, and that this monarchianism may have been intended to please her), and in a far higher way in the Son of David who was born by the Holy Ghost of a Virgin. The Christ, the Saviour, is essentially a man, but the Holy Ghost inspired Him from above. The Father and the Son are one God, whereas Christ is from the earth with a personality of his own. Thus there are two Persons in Christ. The Logos as Wisdom dwelt in the man Jesus, as we live in houses, and worked in Him as inspiration, teaching Him and being with Him, and was united with Him not substantially (or essentially, $\sigma\vartheta\sigma\iota\omega\delta\hat\omega\varsigma$), but qualitatively ($\kappa\alpha\tau\dot\alpha\ \pi\sigma\iota\delta\tau\eta\tau\alpha$). Mary did not bring forth the Word, for she did not exist before the worlds, but a man like to us. Paul denied the inference that there are two Sons. The Son of the Virgin is great by Wisdom, who dwelt in no other so.

Union of two Persons is possible only by agreement of will, issuing in unity of action, and originating by love. By this kind of union Christ had merit; He could have had none had the union been by nature. By the unchangeableness of His will He is like God, and was united to Him by remaining pure from sin. By striving and suffering He conquered the sin of our first parent, and was joined to God, being one with Him in intention and action. God worked in Him to do miracles in order to prove Him the Redeemer and Saviour of the race. By the ever growing and never ceasing movement of friendship He has joined Himself to God so that He can never be separated through all eternity, and His Name is above every Name as a reward of love. Judgment is made over to Him; He may be called "God from the Virgin", "God from Nazareth". He is said to have pre-existed, but this means by predestination only. The baptism of Christ, as usual, was regarded by Paul as a step in His junction with the Logos. If He had been God by nature, Paul argued, there would be two Gods. He forbade hymns to Christ, and openly attacked the older (Alexandrian) interpretations of Scripture.

The party of Paul did not at once disappear. The Council of Nicæa declared the baptism conferred by the Paulianists to be invalid. There is something, though not much, of his teaching in the Lucianist and Arian systems which issued from Antioch. But their Christology was the very opposite of his, which was rather to reappear in a modified form in Theodore of Mopsuestia, Diodorus, Nestorius, and even Theodoret, though these later Antiochenes warmly rejected the imputation of any agreement with the heretic Paul, even in Christology.

It must be regarded as certain that the council which condemned Paul rejected the term $\delta\mu\sigma\sigma\vartheta\sigma\iota\sigma\varsigma$; but naturally only in a false sense used by Paul; not, it seems because he meant by it an unity of Hypostasis in the Trinity (so St. Hilary), but because he intended by it a common substance out of which both Father and Son proceeded, or which it divided between them,—so St. Basil and St. Athanasius; but the question is not clear. The objectors to the Nicene doctrine in the fourth century made copious use of this disapproval of the Nicene word by a famous council.

The fragments are best collected by Routh, "Rell. SS.", III. Further fragments in Pitra, "Analecta sacra", III-IV. The letter of St. Dionysius is spurious. That of six bishops to Paul is usually rejected, but Harnack thinks it genuine, following Hagemann.

HARNACK, *Gesch. der Altchristl. Litt.*, I (1893); BARDENHEWER, *Gesch. der Altkirchlichen litt.*, II (1903); HEFELE, *Councils*, I (tr. 1883); RÉVILLE, *La Christologie de Paul de Samosate* in *Etudes de critique et d'histoire* (Paris, 1896).

JOHN CHAPMAN.

Paul of the Cross, SAINT (PAUL FRANCIS DANEI), b. at Ovada, Genoa, Italy, 3 Jan., 1694; d. in Rome, 18 Oct., 1775. His parents, Luke Danei and Anna Maria Massari, were exemplary Catholics. From his earliest years the crucifix was his book, and the Crucified his model. Paul received his early education from a priest who kept a school for boys, in Cremolino, Lombardy. He made great progress in study and virtue; spent much time in prayer, heard daily Mass, frequently received the Sacraments, faithfully attended to his school duties, and gave his spare time to reading good books and visiting the churches, where he spent much time before the Blessed Sacrament, to which he had an ardent devotion. At the age of fifteen he left school and returned to his home at Castellazzo, and from this time his life was full of trials. In early manhood he renounced the offer of an honourable marriage; also a good inheritance left him by an uncle who was a priest. He kept for himself only the priest's Breviary.

ST. PAUL OF THE CROSS

Inflamed with a desire for God's glory he formed the idea of instituting a religious order in honour of the Passion. Vested in a black tunic by the Bishop of Alessandria, his director, bearing the emblem of our Lord's Passion, barefooted, and bareheaded, he retired to a narrow cell where he drew up the Rules of the new congregation according to the plan made known to him in a vision, which he relates in the introduction to the original copy of the Rules. For the account of his ordination to the priesthood, of the foundation of the Congregation of the Passion, and the approbation of the Rules, see PASSIONISTS. After the approbation of the Rules and the institute the first general chapter was held at the Retreat of the Presentation on Mount Argentaro on 10 April, 1747. At this chapter, St. Paul, against his wishes, was unanimously elected first superior general, which office he held until the day of his death. In all virtues and in the observance of regular discipline, he became a model to his companions. "Although continually occupied with the cares of governing his religious society, and of founding everywhere new houses for it, yet he never left off preaching the word of God, burning as he did with a wondrous desire for the salvation of souls" (Brief of Pius IX for St. Paul's Beatification, 1 Oct., 1852). Sacred missions were instituted and numerous conversions were made. He was untiring in his Apostolic labours and never, even to his last hour, remitted anything of his austere manner of life, finally succumbing to a severe illness, worn out as much by his austerities as by old age.

Among the distinguished associates of St. Paul in the formation and extension of the congregation were: John Baptist, his younger brother and constant companion from childhood, who shared all his labours and sufferings and equalled him in the practice of virtue; Father Mark Aurelius (Pastorelli), Father Thomas Struzzieri (subsequently Bishop of Amelia and afterwards of Todi), and Father Fulgentius of Jesus, all remarkable for learning, piety, and missionary zeal; Venerable Strambi, Bishop of Macerata, and Tolentino, his biographer. Constant personal union with the Cross and Passion of our Lord was the prominent feature of St. Paul's sanctity. But devotion to the Passion did not stand alone, for he carried to a heroic degree all the other virtues of a Christian life. Numerous miracles, besides those special ones brought forward at his beatification and canonization, attested the favour he enjoyed with God. Miracles of grace abounded, as witnessed in the conversion of sinners seemingly hardened and hopeless. For fifty years he prayed for the conversion of England, and left the devotion as a legacy to his sons. The body of St. Paul lies in the Basilica of SS. John and Paul, Rome. He was beatified on 1 October, 1852, and canonized on 29 June, 1867. His feast occurs on 28 April. The fame of his sanctity, which had spread far and wide in Italy during his life, increased after his death and spread into all countries. Great devotion to him is practised by the faithful wherever Passionists are established.

Lives of St. Paul by: STRAMBI in *Oratorian Series* (3 vols., London, 1853); FR. PIUS OF THE NAME OF MARY, tr. by FR. IGNATIUS SPENCER (London and New York); PIUS A SPIRITU SANCTO (London, 1868); and FR. LOUIS OF JESUS AGONIZING (Bordeaux); FR. LUKE C. P., *A great Apostle of the Crucified* (Rome).

ARTHUR DEVINE.

Paul the Hermit, SAINT.—There are three important versions of the Life of St. Paul: (1) the Latin version (*H*) of St. Jerome; (2) a Greek version (*b*), much shorter than the Latin; (3) a Greek version (*a*), which is either a translation of *H* or an amplification of *b* by means of *H*. The question is whether *H* or *b* is the original. Both *a* and *b* were published for the first time by Bidez in 1900 ("Deux versions grecques inédites de la vie de s. Paul de Thèbes", Ghent). Bidez maintains that *H* was the original Life. This view has been attacked by Nau, who makes *b* the original in the "Analect. Bolland." of 1901 (XX, 121–157). The Life, minor details excepted, is the same in either version.

When a young man of sixteen Paul fled into the desert of the Thebaid during the Decian persecution. He lived in a cave in the mountain-side till he was one-hundred-and-thirteen. The mountain, adds St. Jerome, was honeycombed with caves.

When he was ninety St. Anthony was tempted to vain-glory, thinking he was the first to dwell in the desert. In obedience to a vision he set forth to find his predecessor. On his road he met with a demon in the form of a centaur. Later on he spied a tiny old man with horns on his head. "Who are you?" asked Antony. "I am a corpse, one of those whom the heathen call satyrs, and by them were snared into idolatry." This is the Greek story (*b*) which makes both centaur and satyr unmistakably demons, one of which tries to terrify the saint, while the other acknowledges the overthrow of the gods. With St. Jerome the centaur may have been a demon; and may also have been "one of those monsters of which the desert is so prolific." At all events he tries to show the saint the way. As for the satyr he is a harmless little mortal deputed by his brethren to ask the saint's blessing. One asks, on the supposition that the Greek is the original, why St. Jerome changes devils into centaurs and satyrs. It is not surprising that stories of St. Anthony meeting fabulous beasts in his mysterious journey should spring up among people with whom belief in such creatures lingered on, as belief in fairies does to the present day. The stories of the meeting of St. Paul and St. Anthony, the raven who brought them bread, St. Anthony being sent to fetch the cloak given him by "Athanasius the bishop" to bury St. Paul's body in, St. Paul's death before he returned, the grave dug by lions, are among the familiar legends of the Life. It only remains to add that belief in the existence of St. Paul seems to have existed quite independently of the Life.

Besides the writings of BIDEZ and NAU, see BUTLER, *Lausiac Hist.*, etc., pt. i, p. 285, where he criticises Amélineau's view that the Coptic version published by him was the original (Amélineau's view seems to have found no supporters), and maintains the claim of the Latin. In *Journ. of Theolog. Studies*, III, 152, there is a notice concerning Bidez where Amélineau again expresses the same opinion; later in a notice concerning Nau (*ibid.*, V, 151), while still inclining to his old opinion, he says that after reading Nau he is "unable to arrive at a decision." The BOLLANDISTS (I, Jan., 602) gave a Latin translation of a Greek version (the original will be found in *Analect. Bol.*, XI, 563), maintaining it was the original. FUHRMANN in 1750 (*Acta Sincera S. Pauli, etc.*) published, as the original, another Greek version.

F. J. BACCHUS.

Paul the Simple, SAINT.—The story of Paul, as Palladius heard it from men who had known St. Anthony, was as follows: Paul was a husbandman, very simple and guileless. One day, on discovering the infidelity of his wife, he set off to be a monk. He knocked at the door of St. Anthony's cell. This is the substance of the dialogue which ensued: A. "What do you want?" P. "To be a monk." A. "It is quite impossible for you, a man of sixty. Be content with the life of a labourer, giving thanks to God." P. "Whatsoever you teach me I will do." A. "If a monk you must be, go to a cenobium. I live here alone only eating once in five days." With this St. Anthony shut the door, and Paul remained outside. On the fourth day St. Anthony, fearing lest he should die, took him in. He set him to work weaving a rope out of palm leaves, made him undo what he had done, and do it again. When it was evening he asked him if he was ready to eat. Just as St. Anthony liked, was the reply. St. Anthony produced some crusts, took one himself, and gave the old man three. Then followed a long grace—one Psalm said twelve times over, and as many prayers. When each had eaten a crust Paul was told to take another. P. "If you do, I will; if you don't, I won't." A. "I am a monk, and one is enough for me." P. "It is enough for me, for I am going to be a monk." Then came twelve prayers and as many Psalms, followed by a little sleep till midnight, and then again psalms were recited till it was day. Finally Paul got what he wanted. After he had lived with Anthony some months, the saint gave him a cell for himself some miles from his own. In a year's time the grace of healing and casting out devils was bestowed upon Paul. Then follows a story of how he was able to exorcize a fiend over whom even St. Anthony had no power.

ST. PAUL THE HERMIT.

The story of St. Paul in the "Hist. monachorum" is, as regards substantial facts, much the same as that of "Palladius", but the atmosphere is different. In "Palladius" St. Anthony is living quite alone; in the "Historia" he is a kind of abbot of hermits. In "Palladius" he is reluctant to accept Paul; in the "Historia" he invites him to be a monk. In "Palladius" St. Anthony's purpose is to show Paul just what a hermit's life really was; in the "Historia" he subjects him to the rather conventional kinds of tests which any abbot might apply to any postulant. The difference seems to amount chiefly to this:—"Palladius" apparently places the story in the time before, and the "Historia" after St. Anthony began to have disciples. For different anecdotes concerning Paul the reader may be referred to Butler's "Lives of the Saints" or to Tillemont.

BUTLER, *Lausiac Hist. of Palladius*, pt. ii, 69–74, 201; TILLEMONT, *H. E.*, VII, 144; BUDGE, *Paradise of the Holy Fathers*, I, 125 sqq. (the story given in the last is a translation of Palladius).

F. J. BACCHUS.

Paulus Diaconus, also called CASINENSIS, LEVITA, and WARNEFRIDI, historian, b. at Friuli about 720; d. 13 April, probably 799. He was a descendant of a noble Lombard family, and it is not unlikely that he was educated at the court of King Rachis at Pavia, under the direction of Flavianus the grammarian. In 763 we find him at the court of Duke Archis at Benevento, after the collapse of the Lombard kingdom, a monk in the monastery of Monte Cassino, and in 782 in the suite of Charlemagne, from whom he obtained by means of an elegy the release of a brother taken prisoner in 776 in consequence of the Friuli insurrection. After 787 he was again at Monte Cassino, where in all probability he died. His first literary work, evidently while he was still at Benevento, and done at the request of the Duchess Adelperga, was the "Historia Romana", an amplified and extended version of the Roman history of Eutropius, whose work he continued independently in Books XI to XVI, up to the time of Justinian. This compilation, now of no value, but during the Middle Ages diffused in many manuscript editions and frequently consulted, was edited with the work of Eutropius by Droysen in "Mon. Germ. Hist.: Auct. antiq.", II (1879), 4–224. Furthermore, at the instance of Angilram, Bishop of Metz, he compiled a history of the bishops of Metz "Liber de episcopis Mettensibus", or "Liber de ordine et numero episcoporum in civitate Mettensi" extending to 766, in which he gives a circumstantial account of the family and ancestors of Charlemagne, especially Arnulf (P. L., XCV, 699–722).

The most important historical work which has come down to us from his pen is the history of the Lombards, "Historia gentis Langobardorum. Libri VI", the best of the many editions of this work being that of Bethmann and Waitz in "Mon. Germ. Hist.: Script. rerum Langobardarum", (1878), 45–187; school ed. (Hanover, 1878); Ger. tr. Abel (Berlin, 1849; 2nd ed., Leipzig, 1878); Faubert (Paris, 1603); It. tr. Viviani (Udine, 1826). Despite many defects, especially in the chronology, the unfinished work, embracing only the period between 568 and 744, is still of the highest importance, setting forth as it does in lucid style and simple diction the most important facts, and preserving for us many ancient myths and popular traditions replete with an enthusiastic interest in the changing fortunes of the Lombard people. That this work was in constant use until well into the fifteenth century is evident from the numerous manuscript copies, excerpts, and continuations extant. In addition to these historical works, Paulus also wrote a commentary on the Rule of St. Benedict, and a widely-used collection of homilies entitled "Homiliarium", both of which have been preserved only in revised form. Several letters, epitaphs, and poems are still extant, and have been edited by Dümmler in "Mon. Germ. Hist.: Poetæ lat. ævi Carolini", I, 1881.

BETHMANN, *Paulus Diaconus leben und schriften und die geschichtschreibung der Langobarden* in *Archiv der Gesellschaft für älter deutsche Geschichtskunde*, X (Hanover, 1851); WATTENBACH, *Deutschlands Geschichtsquellen*, I (Berlin, 1893), 163–71; POTTHAST, *Bibliotheca historica*, II (Berlin, 1896), 898–905.

PATRICIUS SCHLAGER.

Paulus Venetus, theologian of the Hermits of the Order of Saint Augustine, b. according to the chroniclers of his order, at Udine, about 1368; d. at Venice, 15 June, 1428. He made his religious profession in the Convent of Saint Stephen, Venice, whence the name, Venetus. In 1390 he is said to have been sent to Oxford for his studies in theology, but returned to Italy, and finished his course at Padua. He lectured in the University at Padua during the first quarter of the fifteenth century. His writings, aside from any question of their present worth, show a wide knowledge and interest in the scientific problems of his time. Besides the usual lectures on the four books of "Sentences", sermons, and instructions, he wrote "De Conceptione B. Mariæ Virginis", "De quadratura circuli", "De circulis componentibus mundum", "Logica parva et logica magna". This last, also known as "Logica Duplex", was largely used as a textbook during the fifteenth and sixteenth centuries, and was several times reprinted. Paulus was one of the theologians called to Rome in 1427, by Martin V, to take cognizance of the charges brought against St. Bernardine of Siena, occasioned by the preaching of the "new devotion" to the Holy Name.

LANTERI, *Postrema sæcula sex religionis Augustinianæ* (Tolentino, 1858); ARPE, *Pantheon Augustinianum* (Genoa, 1709).

FRANCIS E. TOURSCHER.

Pavia, DIOCESE OF (PAPIA), in Lombardy, Northern Italy. It is situated in a fertile plain; the city is connected with Milan by the Naviglio canal. It was once famous for the manufacture of organs. Of its many medieval towers, which gave to it the name of "city of the hundred towers", few remain; a covered bridge dating from the fourteenth century is worthy of note. The cathedral was built by Rocchi and Omodeo (1488) on the site of the churches of San Stefano and Santa Maria del Popolo; it contains paintings by Crespi, Gatti, and others; a beautiful silver reliquary of the Holy Thorns, and a carved pulpit by Zanella; the altar of St. Syrus, in the crypt, is by Orseolo. The Church of San Pietro in Ciel d'Oro is the former cathedral, restored in the twelfth century; it receives its present name from the golden background of its mosaics; the body of St. Augustine is preserved in this church; King Luitprand brought it here from Sardinia and concealed it. It was rediscovered in 1695 in a casket of lead and silver, within a marble enclosure; there were lengthy proceedings for its identification; the marble tomb is an exquisite production of the fourteenth century, ordered by the prior Bonifacio, of the family of the marquesses Bottigello; it is adorned with 50 bas-reliefs and 95 statuettes. Boethius is also buried there. Other churches are: Santa Maria del Carmine (1376), a Gothic structure, contains beautiful paintings; San Francesco (1260), also Gothic; Santa Maria di Canepanova (1492), planned by Bramante, an octagonal building with a cupola and beautiful frescoes, contains the mausoleum of the Duke of Brunswick; San Teodoro, Lombard period, under its altar are St. Theodore's relics; San Michele Maggiore (seventh century), where the kings were crowned, the most notable monument of Lombard architecture, contains a crucifix of the eighth century; San Marino, built by King Astolfo, and restored in 1481; Sts. Primo and Feliciano; Santa Maria in Bethlem, a Lombard structure; San Salvatore (seventh century), contains tombs of several Lombard kings; San Lanfranco (1237), contains the tomb of its patron saint, made by order of Cardinal Pallavicino in 1498. Outside the city is the famous Certosa, founded by Gian Galeazzo Visconti; its façade (1491) reflects the Lombard style, but with a marvellous variety of ornament and sculpture; it is divided into three naves by Gothic pillars; the *baldachina* of the altars of the side chapels are all of costly mosaics; the paintings are mostly by Borgognone, although there are some by Perugino, Mantegna, Pordenone, and others; the choir stalls are of inlaid work; the tomb of Gian Galeazzo and the figures taken from the tombs of Lodovico il Moro and of his wife are the most beautiful productions of Lombard sculpture.

Among the secular buildings are: the Castello Visconteo (1360), despoiled by Louis XII, who carried away its library; the university, which grew out of the grammar schools and the schools of Roman and of Lombard law, enlarged by Maria Theresa and Joseph II, with several colleges connected with it, viz. the Ghislieri college (St. Pius V), the Borromeo college (St. Charles), the Gandini college (St. Augustine), and others; and the Museo Civico has a picture gallery, a library, and a collection of copper engravings.

Pavia is the ancient *Ticinum*, founded by the Lævi and Marici, two Ligurian peoples; at a date not well determined it came under Roman power, and was given to the Papia tribe, whence the name of *Papia*, which, however, does not occur before the time of Paulus Diaconus. In A. D. 271, Emperor Aurelian inflicted there a decisive defeat upon the Alamanni; the city was destroyed by Alaric (452); Odoacer, however, transformed it into a stronghold, and stationed there his Heruli and Rugii; Theodoric built a royal palace at Pavia, also an amphitheatre, thermæ etc. Throughout the Gothic War, the city was held by the Goths, although they were defeated in a battle near there in 538. Pavia resisted Alboin, King of the Lombards, for three years, and then became the capital of the Lombard Kingdom, and when it was taken from the Lombards by Charlemagne (battles of Pavia of 754, 755, and 774), it remained the capital of the Kingdom of Italy, where the diets of that realm were held. In the tenth century, the Hungarians brought devastation upon the city on several occasions, especially in 924.

The schools of Pavia were famous in the time of Charlemagne, who took from there the grammarian Petrus Pisanus; in 825 a palatine school was established in the monastery of San Agostino, under the Irishman Dungal. In 901 Berengarius besieged Louis of Provence in Pavia. When Emperor St. Henry II, after defeating Arduin of Ivrea in 1004, was crowned King of Italy at Pavia, the citizens rose against him, and set fire to the town. At his death they destroyed the imperial palace, and resisted Conrad the Salian for two years. The republican Government of the city began at this time, but the period of continual wars against neighbouring cities continued: Milan (1061, 1100), Piacenza, Tortona (1109); Pavia, however, was almost always in alliance with Cremona. On the other hand, it gave assistance to Milan in 1110 against Emperor Henry V, and also in the war of Como, in 1127; but from the beginning of the reign of Barbarossa, it became strongly imperialist, while the emperors were prodigal in bestowing rights and privileges upon the city, e. g. allowing it to elect its own

THE CERTOSA, NEAR PAVIA (LATE XV CENTURY)

consuls. The coins of Pavia were in great demand, while its agriculture and its industries flourished. The city was able in war-time to arm 15,000 infantry and 3000 mounted troops. Pavia remained Ghibelline even under Frederick II (1227), and in 1241 its forces defeated the Pontifical Crusaders under Gregorio da Montelongo. In the second half of the thirteenth century contentions for the lordship of the city arose between the Langosco and the Beccaria families; and this made it possible for Matteo Visconti (1315) to occupy the town, for which, however, the marquesses of Montferrat also contended, until Galeazzo II Visconti in 1359 suppressed the brief popular government that was established by the Augustinian preacher, Jacopo Bussolari (1356–59). From that time on, Pavia belonged to the Duchy of Milan; the Sforzas, however, gave it a Government of its own. In 1499 Louis XII took the city, and thereafter severely punished an insurrection of the town against him. In 1524 Pavia was again besieged unsuccessfully by the French; and, in the following year, the battle that decided the Spanish domination of Milan was fought there, for the taking of Pavia by Lautrec in 1527 had no important consequence. The town underwent another siege by the French in 1655. It was taken by the Austrians in 1706, and again by the French in 1733 and in 1745; the latter, however, were obliged to leave it to the Austrians in 1746, and Pavia followed the fortunes of Lombardy. In 1786, Joseph II established there one of the so-called "general seminaries", suppressed in 1791.

Pavia is the birthplace of: the historian Liutprand, Bishop of Cremona; St. Bernardo Balbi, a collector of decretals; the painter Andreino d'Edesia, a contemporary of Giotto; the canon Zanella, inventor of the bassoon. The Gospel was brought to this city by St. Syrus, according to legend a disciple of St. Peter; but according to the martyrology of Ado, on the authority of an Aquileian martyrology, he was sent by St. Hermagoras, first Bishop of Aquileia. Admitting that Eventius, present at the Council of Aquileia in 381, was the sixth Bishop of Pavia, it may well be that this diocese dates from the second half of the third century; among its other bishops were Ursicinus (before 397); St. Crispinus (432); St. Epiphanius (466), a providential blessing to Italy in the time of Ricimer, Odoacer, and Theodoric; St. Maximus (496); Ennodius (511), a famous orator and poet, decorated by St. Hormisdas with the pallium.

After the Lombard occupation, there was also an Arian bishop at Pavia; he had the church of San Eusebio as cathedral; the last one of these was St. Anastasius, who became a Catholic and sole bishop of the see. After him were: St. Damianus, Biscossia (680), author of a letter against the Monothelites; Armentarius (seventh century) who contended with the Archbishop of Milan regarding metropolitan jurisdiction; St. Petrus (726), a relative of King Aripert, and therefore exiled in his youth by Grimoald; St. Theodorus (745), exiled for unknown reasons, returned only after the victories of Charlemagne; Waldo (791), formerly Abbot of Reichenau; St. Joannes (801); Joannes II (874), to whom John VIII gave the pallium, thereafter given to his successors; Joannes III (884), obtained the use of the cross and of the white horse; Pietro Canepanova (978), chancellor of Otto II, became Pope John XIV; Gulielmo (1073), followed the antipope Guibert, and was deposed; Guido Pipari (1100), more of a warrior than a prelate; Pietro Toscano (1148), a Cistercian, friend of St. Bernard and of St. Thomas à Becket, expelled by Barbarossa, who held the *Conciliabulum* of Pavia against Alexander III in 1159; St. Lanfranc (1180) and St. Bernardo Balbi (1198), famous jurists and canonists; St. Fulco Scotti (1216); Guido de Langosco (1296), also a canonist; Isnardo Tocconi, O.P., administrator of the diocese from 1311 to 1320 and imprisoned as a suspect of heresy, but acquitted; Gulielmo Centuaria (1386), O. Min., noted for his apostolic zeal; Francesco Piccopasio (1427), took a great part in the Council of Basle; Giovanni Castiglioni (1454), became cardinal, and served on several occasions as pontifical legate; Cardinal Jacopo Ammannati (1460), distinguished himself in the defence of the Marches against Sigismondo Malatesta, also a protector of belles-lettres; Cardinal Ascanio Sforza (1479); Cardinal Francesco Alidosio (1505), killed at Ravenna in 1511; Gian M. del Monte (1520), became Pope Julius III; Ippolito de Rubeis (1564), restored the cathedral, founded the seminary, and introduced the reforms of the Council of Trent; he had disputes with St. Charles Borromeo in regard to metropolitan rights, and later became cardinal; St. Alessandro Sauli (1591–93); Jacopo Antonio Morigia (1701); Luigi Tosi (1822), who gave to Mgr Dupuch, Archbishop of Carthage, the forearm of St. Augustine; Pietro M. Ferré (1859), for two years prevented by the new Government from taking possession of his diocese; Lucido M. Parrochi (1871–77), became a cardinal and Vicar Apostolic of Rome.

DETAILS OF FAÇADE OF THE CERTOSA

The councils of Pavia were held in the following years: 850, 855, 876, 879, 889, 997, 998, 1018, 1046, 1114, 1128, 1423, which last was transferred later to Pisa.

The diocese is a suffragan of Milan; it has 82 parishes, 110,300 inhabitants, 4 religious houses of men, and 19 of women, 2 educational establishments for boys, 4 for girls, and 1 tri-weekly publication.

CAPPELLETTI, *Le Chiese d'Italia*, X; CAPSONI, *Memorie stor. di Pavia* (1782); MARRONI, *De ecclesia et episcopis Papiensibus* (Pavia, 1757); MORBIO, *Storia dei municipii italiani* (Pavia and Milan, 1840).

U. BENIGNI.

UNIVERSITY OF PAVIA.—Pavia was, even in Roman times, a literary centre (Ennodius); as the capital of the Lombard kingdom it had its "grammar" schools, and Emperor Lothair erected a "central" school there (825). In the tenth and twelfth centuries there were professors of dialectic and law as well as of literature, and, although the authority of Bologna was then incontestable, the opinions of the "Papienses" were cited with respect. One of these was a certain Lanfranco. Another Lanfranco, who died bishop of the city, had been professor of arts and theology. Until 1361 there was no *Studium Generale* at Pavia; whoever sought legal honours went to Bologna. There were other schools, however, at the beginning of the fourteenth century. In 1361 Galeazzo II obtained from Charles IV a *studium generale* with the privileges accorded to the most renowned universities. Promotions were made by the bishop, who issued the licence to teach. Galeazzo forbade his subjects to study in any other university. In 1389 Boniface IX confirmed its rights and privileges. In 1398 it was transferred to Piacenza, and from 1404 to 1412 it was suspended on account of continued warfare. Re-established by Filippo Maria Visconti in 1412, it excelled in Roman Law, soon surpassing Bologna.

Among the professors of the first epoch may be mentioned: the jurisconsults Cristoforo Castiglioni (*legum monarca*); Castiglione Branda, afterwards cardinal, founder of the Collegio Branda; Catone Sacco, founder of a college for poor students; Giasone del Maino the Magnificent (XV century); Andrea Alciato (from 1536); Gasp. Visconti, afterwards cardinal; Filippo Portalupi, first professor of criminology (1578); Ant. Merenda (1633); the canonists Francesco Bossi, afterwards Bishop of Como, and Trivulzio Scaramuccia, afterwards cardinal. The first teacher of medicine was Augusto Toscani (from 1370); in 1389 the chair of surgery was founded. Other celebrated professors were Giovanni Dondi, who constructed the clock in the Torrione of Padua; Marsiglio S. Sofia (*medicinæ monarca*, XIV century); Francesco Vittuone (1442-43), philosopher and physician; Benedetto da Norcia (1455); Gerolamo Cordano, naturalist and astrologer (d. 1576); Gabriele Carcano, first professor of anatomy. Lectures in astrology (astronomy) were held from 1374. The first to teach mathematics was Francesco Pellacani (1425); in the seventeenth century the professors of mathematics were often chosen from the religious, e. g. the Servites Fil. Ferrari (1646), and Gio. Batt. Drusiano, who first taught military architecture (1645) and assisted in the defence of the city during the French siege of 1655.

Philosophical branches were taught from 1374, the professors of which also taught medicine; in the seventeenth and eighteenth centuries the professors were mostly religious. The study of rhetoric and the classics began in 1389, and in 1399 a chair of Dante was instituted and was held by Filippo da Reggio. Lorenzo Valla, Francesco Filelfo, Giorgio Valla (first professor of Greek literature, 1466), and Demetrios Chalcocondylas (1492) shed lustre on the university during the Renaissance. Hebrew was first taught by Benedetto di Spagna (1491); Bernardo Regazzola (1500), the Antiquary, was one of the founders of archæology. The first professor of theology was the Franciscan Pietro Filargo, afterwards Alexander V; after this many of the professors were Augustinians, as Bonifacio Bottigella; Alberto Crespi (1432), prominent at the Council of Basle; and Blessed Giovanni Porzio, author of many commentaries on the Bible. Others were Francesco della Rovere (1444), afterwards Sixtus IV; Cardinal Gaetano (1498–99); the Orientalist Enrico della Porta, O.P. (1751).

The fame of the university diminished greatly from 1600. In 1763 Maria Theresa reorganized the courses, especially by increasing the number of chairs and adding various institutes and collections. But the theological faculty then became a source of anti-Romanism through the professors Tamburini and Zola; in 1859 it was suppressed. Among the professors of this second epoch were Gandolfi; the gynæcologist Porro; the physiologist Mantegazza; Cesare Lombroso; Golgi, awarded the Nobel prize for his studies on the nervous system; in jurisprudence: Giovanni Silva; Luigi Cremani (1775); Domenico Vario; Romagnosi, the reformer of public law; in the natural sciences: the Abbate Spallanzani (1769); and Alessandro Volta; in mathematics: the Jesuit Boscovich; Mascheroni; Codazza, renowned for his researches on heat and magnetism; in philosophy: the Olivetan Baldinotti (1783); and Ruggero Boughi; in literature: Vincenzo Monti; Ugo Foscolo; and the Orientalist Hager. Connected with the university are a museum of mineralogy, zoology, and comparative anatomy, cabinets of physics, of normal anatomy, and pathology, of physiology, and experimental pathology, various clinics, a chemical laboratory, and a cabinet of numismatics and archæology. There are eighteen burses for graduate study. Two colleges—Ghislieri and Borromeo—are under university supervision. A school of applied engineering and a school of pharmacy are also connected with the university. In 1910 there were 50 professors holding 102 different chairs, besides 103 tutors; the students numbered 1507.

Memorie e documenti per la storia dell' Università di Pavia (Pavia, 1878); DENIFLE, *Die Universitäten des Mittelalters*, I, 572, sqq.; *Cenni storici sulla R. Università di Pavia* (Pavia, 1873).

U. BENIGNI.

Pavillon, NICOLAS, Bishop of Alet, b. at Paris, 1597; d. at Alet, 1677. He joined the community of St-Lazare, founded by St. Vincent de Paul, and, for a time, devoted himself to charities and preaching. His zeal and eloquence caused Richelieu to appoint him to the See of Alet. The thirty-seven years of his episcopate were filled with ceaseless labours for the religious and moral improvement of his diocese; visitation of parishes, holding of synods, foundation of schools, etc. An exaggerated idea of his episcopal responsibilities caused him to oppose pope and king. He was one of the four bishops who refused to sign the formulary imposed by Alexander VII, on the plea that the pope cannot pronounce on facts but only on rights. When Louis XIV commanded submission to the papal order, Pavillon in "Lettre au roi" (1664) declined to recognize his interference. The royal attempt at extending to all the provinces of France the so-called *droit de régale* found in Pavillon a sturdy opponent. He spurned royal threats and ecclesiastical censures and appealed to the pope against both the King of France and the Metropolitan of Narbonne.

His attitude against Alexander VII won him the admiration of Port-Royal. Alet became the Mecca of the Jansenists and the bishop imbibed the errors of Jansenism. From the data of a contemporary pamphlet ("Factum de Messire Vincent Ragot", Paris, 1766) Toreilles shows the strange effects of Jansenist principles on every branch of Pavillon's otherwise zealous administration and on his relations with the nobility, the clergy, the regulars, and the peasantry. He wrote "Rituel d'Alet" (Paris, 1666), condemned by Clement IX, and "Ordonnances et status synodaux" (Paris, 1675).

PARIS, *Vie de M. Pavillon* (Paris, 1738); STE-BEUVE, *Port-Royal* (Paris, 1900), index, s. v.; MARION, *Histoire de l'Eglise*, III (Paris, 1908), 369; TOREILLES, *Nicolas Pavillon* in *Revue du Clergé français* (Oct., 1902).

J. F. SOLLIER.

Pawn Shops. See MONTES PIETATIS.

Pax (OSCULATORIUM, TABULA PACIS, LAPIS PACIS), a tablet to be kissed. The primitive usage in the Church was for the "holy kiss" to be given promiscuously. Later (Const. Apostol., VIII, xxix) men of the laity saluted men with the kiss, while women kissed women. This latter manner of giving the peace among the laity seems to have been maintained till the thirteenth century, when a substitute for the actual kiss was introduced in the shape of a small wooden tablet, or plate of metal (*osculatorium, deosculatorium, asser ad pacem* etc.) bearing an image of the Blessed Virgin, of the titular of the church, or other saint, or more frequently of the crucifixion. The earliest notice of these instruments is in the records of English councils of the thirteenth century (Scudamore, "Notit. Eucharist.", 438). This departure from the prevailing usage is attributed to Cardinal Bona (Rer. Liturg., II, xvi, §7) to the Franciscans. Kissed by the celebrant and cleansed with a linen cloth, the tablet or plate was carried to others to be likewise kissed by them. This ceremony still obtains in low masses (Rubr. Mis., X, n. 3), when the *peace* is thus given to prelates and princes, not to others except in rare cases established by custom. The acolyte or server kneeling at the right of the celebrant presents the tablet. The celebrant kissing it says: "Pax tecum"; the server answers: "Et cum spiritu tuo". The server then carries the instrument in turn to those who are to receive the *peace*, saying to each: "Pax tecum"; each responds, "Et cum spiritu tuo", and then genuflects.

VENABLES in *Dict. Christ. Antiq.*, s. v. *Kiss*; CARP, *Bibliotheca liturg.*, I, 204.

A. B. MEEHAN.

PAX OF THE XV CENTURY (ITALIAN)

Pax in the Liturgy.—*Pax vobis* (or *vobiscum*), like the other liturgical salutations (e. g. *Dominus vobiscum*), is of Scriptural origin. The Gospels contain such forms as: "veniet pax vestra", "pax vestra revertetur ad vos" (Matt., x, 13), "Pax huic domui" (Luke, x, 5), "Pax vobis" (Luke, xxiv, 36; John, xx, 21, 26). The salutation, "Gratia vobis et pax" or "Gratia misericordia et pax", is the opening formula of most of the Epistles of St. Paul and of St. Peter, and occurs also in those of St. John as well as in the Apocalypse. The formula was quoted from the Old Testament by Our Lord and His Apostles (cf. especially "Pax vobiscum", "Pax tecum", Gen., xliii, 23; Judges, vi, 23), and was thus naturally preserved in the liturgy and in Christian epigraphy as a memorial of Apostolic times. Like the *Dominus vobiscum*, it was first used in the liturgy (in the form of *Pax vobis*) by the bishop in welcoming the faithful at the beginning of the Mass before the Collect or the *Oratio*. When the *Confiteor*, *Introit*, *Gloria in excelsis* were added at a later period, the *Pax vobis* or the *Dominus vobiscum* was preserved. The form *Pax vobis* is now employed by bishops and prelates only—*Dominus vobiscum* being used by priests—at the first Collect. Hence the *Dominus vobiscum* became the ordinary introduction to all the orations and most of the prayers. The Greeks have preserved the *Pax omnibus* or *Pax vobiscum*. There was formerly a certain rivalry between the two formulæ, *Pax vobis* and *Dominus vobiscum*, and some councils (notably that of Braga in 563) ordained that both bishops and priests should employ the same form of salutation (for the texts, see the bibliography). Besides this episcopal or sacerdotal salutation, the words *Pax tecum*, *Pax vobis*, or *Pax vobiscum* are used in the Liturgy at the kiss of peace. On such occasions the Liturgy contains prayers or collects *ad pacem* (cf. KISS; Cabrol in "Dict. d'archéol. et de liturgie", s. v. "Baiser de Paix", where all references are given). In the Ambrosian Liturgy, at the end of the Mass, the people are dismissed with the words: "Ite in pace" (cf. "Auctarium Solesmense", 95). Dom Martène (op. cit. in bibliography, III, 171, 174) gives other instances of the use of the word Pax. In Christian epigraphy there is a variety of formulæ: pax; in pace; pax tecum; vivas in pace; requiescat in pace; pax Christi tecum sit; anima dulcissima requiescas in pace; dormit in pace; in locum refrigerii, lucis et pacis (from the formula in the Mass at the Memento of the Dead). See INSCRIPTIONS, EARLY CHRISTIAN; Le Blant, "Inscriptions chrét. de la Gaule", I, 264, etc.; Northcote, "Epitaphs of the Catacombs" (London, 1878), v, and bibliography.

In addition to the works and articles cited in the text, consult: PETER DAMIAN, an opusculum on *Dominus Vobiscum* in *P. L.*, CXLV, 234; ZACCARIA, *Onomasticon*, s. vv. *Pax vobis* and *Salutatio episcopalis*; BONA, *Rerum liturg.*, III, 12, 88 sqq.; SMITH, *Dict. of Christ. Antiq.*, s. v. *Pax* (cf. *Dominus vobiscum*); *De dignitate sacerdotali* (not written by St. Ambrose, as was long believed, but by Gerbert), v, in *P. L.*, XVII, 598, and CXXXIX, 175, contains an important text on this subject; ROCCA, *De salutatione sacerdotis in missa et divinis officiis* in *Thesaurus antiquitat.*, I (Rome, 1745), 236; MARTÈNE, *De antiq. eccles. ritibus*, I, 151 sqq.; MAMACHI, *Origines et antiq. christ.*, IV, 479; III, 17, 19; *Ephemerides liturg.* (Feb., 1910), 108; PROBST, *Die abendländische Messe*, 104, 404, 437; see *Dominus Vobiscum*, V, 114; CABROL in *Dict. d'archéol. chrét.*, s. v. *Acclamations*. For the formula *Pax* and other formulas in funeral epigraphy, cf. INSCRIPTIONS, EARLY CHRISTIAN; KIRSCH, *Die Acclamationen u. Gebete der altchristl. Grabschriften* (Cologne, 1897); IDEM, *Les acclamations des épitaphes chrét. de l'antiquité et les prières liturg. pour les défunts* in *IVe Congrès scientifique des Catholiques* (Fribourg, 1898), 113–22; SYXTO, *Notiones archæol. christ.*, II, *Epigraphia*, 94 sqq.; CABROL, *La prière pour les morts* in *Revue d'apologétique* (15 Sept., 1909); IDEM, *Livre de la prière antique*, 67, 69.

FERNAND CABROL.

Pax Tecum. See KISS.

Pax Vobis. See PAX IN THE LITURGY.

Payeras, MARIANO, b. 10 Oct., 1769, at Inca, Island of Majorca; d. 28 April, 1823. He received the habit of St. Francis at Palma, 5 Sept., 1784; left Spain in Feb., 1793, to join the College of San Fernando, Mexico, which provided missionaries for the Indian missions in California. He was sent to Monterey and stationed at San Carlos, 1796–1798; at Soledad, 1798–1803; at San Diego, 1803–1804; at Purisima Concepcion, 1804–1823. From July, 1815, to April, 1820, Father Payeras held the offices of *presidente* of the missions and *vicario foraneo* of the Bishop of Sonora, to whose jurisdiction California belonged. In 1819 the College of San Fernando elected him *comisario-prefecto* of the missions, in which capacity he, at various times, visited the twenty missions then existing from San Diego to San Rafael, a distance of more than six hundred miles. The zealous prelate also headed various expeditions to the territory of the savages for the purpose of finding suitable sites for new missions. Six months before his death he accompanied an expedition to the Russian settlements in the wilds of Sonoma County, and thereby most probably hastened his demise. In 1819 Fr. Payeras received the thanks of the King of Spain for his services during the Bouchard revolt. While in charge of Purisima he compiled a catechism in the language of the Indians, which was put to use but never published. "There was no friar of better and more evenly balanced ability", says H. H. Bancroft. "It was impossible to quarrel with him. He had extraordinary business ability, was a clear and forcible, as well as a voluminous writer, and withal a man of great strength of mind and firmness of character".

Santa Barbara Mission Archives; Mission Records of Purisima Concepcion; ENGELHARDT, *The Franciscans in California* (Harbor Springs, Mich., 1897); IDEM, *The Missions and Missionaries of California*, II (San Francisco, 1911); BANCROFT, *History of California*, II (San Francisco, 1886).

ZEPHYRIN ENGELHARDT.

Paz, LA. See LA PAZ, DIOCESE OF.

Pázmány, PETER, famous Hungarian ecclesiastic of the seventeenth century; d. 19 March, 1637. He was born of noble blood. His parents were Calvinists; his stepmother, who was a Catholic, turned the boy's spirit towards the Catholic Church. After making his elementary studies in Nagyvárad, where two Jesuits exercised great influence over him, he went to the Jesuit college in Kolozsvár. At the age of thirteen he became a Catholic, and at seventeen entered the Jesuit novitiate. Proceeding to Rome for his higher studies, he studied for four years under Bellarmine. Afterwards he taught philosophy and theology in Gratz, and in 1601 returned to Hungary. He successively became Provost of Turóc, Bishop of Nyitra, in 1616 Archbishop of Esztergom, and lastly Cardinal Primate of all Hungary. Pázmány engaged in a literary warfare with Stephen Magyary, a Protestant preacher, who in a book entitled "The causes of the country's ruin" (Az országokban való sok romlásoknak okairól), published in 1602, declared the Catholic religion to be the principal cause. Pázmány answered him in a work entitled "Reply to Stephen Magyary" (Felelet Magyary Istvánnak), proving that the Protestant religion, and not the Catholic, was the cause. He translated the "Imitation of Christ" and also compiled a prayer-book, still in popular use. In 1605 appeared "Ten arguments proving the falsity of the present science"; in 1609, "Five famous letters to Peter Alvinczy"; in 1613 his great theological and apologetical work, "Hodoegus, or Guide to God's truths" (Hodoegus, vagy Isteni igazságra vezérlö, Kalauz). The first part of the last work was dogmatic, the second part polemical. With unanswerable arguments he showed the truth of the Catholic religion, whose victory in Hungary he secured by this work. Henceforth Protestantism was reduced to personal recriminations and force of arms. In 1636 he published his sermons, which became a model for the priesthood.

Pázmány belongs to the first rank of preachers, his discourses being notable for their logic, rather than beautiful words. By his writings, preaching, but especially by his personal meetings he converted about thirty noble families (e. g. the Zrinyi, Wesselényi, Nádasdy, Rákóczy etc.). These families spent most of their money in converting the people of the lower classes, whom the Reformation had seduced from the true Faith. As archbishop, Pázmány put into effect the decrees of the Council of Trent. He introduced the *Missale Romanum*, and was the great apostle of the celibacy of the clergy. He also displayed great activity in founding schools, building many seminaries for the education of poor students who aspired to the priesthood, and also many elementary and high schools. In 1623 he gave 46,000 dollars toward the building in Vienna of a seminary for Hungarians (the *Pazmaneum*), which is to-day in a very flourishing condition. In 1626 he built a college in Pozsony, the direction of which he placed in the hands of the Jesuits. In 1635 he built an elementary school in the same place, and in 1627 he gave 533 dollars that Hungarian seminarians might be sent to Rome to finish their theological studies. In Nagyszombat he built a seminary and also a college for the children of impoverished nobles. In 1635 he founded the first Hungarian university for the furthering of Catholic ideals; this institution is in Budapest, and is at present (1910) attended by 5000 students. Pázmány ordered that the bishops every year, and the archbishops every four years, should hold a conference, and that the deans and pastors should take an examination every year. As a politician, Pázmány desired Hungary to be a kingdom with a Catholic ruler, and that Hungary and Austria should work together in all dealings with foreign powers, Transylvania being independent. Pázmány's idea was that, with a Catholic Hungarian king, the country would be well protected from the Turks. It was to his earnest efforts that Ferdinand II was partially endebted for his succession to the throne. In 1622 he brought about peace between Gabriel Bethlen (ruler of Transylvania) and Ferdinand II, religious freedom being granted to the Protestants. He battled so long and nobly for Catholicism, and his efforts were crowned with such great success that we may say that he was born in Protestant, but died in Catholic, Hungary.

FRAKNÓI VILMOS, *Pázmány Péter és kora* (*P. Pázmány and his century*, 3 vols., 1867–71); KOVÁCS, *Pázmány Kalauza és Bellarmin Disputatiói* (*The Conductor of Pázmány and the Disputations of Bellarmine*, Kassa, 1908).

A. BANGHA.

Pazzi, MARY MAGDALEN DE', SAINT. See MARY MAGDALEN.

Peace Congresses. I. EARLY HISTORY. — The genesis of the idea of a meeting of representatives of different nations to obtain by peaceful arbitrament a settlement of differences has been traced to the year 1623 in modern history, to a French monk, Eméric Crucé, who wrote a work entitled "The New Cyneas", a discourse showing the opportunities and the means for establishing a general peace and liberty of conscience to all the world and addressed to the monarch and the sovereign princes of the time. He proposed that a city, preferably Venice, should be selected where all the Powers had ambassadors and that there should be a universal union, including all peoples. He suggested careful arrangement as to priority, giving the first place to the pope. Two years after this publication, appeared in Latin the work of Hugo Grotius "On the Right of War and Peace", pleading for a mitigation of some of the barbarous usages of war. William Penn, the founder of Pennsylvania, had a plan for the establishment of a "European Dyet, Parliament or Estates". He was followed by other writers of different nationalities.

Immediately after the dethronement of Napoleon the First a congress of the great European powers met in Vienna, but it could hardly be called a peace congress, as its purpose was rather to adjust the boundaries and limit the sphere of influence of the different nations which had united to overthrow the French emperor. From time to time differences between individual nations or the citizens of one nation and the government of another have been settled by arbitration, but the idea of a World Congress to bring about a reduction of armament and a universal peace is of recent origin.

In 1826, a congress composed of representatives of Spanish-American countries was planned by Bolivar for military as well as political purposes. One of its declared objects was "to promote the peace and union of American nations and establish amicable methods for the settlement of disputes between them". This congress failed, as only four Spanish-American countries were represented and only one ratified the agreement. In 1831, however, Mexico took up the subject and proposed a conference of American Republics "for the purpose of bringing about not only a union and close alliance for defence, but also the acceptance of friendly mediation for the settlement of disputes between them, and the framing and promulgation of a code of penal laws to regulate their mutual relations". It does not appear that anything came of this congress, and in 1847 another was held at Lima, attended by representatives of Bolivia, Chili, Ecuador, New Granada, and Peru, for the purpose of forming an alliance of American republics. The United States was invited but as it was then at war with Mexico it sent no representative. Another congress was held by representatives from the Argentine Republic, Bolivia, Chili, Colombia, Ecuador, Guatemala, Peru, and Venezuela, in 1864. An effort to hold a congress was made by the governments of Chili and Colombia in 1880, "to the end that the settlement by arbitration of each and every international controversy should become a principle of Amercian public law". This congress did not meet, however, owing to a war between Chili and Peru.

In 1881, the President of the United States invited the independent countries of North and South America to meet in a general congress at Washington on 24 November, 1882, "for the purpose of considering and discussing methods of preventing war between the nations of America". This meeting did not take place owing to a variety of reasons, but subsequently, by virtue of an Act of Congress of the United States an invitation was issued by the president to Mexico, the Central and South American Republics, Hayti, Dominican Republic, and Brazil to join in a conference to be held in the city of Washington, the project being to consider: (1) measures tending to preserve the peace and promote the prosperity of the South American States; (2) measures looking to the formation of an American Customs Union; (3) the establishment of regular and frequent communication between the various countries; (4) the establishment of a uniform system of customs regulations, invoices, sanitation of ships, and quarantine; (5) the adoption of a uniform system of weights and measures, and of laws to protect patent rights, copyrights, and trade marks, and for the extradition of criminals; (6) the adoption of a common silver coin; (7) the adoption of a definite plan of arbitration of all questions, disputes, and differences; and (8) such other subjects relating to the welfare of the several States as might be presented by any of them. The congress assembled at Washington on 2 October, 1889. Eighteen American nations, including the United States, had their representatives. The conference adopted a plan of arbitration of international differences, together with various recommendations relating to trade, law, extradition, patents, customs, and sanitary regulations. It further declared arbitration to be a principle of American International Law and obligatory "in all controversies concerning diplomatic and consular privileges, boundaries, territories, indemnities, the right of navigation, and the validity, construction and enforcement of treaties; and that it should be equally obligatory in all other cases, whatever might be their origin, nature or object, with the sole exception of those which in the judgment of one of the nations involved in the controversy, might imperil its independence; but that even in this case, while arbitration for that nation should be optional, it should be obligatory on the adversary power" (7 Moore Int. Law Dig. p. 7). One notable result of the conference was the establishment of the Bureau of the American Republics. All the republics of South America are represented in this bureau, which continues for periods of ten years subject to renewal.

II. LATEST DEVELOPMENTS.—A. *First Hague Conference.*—On 12 August, 1898, in a circular letter addressed to the representatives of different nations, the Emperor of Russia proposed to all governments, which had duly accredited representatives at the imperial court, the holding of a conference to consider the problem of the preservation of peace among nations. During the summer of 1900 the conference assembled at The Hague and on 4 Sept. formal notification of the ratification of the convention for the pacific settlement of international disputes was given by the United States, Austria, Belgium, Denmark, England, France, Germany, Italy, Persia, Portugal, Rumania, Russia, Siam, Spain, Sweden, Norway, and the Netherlands, and subsequently by Japan. A permanent court of arbitration was established at The Hague, composed of representatives of each of the signatory powers appointed for a term of six years. Arbitrators called upon to form a competent tribunal may be chosen from a general list of the members of the court when any of the signatory powers desire to have recourse to the court for a settlement of any difference between them.

The South and Central American republics were not represented at the conference, but at the second International Conference of American States which was initiated by President McKinley and held in the City of Mexico, 22 October, 1901, to 31 January, 1902, a plan was adopted looking to adhesion to The Hague convention, the protocol being signed by all of the delegations except Chili and Ecuador, who subsequently gave their adhesion. The conference authorized the Governments of the United States and Mexico to negotiate with the other signatory powers for the adherence of other American nations. At this conference the project of a treaty for the arbitration of pecuniary claims was adopted, and the signatories agreed for a term of five years to submit to arbitration (preferably to the permanent court at The Hague) all claims for pecuniary loss or damage presented by their respective citizens and not capable of settlement through diplomatic channels, where they were of sufficient importance to warrant the expense of a court of arbitration.

B. *Second Hague Conference.*—A second international peace conference was held at The Hague from 15 June to 18 October, 1907. Forty-four States were represented, including the principal nations of Europe, North and South America, and Asia. The conference drew up thirteen conventions and one declaration. They are as follows: for the pacific settlement of international disputes; respecting the limitation of the employment of force for the recovery of contract debts; relative to the opening of hostilities; respecting the laws and customs of war on land; respecting the rights and duties of neutral powers and persons in case of war on land; relative to the status of enemy merchantships at the outbreak of hostilities; relative to the conversion of merchant-ships into war-ships; relative to the laying of automatic submarine contact mines; respecting bombardment by naval forces in time of war; for the adaptation to naval war of the principles of the Geneva convention; relative to certain restrictions with regard to the exercise of the right of capture in naval war; relative to the creation of an International Prize Court; concerning the rights and duties of neutral powers in naval war; and a declaration prohibiting the discharge of projectiles and explosives from balloons.

The movement towards the settlement of international difficulties by arbitration has made great advances, as will be seen by the foregoing summary. None, however, have attempted to settle by such methods any questions which may touch upon "the vital interests, the independence or the honour" of the different States.

President Taft, in a recent address, has made a plea for negotiation even of the excepted questions, so that there may be an "adjudication of an international arbitration court in every issue which cannot be settled by negotiation no matter what it involves, whether honour, territory or money". The public sentiment of the world upon this subject is crystallizing, and another decade may witness results perhaps even more far-reaching than those that have been already attained.

BALCH, *The New Cyneas of Eméric Crucé* (Philadelphia, 1909); IDEM, *Crucé, l'évolution de l'arbitrage international;* MOORE, *International Law* (from this work the facts relating to American peace congresses have been taken); MOORE, *Digest of International Law;* WILSON, *Hand Book of International Law* (St. Paul, Minn., 1910); SCOTT, *Text of the Peace Conference at The Hague 1907–1909;* HIGGINS, *The Hague Peace Conference.*

WALTER GEORGE SMITH.

Peasants, WAR OF THE (1524–25), a revolt of the peasants of southern and central Germany, the causes of which are disputed as a result of religious and political prejudice. At present the opinion prevails that the revolt was brought about mainly by economic distress. The conditions which must here be taken into consideration are the following. Up to the end of the fourteenth century the peasants enjoyed a relatively advantageous position, even though they did not own their land in fee simple, but held it at a rental, either hereditary or fixed for certain periods. Conditions, however, grew worse. The increase of population due to prosperity coincided in point of time with the development of the economic use of money and its injurious influences. The city overshadowed the country, and at times even exerted dominion over the country districts. International economic conditions also were detrimental to the peasant class. Large quantities of precious metals were drawn from the mines of Peru, Mexico, and Germany, so that the value of money sank about fifty per cent, while prices rose; thus in Thuringia the price of wool was doubled, and the price of merchandise was increased fivefold. On the other hand leases were not reduced or wages raised, but the lords of the land sought to make up their losses by unusually heavy taxation. They extended their authority, increased the services and burdens of the serfs, sought to annul the rights of the market associations, and to do away with the peasants' hereditary lease of their farms, only granting the use of woodland, water, and pasture on condition of heavy rents. Roman law favoured these exactions. Moreover, the military needs and the growing costs of the local governments led to an increase of the taxes. This caused great bitterness of feeling, especially in Würtemberg and Bavaria. To the burdens imposed by the landlord and the territorial sovereign were added imperial taxes, regardless of the economic condition of the poorer classes. The position of the peasants was at its worst in the very small German states, where the landlord was also the sovereign and desired to live like a prince.

Not only peasants but also cities and nobles took part in the great uprising that is known as the War of the Peasants. Of the cities only the smaller were economically connected with the peasants. Large cities, like Frankfort, Würzburg, and Mainz, joined the uprising; but economic conditions do not fully explain their action. It must be assumed, therefore, that external reasons induced the nobility and the cities to combine temporarily with the peasants in the great uprising and that the causes of discontent, which were numerous, varied in the different States. From the end of the fifteenth century great movements for political reform had been in progress, but on account of the selfish policy of the territorial princes all attempts to strengthen the central power had failed, and the Nuremberg Diet of 1524 had completely paralyzed the imperial administration. Part of the rebels desired to reform the empire. Political disorders were intensified by religious. For eight years Luther's attitude had disquieted the people and shaken their religious convictions to their foundations. His declamations about Christian liberty, even if meant in a different sense, increased the ferment. The opponents of the new doctrine regarded Luther, and in part still regard him, as the real instigator of the revolt; the rebels themselves appealed to him in the conviction that they were only carrying out his teachings. It is not surprising that the outbreak took place just at the end of the year 1524. The hope of a national settlement of ecclesiastical reform had come to nought, and the emperor had countermanded the national council, which had been called to meet at Speyer, 1 Sept., 1524. The failure of the efforts for political and ecclesiastical reform must also be included among the causes of the outbreak. Before it is possible to pass a final judgment upon the causes, there must be a wider and more thorough investigation of the religious and intellectual life of the German people before the Reformation.

During the years 1492–1500 there had been sporadic outbreaks in Algäu, Alsace, and in the Diocese of Speyer, but they had been betrayed and suppressed. The revolt of "poor Conrad" against the extortionate taxation of Duke Ulrich of Würtemberg, and the confederation of the Wendic peasants in Carinthia, Carniola, and Styria had also been crushed by the rulers and nobility of these states. The great uprising of the peasants in the second decade of the sixteenth century began in the southern part of the Black Forest. The revolt was under the daring and clear-sighted guidance of Hans Müller of Bulgenbach and, as the rebellion spread over Swabia, Franconia, and Alsace, the power of the rebels steadily grew. They stirred up the people to disorder by means of promises contained in the so-called "Twelve Articles", of which the author is uncertain. They have been ascribed to Pastor Schappler of Memmingen, to Sebastian Lotzer, and to the Pastor of Waldshut, Balthasar Hubmaier, who was under the influence of Münzer. Their demands were economic, social, and religious. The rate of interest, compulsory service to the lord of the manor, and legal penalties they wished mitigated. Other articles demanded the restoration of old German economic conditions, such as the unions of the old marches and the free right of pasturage, fishing, and hunting. Social reform was to culminate in the abolition of serfdom, because Christ made all men free, but obedience to the authorities appointed by God was to be maintained. As regards religion they demanded the right to choose their pastors and to guarantee that the clergy should preach the pure and true Gospel. Thus the moderate element that had a share in preparing these articles had no thought of a radical overthrow of all existing conditions. But in this case, as in all great popular upheavals, the moderation expressed in theory was not carried out.

The mobs that were commanded by the tavern-keeper George Metzler, by Florian Geyer, Wendel Hipler, Jäcklein Rohrbach, and even by the knight, Götz von Berlichingen, often indulged in an unbridled lust of murder and destruction. The best known of these outrages is the horrible murder of Count von Helfenstein on 16 April, 1525. Early in May, 1525, the peasants were everywhere victorious over the nobility. The Bishops of Bamberg and Speyer, the Abbots of Hersfeld and Fulda, the Elector of the Palatinate, and others made concessions of all kinds to their demands. The revolt, however, was at its height and its leaders thought themselves able to carry out their political aims. Several cities joined the uprising, which was to be under the direction of a vigorous and well-organized board of peasants; at Heilbronn a common chancery was to be established for all the rebel bands; the great majority of the rebels under arms were to go home and only a select body was to keep the field. The peasants sought to overthrow their real political opponents, the territorial princes. They planned to reorganize the entire constitution of the empire, a scheme that had been repeatedly discussed since the fourteenth century. The object of their plans of reform was to strengthen the empire and to weaken the power of the territorial princes. The property of the Church was to be secularized, and then used to compensate the feudal lords for the abolition of the feudal burdens. The reforms were then to be carried out under the authority of the empire, such as uniformity of weights and coinage, suppression of custom-duty, restoration of the German law in the courts, etc.

The petty sovereigns now combined and Luther encouraged their intention to crush the rebellion. In April he had advocated peace and had distinguished between justifiable and unjustifiable demands. He now took a different view of the matter. The fanatical mobs directed by Thomas Münzer and Heinrich Pfeifer were spreading destruction in Thuringia by fire and sword, and had destroyed the monasteries of the Harz district and the Thuringian Forest (Michaelstein, Ilsenburg, Walkenried, Kelbra, Donndorf, Rossleben, Memleben, and Reinhardsbrunn). Luther now foresaw the overthrow of State and Church, property and family. Accordingly on 6 May he violently and passionately urged the princes to smite the "murdering and robbing band of the peasants". The hordes commanded by Münzer were defeated on 15 May, 1525, near Frankenhausen by the confederated princes of Saxony, Brunswick, Hesse, and Mansfeld. The prophet Münzer was executed. At about the same time the uprising in southern Germany was subdued. In Alsace the peasants were conquered on 17 May by the united forces of Duke Anton of Lorraine and the Governor of Mörsperg; in Würtemberg they were overthrown near Sindelfingen by the commander of the forces of the Swabian League. The mobs of Odenwald and Rothenburg were utterly crushed on 2 and 4 June; and on 7 June Würzburg had to surrender. The overthrow of the peasants on the upper and middle Rhine required more time. The revolt had taken a more orderly course in Upper Swabia, the Black Forest, and in Switzerland. The north-west and the east were entirely free from the insurrection, for at that time the position of the peasants there was more favourable. Formerly it was thought that after this uprising the condition of the peasants became worse than before, but this view is incorrect. At first, it is true, the severity of martial law had absolute sway; thus, there were 60 executions in Würzburg, and 211 in the whole of Franconia. But the period of terror had also been a lesson to the victors. The condition of the peasants did not grow essentially worse, though it did not greatly improve. Only in a few exceptional cases were reforms introduced, as in Baden and the Tyrol.

ZIMMERMANN, *Geschichte des Bauernkrieges* (Stuttgart, 1845); BAX, *The Peasants' War in Germany* (London, 1899); JANSSEN, *Geschichte des deutschen Volkes* (17th and 18th ed. Freiburg, 1897); STOLZE, *Der deutsche Bauernkrieg* (Halle, 1908); SOMMERLAD, *Bauernkrieg in Handwörterbuch der Staatswissenschaften*, II (3rd ed. Jena, 1909), 653-62; WOLFF, *Der deutsche Bauernkrieg* in *Deutsche Geschichtsblätter*, XI (Gotha, 1909), 61-72.

KLEMENS LÖFFLER.

Peba Indians (OR PEVA), the principal of a small group of cognate tribes, comprising the Peba proper, Caumari, Cauhuachi, Pacaya, and Yagua (Zava by error in Chantre y Herrera), together constituting the Peban linguistic stock, and formerly occupying the country about the confluence of the Javari with the Amazon, in territory held by Peru, but in part claimed also by Ecuador and Colombia. In their primitive condition they resembled the neighbouring Jivaro and Pano, though of less fierce and warlike temper. They held a close friendship with the powerful Omagua of Southern Colombia, and in the eighteenth century formed an important element in the celebrated Jesuit missions of the "Mainas province" of the upper Amazon region. In 1735 (or 1736) the Jesuit Fr. Singler of the Omagua mission with a few Indian companions reached the main village of the Caumari and later that of the Peba, who received him with good will and presented him with their most precious gifts, viz. jars filled with the deadly curari poison used by the hunters for tipping their blowgun arrows. They allowed him to set up a cross in the village and listened with respect to his teaching. Some of both tribes accompanied him to the Omagua mission of San Joaquin, but, their health suffering, they were soon brought back and established in a separate mission called San Ignacio de Pebas, which was placed in charge of Fr. Adan Vidman. Some of the kindred Cauhuachi (Covachi), formerly attached to another Omagua mission, were also brought to San Ignacio, as were later the Yagua. Although nearly related, the tribes differed greatly in temperament. The Peba, according to Fr. Chantre y Herrera, were active and vigorous but rough in manner; the Cauhuachi were equally rude, but more industrious; the Caumari were the neatest and most intelligent; while the Yagua were of restless habit.

In 1754, tribal dissensions culminated in the murder of the resident missionary, Fr. José Casado, by two brothers of the Caumari tribe, resulting in the temporary desertion of the mission of all but the Peba. Fr. José de Vahamonde, a veteran of seventeen years' service in the Amazon forests, was sent to restore order, and under his kindly promises and treatment the fugitives returned and the mission doubled its former number. In spite of smallpox, other epidemic visitations, and the raids of Portuguese slave hunters from Brazil, the mission of San Ignacio de Pebas held its rank until the expulsion of the Jesuits in 1768. It then stood fifth in the list of 33 missions of the Mainas province, with 700 souls, Father Vahamonde being still in charge. Others of the same tribal group were at the mission of San Ignacio de Mainas, and possibly at other missions. On account of the great diversity of dialects the missionaries had introduced the Quichua language of Peru as the common medium of communication. After the expulsion of the Jesuits the missions were continued under Franciscan auspices with some success. When Peru became a separate government in 1821, the missions were neglected and fell into decay. The mission Indians, who had steadily dwindled in number, became scattered and either lost their identity in the mixed population or joined their still wild forest kindred. The small town of Pebas, on the Amazon, now occupies the site of the old mission. The former tribes are extinct or assimilated, with the exception of a remnant of the Yagua, noted for their fine physique, some of whom are about Pebas and the Napo while others dwell on the lower Javari. The greater portion of their tribe was destroyed by smallpox in 1877.

(See also JÍBARO INDIANS; MAINA INDIANS; MAMELUCO; PANO INDIANS.)

CHANTRE Y HERRERA, *Hist. de las Misiones de la Compañia de Jesus en el Marañon Español, 1637-1767* (Madrid, 1901); HERVAS, *Catálogo de las Lenguas*, I (Madrid, 1800); ORTON, *The Andes and the Amazon* (3rd ed., New York, 1876); BRINTON, *The American Race* (New York, 1891); MARKHAM, *Tribes in the Valley of the Amazon* in *Jour. Anthrop. Inst.*, XXIV (London, 1895); GALT, *Indians of Peru* in *Rept. Smithsonian Instn. for 1877* (Washington, 1878); ORDINAIRE. *Les Sauvages du Pérou* in *Revue d'Ethnographie*, VI (Paris, 1887).

JAMES MOONEY.

Pecci, GIOACCHINO. See LEO XIII, POPE.

Pecham (PECCHAM), JOHN, Archbishop of Canterbury, b. about 1240; d. 6 December, 1292. His birthplace was Patcham in Sussex, called in the Middle Ages Pecham (Peccham), in common with Peckham in Surrey and Kent. He received his education from the monks of Lewes, but it is doubtful whether he was a student at Merton College, Oxford. He also studied at Paris, was tutor to the nephew of H. de Andegavia, and later entered the Order of Friars Minor. He succeeded Thomas de Bungay, O.F.M., and taught divinity, being the first to dispute de Quolibet at Oxford; Pecham became ninth Provincial of England (Parkinson says twelfth), and was called to Rome in 1276 and appointed *lector sacri palatii*. When Robert Kilwardby resigned the See of Canterbury, Edward I requested Pecham to take up the cause of Robert Burnell, Bishop of Bath and Wells, and Chancellor of England, but in January, 1279, Pecham himself was elected to that see, and consecrated by Nicholas III. He held a Provincial Council at Reading, 31 July, 1279, in which he carried out the pope's verbal instructions and published fresh enactments against pluralities. In October, 1281, he summoned another Provincial Council to Lambeth, where among other matters his solicitude for the Holy Eucharist is noteworthy. His zeal prompted him to visit every part of his province, uprooting abuses wherever he found them. He compelled the royal chapels which claimed exemption to submit to the visitation. On this occasion he proved that he had inherited the fearless courage of his predecessors, yet retained the royal favour. He intervened with success in behalf of Almeric de Montfort, and had Llewellyn listened to him, he might have averted his own fate and that of his country. His suffragans complained that his zeal had led him beyond the limits of his jurisdiction, and deputed St. Thomas of Hereford to carry their joint appeal to Rome, where apparently it was upheld. At Oxford he renewed the condemnation of certain errors already censured by Robert Kilwardby, many of them containing errors of Averroes, but several of them enunciated by St. Thomas Aquinas, and afterwards commonly accepted in Catholic schools. ("Nineteenth Century and after", January, 1911, p. 74.) In forming an estimate of his character a complete absence of subserviency and an unswerving adherence to principle come into view, but his frequent exertions in favour of the poor and against anything like oppression must not be overlooked. His humility, sincerity, and constancy in the duties of his office, and strict observance of his rule, won for him the admiration of his contemporaries. As the Apostolic protector of his order he defended it and other Mendicant Orders against their enemies. His remains rest in Canterbury Cathedral, but his heart was buried in the church of the Grey Friars, London. A complete list of his writings is published in "British Society of Franciscan Studies" (vol. II, 1909), his letters (720) are found in Martin's "Registrum Epistolarum Fr. Joannis Peckham". He was an excellent poet, some of his poems being attributed to St. Bonaventure, as was also his "Life of St. Antony of Padua" written as Glasberger states, at the bidding of Jerome of Ascoli, and recently identified by F. Hilary, O.S.F.C., in a manuscript in the Capuchin library at Lucerne.

KINGSFORD in *Dict. Nat. Biog.;* WADDING; TRIVET; RODOLPHIUS, *Historia Seraphicæ Religionis;* SBARALEA; LITTLE, *Greyfriars at Oxford;* DENIFLE, *Chartul. Univer. Paris.*

ANDREW EGAN.

Pecock (PEACOCK), REGINALD, Bishop of Chichester, b. in North Wales about 1395; d. at Thorney Abbey about 1460. He was educated at Oriel College, Oxford, where he obtained a fellowship in 1417. During the following years he taught in the schools belonging to Exeter College, obtaining a wide reputation for learning and scholarship. He was ordained priest on 8 March, 1421, and took the degree of bachelor in divinity four years later, about which time he left the university for the court where he won the favour of Humphrey, Duke of Gloucester. In 1431 he was appointed master of Whittington College, London, and rector of St. Michael's-in-Riola. The activity of the London Lollards drew him into controversy against them and at this time he wrote "The Book or Rule of Christian Religion" and "Donet", an introduction to Christian doctrine which was published about 1440. In 1444 he was made Bishop of St. Asaph by papal provision dated 22 April, and on 14 June he was consecrated by Archbishop Stafford. At the same time he took the degree of doctor in divinity at Oxford without any academic act. The bishop's troubles began with a sermon which he preached at St. Paul's Cross in 1447 which gave general offence because of his attempt to justify the bishops for not preaching. The manner of this offended both the agitators whom he attacked and the ecclesiastics whom he defended. Undaunted by the opposition, he summarized his argument in a tract called "Abbreviatio Reginaldi Pecock." It is noteworthy that he incurred in a special degree the resentment of the religious orders. It was unfortunate for Pecock that he was befriended by the unpopular Duke of Suffolk, one of whose last acts before his assassination was to procure the translation of Pecock from St. Asaph's to Chichester, an appointment by which the bishop was attached to the falling house of Lancaster. Soon after he was made a privy councillor, and he was among those who signed the appointment of Richard, Duke of York, as protector during the king's illness.

About 1455 he completed and published his best known work, "The Repressor of Over Much Blaming of the Clergy", written against Lollard doctrine, and about a year later he issued his "Book of Faith". The tendency of these works afforded ground for an attack on him by his theological and political opponents, and on 22 Oct., 1457, Archbishop Bourchier cited Pecock and his accusers to appear before him on 11 Nov. Nine books which he produced were submitted to a commission of theologians who reported adversely on them on the grounds among other reasons that he set the natural law above the authority of the Scriptures, denied the necessity of believing Christ's descent into hell, and belittled the authority of the Church. On 28 Nov., Pecock was sentenced either to complete public abjuration or degradation and death at the stake. Pecock, who all his life had been defending the doctrines of the Church, though possibly in an unwise way, had no intention of a conflict with authority, and abjured first privately, then in public at St. Paul's Cross, a list of errors most of which he had neither held nor taught. The whole proceeding was illegal according to canon law, which required the authority of the Holy See for such a process. This became clear when Pecock appealed to the pope, for Callistus III sent back Bulls of restitution which were equivalent to a condemnation of the Lambeth court. Archbishop Bourchier received these Bulls but refused to act on them and the king was advised to despatch an ambassador to Rome to obtain their revocation. Unfortunately for Pecock Callistus died, and the new pope, Pius II, acting on Pecock's confession, ordered a new trial with the express instructions that in case of conviction he was to be sent to Rome for punishment, or if that were impossible, he was to be degraded and punished in England as the canons decreed. In this document Pecock is said to have already resigned his see of his own accord. His successor John Arundel was appointed on 26 March, 1459, which was before the arrival of the papal brief. There is no indication either that he was sent to Rome or degraded, but there is a document which shows that he was confined in the Abbey of Thorney. There probably he died, though reports differ, but no certain account of his death has been recorded. Space does not permit a statement of Pecock's doctrine, but his intentions were orthodox, and his indiscretions would certainly not have been visited by such severe treatment had it not been for the intrigues of his political enemies. Irregularly they forced from him under fear of death a confession, which Pope Pius, taking it on its merits, naturally regarded as evidence of his guilt.

Bishop Pecock, his Character and Fortunes in *Dublin Review* (January, 1875); LEWIS, *Life of Reynold Pecock* (London, 1744); BABINGTON, Introduction to *The Repressor of Over Much Blaming of the Clergy* in Rolls Series (London, 1860), 2 vols.; COOKE in *Dict. Nat. Biog.*, giving exhaustive list of contemporary and later references; WAGER in *Mod. Lang. Notes*, IX, iv (1894); GAIRDNER, *Lollardy and the Reformation in England* (London, 1908).

EDWIN BURTON.

Pécs. See FÜNFKIRCHEN, DIOCESE OF.

Pectoral (חֹשֶׁן, חֹשֶׁן הַמִּשְׁפָּט, "pectoral of judgment").—The original meaning of the Hebrew term has been lost, and little light is thrown upon it by the early translations. The prevailing equivalent in the Sept. is λόγιον; the Vulgate has *rationale*, whence the literal "rational" of the Douay Version; the rendering in the Authorized Version is "breastplate". In the minute directions given for the distinctive official dress of the high priest in Exodus, xxviii, a section belonging to the priestly code (cf. also Ex., xxxix, 8–21), special prominence is given to the breastplate or pectoral. The divergent description of the same recorded by Josephus ("Antiq.", III, vii, 5 and "Bell.", V, v. 7) is considered less reliable. The main reason of the importance attached to the construction of the pectoral seems to be the fact that it was the receptacle of the sacred oracular lot, the mysterious Urim and Thummim (q. v.), a consideration which renders probable the tentative etymological signification of the original term proposed by Ewald ("Antiquities of

Israel", 294), viz., "the pouch of the Oracle". From Exodus we learn that the material employed was the same substantially as for the ephod (q. v.), viz., gold, blue, purple, and scarlet on a groundwork of fine twined linen, which are the finest and most artistic textile fabrics (cf. also Ecclus., xlv). The form of the pectoral was a square made by the folding in two of the material measuring a cubit in length and a half cubit in breadth. Into this square were fitted by means of gold settings four rows of precious stones, three in a row. On each jewel was inscribed the name of one of the twelve tribes of Israel, whose memory was thus borne continually before the Lord by the high priest in his official functions (see Ex., xxviii, 29).

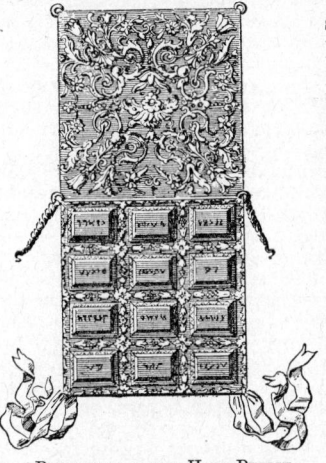

PECTORAL OF THE HIGH PRIEST

Besides the ordinary Commentaries on the Book of Exodus, see ANCESSI, *L'Egypte et Moïse* (Paris, 1875), chapter: *Les Vêtements du Grand Prêtre*; KENNEDY in HASTINGS, *Dict. of the Bible*, s. v. *Breastplate of the High Priest*; BRAUN, *Vest. Sacerd. Heb.* (Amsterdam, 1680).

JAMES F. DRISCOLL.

Pectorale (CRUX PECTORALIS) is the name of the cross used by the pope, cardinals, bishops, abbots, and other prelates entitled to use the pontifical insignia. It is worn on the breast attached to a chain or silken cord, the colour differing, according to the dignity of the wearer, i. e. green, violet, or black. It is made of precious metal, ornamented, more or less, with diamonds, pearls, or similar embellishment, and contains either the relics of some saint, or a particle of the Holy Cross. It is worn over the alb during liturgical functions. The prelate should kiss the cross before putting it on his neck, and while putting it on say the prayer "Munire me digneris" (the origin of which dates back to the Middle Ages), in which he petitions God for protection against his enemies, and begs to bear in mind continually the Passion of Our Lord, and the triumphs of the confessors of the Faith. The pontifical pectoral cross is distinct from the simple cross, the use of which is often permitted by the pope to members of cathedral chapters. Canons, to whom this privilege has been granted, are permitted to wear the cross at choir service only, and not over the alb at liturgical services, unless specially permitted. The pectoral is the latest addition to episcopal ornaments. The custom, however, of wearing a cross on the breast either with or without holy relics, dates back to ancient time and was observed not only by bishops, but also by priests and lay people. The first mention made of the pectoral cross as a part of pontifical ornament is by Innocent III, and its use as such only became customary toward the close of the Middle Ages. As an adornment for bishops we meet it the first time toward the end of the thirteenth century (Durandus), but at that time it was not generally worn by bishops. As Durandus says: "it was left to the discretion of the individual bishop to wear it or not". The Greek bishops also wear a pectoral cross but only over their liturgical vestments (chasuble or *salkos*).

ROHAULT DE FLEURY, *La Messe*, VIII (Paris, 1889); BOCK, *History of Liturgical Vestments*, II (Bonn, 1866); *Kirchenlexicon*, s. v. *Kreuz, 4 Das Pectoralkreuz*; THALHOFER, *Liturgik*, I (Freiburg, 1883); BONA, *Rerum liturg. libri duo*, II (2nd ed. Turin, 1749).

JOSEPH BRAUN.

Pectorius. See AUTUN, DIOCESE OF.

Pednelissus (PETNELISSUS), a titular see in Pamphylia Secunda, suffragan of Perge. In ancient times this city was a part of Pisidia. It is mentioned by Strabo, XII, 570, XIV, 667; Ptolemy, V, 5, 8; Pliny, V, 26, 1; Stephanus Byzantius, s. v.; in the sixth century by Hierocles, "Synecdemus", 681, 12, who locates it in Pamphylia. It is important for its frequent wars with Selge (Polybius, V, 72, etc.). Its coins have two forms of the name, as above (Head, "Historia numorum", 591); other documents frequently give very corrupted forms. The "Notitiæ Episcopatuum" mention the see as late as the thirteenth century; but only two bishops are known; Heraclides, present at the Œcumenical Council of Constantinople, 381, and Martinus, who signed the letter of the bishops of Pamphylia to Emperor Leo (Le Quien, "Oriens christianus", I, 1023). The exact site of the city is unknown and it is identified with several localities; the most probable identification is with the remains of a group of ruins to the south of Tchaudir and to the east of Kizil Keui in Pambóuk ova (cotton field), vilayet of Koniah.

SMITH, *Dict. of Greek and Roman Geogr.*, s. v.; RADET, *Les villes de Pisidie* in *Revue archéologique* (Paris, 1893), 8 sq.; see also the notes of MÜLLER on *Ptolemy*, ed. DIDOT, I, 864.

S. PÉTRIDÈS.

Pedro de Cordova, b. at Cordova, Andalusia, Spain, about 1460; d. on the Island of Santo Domingo, 1525. He studied theology at the University of Salamanca and there joined the Dominicans. About 1510 he went to Santo Domingo, founding the Santa Cruz province of the order. He was a zealous protector of the Indians and a friend of Las Casas. His book, "Doctrina cristiana para instruccion é informacion de los Indios por manera de historia", was printed in 1544 at Mexico by directions of Bishop Zumárraga. It was destined for the education of the Indians, chiefly of the islands, and is one of the earliest books of catechism known to have been composed in America. Fray Pedro was the first inquisitor appointed in the New World. He enjoyed the reputation of a model priest, highly respected by the clergy, the laity, and the Indians.

LAS CASAS, *Historias de las Indias* (Madrid, 1875–76); DÁVILA PADILLA, *Historia de la Fundacion y Discurso de la Provincia de Santiago de México* (Madrid, 1596; Brussels, 1625); YCAZBALCETA, *Bibliografía mexicana* (Mexico, 1886).

AD. F. BANDELIER.

Pedro de Luna (BENEDICT XIII). See LUNA, PEDRO DE.

Peking. See CHINA.

Pelagia, the name of several saints. The old Syrian martyrology (ed. De Rossi-Duchesne, in "Acta SS.", Nov., II; "Martyrol. Hieronym.", lxi) gives the feast of a St. Pelagia of Antioch (in Antiochia Pelagiæ) under the date of 8 October. Further information concerning this martyr, undoubtedly an historical person, is given in a homily of St. John Chrysostom [P. G., L, 479 sqq.; Ruinart, "Acta mart. sincera" (ed. Ratisbon), 540 sqq.]. Pelagia was a Christian virgin fifteen years of age. Soldiers came in search of her, evidently during the Diocletian persecution, in order to force her to offer publicly a heathen sacrifice. She was alone in the house, no one being there to aid her. She came out to the soldiers sent after her and when she learned the order they had to execute, she requested permission to go again into the house in order to put on other clothing. This was granted to her. The virgin who probably knew what was before her was not willing to expose herself to the danger of being dishonoured. She therefore went up to the roof of the house and threw herself into the sea. Thus she died, as St. Chrysostom says, as virgin and martyr, and was honoured as such by the Antiochene Church. St. Ambrose also mentions this St. Pelagia of Antioch ("De virginibus", III, vii, in P. L., XVI, 229;

Epist. XXVII, "Ad Simplicianum", xxxviii, ibid., 1903).

There is a later legend of a Pelagia who is said to have led the life of a prostitute at Antioch and to have been converted by a bishop named Nonnus. According to the story she went to Jerusalem where disguised as a man and under the name of Pelagius she led a life of self-mortification in a grotto on the Mount of Olives. The author of this legend who calls himself the Deacon Jacob has drawn the essential part of his narrative from the forty-eighth homily of St. Chrysostom on the Gospel of St. Matthew. In this homily the preacher relates the conversion of a celebrated actress of Antioch whose name he does not give. As no old authority makes any mention of a Pelagia in Jerusalem, no doubt the alleged converted woman is a purely legendary recasting of the historical Pelagia. In the East the feast of this second Pelagia is observed on the same day (8 October); in the present Roman martyrology the feast of the martyr is observed on 9 June, that of the penitent on 8 October.

On the latter date the Greek Church also celebrates as virgin and martyr still another Pelagia of Tarsus. The Roman martyrology places the feast of this Pelagia on 4 May. There is a legend of later date concerning her. As Tarsus was near Antioch St. Pelagia of Tarsus should probably be identified with the Antiochene martyr, whose feast was also observed in Tarsus and who was afterwards turned into a martyr of Tarsus. Usener's opinion that all these different saints are only a Christian reconstruction of Aphrodite has been completely disproved by Delehaye.

In addition to St. Pelagia of Antioch, taken from the Syrian martyrology, the "Martyrologium Hieronymianum" also mentions on 11 July a martyr Pelagia, the companion in martyrdom of a Januarius, naming Nicopolis in Armenia as the place of martyrdom, and giving a brief account of this saint. She is plainly a different person from the martyr of Antioch. Her name was included by Bede in his martyrology and was adopted from this into the present Roman list of saints.

Acta SS., May, I, 747 sq. (Pelagia of Tarsus); *Acta SS.*, Oct., IV, 261 sq. and *P. G.*, CXVI, 908 sq. (Pelagia of Antioch-Jerusalem); *Bibliotheca hagiographica græca* (2nd ed.), 206; *Bibl. hagiogr. lat.*, II, 959 sq.; USENER, *Legenden der hl. Pelagia* (Bonn, 1879); DELEHAYE, *Les légendes hagiographiques* (Brussels, 1905), 222 sq.

J. P. KIRSCH.

Pelagius I, POPE, date of birth unknown; d. 3 March, 561, was a Roman of noble family; his father, John, seems to have been vicar of one of the two civil "dioceses", or districts, into which Italy was then divided. We first meet with him at Constantinople, in the company of Agapitus I, who, just before his death in that city, appointed Pelagius *apocrisiarius* or nuncio of the Roman Church (536). When, through the intrigues of the Empress Theodora, ever scheming for the advancement of the Monophysite heresy, Silverius, the successor of Agapitus in the See of Rome, had been forcibly deposed and banished from Italy by the Greek general Belisarius, the Emperor Justinian issued strict orders that Silverius should be recalled to Rome, and decreed that, if proved innocent, he should be reinstated. If we are to believe Liberatus, an historian opposed to the Fifth General Council, and hence to Popes Vigilius and Pelagius, the latter was prevailed upon by the empress to travel post haste in order to prevent if possible Silverius's return to Italy. In this mission, however, he failed. Nevertheless, the empress accomplished her will, which resulted in the death of Silverius and the accession of Vigilius, of whom she hoped to make a tool. Pelagius meanwhile acquired great influence with Justinian. He selected the orthodox Paul for the See of Alexandria (540), and had to depose him, and choose a successor two years later (542).

The following year, after having brought about the condemnation of Origen, he returned to Rome. After Justinian published (about 544) his decree on the "Three Chapters" (i. e. brief statements of anathema upon Theodore of Mopsuestia and his writings, upon Theodoret of Cyrus and his writings against St. Cyril of Alexandria and the Council of Ephesus, and upon the letter written by Ibas of Edessa to Maris, Bishop of Hardaschir in Persia), we find Pelagius writing to Ferrandus for his opinion on it, and when Vigilius went to Constantinople (Nov., 545) in obedience to the emperor's orders, he remained as his representative in Rome. The times were hard, for Totila, King of the Goths, had begun to blockade the city. The deacon poured out his private fortune for the benefit of the famine-stricken people, and endeavoured to induce the Gothic king to grant a truce. Though he failed, he afterwards induced Totila to spare the lives of the people when he became master of Rome in Dec., 546. That prince conceived so great an admiration for the Roman deacon that he sent him to Constantinople in order to arrange a peace with Justinian, but the emperor sent him back to say that his general Belisarius was in command in Italy, and that he would decide all questions of peace or war.

Once more the energetic deacon returned to Constantinople, this time to support Vigilius, who was being shamefully treated by the emperor, with a view of making him do his will in the matter of the Three Chapters. Encouraged by Pelagius, Vigilius began to offer a stout resistance to Justinian (551) and issued his first "Constitutum" (May, 553). But in June, after the Fifth General Council of Constantinople, which had condemned the Three Chapters, was over and Pelagius and other supporters of the pope had been thrown into prison, the unfortunate Vigilius gave way, and in his second "Constitutum" (Feb., 554) confirmed the decrees of the Council. Pelagius did not submit at once, but wrote against the opponents of the Three Chapters and blamed the subservience of his superior. At length however he rallied to the pope's side, either because he saw that opposition to him was endangering the unity of the Church, or because, as his adversaries said, he wished to regain Justinian's favour, and by it to succeed Vigilius as pope. It is certain that he did re-enter into the emperor's good graces, shortly before he left Constantinople with the pope, about the beginning of 555. Vigilius died at Syracuse during his return journey (7 June, 555), but it was not till the next year that Pelagius was elected his successor, and consecrated (16 April, 556).

He had no little difficulty in procuring bishops to consecrate him, for there was great opposition to him on account of his change of front regarding the condemnation of the Three Chapters. Some of his enemies even accused him of being responsible for the death of his predecessor. With a view to lessen the ill-feeling against him, he went with the "patrician", Narses, to St. Peter's, and, holding the Gospels and "the Cross of Christ" above his head, he solemnly averred that he had wrought no harm to Vigilius. Then, indirectly to assert the purity of his conduct with reference to his accession to the papacy, he proceeded to denounce simony. His principal aims during his five years' pontificate were to overcome opposition, if not now so much to himself, at any rate to the Fifth General Council, in the West; and to make good the material damage to the Church's property in Italy, brought about by the campaigns between the Greeks and the Goths. Of his personal worth the Romans were again soon convinced, when they saw him use his wealth for their advantage, in the same generous manner as he had done when Totila's blockade had reduced them to the last extremity; as, for example, when they saw him repairing and refurnishing the churches, and reorganizing for the benefit of the poor the possessions and revenues of the Church which the Gothic war, and the long absence of the popes from Rome, had thrown into great confusion.

But Pelagius was not so successful in extinguishing in Italy the schism which the condemnation of the Three Chapters had excited in the West, as he was in winning the confidence of the Romans. The vacillation of Vigilius, and his submission to the will of Justinian, the persecution to which he had been exposed, and the final adhesion of Pelagius himself to his predecessor's decree confirming the Council of Constantinople, embittered the minds of many of the Westerns against the East. They were too angry at the emperor's conduct to realize that with both Vigilius and Pelagius the whole question was rather one of policy and expediency than of religion. Pelagius did all in his power to convince the bishops of Northern Italy, where the schism had taken the deepest hold, that he accepted the first four General Councils as unreservedly as they did, and that the decrees of the recent Council of Constantinople were in no way in real opposition to those of Chalcedon. He pointed out clearly to them that the differences between the two Councils were only on the surface, and not real, and that even if it was not advisable, under the circumstances, to condemn the writings of Theodoret, Theodore, and Ibas, still, as they were *de facto* heretical, there could be no harm in officially declaring that they were such. But the feelings of many had been so aroused that it was impossible to get them to listen to reason. The pope grew impatient, especially when Paulinus, Bishop of Aquileia, had in synod renounced communion with Rome, and excommunicated the great general Narses, the hope of Italy. In several letters he exhorted the "patrician" to use his military power to suppress the schism, and to seize Paulinus. Narses, however, probably on account of the political difficulties with which he was beset, did not move, and it was not till the seventh century that the schism caused in Italy by the condemnation of the Three Chapters was finally healed.

Pelagius, however, in the matter of the Council of Constantinople was more successful in Gaul than in Italy. In reply to a request from the Frankish King Childebert, he sent him a profession of faith, in which he proclaimed his entire agreement with the doctrines of Leo I, and trusted that no untruths about himself might cause a schism in Gaul. Further, in response to a request from the same king, and from Sapaudus, Bishop of Arles, he granted the latter the pallium, and constituted him his vicar over all the churches of Gaul, as his predecessors had been in the habit of so honouring the See of Arles. By these means he prevented any schism from arising in Gaul.

Making use of the "Pragmatic Sanction", which Justinian issued in August, 554, to regulate the affairs of Italy, thrown into hopeless disorder by the Gothic war, Pelagius was able to remedy many of the evils which it had caused. Fragments of a number of his letters, which were brought to light by E. Bishop comparatively recently, give us an insight into his extraordinary activity in this direction. They reveal him organizing ecclesiastical tribunals, suppressing abuses among clerics, to which the disorders of the times had given rise, putting the patrimonies of the Church on a new footing, and meanwhile gathering money and clothes for the poor from Gaul and from "distant islands and countries". Before he died his regulations for the management of the ecclesiastical estates had begun to bear fruit, and we read of revenues beginning to come in to him from various quarters. This "Father of the poor and of his country" was buried in St. Peter's the day after his death, in front of the sacristy.

Liber Pontificalis, ed. DUCHESNE, I (Paris, 1886), *Vit. Vigilii et Pelagii;* LIBERATUS, *Breviarium*, c. xxii etc. in *P. L.*, LXVIII; VICTOR TUNNENSIS, *Chronicon, ibid.;* PROCOPIUS, *De bello Gothico*, ed. DINDORF (Bonn, 1833); or in Latin, MURATORI, *Rerum Italicarum Scriptores*, I, pt. I; FACUNDUS, *De defens. trium capit.* in *P. L.*, LXVII; the letters of PELAGIUS in *P. L.*, LXIX; *Mon. Germ. Hist.: Epistolæ*, III (Berlin, 1892); JAFFÉ, *Regesta*, I (2nd ed., Leipzig, 1888). Modern works: especially DIEHL, *Justinien* (Paris, 1901), 340 etc.; GRISAR, *Hist. de Rome et des Papes* (Paris, 1906), I, pt. II, passim; HODGKIN, *Italy and her Invaders*, IV, V (London, 1895). An account of E. BISHOP'S discovery will be found in MANN, *Lives of the Popes in the early Middle Ages*, III, 233.

HORACE K. MANN.

Pelagius II, date of whose birth is unknown, seemingly a native of Rome, but of Gothic descent, as his father's name was Winigild, d. in Rome, 7 Feb., 590. He succeeded Benedict I, when the Lombards were besieging Rome, but his consecration was delayed in the hope of securing the confirmation of the election by the emperor. But the blockade of Rome by the Lombards, and their control of the great thoroughfares was effective and, after four months, he was consecrated (26 Nov., 579). The most important acts of Pelagius have relation to the Lombards, or to the Istrian schism of the Three Chapters (q. v.). Moved, it would seem, by the words of the new pope, and probably still more by his money and that of the emperor, the Lombards at length drew off from the neighbourhood of Rome. Thereupon, Pelagius at once sent an embassy (in which the deacon Gregory was apparently included) to Constantinople to explain the circumstances of his election, and to ask that succour should be sent to save Rome from the barbarians. But not very much in the way of help for Italy was forthcoming at this period from the exhausted Eastern Roman Empire. Emperor Maurice, it is true, sent somewhat later (c. 584) a new official to Italy with the title of exarch, and with combined civil and military authority over the whole peninsula. But, when he came to Ravenna, this new functionary brought with him only an insufficient military force, and meanwhile both emperor and pope had turned to the Franks.

Towards the beginning of his pontificate (Oct., 580 or 581) Pelagius wrote to Aunacharius (or Aunarius), Bishop of Auxerre, a man of great influence with the different Frankish kings, and begged him to give a practical proof of the zeal he had professed for the Roman Church, by urging them to come to the assistance of Rome. "We believe", he wrote, "that it has been brought about by a special dispensation of Divine Providence, that the Frankish Princes should profess the orthodox faith; like the Roman Emperors, in order that they may help this city, whence it took its rise. . . . Persuade them with all earnestness to keep from any friendship and alliance with our most unspeakable enemies, the Lombards." At length either the prayers of Pelagius, or the political arts of the emperor, induced the Franks to attack the Lombards in Italy. But their zeal for the papal or imperial cause was soon exhausted, and they allowed themselves to be bribed to retire from the peninsula. The distress of the Italians deepened. Pelagius had already sent to Constantinople the ablest of his clergy, the deacon Gregory, afterwards Gregory I, the Great. As the pope's apocrisiary, or nuncio, the deacon had been commissioned to haunt the imperial palace day and night, never to be absent from it for an hour, and to strain every nerve to induce the emperor to send help to Rome. To him Pelagius now dispatched letter after letter urging him to increased exertion. He also implored the new Exarch of Ravenna, Decius (584), to succour Rome, but was told that he was unable to protect the exarchate, still less Rome.

Failing to get help from Ravenna he sent a fresh embassy to Constantinople and exhorted Gregory to act along with it in endeavouring to obtain the desired help. "Here", he wrote, "we are in such straits that unless God move the heart of the emperor to have pity on us, and send us a Master of the soldiery (*magister militum*) and a duke, we shall be entirely at the mercy of our enemies, as most of the district round Rome is without protection; and the army of these most unspeakable people will take possession of the places still held for the empire." Though no imperial troops came to Rome, the exarch succeeded in concluding a truce with the Lombards. Taking advantage of this "peace and quiet", Pelagius II renewed the exertions of his namesake to put an end to the schism caused in Italy by the condemnation of the Three Chapters by Vigilius. The deacon Gregory was recalled from Constantinople, and assisted the pope in the correspondence which was forthwith initiated with Bishop Elias of Grado and the bishops of Istria. In one letter after another the pope bade them remember that the faith of Peter could not be crushed nor changed, and that that faith which he held was the faith of the Council of Chalcedon, as well as of the first three general councils; and, in the most touching terms, he exhorted them to hold to that glorious ecclesiastical unity which they were breaking "for the sake of superfluous questions and of defending heretical chapters". The words of the pope were, however, lost upon the schismatics, and equally without effect was the violence of the Exarch Smaragdus, who seized Severus, the successor of Elias, and, by threats, compelled him to enter into communion with the orthodox bishop, John of Ravenna (588). But as soon as Severus returned to his see, he repudiated what he had done, and the schism continued for some two hundred years longer.

Pelagius was one of the popes who laboured to promote the celibacy of the clergy, and he issued such stringent regulations on this matter, with regard to the subdeacons in the island of Sicily, that his successor Gregory I thought them too strict, and modified them to some extent. But if Gregory had to check the zeal of Pelagius in one direction he emulated it in another. The protest of Pelagius against the assumption of the title "œcumenical" by the Patriarch of Constantinople was repeated with added emphasis by his former secretary. Among the works of piety recorded of Pelagius may be noted his adorning of the Shrine of St. Peter, turning his own house into a hospital for the poor, and rebuilding the Church of St. Lawrence, where may still be seen a mosaic (probably executed by Pelagius) depicting St. Lawrence as standing on the right side of Our Lord. Pelagius fell a victim to the terrible plague that devastated Rome at the end of 589 and was buried in St. Peter's.

Liber Pontif. ed. DUCHESNE, I (Paris, 1886), 309; PAUL THE DEACON, Hist. Longobard. (Berlin, 1879); for the letters of PELAGIUS and GREGORY I see Mon. Germ. Epp., II, III (Berlin, 1892—); GRISAR, Hist. des papes, I, pt. ii (Paris, 1906),—an English translation of this work is to be published shortly; HODGKIN, Italy and her Invaders, V, VI (Oxford, 1896); BARMBY in SMITH, Dict. of Christ. Biog. (London, 1887), s. v.; for the Istrian schism see MANN, Lives of the Popes in the Early Middle Ages, I (London, 1902).

HORACE K. MANN.

Pelagius and Pelagianism.—Pelagianism received its name from Pelagius and designates a heresy of the fifth century, which denied original sin as well as Christian grace.

I. LIFE AND WRITINGS OF PELAGIUS.—Apart from the chief episodes of the Pelagian controversy, little or nothing is known about the personal career of Pelagius. It is only after he bade a lasting farewell to Rome in A. D. 411 that the sources become more abundant; but from 418 on history is again silent about his person. As St. Augustine (De peccat. orig., xxiv) testifies that he lived in Rome "for a very long time", we may presume that he resided there at least since the reign of Pope Anastasius (398–401). But about his long life prior to the year 400 and above all about his youth, we are left wholly in the dark. Even the country of his birth is disputed. While the most trustworthy witnesses, such as Augustine, Orosius, Prosper, and Marius Mercator, are quite explicit in assigning Britain as his native country, as is apparent from his cognomen of Brito or Britannicus, Jerome (Præf. in Jerem., lib. I and III) ridicules him as a "Scot" (loc. cit., "habet enim progeniem Scoticæ gentis de Britannorum vicinia"), who being "stuffed with Scottish porridge" (Scotorum pultibus prægravatus) suffers from a weak memory. Rightly arguing that the "Scots" of those days were really the Irish, H. Zimmer ("Pelagius in Irland", p. 20, Berlin, 1901) has recently advanced weighty reasons for the hypothesis that the true home of Pelagius must be sought in Ireland, and that he journeyed through the southwest of Britain to Rome. Tall in stature and portly in appearance (Jerome, loc. cit., "grandis et corpulentus"), Pelagius was highly educated, spoke and wrote Latin as well as Greek with great fluency and was well versed in theology. Though a monk and consequently devoted to practical asceticism, he never was a cleric; for both Orosius and Pope Zosimus simply call him a "layman". In Rome itself he enjoyed the reputation of austerity, while St. Augustine called him even a "saintly man", vir sanctus; with St. Paulinus of Nola (405) and other prominent bishops, he kept up an edifying correspondence, which he used later for his personal defence.

During his sojourn in Rome he composed several works: "De fide Trinitatis libri III", now lost, but extolled by Gennadius as "indispensable reading-matter for students"; "Eclogarum ex divinis Scripturis liber unus", in the main collection of Bible passages based on Cyprian's "Testimoniorum libri III", of which St. Augustine has preserved a number of fragments; "Commentarii in epistolas S. Pauli", elaborated no doubt before the destruction of Rome by Alaric (410) and known to St. Augustine in 412. Zimmer (loc. cit.) deserves credit for having rediscovered in this commentary on St. Paul the original work of Pelagius, which had, in the course of time, been attributed to St. Jerome (P. L., XXX, 645–902). A closer examination of this work, so suddenly become famous, brought to light the fact that it contained the fundamental ideas which the Church afterwards condemned as "Pelagian heresy". In it Pelagius denied the primitive state in paradise and original sin (cf. P. L., XXX, 678, "Insaniunt, qui de Adam per traducem asserunt ad nos venire peccatum"), insisted on the naturalness of concupiscence and the death of the body, and ascribed the actual existence and universality of sin to the bad example which Adam set by his first sin. As all his ideas were chiefly rooted in the old, pagan philosophy, especially in the popular system of the Stoics, rather than in Christianity, he regarded the moral strength of man's will (liberum arbitrium), when steeled by asceticism, as sufficient in itself to desire and to attain the loftiest ideal of virtue. The value of Christ's redemption was, in his opinion, limited mainly to instruction (doctrina) and example (exemplum), which the Saviour threw into the balance as a counterweight against Adam's wicked example, so that nature retains the ability to conquer sin and to gain eternal life even without the aid of grace. By justification we are indeed cleansed of our personal sins through faith alone (loc. cit., 663, "per solam fidem iustificat Deus impium convertendum"), but this pardon (gratia remissionis) implies no interior renovation or sanctification of the soul. How far the sola-fides doctrine "had no stouter champion before Luther than Pelagius" and whether, in particular, the Protestant conception of fiducial faith dawned upon him many centuries before Luther, as Loofs ("Realencyklopädie für protest. Theologie", XV, 753, Leipzig, 1904) assumes, probably needs more careful investigation. For the rest, Pelagius would have announced nothing new by this doctrine, since the Antinomists of the early Apostolic Church were already familiar with "justification by faith alone" (cf. JUSTIFICATION); on the other hand, Luther's boast of having been the first to proclaim the doctrine of abiding faith, might well arouse opposition. However, Pelagius insists expressly (loc.

cit., 812), "Ceterum sine operibus fidei, non legis, mortua est fides". But the commentary on St. Paul is silent on one chief point of doctrine, i. e. the significance of infant baptism, which supposed that the faithful were even then clearly conscious of the existence of original sin in children.

To explain psychologically Pelagius's whole line of thought, it does not suffice to go back to the ideal of the wise man, which he fashioned after the ethical principles of the Stoics and upon which his vision was centred. We must also take into account that his intimacy with the Greeks developed in him, though unknown to himself, a one-sidedness, which at first sight appears pardonable. The gravest error into which he and the rest of the Pelagians fell, was that they did not submit to the doctrinal decisions of the Church. While the Latins had emphasized the guilt rather than its punishment, as the chief characteristic of original sin, the Greeks on the other hand (even Chrysostom) laid greater stress on the punishment than on the guilt. Theodore of Mopsuestia went even so far as to deny the possibility of original guilt and consequently the penal character of the death of the body. Besides, at that time, the doctrine of Christian grace was everywhere vague and undefined; even the West was convinced of nothing more than that some sort of assistance was necessary to salvation and was given gratuitously, while the nature of this assistance was but little understood. In the East, moreover, as an offset to widespread fatalism, the moral power and freedom of the will were at times very strongly or even too strongly insisted on, *assisting* grace being spoken of more frequently than *preventing* grace (see GRACE). It was due to the intervention of St. Augustine and the Church, that greater clearness was gradually reached in the disputed questions and that the first impulse was given towards a more careful development of the dogmas of original sin and grace (cf. Mausbach, "Die Ethik des hl. Augustinus", II, 1 sqq., Freiburg, 1909).

II. PELAGIUS AND CÆLESTIUS (411–5).—Of far-reaching influence upon the further progress of Pelagianism was the friendship which Pelagius contracted in Rome with Cælestius, a lawyer of noble (probably Italian) descent. A eunuch by birth, but endowed with no mean talents, Cælestius had been won over to asceticism by his enthusiasm for the monastic life, and in the capacity of a lay-monk he endeavoured to convert the practical maxims learnt from Pelagius, into theoretical principles, which he successfully propagated in Rome. St. Augustine, while charging Pelagius with mysteriousness, mendacity, and shrewdness, calls Cælestius (De peccat. orig., xv) not only "incredibly loquacious", but also open-hearted, obstinate, and free in social intercourse. Even if their secret or open intrigues did not escape notice, still the two friends were not molested by the official Roman circles. But matters changed when in 411 they left the hospitable soil of the metropolis, which had been sacked by Alaric (410), and set sail for North Africa. When they landed on the coast near Hippo, Augustine, the bishop of that city, was absent, being fully occupied in settling the Donatist disputes in Africa. Later, he met Pelagius in Carthage several times, without, however, coming into closer contact with him. After a brief sojourn in North Africa, Pelagius travelled on to Palestine, while Cælestius tried to have himself made a presbyter in Carthage. But this plan was frustrated by the deacon Paulinus of Milan, who submitted to the bishop, Aurelius, a memorial in which six theses of Cælestius—perhaps literal extracts from his lost work "Contra traducem peccati"—were branded as heretical. These theses ran as follows: (1) Even if Adam had not sinned, he would have died. (2) Adam's sin harmed only himself, not the human race. (3) Children just born are in the same state as Adam before his fall. (4) The whole human race neither dies through Adam's sin or death, nor rises again through the resurrection of Christ. (5) The (Mosaic) Law is as good a guide to heaven as the Gospel. (6) Even before the advent of Christ there were men who were without sin. On account of these doctrines, which clearly contain the quintessence of Pelagianism, Cælestius was summoned to appear before a synod at Carthage (411); but he refused to retract them, alleging that the inheritance of Adam's sin was an open question and hence its denial was no heresy. As a result he was not only excluded from ordination, but his six theses were condemned. He declared his intention of appealing to the pope in Rome, but without executing his design went to Ephesus in Asia Minor, where he was ordained a priest.

Meanwhile the Pelagian ideas had infected a wide area, especially around Carthage, so that Augustine and other bishops were compelled to take a resolute stand against them in sermons and private conversations. Urged by his friend Marcellinus, who "daily endured the most annoying debates with the erring brethren", St. Augustine in 412 wrote the two famous works: "De peccatorum meritis et remissione libri III" (P. L., XLIV, 109 sqq.) and "De spiritu et litera" (ibid., 201 sqq.), in which he positively established the existence of original sin, the necessity of infant baptism, the impossibility of a life without sin, and the necessity of interior grace (*spiritus*) in opposition to the exterior grace of the law (*litera*). When in 414 disquieting rumours arrived from Sicily and the so-called "Definitiones Cælestii" (reconstructed in Garnier, "Marii Mercatoris Opera", I, 384 sqq., Paris, 1673), said to be the work of Cælestius, were sent to him, he at once (414 or 415) published the rejoinder, "De perfectione justitiæ hominis" (P. L., XLIV, 291 sqq.), in which he again demolished the illusion of the possibility of complete freedom from sin. Out of charity and in order to win back the erring the more effectually, Augustine, in all these writings, never mentioned the two authors of the heresy by name.

Meanwhile Pelagius, who was sojourning in Palestine, did not remain idle; to a noble Roman virgin, named Demetrias, who at Alaric's coming had fled to Carthage, he wrote a letter which is still extant (in P. L., XXX, 15–45) and in which he again inculcated his Stoic principles of the unlimited energy of nature. Moreover, he published in 415 a work, now lost, "De natura", in which he attempted to prove his doctrine from authorities, appealing not only to the writings of Hilary and Ambrose, but also to the earlier works of Jerome and Augustine, both of whom were still alive. The latter answered at once (415) by his treatise "De natura et gratia" (P. L., XLIV, 247 sqq.). Jerome, however, to whom Augustine's pupil Orosius, a Spanish priest, personally explained the danger of the new heresy, and who had been chagrined by the severity with which Pelagius had criticized his commentary on the Epistle to the Ephesians, thought the time ripe to enter the lists; this he did by his letter to Ctesiphon (Ep. cxxliii) and by his graceful "Dialogus contra Pelagianos" (P. L., XXIII, 495 sqq.). He was assisted by Orosius, who, forthwith accused Pelagius in Jerusalem of heresy. Thereupon, Bishop John of Jerusalem "dearly loved" (St. Augustine, "Ep. clxxix") Pelagius and had him at the time as his guest. He convoked in July, 415, a diocesan council for the investigation of the charge. The proceedings were hampered by the fact that Orosius, the accusing party, did not understand Greek and had engaged a poor interpreter, while the defendant Pelagius was quite able to defend himself in Greek and uphold his orthodoxy. However, according to the personal account (written at the close of 415) of Orosius (Liber apolog. contra Pelagium, P. L., XXXI, 1173), the contesting parties at last agreed to leave the final judgment on all questions to the Latins, since both Pelagius and his adversaaries were Latins, and to invoke the decision of Innocent I; meanwhile silence was imposed on both parties.

But Pelagius was granted only a short respite. For in the very same year, the Gallic bishops, Heros of Arles and Lazarus of Aix, who, after the defeat of the usurper Constantine (411), had resigned their bishoprics and gone to Palestine, brought the matter before Bishop Eulogius of Cæsarea, with the result that the latter summoned Pelagius in December, 415, before a synod of fourteen bishops, held in Diospolis, the ancient Lydda. But fortune again favoured the heresiarch. About the proceedings and the issue we are exceptionally well informed through the account of St. Augustine, "De gestis Pelagii" (P. L., XLIV, 319 sqq.), written in 417 and based on the acts of the synod. Pelagius punctually obeyed the summons, but the principal complainants, Heros and Lazarus, failed to make their appearance, one of them being prevented by ill-health. And as Orosius, too, derided and persecuted by Bishop John of Jerusalem, had departed, Pelagius met no personal plaintiff, while he found at the same time a skilful advocate in the deacon Anianus of Celeda (cf. Hieronym., "Ep. cxliii", ed. Vallarsi, I, 1067). The principal points of the petition were translated by an interpreter into Greek and read only in an extract. Pelagius, having won the good-will of the assembly by reading to them some private letters of prominent bishops—among them one of Augustine (Ep. cxlvi)—began to explain away and disprove the various accusations. Thus from the charge that he made the possibility of a sinless life solely dependent on free will, he exonerated himself by saying that, on the contrary, he required the help of God (*adjutorium Dei*) for it, though by this he meant nothing else than the grace of creation (*gratia creationis*). Of other doctrines with which he had been charged, he said that, formulated as they were in the complaint, they did not originate from him, but from Cælestius, and that he also repudiated them. After this hearing there was nothing left for the synod but to discharge the defendant and to announce him as worthy of communion with the Church. The Orient had now spoken twice and had found nothing to blame in Pelagius, because he had hidden his real sentiments from his judges.

III. CONTINUATION AND END OF THE CONTROVERSY (415-8).—The new acquittal of Pelagius did not fail to cause excitement and alarm in North Africa, whither Orosius had hastened in 416 with letters from Bishops Heros and Lazarus. To parry the blow, something decisive had to be done. In autumn, 416, 67 bishops from Proconsular Africa assembled in a synod at Carthage, which was presided over by Aurelius, while fifty-nine bishops of the ecclesiastical province of Numidia, to which the See of Hippo, St. Augustine's see, belonged, held a synod in Mileve. In both places the doctrines of Pelagius and Cælestius were again rejected as contradictory to the Catholic faith. However, in order to secure for their decisions "the authority of the Apostolic See", both synods wrote to Innocent I, requesting his supreme sanction. And in order to impress upon him more strongly the seriousness of the situation, five bishops (Augustine, Aurelius, Alypius, Evodius, and Possidius) forwarded to him a joint letter, in which they detailed the doctrine of original sin, infant baptism, and Christian grace (St. Augustine, "Epp. clxxv-vii"). In three separate epistles, dated 27 Jan., 417, the pope answered the synodal letters of Carthage and Mileve as well as that of the five bishops (Jaffé, "Regest.", 2nd ed., nn. 321-323, Leipzig, 1885). Starting from the principle that the resolutions of provincial synods have no binding force until they are confirmed by the supreme authority of the Apostolic See, the pope developed the Catholic teaching on original sin and grace, and excluded Pelagius and Cælestius, who were reported to have rejected these doctrines, from communion with the Church until they should come to their senses (*donec resipiscant*). In Africa, where the decision was received with unfeigned joy, the whole controversy was now regarded as closed, and Augustine, on 23 September, 417, announced from the pulpit (Serm., cxxxi, 10, in P. L., XXXVIII, 734), "Jam de hac causa duo concilia missa sunt ad Sedem apostolicam, inde etiam rescripta venerunt; causa finita est". (Two synods have written to the Apostolic See about this matter; the replies have come back; the question is settled.) But he was mistaken; the matter was not yet settled.

Innocent I died on 12 March, 417, and Zosimus, a Greek by birth, succeeded him. Before his tribunal the whole Pelagian question was now opened once more and discussed in all its bearings. The occasion for this was the statements which both Pelagius and Cælestius submitted to the Roman See in order to justify themselves. Though the previous decisions of Innocent I had removed all doubts about the matter itself, yet the question of the persons involved was undecided, viz. Did Pelagius and Cælestius really teach the theses condemned as heretical? Zosimus' sense of justice forbade him to punish any one with excommunication before he was duly convicted of his error. And if the steps recently taken by the two defendants were considered, the doubts which might arise on this point, were not wholly groundless. In 416 Pelagius had published a new work, now lost, "De libero arbitrio libri IV", which in its phraseology seemed to verge towards the Augustinian conception of grace and infant baptism, even if in principle it did not abandon the author's earlier standpoint. Speaking of Christian grace, he admitted not only a Divine revelation, but also a sort of interior grace, viz. an illumination of the mind (through sermons, reading of the Bible, etc.), adding, however, that the latter served not to make salutary works possible, but only to facilitate their performance. As to infant baptism he granted that it ought to be administered in the same form as in the case of adults, not in order to cleanse the children from a real original guilt, but to secure to them entrance into the "kingdom of God". Unbaptized children, he thought, would after their death be excluded from the "kingdom of God", but not from "eternal life". This work, together with a still extant confession of faith, which bears witness to his childlike obedience, Pelagius sent to Rome, humbly begging at the same time that chance inaccuracies might be corrected by him who "holds the faith and the see of Peter". All this was addressed to Innocent I, of whose death Pelagius had not yet heard. Cælestius, also, who meanwhile had changed his residence from Ephesus to Constantinople, but had been banished thence by the anti-Pelagian Bishop Atticus, took active steps towards his own rehabilitation. In 417 he went to Rome in person and laid at the feet of Zosimus a detailed confession of faith (Fragments, P. L., XLV, 1718), in which he affirmed his belief in all doctrines, "from the Trinity of one God to the resurrection of the dead" (cf. St. Augustine, "De peccato orig.", xxiii).

Highly pleased with this Catholic faith and obedience, Zosimus sent two different letters (P. L., XLV, 1719 sqq.) to the African bishops, saying that in the case of Cælestius Bishops Heros and Lazarus had proceeded without due circumspection, and that Pelagius too, as was proved by his recent confession of faith, had not swerved from the Catholic truth. As to Cælestius, who was then in Rome, the pope charged the Africans either to revise their former sentence or to convict him of heresy in his own (the pope's) presence within two months. The papal command struck Africa like a bomb-shell. In great haste a synod was convened at Carthage in November, 417, and writing to Zosimus, they urgently begged him not to rescind the sentence which his predecessor, Innocent I, had pronounced against Pelagius and Cælestius, until both had confessed the necessity of interior grace for all salutary thoughts, words, and deeds. At last Zosimus came to a halt. By a rescript of 21 March, 418, he assured them that he had not yet pronounced definitively, but that he was transmitting to Africa all documents bearing on Pelagianism in order to pave the way for a new, joint investigation. Pursuant to the papal command, there was held on 1 May, 418, in the presence of 200 bishops, the famous Council of Carthage, which again branded Pelagianism as a heresy in eight (or nine) canons (Denzinger, "Enchir.", 10th ed., 1908, 101-8). Owing to their importance they may be summarized: (1) Death did not come to Adam from a physical necessity, but through sin. (2) New-born children must be baptized on account of original sin. (3) Justifying grace not only avails for the forgiveness of past sins, but also gives assistance for the avoidance of future sins. (4) The grace of Christ not only discloses the knowledge of God's commandments, but also imparts strength to will and execute them (5) Without God's grace it is not merely more difficult, but absolutely impossible to perform good works. (6) Not out of humility, but in truth must we confess ourselves to be sinners. (7) The saints refer the petition of the Our Father, "Forgive us our trespasses", not only to others, but also to themselves. (8) The saints pronounce the same supplication not from mere humility, but from truthfulness. Some codices contain a ninth canon (Denzinger, loc. cit., note 3): Children dying without baptism do not go to a "middle place" (*medius locus*), since the non-reception of baptism excludes both from "the kingdom of heaven" and from "eternal life". These clearly-worded canons, which (except the last-named) afterwards came to be articles of faith binding the universal Church, gave the death-blow to Pelagianism; sooner or later it would bleed to death.

Meanwhile, urged by the Africans (probably through a certain Valerian, who as *comes* held an influential position in Ravenna), the secular power also took a hand in the dispute, the Emperor Honorius, by rescript of 30 April, 418, from Ravenna, banishing all Pelagians from the cities of Italy. Whether Cælestius evaded the hearing before Zosimus, to which he was now bound, "by fleeing from Rome" (St. Augustine, "Contra duas epist. Pelag.", II, 5), or whether he was one of the first to fall a victim to the imperial decree of exile, cannot be satisfactorily settled from the sources. With regard to his later life, we are told that in 421 he again haunted Rome or its vicinity, but was expelled a second time by an imperial rescript (cf. P. L., XLV, 1750). It is further related that in 425 his petition for an audience with Celestine I was answered by a third banishment (cf. P. L., LI, 271). He then sought refuge in the Orient, where we shall meet him later. Pelagius could not have been included in the imperial decree of exile from Rome. For at that time he undoubtedly resided in the Orient, since, as late as the summer of 418, he communicated with Pinianus and his wife Melania, who lived in Palestine (cf. Card. Rampolla, "Santa Melania giuniore", Rome, 1905). But this is the last information we have about him; he probably died in the Orient. Having received the Acts of the Council of Carthage, Zosimus sent to all the bishops of the world his famous "Epistola tractoria" (418) of which unfortunately only fragments have come down to us. This papal encyclical, a lengthy document, gives a minute account of the entire "causa Cælestii et Pelagii", from whose works it quotes abundantly, and categorically demands the condemnation of Pelagianism as a heresy. The assertion that every bishop of the world was obliged to confirm this circular by his own signature, cannot be proved, it is more probable that the bishops were required to transmit to Rome a written agreement; if a bishop refused to sign, he was deposed from his office and banished. A second and harsher rescript, issued by the emperor on 9 June, 419, and addressed to Bishop Aurelius of Carthage (P. L., XLV, 1731), gave additional force to this measure. Augustine's triumph was complete. In 418, drawing the balance, as it were, of the whole controversy, he wrote against the heresiarchs his last great work, "De gratia Christi et de peccato originali" (P. L., XLIV, 359 sqq.).

IV.—THE DISPUTE OF ST. AUGUSTINE WITH JULIAN OF ECLANUM (419-28).—Through the vigorous measures adopted in 418, Pelagianism was indeed condemned, but not crushed. Among the eighteen bishops of Italy who were exiled on account of their refusal to sign the papal decree, Julian, Bishop of Eclanum, a city of Apulia now deserted, was the first to protest against the "Tractoria" of Zosimus. Highly educated and skilled in philosophy and dialectics, he assumed the leadership among the Pelagians. But to fight *for* Pelagianism now meant to fight *against* Augustine. The literary feud set in at once. It was probably Julian himself who denounced St. Augustine as *damnator nuptiarum* to the influential *comes* Valerian in Ravenna, a nobleman, who was very happily married. To meet the accusation, Augustine wrote, at the beginning of 419, an apology, "De nuptiis et concupiscentia libri II" (P. L., XLIV, 413 sqq.) and addressed it to Valerian. Immediately after (419 or 420), Julian published a reply which attacked the first book of Augustine's work and bore the title, "Libri IV ad Turbantium". But Augustine refuted it in his famous rejoinder, written in 421 or 422, "Contra Iulianum libri VI" (P. L., XLIV, 640 sqq.). When two Pelagian circulars, written by Julian and scouring the "Manichæan views" of the Antipelagians, fell into his hands, he attacked them energetically (420 or 421) in a work, dedicated to Boniface I, "Contra duas epistolas Pelagianorum libri IV" (P. L., XLIV, 549 sqq.). Being driven from Rome, Julian had found (not later than 421) a place of refuge in Cilicia with Theodore of Mopsuestia. Here he employed his leisure in elaborating an extensive work, "Libri VIII ad Florum", which was wholly devoted to refuting the second book of Augustine's "De nuptiis et concupiscentia". Though composed shortly after 421, it did not come to the notice of St. Augustine until 427. The latter's reply, which quotes Julian's argumentations sentence for sentence and refutes them, was completed only as far as the sixth book, whence it is cited in patristic literature as "Opus imperfectum contra Iulianum" (P. L., XLV, 1049 sqq.). A comprehensive account of Pelagianism, which brings out into strong relief the diametrically opposed views of the author, was furnished by Augustine in 428 in the final chapter of his work, "De hæresibus" (P. L., XLII, 21 sqq.). Augustine's last writings published before his death (430) were no longer aimed against Pelagianism, but against Semipelagianism.

After the death of Theodore of Mopsuestia (428), Julian of Eclanum left the hospitable city of Cilicia and in 429 we meet him unexpectedly in company with his fellow exiles Bishops Florus, Orontius, and Fabius, at the Court of the Patriarch Nestorius of Constantinople, who willingly supported the fugitives. It was here, too, in 429, that Cælestius emerged again as the *protégé* of the patriarch; this is his last appearance in history; for from now on all trace of him is lost. But the exiled bishops did not long enjoy the protection of Nestorius. When Marius Mercator, a layman and friend of St. Augustine, who was then present in Constantinople, heard of the machinations of the Pelagians in the imperial city, he composed towards the end of 429 his "Commonitorium super nomine Cælestii" (P. L., XLVIII, 63 sqq.), in which he exposed the shameful life and the heretical character of Nestorius' wards. The result was that the Emperor Theodosius II decreed their banishment in 430. When the

Œcumenical Council of Ephesus (431) repeated the condemnation pronounced by the West (cf. Mansi, "Concil. collect.", IV, 1337), Pelagianism was crushed in the East. According to the trustworthy report of Prosper of Aquitaine ("Chronic.", ad a. 439, in P. L., LI, 598), Julian of Eclanum, feigning repentance, tried to regain possession of his former bishopric, a plan which Sixtus III (432–40) courageously frustrated. The year of his death is uncertain. He seems to have died in Italy between 441 and 455 during the reign of Valentinian III.

V. LAST TRACES OF PELAGIANISM (429–529.)—After the Council of Ephesus (431), Pelagianism no more disturbed the Greek Church, so that the Greek historians of the fifth century do not even mention either the controversy or the names of the heresiarchs. But the heresy continued to smoulder in the West and died out very slowly. The main centres were Gaul and Britain. About Gaul we are told that a synod, held probably at Troyes in 429, was compelled to take steps against the Pelagians. It also sent Bishops Germanus of Auxerre and Lupus of Troyes to Britain to fight the rampant heresy, which received powerful support from two pupils of Pelagius, Agricola and Fastidius (cf. Caspari, "Letters, Treatises and Sermons from the two last Centuries of Ecclesiastical Antiquity", pp. 1–167, Christiania, 1891). Almost a century later, Wales was the centre of Pelagian intrigues. For the saintly Archbishop David of Menevia participated in 519 in the Synod of Brefy, which directed its attacks against the Pelagians residing there, and after he was made Primate of Cambria, he himself convened a synod against them. In Ireland also Pelagius's "Commentary on St. Paul", described in the beginning of this article, was in use long afterwards, as is proved by many Irish quotations from it. Even in Italy traces can be found, not only in the Diocese of Aquileia (cf. Garnier, "Opera Marii Mercat.", I, 319 sqq., Paris, 1673), but also in Middle Italy; for the so-called "Liber Prædestinatus", written about 440 perhaps in Rome itself, bears not so much the stamp of Semipelagianism as of genuine Pelagianism (cf. von Schubert, "Der sog. Prædestinatus, ein Beitrag zur Geschichte des Pelagianismus", Leipzig, 1903). A more detailed account of this work will be found under the article PREDESTINARIANISM. It was not until the Second Synod of Orange (529) that Pelagianism breathed its last in the West, though that convention aimed its decisions primarily against Semipelagianism (q. v.).

All the works of Pelagius, Cælestius and Julian as well as the writings of their adversaries Jerome, Augustine, Orosius, Marius Mercator, etc., which have been quoted in the course of the article, are also the *sources* of the history of the Pelagian heresy. To these must be added the synodal acts of the different councils as far as they are extant. A *Corpus Pelagianum* for later years is furnished by the above-mentioned work of CASPARI. A collection of older documents is found in P. L., XLV, 1609 sqq.; cf. BRUCKNER, *Quellen zur Geschichte des Pelagianismus in Texte und Untersuchungen*, by GEBHARDT AND HARNACK, XV, 3 (Leipzig, 1906). For the *Commentary* on *St. Paul*, cf. RIGGENBACH, *Unbeachtet gebliebene Fragmente des Pelagius-Kommentars zu den Paulinischen Briefen* (Leipzig, 1905); against its genuineness, cf. KLASEN in *Tübinger Theologische Quartalschrift* (1885), 244 sqq., 531 sqq.; its genuineness (with unessential changes) was proved by ZIMMER, *Pelagius in Irland* (Berlin, 1901); cf. SOUTER, *The Commentary of Pelagius on the Epistles of St. Paul: the Problem of its Restoration* (London, 1907); *Journal of Theological Studies* (1906), 568 sqq.; (1907), 526 sqq.; *The Expositor*, I (1907), 455 sqq. For the *history of* Pelagianism, cf. NORIS, *Historia Pelagiana* (Florence, 1673), reprinted in his *Opera*, ed. BERTI, I (Venice, 1729), 1–412. Still valuable is C. W. F. WALCH, *Entwurf einer vollständigen Historie der Ketzereien*, IV (Leipzig, 1768); J. G. WALCH, *De Pelagianismo ante Pelagium* (Jena, 1738); WIGGERS, *Pragmatische Darstellung des Augustinismus und Pelagianismus* (Hamburg, 1833); JACOBI, *Die Lehre des Pelagius* (Leipzig, 1842); WÖRTER, *Der Pelagianismus nach seinem Ursprung und seiner Lehre* (Freiburg, 1874); KLASEN, *Die innere Entwicklung des Pelagianismus* (Freiburg, 1882); ERNST, *Pelagianische Studien* in *Katholik*, II (1884), 225 sqq.; I (1885), 241 sqq.; WARFIELD, *Two Studies in the History of Doctrine: Augustine and the Pelagian Controversy; The Development of the Doctrine of Infant Salvation* (New York, 1897); BRUCKNER, *Julian von Eclanum, sein Leben und seine Lehre* (Leipzig, 1897); HEFELE, *Konziliengeschichte*, II (Freiburg, 1875), 104 sqq.; SCHWANE, *Dogmengeschichte*, II (Freiburg, 1895); HERGENRÖTHER-KIRSCH, *Kirchengeschichte*, I (Freiburg, 1902); TIXERONT, *Histoire des dogmes*, II (Paris, 1909); PETERS in *Kirchenlexikon*, s. v.; LOOFS in *Realencyclopädie für protest. Theologie*, XV (Leipzig, 1904), 747 sqq.; KOCH in *Kirchl. Handlexikon*, s. v.

JOSEPH POHLE.

Pelargus, AMBROSE, theologian, b. at Nidda, Hesse, about 1488; d. at Trier, 1557. Stork (Greek *Pelargon*, whence Pelargus) entered the Dominican order probably at Freiburg, Breisgau. He was famed for his eloquence and admired for the elegance of his writings, being skilled in Latin, Greek, and Hebrew. His polemical efforts were directed principally against the Anabaptists, the Iconoclasts, and those who rejected the Mass. He attended the Diet of Worms (1540) and the Council of Trent in 1546, as theologian and procurator of the Archbishop of Trier. On 10 May, 1546, he addressed the assembled Fathers. When the council was transferred to Bologna in 1547, Charles V, incensed against Pelargus because he had favoured the transfer, induced the archbishop to recall him, but the latter chose him again as his theologian in 1561. His principal works are: "Apologia sacrificii eucharistiæ contra Œcolampadium" (Basle, 1528); "Hyperaspismus, seu apologiæ propugnatio . . ." (Basle, 1529); "Opuscula", against Anabaptists and Iconoclasts (Freiburg, 1534); "Divina S. Joannis Chrysos. Liturgia, e Græco Latine ab Ambrosio Pelargo versa et illustrata" (Worms, 1541); "Inter Pelargum et Erasmum epistolæ" (Cologne, 1539).

QUÉTIF AND ECHARD, *Script. Ord. Præd.*, II (Paris, 1721), 158; PALLAVICINI, *Hist. Conc. Trid.* (Antwerp, 1670), pt. II, bk. X, ii, 6.

D. J. KENEDY.

Pelisson-Fontanier, PAUL, a French writer, b. at Béziers in 1624, of Protestant parents; d. at Versailles, 7 February, 1693. He finished his classical studies at the age of eleven at Castres, studied philosophy at Montauban, law at Toulouse, and, when only nineteen years old, published a Latin translation of, and a commentary on, the first book of Justinian's "Institutes". In 1653 he wrote his "Histoire de l'Académie française", which procured his election to that body. He became secretary to Superintendent Fouquet in 1652, master of accounts at Montpellier in 1659, counsellor of the king in 1660. When Fouquet was discharged, Pelisson stood faithfully by him and was imprisoned in the Bastille (1661), where he remained four years. There he wrote his three "Mémoires" in defence of Fouquet. Liberated in 1666 he was named royal historian by Louis XIV. In 1670 he abjured the Protestant religion, received minor orders and subdiaconate, was given the Abbey of Guieont, and made administrator of divers benefices and disburser of the money destined for needy converts. The charge that he refused the last sacraments on his deathbed is false; he attended to his religious duties to the last. His works include: "Histoire de Louis XIV" (published by Lemascrier, 1749); "Réflexions sur les différends en matière de religion" (1686), against Jurieu and Leibnitz; "Traité de l'Eucharistie" (Paris, 1694), these two works are in Migne, "Démonstrations évangéliques", III; "Prières au Saint-Sacrement" (1734); "Prières sur les épîtres et les évangiles de l'année" (1734).

CHEVÉ, *Dict. des conversions* in MIGNE, *Encycl. théologique*; RÄSS, *Convertiten*, VIII; MARCOU, *Pelisson. Etude sur sa vie et ses œuvres* (Paris, 1859).

GEORGE M. SAUVAGE.

Pella, a titular see and suffragan of Scythopolis in Palæstina Secunda. According to Stephanus Byzantius (s. v.), the town must have been founded by Alexander; in any case it is a Macedonian foundation. Alexander Janneus captured it, and as he was unable to persuade the inhabitants to embrace Judaism, destroyed it (Josephus, "Bel. Jud.", I, iv, 8; "Ant. Jud." XIII, xv, 4); Pompey rebuilt it and reunited it to the Province of Syria ("Bel. Jud." I, vii, 7; "Ant. Jud.", XIV, iv, 4); it became then a part of Decapolis, remained always a Greek town, and formed the northern boundary of Jewish Pareus ("Bel. Jud.", III, iii, 3). As a part of the kingdom of Agrippa it offered in A. D. 66 a safe refuge to the little Christian community of Mt. Sion who, under the leadership of St. Simeon, took refuge there during the revolt of the Jews, and the siege of Jerusalem by the Romans (Eusebius, "H. E.", III, v; Epiphanius, "Haer.", xxix, 7). When, after three years of war and massacres, the second Jewish revolt had been suppressed by Rome (132–5), and Emperor Adrian had rebuilt Jerusalem under the name of "Ælia Capotolina", a part of the community living at Pella re-established themselves by order of the uncircumcised bishop, Mark, on Mount Sion. Nevertheless Christianity persevered at Pella, as testified by Ariston (born there in the second century, and author of the "Dialogue of Jason and Papiscos"), numerous Christian tombs and some inscriptions ("Revue biblique", 1899, VIII, 22). Le Quien (Oriens christianus, III, 697–700) mentions only three bishops: Zebennus in 449; Paul in 518; and Zachary in 532. The ruins of Pella may be seen at Tabakat-Fahil beyond the Jordan and opposite Scythopolis or Beisan; the necropolis and a Christian basilica with three naves are noteworthy.

SMITH, *Dict. of Greek and Roman Geog.*, II, 570; SHUHMAKER, *Pella* (London, 1888); *Echos d'Orient*, III (1899), 83.

S. VAILHÉ.

Pelletier, PIERRE-JOSEPH, b. in Paris, 22 March, 1788; d. there, 19 July, 1842. His father, Bertrand Pelletier, a pharmacist and a follower of Lavoisier, filled several government offices in France after the Revolution, dying at the early age of thirty-six. Like his father, the son showed precocity in science and followed in his steps in the doctrines of Lavoisier. The son's attention was directed to materia medica and to the vegetable alkaloids. He was associated with Caventou in the discovery of quinine in 1820 and without any thought of possible remuneration, if the discovery was kept secret, published his results to the world. It was in 1827 that the Montyon prize of 10,000 francs was awarded to him by the Paris Academy of Science for the discovery, this being the sole reward for so great an achievement. Strychnine was another of his discoveries and his memoir on the subject was published in Paris in 1818. He was professor in the École de pharmacie in Paris and in 1832 became one of its adjunct directors. He was appointed a member of the Conseil de salubrité of Paris and held other positions of honour. In 1840 he was elected to the Academy of Sciences. The natural alkaloid—pelletierine—and three others were named after him by their discoverer, Tauret. Among his works may be cited: "Notice sur la matière verte des feuilles", in collaboration with Caventou (Paris, 1817); "Analyse chimique des quinquinas" (Paris, 1821); "Notice sur les recherches chimiques" (Paris, 1829), etc. Pelletier, as Cauchy testifies, was a convinced Catholic.

La grande encyclopédie; LAROUSSE, *Dictionnaire universel;* KNELLER, *Das Christentum* (2nd ed., Freiburg, 1904).

T. O'CONOR SLOANE.

Pellico, SILVIO, Italian author and patriot, b. at Saluzzio, Italy, 24 June, 1788; d. at Turin, 31 Jan., 1854. His father was a government employee and Silvio spent his youth in different places in Italy, making also a four-years' sojourn in Lyons. At the age of twenty he was in Milan, where he made the acquaintance of several of the best Italian writers, among whom were Monti, Foscolo, and Manzoni. Here he taught French in a school, conducted by the Government, for soldiers' orphans, and when the Austrian authorities deprived him of this post, he served as a private tutor in different families, especially in that of Count Luigi Porro Lambertenghi, one of the leading opponents of Austrian dominion in the land. Lambertenghi founded in 1819 the periodical "Il Conciliatore", which, as a literary organ, voiced the doctrines of the Romantic writers as opposed to those of the Classicist school, and, as a political organ, combatted all foreign domination in Italy. Pellico played an important part in the editing of this periodical. In 1820, with a fellow-worker, Pietro Maroncelli, he incurred suspicion as a member of the Carbonari, and, having been arrested by order of the Austrians, was imprisoned first in the Piombi at Venice and next in the dungeon of San Michele di Murano. After a perfunctory trial he and Maroncelli were condemned to death, but this penalty was soon commuted into one of imprisonment with hard labour, and they were taken to the fortress of Spielberg in Moravia. After eight years of incarceration and much suffering, Pellico was released (1830). During the remainder of his life, broken down by the hardships of imprisonment, he remained entirely aloof from politics, and preferred a life of seclusion.

Pellico is not one of the great Italian authors of the nineteenth century; yet he is one who has endeared himself permanently to the Italian heart by a single document, his prison diary, "Le mie Prigioni". In this work, which rapidly became popular and passed into foreign languages, he relates in simple and unaffected prose his experiences and emotions during the whole period of his confinement. There is no tone of bitterness in his manner; his attitude throughout is that of the genuinely devout and resigned Catholic, and he records with infinite detail and often with profoundly pathetic effect his daily experience in his various prisons. His little account of the spider which he trained to eat from his hand is one of the best remembered passages of modern Italian prose. The very gentleness and homeliness of its narrative made his "Prigioni" the favourite that it is, and well has it been said that the book did more harm to Austria than any defeat on the field of battle. His other writings are: "Liriche", full of religious devotion and patriotic fervour; "Cantiche" or "Novelle poetiche", romantic in inspiration and concerned with medieval life and manners; twelve tragedies; the "Doveri degli uomini", a prose compilation of precepts and example, intended to teach right living to the young; his copious correspondence ("Epistolario"), and a prose version of Byron's "Manfred". Only eight of the tragedies have been published, the most famous of which, "Francesca da Rimini", dealing with the Dantesque tradition, was performed successfully in 1818; it engaged at once the attention of Byron and he translated it into English. The "Francesca" ranks next in importance among his works to the "Prigioni".

Opere (Milan, 1886); *Epistolario* (Florence, 1856); *Le mie Prigioni*, ed. PARAVIA, SONZOGNO, and others; *Poesie e lettere inedite* (Rome, 1898); *Prose e tragedie scelte* (Milan, 1899); RINIERI, *Della vita e delle opere di S. P.* (3 vols., Turin, 1898–1901); BRIANO, *S. P.* (Turin, 1861); PARAVIA in *Revue Contemporaine*, 1853–4; DIDIER in *Revue des Deux Mondes* (Sept., 1842).

J. D. M. FORD.

Pellissier (PELLICIER), GUILLAUME, b. at Melgueil in Languedoc, about 1490; d. at the castle of Montferraud, 1568. He made a brilliant course in law and theology and travelled in France and Italy. In 1527 his uncle, Bishop of Maguelonne, appointed him canon and shortly afterwards his coadjutor. He became the next bishop in 1529. Francis I entrusted him with several important missions; in 1529 he accompanied Louise de Savoie to Cambrai and concluded peace with Charles V. In 1533 at Marseilles he arranged with Clement VII for the marriage of the Duc d'Orléans (Henri II) and Catherine de' Medici. He obtained permission for the translation of his episcopal see from Maguelonne to Montpellier from Paul III in 1536. Four years later he was sent as ambassador to Venice, and brought back a large number of Greek, Syriac, and Hebrew MSS. An ardent Humanist, he was arrested on suspicion of heresy by order of the Parliament of Toulouse, and imprisoned in the castle of Beaucaire, though he easily freed himself from the charge and passed the remainder of his days combatting the Protestant heresy. He was obliged more than once to quit Montpellier, for Aigues-Mortes, and Maguelonne. In 1567 the Protestants destroyed his cathedral. His correspondence was published at Paris (1900); his commentaries on Tacitus are unpublished.

VAISSERE AND DEMI, *Hist. générale de Languedoc.*

T. LATASTE.

Pelotas, DIOCESE OF (PELOTASENSIS), in Brazil, suffragan to Porto Alegre. By a decree of Pius X, dated 15 Aug., 1910, the See of São Pedro do Rio Grande was erected into an archbishopric under the title of Porto Alegre (q. v.) and given four suffragans, three of which were detached from the old diocese. One of these, Pelotas, was formed from twenty-four parishes in the south-eastern portion of Rio Grande do Sul. It includes most of the territory lying near the Lagõa Mirí, and the lower half of the Lagõa dos Patõs. The cathedral church of the new diocese, dedicated to St. Francis of Paula, is at Pelotas, a well-constructed, handsome city, situated on the São Gonçalo. Pelotas, a centre of commercial activity, especially in the cattle trade, contains about 25,000 inhabitants, and has a Jesuit college. Rio Grande, its seaport, twenty-six miles to the south-east, has about 20,000 inhabitants. The other chief centres of population are at Bagé, São Lourenço, São José do Norte, and Boqueirão. The population is almost entirely Catholic.

GALANTI, *Compendio de historia do Brazil*, III, IV (São Paulo, 1902-05).

A. A. MACERLEAN.

Pelouze, THÉOPHILE-JULES, scientist, b. at Valognes, La Manche, 26 Feb., 1807; d. in Paris, 31 May or 1 June, 1867. He began his career as a pharmacist, studying at La Fère. In 1827 he went to Paris and became an assistant to Gay Lussac and Lessaigne. At this period he also occupied a position in the hospital of La Salpêtrière, but resigned to get back to his researches. In 1830 he was a professor in the University of Lille; in 1833 assayer to the Mint, and on the staff of the Polytechnic School in Paris; and later was engaged in the Collège de France, holding the title of professor there until 1851. In 1836 he visited Germany and was associated in his work in organic chemistry with Liebig. In 1837 he succeeded Deyeux as a member of the Academy of Sciences of France. In 1848 he was made president of the Mint Commission, and in 1849 became a member of the Municipal Commission at Paris. He resigned his public positions in 1852.

His work with Liebig included investigations on œnanthic ether, tannic acid, stearin, sugar, etc., and with Frémy, Cahours, and Gélis, on a series of vegetable acids, including mallic and gallic acids, and on petroleum and butyric fermentation. He was the first to synthesize a fatty substance from glycerine and an acid; to isolate tannic acid; to identify beet-root and cane-sugar as being the same; and to make gun-cotton or nitrocellulose in France. Other work by him was devoted to analytical chemistry and the determination of the atomic weights of several of the elements. Discovering a new class of salts (nitro-sulphates) he based thereon a new analytical method for the determination of copper. In 1850 as consulting chemist of the St. Gobain glass works he introduced sodium sulphate as a constituent in glass-making, producing artificial aventurine with chromium as a basis, studying the effect of sunlight on coloured glass, and working on enamels. Many of his papers have been published in the "Annales de Chimie et de Physique" and in the "Comptes Rendus". He published several works: "Traité de Chimie Générale, analytique, Industrielle et agricole" (3 vols., Paris, 1847), in collaboration with Frémy; "Abrégé de Chimie" (Paris, 1848); "Notions générales de Chimie" (Paris, 1853). According to his friend, the Abbé Moigno, he died an edifying Christian death.

POGGENDORFF, *Biographisch-Literarisches Handwörtertuch zur Geschichte der exacten Wissenschaften* (Leipzig, 1863); FIGUIER, *L'Année Scientifique* (*XII Année*), *Comptes Rendus Hebdomadaires des Séances de l'Académie des Sciences*, LXIV (Paris, 1867).

T. O'CONOR SLOANE.

Peltrie, MADELEINE DE LA, *née* CHAUVIGNY, a French noblewoman, and foundress, b. at Caen, 1603; d. at Quebec, 18 November, 1671. In spite of her monastic inclinations, she was forced to wed, at seventeen, Charles de la Peltrie, who died five years later. After ten years of widowhood spent in piety and almsdeeds, Lejeune's "Relation" awakened in her soul an ardent desire for the Canadian mission, which she strove to accomplish notwithstanding fresh opposition from her father. To overcome this, while seemingly complying with her parent's wish to see her remarried, it was arranged that the saintly de Bernière-Louvigny would ask her hand, leaving her free to pursue her generous design. Her father's death intervening, the union was cancelled, though her friend espoused the realization of her plans, duly approved by de Condren and St. Vincent de Paul. She corresponded with the Venerable Marie de l'Incarnation, who recognized her as the soul providentially destined to second her zeal. They reached Quebec, 1 August, 1639, and began together a life of privations and merits inseparable from the rude condition of the colony and the savage nature of their wards. Madame de la Peltrie's charity exerted itself at Sillery, where she stood sponsor for many a dark neophyte. Her intimacy with Jeanne Mance, Maisonneuve, and the other prospective founders of Ville Marie, during the first winter spent near Quebec (1641–42), prompted her to follow them to Montreal, where she was the first communicant at the first Mass celebrated by Father Vimont, S.J. (1642). Deterred from her apparently eccentric plan of visiting the Huron missions, she finally returned to Quebec after an absence of eighteen months, and devoted herself and her fortune wholly and irrevocably to the work of Marie de l'Incarnation. In spite of her entreaties she was never formally admitted to the novitiate, but led the humble and austere life of a true religious, scrupulously following every detail of the observances, and reaching a high degree of contemplative prayer. Governor Courcelles, Intendant Talon, the Indians, and the poor attended her funeral. Besides contributing to the foundation of the Ursuline monastery, she had inaugurated in Quebec, the admirable mission of charity for women of society.

DIONNE, *Serviteurs et Servantes de Dieu au Canada* (Quebec, 1904); *La Vénérable Marie de l'Incarnation* (Paris, 1910); MOTHER STE. CROIX, *Glimpses of the Monastery* (Quebec, 1897).

LIONEL LINDSAY.

Pelusium, titular metropolitan see of Augustamnica Prima in Egypt, mentioned in Ezech., xxx, 15 sq., (A. V. Sin), as the strength or rampart of Egypt against his enemies from Asia, which clearly outlines the eastern frontier of the Delta. *Sin* in Chaldaic, and *Seyân* in Aramaic, means mire, like the Greek Πηλούσιον, which is a translation of it and which, according to Strabo (XVII, i, 21), refers to the mire and the marshes which surrounded the town. The latter was very important, being on the route of the caravans from Africa to Asia, also because its harbour joined the sea to the branch of the Nile called Pelusiac. The Pharaohs put it in a good state of defence. Among its sieges or battles were: the expedition of Nabuchodonosor, 583 B. C.; that of Cambyses who stormed it, 525 B. C. (Herod., III, 10–12); that of Xerxes, 490 B. C., and of Artaxerxes, 460 B. C.; the battle of 373 B. C. between Nectanebus King of Egypt, Pharnabazus, Satrap of Phrygia, and Iphicrates, general of the Athenians. In 333 B. C. the city opened its gates to Alexander; in 173 B. C. Antiochus Epiphanes triumphed under its walls over Ptolemey Philimetor; in 55 B. C. Anthony captured it; and in 31 B. C. Augustus occupied it. The Shah Chosroes took it in A. D. 616, Amru in 640; Baldwin I King of Jerusalem burned it in 1117. The branch of the Nile became choked up and the sea overflowed the region and transformed it into a desert of mud. A hill, covered with ruins of the Roman or Byzantine period and called Tell Farameh, marks the site. There are also the ruins of a fort called Tineh.

The first known bishop is Callinicus, a partisan of Meletium; Dorotheus assisted at the Council of Nicæa; Marcus, Pancratius, and Ammonius (fourth century); Eusebius (first half of the fifth century); George (sixth century). Pelusium became the metropolitan see of Augustamnica when that province was created, mentioned first in an imperial edict of 342 (Cod. Theod., XII, i, 34). The greatest glory of Pelusium is St. Isidore, d. 450. Under the name of Farmah, Pelusium is mentioned in the "Chronicle" of John of Nikiu in the seventh century (ed. Zottenberg, 392, 396, 407, 595).

Le Quien, *Oriens christianus*, II, 531–34; Amélineau, *La géographie de l'Egypte à l'époque copte* (Paris, 1893), 317; Bouvy, *De sancto Isidoro Pelusiota* (Nîmes, 1884).

S. Vailhé.

Pembroke, Diocese of (Pembrokiensis), suffragan of Ottawa, in Canada. The town of Pembroke has a beautiful location on the Ottawa River, about one hundred miles west of the City of Ottawa, in the midst of a rich farming and lumbering district. The locality is mentioned in the early history of Indian missions in Upper Canada; Champlain, when on a voyage of exploration of the Upper Ottawa, pitched his tent where now stands the Pembroke court house. The names of the early missionaries are lost, the first known being those of Fathers Dupins and Bellefeuille, Sulpicians of Montreal, who preached to the Indians of this region in 1836. The foundation of the mission there is ascribed to Father Lynch, and the first resident priest was Father Gillie, under whose direction the first church was begun in 1847. This soon proved inadequate and a more extensive stone structure was erected on a new site. In 1882 when Pembroke was chosen as the see of the new vicariate, plans, eventually carried out, were prepared to transform this church into the Cathedral of St. Columba. The diocese of Pembroke comprises the county of Renfrew, part of each of the counties of Frontenac, Addington, Hastings, and Haliburton, of the district of Nipissing in the Province of Ontario, and the southern part of the county of Pontiac in the Province of Quebec. This territory was separated from the Dioceses of Ottawa, Three Rivers, and St. Boniface, and erected into the Vicariate of Pontiac, 11 July, 1882. This immense district comprised a great portion of northern Ontario and Quebec, extending as far north as Hudson Bay, and east to the district of Keewatin. The work of colonization and development progressed so rapidly that, 4 May, 1898, the vicariate was erected into the Diocese of Pembroke with episcopal see at Pembroke. The remarkable growth of the northern districts, principally through the discovery of immense mineral wealth of gold and silver in the now renowned cobalt region, led to the formation of a new vicariate at Tenniscanning, 22 September, 1908.

Narcisse Zephyrin Lorrain, first Bishop of Pembroke, was born at St. Martin, Laval County, Quebec, 13 June, 1842. His early education was obtained in his own parish school and in 1855 he began his classical studies in the College of St. Therèse, from which he entered the Seminary of St. Therèse. Ordained at Montreal, 4 August, 1867, by Bishop Bourget, for two years he filled the duties of professor and director of his Alma Mater. In 1869 with Bishop Bourget's consent, he was appointed parish priest of Redford then in the Diocese of Albany, New York. He was recalled to Montreal in 1879 and in the following year was appointed vicar-general of that diocese. Two years later he was chosen vicar-general of the new Vicariate of Pontiac, and consecrated Bishop of Cythera, 21 September, 1882, in the church of Notre Dame, Montreal, and on the following day entered Pembroke, where he was to take his residence as Vicar Apostolic of Pontiac. When the vicariate was erected into a diocese he became its first bishop. The works and progress of the diocese under the administration of Bishop Lorrain are proofs of his untiring energy, apostolic zeal, and keen business ability. He visited the Indian missions of the north five times. In 1884 he covered a distance of fifteen hundred miles to the missions of Abbitibbi, Moose Factory, and Albany, and in 1887 in visiting the missions of the St. Maurice he made a voyage of seventeen hundred miles, which like the first and the other three, was for the most part made in canoe or on foot.

The diocese numbers: about 37,000 Catholics; 27 parishes with resident priests, and 15 assistant priests; missions, 34; stations, 17; chapels, 7. Of the clergy 38 are seculars and 4 Oblates of Mary Immaculate. Among the communities of women connected with works of charity and education are: the Grey Nuns of the Cross, Sisters of St. Joseph, Sisters of Providence, Sisters of the Holy Cross, Sisters of the Holy Family. Two large and well-equipped hospitals are conducted by the first mentioned community. The separate school system enjoyed throughout the diocese gives to all a good opportunity for primary and religious instruction, while the higher education of young men is obtained principally at the University of Ottawa. There are 5 academies with 1200 pupils; 71 parochial schools with 13,270 pupils.

H. E. Letang.

Peña (Pegna), Francisco, canonist, b. at Villaroya de los Pinares, near Saragossa, about 1540; d. at Rome, in 1612. He devoted himself to the study of law at Valencia. Later Philip II appointed him auditor of the Rota for Spain, and while at Rome he performed great services not only for his fellow-countrymen but also for the Holy See. He formed one of the commission charged with the preparation of the official edition of the "Corpus juris canonici", published in 1582, and the anonymous notes appended to the edition of the Decretals are attributed to him; he was also concerned in the canonization of several saints: Didacus, Hyacinth, Raymond, Charles Borromeo, and Frances of Rome, publishing biographies of several. His principal works are: "In Directorium Inquisitorum a Nicolao Eimerico conscriptum commentaria" (Rome, 1578); "De officio Inquisitionis" (Cremona, 1655); "In Ambrosii de Vignate tractatum de hæresi commentaria et in Pauli Grillandi de hæreticis et eorum pœnis notæ" (Rome, 1581); "In Bernardi Comensis Dominicani Lucernam inquisitorum notæ et ejusdem tractatum de strigibus" (Rome, 1584); "Responsio canonica ad scriptum nuper editum in causa Henrici Borbonii quo illius fauntores persuadere nituntur episcopos in Francia jure illos absolvere potuisse" (Rome, 1595); "Censura in arrestum Parlamentale Curiæ criminalis Parisiensis contra Joannem Castellum et patres Societatis Jesu" (Rome, 1595); "De temporali regno Christi" (Rome, 1611). His "Decisiones sacræ Rotæ" were published by Urritigoiti (2 vols., Saragossa, 1648–50).

Nicolaus Antonius, *Bibliotheca Hispana nova*, I (Madrid, 1783), 457–58; Schulte, *Die Gesch der Quellen und Lit. des canonischen Rechts*, III (Stuttgart, 1880), 734.

A. Van Hove.

Penal Laws.—This article treats of penal legislation affecting Catholics in English-speaking countries since the Reformation. Separate heads are devoted to the penal laws: I. In England; II. In Scotland; III. In Ireland; IV. In the American Colonies.

I. In England.—By a series of statutes successive sovereigns and Parliaments from Elizabeth to

George III, sought to prevent the practice of the Catholic Faith in England. To the sanguinary laws passed by Elizabeth further measures, sometimes inflicting new disqualifications and penalties, sometimes reiterating previous enactments, were added, until this persecuting legislation made its effects felt in every department of human life. Catholics lost not only freedom of worship, but civil rights as well; their estates, property, and sometimes even lives were at the mercy of any informer. The fact that these laws were passed as political occasion demanded deprived them of any coherence or consistency; nor was any codification ever attempted, so that the task of summing up this long and complicated course of legislation is a difficult one. In his historical account of the penal laws, published at the time when partial relief had only just been granted (see bibliography at end of this section), the eminent lawyer, Charles Butler, the first Catholic to be called to the Bar after the Catholic Relief Act of 1791, and the first to be appointed King's Counsel after the Catholic Emancipation Act, thought it best to group these laws under five heads: (1) Those which subjected Catholics to penalties and punishments for practising their religious worship; (2) those which punished them for not conforming to the Established Church (Statutes of Recusancy); (3) those regulating the penalties or disabilities attending the refusal to take the Oath of Supremacy (1559; 1605; 1689), the declarations against Transubstantiation (Test Act, 1673) and against Popery (1678); (4) the act passed with respect to receiving the sacrament of the Lord's Supper; (5) statutes affecting landed property. For the present purpose, however, it seems preferable to adopt a chronological arrangement, which more clearly exhibits the historical development of the code and the state of the law at any particular period.

The Penal Laws began with the two Statutes of Supremacy and Uniformity by which Queen Elizabeth, in 1559, initiated her religious settlement; and her legislation falls into three divisions corresponding to three definitely marked periods: (1) 1558–70, when the Government trusted to the policy of enforcing conformity by fines and deprivations; (2) 1570–80, from the date of the queen's excommunication to the time when the Government recognized the Catholic reaction due to the seminary priests and Jesuits; (3) from 1580 to the end of the reign. To the first period belong the Acts of Supremacy and Uniformity (1 Eliz. 1 and 2) and the amending statute (5 Eliz. c. 1). By the Act of Supremacy all who maintained the spiritual or ecclesiastical authority of any foreign prelate were to forfeit all goods and chattels, both real and personal, and all benefices for the first offence, or in case the value of these was below £20, to be imprisoned for one year; they were liable to the forfeitures of Præmunire for the second offence, and to the penalties of high treason for the third offence. These penalties of Præmunire were: exclusion from the sovereign's protection, forfeiture of all lands and goods, arrest to answer to the sovereign and Council. The penalties assigned for high treason were drawing, hanging, and quartering; corruption of blood, by which heirs became incapable of inheriting honours and offices, and, lastly, forfeiture of all property. These first statutes were made stricter by the amending act (5 Eliz. c. 1), which declared that to maintain the authority of the pope in any way was punishable by penalties of Præmunire for the first offence and of high treason, though without corruption of blood, for the second. All who refused the Oath of Supremacy were subjected to the like penalties. The Act of Uniformity, primarily designed to secure outward conformity in the use of the Anglican Book of Common Prayer, was in effect a penal statute, as it punished all clerics who used any other service by deprivation and imprisonment, and everyone who refused to attend the Anglican service by a fine of twelve pence for each omission. It should be remembered that the amount of these fines must be multiplied by ten or more to give their modern equivalent.

Coming to the legislation of the second period, there are two acts directed against the Bull of Excommunication: 13 Eliz. c. 1, which, among other enactments, made it high treason to affirm that the queen ought not to enjoy the Crown, or to declare her to be a heretic or schismatic, and 13 Eliz. c. 2, which made it high treason to put into effect any papal Bull of absolution, to absolve or reconcile any person to the Catholic Church, or to be so absolved or reconciled, or to procure or publish any papal Bull or writing whatsoever. The penalties of Præmunire were enacted against all who brought into England or who gave to others *Agnus Dei* or articles blessed by the pope or by anyone through faculties from him. A third act, 13 Eliz. c. 3, which was designed to stop Catholics from taking refuge abroad, declared that any subject departing the realm without the queen's licence, and not returning within six months, should forfeit the profits of his lands during life and all his goods and chattels. The third and most severe group of statutes begins with the "Act to retain the Queen's Majesty's subjects in their obedience" (23 Eliz. c. 1), passed in 1581. This made it high treason to reconcile anyone or to be reconciled to "the Romish religion", prohibited Mass under penalty of a fine of two hundred marks and imprisonment for one year for the celebrant, and a fine of one hundred marks and the same imprisonment for those who heard the Mass. This act also increased the penalty for not attending the Anglican service to the sum of twenty pounds a month, or imprisonment till the fine be paid, or till the offender went to the Protestant Church. A further penalty of ten pounds a month was inflicted on anyone keeping a schoolmaster who did not attend the Protestant service. The schoolmaster himself was to be imprisoned for one year.

The climax of Elizabeth's persecution was reached in 1585 by the "Act against Jesuits, Seminary priests and other such like disobedient persons" (27 Eliz. c. 2). This statute, under which most of the English martyrs suffered, made it high treason for any Jesuit or any seminary priest to be in England at all, and felony for any one to harbour or relieve them. The penalties of Præmunire were imposed on all who sent assistance to the seminaries abroad, and a fine of £100 for each offence on those who sent their children overseas without the royal licence.

So far as priests were concerned, the effect of all this legislation may be summed up as follows: For any priest ordained before the accession of Elizabeth it was high treason after 1563 to maintain the authority of the pope for the second time, or to refuse the oath of supremacy for the second time; after 1571, to receive or use any Bull or form of reconciliation; after 1581, to absolve or reconcile anyone to the Church or to be absolved or reconciled. For seminary priests it was high treason to be in England at all after 1585. Under this statute, over 150 Catholics died on the scaffold between 1581 and 1603, exclusive of Elizabeth's earlier victims.

The last of Elizabeth's laws was the "Act for the better discovery of wicked and seditious persons terming themselves Catholics, but being rebellious and traitorous subjects" (35 Eliz. c. 2). Its effect was to prohibit all recusants from removing more than five miles from their place of abode, and to order all persons suspected of being Jesuits or seminary priests, and not answering satisfactorily, to be imprisoned till they did so.

The hopes of the Catholics on the accession of James I were soon dispelled, and during his reign (1603–25) five very oppressive measures were added to the statute-book. In the first year of his reign there was passed the "Act for the due execution of the statutes against Jesuits, seminary priests, etc" (I Jac. I, iv), by which all Elizabeth's statutes were confirmed with additional aggravations. Thus persons going beyond seas to any Jesuit seminary were rendered incapable of purchasing or retaining any lands or goods in England; the penalty of £100 on everyone sending a child or ward out of the realm, which had been enacted only for Elizabeth's reign, was now made perpetual; and Catholic schoolmasters not holding a licence from the Anglican bishop of the diocese were fined forty shillings a day, as were their employers. One slight relief was obtained in the exemption of one-third of the estate of a convicted recusant from liabilities to penalties; but against this must be set the provision that retained the remaining two-thirds after the owner's death till all his previous fines had been paid. Even then these two-thirds were only to be restored to the heir provided he was not himself a recusant.

The carefully arranged "discovery" of the Gunpowder Plot in 1605 was followed by two statutes of particularly savage character. These were "An Act for the better discovering and repressing of Popish Recusants" (3 Jac. I, iv) and "An Act to prevent and avoid dangers which may grow by Popish Recusants" (3 Jac. I, v). The first of these two wicked laws enacted that all convicted recusants should communicate once a year in the Anglican church under penalties of £20 for the first omission, £40 for the second, and £60 for the third. Moreover the king was to be allowed to refuse the penalty of £20 per month for non-attendance at the Anglican church, and to take in its place all the personal property and two-thirds of the real property of the offender. But the main point of this Act was the new Oath of Allegiance which it prescribed, and which was subsequently condemned by the Holy See. Yet all who refused it were to be subjected to the penalties of Præmunire, except married women, who were to be imprisoned in the common jail. Finally, every householder of whatever religion was liable to a fine of £10 a month for each guest or servant who failed to attend the Anglican church.

The second Act was even worse, and the Catholic historian Tierney justly says of it that it "exceeded in cruelty all that had hitherto been devised for the oppression of the devoted Catholics". It prohibited recusants from remaining within ten miles of the city of London, a provision which it was impossible to carry out; or to remove more than five miles from their usual place of residence till they had obtained licence from four magistrates and the bishop of the diocese or lieutenant of the county. They were disabled from practising as lawyers, physicians, apothecaries; from holding office in any court or corporation; from holding commissions in the army or navy, or any office of emolument under the State; from discharging the duties of executors, administrators, or guardians. Any married woman who had not received the sacrament in the Anglican church for a year before her husband's death forfeited two-thirds of her dower, two-thirds of her jointure, and was debarred from acting as executrix to her husband or claiming any part of his goods. Husbands and wives, if married otherwise than by a Protestant minister in a Protestant church, were each deprived of all interest in the lands or property of the other. They were fined £100 for omitting to have each of their children baptized by the Protestant minister within a month of birth. All Catholics going or being sent beyond the seas without a special licence from king or Privy Council were incapable of benefiting by gift, descent, or devise, till they returned and took the oath of allegiance; and in the meantime the property was to be held by the nearest Protestant heir. And, lastly, every convicted recusant was excommunicated from the Established Church, with the result that they were debarred from maintaining or defending any personal action or suit in the civil courts. Their houses were liable to be searched at any time, their arms and ammunition to be seized, and any books or furniture which were deemed superstitious to be destroyed.

The two remaining statutes of James I were "An Act to cause persons to be naturalized or restored in blood to conform and take the oath of allegiance and supremacy" (7 Jac. I, ii) and "An Act for the reformation of married recusant women, and administration of the oath of allegiance to all civil, military, ecclesiastical and professional persons" (7 Jac. I, vi). The chief effect of this latter act was to cause the oath to be offered to all persons over eighteen, and to empower the committal to prison of any recusant married woman, unless her husband paid £10 a month for her liberty.

During the reign of Charles I the only penal statute was a short "Act to restrain the passing or sending of any to be Popishly bred beyond the Seas" (3 Car. I, iii), which re-enacted the provisions in 3 Jac. I, c. 5, adding that offenders should be disabled from prosecuting any civil actions in law or equity; from acting as guardian, executor, or administrator; receiving any legacy or deed of gift, or bearing any office within the realm. Moreover, such offender was to forfeit all his lands and personal property.

After the Restoration in 1660 an attempt was made by Charles II, not unmindful of the sacrifices Catholics had made in the Stuart cause, to obtain a repeal of the Penal Laws, and a committee of the House of Lords was appointed to examine and report on the question. The matter, however, was allowed to drop; and in the following year both Houses of Parliament joined in petitioning the king to issue a proclamation against the Catholics. Further efforts on the part of the king came to nothing, and matters remained on the same footing till the latter part of his reign, when new statutes of a harassing nature were passed. With the exception of the Corporation Act (13 Car. II, St. 2, c. 1), which was not aimed against Catholics directly, but which provided that no person could hold any municipal office without taking the Oaths of Allegiance and Supremacy and receiving the sacrament in the Protestant church, no new measures were introduced till 1673, when Parliament passed the Test Act (25 Car. II, ii). This required all officers, civil and military, to take the same oaths and to make the Declaration against Transubstantiation. Five years later another Act was passed (30 Car. II, St. 2), which excluded all Catholics from sitting or voting in Parliament, by requiring every member of either House to take the two oaths and to make the blasphemous Declaration against Popery. From this statute, which was entitled "An Act for the more effectual preserving the King's person and government, by disabling Papists from sitting in either House of Parliament", a special exception was made in favour of the Duke of York, afterwards James II.

With the Revolution of 1688 began a new era of persecution. The "Act for further preventing the growth of Popery" (11 & 12 Gul. III, 4), passed in 1699, introduced a fresh hardship into the lives of the clergy by offering a reward of £100 for the apprehension of any priest, with the result that Catholics were placed at the mercy of common informers who harassed them for the sake of gain, even when the Government would have left them in peace. It was further enacted that any bishop or priest exercising episcopal or sacerdotal functions, or any Catholic keeping a school, should be imprisoned for life; that any Catholic over eighteen not taking the Oaths of Supremacy and Allegiance, or making the Declaration against Popery, should be incapable of inheriting or purchasing any lands; and any lands devised to a Catholic who refused to take the oaths should pass to the next of kin who happened to be a Protestant. A reward of £100 was also offered for the conviction of any Catholic sending children to be educated abroad. The cruel operation of this Act, which made itself felt throughout the ensuing century, was extended by a measure passed under Queen Anne (12 Anne, St. 2, c. 14), though Catholics were not generally molested during her reign.

The last penal statutes to be enacted were those of George I. By I Geo., I, St. 2, c. 13, the Hanoverian Succession Oaths were to be taken by all Catholics to whom they were tendered, under penalty of all the forfeitures to which "popish recusant convicts" were liable. The Stuart rising of 1715 was followed by another Act (I Geo., I, St. 2, c. 50) appointing commissioners to inquire into the estates of popish recusants with a view to confiscating two-thirds of each estate. The scope of "An Act to oblige Papists to register their names and real estates" (I Geo., I, St. 2, c. 55) is sufficiently indicated by its title. It added to the expense of all transactions in land, the more galling as Catholics were doubly taxed under the annual land-tax acts. (See also 4 Geo., III, c. 60.) In 1722 was passed "An Act for granting an aid to his Majesty by levying a Tax upon Papists" (9 Geo., I, 18), by which the sum of one hundred thousand pounds was wrung from the impoverished Catholics. Throughout the reign of George II (1727–60) there were no further additions to the penal code and under his successor, George III (1760–1820), the work of repeal was begun.

Even this lengthy enumeration is not absolutely exhaustive, and the Acts here cited contain many minor enactments of a vexatious nature. The task of repeal was a long, slow, gradual, and complicated one, the chief measures of relief being three: The First Catholic Relief Act of 1778, which enabled Catholics to inherit and purchase land and repealed the Act of William III, rewarding the conviction of priests (see Burton, "Life and Times of Bishop Challoner", ch. xxxi); the second Catholic Relief Act of 1791, which relieved all Catholics who took the oath therein prescribed from the operation of the Penal Code (see Ward, "Dawn of the Catholic Revival", viii, xiv-xvi); and the Catholic Emancipation Act of 1829. The only disqualifications against Catholics which appear to be still in force are those which prohibit the sovereign from being or marrying a Catholic, or any Catholic subject from holding the offices of Lord Chancellor, or Lord Lieutenant of Ireland.

The Statutes at Large (various editions, that here cited being London, 1758); Chronological Table and Index of the Statutes (London, 1881); BUTLER, Historical Account of the Laws against Roman Catholics and of the Laws passed for their relief (n. p., 1794); IDEM, Historical Memoirs respecting the English, Irish, and Scottish Catholics (London, 1819); ANSTEY, A Guide to the Laws of England affecting Roman Catholics (London, 1842); MADDEN, The History of the Penal Laws enacted against Roman Catholics (London, 1847); MCMULLAN AND ELLIS, The Reformation Settlement, an Epitome of the Statute and Canon Law thereon (London, 1903).

For the practical working of the Penal Laws and the hardships they inflicted on Catholics reference must be made to English Catholic literature passim. The following are some of the richest sources of information: BRIDGEWATER, Concertatio Ecclesiæ Catholicæ in Anglia (Trier, 1588); DODD, Church History (Brussels, vere Wolverhampton, 1737–42), and much additional information in TIERNEY's edition (London, 1839–43); CHALLONER, Memoirs of Missionary Priests (London, 1740–41); BERINGTON, State and Behaviour of English Catholics from the Reformation to the Year 1781 (London, 1781); MORRIS, Troubles of Our Catholic Forefathers (London, 1872–77); IDEM, The Life of Father John Gerard (London, 1881); FOLEY, Records of the English Province, S. J. (London, 1877–1883); AMHERST, History of Catholic Emancipation (London, 1886); POLLEN, Acts of English Martyrs (London, 1891); MORRIS, Catholic England in Modern Times (London, 1892); ANON, The Position of the Catholic Church in England and Wales during the last two Centuries (London, 1892); THADDEUS, The Franciscans in England (Leamington, 1898); PAYNE, Records of the English Catholics of 1715 (London, 1900); CAMM, Lives of the English Martyrs (London, 1904–05); KIRK, Biographies of English Catholics (London, 1909). Much valuable incidental information on the Penal Code is also to be found in GILLOW, Bibl. Dict. of Eng. Cath. Publications of the Catholic Record Society (London, 1905—) include prison lists, lists of recusants etc.

EDWIN BURTON.

II. IN SCOTLAND.—The first penal statutes were enacted by the Scottish Parliament of 1560, which, on 14 August, passed three statutes; the first abolishing the jurisdiction of the pope, the second repealing all former statutes in favour of the Catholic Church, the third providing that all who said or heard Mass should be punished for the first offence by the confiscation of their goods and by corporal penalties, for the second by banishment from Scotland, for the third by death. A temporary relaxation of these laws was due to Mary Queen of Scots, and a statute was even passed in 1567 giving liberty to every Scotsman to live according to his own religion; but shortly after the Queen's marriage with Bothwell a proclamation was extorted from her on 23 May, 1567, by which severe penalties were renewed against all who refused to conform to Protestantism. After Mary's deposition the Parliament of 1568 passed further acts ratifying the establishment of Protestantism, and prohibiting the exercise of any other ecclesiastical jurisdiction. Lennox's Parliament (1571) decreed the apprehension of all persons possessing papal Bulls or dispensations or gifts and provisions of benefices.

The persecution carried on under these statutes by the Privy Council and by the General Assembly was very severe. The Privy Council issued several proclamations during the next half-century enforcing the penal statutes, forbidding the harbouring of Catholic priests, ordering parents to withdraw their children from Catholic colleges abroad, and rendering husbands liable for the acts of their wives done in support of the Catholic cause. A commission issued in July, 1629, ordered that, should persecuted Catholics take refuge in fortified places, the commissioners should "follow, hunt and pursue them with fire and sword". Though in Scotland there were fewer martyrdoms than in England or Ireland, yet the persecution fell even more heavily on the rank and file of Catholics, and in some respects they suffered outrages not paralleled in England, such as the simultaneous expulsion of all Catholics from their homes which was ordered and carried out in 1629–30. But there were times of comparative tranquillity when the rigour of the law was not enforced.

At the close of the seventeenth century fresh statutes were passed. In May, 1700, an Act of Parliament offered a reward of five hundred merks for the conviction of any priest or Jesuit; the same statute disabled Catholics from inheriting property or educating their children. After the Act of Union, in 1707, the Penal Laws were still enforced. In addition to the provisions already recorded and other sufferings which they shared with English Catholics, there were galling restrictions peculiar to Scotland. The purchase or dissemination of Catholic books was forbidden under pain of banishment and forfeiture of personal property. They could not be governors, school-masters, guardians or factors, and any one who employed them as such was fined a thousand merks. They were fined five hundred merks for teaching "any art, science or exercise of any sort". Any Protestant who became a Catholic forfeited his whole hereditable estate to the nearest Protestant heir.

The first repeal of the Penal Code was effected by the Act for the relief of Scottish Catholics, which received the royal assent in May, 1793, and practically complete liberty was granted to them under the provisions of the Catholic Emancipation Act of 1829.

STOTHERT, ed. GORDON, Catholic Church in Scotland, published anonymously (Glasgow, 1869); BELLESHEIM, tr. HUNTER-BLAIR, History of the Catholic Church in Scotland (Edinburgh, 1887–90); STEWART, The Church of Scotland 1070–1560 (Paisley, 1892), 364 sqq.; FORBES-LEITH, Memoirs of Scottish Catholics during the Seventeenth and Eighteenth Centuries (London, 1909).

EDWIN BURTON.

III. IN IRELAND.—Although the penal laws of Ireland were passed by a Protestant Parliament and aimed at depriving Catholics of their faith, such laws were not the outcome of religious motives only.

They often came from a desire to possess the lands of the Irish, from impatience at their long resistance, from the contempt of a ruling for a subject race. (See IRELAND, *The Anglo-Normans*.) When Henry VIII broke with Rome sectarian rancour came to embitter racial differences. The English Parliament passed the Act of Supremacy, making Henry head of the Church; but the Irish Parliament was less compliant, and did not pass the bill till the legislative powers of the representatives of the clergy had been taken away. And though the Act of Supremacy (1536) was accepted by so many Irish chiefs, they were not followed by the clergy or people in their apostasy. The suppression of monasteries followed, entailing the loss of so much property and even of many lives. Yet little progress was made with the new doctrines either in Henry's reign or in that of his successor, and Mary's restoration of the Faith led the Protestant Elizabeth to again resort to penal laws. In 1559 the Irish Parliament passed both the Act of Supremacy and the Act of Uniformity, the former prescribing to all officers the Oath of Supremacy, the latter prohibiting the Mass and commanding the public use of the Book of Common Prayer. Whoever refused the Oath of Supremacy was dismissed from office, and whoever refused to attend the Protestant service was fined 12 pence for each offence. A subsequent viceregal proclamation ordered all priests to leave Dublin and prohibited the use of images, candles, and beads. For some time these Acts and proclamations were not rigorously enforced; but after 1570, when Elizabeth was excommunicated by the pope, toleration ceased; and the hunting down of the Earl of Desmond, the desolation of Munster, the torturing of O'Hurley and others, showed how merciless the queen and her ministers could be. Elizabeth disliked Parliaments and had but two in her reign in Ireland. She governed by proclamation, as did her successor James, and it was under a proclamation (1611) that the blood of O'Devany, Bishop of Down, was shed. In the next reign there were periods of toleration followed by the false promises of Strafford and the attempted spoliation of Connaught, until at last the Catholics took up arms.

Cromwell disliked Parliaments as much as Elizabeth or James, and when he had extinguished the Rebellion of 1641, he abolished the Irish Parliament, giving Ireland a small representation at Westminster. It was by Acts of this Westminster Parliament that the Cromwellian settlement was carried out, and that so many Catholics were outlawed. As for ecclesiastics, no mercy was shown them under Cromwellian rule. They were ordered to leave Ireland, and put to death if they refused, or deported to the Arran Isles or to Barbadoes, and those who sheltered them at home were liable to the penalty of death. To such an extent was the persecution carried that the Catholic churches were soon in ruins, a thousand priests were driven into exile, and not a single bishop remained in Ireland but the old and helpless Bishop of Kilmore. With the accession of Charles II the Irish Catholics looked for a restoration of lands and liberties; but the hopes raised by the Act of Settlement (1663) were finally dissipated by the Act of Explanation (1665), and the Catholics, plundered by the Cromwellians, were denied even the justice of a trial. The English Parliament at the same time prohibited the importation into England of Irish cattle, sheep, or pigs. The king favoured toleration of Catholicity, but was overruled by the bigotry of the Parliament in England and of the viceroy, Ormond, in Ireland; and if the reign of Charles saw some toleration, it also saw the judicial murder of Venerable Oliver Plunkett and a proclamation by Ormond, in 1678, ordering that all priests should leave the country, and that all Catholic churches and convents should be closed.

The triumph of the Catholics under James II was short-lived. But even when William of Orange had triumphed, toleration of Catholicity was expected. For the Treaty of Limerick (1691) gave the Catholics "such privileges as they enjoyed in the reign of Charles II"; and William was to obtain from the Irish Parliament a further relaxation of the penal laws in existence. The treaty was soon broken. The English Parliament, presuming to legislate for Ireland, enacted that no one should sit in the Irish Parliament without taking the Oath of Supremacy and subscribing to a declaration against Transubstantiation; and the Irish Parliament, filled with slaves and bigots, accepted this legislation. Catholics were thus excluded; and in spite of the declared wishes of King William, the Irish Parliament not only refused to relax the Penal Laws in existence but embarked on fresh penal legislation. Session after session, for nearly fifty years, new and more galling fetters were forged, until at last the Penal Code was complete, and well merited the description of Burke: "as well fitted for the oppression, impoverishment and degradation of a feeble people and the debasement in them of human nature itself as ever proceeded from the perverted ingenuity of man". All bishops, deans, vicars-general, and friars were to leave the country and if they returned, to be put to death. Secular priests at home could remain if they were registered; in 1709, however, they were required to take an oath of abjuration which no priest could conscientiously take, so that registration ceased to be a protection. They could not set up schools at home nor resort to Catholic schools abroad, nor could they receive legacies for Catholic charities, nor have on their churches steeple, cross, or bell.

The laity were no better off than the clergy in the matter of civil rights. They could not set up Catholic schools, nor teach in such, nor go abroad to Catholic schools. They were excluded from Parliament, from the corporations, from the army and navy, from the legal profession, and from all civil offices. They could not act as sheriffs, or under sheriffs, or as jurors, or even as constables. They could not have more than two Catholic apprentices in their trade; they could not carry arms, nor own a horse worth more than £5; they were excluded even from residence in the larger corporate towns. To bury their dead in an old ruined abbey or monastery involved a penalty of ten pounds. A Catholic workman refusing to work on Catholic holy days was to be whipped; and there was the same punishment for those who made pilgrimages to holy wells. No Catholic could act as guardian to an infant, nor as director of the Bank of Ireland; nor could he marry a Protestant, and the priest who performed such a marriage ceremony was to be put to death. A Catholic could not acquire land, nor buy it, nor hold a mortgage on it; and the Catholic landlord was bound at death to leave his estate to his children in equal shares. During life, if the wife or son of such became a Protestant, she or he at once obtained separate maintenance. The law presumed every Catholic to be faithless, disloyal, and untruthful, assumed him to exist only to be punished, and the ingenuity of the Legislature was exhausted in discovering new methods of repression. Viceroys were constantly appealed to to give no countenance to Popery; magistrates, to execute the penal laws; degraded Irishmen called priest-hunters were rewarded for spying upon their priests, and degraded priests who apostatized were rewarded with a government pension. The wife was thus encouraged to disobey her husband, the child to flout his parents, the friend to turn traitor to his friend. These Protestant legislators in possession of Catholic lands wished to make all Catholics helpless and poor. Without bishops they must soon be without priests, and without schools they must necessarily go to the Protestant schools. These hopes however proved vain. Students went to foreign colleges, and bishops came from abroad, facing imprisonment and death. The schoolmaster taught under a sheltering hedge, and the priest said Mass by stealth, watched over by the people, and in spite of priest-hunter and penal laws. Nor were the Catholics won over by such Protestant ministers as they saw, men without zeal and often without faith, not unlike those described by Spenser in Elizabeth's day—"of fleshy incontinency, greedy avarice and disordered lives". In other respects the Penal Laws succeeded. They made the Catholics helpless, ignorant, and poor, without the strength to rebel, the hope of redress, or even the courage to complain.

At last the tide turned. Too poor to excite the cupidity of their oppressors, too feeble to rebel, the Catholics had nevertheless shown that they would not become Protestants; and the repression of a feeble people, merely for the sake of repression, had tarnished the name of England, and alienated her friends among the Catholic nations. In these circumstances the Irish Parliament began to retrace its steps, and concessions were made, slowly and grudgingly. At first the Penal Laws ceased to be rigorously enforced, and then, in 1771, Catholics were allowed to take leases of unreclaimed bog for sixty-one years. Three years later they were allowed to substitute an Oath of Allegiance for the Oath of Supremacy; and in 1778 Gardiner's Act allowed them to take leases of land for 999 years, and also allowed Catholic landlords to leave their estates to one son, instead of having, as hitherto, to divide between all. In 1782 a further Act enabled Catholics to set up schools, with the leave of the Protestant bishop of the place, enabling them also to own horses in the same way as Protestants, and further permitting bishops and priests to reside in Ireland. Catholics were also allowed to act as guardians to children. Grattan favoured complete equality between Catholics and Protestants, but the bigots in Parliament were too strong, and among them were the so-called patriot leaders, Charlemont and Flood. Not till 1792 was there a further Act allowing Catholics to marry Protestants, to practise at the bar, and to set up Catholic schools without obtaining a licence from the Protestant bishop. These concessions were scorned by the Catholic Committee, long charged with the care of Catholic interests, and which had lately passed from the feeble leadership of Lord Kenmare to the more capable leadership of John Keogh. The new French Republic had also become a menace to England, and English ministers dreaded having Ireland discontented. For these reasons the Catholic Relief Bill of 1793 became law. This gave Catholics the parliamentary and municipal franchise, enabled them to become jurors, magistrates, sheriffs, and officers in the army and navy. They might carry arms under certain conditions, and they were admitted to the degrees of Trinity College, though not to its emoluments or higher honours. Two years later the advent of Lord Fitzwilliam as viceroy was regarded as the herald of complete religious equality. But Pitt suddenly changed his mind, and, having resolved on a legislative union, it suited his purpose better to stop further concession. Then came the recall of Fitzwilliam, the rapid rise of the United Irish Society with revolutionary objects, the rebellion of 1798, and the Union of 1800.

From the Imperial Parliament the Catholics expected immediate emancipation, remembering the promises of British and Irish ministers, but Pitt shamefully broke his word, and emancipation was delayed till 1829. Nor would it have come even then but for the matchless leadership of O'Connell, and because the only alternative to concession was civil war. The manner of concession was grudging. Catholics were admitted to Parliament, but the forty-shilling free-holders were disfranchised, Jesuits banished, other religious orders made incapable of receiving charitable bequests, bishops penalized for assuming ecclesiastical titles, and priests for appearing outside their churches in their vestments. Catholics were debarred from being either viceroy or lord chancellor of Ireland. The law regarding Jesuits has not been enforced, but the viceroy must still be a Protestant. Nor was it till the last half-century that a Catholic could be lord chancellor, Lord O'Hagan, who died in 1880, being the first Catholic to fill that office since the Revolution of 1688.

O'Donovan (ed.), *Annals of the Four Masters* (Dublin, 1860); D'Alton, *History of Ireland* (London, 1910); Gilbert, *Viceroys of Ireland* (Dublin, 1865); Hardiman, *Statute of Kilkenny* (Dublin, 1843); Scully, *Penal Laws* (Dublin, 1812); Lecky, *History of Ireland* (London, 1897); *Calendars of State Papers, 1509–1660*; *Journals of the Irish House of Commons*; *Irish Parliamentary Debates, 1781–97*; Moran, *Persecutions of the Irish Catholics* (London, 1900).—See also the authorities quoted in Act of Settlement; Ireland; O'Connell, Daniel; Plunkett, Oliver, Venerable; O'Neill, Hugh.

E. A. D'Alton.

Penal Laws in the English Colonies in America.—*Anglican Establishments.*—The first Virginia Charter in 1606 established the Anglican Church. The second, in 1609, repeated the terms of the establishment and prescribed the Oath of Supremacy. In support of the Establishment, the draconian laws of Governor Dale in 1611 were directed mainly against the moral laxity of the colonists and were soon abrogated. When lawmaking passed to the Colonial Assembly the Establishment was maintained, but penalizing laws were still directed towards the moral uplift of the church. Intolerance of dissent was latent and implicit. Lord Baltimore, refusing as a Catholic to acknowledge the ecclesiastical supremacy of the king, in 1628 was denied temporary residence in the colony. Following this incident a new Act of Uniformity passed the Assembly, fining absentees from service. Another, in 1642, specifically disenfranchised Catholics and enforced the expulsion, within five days, of a priest coming to the colony. Under Governor Berkeley an Act, directed mainly against the Puritan influx, made mandatory the expulsion of Nonconformists; but Puritanism remained, affecting even the Anglican clergy, and gaining a first step toward disestablishment in coercing the Assembly of 1642 to pass a law conferring upon vestries the right of choosing ministers. Under Cromwell this law was confirmed. Toleration was further established, an exception being made against Quakers who, in 1659, were banished and, upon return, were proceeded against as felons. Indeed, their consciences were not relieved from taking oaths and military service until the next century.

The Restoration ended this qualified liberty. In 1661 the old Law of 1642 was revived. The liturgy of the Anglican Church and the catechisms of the canons were prescribed; only ministers ordained by English bishops were allowed in the colony, who alone were to perform marriage services. Children born of marriages otherwise performed were declared illegitimate. Grudgingly enough Virginia recognized the Toleration Act of 1689, and from that time to the Revolution dissenting sects gradually merged into an anti-British political party arrayed against a Tory Establishment, though the prejudice against Catholics in no wise diminished, persisting almost to the Revolution in the curious Act of 1755, "for Disarming Papists", during the French and Indian Wars. Other colonies maintaining the Establishment were North and South Carolina. Penalizing laws were here almost exclusively directed toward enforcing the Establishment upon a growing class of wealthy landowners whose religious indifference to the Tory Church soon arrogated to itself political rather than spiritual independence. Intolerance of Catholics was legally expressed.

Puritan Establishments.—Massachusetts's charter made no mention of religion, and the Puritans were free to construct their absolute theocracy. Episcopacy was repudiated and Congregationalism established. The franchise was limited to church members. Men making active profession of an alien faith were banished. The General Court made provision for a general church tax to be levied and collected by civil officers. In 1631 came the famous law admitting only church members to civic freedom. In 1635 the magistrates were given inquisitional powers over the churches themselves. Congregationalism became law and Church and State were identical. Colonists were compelled to live within easy distance of meeting-houses. Heresy was punished by banishment. Contempt toward ministers merited magisterial reproof, a fine, or standing placarded on a block. In 1656 denial of the Bible meant whipping or banishment, and as late as 1697 a law against "Blasphemy and Atheism" mentions as penalties the pillory, whipping, and boring the tongue with red-hot irons. Catholics of course were not suffered to live in the colony, and Jesuits, if banished, were to be put to death on return. The latter law was never enforced, though latent intolerance may be detected in such an ordinance as that of 1659 making the observance of Christmas a punishable offence. The persecution of Quakers and the inflicting of the death penalty in four instances brought about a rebellion within the colony which, with the endeavour of the Crown to force recognition of the Anglican Church, worked the initial movement in undermining the theocracy. With the appointment of a royal governor the franchise was broadened, Episcopalianism was established, and it was decreed in 1691 that "forever hereafter there shall be liberty of conscience allowed in the worship of God to all Christians (except Papists)".

In Connecticut, Congregationalism under its famous instrument, the Saybrook Platform, became the State religion. But toleration was unstintingly allowed to every other licensed religion. Even laws against Quakers, apparently unenforced, imposed penalties not upon them but upon the communities that harboured them; while the universal "except Papists" phrase is significantly lacking, though in 1743 a law allowed dissenters "being Protestants" to apply for relief.

The short-lived attempt of the settlement at New Haven to found a theocratic colony based upon the Mosaic Law is interesting only in its failure. The famous "Blue Laws", now known to be ironic forgeries, were not much more severe than the Mosaic penalties enforced by the New Haven Legislature, according to their own records. The colony was soon incorporated with that of Connecticut, in whose democratic tolerance it was speedily absorbed.

The first settlers of New Hampshire established a broadly tolerant congregationalism, which allowed civil privileges to be independent of religious belief, but the Puritan establishment was firmly planted throughout the years of the colony's union with Massachusetts. To the influence of this union, perhaps, may be traced the single example of persecution in the colony, that against three Quakers in 1659. In 1679 the union with Massachusetts was dissolved, and a royal governor sought, unsuccessfully, to enforce the establishment of the Anglican Church. The assembly of 1680 fixed the Congregational Establishment. The franchise was limited to Protestants, and subsequent laws, notably those of 1692, 1702, 1714, defined the union of Church and State, allowing the constable to collect the church tax—that from dissenters to go to the support of their own ministers. Under the Toleration Act of 1689 all citizens were obliged to make a declaration against the pope and the doctrines of the Catholic Church.

Changing Establishments.—Under the Duke of York all churches were established with governmental rights, though those of power and induction were placed in the governor's hands. Persecution for conscience's sake seems unrecorded. Much of this tolerant attitude is due to the older Dutch foundation. It was renewed in the "Charter of Liberties", passed by the Assembly in 1683. When the Duke of York came to the throne a faint attempt was made to establish the Anglican Church. Later the council suspended "all Roman Catholics from Command and Places of Trust", and the franchise was soon confined to Protestants. This attitude was given universal royal warrant under the Great Toleration Act, and a supposititious Established Church existed in New York to the American Revolution, suffering the same kind of political opposition that the Establishment endured in Virginia and the Carolinas. The Establishment seized church property and banished Moravians, under the belief that they were "disguised Papists", though its powers began to wane before its downfall with the American Revolution.

The Palatinate of Maryland under the Baltimores furnishes, with the Colony of Rhode Island, the first example in history of a complete separation of Church and State with religious tolerance. Religious freedom was proclaimed in the famous "Act for Church Liberties", passed by the assembly and practically carried out. Under this Catholic toleration a Catholic was fined for "interfering by opprobious reproaches with two Protestants", and Jesuits were refused the privileges of the canon law. The Toleration Act of 1649 denied toleration only to non-Christians and Unitarians, and imposed upon every resident an oath declaring for liberty of conscience. The outcome of the disgraceful Puritan "Plot" resulted in the voiding of the charter, the erection of Maryland as a royal province, and the Episcopal Establishment in 1692. The majority of the colonists were so overwhelmingly non-episcopal that the legislatures never seem to have insisted upon conformity, though they compelled church support. Against Catholics alone persecution endured. They were deprived of all civil and religious rights—the latter only in private homes; the Law of 1704 laid a tax of twenty shillings on every Irish servant imported; while in 1715 it was enacted that children of a Protestant father and a Catholic mother could, in case of the father's death, be taken from the mother. However, the first Catholic church of Baltimore was erected without opposition in 1763, though the rights of the franchise were not extended to Catholics until the American Revolution put an end to all penal enactments.

The Presbyterian and Quaker settlers of the Jerseys, under their proprietors, were granted entire liberty of conscience. But with the assumption of the provinces, the Crown seems to have assumed that, *per se*, the Anglican Church was established, though no specific act to that effect seems to have been passed. At any rate, excepting troubles with Quakers in the French Wars, the annals of New Jersey are free from records of official persecution, though Catholics were disenfranchised when Jersey became a royal province. Georgia with its twoscore years of provincial history excluded "Papists" from its confines. The Anglican Church entered with the Crown and was formally, though unsuccessfully, established by the colonial legislature in 1758, the settlement remaining from the beginning indifferent toward Dissent.

The Free Colonies.—Two colonies, those of Rhode Island and Pennsylvania (with its offspring, Delaware) proclaimed absolute separation of Church and State. The former laboured for long under the accusation of denying citizenship to Catholics, but this charge is probably based on an error of the committee that prepared the revised statutes for the public printer; while the Pennsylvania commonwealth departs from the principles of Rhode Island in restricting the right to hold office to Christians and those who believe in the existence of God. In spite of the protest of Penn, that part of the Test Oath required under the great Toleration Act, excluding Catholics from civil rights, was adopted by the colonial assembly in 1705 and endured until the Revolution, while the Disarming Act was passed, but never enforced.

The only authentic and satisfactory sources for the religious polity of the various colonies are in their own records, many of which may be found in the various State Historical Societies' publications. See also SHEA, *History of the Catholic Church in the United States* (New York, 1888); FISHER, *Colonial Era;* ANDERSON, *History of the Colonial Church;* MEADE, *Old Churches, Ministers, and Families of Virginia* (2 vols., Philadelphia, 1857); COBB, *Rise of Religious Liberty in America* (New York, 1902); HUGHES, *History of the Society of Jesus in North America* (Cleveland, 1910).

JARVIS KEILEY.

Penalty. See CENSURES, ECCLESIASTICAL.

Peñalver y Cardenas, LUIS IGNATIUS, Bishop of New Orleans, Archbishop of Guatemala, son of a wealthy and noble family, b. at Havana, 3 April, 1749; d. there, 17 July, 1810. After studying belles-lettres and philosophy in St. Ignatius College of his native city, he followed there the courses of the University of St. Jerome and in 1771 obtained the degree of Doctor of Theology. Having distinguished himself by his learning and charity, his bishop entrusted him with several missions of an administrative nature, and in 1773 appointed him provisor and vicar-general. When Pius VI, in deference to the prayer of Carlos VI, King of Spain, created Louisiana and the Floridas a diocese, distinct from that of Santiago de Cuba, Luis Peñalver was made its first bishop. He made his entrance into New Orleans on 17 July, 1795, took formal possession of his see, and in the following December published an "Instrucción para el govierno de los párrocos de la diócesis de la Luisiana". He soon began the visitation of his diocese, which then extended over the country known later as the "Louisiana Purchase Territory". On 21 April, 1796, he was at Iberville, on 8 November of the same year at Natchitoches, and at Pensacola on 7 May, 1798. Upon his return in 1799, he drew up a report in which he complained bitterly of the ignorance, irreligion, and the want of discipline which then prevailed in Louisiana.

Bishop Peñalver was promoted to the Archiepiscopal See of Guatemala on 20 July, 1801, and by a Rescript from Rome was empowered to transfer his authority in Louisiana and the Floridas to Canon Thomas Hasset, his vicar-general, and to Rev. Patrick Walsh. After a chase by an English war-vessel, Archbishop Peñalver arrived at Guatemala, where he soon attained to prominence through the interest he manifested in questions that concerned education and the public good. At his own expense he built a hospital and various schools. He resigned his see on 1 March, 1806, and, returning to Havana, devoted the last years of his life to charitable works. At his death he bequeathed $200,000 to the poor and several important legacies to educational institutions.

SHEA, *History of the Catholic Church in the U. S., 1763–1815* (New York, 1888).

JAMES H. BLENK.

Penance (*pœnitentia*) designates (1) a virtue; (2) a sacrament of the New Law; (3) a canonical punishment inflicted according to the earlier discipline of the Church; (4) a work of satisfaction enjoined upon the recipient of the sacrament. These have as their common centre the truth that he who sins must repent and as far as possible make reparation to Divine justice. Repentance, i. e., heartfelt sorrow with the firm purpose of sinning no more, is thus the prime condition on which depends the value of whatever the sinner may do or suffer by way of expiation.

I. THE VIRTUE OF PENANCE.—Penance is a supernatural moral virtue whereby the sinner is disposed to hatred of his sin as an offence against God and to a firm purpose of amendment and satisfaction. The principal *act* in the exercise of this virtue is the detestation of sin, not of sin in general nor of that which others commit, but of one's own sin. The motive of this detestation is that sin offends God: to regret evil deeds on account of the mental or physical suffering, the social loss, or the action of human justice which they entail, is natural; but such sorrow does not suffice for penance. On the other hand, the resolve to amend, while certainly necessary, is not sufficient of itself, i. e., without hatred for sin already committed; such a resolve, in fact, would be meaningless: it would profess obedience to God's law in the future while disregarding the claims of God's justice in the matter of past transgression. "Be converted, and do penance for all your iniquities. . . . Cast away from you all your transgressions . . . and make to yourselves a new heart, and a new spirit" (Ezech., xviii, 30–31; cf. Joel, ii, 12; Jer., viii, 6). In the same spirit St. John the Baptist exhorts his hearers: "Bring forth therefore fruit worthy of penance" (Matt., iii, 8). Such too is the teaching of Christ as expressed in the parables of the Prodigal Son and of the Publican; while the Magdalen who "washed out her sins with her tears" of sorrow, has been for all ages the type of the repentant sinner. Theologians, following the doctrine of St. Thomas (Summa, III, Q. lxxxv, a. 1), regard penance as truly a virtue, though they have disputed much regarding its place among the virtues. Some have classed it with the virtue of charity, others with the virtue of religion, others again as a part of justice. Cajetan seems to have considered it as belonging to all three; but most theologians agree with St. Thomas (ibid., a. 2) that penance is a distinct virtue (*virtus specialis*). The detestation of sin is a praiseworthy act, and in penance this detestation proceeds from a special motive, i. e., because sin offends God (cf. De Lugo, "De pœnitentiæ virtute"; Palmieri, "De pœnitentia", Rome, 1879; theses I–VII.).

Necessity.—The Council of Trent expressly declares (Sess. XIV, c. i) that penance was at all times necessary for the remission of grievous sin. Theologians have questioned whether this necessity obtains in virtue of the positive command of God or independently of such positive precept. The weight of authority is in favour of the latter opinion; moreover, theologians state that in the present order of Divine Providence God Himself cannot forgive sins, if there be no real repentance (St. Thomas, III, Q. lxxxvi, a. 2; Cajetan, ibid.; Palmieri, op. cit., thesis VII). In the Old Law (Ezech., xviii, 24) life is denied to the man who does iniquity; even "his justices which he has done, shall not be remembered"; and Christ restates the doctrine of the Old Testament, saying (Luke, xiii, 5): "except you do penance, you shall all likewise perish." In the New Law, therefore, repentance is as necessary as it was in the Old, repentance that includes reformation of life, grief for sin, and willingness to perform satisfaction. In the Christian Dispensation this act of repentance has been subjected by Christ to the judgment and jurisdiction of His Church, whensoever there is question of sin committed after the reception of Baptism (Council of Trent, sess. XIV, c. i), and the Church acting in the name of Christ not only declares that sins are forgiven, but actually and judicially forgives them, if the sinner already repentant subjects his sins to the "power of the keys", and is willing to make condign satisfaction for the wrong he has done.

II. THE SACRAMENT OF PENANCE.—Penance is a sacrament of the New Law instituted by Christ in which forgiveness of sins committed after baptism is granted through the priest's absolution to those who with true sorrow confess their sins and promise to satisfy for the same. It is called a "sacrament" not simply a function or ceremony, because it is an outward sign instituted by Christ to impart grace to the soul. As an outward sign it comprises the actions of the penitent in presenting himself to the priest and accusing himself of his sins, and the actions of the priest in pronouncing absolution and imposing satisfaction. This whole procedure is usually called, from one of its parts, "confession"; and it is said to take place in the "tribunal of penance", because it is a judicial process in which the penitent is at once the accuser, the person accused, and the witness, while the priest pronounces judgment and sentence. The grace conferred is deliverance from the guilt of sin and, in the case of mortal sin, from its eternal punishment; hence also reconciliation with God, justification. Finally, the confession is made not in the secrecy of the penitent's heart nor to a layman as friend and advocate, nor to a representative of human authority, but to a duly ordained priest with requisite jurisdiction and with the "power of the keys", i. e., the power to forgive sins which Christ granted to His Church.

By way of further explanation it is needful to correct certain erroneous views regarding this sacrament which not only misrepresent the actual practice of the Church but also lead to a false interpretation of theological statement and historical evidence. From what has been said it should be clear: (1) that penance is not a mere human invention devised by the Church to secure power over consciences or to relieve the emotional strain of troubled souls; it is the ordinary means appointed by Christ for the remission of sin. Man indeed is free to obey or disobey, but once he has sinned, he must seek pardon not on conditions of his own choosing but on those which God has determined, and these for the Christian are embodied in the Sacrament of Penance. (2) No Catholic believes that a priest simply as an individual man, however pious or learned, has power to forgive sins. This power belongs to God alone; but He can and does exercise it through the ministration of men. Since He has seen fit to exercise it by means of this sacrament, it cannot be said that the Church or the priest interferes between the soul and God; on the contrary, penance is the removal of the one obstacle that keeps the soul away from God. (3) It is not true that for the Catholic the mere "telling of one's sins" suffices to obtain their forgiveness. Without sincere sorrow and purpose of amendment, confession avails nothing, the pronouncement of absolution is of no effect, and the guilt of the sinner is greater than before. (4) While this sacrament as a dispensation of Divine mercy facilitates the pardoning of sin, it by no means renders sin less hateful or its consequences less dreadful to the Christian mind; much less does it imply permission to commit sin in the future. In paying ordinary debts, as e. g., by monthly settlements, the intention of contracting new debts with the same creditor is perfectly legitimate; a similar intention on the part of him who confesses his sins would not only be wrong in itself but would nullify the sacrament and prevent the forgiveness of sins then and there confessed. (5) Strangely enough, the opposite charge is often heard, viz., that the confession of sin is intolerable and hard and therefore alien to the spirit of Christianity and the loving kindness of its Founder. But this view, in the first place, overlooks the fact that Christ, though merciful, is also just and exacting. Furthermore, however painful or humiliating confession may be, it is but a light penalty for the violation of God's law. Finally, those who are in earnest about their salvation count no hardship too great whereby they can win back God's friendship. Both these accusations, of too great leniency and too great severity, proceed as a rule from those who have no experience with the sacrament and only the vaguest ideas of what the Church teaches or of the power to forgive sins which the Church received from Christ.

Teaching of the Church.—The Council of Trent (1551) declares: "As a means of regaining grace and justice, penance was at all times necessary for those who had defiled their souls with any mortal sin. . . . Before the coming of Christ, penance was not a sacrament, nor is it since His coming a sacrament for those who are not baptized. But the Lord then principally instituted the Sacrament of Penance, when, being raised from the dead, he breathed upon His disciples saying: 'Receive ye the Holy Ghost. Whose sins you shall forgive, they are forgiven them; and whose sins you shall retain, they are retained' (John, xx, 22–23). By which action so signal and words so clear the consent of all the Fathers has ever understood that the power of forgiving and retaining sins was communicated to the Apostles and to their lawful successors, for the reconciling of the faithful who have fallen after Baptism" (Sess. XIV, c. i). Farther on (c. v) the council expressly states that Christ "left priests, His own vicars, as judges (*præsides et judices*), unto whom all the mortal crimes into which the faithful may have fallen should be revealed in order that, in accordance with the power of the keys, they may pronounce the sentence of forgiveness or retention of sins".

Power to Forgive Sins.—It is noteworthy that the fundamental objection so often urged against the Sacrament of Penance was first thought of by the Scribes when Christ said to the sick man of the palsy: "Thy sins are forgiven thee." "And there were some of the scribes sitting there, and thinking in their hearts: Why doth this man speak thus? he blasphemeth. Who can forgive sins, but God only?" But Jesus seeing their thoughts, said to them: "Which is easier to say to the sick of the palsy: Thy sins are forgiven thee; or to say, Arise, take up thy bed and walk? But that you may know that the Son of man hath power on earth to forgive sins, (he saith to the sick of the palsy,) I say to thee: Arise, take up thy bed, and go into thy house" (Mark, ii, 5–11; Matt., ix, 2–7). Christ wrought a miracle to show that He had power to forgive sins and that this power could be exerted not only in heaven but also on earth. This power, moreover, He transmitted to Peter and the other Apostles. To Peter He says: "And I will give to thee the keys of the kingdom of heaven. And whatsoever thou shalt bind upon earth, it shall be bound also in heaven: and whatsoever thou shalt loose on earth, it shall be loosed also in heaven" (Matt., xvi, 19). Later He says to all the Apostles: "Amen I say to you, whatsoever you shall bind upon earth, shall be bound also in heaven; and whatsoever you shall loose upon earth, shall be loosed also in heaven" (Matt., xviii, 18). As to the meaning of these texts, it should be noted: (a) that the "binding" and "loosing" refers not to physical but to spiritual or moral bonds among which sin is certainly included; the more so because (b) the power here granted is unlimited—"*whatsoever* you shall bind, . . . *whatsoever* you shall loose"; (c) the power is judicial, i. e., the Apostles are authorized to *bind* and to *loose;* (d) whether they bind or loose, their action is ratified in heaven. In healing the palsied man Christ declared that "the Son of man has power on earth to forgive sins"; here He promises that what these men, the Apostles, bind or loose on earth, God in heaven will likewise bind or loose. (Cf. also KEYS, POWER OF THE.)

But as the Council of Trent declares, Christ principally instituted the Sacrament of Penance after His Resurrection, a miracle greater than that of healing the sick. "As the Father hath sent me, I also send you. When he had said this, he breathed on them; and he said to them: Receive ye the Holy Ghost. Whose sins you shall forgive, they are forgiven them; and whose sins you shall retain, they are retained" (John, xx, 21–23). While the sense of these words is quite obvious, the following points are to be considered: (a) Christ here reiterates in the plainest terms—"sins", "forgive", "retain"—what He had previously stated in figurative language, "bind" and "loose", so that this text specifies and distinctly applies to sin the power of loosing and binding. (b) He prefaces this grant of power by declaring that the mission of the Apostles is similar to that which He had received from the Father and which He had fulfilled: "As the Father hath sent me". Now it is beyond doubt that He came into the world to destroy sin and that on various occasions He explicitly forgave sin (Matt., ix, 2-8; Luke, v, 20; vii, 47; Apoc., i, 5), hence the forgiving of sin is to be included in the mission of the Apostles. (c) Christ not only declared that sins were forgiven, but really and actually forgave them; hence, the Apostles are empowered not merely to announce to the sinner that his sins are forgiven but to grant him forgiveness—"whose sins you shall forgive". If their power were limited to the declaration "God pardons you", they would need a special revelation in each case to make the declaration valid. (d) The power is twofold—to forgive *or* to retain, i. e., the Apostles are not told to grant or withhold forgiveness indiscriminately; they must act judicially, forgiving or retaining according as the sinner deserves. (e) The exercise of this power in either form (forgiving or retaining) is not restricted: no distinction is made or even suggested between one kind of sin and another, or between one class of sinners and all the rest: Christ simply says "whose *sins*". (f) The sentence pronounced by the Apostles (remission or retention) is also God's sentence—"they are forgiven . . . they are retained".

It is therefore clear from the words of Christ that the Apostles had power to forgive sins. But this was not a personal prerogative that was to cease at their death; it was granted to them in their official capacity and hence as a permanent institution in the Church— no less permanent than the mission to teach and baptize all nations. Christ foresaw that even those who received faith and baptism, whether during the lifetime of the Apostles or later, would fall into sin and therefore would need forgiveness in order to be saved. He must, then, have intended that the power to forgive should be transmitted from the Apostles to their successors and be used as long as there would be sinners in the Church, and that means to the end of time. It is true that in baptism also sins are forgiven, but this does not warrant the view that the power to forgive is simply the power to baptize. In the first place, as appears from the texts cited above, the power to forgive is also the power to retain; its exercise involves a judicial action. But no such action is implied in the commission to baptize (Matt., xxviii, 18-20); in fact, as the Council of Trent affirms, the Church does not pass judgment on those who are not yet members of the Church, and membership is obtained through baptism. Furthermore, baptism, because it is a new birth, cannot be repeated, whereas the power to forgive sins (penance) is to be used as often as the sinner may need it. Hence the condemnation, by the same Council, of any one "who, confounding the sacraments, should say that baptism itself is the Sacrament of Penance, as though these two sacraments were not distinct and as though penance were not rightly called the second plank after shipwreck" (Sess. XIV, can. 2 de sac. pœn.).

These pronouncements were directed against the Protestant teaching which held that penance was merely a sort of repeated baptism; and as baptism effected no real forgiveness of sin but only an external covering over of sin through faith alone, the same, it was alleged, must be the case with penance. This, then, as a sacrament is superfluous; absolution is only a declaration that sin is forgiven through faith, and satisfaction is needless because Christ has satisfied once for all men. This was the first sweeping and radical denial of the Sacrament of Penance. Some of the earlier sects had claimed that only priests in the state of grace could validly absolve, but they had not denied the existence of the power to forgive. During all the preceding centuries, Catholic belief in this power had been so clear and strong that in order to set it aside Protestantism was obliged to strike at the very constitution of the Church and reject the whole content of Tradition.

Belief and Practice of the Early Church.—Among the modernistic propositions condemned by Pius X in the Decree "Lamentabili sane" (3 July, 1907) are the following: "In the primitive Church there was no concept of the reconciliation of the Christian sinner by the authority of the Church, but the Church by very slow degrees only grew accustomed to this concept. Moreover, even after penance came to be recognized as an institution of the Church, it was not called by the name of sacrament, because it was regarded as an odious sacrament" (46): and: "The Lord's words: 'Receive ye the Holy Ghost, whose sins you shall forgive, they are forgiven them, and whose *sins* you shall retain they are retained' (John xx, 22-23), in no way refer to the Sacrament of Penance, whatever the Fathers of Trent may have been pleased to assert" (47). According to the Council of Trent, the consensus of all the Fathers always understood that by the words of Christ just cited, the power of forgiving and retaining sins was communicated to the Apostles and their lawful successors (Sess. XIV, c. i). It is therefore Catholic doctrine that the Church from the earliest times believed in the power to forgive sins as granted by Christ to the Apostles. Such a belief in fact was clearly inculcated by the words with which Christ granted the power, and it would have been inexplicable to the early Christians if any one who professed faith in Christ had questioned the existence of that power in the Church. But if, contrariwise, we suppose that no such belief existed from the beginning, we encounter a still greater difficulty: the first mention of that power would have been regarded as an innovation both needless and intolerable; it would have shown little practical wisdom on the part of those who were endeavouring to draw men to Christ; and it would have raised a protest or led to a schism which would certainly have gone on record as plainly at least as did early divisions on matters of less importance. Yet no such record is found; even those who sought to limit the power itself presupposed its existence, and their very attempt at limitation put them in opposition to the prevalent Catholic belief.

Turning now to evidence of a positive sort, we have to note that the statements of any Father or orthodox ecclesiastical writer regarding penance present not merely his own personal view, but the commonly accepted belief; and furthermore that the belief which they record was no novelty at the time, but was the traditional doctrine handed down by the regular teaching of the Church and embodied in her practice. In other words, each witness speaks for a past that reaches back to the beginning, even when he does not expressly appeal to tradition. St. Augustine (d. 430) warns the faithful: "Let us not listen to those who deny that the Church of God has power to *forgive all sins*" (De agon. Christ., iii). St. Ambrose (d. 397) rebukes the Novatianists who "professed to show reverence for the Lord by reserving to Him alone the power of forgiving sins. Greater wrong could not be done than what they do in seeking to rescind His commands and fling back the office He bestowed. . . . The Church obeys Him in both respects, by binding sin and by loosing it; for the Lord willed that for both the power should be equal" (De pœnit., I, ii, 6). Again he teaches that this power was to be a function of the priesthood. "It seemed impossible that sins should be forgiven through penance; Christ granted this (power) to the Apostles and from the Apostles it has been transmitted to the office of priests" (op. cit., II, ii, 12). The power to forgive extends to all sins: "God makes no distinction; He promised mercy to all and to His priests He granted the authority to pardon *without any exception*" (op. cit., I, iii, 10). Against the same heretics St. Pacian, Bishop of Barcelona (d. 390), wrote to Sympronianus, one of their leaders: "This (forgiving sins), you say, only God can do. Quite true: but what He does through His priests is the doing of His own power" (Ep. I ad Sympron, 6 in P. L., XIII, 1057).

In the East during the same period we have the testimony of St. Cyril of Alexandria (d. 447): "Men filled with the spirit of God (i. e. priests) forgive sins in two ways, either by admitting to baptism those who are worthy or by pardoning the penitent children of the Church" (In Joan., 1, 12 in P. G., LXXIV, 722). St. John Chrysostom (d. 407) after declaring that neither angels nor the archangels have received such power, and after showing that earthly rulers can bind only the bodies of men, declares that the priest's power of forgiving sins "penetrates to the soul and reaches up to heaven". Wherefore, he concludes, "it were manifest folly to condemn so great a power without which we can neither obtain heaven nor come to the fulfilment of the promises. . . . Not only when they (the priests) regenerate us (baptism), but also after our new birth, they can forgive us our sins" (De sacerd., III, 5 sq.). St. Athanasius (d. 373): "As the man whom the priest baptizes is enlightened by the grace of the Holy Ghost, so does he who in penance confesses his sins, receive through the priest forgiveness in virtue of the grace of Christ" (Frag. contra Novat. in P. G., XXVI, 1315).

These extracts show that the Fathers recognized in penance a power and a utility quite distinct from that of baptism. Repeatedly they compare in figurative language the two means of obtaining pardon as two gates of the Church, two beacons of salvation; or, regarding baptism as spiritual birth, they describe penance as the remedy for the ills of the soul contracted after that birth. But a more important fact is that both in the West and in the East, the Fathers constantly appeal to the words of Christ and give them the same interpretation that was given eleven centuries later by the Council of Trent. In this respect they simply echoed the teachings of the earlier Fathers who had defended Catholic doctrine against the heretics of the third and second centuries. Thus St. Cyprian (q. v.) in his "De lapsis" (A. D. 251) rebukes those who had fallen away in time of persecution, but he also exhorts them to penance: "Let each confess his sin while he is still in this world, while his confession can be received, while satisfaction and the forgiveness granted by the priests is acceptable to God" (c. xxix). (See LAPSI.) The heretic Novatian, on the contrary, asserted that "it is unlawful to readmit apostates to the communion of the Church; their forgiveness must be left with God who alone can grant it" (Socrates, "Hist. eccl.", V, xxviii). Novatian and his party did not at first deny the power of the Church to absolve from sin; they affirmed that apostasy placed the sinner beyond the reach of that power—an error which was condemned by a synod at Rome in 251. (See NOVATIANISM.)

The distinction between sins that could be forgiven and others that could not, originated in the latter half of the second century as the doctrine of the Montanists (q. v.), and especially of Tertullian (q. v.). While still a Catholic, Tertullian wrote (A. D. 200–6) his "De pœnitentia" in which he distinguishes two kinds of penance, one as a preparation for baptism, the other to obtain forgiveness of certain grievous sins committed after baptism, i. e., apostasy, murder, and adultery. For these, however, he allows only one forgiveness: "Foreseeing these poisons of the Evil One, God, although the gate of forgiveness has been shut and fastened up with the bar of baptism, has permitted it still to stand somewhat open. In the vestibule He has stationed a second repentance for opening to such as knock; but now once for all, because now for the second time; but never more, because the last time it had been in vain. . . . However, if any do incur the debt of a second repentance, his spirit is not to be forthwith cut down and undermined by despair. Let it be irksome to sin again, but let it not be irksome to repent again; let it be irksome to imperil oneself again, but let no one be ashamed to be set free again. Repeated sickness must have repeated medicine" (De pœn., VII). Tertullian does not deny that the Church can forgive sins; he warns sinners against relapse, yet exhorts them to repent in case they should fall. His attitude at the time was not surprising, since in the early days the sins above mentioned were severely dealt with; this was done for disciplinary reasons, not because the Church lacked power to forgive.

In the minds, however, of some people the idea was developing that not only the exercise of the power but the power itself was limited. Against this false notion Pope Callistus (218–22) published his "peremptory edict" in which he declares: "I forgive the sins both of adultery and of fornication to those who have done penance." Thereupon Tertullian, now become a Montanist, wrote his "De pudicitia" (A. D. 217–22). In this work he rejects without scruple what he had taught as a Catholic: "I blush not at an error which I have cast off because I am delighted at being rid of it . . . one is not ashamed of his own improvement." The "error" which he imputes to Callistus and the Catholics was that the Church could forgive all sins: this, therefore, was the orthodox doctrine which Tertullian the heretic denied. In place of it he sets up the distinction between lighter sins which the bishop could forgive and more grievous sins which God alone could forgive. Though in an earlier treatise, "Scorpiace", he had said (c. x) that "the Lord left here to Peter and through him to the Church the keys of heaven", he now denies that the power granted to Peter had been transmitted to the Church, i. e., to the *numerus episcoporum* or body of bishops. Yet he claims this power for the "spirituals" (*pneumatici*), although these, for prudential reasons, do not make use of it. To the arguments of the "Psychici", as he termed the Catholics, he replies: "But the Church, you say, has the power to forgive sin. This I, even more than you, acknowledge and adjudge. I who in the new prophets have the Paraclete saying: 'The Church can forgive sin, but I will not do that (forgive) lest they (who are forgiven) fall into other sins'" (De pud., XXI, vii). Thus Tertullian, by the accusation which he makes against the pope and by the restriction which he places upon the exercise of the power of forgiving sin, bears witness to the existence of that power in the Church which he had abandoned.

Not content with assailing Callistus and his doctrine, Tertullian refers to the "Shepherd" (*Pastor*), a work written A. D. 140–54, and takes its author Hermas (q. v.) to task for favouring the pardon of adulterers. In the days of Hermas there was evidently a school of rigorists who insisted that there was no pardon for sin committed after baptism (Simil. VIII, vi). Against this school the author of the "Pastor" takes a resolute stand. He teaches that by penance the sinner may hope for reconciliation with God and with the Church. "Go and tell all to repent and they shall live unto God. Because the Lord having had compassion, *has sent me* to give repentance to all men, although some are not worthy of it on account of their works" (Simil. VIII, ii). Hermas, however, seems to give but one opportunity for such reconciliation, for in Mandate IV, i, he seems to state categorically that "there is but one repentance for the servants of God", and further on in c. iii he says the Lord has had mercy on the work of his hands and hath set repentance for them; "and he has entrusted *to me* the power of this repentance. And therefore I say to you, if any one has sinned . . . he has opportunity to repent once". Repentance is therefore possible at least once in virtue of a power vested in the priest of God. That Hermas here intends to say that the sinner could be absolved only once in his whole life is by no means a necessary conclusion. His words may well be understood as referring to public penance (see below), and as thus understood they imply no limitation on the sacramental power itself. The same interpretation applies to the statement of Clement of Alexandria (d. circa A. D. 215): "For God being very merciful has vouchsafed in the case of those who, though in faith, have fallen into transgression, a second repentance, so that should anyone be tempted after his calling, he may still receive a penance not to be repented of" (Stromata, II, xiii).

The existence of a regular system of penance is also hinted at in the work of Clement, "Who is the rich man that shall be saved?", where he tells the story of the Apostle John and his journey after the young bandit. John pledged his word that the youthful robber would find forgiveness from the Saviour; but even then a long serious penance was necessary before he could be restored to the Church. And when Clement concludes that "he who welcomes the angel of penance . . . will not be ashamed when he sees the Saviour", most commentators think he alludes to the bishop or priest who presided over the ceremony of public penance. Even earlier, Dionysius of Corinth (d. circa A. D. 170), setting himself against certain growing Marcionistic traditions, taught not only that Christ has left to His Church the power of pardon, but that no sin is so great as to be excluded from the exercise of that power. For this we have the authority of Eusebius, who says (Hist. eccl., IV, xxiii): "And writing to the Church which is in Amastris, together with those in Pontus, he commands them to receive those who come back after *any fall, whether it be delinquency or heresy*".

The "Didache" (q. v.) written at the close of the first century or early in the second, in IV, xiv, and again in XIV, i, commands an individual confession in the congregation: "In the congregation thou shalt confess thy transgressions"; or again: "On the Lord's Day come together and break bread . . . having confessed your transgressions that your sacrifice may be pure." Clement I (d. 99) in his epistle to the Corinthians not only exhorts to repentance, but begs the seditious to "submit themselves to the presbyters and receive correction so as to repent" (c. lvii), and Ignatius of Antioch at the close of the first century speaks of the mercy of God to sinners, provided they return "with one consent to the unity of Christ and the communion of the bishop". The clause "communion of the bishop" evidently means the bishop with his council of presbyters as assessors. He also says (Ad Philadel.) "that the bishop presides over penance".

The transmission of this power is plainly expressed in the prayer used at the consecration of a bishop as recorded in the Canons of Hippolytus (q. v.): "Grant him, O Lord, the episcopate and the spirit of clemency and the power to forgive sins" (c. xvii). Still more explicit is the formula cited in the "Apostolic Constitutions" (q. v.): "Grant him, O Lord almighty, through Thy Christ, the participation of Thy Holy Spirit, in order that he may have the power to remit sins according to Thy precept and Thy command, and to loosen every bond, whatsoever it be, according to the power which Thou hast granted to the Apostles." (Const. Apost., VIII, 5 in P. G., I, 1073). For the meaning of "episcopus", "sacerdos", "presbyter", as used in ancient documents, see BISHOP; HIERARCHY.

Exercise of the Power.— The granting by Christ of the power to forgive sins is the first essential of the Sacrament of Penance; in the actual exercise of this power are included the other essentials. The sacrament as such and on its own account has a matter and a form and it produces certain effects; the power of the keys is exercised by a minister (confessor) who must possess the proper qualifications, and the effects are wrought in the soul of the recipient, i. e., the penitent who with the necessary dispositions must perform certain actions (confession, satisfaction).

Matter and Form.—According to St. Thomas (Summa, III, lxxiv, a. 2) "the acts of the penitent are the proximate matter of this sacrament". This is also the teaching of Eugenius IV in the "Decretum pro Armenis" (Council of Florence, 1439) which calls the acts "*quasi materia*" of penance and enumerates them as contrition, confession, and satisfaction (Denzinger-Bannwart, "Enchir.", 699). The Thomists in general and other eminent theologians, e. g., Bellarmine, Toletus, Suarez, and De Lugo, hold the same opinion. According to Scotus (In IV Sent., d. 16, q. 1, n. 7) "the Sacrament of Penance is the absolution imparted with certain words" while the acts of the penitent are required for the worthy reception of the sacrament. The absolution as an external ceremony is the matter, and, as possessing significative force, the form. Among the advocates of this theory are St. Bonaventure, Capreolus, Andreas Vega, and Maldonatus. The Council of Trent (Sess. XIV, c. 3) declares: "the acts of the penitent, namely contrition, confession, and satisfaction, are the *quasi materia* of this sacrament". The Roman Catechism (II, v, 13) says: "These actions are called by the Council *quasi materia* not because they have not the nature of true matter, but because they are not the sort of matter which is employed externally as water in baptism and chrism in confirmation". For the theological discussion see Palmieri, op. cit., p. 144 sqq.; Pesch, "Prælectiones

CONFESSIONAL (XIV CENTURY)
Basilica of S. Antonio, Padua

dogmaticæ", Freiburg, 1897; De San, "De pœnitentia", Bruges, 1899; Pohle, "Lehrb. d. Dogmatik". Regarding the form of the sacrament, both the Council of Florence and the Council of Trent teach that it consists in the words of absolution. "The form of the Sacrament of Penance, wherein its force principally consists, is placed in those words of the minister: 'I absolve thee, etc.'; to these words indeed, in accordance with the usage of Holy Church, certain prayers are laudably added, but they do not pertain to the essence of the form nor are they necessary for the administration of the sacrament" (Council of Trent, Sess. XIV, c. 3). Concerning these additional prayers, the use of the Eastern and Western Churches, and the question whether the form is deprecatory or indicative and personal, see ABSOLUTION. Cf. also the writers referred to in the preceding paragraph.

Effect.—"The effect of this sacrament is deliverance from sin" (Council of Florence). The same definition in somewhat different terms is given by the Council of Trent (Sess. XIV, c. 3): "So far as pertains to its force and efficacy, the effect (*res et effectus*) of this sacrament is reconciliation with God, upon which there sometimes follows, in pious and devout recipients, peace and calm of conscience with intense consolation of spirit". This reconciliation implies first of all that the guilt of sin is remitted, and consequently also the eternal punishment due to mortal sin. As the Council of Trent declares, penance requires the performance of satisfaction "not indeed for the eternal penalty which is remitted together with the guilt either by the sacrament or by the desire of receiving the sacrament, but for the temporal penalty which, as the Scriptures teach, is not always forgiven entirely as it is in baptism" (Sess. VI, c. 14). In other words baptism frees the soul not only from all sin but also from all indebtedness to Divine justice, whereas after the reception of absolution in penance, there may and usually does remain some temporal debt to be discharged by works of satisfaction (see below). "Venial sins by which we are not deprived of the grace of God and into which we very frequently fall are rightly and usefully declared in confession; but mention of them may, without any fault, be omitted and they can be expiated by many other remedies" (Council of Trent, Sess. XIV, c. 3). Thus, an act of contrition suffices to obtain forgiveness of venial sin, and the same effect is produced by the worthy reception of sacraments other than penance, e. g., by Holy Communion.

The reconciliation of the sinner with God has as a further consequence the revival of those merits which he had obtained before committing grievous sin. Good works performed in the state of grace deserve a reward from God, but this is forfeited by mortal sin, so that if the sinner should die unforgiven his good deeds avail him nothing. So long as he remains in sin, he is incapable of meriting: even works which are good in themselves are, in his case, worthless: they cannot revive, because they never were alive. But once his sin is cancelled by penance, he regains not only the state of grace but also the entire store of merit which had, before his sin, been placed to his credit. On this point theologians are practically unanimous: the only hindrance to obtaining reward is sin, and when this is removed, the former title, so to speak, is revalidated. On the other hand, if there were no such revalidation, the loss of merit once acquired would be equivalent to an eternal punishment, which is incompatible with the forgiveness effected by penance. As to the further question regarding the manner and extent of the revival of merit, various opinions have been proposed; but that which is generally accepted holds with Suarez (De reviviscentia meritorum) that the revival is complete, i. e., the forgiven penitent has to his credit as much merit as though he had never sinned. See De Augustinis, "De re sacramentaria", II, Rome, 1887; Pesch, op. cit., VII; Göttler, "Der hl. Thomas v. Aquin u. die vortridentinischen Thomisten über die Wirkungen d. Busssakramentes", Freiburg, 1904.

The Minister, i. e., the confessor.—From the judicial character of this sacrament it follows that not every member of the Church is qualified to forgive sins; the administration of penance is reserved to those who are invested with authority. That this power does not belong to the laity is evident from the Bull of Martin V "Inter cunctas" (1418) which among other questions to be answered by the followers of Wyclif and Huss, has this: "whether he believes that the Christian . . . is bound as a necessary means of salvation to confess to a priest only and not to a layman or to laymen however good and devout" (Denzinger-Bannwart, "Enchir.", 670). Luther's proposition, that "any Christian, even a woman or a child" could in the absence of a priest absolve as well as pope or bishop, was condemned (1520) by Leo X in the Bull "Exurge Domine" (Enchir., 753). The Council of Trent (Sess. XIV, c. 6) condemns as "false and as at variance with the truth of the Gospel all doctrines which extend the ministry of the keys to any others than bishops and priests, imagining that the words of the Lord (Matt., xviii, 18; John, xx, 23) were, contrary to the institution of this sacrament, addressed to all the faithful of Christ in such wise that each and every one has the power of remitting sin". The Catholic doctrine, therefore, is that only bishops and priests can exercise the power.

These decrees moreover put an end, practically, to the usage, which had sprung up and lasted for some time in the Middle Ages, of confessing to a layman in case of necessity. This custom originated in the conviction that he who had sinned was obliged to make known his sin to some one—to a priest if possible, otherwise to a layman. In the work "On true penance and false" (De vera et falsa pœnitentia), erroneously ascribed to St. Augustine, the counsel is given: "So great is the power of confession that if a priest be not at hand, let him (the person desiring to confess) confess to his neighbour." But in the same place the explanation is given: "although he to whom the confession is made has no power to absolve, nevertheless he who confesses to his fellow (*socio*) becomes worthy of pardon through his desire of confessing to a priest" (P. L., XL, 1113). Lea, who cites (I, 220) the assertion of the Pseudo-Augustine about confession to one's neighbour, passes over the explanation. He consequently sets in a wrong light a series of incidents illustrating the practice and gives but an imperfect idea of the theological discussion which it aroused. Though Albertus Magnus (In IV Sent., dist. 17, art. 58) regarded as sacramental the absolution granted by a layman while St. Thomas (IV Sent., d. 17, q. 3, a. 3, sol. 2) speaks of it as "quodammodo sacramentalis", other great theologians took a quite different view. Alexander of Hales (Summa, Q. xix, De confessione memb., I, a. 1) says that it is an "imploring of absolution"; St. Bonaventure ("Opera", VII, p. 345, Lyons, 1668) that such a confession even in cases of necessity is not obligatory, but merely a sign of contrition; Scotus (IV Sent., d. 14, q. 4) that there is no precept obliging one to confess to a layman and that this practice may be very detrimental; Durandus of St. Pourcain (IV Sent., d. 17, q. 12) that in the absence of a priest, who alone can absolve in the tribunal of penance, there is no obligation to confess; Prierias (Summa Silv., s. v. Confessor, I, 1) that if absolution is given by a layman, the confession must be repeated whenever possible; this in fact was the general opinion. It is not then surprising that Dominicus Soto, writing in 1564, should find it difficult to believe that such a custom ever existed: "since (in confession to a layman) there was no sacrament . . . it is incredible that men, of their own accord and with no profit to themselves, should reveal to others the secrets of their conscience" (IV Sent., d. 18, q. 4, a. 1). Since, therefore, the weight of theological opinion gradually turned against the practice and since the practice never received the sanction of the Church, it cannot be urged as a proof that the power to forgive sins belonged at any time to the laity. What the practice does show is that both people and theologians realized keenly the obligation of confessing their sins not to God alone but to some human listener, even though the latter possessed no power to absolve.

The same exaggerated notion appears in the practice of confessing to the deacons in case of necessity. They were naturally preferred to laymen when no priest was accessible because in virtue of their office they administered Holy Communion. Moreover, some of the earlier councils (Elvira, A. D. 300; Toledo, 400) and penitentials (Theodore) seemed to grant the power of penance to the deacon (in the priest's absence). The Council of Tribur (895) declared in regard to bandits that if, when captured or wounded, they confessed to a priest or a deacon, they should not be denied communion; and this expression "presbytero vel diacono" was incorporated in the Decree of Gratian and in many later documents from the tenth century to the thirteenth. The Council of York (1195) decreed that except in the gravest necessity the deacon should not baptize, give communion, or "impose penance on one who confessed". Substantially the same enactments are found in the Councils of London (1200) and Rouen (1231), the constitutions of St. Edmund of Canterbury (1236), and those of Walter of Kirkham, Bishop of Durham (1255). All these enactments, though stringent enough as regards ordinary circumstances, make exception for urgent necessity. No such exception is allowed in the decree of the Synod of Poitiers (1280): "desiring to root out an erroneous abuse which has grown up in our diocese through dangerous ignorance, we forbid deacons to hear confessions or to give absolution in the tribunal of penance: for it is certain and beyond doubt that they cannot absolve, since they have not the keys which are conferred only in the priestly order". This "abuse" probably disappeared in the fourteenth or fifteenth century; at all events no direct mention is made of it by the Council of Trent, though the reservation to bishops and priests of the absolving power shows plainly that the Council excluded deacons.

The authorization which the medieval councils gave the deacon in case of necessity did not confer the power to forgive sins. In some of the decrees it is expressly stated that the deacon has not the keys—*claves non habent*. In other enactments he is forbidden except in cases of necessity to "give" or "impose penance", *pœnitentiam dare, imponere*. His function then was limited to the *forum externum;* in the absence of a priest he could "reconcile" the sinner, i. e., restore him to the communion of the Church; but he did not and could not give the sacramental absolution which a priest would have given (Palmieri, Pesch). Another explanation emphasizes the fact that the deacon could lawfully administer the Holy Eucharist. The faithful were under a strict obligation to receive Communion at the approach of death, and on the other hand the reception of this sacrament sufficed to blot out even mortal sin provided the communicant had the requisite dispositions. The deacon could hear their confession simply to assure himself that they were properly disposed, but not for the purpose of giving them absolution. If he went further and "imposed penance" in the stricter, sacramental sense, he exceeded his power, and any authorization to this effect granted by the bishop merely showed that the bishop was in error (Laurain, "De l'intervention des laïques, des diacres et des abbesses dans l'administration de la pénitence", Paris, 1897). In any case, the prohibitory enactments which finally abolished the practice did not deprive the deacon of a power which was his by virtue of his office; but they brought into clearer light the traditional belief that only bishops and priests can administer the Sacrament of Penance. (See below under *Confession*.)

For valid administration, a twofold power is necessary: the power of order and the power of jurisdiction. The former is conferred by ordination, the latter by ecclesiastical authority (see JURISDICTION). At his ordination a priest receives the power to consecrate the Holy Eucharist, and for valid consecration he needs no jurisdiction. As regards penance, the case is different: "because the nature and character of a judgment requires that sentence be pronounced only on those who are subjects (of the judge) the Church of God has always held, and this Council affirms it to be most true, that the absolution which a priest pronounces upon one over whom he has not either ordinary or delegated jurisdiction, is of no effect" (Council of Trent, Sess. XIV, c. 7). Ordinary jurisdiction is that which one has by reason of his office as involving the care of souls; the pope has it over the whole Church, the bishop within his diocese, the pastor within his parish. Delegated jurisdiction is that which is granted by an ecclesiastical superior to one who does not possess it by virtue of his office. The need of jurisdiction for administering this sacrament is usually expressed by saying that a priest must have "faculties" to hear confession (see FACULTIES). Hence it is that a priest visiting in a diocese other than his own cannot hear confession without special authorization from the bishop. Every priest, however, can absolve any one who is at the point of death, because under those circumstances the Church gives all priests jurisdiction. As the bishop grants jurisdiction, he can also limit it by "reserving" certain cases (see RESERVATION) and he can even withdraw it entirely.

Recipient, i. e., the penitent.—The Sacrament of Penance was instituted by Christ for the remission of sins committed after baptism. Hence, no unbaptized person, however deep and sincere his sorrow, can be validly absolved. Baptism, in other words, is the first essential requisite on the part of the penitent. This does not imply that in the sins committed by an unbaptized person there is a special enormity or any other element that places them beyond the power of the keys; but that one must first be a member of the Church before he can submit himself and his sins to the judicial process of sacramental Penance.

Contrition; Attrition.—Without sorrow for sin there is no forgiveness. Hence the Council of Trent (Sess. XIV, c. 4): "Contrition, which holds the first place among the acts of the penitent, is sorrow of heart and detestation for sin committed, with the resolve to sin no more". The Council (ibid.) furthermore distinguishes perfect contrition from imperfect contrition, which is called attrition, and which arises from the consideration of the turpitude of sin or from the fear of hell and punishment. See ATTRITION; CONTRITION, where these two kinds of sorrow are more fully explained and an account is given of the principal discussions and opinions. See also treatises by Pesch, Palmieri, Pohle. For the present purpose it need only be stated that attrition, with the Sacrament of Penance, suffices to obtain forgiveness of sin. The Council of Trent further teaches (ibid.): "though it sometimes happens that this contrition is perfect and that it reconciles man with God before the actual reception of this sacrament, still the reconciliation is not to be ascribed to the contrition itself apart from the desire of the sacrament which it (contrition) includes". In accordance with this teaching Pius V condemned (1567) the proposition of Baius asserting that even perfect contrition does not, except in case of necessity or of martyrdom, remit sin without the actual reception of the sacrament (Denzinger-Bannwart, "Enchir.", 1071). It should be noted, however, that the contrition of which the Council speaks is perfect in the sense that it includes the desire (*votum*) to receive the sacrament. Whoever, in fact, repents of his sin out of love for God must be willing to comply with the Divine ordinance regarding penance, i. e., he would confess if a confessor were accessible, and he realizes that he is obliged to confess when he has the opportunity. But it does not follow that the penitent is at liberty to choose between two modes of obtaining forgiveness, one by an act of contrition independently of the sacrament, the other by confession and absolution. This view was put forward by Peter Martinez (de Osma) in the proposition: "mortal sins as regards their guilt and their punishment in the other world, are blotted out by contrition alone without any reference to the keys"; and the proposition was condemned by Sixtus IV in 1479 (Denzinger-Bannwart, "Enchir.", 724). Hence it is clear that not even heartfelt sorrow based on the highest motives, can, in the present order of salvation, dispense with the power of the keys, i. e., with the Sacrament of Penance.

Confession; Necessity.—"For those who after baptism have fallen into sin, the Sacrament of Penance is as necessary unto salvation as is baptism itself for those who have not yet been regenerated" (Council of Trent, Sess. XIV, c. 2). Penance, therefore, is not an institution the use of which was left to the option of each sinner, so that he might, if he preferred, hold aloof from the Church and secure forgiveness by some other means, e. g., by acknowledging his sin in the privacy of his own mind. As already stated, the power granted by Christ to the Apostles is twofold, to forgive and to retain, in such a way that what they forgive God forgives and what they retain God retains. But this grant would be nullified if, in case the Church retained the sins of a penitent, he could, as it were, take appeal to God's tribunal and obtain pardon. Nor would the power to retain have any meaning if the sinner, passing over the Church, went in the first instance to God, since by the very terms of the grant, God retains sin once committed so long as it is not remitted by the Church. It would indeed have been strangely inconsistent if Christ in conferring this twofold power on the Apostles had intended to provide some other means of forgiveness such as confessing "to God alone". Not only the Apostles, but any one with an elementary knowledge of human nature would have perceived at once that the easier means would be chosen, and that the grant of power so formally and solemnly made by Christ had no real significance (Palmieri, op. cit., thesis X). On the other hand, once it is admitted that the grant was effectual and consequently that the sacrament is necessary in order to obtain forgiveness, it plainly follows that the penitent must in some way make known his sin to those who exercise the power. This is conceded even by those who reject the Sacrament of Penance as a Divine institution. "Such remission was manifestly impossible without the declaration of the offences to be forgiven" (Lea, "History etc.", I, p. 182). The Council of Trent, after declaring that Christ left His priests as His vicars unto whom as rulers and judges the faithful must make known their sins, adds: "It is evident that the priests could not have exercised this judgment without knowledge of the cause, nor could they have observed justice in enjoining satisfaction if (the faithful) had declared their sins in a general way only and not specifically and in detail" (Sess. XIV, c. 5).

Since the priest in the pardoning of sin exercises a strictly judicial function, Christ must will that such tremendous power be used wisely and prudently. Moreover, in virtue of the grant of Christ the priest can forgive all sins without distinction, *quæcumque solveritis*. How can a wise and prudent judgment be rendered if the priest be in ignorance of the cause on which judgment is pronounced? And how can he obtain the requisite knowledge unless it come from the spontaneous acknowledgment of the sinner? This necessity of manifestation is all the clearer if satisfaction for sin, which from the beginning has been part of the penitential discipline, is to be imposed not only wisely but also justly. That there is a necessary connexion between the prudent judgment of the confessor and the detailed confession of sins is evident from the nature of a judicial procedure and especially from a full analysis of the grant of Christ in the light of tradition. No judge may release or condemn without full knowledge of the case. And again the tradition of the earliest time sees in the words of Christ not only the office of the judge sitting in judgment, but the kindness of a father who weeps with the repentant child (Aphraates, "Ep. de Pœnitentia", dem. 7) and the skill of the physician who after the manner of Christ heals the wounds of the soul (Origen in P. G., XII, 418; P. L., XIII, 1086). Clearly, therefore, the words of Christ imply the doctrine of the external manifestation of conscience to a priest in order to obtain pardon.

Confession; Various Kinds.—Confession is the avowal of one's own sins made to a duly authorized priest for the purpose of obtaining their forgiveness through the power of the keys. Virtual confession is simply the will to confess even where, owing to circumstances, declaration of sin is impossible; actual confession is any action by which the penitent manifests his sin. It may be made in general terms, e. g., by reciting the "Confiteor", or it may consist in a more or less detailed statement of one's sins; when the statement is complete, the confession is distinct. Public confession, as made in the hearing of a number of people (e. g. a congregation) differs from private, or secret, confession which is made to the priest alone and is often called auricular, i. e., spoken into the ear of the confessor. We are here concerned mainly with actual distinct confession which is the usual practice in the Church and which so far as the validity of the sacrament is concerned, may be either public or private. "As regards the method of confessing secretly to the priest alone, though Christ did not forbid that any one, in punishment of his crimes and for his own humiliation as also to give others an example and to edify the Church, should confess his sins publicly, still, this has not been commanded by Divine precept nor would it be prudent to decree by any human law that sins, especially secret sins, should be publicly confessed. Since, then, secret sacramental confession, which from the beginning has been and even now is the usage of the Church, was always commended with great and unanimous consent by the holiest and most ancient Fathers; thereby is plainly refuted the foolish calumny of those who make bold to teach that it (secret confession) is something foreign to the Divine command, a human invention devised by the Fathers assembled in the Lateran Council" (Council of Trent, Sess. XIV, c. 5). It is therefore Catholic doctrine, first, that Christ did not prescribe public confession, salutary as it might be, nor did He forbid it; second, that secret confession, sacramental in character, has been the practice of the Church from the earliest days.

Traditional Belief and Practice.—How firmly rooted in the Catholic mind is the belief in the efficacy and necessity of confession, appears clearly from the fact that the Sacrament of Penance endures in the Church after the countless attacks to which it has been subjected during the last four centuries. If at the Reformation or since the Church could have surrendered a doctrine or abandoned a practice for the sake of peace and to soften a "hard saying", confession would have been the first to disappear. Yet it is precisely during this period that the Church has defined in the most exact terms the nature of penance and most vigorously insisted on the necessity of confession. It will not of course be denied that at the beginning of the sixteenth century confession was generally practised throughout the Christian world. The Reformers themselves, notably Calvin, admitted that it had been in existence for three centuries when they attributed its origin to the Fourth Lateran Council (1215). At that time, according to Lea (op. cit., I, 228), the necessity of confession "became a new article of faith" and the canon, *omnis utriusque sexus*, "is perhaps the most important legislative act in the history of the Church" (ibid., 230). But, as the Council of Trent affirms, "the Church did not through the Lateran Council prescribe that the faithful of Christ should confess—a thing which it knew to be by Divine right necessary and established—but that the precept of confessing at least once a year should be complied with by all and every one when they reached the age of discretion" (Sess., XIV, c. 5). The Lateran edict presupposed the necessity of confession as an article of Catholic belief and laid down a law as to the minimum frequency of confession—at least once a year.

In the Middle Ages.—In constructing their systems of theology, the medieval doctors discuss at length the various problems connected with the Sacrament of Penance. They are practically unanimous in holding that confession is obligatory; the only notable exception in the twelfth century is Gratian, who gives the arguments for and against the necessity of confessing to a priest and leaves the question open (Decretum, p. II, De pœn., d. 1, in P. L., CLXXXVII, 1519–63). Peter Lombard (d. about 1150) takes up the authorities cited by Gratian and by means of them proves that "without confession there is no pardon" ... "no entrance into paradise" (IV Sent., d. XVII, 4, in P. L., CXCII, 880–2). The principal debate, in which Hugh of St. Victor, Abelard, Robert Pullus, and Peter of Poitiers took the leading parts, concerned the origin and sanction of the obligation, and the value of the different Scriptural texts cited to prove the institution of penance. This question passed on to the thirteenth century and received its solution in very plain terms from St. Thomas Aquinas. Treating (Contra Gentes, IV, 72) of the necessity of penance and its parts, he shows that "the institution of confession was necessary in order that the sin of the penitent might be revealed to Christ's minister; hence the minister to whom the confession is made must have judicial power as representing Christ, the Judge of the living and the dead. This power again requires two things: authority of knowledge and power to absolve or to condemn. These are called the two keys of the Church which the Lord entrusted to Peter (Matt., xvi, 19). But they were not given to Peter to be held by him alone, but to be handed on through him to others; else sufficient provision would not have been made for the salvation of the faithful. These keys derive their efficacy from the passion of Christ whereby He opened to us the gate of the heavenly kingdom". And he adds that as no one can be saved without baptism either by actual reception or by desire, so they who sin after baptism cannot be saved unless they submit to the keys of the Church either by actually confessing or by the resolve to confess when opportunity permits. Furthermore, as the rulers of the Church cannot dispense any one from baptism as a means of salvation, neither can they give a dispensation whereby the sinner may be forgiven without confession and absolution. The same explanation and reasoning is given by all the Scholastics of the thirteenth and fourteenth centuries. They were in practical agreement as to the necessity of jurisdiction in the confessor. Regarding the time at which confession had to be made, some held with William of Auvergne that one was obliged to confess as soon as possible after sinning; others with Albertus Magnus and St. Thomas that it sufficed to confess within the time limits prescribed by the Church (Paschal Time); and this more lenient view finally prevailed. Further subjects of discussion during this period were: the choice of confessor; the obligation of confessing before receiving other sacraments, especially the Eucharist; the integrity of confession; the obligation of secrecy on the part of the confessor, i. e., the seal of confession. The careful and minute treatment of these points and the frank expression of divergent opinions were characteristic of the Schoolmen, but they also brought out more clearly the central truths regarding penance and they opened the way to the conciliar pronouncements at Florence and Trent which gave to Catholic doctrine a more precise formulation. See Vacandard and Bernard in "Dict. de théol. cath.", s. v. Confession; Turmel, "Hist. de la théologie positive", Paris, 1904; Cambier, "De divina institutione confessionis sacramentalis", Louvain, 1884.

CONFESSIONAL
Church of St. Paul, Antwerp

Not only was the obligation recognized in the Catholic Church throughout the Middle Ages, but the schismatic Greeks held the same belief and still hold it. They fell into schism under Photius (q. v.) in 869, but retained confession, which therefore must have been in use for some time previous to the ninth century. The practice, moreover, was regulated in detail by the Penitential Books (q. v.), which prescribed the canonical penance for each sin, and minute questions for the examination of the penitent. The most famous of these books among the Greeks were those attributed to John the Faster (q. v.) and to John the Monk. In the West similar works were written by the Irish monks St. Columbanus (d. 615) and Cummian, and by the Englishmen Ven. Bede (d. 735), Egbert (d. 767), and Theodore of Canterbury (d. 690). Besides the councils mentioned above (*Minister*) decrees pertaining to confession were enacted at Worms (868), Paris (820), Châlons (813, 650), Tours (813), Reims (813). The Council of Chalcuth (785) says: "if any one (which God forbid) should depart this life without penance or confession he is not to be prayed for". The significant features about these enactments is that they do not introduce confession as a new practice, but take it for granted and regulate its administration. Thereby they put into practical effect what had been handed down by tradition.

St. Gregory the Great (d. 604) teaches: "the affliction of penance is efficacious in blotting out sins when it is enjoined by the sentence of the priest, when the burden of it is decided by him in proportion to the offence after weighing the deeds of those who confess" (In I Reg., III, v, n. 13 in P. L., LXXIX, 207); Pope Leo the Great (440–61), who is often credited with the institution of confession, refers to it as an "Apostolic rule". Writing to the bishops of Campania he forbids as an abuse "contrary to the Apostolic rule" (contra apostolicam regulam) the reading out in public of a written statement of their sins drawn up by the faithful, because, he declares, "it suffices that the guilt of conscience be manifested to priests alone in secret confession" (Ep. clxviii in P. L., LIV, 1210). In another letter (Ep. cviii in P. L., LIV, 1011), after declaring that by Divine ordinance the mercy of God can be obtained only through the supplications of the priests, he adds: "the mediator between God and men, Christ Jesus, gave the rulers of the Church this power that they should impose penance on those who confess and admit them when purified by salutary satisfaction to the communion of the sacraments through the gateway of reconciliation." The earlier Fathers frequently speak of sin as a disease which needs treatment, sometimes drastic, at the hands of the spiritual physician or surgeon. St. Augustine (d. 430) tells the sinner: "an abscess had formed in your conscience; it tormented you and gave you no rest. . . . confess, and in confession let the pus come out and flow away" (In ps. lxvi, n. 6). St. Jerome (d. 420) comparing the priests of the New Law with those of the Old who decided between leprosy and leprosy, says: "likewise in the New Testament the bishops and the priest bind or loose . . . in virtue of their office, having heard various sorts of sinners, they know who is to be bound and who is to be loosed" . . . (In Matt., xvi, 19); in his "Sermon on Penance" he says: "let no one find it irksome to show his wound (vulnus confiteri) because without confession it cannot be healed." St. Ambrose (d. 397): "this right (of loosing and binding) has been conferred on priests only" (De pœn., I, ii, n. 7); St. Basil (d. 397): "As men do not make known their bodily ailments to anybody and everybody, but only to those who are skilled in healing, so confession of sin ought to be made to those who can cure it" (Reg. brevior., 229).

For those who sought to escape the obligation of confession it was natural enough to assert that repentance was the affair of the soul alone with its Maker, and that no intermediary was needed. It is this pretext that St. Augustine sweeps aside in one of his sermons: "Let no one say, I do penance secretly; I perform it in the sight of God, and He who is to pardon me knows that in my heart I repent". Whereupon St. Augustine asks: "Was it then said to no purpose, 'What you shall loose upon earth shall be loosed in heaven'? Was it for nothing that the keys were given to the Church?" (Sermo cccxcii, n. 3, in P. L., XXXIX, 1711). The Fathers, of course, do not deny that sin must be confessed to God; at times, indeed, in exhorting the faithful to confess, they make no mention of the priest; but such passages must be taken in connexion with the general teaching of the Fathers and with the traditional belief of the Church. Their real meaning is expressed, e. g., by Anastasius Sinaita (seventh century): "Confess your sins to Christ through the priest" (De sacra synaxi), and by Egbert, Archbishop of York (d. 766): "Let the sinner confess his evil deeds to God, that the priest may know what penance to impose" (Mansi, Coll. Conc., XII, 232). For the passages in St. John Chrysostom, see Hurter, "Theol. dogmat.", III, 454; Pesch, "Prælectiones", VII, 165.

The Fathers, knowing well that one great difficulty which the sinner has to overcome is shame, encourage him in spite of it to confess. "I appeal to you, my brethren", says St. Pacian (d. 391), ". . . you who are not ashamed to sin and yet are ashamed to confess . . . I beseech you, cease to hide your wounded conscience. Sick people who are prudent do not fear the physician, though he cut and burn even the secret parts of the body" (Parænesis ad pœnit., n. 6, 8). St. John Chrysostom (d. 347) pleads eloquently with the sinner: "Be not ashamed to approach [the priest] because you have sinned, nay rather, for this very reason approach. No one says: Because I have an ulcer, I will not go near a physician or take medicine; on the contrary, it is just this that makes it needful to call in physicians and apply remedies. We [priests] know well how to pardon, because we ourselves are liable to sin. This is why God did not give us angels to be our doctors, nor send down Gabriel to rule the flock, but from the fold itself he chooses the shepherds, from among the sheep He appoints the leader, in order that he may be inclined to pardon his followers and, keeping in mind his own frailty, may not set himself in hardness against the members of the flock" (Hom. "On Frequent Assembly" in P. G., LXIII, 463).

Tertullian had already used the same argument with those who, for fear of exposing their sins, put off their confession from day to day—"mindful more of their shame than of their salvation, like those who hide from the physician the malady they suffer in the secret parts of the body, and thus perish through bashfulness. . . . Because we withhold anything from the knowledge of men, do we thereby conceal it from God? . . . Is it better to hide and be damned than to be openly absolved?" ("De pœnit.", x). St. Cyprian (d. 258) pleads for greater mildness in the treatment of sinners, "since we find that no one ought to be forbidden to do penance and that to those who implore the mercy of God peace can be granted through His priests. . . . And because in hell there is no confession, nor can exomologesis be made there, they who repent with their whole heart and ask for it, should be received into the Church and therein saved unto the Lord" (Ep. lv, "Ad Antonian.", n. 29). Elsewhere he says that many who do not do penance or confess their guilt are filled with unclean spirits; and by contrast he praises the greater faith and more wholesome fear of those who, though not guilty of any idolatrous action, "nevertheless, because they thought of [such action], confess [their thought] in sorrow and simplicity to the priests of God, make the exomologesis of their conscience, lay bare the burden of their soul, and seek a salutary remedy even for wounds that are slight" ("De lapsis", xxvi sqq.). Origen (d. 254) compares the sinner to those whose stomachs are overloaded with undigested food or with excess of humours and phlegm; if they vomit, they are relieved, "so, too, those who have sinned, if they conceal and keep the sin within, they are distressed and almost choked by its humour or phlegm. But if they accuse themselves and confess, they at the same time vomit the sin and cast off every cause of disease" (Homil. on Ps. xxxvii, n. 6, in P. G., XII, 1386). St. Irenæus (130–202) relates the case of certain women whom the Gnostic Marcus had led into sin. "Some of them", he says, "perform their exomologesis openly also [etiam in manifesto], while others, afraid to do this, draw back in silence, despairing to regain the life of God" ("Adv. hær.", I, xiii, 7, in P. G., VII, 591). This etiam in manifesto suggests at least that they had confessed privately, but could not bring themselves to make a public confession. The advantage of confession as against the concealment of sin is shown in the words of St. Clement of Rome in his letter to the Corinthians: "It is better for a man to confess his sins than to harden his heart" (Ep. I, "Ad Cor.", li, 1).

This outline of the patristic teaching shows: (1) that the Fathers insisted on a manifestation of sin as the necessary means of unburdening the soul and regaining the friendship of God; (2) that the confession was to be made not to a layman but to priests; (3) that priests exercise the power of absolving in virtue of a Divine commission, i. e., as representatives of Christ; (4) that the sinner, if he would be saved, must overcome his shame and repugnance to confession. And since the series of witnesses goes back to the latter part of the first century, the practice of confession must have existed from the earliest days. St. Leo had good reason for appealing to the "Apostolic rule" which made secret confession to the priest sufficient without the necessity of a public declaration. Nor is it surprising that Lactantius (d. c. 330) should have pointed to the practice of confession as a characteristic of the true Church: "That is the true Church in which there is confession and penance, which applies a wholesome remedy to the sins and wounds whereunto the weakness of the flesh is subject" ("Div. Inst.", IV, 30).

WHAT SINS ARE TO BE CONFESSED.—Among the propositions condemned by the Council of Trent is the following: "That to obtain forgiveness of sins in the Sacrament of Penance, it is not necessary by Divine law to confess each and every mortal sin which is called to mind by due and careful examination, to confess even hidden sins and those that are against the last two precepts of the Decalogue, together with the circumstances that change the specific nature of the sin; such confession is only useful for the instruction and consolation of the penitent, and of old was practised merely in order to impose canonical satisfaction" (Can. de pœnit., vii). The Catholic teaching consequently is: that all mortal sins must be confessed of which the penitent is conscious, for these are so related that no one of them can be remitted unless all are remitted. Remission means that the soul is restored to the friendship of God; and this is obviously impossible if there remain unforgiven even a single mortal sin. Hence, the penitent, who in confession wilfully conceals a mortal sin, derives no benefit whatever; on the contrary, he makes void the sacrament and thereby incurs the guilt of sacrilege. If, however, the sin be omitted, not through any fault of the penitent, but through forgetfulness, it is forgiven indirectly; but it must be declared at the next confession and thus submitted to the power of the keys.

While mortal sin is the necessary matter of confession, venial sin is sufficient matter, as are also the mortal sins already forgiven in previous confessions. This is the common teaching of theologians, in accord with the condemnation pronounced by Leo X on Luther's assertion, "By no means presume to confess venial sins . . . in the primitive Church, only manifest mortal sins were confessed" (Bull, "Exurge Domine"; Denzinger, "Enchir.", 748). In the constitution "Inter cunctas" (17 Feb., 1304), Benedict XI, after stating that penitents who had confessed to a priest belonging to a religious order are not obliged to reiterate the confession to their own priest, adds: "Though it is not necessary to confess the same sins over again, nevertheless we regard it as salutary to repeat the confession, because of the shame it involves, which is a great part of penance; hence we strictly enjoin the Brothers [Dominicans and Franciscans] to admonish their penitents and in sermons exhort them that they confess to their own priests at least once a year, assuring them that this will undoubtedly conduce to their spiritual welfare" (Denzinger, "Enchir.", 470). St. Thomas gives the same reason for this practice: the oftener one confesses the more is the (temporal) penalty reduced; hence one might confess over and over again until the whole penalty is cancelled, nor would he thereby offer any injury to the sacrament" (IV Sent., d. xvii, q. 3, sol. 5 ad 4).

SATISFACTION.—As stated above, the absolution given by the priest to a penitent who confesses his sins with the proper dispositions remits both the guilt and the eternal punishment (of mortal sin). There remains, however, some indebtedness to Divine justice which must be cancelled here or hereafter (see PURGATORY). In order to have it cancelled here, the penitent receives from his confessor what is usually called his "penance", usually in the form of certain prayers which he is to say, or of certain actions which he is to perform, such as visits to a church, the Stations of the Cross, etc. Almsdeeds, fasting, and prayer are the chief means of satisfaction, but other penitential works may also be enjoined. The quality and extent of the penance is determined by the confessor according to the nature of the sins revealed, the special circumstances of the penitent, his liability to relapse, and the need of eradicating evil habits. Sometimes the penance is such that it may be performed at once; in other cases it may require a more or less considerable period, as, e. g., where it is prescribed for each day during a week or a month. But even then the penitent may receive another sacrament (e. g., Holy Communion) immediately after confession, since absolution restores him to the state of grace. He is nevertheless under obligation to continue the performance of his penance until it is completed.

In theological language, this penance is called satisfaction and is defined, in the words of St. Thomas: "The payment of the temporal punishment due on account of the offence committed against God by sin" (Suppl. to Summa, Q. xii, a. 3). It is an act of justice whereby the injury done to the honour of God is required, so far at least as the sinner is able to make reparation (*pœna vindicativa*); it is also a preventive remedy, inasmuch as it is meant to hinder the further commission of sin (*pœna medicinalis*). Satisfaction is not, like contrition and confession, an essential part of the sacrament, because the primary effect—i. e., remission of guilt and temporal punishment—is obtained without satisfaction; but it is an integral part, because it is requisite for obtaining the secondary effect—i. e., remission of the temporal punishment. The Catholic doctrine on this point is set forth by the Council of Trent, which condemns the proposition: "That the entire punishment is always remitted by God together with the guilt, and the satisfaction required of penitents is no other than faith whereby they believe that Christ has satisfied for them"; and further the proposition: "That the keys were given to the Church for loosing only and not for binding as well; that therefore in enjoining penance on those who confess, priests act contrary to the purpose of the keys and the institution of Christ; that it is a fiction [to say] that after the eternal punishment has been remitted in virtue of the keys, there usually remains to be paid a temporal penalty" (Can. "de Sac. pœnit.", 12, 15; Denzinger, "Enchir.", 922, 925).

As against the errors contained in these statements, the Council (Sess. XIV, c. viii) cites conspicuous examples from Holy Scripture. The most notable of these is the judgment pronounced upon David: "And Nathan said to David: the Lord also hath taken away thy sin: thou shalt not die. Nevertheless, because thou hast given occasion to the enemies of the Lord to blaspheme, for this thing, the child that is born to thee, shall surely die" (II Kings, xii, 13, 14; cf. Gen., iii, 17; Num., xx, 11 sqq.). David's sin was forgiven and yet he had to suffer punishment in the loss of his child. The same truth is taught by St. Paul (I Cor., xi, 32): "But whilst we are judged, we are chastised by the Lord, that we be not condemned with this world". The chastisement here mentioned is a temporal punishment, but a punishment unto salvation.

"Of all the parts of penance", says the Council of Trent (loc. cit.), "satisfaction was constantly recommended to the Christian people by our Fathers". This the Reformers themselves admitted. Calvin (Instit., III, iv, 38) says he makes little account of what the ancient writings contain in regard to satisfaction because "nearly all whose books are extant went astray on this point or spoke too severely". Chemnitius ("Examen C. Trident.", 4) acknowledges that Tertullian, Cyprian, Ambrose, and Augustine extolled the value of penitential works; and Flacius Illyricus, in the "Centuries", has a long list of Fathers and early writers who, as he admits, bear witness to the doctrine of satisfaction. Some of the texts already cited (Confession) expressly mention satisfaction as a part of sacramental penance. To these may be added St. Augustine, who says that "Man is forced to suffer even after his sins are forgiven, though it was sin that brought down on him this penalty. For the punishment outlasts the guilt, lest the guilt should be thought slight if with its forgiveness the punishment also came to an end" (Tract. cxxiv, "In Joann.", n. 5, in P. L., XXXV, 1972); St. Ambrose: "So efficacious is the medicine of penance that [in view of it] God seems to revoke His sentence" ("De pœnit.", 1, 2, c. vi, n. 48, in P. L., XVI, 509); Cæsarius of Arles: "If in tribulation we give not thanks to God nor redeem our faults by good works, we shall be detained in the fire of purgatory until our slightest sins are burned away like wood or straw" (Sermo civ, n. 4).

Among the motives for doing penance on which the Fathers most frequently insist is this: If you punish your own sin, God will spare you; but in any case the sin will not go unpunished. Or again they declare that God wants us to perform satisfaction in order that we may clear off our indebtedness to His justice. It is therefore with good reason that the earlier councils— e. g., Laodicæa (A. D. 372) and Carthage IV (397)— teach that satisfaction is to be imposed on penitents; and the Council of Trent but reiterates the traditional belief and practice when it makes the giving of "penance" obligatory on the confessor. Hence, too, the practice of granting indulgences, whereby the Church comes to the penitent's assistance and places at his disposal the treasury of Christ's merits. Though closely connected with penance, indulgences are not a part of the sacrament; they presuppose confession and absolution, and are properly called an extra-sacramental remission of the temporal punishment incurred by sin. (See INDULGENCES.)

SEAL OF CONFESSION.—Regarding the sins revealed to him in sacramental confession, the priest is bound to inviolable secrecy. From this obligation he cannot be excused either to save his own life or good name, to save the life of another, to further the ends of human justice, or to avert any public calamity. No law can compel him to divulge the sins confessed to him, or any oath which he takes—e. g., as a witness in court. He cannot reveal them either directly—i. e., by repeating them in so many words—or indirectly—i. e., by any sign or action, or by giving information based on what he knows through confession. The only possible release from the obligation of secrecy is the permission to speak of the sins given freely and formally by the penitent himself. Without such permission, the violation of the seal of confession would not only be a grievous sin, but also a sacrilege. It would be contrary to the natural law because it would be an abuse of the penitent's confidence and an injury, very serious perhaps, to his reputation. It would also violate the Divine law, which, while imposing the obligation to confess, likewise forbids the revelation of that which is confessed. That it would infringe ecclesiastical law is evident from the strict prohibition and the severe penalties enacted in this matter by the Church. "Let him beware of betraying the sinner by word or sign or in any other way whatsoever. . . .

we decree that he who dares to reveal a sin made known to him in the tribunal of penance shall not only be deposed from the priestly office, but shall moreover be subjected to close confinement in a monastery and the performance of perpetual penance" (Fourth Lateran Council, cap. xxi; Denzinger, "Enchir.", 438). Furthermore, by a decree of the Holy Office (18 Nov., 1682), confessors are forbidden, even where there would be no revelation direct or indirect, to make any use of the knowledge obtained in confession that would displease the penitent, even though the non-use would occasion him greater displeasure.

These prohibitions, as well as the general obligation of secrecy, apply only to what the confessor learns through confession made as part of the sacrament. He is not bound by the seal as regards what may be told him by a person who, he is sure, has no intention of making a sacramental confession but merely speaks to him "in confidence"; prudence, however, may impose silence concerning what he learns in this way. Nor does the obligation of the seal prevent the confessor from speaking of things which he has learned outside confession, though the same things have also been told him in confession; here again, however, other reasons may oblige him to observe secrecy. The same obligation, with the limitations indicated, rests upon all those who in one way or another acquire a knowledge of what is said in confession—e. g., an interpreter who translates for the priest the words of the penitent, a person who either accidentally or intentionally overhears the confession, an ecclesiastical superior (e. g., a bishop) to whom the confessor applies for authorization to absolve the penitent from a reserved case. Even the penitent, according to some theologians, is bound to secrecy; but the more general opinion leaves him free; as he can authorize the confessor to speak of what he has confessed, he can also, of his own accord, speak to others. But he is obliged to take care that what he reveals shall cast no blame or suspicion on the confessor, since the latter cannot defend himself. In a word, it is more in keeping with the intention of the Church and with the reverence due to the sacrament that the penitent himself should refrain from speaking of his confession. Such, undoubtedly, was the motive that prompted St. Leo to condemn the practice of letting the penitent read in public a written statement of his sins (see above); and it needs scarcely be added that the Church, while recognizing the validity of public confession, by no means requires it; as the Council of Trent declares, it would be imprudent to prescribe such a confession by any human enactment. (For provisions of the civil law regarding this matter, see SEAL OF CONFESSION.)

PUBLIC PENANCE.—An undeniable proof both of the practice of confession and of the necessity of satisfaction is found in the usage of the early Church according to which severe and often prolonged penance was prescribed and performed. The elaborate system of penance exhibited in the "Penitentials" and conciliar decrees, referred to above, was of course the outcome of a long development; but it simply expressed in greater detail the principles and the general attitude towards sin and satisfaction which had prevailed from the beginning. Frequently enough the latter statutes refer to the earlier practice either in explicit terms or by reiterating what had been enacted long before. At times, also, they allude to documents which were then extant, but which have not yet come down to us, e. g., the *libellus* mentioned in the African synods of 251 and 255 as containing *singula capitum placita*, i. e., the details of previous legislation (St. Cyprian, Ep. xxi). Or again, they point to a system of penance that was already in operation and needed only to be applied to particular cases, like that of the Corinthians to whom Clement of Rome wrote his

First Epistle about A. D. 96, exhorting them: "Be subject in obedience to the priests [*presbyteris*] and receive discipline [*correctionem*] unto penance, bending the knees of your hearts" (Ep. I "Ad Cor.", lvii). At the close, therefore, of the first century, the performance of penance was required, and the nature of that penance was determined, not by the penitent himself, but by ecclesiastical authority. (See EXCOMMUNICATION.)

Three kinds of penance are to be distinguished: canonical, prescribed by councils or bishops in the form of "canons" for graver offences. This might be either private, i. e., performed secretly, or public, i. e., performed in the presence of bishop, clergy, and people. When accompanied by certain rites as prescribed in the Canons, it was solemn penance. The public penance was not necessarily canonical; it might be undertaken by the penitent of his own accord. Solemn penance, the most severe of all, was inflicted for the worst offences only, notably for adultery, murder, and idolatry, the "capital sins". The name of *penitent* was applied especially to those who performed public canonical penance. "There is a harder and more grievous penance, the doers of which are properly called in the Church *penitents;* they are excluded from participation in the sacraments of the altar, lest by unworthily receiving they eat and drink judgment unto themselves" (St. Augustine, "De utilitate agendæ pœnit.", ser. cccxxxii, c. iii).

The penitential process included a series of acts, the first of which was confession. Regarding this, Origen, after speaking of baptism, tells us: "There is a yet more severe and arduous pardon of sins by penance, when the sinner washes his couch with tears, and when he blushes not to disclose his sin to the priest of the Lord and seeks the remedy" (Homil. "In Levit.", ii, 4, in P. G., XII, 418). Again he says: "They who have sinned, if they hide and retain their sin within their breast, are grievously tormented; but if the sinner becomes his own accuser, while he does this, he discharges the cause of all his malady. Only let him carefully consider to whom he should confess his sin; what is the character of the physician; if he be one who will be weak with the weak, who will weep with the sorrowful, and who understands the discipline of condolence and fellow-feeling. So that when his skill shall be known and his pity felt, you may follow what he shall advise. Should he think your disease to be such that it should be declared in the assembly of the faithful—whereby others may be edified, and yourself easily reformed—this must be done with much deliberation and the skilful advice of the physician" (Homil. "In Ps. xxxvii", n. 6, in P. G., XII, 1386). Origen here states quite plainly the relation between confession and public penance. The sinner must first make known his sins to the priest, who will decide whether any further manifestation is called for.

Public penance did not necessarily include a public avowal of sin. As St. Augustine also declares, "If his sin is not only grievous in itself, but involves scandal given to others, and if the bishop [*antistes*] judges that it will be useful to the Church [to have the sin published], let not the sinner refuse to do penance in the sight of many or even of the people at large, let him not resist, nor through shame add to his mortal wound a greater evil" (Sermo cli, n. 3). It was therefore the duty of the confessor to determine how far the process of penance should go beyond sacramental confession. It lay with him also to fix the quality and duration of the penance: "Satisfaction", says Tertullian, "is determined by confession; penance is born of confession, and by penance God is appeased" (De pœnit., viii). In the East there existed from the earliest times (Sozomen, H. E., VII, xvi), or at least from the outbreak of the Novatianist schism (Socrates, H. E., V, xix) a functionary known as *presbyter penitentiarius*, i. e., a priest specially appointed on account of his prudence and reserve to hear confessions and impose public penance. If the confessor deemed it necessary, he obliged the penitent to appear before the bishop and his council (*presbyterium*) and these again decided whether the crime was of such a nature that it ought to be confessed in presence of the people. Then followed, usually on Ash Wednesday, the imposition of public penance whereby the sinner was excluded for a longer or shorter period from the communion of the Church and in addition was obliged to perform certain penitential exercises, the *exomologesis*. This term, however, had various meanings: it designated sometimes the entire process of penance (Tertullian), or again the avowal of sin at the beginning, or, finally, the public avowal which was made at the end—i. e., after the performance of the penitential exercises.

The nature of these exercises varied according to the sin for which they were prescribed. According to Tertullian (De pœnit., IX), "*Exomologesis* is the discipline which obliges a man to prostrate and humiliate himself and to adopt a manner of life that will draw down mercy. As regards dress and food, it prescribes that he shall lie in sackcloth and ashes, clothe his body in rags, plunge his soul in sorrow, correct his faults by harsh treatment of himself, use the plainest meat and drink for the sake of his soul and not of his belly: usually he shall nourish prayer by fasting, whole days and nights together he shall moan, and weep, and wail to the Lord his God, cast himself at the feet of the priests, fall on his knees before those who are dear to God, and beseech them to plead in his behalf". At a very early period, the *exomologesis* was divided into four parts or "stations", and the penitents were grouped in as many different classes according to their progress in penance. The lower class, the *flentes* (weeping) remained outside the church door and besought the intercession of the faithful as these passed into the church. The *audientes* (hearers) were stationed in the narthex of the church behind the catechumens and were permitted to remain during the Mass of the Catechumens, i. e., until the end of the sermon. The *substrati* (prostrate), or *genuflectentes* (kneeling), occupied the space between the door and the ambo, where they received the imposition of the bishop's hands or his blessing. Finally, the *consistentes* were so called because they were allowed to hear the whole Mass without communicating, or because they remained at their place while the faithful approached the Holy Table. This grouping into stations originated in the East, where at least the three higher groups are mentioned about A. D. 263 by Gregory Thaumaturgus, and the first or lowest group by St. Basil (Ep. cxcix, c. xxii; ccxvii, c. lvi). In the West the classification did not exist, or at any rate the different stations were not so clearly marked; the penitents were treated pretty much as the catechumens.

The *exomologesis* terminated with the reconciliation, a solemn function which took place on Holy Thursday just before Mass. The bishop presided, assisted by his priests and deacons. A consultation (*concilium*) was held to determine which of the penitents deserved readmission; the Penitential Psalms and the litanies were recited at the foot of the altar; the bishop in a brief address reminded the penitents of their obligation to lead henceforth an upright life; the penitents, lighted candles in hand, were then led into the church; prayers, antiphons, and responses were said, and, finally, the public absolution was given. (See Schmitz, "Die Bussbücher u. die Bussdisciplin d. Kirche", Mainz, 1883; Funk in "Kirchenlex.", s. v. "Bussdisciplin"; Pohle in "Kirchl. Handlex.", s. v. "Bussdisciplin"; Tixeront, "Hist. des dogmes", Paris, 1905; Eng. tr., St. Louis, 1910.) Regarding the nature of this absolution given by the bishop, various opinions have been put forward. According to one view, it was the remission, not of guilt, but of the temporal punishment; the guilt had already been remitted by the absolution which the penitent received in confession before he entered on the public penance. This finds support in the fact that the reconciliation could be effected by a deacon in case of necessity and in the absence of a priest, as appears from St. Cyprian (Ep. xviii).

Speaking of those who had received *libelli* from the martyrs he says: "If they are overtaken by illness, they need not wait for our coming, but may make the *exomologesis* of their sin before any priest, or, if no priest be at hand, before a deacon, that thus, by the imposition of his hands unto penance, they may come to the Lord with the peace which the martyrs had besought us by letters to grant." On the other hand, the deacon could not give sacramental absolution; consequently, his function in such cases was to absolve the penitent from punishment; and, as he was authorized herein to do what the bishop did by the public absolution, this could not have been sacramental. There is the further consideration that the bishop did not necessarily hear the confessions of those whom he absolved at the time of reconciliation, and moreover the ancient formularies prescribe that at this time a priest shall hear the confession, and that the bishop, after that, shall pronounce absolution. But sacramental absolution can be given only by him who hears the confession. And again, the public penance often lasted many years; consequently, if the penitent were not absolved at the beginning, he would have remained during all that time in the state of sin, incapable of meriting anything for heaven by his penitential exercises, and exposed to the danger of sudden death (Pesch, op. cit., p. 110 sq. Cf. Palmieri, op. cit., p. 459; Pignataro, "De disciplina pœnitentiali", Rome, 1904, p. 100; Di Dario, "Il sacramento della penitenza nei primi secoli del cristianesimo", Naples, 1908, p. 81).

The writers who hold that the final absolution was sacramental, insist that there is no documentary evidence of a secret confession; that if this had been in existence, the harder way of the public penance would have been abandoned; that the argument from prescription loses its force if the sacramental character of public penance be denied; and that this penance contained all that is required in a sacrament. (Boudinhon, "Sur l'histoire de la pénitence" in "Revue d'histoire et de littérature religieuses", II, 1897, p. 306 sq. Cf. Hogan in "Am. Cath. Q. Rev.", July, 1900; Batiffol, "Etudes d'histoire et de théologie positive", Paris, 1902, p. 195 sq.; Vacandard in "Dict. de théol.", s. v. "Absolution", 156–61; O'Donnell, "Penance in the Early Church", Dublin, 1907, p. 95 sq.) While this discussion concerns the practice under ordinary circumstances, it is commonly admitted that sacramental absolution was granted at the time of confession to those who were in danger of death. The Church, in fact, did not, in her universal practice, refuse absolution at the last moment even in the case of those who had committed grievous sin. St. Leo, writing in 442 to Theodore, Bishop of Fréjus, says: "Neither satisfaction is to be forbidden nor reconciliation denied to those who in time of need and imminent danger implore the aid of penance and then of reconciliation." After pointing out that penance should not be deferred from day to day until the moment "when there is hardly space either for the confession of the penitent or his reconciliation by the priest", he adds that even in these circumstances "the action of penance and the grace of communion should not be denied if asked for by the penitent" (Ep. cviii, c. iv, in P. L., LIV, 1011). St. Leo states expressly that he was applying the ecclesiastical rule (*ecclesiastica regula*).

Shortly before, St. Celestine (428) had expressed his horror at learning that "penance was refused the dying and that the desire of those was not granted who in the hour of death sought this remedy for their soul"; this, he says, is "adding death to death and killing with cruelty the soul that is not absolved" (Letter to the bishops of the provinces of Vienne and Narbonne, c. ii). That such a refusal was not in accordance with the earlier practice is evident from the words of the Council of Nicæa (325): "With respect to the dying, the ancient canonical law shall now also be observed, namely, that if any one depart from this life, he shall by no means be deprived of the last and most necessary viaticum" (can. xiii). If the dying person could receive the Eucharist, absolution certainly could not be denied. If at times greater severity seems to be shown, this consisted in the refusal, not of absolution, but of communion; such was the penalty prescribed by the Council of Elvira (306) for those who after baptism had fallen into idolatry. The same is true of the canon (22) of the Council of Arles (314) which enacts that communion shall not be given to "those who apostatize, but never appear before the Church, nor even seek to do penance, and yet afterwards, when attacked by illness, request communion". The council lays stress on the lack of proper disposition in such sinners, as does also St. Cyprian when he forbids that they who "do no penance nor manifest heartfelt sorrow" be admitted to communion and peace if in illness and danger they ask for it; for what prompts them to ask [communion] is, not repentance for their sin, but the fear of approaching death" (Ep. ad Antonianum, n. 23).

A further evidence of the severity with which public penance, and especially its solemn form, was administered is the fact that it could be performed only once. This is evident from some of the texts quoted above (Tertullian, Hermas). Origen also says: "For the graver crimes, there is only one opportunity of penance" (Hom. xv, "In Levit.", c. ii); and St. Ambrose: "As there is one baptism so there is one penance, which, however, is performed publicly" (De pœnit., II, c. x, n. 95). St. Augustine gives the reason: "Although, by a wise and salutary provision, opportunity for performing that humblest kind of penance is granted but once in the Church, lest the remedy, become common, should be less efficacious for the sick . . . yet who will dare to say to God: Wherefore dost thou once more spare this man who after a first penance has again bound himself in the fetters of sin?" (Ep. cliii, "Ad Macedonium"). It may well be admitted that the discipline of the earliest days was rigorous, and that in some Churches or by individual bishops it was carried to extremes. This is plainly stated by Pope St. Innocent (405) in his letter (Ep. vi, c. ii) to Exuperius, Bishop of Toulouse. The question had been raised as to what should be done with those who, after a lifetime of licentious indulgence, begged at the end for penance and communion. "Regarding these", writes the pope, "the earlier practice was more severe, the later more tempered with mercy. The former custom was that penance should be granted, but communion denied; for in those times persecutions were frequent, hence, lest the easy admission to communion should fail to bring back from their evil ways men who were sure of reconciliation, very rightly communion was refused, while penance was granted in order that the refusal might not be total. . . . But after Our Lord had restored peace to his Churches, and terror had ceased, it was judged well that communion be given the dying lest we should seem to follow the harshness and sternness of the heretic Novatian in denying pardon. Communion, therefore, shall be given at the last along with penance, that these men, if only in the supreme moment of death, may, with the permission of Our Saviour, be rescued from eternal destruction."

The mitigation of public penance which this passage indicates continued throughout the subsequent period, especially the Middle Ages. The office of *pœnitentiarius* had already (390) been abolished in the East by Nestorius, Patriarch of Constantinople, in consequence of a scandal that grew out of public confession. Soon afterwards, the four "stations" disappeared, and public penance fell into disuse. In the West it underwent a more gradual transformation. Excommunication continued in use, and the interdict (q. v.) was frequently resorted to. The performance of penance was left in large measure to the zeal and good will of the penitent; increasing clemency was shown by allowing the reconciliation to take place somewhat before the prescribed time was completed; and the practice was introduced of commuting the enjoined penance into other exercises or works of piety, such as prayer and almsgiving. According to a decree of the Council of Clermont (1095), those who joined a crusade were freed from all obligation in the matter of penance. Finally it became customary to let the reconciliation follow immediately after confession. With these modifications the ancient usage had practically disappeared by the middle of the sixteenth century. Some attempts were made to revive it after the Council of Trent, but these were isolated and of short duration. (See INDULGENCES.)

IN THE BRITISH AND IRISH CHURCHES.—The penitential system in these countries was established simultaneously with the introduction of Christianity, was rapidly developed by episcopal decrees and synodal enactments, and was reduced to definite form in the Penitentials. These books exerted such an influence on the practice in Continental Europe that, according to one opinion, they "first brought order and unity into ecclesiastical discipline in these matters" (Wasserschleben, "Bussordnungen d. abendländischen Kirche", Halle, 1851, p. 4.—For a different view see Schmitz, "Die Bussbücher u. die Bussdisciplin d. Kirche", Mainz, 1883, p. 187). In any case, it is beyond question that in their belief and practice the Churches of Ireland, England, and Scotland were at one with Rome. The so-called Synod of St. Patrick decrees that a Christian who commits any of the capital sins shall perform a year's penance for each offence and at the end shall "come with witnesses and be absolved by the priest" (Wilkins, "Concilia", I, p. 3). Another synod of St. Patrick ordains that "the Abbot shall decide to whom the power of binding and loosing be committed, but forgiveness is more in keeping with the examples of Scripture; let penance be short, with weeping and lamentation and a mournful garb, rather than long and tempered with relaxations" (Wilkins, ibid., p. 4). For various opinions regarding the date and origin of the synods, see Haddan and Stubbs, "Councils", II, 331; Bury, "Life of St. Patrick", London, 1905. The confessor was called *anmchara* (*animæ carus*), i. e., "soul's friend". St. Columba was *anmchara* to Aidan, Lord of Dalraida, A. D. 574 (Adamnan's "Life of St. Columba", ed. Reeves, p. lxxvi); and Adamnan was "soul's friend" to Finnsnechta, Monarch of Ireland, A. D. 675 (ibid., p. xliii). The "Life of St. Columba" relates the coming of Feachnaus to Iona, where, with weeping and lamentation, he fell at Columba's feet and "before all who were present confessed his sins. Then the Saint, weeping with him, said to him: 'Arise, my son and be comforted; thy sins which thou hast committed are forgiven; because, as it is written, a contrite and humble heart God doth not despise,'" (ibid., I, 30). The need and effects of confession are explained in the Leabhar Breac: "Penance frees from all the sins committed after baptism. Every one desirous of a cure for his soul and happiness with the Lord must make an humble and sorrowful confession; and the confession with the prayers of the Church are as baptisms to him. As sickness injures the body, so sin injures the soul; and as there is a cure for the disease of the body, so there is balm for that of the soul. And as the wounds of the body are shown to a physician, so, too, the sores of the soul must be exposed. As he who takes poison is saved by a vomit, so, too, the soul is healed by confession and declaration of his sins with sorrow, and by the prayers of the Church, and a determination henceforth to observe the laws of the Church of God. . . . Because Christ left to His Apostles and Church, to the end of the world, the power of loosing and binding."

That confession was required before Communion is evident from the penitential ascribed to St. Columbanus, which orders (can. xxx) "that confessions be given with all diligence, especially concerning commotions of the mind, before going to Mass, lest perchance any one approach the altar unworthily, that is, if he have not a clean heart. For it is better to wait till the heart be sound and free from scandal and envy, than daringly to approach the judgment of the tribunal; for the altar is the tribunal of Christ, and His Body, even there with His Blood, judges those who approach unworthily. As, therefore, we must beware of capital sins before communicating, so, also, from the more uncertain defects and diseases of a languid soul, it is necessary for us to abstain and to be cleansed before going to that which is a conjunction with true peace and a joining with eternal salvation". In the "Life of St. Maedoc of Ferns" it is said of the murdered King Brandubh: "And so he departed without confession and the communication of the Eucharist." But the saint restored him to life for a while, and then, "having made his confession and received absolution and the viaticum of the Body of Christ, King Brandubh went to heaven, and was interred in the city of St. Maedoc which is called Ferns, where the kings of that land are buried" (Acta SS. Hib., col. 482). The metrical "Rule of St. Carthach", translated by Eugene O'Curry, gives this direction to the priest: "If you go to give communion at the awful point of death, you must receive confession without shame, without reserve." In the prayer for giving communion to the sick (Corpus Christi Missal) we read: "O God, who hast willed that sins should be forgiven by the imposition of the hands of the priest . . ." and then follows the absolution: "We absolve thee as representatives of blessed Peter, Prince of the Apostles, to whom the Lord gave the power of binding and loosing." That confession was regularly a part of the preparation for death is attested by the Council of Cashel (1172) which commands the faithful in case of illness to make their will "in the presence of their confessor and neighbours", and prescribes that to those who die "with a good confession" due tribute shall be paid in the form of Masses and burial (can. vi, vii).

The practice of public penance was regulated in great detail by the Penitentials. That of St. Cummian prescribes that "if any priest refuses penance to the dying, he is guilty of the loss of their souls . . . for there can be true conversion at the last moment, since God has regard not of time alone, but of the heart also, and the thief gained Paradise in the last hour of his confession" (C. xiv, 2). Other Penitentials bear the names of St. Finnian, Sts. David and Gildas, St. Columbanus, Adamnan. The collection of canons known as the "Hibernensis" is especially important, as it cites, under the head of "Penance" (bk. XLVII), the teaching of St. Augustine, St. Jerome, and other Fathers, thus showing the continuity of the Irish faith and observance with that of the early Church. (See Lanigan, "Eccl. Hist. of Ireland", Dublin, 1829; Moran, "Essays on the Early Irish Church", Dublin, 1864; Malone, "Church Hist. of Ireland", Dublin, 1880; Warren, "The Liturgy and Ritual of the Celtic Church", Oxford, 1881; Salmon, "The Ancient Irish Church", Dublin, 1897.)

IN THE ANGLO-SAXON CHURCH penance was called *behreowsung*, from the verb *hreowan*, whence our word "to rue". The confessor was the *scrift;* confession, *scrift spraec;* and the parish itself was the *scriftscir*, i. e., "confession district"—a term which shows plainly the close relation between confession and the work of religion in general. The practice in England can be traced back to the times immediately following the country's conversion. Ven. Bede (H. E., IV, 23 [25]) gives the story of Adamnan, an Irish monk of the seventh century, who belonged to the monastery of Coldingham, England. In his youth, having committed some sin, he went to a priest, confessed, and was given a penance to be performed until the priest should return. But the priest went to Ireland and died there, and Adamnan continued his penance to the end of his days. When St. Cuthbert (635–87) on his missionary tours preached to the people, "they all confessed openly what they had done, . . . and what they confessed they expiated, as he commanded them, by worthy fruits of penance" (Bede, op. cit., IV, 25). Alcuin (735–804) declares that "without confession there is no pardon" (P. L., C, 337); that "he who accuses himself of his sins will not have the devil for an accuser in the day of judgment" (P. L., CI, 621); that "he who conceals his sins and is ashamed to make wholesome confession, has God as witness now and will have him again as avenger" (ibid., 622). Lanfranc (1005–89) has a treatise, "De celanda confessione", i. e., on keeping confession secret, in which he rebukes those who give the slightest intimation of what they have heard in confession (P. L., CL, 626).

The penitentials were known as *scrift bocs*. The one attributed to Archbishop Theodore (602–90) says: "The deacon is not allowed to impose penance on a layman; this should be done by the bishops or priests" (bk. II, 2): and further; "According to the canons, penitents should not receive communion until their penance is completed; but we, for mercy's sake, allow them to receive at the end of a year or six months" (I, 12). An important statement is that "public reconciliation is not established in this province, for the reason that there is no public penance"— which shows that the minute prescriptions contained in the Penitential were meant for the guidance of the priest in giving penance privately, i. e., in confession. Among the *excerptiones*, or extracts, from the canons which bear the name of Archbishop Egbert of York (d. 766), canon xlvi says that the bishop shall hear no cause without the presence of his clergy, except in case of confession (Wilkins, "Concilia", I, 104). His Penitential prescribes (IX) that "a bishop or priest shall not refuse confession to those who desire it, though they be guilty of many sins" (ibid., 126). The Council of Chalcuth (A. D. 787): "If any one depart this life without penance or confession, he shall not be prayed for" (can. xx). The canons published under King Edgar (960) have a special section "On Confession" which begins: "When one wishes to confess his sins, let him act manfully, and not be ashamed to confess his misdeeds and crimes, accusing himself; because hence comes pardon, and because without confession there is no pardon; confession heals; confession justifies" (ibid., 229). The Council of Eanham (1009): "Let every Christian do as behooves him, strictly keep his Christianity, accustom himself to frequent confession, fearlessly confess his sins, and carefully make amends according as he is directed" (can. xvii, Wilkins, ibid., 289). Among the ecclesiastical laws enacted (1033) by King Canute, we find this exhortation: "Let us with all diligence turn back from our sins, and let us each confess our sins to our confessor, and ever [after] refrain from evil-doing and mend our ways" (XVIII, Wilkins, ibid., 303).

The Council of Durham (c. 1220): "How necessary is the sacrament of penance, those words of the Gospel prove: Whose sins, etc. . . . But since we obtain the pardon of our sins by true confession, we prescribe in accordance with the canonical statutes that the priest in giving penance shall carefully consider the amount of the penance, the quality of the sin, the place, time, cause, duration and other circumstances of the sin; and especially the devotion of the penitent and the signs of contrition." Similar directions are given by the Council of Oxford (1222), which adds after various admonitions: "Let no priest dare, either out of anger or even through fear of death, to reveal the confession of anyone by word or sign . . . and should he be convicted of doing this he ought deservedly to be degraded without hope of relaxation" (Wilkins, ibid., 595). The Scottish Council (c. 1227) repeats these injunctions and prescribes "that once a year the faithful shall confess all their sins either to their own [parish] priest or, with his permission, to some other priest" (can. lvii). Explicit instructions for the confessor are found in the statutes of Alexander, Bishop of Coventry (1237), especially in regard to the manner of questioning the penitent and enjoining penance. The Council of Lambeth (1261) declares: "Since the sacrament of confession and penance, the second plank after shipwreck, the last part of man's seafaring, the final refuge, is for every sinner most necessary unto salvation, we strictly forbid, under pain of excommunication, that anyone should presume to hinder the free administration of this sacrament to each who asks for it" (Wilkins, ibid., 754).

To give some idea of the ancient discipline, the penalties attached to graver crimes are cited here from the English and Irish Penitentials. For stealing, Cummian prescribes that a layman shall do one year of penance; a cleric, two; a subdeacon, three; a deacon, four; a priest, five; a bishop, six. For murder or perjury, the penance lasted three, five, six, seven, ten, or twelve years according to the criminal's rank. Theodore commands that if any one leave the Catholic Church, join the heretics, and induce others to do the same, he shall, in case he repent, do penance for twelve years. For the perjurer who swears by the Church, the Gospel, or the relics of the saints, Egbert prescribes seven or eleven years of penance. Usury entailed three years; infanticide, fifteen; idolatry or demon-worship, ten. Violations of the sixth commandment were punished with great severity; the penance varied, according to the nature of the sin, from three to fifteen years, the extreme penalty being prescribed for incest, i. e., fifteen to twenty-five years. Whatever its duration, the penance included fasting on bread and water, either for the whole period or for a specified portion. Those who could not fast were obliged instead to recite daily a certain number of psalms, to give alms, take the discipline (scourging) or perform some other penitential exercise as determined by the confessor. (See Lingard, "Hist. and Antiq. of the Anglo-Saxon Church", London, 1845; Thurston, "Confession in England before the Conquest" in "The Tablet", Feb. and March, 1905.)

CONFESSION IN THE ANGLICAN CHURCH.—In the Anglican Church, according to the rule laid down in the "Prayer Book", there is a general confession prescribed for morning and evening Service, also for Holy Communion; this confession is followed by a general absolution like the one in use in the Catholic Church. Also in the "Prayer Book" confession is counselled for the quieting of conscience and for the good that comes from absolution and the peace that arises from the fatherly direction of the minister of God. There is also mention of private confession in the office for the sick: "Here shall the sick person be moved to make a special confession of his sins if he feel his conscience troubled with any weighty matter. After which the priest shall absolve him (if he humbly and heartily desire it) after this sort: 'Our Lord Jesus Christ, who has left the power to his Church' etc." Since the beginning of the Oxford Movement confession after the manner practised in the Catholic Church has become more frequent among those of the High Church party. In 1873 a petition was sent to the

Convocation of the Archdiocese of Canterbury asking provision for the education and authorization of priests for the work of the confessional. In the joint letter of the Archbishops of Canterbury and York disapprobation of such course was markedly expressed, and the determination not to encourage the practice of private confession openly avowed. The Puseyites replied citing the authority of the "Prayer Book" as given above. In our time among the High Church folk one notices confessionals in the churches, and one hears of discourses made to the people enjoining confession as a necessity to pardon. Those who hear confessions make use generally of the rules and directions laid down in Catholic "Manuals", and especially popular is the "Manual" of the Abbé Gaume (A. G. Mortimer, "Confession and Absolution", London, 1906).

UTILITY OF CONFESSION.—Mr. Lea ("A History of Auricular Confession", Vol. II, p. 456) says: "No one can deny that there is truth in Cardinal Newman's argument: 'How many souls are there in distress, anxiety and loneliness, whose one need is to find a being to whom they can pour out their feelings unheard by the world. They want to tell them and not to tell them, they wish to tell them to one who is strong enough to hear them, and yet not too strong so as to despise them'"; and then Mr. Lea adds: "It is this weakness of humanity on which the Church has speculated, the weakness of those unable to bear their burdens . . . who find comfort in the system built up through the experience of the ages", etc. It has been made clear that the Church has simply carried out the mind of Christ: "Whatsoever you shall loose shall be loosed"; still we do not hesitate to accept Mr. Lea's reason, that this institution answers in large measure to the needs of men, who morally are indeed weak and in darkness. True Mr. Lea denies the probability of finding men capable of exercising aright this great ministry, and he prefers to enumerate the rare abuses which the weakness of priests has caused, rather than to listen to the millions who have found in the tribunal of penance a remedy for their anxieties of mind, and a peace and security of conscience the value of which is untold. The very abuses of which he speaks at such length have been the occasion of greater care, greater diligence, on the part of the Church. The few inconveniences arising from the perversity of men, which the Church has met with admirable legislation, should not blind men to the great good that confession has brought, not only to the individual, but even to society.

Thinking men even outside the Church have acknowledged the usefulness to society of the tribunal of penance. Amongst these the words of Leibniz are not unknown ("Systema theologicum", Paris, 1819, p. 270): "This whole work of sacramental penance is indeed worthy of the Divine wisdom and if aught else in the Christian dispensation is meritorious of praise, surely this wondrous institution. For the necessity of confessing one's sins deters a man from committing them, and hope is given to him who may have fallen again after expiation. The pious and prudent confessor is in very deed a great instrument in the hands of God for man's regeneration. For the kindly advice of God's priest helps man to control his passions, to know the lurking places of sin, to avoid the occasions of evil doing, to restore ill-gotten goods, to have hope after depression and doubt, to have peace after affliction, in a word, to remove or at least lessen all evil, and if there is no pleasure on earth like unto a faithful friend, what must be the esteem a man must have for him, who is in very deed a friend in the hour of his direst need?"

Nor is Leibniz alone in expressing this feeling of the great benefits that may come from the use of confession. Protestant theologians realize, not only the value of the Catholic theological position, but also the need of the confessional for the spiritual regeneration of their subjects. Dr. Martensen, in his "Christian Dogmatics" (Edinburgh, 1890), p. 443, thus outlines his views: "Absolution in the name of the Father and of the Son and of the Holy Ghost, derived from the full power of binding and loosing which the church has inherited from the apostles, is not unconditional, but depends on the same condition on which the gospel itself adjudges the forgiveness of sins, namely, change of heart and faith. If reform is to take place here, it must be effected either by endeavouring to revive private confession, or, as has been proposed, by doing away with the union between confession and the Lord's Supper, omitting, that is, the solemn absolution, because what it presupposes (personal confession of sin) has fallen into disuse, and retaining only the words of preparation, with the exhortation to self-examination, a testifying of the comfortable promises of the gospel, and a wish for a blessing upon the communicants." Under the head of "Observations" he states: "It cannot easily be denied that confession meets a deep need of human nature. There is a great psychological truth in the saying of Pascal, that a man often attains for the first time a true sense of sin, and a true stayedness in his good purpose, when he confesses his sins to his fellow man, as well as to God. Catholicism has often been commended because by confession it affords an opportunity of depositing the confession of his sins in the breast of another man, where it remains kept under the seal of the most sacred secrecy, and whence the consolation of the forgiveness of sins is given him in the very name of the Lord."

True, he believes that this great need is met more fully with the kind of confession practised in Lutheranism, but he does not hesitate to add: "It is a matter of regret that private confession, as an institution, meeting as it does this want in a regular manner, has fallen into disuse; and that the objective point of union is wanting for the many, who desire to unburden their souls by confessing not to God only but to a fellow-man, and who feel their need of comfort and of forgiveness, which anyone indeed may draw for himself from the gospel, but which in many instances he may desire to hear spoken by a man, who speaks in virtue of the authority of his holy office."

Good bibliographies are given in: POHLE, *Lehrb. d. Dogmatik*, III (Paderborn, 1906); *Dict. de Théol.*, s. v. *Absolution; Confession;* RICHARDSON, *Periodical Articles on Religion* (New York, 1907).

DOCTRINE.—ST. THOMAS, *Sum. Theol.*, III, Q. lxxxiv-xc; BELLARMINE, *De pœnit*, I, 1 sq.; BILLUART, *De pœnit.*, dis. 1, a. 1; COLLET, *Tract. de pœnit.* in MIGNE, *Theol. curs.*, XXII; JENKINS, *The Doctrine and Practice of Auricular Confession* (London, 1783); WISEMAN, *Lectures on the Principal Doctrines and Practices of the Cath. Church* (London, 1844), lect. x; KENRICK, *Theol. dogmatica* (Mechlin, 1858); NAMPON, *Catholic Doctrine as Defined by the Council of Trent* (Philadelphia, 1869); BILLOT, *De ecc. sacramentis*, II (Rome, 1898); WILHELM AND SCANNELL, *A Manual of Cath. Theol.*, II (London, 1909); SCHEEBEN-ATZBERGER, *Dogmatik*, IV (Freiburg, 1903).

HISTORY.—DE L'AUBESPINE, *De veteribus ecc. ritibus* (Paris, 1623); PETAVIUS, *De pœnit. vetere in ecc. ratione diatriba* (Paris, 1624); *P. G.*, XLII, 1037; MORIN, *Commentarius hist. de disciplina in admin. sacram. pœnitentiæ* (Paris, 1651); SIRMOND, *Hist. pœnitentiæ publicæ* (Paris, 1651); BOILEAU, *Hist. confessionis auricularis* (Paris, 1683); MARTÈNE, *De antiq. ecc. ritibus* (Rouen, 1700); CHARDON, *Histoire du sacrement de pénitence* (Paris, 1745); and in MIGNE, *Theol. curs.*, XX; KLEE, *Die Beicht* (Frankfort, 1828); FRANK, *The Bussdisciplin d. Kirche* (Mainz, 1867); PROBST, *Sakramente u. Sakramentalien in den ersten drei christl. Jahrh.* (Tübingen, 1872); SCHWANE, *Dogmengesch.* (Freiburg, 1895), II; FUNK, *Kirchengeschichtl. Abhandlungen u. Untersuchungen*, I (Paderborn, 1897); BRUCKER, *Une nouvelle théorie sur les origines de la pénitence sacramentelle* in *Etudes*, LXXIII (1897); SCHMITZ, *Die Bussbücher u. das kanonische Bussverfahren* (Düsseldorf, 1898); HARENT, *La confession* in *Etudes*, LXXX (1899); KIRSCH, *Zur Gesch. d. kath. Beichte* (Würzburg, 1902); GARTMEIER, *Die Beichtpflicht historisch-dogmatisch dargestellt* (Ratisbon, 1905); O'DOWD, *Notes on Tertullian's De pœnit.* in *Irish Ecc. Record*, XX (1906), 133; RAUSCHEN, *Eucharistie u. Bussakrament in den ersten sechs Jahrh. d. Kirche* (Freiburg, 1908); cf. VACANDARD in *Rev. du clergé français* (15 May, 1908); ESSER, *Articles in Katholik* (1907, 1908); STUFLER, *Articles* in *Zeitschr. f. kathol. Theol.* (1906, 1907, 1908, 1909); O'DONNELL, *The Seal of Confession* in *Irish Theol. Quart.*, V (1910); BRAT, *Les livres pénitentiaux et la pénitence tariffée* (Brignais, 1910).

NON-CATHOLIC.—The Protestant views are stated in the various Confessions of Faith, in explanations of the Thirty-nine Articles, and in commentaries on the Book of Common Prayer.

Good summaries are also given by some Catholic authors, e. g., MÖHLER, *Symbolism*, tr. 1843 (reprint London and New York, 1894); SCHANZ, *Die Lehre d. heiligen Sacramenten* (Freiburg, 1894).—Among Protestant writers, see: PUSEY, *Entire Absolution of the Penitent* (Oxford, 1846); MASKELL, *An Inquiry upon the Doctrine of the Church of England upon Absolution* (London, 1849); BOYD, *Confession, Absolution and the Real Presence* (London, 1867); ACKERMANN, *Die Beichte* (Hamburg, 1853); SIEFFERT, *Die neuesten theolog. Forschungen über Busse u. Glaube* (Berlin, 1896); HARNACK, *Lehrb. d. Dogmengesch.*, I (1894-7); DRURY, *Confession and Absolution* (London, 1903); LOOFS, *Leitfaden d. Dogmengesch.* (4th ed., Halle, 1906); HOLL, *Enthusiasmus u. Bussgewalt beim griechischen Mönchthum* (Leipzig, 1908); LEA, *A History of Auricular Confession* (Philadelphia, 1898) [for criticism of this work see CASEY, *Notes on a Hist. of Auricular Confession* (Philadelphia, 1899)]; BOUDINHON, *Sur l'histoire de la pénitence* in *Revue d'histoire et de littérature religieuses* (1897), 306, 496; VACANDARD, *Le pouvoir des clefs* in *Revue du clergé français*, 1898-99; DOHL, *Étude sur M. Lea* in *Revue critique d'histoire et de littérature* (1898); DELPLACE, *Hist. of Auric. Conf.* in *Am. Eccl. Rev.* (1899); GRAHAM in *Am. Cath. Q. Rev.*, XXXIV (1909)].

See also bibliographies under PENITENTIAL CANONS; SACRAMENT; INDULGENCES.

EDWARD J. HANNA.

Penance, WORKS OF. See MORTIFICATION; REPARATION.

Pendleton, HENRY, controversialist, b. at Manchester; d. in London, Sept., 1557; educated at Brasenose College, Oxford, where he received the degree of Doctor of Divinity, 18 July, 1552. Though he had preached against Lutheranism in Henry VIII's reign, he conformed under Edward VI and was appointed by Lord Derby as an itinerant Protestant preacher. In 1552 he received the living of Blymhill, Staffordshire. He is described as "an able man, handsome and athletic, possessed of a fine clear voice, of ready speech and powerful utterance" (Halley, "Lancashire"). On the accession of Mary he returned to the Catholic Church, and during 1554 received much preferment. He was made canon of St. Paul's and of Lichfield, Vicar of Todenham, Gloucester, and St. Martin Outwich in London; in 1556 he exchanged the latter living for St. Stephen Walbrook. He was appointed chaplain to Bishop Bonner, for whom he wrote two homilies: "Of the Church what it is", and "Of the Authority of the Church". He also wrote "Declaration in his sickness of his faith or belief in all points as the Catholic Church teacheth against sclaunderous reports against him" (London, 1557). Foxe, who purports to record some of his discussions with persons charged with heresy, states that on his death-bed he repented of his conversion; but the authority of this writer can never be accepted without confirming evidence which in this instance, as in so many others, is lacking.

POLLARD in *Dict. Nat. Biog.*; GILLOW, *Bibl. Dict. Eng. Cath.*; FOSTER, *Alumni Oxonienses* (Oxford, 1891); À WOOD, *Athenæ Oxonienses* (London, 1813-20); DODD, *Church History*, I (Brussels vere Wolverhampton, 1737); HENNESSEY, *Novum Repertorium Parochiale Londinense* (London, 1898).

EDWIN BURTON.

Penelakut Indians, a small tribe of Salishan stock, speaking a dialect of the Cowichan language and occupying a limited territory at the south end of Vancouver Island, B. C., with present reservations on Kuper, Tent, and Galiano Islands and at the mouth of Chemainus River, included in the Cowichan agency. From disease and dissipation introduced by the coasting vessels of early days, from changes consequent upon the influx of white immigration about 1858, and from the smallpox visitation upon Southern British Columbia in 1862, they are now reduced in number from 1000 of a century ago to about 250, of whom 140 live at the Penelakut village. They depended upon the sea for subsistence, and in their primitive customs, beliefs, and ceremonials resembled their kindred, the neighbouring Songish, and the cognate Squawmish about the mouth of Fraser River on the opposite coast. Some of them may have come under the teaching of Fr. Demers and the Jesuits as early as 1841, but regular mission work dates from the arrival of the secular priest, Fr. John Bolduc, who was brought over by the Hudson Bay Company in 1843 to minister to the Indians about the newly established post of Camosun, now Victoria. The mission work of the Oblate Fathers in the Vancouver and lower Fraser River region began with Fr. Paul Durieu in 1854. Like most of the Salishan tribes of British Columbia they are now entirely Catholic and of exemplary morality. The Penelakut live by fishing, boat building, farming, labouring work, and hunting; have generally good health and sanitary conditions, fairly good houses, kept neatly, and well-cared-for stock and farm implements. They are an "industrious and law abiding people, temperate and moral, a few of them only being addicted to the use of liquor". The centre of instruction is a Catholic boarding school maintained on Kuper island. (See also SAANICH, SONGISH, SQUAWMISH.)

BANCROFT, *History of British Columbia* (San Francisco, 1887); *Dept. Ind. Affairs, Canada, annual repts.* (Ottawa); *Reports on the Northwestern Tribes of Canada* by various authors in *British Association for the Advancement of Science* (London, 1885-98).

JAMES MOONEY.

Penitentes, LOS HERMANOS (The Penitent Brothers), a society of flagellants existing among the Spanish of New Mexico and Colorado. The subject will be considered under two headings: I. *The Practices of the Penitentes.* II. *Their Origin and History.* I.—*Practices.*—The Hermanos Penitentes are a society of individuals, who, to atone for their sins, practise penances which consist principally of flagellation, carrying heavy crosses, binding the body to a cross, and tying the limbs to hinder the circulation of the blood. These practices have prevailed in Colorado and New Mexico since the beginning of the nineteenth century. Up to the year 1890, they were public; at present they are secret, though not strictly. The Hermanos Penitentes are men; fifty years ago they admitted women and children into separate organizations, which, however, were never numerous. The society has no general organization or supreme authority. Each fraternity is local and independent with its own officers. The chief officer, *hermano mayor* (elder brother), has absolute authority, and as a rule holds office during life. The other officers are the same as those of most secret societies: chaplain, serjeant-at-arms, etc. The ceremony of the initiation, which takes place during Holy Week, is simple, excepting the final test. The candidate is escorted to the *morada* (abode), the home, or council house, by two or more Penitentes where, after a series of questions and answers consisting in the main of prayer, he is admitted. He then undergoes various humiliations. First, he washes the feet of all present, kneeling before each; then he recites a long prayer, asking pardon for any offence he may have given. If any one present has been offended by the candidate, he lashes the offender on the bare back. Then comes the last and crucial test: four or six incisions, in the shape of a cross, are made just below the shoulders of the candidate with a piece of flint.

Flagellation, formerly practised in the streets and in the churches, is now, since the American occupation, confined generally to the *morada* and performed with a short whip (*disciplina*), made from the leaf of the amole weed. Fifty years ago the Hermanos Penitentes would issue from their *morada* (in some places, as Taos, N. M., three hundred strong), stripped to the waist and scourging themselves, led by the *acompañadores* (escorts), and preceded by a few Penitentes dragging heavy crosses (*maderos*); the procession was accompanied by a throng, singing Christian hymns. A wooden wagon (*el carro de la muerte*) bore a figure representing death and pointing forward an arrow with stretched bow. This procession went through the streets to the church, where the Penitentes prayed, continued their scourgings, returned in procession to the *morada*. Other modes of self-castigation were often resorted to;

on Good Friday it was the custom to bind one of the brethren to a cross, as in a crucifixion. At present no "crucifixions" take place, though previous to 1896 they were annual in many places in New Mexico and Colorado. The Penitentes now confine themselves to secret flagellation and occasional visits to churches at night. Flagellation is also practised at the death of a Penitente or of a relative. The corpse is taken to the *morada* and kept there for a few hours; flagellation takes place at the *morada* and during the procession to and from the same.

II.—*Origin and History*.—Flagellation was introduced into Latin America during the sixteenth and seventeenth centuries, though no actual records are found of any organized flagellant societies there until comparatively recent times. In some localities of Mexico, Central, and South America, flagellant organizations, more or less public in their practices, existed until very recently, and still exist in a few isolated places. All these later organizations were regulated and controlled by Leo XIII. The origin of the New Mexican flagellants or *hermanos penitentes* is uncertain, but they seem to have been an outgrowth of the Third Order of St. Francis, introduced by Franciscans in the seventeenth century. Their practices consisted principally in flagellation, without incisions and with no loss of blood, carrying small crosses, and marching in processions with bare feet to visit the churches and join in long prayers. The barbarous customs of the New Mexico Penitentes are of a much later origin. The New Mexican flagellants call their society, "Los hermanos penitentes de la tercer orden de San Francisco", and we know that when the last organization came into prominence in the early part of the nineteenth century, the older organization no longer existed in New Mexico. When their practices reached their worst stage (about 1850–90), the attention of the Church was directed towards them. The society was then very strong among all classes and the ecclesiastical authorities decided to use leniency. In a circular letter to the Penitentes of New Mexico and Colorado in 1886, Archbishop Salpointe of Santa Fé ordered them in the name of the Church to abolish flagellation, and the carrying of heavy crosses, and sent to the different *hermanos mayores* copies of the rules of the Third Order of St. Francis, advising them to reorganize in accordance therewith. His letter and orders were unheeded. He then ordered all the parish priests to see the Penitentes personally and induce them to follow his instructions, but they accomplished nothing. To make matters worse, a Protestant paper, "La hermandad", was published at Pueblo, Colorado, in 1889, which incited the Penitentes to resist the Church and follow their own practices. Archbishop Salpointe, in a circular letter of 1889, then ordered the Penitentes to disband. As a result the society, though not abolished, was very much weakened, and its further growth prevented. In Taos, Carmel, San Mateo, and a few other places they are still numerous, and continue their barbarous practices, though more secretly.

Some important facts concerning the late history of the Penitentes in New Mexico are to be found in *Revista Catolica* (Las Vegas, N. M., 1875–1910, especially 1886–90). No other trustworthy data exist on the subject. Cf. however, *Flagellation in the West of the United States* in *Dublin Review*, V, 114, pp. 178 sqq.; LUMMIS, *The Penitent Brothers* in *Cosmopolitan*, V, 7, pp. 41 sqq.; IDEM, *The Land of poco tiempo* (New York, 1893), 79–108.

AURELIO M. ESPINOSA.

Penitential Canons, rules laid down by councils or bishops concerning the penances to be done for various sins. These canons, collected, adapted to later practice, and completed by suitable directions formed the nucleus of the Penitential Books (see THEOLOGY, MORAL; PENANCE). They all belong to the ancient penitential discipline and have now only an historic interest; if the writers of the classical period continue to cite them, it is only as examples, and to excite sinners to repentance by reminding them of earlier severity. In a certain sense they still survive, for the granting of indulgences (q. v.) is still based on the periods of penance, years, day, and quarantines. The penitential canons may be divided into three classes corresponding to the penitential discipline of the East, of Rome, or of the Anglo-Saxon Churches. (1) In the East, the prominent feature of penance was not the practice of mortification and pious works, though this was supposed; the penance imposed on sinners was a longer or shorter period of exclusion from communion and the Mass, to which they were gradually admitted according to the different penitential "stations" or classes, three in number; for the "weepers" (προσχλαίοντες, *flentes*), mentioned occasionally, were not yet admitted to penance; they were great sinners who had to await their admission outside of the church. Once admitted, the penitents became "hearers" (ἀχροώμενοι, *audientes*), and assisted at the Divine service until after the lessons and the homily; then, the "prostrated" (ὑποπίπτοντες, *prostrati*), because the bishop before excluding them, prayed over them while imposing his hands on them as they lay prostrate; finally the συστάντες, *consistentes*, who assisted at the whole service, but did not receive communion. The penance ended with the admission to communion and complete equality with the rest of the faithful. These different periods amounted in all to three, five, ten, twelve, or fifteen years, according to the gravity of the sins. This discipline, which was rapidly mitigated, ceased to be observed by the close of the fourth century. The relative penitential canons are contained in the canonical letter of St. Gregory Thaumaturgus (about 263; P. G., X, 1019), the Councils of Ancyra (314), Neocæsarea (314–20), Nicæa (325), and the three canonical letters of St. Basil to Amphilochus (Ep. 188, 199, 217 in P. G., XXXII, 663, 719, 794). They passed into the Greek Collections and the Penitential Books. Those laid down by the councils passed to the West in different translations, but were misunderstood or not enforced.

(2) The Roman penitential discipline did not recognize the various "stations", or classes; with this exception it was like the discipline of the East. The penitential exercises were not settled in detail and the punishment properly so called consisted in exclusion from communion for a longer or shorter period. But the practice of admitting to penance only once, which kept the penitents in a fixed order, was maintained longer. The most ancient Western canons relate to the admission or exclusion from public penance; for instance, the decision of Callixtus (Tertullian, "De pudic.", i) to admit adulterers, that of St. Cyril and the Council of Carthage in 251 (Ep. 56) to admit the *lapsi* or apostates, although the Council of Elvira (about 300, Can. 1, 6, 8, etc.) still refused to admit very great sinners. Other canons of this council ordained penances of several years' duration. After Elvira and Arles (314) the penitential canons are rather infrequent. They are more numerous in the councils and decretals of the popes after the close of the fourth century—Siricius, Innocent, and later St. Leo. They reduce the duration of the penance very much, and are more merciful towards the *lapis* or apostates. These texts, with the translations of the Eastern councils, passed into the Western canonical collections.

(3) On the other hand, what is more striking in the penitential canons of Anglo-Saxon and Irish origin, is the particular fixation of the penitential acts imposed on the sinner to insure reparation, and their duration in days, quarantines (*carina*), and years; these consist in more or less rigorous fasts, prostrations, deprivation of things otherwise allowable; also alms, prayers, pilgrimages, etc. These canons, unknown to us in their original sources, are contained in the numerous so-called Penitential Books (*Libri Pænitentiales*) or collections made in, and in vogue from, the seventh century. These

canons and the penitential discipline they represent were introduced to the Continent by Anglo-Saxon missionaries, and were at first received unfavourably (Council of Châlons, 813; Paris, 829); finally, however, they were adopted and gradually mitigated. (See CANONS, COLLECTIONS OF ANCIENT.)

See bibliographies to PENANCE and THEOLOGY, MORAL; MORIN, *Commentarius historicus de disciplina in adminis. sacra. pœnit.* (Paris, 1651); WASSERSCHLEBEN, *D. Bussordnungen d. abendl. Kirche* (Halle, 1851); SCHMITZ, *D. Bussbücher u. d. Bussdisziplin d. Kirche* (Mainz, 1883, 1898); FUNK, *Kirchengeschicht. Abhandl.* I (Paderborn, 1897), 155-209; BALLERINI, *De antiquis collectionibus canonum in P. L.*, XLVI; TARDIF, *Hist. des sources du droit canonique* (Paris, 1887).   A. BOUDINHON.

Penitential Orders, a general name for religious congregations whose members are bound to perform extraordinary works of penance, or to provide others with the means of atoning for grave faults. This class includes such congregations as the Angelicals, Capuchins, Carmelites, Daughters of the Holy Cross of Liège, Third Order of St. Dominic, Order of Fontevrault, Third Order of St. Francis, Daughters of the Good Shepherd, Sisters of the Good Shepherd, Sisters of St. Joseph of Lyons, Magdalens, Sacchetti, etc., which are treated under their separate titles. Likewise all eremitical foundations were, at least in their origin, penitential orders. Other congregations which come under this heading are:—

(1) *Penitents* or *Hermits of St. John the Baptist:* (a) A community near Pampelona in the Kingdom of Navarre, each of the five hermitages being occupied by eight hermits leading a life of mortification and silence, and assembling only for the chanting of the Divine Office. They received the approbation of Gregory XIII (c. 1515), who appointed a provincial for them. Over the light brown habit of rough material confined by a leathern girdle was worn a short mantle, and about the neck a heavy wooden cross. (b) A community founded in France about 1630 by Michel de Sabine for the reform of abuses among the hermits. Only those of the most edifying lives were chosen as members, and rules were drawn up which were approved for their dioceses by the Bishops of Metz and LePuy en Velay. The hermits were under the supervision of a visitator. A member was not permitted to make his final vows until his forty-fifth year, or until he had been a hermit for twenty-five years. Over the heavy brown habit and leathern belt was worn a scapular and a mantle. Similar communities existed in the Dioceses of Geneva and Vienne.

(2) *Ordo pœnitentiæ ss. Martyrum,* or *Ordo Mariæ de Metro de pœnitentia ss. Martyrum,* a congregation which flourished in Poland and Bohemia in the sixteenth century. There are various opinions as to the period of foundation, some dating it back to the time of Pope Cletus, but it is certain that the order was flourishing in Poland and Lithuania in the second half of the thirteenth century, the most important monastery being that of St. Mark at Cracow, where the religious lived under the Rule of St. Augustine. The prior bore the title *prior ecclesiæ S. Mariæ de Metro.* The habit was white, with a white scapular, on which was embroidered a red cross and heart. In a sixteenth-century document the members of this order are referred to as canons regular and mendicants.

(3) *Penitents of Our Lady of Refuge,* also called Nuns or Hospitallers of Our Lady of Nancy, founded at Nancy in 1631 by Ven. Marie-Elizabeth de la Croix de Jésus (b. 30 Nov., 1592; d. 14 Jan., 1649), daughter of Jean-Leonard de Ranfain of Remiremont. After a childhood of singular innocence and mortification she was coerced into a marriage with an aged nobleman named Dubois, whose inhuman treatment of her ceased only with his conversion shortly before his death. Left a widow at the early age of twenty-four, she opened a refuge for fallen women, to whose wants she ministered, assisted by her three young daughters. Her success and the insistence of ecclesiastics encouraged her to ensure the perpetuation of the work by the institution of a religious community (1631), in which she was joined by her daughters and nine companions, including two lay sisters. The new congregation was formally approved by the Holy See in 1634 under the title of Our Lady of Refuge and the patronage of St. Ignatius Loyola, and under constitutions drawn largely from those of the Society of Jesus and in accordance with the Rule of St. Augustine. The institute soon spread throughout France, and by the latter part of the nineteenth century had houses in the Dioceses of Besançon, Blois, Coutances, Marseilles, Rennes, La Rochelle, St-Brieux, Tours, Toulouse, and Valence. The members are divided into three classes (1) those of unblemished lives, bound by a fourth vow to the service of penitents; (2) penitents whose altered life justifies their admission to the community on terms of equality with the first mentioned, save that they are not eligible to office, and that in case the convent is not self-supporting they are required to furnish a small dowry; (3) penitents properly so-called, who observe the same rule as the rest but are without vows or distinctive garb. The habit is reddish brown, with a white scapular. Innocent XI authorized the institution of a special feast of Our Lady of Refuge for 30 January, and the establishment of a confraternity under her patronage.

(4) *Sisters of the Conservatorio di S. Croce della Penitenza* or *del buon Pastore,* also known as *Scalette,* founded at Rome, in 1615, by the Carmelite Domenico di Gesù e Maria, who, with the assistance of Baltassare Paluzzi, gathered into a small house (*conservatorio*) a number of women whose virtue was imperilled, and drew up for them a rule of life. Those desiring to become religious were placed under the Rule of St. Augustine, and, owing to the active interest of Maximilian, Elector of Bavaria, and Cardinal Antonio Barberini, a larger monastery and a church were built for them. External affairs were administered by a prelate known as the vice-protector and his council, and the internal economy by a prioress, but in 1838 the institution was placed under the Sisters of the Good Shepherd. Later a house of training for abandoned girls and a house of correction for erring women were established in connexion with this institution, the latter being enlarged by Pius IX in 1851. The congregation has since been merged into that of the Good Shepherd.

(5) *Ordo religiosus de pœnitentia,* the members of which were called *Scalzetti* or *Nazareni,* founded in 1752 at Salamanca, by Juan Varella y Losada (b. 1724; d. at Ferrara, 24 May, 1769), who had resigned a military career for a life of voluntary humiliation in a house of the Observants at Salamanca. Being urged to found a religious order, he assembled eight companions in community (8 March, 1752) under a rule which he had drawn up the previous year, and for which he obtained the authorization of Benedict XIV. The four foundations which he made in Hungary enjoyed but a brief existence, owing to the regulations of Joseph II, and those in Spain and Portugal did not survive the revolutions in those countries, so that the congregation was eventually confined to Italy. The mother-house is in Rome, where the institute possesses two convents, S. Maria delle Grazie, and S. Maria degli Angeli in Macello Martyrum. The constitutions were confirmed by Pius VI, who granted the congregation the privileges enjoyed by the Franciscans, to which there is a close resemblance in organization and habit. Like the Franciscans, the members take a vow to defend the doctrine of the Immaculate Conception, and, like all mendicant orders, they derive their means of subsistence entirely from contributions, and are forbidden the possession of landed property.

HÉLYOT, *Ordres religieux* (Paris, 1859); HEIMBUCHER, *Orden und Kongregationen* (Paderborn, 1907); (1) DE SABINE, *L'institut réformé des érémites sous l'invocation de s. Jean-Baptiste* (Paris, 1655); (3) *La France eccl.* (1882); *Déclaration de l'Institut de la congrégation de N. D. du Refuge* (Rouen, 1664); (4) PIAZZA, *Eusevologio Romano,* 4, 13.

FLORENCE RUDGE McGAHAN.

Penitential Psalms. See PSALMS.

Penitents, CONFRATERNITIES OF, congregations, with statutes prescribing various penitential works, such as fasting, the use of the discipline, the wearing of a hair shirt, etc. The number of these confraternities increased to such a degree, Rome alone counting over a hundred, that the only way of classifying them is according to the colour of the garb worn for processions and devotional exercises. This consists of a heavy robe confined with a girdle, with a pointed hood concealing the face, the openings for the eyes permitting the wearer to see without being recognized. These confraternities have their own statutes, their own churches, and often their own cemeteries. Aspirants must serve a certain time of probation before being admitted.

(1) *White Penitents.*—The most important group of these is the Archconfraternity of the Gonfalone, established in 1264 at Rome. St. Bonaventure, at that time Inquisitor-general of the Holy Office, prescribed the rules, and the white habit, with the name Recommendati B. V. M. This confraternity was erected in the Church of St. Mary Major by Clement IV in 1265, and four others having been erected in the Church of Ara Cœli, was raised to the rank of an archconfraternity, to which the rest were aggregated. The title of *gonfalone*, or standard-bearer was acquired during the pontificate of Innocent IV, when the members withstood the violence of the Roman nobles and elected a governor of the capitol to represent the pope, then at Avignon. Many privileges and churches were granted to this confraternity by succeeding pontiffs, the headquarters now being the Church of Santa Lucia del Gonfalone. The obligations of the members are to care for the sick, bury the dead, provide medical service for those unable to afford it, and give dowries to poor girls. What distinguishes these White Penitents from those of other confraternities is the circle on the shoulder of the habit, within it a cross of red and white. Other confraternities of White Penitents are those of the Blessed Sacrament at St. John Lateran, the Blessed Sacrament and the Five Wounds at S. Lorenzo in Damaso, the Guardian Angel, etc.

(2) *Black Penitents.*—The chief confraternity in this group is that of Misericordia, or of the Beheading of St. John, founded in 1488 to assist and console criminals condemned to death, accompany them to the gallows, and provide for them religious services and Christian burial. The Archconfraternity of Death provides burial and religious services for the poor and those found dead within the limits of the Roman Campagna. Other confraternities of Black Penitents are those of The Crucifix of St. Marcellus, and of Jesus and Mary of St. Giles.

(3) *Blue Penitents.*—Among the confraternities of this group are those of St. Joseph, St. Julian in Monte Giordano, Madonna del Giardino, Santa Maria in Caccaberi, etc. A number of these confraternities were established in France under the patronage of St. Jerome.

(4) *Grey Penitents*, including besides the Stigmati of St. Francis, the confraternities of St. Rose of Viterbo, The Holy Cross of Lucca, St. Rosalia of Palermo, St. Bartholomew, St. Alexander, etc.

(5) *Red Penitents*, embracing the confraternities of Sts. Ursula and Catherine, the red robe being confined with a green cincture; St. Sebastian and St. Valentine, with a blue cincture; and the Quattro Coronati, with a white cincture, etc.

(6) *Violet Penitents*, the confraternity of the Blessed Sacrament at the Church of St. Andrea della Fratte, under the patronage of St. Francis of Paula.

(7) *Green Penitents*, including the confraternities of St. Rocco and St. Martin at Ripetto, for the care of the sick.

There are many other confraternities which cannot be comprised within any of these groups, because of the combination of colours in their habits. The various confraternities were well represented in France from the thirteenth century on, reaching, perhaps, their most flourishing condition in the sixteenth century.

HÉLYOT, *Ordres religieux*, III (Paris, 1859), 218; MOLINIER, *Institut. et exerc. des confréries des pénitents.*

FLORENCE RUDGE MCGAHAN.

Penne and Atri, DIOCESE OF (PENNENSIS ET ATRIENSIS).—Penne is a city in the Province of Teramo, in the Abruzzi, central Italy; it has an important commerce in leather and in artificial flowers, and within its territory are several springs of medicinal waters, known to the ancients. It is the *Pinna Vestina* of antiquity, the chief city of the Vestini, distinguished for its fidelity to Rome, even in the war of the Marsi. Sulla destroyed the city during the civil war. After the Lombard invasion, it belonged to the Duchy of Benevento, with which it was annexed to the Kingdom of Sicily. In the ninth century it was sacked by the Saracens. According to legend Patrassus, one of the seventy disciples, was the first bishop of this city. The deacon St. Maximus is venerated at the cathedral. The united See of Penne and Atri was erected in 1152. Atri is the ancient Hadria of the Piceni, which became a Roman colony about 282 B. C.; its ancient walls still remain. The cathedral is a fine specimen of the Italian Gothic, and has a campanile nearly 200 feet high. The first bishop of the united sees was Beroaldo; among his successors were: Blessed Anastasio, who died in 1215; the Cistercian Nicolo (1326), held a prisoner for two years by his canons; Tommaso Consuberi (1554), suspected of having conspired against Pius IV, and therefore deposed; Paolo Odescalchi (1586), nuncio to Madrid and Vienna, built the episcopal palace of Atri. Within the territory of these sees is the famous Abbey of San Bartolommeo di Carpineto.

The diocese is immediately subject to the Holy See; it has 95 parishes, 180,790 inhabitants, 4 religious houses of men, and 8 of women, and 4 educational establishments for girls.

CAPPELLETTI, *Le Chiese d'Italia*, XXI; PANSA, *Della diocesi e città di Penne* (1622).

U. BENIGNI.

Pennsylvania, one of the thirteen original United States of America, lies between 39° 43' and 42° 15' N. latitude, and between the Delaware River on the east, and the eastern boundary of Ohio on the meridian 80° 36' W. longitude. It is 176 miles wide from north to south and about 303 miles long from east to west, containing 45,215 square miles, of which 230 are covered by water. It has a shore line on Lake Erie 45 miles in length, and is bounded by New York on the north, New Jersey on the east, Ohio and West Virginia on the west, Delaware, Maryland, and West Virginia on the south. It is the only one of the thirteen original states having no sea coast. About one-third of the state is occupied by parallel ranges and valleys. The mountains average from 1000 to 2000 feet in height. The main ridge, highest on the east, is broken by the north and west branches of the Susquehanna River, which flows through the centre of the state. The Delaware, which is 400 miles in total length, beginning from its origin in Otsego Lake, New York, is navigable for a distance of 130 miles from the sea, and forms the eastern boundary of the state. In the west, the Allegheny and Monongahela unite to form the Ohio. There is a wide range of climate within the geographical limits of the state.

I. HISTORY.—Although Captain John Smith, in 1608, was the first white man to meet natives of Pennsylvania, which he did when he ascended Chesapeake Bay, he never set foot within the limits of the present state. Henry Hudson, on 28 August, 1609, came within the Delaware Capes, but went no farther towards Pennsylvania. The first white man actually to enter the State appears to have been a Frenchman who came from Canada, Etienne Brullé, a companion of Champlain. He explored the valley of the Susquehanna from New York to Maryland in the winter of 1615-16, as is described by Champlain in an account of his voyages. In June, 1610, Captain Samuel Argall, coming from Virginia in search of provisions, entered the Delaware River and gave it its name in honour of the then Governor of Virginia, Lord de la Warr. Captain Cornelius Mey came to the Delaware Capes in 1614 (see NEW JERSEY). Another Dutch captain, Cornelius Hendrickson, came from Manhattan Island and probably navigated the Delaware River as far as the site of Philadelphia in 1616. In 1631, David Pietersen de Vries established a post at Lewes, in Delaware, and later, in 1634, made voyages as far as Tinicum Island and Ridley Creek. For five years after this the Dutch traded on the Delaware River and in 1633 established a post called Fort Beverstrede near Philadelphia. The English Government laid claim to the entire region in 1632 on the ground of first discovery, occupation, and possession, but in April, 1638, an expedition made up partly of Swedes

SEAL OF PENNSYLVANIA

and partly of Dutch, under Peter Minuit, established a post at Fort Christiana on the Brandywine River. This was the first white settlement in the country of the Delaware made by the Swedish Government, and was against the protest of the Dutch Governor of Manhattan. It was but a small colony and lasted only seventeen years. In 1643–44 permanent settlements were made at Tinicum, and in 1651 the Dutch Governor, Peter Stuyvesant, caused Fort Casimer to be built on the present site of New Castle, Delaware, to overawe the Swedes at Christiana. Fort Casimer was occupied by the Swedes in 1654, but they were in their turn driven out by the Dutch, who remained in possession of the Delaware River country until the organization of Penn's colony in 1681.

When William Penn was thirty-six years old, in 1680, his father being dead, there was due him from the Crown the sum of £16,000 for services rendered by his father, Admiral Penn. This was cancelled in 1681 by a gift to him from the Crown of the largest tract of territory that had ever been given in America to a single individual, and in addition he received from the Duke of York all of the territory now included in the State of Delaware, for the sake of controlling the free navigation of the river of that name. This charter, or grant, gave him the title in fee-simple to over 40,000 square miles of territory with the power of adopting any form of government, providing the majority of the colonists consented, and if the freemen could not assemble Penn had the right to make laws without their consent. The new colony was named Pennsylvania. Penn wished the name to be New Wales, or else Sylvania, modestly endeavouring to avoid the special honour implied by prefixing his surname but the king insisted. It has been said, no doubt truthfully, that Penn was impelled by two principal motives in founding the colony: "The desire to found a free commonwealth on liberal and humane principles, and the desire to provide a safe home for persecuted Friends. He was strongly devoted to his religious faith, and warmly attached to those who professed it, but not the less was he an idealist in politics, and a generous and hopeful believer in the average goodness of his fellow men" (Jenkins, "Pennsylvania", I, 204). Penn himself, speaking of the grant by the king, says: "I eyed the Lord in obtaining it, and more was I drawn inward to look to Him, and to owe it to His hand and power than to any other way. I have so obtained it and desire to keep it that I may not be unworthy of His love and do that which may answer His kind providence and serve His truth and people, that an example may be set to the nations. There may be room there but not here for such an holy experiment" (Jenkins, "Pennsylvania", I, 207). He had already shown ability as a colonizer, being concerned in the settlement of New Jersey, where the towns of Salem and Burlington had been laid out before the charter of Pennsylvania was granted.

During practically all of the colonial period, Penn and his descendants governed Pennsylvania through agents or deputy governors. He was the feudal lord of the land, it being his plan to sell tracts from time to time, reserving a small quit-rent or selling outright. Until the American Revolution, in 1776, Penn and his sons held the proprietorship of the Province of Pennsylvania during a period of ninety-four years, excepting only about two years under William III. The colony was organized at the council held at Upland, 3 August, 1681, the deputy governor being William Markham, a cousin of Penn. When Penn himself landed, 28 October, 1682, at New Castle, Philadelphia had been laid out and a few houses had been built. After his landing Penn changed the name of Upland to Chester in honour of the English city. There he summoned the freeholders to meet, and they adopted the "Frame of Government" and ratified "The Laws agreed upon in England". The former instrument provided for a Provincial Council of seventy-two members to be elected by the people. This council was to propose laws to be submitted for the approval of the General Assembly, also to be elected by the people. Thus was formed the first Constitution of Pennsylvania. The laws accepted and re-enacted with many additions became known as "The Great Law". It establishes religious liberty, allowing freedom of worship to all who acknowledge one God, and provides that all members of the Assembly, as well as those who voted for them, should be such as believed Jesus Christ to be the Son of God, the Saviour of the World. The Great Law prohibits swearing, cursing, drunkenness, health-drinking, card-playing, scolding, and lying in conversation. In the preface to the "Frame of Government" may be found the key to Penn's fundamental views on political questions. Thus he wrote: "Governments rather depend upon men than men upon governments; let men be good, and the government cannot be bad; if it be ill they will cure it. Though good laws do well, good men do better; for good laws may want [i. e. lack] good men and be abolished or evaded by ill men; but good men will never want good laws nor suffer ill ones. That, therefore, which makes a good constitution must keep it, viz. men of wisdom and virtue; qualities that, because they descend not with worldly inheritance, must be carefully propagated by a virtuous education of youth. For liberty without obedience is confusion, and obedience without liberty is slavery."

Penn was far in advance of his time in his views of the capacity of mankind for democratic government, and equally so in his broad-minded toleration of differences of religious belief. Indeed, it has been well said that the declaration of his final charter of privileges of 1701 was not alone "intended as the fundamental law of the Province and declaration of religious liberty on the broadest character and about which there could be no doubt or uncertainty. It is a declaration not of toleration but of religious equality and brought within its protection all who professed one Almighty

God,—Roman Catholics, and Protestants, Unitarians, Trinitarians, Christians, Jews, and Mohammedans, and excluded only Atheists and Polytheists." At that time in no American colony did anything approaching to toleration exist. When the provisions of "The Great Law" were submitted to the Privy Council of England for approval they were not allowed; but in 1706 a new law concerning liberty of conscience was passed, whereby religious liberty was restricted to Trinitarian Christians, and when the Constitution of 1776 was adopted, liberty of conscience and worship were extended even further by the declaration that "no human authority can in any case whatever control or interfere with the rights of conscience." It has been said: "There never was in Pennsylvania during the colonial period, to our knowledge, any molestation or interruption of the liberty of Jews, Deists or Unitarians, . . . while the Frame of Government of 1701 . . . guaranteed liberty of conscience to all who confessed and acknowledged 'one Almighty God, the Creator, Upholder and Ruler of the World', and made eligible for office all who believed in 'Jesus Christ the Saviour of the World.'" His toleration of other forms of religious belief was in no way halfhearted and imbued the Society of Friends with feelings of kindness towards Catholics, or at least accentuated those feelings in them. During the time of Lieutenant Governor Gordon a Catholic chapel was erected, which was thought to be contrary to the laws of Parliament, but it was not suppressed pending a decision of the British Government upon the question whether immunity granted by the Pennsylvania law did not protect Catholics. When, during the French War, hostility to France led to an attack upon the Catholics of Philadelphia by a mob after Braddock's defeat, the Quakers protected them.

Penn returned to England in a short time, but made another visit to Pennsylvania in 1699. He returned to England again in 1701, but before his departure a new constitution for the colony was adopted, containing more liberal provisions. This constitution endured until 1776, when a new one was adopted which has since been superseded by three others—the Constitutions of 1790, 1838, and 1873. In 1718 the white population of the colony was estimated at 40,000, of which one-half belonged to the Society of Friends and one-fourth resided in Philadelphia. In 1703 the counties composing the State of Delaware were separated from Pennsylvania. It was not until after the colonial period that the present boundaries of Pennsylvania were settled. Claims were made for portions of the present area of the state on the north, west, and south. Under the charter granted to Connecticut by Charles II, in 1662, the dominion of that colony was extended westward to the South Sea or Pacific Ocean. Although the territory of New York intervened between Connecticut and the present border of Pennsylvania, claim was made by Connecticut to territory now included in Pennsylvania between the fortieth and forty-first parallels of north latitude, and in 1769 a Connecticut company founded a settlement in the valley of Wyoming, and until 1782 the claim of sovereignty was maintained. It was finally settled against Connecticut in favour of Pennsylvania by a commission appointed by mutual agreement of the two states after trial and argument. The controversy between Maryland and Pennsylvania was finally settled in 1774. Lord Baltimore, the founder of Maryland, claimed that the boundaries of his grant extended above the present position of Philadelphia. On the other hand, Penn's contention, if allowed, would have extended the southern limit of Pennsylvania to a point that would have far overlapped the present boundary of Maryland. A litigation in Chancery eventually resulted in a settlement of the boundaries as they now exist. Previous to this final settlement, in the year 1763, Mason and Dixon, two English astronomers, surveyed the western boundary of Delaware and subsequently carried a line westward for the boundary between Pennsylvania and Maryland, setting up a mile-stone at every fifth mile with the arms of the Penn family on the north and Baltimore on the south, intermediate miles being marked with stones having P on one side and M on the other. This line was carried beyond the western extremity of Maryland, and thus it passed into history as marking the line between the northern and southern sections of the whole United States. The difficulty with the western boundary of the state on the Virginia border was settled in 1779 by a commission appointed by the two states. That portion which borders upon Lake Erie, known as the Erie triangle, belonged to New York and Massachusetts. By them it was ceded to the United States, and in 1792 bought from them by Pennsylvania for $151,640. The effect of the settlement of these boundaries was very far-reaching, for if the Connecticut, Maryland, and Virginia claims had been decided adversely to Pennsylvania, there would have been left but a narrow strip of land westward of Philadelphia and eastward of Pittsburg.

Pennsylvania was the scene of some of the most interesting and important events of the French and Indian War during the colonial period, notably the defeat of Braddock at the ford of the Monongahela about seven miles from Fort Duquesne, now the site of Pittsburg. It suffered much from Indian depredations on the western borders. During the early colonial period the mild dealings of the Quakers who controlled the province saved Pennsylvania from many of the ills that befell other colonies from the attacks of the aborigines. Prior to the French and Indian War, the Indians, who had been treated with careful consideration by Penn, were outraged at the unfairness and trickery practised by one of his successors in obtaining title to land extending, on the eastern border of the state, to the region of the Delaware Water Gap, and known as "The Walking Purchase". This, added to the harsh treatment of the frontier settlers, who were for the most part North-of-Ireland immigrants (locally known as Scotch-Irish), resulted in bloody and persistent Indian wars which spread terror throughout the colony and were ended only after several campaigns. The defeat of the Indians by Bouquet and Forbes, and the destruction of the French stronghold, Fort Duquesne, broke the power of the Indians, and the colony was not troubled with them again until the Revolutionary War, when their alliance with the British resulted in the massacre of Wyoming.

When the contest with Great Britain arose, Philadelphia, the chief city of the American Colonies, was chosen as the place for assembling the first Continental Congress. There the Declaration of Independence was drafted and promulgated, and after the Revolution the Government of the United States was seated there until the year 1800, when Washington was made the capital. Philadelphia remained the capital of the state under the Constitution of 1776 until 1812, when it was replaced by Harrisburg. The Convention which drafted the Constitution of the United States assembled at Philadelphia in May, 1787, and presented the draft to Congress on 17 September. On the following day it was submitted to the Assembly of the State of Pennsylvania, by which body the Constitution was ratified on 12 December of the same year, Pennsylvania being the second to approve it. Again, Pennsylvania was the first state to respond to the appeal of President Lincoln for troops at the outbreak of the Civil War. Regiments were sent by Governor Curtin to the garrison at Washington and were largely effective in preventing that city from being captured by the Confederate forces after the first battle of Bull Run. In 1863 General Lee invaded the state, coming from the South by way of the Shenandoah Valley, and was signally defeated in a three days' battle on the 1st,

2d, and 3rd of July at Gettysburg by the Union army under General George G. Meade. This battle has been recognized as the most important in the Civil War, as the success of the Confederate forces would have imperilled Philadelphia and New York and might have led to the final triumph of the Confederacy.

II. ETHNOLOGY AND DENOMINATIONAL STATISTICS. —It has been said of Pennsylvania that no other American colony had "such a mixture of languages, nationalities and religions. Dutch, Swedes, English, Germans, Scotch-Irish and Welsh; Quakers, Presbyterians, Episcopalians, Lutherans, Reformed, Mennonites, Tunkers and Moravians all had a share in creating it" (Fisher). The eastern part of the state, especially the counties immediately adjoining Philadelphia, was settled by a homogeneous population principally of English descent, though there was a large German community near Philadelphia at Germantown. Westward, the County of Lancaster was largely settled by Germans, who brought with them a special knowledge of, and aptitude for, agriculture, with the result that a naturally rich county became one of the most productive in the United States, especially of tobacco and cereals. There is also a large German population in Berks County, where a dialect of the German language is very generally spoken. The first German settlements were made by the Tunkers, now known as Dunkers, or Dunkards, between 1720 and 1729. They were followed by the Schwenkfelders, from the Rhine Valley, Alsatia, Suabia, Saxony, and the Palatinate. Members of the Lutheran Reformed Congregations came between 1730 and 1740. The Moravians settled Bethlehem in 1739, and the so-called Scotch-Irish immigrants from the North of Ireland, settled in Lehigh, Bucks, and Lancaster Counties, and in the Cumberland Valley, between 1700 and 1750. The Welsh came to Pennsylvania previous to 1682, and were the most numerous class of immigrants up to that date. They were assigned a tract of land west of the Schuylkill River, known as "the Welsh Tract", where to this day their geographical names remain.

In 1906 the population of Pennsylvania was the second in size among the states of the Union, being estimated at 6,928,515. Of these 2,977,022 (or 43 per cent) were church members: 1,717,037 Protestants, and 1,214,734 Catholics. The latest census of Catholics (1910) for the entire state shows 1,494,766, of whom 38,235 were coloured. The Protestant denominations in 1906 were divided as follows: Methodists, 363,443; Lutherans, 335,643; Presbyterians, 322,542; Reformed, 181,350; Baptists, 141,694; Episcopalians, 99,021; United Brethren, 55,571; all others, 217,773. The first Protestant Episcopal church (Christ Church) was built in Philadelphia in 1695. Pennsylvania is the second state in the Union in the number of church members and first in the number of church organizations. The value of church property is $173,605,141, being 13 per cent of all the property in the state. Of the entire population in 1906, 57 per cent professed no religion as against 67·2 per cent in 1900. The largest immigration from Ireland to the United States, following the famine of 1847–49, added greatly to the Catholic population of Pennsylvania, which has shown a steady increase. Of recent years missions have been established for the special benefit of the coloured people of Philadelphia, where two churches are now especially devoted to these missions.

III. ECONOMIC CONDITIONS.—A. *Population.*—The United States Census of 1910 gives the population of Pennsylvania as 7,665,111 (a little more than 181·57 to the square mile). Of this number 1,549,008 belonged to Philadelphia and 533,905 to Pittsburg. Thus Philadelphia had maintained its position as the third city of the United States in population, while Pittsburg (with the accession of Allegheny, incorporated with it since the Census of 1900) stood eighth. The Census of 1910 shows an increase of more than 21·62 per cent in the population of the state during the first decade of the twentieth century. The Census report of the foreign-born white and of the coloured population for 1910 (respectively 982,543 and 156,845 in 1900) had not become accessible when this article was prepared. The German and Irish elements exceed by far all other nationalities among the foreign born. In 1910 the largest cities in the state, after Philadelphia and Pittsburg, were Harrisburg, the capital (pop. 64,186), Scranton (129,867), Reading (96,071), Wilkes-Barre (67,105), and Johnstown (55,482). Pennsylvania is entitled to thirty-two representatives in the Congress of the United States and thirty-four votes in the Presidential Electoral College. With the exception of a few cities, the distribution of the population is less dense than in most of the Eastern States. A comparatively small proportion of the population is engaged in agriculture, mining and manufacturing being the principal industries.

B. *Material Resources.*—Until 1880 Pennsylvania was pre-eminent as the lumber state, but its activity in this industry has since been far exceeded in the Southern and North-Western States. In 1900 about 2,313,267 million feet of lumber were cut in Pennsylvania—about one-half of the output of the State of Michigan. In the last ten years the output has decreased. The estimated product for the year 1907 amounted to $31,251,817, at the rate of $18.02 per million feet. Efforts towards conservation and systematic forestry have of late years received considerable impetus. The state is extremely rich in coal, petroleum, natural gas, iron ore, slate, and limestones. Anthracite coal was discovered in Pennsylvania as early as 1768, and the first regular shipments were made in 1820. The anthracite coal fields in the eastern portions of the state are about 500 square miles in area, while the bituminous coal and petroleum fields of the western and north-central sections cover about 9000 square miles. The United States Conservation Commission estimated, in 1910, that there were 117,593,000,000 tons of coal in Pennsylvania. The total output of bituminous coal in 1907 for the Pennsylvanian mines was 149,759,089 American tons (of 2000 lbs. each); of anthracite, 86,279,- 719 Am. tons; so that the state contributed in that year very nearly 50 per cent of the whole output of coal of the United States. In the following year (1908), owing to the general depression in industries, Pennsylvania produced only 118,313,525 tons of bituminous coal. The first oil well in Pennsylvania was discovered in 1860, and in the next following thirty years the state produced 1,006,000,000 barrels of petroleum. The state stands first in the production of coke, the output being normally more than half that of all the United States. The output of pig iron for 1908 was 6,973,621 gross tons, or 43·8 per cent of the entire product of the United States, valued at $110,- 987,346 (about £22,197,468). The first Bessemer steel rails were rolled at Johnstown, Pennsylvania, in 1867. The annual product of iron and steel manufactures is over $200,000,000; they employ 54,000 persons, whose earnings amount to $34,000,000. Pennsylvania also stands first in the production of slate and limestone, contributing two-thirds of the whole output of slate of the United States. It ranks third in the production of sandstone. The total value of its output of quarried stone in 1908 was $4,000,000.

As a manufacturing state, Pennsylvania stands second in the United States. In 1904 it had an invested capital of $1,990,836,988 in manufactures, employing 763,282 wage earners receiving $367,960,890 per annum and producing $1,955,551,332 in value of finished goods, including, besides iron and steel, textiles of various kinds, knitted goods, felt, etc. In 1908 there were 3848 industrial establishments with a total capital of $1,126,406,558, employing 756,600 wage earners, of whom 126,000 were women. This state leads among the Middle States in cotton and exceeds all of the United States in woollen manufactures. The first company to spin yarn by machinery was founded at Philadelphia in 1775. A sale of prints and linens took place in 1789. In 1850 Philadelphia was the leading city of the world in the number of its textile works. In 1899 there were 813 cotton and woollen factories, producing a value of $116,850,782. In 1907, 157 silk plants produced a value of $52,780,830. The agricultural wealth of the state is also considerable, although only 28 per cent of its land is under cultivation. The leading crops are hay, corn, oats, wheat, potatoes, and tobacco, aggregating for the year 1908 a value of $166,173,000. The value of farm animals in 1908 was $145,803,000. The dairy industry in that year, aside from the milk product, was valued at $41,250,000, while tobacco amounted to $3,948,134.

C. *Communications.*—In 1827 the first railroad in the state, nine miles in length, was opened between Mauch Chunk and Summit Hill. In 1842 the Philadelphia and Reading Railroad penetrated the coal regions, and in 1854 the Pennsylvania Railroad between Pittsburg and Philadelphia was opened for traffic. Pennsylvania has 22·96 miles of track for every hundred miles of area. The total assessment of steam railroads operating any portions of their lines within the state is $4,686,281,066—one-third of the assets of all the railroads of the United States. The total earnings for the year ending 13 November, 1908, of the railroads of Pennsylvania subject to taxation were $824,213,593. During that year there were 262,570,546 passengers carried and 81,454,385,026 mile-tons of freight. The street railways show a total capitalization of $484,545,694.

IV. EDUCATION.—A. *General.*—The common school system of education is universal throughout the Commonwealth in every county, township, borough, and city. Each constitutes a separate school district, and new districts are formed as required under the direction of the Court of Quarter Sessions. School directors are elected annually in each district, two qualified citizens being chosen for a term of three years, there being six directors in all. School directors receive no pay, but are exempt from military duty and from serving in any borough or township office. They must hold at least one meeting in every three months and such other meetings as the circumstances of the district may require. It is their duty to establish a sufficient number of common schools for the education of every individual over the age of six years and under the age of twenty-one in their respective districts. They appoint all teachers, fix their salaries, and dismiss them for cause; direct what branches of learning are to be taught in each school, and what books to be used; suspend or expel pupils for cause. They report to the county superintendent, setting forth the number and situation of the schools in their districts, the character of the teachers, amount of taxes, etc. Where land cannot be obtained for schools by agreement of the parties, school directors may enter and occupy such land as they deem fit not exceeding one acre. Free evening schools must be kept open on the application of twenty or more pupils or their parents, for the teaching of orthography, reading, writing, arithmetic, and other branches to pupils who are unable to attend the day schools, for a term of not less than four months in each year. Twenty days' actual teaching constitutes one school month. Schools are closed on Saturdays and legal holidays. High schools may be established in districts having a population of over 5000.

In Penn's charter it was provided that the Government and councils should erect and order all public schools, and before Penn there had been a school taught by Swedes. In 1706 land to the extent of 60,000 acres was set aside for the support of schools. The Constitution of 1790 required the Legislature to provide by law for the establishment of schools throughout the state in such manner that the poor might be taught gratis. The University of Pennsylvania dates from the year 1740. The report of the superintendent of education for the year 1908 shows the number of schools to have been 33,171, taught by 7488 male and 26,525 female teachers, the number of pupils amounting to 1,231,200 and in daily attendance 951,670. The total expenditure for school purposes for that year was more than $34,000,000; the estimated value of school property exceeded $90,000,000. There were in that year thirteen normal schools, seven theological seminaries, three medical colleges, one veterinary college, one college of pharmacy, four dental schools, two law schools, thirty-five colleges and universities, employing 1914 instructors, with an attendance of 12,211 male and 3189 female students.

B. *Catholic.*—Prior to the Revolution, and for some years after it, Philadelphia was the largest city, and St. Mary's the largest Catholic parish in the United States. A parochial school was established in that parish in 1782. This was an English school. Subsequently German schools were established at Goshenhoppen, Berks County, at Lancaster, Hanover, and other places under the auspices of the German Jesuits. In Western Pennsylvania the first Catholic school was established at Sportsman's Hall, Westmoreland County, some time after 1787, where subsequently the Benedictines built St. Vincent's Abbey and College, the mother-house of this religious order in the United States. Father Demetrius Augustine Gallitzin (q. v.) established a Catholic colony in Cambria County in 1799 and in 1800 opened a school at Loretto. The first Catholic church at Pittsburg was built in 1811, and in 1828 a community of the Order of St. Clare, coming from Belgium, established a convent and academy. In 1835 the sisters took charge of the dayschools at Pittsburg and opened an academy for more advanced pupils. They opened a school at Harrisburg in 1828; one at McSherrytown in 1830; one at Pottsville in 1836. The Catholic educational system has been gradually developed since that date until now, in all the dioceses of Pennsylvania, there is a carefully graded system of parochial schools, there being in attendance in the various dioceses 225,224 pupils, who are taught by 2896 religious and lay teachers in 443 schools, irrespective of those who are instructed in the various orphan asylums and charitable institutions of the different dioceses. The course of instruction is graded in the Diocese of Philadelphia, covering Christian doctrine, English, penmanship, arithmetic, algebra, geography, history, civil government, vocal music (including Gregorian), drawing, elementary science. Institutions for higher education are, with a few exceptions, in the hands of the teaching orders and are not an integral part of the parochial school system. The cost of maintenance of the Catholic educational system is defrayed by voluntary contributions.

V. RELIGIOUS CONDITIONS.—A. *Development of the Church.*—The State of Pennsylvania historically coincides with the ecclesiastical Province of Philadelphia, composed of the Archdiocese of Philadelphia and the five suffragan Dioceses of Pittsburg, Erie, Harrisburg, Scranton, and Altoona. (See the special articles on these dioceses respectively.) The Catholic population in Pennsylvania owes its existence mainly to early immigration from Ireland and Germany, though of recent years many Poles, Hungarians, and Italians have swelled its numbers. The first Catholic resident of Philadelphia, a German, came with Daniel Pastorius, the founder of Germantown, in 1683. In 1685 J. Gray, of London, having obtained a grant of land, settled in Pennsylvania, where he changed his name to John Tatham. In 1690 he was appointed Governor of West Jersey, but was unable to take the oath of allegiance to William and Mary. He seems to have been a friend of William Penn. The first priest who can be accurately traced in Pennsylvania was the Reverend John Pierron, of Canada, who in 1673-74 made a tour through Maryland, Virginia, and New England.

The orderly history of the Church in Pennsylvania begins in 1720, when the Rev. Joseph Wheaton, S.J., formed the first parish. The first church, St. Joseph's, was begun in 1733. Its congregation consisted of 22 Irish and 15 Germans, and in 1787 its membership had increased to about 3000. In 1727 there came to Philadelphia 1155 Irish besides their servants. Later in the same year 5600 arrived, and 5655 in 1729. This migration resulted from the unjust laws which were then afflicting the Catholics and Dissenters in Ireland. The same laws drove from the North of Ireland, between 1700 and 1750, some 200,000 Presbyterians, most of whom came to America, and largely to Pennsylvania. In 1771, when Richard Penn succeeded John Penn, in the government of Pennsylvania, the Catholics of Philadelphia, through their rector, the Rev. Robert Harding, presented their congratulations, which were most cordially received. When the Revolution broke out, the comparatively small body of Catholic inhabitants furnished a number of men who attained distinction in the military, naval, or political service, among them being Commodore John Barry, Thomas Fitzsimmons, Stephen Moylan, and George Meade. In 1780, on the occasion of the Requiem Mass for Don Juan de Miralles, the Spanish agent in Philadelphia, Congress assisted in a body together with several general officers and distinguished citizens. After the surrender at Yorktown a Mass of thanksgiving was celebrated in St. Mary's Church, a chaplain of the French Ambassador preaching the sermon.

Prior to the Revolution, as early as 1768, the German Catholics of Philadelphia had obtained property upon which subsequently was erected Holy Trinity Church, which was afterwards incorporated and, in 1789, dedicated. St. Mary's Church, from which Holy Trinity was an offshoot, was dedicated in 1788. The clergy of the United States was reinforced by a body of French priests who arrived at Philadelphia in 1792 and were distributed among various American churches. In 1793 a large number of fugitives came from the French Islands of the West Indies, and it was supposed that an epidemic of yellow fever which broke out soon after was brought by them. All the ministers of the various denominations zealously attended the sick, and many fell victims, including two of the Catholic clergy.

In 1788 Very Rev. John Carroll was elected Bishop of Baltimore with jurisdiction over all the American churches, including Philadelphia. He was consecrated on the 15th of August, 1790, at Lullworth, Dorchester, England.

In 1808 the Diocese of Philadelphia was separated from that of Baltimore (then ruled by Bishop John Carroll), the Dioceses of New York, Boston, and Bardstown being created at the same time. Michael Egan became the first Bishop of Philadelphia, the diocese included the entire State of Pennsylvania and the western and southern parts of New Jersey. In 1843 the Diocese of Pittsburg was established, and took away from Philadelphia a number of the western counties of the state. In 1853 the Diocese of Erie was erected out of the Diocese of Pittsburg, and in the same year the jurisdiction of Philadelphia over a part of New Jersey was transferred to the Diocese of Newark. In 1868 the two Dioceses of Scranton and Harrisburg were created, Philadelphia being left with a jurisdiction confined to the Counties of Berks, Bucks, Carbon, Chester, Delaware, Lehigh, Montgomery, Northampton, and Schuylkill. In 1901 the Diocese of Altoona was constituted out of the Harrisburg territory together with part of that of Pittsburg. In 1875 Philadelphia was made a metropolitan see, Bishop Wood being appointed Archbishop. The first Provincial Council was held on 23 May, 1880.

B. *Laws Relating to Religion*.—By the Constitution of Pennsylvania (Art. I., Sec. 3) it is declared that "All men have a natural and indefeasible right to worship Almighty God according to the dictates of their own consciences; no man can of right be compelled to attend, erect or support any place of worship, or to maintain any ministry against his consent; no human authority can, in any case whatever, control or interfere with the rights of conscience, and no preference shall ever be given by law to any religious establishments or modes of worship". It has been held, however, that Christianity is a part of the common law of Pennsylvania; not Christianity founded on any particular tenets, but Christianity with liberty of conscience to all men (11 S. & R., 394; 26 Pa., 342; 2 How., 199). This liberty does not include the right to carry out every scheme claimed to be part of a religious system. Thus, a Municipal Ordinance forbidding the use of drums by a religious body in the streets of a city is valid (11 Pa., 335). The constitution further provides that "no person who acknowledges the being of a God and a future state of rewards and punishments shall, on account of his religious sentiments, be disqualified to hold any office or place of trust or profit under this commonwealth" (Sec. 4). Therefore, the exclusion of a Sister of Charity from employment as a teacher in the public schools, because she is a Roman Catholic, would be unlawful (164 Pa., 629); now, however, she cannot teach while wearing her religious garb. An Act of Assembly prohibiting the transaction of worldly business on Sunday does not encroach upon the liberty of conscience. It is therefore constitutional. Until a recent Act of Assembly, witnesses in Court were required to believe in a Supreme Being, although their religious opinions were not such as are generally accepted by orthodox Christians. Now, however, it is not necessary that witnesses should have any belief in the existence of a God, their credibility being a question for the jury.

By an Act of Assembly blasphemy and profanity in the use of the names of the Almighty, Jesus Christ, the Holy Spirit, or the Scriptures of Truth, are criminal offences. This is a re-enactment of a provincial law as old as 1700. The sessions of the Legislature are opened with prayer. Christmas Day and Good Friday are among the legal holidays. Five or more persons may form a church corporation for the support of public worship. All churches, meeting houses, or other regular places of stated worship, with the grounds thereto annexed necessary for the occupancy and enjoyment of the same, all burial grounds not used or held for private or corporate profit, together with certain other specified kinds of property devoted to education and benevolence, are exempted from taxation of all sorts. Marriage cannot be solemnized without a licence. Under the Act of 1700, all marriages not forbidden by the law of God are encouraged; but the parents or guardians shall, if conveniently they can, be first consulted, and the parties' freedom from all engagements established. Under the Act of 24 June, 1901 (P. L. 579, Sec. 1), the marriage of first cousins is prohibited, and such marriages are void. The subsequent marriage of parents legitimize their children under the Act of 14 May, 1857. (P. L., 507, Sec. 1.) Since the Act of 11 April, 1848, all property belonging to women before marriage or accruing to them afterwards shall continue as their separate property after marriage. But a woman may not become accommodation indorser, maker, guarantor, or surety for another, nor may she execute or acknowledge a deed or writing, etc. of her real estate unless her husband joins in such mortgage or conveyance (Act of 8 June, 1893). The separate earnings of a married woman are under her separate control and not liable for the debts or obligations of her husband.

Under certain circumstances, a married woman may bring a suit without the intervention of a trustee, but husband and wife cannot sue one another. A married woman may loan money to, and take security from, her husband. A husband is not liable for the wife's debts incurred before her marriage. Absolute divorces may be granted for impotence, bigamy, adultery, cruelty, desertion, force, fraud, or coercion, and for conviction of forgery or infamous crime. The plaintiff must reside within the state for at least one whole year previous to the filing of the petition. A person divorced for adultery cannot marry the paramour during the life of the former husband or wife. Divorces from bed and board are allowed for practically the same causes as absolute divorces. Marriages may be annulled for the usual causes, but proceedings must be taken under the Divorce Acts.

A Board of Public Charities, consisting of five commissioners, is appointed by the governor with the duty of visiting all charitable and correctional institutions at least once a year, examining the returns of the several cities, counties, wards, boroughs, and townships in relation to the support of paupers and in relation to births, deaths, and marriages, and make an annual report as to the causes and best treatment of pauperism, crime, disease, and insanity, together with all desirable information concerning the industrial and material interests of the commonwealth bearing upon these subjects. They have the power of examining the various charitable, reformatory, and correctional institutions, including the city and county jails, prisons, and almshouses, and are required to submit an annual report to the Legislature. Institutions seeking state aid are expected to give notice to the Board, which is to inquire carefully into the grounds for the request and report its conclusions to the Legislature. Before any county prison or almshouse shall be erected the plans must be submitted to the Board.

Prisoners confined in any prison, reformatory, or other institution have the privilege of practising the religion of their choice, and are at liberty to procure the services of any minister connected with any religious denomination in the state, providing such service shall be personal and not interfere with the established order of the religious service in the institution. Established services shall not be of a sectarian character. By an Act of Assembly passed in 1903, the active or visiting committee of any society, existing for the purpose of visiting and instructing prisoners, are constituted official visitors of jails and penitentiaries, and are permitted under reasonable rules and regulations to make visits accordingly.

Intoxicating liquors cannot lawfully be sold in Pennsylvania except under a licence granted by the Court of Quarter Sessions. The sale of liquor on Sunday is forbidden. It is a misdemeanor for any person engaged in the sale or manufacture of intoxicating liquors to employ an intemperate person to assist in such manufacture or sale, or by gift or sale to furnish liquor to anyone known to be of intemperate habits, or to minors, or insane persons. Disregard of a notice not to furnish liquor to intemperate persons issued by a relative renders the party so-selling liable for damages. Any judge, justice, or clergyman who shall perform the marriage ceremony between parties when either is intoxicated shall be guilty of a misdemeanour.

Every person of sound mind who has attained the age of twenty-one years may dispose of his or her real and personal property by will. This includes married women, reserving to the husband his right as tenant by the courtesy and his right to take against the will, and to the wife her right to take against the will. Wills must be in writing and signed at the end either by the testator himself or, in case he is prevented by the extremity of his last illness, by some person in his presence and by his express direction; and in all cases shall be proved by oaths or affirmations of two or more competent witnesses, who need not be attesting witnesses except in the case where the will makes a charitable devise or bequest. In the case of the extremity of the testator's last illness, he may make an oral or nuncupative will for the disposition of his personal property, such will to be made during the last illness in the house of his habitation, or where he has resided for the space of ten days before making his will, or any location where he has been surprised by sickness and dies before returning to his own house. No estate, real or personal, can be bequeathed, devised, or conveyed to any person in trust for any religious or charitable use, except by deed or will, attested by two credible, disinterested witnesses, at least one calendar month before the decease of the testator or alienor. No literary, religious, charitable, or beneficial society, congregation, or corporation may hold real and personal estate to a greater yearly value than $30,000 without express legislative sanction, or on decree of court in special circumstances.

Annual Report Secretary of Internal Affairs (Pa.), pts. III, IV; *Report of Superintendent of Public Instruction* (Pa.) (1908); *Crop Report Secretary of Agriculture* (Pa.) (1909); *Pennsylvania Archives*; HAZARD, *Annals of Pa.* (Philadelphia, 1850); IDEM, *Register of Pennsylvania 1828–36*; *Colonial Records* (1790); PROUD, *History of Pennsylvania* (1797); BARR FERREE, *Pennsylvania, a Primer* (1904); FRANKLIN, *Historical Review of the Constitution and Government of Pennsylvania* (1759); JENKINS, *Pennsylvania* (Philadelphia, 1903); FISHER, *Pennsylvania, Colony and Commonwealth* (1897); IDEM, *Pennsylvania, Province and State* (1899); IDEM, *The Making of Pennsylvania* (1896); KIRLIN, *Catholicity in Philadelphia* (1910); BURNS, *The Catholic School System in the United States* (1908); *The Catholic Directory* (1910); WICKERSHAM, *History of Education in Pennsylvania* (1886); GRIFFIN, *Catholics in the American Revolution*; BOUVIER, *Law Dictionary* (1897); BRIGHTLY-PURDON, *Digest* (1905); DU BOIS, *The Philadelphia Negro* (Philadelphia, 1899); JANNEY, *Life of William Penn* (1852); FISHER, *The True William Penn*; FAUST, *The German Element in the United States* (1909); JACOBS, *Guarantees of Liberty in Pennsylvania* (1907).

WALTER GEORGE SMITH.

Penobscot Indians, the principal tribe of the famous Abnaki confederacy of Maine, and the only one still keeping its name, territory, and tribal identity. The Abnaki confederacy, to which the Penobscot belonged, consisted of a number of small tribes of Algonquian linguistic stock, holding the greater part of the present state of Maine, and closely connected linguistically and politically with the Pennacook of the Merrimac region on the south and with the Maliseet or Etchimin of the St. John river on the north, and more remotely with the Micmac of eastern New Brunswick and Nova Scotia. In all the colonial wars they were active allies of the French against the English, and suffered correspondingly, having dwindled from perhaps 3000 souls in 1600 to about 785 in 1910. Of these the Penobscot number 425, while the rest, all of mixed blood and including the descendants of the broken and incorporated Pennacook, reside, under the name of Abnaki, in the two mission settlements of Saint Francis (335) and Bécancourt (25) in Quebec province, Canada.

The beginning of missionary work among the Abnaki was by the Jesuits Pierre Biard and Enemond Massé, of the French post of Port-Royal (Annapolis, Nova Scotia), in 1611. Two years later a mission establishment was attempted, in connexion with a French post, on Mount Desert island, Maine, but was destroyed by the English commander, Argall, before it was fairly completed. From 1646 to 1657 the Jesuit Fr. Gabriel Druillettes, of the Montagnais Mission, spent much time with the Abnaki, establishing a temporary chapel on the Kennebec, and later drew off many of them to the mission settlements of Canada. In 1688 the Jesuit Fr. Jacques Bigot again took up the work on the Kennebec while in the same year Fr. Louis-Pierre Thury, of the Foreign Missions, established the first regular mission at Panawambskek ("it forks on the white rocks"—Vetromile) or Penobscot, at the falls near the present Oldtown. Here he laboured until his death in 1699, and was succeeded by other priests of the same seminary until 1703, when this mission, like that on the Kennebec, was transferred to Jesuit control, under which it continued, although under constantly greater difficulties, until the fall of Canada in 1763. The most noted incumbent of this earlier period was Fr. Etienne Lauveyat (1718–1729).

From the outbreak of King Philip's war in 1675 up nearly to the close of the French period in 1763 the history of the Abnaki tribes was one of almost unceasing bloody struggle against the English advance. On the side of the English it was a war of extermination, with standing bounties for scalps (or heads), increasing from five pounds in 1675 to forty pounds in 1703 for every scalp of a male above ten years, and at last in 1744 one hundred pounds for the scalp of every male above twelve years of age and fifty for that of a woman or child. Prisoners were sold as slaves (see Williamson). In 1706 Governor Dudley reported that he had not left an Indian habitation or planting field undestroyed. Shortly afterward it was estimated that one-third of the Abnaki had been exterminated by war, disease, or exposure within seven years. In 1722 three hundred men were appointed to destroy the village at Penobscot and four hundred others to ravage constantly throughout the whole Abnaki country. To draw off the Indians from the French interest, efforts were twice made by the English authorities of Massachusetts to persuade them to receive Protestant missionaries, but the offer was rejected. Three times the mission at Norridgewock on the Kennebec, under the devoted Fr. Sebastian Rasles, was attacked and destroyed, and the third time the missionary himself was among the slain. The final result was that the Abnaki who survived withdrew to St. Francis or other mission settlements in Canada, with the exception of the Penobscot, who made a separate treaty of peace in 1749, thus saving themselves and their territory, but forever alienating the affection of their kinsmen by whom they were thenceforth regarded as traitors to the confederacy.

On the outbreak of the Revolution in 1775 the Penobscot, under their chief, Orono, tendered their services to the American cause, at the same time asking that a priest be sent to them, they having then been for nearly forty years without religious instruction. Their offer was accepted and they gave good service throughout the war, but the Massachusetts Government was not then able to find them a priest, owing to the fact that Jesuits and other missionaries had for years been outlawed from New England. When the war was ended the Penobscot made another appeal, this time by a delegation to Bishop Carroll of Maryland, to whom they presented the crucifix of the murdered Fr. Rasles, with the result that in 1785 the Penobscot mission at Oldtown was re-established under Fr. Francis Ciquard, a Sulpician, sent from France for that purpose. He continued with it until 1794, going then to the neighbouring Etchimin (Maliseet). Orono died at Oldtown in 1802. Of later missionaries the most noted is the Jesuit Fr. Eugene Vetromile, stationed at Oldtown from about 1855 to about 1880, author of a small history of the Abnaki and of several works in the language, the most important of which is a manuscript Abnaki Dictionary, now with the Bureau of American Ethnology. The other great dictionary of the language, that of Father Rasles and plundered from the mission in the second attack (1722), was deposited in Harvard University and published in the Memoirs of the American Academy of Arts and Sciences (Cambridge, 1833).

The principal existing Penobscot village, officially known as Oldtown, is on an island in Penobscot river, a few miles above Bangor, and, as indicated by the Indian name, about on the ancient site. The church, dedicated to Saint Anne, is served by a secular priest.

In their aboriginal condition the Abnaki tribes were semi-sedentary, dwelling in villages of communal wigwams covered with bark or woven mats, each village having also a larger central town-house for public gatherings. They cultivated corn and other vegetables, and understood the use of manure. They had also game and fish from the woods and waters. They had the clan system, with fourteen clans (Morgan). Polygamy was rare and tribal government simple. They buried their dead. In general character they were comparatively mild and tractable and not given to extreme cruelty as were the Iroquois. What remains of their mythology has been brought together by Leland in his "Algonquin Legends of New England". The modern Penobscot are entirely Christianized and civilized in habit of living, deriving subsistence by lumbering, boating, hunting, some farming, and the making of Indian wares for sale. They are in friendly touch with their neighbours, the Passamaquoddy band of the Maliseet. See also MISSIONS, CATHOLIC INDIAN, OF THE U. S.; MALISEET INDIANS; RASLES; SAINT FRANCIS MISSION.

LELAND, *Algonquin Legends of New England* (Boston, New York, 1885); the Acadia volumes of the *Jesuit Relations*, ed. THWAITES (73 vols., Cleveland, 1896-1901); *Maine Hist. Soc. Colls.* (first series, 10 vols., Portland and Bath, 1831-1891; second series, 10 vols., Portland, 1890-1899); MAURAULT, *Histoire des Abenakis* (Quebec, 1866); VETROMILE, *The Abnakis and Their History* (New York, 1866); WILLIAMSON, *Hist. of Maine* (2 vols., Hallowell, 1832); SHEA, *Catholic Missions* (New York, 1854).

JAMES MOONEY.

Pension, ECCLESIASTICAL, the right to a certain sum of money to be paid yearly out of the revenues of a church or benefice to a cleric, on account of just reasons approved by an ecclesiastical superior. The term is derived, according to some, from the Latin word *pendeo*, "to depend"; according to others, from the word *pendo*, "to pay". The term *pensio* is sometimes used as synonymous with a certain species of benefice, as when a cleric, by the authority of a superior, receives a perpetual vicarship in a church and is sustained by its revenues. This is looked on as the conferring of a real benefice. In its ordinary acceptation, however, it does not connote the bestowal of a benefice, but refers to the money paid, for a certain time, to a third person from the fruits of a benefice belonging to another, acting under the authorization of an ecclesiastical superior. The obligation to pay such a pension may be incumbent on either the holder of a benefice or on the benefice itself. If the first, then the burden does not pass to his successor; if the second, the obligation lasts as long as the pensioner lives.

As the pope has full power over all benefices, he may impose a pension on any benefice whatsoever, even though it belong to a patron. If, however, the patronage belongs to a royal person, the pope does not usually impose the pension without the patron's consent. For validity, it is not necessary that the pontiff give any cause for his act.

As to the bishop, or anyone inferior to the pope, he may not, generally speaking, impose a perpetual pension on a benefice or increase one already existing, nor may he, in conferring a benefice, make a reservation of a pension to be paid to a third party. It is within the bishop's power, however, to impose a pension, for a reasonable cause, to last for a certain time, even for the life of the holder of the benefice, if he himself consents. In this case, the pension is not imposed upon the benefice, but on its incumbent. The canons forbid the bishop to constitute a pension out of a certain quota of the fruits of a benefice, as a half or a third part, because this has the appearance of a division of the benefice. Just causes for the constitution of a pension by the bishop are: for the sake of peace; for the education of a poor student; for the utility of the Church; for the relief of paupers; for some pious object; for a reward of services rendered; and for the support of a person who resigns a benefice, in which fast case it should be in moderate proportion and not the result of a bargain. For the causes mentioned, a bishop may not impose a pension on a benefice itself, or to have effect after the decease of the incumbent, though some canonists have maintained the contrary. When a bishop confers a benefice, he is not allowed to burden its collation with a pension to be paid to himself, as this would be a simoniacal transaction.

When two beneficiaries interchange benefices, they may not make a pact by which the one receiving the richer post is to pay a pension to the other, but the bishop may make such a stipulation of his own free will on the occasion of the exchange of two beneficiaries. In like manner, while it is simoniacal for an abdicant to stipulate for a pension out of the benefice he resigns, yet he may, for grave cause, request the bishop to give him such a pension, and the bishop may bestow it upon him. Simoniacal pacts are those which are made without the intervention of the proper ecclesiastical authority.

Laymen are incapable of receiving ecclesiastical pensions, and the clerical recipient must not be excommunicate, suspended, or under interdict. Pensions may be transferred to another by the pensioner, if the proper authority sanctions it. The earliest mention of a pension in Church history is said to be that of Domnus of Antioch, who received one out of the revenues of the bishopric, which he had vacated at the time of the Council of Chalcedon in 451.

FERRARIS, *Bibliotheca canonica*, VI (Rome, 1890), s. v. *Pensio*; WERNZ, *Jus decretalium*, II (Rome, 1899).

WILLIAM H. W. FANNING.

Pentacomia, titular see of Palestine, suffragan of Areopolis or Rabbah. It was never a residential see; the Crusaders mistook the "Descriptio orbis romani" of George of Cyprus, where it is mentioned (ed. Gelzer, 53), for a "Notitia episcopatuum", whereas it is a purely civil document. There is a locality of this name in Arabia (op. cit., 54), and a third in Palæstina Prima, now known as Fendacoumieh, near Samaria. Le Quien has made the same error ("Oriens christianus", III, 773), but without discovering the name of one bishop. The site of Pentacomia seems unknown.

S. VAILHÉ.

Pentapolis.—The word, occurring in Wisdom, x, 6, designates the region where stood the five cities (πέντε, πόλις)—Sodom, Gomorrha, Segor (A. V., Zoar), Adama, Seboim—which united to resist the invasion of Chodorlahomor (Gen., xiv), and of which four were shortly after utterly destroyed. This region, which marked the southern limit of the territory occupied by the Canaanites, was included in what was known in old Palestinian geography as the "Kikkar" (i. e. "round" or "oval"; Gen., xiii, 10, 11, 12, etc.; D. V. "the country about the Jordan"; A. V. "the plain"), that is to say probably the lower Jordan Valley and the land around the Dead Sea. The Kikkar was a very fertile country (Gen., xiii, 10). Its fertility caused Lot to settle there (Gen., xiii, 8–13). About the same epoch, or possibly a little earlier, the five kings of the Pentapolis had been defeated in a battle fought in the Valley of Siddim (D. V. "the woodland Vale") by Amraphel (most probably Hammurabi, q. v.), King of Sennaar, Arioch (Rim-Sin), King of Ellasar (Larsa), Chodorlahomor (Kudur-Lagamar), King of Elam and Thadal (Tid al), "king of the nations" (probably countries in the neighbourhood of Elam and in its dependence), and made tributary. Twelve years later the five kings revolting, the Pentapolis was once more invaded by the armies of the East, the territory plundered, and captives led away, among whom were Lot and his household. We read in Gen., xiv, how Abraham went to the rescue of his nephew. The Pentapolis soon recovered from the effects of its defeats, and in its restored prosperity renewed the shameful vices which brought upon it the judgment of God. "The Lord rained upon Sodom and Gomorrha brimstone and fire from the Lord out of heaven, and he destroyed these cities and all the country about, all the inhabitants of the cities and all things that spring from the earth" (Gen., xix, 24–25).

The site of the Pentapolis has been sought in many places around the Dead Sea, even in its very bed. According to the holders of the latter opinion, we should see, in the Biblical description of the destruction of Sodom and Gomorrha, the account of a great geological disturbance which caused a sinking of the country, this forming the bed of the Dead Sea. Travellers pointed out as a remnant of the submerged cities the "Rūjm el-Bâhr", a ledge of rock to the north of the sea, now entirely covered with water, but forming an island or even a peninsula at periods when the lake was considerably lower than now (as, for instance, from 1848 to 1892). Modern geologists, on the other hand, while admitting that disturbances of that character may have occurred in that region in the last fifty or forty centuries, yet with one accord hold that the origin of that body of water goes back to pre-historic times. The site must accordingly be sought elsewhere. There are some, among them Armstrong, Wilson, Conder, Tristram, and recently Dr. Huntington ("Harper's Monthly Magazine", Jan., 1910, pp. 186 sqq.), who, deceived by a certain likeness in names, searched for the Pentapolis to the north of the Dead Sea. Clermont-Ganneau, on the contrary, thought Gomorrha was in the Arabah, about 60 miles south of the Dead Sea (Recueil d'Archéol. Orient., I, pp. 163 sqq.). Most geographers, however, think that the site of the Pentapolis should be sought partly in the shallow bed of the south end of the lake, and partly in its immediate neighbourhood. This view seems to be supported by two serious arguments. First, the name "Jebel Ūsdūm", given to a conspicuous mountain of salt on the south-west shore, echoes apparently a long-standing tradition that Sodom was near by. Second, Segor, the only city that survived the ruin, was known throughout Biblical times (Is., xv, 5; Jer., xlviii, 4) and in the early Christian centuries [Joseph., "Ant.", I, xi, 4; "Bellum jud.", IV, viii, 4; Ptolemy, V, xvii, 5; Euseb., "Onomast.", 231, 261; Madaba Mosaic Map; medieval Arabic geographers (cf. Le Strange, "Palestine under the Moslems", p. 292); crusaders (Guillaume de Tyr, xxii, 30); Segor, then called Zoora, was an episcopal see at the time of the Council of Chalcedon, 451]; it was situated south-east of the Dead Sea, at a distance of 580 stadia (almost 66 miles) from the north shore of the same, and to all appearances should be looked for near the mouth of the Wady Qerahy. The other three cities were possibly north of Segor.

Commentaries on Gen., xix; ARMSTRONG, WILSON, CONDER, *Names and places in the O. T.* (London, 1887); BAEDEKER-BENZIGER, *Palestine and Syria* (4th Engl. ed., Leipzig, 1906); CONDER, *Handbook to the Bible* (London, 1887); LE STRANGE, *Palestine under the Moslems* (London, 1890); ROBINSON, *Biblical Researches in Palestine* (London, 1856); SMITH, *The Historical Geography of the Holy Land* (London, 1894); TRISTRAM, *The Land of Israel* (London, 1872); IDEM, *The Land of Moab* (London, 1873); ABEL, *Une Croisière autour de la Mer Morte* (Paris, 1911); GAUTIER, *Autour de la Mer Morte* (Geneva, 1901); GUÉRIN, *Description de la Palestine, Samarie* (Paris, 1874–1875); BLANKENHORN, *Enstehung und Geschichte des Todten Meeres* in *Zeitschrift des Deutschen Palästina-Vereins*, XIX (1896), 1–64; IDEM, *Noch einmal Sodom und Gomorrha*, *ibid.*, XXI (1898), 63–83; BUHL, *Geographie des Alten Palästina* (Leipzig, 1896).

CHARLES L. SOUVAY.

Pentateuch, in Greek πεντατευχός, is the name of the first five books of the Old Testament. I. NAME.—Though it is not certain whether the word originally was an adjective, qualifying the omitted noun βίβλος, or a substantive, its literal meaning "five cases" appears to refer to the sheaths or boxes in which the separate five rolls or volumes were kept. At what precise time the first part of the Bible was divided into five books is a question not yet finally settled. Some regard the division as antedating the Septuagint translation; others attribute it to the authors of this translation; St. Jerome was of opinion (Ep. 52, ad Paulin., 8; P. L., XXII, 545) that St. Paul alluded to such a division into five books in I Cor., xiv, 19; at any rate, Philo and Josephus are familiar with the division now in question ("De Abrahamo", I; "Cont. Apion.", I, 8). However ancient may be the custom of dividing the initial portion of the Old Testament into five parts, the early Jews had no name indicating the partition. They called this part of the Bible háttôrah (the law), or tôrah (law), or sēphér háttôrah (book of the law), from the nature of its contents (Jos., viii, 34; i, 8; I Esdr., x, 3; II Esdr., viii, 2, 3, 14; x, 35, 37; II Par., xxv, 4); they named it tôráth Mōshéh (law of Moses), sēphér Mōshéh (book of Moses), sēphér tôráth Mōshéh (book of the law of Moses) on account of its authorship (Jos., viii, 31, 32; xxiii, 6; III Kings, ii, 3; IV Kings, xiv, 16; xxiii, 25; Dan., ix, 11; I Esdr., iii, 2; vi, 18; II Esdr., viii, 1; xiii, 1; etc.); finally, the Divine origin of the Mosaic Law was implied in the names: law of Yahweh (I Esdr., vii, 10; etc.), law of God (II Esdr., viii, 18; etc.), book of the law of Yahweh (II Par., xvii, 9; etc.), book of the law of God (Jos., xxiv, 26; etc.). The word *law* in the foregoing expressions has been rendered by νόμος, with or without the article, in the Septuagint version. The New Testament refers to the Mosaic law in various ways: the law (Matt., v, 17; Rom., ii, 12; etc.); the law of Moses (Luke, ii, 22; xxiv, 44; Acts, xxviii, 23); the book of Moses (Mark, xii, 26); or simply, Moses (Luke, xxiv, 27; Acts, xv, 21). Even the Talmud and the older Rabbinic writings call the first part of the Bible the book of the law, while in Aramaic it is simply termed law (cf. Buxtorf, "Lexicon Chaldaicum Talmudicum Rabbinicum", 791, 983; Levy, "Chaldäisches Wörterbuch", 268, 16; Aicher, "Das Alte Testament in der Mischna", Freiburg, 1906, p. 16).

The Greek name πεντατευχός, implying a division of the law into five parts, occurs for the first time about A. D. 150-75 in the letter to Flora by the Valentinian Ptolemy (cf. St. Epiphan., "Hær.", XXXIII, iv; P. G., XLI, 560). An earlier occurrence of the name was supposed to exist in a passage of Hippolytus where the Psalter is called καὶ αὐτὸ ἄλλον πεντάτευχον (cf. edition of de Lagarde, Leipzig and London, 1858, p. 193); but the passage has been found to belong to Epiphanius (cf. "Hippolytus" in "Die griechischen Schriftsteller der ersten drei Jahrhunderte", Leipzig, 1897, t. I, 143). The name is used again by Origen (Comment. in Ev. Jo., t. II; P. G., XIV, 192; cf. P. G., XIII, 444), St. Athanasius (Ep. ad Marcellin., 5; P. G., XXVII, 12), and several times by St. Epiphanius (De mensur. et ponderib., 4, 6; P. G., XLIII, 244). In Latin, Tertullian uses the masculine form *Pentateuchus* (Adv. Marcion., I, 10; P. L., II, 257), while St. Isidore of Seville prefers the neuter *Pentateuchum* (Etym., VI, ii, 1, 2; P. L., LXXXII, 230). The analogous forms Octateuch, Heptateuch, and Hexateuch have been used to refer to the first eight, seven, and six books of the Bible respectively. The Rabbinic writers adopted the expression "the five-fifths of the law" or simply "the five-fifths" to denote the five books of the Pentateuch.

Both the Palestinian and the Alexandrian Jews had distinct names for each of the five books of the Pentateuch. In Palestine, the opening words of the several books served as their titles; hence we have the names: berêshîth, we'ēlleh shemôth or simply shemôth, wáyyíqrâ, wáyedhábbēr, and 'ēlleh háddebārîm or simply debārîm. Though these were the ordinary Hebrew titles of the successive Pentateuchal books, certain Rabbinic writers denote the last three according to their contents; they called the third book tôráth kōhănîm, or law of priests; the fourth, ḥômésh háppîqqûdhîm, or book of census; the fifth, míshnēh thôrah, or repetition of the law. The Alexandrian Jews derived their Greek names of the five books from the contents of either the whole or the beginning of each division. Thus the first book is called Γένεσις κόσμου or simply Γένεσις; the second, Ἔξοδος Αἰγύπτου or Ἔξοδος; the third, Λευειτικόν or Λευιτικόν; the fourth, Ἀριθμοί; and the fifth, Δευτερονόμιον. These names passed from the Septuagint into the Latin Vulgate, and from this into most of the translations of the Vulgate. Ἀριθμοί however was replaced by the Latin equivalent Numeri, while the other names retained their form.

II. ANALYSIS.—The contents of the Pentateuch are partly of an historical, partly of a legal character. They give us the history of the Chosen People from the creation of the world to the death of Moses, and acquaint us too with the civil and religious legislation of the Israelites during the life of their great lawgiver. Genesis may be considered as the introduction to the other four books; it contains the early history down to the preparation of Israel's exit from Egypt. Deuteronomy, consisting mainly of discourses, is practically a summary repetition of the Mosaic legislation, and concludes also the history of the people under the leadership of Moses. The three intervening books consider the wanderings of Israel in the desert and the successive legal enactments. Each of these three great divisions has its own special introduction (Gen., i, 1–ii, 3; Ex., i, 1–i, 7; Deut., i, 1–5); and since the subject matter distinguishes Leviticus from Exodus and Numbers, not to mention the literary terminations of the third and fourth books (Lev., xxvii, 34; Num., xxvi, 13), the present form of the Pentateuch exhibits both a literary unity and a division into five minor parts.

A. GENESIS.—The Book of Genesis prepares the reader for the Pentateuchal legislation; it tells us how God chose a particular family to keep His Revelation, and how he trained the Chosen People to fulfil its mission. From the nature of its contents the book consists of two rather unequal parts; cc. i–xi present the features of a general history, while cc. xii–l contain the particular history of the Chosen People. By a literary device, each of these parts is subdivided into five sections differing in length. The sections are introduced by the phrase 'ēlléh thôledhôth (these are the generations) or its variant zéh sēphér tôledhôth (this is the book of the generations). "Generations", however, is only the etymological meaning of the Hebrew tôledhôth; in its context the formula can hardly signify a mere genealogical table, for it is neither preceded nor followed by such tables. As early Oriental history usually begins with genealogical records, and consists to a large extent of such records, one naturally interprets the above introductory formula and its variant as meaning, "this is the history" or "this is the book of the history." History in these phrases is not to be understood as a narrative resting on folklore, as Fr. von Hummelauer believes ("Exegetisches zur Inspirationsfrage, Biblische Studien", Freiburg, 1904, IX, 4, pp. 26–32); but as a record based on genealogies. Moreover, the introductory formula often refers back to some principal feature of the preceding section, thus forming a transition and connexion between the successive parts. Gen., v, 1, e. g., refers back to Gen., ii, 7 sqq.; vi, 9 to v, 29 sqq. and vi, 8; x, 1 to ix, 18, 19; etc. Finally, the sacred writer deals very briefly with the non-chosen families or tribes, and he always considers them before the chosen branch of the family. He treats of Cain before he speaks of Seth; similarly, Cham and Japhet precede Sem; the rest of Sem's posterity precedes Abraham; Ismael precedes Isaac; Esau precedes Jacob.

Bearing in mind these general outlines of the contents and the literary structure of Genesis, we shall easily understand the following analytical table.

Introduction, Gen., i, 1–ii, 3, consists of the Hexaëmeron; it teaches the power and goodness of God as manifested in the creation of the world, and also the dependence of creatures on the dominion of the Creator.

(1) *General History*, ii, 4–xi, 26.—Man did not acknowledge his dependence on God. Hence, leaving the disobedient to their own devices, God chose one special family or one individual as the depositary of His Revelation.

(a) History of Heaven and Earth, ii, 4–iv, 26.—Here we have the story of the fall of our first parents, ii, 5–iii, 24; of the fratricide of Cain, iv, 1–16; the posterity of Cain and its elimination, iv, 17–26.

(b) History of Adam, v, 1–vi, 8.—The writer enumerates the Sethites, another line of Adam's descendants, v, 1–32, but shows that they too became so corrupt that only one among them found favour before God, vi, 1–8.

(c) History of Noe, vi, 9–ix, 29.—Neither the Deluge which destroyed the whole human race excepting Noe's family, vi, 11–viii, 19, nor God's covenant with Noe and his sons, viii, 20–ix, 17, brought about the amendment of the human family, and only one of Noe's sons was chosen as the bearer of the Divine blessings, ix, 18–29.

(d) History of the Sons of Noe, x, 1–xi, 9.—The posterity of the non-chosen sons, x, 1–32, brought a new punishment on the human race by its pride, xi, 1–9.

(e) History of Sem, xi, 10–26.—The posterity of Sem is enumerated down to Thare the father of Abraham, in whose seed all the nations of the earth shall be blessed.

(2) *Special History*, xi, 27–l, 26.—Here the inspired writer describes the special Providence watching over Abraham and his offspring which developed in Egypt into a large nation. At the same time, he eliminates the sons of Abraham who were not children of God's promise. This teaches the Israelites that carnal descent from Abraham does not suffice to make them true sons of Abraham.

(a) History of Thare, xi, 27–xxv, 11.—This section tells of the call of Abraham, his transmigration into Chanaan, his covenant with God, and His promises.

(b) History of Ismael, xxv, 12–18.—This section eliminates the tribes springing from Ismael.

(c) History of Isaac, xxv, 19–xxxv, 29.—Here we have the history of Isaac's sons, Esau and Jacob.

(d) History of Esau, xxxvi, 1–xxxvii, 1.—The sacred writer gives a list of Esau's posterity; it does not belong to the number of the Chosen People.

(e) History of Jacob, xxxvii, 2–l, 26.—This final portion of Genesis tells of the fate of Jacob's family down to the death of the Patriarch and of Joseph.

What has been said shows a uniform plan in the structure of Genesis, which some scholars prefer to call "schematism". (i) The whole book is divided into ten sections. (ii) Each section is introduced by the same formula. (iii) The sections are arranged according to a definite plan, the history of the lateral genealogical branches always preceding that of the corresponding part of the main line. (iv) Within the sections, the introductory formula or the title is usually followed by a brief repetition of some prominent feature of the preceding section, a fact duly noted and explained by as early a writer as Rhabanus Maurus (Comment. in Gen., II, xii; P. L., CVII, 531–2), but misconstrued by our recent critics into an argument for a diversity of sources. (v) The history of each Patriarch tells of the development of his family during his lifetime, while the account of his life varies between a bare notice consisting of a few words or lines, and a more lengthy description. (vi) When the life of the Patriarch is given more in detail, the account usually ends in an almost uniform way, indicating the length of his life and his burial with his ancestors (cf. ix, 29; xi, 32; xxv, 7; xxxv, 28; xlvii, 28). Such a definite plan of the book shows that it was written with a definite end in view and according to preconceived arrangement. The critics attribute this to the final "redactor" of the Pentateuch who adopted, according to their views, the genealogical framework and the "schematism" from the Priestly Code. The value of these views will be discussed later; for the present, it suffices to know that a striking unity prevails throughout the Book of Genesis (cf. Kurtz, "Die Einheit der Genesis", Berlin, 1846; Delattre, "Plan de la Genèse" in "Revue des quest. hist.", July, 1876; XX, pp. 5–43; Delattre, "Le plan de la Genèse et les générations du ciel et de la terre" in "La science cath.", 15 Oct., 1891, V, pp. 978–89; de Broglie, "Etude sur les généalogies bibliques" in "Le congrès scientif. internat. des catholiques de 1888", Paris, 1889, I, pp. 94–101; Julian, "Etude critique sur la composition de la Genèse", Paris, 1888, pp. 232–50).

B. EXODUS.—After the death of Joseph, Israel had grown into a people, and its history deals no longer with mere genealogies, but with the people's national and religious development. The various laws are given and promulgated as occasion required them; hence they are intimately connected with the history of the people, and the Pentateuchal books in which they are recorded are rightly numbered among the historical books of Scripture. Only the third book of the Pentateuch exhibits rather the features of a legal code. The Book of Exodus consists of a brief introduction and three main parts:

Introduction, i, 1–7.—A brief summary of the history of Jacob connects Genesis with Exodus, and serves at the same time as transition from the former to the latter.

(1) *First Part*, i, 8–xiii, 16.—It treats of the events preceding and preparing the exit of Israel from Egypt.

(a) Ex., i, 8–ii, 25: the Israelites are oppressed by the new Pharao "that knew not Joseph", but God prepares them a liberator in Moses.

(b) iii, 1–iv, 31.—Moses is called to free his people; his brother Aaron is given him as companion; their reception by the Israelites.

(c) v, 1–x, 29.—Pharao refuses to listen to Moses and Aaron; God renews his promises; genealogies of Moses and Aaron; the heart of Pharao is not moved by the first nine plagues.

(d) xi, 1–xiii, 16.—The tenth plague consists in the death of the first-born; Pharao dismisses the people; law of the annual celebration of the pasch in memory of the liberation from Egypt.

(2) *Second Part*, xiii, 17–xviii, 27.—Journey of Israel to Mt. Sinai and miracles preparing the people for the Sinaitic Law.

(a) xiii, 17–xv, 21.—The Israelites, led and protected by a pillar of cloud and fire, cross the Red Sea, but the persecuting Egyptians perish in the waters.

(b) xv, 22–xvii, 16.—The route of Israel is passing through Sur, Mara, Elim, Sin, Raphidim. At Mara the bitter waters are made sweet; in the Desert of Sin God sent quails and manna to the children of Israel; at Raphidim God gave them water from the rock, and defeated Amalec through the prayers of Moses.

(c) xviii, 1–27.—Jethro visits his kinsmen, and at his suggestion Moses institutes the judges of the people.

(3) *Third Part*, xix, 1–xl, 38.—Conclusion of the Sinaitic covenant and its renewal. Here Exodus assumes more the character of a legal code.

(a) xix, 1–xx, 21.—The people journey to Sinai, prepare for the coming legislation, receive the decalogue, and ask to have the future laws promulgated through Moses.

(b) xx, 22–xxiv, 8.—Moses promulgates certain laws together with promises for their observance, and confirms the covenant between God and the people with a sacrifice. The portion xx, 1–xxiii, 33, is also called the Book of the Covenant.

(c) xxiv, 9–xxxi, 18.—Moses alone remains with God on the mountain for forty days, and receives various instructions about the tabernacle and other points pertaining to Divine worship.

(d) xxxii, 1–xxxiv, 35.—The people adore the golden calf; at this sight, Moses breaks the divinely given tables of the law, punishes the idolaters, obtains pardon from God for the survivors, and, renewing the covenant, receives other tables of the law.

(e) xxxv, 1–xl, 38.—The tabernacle with its appurtenances is prepared, the priests are anointed, and the cloud of the Lord covers the tabernacle, thus showing that He had made the people His own.

C. LEVITICUS, called by Rabbinic writers "Law of the Priests" or "Law of the Sacrifices", contains nearly a complete collection of laws concerning the Levitical ministry. They are not codified in any logical order, but still we may discern certain groups of regulations touching the same subject. The Book of Exodus shows what God had done and was doing for His people; the Book of Leviticus prescribes what the people must do for God, and how they must render themselves worthy of His constant presence.

(1) First Part, i, 1–x, 20.—Duties of Israel towards God living in their midst.

(a) i, 1–vi, 7.—The different kinds of sacrifices are enumerated, and their rites are described.

(b) vi, 8–vii, 36.—The duties and rights of the priests, the official offerers of the sacrifices, are stated.

(c) viii, 1–x, 20.—The first priests are consecrated and introduced into their office.

(2) Second Part, xi, 1–xxvii, 34.—Legal cleanness demanded by the Divine presence.

(a) xi, 1–xx, 27.—The entire people must be legally clean; the various ways in which cleanness must be kept; interior cleanness must be added to external cleanness.

(b) xxi, 1–xxii, 33.—Priests must excel in both internal and external cleanness; hence they have to keep special regulations.

(c) xxiii, 1–xxvii, 34.—The other laws, and the promises and threats made for the observance or the violation of the laws, belong to both priests and people.

D. NUMBERS, at times called "In the Desert" by certain Rabbinic writers because it covers practically the whole time of Israel's wanderings in the desert. Their story was begun in Exodus, but interrupted by the Sinaitic legislation; Numbers takes up the account from the first month of the second year, and brings it down to the eleventh month of the fortieth year. But the period of 38 years is briefly treated, only its beginning and end being touched upon; for this span of time was occupied by the generation of Israelites that had been condemned by God.

(1) First Part, i, 1–xiv, 45.—Summary of the happenings before the rejection of the rebellious generation, especially during the first two months of the second year. The writer inverts the chronological order of these two months, in order not to interrupt the account of the people's wanderings by a description of the census, of the arrangement of the tribes, of the duties of the various families of the Levites, all of which occurrences or ordinances belong to the second month. Thus he first states what remained unchanged throughout the desert life of the people, and then reverts to the account of the wanderings from the first month of the second year.

(a) i, 1–vi, 27.—The census is taken, the tribes are arranged in their proper order, the duties of the Levites are defined, the regulations concerning cleanliness in the camp are promulgated.

(b) vii, 1–ix, 14.—Occurrences belonging to the first month: offerings of the princes at the dedication of the tabernacle, consecration of the Levites and duration of their ministry, celebration of the second pasch.

(c) ix, 15–xiv, 45.—Signals for breaking up the camp; the people leave Sinai on the twenty-second day of the second month, and journey towards Cades in the desert Pharan; they murmur against Moses on account of fatigue, want of flesh-meat, etc.; deceived by faithless spies, they refuse to enter into the Promised Land, and the whole living generation is rejected by God.

(2) Second Part, xv, 1–xix, 22.—Events pertaining to the rejected generation.

(a) xv, 1–41.—Certain laws concerning sacrifices; Sabbath-breaking is punished with death; the law of fringes on the garments.

(b) xvi, 1–xvii, 13.—The schism of Core and his adherents; their punishment; the priesthood is confirmed to Aaron by the blooming rod which is kept for a remembrance in the tabernacle.

(c) xviii, 1–xix, 22.—The charges of the priests and Levites, and their portion; the law of the sacrifice of the red cow, and the water of expiation.

(3) Third Part, xx, 1–xxxvi, 13.—History of the journey from the first to the eleventh month of the fortieth year.

(a) xx, 1–xxi, 20.—Death of Mary, sister of Moses; God again gives the murmuring people water from the rock, but refuses Moses and Aaron entrance to the Promised Land on account of their doubt; Aaron dies while the people go around the Idumean mountains; the malcontents are punished with fiery serpents.

(b) xxi, 21–xxv, 18.—The land of the Amorrhites is seized; the Moabites vainly attempt to destroy Israel by the curse of Balaam; the Madianites lead the people into idolatry.

(c) xxvi, 1–xxvii, 23.—A new census is taken with a view of dividing the land; the law of inheritance; Josue is appointed to succeed Moses.

(d) xxviii, 1–xxx, 17.—Certain laws concerning sacrifices, vows, and feasts are repeated and completed.

(e) xxxi, 1–xxxii, 40.—After the defeat of the Madianites, the country across Jordan is given to the tribes of Ruben and Gad, and to half of the tribe of Manasses.

(f) xxxiii, 1–49.—List of encampments of people of Israel during their wandering in the desert.

(g) xxxiii, 50–xxxvi, 13.—Command to destroy the Chanaanites; limits of the Promised Land and names of the men who are to divide it; Levitical cities, and cities of refuge; laws concerning murder and manslaughter; ordinance concerning the marriage of heiresses.

E. DEUTERONOMY is a partial repetition and explanation of the foregoing legislation together with an urgent exhortation to be faithful to it. The main body of the book consists of three discourses delivered by Moses to the people in the eleventh month of the fortieth year; but the discourses are preceded by a short introduction, and they are followed by several appendices.

Introduction, i, 1–5.—Brief indication of the subject matter, the time, and the place of the following discourses.

(1) *First Discourse*, i, 6–iv, 40.—God's benefits are enumerated, and the people are exhorted to keep the law.

(a) i, 6–iii, 29.—The main occurrences during the time of the wandering in the desert are recalled as showing the goodness and justice of God.

(b) iv, 1–40.—Hence the covenant with God must be kept. By way of parenthesis, the sacred writer adds here (i) the appointment of three cities of refuge across the Jordan, iv, 41–43; (ii) an historical preamble, preparing us for the second discourse, iv, 44–49.

(2) *Second Discourse*, v, 1–xxvi, 19.—This forms almost the bulk of Deuteronomy. It rehearses the whole economy of the covenant in two sections, the one general, the other particular.

(a) *The General Repetition*, v, 1–xi, 32.—Repetition of the decalogue, and reasons for the promulgation of the law through Moses; explanation of the first commandment, and prohibition of all intercourse with the gentiles; reminder of the Divine favours and punishments; promise of victory over the Chanaanites; God's blessing on the observance of the Law, His curse on the transgressors.

(b) *Special Laws*, xii, 1–xxvi, 19.—(i) Duties towards God: He is to be duly worshipped, never to be abandoned; distinction of clean and unclean meats; tithes and first-fruits; the three principal solemnities of the year. (ii) Duties towards God's representatives: towards the judges, the future kings, the priests, and Prophets. (iii) Duties towards the neighbour: as to life, external possessions, marriage, and various other particulars.

(3) *Third Discourse*, xxvii, 1–xxx, 20.—A renewed exhortation to keep the law, based on diverse reasons.

(a) xxvii, 1–26.—Command to inscribe the law on stones after crossing the Jordan, and to promulgate the blessings and curses connected with the observance or non-observance of the law.

(b) xxviii, 1–68.—A more minute statement of the good or evil depending on the observance or violation of the law.

(c) xxix, 1–xxx, 20.—The goodness of God is extolled; all are urged to be faithful to God.

(4) *Historical Appendix*, xxxi, 1–xxxiv, 12.

(a) xxxi, 1–27.—Moses appoints Josue as his successor, orders him to read the law to the people every seven years, and to place a copy of the same in the ark.

(b) xxxi, 28–xxxii, 47.—Moses calls an assembly of the Ancients and recites his canticle.

(c) xxxii, 48–52.—Moses views the Promised Land from a distance.

(d) xxxiii, 1–29.—He blesses the tribes of Israel.

(e) xxxiv, 1–12.—His death, burial, and special eulogium.

III. Authenticity.—The contents of the Pentateuch furnish the basis for the history, the law, the worship, and the life of the Chosen People of God. Hence the authorship of the work, the time and manner of its origin, and its historicity are of paramount importance. These are not merely literary problems, but questions belonging to the fields of history of religion and theology. The Mosaic authorship of the Pentateuch is inseparably connected with the question, whether and in what sense Moses was the author or intermediary of the Old-Testament legislation, and the bearer of pre-Mosaic tradition. According to the trend of both Old and New Testament, and according to Jewish and Christian theology, the work of the great lawgiver Moses is the origin of the history of Israel and the basis of its development down to the time of Jesus Christ; but modern criticism sees in all this only the result, or the precipitate, of a purely natural historical development. The question of the Mosaic authorship of the Pentateuch leads us, therefore, to the alternative, revelation or historical evolution; it touches the historical and theological foundation of both the Jewish and the Christian dispensation. We shall consider the subject first in the light of Scripture; secondly, in the light of Jewish and Christian tradition; thirdly, in the light of internal evidence, furnished by the Pentateuch; finally, in the light of ecclesiastical decisions.

A. *Testimony of Sacred Scripture*.—It will be found convenient to divide the Biblical evidence for the Mosaic authorship of the Pentateuch into three parts: (1) Testimony of the Pentateuch; (2) Testimony of the other Old-Testament books; (3) Testimony of the New Testament.

(1) *Witness of the Pentateuch*.—The Pentateuch in its present form does not present itself as a complete literary production of Moses. It contains an account of Moses' death, it tells the story of his life in the third person and in an indirect form, and the last four books do not exhibit the literary form of memoirs of the great lawgiver; besides, the expression "God said to Moses" shows only the Divine origin of the Mosaic laws, but does not prove that Moses himself codified in the Pentateuch the various laws promulgated by him. On the other hand, the Pentateuch ascribes to Moses the literary authorship of at least four sections, partly historical, partly legal, partly poetical.

(a) After Israel's victory over the Amalecites near Raphidim, the Lord said to Moses (Ex., xvii, 14): "Write this for a memorial in a book, and deliver it to the ears of Josue." This order is naturally restricted to Amalec's defeat, a benefit which God wished to keep alive in the memory of the people (Deut., xxv, 17–19). The present pointing of the Hebrew text reads "in *the* book", but the Septuagint version omits the definite article. Even if we suppose that the Massoretic pointing gives the original text, we can hardly prove that *the* book referred to is the Pentateuch, though this is highly probable (cf. von Hummelauer, "Exodus et Leviticus", Paris, 1897, p. 182; Idem, "Deuteronomium", Paris, 1901, p. 152; Kley, "Die Pentateuchfrage", Münster, 1903, p. 217).

(b) Again, Ex., xxiv, 4: "And Moses wrote all the words of the Lord." The context does not allow us to understand these words in an indefinite manner, but as referring to the words of the Lord immediately preceding or to the so-called "Book of the Covenant", Ex., xx–xxiii.

(c) Ex., xxxiv, 27: "And the Lord said to Moses: Write thee these words by which I have made a covenant both with thee and with Israel." The next verse adds: "and he wrote upon the tables the ten words of the covenant." Ex., xxxiv, 1, 4, shows how Moses had prepared the tables, and Ex., xxxiv, 10–26, gives us the contents of the ten words.

(d) Num., xxxiii, 1–2: "These are the mansions of the children of Israel, who went out of Egypt by their troops under the conduct of Moses and Aaron, which Moses wrote down according to the places of their encamping." Here we are informed that Moses wrote the list of the people's encampments in the desert; but where is this list to be found? Most probably it is given in Num., xxxiii, 3–49, or the immediate context of the passage telling of Moses' literary activity; there are, however, scholars who understand this latter passage as referring to the history of Israel's departure from Egypt written in the order of the people's encampments, so that it would be our present Book of Exodus. But this view is hardly probable; for its assumption that Num., xxxiii, 3–49, is a summary of Exodus cannot be upheld, as the chapter of Numbers mentions several encampments not occurring in Exodus.

Besides these four passages there are certain indications in Deuteronomy which point to the literary activity of Moses. Deut., i, 5: "And Moses began to expound the law and to say"; even if the "law" in this text refer to the whole of the Pentateuchal legislation, which is not very probable, it shows only that Moses promulgated the whole law, but not that he necessarily wrote it. Practically the entire Book of Deuteronomy claims to be a special legislation promulgated by Moses in the land of Moab: iv, 1–40; 44–9; v, 1 sqq.; xii, 1 sqq. But there is a suggestion of writing too: xvii, 18–9, enjoins that the future kings are to receive a copy of this law from the priests in order to read and observe it; xxvii, 1–8, commands that on the west side of the Jordan "all the words of this law" be written on stones set up in mount Hebal; xxviii, 58, speaks of "all the words of this law, that are written in this volume" after enumerating the blessings and curses which will come upon the observers and violators of the law respectively, and which are again referred to as written in a book in xxix, 20, 21, 27, and xxxii, 46, 47; now, tne law repeatedly referred to as written in a book must be at least the Deuteronomic legislation. Moreover, xxxi, 9–13 states, "and Moses wrote this law", and xxxi, 26, adds, "take this book, and put it in the side of the ark . . . that it may be there for a testimony against thee"; to explain these texts as fiction or as anachronisms is hardly compatible with the inerrancy of Sacred Scripture. Finally, xxxi, 19, commands Moses to write the canticle contained in Deut., xxxii, 1–43.

The Scriptural scholar will not complain that there are so few express indications in the Pentateuch of Moses' literary activity; he will rather be surprised at their number. As far as explicit testimony for its own, at least partial, authorship is concerned, the Pentateuch compares rather favourably with many other books of the Old Testament.

(2) *Witness of other Old-Testament Books.* (a) *Josue.*—The narrative of the Book of Josue presupposes not merely the facts and essential ordinances contained in the Pentateuch, but also the law given by Moses and written in the book of the law of Moses: Jos., i, 7–8; viii, 31; xxii, 5; xxiii, 6. Josue himself "wrote all these things in the volume of the law of the Lord" (xxiv, 26). Prof. Hoberg maintains that this "volume of the law of the Lord" is the Pentateuch ("Über den Ursprung des Pentateuchs" in "Biblische Zeitschrift", 1906, IV, 340); Mangenot believes that it refers at least to Deuteronomy (Dict. de la Bible, V, 66). At any rate, Josue and his contemporaries were acquainted with a written Mosaic legislation, which was divinely revealed.

(b) *Judges; I, II Kings.*—In the Book of Judges and the first two Books of Kings there is no explicit reference to Moses and the book of the law, but a number of incidents and statements presuppose the existence of the Pentateuchal legislation and institutions. Thus Judges, xv, 8–10, recalls Israel's delivery from Egypt and its conquest of the Promised Land; Judges, xi, 12–28, states incidents recorded in Num., xx, 14; xxi, 13, 24; xxii, 2; Judges, xiii, 4, states a practice founded on the law of the Nazarites in Num., vi, 1–21; Judges, xviii, 31, speaks of the tabernacle existing in the times when there was no king in Israel; Judges, xx, 26–8, mentions the ark of the covenant, the various kinds of sacrifices, and the Aaronic priesthood. The Pentateuchal history and laws are similarly presupposed in I Kings, x, 18; xv, 1–10; x, 25; xxi, 1–6; xxii, 6 sqq.; xxiii, 6–9; II Kings, vi.

(c) *III, IV Kings.*—The last two Books of Kings repeatedly speak of the law of Moses. To restrict the meaning of this term to Deuteronomy is an arbitrary exegesis (cf. III Kings, ii, 3; x, 31); Amasias showed mercy to the children of the murderers "according to that which is written in the book of the law of Moses" (IV Kings, xiv, 6); the sacred writer records the Divine promise of protecting the Israelites "only if they will observe to do all that I have commanded them according to the law which my servant Moses commanded them" (IV Kings, xxi, 8). In the eighteenth year of the reign of Josias was found the book of the law (IV Kings, xxii, 8, 11), or the book of the covenant (IV Kings, xxiii, 2), according to which he conducted his religious reform (IV Kings, xxiii, 1–24); and which is identified with "the law of Moses" (IV Kings, xxiii, 25). Catholic commentators are not at one whether this law-book was Deuteronomy (von Hummelauer, "Deuteronomium", Paris, 1901, pp. 40–60, 83–7) or the entire Pentateuch (Clair, "Les livres des Rois", Paris, 1884, II, p. 557 seq.; Hoberg, "Moses und der Pentateuch", Freiburg, 1905, p. 17 seq.; "Über den Ursprung des Pentateuchs" in "Biblische Zeitschrift", 1906, IV, pp. 338–40).

(d) *Paralipomenon.*—The inspired writer of Paralipomenon refers to the law and the book of Moses much more frequently and clearly. The objectionable names and numbers occurring in these books are mostly due to transcribers. The omission of incidents which would detract from the glory of the Israelite kings or would not edify the reader is not detrimental to the credibility or veracity of the work. Otherwise one should have to place among works of fiction a number of biographical or patriotic publications intended for the young or for the common reader. On their part, the modern critics are too eager to discredit the authority of Paralipomena. "After removing the account of Paralipomena", writes de Wette (Beiträge, I, 135), "the whole Jewish history assumes another form, and the Pentateuchal investigations take another turn; a number of strong proofs, hard to explain away, for the early existence of the Mosaic books have disappeared, the other vestiges of their existence are placed in a different light." A glance at the contents of Paralipomenon suffices to explain the efforts of de Wette and Wellhausen to disprove the historicity of the books. Not only are the genealogies (I Par., i–ix) and the description of worship traced after the data and laws of the Pentateuch, but the sacred writer expressly points out their conformity with what is written in the law of the Lord (I Par., xvi, 40), in the law of Moses (II Par., xxiii, 18; xxxi, 3), thus identifying the law of the Lord with that written by Moses (cf. II Par., xxv, 4). The reader will find similar indications of the existence and the Mosaic origin of the Pentateuch in I Par., xxii, 12 seq.; II Par., xvii, 9; xxxiii, 4; xxxiv, 14; xxv, 12. By an artificial interpretation, indeed, the Books of Paralipomenon may be construed to represent the Pentateuch as a book containing the law promulgated by Moses; but the natural sense of the foregoing passages regards the Pentateuch as a book edited by Moses.

(e) *I, II Esdras.*—The Books of Esdras and Nehemias, too, taken in their natural and commonly accepted sense, consider the Pentateuch as the book of Moses, not merely as a book containing the law of Moses. This contention is based on the study of the following texts: I Esd., iii, 2 sqq.; vi, 18; vii, 14; II Esd., i, 7 sqq.; viii, 1, 8, 14; ix, 3; x, 34, 36; xiii, 1–3. Graf and his followers expressed the view that the book of Moses referrred to in these texts is not the Pentateuch, but only the Priestly Code; but when we keep in mind that the book in question contained the laws of Lev., xxiii, and Deut., vii, 2–4; xv, 2, we perceive at once that the book of Moses cannot be restricted to the Priestly Code. To the witness of the historical books we may add II Mach., ii, 4; vii, 6; Judith, viii, 23; Ecclus., xxiv, 33; xlv, 1–6; xlv, 18, and especially the Preface of Ecclus.

(f) *Prophetic Books.*—Express reference to the written law of Moses is found only in the later Prophets: Bar., ii, 2, 28; Dan., ix, 11, 13; Mal., iv, 4. Among these, Baruch knows that Moses has been commanded to write the law, and though his expressions run parallel to those of Deut., xxviii, 15, 53, 62–4, his threats contain allusions to those contained in other parts of the Pentateuch. The other Prophets frequently refer to the law of the Lord guarded by the priests (cf. Deut., xxxi, 9), and they put it on the same level with Divine Revelation and the eternal covenant of the Lord. They appeal to God's covenant, the sacrificial laws, the calendar of feasts, and other laws of the Pentateuch in such a way as to render it probable that a written legislation formed the basis of their prophetic admonitions (cf. Osee, viii, 12), and that they were acquainted with verbal expressions of the book of the law. Thus in the northern kingdom Amos (iv, 4–5; v, 22 sqq.) and Isaias in the south (i, 11 sqq.) employ expressions which are practically technical words for sacrifice occurring in Lev., i–iii; vii, 12, 16; and Deut., xii, 6.

(3) *Witness of the New Testament.*—We need not show that Jesus and the Apostles quoted the whole of the Pentateuch as written by Moses. If they attributed to Moses all the passages which they happen

to cite, if they ascribe the Pentateuch to Moses whenever there is question of its authorship, even the most exacting critics must admit that they express their conviction that the work was indeed written by Moses. When the Sadducees quote against Jesus the marriage law of Deut., xxv, 5, as written by Moses (Matt., xxii, 24; Mark, xii, 19; Luke, xx, 28), Jesus does not deny the Mosaic authorship, but appeals to Ex., iii, 6, as equally written by Moses (Mark, xii, 26; Matt., xxii, 31; Luke, xx, 37). Again, in the parable of Dives and Lazarus (Luke, xvi, 29), He speaks of "Moses and the prophets", while on other occasions He speaks of "the law and the prophets" (Luke, xvi, 16), thus showing that in His mind the law, or the Pentateuch, and Moses are identical. The same expressions reappear in the last discourse addressed by Christ to His disciples (Luke, xxiv, 44–6; cf. 27): "which are written in the law of Moses, and in the prophets, and in the psalms concerning me". Finally, in John, v, 45–7, Jesus is more explicit in asserting the Mosaic authorship of the Pentateuch: "There is one that accuseth you, Moses . . . for he wrote of me. But if you do not believe his writings, how will you believe my words?" Nor can it be maintained that Christ merely accommodated himself to the current beliefs of his contemporaries who considered Moses as the author of the Pentateuch not merely in a moral but also in the literary sense of authorship. Jesus did not need to enter into the critical study of the nature of Mosaic authorship, but He could not expressly endorse the popular belief, if it was erroneous.

The Apostles too felt convinced of, and testified to, the Mosaic authorship. "Philip findeth Nathanael, and saith to him: We have found him of whom Moses in the law, and the prophets did write." St. Peter introduces a quotation from Deut., xviii, 15, with the words: "For Moses said" (Acts, iii, 22). St. James and St. Paul relate that Moses is read in the synagogues on the Sabbath day (Acts, xv, 21; II Cor., iii, 15). The great Apostle speaks in other passages of the law of Moses (Acts, xiii, 33; I Cor., ix, 9); he preaches Jesus according to the law of Moses and the Prophets (Acts, xxviii, 23), and cites passages from the Pentateuch as words written by Moses (Rom., x, 5–8; 19). St. John mentions the canticle of Moses (Apoc., xv, 3).

B. *Witness of Tradition.*—The voice of tradition, both Jewish and Christian, is so unanimous and constant in proclaiming the Mosaic authorship of the Pentateuch that down to the seventeenth century it did not allow the rise of any serious doubt. The following paragraphs are only a meagre outline of this living tradition.

(1) *Jewish Tradition.*—It has been seen that the books of the Old Testament, beginning with those of the Pentateuch, present Moses as the author of at least parts of the Pentateuch. The writer of the Books of Kings believes that Moses is the author of Deuteronomy at least. Esdras, Nehemias, Malachias, the author of Paralipomena, and the Greek authors of the Septuagint Version consider Moses as the author of the whole Pentateuch. At the time of Jesus Christ and the Apostles friend and foe take the Mosaic authorship of the Pentateuch for granted; neither our Lord nor His enemies take exception to this assumption. In the first century of the Christian era, Josephus ascribes to Moses the authorship of the entire Pentateuch, not excepting the account of the lawgiver's death ("Antiq. Jud.", IV, viii, 3–48; cf. I Procem., 4; "Contra Apion.", I, 8). The Alexandrian philosopher Philo is convinced that the entire Pentateuch is the work of Moses, and that the latter wrote a prophetic account of his death under the influence of a special Divine inspiration ("De vita Mosis", ll. II, III in "Opera", Geneva, 1613, pp. 511, 538). The Babylonian Talmud ("Baba-Bathra", II, col. 140; "Makkoth", fol. IIa; "Menachoth", fol. 30a; cf. Vogüé, "Hist. de la Bible et de l'exégèse biblique jusqu'à nos jours", Paris, 1881, p. 21), the Talmud of Jerusalem (Sota, v, 5), the rabbis, and the doctors of Israel (cf. Fürst, "Der Kanon des Alten Testaments nach den Überlieferungen im Talmud und Midrasch", Leipzig, 1868, pp. 7–9) bear testimony to the continuance of this tradition for the first thousand years. Though Isaac ben Jasus in the eleventh century and Abenesra in the twelfth admitted certain post-Mosaic additions in the Pentateuch, still they as well as Maimonides upheld its Mosaic authorship, and did not substantially differ in this point from the teaching of R. Becchai (thirteenth cent.), Joseph Karo, and Abarbanel (fifteenth cent.; cf. Richard Simon, "Critique de la Bibl. des aut. ecclés. de E. Dupin", Paris, 1730, III, pp. 215–20). Only in the seventeenth century, Baruch Spinoza rejected the Mosaic authorship of the Pentateuch, pointing out the possibility that the work might have been written by Esdras ("Tract. theol.-politicus", c. viii, ed. Tauchnitz, III, p. 125). Among the more recent Jewish writers several have adopted the results of the critics, thus abandoning the tradition of their forefathers.

(2) *Christian Tradition.*—The Jewish tradition concerning the Mosaic authorship of the Pentateuch was brought into the Christian Church by Christ Himself and the Apostles. No one will seriously deny the existence and continuance of such a tradition from the patristic period onward; one might indeed be curious about the interval between the time of the Apostles and the beginning of the third century. For this period we may appeal to the "Epistle of Barnabas" (x, 1–12; Funk, "Patres apostol.", 2nd ed., Tübingen, 1901, I, pp. 66–70; xii, 2–9; *ibid.*, pp. 74–6), to St. Clement of Rome (I Cor., xli, 1; *ibid.*, p. 152), St. Justin ("Apol. I", 59; P. G., VI, 416; I, 32, 54; *ibid.*, 377, 409; "Dial.", 29; *ibid.*, 537), to the author of "Cohort. ad Græc." (9, 28, 30, 33, 34; *ibid.*, 257, 293, 296–7, 361), to St. Theophilus ("Ad Autol.", III, 23; *ibid.*, 1156; 11, 30; *ibid.*, 1100), to St. Irenæus (Cont. hær., I, ii, 6; P. G., VII, 715–6), to St. Hippolytus of Rome ("Comment. in Deut.", xxxi, 9, 31, 35; cf. Achelis, "Arabische Fragmente etc.", Leipzig, 1897, I, 118; "Philosophumena", VIII, 8; X, 33; P. G., XVI, 3350, 3448), to Tertullian of Carthage (Adv. Hermog., XIX; P. L., II, 214), to Origen of Alexandria (Contra Cels., III, 5–6; P. G., XI, 928; etc.), to St. Eusthatius of Antioch (De engastrimytha c. Orig., 21; P. G., XVIII, 656); for all these writers, and others might be added, bear witness to the continuance of the Christian tradition that Moses wrote the Pentateuch. A list of the later Fathers who bear witness to the same truth may be found in Mangenot's article in the "Dict. de la Bible" (V, 74 seq.). Hoberg (Moses und der Pentateuch, 72 seq.) has collected the testimony for the existence of the tradition during the Middle Ages and in more recent times.

But Catholic tradition does not necessarily maintain that Moses wrote every letter of the Pentateuch as it is to-day, and that the work has come down to us in an absolutely unchanged form. This rigid view of the Mosaic authorship began to develop in the eighteenth century, and practically gained the upper hand in the nineteenth. The arbitrary treatment of Scripture on the part of Protestants, and the succession of the various destructive systems advanced by Biblical criticism, caused this change of front in the Catholic camp. In the sixteenth century Card. Bellarmine, who may be considered as a reliable exponent of Catholic tradition, expressed the opinion that Esdras had collected, readjusted, and corrected the scattered parts of the Pentateuch, and had even added the parts necessary for the completion of the Pentateuchal history (De verbo Dei, II, i; cf. III, iv). The views of Genebrard, Pereira, Bonfrère, a Lapide, Masius, Jansenius, and of other notable Biblicists of the sixteenth and seventeenth centuries are equally elastic with regard to the Mosaic authorship of the Pentateuch. Not that they agree with the contentions of our modern Biblical criticism; but they show that to-day's Pentateuchal problems were not wholly unknown to Catholic scholars, and that the Mosaic authorship of the Pentateuch as determined by the Biblical Commission is no concession forced on the Church by unbelieving Bible students.

C. *Voice of Internal Evidence.*—The possibility of producing a written record at the time of Moses is no longer contested. The art of writing was known long before the time of the great lawgiver, and was extensively practised both in Egypt and Babylon. As to the Israelites, Flinders Petrie infers from certain Semitic inscriptions found in 1905 on the Sinaitic peninsula, that they kept written accounts of their national history from the time of their captivity under Ramses II. The Tell-el-Amarna tablets show that the language of Babylon was in a way the official language at the time of Moses, known in Western Asia, Palestine, and Egypt; the finds of Taanek have confirmed this fact. But it cannot be inferred from this that the Egyptians and Israelites employed this sacred or official language among themselves and in their religious documents (cf. Benzinger, "Hebräische Archäologie", 2nd ed., Tübingen, 1907, p. 172 sqq.). It is not merely the possibility of writing at the time of Moses and the question of language that confronts us here; there is the further problem of the kind of written signs used in the Mosaic documents. The hieroglyphic and cuneiform signs were widely employed at that early date; the oldest inscriptions written in alphabetical characters date only from the ninth century B. C. But there can hardly be any doubt as to the higher antiquity of alphabetic writing, and there seems to be nothing to prevent our extending it back to the time of Moses. Finally, the Code of Hammurabi, discovered in Susa in 1901 by the French expedition funded by Mr. and Mrs. Dieulafoy, shows that even in pre-Mosaic times legal enactments were committed to, and preserved in, writing; for the Code antedates Moses some five centuries, and contains about 282 regulations concerning various contingencies in the civic life.

Thus far it has been shown negatively that an historic and legal document claiming to be written at the time of Moses involves no antecedent improbability of its authenticity. But the internal characteristics of the Pentateuch show also positively that the work is at least probably Mosaic. It is true that the Pentateuch contains no express declaration of its entire Mosaic authorship; but even the most exacting of critics will hardly require such testimony. It is practically lacking in all other books, whether sacred or profane. On the other hand, it has already been shown that four distinct passages of the Pentateuch are expressly ascribed to the authorship of Moses. Deut., xxxi, 24-9, is especially to be noted; for it knows that Moses wrote the "words of this law in a volume" and commanded it to be placed in the ark of the covenant as a testimony against the people who have been so rebellious during the lawgiver's life and will "do wickedly" after his death. Again, a number of legal sections, though not explicitly ascribed to the writing of Moses, are distinctly derived from Moses as the lawgiver. Besides, many of the Pentateuchal laws bear evidence of their origin in the desert; hence they too lay an indirect claim to Mosaic origin. What has been said of a number of Pentateuchal laws is equally true of several historical sections. These contain in the Book of Numbers, for instance, so many names and numbers that they must have been handed down in writing. Unless the critics can bring irrefutable evidence showing that in these sections we have only fiction, they must grant that these historical details were written down in contemporary documents, and not transmitted by mere oral tradition. Moreover, Hommel (Die altisraelitische Überlieferung in inschriftlicher Beleuchtung, p. 302) has shown that the names in the lists of the Book of Numbers bear the character of the Arabian names of the second millennium before Christ, and can have originated only in the time of Moses, though it must be admitted that the text of certain portions, e. g., Num., xiii, has suffered in its transmission. We need not remind the reader that numerous Pentateuchal laws and data imply the conditions of a nomadic life of Israel. Finally, both the author of the Pentateuch and its first readers must have been more familiar with the topography and the social conditions of Egypt and with the Sinaitic peninsula than with the land of Chanaan. Cf., e. g., Deut., viii, 7-10; xi, 10 sqq. These internal characteristics of the Pentateuch have been developed at greater length by Smith, "The Book of Moses or the Pentateuch in its Authorship, Credibility, and Civilisation", London, 1868; Vigouroux, "La Bible et les découvertes modernes", 6th ed., Paris, 1896, I, 453-80; II, 1-213, 529-47, 586-91; Idem, "Les Livres Saints et la critique rationaliste", Paris, 1902, III, 28-46, 79-99, 122-6; Heyes, "Bibel und Ægypten", Münster, 1904, p. 142; Cornely, "Introductio specialis in histor. Vet. Test. libros", I, Paris, 1887, pp. 57-60; Poole, "Ancient Egypt" in "Contemporary Review", March, 1879, pp. 757-9.

D. *Ecclesiastical Decisions.*—In accordance with the voice of the triple argument thus far advanced for the Mosaic authorship of the Pentateuch, the Biblical Commission on 27 June, 1906, answered a series of questions concerning this subject in the following way:

(1) The arguments accumulated by the critics to impugn the Mosaic authenticity of the sacred books designated by the name Pentateuch are not of such weight as to give us the right, after setting aside numerous passages of both Testaments taken collectively, the continuous consensus of the Jewish people, the constant tradition of the Church, and internal indications derived from the text itself, to maintain that these books have not Moses as their author, but are compiled from sources for the greatest part later than the Mosaic age.

(2) The Mosaic authenticity of the Pentateuch does not necessarily require such a redaction of the whole work as to render it absolutely imperative to maintain that Moses wrote all and everything with his own hand or dictated it to his secretaries; the hypothesis of those can be admitted who believe that he entrusted the composition of the work itself, conceived by him under the influence of Divine inspiration, to others, but in such a way that they were to express faithfully his own thoughts, were to write nothing against his will, were to omit nothing; and that finally the work thus produced should be approved by the same Moses, its principal and inspired author, and published under his name.

(3) It may be granted without prejudice to the Mosaic authenticity of the Pentateuch, that Moses employed sources in the production of his work, i. e., written documents or oral traditions, from which he may have drawn a number of things in accordance with the end he had in view and under the influence of Divine inspiration, and inserted them in his work either literally or according to their sense, in an abbreviated or amplified form.

(4) The substantial Mosaic authenticity and integrity of the Pentateuch remains intact if it be granted that in the long course of centuries the work has suffered several modifications, as: post-Mosaic additions either appended by an inspired author or inserted into the text as glosses and explanations; the translation of certain words and forms out of an antiquated language into the recent form of speech; finally, wrong readings due to the fault of transcribers, which one may investigate and pass sentence on according to the laws of criticism.

The post-Mosaic additions and modifications allowed by the Biblical Commission in the Pentateuch without removing it from the range of substantial integrity and Mosaic authenticity are variously interpreted by Catholic scholars. (1) We should have to understand them in a rather wide sense, if we were to defend the views of von Hummelauer or Vetter. This latter writer admits legal and historical documents based on Mosaic tradition, but written only in the times of the Judges; he places the first redaction of the Pentateuch in the time of the erection of Solomon's temple, and its last redaction in the time of Esdras. Vetter died in 1906, the year in which the Biblical Commission issued the above Decree; it is an interesting question, whether and how the scholar would have modified his theory, if time had been granted him to do so. (2) A less liberal interpretation of the Decree is implied in the Pentateuchal hypotheses advanced by Hoberg ("Moses und der Pentateuch; Die Pentateuch Frage" in "Biblische Studien", X, 4, Freiburg, 1907; "Erklärung der Genesis", 1908, Freiburg, I–L), Schöpfer (Geschichte des Alten Testamentes, 4th ed., 226 sqq.), Höpfl (Die höhere Bibelkritik, 2nd ed., Paderborn, 1906), Brucker ("L'église et la critique", Paris, 1907, 103 sqq.), and Selbst (Schuster and Holzammer's "Handbuch zur Biblischen Geschichte", 7th ed., Freiburg, 1910, II, 94, 96). The last-named writer believes that Moses left a written law-book to which Josue and Samuel added supplementary sections and regulations, while David and Solomon supplied new statutes concerning worship and priesthood, and other kings introduced certain religious reforms, until Esdras promulgated the whole law and made it the basis of Israel's restoration after the Exile. Our present Pentateuch is, therefore, an Esdrine edition of the work. Dr. Selbst feels convinced that his admission of both textual changes and material additions in the Pentateuch agrees with the law of historical development and with the results of literary criticism. Historical development adapts laws and regulations to the religious, civil, and social conditions of successive ages, while literary criticism discovers in our actual Pentateuch peculiarities of words and phrases which can hardly have been original, and also historical additions or notices, legal modifications, and signs of more recent administration of justice and of later forms of worship. But Dr. Selbst believes that these peculiarities do not offer a sufficient basis for a distinction of different sources in the Pentateuch. (3) A strict interpretation of the words of the Decree is implied in the views of Kaulen (Einleitung, n. 193 sqq.), Kley ("Die Pentateuchfrage, ihre Geschichte und ihre Systeme", Münster, 1903), Flunk (Kirchenlexicon, IX, 1782 sqq.), and Mangenot ("L'authenticité mosaïque du Pentateuque", Paris, 1907; Idem, "Dict. de la Bible", V, 50–119). With the exception of those portions that belong to the time after the death of Moses, and of certain accidental changes of the text due to transcribers, the whole of the Pentateuch is the work of Moses who composed the work in one of the ways suggested by the Biblical Commission.

Finally, there is the question as to the theological certainty of the thesis maintaining the Mosaic authenticity of the Pentateuch. (1) Certain Catholic scholars who wrote between 1887 and 1906 expressed their opinion that the thesis in question is not revealed in Scripture nor taught by the Church; that it expresses a truth not contained in Revelation, but a tenet which may be freely contested and discussed. At that time, ecclesiastical authority had issued no pronouncement on the question. (2) Other writers grant that the Mosaic authenticity of the Pentateuch is not explicitly revealed, but they consider it as a truth revealed formally implicitly, being derived from the revealed formulæ not by a syllogism in the strict sense of the word, but by a simple explanation of the terms. The denial of the Mosaic authenticity of the Pentateuch is an error, and the contradictory of the thesis maintaining the Mosaic authenticity of the Pentateuch is considered *erronea in fide* (cf. Méchineau, "L'origine mosaïque du Pentateuque", p. 34). (3) A third class of scholars considers the Mosaic authenticity of the Pentateuch neither as a freely debatable tenet, nor as a truth formally implicitly revealed; they believe it has been virtually revealed, or that it is inferred from revealed truth by truly syllogistic deduction. It is, therefore, a theologically certain truth, and its contradictory is a rash (*temeraria*) or even erroneous proposition (cf. Brucker, "Authenticité des livres de Moïse" in "Etudes", March, 1888, p. 327; *ibid.*, January, 1897, p. 122–3; Mangenot, "L'authenticité mosaïque du Pentateuque", pp. 267–310).

Whatever effect the ecclesiastical decision concerning the Mosaic authenticity of the Pentateuch may have had, or will have, on the opinion of students of the Pentateuchal question, it cannot be said to have occasioned the conservative attitude of scholars who wrote before the promulgation of the Decree. The following list contains the names of the principal recent defenders of Mosaic authenticity: Hengstenberg, "Die Bücher Moses und Aegypten", Berlin, 1841; Smith, "The Book of Moses or the Pentateuch in its Authorship, Credibility, and Civilisation", London, 1868; C. Schöbel, "Démonstration de l'authenticité du Deutéronome", Paris, 1868; Idem, "Démonstration de l'authenticité mosaïque de l'Exode", Paris, 1871; Idem, "Démonstration de l'authenticité mosaïque du Lévitique et des Nombres", Paris, 1869; Idem, "Démonstration de l'authenticité de la Genèse", Paris, 1872; Idem, "Le Moïse historique et la rédaction mosaïque du Pentateuque", Paris, 1875; Knabenbauer, "Der Pentateuch und die ungläubige Bibelkritik" in "Stimmen aus Maria-Laach", 1873, IV; Bredenkamp, "Gesetz und Propheten", Erlangen, 1881; Green, "Moses and the Prophets", New York, 1883; Idem, "The Hebrew Feasts", New York, 1885; Idem, "The Pentateuchal Question" in "Hebraica", 1889–92; Idem, "The Higher Criticism of the Pentateuch", New York, 1895; Idem, "The Unity of the Book of Genesis", New York, 1895; C. Elliot, "Vindication of the Mosaic Authorship of the Pentateuch", Cincinnati, 1884; Bissel, "The Pentateuch, its Origin and Structure", New York, 1885; Ubaldi, "Introductio in Sacram Scripturam", 2nd ed., Rome, 1882, I, 452–509; Cornely, "Introductio specialis in historicos V. T. libros", Paris, 1887, pp. 19–160; Vos, "Mosaic Origin of the Pentateuchal Codes", London, 1886; Böhl, "Zum Gesetz und zum Zeugniss", Vienna, 1883; Zahn, "Ernste Blicke in den Wahn der modernen Kritik des A. T.", Gütersloh, 1893; Idem, "Das Deuteronomium", 1890; Idem, "Israelitische und jüdische Geschichte", 1895; Rupprecht, "Die Anschauung der kritischen Schule Wellhausens vom Pentateuch", Leipzig, 1893; Idem, "Das Räthsel des Fünfbuches Mose und seine falsche Lösung", Gütersloh, 1894; Idem, "Des Räthsels Lösung oder Beiträge zur richtigen Lösung des Pentateuchräthsels", 1897; Idem, "Die Kritik nach ihrem Recht und Unrecht", 1897; "Lex Mosaica, or the Law of Moses and the Higher Criticism" (by Sayce, Rawlinson, Trench, Lias, Wace, etc.), London, 1894; Card. Meignan, "De l'Éden à Moïse", Paris, 1895, 1–88; Baxter, "Sanctuary and Sacrifice", London, 1896; Abbé de Broglie, "Questions bibliques", Paris, 1897, pp. 89–169; Pelt, "Histoire de l'A. T.", 3rd ed., Paris, 1901, I, pp. 291–326; Vigouroux, "Les Livres Saints et la critique rationaliste", Paris, 1902, III, 1–226; IV, 239–53, 405–15; Idem, "Manuel biblique", 12th ed., Paris, 1906, I, 397–478; Kley, "Die Pentateuchfrage, ihre Geschichte und ihre Systeme", Münster, 1903; Höpfl, "Die höhere Bibelkritik", Paderborn, 1902; Thomas, "The

Organic Unity of the Pentateuch", London, 1904; Wiener, "Studies in Biblical Law", London, 1904; Rouse, "The Old Testament in New Testament Light", London, 1905; Redpath, "Modern Criticism and the Book of Genesis", London, 1905; Hoberg, "Moses und der Pentateuch", Freiburg, 1905; Orr, "The Problem of the Old Testament considered with reference to Recent Criticism", London, 1906.

E. *Opponents of the Mosaic Authorship of the Pentateuch.*—A detailed account of the opposition to the Mosaic authorship of the Pentateuch is neither desirable nor necessary in this article. In itself it would form only a noisome history of human errors; each little system has had its day, and its successors have tried their best to bury it in hushed oblivion. The actual difficulties we have to consider are those advanced by our actual opponents of to-day; only the fact that the systems of the past show us the fleeting and transitory character of the actual theories now in vogue can induce us to briefly enumerate the successive views upheld by the opponents of the Mosaic authorship.

(1) *Abandoned Theories.*—The views advanced by the Valentinian Ptolemy, the Nazarites, Abenesra, Carlstadt, Isaac Peyrerius, Baruch Spinoza, Jean Leclerc are sporadic phenomena. Not all of them were wholly incompatible with the Mosaic authorship as now understood, and the others have found their answer in their own time.—With the work of John Astruc, published in 1753, began the so-called Hypothesis of Documents which was further developed by Eichhorn and Ilgen. But the works of the suspended priest, Alexander Geddes, published in 1792 and 1800, introduced the Hypothesis of Fragments, which in its day was elaborated and championed by Vater, de Wette (temporarily at least), Berthold, Hartmann, and von Bohlen. This theory was soon confronted by, and had to yield to the Hypothesis of Complements or Interpolations which numbered among its patrons Kelle, Ewald, Stähelin, Bleek, Tuch, de Wette, von Lengerke, and for a brief period also Franz Delitzsch. The theory of interpolations again had hardly found any adherents before Gramberg (1828), Stähelin (1830), and Bleek (1831) returned to the Hypothesis of Documents, proposing it in a somewhat modified form. Subsequently, Ewald, Knobel, Hupfeld, Nöldeke, and Schrader advanced each a different explanation of the documentary hypothesis. But all of these are at present only of an historical interest.

(2) *Present Hypothesis of Documents.*—A course of religious development in Israel had been proposed by Reuss in 1830 and 1834, by Vatke in 1835, and by George in the same year. In 1865–66 Graf took up this idea and applied it to the literary criticism of the Hexateuch; for the critics had begun to consider the Book of Josue as belonging to the preceding five books, so that the collection formed a Hexateuch instead of a Pentateuch. The same application was made by Merx in 1869. Thus modified the documentary theory continued in its development until it reached the state described in the translation of the Bible by Kautzsch (3rd ed., with Introduction and Annotations, Tübingen, 1908 sqq.). In itself there is nothing against the assumption of documents written by Moses; but we cannot ascribe with certainty anything of our literary remains to the hands of the Hebrew lawgiver. The beginning of written accounts must be placed towards the end of the time of Judges; only then were fulfilled the conditions which must precede the origin of a literature properly so called, i. e., a general acquaintance with the art of writing and reading, stationary settlement of the people, and national prosperity. What then are the oldest literary remains of the Hebrews? They are the collections of the songs dating from the heroic time of the nation, e. g., the Book of the Wars of the Lord (Num., xxi, 14), the Book of the Just (Jos., x, 12 sqq.), the Book of Songs (III Kings, viii, 53; cf. Budde, "Geschichte der althebr. Literatur", Leipzig, 1906, 17). The Book of the Covenant (Ex., xx, 24–xxiii, 19) too must have existed before the other sources of the Pentateuch. The oldest historical work is probably the book of the Yahwist, designated by J, and ascribed to the priesthood of Juda, belonging most probably to the ninth century B. C.

Akin to this is the Elohim document, designated by E, and written probably in the northern kingdom (Ephraim) about a century after the production of the Yahweh document. These two sources were combined by a redactor into one work soon after the middle of the sixth century. Next follows the lawbook almost entirely embodied in our actual Book of Deuteronomy, discovered in the temple 621 B. C., and containing the precipitate of the prophetic teaching which advocated the abolition of the sacrifices in the so-called high places and the centralization of worship in the temple of Jerusalem. During the Exile originated the Priestly Code, P, based on the so-called law of holiness, Lev., xvii–xxvi, and the programme of Ezechiel, xl–xlviii; the substance of P was read before the post-exilic community by Esdras about 444 B. C. (II Esd., viii–x), and was accepted by the multitude. History does not tell us when and how these divers historical and legal sources were combined into our present Pentateuch; but it is generally assumed that there was an urgent call for a compilation of the tradition and pre-exilic history of the people. The only indication of time may be found in the fact that the Samaritans accepted the Pentateuch as a sacred book probably in the fourth century B. C. Considering their hatred for the Jews, one must conclude that they would not have taken this step, unless they had felt certain of the Mosaic origin of the Pentateuch. Hence a considerable time must have intervened between the compilation of the Pentateuch and its acceptance by the Samaritans, so that the work of combining must be placed in the fifth century. It is quite generally agreed that the last redactor of the Pentateuch completed his task with great adroitness. Without altering the text of the older sources, he did all within man's power to fuse the heterogeneous elements into one apparent (?) whole, with such success that not only the Jews after the fourth century B. C., but also the Christians for many centuries could maintain their conviction that the entire Pentateuch was written by Moses.

(3) *Deficiencies of the Critical Hypothesis.*—As several Pentateuchal critics have endeavoured to assign the last redaction of the Pentateuch to more recent dates, its placement in the fifth century may be regarded as rather favourable to conservative views. But it is hard to understand why the patrons of this opinion should not agree in considering Esdras as the last editor. Again, it is quite certain that the last edition of the Pentateuch must have notably preceded its acceptance on the part of the Samaritans as a sacred book; but is it probable that the Samaritans would have accepted the Pentateuch as such in the fourth century B. C., when the national and religious opposition between them and Jews was well developed? Is it not more probable that the mixed nation of Samaria received the Pentateuch through the priest sent to them from Assyria? Cf. IV Kings, xvii, 27. Or again, as this priest instructed the Samaritan population in the law of the god of the country, is it not reasonable to suppose that he taught them the Pentateuchal law which the ten tribes carried with them when they separated from Juda? At any rate, the fact that the Samaritans accepted as sacred only the Pentateuch, but not the Prophets, leads us to infer that the Pentateuch existed among the Jews before a collection of the prophetic writings was made, and that Samaria chose its sacred book before even Juda

placed the works of the Prophets on the same level with the work of Moses. But this natural inference finds no favour among the critics; for it implies that the historical and legal traditions codified in the Pentateuch, described the beginning, and not the end, of Israel's religious development. The view of Israel's religious development prevalent among the critics implies that the Pentateuch is later than the Prophets, and that the Psalms are later than both. After these general considerations, we shall briefly examine the main principles, the methods, the results, and the arguments of the critical theory.

(a) *Principles of the Critics.*—Without pretending to review all the principles involved in the theories of the critics, we draw attention to two: the historical development of religion, and the comparative value of internal evidence and tradition.

(i) The theory of the historical evolution of Israelitic religion leads us from Mosaic Yahwehism to the ethical monotheism of the Prophets, from this to the universalist conception of God developed during the Exile, and from this again to the ossified Phariseeism of later days. This religion of the Jews is codified in our actual Pentateuch, but has been fictitiously projected backwards in the historical books into the Mosaic and pre-prophetic times.

The idea of development is not a purely modern discovery. Meyer ("Der Entwicklungsgedanke bei Aristoteles", Bonn, 1909) shows that Aristotle was acquainted with it; Gunkel ("Weiterbildung der Religion", Munich, 1905, 64) maintains that its application to religion is as old as Christianity, and that St. Paul has enunciated this principle; Diestel ("Geschichte des A. T. in der christlichen Kirche", Jena, 1869, 56 sqq.), Willmann (Geschichte des Idealismus, 2nd ed., II, 23 sqq.), and Schanz (Apologie des Christentums, 3rd ed., II, 4 sqq., 376) find the same application in the writings of the Fathers, though Hoberg ("Die Forschritte der bibl. Wissenschaften", Freiburg, 1902, 10) grants that the patristic writers often neglect the external forms which influenced the ideas of the Chosen People. The Fathers were not fully acquainted with profane history, and were more concerned about the contents of Revelation than about its historical development. Pesch ("Glaube, Dogmen und geschichtliche Thatsachen" in "Theol. Zeitfragen", IV, Freiburg, 1908, 183) discovers that St. Thomas, too, admits the principle of development in his "Summa" (II–II, Q. i, a. 9, 10; Q. ii, a. 3; etc.). But the Catholic conception of this principle avoids two extremes: (α) the theory of degeneracy, based on the teaching of the early Lutheran theologians (cf. Giesebrecht, "Die Degradationshypothese und die altl. Geschichte", Leipzig, 1905; Steude, "Entwicklung und Offenbarung", Stuttgart, 1905, 18 sqq.); (β) the theory of evolution which dissolves all truth and history into purely natural development to the exclusion of everything supernatural.

It is this latter extreme that is advocated by the Biblical critics. Their description of the early religion of Israel is contradicted by the testimony of the oldest Prophets whose authority is not questioned by them. These inspired seers know of the fall of Adam (Osee, vi, 7), the call of Abraham (Is., xxix, 23; Mich., vii, 20), the destruction of Sodom and Gomorrha (Osee, xi, 8; Is., i, 9; Amos, iv, 11), the history of Jacob and his struggle with the angel (Os., xii, 2 sqq.), Israel's exodus from Egypt and dwelling in the desert (Os., ii, 14; vii, 16; xi, 1; xii, 9, 13; xiii, 4, 5; Am., ii, 10; iii, 1; ix, 7), the activity of Moses (Os., xii, 13; Mich., vi, 4; Is., lxiii, 11, 12), a written legislation (Os., viii, 12), and a number of particular statutes (cf. Kley, "Die Pentateuchfrage", Münster, 1903, 223 sqq.). Again, the theory of development is more and more contradicted by the results of historical investigation. Weber ("Theologie und Assyriologie im Streit um Babel und Bibel", Leipzig, 1904, 17) points out that the recent historical results imply decadence rather than development in ancient oriental art, science, and religion; Winckler ("Religionsgeschichtler und geschichtl. Orient", Leipzig, 1906, 33) considers the evolutionary view of the primitive state of man as false, and believes that the development theory has, at least, been badly shaken, if not actually destroyed by recent Oriental research (cf. Bäntsch, "Altorientalischer und israelitischer Monotheismus", Tübingen, 1906). Köberle ("Die Theologie der Gegenwart", Leipzig, 1907, I, 2) says that the development theory has exhausted itself, reproducing only the thoughts of Wellhausen, and deciding particular questions not in in the light of facts, but according to the postulates of the theory. Finally, even rationalistic writers have thought it necessary to replace the development theory by another more in agreement with historical facts. Hence Winckler ("Ex Oriente lux", Leipzig, 1905–6; Idem, "Der Alte Orient", III, 2–3; Idem, "Die babylonische Geisteskultur in ihren Beziehungen zur Kulturentwicklung der Menschheit" in "Wissenschaft und Bildung", Leipzig, 1907; cf. Landersdorfer in "Historisch-Politische Blätter", 1909, 144) has originated the theory of pan-Babelism according to which Biblical religion is conceived as a conscious and express reaction against the Babylonian polytheistic state religion. It was not the common property of Israel, but of a religious sect which was supported in Babylon by certain monotheistic circles irrespective of nationality. This theory has found powerful opponents in Budde, Stade, Bezold, Köberle, Kugler, Wilke, and others; but it has also a number of adherents. Though wholly untenable from a Christian point of view, it shows at least the weakness of the historical development theory.

(ii) Another principle involved in the critical theory of the Pentateuch supposes that the internal evidence of literary criticism is of higher value than the evidence of tradition. But thus far the results of excavations and historical research have been favourable to tradition rather than to internal evidence. Let the reader only remember the case of Troy, Tiryns, Mycenæ, and Orchomenos (in Greece); the excavations of the English explorer Evans in Crete have shown the historical character of King Minos and his labyrinth; Assyrian inscriptions have re-established the historical credit of King Midas of Phrygia; similarly, Menes of Thebes and Sargon of Agade have been shown to belong to history; in general, the more accurate have been the scientific investigations, the more clearly have they shown the reliability of even the most slender traditions. In the field of New-Testament criticism the call "back to tradition" has begun to be heeded, and has been endorsed by such authorities as Harnack and Deissmann. In the study of the Old Testament too there are unmistakable signs of a coming change. Hommel ("Die altisraelitische Überlieferung in inschriftlicher Beleuchtung", Munich, 1897) maintains that Old-Testament tradition, both as a whole and in its details, proves to be reliable, even in the light of critical research. Meyer ("Die Entstehung des Judentums", Halle, 1896) comes to the conclusion that the foundations of the critical Pentateuchal theory are destroyed, if it can be proved that even part of the impugned Hebrew tradition is reliable; the same writer proves the credibility of the sources of the Books of Esdras (cf. "Grundriss der Geographie und Geschichte des alten Orientes", Munich, 1904, 167 sqq.). S. A. Fries has been led by his critical studies, and without being influenced by dogmatic bias, to accept the whole traditional view of the history of Israel. Cornill and Oettli express the conviction that Israel's traditions concerning even its earliest history are reliable and will withstand the bitterest attacks of criticism; Dawson (cf. Fonck, "Kritik und Tradition im A. T." in "Zeitschrift für katholische Theologie", 1899, 262–81) and others apply to tradition the old principle which has been so frequently misapplied, "magna est veritas, et prævalebit"; Gunkel ("Religionsgeschichtliche Volksbücher", II, Tübingen, 1906, 8) grants that Old-Testament criticism has gone a little too far, and that many Biblical traditions now rejected will be reestablished.

(b) *Critical Method.*—The falsehood of the critical method does not consist in the use of criticism as such, but in its illegitimate use. Criticism became more common in the sixteenth and seventeenth centuries; at the end of the eighteenth it was applied to classical antiquity. Bernheim ("Lehrbuch der historischen Methode", Leipzig, 1903, 296) believes that by this means alone history first became a science. In the application of criticism to the Bible we are limited, indeed, by the inspiration and the canonicity of its books; but there is an ample field left for our critical investigations (Pesch, "Theol. Zeitfragen", III, 48).

Some of the principal sins of the critics in their treatment of Sacred Scripture are the following: (i) They deny everything supernatural, so that they reject not merely inspiration and canonicity, but also prophecy and miracle a priori (cf. Metzler, "Das Wunder vor dem Forum der modernen Geschichtswissenschaft" in "Katholik", 1908, II, 241 sqq.). (ii) They seem to be convinced a priori of the credibility of non-Biblical historical documents, while they are prejudiced against the truthfulness of Biblical accounts. (Cf. Stade, "Geschichte Israel's", I, 86 seq., 88, 101.) (iii) Depreciating external evidence almost entirely, they consider the questions of the origin, the integrity, and the authenticity of the sacred books in the light of internal evidence (Encyl. Prov. Deus, 52). (iv) They overestimate the critical analysis of the sources, without considering the chief point, i. e., the credibility of the sources (Lorenz, "Die Geschichtswissenschaft in ihren Hauptrichtungen und Aufgaben", ii, 329 sqq.). Recent documents may contain reliable reports of ancient history. Some of the critics begin to acknowledge that the historical credibility of the sources is of greater importance than their division and dating (Stärk, "Die Entstehung des A. T.", Leipzig, 1905, 29; cf. Vetter, "Tübinger theologische Quartalschrift", 1899, 552). (v) The critical division of sources is based on the Hebrew text, though it is not certain how far the present Massoretic text differs from that, for instance, followed by the Septuagint translators, and how far the latter differed from the Hebrew text before its redaction in the fifth century B. C. Dahse ("Textkritische Bedenken gegen den Ausgangspunkt der heutigen Pentateuchkritik" in "Archiv für Religionsgeschichte", VI, 1903, 305 sqq.) shows that the Divine names in the Greek translation of the Pentateuch differ in about 180 cases from those of the Hebrew text (cf. Hoberg, "Die Genesis", 2nd ed., p. xxii sqq.); in other words and phrases the changes may be fewer, but it would be unreasonable to deny the existence of any. Again, it is antecedently probable that the Septuagint text differs less from the Massoretic than from the ante-Esdrine text, which must have been closer to the original. The starting point of literary criticism is therefore uncertain.

(vi) It is not an inherent fault of literary criticism that it was applied to the Pentateuch after it had become practically antiquated in the study of Homer and the Nibelungenlied (cf. Katholik, 1896, I, 303, 306 sqq.), nor that Reuss considered it as more productive of difference of opinion than of results (cf. Katholik, 1896, I, 304 seq.), nor again that Wellhausen thought it had degenerated into childish play. Among Bible students, Klostermann ("Der Pentateuch", Leipzig, 1893), König ("Falsche Extreme im Gebiete der neueren Kritik des A. T.", Leipzig, 1885; "Neueste Prinzipien der alt. Kritik", Berlin, 1902; "Im Kampfe um das A. T.", Berlin, 1903), Bugge ("Die Hauptparabeln Jesu", Giessen, 1903) are sceptical as to the results of literary criticism, while Orelli (Der Prophet Jesaja, 1904, V), Jeremias (Das alte Testament im Lichte des Alten Orients, 1906, VIII), and Oettli (Geschichte Israels, V) wish to insist more on the exegesis of the text than on the criss-cross roads of criticism. G. Jacob ("Der Pentateuch", Göttingen, 1905) thinks that the past Pentateuchal criticism needs a thorough revision; Eerdmans ("Die Komposition der Genesis", Giessen, 1908) feels convinced that criticism has been misled into wrong paths by Astruc. Merx expresses the opinion that the next generation will have to revise backwards many of the present historico-literary views of the Old Testament (Religionsgeschichtliche Volksbücher, II, 1907, 3, 132 sqq.).

(c) *Critical Results.*—Here we must distinguish between the principles of criticism and its results; the principles of the historical development of religion, for instance, and of the inferiority of tradition to internal evidence, are not the outcome of literary analysis, but are its partial basis. Again, we must distinguish between those results of literary criticism which are compatible with the Mosaic authenticity of the Pentateuch and those that contradict it. The patrons of the Mosaic authorship of the Pentateuch, and even the ecclesiastical Decree relating to this subject, plainly admit that Moses or his secretaries may have utilized sources or documents in the composition of the Pentateuch; both admit also that the sacred text has suffered in its transmission and may have received additions, in the form of either inspired appendices or exegetical glosses. If the critics, therefore, can succeed in determining the number and the limits of the documentary sources, and of the post-Mosaic additions, whether inspired or profane, they render an important service to the traditional tenet of Pentateuchal authenticity. The same must be said with regard to the successive laws established by Moses, and the gradual fidelity of the Jewish people to the Mosaic law. Here again the certain or even probable results of sane literary and historical criticism will aid greatly the conservative commentator of the Pentateuch. We do not quarrel with the legitimate conclusions of the critics, if the critics do not quarrel with each other. But they do quarrel with each other. According to Merx (*loc. cit.*) there is nothing certain in the field of criticism except its uncertainty; each critic proclaims his views with the greatest self-reliance, but without any regard to the consistency of the whole. Former views are simply killed by silence; even Reuss and Dillmann are junk-iron, and there is a noticeable lack of judgment as to what can or cannot be known.

Hence the critical results, in as far as they consist merely in the distinction of documentary sources, in the determination of post-Mosaic material, e. g., textual changes, and profane or inspired additions, in the description of various legal codes, are not at variance with the Mosaic authenticity of the Pentateuch. Nor can an anti-Mosaic character be pointed out in the facts or phenomena from which criticism legitimately infers the foregoing conclusions; such facts or phenomena are, for instance, the change of the Divine names in the text, the use of certain words, the difference of style, the so-called double accounts of really, not merely apparently, identical events; the truth or falsehood of these and similar details does not directly affect the Mosaic authorship of the Pentateuch. In which results then does criticism clash with tradition? Criticism and tradition are incompatible in their views as to the age and sequence of the documentary sources, as to the origin of the various legal codes, and as to the time and manner of the redaction of the Pentateuch.

(i) *Pentateuchal Documents.*—As to the age and sequence of the various documents, the critics do not agree. Dillmann, Kittel, König, and Winckler place the Elohist, who is subdivided by several writers into the first, second, and third Elohist, before the Yahwist, who also is divided into the first and second Yahwist; but Wellhausen and most critics believe that the Elohist is about a century younger than the Yahwist. At any rate, both are assigned to about the ninth and eighth centuries B. C.; both too incorporate earlier traditions or even documents.

All critics appear to agree as to the composite character of Deuteronomy; they admit rather a Deuteronomist school than single writers. Still, the successive layers composing the whole book are briefly designated by D^1, D^2, D^3, etc. As to the character of these layers, the critics do not agree: Montet and Driver, for instance, assign to the first Deuteronomist cc. i–xxi; Kuenen, König, Reuss, Renan, Westphal ascribe to D^1, iv, 45–9, and v–xxvi; a third class of critics reduce D^1 to xii, 1–xxvi, 19, allowing it a double edition: according to Wellhausen, the first edition contained i, 1–iv, 44; xii–xxvi; xxvii, while the second comprised iv, 45–xi, 39; xii–xxvi; xxviii–xxx; both editions were combined by the redactor who inserted Deuteronomy into the Hexateuch. Cornill arranges the two editions somewhat differently. Horst considers even cc. xii–xxvi as a compilation of pre-existing elements, gathered together without order and often by chance. Wellhausen and his adherents do not wish to assign to D^1 a higher age than 621 B. C., Cornill and Bertholet consider the document as a summary of the prophetic teaching, Colenso and Renan ascribe it to Jeremias, others place its origin in the reign of Ezechias or Manasses, Klostermann identifies the document with the book read before the people in the time of Josaphat, while Kleinert refers it back to the end of the time of the Judges. The Deuteronomist depends on the two preceding documents, J and E, both for his history and his legislation; the historical details not found in these may have been derived from other sources not known to us, and the laws not contained in the Sinaitic legislation and the decalogue are either pure fiction or a crystallization of the prophetic teaching.

Finally, the Priestly Code, P, is also a compilation: the first stratum of the book, both historical and legal in its character, is designated by P^1 or P^g; the second stratum is the law of holiness, H or Lev., xvii–xxvi, and is the work of a contemporary of Ezechiel, or perhaps of the Prophet himself (H, P^2, P^h); besides, there are additional elements springing rather from a school than from any single writer, and designated by Künen as P^3, P^4, P^5, but by other critics as P^s and P^x. Bertholet and Bäntsch speak of two other collections of laws: the law of sacrifices, Lev., i–vii, designated as P^o; and the law of purity, Lev., xi–xv, designated as P^r. The first documentary hypothesis considered P^1 as the oldest part of the Pentateuch; Duston and Dillmann place it before the Deuteronomic code, but most recent critics regard it as more recent than the other documents of the Pentateuch, and even later than Ezech., xliv, 10–xlvi, 15 (573–2 B. C.); the followers of Wellhausen date the Priestly Code after the return from the Babylonian Captivity, while Wildeboer places it either after or towards the end of the captivity. The historical parts of the Priestly Code depend on the Yahwistic and the Elohistic documents, but Wellhausen's adherents believe that the material of these documents has been manipulated so as to fit it for the special purpose of the Priestly Code; Dillmann and Driver maintain that facts have not been invented or falsified by P, but that the latter had at hand other historical documents besides J and E. As to the legal part of P, Wellhausen considers it as an a priori programme for the Jewish priesthood after the return from the captivity, projected backwards into the past, and attributed to Moses; but other critics believe that P has systematized the pre-exilic customs of worship, developing them, and adapting them to the new circumstances.

What has been said clearly shows that the critics are at variance in many respects, but they are at one in maintaining the post-Mosaic origin of the Pentateuchal documents. What is the weight of the reasons on which they base their opinion? (α) The conditions laid down by the critics as prerequisites to literature do not prove that the sources of the Pentateuch must be post-Mosaic. The Hebrew people had lived for, at least, two hundred years in Egypt; besides, most of the forty years spent in the desert were passed in the neighbourhood of Cades, so that the Israelites were no longer a nomadic people. Whatever may be said of their material prosperity, or of their proficiency in writing and reading, the above-mentioned researches of Flinders Petrie show that they kept records of their national traditions at the time of Moses. (β) If the Hebrew contemporaries of Moses kept written records, why should not the Pentateuchal sources be among these documents? It is true that in our actual Pentateuch we find non-Mosaic and post-Mosaic indications; but, then, the non-Mosaic, impersonal style may be due to a literary device, or to the pen of secretaries; the post-Mosaic geographical and historical indications may have crept into the text by way of glosses, or errors of the transcribers, or even inspired additions. The critics cannot reject these suggestions as mere subterfuges; for they should have to grant a continuous miracle in the preservation of the Pentateuchal text, if they were to deny the moral certainty of the presence of such textual changes.

(γ) But would not the Pentateuch have been known to the earlier Prophets, if it had been handed down from the time of Moses? This critical exception is really an argument *e silentio* which is very apt to be fallacious, unless it be most carefully handled. Besides, if we keep in mind the labour involved in multiplying copies of the Pentateuch, we cannot be wrong in assuming that they were very rare in the interval between Moses and the Prophets, so that few were able to read the actual text. Again, it has been pointed out that at least one of the earlier Prophets appeals to a written Mosaic law, and that all appeal to such a national conscience as presupposes the Pentateuchal history and law. Finally, some of the critics maintain that J views the history of man and of Israel according to the religious and the moral ideas of the Prophets; if there be such an agreement, why not say that the Prophets write according to the religious and moral ideas of the Pentateuch? (δ) The critics urge the fact that the Pentateuchal laws concerning the sanctuary, the sacrifices, the feasts, and the priesthood agree with different stages of post-Mosaic historical development; that the second stage agrees with the reform of Josias, and the third with the enactments enforced after the time of the Babylonian Exile. But it must be kept in mind that the Mosaic law was intended for Israel as the Christian law is intended for the whole world; if then 1900 years after Christ the greater part of the world is still un-Christian, it is not astonishing that the Mosaic law required centuries before it penetrated the whole nation. Besides, there were, no doubt, many violations of the law, just as the Ten Commandments are violated to-day without detriment to their legal promulgation. Again there were times of religious reforms and disasters as there are periods of religious fervour and coldness in the history of the Christian Church; but such human frailties do not imply the non-existence of the law, either Mosaic or Christian. As to the particular laws in question, it will be found more satisfactory to examine them more in detail.

(ii) *Pentateuchal Codes.*—The critics endeavour to establish a triple Pentateuchal code: the Book of the Covenant, Deuteronomy, and the Priestly Code. Instead of regarding this legislation as applying to different phases in the forty years' wandering in the desert, they consider it as agreeing with three historical stages in the national history. As stated above, the main objects of this triple legislation are the sanctuary, the feasts, and the priesthood.

(α) *The Sanctuary.*—At first, so the critics say, sacrifices were allowed to be offered in any place where the Lord had manifested his name (Ex., xx, 24–6); then the sanctuary was limited to the one place chosen by God (Deut., xii, 5); thirdly, the Priestly Code supposes the unity of sanctuary, and prescribes the proper religious rites to be observed. Moreover, the critics point out historical incidents showing that before the enforcement of the Deuteronomic law sacrifices were offered in various places quite distinct from the resting place of the ark. What do the defenders of the Mosaic authorship of the Pentateuch answer? First, as to the triple law, it points to three different stages in Israel's desert life: before the erection of the tabernacle at the foot of Mt. Sinai, the people were allowed to erect altars and to offer sacrifices everywhere provided the name of the Lord had been manifested; next, after the people had adored the golden calf, and the tabernacle had been erected, sacrifice could be offered only before the tabernacle, and even the cattle killed for consumption had to be slaughtered in the same place, in order to prevent a relapse into idolatry; finally, when the people were about to enter the promised land, the last law was abolished, being then quite impossible, but the unity of sanctuary was kept in the place which God would choose. Secondly, as to the historical facts urged by the critics, some of them are caused by direct Divine intervention, miracle or prophetic inspiration, and as such are fully legitimate; others are evidently violations of the law, and are not sanctioned by the inspired writers; a third class of facts may be explained in one of three ways: (α') Poels ("Le sanctuaire de Kirjath Jeraim", Louvain, 1894; "Examen critique de l'histoire du sanctuaire de l'arche", Louvain, 1897) endeavours to prove that Gabaon, Masphath, and Kiriath-Jarim denote the same place, so that the multiplicity of sanctuaries is only apparent, not real. (β') Van Hoonacker ("Le lieu du culte dans la législation rituelle des Hébreux" in "Muséeon", April–Oct., 1894, XIII, 195–204, 299–320, 533–41; XIV, 17–38) distinguishes between private and public altars; the public and national worship is legally centralized in one sanctuary and around one altar, while private altars may be had for domestic worship. (γ') But more commonly it is admitted that before God had chosen the site of national sanctuary, it was not forbidden by law to sacrifice anywhere, even away from the place of the ark. After the building of the temple the law was not considered so stringent as to bind under all circumstances. Thus far then the argument of the critics is not conclusive.

(β) *The Sacrifices.*—According to the critics, the Book of the Covenant enjoined only the offering of the first-fruits and the first-born of animals, the redemption of the first-born of men, and a free-will offering on visiting the sanctuary (Ex., xxii, 28–9; xxiii, 15, [Heb., xxiii, 19]); Deuteronomy more clearly defines some of these laws (xv, 19–23; xxvi, 1–11), and imposes the law of tithes for the benefit of the poor, the widows, the orphans, and the Levites (xxvi, 12–5); the Priestly Code distinguishes different kinds of sacrifices, determines their rites, and introduces also incense offering. But history hardly bears out this view: as there existed a permanent priesthood in Silo, and later on in Jerusalem, we may safely infer that there existed a permanent sacrifice. The earliest prophets are acquainted with an excess of care bestowed on the sacrificial rites (cf. Amos, iv, 4, 5; v, 21–2, 25; Osee, *passim*). The expressions of Jeremias (vii, 21–3) may be explained in the same sense. Sin offering was known long before the critics introduce their Priestly Code (Osee, iv, 8; Mich., vi, 7; Ps., xxxix [xl], 7; I Kings, iii, 14). Trespass offering is formally distinguished from sin offering in IV Kings, xiii, 16 (cf. I Kings, vi, 3–15; Is., liii, 10). Hence the distinction between the different kinds of sacrifice is due neither to Ezech., xlv, 22–5, nor to the Priestly Code.

(γ) *The Feasts.*—The Book of the Covenant, so the critics tell us, knows only three feasts: the seven-days' feast of the azymes in memory of the exodus from Egypt, the feast of the harvest, and that of the end of the harvest (Ex., xxiii, 14–7); Deuteronomy ordains the keeping of the feasts at the central sanctuary, adds the Pasch to the feast of the azymes, places the second feast seven weeks after the first, and calls the third, "feast of tabernacles", extending its duration to seven days (Deut., xvi, 1–17); the Priestly Code prescribes the exact ritual for five feasts, adding the feast of trumpets and of atonement, all of which must be kept at the central sanctuary. Moreover, history appears to endorse the contention of the critics: Judges, xxi, 19 knows of only one annual feast in Silo; I Kings, i, 3, 7, 21 testifies that the parents of Samuel went every year to Silo to the sanctuary; Jeroboam I established in his kingdom one annual feast similar to that celebrated in Jerusalem (III Kings, xii, 32–3); the earliest Prophets do not mention the names of the religious feasts; the Pasch is celebrated for the first time after the discovery of Deuteronomy (IV Kings, xxiii, 21–3); Ezechiel knows only three feasts and a sin offering on the first day of the first and the seventh month. But here again, the critics use the argument *e silentio* which is not conclusive in this case. The feast of atonement, for instance, is not mentioned in the Old Testament outside the Pentateuch; only Josephus refers to its celebration in the time of John Hyrcanus or Herod. Will the critics infer from this, that the feast was not kept throughout the Old Testament? History does not record facts generally known. As to the one annual feast mentioned in the early records, weighty commentators are of opinion that after the settlement of the people in the promised land, the custom was gradually introduced of going to the central sanctuary only once a year. This custom prevailed before the critics allow the existence of the Deuteronomic law (III Kings, xii, 26–31), so that the latter cannot have introduced it. Isaias (xxix, 1; xxx, 29) speaks of a cycle of feasts, but Osee, xii, 9 alludes already to the feast of tabernacles, so that its establishment cannot be due to the Priestly Code as the critics describe it. Ezechiel (xlv, 18–25) speaks only of the three feasts which had to be kept at the central sanctuary.

(δ) *The Priesthood.* The critics contend that the Book of the Covenant knows nothing of an Aaronitic priesthood (Ex., xxiv, 5); that Deuteronomy mentions priests and Levites without any hierarchical distinction and without any high priest, determines their rights, and distinguishes only between the Levite living in the country and the Levite attached to the central sanctuary; finally, that the Priestly Code represents the priesthood as a social and hierarchical institution, with legally determined duties, rights, and revenues. This theory is said to be borne out by the evidence of history. But the testimony of history points in the opposite direction. At the time of Josue and the early Judges, Eleazar and Phinees, the son and nephew of Aaron, were priests (Num., xxvi, 1; Deut., x, 6; Jos., xiv, 1 sqq.; xxii, 13, 21; xxiv, 33; Judges, xx, 28). From the end of the time of Judges to Solomon, the priesthood was in the hands of Heli and his descendants (I Kings, i, 3 sqq.; xiv, 3; xxi, 1; xxii, 1) who sprang from Ithamar the younger son of Aaron (I Par., xxiv, 3; cf. I Kings, xxii, 29; xiv, 3; ii, 7 sqq.). Solomon raised Sadoc, the son of Achitob, to the dignity of the high priesthood, and his descendants held the office down to the time of the Babylonian Captivity (II Kings, viii, 17; xv, 24 sqq.; xx, 25; III Kings, ii, 26, 27, 35; Ezech., xliv, 15); that Sadoc too was of Aaronic descent is attested by I Par., vi, 8.

Besides, the Books of Josue and Paralipomenon acknowledge the distinction between priests and Levites; according to I Kings, vi, 15, the Levites handled the ark, but the Bethsamites, the inhabitants of a priestly city (Jos., xxi, 13–6), offered sacrifice.

A similar distinction is made in II Kings, xv, 24; III Kings, viii, 3 sq.; Is., lxvi, 21. Van Hoonacker ("Les prêtres et les lévites dans le livre d'Ezéchiel" in "Revue biblique", 1899, VIII, 180–189, 192–194) shows that Ezechiel did not create the distinction between priests and Levites, but that supposing the traditional distinction in existence, he suggested a division into these classes according to merit, and not according to birth (xliv, 15–xlv, 5). Unless the critics simply set aside all this historical evidence, they must grant the existence of an Aaronitic priesthood in Israel, and its division into priests and Levites, long before the D and P codes were promulgated according to the critical theory. It is true that in a number of passages persons are said to offer sacrifice who are not of Aaronitic descent: Judges, vi, 25 sqq.; xiii, 9; I Kings, vii, 9; x, 8; xiii, 9; II Kings, vi, 17; xxiv, 25; III Kings, viii, 5, 62; etc. But in the first place, the phrase "to offer sacrifice" means either to furnish the victim (Lev., i, 2, 5) or to perform the sacrificial rite; the victim might be furnished by any devout layman; secondly, it would be hard to prove that God committed the priestly office in such a way to Aaron and his sons as not to reserve to himself the liberty of delegating in extraordinary cases a non-Aaronite to perform the priestly functions.

(iii) *Pentateuchal Redaction.*—The four documentary sources of the Pentateuch thus far described were combined not by any one individual; critics require rather three different stages of combination: first, a Yahwistic redactor R^{je} or R^j combined J and E with a view of harmonizing them, and adapting them to Deuteronomic ideas; this happened either before or after the redaction of D. Secondly, after D had been completed in the sixth century B. C., a redactor, or perhaps a school of redactors, imbued with the spirit of D combined the document with JE into JED, introducing however the modifications necessary to secure consistency. Thirdly, a last redactor R^p imbued with the letter and the spirit of P, combined this document with JED, introducing again the necessary changes. The table of nations in Gen., xiv was according to Künen added by this last redactor.

At first sight, one is struck by the complex character of this theory; as a rule, truth is of a more simple texture. Secondly, one is impressed by the unique nature of the hypothesis; antiquity has nothing to equal it. Thirdly, if one reads or studies the Pentateuch in the light of this theory, one is impressed by the whimsical character of the redactor; he often retained what should have been omitted, and omitted what should have been retained. The critics themselves have to take refuge, time and time again, in the work of the redactor, in order to save their own views of the Pentateuch. A recent writer does not hesitate to call the complex redactor *ein genialer Esel*. Fourthly, a truth-loving, straightforward reader is naturally shocked by the literary fictions and forgeries, the editorial changes and subterfuges implied in the critical theory of the Pentateuchal documents and redaction. The more moderate critics endeavour to escape this inconvenience: some appeal to the difference between the ancient and the modern standard of literary property and editorial accuracy; others practically sanctify the means by the end. Oettli considers the dilemma "either the work of Moses or the work of a deceiver" as the expression of sheer imprudence; Kautzsch unctiously points to the depth of the wisdom and the knowledge of God whose ways we cannot fathom, but must admire. The left wing of criticism openly acknowledges that there is no use in hushing up matters; it actually is the result of scientific research that both form and contents of a great part of the Old Testament are based on conscious fiction and forgery.

IV. STYLE OF THE PENTATEUCH.—In some general introductions to the Pentateuch its Messianic prophecies are specially considered, i. e., the so-called *proto-evangelium*, Gen., iii, 15; the blessing of Sem, Gen., ix, 26–7; the patriarchal promises, Gen., xii, 2; xiii, 16; xv, 5; xvii, 4–6, 16; xviii, 10–15; xxii, 17; xxvi, 4; xxviii, 14; the blessing of the dying Jacob, Gen., xlix, 8–10; the Prophecy of Balaam, Num., xxiv, 15 sqq.; and the great Prophet announced by Moses, Deut., xviii, 15–19. But these prophecies belong rather to the province of exegesis than introduction. Again, the text of the Pentateuch has been considered in some general introductions to the work. We have seen already that besides the Massoretic Text we have to take into account the earlier text followed by the Septuagint translators, and the still earlier readings of the Samaritan Pentateuch; a detailed investigation of this subject belongs to the field of textual or lower criticism. But the style of the Pentateuch can hardly be referred to any other department of Pentateuchal study.

As Moses employed no doubt pre-existent documents in the composition of his work, and as he must have made use too of the aid of secretaries, we expect antecedently a variety of style in the Pentateuch. It is no doubt due to the presence of this literary phenomenon that the critics have found so many points of support in their minute analysis. But in general, the style of the work is in keeping with its contents. There are three kinds of material in the Pentateuch: first, there are statistics, genealogies, and legal formularies; secondly, there are narrative portions; thirdly, there are parenetic sections.

No reader will find fault with the writer's dry and simple style in his genealogical and ethnographic lists, in his table of encampments in the desert, or his legal enactments. Any other literary expression would be out of place in records of this kind. The narrative style of the Pentateuch is simple and natural, but also lively and picturesque. It abounds in simple character sketches, dialogues, and anecdotes. The accounts of Abraham's purchase of a burying-ground, of the history of Joseph, and of the Egyptian plagues are almost dramatic. Deuteronomy has its peculiar style on account of the exhortations it contains. Moses explains the laws he promulgates, but urges also, and mainly, their practice. As an orator, he shows a great deal of unction and persuasiveness, but is not destitute of the earnestness of the Prophets. His long sentences remain at times incomplete, thus giving rise to so-called anacolutha (cf. Dt., vi, 10–12; viii, 11–17; ix, 9–11; xi, 2–7; xxiv, 1–4). Being necessarily a popular preacher, he is not lacking in repetitions. But his earnestness, persuasiveness, and unction do not interfere with the clearness of his statements. He is not merely a rigid legislator, but he shows his love for the people, and in turn wins their love and confidence.

Many works referring to the Pentateuch have been cited throughout the course of this article. We shall here add a list of mainly exegetical works, both ancient and modern, without attempting to give a complete catalogue.
PATRISTIC WRITERS.—*Eastern Church:*—ORIGEN, *Selecta in Gen.*, P. G., XII, 91–145; IDEM, *Homil. in Gen.*, *ibid.*, 145–62; IDEM, *Selecta et homil. in Ex., Lev., Num., Deut.*, *ibid.*, 263–818; IDEM, *Fragmenta* in P. G., XVII, 11–36; ST. BASIL, *Homil. in Hexaëmer.* in P. G., XXIX, 3–208; ST. GREGORY OF NYSSA, *In Hexaëmer.* in P. G., XLIV, 61–124; IDEM, *De homin. opific.*, *ibid.*, 124–297; IDEM, *De vita Moysis*, *ibid.*, 297–430; ST. JOHN CHRYS., *Homil. in Gen.* in P. G., LIII, LIV, 23–580; IDEM, *Serm. in Gen.* in P. G., LIV, 581–630; ST. EPHR., *Comment. in Pentat.* in *Oper. syr.*, I, 1–115; ST. CYRIL OF ALEX., *De adoratione in spiritu* in P. G., LXVIII, 133–1125; *Glaphyra* in P. G., LXIX, 13–677; THEODORETUS, *Quæst. in Gen., Ex., Lev., Num., Deut.* in P. G., LXXX, 76–456; PROCOPIUS OF GAZA, *Comment. in Octateuch.* in P. G., LXXXVII, 21–992; NICEPHORUS, *Catena in Octateuch. et libros Reg.* (Leipzig, 1772).
Western Church:—ST. AMBROSE, *In Hexaëmer.* in P. L., XIV, 123–274; IDEM, *De Paradiso terrestri*, *ibid.*, 275–314; IDEM, *De Cain et Abel*, *ibid.*, 315–60; IDEM, *De Noe et arca*, *ibid.*, 361–416;

IDEM, *De Abraham*, ibid., 419–500; IDEM, *De Isaac et anima*, ibid., 501–34; IDEM, *De Joseph patriarcha*, ibid., 641–72; IDEM, *De benedictionibus patriarcharum*, ibid., 673–94; ST. JEROME, *Liber quæst. hebraic.* in Gen. in P. L., XXIII, 935–1010; ST. AUGUSTINE, *De Gen. c. Manich. ll. duo* in P. L., XXXIV, 173–220; IDEM, *De Ger. ad lit.*, ibid., 219–46; IDEM, *De Gen. ad lit. ll. duodecim*, ibid., 245–486; IDEM, *Quæst. in Heptateuch.*, ibid., 547–776; RUFINUS, *De benedictionibus patriarcharum* in P. L., XXI, 295–336; ST. VEN. BEDE, *Hexaëmeron* in P. L., XCI, 9–190; IDEM, *In Pentateuch. commentarii*, ibid., 189–394; IDEM, *De tabernaculo et vasibus ejus*, ibid., 393–498; RHABANUS MAURUS, *Comm. in Gen.* in P. L., CVII, 443–670; IDEM, *Comment. in Ex., Lev., Num., Deut.* in P. L., CVIII, 9–998; WALAFRID STRABO, *Glossa ordinaria* in P. L., CXIII, 67–506.

MIDDLE AGES:—ST. BRUNO OF ASTI, *Expositio in Pentateuch.* in P. L., CLXIV, 147–550; RUPERT OF DEUTZ, *De SS. Trinitate et operib. ejus* in P. L., CLXVII, 197–1000; HUGH OF ST. VICTOR, *Adnotationes elucidatoriæ in Pent.* in P. L., CLXXV, 29–86; HONORIUS OF AUTUN, *Hexaëmeron* in P. L., CLXXII, 253–66; IDEM, *De decem plagis Ægypti*, ibid., 265–70; ABELARD, *Expositio in Hexæmeron* in P. L., CLXXVIII, 731–84; HUGH OF ST. CHER, *Postilla* (Venice, 1588); NICOLAUS OF LYRA, *Postilla* (Rome, 1471); TOSTATUS, *Opera*, I–IV (Venice, 1728); DIONYSIUS THE CARTHUSIAN, *Comment. in Pentateuch.* in *Opera omnia*, I, II (Montreuil, 1896–7).

MORE RECENT WORKS.—*Jewish Writers:*—The *Commentaries* of RASHI (1040–1150), ABENESRA (1092–1167), and DAVID KIMCHI (1160–1235) are contained in the *Rabbinic Bibles;* ABARBANEL, *Comment.* (Venice, 5539 A. M.; 1579 B. C.); CAHEN, French tr. of *Pent.* (Paris, 1831); KALISCH, *Historical and Critical Comment on the Old Test.* (London), *Gen.* (1855); *Lev.* (1867, 1872); *Ex.* (1855); HIRSCH, *Der Pent. übersetzt und erklärt* (2nd ed., Frankfurt, 1893, 1895); HOFFMANN, *Das Buch Lev. übersetzt und erklärt* (Berlin, 1906).

Protestant Writers:—The works of LUTHER, MELANCHTHON, CALVIN, GERHART, CALOVIUS, DRUSIUS, DE DIEU, CAPPEL, COCCEIUS, MICHAELIS, LE CLERC, ROSENMÜLLER, and even of TUCH and BAUMGARTEN, are of minor importance in our days; KNOBEL, *Gen.* (6th ed., by DILLMANN, 1892; tr., Edinburgh, 1897); RYSSEL, *Ex. and Lev.* (3rd ed., 1897); DILLMANN, *Numbers, Deut., Jos.* (2nd ed., 1886); LANGE, *Theologisch-homiletisches Bibelwerk* (Bielefeld and Leipzig): IDEM, *Gen.* (2nd ed., 1877); IDEM, *Ex., Lev., and Numbers* (1874); STOSCH, *Deut.* (2nd ed., 1902); KEIL AND FRANZ DELITZSCH, *Biblischer Comment. über das A. T.:* KEIL, *Gen. and Ex.* (3rd ed., Leipzig, 1878); IDEM, *Lev., Numbers, Deut.* (2nd ed., 1870; tr., Edinburgh, 1881, 1885); STRACK AND ZÖCKLER, *Kurzgefasster Komment. zu den h. Schriften A. und N. T.* (Munich): STRACK, *Gen.* (2nd ed., 1905); IDEM, *Ex., Lev., Numbers* (1894); OETTLI, *Deut.* (1893); NOWACK, *Handkomment. zum A. T.* (Göttingen): GUNKEL, *Gen.* (1901); BÄNTSCH, *Ex., Lev., Numbers* (1903); *Deut.* by STEUERNAGEL (1900); MARTI, *Kurzer Handkommentar z. A. T.* (Freiburg): HOLZINGER, *Gen.* (1898), *Ex.* (1900), *Numbers* (1903); BERTHOLET, *Lev.* (1901), *Deut.* (1899); BÖHMER, *Das erste Buch Mose* (Stuttgart, 1905); COOK, *The Holy Bible according to the Authorised Version*, I–II (London, 1877); SPENCE AND EXELL, *The Pulpit Commentary* (London): WHITELAW, *Gen.;* RAWLINSON, *Ex.;* MEYRICK, *Lev.;* WINTERBOTHAM, *Numbers;* ALEXANDER, *Deut.;* *The Expositor's Bible* (London): DODS, *Gen.* (1887); CHADWICK, *Exod.* (1890); KELLOGG, *Lev.* (1891); WATSON, *Numbers* (1889); HARPER, *Deut.* (1895); *The International Critical Commentary* (Edinburgh): GRAY, *Numbers* (1903); DRIVER, *Deut.* (1895); SPURRELL, *Notes on the Hebrew Text of Gen.* (2nd ed., Oxford, 1896); GINSBURG, *The Third Book of Moses* (London, 1884); DRIVER, *The Book of Gen.* (London, 1904); MACLAREN, *The Books of Ex., Lev., and Numbers* (London, 1906); IDEM, *Deut.* (London, 1906); REUSS, *L'histoire sainte et la loi* (Paris, 1879); KUENEN, HOSYKAAS, AND OORT, *Het Oude Testament* (Leyden, 1900–1).

Catholic Works:—The works of CAJETAN, OLEASTER, STEUCHUS EUGUBINUS, SANTE PAGNINO, LIPPOMANNUS, HAMMER, B. PEREIRA, ASORIUS MARTINENGUS, LORINUS, TIRINIUS, A LAPIDE, CORN. JANSENIUS, BONFRÈRE, FRASSEN, CALMET, BRENTANO, DERESER, and SCHOLZ are either too well known or too unimportant to need further notice. *La Sainte Bible* (Paris): CRELIER, *La Genèse* (1889); IDEM, *l'Exode et le Lévitique* (1886); TROCHON, *Les Nombres et le Deutéronome* (1887–8); *Cursus Scripturæ Sacræ* (Paris): VON HUMMELAUER, *Gen.* (1895); *Ex., Lev.* (1897); *Num.* (1899); *Deut.* (1901); SCHRANK, *Comment. literal. in Gen.* (1835); LAMY, *Comment in l. Gen.* (Mechlin, 1883–4); TAPPEHORN, *Erklärung der Gen.* (Paderborn, 1888); HOBERG, *Die Gen. nach dem Literalsinn erklärt* (Freiburg, 1899); FILLION, *La Sainte Bible*, I (Paris, 1888); NETELER, *Das Buch Genesis der Vulgata und des hebräischen Textes übersetzt und erklärt* (Münster, 1905); GIGOT, *Special Introduction to the Study of the Old Testament*, I (New York, 1901).

A. J. MAAS.

Pentecost. See WHITSUNDAY.

Pentecost (OF THE JEWS), FEAST OF, the second in importance of the great Jewish feasts. The term, adopted from the Greek-speaking Jews (Tob., ii, 1; II Mac., xii, 32; Joseph., "Ant.", III, x, 6; etc.) alludes to the fact that the feast, known in the Old Testament as "the feast of harvest of the firstfruits" (Exod., xxiii, 16), "the feast of weeks" (Exod., xxxiv, 22; Deut., xvi, 10; II Par., viii, 13), the "day of firstfruits" (Num., xxviii, 26), and called by later Jews 'asereth or 'asartha (solemn assembly, and probably "closing festival", Pentecost being the closing festival of the harvest and of the Paschal season), fell on the fiftieth day from "the next day after the sabbath" of the Passover (Lev., xxiii, 11). The interpretation of this passage was early disputed and at the time of Jesus Christ two opinions touching the exact day of the feast were held. Most doctors (and the bulk of the people) understood (on the force of Lev., xxiii, 7) the sabbath spoken of in verse 11 to be the first day of the unleavened bread, Nisan 15; whereas the Sadducees (later also the Karaites) held that the weekly sabbath falling during the Passover festivities was meant (Talmud, Treat. Menach., x, 1–3; Chagiga, ii, 4). Which opinion is more in accordance with the natural meaning of the passage, we shall leave undecided; the dissent is long since over, all Jews celebrating the Pentecost on the fiftieth day after Nisan 16. As the offering of a sheaf of barley marked the beginning of the harvest season, so the offering of loaves made from the new wheat marked its completion. This is no proof that Pentecost was originally a mere nature-festival; but it shows that the Mosaic legislation had in view an agricultural population, to whose special needs and disposition it was perfectly adapted. Since the close of Biblical times, an entirely new significance, never so much as hinted at in Scripture, has been attached by the Jews to the feast: the Pentecost is held to commemorate the giving of the Law on Mount Sinai, which, according to Exod., xix, 1, took place on the fiftieth day after the departure from Egypt. This view, admitted by several Fathers of the Church (St. Jer., "Epist.", lxxviii, 12, P. L., XXII, 707; St. August., "Cont. Faust", xxxii, 12, P. L., XLII, 503; St. Leo, "De Pent. Serm.", I, P. L., LIV, 400), has passed into some modern Jewish liturgical books, where the feast is described as "the day of the giving of the Law" (Maimon. More Neb., iii, 41).

In accordance with this interpretation, modern Jews pass the eve in reading the Law and other appropriate Scriptures. Among them the feast lasts two days, a tradition dating from the difficulty which the Jews of the Diaspora found in ascertaining exactly what day the month begins in Palestine (Talmud, Treat. Pesach., lii, 1; Rosh hashsh., v, 1). On the day of Pentecost no servile work was allowed (Lev., xxiii, 21). The oblation consisted of two loaves of leavened bread made from two-tenths of an ephah (about seven quarts and a fifth) of flour from the new wheat (Lev., xxiii, 17; Exod., xxxiv, 22). The leavened bread could not be placed on the altar (Lev., ii, 11), and was merely waved (D.-V., "lifted"; see OFFERINGS); one loaf was given to the High Priest, the other was divided among the priests who ate it within the sacred precincts. Two yearling lambs were also offered as a peace-offering, and a buck-goat for sin, together with a holocaust of seven lambs without blemish, one calf, and two rams (Lev., xxiii, 18–19). According to Num., xxviii, 26–31, the number of victims to be offered in holocaust on that day differs from the above. The Jews of later times regarded the two enactments as supplementary (Jos., "Ant.", III, X, 6; Talmud, Treat. Menach., iv, 2, 5). The feast was an occasion for social and joyful gatherings (Deut., xvi, 11) and we may infer from the New Testament that it was, like the Passover, attended at Jerusalem by a great home-coming of the Jews from all parts of the world (Act., ii, 5–11).

GREEN, *The Hebrew Feasts* (1886); BÄHR, *Symbolik des Mosaischen Cultus* (Heidelberg, 1839); BENZINGER, *Hebräische Archäologie* (Freiburg, 1894); HITZIG, *Ostern und Pfingsten* (1838); SCHEGG, *Biblische Archäologie* (Freiburg, 1887); SCHÜRER, *Gesch. des Jüdischen Volkes im Zeitalter J. C.* (Leipzig, 1886–90); WELLHAUSEN, *Prolegomena zur Gesch. Israels* (Berlin, 1895); WOGUE, *Catéchisme* (Paris, 1872); IKEN, *Antiquitates Hebraicæ* (Bremen, 1741); RELAND, *Antiquitates Sacræ* (Utrecht, 1741).

CHARLES L. SOUVAY.

Peoria, DIOCESE OF (PEORIENSIS), comprises that part of central Illinois south of the Counties of Whiteside, Lee, Dekalb, Grundy, Kankakee, and north of the Counties of Adams, Brown, Cass, Menard, Sangamon, Nacon, Moultrie, Douglas, and Edgar. It was cut off from the Diocese of Chicago in 1875. Six years later it was enlarged by the addition of Lasalle, Bureau, Henry, Putnam, and Rock Island Counties. Catholicism in this region dates from the days of Father Marquette, who rested at the Indian village of Peoria on his voyage up the Illinois River in 1673. Opposite the present site of the episcopal city, La Salle and Tonti in 1680 built Fort Crèvecœur, in which Mass was celebrated and the Gospel preached by the Recollect Fathers, Gabriel Ribourdi, Zenobius Membre, and Louis Hennepin. With some breaks in the succession, the line of missionaries extends to within a short period of the founding of modern Peoria. In 1839 Father Reho, an Italian, visited Peoria, remaining long enough to build the old stone church in Kickapoo, a small town twelve miles distant. St. Mary's, the first Catholic church in the city proper, was erected by Father John A. Drew in 1846. Among his successors was the poet, Rev. Abram J. Ryan.

Many of the early Irish immigrants came to work on the Illinois and Michigan canal; owing to the failure of the contracting company, they received their pay in land scrip instead of cash, and were thus forced to settle upon hitherto untilled farm-land. These Irish farmers, with the Germans who began to arrive a little later, were the pioneer Catholics whose descendants now constitute the strength of the Church. In more recent years Poles, Slavonians, Slovenians, Croatians, Lithuanians, and Italians have come in considerable numbers to work in the coal mines. They are organized in parishes looked after by priests of their own nationality. The first appointee to the see, Rev. Michael Hurley, requested to be spared the responsibility of organizing and governing the new diocese. After many years of fruitful labour in Peoria, he died, vicar-general in 1898, and was mourned universally in the city and throughout the diocese.

Rt. Rev. John Lancaster Spalding was consecrated first Bishop of Peoria, 1 May, 1877. Born of the distinguished Spalding family, in Lebanon, Kentucky, in 1840, and educated at Bardstown, Mount St. Mary's, Emmittsburg, Louvain, and Rome, his career as pastor in Louisville, Kentucky, as orator, and as author had been marked by signal successes. The promise of his earlier life was more than fulfilled by the long years of his episcopate. Besides creating a new spirit in the Catholic life of the diocese, which found expression in new churches, schools, and institutions of education and charity, he sought fields of larger efforts for his zeal. He laboured earnestly in the cause of Catholic colonization in the West. He preached the truths of life to an ever-increasing and deeply appreciative audience of American people. He ranks high among the educators of the country. The Catholic University of America owes its origin largely to his zeal. Spalding Institute, Peoria, a Catholic school for boys, built and equipped by his generosity, is another monument to his abiding faith in education. His writings are assured of permanent use and admiration by future generations. At the height of his usefulness he was stricken with paralysis on 6 Jan., 1905, and resigned the see, 11 Sept., 1908, residing in Peoria as Archbishop of Scitopolis, to which honour he was raised in 1909.

Right Reverend Edmund M. Dunne, D.D., the second and present Bishop of Peoria, was born at Chicago, 2 Feb., 1864. He began his classical studies at St. Ignatius's College, Chicago, and finished at the Petit Seminaire at Floreffe, Belgium. Completing his theological course at Louvain, he was ordained priest, 24 June, 1887. Later studies in Rome prepared him for the doctor's degree, which was conferred by the Gregorian University in 1890. Eight years of parish work in St. Columbkill's church, Chicago, led to his appointment as pastor of Guardian Angels' Parish. His ministrations among the poor Italians of Chicago were remarkably successful. It was with profound regret that they saw him removed to the chancellorship of the archdiocese, after seven years of unselfish labour. He was consecrated Bishop of Peoria, 1 Sept., 1909.

Statistics: Bishops, 2; mitred abbot, 1; secular priests, 169; regular priests, 43; churches with resident priests, 151; churches, mission, 69; stations, 19; ecclesiastical students, 14; colleges for boys, 4; students, 355; academies for girls, 8; students, 1457; parishes with parochial schools, 69; pupils, 10,672; orphan asylums, 1; orphans, 75; industrial and reform schools, 1; total young people under Catholic control, 12,559; hospitals, 12; homes for the aged, 2; marriages, 1037; baptisms, 4527; burials, 1487; Catholic population, 96,000; number of square miles in diocese, 18,554.

Jas. J. Shannon.

Peoria Indians, a principal tribe of the confederated Illinois Indians (q. v.) having their chief residence, in the seventeenth century, on Illinois river, upon the lake, and about the site of the modern city that bears their name. The first white man ever known to the Illinois was probably the Jesuit Claude Allouez, who met some of them as visitors at his mission on Lake Superior at La Pointe (Bayfield), Wisconsin, in 1667. Six years later Marquette passed through their country, where he soon established a temporary mission. In 1680 the French commander, La Salle, built Fort Crèvecœur on Peoria lake, near the village of the tribe, about the present Rockfort. It was abandoned, but reoccupied in 1684, when a regular mission was begun among the Peoria by Fr. Allouez. His successor in 1687 was Fr. Jacques Gravier, to whom we owe the great manuscript "Dictionary of the Peoria Language", now at Harvard University, the principal literary monument of the extinct Illinois. The Peoria, however, proved obstinate in their old beliefs, and in 1705, at the instigation of the medicine men, Gravier was attacked and dangerously wounded. He narrowly escaped with his life, but died from the effects on 12 Feb., 1708, near Mobile, after having vainly sought a cure in France. The mission continued under other workers, but so late as 1721 the tribe was still almost entirely heathen, although the majority of the Illinois were then Christian. The Peoria shared in the vicissitudes and rapid decline of the Illinois, and in 1832 the remnant of the confederated tribes, hardly 300 souls in all, sold all their claims in Illinois and Missouri and removed to a small reservation on the Osage River, Kansas. In 1854 the remnant of the Wea and Piankishaw of Indiana were consolidated with them, and in 1868 the entire body removed to a tract in north-east Oklahoma, where they now reside, being officially designated as "Peoria and confederated tribes", and numbering altogether only about 200 souls, all mixed-bloods, and divided between Catholic and Methodist. (See also Miami Indians.)

Thwaites (ed.), *The Jesuit Relations* (*Illinois missions*) (73 vols., Cleveland, 1896-1901); Shea, *Catholic Missions* (New York, 1854); Pilling, *Bibliography of the Algonquian Languages* (Washington, 1891); Royce and Thomas, *Indian Land Cessions, Eighteenth Rept. Bur. Am. Eth.*, II (Washington, 1899).

James Mooney.

Pepin the Short, Mayor of the Palace of the whole Frankish kingdom (both Austrasia and Neustria), and later King of the Franks; b. 714; d. at St. Denis, 24 Sept., 768. He was the son of Charles Martel. Pepin and his older brother Carloman were taught by the monks of St. Denis, and the impressions received during their monastic education had a controlling influence upon the relations of both princes to the Church. When the father died in 741 the two brothers began to reign jointly but not without strong opposition, for Griffon, the son of Charles Martel and the Bavarian Sonnichilde, demanded a share in the government. Moreover, the Duke of the Aquitanians and the Duke of the Alamannians thought this a favourable opportunity to throw off the Frankish supremacy. The young kings were repeatedly involved in war, but all their opponents, including the Bavarians and Saxons, were defeated and the unity of the kingdom re-established. As early as 741 Carloman had entered upon his epoch-making relations with St. Boniface, to whom was now opened a new field of labour, the reformation of the Frankish Church. On 21 April, 742, Boniface was present at a Frankish synod presided over by Carloman at which important reforms were decreed. As in the Frankish realm the unity of the kingdom was essentially connected with the person of the king, Carloman to secure this unity raised the Merovingian Childeric to the throne (743). In 747 he resolved to enter a monastery. The danger, which up to this time had threatened the unity of the kingdom from the division of power between the two brothers, was removed, and at the same time the way was prepared for deposing the last Merovingian and for the crowning of Pepin. The latter put down the renewed revolt led by his step-brother Griffon and succeeded in completely restoring the boundaries of the kingdom. Pepin now addressed to the pope the suggestive question: In regard to the kings of the Franks who no longer possess the royal power, is this state of things proper? Hard pressed by the Lombards, Pope Zacharias welcomed this advance of the Franks which aimed at ending an intolerable condition of things, and at laying the constitutional foundations for the exercise of the royal power. The pope replied that such a state of things was not proper. After this decision the place Pepin desired to occupy was declared vacant. The crown was given him not by the pope but by the Franks. According to ancient custom Pepin was then elected king by the nation at Soissons in 751, and soon after this was anointed by Boniface. This consecration of the new kingdom by the head of the Church was intended to remove any doubt as to its legitimacy. On the contrary, the consciousness of having saved the Christian world from the Saracens produced, among the Franks, the feeling that their kingdom owed its authority directly to God. Still this external co-operation of the pope in the transfer of the kingdom to the Carolingians would necessarily enhance the importance of the Church. The relations between the two controlling powers of Christendom now rapidly developed. It was soon evident to what extent the alliance between Church and State was to check the decline of ecclesiastical and civil life; it made possible the conversion of the still heathen German tribes, and when that was accomplished provided an opportunity for both Church and State to recruit strength and to grow.

Ecclesiastical, political, and economic developments had made the popes lords of the *ducatus Romanus*. They laid before Pepin their claims to the central provinces of Italy, which had belonged to them before Liutprand's conquest. When Stephen II had a conference with King Pepin at Ponthion in January, 754, the pope implored his assistance against his oppressor the Lombard King Aistulf, and begged for the same protection for the prerogatives of St. Peter which the Byzantine exarchs had extended to them, to which the king agreed, and in the charter establishing the States of the Church, soon after given at Quiercy, he promised to restore these prerogatives. The Frankish king received the title of the former representative of the Byzantine Empire in Italy, i. e. "Patricius", and was also assigned the duty of protecting the privileges of the Holy See.

When Stephen II performed the ceremony of anointing Pepin and his son at St. Denis, it was St. Peter who was regarded as the mystical giver of the secular power, but the emphasis thus laid upon the religious character of political law left vague the legal relations between pope and king. After the acknowledgement of his territorial claims the pope was in reality a ruling sovereign, but he had placed himself under the protection of the Frankish ruler and had sworn that he and his people would be true to the king. Thus his sovereignty was limited from the very start as regards what was external to his domain. The connexion between Rome and the Frankish kingdom involved Pepin during the years 754–56 in war with the Lombard King Aistulf, who was forced to return to the Church the territory he had illegally held. Pepin's commanding position in the world of his time was permanently secured when he took Septimania from the Arabs. Another particularly important act was his renewed overthrow of the rebellion in Aquitaine which was once more made a part of the kingdom. He was not so fortunate in his campaigns against the Saxons and Bavarians. He could do no more than repeatedly attempt to protect the boundaries of the kingdom against the incessantly restless Saxons. Bavaria remained an entirely independent State and advanced in civilization under Duke Tassilo. Pepin's activity in war was accompanied by a widely extended activity in the internal affairs of the Frankish kingdom, his main object being the reform of legislation and internal affairs, especially of ecclesiastical conditions. He continued the ecclesiastical reforms commenced by St. Boniface. In doing this Pepin demanded an unlimited authority over the Church. He himself wished to be the leader of the reforms. However, although St. Boniface changed nothing by his reformatory labours in the ecclesiastico-political relations that had developed in the Frankish kingdom upon the basis of the Germanic conception of the State, nevertheless he had placed the purified and unified Frankish Church more definitely under the control of the papal see than had hitherto been the case. From the time of St. Boniface the Church was more generally acknowledged by the Franks to be the mystical power appointed by God. When he deposed the last of the Merovingians Pepin was also obliged to acknowledge the increased authority of the Church by calling upon it for moral support. Consequently the ecclesiastical supremacy of the Frankish king over the Church of his country remained externally undiminished. Nevertheless by his life-work Pepin had powerfully aided the authority of the Church and with it the conception of ecclesiastical unity. He was buried at St. Denis where he died. He preserved the empire created by Clovis from the destruction that menaced it; he was able to overcome the great danger arising from social conditions that threatened the Frankish kingdom, by opposing to the unruly lay nobility the ecclesiastical aristocracy that had been strengthened by the general reform. When he died the means had been created by which his greater son could solve the problems of the empire. Pepin's policy marked out the tasks to which Charlemagne devoted himself: quieting the Saxons, the subjection of the duchies, and lastly the regulation of the ecclesiastical question and with it that of Italy.

HAHN, *Jahrbücher des fränkischen Reiches 741–752* (Berlin, 1863); OELSNER, *Jahrbücher des fränkischen Reiches unter König Pippin* (Leipzig, 1871); MÜHLBACHER, *Deutsche Geschichte unter der Karolingern* (Stuttgart, 1896); PARIS, *La légende de Pépin le Bref* in *Mélanges* (Havre, 1895); KAMPERS, *Karl der Grosse* (Mainz, 1910).—Of the large bibliography concerning the question of the Donation of Pepin may be mentioned: SCHEFFER-BOICHORST, *Pepins und Karls d. Gr. Schenkungsversprechen* in *Mitteilungen des Osterr. Instituts für Geschichtsforschung*, V; MARTENS, *Die drei unächten Kapitel der Vita Hadrians I* in *Theolog. Quartalschrift*, LXVIII; SCHNÜRER, *Die Entstehung des Kirchenstaats* (Cologne, 1894); MARTENS, *Beleuchtung der neuerten Kontroversen über die römische Frage unter Pippin und Karl d. Gr.* (Münster, 1898); CRIVELLUCCI, *Delle Origini dello Stato Pontificio* in *Studi storici*, X, XI, XII.

FRANZ KAMPERS.

Pepuzians. See MONTANISTS.

Peratæ. See GNOSTICISM.

Percy, JOHN (*alias* JOHN FISHER), b. at Holmeside, Durham, 27 Sep., 1569; d. at London, 3 Dec., 1641. Converted when only fourteen years, he went first to Reims, in 1586, then to the English College, Rome, 1589–94. Returning to Belgium, he entered the Jesuit novitiate, 2 May, 1594, and then set out for England in 1596. He was, however, arrested by the Dutch, tortured, and sent prisoner to London. He managed to escape, and became the companion of Father Gerard in several adventures. He was seized at Harrowden (November, 1605) at the time of the Gunpowder Plot, but was eventually banished at the request of the Spanish ambassador (1606). Retiring to Belgium he was for a time head of the English Jesuits, then professor of Scripture at Louvain, after which he returned again to England, and was again imprisoned and condemned to death (1610). He had already begun to write on current controversies, and when James I desired a series of disputations in 1622, Percy, who was then in a prison in London, was required to defend the Catholic side. In these disputations King James himself and Laud took a leading part. As a result of these disputations, Mary Countess of Buckingham, and Chillingworth became converts to the Church. These controversies were afterwards printed and discussed by Percy and Floyd on the Catholic side, and by Laud, Francis White, John White, Featley, and Wotton on the Protestant. Percy was eventually released in 1625 and ordered to banishment in 1635, but he was suffered to remain in London till his death.

FOLEY, *Records of the English Province S. J.* (London, 1877); SOMMERVOGEL, *Bibliothèque de la C. de J.* (Paris, 1892); LAUD, *Conference with Fisher the Jesuit* (London, 1901).

J. H. POLLEN.

Peregrine Latiosi, SAINT. See SERVITE ORDER.

Peregrinus.—The canons of Priscillian, prefixed to the Epistles of St. Paul in many (chiefly Spanish) MSS., are preceded by an introduction headed "Prœmium sancti Peregrini episcopi in epistolas Pauli Apostoli", in which it is explained that the canons were not written by St. Jerome but by Priscillian, and that they are given in an expurgated edition. The prologue of Priscillian himself to his canons follows; it shows none of the characteristics of style found in the tractates of Priscillian; it has presumably been rewritten by Peregrinus, if the tractates are genuine.

The Codex Gothicus of the cathedral of Leon contains a prayer, and the words "et Peregrini f. o karissimi memento". The preface of St. Jerome to his lost translation of the Books of Solomon from the Septuagint occurs in some MSS. after his preface to his translation of those books from the Hebrew; in most of these MSS. (Spanish, or under Spanish influence) a note is appended explaining that both prefaces are given because, to the Vulgate text which follows, there have been added in the margin the additions found in the Septuagint; then come the words "et idcirco qui legis semper Peregrini memento". The Stowe codex of St. John also has a subscription, in which the writer describes himself as "Sonid Peregrinus". Sonid is said to be Celtic for a warrior; it reminds us of "Vincentius", and St. Vincent of Lerins in fact wrote his Commonitorium under the pseudonym of Peregrinus. But he cannnot be identified with the Spanish Peregrinus, as he was not a bishop. The latter has been identified by Schepss, Berger, Fritsche, and Künstle with Bachiarius, a Spaniard who left his country, and is fond of speaking of his *peregrinatio*; he was accused of Priscillianism, and defended his own orthodoxy; but he was a monk, and we do not know that he ever became a bishop. It is however most probable that the Spanish Peregrinus lived at the beginning of the fifth century, and he cannot be later than the eighth. Künstle is wrong in attributing to him the Pseudo-Jerome's prologue to the Catholic Epistles.

SCHEPSS, *Priscilliani quæ supersunt,* C. S. E. L., XVIII (Vienna, 1889), 179; BERGER, *Histoire de la Vulgate* (Paris, 1893); FRITSCHE in *Zeitschr. für Kirchengesch.*, XVII (1897), 212; KÜNSTLE, *Das Comma Johanneum* (Freiburg im Br., 1905); CHAPMAN, *Early history of the Vulgate Gospels* (Oxford, 1908).

JOHN CHAPMAN.

Pereira (PEREYRA, PERERA, PERERIUS), BENEDICT, philosopher, theologian, and exegete, b. about 1535, at Ruzafa, near Valencia, in Spain; d. 6 March, 1610, at Rome. He entered the Society of Jesus in 1552 and taught successively literature, philosophy, theology, and Sacred Scripture in Rome. He published eight works, and left a vast deal of manuscript. (Sommervogel, *infra*, mentions twelve sets.) The main difficulties of Genesis are met in "Commentariorum et disputationum in Genesim tomi quattuor" (Rome, 1591–99). This is a mine of information in regard to the Deluge, ark of Noe, tower of Babel, etc., and is highly esteemed by Biblical scholars, even by men of the critical bias of Richard Simon (Histoire critique du Vieux Testament, III, xii). The "Commentariorum in Danielem prophetam libri sexdecim" (Rome, 1587) are much less diffuse, and evidence the critical acumen, untiring energy, and historical research of the author. Other writings of importance published by Pereira were five volumes of exegetical dissertations on: "Exodus", 137 dissertations (Ingolstadt, 1601); "The Epistle to the Romans", 188 dissertations (Ingolstadt, 1603); "The Apocalypse", 183 dissertations (Lyons, 1606); "The Gospel of St. John", 214 dissertations on the first nine chapters (Lyons, 1608); 144 dissertations on five following chapters (Lyons, 1610). To the fourth volume of the dissertations is appended a curious work of twenty-three dissertations to show that Mohammed was not the Antichrist of the Apocalypse and of Daniel.

SOMMERVOGEL, *Bibl. de la Compagnie de Jésus*, VI, 499–507; IX, 764; HURTER, *Nomenclator*, I (Innsbruck, 1892), 182.

WALTER DRUM.

Peretti, FELICE. See SIXTUS V, POPE.

Perez, JUAN, d. before 1513. At one time he held the office of *contador* or accountant to the Queen of Spain, showing he was of noble family. Later he entered the Franciscan Order and distinguished himself for piety and learning. Queen Isabella chose him for her confessor. Finding court life distracting he asked permission to retire to his monastery. Soon after he was elected guardian of the convent, half a league from Palos in Andalusia, La Rábida (Arabian for hermitage, because it had once served as a Mohammedan place of retreat). In 1200 it came into the hands of the Knights Templar, who in 1221 ceded it to the Friars Minor. Father Francisco Gonzaga, Superior General of the Order (1579–87), declares that La Rábida became a Franciscan monastery in 1261; and that it belonged to the Franciscan Custody of Seville, which by Decree of Alexander VI, 21 Sept., 1500, was raised to the rank of a province. The convent remained in charge of the Friars Minor without interruption until the general confiscation of religious houses in 1835. It is now the property of the nation, and used as a museum.

Here Christopher Columbus in 1484 or 1485 made the acquaintance of Perez. Father Antonio de Marchena, a cosmographer of some note, lived here, and in him the navigator discovered a man bent on the project of discovering a new world. The historian Francisco Lopez Gomara (q. v.) in 1552 seems to have started the blunder, copied by almost every subsequent writer on the subject, of making the two names Perez and Marchena serve to describe one and the same person by speaking of the Father Guardian of La Rábida as Father Juan Perez de Marchena. Both fathers materially assisted Columbus, who acknowledges his obligation in one of his letters to the king and queen. He writes that everybody ridiculed him save two friars, who always remained faithful. Navarrete, indeed, claims that Columbus in this passage spoke of Perez, the Franciscan, and Diego de Deza, the Dominican. As the latter was Bishop of Palencia when the navigator wrote his letter, and Columbus on all other occasions speaks of him as Bishop of Palencia, or lord bishop, it would seem strange that in this one instance he should omit the title. Deza aided Columbus to the best of his ability among the scientists of Salamanca; but he could not prevent the adverse decision of the Spanish Court. It was Juan Perez who persuaded the navigator not to leave Spain without consulting Isabella, when, footsore and dispirited, he arrived at La Rábida, determined to submit his plan to the King of France. At the invitation of the queen, Perez made a journey to Santa Fé for a personal interview with her. As a result Columbus was recalled, and with the assistance of Cardinal Mendoza and others his demands were finally granted.

When the navigator at last on 3 August, 1492, set sail in the Santa Maria, Perez blessed him and his fleet. Some writers assert that Perez accompanied his illustrious friend on the first voyage, but the silence of Columbus on this point renders the claim improbable. It appears certain, however, that Perez joined his friend on the second voyage in 1493. The earliest and best writers also agree: that when the second expedition reached Haiti, Father Perez celebrated the first Mass in the New World at Point Conception on 8 Dec., 1493, in a temporary structure; that this was the first church in America; and that Father Perez preserved the Blessed Sacrament there. He also became the guardian of the first convent which Columbus ordered to be erected at Santo Domingo. There all trace of him is lost. Whether he returned to La Rábida or died in America is uncertain. All we know is that, in the legal dispute between Diego and Columbus, the royal fiscal, Dr. Garcia Hernandez, testified in 1513 that Father Perez was then dead.

GONZAGA, *De Origine Seraphicæ Religionis Franciscanæ*, II (Rome, 1587); LAS CASAS, *Historia de las Indias* (Madrid, 1875); DAZA, *Cronica General* (Valladolid, 1611); OLMO, *Arbol Serafico* (Barcelona, 1703); MELENDEZ, *Tesoros Verdaderos de las Indias* (Rome, 1681); HAROLD, *Epitome Annalium Ordinis Minorum* (Rome, 1662); COLL, *Colón y La Rábida* (Madrid, 1892); IRVING, *Life and Voyages of Christopher Columbus* (New York, 1868); TARDUCCI, *Life of Christopher Columbus*, tr. BROWNSON (Detroit, 1891); CIVEZZA, *Storia Universale*, V (Rome, 1861); CLARKE, *Old and New Lights on Columbus* (New York, 1893).

ZEPHYRIN ENGELHARDT.

Pérez de Hita, GINÉS, Spanish writer, b. at Murcia. Little is known of his life except that he lived during the second half of the sixteenth century, and probably took part in campaigns against the Moors in 1560 and following years. The work that has made him famous is his "Guerras civiles de Granada". It is in reality two separate works, dealing with events and persons separated in point of time by more than half a century. The first, when it was printed, contained the following note: "History of the Zegries and Abencerrages, Moorish bands of Granada; of the civil war which occurred at Vega between the Christians and the Moors, and was won by King Ferdinand V; now newly published in an Arabic book, the author of which is a Moor named Aben-Hamin of Granada; translated into Spanish by Ginés Pérez" (Zaragoza, 1595; Valencia, 1597). Not even the Arabic origin of this book is genuine nor is it a real history, but merely a novel founded upon fact. Pérez de Hita did not live when the Moors were in the height of their power in Granada, but, as he served in campaigns against the Moors, he was able to study their customs and ideas, and witness the remains of their glory. The second work deals with the Moorish uprising, and was published at Barcelona in 1619. This part passed through many editions, among which the later ones are that published in Madrid, 1833, and the one forming part (vol. III) of "La Biblioteca de Autores Españoles" of Rivadeneira. The first may be characterized as an historical novel, while the second may be called a history partaking of the nature of the novel. A striking peculiarity of Pérez de Hita is that he uses the language of to-day, and we look almost in vain for an archaic form. The phraseology is modern, and the diction is pure, terse, and sonorous.

BUENAVENTURA CARLOS ARIBAU in *Biblioteca de Autores Españoles*, III (Madrid, 1848).

VENTURA FUENTES.

CONVENT OF LA RÁBIDA

Perfection, CHRISTIAN AND RELIGIOUS.—A thing is perfect in which nothing is wanting of its nature, purpose, or end. It may be perfect in nature, yet imperfect inasmuch as it has not yet attained its end, whether this be in the same order as itself, or whether, by the will of God and His gratuitous liberality, it be entirely above its nature, i. e. in the supernatural order. From Revelation we learn that the ultimate end of man is supernatural, consisting in union with God here on earth by grace and hereafter in heaven by the beatific vision. Perfect union with God cannot be attained in this life, so man is imperfect in that he lacks the happiness for which he is destined and suffers many evils both of body and soul. Perfection therefore in its absolute sense is reserved for the kingdom of heaven.

CHRISTIAN PERFECTION is the supernatural or spiritual union with God which is possible of attainment in this life, and which may be called relative perfection, compatible with the absence of beatitude, and the presence of human miseries, rebellious passions, and even venial sins to which a just man is liable without a special grace and privilege of God. This perfection consists in charity, in the degree in which it is attainable in this life (Matt., xxii, 36-40; Rom., xiii, 10; Gal., v, 14; I Cor., xii, 31, and xiii, 13). This is the universal teaching of the Fathers and of theologians. Charity unites the soul with God as its supernatural end, and removes from the soul all that is opposed to that union. "God is charity; and he that abideth in charity abideth in God, and God in him" (I John, iv, 16). Suarez explains that perfection can be attributed to charity in three ways: (1) *substantially* or *essentially*, because the essence of union with God consists in charity for the habit as well as for the endeavour or pursuit of perfection; (2)

principally, because it has the chief share in the process of perfection; (3) *entirely*, for all other virtues necessarily accompany charity and are ordained by it to the supreme end. It is true that faith and hope are prerequisites for perfection in this life, but they do not constitute it, for in heaven, where perfection is complete and absolute, faith and hope no longer remain. The other virtues therefore belong to perfection in a secondary and accidental manner, because charity cannot exist without them and their exercise, but they without charity do not unite the soul supernaturally to God. (Lib. I, De Statu Perfectionis, Cap. iii).

Christian perfection consists not only in the habit of charity, i. e. the possession of sanctifying grace and the constant will of preserving that grace, but also in the pursuit or practice of charity, which means the service of God and withdrawal of ourselves from those things which oppose or impede it. "Be it ever remembered", says Reginald Buckler, "that the perfection of man is determined by his actions, not by his habits as such. Thus a high degree of habitual charity will not suffice to perfect the soul if the habit pass not into act. That is, if it become not operative. For to what purpose does a man possess virtue if he uses it not? He is not virtuous because he can live virtuously but because he does so." (The Perfection of Man by Charity. Ch. vii, p. 77.)

The perfection of the soul increases in proportion with the possession of charity. He who possesses the perfection which excludes mortal sin obtains salvation, is united to God, and is said to be just, holy, and perfect. The perfection of charity, which excludes also venial sin and all affections which separate the heart from God, signifies a state of active service of God and of frequent, fervent acts of the love of God. This is the perfect fulfilment of the law (Matt., xxii, 37), as God is the primary object of charity. The secondary object is our neighbour. This is not limited to necessary and obligatory duties, but extends to friends, strangers, and enemies, and may advance to a heroic degree, leading a man to sacrifice external goods, comforts and life itself for the spiritual welfare of others. This is the charity taught by Christ by word (John, xv, 13) and example. (See LOVE, THEOLOGICAL VIRTUE OF.)

RELIGIOUS PERFECTION.—Christian perfection, or the perfection of charity as taught by our Saviour, applies to all men, both secular and religious, yet there is also religious perfection. The religious state is called a school (*disciplina*) of perfection and it imposes an obligation, more strict than that of the secular state, of striving after perfection. Seculars are obliged to perfection by the observance of the precepts or commandments only; while religious are obliged to observe also the evangelical counsels to which they freely bind themselves by the vows of poverty, chastity, and obedience. The counsels (see COUNSELS, EVANGELICAL) are the means or instruments of perfection in both a negative and positive sense. *Negatively*: the obstacles in the way of perfection, which are (I John, i, 16) concupiscence of the eyes, concupiscence of the flesh, and pride of life, are removed by the vows of poverty, chastity, and obedience, respectively. *Positively*: the profession of the counsels tends to increase the love of God in the soul. The affections, freed from earthly ties, enable the soul to cling to God and to spiritual things more intensely and more willingly, and thus promote His glory and our own sanctification, placing us in a more secure state for attaining the perfection of charity.

It is true that seculars who also tend to perfection have to perform many things that are not of precept, but they do not bind themselves irrevocably to the evangelical counsels. It is, however, expedient only for those who are called by God to take upon themselves these obligations. In no state or condition of life is such a degree of perfection attainable that further progress is not possible. God on his part can always confer on man an increase of sanctifying grace, and man in turn by cooperating with it can increase in charity and grow more perfect by becoming more intimately and steadfastly united to God.

BUCKLER, *The Perfection of Man by Charity* (London, 1900); DEVINE, *A Manual of Ascetical Theology* (London, 1902); IDEM, *Convent Life* (London, 1904); ST. FRANCIS DE SALES, *Treatise on the Love of God* (Dublin, 1860); SUAREZ, *De religione*, tr. 7, L. I.; ST. THOMAS, *Summa*, II-II, Q. clxxxiv; IDEM, *Opus De perfectione vitæ spiritualis*; VERMEERSCH, *De religiosis institutis et personis tractatus canonico moralis* (Rome, 1907); RODRIGUEZ, *The Practice of Christian and Religious Perfection* (New York); HUMPHREY, *Elements of Religious Life* (London, 1905).

ARTHUR DEVINE.

Perfectionists. See SOCIALISTIC COMMUNITIES.

Pergamus, titular see, suffragan of Ephesus. This city was situated on the banks of the Selinus. It was at first a city of refuge, as its name indicates, for the people of the plain, and has been regarded as a colony of Arcadians. The Greek historians have reconstructed for it a complete history because they confused it with the distant Teuthrania. It is mentioned for the first time by Xenophon ("Anab.", VII, viii, 8; "Hellen.", III, i, 6). Captured by Xenophon in 399 and immediately recaptured by the Persians, it was severely punished in 362 after a revolt. It did not become important until Lysimachus, King of Thrace, took possession, 301 B. C. His lieutenant Philetairos enlarged the town, which in 281 he made the capital of the new kingdom which he founded. In 261 he bequeathed his possessions to his nephew Eumenius I (263–41 B. C.), who increased them greatly, leaving as heir his cousin Attalus I (241–197 B. C.).

Its highest prosperity was reached under his son Eumenius II (197–59 B. C.). He founded a school of sculpture, built in memory of his exploits a magnificent marble altar adorned with a battle of the giants (Ampelius, "Miracula Mundi", 14), the splendid remains of which are in the museum of Berlin, and finally founded the celebrated library. Attalus III at his death in 133 B. C. bequeathed his kingdom to Rome. Aristonicus, natural son of Eumenius II, endeavoured to restore the monarchy, but he was captured in 129 B. C. by Perpenna, and the kingdom was annexed to the Roman Empire under the name of Asia Propria. It is worthy of mention that parchment was discovered there, and that the physician Galen was a native.

The Apocalypse (ii, 12), mentions the martyr Antipas in connexion with Pergamus. Gaius, to whom was addressed the Third Epistle of St. John, became bishop of this city, according to the Apostolic Constitutions (vii, 46). Attalus, martyred at Lyons under Marcus Aurelius, was a native of Pergamus. Eusebius of Cæsarea (Hist. eccl., IV, 15, 48), mentions the martyrs Carpus, Papylus, and Agathonice, executed in March, 250. Out of a population of 120,000 inhabitants which Pergamus then possessed, a large number were Christians. Among its bishops may be mentioned: Theodotus who about 150 was active against the Gnostic sect of Colorbasiani; Eusebius, present at the Councils of Sardica and Philippopolis in 344; Dracontius, deposed in 360 at the Council of Constantinople; Philip, present at the Council of Ephesus in 431; Eutropius, at the Robber Synod of 449; John, d. about 549; Theodore, at the Sixth Œcumenical Council in 681; Basil, at the Seventh in 787; Methodius at the Eighth in 878; George, living in 1256; Arsenius, 1303–16. Pergamus was a suffragan of Ephesus until the twelfth century, when it became a metropolitan see. Although long occupied by the Turks the town was still a metropolis in 1387, when the title was removed and it became once more a diocese (Miklosich and Müller, "Acta patriarchatus Constantinopolitani", II, 103, 397). The diocese itself soon disappeared.

In 610 the body of Emperor Phocas was burned in a brazen ox brought from Pergamus. In the seventh century an Armenian colony, much attached to Monophysitism, and from which sprang the Byzantine Emperor Philippicus Bardanes (711–13), established itself there. In 716 the Arab general Maslama captured the town. From this period dates its decline. It was rebuilt on a smaller scale and formed part of the theme of Thrakesion. Constantine Porphyrogenitus still speaks of it (De themat., I, 24, 5–13) as a brilliant city of Asia. In 1197 the French of the Second Crusade halted there. The town had already suffered from Turkish incursions. It then became the capital of the theme of Neocastra, and a stronghold against the sultans of Iconium. In 1306 the Emir of Karasi captured it from the Greeks, but thirty years later Sultan Orkhan took it from him. Save for the temporary occupation of Timur-Leng in 1402, it has since belonged to the Osmanlis. Under the name of Bergama it now forms a caza of the vilayet of Smyrna and numbers 20,000 inhabitants, of whom 10,000 are Turks, 700 Jews, and 9,300 Christians (300 Armenians and 9000 Greek schismatics). The latter have two schools for boys and girls, with about 800 pupils, and five churches. The remains of three ancient churches have been discovered, among them the magnificent basilica of St. John. The church of St. Sophia was converted into a mosque in 1398.

Le Quien, *Oriens christianus*, I, 713–16; III, 957–60; van Cafellen, *De regibus et antiquitatibus pergamenis* (Amsterdam, 1840); Imhoof-Blumer, *Die Münzen der Dynastie von Pergamon* (Berlin, 1884); Urlichs, *Pergamon, Geschichte und Kunst* (Leipzig, 1883); Conze, Humann and Bonn, *Die Ergebnisse der Ausgrabungen zu Pergamon* (Berlin, 1880–88); Pedroli, *Il regno di Pergamo* (Turin, 1896); Humann, *Führer durch die Ruinen von Pergamon* (Berlin, 1887); *Altertümer von Pergamon* (8 vols., Berlin); Conze, *Pro Pergamo* (Berlin, 1898); *Pergamon* in Baumeister, *Denkmäler des klassischen Altertums*, II, 1206–87; Ussing, *Pergamos, seine Geschichte und Monumenta* (Berlin, 1899); Collignon et Pontremoli, *Pergame* (Paris, 1900); *Acad. des Inscriptions et Belles-Lettres* (Paris, 1901), 823–30; Cardinali, *Il regno di Pergamo* (Rome, 1906); Gelzer, *Pergamon unter Byzantinern und Osmanen* (Berlin, 1903); Cuinet, *La Turquie d'Asie*, III, 472–78; Lampakès, *Les sept astres de l'Apocalypse* (Athens, 1909), 251–300; Ramsay, *The Seven Churches of Asia*; *Journal of Hellenic Studies*, passim.

S. Vailhé.

Perge, titular metropolitan see in Pamphylia Secunda. Perge, one of the chief cities of Pamphylia, was situated between the Rivers Catarrhactes (Duden sou) and Cestrus (Ak sou), 60 stadia from the mouth of the latter; now the village of Murtana on the Suridjik sou, a tributary of the Cestrus, in the vilayet of Koniah. Its ruins include a theatre, a palæstra, a temple of Artemis, and two churches. The very famous temple of Artemis was located outside the town. Sts. Paul and Barnabas came to Perge during their first missionary journey, but probably stayed there only a short time, and do not seem to have preached there (Acts, xiii, 13); it was there that John Mark left St. Paul to return to Jerusalem. On his return from Pisidia St. Paul preached at Perge (Acts, xiv, 24). The Greek "Notitiæ episcopatuum" mentions the city as metropolis of Pamphylia Secunda until the thirteenth century. Le Quien (Oriens christ., I, 1013) gives 11 bishops: Epidaurus, present at the Council of Ancyra (314); Callicles at Nicæa (325); Berenianus, at Constantinople (426); Epiphanius at Ephesus (449), at Chalcedon (451), and signer of the letter from the bishops of the province to Emperor Leo (458); Hilarianus, at the Council of Constantinople (536); Eulogius, at Constantinople (553); Apergius, condemned as a Monothelite at Constantinople (680); John, at the Trullan Council (692); Sisinnius Pastillas about 754, an Iconoclast, condemned at Nicæa (787); Constans, at Nicæa (787); John, at Constantinople (869).

Ramsay in *Journal of Hellenic Studies* (1880), 147–271; Hill, *Catalogue of the British Museum: Pamphylia* (London, 1897), 129–31; Idem, *Catalogue of the Greek coins of Lycion: Pamphylia* (London, 1897), 119–42; Lanckoroński, *Les villes de la Pamphylie et de la Pisidie*, I (Paris, 1890), 35–67.

S. Pétridès.

Pergola. See Cagli e Pergola, Diocese of.

Pergolesi, Giovanni Battista, b. at Naples, 3 Jan., 1710; d. 16 March, 1736, at Pozzuoli, near Naples. This young man of delicate and poetic musical gifts might have done great things for the music of the Church had he not lived when composers were trying to serve two masters. Of frail constitution, he shortened his career by irregular conduct. At an early age he entered the Conservatory "dei poveri di Gesù Christo" in his native city, studied the violin under Domenico Matteis and afterwards enjoyed the guidance in composition of Gaetano Greco, Francesco Durante, and Francesco Feo. As a student he attracted attention by his sacred drama "San Guglielmo d'Aquitania" but, following the trend of his time, he devoted the next few years to the theatre, producing with more or less success "La Sallustia", "Amor fa l'uomo cieco", and "Recimero". He was not satisfied with these latter achievements, and when Naples was visited by an earthquake, Pergolesi was commissioned to write a mass for the solemn services of thanksgiving in the church of Santa Maria della Stella. Through this work for two five-part choirs and two orchestras, he became known as one of the most resourceful composers of the Neapolitan school. Shortly after he produced another mass for two choirs and later a third and fourth. Then the young master once more yielded to the allurements of the theatre. The intermezzo, "Serva padrona", survived his more pretentious works of this period. Although requiring for performance but two singers and a quartette of stringed instruments, it had instantaneous and lasting success. The last two years of his life Pergolesi devoted almost entirely to the interpretation of liturgical texts (masses, a "Salve Regina", etc.), almost all of them for chorus and orchestra. The work, by which he is most remembered, is the "Stabat mater" for two-part choir and stringed orchestra and organ, which he wrote shortly before his death for the Minorite monastery of San Luigi in Naples. Requiring great flexibility of execution on the part of the vocalists, it especially displays the author's chief characteristic, namely, delicacy and tenderness of feeling and exquisite workmanship. Though of lasting artistic value, Pergolesi's compositions are not available for liturgical purposes because for the most part they partake of the nature and form of contemporaneous operatic productions. They are better suited for performance at sacred concerts. The latest arrangement of Pergolesi's "Stabat mater", for chorus and modern orchestra, is by Alexis Lwow.

Boyer, *Notice sur la vie et les ouvrages de Giovanni Battista Pergolesi* in Mercure de France (Paris, 1772); Blasis, *Biografia di Pergolesi* (Naples, 1817); Faustini-Fasini, *Giovanni Battista di Pergolesi attraverso i suoi biografi* (Naples, 1900); Villarosa, *Littera biografica* (Naples, 1831); Idem, *Memorie di compositori di musica del regno di Napoli* (Naples, 1840).

Joseph Otten.

Pericope. See Gospel in the Liturgy; Lessons in the Liturgy.

Pericui Indians, a rude and savage tribe, of unknown linguistic affinity, formerly occupying the extreme southern end of the peninsula of California. With the neighbouring and allied tribe, the Cora, they numbered originally about 4000 souls. In general habit they closely resembled the Guaicuri (q. v.) as described by Baegert, but exceeded them in intractable savagery, being in chronic hostility, not only with the Spaniards, but with most of the other tribes of the adjacent region. In 1720 the Jesuit Fathers Bravo and Ugarte founded among them the mission of Nuestra Señora del Pilar, at La Paz, followed in a few years by several other Jesuit establishments. In 1734 under the leadership of two chiefs of negro origin, the two tribes revolted against the strictures of the missionaries upon polygamy and other immoralities, butchered Fathers Carranco and Tamaral, with a number of the mission followers, and plundered and burned the missions of Santiago, San José, Santa Rosa, and La Paz. For some time there was danger of an outbreak throughout the whole peninsula, but order was restored and mission work resumed. From 1742 to 1748, a series of epidemic visitations, probably smallpox, reduced them to one-sixth of their former number, and two of the four missions were abandoned. In 1769 another pestilential visitation wasted their numbers and provoked another outbreak, which was suppressed by Governor Gonzalez in person. By 1772 less than 400 remained alive and these were hopelessly diseased from contact with the pearl fishers and Spanish soldiery. Missions were continued at San José and La Paz (Todos Santos) under Franciscan and Dominican auspices into the last century, but the tribe is long since extinct.

For bibliography see GUAICURI INDIANS.

JAMES MOONEY.

Périgueux, DIOCESE OF (PETROCORICENSIS), comprises the Department of Dordogne and is suffragan to the Archbishopric of Bordeaux. By the Concordat of 1801, the Dioceses of Périgueux and Sarlat were united to the See of Angoulême; in 1821 Périgueux was again the seat of a bishopric which united the former Dioceses of Périgueux and Sarlat, excepting 60 parishes given to Agen and Angoulême and 49 parishes which had once belonged to Limoges, Cahors, and Tulle.

The Martyrology of Ado gives St. Front as the first Bishop of Périgueux; St. Peter is said to have sent him to this town with the St. George to whom later traditions assign the foundation of the church of Le Puy (q. v.). Subsequent biographies, which appeared between the tenth and thirteenth centuries, make St. Front's life one with that of St. Fronto of Nitria, thereby giving it an Egyptian colouring. At all events we know by the Chronicle of Sulpicius Severus that a Bishop of Périgueux, Paternus, was deposed for heresy about 361. Among the bishops are: Raymond V, Cardinal of Pons (1220–1223); the future cardinal, Blessed Elie de Bourdeilles (1447–1468); Claude de Longwy, Cardinal of Givry (1540–1547); the future Cardinal Gousset (1836–1840), subsequently Archbishop of Reims.

The Abbey of Saint-Sauveur of Sarlat, later placed under the patronage of St. Sacerdos, Bishop of Limoges, seems to have existed before the reigns of Pepin the Short and Charlemagne who came there in pilgrimage and because of their munificence deserved to be called "founders" in a Bull of Eugene III (1153). About 936 St. Odo, Abbot of Cluny, was sent to reform the abbey. The abbey was made an episcopal see by John XXII, 13 Jan., 1318.

Among the bishops of Sarlat were Cardinal Nicolas de Gaddi (1535–1546) and the preacher Jean de Lingendes (1639–1650).

Vesuna (subsequently Périgueux) was in the fifth century the site of an important school; it had distinguished professors: Paulinus the rhetorician; his son Paulinus the poet, who wrote (between 465 and 470) a poem on the life of St. Martin and another poem on the miraculous cure of his grandson by St. Martin; two named Anthedius; and Lupus, poet, rhetorician, and mathematician. Two provincial synods of Bordeaux were held at Périgueux in 1368 and 1856.

The history of the church of St. Front of Périgueux gave rise to numerous discussions between archæologists. Félix de Verneihl claims that St. Front was a copy of St. Mark's (Venice); Quicherat, that it was copied from the church of the Holy Apostles of Constantinople. M. Brutails is of opinion that if St. Front reveals an imitation of Oriental art, the construction differs altogether from Byzantine methods. The dates 984–1047, often given for the erection of St. Front, he considers too early; he thinks that the present church of St. Front was built about 1120–1173, in imitation of a foreign monument by a native local school of architecture which erected the other domed buildings in the south-west of France.

St. Vincent de Paul was ordained priest 23 Sept., 1600, by Bourdeilles, Bishop of Périgueux. Fénelon (q. v.), born in the Diocese of Sarlat, was titular of the priory of Carinac which his uncle François de Salignac, Bishop of Sarlat, had given him. The Church of Périgueux is the only one in France to celebrate the feast of Charlemagne (28 Jan.). This Church has a special veneration for Saints Silanus, Severinus, Severianus, and Frontasius, martyrs, disciples of St. Front; St. Mundana, martyr, mother of St. Sacerdos, Bishop of Limoges (sixth century); the Benedictine St. Cyprian, Abbot of the Périgueux monastery (sixth century); St. Sour (Sorus), a hermit who died about 580, founder of the Abbey of Terrasson. The Carmelite monk St. Peter Thomas (1305–1366), a native of Salles in the Diocese and Patriarch of Constantinople, died in Cyprus during the crusade which for a short time gave Alexandria to the Christians.

THE CATHEDRAL, PÉRIGUEUX

The Diocese of Périgueux has a remarkable relic: Pierre Raoul or Gérard, a parish priest in Périgord, brought back after the first crusade the Holy Shroud of Christ, entrusted to him by a dying ecclesiastic of Le Puy, who himself obtained this relic from the legate Adhémar de Monteil. The Cistercians who founded the monastery of Cadouin in 1115 had a church erected in honour of this relic; its cloister, a marvel of art, was consecrated in 1154. Notwithstanding the strict rules of the order interdicting the use of gold vases, the Chapter of Cîteaux permitted a gold reliquary for the Holy Shroud. As early as 1140, the Holy See instituted a confraternity in honour of the Holy Shroud, thought to be the oldest in France. St. Louis in 1270 venerated the Holy Shroud at Cadouin; Charles VI had it exposed for one month in Paris; Louis XI founded at Cadouin in 1482 a daily Mass. Bishop Lingendes in 1444 held an official investigation which asserted the authenticity of the relic. The other chief places of pilgrimage are: at Belvès, a shrine of Notre-Dame de Capelou, mentioned in 1153 in a Bull of Eugene III. Notre-Dame de Fontpeyrines; Notre-Dame du Grand Pouvoir at Périgueux, dating back to 1673; Notre-Dame des Vertus, dating back to 1653; Notre-Dame de Temniac, near Sarlat, a shrine where Clement V established a priory; Notre-Dame de Coulaures; Notre-Dame des Ronces at Nontron, dating back to the beginning of the seventeenth century.

Prior to the enforcement of the Law of 1901, there were in the Diocese of Périgueux, Capuchins, Carthusians, Trappists, Sulpicians, and various orders of teaching Brothers. The Congregation of Sisters of St. Martha, founded in 1643 (mother-house at Périgueux), is an important nursing and teaching order. The convent of Clarisses of Notre-Dame de la Garde, at Périgueux, was founded by two nuns whom St. Clare had personally sent from Assisi. At the beginning of the twentieth century the Diocese of Périgueux had the following religious institutions: 15 infant schools, 1 orphanage for boys, 5 orphanages for girls, 4 houses of shelter, 25 hospitals or asylums, 3 houses of visiting nurses, 1 house of retreat. In 1905 (the end of the period covered by the Concordat) the diocese had a population of 452,951 inhabitants, with 69 parishes, 467 succursal parishes, and 45 vicariates supported by the State.

Gallia Christiana (nova), II (1720), 1446, 1487, 1508, 1533 and instrum., 485–500; DUCHESNE, *Fastes épiscopaux*, II; LABROUE, *L'école de Périgueux au V° siècle: poètes et rhéteurs* (Paris, 1903); DUPUY, *L'Estat de l'Eglise du Périgord depuis le christianisme*, ed. AUDIERNE (2 vols., Périgueux, 1842–1843); BERNARET, *Organisation des deux diocèses du Périgord* in Bulletin de la soc. hist. et arch. du Périgord, I and III (Périgueux, 1874 and 1876); VILLEPELET, *Hist. de la ville de Périgueux et de ses institutions municipales jusqu'au traité de Brétigny* (Périgueux, 1908); BRUTAILS, *La Question de Saint-Front* (Caen, 1895); DE LA NAUZE, *Hist. de l'église de Sarlat* (Paris, 1857); TARDE, *Chroniques contenant l'hist. religieuse et politique de la ville et du diocèse de Sarlat depuis les origines jusqu'aux premières années du XVII° siècle*, ed. DE GÉRARD (Paris, 1887); MAYJONADE, *Le Saint Suaire de Cadouin* (Paris, 1905); ROUMEJOUX, BOSREDON, and VILLEPELET, *Bibliographie générale du Périgord* (5 vols., Paris, 1898, 1902).

GEORGES GOYAU.

Periodi (PETRI), the name under which the Pseudo-Clementine writings are quoted by Epiphanius, Jerome, and the "Philocalia". See CLEMENTINES.

Periodical Literature, CATHOLIC.—The invention of printing, besides exerting a great influence on literature in general and on education, gave birth to a new species of literature: publications appearing at intervals either regular or irregular. These sheets, or broadsides as they were called, dealing mostly with religious and political events, can be traced back to the year 1493. The oldest existing broadsides were published in Germany, the earliest Italian periodicals were the "Notizie scritte" of Florence, which were called *Gazetta* from the coin paid for reading them. These early precursors of the modern newspaper were of course very rudimentary, and without any set form or scheme. From the first, however, religious interests found an echo in them. The broadsides were later succeeded by the "relations" and the title of the Jesuit "Relations", which has become almost a household word in American history, shows how early the Church authorities appreciated the possibilities of this new kind of periodical publication. In the present article the reader will find not only a history of Catholic periodical literature in the most prominent countries of the western world, but also an account of its present status.

Our article treats of periodical literature whether appearing daily, weekly, semi-weekly, monthly, quarterly, or annually. It includes not merely the political newspaper, of which the American daily is the most characteristic specimen, but also the weekly, of which the London "Tablet" and the New York "America" may serve as types; the monthly, dealing mostly with historical, scientific, religious, and literary subjects, for which the English "Month" or the French "Correspondant" may be cited as examples; the quarterly, of which there are two kinds, the one being more general in character, the other treating of special sciences and interests. Of the former class the "Dublin Review" may be adduced as an instance; of the latter there is a great variety extending from such publications as the "Revue des Questions Scientifiques" to the special reviews on dogmatic and moral theology, canon law, the history of religious orders, and even hagiography, like the "Analecta Bollandiana". It will be perceived at once that many of the last mentioned publications appeal only to a very limited public and that in their case the circulation of 500 may be evidence of great merit and influence, though the number of their subscribers is small compared with the thousands of patrons of which our dailies and some of our magazines can boast.

In order to enable the reader to appreciate justly the information laid before him below, we submit the following general remarks:—(1) Prior to the middle of the eighteenth century and in fact almost up to the time of the French Revolution, all the periodicals published in a country reflected the spirit of the religion dominant in that country; in other words, in Catholic countries they were animated by the Catholic spirit and may be regarded as a part of Catholic literature. (2) Even in the nineteenth century, and especially during its first half, the Press of the various countries of the western world largely represented the feelings and ideas of the majority of their inhabitants. Thus at the present time, the Spanish journals are largely written from the Catholic point of view. (3) The daily journals of continental Europe still differ markedly from the typical American daily. The latter aims above all at gathering and printing the political, social, including criminal and economical, news of the day, while art, literature, and religion occupy a secondary rank and the editorials have grown gradually less important. In continental Europe, editorial articles, feuilletons, and varied essays often fill much more space than telegraphic and other news. This state of things accounts for the fact that the continental European journal requires much less capital than a great American daily. It also explains, why, in general, the non-Catholic European Press is characterized by much greater animosity to the Church and why Catholic dailies are more easily established and supported in some of the European countries. (4) The European weekly Press hardly makes any effort to publish contemporary news. The Catholic weeklies confine themselves for the most part to the discussion of topics, either purely religious or involving ecclesiastical interests.

The following articles have been written by men specially well-informed on the Press of their several countries, deserving of every confidence.

AUSTRIA.—The Catholic Press is represented in Austria by 140 newspapers and 152 other periodicals. Of the former, 79 are in German; 22 in the Czech, or Bohemian, language; 16 in Polish; 3 in Ruthenian; 8 in Slovenian; 5 in Croatian; 7 in Italian. The 79 German newspapers are distributed as follows: Lower Austria, 22; Upper Austria, 12; Salzburg, 3; Styria, 6; Tyrol, 13; Vorarlberg, 3; Bohemia, 9; Moravia, 5; Silesia, 1; Carinthia, 4; Carniola, 1. Of the Czech newspapers, 12 are published in Bohemia, 10 in Moravia; the Polish are published in Silesia (4), Galicia (11), and Bukowina (1); the Ruthenian are all published in Galicia; the Slovenian, 1 in Carinthia, 4 in Carniola, 2 in Görz, and 1 in Istria; the Croatian, 4 in Dalmatia and 1 in Istria; the Italian, 3 in the Tyrol, 2 in Görz, and 2 in Istria. The other periodicals are distributed as follows: Lower Austria, 33; Upper Austria, 8; Salzburg, 5; Styria, 7; the Tyrol, 11; Vorarlberg, 4; Bohemia, 31; Moravia, 18; Silesia, 5; Galicia, 26; Bukowina, 1; Carinthia, 1; Carniola, 11; Görz and Gradisca, 1; Istria, including Triest, 5; Dalmatia, 1.

The distribution of the Catholic daily papers is as

follows: Lower Austria, 4, of which 2 appear twice daily. Of these the "Reichspost" (Dr. Funder, editor-in-chief) is issued twice daily, and prints 16,000 copies to each edition; "Vaterland" (P. Siebert, editor-in-chief), two editions daily of 2500 copies each; "Neuigkeits-Weltblatt", August Kirsch, owner, 5000 copies to each edition; "Neue Zeitung", 50,000 copies to each edition. All these papers are published at Vienna. Upper Austria has the "Linzer Volksblatt", 4500 copies to each edition; in Salzburg, the "Salzburger Chronik", 3500 copies; in Styria, the "Grazer Volksblatt", 8500 copies; the "Kleine Zeitung", 26,000 copies to an edition, the last two published at Graz. In the Tyrol 3 daily papers are published: at Innsbruck the "Allgemeiner Tiroler Anzeiger", with an edition of 3000 copies, and the "Neue Tiroler Stimmen", with an edition of 1500 copies; at Trent, the Italian "Trentino", with an edition of 5000 copies. At Bregenz in Vorarlberg is published the "Vorarlberger Volksblatt", with an edition of 3500 copies. Bohemia has only one daily in the Czech language, the "Čech" of Prague, with an edition of 3800 copies; in Moravia, the Czech "Hlas" is published at Brünn, 2000 copies to an edition. Polish papers are the "Czas", published at Lemberg, 5000 copies twice daily; the "Gazeta Lwowska", 2000 copies to an edition; the "Gazeta Narodova", published at Lemberg, 4500 copies; the "Glos narodu", published at Cracow, 8800 copies twice daily; two other papers at Lemberg are the "Ruslau" and the "Przeglad", each 5000 copies to an edition. At Klagenfurt in Carinthia is published the "Kärntner Tagblatt", edition of 2000 copies; at Laibach in Carniola, the Slovenian "Slovenec", edition of 3700 copies; at Triest, the Italian "Giornale". In Dalmatia the "Hrvatska kruna" is published in Croatian, with an edition of 9000 copies.

The local Press, weekly and monthly, is very large; this is especially the case in the Alpine provinces and northern Bohemia. The learned periodicals show work of high quality. Among them should be mentioned: the "Kultur", published at Vienna by the Leo-Gesellschaft, and the "Allgemeines Literaturblatt", also the "Correspondenzblatt für den Clerus", edition of 7000 copies, the "Theologischpraktische Quartalschrift", published at Linz, edition of 12,000 copies; "Anthropos" at Salzburg, "Christliche Kunstblätter" at Linz, "Kunstfreund" at Innsbruck, "Immergrün" at Warnsdorf, "Vlast" at Prague. As regards illustrated family periodicals the non-Catholic Press is decidedly in the lead.

The actual condition of the Catholic Press in Austria is far from satisfactory, though by no means hopeless. Its defects are fully recognized by those who are best able to remedy them. The daily papers, in particular, suffer from the lack of funds. There is no wealthy Catholic middle class, the prosperous city population being to a great extent (politically at least) anti-Catholic, while most of the zealous Catholics are found among the rural population, who, in Austria, care little for newspapers. This state of things renders Catholic journalism an uninviting field for business investment, and the dearth of capital employed in Catholic journalism as business enterprise is only inadequately supplied by donations from the nobility and clergy, who have neither the inclination nor the experience to secure an advantageous employment of the funds subscribed by them. Subsisting on these slender contributions by supporters of the party, the Catholic papers are unable to make any efforts for their own improvement or for the increase of their circulation by advertising; they are party institutions, not business enterprises, and have to be satisfied with keeping their expenditures down to the limits of the party contributions. At the same time, the conduct of the papers is in the hands of persons who, besides having no pecuniary interest in pushing them as enterprises, generally lack journalistic training. This technical inferiority, indeed, affects the whole working value of the Austrian Catholic Press; the remuneration of contributors, as well as of editors, being considerably below the standard of the Liberal Press, the best talent of the country avoids Catholic journalism and enlists itself in the service of the opposition. Lastly, its financial weakness places the Catholic Press at a serious disadvantage in regard to the supply of scientific matter and foreign news, both of which are abundantly commanded by the affluent Liberal Press.

These enormous difficulties are to some extent counteracted, it is true, by Catholic zeal and self-sacrifice, but the strain of ceaseless effort necessarily results in a lack of effective force. External difficulties aggravate the disheartening conditions. The control of public affairs by a Liberal Press lasted so long that the whole reading public, good Catholics included, became habituated to it, and this acquiescence in a wrong state of things resulted in intellectual inertia. Only in the first decade of the present century did the more practically Catholic elements begin to realize that those aristocratic-conservative influences which are popularly regarded as reactionary are not necessarily the most favourable to Catholic interests. The Christian-Socialist popular party has taken up the Catholic programme and thus opened a way for it among the masses; a spirited agitation resulted in diminishing the political power of the Liberal Press; but, in spite of all this, the public, long accustomed to the style of Liberal journalism, find Catholic periodicals lacking in piquancy.

One more external difficulty with which Catholic periodical literature in Austria—in contrast to the conditions of United Germany—has to contend, is the multiplicity of races and languages among the populations of the empire. The national rivalries are not always held in check by the profession of a common faith. The Catholics of each race insist upon maintaining distinct Catholic periodicals in their respective languages; hence a large number of periodicals each with a circulation far too small to ensure success. This difficulty has recently increased rather than diminished. The "Vaterland", e. g., a Vienna periodical, formerly read by Catholics throughout the Austrian crown lands, irrespective of their own national languages, has now had its circulation curtailed through this cause. And in general it may be said that no Catholic paper in Austria can count upon a circulation among all Catholics under the Austrian Crown; a separate Press has to be organized for the Catholics of each language.

The result of all these internal and external difficulties is the present embarrassed position of the Catholic Press of Austria. Attempts have been made, with the best intentions, at various times, by individuals, corporate bodies, and congresses; all, however, have failed of lasting success, because they lacked system and organization. It is greatly to the credit of some that this defect was finally recognized, and an effort made to correct it, by the Pius-Verein. As attempts to obtain money for the Press from the few rich have failed, a constant appeal is made to the great mass of people of small means, and large sums are thus collected. In this way the question of means is to be settled. By constant agitation, or by frequent meetings, local groups, and confidential agents, the apathy of the people is to be ended.

Although the condition, taken as a whole, of the Catholic Press in Austria is not prosperous, still the great efforts that have been made of late years and are still making with ever-increasing zeal, at the present time, justify the hope that the apathy of large sections of the reading public may be overcome, an appreciation aroused of the importance of a Press that is honourable and steadfast in the Faith. Only when this is attained will the sacrifices in money and labour that have been made for many years for the sake of the Catholic Press bear fruit, and a powerful press will be the strongest protection against the opponents of the Church in Austria.

ANTON WEIMAN.

BELGIUM.—*Historical Outline of the Press in Belgium.*—Periodical literature in Belgium may be traced back to 1605, when the Archduke and Archduchess Albert and Isabella granted Abraham Verhoeven of Antwerp the privilege of publishing his newspaper "Nieuwe Tijdingen". But it is in the Dutch period of Belgian history that Catholic literature really originated. At that time appeared the "Spectateur Belge" of Father de Foere, which several times provoked the anger of William I; the "Courrier de la Meuse", founded at Liège in 1820 by Kersten; the "Catholique des Pays-Bas" and the "Vaderland", both founded at Ghent by de Neve; the "Politique de Gand", the "Noord-Brabantier", all showing remarkable zeal in defending the Catholic Church at a time when Catholic journalists were threatened with imprisonment. A few years after the establishment of Belgian independence the "Courrier de la Meuse" was transferred from Liège to Brussels, and took the name of "Journal de Bruxelles". Long afterwards under the editorship of the Baron Prosper de Haulleville (d. 1899) it became the leading Catholic organ; but now it has lost its prominence.

Causes which stopped its Development.—The Revolution of 1830 brought Belgium the liberty of the press. The majority of the population and of the National Congress were Catholics, but the Catholic Press from 1830 to 1874 improved very slowly. The first cause of this was the disagreement between the Catholics and the Catholic Liberals; the next was the neglect of the old and the establishment of new publications. Among the new publications were "Le nouveau conservateur belge", an ecclesiastical and literary magazine, founded in 1830 and discontinued in 1835; the "Messager des sciences historiques et des arts de la Belgique", founded in 1833 and discontinued in 1896; the "Revue Belge" of 1834, which lasted only a few years; the "Revue catholique de Louvain", devoted to religious controversy, history, and apologetics; from 1843 till 1884 it counted among its contributors the foremost professors of the University of Louvain. Another obstacle to the growth of the Catholic Press is the fact that the people of Belgium consist of two races with different languages, customs, and habits. Also the competition of French journals injured the growth of the Belgian press. French periodicals and newspapers appear in Brussels almost at the same time as in Paris. Besides their intrinsic merits, they have the advantage of being fashionable. Moreover, many Belgian writers have contributed to French periodicals. As an instance we may name the "Mélanges théologiques", a review of moral theology and canon law founded by a society of Belgian ecclesiastics at Liège in 1847. This magazine removed to Paris in 1856, where it was styled "Revue Théologique", and was conducted by a committee of French and Belgian priests. In 1861 it settled at Louvain, and there continued many years.

Present State.—About the middle of the last century, the religious question became prominent in Belgium. Catholics felt the need of a vigorous defence against irreligion and Freemasonry. New life was infused into the Catholic Press and to-day its condition is more satisfactory.

(1) *Dailies.*—Out of a total of 86 political daily papers 38 are Catholic. In consequence of the constant political activity all the important towns, even the suburbs of Brussels, have their local daily papers. Bruges has "La Patrie"; Charleroi, "Le Pays Wallon", a democratic journal of wide and vigorous efficiency; Liège, the "Gazette de Liège", which under editorship of Demarteau (1909) has reached a larger circulation than all the other Liège newspapers together. The "Bien Public", founded at Ghent in 1853 by Senator Lammens, Count de Hemptine, and others, circulates in all the provinces of Belgium, especially among the clergy. Its chief editor, Count Verspeyen, who has just celebrated his fiftieth anniversary as a journalist, has secured for it a well-deserved reputation on thoroughly Catholic lines. The most influential Catholic journal in Belgium is the "Patriote", founded in Brussels in 1883 by M. Jourdain, which with its local issue the "National" has a circulation of 180,000. His bold and skilful attacks brought about the downfall of the Liberal Government in 1884. The "XXᵉ Siècle", founded also in Brussels by the late Duke d'Ursel, the present ministers Helleputte, de Brocqueville, and others, is more democratic. In Brussels also is published "Het Nieuws van den Dag", the most popular newspaper among the Flemings.

(2) *Weeklies.*—Of the 1200 Belgian weeklies, the Catholics certainly control more than one-half. Each important locality has its political and illustrated weeklies. Many parishes have their "Bulletin paroissial". Each diocese publishes its "Semaine religieuse". In Mechlin the organ of the archbishopric, which is styled "La Vie diocésaine", receives contributions from Cardinal Mercier.

(3) *Reviews and Magazines.*—About a thousand reviews and magazines are published in Belgium, many of them by Catholics.

(a) Theology and Religion.—The "Revue théologique" mentioned above was replaced in 1907 by the "Nouvelle revue théologique", edited by Father Besson. Besides this small but useful review, about 150 periodicals of various descriptions treat of theology, apologetics, missions, special devotions etc. The Jesuits have their "Missions belges de la Compagnie de Jésus", a well-illustrated monthly magazine, which in 1899 took the place of the old "Précis historiques", founded by Father Terwecoren. The Fathers of Scheut (near Brussels) have their "Missions en Chine, au Congo et aux Philippines". Other religious congregations and some large monasteries issue reports of their pious works, or reviews of piety, of liturgy, hagiography, etc.

(b) Scientific Reviews.—The Catholic standard scientific review is the "Revue des questions scientifiques", a large quarterly to which is joined a smaller one of a more technical character. Both were founded in 1877 by Father Carbonnelle, S.J., and a Franco-Belgian committee of prominent Catholic scientists. Their motto: *Nulla unquam inter fidem et rationem vera dissensio esse potest* (Conc. Vatican.) found a practical confirmation in the sound scientific character of the whole series. The present editors are Prof. Mansion and Father Thirion. The "Revue néo-scolastique" was founded in 1894 by Cardinal Mercier, while directing his Institut de philosophie thomiste at Louvain, with which it is closely connected (quarterly: present editor, Prof. de Wulf). With the same institution is connected the "Revue catholique de droit", of Prof. Crahay of Liège, and the "Revue sociale catholique", of Mgr Deploige, Prof. Thiery, Prof. Defourny, and others. At Louvain also appear some special scientific reviews, such as the "Revue médicale" and the celebrated magazine of cytology entitled "La Cellule" of the late Canon Carnoy (present editor, Prof. Gilson). Also some philosophical reviews: "Le Muséon" of the late Mgr de Harlez, continued by Prof. Colinet, Prof. Lefort, and others; "Le Musée belge" of Prof. Collard and Prof. Waltzing (the latter of the Liège University); the "Leucensche Bijdragen" (for Dutch philology), edited by Prof. Colinet, Lecoutere, and others. There is also the Belgian law review, "Revue pratique des sociétés civiles", founded by Prof. Nyssens, Minister of Labour, and continued by Prof. Corbiau. Outside of Louvain, we notice "Mathesis" (Prof. Mansion of Ghent); the "Courrier littéraire et mathématique", edited by Prof. H. Gelin and the present writer as a guide for preparing for public examinations.

(c) *Historical Reviews.*—The largest is the important "Revue d'histoire ecclésiastique", a quarterly founded in 1900 by Canon Cauchie and Canon Ladeuze, now Mgr Ladeuze, Rector of Louvain University. Others are: the "Revue bénédictine", which in 1895 took the place of the "Messager des fidèles", edited since 1884 at the Benedictine Abbey of Maredsous by Dom Gerard van Caloen; the "Archives Belges" (Prof. G. Kurth, at Liège, since 1899); the "Analectes pour servir à l'histoire de l'Ordre de Prémontré", edited at the Park Abbey (Louvain) by Father van Waffelghem. Mention should also be made of the "Analecta Bollandiana" (see BOLLANDISTS).

(d) *Literature.*—The "Revue Générale", though it deals, according to its title, with all matters of common interest, is chiefly a literary review. This monthly publication, founded in 1863, reckoned among its ordinary contributors the distinguished statesmen Malou, Deschamps, and Nothomb, Deputy Coomans, Prof. de Monge, the publicist Prosper de Haulleville etc. To-day the parliamentary leader, M. Ch. Woeste, makes it the vehicle of his political views. M. Eug. Gilbert regularly contributes to it a most valuable literary chronicle. With this magazine we may mention the "Dietsche Warande en Belfort". Other Catholic literary reviews are: "Le Magasin Littéraire", of Ghent; "La Lutte" and "Le Journal des gens de lettres belges", of Brussels, which have pleaded for Catholic art, but have been succeeded by younger magazines such as "Durandal", a monthly illustrated review edited by Abbé Moeller, "Le Catholique", and "La Revue Jeune".

(e) *Art Reviews.*—Most of these literary reviews touch upon art questions, but there are also "Revue de l'art chrétien", a review of medieval archæology; the "Courrier de Saint Grégoire" and "Musica sacra" which aims at promoting the use of sound music in Church services; "Le Bulletin de la Société d'art et d'histoire du diocèse de Liège", of which Mgr Rutten, now Bishop of Liège, was the president for a long time; the "Bulletin des métiers d'art", which serves as the organ of the St. Luke schools, founded by Brother Marès for teaching the technical arts on Christian principles. ATH. GLOUDEN.

CANADA.—Under the French domination, periodical literature, still in its infancy in France even as late as the close of the eighteenth century, was totally unknown in Canada. The first newspapers founded in the colony, the "Quebec Gazette" (1764) and the "Montreal Gazette" (1778), both weeklies with a double-column page alternately in English and in French, without being professedly Catholic, were not unfriendly towards the Church.

PROVINCE OF QUEBEC, OR LOWER CANADA.—The first periodical of importance was "Le Canadien", founded in Quebec (1806) by Pierre Bédard. Although essentially political and patriotic, nevertheless by its vindication of religious as well as civil liberty, and owing to the unexceptionable Catholicism of the French Canadian population whose interests it represented, "Le Canadien" may safely be styled a Catholic organ. This same principle applies to the greater number of French papers published in Canada. After a series of suppressions and interruptions, "Le Canadien" (first weekly, then daily) lasted for over fifty more years, during a long period of which its chief editor was Etienne Parent, whose valiant pen ably defended the rights of his fellow-citizens and helped to maintain their national dignity and autonomy.

Next in order of importance, if not of date, follows "La Minerve" (first weekly, then daily), founded in Montreal (1826) by Augustin-Norbert Morin. It had a career of seventy years, and numbered among its ablest editors Antoine Gérin-Lajoie, Raphael Bellemare, and Joseph Tassé. The chief organ of the English-speaking Catholics was the "True Witness" (weekly), founded in Montreal (1850) by George E. Clerk, a convert from Anglicanism, who loyally and generously served the cause of the True Faith during his prolonged editorship. The "True Witness" had been preceded by the short-lived "Irish Vindicator" of Montreal (1828), and still exists under the lately assumed name of "The Tribune".

In 1857 was founded in Quebec "Le Courrier du Canada" (first weekly, then daily). It had an honourable and fruitful career of forty-five years under the leadership of such learned, vigorous, and elegant writers and uncompromising Catholics as Doctor Joseph Charles Taché, Auguste-Eugène Aubry, and Thomas Chapais. Montreal gave birth to two entirely Catholic daily papers: "Le Nouveau-Monde" (1867–81) with the Honourable Alphonse Desjardins as chief editor, and "L'Etendard" (1883–) under the direction of the Honourable Senator Anselme Trudel. A weekly, "Les Mélanges Religieux", founded in Montreal (1839) by Reverend J. C. Prince, lasted till 1846. "L'Opinion Publique", an illustrated weekly, published in Montreal for fourteen years (1870–83) counted many brilliant *littérateurs* among its contributors. Most noteworthy among the monthlies are, in order of date, "Le Journal de l'Instruction Publique", founded in Montreal (1857) by the Honourable Pierre-J.-O. Chauveau, a distinguished orator and writer, who was its chief editor until its cessation (1878); "Les Soirées Canadiennes", Quebec (1861–5); "Le Foyer Canadien", Quebec (1863–6); "La Revue Canadienne", Montreal (1864), still flourishing under the direction of the Montreal branch of the University of Laval; "Le Canada Français", semi-monthly, edited by the parent University of Quebec (1888–91). These five reviews form a collection replete with the best productions of French Canadian literature.

For divers reasons, the Catholic Press in Lower Canada, in fact throughout the whole Dominion, with the exception of a few short-lived ventures, cannot boast of a daily newspaper published in the English language. In the Province of Quebec the only organ of the English-speaking Catholics is the above mentioned "Tribune" (weekly). Of the existing French Catholic dailies, "L'Action Sociale", founded in Quebec (1907) by Archbishop L.-N. Bégin, is totally independent of politics, appreciating men and events from an exclusively Catholic and non-partisan viewpoint; its present circulation, comprising the weekly edition, is 28,000, as compared with the 90,000 of the non-Catholic "Montreal Star". Another, "Le Devoir", advocating nationalism, founded in Montreal (1909) and directed by Henri Bourassa, has also a good circulation. The foremost weekly, still in existence, is "La Vérité", founded in Quebec (1881) by Jules-Paul Tardivel, who has been called the Canadian Veuillot. This paper, during the career of its founder, exerted a considerable influence on Catholic opinion. "Le Courrier de St-Hyacinthe" (1853), "Le Journal de Waterloo" (1879), "Le Bien Public", Three-Rivers (1909), all weeklies still in operation, deserve a special mention for their soundness of judgment and dutiful submission to the guidance of the spiritual authority. Among the existing monthlies may be mentioned "Le Naturaliste Canadien", Quebec, founded by the Abbé Léon Provancher (1868), the only Catholic scientific review in Canada; "La Nouvelle-France", a high-class review with a comprehensive programme; "Le Bulletin du Parlerfrançais", a technical review of a chiefly philological character, both founded in Quebec in 1902; "L'Enseignement Primaire", a pedagogical review, now in its thirty-second year, published in Quebec, and distributed by the Government to all the Catholic primary schools of the province, renders good service to the cause of elementary education. The outlook of the Catholic Press in the old French province seems very hopeful, thanks to the improvement of higher education, to the inculcation of a more thorough Catholic spirit, and a more dutiful compliance with the directions of the Vicar of Christ.

ONTARIO.—The first Catholic paper published in Upper Canada was the "Catholic", founded and edited in Kingston (1830) by Very Rev. William Peter MacDonald, and published later in Hamilton (1841–44). In 1837 Toronto had its first Catholic organ, "The Mirror", which lasted till 1862. It was followed successively by "The Canadian Freeman" (1858–63), under the editorship of J. J. Mallon and James G. Moylan; "The Irish Canadian", established by Patrick Boyle (1863–92; 1900–01); "The Tribune" (1874–85), with the Hon. Timothy Warren Anglin for its latest editor; "The Catholic Record", London (1878), is by far the most flourishing Catholic weekly in Canada, with its circulation of 27,000. Toronto likewise claims the following noteworthy Catholic periodical: "The Catholic Weekly Review" (1887–93); its editors were successively F. W. G. Fitzgerald, H. F. McIntosh, P. DeGruchy, Revs. F. W. Flannery and J. D. McBride; in 1893 it was merged into the "Catholic Register", whose editors were, in order of date, Rev. Doctor J. R. Teefy, J. C. Walsh, and P. P. Cronin. In 1908, under the title of "Register-Extension", it became the organ of the Catholic Church Extension Society, under the editorship of Rev. A. E. Burke, D.D.

MARITIME PROVINCES.—*Nova Scotia*.—Though Halifax can boast of the first newspaper in Canada, now including the Maritime Provinces (the "Royal Gazette", 1752), the first Catholic periodical, "The Cross", was founded only in 1845, by the future Archbishop W. Walsh, and lasted till 1857. By far the most important Catholic organ of the province is "The Casket" (weekly), of Antigonish, founded in 1852 and still in full activity. Its editorial chair was successively filled by the learned theologians, Doctors M. McGregor, N. McNeil, and Alex. McDonald, the two last named since appointed respectively to the Sees of Vancouver and Victoria, British Columbia. Sureness of doctrine and vigilance in denouncing contemporary errors are its chief characteristics.

New Brunswick.—"The Freeman", a political paper, was founded in St. John, 1851, with Hon. T. W. Anglin as editor. He was succeeded by W. R. Reynolds. Under the name of "The New Freeman" since 1902, its character is exclusively Catholic. While strongly advocating temperance and total abstinence, it strives to enlighten non-Catholics and to foster vocations for the priesthood. French Acadian journalism is chiefly represented by "Le Moniteur Acadien", founded at Shediac (1866), and "L'Evangeline", of Moncton.

Prince Edward Island.—The first Catholic paper of the island was the "Palladium" (1843–5). It was followed by the "Examiner" (1847–67), both edited by Edward Whelan. Then came "The Vindicator" (1862–4), strictly non-political, to be succeeded by "The Charlottetown Herald", still in existence.

NORTH-WEST PROVINCES.—Catholic journalism in the north-west begins in 1871 with "Le Métis", the organ of the half-breeds, under the editorship of Hon. J. Royal. Next comes "Le Manitoba", a valiant champion of the Catholic schools, founded by Hon. J. Bernier, and now edited by his son. The first Catholic paper in English was "The North-West Review", begun in 1885, long edited by Rev. L. Drummond, S.J., and still fighting the good fight. The German Catholics have also their organ, "West Canada", and the Poles their "Gazeta Katolicka". These three papers are issued by the same printing-house in Winnipeg, under the patronage of the present Archbishop of St. Boniface (1911). A Ruthenian Catholic paper will shortly appear under the same auspices. "Le Patriote" began publication in 1910, at Duck Lake, Sask. Edmonton, Alta, has "Le Courrier de l'Ouest", and Vancouver, British Columbia, "The Western Catholic".

TURCOTTE, *Le Canada sous l' Union* (Quebec, 1871); DIONNE, *Inventaire chronologique* (Quebec, 1905); MORICE, *Hist. of the Catholic Church in Western Canada* (Toronto, 1909); HOPKINS, *Canada* (Quebec, 1899).

LIONEL LINDSAY.

ENGLAND.—Not until the toleration acts of the early nineteenth century and the Catholic revival incident upon the immigration of the French clergy, were English Catholics in any position to conduct a periodical literature of their own, though occasional pamphlets on various questions of Catholic interest had been issued. With the agitation over the Veto and Emancipation, a beginning was made with a monthly review, the pioneer Catholic publication of the kind, "Andrews' Orthodox Journal", first issued in 1812 by Eusebius Andrews, a Catholic printer and bookseller of London. It had but a few years of chequered existence, as there was not a sufficiently large reading public to make it self-supporting. The real beginnings of Catholic periodical literature were made more than twenty years later, by which time the growth of the Catholic body in its newly won freedom, the progress of Catholic education, and the interest excited by the Tractarian movement had all combined to supply a wider circle of readers. A great step was taken by Wiseman and O'Connell in the foundation of a quarterly, the "Dublin Review" (1836). The fame of the "Edinburgh" suggested a territorial title, and Dublin was chosen as a great Catholic centre, though from the first it was edited and published in London. The review was intended to provide a record of current thought for educated Catholics and at the same time to be an exponent of Catholic views to non-Catholic inquirers. Beginning before the first stirrings of the Oxford Movement, it presents a record of the intellectual life of the century and produced articles which had an immense influence upon the religious thought of the times. It was in the August of 1839 that an article by Wiseman on the Anglican Claim caught the attention of Newman. Impressed by the application of the words of St. Augustine, *securus judicat orbis terrarum*, which interpreted and summed up the course of ecclesiastical history, he saw the theory of the *Via media* "absolutely pulverized" (Apologia, 116–7). It was a turning point for Newman and for the whole course of the Oxford Movement, and the incident is worth remembering as an example of the power of a good Catholic Press. Gradually the Tractarian converts appeared in the lists of contributors: Ward (q. v.), Oakeley, Marshall, Morris, Christie, Formby, Capes, Allies (q. v.), Anderson (q. v.), Manning (q. v.), and a glance through the volumes of the "Dublin" will reveal names prominent in the great religious, scientific, and literary movements of the century. During the sixties and the early seventies it was under the vigorous direction of Dr. W. G. Ward. After his retirement it was edited by Dr. Hedley, afterwards Bishop of Newport, and then acquired by Cardinal Manning, who appointed Canon Moyes editor. It is now the property and under the direction of Mr. Wilfrid Ward, son of its famous editor.

The first issue of the annual "Catholic Directory" appeared in 1837. Owing to the Oxford Movement, the forties were a time of marked literary activity. In 1840 two new enterprises were inaugurated. Mr. Dolman, a Catholic publisher in London who had issued a number of really important books including the writings of Lingard and Husenbeth, produced in "Dolman's Magazine" a high class literary monthly, and on 16

May, 1840, Frederick Lucas (q. v.) became the pioneer of the Catholic newspaper Press in England by publishing the first number of "The Tablet", a weekly newspaper and review. Lucas was a strong man, and regarded his work as founder and editor of a Catholic paper as a sacred mission. He threw into it all his zeal and energy, realizing the enormous possibilities for good of the religious Press when many were hopelessly blind to such considerations. His uncompromising views led to difficulties with his financial supporters, but he emerged triumphant. For awhile after the crisis of 1848 Lucas, then active in Irish politics, removed "The Tablet" office to Dublin, but it was brought back to London by the new proprietors, into whose hands it passed when failing health compelled Lucas to give up the editorship. It was not easy to replace such a man. He had not been content to chronicle events; he had influenced them. For many years after his death, in 1855, "The Tablet" was a mere humdrum record of news. Among the distinguished editors was Cardinal Vaughan (q. v.) who conducted the "Tablet" during the stormy discussions on Papal Infallibility and the Vatican Council. When he became Bishop of Salford, he placed the editorship in the hands of Mr. Elliot Ranken, who was succeeded by Mr. Snead-Cox, the present editor. "The Tablet", besides championing the Catholic cause, assists in the propagation of the Faith in far-off lands, as under the terms of the trust created by the late Cardinal Vaughan its profits go to the support of St. Joseph's Missionary College, of which he was the founder.

Two other notable periodicals were founded in the forties. "The Tablet" was a sixpenny paper, reduced to its present price, five pence, on the abolition of the newspaper stamp duty. Its price put it beyond the reach of tens of thousands of Catholic workers. To supply them with a penny magazine Mr. Bradley in 1846 founded "The Lamp". It gave much of its space to Catholic fiction, descriptive articles, and the like, and ventured on an occasional illustration, a portrait or a picture of a new church; but it also supplied news and reported in full Wiseman's lectures and other notable Catholic utterances. For years it struggled with lack of capital, and for awhile Bradley edited his paper from his room in the debtors' prison at York. His name deserves honourable record as the pioneer of the popular Catholic Press. The other paper, "The Rambler", of which the first issue appeared on 1 January, 1848, was intended to be a high class weekly review of literature, art, and science. In 1859, Lord Acton (q. v.), who had then just returned from the Continent, succeeded Newman in the editorship. The price, sixpence, limited its public and in 1862 it became a quarterly under the title of "The Home and Foreign Review". In its last years this review, which had once done good service, was a source of trouble and disedification, but its sale, which dwindled yearly, was largely among Anglicans and other non-Catholics. In the mid years of the nineteenth century the abolition of the various taxes on newspapers and the cheapening of the processes of production led to the coming of the penny newspapers. The first Catholic penny paper with permanent success was "The London Universe". Its origin was connected with the earlier activity of Lucas, who successfully advocated the introduction of the Conferences of St. Vincent de Paul into England. It was a group of members of the London Conferences who produced "The Universe". Speaking to their president, Mr. George Blount, one evening in 1860, Cardinal Wiseman, after alluding to the flood of calumny then poured out in the Press against the Holy See, said: "Cannot the Society of St. Vincent de Paul do something to answer those frightful calumnies, by publishing truths, as M. Louis Veuillot is doing in Paris in 'L'Univers'? We want a penny paper, and now that the tax has been removed it should be possible." It was decided that, though the society, as such, could not found a newspaper, a committee of its members should undertake the task. It included George Blount, Stuart Knill (afterwards the first Catholic Lord Mayor of London), Viscount Fielding (Lord Denbigh), Viscount Campden (Lord Gainsborough), Sidney Lescher, Archibald Dunn, Arthur à Beckett, and George J. Wigley, the London correspondent of the Paris "Univers". Wigley secured a foreign news service for the projected paper from M. Veuillot's Paris office, and at his suggestion the name of "The Universe" was chosen. Mr. Denis Lane undertook the printing, Mr. Dunn the editorship, and on 8 December, 1860, the first Catholic penny paper in England was started. At first it was strictly non-political. The editor and staff gave their services gratuitously, but even with this help expenses were greater than receipts. To attract a larger circulation political articles were inserted, which led to the resignation of the greater part of the staff. Mr. Lane then took over the paper and conducted it for many years as a Catholic paper, giving a general support to the Liberals and the Irish national cause. He had always a priest as "theological editor"; amongst those who thus assisted him were Father W. Eyre, S.J., Father Lockhart, and Cardinal Manning. The movement for the rescue of destitute Catholic children originated in "The Universe" office. It has lately celebrated its fiftieth anniversary, and has amalgamated with another paper, "The Catholic Weekly", founded to give a record of Catholic news without any party politics. "The Universe" has thus reverted to its original programme.

"The Lamp" was reorganized about the same time and had for some years a prosperous existence as a popular magazine. Fathers Rawes and Caswall, Lady Georgiana Fullerton, Miss Drane, Cecilia Caddell were among its contributors. In 1864 Miss Taylor founded "The Month", at first an illustrated magazine giving much of its space to fiction and the lighter forms of literature. When she founded her first community of nuns (Poor Servants of the Mother of God), her magazine passed to the Jesuits, and under the able editorship of the late Father Henry J. Coleridge, "The Month" became a high-class review. It had many notable contributors, and in its pages Newman's "Dream of Gerontius" first appeared. Numerically, the main strength of English Catholicism has always been in the North, and after the foundation of "The Universe" several efforts were made to produce a Catholic penny paper in Lancashire. Three successive enterprises had a brief career. A fourth, a paper known as "The Northern Press" was barely existing, when, in 1867, it was taken over by a remarkable man, the late Father James Nugent of Liverpool. He renamed it "The Catholic Times" and gradually made it the most widely circulated Catholic paper in England. Printed for many years by the boys of the refuge he had founded in Liverpool, when it became a profit-earning paper it helped support this work of charity. Offices were opened in Manchester and London. A special London edition was produced, and in 1878 a Christmas supplement issued under the title of "The Catholic Fireside" was so successful that it was continued as a monthly penny magazine; in 1893 it was made a weekly publication. "The Catholic Times" appeals largely to the Catholics of Irish descent in Great Britain, and has always championed the Nationalist cause. It gives considerable space to reviews and literary matter, and has a well organized service of correspondents. Mr. P. L. Beazley, the present editor, has directed it for twenty-seven years and is now the dean of Catholic journalism.

In the sixties other papers were founded, for awhile fairly prosperous, though they never won the established position of "The Catholic Times" and "The Tablet". "The Weekly Register" was a threepenny paper, of much the same character as "The Tablet", but favouring the Liberals and Nationalists. Later, under the editorship of Charles Kent and then of Mr. Wilfrid Meynell, it had a marked literary quality, but in England it is found that no paper is a permanent success at any price between the popular penny and the sixpence that gives a margin of profit on a moderate circulation. "The Weekly Register" has ceased to exist and with it "The Westminster Gazette", whose name is now that of a London evening paper. The "Westminster" was owned and edited by Pursell, afterwards biographer of Manning. During the months of newspaper controversy that preceded the definition of Papal Infallibility the "Westminster" was "non-opportunist", and Cardinal Vaughan, while he avoided all controversy on the subject in "The Tablet", contributed, week after week, letters to the "Westminster", combating its editorial views. It never had much circulation, and Vaughan was able a few years later to end its competition by buying and stopping it. The late Father Lockhart edited for some years "Catholic Opinion", a penny paper giving extracts from the Catholic Press at home and abroad. After his death it was amalgamated with "The Catholic Times". A remarkable development in connexion with the popular Press is that directed by Mr. Charles Diamond, for some time a member of the Irish Parliamentary party, who started (1884) "The Irish Tribune" in Newcastle-on-Tyne. Shortly after, he purchased two other Catholic papers, the Glasgow "Observer" and the Preston "Catholic News", which were in difficulties for want of capital. He then formed the idea of working several papers from a common centre, much of the matter being common to all, but each appearing under a local title and having several columns of special matter of local interest. He now issues "The Catholic Herald" from London, as the centre of the organization, and thirty-two other local weekly papers in various towns of England, Wales, and Scotland. He also produces on the same system ten different parish magazines and "The Catholic Home Journal", with which the old "Lamp" has been amalgamated.

There are a considerable number of minor Catholic monthlies, mostly founded in recent years to advocate and promote special objects. The "Annals of the Propagation of the Faith" and "Illustrated Catholic Missions" specialize on the news of the mission field. "Catholic Book Notes", a monthly issued by the Catholic Truth Society and edited by Mr. James Britten, is an admirable record of current literature and a model of scholarly and thoroughly honest reviewing. "The Second Spring", edited by Father Philip Fletcher, is a record of the work of the Ransom League for the conversion of England. "The Crucible" is a monthly review of social work for Catholic women. There are a number of devotional magazines issued by various religious orders, the most widely circulated of which is the "Messenger of the Sacred Heart", edited by the Jesuits. There are also several college magazines, some of which produce work of a high literary standard. It might be a gain if there were more concentration and fewer publications with larger circulation. Many of these have a comparatively small circle of readers; even the most widely circulated Catholic publication in England has an issue that falls far below that of its more powerful non-Catholic competitors. The result is that the scale of pay in Catholic journalism is below the ordinary press standards, and many Catholic writers in working for the Catholic Press are making a continual sacrifice; but the standard of work produced has steadily risen, and the Catholic Press in England to-day, with all its deficiencies and difficulties, is doing most useful work and exercises an ever growing influence.

The foregoing article is based on personal knowledge and on information kindly supplied by the editors of various publications. The following may be consulted: LUCAS, *The Life of Frederick Lucas, M. P.* (London, 1886); SNEAD-COX, *Life of Cardinal Vaughan* (London, 1910); GASQUET, *Lord Acton and his Circle* (London, 1906); WARD, *Life and Times of Cardinal Wiseman* (London, 1897); IDEM, *W. G. Ward and the Oxford Movement* (London, 1889); IDEM, *W. G. Ward and the Catholic Revival* (London, 1893).

A. HILLIARD ATTERIDGE.

FRANCE.—The first periodical published in France was the "Gazette de France", founded in May, 1631, by the physician Théophraste Renaudot. It first appeared weekly, in four pages; in 1632 it had eight pages divided into two parts, one called the "Gazette", the other "Nouvelles ordinaires de divers endroits". It soon had a monthly supplement, entitled "Relations des nouvelles du monde reçues dans tout le mois", and then additional pages called "Extraordinaires". From 1652 to 1665 the "Muse Historique", edited by Loret, related in verse the happenings of each week. The "Mercure Galant", founded in 1672 by Donneau de Visé, was a literary and political journal which in 1724 became the "Mercure de France". In 1701, in opposition to the "Nouvelles de la République des Lettres", which the philosopher Bayle edited from Holland, appeared a publication called "Mémoires pour servir à l'histoire des sciences et des beaux arts, recueillis par l'ordre de S. A. Mgr. le prince souverain de Dombes". It was edited by the Jesuits and is known in history as the "Journal de Trévoux", and was maintained until the suppression of the Society of Jesus. The "Année Littéraire", edited by Fréron (1754–76), was a formidable opponent of the *philosophes*, and especially of Voltaire, whose doctrines it combatted. It was published every ten days. An Anglo-French paper, the "Courrier de Londres", was founded in London in 1776. It appeared twice a week, and was very influential in developing the Revolutionary spirit. The first French daily was founded in 1777 and was called the "Journal de Paris ou la Poste du soir". The "Gazette de France" became a daily in 1792.

At the beginning of the eighteenth century twenty journals were printed in Paris, and at the outbreak of the Revolution this number had been trebled. Between May, 1789, and May, 1793, about a thousand periodicals saw the light. The most important organ of the Royalist opposition was called the "Actes des Apôtres", to which such writers as Rivarol, Bergasse, and Montlosier contributed under the editorship of Peltier. Under the Directory forty journals suspected of Royalism were suppressed, and their editors deported. The Consulate would tolerate only thirteen political dailies, and the First Empire only four. The "Journal des Débats", owing to the idea of its founders, the Bertin brothers, of uniting with it a literary *feuilleton* written by the critic Geoffroy, took first rank under the Empire. Geoffroy's influence was important from a religious point of view, for in his *feuilletons* he voluntarily treated all the philosophical questions, and carried on a most intelligent campaign against Voltaireanism.

Under the Restoration Catholicism was defended by the "Gazette de France", the "Quotidienne", the "Mémorial religieux", the "Défenseur", the "Catholique", the "Correspondant", the "Mémorial", and the "Conservateur". The last-named was one of the most important; Châteaubriand, Bonald, Lammenais, and the Cardinal de La Luzerne were among its contributors. But even then the divisions among Catholics weakened the influence of their Press. Under the Restoration the Voltairean spirit had in the Press of the Left a representative who was very formidable to religious ideas, namely the pamphleteer Paul-Louis Courrier. The Gallican spirit was represented in the "Drapeau Blanc" by the Comte de Montlosier, while the Monarchist journal, the "Constitutionnel", in order to retain a certain clientele, systematically published, several times a week, absurd and calumniating tales concerning the clergy. The systematic Anticlerical Press in France dates from the period of the

Restoration, and at the same time a large section of the Monarchist press was hostile to the Church. In his book on the "Congregation" M. Geoffroy de Grandmaison has drawn up a list of eighteen anticlerical articles published by the "Constitutionnel" in the single month of September, 1826.

Under the Monarchy of July the first noteworthy incident was the publication of the "Avenir" (see LAMENNAIS). The Legitimist Press, of Catholic tendencies, offered a vigorous opposition to the Monarchy of July, the chief organs being the "Quotidienne" (see LAURENTIE) and the old "Gazette", of which the Abbé de Genonde was long the principal editor. Crétineau-Joly (q. v.) issued a provincial journal, the "Gazette du Dauphiné", a fearless instrument of Catholic and Legitimist propaganda. The first really serious attempt at Catholic journalism belongs to this period. On Sunday, 3 Nov., 1833, appeared the first number of the "Univers religieux, politique, scientifique et littéraire". Its motto was: "Unity in what is certain, liberty in what is doubtful, charity, truth, and impartiality in all." It was founded by the Abbé Migne. Offsetting the "Ami de la Religion" and the "Journal des villes et des campagnes", which were of Gallican tendencies, the "Univers", with which the "Tribune", founded by Bailly, was soon merged, represented the most distinctly Roman tendency. Montalembert became associated with the "Univers" in 1835; Louis Veuillot contributed to it his first article in 1839. The "Univers", as the centre of the Catholic campaigns for liberty of instruction, assured a widespread circulation to the claims of the bishops and the speeches of Montalembert and Lacordaire. The "Opinion Publique", founded in 1848 by Alfred Nettement, was a Royalist Catholic journal, which was assured a literary reputation by the contributions of Barbey d'Aurevilly and Armand de Pontmartin. In the same year, at the instance of Ozanam and the Abbé Maret, Lacordaire founded the "Ere Nouvelle", which within three months received 3200 subscriptions, chiefly among the younger clergy, but which did not last long.

Under the Second Empire several very serious discussions occupied the attention of the Catholic Press: viz., the use of the pagan classics in secondary studies (see GAUME); the controversy aroused by the baptism of the Jewish child Mortara, of Bologna, who had been baptized during a serious illness by a Christian servant without the knowledge of his parents, and subsequently reared as a Christian at the command of the Pontifical Government; and the discussions concerning the Roman question. In the course of the discussions on the last-named topic the "Univers" was suppressed by an imperial decree of 29 Jan., 1860, as being guilty of having "compromised public order, the independence of the State, the authority and the dignity of religion". It reappeared 15 April, 1867, and played a very important part during the years preceding the Vatican Council. The "Français", founded 1 April, 1868, by Augustin Cochin and Mgr Dupanloup, received contributions from the Duc de Broglie, M. Thureau-Dangin (at present permanent secretary of the French Academy), and the future minister Buffet, and was constantly engaged in controversy with the "Univers".

The law of 29 July, 1881, definitely established the complete freedom of the press, and submitted to juries formed of simple citizens the political suits brought by officials against newspapers. The law of 1893 against Anarchist abuses was a restriction of the absolute liberty of the Press, but this law is seldom enforced. The characteristic fact of the history of the Press under the Third Republic is the development of five-centime journals, inaugurated as early as 1836 by the foundation of the "Presse" under the auspices of Emile de Girardin.

At the present time the two Catholic journals of Paris are the "Univers" and the "Croix". For the former, see FRANCE. The "Croix" is published by the Maison de la Bonne Presse, which originated in the foundation in 1873 of the "Pèlerin", a bulletin of societies and an organ of pilgrimages, which in 1867 became an illustrated journal, amusing and sometimes satirical; its present circulation is 300,000. In 1880 a monthly review, the "Croix", was founded, which became a daily in June, 1883, after the second penitential crusade to the Holy Places organized by the Assumptionists. After the Associations Law the Maison de la Bonne Presse was purchased in 1900 by M. Paul Féron-Vrau; it employs a staff of about 600 persons. For its great journal, the "Croix", it has throughout the country more than 10,000 committees and nearly 50,000 promoters. It has more direct subscriptions than any Parisian journal, and its circulation places it fourth in rank. It costs one sou (five centimes), and since 1 Jan., 1907, has had six large pages. For purposes of propaganda there is a smaller paper issued daily, which is delivered in quantities to the clergy for 8 or 9 centimes weekly. The "Croix du Dimanche", appearing weekly, besides the news of the week, gives agricultural information in a supplement called the "Laboureur". The "Croix illustrée" has appeared since 24 Dec., 1900, and soon reached a circulation of 50,000 copies. The Ligue de l'Ave Maria, founded Oct., 1888, under the inspiration of Admiral Guicquel des Touches, has had a monthly, the "Petit Journal bleu", since 1897, with a circulation of over 100,000. Its direct subscription price is only 25 centimes yearly, and a number of copies for propaganda may be secured for a half-centime per copy.

The Maison de la Bonne Presse also publishes the "Action Catholique" (founded 1899), a monthly review; the "Chronique de la Bonne Presse", a weekly, founded 25 April, 1900, to give information concerning the movement of ideas in the Press; the "Conférences", a semi-monthly review which supplies accounts of conferences; the "Fascinateur", which gives notes on photographic slides and views for Catholic conferences; the "Cosmos", a popular scientific review, founded by the Abbé Moigno in 1852; the "Contemporains", founded in 1892, which each week gives the biography of some celebrated person; "Echos d'Orient", founded in 1896 and devoted to Oriental and Byzantine questions; "Questions Actuelles", a weekly, founded in 1887, which publishes all recent documents bearing on political and religious questions; the "Revue d'Organization et de Défense Religieuse", founded in 1908, a semi-monthly review, which studies religious questions from a legal standpoint; the "Mois Littéraire et Pittoresque", a popular review founded in 1899; the "Vies des Saints", founded in 1880; "Noël", for children, founded in 1895; and two reviews devoted to the two capitals of Christendom: "Rome", founded Dec., 1903; and "Jérusalem", founded July, 1904. In a single year 350,000 letters reach the Maison de la Bonne Presse.

Another Parisian Catholic daily is the "Démocratie", founded by M. Sangnier, former president of the "Sillon". The first number appeared a few days previous to the Encyclical of Pius X on the "Sillon" (Aug., 1910), and the publication has continued with the authority of Cardinal Merry del Val. The "Libre Parole", an anti-Semitic journal founded in 1891 by M. Edouard Drumont, has since 1910 been marked by a Catholic tendency owing to the collaboration of several members of the Association Catholique de la Jeunesse Française. At Saint-Maixent (Deux-Sèvres) has been founded the Maison de la Bonne Presse de l'Ouest, which publishes parochial bulletins and almanacs. The circulation of the bulletins equalled (1908) nearly 100,000 monthly copies for 300 parishes, that of yearly almanacs nearly 200,000 copies for more than 800 parishes.

By means of fourteen combinations the "Croix" of

Paris is transformed into a local journal, partly general in character, but always retaining its title of the "Croix". Under the title of "Liberté pour tous", the Maison de la Bonne Presse de l'Ouest publishes a four-page journal; two pages forming the common section figure in all the local journals which wish to borrow them, the other two form the special section and vary according to locality. In August, 1905, M. Paul Féron-Vrau founded the "Presse Régionale", a society for the creation or purchase in each diocese of a number of Catholic journals. At present this society owns the "Express de Lyon", the "Nouvelliste de Bretagne" at Rennes, the "République de l'Isère" at Grenoble, the "Journal d'Amiens", the "Express de l'Ouest" at Nantes, the "Eclair de l'Est" at Nancy, and the "Eclair Comtois" at Besançon.

The "Nouvellistes", which are journals with Royalist tendencies, are all Catholic. Bordeaux, Rennes, and Rouen have such publications. The best known is the "Nouvelliste de Lyon", noted for its political news. In the north the Catholics have numerous local journals; the Lille "Dépêche", the "Journal de Roubaix", and the "Croix du Nord" have together about 170,000 subscribers. The "Ouest-Eclair" has a wide circulation in Catholic Brittany. The departments of the South have no Catholic journal capable of combating seriously with the "Dépêche de Toulouse", a radical anticlerical journal and one of the most powerful political organs in France. The organization of the "Presse pour tous", founded in 1903 by Mme Taine, widow of the celebrated philosopher, collects subscriptions for the distribution of good papers among study circles or shops having many customers.

The Catholics of France founded in 1905 the "Agence de la Presse nouvelle", a telegraphic agency for Catholic news. It supplied the news for 1908 to about one hundred papers. There is also a religious and social information-bureau, the object of which is to centralize the religious news of various countries, and which as early as 1908 had correspondents in forty-two dioceses. The most important French Catholic review is the "Correspondant", issued on the 10th and 25th of every month. It was at first (March, 1829) a semi-weekly paper. Its founders were Carné, Cazalès, and Augustin de Meaux, and its motto was Canning's words: "Civil and religious liberty throughout the world". Its object was to reconcile Catholicism and modern ideas. During the Monarchy of July it underwent various vicissitudes. In 1853 Montalembert wished to build it up in order to offset the influence of Louis Veuillot and the "Univers", and he secured the co-operation of Albert de Broglie, Falloux, and Dupanloup. Its frequent praise of English parliamentary institutions aroused the suspicions of the empire. The "Correspondant" was at one with the "Univers" in defending the temporal power of the pope, and also felt at times the harshness of the imperial police. During the Vatican Council there was sharp conflict between the "Univers", which was for Infallibility, and the "Correspondant", which was against it. Under the Third Republic the "Correspondant" was successively edited by MM. Léon Lavedan, Etienne Lamy, of the French Academy, and Etienne Trogau, and endeavoured to show, according to the terms of its programme of 1829, that Catholicism "still holds within its fruitful breast the wherewithal to satisfy all the needs, wishes, and hopes of humanity". The "Bulletin de la Semaine", published since 1905, gives weekly a number of documents and articles of present interest on religious questions. Founded by M. Imbart de La Tour, this paper, while not concerning itself with dogmatic questions, recalls in certain respects, by the spirit of its religious policy, the tendency of the "Correspondant" during the pontificate of Pius IX.

In 1856 the Jesuits Charles Daniel and Jean Gagarin founded the "Etudes de théologie, de philosophie et d'histoire", with the aim of furthering Russia's return to the Catholic Church. This soon became a semi-monthly, dealing with all important religious questions and entitled "Etudes religieuses, historiques et littéraires, publiées par des Pères de la Compagnie de Jésus". Consequent on the decrees of 1880 against congregations it was suspended, but resumed publication in 1888. In 1910 was founded the "Recherches", wherein the Fathers of the Society of Jesus treat the most interesting problems of religious knowledge. The Assumptionists own the "Revue Augustinienne"; the Dominicans the "Revue Thomiste" (1893), and the "Revue de la Jeunesse" (1909), published in Belgium. Since 1892 the Dominicans of Jerusalem have owned the "Revue Biblique". The Institut Catholique of Paris has a bulletin; many of the professors of the Catholic University of Lyons contribute to the "Université Catholique" of that city. The Catholic University of Angers has the "Revue des Facultés Catholiques de l'Ouest"; the Institut Catholique of Toulouse the "Bulletin d'histoire et littérature religieuse". There are two Catholic philosophical reviews: the "Revue de Philosophie", founded in 1900 by M. Peillaube, in connexion with the school of philosophy which is striving for a compromise between Thomism and contemporary results in physiology and psychology; and the "Annales de philosophie chrétienne", founded in 1828 by Augustin Bonnetty. The chief editors of the latter are MM. Laberthonnière and Maurice Blondel, and its motto the saying of St. Augustine: "Let us seek as those who would find, and find as those who would still seek".

The "Revue des Questions Historiques", founded in 1866, does great credit to Catholic learning. Its present editor is M. Jean Guiraud, professor at the University of Besançon. Since 1907 the French Benedictines who have emigrated to Belgium have created the "Revue Mabillon", an important review of Benedictine history. The "Revue d'histoire de l'Eglise de France" (Analecta Gallicana) was founded in 1910. The two chief reviews for the clergy are the "Ami du clergé", published at Langres since 1878, and the "Revue du Clergé Français", published at Paris since 1894. The "Revue pratique d'Apologétique", founded in 1905, is edited by Mgr Baudrillart, rector of the Paris Institut Catholique. A characteristic of recent years is the issue of political and social bulletins published by various female Catholic sodalities and intended for Catholic women. One of the chief reviews of the Catholic social movement is the "Chronique sociale de France" (formerly "Chronique du Sud-Est"), the organ of the group which organized the Semaines sociales. A powerful movement of Catholic social journalism is due to the bureaux of the Action populaire organized at Reims (see FRANCE). The periodical yellow pamphlets issued by the Action Populaire between 1903 and 1911 have reached the number of 236. Besides its annual "Guides sociaux" it publishes a theoretical review of social studies, founded in 1876 by the organization of Catholic workmen as the "Association Catholique", now called the "Mouvement social, revue catholique internationale". It issues a popular social review called the "Revue verte", or "Revue de l'Action populaire". Finally, the Action populaire publishes "Brochures périodiques d'Action religieuse", which are unquestionably the most interesting sources of information with regard to the undertakings of the Church of France since its separation from the State.

TAVERNIER, *Du journalisme, son histoire, son rôle politique et religieux* (Paris, 1902); *Guide d'Action Religieuse*, published by the Action populaire of Reims (1908).

GEORGES GOYAU.

GERMANY.—The Catholic periodical press of Germany is a product of the nineteenth century. It is only within the last forty years that it has become important by its circulation and its ability. A number of Catholic journals are, however, much older.

The oldest, the "Augsburg Postzeitung", was founded in 1695, and five others were established in the eighteenth century. Of those which were founded in the early part of the nineteenth century the most important is the "Westfälischer Merkur", established at Münster in 1822, which at first, it is true, had a Liberal tendency. Until 1848 Catholic journalism did not prosper. In this reactionary period the severe censorship of the government authorities was a drawback to the Press in general; Catholic journals were viewed in an even less friendly spirit than the others. In Würtemberg and Hesse no Catholic journals were allowed to be published. Up to the second and third decades of the nineteenth century, on the other hand, the Catholics themselves seemed to be in a condition of intellectual torpor. For the most part, the clergy were under the influence of Protestantism and the prevailing philosophy of the times. Cultured society, the Catholic no less than the Protestant, was under the influence of the "all-embracing religion of humanity", which diluted Christianity.

The "Theologische Zeitschrift" of Bamberg, edited by J. J. Batz and Father Brenner, may be regarded as the oldest periodical, but its existence lasted only from 1809 to 1814. It was followed by the "Katholische Literaturzeitung", first edited by Father K. Felder, then by Kaspar Anton von Mastiaux, who was succeeded by Friedrich von Kerz and Anton von Besnard (1810–36). The oldest of the periodicals still in existence is the "Tübinger Theologische Quartalschrift", founded in 1819, which has always had a high reputation on account of its genuinely scholarly spirit. Among its editors have been Hirscher, Möhler, Kuhn, Hefele, Welte, Linsemann, Funke, and Schanz, names of the highest repute in the history of theology. In 1821 the "Katholik" was founded by Andreas Räss and Nikolaus Weis, afterwards Bishops of Strasburg and Speyer respectively. The purpose was stated to be "to offer the necessary opposition to the attacks, partly open, partly concealed, against the Church, by orthodox articles on the doctrines of faith and morals, Church history and liturgy, the training of children, devotional exercises by the people, and all that belongs to the Catholic Faith". The chief collaborator in 1824–26 was the great publicist Joseph von Görres, but the responsible editors were G. Scheiblein and Fr. L. Br. Liebermann. In 1827, Weis again became the chief editor. He was followed by Franz Xaver Dieringer (1841–43); Franz Sausen (1844–49); Johann Baptist Heinrich and Christoph Moufang (1850–90); Michael Raich (1891–1906); Joseph Becker and Joseph Selbst (from 1907). Since the appearance of the new Scholasticism the "Katholik" has been its exponent.

The Catholic movement was greatly aided by the arrest in 1837 of the Archbishops of Cologne and Posen-Gnesen, von Droste-Vischering and von Dunin. Connected with this is the founding of the "Historisch-politische Blätter", by Georg Phillips and Guido Görres in 1838. This periodical contended against false theories of the state, ecclesiastical Liberalism, and the writing of history from a Protestant point of view. Distinguished publicists such as Joseph Görres, father of Guido, and the converted jurist Karl Ernst Jarck collaborated on the journal and gained for it a lasting influence. Up to 1871 it was the most prominent journalistic organ of the Catholics. Its position in politics was that of Greater Germany. After the death of Görres (1852) the chief editor was Edmund Jörg; the assistant editor from 1858 up to Jörg's death in 1901 was Franz Binder. From 1903 Binder and Georg Jochner have shared the editorial responsibility. Other periodicals were only short-lived, as the Hermesian "Zeitschrift für Philosophie und katholische Theologie" that existed from 1833 to 1852; the "Jahrbücher für Theologie und christliche Philosophie" (1834–47), edited by the theological faculty of Giessen; the "Zeitschrift für Theologie", edited at Freiburg in 1839–49; the "Archiv für theologische Literatur", edited by Dollinger, Haneberg, etc., from 1842 to 1843; the "Katholische Zeitschrift für Wissenschaft und Kunst", edited by Dieringer 1844–46, and the continuation of this periodical, the "Katholische Vierteljahrsschrift für Wissenschaft und Kunst", 1847–49. In addition there were various church weeklies.

The year 1848 and the political and religious emancipations which it brought were of much importance for Catholic life and the Catholic press. The freedom of the Press enabled the journals to express public opinion. From this time on each important periodical became the advocate of some definite political idea. Moreover, another result of 1848 was freedom of association, of which the Catholics at once made use to the largest possible extent. An increase in the circulation of the journals already existing and the founding of new ones was very materially aided by the Catholic societies. A rich Catholic life arose and came into public notice with unexpected power. Thus in the years directly succeeding 1848 a large number of new periodicals appeared. Among them were, to mention only the more important, the "Echo der Gegenwart" of Aachen; the "Rheinische Volkshalle" of Cologne, which, from 2 Oct., 1849, took the name of "Deutsche Volkshalle"; the "Mainzer Journal", edited by Franz Sausen: the "Deutsches Volksblatt" of Stuttgart; the "Niederrheinische Volkszeitung" of Krefeld; in 1849 the "Westfälisches Volksblatt" of Paderborn; in 1852 the "Münsterische Anzeiger"; in 1853 the "Rheinischen Volksblätter" of Cologne; in 1854 the "Neue Augsburger Zeitung"; in 1856 the "Bayrischer Kurier" of Munich. In addition the conference of bishops held at Würzburg (November, 1848) expressed the wish that there should be founded in all dioceses Sunday papers containing edifying and instructive matter. Of such journals the one that attained the most importance was the "Frankfurter katholisches Kirchenblatt". The most important journals during the fifth decade of the nineteenth century were the "Deutsche Volkshalle" of Cologne, the "Mainzer Journal", and the "Deutsches Volksblatt". The "Deutsche Volkshalle" was suppressed 10 July, 1855, because its attitude towards the Government had not been friendly. Its place was taken by a journal planned on a large scale, the "Deutschland" of Frankfort, founded in 1855 by the city parish priest and well-known writer, Beda Weber. After two years it ceased, not from lack of vitality, but on account of bad financial management. The "Kölnische Blätter", issued from 1 April, 1860, by J. P. Bachem of Cologne, had a more fortunate fate. From 1 Jan., 1869, this well-edited paper bore the name of "Kölnische Volkszeitung". Further, during the sixties appeared the "Freiburger Bote" (1865); the "Fränkische Volksblatt" of Würzburg (1867); the "Essener Volkszeitung" (1868); the "Osanbrücker Volkszeitung" (1868); and the "Schlesische Volkszeitung" (1869).

In 1862 the "Literarischer Handweiser" was founded at Münster by Franz Hülskamp and Hermann Rump, to give information concerning the latest literary publications. From 1876, after Rump's death, Hülskamp edited it alone; from 1904 it has been edited by Edmund Niesert. The "Chilianeum", a general review for "learning, art, and life" was founded at Würzburg and edited by J. B. Stamminger; the review had excellent collaborators, but lived only from 1862 to 1869. During the sixties there was also established the organ of the German Jesuits, the "Stimmen aus Maria-Laach", which originally (from 1865) appeared at irregular intervals as pamphlets on burning questions of Catholic principles. It was called into existence by the storm against the Syllabus and the Encyclical of 8 Dec., 1864. From 1871 it has been issued regularly and has included within the scope of its observation all important questions and events. Its circle of collaborators includes the most noted German Jesuits, as Alexander Baumgartner (now deceased), Stephan Beissel, Viktor Cathrein, Franz Ehrle, Wilhelm Kreiten (now deceased), Augustin Lehmkuhl, Christian and Tilmann Pesch, etc. In 1866 the excellent "Theologisches Literaturblatt" of Bonn was founded, but after 1870 it became an organ of the Old Catholics.

The *Kulturkampf* now broke out, which consolidated the Catholics, and impressed on them most powerfully the necessity of a press of their own. Consequently the larger number of Catholic periodicals have appeared from the seventies on. Simultaneous with the occurrence of the *Kulturkampf* was the founding of the Centre Party (Dec., 1870). Since then a Catholic paper and a paper that is the organ of the Centre Party are with very few exceptions identical. During the exciting years of the ecclesiastico-political struggle small papers particularly, such as the "Kaplanspresse" (curate's press), shot up like mushrooms. On 1 Jan., 1871 the "Germania" newspaper appeared at Berlin, as the new and most important organ of the Centre Party; it was founded as a company by members of the Catholic societies of Berlin with the active and praiseworthy aid of the embassy councillor Friedrich Kehler (d. 1901). Up to 1878 Paul Majunke (d. 1899) wrote for it articles that were exceedingly sharp and contentious in tone. He was followed as editor up to 1881 by the learned and more moderate Dr. Adolf Franz, who was succeeded by Theodor Stahl, Dr. Eduard Marcour, and, from 1894, Hermann ten Brink. Besides the "Germania" and the "Kölnische Volkszeitung", which latter has been edited from 1876 by Dr. Hermann Cardauns with great skill and intelligence, there are important provincial periodicals that maintain Catholic interests. Of these should be mentioned: the "Deutsche Reichszeitung" founded at Bonn in 1872; the "Düsseldorfer Volksblatt", that developed greatly under the editorial guidance of Dr. Eduard Hüsgen; the "Niederrheinische Volkszeitung" of Krefeld; the "Essener Volkszeitung"; the "Trierische Landeszeitung", founded in 1873 by the energetic chaplain Georg Friedrich Dasbach (d. 1907); the "Westfälischer Merkur" of Münster, edited by J. Hoffmann and Chaplain Karl Böddinghaus; the "Tremonia" of Dortmund, founded in 1875; the "Münsterischer Anzeiger"; the "Westfälisches Volksblatt" of Paderborn; the "Schlesische Volkszeitung" of Breslau, edited by Dr. Arthur Hager, one of the "most dashing champions of the Centre Party"; the "Deutsches Volksblatt" of Stuttgart; the "Mainzer Journal"; the "Badischer Beobachter"; the "Augsburger Postzeitung"; the "Bayerischer Kurier" of Munich. The editors had to make great personal sacrifices, for the legal actions against them for violations of the press laws, the confiscations, fines, and imprisonments were almost endless. It must be acknowledged that there were some editorial elements whose speech and method of fighting did no honour to their cause. Among the weekly papers the "Katholisches Volksblatt" of Mainz had a large circulation (35,000), and great influence in Southern Germany; the "Schwarzes Blatt" was published at Berlin as a paper of general scope for the common people.

It was in the era of the *Kulturkampf* (1875) that the first large illustrated family periodical "Der Deutsche Hausschatz" was founded at Ratisbon; it had a large circulation and was edited 1875–88 by Venanz Müller; 1888–98 by Heinrich Keiter; at present by Dr. Otto Denk. A new literary journal was also established in 1875 by the secular priest J. Köhler under the name of the "Literarische Rundschau für das katholische Deutschland". From this time on the Catholic Press has steadily grown. The number of political newspapers and ecclesiastico-political Sunday papers was: in 1880, 186; in 1890, 272; in 1900, 419; in 1908, 500. In Prussia alone the Catholic periodicals numbered in 1870, 49; in 1880, 109; in 1890, 149; in 1900, 270. The number of Catholic periodicals appearing in Germany in 1890 was 143. Since this date the number has more than doubled.

The present condition of the Catholic Press is as follows: (1) Daily political newspapers, 278; political newspapers appearing four times weekly, 14; three times weekly, 134; twice weekly, 83; once weekly, 64; in addition there are 19, the time of appearance of which is unknown, making altogether 592. In regard to the extent of the circulation of these newspapers, statements as to the issue have been given by the publishers of 338 of them. The total issue of all for one number amounts to 1,938,434. The issue printed by the remaining 254 can be averaged as 1500 for each number, altogether as 381,000. According to this all the political newspapers taken together issue a total edition of 2,319,434 for one number. In 1880 the number of subscribers to the Catholic papers was estimated at 596,000; in 1890 Keiter estimated it at over 1,000,000. The growth, therefore, was very large. Unfortunately, a comparison with the Protestant Press cannot be made, because comprehensive statistics are lacking, and because there is some uncertainty as to just what would be meant by a "Protestant newspaper". Yet it may be accepted that the Catholic Press would equal it in the number of its organs and subscribers.

An important Catholic newspaper is the "Kölnische Volkszeitung", which appears three times daily; the editor-in-chief from 1907 is Dr. Karl Hoeber, the publisher J. P. Bachem of Cologne; circulation 26,500 copies. Its quiet, dignified, conciliatory tone, combined with firmness of principle, has gained for it the respect of all, especially the cultured circles, and its influence extends far beyond the limits of Germany. The "Germania" is next to it in reputation; the editor-in-chief of the "Germania" is Hermann ten Brink, the publisher. Financially it is less favourably situated than the Cologne journal, because being published in a Protestant city, it lacks advertisements. In 1882 its circulation was 7000 copies; its present circulation is unknown, but it is probably from 12,000 to 14,000. The other newspapers previously mentioned in speaking of the *Kulturkampf* have also prospered and developed, with the possible exception of the "Westfälischer Merkur", which has declined somewhat. The one with the largest number of subscribers is the "Essener Volkszeitung" (54,500).

(2) There are published in the German Empire over 300 Catholic periodicals, which have about 5,000,000 subscribers. Among these are: (a) General reviews, 8. The most important, finest in tone, contents, and artistic execution is the monthly "Hochland", founded in 1903 and edited by Karl Muth; the publisher is J. Kösel of Munich, and an edition contains 10,000 copies. The list of collaborators contains the names of Bäumker, Cardauns, Finke, Grauert, von Handel-Mazzetti, von Hertling, Kiefl, Mausbach, Pastor, Schanz (now deceased), Schell (now deceased), Schönbach, Spahn, Streitberg, Willmann. The monthly called "Der Aar", founded in 1910, seeks to compete with the "Hochland", but falls a little below the other; the editor is Dr. Otto Denk, the publisher is Pustet at Ratisbon. The semi-monthly "Die Historisch-politische Blätter", published by Riedel at Munich, edition 3000 copies, and the "Stimmen aus Maria-Laach", published ten times a year by Herder at Freiburg, edition 5200 copies, are carried on, on the same lines as heretofore. The "Allgemeine Rundschau", a semi-monthly edited and published by Dr. Armin Kausen at Munich, devotes itself to the living questions of political and religious life. It specially combats immorality in life and art.

(b) Theological reviews, 10, diocesan and parochial papers, about 20. A description has already been given of the "Theologische Quartalschrift", published by Laupp at Tübingen, edition 630 copies; and the "Katholik", published by Kirchheim at Mainz, edition 800 copies. A good periodical for theological literature is the "Theologische Revue", edited by Prof. Diekamp, published by Aschendorff at Münster, edition 950 copies.

(c) Family and religious-popular periodicals, 90. The subscription list of the oldest and highest in repute of this class, the "Deutsche Hausschatz", has declined; it is published by Pustet at Ratisbon, and its edition in 1900 was 38,000 copies; in 1908, 28,000; the number of copies forming an edition at present is unknown. Large circulations are enjoyed by: the "Stadt Gottes", edited by the Society of the Word of God, at Steyl, edition 140,000 copies; the "Christliche Familie", edited by Dr. Jos. Burg, published by Fredebeul and Koenen at Essen, edition 150,000 copies; the "Katholisches Sonntagsblatt" of Stuttgart, edition 75,000 copies.

(d) Legal, national, and socio-economic, 6; among these is the "Archiv für katholisches Kirchenrecht", founded by Ernst von Moy in 1857, edited later by Friedrich H. Vering, and at present by Franz Heiner, published by Kirchheim at Mainz.

(e) Scientific periodicals, 3. The most important of these is "Natur und Offenbarung", edited by Dr. Forch, published by Aschendorff at Münster, edition 900 copies; (f) Philosophical periodicals, 2; (g) Educational periodicals, 34; (h) Historical periodicals, 10. Among these one of general importance is the "Historisches Jahrbuch der Görresgesellschaft", founded in 1880. Its former editors are: Hüffer, Hermann Grauert, Joseph Weiss; its present editor is Max Jansen; it is published by Herder at Munich, edition about 750 copies.

(i) Periodicals for historical art, 6. Among these are the two illustrated monthlies "Zeitschrift für christliche Kunst", edited by Prof. Dr. Schnütgen, published by Schwann at Düsseldorf, edition 900 copies; and "Die christliche Kunst", edited by J. Staudhamer, published by the Society for Christian Art of Munich, edition 6400 copies; (j) Periodicals for church music, 8.

(k) Literary journals, 18. Among these are the "Literarischer Handweiser", published by Theissing at Münster, and the "Literarische Rundschau für das katholische Deutschland", edited by Prof. Joseph Sauer, published by Herder at Freiburg; (l) Missionary periodicals, 14; (m) Periodicals for children and youth, 21; (n) Periodicals issued by Catholic associations, 24.

Up to the present time the growth of the Catholic Press of Germany has been both rapid and steady. As the Catholics in Germany number about 21,000,000, there is room for an increase in the sales of these periodicals, and their circulation will probably grow still larger. On the other hand an increase in the number of organs is less necessary and desirable. The effort should rather be made to overcome the decided disparity between quantity and quality. There are, perhaps, no more than a dozen Catholic dailies which have a really high value. Most of the others limit themselves to a systematic use of correspondence, the collection of notices, and polemics that are not always very skilful; they are also, in part, so monotonous that they can only be enjoyed by an unassuming circle of readers. The relatively small subscription lists of the really important journals and the undue number of small periodicals show that the cultivated classes satisfy their need of reading in part with non-Catholic periodicals. The case is the same with the family papers. An issue of 10,000 copies is very small for so excellent a review as "Hochland". The satisfaction expressed in each succeeding edition of Keiter's "Handbuch der katholischen Presse" over the growth of the Catholic press refers only to quantity. In regard to quality there is little choice.

KLEMENS LÖFFLER.

HOLLAND.—Towards the end of the eighteenth century the grinding oppression, under which the Catholic Faith in the Northern Netherlands had laboured so long, began to grow less marked, and the Catholics, upon whose printing-presses the Government had always kept a vigilant eye, now ventured to assert themselves more in public life and even to issue periodicals in order to proclaim and uphold their religious principles. The first attempt was on a most modest scale and appeared under the title of "Kerkelijke Bibliotheek" (6 vols., 1794–96), followed by the "Mengelingen voor Roomsch-Catholijken" (5 vols., 1807–14), edited by Prof. J. Schrant, Rev. J. W. A. Muller, and Prof. J. H. Lexius. But the man who inspired Catholic periodical literature with life and vigour and brought it to comparative perfection was Joachim George le Sage ten Broek (d. 1847), a convert from Protestantism (1806) and known in Holland as the "Father of the Roman Catholic Press". In 1818 he founded "De Godsdienstvriend" (102 vols., 1818–69), containing articles of local interest, recent ecclesiastical intelligence, and especially moderate polemics against Protestant and Liberal pretensions, by which he united the efforts of the Catholics in their struggle for emancipation. Assisted by his adopted son, Josué Witz, Le Sage displayed a great and wonderful energy not only in his books, but also in several serials, edited by him or at least with his collaboration, viz., the works of the "R. Cath. Maatschappy" (1821–2), suppressed in 1823, the "R. Kath. Bibliotheek" (6 vols., 1821–6), the "Godsdienstige en zedekundige mengelingen" (1824–8), the "Bijdragen tot de Godsdienstvriend" (2 vols., 1824–7), "De Ultramontaan" (5 vols., 1826–30) with its sequels, "De Morgenstar" (2 vols., 1831–2) and "De Morgenstar der toekernst" (7 vols., 1832–5), finally, "De Correspondent" (3 vols., 1833–4) continued later by Josué Witz in the "Catholijke Nederlandsche Stemmen" (22 vols., 1835–56), appearing under the title of "Kerkelijke Courant" from 1857 till 1873. Besides this in 1844 Witz started a popular magazine, "Uitspanningslectuur" (40 vols., 1844–52). In the mean time other serials were published in the Catholic interest, viz., "Minerva" (6 vols., 1818–20), continued in "De Katholijke" (3 vols., 1822–4), "Katholikon" (3 vols., 1828–30), "De Christelijke Mentor" (2 vols., 1828–9), "Magazijn voor R.-Katholieken" (9 vols., 1835–45), and "Godsdienstig, geschied-en letterkundig Tijdschrift" (2 vols., 1838–39), but none of these survived. A new generation of Catholic writers soon arose, by whom the struggle for emancipation was continued on a more scientific basis.

In 1842 F. J. van Vree, later Bishop of Haarlem, Th. Borret, C. Broere, J. F. Leesberg, and others founded the best and oldest of the periodicals still existing, "De Katholiek" (138 vols., 1842–1910). This periodical in the course of time introduced many new features which have increased its usefulness, the most important being the admission of lengthier articles contributed by prominent Catholic scholars. A fresh impetus in the field of art and literature was given by Jos. Alberdingk Thijm's "Dietsche Warande" (27 vols., 1855–90) and his more popular "Volksalmanak" (50 vols., 1852–1901), the later issues being entitled "Jaarboekje" (7 vols., 1902–08) and finally consolidated with the "Annuarium der Apologetische Vereeniging Petrus Canisius" (2 vols., 1909–10). Under Thijm's direction two eminent writers were formed: Dr. H. J. Schaepman, poet and politician, and Dr. W. Nuijens, the historian, who, having jointly founded the "Kath. Nederl. Brochurenvereeniging" (27 brochures, 1869–70), transformed it later into the more scientific monthly "Onze Wachter" (23 vols., 1874–85), combined with "De Wachter" (6 vols., 1871–3), afterwards named "De Katholiek" in 1885. Meanwhile "De Wachter" (12 vols., 1874–85), more especially devoted to studies of Dante, continued to exist under the editorship of J. Bohl and was finally merged in "De wetenschappelijke Nederlander" in which the Rev. J. Brouwers published many interesting Essays (8 vols., 1881–90). Recently "De Katholiek" has found powerful competitors in "Van onzen tijd" (at first a monthly, 15 vols., 1900–10; then a weekly, 1 vol., 1910–1911) and in the "Annalen der vereeniging tot het bevorderen van de beoefening der wetenschap onder de katholieken in Nederland" (2 vols., 1907–10), which contain articles of a most scholarly character. In this country as elsewhere the Jesuits have edited a periodical of their own, the valuable "Studiën. Tijdschrift voor godsdienst, wetenschap, letteren" (74 vols., 1868–1910), while in "De katholieke missiën" (35 vols., 1876–1910) they have kept up a lively interest in the foreign missions, towards which Holland has always been so generous.

In the field of purely historical research there are the "Bijdragen voor de geschiedenis van het bisdom van Haarlem" (33 vols., 1873–1910) and the "Archief voor heb aarbsbisdom Utrecht" (36 vols., 1875–1910), which together with the historical contributions appearing in the other periodicals fully answer the existing interest; it was this that led to the early collapse of the "Geschiedkundige Bladen" (4 vols., 1905–6). No better fate awaited the only periodical on ecclesiastical art, "Het Gildeboek" (3 vols., 1873–81; "Verslagen", 11 vols., 1886–90) edited by Mgr van Henkelum, dean of St. Bernulph's Guild, but its work is still carried on in part by the Belgian-Dutch review "Sint Lucas" (2 vols., 1908–10). "De katholieke Gids" (20 vols., 1889–1908), a monthly, the contents of which were never of any great moment, met a similar fate; as did the weekly "Stemmen onzer Eeuw" (1905–06), while the only educational paper "Opvoeding en Onderwijs" (2 vols., 1908–10), recently founded, seems already to be on the wane. Among the apologetic papers there are some that deserve special mention: "Het Dompertje van den onden Valentijn" (32 vols., 1867–1900), succeeded by "Het nieuwe Dompertje" (4 vols., 1901–4), and "Het Dompertje" (6 vols., 1905–10), the works of the "Willibrordus-vereeniging" (180 brochures, 1896–1910), the series "Geloof en Wetenschap" (36 booklets, 1904–10) as well as the publications issued by the "Apologetische vereeniging Petrus Canisius" (some 40 booklets, 1906–10). Among the apologetic journals may also be reckoned "Boekenschouw" (5 vols., 1906–10; formerly called "Lectuur", 2 vols., 1904–5), a critical book review. The "Central Office for Social Action" at Leiden issues no fewer than four periodicals under the chief editorship of P. J. Aalberse: the excellent "Katholiek sociaal Weekblad" (9 vols., 1902–10), the "Volksbibliotheek" (25 numbers, 1905–10), the "Politieke en Sociale studiën", at first two separate serials, now united (3 and 5 vols., 1906–10), and the "Volkstijdschrift" (27 numbers, 1909–10). Sobriëtas (4 vols., 1907–10) is the chief organ of the Catholic temperance movement.

In addition Holland possesses a flourishing exclusively theological monthly, "Nederlandsche Katholieke stemmen" (10 vols., 1901–10), which is a continuation of an older ecclesiastical paper of the same name (22 vols., 1879–1900). The "Sint-Gregoriusblad" (35 vols., 1876–1910) is devoted to church music, while the "Koorbode" (5 vols., 1906–10) upholds the modern movements. The Catholic university students have their "Annuarium der R. Kath. studenten" (8 vols., 1902–10), and recently they started a weekly paper "Roomsch Studenten-blad" (1 vol., 1910–1). Finally Catholic ladies have the Belgian-Dutch magazine, "De Lelie" (2 vols., 1909–10). Besides those already mentioned there are some fifty other periodicals some of which supply entertaining literature, such as the "Katholieke Illustratie" (44 vols., 1867–1910) and the "Leesbibliotheek voor christelijke huisgezinnen" (56 vols., 1856–1910), while others, mostly published for the benefit of the foreign missions, are of a devotional character. Mention must be made of the annual Catholic directories of Holland. The first of these was the "Almanach du clergé catholique" (7 vols., 1822–29), issued when Holland and Belgium were politically united. Then came the "R.-Kath. Jaarboek" (9 vols., 1835–44), succeeded by "Kerkelijk Nederland" (10 vols., 1847–56), together with the interesting "Handboekje voor de zaken der R.-Kath. eeredienst" (by J. C. Willemse, 32 vols., 1847–80), while the statistics of more modern times and the present day and all desirable information can be found carefully arranged in the "Pius-almanak" (36 vols., 1875–1910), which had a temporary rival in "Onze Pius-almanak" (6 vols., 1900–05).

Among the journals the three most prominent dailies are: "De Tijd", started by the Rev. J. A. Smits, J. W. Cramer, and P. van Cranenburgh in 1846, which is considered the chief leader and representative of public opinion amongst Catholics; the more militant "De Maasbode", founded in 1868, and the democratic "Het Centrum", begun in 1884. All these Dutch papers and periodicals are irreproachably orthodox. As to the circulation the dailies enjoy, no figures are available. But "De Voorhoede", a weekly paper established in 1907, is known to have an edition of 25,000 copies. In all, Holland has 15 Catholic dailies, of which only "De Maasbode" issues a morning and an evening edition (since 1909). In addition to these there are 31 papers published more than once a week, with 76 weeklies and some 70 monthlies.

BONAV. KRUITWAGEN.

INDIA.—See INDIA.

IRELAND.—Owing to the ferocity of the penal laws, such a thing as Catholic periodical literature was impossible in Ireland during the seventeenth and eighteenth centuries. It was not until 1793 that any notable relaxation was made in the disabilities under which Irish Catholics laboured, and the only form of literature, even in the first quarter of the nineteenth century, was polemical. The sporadic pamphlets issued by the leaders of the Catholic Committee, especially in regard to the Veto question and the Quarantotti rescript, can scarcely be regarded as periodical literature, nor yet the able series of "Letters of Hierophilus" (1820–23) by Bishop Doyle. After Catholic Emancipation (1829), Irish Catholics began to use the power of the press. In 1834 the "Catholic Penny Magazine" was started as a weekly, published by Caldwell of Dublin. The first number was issued in February, 1834, and the last in December, 1835. A new era opened with the foundation of the "Dublin Review" in May, 1836, a journal Irish in more than name, its founders being Dr. Nicholas Wiseman and Daniel O'Connell. Twice subsequently O'Connell made a personal appeal on its behalf. The first editor, to whom Cardinal Wiseman gives the original credit of the project, was W. Michael Quin (q. v.). In a short time it came under the control of W. Henry R. Bagshawe, but he was rather sub-editor with ample authority under Dr. Wiseman. The history of the "Review" belongs to the English section of this article, but Ireland can claim a great share in this arduous enterprise. At least one-half, often much more, of the literary matter of the original series was produced in Ireland; and Irish topics, political, social, educational, or literary, constituted a large part of the contents. Dr. C. W. Russell of Maynooth was the chief support of Dr. Wiseman who, writing in January, 1846, calls him editor. When Dr. W. G. Ward became proprietor, the editorial work was done by another Irishman, John Cashel Hoey. An Irish editor of a later date was Mgr Moyes. A number of influential Ulster Catholics established the Belfast "Vindicator", in 1839, with Charles Gavan Duffy as editor, whose successor in 1842 was Kevin T. Buggy. This, though an able weekly, ceased soon after 1844. In 1840, a magazine, entitled "The Catholic Luminary", was established in Dublin, which appeared every alternate Saturday, was managed by a committee of priests and laymen, the subscription price being eight shillings yearly, and lasted from 20 June to 19 December, 1840.

Its successor was the "Catholic Magazine", published by James Duffy in 1847, a monthly journal devoted to national literature, arts, antiquities, etc. Although ably conducted by Denis Florence MacCarthy, Richard D. Williams, and Father Kenyon, it declined in 1848, owing to political excitement, and ceased publication in the following December. A weekly paper, entitled "Catholic Advocate", was issued in 1851, but only one number was published. James Duffy ventured on another monthly, called "Duffy's Fireside Magazine", which ran from 1851–54. He also published a weekly magazine, "The Catholic Guardian", devoted to national and religious literature, but it ceased after forty-three numbers, the last issue being dated 20 Nov., 1852. Frederick Lucas, a convert from Quakerism, had founded the "Tablet", the first number of which appeared 16 May, 1840. After some years he came to know Irishmen like Gavan Duffy and John O'Hagan; and, as he was dissatisfied with the support given by English Catholics, he transferred the "Tablet" to Dublin at the end of 1849. After his death (1855) it was transferred back to London. The "Catholic Layman", a monthly polemical magazine, price one shilling, ran from 1852 to 1854. The "Catholic University Gazette", a weekly paper under the auspices of Cardinal Newman, had a brief existence from June, 1854, until the end of August, 1855. Its price was but one penny. Another weekly, the "Irish Catholic Magazine", edited by W. J. O'Neill Daunt, ran from January to August, 1856. The "Harp", edited by M. J. McCann, was issued in 1859. It was an excellent Catholic monthly, but had a sporadic existence under varying titles, and finally disappeared in February, 1864. Among its contributors were Canon O'Hanlon, Dr. R. D. Joyce, Dr. Sigerson, Dr. Campion, and John Walsh. McCann, still remembered as the author of the song "O'Donnell Abu", died in London in 1883. In July, 1860, James Duffy founded the "Hibernian Magazine", edited by Martin Haverty, a distinguished alumnus of the Irish College, Rome. It was a monthly, price eight pence, and ran for two years. The contributors included Father C. P. Meehan, Prof. Kavanagh, D. F. MacCarthy, Dr. O'Donovan, William Carleton, D'Arcy Magee, and W. J. Fitzpatrick, and the articles were all signed. It ceased after two years, but a second series was started in 1862, with Father Meehan as editor, which extended to six volumes and ended in June, 1865. A higher-class magazine was "Atlantis", the official literary organ of the Catholic University, of which four volumes appeared between the years 1859 and 1861, the contributors being Cardinal Newman, O'Curry, John O'Hagan, and others. In 1870 Father Robert Kelly, S.J., founded the "Monitor", a small penny monthly, mainly as a temperance organ. Its success was so great that he issued it in an enlarged form as the "Illustrated Monitor" in 1873. Father Kelly died 15 June, 1876, but the publication was continued by the publisher, Joseph Dollard. It steadily declined in 1877, and came to an abrupt end in 1878. In June, 1906, Mgr O'Riordan edited a really high-class quarterly, the "Seven Hills Magazine", published by Duffy of Dublin, but it also ceased with the issue of September, 1908.

In regard to existing periodicals, there is no distinctively Catholic daily paper in Ireland, but the "Freeman's Journal" is frankly Catholic in tone, and gives prominence to Catholic topics. As to the weeklies, there is but one, the "Irish Catholic", founded by T. D. Sullivan in 1888. Its first editor was Robert Donovan (now professor in the National University), who after five weeks was replaced by W. F. Dennehy in August of the same year. It may be described as a Conservative-National organ, supporting the Irish hierarchy in their corporate decisions on all religious and political matters. In 1890, at the time of the Parnell "split", it loyally stood by the bishops. In 1891, the "Nation" was merged into the "Irish Catholic" and in 1897 it became a daily. Though the "Daily Nation" ceased in 1900, the "Irish Catholic" continued as a weekly, with Mr. Dennehy as editor and publisher. It remains unconnected with any of the existing political parties, but is markedly opposed to any union with British Liberalism and Radicalism. The paper has a circulation throughout Great Britain, America, and the colonies. Among monthlies the "Irish Ecclesiastical Record" can claim premier place. Founded in March, 1864, by Cardinal Cullen, who appointed Rev. Dr. Conroy and Rev. Dr. Moran as editors, it was to be a link between Ireland and Rome, and its policy was expressed in its motto: "Ut Christiani, ita et Romani sitis". In 1871, both of the editors were raised to the episcopate, Dr. Conroy to Ardagh, and Dr. Moran (now Cardinal Primate of Australia) to Ossory. Dr. Verdon and Dr. Tynan edited it for over four years, and Dr. Walsh took charge of it for the last six months of 1876, when it was allowed to lapse. A third series was started in 1880, with Dr. Carr (now Archbishop of Melbourne) as editor, and published from Maynooth College. Dr. Healy (now Archbishop of Tuam) was editor from 1883 to 1884, after whom came Dr. Browne (Bishop of Cloyne), who worked zealously for ten years. In 1894, Rev. Canon Hogan became editor. A mere glance at the twenty-nine volumes of the "Record" is sufficient to vindicate its long existence, and the list of contributors includes some of the greatest names in theology, liturgy, canon law, Church history, Scripture, etc. The "Irish Monthly", founded in July, 1873, can boast the longest continuous existence of any Irish Catholic magazine, and, moreover, it enjoys the unique distinction of having had but one editor in thirty-eight years, namely Rev. Matthew Russell, S.J. It is not too much to say that Father Russell's personality has been the secret of the popularity of this magazine, and the list of contributors includes Lady Fullerton, Sir C. Gavan Duffy, Judge O'Hagan, Aubrey de Vere, D. F. MacCarthy, Rev. Dr. Russell, Rev. Dr. O'Reilly, S.J., Rev. Ignatius Ryder, Father Bridgett, C.SS.R., Mother Raphael Drane, Lady Gilbert (Rose Mulholland), Rev. T. A. Finlay, S.J., Archbishop Healy, Rev. D. Bearne, S.J., and a host of others. Among the writers discovered by the "Irish Monthly" are: Oscar Wilde, "M. E. Francis", Lady Gilbert, Katherine Tynan, Hilaire Belloc, Alice Furlong, and Francis Wynne, author of "Whisper". Intended for lay readers, it is always bright, readable, and healthy. The "New Ireland Review", founded March, 1894, is a purely literary monthly, the successor of the short-lived "Lyceum", founded and edited by Rev. T. A. Finlay, S.J., in 1890. Its contributors included the most distinguished clerical and lay writers, and it continued as a powerful Catholic organ, with special reference to history and economics—under the able editorship of Father Finlay—until it ceased with the February number, 1911. "The Irish Rosary", founded in April, 1897, as a small magazine, edited by the Irish Dominicans, was enlarged to eighty pages in 1901, and its scope widened. Father Ambrose Coleman, O.P., who became editor in 1903, added a certain journalistic tone to it, thus making it bright and up-to-date. The present editor is Father Finnbar Ryan, O.P. Among its contributors are many able Dominican writers, well-known laymen like Professor Stockley, Dr. Fitzpatrick, R. F. O'Connor, Shane Leslie, Jane Martyn, S. M. Lyne, Sister Gertrude, and Nora O'Mahony. The only quarterly is the "Irish Theological Quarterly", founded in January, 1906, by six Maynooth professors, one of whom (Dr. McKenna) has since become Bishop of Clogher. Ably conducted, it keeps thoroughly abreast of all theological and Scriptural matters.

POWER, *Irish Literary Enquirer* (London, 1867); FLOOD, *Irish Catholic Periodicals* (MS.); CASARTELLI in *Dublin Review* (April, 1896).

W. H. GRATTAN-FLOOD.

ITALY.—Without going back to the *Acta Diurna*, *Acta Senatus*, or *Acta publica*, existing in Rome in Cæsar's time, the modern newspaper had its birth in Venice. From the first years of the sixteenth century we learn of journals issued in that city every two or three days, sometimes even daily, under the surveillance of the Government. These sheets, called *Avvisi*, for the most part in manuscript, were distributed among the governors of provinces and the ambassadors to foreign courts; they were later read in public, and sold after the reading for a *gazzetta* (14.6 gazzettas =1 lira), hence the name "gazette". At first these journals had an official character; but in 1538, during the Turkish War, their publication was entrusted to private enterprise, though they continued to be supervised by the Government. Under these new auspices journalism was carried on without serious competition up to the first decades of the eighteenth century.

It was natural that the example of Venice should be imitated elsewhere, but in Italy its functions were mainly confined to pandering to a scandal-loving public. In Rome this was carried to such a degree that in 1578 Greogry XIII issued a Bull of excommunication against the journalists who propagated the true and false scandals of society and the court. After Venice came Florence, where they printed *Notizie* or *Gazzetta*. In Rome the first permanent journal was "Il Diario de Roma", begun in 1716 during the war against the Turks in Hungary, printed by Luca and Giovanni Cracas, hence its familiar name "Il Cracas". After 1718 it was published twice a week, with a supplement. At the end of the eighteenth century, the subscription was 24 *paoli* (12 lira) per annum. Towards the middle of the eighteenth century a more intense journalistic life became manifest in Venice. In 1760 another journal, the "Gazzetta Veneta" appeared, edited by Gaspere Gozzi, who in the succeeding year founded a literary review called the "Osservatore Veneto". The directorship of the "Gazzetta Veneta" was then assumed by the priest Chiari; this paper survived until 1798, though its title was changed a number of times.

The following papers also deserve mention: the "Diario Veneto" (1765); the "Gazzetta", with sub-title "Notizie del mondo" (1769); the "Novellista Veneto" (1775, daily); "Avvisi Pubblici de Venezia" (1785); the "Gazzetta delle Gazzette" (1786), the only one that also treated of political questions; the "Nuovo Postiglione" (1789). From 1768 to 1791 the "Gazzetta Fiorentina" was circulated at Florence. Besides the foregoing, a number of scientific and literary journals made their appearance. The first of these is the "Giornale dei letterati", founded in Rome by the learned Benedetto Bocchini (1650–1700). In 1718 the "Giornale dei letterati d'Italia" of Apostolo Zeno appeared at Venice, where also in the same year Pavini translated from the French the "Mercurio Storico". To these was added in 1724 the "Gran Giornale d'Europa", later the "Foglio per le Donne", the "Influssi" of Pasiello, the "Diario" of Cristoforo Zane (1735), and the "Giornale enciclopedico" (1777–87). The "Osservatore" of Gozzi, already mentioned, belongs to this category. The most famous literary journal of this epoch was the "Frusta" of Barretti at Turin, which unceasingly attacked the decadent literature of the times. Other literary and educational periodicals were: the "Analisi ragionata dei libri nuovi", published in Naples, later changed its title to "Giornale letterario" (1793–99). We may mention also the *raccolte* (collections) of various works and dissertations, which were published in a number of cities. Such was the "Raccolta Milanese", the "Opuscoli" of Calogerà at Pisa, the "Simbole" by Gori, even the "Saggi", etc. of the various academies in the cities of Italy. Beginning with 1710, Cracas printed a species of almanac, the "Notizie per l'anno"; while the Roman "Calendario" was the precursor of the "Gerarchia Cattolica" of to-day.

With the French Revolution, other papers were founded throughout Italy to advocate the new regime. In Venice in 1797 was printed the "Monitore lombardo-veneto-traspadano"; the "Libero Veneto"; the "Italiano rigenerato"; and the "Raccolta delle carte pubbliche". When Venice became Austrian, these journals disappeared, and the former "Gazzetta Urbana" became the "Gazzetta Veneta privilegiata" (1799). The "Diario di Roma" was discontinued from the close of 1798 until October of the succeeding year, again from 1808 to 1814, and from this last date continued up to the middle of the century. During the first French occupation the "Monitore di Roma" was published in Rome; the "Gazzetta Romana", founded in 1808 and edited in two languages, was followed in 1809 by the "Giornale del Campidoglio", and in 1812 by the "Giornale politico del dipartamento di Roma", containing treatises on antiquities and the results of excavations, and other items of interest. Mention may also be made of the "Giornale patriotico della Repubblica Napolitana".

The pre-revolutionary journals were all Catholic. In the Reign of Terror the publication of Catholic journals became impossible. During the time of the Restoration the government in Italy held the censorship of the press in regard to all questions of political import; but journals were free to exert themselves in behalf of Catholicism. Foreign books, however, were circulated, propagating the political, social, and religious maxims of the Revolution. Thus the need of a conservative Catholic press made itself felt. The first to appear upon the field was in 1831, the "Voce della Verità" of Modena, founded under the auspices of Duke Francis V, and under the directorship of Antonio Parenti and Professor Bartolommeo Veratti. These journals continued to appear only until 1841. In this year Ballerini founded the "Amico Cattolico" at Milan. The Revolution of 1848 (although signalized by the founding at Rome of the "Pallade" and the satirical paper "Don Pirlone"; at Piacenza, the "Eridano", representing the Provisional Government, the "Tribuno" representing the Opposition), made the necessity of good papers very urgent. On the return of Pius IX the "Giornale di Roma" was founded at Rome (1850–65), to which was added an evening paper, the "Osservatore Romano", which, when the "Giornale" was suspended, became the organ of the Pontifical Government.

At Turin the "Armonia" was founded in 1849, which fought strenuously for the cause of the Church. The "Unità Cattolica" appeared in 1862, directed by Margotti, and the "Armonia" was transferred to Florence; at Genoa the "Eco d'Italia" was established in 1849, an illustrated daily paper, still published under the name of "Liguria del Popolo". At Locarno, Canton of Ticino, Switzerland, the "Credente Cattolico" appeared in 1856; in the same year the "Osservatore Bolognese", at Bologna founded by Fangarezzi, Casoni, Acquaderni, etc., afterwards suppressed in 1859 by the provisional Government; in Florence the "Contemporaneo" (1857), founded by Stefano San Pol; in Naples, beginning in 1860, was published the "Omnibus", directed by Vincenzo Torello. After the annexation of a large part of Italy to Sardinia, when the influence of a Catholic Press was urgently needed, its freedom was continually hampered by all sorts of petty vexations. Papers that had been suppressed reappeared under other names. This persecution is explained either by the sectarian spirit of those in power, or by the impression then prevailing that the Catholic party was the declared enemy of the new Government. Thus there appeared at Bologna in 1861 the "Eco delle Romagne", substituted for the "Osservatore Bolognese", which in turn was suppressed in 1863 and succeeded by the "Patriotto Cattolico", followed again by the "Conservatore" (1868), and by the "Unione" (1878). A similar fate befell the "Osservatore Lombardo" of Brescia (1862–63). The "Difensore" of Modena was similarly treated and suppressed in 1867; and the year following Mgr Balan founded the "Diritto Cattolico", still published. In Florence the "Contemporaneo" succeeded to the "Corriere Toscano". In Venice the "Veneto Cattolico" appeared in 1866, and in 1867 assumed the name of "Difesa", which still survives. The "Osservatore Cattolico" was founded at Milan in 1864, and was entrusted to the editorship of Don Albertario. This journal undertook the refutation of the Rosminian doctrines, and was a faithful advocate of the papal policy. At this period religious papers were founded in other cities of Italy: the "Libertà", at Locarno (1866); the "Voce Cattolica" (1866); the "Gazzetta di Mondovì" (1868); the "Libertà Cattolica" of Naples (1867); the "Sicilia Cattolica" of Palermo (1868); the "Genio Cattolico" of Reggio Emilia (1869).

Meanwhile Pius IX felt the need at Rome of a politico-religious organ for the support of his own programme, for the refutation of pernicious doctrines, and to serve as a medium of official communication to the Catholic world. This was realized by the foundation of the "Correspondance de Rome", and the "Acta Sanctæ Sedis" (1865). The chief principles of the "Correspondance" were the support of the Holy See and opposition to the Liberal Catholics and Opportunists. In 1870 this paper was moved to Geneva by Mgr Mermillod, where it altered its title to "Correspondance de Genève". It then became an instrument of Blome in his vigorous campaign against Bismarck, especially during the *Kulturkampf*. This paper supported the intransigent party favoured by the pope, though it failed to obtain the sympathy of Cardinal Antonelli. At the death of Pius IX the condition of Catholic journals was very favourable. They were perhaps inferior to the papers of their opponents in form, but were unrivalled as to the ability of their writers and the vigour and intelligence of their polemics. Among these the "Unità Cattolica" was especially distinguished.

The year 1870 beheld a revival of governmental and sectarian opposition to Catholic journals, which, however, increased in number despite the hostility manifested toward them. This was particularly the case with those papers of periodical issue. Thus in Rome in this year was founded the "Voce della Verità" (which ceased in 1904); the "Eco del Litorale" at Gorizia; the "Amico del Popolo", at Lucca (1872); the "Discussione", at Naples (1873); the "Verona Fedele", at Verona; the "Cittadino", at Genoa (1873); at Turin the "Corriere Nazionale" (1873), which in 1894 was fused with the "Italia Reale", and was founded after the transfer to Florence of the "Unità Cattolica"; at Venice the "Berico" (1876); at Udine the "Cittadino Italiano" (1878); at Perugia the "Paese" (1876); at Treviso the "Vita del Popolo", etc.

Leo XIII also realized the need of a papal journal through which he could communicate with the foreign press, and he consequently created the "Journal de Rome"; this paper did not fulfil his expectations, so it was succeeded by the "Moniteur de Rome" (1881–95). The most prominent developments of Italian journalism of the last few years are the union of the "Osservatore Cattolico" of Milan with the "Lega Lombarda" (founded in 1884), which two papers were fused as the "Unione". Another event in Italian journalism was the foundation of the "Momento" at Turin, and the alliance formed by the "Corriere d'Italia" (1905, originally called "Giornale di Roma") with the "Avvenire d'Italia" of Bologna and with the "Corriere della Sicilia" (Palermo). The "Correspondance de Rome", founded in 1907 with the title "Corrispondenza Romana", has a scope similar to the paper of the same name under Pius IX. Like its prototype, though not official in character, it is an echo of the Vatican.

Before we consult the actual statistics of the Catholic press of Italy it may be well to survey the history of that class of Catholic periodicals which comprises literature and erudition to the exclusion of politics. Among these periodicals, we may mention first the "Giornale arcadico" of Rome (1819–68), revived in 1888 with the title "Arcadia", and in 1898 reassuming its former title. Then came the "Tiberino" (1833); the "Album" (1834), illustrated and treating largely of the biographies of contemporaneous men; the "Rivista" (1831), devoted to the theatre; the "Giornale Ecclesiastico" (1825), a periodical devoted to canon law, in 1835 issued again as the "Annali delle scienze religiose", directed by Mgr Antonio de Luca and recognized as the organ of the Academy of the Catholic Religion. In 1865 de Rossi founded the "Bullettino di Archeologia Cristiana", reappearing as the "Nuovo Bullettino" etc. In Modena, to the labours of Veratti already mentioned were added the "Memorie di Religione"; the "Opuscoli religiosi, letterari e morali"; the "Strenne filologiche"; in 1858 he founded there a collection of "Letture amene ed oneste". Under the title of "Letture Cattoliche" and similar titles, periodicals existed in various cities, Padua, Naples, Genoa, Turin (this last founded by Don Bosco), etc.

Among the periodicals of an earlier date we must cite the "Giornale scientifico letterario" and the "Rivista di scienze, lettere e arti". Strictly religious periodicals, such as "Settimane Religiose", etc. were printed in many cities, often for the benefit of some sanctuary or in behalf of some pious work. The "Donna e la Famiglia" (Genoa, 1862), which had a fashion supplement; the "Consigliere delle Famiglie" (Genoa, 1879); the "Missione della Donna" (Sciacca, 1875), were published for circulation in families. At the present time we should name especially the "Pro Familia" (Bergamo, splendidly illustrated). In many cities (Turin, Genoa, Massa Carrara, etc.) papers were published for workmen; others were devoted especially to the peasants. For education and the cause of Christian schools were founded the "Scuola Italiana Moderna" (Milan, 1893) and the "Vittorino da Feltre" (Feltre, 1890). The "Museo delle Missioni Cattoliche" (Turin, 1857); the "Missioni cattoliche" (Milan); the "Missioni francescane in Palestina" (Rome); the "Oriente Serafico" (Assisi, 1889); "Gerusalemme" (Genoa, 1877) and other bulletins of this kind indicate their subject-matter by their titles. With the periodical "La Scienza e la Fede" Sanseverino, the celebrated philosopher of Naples, assisted by Signoriello and by d'Amelio, carried on a propaganda for the philosophy and theology of St. Thomas.

The periodical "Scienza Italiana", founded in 1814 by the Jesuit Cornoldi and the physician Venturini, had a similar scope. After the encyclical "Æterni Patris" various other periodicals of this kind appeared, such as the "Eco di S. Tommaso d'Aquino" (Parma, 1879); "Divus Thomas" (Piacenza, 1880); the "Favilla" (Palermo); finally the "Rivista Neotomistica" was founded at Florence (1910). The

"Catechista Cattolico" (Piacenza, 1877), and the "Risveglio del catechismo" (Chieri, 1893), the "Predicatore Cattolico" (Giarre), the "Poliantea oratoria" (Caltagirone, 1881), the "Crisostomo" (Rome) express their subjects in their titles, as also the "Monitore Liturgico" (Macerata, 1888), the "Ephemerides liturgicæ" (Rome, 1887), the "Rassegna Gregoriana" (Rome), the "Scuola Veneta di Musica Sacra" of Tebaldini, etc. The "Bessarione" (1897) is devoted to Oriental Christian studies. The "Scuola Cattolica", founded by Cardinal Parocchi (1878), embraces all branches of theology and discipline. For social studies made after the encyclical "Rerum Novarum" in 1892, Benigni founded the "Rassegna sociale" (Perugia, afterwards Genoa); and in the next year Mgr Talamo began the "Rivista internazionale di scienze sociali", etc. In 1898 Murri founded a periodical of social studies, the "Cultura sociale", which deviated into forbidden tendencies of thought.

Historical periodicals are: "Rivista storica" of Pavia (now at Saronne); the "Muratori" (Pubblicazione di testi per la storia d'Italia); the "Rivista storica benedettina"; the "Archivum franciscanum historicum" (Rome); the "Miscellanea francescana" of Mgr Faloci Pulignani (Foligno, 1887); the "Miscellanea di Storia Ecclesiastica e studi ausiliari" (Rome, 1904–07), and the "Rivista storico-critica delle scienze teologiche" (Rome, 1905), recently condemned by the Holy Office. Among the existing scientific and literary reviews, the oldest and most widely-circulated is the "Civiltà Cattolica", conducted by priests of the Society of Jesus, forming a community by themselves, and directly subject to the general. This was founded in 1850 under the auspices of Pius IX. Among the founders and early writers Bresciani, Curci, Brunengo, Taparelli, Cornoldi, Liberatore, etc. won distinction. Mention must be made of "Acta Apostolicæ Sedis", the official bulletin of the Holy See, founded by *motu proprio* in 1908, in which are published the Bulls, Constitutions, Encyclicals, and other acts of the pope, together with the Decrees of the Roman Congregations. Several periodicals of the same kind are and have been published in Rome, such as the "Nuntius Romanus" (1882–1904), the "Analecta Ecclesiastica" (1893), the "Acta Pontificia", etc., besides the "Acta S. Sedis" already mentioned. The "Monitore Ecclesiastico", founded in Conversano by Mgr Gennari, afterwards cardinal, not only gives the more important pontifical news, but treats of moral theology and canon law, and publishes decisions concerning ecclesiastical matters." The "Nuova Rivista delle Riviste" of Macerata gives a digest of important articles appearing in national and foreign periodicals upon matters of interest to the clergy. Finally it is necessary to note satirical and humorous periodicals. Among these the "Vespra" of Florence and the "Frusta" of Rome were well-known for a time, but ceased on account of the frequent actions for damages brought against them. With these may be classed the "Follia" of Naples, the "Mulo" of Bologna, and the "Bastone" of Rome.

The above statistics have been largely gathered from the "Annuario Ecclesiastico" which undertakes to register all Catholic papers published throughout Italy. This registration, however, is neither complete nor exact, some existing periodicals being omitted, whilst others that have stopped publication are still on the list. Moreover the "Annuario Ecclesiastico" does not inform us whether the journal is a daily or a weekly. This being the case, it is well to note that a number of so-called daily journals appear at the most only three times a week. Of such there were three published at Rome and two published at Turin and Genoa. Besides the above mentioned there are 101 political and social journals issued several times a month; 81 religious periodicals appearing once or twice a month; five periodicals of general erudition; and five devoted to philosophical and theological studies, in which class might be included the "Rivista Rosminiana"; and ten reviews consecrated to canon law. This last enumeration comprises a few bulletins of episcopal courts. Apart from the foregoing there are also two reviews devoted to preaching; six to missionary interests; three to education; and one to social studies. Other periodicals may be counted among Catholic ones by the notably Catholic character of their managers: such as the "Rivista di Matematiche", etc., founded by Tartellini, then professor in the University of Rome; now edited by Cardinal Maffi. Among the political and social reviews it must be observed that two tendencies existed, one decidedly liberal, and the other absolutely papal. The first dealt with the "Roman Question" as obselete. It advocated a larger individual liberty and independence from the particular views of the Holy See and the episcopate in politics and social matters. The reviews taking this liberal attitude never failed however to profess their allegiance and obedience to authority. On the other hand there existed the papal press, which might be characterized by its perfect submission to and advocacy of the prevailing opinions of the Vatican and the episcopate. To this last class belong: the "Riscossa" of Braganze (Mgr Scotton); the "Unità Cattolica" (Florence); the "Italia Reale" (Turin); the "Liguria" (Genoa); the "Difesa" (Venice); the "Osservatore Romano" (Rome); the "Libertà" (Naples); the "Correspondance de Rome", and some other small sheets.

With regard to the geographical distribution of the Catholic press, there is an enormous disproportion between the north and the south. Southern Italy (Naples and Palermo) has only two daily papers. But even in the North there are large cities without a daily Catholic publication, e. g., Padua and Ancona, while Ravenna and Rimini have not even a weekly one. The need of weekly journals is naturally felt still more in Southern Italy.

FERRANDINA, *Censimento della stampa Cattolica* (Asti, 1893); GIACCHI, *Il giornalismo in Italia* (Rome, 1883); CASONI, *Cinquant' anni di giornalismo* (Bologna, 1907); CHIAUDANO, *Il giornalismo cattolico* (Turin, 1910); SANTELENA, *Giornali veneziani nel settecento* (Venice, 1908); CHIERICI, *Il quinto potere a Roma: storia dei giornali e giornalisti romani* (Rome, 1905); ROVITO, *Dizionario dei letterati e giornalisti italiani contemporanei* (Naples, 1907); DELLA CASA, *I Nostri* (Treviso, 1903), lives of illustrious Catholic pressmen.

U. BENIGNI.

MEXICO.—*Colonial Period.*—During the administration of the viceroy Baltasar de Zúñiga Guzmán de Sotomayor, Marqués de Valero, the first newspaper, supervised by J. Ignacio María de Castorena y Ursúa (precentor of the Cathedral of Mexico and afterwards Bishop of Yucatan), was published in Mexico, January, 1722, with the heading "Gaceta de México y Noticias de Nueva España que se imprimirán Cada mes y comienzan desde primero de Enero de 1722" (Gazette of Mexico and notices of New Spain, which will be published every month, and which will begin the first of January, 1722). Later the name was changed to "Florilegio Historial de México etc.", and in June of this year the enterprise was abandoned. In the numbers published, the news items were arranged according to the principal cities of the colony. With the second issue brief notices of the books being published in Mexico and Spain were added and also accounts of important events in Lower California and the principal cities of Europe. In January, 1728, the second publication, the "Compendio de Noticias Mexicanas", edited by J. Francisco Sahagún de Arévalo Ladrón de Guevara, appeared. This continued in circulation until November, 1739, when it was succeeded by the "Mercurio de Mexico", edited by the same person. The "Mercurio" was issued monthly and in the same form as the "Gaceta" and "Florilegio". Among its news items were, accounts of religious festivals, *autos de fé*, competitions for the university faculties, European events, shipping news at the port of Vera Cruz, and news from the Philippines, China, and even Morocco. When there was an abundance of news a fortnightly issue appeared. The desire to keep readers informed on the most important events connected with the Spanish Monarchy, e. g., the conquest of the Kingdom of Naples, is evident. In 1742 the "Mercurio" discontinued publication and no paper existed until 1784, when the new "Gaceta de México", edited by M. A. Valdés, appeared and continued without interruption until 1809. It was issued bi-monthly, modelled more or less on the gazettes of 1722 and 1728; it indicated the price of bread and meat in the City of Mexico and published officially and integrally the royal orders. To Ignacio Bartolache and the Rev. José Antonio Alzate (q. v.), well-known Mexican writers of the eighteenth century, is due the honour of having issued the first scientific publications. The former published (1772) the "Mercurio Volante", which was short-lived; it was characterized as a newspaper giving curious and important notices upon various matters bearing on physics and medicine ("con noticias curiosas é importantes sobre varios asuntos de Física y Medicina"). Alzate began (1768) the "Diario Literario de México"; this was suppressed, but reappeared on 26 October under the title of "Asuntos Varios Sobre Ciencias y Artes". After eleven numbers were published it was again suppressed, only to reappear (1787) under the title of "Observaciones sobre Física, Historia Natural y Artes Utiles", fourteen numbers of which were issued. In January, 1788, the famous "Gaceta de Literatura" appeared and was issued monthly, though with some irregularity, until 1799. This publication was a literary and scientific review; all subjects were examined and discussed by the learned priest-editor. Here might be read with benefit articles on medicine, botany, mineralogy, Mexican archæology, architecture, philosophy, ethnology, jurisprudence, physics, astronomy, topography, etc. The files are a veritable encyclopedia, and the number and variety of the subjects treated, as well as the scholarly manner in which they are handled, are evident proof of Father Alzate's remarkable erudition. On 1 October, 1805, Jacobo Villaurrutia established the "Diario de México", the first daily paper published in the colony; it was issued every day, including holidays, until 1816. Among its contributors were Navarette, Sánchez de Tagle, Barguera, Anastasio Ochoa, and Lacunza y Burazábal. The "Gaceta del Gobierno de México", founded in 1810, was the official organ of the viceregal Government until 1821.

Period of the War of Independence.—The first newspaper devoted to the cause of independence was the "El Despertador Méxicano", edited by Francisco Severo Maldonado. It was begun on 20 December, 1810, but did not last long. The second newspaper controlled by the insurgents was the "Ilustrador Nacional". The editor, Dr. José María Cos, made the type from wood and mixed indigo for the printing ink. When he was able to procure metal type, he continued to publish his newspaper under the title "El Ilustrador Americano". It lasted from May, 1812, until April, 1813. The viceregal Government and the ecclesiastical authorities rigidly prohibited it. The latter obliged the faithful to give up their copies, and denounced those who retained any. The third newspaper, "El Correo Americano del Sur", appeared in February, 1813. The priest, José María Morelos, after conquering Oaxaca and organizing his government, established it and confided the editing first to J. M. de Herrera, formerly parish priest of Huamustitlán, and afterwards to the lawyer, Carlos M. Bustamante. The paper was issued every Thursday until 27 May of the same year. Upon the proclamation of the freedom of the press, two newspapers, "El Juguetillo" and "El Pensador Méxicano", edited respectively by C. M. Bustamante and Joaquín Fernández de Lizardi, appeared; they fearlessly attacked the abuses of the viceregal Government. The "Juguetillo" published only six numbers, and both were suppressed by the Viceroy Venegas in December, 1812. Lizardi was imprisoned, but was liberated shortly afterwards, and continued the publication of his paper, eliminating, however, its offensive tone. Bustamante escaped imprisonment and published two more numbers of the "Juguetillo", the last in 1821. Among other newspapers published during this period may be mentioned: "Clamores de la Fidelidad Americana", published in Yucatan by José Matías Quintana, for which he was imprisoned; the "Boletín Militar", published by General Mina from the printing-press which he carried with his expedition; the army of Iturbide published several sheets, "El Méxicano Independiente", "Ejército Imperial de las Tres Garantías", "Diario Político Militar Méxicano". The "Centinela contra Seductores" was an anti-insurgent paper, issued towards the end of 1810; the "Especulador Patriotico" (1810–11), a weekly dedicated to the Viceroy Venegas. J. M. Wenceslas Sánchez de la Barquera issued several interesting papers, including "Semanario económico de noticias curiosas y eruditas sobre Agricultura y demás Artes y Oficios" (1808–10); "El Correo de los Niños" (1813), the first juvenile paper published in Mexico; and "El Amigo de los Hombres" (1815). The "Noticioso General" (1815–22), the largest newspaper of the colony, published official documents and news of all kinds. At first it was issued every fortnight, but afterwards it appeared on Monday, Wednesday, and Friday.

After the War of Independence.—When the Independence of Mexico was established newspapers were multiplied. Some approved, others condemned, the new regime, according to the policies adopted by the new Government. Carlos María Bustamante published (1821–26) thirty numbers of "La Avispa de Chilpancingo", attacking the Iturbide administration. In 1822 were published "El Sol" and "El Correo de la Federación", organs respectively of the Freemasons of the Scottish (centralistic), and York (federalistic), Rite. The Liberals controlled two important publications, "El Siglo XIX" and "El Monitor Republicano". Gómez Pedraza, Otero, Payno, de la Rosa, Zarco Vigil, and others contributed to the first, and to the second, which was even more radical in its ideas, Florencio Castillo, Valente, Baz, Mateos etc., and Castelar as Spanish correspondent. The Conservatives published "La Sociedad" (edited by José M. Roa Barcena) and "La Cruz" (edited by Ignacio Aguilar y Marocho). The first number of "La Cruz" appeared on 1 Nov., 1855; its heading states that "it is an exclusively religious paper, founded *ex-professo* to diffuse orthodox doctrines, and to defend and vindicate them against the prevalent errors". In its prologue it sums up the situation of that time, deplores the attacks on the Church, and the satires against the clergy; it urges the faithful to prepare themselves for the struggle in defence of religion. The paper had four divisions; the first explained the teachings of the Church on points which circumstances deemed it most opportune to treat; the second refuted all errors advanced against this teaching; the third published short essays on religious subjects; the fourth gave accounts of all notable events, in the Republic and in other countries, that had a bearing on the special object of the publication. Unfortunately this weekly lasted only until 29 July, 1858. Its battles against the Liberals were sharp and brilliant, and its contributors gave striking examples of their learning and profound adhesion to the teaching of the Church. During the civil wars the Press in many instances, particularly during the heated discussions that characterized the period prior to the Constitution of 1857, deserted its office of peacemaker and seemed to have for its only object the arousing of political enmities. And it was not without danger that a journalistic career was followed in those days. The "Veracruzano" of 7 October, 1862, referring to the overthrow of the Government of Miramón and the capture of the capital of Mexico by Juárez (1 Jan., 1861), announced the assassination of Vicente Segura, editor of "Diaro de Avisos" and political antagonist of the victorious party, declaring that "in this truly significant manner demagogism fulfilled the first of the guarantees of the system of Liberalism, freedom of the press". Notwithstanding the risks involved in the expression of animus in connexion with this crime, several publications endeavoured to stem the torrent of pernicious ideas which had been loosed. The editor of the "Pajaro Verde" had to close his establishment; and the principal contributor to "El Amigo del Pueblo" was imprisoned. A Spaniard, suspected of circulating pamphlets, was, without proof of any sort, thrown into prison. His printing-press was confiscated, and later he was exiled.

During the Empire of Maximilian.—Four papers, the "Diario del imperio", "L'Ere Nouvelle", "La Razón", and "L'Estafette", supported more or less openly by the Imperial Government, may be mentioned. In their attitude towards religion (favourable or unfavourable, according to the dictates of the members of the imperial cabinet) they lacked the freedom and independence which make a paper the representative of the sentiments of the people. Some independent journals ("La Sociedad") were also issued, and from time to time published articles which called the attention of the Imperial Government to their columns.

The Present Time.—After the fall of the empire and especially since the presidential tenure of office of General Porfirio Diaz, the Catholic Press has enjoyed a little more freedom. With the exception of the local papers published in the various states, which did not cease to work for the cause ("El Amigo de la Verdas" of Pueblo and others), the first newspaper to continue the traditions of the Catholic journalists of other days was "La Voz de Mexico" (1870–1900). It counted many distinguished writers on its staff, and, as a paper which had never been aught but loyal to the cause it had espoused, it earned the respect and good will of everyone. Shortly before it ceased publication, "El Pais" (now in its twelfth year, and an active defender of Catholic interests) was founded. "El Nacional", another Catholic paper, published for a number of years, rendered good service to the Catholic cause. On 1 July, 1883, Victoriano Agueros founded "El Tiempo", which is undoubtedly the most important of all political daily papers of the republic supporting Catholic interests. In two years its circulation increased from 1000 to 6000 copies. By the vigour with which it attacked the errors of the government of Manuel González it won great popularity, but this attitude won persecution for the editor and contributors, who were several times imprisoned. In 1887 the editorial office was closed and publication suspended for eleven days. But to-day the paper defends its ideals as undauntedly as before. The literary edition (begun in 1883), published every Sunday and to which many notable writers, including Ipandro Arcáico (Arcadian name of the Bishop of S. Luis Potosi), Joaquín García Icazbalceta, J. María Roa Barcena, José Sebastián Segura, and others contributed, gave prominence to the work of many native authors, which would otherwise have remained unpublished. Its columns have always been open to the discussion of all questions contributing to the progress and aggrandizement of Mexico. An illustrated Sunday edition, "El Tiempo Ilustrado", has also been added to the publications connected with "El Tiempo". Among the illustrated monthly reviews may be mentioned "El Mensajero del Corazón de Jesús", which has received much favourable notice.

The principal organ of the Liberal party, "El Liberal", has the largest circulation of any newspaper in the Republic.

León, *Bibliografía mexicana del siglo XVIII* (Mexico, 1902–7); Obregón, *México viejo: La prensa colonial* (Mexico, 1900); Alzate, *Gaceta de Literatura* (4 vols., Puebla, 1831); *México á través de los siglos*, 5 vols.; Icazbalceta, *Biographía de D. C. M. Bustamante* (Mexico, 1853); Ramos y Duarte, *Diccionario de curiosidades históricas* (Mexico, 1899); *Le Mexique au début du XX siècle* (2 vols., Paris, 1905); *México, su evolución social* (3 vols., Mexico, 1901); *Colección de La Cruz* (7 vols.); Lefevre, *Hist. de l'intervention française au Mexique* (Brussels and London,1869); Arrangoiz, *México desde 1808 hasta 1867* (Madrid, 1872); García Cubas, *El Libro de mis recuerdos* (Mexico, 1904); Figueroa Domenech, *Guía general descriptiva de la República Méxicana* (Mexico, 1899); Cavo, *Los tres siglos de México* (Jalapa, 1870).

Camillus Crivelli.

POLAND.—There was a period of slow development from 1831 to 1864, and a period of progress from 1864 to the present day. During the first period there were published at Warsaw 5 daily papers, 14 weeklies, and 1 monthly periodical; in Galicia, 3 daily papers, 3 semi-weeklies, and 3 weeklies; in the Grand Duchy of Posen, 1 daily paper; in Austrian Silesia, 1 weekly. Several of these that appeared before 1863 are still published. The Polish Press reflects the political conditions of the countries that have annexed the territory of Poland. In Galicia (Austria) it is entirely free; in Russia it is subject to a severe censorhsip, which is also the case in Germany.

One of the oldest publications in Galicia is the "Czas" (Time), daily, the organ of the Conservative party, and well edited from the literary as well as from the political point of view. Its publication began in 1848. In 1866 there appeared the "Przegląd polski" (Polish Review), which had from its beginning the collaboration of Count Stanislas Tarnowski and Stanislas Koźmian. It remains the most important historical and literary periodical of Poland. The "Czas" and the "Przegląd polski" have always maintained a strictly Catholic character. In 1867 Julius Starkla and Thaddeus Romanowicz established at Lemberg the "Dziennik Literacki" (Literary Journal), which had a short life; John Dobrzański founded the "Gazeta Narodowa" (National Gazette), to which was united in 1869 the "Dziennik Polski" (Polish Journal). In 1871 Rev. Edward Podolski established the "Przegląd lwowski" (Lemberg Review), which strenuously defended Catholic interests during its existence. In the same city there appeared the "Gazeta Lwowska" (Lemberg Gazette), the organ of the imperial viceroy in Galicia. In 1884 the Polish Jesuits began at Cracow the publication of the "Przegląd powszechny" (Universal Review), a periodical still published, and which has rendered important services to the Catholic cause from the scientific and literary points of view. In the same city there was published from 1881 to 1886 the "Przegląd literacki i artystyczny" (Literary and Artistic Review). In 1894 in the whole of Austria there were published 126 Polish periodicals and daily papers, of which 65 appeared at Lemberg and 29 at Cracow. At Lemberg the daily papers were the "Dziennik polski", the "Gazeta lwowska", the "Gazeta narodowa", the "Kurjer Lwowski", and the "Przegląd". There were two Catholic weeklies, the "Gazeta katolicka" and the "Tygodnik katolicki". At the present time the Catholic Press is chiefly represented by the "Gazeta kościelna" (Ecclesiastical Gazette), a small semi-weekly, poor in doctrine and immersed in politics. From the scientific standpoint the most important periodical is the "Kwaltarnik hystoryczny" (Tri-monthly historical periodical), which began publication in 1886, and the numbers of which constitute a valuable collection of historical works. No less important are the "Pamietniki literacki" (Literary Monuments), the "Ateneum polskie", the "Kosmos" (the organ of the society of naturalists of Lemberg), and the "Nasz kraj". In 1911 there appeared the only philosophical periodical of Galicia, the "Ruch filozoficzny" (Philosophical Movement).

At Cracow, besides the "Czas", there are the "Nowa Reforma" and the "Głos narodu" (Voice of the People), an organ of the clergy and of the militant Catholic party. The Socialists publish there the "Naprzód" (Forward), the official organ of their party, and the monthly periodical "Krytyka". In recent years there has been established the "Swiat Slowianski" (Slav World), the organ of the Slav club of Cracow, containing valuable information relating to the various Slav countries. The Academy of Sciences of Cracow publishes a "Bulletin international", monthly; and the "Rozprawy" (Dissertations) of mathematics, physics, and biology. Daily papers and periodicals are published also in the other Galician cities of Tarnow, Rzeszowo, Sambor, Stanislaw, Jaroslaw, and Przemysl.

One of the oldest Polish daily papers existing in Prussia is the "Dziennik poznański" (Posen Journal), established in 1859. From 1845 to 1865 there appeared the "Przegląd poznański", an ardent defender of Catholicism, edited by Rev. John Koźmian; in 1860 Rev. John Prusinowski published the "Tygodnik katolicki" (Illustrated Week). In 1865 Louis Rzepecki began the publication of the scientific periodical "Oświata" (Culture), which, however, had only a short life, and was followed by the "Przegląd Wielkopolski" (Review of Great Poland), edited by Emilius Kierski. In 1870 Edmond Callier founded the "Tygodnik Wielkopolski", to which the best Polish writers contributed. The "Kurjer Poznański", established by Theodor Zychliński in 1872, also acquired great importance. In 1894 there were published in Prussia and in the Grand duchy of Posen the following daily papers: the "Dziennik poznański", the "Goniec wielkopolski", the "Kurjer poznański", the "Orędownik" (Advocate), and the "Wielkopolanin". The "Przegląd poznański" resumed its publications under the direction of Wladislaw Rabski, while other daily papers were published at Danzig, Thorn, Pelplin, and Allenstein. In 1909, under the direction of Wladislaw Hozakowski, rector of the seminary of Posen, there was published the "Unitas", a monthly periodical for the clergy, well edited from the theological standpoint.

In 1841 the publication of the "Biblioteka Warszawska", a monthly periodical dedicated especially to literature, began in Russian Poland. Its excellence is still maintained. In 1904 there were published in Warsaw 9 dailies, 33 weeklies, 7 fortnightlies, and 5 monthly periodicals. At the present time there are published in Warsaw the "Dzien" (Day); the "Dziennik powszechny" (Universal Journal); the "Głos Warszawski" (Voice of Warsaw); "Głos poranny" (Voice of Morning); the "Kurjer polski"; "Kurjer Warszawski"; "Nowa Gazeta"; "Przegląd poranny"; "Widomości Codzienne" (Daily News); "Slovo" (Word), a Nationalist paper that has great influence; and the "Warszawska Gazeta". Other dailies are published at Lublin, Kieff ("Dziennik kijowski"), at Vilna ("Kurjer litewski" and "Goniec Wilenski"), at Lodz, and at St. Petersburg. Among the periodicals, besides the "Biblioteka Warszawska", mention should be made of the "Biesiada literacka" (Literary Banquet), splendidly illustrated; the "Kultura", hostile to Catholicism; the "Przegląd filozoficzny" (Philosophical Review), a quarterly publication; the "Przegląd historyczny" (Historical Review), scientific, twice monthly; the "Swiat" (World), an illustrated weekly; and the "Tygodnik illustrowane". The Catholic press until two years ago was represented by the "Przegląd katolicki", of Warsaw, a publication of very little value theologically, and dedicated more to politics. This paper was the one most read by the clergy. Count Roger Lubieński established the "Wiara" (Faith), a weekly devoted to ecclesiastical news; and these two publications are now united into one. A scientifically important periodical, the "Kwartalnik teologiczny", lasted only a few years. At the present time, of the daily papers or periodicals for the clergy, or having a strictly Catholic programme, those most read are: the "Polakkatolik"; the "Myśl katolicka", of Censtochowa; and the "Atheneum kaptanskie", of the seminary of Wloslawek, a monthly scientific publication.

In Russia the Lithuanians publish at Vilna the "Litwa" (Lithuania) in defence of their nationality; while the Jews publish at Warsaw the "Izraelita", a weekly. The "Przewodnik bibliograficzny" (Bibliographical Guide) of Cracow, a monthly publication, and the "Przegląd bibliograficzny" of Przemysl are bibliographical periodicals which mention all Polish writings that appear, of all writings that concern Poland, and of the writings that are published in the principal Polish reviews. The number of scientific periodicals devoted to medicine, veterinary surgery, pharmaceutics, architecture, the fine arts, heraldry, archæology, philology, etc., is about 100, which is proof of the intense scientific work of the Poles, who, notwithstanding their difficult political conditions, co-operate with much ardour in modern scientific movements. The Mariavites have a special organ, "Maryawita"; and their "Wiadomości" appears twice each week. At Warsaw there is published the tri-monthly periodical "Myśl niepolegta" (Independent Thought), full of vulgar calumnies and accusations against Catholicism.

In 1864 Polish fugitives established the "Ojczyna" (Native Land) at Leipzig, the "Przyszłość" (The Future) at Paris, and the "Przegląd powszechny" at Dresden. At Chicago, U. S. A., the chief centre of Polish emigration, are published the "Dziennik chicagoski", the "Dzieńświety" (Holy Day), the "Gazeta katolicka", the "Gazeta polska", the "Nowe Życie" (New Life), the "Sztandar", "Tygodnik naukowo-powieściowy", "Wiara i ojczyna", "Zgoda", and "Ziarno", a musical publication. Other papers are published at Milwaukee, Buffalo, New York, Detroit, Philadelphia, Winona, Cleveland, Toledo, Baltimore, Pittsburg, Stevens Point, Manitowoc, Mohanoy City, and Wilkes-Barre. Brazil also has a Polish publication.

CHMIELOWSKI, *Zarys najnowszej literatury polskiej* (Cracow, 1895), 3–213; NAGLA, *Dziennikarstwo polskie w Ameryce i jego 30-letnie dzieje* (Polish Periodical Literature in America, and its history for 30 years) (Chicago, 1894). AURELIO PALMIERI.

PORTUGAL.—An ephemeral news-sheet appeared in 1625, and a monthly gazette relating the progress of the War of Independence commenced in 1641, but Portuguese periodical literature really begins with the "Gazeta de Lisboa", founded by José Freire de Monterroyo Mascarenhas, which lasted from 1715 until 1760. Until the end of the eighteenth century any differences of opinion in matters of faith which might exist were not discussed in print, but, notwithstanding the censorship, French ideas began to filter into Portugal, and early in the nineteenth century the press began to be divided between Liberal and Absolutist; the former advocating radical changes in State and Church, the latter defending Absolutism in politics, and Catholic orthodoxy. In 1798 appeared the "Mercurio" to combat the French Revolution, and this was followed by other anti-French journals, among them the "Observador Portuguez". On the Liberal side came the "Investigador Portuguez" in 1811 and the "Portuguez" in 1814, both published in London, from which city the Liberal exiles directed their assaults on the old regime. These attacks were met by the "Expectador Portuguez". The Revolution of 1820 gave a great stimulus to journalism, and the "Diario do Governo" began to be issued in that year. At first the Liberal papers were rather anti-Absolutist than anti-Catholic, but the Civil War led to the formation of two political camps, and Liberalism in politics came to mean Liberalism in religion. The activity of Freemasonry and the unprogressive ideas of the Absolutists were the causes. As early as 1823 the "Archivo da Religião Christã" was founded "to combat error and impiety", but the papers of this period were devoted almost entirely to politics, all being very violent. Among those which argued for a constitution, the "Portuguez", directed by Garrett, showed the greatest literary skill. The year 1827 saw the issue of an avowedly anti-clerical print, while the defence of Throne and Altar was carried on by the redoubtable Father José Agostinho de Macedo (q. v.) in the "Besta Esfolada" (Flayed Beast) and many other periodicals of a most bellicose character. From 1829 to 1833 the "Defensor dos Jesuitas" was issued to defend the Society, which fell with the other orders when the Liberals triumphed and Dom Miguel lost his throne.

The constitutional monarchy had an anti-clerical character from the first, and most of the papers took on the same tone. A Catholic Press became an absolute necessity, but as its supporters were mostly Miguelists, it was too political, and never exercised much religious influence over the nation. "The Peninsula", organ of the Miguelist exiles, supported the Catholic Absolutist cause until 1872, and the "Nação", of the same party, still exists. From 1840 to 1892 the chief Radical paper was the "Revolução de Septembro". The purely religious organs included the "Annaes da Propagação da Fé" (1838); the "Cruz", an Oporto weekly; and the "Atalaia Catholica", printed at Braga; but the other Catholic papers had a short life, though the "Bem Publico" (Public Weal) lasted from 1859 to 1877. In 1863 came the "Boletim do Clero e do Professorado", a pedagogic paper, in 1866 the "União Catholica", a religious and literary weekly, and in 1871 the "Fé". The "Palavra" of Oporto was founded in 1872, and in 1874 the "Mensageiro do Coração de Jesus", the monthly organ of the Apostleship of Prayer, which in 1881 slightly changed its title. In 1883 was founded the "Instituições Christãs", a fortnightly religious and scientific review, which, however, ceased in 1893; in 1885 the "Clero Portuguez", a weekly ecclesiastical review; and in 1889 the "Voz do Evangelho", a monthly. While the Catholic papers lacked support, the secular press was expanding rapidly, and developed a more and more irreligious, or at least indifferentist, character. This is even more true of the Republican papers. It would take too much space even to name the principal secular newspapers, but it is enough to say that they favoured the subjection of Church to State and defended the laws of Aguiar ("Kill-friars") which suppressed the religious orders. This attitude has become more marked since the Revolution, nearly all the Monarchical papers having ceased publication, or passed over to the Republicans, who are mostly anti-Catholic.

The present Catholic Press consists of the following papers: *Dailies.*—The "Palavra", with a circulation of 12,000 and the "Correio do Norte", with 6,000, both at Oporto. The "Portugal" of Lisbon had a circulation of 11,500, but ceased when the Republic was proclaimed. The circulation of the irreligious "Seculo" and "Mundo" is no doubt greater than that of the three Catholic dailies combined. *Weeklies.*—The publishing house, "Veritas", at Guarda, prints a paper which appea.s under distinct titles in various provincial towns. Lisbon has the "Bem Publico", Guimarães the "Restauração", Oporto the "Ensino", and Vizeu the "Revista Catholica". *Monthlies.*— The "Novo Mensageiro do Coração de Jesus", published by the Jesuits, ceased when the Society was expelled in October, 1910; the "Voz de Santos Antonio", a Franciscan print, had already been suspended by order of the Holy See for its Modernism, and the only existing review of importance is the "Rosario", issued by the Irish Dominicans at Lisbon.

If the Catholic Press limits itself in future to religious and social action, and lays aside the old methods in which it identified religion with the monarchy, it may regain some influence over those who have not altogether lost Christian sentiments. For some years before the Revolution it was too political and fought the enemies of the Church with their own arms.

EDGAR PRESTAGE.

SCOTLAND.—No Catholic periodical of any kind seems to have made its appearance in Scotland until after the Emancipation Act of 1829. Three years subsequent to the passing of that act, namely in April, 1832, James Smith, an Edinburgh solicitor, and father of William Smith (Archbishop of St. Andrews and Edinburgh, 1885–92), started a monthly journal called the "Edinburgh Catholic Magazine", editing it himself. The publication was suspended with the number of November, 1833, but was resumed in February, 1837. In April, 1838, however, Mr. Smith having removed to England, the word "Edinburgh" was dropped from the title of the magazine, which continued to be published in London until the end of 1842. More than fifty years later another monthly magazine, the "Scottish Catholic Monthly", was established and edited by Goldie Wilson. It existed for three years, from October, 1893, until December, 1896. The Benedictines of Fort Augustus founded and conducted a magazine called "St. Andrew's Cross", from August, 1902, to November, 1903, as a quarterly, and from January, 1904, to December, 1905, as a monthly, after which it was discontinued. The French Premonstratensian Canons, who made a foundation in the Diocese of Galloway in 1889, and remained there for a few years, published for a short time, at irregular intervals, a periodical called the "Liberator", which was something of a literary curiosity, being written in English by French fathers whose acquaintance with that language was very rudimentary. A quarterly magazine, called "Guth na-Bliadhna" (the "Voice of the Year"), was started in 1904 by the Hon. R. Erskine, a convert to Catholicism, who still (1911) edits it. The articles, which are of Catholic and general interest, are nearly all written in the Gaelic language. A little monthly, called the "Catholic Parish Magazine", is printed in Glasgow, and is localized (with parochial news) for a number of missions in Glasgow and Galloway.

No Catholic daily paper has ever been published in Scotland, although the possibility of successfully conducting such a paper, in Glasgow, has been more than once under consideration. Of weekly papers the first issued seems to have been the "Glasgow Free Press", which came into Catholic hands about 1850, and was published, under various editors, for several years. The "Northern Times" was started in opposition to this, but only survived about eighteen months. The "Irish Exile", another weekly, was started in 1884, and ran for about eighteen months. Finally, in 1885, the "Glasgow Observer" came into existence, and is now, with its affiliated papers, printed for circulation in Edinburgh, Aberdeen, Dundee, and Lanarkshire, the only Catholic weekly published in Scotland. The Glasgow "Star", which was started in 1895, and was conducted for some years in the interest of the publicans, in opposition to the temperance policy of the "Observer", was finally (in 1908) acquired by the latter paper, which now issues it mid-weekly.

D. O. HUNTER-BLAIR.

SPAIN.—The periodical Press in Spain began to exist early in the history of that country. The "Enciclopedia Hispano-Americana", in the article "periodismo", mentions news publications as early as the time of Charles V; and "El Mundo de los periodicos", of 1898–99 (p. 945), gives 1661 as the date when the first periodical appeared in Spain. The publication of this kind of literature continued to develop in succeeding years until it reached a maximum in 1762, when fourteen periodicals were published; the number then diminished until, in 1780, it had sunk to two, increasing once more to fourteen in 1786. The publications of this period treated of political, commercial, and literary matters, though such a periodical as the "Apologista Universal", believed to have been edited by Fray Pedro de Centeno, denounced abuses and refuted errors.

The Catholic Press as we now have it did not exist until a later period, when the attacks of gallicizing Liberals and Voltaireans upon the Catholic Religion roused Catholics to defend the traditional doctrines. The liberty of the Press decreed by the Cortes of Cadiz, in 1812, resulted in a remarkable ebullition among Liberal writers, and in 1814 the number of periodicals amounted to twenty-three, while Father Alvarado, the Dominican, wrote his famous articles, under the title "Cartas de un filósofo rancio" (Letters of a Soured Philosopher), against the new doctrines which the French Revolutionists had planted in Spain, and the nascent Liberal Press were striving to popularize. At this time, too (1813–15), Fray Agustin de Castro, the Hieronymite, edited "La Atalya de la Mancha" (The Watch-Tower of La Mancha). On 25 April, 1815, a decree of Ferdinand VII prohibited the publication of any periodical except "La Gaceta" and "El Diario de Madrid". But when the Constitution of 1820 proclaimed the liberty of the Press, the number of Liberal periodicals rose to sixty-five. Mesonero Romanos, in his "Recollections of a Septuagenarian" (Madrid, 1880), p. 453, speaking of this era in Spanish history, uses the expression: "the indiscreet attempt made by the political press in the turbulent constitutional period of 1820–23". No Catholic periodicals were published at this time, since, as the same author tells us (p. 232), "The Serviles and Absolutists maintained a complete silence as the only means of avoiding the attacks of the journalists". It must be borne in mind that the Catholics of that time were, as a general rule, Absolutists. In 1823 the king was again absolute, and once more he silenced the Press, which declined for a number of years, until the triumph of Liberalism during the regency of Doña Cristina gave it new life. The number of periodicals reached forty in 1837, and constantly increased thereafter.

Among the Catholic periodicals which appeared during the reign of Isabella II, may be mentioned the Carlist publications, "El Católico" and "La Esperanza", the latter founded by Pedro de la Hoz. "El Pensamiento de la nación" was edited by the famous philosopher Balmez, who had begun his career as a journalist with "La Civilización", published at Barcelona, in collaboration with Ferrer y Subirana, before leaving him to found "Sociedad". Navarro Villoslada was the editor of "El Pensamiento Español", and such distinguished writers as Gabino Tejado, Juan M. Orti y Lara, and Suarez Bravo were among its contributors. Candido Nocedal founded "La Constancia", a shortlived publication, in which the distinguished Catholic journalist and writer Ramón Nocedal made his first efforts. All these periodicals disappeared during the period of the Revolution. After the Revolution, and when the Carlist War had been brought to a conclusion, Candido Nocedal, having, with other moderate members of the Isabellist Party, joined the Carlists, founded "El Siglo Futuro" in 1874. Vicente de la Hoz, son of the former editor of "La Esperanza", founded "La Fé", and Suarez Bravo "El Fenix", which lasted only two years. Alejandro Pidal revived "La España Católica", which had existed before the Revolution. At Seville there appeared "El Diario de Sevilla", which will always be associated with the name of that illustrious writer Padre Francisco Mateos Gago. Upon the death of Candido Nocedal, who had been the leader of the Carlist Party since the end of the Civil War, differences arose between his son Ramón and the other chiefs of that party, which gave rise to the "Burgos Manifesto" of 1888. The Carlists separated from the Integrists, who were led by Ramón Nocedal. That same year, 1888, saw the first appearance of "El Correo Español", now (1910) the organ of Don Jaime's party. In 1897 "El Universo" was founded by Juan M. Orti, who, a few years earlier, had left the Intergist Party.

Forty-eight Catholic dailies are now published in Spain. They may be grouped as Integrist, Jaimist, and Independent. The first and second of these groups represent the two Traditionalist parties; the third is formed of those journals which maintain Catholic doctrines without adhering to any political party. Of the forty-eight, eleven are Integrist, eleven Jaimist, and the remainder Independent. The most important are "El Siglo Futuro", Integrist, founded in 1874, now edited by Manuel Senante, a member of the Cortes; "El Correo Español", Jaimist, founded in 1888, owned by the Duke of Madrid, edited by Rafael Morales; "El Universo", founded in 1899, owned by the Junta Social de Acción Católica, edited by Rufino Blanco (these three published at Madrid); "La Gaceta del Norte", founded in 1901, published at Bilbao, edited by José Becerra. The number of copies printed by these papers naturally varies with circumstances; it is safe to say, however, that on an average "El Siglo Futuro" prints 7000 copies; "El Correo Español", 18,000; "El Universo", 14,000; "La Gaceta del Norte", 12,000. Against this the anti-Catholic dailies publish: "El Pais", Socialist Republican, 18,000 copies; "El Heraldo de Madrid", 70,000; "El Liberal", 40,000. The Moderate periodicals—e. g., "A. B. C.", "La Correspondencia de España", and "La Epoca", the organ of the Conservative Party—have a large number of readers.

The other Catholic periodicals are: 2 tri-monthly; 7 bi-weekly; 63 weekly; 5 published every ten days; 9 semi-monthly; 9 monthly. Of these 11 are Catholic-social; 9 Integrist; 19 Jaimist; the rest Independent. The illustrated papers worthy of mention among them are "La Lectura Dominical" (Sunday Reading), organ of the Apostolate of the Press, "El Iris de Paz", conducted by the Missionary Sons of the Immaculate Heart of Mary, at Madrid; "La Hormiga de Oro" (The Golden Ant), Catholic illustrated, Barcelona; "La Revista Popular", edited by Felix Saeda y Salvany, Barcelona. There are twenty-four semi-monthly and seventy-four monthly reviews published in Spain; twenty-eight of them deal with social questions, one is devoted to Spanish Sacred Music, four deal with ecclesiastical sciences in general, while the remainder handle religious and literary topics. About twelve of these are illustrated, the principal being: "La Ciudad de Dios", founded in 1881, a semi-monthly review conducted by the Augustinian Fathers of the Escorial, and including among its notable contributors the late Padre Camara, formerly Bishop of Salamanca; "Razón y Fe", founded in 1901, a monthly review published by the Jesuit Fathers at Madrid; "Revista de Estudios Franciscanos", founded 1907, published by the Capuchin Fathers at Sarria (Barcelona), and including among its most noteworthy contributors Padre Francisco Esplugas; "La Ciencia Tomista", bi-weekly, founded in March, 1910, published by the Dominican Fathers; "El Mensajero del Corazón de Jesus" (Messenger of the Sacred Heart), a monthly review, founded in 1869 by Father de la Ramière, and now edited by Padre Remigio Vilarino. (Padre Coloma, S.J., a member of the Academy of the Language, and celebrated as a novelist, has published in "El Mensajero" his most notable works.) "Revista Católica de Cuestiones Sociales", founded in 1895, at Madrid, organ of the general association of the "Dames de la buena prensa", edited by José Ignacio de Molina. "Revista Social Hispano-Americana", founded in 1902, semi-monthly publication of the "Acción Popular", Barcelona.

It is difficult to say anything with certainty as to the future of the Catholic Press in Spain, though there is reasonable ground for a hopeful view. The one thing evident is that, within the last few years, the number of Catholic publications in this country has considerably increased, and that an active propaganda is in progress in favour of the Catholic Press. Many Catholics, it seems, are awakening from their lethargy and are beginning to realize the necessity of using every possible means to counteract the pernicious effect of the evil press. The "Asociación de la Buena Prensa", organized with the approval of Cardinal Spinola, Archbishop of Seville, has already (1910) held two conferences. A Catholic agency has been formed to supply news to Catholic periodicals, and some of the new periodicals, such as "La Gaceta del Norte", give much information and are equipped with excellent typographic facilities.

Manuel del Propaganda (Seville, 1908); CASAS, *Anuario de la prensa católica Hispano-Portuguesa* (Orense, 1909); CRIADO, *Las ordenes religiosas en el periodismo español* (Madrid, 1907); PELAEZ, *La importancia de la prensa* (Barcelona, 1907); IDEM, *La Cruzada de la Buena Prensa* (Barcelona, 1908); DUESO, *Escándalo, Escándalo* (Madrid, 1907); *La Agencia Católica de información* (Saragossa, 1910).

ENRIQUE JIMÉNEZ.

SWITZERLAND.—The history of Swiss journalism goes back to the beginning of the seventeenth century, the first Swiss newspaper being issued at Basle in 1610. It is significant that the early newspapers of Switzerland, which was at that time only nominally free, hardly discussed political matters excepting those of foreign countries and this was the case until well into the eighteenth century. The censorship exercised at that time was so strict that it did not seem advisable to raise questions concerning home matters. Even in the middle of the eighteenth century, writers of objectionable articles were bluntly notified to give up writing for newspapers. The political newspaper did not appear until at the close of the eighteenth and the beginning of the nineteenth century, when the freedom of the Press was gradually allowed. This freedom, however, for a long time existed chiefly in the Protestant cantons. Catholic journalism in the present sense is a recent growth, and does not extend farther back than the third decade of the last century, when the first Catholic newspapers appeared at Lucerne and St. Gall. The reasons for this were partly of a political and partly of an economic character. Switzerland is a federation of twenty-five cantons, each of which up to 1848 was absolutely sovereign and up to 1874 was practically sovereign. Even now the cantons possess many of the rights of sovereignty, though not as many as the States of the American Union. Hence the political Press has mainly a cantonal or local character, dealing with the interests of the sub-divisions of a small state.

All the Catholic cantons are relatively small, some of them not having more than 20,000 or 30,000 inhabitants. Moreover, the population is mostly rural. Except Lucerne and Fribourg, they do not contain important cities, and, finally, the Catholic party for many years totally misjudged the importance and influence of the political Press in general, and let itself be outstripped by their opponents. The first strong impulse to the founding of a Catholic Press was given by the civil war of 1847, called the war of the *Sonderbund;* the war ended with the defeat of the seven Catholic cantons, which placed them largely at the mercy of a violent Liberalism. This was still more the case in the cantons made up of Catholic and Protestant districts. The Catholic Press grew very rapidly during the sixth decade of the past century and still more so during the Swiss *Kulturkampf* of the seventies. More recently a large emigration of Catholics into Protestant cantons led to the founding of Catholic newspapers in these cantons. Switzerland has now a Catholic Press in the Catholic cantons, in those where Catholics and Protestants are on a parity, and in the Protestant cantons.

The statistics are as follows: In 1911 Switzerland had 399 political newspapers, of which 64 were Catholic. Of these Catholic papers, 1 is issued 7 times a week, 10 are issued 6 times weekly, 1 is issued 5 times weekly, 3 appear 4 times weekly, 22 appear 3 times, 13 appear twice weekly, and 14 once a week. 50 are published in German, 9 in French, 4 in Italian, and 1 in Rhæto-Romanic. The number of copies issued at an edition are, taken altogether, as follows: the 4 daily papers, including 1 issued 5 times weekly, have a circulation of 52,000 copies; 3 that appear 4 times weekly, 8000 copies; 22 appearing 3 times weekly, 57,000; 13 appearing twice weekly, 30,000; 14 appearing once a week, 60,000. Thus the 64 Catholic papers have a total circulation of 207,000. The Canton of Aargau has 6; Appenzell Outer Rhodes, none; Appenzell Inner Rhodes, 1; half-canton of Basel-Stadt, 1; half-canton of Basel-Land, none; Berne, 3; Fribourg, 4; St. Gall, 12; Geneva, 1; Glarus, 1; Grisons, 3; Lucerne, 5; Neuchâtel, none; Schaffhausen, 1; Schwyz, 5; Solothurn, 3; Ticcino, 3; Thurgau, 1; half-canton of Nidwald, 1; half-canton of Obwald, 1; Uri, 1; Vaud, none; Valais, 5; Zug, 1; Zurich, 4. The Catholic cantons have 28 Catholic papers, including 3 dailies, the cantons having parity, 27, including 5 dailies; the Protestant cantons, 9, including 4 dailies and 1 appearing 5 times weekly.

Although the Catholic Press of Switzerland has grown enormously in the last thirty years, and need not fear comparison with that of other countries, even entirely Catholic, yet the result is much less satisfactory and even disappointing if we compare the Catholic with the anti-Catholic press. According to the census of 1910 Switzerland has in round numbers 3,700,000 inhabitants. Of these about 1,500,000 are Catholics. From this we should deduct the liberal Catholics, a fairly large element, and the foreign workmen, Italian men and women, journeymen-mechanics, servants, etc., that are only temporary residents. Consequently only about 1,200,000 Catholics can be taken into consideration for the present purpose. We shall compare only the dailies. A comparison between the weekly papers would not yield a much better result, as is evident from the fact that there are only 64 Catholic political papers to counterbalance 399 non-Catholic, and for 269 non-Catholic weeklies that appear 1 to 4 times weekly there are only 53 Catholic ones. The daily non-Catholic Press of Switzerland includes 67 newspapers; of these 44 are extreme Liberal, that is, hostile to the Church and in part disposed to renew the *Kulturkampf;* 3 of these appear twice a day, total circulation, 244,000; 7 Liberal-Conservative, Protestant in faith, and generally friendly to Catholics, total circulation 46,000; 10 Social-Democratic and belonging to the Democratic party of the Left, partly hostile to Catholics but not inclined to carry on a *Kulturkampf*, total circulation 54,000; 7 politically indifferent, total circulation 164,000. Taken altogether, as before said, 67 papers with a total circulation of 508,000, opposed to which are 12 Catholic dailies, one of which appears 5 times weekly, with a total circulation of 52,000. In proportion to the population there should be at least 20 with a circulation of 150,000. The total circulation of all the 64 Catholic Swiss papers is 207,000 copies, not the half of the total circulation of the non-Catholic dailies, and the total circulation of the extreme Liberal dailies alone is much larger than the total circulation of all the Catholic papers taken together. It should be further added that up to now the Catholic Press contains no paper of two daily editions, and that the best non-Catholic newspapers exceed the Catholic ones in copiousness of matter, etc. It is also worthy of notice that the Catholic daily with the largest circulation, the "Vaterland", has about 11,000 subscribers among Catholics, while among the 63,000 subscribers to the politically and ecclesiastically indifferent "Zürcher Tagesanzeiger", there are about 20,000 Catholics. Again, it is not a Catholic weekly that has the largest circulation among Catholics, but it is the rather Liberally inclined "Schweiz. Wochenzeitung" of Zurich. Yet the Catholic party is the second in strength in Switzerland.

But the Liberal and Protestant parties are socially and economically in a far better position, they control the larger part of the cities, while the majority of the Catholic population represent the country and mountain districts, which have less need of a daily paper. On the other hand, the daily Press of the Social Democratic party and of the Democratic party of the Left have a total circulation of 54,000, although they draw their readers almost entirely from the lower classes of the population. However, the Swiss Catholic Press is earnest, courageous, and on the whole is able and efficient, and exerts a greater influence than is the case with the greater part of the Liberal Press. The principal Catholic newspapers of Switzerland are: the "Vaterland", founded at Lucerne in 1873; the "Neuen-Zürcher Nachrichten", established at Zurich in 1904; the "Ostschweiz", in 1874 at St. Gall; the "Basler Volksblatt", in 1873 at Basle; and the "Liberté", in 1865 at Fribourg. Among the pioneers, now deceased, of the Catholic Press of Switzerland special mention should be made of: Bishop Augustinus Egger, Landamman Baumgartner, and Joseph Gmür of St. Gall, Schultheiss von Segesser of Lucerne, Landamman Hänggi of Solothurn, the episcopal commissary von Ah, and Landamman Th. Wirz of Obwald, Mgr Jurt of Basle, and Canon Schorderet of Fribourg. Among Catholic periodicals the following should be mentioned: "Die schweiz. Kirchenzeitung", of Lucerne, a theological review that has a high reputation among the German clergy also: the "Schweiz. Rundschau", issued at Stans, a Catholic scientific and literary review; the "Schweiz. sozialpolit. Blätter", of Fribourg; the "Alte und Neue Welt", of Einsiedeln, an illustrated Catholic family paper, which has a large circulation also in Germany and Austria; the "Zukunft", of Einsiedeln, a Catholic review for the Swiss associations for young men; various religious Sunday papers for the people; an illustrated supplement for Catholic newspapers; a large number of Catholic calendars, as well as the organs of Catholic societies, etc. The five papers for Catholic workmen and working women have been included among the political newspapers.

GEORG BAUMBERGER.

THE UNITED STATES.—According to "The Official Catholic Directory" for 1911, there are 321 Catholic periodicals published in the United States. Of these about two-thirds, or 201, are printed in English, 51 in German, 24 in French, 24 in Polish, 7 in Bohemian, 5 in Italian, 2 in Slavonic, 2 in Magyar, 2 in Dutch, 1 in Croatian, 1 in Spanish, 1 in an Indian dialect. These make up 13 dailies, 115 weeklies, 128 monthlies, 29 quarterlies, 2 bi-weeklies, 5 semi-weeklies, 4 semi-monthlies, 9 bi-monthlies, and 16 annuals. Of the dailies 7 are French, 4 Polish, 2 German, and 1 Bohemian; none is English. The French Canadians of Maine, Massachusetts, and Rhode Island support seven dailies, eleven weeklies, one semi-weekly, one monthly, and a quarterly, all of which are printed in French. From 1809 to 1911 some 550 Catholic periodicals were started in the United States, but only five of those published during the first half of the nineteenth century survive. Several attempts have been made to establish a news association of Catholic papers, notably at Cincinnati, in May, 1890, but nothing practical came of these efforts.

According to localities the Catholic publications are divided up as follows: Alabama, 2; Arizona, 1; Arkansas, 1; California, 9; Colorado, 2; Connecticut, 5; Delaware, 4; District of Columbia, 7; Illinois, 30; Indiana, 14; Iowa, 8; Kansas, 4; Kentucky, 5; Louisiana, 2; Maine, 2; Maryland, 10; Massachusetts, 15; Michigan, 11; Minnesota, 7; Missouri, 15; Montana, 1; Nebraska, 2; New Hampshire, 1; New Jersey, 4; New Mexico, 1; New York, 61; North Carolina, 2; Ohio, 23; Oregon, 7; Pennsylvania, 29; Rhode Island, 1; South Carolina, 2; Tennessee, 2; Texas, 6; Utah, 1; Washington, 2; West Virginia, 1; Wisconsin, 21.

Many publications advocating Irish interests are, and have been, edited by Catholics and addressed to a Catholic constituency, but they are secular political enterprises, and are not to be properly enumerated under the head of religious publications (see IRISH, THE, IN COUNTRIES OTHER THAN IRELAND.—I. IN THE UNITED STATES).

Newspapers.—The first Catholic newspaper printed in the United States was due to the enterprise of Father Gabriel Richard, of Detroit, Michigan. In 1808 he visited Baltimore, and while there bought a printing press and a font of type which he sent over the mountains to Detroit (then a frontier town) and set up in the house of one Jacques Lasselle, in the suburb of Springwells. On this press, the lever of which is still preserved in the museum of the Michigan Historical Society, he printed, on 31 August, 1809, the first issue of "The Michigan Essay, or Impartial Observer", containing sixteen columns and a half in English, and one column and a half in French, on miscellaneous topics. There is no local news included in its contents and only one advertisement, that of St. Anne's school, Detroit. The imprint says the paper was printed and published by James M. Miller, but under the direction of Father Richard. It was to appear every Thursday; only one issue, however, was made, and of this but five copies are extant. The next journalistic effort was in New York, where Thomas O'Connor, father of the jurist Charles O'Conor (q. v.), began, 10 December, 1810, a weekly called the "Shamrock, or Hibernian Chronicle", which ceased publication 17 August, 1817. It was revived as a monthly called "The Globe" in 1819 and lasted a year. His pen, says his son, "was ever directed in vindicating the fame of Ireland, the honour of our United American States, or the truth and purity of his cherished mother the Apostolic Church". Although these two papers were not distinctively religious journals, they were Catholic in tone and teaching, as might be expected from their Catholic direction.

Bishop England of Charleston (see ENGLAND, JOHN) follows, in 1822, with his "United States Catholic Miscellany". "The writer would add", says the bishop, in a history of his diocese which he published while on a visit to Dublin, in 1832, "that during upwards of ten years he and his associates have, at a very serious pecuniary loss, not to mention immense labour, published a weekly paper, 'The United States Catholic Miscellany', in which the cause of Ireland at home and Irishmen abroad, and of the Catholic religion through the world, has been defended to the best of their ability. This paper is published every week on a large sheet of eight pages containing twenty-four pages of letter press, in the city of Charleston." Its publication ceased in 1861, as a result of the War of Secession. One of the bishop's most efficient assistants in this enterprise was his sister Johanna, a woman of fine culture and much mental vigour, who has never received proper credit for all the variety of solid work she did on the paper. With the second quarter of the nineteenth century came the great influx of Catholic immigrants and a consequent development of the Catholic Press. The pioneer journal of this era was "The Truth Teller", the first number of which appeared in New York, on 2 April, 1825, with the imprint of W. E. Andrews & Co., which was continued on the first six issues of the paper. William Eusebius Andrews (q. v.) was the English publisher who was so active in England, during Bishop Milner's time, and his connexion with the New York venture is now explainable only as he was then printing a "Truth Teller" in London. In the issue of 19 October, 1825, William Denman (q. v.) and George Pardow are given as the proprietors of the New York "Truth Teller", and so continued until 2 January, 1830, when Pardow sold his interest to Denman, and the latter remained its sole proprietor until 31 March, 1855, when he disposed of it to the owners of the "Irish American", who shortly after merged it in that paper.

Denman, in the early days of the "Truth Teller", had the assistance, as contributors, of the Rev. Dr. John Power, rector of St. Peter's Church, the Rev. Thomas Levins, a former Jesuit and a man of ripe learning and ability, Dr. William James MacNeven (q. v.), the Rev. Joseph A. Schneller, the Rev. Felix Varela, and Thomas O'Connor, but the paper becoming tainted with trusteeism (see TRUSTEE SYSTEM), and opposing Bishop Dubois, a rival, the "Weekly Register and Catholic Diary" was started on 5 October, 1833, by Fathers Schneller and Levins. It lasted three years, and was succeeded, in 1839, by the "Catholic Register", which, the next year, was combined with the "Freeman's Journal", then a year old. The editors at first were James W. and John E. White, nephews of Gerald Griffin, the Irish novelist. Eugene Casserly (q. v.) and John T. Devereux succeeded them, and in 1842 Bishop Hughes took the paper to keep it alive, and made his secretary, the Rev. James Roosevelt Bayley (afterwards Archbishop of Baltimore), its editor. In 1848 the bishop offered to give the paper to Orestes A. Brownson (q. v.), but soon after sold it to James A. McMaster (q. v.), the latter borrowing the money for its purchase from George Hecker, a brother of the Rev. Isaac T. Hecker (q. v.), founder of the Paulists. McMaster continued as its editor and proprietor until his death, 29 Dec., 1886. In 1861, because of its violent State's Rights editorials, it was suppressed by the Government, and did not resume publication until 19 April, 1862. Maurice Francis Egan was editor of the paper for two years after McMaster's death, and in 1894 the Rev. Dr. Louis A. Lambert (b. at Allenport, Pennsylvania, 11 February, 1835; d. at Newfoundland, New Jersey, 25 September, 1910) took the position and so continued until his death.

New York City was, during the first half of the nineteenth century, the leader in Catholic journalism. The pioneer papers devoted their space mainly to controversial articles explanatory of the truths of the Faith, and in defence of the teachings of the Church in answer to attack and calumny. The assaults of the Native American and Know-nothing periods also largely engaged their attention. In this they were assisted by a number of journals not strictly religious, but political and social, edited by Catholics, and for a numerous constituency Irish by birth or descent. Of these the oldest, "The Irish American", founded 12 August, 1849, by Patrick Lynch (b. at Kilkenny, Ireland, 1811; d. in Brooklyn, New York, May, 1857); edited from 1857 until 1906 by his step-son Patrick J. Meehan (b. at Limerick, Ireland, 17 July, 1831; d. Jersey City, New Jersey, 20 April, 1906), with the "Catholic Telegraph" of Cincinnati (founded 1831), "Pilot" of Boston (1837), "Freeman's Journal" of New York (1840), and "Catholic" of Pittsburg (1846), alone survive in 1911, of the many Catholic papers in existence in the United States during the first half of the nineteenth century. In October, 1848, Thomas D'Arcy McGee began in New York a paper called "The Nation" which lasted until June, 1850, its end being hastened by McGee's violent controversy with Bishop Hughes. Another venture of his, "The American Celt", completed in June, 1857, had a peripatetic existence of four years—in Boston, Buffalo, and New York—when it was purchased by D. & J. Sadlier and made over into a new paper, "The Tablet", the first number of which appeared on 5 June of that year, with Bernard Doran Killian as its editor. His successors in that position, until the paper died in 1893, included Dr. J. V. Huntington, William Denman, Mrs. M. A. Sadlier, Dr. Henry J. Anderson, O. A. Brownson, Lawrence Kehoe, and D. P. Conyngham. Archbishop Hughes started, in 1859, as his personal organ, "The Metropolitan Record", which ceased publication in 1873. During all this time John Mullaly was its editor.

In 1872 "The Catholic Review", a paper combining the ideals of progressive modern journalism under the direction of a man who had had practical newspaper training, was begun by Patrick V. Hickey (b. in Dublin, Ireland, 14 Feb., 1846; d. in Brooklyn, New York, 21 Feb., 1889). For a time it met with success as a high-class weekly, and, to meet the demand for a cheap popular paper, Hickey printed also, in 1888, "The Catholic American" and the "Illustrated Catholic American". After his death, the Rev. J. Talbot Smith edited "The Review", which ceased to exist in 1899. Mr. Herman Ridder founded "The Catholic News" in 1886, and it is notable that the historian Dr. John Gilmary Shea closed his long and splendid career as its editor, 22 Feb., 1892. The "News" attained a very large and widespread circulation as a medium of entertaining and instructive reading matter for the masses under the business management of Henry Ridder and the editorial direction of Michael J. Madigan.

Several attempts have been made to establish a paper in the Diocese of Brooklyn, notably the "Catholic Examiner", in 1882, and the "Leader", in 1884. Both were shortlived. In June, 1908, the "Tablet" was started. In February, 1909, it was made a diocesan organ and purchased by a company made up of diocesan priests. Albany had a "Catholic Pioneer" in 1853, followed by several other ventures with brief existences. The "Catholic Sun" of Syracuse, in 1892, succeeded the "Catholic Reflector" of the early sixties and the equally shortlived "Vindicator" and "Sentinel". The "Sun" is also circulated as the "Catholic Chronicle" in Albany and the "Catholic Light" in Scranton, Penn. The Newark, New Jersey, "Monitor" was begun in September, 1906. Buffalo, New York, also had several experiences, beginning with D'Arcy McGee's "American Celt", in 1852, and culminating in the "Catholic Union and Times", the "Union" starting in 1872, and being combined later with the "Times", founded in 1877 by the Rev. Louis A. Lambert at Waterloo. For most of the years of its progress the editor was the Rev. Patrick Cronin (b. in Ireland, 1835; d. at North Tonawanda, New York, 12 Dec., 1905), a forceful and able writer and a recognized leader among the Irish-American element in the United States.

The Catholic papers of Philadelphia start with the Hogan schism (see CONWELL, HENRY), the "Catholic Herald and Weekly Register" being issued 30 Nov., 1822, by E. F. Crozet to support the rebellious priest. To offset its influence and assist Bishop Conwell, the "Catholic Advocate and Irishman's Journal" was started 22 Feb., 1823. In August, 1822, the "Erin", a national paper, was first issued. These were followed in 1833 by the "Catholic Herald", which had a stormy existence under the editorial management of a convert, Henry Major, who was a professor in the diocesan seminary. Disappointed in his ambition, Major relapsed to Episcopalianism, though he repented in his last illness. He was a bitter antagonist of Orestes A. Brownson in the controversies that were carried on during the fifties by the editors of the Catholic publications of that period. Another "Catholic Herald" was issued 22 June, 1872, by Marc F. Vallette, and had a brief existence. The "Catholic Standard", started 6 June, 1866, was suspended 20 Feb., 1867, but resumed publication on 22 June of the same year. Its first editor was the Rev. Dr. James Keogh; others were Mark Wilcox, George D. Wolf, and F. T. Furey. In 1874 Hardy & Mahony became its publishers, and 7 Dec., 1895, it combined (under the title of "Catholic Standard and Times") with the "Catholic Times", a rival which had the Rev. Louis A. Lambert as editor, and the first number of which was dated 3 Dec., 1892. Its news, editorials, and correspondence are regarded as authoritative, and frequently quoted by the secular Press. A monthly, the "Irish Catholic Benevolent Union Journal", with Martin I. J. Griffin as editor, began in March, 1873; had its title changed in March, 1894, to "Griffin's Journal", and suspended in July, 1900.

Bishop Michael O'Connor, of Pittsburg, founded (16 March, 1844) "The Pittsburg Catholic". Its manager and proprietor was J. F. Boylan, with whom was associated a printer named Jacob Porter, a convert. On 30 June, 1847, Porter and Henry McNaughton bought the paper with which Porter retained his connexion until 1889. He died in his eighty-third year, 14 January, 1908. An early editor was the Rev. Hugh P. Gallagher, president of the Pittsburg seminary, born in County Donegal, Ireland, in 1815, and ordained priest in 1840. In 1852 he went to San Francisco, where he started the "Catholic Standard" the following year. He died there in 1883. The "Catholic Observer" of Pittsburg dates from 1899. The "Emerald Vindicator" began at Pittsburg, May, 1882, moved to Norfolk, Virginia, in August, 1888, suspended in July, 1889. During the seventies, under Bishop Mullen's patronage the "Lake Shore Visitor" was published at Erie, Pennsylvania, for several years.

Bishop Fenwick, feeling that a journalistic organ was needed in Boston, started "The Jesuit, or Catholic Sentinel", the first number of which was dated 5 September, 1829. "The rapid increase and respectability of Roman Catholics in Boston and throughout the New England States", says the prospectus, "loudly calls for the publication of a Newspaper, in which the Doctrine of the Holy Catholic Church, ever the same, from the Apostolic Age down to our time, may be truly explained, and moderately, but firmly defended." Objection having been made that the name "The Jesuit" was prejudicial to the increase of circulation. Bishop Fenwick, after four months, allowed the title to be changed to "The Catholic Intelligencer", but in a short time went back to the original style. This did not improve conditions, and, on 27 December, 1834, another title, "The Irish and Catholic Sentinel", was announced; during 1835, however, the paper was called "The Literary and Catholic Sentinel", and on 2 January, 1836, evolved into "The Boston Pilot", a name subsequently changed to "The Pilot". The first editors were George Pepper and Dr. J. S. Bartlett, and the printers and publishers Patrick Donahoe and Henry L. Devereux. Patrick Donahoe (q. v.), who became connected with "The Pilot", in 1835, by the withdrawal of Devereux, assumed the ownership of the enterprise, which in the course of a few years grew into a most important paper of national circulation and influence, advocating Catholic and Irish interests. The editors under whose direction this success was attained were Thomas D'Arcy McGee, the Rev. J. P. Roddan, the Rev. Joseph M. Finotti (q. v.), John Boyle O'Reilly, James J. Roche, and Katherine E. Conway. Over the pen name of "Laffan", Michael Hennessy, of the editorial staff of the New York daily "Times" (b. at Thomastown, Co. Kilkenny, Ireland, 8 Sept., 1833; d. in Brooklyn, New York, 23 July, 1892), contributed for years weekly articles on Catholic and Irish historical and genealogical topics that had a very wide popularity. The Rev. John P. Roddan was a Boston priest educated at the Propaganda, Rome, and on his return home made pastor at Quincy, Mass., where, in addition to his pastoral duties, he edited "The Pilot". He was a friend of Orestes A. Brownson, and wrote many articles for his "Review". Boyle O'Reilly's connexion with "The Pilot" began about 1870, and continued till his death in 1890. On the failure of Patrick Donahoe's bank and publishing house in 1876, Archbishop Williams came to his rescue and purchased a three-fourths interest in "The Pilot" for the benefit of the depositors in the bank. O'Reilly held the other fourth, and was given the business as well as the editorial management. In 1890 the venerable Patrick Donahoe, who had bravely gone to work to rehabilitate his fortunes, was able to buy back "The Pilot" and resumed its management, which he held until his death, 18 March, 1891. In June, 1908, Archbishop O'Connell bought "The Pilot" from the Donahoe family and made it the official diocesan organ of the diocese and a distinctively Catholic journal.

When Orestes A. Brownson became a Catholic he attended the church in East Boston of which the Rev. Nicholas O'Brien was pastor. Father O'Brien in 1847 persuaded Brownson to join him in the publication of "The Catholic Observer". He soon proved his unfitness for the management of the paper, which suspended after two years' existence. In 1888 a number of priests organized a corporation which began the publication of "The Sacred Heart Review". Under the direction of Mgr John O'Brien it attained a great reputation for enterprise and literary merit. Another Boston paper, "The Republic", was started in 1881 by Patrick Maguire, but more as a political, than a strictly Catholic organ. In Connecticut Bishop Fenwick was even earlier with his journalistic venture than he was in Boston, for the "Catholic Press" was begun in Hartford, on 11 July, 1829. In its office he started the first Sunday school, 19 July, 1829, and there, too, Mass was offered up for the few Catholics composing the pioneer colony. The "Press" did not long survive, and its successor did not arrive until 1876, when the "Connecticut Catholic" was begun. Twelve years later Bishop Tierney purchased this paper and made it, as the "Catholic Transcript", official diocesan property, with the Rev. T. S. Duggan as editor. In Rhode Island the Providence "Visitor" dates from 1877.

The "Catholic Mirror" was established at Baltimore in 1849, and, as an expression of Southern opinion and the diocesan organ, had, in its early years, considerable influence. After the War, however, its prestige waned, and, in spite of several efforts to keep it alive, it suspended in 1908. Kentucky's first Catholic paper, the "Catholic Advocate", was founded in 1835 by Ben. J. Webb, then foreman printer of the Louisville "Journal", encouraged in the scheme by the Rev. Dr. Reynolds and the Rev. Dr. Martin J. Spalding. It took the place of the "Minerva", a monthly magazine, founded in 1834, and edited by the faculty of St. Joseph's College, Bardstown. In the old "Advocate" many of the most valuable papers written by Bishop Spalding first appeared. In May, 1858, it was succeeded by the "Catholic Guardian", started in Louisville by the members of the local Particular Council of the St. Vincent de Paul Society, which had a fair success, but was forced to suspend by the Civil War in July, 1862. The "Catholic Advocate" was revived later as the "Central Catholic Advocate", and in 1896 the "Midland Review" was started to rival it. There was not room for both so the new absorbed the old journal; but, in spite of the fact that the publication was high-class, it died after a checkered existence of five years. Its editor was a versatile writer of both poetry and prose, Charles J. O'Malley, who left the "Angelus" magazine of Cincinnati to edit the Louisville paper. When he found that his field there was too limited for any practical success, he took the editorial management of the "Catholic Sun" of Syracuse, N. Y., whence he went to Chicago to take charge of the "New World", in which position he died 26 March, 1910. He was born in Kentucky 9 February, 1857. In the period before the Civil War, the "Advocate" and the Baltimore "Mirror" were important and influential factors in Catholic affairs. The Louisville "Catholic Record", a diocesan organ, dates from 1878.

Other Southern papers are the New Orleans "Morning Star", established in 1867, and of which two poets, the Rev. Abram J. Ryan and James R. Randall, were at times editors; "The Southern Catholic", begun in 1874 at Memphis, Tenn., suspended, and followed by the "Catholic Journal". In Missouri "The Shepherd of the Valley" started at St. Louis in 1832 with a convert, R. A. Bakewell, as its editor. It suspended in 1838, was revived in 1851, and lasted three years longer. Bakewell, who died in 1909, created much trouble by his editorials, which were used for years as anti-Catholic ammunition by the Native American and Know-nothing politicians. It was the time of O'Connell's Irish agitation for repeal of the union with England, and the Revolutionary movement of 1848, and he also antagonized the Irish-American element. Although the Catholic constituency, to which their publications appealed, was mainly Irish, many of these convert editors went out of their way to offend Irish susceptibilities. Bakewell's denunciations of Thomas Francis Meagher, John Mitchell, the Rev. Dr. Cahill, and other popular Irishmen enraged "my Irish constituents", he tells Brownson, in a letter dated 7 January, 1853. Brownson, in an article in his "Review" of July, 1854, on Native-Americanism raised a storm by the manner in which he referred to the Irish element. After it was printed, Father Hecker, founder of the Paulists, wrote to him: "The Irish prelates and priests have become mighty tender on the point of Nationality. Your dose on Native-Americanism has operated on them and operated powerfully, and especially at the West. They felt sore, and let me add also weak from its effects. . . . The truth is, I fear, that there may before long come a collision on this point in our Church. The American element is increasing steadily in numerical strength, and will in time predominate; and at the present moment, on account of the state of the public mind, has great moral weight, and this in itself must excite unpleasant feelings on the other side." The "Western Watchman" of St. Louis, Missouri, edited and controlled by the Rev. D. S. Phelan, may be called the last of the old style personal organs, and has been running a strenuous course since 1865. In 1846 a predecessor, the "Catholic News Letter", began an existence of three years, and in 1878 a stock company was formed which combined an existing weekly, the "Catholic World", until then published in Illinois, with the "Church Progress" as a rival to the "Watchman". For several years Condé B. Pallen held the position of editor of the "Progress".

The Cincinnati "Catholic Telegraph", established in 1831, now the oldest surviving Catholic publication of the United States, enjoyed during the early years of Bishop Purcell's administration a national reputation under the editorial direction of his brother, the Rev. Edmund Purcell, the Rev. S. H. Rosecranz, and the Rev. J. F. Callaghan. Bishop Gilmour, of Cleveland, was a strong advocate of the value of a Catholic paper, and, beginning in 1874, spent a considerable amount of money, time, and personal effort in trying to establish the "Catholic Universe" in his cathedral city. Manly Tello was the editor during its early years. The "Catholic Columbian" of Columbus started in 1875, and the "Record" of Toledo in 1905.

The best known and most widely circulated Western publication is the "Ave Maria", a scholarly literary weekly, founded by Father Sorin of the Congregation of the Holy Cross, at Notre Dame, Indiana, in 1865. For the first issues the editor was Father Gillespie, C.S.C., and his sister, the well known Mother Mary St. Angela Gillespie (see GILLESPIE, ELIZA MARIA), was a frequent auxiliary. In 1874 the Rev. Daniel E. Hudson, C.S.C., took charge. An early venture in Chicago was the "Western Tablet", in 1852, under the editorial direction of a convert, M. L. Linton. Another editor was James A. Mulligan, more famous as the colonel of the 23rd Illinois volunteers of the Civil War (the Western Irish Brigade). He was born at Utica, New York, 25 June, 1830, and went to Chicago in 1836. He studied law before becoming an editor. His heroic defence of Lexington, Ky., in September, 1861, where, with 2800 men, he withstood an army of 22,000, made him a popular hero. He died, 26 July, 1864, from wounds received two days before at the battle of Kernstown, Va. The "Western Tablet" did not survive, and it had several ill-starred successors until the "New World" appeared in 1892. Three years later the "Western Catholic" was printed at Quincy, Ill. The "Michigan Catholic" of Detroit dates from 1872. In October, 1869, the "Star of Bethlehem" was established as a monthly at Milwaukee, Wisconsin, by the St. Louis Brothers. Two years later they sold the paper to the "Catholic Vindicator", which had been established in November, 1870, at Monroe, Wis., by Dr. D. W. Nolan and the Rev. John Casey. The "Catholic Vindicator" and "Star of Bethlehem" were consolidated, and established in Milwaukee, November, 1871. In November, 1878, Edward A. Bray and the Rev. G. L. Willard, having purchased the "Catholic Vindicator" from Dr. D. W. Nolan, changed the name to the "Catholic Citizen". In 1880 H. J. Desmond undertook its editorial management.

Other Western papers are the "Catholic Tribune", Dubuque, Iowa (1899); "Intermountain Catholic", Salt Lake City, Utah (1899); the "Catholic Bulletin", St. Paul, Minn. (1911); "True Voice", Omaha, Neb. (1903); "Catholic Register", Kansas City, Mo. (1899); "Catholic Sentinel", Portland, Oregon (1870). In San Francisco, Cal., the "Monitor" is one of the veterans dating as far back as 1852. Later enterprises are the "Leader" of the same city (1902); the "Catholic Herald" of Sacramento (1908); and "Tidings" of Los Angeles (1895).

Magazines and Periodicals.—The first Catholic magazine was the "Metropolitan, or Catholic Monthly Magazine" issued at Baltimore, Md., January, 1830. It lived a year. Another "Metropolitan" began in February, 1853, but also failed to make a permanent impression. In January, 1842, the "Religious Cabinet", a monthly, edited by Rev. Dr. Charles J. White and Rev. James Dolan, was started in Baltimore. After a year its title was changed to the "United States Catholic Magazine", which lasted until 1847. The Rev. Dr. White and Dr. J. V. Huntington were its most noted editors, and the contributors included Archbishop M. J. Spalding, Bishop Michael O'Connor, the Rev. Dr. C. C. Pise, and B. N. Campbell. In New York the "Catholic Expositor", edited by the Rev. Dr. Charles C. Pise and the Rev. Felix Varela, lasted three years (1842–44). Father Varela was also instrumental in the publication in New York, by C. H. Gottsberger, of the "Young Catholic's Magazine" in March, 1838; it was suspended in February, 1840. The "National Catholic Register", a monthly, the first issue of which appeared at Philadelphia, in January, 1844, did not last long.

When Father Hecker started the "Catholic World", in 1865, its editor for the first five years was John R. G.

Hassard (q. v.), and the publisher Lawrence Kehoe (b. in Co. Wexford, Ireland, 24 July, 1832; d. in Brooklyn, New York, 20 Feb., 1890). To the latter was due much of the early success of the magazine and of the Catholic Publication Society. Under the patronage of the Christian Brothers the "De La Salle Monthly" was begun in 1867. Its name was later changed to the "Manhattan Monthly" and the Irish patriot and poet John Savage was for a time its editor. The "Young Crusader" of Boston (1868), "Catholic Record", Philadelphia (1871), "Central Magazine", St. Louis (1872), "Donahoe's Magazine", Boston (1878), follow in the list of failures. The "Rosary Magazine," begun by the Dominicans in New York, in 1891, was transferred to Somerset, Ohio. The Sisters of Mercy have published, since 1908, at Manchester, New Hampshire, "The Magnificat". In April, 1866, the Rev. B. Sestini, S.J., founded the "Messenger of the Sacred Heart" at Georgetown, D. C.; thence it was moved to Woodstock, Md., next to Philadelphia, and finally to New York, in 1893. Later, in 1907, the "Messenger of the Sacred Heart" was devoted entirely to the interests of the Confraternity of the Sacred Heart, and the "Messenger", a separate magazine of general literary character, was issued. The latter publication, in April, 1910, was changed to a weekly review, "America", which, by authority of the General of the Society of Jesus, was made the joint work of the provincials of the Society in North America. It took immediate rank as an exponent of Catholic opinion with a national scope and circulation. The Rev. John J. Wynne, S.J., was its founder and first editor-in-chief. The Catholic University, Washington, publishes two magazines, the "Catholic University Bulletin" and the "Catholic Educational Review" (1911), and nearly all the Catholic colleges and the academies have monthlies edited and compiled by the students.

For historical work Philadelphia has two quarterly magazines, "American Catholic Historical Researches" and "Records of the American Catholic Historical Society". New York has one, "Historical Records and Studies", of the United States Catholic Historical Society. When the reading-circle movement began, Warren E. Mosher (b. at Albany, N. Y., 1860; d. at New Rochelle, N. Y., 22 March, 1906), who was one of the founders of the Catholic Summer School, started the "Catholic Reading Circle Review". This title was later changed to "Mosher's Magazine", but the periodical did not survive its founder. The "Catholic Fortnightly Review", of Techny, Ill., edited by Arthur Preuss, and the "St. John's Quarterly", of Syracuse, N. Y., edited by the Rev. Dr. J. F. Mullany, are personal organs of the editors. "Benziger's Magazine", New York, 1898, and "Extension", Chicago, 1907, are illustrated monthlies. The "Ecclesiastical Review", Philadelphia (1889), supplies a varied and interesting quantity of professional information for the clergy. An attempt was made to offer from the same office in "The Dolphin", a similarly important publication for the laity, but it failed to attract the necessary support. Another failure, for a like reason, was made in New York in the "New York Review, a journal of Ancient Faith and Modern Thought", issued bi-monthly from St. Joseph's Seminary, Dunwoodie, June, 1905—May-June, 1908.

The first quarterly review established in the United States was the "American Review of History and Politics", founded by a Catholic, Robert Walsh, at Philadelphia, and of which two volumes were published (1811–12). Walsh was born at Baltimore, Md., in 1784, and educated at Georgetown College. He was a man of great literary ability, and died United States consul at Paris, 7 Feb., 1859. The first and most important Catholic quarterly was "Brownson's Quarterly Review", which Orestes A. Brownson began in January, 1844, at Boston (moved to New York, 1855), after his conversion. He suspended its publication in 1864 "because he was unwilling", he said, "to continue a periodical which had not the full confidence of the Catholic hierarchy". It was revived in 1873, and finally ceased publication in October, 1875, with the statement: "I discontinue the Review solely on account of my precarious health and the failure of my eyes." The first number of the "American Catholic Quarterly Review" was issued at Philadelphia, in January, 1876, and the Rev. James A. Corcoran (q. v.), George D. Wolf, and Archbishop Patrick John Ryan are notable as its editors. The "Globe Review", of Philadelphia, edited by the erratic William Henry Thorne, had a short career of violent iconoclastic character.

Special Organs.—The fraternal organizations have their special organs—as, for example, the "National Hibernian" (Washington, 1900), of the Ancient Order of Hibernians—which devote their pages to the interests of the social organizations which they represent. The German Catholic Press, led by two influential dailies, has made much more substantial and practical progress than its English contemporaries. Prominent among the editors who contributed to these achievements were Dr. Maximilian Oertel (q. v.) and Edward Frederic Reinhold Preuss (b. at Königsberg, Germany, 10 July, 1834; d. at St. Louis, Missouri, July, 1904). There are sixty-nine Polish papers printed in the United States, twenty odd being thoroughly Catholic, and the others ranging from neutrality to violent anti-clericalism. Of the nine dailies four are distinctively Catholic. The oldest paper is the "Gazeta Katolicka", founded by Father Barzynski. He also founded, in 1889, the "Dziennik Chicagoski" (Chicago Daily News), the controlling interest in which is owned by the Resurrectionist Fathers. There are eighteen Polish papers printed in Chicago, four of them dailies, and of the eighteen seven are Catholic. The Bohemians have a number of prosperous periodicals including 1 daily, 1 semi-weekly, 2 weeklies, 1 monthly, and 1 bi-monthly. (See also BOHEMIANS IN THE UNITED STATES; FRENCH CATHOLICS IN THE UNITED STATES; GERMANS IN THE UNITED STATES.—*The Press;* ITALIANS IN THE UNITED STATES.—*Religious Organizations;* POLES IN THE UNITED STATES.)

FINOTTI, *Bibliographia Cath. Americana* (New York, 1872); *Brownson's Quarterly Review* (New York, Jan., 1849); MIDDLETON in *Records of Am. Cath. Hist. Soc.* (Philadelphia, Sept., 1893; March, 1908); GRIFFIN in *Catholic Hist. Researches* (Philadelphia); U. S. CATH. HIST. SOC., *Cath. Hist. Records and Studies*, III (New York, Jan., 1903), part i; MURRAY, *Popular Hist. of Cath. Church in U. S.* (New York, 1876); *Catholic Citizen* (Milwaukee, Wis.), files; *Catholic News* (New York, 11 and 18 April, 1908); H. F. BROWNSON, *Brownson's Middle Life;* IDEM, *Later Life* (Detroit, 1899–1900); *Catholic Directory,* files; MESSMER, *Works of the Rt. Rev. John England* (Cleveland, 1908); KEHOE, *Works of Most Rev. John Hughes* (New York, 1864); BAYLEY, *Brief Sketch of Hist. of Cath. Church on the Island of New York* (New York, 1870); MULLANY, *Catholic Editors I Have Known* in *St. John's Quarterly* (Syracuse, 1910–11), files.

THOMAS F. MEEHAN.

Peripatetic School. See ARISTOTLE.

Perjury (Lat. *per*, through and *jurare*, to swear) is the crime of taking a false oath (q. v.). To the guilt of the sin of lying it adds an infraction of the virtue of religion. An oath properly taken is an act of worship because it implies that God as witness to the truth is omniscient and infallible. Hence the wickedness of invoking the Divine testimony to confirm an untruth is specially criminal. Prescinding from cases of ignorance or insufficient deliberation this sin is reputed to be always mortal. When in doubt one cannot without perjury swear to a thing as certain. When mental reservation is permissible it is lawful to corroborate one's utterance by an oath, if there be an adequate cause. It is obvious, however, that if in general it be true that there is need of caution in the use of mental reservations lest they be simply lies, there will be an additional motive for care when they are to be distinguished with the solemnity of an oath. According to the common doctrine as to co-operation in another's sin, it would be a grievous offense to require a person to take an oath when we know he is going to perjure himself. This teaching, however, does not apply to cases in which justice or necessity demand that a statement be sworn to. Hence, for instance, a trial judge may insist that evidence be presented under oath even though it be clear that much or all of the testimony is false. Perjury, according to the divisions in vogue in Canon Law, belongs to the category of crimes called mixed. These may fall under the cognizance of either the ecclesiastical or civil court, according as they are reputed to work damage either to the spiritual or civil commonwealth. No canonical penalty is incurred by one guilty of perjury, at least directly. When, however, a person has been convicted of it before a competent tribunal and sentence imposed, he is esteemed infamous (*infamia juris*) and therefore irregular.

TAUNTON, *The Law of the Church* (London, 1906); SLATER, *Manual of Moral Theology* (New York, 1908); BALLERINI, *Opus Theologicum Morale* (Prato, 1899).

JOSEPH F. DELANY

Perlo, PHILIP. See KENIA, VICARIATE APOSTOLIC OF.

Permaneder, FRANZ MICHAEL, canonist, b. at Traunstein, Bavaria, 12 Aug., 1794; d. at Ratisbon, 10 Oct., 1862. He studied theology and jurisprudence at Landshut and in 1818 was ordained to the priesthood at Ratisbon. He was appointed in 1834 professor of church history and canon law at the "Lyceum" of Freising, and in 1847 joined the theological faculty of the University of Munich. He was contributor to the first edition of the "Kirchenlexicon", and also wrote: "Handbuch des gemeingültigen katholischen Kirchenrechts mit steter Rücksicht auf Deutschland" (Landshut, 1846); "Die kirchliche Baulast" (Munich, 1853); "Bibliotheca patristica" (incomplete; Landshut, 1841–44); a continuation of the "Annales almæ literarum universitatis Ingolstadii" (Munich, 1859).

SCHULTE, *Geschichte der Quell. u. Lit. des Kan. Rechts*, III (Stuttgart, 1880), i, 356–57.

N. A. WEBER.

Pernter, JOSEPH MARIA, scientist, b. at Neumark, Tyrol, 15 March, 1848; d. at Arco, 20 Dec., 1908. He entered the Society of Jesus after graduation from the Gymnasia at Bozen and Meran. For a time he acted as professor of physics at Kalocsa and Kalksburg. In 1877 he was obliged to leave the order, on account of an ailment in his head. He then studied physics at the University of Vienna and received the doctor's degree. After entering the Central Institute as volunteer in October, 1878, Pernter became assistant in 1880, and adjunct in 1884; in 1885 he also began to act as a *privatdozent* at the university. In 1890 he was called to the University of Innsbruck in the capacity of extraordinary professor, and in 1893 was appointed ordinary professor of cosmic physics. At Innsbruck he began a number of works including papers on the conditions of wind, humidity, radiation, and meteorological optics. In his most important work "Atmospherische Optik", he collected all published treatises and also supplied original papers necessary to complete certain subjects. Unfortunately he died before he had finished this valuable publication. His German translation of Abercromby's work, "The weather", is also noteworthy.

In 1897 Pernter became professor at the University of Vienna, and director of the Central Meteorological Institute. He reorganized the institute and extended it considerably, increasing the staff from fifteen to thirty-one. He made it possible for the institute to take part in balloon ascents for scientific purposes. A laboratory, a printing office, a reading room, etc., were added, also a bureau for seismic observations. Instruments for recording earth tremors were set up, and the institute supervised the network of stations for the study of earthquakes, its name being changed to "Zentralanstalt für Meteorologie und Geodynamik". He introduced various improvements in practical weather forecasting, such as the free delivery of forecasts in the summer to all telegraph stations. During his directorate were introduced the experiments on so-called "weather-shooting", as a prevention of the dangers due to hail. These experiments created considerable excitement in the agricultural circles of Austria and Italy. Pernter examined the matter carefully and fearlessly, and came to a conclusion that proved to be the deathblow of this practice.

He was kind towards his subordinates and interested in their welfare. It will take some time before a full appreciation is had of all that he accomplished for the institute. The most important of his numerous political papers is "Voraussetzungslose Forschung, freie Wissenschaft und Katholizismus", published during the Mommsen agitation. In this essay he sought to prove the possibility of combining strict religious faith with exact research. Pernter was also one of the founders of the "Leo-Gesellschaft" in Vienna and of the branch at Innsbruck. These societies have suffered a great loss, because he took an active part as long as he could in all their work and propaganda. During the last years of his life he was a victim to sclerosis of the arteries, which especially affected his heart. He suffered very much through weakness of the heart, difficulty of breathing, and occasional fainting spells. He was also depressed by the sickness and death of his beloved young daughter and of his wife. These numerous blows combined to hasten his end.

WILHELM TRABERT.

Perpetua, SAINT. See FELICITAS AND PERPETUA, SAINTS.

Perpetual Adoration. See ADORATION, PERPETUAL.

Perpetual Adoration, RELIGIOUS OF (Belgium), a congregation with simple vows, founded at Brussels, 1857, by Anna de Meeus, daughter of Count Ferdinand de Meeus, for whose head a price was offered by the insurgents during the Revolution of 1830. In 1843 Mlle de Meeus, then twenty years of age, at the request of the rector visited the sacristy of the church near their chateau and other churches. Impressed by the miserable state of the vestments and all that pertained to the altar, she found the inspiration of her life's work. Considering the poverty and neglect of Jesus Christ in the Blessed Sacrament and desiring to make reparation to Him, she conceived the idea of an association with the object of reviving faith in the Real Presence: by adoration, night and day; persons undertaking to make monthly an hour of adoration, and give yearly an offering for the benefit of poor churches; by working to enhance the dignity of Divine worship by providing the necessaries for the becoming celebration of the sacred mysteries. The Association of Perpetual Adoration and Work for Poor Churches was organized in 1848 under the direction of Rev. Jean Baptiste Boone, S.J., "the apostle of Brussels". The necessity was soon felt that a religious body should be its centre and support, one which would be wholly devoted to the propagation of the knowledge, love, and adoration of the Blessed Sacrament.

As no community existed which made this work its special vocation, the project of a new religious institute was formed and realized when Mlle de Meeus, directed by Father Boone, founded the Religious of the Perpetual Adoration. The constitutions were definitively approved by Pius IX (March, 1872). The religious must not only be adorers but also missionaries of the Blessed Sacrament, devoting themselves to all that, compatible with a life of retirement, can further Its glory: religious instruction, preparation for first Communion, retreats, etc. Their churches with the Blessed Sacrament exposed are always open to the public. By their principal work, the association, they strive to increase love for the Blessed Sacrament, by hours of adoration, grants of vestments to poor churches, the Forty Hours Devotion, etc. The association spread rapidly throughout the world (in America it is frequently called "Tabernacle Society"). In 1853 it was erected an archassociation with power to affiliate others. The decree of Leo XIII transferring it to Rome (February, 1879) declares: "The archassociation is one with the institute in name and in its object, it is subordinate to the institute as to its head, and must be subordinate to it in virtue of the constitutions approved by the Holy See". The archassociation was raised to the rank of *prima primaria*, July, 1895. The institute has many houses in Europe. In August, 1880, it was introduced into England by Cardinal Herbert Vaughan, then Bishop of Manchester. Its first foundation in America was at Washington, D. C., October, 1900.

C. L. Martin.

Perpetual Adoration, Religious of the, a contemplative religious congregation, founded in 1526 by Sister Elizabeth Zwirer (d. 1546), at Einsiedeln, Switzerland, and following the Benedictine rule. At the beginning of the year 1789 they commenced the practice of adoration of the Blessed Sacrament during the day before the closed tabernacle. A lay association was established, the members of which contributed a small sum of money for the expenses of the sanctuary necessitated by perpetual adoration. On 2 May, 1798, during the French invasion the sisters were expelled and their monastery ruined. Five years later, after the Concordat of Napoleon, the community returned. Acting on the advice of their confessor, Father Pierre Perrot, the sisters, on 8 January, 1846, began the practice of adoration by night as well as by day. In 1852 to signify their devotion to the Blessed Sacrament, they decided to wear a figure of an ostensorium on the breast of their habit. In 1859 Empress Elizabeth of Austria presented the monastery with a magnificent chalice and a reliquary. A new church was opened in 1882, and is adorned with three beautiful paintings, representing the adoration of Christ. The convent at Einsiedeln is the only house of its kind, and has its own novitiate. In 1909 the community numbered 46 professed sisters and 5 novices.

Arthur Letellier.

Perpetual Adoration, Sisters of the (Quimper, France), an institute of nuns devoted to perpetual adoration of the Blessed Sacrament and to the education of orphan children; founded at Quimper (Brittany), by Abbé François-Marie Langrez (b. at Saint Servan, 20 July, 1787; d. at Quimper, 10 August, 1862). In early youth François-Marie had been an apprentice rope-maker, but he began to study the classics at sixteen, and was ordained 19 December, 1812. In December, 1821, he conceived the first idea of the work he subsequently founded. Two poor homeless little girls crossed his path. He confided them to Marguerite Le Maître, a domestic servant. Other orphans were found and sheltered. In 1826 Marguerite's home contained an oratory and was provided with a dormitory holding thirty beds. Three years later she received her first two co-labourers, and on 21 November, 1829, the first chapel of the institute was opened. In 1832, Mlle Olympe de Moëlien, in whose family Marguerite Le Maître had been a servant when she began her charitable work, entered the little society, being made superioress, 10 March, 1833. On 20 January, 1835, Mère Olympe and her companions first put on the religious habit. In September, 1835 a tentative rule of life was drawn up by Abbé Langrez. In March, 1836, the first sisters made their vows. On 27 March, 1837, Sister Marguerite Le Maître died. Adoration of the Blessed Sacrament which was begun in March, 1836, did not become perpetual, day and night, till 1843, eight days after the death of Mère Olympe, who left after her a great reputation for sanctity. At that time the community numbered 11 choir sisters, 4 postulants, and had charge of 70 children. In 1845 their rule was approved by Mgr Graveran, Bishop of Quimper. A little later they were recognized by the Government under the title of Sisters of the Perpetual Adoration. On 10 May, 1851, a house was founded at Recouvrance, transferred, 28 October, 1856, to Coat-ar-Guéven, near Brest. This and the house at Quimper are the only ones that practise perpetual adoration. In 1882, the institute contained 400 orphan girls and 128 religious. Since its foundation, it has received 1754 orphan girls, of whom 1000 have embraced the religious life in different congregations.

Arthur Letellier.

Perpetual Adorers of the Blessed Sacrament (Sacramentines).—Anton Le Quien, b. in Paris, 23 Feb., 1601, the founder of the first order exclusively devoted to the practice of Perpetual Adoration, entered the Dominican Order, and after ordination was named master of novices at Avignon, and later prior of the convent at Paris. "During the seventeenth century", we read in his works, edited by Potton, "we find only two religious orders that have Perpetual Adoration. The first is that of the Sisters of the Blessed Sacrament, founded by Père Antoine, O.P.; the second that of the Benedictine Adoratrices, founded first at Paris and afterwards in several other cities, by the celebrated Mother Mechtilde. This religious, supported by powerful protectors, easily accomplished her task. Perpetual Adoration began among her daughters in 1654, while the Sisters of the Blessed Sacrament received the privilege of reserving the Blessed Sacrament only in 1659. But Père Antoine had begun the establishment of the Sisters of the Blessed Sacrament about 1639, while Mère Mechtilde's work appears, according to Hélyot, to date back no further, even in project, than 1651. Père Antoine may, then, be considered as possessing priority, especially as his order was intended solely for the worship of the Holy Eucharist, while that of Mère Mechtilde, although in existence, was adapted to that end only at a later period". Migne's "Dictionnaire des Ordres religieux" mentions no religious order exclusively destined for the worship of the Blessed Sacrament, except that of Père Antoine, and that of the Adoration Réparatrice, established in France for the first time in 1848.

In 1639 Père Antoine began his work at Marseilles. Sister Anne Negrel was named the first superioress. But the definitive establishment of the religious took place only in 1659–60, when Mgr de Puget, Bishop of Marseilles, erected them into a congregation under the title of Sisters of the Blessed Sacrament. The final formalities for the approval of the order having been concluded in Rome (1680), Innocent XI expedited a Brief, which could not be put in execution because of a change of bishop. Innocent XII issued a new Brief the same year in which the Apostolic Process was opened for the canonization of its founder. The only foundation of the order in the eighteenth century was made at Bollène (Vaucluse) in 1725. Sixty years later, under the government of Mère de La Fare, this monastery had the honour of offering to God thirteen victims, who succeeded one another on the scaffold, from the fifth to the twenty-sixth of July, 1794. The process for the canonization of these martyrs was opened at Rome, January, 1907.

Mère de La Fare, having escaped the guillotine,

gathered together her community in 1802, and made a foundation at Avignon in 1807. The same year a Sacramentine of Marseilles founded a convent at Aix-en-Provence. In 1816 the convent of Marseilles was reopened, and Mère de La Fare made a new foundation at Carpentras. In 1859 six religious of Aix founded a house at Bernay, Normandy, and in 1863 some Sisters from Bollène founded a convent of Perpetual Adoration at Taunton, England. Oxford also has a foundation. All the houses of this order are autonomous and dependent on the ordinary of the diocese, who is their superior. In consequence of the persecution of religious congregations in France, the Sacramentines of Marseilles were obliged to abandon their convent. The four other houses of Southern France, being authorized by the Government, still subsist, though their boarding-school is closed. The Sacramentines of Bernay at the time of the expulsion, July, 1903, were compelled to close their boarding-school and go into exile. Thirteen of the sisters retired to Belgium, and founded a house at Hal. The rest of the community settled in England at Whitson Court, Newport, Monmouthshire. Their existence is precarious, for they are not permitted to open a school. Their days are spent in prayer, adoration, and the making of altar-breads, vestments, and church ornaments. In March, 1911, the Sacramentines were permitted by Archbishop Farley to open a house in Holy Trinity parish, Yonkers, New York.

HÉLYOT, *Histoire des Ordres*, IV, 421 sq.; HEIMBUCHER, *Die Orden u. Kongregationen*, s. v. *Sakramentinerinnen*.

A. LETELLIER.

Perpetual Help, SISTERS OF OUR LADY OF, a congregation founded in the parish of St. Damien, Bellechasse, P. Q., Canada, 28 August, 1892, by Abbé J. O. Brousseau. The institute devotes itself to the following works: the instruction of children, particularly in country and city parochial schools; the education of orphans and the maintenance of agricultural orphanages in which, together with religious instruction and a good education, children may be given a taste for farming; the care of the aged and infirm of both sexes.

Abbé J. O. Brousseau laboured earnestly to secure funds for the new foundation and to overcome the obstacles to its progress. The pastors of a number of parishes in the Diocese of Quebec authorized him to seek pecuniary aid, on condition that he would admit some of their aged poor and orphans to his institutions. Among those who coöperated with him was Mlle Virginie Fournier, born at St. Joseph de Lévis but a resident of Fall River, Mass., a woman of experience and courage. She became the first superior of the little community which as Mère St. Bernard she governed for six years, with great success. From the first year of the community's existence, the sisters have conducted the principal schools of the parish of St. Damien. The demand for these religious educators increased and, in 1907, having no more disengaged subjects, they were obliged to refuse the direction of seventeen municipal schools. The first profession occurred on 27 March, 1897, when fifteen sisters pronounced the three vows of religion for a year, renewing them annually until the taking of their perpetual vows on 10 July, 1908. The congregation recruits its members from all classes of society, poverty being no obstacle. None are received save those of upright intention, sound judgment, a well-disposed will, and sufficiently robust health. To accept subjects under fifteen years of age and over thirty, widows or persons having already taken either temporary or perpetual vows in another religious community, it is necessary to have the permission of the Holy See. The dower is fixed at a hundred dollars; in default of this the aspirant must promise to give instead what will later revert to her by right of inheritance, bequest, or in any other legitimate way. The period of postulantship lasts six months, that of noviceship eighteen months, and after six years, permanent vows are taken.

The institute has so far confined its activities to the Diocese of Quebec. In 1907–08, the constitutions were recast and made conformable to the observations in the "Guide canonique" by Mgr Battandier, the superior-general and her councilors being directed in this work by the Rev. Charles Gonthier, S.J., of Montreal. At present the congregation conducts 21 schools in the Province of Quebec, with 2532 pupils, 1 hospital with 44 inmates, and 35 sisters, and has charge of 50 orphans. The order numbers (1911) 112 professed sisters, 8 novices, and 12 postulants.

SISTER ST. IGNACE DE LOYOLA.

Perpetual Succour, OUR LADY OF.—The picture of Our Lady of Perpetual Succour is painted on wood, with background of gold. It is Byzantine in style and is supposed to have been painted in the thirteenth century. It represents the Mother of God holding the Divine Child while the Archangels Michael and Gabriel present before Him the instruments of His Passion. Over the figures in the picture are some Greek letters which form the abbreviated words Mother of God, Jesus Christ, Archangel Michael, and Archangel Gabriel respectively. It was brought to Rome towards the end of the fifteenth century by a pious merchant, who, dying there, ordered by his will that the picture should be exposed in a church for public veneration. It was exposed in the church of San Matteo, Via Merulana, between St. Mary Major and St. John Lateran. Crowds flocked to this church, and for nearly three hundred years many graces were obtained through the intercession of the Blessed Virgin. The picture was then popularly called the Madonna di San Matteo. The church was served for a time by the Hermits of St. Augustine, who had sheltered their Irish brethren in their distress. These Augustinians were still in charge when the French invaded Rome (1812) and destroyed the church. The picture disappeared; it remained hidden and neglected for over forty years, but a series of providential circumstances between 1863 and 1865 led to its discovery in an oratory of the Augustinian Fathers at Santa Maria in Posterula.

The pope, Pius IX, who as a boy had prayed before the picture in San Matteo, became interested in the discovery and in a letter dated 11 Dec., 1865 to Father General Mauron, C.SS.R., ordered that Our Lady of Perpetual Succour should be again publicly venerated in Via Merulana, and this time at the new church of St. Alphonsus. The ruins of San Matteo were in the grounds of the Redemptorist Convent. This was but the first favour of the Holy Father towards the picture. He approved of the solemn translation of the picture (26 April, 1866), and its coronation by the Vatican Chapter (23 June, 1867). He fixed the feast as *duplex secundæ classis*, on the Sunday before the Feast of the Nativity of St. John the Baptist, and by a decree dated May, 1876, approved of a special office and Mass for the Congregation of the Most Holy Redeemer. This favour later on was also granted to others. Learning that the devotion to Our Lady under this title had spread far and wide, Pius IX raised a confraternity of Our Lady of Perpetual Succour and St. Alphonsus, which had been erected in Rome, to the rank of an arch-confraternity and enriched it with many privileges and indulgences. He was amongst the first to visit the picture in its new home, and his name is the first in the register of the archconfraternity. Two thousand three hundred facsimiles of the Holy Picture have been sent from St. Alphonsus's church in Rome to every part of the world. At the present day not only altars, but churches and dioceses (e. g. in England, Leeds and Middlesborough; in the United States, Savannah) are dedicated to Our Lady of Perpetual Succour. In some places, as in the United States, the title has been translated Our Lady of Perpetual Help.

Beata Virgo de Perpetuo Succursu, id est, de antiqua et prodigiosa Imagine in Ecclesia S. Alphonsi de Urbe Cultui reddita, necnon ae Archisodalitate sub titulo B. M. V. de Perpetuo Succursu et S. Alphonsi M. de Liguorio canonice erecta (Rome, 1876).

J. MAGNIER.

Perpetuus, SAINT, eighth Bishop of Tours, d. 1 January, or 8 December, 490, or 8 April, 491. He was a member of the illustrious family which produced St. Eustachius, who had been his predecessor, and also Saint Volusianus, who became his successor in the same episcopal see. Appointed about 460, he guided the Church of Tours for thirty years, and it is apparent, from what little information we have, that during his administration Christianity was considerably developed and consolidated in Touraine. Shortly after his elevation, St. Perpetuus presided at a council in which eight bishops who were reunited in Tours on the Feast of St. Martin had participated, and at this assembly an important rule was promulgated relative to ecclesiastical discipline. He maintained a careful surveillance over the conduct of the clergy of his diocese, and mention is made of priests who were removed from their office because they had proved unworthy. He built monasteries and various churches, but above all he desired to replace by a beautiful basilica (470) the little chapel that Saint Britius had constructed, to protect the tomb of St. Martin. The will of St. Perpetuus was published for the first time in 1661 by Dom Luc d'Achéry in his "Spicilegium". This curious historical monument belonging to the end of the fifth century gives us an excellent idea of the sanctity of its author.

BARONIUS, *Ann.* (1595), 47–52, 482; BOURASSÉ, *Le testament de S. Perpétue, évêque de Tours*, in *Bull. de la Soc. arch. de Touraine*, II (Tours, 1871–3), 256; CEILLIER, *Hist. gén. des auteurs sacr. et eccl.*, XV (Paris, 1748), 189–95; HENSCHENIUS, in *Act. SS. Bolland.*(1675), Apr., I, 748–52; *Hist. litt. de la France*, II (Paris, 1735), 619–27; ROBOTTI DEL FISCALE, *Cenni stor. intorno al glor. vescovo di Tours, S. Perpetuo* (Alessandria, 1859); TILLEMONT, *Mém. pour servir à l'hist. ecclés.*, XVI (Paris, 1712), 770–3.

LÉON CLUGNET.

Perpignan, DIOCESE OF (PERPINIANUM), comprises the Department of Pyrénées Orientales; created by the union of the ancient See of Elne, part of the Diocese of Urgel known as French Cerdagne, three cantons of the former Diocese of Alet, and two villages of the ancient Diocese of Narbonne. This department was united in 1802 to the Diocese of Carcassonne; by the Concordat of 1817 it received a special see. This see, though it continued the aforesaid ancient See of Elne, was located at Perpignan, where the bishops of Elne had resided since 1601 in virtue of a Bull of Clement VIII. Elne was a suffragan of Narbonne until 1511; from 1511 to 1517 it was directly subject to the Holy See; in 1517 it became again a suffragan of Narbonne; a Decree of the Council of Trent made it a suffragan of Tarragona; after 1678 it was again a suffragan of Narbonne. The See of Perpignan as it was re-established in 1817 is suffragan to Albi.

The first known Bishop of Elne is Dominus, mentioned in 571 in the Chronicle of John of Biclarum. Among others are Cardinal Ascanio Maria Sforza (1494–95), Cardinal Cæsar Borgia (1495–98), Cardinal François de Loris (1499–1506), Cardinal Jacques de Serra (1506–12), Cardinal Hieronimo Doria (1530–33), Olympe Gerbet (1854–64). The Cathedral of Elne (eleventh century) and the adjoining cloister are rich examples of elaborate medieval ornamentation. In the later Middle Ages, and under the influence of Roman law, Roussillon witnessed certain offensive revivals of ancient slavery; this is proved by numerous purchase deeds of Mussulman, and even Christian, slaves, dating back to the fourteenth and fifteenth centuries. The diocese honours especially St. Vincent de Collioure, martyr (end of third century); and St. Eulalia and St. Julia, virgins and martyrs (end of third century). In memory of former ties with the metropolis of Tarragona, the Church of Perpignan honours several Spanish saints: St. Fructuosus, Bishop of Tarragona, and his deacons Augurius and Eulogius, martyred at Tarragona in 259; some martyrs of the Diocletian persecution (end of third century); Justa and Rufina of Seville; Felix and Narcissus of Gerona; Aciselus and Victoria of Cordova; Leocadia, of Toledo; St. Ildefonsus (607–67), Archbishop of Toledo.

The Benedictine Dom Briard (1743–1828), who continued the important series of "Historiens de France", belonged to Perpignan. At Perpignan Benedict XIII (Pedro de Luna) held a council 1 Nov., 1408, to rally his partisans; they gradually melted away and on 1 Feb., 1409, the eighteen remaining bishops advised

THE CATHEDRAL, PERPIGNAN

the antipope to send ambassadors to Pisa to negotiate with Gregory XII. Numerous councils were held at Elne: in 1027, 1058, 1114, 1335, 1337, 1338, 1339, 1340, and 1380. The council held in 1027 decreed that no one should attack his enemy from Saturday at nine o'clock to Monday at one; and that Holy Mass be said for the excommunicated for a space of three months, to obtain their conversion. The author of "l'Art de verifier les Dates" wrongly maintains that the Council of Elvira was held at Elne. The chief places of pilgrimage of the diocese are: Notre-Dame du Château d'Ultréra, at Sorède; Notre-Dame de Consolation, at Collioure; Notre-Dame de Font Romeu, at Odeillo; Notre-Dame de Força-Réal, near Millas; Notre-Dame de Juigues, near Rivesaltes; the relics of Sts. Abdon and Sennen at Arles on the Tech. Prior to the application of the law of 1901, the Diocese of Perpignan had Capuchin Fathers and various orders of teaching Brothers. The Sisters of the Most Holy Sacrament, mother-house at Perpignan, are a nursing and teaching order. At the beginning of the twentieth century the religious congregations directed in the diocese 1 infant school, 13 day nurseries, 1 boys' orphanage, 2 girls' orphanages, 8 hospitals or asylums, and 2 houses for the care of the sick in their own homes. In 1905 there were 212,121 inhabitants, 26 parishes, 197 succursal parishes, and 43 vicariates subventioned by the state.

Gallia Christiana, nova, VI (1739), 1030–79, Instr., 474–97; DUCHESNE, *Fastes Épiscopaux;* PUIGGARI, *Catalogue Biographique des évêques d'Elne*(Perpignan, 1842); GAZANYOLA, *Histoire du Rous-*

sillon (Perpignan, 1857); DE BARTHÉLEMY, *Etudes sur les établissements monastiques du Roussillon* (Paris, 1857); TOLRA DE BORDAS, *L'ordre de Saint François d'Assise en Roussillon, fragments et récits sur l'histoire ecclésiastique du diocèse d'Elne* (Paris, 1884); BRUTAILS, *Etude sur l'esclavage en Roussillon du XIIe au XVIIe siècle* (Paris, 1886); IDEM, *Monographie de la Cathédrale et du Cloître d'Elne* (Perpignan, 1887); TOREILLES, *Perpignan pendant la Révolution* (3 vols., 1896–97); BORRALLO, *Promenades archéologiques; Elne et sa cathédrale* (Perpignan, 1909); DE BEAULIEU, *Les Sanctuaires de la Vièrge en Roussillon* (2 vols., Perpignan, 1903–04).

GEORGES GOYAU.

UNIVERSITY OF PERPIGNAN.—Peter IV of Aragon (1327–87), having conquered (1344) the town of Perpignan and reunited to his estates the Kingdom of Majorca, of which Perpignan was the capital, compensated that city for its loss of power by founding, at the request of the magistrates, 20 March, 1349, the University of Perpignan, for the teaching of civil and canon law, and other arts and sciences. In the charter he praised "the deep learning of the professors of Perpignan". By the Bull of 28 November, 1379, the antipope Clement VII confirmed the foundation and privileges, and the university, in a petition addressed to him in 1393, declared him its founder: "Pater et Genitor". In 1381 John I, son of Peter IV, granted permission to the city authorities to build the university near the royal castle. The institution spread in Perpignan an atmosphere of learning, the study of law being specially developed. Theology was taught there during the first years of the fourteenth century, but it was not until 21 July, 1447, that the faculty of theology was created by a Bull of Nicholas V and it did not receive its statutes until 1459. The university disappeared in 1793.

RASHDALL, *Universities*, I (Oxford, 1895), 90; FOURNIER, *Statuts des Universités françaises*, II (Paris, 1891), 651–716; DENIFLE, *Die Entstehung der Universitäten*, I (Berlin, 1885), 515–17; VIDAL, *Histoire de la ville de Perpignan* (Paris, 1897).

GEORGES GOYAU.

Perraud, ADOLPHE, cardinal and academician; b. at Lyons, France, 7 Feb., 1828; d. 18 Feb., 1906. He had a brilliant career at the lycées Henri IV and St. Louis, and entered the Ecole normale, where he was strongly influenced by Gratry. In 1850 he secured the fellowship of history and for two years he taught at the lycée of Angers. In 1852 he abandoned teaching to embrace the sacerdotal state. He returned to Paris where he joined the Oratory which was then being reorganized by Gratry and Abbé Pététot, curé of St. Roch. On his ordination in 1855 after a sojourn at Rome he was appointed professor of history and prefect of religion at the *petit séminaire* of St. Lô which had just been confided to the Oratory. At the same time he devoted himself to preaching, for which purpose he was recalled to Paris. In 1860 he visited Ireland, after which he wrote "Contemporary Ireland" (1862). In 1865 he defended a theological thesis at the Sorbonne, where in 1866 he became professor of ecclesiastical history and dealt brilliantly with the history of Protestantism. He was appointed (1870) by E. Ollivier a member of the Committee of Higher Education. In 1870 he was a chaplain in MacMahon's army, and after the war preached at St. Philippe du Roub and at St. Augustine. Made Bishop of Autun in 1874 despite his liberal tendencies, he interested himself especially in working-men. After the catastrophe of Montceau les mines, in which twenty-two miners perished, he preached the funeral sermon; he gave several Lenten courses in his cathedral and preached the funeral sermons of Cardinal Guibert, Cardinal Lavigerie, and MacMahon. He was actively concerned in the improvement of clerical studies in which connexion his sermon (1879) on "the Church and light" caused a great sensation; after the Congress of Brussels (1894) he was named honorary president of the Society for the Encouragement of Higher Studies among the Clergy. Elected to the French Academy in 1882 to replace Barbier, in 1885 he welcomed Duruy and in 1889 delivered the discourse on the prizes of virtue. Having been superior-general of the Oratory from 1884, he resigned in 1901 in order not to sign the request for authorization of his congregation. He was created cardinal *in petto*, 16 Jan., 1893, the creation being published at the Consistory of 1895. At the conclave of 1903 he energetically opposed the movement of exclusion directed against Rampolla by Puczina, Archbishop of Cracow, in the name of the Austrian Government. His works consist of the "Etudes sur l'Irlande contemporaine" (Paris, 1862); "L'Oratoire de France au XVIIe siècle" (1865); "Paroles de l'heure présente" (1872); "Le Cardinal de Richelieu" (1872); also oratorical works.

BAUDRILLART, *Le Cardinal Perraud* in *Le Correspondant* (25 Feb., 1906); MATHIEU, *Discours de réception à l'Académie Française* (5 Feb., 1907); CHAUVIN, *L'Oratoire*.

J. LATASTE.

Perrault, CHARLES, writer, b. in Paris, 12 Jan., 1628; d. 16 May, 1703. His first literary attempts were a parody of the sixth book of Virgil's Æneid, and a short poem, "Les Ruines de Troie ou l'Origine du Burlesque." After being a lawyer for some time, he was appointed chief clerk in the king's building, superintendent's office (1664). He suggested to his brother Claude, an architect, to build the Louvre's colonnade, and induced Colbert to establish a fund called *Liste des Bienfaits du Roi*, to give pensions to writers and savants not only in France but in Europe. He took part in the creation of the Academy of Sciences as well as the restoration of the Academy of Painting. When the Academy of Inscriptions and Belles-Lettres was founded by Colbert (1663), he was made secretary for life. Having written but a few poems, he was elected to the French Academy in 1671, and on the day of his inauguration he caused the public to be admitted to the meeting, a privilege that has ever since been continued. As a poet, he attempted to revive the old epic, adapting it to a Christian subject, in "Saint-Paulin" (1686). His preface to "Le siècle de Louis le Grand", soon followed by "Parallèle des Anciens et des Modernes", started the famous literary quarrel of Ancients and Moderns, which led to endless controversy with Boileau; he stood for the Moderns, while Bossuet, Fénelon, and Boileau fought for the Ancients. All his literary productions were surpassed by a little masterpiece that gave him a lasting popularity: "Contes de ma Mère l'Oye, ou Histoires du temps passé" (1697), a collection of fairy tales which, while displaying no special originality, were treated in a very skilful manner. His complete works were published in Paris, 1697–98, in one volume.

Mémoires (Paris, 1759); GIRAUD, *Lettre critique* (Paris, 1864); BARINE in *Revue des Deux Mondes* (Dec., 1890); BRUNETIÈRE, *Manuel de l'histoire de la littérature française* (Paris, 1899).

LOUIS N. DELAMARRE.

Perrault, CLAUDE, b. at Paris, 1613; d. there, 1688. He built the main eastern façade of the Louvre, known as the "Colonnade". His extraordinary talent and versatility brought up on him much enmity and detraction, especially in his architectural work. He achieved success as physician and anatomist, as architect and author. As physician and physicist, he received the degree of doctor from the University of Paris, became one of the first members of the Academy of Sciences founded in 1666, and repeatedly won prizes for his thorough knowledge of physics and chemistry. He was the author of a series of treatises on physics and zoology, as well as on certain interesting machines of his own invention.

Colbert induced him to translate Vitruvius, and this work inspired him with enthusiasm for architecture. Like his contemporary, Blondel, he contributed to revive the feeling for the rules and principles in architecture. His Vitruvius with a good commentary and tables appeared in 1673, and an epitome of it in 1674. The same aims were pursued in his "Ordonnance des cinq espèces des colonnes selon la méthode des anciens" (1683). Perrault's architectural drawings are regarded as excellent pieces of work; before the burning of the Louvre in 1871 there were preserved there, besides his drawings for the Vitruvius, two folio volumes containing among other things the designs for the Louvre, which had been published by the master's brother, Charles Perrault.

In his completed buildings, much fault is found, e. g. in the Observatoire, the astronomical observatory of Paris, although in certain parts we find traces of his later mastery. Perrault's design for a triumphal arch on Rue St-Antoine was preferred to the designs of Lebrun and Leveau, but was only partly executed in stone. When the arch was taken down, it was found that the ingenious master had devised a means of so uniting the stones without the use of mortar that it had become an inseparable mass. In the competition for the colonnade of the Louvre he was successful over all rivals, even Bernini, who had been summoned from Italy expressly for that purpose. This work claimed his attention from 1665 to 1680, and established his reputation. He was required to demonstrate the feasibility of his plans by constructing a model. Perrault is reproached with lacking in consideration for the work of his predecessors, and with positively depreciating the same. The whole palace could not be completed at the time, but the colonnade became widely celebrated. The simple character of the ground floor sets off the Corinthian columns, modelled strictly according to Vitruvius, and coupled on a plan which Perrault himself devised. Perrault built the church of St-Benoît-le-Bétourné, designed a new church of Ste-Geneviève, and erected an altar in the Church of the Little Fathers, all in Paris.

BERTY, *Les grands architectes français* (Paris, 1860); LANCE, *Dict. des architectes français* (Paris, 1873); VON GEYMÜLLER, *Die Baukunst der Renaissance in Frankreich* (Stuttgart, 1898–1901).

G. GIETMANN.

Perreyve, HENRI, b. at Paris, 11 April, 1831; d. there, 18 June, 1865. His father was professor at the Faculté de Droit. He received his classical education at the Collège Saint-Louis. According to his father's wish he studied law, but having finished his legal course he studied philosophy and theology. He then became closely united with Charles and Adolphe, later Cardinal Perraud, and this small group with Father Gratry, under the guidance of Father Pététol, began the restoration of the Oratory in France. He was ordained priest in 1858, appointed chaplain to the Lycée Saint-Louis in 1860, and one year later was called to the professorship of ecclesiastical history at the Sorbonne. For some time he was forced by illness to abandon his lectures.

He had been united in intimate friendship with the great Catholic leaders of the time in France, including Ozanam, Montalembert, Cochin, and especially Lacordaire. By his kind and affectionate nature Perreyve exercised a great influence on those around him, especially on young men.

Among his works were: "De la critique des Evangiles" (Paris, 1859); "Entretiens sur l'Eglise catholique" (2 vols., Paris, 1901); "La Journée des malades" (Paris, 1908); "Biographies et panégyriques" (Paris, 1907); "Souvenirs de première communion" (Paris, 1899); "Sermons" (Paris, 1901); "Deux roses et deux Noëls" (Paris, 1907); "Méditations sur l'Evangile de Saint Jean" (Paris, 1907); "Méditations sur les saints ordres" (Paris, 1901). Some of his letters have also been published in book form.

GRATRY, *Henri Perreyve* (London, 1872); BERNARD, *Les derniers jours de l'abbé Perreyve*. GEORGE M. SAUVAGE.

Perrone, GIOVANNI, Jesuit theologian, b. at Chieri, Italy, 11 March, 1794; d. at Rome, 28 Aug., 1876. After studying theology and obtaining the doctorate at Turin, he entered the Society of Jesus on 14 December, 1815. The Society had been re-established by Pius VII only a year before, and Perrone was very soon appointed to teach theology at Orvieto. A few years later he was made professor of dogmatic theology in the Roman College, and held this post till the Roman Republic of 1848 forced him to seek refuge in England. After an exile of three years, Perrone again took the chair of dogma in the Roman College, and, excepting the years of his rectorship at Ferrara, taught theology till prevented by old age. He was consultor of various congregations and was active in opposing the errors of George Hermes, as well as in the discussions which ended in the dogmatic definition of the Immaculate Conception (cf. "Annali delle scienze religiose", VII). Of Perrone's many writings, the most important is the "Prælectiones Theologicæ", which has reached a thirty-fourth edition in nine volumes. The compendium which Perrone made of this work has reached its forty-seventh edition in two volumes. His complete theological lectures were published in French and have run through several editions; portions have been translated into Spanish, Polish, German, Dutch, and other languages. Sommervogel mentions forty-four different works by this great fellow-professor of Passaglia and Franzelin in the Roman College.

SOMMERVOGEL, *Bibliothèque de la Compagnie de Jésus*, VI, 558–571; HURTER in *Kirchenlexikon*, s. v.

WALTER DRUM.

Perry, STEPHEN JOSEPH, b. in London, 26 August, 1833; d. 27 Dec., 1889. He belonged to a well-known Catholic family. His schooling was first at Gifford Hall, and then at the Benedictine College, Douai, whence he proceeded to Rome to study for the priesthood. Having resolved to enter the Society of Jesus, he made his novitiate (1853–5) first at Hodder, and then at Beaumont Lodge, after which he pursued his studies at St. Acheul, near Amiens, and at Stonyhurst. In consequence of his marked bent for mathematics, he was sent to attend the lectures of Professor De Morgan, in London, and those of Bertrand, Lionville, Delaunay, Cauchy, and Serret, in Paris. In the autumn of 1860 he was recalled to Stonyhurst to teach physics and mathematics, likewise taking charge of the observatory.

In 1863 he commenced his theological studies at St. Beuno's, N. Wales, and was ordained in 1866. He resumed his former duties at Stonyhurst, which during the rest of his life were uninterrupted, save by special scientific engagements. In company with Fr. Walter Sidgreaves, he made magnetic surveys, in 1868 of Western, in 1869 of Eastern, France, and in 1871 of Belgium. In 1870 he went in charge of a government expedition to observe a solar eclipse at Cadiz; at Carriacou (West Indies) in 1886; at Moscow in 1887; and at the Salut Islands in 1889, on which journey he lost his life.

In 1874 he headed a party similarly sent to Kerguelen in the South Indian Ocean, to observe a transit of Venus, when he also took a series of observations to determine the absolute longitude of the place, and others for the magnetic elements, not only at Kerguelen itself, but, on his way to and fro, at the Cape, Bombay, Aden, Port Said, Malta, Palermo, Rome, Naples, Florence, and Moncalieri. He likewise drew up a Blue-book on the climate of "The Isle of Desolation", as Kerguelen was called by Captain Cook.

In 1882 he went again with W. Sidgreaves, to observe a similar transit in Madagascar, and he again took advantage of the occasion for magnetic purposes. In 1874 he became a Fellow of the Royal Society.

At Stonyhurst, while he greatly developed the meteorological work of the observatory, and in the province of astronomy made frequent observations of Jupiter's satellites, of stellar occultations, of comets, and of meteorites, it was in the department of solar physics that he specially laboured, particular attention being paid to spots and faculæ. For observation in illustration of these an ingenious method was devised and patiently pursued. Father Perry was, moreover, much in request as a lecturer. He died while actually performing the duty assigned him in conducting an eclipse expedition in the pestilential group misnamed the "Isles de Salut". The observation on this occasion was exceedingly successful, and Father Perry, though already severely indisposed, managed to perform his part without interruption. As soon as it was over, however, he became alarmingly worse, and having got on board H.M.S. "Comus", which had been detailed for the service, he died at sea five days later, 27 Dec., 1889. He was buried in the Catholic cemetery at Georgetown, Demerara.

An account of his life and scientific works by CORTIE is published by the CATHOLIC TRUTH SOCIETY.

JOHN GERARD.

Persecution.—GENERAL.—Persecution may be defined in general as the unlawful coercion of another's liberty or his unlawful punishment, for not every kind of punishment can be regarded as persecution. For our purpose it must be still further limited to the sphere of religion, and in that sense persecution means unlawful coercion or punishment for religion's sake.

The Church has suffered many kinds of persecution. The growth and the continued existence of Christianity have been hindered by cultured paganism and by savage heathenism. And in more recent times agnosticism has harassed the Church in the various states of America and Europe. But most deplorable of all persecutions have been those that Catholicism has suffered from other Christians. With regard to these it has to be considered that the Church herself has appealed to force, and that, not only in her own defence, but also, so it is objected, in unprovoked attack. Thus by means of the Inquisition (q. v.) or religious wars she was herself the aggressor in many instances during the Middle Ages and in the time of the Reformation. And even if the answer be urged that she was only defending her own existence, the retort seems fairly plausible that pagan and heathen powers were only acting in their own defence when they prohibited the spread of Christianity. The Church would therefore seem to be strangely inconsistent, for while she claims toleration and liberty for herself she has been and still remains intolerant of all other religions.

In answer to this objection, we may admit the fact and yet deny the conclusion. The Church claims to carry a message or rather a command from God and to be God's only messenger. In point of fact it is only within recent years, when toleration is supposed to have become a dogma, that the other "champions of Revelation" have abandoned their similar claims. That they should abandon their right to command allegiance is a natural consequence of Protestantism; whereas it is the Church's claim to be the accredited and infallible ambassador of God which justifies her apparent inconsistency. Such intolerance, however, is not the same as persecution, by which we understand the unlawful exercise of coercion. Every corporation lawfully constituted has the right to coerce its subjects within due limits. And though the Church exercises that right for the most part by spiritual sanctions, she has never relinquished the right to use other means. Before examining this latter right to physical coercion, there must be introduced the important distinction between pagans and Christians. Regularly, force has not been employed against pagan or Jew: "For what have I to do to judge them that are without?" (I Cor., v, 12); see JEWS AND JUDAISM: *Judaism and Church Legislation.*

Instances of compulsory conversions such as have occurred at different periods of the Church's history must be ascribed to the misplaced zeal of autocratic individuals. But the Church does claim the right to coerce her own subjects. Here again, however, a distinction must be made. The non-Catholic Christians of our day are, strictly speaking, her subjects; but in her legislation she treats them as if they were not her subjects. The "Ne temere", e. g., of Pius X (1907), recognizes the marriages of Protestants as valid, though not contracted according to Catholic conditions: and the laws of abstinence are not considered to be binding on Protestants. So, with regard to her right to use coercion, the Church only exercises her authority over those whom she considers personally and formally apostates. A modern Protestant is not in the same category with the Albigenses or Wyclifites. These were held to be personally responsible for their apostasy; and the Church enforced her authority over them. It is true that in many cases the heretics were rebels against the State also; but the Church's claim to exercise coercion is not confined to such cases of social disorder. And what is more, her purpose was not only to protect the faith of the orthodox, but also to punish the apostates. Formal apostasy was then looked upon as treason against God—a much more heinous crime than treason against a civil ruler, which, until recent times, was punished with great severity. (See APOSTASY; HERESY.) It was a poisoning of the life of the soul in others (St. Thomas Aquinas, II-II, Q. xi, articles 3, 4.)

There can be no doubt, therefore, that the Church claimed the right to use physical coercion against formal apostates. Not, of course, that she would exercise her authority in the same way to-day, even if there were a Catholic State in which other Christians were personally and formally apostates. She adapts her discipline to the times and circumstances in order that it may fulfil its salutary purpose. Her own children are not punished by fines, imprisonment, or other temporal punishments, but by spiritual pains and penalties, and heretics are treated as she treated pagans: "Fides suadenda est, non imponenda" (Faith is a matter of persuasion, not of compulsion)—a sentiment that goes back to St. Basil ("Revue de l'Orient Chrétien", 2nd series, XIV, 1909, 38) and to St. Ambrose, in the fourth century, the latter applying it even to the treatment of formal apostates. It must also be remembered that when she did use her right to exercise physical coercion over formal apostates, that right was then universally admitted. Churchmen had naturally the ideas of their time as to why and how penalties should be inflicted. Withal, the Roman Inquisition (q. v.) was very different from that of Spain, and the popes did not approve the harsh proceedings of the latter. Moreover, such ideas of physical coercion in matters spiritual were not peculiar to Catholics (see TOLERATION). The Reformers were not less, but, if anything, more, intolerant (see INQUISITION). If the intolerance of Churchmen is blamable, then that of the Reformers is doubly so. From their own standpoint, it was unjustifiable. First, they were in revolt against the established authority of the Church, and secondly they could hardly use force to compel the unwilling to conform to their own principle of private judgment. With this clear demarcation of the Reformer's private judgment from the Catholic's authority, it hardly serves our purpose to estimate the relative violence of Catholic and Protestant Governments during the times of the Reformation. And yet it is well to remember that the methods of the maligned Inquisition in Spain and Italy were far less destructive of life than the religious wars of France and Germany. What is, however, more to our purpose is to notice the outspoken intolerance of the Protestant leaders; for it gave an additional right to the Church to appeal to force. She was punishing her defaulting subjects and at the same time defending herself against their attacks.

Such compulsion, therefore, as is used by legitimate

authority cannot be called persecution, nor can its victims be called martyrs. It is not enough that those who are condemned to death should be suffering for their religious opinions. A martyr is a witness to the truth; whereas those who suffered the extreme penalty of the Church were at the most the witnesses to their own sincerity, and therefore unhappily no more than pseudo-martyrs. We need not dwell upon the second objection which pretends that a pagan government might be justified in harassing Christian missionaries in so far as it considered Christianity to be subversive of established authority. The Christian revelation is the supernatural message of the Creator to His creatures, to which there can be no lawful resistance. Its missionaries have the right and the duty to preach it everywhere. They who die in the propagation or maintenance of the Gospel are God's witnesses to the truth, suffering persecution for His sake.

SYDNEY SMITH, *The Pope and the Spanish Inquisition* in *The Month*, LXXIV (1892), 375-99; cf. *Dublin Review*, LXI (1867), 177-78; KOHLER, *Reform und Ketzerprocess* (Tübingen, 1901); CAMUT, *La Tolérance protestante* (Paris, 1903); RUSSELL, *Maryland; The Land of Sanctuary* (Baltimore, 1907); PAULUS, *Zu Luthers These über die Ketzerverbrennung* in *Hist. Polit. Blätter*, CXL (1908), 357-67; MOULARD, *Le Catholique et le pouvoir coercitif de l'Eglise* in *Revue pratique de l'Apologétique*, VI (1908), 721-36; KEATING, *Intolerance, Persecution, and Proselytism* in *The Month*, CXIII (1909), 512-22; DE CAUZONS, *Histoire de l'Inquisition en France*, I (Paris, 1909).

OUTLINE OF PRINCIPAL PERSECUTIONS.—The brief outline here given of persecutions directed against the Church follows the chronological order, and is scarcely more than a catalogue of the principal formal and public onslaughts against Catholicism. Nor does it take into account other forms of attack, e. g., literary and social persecution, some form of suffering for Christ's sake being a sure note of the True Church (John, xv, 20; II Tim., iii, 12; Matt., x, 23). For a popular general account of persecutions of Catholics previous to the nineteenth century see Leclercq, "Les Martyrs" (5 vols., Paris, 1902-09).

Roman Persecutions (52-312). The persecutions of this period are treated extensively under MARTYR. See also MARTYRS, ACTS OF THE, and the articles on individual martyrs or groups of martyrs (MARTYRS, THE TEN THOUSAND; FORTY MARTYRS; AGAUNUM, for the Theban Legion). An exhaustive and reliable work is Allard, "Les Persécutions" (5 vols., Paris, 1885); also his "Ten Lectures on the Martyrs" (New York, 1907); and for an exhaustive literature see Healy, "The Valerian Persecution" (Boston).

Under Julian the Apostate (361-63).—Constantine's edict of toleration had accelerated the final triumph of Christianity. But the extreme measures passed against the ancient religion of the empire, and especially by Constans, even though they were not strictly carried out, roused considerable opposition. And when Julian the Apostate (361-63) came to the throne, he supported the defenders of paganism, though he strove to strengthen the old religion by recommending works of charity and a priesthood of strictly moral lives which, a thing unheard of, should preach and instruct. State protection was withdrawn from Christianity, and no section of the Church favoured more than another, so that the Donatists and Arians were enabled to return.

All the privileges formerly granted to clerics were repealed; civil jurisdiction taken from the bishops, and the subsidies to widows and virgins stopped. Higher education, also, was taken out of the hands of Christians by the prohibition of anyone who was not a pagan from teaching classical literature. And finally, the tombs of martyrs were destroyed. The emperor was afraid to proceed to direct persecution, but he fomented the dissensions among the Christians, and he tolerated and even encouraged the persecutions raised by pagan communities and governors, especially in Alexandria, Heliopolis, Maiouma, the port of Gaza, Antioch, Arethusa, and Cæsarea in Cappadocia (cf. Gergory of Nazianzus, Orat. IV, 86-95; P. G., XXXV, 613-28). Many, in different places, suffered and even died for the Faith, though another pretext was found for their death, at least by the emperor. Of the martyrs of this period mention may be made of John and Paul (q. v.), who suffered in Rome; the soldiers Juventinus and Maximian (cf. St. John Chrysostom's sermon on them in P. G., L, 571-77); Macedonius, Tatian, and Theodulus of Meros in Phrygia (Socrates, III, 15; Sozomen, V, 11); Basil, a priest of Ancyra (Sozomen, V, 11). Julian himself seems to have ordered the executions of John and Paul, the steward and secretary respectively of Constantia, daughter of Constantine. However, he reigned only for two years, and his persecution was, in the words of St. Athanasius, "but a passing cloud".

SOZOMEN, *Hist. Eccl.*, V, 11; SOCRATES, III, 15; AMMIANUS MARCELLINUS, XXI-XXV; TILLEMONT, *Mémoires*, VII, 322-43; 717-45; LECLERCQ, *Les Martyrs*, III (Paris, 1904); ALLARD, *Le Christianisme et l'empire romain de Néron à Théodore* (Paris, 1897), 224-31; IDEM, *Julien l'Apostat*, III, 52-102; 152-158 (Paris, 1903); DUCHESNE, *Histoire ancienne de l'Eglise*, II (Paris, 1907), 328-35.

In Persia.—When the persecution of Christianity was abandoned by the Roman Government, it was taken up by Rome's traditional enemy, the Persians, though formerly they had been more or less tolerant of the new religion. On the outbreak of war between the two empires, Sapor II (310-80), under the instigation of the Persian priests, initiated a severe persecution of the Christians in 339 or 340. It comprised the destruction or confiscation of churches and a general massacre, especially of bishops and priests. The number of victims, according to Sozomen (Hist. Eccl., II, 9-14), was no less than 16,000, among them being Symeon, Bishop of Seleucia; there was a respite from the general persecution, but it was resumed and with still greater violence by Bahram V (420-38), who persecuted savagely for one year, and was not prevented from causing numerous individual martyrdoms by the treaty he made (422) with Theodosius II, guaranteeing liberty of conscience to the Christians. Yezdegerd II (438-57), his successor, began a fierce persecution in 445 or 446, traces of which are found shortly before 450. The persecution of Chosroes I from 541 to 545 was directed chiefly against the bishops and clergy. He also destroyed churches and monasteries and imprisoned Persian noblemen who had become Christians. The last persecution by Persian kings was that of Chosroes II (590-628), who made war on all Christians alike during 627 and 628. Speaking generally, the dangerous time for the Church in Persia was when the kings were at war with the Roman Empire.

SOZOMEN, op. cit., 9-14; *Acta Sanctorum Martyrum*, ed. ASSEMANI, I (Rome, 1748), Syriac text with Lat. tr.; *Acta Martyrum et Sanctorum*, II, III, IV, ed. BEDJAN (Leipzig, 1890-95), Syriac text (for discussion of these two authorities see DUVAL, *Littérature syriaque* (Paris, 1899), 130-43).
A list of martyrs who suffered under Sapor II was first published by WRIGHT and reproduced in the *Martyrologium Hieronymianum* by DE ROSSI AND DUCHESNE in *Acta SS.*, Nov., II, part I, lxiii (Brussels, 1894); HOFFMANN, *Auszüge aus syrischen Akten persischer Martyrer*, text, tr., and notes (Leipzig, 1886); LECLERCQ, op. cit., III; DUVAL, *Littérature syriaque* (Paris, 1897), 129-47; LABOURT, *Le Christianisme dans l'empire perse* (Paris, 1904); DUCHESNE, op. cit. (Paris, 1910), 553-64.

Among the Goths.—Christianity was introduced among the Goths about the middle of the third century, and "Theophilus Episcopus Gothiæ" was present at the Council of Nicæa (325). But, owing to the exertions of Bishop Ulfilas (340, d. 383), an Arian, Arianism was professed by the great majority of the Visigoths of Dacia (Transylvania and West Hungary), converts from paganism; and it passed with them into Lower Mœsia across the Danube, when a Gothic chieftain, after a cruel persecution, drove Ulfilas and his converts from his lands, probably in 349. And subsequently, when in 376 the Visigoths, pressed by the Huns, crossed the Danube and entered the Roman Empire, Arianism was the religion practised by the

Emperor Valens. This fact, along with the national character given to Arianism by Ulfilas (q. v.), made it the form of Christianity adopted also by the Ostrogoths, from whom it spread to the Burgundians, Suevi, Vandals, and Lombards.

The first persecution we hear of was that directed by the pagan Visigoth King Athanaric, begun about 370 and lasting for two, or perhaps six, years after his war with Valens. St. Sabas was drowned in 372, others were burnt, sometimes in a body in the tents which were used as churches. When, in the fifth and sixth centuries, the Visigoths invaded Italy, Gaul, and Spain, the churches were plundered, and the Catholic bishops and clergy were often murdered; but their normal attitude was one of toleration. Euric (483), the Visigoth King of Toulouse, is especially mentioned by Sidonius Apollinaris (Ep. vii, 6) as a hater of Catholicism and a persecutor of the Catholics, though it is not clear that he persecuted to death. In Spain there was persecution at least from time to time during the period 476–586, beginning with the aforesaid Euric, who occupied Catalonia in 476. We hear of persecution by Agila (549–554) also, and finally by Leovigild (573–86). Bishops were exiled and church goods seized. His son Hermenigild, a convert to the Catholic Faith, is described in the seventh century (e. g. by St. Gregory the Great) as a martyr. A contemporary chronicler, John of Biclaro, who had himself suffered for the Faith, says that the prince was murdered in prison by an Arian, Sisibert; but he does not say that Leovigild approved of the murder (see Hermingild; and Hodgkin, "Italy and her Invaders", V, 255). With the accession of Reccared, who had become a Catholic, Arianism ceased to be the creed of the Spanish Visigoths.

As for the Ostrogoths, they seem to have been fairly tolerant, after the first violences of the invasion. A notable exception was the persecution of Theodoric (524–26). It was prompted by the repressive measures which Justin I had issued against the Arians of the Eastern Empire, among whom Goths would of course be included. One of the victims of the persecution was Pope John I, who died in prison.

Kauffman, *Aus der Schule des Wulfila: Auxentii Dorostorensis Epistola de fide, vita et obitu Wulfila* (Strasburg, 1899); Auxentius's account is also found in Waitz, *Ueber das leben und die lehre des Ulfila* (Hanover, 1840); Hodgkin, *Italy and her Invaders*, I (Oxford, 1892), 80-93; Duchesne, *op. cit.*, II (Paris, 1908); Scott, *Ulfilas, Apostle of the Goths* (Cambridge, 1885).

For Visigoths: Socrates, *op. cit.*, IV, 33; Contemporary letter on *St. Sabas*, Acta SS., 12 April; see also later document on *St. Nicetas*, *ibid.*, 15 Sept., and Hodgkin, *op. cit.*, I, 1, 175; Dahn, *Urgeschichte der germanischen und romanischen Volker*, I (Berlin, 1881), 426 sq., for Athanaric's persecution; Sidonius Apollinaris, ep. vii, 6 in *Mon. Germ. Hist.: Auct. Antiq.*, VIII, Hodgkin, *op. cit.*, II, 484, for Euric; John of Biclaro in *Mon. Germ. Hist.: Auct. Antiq.*, XI, 211; Gorres, *Kirche und Staat im Westgotenreich von Eurich bis Leovigild* in *Theol. Stud. u. Krit.* (Gotha, 1893), 708-34; Gams, *Kirchengeschichte Spaniens*, I, II (Augsburg, 1862), 4; Leclercq, *L'Espagne chrétienne* (Paris, 1906); Aschbach, *Gesch. der Westgoten* (Frankfort, 1827).

For Ostrogoths: *Vita S. Severini* in *Mon. Germ. Hist.: Auct. Antiq.*, 1; Papencordt, *Gesch. der stadt Rom.* (Paderborn, 1857), 62 sq.; Pfeilschrifter, *Der Ostrogotenkönig Theodoric der Grosse und die Katholische Kirche* in *Kirchengeschichtliche Studien*, III (Münster, 1896), 1, 2; Grisar, *Geschichte Roms und der Papste im Mittelalter*, I (Freiburg im Br., 1901), 86, 481.

For general account of Goths and Catholicism, see Uhlhorn, *Kämpfe und Siege des Christentums in der germanischen Welt* (Stuttgart, 1898).

Among the Lombards.—St. Gregory the Great, in parts of his "Dialogues", describes the sufferings which Catholics had to endure at the time of the Lombard invasion under Alboin (568) and afterwards. But on the whole, after Autharis's death (590) the Lombards were not troublesome, except perhaps in the Duchies of Benevento and Spoleto. Autharis's queen, Theudelinda, a Catholic princess of Bavaria, was able to use her influence with her second husband, Agilulf, Autharis's successor, so that he, although probably remaining an Arian, was friendly to the Church and allowed his son to be baptized a Catholic (see Lombardy).

St. Gregory the Great, *Dialogues*, III, 27, 28, 37, 39; IV, 21-23, see Hodgkin, *op. cit.*, VI, 97, 104; Paul the Deacon, *Historia Langobardorum*, I-IV in *Mon. Germ. Hist.: Script. Langob. et Ital.* (Hanover, 1878), 45 sq., see Hodgkin, *op. cit.*, V, 68-80; Dahn, *op. cit.*; Grisar, *op. cit.*

Among the Vandals.—The Vandals, Arians like the Visigoths and the others, were the most hostile of all towards the Church. During the period of their domination in Spain (422–29) the Church suffered persecution, the details of which are unknown. In 429, under the lead of Genseric, the Goths crossed over to Africa, and by 455 had made themselves masters of Roman Africa. In the North, the bishops were driven from their sees into exile. When Carthage was taken in 439 the churches were given over to the Arian clergy, and the bishop Quodvultdeus (a friend of St. Augustine) and the greater part of the Catholic clergy were stripped of what they had, put on board unseaworthy ships, and carried to Naples. Confiscation of church property and exile of the clergy was the rule throughout the provinces of the North, where all public worship was forbidden to Catholics. In the provinces of the South, however, the persecution was not severe. Some Catholic court officials, who had accompanied Genseric from Spain, were tortured, exiled, and finally put to death because they refused to apostatize. No Catholic, in fact, was allowed to hold any office.

Genseric's son, Huneric, who succeeded in 477, though at first somewhat tolerant, arrested and banished under circumstances of great cruelty nearly five thousand Catholics, including bishops and clergy, and finally by an edict of 25 Feb., 484, abolished the Catholic worship, transferred all churches and church property to the Arians, exiled the bishops and clergy, and deprived of civil rights all those who would not receive Arian baptism. Great numbers suffered savage treatment, many died, others were mutilated or crippled for life. His successor, Guntamund (484–96), did not relax the persecution until 487. But in 494 the bishops were recalled, though they had afterwards to endure some persecution from Trasamund (496–523). And complete peace came to the Church at the accession of Genseric's son Hilderic, with whom the Vandal domination ended (see Africa).

Idatius in *Mon. Germ. Hist.: Auct. Antiq.*, XI, 13-36; Migne, P. L., LI; Victor Vitensis, *Historia persecutionis Africanæ provinciæ*, ed. Halm in *Mon. Germ. Hist.*, *loc. cit.*, III; Petschenig, *Corpus Script. eccles. lat.*, VII (Vienna, 1881); Migne, P. L., LVII; Prosper, *Chronicon* in *Mon. Germ. Hist.*, loc. cit., IX; Migne, P. L., LI; Ruinart, *Hist. persec. Vand.* in P. L., LVIII; Papencordt, *Gesch. der Vandalischen Herrschaft in Afrika* (Berlin, 1837); Dahn, *op. cit.*; Hodgkin, *op. cit.*, II, 229-30, 269-82; Leclercq, *L'Afrique chrétienne*, II (Paris, 1904); Idem, *Les Martyrs*, III (Paris, 1904); Duchesne, *op. cit.*, III, 625-45.

In Arabia.—Christianity penetrated into South Arabia (Yemen) in the fourth century. In the sixth century the Christians were brutally persecuted by the Jewish King Dunaan, no less than five thousand, including the prince, Arethas, being said to have suffered execution in 523 after the capture of Nagra. The Faith was only saved from utter extinction at this period by the armed intervention of the King of Abyssinia. And it did in fact disappear before the invading forces of Islam.

Fell, *Die Christenverfolgung in Südarabien* in *Zeitsch. der deutschen morgent. Gesellschaft* (1881), XXV. (See Arabia.)

Under the Mohammedans.—With the spread of Mohammedanism in Syria, Egypt, Persia, and North Africa, there went a gradual subjugation of Christianity. At the first onset of invasion, in the eighth century, many Christians were butchered for refusing to apostatize; afterwards they were treated as helots, subject to a special tax, and liable to suffer loss of goods or life itself at the caprice of the caliph or the populace. In Spain the first Mohammedan ruler to institute a violent persecution of the Christians was the viceroy Abderrahman II (821–52). The persecution was begun in 850, was continued by Mohammed (852–87)

XI.—45

and lasted with interruptions till 960, when the Christians were strong enough to intimidate their persecutors. The number of martyrs was small, Eulogius, Archbishop of Toledo (11 March, 859), who has left us an account of the persecution, being himself the most famous (see MOHAMMED AND MOHAMMEDANISM).

PARGOIRE, *L'Eglise byzantine* (Paris, 1905), 153–6, 275–9; LECLERCQ, *L'Afrique chrétienne*, II (Paris, 1904); IDEM, *Les Martyrs*, IV (Paris, 1905). For Spain: see EULOGIUS and Bibliography; *Vita S. Eulogii*, by ALVARUS in *P. L.*, CXV, 705 sq.; EULOGIUS, *Memoriale Sanctorum seu libri III de martyribus cordubensibus*; MIGNE, *P. L.*, CXV, 731; DOZY, *Histoire des Mussulmans d'Espagne*, II (Leyden, 1861); GAMS, *Kirchengesch. Spaniens*, II (Ratisbon, 1864); HAINES, *Christianity and Islam in Spain, 756–1031* (London, 1889); LECLERCQ, *L'Espagne chrétienne* (Paris, 1906).

Under the Iconoclasts.—The troubles brought on the Church of the East by the Iconoclastic emperors cover a period of one hundred and twenty years. Leo III (the Isaurian) published two edicts against images about 726 and 730. The execution of the edicts was strenuously resisted. Popes Gregory II and III protested in vigorous language against the autocratic reformer, and the people resorted to open violence. But Constantine V (Copronymus, 741–75) continued his father's policy, summoning a council at Constantinople in 754 and then persecuting the orthodox party. The monks formed the especial object of his attack. Monasteries were demolished, and the monks themselves shamefully maltreated and put to death. Under Constantine VI (780–97), through the influence of his mother, the regent Irene, the Seventh Œcumenical Council was summoned in 787, and rescinded the decrees of Copronymus's Council. But there was a revival of the persecution under Leo V (813–20), the bishops who stood firm, as well as the monks, being the special objects of his attack, while many others were directly done to death or died as a result of cruel treatment in prison. This persecution, which was continued under Michael II (820–29), reached its most fierce phase under Theophilus (829–42). Great numbers of monks were put to death by this monarch; but at his decease the persecutions ended (842) (see ICONOCLASM).

Theodori Studitæ Epistola, P. G., XCIX; TOUGARD, *La Persécution iconoclaste d'après la correspondance de S. Théodore Studite* in *Revue des Questions historiques*, L (1891), 80, 118; HERGENROTHER, *Photius*, I, 226 sqq. (Ratisbon, 1867); LOMBARD, *Constantin V, Empereur des Romains* (Paris, 1902); PARGOIRE, *L'Eglise byzantine de 527–847* (Paris, 1905), contains abundant references to lives and acts of martyrs.

MODERN PERIOD.—We have reviewed the persecutions undergone by the Church during the first millennium of her existence. During her second millennium she has continued to suffer persecution in her mission of spreading the Gospel, and especially in Japan and China (see MARTYRS, JAPANESE; MARTYRS IN CHINA). She has also had to face the attacks of her own children, culminating in the excesses and religious wars of the Reformation.

For an account of the persecutions of Irish, English, and Scotch Catholics, see ENGLAND; IRELAND; SCOTLAND; PENAL LAWS; and the numerous articles on individual martyrs, e. g. EDMUND CAMPION, BLESSED; PLUNKETT, OLIVER, VENERABLE.

Poland.—Within the last century, Poland has suffered what is perhaps the most notable of recent persecutions. Catholicism had continued to be the established religion of the country until the intervention of Catherine II of Russia (1762–96). By means of political intrigues and open hostility, she first of all secured a position of political suzerainty over the country, and then effected the separation of the Ruthenians from the Holy See, and incorporated them with the Orthodox Church of Russia. Nicholas I (1825–55), and Alexander II (1855–81), resumed her policy of intimidation and forcible suppression. The latter monarch especially showed himself a violent persecutor of the Catholics, the barbarities that were committed in 1863 being so savage as to call forth a joint protest from the Governments of France, Austria, and Great Britain. After his death the Catholics were granted a certain measure of toleration, and in 1905 Nicholas II granted them full liberty of worship (see POLAND; RUSSIA).

For the persecution of Catholics in the Ottoman Empire see TURKEY.

In modern times, however, a new element has been added to the forces opposing the Church. There have indeed been occasional recrudescences of the "Reformers", violence dictated by a frenzied fear of Catholic progress. Such were for instance the Charleston and Philadelphia disturbances in 1834 and 1844, and the "No Popery" cries against the establishment of the Catholic hierarchy in England and Holland in 1850 and 1853. But this was no more than the spirit of the Reformation. For the attitude of the South American republics during the nineteenth century, see the articles on those countries.

Liberalism.—A new spirit of opposition appears in the so-called "Liberalism" and in Free Thought, whose influence has been felt in Catholic as well as Protestant countries. Its origin is to be traced back to the infidel philosophy of the eighteenth century. At the end of that century it had grown so strong that it could menace the Church with armed violence. In France six hundred priests were murdered by Jourdan, "the Beheader", in 1791, and in the next year three hundred ecclesiastics, including an archbishop and two bishops, were cruelly massacred in the prisons of Paris. The Reign of Terror ended in 1795. But the spirit of infidelity which triumphed then has ever since sought and found opportunities for persecution. And it has been assisted by the endeavours of even so-called Catholic governments to subordinate the Church to the State, or to separate the two powers altogether. In Switzerland the Catholics were so incensed by the attacks of the Liberal party on their religious freedom that they resolved on an appeal to arms. Their *Sonderbund* (q. v.) or "Separate League" was at first successful in the war of 1843, and in spite of its final defeat by the forces of the Diet in 1847 the result has been to secure religious liberty throughout Switzerland. Since that time the excitement caused by the decree on Papal Infallibility found vent in another period of hostile legislation; but the Catholics have been strong enough to maintain and reinforce their position in the country.

In other countries Liberalism has not issued in such direct warfare against the Church; though the defenders of the Church have often been ranged against revolutionaries who were attacking the altar along with the throne. But the history of the nineteenth century reveals a constant opposition to the Church. Her influence has been straitened by adverse legislation, the monastic orders have been expelled and their property confiscated, and, what is perhaps most characteristic of modern persecution, religion has been excluded from the schools and universities. The underlying principle is always the same, though the form it assumes and the occasion of its development are peculiar to the different times and places. Gallicanism in France, Josephinism in Austria, and the May Laws of the German Empire have all the same principle of subordinating the Church to the Government, or separating the two powers by a secularist and unnatural divorce. But the solidarity of Catholics and the energetic protests of the Holy See succeeded often in establishing Concordats to safeguard the independent rights of the Church. The terms of these concessions have not always been observed by Liberal or Absolutist Governments. Still they saved the Church in her time of peril. And the enforced separation of Church from State which followed the renunciation of the Concordats has taught the Catholics in Latin countries the dangers of Secularism (q. v.) and how they must defend their rights as members of a Church which transcends the limits of states and nations, and acknowledges an authority beyond the reach of political legislation. In the Teutonic countries, on the other hand, the Church does not loom so large a target for the missiles of her enemies. Long years of persecution have done their work, and left the Catholics with a greater need and a greater sense of solidarity. There is less danger of confusing friend and foe, and the progress of the Church is made more apparent.

BRÜCK-KISSLING, *Gesch. der kath. Kirche im neunzehnten Jahrh.* (5 vols., Mainz and Münster, 1908); MACCAFFREY, *History of the Catholic Church in the Nineteenth Century* (2 vols., Dublin, 1909); GOYAU, *L'Allemagne religieuse* (3 vols., Paris, 1906).

JAMES BRIDGE.

Persecutions, COPTIC (ACCORDING TO GREEK AND LATIN SOURCES).—During the first two centuries the Church of Alexandria seems to have been freer from official persecution at the hands of the Roman Government than its sister churches of Rome and Antioch. Two causes may have contributed to this: (1) the privileged political and religious status in Egypt of Jews from whom the Government found it difficult to distinguish the Christians; (2) Roman citizenship having never been extended to the Egyptians, except in a few individual cases, the inhabitants of Egypt were free from the obligations of the Roman state religion and consequently there was no reason for persecution. For it is well known that the only cause of the persecutions in the first and second centuries was the incompatibility of the Christian faith with the state religion, which every Roman citizen, the Jews excepted, was obliged to practice, though free otherwise to follow any other form of religion he chose.

PERSECUTION OF SEVERUS (200–11).—But when Septimius Severus by a special edict (about A. D. 200) forbade under severe punishment "to make Jews and Christians", the law applied to all subjects of the Roman Empire whether citizens or not; the Egyptian Church with its famous catechetical school of Alexandria, and the fresh impulse given by Demetrius to the diffusion of Christianity throughout the country, seem to have attracted the attention of the emperor, who had just visited Egypt. The school broke up just at that time; and its director, Clement of Alexandria, being obliged to leave Egypt, the youthful Origen attempted to reorganize it. He was soon arrested by the newly-appointed prefect Aquila. Shortly before, under Lætus, his father Leonidas had been the first victim of the persecution. Origen had earnestly encouraged him to stand firm in his confession, and was himself now longing for a martyr's death. His desire was frustrated through the efforts of his mother and friends. But he had the consolation of assisting and encouraging a number of his pupils who died for the faith. Plutarch, who had been his first disciple, Serenus (burnt), Heraclides, a catechumen, and Hero, a neophyte (both beheaded), a woman, Herais, a catechumen (burnt), another, Serenus (beheaded), and Basilides, a soldier attached to the office of Aquila. Potamiæna, a young Christian woman, had been condemned to be sunk by degrees in a cauldron of boiling pitch and was being led to death by Basilides, who on the way protected her against the insults of the mob. In return for his kindness the martyr promised him not to forget him with her Lord when she reached her destination. Soon after Potamiæna's death Basilides was asked by his fellow-soldiers to take a certain oath; on answering that he could not do it, as he was a Christian, at first they thought he was jesting, but seeing he was in earnest they denounced him and he was condemned to be beheaded. While waiting in jail for his sentence to be carried out some Christians (Origen being possibly one of them) visited him and asked him how he happened to be converted; he answered that three days after her death, Potamiæna had appeared to him by night and placed a crown on his head as a pledge that the Lord would soon receive him into his glory.

Potamiæna appeared to many other persons at that time, calling them to faith and martyrdom (Euseb., "Hist. Eccl.", VI, iii–v). To these conversions, Origen, an eyewitness, testifies in his "Contra Celsum" (I, 46; P. G., XI, 746). Marcella, mother of Potamiæna, who likewise perished by fire, is the only other martyr whose name is recorded in authentic sources, but we are told of legions of Christians that were sent to Alexandria from all points of Egypt and Thebaid as picked athletes directed to the greatest and most famous arena of the world (Euseb., "Hist. Eccl.", VI, i).

PERSECUTIONS OF DECIUS (249–51).—Severus died in 211. Authentic sources mention no further official persecution of the Christians of Egypt until the edict of Decius, A. D. 249. This enactment, the exact tenor of which is not known, was intended to test the loyalty of all Roman subjects to the national religion, but it contained also a special clause against the Christians, denouncing the profession of Christianity as incompatible with the demands of the State, proscribing the bishops and other church officials, and probably also forbidding religious meetings. Disobedience to the imperial orders was threatened with severe punishments, the nature of which in each individual case was left to the discretion or zeal of the magistrates (see Gregg, "Decian Persecution", 75 sqq.). During the long period of peace the Egyptian Church had enjoyed since Severus' death it had rapidly increased in numbers and wealth, much, it seems, to the detriment of its power of endurance. And the fierce onslaught of Decius found it quite unprepared for the struggle. Defections were numerous, especially among the rich, in whom, says St. Dionysius, was verified the saying of Our Lord (Matt., xix, 23) that it is difficult for them to be saved (Euseb., "Hist. Eccl.", VI, xli, 8). Dionysius was then the occupant of the chair of St. Mark. The particulars of the persecution, and of the popular outbreak against the Christians in Alexandria (A. D. 249) are known to us almost exclusively from his letters as preserved by Eusebius (see DIONYSIUS OF ALEXANDRIA). Decius' death in A. D. 251 put an end to the persecution.

PERSECUTION OF VALERIAN (257–61).—The persecution of Valerian was even more severe than that of Decius. Dionysius who is again our chief authority lays the responsibility for it to the emperor's chief counselor, Macrianus "teacher and ruler of the Magi from Egypt" (Euseb., "Hist. eccl.", VII, x, 4). A first edict published in 257 ordered all bishops, priests, and deacons to conform with the state religion under penalty of exile and prohibited the Christians from holding religious assemblies under penalty of death (Healy, "Valerian Persecution", 136). In 258 a second edict was issued sentencing to death bishops, priests, and deacons, and condemning laymen of high rank to degradation, exile, and slavery, or even death in case of obstinacy, according to an established scale of punishments (Healy, ibid., 169 sq.), confiscation of property resulting *ipso facto* in every case. Dionysius was still in the chair of St. Mark. On receipt of the first edict Æmilianus, then Prefect of Egypt, immediately seized the venerable bishop with several priests and deacons and on his refusal to worship the gods of the empire exiled him to Kephro in Libya. There he was followed by some brethren from Alexandria and others soon joined him from the provinces of Egypt, and Dionysius managed not only to hold the prohibited assemblies but also to convert not a few of the heathens of that region where the word of God had never been preached. Æmilianus was probably ignorant of these facts which even under the provisions of the first edict made the bishop and his companions liable to capital punishment. Desiring however to have all the exiles in one district nearer at hand where he could seize them all without difficulty whenever he wished, he ordered their transfer to Mareotis, a marshy district south-west of Alexandria, "a country", Dionysius says, "destitute of brethren and exposed to the annoyances of the travelers and incursions of robbers", and assigned them to different villages throughout that desolate region. Dionysius and his companions were stationed at Colluthion, near the highway, so they could be seized first. This new arrangement, which had caused no small apprehension to Dionysius, turned out much better than the former one. If intercourse with Egypt was more difficult, it was easier with Alexandria; Dionysius had the consolation of seeing his friends more frequently, those who were nearer to his heart, and he could hold partial meetings with them as was customary in the most remote suburbs of the capital (Euseb., "Hist. eccl.", VII, xi, 1–7). This is unfortunately all we know of Valerian persecution in Egypt. The portion of Dionysius' letter to Domitius and Didymus in which Eusebius refers to the persecution of Valerian (loc. cit., VII, xx) belongs rather to the Decian times. It is to be regretted that Eusebius did not preserve for us in its entirety Dionysius' letter "to Hermammon and the brethren in Egypt, describing at length the wickedness of Decius and his successors and mentioning the peace under Gallienus".

Immediately after Valerian's capture by the Persians (260?) his son Gallienus (who had been associated with him in the empire for several years) published edicts of toleration if not of recognition in favour of the Christians (see McGiffert's note 2 to Eusebius, "Hist. eccl.", VII, xiii). But Egypt having fallen to the lot of Macrianus it is probable that he withheld the edicts or that the terrible civil war which then broke out in Alexandria between the partisans of Gallienus and those of Macrianus delayed their promulgation. After the usurper's fall (late in 261 or early in 262), Gallienus issued a rescript "to Dionysius, Pinnas, Demetrius, and the other bishops" to apprise them of his edicts and to assure them that Aurelius Cyrenius, "chief administrator of affairs", would observe them (Euseb., "Hist. eccl.", VII, xiii; and McGiffert, note 3).

Persecutions of Diocletian (303–5) and Maximinus (a. d. 305–13).—For reasons on which sources either disagree or are silent (see Duchesne, "Hist. anc. de l'église", II, 10 sq.; McGiffert in "Select Lib. of Nicene and Post-Nicene Fathers, N. S.", I, 400), Diocletianus, whose household was full of Christians, suddenly changed his attitude towards Christianity and initiated the longest and bloodiest persecutions against the Church. Lactantius informs us (De mort. persec., IX) that Diocletian acted on the advice of a council of dignitaries in which Galerius played the principal part. It was in a. d. 303, the nineteenth year of his reign, and the third of Peter Alexandrinus as Bishop of Alexandria. Egypt and Syria (as part of the Diocese of Orient) were directly under the rule of Diocletian. This general outbreak had been preceded for three years at least by a more or less disguised persecution in the army. Eusebius says that a certain *magister militum* Veturius, in the sixteenth year of Diocletian, forced a number of high rank officers to prove their loyalty by the usual test of sacrificing to the gods of the empire, on penalty of losing their honours and privileges. Many "soldiers of Christ's kingdom" cheerfully gave up the seeming glory of this world and a few received death "in exchange for their pious constancy" (Euseb., "Hist. eccl.", VIII, iv; "Chron.", ed. Schöne, II, 186 sq.). On 23 February, 303, the Church of Nicomedia was torn down by order of the emperors. The next day (thus Lact., op. cit., xiii. Euseb. says "in March, on the approach of the Passion"), a first edict was published everywhere ordering the churches to be destroyed, the Holy Scriptures to be burned, and inflicting degradation on those in high rank and slavery on their households. Two other edicts soon followed, one ordering the imprisonment of all church officials, the other commanding them to sacrifice to the gods (Euseb., op. cit., VIII, ii, 4, 5; vi, 8, 10). In 304, while Diocletian was seriously ill, a fourth edict was issued commanding all the people to sacrifice at once in the different cities and offer libations to the idols (Euseb., "Mart. Pal.", III, i). On 1 May, 305, both Diocletian and Maximian Herculius retired officially from the public life and a tetrarchy was organized with Galerius and Constantius as Augusti and Severus and Maximinus Daia as Cæsars; and a new apportionment of the empire was made, Egypt and Syria with the rest of the Diocese of Orient going to Maximinus. Superstitious in the extreme, surrounded by magicians without whom he did not venture to move even a finger, ferocious and dissolute, Maximinus was far more bitter against the Christians than Galerius himself.

To give a fresh impetus to the persecution, he published again (305) in his provinces, in his own name, the fourth edict which had been issued the year before by all the members of the tetrarchy, thus making it clear that no mercy was to be expected from him (Euseb., "Mart. Pal.", IV, viii). In 307, after the death of Constantius, his son Constantine was made second Cæsar and Severus promoted to the rank of Augustus. The following year Severus, defeated by Maxentius, was obliged to take his own life and his place and rank was given by Galerius to Licinius. Maximinus then assumed the title of Augustus against the wish of Galerius who nevertheless had to recognize him and bestowed the same title on Constantine. It was probably on the occasion of this quarrel with Galerius that Maximinus for a short while in the summer of 308 relaxed somewhat his measures against the Christians. "Relief and liberty were granted to those who for Christ's sake were labouring in the mines of the Thebaid" (Mart. Pal., IX, i). But suddenly in the autumn of the same year he issued another edict (so-called fifth edict) ordering the shrines of the idols to be speedily rebuilt and all the people, even infants at the breast, to be compelled to sacrifice and taste of the offerings. At the same time he commanded the things for sale in the markets to be sprinkled with the libations from the sacrifices, the entrance to the public baths to be contaminated similarly (Mart. Pal., IX, ii). And when three years later (April, 311) Galerius, devoured by a terrible disease and already on the point of death, finally softened toward the Christians and asked them to pray to their God for his recovery, Maximinus significantly kept aloof (Hist. eccl., VIII, xvii). His name does not appear with those of Galerius, Constantinus, and Licinius, in the heading of the edict of toleration, which, moreover, was never promulgated in his provinces. However, probably to placate his two colleagues on the occasion of a new apportionment of the power as a result of Galerius' death, he told his chief official, Sabinus, to instruct the governors and other magistrates to relax the persecution. His orders received wider interpretation than he expected, and while his attention was directed by the division of the Eastern empire between himself and Licinius, the confessors who were awaiting trial in the prisons were released and those who had been condemned to the mines returned home in joy and exultation.

This lull had lasted about six months when Maximinus resumed the persecution, supposedly at the request of the various cities and towns who petitioned him not to allow the Christians to dwell within their walls. But Eusebius declares that in the case of Antioch the petition was Maximinus' own work, and that the other cities had sent their memorials at the solicitation of his officials who had been instructed by himself to that effect. On that occasion he created in each city a high-priest whose office it was to make daily sacrifices to all the (local) gods, and with the aid of the priests of the former order of things, to restrain the Christians from building churches and holding religious meetings, publicly or privately (Eusebius, op. cit., IX, ii, 4; Lactant., op. cit., XXXVI). At the same time everything was done to excite the heathens against the Christians. Forged Acts of Pilate and of Our Lord, full of every kind of blasphemy against Christ, were sent with the emperor's approval to all the provinces under him, with written commands that they should be posted publicly in every place and that the schoolmasters should give them to their scholars instead of their customary lessons to be studied and learned by heart (Euseb., op. cit., IX, v). Members of the hierarchy and others were seized on the most trifling pretext and put to death without mercy. In the case of Peter of Alexandria no cause at all was given. He was arrested quite unexpectedly and beheaded without explanation as if by command of Maximinus (ibid., IX, vi). This was in April, 312, if not somewhat earlier. In the autumn of the same year Constantine defeated Maximinus and soon after conjointly with Licinius published the edict of Milan, a copy of which was sent to Maximinus with an invitation to publish it in his own provinces. He met their wishes half way, publishing instead of the document received an edict of tolerance, but so full of false, contradictory statements and so reticent on the points at issue, that the Christians did not venture to hold meetings or even appear in public (Euseb., "Hist. eccl.", IX, ix, 14–24). It was not, however, until the following year, after his defeat at Adrianople (30 April, 313) at the hands of Licinius, with whom he was contending for the sole supremacy over the Eastern empire, that he finally made up his mind to enact a counterpart of the edict of Milan, and grant full and unconditional liberty to the Christians. He died soon after, consumed by "an invisible and God-sent fire" (Hist. eccl., IX, x, 14). Lactantius says he took poison at Tarsus, where he had fled (op. cit., 49).

EFFECTS OF THE PERSECUTIONS.—On the effects of the persecutions in Egypt, Alexandria, and the Thebaid in a general way we are well informed by ocular witnesses, such as Phileas, Bishop of Thmuis, in a letter to his flock which has been preserved by Eusebius (Hist. eccl., VIII, x), who visited Egypt towards the end of the persecution, and seems to have been imprisoned there for the faith. Eusebius speaks of large numbers of men in groups from ten to one hundred, with young children and women put to death in one day, and this not for a few days or a short time, but for a long series of years. He describes the wonderful ardour of the faithful, rushing one after another to the judgment seat and confessing themselves Christians, the joy with which they received their sentence, the truly Divine energy with which they endured for hours and days the most excruciating tortures; scraping, racking, scourging, quartering, crucifixion head downwards, not only without complaining, but singing and offering up hymns and thanksgiving to God till their very last breath. Those who did not die in the midst of their tortures were killed by the sword, fire, or drowning (Euseb., "Hist. eccl.", VIII, viii, 9). Frequently they were thrown again into prison to die of exhaustion or hunger. If perchance they recovered under the care of friends and were offered their freedom on condition of sacrificing, they cheerfully chose again to face the judge and his executioners (Letter of Phileas, ibid., 10). Not all, however, received their crowns at the end of a few hours or days. Many were condemned to hard labour in the quarries of Porphyry in Assuan, or, especially after A. D. 307, in the still more dreaded copper mines of Phûnon (near Petra, see Revue Biblique, 1898, p. 112), or in those of Cilicia. Lest they should escape, they were previously deprived of the use of their left legs by having the sinews cut or burnt at the knee or at the ankle, and again their right eyes were blinded with the sword and then destroyed to the very roots by fire. In one year (308) we read of 97, and again of as many as 130, Egyptian confessors thus doomed to a fate far more cruel than death, because of the remoteness of the crown they were impatient to obtain and the privation of the encouraging presence and exhortations of sympathetic bystanders (Mart. Pal., VIII, i, 13).

God in at least two instances related by Eusebius inspired the tyrant to shorten the conflict of those valiant athletes. At his command forty of them, among whom were many Egyptians, were beheaded in one day at Zoara, near Phûnon. With them was Silvanus of Gaza, a bishop who had been ministering to their souls. On the same occasion, Bishops Peleus and Nilus, a presbyter, and a layman, Patermuthius, all from Egypt, were condemned to death by fire probably at Phûnon, A. D. 309 (Euseb., "Mart. Pal.", XIII, Cureton, pp. 46–8). Besides Peter of Alexandria, but a few of the many who suffered death illustriously at Alexandria and throughout Egypt and the Thebaid are recorded by Eusebius, viz., Faustus, Dius, and Ammonius, his companions, all three presbyters of the Church of Alexandria, also Phileas, Bishop of Thmuis and three other Egyptian bishops; Hesychius (perhaps the author of the so-called Hesychian recension, see Hastings, "Dict. of the Bible", IV, 445), Pachymius, and Theodorus (Hist. eccl., VIII, xiii, 7); finally Philoromus, "who held a high office under the imperial government at Alexandria and who administered justice every day attended by a military guard corresponding to his rank and Roman dignity" (ibid., ix, 7). The dates of their confessions, with the exception of that of St. Peter (see above) are not certain.

EGYPTIAN MARTYRS IN SYRIA AND PALESTINE.— Among these, Eusebius mentions Pæsis and Alexander, beheaded at Cæsarea in 304, with six other young confessors. Hearing that on the occasion of a festival the public combat of the Christians who had lately been condemned to the wild beasts would take place, they presented themselves, hands bound, to the governor and declared themselves Christians in the hope of being sent to the arena. But they were thrown in prison, tortured, and finally were beheaded (Mart. Pal., IV, iii). Elsewhere we read of five young Egyptians who were cast before different kinds of ferocious beasts, including bulls goaded to madness with red-hot irons, but none of which would attack the athletes of Christ who, though unbound, stood motionless in the arena, their arms stretched out in the form of a cross, earnestly engaged in prayer. Finally they were also beheaded and cast into the sea (Hist. eccl., VIII, vii). We must also mention with Eusebius a party of Egyptians who had been sent to minister to the confessors in Cilicia. They were seized as they were entering Ascalon. Most of them received the same sentence as those whom they had gone to help, being mutilated in their eyes and feet, and sent to the mines. One, Ares, was condemned to be burnt, and two, Probus (or Primus) and Elias, were beheaded, A. D. 308 (Mart. Pal., X, i). The following year five others who had accompanied the confessors to the mines in Cilicia were returning to their homes when they were arrested as they were passing the gates of Cæsarea, and were put to death after being tortured, A. D. 309 (ibid., vi–xiii).

We close this section with the name of Ædesius, a young Lycian and brother of Apphianus (Mart. Pal., IV). He had been condemned to the mines of Palestine. Having somehow been released, he came to Alexandria and fell in with Hierocles, the governor, while he was trying some Christians. Unable to contain his indignation at the sight of the outrages inflicted by this magistrate on the modesty of some pure women, he went forward and with words and deeds overwhelmed him with shame and disgrace. Forthwith he was committed to the executioners, tortured and cast into the sea (Mart. Pal., V, ii–iii). This glorious page of the history of the Church of Egypt is not of course quite free from some dark spots. Many were overcome by the tortures at various stages of their confessions and apostatized more or less explicitly. This is attested by the "Liber de Pœnitentia" of Peter of Alexandria, dated from Easter, 306 (published in Routh, Reliquiæ Sacræ, 2nd ed., IV, 23 sqq.). (See Lapsi.)

Persecution of Diocletian in the Acts of Martyrs of the Coptic Church.—The Acts of Martyrs of Egypt in their present form have been, with few exceptions, written in Coptic, and were currently read in the churches and monasteries of Egypt at least from the ninth to the eleventh century. Later they were, like the rest of the Coptic literature, translated into Arabic and then into Ethiopic for the use of the Abyssinian Church. The Coptic Acts have often come down to us both in Bohairic and in Sahidic, those in the latter dialect being as a rule fragmentary, as most of its literature. Where we have the same Acts in two or more dialects or languages, it generally happens that the various versions represent more or less different recensions, and this is sometimes the case even between two copies of the same Acts in the same language. The greater part of the extant Bohairic Acts have been published with a French translation by the present writer of this article in "Les Actes des Martyrs de l'Égypte", etc., I (here = H), and by J. Balestri and the present writer, with a Latin translation, in "Acta Martyrum", I (here = B-H). Two of the Arabic Acts have appeared in French translation only, and without indication of the MSS. from which they were taken, under the name of E. Amélineau in "Contes et romans", etc., II (here = A). For the publication of some of the Ethiopic Acts we are indebted to E. Pereira in "Acta Martyrum", I (here = P).

Unlike the Acts of martyrs of the other churches, those of the Coptic Church, almost without any exception, contain some historical data of a more general character, which are as the background of the narrative proper. Put side by side, the data furnished by the various Acts of martyrs referred to the persecution of Diocletian prove on careful examination to constitute just such an outline of the history of that persecution as could result from a condensed compilation of the writings of Eusebius. Indeed it seems as though each individual writer of those Acts had before his eyes a compilation of that nature and took from it just what best served his purpose. Sometimes the original text is almost literally rendered in Coptic (and what is still more surprising in Arabic or in Ethiopic), with here and there an occasional distortion owing to the failure on the part of the translator to grasp the right meaning of a difficult or obscure passage; sometimes it is paraphrased; frequently it has been amplified or developed, and still more frequently we find it more or less curtailed. In other cases several passages have been condensed into one, so as to make appear simultaneous facts chronologically distinct. Finally, it not seldom occurs that a paragraph or even a short passage of Eusebius has been transformed into a real historical romance. In the latter case all proper names are fictitious, and the same historical character appears under various names. Antiochia is universally substituted for Nicomedia as the capital of the eastern empire. Naturally also some violence is inflicted on the original at the point where the romance is grafted upon it. A few examples will suffice to illustrate our view and at the same time we hope to show its correctness.

Bringing together the data furnished by the "Acts of Claudius" (P., 175, and A., 3), and Theodore Stratelates (B-H, 157), we can easily reconstruct the primitive Coptic version of the beginning of the persecution as follows: In the nineteenth year of Diocletian, as the Christians were preparing to celebrate the Passion, an edict was issued everywhere, ordering their churches to be destroyed, their Holy Scriptures burnt, and their slaves liberated, while other edicts were promulgated demanding the imprisonment and punishment of the ministers of the Christian Church unless they sacrificed to the gods. This is unmistakably a translation of Eusebius, "Hist. eccl.", VIII, ii, 4–5, and although it shows three omissions, viz., the indication of the month; the mention that this was the first edict, and the third provision of the edict, together with the wrong translation of the fourth clause, however, two of the omissions are supplied by the "Acts of Epime" (B-H, 122; comp. Didymus H., 285), in which we find as heading of the general edict (fourth edict, see p. 707c) these curious words: *This was the first edict [apographê] that was against all the saints. He [the king] got up early on the first day of the month of Pharmuthi* [27 March–25 April], *as he was to pass into a new year and wrote an edict [diatagma] etc.* It needs but a superficial comparison between Eusebius, "Hist. eccl.", VIII, ii, 4–5, and "Mart. Pal.", III, i, to see that the italics in the Coptic version above belong to the former passage, while the rest represent a distorted rendering of the latter. The Coptic has even retained to some extent the difference of style in the two places, having *apographê* for *graphê* in the first case and *diatagma* for *prostagma* in the latter. The other omission, viz., the third clause of the edict, may be lurking in some other text already extant or yet to be discovered. As for having misunderstood the fourth clause of the edict, the Coptic compiler may well be forgiven his error in view of the divergence of opinion still obtaining among scholars as to the right interpretation of this somewhat obscure passage. (See McGiffert on the passage, note 6. In this case, as the reader may have observed, we have departed from McGiffert's translation in supplying "their" before "household", thus making this fourth clause in reality a continuation of the third one.)

Here is now another passage in which the text of Eusebius is gradually transformed so as to lose practically everything of its primitive aspect. In the "Acts of Theodore the Eastern" (one of the most legendary compositions in the Coptic Martyrology), we read that Diocletian, having written the edict, handed it to one of the magistrates, Stephen by name, who was standing by him. Stephen took it and tore it up in the presence of the king. Whereupon the latter grasped his sword and cut Stephen in twain, and wrote the edict over again which he sends all over the world (P., 120 sq.). The legend process has begun, to say the least. Yet everybody will recognize in this story a translation, distorted as it may be, of Eusebius, VIII, v (those in Nicomedia). As in Eusebius it is a man in high rank who tears the edict. Only in Eusebius the edict was posted up instead of being handed by the emperor, and the act took place "while two of the emperors were in the same city" not "in the presence of the emperor"; finally, Eusebius does not say with what death the perpetrator of the act met (Lactantius, "De mort. persec.", XIII, says he was burnt). In the "Acts of Epime", the legend takes another step forward. A young soldier of high rank, seeing the edict (posted up) takes off his sword-belt and presents himself to the king. The king asks him who he is. The soldier answers that he is Christodorus, son of Basilides the Stratelates, but that henceforth he shall not serve an impious king, but confess Christ. Then the king takes the sword of one of the soldiers and runs it through the young man (B-H, 122 sq.). There is almost nothing left of Eusebius' account of this story. In fact it looks as if the writer of the "Acts of Epime" had taken it from those of Theodore the Eastern, or some other already distorted version of the Eusebian account, and spoiled it still more in his effort to conceal his act of plagiarism.

We could cite many more passages of the Acts of martyrs of Egypt, thus reproducing more or less exactly, yet unmistakably, the account of the persecution of Diocletian as given by Eusebius. In fact almost every chapter of the eighth book of his "History" is represented there by one or more passages, also some chapters of the seventh and ninth books, and of the book on the Martyrs of Palestine, so that there can be no serious doubt as to the existence of a Coptic history of the persecution of Diocletian based on Eusebius. This may have been a distinct work, or it may have been part of the Coptic church history, in twelve books, of which considerable fragments are known to be extant (see EGYPT, *History*). From that same Coptic church history were taken, possibly, the several excerpts from Eusebius to be found in the "History of the Patriarchs" of Severus of Ashmunein (EGYPT, p. 362d), and it might be one of the Coptic and Greek works to which this author refers as having been used by him [Graffin-Nau, "Patrologia Orientalis", I, 115; cf. Crum, "Proceedings of the Society of Biblical Archæology", XXIV (1902), 68 sqq.]. However, it seems more likely that the Coptic and Greek works spoken of by Severus were lives of the individual patriarchs, the compilers of which may have used either Eusebius' original text or more probably the Coptic work in question.

There are also in the Acts of martyrs of Egypt clear traces of other sources of information as to the persecution of Diocletian. This is generally the case with some of the more legendary pieces. For instance, in the introduction to the "Acts of Epime", we read that Diocletian, formerly a Christian (probably here confused with Julian the Apostate), apostatized and made for himself seventy gods, calling the first of them Apollo, and so on. Then he called a council of dignitaries of the empire and told them that Apollo and the rest of the gods had appeared to him, and demanded a reward for having restored him to health and given him the victory. In behalf of all, Romanus the Stratelates suggested to oblige all the subjects of Diocletian to worship his gods under penalty of death. Is it not clear that the first author of the narrative must have read in some form or other the ninth chapter of Lactantius' "De mortibus persecutorum"? In what other source could we have found that Diocletian acted on the advice of a council, and that of Apollo, no matter whether the god volunteered his advice or Diocletian sought it? Can it be a mere coincidence that both Lactantius and the Coptic writer explain practically in the same way Diocletian's determination to persecute the Christians?

EUSEBIUS, *Historia ecclesiastica* in *P. G.*, XX; IDEM, *De martyribus Palæstinæ* (*ibid.*); both works also, in English tr. (which we follow) with *Prolegomena* and notes by McGIFFERT in *Select Library of Nicene and Post-Nicene Fathers of the Christian Church*, new series, I (Oxford, 1890); LACTANTIUS, *De morte persecutorum* in *P. L.*, VII; GREGG, *The Decian Persecution* (Edinburgh, 1897); HEALY, *The Valerian Persecution* (Boston, 1905); MASON, *The Persecution of Diocletian* (Cambridge, 1876); SCHOENAICH, *Die Christenverfolgung des Kaisers Decius* (Jauer, 1907); TILLEMONT, *Mémoires pour servir à l'histoire ecclésiastique des six premiers siècles*, III–V; HYVERNAT, *Les actes des martyrs de l'Égypte tirés des manuscrits coptes de la bibliothèque Vaticane, etc.*, I (Paris, 1886–87); BALESTRI AND HYVERNAT, *Acta Martyrum*, I in *Corpus Scriptorum Christianorum Orientalium: Scriptores Coptici*, I (third series, Paris, 1907); PEREIRA, *Acta Martyrum, ibid., Scriptores Æthiopici*, XXVIII (second series, Paris, 1907); AMÉLINEAU, *Contes et romans de l'Égypte chrétienne* (Paris, 1888). For a complete bibliography of the material at hand see BOLLANDISTS (PEETERS), *Bibl. Hagiogr. Orient.* (Brussels, 1910). The only important addition to be made to this very useful work is the recent publication of WINSTEDT, *Coptic texts on Saint Theodore the General, St. Theodore the Eastern, etc.* (with English tr., London, 1910).

H. HYVERNAT.

Perseverance, FINAL (*perseverantia finalis*), is the preservation of the state of grace till the end of life. The expression is taken from Matt., x, 22, "He that shall persevere unto the end, he shall be saved." A temporary continuance in grace, be it ever so long, evidently falls short of the obvious meaning of the above phrase, if it fails to reach the hour of death. On the other hand the saying of St. Matthew does not necessarily imply a lifelong and unbroken continuance in grace, since it is of faith that lost grace can be recovered. Between the temporary continuance or imperfect perseverance and the lifelong continuance or most perfect perseverance there is room for final perseverance as commonly understood, i. e., the preservation of grace from the last conversion till death. It may be viewed as a power or as an actual fact. As a power it means the ensemble of spiritual means whereby the human will is enabled to persevere unto the end if it duly co-operates. As an actual fact it means the *de facto* preservation of grace and implies two factors, one internal, i. e., the steadfast use of the various means of salvation, the other external, i. e., the timely coming of death while the soul is at peace with God. Theologians, aptly or not, call the former active and the latter passive perseverance. There may be passive perseverance without active, as when an infant dies immediately after Baptism, but the normal case, which alone is considered here, is that of a good death crowning a greater or lesser duration of well-doing. By what agency the combined stability in holiness and timeliness of death are brought about is a problem long debated among Christian writers. The Semipelagians of the fifth century, while forsaking the sweeping ethical naturalism of Pelagius and admitting on principle the graces of the will, contended nevertheless, that the final perseverance of the justified was sufficiently accounted for by the natural power of our free will; if sometimes, in order to tally with conciliar definitions, they called it a grace, it was but a misnomer, as that grace could be merited by man's natural exertions. Oppositely, the Reformers of the sixteenth century, partly followed by the Baianist and Jansenist school, so minimized the native power and moral value of our free will as to make final perseverance depend on God alone, while their pretended fiducial faith and inadmissibility of grace led to the conclusion that we can, in this world, have absolute certainty of our final perseverance.

The Catholic doctrine, outlined by St. Augustine, chiefly in "De dono perseverantiæ" and "De correptione et gratia", and the Council of Orange in Southern Gaul, received its full expression in the Council of Trent, sess. VI, c. xiii, can. 16 and 22: (1) The power of persevering.—Canon 22 (Si quis dixerit justificatum vel sine speciali auxilio Dei in accepta justitia perseverare posse, vel cum eo non posse, anathema sit), by teaching that the justified cannot persevere without a special help of God, but with it can persevere, not only condemns both the naturalism of the Semipelagians and the false supernaturalism of the Reformers but also clearly implies that the power of perseverance is neither in the human will alone nor in God's grace solely, but in the combination of both, i. e., Divine grace aiding human will, and human will co-operating with Divine grace. The grace in question is called by the Council "a special help of God", apparently to distinguish it both from the concurrence of God in the natural order and habitual grace, neither of which were denied by the Semipelagians. Theologians, with a few exceptions, identify this special help with the sum total of actual graces vouchsafed to man. (2) Actual perseverance.—The Council of Trent, using an expression coined by St. Augustine, calls it (*magnum usque in finem perseverantiæ donum*) the great gift of final perseverance. "It consists", says Newman, "In an ever watchful superintendence of us on the part of our All-Merciful Lord, removing temptations which He sees will be fatal to us, succouring us at those times when we are in particular peril, whether from our negligence or other cause, and ordering the course of our life so that we may die at a time when He sees that we are in the state of grace." The supernatural character of such a gift is clearly asserted by Christ: "Holy

Father, keep them in thy name whom thou has given" (John, xvii, 11); by St. Paul: "he, who hath begun a good work in you, will perfect it unto the day of Christ Jesus" (Phil., i, 6); and by St. Peter: "But the God of all grace, who hath called us unto his eternal glory in Christ Jesus, after you have suffered a little, will himself perfect you, and confirm you, and establish you" (I Pet., v, 10). The extreme preciousness of that supernatural gift places it alike beyond our certain knowledge and meriting power.

That we can never in this life be certain of our final perseverance is defined by the Council of Trent, Sess. VI, can. xvi: "Si quis magnum illud usque in finem perseverantiæ donum se certo habiturum, absoluta et infallibili certitudine dixerit, nisi hoc ex speciali revelatione didicerit, anathema sit". What places it beyond our meriting power is the obvious fact that revelation nowhere offers final perseverance, with its retinue of efficacious graces and its crown of a good death, as a reward for our actions, but, on the contrary, constantly reminds us that, as the Council of Trent puts it, "the gift of perseverance can come only from Him who has the power to confirm the standing and to raise the fallen". However, from our incapacity to certainly know and to strictly merit the great gift, we should not infer that nothing can be done towards it. Theologians unite in saying that final perseverance comes under the impetrative power of prayer and St. Liguori (Prayer, the great means of Salvation) would make it the dominant note and burden of our daily petitions. The sometimes distressing presentation of the present matter in the pulpit is due to the many sides of the problem, the impossibility of viewing them all in one sermon, and the idiosyncrasies of the speakers. Nor should the timorousness of the saints, graphically described by Newman, be so construed as to contradict the admonition of the Council of Trent, that "all should place the firmest hope in the succour of God". Singularly comforting is the teaching of such saints as St. Francis de Sales (Camus, "The Spirit of St. Francis de Sales", III, xiii) and St. Catherine of Genoa (Treatise of Purgatory, iv). They dwell on God's great mercy in granting final perseverance, and even in the case of notorious sinners they do not lose hope: God suffuses the sinners' dying hour with an extraordinary light and, showing them the hideousness of sin contrasting with His own infinite beauty, He makes a final appeal to them. For those only who, even then, obstinately cling to their sin does the saying of Ecclus., v, 7, assume a sombre meaning "mercy and wrath quickly come from him, and his wrath looketh upon sinners". (See GRACE.)

ST. THOMAS, *Summa theologica*, I-II, Q. cxiv, a. 9; WILHELM AND SCANNELL, *A Manual of Catholic Theology*, II (London, 1901), 242; HUNTER, *Outlines of Dogmatic Theology*, III (New York, 1894), 47; NEWMAN, *Perseverance in Grace* in *Discourses to Mixed Congregations* (London and New York, 1906); LABAUCHE, *L'homme dans l'état de grâce* in *Leçons de théologie dogmatique* (Paris, 1908); BAREILLES, *Le catéchisme romain* (Montréjeau, 1906-10), III, 417, and VI, 434. See also current theological treatises *De gratia*. J. F. SOLLIER.

Persia.—The history, religion, and civilization of Persia are offshoots from those of Media. Both Medes and Persians are Aryans; the Aryans who settled in the southern part of the Iranian plateau became known as Persians, while those of the mountain regions of the north-west were called Medes. The Medes were at first the leading nation, but towards the middle of the sixth century B. C. the Persians became the dominant power, not only in Iran, but also in Western Asia.

Persia (in Heb. פרס, in the Sept. Περσίς, in the Achæmenian inscriptions *Parsa*, in Elamitic *Parsin*, in modern Persian *Fars*, and in Arabic *Fars*, or *Fâris*) was originally the name of a province in Media, but afterwards—i. e., towards the beginning of the fifth century B. C.—it became the general name of the whole country formerly comprising Media, Susiana, Elam, and even Mesopotamia. What we now call Persia is not identical with the ancient empire designated by that name. That empire covered, from the sixth century B. C. to the seventh of our era, such vast regions as Persia proper, Media, Elam, Chaldea, Babylonia, Assyria, the highlands of Armenia and Bactriana, North-Eastern Arabia, and even Egypt. Persia proper is bounded on the north by Transcaucasia, the Caspian Sea, and Russian Turkestan; on the south by the Indian Ocean and the Persian Gulf; on the east by Russian Turkestan, Afghanistan, and Beluchistan, and on the west by Asiatic Turkey and the Persian Gulf; it is over one-fifth as large as the United States (excluding Alaska) and twice as large as Germany, having an area of about 642,000 square miles. The whole country occupies a plateau varying in height from 3000 to 5000 feet, and subject to wide extremes of climate, its northern edge bordering on the Caspian Sea and the plain of Turkestan, its southern and south-western on the Persian Gulf and the plains of Mesopotamia. The ancient Persians were vigorous and hardy, simple in manners, occupied in raising cattle and horses in the mountainous regions, and agriculture in the valleys and plains. The four great cities were Ecbatana, in the north, Persepolis in the east, Susa in the west, and Seleucia-Ctesiphon in the south-west. The provinces and towns of modern Persia will be given below.

I. HISTORY.—Historians generally assign the beginnings of Persian history to the reign of Cyrus the Great (550–529 B. C.), although, strictly speaking, it should begin with Darius (521–485 B. C.). Cyrus was certainly of Persian extraction, but when he founded his empire he was Prince of Elam (Anzan), and he merely added Media and Persia to his dominion. He was neither by birth nor religion a true Persian, for both he and Cambyses worshipped the Babylonian gods. Darius, on the other hand, was both by birth and religion a Persian, descended, like Cyrus, from the royal Achæmenian house of Persia, and a follower of the Zoroastrian faith. The ancestors of Darius had remained in Persia, whilst the branch of the family of which Cyrus was a member had settled in Elam. The history of Persia may be divided into five great periods, each represented by a dynasty: A. The Achæmenian Dynasty, beginning with the kingdom of Cyrus the Great and ending with the Macedonian conquest (550–331 B. C.); B. The Greek, or Seleucian, Dynasty (331–250 B. C.); C. The Parthian Dynasty (250 B. C.–A. D. 227); D. The Sassanian Dynasty (A. D. 227–651); E. The Mohammedan period (A. D. 651 to the present).

A. *The Achæmenian Dynasty* (550–331 B. C.).—Towards the middle of the sixth century B. C., and a few years after the death of Nebuchadnezzar (Nabuchodonosor) the Great, King of Babylon (605–562 B. C.), Western Asia was divided into three kingdoms: the Babylonian Empire, Media, and Lydia; and it was only a question of time which of the three would annihilate the other two. Astyages (585–557 B. C.), the successor of Cyaxares (625–585 B. C.), being engaged in an expedition against Babylonia and Mesopotamia, Cyrus, Prince of Anzan, in Elam, profiting by his absence, fomented a rebellion in Media. Astyages, hearing of the revolt, immediately returned, but was defeated and overthrown by Cyrus, who was proclaimed King of Media. Thus, with the overthrow of Astyages and the accession of Cyrus to the throne, the Median Empire passed into the hands of the Persians (550 B. C.). In 549, Cyrus invaded Assyria and Babylonia; in 546 he attacked Crœsus of Lydia, defeated him, and annexed Asia Minor to his realm; he then conquered Bactriana and, in 539, marched against Babylon. In 538 Babylon surrendered, Nabonidus fled, the Syro-Phœnician provinces submitted, and Cyrus allowed the Hebrews to return to Palestine. But in 529 he was killed in battle, and was succeeded by Cambyses, the heir apparent, who put his brother

Smerdis to death. In 525 Cambyses, aided by a Phœnician fleet, conquered Egypt and advanced against the Sudan, but was compelled to return to Egypt. On his way home, and while in Syria, being informed that Gaumata, a Magian, pretending to be the murdered Smerdis, had seized the throne, Cambyses committed suicide (522) and was succeeded, in 521, by Darius Hystaspes, who, with six other princes, succeeded in overthrowing the usurper Gaumata.

With the accession of Darius, the throne passed to the second line of descendants of Teispes II, and thus the Elamite dynasty came to an end. This was soon followed by a general revolt in all the provinces, including Babylon, where a son of Nabonidus was proclaimed king. Susiana also rose up in arms, and Darius was confronted with the task of reconquering the empire founded by Cyrus. In 519 Babylon was conquered, all the other provinces, including Egypt, were pacified and the whole empire reorganized and divided into satrapies with fixed administration and taxes. In 515 the Asiatic Greeks began to rebel, but were crushed by Darius. Thence he marched to the Indus and subjugated the country along its banks. In 499 the Ionians revolted, but were defeated and the city of Miletus destroyed (494 B. C.). In 492 Mardonius, one of Darius's generals, set out to reconquer Greece, concentrating all his forces in Cilicia; but the Persians were defeated at Marathon (490 B. C.). In 485 Darius was succeeded by his son, Xerxes I, who immediately set out to reconquer Egypt and Babylon, and renewed the war against Greece. After the indecisive battles of Thermopylæ and Artemisium, he was defeated by Themistocles at Salamis near Athens (480). During the years 479–465, Xerxes met with constant reverses; he gradually lost Attica, Ionia, the Archipelago, and Thrace, and at last was assassinated by Artabanus and Artaxerxes. The latter, becoming king as Artaxerxes I, in 464 quelled revolts in Bactria and Egypt in the year 454. In 449, the Persian fleet and army having been again defeated near Salamis, in Cyprus, a treaty of peace was made between Persia and Athens. Artaxerxes died in 424 and was succeeded by his eldest son, Xerxes II, who reigned but forty-five days and was murdered by his half-brother Sogdianus. Sogdianus reigned six months and was murdered by Ochus, who ascended the throne in 423 as Darius II Nothus (the Bastard).

In 412, Darius II compelled Sparta to recognize Persian suzerainty over the Greek cities of Asia Minor, and reconquered the cities of Ionia and Caria. On his death, in 404, Arsaces, his eldest son, ascended the throne as Artaxerxes II, and quelled revolts in Cyprus, Asia Minor, and Egypt. But in the last seven years of his reign, Egypt and Asia Minor became once more independent. He died in 359 and was succeeded by his son Ochus, known as Artaxerxes III. In this same year, the Persians were defeated in Egypt and lost Phœnicia and Cyprus (352); but in 345–340, Artaxerxes succeeded in conquering and crushing Sidon, Cyprus, and Egypt. In 338 he was murdered and was succeeded by his youngest son, Arses, who was in his turn put to death by the eunuch Bagoas (335), and was succeeded by Codomannus, great-grandson of Darius II, who assumed the name of Darius III. In 334 Alexander, the son of Philip of Macedon, began his career of conquest by subduing all Asia Minor and Northern Syria. After conquering Tyre, Phœnicia, Judea, and Egypt in 332, he invaded Assyria, and at Arbela, in 331, defeated Darius and his vast army, thus putting an end to the Achæmenian dynasty. Darius III fled to Media, where he was seized and murdered by Bessus, Satrap of Bactria (330), while Alexander entered Babylon and Susa, and subdued the provinces of Elam, Persia, and Media. Bessus, the murderer of Darius, who had proclaimed himself King of Persia under the name of Artaxerxes IV, fell into Alexander's hands and was put to death (330 B. C.).

B. *The Greek, or Seleucian, Dynasty* (331–250 B. C.). —With Alexander's signal victory over Darius III at Arbela (Guagamela), in 331, the Achæmenian Kingdom of Persia came to an end. Alexander founded more than seventy cities in which he planted Greek and Macedonian colonies. But the great conqueror, greedy for sensual pleasures, plunged into a course of dissipation which ended in his death, 13 June, 323. Dissension and civil wars broke out at once in every quarter of the vast empire, from India to the Nile, and lasted for nearly forty-two years. Perdiccas, the regent of Babylon during the minority of Alexander's son, was soon assassinated, and his power claimed by Pitho, Satrap of Media; but Pitho was displaced by a conspiracy of the other satraps, who, in 316, chose Eumenes to occupy the throne of Alexander. Eumenes was betrayed into the hands of Antigonus, another great Macedonian general, who again was obliged, in 312, to yield to Seleucus, one of the Alexandrian generals, founder of the Seleucid dynasty. He built the city of Seleucia, on the Tigris, making it the capital of the Persian, or rather Græco-Persian, Empire. The great disturbing element during the Seleucian period was the rivalry between Greeks and Macedonians, as well as between cavalry and infantry. The Greek colonists in Bactria revolted against Macedonian arrogance and were with difficulty pacified by Seleucus Nicator. But the dissatisfaction continued, and, in the reign of Antiochus II, about 240 B. C., Diodotus, Satrap of Bactria, revolted and founded a separate Greek state in the heart of Central Asia. This Kingdom of Bactria presents one of the most singular episodes in history. A small colony of foreigners, many hundred miles from the sea, entirely isolated, and numbering probably not over thirty-five thousand, not only maintained their independence for about one hundred years in a strange land, but extended their conquests to the Ganges, and included several hundred populous cities in their dominions.

The reign of Seleucus Nicator lasted from 312 to 280 B. C. His first care was to reorganize his empire and satrapies (seventy-two in number), which yielded him an annual revenue equivalent to about twenty million dollars. In 289 he removed the seat of government from Seleucia to Antioch, in Syria. But, as it was impossible to govern properly so extensive an empire from so distant a capital, he found it advisable to make over the upper satrapies to Antiochus, his son, giving him Seleucia as his capital (293 B. C.). In 280, however, Seleucus was assassinated and was succeeded by his son, Antiochus I (called Soter), whose reign of twenty-one years was devoid of interest. His second son, Antiochus II (called Theos), succeeded him in 261, a drunken and dissolute prince, who neglected his realm for the society of unworthy favourites. During his reign, north-eastern Persia was lost to the empire, and some Bactrians, emboldened by the weakness and effeminacy of Antiochus, and led by the brothers, Arsaces and Tiridates, moved west into Seleucid territory, near Parthia. Phereeles, the Seleucid satrap, having insulted Tiridates, was slain, and Parthia freed from the Macedonians. Arsaces, the brother of Tiridates, was proclaimed first King of Parthia in 250 B. C., and the Seleucid dynasty fell into decay.

C. *The Arsacid, or Parthian Dynasty* (250 B. C. –A. D. 216).—The founding of the Parthian monarchy marks the opening of a glorious era in the history of Persia. The Parthians, though inferior in refinement, habits, and civilization to the Persians proper, form, nevertheless, a branch of the same stock. They were originally a nomadic tribe and, like the Persians, followers of Zoroaster. They had their own customs, and were famous for their horsemanship, their armies being entirely composed of cavalry, completely clad in chain armour and riding without saddles. They left few records; indeed, we really know very little of the internal history of the Parthians, and would have known still less but for the frequent wars between them and the Greeks and Romans. Numbers of Parthian coins are still found in northern Persia and have been of great value to the historian who, thousands of years later, has tried to put together the disjointed history of this dynasty. Amid the faint and confused outlines which alone remain to record the career of the mighty Parthian race which for over four hundred years ruled in Persia with a rod of iron, and which repeatedly hurled back the veteran legions of Rome, we are able to discern two or three grand figures and some events that will be remembered while the world lasts.

Of these heroes of Parthia the most important was Mithridates the Great, who not only repaired the losses the empire had sustained in its conflicts with the Seleucids, but carried the conquests of Parthia as far as India in one direction, and the banks of the Euphrates in the other. Parthians and Romans met for the first time, not for war, but to arrange a treaty of peace between the two great powers of that age. Soon after this event Demetrius III, head of the Seleucian dynasty, was forced to surrender, with his entire army, to Mithridates, and ended his days in captivity. Armenia also fell under the Parthian domination during the reign of Mithridates. The coins of Mithridates are very numerous and clearly cut; the design shows the portrait of that monarch, with a full beard and strongly marked, but pleasing, features. His immediate successors were men of an entirely different stamp, and Tigranes, King of Armenia, was able, not only to revolt, but to rob Parthia of some of her western provinces. In time Phraates succeeded to the throne of the Arsacids and, by calling for aid from the Romans, caused the overthrow of Tigranes; but the haughty republic of the West granted its assistance with such ill grace that years of warfare resulted. Phraates was murdered by his two sons. Orodes, as the Latins called him (Huraodha, in the Perso-Parthian tongue) ascended the throne; but to avoid dissension it was agreed that his brother, Mithridates, should rule over Media as an independent king. It was not long before civil war broke out between the two, and in the end Mithridates was taken and put to death in the presence of his brother. In 54 B. C., the civil wars of Rome having ceased for a while, Crassus, who with Cæsar and Pompey, shared the authority in the republic, took command of the Roman armies in Asia. He needed but the merest pretext to invade and attack Parthia; the easy victories of Pompey in Armenia led him to imagine that he had but to reach the borders of the Persian Empire and it would fall helpless into his grasp. He was a brave man, and led sixty thousand of the best troops in the world, but his contempt of the enemy, and the greed of gold for which he was notorious, brought him into a terrible catastrophe. The chief general of Orodes was Surenas, the first nobleman of the empire. On 16 June, 54 B. C., the Romans and the Parthians met at Carræ, near the sources of the Euphrates. Surenas concealed the mass of his army behind the hills, allowing the Romans to see at first only his heavy cavalry. Little suspecting the actual force of the enemy, Publius Crassus, son of the general, charged with the cavalry. The Parthians, following their usual tactics, broke and fled as if in dismay. When they had drawn the Romans far enough from the main body, the entire army of Surenas re-formed, surrounded them, and cut them to pieces. After this success, the Parthians hovered on the flanks of the Roman infantry, annoying them with missiles. Of the great army which Crassus had led into Asia not twenty thousand survived, and of these ten thousand were taken captive and settled by Orodes in Margiana. Orodes himself, after a long reign, during which Parthia attained the climax of her power, was strangled in his eightieth year by his son Phraates. He was the first Parthian king to assume the title of "King of Kings".

Phraates, his successor, removed the seat of government from the north of the empire to Taisefoon, or, as the Greeks called it, Ctesiphon, a suburb of Seleucia, which continued to be the capital until the Mohammedan conquest, more than six hundred years later. Hatra, in that vicinity, also acquired importance under the Parthian kings, who caused a splendid palace to be erected there. Phraates was eminently successful in his military operations, although steeped in crime. Besides murdering his father, he had caused all his near relations to be put to death, to ensure his own position on the throne. Phraates soon had another Roman war on his hands. Before the death of Orodes, that monarch had associated with him his son Pacorus, a soldier and statesman, who conquered Syria and ruled both there and in Palestine with a mildness which contrasted favourably with the severity of the Roman governors expelled by him. But Pacorus was finally defeated and killed by the Roman consul, Ventidius, and the territories he had captured on the coast of the Mediterranean were lost to Parthia. In the year 33 B. C. Mark Antony began a campaign against the Parthians, whom the Romans never forgave for the crushing defeat at Carræ. His army numbered one hundred thousand men, including no less than forty thousand cavalry intended to cope with the terrible horsemen of Parthia. To oppose this immense force, Phraates could collect only forty thousand cavalry; but he immediately began operations by surprising the baggage trains of the enemy, and cutting to pieces the escort of seven thousand five hundred men. Antony was at the time engaged in besieging Phraaspa. He was obliged to abandon the siege, but the pursuit of the Parthians was so vigorous that the Roman general was hardly able to reach the frontier of Armenia after losing thirty thousand of his best troops. For one hundred years after this, Rome dared not again attack Parthia; and when, in later ages, her legions repeated the attempts to penetrate into the heart of Persia, they invariably failed.

Phraates was dethroned by a conspiracy of his brother Tiridates. He fled to Tourân, or Scythia, of which we hear so often in the legendary history of Persia. There he succeeded in raising an immense army of Tatars, and, hurling the usurper from power, forced him to seek an asylum at Rome, where he endeavoured to obtain assistance from the Romans, promising important concessions in return. But his offers were declined. A century later, Trajan invaded Parthia, but, in spite of some early successes, was forced to retire to Syria. Vologeses II is memorable for his death, A. D. 148, at the age of ninety-six, after a reign of seventy-one years. During the reign of Vologeses III Western Persia was invaded by Cassius, the Roman consul. Vologeses was defeated in a great battle, and Cassius penetrated as far as Babylonia, the capital of which was Seleucia, a most flourishing city, with a population of over four hundred thousand. Cassius sacked and burned Seleucia, completely wiping it out of existence. Parthia never recovered from the effects of this last war with Rome. The dynasty which had founded the greatness of the Parthian empire had become enervated by its successes. In 216 the war with Rome was renewed. King Artabanus had put down several rivals and reduced the greater part of the Parthians under his power. Macrinus, the Roman Emperor, suffered two crushing defeats from Artabanus, and was obliged to purchase peace by paying an indemnity of 50,000,000 denarii (about $9,000,000) at the very time when the doom of Parthia was impending. With the death of Artabanus, A. D. 216, the Parthian dynasty came to an end.

D. *The Sassanian Dynasty* (A. D. 227-651).—The immediate causes which brought about the overthrow of the Parthian kingdom and the establishment of the dynasty of Sassan in its stead are not known. The new dynasty of the Sassanids was a more genuine representative of the civilized Iranian race than the Parthian Arsacidæ, especially as far as religion was concerned. The founder of the Sassanian dynasty, Ardashir Papakan (Artaxerxes, son of Papak), was born at Persis, in central Iran; his family claimed descent from a mythical ancestor, Sassan, and he was therefore of the priestly caste. Babek, the father of Ardashir, seems to have founded a small kingdom at Persis, and to have annexed the territories of other lesser princes, thus gradually encroaching on various Parthian provinces. Vologeses V, the last king of the Arsacid dynasty of Parthia, declared war against the rising chief, but was defeated and put to death by Ardashir A. D. 227. Thus the Parthian Empire passed into the hands of the Sassanian dynasty. The surviving Arsacids fled to India, and all the provinces accepted Ardashir's rule without resistance. It was in fact the beginning of a new national and religious movement, the new dynasty being looked upon as the true and genuine successor of the old and noble Achæmenian dynasty, and of the Zoroastrian religion.

One of the first acts of Ardashir was to send an embassy to Rome demanding that the whole of Western Asia should be ceded to him. Soon afterwards, in 230, he sought to regain the lost provinces of Mesopotamia by force of arms. The emperor, Alexander Severus, opposed the advance of Ardashir's army, but was only partly successful. Ardashir devoted the remaining years of his reign to founding new towns, schools, and temples, and to reorganizing the judicial system of the courts and the army. Everywhere were evidences of a new development of the true Iranian spirit; and it was not long before the Persian nation deemed itself sufficiently strong once more to enforce its old claims to the sovereignty of Western Asia. Sapor I, the son of Ardashir, who reigned from 240 to 273, renewed the war with Rome, first against Gordian, then against Valerian. The latter emperor was treacherously seized at a conference in 260, and spent the rest of his life in a Persian prison subject to most barbarous ill-usage. Sapor then conquered Syria and destroyed Antioch, but was finally driven back by Odenathus, King of Palmyra. After the death of Odenathus the war was continued by his widow, Zenobia, who was so elated by her success that she attempted to found an independent Syrian empire under the leadership of Palmyra, but was defeated and taken prisoner by the Romans under Aurelian.

The third Sassanid king, Hormuz, reigned only one year; his successor, Bahram I (274-77), continued the war with Zenobia and afterwards with Aurelian. But this war terminated, without any result, at the death of Aurelian, in 275. During this period, the revival of the Zoroastrian religion became a movement of great importance. Having attained ascendancy in Persia under the early Sassanid kings, it grew very intolerant, persecuting alike heathen and Christian. It first turned against Mani, the founder of Manichæism, and his followers, under Bahram I. Mani himself, at first in favour at the Persian Court, was crucified about the year 275. Under the next king, Bahram II (277-94), Persia suffered severe reverses from the Roman Emperor Carus, the capital city, Ctesiphon, even falling into the hands of the Romans. Bahram III, son of Bahram II, reigned only eight months, and was succeeded by his younger brother, Narsi I, who renewed the war with Rome with disastrous results. He was succeeded by his son, Hormuz II (303-10), and he, again, by Sapor II (310-81). It was in the latter reign that the Christians in Persia suffered serious persecution. During the early years of Sapor II the Christian religion received formal recognition from Constantine, and there is no doubt that this identification of the Church with the Roman Empire was the chief cause of its disfavour in Persia. Moreover, there is evidence that Christianity had spread widely in the Persian dominions, and every Christian was suspected of disaffection towards the Persian king and secret attachment to the Roman Empire, the more so because even the Persian-speaking Christians employed the Syriac language in their worship. Probably this feeling of suspicion was increased by the letter which Constantine wrote to Sapor (Theod., "H. E.", I, xxv), asking protection for the Christians resident in Persia. (See III, below.) To this period belongs Aphraates, a converted Persian noble, a writer of homilies. When Constantine was dead, and the Magi had attained complete ascendancy over the Persian king, a persecution ensued which was far more severe than any of those of the Roman Emperors.

This attack upon the Christians was but part of Sapor's anti-Western policy. In 350 he openly declared war against Rome, and marched on Syria. The first important action was the siege of Nisibis, where the famous Jacob, founder of the school of Nisibis, was then bishop. The siege lasted seventy days, and then the Persians having built a dam across the River Mygdonius, the waters broke down the wall. The siege was unsuccessful, however, and the campaign ended in a truce. Julian, who became emperor in 361, determined to invade the dominions of Sapor. In March, 363, he set out from Antioch to march towards Carræ. From the latter point two roads led to Persia: one through Nisibis to the Tigris, the other turning south along the Euphrates and then crossing the lower Tigris. Julian chose the second of these and, passing through Callinicum, Carchemish, and Zaitham, reached the Persian capital, Ctesiphon, where he was met with proposals of peace from Sapor, but refused them. After crossing the Tigris, he burned his ships to prevent their falling into the hands of the enemy; but the result was something like a panic amongst his followers. Supplies ran short, and the army entered the desert, where it seems to have lost its way. There had been no battle as yet, but almost daily skirmishes with the light-armed Persian cavalry. In one of these skirmishes Julian was slain by a javelin, whether thrown by one of the enemy or by one of his own followers has never been known. The soldiers at once elected Jovian, one of Julian's generals, and he began his reign by making a thirty years' truce with Persia. The Persians were to supply guides and food for the retreat, while the Romans promised to surrender Nisibis and give up their protectorate over Armenia and Iberia, which became Persian provinces. The surrender of Nisibis put an end to the school established there by Jacob, but his disciple Ephraim removed to Edessa, and there re-established the school, so that Edessa became once more the centre of Syriac intellectual life. With this school must be connected the older Syriac martyrologies, and many of the Syriac translations and editions of Greek church manuals, canons, and theological writers. Thus were preserved Syriac versions of many important works, the original Greek of which is lost.

In spite of this thirty years' truce, the Persians for a time kept up a petty warfare, the Romans acting on the defensive. But as age rendered Sapor helpless, this warfare died out. Sapor died in 380, at the age of seventy; being a posthumous son, he had spent his whole life on the throne. During the reigns of Sapor III and Bahram IV Persia remained at peace. In 379 the Emperor Theodosius the Great received an embassy from Persia proposing friendly relations. This was mainly due to the fact that the Persians had difficulties on their northern and eastern frontiers, and wished to have their hands free in the west. Incidentally, it may be noted that the flourishing period of the "middle school", under the leadership of Dorotheus, and the spread of monasticism through Persia and Mesopotamia were contemporary with the disastrous expedition and peace of Jovian. The great bishop, Jacob of Nisibis, forms a connecting link between all three: as bishop he was contemporary with Sapor II; he encouraged Nisibis in its first resistance to the army of Sapor; his school at Nisibis was modelled on that of Diodorus at Antioch, and he was the patron and benefactor of the monastery founded by Awgin on Mount Izla.

In 399 Bahram IV was succeeded by his younger brother Yezdegerd (399–420). Early in this reign Maruthas, Bishop of Maiperkat, in Mesopotamia, was employed by the Roman Emperor as envoy to the Persian Court. Maruthas quickly gained great influence over the Persian king, to the annoyance of the Zoroastrian magi, and Yezdegerd allowed the free spread of Christianity in Persia and the building of churches. Nisibis once more became a Christian city. The Persian Church at this period seems to have received, under Maruthas (q. v.), the more developed organization under which it lived until the time of the Mohammedan conquest. (See III, below.) Later in the reign of Yezdegerd, the Persian bishop, Abdas of Susa, was associated with Maruthas, and, by his impetuosity, put an end to the good relations between the Persian king and the Christians. Abdas destroyed one of the fire temples of the Zoroastrians; complaint was made to the king, and the bishop was ordered to restore the building and make good all damage that he had committed. Abdas refused to rebuild a heathen temple at his own expense. The result was that orders were issued for the destruction of all churches, and these were carried out by the Zoroastrians, who had regarded with great envy the royal favour extended to Maruthas and his co-religionists. Before long the destruction of churches developed into a general persecution, in which Abdas was one of the first martyrs. When Yezdegerd died in 420, and was succeeded by his son Bahram V, the persecution continued, and large numbers of Christians fled across the frontier into Roman territory. A bitter feeling between Persia and Rome grew out of Bahram's demand for the surrender of the Christian fugitives, and war was declared in 422. The conflict commenced with Roman success in Armenia and the capture of a large number of Persian prisoners; the Romans then advanced into Persia and ravaged the border province of Azazena, but the seat of war was soon transferred to Mesopotamia, where the Romans besieged Nisibis. The Persians, hard pressed in this siege, called in the Turks to their assistance, and the united armies marched to the relief of the city. The Romans were alarmed at the news of the large numbers of the Persian forces and raised the siege, but soon afterwards, when the Turks had retired, there was a general engagement in which the Romans inflicted a crushing defeat upon their adversaries, and compelled them to sue for peace. Although the latter half of the fourth and the beginning of the fifth century was a period of so much distress in the Eastern provinces, which were exposed to the growing ambition of Persia, it was a time of extension of the Christian Church and of literary activity. This literary and ecclesiastical development led to the formation of a Syriac literature in Persia (Syriac being the liturgical language of the Persian Church), and ultimately of a Christian Persian literature.

Towards the middle of the fifth century, the Persian Emperor Yezdegerd (442–59) was compelled to turn his attention to the passes of the Caucasus; troops of Huns and Scythians had already broken through into Iran. Peroses (Firuz), his successor, made war on the nomads of the Caspian regions, and in 484 lost his life in battle with them. Four years later the throne of Persia was occupied by Qubad I, who reigned from 488 to 531. During this reign there developed in Persia a new sect of the Fire-worshippers (the Mazdakeans), who were at first favoured by the king, but who subsequently involved the empire in serious complications. The last decade of Qubad's reign was chiefly occupied by wars with the Romans, in which he found a good means for diverting the attention of his people from domestic affairs. During the very last days of his life Qubad was compelled once more to lead an army to the West to maintain Persia's influence over Lasistan in southern Caucasia, the prince of which country had become a convert to Christianity, and consequently an ally of the Byzantine Empire. It was during the same reign that the Nestorians began to enter more fully into Persian life, and under him that they began their missionary expansion eastwards. About the year 496 the patriarchal See of Seleucia-Ctesiphon fell into the hands of the Nestorians, and henceforth the Catholicos of Seleucia became the Patriarch of the Nestorian Church of Persia, Syria, China, and India. After the death of Qubad the usual quarrels as to the succession arose, and finally ended, in 531, with the accession of Chosroes I Anushirwân, whom Qubad had looked upon as the most capable of his sons. Chosroes was a champion of the ancient Iranian spirit, a friend of the priest class, and an irreconcilable enemy of the Mazdakites, who had chosen one of his numerous brothers as their candidate for the throne. During his reign the Persian Empire attained the height of its splendour; indeed, the government of Chosroes I, "the Just", was both equitable and vigorous. One of his first acts was to make peace with Byzantium, the latter agreeing to pay a large contribution towards the fortification of the Caucasian passes. In addition to strengthening the Caucasus, Chosroes also sought to fortify the north-eastern frontier of his empire by constructing a great wall, and he asserted his claims to a portion of north-western India by force of arms, but soon turned his attention once more to the West. In 531 he proclaimed a general toleration, in which not only Christians, but also Manichæans and Mazdakites, were included.

The period 532–39 was spent in the extension and strengthening of the eastern frontiers of Persia. In 539 Chosroes returned to Ctesiphon, and was persuaded by the Bedouin Al Mondar to renew Qubad's attempted conquest of Syria. The pretext was that Justinian was aiming at universal dominion, but there is no doubt that the real reason was that Al Mondar remembered the ease with which he had once plundered Syrian territory. In 540 the Persians invaded Syria and captured the city of Shurab. The prisoners taken from this city were released at the request of Candidus, bishop of the neighbouring town of Sergiopolis, who undertook to pay a ransom of 200 pounds of gold. Then Chosroes took Mabbogh, which paid a ransom, then Berœa, and finally proceeded against Antioch itself, which was captured after a short resistance. From Antioch Chosroes carried off many works of art and a vast number of captives. On his way homewards he made an attack upon Edessa, a city generally regarded as impregnable, but was taken ill during the siege.

During Chosroes's illness trouble occurred in Persia. He had married a Christian wife, and his son Nushizad was also a Christian. When the king was taken ill at Edessa a report reached Persia that he was dead, and at once Nushizad seized the crown. Very soon the rumour was proved false, but Nushizad was persuaded by persons who appear to have been in the pay of Justinian to endeavour to maintain his position. The action of his son was deeply distressing to Chosroes; but it was necessary to take prompt measures, and the commander, Ram Berzin, was sent against the rebels. In the battle which followed Nushizad was mortally wounded and carried off the field.

In his tent he was attended by a Christian bishop, probably Mar Aba, and to this bishop he confessed his sincere repentance for having taken up arms against his father, an act which, he was convinced, could never win the approval of Heaven. Having professed himself a Christian he died, and the rebellion was quickly put down.

Mar Aba was probably the Nestorian Catholicos from 536 to 552. He was a convert from Zoroastrianism, and had studied Greek at Nisibis and Edessa, making use of his knowledge to prepare and publish a new version of the Old Testament. This appears to have been a total failure, for the Nestorians, unlike the Jacobites, steadily adhered to the Peshito. On being appointed catholicos he established a school at Seleucia, which soon became a great centre of Nestorian scholarship. He wrote commentaries, homilies, and letters, the two former classes of work representing, no doubt, the substance of his teaching in the school which he founded. Hymns are extant which are ascribed to him. Chosroes, after his return from Syria, taunted Mar Aba with professing a type of Christianity unknown to the rest of the world. But Mar Aba did much to remove the more marked peculiarities of the Nestorian schism, especially again enforcing celibacy amongst the bishops. From time to time he held discussions with Chosroes, until on one occasion, being tactless enough not to be convinced by the arguments of the sovereign, he was sentenced to banishment. As he disobeyed the decree, he was cast into prison, where he died in 552. In 542 Chosroes claimed from Bishop Candidus the payment of the sum to which he had pledged himself as ransom for the captives taken at Shurab; but the bishop was unable to raise the money; in fact he confessed that he had only made the promise in the expectation that the Government would find part of the sum required, and this had not been done. Therefore Candidus was put to death. In the course of the same year Chosroes advanced south and attacked Jerusalem, but was repulsed by Belisarius.

Mar Aba's foundation of a school at Seleucia seems to have suggested to Chosroes the idea of founding a Zoroastrian school similar to it and to the Christian instructions at Edessa and Nisibis. In pursuance of this plan the king opened a college at Djundi Shapur, and here many Greek, Syrian, and Indian works were translated into Persian, and the ancient laws of Persia were rendered into the vernacular dialect (Pahlavi). Meanwhile the school at Seleucia became a centre of Nestorian life. It was a period during which the Nestorians were returning to a greater conformity to the usages of the rest of Christendom. We have already mentioned Mar Aba's restoration of celibacy, at least as far as the bishops were concerned. About the same time two distinguished monks, both bearing the name of Abraham of Kashkar, introduced reforms into monastic life which also tended towards conformity with the practices of the Church within the Roman Empire. Probably this tendency to conformity was due to increase of Greek influence observable during the reign of Chosroes, and the contact with the empire due to the invasion of Syria; nevertheless the Nestorians remained a distinct body.

Meanwhile the Catholicos Mar Aba had died, and Chosroes appointed his favourite physician, Joseph, as Bishop of Seleucia (552). Many strange stories are related of his cruelty as bishop; after three years he was deposed on a petition of the Christians of Seleucia. He lived twelve years after his deposition, and during that period no catholicos was appointed. About the same time the indefatigable Jacob Burdeana consecrated Achudemma as Jacobite bishop in Persia, and made a proselyte of a member of the royal family. Amongst the Persians it was never permitted to make converts from the state religion. The Jacobites however were of little importance so far east, where Nestorianism was the prevailing type of Christianity. After the death of Joseph in 567, Ezechiel, a disciple of Mar Aba, was appointed Catholicos of Seleucia, under whom lived the *periodeutes* Bodh, the translator into Syriac of the Indian tales known as "Kalilah and Dimnah". It is noteworthy that the Nestorians were beginning to take an interest in Indian literature, an interest probably to be referred to the influence of the Djundi Shapur school.

Chosroes was succeeded by his son Hormuz (579–90). For the first three years of his reign Hormuz was guided by the statesman-philosopher Buzurg, but after his retirement Hormuz gave himself up to every form of self-indulgence and tyranny. Under these conditions the power of Persia declined, and the land suffered invasion on the north, east, and west. To check the Byzantines, Bahram, a general who had distinguished himself under Chosroes, was sent to invade Colchis, but he was defeated and recalled in disgrace. Knowing that this was equivalent to sentence of death, Bahram revolted, and succeeded in capturing Hormuz, whom he put to death. Chosroes, the king's son, fled and was well received by Probus, Governor of Circesium, and afterwards by the Emperor Mauritius. With the help of the Romans this younger Chosroes defeated Bahram, and became king as Chosroes II. As he owed his kingdom and his wife to the Emperor Mauritius, Chosroes was devoted to the dynasty then reigning at Constantinople. Although not himself a Christian, he paid honour to the Blessed Virgin and to the martyrs Sergius and Bacchus, two saints popular among the Syrians, while his wife was an ardent Jacobite.

In 604 the Roman Emperor Mauritius was assassinated, and the Persian king resolved to attack the empire in order to avenge his benefactor. In 604 the Persians again invaded the eastern provinces and took the city of Daras. The invasion of Chosroes II was the severest blow that the Byzantine power in Asia had to endure, previous to the rise of Islam. After five years of war Chosroes II reached Constantinople. It was not a mere plundering expedition, but a serious invasion whose success clearly proved the growing weakness of the Byzantine Empire. Next year (606) the invaders reached Amida; in 607 they were at Edessa; in 608 at Aleppo; and by 611 they had conquered all northern Syria, and established themselves at Antioch. They then turned south and conquered Palestine. In 615 Jerusalem revolted, but was cruelly punished, some 17,000 persons being put to death, and about 35,000 led away captive. The fragment of the True Cross, the most precious relic of the city, was carried off. Next year (616) the Persians took Alexandria, and in 617 besieged Constantinople. Although the imperial city was not taken, Asia Minor remained in the hands of the Persians until 624.

Chosroes II was repelled, not by the Romans, but by a people who were yearly growing more powerful, and were destined ultimately to displace both Rome and Persia in Asia—the Arabs. Chosroes II had a harem of 3000 wives, as well as 12,000 female slaves, but he now demanded as wife Hadiqah, the daughter of the Christian Arab Na'aman, himself the son of Al Mondir. Na'aman refused to permit his Christian daughter to enter the harem of a Zoroastrian, and for this refusal he was trampled to death by an elephant, whilst Hadiqah took refuge in a convent. The news of this outrage upon an Arab provoked all the Bedouin tribes, and the Arabs revolted. Chosroes II was totally defeated, and fled to the Emperor Heraclius. This victory made a great impression upon the Arab mind, and probably led to the Mohammedan conquests.

E. *The Mohammedan and Modern Periods* (A. D. 651–1911).—During the reign of Yezdegerd III, the successor of Chosroes II, and the last of the Sassanian kings, the Arab invaders attacked Persia and its Mesopotamian territories more and more boldly. In 650 Khâlid, one of the Arab generals, assuming the offensive, defeated the Persian troops on the border of the Euphrates valley. The Christians of this region soon submitted to him. Then the Arabs invaded the country about the Tigris. In 634 Abu Ubaid of Taif, to whom Khâlid assigned the task of annexing Persia, was utterly defeated and slain by the Persians, who, however, were routed in 635–66 by Caliph Omar at Bowaib. Towards the close of the year 636, or in 637, they were again defeated by the Arabs, under Sa'd, at Kadisiyya. The victorious Arabs entered Babylonia and took Seleucia after a lengthy siege. Thence they crossed the Tigris and fell on Ctesiphon, Yezdegerd fleeing towards the Medo-Babylonian frontier. Meantime another army of Arabs had occupied Lower Irâk and entered Susiana. The decisive and final victory took place in 640–42 at Nehavend, near Ecbatana, when the great Persian Empire and the Sassanian dynasty were completely destroyed.

During the reigns of Omar, Othman, and Ali, the first caliphs and successors of Mohammed, as well as under the Omayyads (634–720), Persia was ruled by deputy governors; but on the accession of the Abbasides (A. D. 750), Bagdad became their capital, and Khorasan their favourite province, and thus the very heart of the former territory of the Persian Empire became the centre of the caliphate. But their rule soon became merely a nominal one, and ambitious governors established independent principalities in various parts of Persia. Many of these dynasties were short-lived; others lasted for a considerable period and were powerful kingdoms. For the next two centuries Persia was subject to the caliphs. But in 868 an adventurer named Soffar, who had been a pewterer and afterwards a bandit, gathered a native force and expelled the viceroys of the caliph, founding a dynasty known as the Soffarides. In the beginning of the tenth century Persia was divided between the families of Samani and Dilami, the first of which reigned over eastern Persia and Afghanistan, and the second over the rest of the country. Under these dynasties Persia fell beneath the yoke of the Seljuks, and was ruled by Togrul Beg, Alp Arslan, and Malek Shah, all of whom were conquerors greatly celebrated in oriental history. Their dynasty declined and perished in the twelfth century. After a long period of anarchy Persia was overrun and conquered by the Mongols led by Hulaku Khan, grandson of Yenghis (1258), who established the seat of his empire at Maragha in Azerbejan.

The next important event in the history of Persia was its conquest and devastation by Timur-Leng toward the end of the fourteenth century. Under his successors civil war prevailed almost continually, until in the beginning of the sixteenth century Ismail, a descendant of a famous saint, Sheik Suffi, founded the Suffavean dynasty. He died in 1523, and was succeeded by his son Tamasp, whose reign of fifty-three years was very prosperous. Abbas, who ascended the throne about 1587, was a still greater sovereign, though to his family he proved a sanguinary tyrant. After his death in 1628 the Suffavean dynasty gradually declined, and was at length overthrown by the Afghans, who conquered Persia in 1722, and ruled it for seven years with much tyranny, till they were expelled by the celebrated Nadir Shah, who ascended the throne in 1736. His reign was memorable for his success over foreign enemies and for his cruelty to his family and people. After his death in 1747 a series of revolutions occurred, and order was not fully restored till toward the close of the century, when Agha Mohammed, first of the reigning dynasty of Kadjars, became shah. His successors have been Feth-Ali (1797–1834), Mohammed (1835–48), and Nasr-ed-Din, who succeeded in 1848, being then 18 years old. Persia has been involved in three wars since the accession of this dynasty. Of these, two were with Russia, the first ending in 1813, and the second in 1828, both of them having been disastrous to Persia, which lost Georgia, Mingrelia, Erivan, Nakhitchevan, and the greater part of Talish, the Russian frontier being advanced to Mount Ararat and the left bank of the Aras; the third war was with Great Britain, and was begun in 1856 owing to a series of disputes between officials of the Persian Government and the British minister at Teheran. After repeated victories of the British troops in the south of Persia under Generals Outram and Havelock, it was terminated on 4 March, 1857, by a treaty signed at Paris, favourable to the demands of the British. In 1860 pestilence and famine devastated parts of the country; and a still greater famine in 1870 and 1871 is believed to have caused the death of two million persons. In the summer of 1873 Nasr-ed-Din made a tour through Europe, visiting Vienna, Paris, and London, and in 1878 visited Russia. In 1889 he again made a tour of Europe. As a ruler he was energetic and severe. He was largely under the influence of the Russian Court, though for a time after the failure of his attempt to restore the Persian dominion over Herat he maintained a somewhat friendly attitude toward Great Britain. He sternly repressed revolts and conspiracies, but, through the sale of the tobacco monopoly to English speculators, he offended many of his subjects, and his unpopularity was increased by the scarcity of food in several of the provinces in subsequent years. In 1896 he was assassinated as he was entering a shrine near Teheran, and was succeeded by his son, Muzaffer-ed-Din.

The new shah introduced several reforms in his kingdom, and, aided by twelve ministers, assumed personally the government of the empire. He visited Europe in 1900 and narrowly escaped assassination in Paris. He became very friendly with Russia, to whom his friendship proved beneficial. In 1905 a revolution took place in Persia in which royal princes and mullahs took part. They left the capital and took refuge at Khum, demanding reform and a parliamentary government. The shah hesitated at first, but finally decided to convoke a Majlis, 5 August, 1906. This was opposed by the court party, but Muzaffer-ed-Din succeeded in forcing upon the reactionaries the establishment of a parliament. On 4 January, 1907, he died and was succeeded by his son, Mohammed-Ali-Mirza (8 January, 1907), who from the very first day of his reign was involved in difficulties with the Parliament. He was unduly influenced by Russia, and was at times reluctant to conform with the demands of the Reform and Parliamentary party. Unrest and antagonism were everywhere visible, and the tension was such that a political revolution seemed impending. Meanwhile Parliament was several times suppressed and reconvoked; various provinces rebelled and Teheran was at one time in a state of siege. Finally Mohammed-Ali-Mirza was forced to abdicate (1909) and was succeeded by his son, Ahmed Mirza, a boy of twelve years.

Till 1906 the Government of Persia was an absolute monarchy. The shah was assisted by a grand vizier and several ministers. His will was absolute, and that of the *imams*, or priests, was paramount. To-day, however, it is divided into three departments, viz., the Court; the Ministerial Departments; and the National Assembly, or Parliament (Majlis). Theoretically, however, the shah is still the "king of kings" and the supreme ruler, executive, and counsellor in every department. The country is divided into five great *mamlikats*, or large provinces, viz., Azerbedjan, Farsistan, Ghilan, Khorasan, and Kirman (their corresponding capitals being: Tabriz, Shirza, Resht, Meshhed, and Kirman), and thirty vilayets, or smaller provinces. The present capital of the empire is Teheran. The Governorship of Azerbedjan is always given to the heir apparent, and the governors of the other provinces are appointed by the shah for a term of one year. In all large towns there are sub-governors and village masters. The latter are really the tax-collectors. The rate of taxation varies in different parts of the country. The tax on personal property is light, while the income tax is still lighter, being paid chiefly in kind. Justice is administered partly by the shah and partly by the courts and the *imams*.

Statistics.—The area of modern Persia is about 635,000 square miles, a large part being desert; the population is about 9,000,000, one-fourth of whom are nomads. The estimated population of the principal cities is: Teheran, 280,000; Tabriz, 200,000; Ispahan, 70,000; Meshhed, 60,000; Kirman, 60,000; and Yezd, 45,000. The principal imports, which amount yearly to about 450,000,000 krans (a kran is equivalent to 7 cents of U. S. A. money), are cotton fabrics, sugar, tea, woollens, petroleum, iron and steel goods, and the precious metals. The principal exports, which amount to about 400,000,000 krans annually, are fruits, carpets, cotton, fish, rice, silk and cocoons, rubber, wool, opium, hides and skins, copper, cereals, and living animals. The modern Persians are Mohammedans. Of these, nearly seven-eighths are Shiites, and only one-eighth Sunnites. Besides, there are about 9000 Parsis, or followers of Zoroaster, 40,000 Jews, 50,000 Armenians, 25,000 Nestorians, and 10,000 Chaldeans (Catholic). Concerning the religion of the ancient Persians, from the time of the Achæmenian dynasty down to the end of the Sassanian period, covering about twelve centuries (sixth cent. B. C.–seventh cent. A. D.), see ZOROASTRIANISM; the official religion of the medieval and modern Persians is Mohammedanism (q. v.).

II. PERSIAN LANGUAGE AND LITERATURE.—The term Persian, as applied both to the people and their language, has now a wider significance than it originally bore. A more appropriate term would be Iran or Iranian. The early inhabitants of Iran were Aryans, and their languages and dialects, for the last three or four thousand years, belong to the so-called Aryan family. Even the Persian language of to-day, notwithstanding the immense influence exercised upon it by Arabic, is still the lineal offspring of the language spoken by Cyrus, Darius, and the Sassanian kings. This continuity, however, is broken by two great gaps, occasioned by the Greek and Parthian invasions on the one hand, and by the Mohammedan domination on the other, viz., from 331 B. C.–A. D. 227; and 635 and the following years respectively.

The history of the Persian language falls, therefore, into three well-defined periods, as follows: *The Achæmenian Period* (550–331 B. C.), represented by the edicts and proclamations contained in the Persian cuneiform inscriptions, which, though of considerable extent, are similar in character and style and yield a vocabulary of about 400 words. The language represented by these inscriptions, deciphered by Grotefend, Sir H. Rawlinson, Hincks, Oppert, and others towards the middle of the last century, is generally called Old Persian. *The Sassanian Period* (A. D. 227–651), represented by inscriptions on monuments, medals, gems, seals, and coins, and by a literature estimated as equal in bulk to the Old Testament. This literature is entirely Zoroastrian and almost entirely theological and liturgical. The language in which it is written is little more than a very archaic form of the present language of Persia devoid of the Arabic element. It is generally known as Pahlavi, or Middle Persian. Properly speaking, the term Pahlavi applies rather to the script than the language. *The Mohammedan Period* (from about A. D. 900 until the present day), represented by the Persian language as it was spoken by the Persians after the Arab conquest, and after the adoption of the Mohammedan religion by the vast majority of the inhabitants of Persia. The difference between Late Pahlavi and the earliest form of Modern Persian was, save for the Arabic element generally contained in the latter, merely a difference of script. This is generally called Modern Persian, or Neo-Persian. Of Modern Persian there are many dialects spoken in different parts of Persia at the present day. The principal ones are those spoken in Mazandarán, Ghilan, and Talish in the north; Samnân in the northeast; Kashán, Quhrûd and Na'in in the centre, with the peculiar Gabri dialect spoken by the Zoroastrians inhabiting Yezd, Kirman, Rafsinján, etc. Siwand in the south; Luristan, Behbehân and Kurdistan in the west; and the Sistáni and Bakhtiyari idioms.

In Persian literature we recognize four epochs, comprising (1) The Old Persian cuneiform inscriptions of the Achæmenian kings. (2) The Avesta, the Sacred Books of the Zoroastrians, believed by many to date from Zoroaster's own time (about sixth cent. B. C.). (3) The Pahlavi literature, including the contemporary Sassanian inscriptions. (4) The Post-Mohammedan, or Modern Persian, literature of the last thousand years, which alone is usually called and understood as Persian literature. To this last may be added the large Arabic literature produced by Persians. The literature of the first period is very scanty, consisting mainly of the Achæmenian inscriptions written in the simplest form of the cuneiform script; principal among which is the famous trilingual inscription of Darius the Great (521–486 B. C.), engraved in the rock on Mount Behistun, near Hamadan, and memorable in the annals of Assyriology for furnishing scholars with the real clue for describing and interpreting the Assyro-Babylonian language and inscriptions (see ASSYRIA). Most of these Achæmenian inscriptions date from about the end of the sixth century B. C., although we have specimens as late as Artaxerxes Ochus (359–38 B. C.). Very similar to this Old Persian dialect is the language in which the Sacred Books of the Zoroastrians, generally but improperly called the Zend-Avesta, are written. This Zoroastrian, or Avestan, literature is theological and liturgical in character, and its production goes back perhaps to the sixth century B. C., although in its present form it includes many later accretions and redactions, mostly of post-Christian times and coinciding with the period of the Sassanian dynasty (see AVESTA). During the Parthian, or Arsacid dynasty, no literature was produced, except the few inscriptions and coins written in Greek.

The Pahlavi literature consists of inscriptions, coins, and several religious, legendary, historical, and literary productions. The inscriptions and the coins belong to the Sassanian dynasty, while the rest extends from their time till about the tenth century. Prof. West divides Pahlavi literature into three classes: (1) Pahlavi translations of Avesta texts, represented by twenty-seven works, estimated to contain about 141,000 words; (2) Pahlavi texts on religious subjects, represented by fifty-five works, estimated to contain an aggregate of about 446,000 words, mostly commentaries, prayers, traditions, admonitions, injunctions, pious sayings, etc.; (3) Pahlavi texts on non-religious subjects, represented by only eleven works, comprising in all about 41,000 words, but forming by far the most interesting part of Pahlavi literature, as they contain the record of the early legendary history of Iran and Persia, which forms the background of the great epic of Firdûsi, the "Shahnameh", or "Book of Kings".

The Modern, or Mohammedan, Persian literature extends from about the tenth century A. D. till our own days, and is by far the richest of the four. The rise, development, and progress of Modern Persian literature is intimately connected with the rise, development, and progress of Arabian, or Mohammedan, religious life and literature. The beginning of the ninth century may be said to be the starting-point of the modern national Persian independence and literature. The earliest writer of this period was a poet, Abbâs by name, who composed in A. D. 809 a poem in honour of the Abbasid Caliph, Ma mûn. Abbas's first poetical effort was improved upon by men like Hanzalah, Hakim Firuz, and Abu-Salik, who began to imitate the Arabic *qasîdah* form of poetical composition. These were soon followed by a dozen other poets who wrote some beautiful lyric and elegiac poetry. The earliest Persian prose writer was Bal'ami who, by order of Shah Mansûr I, translated into Persian, in 936, the Arabic universal history of Tábari (224–310 A. H.). Others translated Tábari's great "Commentary" on the Koran from Arabic into Persian. This was followed by Abu Mansûr Muwaffak's book on medicine and by the great philosopher, Avicenna (d. 1037), himself a Persian by birth, who wrote some of his works in Persian and some in Arabic. But the greatest of all Modern Persian poets, the forerunner and father of Modern Persian poetry, and the Homer of Persian epic— equal indeed in power of imagination, wealth of poetical descriptions, and elevated style to any old or modern poet—is Firdûsi (A. D. 940–1020), the author of the "Shahnameh" or "Book of Kings", on which the author laboured for thirty-five years. It is about eight times as long as the Iliad and contains a lengthy detailed description of all the historical and legendary wars, conquests, heroes, traditions, and customs of ancient and Sassanian Iran. Firdûsi had many imitators, such as the author of the "Garshaspnáma", 'Ali ibn Ahmad Asadi (about 1066), written in 9000 distichs; of the "Sámnáma", in which the heroic deeds of Rustem's grandfather are celebrated, and which equals in length the "Shahnameh" itself; the "Sa-'hanhírnáma", the "Farámurznáma", the "Bánú-Gusháshpnáma", the "Barsúnáma", the "Shahriyarnáma", the "Bahmannáma", the various "Iskandarnámas", the "Bustani-Khayâl" (a romance in fifteen volumes), the "Anbiyánáma" and many other epopees, all written within the period A. D. 1066–1150.

During the last four or five centuries, several other epic writers flourished in Persia such as Mu'in Almiskin (d. 1501), who wrote in prose the epic of Hatim Tay, the celebrated Arabian chief; Hatifi (d. 1521), the author of "Timurnáma", or the epic of Tamerlane; Kasimi (d. about 1561), Kamali of Sabawar, Ishrâfi, and the authors of the "Shahinshahnáma" and the "Georgenáma". Romantic fiction was also cultivated with success by such writers as Nizami of Ganja (1141–1203), 'Am'ak of Bokhara (d. 1149), author of the romance of Yusuf and Zuleikha, Jam'i (d. 1492), Mauji Kasim Khan (d. 1571), Nazim of Herat (d. 1670), and Shaukat, Governor of Shiraz, who flourished towards the beginning of the nineteenth century. The best known Persian writers of encomium and satire are: Abul-Faraj Runi, Mas'ûd ibn Sa'd ibn Salmân (about 1085), Adib Sabir (about 1145), Jauhari, Amir Mu'izzi (d. 1147), Rashid Watwat (d. 1172), Abd-Alwasi Jabali, Hasan Ghaznavi (d. 1169), Auhad-Uddin Anwarí (d. about 1196), Suzani of Samarkand (d. 1174) and his contemporaries, Abu-Ali Shatranji, Lami' of Bokhara, Khakáni (d. 1199), the greatest rival of Anwari, Ubaid Zakani (d. 1370), Mujir-Uddin Bailakani (d. 1198), Zahir Fairabi (d. 1202), Athir Akhsikati (d. 1211), Kamal-uddin Isfahani (d. 1237), and Saif-uddin Isfarangi (d. 1267).

Didactic and mystic poetry was very successfully cultivated by several Persian poets, principal among whom are Sheikh Abu Sa'îd ibn Abu-l-Khair of Khorasan (968–1049), the contemporary of Firdûsi and the inventor of the ruba'i, or quatrain, form of poetical composition; Omar Khayyám, the famous astronomer and the celebrated author of the Rubáiyát, made famous by Fitzgerald's translation, Afdaluddin Kashi (d. 1307), Násir ibn Khosrau (d. about 1325), 'Ali ibn 'Uthmân al-jullâbi (d. about 1342), Hakim Sana'i of Ghanza (about 1130), Jelal-uddin Rumi (1207–73), "the most uncompromising Sufic follower, and the greatest pantheistic writer of all ages", Farîd-uddin 'Attaŕ (d. 1230), and many others. But the greatest and most moderate of all Persian Sufic poets was Sa'di (d. about 1292), "whose two best-known works, the 'Bustân', or 'Fruit-garden', and the 'Gulistân', or 'Rose-garden', owe their great popularity both in the East and the West to the purity of their spiritual thoughts, their sparkling wit, charming style, and the very moderate use of mystic theories". Later didactic and mystic poets are Nizari (d. 1320), Kátibi (d. 1434), Hairati (d. 1554), Iami' (d. 1487), Sana'i, Iraki (d. about 1309), Ḥusaini (d. 1318), Maḥmud Shabistari (d. 1320), Auḥadi (d. 1338), Kasim Ánvâr (d. 1434), Ahlí of Shiraz (d. 1489), Hilali (d. 1532), Baha'-uddin 'Âmili (d. 1621), and many others. Like the Arabs, the Persians cultivated with immense success lyric poetry and the description and idealization of the pleasures of love, of women, of wine, and of the beauties of nature. The prince of these lyric poets is Hâfiz (d. 1389). He had many imitators, such as Salmán of Sáwa (d. about 1377), Kamâl Khujandi, Muhammed Shirin Maghribi (d. 1406), Ni'mat-ullah Wali (d. 1431), Kasimi-Anwâr, Amir Shâhi (1453), Banna'i (d. 1512), Baba Fighani of Shirâz (d. 1519), Nargisi (d. 1531), Lisâni (d. 1534), Ahlî of Shiraz (d. 1535), Nau'i (d. 1610), and innumerable others who strove, more or less successfully, to imitate Hâfiz as well as Iamí and Nizámi. To more recent date belong the poets Zulali (d. 1592), Sa'ib (d. 1677), and Hatif of Isfahân (d. about 1785).

Persian literature is not very rich in historical and theological works, and even the comparatively small number of these is generally based on Arabic Mohammedan historical and theological productions. Finally, it must not be forgotten that from about the eighth or ninth century A. D. till about the fifteenth some of the greatest Mohammedan theologians, historians, philosophers, grammarians, lexicographers, and philologists, who wrote in Arabic, were of Persian origin. It must also be noted that owing to the constant and intimate social, political, literary, and religious intercourse between Arabs and Persians, especially during the Abbasid dynasty, Modern Persian, especially in its vocabulary, has been very extensively affected by Arabic, so much so that a perfect knowledge of Modern Persian is impossible without the knowledge of Arabic. Persian, also, in its turn, especially during the last four or five centuries, has very perceptibly affected the Turkish language.

III. CHRISTIANITY IN PERSIA.—A. *From the Apostolic Age to the Thirteenth Century*.—The beginning of Christianity in Persia may well be connected with what we read in Acts (ch. ii, v. 9) viz., that on the Day of Pentecost there were at Jerusalem "Parthians, and Medes, and Elamites, and inhabitants of Mesopotamia". These, doubtless, on their return home, announced to their countrymen the appearance of the new religion. Early ecclesiastical traditions, furthermore, both foreign and local, tenaciously maintain that Peter and Thomas preached the Gospel to the Parthians; that Thaddæus, Bartholomew, and Addeus, of the Seventy, evangelized the races of Mesopotamia and Persia, and that Mari, a noble Persian convert, succeeded Addai (Addeus) in the government of the Persian Christian communities. He is said to have been succeeded by the bishops Abrês, Abraham, Jacob, Ahadabuhi, Tomarsa, Shahlufa, and Papa, which brings us down to the end of the third century. When we read in later Syriac documents that towards the beginning of the third century the Christians in the Persian empire had some three hundred and sixty churches, and many martyrs, it is not difficult to imagine even if we discount the many legendary elements in these traditions, how vigorous and how successful the early Christian propaganda must have been in those distant regions.

Owing to the toleration of the Parthian Kings, Christianity kept slowly but steadily advancing in various parts of the empire. With the advent of the Sassanian dynasty, however (A. D. 226–641), Christianity was often subjected to very severe trials. Its chief opponents were the Zoroastrian Magi and priestly schools, as well as the numerous Jews scattered through the empire. The Sassanian kings in general espoused the cause of Zoroastrianism, which under them became once more the official religion; and, though some of this dynasty favoured Christianity, the national feeling always clung to the ancient creed. Many thousands of Persians embraced Christianity, but Persia remained the stronghold of Zoroastrianism, and there never arose an indigenous Persian Church, worshipping in the Persian language and leavening the whole nation. The Persian Church was of Syrian origin, traditions, and tendencies, and, for about three centuries, regarded Antioch as the centre of its faith and the seat of authority. When the Christian religion was accepted by Constantine (A. D. 312), it was naturally regarded by the Persian emperors as the religion of their rivals, the Romans. Religious and national feeling thus united against it, and bitter persecutions continued in Persia for a century after they had ceased in the Roman Empire. Some of these persecutions—notably that under Sapor II—were as terrible as any which the Christians of the West had experienced under the Emperor Diocletian.

Notwithstanding these obstacles, the Christian religion kept steadily growing. Towards the beginning of the fourth century the head of the Persian Church selected the city of Seleucia-Ctesiphon, the capital of the empire, for his metropolitan see. Under his jurisdiction were several bishops, one of whom, John by name, was present at the Council of Nicæa (325). In 410, a synod of Christians was held at the Persian capital. In 420 there were metropolitans at Merv and Herat. King Yezdegerd himself sent the Patriarch of the Persian Church on a mission to the Roman emperor. Between 450 and 500 the Nestorians, persecuted in the Roman Empire, fled to Persia for protection, and in 498 the whole Persian Church declared in favour of Nestorianism. Henceforth the history of Christianity in Persia is their history. In the next two centuries the Persian Church kept steadily increasing till it rivalled, and perhaps surpassed, in extent, power, and wealth any other national Christian Church; having a hierarchy of two hundred and thirty bishops, scattered over Assyria, Babylonia, Chaldea, Arabia, Media, Khorasan, Persia proper, the very deserts of Turkestan, the Oasis of Merv, both shores of the Persian Gulf, and even beyond it, in the Islands of Socotra, and Ceylon, through the coasts of Malabar, and at last China and Tatary. Mgr Duchesne rightly observes that "the dominion of the 'Catholicos' of Seleucia was of no mean dimensions, and by the extension of his jurisdiction this high ecclesiastical dignitary figures in the same light as the greatest of the Byzantine patriarchs. We might almost go further and say that, inasmuch as we can compare the Persian Empire to the Roman, the Persian Church may be compared to the Church of the great western Power" ("The Churches Separated from Rome", tr. Mathew, New York, 1907, p. 16).

The history of Christianity in the Sassanian empire shows that there has been a very active and successful propaganda among the Iranians. We read of Christians among the landlord class about Mosul and in the mountain region east of that city. Some of the Christians were of high rank. The last Chosroes was killed in an insurrection headed by a Christian whose father had been the chief financial officer of the realm. Some of the patriarchs of the Nestorian Church were converts, or sons of converts, from Magianism. While numerous, however, the Persian Christians were not organized into a national Church. There were certain differences between them and the Nestorians farther west, and these differences were the beginnings of ecclesiastical independence, but the patriarchs asserted their authority in the end. Syriac was the ecclesiastical and theological language and even in Persia proper there was at most a very scanty Christian literature; even the Scriptures had not been translated into the vernacular.

It is clear that Christianity was widely diffused in Persia, that in some localities the Christians were very numerous, and that the Christian religion continued to spread after the rise of Mohammedanism. The two forces which had most to do with this spread of Christianity were commerce and monasticism. Christian merchants had a share in the wholesale trade of Asia: trade with India opened the way for the early introduction of Christianity there, and the hold which Christianity acquired on the shores of the Persian Gulf was probably due to the Indian and Arabian trade routes. The strong rule of the early Abbasid caliphs gave opportunity for the development of commerce. The position of the Christians at the capital as bankers and merchants would give them a share in this trade. Christian artisans, including goldsmiths and jewellers, would find employment in the large cities. In his account of the mission of the Nestorian monks, Thomas of Marga relates that the Patriarch Timothy sent his missionary with a company of merchants who were journeying together to Mugan (the plain of Mugan?) on the River Aras (Araxes).

Monasticism was imported into Mesopotamia in the fourth century by monks from Egypt. The legendary account of Mar Awgin, or St. Eugenius, relates that his monastery near Nisibis contained three hundred and fifty monks, while seventy-two of his disciples established each a monastery. The number of monasteries increased rapidly in the fourth and fifth centuries. In the sixth century there was a movement in the Nestorian Church against the enforced celibacy of the higher clergy and against celibate monks, but celibacy won the day, and monasticism was firmly established. The monks must have been numbered by hundreds, if not thousands, for, in addition to the numerous monasteries in Mesopotamia and the regions north of the Tigris, there were scattered monasteries in Persia and Armenia. Besides the cenobites, living in large communities, there were numerous solitaries living in caves or rude huts. These were influential enough among the Qatrayi, on the Persian Gulf, to call for a separate letter from the Patriarch Ishuyabh I. Some of these monks must have been full of real missionary zeal, although of course the prevailing and distinctive spirit of their institute was contemplative rather than missionary.

Yet, in spite of all, Christianity failed, and Islam succeeded in gaining the Iranian race. This failure of Christianity was not wholly due to the success of Islam: internal dissensions, ambition, dishonesty, and corruption among the clergy greatly contributed to the gradual dissolution of this wonderful Church. Under the Arabs, the Christians of Persia were not in wholly unfavourable circumstances. Indeed, the first two centuries of Mohammedan domination, especially under the Abbassids, were the most glorious period in the history of the Persian Church. It is true that at times the Christians were liable to excessive exactions and to persecutions, but they were recognized as the People of the Book; and the Nestorians were especially privileged, and held many offices of trust. The missionary work was carried on and extended. It could not take much root in Persian soil after the Persians became Moslems, but it gained more and more influence in Tatary and China, beyond the limits of Mohammedan conquest. This was a period of comparative peace in those regions, and of the greatest missionary zeal and enterprise on the part of the Nestorians, who planted churches in Transoxiana as far as Kashgar, in the regions of Mongolia, and throughout Northern China. To attest this fact there are extensive Christian graveyards containing memorials of the Turkish race on the borders of China, and the monument of Si-ngan-fu, in Shensi, giving the history of the Nestorian Mission in China for 145 years (A. D. 636–781). Timotheus, a patriarch of the Church for forty years, was zealously devoted to missionary work, and many monks traversed Asia. In the eleventh and twelfth centuries there were large Christianized communities. A Mogul prince, Unkh Khan, gave the name to the celebrated Prester John, and his successors were nominal Christians till overthrown by Jenghis Khan. The names of twenty-five metropolitan sees, from Cyprus in the west to Pekin in the east, are recorded, and their schools were spread far and wide through Western and parts of Central Asia.

B. *From Jenghis Khan to the Present Time.*—The last of the race of Christian kings—probably Christian only in name—was slain by Jenghis Khan about A. D. 1202. Jenghis had a Christian wife, the daughter of this king, and he was tolerant towards the Christian faith. In fact the Mogul conquerors were without much religion, and friendly towards all creeds. The wave of carnage and conquest swept westward, covered Persia, and overwhelmed the Caliph of Bagdad in 1258. This change was for a time favourable to Christianity, as the rulers openly declared themselves Christians or were partial to Christianity. The patriarch of the Nestorians was chosen from people of the same language and race as the conquerors; he was a native of Western China; he ruled the Church through a stormy period of seven reigns of Mogul kings, had the joy of baptizing some of them, and for a time hoped that they would form such an alliance with the Christians of Europe against the Mohammedans as should open all Asia, as far as China, to Christianity. This hope did not last long; it ended in a threat of ruin: the Nestorians were too degraded, ignorant, and superstitious to avail themselves of their opportunity. After a time of vacillation the Moguls found Mohammedanism better suited to their rough and bloody work. The emperor, having decided, flung his sword into the scale, and at his back were 100,000 warriors. The whole structure of the Nestorian Church, unequal to the trial, crumbled under the persecutions and wars of the Tatars. With Timur-Leng (A. D. 1379–1405) came their utter ruin. He was a bigoted Moslem, and put to the sword all who did not escape to the recesses of the mountains. Thus did Central Asia, once open to Christian missions, see the utter extermination of the Christians, not a trace of them being left east of the Kurdish Mountains. The Christian faith was thrown back upon its last defences in the West, where hunted and despised, its feeble remnant of adherents continued to retain, as it were, a death-grip on their churches and worship.

During the last five centuries Christianity has been simply a tolerated but oppressed and despised faith in Persia. From the invasions of Timur-Leng until the accession of Abbas the Great (1582), a period of two hundred years, its history is almost a blank. In 1603 some Armenian chiefs appealed to Shah Abbas for protection against the Turks: he invaded Armenia, and in the midst of the war decided to devastate it, that the Turks might be without provisions. From Kars to Bayazid the Armenians were driven before the Persian soldiery to the banks of the Aras, near Julfa. Their cities and villages were depopulated. From every place of concealment they were driven forth. Convents were plundered, and their inmates driven out. The captives were forced to cross the Aras without proper transports. Many women and children, sick and aged, were carried away by the swift current. Two chiefs were beheaded to hasten the progress. Women were carried off to Persian harems. Through unfrequented paths, and with untold hardships, they reached their destinations. The principal colony, five thousand souls, was settled at New Julfa, near Ispahan, where they were granted many privileges. Both Armenians and Georgians were scattered through Central Persia, and some of their descendants are villagers in the Bakhtiyari country. A colony of seven thousand was planted at Ashraf, in Mezanderan, where malaria destroyed the greater portion of them; the remnant were restored to Armenia in the reign of Safi Shah. The colony at Julfa (now known as Tulfa, on the River Zendeh) prospered greatly and became very wealthy by trade and the arts.

Under the Safavean kings, the Christians of Azarbedjan and Transcaucasia suffered much from the wars of the Turks and Persians. Both banks of the Arras were generally in the hands of the Persians. Some of the shahs were tolerant, and the Christians prospered; some overtaxed them. The last, Shah Sultan Husain, oppressed them: he repealed the law of retaliation, whereby a Christian could exact equivalent punishment from a Mussulman criminal; he enacted that the price of a Christian's blood should be the payment of a load of grain. Julfa was subjected to great suffering at the time of the invasion of the Afghan Mahmud. It was captured, and a ransom of seventy thousand tomans and fifty of the fairest and best-born maidens exacted. The grief of the Armenians was so heartrending that many of the Afghans were moved to pity and returned the captives. When Mahmud subsequently became a maniac the Armenian priests were called in to pray over him and exorcise the evil spirit. Nadir Shah continued to oppress the Armenians, ostracized them, and interdicted their worship. On this account many emigrated to India, Bagdad, and Georgia. About eighty villages remained between Hamadan and Ispahan. Under the Kajar dynasty the state of the Christians is better known. Notices of them abound in the narrations of travellers of the period. Agha Mohammed, founder of the Kajar dynasty, sacked Tiflis and transported many Georgians into Persia. Others went to Russia. Their descendants, mostly Mohammedans, are frequently met occupying high positions in the Government.

At the time of the Russian war, early in the nineteenth century, nine thousand families of Armenians and many Nestorians emigrated from Azarbedjan. Some were induced to come back by Abbas Mirza, under the protection of the English. Those in Tabriz were exempted from taxes and had the right to appeal to the British consul. This right of protection was afterwards withdrawn, and finally, after many vain protests on the part of the Armenians, the exemption from taxes was annulled in A. D. 1894. The condition of Christians in Persia under Nasred-Din and his successors, down to the present time, will be described in the following section.

C. *Catholic Missions.*—The history of Catholic missions in Persia is intimately connected with the various attempts made by the Nestorians, in the last nine centuries, to join the Catholic Church. In some cases, these movements were the results of efforts made by the early Franciscan and Dominican, and, after them, the Jesuit missionaries. In 1233 the Nestorian catholicos, Sabarjesus, sent to Pope Gregory IX an orthodox profession of faith and was admitted to union with the Church of Rome. The same was done, in 1304, by Jabalaha (1281–1317) during the pontificate of Benedict XI. In 1439 Timotheus, Nestorian

Metropolitan of Tarsus and Cyprus, renounced Nestorianism, and in 1553 the patriarch John Sulaka visited Rome and submitted to Pope Julius III his profession of faith, as a result of which several thousand Nestorians of Persia became Catholics. His successor, Ebedjesus, followed his example, visited Rome, and assisted at the last (twenty-fifth) session of the Council of Trent. In 1582 Simeon Denha was elected patriarch of the converted Nestorians, henceforth called simply Chaldeans, and, owing to Turkish persecution, he transferred the patriarchal see to Urumiah in Persia. Shortly afterwards, he received the pallium from Gregory XIII through Laurent Abel, Bishop of Sidon, who was commissioned by the pope to investigate the condition of the various churches of the East. Mar Denha's successors, Simeon VIII, IX, X, XI, and XII, all remained faithful to Rome, and fixed their patriarchal see at Urumiah and Khosrowa; Simeon IX, in fact, in a letter to Pope Innocent X, informs him that the Nestorian Uniats, or Chaldeans, under his patriarchal jurisdiction numbered some 200,000 souls. Simeon XI sent his profession of faith to Alexander VII (elected 1653); and Simeon XII, to Clement X (1670). From 1670 to 1770 the relations between the Nestorian patriarchs and Rome were suspended.

But in 1770 one of the successors of Simeon XII addressed a letter to Pope Clement XIV in which he expresses his intention of resuming once more orthodox and friendly relations with Rome. The successors of this patriarch, however, completely severed their relations with Rome, and transferred their patriarchal residence from Urumiah to Kotchanes, in Kurdistan, which became thenceforward the see of the Nestorian patriarchs. Meanwhile, the many thousand Nestorian Uniats, or Chaldeans, who remained faithful to the Catholic Faith selected for themselves an independent Catholic patriarch, who was confirmed with all the patriarchal privileges by Innocent XI on 20 May, 1681. To his successor, Joseph I, was given the title of "Patriarch of Babylon", i. e. of Seleucia-Ctesiphon, the ancient patriarchal see of the Nestorian Church. In 1695 he resigned and went to Rome, where he shortly afterwards died. His successors were Joseph II, III, IV, V, and VI, all belonging to the same family of Mar Denha. They governed the Chaldean Church during the eighteenth century, and their patriarchal residence was transferred from Persia to Mesopotamia—to Diarbekir, Mosul, and Amida successively.

Beginning with the early years of this century, several Capuchin (1725) and Dominican (1750) missionaries were sent to Mosul, and through their efforts and zeal all traces of Nestorianism disappeared from the Chaldean Church in Mesopotamia. After the death of Joseph VI the Congregation of Propaganda decreed that henceforth but one Chaldean patriarch should be acknowledged. Leo XII confirmed the decree, and Pius VIII put it into execution, 5 July, 1830, by creating Mar Hanna (Yuhanna Hormuz) the sole and only legitimate patriarch of the Chaldeans. He transferred his patriarchal see from Diarbekir to Bagdad, where he died in 1838. His successor, Isaiade Yakob, who resided at Khosrowa, near Salamas, in Persia, resigned in 1845, and was succeeded, in 1848, by Joseph Audo, who died in 1878, and was succeeded by Elia Abbolionan, who died in 1894 and was succeeded by Ebedjesus Khayyat, after whose death at Bagdad, in 1899, the patriarchal dignity was conferred in 1900 upon the present incumbent, Joseph Emanuel. The official title and residence of the Chaldean patriarchs is that of Babylon, but for administrative reasons they reside at Mosul, from which centre they govern 5 archdioceses and 10 dioceses, containing 100,000 souls.

The history of European Catholic missions in Persia dates from the time of the Mongolian rule, in the thirteenth and fourteenth centuries, when several embassies of Dominicans and Franciscans were sent by the popes to the Mongol rulers both in Central Asia and in Persia; and although their noble efforts brought no permanent results, they paved the way for future and more successful Catholic propaganda. In the early part of the seventeenth century, political aims led the kings of Persia to contract friendly relations with Europe. This gave a new impetus to Catholic missionary enterprise, and Carmelite, Minorite, and Jesuit missionaries were well received by Shah Abbas the Great, who allowed them to establish missionary stations all through his dominion. Ispahan was made the centre, and several thousand Nestorians returned to the Catholic Church. These missionaries were soon followed by Augustinians and Capuchins, who enlarged their missionary field, extending it to Armenians and Mohammedans as well. The most distinguished of these missionaries was Father de Rhodes of Avignon, the Francis Xavier of Persia, who became the best beloved man in Ispahan. On his death in 1646 the shah himself, with his court and nobles, as well as the largest part of the population of Ispahan, attended his funeral. He was called by them "The Saint". After his death, the city of Ispahan was created an episcopal see, the first incumbent of which was the Carmelite Thaddeus. Under Nadir Shah and Shah Sultan Husain, however, the tide turned again, and persecution followed. The missionaries were forced to flee, and thousands of Christians were compelled either to migrate or to apostatize. This was in the early part of the eighteenth century. A hundred years later missionary work recommenced, and thousands of Nestorians were converted to the Catholic Faith.

The second epoch of Catholic missionary work in Persia was begun in 1840 by the Lazarists, in consequence of the representations of Eugene Boré, a French savant and a fervent Catholic, who in 1838 was sent to Persia on a scientific mission by the French Academy and the Minister of Public Instruction. He himself founded four schools, two in Tabriz and Ispahan for the Armenians, and two in Urumiah and Salamas for the Chaldeans. Condescending to his advice and instructions, the Congregation of Propaganda confided the establishment of the new mission to the Lazarists, who were joined later on by the French Sisters of Charity. The first Lazarist missionary was Father Fornier, who arrived at Tabriz in 1840 as prefect Apostolic. He was joined in the following year by two other fathers of the same society, Darnis and Cluzel, who took immediate charge of the school founded by M. Boré and already attended by sixty pupils. Two years later, yielding to strong opposition on the part of the schismatical Armenian clergy, Darnis left Tabriz and established himself at Urumiah, while Cluzel remained at Ispahan, and Fornier in Tabriz. Cluzel was soon afterwards joined by Darnis in Urumiah, the latter having left the school at Ispahan in charge of Giovanni Derderian, a most zealous Armenian Catholic priest who was subsequently elected bishop of that see, but did not live to receive consecration.

On arriving at Urumiah, the first Lazarists found the American Protestant missionaries already well established in that city, but soon outstripped them in influence and zeal, as is shown by the fact that within two years the number of pupils in the Catholic school increased from 200 to over 400, with two churches, one in Urumiah and the other in Ardishai, the most populous village in the vicinity of Urumiah. Here again the Catholic missionaries were persecuted; owing to the intrigues of the Russian consul and the opposition of the Nestorians, they were compelled to leave their stations, while a fourth Lazarite, Father Rouge, had meanwhile arrived and established a new mission at Khosrowa. With the establishment, however, of a new French representative at the Persian Court, M. de Sartiges, the Lazarists were permitted by the Persian Government to continue their work unmolested, Father Cluzel having become a great favourite with Mirza Aghasi, the prime minister. In 1863, Father Rouge died at Urumiah and was succeeded by a native Chaldean priest, Father Dbigoulim, who had joined the Lazarist Order. In 1852, Father Varèse was sent to Urumiah, and in 1856 was followed by eight French Sisters of Charity. Meanwhile, Mgr Trioche, Apostolic Delegate of Mesopotamia, sent Dom Valerga (afterwards Latin Patriarch of Jerusalem) to Khosrowa, where he built a magnificent stone church. Darnis and Cluzel soon afterwards established there a seminary to train indigenous candidates for the priesthood, teaching them Latin, French, Syriac, and Armenian, as well as theology.

Some of the seminarians became secular priests, others joined the Lazarists, among the latter being Dbigoulim, Paul Bedjan now residing in Belgium, and famous in the scientific world for his admirable edition of some twenty-five volumes of Syriac texts and literature, and Dilou Solomon. In 1852, Father Terral, a new arrival, took charge of the seminary and a few years later became superior of the mission. Besides the seminary, two other colleges were opened, one for boys, the other for girls, the latter under the care and direction of the newly-arrived Sisters of Charity. To these were soon added one hospital and one orphan asylum, where all—Mohammedans, Nestorians, Armenians, and Catholics—were gratuitously admitted and cared for. This splendid work evoked the admiration of Shah Nasr-ed-Din himself, and he contributed a yearly allowance of 200 tomans ($400) towards the maintenance of the two institutions. Soon after, two more hospitals were opened, one at Urumiah and one at Khosrowa. In 1858 Father Darnis died at the age of forty-four, and in his place several new missionaries were sent. In 1862 the Lazarists established themselves permanently at Teheran under the able direction of Fathers Varèse and Plagnard, who soon built there a church and a mission house around which the European colony of Teheran gathered, and which soon afterwards became the most beautiful residential section of the Persian capital. In 1874 the Sisters of Charity established themselves at Teheran with a house, a hospital, and two schools.

The crowning event in the history of Catholic missions in Persia, however, took place in 1872, when the Prefecture Apostolic of Persia was raised to the dignity of an Apostolic Delegation, with Mgr Cluzel as its first incumbent. In 1874 he was consecrated, in Paris, Archbishop of Heraclea, and assumed the functions of Apostolic Delegate of Persia and Administrator of the Diocese of Ispahan, thus withdrawing the Persian Mission from the jurisdiction of the Apostolic Delegation of Mesopotamia. On his arrival in Persia, Mgr Cluzel was immediately acknowledged by the shah, decorated with the insignia of the Lion and Sun, and officially confirmed, by a special imperial firman, as the representative of the Father of the Faithful. During the seven years of his episcopal activity in Persia, the Lazarist mission made wonderful progress with the Chaldeans and Nestorians. A great cathedral was built at Urumiah, and many new schools were opened in the neighbouring villages. Mgr Cluzel died in 1882 and was succeeded by Mgr Thomas, who built a preparatory school for the seminary of Khosrowa and successfully introduced celibacy among the native Catholic Chaldean clergy. Ill-health, however, compelled him to retire, and he was succeeded by Mgr Montety, who also had to resign for the same reason, and was succeeded, in 1896, by the present delegate Apostolic, Mgr Lesné, titular Archbishop of Philippopoli. Under his able administration, the Catholic mission has made further progress, extending its beneficial work far beyond the limits of Persia proper, into Sina, the Taurus mountains, and the regions of Persian Kurdistan and Armenia.

The latest statistics are as follows: Catholics of the Latin Rite, 350; Catholic Chaldeans, about 8000, with 52 native priests and 3 dioceses; Nestorians, about 35,000; Catholic Armenians, about 700, with 5 priests; Protestants, about 5000.—Catholic missions: Lazarist Fathers, 19, with 5 mission stations; churches and chapels, 48; seminaries, 2, with 17 students; schools, 55, with 800 pupils; hospitals, 3; religious houses, 3—2 for men, with 18 religious, and 1 for women, with 37 sisters.

D. *Non-Catholic Missions.*—The earliest Protestant missionaries in Persia were Moravians who in 1747 came to evangelize the Guebers, but owing to political disturbances were compelled to withdraw. The next missioner was Henry Martin, a chaplain in the British army in India, who, in 1811, went to Persia and remained at Shiraz but eleven months, having completed there, in 1812, his Persian translation of the New Testament. After many trials and much opposition, especially from the Mohammedan mullahs, or priests, he was forced to leave the country, and died at Tokat, in Asia Minor, on his way back to England. The next labourer was a German, the Rev. C. G. Pfander, of the Basle Missionary Society, who visited Persia in 1829; after some years of fruitless labour in Kirmanshah and Georgia he too had to leave the country, and died in 1869 at Constantinople. He is well known for his book "Mizan-ul-Hakk" (The Balance of Truth), in which he points out the superiority of Christianity over Mohammedanism. In 1833 another German missionary, the Rev. Frederic Haas, with some colleagues, being forced to leave Russia, entered Persia and for a time made their headquarters at Tabriz; but they also had to leave the country. In 1838, the Rev. W. Glen, a Scottish missionary, entered Persia and spent four years at Tabriz and Teheran, occupied mainly in completing and revising his own Persian translation of the Old Testament. The work of all these missions was principally directed to the conversion of Mohammedans and was therefore, as such attempts have generally proved, a complete failure.

The first organized Protestant missionary attempt among the Nestorian Christians of Persia took place in 1834, when the American Board of Commissioners of Foreign Missions (Congregational) commissioned Justin Perkins and his wife, and Asahel Grant (1835) and his wife to establish a mission among the Persian Nestorians. Between 1834 and 1871 some fifty-two missionaries, we are told, were sent by the A. B. C. F. M. into Persia. Among these American missionaries were several physicians who, by ministering gratuitously to the poor Nestorians, made some progress. In 1870 the work of the A. B. C. F. M. was transferred to the Board of Missions of the American Presbyterian Church, and the mission was divided into those of Eastern and Western Persia, the former including Tabriz, Teheran, Hamadan, Resth, Kazwin, and Kirmanshah; the latter, the Province of Azarbedjan (Urumiah, Khosrowa) and parts of Kurdistan, Caucasus, and Armenia. The work has been, and still is, more of a humanitarian and semi-educational character than moral or religious. About $600,000 was expended on this mission between 1834 and 1870, a larger amount between 1870 and 1890, and about one million dollars from 1890 to the present time, i. e., over two million dollars altogether. Yet it is extremely doubtful whether any results commensurate with this vast expenditure have been accomplished. The latest statistics (1909) are as follows: Missionaries, 37 (including 6 male and 3 female physicians); 35 native ministers; 7000 adherents; 3000 communicants; 2692 pupils distributed among 62 schools; 4 hospitals. The Church Missionary Society, established in 1869, has stations in Kirman, Yezd, Shiraz, and at Ispahan. The work is mainly medical and educational. The statistics are: 33 missionaries, including 4 male and 5 female physicians; native clergy, 1; native teachers, 28; Christians, 412; communicants, 189; schools, 8, with 409 scholars; hospitals, 6. The British and Foreign Bible Society also does an extensive work in Southern Persia.

The greatest competitor of the two above-mentioned missionary societies is the Anglican mission known as "The Assyrian Mission", which was established in 1884 by Archbishop Benson of Canterbury with headquarters at Urumiah and Kotchanes, the seat of the Nestorian patriarch, and having for its principal aim the union of the Nestorian with the Anglican Church. It is interesting to read an estimate of the work of this mission from the pen of an American Presbyterian missioner: it repudiates the name *Protestant*, and has for its avowed object the strengthening of the Nestorian Church to resist Catholic influences on the one hand and Protestant on the other. It has a strong force of missionaries, who wear the garb of their order, and are under temporary vows of celibacy and obedience. Its present statistics are: missionaries, 2; schools, 30, with 470 scholars, besides 12 distinctly Nestorian schools in various sections of Kurdistan. This mission originated in 1842, when "Archbishop Howley, with the assistance of the Society for the Propagation of the Gospel, sent the Rev. G. P. Badger to Mosul, to begin work among the mountain Nestorians. Just at that time the Kurdish sheikh, Berd Khan, was raging in the mountains of Kurdistan. The general confusion and disorder were such that Badger had to return in despair to England within a year" (Richter, "History of Protestant Missions in the Near East", 1910). Thirty-four years later the Rev. E. L. Cutts was sent to Kurdistan, but left within a year. The Scandinavian Wahl, however, remained for five years (1880–85) in the heart of Kurdistan amidst great privations. After the organization of "The Assyrian Mission", in 1886, one of its missionaries settled at Kotchhannes, some 7000 feet above sea-level, while its headquarters were established at Urumiah.

Many other small Protestant enterprises have lately sprung up in Persia, especially at Urumiah. The United Lutheran Church of America maintains a few *kashas* (Nestorian priests), and in 1905, sent an American missionary, the Rev. Mr. Fossum, to superintend the work. A Syrian congregation at Urumiah, having left the Russian Church, has joined this mission. The Swedish-American "Augustana Synode" employs a *kasha*, who conducts two day-schools. The Evangelical Association for the Advancement of the Nestorian Church, founded at Berlin in 1906, employs a *kasha* who has had a Lutheran training in Germany. He co-operates to some degree with the Anglicans, and has added a fourth to the already existing mission printing establishments at Urumiah. For ten years Dr. Lepsius's German "Orientmission" maintained outside Urumiah an orphanage for Syrian fugitives from the mountains, but it is to be closed soon. The English Plymouth Brethren employ three or four *kashas* in the "Awishalum" Mission, named after the chief representative of the mission in Persia, Awishalum [Absolom] Seyad. There are also small missions connected with the American Dunkards, the Holiness Methodists, the American Southern Baptists and Northern Baptists, and the English Congregationalists.

The latest non-Catholic missionary enterprise in Persia was that of the Russians, in 1898. The aim of this mission is more political than educational or religious, and the extraordinary readiness with which several thousand Nestorians flocked to the Russian Orthodox Church is explained by the fact that the Nestorians were very anxious for foreign protection against the tyranny of Persia and Turkey.

I. HISTORY, ETC.—MASPERO, *The Passing of Empires* (London, 1899); DIEULAFOY, *La Perse, la Chaldée, et la Susiane* (Paris, 1889); BENJAMIN, *Persia and the Persians* (Boston, 1887); RAWLINSON, *The Sixth and Seventh Great Monarchies of the Ancient Eastern World* (London, 1886); DE RAGOZIN, *History of Media* (London, 1802); BENJAMIN, *History of Persia* (London, 1892); RAWLINSON, *History of Parthia* (London, 1890) (these three in the *History of the Nations* series); MALCOLM, *History of Persia* (London, 1829); BARBIER DE MEYNARD, *Dictionnaire géographique, historique et littéraire de la Perse* (Paris, 1861); WATSON, *History of Persia from the Beginning of the Nineteenth Century* (London, 1873); PIGGOT, *Persia, Ancient and Modern* (London, 1874); JUSTI, *Geschichte des alten Persiens* (Berlin, 1879); NÖLDEKE, *Aufsätze zur persischen Geschichte* (Leipzig, 1887); GUTSCHMIED, *Geschichte Irans und seiner Nachbarländer* (Tübingen, 1888); JUSTI AND HORN in GEIGER AND KUHN, *Grundriss der iranische Philologie*, II (Strasburg, 1897–1900); CHRISTENSEN, *L'Empire des Sassanides, le peuple, l'état, la cour* (Copenhagen, 1907); CURZON, *Persia and the Persian Question* (London, 1892); DE MORGAN, *Mission scientifique en Perse* (Paris, 1894); SYKES, *Ten Thousand Miles in Persia* (London, 1902); JACKSON, *Persia, Past and Present* (New York, 1906).—On Persian Art: DIEULAFOY, *L'Art antique de la Perse* (Paris, 1884); PERROT AND CHIPIEZ, *History of Art in Persia* (London, 1892); GAYET, *L'Art persane* (Paris, 1895); AUBIN, *La Perse d'aujourd'hui* (Paris, 1908).

II. LANGUAGE AND LITERATURE.—HAMMER, *Geschichte der schönen Redekünste Persiens mit einer Blütenlese* (Vienna, 1818); OUSELEY, *Biographical Notices of Persian Poets* (London, 1846); PIZZI, *Storia della letteratura Persiana* (Turin, 1894); IDEM, *L'Epopea persiana* (Turin, 1887); REED, *Persian Literature, Ancient and Modern* (Chicago, 1893); CHODZKO, *Specimens of the Popular Poetry of Persia* (London, 1842); MOHL, *Le Shah-Nameh de Firdousi* (Paris, 1876–78); ROGERS, *The Shah-Namah of Fardusi* (London, 1907); DOLE AND WALKER, *Flowers from Persian Poets* (New York, 1901); HORN, *Geschichte der persischen Literatur* (Leipzig, 1901); and above all, BROWNE, *Literary History of Persia*, I (London, 1902), II (1906).—See also bibliographies to AVESTA and AVESTA, THEOLOGICAL ASPECTS OF.

III. CHRISTIANITY IN PERSIA.—A. Earlier Periods.—TABARI, *Geschichte der Persen und Araber zur Zeit der Sassaniden*, ed. NÖLDEKE (Leyden, 1879); BARHEBRÆUS, *Chronicon Ecclesiasticum*, ed. ABBELOOS-LAMY (Louvain, 1874); ASSEMANI, *Bibliotheca Orientalis* (Rome, 1719–28), especially III, pts. i, ii; BEDJAN, *Acta Martyrum et Sanctorum* (Leipzig, 1890–99); HOFFMAN, *Auszüge aus Syrischen Akten persischer Märtyrer* (Leipzig, 1886); THOMAS OF MARGA, *Book of Governors*, ed. BUDGE (London, 1893); BEDJAN, Fr. tr. CHABOT, *Jabalaha: Vie de Jabalaha*, etc. (Paris, 1895); WRIGHT, *A Short History of Syriac Literature* (London, 1891); DUVAL, *Littérature Syriaque* (Paris, 1899); DUCHESNE, tr. MATHEW, *Churches Separated from Rome* (New York, 1907); BURKITT, *Early Eastern Christianity* (New York, 1904); LABOURT *Le Christianisme dans l'empire perse sous la dynastie Sassanide* (Paris, 1904); ADENEY, *The Greek and Eastern Churches* (New York, 1908); SHEDD, *Islam and the Oriental Churches* (Philadelphia, 1904); O'LEARY, *The Syriac Church and Fathers* (London, 1909); WIGRAM, *An Introduction to the History of the Assyrian Church, 100–640 A. D.* (London, 1910); BARTHOLD, *Zur Geschichte des Christenthums in Mittel-Asien bis zur mongolischen Eroberung* (Tübingen, 1901).

B. Catholic Missions.—*Annales de la Congrégation de la Mission;* CHARDIN, *Voyages en Perse et autres lieux de l'Orient* (Amsterdam, 1711); *Mémoires des Jésuites d'Ispahan;* PIOLET, *La France au dehors, ou Les Missions catholiques françaises au XIXe siècle*, I: *Missions d'Orient* (Paris, 1900), 185–222; MILLER-SIMONIS, *Du Caucase au Golfe Persique* (Paris, 1892); GIAMIL, *Genuinæ relationes inter syros orientales seu chaldæos et romanos pontifices* (Rome, 1900); *Missiones catholicæ cura S. C. de Prop. Fide descriptæ* (Rome, annual).

C. Non-Catholic Missions.—PERKINS, *Residence of Eight Years in Persia* (Andover, 1843); IDEM, *Missionary Life in Persia* (Boston, 1861); GUEST, *Story of a Consecrated Life* (London, 1870); ANDERSON, *History of the Missions of the A. B. C. F. M. Oriental Missions* (Boston, 1874); BASSETT, *Persia: Eastern Mission* (Philadelphia, 1890); WILSON, *Persian Life and Customs* (Chicago, 1895); IDEM, *Persia: Western Mission* (Philadelphia, 1896); RICHTER, *A History of Protestant Missions in the Near East* (New York, 1910), 279–337; RILEY, *Progress and Prospects of the Archbishop of Canterbury's Mission* (London, 1889); MACLEAN AND BROWNE, *The Catholicos of the East and His People* (London, 1892); LAWRENCE, *Modern Missions in the East* (New York, 1895).

GABRIEL OUSSANI.

Persico, IGNATIUS, cardinal, b. 30 Jan., 1823, at Naples, Italy; d. 7 Dec., 1896. He entered the Capuchin Franciscan Order on 25 April, 1839. Immediately after ordination he was sent in November, 1846, to Patna, India. The vicar Apostolic, Anastasius Hartmann, made him his *socius* and confidant. In 1850 Persico accompanied Bishop Hartmann to Bombay, when he was transferred to that vicariate, and assisted him in founding a seminary and establishing the "Bombay Catholic Examiner". At the time of the Goanese schism in 1853, the bishop sent Persico to Rome and London to lay the Catholic case before the pope and the British Government. He obtained British recognition for Catholic rights.

He was consecrated bishop on 8 March, 1854, and nominated bishop-auxiliary to Bishop Hartmann; but the next year he was appointed visitor of the Vicariate of Agra, and afterwards vicar Apostolic of that district. During the Indian Mutiny he was several times in danger of his life. The anxieties of this period told upon his health and in 1860 he was compelled to return to Italy. Sent in 1866 on a mission to the United States, he took part in the Council of Baltimore. On 20 March, 1870, he was nominated Bishop of Savannah; but his health again failing, he resigned in 1873. In 1874 he was sent as Apostolic delegate to Canada; and in 1877 he was commissioned to settle the affairs of the Malabar schism. On 26 March, 1879, he was appointed Bishop of Aquino in Italy; but in March, 1887, he was promoted to the titular Archbishopric of Tamiatha and sent as Apostolic delegate to Ireland to report upon the relations of the clergy with the political movement. He quickly saw that the question must be considered not merely in relation to present politics but also in relation to the past history of Ireland, and he delayed his final report in order to consider the question in this broader aspect. Meanwhile the Holy See issued its condemnation of the Plan of Campaign. Persico returned to Rome much disappointed. He was at once nominated Vicar of the Vatican Chapter. On 16 January, 1893, he was created cardinal priest of the title of St. Peter in Chains.

Analecta Ord. Min. Capp., XII, 30–32; see also letters of PERSICO in *United Irishman* (23 April, 1904).

FATHER CUTHBERT.

Person.—The Latin word *persona* was originally used to denote the mask worn by an actor. From this it was applied to the rôle he assumed, and, finally, to any character on the stage of life, to any individual. This article discusses (1) the definition of "person", especially with reference to the doctrine of the Incarnation; and (2) the use of the word *persona* and its Greek equivalents in connexion with the Trinitarian disputes. For the psychological treatment see PERSONALITY.

(1) *Definition.*—The classic definition is that given by Boethius in "De persona et duabus naturis", c. ii: *Naturæ rationalis individua substantia* (an individual substance of a rational nature). "Substance" is used to exclude accidents: "We see that accidents cannot constitute person" (Boethius, op. cit.). *Substantia* is used in two senses: of the concrete substance as existing in the individual, called *substantia prima*, corresponding to Aristotle's οὐσία πρώτη; and of abstractions, substance as existing in genus and species, called *substantia secunda*, Aristotle's οὐσία δευτέρα. It is disputed which of the two the word taken by itself here signifies. It seems probable that of itself it prescinds from *substantia prima* and *substantia secunda*, and is restricted to the former signification only by the word *individua*.

Individua, i. e., *indivisum in se*, is that which, unlike the higher branches in the tree of Porphyry, genus and species, cannot be further subdivided. Boethius in giving his definition does not seem to attach any further signification to the word. It is merely synonymous with *singularis*.

Rationalis naturæ.—Person is predicated only of intellectual beings. The generic word which includes all individual existing substances is *suppositum*. Thus person is a subdivision of *suppositum* which is applied equally to rational and irrational, living and non-living individuals. A person is therefore sometimes defined as *suppositum naturæ rationalis*.

The definition of Boethius as it stands can hardly be considered a satisfactory one. The words taken literally can be applied to the rational soul of man, and also to the human nature of Christ. That St. Thomas accepts it is presumably due to the fact that he found it in possession, and recognized as the traditional definition. He explains it in terms that practically constitute a new definition. *Individua substantia* signifies, he says, *substantia, completa, per se subsistens, separata ab aliis*, i. e., a substance, complete, subsisting *per se*, existing apart from others (III, Q. xvi, a. 12, ad 2um). If to this be added *rationalis naturæ*, we have a definition comprising the five notes that go to make up a person: (a) *substantia*—this excludes accident; (b) *completa*—it must form a complete nature; that which is a part, either actually or "aptitudinally" does not satisfy the definition; (c) *per se subsistens*—the person exists in himself and for himself; he is *sui juris*, the ultimate possessor of his nature and all its acts, the ultimate subject of predication of all his attributes; that which exists in another is not a person; (d) *separata ab aliis*—this excludes the universal, *substantia secunda*, which has no existence apart from the individual; (e) *rationalis naturæ*—excludes all non-intellectual *supposita*. To a person therefore belongs a threefold incommunicability, expressed in notes (b), (c), and (d). The human soul belongs to the nature as a part of it, and is therefore not a person, even when existing separately. The human nature of Christ does not exist *per se seorsum*, but *in alio*, in the Divine Personality of the Word. It is therefore communicated by assumption and so is not a person. Lastly the Divine Essence, though subsisting *per se*, is so communicated to the Three Persons that it does not exist apart from them; it is therefore not a person.

Theologians agree that in the Hypostatic Union the immediate reason why the Sacred Humanity, though complete and individual, is not a person is that it is not a subsistence, not *per se seorsum subsistens*. They have, however, disputed for centuries as to what may be the ultimate determination of the nature which if present would make it a subsistence and so a person, what in other words is the ultimate foundation of personality. According to Scotus, as he is usually understood, the ultimate foundation is a mere negation. That individual intellectual nature is a person which is neither of its nature destined to be communicated—as is the human soul—nor is actually communicated—as is the Sacred Humanity. If the Hypostatic Union ceased, the latter would *ipso facto*, without any further determination, become a person. To this it is objected that the person possesses the nature and all its attributes. It is difficult to believe that this possessor, as distinct from the objects possessed, is constituted only by a negative. Consequently, the traditional Thomists, following Cajetan, hold that there is a positive determination which they call the "mode" of subsistence. It is the function of this mode to make the nature incommunicable, terminated in itself, and capable of receiving its own *esse*, or existence. Without this mode the human nature of Christ exists only by the uncreated *esse* of the Word.

Suarez also makes the ultimate foundation of personality a mode. In his view, however, as he holds no real distinction between nature and *esse*, it does not prepare the nature to receive its own existence, but is something added to a nature conceived as already existing. Many theologians hold that the very concept of a mode, viz., a determination of a substance really distinct from it but adding no reality, involves a contradiction. Of more recent theories that of Tiphanus ("De hypostasi et persona", 1634) has found many adherents. He holds that a substance is a *suppositum*, an intelligent substance a person, from the mere fact of its being a whole, *totum in se*. This totality, it is contended, is a positive note, but adds no reality, as the whole adds nothing to the parts that compose it. In the Hypostatic Union the human nature is perfected by being assumed, and so ceases to be a whole, being merged in a greater totality. The Word, on the other hand, is not perfected, and so remains a person. Opposing theologians, however, hold that this notion of totality reduces on analysis to the Scotistic negative. Lastly the neo-Thomists, Terrien, Billot, etc., consider personality to be ultimately constituted by the *esse*, the actual existence, of an intelligent substance. That which subsists with its own *esse* is by that very fact incommunicable. The human nature of Christ is possessed by the Word and exists by His infinite *esse*. It has no separate *esse* of its own and for this reason is not a person. The *suppositum* is a *suppositum* as being *ens* in the strictest sense of the term. Of all Latin theories this appears to approach most nearly to that of the Greek fathers. Thus in the "Dialogues of the Trinity" given by Migne among the works of St. Athanasius, the author, speaking of person and nature in God, says: Ἡ γὰρ ὑπόστασις τὸ εἶναι σημαίνει ἡ δὲ θεότης τὸ τί εἶναι (Person denotes *esse*, the Divine nature denotes the quiddity; M. 28, 1114). An elaborate treatment is given by St. John Damascene, Dial. xlii.

(2) *The use of the word persona and its Greek equivalents in connexion with the Trinitarian disputes.*—For the constitution of a person it is required that a reality be subsistent and absolutely distinct, i. e. incommunicable. The three Divine realities are relations, each identified with the Divine Essence. A finite relation has reality only in so far as it is an accident; it has the reality of inherence. The Divine relations, however, are in the nature not by inherence but by identity. The reality they have, therefore, is not that of an accident, but that of a subsistence. They are one with *ipsum esse subsistens*. Again every relation, by its very nature, implies opposition and so distinction. In the finite relation this distinction is between subject and term. In the infinite relations there is no subject as distinct from the relation itself; the Paternity *is* the Father—and no term as distinct from the opposing relation; the Filiation *is* the Son. The Divine realities are therefore distinct and mutually incommunicable through this relative opposition; they are subsistent as being identified with the subsistence of the Godhead, i. e. they are persons. The use of the word *persona* to denote them, however, led to controversy between East and West. The precise Greek equivalent was πρόσωπον, likewise used originally of the actor's mask and then of the character he represented, but the meaning of the word had not passed on, as had that of *persona*, to the general signification of individual. Consequently *tres personæ*, τρία πρόσωπα, savoured of Sabellianism to the Greeks. On the other hand their word ὑπόστασις, from ὑπό-ἵστημι, was taken to correspond to the Latin *substantia*, from *sub-stare*. *Tres hypostases* therefore appeared to conflict with the Nicæan doctrine of unity of substance in the Trinity. This difference was a main cause of the Antiochene schism of the fourth century (see MELETIUS OF ANTIOCH). Eventually in the West, it was recognized that the true equivalent of ὑπόστασις was not *substantia* but *subsistentia*, and in the East that to understand πρόσωπον in the sense of the Latin *persona* precluded the possibility of a Sabellian interpretation. By the First Council of Constantinople, therefore, it was recognized that the words ὑπόστασις, πρόσωπον, and *persona* were equally applicable to the three Divine realities. (See INCARNATION; NATURE; SUBSTANCE; TRINITY.)

BOETHIUS, *De Persona et Duabus Naturis*, ii, iii, in *P. L.*, LXIV, 1342 sqq.; RICKABY, *General Metaphysics*, 92–102, 279–97 (London, 1890); DE REGNON, *Etudes sur la Trinité*, I, studies i, iv; ST. THOMAS AQUINAS, III, Q. xvi, a. 12; *De Potentia*, ix, 1–4; TERRIEN, *S. Thomæ Doctrina de Unione Hypostatica*, bk. I, c. vii; bk. III, cc. vi-vii (Paris, 1894); FRANZELIN, *De Verbo Incarnato*, sect. III, cc. iii-iv (Rome, 1874); HARPER, *Metaphysics of the School*, vol. I, bk. III, c. ii, art. 2 (London, 1879).

L. W. GEDDES.

Person, ECCLESIASTICAL.—In its etymological sense this expression signifies every person who forms a part of the external and visible society which constitutes the Church, and who has not been canonically expelled therefrom. But the expression is rarely used in this sense; customarily it indicates persons whom a special tie connects with the Church, either because they have received ecclesiastical tonsure, minor, or higher orders, and are a fortiori invested with a power of jurisdiction; or because they have taken vows in a religious order or congregation approved by the Church. This more intimate union with the Church involves particular duties which are not incumbent on the general faithful (see CLERIC).

SCHERER, *Handbuch des Kirchenrechts*, I (Graz, 1886), 309–12.

A. VAN HOVE.

Persona Gobelinus. See GOBELINUS.

Personality.—It is proposed in this article to give an account (1) of the physical constituents of personality in accordance with the scholastic theory; (2) of concepts of personality that conflict with the theory; (3) of abnormalities of consciousness with reference to their bearing on theories of personality.

(1) THE PHYSICAL CONSTITUENTS OF PERSONALITY.—A man's personality is that of which he has cognizance under the concept of "self". It is that entity, substantial, permanent, unitary, which is the subject of all the states and acts that constitute his complete life. An appeal to self-consciousness shows us that there is such a subject, of which thought, will, and feeling are modifications. It is substantial, i. e. not one or all of the changing states but the reality underlying them, for our self-consciousness testifies that, besides perceiving the thought, it has immediate perception in the same act of the subject to whom the thought belongs. Just as no motion can be apprehended without some sort of apprehension of the object moved, so the perception of thought carries with it perception of the thinker. The changing states are recognized as determinations of the "self", and the very concept of a determination involves the presence of something determined, something not itself a determination, i. e. a substance. It is permanent, in that though one may say, "I am completely changed", when referring to a former state, still one knows that the "I" in question is still the same numerically and essentially, though with certain superadded differences.

This permanence is evident from a consideration of our mental processes. Every act of intellectual memory implies a recognition of the fact that I, thinking now, am the "self" as the one who had the experience which is being recalled. My former experiences are referred to something which has not passed as they have passed, to my own self or personality. From this permanence springs the consciousness of self as a unitary principle. The one to whom all the variations of state belong is perceived as an entity complete in itself and distinguished from all others. Unity of consciousness does not constitute but manifests unity of being. The physical principle of this permanence and unity is the simple, spiritual, unchanging substance of the rational soul. This does not mean, however, that the soul is identical with the personal self. There are recognized as modifications of the self not merely acts of thought and volition, but also sensations, of which the immediate subject is the animated body. Even in its own peculiar sphere the soul works in conjunction with the body; intellectual reasoning is accompanied and conditioned by sensory images. A man's personality, then, consists physically of soul and body. Of these the body is what is termed in scholastic language the "matter", the determinable principle, the soul is the "form", the determining principle. The soul is not merely the seat of the chief functions of man—thought and will; it also determines the nature and functioning of the body. To its permanence is due the abiding unity of the whole personality in spite of the constant disintegration and rebuilding of the body. Though not therefore the only constituent of personality, the soul is its formal principle. Finally, for the complete constitution of personality this *compositum* must exist in such a way as to be "subsistent" (see PERSON).

(2) NON-SCHOLASTIC THEORIES OF PERSONALITY. —Many modern schools of philosophy hold that personality is constituted not by any underlying reality which self-consciousness reveals to us, but by the self-consciousness itself or by intellectual operations. Locke held that personality is determined and constituted by identity of consciousness. Without denying the existence of the soul as the substantial principle underlying the state of consciousness, he denied that this identity of substance had any concern with personal identity. From what has been said above it is clear that consciousness is a manifestation, not the principle, of that unity of being which constitutes personality. It is a state, and presupposes something of which it is a state. Locke's view and kindred theories are in conflict with the Christian revelation, in that, as in the Incarnate Word there are two intellects and two "operations", there are therefore two consciousnesses. Hence accepting Locke's definition of personality there would be two persons.

From Locke's theory it was but a step to the denial of any permanent substance underlying the perceived states. For Hume the only knowable reality consists in the succession of conscious thoughts and feelings. As these are constantly changing it follows that there is no such thing as permanence of the Ego. Consequently, the impression of abiding identity is a mere fiction. Subsequent theorists however, could not acquiesce in this absolute demolition; an explanation of the consciousness of unity had somehow to be found. Mill therefore held personality to consist in the series of states "aware of itself as a series". According to James, personality is a thing of the moment, consisting in the thought of the moment: "The passing thought is itself the thinker". But each thought transmits itself and all its content to its immediate successor, which thus knows and includes all that went before. Thus is established the "stream of consciousness" which in his view constitutes the unity of the Ego. Besides the fundamental difficulties they share in common, each of these theories is open to objections peculiar to itself. How can a number of states, i. e. of events *ex hypothesi* entitatively distinct from one another, be collectively conscious of themselves as a unity? Similarly, in the theory of James, successive thoughts are distinct entities. As therefore no thought is ever present to the one preceding it, how does it know it without some underlying principle of unity connecting them?

Again, James does not believe in unconscious states of mind. In what sense then does every thought "know" all its predecessors? It is certainly not conscious of doing so. But the objection fundamental to all these theories is that, while pretending to account for all the phenomena of self-consciousness, its most important testimony, namely that to a self who is not the thought, who owns the thought, and who is immediately perceived in the act of reflexion upon the thought, is treated as a mere fiction. Against any such position may be urged all the arguments for the permanent and unitary nature of the self. The modern school of empirical psychologists shows a certain reaction against systems which deny to personality a foundation in substance. Thus Ribot: "Let us set aside the hypothesis which makes of the Ego 'a bundle of sensations', or states of consciousness, as is frequently repeated after Hume. This is ... to take effects for their cause" (Diseases of Personality, 85). For them the unity of the Ego rests merely on the unity of the organism. "The organism, and the brain, as its highest representation, constitute the real personality" (op. cit., 154). A system which ignores the existence of the human soul fails to account for the purely intellectual phenomena of consciousness, abstract ideas, judgment, and inference. These require a simple, i. e. non-extended, and therefore immaterial principle. The various theories we have been considering make the whole personality consist in what is really some part of it. Its substantial constituents are soul and body, its accidental constituents are all the sensations, emotions, thoughts, volitions, in fact all the experiences, of this *compositum*.

(3) ABNORMALITIES OF CONSCIOUSNESS.—We may here review briefly some forms of what are known as "disintegrations of personality", and consider to what extent they affect the scholastic theory of the constitution of the person. In double or multiple personality there are manifested in the same individual two or more apparently distinct series of conscious states. There is a break not merely of character and habit, but of memory also. Thus in 1887 a certain Ansel Bourne disappeared from his home at Coventry, Rhode Island, and two weeks later set up business as A. J. Browne, a baker, at Norristown, Pennsylvania. This new "personality" had no knowledge of Ansel Bourne. After eight weeks he one morning woke up to find himself again Ansel Bourne. The adventures, even the existence, of A. J. Browne were a vanished episode. Subsequently under hypnotic influence the latter "personality" was recalled, and recounted its adventures. The phenomena of double personality may also be recurrent apart from hypnosis. In such cases the two states reappear alternately, each having the chain of memories proper to itself. The instance most frequently cited is that of "Felida X", observed for many years by Dr. Azam. Two states of consciousness alternated. In state II she retained memory of what happened in state I, but not vice versa. Her character in the two states was widely different. Frequently in such cases the character in the second state tends to become more like the character in the original state, appearing finally as a blend of the two, as in the case of Mary Reynolds (cf. "Harper's Magazine", May, 1860).

In "multiple personality" the most extraordinary abnormalities of memory and character occur. In the case of "Miss Beauchamp" (Proceedings of the Society for Psychical Research, xv, 466 sq.), besides the original personality, there were no less than four other states periodically reappearing, different from one another in temperament, and each with a continuous memory. Owing to a mental shock in 1893 Miss Beauchamp's character changed, though memory remained continuous. This state was afterwards called B I. Under hypnotism two other states manifested themselves B II, and B III. Of these B III ("Sally") practically developed an independent existence, and continually manifested itself apart from hypnotic suggestion. B I had no memory of B II or B III. B II knew B I, but not B III, while B III knew both the others. Eventually in 1899 after another mental shock there appeared a fourth "personality" B IV, whose memory presented a complete blank from the "disappearance" of the original Miss Beauchamp after the first shock till the appearance of B IV after the second, six years later. Her character was, however, very unlike that of the original personality. B III had memory of all that happened to B IV, but did not know her thoughts. Furthermore, B III was exceedingly jealous both of her and of B I, and played spiteful tricks on them. In connexion with these phenomena, the theory has been proposed that the original personality became "disintegrated" after the first shock, and that B I and B IV are its components, while B II and B III are varying manifestations of the "subliminal self".

Sometimes again the phenomena of "double personality" are manifested in an individual, not in alternating periods, but simultaneously. Thus M. Taine cites the case of a lady who while continuing a conversation would write a whole page of intelligent and connected matter on some quite alien subject. She had no notion of what she had been writing, and was frequently surprised, sometimes even alarmed, on reading what she had written.

In dealing with the problems suggested by such phenomena, one must first of all be sure that the facts are well attested and that fraud is excluded. It should also be noted that these are abnormal conditions, whereas the nature of personality must be determined by a study of the normal individual. Nor is it permissible even in these exceptional cases to infer a "multiple" personality, so long as the phenomena can be explained as symptoms of disease in one and the same personality.

The various groups of phenomena enumerated above would merit the title of different "personalities", if it could be shown (a) that personality is constituted by functioning as such, and not by an underlying substantial principle, or (b) that, granted that there be a formal principle of unity, such cases showed the presence in the individual, successively or simultaneously, of two or more such principles, or (c) that the principle was not simple and spiritual but capable of division into several separately functioning components. The hypothesis that functioning, as such, constitutes personality has already been shown insufficient to account for the facts of normal consciousness, while the other theories are opposed to the permanence and simplicity of the human soul. Nor are any of these theories necessary to account for the facts. The soul not being a pure spirit but the "form" of the body, it follows that while it performs acts in which the body has no share as a *cause*, still the soul is *conditioned* in its activity by the state of the physical organism. Now, in the case of non-simultaneous double personality, the essential feature is the break of memory. Some experiences are not referred to the same "self" as other experiences; in fact, the memory of that former self disappears for the time being. Concerning this one may remark that such failures of memory are exaggerated; there is no complete loss of all that has been acquired in the former state. Apart from the memory of definite facts about oneself there remains always much of the ordinary intellectual possession. Thus the baker "A. J. Browne" was able to keep his accounts and use the language intelligently. That he could do so shows the permanence of the same intellectual and therefore non-composite principle. The disappearance from his memory of most of his experiences merely shows that his physical organism, by the state of which the action of his soul is conditioned, was not working in the normal way.

In other words, while the presence of any form of intellectual memory shows the continuance of a permanent spiritual principle, the loss of memory does not prove the contrary; it is merely absence of evidence either way. Thus the theory that the soul acts as the "form" of the body explains the two partially dissevered chains of memory. What sort of change in the nervous organism would be necessary to account for the calling up of two completely different sets of experiences, as occurs in double personality, no psychologists, even those who consider the physical organism the sole principle of unity, pretend to explain satisfactorily. It may be remarked that such manifestations are almost always found in hysterical subjects, whose nervous organization is highly unstable, and that frequently there are indications which point to definite lesion or disease in the brain.

The alleged cases of simultaneous double personality, manifested usually by speech in the case of one and writing in the case of the other, present special difficulty, in that there is question not of loss of memory of an action performed, but of want of consciousness of the action during its actual performance. There are certainly degrees of consciousness, even of intellectual operation. The doubt therefore always remains as to whether the so-called unconscious writing, if really indicative of mental operation, be literally unconscious or only very faintly conscious. But there is a further doubt, namely, as to whether the writing of the "secondary personality" is intellectual at all at the moment. The nervous processes of the brain being set in motion may run their course without any demand arising for the intellectual action of the soul. In the case of such highly nervous subjects, it is at least possible that images imprinted on the nervous organism are committed to writing by purely automatic and reflex action.

Finally, there remains a sense in which phenomena of the same nature as those we have been considering may be indicative of the presence of a second personality, e. g. when the body is under the influence of an alien spirit. Possession is something the possibility of which the Church takes for granted. This, however, would not imply a true double personality in one individual. The invading being would not enter into composition with the body to form one person with it, but would be an extrinsic agent communicating local motion to a bodily frame which it did not "inform". (See CONSCIOUSNESS; SOUL.)

MYERS, *Human Personality and its Survival of Bodily Death*, I (London, 1903), ii, and appendix; RIBOT, *Les Maladies de la Personnalité* (Paris, 1885), tr. *The Diseases of Personality* (Chicago, 1906); MAHER, *Psychology* (London, 1903); ROURE, *Etudes*, LXXV, 35, 492, 636; RICHMOND, *An Essay on Personality as a Philosophical Principle* (London, 1900); ILLINGWORTH, *Personality, Human and Divine* (London, 1894), i, ii; HARPER, *Metaphysics of the School*, bk. V (London, 1879), ii, iii; BINET, *Les Altérations de la Personnalité* (Paris, 1892), tr. (London, 1896); *On Double Consciousness* (Chicago, 1905).

L. W. GEDDES.

Persons (also, but less correctly, PARSONS), ROBERT, Jesuit, b. at Nether Stowey, Somerset, 24 June, 1546; d. in Rome, 15 April, 1610.

I. EARLY LIFE.—His parents were of the yeoman class (for the controversy about them, see below "Memoirs", pp. 36–47), but several of his many brothers rose to good positions. By favour of the local parson, John Hayward (once a monk at Taunton), Robert was sent to St. Mary's Hall, Oxford (1562). After taking his degrees with distinction he became fellow and tutor at Balliol (1568); but 13 Feb., 1574, he was forced to resign, partly because of his strong Catholic leanings, partly through college quarrels. Before long, he went abroad, and was reconciled, probably by Father William Good, S.J., and after a year spent in travel and study, he became a Jesuit at Rome (3 July, 1575).

ROBERT PARSONS (PERSONS)

II. ENGLISH MISSION, 1579–1581.—At Rome he suggested the English mission for the Society, and when the students of the English College (q. v.) there came into difficulties with their first rector, he exerted himself to maintain peace, and proposed the "oath of the missions", an idea which was taken up, and is now in vogue throughout the Church. When the college was entrusted to the Jesuits, he was temporarily installed as rector (19 March, 1579). Dr. Allen (q. v.) came to Rome, 10 Oct., 1579, to complete the college arrangements, already so well begun, and at his instance the Jesuit mission to England was decided upon (Dec., 1579). The year of mission in England (12 June, 1580, to late August, 1581) was the most useful of Persons's life. Ever at the post of danger, he yet managed to avoid seizure, while he organized means of missionary enterprise not for Jesuits only but for the whole country. Laymen and secular priests carried out his plans with whole-hearted enthusiasm, and deserve unstinted praise for the results that followed. Persons not only preached, confessed, arranged missionary tours, and posts, he also wrote books and pamphlets, and set up his "magic press" (q. v., Brinkley, Stephen), which printed and set forth Campion's "Decem Rationes", while several books of his own, answers to onslaughts of Protestants, were brought out within a few days of the attack. Considering the losses previously incurred through want of courage and energy, it would be impossible to praise this pioneer work too highly. But later on the missionary methods had to be modified: the presses were transferred abroad, and the challenges to disputation were dropped. Though not initiated by Persons, they had been subsequently approved by him. (See COUNTER-REFORMATION, VII. *England;* EDMUND CAMPION, BLESSED.)

III. POLITICS, 1582–84.—After Campion had been taken (17 July, 1581) and the press captured (8 August), Persons slipped across to France hoping to do some business with Allen, to set up a new press, and return. The press was begun again under George Flinton at Rouen, but Persons never saw England again, and found himself in entirely new circumstances, which led to new, and much less desirable results. He was now living under the French Provincial Père Claude Matthieu, an advocate of armed resistance to the Huguenots; and he was necessarily under the influence of the King of Spain and the Duke of Guise, afterwards the leader of "La Sainte Ligue" and the champion of Mary Stuart. A great change too had come over her fortunes. Esmé Stuart, Sieur d'Aubigny, created Duke of Lennox, the favourite of the youthful King James, espoused her side (7 March, 1582). Never had she had such an ally, who actually controlled the chief ports of Scotland, and enjoyed the king's entire confidence. Father William Crichton, S.J., an enthusiastic Scot, who had just gone to Edinburgh as a missioner, was completely carried away by the prospect, and returned at once to lay Lennox's offers before the Duke of Guise. Persons and Allen were summoned for advice, and a meeting was held in Paris (18–24 May), in which both they and the papal nuncio, and the Archbishop of Glasgow took part. Everyone agreed that the King of Spain and the pope should be called upon to help. If they did not, there was no chance of Lennox maintaining his position for long, with England and the Scottish Kirk allied against him. The congress decided that Persons should go to Philip, and Crichton to Pope Gregory; and though the two Jesuits demurred, as having other orders from their superiors, the papal nuncio insisted and his authority of course prevailed. Persons now undertook two journeys, to Philip in Spain (June–Oct., 1582) and to Rome (Sept., 1583). Pope Gregory fully approved the plans, but the king always refused to consent, with qualifications, however, which led Allen and Persons to hope on till the beginning of 1584, by which time Lennox had fallen, and the other favourable circumstances had ceased. Looking back we now recognize how great Father Persons's error was; but it is also easy to see that with the approbation of the pope and of Allen and the other leading English Catholics living abroad, he had many excuses. He certainly did not contemplate the subjection of his country, but its liberation from an insufferable burden of persecution (see also ARMADA, THE SPANISH, IV. *Catholic Co-operation*).

IV. SPAIN, 1588–97.—Recalled to Rome in 1585, he was professed there (7 May, 1587) and sent to Spain at the close of 1588, to conciliate King Philip, who was offended with Father Acquaviva. Persons was successful, and then made use of the royal favour to found the seminaries of Valladolid, Seville, and Madrid (1589, 1592, 1598) and the residences of San-Lucar, and of Lisbu (which became a college in 1622). Already in 1582 he had founded a school at Eu, the first English Catholic boys' school since the Reformation; and he now succeeded in establishing at St. Omers (1594) a larger institution to which the boys from Eu were transferred, and which, after a long and romantic history, still flourishes at Stonyhurst (q. v.). Whilst in Rome and Spain Persons wrote several still extant State papers, which show that he was still in favour of armed intervention on behalf of the English Catholics, but his main policy was to wait for the next succession, when he expected there would be a variety of claimants, for it was one of Elizabeth's manias to leave the succession an open question. Persons thought that a Catholic successor and by preference the Infanta (who was a representative of the house of Lancaster) would have a fair chance. On this topic there appeared in 1594, under the pseudonym of N. Dolman, the important "Conference on the next succession". The penman was really Richard Verstegan (q. v.; see also, Record Office,"Dom. Eliz.", 252, n. 66, and Vatican Archives, "Borghese", 448, ab, f. 339) but both Cardinal Allen and Sir Francis Englefield had helped and approved, while Persons had also revised the MS. and rewritten many passages. The book was a manifesto of his party, and though declining the authorship, he always defended its principle, which was the people's right of participation in the settlement of a ruler, as opposed to the Gallican theory of the Divine right of kings. (See ORIGIN OF GOVERNMENT; GALLICANISM.) But though Persons's theory is praiseworthy, his practical conclusion (mentioned above) was illusory. Owing to the unpopularity of Spain, the book was very badly received, and he could not effectively prevent its popular attribution to himself. Ten years earlier (1584) another political publication in favour of Mary Queen of Scots, widely known as "Leicester's Commonwealth", had also been popularly ascribed to him; presumably because he very unwisely allowed a Jesuit lay-brother, Ralph Emerson, to take the first consignment of them to England, where they were seized. The real author was probably Charles Arundel.

V. THE APPELLANTS, 1598–1603.—Cardinal Allen died in 1594 and after he had gone, the English Catholics were tried by a series of the most distressing disturbances, which originated in the misery and consequent discontent of the exiles, and which gradually affected the seminaries, the clergy, and even the Catholic prisoners. Allen had ruled by personal influence; and left no successor. The clergy were without superior or organization. Persons returned to Rome (April, 1597) to quiet the disturbances at the English College, which no one else could calm. He was immediately and remarkably successful; and there was talk of making him a cardinal. But, as the pope never intended to do so, it is unnecessary to discuss what might have happened had he received that dignity. Cardinal Cajetano, the Protector, now ordered him to draw up a scheme of government for the rest of the clergy. His first idea was to establish an archbishop in Flanders, and a bishop in England, but considering the fury of the persecution a hierarchy of priests was preferred. In England an archpriest with assistants was appointed (7 March, 1598); in Flanders, Spain, and Rome, "Prefects of the Mission", while the nuncio in Flanders was to be the vicegerent of the cardinal-protector, with supreme jurisdiction. In point of fact it was found more convenient to deal directly with the archpriest, George Blackwell, who, albeit a good scholar and an amiable man, had not the skill and experience necessary to calm the disputes then raging, and his endeavours turned the complainants against himself. An appeal was carried against him to Rome; but was decided in his favour, 6 April, 1599. But Father Persons, who had defended him, misunderstood the nature of the opposition, and treated the appellant envoys like recalcitrant scholars, and Blackwell misused his victory. A second appeal ensued (Nov., 1600), which was backed up by the publication of many books, some of which contained scandalous attacks on Father Persons, who defended himself in two publications "A briefe Apologie" (St. Omers?, 1601), and the "Manifestation" (1601). The appellants were patronized by the French ambassador, the archpriest by the Spanish, and the debate grew very warm, Father Persons's pen being busily engaged the whole time. Clement VIII in the end maintained the archpriest's authority, but justified the grounds of the appeal, ordering that six of the appellant party should be admitted among the assistants, cancelled the instruction which commanded the archpriest to seek the advice of the Jesuit superior in matters of greater moment, and forbade all further books on either side. Thus the appellants won the majority of points, and a party supported by France, but hostile to Persons, became influential among the English clergy.

VI. CONCLUSION, 1602–10.—Persons remained till his death rector of the English College, but he nearly lost that post in 1604. Clement VIII had been told by the French ambassador that James would be favourably impressed, if he proved his independence of the Jesuits, by sending Father Persons away. Persons, as it happened, was ill, and had to go to Naples (Nov., 1604); whereupon the pope gave orders for him not to return. But the pontiff himself died 3 March, 1605, and his successor, Paul V, reversed his policy, which was unpopular at Perth. Persons returned to his post, and enjoyed full papal favour until his death. Father Persons's greatest work, his "Christian Directory" [originally called "The Book of Christian Exercise", and known as "The Book of Resolution" (Rouen, 1582), with innumerable editions and translations], had been conceived during his heroic mission in England. His edition of Sander's "De Schismate Anglicano" (Rome, 1506) had also an immense circulation. His later works, were controversial, written with wonderful vigour, irony, incisiveness, and an easy grasp of the most complex subjects; but they lack the deep sympathy and human interest of his missionary books. Father Persons was a man of great parts, eloquent, influential, zealous, spiritual, disinterested, fearless. Yet he had some of the defects of his qualities. He was masterful, sometimes a special pleader, and greater as a pioneer or sectional leader than as *Generalissimo*. Though his services in the mission field, and in the education of the clergy were priceless, his participation in politics and in clerical feuds cannot be justified except in certain aspects.

PERSONS, *Memoirs* (CATHOLIC RECORD SOCIETY), II, IV (London, 1906, 1907); MORE, *Historia Provinciæ Anglicanæ* (St. Omers, 1660); KNOX, *Letters of Cardinal Allen* (London, 1882); POLLEN, *Politics of English Catholics* in *The Month* (1902–04); KRETZSCHMAR, *Invasionsprojecte der katholischen Mächte gegen England* (Leipzig, 1892); MEYER, *England und die katholische Kirche unter Elizabeth* (Rome, 1911); BELLESHEIM, *Cardinal Allen und die englische Seminare* (Mainz, 1885); DODD-TIERNEY, *Church History of England* (London, 1838); LAW, *Appellant Controversy* (CAMDEN SOCIETY, 1896, 1898); COUZARD, *Une ambassade à Rome sous Henri IV* (Paris, 1900?); LAFLEUR DE KERMAINGANT, *Christophe de Harlay, comte de Beaumont* (Paris, 1895); OSSAT, *Letters*, in various editions by AMELOT DE LA HOUSSAIE (Amsterdam, 1708); DÉGERT (Paris, 1894), TAMIREZ DE LARROQUE (Paris, 1872), etc.; DE FRESNE, *Ambassades* (Paris, 1635); SOMMERVOGEL, *Bibl. de la C. de J.; Bibl. Dict. Eng. Cath.; Dict. Nat. Biog.*

J. H. POLLEN.

Perth (SCOTLAND). See DUNKELD.

Perth (PERTHENSIS), DIOCESE OF, in Western Australia, suffragan to Adelaide; bounded on the north by parallel 31° 20′ S. lat. (the Moore River), east to 120° E. long., and thence by parallel 29° S. lat. to the border of South Australia, its eastern boundary, on the south and west by the ocean. The first Catholics, Irish emigrants, settled about seventy-five years ago near the present city of Perth. As they had no priest, Archbishop Polding of Sydney appointed Rev. John Brady his vicar-general for the western portion of Australia. A native of Cavan, Father Brady had laboured for twelve years in Mauritius, before going to Australia in February, 1838. With Fr. John Joostens, a former Dutch chaplain in Napoleon's forces, and Patrick O'Reilly, a catechist, he reached Albany, 4 November, 1843, and Perth, 13 December, 1843. Land for a church, presbytery, and school was donated by Governor Hutt, and the foundation stone of the church laid, 27 December, 1843. Shortly afterwards Fr. Brady went to Europe to procure aid, and was ordained bishop at Rome, 18 May, 1845. He returned with some missionaries, including six Sisters of Mercy from Carlow, Ireland, under Mother Ursula Frayne, reaching Fremantle in January, 1846.

The early days of the mission were days of suffering and poverty. In 1848 the scattered Catholic population, which was extremely poor, numbered only 306 out of 4600 whites. The bishop soon sent Fr. Confalonieri with two catechists, James Fagan and Nicholas Hogan, to Port Essington to convert the native northern blacks. The catechists were drowned in a shipwreck on the voyage, but Fr. Confalonieri was spared to labour for two years, till his death by fever at Victoria, Melville Island, when he had converted over 400 blacks. An attempt to found a southern native mission failed for want of resources. A central mission was confided to two Spanish Benedictines, Dom Serra and Dom Salvado. In March, 1847, they established a monastery, now New Norcia (q. v.), 84 miles from Perth. The first diocesan synod was held there, 13 March, 1848, attended by the bishop and his three priests. The mission sinking heavily in debt, Dom Salvado was sent to Europe for funds. He returned January, 1849, but his resources were applied to New Norcia alone. Dom Serra, who had also gone to Europe, had while there been made Bishop of Port Victoria. Worn out by toil and anxiety, Dr. Brady applied for a coadjutor, and Dom Serra was transferred from Port Victoria to the titular See of Daulia and appointed to administer the temporalities of Perth. He arrived there from Europe with a large contingent of Benedictines in 1849. Dissension broke out between the laity and the Spanish monks, and Dr. Brady, unable to bear the strain, returned to Ireland in 1852; he died in France, 2 December, 1871. While he was in Perth, Dr. R. R. Madden, the historian, was appointed colonial secretary, the first Catholic to hold that office in the colonies. On Corpus Christi, 10 June, 1854, the first two black children received Holy Communion at Perth. In 1859 Fr. Martin Griver was made administrator of the diocese. In 1862 Dom Serra returned to Spain, where he died in 1886.

On 10 October, 1869, Fr. Griver was named Bishop of Tloa and Administrator Apostolic of Perth. In July, 1873, he became Bishop of Perth. In 1863 churches were erected at Fremantle, Guildford, and York. The cathedral of Perth, begun in that year, was dedicated on 29 January, 1865. In 1867 the Sisters of Mercy established an orphanage at Perth. In 1882 the diocese contained 8500 Catholics, with 1300 children in the parochial schools. Bishop Griver died on 1 November, 1886. Born at Granollers in Spain, 11

November, 1810, he studied medicine, but later joined the priesthood and went out with Dom Serra in 1849. He laboured strenuously in building up the diocese, and was a man of wonderful asceticism; after his death a wooden cross twelve inches long was found attached to his shoulders, fastened permanently into his flesh by five iron spikes. Dr. Matthew Gibney, who had been appointed Bishop of Scythopolis and Coadjutor of Perth *cum jure successionis*, was consecrated at Perth, 23 January, 1887. Under his guidance the diocese made rapid progress, as in his earlier days, so during his episcopate, he was an ardent apostle of religious education for children. He introduced all the religious congregations mentioned below, except the Sisters of Mercy and the Sisters of St. Joseph. In 1889, with two Vincentians, he gave a mission throughout the whole of his diocese. In 1890 he set out for Beagle Bay, where he established a successful native mission, under the care of the Trappists, who were later replaced by the Pallotine Fathers and the Sisters of St. John of God from Subiaco, Perth. Owing to advanced years, Dr. Gibney resigned his see and has been succeeded by Most Reverend P. J. Clune, C.SS.R. (1911). Dr. Clune, born in Clare, Ireland, 1863, was ordained for the Diocese of Goulbourn (q. v.) 24 June, 1886. In 1892 he returned to Ireland, and became a Redemptorist. After being stationed at Dundalk and Limerick, he was sent to Wellington, New Zealand, as rector of the Redemptorist monastery; after which he was superior at North Perth till his election as bishop. From the original Diocese of Perth, three additional ecclesiastical districts have been formed: New Norcia (1847); the Vicariate Apostolic of Kimberley (1887); and the Diocese of Geraldton (1898).

Statistics of religious congregations.—Men: Oblates of Mary Immaculate (1894), 2 houses, 11 members; Redemptorists (1894), 1 monastery, 8 members; Irish Christian Brothers (1894), 4 houses, 18 members. Women: Sisters of Mercy (1846), 12 houses, 153 nuns; Sisters of St. Joseph of the Apparition (1855), 6 houses, 46 nuns; Sisters of St. John of God (1885), 4 houses, 43 nuns; Sisters of Notre-Dame des Missions (1887), 4 houses, 22 nuns; Presentation Sisters (1900), 3 houses, 12 nuns; Sisters of St. Joseph of the Sacred Heart (1890), 5 houses, 16 nuns; Institute of the Blessed Virgin Mary, or Loreto Nuns (1897), 2 houses, 26 professed sisters. There are 22 high schools (3 boys', 19 girls'), with 1238 pupils; 43 primary schools with 5230 pupils; teachers engaged, 408; 1 boys' orphanage; 1 girls' orphanage; 1 boys' industrial school; 1 girls' reformatory; 1 Magdalene Asylum; 2 hospitals (these charitable institutes contain 413 inmates); 26 ecclesiastical districts; 51 churches; 44 secular and 13 regular priests; 27 brothers; 366 nuns; 54 lay teachers and a Catholic population of 45,000.

MORAN, *Hist. of the Catholic Church in Australasia* (Sydney, s. d.), 553–91; 969–79; *Australasian Catholic Directory* (Sydney, 1910).

A. A. MACERLEAN.

Pertinax, PUBLIUS HELVIUS, Roman Emperor (31 Dec., 192), b. at Alba Pompeia, in Liguria, 1 August, 126; d. at Rome 28 March, 193. A freedman's son, he taught grammar at Rome before entering the army. Because of his military ability and his competence in civil positions, he was made prætor and consul. His services in the campaign against Avidius Cassius led Marcus Aurelius to give Pertinax the chief command of the army along the Danube, a position he filled with such distinction that Marcus Aurelius made him successively governor of Mœsia, Dacia, and Syria.

Commodus first made him commander-in-chief of the troops in Britain, then appointed him governor in Africa, and finally made him prefect of the city of Rome. On account of a conspiracy against Commodus many innocent persons, including Pertinax, were banished. After the strangling of Commodus, Pertinax was proclaimed emperor by the soldiers at the suggestion of Lætus, prefect of the prætorian guard. Pertinax had himself elected as head of the State once more by the senators and revived the title "Princeps Senatus"; on the first day of his reign he assumed the title "Pater Patriæ". Pertinax strove to restore order in the administration of the State. By selling at auction the costly furniture and plate of Commodus and by a frugal administration, before three months he was able to make gifts of money to the people and give to the prætorian guard the promised largess. He also was able to resume public works. He separated public lands from those belonging to the emperor, endeavoured to bring about the resettling of deserted estates, to recall those arbitrarily banished, and to bring informers to trial. He refused the title of Augusta for his wife, or that of Cæsar for his son until he had earned the honour. When the prætorians saw that the emperor meant to restore the ancient discipline and when the prefect Lætus noticed that he strove to limit his own influence, he aroused the soldiers of the guard against the emperor. After suppressing the revolt of the consul, Sossius Falco, Pertinax declined to put him to death, though the Senate had decreed his execution. Several prætorians were suspected of being members of the conspiracy; Lætus had these put to death without any trial and made the soldiers believe that it was done by imperial command. The prætorians now resolved to depose Pertinax. One evening a mob of about two hundred soldiers went to the palace to murder the emperor. The latter came out to them without arms in the hope of quieting them by his personal influence. His words impressed the mutineers and they put their swords back in the scabbards, when suddenly a Tongrian cavalryman fell upon Pertinax and stabbed him in the breast. This incited the others who fell upon Pertinax; the emperor's head was put on a lance and carried through the streets of the city to the camp. Severus, the second successor of Pertinax, deified him.

SCHILLER, *Gesch. der röm. Kaiserzeit*, I, pt. II (Gotha, 1883); VON DOMASZEWSKI, *Gesch. der röm. Kaiser* (Leipzig, 1909).

KARL HOEBER.

Peru, a republic on the west coast of South America, founded in 1821 after the war of independence, having been a Spanish colony. It is difficult to ascertain the true origin of the word "Peru", as the opinions advanced thereon are vague, numerous, and conflicting. Almost all, however, derive it from the terms "Beru", "Pelu", and "Biru", which were, respectively, the names of an Indian tribe, a river, and a region. Prescott asserts that "Peru" was unknown to the Indians, and that the name was given by the Spaniards. Peru's territory lies between 1° 29′ N. and 19° 12′ 30″ S. lat., and 61° 54′ 45″ and 81° 18′ 39″ W. long. Bounded by Ecuador on the north, Brazil and Bolivia on the east, Chile on the south, and the Pacific Ocean on the west, its area extends over 679,000 sq. miles. The Andean range runs through Peru from S. E. to N. W., describing a curve parallel to the coast.

HISTORY.—However true the fact may be that gold was the object uppermost in the minds of the Spanish conquerors of the New World, it is a matter of history that in that conquest, from the northernmost confines of Mexico to the extreme south of Chile, religion always played a most important part, and the triumphant march of Castile's banner was also the glorious advance of the sign of the Saviour. That religion was the key-note of the American Crusades is evident from the history of their origin; the sanction given them by the Supreme Pontiff; the throng of self-devoted missionaries who followed in the wake of the conquerors to save the souls of the conquered ones; the reiterated instructions of the Crown, the great purpose of which was the conversion of the natives; and from the acts of the soldiers themselves (Prescott,

"Conquest of Peru", II, iii). The first news of the existence of the great Empire of the Incas reached the Spaniards in the year 1511, when Vasco Nuñez de Balboa, the discoverer of the Pacific Ocean, was engaged in an expedition against some Indian tribes in the interior of Darien. Perhaps the glory of conquering Peru would have fallen upon Balboa had not the jealousy of his chief, Pedro Arias de Avila, Governor of Panama, cut short his brilliant career. The second attempt to reach the coveted domain of the Incas was made in 1522, when Pascual de Andagoya started south from Panama, but he was compelled by ill health to return. Francisco Pizarro, after two unsuccessful expeditions (1524–25 and 1526–27) and a trip to Spain for the purpose of interesting Charles V in the undertaking, finally started the actual work of invading Peru, sailing from Panama in January, 1531. (See PIZARRO, FRANCISCO.)

When the persistent commander finally reached the country in 1532, the vast Inca empire is said to have extended over more than one-half of the entire South American continent. He found a people highly civilized, with excellent social and political institutions, who had developed agriculture to a remarkable degree through a splendid system of irrigation. They worshipped the sun as embodying their idea of a supreme being who ruled the universe. This worship was attended by an elaborate system of priestcraft, ritual, animal sacrifices, and other solemnities. After the conquest had been consummated (1534), Father Vicente Valverde, one of the five Dominicans who had accompanied the conqueror from Spain, was nominated Bishop of Cuzco and soon afterwards confirmed by Paul III, his jurisdiction extending over the whole territory of the newly-conquered domain. He was assassinated by the Indians of Puna, off Guayaquil, in 1541 when returning to Spain. Upon taking Cuzco, the capital of the empire, Pizarro provided a municipal government for the city, and encouraged its settlement by liberal grants of lands and houses. On 5 Sept., 1538, Bishop Valverde laid the foundations of the cathedral, and later a Dominican monastery was erected on the site of the Incaic temple of the sun, a nunnery was established, and several churches and monasteries built. The Dominicans, the Brothers of Mercy, and other missionaries actively engaged in propagating the Faith among the natives. Besides the priests that Pizarro was required to take in his own vessels, the succeeding ships brought additional numbers of missionaries, who devoted themselves earnestly and disinterestedly to the task of spreading the religion of Christ among the Indians. Their conduct towards them was in marked contrast to that of the conquerors, whose thirst for gold was never satiated, and who, having ransacked the villages and stripped the temples of their gold and silver ornaments, had enslaved the Indians, forcing them to work in the mines for their benefit.

At the outset and for several years thereafter the missionaries had to labour under almost unsurmountable obstacles, such as the uprising of the Inca Manco (a brother of Atahualpa, whom Pizarro had placed on the vacant throne) and the first civil wars among the conquerors themselves. These culminated in the execution of Diego de Almagro (1538) by order of Pizarro, and the assassination of the latter by the former's son, and were followed by other no less bloody conflicts between Cristobal Vaca de Castro (the newly-appointed governor) and Almagro's son (1543), and Gonzalo Pizarro and Blasco Nuñez de Vela, the first viceroy (1544–45). The news of this, the most formidable rebellion that had so far been recorded in the history of Spain, caused a great sensation at the Court. Father Pedro de la Gasca was selected for the delicate task of pacifying the colony. Provided with unbounded powers, Gasca reached Peru in July, 1546, and scarcely three years had elapsed when he accomplished the great object of his mission. Having restored peace, his next step was to ameliorate the condition of oppressed natives, in doing which he went farther than was agreeable to the wishes of the colonists. Other reforms were introduced by the far-seeing priest, thus placing the administration upon a sound basis and facilitating a more stable and orderly government by his successors. Upon his return to Spain he was raised to the Bishopric of Palencia, which diocese he administered until 1561, when he was promoted to the vacant See of Siguenza. He died in 1567 at the age of seventy-one. Unfortunately, the disturbances of the country were renewed on the departure of Gasca. The most serious uprising was that

CHURCH OF LA COMPAÑIA, AREQUIPA, PERU

of Francisco Fernandez Girón (1550–54) during the regime of the second viceroy, Antonio de Mendoza. Girón's execution (Dec., 1554) put an end to the last of the civil wars among the conquerors; and through the conciliatory and energetic measures of Andrés Hurtado de Mendoza, the third viceroy, the country was at last pacified, and the authority of Spain firmly established.

The Dominicans were the first ministers of the Gospel to come to Peru, and did splendid and efficient work in Christianizing the natives. They built many churches, monasteries, convents, and colleges, and acquired considerable prominence in ecclesiastical matters during the seventeenth century. Saint Rose of Lima (1586–1617), the patron of the Peruvian capital, was educated in one of their nunneries, and lived there until her death. The Franciscan fathers were also among the pioneer missionaries of Peru, and were prominent for their unceasing labours in the remotest wilds of South America. One of them, Saint Francis Solanus, made a journey from Peru to the Paraguayan Chaco, preaching to the tribes in their own dialects (1588–89). The Franciscan churches and buildings are among the handsomest in the country. Likewise, the good work of the Order of Saint Augustine stands high in the annals of Peruvian church history. Of the several temples and convents erected by the order during the viceroyalty, the church of Our Lady of Mercy is one of the most attractive in Lima. In 1567, at the earnest request of Philip II, Saint Francis Borgia, then General of the Society of Jesus, sent the first Jesuits to Peru under Father Geronimo Ruiz Portillo, who with his six companions arrived at Callao on 28 March, 1568, and entered Lima on 1 April. As in Paraguay and other parts of South America, the work of the Jesuits in Peru was most effective in propagating the Faith among the Indians as well as in educating them. After establishing a convent, a seminary, and a church in Lima, they built temples and schools in almost all the towns. At Juli, on the shores of Titicaca Lake, they founded a training school for missionaries (1577), where the novices were taught the native dialects. At that time the first printing press in South America was introduced by the order. Among their number were several of the most famous educators, historians, scientists, geographers, naturalists, and literary men of the period. Their educational institutions soon became renowned, not only in the American colonies, but also in Spain and Europe. The great and redeeming work of the Jesuits was flourishing when the decree of Charles III of 1769, ordering their expulsion from the Spanish domains, reached Peru and was executed by the Viceroy Manuel de Amat.

The Dominican Geronimo de Loayza, first Bishop of Lima (1546–1575), was succeeded by Saint Toribio de Mogrovejo (1538–1606). Nominated to the See of Lima in 1578, he entered that capital on 24 May, 1581. He learned the Quichua language thoroughly in order to find out for himself the real condition and actual wants of the Indians, whose interests he protected and promoted with the greatest zeal and care. Such was his activity that within comparatively few years he held fourteen synods and three councils, through which many beneficial reforms were instituted; and personally visited twice the whole territory under his jurisdiction, comprising at that time the greater portion of the South American continent. These tours of inspection he made on foot and accompanied only by two of his secretaries. He had scarcely started on his third journey when death surprised him on 23 March, 1606. Among other works which stand as a lasting monument to his memory are the Seminary of Saint Toribio and the Convent of Santa Clara in Lima. The Holy Office was established in Peru in 1570, during the regime of the viceroy Francisco de Toledo, the tribunal of the Inquisition sitting at Lima and extending its jurisdiction over the Captaincy-General of Chile, the Presidency of Quito, the Viceroyalty of Buenos Ayres, and part of the Viceroyalty of New Granada. It was abolished on 23 Sept., 1813, when the Viceroy Abascal enforced the order to that effect, enacted by the Cortes of Cadiz on 22 Feb. of the same year. But shortly after Ferdinand VII was restored to the throne of Spain, the inquisition was re-established in Peru (16 Jan., 1815) and operated until its definite abolition in 1820, when the struggle for freedom had assumed full sway. By an express provision, the jurisdiction of the Holy Office never comprised the Indians, who continued under the authority of the bishops and the ordinary courts.

For nearly three centuries, Peru was ruled by thirty-eight viceroys, or, in their stead, the government was temporarily exercised by the Audiencia Real of Lima, founded in 1544. As the representative of the King of Spain the viceroy was vested with almost absolute powers, and besides his executive functions he discharged those of Vice-Patron of the Church, President of the Audiencia, captain-general of the army, and Superintendent of the Royal Exchequer. The movement for emancipation in Peru began early in the nineteenth century, but the first attempts were repressed with considerable severity, and it was not until 28 July, 1821, that independence was declared. The defeat of the royalists at the battle of Ayacucho (9 Dec., 1824) put an end to the Spanish rule. Under the independent government, the executive assumed the same rights of patronage vested in the viceroy, and the five different constitutions adopted since the establishment of the republic recognized the Roman Catholic religion as the official church of the country with exclusion of any other.

POPULATION.—The last census of Peru was taken in 1876, hence the present population of the republic is known only approximately. According to the enumeration of that year, the number of inhabitants was 2,676,000. Recent estimates have, however, been made (1906) that show the population to have increased to 3,547,829. Of this total fifty per cent. is formed by Indians; fifteen per cent. by whites, mostly the descendants of Spaniards; three per cent. by negroes; one per cent. by Chinese and Japanese; and the remaining thirty-one per cent. by the offspring of intermarriage between the different races. According to the "Annuario Ecclesiastico" of Rome (1909), the Catholic population of Peru is 3,133,830, distributed as follows among the various dioceses: Lima, 606,900; Arequipa, 270,460; Ayacucho, 200,610; Chachapoyas, or Maynas, 95,370; Cuzco, 480,680; Huánuco, 288,100; Huaraz, 350,000; Puno, 260,810; Trujillo, 580,900.

ECCLESIASTICAL DIVISIONS.— The ecclesiastical Province of Peru comprises: one archdiocese, Lima, erected in 1543 and raised to metropolitan rank in 1546; nine suffragan dioceses, enumerated in order of seniority: Cuzco, 1536; Arequipa, 1609; Ayacucho, formerly Huamanga, 1615; Trujillo, 1616; Chachapoyas, or Maynas, 1843; Huánuco, 1865; Puno, 1865; Huaraz, 1900; and three prefectures Apostolic: San Leon de Amazonas, 1900; San Francisco del Ucayali, 1900; and Santo Domingo del Urubamba, 1900. The cathedral and episcopal residences are situated in the capital city of Lima. There are 66 parish churches in the Archdiocese of Lima, 85 in Cuzco, 71 in Arequipa, 102 in Trujillo, 87 in Ayacucho, 44 in Chachapoyas, 58 in Huánuco, 52 in Puno, and 48 in Huaraz. The number of additional churches and public chapels is perhaps about three times this number, as each parish has three or four churches besides the parish church. The number of secular priests corresponds to the number of parishes, approximately one-fourth of the entire number, when the number of assistant parish priests, chaplains, and priests without regular appointments are taken into consideration. The religious orders, both male and female, are well represented. In the Archdiocese of Lima the Franciscans have three convents, and the Lazarists, Redemptorists, Fathers of the Sacred Hearts of Jesus and Mary, Jesuits, Mercedarians, Augustinians, and Fathers of St. Camillus one each. Among the women, the Tertiaries of St. Francis have five convents; the Sisters of St. Joseph of Cluny four; the Dominicans, Carmelites, Conceptionists, Salesians, Religious of the Sacred Heart, and of the Sacred Hearts of Jesus and Mary two each; the Poor Clares, Bernardines, Capuchinesses, and Augustinians one each.

In the various dioceses many religious houses are to be found. Cuzco: Franciscans two, Dominicans, Mercedarians, Poor Clares, Carmelites, Dominican nuns, Sisters of the Sacred Hearts of Jesus and Mary, one each; Arequipa: Franciscans two, Jesuits, Lazarists, Salesians, Dominicans, Mercedarians, Dominican nuns, Carmelites, Sisters of the Sacred Hearts of Jesus and Mary one each; Trujillo: Franciscans two, Lazarists, Conceptionists, Carmelites, Poor Clares, Tertiaries of St. Dominic one each; Ayacucho: Redemptorists, Franciscans, Carmelites, Poor Clares one each; Huánuco: Franciscans, Tertiaries of St. Francis (women), Conceptionists one each; Huaraz: Franciscans, Sisters of Our Lady of Lourdes, Tertiaries of St. Francis (women) each one. The Dioceses of Chachapoyas and Puno have no religious houses. The three prefectures Apostolic, in the north, centre, and south of the republic, are under the care of the Augustinians, Franciscans, and Dominicans, who work principally for the conversion of the infidel native tribes. The Government allows a small subsidy for the maintenance of these missions, but their greatest source of income is derived from the "Propagación de la Fe en el Oriente del Perú". This pious association has spread over the whole republic and collects the contributions of the faithful, which are, relatively speaking, very abundant. Each diocese has its own diocesan seminary for the education of its priests. The Franciscans are in charge of the seminaries of the dioceses of Cuzco and Ayacucho, the Lazarists of those of Trujillo and Arequipa, the Fathers of the Sacred Hearts of Jesus and Mary of that of Huaraz, and the rest are under the care of the seculars. The Government does not claim supervision over the seminaries, which are under the control of the respective bishops.

CHARITIES.—There are some thirty hospitals in Peru administered by various charitable societies, one old people's home, one orphan asylum, and several congregations especially dedicated to charitable works, besides a great number of private associations devoted to the work of gratuitous teaching, visiting the sick poor in their homes, legalizing illicit unions, etc.

LAWS.—*Religion*.—The constitution, promulgated on 10 Dec., 1860, expressly provides that the nation profess the Roman Catholic religion; that the State protect it and does not permit the public exercise of any other (Art. 4). There is, however, no interference in personal religious beliefs, and there are Protestant churches in the republic. Under the Organic Law of 17 Sept., 1857 (Arts. 49–54), the prefects of departments are given certain supervisory powers over ecclesiastical affairs connected with the national patronage. Article 94 of the Constitution, on the duties of the president of the republic, establishes that the chief magistrate shall: exercise the ecclesiastical patronage according to law; nominate for archbishops and bishops, with the approval of Congress, those who have been chosen according to law; nominate church dignitaries, canons, curates, and incumbents of ecclesiastical benefices; conclude concordats with the Apostolic See, according to instructions given by Congress; grant or refuse, with the assent of Congress, passage to decrees of councils, or pontifical Bulls, Briefs, and Rescripts; but in case that these affect matters in litigation, the supreme court of justice of the republic must be previously heard.

Article 1358 of the Civil Code in force, under which the Church and religious orders were prohibited from disposing of their property without the consent of the Government, was repealed, 30 Sept., 1901. Hence the Church in Peru, as a juridical entity, can acquire and possess property of all kinds, as well as contract obligations and exercise civil or criminal action, according to the statutes of the country, the concordat, and the ecclesiastic canons and discipline. Temples and all places of worship are exempt from taxation, but other church property yielding a revenue of $100 or more is subject to the ecclesiastical tax according to the Regulation of 20 Dec., 1886. Arts. 83 to 94 of the Civil Code refer to clergymen and religious, containing a definition of who are such; the qualifications necessary for the profession; their exemption from public services; the recovery of civil rights by religious upon their secularization, etc. The religious orders are governed by the Regulations for Regulars (*Reglamento de Regulares*), approved by Resolution of 12 Jan., 1872. Although the modern law obliges all citizens to military duty, there has never been a case where it has been applied to priests or seminarists. No special exemption is granted to clerics in regard to trials; they are tried in the public courts, civil or criminal, as the case may be. There is no law enforcing the observance of holy days, although in the capital a particular ordinance exists which requires that stores be closed on Sundays and Holy Days. Processions and other public acts of worship may be held without interference from the Government. The administration of the different branches of the Church in Peru, in so far as the national patronage is concerned, is entrusted to the Minister of Justice, Worship, and Public Instruction. The fiscal budget assigns the sum of $100,000 for the maintenance of the Church, including the salaries of prelates, rectors, etc.

WILLS AND TESTAMENTS.—The procedure that obtains in Peru is similar to that in force in Spain, being based upon the Roman law. According to the Civil Code, wills may be either open or closed. An open will (*testamento abierto*) may be executed in a public instrument, i. e., before a notary public, in a private document, or verbally (Arts. 651–656). There are, besides, special forms of wills, such as the military, the maritime, and others, in which, on account of the unusual circumstances attending upon each particular case, the ordinary formalities of law are dispensed with, and others of a less restrictive nature prescribed instead (Arts. 674–681). A closed will (*testamento cerrado*) must be duly sealed by the testator himself. A foreigner owning property in Peru must testate according to the provisions of the Civil Code (Art. 692); and if he have an estate abroad he may dispose of it by will executed in accordance with the laws of the country wherein such estate may be located, or with those of his native land (Art. 693), provided he have no rightful heir or heirs in Peru (Art. 695). The substantive law governing wills and testaments, succession, etc. is contained in Arts. 651 to 954 of the Civil Code.

Cemeteries are under the authority of charitable associations and the parish priests. Under the Resolutions of 20 Nov., 1868 and 19 Jan., 1869, the Municipal Councils of the republic are instructed to establish and maintain laic cemeteries for the burial of persons not belonging to the Catholic Church.

Marriage and Divorce.—The Peruvian Civil Code expressly prescribes that marriages in the republic must be performed with the formalities established by the Council of Trent; but in order to enable non-Catholics to marry in the country a law was enacted on 23 Dec., 1897, empowering the *Alcaldes* (mayors) of the Provincial Councils to solemnize marriages. Divorce in Peru, as established by Arts. 191 seq. of the Civil Code, is not absolute, i. e., does not terminate the bond of union. Marriage can only be nullified through the regular ecclesiastical procedure, if by reason of canonical disabilities, or through the ordinary courts of justice, if on account of civil impediments. Sec. III of the Civil Code (Arts. 120–217) is devoted to the subject of matrimony, including divorce.

Schools.—Education in Peru is a national institution under the Department of Justice, Public Instruction, and Worship, but is also given by private establishments, of which there are several maintained by religious orders. It is divided into primary, secondary, and academic. Primary instruction was, until 1905, when the new public education law went into effect, in the hands of the municipalities, but in view of their limited resources the national Government found it necessary to take charge of it. It is free and compulsory and is given in about 2500 public schools, with 3105 teachers, and an attendance of 162,298 pupils (1909). Secondary education is furnished by thirty government colleges and several private institutions. Academic instruction is afforded by the universities of the republic. Foremost among them is the University of Saint Mark, founded at Lima in 1574, which has faculties of theology, law, medicine, letters, sciences, and political economy. There are also the Universities of Saint Thomas of Cuzco, Saint Thomas of Trujillo, and Saint Augustine of Arequipa. Normal, agricultural, and manual training schools are largely attended.

LORENTE, *Historia del Perú* (Lima, 1863-76); PRESCOTT, *History of the Conquest of Peru* (Boston, 1859); RAIMONDI, *El Perú* (Lima, 1890-1902); BERMÚDEZ, *Anales de la Catedral de Lima* (Lima, 1903); ENOCK, *The Andes and the Amazon* (London, 1908); IDEM, *Peru* (New York, 1908); WRIGHT, *The Old and New Peru* (Philadelphia, 1908); GARLAND, *Peru in 1906* (Lima, 1907); SEEBEE, *Notes on Peru* (London, 1901); *Bulletin of the Pan-American Union* (August, 1910).

J. MOREN-LACALLE.

Perugia, ARCHDIOCESE OF (PERUSINA), in Umbria, Central Italy. The city is situated on a hill on the right of the Tiber. The Gothic cathedral is of the fourteenth century, its façade being yet unfinished; it contains paintings by Baroccio, Manni, and Signorelli; there is a marble sarcophagus in which are the remains of Urban IV and Martin IV; in the chapel del Santo Anello is preserved an onyx ring, which is said to have been the marriage ring of Our Lady, and which was venerated first at Chiusi, where it was stolen, and then taken to Perugia in the fifteenth century; in the chapter library is preserved a codex of the Gospel of St. Luke, of the sixth century. Other churches are: San Pietro dei Cassinesi, the church of a monastery founded by St. Peter Vincioli about 1000; San Ercolano, the high altar of which is made of an ancient sarcophagus; Sant' Angelo, a round building, dating from the sixth century; the Madonna della Luce, a graceful little temple by Galeazzo Alessio; San Francesco del Prato, now the seat of the "Accademia" of fine arts. The university, founded in 1320, has three faculties, and contains a museum of Etruscan, Roman, and Christian antiquities, with many sculptures and inscriptions, among the latter, the "Tabulæ Perusinæ", discovered in 1822. The most notable ancient monuments of the town are the Porta Augusta; the tomb of the Volumnii, which was discovered in 1840 by Vermiglioli; and the Etruscan walls.

Perugia was among the most important cities of the Etruscans, with whom it took part in the wars against Rome in 310 and 295 B. C., as also in the Samnite War. The Perugian War (41 B. C.) is famous; the troops of Anthony were shut up here, where they were compelled to surrender. During the Gothic War, Perugia suffered various sieges, by the Byzantines in 537 and in 552, and by the Goths in 546 and 548. The Lombards at the time of their first incursion had taken possession of the city, but in 592 it came again under the Byzantine power and was made the seat of a *dux*. In 749 it was besieged by the Lombard King Rachis, who, however, was persuaded by Pope Zacharias to raise the siege. Pepin gave the city to the Holy See. From the beginning of the eleventh century, Perugia was established as a free commune and was in struggles with the neighbouring cities of Umbria and of Tuscany (Chiusi, 1012; Cortona, 1049; Assisi, 1054; Todi, 1056; Foligno, 1080 and 1090); it was governed by consuls (from 5 to 16), for whom were substituted in 1303 the *priori delle arti;* after 1174 there was a *podestà*, and later a *capitano del popolo*.

Perugia, friendly to Florence and faithful to the Holy See, was essentially a Guelph city, and in the thirteenth century the popes established their residence here for a long time; four of them were elected here (Honorius III, Honorius IV, Celestine V, and Clement V). On the other hand, continuing its wars with neighbouring cities (Spoleto, from 1324, was besieged for two years), Perugia extended its sovereignty over the greater portion of Umbria, and over a part of Tuscany. In 1375 it was among the first cities that revolted against Gregory IX at the instance of the Florentines. Meanwhile, there had been formed two parties: the Raspanti (the popular party) and the Beccarini (the party of the nobles), and between them they had made it possible for Biondo Michelotti to become lord of the city in 1390; he, however, was killed in 1393, and then Gian Galeazzo Visconti took possession of the town; but in 1403 it became subject to Boniface IX. Afterwards it fell into the power of Ladislao di Napoli; in 1416 the city was taken by Braccio da Montone, who was recognized as lord of Perugia by Martin V. At his death in 1424 the nobles came into power, but contention soon developed among them, and eventually the Baglioni made away with the Oddi family. Finally, Gian Paolo Baglione became a tyrant of the city, making himself detested by his cruelty and dissolute habits. He was reduced to order in 1506 by Julius II; but fresh cruelties against his own relations led to his decapitation by order of Leo X in 1520; Perugia then came once more into immediate dependency upon the Holy See.

In 1534 Rodolfo Baglione set fire to the Apostolic palace, and the vicelegate was slain; and no sooner had order been established after these events, than a rebellion broke out on account of the tax on salt, which Paul III had increased in 1540; Perugia declared itself a "city of Christ", and confided its keys to the care of a crucifix. On 5 July, however, it was compelled to surrender to the troops of Pierluigi Farnese and lost its freedom. Paul III built a fortress to prevent further revolts of the Perugians, while Julius III restored to them the greater part of their privileges. In the rebellion of 1848, the first act of the Perugians was to demolish the tower of Paul III. In 1859 there was a provisional Government established, but the Pontifical troops soon took possession of the city, though they did not commit the acts of cruelty of which they have been accused. Finally in 1860 General de Sonnaz took possession of the town in the name of the King of Sardinia.

Blessed John of Perugia, one of the first companions of St. Francis, died in 1230. In the martyrologies are found the names of the martyrs Constantius (Constantinus, whom some believe to have been a bishop), Florentius, and Felicissimus, who died at Perugia. Under Decius one Decentius was bishop, according to the tradition; but the first bishop of whom there is any certain knowledge was St. Herculanus, killed by King Totila in 546; many admit there were two bishops and saints of this name, of whom the first is said to have died either in one of the great persecutions or under Julian the Apostate (Cappelletti).

St. Herculanus was succeeded by Joannes, who consecrated Pope Pelagius I (566); Aventius (591); Laurentius (649); Benenatus (679); St. Asclepiodorus (about 700), whose relics were later taken to Metz; Conon (998) and Andreas (1033), who had various controversies with the abbots of San Pietro; Joannes (1105), who consecrated the monastery of Monte Corona; Vivianus, who was present at the council of 1179; Giovanni (1206), who gave a convent to St. Francis; Salvio de' Salvi (1231), a pious and learned prelate, who restored San Stefano, the ancient cathedral; Francesco Poggi, O. Min. (1312), who built S. Domenico nuovo; Andrea Bontempi (1339), a cardinal, and legate general of Umbria; Andrea Giovanni Baglione (1434), who filled several convents with reformed religious; Dionisio Vannucci (1482), who erected the altar of the chapel del Sacro Anello; Giovanni Lopez (1492), a cardinal who enjoyed influence under Alexander VI; Trilo Baglione (1501), deposed by Alexander VI for having taken up arms against Cæsar Borgia and restored to his see by Julius II; Antonio Ferreri (1506), who suspected by Julius II died in the Castle of S. Angelo in 1508; Cardinal Agostino Spinola (1510), under whom the canons of the cathedral, who since the twelfth century had lived according to the Rule of St. Augustine, were

PERUGIA

THE PORTA URBICA ETRUSCA

PIAZZA DEL MUNICIPIO FROM THE CATHEDRAL

THE MUNICIPAL BUILDING (XIV CENTURY)

VIA DEL CARDELLINO, WITH ARCH OVER WHICH THE APPIAN WAY PASSES

relieved of that rule; Jacop Soimonetti (1535), a cardinal; Fulvio Corneo (1550), reformer of the diocese and founder of the seminary; Ippolito Corneo (1553), who established a house of reform, and a monastery for poor young men; Giulio Oradini (1562), who founded a college for clerks; Napoleone Comitoli (1591), the founder of other charitable institutions; M. Ant. Ausidei (1726), who embellished the cathedral; Alessandro M. Odoardi (1776), a zealous prelate, who discovered the body of St. Costanzo; Camillo Campanelli (1804), who took the oath of allegiance to Napoleon; Carlo Filesio Cittadini (1818), who distinguished himself by his firmness and prudence against the Provisional Government of 1831, and by his generosity saved the city from pillage at that time; Gioacchino Pecci (1846), who became Leo XIII, and who made Perugia an archdiocese without suffragans.

The archdiocese has 199 parishes, with 100,900 inhabitants, 9 religious houses of men, 21 of women, and 1 Catholic weekly publication.

CAPPELLETTI, *Le Chiese d' Italia*, V; VERMIGLIOLI, *Bibliografia storico-perugina* (Perugia, 1823); BARLOTI, *Storia di Perugia* (Perugia, 1843); FABRETTI, *Cronache di Perugia* (Turin, 1892); BONAZZI, *Storia di Perugia* (1875); *Bullettino della Soc. di Storia Patria per l' Umbria* (Perugia, 1886).

U. BENIGNI.

UNIVERSITY OF PERUGIA.— One of the "free" universities of Italy, was erected into a *studium generale* on 8 Sept., 1308, by the Bull "Super specula" of Clement V. A school of arts existed about 1200, in which medicine and law were soon taught. Before 1300 there were several *universitates scholiarum*. Jacobus de Belviso, a famous civil jurist, taught here from 1316 to 1321. By Bull of 1 Aug., 1318, John XXII granted the privilege of conferring degrees in civil and canon law, and on 18 Feb., 1321, in medicine and arts.

On 19 May, 1355, the Emperor Charles IV issued a Bull confirming the papal erection and raising it to the rank of an imperial university. This unusual mark of favour was given to assist Perugia after the terrible plague years 1348–49. In 1362 the Collegium Gregorianum (later called the *Sapienza vecchia*) was founded by Cardinal Nicolo Capocci for the maintenance of forty youths. Gregory XI by Brief of 11 Oct., 1371 gave the privileges of a *studium generale* to this new faculty of theology. This faculty was suppressed and its property merged in the university in 1811. To this foundation the *Sapienza nuova* was transferred in 1829. The latter was founded by Benedetto Guidalotti, Bishop of Recanti in 1426, with Martin V's approval, as the Collegio di S. Girolamo. It was a free hostel for impecunious strangers who wished to study law and medicine. Suppressed by the French in 1798, it was reopened in 1807 by Pius VII as the Collegio Pio. In the Constitution of 27 Aug., 1824, Leo XII made this the chief college of the university. Since the time of Napoleon I the university has occupied the old Olivetan convent of Monte Morcino. There was a faculty of mathematics down to 1884. The statutes are modelled upon those of Bologna. The number of students at different dates were: 1339, 142; 1881, 79; 1911, 350. Among its eminent teachers were: the canonist Johannes Andreas; Cino da Pistoia (1270–1336), poet and jurist; his pupil Bartolus (1314–27),

XI.—47

famous civil jurist; his pupil Baldus; Albericus Gentilis, founder of the science of international law; and Francesco della Rovere (Sixtus IV). Among its students were: Nicholas IV, Gregory XI, Innocent VII, Martin V, Pius III, Julius II, Julius III, Urban VII, Gregory XIV, Clement VIII, and Paul V.

Statistics (1911):—Expenditure, 295,470 lire; receipts, 285,748 lire; examination fees, 5948 lire; faculty of jurisprudence, 11 professors; faculty of medicine, 13; school of pharmacy 5; school of veterinary medicine, 3. A large number of institutions are connected with the university, e. g., an obstetric training college, laboratories for general chemistry and for pharmacy, etc., also the meteorological observatory (founded 1800). The library has over 54,000 volumes. The museum contains vases, bronzes, and sculptures, and many valuable Etruscan and Roman antiquities.

BINI, *Mem. istoriche della Perugina università degli studi* (Perugia, 1816); PADELLETTI, *Contributo alla storia dello Studio di Perugia nei secoli 14 e 15* (Bologna, 1873); ROSSI, *Doc. per la storia dell' università di Perugia* in *Giornale di erudizione artistica*, IV–VI (Perugia, 1875–77), 2nd series, II (Perugia, 1883); RASHDALL, *The Universities of Europe in the Middle Ages*, II, I (Oxford, 1895), 40–43.

C. F. WEMYSS BROWN.

Perugino (PIETRO VANNUCCI), Italian painter, founder of the Umbrian school, b. at Città della Pieve in 1446; d. at Fontignano near Perugia in February, 1524. He was called Perugino, although he often signed his name Petrus de Castro Plebis. He studied art at Perugia, where he found an earlier school, that of Nicolo Alunno and Boccati da Camerino, already remarkable for the pure expression of the sentiment and animation of the interior life. Perugino adopted this tradition, adding to it the decorative taste of his master, Fiorenzo di Lorenzo, and influenced by the powerful style of Piero della Francesca. In 1472 he went to Florence, where he was the comrade of Leonardo in Verrocchio's studio, the most active centre and laboratory of the methods of the Renaissance. Here Perugino acquired knowledge whereby he expressed his ideas in an imperishable manner. He learned construction, became a master of perspective, and in style followed a fixed formula, which was much admired. Unfortunately his early works are lost. His frescoes in the Palazzo Pubblico in Perugia (1475) and those in Cerqueto have been destroyed or ruined. His earliest extant picture is the "Delivery of the Keys to St. Peter" (1482), in the Sistine Chapel at Rome, where three other frescoes were later destroyed to make room for the "Last Judgment" of Michelangelo. Perugino then held a foremost place in the Italian school, and to-day his one remaining fresco shines as a masterpiece among the more brilliant inventions of the Florentine school. It engendered numerous works of art, and Raphael, Perugino's great pupil, was mindful of it in the "Sposalizio", the most exquisite work of his youth.

Within the next fifteen years (1484–99) Perugino attained his greatest success. His work was most in demand for religious pictures, and he went from city to city painting altar-pieces or ecclesiastical frescoes. In 1491–2, having gone to Rome to paint the decoration (no longer extant) of the palace of the Cardinal de' Medicis, he executed the delightful picture in the Villa Albani, the "Adoration of the Holy Child" (1491).

Except for some journeys to Perugia, Venice, and Tano, Florence was his centre of operations for that period. To it belong the "Crucifixion" and the "Gethsemane" of the Florence Accademia; the famous "Pietà" of the same museum; the "Taking down from the Cross" of the Pitti (1495); the "Vision of St. Bernard" in the Museum of Munich; but the most wonderful of these works is the great fresco of the "Crucifixion" in Sta Maddalena dé Pazzi (1496). The beauty of the faces, the stirring gravity of the scene, the finish of the colouring, and the perfection of the landscape rank this picture first among Perugino's works in Italy. The triptych of the "Nativity" (1500) at London is a miniature of this fresco almost equal to it in beauty. Perugino shows himself an incomparable landscape artist in the pictures of his best period; he was an eminent master of the painting of the atmosphere. He derives his expression from the rarest artistic qualities, from a finished composition, spacing of figures, use of oils, and deep, harmonious colouring, thereby achieving an effect of depth and fullness. In his masterpieces, though he transforms the reality to a great extent, he is nevertheless very true to nature. He copies the nude quite as accurately as the most able of the Florentines, as is seen in the wonderful "St. Sebastian" of the Louvre, and he is capable of the most exact and close veracity, for example, the two admirable heads of Carthusians at the Florence Accademia, which suffice to place him in the front rank of portrait painters. Perugino is one of the greatest and most popular artists of Italy and his work is distinctive for the creation of the "pious picture".

The decoration of the Cambio, or Bourse of Perugia (1499), marks the beginning of a period of decline. The effect of this hall decorated with frescoes on the four walls and with arabesques on the ceiling is very charming, but the conception is extremely arbitrary, and the composition worthless and insignificant. Ancient heroes, prophets, and sibyls all have the same disdainful expression; the whole is neutral, abstract, vague. The artist replaces all semblance of thought, conscience, and effort with an appearance of sentiment which is merely sentimentality. Thenceforth Perugino is a deplorable example of a great artist who destroys himself by subordination to mere handicraft. Unquestionably he had a sublime period in his life, when he first endowed incomparable plastic bodies with an unlooked-for expression of the infinite and the divine, but he soon abused this oft-repeated formula, the arrangement became purely schematic, the figures stereotyped, the colouring sharp and acidulous, and all emotion evaporated. The only part of his genius that persisted to the end was an eye enamoured of the skies and light. This decline was clearly evident in 1504, when Isabella d'Este ordered the artist to paint the "Combat of Love and Chastity", now in the Louvre. At this time art was achieving its most glorious conquests, as testified by the two famous cartoons of Leonardo and Michelangelo (1506) at Florence. The works of his last twenty years, frescoes and altar-pieces, are scattered through Umbria, at Perugia, Spello, Siena etc. They add nothing to his glory. The ceiling which he painted for Julius II in 1508 in the Camera dell' Incendio at the Vatican has at least a high decorative value. In 1521 the old artist worked once more in collaboration with Raphael. The latter had left an unfinished fresco at S. Spirito at Perugia and after his death Perugino was commissioned to finish it. Nothing shows more clearly the moral difference between these two geniuses, the wonderful progress and self-development of Raphael, the immobility and intellectual apathy of his master. The latter died of the pest at the age of seventy-eight.

VASARI, *Le Vite*, ed. MILANESI (Florence, 1878); MARCHESI, *Il Cambio di Perugia* (Pratro, 1853); PASSAVANT, *Raphael d' Urbin et son père* (Paris, 1860); *Essai sur les peintres de l'Ombrie* (1860);
MORELLI, *Italian painters* (London, 1892–3); BRUNAMONTI, *Pietro Perugino* in *Rivista Contemporanea* (1889); BRAGHIROLLI, *Notizie e documenti inediti intorno a Pietro Vanucci* (Perugia, 1874); BURCKHARDT, *Art Guide to Painting in Italy* (London, 1879); BROUSSOLLE, *Pèlerinages ombriens* (Paris, 1896); *La Jeunesse de Perugin* (Paris, 1901); BERENSON, *Central Italian painters* (London, 1897); WILLIAMSON, *Perugino* (London, 1903).

LOUIS GILLET.

Peruzzi, BALDASSARE, architect and painter, b. at Siena, 7 March, 1481; d. at Rome, 6 Jan., 1537. He derived much benefit from the years of apprenticeship under Bramante, Raphael, and Sangallo during the erection of St. Peter's. An evidence of his genius for independent work is the Palazzo Massimi alle Colonne, which he began in 1535. Almost all art critics ascribe also to him the Villa Farnesina. In this, two wings branching off from a central hall, a simple arrangement of pilasters, and a beautiful frieze on the exterior of the building, airy halls, and a few splendid rooms are combined in excellent taste. The paintings which adorn the interior are for the most part by Peruzzi. The decoration of the façade, the work of Peruzzi, has almost entirely perished. To decorate this villa on the Tiber a number of second-rate artists were employed, and just as the style of the villa in no wise recalls the old castellated type of country-house, so the paintings in harmony with the pleasure-loving spirits of the time were thoroughly antique and uninspired by Christian ideas. It seems that Raphael designed the composition of the story of Amor and Psyche as a continuation of the Galatea. On a plate-glass vault Peruzzi painted the firmament, with the zodiacal signs, the planets, and other heavenly bodies, his perspective being so skilful as to deceive even the eye of Titian. The close proximity of Raphael's work has overshadowed Peruzzi in the ceiling decoration of the Stanza d'Eliodoro in the Vatican. While Raphael designed the mural paintings and, it may be, the entire plan for the decoration of the hall, it is certain that the tapestry-like frescoes on the ceiling are to be ascribed to Peruzzi. Four scenes represent God's saving omnipotence as shown in the case of Noe, Abraham, Jacob, and Moses. The manifestation of the Lord in the burning bush and the figure of Jehovah commanding Noe to enter the ark were formerly considered works of Raphael. But some time before, Peruzzi had produced for the church of S. Croce in Gierusalemme a mosaic ceiling, the beautiful keystone of which represented the Saviour of the world. Other paintings ascribed to him are to be found in S. Onofrio and S. Pietro in Mostorio. That Peruzzi improved as time went on is evident in his later works, e. g., the "Madonna with Saints" in S. Maria della Pace at Rome, and the fresco of Augustus and the Triburtine Sibyl in Fontegiusta at Siena. As our master interested himself in the decorative art also, he exercised a strong influence in this direction, not only by his own decorative paintings but also by furnishing designs for craftsmen of various kinds.

REDTENBACHER, *Peruzzi und seine Werke* (Karlsruhe, 1875); WEESE, *Baldassare Peruzzi's Anteil an dem malerischen Schumcke der Villa Farnesina* (Leipzig, 1894); RICHTER, *Siena* (Leipzig); STEINMANN, *Rom in der Renaissance* (Leipzig); GRUNER, *Fresco Decorations and Stuccoes of Churches and Palaces in Italy* (London, 1854).

G. GIETMANN.

Pesaro, DIOCESE OF (PESAURENSIS), in central Italy. The city is situated at the mouth of the river Foglia, on the Adriatic Sea. The industries of the town include fisheries, agriculture, the manufacture of majolicas, the working of sulphur and lignite coal mines, bituminous schist, and marble. The cathedral (San Francesco) has a beautiful Gothic portal and a "Coronation of the Madonna", by Bellini; the church of San Domenico is a work of Fra Paolo Belli; in the latter is the mausoleum of the poet Giulio Perticari. The Palazzo Ducale was begun by Laurana before 1465, and was finished by the Gengas, father and son.

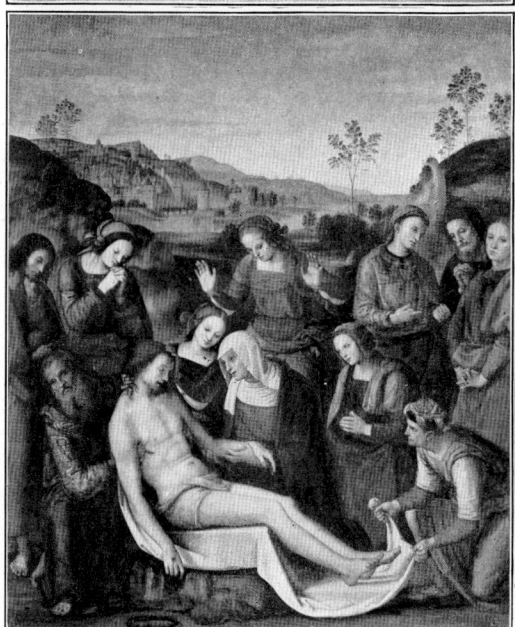

PERUGINO

MADONNA WITH FOUR SAINTS
VATICAN, ROME

PREPARATION FOR THE TOMB
PITTI PALACE

MADONNA ADORING THE INFANT CHRIST (DETAIL)
PITTI PALACE

VISION OF ST. BERNARD
PINAKOTHEK, MUNICH

In the Almerici palace is a museum of ancient inscriptions, coins, and ivory carvings, a collection of majolica, a small picture gallery, and the Olivieri library. Beside the episcopal residence is the ancient *duomo*, now closed, and the remains of a Christian nymphæum. Outside the city is the Villa Imperiale, built by Alessandro Sforza (1469). Among the scientific institutions mention should be made of the Liceo Musicale, dedicated to Rossini, a native of Pesaro. Of the charitable institutions, the infant asylum dates from 1257, and the retreat for penitent women from 1619.

At the beginning of the fourth century B. C., Pesaro was occupied by the Senones, who were driven from there in 283. The town became a colony in 184. During the Gothic War, it underwent frequent sieges. In the eighth century Pesaro fell four times into the hands of the Lombards, and finally was annexed to the Pontifical States. Giovanni Malatesta, the Lame, became *podestà* of Pesaro in 1285. Galeazzo Malatesta, having no children, gave Pesaro as a dower to his niece, Costanza Varano, wife of Alessandro Sforza, and the latter was confirmed in the possession of the city by the Holy See in 1447. Costanzo Sforza (1473) fought against the pope in the service of Florence, and left the duchy to his natural son Giovanni (1481); the latter married Lucrezia Borgia, from whom he was eventually separated. Costanzo II inherited the duchy in 1510, under the tutelage of his uncle Galeazzo, but in 1512 Julius II gave Pesaro to Francesco M. della Rovere, Duke of Urbino, and the city remained united to this duchy, of which it became the capital. In 1860 the town was valiantly defended by 800 men of the Pontifical troops against the army of Cialdini, but it was compelled to surrender.

The Blessed Francis of Pesaro (1350) and the Blessed Michelina Metelli (1356) were of this city; the first is buried in the cathedral, and the second in the church of the Conventuals; other natives of Pesaro were the Blessed Santo, O. Min., who died in 1393; Blessed Pietro Giacomo (1496), an Augustinian, and Blessed Serafina Sforza (1478), wife of the Duke Alessandro Sforza; at the cathedral is the body of the Blessed Felice Meda (d. 1444). The people of Pesaro have great veneration for St. Terentius, a martyr of uncertain date. The first bishop, St. Florentius, is said to have governed this see in the middle of the second century, while the bishop, St. Decentius, according to tradition, suffered martyrdom under Diocletian; Bishop Heraclianus was at the Council of Sardica in 343. Other bishops were Germanus, who went with Cresconius di Todi to Constantinople in 497 as legate of Anastasius II; Felix, whom St. Gregory the Great brought to trial; Maximus (649); Benenatus, a legate to the Sixth General Council (680); Stabilinus (769); Adelberto (998), founder of the monastery of S. Tommaso in Folgia, where Clement II died in 1047; Pietro (1070), who was deposed, being a partisan of the schism of Barbarossa; Bartolomeo (1218); Omodio (1346); Biagio Geminelli (1354); Leale Malatesta (1370), who was the first to convoke a diocesan synod; Cardinal Antonio Casini (1406); Giulio Simonetti (1560), was at the Council of Trent, and founded the seminary; Gian Lucido Palombara (1658), consecrated the new cathedral; Umberto Radicati (1742), held an important diocesan synod; Cardinal Gennaro Ant. de' Simoni (1775); and Andrea Mastai-Ferretti (1806).

The diocese is a suffragan of Urbino; it has 39 parishes, 47,000 inhabitants, 9 religious houses of men, 7 of women, 2 educational establishments for male students, and 4 for girls.

CAPPELLETTI, *Le Chiese d'Italia*, III; MARCOLINI, *Notizie storiche della provincia di Pesaro e Urbino* (2nd ed., Pesaro, 1883).

U. BENIGNI.

Pescennius Niger, Emperor of Rome (193-194). He was a native of central Italy, and during the reigns of Marcus Aurelius and Commodus had kept the Germans from invading Roman territory. In 192 he suppressed an outbreak of the Jews and Saracens. After the death of Pertinax the prætorian guards proclaimed Didius Julianus emperor; the troops in Britain elected Clodius Albinus; those on the Danube chose Lucius Septimius Severus; and the soldiers in Syria elected the governor of that province, Caius Pescennius Niger Justus. Septimius Severus advanced to Rome with the Pannonian legions. Julianus was killed, and the senate acknowledged Severus. Severus now made Albinus practically a co-emperor. Forthwith he addressed himself against Pescennius Niger. The latter had many adherents at Rome. Moreover, Antioch, where the proclamation of the rival emperor had been issued, aspired to the same position as Rome. Pescennius gained the support of the petty Oriental rulers. In preparation for the advance of Severus he appointed the able proconsul of the Province of Asia, Asellius Æmilianus, as his chief of staff. The ports of Asia were closed; the passes over the Taurus mountains were fortified; and Byzantium was garrisoned.

Severus also had made far-reaching preparations. Troops were sent to Africa and the seasoned army of the Danube was brought together. The advance guards of the opposing armies met at Perinthus, the capital of Thrace. The soldiers of Severus were repulsed. Severus, however, proceeded with his main army across the Bosporus and by way of Candeto near Cyzicus. Here in 194 a battle took place in which Æmilianus was slain. Niger himself now hastened to the scene but was defeated near Nicæa, with the result that most of the cities of the Province of Asia came into the hands of Severus. Niger fled to reach Antioch. The possession of this city was decided by a battle fought south of Issus in which Pescennius Niger was defeated. While making his escape to the Parthians he was overtaken and killed towards the end of 194. His severed head was exhibited by order of Severus before the besieged city of Byzantium. Severus mercilessly punished Niger's adherents, whether private individuals or cities. Byzantium did not surrender until 196. Severus was also successful against the vassal states of the Parthians, Adiabene and Osrhoene. For the time being the Roman Province of Osrhoene was established.

For bibliography see PERTINAX.

KARL HOEBER.

Pesch, TILMANN, a Jesuit philosopher, b. at Cologne, 1 Feb., 1836; d. at Valkenburg, Holland, 18 Oct., 1899. He became a Jesuit on 15 October, 1852, and made his novitiate at Friedrichsburg near Münster; he studied classics two years at Paderborn, philosophy two years at Bonn; taught four years at Feldkirch, Switzerland; studied theology one year at Paderborn and three years at Maria-Laach, after which he made his third year of novitiate at Paderborn. He then taught philosophy at Maria-Laach (1867-69). From 1870 till 1876 he worked in the ministry, and again taught philosophy eight years (1876-84), at Blyenbeck. The literary activity of Pesch began in 1876. He contributed to "Philosophia Lacensis"; "Institutiones philosophiæ naturalis" (1880); "Institutiones logicales" (1888); "Institutiones psychologicæ" (1896-98). The last fifteen years of his life were devoted entirely to writing and to the ministry. By publishing treatises in German, Pesch helped much to spread Catholic truth. Such treatises were "Weltphänomenon" (1881), "Welträtsel" (1884), "Seele und Leib" (1893), and "Christliche Lebensphilosophie" (1895). The last work reached its fourth edition within three years. Besides these more scholarly writings, he published popular philosophic and apologetic articles and pamphlets. The most important of these were the articles published in the "Germania" above the pseudonym "Gottlieb"; they were later arranged in two volumes, "Briefe aus Hamburg" (1883), and "Der Krach von Wittenberg" (1889), refuting the usual calumnies against the Church. His most popular book was "Das Religiöse Leben", of which thirteen large editions have appeared. During all this period of literary activity, Pesch was tireless as a missioner in Germany. He was often arrested under charge of being a Jesuit. Pesch taught the best in Scholasticism, but appreciated what was good in other systems of philosophy. His Latin writings contain the latest results of natural science applied to the illustration of truth by scholastic methods.

Mitteilungen aus der deutschen Provinz (Roermond), n. 8, 721; THOELEN, *Menologium oder Lebensbilder aus der Geschichte der deutschen Ordensprovinz der Gesellschaft Jesu* (Roermond, 1901), 602.

WALTER DRUM.

Peschitto. See MANUSCRIPTS OF THE BIBLE; VERSIONS OF THE BIBLE.

Pescia, DIOCESE OF (PISCIENSIS), in Tuscany, Italy, on the Rivers Pescia Maggiore and Pescia Minore, situated in a fertile plain; its textile industry is

CATHEDRAL, PESCIA
Rebuilt in 1693, the campanile in 1306

considerable. The cathedral is very ancient, but was restored by Ferri in 1663; it contains beautiful paintings by Gabbaini and the mausoleum of Baldassare Turini. Other churches are S. Michele and S. Stefano, anterior to the twelfth century, and S. Francesco, which dates from 1211. The earliest mention of Pescia is of the eighth century; later it belonged to the Republic of Lucca until the fourteenth century, when it was conquered by the Florentines, who defended it effectively in 1430 against Francesco Sforza. In 1554 Pietro Strozzi, an exile from Florence, became master of Pescia, but he was compelled to surrender to Duke Cosimo de' Medici. Pescia is the home of the Ammannati family, and of the painter Mariano da Pescia. In 1519 Leo X withdrew it from the jurisdiction of Lucca, raising it to the dignity of a prelacy *nullius*; and in 1726 it was made a diocese, suffragan of Pisa. Its first bishop was Bartolommeo Pucci (1728); among his successors should be mentioned Francesco Vicenti (1773–1801), who in 1784 founded the seminary. The diocese has 36 parishes, with 70,504 inhabitants; 5 religious houses of men, and 10 of women; 2 educational institutions for male students, and 8 for girls; and 1 Catholic weekly publication.

CAPPELLETTI, *Le Chiese d'Italia*, XXI; PUCCINELLI, *Storia di Pescia*.

U. BENIGNI.

Pessimism.—I. A TEMPER OF MIND.—In popular language the term pessimist is applied to persons who habitually take a melancholy view of life, to whom painful experiences appeal with great intensity, and who have little corresponding appreciation of pleasurable ones. Such a temper is partly due to natural disposition, and partly to individual circumstances. According to Caro (after von Hartmann), it is especially prevalent in periods of transition, in which old ways of thought have lost their hold, while the new order has not yet made itself fully known, or has not secured general acceptance for its principles. In such a state of things men's minds are driven in upon themselves; the outward order appears to lack stability and permanence, and life in general tends consequently to be estimated as hollow and unsatisfactory. Metchnikoff attributes the pessimistic temper to a somewhat similar period in the life history of the individual, viz.:—that of the transition from the enthusiasm of youth to the calmer and more settled outlook of maturity. It may be admitted that both causes contribute to the low estimate of life which is implied in the common notion of the pessimistic temperament. But this temperament seems to be far from rare at any time, and to depend upon causes too complex and obscure for exhaustive analysis. The poetic mind has very generally emphasized the painful aspect of life, though it is seldom wholly unresponsive to its pleasurable and desirable side. With Lucretius, however, life is a failure and wholly undesirable; with Sophocles, and still more with Æschylus, the tragic element in human affairs nearly obscures their more cheerful aspect: "It is best of all never to have been born"; the frank and unreflective joy in living and in the contemplation of nature, which runs through the Homeric poems, and is apparent in the work of Hesiod and that of the Greek lyrists, is but seldom found among those who look below the surface of things. In proportion as human affairs outgrew the naïve simplicity of the early periods of history, the tendency to brood over the perplexities of emerging spiritual and social questions naturally increased. Byron, Shelley, Baudelaire and Leconte de Lisle, Heine and Leopardi are the poets of satiety, disillusion, and despair, as the genius of Goethe and Browning represents the spirit of cheerfulness and hope.

At the present moment it would seem that the variety of interests which science and education have brought within the reach of most persons, and the wide possibilities opened up for the future, have done much to discourage pessimistic feelings and to bring about the prevalence of a view of life which is on the whole of an opposite character. We must not, indeed, expect that the darker aspect of the world will ever be wholly abolished, or that it will ever cease to impress itself with varying degrees of intensity upon different temperaments. But the tendency of the present day is undoubtedly in the direction of that cheerful though not optimistic view of life which George Eliot called Meliorism, or the belief that though a perfect state may be unattainable, yet an indefinitely extended improvement in the conditions of existence may be looked for, and that sufficient satisfaction for human energy and desire may be found in the endeavour to contribute to it.

II. A SCHOOL OF PHILOSOPHY.—As a philosophical system, Pessimism may be characterized as one of the many attempts to account for the presence of evil in the world (see EVIL). Leibniz held that "metaphysical" evil is necessarily involved in the creation of finite existences, and that the possibility of sin and consequent suffering is inalienable from the existence of free and rational creatures. The principle from which evil arises is thus made to be an integral part of the actual constitution of nature, though its development is regarded as contingent. With Schopenhauer, the originator of Pessimism as a system, as with those who have accepted his qualitative estimate of the value of existence, evil in the full sense is not merely, as with Leibniz, a possible development of certain fundamental principles of nature, but is itself the fundamental principle of the life of man. The world is essentially bad and "ought not to be".

Schopenhauer holds that all existence is constituted by the objectivization of will, which is the sole and universal reality. Will is blind and unconscious until it is objectivized in human beings, in whom it first attains to consciousness, or the power of representation (*Idea; Vorstellung*). Hence arises the constant suffering which is the normal condition of human life. The essential nature of will is to desire and strive; and the consciousness of this perpetual unfulfilled desire is pain. Pleasure is merely an exception in human experience, the rare and brief cessation of the striving of the will, the temporary absence of pain. This theory recalls that of Plato ("Phædo") who regarded pleasure as the mere absence of pain; and the conception of conscious life as essentially painful and undesirable is nearly identical with the Buddhist notion (quoted with approval by Schopenhauer) that conscious existence is fundamentally and necessarily evil. Hence, further, comes the ethical theory of Schopenhauer, which may be summed up as the necessity for "denying the Will to live". Peace can be attained only in proportion as man ceases to desire; thus the pain of life can be minimized only by an ascetic renunciation of the search after happiness, and can be abolished only by ceasing to live. On the same principle, the poet Leopardi extolled suicide; and Mainländer took his own life.

Schopenhauer's philosophical system of Monism has generally been regarded as in a great degree purely fanciful and self-contradictory. The teleological function attributed to the unconscious will, which produces phenomenal existence through the intervention of quasi-Platonic ideas, is obviously out of place; and the notion that we can through consciousness perceive will as apart from consciousness in our automatic bodily functions and thence also in the external world, creates a confusion between the rational will which we know in ourselves as the cause of action, and mere tendency or instinct, for which the characteristics of will are arbitrarily assumed.

Von Hartmann endeavoured to improve upon Schopenhauer by taking the unconscious (*Unbewusst*) as the foundation of reality. Will and idea are with him twin functions of the unconscious, which energizes both in them and apart from them. The idea becomes conscious through its opposition to will, and from this opposition arises the incurable, because essential, evil of life. In order to induce men to continue to exist, the unconscious leads them on to the pursuit of an unattainable happiness. The delusion presents itself in three successive forms, or stages, corresponding to the childhood, youth, and manhood of the race. In the first stage happiness is considered as attainable in the present life; in the second it is relegated to a transcendental future beyond the grave, and in the third (the present day) it is looked forward to as the future result of human progress. All are equally delusive; and there occurs, as a necessary consequence, at the end of each stage, and before the discovery of the next, the "voluntary surrender of individual existence" by suicide; and when, in its old age, the race has discovered the futility of its hopes it will desire nothing but unconsciousness and so will cease to will, and therefore to be.

Meanwhile, the moral duty of man is to co-operate in the cosmic process which leads to this end. He is "to make the ends of the Unconscious his own ends", to renounce the hope of individual happiness, and so by the suppression of egoism to be reconciled with life as it is. Here von Hartmann claims to have harmonized Optimism and Pessimism, by finding in his own Pessimism the strongest conceivable impulse to effective action. With von Hartmann, life is not, as with Schopenhauer, essentially painful; but pain predominates greatly over pleasure: and the world is the outcome of a systematic evolution, by which the end of the unconscious will eventually be attained in the return of humanity into the peace of unconsciousness. The world is not, as Schopenhauer considered it, the worst possible, but the best, as is shown by the adaptation of means to ends in the evolutionary process. Nevertheless it is altogether bad, and had better not have been.

The unconscious of von Hartmann is involved in the same self-contradiction as the will of Schopenhauer. It is difficult to attach any real significance to the conception of consciousness as a function of the unconscious, or to that of purposive action by the unconscious. Considered simply as a reasoned basis for a doctrine of Pessimism, von Hartmann's system appears much like a Gnostic mythology, or such quasi-mystical imagery as that of Jacob Boehme, representing the pessimistic aspect of the actual world. From this point of view it may be said that both Schopenhauer and Hartmann rendered some service by emphasizing the perpetual contrast between desire and achievement in human affairs, and by calling attention to the essential function of suffering in human life. Schopenhauer and von Hartmann stand alone as the originators of metaphysical systems of an essentially pessimistic character. The subject has also, however, been treated from a philosophical standpoint by Bahnsen, Mainländer, Duprel, and Preuss, and has been discussed from a more or less optimistic point of view by Dühring, Caro, Sully, W. James, and many others. The extravagant speculations of Nietzsche are to a great extent founded on his early sympathy with the point of view of Schopenhauer.

The view to be taken of the contention of Pessimism depends mainly on whether the question can be settled by an estimate—supposing that one can be formed—of the relative amount of pleasure and pain in average human life. It may well be thought that such a calculus is impossible, since it must obviously depend in a great degree on purely subjective and therefore variable considerations. Pleasure and pain vary indefinitely both in kind and intensity with persons of differing idiosyncrasies. Life, it is contended, may still be happy, even though its pains may exceed its pleasures; or it may be worthless even if the reverse is the case. The point of view involves a judgment of values, rather than a quantitative estimate of pleasure and pain. The true pessimistic estimate of life would be that it is rather unhappy, because it is worthless, than worthless because it is unhappy. But again, values can be estimated or judged only according to the degree of personal satisfaction they imply; and we are brought back to a merely subjective view of the value of life, unless we can discover some absolute standard, some estimate of the comparative importance of its pleasures and pains which is invariable and the same for all. Such a standard of value is to be found in religious belief, and exists in its most complete form in the faith of Catholics. Religion fixes the scale of values by reference not to varying individual sensibilities, but to an eternal law which is always ideally and may be actually the reason of the individual judgment. Moreover, the recognition of such an absolute standard itself provides an absolute satisfaction, arising from action in accordance with it, which cannot exist in the absence of such recognition, and which is only travestied by Schopenhauer's pseudo-mystical delight in contemplating the "kernel of things", or by von Hartmann's personal adoption of the assumed "ends" of the unconscious.

Thus the Christian law of duty gives to action, in itself possibly quite the reverse of pleasurable, a value far outweighing that of the satisfaction arising from any specific pleasure, whether sensuous or intellectual. The inevitable Christian tendency to depreciate satisfaction arising from pleasure as against the performance of duty has caused Christianity to be classified as a system of Pessimism. This is, for example, the view taken of it by Schopenhauer, who declares that "Optimism is irreconcilable with Christianity", and that true Christianity has throughout that ascetic fundamental character which his philosophy explains as the denial of the will to live.

Von Hartmann, in like manner, rejecting as mythical the foundation of the Christian Faith and its hope of the hereafter, takes its historical and only important content to be the doctrine that "this earthly vale of tears has in itself no value whatever, but that, on the contrary, the earthly life is composed of tribulation and daily torment." It can hardly be disputed that the Christian view of life in itself is scarcely less pessimistic than that of Schopenhauer or Hartmann; and its pains are regarded as essentially characteristic of its present condition, due to the initial misdirection of human free-will. No estimate of the essential painfulness of human life could well exceed that of the "Imitatio Christi" (see, e. g., III, xx). But the outlook is profoundly modified by the introduction of the "eternal values" which are the special province of Christianity. The unhappiness of the world is counterbalanced by the satisfaction which arises from a peaceful conscience, and a sense of harmony between individual action and eternal law; faith and love contribute an element of joy to life which cannot be destroyed, and may even be enhanced, by temporal suffering; and in some cases at least the delights of supernatural mystical contemplation reduce merely natural pain and pleasure to comparative insignificance.

SCHOPENHAUER, *The World as Will and Idea*, tr. HALDANE AND KEMP (London, 1886); VON HARTMANN, *The Philosophy of the Unconscious*, tr. COUPLAND (London, 1893); BENEKE, *Neue Grundlegung zur Metaphysik* (Berlin, 1822); DÜHRING, *Der Werth des Lebens* (Leipzig, 1881); MAINLÄNDER, *Philosophie der Erlösung* (Berlin, 1886); CHALLEMEL-LACOUR, *Etudes et réflexions d'un pessimiste* (Paris, 1901); CARO, *Le pessimisme au XIXe siècle* (Paris, 1878); PIERENS-GEVAERT, *La tristesse contemporaine* (Paris, 1899); JAMES, *The Will to Believe* (Philadelphia, 1896); IDEM, *Pragmatism*: lecture VIII (London, 1897); SULLY, *Pessimism* (London, 1901); SCHILLER, *The Relation of Pessimism to Ultimate Philosophy* in *International Journal of Ethics*, VIII (1897); RENOUVIER, *Notre pessimisme* in *La crit. philos.* (1872); WENLEY, *Aspects of Pessimism* (London, 1894); MALLOCK, *Is Life Worth Living?* (London, 1879); MÜNSTERBERG, *The Eternal Values* (Boston, 1909); METCHNIKOFF, *The Prolongation of Life* (tr. London, 1907).

A. B. SHARPE.

Pessinus (πεσσινοῦς), titular see of Galatia Secunda. Pessinonte, on the southern slope of Mt. Dindymus and the left bank of the Sangarius, was an ancient city, having commercial but chiefly religious importance, owing to the cult of Cybele under the title of Agdistis, whose statue, or rather a stone supposed to represent her, was considered to have fallen from heaven. The Galli, priests of the temple, flourished under the Assyrians, Lydians, and Persians. The city passed to the kings of Pergamus, one of whom rebuilt the temple; about 278 B. C. it became the capital of the Tolistoboii, one of the three Gallic tribes which founded the Kingdom of Galatia. As early as 204 B. C. the Romans sent an embassy to procure the statue which they placed in the temple of Victory on the Palatine, but the cult of the goddess continued. In 189 B. C. the Galli sent an embassy to the consul Manlius, encamped on the banks of the Sangarius, and later Julian the Apostate made a pilgrimage to Pessinus. Under the Romans the city declined. After Constantine it was the metropolis of Galatia Secunda or Salutaris. Ten bishops are known: Demetrius, the friend and defender of St. John Chrysostom, who died in exile; Pius, present at the Council of Ephesus (431); Theoctistus, at Chalcedon (451); Acacius, at Constantinople (536); George, about 600; John, at Constantinople (692); Gregory, at Nicæa (787); Eustratius, at Constantinople (879); Nicholas, present at the Council of Constantinople (1054), at which Michael Cærularius proclaimed the rupture with Rome. The "Notitiæ episcopatuum" mention the see until the middle of the fourteenth century. The ruins of a theatre, the temples of Cybele and of Æsculapius are at Bala Hissar, nine or ten miles from Sivri Hissar, chief town of the caza of the vilayet of Angora. Some Christian inscriptions have been discovered.

LE QUIEN, *Oriens christ.*, I, 489; SMITH, *Dict. of Greek and Roman geog.*, s. v.; *Bibl. des auteurs anciens*; HAMILTON, *Researches*, I 438, seq.; LEAKE, *Asia Minor*, 82 seq.; TEXIER, *Asie mineure*, 473–9; PERROT, *Galatie et Bithynie*, 207 seq.

S. PÉTRIDÈS.

Pestalozzi and Pestalozzianism.—Johann Heinrich Pestalozzi, one of the greatest pioneers of modern education, b. at Zurich, Switzerland, 12 January, 1746; d. at Brugg, 17 February, 1827. Descended from a Calvinist family and destined to become a preacher, Pestalozzi abandoned this project for the study of law. He was greatly influenced by Rousseau's "Social Contract" and "Emile", and tried to carry into practice some of that author's ideas. He first took up farming at Neuhof (New Farm), but failed through lack of practical talent. He then gathered at Neuhof (1774) waifs and castaways, who were to work in his spinning-mill and to receive in turn some industrial and moral training. Unbusinesslike methods led to financial difficulties and the closing of the establishment in 1780. Evil days then followed for Pestalozzi and his heroic wife who had sacrificed all her property for his schemes; sometimes they lacked bread and fuel, and illness added to their suffering. Sympathizing with the poor peasantry, Pestalozzi developed a plan for elevating their condition through education. In 1781 appeared his "Lienhard und Gertrud", a simple story which shows how a village was regenerated through the efforts of a good pastor, an able magistrate, a zealous teacher, and chiefly through the influence of Gertrude, a perfect wife and mother, who becomes the Good Samaritan of the village. This book, eagerly read wherever German was understood, made its author famous. In 1798 Pestalozzi determined to become a schoolmaster himself. The village of Stanz had been burnt by the French soldiers, and many children wandered about destitute, exposed to physical and moral ruin. Pestalozzi was made the head of an institution at Stanz in which the orphans were to be trained. When, in the following year, the French army needed the building for a hospital, the orphans' school came to a sudden end.

Pestalozzi then opened a school in the Castle of Burgdorf, and there laboured zealously from 1799 to 1804, though hampered by jealousies and misunderstandings. With this institution he connected a normal school, the first in the Protestant cantons of Switzerland; the Catholics already possessed one, in the monastery of St. Urban, Canton of Lucerne. At Burgdorf Pestalozzi wrote "Wie Gertrud ihre Kinder lehrt" (How Gertrude Teaches her Children), which, better than any other of his books, explains his educational aims and methods. When sent to Paris as one of the Swiss delegates, he tried to interest the First Consul in his educational work, but Napoleon declared that he would not be bothered about questions of A B C. In 1804 Pestalozzi, driven out of the Castle of Burgdorf, transferred his school to Munchenbuchsee, and thence to Yverdun. Eager students of pedagogy flocked to Yverdun from Prussia, Russia, France, Italy, Spain, England, and other countries, among the rest Fröbel, Herbart, von Raumer, and Ritter. But Pestalozzi's lack of organizing talent and dissensions among his teaching staff led to the decline and finally to the closing of the establishment (1825).

Pestalozzi's career is almost a puzzle. All his undertakings proved failures, and yet he is the most influential of modern educators. There was nothing attractive in his external appearance. He had read very few books, possessed neither philosophical penetration nor mastery of method, and entirely lacked talent for organization. A keen observer at Yverdun declared that he would not have been able to conduct successfully a small village school. That, in spite of all these drawbacks, he exerted a profound influence on modern education was due chiefly to his self-sacrificing love for children, and his enthusiasm for educational work. This enthusiasm became an inspiration, almost an infection for all those who came in contact with "Father Pestalozzi", as they affectionately called him. He created a new educational spirit, interest in education, and a new school atmosphere, namely, love for the children. He himself said that he intended to "psychologize instruction", and he may be called the originator of the modern psychological tendency in education. The foundation of instruction he finds in *Anschauung*, which has been inadequately rendered in English by "sense-impression" or "observation", and is perhaps better expressed by "intuition". The object lesson is the core of the whole system, and exercises are based more on the study of objects than of words. Pestalozzi's system has been severely criticized by some and extravagantly praised by others; his work is overestimated by those who call him the "father of the elementary school", although it must be admitted that he did much to improve it. Some of his principles involved contradictions, not a few of his methods were one-sided and even unsound; but his ideas, stripped of their eccentricities by his disciples, became prominent features in modern education. Herbart and Fröbel supplemented his work—the former by developing the psychology of education, the latter by originating the kindergarten system. The school systems of Prussia and other European states embodied many of Pestalozzi's ideas; in England a modified Pestalozzianism was carried into practice by Dr. Mayo. Pestalozzian ideas were transplanted to America by one of Pestalozzi's assistants, the Alsatian Joseph Neef (wrongly called a priest, e. g. in Schmid's "Gesch. der Erz.", V, ii, 580), who opened a school in Philadelphia in 1808, and later taught at New Harmony, Indiana. Horace Mann was influenced by Pestalozzian principles; so was the "Oswego Movement", which emphasized the use of objects as the foundation of instruction and greatly determined the character of American normal-school training. "For the most part, so far as principle is concerned, American schools are yet upon the Pestalozzian basis, though the special methods of applying these principles have been much improved" (Monroe, "Hist. of Ed.", 669).

One of the weakest points in Pestalozzi's system was his attitude towards religion. Through the influence of the writings of Rousseau he had lost the strict religious views of his Calvinist family, and, while he still believed in a personal God and Divine Providence, his was a rationalistic and merely natural religion. Although he always spoke most reverently of the Bible and of Christ, he never attained to a clear recognition of the Divinity of Christ, but remained outside dogmatic Christianity. His disciples are divided into two schools—one rationalistic, led by Diesterweg, the other Christian, which follows Pestalozzian methods of instruction without adopting his religious views. To the latter school belong some prominent Catholic educators, as Bishop Sailer of Ratisbon and Bernard Overberg, the reformer of education in Westphalia. In dealing with Catholics, and in speaking of things Catholic, Pestalozzi invariably showed tact and consideration; he never forgot that he had received kind treatment from Catholics at Stanz at a time when he was distrusted by some and ridiculed as a visionary by others. "You will hardly believe", he wrote to a friend, "that it was the Capuchin Friars and the nuns of the Convent that showed the greatest sympathy with my work."

The vast bibliography on Pestalozzi is collected by ISRAEL in *Monumenta Germaniæ Pædagogica*, XXV, XXIX, XXXI; PESTALOZZI, *Sämtliche Werke*, ed. SEYFFARTH (12 volumes, 1899—). Many separate editions of *Lienard u. Gertrud*, and *Wie Gertrud ihre Kinder lehrt*—English translation (Boston, 1885; Syracuse, 1898); ed. BÜRGEL AND BECK, with German notes for Catholic teachers and normal-school pupils (Paderborn, 1887, 1892). Translation of other works and articles of Pestalozzi, in *Barnard's Journal*, II-VII, XIII, XXX, XXXI. Biographies, etc. in English by DE GUIMPS (Syracuse, 1889); KRUESI (New York, 1875); PINLOCHE (New York, 1901); HOLMAN (London and New York, 1908). Consult also QUICK, *Educational Reformers* (New York, 1890); MONROE, *Hist. of Education* (New York, 1906). Of the numerous biographies in German, the latest, and probably the best, is that by HEUBAUM (Berlin, 1910).

ROBERT SCHWICKERATH.

Pétau, DENIS (DIONYSIUS PETAVIUS), one of the most distinguished theologians of the seventeenth century, b. at Orléans, 1583; d. at Paris, 11 December, 1652. He studied first at Orléans, then at Paris, where he successfully defended his theses for the degree of Master of Arts, not in Latin, but in Greek. After this he followed the theological lectures at the Sorbonne, and, on the advice of Ysambert, successfully applied for the chair of philosophy at Bourges. At Paris he became very intimate with Isaac Casaubon (see Letters MXXIV, MXXVIII, MXXXVIII, MXLIV), librarian at the Bibliothèque Royale, where he spent all his spare time studying the ancient Greek manuscripts. At Orléans he was ordained deacon and presented with a canonry. After spending two years at Bourges he returned to Paris, and entered into relations with Fronton du Duc, the editor of St. John Chrysostom. In 1605 he became a Jesuit, taught rhetoric at Reims (1609), La Flèche (1613), and at the College of Paris (1618). During this last period he began a correspondence with the Bishop of Orléans, Gabriel de Laubépine (Albaspinæus), on the first year of the primitive Church. From 1622 he taught positive theology for twenty-two years. During this time he was about to leave France on two occasions—first, to teach ecclesiastical history at Madrid at the invitation of Philip IV (1629), secondly to become a cardinal at Rome where Urban VIII wanted him (1639). At sixty years of age he stopped teaching, but retained his office of librarian, in which he had succeeded Fronton du Duc (1623), and consecrated the rest of his life to his great work, the "Dogmata theologica". The virtues of Pétau were not inferior to his talent; he was a model of humility and regularity, and, in spite of his feeble health, practised continual and severe mortifications. His ardent zeal for the Church inspired a rare talent to which his numerous works bear evidence; he devoted himself to the study of literature (Greek and Latin poets) and to other more erudite forms of learning.

The complete list of his works fills twenty-five columns in Sommervogel: he treats of chronology, history, philosophy, polemics, patristics, and history of dogma. The first edition of the works of Synesius appeared in 1612, undertaken ten years earlier at the advice of Casaubon ("Synesii episcopi Cyrenensis opera", new ed., 1633); in 1613 and 1614 the discourses of Themistius and Julian (new ed., 1630); in 1616 the "Breviarium historicum Nicephori"; then, after some poetical and oratorical works, an edition of

St. Epiphanius in two volumes (1622; new ed., 1632), which had been undertaken at the advice of Jacques Gretser, S.J., and was originally intended only as a revised translation of Janus Cornarius. In 1622 and 1623 appeared the "Mastigophores", three pamphlets, and the notes dealing with Saumaise's "Tertullian", a bitter polemical work. Among his previous writings, Pétau had inserted some masterly dissertations on chronology; in 1627 he brought out his "De doctrina temporum", and later the "Tabulæ chronologicæ" (1628, 1629, 1633, 1657). It surpassed Scaliger's "De Emendatione temporum" (Paris, 1583), and prepared the ground for the works of the Benedictines. A summary of it appeared in 1633 (1635, 1641, etc.) under the title of "Rationarium temporum", of which numerous reprints and translations into French, English, and Italian have been made. About the same time (1636–44) appeared poetical works in Greek and in Latin and dissertations (often of a polemical nature) against Grotius, Saumaise, Arnauld, etc. His paraphrase of the Psalms in Greek verse was dedicated to Urban VIII (in 1637). Finally there appeared in 1643 the first three volumes of the "Dogmata theologica" (dated 1644); the fourth and fifth volumes were published in 1650. The work was incomplete at the death of the author, and, despite several attempts, was never continued. Numerous editions of the "Dogmata theologica" have been published, including that by the Calvinist Jean le Clerc (Clericus, alias Theophile Alethinus), published in Antwerp (Amsterdam) in 1700; the last edition was brought out in eight volumes by J. B. Fournials (Paris, 1866–8). In 1757 F. A. Zaccaria, S.J. republished the work in Venice with notes, dissertations, etc.; in 1857 Passaglia and Schrader undertook a similar work, but they produced only the first volume. His letters, "Epistolarum libri tres", were published after his death; though far from being complete, they give an idea of his close acquaintance with the most famous men in France, Holland, Italy, etc.; they also furnish valuable information on the composition of his works and his method.

The reputation Pétau enjoyed during his lifetime was especially due to his work on chronology; numerous eulogies were pronounced on him by his contemporaries, such as Huet, Valois, Grotius, Isaac Voss, F. Clericus, Noris, etc. His chronological work has long since been surpassed, and a list of errors—inevitable at the period—could be drawn up even in the case of this man who boasted that he counted no less than eight thousand mistakes in the "Annals" of Baronius. But the great glory, which in the eyes of posterity surrounds the name of Pétau, is due to his patristic works and his importance in the history of dogma. With good reason he may be styled the "Father of the History of Dogma". The success of his work in this sphere was slow to make itself felt—it brought on the author accusations even from within his order—but it was highly esteemed by his pupils and far-seeing friends (e. g., H. Valois, Huet, etc.).

To form an opinion of Pétau's work it is necessary to go back to the period in which he wrote. It is far from being perfect and his criticism is more than once at fault. But his merit increases in spite of his shortcomings, when it is remembered that he had at hand only very imperfect editions of the Fathers, all inferior to the great masterpieces of the Benedictines; that many of the known texts only existed in translations, or in late and poorly studied manuscripts; that his predecessors in this line were few and practically everything had to be created. What he wanted had already been outlined by Melchior Cano in his work "De locis theologicis". Here we pass from theory to practice and we find a master at once. The originality of Pétau's work has been questioned; it may have been inspired, it is said, by a similar treatise of Oregius (d. 1635), as Zöckler maintains, or by the "Confessio catholica" of John Gerhard (d. 1627), as conjectured by Eckstein. But the "Confessio catholica" has a quite different aim, as is stated on the very first page; whole treatises, as for instance that on Christ, have but scanty quotations from three or four Fathers of the Church, and present nothing similar to the long historical developments of the sixteen books "De Incarnatione Verbi" of Pétau. The relationship with Cardinal Aug. Oregius, which rests solely on a conversation of a religious of the Minims of Dijon related in the "Voyage littéraire de deux Bénédictins" (Paris, 1717, p. 147), has been examined in detail and completely disposed of by F. Oudin, S.J. in the "Mémoires de Trévoux" (July, 1718, pp. 109–33).

The state of religious strife during the days succeeding the Council of Trent drew all minds towards the primitive ages of the Church concerning which certain ancient documents were being discovered, while the excessive subtlety of many Scholastics of the decadence instigated a return towards positive sources. Pétau was no doubt inspired by the same ideas, but the execution of the work is completely his own. His aim and purpose are set forth by his dedicatory letter to the General of the Jesuits (Epist., III, liv), and in several parts of his "Prolegomena" (cf. I, i). His method reveals all the resources which the sciences of history and philosophy have furnished to the theologians. He declares his opinion with full liberty as, e. g., concerning the opinion of St. Augustine on the problem of predestination, or the ideas on the Trinity of the ante-Nicene writers. Even for those who do not follow his historical plan the work has furnished a copious supply of documents; for theologians it has been a store of patristic arguments. We may here add that Pétau, like Cano, took the greatest pains with his literary style. He exaggerates the faults of Scholasticism; but on the other hand he defends it against the accusations of Erasmus. We still find the controversialist in the author of the "Dogmata"; after giving the history of each dogma, he adds the refutation of new errors. In his polemical writings his style was bitter; here and there he is more gentle, as when engaged in discussions with Grotius, who was drawing near the Catholic Faith. The memory of Pétau was celebrated the day after his death by Henri Valois, one of his best pupils, and by L. Allatius in a Greek poem composed at the request of Cardinal Barberini.

OUDIN, *Denis Pétau* in NICERON, *Mémoires pour servir à l'hist. des hommes illustres*, XXXVII (1737), 81, and in *Mémoires de Trévoux* (July, 1718); GODET AND TURMEL, *Revue du clergé français*, XXIX (1902), 161, 372, 449; CHATELLAIN, *Le Père Denis Pétau d'Orléans* (1884); STANONIK, *Dionysius Petavius* (Graz, 1876); SOMMERVOGEL, *Bibl. des écriv. S. J.*, VI (1895); KUHN, *Ehrenrettung des D. Petavius u. der kathol. Auffassung der Dogmengesch.* in *Tübinger theolog. Quartalschrift.*, XXXII (1850), 249.

J. DE GHELLINCK.

Peter, SAINT, Prince of the Apostles.—The life of St. Peter may be conveniently considered under the following heads: I. Until the Ascension of Christ; II. St. Peter in Jerusalem and Palestine after the Ascension; III. Missionary Journeys in the East; The Council of the Apostles; IV. Activity and Death in Rome; Burial-place; V. Feasts of St. Peter; VI. Representations of St. Peter.

I. UNTIL THE ASCENSION OF CHRIST.—St. Peter's true and original name was Simon (Σίμων), sometimes occurring in the form Συμεών (Acts, xv, 14; II Pet., i, 1). He was the son of Jona (Johannes) and was born in Bethsaida (John, i, 42, 44), a town on Lake Genesareth, the position of which cannot be established with certainty, although it is usually sought at the northern end of the lake. The Apostle Andrew was his brother, and the Apostle Philip came from the same town. Simon settled in Capharnaum, where he was living with his mother-in-law in his own house (Matt., viii, 14; Luke, iv, 38) at the beginning of Christ's public ministry (about A. D. 26–28). Simon was thus married, and, according to Clement of

Alexandria (Stromata, III, vi, ed. Dindorf, II, 276), had children. The same writer relates the tradition that Peter's wife suffered martyrdom (ibid., VII, xi, ed. cit., III, 306). Concerning these facts, adopted by Eusebius (Hist. Eccl., III, xxxi) from Clement, the ancient Christian literature which has come down to us is silent. Simon pursued in Capharnaum the profitable occupation of fisherman in Lake Genesareth, possessing his own boat (Luke, v, 3). Like so many of his Jewish contemporaries, he was attracted by the Baptist's preaching of penance and was, with his brother Andrew, among John's associates in Bethania on the eastern bank of the Jordan. When, after the High Council had sent envoys for the second time to the Baptist, the latter pointed to Jesus who was passing, saying "Behold the Lamb of God", Andrew and another disciple followed the Saviour to his residence and remained with Him one day.

Later, meeting his brother Simon, Andrew said "We have found the Messias", and brought him to Jesus, who, looking upon him, said: "Thou art Simon the son of Jona: thou shalt be called Cephas, which is interpreted Peter". Already, at this first meeting, the Saviour foretold the change of Simon's name to Cephas (Κηφᾶς; Aramaic Kīphā, rock), which is translated Πέτρος (Lat., *Petrus*) a proof that Christ had already special views with regard to Simon. Later, probably at the time of his definitive call to the Apostolate with the eleven other Apostles, Jesus actually gave Simon the name of Cephas (*Petrus*), after which he was usually called Peter, especially by Christ on the solemn occasion after Peter's profession of faith (Matt., xvi, 18; cf. below). The Evangelists often combine the two names, while St. Paul uses the name Cephas. After the first meeting Peter with the other early disciples remained with Jesus for some time, accompanying Him to Galilee (Marriage at Cana), Judæa, and Jerusalem, and through Samaria back to Galilee (John, ii–iv). Here Peter resumed his occupation of fisherman for a short time, but soon received the definitive call of the Saviour to become one of His permanent disciples. Peter and Andrew were engaged at their calling when Jesus met and addressed them: "Come ye after me, and I will make you to be fishers of men". On the same occasion the sons of Zebedee were called (Matt., iv, 18–22; Mark, i, 16–20; Luke, v, 1–11; it is here assumed that Luke refers to the same occasion as the other Evangelists). Thenceforth Peter remained always in the immediate neighbourhood of Our Lord. After preaching the Sermon on the Mount and curing the son of the centurion in Capharnaum, Jesus came to Peter's house and cured his wife's mother, who was sick of a fever (Matt., viii, 14–15; Mark, i, 29–31). A little later Christ chose His Twelve Apostles as His constant associates in preaching the Kingdom of God.

Among the Twelve Peter soon became conspicuous. Though of irresolute character, he clings with the greatest fidelity, firmness of faith, and inward love to the Saviour; rash alike in word and act, he is full of zeal and enthusiasm, though momentarily easily accessible to external influences and intimidated by difficulties. The more prominent the Apostles become in the Evangelical narrative, the more conspicuous does Peter appear as the first among them. In the list of the Twelve on the occasion of their solemn call to the Apostolate, not only does Peter stand always at their head, but the surname *Petrus* given him by Christ is especially emphasized (Matt., x, 2: "Duodecim autem Apostolorum nomina hæc: Primus Simon qui dicitur Petrus . . ."; Mark, iii, 14–16: "Et fecit ut essent duodecim cum illo, et ut mitteret eos prædicare . . . et imposuit Simoni nomen Petrus"; Luke, vi, 13–14: "Et cum dies factus esset, vocavit discipulos suos, et elegit duodecim ex ipsis (quos et Apostolos nominavit): Simonem, quem cognominavit Petrum . . ." On various occasions Peter speaks in the name of the other Apostles (Matt., xv, 15; xix, 27; Luke, xii, 41, etc.). When Christ's words are addressed to all the Apostles, Peter answers in their name (e. g., Matt., xvi, 16). Frequently the Saviour turns specially to Peter (Matt., xxvi, 40; Luke, xxii, 31, etc.).

Very characteristic is the expression of true fidelity to Jesus, which Peter addressed to Him in the name of the other Apostles. Christ, after He had spoken of the mystery of the reception of His Body and Blood (John, vi, 22 sqq.) and many of His disciples had left Him, asked the Twelve if they too should leave Him; Peter's answer comes immediately: "Lord, to whom shall we go? thou hast the words of eternal life. And we have believed and have known, that thou art the Holy One of God" (Vulg. "thou art the Christ, the Son of God"). Christ Himself unmistakably accords

STATUE OF ST. PETER ENTHRONED (III CENTURY)
Crypt of St. Peter's, Rome

Peter a special precedence and the first place among the Apostles, and designates him for such on various occasions. Peter was one of the three Apostles (with James and John) who were with Christ on certain special occasions—the raising of the daughter of Jairus from the dead (Mark, v, 37; Luke, viii, 51); the Transfiguration of Christ (Matt., xvii, 1; Mark, ix, 1; Luke, ix, 28); the Agony in the Garden of Gethsemani (Matt., xxvi, 37; Mark, xiv, 33). On several occasions also Christ favoured him above all the others; He enters Peter's boat on Lake Genesareth to preach to the multitude on the shore (Luke, v, 3); when He was miraculously walking upon the waters, He called Peter to come to Him across the lake (Matt., xiv, 28 sqq.); He sent him to the lake to catch the fish in whose mouth Peter found the stater to pay as tribute (Matt., xvii, 24 sqq.).

In especially solemn fashion Christ accentuated Peter's precedence among the Apostles, when, after Peter had recognized Him as the Messias, He promised that he would be head of His flock. Jesus was then dwelling with His Apostles in the vicinity of Cæsarea Philippi, engaged on His work of salvation. As Christ's coming agreed so little in power and glory with the expectations of the Messias, many different views concerning Him were current. While journeying along with His Apostles, Jesus asks them: "Whom do men say that the Son of man is?" The Apostles answered: "Some John the Baptist, and other some Elias, and others Jeremias, or one of the prophets". Jesus said to them: "But whom do you say that I am?" Simon said: "Thou art Christ, the Son of the living God". And Jesus answering said to him: "Blessed art thou, Simon Bar-Jona: because flesh and blood hath not revealed it to thee, but my Father who is in heaven. And I say to thee: That thou art Peter [Kīphā, a rock]; and upon this rock [Kīphā] I will build my church [ἐκκλησίαν], and the gates of hell shall not prevail against it. And I will give to thee the keys of the kingdom of heaven. And whatsoever thou shalt bind upon earth, it shall be bound also in heaven: and whatsoever thou shalt loose on earth, it shall be loosed also in heaven". Then he commanded his disciples, that they should tell no one that he was Jesus the Christ (Matt., xvi, 13–20; Mark, viii, 27–30; Luke, ix, 18–21).

By the word "rock" the Saviour cannot have meant Himself, but only Peter, as is so much more apparent in Aramaic in which the same word (Kīphā) is used for "Peter" and "rock". His statement then admits of but one explanation, namely, that He wishes to make Peter the head of the whole community of those who believed in Him as the true Messias; that through this foundation (Peter) the Kingdom of Christ would be unconquerable; that the spiritual guidance of the faithful was placed in the hands of Peter, as the special representative of Christ. This meaning becomes so much the clearer when we remember that the words "bind" and "loose" are not metaphorical, but Jewish juridical terms. It is also clear that the position of Peter among the other Apostles and in the Christian community was the basis for the Kingdom of God on earth, that is, the Church of Christ. Peter was personally installed as Head of the Apostles by Christ Himself. This foundation created for the Church by its Founder could not disappear with the person of Peter, but was intended to continue and did continue (as actual history shows) in the primacy of the Roman Church and its bishops. Entirely inconsistent and in itself untenable is the position of Protestants who (like Schnitzer in recent times) assert that the primacy of the Roman bishops cannot be deduced from the precedence which Peter held among the Apostles. Just as the essential activity of the Twelve Apostles in building up and extending the Church did not entirely disappear with their deaths, so surely did the Apostolic Primacy of Peter not completely vanish. As intended by Christ, it must have continued its existence and development in a form appropriate to the ecclesiastical organism, just as the office of the Apostles continued in an appropriate form. Objections have been raised against the genuineness of the wording of the passage, but the unanimous testimony of the manuscripts, the parallel passages in the other Gospels, and the fixed belief of pre-Constantine literature furnish the surest proofs of the genuineness and untampered state of the text of Matthew (cf. "Stimmen aus Maria-Laach", I, 1896, 129 sqq.; "Theologie und Glaube", II, 1910, 842 sqq.).

In spite of his firm faith in Jesus, Peter had so far no clear knowledge of the mission and work of the Saviour. The sufferings of Christ especially, as contradictory to his worldly conception of the Messias, were inconceivable to him, and his erroneous conception occasionally elicited a sharp reproof from Jesus (Matt., xvi, 21–23; Mark, viii, 31–33). Peter's irresolute character, which continued notwithstanding his enthusiastic fidelity to his Master, was clearly revealed in connexion with the Passion of Christ. The Saviour had already told him that Satan had desired him that he might sift him as wheat. But Christ had prayed for him that his faith fail not, and, being once converted, he confirms his brethren (Luke, xxii, 31–32).

Peter's assurance that he was ready to accompany his Master to prison and to death, elicited Christ's prediction that Peter should deny Him (Matt., xxvi, 30–35; Mark, xiv, 26–31; Luke, xxii, 31–34; John, xiii, 33–38). When Christ proceeded to wash the feet of His disciples before the Last Supper, and came first to Peter, the latter at first protested, but, on Christ's declaring that otherwise he should have no part with Him, immediately said: "Lord, not only my feet, but also my hands and my head" (John, xiii, 1–10). In the Garden of Gethsemani Peter had to submit to the Saviour's reproach that he had slept like the others, while his Master suffered deadly anguish (Mark, xiv, 37). At the seizing of Jesus, Peter in an outburst of anger wished to defend his Master by force, but was forbidden to do so. He at first took to flight with the other Apostles (John, xviii, 10–11; Matt., xxvi, 56); then turning he followed his captured Lord to the courtyard of the High Priest, and there denied Christ, asserting explicitly and swearing that he knew Him not (Matt., xxvi, 58–75; Mark, xiv, 54–72; Luke, xxii, 54–62; John, xviii, 15–27). This denial was of course due, not to a lapse of interior faith in Christ, but to exterior fear and cowardice. His sorrow was thus so much the greater, when, after his Master had turned His gaze towards him, he clearly recognized what he had done. In spite of this weakness, his position as head of the Apostles was later confirmed by Jesus, and his precedence was not less conspicuous after the Resurrection than before.

The women, who were the first to find Christ's tomb empty, received from the angel a special message for Peter (Mark, xvi, 7). To him alone of the Apostles did Christ appear on the first day after the Resurrection (Luke, xxiv, 34; I Cor., xv, 5). But, most important of all, when He appeared at the Lake of Genesareth, Christ renewed to Peter His special commission to feed and defend His flock, after Peter had thrice affirmed his special love for his Master (John, xxi, 15–17). In conclusion Christ foretold the violent death Peter would have to suffer, and thus invited him to follow Him in a special manner (ibid., 20–23). Thus was Peter called and trained for the Apostleship and clothed with the primacy of the Apostles, which he exercised in a most unequivocal manner after Christ's Ascension into Heaven.

II. St. Peter in Jerusalem and Palestine after the Ascension.—Our information concerning the earliest Apostolic activity of St. Peter in Jerusalem, Judæa, and the districts stretching northwards as far as Syria is derived mainly from the first portion of the Acts of the Apostles, and is confirmed by parallel statements incidentally in the Epistles of St. Paul. Among the crowd of Apostles and disciples who, after Christ's Ascension into Heaven from Mount Olivet, returned to Jerusalem to await the fulfilment of His promise to send the Holy Ghost, Peter is immediately conspicuous as the leader of all, and is henceforth constantly recognized as the head of the original Christian community in Jerusalem. He takes the initiative in the appointment to the Apostolic College of another witness of the life, death, and resurrection of Christ to replace Judas (Acts, i, 15–26). After the descent of the Holy Ghost on the feast of Pentecost, Peter standing at the head of the Apostles delivers the first public sermon to proclaim the life, death, and resurrection of Jesus, and wins a large number of Jews as converts to the Christian community (ibid., ii, 14–41). First of the Apostles he worked a public miracle, when with John he went up into the temple and cured the lame man at the Beautiful Gate. To the people crowding in amazement about the two Apostles, he preaches a long sermon in the Porch of Solomon, and brings new increase to the flock of believers (ibid., iii, 1–iv, 4).

In the subsequent examinations of the two Apostles before the Jewish High Council, Peter defends in undismayed and impressive fashion the cause of Jesus and the obligation and liberty of the Apostles to preach the Gospel (ibid., iv, 5-21). When Ananias and Sapphira attempt to deceive the Apostles and the people, Peter appears as judge of their action, and God executes the sentence of punishment passed by the Apostle by causing the sudden death of the two guilty parties (ibid., v, 1-11). By numerous miracles God confirms the Apostolic activity of Christ's confessors, and here also there is special mention of Peter, since it is recorded that the inhabitants of Jerusalem and neighbouring towns carried their sick in their beds into the streets so that the shadow of Peter might fall on them and they might be thereby healed (ibid., v, 12-16). The ever-increasing number of the faithful caused the Jewish supreme council to adopt new measures against the Apostles, but "Peter and the Apostles" answer that they "ought to obey God rather than men" (ibid., v, 29 sqq.). Not only in Jerusalem itself did Peter labour in fulfilling the mission entrusted to him by his Master. He also retained connexion with the other Christian communities in Palestine, and preached the Gospel both there and in the lands situated farther north. When Philip the Deacon had won a large number of believers in Samaria, Peter and John were deputed to proceed thither from Jerusalem to organize the community and to invoke the Holy Ghost to descend upon the faithful. Peter appears a second time as judge, in the case of the magician Simon, who had wished to purchase from the Apostles the power that he also could invoke the Holy Ghost (ibid., viii, 14-25). On their way back to Jerusalem, the two Apostles preached the joyous tidings of the Kingdom of God. Subsequently, after Paul's departure from Jerusalem and conversion before Damascus, the Christian communities in Palestine were left at peace by the Jewish council.

STATUE OF ST. PETER
St. Peter's, Rome

Peter now undertook an extensive missionary tour, which brought him to the maritime cities, Lydda, Joppe, and Cæsarea. In Lydda he cured the palsied Eneas; in Joppe he raised Tabitha (Dorcas) from the dead; and at Cæsarea, instructed by a vision which he had in Joppe, he baptized and received into the Church the first non-Jewish Christians, the centurion Cornelius and his kinsmen (ibid., ix, 31-x, 48). On Peter's return to Jerusalem a little later, the strict Jewish Christians, who regarded the complete observance of the Jewish law as binding on all, asked him why he had entered and eaten in the house of the uncircumcised. Peter tells of his vision and defends his action, which was ratified by the Apostles and the faithful in Jerusalem (ibid., xi, 1-18).

A confirmation of the position accorded to Peter by Luke, in the Acts, is afforded by the testimony of St. Paul (Gal., i, 18-20). After his conversion and three years' residence in Arabia, Paul came to Jerusalem "to see Peter". Here the Apostle of the Gentiles clearly designates Peter as the authorized head of the Apostles and of the early Christian Church. Peter's long residence in Jerusalem and Palestine soon came to an end. Herod Agrippa I began (A. D. 42-44) a new persecution of the Church in Jerusalem; after the execution of James, the son of Zebedee, this ruler had Peter cast into prison, intending to have him also executed after the Jewish Pasch was over. Peter, however, was freed in a miraculous manner, and, proceeding to the house of the mother of John Mark, where many of the faithful were assembled for prayer, informed them of his liberation from the hands of Herod, commissioned them to communicate the fact to James and the brethren, and then left Jerusalem to go to "another place" (Acts, xii, 1-18). Concerning St. Peter's subsequent activity we receive no further connected information from the extant sources, although we possess short notices of certain individual episodes of his later life.

III. MISSIONARY JOURNEYS IN THE EAST; COUNCIL OF THE APOSTLES.—St. Luke does not tell us whither Peter went after his liberation from the prison in Jerusalem. From incidental statements we know that he subsequently made extensive missionary tours in the East, although we are given no clue to the chronology of his journeys. It is certain that he remained for a time at Antioch; he may even have returned thither several times. The Christian community of Antioch was founded by Christianized Jews who had been driven from Jerusalem by the persecution (ibid., xi, 19 sqq.). Peter's residence among them is proved by the episode concerning the observance of the Jewish ceremonial law even by Christianized pagans, related by St. Paul (Gal., ii, 11-21). The chief Apostles in Jerusalem—the "pillars", Peter, James, and John—had unreservedly approved St. Paul's Apostolate to the Gentiles, while they themselves intended to labour principally among the Jews. While Paul was dwelling in Antioch (the date cannot be accurately determined), St. Peter came thither and mingled freely with the non-Jewish Christians of the community, frequenting their houses and sharing their meals. But when the Christianized Jews arrived in Jerusalem, Peter, fearing lest these rigid observers of the Jewish ceremonial law should be scandalized thereat, and his influence with the Jewish Christians be imperilled, avoided thenceforth eating with the uncircumcised.

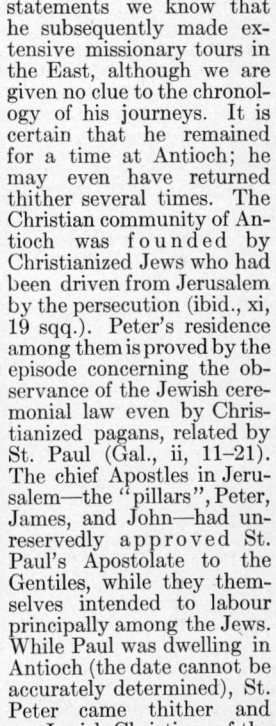

His conduct made a great impression on the other Jewish Christians at Antioch, so that even Barnabas, St. Paul's companion, now avoided eating with the Christianized pagans. As this action was entirely opposed to the principles and practice of Paul, and might lead to confusion among the converted pagans, this Apostle addressed a public reproach to St. Peter, because his conduct seemed to indicate a wish to compel the pagan converts to become Jews and accept circumcision and the Jewish law. The whole incident is another proof of the authoritative position of St. Peter in the early Church, since his example and conduct was regarded as decisive. But Paul, who rightly saw the inconsistency in the conduct of Peter and the Jewish Christians, did not hesitate to defend the immunity of converted pagans from the Jewish Law.

Concerning Peter's subsequent attitude on this question St. Paul gives us no explicit information. But it is highly probable that Peter ratified the contention of the Apostles of the Gentiles, and thenceforth conducted himself towards the Christianized pagans as at first. As the principal opponents of his views in this connexion, Paul names and combats in all his writings only the extreme Jewish Christians coming "from James" (i. e., from Jerusalem). While the date of this occurrence, whether before or after the Council of the Apostles, cannot be determined, it probably took place after the council (see below). The later tradition, which existed as early as the end of the second century (Origen, "Hom. vi in Lucam"; Eusebius, "Hist. Eccl.", III, xxxvi), that Peter founded the Church of Antioch, indicates the fact that he laboured a long period there, and also perhaps that he dwelt there towards the end of his life and then appointed Evodius, the first of the line of Antiochian bishops, head of the community. This latter view would best explain the tradition referring the foundation of the Church of Antioch to St. Peter.

It is also probable that Peter pursued his Apostolic labours in various districts of Asia Minor, for it can scarcely be supposed that the entire period between his liberation from prison and the Council of the Apostles was spent uninterruptedly in one city, whether Antioch, Rome, or elsewhere. And, since he subsequently addressed the first of his Epistles to the faithful in the Provinces of Pontus, Galatia, Cappadocia, and Asia, one may reasonably assume that he had laboured personally at least in certain cities of these provinces, devoting himself chiefly to the Diaspora. The Epistle, however, is of a general character, and gives little indication of personal relations with the persons to whom it is addressed. The tradition related by Bishop Dionysius of Corinth (in Eusebius, "Hist. Eccl.", II, xxviii) in his letter to the Roman Church under Pope Soter (165-74), that Peter had (like Paul) dwelt in Corinth and planted the Church there, cannot be entirely rejected. Even though the tradition should receive no support from the existence of the "party of Cephas", which Paul mentions among the other divisions of the Church of Corinth (I Cor., i, 12; iii, 22), still Peter's sojourn in Corinth (even in connexion with the planting and government of the Church by Paul) is not impossible. That St. Peter undertook various Apostolic journeys (doubtless about this time, especially when he was no longer permanently residing in Jerusalem) is clearly established by the general remark of St. Paul in I Cor., ix, 5, concerning the "rest of the apostles, and the brethren [cousins] of the Lord, and Cephas", who were travelling around in the exercise of their Apostleship.

Peter returned occasionally to the original Christian Church of Jerusalem, the guidance of which was entrusted to St. James, the relative of Jesus, after the departure of the Prince of the Apostles (A. D. 42-44). The last mention of St. Peter in the Acts (xv, 1-29; cf. Gal., ii, 1-10) occurs in the report of the Council of the Apostles on the occasion of such a passing visit. In consequence of the trouble caused by extreme Jewish Christians to Paul and Barnabas at Antioch, the Church of this city sent these two Apostles with other envoys to Jerusalem to secure a definitive decision concerning the obligations of the converted pagans (see JUDAIZERS). In addition to James, Peter and John were then (about A. D. 50-51) in Jerusalem. In the discussion and decision of this important question, Peter naturally exercised a decisive influence. When a great divergence of views had manifested itself in the assembly, Peter spoke the deciding word. Long before, in accordance with God's testimony, he had announced the Gospels to the heathen (conversion of Cornelius and his household); why, therefore, attempt to place the Jewish yoke on the necks of converted pagans? After Paul and Barnabas had related how God had wrought among the Gentiles by them, James, the chief representative of the Jewish Christians, adopted Peter's view and in agreement therewith made proposals which were expressed in an encyclical to the converted pagans.

The occurrences in Cæsarea and Antioch and the debate at the Council of Jerusalem show clearly Peter's attitude towards the converts from paganism. Like the other eleven original Apostles, he regarded himself as called to preach the Faith in Jesus first among the Jews (Acts, x, 42), so that the chosen people of God might share in the salvation in Christ, promised to them primarily and issuing from their midst. The vision at Joppe and the effusion of the Holy Ghost over the converted pagan Cornelius and his kinsmen determined Peter to admit these forthwith into the community of the faithful, without imposing on them the Jewish Law. During his Apostolic journeys outside Palestine, he recognized in practice the equality of Gentile and Jewish converts, as his original conduct at Antioch proves. His aloofness from the Gentile converts, out of consideration for the Jewish Christians from Jerusalem, was by no means an official recognition of the views of the extreme Judaizers, who were so opposed to St. Paul. This is established clearly and incontestably by his attitude at the Council of Jerusalem. Between Peter and Paul there was no dogmatic difference in their conception of salvation for Jewish and Gentile Christians. The recognition of Paul as the Apostle of the Gentiles (Gal., ii, 1-9) was entirely sincere, and excludes all question of a fundamental divergence of views. St. Peter and the other Apostles recognized the converts from paganism as Christian brothers on an equal footing; Jewish and Gentile Christians formed a single Kingdom of Christ. If therefore Peter devoted the preponderating portion of his Apostolic activity to the Jews, this arose chiefly from practical considerations, and from the position of Israel as the Chosen People. Baur's hypothesis of opposing currents of "Petrinism" and "Paulinism" in the early Church is absolutely untenable, and is to-day entirely rejected by Protestants.

IV. ACTIVITY AND DEATH IN ROME; BURIAL PLACE.—It is an indisputably established historical fact that St. Peter laboured in Rome during the last portion of his life, and there ended his earthly course by martyrdom. As to the duration of his Apostolic activity in the Roman capital, the continuity or otherwise of his residence there, the details and success of his labours, and the chronology of his arrival and death, all these questions are uncertain, and can be solved only on hypotheses more or less well-founded. The essential fact is that Peter died at Rome: this constitutes the historical foundation of the claim of the Bishops of Rome to the Apostolic Primacy of Peter.

St. Peter's residence and death in Rome are established beyond contention as historical facts by a series of distinct testimonies extending from the end of the first to the end of the second centuries, and issuing from several lands. That the manner, and therefore the place of his death, must have been known in widely-extended Christian circles at the end of the first century is clear from the remark introduced into the Gospel of St. John concerning Christ's prophecy that Peter was bound to Him and would be led whither he would not: "And this he said, signifying by what death he should glorify God" (John, xxi, 18-19, see above). Such a remark presupposes in the readers of the Fourth Gospel a knowledge of the death of Peter. St. Peter's First Epistle was written almost undoubtedly from Rome, since the salutation at the end reads: "The church that is in Babylon, elected together with you, saluteth you: and so doth my son Mark" (v, 13). Babylon must here be identified with the Roman capital; since Babylon on the Euphrates, which lay in ruins, or New Babylon (Seleucia) on the Tigris, or the Egyptian Babylon near Memphis, or Jerusalem cannot be meant, the reference must be to Rome, the only city which is called Babylon elsewhere in ancient Christian literature (Apoc., xvii, 5; xviii, 10; "Oracula Sibyl.", V, verses 143 and 159, ed. Geffcken, Leipzig, 1902, 111).

From Bishop Papias of Hierapolis and Clement of Alexandria, who both appeal to the testimony of the old presbyters (i. e., the disciples of the Apostles), we learn that Mark wrote his Gospel in Rome at the request of the Roman Christians, who desired a written memorial of the doctrine preached to them by St. Peter and his disciples (Eusebius, "Hist. Eccl.", II, xv; III, xl; VI, xiv); this is confirmed by Irenæus (Adv. hær., III, i). In connexion with this information concerning the Gospel of St. Mark, Eusebius, relying perhaps on an earlier source, says that Peter described Rome figuratively as Babylon in his First Epistle. Another testimony concerning the martyrdom of Peter and Paul is supplied by Clement of Rome in his Epistle to the Corinthians (written about A. D. 95-97),wherein he says (v): "Through zeal and cunning the greatest and most righteous supports [of the Church] have suffered persecution and been warred to death. Let us place before our eyes the good Apostles—St. Peter, who in consequence of unjust zeal, suffered not one or two, but numerous miseries, and, having thus given testimony (μαρτυρήσας), has entered the merited place of glory". He then mentions Paul and a number of elect, who were assembled with the others and suffered martyrdom "among us" (ἐν ἡμῖν, i. e., among the Romans, the meaning that the expression also bears in chap. lv). He is speaking undoubtedly, as the whole passage proves, of the Neronian persecution, and thus refers the martyrdom of Peter and Paul to that epoch.

In his letter written at the beginning of the second century (before 117), while being brought to Rome for martyrdom, the venerable Bishop Ignatius of Antioch endeavours by every means to restrain the Roman Christians from striving for his pardon, remarking: "I issue you no commands, like Peter and Paul: they were Apostles, while I am but a captive" (Ad. Rom., iv). The meaning of this remark must be that the two Apostles laboured personally in Rome, and with Apostolic authority preached the Gospel there. Bishop Dionysius of Corinth, in his letter to the Roman Church in the time of Pope Soter (165-74), says: "You have therefore by your urgent exhortation bound close together the sowing of Peter and Paul at Rome and Corinth. For both planted the seed of the Gospel also in Corinth, and together instructed us, just as they likewise taught in the same place in Italy and at the same time suffered martyrdom" (In Eusebius, "Hist. Eccl.", II, xxviii). Irenæus of Lyons, a native of Asia Minor and a disciple of Polycarp of Smyrna (a disciple of St. John), passed a considerable time in Rome shortly after the middle of the second century, and then proceeded to Lyons, where he became bishop in 177; he described the Roman Church as the most prominent and chief pre-

ST. PETER RECEIVING THE KEYS
Perugino, Sistine Chapel, Rome

server of Apostolic tradition, as "the greatest and most ancient church, known by all, founded and organized at Rome by the two most glorious Apostles, Peter and Paul" (Adv. hær., III, iii; cf. III, i). He thus makes use of the universally known and recognized fact of the Apostolic activity of Peter and Paul in Rome, to find therein a proof from tradition against the heretics.

In his "Hypotyposes" (Eusebius, "Hist. Eccl.", IV, xiv), Clement of Alexandria, teacher in the catechetical school of that city from about 190, says on the strength of the tradition of the presbyters: "After Peter had announced the Word of God in Rome and preached the Gospel in the spirit of God, the multitude of hearers requested Mark, who had long accompanied Peter on all his journeys, to write down what the Apostles had preached to them" (see above). Like Irenæus, Tertullian appeals, in his writings against heretics, to the proof afforded by the Apostolic labours of Peter and Paul in Rome of the truth of ecclesiastical tradition. In "De Præscriptione", xxxv, he says: "If thou art near Italy, thou hast Rome where authority is ever within reach. How fortunate is this Church for which the Apostles have poured out their whole teaching with their blood, where Peter has emulated the Passion of the Lord, where Paul was crowned with the death of John" (*scil.* the Baptist). In "Scorpiace", xv, he also speaks of Peter's crucifixion. "The budding faith Nero first made bloody in Rome. There Peter was girded by another, since he was bound to the cross". As an illustration that it was immaterial with what water baptism is administered, he states in his book ("On Baptism", ch. v) that there is "no difference between that with which John baptized in the Jordan and that with which Peter baptized in the Tiber"; and against Marcion he appeals to the testimony of the Roman Christians, "to whom Peter and Paul have bequeathed the Gospel sealed with their blood" (Adv. Marc., IV, v).

The Roman, Caius, who lived in Rome, in the time of Pope Zephyrinus (198–217), wrote in his "Dialogue with Proclus" (in Eusebius, "Hist. Eccl.", II, xxviii), directed against the Montanists: "But I can show the trophies of the Apostles. If you care to go to the Vatican or to the road to Ostia, thou shalt find the trophies of those who have founded this Church". By the trophies (τρόπαια) Eusebius understands the graves of the Apostles, but his view is opposed by modern investigators, who believe that the place of execution is meant. For our purpose it is immaterial which opinion is correct, as the testimony retains its full value in either case. At any rate the place of execution and burial of both were close together; St. Peter, who was executed on the Vatican, received also his burial there. Eusebius also refers to "the inscription of the names of Peter and Paul, which have been preserved to the present day on the burial-places there" (i. e. at Rome). There thus existed in Rome an ancient epigraphic memorial commemorating the death of the Apostles. The obscure notice in the Muratorian Fragment ("Lucas optime theofile conprindit quia sub præsentia eius singula gerebantur sicuti et semote passionem petri evidenter declarat", ed. Preuschen, Tübingen, 1910, p. 29) also presupposes an ancient definite tradition concerning Peter's death in Rome. The apocryphal Acts of St. Peter and the Acts of Sts. Peter and Paul likewise belong to the series of testimonies of the death of the two Apostles in Rome (Lipsius, "Acta Apostolorum apocrypha", I, Leipzig, 1891, pp. 1 sqq., 78 sqq., 118 sqq., cf. Idem, "Die apokryphen Apostelgeschichten und Apostellegenden", II, i, Brunswick, 1887, pp. 84 sqq.).

In opposition to this distinct and unanimous testimony of early Christendom, some few Protestant historians have attempted in recent times to set aside the residence and death of Peter at Rome as legendary. These attempts have resulted in complete failure. It was asserted that the tradition concerning Peter's residence in Rome first originated in Ebionite circles, and formed part of the Legend of Simon the Magician, in which Paul is opposed by Peter as a false Apostle under Simon; just as this fight was transplanted to Rome, so also sprang up at an early date the legend of Peter's activity in that capital (thus in Baur, "Paulus", 2nd ed., 245 sqq., followed by Hase and especially Lipsius, "Die quellen der römischen Petrussage", Kiel, 1872). But this hypothesis is proved fundamentally untenable by the whole character and purely local importance of Ebionitism, and is directly refuted by the above genuine and entirely independent testimonies, which are at least as ancient. It has moreover been now entirely abandoned by serious Protestant historians (cf., e. g., Harnack's remarks in "Gesch. der altchristl. Literatur", II, i, 244, n. 2). A more recent attempt was made by Erbes (Zeitschr. für Kirchengesch., 1901, pp. 1 sqq., 161 sqq.) to demonstrate that St. Peter was martyred at Jerusalem. He appeals to the apocryphal Acts of St. Peter, in which two Romans, Albinus and Agrippa, are mentioned as persecutors of the Apostles. These he identifies with the Albinus, Procurator of Judæa, and successor of Festus, and Agrippa II, Prince of Galilee, and thence concludes that Peter was condemned to death and sacrificed by this procurator at Jerusalem. The untenableness of this hypothesis becomes immediately apparent from the mere fact that our earliest definite testimony concerning Peter's death in Rome far antedates the apocryphal Acts; besides, never throughout the whole range of Christian antiquity has any city other than Rome been designated the place of martyrdom of Sts. Peter and Paul.

Although the fact of St. Peter's activity and death in Rome is so clearly established, we possess no precise information regarding the details of his Roman sojourn. The narratives contained in the apocryphal literature of the second century concerning the supposed strife between Peter and Simon Magus belong to the domain of legend. From the already mentioned statements regarding the origin of the Gospel of St. Mark, we may conclude that Peter laboured for a long period in Rome. This conclusion is confirmed by the unanimous voice of tradition which, as early as the second half of the second century, designates the Prince of the Apostles the founder of the Roman Church. It is widely held that Peter paid a first visit to Rome after he had been miraculously liberated from the prison in Jerusalem; that, by "another place", Luke meant Rome, but omitted the name for special reasons. It is not impossible that Peter made a missionary journey to Rome about this time (after 42 A. D.), but such a journey cannot be established with certainty. At any rate, we cannot appeal in support of this theory to the chronological notices in Eusebius and Jerome, since, although these notices extend back to the chronicles of the third century, they are not old traditions, but the result of calculations on the basis of episcopal lists. Into the Roman list of bishops dating from the second century, there was introduced in the third century (as we learn from Eusebius and the "Chronograph of 354") the notice of a twenty-five years' pontificate for St. Peter, but we are unable to trace its origin. This entry consequently affords no ground for the hypothesis of a first visit by St. Peter to Rome after his liberation from prison (about 42). We can therefore admit only the possibility of such an early visit to the capital.

The task of determining the year of St. Peter's death is attended with similar difficulties. In the fourth century, and even in the chronicles of the third, we find two different entries. In the "Chronicle" of Eusebius the thirteenth or fourteenth year of Nero is given as that of the death of Peter and Paul (67–68); this date, accepted by Jerome, is that generally held. The year 67 is also supported by the statement, also accepted by Eusebius and Jerome, that Peter came to Rome under the Emperor Claudius (according to Jerome, in 42), and by the above-mentioned tradition of the twenty-five years' episcopate of Peter (cf. Bartolini, "Sopra l'anno 67 se fosse quello del martirio dei gloriosi Apostoli", Rome, 1868). A different statement is furnished by the "Chronograph of 354" (ed. Duchesne, "Liber Pontificalis", I, 1 sqq.). This refers St. Peter's arrival in Rome to the year 30, and his death and that of St. Paul to 55.

Duchesne has shown that the dates in the "Chronograph" were inserted in a list of the popes which contains only their names and the duration of their pontificates, and then, on the chronological supposition that the year of Christ's death was 29, the year 30 was inserted as the beginning of Peter's pontificate, and his death referred to 55, on the basis of the twenty-five years' pontificate (op. cit., introd., vi sqq.). This date has however been recently defended by Kellner ("Jesus von Nazareth u. seine Apostel im Rahmen der Zeitgeschichte", Ratisbon, 1908; "Tradition geschichtl. Bearbeitung u. Legende in der Chronologie des apostol. Zeitalters", Bonn, 1909). Other historians have accepted the year 65 (e. g., Bianchini, in his edition of the "Liber Pontificalis" in P. L., CXXVII, 435 sqq.) or 66 (e. g. Foggini,

ST. PETER
RIBERA (SPAGNOLETTO), THE PRADO, MADRID

"De romani b. Petri itinere et episcopatu", Florence, 1741; also Tillemont). Harnack endeavoured to establish the year 64 (i. e. the beginning of the Neronian persecution) as that of Peter's death ("Gesch. der altchristl. Lit. bis Eusebius", pt. II, "Die Chronologie", I, 240 sqq.). This date, which had been already supported by Cave, du Pin, and Wieseler, has been accepted by Duchesne (Hist. ancienne de l'église, I, 64). Erbes refers St. Peter's death to 22 Feb., 63, St. Paul's to 64 ("Texte u. Untersuchungen", new series, IV, i, Leipzig, 1900, "Die Todestage der Apostel Petrus u. Paulus u. ihre röm. Denkmäler"). The date of Peter's death is thus not yet decided; the period between July, 64 (outbreak of the Neronian persecution), and the beginning of 68 (on 9 July Nero fled from Rome and committed suicide) must be left open for the date of his death. The day of his martyrdom is also unknown; 29 June, the accepted day of his feast since the fourth century, cannot be proved to be the day of his death (see below).

Concerning the manner of Peter's death, we possess a tradition—attested to by Tertullian at the end of the second century (see above) and by Origen (in Eusebius, "Hist. Eccl.", II, i)—that he suffered crucifixion. Origen says: "Peter was crucified at Rome with his head downwards, as he himself had desired to suffer". As the place of execution may be accepted with great probability the Neronian Gardens on the Vatican, since there, according to Tacitus, were enacted in general the gruesome scenes of the Neronian persecution; and in this district, in the vicinity of the Via Cornelia and at the foot of the Vatican Hills, the Prince of the Apostles found his burial-place. Of this grave (since the word τρόπαιον was, as already remarked, rightly understood of the tomb) Caius already speaks in the third century. For a time the remains of Peter lay with those of Paul in a vault on the Appian Way, at the place *ad Catacumbas*, where the Church of St. Sebastian (which on its erection in the fourth century was dedicated to the two Apostles) now stands. The remains had probably been brought thither at the beginning of the Valerian persecution in 258, to protect them from the threatened desecration when the Christian burial-places were confiscated. They were later restored to their former resting-place, and Constantine the Great had a magnificent basilica erected over the grave of St. Peter at the foot of the Vatican Hill. This basilica was replaced by the present St. Peter's in the sixteenth century. The vault with the altar built above it (*confessio*) has been since the fourth century the most highly venerated martyr's shrine in the West. In the substructure of the altar, over the vault which contained the sarcophagus with the remains of St. Peter, a cavity was made. This was closed by a small door in front of the altar. By opening this door the pilgrim could enjoy the great privilege of kneeling directly over the sarcophagus of the Apostle. Keys of this door were given as precious souvenirs (cf. Gregory of Tours, "De gloria martyrum", I, xxviii).

The memory of St. Peter is also closely associated with the Catacomb of St. Priscilla on the Via Salaria. According to a tradition, current in later Christian antiquity, St. Peter here instructed the faithful and administered baptism. This tradition seems to have been based on still earlier monumental testimonies. The catacomb is situated under the garden of a villa of the ancient Christian and senatorial family, the Acilii Glabriones, and its foundation extends back to the end of the first century; and since Acilius Glabrio (q. v.), consul in 91, was condemned to death under Domitian as a Christian, it is quite possible that the Christian faith of the family extended back to Apostolic times, and that the Prince of the Apostles had been given hospitable reception in their house during his residence at Rome. The relations between Peter and Pudens, whose house stood on the site of the present titular church of Pudens (now Santa Pudentiana) seem to rest rather on a legend.

Concerning the Epistles of St. Peter, see PETER, EPISTLES OF SAINT; concerning the various apocrypha bearing the name of Peter, especially the Apocalypse and the Gospel of St. Peter, see APOCRYPHA. The apocryphal sermon of Peter (κήρυγμα), dating from the second half of the second century, was probably a collection of supposed sermons by the Apostle; several fragments are preserved by Clement of Alexandria (cf. Dobschütz, "Das Kerygma Petri kritisch untersucht" in "Texte u. Untersuchungen", XI, i, Leipzig, 1893).

V. FEASTS OF ST. PETER.—As early as the fourth century a feast was celebrated in memory of Sts. Peter and Paul on the same day, although the day was not the same in the East as in Rome. The Syrian Martyrology of the end of the fourth century, which is an excerpt from a Greek catalogue of saints from Asia Minor, gives the following feasts in connexion with Christmas (25 Dec.): 26 Dec., St. Stephen; 27 Dec., Sts. James and John; 28 Dec., Sts. Peter and Paul. In St. Gregory of Nyssa's panegyric on St. Basil we are also informed that these feasts of the Apostles and St. Stephen follow immediately after Christmas. The Armenians celebrated the feast also on 27 Dec.; the Nestorians on the second Friday after the Epiphany. It is evident that 28 (27) Dec. was (like 26 Dec. for St. Stephen) arbitrarily selected, no tradition concerning the date of the saints' death being forthcoming. The chief feast of Sts. Peter and Paul was kept in Rome on 29 June as early as the third or fourth century. The list of feasts of the martyrs in the Chronograph of Philocalus appends this notice to the date: "III. Kal. Jul. Petri in Catacumbas et Pauli Ostiense Tusco et Basso Coss." (=the year 258). The "Martyrologium Hieronyminanum" has, in the Berne MS., the following notice for 29 June: "Romæ via Aurelia natale sanctorum Apostolorum Petri et Pauli, Petri in Vaticano, Pauli in via Ostiensi, utrumque in catacumbas, passi sub Nerone, Basso et Tusco consulibus" (ed. de Rossi—Duchesne, 84).

The date 258 in the notices shows that from this year the memory of the two Apostles was celebrated on 29 June in the Via Appia *ad Catacumbas* (near San Sebastiano fuori le mura), because on this date the remains of the Apostles were translated thither (see above). Later, perhaps on the building of the church over the graves on the Vatican and in the Via Ostiensis, the remains were restored to their former resting-place: Peter's to the Vatican Basilica and Paul's to the church on the Via Ostiensis. In the place *Ad Catacumbas* a church was also built as early as the fourth century in honour of the two Apostles. From 258 their principal feast was kept on 29 June, on which date solemn Divine Service was held in the above-mentioned three churches from ancient times (Duchesne, "Origines du culte chrétien", 5th ed., Paris, 1909, 271 sqq., 283 sqq.; Urbain, "Ein Martyrologium der christl. Gemeinde zu Rom an Anfang des 5. Jahrh.", Leipzig, 1901, 169 sqq.; Kellner, "Heortologie", 3rd ed., Freiburg, 1911, 210 sqq.). Legend sought to explain the temporary occupation by the Apostles of the grave *Ad Catacumbas* by supposing that, shortly after their death, the Oriental Christians wished to steal their bodies and bring them to the East. This whole story is evidently a product of popular legend. (Concerning the Feast of the Chair of Peter, see CHAIR OF PETER.)

A third Roman feast of the Apostles takes place on 1 August: the feast of St. Peter's Chains. This feast was originally the dedication feast of the church of the Apostle, erected on the Esquiline Hill in the fourth century. A titular priest of the church, Philippus, was papal legate at the Council of Ephesus in 431. The church was rebuilt by Sixtus III (432–40) at the expense of the Byzantine imperial family. Either the solemn consecration took place on 1 August, or this was the day of dedication of the earlier church. Perhaps this day was selected to replace the heathen festivities which took place on 1 August. In this church, which is still standing (S. Pietro in Vincoli), were probably preserved from the fourth century St. Peter's chains, which were greatly venerated, small filings from the chains being regarded as precious relics. The church thus early received the name *in Vinculis*, and the feast of 1 August became the the feast of St. Peter's Chains (Duchesne, op. cit., 286 sqq.; Kellner, loc. cit., 216 sqq.). The memory of both Peter and Paul was later associated also with two places of ancient Rome: the Via Sacra, outside the Forum, where the magician Simon was said to have been hurled down at the prayer of Peter, and the prison *Tullianum*, or *Carcer Mamertinus*, where the Apostles were supposed to have been kept until their execution. At both these places, also, shrines of the Apostles were erected, and that of the Mamertine Prison still remains in almost its original form from the early Roman time. These local commemorations of the Apostles are based on legends, and no special celebrations are held in the two churches. It is, however, not impossible that Peter and Paul were actually confined in the chief prison in Rome at the fort of the Capitol, of which the present *Carcer Mamertinus* is a remnant.

VI. REPRESENTATIONS OF ST. PETER.—The oldest extant is the bronze medallion with the heads of the Apostles; this dates from the end of the second or the beginning of the third century, and is preserved in the Christian Museum of the Vatican Library. Peter has a strong, roundish head, prominent jaw-bones, a receding forehead, thick, curly hair and beard. (See illustration in CATACOMBS.) The features are so individual that it partakes of the nature of a portrait. This type is also found in two representations of St. Peter in a chamber of the Catacomb of Peter and Marcellinus, dating from the second half of the third century (Wilpert, "Die Malerein der Katakomben Rom", plates 94 and 96). In the paintings of the catacombs Sts. Peter and Paul frequently appear as interceders and advocates for the dead in the representations of the Last Judgment (Wilpert, 390 sqq.), and as introducing an Orante (a praying figure representing the dead) into Paradise.

In the numerous representations of Christ in the midst of His Apostles, which occur in the paintings of the catacombs and carved on sarcophagi, Peter and Paul always occupy the places of honour on the right and left of the Saviour. In the mosaics of the Roman basilicas, dating from the fourth to the ninth centuries, Christ appears as the central figure, with Sts. Peter and Paul on His right and left, and besides these the saints especially venerated in the particular church. On sarcophagi and other memorials appear scenes from the life of St. Peter: his walking on Lake Genesareth, when Christ summoned him from the boat; the prophecy of his denial; the washing of his feet; the raising of Tabitha from the dead; the capture of Peter and the conducting of him to the place of execution. On two gilt glasses he is represented as Moses drawing water from the rock with his staff; the name Peter under the scene shows that he is regarded as the guide of the people of God in the New Testament.

Particularly frequent in the period between the fourth and sixth centuries is the scene of the delivery of the Law to Peter, which occurs on various kinds of monuments. Christ hands St. Peter a folded or open scroll, on which is often the inscription *Lex Domini* (Law of the Lord) or *Dominus legem dat* (The Lord gives the law). In the mausoleum of Constantina at Rome (S. Costanza, in the Via Nomentana) this scene is given as a pendant to the delivery of the Law to Moses. In representations on fifth-century sarcophagi the Lord presents to Peter (instead of the scroll) the keys. In carvings of the fourth century Peter often bears a staff in his hand (after the fifth century, a cross with a long shaft, carried by the Apostle on his shoulder), as a kind of sceptre indicative of Peter's office. From the end of the sixth century this is replaced by the keys (usually two, but sometimes three), which henceforth became the attribute of Peter. Even the renowned and greatly venerated bronze statue in St. Peter's possesses them; this, the best known representation of the Apostle, dates from the last period of Christian antiquity (Grisar, "Analecta romana", I, Rome, 1899, 627 sqq.).

BIRKS, *Studies of the Life and Character of St. Peter* (London, 1887); TAYLOR, *Peter the Apostle*, new ed. by BURNET AND ISBISTER (London, 1900); BARNES, *St. Peter in Rome and his Tomb on the Vatican Hill* (London, 1900); LIGHTFOOT, *Apostolic Fathers*, 2nd ed., pt. I, vol. II (London, 1890), 481 sq., *St. Peter in Rome*; FOUARD, *Les origines de l'Eglise: St. Pierre et les premières années du christianisme* (3rd ed., Paris, 1893); FILLION, *Saint Pierre* (2nd ed., Paris, 1906); collection *Les Saints*; RAMBAUD, *Histoire de St. Pierre apôtre* (Bordeaux, 1900); GUIRAUD, *La venue de St Pierre à Rome* in *Questions d'hist. et d'archéol. chrét.* (Paris, 1906); FOGGINI, *De romano D. Petri itinere et episcopatu* (Florence, 1741); RINIERI, *S. Pietro in Roma ed i primi papi secundo i più vetusti cataloghi della chiesa Romana* (Turin, 1909); PAGANI, *Il cristianesimo in Roma prima dei gloriosi apostoli Pietro e Paolo, e sulle diverse venute de' principi degli apostoli in Roma* (Rome, 1906); POLIDORI, *Apostolato di S. Pietro in Roma* in *Civiltà Cattolica*, series 18, IX (Rome, 1903), 141 sq.; MARUCCHI, *Le memorie degli apostoli Pietro e Paolo in Roma* (2nd ed., Rome, 1903); LECLER, *De Romano S. Petri episcopatu* (Louvain, 1888); SCHMID, *Petrus in Rom oder Novæ Vindiciæ Petrinæ* (Lucerne, 1892); ESSER, *Des hl. Petrus Aufenthalt, Episkopat und Tod in Rom* (Breslau, 1889); KNELLER, *St. Petrus, Bischof von Rom* in *Zeitschrift f. kath. Theol.*, XXVI (1902), 33 sq., 225 sq.; MARQUARDT, *Simon Petrus als Mittel und Ausgangspunkt der christlichen Urkirche* (Kempten, 1906); GRISAR, *Le tombe apostoliche al Vaticano ed alla via Ostiense* in *Analecta Romana*, I (Rome, 1899), 259 sq.

J. P. KIRSCH.

Peter, EPISTLES OF SAINT.—These two Epistles will be treated under the following heads: I. Authenticity; II. Recipients, occasion, and object; III. Date and place of composition; IV. Analysis.

I. FIRST EPISTLE.—A. *Authenticity*.—The authenticity, universally admitted by the primitive Church, has been denied within the past century by Protestant or Rationalist critics (Baur and the Tübingen School, Von Soden, Harnack, Jülicher, Hilgenfeld, and others), but it cannot seriously be questioned. It is well established: (1) by extrinsic arguments: (a) Quotations from or allusions to it are very numerous in writings of the first and second centuries, e. g., Justin's letter to the Churches of Lyons and Vienne, Irenæus, Clement of Alexandria, Papias, Polycarp, Clement of Rome, the "Didache", the "Pastor" of Hermas, and others. The Second Epistle of St. Peter, admitted to be very ancient even by those who question its authenticity, alludes to an earlier Epistle written by the Apostle (iii, 1). The letter therefore existed very early and was considered very authoritative. (b) Tradition is also unanimous for St. Peter's authorship. In the second and third centuries we have much explicit testimony to this effect. Clement and Origen at Alexandria, Tertullian and Cyprian in Africa, the Peshitto in Syria, Irenæus in Gaul, the ancient Itala and Hippolytus at Rome all agree in attributing it to Peter, as do also the heretics, Basilides and Theodore of Byzantium. (c) All the collections or lists of the New Testament mention it as St. Peter's; the Muratorian Canon, which alone is at variance with this common tradition, is obscure and bears evident marks of textual corruption, and the subsequent restoration suggested by Zahn, which seems much more probable, is clearly favourable to the authenticity. Moreover Eusebius of Cæsarea does not hesitate to place it among the undisputed Scriptures.

(2) By intrinsic arguments.—Examination of the Epistle in itself is wholly favourable to its authenticity; the author calls himself Peter, the Apostle of Jesus Christ (i, 1); Mark, who, according to the Acts

of the Apostles, had such close relations with Peter, is called by the author "my son" (v, 13); the author is represented as the immediate disciple of Jesus Christ (i, 1; v, 9, 11–14); he exercises from Rome a universal jurisdiction over the whole Church (v, 1). The numerous places in which he would appear to be the immediate witness of the life of Christ (i, 8; ii, 21–24; v, 1), as well as the similarity between his ideas and the teaching of the Gospels, are eloquently in favour of the Apostolic author (cf. Jacquier, 251). Finally, some authors consider that the Epistle and the sermons of St. Peter related in the Acts show an analogy in basis and form which proves a common origin. However, it is probable if not certain that the Apostle made use of an interpreter, especially of Sylvanus; St. Jerome says: "The two Epistles attributed to St. Peter differ in style, character, and the construction of the words, which proves that according to the exigencies of the moment St. Peter made use of different interpreters" (Ep. cxx ad Hedib.). Peter himself seems to insinuate this: Διὰ Σιλουανοῦ ὑμῖν . . . ἔγραψα (v, 12), and the final verses (12–14) seem to have been added by the Apostle himself. Without denying that Peter was able to use and speak Greek, some authors consider that he could not write it in the almost classic manner of this Epistle. Nevertheless it is impossible to determine exactly the share of Sylvanus; it is not improbable that he wrote it according to the directions of the Apostle, inserting the ideas and exhortations suggested by him.

Objections: (a) The relation between the First Epistle of Peter and the Epistles of Paul, especially Romans and Ephesians, does not prove, as has been claimed (Jülicher), that the Epistle was written by a disciple of Paul. This relation, which has been much exaggerated by some critics, does not prove a literary dependence nor prevent this Epistle from possessing a characteristic originality in ideas and form. The resemblance is readily explained if we admit that Peter employed Sylvanus as interpreter, for the latter had been a companion of Paul, and would consequently have felt the influence of his doctrine and manner of speaking. Moreover, Peter and Sylvanus were at Rome, where the letter was written, and they would naturally have become acquainted with the Epistles to the Romans and the Ephesians, written some months before and intended, at least in part, for the same readers. (b) It has been claimed that the Epistle presupposes an official and general persecution in the Roman Empire and betokens a state of things corresponding to the reign of Vespasian, or even that of Domitian or Trajan, but the data it gives are too indefinite to conclude that it refers to one of these persecutions rather than to that of Nero; besides, some authors consider that the Epistle does not at all suppose an official persecution, the allusions being readily explained by the countless difficulties and annoyances to which Jews and pagans subjected the Christians.

B. *Recipients of the Epistle; Occasion and Object.*—It was written to the faithful of "Pontus, Galatia, Cappadocia, Asia, and Bithynia" (i, 1). Were these Christians converted Jews, dispersed among the Gentiles (i, 1), as was held by Origen, Didymus of Alexandria, etc., and is still maintained by Weiss and Kuhl, or were they in great part of pagan origin? The latter is by far the more common and the better opinion (i, 14; ii, 9–10; iii, 6; iv, 3). The argument based on i, 7, proves nothing, while the words "to the strangers dispersed through Pontus" should not be taken in the literal sense of Jews in exile, but in the metaphorical sense of the people of God, Christians, living in exile on earth, far from their true country. The opinions of authors admitting the authenticity are divided with regard to the historical circumstances which occasioned the Epistle, some believing that it was written immediately after Nero's decree proscribing the Christian religion, in which case the difficulties to which Peter alludes do not consist merely of the calumnies and vexations of the people, but also include the judicial pursuit and condemnation of Christians (iv, 14–16; v, 12; ii, 23; iii, 18), while iv, 12, may be an allusion to the burning of Rome which was the occasion of Nero's decree. This is the opinion of Hug, Gloire, Batiffol, Neander, Grimm, Ewald, Allard, Weiss, Callewaert, etc., while others date the Epistle from the eve of that decree (Jacquier, Brassac, Fillion, etc.). The Epistle, they say, having been written from Rome, where the persecution must have raged in all its horror, we naturally look for clear and indisputable indications of it, but the general theme of the Epistle is that the Christians should give no occasion to the charges of the infidels, but that by their exemplary life they should induce them to glorify God (ii, 12, 15; iii, 9, 16; iv, 4); besides, the way of speaking is generally hypothetical (i, 6; iii, 13–14; iv, 14), there being no question of judges, tribunals, prison, tortures, or confiscation. The Christians have to suffer, not from authority, but from the people among whom they lived.

The Apostle Peter wrote to the Christians of Asia to confirm them in the Faith, to console them amid their tribulations, and to indicate to them the line of conduct to follow in suffering (v, 2). Except for the more dogmatic introduction (i, 3–12) and a few short instructions strewn throughout the letter and intended to support moral exhortations, the Epistle is hortatory and practical. Only an absurd *a priori* argument could permit the Tübingen critics to assert that it had a dogmatic object and was written by a second-century forger with the intention of attributing to Peter the doctrines of Paul.

C. *Place and Date of Composition.*—The critics who have denied Peter's sojourn at Rome must necessarily deny that the letter was written from there, but the great majority of critics, with all Christian antiquity, agree that it was written at Rome itself, designated by the metaphorical name Babylon (v, 13). This interpretation has been accepted from the most remote times, and indeed no other metaphor could so well describe the city of Rome, rich and luxurious as it was, and given over to the worship of false gods and every species of immorality. Both cities had caused trouble to the people of God, Babylon to the Jews, and Rome to the Christians. Moreover this metaphor was in use among the early Christians (cf. Apoc., xiv, 8; xvi, 19; xvii, 5; xviii, 2, 10, 21). Finally, tradition has not brought us the faintest memory of any sojourn of Peter at Babylon. The opinions of critics who deny the authenticity of the Epistle range from A. D. 80 to A. D. 160 as the date, but as there is not the slightest doubt of its authenticity they have no basis for their argument. Equally diverse opinions are found among the authors who admit the authenticity, ranging from the year A. D. 45 to that accepted as that of the death of Peter. The most probable opinion is that which places it about the end of the year 63 or the beginning of 64; and St. Peter having suffered martyrdom at Rome in 64 (67?) the Epistle could not be subsequent to that date; besides, it assumes that the persecution of Nero, which began about the end of 64, had not yet broken out (see above). On the other hand the author frequently alludes to the Epistle to the Ephesians, making use of its very words and expressions; consequently the Epistle could not be prior to 63, since the Epistle to the Ephesians was written at the end of Paul's first captivity at Rome (61–63).

D. *Analysis.*—The Epistle as a whole being but a succession of general ideas without close connexion, there can be no strict plan of analysis. It is divided as follows: the introduction contains, besides the address (superscription and salutation, i, 7), thanksgiving to God for the excellence of the salvation and regeneration to which He has deigned to call the Christians (3–12). This part is dogmatic and serves as a basis for all the moral exhortations in the body of the Epistle. The body of the Epistle may be divided into three sections: (a) exhortation to a truly Christian life (i, 13–ii, 10), wherein Peter successively exhorts his readers to holiness in general (13–21), to fraternal charity in particular (i, 22–ii, 1), to love and desire of the true doctrine; thus they shall be living stones in the spiritual house of which Christ is the cornerstone, they shall be the royal priesthood and the chosen people of the Lord (2–10). (b) Rules of conduct for Christians living among pagans, especially in time of persecution (ii, 11–v, 19). Let their conduct be such that the infidels themselves shall be edified and cease to speak evil of the Christians (11–12). This general principle is applied in detail in the exhortations relating to obedience to civil rulers (13–17), the duties of slaves to their masters (18–25), the mutual duties of husband and wife (iii, 1–7). With regard to those who, not having the same faith, calumniate and persecute the Christians, the latter should return good for evil, according to the example of Christ, who though innocent suffered for us, and who preached the Gospel not only to the living, but also to the spirits that were in prison (8–22). The Apostle concludes by repeating his exhortation to sanctity in general (iv, 1–6), to charity (7–11), to patience and joy in suffering for Christ (12–19). (c) Some special recommendations follow (v, 1–11): let the ancients be careful to feed the flock entrusted to their keeping (1–4); let the faithful be subject to their pastor (5a); let all observe humility among themselves (5b); let them be sober and watchful, trusting the Lord (6–11).

In the epilogue the Apostle himself declares that he has employed Sylvanus to write the letter and affirms that the Divine grace possessed by his readers is the true grace (12); he addresses to them the salutations of the Church in Rome and those of Mark (13), and gives them his Apostolic blessing.

SECOND EPISTLE.—A. *Authenticity*.—In the present state of the controversy over the authenticity it may be affirmed that it is solidly probable, though it is difficult to prove with certainty. (1) Extrinsic arguments.—(a) In the first two centuries there is not in the Apostolic Fathers and other ecclesiastical writers, if we except Theophilus of Antioch (180), a single quotation properly so called from this Epistle; at most there are some more or less probable allusions in their writings, e. g., the First Epistle of St. Clement of Rome to the Corinthians, the "Didache", St. Ignatius, the Epistle of Barnabas, the "Pastor" of Hermas, the Epistle of Polycarp to the Philippians, the Dialogue of St. Justin with Trypho, St. Irenæus, the Clementine "Recognitions", the "Acts of Peter", etc. The Epistle formed part of the ancient Itala, but is not in the Syriac. This proves that the Second Epistle of Peter existed and even had a certain amount of authority. But it is impossible to bring forward with certainty a single explicit testimony in favour of this authenticity. The Muratorian Canon presents a mutilated text of I Peter, and Zahn's suggested restoration, which seems very probable, leaves only a doubt with regard to the authenticity of the Second Epistle.

(b) In the Western Church there is no explicit testimony in favour of the canonicity and Apostolicity of this Epistle until the middle of the fourth century. Tertullian and Cyprian do not mention it, and Mommsen's Canon (360) still bears traces of the uncertainty among the Churches of the West in this respect. The Eastern Church gave earlier testimony in its behalf. According to Eusebius and Photius, Clement of Alexandria (d. 215) commented on it, but he seems not to have ranked it with the first. It is found in the two great Egyptian versions (Sahidic and Bohairic). It is probable that Firmilian of Cæsarea used it and ascribed it to St. Peter, as Methodius of Olympus did explicitly. Eusebius of Cæsarea (340), while personally accepting II Peter as authentic and canonical, nevertheless classes it among the disputed works (ἀντιλεγόμενα), at the same time affirming that it was known by most Christians and studied by a large number with the other Scriptures. In the Church of Antioch and Syria at that period it was regarded as of doubtful authenticity. St. John Chrysostom does not speak of it, and it is omitted by the Peshitto. That the Epistle formerly accepted in that Church (Theophilus of Antioch) was not yet included in the canon was probably due to dogmatic reasons.

(c) In the second half of the fourth century these doubts rapidly disappeared in the Churches of the East owing to the authority of Eusebius of Cæsarea and the fifty copies of the Scriptures distributed by command of Constantine the Great. Didymus of Alexandria, St. Athanasius, St. Epiphanius, St. Cyril of Jerusalem, St. Gregory Nazianzen, the Canon of Laodicea, all regard the letter as authentic. The addition to the text of Didymus, according to which it was the work of a forger, seems to be the error of a copyist. So in the West relations with the East and the authority of St. Jerome finally brought about the admission of its authenticity. It was admitted to the Vulgate, and the synod convoked by Pope Damasus in 382 expressly attributes it to St. Peter.

(2) Intrinsic arguments.—If tradition does not appear to furnish an apodictic argument in favour of the authenticity, an examination of the Epistle itself does. The author calls himself Simon Peter, servant and Apostle of Jesus Christ (i, 1), witness of the glorious transfiguration of Christ (i, 16–18); he recalls the prediction of His death which Christ made to him (i, 14); he calls the Apostle Paul his brother, i. e., his colleague in the Apostolate (iii, 15); and he identifies himself with the author of the First Epistle. Therefore the author must necessarily be St. Peter himself or some one who wrote under his name, but nothing in the Epistle forces us to believe the latter. On the other hand there are several indications of its authenticity: the author shows himself to be a Jew, of ardent character, such as the New Testament portrays St. Peter, while a comparison with the ideas, words, and expressions of the First Epistle affords a further argument in favour of the identity of the author. Such, at least, is the opinion of several critics.

In examining the difficulties raised against the authenticity of the Epistle, the following facts should be remembered: (a) This Epistle has been wrongly accused of being imbued with Hellenism, from which it is even farther removed than the writings of Luke and the Epistles of Paul. (b) Likewise the false doctrines which it opposes are not the full-blown Gnosticism of the second century, but the budding Gnosticism as opposed by St. Paul. (c) The difference which some authors claim to find between the doctrine of the two Epistles proves nothing against the authenticity; some others have even maintained that comparison of the doctrines furnishes a new argument in favour of the author's identity. Doubtless there exist undeniable differences, but is an author obliged to confine himself within the same circle of ideas? (d) The difference of style which critics have discovered between the two Epistles is an argument requiring too delicate handling to supply a certain conclusion, and here again some others have drawn from a similarity of style an argument in favour of a unity of authorship. Admitting that the manner of speaking is not the same in both Epistles, there is, nevertheless, not the slightest difficulty, if it be true as St. Jerome has said (see above under FIRST EPISTLE), that in the composition of the two Epistles St. Peter made use of different interpreters. (e) It is also incorrect to say that this Epistle supposes the Epistle of St. Paul to have been already collected (iii, 15–16), for the author does not say that he knew all the Epistles of St. Paul. That he should have regarded Paul's letters as inspired forms a difficulty only to those who do not admit the possibility of a revelation made to Peter on this point. Some authors have also wrongly contested the unity of the Epistle, some claiming that it consists of two distinct epistles, the second beginning with ch. iii, others maintaining that the ii, 1–iii, 2, has been interpolated. Recently M. Ladeuze (Revue Biblique, 1905) has advanced an hypothesis which seems to end numerous difficulties: by an involuntary error of a copyist or by accidental transposition of the leaves of the codex on which the Epistle was written, one of the parts of the Epistle was transposed, and according to the order of sections the letter should be restored as follows: i–ii, 3a; iii, 1–16; ii, 3b–22; iii, 17–18. The hypothesis seems very probable.

Relations of II Peter with the Epistle of Jude.— This Epistle has so much in common with that of Jude that the author of one must have had the other before him. There is no agreement on the question of priority, but the most credited opinion is that Peter depends on Jude (q. v.).

B. *Recipients, Occasion, and Object.*—It is believed that this Epistle, like the First, was sent to the Christians of Asia Minor, the majority of whom were converted Gentiles (iii, 1–2; ii, 11–12; etc.). False teachers (ii, 1), heretics and deceivers (iii, 3), of corrupt morals (ii, 1) and denying the Second Advent of Christ and the end of the world, sought to corrupt the faith and the conduct of the Christians of Asia Minor. Peter wrote to excite them to the practice of virtue and chiefly to turn them away from the errors and bad example of the false teachers.

C. *Date and Place of Composition.*—While those who reject the authenticity of the Epistle place it about 150, the advocates of its authenticity maintain that it was written after 63–4, the date of the First Epistle, and before 64–5, the date believed to be that of the death of St. Peter (i, 14). Like the First, it was written at Rome.

D. *Analysis.*—In the exordium the Apostle, after the inscription and salutation (i, 1–2), recalls the magnificent gifts bestowed by Jesus Christ on the faithful; he exhorts them to the practice of virtue and all the more earnestly that he is convinced that his death is approaching (3–15). In the body of the Epistle (i, 16–iii, 13) the author brings forward the dogma of the second coming of Christ, which he proves, recalling His glorious transfiguration and the prediction of the Prophets (i, 16–21). Then he inveighs against the false teachers and condemns their life and doctrines: (a) They shall undergo Divine chastisement, in proof of which the Apostle recalls the punishment inflicted on the rebel angels, on the contemporaries of Noe, on the people of Sodom and Gomorrha (ii, 1–11). (b) He describes the immoral life of the false teachers, their impurity and sensuality, their avarice and duplicity (12–22). (c) He refutes their doctrine, showing that they are wrong in rejecting the second coming of Christ and the end of the world (iii, 1–4), for the Judge shall certainly come and that unexpectedly; even as the ancient world perished by the waters of the flood so the present world shall perish by fire and be replaced by a new world (5–7). Then follows the moral conclusion: let us live holily, if we desire to be ready for the coming of the Judge (8–13); let us employ the time given us to work out our salvation, even as Paul taught in his Epistles which the false teachers abuse (14–17). Verse 18 consists of the epilogue and doxology.

Drach-Bayle, *Epîtres catholiques* (Paris, 1873); Hundhausen, *Die beiden Pontificalhereiben des Apostelfürsten Petrus* (Mainz, 1878); Cornely, *Hist. et crit. introductio in U. T. libros sacros*, III, *Introductio specialis* (Paris, 1886); Beelen, *Het niewe Testament* (Bruges, 1891); Jülicher, *Einleitung in das neue Testament* (1894); Kühl, *Briefe Petri und Judæ* (Göttingen, 1897); Hort, *The First Epistle of St. Peter* (London, 1898); von Soden, *Briefe des Petrus* (Freiburg, 1899); Harnack, *Gesch. der altchrist. Literatur, die Chronologie* (Leipzig, 1900); Monnier, *La première épître de Pierre* (Macon, 1900); Zahn, *Grundriss der Gesch. des neutestamntlichen Kanons* (Leipzig, 1901); Trankle, *Einleitung in das neue Test.* (Freiburg, 1901); Bigg, *A Critical and Exegetical Commentary on the Ep. of St. Peter and St. Jude* (Edinburgh, 1902); Ceulemans, *Comment. in epist. catholicas et apocalypsim* (Mechlin, 1904); Henkel, *Der zweite Brief des Apostelfürsten Petrus geprüft auf seine Echtheit* (Freiburg, 1904); Belser, *Einleitung in das neue Test.* (Freiburg, 1905); Calmes, *Epîtres cathol. Apocalypse* (Paris, 1905); Weiss, *Der erste Petrusbrief und die neuere Kritik* (Lichterfelde, 1906); Dillenseger, *L'authenticité de la II Petri in Mélanges de la faculté orientale* (Beirut, 1907); Callewaert in *Revue d'hist. ecclés.* (Louvain, 1902, 1907); Jacquier, *Hist. des livres du N. Test.* (Paris, 1908); Brassac, *Manuel bibl.* (Paris, 1909); Vansteenkiste-Camerlynck, *Comment. in epist. cathol.* (Bruges, 1909).

A. Van der Heeren.

Peter, Gospel of Saint. See Apocrypha, subtitle III.

Peter, Sarah, philanthropist, b. at Chillicothe, Ohio, U. S. A., 10 May, 1800; d. at Cincinnati, 6 Feb., 1877. Her father, Thomas Worthington, was Governor of Ohio, 1814–18, and also served in the United States Senate. On 15 May, 1816, she married Edward King, son of Rufus King of New York, who died 6 Feb., 1836; and in October, 1844, she married William Peter, British consul at Philadelphia, who died 6 Feb., 1853. During her residence at Philadelphia she founded, 2 Dec., 1850, the School of Design for Women. Returning to Cincinnati she spent most of her remaining years as a patron of art, and in works of charity and philanthropy. She became a convert at Rome in March, 1855, being instructed there by Mgr Mermillod. The foundations of the Sisters of the Good Shepherd, the Sisters of Mercy, the Little Sisters of the Poor in Cincinnati, and other institutions owed much to her generosity. In 1862 she volunteered as a nurse, and went with the sisters who followed Grant's army in the south-west after the battle of Pittsburg Landing.

King, *Memoirs of the Life of Mrs. Sarah Peter* (Cincinnati, 1889); *Catholic Telegraph* (Cincinnati), files; *Freeman's Journal* (New York), files.

Thomas F. Meehan.

Peter, Tomb of Saint. See St. Peter, Tomb of.

Peter Arbues, Saint. See Peter of Arbues, Saint.

Peter Baptist and Twenty-five Companions, Saints, d. at Nagasaki, 5 Feb., 1597. In 1593 while negotiations were pending between the Emperor of Japan and the Governor of the Philippine Islands, the latter sent Peter Baptist and several other Franciscans as his ambassadors to Japan. They were well received by the emperor, and were able to establish convents, schools, and hospitals, and effect many conversions. When on 20 Oct., 1596, a Spanish vessel of war, the "San Felipe", was stranded on the isle of Tosa, it became, according to Japanese custom, the property of the emperor. The captain was foolish enough to extol the power of his king, and said that the missionaries had been sent to prepare for the conquest of the country. The emperor became furious, and on 9 Dec., 1596, ordered the missionaries to be imprisoned. On 5 Feb., 1597, six friars belonging to the First Order of St. Francis (Peter Baptist, Martin of the Ascension, Francis Blanco, priests; Philip of Jesus, cleric; Gonsalvo Garzia, Francis of St. Michael, laybrothers), three Japanese Jesuits (Paul Miki, John Goto, James Kisai) and seventeen native Franciscan Tertiaries were crucified. They were beatified 14 Sept., 1627, by Urban VIII, and canonized 8 June, 1862, by Pius IX.

Leon, *Lives of the Saints and Blessed of the Three Orders of St. Francis*, I (Taunton, 1885), 169–223; Wadding, *Ann. Min.*, 98–104, 261–81; *Acta SS.*, Feb., I, 729–770; Inés, *Crónica de la provincia de San Gregorio Magno de Religiosos Descalzos de N.S.P. San Francisco en las islas Filipinas, China, Japón etc.*, I (Manila, 1892); Martínez, *Compendio histórico de la apostólica provincia de San Gregorio de Filipinas* (Madrid, 1756); Bouix, *Histoire des 26 martyrs du Japon crucifiés à Nangasaqui* (Paris, Lyons, 1682); Deplace, *Le Catholicisme au Japon; II, L'Ere des Martyres 1593–1660* (Brussels, 1909).

Ferdinand Heckmann.

Peterborough Abbey, Benedictine monastery in Northamptonshire, England, known at first as Medeshamstede, was founded about 654 by Peada, King of the Mercians, who appointed as first abbot, Saxulf. Peada's church and monastery were completely destroyed by the Danes in 870. The circumstantial account of this event, given in Abbot John's chronicle, is fictitious, but the fact of the abbey's destruction is certain. In 970, in the monastic revival associated with the name of St. Dunstan, the monastery was rebuilt through the efforts of Ethelwold, Bishop of Winchester, with the aid of King Edgar. Part of the foundations were laid bare in 1887, when the central tower of the present cathedral was rebuilt, and its dimensions seem to have been about half those of the present building. The abbey suffered both from fire and pillage in the unsettled period preceding the Norman conquest, and in 1116 during the abbacy of Dom John of Sais a great conflagration destroyed the monastic buildings with the little town that had grown up around them. The work of rebuilding, begun by Abbot John, ceased at his death, in 1125. Martin de Bec, successor of Abbot Henry of Anjou, pushed the work forward, and the presbytery of the new church was finished and entered upon by the monks about 1140. The work of building went on steadily until 1237, when the completed church was consecrated by Robert Grostête, Bishop of Lincoln. When the monastery was surrendered to King Henry VIII in 1541 the church was spared from destruction, because it contained the remains of his first wife. It then became the cathedral of the new Diocese of Peterborough, and the last abbot, John Chambers, was rewarded for his compliance to the royal demands by being made the first bishop. Though the great church was begun during the Norman period, a considerable portion belongs to the thirteenth century. This is true in particular of the glorious west front, which Fergusson and Freeman agree in calling the grandest and most original in Europe. It consists of three huge arches, supported on triangular columns and enriched with a number of delicate shafts, which open into a long narthex or portico, extending the whole width of the building. The interior has a nave of eleven bays (228 ft.), with transepts and presbytery terminating in a circular apse. The original ambulatory, round the east end, was replaced in the late fifteenth century by a square-ended chapel, of great delicacy, in the Perpendicular style. The total interior length is 426 ft., interior height 78 ft., length of transepts 185 ft. Much controversy has been aroused over the rebuilding of the central tower and the restoration of the west front, but both these works were inevitable and have been carried out with the greatest regard for the designs of the original architects.

DUGDALE, *Monasticon Anglicanum*, I (London, 1817), 344–404; GUNTON, *History of the Church of Peterborough* (London, 1686); TANNER, *Notitia Monastica* (London, 1744), 371–373; *Historiæ cænobii Burgensis scriptores varii*, ed. SPARKE in *Hist. Angl. Scriptores*, iii (London, 1723), 1–256; ELIAS OF TRIKINGHAM, *Annales*, ed. PEGGE (London, 1789); *Chronicon Angliæ Petriburgense, 654–1368*, ed. GILES (London, 1845); *Chronicon breve Ecclesiæ Petriburgensis, 1074–1181*, ed. STAPLETON (London, 1849); BROWNE-WILLIS, *Survey of English Cathedrals*, III (London, 1730), 475; BRITTON, *History and Antiquities of Peterborough Cathedral* (London, 1836); SWEETING, *The Cathedral Church of Peterborough* (London, 1898).

G. ROGER HUDLESTON.

Peterborough, DIOCESE OF (PETERBOROUGHENSIS), in the Province of Ontario, Canada, comprises the Counties of Peterborough, Northumberland, Durham, and Victoria, with the Districts of Muskoka and Parry Sound. It was erected by Leo XIII, 11 July, 1882, by detaching the four former counties from the Diocese of Kingston and uniting them with the Vicariate of Northern Canada, which then included the Districts of Muskoka, Parry Sound, Nipissing, Algoma, and Thunder Bay. Rt. Rev. John Francis Jamot, at that time Vicar Apostolic of Northern Canada, was appointed first bishop. The new diocese then extended about 1110 miles from south-east to north-west, and its southern limit reached to Lakes Superior and Huron, the Georgian Bay, and a part of Lake Ontario. Bishop Jamot was born in France in 1828, and came to the Diocese of Toronto in 1853. After serving in the parish of Barrie for several years he was transferred to St. Michael's Cathedral, Toronto, and appointed chancellor and vicar-general of the diocese. In 1874 he was appointed Bishop of Sarepta and Vicar Apostolic of Northern Canada, where he displayed zeal and energy in seeking out the Catholics of his extensive vicariate. When in 1882 the Diocese of Peterborough was formed the total Catholic population was about 30,000, of whom 5000 were Indians, with 47 churches and 25 priests, of whom 11 were Jesuits attending the western part of the diocese and the Indian Missions. After the erection of the Diocese of Peterborough in 1882 Bishop Jamot moved his see from Bracebridge to the city of Peterborough, where he died 4 May, 1886. Rt. Rev. Thomas Joseph Dowling, then Vicar General of the Diocese of Hamilton, succeeded him and was consecrated 1 May, 1887. He continued the many good works of his predecessor and after two years was transferred to the Diocese of Hamilton. The third bishop, Rt. Rev. Richard Alphonsus O'Connor, was consecrated 1 May, 1889. He was born at Listowel, Co. Kerry, Ireland, 15 April, 1838, came to Canada in 1841 with his parents, and settled at Toronto. He was one of the first students in St. Michael's College, Toronto, and made his theological course in the Grand Seminary, Montreal. On 2 August, 1861, he was ordained priest in St. Michael's Cathedral, Toronto, and, after serving in various parishes as pastor, and for eighteen years as Dean of Barrie, he was appointed Bishop of Peterborough by Leo XIII, 11 Jan., 1889.

During the administration of Bishop O'Connor the western part of the diocese increased rapidly in population, and, that religion might keep pace with the material progress of the country, many churches and schools were built. On account of the large influx of settlers into New Ontario, which embraced the western part of the Diocese of Peterborough, and the development of that district in agriculture, commerce, mining, and manufacturing industries, a brief dated 14 Nov., 1904, of Pius X constituted the new Diocese of Sault Ste Marie by detaching from the Diocese of Peterborough the western part of the District of Nipissing, with the Districts of Algoma and Thunder Bay. There was then a population of 27,000 Catholics, with 35 priests and 64 churches, in the new Diocese of Sault Ste Marie; and 24,000 Catholics, with 29 priests and 45 churches, in the portion left to Peterborough. The city of Peterborough has a population of about 18,000, about one-fourth of whom are Catholics, with two churches, one hospital, one House of Providence, an orphanage, and the largest total abstinence society in Canada, numbering over 1000 men. In the diocese are many Catholic schools, conducted chiefly by the Sisters of St. Joseph, who have a motherhouse and novitiate in the cathedral city, and have charge of the hospitals, House of Providence, and orphanage. They also conduct a select academy at Lindsay, besides directing the day school for girls. In Peterborough there are three large schools, with 19 teachers, 17 of whom are Sisters of St. Joseph. At present the Catholic population of the diocese is about 26,000, with 29 secular priests, 3 Jesuit Fathers, 50 churches, 2 hospitals, one House of Providence, and one orphanage.

R. A. O'CONNOR.

Peter Canisius (KANNEES, KANYS, probably also DE HONDT), BLESSED, b. at Nimwegen in the Netherlands, 8 May, 1521; d. in Fribourg, 21 November, 1597. His father was the wealthy burgomaster, Jacob Canisius; his mother, Ægidia van Houweningen, died shortly after Peter's birth. In 1536 Peter was sent to Cologne, where he studied arts, civil law, and theology at the university; he spent a part of 1539 at the University of Louvain, and in 1540 received the degree of Master of Arts at Cologne. Nicolaus van Esche was his spiritual adviser, and he was on terms of friendship with such staunch Catholics as Georg of Skodborg (the expelled Archbishop of Lund), Johann Gropper (canon of the cathedral), Eberhard Billick (the Carmelite monk), Justus Lanspergius, and other Carthusian monks. Although his father desired him to marry a wealthy young woman, on 25 February, 1540 he pledged himself to celibacy. In 1543 he visited Peter Faber and, having made the "Spiritual Exercises" under his direction, was admitted into the Society of Jesus at Mainz, on 8 May. With the help of Leonhard Kessel and others, Canisius, labouring under great difficulties, founded at Cologne the first German house of the order; at the same time he preached in the city and vicinity, and debated and taught in the university. In 1546 he was admitted to the priesthood, and soon afterwards was sent by the clergy and university to obtain assistance from Emperor Charles V, the nuncio, and the clergy of Liège against the apostate Archbishop, Hermann von Wied, who had attempted to pervert the diocese. In 1547, as the theologian of Cardinal Otto Truchsess von Waldburg, Bishop of Augsburg, he participated in the general ecclesiastical council (which sat first at Trent and then at Bologna), and spoke twice in the congregation of the theologians. After this he spent several months under the direction of Ignatius in Rome. In 1548 he taught rhetoric at Messina, Sicily, preaching in Italian and Latin. At this time Duke William IV of Bavaria requested Paul III to send him some professors from the Society of Jesus for the University of Ingolstadt; Canisius was among those selected.

On 7 September, 1549, he made his solemn profession as Jesuit at Rome, in the presence of the founder of the order. On his journey northward he received, at Bologna, the degree of doctor of theology. On 13 November, accompanied by Fathers Jaius and Salmeron, he reached Ingolstadt, where he taught theology, catechized, and preached. In 1550 he was elected rector of the university, and in 1552 was sent by Ignatius to the new college in Vienna; there he also taught theology in the university, preached at the Cathedral of St. Stephen, and at the court of Ferdinand I, and was confessor at the hospital and prison. During Lent, 1553 he visited many abandoned parishes in Lower Austria, preaching and administering the sacraments. The king's eldest son (later Maximilian II) had appointed to the office of court preacher, Phauser, a married priest, who preached the Lutheran doctrine. Canisius warned Ferdinand I, verbally and in writing, and opposed Phauser in public disputations. Maximilian was obliged to dismiss Phauser and, on this account, the rest of his life he harboured a grudge against Canisius. Ferdinand three times offered him the Bishopric of Vienna, but he refused. In 1557 Julius III appointed him administrator of the bishopric for one year, but Canisius succeeded in ridding himself of this burden (cf. N. Paulus in "Zeitschrift für katholische Theologie", XXII, 742–8). In 1555 he was present at the Diet of Augsburg with Ferdinand, and in 1555–56 he preached in the cathedral of Prague. After long negotiations and preparations he was able to open Jesuit colleges at Ingolstadt and Prague. In the same year Ignatius appointed him first provincial superior of Upper Germany (Swabia, Bavaria, Bohemia, Hungary, Lower and Upper Austria). During the winter of 1556–57 he acted as adviser to the King of the Romans at the Diet of Ratisbon and delivered many sermons in the cathedral. By the appointment of the Catholic princes and the order of the pope he took part in the religious discussions at Worms. As champion of the Catholics he repeatedly spoke in opposition to Melanchthon. The fact that the Protestants disagreed among themselves and were obliged to leave the field was due in a great measure to Canisius. He also preached in the cathedral of Worms.

During Advent and Christmas he visited the Bishop of Strasburg at Zabern, started negotiations for the building of a Jesuit college there, preached, explained the catechism to the children, and heard their confessions. He also preached in the cathedral of Strasburg and strengthened the Catholics of Alsace and Freiburg in their faith. Ferdinand, on his way to Frankfort to be proclaimed emperor, met him at Nuremburg and confided his troubles to him. Then Duke Albert V of Bavaria secured his services; at Straubing the pastors and preachers had fled, after having persuaded the people to turn from the Catholic faith. Canisius remained in the town for six weeks, preaching three or four times a day, and by his gentleness he undid much harm. From Straubing he was called to Rome to be present at the First General Congregation of his order, but before its close Paul IV sent him with the nuncio Mentuati to Poland to the imperial Diet of Pieterkow; at Cracow he addressed the clergy and members of the university. In the year 1559 he was summoned by the emperor to be present at the Diet of Augsburg. There, at the urgent request of the chapter, he became preacher at the cathedral, and held this position until 1566. His manuscripts show the care with which he wrote his sermons. In a series of sermons he treats of the end of man, of the Decalogue, the Mass, the prophecies of Jonas; at the same time he rarely omitted to expound the Gospel of the day; he spoke in keeping with the spirit of the age, explained the justification of man, Christian liberty, the proper way of interpreting the Scriptures, defended the worship of saints, the ceremonies of the Church, religious vows, indulgences, urged obedience to the Church authorities, confession, communion, fasting, and almsgiving; he censured the faults of the clergy, at times perhaps too sharply, as he felt that they were public and that he must avoid demanding reformation from the laity only. Against the influence of evil spirits he recommended the means of defence which had been in use in the Church during the first centuries—lively faith, prayer, ecclesiastical benedictions, and acts of penance. From 1561–52 he preached about two hundred and ten sermons, besides giving retreats and teaching catechism. In the cathedral his confessional and the altar at which he said Mass were surrounded by crowds, and alms were placed on the altar. The envy of some of the cathedral clergy was aroused, and Canisius and his companions were accused of usurping the parochial rights. The pope and bishop favoured the Jesuits, but the majority of the chapter opposed them. Canisius was obliged to sign an agreement according to which he retained the pulpit but gave up the right of administering the sacraments in the cathedral.

In 1559 he opened a college in Munich; in 1562 he appeared at Trent as papal theologian. The council was discussing the question whether communion should be administered under both forms to those of the laity who asked for it. Lainez, the general of the Society of Jesus, opposed it unconditionally. Canisius held that the cup might be administered to the Bohemians and to some Catholics whose faith was not very firm. After one month he departed from Trent, but he continued to support the work of the Fathers by urging the bishops to appear at the council, by giving expert opinion regarding the Index and other matters, by reports on the state of public opinion, and on newly-published books. In the spring of 1563 he rendered a specially important service to the Church; the emperor had come to Innsbruck (near Trent), and had summoned thither several scholars, including Canisius, as advisers. Some of these men fomented the displeasure of the emperor with the pope and the cardinals who presided over the council. For months Canisius strove to reconcile him with the Curia. He has been blamed unjustly for communicating to his general and to the pope's representatives some of Ferdinand's plans, which otherwise might have ended contrary to the intention of all concerned in the dissolution of the council and in a new national apostasy. The emperor finally granted all the pope's demands and the council was able to proceed and to end peacefully. All Rome praised Canisius, but soon after he lost favour with Ferdinand and was denounced as disloyal; at this time he also changed his views regarding the giving of the cup to the laity (in which the emperor saw a means of relieving all his difficulties), saying that such a concession would only tend to confuse faithful Catholics and to encourage the disobedience of the recalcitrant.

In 1562 the College of Innsbruck was opened by Canisius, and at that time he acted as confessor to the "Queen" Magdalena (declared Venerable in 1906 by Pius X; daughter of Ferdinand I, who lived with her four sisters at Innsbruck), and as spiritual adviser to her sisters. At their request he sent them a confessor from the society, and, when Magdalena presided over the convent, which she had founded at Hall, he sent her complete directions for attaining Christian perfection. In 1563 he preached at many monasteries in Swabia; in 1564 he sent the first missionaries to Lower Bavaria, and recommended the provincial synod of Salzburg not to allow the cup to the laity, as it had authority to do; his advice, however, was not accepted. In this year Canisius opened a college at Dillingen and assumed, in the name of the order, the administration of the university which had been founded there by Cardinal Truchsess. In 1565 he took part in the Second General Congregation of the order in Rome. While in Rome he visited Philip, son of the Protestant philologist Joachim Camerarius, at that time a prisoner of the Inquisition, and instructed and consoled him. Pius IV sent him as his secret nuncio to deliver the decrees of the Council of Trent to Germany; the pope also commissioned him to urge their enforcement, to ask the Catholic princes to defend the Church at the coming diet, and to negotiate for the founding of colleges and seminaries. Canisius negotiated more or less successfully with the Electors of Mainz and Trier, with the Bishops of Augsburg, Würzburg, Osnabrück, Münster, and Paderborn, with the Duke of Jülich-Cleves-Berg, and with the City and University of Cologne; he also visited Nimwegen, preaching there and at other places; his mission, however, was interrupted by the death of the pope. Pius V desired its continuation, but Canisius requested to be relieved; he said that it aroused suspicions of espionage, of arrogance, and of interference in politics (for a detailed account of his mission see "Stimmen aus Maria-Laach", LXXI, 58, 164, 301).

At the Diet of Augsburg (1566), Canisius and other theologians, by order of the pope, gave their services to the cardinal legate Commendone; with the help of his friends he succeeded, although with great difficulty, in persuading the legate not to issue his protest against the religious peace, and thus prevented a new fratricidal war. The Catholic members of the diet accepted the decrees of the council, the designs of the Protestants were frustrated, and from that time a new and vigorous life began for the Catholics in Germany. In the same year Canisius went to Wiesensteig, where he visited and brought back to the Church the Lutheran Count of Helfenstein and his entire countship, and where he prepared for death two witches who had been abandoned by the Lutheran preachers. In 1567 he preached the Lenten sermons in the cathedral of Würzburg, gave instruction in the Franciscan church twice a week to the children and domestics of the town, and discussed the founding of a Jesuit college at Würzburg with the bishop. Then followed the diocesan synod of Dillingen (at which Canisius was principal adviser of the Bishop of Augsburg), journeys to Würzburg, Mainz, Speyer, and a visit to the Bishop of Strasburg, whom he advised, though unsuccessfully, to take a coadjutor. At Dillingen he received the application of Stanislaus Kostka to enter the Society of Jesus, and sent him with hearty recommendations to the general of the order at Rome. At this time he successfully settled a dispute in the philosophical faculty of the University of Ingolstadt. In 1567 and 1568 he went several times to Innsbruck, where in the name of the general he consulted with the Archduke Ferdinand II and his sisters about the confessors of the archduchesses and about the establishment of a Jesuit house at Hall. In 1569 the general decided to accept the college at Hall.

During Lent of 1568 Canisius preached at Ellwangen, in Würtemberg; from there he went with Cardinal Truchsess to Rome. The Upper German province of the order had elected the provincial as its representative at the meeting of the procurators; this election was illegal, but Canisius was admitted. For months he collected in the libraries of Rome material for a great work which he was preparing. In 1569 he returned to Augsburg and preached Lenten sermons in the Church of St. Mauritius. Having been a provincial for thirteen years (an unusually long time) he was relieved of the office at his own request, and went to Dillingen, where he wrote, catechized, and heard confessions, his respite, however, was short; in 1570 he was obliged again to go to Augsburg. A year later he was compelled to move to Innsbruck and to accept the office of court preacher to Archduke Ferdinand II. In 1575 Gregory XIII sent him with papal messages to the archduke and to the Duke of Bavaria. When he arrived in Rome to make his report, the Third General Congregation of the order was assembled and, by special favour, Canisius was invited to be present. From this time he was preacher in the parish church of Innsbruck until the Diet of Ratisbon (1576), which he attended as theologian of the cardinal legate Morone. In the following year he supervised at Ingolstadt the printing of an important work, and

BLESSED PETER CANISIUS BEFORE THE EMPEROR FERDINAND I
AND CARDINAL OTTONE

CESARE FRACASSINI, VATICAN GALLLERY OF MODERN ART

induced the students of the university to found a sodality of the Blessed Virgin. During Lent, 1578, he preached at the court of Duke William of Bavaria at Landshut. The nuncio Bonhomini desired to have a college of the society at Fribourg; the order at first refused on account of the lack of men, but the pope intervened and, at the end of 1580, Canisius laid the foundation stone. In 1581 he founded a sodality of the Blessed Virgin among the citizens and, soon afterwards, sodalities for women and students; in 1582 schools were opened, and he preached in the parish church and in other places until 1589.

The canton had not been left uninfluenced by the Protestant movement. Canisius worked indefatigably with the provost Peter Schnewly, the Franciscan Johannes Michel, and others, for the revival of religious sentiments amongst the people; since then Fribourg has remained a stronghold of the Catholic Church. In 1584, while on his way to take part in another meeting of the order at Augsburg, he preached at Lucerne and made a pilgrimage to the miraculous image of the Blessed Virgin at Einsiedeln. According to his own account, it was then that St. Nicholas, the patron saint of Fribourg, made known to him his desire that Canisius should not leave Fribourg again. Many times the superiors of the order planned to transfer him to another house, but the nuncio, the city council, and the citizens themselves opposed the measure; they would not consent to lose this celebrated and saintly man. The last years of his life he devoted to the instruction of converts, to making spiritual addresses to the brothers of the order, to writing and re-editing books. The city authorities ordered his body to be buried before the high altar of the principal church, the Church of St. Nicolaus, from which they were translated in 1625 to that of St. Michael, the church of the Jesuit College.

Canisius held that to defend the Catholic truths with the pen was just as important as to convert the Hindus. At Rome and Trent he strongly urged the appointment at the council, at the papal court, and in other parts of Italy, of able theologians to write in defence of the Catholic faith. He begged Pius V to send yearly subsidies to the Catholic printers of Germany, and to permit German scholars to edit Roman manuscripts; he induced the city council of Fribourg to erect a printing establishment, and he secured special privileges for printers. He also kept in touch with the chief Catholic printers of his time—Plantin of Antwerp, Cholin of Cologne, and Mayer of Dillingen—and had foreign works of importance reprinted in Germany, for example, the works of Andrada, Fontidonio, and Villalpando in defence of the Council of Trent.

Canisius advised the generals of the order to create a college of authors; urged scholars like Bartholomæus Latomus, Friedrich Staphylus, and Hieronymus Torrensis to publish their works; assisted Onofrio Panvinio and the polemic Stanislaus Hosius, reading their manuscripts and correcting proofs; and contributed to the work of his friend Surius on the councils. At his solicitation the "Briefe aus Indien", the first relations of Catholic missioners, were published (Dillingen, 1563–71); "Canisius", wrote the Protestant preacher, Witz, "by this activity gave an impulse which deserves our undivided recognition, indeed which arouses our admiration" ("Petrus Canisius", Vienna, 1897, p. 12).

The latest bibliography of the Society of Jesus devotes thirty-eight quarto pages to a list of the works published by Canisius and their different editions, and it must be added that this list is incomplete. The most important of his works are described below; the asterisk signifies that the work bears the name of Canisius neither on the title page nor in the preface. His chief work is his triple "Catechism". In 1551 King Ferdinand I asked the University of Vienna to write a compendium of Christian doctrine, and Canisius wrote (Vienna, 1555), at first for advanced students, his "Summa doctrinæ christianæ . . . in usum Christianæ pueritiæ", two hundred and eleven questions in five chapters (the first edition appeared without the name of the author, but later all three catechisms bore his name); then a short extract for school children, "Summa . . . ad captum rudiorum accommodata" (Ingolstadt, 1556), was published as an appendix to the "Principia Grammatices"; his catechism for students of the lower and middle grades, "Parvus Catechismus Catholicorum" (later known as "Institutiones christianæ pietatis" or "Catechismus catholicus"), is an extract from the larger catechism, written in the winter of 1557–58. Of the first Latin edition (Cologne, 1558), no copy is known to exist; the German edition appeared at Dillingen, 1560. The "Summa" only received its definite form in the Cologne edition of 1556; it contains two hundred and twenty-two questions, and two thousand quotations from the Scriptures, and about twelve hundred quotations from the Fathers of the Church are inscribed on the margins; later all these quotations were compiled in the original by Peter Busæus, S.J., and appeared in four quarto volumes under the title "Authoritates Sacræ Scripturæ et Sanctorum patrum" etc. (Cologne, 1569–70); in 1557 Johannes Hasius, S.J., published the same work in one large folio volume, entitled "Opus catechisticum", for which Canisius wrote an introduction. The catechism of Canisius is remarkable for its ecclesiastically correct teachings, its clear, positive sentences, its mild and dignified form. It is to-day recognized as a masterpiece even by non-Catholics, e. g., the historians Ranke, Menzel, Philippson, and the theologians Kawerau, Rouffet, Zerschwitz.

Pius V entrusted Canisius with the confutation of the Centuriators of Magdeburg (q. v.). Canisius undertook to prove the dishonesty of the centuriators by exposing their treatment of the principal persons in the Gospel —John the Baptist, the Mother of God, the Apostle St. Peter—and published (Dillingen, 1571) his next most important work, "Commentariorum de Verbi Dei corruptelis liber primus: in quo de Sanctissimi Præcursoris Domini Joannis Baptistæ Historia Evangelica . . . pertractatur". Here the confutation of the principal errors of Protestantism is exegetical and historical rather than scholastical; in 1577 "De Maria Virgine incomparabili, et Dei Genitrice sacrosancta, libri quinque" was published at Ingolstadt. Later he united these two works into one book of two volumes, "Commentariorum de Verbi corruptelis" (Ingolstadt, 1583, and later Paris and Lyons); the treatise on St. Peter and his primacy was only begun; the work on the Virgin Mary contains some quotations from the Fathers of the Church that had not been printed previously, and treats of the worship of Mary by the Church. A celebrated theologian of the present day called this work a classic defence of the whole Catholic doctrine about the Blessed Virgin (Scheeben, "Dogmatik", III, 478); in 1543 he published (under the name of Petrus Nouiomagus) *"Des erleuchten D. Johannis Tauleri, von eym waren Euangelischen leben, Göttliche Predig. Leren" etc., in which several writings of the Dominican mystic appear in print for the first time. This was the first book published by a Jesuit. "Divi Cyrilli archiepiscopi Alexandrini Opera" (Latin translation, 2 fol. vols., Cologne, 1546); "D. Leonis Papæ huius nominis primi . . . Opera" (Cologne, 1546, later reprinted at Venice, Louvain, and Cologne), Leo is brought forward as a witness for the Catholic teachings and the discipline of the Church against the innovators; "De consolandis ægrotis" (Vienna, 1554), exhortations (Latin, German, and Italian) and prayers, with a preface by Canisius; *"Lectiones et Precationes Ecclesiasticæ" (Ingolstadt, 1556), a prayer-book for students, reprinted more than thirty times under the titles of "Epistolæ et Evangelia" etc.; *"Principia grammatices" (Ingolstadt, 1556); Hannibal Codrett's Latin Grammar, adapted for German students by Canisius, reprinted in 1561, 1564 and 1568; *"Ordnung der Letaney von vnser lieben Frawen" [Dillingen (1558)], the first known printing of the Litany of Loreto, the second (Macerata, 1576) was most probably arranged by Canisius; *"Vom abschiedt des Coloquij zu Wormbs" (s. l. a., 15–58?).

*"Ain Christlicher Bericht, was die hailige Christliche Kirch . . . sey" (Dillingen, 1559), translation and preface by Canisius (cf. N. Paulus in "Historisch-polit. Blätter", CXXI, 765); "Epistolæ B. Hieronymi . . . selectæ" (Dillingen, 1562), a school edition arranged and prefaced by Canisius and later reprinted about forty times; *"Hortulus Animæ" (q. v.), a German prayer-book arranged by Canisius (Dillingen, 1563), reprinted later, probably published also in Latin by him. The "Hortuli" were placed later on the Index *nisi corrigantur*; *"Von der Gesellschaft Jesu Durch. Joannem Albertum Wimpinensem" (Ingolstadt, 1563), a defence of the order against Chemnitz and Zanger, the greater part of which was written by Canisius; "Institutiones, et Exercitamentas Christianæ Pietatis" (Antwerp, 1566), many times reprinted, in which Canisius combined the catechism for the middle grades and the "Lectiones et Precationes ecclesiasticæ" (revised in Rome); "Beicht- und Communionbüchlein" [Dillingen, 1567 (?), 1575, 1579, 1582, 1603; Ingolstadt, 1594, etc.]; "Christenliche . . . Predig von den vier Sontagen im Aduent, auch vonn dem heiligen Christag" (Dillingen, 1570).

At the request of Ferdinand II of Tyrol, Canisius supervised the publishing of *"Von dem hoch vnd weitberhümpten Wunderzeichen, so sich . . . auff dem Seefeld . . . zugetragen" (Dillingen, 1580), and wrote a long preface for it; then appeared "Zwey vnd neuntzig Betrachtung vnd Gebett, dess . . . Bruders Clausen von Vnterwalden" (Fribourg, 1586); "Manuale Catholicorum. In usum pie precandi" (Fribourg, 1587); "Zwo . . . Historien . . . Die erste von . . . S. Beato, ersten Prediger in Schweitzerland. Die andere von . . . S. Fridolino, ersten Prediger zu Glaris vnd Seckingen" (Fribourg, 1590): in this, the first of the popular biographies of the saints especially worshipped in Switzerland, Canisius does not give a scholarly essay, but endeavours to strengthen the Catholic Swiss in their faith and arouse their piety; "Notæ in Evangelicas lectiones, quæ per totum annum Dominicis diebus . . . recitantur" (Fribourg, 1591), a large quarto volume valuable for sermons and meditations for the clergy; "Miserere, das ist: Der 50. Psalm Davids . . . Gebettsweiss . . . aussgelegt" (Munich, 1594, Ingolstadt, 1594); "Warhafte Histori . . . Von Sanct Moritzen . . . vnd seiner Thebaischen Legion . . . Auch insonderheit von Sanct Vrso" (Fribourg, 1594); *"Catholische Kirchengesäng zum theil vor vnd nach dem Catechismo zum teil sonst durchs Jahr . . . zusingen" (Fribourg, 1596); "Enchiridion Pietatis quo ad precandum Deum instruitur Princeps" (s. l., 1751), dedicated by Canisius in 1592 to the future emperor, Ferdinand II (Zeitschrift für katholische Theologie, XIV, 741); "Beati Petri Canisii Exhortationes domesticæ", mostly short sketches, collected and edited by G. Schlosser, S.J. (Roermond, 1876); "Beati Petri Canisii Epistulæ et Acta": 1541–65, edited by O. Braunsberger, S.J. (4 vols., Freiburg im Br., 1896–1905). There still remain unpublished four or five volumes containing eleven hundred and ninety-five letters and *regesta* written to or by Canisius, and six hundred and twenty-five documents dealing with his labours.

"Peter Canisius", says the Protestant professor of theology, Krüger, "was a noble Jesuit; no blemish stains his character" ("Petrus Canisius" in "Geschichte u. Legende", Giessen, 1898, 10). The principal trait of his character was love for Christ and for his work; he devoted his life to defend, propagate, and strengthen the Church. Hence his devotion to the pope. He did not deny the abuses which existed in Rome; he demanded speedy remedies; but the supreme and full power of the pope over the whole Church, and the infallibility of his teaching as Head of the Church, Canisius championed as vigorously as the Italian and Spanish brothers of the order. He cannot be called an "Episcopalian" or "Semi-Gallican"; his motto was "whoever adheres to the Chair of St. Peter is my man. With Ambrose I desire to follow the Church of Rome in every respect". Pius V wished to make him cardinal. The bishops, Brendel of Mainz, Brus of Prague, Pflug of Naumburg, Blarer of Basle, Cromer of Ermland, and Spaur of Brixen, held him in great esteem. St. Francis of Sales sought his advice by letter. He enjoyed the friendship of the most distinguished members of the College of Cardinals—Borromeo, Hosius, Truchsess, Commendone, Morone, Sirlet; of the nuncios Delfino, Portia, Bonhomini and others; of many leading exponents of ecclesiastical learning; and of such prominent men as the Chancellor of the University of Louvain, Ruard Tapper, the provost Martin Eisengrein, Friedrich Staphylus, Franz Sonnius, Martin Rithovius, Wilhelm Lindanus, the imperial vice-chancellors Jacob Jonas and Georg Sigismund Seld, the Bavarian chancellor Simon Thaddæus Eck, and the Fuggers and Welsers of Augsburg. "Canisius's whole life", writes the Swiss Protestant theologian Gautier, "is animated by the desire to form a generation of devout clerics capable of serving the Church worthily" ("Etude sur la correspondance de Pierre Canisius", Geneva, 1905, p. 46). At Ingolstadt he held disputations and homiletic exercises among the young clerics, and endeavoured to raise the religious and scientific standard of the Georgianum. He collected for and sent pupils to the German College at Rome and provided for pupils who had returned home. He also urged Gregory XIII to make donations and to found similar institutions in Germany; soon papal seminaries were built at Prague, Fulda, Braunsberg, and Dillingen. At Ingolstadt, Innsbruck, Munich, and Vienna schools were built under the guidance of Canisius for the nobility and the poor, the former to educate the clergy of the cathedrals, the latter for the clergy of the lower grades. The reformed ordinances published at that time for the Universities of Cologne, Ingolstadt, and Vienna must be credited in the main to his suggestions.

With apostolic zeal he loved the Society of Jesus; the day of his admission to the order he called his second birthday. Obedience to his superiors was his first rule. As a superior he cared with parental love for the necessities of his subordinates. Shortly before his death he declared that he had never regretted becoming a Jesuit, and recalled the abuses which the opponents of the Church had heaped upon his order and his person. Johann Wigand wrote a vile pamphlet against his "Catechism"; Flacius Illyricus, Johann Gnypheus, and Paul Scheidlich wrote books against it; Melanchthon declared that he defended errors wilfully; Chemnitz called him a cynic; the satirist Fischart scoffed at him; Andreæ, Dathen, Gallus, Hesshusen, Osiander, Platzius, Roding, Vergerio, and others wrote vigorous attacks against him; at Prague the Hussites threw stones into the church where he was saying Mass; at Berne he was derided by a Protestant mob. At Easter, 1568, he was obliged to preach in the Cathedral of Würzburg in order to disprove the rumour that he had become a Protestant. Unembittered by all this, he said, "the more our opponents calumniate us, the more we must love them". He requested Catholic authors to advocate the truth with modesty and dignity without scoffing or ridicule. The names of Luther and Melanchthon were never mentioned in his "Catechism". His love for the German people is characteristic; he urged the brothers of the order to practise German diligently, and he liked to hear the German national hymns sung. At his desire St. Ignatius decreed that all the members of the order should offer monthly Masses and prayers for the welfare of Germany and the North. Ever the faithful advocate of the Germans at the Holy See, he obtained clemency for them in questions of ecclesiastical censures, and permission to give extraordinary absolutions and to dispense from the law of fasting. He also wished the Index to be modified that German confessors might be authorized to permit the reading of some books, but in his sermons he warned the faithful to abstain from reading such books without permission. While he was rector of the University of Ingolstadt, a resolution was passed forbidding the use of Protestant textbooks and, at his request, the Duke of Bavaria forbade the importation of books opposed to religion and morals. At Cologne he requested the town council to forbid the printing or sale of books hostile to the Faith or immoral, and in the Tyrol had Archduke Ferdinand II suppress such books. He also advised Bishop Urban of Gurk, the court preacher of Ferdinand I, not to read so many Protestant books, but to study instead the Scriptures and the writings of the Fathers. At Nimwegen he searched the libraries of his friends, and burned all heretical books. In the midst of all these cares Canisius remained essentially a man of prayer; he was an ardent advocate of the Rosary and its sodalities. He was also one of the precursors of the modern devotion of the Sacred Heart.

During his lifetime his "Catechism" appeared in more than 200 editions in at least twelve languages. It was one of the works which influenced St. Aloysius Gonzaga to enter the Society of Jesus; it converted, among others, Count Palatine Wolfgang Wilhelm of Neuburg; and as late as the eighteenth century in many places the words "Canisi" and catechism were synonymous. It remained the foundation and pattern for the catechisms printed later. His preaching also had great influence; in 1560 the clergy of the cathedral of Augsburg testified that by his sermons nine hundred persons had been brought back to the Church, and in May, 1562, it was reported the Easter communicants numbered one thousand more than in former years. Canisius induced some of the prominent Fuggers to return to the Church, and converted the leader of the Augsburg Anabaptists. In 1537 the Catholic clergy had been banished from Augsburg by the city council; but after the preaching of Canisius public processions were held, monasteries gained novices, people crowded to the jubilee indulgence, pilgrimages were revived, and frequent Communion again became the rule. After the elections of 1562 there were eighteen Protestants and twenty-seven Catholics on the city council. He received the approbation of Pius IV by a special Brief in 1561. Great services were rendered by Canisius to the Church through the extension of the Society of Jesus; the difficulties were great: lack of novices, insufficient education of some of the younger members, poverty, plague, animosity of the Protestants, jealousy on the part of fellow-Catholics, the interference of princes and city councils. Notwithstanding all this, Canisius introduced the order into Bavaria, Bohemia, Swabia, the Tyrol, and Hungary, and prepared the way in Alsace, the Palatinate, Hesse, and Poland. Even opponents admit that to the Jesuits principally is due the credit of saving a large part of Germany from religious innovation. In this work Canisius was the leader. In many respects Canisius was the product of an age which believed in strange miracles, put witches to death, and had recourse to force against the adherents of another faith; but notwithstanding all this,

Johannes Janssen does not hesitate to declare that Canisius was the most prominent and most influential Catholic reformer of the sixteenth century (Geschichte des deutschen Volkes, 15th and 16th editions, IV, p. 406). "Canisius more than any other man", writes A. Chroust, "saved for the Church of Rome the Catholic Germany of to-day" (Deutsche Zeitschrift für Geschichtswissenschaft, new series, II, 106). It has often been declared that Canisius in many ways resembles St. Boniface, and he is therefore called the second Apostle of Germany. The Protestant professor of theology, Paul Drews, says: "It must be admitted that, from the standpoint of Rome, he deserves the title of Apostle of Germany" ("Petrus Canisius", Halle, 1892, p. 103).

Soon after his death reports spread of the miraculous help obtained by invoking his name. His tomb was visited by pilgrims. The Society of Jesus decided to urge his beatification. The ecclesiastical investigations of his virtues and miracles were at first conducted by the Bishops of Fribourg, Dillingen, and Freising (1625–90); the apostolic proceedings began in 1734, but were interrupted by political and religious disorders. Gregory XVI resumed them about 1833; Pius IX on 17 April, 1864, approved of four of the miracles submitted, and on 20 November, 1869, the solemn beatification took place in St. Peter's at Rome. In connexion with this, there appeared between 1864–66 more than thirty different biographies. On the occasion of the tercentenary of his death, Leo XIII issued to the bishops of Austria, Germany, and Switzerland his much-discussed "Epistola Encyclica de memoria sæculari B. Petri Canisii"; the bishops of Switzerland issued a collective pastoral; in numerous places of Europe and in some places in the United States this tercentenary was celebrated and about fifty pamphlets were published. In order to encourage the veneration of Canisius there is published at Fribourg, Switzerland, monthly since 1896, the "Canisius-Stimmen" (in German and French). The infirmary of the College of St. Michael, in which Canisius died, is now a chapel. Vestments and other objects which he used are kept in different houses of the order. The Canisius College at Buffalo possesses precious relics. In the house of Canisius in the Broersstraat at Nimwegen the room is still shown where he was born. Other memorials are: the Canisius statue in one of the public squares of Fribourg, the statue in the cathedral of Augsburg, the Church of the Holy Saviour and the Mother of Sorrows, recently built in his memory in Vienna, and the new Canisius College at Nimwegen. At the twenty-sixth general meeting of German Catholics held at Aachen, 1879, a Canisius society for the religious education of the young was founded. The general prayer, said every Sunday in the churches originated by Canisius, is still in use in the greater part of Germany, and also in many places in Austria and Switzerland. Various portraits of Canisius exist: in the Churches of St. Nicolaus and St. Michael at Fribourg; in the vestry of the Augsburg Cathedral; in the Church of St. Michael at Munich; in the town hall at Nimwegen; in the town hall at Ingolstadt; in the Cistercian monastery at Stams. The woodcut in Pantaleo, "Prosopographia", III (Basle, 1566), is worthless. Copper-plates were produced by Wierx (1619), Custos (1612), Sadeler (1628), Hainzelmann (1693), etc. In the nineteenth century are: Fracassini's painting in the Vatican; Jeckel's steel engraving; Leo Samberger's painting; Steinle's engraving (1886). In most of these pictures Canisius is represented with his catechism and other books, or surrounded by children whom he is instructing. (See DOCTRINE, CHRISTIAN; COUNTER-REFORMATION; SOCIETY OF JESUS.)

B. P. Canisii Epist. et Acta, ed. BRAUNSBERGER (5 vols., Freiburg im Br., 1896–1905), s. v. *Confessiones* and *Testamentum;* the Beatification Acts (some printed as manuscripts in only a few copies, the others unprinted); *Mon. Hist. Societatis Jesu: Chronicon Polanci, Epistolæ quadrimestres mittæ* etc., so far about thirty volumes (Madrid, 1894—). Of the complete biographies, the following are the most important: RADERUS, *De Vita Canisii* (Munich, 1614); SACCHINUS, *De vita et rebus gestis P. Petri Canisii* (Ingolstadt, 1616); BOERO, *Vita del Beato Pietro Canisio* (Rome, 1864); RIESS, *Der selige Petrus Canisius* (Freiburg, 1865); LE BACHELET in *Dict. de Théol. Cath.* (Paris, 1905), s. v. *Canisius*. Biographies, in German: by PRATISS (Vienna, 1865), MARCOUR (Freiburg, 1881), PFÜLF (Einsiedeln, 1897), MEHLER (Ratisbon, 1897); in Latin by PYTHON (Munich, 1710); in French by DORIGNY (Paris, 1707), SÉGUIN (Paris, 1864), BOVET (Fribourg, 1865, 1881), DE BERTIGNY (Fribourg, 1865), MICHEL (Lille, 1897); in Dutch by DE SMIDT (Antwerp, 1652), SÉGUIN-ALLARD (Nimwegen, 1897); in Italian by FULIGATTI (Rome, 1649), ODDI (Naples, 1755); in Spanish by NIEREMBERG (Madrid, 1633), GARCIA (Madrid, 1865). Cf. also KROSS, *Der selige Petrus Canisius in Oesterreich* (Vienna, 1898), from manuscript sources; REISER, *B. Petrus Canisius als Katechet* (Mainz, 1882); ALLARD, *Canisiana*, from the Dutch *Studien* (Utrecht, 1898–99); BRAUNSBERGER, *Entstehung u. erste Entwicklung d. Katechismen d. seligen Petrus Canisius* (Freiburg, 1893); SOMMERVOGEL, *Bibliothèque de la C. de J.* (new ed., Brussels and Paris, 1890–1900), II, 617–88; VIII, 1974–83; DUHR, *Gesch. d. Jesuiten in den Länden deutscher Zunge*, I (Freiburg, 1907); various *Nuntiature Reports* of Germany and Switzerland published by STEINHERZ, SCHELLHASS, HANSEN, STEFFENS-REINHARDT, etc.   OTTO BRAUNSBERGER.

Peter Cantor, theologian, b. probably at Gisberoi, near Beauvais, France; d. at Long Pont Abbey, 22 Sept., 1197. He was a member of the Hosdenc family; when still young he went to Reims, which may possibly have been his birthplace, and was educated at the cathedral school. He was a professor for many years, canon of the cathedral, and would seem to have had also the office of *cantor* or *succentor*.

Towards 1170, we find Peter as canon and professor of theology of the cathedral school at Paris, where in 1180 he is again invested with the office of cantor, for his predecessor appears on the documents for the last time in 1180, whilst mention is first made of him in 1184. This is what caused him to be designated Petrus Cantor, Cantor Parisiensis, or simply Cantor; and his name is found on many charters. At the same time, his capabilities led him to be frequently chosen by the popes as a judge, e. g., at Troyes in 1188, and also during 1196 and 1197 at Compiègne for the royal divorce case with Ingeberge. In 1191 the people and clergy of Tournai chose him for their bishop, but his election was annulled by Bishop Guillaume de Champagne of Reims. At the death of Maurice de Sully in 1196, it is said that he was elected Bishop of Paris, but refused the dignity.

In 1196 Peter was elected dean of the cathedral chapter of Reims. Whilst on his journey from Paris to Reims, Peter visited the Cistercians at Long Pont Abbey, was taken ill there, died, and was buried, probably wearing the habit of the order. In the Cistercian menology he is honoured as one of themselves (19 May).

He left commentaries or glosses on all the Old Testament Books, except Judith, Esther, Tobias, and Leviticus; the best are those on the Psalms. In like manner he also wrote glosses on the whole of the New Testament, following the Harmony of the Four Gospels which, under the name of Ammonius, or Tatian, was much in use during the Middle Ages. His commentaries on the Gospels and on the Apocalypse are perhaps the most worthy of praise; that on St. Paul may be described as an interlinear gloss; in it scholastic discussions are often introduced à propos of certain subjects as they are suggested by the text. This style of writing commentaries was by no means new to the age in which he lived, and it is more and more developed at this period. None of these works were printed, not even an introduction or treatise which he wrote on the Bible in twenty folio pages variously entitled: "De tropis theologicis", "De contrarietate scripturæ", or "De tropis loquendi"; in it he lays down rules for the solution of contradictions that may seem to exist between different passages of the Bible. Traces of it may be found in Peter's commentaries and annotations on the Bible; the rules of Ticonius are sometimes found following on the "De tropis" of Peter.

There are two other unpublished works, namely, the "Summa de sacramentis et animæ consiliis", which though lengthy is nevertheless precious for its varied information on the institutions and religious customs of the time; he develops at great length the moral side of the question, especially when writing on the Sacrament of Penance. He purposely leaves aside matters already discussed by Peter Lombard, for as he himself says it is his intention to complete them. The "Distinctiones" or "Summa quæ dicitur Abel" is a theological dictionary arranged in alphabetical order, "Abel" being the first word, in which is found a short résumé of the ideas, doctrines, and theories of the time; with this as title, he wrote a valuable document which is still to be found in many manuscripts (Paris, Rome, Bruges, etc.). Pitra has published portions of it ("Spicilegium Solesmense", III, I, 308; "Analecta Sacra," II, 6–154, 585–628).

The "Verbum Abbreviatum", his only work that was entirely printed, with the "Contra Monachos proprietarios" which in Migne forms the matter of chapter cliii and written before 1187, is not a course of ethics or asceticism, but a book addressed chiefly to the clergy and more in particular to monks, wherein he exhorts to the practice of virtue; his sources are the Bible, the writings of the Fathers, and profane authors. What he says about manners, customs, etc., is very instructive for the time in which he wrote. As in the "Summa de Sacramentis", so here are found scholastic theories side by side with practical remarks on daily life from a religious point of view (1st ed., Mons, 1639; Migne, P. L., CCV, 23). Some sermons are also ascribed to Peter, but only those which are in the form of detached chapters of the "Verbum abbreviatum" are known.

Hist. littér. de la France, XV; HAURÉAU, *Notices et extraits de quelques manuscrits,* I, 76, 224, etc.; II, 14, etc.; V, 4–7, etc.; SCHMID-GUTJAHR, *Petrus Cantor* (Graz, 1899); DENIFLE-CHATELAIN, *Chartularium Universitatis Parisiensis,* I, 13, 46; *Bibliothèque de l'Ecole des Chartes* (1840), 398.

J. DE GHELLINCK.

Peter Celestine, SAINT. See CELESTINE V, SAINT, POPE.

Peter Cellensis (DE LA CELLE), Bishop of Chartres, b. of noble parentage in Champagne; d. at Chartres, 20 February, 1183. He was educated in the monastery of St. Martin-des-Champs at Paris, became a Benedictine, and in 1150 was made Abbot of La Celle near Troyes, whence his surname, Cellensis. In 1162 he was appointed Abbot of St. Rémy at Reims, and in 1181 he succeeded John of Salisbury as Bishop of Chartres. He was highly esteemed by men like John of Salisbury, Thomas à Becket, Archbishop Eskil, Eugene III, and especially Alexander III. His literary productions were edited by Janvier (Paris, 1671) and reprinted in P. L., CCII, 405–1146. They consist of 177 epistles, 95 sermons, and 4 treatises entitled: (1) "De panibus ad Joannem Sarisberiensem"; (2) "Mosaici tabernaculi mysticæ et moralis expositionis libri duo"; (3) "De conscientia"; (4) "De disciplina claustrali ad Henricum I, Campaniæ Comitem". His epistles, which are valuable from an historical standpoint, were edited separately by Sirmond (Paris, 1613). His sermons and treatises are extremely bombastic and allegorical.

GILLET, *De Petro Cellensi, abbate Sancti Remigii Remensis et Camotensi episcopo dissertatio* (Paris, 1881); GEORGES, *Pierre de Celles, sa vie et ses œuvres* (Troyes, 1857); *Hist. litt. de la France,* XIV, 236–67; ZIEGELBAUER, *Hist. rei literariæ O. S. B.,* III, 162–65; CEILLIER, *Hist. gén. des auteurs sacrés,* XIV (Paris, 1863), 680–13.

MICHAEL OTT.

Peter Chrysologus, SAINT, b. at Imola, 406; d. there, 450. His biography, first written by Agnellus (Liber pontificalis ecclesiæ Ravennatis) in the ninth century, gives but scanty information about him. He was baptized, educated, and ordained deacon by Cornelius, Bishop of Imola, and was elevated to the Bishopric of Ravenna in 433. There are indications that Ravenna held the rank of metropolitan before his time. His piety and zeal won for him universal admiration, and his oratory merited for him the name Chrysologus. He shared the confidence of Leo the Great and enjoyed the patronage of the Empress Galla Placidia. After his condemnation by the Synod of Constantinople (448), the Monophysite Eutyches endeavoured to win the support of Peter, but without success.

A collection of his homilies, numbering 176, was made by Felix, Bishop of Ravenna (707–17). Some are interpolations, and several other homilies known to be written by the saint are included in other collections under different names. They are in a great measure explanatory of Biblical texts and are brief and concise. He has explained beautifully the mystery of the Incarnation, the heresies of Arius and Eutyches, the Apostles' Creed, and he dedicated a series of homilies to the Blessed Virgin and St. John the Baptist. His works were first edited by Agapitus Vicentinus (Bologna, 1534), and later by D. Mita (Bologna, 1634), and S. Pauli (Venice, 1775)—the latter collection having been reprinted in P. L., LII. Fr. Liverani ("Spicilegium Liberianum", Florence, 1863, 125 seq.) edited nine new homilies and published from manuscripts in Italian libraries different readings of several other sermons. Several homilies were translated into German by M. Held (Kempten, 1874).

BARDENHEWER, *Patrology*, tr. SHAHAN, 526 sqq.; DAPPER, *Der hl. Petrus Chrysologus* (Cologne, 1867); STABLEWSKI, *Der heilige Kirchenvater Petrus von Ravenna Chrysologus* (Posen, 1871); LOOSHORN, *Der hl. Petrus Chrysologus und seine Schriften* in *Zeitschrift f. kathol. Theol.*, III (1879), 238 seq.; WAYMAN, *Zu Petrus Chrysologus* in *Philologus*, LV (1896), 464 seq.

IGNATIUS SMITH.

Peter Claver, SAINT, the son of a Catalonian farmer, was b. at Verdu, in 1581; d. 8 September, 1654. He obtained his first degrees at the University of Barcelona. At the age of twenty he entered the Jesuit novitiate at Tarragona. While he was studying philosophy at Majorca in 1605, Alphonsus Rodriguez, the saintly door-keeper of the college, learned from God the future mission of his young associate, and thenceforth never ceased exhorting him to set out to evangelize the Spanish possessions in America. Peter obeyed, and in 1610 landed at Cartagena, where for forty-four years he was the Apostle of the negro slaves. Early in the seventeenth century the masters of Central and South America afforded the spectacle of one of those social crimes which are entered upon so lightly. They needed labourers to cultivate the soil which they had conquered and to exploit the gold mines. The natives being physically incapable of enduring the labours of the mines, it was determined to replace them with negroes brought from Africa. The coasts of Guinea, the Congo, and Angola became the market for slave dealers, to whom native petty kings sold their subjects and their prisoners. By its position in the Caribbean Sea, Cartagena became the chief slave-mart of the New World. A thousand slaves landed there each month. They were bought for two, and sold for 200 écus. Though half the cargo might die, the trade remained profitable. Neither the repeated censures of the pope, nor those of Catholic moralists could prevail against this cupidity. The missionaries could not suppress slavery, but only alleviate it, and no one worked more heroically than Peter Claver.

Trained in the school of Père Alfonso de Sandoval, a wonderful missionary, Peter declared himself "the slave of the negroes forever", and thenceforth his life was one that confounds egotism by its superhuman charity. Although timid and lacking in self-confidence, he became a daring and ingenious organizer. Every month when the arrival of the negroes was signalled, Claver went out to meet them on the pilot's boat, carrying food and delicacies. The negroes, cooped up in the hold, arrived crazed and brutalized by suffering and fear. Claver went to each, cared for him, and showed him kindness, and made him understand that henceforth he was his defender and father. He thus won their good will. To instruct so many speaking different dialects, Claver assembled at Cartagena a group of interpreters of various nationalities, of whom he made catechists. While the slaves were penned up at Cartagena waiting to be purchased and dispersed, Claver instructed and baptized them in the Faith. On Sundays during Lent he assembled them, inquired concerning their needs, and defended them against their oppressors. This work caused Claver severe trials, and the slave merchants were not his only enemies. The Apostle was accused of indiscreet zeal, and of having profaned the Sacraments by giving them to creatures who scarcely possessed a soul. Fashionable women of Cartagena refused to enter the churches where Father Claver assembled his negroes. The saint's superiors were often influenced by the many criticisms which reached them. Nevertheless, Claver continued his heroic career, accepting all humiliations and adding rigorous penances to his works of charity. Lacking the support of men, the strength of God was given him. He became the prophet and miracle worker of New Granada, the oracle of Cartagena, and all were convinced that often God would not have spared the city save for him. During his life he baptized and instructed in the Faith more than 300,000 negroes. He was beatified 16 July, 1850, by Pius IX, and canonized 15 Jan., 1888, by Leo XIII. His feast is celebrated on the ninth of September. On 7 July, 1896, he was proclaimed the special patron of all the Catholic missions among the negroes. Alphonsus Rodriguez was canonized on the same day as Peter Claver.

Lives of the saints by DE ANDRADA (Madrid, 1657), DOMINGUEZ, DE LARA, SUÁREZ, FERNÁNDEZ, FLEURIAN; SOMMERVOGEL, *Bibl. de la Comp. de Jésus* (Brussels, 1890—); WASER (Paderborn, 1852); SOLÁ (Barcelona, 1888); HÖVER (Dulmen, 1888); an excellent article by LEHMKUHL in *Stimmen aus Maria-Laach*, XXIV, 380 sqq.

PIERRE SUAU.

Peter Comestor, theological writer, b. at Troyes, date unknown; d. at Paris about 1178. He was first attached to the Church of Notre-Dame at Troyes and habitually signed himself as "Presbyter Trecensis". Before 1148 he became dean of the chapter and received a benefice in 1148. About 1160 he formed one of the Chapter of Notre-Dame at Paris, and about the same year he replaced Eudes (Odon) as chancellor. At the same time he had charge of the theological school. It was at Paris that Peter Comestor composed and certainly finished his "Historia Scholastica"; he dedicated it to the Bishop of Sens, Guillaume aux Blanches Mains (1169–76). Alexander III ordered Cardinal Peter of St. Chrysogonus to allow the chancellor Peter to exact a small fee on conferring the licence to teach, but this authorization was altogether personal. A short time afterwards the same cardinal mentioned the name of Peter to Alexander III, as among the three most cultured men of France. The surname of "Comestor", given to Peter during his life, also proves the esteem in which his learning was held: he was a great bookworm; he often refers to his surname in his sermons and in the epitaph said to be composed by him: "Petrus eram . . . dictusque comestor, nunc comedor." He afterwards withdrew to the Abbey of St. Victor and made profession of canonical life. He was buried at St. Victor; and the necrology of the canons mentions him as one of themselves (21 October). His works include commentaries on the Gospels, allegories on Holy Scripture, and a moral commentary on St. Paul, all of which are as yet unpublished.

His "Historia Scholastica" is a kind of sacred

history, composed for students, and at their own request. The author begins the sacred narrative at the Creation, and continues it to the end of the incidents related in the Acts of the Apostles; all the books of the Bible are contained therein, except those whose nature is purely didactic, the Book of Wisdom, the Psalms, the Prophets, the Epistles, etc. The discourses are abbreviated. He borrows frequently from profane authors, especially from Flavius Josephus for the beginning of the Gospels, and very often the text is as though paraphrased in a commentary where all data, cosmological and physical, philosophical, theological, allegorical, historical, geographical, etc., are found. It is easy to understand, of course, that there are numerous inaccuracies and fables. The work consists of twenty books and often small "additions" supply geographical or etymological appendixes at the end of the chapters. This Biblical history met with great success, as witness the large number of manuscripts, the mention of his name in all the libraries of the Middle Ages, the lists of classical books for the universities and schools, the quotations and the eulogies with which the name of its author is everywhere accompanied (cf. the canonist Huguccio, about 1190) and its numerous translations. In the fifteenth century, the work was still in great demand, as can be seen by the editions made before 1500 of the Latin text, or of the French translation (Strasburg, 1469, 1483, 1485, 1847; Reutlingen, 1473; Lyons, 1478; Basle, 1486; Paris, 1487, etc.). Migne (P. L., CXCVIII, 1053-1844) reproduces the Madrid edition of 1699.

The sermons of Peter Comestor have been left to us in numerous manuscripts, often under other names, but the complete and continued series has not yet been published. We ought to mention here a series of fifty-one sermons placed wrongly under the name of Peter of Blois and printed among his works (Migne, CCVII, and CCVIII, 1721, etc.); some figure also in the works of Hildebert de Mans (Migne, CLXXI, sermon 7, 15, 17, 21, 22, 23, etc.). The sermon in which the word "transubstantiation" occurs, the 93rd (not the 73rd), is not Hildebert's but Peter Comestor's; let us remark, however, that the word is already found in Roland Bandinelli (Alexander II) before 1150. Other collections, like that of the 114 sermons copied at St. Victor before 1186, are still unpublished, more than twelve manuscripts are in the libraries of Paris, and all has not yet been unravelled in this assortment. As a preacher, Peter was subtle and pedantic in his style, in keeping with the taste of his time and of his audience of scholars and professors assembled around the pulpit of the chancellor. The sermons attributed to him during his stay at St. Victor are simple in style, instructive, and natural in tone. Also some verses are attributed to Peter Comestor and a collection of maxims entitled "Pancrisis", perhaps that which still exists in a manuscript of Troyes.

Hist. litt. de la France, XIV, 12-17; DENIFLE-CHÂTELAIN, *Chartul. Univ.*, I (Paris), 8; FOURIER-BONNARD, *Hist. de l'abb. de Saint-Victor* (Paris, 1907), 123, etc.; FÉRET, *La Faculté de Théol. de Paris*, I (Paris, 1894), 42-48; BOURGAIN, *La Chaire Française au XIIe siècle* (Paris, 1879), 123; HAURÉAU, *Notices et Extraits de quelques manuscrits*, I, 28, 37, etc.; II, 18, 80, etc.; IV, 2, 3, etc.

J. DE GHELLINCK.

Peter Damian (or DAMIANI) SAINT, Doctor of the Church, Cardinal-Bishop of Ostia, b. at Ravenna "five years after the death of the Emperor Otto III," 1007; d. at Faenza, 21 Feb., 1072. He was the youngest of a large family; his parents were noble, but poor. At his birth an elder brother protested against this new charge on the resources of the family with such effect that his mother refused to suckle him and the babe nearly died. A family retainer, however, fed the starving child and by her example and reproaches recalled his mother to her duty. Left an orphan in early years, he was at first adopted by an elder brother, who ill-treated and under-fed him while employing him as a swineherd. The child showed signs of great piety and of remarkable intellectual gifts, and after some years of this servitude another brother, who was archpriest at Ravenna, had pity on him and took him away to be educated. This brother was called Damian, and it is generally accepted that St. Peter added this name to his own in grateful recognition of his brother's kindness. He made rapid progress in his studies, first at Ravenna, then at Faenza, finally at the University of Parma, and when about twenty-five years old was already a famous teacher at Parma and Ravenna. But, though even then much given to fasting and to other mortifications, he could not endure the scandals and distractions of university life and decided (about 1035) to retire from the world. While meditating on his resolution he encountered two hermits of Fonte-Avellana, was charmed with their spirituality and detachment, and desired to join them. Encouraged by them Peter, after a forty days' retreat in a small cell, left his friends secretly and made his way to the hermitage of Fonte-Avellana (q. v.). Here he was received, and, to his surprise, clothed at once with the monastic habit.

Both as novice and as professed religious his fervour was remarkable and led him to such extremes of penance that, for a time, his health was affected. He occupied his convalescence with a thorough study of Holy Scripture and, on his recovery, was appointed to lecture to his fellow-monks. At the request of Guy of Pomposa and other heads of neighbouring monasteries, for two or three years he lectured to their subjects also, and (about 1042) wrote the life of St. Romuald for the monks of Pietrapertosa. Soon after his return to Fonte-Avellana he was appointed *economus* of the house by the prior, who also pointed him out as his successor. This, in fact, he became in 1043, and he remained prior of Fonte-Avellana till his death. His priorate was characterized by a wise moderation of the rule, as well as by the foundation of subject-hermitages at San Severino, Gamugno, Acerata, Murciana, San Salvatore, Sitria, and Ocri. It was remarkable, too, for the introduction of the regular use of the discipline, a penitential exercise which he induced the great abbey of Monte Cassino to imitate. There was much opposition outside his own circle to this practice, but Peter's persistent advocacy ensured its acceptance to such an extent that he was obliged later to moderate the imprudent zeal of some of his own hermits. Another innovation was that of the daily siesta, to make up for the fatigue of the night office. During his tenure of the priorate a cloister was built, silver chalices and a silver processional cross were purchased, and many books added to the library. (See FONTE-AVELLANA.)

Although living in the seclusion of the cloister, Peter Damian watched closely the fortunes of the Church, and like his friend Hildebrand, the future Gregory VII (q. v.), he strove for her purification in those deplorable times. In 1045 when Benedict IX resigned the supreme pontificate into the hands of the archpriest John Gratian (Gregory VI), Peter hailed the change with joy and wrote to the pope, urging him to deal with the scandals of the Church in Italy, especially with the evil bishops of Pesaro, of Citta di Castello, and of Fano. (See BENEDICT IX; GREGORY VI.) He was present in Rome when Clement II crowned Henry III and his wife Agnes, and he also attended a synod held at the Lateran in the first days of 1047, in which decrees were passed against simony. After this he returned to his hermitage (see CLEMENT II; DAMASUS II). Pope St. Leo IX (q. v.) was solemnly enthroned at Rome, 12 Feb., 1049, to succeed Damasus II, and about two years later Peter Damian published his terrible treatise on the vices of the clergy, the "Liber Gomorrhianus", dedicating it to the pope. It caused a great stir and aroused not a little enmity against its author. Even the pope, who had at first praised the work, was persuaded that it was exaggerated and his coldness drew from Damian a vigorous letter of protest. Meanwhile the question arose as to the validity of the ordinations of simoniacal clerics. The prior of Fonte-Avellana was appealed to and wrote (about 1053) a treatise, the "Liber Gratissimus", in favour of their validity, a work which, though much combatted at the time, was potent in deciding the question in their favour before the end of the twelfth century. In June, 1055, during the pontificate of Victor II (q. v.), Damian attended a synod held at Florence, where simony and clerical incontinence were once more condemned. About two years later he fell ill at Fonte-Avellana and nearly died, but suddenly, after seven weeks of pain, recovered, as he believed, through a miracle.

During his illness the pope died, and Frederic, abbot of Monte Cassino, was elected as Stephen X. In the autumn of 1057, Stephen X determined to create Damian a cardinal. For a long time he resisted the offer, but was finally forced, under threat of excommunication, to accept, and was consecrated Cardinal-Bishop of Ostia on 30 Nov., 1057. In addition he was appointed administrator of the Diocese of Gubbio. The new cardinal was impressed with the great responsibilities of his office and wrote a stirring letter to his brother-cardinals, exhorting them to shine by their example before all. Four months later Pope Stephen died at Florence and the Church was once more distracted by schism. The Cardinal of Ostia was vigorous in his opposition to the antipope Benedict X, but force was on the side of the intruder and Damian retired to Fonte-Avellana. (See NICHOLAS II; GREGORY VII.)

About the end of the year 1059 Peter was sent as legate to Milan by Nicholas II. The Church at Milan had been, for some time, the prey of simony and incontinence. So bad was the state of things, that benefices were openly bought and sold and the clergy publicly "married" the women they lived with. But the faithful of Milan, led by St. Ariald the Deacon and St. Anselm, Bishop of Lucca, strove hard to remedy these evils. At length the contest between the two parties became so bitter that an appeal was made to the Holy See to decide the matter. Nicholas II sent Damian and the Bishop of Lucca as his legates. But now the party of the irregular clerics took alarm and raised the cry that Rome had no authority over Milan. At once Peter took action. Boldly confronting the rioters in the cathedral, he proved to them the authority of the Holy See with such effect that all parties submitted to his decision. He exacted first a solemn oath from the archbishop and all his clergy that for the future no preferment should be paid for; then, imposing a penance on all who had been guilty, he re-instated in their benefices all who undertook to live continently. This prudent decision was attacked by some of the rigourists at Rome, but was not reversed. Unfortunately, on the death of Nicholas II, the same disputes broke out; nor were they finally settled till after the martyrdom of St. Ariald in 1066. Meanwhile Peter was in vain pleading to be released from the cares of his office. Neither Nicholas II nor Hildebrand would consent to spare him.

In July, 1061, the pope died and once more a schism ensued. Damian used all his powers to persuade the antipope Cadalous (q. v.) to withdraw, but to no purpose. Finally Hanno, the Regent of Germany, summoned a council at Augsburg at which a long argument by St. Peter Damian was read and greatly contributed to the decision in favour of Alexander II (q. v.). In 1063 the pope held a synod at Rome, at which Damian was appointed as legate to settle the dispute between the Abbey of Cluny and the Bishop of Mâcon. He proceeded to France, summoned a council at Châlon-sur-Saône, proved the justice of the contentions of Cluny, settled other questions at issue in the Church of France, and returned in the autumn to Fonte-Avellana. While he was in France the antipope Cadalous had again become active in his attempts to gain Rome, and Damian brought upon himself a sharp reproof from Alexander and Hildebrand for twice imprudently appealing to the royal power to judge the case anew. In 1067 the cardinal was sent to Florence to settle the dispute between the bishop and the monks of Vallombrosa, who accused the former of simony. His efforts, however, were not successful, largely because he misjudged the case and threw the weight of his authority on the side of the bishop. The matter was not settled till the following year by the pope in person. In 1069 Damian went as the pope's legate to Germany to prevent King Henry from repudiating his wife Bertha. This task he accomplished at a council at Frankfort and returned to Fonte-Avellana, where he was left in peace for two years.

Early in 1072 he was sent to Ravenna to reconcile its inhabitants to the Holy See, they having been excommunicated for supporting their archbishop in his adhesion to the schism of Cadalous. On his return thence he was seized with fever near Faenza. He lay ill for a week at the monastery of Santa Maria degl' Angeli, now Santa Maria Vecchia. On the night preceding the feast of the Chair of St. Peter at Antioch, he ordered the office of that feast to be recited and at the end of Lauds he died. He was at once buried in the monastery church, lest others should claim his relics. Six times has his body been translated, each time to a more splendid resting-place. It now lies in a chapel dedicated to the saint in the cathedral of Faenza in 1898. No formal canonization ever took place, but his cultus has existed since his death at Faenza, at Fonte-Avellana, at Monte Cassino, and at Cluny. In 1823 Leo XII extended his feast (23 Feb.) to the whole Church and pronounced him a Doctor of the Church. The saint is represented in art as a cardinal bearing a discipline in his hand; also sometimes he is depicted as a pilgrim holding a papal Bull, to signify his many legations.

Acta SS. Boll., III, Feb. (Venice, 1736), 406–27; BIRON, St. Pierre Damien, 1007–72 (Paris, 1908); CAPECELATRO, Storia di San Pier Damiano (Rome, 1887); KLEINERMANNS, Der heilige Petrus Damiani (Steyl, 1882); LADERCHI, Vita S. Petri Damiani (3 vols., Rome, 1702); MABILLON, Acta SS. O.S.B., Sæc. VI, P. ii (Venice, 1733), 253–273; MARTIN, Saint Léon IX, 1002–54 (Paris, 1904); MIGNE, Dictionnaire de Patrologie, V (Paris, 1864), 959–1000; P. L., CXLIV, CXLV (Paris, 1867); MITTARELLI ET COSTADONI, Annales Camaldulenses, II (Venice, 1756), 40–359; NEUKIRCH, Das Leben des Petrus Damiani . . . bis zur . . . 1059 (Göttingen, 1875); PFÜLF, Damiani's Zwist mit Hildebrand in Stimmen aus Maria-Laach, XLI (1891), 281–307, 400–416, 508–525; ROTH, Der heilige Petrus Damiani, O.S.B., in Studien O. S. B., VII (1886), i, 110–134; ii, 357–374; iii, 43–66; iv, 321–336; VIII (1887), i, 56–64; ii, 210–216.

LESLIE A. ST. L. TOKE.

Peter de Blois, statesman and theologian, b. at Blois about 1130; d. about 1203. He appears to have first studied at Tours, and was, perhaps, the disciple of Jean de Salisbury, who taught in Paris from 1140 to 1150; he studied law in Bologna, and theology in Paris, where he taught the liberal arts. In 1167 Count Stephen du Perche brought him to Sicily (1167). Here he became preceptor of the king, guardian of the royal seal, and one of the queen's principal counsellors. But the favouritism shown the foreigner excited the jealousy of the nobles and he was obliged to leave Sicily (1169). After several years in France, he went to England, where he became one of Henry II's diplomatic agents and was charged with negotiations with the pope and the King of France. In 1176 he became chancellor of the Archbishop of Canterbury and Archdeacon of Bath. He became entangled in the disputes between the archbishop and the monks of his diocese and, in this connexion, was sent to Rome in 1177, and to Verona in 1187, on diplomatic missions to the popes. After the death of Henry II (1189), he fell into disgrace, and he speaks in his letters of Richard the Lion Hearted as the "new Pharaoh". He entered the service of Queen Eleanor of Aquitaine, to whom he was secretary (1190-95), and was made Archdeacon of London. But his revenue from this benefice scarcely sufficed for his living and he wrote to Innocent III to this effect in one of the last letters (1198) he has left us. His material status was hardly in keeping with the great authority he exercised in England towards the end of the reign of Henry II, in affairs of the State, or of the Church. Not only was he the king's chief counsellor, but many bishops consulted him and obtained his advice on important matters regarding their dioceses.

He wrote numerous letters, models of his epoch, but full of the bad taste of the twelfth century. He wrote also numerous treatises. He continued the "History of the Monastery of Croyland of Ingulf" (901 to 1135). Unfortunately, the "History of Henry II" has been lost (De rebus gestis Henrici II). His other writings are sermons, commentaries on the Scripture, moral and ascetic treatises, in which he attacks with blunt frankness the morals of the English and Aquitainian bishops (treatise entitled, "Quales sunt"). In 1189, after the taking of Jerusalem by Saladin, he composed his "De hierosolymitana peregrinatione acceleranda" (P. L. CCVII, 1057), wherein he censures the indifferent faith of the princes who deferred the undertaking of the crusade, and threatens them with seeing the mission which they have deserted accomplished by the people. He also composed an "Instruction on the Faith" which Alexander III sent to the Sultan of Iconium. In several of his letters he returns to the question of the crusade. His works were edited by Giles in "Patres Ecclesiæ Anglicanæ", 4 vols. (Oxford, 1846-47), and in P. L., CCVII (4 vols., Paris).

CEILLIER, *Hist. des Auteurs ecclés.*, XXIII (Paris, 1763), 206–24; *Hist. Litt. de la France*, XV (Paris, 1820), 341–413; MICHAUD, *Bibliothèque des Croisades*, III (Paris, 1829), 250; NORGATE, *England under the Angevin Kings*, II (London, 1887); CHALANDON, *Hist. de la domination normande en Italie et en Sicile*, II (Paris, 1907); MOLINIER, *Les Sources de l'hist. de France*, pt. II (Paris, 1902), 203, dealing with Peter's *Ars dictaminis*.

LOUIS BRÉHIER.

Peter de Honestis, b. at Ravenna about 1049; d., 29 March, 1119. Among his ancestors was the great St. Romuald, founder of the Camaldolese monks. All his life Peter fasted every Saturday in honour of Our Lady, and strongly recommended this practice to his religious. He styled himself *Petrus peccator*. He lived for some years in the Holy Land. When returning a great storm arose in the Adriatic and the ship was in imminent danger. Peter made a vow to build a church in honour of Our Lady should he safely reach the harbour. In fulfilment of his promise he built a church and monastery on the family property. Near by there was a small community of clerics, and Peter having joined them, was soon after made their superior, and with them removed to the church and monastery he had built, in 1099. His name is associated with the sodality called "The Children of Mary", established in honour of a miraculous picture of Our Lady, now called "Madonna Greca", which tradition says came from Constantinople. The number of his religious increasing, Peter gave them some statutes grounded on the rule of St. Augustine. These were approved by Paschal II, and having afterwards been adopted by many other communities of Canons Regular, the Portuensis Congregation was formed. By common consent Peter has always been called Blessed. In former times his office and feast used to be celebrated at Ravenna; the process of his beatification is now before the Holy See.

PENNOTTO, *Generalis Sacri Ordinis Canonicorum-Clericorum Historia Tripartita* (Rome, 1642); *Bullarium Lateranense* (Rome, 1727); *Storia della Madonna Greca, da D. P. S.* (Ravenna, 1887); *Vita del Beato Pietro degli Onesti* (Ravenna, 1893); *Pia associazione mondiale, fondata nel 1100 dal B. Pietro degli Onesti: Breve storia della Madonna Greca* (Ravenna, 1891).

A. ALLARIA.

Peter de Regalado (REGALATUS), SAINT, Friar Minor and reformer, b. at Valladolid, 1390; d. at Aguilera, 30 March, 1456. His parents were of noble birth and conspicuous for their wealth and virtue. Having lost his father in his early youth, he was piously educated by his mother. At the age of ten years Peter begged to be admitted into the Seraphic Order, which favour was granted him three years afterwards in the convent of his native town. In 1404 he became one of the first disciples of Peter de Villacreces, who in 1397 had introduced into Spain the reform of the Observance of which he became one of the most zealous propagators. In the newly-founded convent at Aguilera Peter found the life of solitude, prayer, and eminent poverty, which had always been the greatest object of his desire. In 1415 he became superior of the convent at Aguilera and, on the death of Peter de Villacreces (1422), also of that at Tribulos or del Abroyo. He observed nine Lents, fasting on bread and water, and was endowed with the gift of miracles and prophecy and of every virtue. When his body was exhumed thirty-six years after his death, at the instance of Isabella the Catholic, it was found incorrupt and placed in a more precious tomb. He was beatified by Innocent XI, 11 March, 1684, and canonized by Benedict XIV, 29 June, 1746. His feast is celebrated 13 May, the day of the translation of his body. In art he is represented with flames bursting from his heart.

CLARY, *Lives of the Saints and Blessed of the Three Orders of St. Francis*, II (Taunton, 1886), 150–9; DAZA, *Excelencias de la ciudad de Valladolid, con la vida y milagros de s. fray Pedro Regalado etc.* (Valladolid, 1627), Lat. tr. in *Act. SS.*, III, March, 850–64; *Relatio pro canonizatione*, ibid., 864–70; WADDING, *Ann. Min.*, XII, 2–9, 445–74; BERGUIN, *St. Pierre Régalat, prêtre de l'ordre des Frères Mineurs de l'Observance, restaurateur de la discipline régulière en Espagne* (Périgueux, 1898).

FERDINAND HECKMANN.

Peter de Vinea (DE VINEIS, DELLA VIGNA), b. at Capua about 1190; d. 1249. Peter's legal learning and the elegance of his Latin style in course of time made him the most prominent statesman of public affairs at the court of Frederick II. Frederick's political views, which aimed at absolutism in Church and State, he succeeded in strengthening in every direction. In his capacity as chief judge of the court he took a prominent part in the administration of justice and legislation in Sicily. Perhaps he was also associated with Archbishop James of Capua in drawing up the new code of laws for the Kingdom of Sicily, called the "Constitutions of Melfi" and issued in 1231 by order of Frederick. Probably Peter was the emperor's ambassador at the Council of Lyons in 1245. Certain it is that in the same year, as the envoy of the emperor, he sought the mediation of St. Louis in the conflict that was developing between Church and State.

About this date he was already, along with Thaddeus of Suessa, the real director of the imperial chancellery. In 1247 he was made imperial prothonotary and logothete of the Kingdom of Sicily and thus the sole head of the imperial chancellery. This important position in the State was his ruin. He sought to enrich himself and his family. His embezzlements went so far that, as the emperor himself said, they led to a financial disaster which might have become dangerous to the empire. Just at the time that Frederick made this discovery at Cremona in February, 1249, a physician attempted to give the emperor a poisoned drink. Peter was suspected of being privy to the plot. This report, based on a statement of Matthew of Paris, has been even recently credited by Gerdes, while Hampe rejects it. Dante, however, goes too far when, in the "Inferno" (xiii, 55 sqq.), he allows Peter to say that he has never broken faith with the emperor. Frederick, on his return to Sicily, ordered his one-time confidant to be put in chains. Peter was forced to retire to Etruria where Frederick had him imprisoned at San Miniato and had his eyes put out. He is said to have committed suicide here. His letters, a part of which were printed in the sixteenth century, are of great interest. He was also esteemed as a poet. His poems contain many violent satires on the clergy.

HUILLARD-BRÉHOLLES, *Vie et correspondance de Pierre de la Vigne* (Paris, 1865); CAPASSO AND TANELLI, *Pietro della Vigna* (Caserta, 1882); HANAUER, *Material zur Beurteilung der Petrus de Vinea-Briefe* in *Mitteilungen des Oestrr. Institut*s, XXI; as to the manuscripts of the letters cf. *Archiv für deutsche Gesch.*, VII (1839), 890 sqq.; PETRUS DE VINEA, *Epistolarum libri VI*, ed. ISELIUS (2 vols., Basle, 1740); GERDES, *Gesch. der Hohenstaufen und ihrer Zeit* (Leipzig, 1908); HAMPE, *Deutsche Kaisergesch. in der Zeit der Salier und Staufer* (Leipzig, 1909); WATTENBACH, *Deutschlands geschichtsquellen im Mittelalter* (Stuttgart, 1894); WINKELMANN, *Jahrbücher der deutschen gesch. unter Friedrich II* [2 vols. up to 1233 (Leipzig, 1889 and 1897)].

F. KAMPERS.

Peter Faber (FAVRE or LE FÈVRE), BLESSED, b. 13 April, 1506, at Villaret, Savoy; d. 1 Aug., 1546, in Rome. As a child he tended his father's sheep during the week, and on Sunday he taught catechism to other children. The instinctive knowledge of his vocation as an apostle inspired him with a desire to study. At first he was entrusted to the care of a priest at Thônes, and then to a neighbouring school. Although without any definite plans for the future, he resolved to go to Paris. His parents consented to the separation, and in 1525 Peter arrived in Paris. Here he acquired the learning he desired, and found quite unexpectedly his real vocation. He was admitted gratuitously to the college of Sainte-Barbe, and shared the lodging of a student from Navarre, Francis Xavier, the future saint, in a tower which still existed in 1850. They became intimately attached to each other, receiving on the same day in 1530 the degree of master of arts. At the university he also met St. Ignatius Loyola (q. v.) and became one of his associates. He was ordained in 1834, and received at Montmartre, on 15 August of the same year, the vows of Ignatius and his five companions. To these first six volunteers, three others were to attach themselves. Ignatius appointed them all to meet at Venice, and charged Faber to conduct them there. Leaving Paris 15 Nov., 1536, Faber and his companions rejoined Ignatius at Venice in Jan., 1537. Ignatius then thought of going to evangelize the Holy Land, but God had destined him for a vaster field of action.

After Ignatius, Faber was the one whom Xavier and his companions esteemed the most eminent. He merited this esteem by his profound knowledge, his gentle sanctity, and his influence over souls. Faber now repaired to Rome, and after some months of preaching and teaching, the pope sent him to Parma and Piacenza, where he brought about a revival of Christian piety. Recalled to Rome, Faber was sent to Germany to uphold Catholicism at the Diet of Worms. In reality the diets which the Protestants were enabled to hold through the weakness of Charles accomplished no good. From the Diet of Worms, convoked in 1540, he was called to that of Ratisbon in 1541. Faber was startled by the ruin which Protestantism had caused in Germany, and by the state of decadence presented by Catholicism; and he saw that the remedy did not lie in discussions with the heretics, but in the reform of the faithful—above all, of the clergy. For ten months, at Speyer, at Ratisbon, and at Mainz, he conducted himself with gentleness and success. It was above all by the Spiritual Exercises that he accomplished most of his conversions. Princes, prelates, and priests revealed their consciences to him, and people were astounded by the efficacy of an apostolate accomplished so rapidly. Recalled to Spain by St. Ignatius, Faber tore himself away from the field where he had already gathered such a harvest, and won Savoy, which has never ceased to venerate him as a saint; but he had hardly been in Spain six months when by order of the pope he was again sent to Germany. This time for nineteen months Faber was to work for the reform of Speyer, Mainz, and Cologne— a thankless task. However, he gained the ecclesiastics little by little, changed their hearts, and discovered in the young many vocations. That he decided the vocation of Bl. Peter Canisius is in itself sufficient to justify his being called the Apostle of Germany. The Archbishop of Cologne, Herman of Wied, was already won over by the heresy which he was later publicly to embrace. It was also at Cologne that Faber especially exercised his zeal. After spending some months at Louvain, in 1543, where he implanted the seeds of numerous vocations among the young, he returned to Cologne, and there it may be said that he extirpated all heresy. But he was forced by obedience to leave Germany in August, 1544, going at first to Portugal, later to Spain. At the court of Lisbon and that of Valladolid, Faber was an angel of God. He was called to the principal cities of Spain, and everywhere inculcated fervour and fostered vocations. Let it suffice to mention that of Francis Borgia, which he, more than anyone else, was the means of strengthening. Faber, at forty, was wasted by his incessant labours and his unceasing journeys always made on foot. The pope, however, thought of sending him to the Council of Trent as theologian of the Holy See; John III wanted him to be made Patriarch of Æthopia. Called to Rome, Faber, weakened by fever, arrived there 17 July, 1546, to die in the arms of St. Ignatius, the first of the following August. Those who had known him already invoked him as a saint. Saint Francis de Sales, whose character recalled that of Faber's, never spoke of him except as a saint. He was beatified, 5 September, 1872; his feast is kept on 8 August.

Memoriale B. Petri Fabri, ed. BOUIX (Paris, 1873); *Cartas y otros escritos del B. Pedro Fabro* (Bilbao).

PIERRE SUAU.

Peter Fourier, SAINT, known as LE BON PÈRE DE MATTAINCOURT, b. at Mirecourt, Lorraine, 30 Nov., 1565; d. at Gray, Haute-Saône, 9 Dec., 1640. At fifteen he was sent to the University of Pont-à-Mousson. His piety and learning led many noble families to ask him to educate their sons. He became a Canon Regular in the Abbey of Chaumousey and was ordained in 1589. By order of his abbot he returned to the university and became proficient in patristic theology; he knew the "Summa" of St. Thomas by heart. In 1597 he was made parish priest of Mattaincourt, a corrupt district threatened with the new heresy. By his prayers, instructions, and good example, religion was soon restored. Fourier did not neglect the temporal interests of his parishioners; to help those who through ill-fortune had fallen into poverty, he established a kind of mutual help bank. He instituted three sodalities, of St. Sebastian for men, of the Holy Rosary for women, and of the Immaculate Conception for girls, or "Children of Mary". He composed some dialogues which treated of the virtues opposed to the vices most common among his people. These dialogues the children delivered every Sunday in pub-

ST. PETER FOURIER

lic. To perpetuate his work, Peter founded in 1598 an order of women, the Congregation of Notre-Dame, who teach poor girls gratuitously. The institute spread and with some modifications was introduced into America by the Ven. Marguerite Bourgeoys (d. 1700).

In 1621, by order of the Bishop of Toul, Fourier undertook the reform of the canons regular in Lorraine who in 1629 formed the Congregation of Our Saviour. Of this congregation he was made superior general in 1632. He wished his brother canons to do for boys what his nuns were doing for girls. In 1625 Peter was entrusted with the conversion of the Principality of Salm, near Nancy, which had gone over to Calvinism. In six months all the Protestants, whom he called "poor strangers", had returned to the Faith. On account of his attachment to the House of Lorraine he was driven into exile at Gray, where he died. In 1730 Benedict XIII published the Decree of his Beatification, and Leo XIII canonized him in 1897.

BEDEL, *La vie du Très Révérend Père Pierre Fourier, dit vulgairement, Le Père de Mettaincourt* (1645); CHAPIA, *Idea boni parochi et perfecti religiosi*; VUILLIMIN, *La Vie de St. Pierre Fourier* (Paris, 1897).

A. ALLARIA.

Peter Fullo, intruding Monophysite Patriarch of Antioch; d. 488. He received the Greek surname Γναφεύς (Latin, *Fullo*) from his trade of fuller of cloth, which he practised when a monk at the monastery of the Accœmeti in the Diocese of Chalcedon. Expelled from his monastery on account of his dissolute life and his heretical doctrines, he went to Constantinople where the future Emperor Zeno obtained for him the position of presbyter at the church of St. Bassa in Chalcedon. Driven thence by the populace, he accompanied Zeno to Antioch, incited the people against their patriarch, Martyrius, and, upon the latter's resignation, usurped the see in 470. He gained the favour of the Monophysites by adding to the Trisagion the words ὁ σταυρωθεὶς δι' ἡμᾶς (who wast crucified for us) in the monophysite sense that the Father and the Holy Ghost were crucified with the Son. In 471 he was deposed by the Emperor, but he again usurped the see in 476 to be deposed a second time and banished in 478. The usurping Emperor Basilicus reinstated him in 485 and he held the see until his death. (See MONOPHYSITES AND MONOPHYSITISM.)

VALESIUS (VALOIS), *De Petro Antiocheno episcopo qui Fullo cognominatus est de synodis adversus eum collectis*, appendix to his ed. of EVAGRIUS, *Hist. eccl.* (Paris, 1673), reprinted in *P. G.*, LXXXVI, 2885-95; TILLEMONT, *Hist. des empereurs*, VI, 404-7; THEODORUS LECTOR, *Hist. eccl.*, I, xx-xxii; THEOPHANES, *Chronographia*, ad ann. 456, 467, 469, 482; LIBERATUS, *Breviarium*, xviii; xviii; LE QUIEN, *Oriens christ.*, II (Paris, 1740), 724-5.

MICHAEL OTT.

Peter Gonzalez, SAINT, popularly known as ST. ELMO, b. in 1190 at Astorga, Spain; d. 15 April, 1246, at Tuy. He was educated by his uncle, Bishop of Astorga, who gave him when very young a canonry. Later he entered the Dominican Order and became a renowned preacher; crowds gathered to hear him and numberless conversions were the result of his efforts. He accompanied Ferdinand III of Leon on his expeditions against the Moors, but his ambition was to preach to the poor. He devoted the remainder of his life to the instruction and conversion of the ignorant and of the mariners in Galicia and along the coast of Spain. He lies buried in the cathedral of Tuy and was beatified in 1254 by Innocent IV. St. Elmo's fire is a pale electrical discharge sometimes seen on stormy nights on the tips of spires, about the decks and rigging of ships, in the shape of a ball or brush, singly or in pairs, particularly at the mastheads and yardarms. The mariners believed them to be the souls of the departed, whence they are also called corposant (*corpo santo*). The ancients called them Helena fire when seen singly, and Castor and Pollux when in pairs.

BUTLER, *Lives of the Saints*; HARRIS, *The Dioscuri in Christian Legends* (London, 1903); DRESSEL, *Lehrbuch der Physik* (Freiburg, 1895).

FRANCIS MERSHMAN.

Peter Igneus (PETER ALDOBRANDINI), BLESSED, an Italian monk of the Benedictine congregation of the Vallombrosians, and Cardinal-Bishop of Albano; d. c. 1089. The struggle waged against simony in the eleventh century led to violent scenes in several Italian cities. At Florence Bishop Peter Mezzobarbo, known also as Peter of Pavia, was publicly accused of simoniacal acquisition of the episcopal dignity. As he strenuously denied the charge and had numerous and prominent supporters, the controversy caused intense agitation at Florence. The Vallombrosian monks were his chief accusers, and upon the insistence of the people for proof, the judgment of God, or trial by fire, was resorted to. The Abbot St. John Gualbert designated for the test Peter Aldobrandini, who successfully underwent the ordeal (1068), hence called "Igneus", or Fire-tried. This triumph of the monks was followed by confession on the part of the bishop. Peter Igneus subsequently became abbot, and in 1074 Cardinal-Bishop of Albano. During the pontificate of Gregory VII he was entrusted with important missions. In 1079 he proceeded to Germany as papal legate with the Bishop of Padua to mediate between the rivals Henry IV and Rudolf of Suabia. Upon the renewal of the excommunication against Henry IV at Salerno in 1084, Gregory VII designated him as one of the two envoys sent to France for the promulgation of the sentence.

Acta SS., July, III (Paris, 1867), 340-44; MANN, *Lives of the Popes*, VI (St. Louis, 1910), 302.

N. A. WEBER.

Peter Lombard, theologian, b. at Novara (or perhaps Lumello), Italy, about 1100; d. about 1160-64. He studied first at Bologna, later on at Reims and Paris. St. Bernard, who had provided for his wants at Reims, gave him a letter of recommendation to the Abbot of St. Victor, Gilduin (1114-55). To judge from this letter, his stay at Paris was to be short: "per breve tempus usque ad Nativitatem Virginis". There is no evidence of his having gone back to Italy. We learn from John of Cornwall, his pupil, that he assiduously studied the works of Abelard, whose lectures he had probably followed about 1136. His own writings show the influence of his master. In 1148, he was at Reims in company with Robert of Melun, both being called "magistri scholares" by Otto of Freisingen; and he joined Adam du Petit-Pont, Hughes of Amicus, and others, in theological discussions with Gilbert de la Porrée. About the same time (1145-51) he wrote his "Book of Sentences". He was then professor at the school of Notre Dame.

He was acquainted before this date with the works of Gratian the canonist, for he utilizes the "Decretum" in his "Sentences". About the same time he had in his hands the newly-finished translation of St. John Damascene by Burgundio of Pisa; all these details show the care he had to enlarge the circle of his knowledge. In 1152 Eugene III had a prebendaryship conferred on him by the Archbishop of Beauvais (Jaffé-Wattenbach, 9534). In 1158 or 1159 he was appointed Archbishop of Paris; but held the office for a short time only, being succeeded by Maurice de Sully, the builder of the present Cathedral of Notre Dame, in 1160 or 1161. He died some time after, but the exact date is unknown; it could not have been later than 1164; in the years that follow we sometimes meet his name in the cartulary of Notre Dame of Paris: the house he lived in is put up for sale; his original copy of the "Sentences" is bequeathed by Stephen Langton, Archbishop of Canterbury, to the library of Notre Dame. The old legend that makes him the brother of Gratian of Bologna and of Peter Comestor has no foundation whatever.

The works of Peter Lombard include: (1) "Commentaries on the Psalms and St. Paul" which have come down to us in quite a number of manuscripts. They are chiefly a compilation of patristic and medieval exegesis, after the manner of the professors of the age and of the old "Catenæ"; (2) "Sermons", which are also found in quite a number of manuscripts; they are rather dry, often allegorical, and always very methodical in their divisions; several of them are printed among the works of Hildebert du Mans and others; extracts of others have been published by Protois (cf. infra); (3) The "Sentences" ("Quatuor libri Sententiarum"). It is this theological work above all that made the name of Peter Lombard famous, and gives him a special place in the history of theology in the Middle Ages. Henceforth he is called the "Magister Sententiarum", or simply the "Magister". The work is divided into four books. In a long series of questions it covers the whole body of theological doctrine and unites it in a systematized whole. Towards the thirteenth century, the various books were divided into *distinctiones* (an old Latin word that first meant a pause in reading, then a division into chapters), though the author had done nothing more than to have the questions follow one another; in the manuscripts, these questions do not always bear the same title.

The first book treats of God and the Blessed Trinity, of God's attributes, of Providence, of predestination, and of evil; the second, of the creation, the work of the six days, the angels, the demons, the fall, grace, and sin; the third, of the Incarnation, the Redemption, the virtues, and the Ten Commandments; the fourth, of the sacraments in general, the seven sacraments in particular, and the four last things, death, judgment, hell, and heaven. The "Book of Sentences" was written about 1150. In any case it was subsequent to the composition of the "Decretum" of Gratian of Bologna, which dates from about 1140 and contains pages that bear a striking likeness to the "Sentences". A careful examination of the texts cited in each author, in the same order, with the same inaccuracies or the same changes, Peter Lombard's citation of some "Dicta Gratiani", and his opposition to some of Gratian's opinions (e. g. on the question of the essence of marriage)—all these facts prove the priority of the "Decretum" to the "Sentences"; the old view of the canonist Schulte has been abandoned for that of P. Fournier, who has demonstrated Peter's dependence on Gratian. A manuscript of the "Sentences" written in 1158 still exists, but there is every reason to believe that the work was finished some eight years earlier.

On the other hand, Gandulph of Bologna, who has been credited with having inspired Peter, is later than the Lombard; he utilized, transcribed, or synopsized parts of the work of the "Magister Sententiarum". The method and purpose of the book found their explanation in the intellectual movement of the times: arguments from authority laying down the doctrine, and dialectics which reasons about dogma or conciliates the "Auctoritates" (as Abelard advised), are the most striking features in its composition. This work may be looked upon as the result of the two tendencies of the period: the one indulging, sometimes too much, in speculation, the other recurring to authority. It must be confessed that Peter Lombard tried to steer a middle course between these opposing tendencies. From Abelard, whose work had hardly lost its fascination in spite of the condemnations of Soissons and Sens, he borrows freely; but he is on guard against Abelard's errors. He has no desire to make Christian doctrine a matter for controversy after the manner of the "garruli ratiocinatores" against whom he has to defend himself. But he has no hesitation in exposing in a reasoned way the different points of doctrine: it is but the method followed with still greater success and depth by St. Thomas. He makes full use of the Bible and the Fathers, but he never goes to the point of refusing reason its due rôle. It is here that the works of the School of St. Victor are especially serviceable to him: he borrows considerably from Hugo's "De Sacramentis", as well as from the "Summa Sententiarum", which, though not written by Hugo, is very much indebted to him. In addition to the foregoing, mention must be made of Abelard, Gratian, Ivo of Chartres, and Alger of Liège as the chief sources of the "Liber Sententiarum".

Among the Fathers of the Church Augustine is quoted about ten or fifteen times as often as Ambrose, Jerome, or Hilary; the Greek Fathers, with the exception of John Damascene, who is quoted about twenty-five times, are scarcely represented; the ante-Nicene writers, except Origen, are mentioned on no more than five or six occasions; nevertheless, one may say that the "Sentences", with Gratian's work, are the chief sources whence many theologians of the Middle Ages drew their knowledge of the Fathers. Peter's work is mainly a compilation. Whole "distinctions" have been traced in detail to their sources; scarcely more than ten lines have been found to be original. He makes no secret of this; his plan was to write a kind of *Corpus* which would save the trouble of looking up many different volumes. But this fact cannot blind us to the merits of his work; he opposed the excesses of the dialecticians and at the same time found a *via media* to calm the fears of those who advocated a complete separation of reason and dogma. He arranged traditional doctrines and theories in a system and summarized the controversies of the time and the opinions involved in the different questions. Besides, his attempted solutions of many questions roused the students' curiosity and led the professors to comment on him. On the whole and in spite of his connexion with Abelard, he is orthodox; a proposition of his on "Christological nihilism" was condemned by Alexander III; other theses were abandoned in the century that followed; St. Bonaventure mentions eight of them and the University of Paris later added others. But the success of the book was incontestable; down to the sixteenth century it was the textbook in the university courses, upon which each future doctor had to lecture during two years.

The want of originality and the refusal of the "Magister" to decide upon many points between two solutions were very favourable to the work of the masters who commented upon him. But the success of Peter Lombard was not immediate. Attacked sometimes during his lifetime, as Maurice of Sully among others relates, after his death he was bitterly inveighed against, especially by Gautier of St. Victor and by Joachim of Flora. This opposition even went so far as to try to get his writings condemned. In 1215 at the Lateran Council these attempts were baffled, and the second canon began a profession of faith in these words: "Credimus cum Petro [Lombardo]". The exegetical work and the "Sentences" of Peter Lombard have often been printed: the commentaries upon the Epistles of St. Paul in 1474, etc.; the "Sentences" were printed in 1472 and for the last time in 1892 (Paris). Migne contains these three works (P. L., CXCI, CXCII). The best edition of the "Sentences" is that which is found in the commentary of St. Bonaventure (Opera S. Bonaventuræ, Quaracchi, 1885, I–IV).

Hist. litt. de la France, XII; PROTOIS, *Pierre Lombard* (Paris, 1880); BALTZER, *Die Sentenzen des Petrus Lombardus* (Leipzig, 1902); ESPENBERGER, *Die Philosophie des Petrus Lombardus* (Münster, 1901); DE GHELLINCK, *The Book of Sentences* in *Dublin Review* (1910); *Mediæval Theology* in *American Catholic Quarterly Review* (1908); *Revue des Questions historiques* (July, 1910); *Revue Néo-scolastique* (1909).

J. DE GHELLINCK.

Peter-Louis-Marie Chanel, BLESSED, b. at Cuet, Diocese of Belley, France, 1802; d. at Futuna, 28 April, 1841. He was ordained priest in 1827, and engaged in the parochial ministry for a few years; but the reading of letters of missionaries in far-away lands inflamed his heart with zeal, and he resolved to devote his life to the Apostolate. In 1831 he joined the Society of Mary, and in 1836 he embarked for Oceania.

He was assigned by his bishop to the Island of Futuna, and landed in Nov., 1837. No Christian missionary had ever set foot there, and the difficulties Peter encountered amidst those savage tribes were almost incredible. Nevertheless, he was beginning to see the results of his efforts, when Niuluki, king and also pontiff of the island, already jealous of the progress of the new religion, was exasperated by the conversion of his son and daughter. At his instigation, one of the ministers gathered some of the enemies of Christianity and Peter was cruelly assassinated without uttering a word of complaint. Through his death, the venerable martyr obtained what he had so ardently desired and earnestly worked for, the conversion of Futuna. In 1842, two Marist missionaries resumed his work, and nowhere has the preaching of the Gospel produced more wonderful results. Peter was declared Venerable by Pius IX in 1857, and beatified by Leo XIII on 17 November, 1889.

BOURDIN, *Vie du Vén. Serviteur de Dieu Pierre-Marie-Louis Chanel* (Lyons, 1867); NICOLET, *Life of Blessed P. M. L. Chanel* (Dublin, 1890); *Quelques guérisons et grâces signalées obtenues par l'intercession du Bienheureux P. M. L. Chanel* (Lyons, 1891); HERVIER, *Les Missions Maristes en Océanie* (Paris, 1902); *Life of the Ven. Fr. Colin, Founder and First Superior General of the Society of Mary* (St. Louis, 1909). JOSEPH FRERI.

Peter Mongus (μογγός, "stammerer", or "hoarse"), intruded Monophysite patriarch of Alexandria (d. 490). Under Timothy Ailuros, who was made patriarch by the Egyptian Monophysites after Chalcedon (454–460), Peter Mongus was an ardent adherent of that party. As Timothy's deacon he took part in the persecution of the Melchites. Timothy Ailuros was expelled from the patriarchal throne in 460 and the orthodox Timothy Salophakiolos was set up by the government instead (460–75). In 475 another revolution recalled Ailuros, who held his place till death (477). His party thereupon elected Peter Mongus to succeed him. The Emperor Zeno (474–91) sentenced Mongus to death; he escaped by flight. Meanwhile Salophakiolos returned and reigned till his death (481). The Melchites chose John Talaia to succeed (481–82: see JOHN TALAIA). Peter Mongus, always claiming to be patriarch, now comes forward again. John had quarrelled with Acacius, patriarch of Constantinople, and refused to sign Zeno's Henoticon (482; see HENOTICON); so he was expelled, the emperor changed his attitude, and supported Mongus (482). Talaia fled to Rome, Mongus took possession of the see, and sent notice of his succession to Rome, Antioch, and Constantinople. He had signed the Henoticon and was therefore inserted in Acacius's diptychs as Patriarch of Alexandria. But the pope (Felix II or III, 483–92) defended Talaia's rights in two letters to Acacius.

From this time Mongus became the chief champion of all Monophysites. He held a synod to condemn Chalcedon, and desecrated the tombs of Proterios and Salophakiolos, his Melchite predecessors. He was excommunicated repeatedly by the pope. It was communion with Mongus and the acceptance of the Henotikon that caused the Acacian schism of Constantinople (484–519). When Acacius died and was succeeded by Flavitas (or Fravitas, 489–90) Mongus wrote to the new patriarch again condemning Chalcedon and encouraging him in his schism with Rome. He died in 490 and was succeeded by another Monophysite, Athanasius II (490–96). For a long time after his death the name of Peter Mongus was still a party word. To read it in the diptychs (of the dead) was a kind of profession of Monophysitism; the first condition of reunion with Rome and the Catholic world generally was to erase it, with that of Dioscurus and the other great champions of the heresy. In the line of Alexandrine patriarchs Mongus is counted as Peter III. He is said to have written many books, of which however nothing remains. A pretended correspondence between him and Acacius (in Coptic) is proved to be spurious by Amélineau in the "Mémoires publiés par les membres de la mission archéologique française au Caire", IV (Paris, 1888), 196–228.

Mongus takes an important place in any history of Monophysitism, as EVAGRIUS, *Chronicon Paschale* in P. G., XCII; LIBERATUS. See also GUTSCHMID, *Verzeichniss der Patriarchen von Alexandrien* in *Kleine Schriften*, II (Leipzig, 1890), 395–525; HEFELE-LECLERCQ, *Histoire des Conciles*, II (Paris, 1908), 916–26; NEALE, *History of the Holy Eastern Church*, II (London, 1847), 21–24. ADRIAN FORTESCUE.

Peter Nolasco, SAINT, b. at Mas-des-Saintes-Puelles, near Castelnaudary, France, in 1189 (or 1182); d. at Barcelona, on Christmas Day, 1256 (or 1259). He was of a noble family and from his youth was noted for his piety, almsgiving, and charity. Having given all his possessions to the poor, he took a vow of virginity and, to avoid communication with the Albigenses, went to Barcelona.

At that time the Moors were masters of a great part of the Iberian peninsula, and many Christians were detained there and cruelly persecuted on account of the Faith. Peter ransomed many of these and in doing so consumed all his patrimony. After mature deliberation, moved also by a heavenly vision, he

ST. PETER NOLASCO AND ST. RAYMOND OF PEÑAFORT
Francisco Zurbaran, Louvre

resolved to found a religious order (1218), similar to that established a few years before by St. John de Matha and St. Felix de Valois, whose chief object would be the redemption of Christian slaves. In this he was encouraged by St. Raymond Peñafort and James I, King of Aragon, who, it seems, had been favoured with the same inspiration. The institute was called Mercedarians (q. v.) and was solemnly approved by Gregory IX, in 1230. Its members were bound by a special vow to employ all their substance for the redemption of captive Christians, and if necessary, to remain in captivity in their stead. At first most of these religious were laymen as was Peter himself. But Clement V decreed that the master general of the order should always be a priest. His feast is celebrated on the thirty-first of January.

Acta SS.; DE VARGAS, *Chronica sancti et militaris ordinis B. M. de Mercede* (Palermo, 1619); GARI Y SIUMELL, *Bibliotheca Mercedaria* (Barcelona, 1875); MARIN, *Histoire de l'église* (Paris, 1909). A. ALLARIA.

Peter of Alcántara, SAINT, b. at Alcántara, Spain, 1499; d. 18 Oct., 1562. His father, Peter Garavita, was the governor of the place, and his mother was of the noble family of Sanabia. After a course of grammar and philosophy in his native town, he was sent, at the age of fourteen, to the University of Salamanca. Returning home, he became a Franciscan in the convent of the Stricter Observance at Manxarretes in 1515. At the age of twenty-two he was sent to found a new community of the Stricter Observance at Badajoz. He was ordained priest in 1524, and the following year made guardian of the convent of St. Mary of the Angels at Robredillo. A few years later he began preaching with much success. He preferred to preach to the poor; and his sermons, taken largely from the Prophets and Sapiential Books, breathe the tenderest human sympathy. The reform of the "Discalced Friars" had, at the time when Peter entered the order, besides the convents in Spain, the Custody of Sta. Maria Pietatis in Portugal, subject to the General of the Observants.

Having been elected minister of St. Gabriel's province in 1538, Peter set to work at once. At the chap-

ST. PETER OF ALCÁNTARA
Claudio Coello, Pinakothek, Munich

ter of Plasencia in 1540 he drew up the Constitutions of the Stricter Observants, but his severe ideas met with such opposition that he renounced the office of provincial and retired with Father John of Avila into the mountains of Arabida, Portugal, where he joined Father Martin a Santa Maria in his life of eremitical solitude. Soon, however, other friars came to join him, and several little communities were established, Peter being chosen guardian and master of novices at the convent of Pallais. In 1560 these communities were erected into the Province of Arabida. Returning to Spain in 1553 he spent two more years in solitude, and then journeyed barefoot to Rome, and obtained permission of Julius III to found some poor convents in Spain under the jurisdiction of the general of the Conventuals. Convents were established at Pedrosa, Plasencia, and elsewhere; in 1556 they were made a commissariat, with Peter as superior, and in 1561, a province under the title of St. Joseph. Not discouraged by the opposition and ill-success his efforts at reform had met with in St. Gabriel's province, Peter drew up the constitutions of the new province with even greater severity. The reform spread rapidly into other provinces of Spain and Portugal.

In 1562 the province of St. Joseph was put under the jurisdiction of the general of the Observants, and two new custodies were formed: St. John Baptist's in Valencia, and St. Simon's in Galicia (see FRIARS MINOR). Besides the above-named associates of Peter may be mentioned St. Francis Borgia, Blessed John of Avila, and St. Louis of Granada. In St. Teresa, Peter perceived a soul chosen of God for a great work, and her success in the reform of Carmel was in great measure due to his counsel, encouragement, and defence. (See CARMELITES.) It was a letter from St. Peter (14 April, 1562) that encouraged her to found her first monastery at Avila, 24 Aug. of that year. St. Teresa's autobiography is the source of much of our information regarding Peter's life, work, and gifts of miracles and prophecy.

Perhaps the most remarkable of Peter's graces were his gift of contemplation and the virtue of penance. Hardly less remarkable was his love of God, which was at times so ardent as to cause him, as it did St. Philip Neri, sensible pain, and frequently rapt him into ecstasy. The poverty he practised and enforced was as cheerful as it was real, and often let the want of even the necessaries of life be felt. In confirmation of his virtues and mission of reformation God worked numerous miracles through his intercession and by his very presence. He was beatified by Gregory XV in 1622, and canonized by Clement IX in 1669. Besides the Constitutions of the Stricter Observants and many letters on spiritual subjects, especially to St. Teresa, he composed a short treatise on prayer, which has been translated into all the languages of Europe. His feast is 19 Oct. (See PASCAL BAYLON, SAINT; PETER BAPTIST, SAINT; JAPANESE MARTYRS.)

Lives by JOHN OF SANTA MARIA, *Min. Obs. Ale. Chron. Prov. S. Jos.*, l, I; and MARCHESIO (Rome, 1667); PAULO, *Vita S. Petri Alc.* (Rome, 1669); WADDING, *Annales, an. 1662;* LEO, *Lives of the Saints and Blessed of the Three Orders of St. Francis,* IV (Taunton, 1888); *Acta SS.*, Oct., VIII, 636 sq.

NICHOLAS REAGAN.

Peter of Alexandria, SAINT, became Bishop of Alexandria in 300; martyred Nov., 311. According to Philip of Sidetes he was at one time head of the famous catechetical school at Alexandria. His theological importance lies in the fact that he marked, very probably initiated, the reaction at Alexandria against extreme Origenism.

When during the Diocletian persecution Peter left Alexandria for concealment, the Meletian schism broke out. There are three different accounts of this schism: (1) According to three Latin documents (translations from lost Greek originals) published by Maffei, Meletius (or Melitius), Bishop of Lycopolis, took advantage of St. Peter's absence to usurp his patriarchal functions, and contravened the canons by consecrating bishops to sees not vacant, their occupants being in prison for the Faith. Four of them remonstrated, but Meletius took no heed of them and actually went to Alexandria, where, at the instigation of one Isidore, and Arius the future heresiarch, he set aside those left in charge by Peter and appointed others. Upon this Peter excommunicated him. (2) St. Athanasius accuses Meletius not only of turbulent and schismatical conduct, but of sacrificing, and denouncing Peter to the emperor. There is no incompatibility between the Latin documents and St. Athanasius, but the statement that Meletius sacrificed must be received with caution; it was probably based upon rumour arising out of the immunity which he appeared to enjoy. At all events nothing was heard about the charge at the Council of Nicæa. (3) According to St. Epiphanius (Haer., 68), Meletius and St. Peter quarrelled over the reconciliation of the *lapsi* (q. v.), the former inclining to sterner views. Epiphanius probably derived his information from a Meletian source, and his story is full of historical blunders. Thus, to take one example, Peter is made a fellow-prisoner of Meletius and is martyred in prison. According to Eusebius his martyrdom was unexpected, and therefore not preceded by a term of imprisonment.

There are extant a collection of fourteen canons issued by Peter in the third year of the persecution dealing chiefly with the *lapsi*, excerpted probably from an Easter Festal Epistle. The fact that they were ratified by the Council of Trullo, and thus became part of the canon law of the Eastern Church, probably accounts for their preservation. Many MSS. contain a fifteenth canon taken from writing on the Passover. The cases of different kinds of lapsi were decided upon in these canons.

The Acts of the martyrdom of St. Peter are too late to have any historical value. In them is the story of Christ appearing to St. Peter with His garment rent, foretelling the Arian schism. Three passages from "On the Godhead", apparently written against Origen's subordinationist views, were quoted by St. Cyril at the Council of Ephesus. Two further passages (in Syriac) claiming to be from the same book, were printed by Pitra in "Analecta Sacra", IV, 188; their genuineness is doubtful. Leontius of Byzantium quotes a passage affirming the two Natures of Christ from a work on "The Coming of Christ", and two passages from the first book of a treatise against the view that the soul had existed and sinned before it was united to the body. This treatise must have been written against Origen. Very important are seven fragments preserved in Syriac (Pitra, op. cit., IV, 189-93) from another work on the Resurrection, in which the identity of the risen with the earthly body is maintained against Origen.

Five Armenian fragments were also published by Pitra (op. cit., IV, 430 sq.). Two of these correspond with one of the doubtful Syriac fragments. The remaining three are probably Monophysite forgeries (Harnack, "Altchrist. Lit.", 447). A fragment quoted by the Emperor Justinian in his Letter to the Patriarch Mennas, purporting to be taken from a Mystagogia of St. Peter's, is probably spurious (see Routh, "Reliq. Sac.", III, 372; Harnack, op. cit., 448). The "Chronicon Paschale" gives a long extract from a supposed writing of Peter on the Passover. This is condemned as spurious by a reference to St. Athanasius (which editors often suppress) unless, indeed, the reference is an interpolation. A fragment first printed by Routh from a Treatise "On Blasphemy" is generally regarded as spurious. A Coptic fragment on the keeping of Sunday, published by Schmidt (Texte und Untersuchung., IV) has been ruled spurious by Delehaye, in whose verdict critics seem to acquiesce. Other Coptic fragments have been edited with a translation by Crum in the "Journal of Theological Studies" (IV, 287 sqq.). Most of these come from the same manuscript as the fragment edited by Schmidt. Their editor says: "It would be difficult to maintain the genuineness of these texts after Delehaye's criticisms (Anal. Bolland., XX, 101), though certain of the passages which I have published may indicate interpolated, rather than wholly apocryphal compositions."

ROUTH, *Reliq. Sac.*, III, 319-72, gives most of the passages attributed to St. Peter. A translation of many of these, as well as of the martyrdom, will be found in CLARKE, *Ante-Nicene Christ. Library*, in vol. containing works of METHODIUS. For the Meletian schism: HEFELE, *Hist. of Councils*, tr. I, 341 sq. The best editions of the Canons is LAGARDE, *Reliq. Juris Eccles.*, 63-73. The latest edition of the martyrdom is VITEAU, *Passions des saints Ecaterine et Pierre d'Alexandrie, Barbara et Anysia* (Paris, 1897). See HARNACK, *Altchrist. Lit.*, 443-49; and *Chronologie*, 71-75. BARDENHEWER, *Gesch. d. altkirch. Lit.*, II, 203 sq. RADFORD, *Three Teachers of Alexandria: Theognostus, Pierius and Peter* (Cambridge, 1908).

F. J. BACCHUS.

Peter of Aquila (SCOTELLUS), Friar Minor, theologian and bishop, b. at Aquila in the Abruzzi, Italy, towards the end of the thirteenth century; d. at Trivento, 1361. In 1334 he figures as master of theology and provincial of his order in Tuscany. In 1334 he was appointed confessor of Queen Joan I of Naples and shortly afterwards inquisitor of Florence. His servants having been punished by public authority, the inquisitor excommunicated the priors and placed the town under interdict. On 12 February, 1347, Peter was named Bishop of S. Angelo de Lombardi in Calabria, and on 30 May, 1348, was transferred to Trivento. He was an able interpreter of Scotus, and was called "Doctor sufficiens". His chief works are commentaries on the four books of Sentences, which being a compendium of the doctrine of Scotus were called "Scotellum", whence the author's surname "Scotellus". The commentaries have passed through various editions, the first by Peter Drach, at Speier, 1480, and recently by Paolini (Genoa, 1907-09).

EUBEL, *Bullarium Franciscanum*, VI (Rome, 1902), 192, 214; *Analecta Franciscana*, IV (Quaracchi, 1906), 339, 530; WADDING, *Annales Minorum*, ad a. 1343, n. 35; ad a. 1346, nn, 4, 5; IDEM, *Scriptores Ord. Min.* (Rome, 1806), 187; SBARALEA, *Supplem. ad Script. Ord. Min.* (Rome, 1806), 583; MAZZUCHELLI, *Gli scrittori d'Italia*, II (Brescia, 1753), 902-3; CAPPELLETTI, *Le chiese d'Italia*, XX (Venice, 1866), 551.

LIVARIUS OLIGER.

Peter of Arbues (correctly, PETER ARBUES), SAINT, b. in 1441 (or 1442); d. 17 Sept., 1485. His father, a nobleman, was Antonio Arbues, and his mother's name was Sancia Ruiz. He studied philosophy, probably at Huesca, but later went to Bologna, where in the Spanish college of St. Clement he was regarded as a model of learning and piety, and was graduated in theology and law. Returning to Spain he became a canon regular at Saragossa, where he made his religious profession in 1474. About that time Ferdinand and Isabella had obtained from Sixtus IV a Bull to establish in their kingdom a tribunal for searching out heretics, and especially Jews who after having received baptism had relapsed openly or secretly into Judaism; these were known as Marranos. The famous Thomas Torquemada, in 1483, was appointed grand inquisitor over Castile and, being acquainted with the learning and virtue of Peter Arbues, named him inquisitor provincial in the Kingdom of Aragon (1484). Peter performed the duties with zeal and justice. Although the enemies of the Inquisition accuse him of cruelty, it is certain that not a single sentence of death can be traced to him (see INQUISITION). The Marranos, however, whom he had punished hated and resolved to do away with him. One night while kneeling in prayer before the altar of Our Lady in the metropolitan church, where he used to recite the office with his brother canons, they attacked him, and hired assassins inflicted several wounds from which he died two days after. He was canonized by Pius IX, in 1867.

BOLLANDISTS, *Proprium Festorum Hispanorum;* LUZZI, *Vita di S. Pietro de Arbues Canónico Regolare* (Rome, 1867).

A. ALLARIA.

Peter of Auvergne, philosopher and theologian; d. after 1310. He was a canon of Paris; some biographers have thought that he was Bishop of Clermont (Gallia Christ., II, 283), because a Bull of Boniface VIII of the year 1296 names as canon of Paris, Peter of Croc (Cros), already canon of Clermont (Thomas, in "Mélanges d'arch. et d'hist.", Paris, 1882, II, 117-20); but it is more likely that they are distinct. Peter of Auvergne was in Paris in 1301 (Script. Prædicat., I, 489), and, according to several accounts, was a pupil of St. Thomas. In 1279, while the various nations of the University of Paris were quarrelling about the rectorship, Simon of Brion, papal legate, appointed Peter of Auvergne to that office; in 1296 he was elected to it.

His published works are: "Supplementum Commentarii S. Thomæ in tertium et quartum librum de cælo et mundo" (in "Opera S. Thomæ", II, *ad finem*); commentaries on Aristotle's "Meteororum"; "De Juventute et senectute"; "De longitudine et brevitate vitæ"; "De motu animalium". He has been credited with a supplement to the "Summa" of St. Thomas, but there is no scientific warrant for this. Peter also left numerous treatises which are either at the Biblioth. Nationale, or at l'Arsenal of Paris: "Sex quodlibeta", long discussions after the manner of St. Thomas; "Sophisma Determinatum"; "Quæstiones super totam logicam veterem Arist."; "Quæstiones

ST. PETER MARTYR ENJOINING SILENCE
FRA ANGELICO, CONVENT OF SAN MARCO, FLORENCE

super Perphyrium"; "In Arist. Metaphysicam"; "In libros Politicorum"; "De somno et vigilia"; "De veget. et plantis"; "De anima".

WADDING, Script. Minor. (1690), 279; DU BOULAY, Hist. Univ. de Paris, III (Paris, 1666), 709; Hist. ant. eccl. XIV (Paris, 1701), 214; QUÉTIF-ECHARD, Script. Præd., I (Paris, 1719), 489; OUDIN, Comm. de script. eccl., III (Paris, 1722), 927; FABRICIUS, Bibl. med. æt., V (Paris, 1736), 711; LAJARD in Hist. litt. de France, XXV (Paris, 1869), 93, 114; DENIFLE, Cart. Univ. Paris, I (Paris, 1889), 930; II, 69, 90; FÉRET, La Faculté de théologie de Paris, III (Paris, 1896), 221–7.
JOSEPH DEDIEU.

Peter of Bergamo (ALMADURA), theologian, date of birth unknown; d. at Placentia, in 1482. He entered the Dominican Order in his native town, and completed his studies at the University of Bologna, where he received his degree. In the Dominican House of Studies he filled the offices of Master of Students and Bachelor of the Studium. The people of Piacenza venerated him as a saint, and Fr. Leander Alberti states that miracles were wrought through his intercession. His remains were deposited in a crypt under the high altar of the chapel of St. Thomas. All of his writings that have come down to us deal with the works of St. Thomas: "Index universalis in omnia opera D. Th. de Aquino" (Bologna, 1475) and "Concordantiæ locorum doct. Angel. quæ sibi invicem adversari videntur" (Basle, 1478), combined under the title, "Tabula in libros . . . cum additionibus conclusionum, concordantiis locorum et S. Script. auctoritatibus" (Venice, 1497; Rome, 1535). In the edition of St. Thomas's works published by order of St. Pius V all Almadura's indices, etc, appear under the name: "Tabula aurea exim. doct. Fr. Petri de Bergamo . . . in omnes libros, opuscula et commentaria D. Th. Aquin. . . ." (Rome, 1570). This "Tabula aurea" was republished as vol. XXV of the Parma edition of St. Thomas's works (Parma, 1873).

QUÉTIF and ECHARD, Script. Ord. Praed., 1 (Paris, 1719), 863; TOURON, Hist. des hommes illustres de l'Ordre de S. Dom., III (Paris, 1746), 529; ALBERTI, De viris illus. Ord. Præd. (Bologna, 1517); Descrittione di tutta Italia (Bologna, 1550).
D. J. KENEDY.

Peter of Bruys. See PETROBRUSIANS.

Peter of Ghent. See MEXICO.

Peter of Pisa, BLESSED. See HIERONYMITES.

Peter of Poitiers, French scholastic theologian, b. at Poitiers or in its neighbourhood about 1130; d. in Paris in 1215. He studied at the University of Paris, where he became professor of theology and lectured for thirty-eight years. In 1169 he succeeded Peter Comestor in the chair of scholastic theology. His lectures were so brilliant as to inspire the enmity of Gauthier de St-Victor, one of the bitterest opponents of Scholasticism, who ranked him with Gilbert de la Porrée, Abelard, and Peter Lombard in the pamphlet wherein he tries to throw ridicule on the four doctors, under the name of the "Four Labyrinths of France". In 1179 he published five books of sentences which are a synopsis of his lectures. His doctrine is orthodox, but, though containing no condemned proposition, it exhibits more vain subtility than real theology based on Holy Scripture. Those who accuse Scholasticism of being a mere logomachy can find arguments in the writings of Peter of Poitiers. He wrote commentaries, still unedited, on Exodus, Leviticus, Numbers, and the Psalms. A chronological and genealogical abridgment of the Bible is attributed to him, but the authorship is uncertain. As Chancellor of the Church of Paris he displayed great zeal on behalf of poor students, and to supply their want of text-books, which were very expensive, he had a kind of synopsis engraved on the walls of the classrooms for their assistance. In 1191 he was appointed by Celestine III to settle a dispute between the Abbeys of St-Eloi and St-Victor. He was a constant correspondent of Celestine III and Innocent III. Certain writers erroneously believe that he died Bishop of Embrun; the "Gallia Christiana Nova" shows that he was only Chancellor of Paris. His works were published by Dom Mathoud with those of Robert Pullus (Paris, 1855).

DU BOULAY, Hist. de l'université de Paris, II; Gallia Christiana, VII; Bibliothèque latine du moyen âge (Paris, 1759).
J. LATASTE.

Peter of Sebaste, SAINT, bishop, b. about 340; d. 391. He belonged to the richly blest family of Basil and Emmelia of Cæsarea in Cappadocia, from which also sprang St. Macrina the Younger (q. v.) and the two great Cappadocian doctors, Basil of Cæsarea and Gregory of Nyssa. He was the youngest of a large family, and Macrina, his eldest sister, exercised a great influence over his religious training, acting as his instructress in the way of Christian perfection, and directing him towards the spiritual and ascetic life. Renouncing the study of the profane sciences, he devoted himself to meditation on Holy Writ and the cultivation of the religious life. Shortly after his brother's elevation to the episcopal See of Cæsarea, Peter received from him priestly ordination, but subsequently, withdrawing from active affairs, resumed the life of a solitary ascetic. He assisted his sister towards the attainment of her life's object, and aided her and her mother in their monastic establishment after his father's death (Gregory of Nyssa, "Vita s. Macrinæ"). About 380–81 he was elevated to the See of Sebaste in Armenia and, without displaying any literary activity, took his stand beside his brothers Basil and Gregory in their fight against the Arian heresy (Theodoret, "H. E.", IV, xxvii). In his life and episcopal administration he displayed the same splendid characteristics as Basil. Linked together in the closest manner with his brothers, he followed their writings with the greatest interest. At his advice Gregory of Nyssa wrote his great work "Against Eunomius", in defence of Basil's similarly named book answering the polemical work of Eunomius. It was also at his desire that Gregory wrote the "Treatise on the Work of the Six Days", to defend Basil's similar treatise against false interpretations and to complete it. Another work of Gregory's, "On the Endowment of Man", was also written at Peter's suggestion, and sent to the latter with an appropriate preface as an Easter gift in 397. We have no detailed information concerning his activity as a bishop, except that he was present at the Œcumenical Council of Constantinople in 381. After his death in 391 he was venerated as a saint. His feast falls on 8–9 January.

Acta SS., I Jan., 588–590; BUTLER, Lives of the Saints, I, 9 Jan.; see bibliography under BASIL THE GREAT and GREGORY OF NYSSA.
J. P. KIRSCH.

Peter of Verona, SAINT, b. at Verona, 1206; d. near Milan, 6 April, 1252. His parents were adherents of the Manichæan heresy, which still survived in northern Italy in the thirteenth century. Sent to a Catholic school, and later to the University of Bologna, he there met St. Dominic, and entered the Order of the Friars Preachers. Such were his virtues, severity of life and doctrine, talent for preaching, and zeal for the Faith, that Gregory IX made him general inquisitor, and his superiors destined him to combat the Manichæan errors. In that capacity he evangelized nearly the whole of Italy, preaching in Rome, Florence, Bologna, Genoa, and Como. Crowds came to meet him and followed him wherever he went; and conversions were numerous. He never failed to denounce the vices and errors of Catholics who confessed the Faith by words, but in deeds denied it. The Manichæans did all they could to compel the inquisitor to cease from preaching against their errors and propaganda. Persecutions, calumnies, threats, nothing was left untried.

When returning from Como to Milan, he met a certain Carino who with some other Manichæans had plotted to murder him. The assassin struck him with an axe on the head with such violence, that the holy man fell half dead. Rising to his knees he recited the first article of the Symbol of the Apostles, and offering his blood as a sacrifice to God, he dipped his fingers in it and wrote on the ground the words: "Credo in Deum". The murderer then pierced his heart. The body was carried to Milan and laid in the church of St. Eustorgio, where a magnificent mausoleum, the work of Balduccio Pisano, was erected to his memory. He wrought many miracles when living, but they were even more numerous after his martyrdom, so that Innocent IV canonized him on 25 March, 1253.

MARCHESE, *Vita di S. Pietro Martire* (Fiesole, 1894); HINDS, *A Garner of Saints* (London, 1900); PERRENS, *St Pierre martyr et l'hérésie des Patarins à Florence* in *Rev. Histor.*, II (1876), 337–66; *Acta SS.* (1678), April, III, 678–86.

A. ALLARIA.

Peter's Chains, FEAST OF. See PETER, SAINT.

Peterspence, otherwise known to the Anglo-Saxons as "Romfeoh" or "Romescot", is the name traditionally given to an annual contribution or tribute (originally of a penny from each householder holding land of a certain value) paid to the exchequer of the Holy See by various peoples of Christendom. In the Middle Ages this form of contribution seems almost to have been confined to England and some few other northern nations, and it was unquestionably in England that it took its rise. Neglecting some vague and unreliable traditions which ascribed the origin of "Romescot" to Ini, King of Wessex, in 727, we are possibly on firmer ground if we identify the beginnings of this contribution with a sum of 365 mancuses yearly, promised by Offa of Mercia, and confirmed to the pope's legates at the Synod of Chelsea in 787. The promise is mentioned in an extant letter from Pope Leo III to Kenulf, Offa's successor (Haddan and Stubbs, "Councils", III, 445, 525; cf. ibid., 538). It is stated that the money was to be applied to the relief of the poor and to providing lights for the churches of Rome and, rather strangely, nothing is said of the support of the Anglo-Saxon School ("Schola Saxonum") in the Borgo, which Pope Alexander II and later chroniclers closely associated with the beginnings of Peterspence. Again it seems certain that Ethelwulf after his visit to Rome with his son Alfred (c. 855) ordered that three hundred mancuses were to be sent to the Holy See each year (Asser, ed. Stevenson, 15, 211). Whether this was a new grant, or a confirmation of the tribute of Offa, is not clear (cf. Liebermann, "Ueber die Leges Eadwardi", 55); neither is it certain whether this sum of 300 mancuses was to be provided out of the royal exchequer or collected in pennies from the people. We only know that not long afterwards, during the reign of Alfred, the Anglo-Saxon Chronicle speaks of the conveyance to Rome of "the donation of the Wessex folk and their king" (cf. Chron. Æthelwardi, A. D. 888), and that in the code known as the "Dooms of Edward and Guthrum", which no doubt represents the legislation of Alfred's reign, we find for the first time explicit mention of "Romfeoh" as a contribution paid by the people. Under Edmund (941–46), at a great council of the clergy and laity held in London at Easter time, "Romfeoh" was declared to be one of the dues which must be paid by every man under pain of excommunication, and a later ordinance under Edgar speaks of it as the "hearth-penny" and enjoins with threats of heavy penalties that it must be paid by St. Peter's Massday, i. e. "Lammas", the feast of St. Peter's Chains (1 August). That the tax was in fact collected and sent to Rome in coins of small value, archæological evidence has proved. In 1883 a hoard of 835 coins was discovered in Rome, apparently near the site of one of the old papal palaces. Almost all these pieces without exception were Anglo-Saxon silver pennies, 217 of them bearing the imprint of King Edward the Elder, and 393 that of Athelstan, none of them being later than the year 947.

There can be no doubt that this find represents an instalment of Peterspence sent to Rome just as it had been collected; and the conclusion is confirmed by some other archæological discoveries of earlier date. A remarkable letter of King Cnut, written from Rome in 1027 to his people in England, expresses in solemn terms his devotion to the Holy See and enjoins that Peterspence and some other ecclesiastical taxes should be paid before his return to England. "Cnut", says Dr. Jensen, "undoubtedly renewed and confirmed the donation from England to the papal court on the occasion of this pilgrimage to Rome." The manner of levying the tax is, however, imperfectly understood, for, as Liebermann has shown (Eng. Hist. Rev., 1896, p. 746), M. Fabre is mistaken in supposing that he has found the text of Cnut's agreement in the "Liber Censuum". In spite of Cnut's good will, considerable negligence about the payment of Peterspence continued under the later Anglo-Saxon kings. After the Norman Conquest, St. Gregory VII addressed a formal demand to King William in 1074. "Concerning the Peterspence to be collected in England", he wrote, "we charge you to watch over it as if it were your own revenue." After some delays the Conqueror wrote a conciliatory reply and, while refusing feudal homage to the papacy as not justified by any precedent, he formally recognized the claim to Peterspence and promised that the arrears should be made up. But though the contribution on the whole was paid, and though various efforts and accommodations were made by the popes and their representatives in England, it seems clear that the collection of Peterspence was at hardly any time carried out in a way that was satisfactory to the Holy See. Innocent III on 28 Jan., 1214, wrote indignantly to the English bishops that "certain prelates having collected these pence [*denarios*] in our name, have not been ashamed to retain the greater part for themselves. They paid us only 300 marks, usurping for their own use 1000 marks or more" (Potthast, "Regesta", no. 2635). This language, as Dr. Jensen forcibly urges, seems inconsistent with the idea of any formal composition assented to by the Holy See, in virtue of which the popes agreed to farm the whole proceeds of Peterspence for a payment of 300 marks. It seems, however, that this annual payment of a sum of 300 (or more strictly 299 marks) was the solution practically arrived at, and we even know the proportions in which this amount was levied upon the different dioceses of England.

Another point to be noted is that both before and after the surrender of the kingdom by King John, who made England the fief of the Holy See (see ENGLAND), a certain confusion seems sometimes to have existed between Peterspence and the feudal tribute, called in Latin *census*, which was paid as the price of the papal protection. The two, however, were really quite distinct. In 1317 Edward II acknowledged that the annual feudal tribute of 1000 marks had not been paid for twenty-four years, and his agents undertook solemn engagements to pay off the arrears by instalments. This promise was never fulfilled. Edward III paid this tribute for a time, but would not accept any responsibility for any outstanding debts. After 1343 no further payments were made, and in 1366 the tribute was formally repudiated, and abolished by Parliament. On the other hand the sum of 300 marks, which was annually due to the pope as Peterspence, can be shown to have been collected and sent at least intermittently down to Henry VIII's breach with Rome. It was abolished in 1534, and though temporarily revived under Mary, it was not found possible at that time to levy it throughout England.

In Sweden, Norway, and Iceland, countries whose religious traditions can be shown in a number of different ways to have been borrowed from England, it seems clear that a contribution of a penny from every household was made not unwillingly. Adrian IV, who before he was made pope had visited Scandinavia and regulated the payment of this tax, desired also, if we may accept the authenticity of the Bull, "Laudabiliter", to extend it to Ireland. In any case there had no doubt existed in Rome, from the time of Gregory VII and probably earlier, some vague tradition that this payment of a *denarius* per household had been sanctioned by Charlemagne. But in many parts of the world, as, for example, Portugal, the Two Sicilies, Poland, etc., it is not always easy to distinguish the Peterspence proper from the feudal tribute above referred to, which was the price of papal protection.

The payment of anything resembling Peterspence seems nowhere to have survived the Reformation. But at the time when Pius IX, driven from Rome by the Revolutionaries, took refuge at Gaeta, the Comte de Montalembert is said to have taken the lead in organizing a Catholic Committee in France, which, working in harmony with the bishops, was eventually successful in collecting a very substantial subsidy for the pope under the name of the "denier de Saint Pierre" (Daux, p. 46). Others assign the beginnings of the work to a voluntary contribution organized at Vienna in 1860 by the "Confraternity of St. Michael" which spread first to Ireland and then to the rest of the world. Certain it is that already in the sixties large amounts were being sent to Rome as Peterspence from France, Belgium, Germany, Ireland, and many other countries. Since the occupation of Rome by the Italian Government and the rejection by Pius IX of the Law of Guarantees, the sums paid as Peterspence have become one of the principal sources of income of the Holy See. Accurate statistics are wanting, but it was stated in 1866 that the total receipts under this one head amounted to about £360,000 ($1,800,000) annually. At one time after the occupation of Rome something near £800,000 ($4,000,000) is said to have been sent to Rome as Peterspence in one year; but these figures have very much fallen off of late owing to the persecution of the Church in France and the severe strain now made upon the resources of Catholics in that country. For the most part the contributions made under this head are sent to Rome through the bishops, but in the collection of funds the most important part of the work is done by various "Peterspence Associations", that of St. Michael and that of "Le Denier de Saint Pierre" being the best known. The members of these organizations pledge themselves to make some very small minimum contribution; they solicit the subscription of others; and they unite in certain exercises of piety, which are richly indulgenced.

JENSEN in the *Transactions of the Royal Historical Society*, New Series, XV (1901), 171–247; XIX (1905), 209–277; JENSEN, *Der englische Peterspfennig und die Lehnsteuer aus England und Irland* (Heidelberg, 1903); FABRE, *Le "Liber Censuum" de l'Eglise romaine* (Paris, 1892), FABRE in *Mélanges G. B. de Rossi* (Paris, 1892), 159 sq.; FABRE, *Der Peterspfennig als Einnahmequelle der eng. Krone* in *Zeitschrift f. Socialgesch.* (1896), 459 sq.; LIEBERMANN in *English Historical Review* (1896); DAUX, *Le Denier de Saint Pierre* (Paris, 1907); HERGENRÖTHER in *Kirchenlex.*, I, 77; LINGARD, *History of England*; IDEM, *Antiquities of the Anglo-Saxon Church*. HERBERT THURSTON.

Peterssen, GERLAC (GERLACUS PETRI), b. at Deventer, 1377 or 1378; d. 18 Nov., 1411. He entered the Institution of the Brethren of Common Life, and devoted his time to calligraphy, transcription of manuscripts, education, and prayer. He became connected with many illustrious contemplative men, e. g. John Ruysbroeck; Florent Radewyn; Henry Kalkar; Gerard of Zutphen; Thomas and John a Kempis, and John Vos of Huyden. When Radewyn founded a monastery of regular canons at Windejheim, in 1386, Gerlac followed him, and remained there till 1403 as a simple clerk; he had no other employment than that of a sexton. He has been called another Kempis, and several critics have ascribed to Kempis words or theories which belong to Gerlac. Gerlac left his brethren to come back to his cell, where, as he said, "somebody was waiting for him". It has been maintained that the "Imitation" reproduced several ideas and the general spirit of Gerlac's ascetic works. In fact, Thomas a Kempis inserted into the work, a copy of which he wrote in 1441, the passage of the "Soliloquies" where Gerlac says that he would feel no pain, if necessary for the greater glory of God, to be in hell for ever. This passage is an interpolation, which was soon deleted from the "Imitation". The difference between the ascetic theories of Gerlac and those of the author of the "Imitation" are numerous and deep enough to make any similarities apparent.

Works: "Breviloquium de accidentiis exterioribus" (before 1403); "De libertate spiritus"; "Soliloquium cum Deo ignitum" (Cologne, 1616; Flemish tr., 1623; Fr., 1667; It., 1674; Sp., 1686).

FABRICIUS, *Bibl. m. æ.*, V (1736), 770; FOPPENS, *Bibl. Belgica*, I (1739), 364; GRAESSE, *Trésor* (1862), III, 58; PAQUOT, *Hist. litt. Pays-Bas*, XVIII (1770), 35–36. JOSEPH DEDIEU.

Peter the Hermit, b. at Amiens about 1050; d. at the monastery of Neufmoutier (Liège), in 1115. His life has been embellished by legend, and he has been wrongly credited with initiating the movement which resulted in the First Crusade. While the contemporary historians mentioned him only as one of the numerous preachers of the crusade, the later chroniclers, Albert of Aix-la-Chapelle and above all William of Tyre, gave him an all-important rôle. According to Albert of Aix Peter having led during some years the rigorous life of a hermit undertook a pilgrimage to Jerusalem and suffered much at the hands of the Turks. One day when he was asleep in the Basilica of the Holy Sepulchre, Our Lord appeared to him and ordered him to ask for credentials from the Patriarch of Jerusalem and to go to Europe proclaiming the miseries which had befallen the Christians of the Orient. Peter obtained the patriarchal letters and sought Urban II, who, moved by his recital, came to preach the crusade at Clermont ("Histor. Hierosol.", I, 2). According to William of Tyre (I, II), it was of his own accord that Peter went to find the pope. The pilgrimage of Peter is mentioned by Anna Comnena (Alexiad, X, 8), who, born in 1083, could know nothing of this history except through tradition; she relates, however, that he could not get as far as Jerusalem, and that, resolved to undertake a second pilgrimage, he conceived the idea of preaching a crusade in order to be able to go to the Holy Sepulchre attended by a goodly company. It is evidently absurd to ascribe the Crusades to such an insignificant cause. Because of the silence of contemporaries and the later contradictory accounts, even the fact of the pilgrimage of Peter is doubtful, while it is impossible to assign to him the rôle of promoter of the crusade. The merit of this belongs solely to Pope Urban II (see CRUSADES). Writers like Albert of Aix wished to deprive the pope of this honour in order to attribute it to the ascetics so popular at that time in Europe. It is absolutely certain that it was only after the Council of Clermont that Peter commenced to preach the crusade.

In March, 1096, he led one of the numerous bands going to the East; his enthusiastic eloquence is described by the chroniclers. He arrived with his army at Constantinople 1 August, 1096. After a toilsome march as far as Nicomedia Peter pitched his camp at Civitot and seeing his army without resources returned to Constantinople to solicit help from the Emperor Alexius. During his absence, the crusaders, commanded by Walter the Penniless, were massacred by the Turks near Nicæa (Oct., 1096). Peter assembled the remnants of his band and in May, 1097, joined the army of Godfrey of Bouillon near Nicomedia. After this he had but an unimportant part. In Jan., 1098, at the siege of Antioch, he even attempted to desert the army, but was prevented by Tancred. In spite of this cowardice he was one of the envoys sent to Kerbûga. On his return to Europe he founded the monastery of Neufmoutier. See CRUSADES.

D'OULTREMAN, *La vie du Vénérable Pierre l'Ermite* (Mons, 1612), reprinted (Clermont, 1895), gives the traditional point of view; HAGENMEYER, *Peter der Eremite* (Leipzig, 1879), Fr. tr., *Le vrai et le faux sur Pierre l'Ermite* (Paris, 1879); KURTH, *Pierre l'Ermite* (Liège, 1892); DONNET, *Pierre l'Hermite et la famille Lhermite d'Anvers* (Antwerp, 1893). LOUIS BRÉHIER.

Peter the Venerable, ABBOT OF CLUNY. See MONTBOISSIER, PETER OF, BLESSED.

Peter Urseolus (ORSEOLO), SAINT, b. at Rivo alto, Province of Udina, 928; d. at Cuxa, 10 January, 987 (997 is less probable). Sprung from the wealthy and noble Venetian family, the Orseoli, Peter led from his youth an earnest Christian life. In the service of the republic, he distinguished himself in naval battles against the pirates. In 946 he married a noble Venetian lady, Felicitas; a son of this marriage, who bore the same name as his father, also became Doge of Venice (991–1009). On 11 Aug., 976, the Doge Pietro Candiano fell a victim to a conspiracy, whose members, in their anxiety to obtain possession of him, set fire to his palace, thereby destroying not only this building, but also the churches of San Marco, San Teodoro, and Santa Maria di Zobenigo, as well as about three hundred houses. On the following day Pietro Orseolo was chosen doge in San Pietro di Castello, but it was only out of regard for his obligations towards his native land that he allowed himself to be prevailed upon to accept the office. The tradition recorded by Peter Damian (Vita s. Romualdi, V, in P. L., CXLIV, 960), that Peter had taken part in the conspiracy and that his later retirement from the world was due to his desire to expiate therefor, is without foundation. As one might expect from his personal piety, the new doge showed himself a zealous patron of churches and monasteries as well as an able ruler. He had the doge's palace and the church of San Marco rebuilt at his own expense, procuring in Constantinople for the latter the first golden altar-covering (*Pala d'oro*), and bequeathed one thousand pounds to persons injured by the fire and a similar sum to the poor. He renewed the treaty with Capodistria, and succeeded in averting from the republic the vengeance of Candiano's family, especially of his wife Waldrada, niece of Empress Adelaide, and his son Vitalis, Patriarch of Grado. About this time, through the influence of Abbot Guarinus of Cuxa (a Benedictine monastery at the foot of the Pyrenees, in the territory of Roussillon), he decided to enter a monastery, leaving Venice secretly with the abbot and two companions in the night of 1–2 September, 987. As a monk in the abbey of Cuxa, he presented to his spiritual brothers a model of humility, zeal for prayer, and charity. For a period he was under the spiritual guidance of St. Romuald (q. v.). As early as the eleventh century the veneration of Peter Urseolus as a saint was approved by the Bishop of Elne. In 1731 Clement XII ratified this cult, and appointed 14 January as his feast.

MABILLON, *Acta SS. ordinis s. Benedicti*, V, 878 sqq.; *Bibliotheca hagiographica latina*, II, 986; TOLRA, *St Pierre Orséolo* (Paris, 1897); SCHMID, *D. hl. Petrus Orseolo, Doge von Venedig u. Benedictiner*, in *Studien und Mitteilungen aus dem Bened. u. Cisterzienserorden* (1901), 71 sq., 251 sq.; KRETSCHMAY, *Gesch. von Venedig*, I (Gotha, 1905), 115 sq., 438 sq. J. P. KIRSCH.

Petinessus (PITNISUS), titular see in Galatia Secunda (Salutaris). This city is mentioned by Strabo, XII, 567; Ptolemy, V, 4, 10; Hierocles, "Synecdemus", 697, 7, and Stephanus Byzantius, s. v. According to the first of these authors it was situated in the salt desert, to the west of Lake Tatta (at the present time Touz Gueul), between Lycaonia and Haimama. The "Notitiæ episcopatuum" mention it among the suffragan sees of Pessinus, created by Theodosius between 386 and 395, and existing as late as the thirteenth century. There is a record of but one bishop, Pius, present at the Council of Chalcedon, 451 (Le Quien, "Oriens christianus", I, 493). The exact name and position of the city, which differs greatly according to various documents, is not known. Ramsay (Asia Minor, 227), mentions the place as near the site of Piri Begli or a little to the east of it.

S. PÉTRIDÈS.

Petit, JEHAN (LE PETIT). See JOHN PARVUS.

Petit-Didier, MATTHIEU, Benedictine theologian and ecclesiastical historian, b. at Saint-Nicolas-du-Port in Lorraine, 18 December, 1659; d. at Senones, 15 July (June?), 1728. After studying at the Jesuit college at Nancy he joined the Benedictine Congregation of St-Vannes, in 1675, at the monastery of St-Mihiel. In 1682 he was appointed professor of philosophy and theology. In 1699 he was canonically elected Abbot of Bouzonville, but could not take possession because the Duke of Lorraine had given the abbey *in commendam* to his own brother. He was elected Abbot of Senones in 1715, but got possession only after a lengthy dispute with another claimant. He became president of his congregation in 1723 and two years later Benedict XIII appointed him Bishop of Acra *in partibus infidelium* in reward for his opportune "Traité sur l'autorité et l'infaillibilité du pape" (Luxemburg, 1724). The work was forbidden in France and Lorraine by the Parliaments of Paris and Metz; it was translated into Italian (Rome, 1746); and into Latin by Gallus Cartier, O.S.B. (Augsburg, 1727, it is printed also in Migne, "Cursus theol.", IV, 1141–1416). The work was especially pleasing to the pope, because Petit-Didier, misled by the "Declaration of the French Clergy" in 1682, had formerly been an appellant from the Constitution "Unigenitus". The remaining works of Petit-Didier are: "Remarques sur la Bibliothèque ecclésiastique de M. Dupin" (Paris, 1691–93), in which he points out many errors; "Dissertation historique et théologique dans laquelle on examine quel a été le sentiment du Concile de Constance et des principaux Théologiens qui y ont assisté, sur l'autorité du pape et sur son infaillibilité" (Luxemburg, 1724), in which the author defends the opinion that the decree of the Council of Constance concerning the superiority of a general council over the pope was intended only for the time of a schism; "Dissertationes historico-critico-chronologicæ in Vetus Testamentum" (Toul, 1699); "Justification de la morale et de la discipline de Rome et de toute l'Italie" (1727), a reply to an anonymous treatise entitled: "La morale des Jésuites et la constitution Unigenitus comparée à la morale des payens".

His brother, JEAN-JOSEPH, a Jesuit theologian and canonist, was born at Saint-Nicolas-du-Port in Lorraine, on 23 October, 1664; and died at Pont-à-Mousson, on 10 August, 1756. Entering the Society of Jesus, 16 May, 1683, he was professed 2 February, 1698, and taught belles-lettres, philosophy, and canon law at Strasburg from 1694 to 1701, and theology at Pont-à-Mousson from 1704 to 1708. About 1730 he became the spiritual director of Duchess Elizabeth-Charlotte of Lorraine. A few years later he returned to the Jesuit house at Saint-Nicolas where he spent the remainder of his life. His chief works are: "De justitia, jure et legibus" (Pont-à-Mousson 1704); "Remarques sur la théologie du R. P. Gaspard Juenin" (1708), a refutation of the Jansenistic errors of Juenin; "Les Saints enlevez et restituez aux Jesuites" (Luxemburg, 1738), concerning Saints Francis Xavier and John Francis Regis; "Traité de la clôture des maisons religieuses de l'un et de l'autre sexe" (Nancy, 1742); "Recueil de Lettres critiques sur les Vies des Saints du Sieur Baillet" (Cologne, 1720); "Les prets par obligation stipulative d'interest usités en Lorraine et Barrois" (Nancy, 1745), a canonical treatise; "Sancti Patris Ignatii de Loyola exercitia spiritualia tertio probationis anno per mensem a Patribus Societatis Jesu obeunda" (Prague, 1755; Paris, 1889).

ZIEGELBAUER, *Historia rei literariæ O. S B.* (Augsburg, 1754), III, 455–7, II, 154–5; CALMET, *Bibl. Lorraine* (Nancy, 1751), 724–35; HURTER, *Nomenclator literarius* (Innsbruck, 1910), 1108–10; SOMMERVOGEL, *Bibl. de la Compagnie de Jésus*, IV (Brussels, 1895), 624–7.
MICHAEL OTT.

Petite Eglise, LA. See NAMUR, DIOCESE OF.

Petitions to the Holy See.—I. MODE OF PETITIONING.—Faculties, indults, dispensations, and other favours, the granting of which is reserved to the Holy See, must be asked by means of a petition in writing presented to the sovereign pontiff, regularly through the medium of one of the Sacred Congregations of the Roman Curia. Under the new constitution of the Roman Curia by Pius X, any private person may personally approach and petition the Holy See. But it is always well, and often necessary, to present commendatory letters of the petitioner's ordinary, as in the case of faculties, dispensations, and such like. It is also frequently advisable to make use of an agent in Rome, who can attend to the matter personally. For this purpose any trustworthy man may be chosen, provided he be acceptable to the Sacred Congregation with which he has to treat. (Cf. Const., "Sapienti Consilio", Normæ communes, c. ix.)

II. FORM AND CONTENTS OF THE PETITION.—The petition should be written on a double sheet of white paper of the foolscap or large quarto size; and the text should pass, if its length renders this necessary, from the first to the second page, and so on, as in a printed book, no intermediate page being left blank. The official languages of the Curia are still Latin, Italian, and French; but documents in English, German, Spanish, and Portuguese are now authorized (cf. Const. "Sapienti Consilio", Normæ peculiares, c. vi., n. 5.). It is fitting, however, that petitions sent by episcopal curiæ and by ecclesiastics in general, and those that have reference to the sacraments, should be written in the Church's official language, Latin. The petition should be addressed to the pope himself, and should therefore begin with the words "Beatissime Pater" (Most Holy Father). The petitioner should then give his full name, place of residence, and diocese. (These are omitted in petitions to the Sacred Penitentiary.) Next should follow a clear and concise statement of the favour desired, the reasons for the petition, and all the information necessary to enable the Holy See to arrive at its decision. The omission of material facts or the commission of substantial errors in the petition may invalidate the dispensation or indult granted. Thus, petitions for matrimonial dispensations must express: (1) the Christian names and surnames of the petitioners; (2) the diocese of origin or actual domicile; (3) the exact nature of the impediment; (4) the degree of consanguinity, affinity, etc.; (5) the number of the impediments; (6) various circumstances (Instruction of S. Congr. of Propaganda, 9 May, 1877). The petition should not be concluded in the form of a letter, but with the abbreviated formula "Et Deus, etc." or "Quare, etc." At the foot of the petition the address of the person to whom the reply is to be sent (if it is not to be transmitted through an agent) should be written.

III. DESTINATION OF VARIOUS PETITIONS.—All petitions in matrimonial cases are dealt with by the Congr. de disciplina Sacramentorum, except those that have to do with the internal forum (i. e., confessional and occult cases), which go to the Sacred Penitentiary, and those into which the impediment *mixtæ religionis* or *disparitatis cultus* enters, which fall under the jurisdiction of the Holy Office. The Congr. de disciplina Sacramentorum has charge, too, of all else connected with the sacraments and the Mass, with the exception of their rites and ceremonies, the regulation of which belongs to the Congregation of Rites. Hence petitions for the solution of liturgical difficulties should be sent to the latter Congregation; petitions, e. g., for a private oratory, reservation of the Blessed Sacrament, non-fasting communion, etc., to the former. The Congregation of the Council deals with petitions relating to the commandments of the Church, ecclesiastical discipline, confraternities, and the administration of church property. All matters concerning religious, whether individuals or communities, with one or two exceptions, are in the hands of the Congr. de Religiosis. Finally, all the business of those countries which still remain subject to the Congr. of Propaganda, is transacted through that Congregation, with the exception of the affairs of religious as such.

Constitutio Sapienti Consilio: Normæ communes et peculiares in *Acta Apostolicæ Sedis*, I, 7; CAPPELLO, *De Curia Romana juxta reformationem a Pio X sapientissime inductam*, I (Rome, 1911), ii, 3; KONINGS-PUTZER, *Commentarium in facultates apostolicas* (New York, 1898), 63–8; GASPARRI, *De matrimonio*, I (Paris, 1904), iii, 4, § 2, 3°; DE BECKER, *De sponsalibus et matrimonio* (Louvain, 1903),'sect. v, c. iii, §§ 1, 2 ; ZITELLI, *De dispensationibus matrimonialibus* (Rome, 1887), iv.
CHARLES CRONIN.

Petra, titular metropolitan see of Palæstina Tertia. Under the name of Sela (the rock) this region is described in Abdias (i, 3 sqq.) as an eagle's nest on the mountain top. It is also referred to in Isaias (xlii, 11), IV Kings (xiv, 7), and II Par. (xxv, 11). In the two last-mentioned passages it is related that towards the end of the ninth century B. C. Amasias, King of Jerusalem, vanquished the Edomites, captured Sela, and cast from "the steep of a rock" 10,000 captives, who were dashed to pieces. He then called Sela Ioqteel (Jectehel), of which there is no trace in history. If these Biblical texts really relate to Petra, others in which there is mention of Sela refer to other localities. Petra was not then the capital city of the Kingdom of Edom. This rank was held by Bosra, and Petra seems to have been a city of refuge whither in times of danger the chieftains fled with their treasures and dwelt in the caverns as in houses.

When the Rock was spoken of in 312 B. C. by Diodorus Siculus (XIX, 94–100), it was no longer inhabited by Edomites, who had been crowded into Southern Palestine, but by Arabian merchants, the Nabatæans or the Nabajoth of the Bible (Gen., xxv, 13; xxviii, 9; xxxvi, 3; Is., lx, 7). It is difficult to determine when they began to occupy the region. When conquered by Asurbanipal (640 B. C.), the Nabaitu were a powerful North-Arabian tribe which had fought its way as far as the countries of Edom, Moab, and Ammon. In the fourth century B. C. the Nabatæans were masters of the country and served as commercial intermediaries between Arabia and Egypt, and between Arabia and Syria. The wealth secured in Petra attracted the covetousness of Athenes, general of Antigonus (312 B. C.). He took it by surprise in the absence of the men, who on their return surprised the Greeks, massacred them, and sent presents to Antigonus that they might be free to continue their commerce. A second attempt, made by Demetrius, son of Antigonus, was equally unsuccessful (Diod. Sic., XIX, 94–100). There was then formed a Nabatæan kingdom of which Petra was the capital and which extended from Arabia Felix to Hauran. The first known king was Aretas I (II Mach., v, 8). The following, according to M. Dussand in the "Journal Asiatique" (Paris, 1904, pp. 189–338), is the list of known sovereigns: Aretas I (169 B. C.); Aretas II (110–96); Obodas I (about 90); Rabel I (about 87); Aretas III (87–62); Obodas II (about 62–47); Malichus I (about 47–30); Obodas III (30–9); Aretas IV (9 B. C.–A. D. 40); Malichus II (40–75); Rabel II (75–101); Malichus III (101–106). Aretas III gave Petra its Græco-Roman character. From his reign and that of Aretas IV date most of the beautiful buildings still preserved. Petra was definitely annexed to the Roman Empire in A. D. 106 by

Cornelius Palma, lieutenant of Trajan. From it was formed the Province of Arabia, "redacta in formam provinciæ Arabia", as Trajan's sign-posts read, extending from Bostra in Hauran to the Red Sea. In 295 the province was divided into Arabia Augusta Libanensis on the north, with Bostra as metropolis, and Arabia on the south, with Petra as metropolis. Twelve years later Southern Arabia was united with the Province of Palestine to be again detached in the second half of the fourth century (between 358 and 390), and to constitute thenceforth Palæstina Tertia or Palæstina Salutaris, with Petra as metropolis. The custom arose of calling it Arabia Petræa, because of the city of Petra, and not with the implication that the region was rocky, for it is rather fertile. After a visit from the Emperor Hadrian Petra took the surname of Hadriana, found on the coins and on some inscriptions.

Christianity was introduced into Petra doubtless at an early date, for in the time of Strabo, who has described the country (XIV, iv, 21 sq.), Greek and Latin merchants flocked thither. Among its bishops Le Quien (Oriens christ., III, 721-8) mentions St. Asterius, whose feast is celebrated on 20 June, one of the defenders of the Council of Nicæa and St. Athanasius; his contemporary Germanus, probably an Arian; John (457); Theodore (536), biographer of St. Theodosius the Cenobite; Athenogenes, a relative of the Emperor Maurice (end of the sixth century). An inscription indicates likewise a bishop by the name of Jason (probably fifth century). The Diocese of Petra in Palestine, mentioned by Le Quien (ibid., III, 663-70), who relied on a faulty text of St. Athanasius, never existed. In the time of John Moschus (seventh century) Petra was a flourishing monastic centre, but the decline of the city was even then far advanced, because the direction of commerce had changed and the prosperity of Palmyra had injured that of Petra. When the Franks took possession of the country in the twelfth century and founded their Trans-Jordanic principality they established somewhat prior to 1116 a stronghold called "Li Vaux Moyse", a translation of the Arabic name Ouadi-Moussa, the ruins of which have been discovered near the village of El-Dji. It was captured by the Arabs, first in 1144 and definitively in 1188. The Latin archdiocese, called Petra Deserti, which was established by the crusaders in 1168, must not be confused with our Petra; the former is Charac-Moba, the ancient capital of the Moabites, now El-Kerac (Le Quien, ibid., III, 1305; Du Cange, Les familles d'Outre-mer, Paris, 1859, p. 755; Eubel, Hierarchia catholica medii ævi, I, 418).

Petra, now Ouadi-Moussa, is completely ruined. Of the Græco-Roman city there remain, besides the theatre hewn from the rock, only shapeless ruins; but the tombs dug in the sides of the mountain surrounding the city are one of the wonders of the world. There are more than 3000, of different periods. Archæology, it is true, regards some of them as temples. As the red sandstone from which the tombs are hewn is veined with a variety of colours, and as the light is dazzling, this city of the dead presents the appearance of a veritable fairy-land, the like of which is not to be seen elsewhere in the world. Recently the high place and the site of the altar of sacrifice have been discovered.

When the late Archbishop of New York, Michael Augustine Corrigan, was coadjutor to Cardinal McCloskey, his titular see was that of Petra.

LABORDE, *Voyage dans l'Arabie Pétrée* (Paris, 1830-34); WILSON, *The Lands of the Bible*, I (Edinburgh), 291-336; STANLEY, *Sinai and Palestine* (London, 1860), 87-98; PALMER, *The Desert of Exodus*, II (London, 1871); LIBBEY, *The Jordan Valley and Petra* (New York, 1905); LUYNES, *Voyage d'exploration à la Mer Morte* etc. (Paris, 1871), 274; BUHL, *Gesch. der Edomiter* (Leipzig, 1893); BRUNNOW AND DOMASZEWSKI, *Die Provincia Arabia*, I (Strasburg, 1904); MUSIL, *Arabia Petræa*, II (Vienne, 1907); DALMAN, *Petra und seine Felsheiligtümer* (Leipzig, 1908); SARGENTON-GALICHON, *Sinai, Maân, Pétra* (Paris, 1904); *Revue Biblique* (1897; 1898; 1902; 1903); KERGORLAY, *Sites délaissés d'Orient* (Paris, 1911), 91-154.

S. VAILHÉ.

Petrarch, FRANCESCO, Italian poet and humanist, b. at Arezzo, 20 July, 1304; d. at Arquá, 19 July, 1374. His father, Petracco or Petraccolo (a name which the son adopted as his cognomen, changing it to Petrarca) came of a family belonging originally to the region of the Valdarno, but already settled for some time at Florence. There Ser Petracco acted as clerk of one of the courts of justice, but with other White Guelphs he was banished in 1302, and went to Arezzo. Francesco's earliest years were spent chiefly at Incisa in the ancestral district of the Valdarno. In 1310 his father transferred their abode to Pisa, whence the family went to Avignon in France, which had been for about six years the papal residence. Between 1315 and 1319 the lad was trained at Carpentras under the tutelage of the Italian Convenevole da Prato. His father intended him for the legal profession, and sent him for the necessary studies to Montpellier (1319-23) and to Bologna (1323-5). Francesco disliked the career chosen for him, and devoted himself as much as possible to belles-lettres, thereby so incensing his father that, upon one occasion, the latter burned a number of his favourite ancient authors. When Ser Petracco died in 1323, Francesco returned to Avignon and took minor orders, which permitted him to enjoy church benefices and only bound him to the daily reading of his Office. He entered rather freely into the gay and fashionable life at Avignon, and there on Good Friday (1327) he saw for the first time Laura, the lady who was to be the inspiration of his most famous work. In spite of what he himself says as to his first encounter with Laura, many persons have doubted her real existence. The majority of critics, however, believe that she was truly a lady in the flesh, and some identify her with a certain Laura, the wife of Hugues de Sade (d. 1348). There would seem to be little chance for romance in such an attachment, yet the weight of authority is in favour of regarding it as a genuine one productive of true and poignant emotion in Petrarch, however Platonic it may have remained.

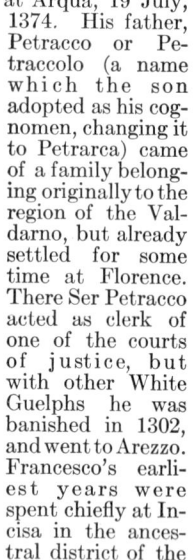

About 1330 the poet began a period of restless

wandering, and in 1333 he made a journey through northern France and through Germany, recording his observations and experiences in his letters. Back at Avignon for a while, and now invested with a canonical benefice, he set forth for Italy, in 1336, in the company of some members of the Colonna family, with which he had been closely allied for some time past, and in January, 1337, he entered Rome for the first time. By the end of the year he appears to have settled in Vaucluse, and there he found the peace and the inspiration that produced so many of his best lyrics. Accepting an invitation to go to Rome on Easter Sunday, 1341, he was publicly crowned as poet and historian in the Capitol. For a number of years he wandered about from one Italian city to another, seeking the codices that preserved the priceless literary works of antiquity (he certainly discovered works of Cicero and parts of the "Institutiones" of Quintilian), and occasionally occupying clerical posts. He formed a friendship with Cola di Rienzi, and in 1347 saluted him in verse as the restorer of the order of the ancient Roman Republic. A friendship of greater importance was that which he now contracted with Boccaccio, who, like himself, desired to promote humanistic studies and researches. Refusing an offer to assume the rectorship of the Florentine Studio (or University) just established, he resumed his peregrinations, spending a good part of the time at Venice, and accompanied there for a while by Boccaccio and by Leo Pilatus, from whom both he and Boccaccio had hoped to gain some direct knowledge of Greek and its literature. The transfer of the pontifical Court back to Rome in 1367 filled him with unbounded joy.

As a scholar, Petrarch possessed encyclopedic knowledge, and much of this he has set down in his Latin works, which constitute the larger part of his production in both prose and verse. They include the "Africa" in hexameters, dealing with the Second Punic war and especially with the adventures of Scipio Africanus, in pseudo-epic fashion and in a way which hardly elicits our admiration, although the author deemed it his greatest work; the "Carmen bucolicum" made up of twelve eclogues; the "Epistolæ metricæ" in three books of hexameters, interesting for the autobiographical matter which they contain; several moral treatises, such as the "De contemptu mundi", which consists of three dialogues between the author and St. Augustine, both of them in the presence of Truth; the "De vita solitaria"; the "De ocio religiosorum", praising monastic life, etc.; some "Psalmi pœnitentiales" and some prayers; a number of historical and geographical works, among which figure the "Rerum memorandarum libri quattuor" and the "De viris illustribus", treating of illustrious men from Romulus down to Titus; some invectives (especially the "Invectiva in Gallum", assailing the French); a few orations; and finally his very many letters, which cover the whole course of his life from 1325 to the end, and one of the most interesting of which is the "Epistola ad posteros", written after 1370, and furnishing an autobiography of considerable importance. A Latin comedy, "Philologia", has not yet been discovered.

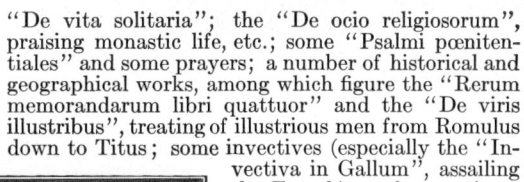

FRANCESCO PETRARCH
Painting by Andrea del Castagno
Convent of Sant' Apollonia, Florence

In spite of the magnitude of Petrarch's composition in Latin and the stress which he put upon it himself, his abiding fame is based upon his Italian verse, and this forms two notable compilations, the "Trionfi" and the "Canzoniere". The "Trionfi", written in *terza rima*, and making large use of the vision already put to so good stead by Dante, is allegorical and moral in its nature. In the "Trionfi" we have a triumphal procession in which there take part six leading allegorical figures: Love, Chastity, Death, Fame, Time, and Divinity. Chastity triumphs over its predecessor, and finally Divinity triumphs over them all and remains supreme, as the symbol of peace, eternal life, and the everlasting union of the poet with his beloved Laura. The "Canzoniere", the poet's masterpiece, and one of the imperishable monuments of the world's literature, was first put into shape by the author and made known by him under the title of "Rerum vulgarium fragmenta". It consists of sonnets (and these are the more numerous) of *canzoni*, of *sestine*, of *ballate*, and of madrigals. The love motive prevails in the majority of these, but political and patriotic feeling regulates some of the most famous of them, and still others are infused with moral and other

TOMB OF PETRARCH
At Aqua near Padua

sentiments. Some lyrics bearing apparent relations to the "Canzoniere", but excluded by the poet from its final make-up, have been published under the title of "Extravaganti". In the strictly amorous part of the "Canzoniere", Petrarch sings of his lady living and dead, and, reviving in his psychological manner the methods of the earlier *dolce stil nuovo* School, particularly reflects the spirit of Cino da Pistoia. But all is not imitation on the part of his Muse; his inner man is expressed in even greater degree than the literary formalism which he owed to his predecessors of the thirteenth and the early fourteenth century. Still it must be admitted that the very refinement of his verse-form and the constant repetition of emotions, that vary but slightly one from the other, tend inevitably to pall upon us. The "Canzoniere" and the "Trionfi" begot for Petrarch legions of followers in Italy, and Petrarchism, as the imitation of his manner was termed, continued down into the Renaissance, growing less according as the numberless disciples took to imitating one another rather than the master directly, until Bembo started a propaganda in favour of copying only the original model.

MARSAND, *Biblioteca Petrarchesca* (Milan, 1826); HORTIS, *Catalogo delle opere di Petrarca* (Trieste, 1874); FERRAZZI, *Bibliografia Petrarchesca* (Bassano, 1887); FISKE, *Handlist of Petrarch Editions in the Florentine Public Libraries* (Florence, 1886); D'ANCONA AND BACCI, *Manuale della letteratura italiana*, I (Florence, 1895). Of the Latin works the *Africa* has been published critically by CORRADINI (Padua, 1874); the *Poemata minora* by ROSSETTI (Milan, 1829–34); and many of the *Epistolæ* by FRACASSETTI (Florence, 1859–63; It. tr. Florence, 1863–67). There have been many editions of the Italian lyrics; a notable one is that of CARDUCCI and FERRARI (Florence, 1899). All the leading accounts of Italian literary history deal fully with Petrarch—see among others: GASPARY, *Storia della let. ital.*, I (Turin, 1887); DE SANCTIS, *Saggio critico sul Petrarca* (Naples, 1869); IDEM, *Studi critici* (Naples, 1890); BARTOLI, *Storia della let. ital.*, VII (Florence, 1884); VOIGT, *Die Wiederbelebung des classischen Alterthums* (2nd ed., Berlin, 1880), and NOLHAC, *Pétrarque et l'humanisme* (Paris, 1892), treat of his humanistic endeavours. See further: MÉZIÈRES, *Pétrarque* (Paris, 1867); KOERTING, *Petrarcas Leben und Werke* (Leipzig, 1878).

J. D. M. FORD.

Petre, FAMILY OF.—The Petres are one of those staunch and constant families, which have played a great part in the preservation of the Catholic Faith in England. There is no volume of the "Catholic Record Society" (London) which does not contain references to their name, sometimes by scores; Gillow gives biographies of fifteen, Kirk of ten; the Jesuits count twelve in their order, and there are eighteen in the current "Catholic Who's Who" (London).

The fortunes of the Petres were, oddly enough, built up on the ruins of the monasteries. Sir William Petre, with the pliability of his age, held the confidential post of secretary of State through the revolutionary changes of Henry VIII, Edward VI, Mary, and Elizabeth. His later years were probably more orthodox; his widow, the patroness of the martyr, Blessed John Payne (q. v.), was certainly a loyal Catholic. His son, John, was created a baron by James I, and with his grandson William (d. 1637) Catholicism, which had not hitherto been professed by the heads of the house, was publicly acknowledged. William, fourth Lord, who had distinguished himself in the civil wars, died a martyr's death in the tower of London, 5 Jan., 1684, accused of complicity in Oates's Plot. Robert Edward, the ninth Baron (1742–1801), played a leading part in the struggles for Catholic Emancipation. He was, however, though a practical, and on the whole a good, Catholic, tainted by some of the Liberalistic ideas then prevalent, and failed as chairman of the Catholic Committee in the loyalty due to the bishops. He was also reputed to have been Grand Master of the Freemasons. But Masonry had not then been censured with the clearness with which it has been condemned since. William Joseph (b. 1847; d. 1893), a domestic prelate, and thirteenth Baron, devoted many years to Catholic liberal education, founding and maintaining a school at Woburn Park (1877–84) and defended his theories of education in several pamphlets. The family has also produced two bishops, Francis (b. 1692; d. 1775) and Benjamin (b. 1672; d. 1758), who were respectively coadjutors of Bishop Dicconson in the Northern District and of Dr. Challoner in the Southern.

SIR EDWARD PETRE, BARONET, S.J., and privy councillor (1631–99), fills more space in history than any of his family, owing to the multiplicity of attacks made upon him as a chaplain and adviser of James II. Petre's unpopularity as a Jesuit was so great that it harmed the king's cause; but if we regard his conduct by itself, no serious fault has yet been proved against him. If we cannot yet confidently acquit him of all blame, that is chiefly because first-hand evidence is very deficient; but the nearer we get to first-hand evidence, the better does Petre's conduct appear. Before James's accession (6 Feb., 1685) he had shown good, but not extraordinary, virtue and ability, and was then vice-provincial of his order. James soon made him clerk of the closet, but without any political power. On 9 Oct. the king wrote to ask the pope to make him a bishop *in partibus*, and the pope refused (24 Nov., 1685). The first application made little or no stir; it did not even reach the ear of the general of the Jesuits till the pope told him of it, 22 May, 1686. At that time Lord Castlemaine, having arrived in Rome as James's ambassador, had renewed the application, while James urged it forcibly on Mgr. d'Adda, the papal nuncio in London (28 June). But if the pope was rightly immovable, the king was characteristically obstinate.

Next year (1687) Castlemaine renewed the petition with a doggedness that "excited the bile" of the pontiff (March). James backed up the application by letters of 16 June and 24 Sept., and now requested that Petre be made a cardinal; but the pope (16 Aug., 22 Nov.) steadily refused. Such urgency was certain to be attributed to Petre's ambition, and the general of the order wrote pressingly (22 Nov., 20 Dec., and 10 Jan., 1688) for explanations. James himself now sent letters in Petre's defence to pope and general (22 Dec.), while the provincial and Petre also wrote, setting forth all they had done to persuade James to desist. All these letters are unfortunately lost, except those from the king. We know, however, that they completely vindicated Petre's character in the eyes of the pope and of the general. A further cause of irritation, however, had been given by the admission of Petre to the rank of privy councillor (11 Nov., 1687), and the oath of allegiance taken on that occasion, though not objected to in the case of the other Catholic lords, was much commented upon, and laid before the pope. But a better understanding now prevailed at Rome, and the incident dropped.

In England, on the other hand, after his nomination as privy councillor, the popular charges against him became more insulting than ever, and reached their height in the insinuations made about the birth of the prince (James Francis Stuart). Though the worst of these charges stand self-refuted, it is to be regretted that want of documents prevents our defending the father against others, though the presumptions are generally in his favour. If, as it is said, he persuaded James to dismiss the Countess of Dorchester (Mrs. Sedley), he may be said to have deserved his place at Court. If James had taken his advice and stayed on at Westminster, the fortunes of his house would probably have ended differently. Like everyone in James's entourage, Petre at first believed in Sunderland, but he was also among the first to detect that minister's duplicity, and to break with him. Setting aside prejudiced witnesses (and it will be remembered that there was a party against him, even among Catholics), and studying those in sympathy with the Jesuit, we seem to perceive in him a steadfast, kind-hearted English priest, devoting himself with energy to the opportunities for spiritual good that opened out before him. With little gift for politics, nor paying much heed to them, he was nevertheless severely blamed when things went wrong. He was also regardless, almost callous, as to what was said about him by friend or foe.

HOWARD AND BURKE, *Genealogical Collections illustrating the history of Roman Catholic families of England*, I (London, 1887); G. E. C[OKAYNE], *Peerage of England*, VI (London, 1895), 247; IDEM, *Baronetage*, II, 247; FOLEY, *Records of the English Province S. J.* (London, 1879), V and VII; DÜHR, *Jesuitenfabeln* (Freiburg im Br., 1891), 170 (the article *Petre* is omitted in later editions); LONGRIDGE, *Guilt or Innocence of Father Petre* in *The Month* (Sep., 1886 to March, 1887). Transcripts of the dispatches of the

TRIUMPH OF FAME

AFTER A XV-CENTURY MS. IN THE RICCARDIANA, FLORENCE

Petrobrusians, heretics of the twelfth century so named from their founder Peter of Bruys. Our information concerning him is derived from the treatise of Peter the Venerable against the Petrobrusians and from a passage in Abelard. Peter was born perhaps at Bruis in south-eastern France. The history of his early life is unknown, but it is certain that he was a priest who had been deprived of his charge. He began his propaganda in the Dioceses of Embrun, Die, and Gap, probably between 1117 and 1120. Twenty years later the populace of St. Gilles near Nîmes, exasperated by his burning of crosses, cast him into the flames. The bishops of the above-mentioned dioceses suppressed the heresy within their jurisdiction, but it gained adherents at Narbonne, Toulouse, and in Gascony. Henry of Lausanne, a former Cluniac monk, adopted the Petrobrusians' teaching about 1135 and spread it in a modified form after its author's death. Peter of Bruys admitted the doctrinal authority of the Gospels in their literal interpretation; the other New-Testament writings he probably considered valueless, as of doubtful Apostolic origin. To the New-Testament Epistles he assigned only a subordinate place as not coming from Jesus Christ Himself. He rejected the Old Testament as well as the authority of the Fathers and of the Church. His contempt for the Church extended to the clergy, and physical violence was preached and exercised against priests and monks. In his system baptism is indeed a necessary condition for salvation, but it is baptism preceded by personal faith, so that its administration to infants is worthless. The Mass and the Eucharist are rejected because Jesus Christ gave His flesh and blood but once to His disciples, and repetition is impossible. All external forms of worship, ceremonies and chant, are condemned. As the Church consists not in walls, but in the community of the faithful, church buildings should be destroyed, for we may pray to God in a barn as well as in a church, and be heard, if worthy, in a stable as well as before an altar. No good works of the living can profit the dead. Crosses, as the instrument of the death of Christ, cannot deserve veneration; hence they were for the Petrobrusians objects of desecration and were destroyed in bonfires.

PETER THE VENERABLE, *Epistola sive tractatus adversus petrobrusianos hæreticos* in *P. L.*, CLXXXIX, 719–850; ABELARD, *Introductio ad theologiam*, II, iv, in *P. L.*, CLXXVIII, 1056; VERNET in *Dict. théol. cath.*, II, 1151–56; FUNK, *Manual of Church History*, tr. CAPPADELTA, I (St. Louis, 1910), 354–5.

N. A. WEBER.

Petronilla, SAINT, virgin, probably martyred at Rome at the end of the first century. Almost all the sixth- and seventh-century lists of the tombs of the most highly venerated Roman martyrs mention St. Petronilla's grave as situated in the Via Ardeatina near Sts. Nereus and Achilleus (De Rossi, "Roma sotterranea", I, 180–1). These notices have been completely confirmed by the excavations in the Catacomb of Domitilla. One topography of the graves of the Roman martyrs, "Epitome libri de locis sanctorum martyrum", locates on the Via Ardeatina a church of St. Petronilla, in which Sts. Nereus and Achilleus, as well as Petronilla, were buried (De Rossi, loc. cit., 180). This church, built into the above-mentioned catacomb, has been discovered, and the memorials found in it removed all doubt that the tombs of the three saints were once venerated there (De Rossi in "Bullettino di archeol. crist.", 1874 sq., 5 sqq.). A painting, in which Petronilla is represented as receiving a deceased person (named Veneranda) into heaven, was discovered on the closing stone of a tomb in an underground crypt behind the apse of the basilica (Wilpert, "Die Malereien der Katakomben Roms", Freiburg, 1903, plate 213; De Rossi, ibid., 1875, 5 sqq.). Beside the saint's picture is her name: *Petronilla Mart.* (yr). That the painting was done shortly after 356, is proved by an inscription found in the tomb. It is thus clearly established that Petronilla was venerated at Rome as a martyr in the fourth century, and the testimony must be accepted as certainly historical, notwithstanding the later legend which recognizes her only as a virgin (see below). Another known, but unfortunately no longer extant, memorial was the marble sarcophagus which contained her remains, under Paul I (q. v.; 757–65) translated to St. Peter's. In the account of this in the "Liber Pontificalis" (ed. Duchesne, I, 466) the inscription carved on the sarcophagus is given thus: *Aureæ Petronillæ Filiæ Dulcissimæ* (of the golden Petronilla, the sweetest daughter). We learn, however, from extant sixteenth-century notices concerning this sarcophagus that the first word was *Aur.* (*Aureliæ*), so that the martyr's name was Aurelia Petronilla. The second name comes from Petro or Petronius, and, as the name of the great-grandfather of the Christian consul, Flavius Clemens, was Titus Flavius Petronius, it is very possible that Petronilla was a relative of the Christian Flavii, who were descended from the senatorial family of the Aurelii. This theory would also explain why Petronilla was buried in the catacomb of the Flavian Domitilla. Like the latter, Petronilla may have suffered during the persecution of Domitian, perhaps not till later.

In the fourth-century Roman catalogue of martyrs' feasts, which is used in the "Martyrologium Hieronymianum", her name seems not to have been inserted. It occurs in the latter martyrology (De Rossi-Duchesne, "Martyrol. Hieronym.", 69), but only as a later addition. Her name is given under 31 May and the Martyrologies of Bede and his imitators adopt the same date (Quentin, "Les martyrologes historiques", Paris, 1908, 51, 363 etc.). The absence of her name from the fourth-century Roman calendar of feasts suggests that Petronilla died at the end of the first or during the second century, since no special feasts for martyrs were celebrated during this period. After the erection of the basilica over her remains and those of Sts. Nereus and Achilleus in the fourth century, her cult extended widely and her name was therefore admitted later into the martyrology. A legend, the existence of which in the sixth century is proved by its presence in the list of the tombs of the Roman martyrs prepared by Abbot John at the end of this century (De Rossi, "Roma sotterranea", I, 180), regards Petronilla as a real daughter of St. Peter. In the Gnostic apocryphal Acts of St. Peter, dating from the second century, a daughter of St. Peter is mentioned, although her name is not given (Schmid, "Ein vorirenäische gnostisches Originalwerk in koptischer Sprache" in "Sitzungsber. der Berliner Akademie", 1896, 839 sqq.; Lipsius, "Die apokryphen Apostelgeschichten u. Apostellegenden", II, i, Brunswick, 1887, 203 sqq.). The legend being widely propagated by these apocryphal Acts, Petronilla was identified at Rome with this supposed daughter of St. Peter, probably because of her name and the great antiquity of her tomb. As such, but now as a virgin, not as a martyr, she appears in the legendary Acts of the martyrs Sts. Nereus and Achilleus and in the "Liber Pontificalis" (loc. cit.). From this legend of St. Nereus and Achilleus a similar notice was admitted into the historical martyrologies of the Middle Ages and thence into the modern Roman Martyrology. In 757 the coffin containing the mortal remains of the saint was transferred to an old circular building (an imperial mausoleum dating from the end of the fourth century) near St. Peter's. This building was altered and became the Chapel of St. Petronilla (De Rossi, "Inscriptiones christianæ urbis Romæ", II, 225). The saint subsequently appears as the special patroness of the treaties concluded between the popes and the Frankish emperors. At the rebuilding of St. Peter's in the sixteenth century, St. Petronilla's remains were translated to an altar (still dedicated to her) in the upper end of the right side-aisle (near the cupola). Her feast falls on 31 May.

DE ROSSI, *Sepolcro di S. Petronilla nella basilica in via Ardeatina e sua traslazione al Vaticano* in *Bullettino di arch. crist.* (1878), 125 sq. (1879), 5 sq.; DUMAZ, *La France et sainte Pétronille* in *Annales de St. Louis des Français* (1899), 517 sq.; URBAIN, *Ein Martyrologium der christl. Gemeinde zu Rom* (Leipzig, 1901), 152; DUFOURCQ, *Les Gesta Martyrum romains*, I (Paris, 1900), 251 sq.

J. P. KIRSCH.

Petronius, SAINT, Bishop of Bologna, date of birth unknown; d. before 450. The only certain historical information we possess concerning him is derived from a letter written by Bishop Eucherius of Lyons (d. 450–5) to Valerianus (in P. L., L, 711 sqq.) and from Gennadius' "De viris illustribus", XLI (ed. Czapla, Münster, 1898, p. 94). Eucherius writes that the holy Bishop Petronius was then renowned in Italy for his virtues. From Gennadius we receive more detailed information: Petronius belonged to a noble family whose members occupied high positions at the imperial Court at Milan and in the provincial administrations at the end of the fourth and the beginning of the fifth centuries. His father (also named Petronius) was probably *præfectus prætorio*, since a Petronius filled this office in Gaul in 402–8. Eucherius seems to suggest (P. L., 719) that the future bishop also held an important secular position. Even in his youth Petronius devoted himself to the practices of asceticism, and seems to have visited the Holy Places in Jerusalem, perhaps on a pilgrimage. About 432 he was elected and consecrated Bishop of Bologna, where he erected a church to St. Stephen, the building scheme of which was in imitation of the shrines on Golgotha and over the Holy Sepulchre in Jerusalem. The buildings belong approximately to the period when Leo I had basilicas erected in Rome and Galla Placidia in Ravenna. Petronius is believed to have written a work on the life of the Egyptian monks (Vitæ patrum Ægypti monachorum); the author of this work, however, is Rufinus of Aquileia. The treatise "De ordinatione episcopi", bearing the name of Petronius as author, is by the elder Petronius, who was a man of eloquence and wide acquaintance with the secular sciences. Morin has published a sermon entitled "In die ordinationis vel Natale episcopi" (Revue bénédictine, 1897, 3 sq.), which Gennadius ascribes to Bishop Petronius of Verona, whom Czalpa holds is Petronius of Bologna, but this assignment is not certain. According to Gennadius, Petronius died during the reign of Emperor Theodosius and Valentinian, i. e., before 450. In the twelfth century appeared a legendary life of the saint, whose relics were discovered in 1141. Shortly afterwards a church was erected in his honour at Bologna; a second, planned on a large scale, was begun in 1390, and built as far as the cross-aisle. In 1659 the building was resumed and the glorious Italian-Gothic church completed as it stands to-day. The feast of St. Petronius is celebrated on 4 October.

Acta SS., II, Oct., 454 sqq.; MELLONI, *Atti o memorie di S. Petronio* (Bologna, 1784); BOLLAND, *Bibl. hag. lat.*, II (1901), 965–6; MORIN, *Deux petits discours d'un évêque Petronius du Ve siècle* in *Revue bénédictine* (1897), 1 sqq.; CZAPLA, *Gennadius als Literarhistoriker* (Münster, 1898), 94 sqq.; LANZONI, *San Petronio, vescovo di Bologna nella storia e nella legenda* (Rome, 1907)

J. P. KIRSCH.

Petropolis, DIOCESE OF (PETROPOLITANENSIS), in the Province of Rio de Janeiro, Brazil, erected 11 Feb., 1895. The see founded by Leo XIII, 21 May, 1893, at Nictheroy, and transferred to Petropolis 11 Feb., 1895, was retransferred to Nictheroy in 1908. The city of Petropolis was founded by the Emperor of Brazil in 1845, as a colony for German immigrants and named in honour of Dom Pedro; it is a delightful summer resort. In 1894 it was made the capital of the State of Rio de Janeiro. Nictheroy is situated on the Bay of Rio de Janeiro. In 1834, when the city of Rio de Janeiro was formed into a "municipio neutro" and separated from the rest of the state, Nictheroy became the capital of the province and remained so until 1894. The first bishop, François de Rogo Maia, b. at Pernambuco, 29 Sept., 1849, was elected in Sept., 1893. The second bishop, Jean-François Braga, b. at Pelotas, Diocese of St. Pierre de Rio Grande, 24 Aug., 1867, cons. 24 Aug., 1902; transferred to the See of Curityba, 1907. The present bishop, Augustin-François Bennassi, b. at Rio de Janeiro, 17 Nov., 1868, was elected 13 March, 1908, and cons. 10 May following. Statistics: area, 15,548 square miles; Catholic population, 1,000,300 (Protestants, about 9000); 123 parishes, 100 filial churches or chapels, 89 secular and 35 regular priests, 3 colleges, and one technical school.

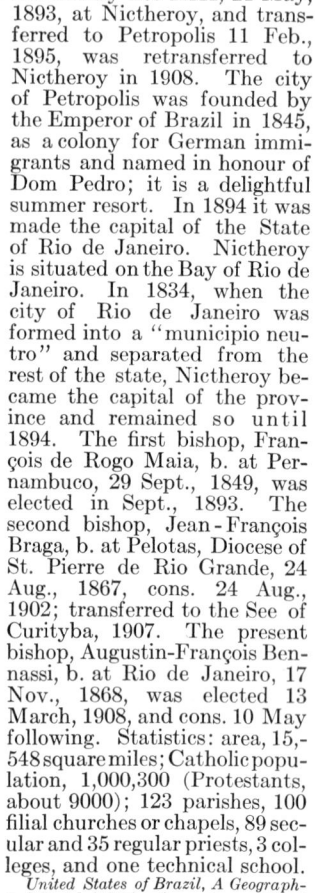

United States of Brazil, A Geographical Sketch (1901); *Annuaire pontifical catholique* (Paris, 1910).

J. ZEVELY.

ST. PETRONIUS
Church of S. Domenico, Bologna
School of Michelangelo

Petrucci, OTTAVIO DEI, inventor of movable metal type for printing mensural and polyphonic music, b. at Fossombrone near Urbino, Italy, 18 June, 1466; d. there, 7 May, 1539. In 1498 he secured from the City Council of Venice a twenty years' patent for the exploitation of his invention. Beginning in 1501, he continued his publications for ten years at Venice, after which he turned his establishment over to Amadeo Scotti and Niccolò da Rafael. He afterwards secured from the papal authorities a fifteen years' privilege or license for the Papal States. From 1513 to 1523 he operated a music-printing establishment in his native city, Fossombrone.

Until 1901 Petrucci was considered as the pioneer in the use of the movable metal type for the printing of liturgical books, but Dom Rafael Molitor, in his "Nachtridentinische Choralreform" (Leipzig, 1901, I, 94), demonstrates that it was Ulric Han, or Hahn, a native of Ingolstadt, residing at Rome, who printed the first Missal in metal type notes in 1476. Petrucci's great advance consisted in the triple process (i. e., first the text and initials, then the lines, and lastly the notes) and the wonderful neatness and perfection with which the printing was done, so that his publications have not only survived but have been unequalled by any of his successors. They were surpassed in distinctness only by a perfected engraving process of the eighteenth century. His work was of the greatest importance for the dissemination and preservation of the polyphonic compositions of his time, especially those of the Netherlands masters. In the libraries of Bologna, Treviso, the Paris Conservatoire, Venice, Vienna, Berlin, Munich, collections are preserved containing *frottole, chansons*, motets, and masses by contemporary masters, such as Josquin Deprés, Hayne, de Orto, Obrecht, La Rue, Busnois, Compère, Ghisclin, Agricola, Isaac, Okeghem, Tinctoris, and a host of others, many of whom would probably have been altogether forgotten but for these remarkable prints, now four hundred years old.

RIEMANN, *Geschichte der Musik*, II (Leipzig, 1907), i; IDEM, *Musiklexikon* (Leipzig, 1905); MOLITOR, *Nachtridentinische Choralreform*, I (Leipzig, 1901); MENDEL, *Musiklexikon*, VIII (Leipzig, 1877).

JOSEPH OTTEN.

Petrus a Tarentasia. See INNOCENT V, BLESSED, POPE.

Petrus Alfonsus, converted Jew and controversialist, b. at Huesca, in the former Kingdom of Aragon, 1062; d. 1110. Previous to his conversion he was known as Moses Sephardi (the Spaniard). King Alfonso I of Aragon, whose physician-in-ordinary he became, stood sponsor at his baptism, which he received in his native town on St. Peter's day (29 June, 1106). In honour of this saint and of his sponsor he chose the name Petrus Alfonsus. As his conversion was attributed by his former co-religionists to ignorance or dishonourable motives, he published a justification in a Latin work consisting of twelve dialogues between a Jew and a Christian. These dialogues were first printed at Cologne in 1536, and have since frequently been re-edited. A second work of Petrus Alfonsus, based on Arabic sources, is entitled "Ecclesiastical Discipline" (Disciplina Clericalis). It has been translated into several languages and is preserved in numerous manuscripts. Labouderie, Vicar-General of Avignon, published it at Paris in 1824 with a French translation of the fifteenth century. Another edition by F. W. V. Schmidt appeared at Berlin in 1827. The text of both works of Petrus Alfonsus, preceded by biographical notices, may be found in Migne, CLVII, 527–706.

CEILLIER, *Auteurs ecclésiast.*, XIV (Paris, 1863), i, 170–73; KOHUT in *Jewish Encycl.*, I, 377; DOUCE in BOHN'S *Antiq. Libr.*, X (London, 1848), 39–44.

N. A. WEBER.

Petrus Aureoli. See AUREOLI.

Petrus Bernardinus, Florentine heretic, b. at Florence about 1475; d. 1502. His parents were common folk, and he himself lacked all higher education. But he attached himself with fanatical zeal to Savonarola, and, by diligent attendance at his sermons and zealous study of his writings, acquired a wide but superficial theological knowledge. Peter preached to the people in the public squares of Florence and, during the lifetime of Savonarola and after his death, he propagated secretly eccentric and revolutionary doctrines. According to him, the Church must be renewed with the sword; until this was accomplished, there was no need to confess, since all priests, secular and regular, were unworthy. According to the Florentine chronicler, Cerretani, about twenty adherents of Savonarola formed a secret society and elected Peter pope. The latter, who was then twenty-five years old, assumed special ecclesiastical functions and anointed his followers with oil (the alleged anointment of the Holy Ghost). The members attended no Divine Service, but during their meetings prayed in spirit under the leadership of Peter, whom they regarded as a prophet. The association was discovered by the archbishop and at his request the Council of Florence proscribed its meetings. In 1502 the members left the town secretly and proceeded to Mirandola where Count Gian Francesco, a zealous supporter of Savonarola, gave them a friendly reception. When, a little later, the count was besieged by two of his brothers, who claimed Mirandola, Peter declared it God's will that Gian Francesco should overcome his enemies. However, Mirandola was taken and the count lost his territory in August, 1502. The sectaries falling into the hands of the victors, Peter and some of his companions were burned as heretics; the remainder were expelled or dispatched to Florence. The attempts of Protestant historians to stamp Peter as a forerunner of the Reformation cannot be historically justified.

PASTOR, *History of the Popes*, tr. ANTROBUS, V (St. Louis, 1902), 214–16.

J. P. KIRSCH.

Petrus Diaconus, the name of several men of note in ecclesiastical history and literature.

(1) One of the Scythian monks who appeared in 519 before Pope Hormisdas in connexion with the Theopaschite controversy. He wrote concerning this question his treatise "De incarnatione et gratia", at the same time directed against the teaching of Faustus of Riez respecting grace and addressed to St. Fulgentius of Ruspe; in P. L., LXII, 83–92; Bardenhewer, tr. Shahan, "Patrology", 548, 1908. (St. Louis).

(2) A disciple and friend of Gregory the Great; d. at Rome 12 March, 605 or 606. His questioning occasioned the composition of Gregory's "Dialogues". He is also authority for the statement that the Holy Spirit sometimes hovered in the form of a dove over the great pope's head.

Acta SS., March, II, 208–9; MANN, *Lives of the Popes*, I (St. Louis, 1902), i, 243–44.

(3) A monk of Monte Cassino known also as Petrus Subdiaconus; d. c. 960. He was subdeacon of the church of St. Januarius at Naples, and he continued the history of this diocese (Gesta episc. Neap.), an anonymous work which had already been added to by John the Deacon. He wrote the lives of several saints, including, according to some critics, that of Athanasius, Bishop of Naples ("Vita et translatio Athanasii ep. Neap.").

(4) Another monk of Monte Cassino, also called "the Librarian" (Bibliothecarius), b. c. 1107 at Rome; d. probably c. 1140. A descendant of the Counts of Tusculum, he was offered in 1115 to the monastery of Monte Cassino. About 1127 he was forced to leave the abbey and retired to the neighbouring Atina, seemingly because he was an adherent of the Abbot Oderisius. In 1137 he was allowed to return to Monte Cassino. That same year he appeared before Emperor Lothair II, then in Italy, on behalf of his monastery. The sovereign was so pleased with him that he appointed him his chaplain and secretary, and would probably have attached him permanently to his person had not Abbot Wibald considered Peter's return necessary to the abbey. At Monte Cassino Peter became librarian and keeper of the archives, of which he compiled a register. Besides continuing the chronicle of Monte Cassino by Leo Marsicanus (or Ostiensis) from 1075 to 1138, he wrote several historical works: "De viris illustribus Casinensibus"; "De ortu et obitu justorum Casinensium"; "De Locis sanctis"; "Disciplina Casinensis"; "Rhythmus de novissimis diebus". Peter forged, under the name of Gordian, the Passion of St. Placidus. He is vain and occasionally untruthful, but an entertaining writer. His works are in P. L., CLXXIII, 763–1144.

P. L., CLXXIII, 462–80; BALZANI, *Early Chroniclers of Europe, Italy* (London, 1883), 174–80; MANN, *Lives of the Popes*, VII (St. Louis, 1910), 218.

N. A. WEBER.

Petrus de Natalibus, bishop, author of a collection of lives of the saints; date of birth unknown; d. between 1400 and 1406. No details of the early life of this hagiographer have been handed down to us. A Venetian, he consecrated himself to the ecclesiastical state, becoming a canon in Equilio (Jesolo). On 5 July, 1370, he was elevated to the episcopal see of that city. Details are also lacking regarding his pastoral activity. The last mention of him refers to the year 1400, and in 1406, another appears as Bishop of Equilio; the date of his decease, therefore, must be set between these two years (Eubel, "Hierarchia catholica medii ævi", I, 250). He is chiefly known as the author of "Legends of the Saints" in twelve books, a very valuable work with a wide circulation. In his arrangement of the various lives he follows the calendar of the Church. The collection, first printed in Vicenza, 1493, went through many editions, the last of which (the eighth) appeared in Venice, 1616.

FABRICIUS, *Bibliotheca mediæ et infimæ ætatis*, ed. MANSI, V, 93; POTTHAST, *Bibliotheca historica medii ævi*, 2nd ed., II, 918.

J. P. KIRSCH.

Petrus de Palude. See PALUDANUS.

Petrus Juliani. See JOHN XXI, POPE.

Petun Nation, one of the three great divisions of the Huron Indians, the other two being the Hurons proper and the Neutrals. What was common to the three in name, country, population, government, religion, history, etc., previous to their dispersion by the Iroquois, is to be found under the heading of HURON INDIANS. In that article the fate of the Neutrals after the disastrous event and the migration of the Hurons proper were treated in full. Seeing that the Petun or Tobacco Nation, as soon as their scattered remnants had gradually drifted together, became known to the English colonists as the Dionondadies or Wyandots, which latter name they bear exclusively at the present day, what concerns their migrations in the West has been collected under the article WYANDOT INDIANS.

ARTHUR EDWARD JONES.

Peuerbach (also PEURBACH, PURBACH, PURBACHIUS), GEORGE VON, Austrian astronomer, b. at Peuerbach near Linz, 30 May, 1423; d. in Vienna, 8 April, 1461. His real family name, as well as his early schooling, is unknown. About the year 1440 he received the degree of master of philosophy and the free arts, *cum insigni laude*, at the University of Vienna. His teacher in mathematics was probably Johann von Gmünden. In 1448 he went on a trip to Italy for the sake of study. There Bianchini of Ferrara and Cardinal Nicholas of Cusa, then in Rome, became interested in the young man and induced him to lecture on astronomy at the University of Ferrara. He refused offers of professorships at Bologna and Padua, and also the appointment as court astronomer to King Ladislaus of Hungary, but went back to Vienna in 1450 to teach. He lectured on philology and classical literature. His scientific teaching was done chiefly in private, his most famous pupil being Johann Müller of Königsberg, later known as Regiomontanus. Peuerbach has been called the father of observational and mathematical astronomy in the West. He began to work up Ptolemy's "Almagest", replacing chords by sines, and calculating tables of sines for every minute of arc for a radius of 600,000 units. This was the first transition from the duodecimal to the decimal system. His observations were made with very simple instruments, an ordinary plumb-line being used for measuring the angles of elevation of the stars. Cardinal Bessarion invited him to Rome to study Ptolemy in the original Greek and not from a faulty Latin translation. He accepted on condition that Müller go with him. On account of the master's death the pupil went alone to complete the work.

Peuerbach is also noted for his great attempt to reconcile the opposing theories of the universe, the so-called homocentric spheres of Eudoxus and Aristotle, with Ptolemy's epicyclic trains. This work, "Theoricæ, etc.", had an enormous success and remained the basis of academic instruction in astronomy until years after Copernicus had swept away all these hypotheses. Twenty works are known. Among these the following are the most important: "Theoricæ novæ planetarum, id est septem errantium siderum nec non octavi seu firmamenti" (1st ed., Nuremberg, 1460, followed by many others in Milan and Ingolstadt); "Sex primi libri epitomatis Almagesti", completed by Regiomontanus (Venice, 1496; Basle, 1534; Nuremberg, 1550); "Tabulæ eclypsium super meridiano Viennensi" (2nd ed., Vienna, 1514); "Quadratum geometricum meridiano" (Nuremberg, 1516); "Nova tabula sinus de decem minutis in decem per multas, etc.", completed by Regiomontanus (Nuremberg, 1541).

FIEDLER, *Peuerbach und Regiomontanus* in *Jahresbericht des K. Kathol. Gymn. zu Leobschütz*, L (1870); WOLF, *Gesch. d. Astr.* (Munich, 1877); GUNTHER, *Allg. Deutsche Biogr.*, XXV (Leipzig, 1887), 559.

WILLIAM FOX.

Peutinger, CONRAD, antiquarian and humanist, b. at Augsburg, 14 Oct., 1465; d. 28 Dec., 1547. As a young man he studied law and belles-lettres at Padua, Bologna, and Florence. At Rome his enthusiasm for antiquity was awakened. Returning to Germany he entered the service of his native city in 1490, receiving the definite appointment of syndic in 1497. To the end of his life he served the city in various capacities and always with distinction. He enjoyed the friendship and special confidence of the Emperor Maximilian, who frequently employed him on missions of a diplomatic or literary nature. Through this friendship Peutinger obtained for Augsburg valuable privileges, notably in 1506 while he stayed with Maximilian in Vienna and Hungary, where he took a leading part in the negotiations between the emperor and his rebellious Hungarian subjects. In 1512 he acted as intermediary between the emperor and the Republic of Venice. Moreover, through his connexions with influential men in Germany, as well as in Italy and France, Peutinger was able to procure for his imperial friend much valuable information concerning current events. He was frequently occupied with furthering the literary and artistic plans of his patron; thus he had much to do with arranging for the designs and wood-cuts used in the sumptuous editions of Maximilian's poems "Weisskunig" and "Teurdank". After the death of Maximilian (1519) Peutinger continued to serve under Charles V. He represented his native city at the Diet of Worms (1521). Towards Luther his attitude was at first entirely sympathetic, but he refused to break with the Church, and maintained a conservative attitude which made him an object of distrust to the adherents of the Reformation. At the Diet of Augsburg (1530) he presented the protest in the name of the city against the imperial decree, but when, in 1534, it was proposed to carry out the religious innovations without regard to the desires of the Catholic clergy, Peutinger advised against it, putting his trust in a plenary council to restore the lost Church unity. His advice was not heeded, and so he retired with a pension and henceforth devoted himself almost exclusively to his studies. In 1538 he was made a patrician, and a few days before his death he was ennobled.

Of his literary work only a part has been published. In Augsburg he had collected a rich store of ancient Roman inscriptions, the historical value of which he had learned to realize while a student in Italy. At the suggestion of Maximilian these were published in 1505 under the title "Romanæ vetustatis fragmenta in Augusta Vindelicorum et ejus diœcesi" (2nd ed., 1520, Mainz). In the "Sermones convivales de finibus Germaniæ contra Gallos", which goes under Peutinger's name, the ancient boundaries of Gaul and Germany are discussed. Peutinger also published many important sources for German history, among them the history of the Goths by Jordanes, that of the Langobards by Paulus Diaconus, and the "Chronicon Urspergense" (see KONRAD VON LICHTENAU), all of which appeared in 1515. The famous "Tabula Peutingeriana", a thirteenth-century copy of an old Roman map of the military roads of the empire, is not properly called after Peutinger, to whom it was bequeathed by its discoverer, Conrad Celtes. Peutinger intended to publish it, but died before he could carry out his plan. Peutinger's magnificent collection of MSS., coins, and inscriptions remained in his family until 1714, when the last descendant, Ignace Peutinger, bequeathed it to the Jesuits of Augsburg. After the suppression of the order, part of it went to the town library, and part to Vienna.

LOTTER, *Historia vitæ atque meritorum Conradi Peutingeri* (1729), revised edition by VEITH (Augsburg, 1783); HERBERGER, *C. P. in seinem Verhältnisse zum Kaiser Maximilian I* (Augsburg, 1851); GEIGER, *Renaissance und Humanismus* in ONCKEN, *Allgemeine Weltgeschichte*, II, 8 (Berlin, 1882), 370–372; LIER in *Allgemeine Deutsche Biographie*, XXV (Leipzig, 1887), 561–8.

ARTHUR F. J. REMY.

Peyto (PETO, PETOW), WILLIAM, cardinal; d. 1558 or 1559. Though his parentage was long unknown, it is now established that he was the son of Edward Peyto of Chesterton, Warwickshire, and Goditha, daughter of Sir Thomas Throckmorton of Coughton. He was educated by the Grey Friars and took his degree of B. A. at Oxford; but he was incorporated in Cambridge university, 1502-3, and became M. A. there in 1505. He was elected fellow of Queen's College in 1506, and on 14 June, 1510, was incorporated M. A. at Oxford. Entering the Franciscan Order, he became known for his holiness of life, and was appointed confessor to Princess Mary. Later on he was elected Provincial of England and held that office when in 1532 he denounced the divorce of Henry VIII in the king's presence. He was imprisoned till the end of that year, when he went abroad and spent many years at Antwerp and elsewhere in the Low Countries, being active on behalf of all Catholic interests. In 1539 he was included in the Act of Attainder passed against Cardinal Pole and his friends (31 Hen. VIII, c. 5), but he was in Italy at the time and remained there out of the king's reach. On 30 March, 1543, Paul III nominated him Bishop of Salisbury. He could not obtain possession of his diocese, nor did he attempt to do so, on the accession of Queen Mary in 1553, but resigned the see and retired to his old convent at Greenwich. There he remained till Paul IV, who had known him in Rome and highly esteemed him, decided to create him cardinal and legate in place of Pole. But as Peyto was very old and his powers were failing, he declined both dignities. He was, however, created cardinal in June, 1557, though Queen Mary would not allow him to receive the hat, and the appointment was received with public derision. It was a tradition among the Franciscans that he was pelted with stones by a London mob, and so injured that he shortly afterwards died (Parkinson, op. cit. below, p. 254). Other accounts represent him as dying in France. The date frequently assigned for his death (April, 1558) is incorrect, as on 31 October, 1558, Queen Mary wrote to the pope that she had offered to reinstate him in the Bishopric of Salisbury on the death of Bishop Capon, but that he had declined because of age and infirmity.

COOPER, *Athenæ Cantabrigienses*, I (Cambridge, 1858), giving new particulars as to his family and his university career; WOOD, *Athenæ Oxonienses*, ed. BLISS (London, 1813–20); PARKINSON, *Collectanea Anglo-Minoritica* (London, 1726); DODD, *Church History* (Brussels *vere* Wolverhampton, 1737–42); BRADY, *Episcopal Succession*, I, II (Rome, 1877); GASQUET, *Henry VIII and the English Monasteries* (London, 1888); GAIRDNER in *Dict. Nat. Biog.*, citing state papers, but otherwise an imperfect and defective account; GILLOW in *Bibl. Dict. Eng. Cath.*, s. v.; STONE, *Mary the First* (London, 1901); HAILE, *Life of Cardinal Pole* (London, 1910).

EDWIN BURTON.

Pez (1) BERNHARD, historian, b. 22 February, 1683, at Ybbs near Melk; d. 27 March, 1735, at Melk, southern Austria. Bernhard studied at Vienna and Krems, and in 1699 entered the Benedictine monastery at Melk. Having devoted himself to the classic languages, he was made professor in the monastery school in 1704, and in the same year went to the University of Vienna, where he studied theology, and in 1708, was ordained priest. He now zealously devoted himself to the study of history, and in 1713, became librarian at Melk. As a model for his historical works he followed the French Benedictines of St. Maur. He studied the archives of the order at Melk and Vienna, and in 1715–17 he, with his brother whose interest in historical subjects he had excited, searched for manuscripts in the Austrian, Bavarian, and Swabian monasteries. In 1716 he published a plan for a universal Benedictine library, in which all the authors of the order, and their works, should be catalogued and reviewed. He obtained from the monasteries of his order no less than seven hundred and nine titles. He also had friendly literary relations with Johann v. Eckhart, Schannat, Uffenbach, Schmincke, Mosheim, Lünig etc. In 1728 he accompanied Count Sinzendorf to France, where he made the acquaintance of Montfaucon, Martène, Durand, Le Texier, Calmet etc., and enriched his collection from the libraries of the order. His chief works are: "Thesaurus anecdotorum novissimus" (6 fol. vol., Augsburg, 1721–9), a collection of exegetic, theological, philosophical, ascetic, and historical literary sources; "Bibliotheca ascetica" (12 vols., 1723–40), containing the sources of ascetic literature; "Bibliotheca Benedictino-Maruiana" (1716). In a controversy with the Jesuits he defended his order with the "Epistolæ apologeticæ pro Ordine S. Benedicti", 1716. In 1725 he published "Homilien des Abtes Gottfried von Admont (1165)", in two vols., and the minor philosophical works of Abbot Engelbert von Admont. His proposed monumental work, "Bibliotheca Benedictina Generalis", was never completed. His manuscript material is partly made use of in the "Historia rei literariæ O.S.B." by Ziegelbauer-Legipont (1754). His manuscripts are preserved at Melk.

(2) HIERONYMUS, b. 24 February, 1685, at Ybbs; d. 14 October, 1762, at Melk. In 1703 he entered the novitiate at Melk and was ordained in 1711. He became a valuable assistant to his brother, after whose death he became librarian. His principal works are: "Scriptores rerum Austriacarum", 1721–45, in three volumes, a collection of over one hundred sources, even to-day valuable for Austrian history; "Acta S. Colomanni" (1713); "History of St. Leopold" (1746).

ZIEGELBAUER-LEGIPONT, *Hist. rei lit. O. S. B.* (Augsburg, 1754), I, 446–50, III, 466–76; WURZBACH, *Biog. Lex. des Kaiserthums Oesterreich*, XXII (Vienna, 1870), 145–50; KRONES in *Allgem. deut. Biog.* s. v.; KATSCHTHALER, *Ueber Bernhard Pez und dessen Briefwechsel* (Melk, 1889); HURTER, *Nomen. lit. theologiæ catholicæ*, 3rd ed., III (Innsbruck, 1910), 1141–5, 1553.

KLEMENS LÖFFLER.

Pfanner, FRANZ, abbot, b. at Langen, Vorarlberg, Austria, 1825; d. at Emmaus, South Africa, 24 May, 1909. In 1850 he was ordained priest and was given a curacy in his native diocese. Nine years later he was appointed an Austrian army chaplain in the Italian campaign against Napoleon III, but the war was over before he could take up his appointment. After serving as chaplain to the Sisters of Mercy at Agram for several years, he went to Rome, and there saw the Trappists for the first time. Whilst waiting for his bishop's permission to join this order, he went on a pilgrimage to the Holy Land. In November, 1864, he was professed at the Trappist monastery of Marienwald in Austria, and was made sub-prior a few weeks later. He again went to Rome in 1866, where he reorganized the well-known monastery at Tre Fontane. Then he conceived the idea of a foundation in Turkey. The difficulties seemed insuperable, but in 1869 he was able to open the monastery of Mariastern in Bosnia, which was raised to the status of an abbey in 1879. In that year Bishop Richards of the Eastern Vicariate of the Cape of Good Hope was in Europe, seeking Trappists to evangelize the Kafirs and to teach them to work. When all others had declined the invitation, Abbot Franz resolved to relinquish his settled abbey and face fresh difficulties in South Africa. At the end of July, 1880, he arrived at Dunbrody, the place purchased by Bishop Richards for the work. But on account of the drought, winds and baboons, he declared the site unsuitable after a trial of several years. With the permission of Bishop Jolivet, O.M.I., of the Natal Vicariate, he then (December, 1882) bought from the Land Colonization Company a part of the farm Zoekoegat, near Pinetown. The fine monastery of Mariannhill was built here, and it soon became the centre of a great work of civilization. Finding the need of a sisterhood to teach the Kafir girls, with characteristic energy he founded the Sisters of the Precious Blood, who number more than 300. In 1885 Mariannhill was created an abbey, and Prior Franz Pfanner elected the first mitred abbot. But in 1893 he resigned his prelacy and began life again in the mission station of Emmaus, where he remained until his death.

The missionary methods of Abbot Franz and his successors have won the approval of all those interested in the natives of South Africa. Such various authorities as Mark Twain and the last Prime Minister of the Cape have spoken enthusiastically of the work. It has prospered exceedingly. At the date of Abbot Franz's death there were 55 priests, 223 lay-brothers and 326 nuns working in 42 mission stations among the natives. Only a few months before Abbot Franz's death the Holy See, at the petition of the Trappists of Mariannhill, made a considerable change in their status. The Cistercian Rule in its rigour, for which Abbot Pfanner was most zealous, was found to be an obstacle to missionary development in some particulars. Hence the name of the order was changed to that of the Missionary Religious of Mariannhill, and they were given a milder rule on a three years' trial, after which the whole subject will again be submitted to the judgment of the Holy See.

For bibliography, see MARIANNHILL.

SIDNEY R. WELCH.

Pfefferkorn, JOHANNES, a baptized Jew, b. probably at Nuremberg, 1469; d. at Cologne, between 1521 and 1524. In 1505, after many years of wandering, he, together with his wife and children, was converted to Christianity at Cologne. He soon became known through his efforts for the conversion of the Jews and his controversy with Reuchlin. In "Der Judenspiegel" (Cologne, 1507), he demanded that the Jews should give up the practice of usury, work for their living, attend Christian sermons, and do away with the Books of the Talmud, which caused such hatred against Christianity. On the other hand, he condemned the persecution of the Jews as an obstacle to their conversion, and defended them against the charge of murdering Christian children for ritual purposes. Bitterly opposed by the Jews on account of this work, he virulently attacked them in: "Wie die blinden Jüden ihr Ostern halten" (1508); "Judenbeicht" (1508); and "Judenfeind" (1509). Convinced that the principal source of the obduracy of the Jews lay in their books, he tried to have them seized and destroyed. He obtained from several Dominican convents recommendations to Kunigunde, the sister of the Emperor Maximilian, and through her influence to the emperor himself. On 19 August, 1509, Maximilian ordered the Jews to deliver to Pfefferkorn all books opposing Christianity. Pfefferkorn began the work of confiscation at Frankfort-on-the-Main; thence he went to Worms, Mainz, Bingen, Lorch, Lahnstein, and Deutz. But a new imperial mandate of 10 Nov., 1509, gave the direction of the whole affair to the Elector and Archbishop of Mainz, Uriel von Gemmingen, with orders to secure opinions from the Universities of Mainz, Cologne, Erfurt, and Heidelberg, from the inquisitor Jakob Hochstraten of Cologne, from the priest Victor von Carben, and from Johann Reuchlin. Pfefferkorn, in order to vindicate his action and to gain still further the good will of the emperor, wrote "In Lob und Eer dem allerdurchleuchtigsten grossmechtigsten Fürsten und Herrn Maximilian" (Cologne, 1510). In April he was again at Frankfort, and with the delegate of the Elector of Mainz and Professor Hermann Ortlieb, he undertook a new confiscation.

Hochstraten and the Universities of Mainz and Cologne decided (Oct., 1510) against the Jewish books. Reuchlin declared that only those books obviously offensive (as the "Nizachon" and "Toldoth Jeschu") should be destroyed. The elector sent all the answers received at the end of October to the emperor through Pfefferkorn. Thus informed of Reuchlin's vote Pfefferkorn was greatly excited, and answered with "Handspiegel" (Mainz, 1511), in which he attacked Reuchlin unmercifully. Reuchlin complained to the Emperor Maximilian, and he answered Pfefferkorn's attack with his "Augenspiegel", against which Pfefferkorn published his "Brandspiegel". In June, 1513, both parties were silenced by the emperor. Pfefferkorn however published in 1514 a new polemic, "Sturmglock", against both the Jews and Reuchlin. During the controversy between Reuchlin and the theologians of Cologne, Pfefferkorn was assailed in the "Epistolæ obscurorum virorum" by the young Humanists who espoused Reuchlin's cause. He replied with "Beschirmung", or "Defensio J. Pepericorni contra famosas et criminales obscurorum virorum epistolas" (Cologne, 1516), "Streitbüchlein" (1517). When in 1520 Reuchlin's case was decided in Rome by the condemnation of "Augenspiegel", Pfefferkorn wrote as an expression of his triumph "Ein mitleidliche Klag" (Cologne, 1521). Pfefferkorn was a fanatic and his public and literary life had little of sympathy or grace, but he was certainly an honourable character and the caricature which his opponents have drawn of him is far from true.

GEIGER, *Pfefferkorn* in *Jüdische Zeitschrift für Wissenschaft und Leben*, VII (1869), 293–307; IDEM, *Joh. Reuchlin* (Leipzig, 1871), 209–454; IDEM, *Der Kampf gegen die Bücher der Juden am Anfange des 16. Jahrhunderts in seiner Beziehung auf Frankfurt* in *Archiv für Frankfurts Geschichte und Kunst*, new series, IV (1869), 208–17; ROTH, *Der Kampf um die Judenbücher und Reuchlin vor der theologischen Fakultät zu Mainz 1509–1513* in *Der Katholik*, II (1909), 4th series, XL, 139–44; JANSSEN, *Geschichte des deutschen Volkes*, II (Freiburg, 1897), 43 sq.

FRIEDRICH LAUCHERT.

Pfister, ADOLF, educationist, b. at Hechingen in Hohenzollern, 26 Sept., 1810; d. at Ober-Dischingen in Würtemberg, 29 April, 1878. He was educated at the Latin school at Hechingen, at the Lyceum of Rastatt, and later at Sasbach. He then studied theology at the Grand Seminary of Strasburg, and was ordained to the priesthood, 25 May, 1833, at Freiburg. After serving for five months as curate at Sasbach, and for a year as assistant at the cathedral of Freiburg, he returned to Hohenzollern, and, from 1835 to 1838, was curate at Steinhofen near Hechingen. In 1838 he obtained civic rights in Würtemberg, and as a priest of the Diocese of Rottenburg, he was pastor first in Dotternhausen; 31 Jan., 1839, at Rosswangen; 11 May, 1841, at Risstissen; from 1851 also school inspector in Ehingen. On 12 Aug., 1867, the Catholic theological faculty of Tübingen granted him the degree of Doctor of Theology. In May, 1877, he withdrew to Ober-Dischingen. In 1857 he founded the "Rottenburger Kirchenblatt", which he published for three years. From 1860 he edited the "Katholisches Schulwochenblatt" Spaichingen), which, together with Hermann Rolfus, he continued as "Süddeutsches katholisches Schulwochenblatt" (1861–67), and with J. Haug and Fr. J. Knecht as "Magazin für Pädagogik" (1868–72). But his most valuable work was the editing with Rolfus of the "Real-Encyclopädie des Erziehungs- und Unterrichtswesens nach katholischen Principien" (4 vols., Mainz, 1863–66; 2nd ed., 1872-1874; a 5th vol., "Ergänzungsband", was published by Rolfus alone in 1884 after Pfister's death). Among Pfister's other writings may be mentioned: "Unterricht über das Werk der Glaubensverbreitung" (Freiburg, 1850); a German translation of Thomas à Kempis, "Vier Bücher von der Nachfolge Christi" (Freiburg, 1860; 4th ed., 1873); and "Kinderlegende" (Freiburg, 1863); he also compiled several prayer-books.

ROLFUS AND PFISTER, *Real-Encyclopädie des Erziehungs- und Unterrichtswesens, Ergänzungsband* (Mainz, 1884), 265–7; KEHREIN, *Biographisch-literarisches Lexicon der katholischen deutschen Dichter, Volks- und Jugendschriftseller im 19. Jahrhundert*, II (Würzburg, 1871), 9; NEHER, *Personal-Katalog der Geistlichen des Bisthums Rottenburg* (3rd ed., Schwäbisch Gmünd, 1894), 54.

FRIEDERICH LAUCHERT.

Pflug, JULIUS VON, last Catholic Bishop of Naumburg-Zeitz, b. at Eythra, near Leipzig, 1499; d. at Zeitz, 3 Sept., 1564. He was the son of Cæsar von Pflug, who acted as commissary for the Elector of Saxony in the religious disputation at Leipzig in 1519. Julius entered college at Leipzig, when only eleven years of age, continued his studies at Padua, and finished them in 1521 at Bologna, obtaining the degree of Doctor of Laws. At Leipzig he was the pupil of Peter Mosellanus, and at Padua of Lazaro Buonamico. He had received benefices at Mainz and Merseburg, and on his return was made dean of the cathedral of Meissen and provost at the collegiate church of Zeitz. The times in which he lived were full of troubles; Luther and his adherents were using every energy in spreading their religious views, and were supported in their work by the civil power. Pflug himself had received an education in accordance with the humanistic ideals then prevalent, while his theological knowledge, mostly self-acquired, was not very profound. He was gifted with rare diplomatic talents, and, being naturally inclined to peace and harmony, he was willing to make sacrifices even in matters of doctrine and discipline. Hence his presence was requested for nearly every theological conference held for the purpose of finding some lines of conformity in doctrine between the Catholics and Evangelicals. Thus we find him engaged at Leipzig in 1534, together with Behus and Türk against Melanchthon and Brück. In 1539 he was similarly employed by the Bishop of Meissen when the Elector of Saxony was introducing Protestantism into this diocese. It seems that, by order of the bishop, Pflug and Wicel composed a treatise giving four articles of belief, "which every Christian is bound to accept". This produced no pacifying effect, nor did the personal interview between the elector and Pflug, but rather brought about Pflug's loss of favour with John Frederick of Saxony.

On 6 January, 1541, Philip, Bishop of Naumburg, died at Freising, and ten days later the chapter received the news. Dreading the interference of the elector, the chapter ordered the occupation of the palace at Zeitz which held the treasures of the diocese, and on the twentieth of the same month proceeded to the election of a successor, at which Pflug was the unanimous choice. The apprehensions of the chapter were entirely justified, for John Frederick had determined to fill any vacancy and give no chance for an election. Pflug was at the time with Cardinal Albrecht of Mainz whose position brought him into close contact with the emperor. Pflug was informed of his election, and was earnestly requested not to refuse acceptance. At the imperial court he was considered the proper person to defend the independence of the diocese even against the elector. John Frederick received notice of the death of Philip on 23 January, and on the next day news of the election. He would not permit Pflug to take possession, and immediately issued orders to the city council that, until further orders, no allegiance be offered the new bishop. In the following year, on 20 January, he ordered Luther to ordain Nicholas von Amsdorf as Bishop of Naumburg. In the meantime Pflug was employed to further the reformatory projects of the emperor, and appeared in April, 1541, at the religious colloquy at Ratisbon. The book published at this meeting and the imperial edict of 29 June, 1541, called the Interim of Ratisbon, gave little satisfaction to either party: Luther and the elector wanted larger concessions, while the Catholics claimed that too much had been granted. Pflug and Gropper tried to justify themselves in a pamphlet. After the victory of Mühldorf, 24 April, 1547, over the combined forces of the Smalkaldic League, Pflug was able to enter his diocese, which had become almost entirely Protestant. He did his best to bring back the people to the Catholic faith, but in vain. He was permitted to hold Catholic service only in the cathedral of Naumburg and in the collegiate church at Zeitz; the monasteries and their property remained secularized. He removed the Evangelical preachers from some of the churches, but the civil authorities restored them to their positions.

In 1549 he called the pastors to Zeitz to find out their qualifications. He found a sad condition of affairs: all the priests were married with one exception, and willing rather to lose their pastorates than to give up their wives. He applied to other bishops to obtain unmarried priests, but they were unable to assist him, and thus he reported to Pope Julius III. Under this pressure he had a petition drawn up to the Cardinals Mendoza and Pole asking the toleration of married priests, though personally he preferred the unmarried clergy. Similarly he had on a former occasion expressed his opinion that many wavering minds might be kept in communion with the Church if the Holy Eucharist were administered to the laity under both species. His plan to establish a Catholic educational institution for aspirants to the clerical state failed, but he assisted students at Catholic colleges out of his own scanty income. He no longer expected any good results from disputations with the Protestants, though he was present in December, 1547, at Jüterbogk and in August, 1548, at Pegau, and assisted in framing the Interim of Augsburg. In November, 1551, he made his appearance at the Council of Trent, but on account of ill-health remained only a short time. In 1553 the elector introduced a Protestant consistory into Zeitz, and gave the cathedral of Naumburg to the common use of Catholics and Protestants. In 1559 Pflug expressed a desire for a coadjutor with the right of succession, and in 1561 he wished to resign in favour of Peter von Naumark, dean of the cathedral, but received no answer. For the temporal welfare of his diocese he made many useful regulations, lightened the burdens of the people after the ravages of the war, ordered the highways and forests to be cleared of the prowling bands of robbers, and regulated the wages and time of labour. Though Pflug has been accused of crypto-Lutheranism, no charges have ever been made against his priestly character. After death he was buried in his church at Zeitz. He wrote many treatises in Latin and

German on theological and kindred subjects. Their titles may be found in Ersch und Gruber, 3 Sect., XXI, 251. In the same work there is a biography from a Catholic standpoint, and another from a Protestant view. Some 115 letters of his are in the "Epistolæ Petri Mosellani . . . ad Julium Pflugium" (ed. Müller, Leipzig, 1802).

WEBER in *Kirchenlex.*; *Allgem. Deutsche Biogr.*; PASTOR, *Die kirchl. Reunionsbestrebungen während der Regierung Karls V* (Freiburg, 1879); JANSSEN, *Gesch. des deutschen Volkes*, III, 5, 459 seq.; IV, 25, 152; HOFFMANN, *Naumburg im Zeitalter der Reformation* (Leipzig, 1901); HURTER, *Nomenclator*.

FRANCIS MERSHMAN.

Pforta, a former Cistercian monastery (1137–1540), near Naumburg on the Saale in the Prussian province of Saxony. The monastery was at first situated in Schmölln on the Sprotta, near Altenburg. Count Bruno of Pleissengau founded there, in 1127, a Benedictine monastery and endowed it with 1100 "hides" of land. This foundation not being successful, Bishop Udo I of Naumburg, a relative of Bruno, on 23 April, 1132, replaced the Benedictines by Cistercian monks from the monastery of Walkenried. The situation here proved undesirable, and in 1137 Udo transferred the monastery to Pforta, and conferred upon it 50 hides of arable land, an important tract of forest, and two farms belonging to the diocese. For this fact we have Udo's own statement in a proclamation of 1140. The place was called Pforta (Porta) on account of its location in the narrow valley which was the entrance into Thuringia. The patroness of the abbey was Our Lady, and the first abbot, Adalbert, 1132–1152. Under the third abbot, Adelold, two convents were founded from it, in the Mark of Meissen and in Silesia, and in 1163, Alt-Celle and Leubus (q. v.) were also established in the latter province. At this period the monks numbered about eighty. In 1205 Pforta sent a colony of monks to Livonia, founding there the monastery of Dünamünde. The abbey was distinguished for its excellent system of management, and after the first 140 years of its existence its possessions had increased tenfold. Little is known regarding the spiritual life of the abbey, as the monks left no chronicles. At the end of the thirteenth and the beginning of the fourteenth century, though a period of strife, the monastery flourished with redoubled vigour. The last quarter of the fourteenth century witnessed, however, the gradual decline of its prosperity, and also the relaxation of monastic discipline. When Abbot Johannes IV was elected in 1515, there were forty-two monks and seven lay brothers who later revolted against the abbot; an inspection which Duke George of Saxony caused to be made revealed the fact that morality had ceased to exist in the monastery. The last Abbot, Peter Schederich, was elected in 1533. When the Catholic Duke George was succeeded by his Protestant brother Henry, the monastery was suppressed (9 November, 1540), the abbot, eleven monks, and four lay brothers being pensioned. In 1543, Duke Moritz opened a national school in the abbey, appropriating for its use the revenues of the suppressed monastery of Memleben. At first the number of scholars was 100, in 1563 fifty more were able to be accommodated. The first rector was Johann Gigas, renowned as a lyric poet. Under Justinus Bertuch (1601–1626) the school attained the zenith of its prosperity. It suffered greatly during the Thirty Years' War, in 1643, there being only eleven scholars. Among its pupils may be mentioned the poet, Klopstock, and the philosopher, Fichte. Since 1815 Pforta belongs to Prussia, and even at the present day the school is held in high esteem. The church was built in the thirteenth century; it is a cross-vaulted, colonnaded basilica with an extraordinarily long nave, a peculiar western façade, and a late Romanesque double-naved cloister. What remains of the original building (1137–40) is in the Romanesque style, while the restoration (1251–1268) belongs to the early Gothic.

WOLFF, *Chronik des Klosters Pforta*, I, II (Leipzig, 1843–46); CORSSEN, *Altertümer und Kunstdenkmäle des Cistercienserklosters St. Marien und der Landesschule zur Pforte* (Halle, 1868); BOEHME, *Pforte in seiner kulturgeschichtlichen Bedeutung während des 12. und 13. Jahrhunderts* (Halle, 1888); *Urkundenbuch des Klosters Pforte bearb. von Boehme*, I (Halle, 1893–1904).

KLEMENS LÖFFLER.

Phacusa, titular see and suffragan of Pelusium, in Augustamnica Prima. Ptolemy (IV, v, 24) makes it the suffragan of the nomos of Arabia in Lower Egypt; Strabo (XVII, i, 26) places Phacusa at the beginning of the canal which empties into the Red Sea; it is described also by Peutinger's Table under the name of Phacussi, and by the "Anonymus" of Ravenna (130), under Phagusa. In the list of the partisan bishops of Meletius present at the Council of Nicæa in 325 may be found Moses of Phacusa (Athanasius, "Apologia contra Arian.", 71); he is the only titular we know of. Ordinarily, Phacusa is identified with the modern Tell-Fakus; Brugsch and Navilla, in "Goshen and the Shrine of Saft el-Henneh" (London, 1885), place it at Saft about twelve miles from there.

ROUGÉ, *Géographie ancienne de la Basse Egypte* (Paris, 1891), 137–39.

S. VAILHÉ.

Phalansterianism. See COMMUNION; SOCIALISM.

Pharao (פרעה, *Par'o*, or, after a vowel, *Phar'o*; Gr. Φαραώ; Lat. Pharao), the title given in Sacred Scripture to the ancient kings of Egypt. The term is derived from the Egyptian Per'o, "great house", which originally designated the royal palace, but was gradually applied to the Government and then to the ruler himself, like the Vatican and the Quirinal, for instance, in modern times. At the period of the eighteenth dynasty (sixteenth to fourteenth cent. B. C.) it is found in common use as a reverential designation of the king. About the beginning of the twenty-second dynasty (tenth to eighth cent. B. C.), instead of being used alone as heretofore, it began to be added to the other titles before the king's name, and from the twenty-fifth dynasty (eighth to seventh cent. B. C.) it was, at least in ordinary usage, the only title prefixed to the royal appellative. Meanwhile the old custom of referring to the sovereign simply as Per'o still obtained in narratives. The Biblical use of the term reflects Egyptian usage with fair accuracy. The early kings are always mentioned under the general title Pharao, or Pharao the King of Egypt; but personal names begin to appear with the twenty-second dynasty, though the older designation is still used, especially when contemporary rulers are spoken of. The absence of proper names in the first books of the Bible is no indication of the late date of their composition and of writer's vague knowledge of Egyptian history, rather the contrary. The same is true of the use of the title Pharao for kings earlier than the eighteenth dynasty, which is quite in keeping with Egyptian usage at the time of the nineteenth dynasty.

The first king mentioned by name is Sesac (Sheshonk I), the founder of the twenty-second dynasty and contemporary of Roboam and Jeroboam (III Kings, xi, 40; II Par., xii, 2 sqq.). Pharao is not prefixed to his name probably because the Hebrews had not yet become familiarized with the new style. The next, Sua, or So, ally of Osee, King of Israel (IV Kings, xvii, 4), is commonly identified with Shabaka, the founder of the twenty-fifth dynasty, but he was probably an otherwise unknown local dynast prior to Shabaka's reign. Winckler's opinion that he was a ruler of Musri in North Arabia, though accepted by many, is without sufficient foundation. Tharaca, who was the opponent of Sennacherib, is called King of Ethiopia (IV Kings, xix, 9; Is., xxxvii, 9), and hence is not given the title Pharao which he bears in Egyptian documents. Nechao, who defeated Josias (IV

Kings, xxiii, 29 sqq.; II Par., xxxv, 20 sqq.), and Ephree, or Hophra, the contemporary of Sedecias (Jer., xliv, 30), are styled Pharao Nechao and Pharao Ephree, according to the then Egyptian usage.

Unnamed Pharaos of the Bible. (1) The Pharao of Abraham.—The uncertainties attaching to ancient chronology make it impossible to determine the identity of the Pharao who ruled over Egypt when Abraham arrived in the country. The Massoretic text gives 1125 years between Abraham's migration to Chanaan and the building of the temple, whereas the Septuagint allows 870 (see CHRONOLOGY). As the building is placed about 1010 B. C. by some scholars, and about 969 B. C. by others, the date of Abraham's migration would be 2135 or 2094 B. C. for the Massoretic text, and 1880 or 1839 B. C. for the Septuagint. Ancient Egyptian chronology is as uncertain as that of the Bible. If Meyer's dates, adopted in the article EGYPT, are correct, Abraham's journey to Egypt would have to be referred to the reign of one of the Mentuhoteps of the eleventh dynasty, or to that of either Usertesen (Sesostris) III, or Amenemhet III of the twelfth. (2) The Pharao of Joseph.—It is generally admitted that Joseph held office under one of the shepherd, or Hyksos, kings, who ruled in Egypt between the twelfth and eighteenth dynasties, and were finally expelled by Ahmose I shortly after 1580. The length of their rule is unknown, but probably it did not last much over a hundred years. Joseph's tenure of office would accordingly be placed in the seventeenth century B. C. If the Exodus took place at the beginning of the reign of Merneptah, i. e., about 1225, as most scholars now maintain, and the sojourn of the Israelites in Egypt lasted 430 years, as stated in the Massoretic text (Ex., xii, 40), the time would be about 1665. The names of four Hyksos kings are known to us from Egyptian monuments, a Khian and three Apophises. George Syncellus states that in his time (eighth cent. A. D.) there was a general consensus that the Pharao of Joseph was Apophis, probably Apophis II, the most important of the three. This opinion is possibly true, but the history of the period is too obscure to allow a definite statement.

(3) The Pharao of the Oppression and of the Exodus. (See ISRAELITES.)

(4) The other Pharaos.—The Pharao with whom Adad sought refuge in the time of David (III Kings, xi, 17) was a king of the twenty-first dynasty, either Paynozem or Amenemopet. Solomon's father-in-law (III Kings, iii, 1) may have been Amenemopet, Siamon, or Pesibkhenno II. The Pharao mentioned in IV Kings, xviii, 21 and Is., xxxvi, 6 is by many thought to be Tharaca; but if the expedition of Sennacherib occurred in 701, as is generally held, there is little doubt that Shabaka, or possibly Shabataka, is the Pharao referred to. Tharaca came to the throne some years later, and the title King of Ethiopia (IV Kings, xix, 9; Is., xxxvii, 9) is given to him by anticipation. The unnamed Pharao of Jer., xxv, 19, is probably Nechao, who is certainly meant in xlvi, 17, and xlvii, 1; elsewhere Ephree is intended. The latter is also the Pharao of Ezechiel.

See the literature mentioned under the articles to which reference has been made.
F. BECHTEL.

Pharbætus, titular see and suffragan of Leontopolis, in Augustamnica Secunda. This name is merely the transcription, with the Coptic article P, of the native name *Harbait* or *Harbet*, a name which is moreover reproduced under the form Κάρβενθος in George of Cyprus ("Descriptio orbis romani", ed. Gelzer, 706). It is the capital of the nome of this name in Lower Egypt described by Herodotus (II, 166); Strabo, XVII, i, 20; Pliny, V, 9, 11. There is a record of Bishop Arbetion at Nicæa in 325 (Gelzer, "Patrum nicænorum nomina", LX), and Bishop Theodorus in 1086 (Renaudot, "Historia patriarcharum alexandrinorum", 458), but it is possible that the latter was bishop of another Pharbætus situated further to the west, and which according to Vansleb was equally a Coptic see. John of Nikiu (Chronicle, CV) relates that under the Emperor Phocas (602–10) the clerics of the province killed the Greek governor Theophilus. Pharbætus is now called Horbeït, north of Zagazig in the Province of Sharqyeh; it has about 520 inhabitants.

GELZER, *Georgii Cyprii Descriptio orbis romani*, 114-16; ROUGÉ, *Géographie ancienne de la Basse Egypte* (Paris, 1891), 66-74; AMÉLINEAU, *La Géographie de l'Egypte à l'époque copte* (Paris, 1893), 330.
S. VAILHÉ.

Pharisees, a politico-religious sect or faction among the adherents of later Judaism, that came into existence as a class about the third century B. C. After the exile, Israel's monarchial form of government had become a thing of the past; in its place the Jews created a community which was half State, half Church. A growing sense of superiority to the heathen and idolatrous nations among whom their lot was cast came to be one of their main characteristics. They were taught insistently to separate themselves from their heathen neighbours. "And now make confession to the Lord the God of your fathers, and do his pleasure, and separate yourselves from the people of the land, and from your strange wives" (I Esd., x, 11). Intermarriage with the heathen was strictly forbidden and many such marriages previously contracted, even of priests, were dissolved in consequence of the legislation promulgated by Esdras. Such was the state of things in the third century when the newly introduced Hellenism threatened Judaism with destruction. The more zealous among the Jews drew apart calling themselves *Chasidim* or "pious ones", i. e., they dedicated themselves to the realization of the ideas inculcated by Esdras, the holy priest and doctor of the law. In the violent conditions incidental to the Machabean wars these "pious men", sometimes called the Jewish Puritans, became a distinct class. They were called Pharisees, meaning those who separated themselves from the heathen, and from the heathenizing forces and tendencies which constantly invaded the precincts of Judaism (I Mach., i, 11; II Mach., iv, 14 sq.; cf. Josephus Antiq., XII, v, 1).

During these persecutions of Antiochus the Pharisees became the most rigid defenders of the Jewish religion and traditions. In this cause many suffered martyrdom (I Mach., i, 41 sq.), and so devoted were they to the prescriptions of the Law that on one occasion when attacked by the Syrians on the Sabbath they refused to defend themselves (I Mach., ii, 42; ibid., v, 3 sq.). They considered it an abomination to even eat at the same board with the heathens or have any social relations with them whatsoever. Owing to their heroic devotedness their influence over the people became great and far-reaching, and in the course of time they, instead of the priests, became the sources of authority. In the time of Our Lord such was their power and prestige that they sat and taught in "Moses' seat". This prestige naturally engendered arrogance and conceit, and led to a perversion in many respects of the conservative ideals of which they had been such staunch supporters. In many passages of the Gospels, Christ is quoted as warning the multitude against them in scathing terms. "The scribes and the Pharisees have sitten in the chair of Moses. All things therefore whatsoever they shall say to you, observe and do: but according to their works do ye not; for they say and do not. For they bind heavy and insupportable burdens, and lay them on men's shoulders; but with a finger of their own they will not move them. And all their works they do for to be seen of men. For they make their phylacteries broad, and enlarge their fringes. And they love the first places at feasts, and the first chairs in the synagogues. And salutations in the market place, and to be called by men, Rabbi" (Matt., xxiii, 1-8). Then follows the terrible arraignment of the scribes and Pharisees for their hypocrisy, their rapacity, and their blindness (ibid., 13-36).

After the conflicts with Rome (A. D. 66-135) Pharisaism became practically synonymous with Judaism. The great Maccabean wars had defined Pharisaism: another even more terrible conflict gave it a final ascendancy. The result of both wars was to create from the second century onward, in the bosom of a tenacious race, the type of Judaism known to the western world. A study of the early history of Pharisaism reveals a certain moral dignity and greatness, a marked tenacity of purpose at the service of high, patriotic, and religious ideals. As contrasted with the Sadducees (q. v.), the Pharisees represented the democratic tendency; contrasted with the priesthood, they stood for both the democratic and the spiritualizing tendency. By virtue of the Law itself the priesthood was an exclusive class. No man was allowed to exercise a function in the Temple unless he was able to trace his descent from a priestly family. The Pharisees consequently found their main function in teaching and preaching. Their work was chiefly connected with the synagogues, and embraced the schooling of children and missionary efforts among the heathen tribes. Thus, in a sense, Pharisaism helped to clear the ground and prepare the way for Christianity. It was the Pharisees who made idealized nationalism, based upon the monotheism of the prophets, the very essence of Judaism. To them we are indebted for the great apocalypses, Daniel and Enoch, and it was they who made common the belief in the resurrection and future reward. In a word, their pedagogical influence was an important factor in training the national will and purpose for the introduction of Christianity. This great work, however, was marred by many defects and limitations. Though standing for the spiritualizing tendency, Pharisaism developed a proud and arrogant orthodoxy and an exaggerated formalism, which insisted on ceremonial details at the expense of the more important precepts of the Law (Matt., xxiii, 23-28). The importance attached to descent from Abraham (Matt., iii, 9) obscured the deeper spiritual issues and created a narrow, exclusive nationalism incapable of understanding a universal Church destined to include Gentile as well as Jew. It was only through the revelation received on the road to Damascus, that Saul the Pharisee was enabled to comprehend a church where all are equally the "seed of Abraham", all "one in Christ Jesus" (Gal., iii, 28-9). This exclusivism, together with their over valuation of external levitical observances, caused the Pharisees to be ranged in opposition to what is known as prophetism, which in both the Old and New Testament places the main emphasis on character and the religious spirit, and thus they incurred not only the vehement reproaches of the Precursor (Matt., iii, 7 seq.), but also of the Saviour Himself (Matt., xxiii, 25 seq.).

The Pharisees are seen at their best when contrasted with the Zealots on one hand, and with the Herodians on the other. Unlike the Zealots, it was their policy to abstain from the appeal to armed force. It was their belief that the God of the nation controlled all historic destinies, and that in His own good time He would satisfy the long frustrated desires of His chosen people. Meanwhile the duty of all true Israelites consisted in whole-hearted devotion to the Law, and to the manifold observances which their numerous traditions had engrafted upon it, joined to a patient waiting for the expected manifestation of the Divine Will. The Zealots on the contrary bitterly resented the Roman domination and would have hastened with the sword the fulfilment of the Messianic hope. It is well known that during the great rebellion and the siege of Jerusalem, which ended in its destruction (A. D. 70), the fanaticism of the Zealots made them terrible opponents not only to the Romans, but also to the other factions among their own countrymen. On the other hand, the extreme faction of the Sadducees, known as the Herodians, was in sympathy with the foreign rulers and pagan culture, and even looked forward to a restoration of the national kingdom under one of the descendants of King Herod. Yet we find the Pharisees making common cause with the Herodians in their opposition to the Saviour (Mark, iii, 6; xii, 13, etc.).

GIGOT, *Outlines of New Testament History* (New York, 1902), 74 sqq.; LE CAMUS, *L'Œuvre des Apôtres*, I (Paris, 1905), 133; FARRAR, *The Life and Work of St. Paul* (New York, 1880), 26-39; EATON in HASTINGS, *Dict. of the Bible*, s. v.; EDERSHEIM, *The Life and Times of Jesus the Messiah*, passim.

JAMES F. DRISCOLL.

Pharsalus, titular see and suffragan of Larissa in Thessaly. The city is mentioned for the first time after the Persian war. In 445 B. C. it was unsuccessfully besieged by the Athenian Myronides (Thucyd., I, III), in 395 it was seized by Midias, tyrant of Larissa (Diodorus Siculus, XIV, 82), and it was finally forced to submit to Jason of Pheræ (Xenoph., "Hellen.", VI, 1, 2); in 191 the consul Acilius Glabrio made it over to Antiochus, King of Syria. It is specially famous for the victory of 9 August, 48 B. C., won by Cæsar from Pompey, after the latter had killed 15,000 men. At the time of Pliny (Hist. Nat., IV, 15) it was a free city. In the sixth century A. D. it was made a port of Thessaly ("Hieroclis Synecdemus", ed. Burckhardt, 642, 13); in the time of Constantine Porphyrogenetus, it belonged to the theme of Macedonia (op. cit., 50, 6). In 1881 it was ceded by Turkey with Thessaly to Greece. Of the three Greek bishops mentioned by Le Quien (Oriens christianus, II, 116), it is doubtful if the first belonged to this see, but this list could easily be completed. At the beginning of the tenth century Pharsalus still remained suffragan of Larissa (Gelzer, "Ungedruckte . . . Texte der Notitiæ Episcopatuum", 557); about 970 (op. cit., 572) it became an autocephalous archbishopric; in 1300 it was elevated by Andronicus II to metropolitan dignity; at the close of the fifteenth century it was again suffragan of Larissa. Later it was united to the Diocese of Phanarion, and was suppressed only to be replaced (1900) by the Sees of Phanarus and Thessaliotides. Pharsala numbers 2500 inhabitants, of whom nearly half are Turks. The Greeks were defeated there in 1897.

LEAKE, *Northern Greece*, IV, 484; SMITH, *Dict. of Greek and Roman Geography*, s. v.

S. VAILHÉ.

Phaselis, titular see in Lycia, suffragan of Myra. The city was a Doric colony on the Pamphylian Gulf. Situated on an isthmus separating two harbours, it owed to this fortunate location the fact that it became an important centre of commerce between Greece, Asia, Egypt, and Phœnicia, although it did not belong to the confederation of Lycian cities. The pirates of Cilicia were allied with it, first through business intercourse, then by treaty. After the capture of Olympus P. Servilius laid siege to it. It was defended by Zenicetus, who, being unable to hold it, set fire to the city and plunged into the flames together with his companions. Phaselis recovered from this disaster. However, as early as the Roman period the little harbour had become a swamp exhaling pestilential vapours, and the situation grew worse until the city was in complete decay. There was a temple of Athene at Phaselis, where the lance of Achilles was exhibited. It was the birthplace of the poet and orator Theodectes. It was also renowned for its roses, from which the essence was extracted. There was invented the bark called φάσηλος which figures on all the coins of the city. There was a Roman colony at Phaselis about 139 B. C., for the Romans wrote to the inhabitants to send help to Simon Machabeus and the Jews (I Mach., xv, 23). Only two of its bishops are known: Fronto at Chalcedon (451); and Aristodemus, who in 458 signed the letter from the bishops of Lycia to the Emperor Leo. At the Council of Nicæa (787), the absent bishop was represented by the deacon John. The see is mentioned in the "Notitiæ episcopatuum" until the thirteenth century. The ruins of Phaselis are at Tekir Ova in the vilayet of Koniah; they belong to the Roman period, the most important being a theatre. There are also numerous sarcophagi.

LE QUIEN, *Oriens christianus*, I, 985; BEAUFORT, *Karamania*, 53–65; FELLOWS, *Asia Minor*, 211 sqq.; LEAKE, *Asia Minor*, 190; TEXIER, *Asie mineure*, 697–99; HILL, *Catalogue of Greek Coins in the British Museum: Lycia*, p. lxvii.

S. PÉTRIDÈS.

Phasga (A. V. PISGAH).—Whether the word in Hebrew is a proper or a common noun is not clear; certain it is at any rate that it designates a mountain of the Abarim range (Deut., xxxii, 49), east of the Jordan (Deut., iv, 49), in the land of Moab (Num., xxi, 20), "over against Jericho" (Deut., xxxiv, 1), above Yeshimon [Num., xxi, 20; D. V. "which looketh towards the desert" ('Ain Suweimeh)], east of the north end of the Dead Sea (Deut., iv, 49; Jos., xii, 3), in connexion with Mount Nebo, and commanding an extensive view of the Holy Land (Deut., xxxii, 49; xxxiv, 1–4), on the south-east border of which it stood (Deut., iv, 49). From all these indications it appears that Phasga is no other than Mount Nebo itself (Jebel Neba, south-west of Hesban or Hesebon), or, better still, the western peak of the mountain, Ras Ṣiâghâ. On its slopes the Israelites pitched their camp (Num., xxi, 20); in the "field of Sophim" (D. V. "a high place") on the mountain Balaam uttered his second oracle about Israel (Num., xxiii, 11–24); lastly from the top of Phasga, Moses surveyed the Promised Land.

BIRCH, *The Prospect from Pisgah* in *Pal. Explor. Fund Quart. Stat.* (London, 1898); CONDER, *Heth and Moab* (London, 1889); SMITH, *Historical Geography of the Holy Land* (London, 1894); TRISTRAM, *The Land of Moab* (London, 1874); LAGRANGE, *Itinéraire des Israélites: De la Frontière de Moab aux Rives du Jourdain* in *Revue Biblique* (1900), 443–449.

CHARLES L. SOUVAY.

Phenomenalism (φαινόμενον) literally means any system of thought that has to do with appearances. The term is, however, usually restricted to the designation of certain theories by which it is asserted: (1) that there is no knowledge other than that of phenomena—denial of the knowledge of substance in the metaphysical sense; or (2) that all knowledge is phenomenal—denial of the thing-in-itself and assertion that all reality is reality directly or reflectively present to consciousness.

(1) The first form of Phenomenalism reaches its full statement in Hume, though its logical development can be traced back through Berkeley and Locke to Descartes. It consists in the theory that substance is merely a relation between ideas; that its existence, as a reality, is incapable of intuitive or demonstrative certainty. The origin of the idea of substance can be explained on the basis of the imagination (Hume). The transient mental, or world, phenomena are related in the imagination to a supposed substrate—a fictitious ground, permanent and inert — which accounts for their appearance. The theory destroys metaphysics and replaces it with epistemology. This is quite in keeping with Hume's Associationism in psychology. The "Treatise on Human Nature" admits ideas and impressions, together with the association of these elements according to the well-known laws (see ASSOCIATION; PSYCHOLOGY); and nothing more than this is given or is necessary to explain whatever is found in consciousness. For substance (as well as causality, etc.) can be explained adequately as the result of ideas that have been frequently present in conjunction. Hume restricted these views to exact experimental science, and safeguarded the ordinary experience of life by asserting that the concepts of substance, etc., are accompanied by a natural belief, or conviction, of their reality arising from feeling. His doctrine was widely accepted in France, and in Germany became the ideological forerunner of Kant's "Kritik". Though at once labelled Scepticism in England, on account of its consequences in natural theology, it is a frankly consistent Empiricism (q. v.) quite in place in the evolution of the school of English thought. Where Locke, criticizing the ideogeny of Descartes, and admitting the part of empirical experience in the formation of ideas, left the metaphysical material substance and the metaphysical soul, as realities, uncriticized, Berkeley, developing his position further, taught that the supposed existence of the material world was not only indemonstrable, but false. Only spirits, with their ideas and volitions, exist. *Esse* of the material is *percipi*: and the regularity of nature is no more than the order of ideas as produced in us by another spirit, namely, God. Hume's position is but a step further than this. Soul, or mind, as substance, is no more real than body. Here the Phenomenalism of Berkeley becomes logically complete.

Quite consistent with this conception is the statement of Huxley that mind is only the collection of perceptions united by certain relations between them (see Huxley, "Hume, a Biography", II, ii, p. 64), or that of Taine, the Positivist, that the Ego is no more than a luminous sheaf, having no other reality than the lights that compose it (see Taine, "*De l'intelligence*", I, pref., p. 11). As we shall show, the opposition of Hume to the concept of substance seems to rest upon a misunderstanding: for he admits (Treatise I, part 4, sect. 1) "something" that is accountable for impressions and "something" that is impressed (body, mind). Huxley seems but to popularize by his simile the conception of the Scotch philosopher, that there is no mind or soul (as substance) apart from its acts. Huxley compares the soul to a republic in which the members are united by their manifold ties and mutual relationships as citizens. This leaves the impressions and ideas substantial and makes of the mind what Scholastics would call an "accidental" unity, and of the substance (soul) a "permanent possibility of sensations", as Mill expresses it. Max Müller has dealt with this notion in his "Science of Thought" (248) where he observes that such terms as *possibility* express a common quality that is always *of something*, from which we have abstracted them. To call mind a "possibility" is at the same time to deny that it is a substance and to assert of it a quality belonging to substance, which would seem to be contradictory.

The idealistic standpoint of Hume, together with the doctrine of Positivism (q. v.), has had so great an influence upon modern thought that it will be well to show in what the misunderstanding, already referred to, consists. As Cardinal Mercier points out ("Ontologie", 1902, p. 263), it is incredible that such thinkers as Hume and Kant, Mill, Spencer, Wundt, Paulsen, Comte, Renouvier, Bergson, and others, should have so totally misunderstood the substantiality of things and of the Ego as to profess a Phenomenalism contradictory to the doctrine of the School. On the other hand, it is no less incredible that philosophers like Aristotle, St. Thomas, and the Schoolmen, should have "been at fault in their interpretation of an elementary truth of common sense". On the face of it, a misunderstanding seems probable. To what was this due? First, to the doubt cast by Descartes upon the truth and validity of our notions of substance; second, to the observation of Locke, that we are incapable of directly attaining to substance. If thought could immediately conceive the substance of a thing, we ought to be able to deduce all its properties from that conception. Third, to the explanation advanced by Hume, of the origin of the idea of substance by habit. These three steps form a sequence in the development of Idealism. Fourth, to the Positivism, for which this paved the way, as expressed by Comte and Mill. The various schools of thought that may be grouped under Phenomenalism: plain Empiricism, as taught by Hume; Agnosticism, as advanced by Spencer and Huxley; Positivism, represented by Comte, Littré, Taine, and Mill; all share in the misunderstanding initiated by Descartes with regard to the nature of substance as put forward by the School. The Criticism of Kant may well be included with them, as limiting the object of human knowledge to experience, or phenomenal appearance —although some knowledge as to the noumenon is reached by way of the postulates of the practical reason—the three ideas, soul, world, God. So also may be included the neo-critical movement of Renouvier.

It is important that this misunderstanding should be cleared up. Scholasticism indeed maintains that we have a direct but confused and implicit intuition of substance. We grasp the reality of "something that can exist by itself". "Every perception is a substance, and every part of a perception is a distinct substance" (Hume, "*Treatise*", I, part 4, sect. 5). Thus far the Empiricist agrees with the Scholastic. But upon analysis and reflection, the latter maintains, the distinction between substance and accident emerges. What at first appeared to exist in itself, is seen to exist in something else. That something else is then perceived to be substance; and what before was taken for it, is seen to be accident or phenomenon. Further, as against the criticism of Locke, it is to be remarked that Scholastic philosophy does not claim for the intelligence a direct experience of the specific nature of substance. On the contrary, it relies entirely upon induction to establish such nature. To the objection that induction gives us no knowledge other than of the phenomenal, it answers that we know at least this of the specific substance—that it is the subject of certain observed modifications and the cause of certain observed effects. One further point that is interesting in this connexion is the unfortunate attribution of inertia to substance. Paulsen writes that the soul is not inert as is the atom, thereby sharing the opinion of Wundt. This idea of substance as an inert substrate is also traceable to the Cartesian philosophy, which is thus upon two counts the parent of Phenomenalism. It is hardly necessary to point out that Scholasticism does not regard either the soul or the material atom as inert, except by a mental abstraction which is practised upon the idea of nature (as immanent activity) to reach the simple conception of "that which is capable of existing in itself" (see SUBSTANCE).

(2) The second form of Phenomenalism may be found in the doctrine of Fichte and of the school that develops his ideas; as well as in certain tendencies and developments of the system of thought known as Pragmatism (q. v.). With Fichte, the thing-in-itself of Kant disappears as the ground of experience, and its place is taken by consciousness determining itself. That things are and are known implies a double series, real and ideal, for which Dogmatism is incapable of accounting. There is nothing else, as a ground, than a "being posited" by consciousness. But consciousness is aware of itself, knowing its activity, and the nature of this activity. In this conception the real—the functions of consciousness —is paralleled by the ideal—knowledge of these functions. The thing-in-itself is no longer necessary to explain the possibility of knowledge, which here becomes the explanation of the original relation of consciousness to itself. The object has no existence, save for the subject. Fichte's philosophy has much influenced later thought in Germany as elsewhere.

The attempt made by Schelling to avoid the contradiction between his doctrine and that of Kant resulted in a form of idealistic Phenomenalism (developed further by Novalis and von Schlegel), and ultimately in a neo-Spinozaistic Pantheism. Hegel's Idealism is a logical, or metaphysical, one, in which the only reality (spirit) "becomes" in a process-form of dialectic. In the thesis, antithesis, and synthesis of Absolute mind, the return to consciousness takes the form of phenomena, as spirit becoming apparent to itself. With Schopenhauer, who begins his "Die Welt als Wille und Vorstellung" with these words: " 'The world is my idea':—this is a truth which holds good for everything that lives and knows . . ." it would seem that a transition from idealistic Phenomenalism to modern "scientific" Realism is in progress.

Pragmatism is the most recent form of Empiricism, and as such belongs to the first form of Phenomenalism noticed above; but its psychologic attitude, and the subjectivist developments it displays, make it perhaps more fitting to mention it here. For the system as a whole the truth of reality rests upon the subjective feeling of certainty (see EPISTEMOLOGY). The answers given as to why this should be are because of (1) an a priori constitution of mind, of transcendental order and for all individuals; (2) utility, coherence, or vital experience (James, Leroy, Schiller); or (3) an act of the will (Ribot). The first two accounts of the psychological fact of certainty insensibly give place to the third, which is the last word of psychological Subjectivism, except one: and that one is the theory of Solipsism. It will be observed that this line of development is one of an elaboration of a voluntaristic form of Phenomenalism. Where Schiller (Studies in Humanism) writes that the basis of fact accepted by Pragmatism depends upon its "acceptance"; "that it (acceptance) is fatal to the chimera of a 'fact' for us existing quite independently of our 'will' ", and James (Pragmatism) "Why may they (our acts) not be the actual . . . growing-places . . . of the world—why not be the workshop of being where we catch fact in the making, so that nowhere may the world grow any other kind of way than this?" Solipsism goes but one step further in declaring that there is no absolute Ego nor absolute non-Ego. There is no more than the individual consciousness (cf. von Schubert Soldern). Admitting the principles, an escape from such a conclusion is difficult. The pure experience of Avenarius, the *reine Erfahrung* for you and for me, is theoretic and inevident. Indeed Humanism itself, as advanced by Schiller, seems to be but a kind of Solipsism. The data of thought are immanent, and we only organize them; but Schiller gives no indication of their origin; indeed he says it is absurd to ask whence the given of thought derives. The whole modern school of Immanence (q. v.) belongs to the development of this form of Phenomenalism.

ST. THOMAS, *Opera* (Parma, 1854), especially the *De veritate*; AVENARIUS, *Philosophie als Denken, etc. Prolegomena zur einer Kritik der reinen Erfahrung* (Leipzig, 1878); BERGSON, *Essai sur les données immédiates de la conscience* (Paris, 1889); BERKELEY, *Works*, ed. FRASER (Oxford, 1901); BRADLEY, *Appearance and Reality* (London, 1893); CATOR, *Subjectivism and Solipsism* in *Dublin Review* (July, 1903); COMTE, *Cours de philosophie positive* (Paris, 1830-42); DESCARTES, *Œuvres*, published by COUSIN (Paris, 1824-6); FICHTE, *Sämmtliche Werke* (Berlin); HUME, *Philosophical Works*, ed. GREEN AND GROSE (London, 1878); HUXLEY, *Hume, A Biography* (London, 1878); JAMES, *Pragmatism* (London, 1907); KANT, *Werke*, ed. ROSENKRANZ AND SCHUBERT (Leipzig, 1838-40); LOCKE, *An Essay Concerning Human Understanding* (London, 1881); MCCOSH, *Agnosticism of Hume and Huxley* (London, 1884); JAMES MILL, *Analysis of the Phenomena of the Human Mind*, with notes by J. S. MILL (London, 1869); J. S. MILL, *An Examination of Sir William Hamilton's Philosophy* (London, 1889); RENOUVIER, *Essais de critique générale* (Paris, 1854-64); RIBOT, *Essai sur l'imagination créatrice* (Paris, 1900); SCHILLER, *Studies in Humanism* (London, 1907); VON SCHUBERT SOLDERN, *Ueber Transcendenz des Objects und Subjects* (Leipzig, 1882); IDEM, *Grundlagen einer Erkenntnisstheologie* (Leipzig, 1884); WINDELBAND, *Hist. of Phil.*, tr. TUFTS (New York, 1907).

FRANCIS AVELING.

Philadelphia, titular see in Lydia, suffragan of Sardes. The city was founded by Philadelphus, King of Pergamon (159–38 B. C.), in the vicinity of Callatebus on the left bank of the Cogamus (Kouzou Tchai); its location was most favourable for commercial and strategical purposes. In 133 B. C. it became a Roman possession. It was subject to earthquakes, and at the time of Augustus was almost in ruins; but, quickly restored, was of commercial importance as late as the Byzantine period. Its wines were famous; its coins bore the image of Bacchus or a bacchante. On the coins of the first century the city is called Neocæsarea, under Vespasian it received the cognomen of Flavia. During the eleventh and succeeding centuries it was repeatedly captured by and retaken from the Turks until it was definitively conquered by Bajazet in 1390. In the seventeenth century it had 8000 inhabitants, of whom 2000 were Christians. To-day it has about 15,000, including 3500 Greeks. The Turks called it Ala Sheir; it is the capital of the caza of the vilayet of Smyrna, is still, on account of its fertility, an important agricultural and commercial centre; and is a railway station between Smyrna and Dinair. It possesses numerous ruins, a theatre, stadium, two walls, many Byzantine churches, etc. and has mineral springs. Christianity was introduced into Philadelphia in Apostolic times. According to the "Apostolic Constitutions" (VII, xlvi), its first bishop Demetrius must have been appointed by St. John. The apologist St. Miltiades mentions a prophetess Ammia who must have belonged to the primitive Church of Philadelphia (Eusebius, "Hist. Eccl.", V, xvii). One of the seven letters of the Apocalypse is addressed to the Bishop of Philadelphia (Apoc., i, ii, iii, 7–13). This bishop was highly commended, and while the writer recognizes that the community is small, he tells us that the Jews who tried to disturb it were valiantly resisted by its faithful pastors. St. Ignatius of Antioch later sent to the Christians of Philadelphia an interesting letter warning them against the Jews (Funk, "Die apostolischen Väter", Tübingen, 1901, pp. 98–102). The ancient "Notitiæ" place Philadelphia among the most important suffragans of Sardes. Under Andronicus Palæologus it was raised to metropolitan rank, and has continued such among the Greeks, its jurisdiction, since the fourteenth century, extending over many neighbouring sees, later obliterated by the Turkish conquest. Among its bishops or metropolitans, of whom Le Quien (Oriens christ., I, 867 sq.) gives a very incomplete list, may be mentioned: Hetimasius, present at the Council of Nicæa (325); Cyriacus, at the Council of Philippopolis (344); Theodosius, deposed at the Council of Seleucia (359); Theophanes, present at the Council of Ephesus (431); Asianus (458); Eustathius (518); John, present at the Council of Constantinople (680); Stephanus at Nicæa (787); Michael under Leo the Armenian; Theoleptus at the end of the thirteenth and in the fourteenth century, hymn writer, orator, and master of the famous Barlaam (P. G., CXLIII, 381 sq.); Macarius Chrysocephalas (1345) wrote homilies (ibid., CL, 227 sq.); Gabriel Severus (1577) wrote works against the Latins and resided, as did his six successors, at Venice; Gerasimus Blachus (1679), author of numerous works; Meletius Typaldus (1685), deposed for becoming a Catholic.

ARUNDELL, *Discoveries in Asia Minor*, I, 34; CHANDLER, *Travels*, 310 sq.; SMITH, *Dict. of Greek and Roman Geogr.*, s. v.; LE CAMUS, *Les sept Eglises de l'Apocalypse* (Paris, 1896), 203–16; FILLION in VIGOUROUX, *Dict. de la Bible*, s. v.; WACHTER, *Der Verfall des Griechentums im XIV. Jahrhundert in Kleinasien* (Leipzig, 1903), 44 sq.; LAMPAKES, *The Seven Stars of the Apocalypse* (Athens, 1909), 365–414, in Greek; RAMSAY, *The Seven Churches of Asia* (London, 1908).

S. PÉTRIDÈS.

Philadelphia, ARCHDIOCESE OF (PHILADELPHIENSIS), diocese established in 1808; made an archdiocese, 12 Feb., 1875, comprises all the city and county of Philadelphia, and the counties of Berks, Bucks, Carbon, Chester, Delaware, Lehigh, Montgomery, Northampton, and Schuylkill, an area of 5043 square miles, in the southeastern portion of the State of Pennsylvania. The population of this area, according to the United States Census, in 1910, was 2,712,708, of which number 1,549,008 belonged to the City of Philadelphia. This city, the capital of the archdiocese, was, until 1800, the capital of the United States. It is the third city in the United States in population; its wealth invested in manufacturing industries exceeds $500,000,000, and it is the leading American city in shipbuilding, the manufacture of locomotive engines, street-railway cars, carpets, leather, oilcloth, and several other important commodities. In 1909 the foreign commerce of Philadelphia amounted to $150,504,095.

HISTORY.—Penn's colony, founded in 1682, as a "holy experiment", by which each man could without molestation worship God according to the dictates of his own conscience (see PENNSYLVANIA), soon became a welcome haven of refuge to the persecuted Catholics of the neighbouring colonies. Since the missionary priests, mainly Jesuits, watched over the movements of the members of their scattered flocks, it is not surprising that in their frequent journeyings between New York and Maryland they should find opportunity to gather the faithful in the house of a Catholic for the celebration of the sacred mysteries and preaching the Word of God. There was a steady growth in the number of Catholics throughout the colony, including some distinguished converts. Repeated complaints were made to London, that the "Popish Mass" was read publicly at Philadelphia; but Penn's "Fundamental" shielded the Catholics in his province from molestation. The first resident priest in Philadelphia was Father Joseph Greaton, S.J., who began his labours among the missions of Maryland and Pennsylvania in 1720. His first concern was to build a chapel and rectory. With this object he bought the ground where the first public chapel was erected in Philadelphia, and where still stands old St. Joseph's church, near Fourth and Walnut Streets. In 1741 Father Greaton received an assistant in the person of Rev. Henry Neale, S.J. Welcome financial aid came to the Pennsylvania missions through the bounty of Sir John James, of London, who made a bequest in their favour. The German immigrants were looked after by two missionaries from the Fatherland, Rev. Theodore Schneider of Heidelberg, who resided in Berks Co., at Goshenhoppen, and Father Wappeler of Westphalia, who attended the Catholics of Conewago and Lancaster. Father Neale died 5 May, 1748; and the aged Greaton retired to Maryland, where he ended his saintly career, 19 Aug., 1753.

The second pastor of Philadelphia was Father Robert Harding, born in Nottinghamshire, England, 6 Oct., 1701, who, having entered the Society of Jesus, came to America in 1732. He assumed charge of Philadelphia in 1749 and laboured with intelligence and success for twenty-three years. During the excitement of the French and Indian War charges of disloyalty were brought against the Catholics, but passed away without causing suffering. Father Harding estimated the Catholics of Philadelphia as about 2000. Another deserving labourer in the vineyard was the German Jesuit, Father Steinmeyer, known in the colony as Ferdinand Farmer. He laboured first at Lancaster among the Germans, afterwards as assistant to Father Harding. He is described as a philosopher and astronomer, and in 1779 was a trustee of the University of Pennsylvania. Father Harding purchased land for a new church and cemetery. The church was opened in 1763 as St. Mary's; it became the parish church, St. Joseph's remaining a chapel. Father Harding died 1 Sept., 1772, and was interred at St. Mary's. He was succeeded by the Rev. Robert Molyneux, who, together with Father Farmer, skilfully guided the infant

Church during the stormy days of the Revolution. Like the majority of their flock, they remained neutral, till the coming of the French allies called for repeated services on occasions of joy or sorrow; the addresses, however, were mostly delivered by the chaplain to the French ambassador.

At the end of the war Father Molyneux opened the first Catholic parish school. In Oct., 1785, the sacrament of Confirmation was administered for the first time in Philadelphia by the Very Rev. John Carroll, prefect Apostolic. On 17 Aug. of the following year Father Farmer passed to his reward. His funeral was attended by the American Philosophical Society, the professors and trustees of the University of Pennsylvania, and by large numbers of non-Catholics. No one had done so much to make the Catholic religion respected by the residents of New Jersey and Pennsylvania. Father Molyneux soon after retired from active service and was succeeded by the Rev. Francis Beeston, who built the presbytery of St. Joseph's which is still occupied by the clergy. In 1788 a number of German Catholics agitated for a new distinctively German church: Dr. Carroll reluctantly consented, warning them against a feeling of separatism and admonishing them that they could not be permitted to name their own pastors. In 1795 the German church was ready for occupancy, and was named Holy Trinity, being, it is said, the last building for public purposes erected in Philadelphia of alternate red and black glazed brick. This church gave great trouble to Bishop Carroll, on account of the pretensions of the trustees, and had to be placed under interdict. The three churches now built, St. Joseph's, St. Mary's, and Holy Trinity, were all in the southern part of the city. Provision had to be made for the Catholics living in what was then the extreme northern section. Opportunely, the Augustinians were seeking to found a house in the United States, and to them the new congregation was entrusted. In 1796 the Rev. Matthew Carr, O.S.A., issued an appeal to the inhabitants of Philadelphia and received a generous response. President Washington figures in the list of subscribers, for $50, Commodore Barry, for $150, and Stephen Girard, for $40. After many vicissitudes, "the largest church in Philadelphia" was dedicated under the invocation of St. Augustine, 7 June, 1801. When Father Carr removed to his new residence near St. Augustine's, the trustees of St. Mary's petitioned the bishop to send them a pastor capable of sustaining the dignity of "the leading church in the United States". The bishop found them the priest they were looking for in the person of the Rev. Michael Egan, a Franciscan stationed at Lancaster. He had come to America in order to establish in this country a house of his order, but found the time premature and became a missionary priest under the jurisdiction of Bishop Carroll. He was ably assisted at St. Mary's by Father Rossiter.

The time having arrived when Philadelphia should be erected into an episcopal see, Pius VII, by Bulls dated 8 April, 1808, designated the diocese as including "the entire two States of Pennsylvania and Delaware, and the western and southern part of the State of New Jersey". An accompanying Brief appointed Father Michael Egan (q. v.) to be the first occupant of the see. Owing to the existing political conditions in Europe, the Briefs did not reach Baltimore until 1810, and during the interval Father Egan remained in Philadelphia as vicar-general to Bishop Carroll. On 10 Nov., 1808, there arrived in Philadelphia the Dominican Father William Vincent Harold, who came from Ireland recommended by the Archbishop of Dublin and other dignitaries. Bishop Egan accepted him with eagerness, and the eloquent preacher soon became a great favourite. Bishop Egan having been consecrated at Baltimore, 28 Oct., 1810, made Father Harold his vicar-general and took up his residence at St. Joseph's with him and an uncle of his, the Rev. James Harold, who had arrived from Ireland in March, 1811. Relations between the bishop and the Harolds became strained for domestic reasons not well explained. Trouble arose between the clergy and the trustees, and the Harolds returned to Europe. After a troubled administration of three years and nine months Bishop Egan died at the age of fifty-three. The trustees of St. Mary's had acquired for themselves such a reputation for insubordination, that it was no easy matter to find any one willing to take up the burden of the episcopate. Fathers Maréchal, DeBarth and David declined to accept.

Finally, after an interval of five years, the Holy See selected the vicar-general of Armagh, Ireland, the Very Rev. Henry Conwell, seventy-two years old. He was consecrated in London by Bishop Poynter, 24 Sept., 1820, and arrived in Philadelphia on 25 Nov., of that year. A very disagreeable duty was awaiting him in the case of the Rev. William Hogan, a priest of Albany whom the administrator had imprudently admitted to the diocese without sufficient inquiry or credentials. Bishop England states that he was "deficient in the most common branches of an English education". But he was a man of fine personal presence, a fluent talker, a born demagogue, and able to preach on topics which tickled the ears of men whose religion was a matter of fashion. A clear and impartial narrative of the Hogan Schism is found in Father Kirlin's excellent work, "Catholicity in Philadelphia". (See also CONWELL, HENRY.) It remains a question whether the Hogan schism, which engrossed the interest of Catholics throughout the entire nation, did not do more good than harm. It focussed the attention of Catholics and non-Catholics on the important question of episcopal rights. While some lukewarm Catholics fell away from the Church, the body of the faithful rallied to their pastors with ardour and increased intelligence. The question of lay interference in the administration of the affairs of the Church was settled for all time in Philadelphia. The repudiation by the Holy See and by the hierarchy of the United States of the compromise of 9 Oct., 1826, in which Bishop Conwell surrendered to the already beaten trustees several episcopal rights, ended forever in these States the tyranny of trusteeism.

On 7 July, 1830, there arrived in the city of Philadelphia a man who was to shed lustre on the diocese and on the United States, Francis Patrick Kenrick (q. v.). Having been appointed coadjutor of the diocese, he found a valuable lieutenant in the person of the Rev. John Hughes, a man five or six months his junior, who remained Bishop Kenrick's right hand and secretary until his own elevation to the See of New York. After fruitless admonitions to the trustees of St. Mary's, the administrator, on 16 April, 1831, closed the church and cemeteries of St. Mary's. On 18 May the trustees surrendered, and on 28 May the church was reopened. In 1832 Bishop Kenrick opened what eventually became the diocesan seminary of St. Charles Borromeo, the beneficent results of which were soon apparent. During the first two years of this administration the number of churches was doubled, the first addition being the church of St. John the Evangelist built by Father John Hughes and dedicated 8 April, 1832, which was soon followed by that of St. John Baptist, Manayunk, with the Rev. Thomas Gegan as first pastor. On 8 April, 1833, was laid the cornerstone of St. Michael's church at Kensington, organized by the Rev. Terence J. Donoghue.

When the awful cholera scourge visited Philadelphia in 1832, the intrepidity of the priests and sisters presented an example of heroic Christian charity which was long remembered. On 14 May, 1837, death called away one of the most valiant priests of the city, Father Michael Hurley, O.S.A., who almost from the beginning of the century had given great edification by his zeal and saintly life. Later in the same year the Rev. John Hughes was elevated to the episcopal See of New York. About the same time St. John's became the cathedral. In 1839 the parish of St. Francis Xavier was founded for the Fairmount district, and St. Patrick's church was organized for the Schuylkill suburb. The following year saw the founding of St. Philip's in the extreme south. Its first pastor was the Rev. John P. Dunn. In 1842 the Germans of Kensington were provided for by the building of St. Peter's and the installation of the Redemptorist Fathers. In 1843 the church of St. Paul was opened in Moyamensing by the Rev. Patrick F. Sheridan. To the north, the church of St. Stephen was built near the spot in Nicetown where the first Masses were celebrated by itinerant missionaries. On 15 Nov., 1846, St. Anne's church at Port Richmond was dedicated by Father Gartland of St. John's, Bishop Hughes of New York preaching the sermon. During the year 1845, St. Joachim's was founded at Frankford by the Rev. Dominic Forrestal. On the Feast of Sts. Peter and Paul, 29 June, 1846, the bishop issued a pastoral letter announcing his determination to build a cathedral. He chose for the site a plot of ground adjoining the seminary at Eighteenth and Race Streets. The architect was Napoleon Lebrun. It was the bishop's intention to avoid running into debt, so the cathedral was long in building. In 1848 he founded the church of the Assumption, with the convert, Charles I. H. Carter, for pastor. The ancient suburb of Germantown contained very few Catholics, but the Lazarist Fathers, who conducted the seminary, were willing to assume the risk of building a church in that section, and the church of St. Vincent de Paul was opened for worship on 13 July, 1851, the first pastor being the Rev. M. Domenec, afterwards Bishop of Pittsburg. In 1849 a church was built at Holmesburg and named St. Dominic, the Rev. Charles Dominic Berrill, O.P., being appointed pastor. In 1850 the parish of St. James, in West Philadelphia, was founded by the Rev. J. V. O'Keefe, who took a census and discovered forty Catholic adults in the district. The last evidence in Philadelphia of Bishop Kenrick's activity was the church of St. Malachy, the cornerstone of which he blessed 25 May, 1851. Before its completion he was transferred to the metropolitan See of Baltimore. The western portion of Pennsylvania was formed into the Diocese of Pittsburg, 8 Aug., 1843, with the Rt. Rev. M. O'Connor, D.D., for its first bishop. (For the burning of Catholic churches in the Philadelphia riots of 1844, see KNOWNOTHINGISM.)

The fourth Bishop of Philadelphia, John Nepomucene Neumann, was consecrated 28 March, 1852. (See NEUMANN, JOHN NEPOMUCENE, VENERABLE.) Ten churches sprang up during the first year of his episcopate. The constant topic of his exhortations was the necessity of parish schools. Failing to bring the contumacious trustees of Holy Trinity to their senses, he undermined their influence by putting up the church of St. Alphonsus. On 19 Oct., 1854, he left for Rome to assist at the proclamation of the dogma of the Immaculate Conception, and he returned in March, 1855. On 26 April, 1857, the Rt. Rev. James Frederick Wood was consecrated in the cathedral of Cincinnati as coadjutor to the Bishop of Philadelphia. Bishop Wood was acknowledged by the financial world as thoroughly acquainted with every phase of the banking business, which had been the occupation of his earlier years. At a meeting of the clergy, Bishop Neumann announced that the work of completing the cathedral had been committed to his coadjutor. In October, 1857, he held his last synod: there were 114 priests present, and 32 had been excused from attendance.

James Frederick Wood, the fifth bishop of the diocese, was born at Philadelphia 27 April, 1813. His father, James Wood, was an English merchant and had his child baptized by a minister of the Unitarian sect. In 1827 James Wood and his family removed to Cincinnati, where the boy obtained a position as clerk in a bank. Eleven years later (7 April, 1838), in his twenty-fifth year, the future bishop was received into the Catholic Church by Bishop Purcell, and next year he was sent to Rome to prosecute his studies at the College of the Propaganda, where he was ordained to the priesthood by Cardinal Fransoni, 25 March, 1844. After a short term as assistant at the cathedral of Cincinnati, he was appointed pastor of St. Patrick's church. Though the main object of his appointment to Philadelphia was to relieve Bishop Neumann of the temporal cares of the diocese, yet he by no means confined his efforts to that sphere. He was zealous in preaching the Word of God and gave confirmation in all the churches. On the death of Bishop (Venerable John Nepomucene) Neumann, which took place on 5 January, 1860, the Catholic population of the diocese, which still included Delaware, was estimated at 200,000 souls. There were 157 churches (besides 9 in course of erection) and 7 chapels, attended by 147 priests. The preparatory seminary at Glen Riddle, under the Rev. J. F. Shanahan, and the theological seminary adjoining the cathedral, under the Rev. Wm. O'Hara, D.D., were in a flourishing condition. There were 36 parish schools, attended by 8710 pupils. The diocese was well supplied with colleges, academies, asylums, hospitals, and religious orders of both sexes. In the first year of his administration Bishop Wood established, at the two extreme ends of the city, the parishes of the Annunciation and All Saints, Bridesburg.

The bishop had the erection of the cathedral well in hand, when the outbreak of the Civil War came to retard its completion. Nothing daunted, however, he continued his efforts and on 20 Nov., 1864, had the happiness to sing the first Mass in the immense edifice. Scarcely had he finished the cathedral, when he purchased a large tract of land just outside the city limits, as the site of a new seminary. The pastoral letter in which he announced the purchase at Overbrook is dated 8 Dec., 1865; on 16 Sept., 1871, the beautiful building was filled with 128 students from the two old seminaries. During his visit to Rome, in 1867, he petitioned the Holy See for the creation of the Dioceses of Scranton and Harrisburg, and his wish was granted 3 March, 1868. He was prominent at the Second Plenary Council of Baltimore, and, indeed, at every assembly of the hierarchy his counsels were reverently listened to. He attended the Council of the Vatican, but being in poor health left Rome early in March. He took a great interest in the newly established North American College, wisely insisted that the funds of the college should be kept in America, and was unanimously appointed treasurer of the board.

On 15 Oct., 1873, with all possible pomp, Bishop Wood consecrated the diocese to the Sacred Heart of Jesus. In 1875 he was prostrated by rheumatism; a journey to the South gave him slight relief; and when the instruments arrived creating him archbishop and making Philadelphia a metropolitan see, it was with evident pain he went through the long ceremony of the conferring of the pallium. He had wonderful recuperative powers, however, and in 1877 went to Rome with $30,000 Peter's pence to assist at the celebration of the golden jubilee of Pius IX's episcopate. Recovering from another bad attack in Rome, he returned home. On 23 May, 1880, he presided over the First Provincial Council of Philadelphia. After this he was for the most part confined to his room, where, however, he continued to transact business with his usual energy. His end came on 20 June, 1883. The entire City of Philadelphia turned out to show its affection for one whom it regarded as its most distinguished citizen. Archbishop Wood is buried with the other bishops of the diocese in the crypt beneath the cathedral. He had administered the Sacrament of Confirmation to 105,000 persons. In 1868, in the curtailed diocese, there were 76 churches and 21 chapels; at his death there were 127 churches and 53 chapels. He found, in 1858, 33 parish schools in this section; he left 58.

The choice of a successor to Archbishop Wood demanded thought on the part of the Roman authorities, and they took a year to come to a decision. At first they seemed to consider favourably the venerable Bishop O'Hara of Scranton, who, as rector of the seminary and vicar-general of the diocese, had done valuable service in Philadelphia. There is little doubt that he would have been selected, had it not been for his seventy odd years. The deliberations of Propaganda finally concluded with the choice of the coadjutor of St. Louis; the Rt. Rev. Patrick John Ryan, who was in his fifty-second year, had administered an important diocese for ten years, and seemed to lack no qualification demanded by so eminent a metropolitan see as Philadelphia. (See RYAN, PATRICK J.)

On 20 Aug., 1884, he took formal possession of his archiepiscopal see and received the homage of 250 priests of the diocese. In November of that year he opened the proceedings of the Third Plenary Council, and on 4 January, 1885, was invested with the pallium. After 24 Feb., 1897, he was ably assisted by his auxiliary bishop, the Rt. Rev. Edmond F. Prendergast. On the death of Archbishop Ryan, which took place on 11 February, 1911, Bishop Prendergast assumed the administration of the diocese.

Philadelphia is also the residence of the Rt. Rev. Soter Stephen Ortynski, the Ruthenian Greek Catholic bishop for the United States (see GREEK CATHOLICS IN THE UNITED STATES).

There is probably no diocese in the world better provided with institutions of religion, education, and charity than Philadelphia. The parish school system is admirably organized. There are 141 schools teaching 63,612 children. There are 149 ecclesiastical students preparing for the priesthood, and there is never a lack of vocations. The Catholic population of the diocese was estimated in 1910 at 525,000, whose spiritual needs are supplied by 582 priests, regular and secular. There are 434 churches, chapels, and stations. The religious institutes established in the diocese are: Redemptorist Fathers (14), Augustinian Fathers (Villanova and six other establishments, 33 fathers), Congregation of the Holy Ghost (4 houses, 1 novitiate, 1 industrial school, 15 fathers), Vincentian Fathers (3 houses, 1 seminary, 24 fathers), Society of Jesus (2 houses, 1 college, 22 fathers), Christian Brothers (10 houses, 89 brothers). There are in the diocese (1911) 2565 religious women, novices, and postulants and 11 schools for girls under the care of religious women. The religious institutes for women are: Sisters of the Blessed Sacrament, Sisters of Charity, Sisters of Christian Charity, Felician Sisters, Franciscan Tertiaries, Missionary Sisters of the Third Order of St. Francis, Sisters of the Good Shepherd, Sisters of the Holy Child Jesus, Sisters of the Most Holy Family of Nazareth, Sisters-Servants of the Immaculate Heart, Discalced Carmelites, Sisters of St. Joseph, Sisters of Mercy (Philadelphia foundation and Scranton foundation), School Sisters of Notre Dame, Sisters of Notre Dame (Namur), Little Sisters of the Poor, Religious of the Sacred Heart, Sisters of St. Dominic, Bernardine, Sisters of St. Francis (Polish), Missionary Sisters of the Sacred Heart, Poor Handmaids of Jesus Christ, Filiæ Mariæ.

SHEA, *Hist. of the Cath. Church in the U. S.* (New York, 1886–92); MAHONY, *Historical Sketches of the Cath. Churches and Institutions of Philadelphia*; KIRLIN, *Catholicity in Philadelphia* (Philadelphia, 1909); *Catholic Standard and Times*, files; *Am. Cath. Hist. Researches; Official Cath. Directory* (1911).

JAMES F. LOUGHLIN.

Philanthropinism, the system of education educed from the ideas of Rousseau and of the German "Enlightenment", and established by Basedow on the basis of "philanthropy". Johann Bernhard Basedow (b. at Hamburg, 11 Sept., 1723; d. at Magdeburg, 25 July, 1790) was a pupil at the school of Hamburg under the free-thinker Hermann Samuel Reimarus, studied theology at Leipzig, became (1749) a tutor in a noble family in Holstein, and (1753) professor at the academy for young noblemen at Soroe on the Island of Zealand, Denmark. In 1761 he was removed from this position on account of his Rationalistic opinions and appointed professor in a school at Altona. Here he published his "Methodenbuch für Väter und Mütter der Familien und Völker" (Altona and Bremen, 1770; 3rd ed., 1773), in which he presented in detail his ideas for the improvement of the school-system. This work and his "Agathokrator oder von der Erziehung künftiger Regenten" (Leipzig, 1771) attracted the attention of Prince Leopold Friedrich Franz of Anhalt-Dessau. In 1771 the prince called Basedow to Dessau, where he wrote his "Elementarwerk" (4 vols. with 100 copper-plates, Dessau, 1774; 2nd ed., Leipzig, 1785) which, in a form suitable to modern times, sought to present the idea carried out in the "Orbis pictus" of Comenius, of uniting the pictures of the things with the notions of them, by giving with pictures all the material essential for training children. In 1774 he opened a model school at Dessau, the "Philanthropinum".

As the name signifies, it was to be a school of philanthropy for teachers and pupils. In contrast to the severe discipline of earlier days, children were to be trained in a friendly and gentle manner, instruction was to be made attractive, study as easy and pleasant as possible. The standard in forming the course of study was the practical and useful. Languages were to be taught more by practice and speaking than by the learning of grammatical rules, Latin, German, and French being regarded as the most important. Special attention was also given to the more practical studies, as arithmetic, geometry, geography, drawing, and natural science. Basedow and his successors deserve credit for their improvement of methods and educational appliances. Special stress was laid on physical development. The fact that children belonged to a particular nation or religious confession was disregarded; education was to produce cosmopolites. Religious instruction was to be replaced by the teaching of a universal natural morality. Among the teachers who aided Basedow in this school was Christian Heinrich Wolke, who had been his assistant before this in preparing the "Elementarwerk". Basedow, although a fine pedagogist, lacked the personal qualities necessary for conducting such an institution, and retired in 1776. His place was taken (1776–77) by Joachim Heinrich Campe (1746–1818), who was later a prolific writer on subjects connected with Philanthropinism, and is best known by his German version of Robinson Crusoe called "Robinson der Jüngere"; his most important work is "Allgemeine Revision des gesammten Schul- und Erziehungswesens" (16 vols., 1785–91). For a short time after Campe had retired, Basedow, assisted by Wolke, was once more the head of the school. Among the others who taught for a time at this institution were Ernst Christian Trapp (1745–1818), who sought to systematize the philanthropinist principles and theories in his "Versuch einer Pädagogik" (Berlin, 1780); Salzmann (see below), and Louis Henry Ferdinand Olivier (1759–1815). In 1793 this first "Philanthropinum" ceased to exist.

Those who held Basedow's pedagogical opinions were called *Philanthropen*, or *Philanthropisten*. In imitation of the school at Dessau institutions called *Philanthropin* were established at various places. The only *Philanthropin* that prospered and still exists was that founded by Salzmann at Schnepfenthal in the Duchy of Gotha. Christian Gotthilf Salzmann (b. at Sömmerda near Erfurt, 1 June, 1744; d. at Schnepfenthal, 31 Oct., 1811) was one of the most distinguished pedagogues of the Philanthropinist school, and probably the most interesting personality among all its representatives. He was originally a Protestant pastor at Erfurt; then, after writing on educational subjects for some time, he became the teacher of religion at the Philanthropin at Dessau (1781–84), and in 1784 founded his own school at Schnepfenthal, which he conducted until his death. Like the entire Philanthropinist school, his religious opinions were rationalistic. The best known of his writings are "Krebsbüchlein oder Anweisung zu einer unvernünftigen Erziehung der Kinder" (Erfurt, 1780, and frequently reprinted), a satirical account of the results of a wrong education; "Ameisenbüchlein oder Anweisung zu einer vernünftigen Erziehung der Erzieher" (Schnepfenthal, 1806); "Konrad Kiefer oder Anweisung zu einer vernünftigen Erziehung der Kinder" (Erfurt, 1796). The most important of Salzmann's assistants was Johann Christoph Friedrich Guts-Muths (1759–1839), who was the teacher of geography at Salzmann's school; one of his pupils was the celebrated geographer Karl Ritter, the first pupil of the school at Schnepfenthal. Guts-Muths, however, is best known for his work in gymnastics. Friedrich Eberhard von Rochow (1734–1805) advocated views similar to those of the Philanthropinists, but, unlike the actual members of this school, did much for the improvement of primary education; his "Kinderfreund" (1775, and many later editions) was a widely used school-book. Finally Christian Felix Weisse (1726–1804), a voluminous writer for children, exerted great influence through his "Kinderfreund" (24 vols., 1775–84), a weekly publication for children.

PINLOCHE, *La réforme de l'éducation en Allemagne au 18e siècle, Basedow et le philanthropinisme* (Paris, 1889); PINLOCHE AND RAUSCHENFELS, *Gesch. des Philanthropinismus* (Leipzig, 1896); THALHOFER, *Die sexuelle Pädagogik bei den Philanthropen* (Kempten, 1907); ROLFUS AND PFISTER, *Real-Encyclopädie des Erziehungs- und Unterrichtswesens*, IV (2nd ed., Mainz, 1874), 1–15; KELLNER, *Kurze Gesch. der Erziehung und des Unterrichts* (6th ed., Freiburg im Br., 1881), 141–56; PAULSEN, *Gesch. des gelehrten Unterrichtes auf den deutschen Schulen und Universitäten*, II (2nd ed., Leipzig, 1897), 46–63; BAUMGARTNER, *Gesch. der Pädagogik* (Freiburg im Br., 1902), 166–72; KRIEG, *Lehrbuch der Pädagogik* (2nd ed., Paderborn, 1900), 145–47; BASEDOW, *Ausgewählte Schriften*, ed. GÖRING in *Bibliothek pädagogischer Klassiker* (Langensalza, 1880); SALZMANN, *Ausgewählte Schriften*, ed. ACKERMANN in *Bibliothek pädagogischer Klassiker* (2 vols., Langensalza, 1889–91); SALZMANN, *Krebsbüchlein und Ameisenbüchlein*, ed. WIMMERS in *Sammlung der bedeutendsten pädagogischen Schriften*, VI (Paderborn, 1890; 2nd ed., 1894; 9th ed., 1891).

FRIEDRICH LAUCHERT.

Philastrius, SAINT, Bishop of Brescia, d. before 397. He was one of the bishops present at a synod held in Aquileia in 381. St. Augustine met him at Milan about 383, or perhaps a little later (St. Augustine, Ep. ccxxii). He composed a catalogue of heresies (Diversarum Hereseon Liber) about 384. Among the writings of St. Gaudentius (q. v.) was a sermon purporting to be preached on the fourteenth anniversary of St. Philastrius's death. According to this sermon, Philastrius's life began with a great act of renunciation, for which he might fitly be compared to Abraham. Later he was ordained priest, and travelled over nearly the whole Roman world (circumambiens Universum pene ambitum Romani Orbis), preaching against pagans, Jews, and heretics, especially the Arians. Like St. Paul he carried in his body the "stigmata" of Christ, having been scourged for his zeal against the last-named heretics. At Milan he was a great stay of the Catholic party in the time of St. Ambrose's Arian predecessor. At Rome he held both private and public disputations with heretics, and converted many. His wanderings ceased when he was made Bishop of Brescia.

Doubts were first raised by Dupin as to the genuineness of this sermon, and these have been reiterated by Marx, the latest editor of Philastrius, who thinks the sermon a forgery of the eighth or ninth century. The chief objection to its genuineness, rather a weak one, seems to be that it is not found in the MSS. containing the undoubted sermons of St. Gaudentius. Marx was answered by Knappe, "Ist die 21 Rede des hl. Gaudentius (Oratio B. Gaudentii de Vita et Obitu B. Filastrii episcopi prædecessoris sui) echt? Zugleich ein Betrag zur Latinität des Gaudentius" (Osnabrück), who endeavours to prove the genuineness of the sermon in question by linguistic arguments. His Bollandist reviewer thinks he has made a strong case (Anal. Boll., XXVIII, 224). Philastrius's "Catalogue" of heresies would have little value, were it not for the circumstance discovered by Lipsius that for the Christian heresies up to Noetus the compiler drew from the same source as Epiphanus, i. e. the lost Syntagma of Hippolytus. By the aid, therefore, of these two and the Pseudo-Tertullian "Adv. Hær.", it has been possible in great measure to reconstruct the lost treatise of Hippolytus. The first edition of the "Catalogue" was published at Basle (1528); the latest, ed. Marx, in the Vienna "Corp. Script. Eccl. Lat." (1898).

TILLEMONT, H. E., VIII, 541 sq.; CEILLIER, *Hist. des Auteurs Eccles.*, VI, 739 sq.; LIPSIUS, *Zur Quellenkritik des Epiphanus* (Vienna, 1865); IDEM, *Quellen der ält. Ketzergesch.* (Leipzig, 1875); HARNACK, *Quellenkritik der Gesch. des Gnosticismus* (Leipzig, 1874); KUNZE, *De hist. Gnosticismi fontibus novæ quæst. criticæ* (Leipzig, 1894).

F. J. BACCHUS.

Philemon (Gr. φιλήμων), a citizen of Colossæ (q. v.), to whom St. Paul addressed a private letter, unique in the New Testament, which bears his name. As appears from this epistle, Philemon was his dear and intimate friend (verses 1, 13, 17, 22), and had been converted most probably by him (verse 19) during his long residence at Ephesus (Acts, xix, 26; cf. xviii, 19), as St. Paul himself had not visited Colossæ (Col., ii, 1). Rich and noble, he possessed slaves; his house was a place of meeting and worship for the Colossian converts (verse 2); he was kind, helpful, and charitable (verses 5, 7), providing hospitality for his fellow-Christians (verse 22). St. Paul calls him his fellow-labourer (συνεργός, verse 1), so that he must have been earnest in his work for the Gospel, perhaps first at Ephesus and afterwards at Colossæ. It is not plain whether he was ordained or not. Tradition represents him as Bishop of Colossæ (Const. Apost., VII, 46), and the Menaia of 22 November speak of him as a holy apostle who, in company with Appia, Archippus, and Onesimus had been martyred at Colossæ during the first general persecution in the reign of Nero. In the address of the letter two other Christian converts, Appia and Archippus (Col., iv, 17), are mentioned; it is generally believed that Appia was Philemon's wife and Archippus their son. St. Paul, dealing exclusively in his letter with the domestic matter of a fugitive slave, Onesimus, regarded them both as deeply interested. Archippus, according to Col., iv, 17, was a minister in the Lord, and held a sacred office in the Church of Colossæ or in the neighbouring Church of Laodicæa.

PHILEMON, EPISTLE TO.—A. *Authenticity*.—External testimony to the Pauline authorship is considerable and evident, although the brevity and private character of the Epistle did not favour its use and public recognition. The heretic Marcion accepted it in his "Apostolicon" (Tertullian, "Adv. Marcion", V, xxi); Origen quotes it expressly as Pauline ("Hom.", XIX, "In Jerem.", II, 1; "Comment. in Matt.", Tract. 33, 34); and it is named in the Muratorian Fragment as well as contained in the Syriac and old Latin Versions. Eusebius includes Philemon among the *homologoumena*, or books universally undisputed and received as sacred. St. Chrysostom and St. Jerome, in the prefaces to their commentaries on the Epistle, defend it against some objections which have neither historical nor critical value. The vocabulary (ἐπίγνωσις, παράκλησις τάχα), the phraseology, and the style are unmistakably and thoroughly Pauline, and the whole Epistle claims to have been written by St. Paul. It has been objected, however, that it contains some words nowhere else used by St. Paul (ἀναπέμπειν, ἀποτίνειν, ἄχρηστος, ἐπιτάσσειν, ξενία, ὀνίνασθαι, προσοφείλειν). But every Epistle of St. Paul contains a number of ἅπαξ λεγόμενα employed nowhere else, and the vocabulary of all authors changes more or less with time, place, and especially subject-matter. Are we not allowed to expect the same from St. Paul, an author of exceptional spiritual vitality and mental vigour? Renan voiced the common opinion of the critics when he wrote: "St. Paul alone, it would seem, could have written this little masterpiece" (St. Paul, p. xi).

B. *Date and place of writing.*—It is one of the four Captivity Epistles composed by St. Paul during his first imprisonment in Rome (see COLOSSIANS; EPHESIANS; PHILIPPIANS, EPISTLES TO THE; Philem., 9, 23). Colossians, Ephesians, and Philippians are closely connected, so that the general opinion is that they were written and despatched at the same time, between A. D. 61–63. Some scholars assign the composition to Cæsarea (Acts, xxiii–xxvi, A. D. 59–60), but both tradition and internal evidence are in favour of Rome.

C. *Occasion and purpose.*—Onesimus, most likely only one of many slaves of Philemon, fled away and, apparently before his flight, defrauded his master, and ran away to Rome, finding his way to the hired lodging where Paul was suffered to dwell by himself and to receive all that came to him (Acts, xxviii, 16, 30). It is very possible he may have seen Paul, when he accompanied his master to Ephesus. Onesimus became the spiritual son of St. Paul (verses 9, 10), who would have retained him with himself, that in the new and higher sphere of Christian service he should render the service which his master could not personally perform. But Philemon had a prior claim; Onesimus, as a Christian, was obliged to make restitution. According to the law, the master of a runaway slave might treat him exactly as he pleased. When retaken, the slave was usually branded on the forehead, maimed, or forced to fight with wild beasts. Paul asks pardon for the offender, and with a rare tact and utmost delicacy requests his master to receive him kindly as himself. He does not ask expressly that Philemon should emancipate his slave-brother, but "the word emancipation seems to be trembling on his lips, and yet he does not once utter it" (Lightfoot, "Colossians and Philemon", London, 1892, 389). We do not know the result of St. Paul's request, but that it was granted seems to be implied in subsequent ecclesiastical tradition, which represents Onesimus as Bishop of Berœa (Constit. Apost., VII, 46).

D. *Argument.*—This short letter, written to an individual friend, has the same divisions as the longer letters: (a) the introduction (verses 1–7); (b) the body of the Epistle or the request (verses 8–22); (c) the epilogue (verses 23–25). (a) The introduction contains (1) the salutation or address: Paul, "prisoner of Christ Jesus, and Timothy" greet Philemon (verse 1), Appia, Archippus, and the Church in their house (verse 2), wishing them grace and peace from God our Father and the Lord Jesus Christ (verse 3); (2) the thanksgiving for Philemon's faith and love (verses 4–6), which gives great joy and consolation to the Apostle (verse 7). (b) The request and appeal on behalf of the slave Onesimus. Though he could enjoin Philemon to do with Onesimus that which is convenient (verse 8), for Christian love's sake, Paul "an aged man and now also a prisoner of Jesus Christ" (verse 9) beseeches him for his son Onesimus whom he had begotten in his bonds (verse 10). Once he was not what his name implies (helpful); now, however, he is profitable to both (verse 11). Paul sends him again and asks Philemon to receive him as his own heart (verse 12). He was desirous of retaining Onesimus with himself that he might minister to him in his imprisonment, as Philemon himself would gladly have done (verse 13), but he was unwilling to do anything without Philemon's decision, desiring that his kindness should not be as it were "of necessity but voluntary" (verse 14). Perhaps, in the purpose of Providence, he was separated from thee for a time that thou mightest have him for ever (verse 15), no longer as a slave but more than a slave, as a better servant and a beloved Christian brother (verse 16). If, therefore, thou regardest me as a partner in faith, receive him as myself (verse 17). If he has wronged thee in any way, or is in thy debt, place that to my account (verse 18). I have signed this promise of repayment with my own hand, not to say to thee that besides (thy remitting the debt) thou owest me thine own self (verse 19). Yea, brother, let me have profit from thee (σοῦ ὀναίμην) in the Lord, refresh my heart in the Lord (verse 20). Having confidence in thine obedience, I have written to thee, knowing that thou wilt do more than I say (verse 21). But at the same time, receive me also and prepare a lodging for me: for I hope that through your prayers I shall be given to you (verse 22). (c) The epilogue contains (1) salutations from all persons named in Col., iv, 10–14 (verses 23–24), and (2) a final benediction (verse 25). This short, tender, graceful, and kindly Epistle has often been compared to a beautiful letter of the younger Pliny (Ep. IX, 21) asking his friend Sabinian to forgive an offending freedman. As Lightfoot (Colossians and Philemon, 383 sq.) says: "If purity of diction be excepted, there will hardly be any difference of opinion in awarding the palm to the Christian apostle".

E. *Attitude of St. Paul towards slavery.*—Slavery was universal in all ancient nations and the very economic basis of the old civilization. Slaves were employed not only in all the forms of manual and industrial labour, but also in many functions which required artistic skill, intelligence, and culture; such was especially the case in both the Greek and the Roman society. Their number was much greater than that of the free citizens. In the Greek civilization the slave was in better conditions than in the Roman; but even according to Greek law and usage, the slave was in a complete subjection to the will of his master, possessing no rights, even that of marriage. (See Wallon, "Hist. de l'Esclavage dans l'Antiquité", Paris, 1845, 1879; SLAVERY.) St. Paul, as a Jew, had little of pagan conception of slavery; the Bible and the Jewish civilization led him already into a happier and more humane world. The Bible mitigated slavery and enacted a humanitarian legislation respecting the manumission of slaves; but the Christian conscience of the Apostle alone explains his attitude towards Onesimus and slavery. On the one hand, St. Paul accepted slavery as an established fact, a deeply-rooted social institution which he did not attempt to abolish all at once and suddenly; moreover, if the Christian religion should have attempted violently to destroy pagan slavery, the assault would have exposed the Roman empire to a servile insurrection, the Church to the hostility of the imperial power, and the slaves to awful reprisals. On the other hand, if St. Paul does not denounce the abstract and inherent wrong of complete slavery (if that question presented itself to his mind, he did not express it), he knew and appreciated its actual abuses and evil possibilities and he addressed himself to the regulations and the betterment of existing conditions. He inculcated forbearance to slaves as well as obedience to masters (Eph., vi, 5–9; Col., iii, 22; iv, 1; Philem., 8–12, 15, 17; I Tim., vi, 1; Tit., ii, 9). He taught that the Christian slave is the Lord's freedman (I Cor., vii, 22), and vigorously proclaimed the complete spiritual equality of slave and freeman, the universal, fatherly love of God, and the Christian brotherhood of men: "For you are all the children of God by faith in Christ Jesus. For as many of you as have been baptized in Christ, have put on Christ. There is neither Jew nor Greek, there is neither bond nor free: there is neither male nor female. For you are all one in Christ Jesus" (Gal., iii, 26-28; cf. Col., iii, 10-11). These fundamental Christian principles were the leaven which slowly and steadily spread throughout the whole empire. They curtailed the abuses of slavery and finally destroyed it (Vincent, "Philippians and Philemon", Cambridge, 1902, 167).

In addition to works referred to, consult Introductions to the New Testament. CATHOLIC: TOUSSAINT in VIGOUROUX, *Dict. de la Bible*, s. vv. *Philémon; Philémon, Epître à;* VAN STEENKISTE, *Commentarius in Epistolas S. Pauli*, XI (Bruges, 1896); ALLARD, *Les esclaves chrétiens* (Paris, 1900); PRAT, *La Théologie de S. Paul* (Paris, 1908), 384 sq.; NON-CATHOLIC: OLTRAMARE, *Commentaire sur les Epîtres de S. Paul aux Colossiens, aux Ephésiens et à Philémon* (Paris, 1891); VON SODEN, *Die Briefe an die Kolosser, Epheser, Philemon* in *Hand-Commentar zum N. T.*, ed. HOLTZMANN (Freiburg, 1893); SHAW, *The Pauline Epistles* (Edinburgh, 1904); WOULE, *The Epistles to the Colossians and to Philemon* (Cambridge, 1902).

A. CAMERLYNCK.

Philibert, SAINT. See JUMIÈGES, ABBEY OF.

Philip, SAINT, APOSTLE.—Like the brothers, Peter and Andrew, Philip was a native of Bethsaida on Lake Genesareth (John, i, 44). He also was among those surrounding the Baptist when the latter first pointed out Jesus as the Lamb of God. On the day after Peter's call, when about to set out for Galilee, Jesus met Philip and called him to the Apostolate with the words, "Follow me". Philip obeyed the call, and a little later brought Nathaniel as a new disciple (John, i, 43-45). On the occasion of the selection and sending out of the twelve, Philip is included among the Apostles proper. His name stands in the fifth place in the three lists (Matt., x, 2-4; Mark, iii, 14-19; Luke, vi, 13-16) after the two pairs of brothers, Peter and Andrew, James and John. The Fourth Gospel records three episodes concerning Philip which occurred during the epoch of the public teaching of the Saviour: (1) Before the miraculous feeding of the multitude, Christ turns towards Philip with the question: "Whence shall we buy bread, that these may eat?" to which the Apostle answers: "Two hundred pennyworth of bread is not sufficient for them, that every one may take a little" (vi, 5-7). (2) When some heathens in Jerusalem came to Philip and expressed their desire to see Jesus, Philip reported the fact to Andrew and then both brought the news to the Saviour (xii, 21-23). (3) When Philip, after Christ had spoken to His Apostles of knowing and seeing the Father, said to Him: "Lord, shew us the Father, and it is enough for us", he received the answer: "He that seeth me, seeth the Father also" (xiv, 8-9). These three episodes furnish a consistent character-sketch of Philip as a naïve, somewhat shy, sober-minded man. No additional characteristics are given in the Gospels or the Acts, although he is mentioned in the latter work (i, 13) as belonging to the Apostolic College.

The second-century tradition concerning him is uncertain, inasmuch as a similar tradition is recorded concerning Philip the Deacon and Evangelist—a phenomenon which must be the result of confusion caused by the existence of the two Philips. In his letter to St. Victor, written about 189-98, Bishop Polycrates of Ephesus mentions among the "great lights", whom the Lord will seek on the "last day", "Philip, one of the Twelve Apostles, who is buried in Hieropolis with his two daughters, who grew old as virgins", and a third daughter, who "led a life in the Holy Ghost and rests in Ephesus." On the other hand, according to the Dialogue of Caius, directed against a Montanist named Proclus, the latter declared that "there were four prophetesses, the daughters of Philip, at Hieropolis in Asia, where their and their father's grave is still situated." The Acts (xxi, 8-9) does indeed mention four prophetesses, the daughters of the deacon and "Evangelist" Philip, as then living in Cæsarea with their father, and Eusebius, who gives the above-mentioned excerpts (Hist. eccl., III, xxxii), refers Proclus' statement to these latter. The statement of Bishop Polycrates carries in itself more authority, but it is extraordinary that three virgin daughters of the Apostle Philip (two buried in Hieropolis) should be mentioned, and that the deacon Philip should also have four daughters, said to have been buried in Hieropolis. Here also perhaps we must suppose a confusion of the two Philips to have taken place, although it is difficult to decide which of the two, the Apostle or the deacon, was buried in Hieropolis. Many modern historians believe that it was the deacon; it is, however, possible that the Apostle was buried there and that the deacon also lived and worked there and was there buried with three of his daughters, and that the latter were afterwards erroneously regarded as the children of the Apostle. The apocryphal "Acts of Philip," which are, however, purely legendary and a tissue of fables, also refer Philip's death to Hieropolis. The remains of the Philip who was interred in Hieropolis were later translated (as those of the Apostle) to Constantinople and thence to the church of the Dodici Apostoli in Rome. The feast of the Apostle is celebrated in the Roman Church on 1 May (together with that of James the Younger), and in the Greek Church on 14 November.

Acta SS., May, I, 11-2; BATIFFOL in *Analecta Bollandiana*, IX (1890), 204 sqq.; LIPSIUS, *Die apokryphen Apostelgeschichten und Apostellegenden*, II, II (Brunswick, 1884), 1 sqq.; *Bibl. hagiogr. latina*, II, 991; on the two Philips cf. ZAHN in *Forschungen zur Gesch. des neutestamentl. Kanons*, VI (Erlangen, 1900), 158 sqq.

J. P. KIRSCH.

J. J. Little & Ives Co.
New York—Printers.
J. F. Tapley Co.
New York—Binders.